HISTORICAL STATISTICS OF CANADA

HISTORICAL STATISTICS OF CANADA

M.C.URQUHART

EDITOR

K.A.H.BUCKLEY

ASSISTANT EDITOR

Sponsored by Canadian Political Science Association

and Social Science Research Council of Canada

CAMBRIDGE: AT THE UNIVERSITY PRESS

TORONTO: THE MACMILLAN COMPANY OF CANADA LTD

1965

R317.1
Urquhart

Published (in Canada) by
The Macmillan Company of Canada Limited
70 Bond Street, Toronto 2

Published (in the rest of the world) by
The Syndics of the Cambridge University Press

Bentley House, 200 Euston Road, London, N.W.1
American Branch: 32 East 57th Street, New York, N.Y. 10022
West African Office: P.O. Box 33, Ibadan, Nigeria

Printed in Great Britain at the University Printing House, Cambridge
(Brooke Crutchley, University Printer)

CONTENTS

SECTION CHIEFS AND PANEL MEMBERS

The affiliation of the section chiefs, panel members and others who helped directly in the preparation of the volume is that at the time that the main work of preparing the material was done. Some of those listed will have a different affiliation at the time the volume appears.

Section A: Population and Migration

Section Chief:

K. A. H. BUCKLEY. Department of Economics and Political Science, University of Saskatchewan.

Panel members:

A. H. LeNeveu. Chief, Analysis Immigration and Citizenship Statistics Section, Census Division, Dominion Bureau of Statistics.

J. P. Delisle. Chief, Statistics Section, Administrative Services, Department of Citizenship and Immigration.

Mrs Helen Buckley. Center of Community Studies, University of Saskatchewan.

Section B: Vital Statistics, Health and Welfare

Section Chief:

Jacques Henripin. Department of Economics, University of Montreal.

Panel members:

Gordon H. Josie. Principal Research Officer, Research and Statistics Division, Department of National Health and Welfare.

Joseph W. Willard. Deputy Minister, Department of National Health and Welfare.

F. F. Harris. Director, Health and Welfare Division, Dominion Bureau of Statistics.

Yves Martin. Faculty of Social Sciences, Laval University.

Section C: The Labour Force

Section Chief:

K. A. H. Buckley. Department of Economics and Political Science, University of Saskatchewan.

Panel members:

W. A. Nesbitt. Chief, Processing and Analysis Section, Special Surveys Division, Dominion Bureau of Statistics.

A. H. LeNeveu. Chief, Analysis Immigration and Citizenship Statistics Section, Census Division, Dominion Bureau of Statistics.

G. V. Haythorne. Deputy Minister, Department of Labour, Ottawa.

Section D: Wages and Working Conditions

Section Chief:

Douglas Hartle. Department of Political Economy, University of Toronto.

Panel members:

C. H. Curtis. Department of Political and Economic Science, Queen's University.

J. C. Weldon. Department of Economics and Political Science, McGill University.

Section E: National Income and the Capital Stock

Section Chief:

M. C. Urquhart. Department of Political and Economic Science, Queen's University.

Panel member:

Simon Goldberg. Assistant Dominion Statistician, Dominion Bureau of Statistics.

Acknowledgement:

H. J. Adler. Assistant Director, National Income and Balance of Payments Division, Dominion Bureau of Statistics.

Section F: The Balance of International Payments, International Indebtedness and Foreign Trade

Section Chief:

Herbert Marshall. Dominion Statistician, Retired.

Panel members:

F. A. Knox. Department of Political and Economic Science, Queen's University.

George Watts. Research Department, Bank of Canada.

C. D. Blyth. Director, National Income and Balance of Payments Division, Dominion Bureau of Statistics.

A. E. Safarian. Department of Economics and Political Science, University of Saskatchewan.

Section G: Government Finance

Section Chief:

J. H. Perry. Director, Canadian Tax Foundation, Toronto.

Panel members:

J. Lowther. Commissioner of Finance, City of Ottawa.

G. A. Wagdin. Director, Public Finance and Transportation Division, Dominion Bureau of Statistics.

J. Howes. Secretary, Metropolitan Study Committee, Vancouver, British Columbia.

H. R. Balls. Comptroller of the Treasury, Department of Finance, Ottawa.

Acknowledgement:

Miss E. R. Cram. Chief, Public Finance Section, Dominion Bureau of Statistics.

Section H: Banking and Finance

Section Chief:

E. P. Neufeld. Department of Political Economy, University of Toronto.

Acknowledgement:

P. A. T. Campbell.

Section J: Price Indexes

Section Chief:

A. ASIMAKOPULOS. Department of Economics and Political Science, McGill University.

Panel members:

J. WELDON. Department of Economics and Political Science, McGill University.

L. E. ROWEBOTTOM. Assistant to the Dominion Statistician, Dominion Bureau of Statistics.

W. C. HOOD. Department of Political Economy, University of Toronto.

Acknowledgements:

F. CURRY. Chief, Retail Prices Section, Prices Division, Dominion Bureau of Statistics.

K. WALLACE. Chief, Wholesale Prices Section, Prices Division, Dominion Bureau of Statistics.

Miss B. J. EMERY. National Accounts and Balance of Payments Division, Dominion Bureau of Statistics.

Section K: Lands and Forests

Section Chief:

G. K. GOUNDREY. Department of Political Economy, University of Alberta.

Panel members:

VERNON FOWKE. Department of Economics and Political Science, University of Saskatchewan.

A. L. BEST. Department of Forestry, Ottawa.

Section L: Agriculture

Section Chief:

D. L. MACFARLANE. Macdonald College, McGill University.

Panel members:

J. W. CHANNON. Grain Division, Department of Trade and Commerce, Ottawa.

J. A. DAWSON. Economics Division, Department of Agriculture, Ottawa.

R. S. ELLIS. Chief, Census of Agriculture Section, Census Division, Dominion Bureau of Statistics.

W. F. EWERT. Chief, Livestock and Animal Products Section, Agriculture Division, Dominion Bureau of Statistics.

A. D. HOLMES. Director, Prices Division, Dominion Bureau of Statistics.

C. V. PARKER. Director, Agriculture Division, Dominion Bureau of Statistics.

W. D. PORTER. Assistant Director, Agriculture Division, Dominion Bureau of Statistics.

J. B. RUTHERFORD. Assistant Director, Economics Service, Department of Fisheries, Ottawa.

Section M: Fisheries

Section Chief:

H. S. GORDON. Department of Economics, Carleton University.

Panel members:

W. C. MACKENZIE. Director, Economics Service, Department of Fisheries, Ottawa.

J. B. RUTHERFORD. Assistant Director, Economics Service, Department of Fisheries, Ottawa.

R. E. JOHNSON. Chief, Fisheries Section, Dominion Bureau of Statistics.

Acknowledgements:

D. A. MACLEAN. Economics Service, Department of Fisheries.

Section N: Minerals and Fuel

Section Chief:

JOHN DAVIS. British Columbia Electric Company Limited, Vancouver, British Columbia.

Panel members:

A. R. DEIR. Chief, Mineral Statistics Section, Dominion Bureau of Statistics.

W. K. BUCK. Chief, Mineral Resources Division, Mines and Technical Surveys Department, Ottawa.

R. D. HOWLAND. Commissioner, Royal Commission on Energy.

C. L. O'BRIAN. Chairman, Dominion Coal Board.

L. S. EVANS. Chief, Communications, Distribution and Transmission Section, Dominion Bureau of Statistics.

Section P: Electric Power

Section Chief:

JOHN DAVIS. British Columbia Electric Company Limited, Vancouver, British Columbia.

Panel members:

R. D. HOWLAND. Commissioner, Royal Commission on Energy.

C. L. O'BRIAN. Chairman, Dominion Coal Board.

R. L. BORDEN. Chief, Communications, Distribution and Transmission Section, Dominion Bureau of Statistics.

S. A. WAGDIN. Director, Public Finance and Transportation Division, Dominion Bureau of Statistics.

Section Q: Manufactures

Section Chief:

ARTHUR J. R. SMITH. Director of Research, Private Planning Association of Canada, Montreal.

Panel members:

T. VOUT. Economist, Prime Minister's Office.

V. R. BERLINGUETTE. Assistant to Director, and Chief, Manufactures Section, Industry and Merchandising Division, Dominion Bureau of Statistics.

D. H. FULLERTON. President, Fullerton, MacKenzie and Associates Limited, Investment Consultants.

JOHN DALES. Department of Political Economy, University of Toronto.

A. COHEN. Assistant Director, Industry and Merchandising Division, Dominion Bureau of Statistics.

Section R: Construction and Housing

Section Chief:

K. A. H. BUCKLEY. Department of Economics and Political Science, University of Saskatchewan.

Panel members:

Mrs HELEN BUCKLEY. Center of Community Studies, University of Saskatchewan.

ALBERT GORACZ. Economist, Central Mortgage and Housing Corporation.

DEREK KNIGHT. Supervisor, Economic Research Department, Central Mortgage and Housing Corporation.

D. A. TRAQUAIR. Business Finance Division, Dominion Bureau of Statistics.

Section S: Transportation and Communication

Section Chief:

J. L. McDougall. School of Business, Queen's University.

Panel members:

John Stenason. Director of Economic Research, Canadian Pacific Railway Co.

R. A. Bandeen. Senior Staff Officer, Planning, Department of Research and Development, Canadian National Railways.

G. A. Richardson. Chief, Transportation and Public Utilities Section, Dominion Bureau of Statistics.

C. S. Carter. Chief Statistician, Bell Telephone Company of Canada.

A. W. Currie. Department of Political Economy, University of Toronto.

K. W. Studnicki-Gizbert. Chief, Economics Division, Air Transport Board, Ottawa.

A. L. Brown. Chief, Transportation Section, Dominion Bureau of Statistics.

Adam Jaworski. Economic Policy and Research Branch, Department of Transport.

N. M. Griffith. Comptroller, Post Office Department, Ottawa.

Section T: Internal Trade and Service

Section Chief:

M. C. Urquhart. Department of Political and Economic Science, Queen's University.

Acknowledgements:

J. C. Brierley. Merchandising Section, Retail Trade, Dominion Bureau of Statistics.

G. Snyder. Merchandising Section, Retail Trade, Dominion Bureau of Statistics.

Section V: Education

Section Chief:

R. W. B. Jackson. Director, Department of Educational Research, Ontario College of Education, University of Toronto.

Panel members:

Charles Bilodeau. Department of Education, Quebec.

Oswald Hall. Department of Political Economy, University of Toronto.

C. E. Hendry. School of Social Work, University of Toronto.

E. F. Sheffield. Canadian Universities Foundation.

F. E. Whitworth. Education Division, Dominion Bureau of Statistics.

Acknowledgements:

Willard Brehaut. Department of Educational Research, Ontario College of Education, University of Toronto.

N. LeSeelleur. Education Division, Dominion Bureau of Statistics.

R. D. Mitchener. Education Division, Dominion Bureau of Statistics.

Section W: Politics and Government

Section Chief:

Norman Ward. Department of Economics and Political Science, University of Saskatchewan.

Acknowledgements:

Charles Dunlop. Department of Economics and Political Science, University of Saskatchewan.

J. E. Hodgetts. Department of Political and Economic Science, Queen's University.

Howard Scarrow. University of Michigan.

Section Y: Justice

Section Chief:

Nicolas Zay. Director of Research, School of Social Work, University of Montreal.

Panel members:

W. A. Magill. Chief, Judicial Section, Dominion Bureau of Statistics.

P. J. Giffen. Department of Political Economy, University of Toronto.

B. R. Blishen. Department of Anthropology and Sociology, University of British Columbia.

Stuart Ryan. Faculty of Law, Queen's University.

Special acknowledgement:

W. A. Magill. Chief, Judicial Section, Dominion Bureau of Statistics.

FOREWORD

This volume has been long awaited by scholars and by many others, both at home and abroad, who are concerned with the economic, social and political affairs of Canada. The scope of the data and its presentation constitute a major contribution to scholarship in the social sciences. The preparation of the volume was carried out under the joint sponsorship of the Social Science Research Council of Canada and the Canadian Political Science Association. The Social Science Research Council made the initial grant required to start the project.

The two sponsoring bodies appointed a Policy Committee to supervise the planning of the project and to arrange for its financing. The project was an extensive co-operative undertaking. It included the efforts of a large number of individual scholars and experts, and the assistance, both financial and otherwise, of a large number of official and private bodies. This help and participation is specifically acknowledged and described in the preface. On behalf of the Policy Committee and the sponsoring bodies I wish to express our gratitude and satisfaction for the help which was so readily given by so many.

A very special debt of gratitude is due to the editor, Professor M. C. Urquhart, and to the assistant editor, Professor K. A. H. Buckley. Their skill and a substantial part of their time over the past several years have been devoted to the detailed organization and management of this large and complex project. In large measure, the publication of this volume is the result of their indefatigable and invaluable contribution.

JOHN J. DEUTSCH
Chairman, Policy Committee,
Historical Statistics Project

OTTAWA
12 November 1964

PREFACE

The primary, but not the only, object of this volume is to present, in one place, a wide range of statistical time series, along with material describing the series, covering where possible the period from 1867 to 1960. These data are of interest especially to persons doing analytical work in the social sciences, but they should also be of use to a much wider group, indeed, to all who are interested in the quantitative aspects of the social and economic history of Canada.

The text accompanying the tables is an integral part of each section. In addition to giving the sources of the data, it is designed to give a sufficient description of the content of the individual time series that the general user may be able to use them without reference to the basic sources. It also provides a good deal of description of the way in which the data have originated and have been processed. These descriptions along with, in many instances, more direct evaluation of individual series provide some basis on which to judge the reliability of the data.

The Data

Nearly all the data have appeared elsewhere before. They are covered here for three reasons. First, data ranging as broadly as those given here are not commonly found in one document. Secondly, the data for the various parts of even one statistical time series usually must be obtained from more than one publication: in some cases the data for individual years are available only in a series of annual or periodic reports each of which provides information for a single year or perhaps for two or three years; in other cases one report may carry the data for several years out of the whole period covered, but it is still necessary to consult several reports to complete the whole span of the series. Further, data of one report have sometimes been revised in later publications, and one not familiar with the sources might be led into using an obsolete series for lack of knowledge of the revised one; in addition, owing to misprints, there may be conflicts of data given in one number of a series of reports with those in other numbers. Thirdly, a number of the series or parts of them came from documents that are now rare, and a special effort has been made to present the data from such sources.

Owing to limitations of space the data are predominantly, though not invariably, for aggregates that are broad with respect both to the subject matter covered and to the detail given by regions. In the latter regard, national aggregates predominate; but a considerable amount of material is given either for the five regions commonly used in presentation of Canadian data—the Atlantic Provinces, Quebec, Ontario, the Prairie Provinces, British Columbia—or for individual provinces; and in rarer instances, as in the fisheries or in water transport, a somewhat different regional breakdown is used as required by the nature of the operations which the data cover.

Most of the data are from published sources of which public documents form the greatest part, though a considerable amount of material has also been obtained from privately prepared data. The limited amount of unpublished material used is, in the main, from government sources and particularly from the Dominion Bureau of Statistics: only a very small amount of material is from private, unpublished sources.

The specialized worker may require the data in more detail than can be given here, or may wish more information on the nature of the data than could be given in this volume, and recourse to the original sources of these series or to other sources of related material may be necessary. The source references given here should be a useful starting-point for the specialist in his further inquiries. In all cases the specific sources used have been cited and, when feasible, the specific page number in the source is given.

Unfortunately, in some cases, and especially when the data are based upon individual volumes of a long series of annual reports, citations of each individual document and page would have taken more space than could be devoted to them; even in these cases, however, the specific series of documents used are properly cited.

The statistical data of this volume are almost invariably as given in the source document, and no attempt has been made to prepare derived series having greater continuity than that provided by the data of the sources. For example, if in the source material one series overlaps in time with another that covers approximately the same phenomena, the data have not been linked to present a continuous series unless this has already been done in the source. Rather, if possible, a period of overlap is given for the two series and the reader may use his own judgement about how best to link them.

With the exception of a few statistics of colonial times, the aim was to cover the period from Confederation in 1867 to 1960. Many series, of course, do not go back as far as 1867 and a number of series end before 1960. Generally, series that began later than the end of the Second World War are not included since they are ordinarily readily available, frequently in their entirety, in one volume.

The greater number of the series contain annual data with, however, some notable exceptions: data obtained from the decennial census are for every tenth year; a limited amount of data is available for each fifth year from quinquennial censuses; some data, such as election results, from their very nature appear irregularly; in a few cases averages for a number of years are given; and to conserve space some series in the section on education are given for every fifth year.

Format

The planning of this volume was helped by the availability of its counterparts for the United States: United States Bureau of the Census, *Historical Statistics of the United States, Colonial Times to 1957* (Washington D.C., U.S. Government Printing Office, 1960), and its predecessor published in 1949. The format is similar. The material is presented in twenty-one sections, each devoted to a single field; the fields covered are given in the Table of Contents. Within each section a descriptive text gives the sources of the data, describes their attributes and in many of the sections tells in general terms of the way in which they were originally derived. The text is followed by the statistical tables. In these tables each series may be identified by an initial letter which denotes the section in which it falls, and then by a series number, the series being numbered consecutively beginning with Series 1 in each section.

Several other features of the format require attention. First, near the beginning of each section a bibliography of the published sources of data is given with the detail necessary to permit one to find the source in a library card catalogue. Within each section, later and more specific reference to sources is given in an abbreviated form, but the reader may obtain the information necessary for finding the source documents by referring to the earlier bibliography. References to other publications than those used as sources for the statistical data are given in full detail at the place where reference to them is first made.

Secondly, the empty cells in the statistical tables have various meanings. They may mean that the data are not available, that the entries are zero, or that the quantities were so small that when the data were rounded to thousands, millions, or other magnitudes these particular entries were rounded to zero. It is expected that the user will ordinarily be able to tell from adjacent entries what empty cells mean. In instances where the meaning of an empty cell is not readily discernible from such adjacent data it is explained in the text.

Thirdly, the footnotes to the tables are ordinarily used to indicate characteristics of the data for particular years within a series or a group of series. If an attribute applies to a series throughout its length the appropriate note is given in the descriptive text.

Fourthly, the assignment of series to particular sections was in some degree arbitrary; several of the series are related to the material of two or more sections. The practice followed was to assign the series to the section to which it seemed most closely related. Some cross-references to related material in other sections are made in the text of the various sections. But the most comprehensive cross-referencing is done in the index.

Finally, some data are given in appendices to various of the sections. In many instances the data in the appendices are of a lower order of reliability than those of the preceding tables of their respective sections; in some cases they give data for the colonial period; in others they came from private but unpublished sources.

Genesis of the Volume

The project of which this volume is the end result had its origins in a recommendation of the Committee on Statistics of the Canadian Political Science Association. The establishment of this Committee had been authorized in June 1958 to examine what action, if any, might be taken to help the user of statistics in the social sciences for purposes of scholarly research. The Committee held its first meeting in the late summer of 1958, at which time it was decided to examine the availability of data for a volume of historical statistics. K. A. H. Buckley was asked to report on the matter at a subsequent meeting. After Committee study of a favourable report by Buckley, M. C. Urquhart was asked to explore the possibility of finding enough people willing to participate in the project to ensure that it could be carried out, and to explore the possibilities of obtaining material support for it. Following on his report that the project seemed feasible on both grounds, a recommendation of the Committee to the Association that it sponsor the project along with the Social Science Research Council of Canada was approved by both bodies in June 1959. The Social Science Research Council made a grant for initiating the project, and additional support both in cash and in kind was obtained from various bodies denoted below.

Organization and Procedures

A Policy Committee was appointed to assume ultimate responsibility for the project on behalf of the sponsoring bodies, to review and approve the operating plans of the project, to approve its budget and to plan its financing. This Committee consisted of J. J. Deutsch (Chairman), E. F. Beach, S. D. Clark, M. C. Urquhart and K. A. H. Buckley. The active management of the project was carried out by the editor, M. C. Urquhart, with the help of K. A. H. Buckley, the assistant editor. In addition to attending to the details of organizing the project and taking the initial steps in arranging support for the project, it was their responsibility to see that the posts of section chiefs were filled, that members of panels for each section were appointed and that the subject-matter of the sections was collated to assure a balanced presentation within the framework of the whole volume, as well as to do the final editing.

The material of the volume is the product of the co-operative effort of many interested persons with specialized competence in the particular subjects covered. For each of the twenty-one sections of subject-matter a section chief assumed the responsibility. Each section chief had an advisory panel to advise in the selection of the time series to be included in his section. Typically, he had an assistant for at least three months, or the equivalent in other forms of assistance. In addition to selecting the relevant data with the aid of his panel and presenting them in tabular form, the section chief prepared a descriptive text for his section.

Collation of the material in the various sections came at two stages. First, after the section chiefs had prepared the initial lists of the material that they proposed for their sections the editors collated all the proposals, in order to avoid duplication, on the one hand, and to suggest material that might be added since it was not appearing elsewhere, on the other hand. Secondly, much of the work of the final editing had the same objectives. In addition, section chiefs and editors maintained close contact throughout the preparation of the material.

The first stages of selection of series and the initial collation by the editors were done during the winter of 1959–60. The most active period of work by the section chiefs and their assistants was during the summer of 1960 when most of the preparation of the tables and work on the text was done. Some of the sections reached the editors' hands in 1960 and nearly all were in during 1961. The work of the editors proceeded throughout and was completed by early 1963.

There are some regrettable shortcomings in this book. Despite the limitations of space, some additional series might well have been prepared had resources permitted. In the main, they are of the kind that require the preparation of data year by year from annual reports. And, though a considerable amount of such work has been done for this volume, it was not possible to do more. In addition, there are, no doubt, some oversights of apparently obvious material. These shortcomings exist in part because editors and section chiefs worked on a part-time basis, carrying the work with their regular appointments at the same time. There was no person employed full-time throughout the life of the project.

Financial Support and Other Acknowledgements

The project received financial and other support, which is gratefully acknowledged, from a wide number of public and private bodies. First, direct financial help was provided by: the Social Science Research Council of Canada; The Canada Council; the Central Mortgage and Housing Corporation in its administration of research funds provided by the National Housing Act; the Bank of Canada; the Canadian Bankers' Association. Secondly, a number of posts, each of three months' duration, were made available in the summer of 1960 for the support of section chiefs and of their assistants by the following federal departments or agencies: Department of Agriculture; Department of Finance; Department of Labour; Department of National Health and Welfare; Bank of Canada; Dominion Bureau of Statistics. Thirdly, assistance on particular parts of the project through work done by their own personnel was provided by the following federal bodies: Department of Agriculture; Department of Finance; Department of Fisheries; Department of National Health and Welfare; Central Mortgage and Housing Corporation; Dominion Bureau of Statistics. Fourthly, the Bell Telephone Company prepared the data on telephones; an officer of the Department of Transport prepared the data on air transport; and the Post Office Department provided the data on the post office. Fifthly, Queen's University provided a considerable amount of office space and other facilities for the editorial work. Finally, the material prepared by some section chiefs was in part obtained from work they had done on other research projects.

It would be ungracious not to make special mention of the contribution of the Dominion Bureau of Statistics to the project. In addition to the substantial amount of help noted above, many people in the Bureau gave a great deal of assistance in providing material, in serving as panel members, in discussing material with editors and section chiefs, in checking much of the material, in reading manuscripts and proofs, and in many other ways. Without this help the volume would have been much less substantial and accurate. And, of course, a very large part of the data comes from publications of the Dominion Bureau of Statistics.

Mention should also be made of the contributions of those persons who participated directly in the preparation of the material. While section chiefs received modest honoraria they were far from a consideration for the services performed. The time of panel members, in some cases very considerable, and of many other persons in the public service and in private life was also donated to the project.

The editors wish also to make some personal acknowledgements. The help of Mrs M. E. Arrowsmith in their work was well-nigh indispensable; her assiduous care, perceptiveness and judgement, from the time the individual manuscripts were first received from section chiefs until the last of the final manuscript went to the publisher, are responsible for a large part of the merits of the volume as it appears. The advice and encouragement of Mr K. W. Taylor at all stages of the project was greatly appreciated. And there are the debts, too numerous to be mentioned, to those who assisted in checking data, in typing and in proof-reading.

Finally, there are the grateful acknowledgements to publishers and authors of privately prepared material, and to private companies or organizations that provided material directly. Permission to use material identified by specific citation in the body of the volume was kindly granted by the following publishers or organizations:

Bowes and Bowes Publishers, Limited
The Copp Clark Publishing Company, Limited
Harvard University Press
The Macmillan Company of Canada Limited
Princeton University Press
Ryerson Press
Southam-MacLean Publications Limited
University of Toronto Press
Canadian Journal of Economics and Political Science (University of Toronto Press)
Population Studies (Population Investigation Research Centre, London School of Economics)
Canadian Journal of Public Health
Canadian Parliamentary Guide (Pierre Normandin)
Encyclopedia Canadiana (The Grolier Society of Canada Limited)
Canadian Bankers' Association
Canadian Dental Association
Canadian Nurses Association
Canadian Tax Foundation
Carnegie Endowment for International Peace
Dun and Bradstreet of Canada, Limited
International Pacific Halibut Commission
Montreal and Canadian Stock Exchanges
Toronto Stock Exchange
Newsprint Association of Canada

Information was kindly provided by a number of private companies and other organizations, which are identified in the source references in the text.

Grateful acknowledgement is also made to the individual authors of the privately prepared material, whose names appear in source references in the body of the text and who have provided permission for the use of the material.

Responsibility

While the selection and presentation of data were matters of continuous consultation between editors and section chiefs, the editors must assume responsibility for the final form and contents of volume. In the final editing process changes were made in some section material to make it consistent with the general form adopted, and in cases some material was added or deleted to eliminate residual duplications among sections and to fill in obvious gaps.

M. C. URQUHART

SECTION A: POPULATION AND MIGRATION

KENNETH BUCKLEY, *University of Saskatchewan*

The statistics of this section are in four main divisions. Series A1–199 are population statistics from the Census of Canada from 1851 to 1956. Series A200–220 are records of internal migrants and estimates of internal migration of the native-born population from 1871 to 1951 based upon the Census of Canada. Series A221–253 present private and official estimates of inter-provincial migration and net migration from 1851 to 1956. Series A254–347 are statistics of immigration based upon the official records of immigration.

The official published sources of the statistics in this section are:

Dominion Bureau of Statistics, *Census of Canada*, decennial census, 1871 to 1951 (Ottawa, Queen's Printer), prepared by the Dominion Bureau of Statistics for censuses 1921 to 1951, and by the Census Office, in the Department of Agriculture from 1871 to 1912 and in the Department of Trade and Commerce until the Census Office became part of the Dominion Bureau of Statistics in 1918; Dominion Bureau of Statistics, *Census of Canada, 1956* (Ottawa, Queen's Printer) given in *Census Bulletins*; Dominion Bureau of Statistics, *Canada Year Book*, annual since 1905 (Ottawa, Queen's Printer), succeeding the *Statistical Year Book*, annual 1885 to 1904; Department of Citizenship and Immigration, *Annual Report, 1959–60* (Ottawa, Queen's Printer, 1960).

Unpublished data in various department files were also used extensively. Use of reports on immigration appearing at various times in the annual reports of the Departments of Agriculture, of the Interior, of Immigration and Colonization, and of Mines and Resources for the material in the text is designated in the general note on immigration appearing below.

In addition to the official records, private estimates from the following sources were used:

Kenneth Buckley, 'Historical Estimates of Internal Migration', *Canadian Political Science Association, Conference on Statistics, 1960, Papers* (Toronto, University of Toronto Press, 1962), pp. 1–37; Nathan Keyfitz, 'The Growth of Canadian Population', *Population Studies*, vol. IV, no. 1 (June 1950), pp. 47–63; Duncan M. McDougall, 'Immigration into Canada', *Canadian Journal of Economics and Political Science*, vol. 27, no. 2 (May 1961), p. 51.

POPULATION (Series A1–199)

General note

The population statistics in this subsection are from the census of 1956 and from the decennial censuses from 1851 to 1961. The series apply, in the main, to the present geographic areas of the provinces and the country. Exceptions in the areas covered are noted in the following commentaries and in footnotes to the tables, and only the effects of three boundary changes and a change in the areas enumerated are noted at this point. Firstly, Newfoundland is included in the annual data for 1949 to 1961 only and in the census data for 1951, 1956 and 1961 only. Secondly, Alberta and Saskatchewan were enumerated with the Northwest Territories in the censuses of 1871 to 1901; after their establishment as provinces in 1905 they were shown separately and the 1901 census data, but not those of earlier

censuses, were recast to separate the population within the areas of the newly formed provinces. For this reason recorded population of the Northwest Territories shows a substantial drop between the censuses of 1891 and 1901. Thirdly, with the Boundaries Extension Act of 1912 the areas of Ontario, Quebec and Manitoba were substantially increased, though the added areas did not contain large numbers of persons. In the reports of the 1921 census and thereafter the populations given for Ontario, Quebec and Manitoba in 1911 were adjusted to include those living in the areas added by the 1912 extensions, and these adjusted figures are used in the series presented in this section. Of the decline in population of 13,622 shown for the Northwest Territories between the 1901 and 1911 censuses, 11,974 persons are accounted for by the extension of boundaries by the act of 1912. Fourthly, the 'unorganized territories' of Keewatin, Athabaska, Mackenzie and Yukon were enumerated for the first time in the census of 1901 (see *Census, 1901*, vol. I, p. xiii and p. 5). For a list of changes in area of the provinces and country see series K1–2.

The census of population and agriculture has been long established in Canada. The first was taken in 1666. It was followed by 36 censuses during the French regime. After the British occupation in 1759 censuses were taken, although less frequently, until 1824. In that year an annual census was introduced in Upper Canada (Ontario) and continued until the Act of Union in 1841. In the same period five censuses were taken in Lower Canada (Quebec), seven in the Assiniboine and Red River District (Manitoba) and several were taken in the four Atlantic provinces. A complete chronological summary of Canadian censuses and the population recorded by each one and population estimates based upon numerous surveys from 1605 to 1931 may be found in *Census, 1931*, vol. I, pp. 133–53. This is an expansion and revision of the chronology prepared by J. C. Taché which appears in the Introduction, *Census, 1871*, vol. IV. The latter volume also contains summaries of each census included in Taché's chronology.

Census acts were passed by the Province of Canada in 1841 and 1842 which provided for the census of Upper Canada in 1842 and of Lower Canada in 1844. An act of 1851 provided for a census of Canada in January 1852, April 1861 and decennially thereafter. Following Confederation, legislation in 1870 (23 Vic., C. 21) provided for a census in April 1871 of the four federated provinces. The Act was amended in 1871 to extend its application 'to all Territory beyond the four Provinces of Ontario, Quebec, Nova Scotia and New Brunswick, now forming part of the Dominion of Canada...', and amended again in 1879 to provide that '...a Census shall be taken in the year 1881, and then in every tenth year thereafter.' A census of Manitoba and the Territories was undertaken in 1886, of Manitoba in 1896, and of Manitoba, Saskatchewan and Alberta in 1906, 1916, 1926, 1936 and 1946. In 1956 this quinquennial census was not taken, but a more limited census of Canada as a whole was done.

From the outset the decennial census has been carried out under the superintendence of a chief census officer or committee with district commissioners and census enumerators in the field. In late 1851, for example, 83 commissioners were appointed and they, in turn, selected 1,073 enumerators to conduct the census of the Province of Canada. All were furnished with printed instructions and specimen schedules to illustrate procedures (see *Census of Canada, 1851-2*, vols. I-II, p. iii). Under Taché's direction enumeration in 1871 was greatly improved with the appointment of thirteen census officers some months before census field-work began 'to assist in preparation, and afterwards to superintend the work of the Commissioners and Enumerators, each within a group of districts assigned to him'. All field-workers were given a series of oral instruction, the 206 commissioners by the officers, the 2,789 enumerators by the commissioners (see Taché's letter of submittal to the Minister of Agriculture and p. xii, *Census, 1871*, vol. I). This general approach was extended and improved in subsequent decades. The major improvements came after the establishment of a permanent census staff in 1905 (see below). Before that date the entire census staff was newly recruited prior to each census. For an account of the extensive planning for and execution of the contemporary census, see *Census, 1951*, vol. XI.

Initially the census was the responsibility of the Ministry of Agriculture. In 1905 the Census Act of 1871 and its amendments were consolidated with the General Statistics Act (R.S. Canada, 1886, C. 59) and provision was made for the establishment of a permanent Census and Statistics Office of Canada. In 1912 this agency was transferred to the Ministry of Trade and Commerce. Later it became part of the Dominion Bureau of Statistics, created in 1918 by an act effecting a complete consolidation of existing statistical legislation (8-9 Geo. V, C. 43: short title, The Statistics Act).

The census of Canada has always been taken on the *de jure* principle whereby each person is enumerated as belonging to the locality in which he or she regularly lives. This principle is consistent with the fundamental legal reason for the census, which is to determine decennially the representation of each province in the federal House of Commons. Since 1911 the census has been taken on a day in June, usually on or near 1 June. Before 1911 the census was taken in March or April on a date close to 1 April of the census year. For detailed descriptions of the history, procedures, scope and uses of the census see *Administrative Report* by the Dominion Statistician, *Census, 1951*, vol. XI and, same title, *Census, 1931*, vol. I, pp. 29-96.

It is not possible to comment in a general way upon the accuracy of the successive censuses, although anomalies and inconsistencies have been pointed out over the past century. The censuses of 1851 and 1861 are not full enumerations and D.B.S. suggests that the underenumeration is about 100,000. This guess is discussed in the note to series A2-14 below. The census of 1851 was taken with greater care in Lower Canada than in Upper Canada 'where, unfortunately, many of the Enumerators proved themselves wholly unfit...the negligence and ignorance displayed...has added materially to the labours of the Office [of Registration and Statistics]...'. The introduction refers to '...a very general feeling...that the census had...reference to taxation....Enumerators were frequently received most ungraciously, and the information sought was, not only partially, but, in some cases, altogether withheld'. (*Census, 1851-2*, vols. I-II, p. iv.) However, the census of agriculture suffered more than the census of population from this cause (*ibid.*, p. vi).

The census of 1861 was the subject of an able and critical study by John Langton. Langton, who had been Auditor in the Province of Canada and became the Deputy Minister of Finance following Confederation, delivered a paper to the Literary and Historical Society of Quebec, March 1864, on his findings (see the Society's *Transactions*, 1863-4, New Series, no. 2 (Quebec, 1864), pp. 105-24). His criticism was levelled less at the enumeration than at the work of the clerical staff which he checked. He read the paper '...partly with the objective of showing what results may be considered as at least approximately correct, and partly to warn others from wasting as much time as I have done on those parts which can do nothing but mislead' (p. 105). He states: 'I do not think that there is any reason to doubt the numbers living, the proportion of males and females, and of married and single very nearly representing the true state of the population; and the ages, would, probably, be not very far wrong, though there is much more doubt upon this subject' (p. 106). The bulk of his paper is devoted to a demonstration of the imperfection of the data on vital statistics. He concludes that: 'It is hardly possible to expect any much better result to follow from the returns of enumerators, who have had no experience in the work expected of them, and from submitting their schedules to a body of extra clerks, called in for the occasion, who appear to have worked without concert, and almost without supervision' (p. 121).

Taché introduced the procedure of instructing and supervising the field staff but his and each following census have had their critics who, it was assumed, were for the most part wrong. (See, for example, the long reply to critics in *Census, 1881*, vol. IV, pp. xii-xxvi and, for a more recent example, the remarks of the Dominion Statistician, *Census, 1931*, vol. I, p. 54.)

The attack upon the census of 1891 by the Liberal opposition was particularly bitter and, while certainly partisan, did have some degree of substance. The charges are summarized by Sir Richard Cartwright in his *Reminiscences* (Toronto, 1912), pp. 325-9. Although the rule was introduced in that census that persons out of the country more than twelve months should not be counted as residents, *de jure* (*Census, 1891*, vol. I, p. x), it was charged that many emigrants were counted. Later, 'when we [the Liberals] took the census in 1901 I caused this matter to be investigated, with the result that we found that in twenty constituencies in Quebec the census enumerators in 1891 had reported some forty thousand more people than the clergy had been able to discover the January previous'. Assuming that the clergy were accurate and that this sample was representative, Cartwright estimated a possible overenumeration of 250 to 300 thousand persons in central and eastern Canada. However, in the nature of the case, this kind of criticism is unconvincing. That the number of industrial establishments was inflated in 1891 can be demonstrated on the basis of internal evidence in successive censuses of industry. (Other totals in the census of industry are probably not much affected by this overenumeration.) But paying enumerators on the basis of numbers of establishments reported, as in 1891, might, by itself, explain the bias without the support of Cartwright's charges of a Conservative conspiracy.

In general, censuses fall short of their goal of complete enumeration. Extensive training of enumerators will reduce inconsistencies and discrepancies. The size of the errors, unlike sampling errors, cannot be determined by an analysis of the census data themselves. The probable size of discrepancies and also the inconsistencies may be determined by comparisons with independent estimates of the same magnitudes. An exposition of the comparative checks made for a contemporary census appears in *Census, 1951*, vol. XI, pp. 79-93. The agency employed to make these checks is the Canadian Labour Force Survey. While the checks are far from exhaustive, the analysis of the results illustrates the problems of all censuses, and indicates the degree of accuracy to be expected in the census of recent times.

A1. Estimated population of Canada, 1867 to 1961

SOURCE: for 1867 to 1951, *Census, 1951*, vol. X, appendix A, p. 4; for 1952 to 1956, *Canada Year Book, 1959*, p. 162; for 1957 to 1961, D.B.S., Census Division, Analysis Section. The figure for 1961 is the final census figure and the figures for 1957 to 1960 are the final revised figures prepared after the 1961 census figure was available.

The estimates of the population of Canada for intercensal years since 1867 are derived by two methods: one method for the period 1867 to 1931, another for the period since 1932.

The methods of estimation for the earlier period involved three steps. A graduated annual population series for each decade from 1841 to 1931 was obtained by fitting smooth curves to successive sets of three decennial census figures of total population, that is, population at the beginning and end of the decade in question and at the date of the following decennial census. Then an estimate of the primary trend of population was obtained by running a logistic curve through the graduated annual series. This was assumed to yield a series of annual 'normal increases'. Fluctuations in these increases were introduced to achieve the final intercensal estimates. 'The controls for the fluctuations taken were: (1) the immigrant arrivals up to June 1 of the year calculated; (2) the arrivals of the second year preceding, and (3) the average yearly arrivals of the third to seventh years preceding the year calculated' (*Census, 1951*, vol. X, appendix A, p. 3).

The last two steps in this method of interpolation are supported by the following argument: 'Reason as well as observation showed that the yearly fluctuations were largely, if not wholly, due to immigration and emigration (natural increase alone would tend to produce smooth yearly increases). It was also observed that the immigrant arrivals during the two years immediately preceding the census years were more largely represented in the increase in the immigrant population during the decade than the arrivals of the remaining eight years' (*Census, 1951*, vol. X, appendix A, p. 3). The final two steps were employed 'to obtain adequate weights for these considerations...'.

The estimates for the period 1867 to 1931 were made by M. C. MacLean and were published for the first time along with a note on the method in *Canada Year Book, 1932*, pp. 108–10. The 'normal' population series based upon two logistic cycles, before and after 1891, may be found in the same source. A slightly condensed version of the methodological note has appeared in subsequent censuses.

MacLean subscribed to a Pearl and Reed type logistic theory of population growth which he developed at length in 'The Growth of Population in Canada', *Census of Canada, 1931*, vol. I, pp. 99–132. He also subscribed to the so-called displacement theory of immigration stating, for example, that it '...is remarkable that a negative weight was obtained for number (3) [the third control cited above], confirming the belief that where the population was increasing faster than normal the excess was thrown out within a short period' (*Canada Year Book, 1932*, p. 109).

The logistic theory and the displacement theory have been severely criticized. For a summary of criticism unfavourable to the former and citations of the relevant bibliography, see 'History of Population Theories' by the Population Division, United Nations, in J. J. Spengler and P. D. Duncan, editors, *Population Theory and Policy* (Glencoe, 1956), pp. 30–2, 52–3. With respect to the shortcomings of the displacement theory, see Mabel Timlin, *Does Canada Need More People?* (Toronto, 1951). Also, the assumption that 'natural increase alone would tend to produce smooth yearly increases' (*Canada Year Book, 1932*, p. 109) from 1867 to 1931 is questionable. Both births and

deaths may have been subject to long swings of the type established by Simon Kuznets in the United States ('Long Swings in the Growth of Population and in Related Economic Variables', *Proceedings of the American Philosophical Society*, February 1958, 102, no. 1, pp. 25–52), and which are also clearly evident in the flow of births of the Roman Catholic population of Quebec (see Kenneth Buckley, 'The Role of Staple Industries in Canada's Economic Development', *Journal of Economic History*, vol. XVII, December 1958, p. 449). The reliability of the movement of the annual interpolations must remain in doubt until further research has established more firmly the probable levels of births, deaths and emigration in the period prior to 1931. In addition there is the problem of the uncertainty of variation in the degree of underenumeration in the successive census benchmarks, which has not been systematically investigated.

The annual series from 1932 to the present is on much firmer ground. 'Estimates are constructed for the total population of Canada and the provinces and are available shortly after the date to which they apply, June 1, of each year. As final figures on the components of population change are not ready at that date, the number of births, deaths and immigration are partly filled in by extrapolation...' (*Census, 1951*, vol. X, appendix A, p. 1). Working forward from the last census, annual births and immigration are added, deaths and emigration subtracted. Any errors in previous extrapolations, which may become evident as final figures on births, deaths, etc., become available, are compensated for in current extrapolations to avoid a cumulative error. The earlier estimates are not themselves revised until the subsequent census year, at which time final estimates for the intercensal decade are prepared. A major weakness in the estimates is the lack of a comprehensive record of annual emigration. Canada does not record emigration. The statistics of emigration are based upon immigrants to United States and the United Kingdom reporting Canada as the country of last permanent residence (see *Canada Year Book, 1961*, p. 165). An allowance is made for emigration to other countries (see below, p. 9).

In addition to the extrapolations described above, which are only corrected at census dates, the Dominion Bureau of Statistics also publishes a statement of the annual population and the components of population change in which the previous estimates for each year since the last census are revised on the basis of the latest information available (see, for example, *Canada Year Book, 1957–58*, p. 118). Since this statement is based upon the latest figures available at the time of publication, it is the better source of year to year changes in population.

Annual estimates of provincial populations since 1867 and a description of the method used to obtain them may also be found in the sources listed at the beginning of this note.

One discrepancy appears in the source used and in all other sources of this series. Population in 1931 rounded to the nearest thousand is always shown as 10,376. The population in 1931 was 10,376,786 (see series A2).

A2–14. Population of Canada by province, census dates, 1851 to 1961

SOURCE: for 1851 to 1951, *Census, 1951*, vol. X, table 1, p. 11; for 1956, vol. I, table 1, p. 1-1; for 1961, D.B.S., Census Division, Analysis Section; also see *Census, 1941*, vol. I, table 1, p. 5.

Apart from Newfoundland, which is not included in the table prior to 1951, and the qualifications noted in the general note to series A1–199 the figures apply to the present area of Canada. The population of Newfoundland and other data from the eleven censuses taken by the Newfoundland government from 1836 to 1945 may be found in *Canada Year Book, 1950*, pp. 171–5.

With respect to the consistency of the individual series, two issues deserve comment. One is the extent of the under-enumeration of the population in the western territories in the earlier censuses, which is discussed below. The other is differential enumeration in subsequent censuses about which little of use can be said. Evidence of differential underenumeration can be demonstrated for certain classifications. Keyfitz, for example, emphasizes the problem and especially the under-enumeration of children 0–4 in the earlier censuses ('The Growth of Canadian Population', p. 62). In censuses since 1921 the apparent decennial survival ratios of the age 0–4 group of native-born children consistently exceed unity, suggesting that underenumeration of that class may still be characteristic of the census. It may also reflect an exaggeration of the 5–9 age group through a consistent reporting of four-year-olds as five. Other illustrations could be cited, but, at the present stage of population research in Canada, no general conclusions can be made on possible variations in the degree of underenumeration in the successive censuses.

The figures in series A2–14 were taken from the 1951 and 1956 census volumes. The same figures to 1941 are shown in *Census, 1941*, vol. 1, table 1, p. 5 with the following note: 'Manitoba, British Columbia and the Northwest Territories were only partially covered in 1851 and 1861. It is probable that these areas contained 100,000 persons including Indians in these two decades who are not included in the figures shown.' The figures shown are as follows:

Year	Manitoba	British Columbia	Territories	Total
1871	25,228	36,247	48,000	109,475
1861	—	51,524	6,691	58,215
1851	—	55,000	5,700	60,700

The footnote apparently means that we should add about 100,000 to the totals shown for 1851 and 1861 to get an approximation of decennial changes from 1851 and 1871; but the decline from 158,000 in 1861 (if it is accepted that the underenumeration was 100,000 persons) to 109,000 in 1871 rules out that interpretation unless there was also a very large underenumeration in 1871, which is unlikely. Another interpretation implies that the figures exclude a large number of Indians. For example, Keyfitz states: 'There is a suspicion...that the official figures for 1851 and 1861 may be short as much as 100,000, largely through an undercount of aborigines' (Keyfitz, p. 47 n.). One needs only to consult the sources of the official figures to question seriously this interpretation because the figures are based largely upon estimates of the Indian population and the totals are not far below the only reasonably firm benchmark estimate that we have, namely the estimates of the Indian population made by J. C. Taché which he published in the Introduction, *Census, 1871*, vol. IV, pp. lxii–lxxxiv.

The Indian population of provinces east of Manitoba was enumerated by the *Census, 1871*. Taché, using the sources available, estimated the western Indian population at 79,000. As a result of a limited enumeration in 1881, his estimate for British Columbia was raised by 2,661 (*Census, 1881*, vol. IV, p. 132) which, along with other population of 27,814 in 1871, yields the total of 109,475 still shown for 1871.

Taché's estimate appears reasonable. Adding the Indians enumerated in the east in 1871, he obtained a total of 102,358. With a more complete enumeration in 1881 and filling the gaps with Taché's estimates, Indians totalled 108,547. Of this total, 34,000 were based upon Taché's 1871 estimates and the procedure was justified by a comparison of sub-districts estimated in 1871 and enumerated in 1881 (*Census, 1881*, vol. 1, p. xiv). In 1901, when a major effort was made to enumerate the un-

organized territories (*Census, 1901*, vol. 1, p. xiii), 93,460 Indians and 34,481 Métis were enumerated. With respect to the Indian population before 1871, Taché examined and discussed at some length (*Census, 1871*, vol. IV, pp. xxiv ff.) estimates made by the Hudson's Bay Company for the year 1857 and found these consistent with his own results.

Taché's estimate of the Indian population living west of Ontario in 1871 plus the 2,661 mentioned above is 81,661. The 55,000 shown for British Columbia in 1851 is an estimate of the Indian population made in that year (*Census, 1931*, vol. 1, p. 150). The 5,700 shown for the Territories in 1851 appears to be an interpolation of two censuses of Assiniboine and Red River District which recorded 5,391 persons in 1849 and 6,691 in 1861 (*ibid.*, pp. 150–1 and *Census, 1871*, vol. IV, p. 175, pp. 242–4). In the 1856 census approximately 80 per cent of the heads of families were reported as native-born. One may assume that most of these were Métis and that several hundred were Indians (*Census, 1871*, vol. IV, p. lxxxiv).

The figure shown for the Territories in 1861 is the total of the 1856 census of Assiniboine and Red River given above. The 51,524 shown for British Columbia in 1861 is the sum of three estimates: an Indian population of 37,900 in 1861, and estimates by Governor Douglas of the population of Vancouver Island in 1861 of 3,024 and of the mainland in 1858 of 10,600. The last two estimates exclude Indians.

Following news of gold discoveries on the Fraser in 1856 the population increased sharply to between 25,000 and 30,000 by August 1859. It has been estimated that there were 17,000 persons excluding Indians in the area in 1859 and that by 1861 the total had fallen to 5,000 (Easterbrook and Aitken, *Canadian Economic History* (Toronto, 1956), pp. 335–7).

Turning to the figures shown for 1871, we find the following components in each area: in Manitoba, 13,000 Indians, other population 12,228; in British Columbia, 25,661 Indians and 10,586 other population; in the Territories, 43,000 Indians and 5,000 others. The estimate of British Columbia Indians is based largely upon Taché's work. Another estimate of 29,375, *Census, 1931*, vol. 1, p. 151, was not incorporated in the census of Canada. The 'other' populations in British Columbia and Manitoba were enumerated; the remainder of the total was estimated. Grouping the figures for western areas and including Métis with the population of other origin we get the following results:

Year	Indian	Other population	Total
1871	81,661	27,814	109,475
1861	43,500	14,715	58,215
1851	55,000	5,700	60,700

With respect to Indian population, it appears that a guess of an undercount of 30,000 in 1851 and 40,000 in 1861 would be closer to the truth than the additions implied by the 100,000 suggested in the census of 1941, even with a liberal allowance for the underenumeration of other population. The difference is not large relative to the total population of Canada at the time. It is important, however, when the issue is one of decennial changes in Canada's population from 1851 to 1871.

Eskimoes were not enumerated in the early censuses. The series entitled Native Indians and Eskimoes (series A109) until 1911 is the same as reported by the Indian Affairs Branch for Indians alone. Thereafter the coverage of Eskimoes increased from about 3,000 to the 11,000 reported in 1956 by the Department of Northern Affairs and National Resources (see *Canada Year Book, 1957–8*, p. 149 ff.).

A 15–19. Population, rural and urban, census dates, 1871 to 1956

SOURCE: for 1871 to 1951, basis 1941 definition, *Census, 1951*, vol. I, table 13; for 1901 to 1956, basis 1956 definition, *1956 Census Bulletin*, 3–2, table I, pp. 2–26.

Three definitions of urban and rural population have been used in the censuses of Canada. Two of these are relevant to this table; all three are used in series A 25–27.

In 1941 and in all earlier censuses, the population living in all incorporated cities, towns and villages, of any size, was counted as urban. The rest of the population was rural. Owing to differences among the provinces in the laws governing incorporation, and also because some large and essentially urban populations, especially parts of the metropolitan areas, were not incorporated and therefore classified as rural until 1941, the definition of urban was altered in 1951. Figures based upon the 1941 definition are presented because they provide the longest available historical series.

In the 1951 census all places of 1,000 population and over, whether incorporated or not, were defined as urban, plus the population living in the fringe areas of fourteen cities defined as metropolitan areas for census purposes (see *Census, 1951*, vol. I, appendix A, p. 4 and pp. 15–28). This change in definition resulted in a net increase of 687,000 in the population classified as urban in 1951: an increase of 851,130 persons in metropolitan fringe areas that were not incorporated, an increase of 265,584 persons in other unincorporated places of over 1,000 population and a decrease of 429,683 persons living in incorporated places of less than 1,000 population (see *Census, 1951*, vol. x, pp. 33–5). A rural series based upon the 1951 definition appears in series A 25–27 because it provides the longest available census series distributing the rural population between farm and nonfarm.

The 1956 census extended the definition of urban to include the population in the unincorporated fringe of 'other major areas'. These are areas in which the largest incorporated unit has a population in excess of 25,000. Also, fringe areas of metropolitan areas were redefined to include the whole of most surrounding municipalities instead of only part. This new definition had the effect of raising further the total defined as urban in 1951, as compared with the 1941 definition, by 244,721, of whom 153,993 were in other major urban areas.

It is pointed out in a footnote to series A 16–17 that for these series only 1951 is strictly comparable to 1956. In 1941 the urban figure given in the table does not include the population of the unincorporated suburbs of 'other major urban areas'. The figure is therefore possibly 2 per cent lower than it would be if the 1956 definition were followed precisely. The figures from 1901 to 1931 have also been adjusted to conform with the 1956 definition but less completely than in 1941. The following adjustments were made: the population of incorporated centres of less than 1,000 was excluded; some part of the 'urban fringes' surrounding larger cities later defined as parts of the census metropolitan areas was included. However, no addition was made for population living in unincorporated places in excess of 1,000 persons from 1901 to 1931. For further comment, see *1956 Census Bulletin*, 3–2, pp. 2–5.

Sources for the rural-urban breakdown on the 1951 definition of urban are as follows:

for 1956, *1956 Census Bulletin*, 1–7, inside front cover; for 1951, *Census, 1951*, vol. I, table 13; for 1941, *Census, 1951*, vol. x, table VI, p. 40.

A sex breakdown of the urban and rural populations is available back to 1871 on the 1941 definition. On the 1951 and 1956 definitions there are sex breakdowns only for single census years. See series A 44–59 for urban-rural by age and sex, 1921 to 1956.

A 20–24. Population in incorporated centres of 1,000 persons and over, by size groups, census dates, 1871 to 1956

SOURCE: for places 5,000 and over in 1871 and 1881, *Census, 1921*, vol. I, table 12; for 1891, *Census, 1951*, vol. x, table IV, p. 37; for 1901 to 1956, *1956 Census Bulletin*, 3–2, table 2, pp. 2–27. See also *Census, 1941*, vol. I, table 7, pp. 583–91.

Additions for centres from 1,000 to 4,999 (footnote 3) in 1871 and 1881 were made on the basis of data in the 1921 census table cited above which provides an historical series of the populations of all cities, towns and villages having a population of 1,000 or over in 1921. The 1881 census table cited above shows the populations in 1871 and 1881 of centres 5,000 and over in 1881. These were classified into three size groups and added to obtain the totals shown in the table. It is assumed that it is unlikely that any centre of 5,000 or more in 1871 declined below 5,000 by 1881.

It was pointed out in the note to series A 15–19 that the 1941 definition of urban covered all incorporated centres. Consequently the difference between series A 18 and series A 20 is a measure of incorporated centres of less than 1,000 population. Volume x, table IV, p. 37 of the 1951 *Census* supplies figures for these centres from 1891 to 1951. However, that table does not include Yukon, Northwest Territories or Newfoundland in its coverage.

A 25–27. Rural population, farm and nonfarm, census dates, 1931 to 1956

SOURCE: for figures based upon the 1941 definition, *Census, 1951*, vol. x, table IX, p. 46; for 1951 definition, *Census, 1951*, vol. x, table VIII, p. 45; for 1956 definition, *1956 Census Bulletin*, 3–2, table XI, pp. 2–21.

Total rural on the basis of the 1956 definition, series A 25, is the same as series A 17. See note to series A 15–19 for the three definitions of rural and urban used by the census.

The farm and rural nonfarm populations are available in three censuses with one modification of the 1951 definition of rural. On that definition unincorporated centres of 1,000 or over are classified as urban. However, they were classified as rural in 1931 and 1941 and cannot be segregated. They are therefore included in the 1951 total of 'rural nonfarm' in the table to make the three figures conceptually comparable.

A farm-nonfarm breakdown for 1951 and 1956 on the 1951 definition, including Newfoundland, Yukon and Northwest Territories, may be obtained in *1956 Census Bulletin*, 1–7, inside cover, and *Census, 1951*, vol. I, table 15; and for 1941 and 1951 almost the same in *Census, 1951*, vol. x, table 6. The series appearing in this volume have the advantage that they can be projected back to 1931. See also the note to series A 15–19.

Total rural, basis the 1941 definition, series A 25, does not agree with rural totals in series A 19 because the former does not include Yukon, Northwest Territories and Newfoundland.

Estimates of farm and rural nonfarm population for selected years, 1920 to 1951, may be found in O. J. Firestone, *Canada's Economic Development 1867–1953* (London, 1958), p. 60.

A 28–43. Population, by age and sex, census dates, 1851 to 1956

SOURCE: for 1851 to 1871, Nathan Keyfitz, 'The Growth of Canadian Population', table 3, p. 50; for 1881 and 1891, *Census, 1941*, vol. I, table 12; for 1901 to 1951, *Census, 1951*, vol. I, table 19; for 1956, *1956 Census Bulletin*, 1–9, table 16.

The totals from 1851 to 1956 agree with the total populations shown in series A2–14. The note to the latter table should be consulted with respect to the question of coverage.

Persons whose ages were not stated have been assigned to various age groups by two methods. Prior to 1941 the total 'age not stated' in each census was prorated on the basis of the distribution of the remaining population. See *Census, 1931*, vol. I, table 8, p. 387, for the numbers so distributed from 1851 to 1931 and pp. 197–8 for a discussion of some of their attributes. Beginning with the 1941 census the method used to distribute 'age not stated' has been much more precise. The unstated ages were assigned before any tabulations were made on the basis of all other relevant information available in the census schedules. See 'Unstated Ages', *Census, 1941*, vol. I, pp. 120–7. The same section also deals with the question of accuracy of reporting age in 1941 and in previous censuses. The totals of 'age not stated' in each census from 1881 to 1941 are also shown (*ibid.*, p. 120).

All figures in series A28–43 have been rounded to the nearest thousand. As a result the components do not always add precisely to the totals shown.

A44–59. Population, by age and sex, urban and rural, census dates, 1921 to 1956

SOURCE: *Census, 1921*, vol. II, table 7; *Census, 1931*, vol. III, table 1; *Census, 1941*, vol. II, table 21; *Census, 1951*, vol. I, table 21; *1956 Census Bulletin*, 1–9, table 17.

Footnotes to the series A44–59 indicate the definitions of urban and rural employed. See the note to series A15–19 for these definitions.

With a few exceptions due to rounding, totals in series A44 agree with totals in series A15–19 and A28.

In 1921 and 1931, persons whose ages were not stated have been distributed by age (see note to series A28–43) and by rural and urban. In rounding, series A45–59 do not add across to totals given in series A44 in 1921 and 1931. The numbers of 'age not stated' *before* rounding were as follows: in 1921, urban male, 5,536, female, 5,095; rural male, 6,052, female, 4,579; in 1931, urban male, 1,725, female, 691; rural male, 986, female, 369.

A60–74. Population, by marital status and sex, census dates, 1871 to 1956

SOURCE: for population, all ages, *Census, 1941*, vol. I, table 18; for population 15 years and over for 1891 to 1931, *Census, 1941*, vol. I, table 20; for 1941 and 1951, *Census, 1951*, vol. X, table 17; for 1956, *1956 Census Bulletin*, 1–12, table 28.

The table shows marital status of the population 15 years of age and over for census years from 1891 to 1956 with the exception of 1901 when the classification by age was not available. To fill this gap and provide an overlap with 1891 the marital status of the whole population is shown from 1871 to 1901. In each census year persons whose marital status is not stated have been assigned to the various categories by supplementary information in 1951 and 1956 and by simple proration in all prior censuses with the single exception noted in footnote 3 of the table.

With two exceptions, the 'married' cover all married, whether or not they are living together. In 1911 and 1921 the 'permanently separated' were included with the 'divorced'.

A75–113. Origins of the population, census dates, 1871 to 1951

SOURCE: for 1871 to 1921, *Canada Year Book, 1948–49*, p. 154; for 1931 to 1951, *Canada Year Book, 1957–58*, p. 137.

In each census since Confederation an attempt has been made to establish the origin of the population. Until 1951 the term 'racial origin' was used. Actually the concept has been a mixture of biological, cultural and geographic attributes. At each census from 1871 to 1941 with the exception of 1891, when the question on origin was limited to French and 'other', fairly stable rules were followed in the enumeration. Indian, Eskimo, Negro, Chinese, Japanese and East Indian were distinguished by colour. For those of European descent the classification was essentially cultural and geographic. The distinction among Ukrainian, Polish and Russian was a combination of language and geography. For Jews the criterion was primarily religion.

For persons of mixed derivation, in the case of those of European descent, the line is through the father. For Indians and in 'the case of the black or yellow races, persons deriving through either parent are so named' (*Census, 1931*, vol. I, p. 45). The term 'half-breed' appears in the censuses of 1871, 1901 and 1941. Series A109, Indians and Eskimoes, includes two so recorded in the five eastern provinces in 1871 and 34,481 recorded in 1901 (see *Canada Year Book, 1932*, p. 938). In 1941, 35,416 persons of mixed Indian and European descent are included with 'other', series A111.

A revised concept of origin was introduced in the 1951 census in the attempt to continue '...to distinguish groups in the population having similar cultural characteristics, based on a common heritage...' and despite the fact that '...the value of the census inquiry on origin...has often been debated' (*Census, 1951*, vol. X, pp. 131–2). The statement also adds '...there is no doubt that the accuracy of the origin inquiry varies somewhat inversely to the number of generations which a person must go back for the time period in which his ancestors came to this continent. Intermarriage between different ethnic groups and the gradual assimilation of immigrants add to the problem of many persons in reporting their origin...' (*ibid.*, p. 133).

A major change in 1951 was to extend the rule governing mixed origins for the European population to all others. All Indians living on reserves were recorded as 'Native Indians'. Others who were in part Indian, Negro, Chinese, Japanese, etc., were assigned an origin determined by tracing the descent through the father's lineage. In addition a new category of 'unknown origin' was established. Moreover, anyone who insisted that his origin was 'Canadian' or 'American' was recorded as such. 71,759 'unknown' and 14,152 Americans are included among 'other', series A111 in 1951.

For a more detailed discussion of the origin concept, consult N. B. Ryder, 'The Interpretation of Origin Statistics', *Canadian Journal of Economics and Political Science*, vol. 21, no. 4 (November 1955), pp. 466–79; *Census, 1951*, vol. X, pp. 131–3, 152–6; *Census, 1941*, vol. I, pp. 218–19, 246–50; introduction to W. B. Hurd's census monograph, *Racial Origins and Nativity of the Canadian People, Census, 1931*, vol. XIII; and *Census, 1931*, vol. I, pp. 45–6.

A114–132. Principal religious denominations of the population, census dates, 1871 to 1951

SOURCE: for 1871 to 1921, *Canada Year Book, 1948–49*, p. 155; for 1931 to 1951, *Canada Year Book, 1957–58*, p. 137.

At each census from 1871 to 1951, enumerators were given the following, or a similar, instruction: 'Report the specific religious body, denomination, sect or community of which the person is a member or which the person adheres to or favours' (*Census, 1951*, vol. X, p. 157). In the table the historical growth of all of the principal denominations—that is, of 200,000 or more adherents—and of seven of the thirteen so-called smaller denominations—10,000 to 200,000 adherents—are shown. The other six smaller denominations have been combined with a multitude of the smallest denominations in the 'other' category, series A130. The 'not stated' totals from 1871 to 1941 are shown separately. In another source the 'not stated' have been assigned to the stated denominations on a proportional basis. The same source (*Census, 1951*, vol. X, pp. 159–60) also provides historical series for the six other smaller denominations not shown separately here.

A133–142. Population, Canadian, other British and foreign-born, by sex, census dates, 1871 to 1951

SOURCE: for totals from 1871 to 1951, *Census, 1951*, vol. I, table 44; for sex breakdown in 1911, Dominion Bureau of Statistics, unpublished data, Folio CXL; for sex breakdown in 1921, 1931, 1941, *Census, 1941*, vol. I, table VII, p. 177; for sex breakdown in 1951, *Census, 1951*, vol. I, table 45.

Series A133–142 and the three tables which follow deal with various attributes of native- and foreign-born population. The present note applies to all of them. The tables presented are mutually consistent although a minor difficulty arises because of an inconsistency in the treatment of 'birthplace not stated' which is common to them all. This classification does not appear in the 1951 census where maximum use was made of other information in the census schedules to assign a place of birth to all persons in the category.

The synthetic character of the population census of the western provinces in 1871 has been reviewed in the note to series A2–14 and is reflected in footnote 4 of series A133–142. Though the estimates for British Columbia and Northwest Territories were not included in the 'Canadian-born' in 1871, Indians in these areas are included in later censuses.

In 1871, 1881 and 1891, there were 1,828, 6,334 and 3,491 persons, respectively, reported as 'place of birth not stated' (see *Canada Year Book, 1910*, p. 2). Canadian, other British and foreign-born components of these totals cannot be distinguished. They are included with the Canadian-born in series A134–136. Beginning with the 1901 census, much larger totals of 'birthplace not stated' appear in the census and the individual components are distinguished and can be assigned as Canadian, other British or foreign-born. The Canadians, however, cannot be assigned to a province nor the British and foreign-born to a specific country. (See *Canada Year Book, 1913*, p. 73; *Canada Year Book, 1943–44*, p. 114; *Census, 1931*, vol. I, table II n., p. 215.) Footnote 1, series A170–199, shows the number of British-born for whom country of birth is unknown. The 'not stated' for the foreign-born are included with 'other foreign-born' in the census figures until 1931. In 1941 a small number (945) are not assigned to any category (see footnote 3, series A133–142). In 1951 the 'not stated' were assigned to countries before tabulations were made.

Persons who were born at sea have been classified among 'other' under either 'British Possessions' or 'British Commonwealth'. See *Canada Year Book, 1950*, p. 162 and *Census, 1931*, vol. I, table I, p. 214 for the relevant footnotes.

Newfoundland-born were shifted from other British to Canadian-born in 1951. In the same census, persons born in the Republic of Ireland were shifted from British to other foreign-born. Prior to 1951 both are included with other British.

A143–154. Population, by birthplace and sex, rural and urban, census dates, 1921 to 1951

SOURCE: for 1921, *Census, 1941*, vol. I, table VII, p. 177; for 1931, *Census, 1931*, vol. IV, table 5; for 1941, *Census, 1941*, vol. II, table 42; for 1951, *Census, 1951*, vol. I, table 46.

Totals, male and female, were added from the sources cited for the three birthplace classifications in 1931, 1941 and 1951. The results agreed with totals shown in series A133–142. This was not true for the comparable table in the 1921 census. Totals, by birthplace and sex, differed slightly from those taken from

the 1941 census but the differences are so small that they disappear when figures are rounded to the nearest thousand as in series A155–169. The figures shown in the table for 1921, which agree with totals in series A133–142, were calculated from the 1941 census table, cited above, which gives a percentage distribution by birthplace and rural-urban.

The totals of rural and urban population that may be derived from this table for 1951 are the same as those given in series A15–19 and, allowing for 'birthplace not stated', for 1941 (see footnote 3, series A143–154). Minor discrepancies exist in the rural-urban breakdowns obtained from earlier censuses. Series A15–19 are from the 1951 census. Total populations are the same in both but series A143–154 show a total 1,740 higher than series A15–19 in urban and 1,740 lower in rural in 1931 and a total of 2,450 higher in urban and 2,450 lower in rural in 1921.

See the note to series A133–142 for a description of other attributes of the birthplace series.

A155–169. Population, Canadian, other British and foreign-born, by age and sex, census dates, 1911 to 1951

SOURCE: for sex and age distribution in 1911, Dominion Bureau of Statistics, unpublished data, Folio CXL; *Census, 1921*, vol. II, table 10; *Census, 1931*, vol. III, table 23; *Census, 1941*, vol. III, table 18; *Census, 1951*, vol. II, table 10.

Detailed age distributions are available in the sources cited. They were added to provide the condensed distributions shown in this volume.

See the note to series A133–142 for a description of the census birthplace series.

A170–199. Country of birth of other British-born and foreign-born population, census dates, 1871 to 1951

SOURCE: *Census, 1951*, vol. I, table 44.

Some details available in the source have been eliminated for reasons of space. In 1951 other British Commonwealth, with the population born in each in brackets, includes: Australia (4,161), India and Pakistan (3,934), South Africa (2,057), West Indies (3,888), Other (6,527). In 1951 Scandinavia, with population born there, includes: Norway (22,969), Sweden (22,635), Denmark (15,679), Iceland (3,239). The totals of other British-born in 1901, 1911 and 1921, including those for whom countries of birth are unknown, are shown in series A137.

See the note to series A133–142 for a discussion of the census series on countries of birth.

INTERNAL MIGRATION (Series A200–220)

A200–210. Province of residence and province of birth of native-born internal migrants in Canada, census dates, 1871 to 1951

SOURCE: Buckley, 'Historical Estimates of Internal Migration', table 1, pp. 6–7.

The figures cover the Canadian-born migrants whose province of birth was stated in the respective censuses. For persons whose province of birth was not stated, by provinces, 1871 to 1941, see Buckley, 'Historical Estimates of Internal Migration', table 16, p. 37, and for a detailed distribution of the totals of series A200–210 by provinces, see *ibid.*, tables 5–14, pp. 15–35. For the purpose of series A200–210 any Canadian-born person not living in the province of his or her birth is termed a native-born internal migrant (see note to series A211–220). Panel A shows the number of persons living in each province who were born in another province. Panel B shows the number of persons not living in the province of birth by the province in which they were born.

A 211–220. Estimates of net internal migration of native-born in Canada by intercensal intervals, 1871 to 1951

SOURCE: Buckley, 'Historical Estimates of Internal Migration', table 3, pp. 10–11.

Intercensal changes in the totals of the two panels of series A 200–210 provide estimates of the in-migration and out-migration of the native-born population by provinces and by decades. In turn, the differences in these components of internal migration provide estimates of *net* internal migration by decades. Only net migration is shown here. In the second panel net migration is expressed as a rate per thousand of native population. The population bases used to calculate the rates of net migration are the average of the native-born populations in successive censuses who reported province of birth (see Buckley, p. 14 and table 15, p. 36). The source presents a discussion of the uses of and the biases inherent in estimates of net migration derived by this method.

For a comparison of the present estimates of net migration of the native-born adjusted for in-migration of the foreign-born with Keyfitz's estimates of net migration by provinces (series A 221–232), which include the net migration of both native and foreign-born, see Buckley, pp. 12–13.

INTERPROVINCIAL AND INTERNATIONAL MIGRATION (Series A 221–253)

A 221–232. Estimates of changes in the population ten years and over of the provinces through natural increase and migration, by decades, 1881 to 1941

SOURCE: Keyfitz, 'The Growth of Canadian Population', pp. 47–63.

Keyfitz applied life-table survival ratios to the population distributed by age and sex to obtain intercensal estimates of the natural increase and net migration of the national population aged 10 and over from 1851 to 1941 and of the provincial populations from 1881 to 1941. The estimates for the latter period are shown in series A 221–232. The national estimates for the period 1851 to 1881 appear in series A 244–248. When applied to the distribution of population in one census, the survival ratios yield the expected population ten years and over in the subsequent census year by age and sex. The difference between the expected and actual population 10 years and over gives an estimate of net migration by age and sex. English Life Tables were used to obtain the trend in past mortality in order to project Canadian survival rates back from 1931–41 to 1851. 'The Canadian Life Tables were used...to obtain probabilities of survival for 5-year age groups, and the ratios of the Canadian to the English (age by age) for the average of 1931–41 were used as factors to modify the latter back to the earliest period...' (Keyfitz, p. 49).

Given the net migration for Canada as a whole and the official record of immigration, estimates of emigration by decades may be obtained as a residual. These estimates may be found in the source cited.

In addition to estimates of natural increase and the components of migration, Keyfitz also estimated total births during each pre-censal decade and, with the estimates of deaths implicit in his method, constructed a population balance sheet showing the four components of population change by decades since 1851 (see series A 244–248).

Keyfitz did not attempt to estimate net migration of persons under 10 years living at the end of each census interval. Among other limitations of the estimates, he emphasized the problem of differential enumeration and especially the problem of under-enumeration of children aged 0–4 years in the earlier censuses which results in a 'consistently heavy apparent in-migration at ages 10–14' (Keyfitz, p. 62).

Keyfitz distributed the 'age not stated' totals in proportion to the 'age stated' in each census. The sizes of the 'not stated' groups, which were large in the earlier censuses, are shown in his source, which was *Census, 1931*, vol. 1, table 8 for census years prior to 1941. His distributions are precisely the same in 1931 and 1941 as those shown in series A 28–43. From 1881 to 1921, the various age categories sometimes differ by one or two thousand. Keyfitz is the source for the age and sex distributions from 1851 to 1871 shown in series A 28–43.

A 233–243. Changes in the population through natural increase and migration, by province, by intercensal intervals, 1931 to 1956

SOURCE: *Canada Year Book, 1957–58*, p. 120.

Following the establishment of the Dominion Bureau of Statistics under the Statistics Act of 1918, a plan was devised to compile national vital statistics through the co-operative efforts of D.B.S. and the nine provincial offices of vital statistics. In 1921 the first summary report covering eight provinces was published. Beginning in 1926 all (nine) provinces had entered the registration area (*Canada Year Book, 1948–49*, p. 186). With national coverage of annual births and deaths, net migration, by provinces, for intercensal intervals, has been estimated as a residual by D.B.S. These estimates of net migration are given in series A 233–243.

A 244–253. Estimates of components of changes in population ten years and over, Canada, by decades, 1851 to 1921

SOURCE: Keyfitz, 'The Growth of Canadian Population', p. 51; McDougall, 'Immigration into Canada', p. 172.

McDougall employed the same general method as Keyfitz but adopted quite different assumptions to estimate the components of population change in Canada from 1851 to 1921. The two estimates are presented together in series A 244–253.

McDougall constructed a new life table and made independent estimates of total immigration to Canada rather than use the official record of total immigration as Keyfitz did. His defence of his assumptions with respect to mortality and immigration in the period 1851 to 1921 is developed at length in the article cited above. A comment by Keyfitz appears in the same issue of *C.J.E.P.S.*, pp. 242–3.

McDougall accepted the survival rates of the white population of the limited registration area of the United States in the decade 1901 to 1910 as a primary benchmark. He extrapolated these rates to 1851–61 using the English Life Tables and obtained rates for the period 1910 to 1930 on a straight-line interpolation between the United States Table, 1901–10, and the Canadian Life Table, 1930–32. The end result is lower survival rates, hence smaller natural increase and greater net migration, than in the Keyfitz estimates.

McDougall used data from the records of emigration of a sample of countries in which the bulk of Canada's immigrant population originated supplemented by the records of immigration of the United States to obtain his estimates of immigration to Canada. The detailed procedure, described in the source, is too lengthy and complex to describe here. The result is an estimate of total immigration from 1851 to 1921 considerably below the official series, A 254, namely 4,186 thousand as compared to 5,351 thousand. This difference may be conceived as a difference in definition—as Keyfitz points out in his comment—with McDougall treating as transients those persons who are treated by Keyfitz as immigrants and then as emigrants when they leave the country after a short residence or perhaps even after merely travelling through Canada. The gross flows are affected very significantly but net migration not at all by this difference in definitions. The more fundamental difference lies in the respective assumptions concerning the levels of mortality from 1851 to 1921. On the evidence presented thus far the questions at issue cannot be regarded as settled and for that reason both estimates are presented here. In his study, *Canada's Economic Development, 1867–1953*, pp. 240–9, O. J. Firestone uses a different and quite promising approach to the same problem (see the note to series B82–91 in section B).

For the Keyfitz assumptions, see the note to series A221–232. See the note to series A254 for a summary of the criticism of the official immigration series. For comments on the problem of underenumeration in the census benchmarks, see the general note to this subsection on population and the note to series A2–14. For comments on the source and possible degree of bias in Firestone's estimates for the nineteenth century, see *American Economic Review*, LXIX, vol. 59 (June 1959), pp. 431–3 and the note to series B86 and B87. For Firestone's method and his estimates in the period 1900 to 1921, see series B86 and B87 and Dr. Henripin's note to the table.

IMMIGRATION (Series A254–347)

General note

The federal Department of Agriculture supervised immigration until 1892 when the Immigration Branch was moved to the Department of the Interior to coordinate the administration of immigration and western land settlement. The federal Department of Agriculture, created by legislation in 1868 (31 Vic., C. 53), was a continuation of the Department of Agriculture of the Province of Canada which, in 1862 (25 Vic., C. 7), replaced the Bureau of Agriculture established in 1852 (16 Vic., C. 11 and C. 18). The Minister who administered the Bureau was also chairman of the Board of Registration and Statistics, responsible for the census, and, by the legislation of 1862, was specifically assigned 'the official superintendence and management of all matters relative to Immigration...'. From the outset the promotion of immigration was the primary task of the Bureau and its successor. (See V. C. Fowke, *Canadian Agricultural Policy, The Historical Pattern* (Toronto, University of Toronto Press, 1946), pp. 111–21, 165–73.) Accordingly, the official record of immigrant arrivals intending to settle in Canada begins with the year 1852. There are earlier data in official sources on total immigrants arriving at and emigrants sailing to British North American seaports and some of these are cited in the note to series A254.

Immigration was under the control of the Department of the Interior from 1892 until October 1917, when the Immigration Branch became the Department of Immigration and Colonization and continued as an independent department until 1936. In December of that year the Department became the Immigration Branch of the Department of Mines and Resources. In January 1950 immigration was again shifted and became the Immigration Branch of the Department of Citizenship and Immigration. The Statistics Section of that Department, the annual reports of the several Departments listed above and *Canada Year Book* are the basic sources of the statistics of immigration presented in this subsection.

Immigration statistics in Canada have been for the most part a by-product of legislation to control the solicitation and transportation of immigrants and their reception at ports of entry and to protect the resident population against communicable diseases and charitable burdens and the immigrants against physical and economic exploitation at the hands of transportation companies and the crimps and land jobbers who found them an easy mark. The first federal Immigration Act, 1869, two years after Confederation, embodied principles developed in Imperial and Colonial legislation dating back to the eighteen-twenties. (See *Canada Year Book, 1957–58*, for a summary of the growth of immigration legislation.) But under this and under subsequent legislation no provisions were made for adequate statistical controls, with the result that the accuracy of immigration statistics prior to the nineteen-twenties must be seriously questioned. The major problems and inconsistencies are indicated in the notes to the tables. A major weakness in the migration statistics is the lack of emigration statistics which have not been collected in Canada. A partial direct estimate of emigration is made on the basis of information supplied by immigration officials of the United States and the United Kingdom and, in recent years, the United Nations Statistical Branch.

A degree of statistical control at seaports was implicit in immigration legislation. The following description was obtained by correspondence with J. P. Delisle, Chief of the Statistics Section of the Department:

No passenger was to debark until a passenger list supplied by the master of the vessel had been checked and the ship inspected by quarantine officers. The passenger list was to include the names of heads of families and the number of persons accompanying them, occupation, country of origin and destination; also the names and similar details for all single persons.

Immigration statistics were compiled from the passenger lists (better known as ships' manifests) at seaports and submitted to Immigration headquarters. These manifests, introduced at the ports of Quebec (May 1865), Halifax (January 1881), Saint John, N.B. (January 1900) and at other seaports as the need arose, remained the only source documents for statistical purposes until 1921 at which time an individual record of entry was introduced and used for statistical compilation until January 1925. Then seaports reverted to the use of the manifest (which remained in existence until 1951) and turned over to the Statistical Unit of the Immigration Branch in Ottawa the responsibility of compiling statistics from the manifests.

At border points, official records of entry began in 1908 and consisted of a chronological list of arrivals prepared at every port. In 1919 the use of an individual card of entry was introduced but it was replaced in 1925 by a monthly return, listing all immigrant arrivals at the various ports along the International Boundary.

In 1952 a landing card came into use at border points and seaports to meet the needs of the Landing Records Section and the Statistical Unit in Ottawa. The introduction of this document has coincided with the compilation of more detailed statistical tables than the ship's manifests or the monthly immigration returns had ever permitted. This card system is still in existence.

At border points prior to 1908 travellers by land created particular problems. Numbers of immigrant settlers were to be reported to the Department of Agriculture in Ottawa by the immigration agents stationed in cities like Hamilton, London, Winnipeg, etc. The individual reports of these agents appear in the annual reports of the Department. This method introduced possibilities both of exaggeration, for example, counting transients from the State of New York to Michigan as immigrants, and of undercounting, for example, not recording wagon movements into Saskatchewan and Alberta. Canadians returning from the United States were also included in the original records of immigrant arrivals (see note to series A254), and a subsequent adjustment of the record was made to eliminate their estimated numbers from 1904 to 1924.

In addition to the reports of the immigration agents at or near border points and at seaports, another important source of the estimates beginning in 1873 was the custom houses. The Minister of Agriculture in that year added in '...returns from the Custom Houses along the frontier...[of] ascertained arrivals from the entries of settlers' goods' (*Sessional Papers, 1875*, vol. VIII, no. 8, p. iv). The importance of these are described in the note to series A254.

Many of the immigration series presented in this volume were obtained directly from the ledgers of the Immigration Branch owing to the fact that most of the published sources show the data since 1900 on a fiscal year basis. The figures presented here are, with some exceptions, calendar year figures for longer time periods than have been published hitherto.

A254. Immigrant arrivals in Canada, 1852 to 1960

SOURCE: for 1852 to 1959, *Annual Report, 1959–60*, Department of Citizenship and Immigration, Ottawa, 1960, p. 28; for 1960, files of the Department.

The conceptual consistency and the reliability of Canada's immigration statistics have never been thoroughly investigated. To treat the issue of internal consistency of series A254, one must break the series into at least eight segments, 1852 to 1865 1866 to 1872, 1873 to 1891, 1892 to 1896, 1897 to 1903, 1904 to 1925, 1926 to 1960, and consider each in turn.

Prior to 1936 it was the usual practice to publish, in the *Canada Year Book* and in the annual reports of the Immigration Branch, fiscal year totals back to 1901 and calendar year totals from 1900 back to 1881 with a breakdown of immigrant arrivals from the United Kingdom, the United States and from other countries. Calendar year totals since 1852 first appeared in *Canada Year Book, 1936*, p. 186. The totals for the period 1852 to 1865 are very close to the original estimates of A. C. Buchanan which appear in the *Journals of the Legislative Assembly of the Province of Canada*, 1854 to 1865. The basic record of the overseas immigrants was the total immigrant arrivals in the St. Lawrence River. This series, which is available annually back to 1849 and quinquennially back to 1829 and which provides classifications by sex, adult and child, country of origin and occupation, invariably appeared in the annual report of the Quebec immigration agent. (See, for example, *Sessional Papers, 1885*, vol. 14, no. 7, S.P. no. 12, p. 9.) Ferenczi compiled an annual series from 1827 to 1848 from British sources which agrees roughly with the quinquennial statements (see Imre Ferenczi, *International Migrations* (New York, 1929), vol. I, pp. 360–2). The statements of intention of the individual immigrants were accepted by the immigration agents to determine the portion of total arrivals planning to settle in Canada. To these were added the number of arrivals from the United States estimated by the agents.

Initially the estimate of arrivals from the United States was clearly a rough guess. In 1854, for example, the figure was placed at 6,000 to 7,000 (Canada Assembly, *Journal, 1854–55*, vol. 13, app. 13, app. (DDD), 16th page). Deducting from arrivals at Quebec those who came from the Maritimes and adding 7,000, one gets 37,326 for total immigration. The current official record for that year is 37,263. In 1856 a single total of the United States movement is secured by the addition of estimates of the movement at six entry points with the largest movement via the Suspension Bridge at Niagara. This general method was followed thereafter. (See, for example, Canada Assembly, *Journal, 1861*, vol. 21, 7th page.) These estimates were made by immigration agents. In one year, 1865, the current official figure is the same as the original figure of arrivals to the province of Canada. No addition was made for the arrivals at Maritime ports (for immigrants landed at Maritime ports, see Ferenczi, p. 369). The estimated immigration from the United States is given in the *Journals* and, in my opinion, the figures are subject

in some degree to the same kind of inflation as later figures (see below).

The record was critically reviewed in the years immediately following Confederation. The published estimate for the province of Canada in 1866 was revised, an addition was made for arrivals at Maritime ports, and the new series was carried forward to 1872. The following quotations of evidence given by J. C. Taché, the Deputy Minister of Agriculture, are from the first report of the Standing Committee on Immigration and Colonization, Canada, *House of Commons Journals, 1867–68*, vol. I, app. 8, pp. 7–8. 'The immigrants on their arrival at the place where an agent is located, are met by the Agent whose duties are to see that the laws which protect the immigrant are fully complied with....The immigrants coming up the St. Lawrence are first visited at the Quarantine station at Grosse Isle...'. Referring to 'passage money', that is, assistance to proceed inland, he stated: 'The great bulk of the immigrants so transported, I have every reason to believe, and for many I have evidence of it, have been immigrants bound for the United States.... It is a notorious fact that many immigrants are advised before leaving Europe, by agents of forwarding companies or by friends, who have preceded them by way of the St. Lawrence, to plead poverty on their reaching Quebec or other places....'

To the question 'Are the returns made by the Immigrant Agents of the number of immigrants who settle in Canada reliable?' Taché replied that they '...are far from correct. So much so that...the late...Minister of Agriculture...withheld this information from the body of the Departmental Report for 1865...'.

The Committee's report continues (pp. 8–9):

In...June and July, 1866, a Departmental enquiry was made into the same subject, and the result was again to prove the total incorrectness of those returns, and the extreme difficulties, if not impossibilities, encountered by our Agents in the way of collecting correct information....The almost only basis of such calculations is the mere *ipse dixit* of the immigrants, who all think it is their immediate interest to represent themselves as intending settlers for Canada. Another great source of error arises from the fact that quite a number...after a short sojourn in the country, leave it again to emigrate toward the neighboring states.

Use of customs entries to record immigration from the United States was first suggested in the report for 1865 (Assembly, *Journal, 1866*, vol. 26, app. 2, S.P. no. 5, p. 7). The original estimate of total immigration for 1866 was 20,000 which included 7,279 from the United States reported by customs, 4,303 from overseas arriving via Quebec, with the remainder coming from the United States being estimated by the agents (*Sessional Papers, 1867–68*, vol. I, no. 3, appendix to the Report of the Minister of Agriculture, pp. 7–8). However, the customs source was not used in the revised estimate of total immigration of 10,091. (The figure of 11,427 for 1866 in series A254 includes 1,336 arrivals at Maritime ports.) The agents' estimate of the other movement from the United States was also revised downward.

This stricter approach to estimating immigrants from the United States was continued until 1872. In reply to questions on the immigration of that year, Mr. Love, Secretary of the Department of Agriculture, suggested that the United States immigration was now probably understated. United States arrivals at many agencies 'were not entered in the statements of numbers of immigrants as kept by the Department, which were, with very little exception, confined to those who come from beyond the sea' (*House of Commons Journals, 1873*, vol. VI, app. 7, p. 5). While the phrase 'with very little exception' overstates the case, the quotation does suggest the concern felt about arrivals from the United States. In 1873 the estimate obtained from the reports of the immigration agents was raised by the returns of custom houses along the frontier (*Sessional Papers, 1875*, vol. VIII, no. 8, p. iv). This was a significant change in the method of estimation, accounting for 8,971 of the total immigration of 50,050 in 1873, 35,191 of 103,824 in 1884, 33,518 of 75,067 in 1890. After a gap of five years from 1892 to 1896, when no arrivals from the United States were recorded, the returns from customs declined. They stood at 7,193 of 189,064 in 1905–6. Thereafter the category was not shown separately but was still included in the total immigration from the United States shown in the annual reports (see *Sessional Papers, 1891*, vol. XXIV, no. 4, p. xxxvi and *Report of the Superintendent of Immigration*, Sessional Paper no. 25, 1906, pp. 4–5).

Series A 254 is therefore on a different but conceptually consistent basis from 1873 to 1891. In the annual reports of the Department of Immigration and Colonization (see, for example, *Report, 1926–27*, p. 9) and in the *Canada Year Book* (see the issues for 1936 and 1950, p. 186), it was long the standard practice to show total arrivals from the United States beginning with 1881 with a note to the effect that the figures included non-immigrants as well as immigrants. This was also true prior to 1881. Total arrivals from 1881 to 1891 were 968,000, of which 580,000 are recorded as having come from the United States. From 1875 to 1880, of a total of 189 thousand, 115 thousand were recorded via the Suspension Bridge, via Manitoba and the customs houses. In both periods United States arrivals at about 60 per cent of the total are similarly inflated.

From 1892 to 1896 the attempt to measure immigrant arrivals from the United States was abandoned. Since there are no statistics of the movement, series A 254 is on a different basis in those five years.

Estimation of immigrants from the United States was resumed in 1897 and continued until 1932–3 when a major revision of the series was undertaken. In the fiscal year 1924–5, returning Canadians were segregated and the record published independently for the first time (see series A 338–341). 'For a number of years prior to 1924 some persons readmitted to Canada as formerly resident in the Dominion were included in the immigration returns.... The necessary revisions have been made in these tables in the present report' (*Report of the Department of Immigration and Colonization, 1932–33*, p. 8). This revision was carried back to 1903–4, but the conceptual problem was much older than that. For example, '...in 1874 there was an unusually large number of immigrants from the United States, as ascertained from entries of settlers' goods at Custom Houses.... The number was 14,110; a considerable number of these were understood to be repatriated Canadians' (Canada, *House of Commons Journals, 1875*, vol. 9, app. 4, p. 1). In 1873, '...8,971 came to us from the United States, and are for the most part supposed to be Canadians returned to their homes' (Canada, *House of Commons Journals, 1874*, vol. 8, app. 7, p. 2).

The numbers from the United States from 1897 to 1902 may have been considered too small to warrant adjustment but that is not true of 1903. The total in fiscal 1902–3 is 49,473. Fiscal 1903–4 before the revision was 45,171; after revision it became 40,739, a change of 4,432. This revision makes the number of immigrants in fiscal 1903–4 from all countries appear to decline by 2,500; before the revision the series showed a rise of about 2,000. For this reason the calendar year figures from 1897 to 1903 in series A 254 cannot be taken as consistent with the series after 1904.

The revision of 1932–3 resulted in the loss of some classifications of immigrants from the United States prior to 1925.

The overseas totals prior to 1925 are also not so reliable as those after because it was not until 1925 that the responsibility of compiling statistics from the manifests was shifted from the seaports to the Statistical Unit of the Immigration Branch (see the general note). Hence, for at least three reasons the immigration statistics after 1925 are superior to the earlier series. The introduction of the landing-card system in 1952 (see general note) marks the last stage in the development of immigration statistics and coincided with the presentation in the annual reports of the Department of more precise and detailed statistics than earlier methods permitted.

CONCLUDING NOTE: The figure for 1867 in series A 254 should be 10,666, not 14,666 as usually shown. The figure is obtained by subtracting from the total the arrivals of those who come from overseas and go on to the United States. This was done correctly in the original report (*Sessional Papers, 1869*, vol. II, no. 6, S.P. no. 76, p. 5). In the next report a misprint occurs and the figure 14,666 is carried over to all subsequent reports. See *Sessional Papers, 1870*, vol. III, no. 6, S.P. no. 80, p. 3 for the relevant aggregates and the error.

The record of immigration from overseas since 1852 has been assembled on a uniform basis. Statements of intention to settle in Canada may not have been always truthful, and many intending settlers from overseas may have moved on to the United States after a short-term residence. One's view of the seriousness of these two problems depends upon the issue of defining an immigrant (see note to series A 244–253). A more serious problem is the inconsistency in the record of immigrants from the United States demonstrated above. In my opinion this series is exaggerated from 1852 to 1865. It is at a more appropriate level from 1866 to 1872, and then grossly exaggerated from 1873 to 1891. There is no record at all from 1892 to 1896. The record from 1897 to 1903 has not been adjusted for returning Canadians and the adjustment for this component from 1904 to 1925 is based upon estimates. In this latter period the original record was obtained by improved methods beginning in 1908.

The quality of the statistics of all immigrants was improved in the period 1926 to 1951 and further improved in the period 1952 to the present.

A 255–272. Immigration to Canada by intended occupations and dependents, 1953 to 1960

SOURCE: files of the Department of Citizenship and Immigration.

The present classification of occupations, introduced in 1953, is based upon the classification of the 1951 census of Canada. It replaced an older classification (see notes to series A 273–283 and series A 284–299 below) which showed only major occupation groups. The detailed classifications underlying each major class shown here may be found in the annual reports of the Department.

The intended occupation usually coincides with the last full-time occupation of the immigrant. Recent surveys have indicated that two or three years may go by before the immigrant has the opportunity to work in the field of his choice. Recent labour-force surveys have also revealed that labour-force participation by female immigrants is higher than these statistics of intended occupations would imply.

A 273–283. Immigration to Canada by intended occupations and dependents, 1932 to 1952

SOURCE: the files of the Department of Citizenship and Immigration.

See note to series A 284–299. This table is provided as a link between series A 255–272 and series A 284–299 which takes the occupational distribution, on a broad group basis, back to 1904 for immigrants from overseas and back to 1912 for total immigrants.

A284–299. Immigration to Canada by occupational groups, sex of adults, children, from overseas and the U.S.A., and from overseas, 1904 to 1951

SOURCE: the files of the Department of Citizenship and Immigration.

The following information was supplied by the Immigration Branch. This table was designed to emphasize occupational groups and does not distinguish precisely between the gainfully occupied and the not gainfully occupied (dependents and others) as series A273–283 was designed to do. Hence it is not possible, *from this table*, to discern exactly how many immigrants were intending to seek gainful employment and how many were not. However, the table does provide an *indication* of how immigrants were divided between the two categories, and in this connection the following points should be borne in mind:

The series shown in this and in the preceding table add to the same totals (all immigrant arrivals) and the class totals can be compared in the years of overlap to estimate the dependents included under the class headings of series A284–299.

Every adult male in each of the occupational classes except in 'Others and unclassified' was gainfully occupied. Some of the adults included in 'Others and unclassified' were also gainfully occupied (for example, professionals were included in that class), but a number were not gainfully occupied (for example, retired persons and students were also put under that heading).

All female domestics were gainfully occupied.

As for other adult females, a certain number were intending to become gainfully occupied in Canada. They would likely have been proportionally largest in 'Trading' and lowest in 'Others and unclassified'. In all groups the percentage of gainfully occupied would likely be smaller in the earlier years.

Before 1 April 1925 all children (persons thirteen years of age and under) were dependents. After that date a number of persons classed as children (seventeen years of age and under) would have intended to take jobs. There are probably some in each class except 'Female domestics', with the largest percentage in 'Farming'.

In the 'Others and unclassified' group, the adult males are principally professionals, students and retired persons. The adult females and the children are probably for the most part those arriving after the householder. The category also includes students and retired persons, and wives and children of males in this group. It is therefore assumed that the majority of the class are not intending to seek a gainful occupation.

During the whole period covered by the table, males who would now be classified as domestics were classified as 'Unskilled and semi-skilled labourers'.

Female domestic immigrants under eighteen years of age, 1930 to 1951

	From			From	
Year	Overseas	United States	Year	Overseas	United States
1951	88	0	1940	61	9
			1939	113	3
1950	77	1	1938	182	0
1949	98	0	1937	137	0
1948	127	1	1936	75	1
1947	101	2			
1946	72	4	1935	63	0
			1934	65	4
1945	85	2	1933	71	8
1944	63	3	1932	76	11
1943	57	2	1931	211	23
1942	41	5			
1941	75	8	1930	1,116	47

The low age limit for children prior to 1 April 1925 (see footnote 2, series A284–299) implies that no children are included under female domestics before 1925. An indeterminable number are included from 1926 to 1929. The numbers of female domestics under 18, that is, children included in series A285 from 1930 to 1951 were as shown in the preceding table.

A300–315. Immigration to Canada by age, sex and marital status, 1933 to 1960

SOURCE: the files of the Department of Citizenship and Immigration.

Greater detail on age distribution of immigrants may be found in the annual reports of the Immigration Branch. The compression of detail given here was governed by the nature of the age distribution itself and by the compressions of the age distributions of the foreign born, series A155–169, and of the labour force, series C70–84 and series C85–97.

A316–336. Ethnic origin of all immigrants to Canada, from overseas and the U.S.A., and from overseas, 1901 to 1925

SOURCE: the files of the Department of Citizenship and Immigration.

The classification of immigrants from the United States prior to 1926 was lost as a result of the revision of the statistics in 1932–33 (see general note). The total immigrant arrivals from the United States since 1903–4 are shown in series A337. The distribution of all immigrants between overseas and the United States, 1926 to the present, may be found in the annual reports of the Immigration Branch.

The usefulness of the origin statistics has occasionally been questioned. However, the classification is not an arbitrary one. It does reflect what the immigrants themselves believe to be their origin. Prior to 1914 the question on racial origin, the term then in use, was essentially one of nationality. After 1918 greater emphasis was placed upon cultural factors. The term 'ethnic origin' replaced 'racial origin' in 1955 but the emphasis was not changed. Both expressions refer to the social or cultural group to which the immigrant belongs or feels he belongs. The immigrants are left with a great deal of discretion and they are classified according to the answers they give.

Other classifications, which can be maintained more consistently, including country of last permanent residence and country of citizenship, have been employed by the Immigration Branch in recent years. These series may be found in the annual reports of the Branch.

A337. Immigrant arrivals from the United States, 1904 to 1960

SOURCE: the files of the Department of Citizenship and Immigration.

For a discussion of the record of immigrant arrivals from the United States since 1852 and its revision in 1932–33 for the period since 1904 see the general note to this subsection and note to series A254.

A338–341. Canadians returning from the United States, 1925 to 1960

SOURCE: the figures were obtained from the files of the Department of Citizenship and Immigration.

'A movement not included in the immigration figures is that of returned Canadians. Since April 1924, a record has been kept of the number of Canadian citizens returning...after an absence in the United States, who left Canada with the intention of making their permanent home in the United States and subsequently returned...declaring their intention of again taking up permanent residence....Persons who left Canada on visits or for other temporary purpose, have not been included' (*Report of the Department of Immigration and Colonization, 1926–27*, p. 6). The meaning of 'temporary purpose' is amplified in the following: 'Not all immigrants are of non-Canadian birth; a few Canadian born who subsequently obtained domicile or citizenship in another country but still later, returned to Canada are now "immigrants", the Immigration Department so regarding any Canadian who has lived three or more years in another country, if and when he resumes residence in Canada. The Department...since 1924 also maintains statistics of "returned Canadians" from the United States, i.e., of Canadians (apart from students and travellers) who have gone to the United States for seasonal or other employment, but have returned within a three-year period' (*Census, 1931*, vol. I, p. 43).

It is believed, however, by the Economic and Social Research Division of the Department of Citizenship and Immigration that these series understate the backflow.

The category of 'returned Canadians' is not included in the totals of series A254 from 1904 to 1960 (see note to series A254).

A 342–347. Persons deported, including accompanying persons, after admission, by principal causes, 1903 to 1960

SOURCE: the files of the Department of Citizenship and Immigration.

Persons who may be deported in addition to persons with the status of landed immigrants include some nonimmigrants or persons without status such as deserting seamen and stowaways.

Series A1. *Estimated population of Canada, 1867 to 1961*

(thousands)

Year[1,2]	Total population	Year	Total population	Year	Total population	Year	Total population	Year	Total population	Year	Total population
	1		1		1		1		1		1
1961	18,238	1944	11,946	1928	9,835	1912	7,389	1896	5,074		
1960	17,870	1943	11,795	1927	9,637	1911	7,207				
1959	17,483	1942	11,654	1926	9,451			1895	5,026	1880	4,255
1958	17,080	1941	11,507			1910	6,988	1894	4,979	1879	4,185
1957	16,610			1925	9,294	1909	6,800	1893	4,931	1878	4,120
1956	16,081	1940	11,381	1924	9,143	1908	6,625	1892	4,883	1877	4,064
		1939	11,267	1923	9,010	1907	6,411	1891	4,833	1876	4,009
1955	15,698	1938	11,152	1922	8,919	1906	6,097				
1954	15,287	1937	11,045	1921	8,788			1890	4,779	1875	3,954
1953	14,845	1936	10,950			1905	6,002	1889	4,729	1874	3,895
1952	14,459			1920	8,556	1904	5,827	1888	4,678	1873	3,826
1951	14,009	1935	10,845	1919	8,311	1903	5,651	1887	4,626	1872	3,754
		1934	10,741	1918	8,148	1902[1]	5,494	1886	4,580	1871	3,689
1950	13,712	1933	10,633	1917	8,060	1901	5,371				
1949[2]	13,447	1932	10,510	1916	8,001			1885	4,537	1870	3,625
1948	12,823	1931	10,376			1900	5,301	1884	4,487	1869	3,565
1947	12,551			1915	7,981	1899	5,235	1883	4,430	1868	3,511
1946	12,292	1930	10,208	1914	7,879	1898	5,175	1882	4,375	1867	3,463
1945	12,072	1929	10,029	1913	7,632	1897	5,122	1881	4,325	—	—
										—	—

[1] From 1867 to 1901 the figures apply to 1 April; from 1902 to 1961 the figures apply to 1 June.   [2] The population of Newfoundland is included beginning in 1949.

Series A2–14. *Population of Canada, by province, census dates, 1851 to 1961*

Year	Canada	Newfoundland	Prince Edward Island	Nova Scotia	New Brunswick	Quebec	Ontario	Manitoba	Saskatchewan	Alberta	British Columbia	Yukon	Northwest Territories
	2	3	4	5	6	7	8	9	10	11	12	13	14
1961	18,238,247	457,853	104,629	737,007	597,936	5,259,211	6,236,092	921,686	925,181	1,331,944	1,629,082	14,628	22,998
1956	16,080,791	415,074	99,285	694,717	554,616	4,628,378	5,404,933	850,040	880,665	1,123,116	1,398,464	12,190	19,313
1951	14,009,429	361,416	98,429	642,584	515,697	4,055,681	4,597,542	776,541	831,728	939,501	1,165,210	9,096	16,004
1941	11,506,655	—	95,047	577,962	457,401	3,331,882	3,787,655	729,744	895,992	796,169	817,861	4,914	12,028
1931	10,376,786	—	88,038	512,846	408,219	2,874,662	3,431,683	700,139	921,785	731,605	694,263	4,230	9,316
1921	8,787,949[1]	—	88,615	523,837	387,876	2,360,510	2,933,662	610,118	757,510	588,454	524,582	4,157	8,143
1911	7,206,643	—	93,728	492,338	351,889	2,005,776	2,527,292	461,394	492,432	374,295	392,480	8,512	6,507
1901	5,371,315	—	103,259	459,574	331,120	1,648,898	2,182,947	255,211	91,279	73,022	178,657	27,219	20,129
1891	4,833,239	—	109,078	450,396	321,263	1,488,535	2,114,321	152,506	—[2]	—[2]	98,173	—	98,967
1881	4,324,810	—	108,891	440,572	321,233	1,359,027	1,926,922	62,260	—	—	49,459	—	56,446
1871	3,689,257	—	94,021	387,800	285,594	1,191,516	1,620,851	25,228	—	—	36,247	—	48,000
1861	3,229,633	—	80,857	330,857	252,047	1,111,566	1,396,091	—[2]	—	—	51,524[3]	—	6,691[3]
1851	2,436,297	—	62,678[4]	276,854	193,800	890,261	952,004	—	—	—	55,000[3]	—	5,700[3]

[1] Includes 485 members of the Royal Canadian Navy whose province of residence is not known.   [2] Included with Northwest Territories.   [3] For the discussion of the ambiguities and underenumeration contained in these figures consult the note to this table.   [4] 1848 figure.

Series A15–19. *Population, rural and urban, census dates, 1871 to 1956*

Year	Total population	1956 definition[1]		1941 definition	
		Urban	Rural	Urban	Rural
	15	16	17	18	19
1956	16,080,791	10,714,855	5,365,936	9,286,126	6,794,665
1951[2]	14,009,429	8,817,637	5,191,792	7,941,222	6,068,207
1941	11,506,655	6,548,326	4,958,329	6,252,416	5,254,239
1931	10,376,786	5,574,005	4,802,781	5,572,058	4,804,728
1921	8,787,949	4,257,443	4,530,506	4,352,122	4,435,827
1911	7,206,643	3,147,297	4,059,346	3,272,947	3,933,696
1901	5,371,315	1,990,162	3,381,153	2,014,222	3,357,093
1891	4,833,239	—	—	1,537,098	3,296,141
1881	4,324,810	—	—	1,109,507	3,215,303
1871	3,689,257	—	—	722,343	2,966,914

[1] For 1951 the figures of urban population are adjusted exactly according to the 1956 definition. The remainder of the total population represents rural. The reason for lack of strict comparability with early censuses is explained in the notes to this table.

[2] Including Newfoundland beginning in 1951. The total population of Newfoundland in 1951 is distributed as follows: basis 1956 definition, urban, 154,359; rural, 207,057; total 361,416; and basis 1941 definition, urban, 104,377; rural, 257,039; total 361,416.

Series A 20–24. *Population in incorporated centres of 1,000 persons and over, by size groups, census dates, 1871 to 1956*

Year	Total	100,000 persons and over	30,000–99,999 persons	5,000–29,999 persons	1,000–4,999 persons
	20	**21**	**22**	**23**	**24**
1956[1]	8,842,206	3,661,994	1,394,055	2,511,245	1,274,912
1951[1]	7,511,539	3,260,939	1,147,888	1,947,128	1,155,584
1941	5,853,603	2,645,133	928,367	1,370,375	909,728
1931	5,160,901	2,328,175	696,680	1,305,304	830,742
1921	3,977,064	1,658,697	495,566	1,057,965	764,836
1911	3,007,576	1,080,960	488,748	782,771	655,097
1901	1,867,260	475,770	343,266	503,187	545,037
1891[2]	1,440,605	397,865	224,760	390,670	427,310
1881[2]	—[3]	140,747	220,922	298,371	—[3]
1871[2]	—[3]	107,225	115,791	228,354	—[3]

[1] Including Newfoundland beginning in 1951.
[2] Not including Yukon and the Northwest Territories. There were no centres of 1,000 persons and over in Yukon and Northwest Territories in earlier census years.

[3] Centres of 1,000–4,999 were estimated as follows: 1881, 316,000; 1871, 196,000.

Series A 25–27. *Rural population, farm and nonfarm, census dates, 1931 to 1956*

Year	Total rural	Nonfarm	Farm
	25	**26**	**27**
	1956 definition[1]		
1956	5,365,936	2,734,349	2,631,587
1951	5,191,792	2,422,506	2,769,286
	1951 definition[2]		
1951	5,375,328	2,559,633	2,815,695
1941	5,236,164	2,123,396	3,112,768
1931	4,907,833	1,670,116	3,237,717
	1941 definition[2]		
1951	5,789,686	2,955,815	2,833,871
1941	5,239,094	2,122,172	3,116,922

[1] Includes Yukon, Northwest Territories and Newfoundland.

[2] Excludes Yukon, Northwest Territories and Newfoundland.

Series A28–43. *Population, by age and sex, census dates, 1851 to 1956*

(thousands)

Year[1]	Sex	Total population	Under 5 years	5–9 years	10–14 years	15–19 years	20–24 years	25–29 years	30–34 years	35–39 years	40–44 years	45–49 years	50–54 years	55–59 years	60–64 years	65–69 years	70 years and over
		28	29	30	31	32	33	34	35	36	37	38	39	40	41	42	43
1956[1]	Both sexes	16,081	1,984	1,807	1,435	1,162	1,129	1,198	1,216	1,114	1,025	879	733	629	525	464	780
	Male	8,152	1,012	920	732	587	567	606	603	556	523	456	382	322	266	238	385
	Female	7,929	972	887	703	576	562	592	614	559	503	423	351	307	259	227	395
1951[1]	Both sexes	14,009	1,722	1,398	1,131	1,058	1,089	1,131	1,043	999	869	745	663	571	506	433	653
	Male	7,089	879	714	575	532	538	553	513	504	446	388	340	293	264	228	323
	Female	6,921	843	684	556	526	551	578	530	496	423	357	322	278	242	205	330
1941	Both sexes	11,507	1,052	1,046	1,101	1,120	1,032	967	844	760	677	635	592	507	407	308	460
	Male	5,901	534	529	556	565	518	488	432	396	349	333	316	275	219	163	228
	Female	5,606	518	517	545	555	514	479	412	363	328	303	276	232	189	145	232
1931	Both sexes	10,377	1,075	1,133	1,074	1,040	912	787	709	689	646	586	489	367	295	231	345
	Male	5,375	543	573	543	526	464	411	368	359	348	322	268	199	157	121	174
	Female	5,002	531	560	531	514	448	376	341	329	298	264	221	168	138	110	171
1921	Both sexes	8,788	1,059	1,050	914	805	713	688	655	634	529	436	363	281	240	172	248
	Male	4,530	534	529	462	405	352	349	344	343	287	238	196	149	127	91	124
	Female	4,258	525	521	452	400	361	340	310	291	241	199	167	133	113	82	124
1911	Both sexes	7,207	890	785	702	686	712	663	559	471	392	333	287	214	179	132	204
	Male	3,822	450	396	356	355	390	374	313	260	215	180	154	114	95	68	103
	Female	3,385	440	389	346	331	322	289	246	211	177	153	133	100	84	64	101
1901	Both sexes	5,371	646	618	583	557	515	430	369	336	294	242	206	162	142	106	165
	Male	2,752	326	313	297	283	260	220	192	176	155	127	107	83	74	55	84
	Female	2,620	320	306	285	275	255	209	177	160	139	115	99	79	69	52	81
1891	Both sexes	4,833	611	592	554	521	482	395	326	275	235	198	173	131	121	85	135
	Male	2,460	309	300	282	262	242	199	167	142	121	102	89	68	63	45	70
	Female	2,373	302	292	272	259	240	196	158	132	114	96	84	64	58	40	65
1881	Both sexes	4,325	599	562	513	483	436	337	265	232	196	171	143	112	98	69	109
	Male	2,189	304	284	262	240	215	168	134	117	100	88	73	58	53	37	57
	Female	2,136	295	278	251	243	221	169	132	115	97	83	70	54	46	32	52
1871	Both sexes	3,689	541	519	476	408	351	282	223	188	158	139	113	90	69	56	79
	Male	1,869	276	264	243	202	172	138	111	94	81	72	60	48	38	31	43
	Female	1,820	265	255	233	206	179	144	112	94	77	67	53	42	31	25	36
1861	Both sexes	3,230	543	429	399	374	304	254	200	161	136	110	89	71	58	42	56
	Male	1,660	277	218	203	187	154	129	103	84	72	59	48	38	32	24	30
	Female	1,570	266	211	196	187	150	125	97	77	64	51	41	33	26	18	26
1851	Both sexes	2,436	451	346	298	277	223	184	145	118	101	81	64	49	35	23	42
	Male	1,250	233	173	152	136	112	93	75	62	54	43	35	27	19	13	22
	Female	1,186	218	173	146	141	111	91	70	56	47	38	29	22	16	10	20

[1] Includes Newfoundland beginning in 1951.

Series A44–59. *Population, by age and sex, urban and rural, census dates, 1921 to 1956*

(thousands)

Year	Locale and sex	Total	0–4 years	5–9 years	10–14 years	15–19 years	20–24 years	25–29 years	30–34 years	35–39 years	40–44 years	45–49 years	50–54 years	55–59 years	60–64 years	65–69 years	70 years and over
		44	45	46	47	48	49	50	51	52	53	54	55	56	57	58	59
1956[1]	Urban																
	male	5,299	644	569	435	344	374	426	426	384	357	307	254	211	172	152	242
	female	5,416	621	551	423	365	410	437	450	402	362	303	250	218	184	162	281
	Rural nonfarm																
	male	1,442	196	175	134	110	104	103	100	91	83	72	59	51	43	42	79
	female	1,293	187	170	129	100	86	89	90	81	70	57	46	43	39	37	68
	Farm																
	male	1,411	172	175	163	132	89	76	77	81	82	77	69	61	50	43	63
	female	1,220	164	166	151	111	66	66	74	76	71	63	55	47	36	28	47
1951[2]	Urban																
	male	4,222	504	389	301	289	330	358	328	320	281	242	213	181	163	137	187
	female	4,406	484	376	296	317	382	401	359	336	287	240	218	188	164	138	218
	Rural nonfarm																
	male	1,339	188	148	113	100	99	100	94	91	78	65	56	48	45	43	71
	female	1,214	180	142	111	91	88	95	89	80	64	51	46	41	38	36	62
	Farm																
	male	1,527	187	176	161	144	109	94	91	93	86	81	72	64	57	48	65
	female	1,301	179	167	149	117	81	83	82	80	72	66	58	49	39	31	49
1941[3]	Urban																
	male	3,079	250	248	270	284	275	272	241	221	195	186	176	149	116	83	115
	female	3,174	242	244	270	303	315	297	254	221	200	184	168	139	113	86	138
	Rural																
	male	2,822	284	281	286	281	243	217	190	176	154	147	140	126	102	80	114
	female	2,432	276	273	274	252	200	182	158	142	128	119	108	93	75	59	94
1931[3]	Urban																
	male	2,773	260	278	265	257	236	221	205	202	196	179	146	104	79	59	82
	female	2,801	255	275	266	286	274	231	207	200	181	158	132	97	79	63	96
	Rural																
	male	2,602	283	294	278	268	228	189	163	157	152	143	121	96	78	62	91
	female	2,201	276	286	266	229	173	145	133	129	117	105	90	71	58	47	75
1921[3]	Urban																
	male	2,147	238	241	207	179	164	175	178	177	147	118	95	70	58	40	53
	female	2,205	235	242	211	203	203	196	178	164	135	109	91	70	61	42	61
	Rural																
	male	2,383	295	288	254	224	187	173	165	165	140	118	100	78	68	50	71
	female	2,054	289	278	241	196	157	143	132	126	106	90	76	62	52	39	62

[1] Based on 1956 definition of urban. Includes Newfoundland.
[2] Based on 1951 definition of urban. Includes Newfoundland.
[3] 1941, 1931 and 1921 based on 1941 definition of urban.

Series A60–74. *Population, by marital status and sex, census dates, 1871 to 1956*

Year	Total			Single			Married[1]			Widowed			Divorced		
	Both sexes	Male	Female	Both sexes	Male	Female	Both sexes	Male	Female	Both sexes	Male	Female	Both sexes	Male	Female
	60	61	62	63	64	65	66	67	68	69	70	71	72	73	74
						Population, 15 years and over									
1956[2]	10,855,581	5,488,060	5,367,521	2,960,929	1,691,761	1,269,168	7,146,673	3,586,641	3,560,032	711,211	194,722	516,489	36,768	14,936	21,832
1951[2]	9,758,712	4,920,815	4,837,897	2,821,788	1,579,351	1,242,437	6,261,578	3,141,754	3,119,824	643,348	186,595	456,753	31,998	13,115	18,883
1941	8,308,104	4,281,237	4,026,867	3,032,324	1,703,795	1,328,529	4,736,585	2,400,100	2,336,485	525,163	170,773	354,390	14,032	6,569	7,463
1931	7,095,010	3,715,527	3,379,483	2,671,820	1,522,491	1,149,329	3,978,012	2,039,918	1,938,094	437,731	149,063	288,668	7,447	4,055	3,392
1921	5,764,598	3,004,173	2,760,425	2,062,520	1,177,952	884,568	3,337,535	1,702,526	1,635,009	357,132	120,020	237,112	7,411	3,675	3,736
1911	4,830,093	2,619,817	2,210,276	1,952,341	1,182,167	770,174	2,602,295	1,345,386	1,256,909	271,031	90,121	180,910	4,426	2,143	2,283
1901[3]	—	—	—	—	—	—	—	—	—	—	—	—	—	—	—
1891	3,075,749	1,569,502	1,506,247	1,295,937	710,576	585,361	1,588,023	796,149	791,874	191,789	62,777	129,012	—	—	—
						Population, all ages									
1901	5,371,315	2,751,708	2,619,607	3,312,593	1,748,582	1,564,011	1,833,043	928,952	904,091	225,018	73,837	151,181	661	337	324
1891	4,833,239	2,460,471	2,372,768	3,053,392	1,601,541	1,451,851	1,588,055	796,153	791,902	191,792	62,777	129,015	—	—	—
1881	4,324,810	2,188,854	2,135,956	2,784,396	1,447,415	1,336,981	1,380,084	690,544	689,540	160,330	50,895	109,435	—	—	—
1871[4]	3,689,257	1,869,264	1,819,993	2,366,876	1,226,347	1,140,529	1,119,659	560,075	559,584	118,475	37,874	80,601	—	—	—

[1] Includes all married persons whether or not they are living together.
[2] Includes Newfoundland.
[3] Classification by age and marital status not available for 1901.
[4] Total includes total population of British Columbia and Northwest Territories for which marital status not available.

U & B

Series A75–113. *Origins of the population, census dates, 1871 to 1951*

Series no.	Origin	1871[1]	1881	1901	1911	1921	1931	1941	1951
75	British	2,110,502	2,548,514	3,063,195	3,999,081	4,868,738	5,381,071	5,715,904	6,709,685
76	English	706,369	881,301	1,260,899	1,871,268	2,545,358	2,741,419	2,968,402	3,630,344
77	Irish	846,414	957,403	988,721	1,074,738	1,107,803	1,230,808	1,267,702	1,439,635
78	Scottish	549,946	699,863	800,154	1,027,015	1,173,625	1,346,350	1,403,974	1,547,470
79	Other	7,773	9,947	13,421	26,060	41,952	62,494	75,826	92,236
80	Other European	1,322,813	1,598,386	2,107,327	3,006,502	3,699,846	4,753,242	5,526,964	6,872,889
81	French	1,082,940	1,298,929	1,649,371	2,061,719	2,452,743	2,927,990	3,483,038	4,319,167
82	Austrian	—	—	10,947[2]	44,036	107,671	48,639	37,715	32,231
83	Belgian	—	—	2,994	9,664	20,234	27,585	29,711	35,148
84	Czech and Slovak	—	—	—	—	8,840	30,401	42,912	63,959
85	Danish	—[3]	—[3]	—[3]	—[3]	21,124	34,118	37,439	42,671
86	Finnish	—	—	2,502	15,500	21,494	43,885	41,683	43,745
87	German	202,991	254,319	310,501	403,417	294,635	473,544	464,682	619,995
88	Greek	39	—	291	3,614	5,740	9,444	11,692	13,966
89	Hungarian	—	—	1,549[4]	11,648	13,181	40,582	54,598	60,460
90	Icelandic	—[3]	—[3]	—[3]	—[3]	15,876	19,382	21,050	23,307
91	Italian	1,035	1,849	10,834	45,963	66,769	98,173	112,625	152,245
92	Jewish	125	667	16,131	76,199	126,196	156,726	170,241	181,670
93	Lithuanian	—	—	—	—	1,970	5,876	7,789	16,224
94	Netherlander	29,662	30,412	33,845	55,961	117,505	148,962	212,863	264,267
95	Norwegian	—[3]	—[3]	—[3]	—[3]	68,856	93,243	100,718	119,266
96	Polish	—	—	6,285	33,652	53,403	145,503	167,485	219,845
97	Romanian	—	—	354[5]	5,883	13,470	29,056	24,689	23,601
98	Russian	607[6]	1,227[6]	19,825	44,376	100,064	88,148	83,708	91,279
99	Scandinavian	1,623	5,223	31,042	112,682	—[7]	—[7]	—[7]	—[7]
100	Swedish	—[3]	—[3]	—[3]	—[3]	61,503	81,306	85,396	97,780
101	Ukrainian	—	—	5,682	75,432	106,721	225,113	305,929[8]	395,043
102	Yugoslavic	—	—	—	—	3,906	16,174	21,214	21,404
103	Other	3,791	5,760	5,174	6,756	17,945	9,392	9,787	35,616
104	Asiatic	4	4,383	23,731	43,213	65,914	84,548	74,064	72,827
105	Chinese	—	4,383	17,312	27,831	39,587	46,519	34,627	32,528
106	Japanese	—	—	4,738	9,067	15,868	23,342	23,149	21,663
107	Other	4	—	1,681	6,315	10,459	14,687	16,288	18,636
108	Other Origins	52,442	173,527	177,062	157,847	153,451	157,925	189,723	354,028
109	Native Indian and Eskimo	23,037	108,547	127,941	105,611	113,724	128,890	125,521	165,607
110	Negro	21,496	21,394	17,437	16,994	18,291	19,456	22,174	18,020
111	Other	348	2,780	145	18,310	187	681	36,753[9]	} 170,401
112	Not stated	7,561	40,806	31,539	16,932	21,249	8,898	5,275	}
113	Totals	3,485,761	4,324,810	5,371,315	7,206,643	8,787,949	10,376,786	11,506,655	14,009,429

[1] Includes the four original provinces of Canada only.
[2] Includes Bohemian, Bukovinian and Slavic.
[3] Included under Scandinavian.
[4] Includes Lithuanian and Moravian.
[5] Includes Bulgarian.
[6] Includes Finnish and Polish.
[7] Since 1921 Scandinavian has been divided into Danish, Icelandic, Norwegian and Swedish.
[8] Includes Bukovinian, Galacian and Ruthenian.
[9] Includes 35,416 Métis.

Series A114–132. *Principal religious denominations of the population, census dates, 1871 to 1951*

Series no.	Religious denomination	1871	1881	1891	1901	1911	1921	1931	1941	1951
114	Anglican	501,269	574,818	646,059	681,494	1,043,017	1,407,780	1,639,075	1,754,368	2,060,720
115	Baptist	243,714	296,525	303,839	318,005	382,720	421,730	443,944	484,465	519,585
116	Congregationalist	21,829	26,900	28,157	28,293	34,054	30,730	694[1]	—[2]	—[2]
117	Evangelical Church	4,701	—	—	10,193	10,595	13,905	22,239	37,064	50,000
118	Greek Orthodox[3]	18	—	—	15,630	88,507	169,832	102,529	139,845	172,271
119	Jewish	1,115	2,393	6,414	16,401	74,564	125,197	155,766	168,585	204,836
120	Lutheran	37,935	46,350	63,982	92,524	229,864	286,458	394,920	401,836	444,923
121	Mennonite (includes Hutterite)[4]	—	—	—	31,797	44,625	58,797	88,837	111,554	125,938
122	Methodist	578,161	742,981	847,765	916,886	1,079,993	1,159,246	—[2]	—[2]	—[2]
123	Mormon	—	534	—	6,891	15,971	19,622	22,041	25,328	32,888
124	Pentecostal	—	—	—	—	513	7,003	26,349	57,742	95,131
125	Presbyterian	574,577	676,165	755,326	842,531	1,116,071	1,409,406	872,428[1]	830,597[1]	781,747[1]
126	Roman Catholic	1,532,471	1,791,982	1,992,017	2,229,600	2,833,041	3,389,626	4,102,960	4,806,431	6,069,496
127	Salvation Army	—	—	13,949	10,308	18,834	24,733	30,773	33,609	70,275
128	Ukrainian (Greek) Catholic	—	—	—	—	—	—	186,879[5]	185,948[5]	190,831
129	United Church of Canada	—	—	—	—	—	8,728	2,021,065	2,208,658	2,867,271
130	Other	66,080	79,927	95,464	127,540	201,784	235,897	250,245	243,466	} 322,017
131	Not stated	126,853[6]	86,769	80,267	43,222	32,490	19,259	16,042	17,159	}
132	Totals	3,689,257	4,324,810	4,833,239	5,371,315	7,206,643	8,787,949	10,376,786	11,506,655	14,009,429

The figures for 1931 to 1951 opposite Congregationalist and Presbyterian are the numbers of those denominations not included in United Church of Canada.
[2] Included in the United Church of Canada.
[3] Greek Orthodox and Greek Catholic combined under the term 'Greek Church' in 1921 and prior years.
[4] Mennonites were included with Baptists in 1871 and 1881; in 1891 they were included with 'other denominations'.
[5] Includes 'other Greek Catholics'.
[6] Includes 109,475 population in Manitoba, British Columbia and the Northwest Territories who were largely Indian and hence likely pagan.

Series A133–142. *Population, Canadian, other British and foreign-born, by sex, census dates, 1871 to 1951*

Year	Total population	Canadian-born			Other British-born[1]			Foreign-born		
		Total	Male	Female	Total	Male	Female	Total	Male	Female
	133	**134**	**135**	**136**	**137**	**138**	**139**	**140**	**141**	**142**
1951	14,009,429	11,949,518[2]	6,001,035[2]	5,948,483[2]	933,049	462,640	470,409	1,126,862	625,198	501,664
1941	11,506,655[3]	9,487,808	4,794,439	4,693,369	1,003,769	527,423	476,346	1,014,133	577,906	436,227
1931	10,376,786	8,069,261	4,076,001	3,993,260	1,184,830	631,411	553,419	1,122,695	667,129	455,566
1921	8,787,949	6,832,224	3,443,109	3,389,115	1,065,448	567,068	498,380	890,277	519,466	370,811
1911	7,206,643	5,619,682	2,849,442	2,770,240	834,229	501,626	332,603	752,732	470,927	281,805
1901	5,371,315	4,671,815	—	—	421,051	—	—	278,449	—	—
1891	4,833,239	4,189,368	—	—	490,573	—	—	153,298	—	—
1881	4,324,810	3,721,826	—	—	478,615	—	—	124,369	—	—
1871	3,689,257[4]	3,010,803	—	—	498,953	—	—	95,254	—	—

[1] Other British-born covers England and Wales, North Ireland, Scotland, the Lesser Isles and Other British Commonwealth (1951 *Census*). For breakdown, see series A170–176. Previous to 1951, the item 'Other British-born' includes also Newfoundland and the Republic of Ireland.
[2] Includes Newfoundland.
[3] Total population in 1941 includes 945 'birthplace not stated'.
[4] Total population in 1871 includes 84,247 population, largely Indians, in British Columbia and the Northwest Territories for whom birthplace is unknown. For discussion of 'not stated' in all years see the note to this table.

Series A143–154. *Population, by birthplace and sex, rural and urban,[1] census dates, 1921 to 1951*

Year	Canadian-born[2]				Other British-born[2]				Foreign-born			
	Rural		Urban		Rural		Urban		Rural		Urban	
	Male	Female	Male	Female	Male	Female	Male	Female	Male	Female	Male	Female
	143	**144**	**145**	**146**	**147**	**148**	**149**	**150**	**151**	**152**	**153**	**154**
1951	2,526,344	2,257,036	3,474,691	3,691,447	99,783	86,526	362,857	383,883	240,484	171,003	384,714	330,661
1941[3]	2,358,768	2,097,622	2,435,671	2,595,747	175,604	138,372	351,819	337,974	287,014	196,442	290,892	239,785
1931	2,047,970	1,829,124	2,028,031	2,164,136	220,574	159,927	410,837	393,492	333,477	211,916	333,652	243,650
1921	1,879,938	1,704,725	1,563,171	1,684,390	212,083	157,986	354,985	340,394	291,420	192,080	228,046	178,731

[1] 1951 definition of urban in 1951; 1941 definition all previous years. See note to series A15–19.
[2] In 1951, 'Canadian-born' includes Newfoundland. In other years, Newfoundland is under 'Other British-born'.
[3] Excludes 945 whose birthplace is not stated: rural, 417; urban, 528; males, 768; females, 177.

Series A155–169. *Population, Canadian, other British and foreign-born, by age and sex, census dates, 1921 to 1951*

(thousands)

Year	All ages			Under 15 years			15–24 years			25–64 years			65 years and over		
	Both sexes	Males	Females	Both sexes	Males	Females	Both sexes	Males	Females	Both sexes	Males	Females	Both sexes	Males	Females
	155	**156**	**157**	**158**	**159**	**160**	**161**	**162**	**163**	**164**	**165**	**166**	**167**	**168**	**169**
	Canadian-born														
1951[1]	11,950	6,001	5,948	4,154	2,118	2,036	2,046	1,019	1,027	5,058	2,528	2,530	691	336	355
1941[2]	9,488	4,794	4,693	3,149	1,594	1,555	2,016	1,014	1,002	3,794	1,925	1,869	529	261	268
1931[3]	8,069	4,076	3,993	3,129	1,580	1,548	1,662	834	828	2,854	1,448	1,406	422	211	211
1921[3]	6,833	3,443	3,389	2,834	1,429	1,405	1,177	583	594	2,490	1,264	1,226	312	157	155
1911[3]	5,620	2,849	2,770	2,130	1,074	1,056	1,068	537	531	2,165	1,109	1,057	240	119	121
	Other British and foreign-born														
1951	2,060	1,088	972	96	50	46	101	50	50	1,468	772	696	395	215	180
1941[2]	2,018	1,105	913	50	25	25	136	69	67	1,593	882	712	239	130	109
1931[3]	2,308	1,299	1,009	152	78	74	289	155	134	1,711	982	729	154	83	71
1921[3]	1,956	1,087	869	185	95	91	336	171	165	1,326	763	563	107	57	50
1911[3]	1,587	973	614	241	124	117	318	200	118	913	582	332	94	50	44

[1] Including Newfoundland. Prior to 1951 persons born in Newfoundland are included under heading 'Other British and foreign-born'.
[2] Not including some portion of the 768 males and 177 females whose place of birth was not stated.
[3] All ages includes 'age not stated'.

Series A170–199. *Country of birth of other British-born and the foreign-born population, census dates, 1871 to 1951*

Year	Total all countries[1]	England and Wales	Scotland	Northern Ireland[2]	Lesser Isles	Newfound-land	Other British Common-wealth	United States	Europe Total	Republic of Ireland[2]
	170	171	172	173	174	175	176	177	178	179
1951	2,059,911	627,551	226,343	56,685	1,903	—[3]	20,567	282,010	801,618	24,110
1941	2,017,902	635,221	234,824	86,126	3,954	25,837	17,807	312,473	653,705	—
1931	2,307,525	746,212	279,765	107,544	5,421	26,410	19,478	344,574	714,462	—
1921	1,955,725	700,442	226,481	93,301	4,807	23,103	17,226	374,022	459,325	—
1911	1,586,961	519,401	169,391	92,874	2,860	15,469	14,526	303,680	404,941	—
1901	699,500	203,803	83,631	101,629	956	12,432	3,771	127,899	125,549	—
1891	643,871	219,688	107,594	149,184	1,269	9,336	3,502	80,915	53,841	—
1881	602,984	169,504	115,062	185,526	814	4,596	3,113	77,753	39,161	—
1871	594,207	147,081	125,450	223,212	852	—[3]	2,358	64,613	28,699	—

Year	Scandinavia	France	Belgium	Netherlands	Germany	Austria and Hungary	Czecho-slovakia	Switzerland	Italy	Greece
	180	181	182	183	184	185	186	187	188	189
1951	64,522	15,650	17,251	41,457	42,693	70,527	29,546	6,414	57,789	8,594
1941	72,473	13,795	14,773	9,923	28,479	82,526	25,564	5,505	40,432	5,871
1931	90,042	16,756	17,033	10,736	39,163	65,914	22,835	6,076	42,578	5,579
1921	64,795	19,247	13,276	5,827	25,266	65,028	4,322	3,479	35,531	3,769
1911	61,240	17,619	7,975	3,808	39,577	78,088	1,689	—	34,739	2,640
1901	18,388	7,944	2,280	385	27,300	28,407	—	1,211	6,854	213
1891	7,827	5,381	—	—	27,752	—	—	—	2,795	—
1881	2,076	4,389	—	—	25,328	—	—	—	777	—
1871	588	2,908	—	—	24,162	102	—	—	218	—

Year	U.S.S.R.	Poland	Finland	Romania	Yugoslavia	Other	China	Japan	Other	Other countries
	190	191	192	193	194	195	196	197	198	199
1951	188,292	164,474	22,035	19,733	20,912	7,619	24,166	6,239	6,740	6,089
1941	124,402	155,400	24,387	28,454	17,416	4,305	29,095	9,462	5,886	3,512
1931	133,869	171,169	30,354	40,322	17,110	4,920	42,037	12,261	6,310	3,051
1921	112,412	65,304	12,156	22,779	1,946	4,188	36,924	11,650	5,062	3,294
1911	89,984	31,373	10,987	18,271	—	6,951	27,083	8,425	5,438	3,165
1901	31,231		—	1,066	—	270	17,043	4,674	1,863	1,421
1891	9,222	695	—	—	—	169	9,129	—	—	9,413
1881		6,376	—	—	—	215	—	—	—	7,455
1871		416	—	—	—	305	—	—	—	1,942

[1] The totals for all countries in 1901, 1911 and 1921 include 14,829, 19,708 and 88, respectively, 'other British-born' whose countries of birth are unknown.

[2] Prior to 1951, the Republic of Ireland is included with Northern Ireland.

[3] Included with Canadian-born.

Series A 200–210. *Province of residence and province of birth of native-born internal migrants in Canada, census dates, 1871 to 1951*

(thousands of persons)

Year	Total[1]	Prince Edward Island	Nova Scotia	New Brunswick	Quebec	Ontario	Manitoba	Saskatchewan	Alberta	British Columbia	Yukon and Northwest Territories
	200	201	202	203	204	205	206	207	208	209	210
Panel A: Migrants by province of residence											
1951	1364.2	5.4	38.6	34.6	155.8	390.9	96.9	106.7	170.2	357.0	8.2
1941	916.7	2.8	24.1	25.3	109.5	218.0	87.8	125.0	124.3	197.3	2.5
1931	783.5	2.5	15.8	23.6	79.4	145.4	89.2	160.0	125.0	140.7	2.0
1921	684.1	2.0	16.1	20.4	46.2	108.4	95.6	169.0	119.1	106.1	1.2
1911	537.3	1.7	11.7	13.5	28.8	77.5	92.4	140.1	86.4	83.1	2.0
1901	298.1	2.5	11.2	12.7	25.2	71.6	81.1		41.8[2]	39.8	12.2[2]
1891	210.1	3.3	8.7	12.2	19.3	68.6	57.4		20.6[2]	20.2	—[2]
1881	130.2	4.1	6.9	12.3	13.2	57.9	31.0		2.1	2.8	—
1871	67.8	—	4.0	7.9	8.8	47.2			0	—	—
Panel B: Migrants by province of birth											
1951	1364.2	26.8	97.6	89.7	215.1	306.7	188.6	268.4	121.0	47.9	2.5
1941	916.7	18.6	55.7	51.7	158.1	288.1	122.1	135.9	65.6	19.9	1.0
1931	783.5	17.0	52.3	42.9	154.2	315.5	89.7	59.9	36.5	14.5	.7
1921	684.1	17.3	43.0	33.3	145.2	330.2	60.0	27.2	17.1	10.1	.7
1911	537.3	14.0	32.3	26.0	113.1	296.6	38.3	6.3	4.8	3.4	2.5
1901	298.1	9.1	18.9	16.6	85.5	143.3	10.9		12.4[2]	1.2	—[2]
1891	210.1	6.7	18.5	13.7	75.1	88.6	5.8		1.3	.5	—
1881	130.2	5.8	14.4	10.6	58.7	32.3	1.6		6.6	.1	—
1871	67.8	—	9.5	7.2	43.3	7.5			.4	—	—

[1] Series A 200 may not be the exact sum of series A 201–210, as a result of rounding.

[2] Data for Yukon and Northwest Territories are included with Saskatchewan and Alberta for this and earlier years.

Series A 211–220. *Estimates of net internal migration of native-born in Canada by intercensal intervals, 1871 to 1951*

Year	Prince Edward Island	Nova Scotia	New Brunswick	Quebec	Ontario	Manitoba	Saskatchewan	Alberta	British Columbia	Yukon and Northwest Territories
	211	212	213	214	215	216	217	218	219	220
Panel A: Thousands of migrants[1]										
1941–51	− 5.6	−27.4	−28.8	−10.8	+154.3	−57.5	−150.7	− 9.4	+131.7	+ 4.2
1931–41	− 1.3	+ 4.8	− 7.0	+26.3	+100.3	−33.8	−111.0	−29.9	+ 51.3	+ .3
1921–31	+ .8	− 9.6	− 6.4	+24.1	+ 51.4	−36.1	− 41.8	−13.5	+ 30.2	+ .8
1911–21	− 3.0	− 6.3	− .5	−14.6	− 2.7	−18.5	+ 8.0	+20.4	+ 16.3	+ 1.0
1901–11	− 5.7	−12.9	− 8.4	−24.0	−147.3	−16.0		+184.9	+ 41.1	− 11.6
1891–1901	− 3.1	+ 2.1	− 2.5	− 4.5	− 51.7	+18.5		+ 22.3[2]	+ 18.9	— [2]
1881–91	− 1.8	− 2.3	− 3.2	−10.2	− 45.6	+22.2		+ 23.8	+ 17.0	—
1871–81[3]	—	− 2.0	+ 1.0	−11.1	− 14.2			− 4.1	—	—
Panel B: Migration per thousand native population[1]										
1941–51	−60	−48	−62	− 3	+ 45	−100	−230	−15	+197	+231
1931–41	−15	+10	−17	+ 9	+ 35	− 68	−176	−62	+116	+ 20
1921–31	+ 9	−20	−17	+10	+ 21	− 85	− 79	−37	+ 95	+ 76
1911–21	−34	−13	− 1	− 7	− 1	− 57	+ 23	+86	+ 75	+106
1901–11	−59	−29	−26	−14	− 76	− 71		+743	+308	−853
1891–1901	−31	+ 5	− 8	− 3	− 29	+128		+244[2]	+242	— [2]
1881–91	−18	− 6	−11	− 8	− 28	+283		+355	+371	—
1871–81	—	− 5	+ 4	− 9	− 11	—		—	—	

[1] Excluding Canadian-born whose province of birth is not stated.

[2] Data for Yukon and Northwest Territories are included with Saskatchewan and Alberta for this and earlier years.

[3] For 1871 to 1881 the figures do not add to zero because of incomplete data for 1871.

Series A221–232. *Estimates of changes in the population ten years and over of the provinces through natural increase and migration, by decades, 1881 to 1941*

(thousands)

Decade	Population and changes	Canada	Prince Edward Island	Nova Scotia	New Brunswick	Quebec	Ontario	Manitoba	Saskat-chewan	Alberta	British Columbia	Yukon	Northwest Territories
		221	222	223	224	225	226	227	228	229	230	231	232
1901–41	Natural increase	4,488	39	243	219	1,600	1,137	335	440	304	162	− 1	9
	Net migration	+819	−42	−133	−111	−170	+324	+ 84	+218	+290	+395	−21	−15
1941	Population 10 +	9,409	76	464	359	2,631	3,188	606	723	646	703	4	9
1931–41	Natural increase	1,352	9	60	62	495	322	89	156	109	48	—	2
	Net migration	−112	− 2	+ 2	− 13	− 32	+ 75	− 41	−138	− 35	+ 72	—	—
1931	Population 10 +	8,169	69	402	310	2,168	2,791	558	705	572	583	4	7
1921–31	Natural increase	1,389	9	69	61	443	338	116	173	116	62	4	2
	Net migration	+103	− 9	− 70	− 43	− 10	+129	− 10	− 5	+ 22	+101	—	− 1
1921	Population 10 +	6,677	69	403	292	1,735	2,324	452	537	434	420	4	6
1911–21	Natural increase	1,036	9	62	52	378	259	82	93	64	36	—	1
	Net migration	+113	−14	− 37	− 25	− 99	+ 46	+ 24	+ 78	+ 85	+ 58	− 4	—
1911	Population 10 +	5,528	74	378	265	1,456	2,019	346	366	285	326	8	5
1901–11	Natural increase	711	12	52	44	284	218	48	18	15	16	− 1	4
	Net migration	+715	−17	− 28	− 30	− 29	+ 74	+111	+283	+218	+164	−17	−14
1901	Population 10 +	4,101	79	354	251	1,201	1,727	187	65[1]	52[1]	146	26[1]	15
1891–1901	Natural increase	654	14	50	43	249	245	30	—	—	8	—	17[1]
	Net migration	−181	−17	− 40	− 32	−121	−144	+ 48	—	—	+ 58	—	+68
1891	Population 10 +	3,628	82	344	240	1,073	1,626	109	—	—	80	—	73
1881–91	Natural increase	669	16	60	48	235	282	13	—	—	5	—	13
	Net migration	−205	−14	− 43	− 44	−132	− 84	+ 52	—	—	+ 37	—	+21
1881	Population 10 +	3,164	80	327	236	970	1,428	44	—	—	38	—	39

[1] Series A232 includes data for Saskatchewan, Alberta and Yukon for years 1881 to 1901.

Series A233–243. *Changes in the population through natural increase and migration, by province, by intercensal intervals, 1931 to 1956*

Decade	Population change	Canada[1]	Newfound-land	Prince Edward Island	Nova Scotia	New Brunswick	Quebec	Ontario	Manitoba	Saskat-chewan	Alberta	British Columbia
		233	234	235	236	237	238	239	240	241	242	243
1951–56	Natural increase	1,471,766	52,892	8,920	63,156	59,812	474,516	431,913	73,651	85,978	119,307	98,006
	Net migration	+599,596	+766	− 8,064	−11,023	−20,893	+98,181	+375,478	− 152	− 37,041	+64,308	+135,248
1941–51	Natural increase	1,972,394	—	15,802	103,512	99,904	736,058	505,034	107,510	135,106	150,303	116,527
	Net migration	+168,964	—	−12,420	−38,890	−41,608	−12,259	+304,853	−60,713	−199,370	− 6,971	+230,822
1931–41	Natural increase	1,221,787	—	9,681	57,268	59,359	459,211	278,488	78,083	131,752	106,405	41,100
	Net migration	− 91,918	—	− 2,672	+ 7,848	−10,177	− 1,991	+ 77,484	−48,478	−157,545	−41,841	+ 82,498

[1] Includes the Yukon and Northwest Territories. Newfoundland is included for 1951 to 1956 only.

Series A244–253. *Estimates of components of changes in population ten years and over, Canada, by decades, 1851 to 1921*

(thousands)

Decade	Keyfitz estimates					McDougall estimates				
	Natural increase	Net migration	Population 10 and over end of decade	Immigration	Emigration	Natural increase	Net migration	Population 10 and over end of decade	Immigration	Emigration
	244	245	246	247	248	249	250	251	252	253
1911–21	916[1]	+233	6,677	1,592	1,360	841[1]	+306	6,679[2]	1,373	1,067
1901–11	711	+715	5,528	1,782	1,066	631	+794	5,532[2]	1,111	317
1891–1901	654	−181	4,101	326	507	595	−115	4,107[2]	249	364
1881–91	669	−205	3,628	903	1,108	617	−154	3,628	448	602
1871–81	619	− 85	3,164	353	438	575	− 40	3,164	253	293
1861–71	563	−191	2,630	186	376	543	−170	2,630	266	436
1851–61	495	+123	2,258	209	86	464	+154	2,258	486	332

[1] Allows for 120,000 additional deaths imputed to World War I.

[2] The differences in total population figures result from McDougall's use of *Census, 1951*, vol. I, table 19. Keyfitz used *Census, 1931*, vol. I, table 8, p. 387.

Series A254. *Immigrant arrivals in Canada, 1852 to 1960*

Year	Numbers 254	Year	Numbers 254	Year	Numbers 254	Year	Numbers 254	Year	Numbers 254	Year	Numbers 254
1960	104,111	1940	11,324	1920	138,824	1900	41,681	1880	38,505	1860	6,276
1959	106,928	1939	16,994	1919	107,698	1899	44,543	1879	40,492	1859	6,300
1958	124,851	1938	17,244	1918	41,845	1898	31,900	1878	29,807	1858	12,339
1957	282,164	1937	15,101	1917	72,910	1897	21,716	1877	27,082	1857	33,854
1956	164,857	1936	11,643	1916	55,914	1896	16,835	1876	25,633	1856	22,544
1955	109,946	1935	11,277	1915	36,665	1895	18,790	1875	27,382	1855	25,296
1954	154,227	1934	12,476	1914	150,484	1894	20,829	1874	39,373	1854	37,263
1953	168,868	1933	14,382	1913	400,870	1893	29,633	1873	50,050	1853	29,464
1952	164,498	1932	20,591	1912	375,756	1892	30,996	1872	36,578	1852	29,307
1951	194,391	1931	27,530	1911	331,288	1891	82,165	1871	27,773	—	—
1950	73,912	1930	104,806	1910	286,839	1890	75,067	1870	24,706	—	—
1949	95,217	1929	164,993	1909	173,694	1889	91,600	1869	18,630	—	—
1948	125,414	1928	166,783	1908	143,326	1888	88,766	1868	12,765	—	—
1947	64,127	1927	158,886	1907	272,409	1887	84,526	1867	10,666[1]	—	—
1946	71,719	1926	135,982	1906	211,653	1886	69,152	1866	11,427	—	—
1945	22,722	1925	84,907	1905	141,465	1885	79,169	1865	18,958	—	—
1944	12,801	1924	124,164	1904	131,252	1884	103,824	1864	24,779	—	—
1943	8,504	1923	133,729	1903	138,660	1883	133,624	1863	21,000	—	—
1942	7,576	1922	64,224	1902	89,102	1882	112,458	1862	18,204	—	—
1941	9,329	1921	91,728	1901	55,747	1881	47,991	1861	13,589	—	—

[1] See the concluding note to series A254 on this figure for 1867.

Series A255–272. *Immigration to Canada by intended occupations and dependents, 1953 to 1960*

Year	Total immigration 255	Workers Total 256	Managerial 257	Professional 258	Clerical 259	Transport and communication 260	Commercial and financial 261	Service 262	Agriculture 263	Logging, fishing and trapping 264	Mining 265	Manufacturing, mechanical and construction 266	Labourers 267	Not stated 268	Dependents Total 269	Wives 270	Children 271	Other 272
From overseas and the United States																		
1960	104,111	53,573	825	7,436	5,860	1,223	2,152	8,763	5,321	188	479	13,551	7,482	293	50,538	20,654	24,626	5,258
1959	106,928	53,551	837	6,947	5,459	999	2,107	9,740	4,965	123	248	12,792	8,940	394	53,377	21,223	26,133	6,021
1958	124,851	63,078	944	7,553	6,745	1,229	2,229	11,501	5,071	169	344	17,476	9,388	429	61,773	24,795	30,444	6,534
1957	282,164	151,511	1,216	16,040	16,829	5,254	6,559	17,574	10,838	827	1,866	54,376	19,471	661	130,653	52,533	70,673	7,447
1956	164,857	91,039	996	9,343	9,492	2,255	3,823	13,800	7,500	505	1,144	29,264	12,482	435	73,818	30,547	38,461	4,810
1955	109,946	57,987	1,404	7,159	5,775	1,190	2,146	9,588	7,036	260	254	15,117	7,687	371	51,959	21,637	25,397	4,925
1954	154,227	84,376	1,633	8,350	6,775	1,938	2,735	11,974	10,920	335	428	25,699	13,011	578	69,851	28,897	35,503	5,451
1953	168,868	91,133	1,176	8,845	6,339	1,855	3,185	13,766	17,250	415	464	26,492	10,380	966	77,735	31,343	41,253	5,139
From overseas																		
1960	92,864	49,192	275	5,808	5,360	1,129	1,778	8,414	5,095	157	463	13,011	7,417	285	43,672	18,081	21,131	4,460
1959	95,590	49,370	305	5,502	4,998	916	1,670	9,416	4,764	91	236	12,214	8,875	383	46,220	18,562	22,424	5,234
1958	114,005	58,862	379	6,277	6,249	1,096	1,859	11,174	4,898	140	322	16,726	9,334	408	55,143	22,274	27,061	5,808
1957	271,156	147,181	617	14,886	16,365	5,125	6,137	17,245	10,702	747	1,815	53,526	19,382	634	123,975	49,910	67,227	6,838
1956	155,080	87,189	441	8,322	9,027	2,157	3,411	13,508	7,351	429	1,113	28,650	12,368	412	67,891	28,171	35,481	4,239
1955	99,554	53,803	486	6,037	5,334	1,083	1,771	9,312	6,846	194	235	14,572	7,613	320	45,751	19,053	22,361	4,337
1954	144,117	80,205	811	7,269	6,331	1,831	2,355	11,735	10,709	277	390	25,095	12,924	478	63,912	26,417	32,694	4,801
1953	159,489	87,129	704	7,664	5,943	1,749	2,739	13,566	17,037	379	432	25,791	10,312	813	72,360	29,041	38,836	4,483

Series A273–283. *Immigration to Canada by intended occupations and dependents, 1932 to 1952*

Year	Total	Skilled	Unskilled and semi-skilled	Farming	Clerical	Pro-fessional	Trading	Domestic servants	Dependent wives	Dependent children	Others[1]
	273	274	275	276	277	278	279	280	281	282	283
From overseas and the United States											
1952	164,498	22,034	19,586	16,971	6,900	7,054	3,402	7,556	31,011	42,999	6,985
1951	194,391	33,682	31,007	25,890	5,317	4,001	2,956	6,531	34,938	44,667	5,402
1950	73,912	6,351	6,973	15,520	2,417	1,628	1,704	2,622	14,368	18,671	3,658
1949	95,217	9,313	9,584	19,139	2,893	1,879	2,043	4,551	18,827	22,574	4,414
1948	125,414	15,990	16,445	19,799	4,689	2,288	2,984	8,303	22,798	26,430	5,688
1947	64,127	9,395	9,056	4,550	4,066	1,954	2,900	1,989	12,233	11,438	6,546
1946	71,719	3,143	1,530	1,120	1,617	1,368	1,676	596	36,295	20,366	4,008
1945	22,722	1,236	1,189	410	659	560	625	555	9,362	6,556	1,570
1944	12,801	625	785	272	383	382	325	421	4,498	3,898	1,212
1943	8,504	671	538	189	393	355	226	423	2,380	2,149	1,180
1942	7,576	517	340	187	315	339	213	457	1,942	1,739	1,527
1941	9,329	612	444	231	310	392	288	631	1,967	1,821	2,633
1940	11,324	765	594	467	318	536	443	593	2,685	2,709	2,214
1939	16,994	655	376	2,312	293	635	585	778	4,264	4,825	2,271
1938	17,244	571	372	2,066	272	502	588	977	4,316	5,685	1,895
1937	15,101	541	452	1,410	312	431	509	786	3,946	4,948	1,766
1936	11,643	436	302	906	194	332	403	581	3,095	3,890	1,504
1935	11,277	418	270	778	235	341	375	516	2,880	3,881	1,583
1934	12,476	565	343	830	284	358	530	571	3,264	4,100	1,631
1933	14,382	644	448	1,098	257	359	693	604	3,649	4,639	1,991
1932	20,591	1,028	537	1,923	369	467	967	751	4,940	7,349	2,260
From overseas											
1952	155,192	21,372	19,144	16,734	6,491	5,673	2,896	7,494	28,637	40,635	6,116
1951	186,659	32,988	30,551	25,639	4,858	3,390	2,444	6,477	32,949	42,793	4,570

[1] 'Others' includes workers and nonworkers, namely, not stated, not known, retired, fiancées, students over 18. The majority would be nonworkers.

Series A284–299. *Immigration to Canada by occupational groups, sex of adults, children, from overseas and the United States, and from overseas, 1904 to 1951*

Year	Total			Farming		Mining		Trading		Skilled mechanics		Unskilled and semi-skilled labourers		Female domestic	Others and unclassified	
	Males	Females[1]	Children[2]	Males	Females	Males	Females	Males	Females	Males	Females	Males	Females		Males	Females
	284	285	286	287	288	289	290	291	292	293	294	295	296	297	298	299
From overseas and the United States																
1951	95,818	53,327	45,246	25,170	7,257	3,018	382	5,692	4,519	32,086	11,814	25,405	6,275	6,531	4,447	16,549
1950	30,700	24,250	18,962	15,027	4,549	533	90	2,697	2,275	5,821	2,706	4,550	2,665	2,622	2,072	9,343
1949	39,044	33,055	23,118	18,118	6,456	1,232	61	2,998	2,891	8,336	4,219	5,938	3,237	4,551	2,422	11,640
1948	52,986	45,319	27,109	18,370	7,169	2,888	63	4,345	4,747	14,031	7,292	10,416	4,179	8,303	2,936	13,566
1947	27,281	24,890	11,956	4,174	1,923	429	41	4,211	3,910	8,546	3,122	7,363	1,684	1,989	2,558	12,221
1946	9,934	40,894	20,891	1,069	424	59	11	2,429	1,440	2,962	806	1,226	363	596	2,189	37,254
1945	4,259	11,707	6,756	398	186	77	4	811	662	1,173	251	949	186	555	851	9,863
1944	2,391	6,319	4,091	260	123	69	4	387	400	590	143	522	152	421	563	5,076
1943	2,113	4,123	2,268	182	73	15	3	307	391	635	172	374	144	423	600	2,917
1942	2,280	3,475	1,821	172	70	21	10	289	310	485	145	242	86	457	1,071	2,397
1941	3,851	3,572	1,906	217	73	19	2	411	294	583	175	403	41	631	2,218	2,356
1940	3,939	4,587	2,798	435	173	33	5	588	363	715	239	531	59	593	1,637	3,155
1939	4,866	6,936	5,192	1,997	1,236	34	8	712	437	601	271	317	63	778	1,205	4,143
1938	4,142	6,982	6,120	1,730	1,052	37	11	716	383	507	232	296	67	977	856	4,260
1937	3,573	6,263	5,265	1,223	728	53	17	662	366	483	191	349	74	785	803	4,102
1936	2,691	4,906	4,046	818	478	31	10	522	237	408	165	255	54	575	657	3,387
1935	2,550	4,593	4,134	727	336	33	4	516	233	381	137	215	52	511	678	3,383
1934	2,998	5,107	4,371	766	315	48	8	698	291	487	183	272	49	554	727	3,776
1933	3,691	5,749	4,942	1,020	422	54	16	817	368	585	207	363	70	596	852	4,149
1932	5,429	7,259	7,903	1,568	656	55	9	1,180	476	947	354	426	100	745	1,253	5,006
1931	7,280	9,728	10,522	2,048	888	62	13	1,581	730	1,422	493	695	167	1,639	1,472	6,032
1930	44,078	32,882	27,846	27,429	4,533	231	30	3,750	1,764	5,971	1,850	4,204	809	13,171	2,493	11,888
1929	75,814	48,945	40,234	46,124	7,381	710	113	5,744	2,499	10,815	2,837	9,226	1,609	18,177	3,195	16,329
1928	95,377	39,809	31,597	61,160	6,160	689	119	4,057	1,655	7,198	1,971	5,534	973	16,154	2,768	12,777
1927	88,213	38,722	31,949	67,599	7,253	722	112	3,686	1,570	6,738	1,991	6,364	1,128	15,380	3,104	11,288
1926	74,272	33,910	27,802	55,421	6,577	1,101	105	2,998	1,422	6,141	1,913	5,790	1,019	13,043	2,821	9,831
1925	38,561	25,341	21,005	25,275	4,532	610	10	2,452	1,271	3,937	1,240	3,769	754	9,404	2,518	8,130
1924	65,619	36,609	21,936	38,166	6,043	1,446	168	4,056	2,639	8,943	2,343	11,192	1,412	13,381	1,816	10,623
1923	77,373	35,501	20,855	38,705	5,112	2,729	283	4,432	2,252	15,914	3,348	12,866	1,297	12,627	2,727	10,582
1922	28,881	22,296	13,047	15,542	4,105	877	111	1,493	813	4,540	1,427	2,850	465	6,332	3,579	9,043
1921	39,681	32,617	19,430	20,176	6,016	658	122	3,299	1,556	5,712	2,482	4,267	1,174	7,998	5,569	13,269
1920	65,528	46,991	26,305	26,399	6,998	1,991	375	4,528	2,507	14,398	5,060	10,123	2,556	10,205	8,089	19,290
1919	36,434	46,955	24,309	16,416	5,276	604	157	1,671	1,149	7,355	2,595	3,457	946	4,803	6,931	32,029
1918	21,021	11,515	9,309	8,538	2,955	259	40	1,369	588	2,874	810	3,637	348	1,087	4,344	5,687
1917	47,333	14,050	11,527	20,152	3,790	748	52	2,056	602	9,534	1,301	11,530	513	1,692	3,313	6,100
1916	31,004	15,177	9,733	11,230	2,670	497	46	1,412	673	8,899	2,270	6,068	585	3,487	2,898	5,446
1915	17,498	11,505	7,662	7,475	2,492	257	42	826	474	4,569	1,264	1,951	488	2,385	2,420	4,360
1914	80,105	41,275	29,104	27,715	8,685	1,508	419	3,836	2,031	12,082	6,468	30,120	4,650	10,582	4,844	8,440
1913	241,176	92,740	66,883	67,556	15,331	4,326	996	15,441	5,339	40,787	17,426	103,578	13,308	24,547	9,488	15,793
1912	225,587	86,291	63,878	78,248	17,887	4,642	990	14,516	4,409	35,177	15,612	84,160	12,204	22,109	8,844	13,080

Series A 284–299. *Immigration to Canada by occupational groups, sex of adults, children, from overseas and the United States, and from overseas, 1904 to 1951 (continued)*

Year	Total Males	Total Females[1]	Total Children[2]	Farming Males	Farming Females	Mining Males	Mining Females	Trading Males	Trading Females	Skilled mechanics Males	Skilled mechanics Females	Unskilled and semi-skilled labourers Males	Unskilled and semi-skilled labourers Females	Female domestic	Others and unclassified Males	Others and unclassified Females
	284	285	286	287	288	289	290	291	292	293	294	295	296	297	298	299
									From overseas							
1951	93,133	50,206	43,320	24,930	7,170	3,004	377	5,024	4,004	31,434	11,571	25,067	6,129	6,477	3,674	14,478
1950	27,878	21,164	17,071	14,764	4,459	513	84	1,813	1,778	5,150	2,486	4,178	2,479	2,585	1,460	7,293
1949	36,197	29,953	21,323	17,846	6,340	1,216	58	2,251	2,443	7,604	4,002	5,514	3,034	4,530	1,766	9,546
1948	50,278	42,271	25,484	17,982	7,001	2,865	53	3,703	4,326	13,341	7,049	10,055	4,005	8,273	2,332	11,564
1947	23,731	21,236	9,720	3,677	1,722	397	30	3,261	3,340	7,730	2,842	6,911	1,554	1,924	1,755	9,824
1946	6,273	36,785	17,192	431	166	28	4	1,516	886	2,249	587	791	243	539	1,258	34,360
1945	2,332	8,904	5,092	55	10	65	4	352	345	775	138	736	97	513	349	7,797
1944	1,211	4,222	2,859	25	14	62	3	153	179	368	71	416	95	392	187	3,468
1943	1,007	1,940	1,156	22	8	12	3	111	186	356	96	241	84	367	265	1,196
1942	718	1,205	555	21	7	14	8	89	91	186	53	128	34	352	280	660
1941	930	1,224	581	34	13	10	—	116	98	173	50	257	9	510	340	544
1940	1,354	1,752	1,084	117	61	10	2	185	151	198	78	358	20	431	486	1,009
1939	3,202	4,474	3,669	1,669	1,097	14	4	363	249	302	148	198	35	676	656	2,265
1938	2,449	4,624	4,338	1,342	882	18	5	256	165	252	114	192	36	873	389	2,549
1937	1,871	3,997	3,678	886	574	22	5	220	123	196	81	214	32	711	333	2,471
1936	1,326	2,866	2,575	508	325	14	6	191	70	189	65	138	21	517	286	1,862
1935	1,062	2,574	2,350	359	162	11	—	185	86	157	46	113	27	426	237	1,827
1934	1,095	2,881	2,429	317	103	12	2	182	81	214	98	143	20	454	227	2,123
1933	1,073	2,735	2,074	315	88	9	7	181	81	184	66	172	22	457	212	2,014
1932	1,238	2,942	2,702	366	106	13	3	210	108	203	80	191	28	520	255	2,097
1931	2,350	5,199	4,786	697	282	32	7	371	205	481	159	343	76	1,308	426	3,162
1930	33,855	26,778	18,541	23,722	3,457	180	24	1,859	971	3,670	1,202	3,354	595	12,494	1,070	8,035
1929	60,251	40,754	32,136	41,632	6,239	547	94	3,199	1,435	6,469	1,899	6,755	1,252	17,554	1,649	12,281
1928	80,387	32,604	23,859	69,368	4,786	487	84	2,091	902	3,688	1,252	3,491	663	15,553	1,262	9,364
1927	76,165	32,920	25,981	62,453	5,992	572	101	2,269	1,036	4,617	1,498	4,607	869	14,858	1,647	8,566
1926	63,557	28,701	22,782	50,163	5,340	937	96	2,043	1,056	4,367	1,519	4,503	812	12,469	1,544	7,409
1925	29,092	21,263	16,835	20,543	3,445	482	6	1,573	927	2,588	960	2,478	623	8,973	1,428	6,329
1924	56,563	32,677	18,882	33,922	4,893	1,263	149	2,947	2,191	7,573	2,086	10,115	1,265	13,003	743	9,090
1923	67,981	31,410	17,622	33,986	3,893	2,551	254	3,451	1,829	14,745	3,097	11,569	1,120	12,166	1,679	9,051
1922	19,563	17,834	9,293	9,725	2,386	722	87	875	580	3,409	1,180	2,379	371	5,849	3,894	7,381
1921	26,553	26,746	14,541	12,667	3,924	529	105	2,320	1,168	3,936	2,095	3,207	968	7,453	3,894	11,033
1920	41,201	38,424	19,011	15,271	4,140	1,609	320	3,089	1,972	9,183	4,115	6,520	2,072	9,490	5,529	16,315
1919	12,492	37,300	15,777	3,410	1,749	232	102	807	778	2,108	1,295	1,586	657	4,059	4,349	28,660
1918	4,454	3,637	1,985	377	165	12	9	402	110	289	200	854	89	274	2,520	2,790
1917	2,565	2,994	1,614	466	194	32	7	185	88	351	165	940	105	640	591	1,795
1916	3,741	7,132	3,262	896	642	35	22	251	351	702	930	1,354	252	2,716	503	2,219
1915	3,321	5,711	3,336	1,197	741	75	26	256	297	444	488	420	275	1,766	929	2,118
1914	52,107	29,258	18,906	13,536	4,273	1,038	360	2,496	1,554	5,750	4,795	26,624	4,014	9,474	2,663	4,788
1913	181,202	72,782	49,103	44,475	9,281	2,743	860	12,210	4,324	27,223	14,856	89,246	11,819	22,748	5,305	8,894
1912	145,580	65,213	44,868	50,279	10,236	2,964	842	11,448	3,530	21,206	12,926	54,217	9,526	20,447	5,466	7,706
1911	122,061	57,883	39,316	47,050	11,136	2,488	737	9,896	2,590	11,053	5,755	40,692	9,719	18,410	10,882	9,536
1910	104,432	43,696	30,361	45,197	10,036	3,586	757	7,964	2,268	18,554	7,481	24,689	4,005	14,217	4,442	4,932
1909	52,293	23,625	17,367	19,372	4,948	2,155	464	4,271	1,276	9,464	4,509	15,186	2,007	7,705	1,845	2,716
1908	48,822	24,007	18,747	16,445	4,334	1,389	472	4,869	2,130	9,844	5,631	14,614	2,052	6,711	1,661	2,677
1907	136,298	44,854	39,673	30,227	6,497	2,904	736	9,890	3,660	33,059	13,148	56,701	5,882	10,755	3,517	4,176
1906	90,170	32,126	29,965	26,182	6,096	2,487	663	5,807	2,073	23,804	8,859	29,167	4,418	7,381	2,723	2,636
1905	61,238	20,928	19,364	22,576	5,006	1,291	361	3,142	1,128	16,667	4,965	15,283	2,043	5,313	2,279	2,112
1904	55,803	18,426	17,073	20,797	4,717	2,128	442	3,366	649	12,965	2,640	15,735	1,915	4,422	812	3,641

[1] From 1930 to 1951 females include some female domestics who were under 18 years. See the commentary for the numbers included.

[2] Prior to approximately the end of 1910 persons 11 years of age or under were classed as children. Thereafter, until 1 April 1925, persons 13 years of age or under were classed as children. From 1 April 1925 to 31 December 1951 all persons 17 years or under with the exception of female domestics were classed as children. Some children may have had occupations but they are not included in the occupational totals in the table.

Series A 300–315. *Immigration to Canada by age, sex and marital status, 1933 to 1960*

Year	All ages		0–14 years		15–19 years				20–39 years				40 years and over			
					Males		Females		Males		Females		Males		Females	
	Males	Females	Males	Females	Married	Other	Married	Other	Married	Other	Married	Other	Married	Other	Married	Other
	300	301	302	303	304	305	306	307	308	309	310	311	312	313	314	315
1960	51,018	53,093	11,625	11,105	36	4,145	998	3,403	12,812	15,505	16,330	11,924	5,881	1,014	5,301	4,032
1959	51,476	55,452	12,531	11,675	46	4,387	934	3,685	12,560	14,413	16,615	12,552	6,490	1,049	5,742	4,249
1958	60,630	64,221	14,599	13,584	56	5,136	1,072	4,412	14,934	17,576	19,704	14,503	7,196	1,133	6,518	4,428
1957	154,226	127,938	34,337	32,049	129	10,753	1,665	7,382	47,314	44,901	48,227	21,374	14,595	2,197	11,323	5,918
1956	89,541	75,316	18,879	17,334	62	7,208	1,019	4,735	24,508	29,182	25,947	15,059	8,221	1,481	6,934	4,288
1955	56,828	53,118	12,334	11,292	46	4,456	698	3,254	14,290	18,504	17,571	11,157	5,935	1,263	5,574	3,572
1954	84,531	69,696	17,222	15,876	68	6,407	673	4,159	22,563	27,669	23,835	13,856	9,093	1,509	7,382	3,915
1953	91,422	77,446	19,901	18,420	60	7,294	628	5,030	24,128	27,188	25,799	14,558	11,037	1,814	8,581	4,430
1952	89,849	74,649	20,743	18,912	41	6,093	456	3,083	23,334	25,359	26,010	11,952	12,066	2,213	8,818	4,518
1951	120,166	74,225	20,700	18,774	52	8,796	600	3,820	33,453	39,593	27,293	9,952	14,541	3,031	9,135	4,651
1950	40,987	32,925	8,421	7,668	24	3,520	276	1,876	9,749	11,631	10,113	4,897	6,269	1,373	4,841	3,254
1949	51,162	44,055	10,214	9,595	16	3,739	372	2,820	12,720	14,910	13,671	7,125	7,864	1,699	6,367	4,105
1948	67,090	58,324	11,862	11,211	23	4,323	343	3,919	16,043	22,536	16,293	13,387	9,771	2,532	7,959	5,212
1947	33,435	30,692	5,162	4,907	18	1,600	369	1,949	8,536	11,646	8,326	6,910	5,245	1,228	4,467	3,764
1946	20,483	51,236	9,998	9,466	14	793	3,504	1,121	4,191	2,336	30,466	2,656	2,489	662	2,487	1,536
1945	7,701	15,021	3,237	3,019	6	443	804	657	1,421	983	7,715	1,196	1,268	343	951	679
1944	4,494	8,307	1,907	1,749	4	338	329	554	681	483	3,539	841	828	253	722	573
1943	3,290	5,214	995	917	3	365	160	445	581	424	1,654	847	700	222	654	537
1942	3,208	4,368	784	746	4	356	99	371	526	636	1,347	728	656	246	581	496
1941	4,791	4,538	810	816	1	453	92	455	785	1,704	1,302	794	762	276	624	455
1940	5,371	5,953	1,221	1,176	2	375	89	444	914	1,348	1,687	827	1,101	410	1,010	720
1939	7,681	9,313	2,284	2,027	3	812	96	758	1,417	1,191	2,851	1,154	1,566	408	1,399	1,028
1938	7,416	9,828	2,682	2,457	3	807	133	829	1,375	1,063	3,043	1,258	1,160	326	1,239	869
1937	6,300	8,801	2,255	2,248	3	602	106	632	1,126	995	2,849	1,085	1,012	307	1,076	805
1936	4,818	6,825	1,846	1,735	—	383	74	436	784	735	2,269	913	815	255	814	584
1935	4,656	6,621	1,886	1,762	2	338	79	414	645	754	2,160	853	767	264	696	657
1934	5,159	7,317	1,911	1,953	3	391	80	414	748	923	2,496	982	862	321	772	620
1933	6,191	8,191	2,234	2,157	2	407	106	474	995	1,061	2,645	1,126	1,116	376	961	722

Series A316–336. *Ethnic origin of all immigrants to Canada, from overseas and the United States, and from overseas, 1901 to 1960*

Year[1]	British					Northwest Europe			Central Europe		
	English	Scottish	Irish	Welsh	British not elsewhere stated	French	Belgian and Dutch	Scandina-vian	German and Austrian including Luxembourg	Balkan states	Czechoslo-vakian and Swiss
	316	317	318	319	320	321	322	323	324	325	326
						From overseas and the United States					
1960	15,601	6,130	4,012	692	—	2,940	6,759	2,261	13,444	5,087	1,031
1959	15,034	5,526	3,834	563	—	2,622	6,528	2,532	13,277	3,682	886
1958	20,224	6,713	4,792	760	—	3,292	8,950	3,089	16,839	7,892	1,053
1957	75,546	24,533	15,828	2,629	—	6,214	15,531	10,471	33,682	35,954	1,718
1956	35,204	11,987	8,242	1,154	—	3,768	10,400	5,361	30,978	6,509	1,462
1955	22,422	7,289	4,910	846	—	2,941	8,343	2,907	21,460	2,040	1,034
1954	29,617	11,534	7,748	1,075	—	3,489	18,037	3,240	34,983	2,450	1,404
1953	31,018	11,317	8,669	958	—	3,830	22,235	3,406	39,853	3,304	1,466
1952	29,341	11,693	5,901	937	—	5,000	22,890	4,242	29,344	4,234	2,323
1951	21,348	10,002	3,373	638	—	6,949	22,060	6,671	33,234	9,958	4,295
1950	11,068	3,928	2,322	327	—	1,929	8,107	1,606	6,642	3,171	1,950
1949	16,116	6,180	3,527	537	—	1,906	8,753	1,700	6,721	3,623	2,467
1948	32,441	11,590	5,096	981	—	1,884	11,516	1,406	3,713	4,672	1,801
1947	30,346	8,696	4,006	1,035	—	1,524	4,364	816	1,186	407	503
1946	42,197	10,209	4,632	1,294	—	3,229	3,182	879	1,298	262	378
1945	13,831	2,469	1,878	273	—	1,295	301	361	584	106	110
1944	7,888	1,254	1,112	127	—	860	175	219	320	67	51
1943	4,661	902	896	88	—	701	141	148	314	55	54
1942	3,656	971	813	88	—	660	157	208	290	36	71
1941	4,247	1,129	1,069	140	—	792	245	251	400	64	106
1940	5,048	1,350	1,156	135	—	949	295	304	432	163	186
1939	4,261	1,384	1,071	127	—	930	632	327	1,586	719	1,116
1938	4,163	1,365	1,130	130	—	1,049	535	325	1,102	1,348	1,772
1937	3,736	1,314	1,017	102	—	871	332	338	1,137	1,170	1,480
1936	3,049	1,133	854	105	—	833	305	249	792	800	768
1935	3,089	1,204	895	88	—	840	272	300	725	705	590
1934	3,491	1,198	1,021	115	—	903	228	307	945	785	723
1933	4,301	1,700	1,316	126	—	1,337	240	362	1,213	769	520
1932	6,461	2,612	1,886	184	—	2,832	328	628	1,842	592	423
1931	9,417	3,825	2,748	371	—	2,938	405	723	2,389	841	517
1930	24,789	11,996	7,876	1,116	—	5,084	2,032	4,709	13,544	5,349	3,327
1929	43,287	23,207	14,478	3,586	—	5,187	2,932	10,820	17,919	8,315	3,834
1928	37,662	18,532	12,523	3,316	—	4,605	3,596	12,132	17,964	11,409	6,171
1927	34,056	17,569	11,857	2,204	—	3,834	5,079	14,363	15,845	9,563	5,930
1926	30,593	16,339	11,425	1,568	—	2,882	4,126	8,584	13,791	9,909	5,524
						From overseas					
1925	18,647	10,039	5,779	897	95	457	1,985	3,092	6,621	5,211	2,185
1924	28,276	17,305	10,760	1,271	2,068	351	3,325	7,880	2,727	5,931	3,630
1923	35,783	25,107	8,231	989	5,391	324	2,166	6,016	1,364	1,039	3,461
1922	17,729	9,531	3,217	528	1,599	289	418	1,444	204	618	237
1921	26,407	12,551	4,108	744	557	364	818	1,623	208	1,170	360
1920	49,248	19,486	6,122	951	1,353	984	2,766	1,585	153	801	487
1919	43,973	10,148	2,506	624	678	1,486	1,005	563	30	22	86
1918	3,614	659	155	56	912	136	97	215	—	1	9
1917	1,987	406	199	40	1,482	130	141	470	1	—	14
1916	5,411	2,139	947	99	1,544	192	250	894	18	9	29
1915	6,672	1,952	865	117	301	191	406	526	48	10	49
1914	35,801	9,430	3,942	706	876	1,568	2,230	2,622	3,632	6,173	412
1913	113,004	31,426	10,542	2,012	1,414	2,668	4,476	5,543	8,942	7,660	738
1912	104,226	30,413	9,242	1,978	1,760	2,673	3,028	5,191	6,256	10,715	573
1911	99,200	34,686	8,419	1,771	3,694	2,169	2,785	5,239	9,284	3,792	517
1910	76,976	27,938	6,432	1,292	3,217	1,980	2,341	5,804	10,963	3,305	521
1909	35,087	13,010	3,647	600	3,804	1,633	1,464	3,529	4,742	2,354	288
1908	39,805	11,676	3,718	528	2,785	1,944	1,255	1,848	3,144	2,592	180
1908[1]	90,830	22,223	6,547	1,032	3,758	2,671	2,426	4,073	4,262	6,978	195
1907[1]	41,156	10,729	3,404	502	1,308	1,314	1,044	2,296	2,451	1,342	112
1906[1]	65,135	15,846	797	5,018	945	1,648	1,495	3,859	3,120	2,580	172
1905	48,847	11,744	770	3,998	528	1,743	1,077	4,118	3,596	2,383	150
1904	36,003	10,552	691	3,128	655	1,534	1,027	4,203	3,501	3,312	128
1903	32,087	7,046	423	2,236	406	937	526	5,448	2,668	4,273	73
1902	12,783	2,853	312	1,311	16	431	258	2,451	1,368	1,600	17
1901	9,331	1,476	70	933	3	360	157	1,750	1,212	721	30

Series A316–336. *Ethnic origin of all immigrants to Canada, from overseas and the United States, and from overseas, 1901 to 1960*
(continuation)

Year[1]	Eastern Europe			Southern Europe			Other origins			
	Union of Soviet Socialist Republics	Polish	Baltic States	Italian	Greek	Other Southern Europe	Jewish	Chinese and Japanese	Other Asian[2]	Other origins
	327	328	329	330	331	332	333	334	335	336
From overseas and the United States										
1960	581	3,401	1,455	21,690	5,093	6,645	2,964	1,571	1,371	1,383
1959	548	3,960	1,297	27,223	5,035	5,416	3,395	2,783	1,510	1,277
1958	657	3,171	1,809	28,878	5,476	3,370	2,895	2,823	1,519	649
1957	972	3,096	3,734	29,763	5,706	6,686	6,037	1,871	1,332	861
1956	866	2,438	1,852	30,064	5,274	2,942	2,190	2,227	1,169	770
1955	857	2,073	1,393	20,545	3,057	2,150	1,660	2,704	810	505
1954	1,129	2,461	1,760	24,857	2,956	2,549	2,036	2,031	558	313
1953	1,484	3,308	2,605	24,547	2,112	1,625	4,300	1,985	515	331
1952	3,968	5,638	5,504	21,554	1,750	1,332	5,682	2,327	594	244
1951	9,254	13,078	12,954	24,532	2,918	2,527	7,167	2,711	492	230
1950	4,468	6,732	5,236	9,246	913	1,064	3,006	1,759	259	179
1949	7,539	12,359	8,334	7,936	774	450	5,047	816	182	250
1948	11,482	13,915	9,531	3,352	775	890	9,892	82	138	257
1947	2,374	2,735	2,113	298	711	133	2,424	23	213	220
1946	384	730	98	320	108	131	2,100	11	64	213
1945	119	332	47	132	38	45	654	—	29	118
1944	75	106	17	74	16	30	310	—	23	77
1943	56	72	28	76	15	15	203	1	22	56
1942	47	77	29	48	18	21	311	—	19	56
1941	62	117	29	70	31	29	446	4	12	86
1940	67	112	58	178	61	52	638	44	29	67
1939	1,936	439	147	262	140	21	1,763	44	53	36
1938	2,070	633	143	428	130	28	748	57	50	38
1937	1,359	675	151	481	110	37	559	147	46	39
1936	909	414	122	349	92	34	659	103	47	26
1935	582	447	94	392	67	18	803	70	65	31
1934	648	436	127	375	58	24	869	127	65	31
1933	472	410	117	365	53	21	781	107	82	90
1932	586	474	120	435	71	40	747	120	115	95
1931	652	680	212	633	66	42	670	174	93	134
1930	9,256	5,207	3,558	1,327	575	104	4,220	218	217	302
1929	11,867	6,424	5,852	1,514	741	158	4,001	181	201	489
1928	17,325	8,583	5,743	1,114	770	154	4,059	536	209	380
1927	12,179	8,481	6,252	4,617	610	130	5,184	513	280	340
1926	10,795	5,552	5,738	2,683	319	122	4,867	443	403	319
From overseas										
1925	3,077	1,952	1,698	1,652	214	86	2,637	424	381	61
1924	5,594	2,908	6,363	2,676	215	37	5,428	517	696	164
1923	3,668	4,157	255	6,062	294	1,161	9,494	1,215	687	149
1922	206	2,758	785	2,030	187	73	3,385	1,205	163	84
1921	513	2,853	460	2,508	195	76	8,731	3,213	270	111
1920	1,441	3,544	1,198	3,927	297	362	1,335	1,854	479	263
1919	44	24	25	717	31	413	74	2,977	18	125
1918	45	2	15	60	5	14	25	4,024	2	30
1917	32	—	129	327	59	204	38	1,434	12	68
1916	27	15	276	713	274	160	137	866	13	122
1915	43	7	91	365	124	10	73	462	7	49
1914	13,110	2,373	637	7,365	1,506	821	4,279	2,281	226	281
1913	47,665	13,339	3,508	27,704	898	1,727	11,574	7,184	726	408
1912	35,065	10,077	2,135	14,265	1,523	293	6,885	7,667	1,357	339
1911	18,661	6,028	1,637	7,218	584	230	5,044	7,371	628	303
1910	9,610	5,454	2,262	8,181	784	195	5,060	5,077	739	408
1909	4,405	4,092	1,348	6,919	461	38	2,779	2,127	772	186
1908	3,649	7,346	453	4,006	174	40	2,504	3,021	743	165
1908[1]	7,193	15,861	1,212	11,212	1,053	64	7,712	9,485	4,472	1,215
1907[1]	2,230	2,685	1,049	5,114	545	36	6,584	2,134	2,913	978
1906[1]	3,418	6,381	1,103	7,959	254	20	7,127	1,940	1,206	1,245
1905	1,914	7,671	1,323	3,473	98	12	7,715	354	841	568
1904	1,955	8,398	845	4,445	191	7	3,727	—	545	313
1903	5,505	8,656	1,734	3,371	193	9	2,066	—	1,090	137
1902	2,479	6,550	1,292	3,828	161	1	1,015	2	1,269	994
1901	1,044	4,702	682	4,710	81	14	2,765	13	662	446

[1] For 1901 to 1906, fiscal year ending 30 June of the year given. Nine months for 1907 ending 31 March. Fiscal year ending 31 March 1908. Calendar year 1908 to 1960.

[2] Including immigrants of Egyptian origin.

Series A 337. *Immigrant arrivals from the United States, 1904 to 1960*

Year	Number 337	Year	Number 337	Year	Number 337	Year	Number 337	Year	Number 337	Year	Number 337
1960	11,247	1950	7,799	1940	7,134	1930	25,632	1920	40,188	1910	108,300
1959	11,338	1949	7,744	1939	5,649	1929	31,852	1919	42,129	1909	80,409
1958	10,846	1948	7,381	1938	5,833	1928	29,933	1918	31,769	1908	51,750
1957	11,008	1947	9,440	1937	5,555	1927	23,818	1917	65,737	1907	51,584
1956	9,777	1946	11,469	1936	4,876	1926	20,944	1916	41,779	1906	59,392
1955	10,392	1945	6,394	1935	5,291	1925	17,717	1915	24,297	1905	39,935
1954	10,110	1944	4,509	1934	6,071	1924	16,042	1914	50,213	1904	39,950
1953	9,379	1943	4,401	1933	8,500	1923	16,716	1913	97,712		
1952	9,306	1942	5,098	1932	13,709	1922	17,534	1912	120,095		
1951	7,732	1941	6,594	1931	15,195	1921	23,888	1911	112,028		

Series A 338–341. *Canadians returning from the United States, 1925 to 1960*

Year	Total[1] 338	Canadian-born citizens 339	British who had acquired Canadian domicile 340	Naturalized Canadian citizens 341	Year	Total 338	Canadian-born citizens 339	British who had acquired Canadian domicile 340	Naturalized Canadian citizen 341
1960	5,233	—	—	—	1940	4,990	4,705	207	78
1959	5,243	—	—	—	1939	4,610	3,572	565	473
1958	5,297	—	—	—	1938	4,659	4,016	333	310
1957	5,426	—	—	—	1937	5,167	4,443	377	347
1956	4,740	—	—	—	1936	5,168	4,649	297	222
1955	3,942	—	—	—	1935	6,378	4,961	632	785
1954	4,516	—	—	—	1934	7,272	5,926	739	607
1953	4,606	—	—	—	1933	10,209	9,330	457	422
1952	4,707	—	—	—	1932	18,220	16,801	809	610
1951	3,635	—	—	—	1931	20,352	18,503	1,135	714
1950	3,518	3,372	77	69	1930	31,608	28,230	2,176	1,202
1949	4,050	3,907	53	90	1929	30,479	27,328	2,265	886
1948	5,678	4,438	1,077	163	1928	34,120	30,436	2,674	1,010
1947	8,970	6,746	1,972	252	1927	42,078	36,838	3,560	1,680
1946	5,177	4,535	558	84	1926	62,293	53,736	5,792	2,765
1945	2,689	2,484	172	33	1925	39,987	33,774	3,658	2,555
1944	2,210	2,070	120	20					
1943	2,333	2,225	93	15					
1942	3,467	3,269	170	28					
1941	3,564	3,372	133	59					

[1] A breakdown of the total is not available after 1950.

Series A 342–347. *Persons deported,[1] including accompanying persons, after admission, by principal causes, 1903 to 1960*

Year	Total 342	Medical causes 343	Public charges 344	Criminal causes 345	Other civil causes 346	Accompanying deported persons 347	Year	Total 342	Medical causes 343	Public charges 344	Criminal causes 345	Other civil causes 346	Accompanying deported persons 347
1960	571	66	15	200	246	44	1930	3,963	600	2,106	591	107	559
1959	744	107	10	228	337	62	1929	1,964	650	444	441	194	235
1958	655	81	7	168	346	53	1928	1,886	519	430	426	257	254
1957	506	55	10	145	277	19	1927	1,585	470	354	447	149	165
1956	604	90	21	165	292	36	1926	1,716	410	506	453	189	158
1955	860	147	24	205	403	81	1925	1,686	420	543	520	58	145
1954	902	126	26	266	403	81	1924	2,106	649	775	511	93	78
1953	786	121	18	149	452	46	1923	1,632	282	679	543	76	52
1952	580	54	23	102	400	1	1922	2,046	313	950	630	105	48
1951	461	40	14	85	322	—	1921	1,044	133	236	586	52	37
1950	392	47	31	100	209	5	1920	655	123	158	334	22	18
1949	415	48	27	94	243	3	1919	454	70	103	236	35	10
1948	354	33	18	120	181	2	1918	527	39	91	274	84	39
1947	368	33	8	143	184	—	1917	605	98	161	277	60	9
1946	343	16	10	114	203	—	1916	1,243	206	635	329	68	5
1945	256	28	1	92	135	—	1915	1,734	379	789	404	128	34
1944	181	17	3	104	57	—	1914	1,834	570	715	376	163	10
1943	246	17	2	107	118	2	1913	1,281	370	392	334	169	16
1942	244	20	—	85	137	2	1912	959	229	343	242	128	17
1941	516	12	2	74	423	5	1911	784	222	289	172	83	18
1940	392	14	8	96	273	1	1910	734	212	348	130	44	—
1939	413	33	29	113	233	5	1909	1,748	467	1,074	115	71	21
1938	439	38	45	101	243	12	1908	825	384	309	68	38	26
1937	421	44	51	106	187	33	1907	201	126	28	12	—	35
1936	605	52	135	124	238	56	1906	137	110	18	1	4	4
1935	675	90	133	251	168	33	1905	86	58	19	8	—	1
1934	1,701	181	880	288	196	156	1904	85	61	19	1	1	3
1933	5,138	316	3,541	584	238	459	1903	67	49	14	—	—	4
1932	7,647	560	5,217	909	290	671							
1931	6,583	730	4,084	1,022	261	486							

[1] Data do not include persons rejected at ports of entry after examination.

SECTION B: VITAL STATISTICS, HEALTH AND WELFARE

JACQUES HENRIPIN, *University of Montreal*

The statistics in the tables of section B are in three divisions. Series B 1–107 contain data on Vital Statistics, series B 108–227 on Health, and series B 228–270 on Social Welfare. In addition, series B 271–277, which are an appendix to this section, give data on vital statistics of the Catholic population of the Province of Quebec, 1608 to 1890.

The source references for Vital Statistics (series B 1–107) are:

Dominion Bureau of Statistics, Health and Welfare Division, *Vital Statistics*, annual since 1921 (Ottawa, Queen's Printer); Dominion Bureau of Statistics, *Canadian Vital Statistics Trends 1921–1954*, Reference Paper No. 70 (Ottawa, Queen's Printer, 1956); Dominion Bureau of Statistics, *Canadian Life Tables 1950–52, 1955–57*, Reference Paper (Ottawa, Queen's Printer, 1960); Dominion Bureau of Statistics, *Canada Year Book, 1936* (Ottawa, King's Printer, 1936); Dominion Bureau of Statistics, *Census of Canada, 1951*, vol. I (Ottawa, Queen's Printer); Dominion Bureau of Statistics, *Canadian Statistical Review*, monthly (Ottawa, Queen's Printer); Province of Quebec, Bureau of Statistics, *Statistical Year Book*, annual since 1913 (Quebec, Queen's Printer); Province of Quebec, *Annual Report of the Provincial Bureau of Health*, annual from 1922–23 to 1934–35 (Quebec, King's Printer); Province of Quebec, *Twenty-eighth Annual Report of the Superior Board of Health for the Year 1921–22* (Quebec, King's Printer); City of Montreal, *Report of the Municipal Department of Hygiene*, annual to 1917, followed by *Report of the Department of Health*, annual from 1918 (Montreal); Central Mortgage and Housing Corporation, *Canadian Housing Statistics, 1961* (Ottawa, 1962); O. J. Firestone, *Canada's Economic Development 1867–1953*, Income and Wealth Series VII, International Association for Research in Income and Wealth (London, Bowes & Bowes, 1958); Nathan Keyfitz, 'The Growth of Canadian Population', *Population Studies*, vol. IV, no. 1 (June 1950), pp. 47–63.

The source references for Health (series B 108–227) are:

Department of National Health and Welfare, Research Division, *Survey of Physicians in Canada, June 1954*, Memo no. 2, General Series, 6th edition (Ottawa, Queen's Printer, 1955); Department of National Health and Welfare, Research Division, *Government Expenditures and Related Data on Health and Social Welfare*, Social Security Series, Memo No. 14, 2nd and 3rd editions (Ottawa, Queen's Printer, 1955 and 1960); Department of National Health and Welfare, *Voluntary Medical Care Insurance, A Study of Non-Profit Plans in Canada*, General Series no. 4 (Ottawa, Queen's Printer, 1954); Department of National Health and Welfare, *Voluntary Hospital and Medical Insurance in Canada, 1955, 1956, 1957, 1958*, Health Care Series no. 6, 10, 11 and 13 (Ottawa, Queen's Printer, 1957, 1958, 1959, 1961); Dominion Bureau of Statistics, *Notifiable Diseases*, annual (Ottawa, Queen's Printer); Dominion Bureau of Statistics and Department of National Health and Welfare, *Canadian Sickness Survey*, no. 10 (Ottawa, Queen's Printer, February 1957); Dominion Bureau of Statistics, *Hospital Statistics*, annual since 1932, in two volumes since 1952 (Ottawa, Queen's Printer); Dominion Bureau of Statistics, *Mental Health Statistics*, annual since 1932 (Ottawa, Queen's Printer); Dominion Bureau of Statistics, *Tuberculosis Statistics*, annual since 1937 (Ottawa, Queen's Printer)—see also *Tuberculosis Statistics, Financial Supplement*; Province of Ontario, Department of Health, *A Survey of Public General Hospitals in Ontario*, Part II: *General Statistics*, Part III: *Financial Statistics* (Toronto, King's Printer,

1939); Province of Quebec, Bureau of Statistics, *Statistical Year Book*, annual since 1913 (Quebec, Queen's Printer); *Census of Canada*, various years; Canadian Dental Association, *Statistical Data re Dentists in Canada*, annual (Toronto); Canadian Dental Association, *Canadian Dental Students Register*, annual (Toronto); Canadian Nurses Association, *Facts and Figures About Nursing in Canada, 1960*; Canadian Nurses Association, *Information on Nurses and Nursing in Canada, 1950*; E. H. Lossing, 'Reporting of Notifiable Diseases', *Canadian Journal of Public Health* (November 1955).

The source references for Social Welfare (series B 228–270) are:

Dominion Bureau of Statistics, *Canada Year Book*, annual since 1905 (Ottawa, Queen's Printer); Department of National Health and Welfare, *Annual Report, 1959* (Ottawa, Queen's Printer, 1959); Department of National Health and Welfare, Research Division, *Government Expenditures and Related Data on Health and Social Welfare*, Social Security Series, Memo No. 14, 2nd and 3rd editions (Ottawa, Queen's Printer, 1955 and 1960); Dominion Bureau of Statistics, *National Accounts, Income and Expenditure, 1926–56, 1957, 1958, 1961* (Ottawa, Queen's Printer); Dominion-Provincial Conference on Reconstruction, *Comparative Statistics of Public Finance* (Ottawa, King's Printer, 1945); Royal Commission on Dominion-Provincial Relations, Book III: *Documentation* (Ottawa, King's Printer, 1940); Royal Commission on Dominion-Provincial Relations, appendix 6, *Public Assistance and Social Insurance*, by A. E. Grauer (Ottawa, King's Printer, 1939).

VITAL STATISTICS (Series B 1–107)

General note

The general order of the material presented in this section is from more recent and more complete to older and more fragmentary data. Vital statistics have been collected by the Dominion Bureau of Statistics on a national basis in Canada since 1921 except for the Province of Quebec, which entered the system in 1926, and Newfoundland, which entered in 1949 when it joined Confederation. But the Dominion Bureau of Statistics has published some series beginning in 1921 which cover the present territory of Canada.

National estimates for earlier years presented here are based mainly on two works, one by N. Keyfitz, the other by O. J. Firestone (see references above). We have added to these estimates series relating to the most important vital statistics rates for the Province of Quebec and a series on death rates for the city of Montreal. These last series come from registration records of vital statistics and they are given to provide a basis to compare the estimates for Canada with figures originating from registration. The reason for choosing the Province of Quebec and the City of Montreal is that Quebec is the only province where registration was reasonably complete during the latter part of the nineteenth century. And it appears that the same is true of the City of Montreal. Death rates based on registration in other provinces, for instance, would give quite unacceptable figures and the same is probably true for the number of births reported. The Province of Quebec, indeed, offers an uncommon and most valuable source of information on the number of births, marriages and deaths: there is a practically complete record of these events for the Catholic population of this province since 1608, the date of the foundation of New France, up to 1883. This material is presented briefly at the end of this chapter with roughly calculated rates for ten-year periods.

In Canada, the registration of births, deaths and marriages is a responsibility of the provinces and is compulsory. But under a Dominion-Provincial agreement, since 1921 the Dominion Bureau of Statistics has made the compilations and calculated the rates. The Dominion Bureau of Statistics also provides annual estimates of the population by age and sex (see D.B.S., *Population Estimates, 1921–1952*, Reference Paper No. 40 (Ottawa, Queen's Printer, 1953) and *Population Estimates, 1952–1956*, Supplement to Reference Paper No. 40). The intercensal estimates are revised after each census and the rates are readjusted accordingly. In 1945 a new agreement was adopted which provided for the establishment of a Vital Statistics Council, the task of which is to work towards the improvement of legislation, registration techniques and the quality of Canadian vital statistics.

There is no systematic evaluation of the completeness of registration but occasional tests exist. One of these is the administration of the family allowances programme which indicates that birth registration is now practically complete. For earlier years the 1931 and 1941 censuses have been used to evaluate the underregistration of births. According to Enid Charles (see *The Changing Size of the Family in Canada*, 1941 Census Monograph (Ottawa, King's Printer, 1948), p. 290) the underregistration of births in Canada varies greatly from one province to another. She estimates the total underregistration at 3 per cent in 1941 and 5 per cent in 1930 to 1932. There is no comparable check for deaths and marriages but it is believed that the records are virtually complete.

The population basis for the calculation of rates in this section includes the armed forces abroad. But deaths among these are not counted even when they are computed on the basis of place of residence. Marriages celebrated abroad are not counted either, since marriages are classified according to place of occurrence.

B1–14. Live births, crude birth rate, age-specific fertility rates, gross reproduction rate and percentage of births in hospital, Canada, 1921 to 1960

SOURCE: for 1921 to 1958, D.B.S., *Vital Statistics, 1958*: table 8, p. 95, for total number of live births and birth rate; table 14, p. 100, for number and proportion of illegitimate births; table 13, p. 99, for fertility rates by age of mother, total fertility rate and gross reproduction rate; table 11, p. 98, for percentage of births occurring in hospital; for 1959 and 1960, D.B.S., *Vital Statistics, 1960*. These figures and rates are given by province in the same publications.

All rates for 1957 to 1960 were calculated by the Vital Statistics Branch, Health and Welfare Division, D.B.S., on the basis of the final revised population figures prepared after the 1961 census count was known.

B1. The criteria adopted for defining live births and stillbirths were changed in 1955. Before this date a live birth was defined as the birth of a child who breathes after the body of the foetus is outside the body of the mother. Since 1955, following the definition of the World Health Organization, a live birth is the complete expulsion from its mother of a product of conception which, after such separation, breathes or shows any other evidence of life.

B2–3. Illegitimate births are births for which parents reported themselves as not having been married to each other at the time of birth or registration. In the case of Ontario, since 1949, they are births for which the marital status of the mother was reported as single.

B5–11. The age-specific fertility rates are the annual number of births to women in a specified age group per 1,000 female population of that age group.

B12. The total fertility rate is the sum of the fertility rates of women at each year of age. This sum represents the number of children that a thousand women would have throughout their lifetime, assuming no mortality, if they experienced at each age the fertility observed during the year for which the age-specific fertility rates have been calculated.

B13. The gross reproduction rate is similar to the total fertility rate except that only female children are considered. It represents the number of daughters a cohort of a thousand women would have during their lives under the same hypotheses as for the total fertility rate.

B15–22. Total number of deaths, crude and standardized death rates by sex, natural increase and rate, Canada, 1921 to 1960

SOURCE: for 1921 to 1958, D.B.S., *Vital Statistics, 1958*: table 20, p. 109, for total number of deaths; table 25, pp. 116–21, for gross death rates; table 26, pp. 122–3, for standardized death rates; table 5, p. 73, for natural increase; for 1959 and 1960, D.B.S., *Vital Statistics, 1960*. The same data can be found by province in the same publication.

All rates for 1957 to 1960 were calculated on final revised population estimates (see the note to series B1–14).

B19–20. Standardized death rates are death rates corrected for differences in age composition. The 1956 census population was chosen as the standard age distribution. The age-specific death rates actually observed in a given year were applied to the age distribution of this standard population and a total death rate was computed for each year and each sex.

B23–34. Average age-specific death rates, both sexes, Canada, for five-year periods, 1921 to 1960

SOURCE: D.B.S., Health and Welfare Division, Vital Statistics Section, special and nonpublished tabulation. Death rates by age groups are regularly published in each annual *Vital Statistics* report for the current year and for each province. In *Vital Statistics, 1958*, table J, p. 34, age-specific death rates are presented for selected five-year periods with a different age grouping from 1926 to 1958.

All rates from 1957 to 1960 were calculated on final revised population estimates (see the note to series B1–14).

B35–50. Average annual number of deaths and death rates for leading causes of death, Canada, for five-year periods, 1921 to 1960

SOURCE: D.B.S., Health and Welfare Division, Vital Statistics Section, special and nonpublished tabulation. Number of deaths and death rates by cause and sex are regularly published in each annual *Vital Statistics* report for the current year for each province on the basis of the intermediate international list of causes of deaths. They are also published for Canada by sex and age groups and, for 1958, by sex, age groups and marital status. In *Vital Statistics, 1958*, table K, p. 35, death rates for selected groups of causes are presented for five-year periods from 1926 to 1958.

All rates from 1957 to 1960 were calculated on final revised population estimates (see the note to series B1–14).

Comparison of rates between years should be made with caution. The system of classification of deaths by cause has to change from time to time to be consistent with current medical knowledge and terminology and discontinuities are introduced into the time trends of death rates for certain causes of death (see Dunn and Shackley, 'Comparison of Cause-of-Death Assignments by the 1929 and 1938 Revisions of the International

List: Deaths in the United States, 1940', U.S. Bureau of the Census, *Vital Statistics—Special Reports*, vol. 19, no. 14, pp. 153–278, 1944). In Canada, the D.B.S. Vital Statistics Section has adopted the different revisions of the international list as follows: third revision, 1921 to 1930; fourth revision, 1931 to 1940; fifth revision, 1941 to 1949; sixth revision, 1950 to 1957; seventh revision, 1958 to 1960.

B51–58. Stillbirths and rate, infant deaths and rate by sex, neo-natal death rate and maternal mortality rate, Canada, 1921 to 1960

SOURCE: for 1921 to 1958, D.B.S., *Vital Statistics, 1958*: table 19, p. 106, for stillbirths; table 32, pp. 187–9, for infant deaths and rates; table 37, p. 203, for neo-natal death rate; table 40, p. 213, for maternal mortality; for 1959 and 1960, D.B.S., *Vital Statistics, 1960*. In the same publication, these data are also given for each province; for the current year, infant deaths are given by sex and month of death for selected causes of death and by sex and age for selected causes of death. Neo-natal deaths and rates are also given for selected causes of death, as well as maternal mortality.

B51–52. Since 1955, stillbirths are defined as the birth of a foetus, after at least 28 weeks of pregnancy, which, after complete separation from the mother, does not show any sign of life. Prior to this date a stillbirth was defined as the birth of a foetus, after at least 28 weeks of pregnancy, which, after complete separation from the mother, does not breathe (see note to series B1). The registration of stillbirths is probably less complete than for live births and the criteria for defining a stillbirth are more or less subject to medical practice.

B53–57. Neo-natal deaths are included in infant deaths. Neo-natal deaths until 1950 included deaths under one calendar month; since 1951 they include deaths under 28 days.

B59–64. Average annual infant death rates for selected causes, Canada, for five-year periods, 1931 to 1960

SOURCE: D.B.S., Vital Statistics Section, special and nonpublished tabulation. Numbers and rates of infant deaths by cause are regularly published in the *Vital Statistics* reports for current year and for each province.

The same remarks as the ones given for series B35–50 would apply here, probably with still greater emphasis on the lack of comparability of rates between periods, particularly for immaturity.

B65–74. Life expectancy by sex, at selected ages, Canada, census years, 1871 to 1956

SOURCE: D.B.S., *Canadian Vital Statistics Trends, 1921–54*, tables 32 and 33, pp. 50–4, for the years 1871 to 1951; D.B.S., *Vital Statistics, 1958*, table 51, p. 228, for 1956.

The life expectancy at a specified age is the average number of years to be lived by members of a hypothetical cohort of individuals, assumed to be subject throughout the remainder of their lives to the age-specific mortality rates observed in a given time period. Figures for 1871, 1881 and 1921 are interpolated from original figures which were not given for the ages appearing in our table. They are to be interpreted with caution because of difficulties in registration of deaths in these early years. For more details on the computation of life expectancy for these years, see D.B.S., *Canadian Abridged Life Tables, 1871, 1881, 1921, 1931* (Ottawa, King's Printer, 1939).

B75–81. Number of marriages and rate, average age at marriage for brides and bridegrooms, number of divorces and rate, net family formation, Canada, 1921 to 1960

SOURCE: for 1921 to 1955, D.B.S., *Vital Statistics, 1958*: table 43, p. 219, for marriages; tables 44 and 45, p. 220, for age at marriage; table 50, p. 226, for divorces; for 1956 to 1960, D.B.S., *Vital Statistics, 1960*. In this publication, these series are also given for each province. A table is regularly published giving, for the current year, the religion of brides by religion of grooms. Source of net family formation: for 1951 to 1960, Central Mortgage and Housing Corporation, *Canadian Housing Statistics, 1961*; for 1921 to 1950, Firestone, *Canada's Economic Development 1867–1953*, pp. 240–1.

All rates for 1957 to 1960 were calculated on final revised population estimates (see the note to series B1–14).

Net family formation is the number of marriages, plus married female immigrants, less deaths of married persons, less married female emigrants, less divorces. Marriages, married female immigrants, deaths of married persons, divorces are obtained from registration statistics; married female emigrants are assumed to be one-fifth of the total number of emigrants (see Firestone, *Residential Real Estate in Canada* (Toronto, 1951), pp. 436–7).

B82–91. Estimated births, deaths, natural increase, marriages (number and rates), immigration, emigration, Canada, 1900 to 1920

SOURCE: Firestone, *Canada's Economic Development, 1867–1953*, table 83, pp. 240–1. A great deal of computation is involved in these estimates. They are described in Firestone's work, pp. 244–7, and were made by the Economic Research Department of the Central Mortgage and Housing Corporation. Here is a brief note on the method used:

Population data used to calculate rates for census years are from decennial censuses. For intercensal years, they are estimates made by the Dominion Bureau of Statistics, published in the *Canada Year Book, 1936*, p. 141. The method used is described in the *Canada Year Book, 1932*, pp. 108–9. These estimates were then converted to a year-end basis by linear interpolation.

For 1900 to 1920, data on deaths were obtained from provincial reports of deaths registered. Where data were lacking, estimates were based on the death rate for neighbouring provinces.

Marriage data for Quebec 1900 to 1920 are from the *Statistical Year Book*, Province of Quebec, 1921, p. 54. For other provinces, marriage registration was available for almost the whole period or for scattered years in the journals, sessional papers or annual reports. Where data were lacking estimates were based on marriage rates for comparable provinces.

Immigration data are those published in the *Canada Year Book*. The estimates of emigration are calculated by subtracting from the sum of births and immigrants, the sum of deaths and the annual population increase.

Firestone's estimates for the period 1867 to 1900 are not published here since it is his intention to revise them. Births for that period were underestimated for at least three reasons: (1) underenumeration of persons of less than one year at the censuses; (2) underregistration of deaths of children of this age group during the year preceding the census; (3) the proportion of these deaths added to the number of surviving children under one year at the census. A comparison of the method used for the provinces other than Quebec and the registration of Quebec Catholic births can be made. On the basis of this comparison, and if we assume that the error produced by the three factors mentioned above is of the same magnitude in other provinces as in Quebec, the earlier estimates published in Firestone's work should be multiplied by 1.10 in 1870, 1.16 in 1880, 1.11 in 1890 and 1.03 in 1900.

Births estimates for the years 1900 to 1920 were adjusted with Keyfitz's estimates (see note to series B100–107) and are probably much better, but still Keyfitz's estimates are subject to the underenumeration of children 0–9 years of age at censuses.

Deaths and death rates also are most probably underestimates. A comparison of the rates given in series B 89 and the rates for the Province of Quebec, series B 93, or the rates calculated from Keyfitz's data in series B 100–107 would suggest such a conclusion.

As to marriages, one can only speculate on the completeness of registration.

B 92–99. Birth, death, marriage and infant mortality rates, death rates for selected causes for the Province of Quebec, death rate in the City of Montreal, 1867 to 1920

SOURCE: Number of births and population for the years 1867 to 1883 are the estimates made by the Economic Research Department of the Central Mortgage and Housing Corporation. Population estimates for calculating all rates of 1884 to 1920 are from the *Canada Year Book, 1936*, p. 141. They were adjusted in the source for nonreporting municipalities. Number of births, marriages and deaths for 1884 to 1920 are from the *Statistical Year Book* of Quebec: *1921*, pp. 54, 57, for the years 1884 to 1909; *1925*, table 144, p. 103, for the years 1910 to 1911; *1928*, table 42, p. 66, for the years 1912 to 1920. Infant mortality rates are from the *Statistical Year Book* of Quebec: *1921*, p. 60, for 1900 to 1909; *1925*, table 153, p. 108, for 1910 to 1912; *1928*, table 52, p. 72, for 1913 to 1920. Death rates for specified causes are the ones which are published in the *Twenty-eighth Annual Report of the Superior Board of Health for the year 1921–22*, tables 10 and 16, pp. 139–49. Rates for a few other causes are also given in the same publication.

B 99. Death rate for Montreal, 1872 to 1920, are from *Report of the Municipal Department of Hygiene and Statistics* of the City of Montreal: *1914*, pp. 168–9, for the years 1872 to 1914; different years for 1915 to 1920. Infant mortality rate and death rates for communicable diseases are also given in this publication but are not reproduced here.

The reasons for publishing these series on the Province of Quebec and the City of Montreal here is that the data relating to these regions are based on a good registration system, which is probably unique in Canada for these early years.

B 100–107. Number of births, deaths, immigrants and emigrants; birth and death rates for intercensal periods; number of children aged under 5 years per 1,000 women aged 15–44, Canada, 1851 to 1961

SOURCE: for 1851 to 1951, D.B.S., *Canadian Vital Statistics Trends, 1921–1954*, tables 1–2, pp. 7, 9; for the period 1951 to 1956, births and deaths figures are from *Vital Statistics, 1951* and *1956*, immigration figures are from *Canadian Statistical Review*; for the period 1956 to 1961, births and deaths figures compiled by the Vital Statistics Section, D.B.S.

The original estimates for 1851 to 1921 were made by Nathan Keyfitz (see 'The Growth of Canadian Population') and were revised slightly in the above source. The method used by Keyfitz was to apply survival rates to the respective age groups of the Canadian population as given by the censuses, using modified English life tables. The difference between the actual population at the next census and the expected population is attributed to net migration. Knowing immigration, which was registered, emigration could be calculated as a residual. This method assumes that there was no migration of persons aged 0–9 at the end of an intercensal period, during that period. Net migration itself is a residual and its correctness is dependent upon the validity of the survival rates chosen. In the same article by Keyfitz, net migration is estimated for each province from 1881 to 1941, for each ten-year period. For a comparison with estimates made by applying a quite different trend of survival rates, see series A 249–253.

For the period 1921 to 1956, vital statistics records have been used together with immigration records. The results of the two methods can be compared for the periods 1921 to 1931 and 1931 to 1941. They do not differ greatly.

Average annual rates of births and deaths have been calculated by relating one-tenth of the estimated or registered number of births and deaths respectively to the arithmetic mean of the population at both ends of the period.

For the computation of the number of children under five per 1,000 women 15–44, no correction has been made for the under-registration of children at the censuses, which is believed to be greater than for the total population.

HEALTH (Series B 108–227)

General note

Data on physicians, dentists and nurses are presented first. They are followed by rates of notifiable diseases as reported to the Dominion Bureau of Statistics since 1926. Eight tables on hospitals and patients follow. Annual data on hospitals were not collected on a national basis in Canada before 1932. For the earlier periods, a limited amount of information can be found in the censuses from 1871 to 1901. The intermediate period will be covered here by data for the Provinces of Ontario and Quebec. They are much more abundant than can be found in the censuses mentioned and give an idea of the conditions that prevailed at the beginning of the century. Even today not all hospitals report on the movement of their patients and beds available and fewer still report financial information.

According to type of service, hospitals are classified in four main categories: general, mental, tuberculosis and other special. But each of these categories may also be subdivided into public, private and federal hospitals. A few remarks should be added on these categories. When hospitals offer more than one type of service, the predominant type is applied to the entire hospital with one exception: if an institution contains a 'general' unit, it will be classed as general. 'Other special' category includes: chronic, communicable disease, convalescent, maternity, ortho-paedic hospitals and unclassified hospitals. A public hospital is 'one which is not operated for profit, accepts all patients regardless of their ability to pay, and is recognized as a public hospital by the province in which it is located' (D.B.S., *Hospital Statistics*, vol. 1, 1956, p. 10). Private hospitals are those set up with restrictions on admissions; usually they are established for profit and accept paying patients only. Federal hospitals are those set up and operated by departments of the federal government for the care of special groups of patients (e.g. veterans, Indians, mariners, servicemen). Almost all mental and tuberculosis beds are in public hospitals. The great majority of 'general beds' are also in public hospitals but a significant amount are in federal hospitals. 'Other special' beds is the only category where there is a significant proportion of beds in private hospitals (approximately 20 per cent).

For the period 1932 to 1960 five tables are presented. The first gives a general idea of the number of hospitals and beds for all categories of hospitals operating. Each of the three following tables is devoted to each category. For 'general' and 'special' hospitals, only reporting hospitals are included. It is believed that all mental and tuberculosis hospitals report the movement of their patients. Another table gives financial data for each category of public hospitals.

The last two tables of this subsection relate to governments' expenditures on health and to persons enrolled in nonprofit medical insurance plans.

B108–115. Number of physicians, dentists and nurses, population per physician, dentist and nurse, number of graduates of medical and dental schools, Canada, 1871 to 1960

B108–110. Physicians and graduates. SOURCE: for 1901 to 1954, D.N.H.W., *Survey of Physicians in Canada* (1954), pp. 10, 18; for the years 1881 and 1891, *Census, 1921*, vol. IV, p. 6; for 1871, *Census, 1871*, vol. II, p. 341. Figures on physicians for 1943 to 1959 are based on individual records of Canadian doctors kept by the Department of National Health and Welfare; for other years, they are census figures. In the *Survey of Physicians*, the distribution of physicians is given by province, sex, age groups, nature of major work and urban concentration. The records of the Department of Health and Welfare are checked periodically by surveys; six were made between 1943 and 1954.

B111–113. Dentists and graduates. SOURCE: for number of dentists: 1947 to 1960. *Statistical Data re Dentists*; for other years, *Census of Canada: 1941*, vol. VII, p. 32; *1931*, vol. VII, p. 72; *1921*, vol. IV, p. 6; *1871*, vol. II, p. 337; for number of graduates, *Canadian Dental Students Register*. In the two publications of the Canadian Dental Association, data are presented on distribution of dentists by province, sex, specialty, on deaths, retirements, additions, relocations of dentists, on distribution of students by province and university and on average cost for a four-year course.

B114–115. Nurses. SOURCE: for 1951 to 1959, *Facts and Figures About Nursing*; for 1941 to 1950, *Information on Nurses and Nursing*; for other years, *Census of Canada: 1931*, vol. VII, p. 72; *1921*, vol. IV, p. 6. Other data on distribution by province, sex, major field, institutions, students, nurse migrations are given in *Facts and Figures About Nursing*.

B116–124. Annual rates of notifiable diseases, Canada, 1926 to 1960

SOURCE: special tabulation prepared by D.B.S., Health and Welfare Division. These data are published in D.B.S., *Notifiable Diseases*, by four-week periods.

These rates are based on reports to their respective provincial governments of local medical officers of health on notifiable diseases reported to them. Each provincial officer of health consolidates these reports and submits them to D.B.S. The reporting of notifiable diseases on a national level was affected by provincial differences in lists of reportable diseases, variations between provinces concerning exact international categories associated with each reportable disease and the proportion of cases reported by physicians.

There is evidence that the number of cases reported is far from being complete. In the national survey on sickness conducted in Canada during 1950 to 1951, the number of persons reporting illness as commencing during the survey year for the same diseases as those reported here is much greater. The ratio of the number of cases reported through health authorities to the number of cases reported in the survey is as follows: measles, 13.8 per cent; whooping cough, 10.9 per cent; chickenpox, 17.3 per cent; mumps, 13.9 per cent; German measles, 17.1 per cent (see Lossing, 'Reporting of Notifiable Diseases', pp. 444–8; also, *Canadian Sickness Survey, 1950–51*, no. 10, table 7). At least the figures in the table presented here may represent the evolution of each disease. But in the paper quoted above, the author says that reporting is probably more incomplete during epidemic periods than during periods of lesser incidence.

B125–137. Number of hospitals operating and reporting, rated bed capacity, number of beds per 1,000 population, by category of hospitals; number of bassinets in public and federal hospitals, Canada, 1932 to 1960

SOURCE: special tabulations prepared by the Health and Welfare Division, Institution Section, of the Dominion Bureau of Statistics.

Most of these figures are published, sometimes in another form, in the following annual D.B.S. publications: *Hospital Statistics* (2 volumes since 1952, one on general information, the other on financial information), *Mental Health Statistics* and *Tuberculosis Statistics*. These publications contain much more information than can be given here. Data are given by province and cover also service and educational facilities. For mental hospitals, they cover information on age, sex, marital status, residence, education, origin, occupation, industry, diagnoses of patients admitted. Comparable data are also given for tuberculosis hospitals.

B130–133. Rated bed capacity 'is a theoretical number, representing the number of beds that could be placed in a given hospital structure if a standard number of square feet were allowed for each bed. This number may be equal to or be greater or less than the actual number of beds in regular use (referred to as "beds set up").... It is not possible to ascertain to what extent standards have been scrupulously applied (by provinces or hospitals) but it is known that their application is becoming more general' (see *Hospital Statistics, 1956*, p. 9).

It must be pointed out that, except for most recent years, data on bed capacity were collected for beds set up and not for rated capacity. Moreover, beds set up were usually overestimated. In these conditions, the D.B.S. estimates of rated bed capacity should be interpreted cautiously.

Data on public and private mental hospitals include psychiatric units. These are units, within a hospital or sanatorium, which are organized for the treatment of patients with psychiatric disorders. Treatment in these units is generally more intensive and shorter than in mental hospitals.

B138–148. Public general and special allied hospitals: number of beds and cribs, movement of patients, expenditure per patient-day, full-time personnel, Canada, 1932 to 1960

SOURCE: same as for B125–137.

It should be noted that these series refer to public hospitals reporting only and that the admissions include admissions in psychiatric units of these hospitals. Percentage occupancy is the ratio of the average number of patients to bed capacity. This ratio is affected by possible errors in bed capacity estimates, and it is possible that the real trend of occupancy be in the direction opposite to that shown.

B149–158. Mental institutions: movement of patients, cost per patient-day, full-time personnel, Canada, 1932 to 1960

SOURCE: same as for B125–137.

B159–169. Public and federal tuberculosis institutions: number of beds, movement of patients, cost per patient-day, full-time personnel, Canada, 1937 to 1960

SOURCE: same as for B125–137.

B161. A first admission is that of a patient who had never been a patient in a tuberculosis institution.

B162. A readmission 'to continue treatment' is that of a patient (1) for whom treatment had been postponed on a previous discharge, or (2) who had been discharged against medical advice more than 30 days prior to the readmission.

B163. 'Reviews out' are separations of 'reviews in'. A 'review in' is the admission, after previous discharge from a tuberculosis institution, of a patient found not to have active tuberculosis, and subsequently discharged within 30 days. If a patient has active tuberculosis or if he is not discharged within 30 days, he is classed as a readmission.

B170–181. Financial statistics of public health institutions, Canada, 1932 to 1960

SOURCE: same as for B125–137. It should be noted that the number of hospitals reporting financial data is not the same as the number of hospitals reporting bed capacity and movement of patients. The difference can be measured by comparing number of beds in series B170, 174 and 178 with series B138, 139, 131 and 132.

For public general and special hospitals, grants by governments do not comprise all money received by hospitals from government sources. In addition to the grants, payments are made on behalf of patients and the figures given do not include these. For public mental and public tuberculosis institutions, grants by governments constitute a better measure of government money received.

B182–194. Public general hospitals; number of hospitals and beds, beds per 1,000 population, patients treated, average days' stay per patient, operating costs and distribution of income, Ontario, quinquennial years, 1900 to 1935

SOURCE: Ontario, Department of Health, *A Survey of Public General Hospitals*, Part II, pp. 36, 38, 39; Part III, pp. 14, 19. In Part III data are given on rates of per diem grants for indigent patients (pp. 2, 3) and different rates of income or cost per patient or per capita.

Public general hospitals do not include convalescent hospitals and homes for incurables. According to the source they do include Red Cross outpost hospitals. A footnote to appendix I, p. 31 of Part III, which gives income from various sources states that income on Red Cross outpost hospitals is included beginning in 1924.

B187. Average days' stay per patient treated is based on total patients treated and not on number of discharges.

B188–189. Operating costs include interest and sinking fund charges but no depreciation. They cover all costs and are not limited to those for in-patients. In the calculation of operating costs per patient-day, each infant-day is taken as being equivalent to one adult-day.

B190–194. Income from patients (B190) does not include per diem grants by provincial or municipal governments. Municipal grants are mainly made as a per diem payment for indigents. From 1929 onward in the source, which gives the data for each year, small 'other grants', averaging less than 10 per cent of the maintenance grants, are given. Provincial grants are all on a per diem basis for indigents, with one exception. Until 1930 the provincial government's practice 'was to extend the statutory grants for indigent patients to *all* patients for a period to ten years following the establishment of each hospital' (part III, p. 1, italics in the original). These special grants carried on into the nineteen-thirties for any hospital established by 1930. Their purpose was to provide some contribution towards the capital cost of the hospital. It is stated in the source, however, that 'The major portion of capital costs have been provided by the voluntary bodies responsible for the establishment of the hospital, assisted in many cases by the municipality...' (part III, p. 1).

B195–215. Miscellaneous statistics relating to hospitals in the Province of Quebec, quinquennial years, 1885 to 1930

SOURCE: Quebec, *Statistical Year Book*, most of the data from 1932 edition, pp. 174–81 and 1927 edition, pp. 206–16.

B216–219. Number of institutions and of inmates in lunatic asylums and hospitals, Canada, 1871, 1881, 1891 and 1901

SOURCE: *Census of Canada*: *1901*, vol. IV, p. 357; *1891*, vol. IV, table S; *1881*, vol. II, table XX; *1871*, vol. II, table XIX.

B220–224. Government expenditures on health, Canada, 1933 to 1960

SOURCE: D.N.H.W., *Government Expenditures on Health and Social Welfare*, for 1947 to 1958, 3rd edition, table 16, p. 45; for 1959, 1960 and for 1933 to 1943, nonpublished tabulation prepared at the Department of National Health and Welfare, Research and Statistics Division. The original sources are: (1) for 1947 to 1958: *Public Accounts of Canada* for the fiscal years ended 31 March 1948 to 1959; D.B.S., *Financial Statistics of Provincial Governments, 1947 to 1958*; D.B.S., *Financial Statistics of Municipal Governments, 1947 to 1952*; *Quebec Statistical Year Book, 1950 to 1953*; D.B.S., *Comparative Statistics of Public Finance, 1945 and 1951 to 1959*; and data supplied by the National Income Section of the D.B.S.; (2) for 1933 to 1943: Dominion-Provincial Conference on Reconstruction of 1945, *Comparative Statistics of Public Finance*, table 10, pp. 37–45.

For the years 1947 to 1960, the figures correspond to net ordinary and capital expenditures, including administrative costs. For municipal governments, the amounts exclude capital expenditures out of ordinary revenue and capital expenditures out of capital funds for the years 1947 to 1952. They do not include capital expenditures out of capital funds for the Province of Quebec, 1947 to 1960. Provincial expenditures include health benefits under workmen's compensation programmes. Municipal expenditures exclude sanitation and waste removal. For 1933 to 1943, Veterans' and Workmen's Compensation expenditures are totally excluded.

In the publication *Government Expenditures on Health and Social Welfare*, data are given by province and for more detailed items or functions.

B225–227. Estimated enrolment in nonprofit medical insurance plans, Canada, at 31 December, 1937 to 1960

SOURCE: for 1937 to 1953, D.N.H.W., *Voluntary Medical Care Insurance, A study of Non-Profit Plans in Canada*, pp. 29, 47, 187; for 1954, 1959 and 1960, unpublished compilation, D.N.H.W., Research and Statistics Division; for 1955, *Voluntary Hospital and Medical Insurance in Canada, 1955*, table 4, Canada, series II; for 1956, *Voluntary Hospital and Medical Insurance in Canada, 1956*, p. 19; for 1957, *Voluntary Medical Insurance in Canada, 1957*, table 4, Canada; for 1958, *Voluntary Medical Insurance in Canada, 1958*.

The material relating to enrolment has been assembled in co-operation with the nonprofit plans. The first plan was introduced in 1937, in Ontario. A 'comprehensive' plan is 'one which provides a wide range of benefits, including payments for each of the following services: physicians' calls in office, home and hospitals consultations; surgical operations and procedures; confinements; anaesthesia; and X-ray, laboratory and other diagnostic procedures'. A 'limited' plan is 'one which provides only a limited selection of these benefits such as surgical and obstetrical care, with or without medical (non-surgical) care in hospital' (see D.N.H.W., *Voluntary Medical Care Insurance*, etc., p. 24).

The figures give the number of persons covered.

In addition to enrolment in nonprofit plans which are covered in the data of series B225–227 there are private plans carried, in the main, with insurance companies. In 1957 the number in such private plans reported in *Voluntary Medical Insurance in Canada, 1957* was 3,688,100 persons. The unduplicated total number covered by nonprofit and reported private plans was 7,301,433 persons.

SOCIAL WELFARE (Series B228–270)

General note

It would probably be impossible to produce statistical data on all forms of social welfare in Canada. Not to mention the difficulties related to the definition of social welfare itself, many activities in this field are conducted by private agencies and it would be almost impossible to collect statistics on all of them. Were it possible, the lack of comparability among different data would probably deprive national aggregates of any precise meaning. Data presented in this section are limited to governments' social welfare activities. Not all of them are included. Except for series B266–270, which cover total expenditures on social welfare by the three levels of governments, the data relate almost exclusively to income maintenance programmes. Even among those, some are not included for different reasons. Workmen's compensation and unemployment insurance programmes are treated in Section D, Wages and Working Conditions. Allowances for disabled persons and unemployment assistance programmes—both federal-provincial programmes—started only in 1955 and 1956 respectively; moreover, the federal Prairie Farm Assistance programme and the provincial programmes for child care protection have been neglected.

In order that the reader can have an idea of the importance of these programmes, a few figures will be given here for one recent year:

(a) *Federal programme*

    1. Unemployment insurance

        Persons insured, June 1959:   4,072,900

        Amount of benefit paid in 1959: $406,097,000

(b) *Federal-provincial programmes*

    1. Allowances for disabled persons

        Recipients in March 1960:   49,889

        Federal government contribution in 1959–60: $16,050,514

    2. Unemployment assistance

        Recipients in March 1960:   321,059

        Federal government contribution in 1959–60: $36,579,658

(c) *Provincial programmes*

    1. Workmen's compensation

        Compensation paid (including medical services) in 1959: $113,219,602

    2. Child welfare

        Expenditures in 1958–9: $23,216,000

These figures are from D.B.S., *Canada Year Book*, *1961* except for child welfare expenditures from D.N.H.W., *Government Expenditures on Health and Social Welfare*, *1947 to 1959*, 3rd edition, appendix 10.

The general order of the data is as follows: the first tables, series B228–265, relate to particular programmes except for series B263 and 265 which relate to provincial and municipal grants to private noncommercial institutions; the last table gives expenditures on social welfare by level of government.

B228–242. Family allowances, old age security and old age assistance, Canada, 1945 to 1960

SOURCE: *Canada Year Book*, different years, chapter on Public Health, Welfare and Social Security. See also D.N.H.W., *Annual Report*. Data for each province are also given in these publications.

Family allowances were introduced in 1945 and old age security in 1952. These programmes are administered by the federal government and provide universal payments without means tests to children under 16 years of age and adults aged 70 years and over respectively. Old age assistance is a federal-provincial programme administered by the province which provides assistance to persons aged 65–69 who are in need as demonstrated by a means test. The federal contribution may not exceed 50 per cent of the total assistance, with a maximum on which the federal share was calculated of: $40 prior to 1 July 1957; $46 from 1 July 1957 to 31 October 1957; $55 from 1 November 1957 to 1960. The old age security and old age assistance programmes covered in these series began in 1952. They succeeded a prior old age pension programme for which the data are given in series B243–246.

B243–250. Old age pensions and pensions for the blind: average monthly pension, number of pensioners, per cent of pensioners to population and federal contribution, Canada, 1928 to 1960

SOURCE: *Canada Year Book*, different years, chapter on Public Health, Welfare and Social Security. See also D.N.H.W., *Annual Report*. Data for each province are also given in these publications.

The old age pensions were paid jointly by the federal and provincial governments. Old age pensions started in 1927 and became effective in the different provinces on various dates between 1927 and 1936. Pensions were paid under this programme to persons aged 70 and over who were in need. In 1952 this system was replaced by the old age security programme (see note to series B228–242). Pensions for the blind were started in 1937 and are paid to persons who are in need and whose age is above a certain number of years which varied through the years. Under these two programmes the federal contribution might not exceed 75 per cent of the total pension, with a maximum on which the federal contribution was calculated of: $40 prior to 1 July 1957; and, for the blind, $46 from 1 July 1957 to 31 October 1957; $55 from 1 November 1957 to 1960.

B251–255. Federal government annuities: contracts issued, money received and paid and number and value of contracts in force, Canada, 1909 to 1960

SOURCE: *Canada Year Book*, various years.

B256–259. Veterans expenditure: total expenditures, pensions, war allowances, hospital and medical services, Canada, 1934 to 1961

SOURCE: for the years 1948 to 1959, D.N.H.W., *Government Expenditures on Health and Social Welfare*, 2nd edition, appendices 1–3, pp. 48–55, 3rd edition, appendices 1–3 (for original sources, see series B220–224); for the years 1934 to 1947 and 1960 and 1961, nonpublished data supplied by the Department of National Health and Welfare, Research and Statistics Division. The original sources for the period 1934 to 1947 are: (1) for 1939 to 1947, *Public Accounts*; (2) for 1934 and 1938, Dominion-Provincial Conference on Reconstruction of 1945, *Comparative Statistics of Public Finance*, table 10, pp. 37–45 (item called: 'veterans pensions and after-care'). The number of different categories of recipients is given in the *Canada Year Book*.

Series B259 includes capital expenditures on hospitals.

B260–265. Provincial and municipal transfer payments for selected social welfare programmes, Canada, 1926 to 1960

SOURCE: for series B261: for 1959 and 1960, unpublished compilation D.N.H.W., Research and Statistics Division; for 1947 to 1958, D.N.H.W., *Government Expenditures on Health and Social Welfare*, 2nd edition, table 9, p. 21, 3rd edition, appendix 10; for 1933 to 1943, Dominion-Provincial Conference on Reconstruction of 1945, *Comparative Statistics of Public Finance*, table 10, pp. 37–45; for all other series: D.B.S., *National Accounts, Income and Expenditure*, *1926–56*, table 44, pp. 82–3 and same publication, *1961*, table 44.

Provincial and municipal direct relief figures presented in series B260–265 are different from the ones appearing in Dominion-Provincial Conference on Reconstruction, *Compara-*

tive Statistics of Public Finance, table 10 and Royal Commission on Dominion-Provincial Relations, book III, *Documentation*, table 19. The latter figures follow.

Provincial and municipal direct relief
(millions of dollars)

Year	Provincial	Municipal
1943	4	3
1941	10	5
1939	43	16
1937	61	20
1933	36	23
1930	4	3

SOURCE: Dominion-Provincial Conference on Reconstruction, *Comparative Statistics of Public Finance*, table 10; Royal Commission on Dominion-Provincial Relations, book III, *Documentation*, table 19.

Information on relief programmes could be completed by the data given in Grauer's study, *Public Assistance and Social Insurance*, prepared for the Royal Commission on Dominion-Provincial Relations. Some of these data will be given in the two following tables.

Number of persons on unemployment and drought relief reported by the provinces and federal departments, Canada, 1932 to 1937
(thousands)

Year	Highest and lowest month	Direct relief Non-drought areas	Direct relief Drought areas	Other relief projects	Total Number	Total Percentage of population
1937	March	1,046	168	79	1,293	11.6
	August	573	144	42	759	6.8
1936	March	1,240	158	75	1,473	13.4
	September	874	100	57	1,031	9.3
1935	March	1,172	179	118	1,469	13.4
	September	886	19	60	965	8.8
1934	March	1,206	152	146	1,504	13.9
	September	825	106	92	1,023	9.4
1933	April	1,428	90	72	1,590	14.9
	September	920	49	83	1,053	9.9
1932	December	1,170	72	56	1,299	12.4
	May	457	140	66	662	6.3

SOURCE: Grauer, *Public Assistance and Social Insurance*, p. 12.

Relief disbursements by years ending 31 March, Canada, 1931 to 1937
(millions of dollars)

Fiscal year ending 31 March	Disbursements through provincial and municipal agencies, funds provided by: Dominion	Provinces	Municipal	Total	Disbursements by Dominion through its own agencies	Total disbursements
1937	66	38	23	127	26	153
1936	73	40	22	135	38	173
1935	64	57	21	142	17	159
1934	37	42	22	101	7	108
1933	49	26	19	94	4	98
1932	44	29	20	93	7	100
1931	3	9	9	21	1	22
Total	336	241	136	713	100	813

SOURCE: Grauer, *Public Assistance and Social Insurance*, p. 16.

Figures on number of recipients of mothers' allowances and amounts paid are published for each province in the *Canada Year Book*.

Private noncommercial institutions include universities, hospitals and the like.

B266–270. Government expenditures on social welfare, by level of government and *per capita*, Canada, 1913 to 1960

SOURCE: for 1959 and 1960, unpublished data D.N.H.W., Research and Statistics Division; for 1947 to 1958, D.N.H.W., *Government Expenditures on Health and Social Welfare*, 3rd edition, tables 3, 8, 12,

pp. 11, 31, 43, respectively (for original sources, see series B220–224); for 1933 to 1943, nonpublished data of the Department of National Health and Welfare, Research Division, based on Dominion-Provincial Conference on Reconstruction, *Comparative Statistics of Public Finance*, table 10, pp. 37–45; for 1913 to 1930, nonpublished data of same source, based on Royal Commission on Dominion-Provincial Relations, book III, *Documentation*, table 19 and on figures supplied by D.B.S., National Income Section for workmen's compensation.

For the years 1947 to 1960, figures relate to ordinary and capital expenditures, including administrative costs. Federal expenditures include income maintenance payments, welfare services and grants. Provincial expenditures include expenditures on cash benefits under workmen's compensation programmes but exclude debt retirement expenditures. Municipal expenditures exclude capital expenditures out of ordinary revenue and capital expenditures out of capital funds for the years 1947 to 1952. They exclude capital expenditures out of capital fund for the Province of Quebec for all years.

The principal difference between figures for 1933 to 1943 (Conference on Reconstruction) and those for 1913 to 1930 (Royal Commission on Dominion-Provincial Relations) are as follows: in the first one, amounts under 'relief' are limited to expenditures for direct relief and to provincial contributions to municipal relief works; whereas the second one adds some expenditures on highways, public domain, etc. Figures for 1913 to 1930 might also include expenditures on health.

APPENDIX TO SECTION B

EARLY VITAL STATISTICS FOR THE PROVINCE OF QUEBEC (Series B271–277)

B271–277. Births, marriages and deaths for the Roman Catholic population of the Province of Quebec: numbers and average annual rates, by decades, 1608 to 1890.

SOURCE: for population: *Census of Canada, 1871, 1881 and 1891*; for vital statistics: *Census, 1871*, vol. V, part II, table I, pp. 162–3, for 1608 to 1875; *Census, 1881*, vol. IV, part II, table II, p. 144, for 1876 to 1883; Province of Quebec, *Statistical Year Book, 1921*, p. 51, for 1884 to 1890. In the *1871 Census*, vol. V, part II, data on the number of births, marriages, and deaths for the Catholic population of the Province of Quebec are also given, by year and by county or region. The same data are also given for the Catholic population of the City of Quebec, with important additions for each year of the period 1771 to 1870. These additions are number of deaths, by single day of age for the first month, by month of age for the first year of life and by individual year of age for the rest of the life.

The rates of series B275–277 have been computed by the author, by relating one-tenth of the number of events during a decade to the estimated population at the middle of the period. This method gives rates that are higher by 1 per cent approximately than the rates that would be obtained if the same number of events was related to the arithmetic mean of the annual population figures of the period. Population has been estimated by interpolation on semilogarithmic paper. There are no data on Catholic population between 1765 and 1844.

The registration of vital statistics for this population is thought to have been practically complete. Original information comes from parish registers, which were kept with great care and completeness. They could be checked by transcripts which exist since 1678 when the French government passed an ordinance requiring the priests to forward a copy of each act to the clerk of the Royal Judge.

Series B1-14. *Live births, crude birth rate, age-specific fertility rates, gross reproduction rate and percentage of births in hospital, Canada, 1921 to 1960*

(all fertility rates based on live births per thousand women for the specified group)

Year	Total number	Number illegitimate[6]	Percentage illegitimate[6]	Crude birth rate[1]	15–19 years	20–24 years	25–29 years	30–34 years	35–39 years	40–44 years	45–49 years	Total fertility rate[2]	Gross reproduction rate (per thousand women)[2]	Percentage of births occurring in hospital[3]
	1	**2**	**3**	**4**	**5**	**6**	**7**	**8**	**9**	**10**	**11**	**12**	**13**	**14**
1960	478,551	20,413	4.3	26.8	59.8	233.5	224.4	146.2	84.2	28.5	2.4	3,895	1,893	94.6
1959	479,275	20,221	4.2	27.4	60.4	233.8	226.7	147.7	87.3	28.5	2.7	3,935	1,915	93.1
1958	470,118	19,027	4.0	27.5	59.2	226.5	223.3	147.9	87.6	28.9	2.7	3,880	1,886	91.7
1957	469,093	18,629	4.0	28.2	60.2	227.1	224.1	149.4	90.7	30.7	2.8	3,925	1,907	90.2
1956	450,739	17,510	3.9	28.0	55.9	222.2	220.1	150.3	89.6	30.8	2.9	3,858	1,874	88.4
1955	442,937	17,034	3.8	28.2	54.2	218.3	215.1	153.8	89.8	32.3	2.9	3,831	1,863	86.5
1954	436,198	16,947	3.9	28.5	54.3	217.4	213.2	156.5	88.5	32.4	3.2	3,828	1,861	84.6
1953	417,884	16,064	3.8	28.1	52.0	208.2	208.4	153.2	88.1	31.2	2.9	3,721	1,812	83.4
1952	403,559	15,174	3.8	27.9	50.4	201.0	205.2	150.7	87.4	30.7	2.8	3,641	1,763	81.4
1951	381,092	14,537	3.8	27.2	48.1	188.7	198.8	144.5	86.5	30.9	3.1	3,503	1,701	79.1
1950	372,009	14,510	3.9	27.1	46.0	181.3	200.6	141.3	87.9	30.8	3.0	3,455	1,678	76.0
1949	367,092	14,390	3.9	27.3	45.2	181.5	201.2	139.7	88.8	31.5	3.2	3,456	1,678	74.3
1948	359,860	15,302	4.3	27.3	43.2	181.1	197.6	141.4	89.0	32.6	3.3	3,441	1,676	72.3
1947	372,589	14,912	4.0	28.9	42.6	189.1	206.4	150.5	93.1	34.1	3.3	3,595	1,753	71.0
1946	343,504	14,102	4.1	27.2	36.5	169.6	191.4	146.0	93.1	34.5	3.8	3,374	1,640	67.6
1945	300,587	13,394	4.5	24.3	31.6	143.3	166.8	134.3	90.3	33.5	3.7	3,018	1,462	63.2
1944	293,967	12,409	4.2	24.0	31.3	143.3	168.7	134.1	88.1	33.0	3.4	3,010	1,457	61.0
1943	292,943	11,944	4.1	24.2	32.1	146.8	175.4	131.9	86.5	31.9	3.5	3,041	1,478	54.7
1942	281,569	11,531	4.1	23.5	32.0	145.1	168.7	128.0	83.0	32.3	3.6	2,964	1,434	53.7
1941	263,993	10,430	4.0	22.4	30.7	138.4	159.8	122.3	80.0	31.6	3.7	2,832	1,377	48.9
1940	252,577	9,822	3.9	21.6	29.3	130.3	152.6	122.8	81.7	32.7	3.7	2,766	1,348	45.3
1939	237,991	9,346	3.9	20.6	27.2	119.7	144.0	120.4	83.0	32.6	3.9	2,654	1,294	41.7
1938	237,091	9,452	4.0	20.7	26.9	121.2	145.3	123.9	84.8	34.0	4.1	2,701	1,314	39.4
1937	227,869	8,843	3.9	20.1	25.6	113.6	142.2	123.4	85.3	34.7	4.2	2,646	1,286	36.4
1936	227,980	8,917	3.9	20.3	25.7	112.1	144.3	126.5	90.0	36.3	4.4	2,696	1,310	34.5
1935	228,396	8,527	3.7	20.5	26.5	112.5	148.5	128.6	92.6	37.3	4.9	2,755	1,346	32.3
1934	228,296	8,321	3.6	20.7	26.2	113.1	151.2	133.1	93.0	39.2	4.9	2,803	1,368	30.0
1933	229,791	8,644	3.8	21.0	27.4	117.8	155.6	132.8	94.9	39.3	5.1	2,864	1,394	28.5
1932	242,698	8,655	3.6	22.5	28.7	129.6	168.3	140.6	100.5	43.7	5.5	3,084	1,499	27.5
1931	247,205	8,543	3.5	23.2	29.9	137.1	175.1	145.3	103.1	44.0	5.5	3,200	1,555	26.8
1930	250,335	8,255	3.3	23.9	30.5	143.0	176.0	148.0	106.7	46.6	5.5	3,282	1,599	26.6
1929	242,226	7,670	3.2	23.5	30.3	139.9	172.5	144.2	104.8	46.2	5.4	3,217	1,565	24.5
1928	243,616	7,436	3.1	24.1	30.2	140.3	172.8	149.9	111.0	48.8	5.9	3,294	1,604	21.5
1927	241,149	6,865	2.8	24.3	29.6	140.0	173.6	151.2	113.8	49.4	6.2	3,319	1,609	19.3
1926	240,015	6,307	2.6	24.7	29.0	139.9	177.4	153.8	114.6	50.7	6.0	3,357	1,628	17.8
1925	249,365	4,201[4]	2.6[4]	26.1	—	—	—	—	—	—	—	—	—	—
1924	251,351	3,848[4]	2.3[4]	26.7	—	—	—	—	—	—	—	—	—	—
1923	247,404[5]	3,556[4]	2.2[4]	26.7[1]	—	—	—	—	—	—	—	—	—	—
1922	259,825[5]	3,515[4]	2.1[4]	28.3[1]	—	—	—	—	—	—	—	—	—	—
1921	264,879[5]	3,334[4]	2.0[4]	29.3[1]	—	—	—	—	—	—	—	—	—	—

[1] Number of live births per thousand population; excludes Yukon and Northwest Territories, 1921 to 1923.

[2] Data for Yukon and Northwest Territories not available prior to 1950; Newfoundland excluded throughout.

[3] Excluding the province of Newfoundland; excludes Yukon and Northwest Territories, 1926 to 1949.

[4] Excluding the province of Quebec, 1921 to 1925; excluding Newfoundland 1921.

[5] Excludes Yukon and Northwest Territories.

[6] Excludes Yukon and Northwest Territories prior to 1950.

Series B 15–22. *Total number of deaths, crude and standardized death rates by sex, natural increase and rate, Canada, 1921 to 1960*
(all rates are per thousand population)

Year	Total number of deaths	Crude death rates			Standardized death rates[1]		Natural increase	
		Male[1]	Female[1]	Both sexes	Male	Female	Number	Rate
	15	16	17	18	19	20	21	22
1960	139,693	9.0	6.6	7.8	9.1	6.4	338,858	19.0
1959	139,913	9.2	6.8	8.0	9.3	6.7	339,362	19.4
1958	135,201	9.1	6.7	7.9	9.3	6.6	334,917	19.6
1957	136,579	9.5	6.9	8.2	9.6	6.9	332,514	20.0
1956	131,961	9.4	7.0	8.2	9.4	7.0	318,778	19.8
1955	128,476	9.4	6.9	8.2	9.4	6.9	314,461	20.0
1954	124,855	9.3	7.0	8.2	9.3	7.0	311,343	20.3
1953	127,791	9.8	7.4	8.6	9.8	7.5	290,093	19.5
1952	126,385	10.0	7.5	8.7	9.9	7.6	277,174	19.2
1951	125,823	10.1	7.8	9.0	10.0	8.0	255,269	18.2
1950	124,220	10.1	7.9	9.1	10.1	8.1	247,789	18.0
1949	124,567	10.3	8.1	9.3	10.3	8.3	242,525	18.0
1948	122,974	10.4	8.3	9.3	10.4	8.5	236,886	18.0
1947	121,503	10.4	8.3	9.4	10.6	8.7	251,086	19.5
1946	118,785	10.3	8.4	9.4	10.7	9.0	224,719	17.8
1945	117,325	10.3	8.5	9.5	10.9	9.2	183,262	14.8
1944	120,393	10.5	8.9	9.8	11.3	9.7	173,574	14.2
1943	122,640	10.9	9.2	10.1	11.8	10.1	170,303	14.1
1942	117,110	10.6	8.8	9.8	11.6	9.8	164,459	13.7
1941	118,797	10.8	9.1	10.1	12.0	10.3	145,196	12.3
1940	114,717	10.5	9.0	9.8	11.8	10.2	137,860	11.8
1939	112,729	10.4	9.0	9.7	11.8	10.4	125,262	10.9
1938	110,647	10.3	8.9	9.7	11.8	10.4	126,444	11.0
1937	118,019	10.9	9.7	10.4	12.7	11.4	109,850	9.7
1936	111,111	10.2	9.3	9.9	12.0	11.0	116,869	10.4
1935	109,724	10.2	9.2	9.9	12.1	11.0	118,672	10.6
1934	105,277	10.0	8.9	9.5	11.9	10.8	123,019	11.2
1933	105,603	10.0	9.2	9.7	12.0	11.2	124,188	11.3
1932	108,161	10.3	9.5	10.0	12.5	11.6	134,537	12.5
1931	108,446	10.5	9.6	10.2	12.7	11.7	138,759	13.0
1930	113,283	11.2	10.2	10.8	13.5	12.4	137,052	13.1
1929	117,622	11.8	10.8	11.4	14.3	13.3	124,604	12.1
1928	113,176	11.6	10.6	11.2	14.0	13.0	130,440	12.9
1927	109,104	11.4	10.4	11.0	13.8	12.7	132,045	13.3
1926	111,055	11.9	10.9	11.4	14.3	13.4	128,960	13.3
1925	102,528	10.3	9.5	10.7	12.5	11.7	146,837	15.4
1924	102,820	10.3	9.6	10.9	12.6	11.9	148,531	15.8
1923	108,858[2]	11.0	10.4	11.8[2]	13.5	12.9	138,546[2]	14.9[2]
1922	106,068[2]	11.0	10.3	11.6[2]	13.4	12.6	153,757[2]	16.7[2]
1921	104,531[2]	10.9	10.2	11.6[2]	13.3	12.4	160,348[2]	17.7[2]

[1] Excluding the Province of Quebec for 1921 to 1925, Newfoundland for 1921 to 1948 and Yukon and Northwest Territories for 1921 to 1949.   [2] Excluding Yukon and Northwest Territories.

Series B 23–34. *Average age-specific death rates, both sexes, Canada, for five-year periods, 1921 to 1960*
(per thousand population)

Period[1]	All ages	0 years	1–4 years	5–14 years	15–24 years	25–34 years	35–44 years	45–54 years	55–64 years	65–74 years	75–84 years	85 years and over
	23	24	25	26	27	28	29	30	31	32	33	34
1960	7.8	28.3	1.2	.5	1.0	1.2	2.3	6.0	15.0	35.5	86.8	207.4
1959	8.0	29.6	1.2	.6	1.0	1.3	2.3	6.0	15.2	36.7	89.1	211.3
1956–60	8.0	31.3	1.3	.5	1.0	1.3	2.3	6.1	15.4	36.2	88.7	208.7
1951–5	8.5	37.5	1.7	.7	1.1	1.5	2.6	6.6	15.9	36.9	90.6	213.1
1946–50[1]	9.3	49.0	2.4	.9	1.5	1.8	3.2	7.2	16.7	39.3	93.6	213.5
1941–5	9.8	61.0	3.6	1.2	1.9	2.4	3.8	7.7	17.3	41.1	102.0	233.0
1936–40	9.8	70.8	5.0	1.5	2.2	2.9	4.4	8.0	17.7	42.2	103.2	227.5
1931–5	9.8	80.7	5.5	1.5	2.5	3.4	4.7	8.2	17.7	42.1	103.2	225.2
1926–30	11.1	26.7		2.2	3.3	4.0	5.5	8.7	18.3	44.7	109.6	255.1
1921–5[1]	10.3	23.5		2.2	3.1	3.9	5.2	8.2	17.6	43.2	105.7	243.5

[1] Excluding Quebec, 1921 to 1925, Newfoundland, 1921 to 1948 and Yukon and Northwest Territories, 1921 to 1949.

Series B35–50. *Average annual number of deaths and death rates for leading causes of death, Canada, for five-year periods, 1921 to 1960*

(all rates are per 100,000 population)

Period[1]	Cardiovascular renal diseases, 330–4, 400–68, 592–4* Number	Rate	Cancer, 140–205* Number	Rate	Accidents, 800–962* Number	Rate	Tuberculosis, 001–019* Number	Rate	Diseases of early infancy,[2] 760–76* Number	Rate	Influenza, bronchitis and pneumonia,[2] 480–3, 490–3, 500–2, 763* Number	Rate	Gastritis, duodenitis, enteritis and colitis, 543, 571, 572* Number	Rate	Communicable diseases,[3] 055, 056, 085, 050, 040, 041* Number	Rate
	35	36	37	38	39	40	41	42	43	44	45	46	47	48	49	50
1960	70,754	395.9	23,181	129.7	9,403	52.6	823	4.6	7,085	39.6	7,223	40.4	974	5.5	149	0.8
1959	70,152	401.3	22,243	127.2	9,439	54.0	959	5.5	7,453	42.6	8,227	47.1	995	5.7	145	0.8
1956–60	68,083	399.9	21,895	128.6	9,385	55.1	1,050	6.2	7,527	44.2	7,652	44.9	964	5.7	195	1.1
1951–5	61,522	414.0	19,120	128.7	8,531	57.4	2,175	14.6	7,355	49.5	6,816	45.9	1,152	7.8	376	2.5
1946–50[1]	53,466	413.0	16,737	129.3	7,624	58.9	4,803	37.1	7,543	58.3	7,159	55.3	1,840	14.2	639	4.9
1941–5	47,498	403.3	14,521	123.3	7,139	60.6	5,898	50.1	6,740	57.2	8,139	69.1	2,261	19.2	1,145	9.7
1936–40	37,617	337.6	12,682	113.8	6,225	55.9	6,265	56.2	6,708	60.2	10,864	97.5	2,690	24.1	1,733	15.6
1931–5	31,559	297.5	10,699	100.9	5,555	52.4	6,950	65.5	7,900	74.5	10,674	100.6	3,757	35.4	1,888	17.8
1926–30	26,818	273.1	8,638	88.0	5,772	58.8	7,884	80.3	9,597[4]	97.7	13,138	133.8	5,387	54.9	3,436	35.0
1921–5	20,008	221.9	6,848	75.9	4,643	51.5	7,671	85.1	10,009[4]	111.0[4]	12,722	141.1	6,514	72.2	4,251	47.1

* Numbers refer to categories of the International Statistical Classification of Diseases, Injuries and Causes of Death (Seventh Revision), although these may not be strictly comparable over the period for some diseases.
[1] Newfoundland included in 1949 and following years. Yukon and Northwest Territories included in 1950 and following years.

[2] Pneumonia of the newborn included in both 'Diseases of early infancy' and 'Influenza, bronchitis and pneumonia' for all years (except for the Province of Quebec, 1921 to 1925).
[3] Diphtheria, whooping cough, measles, scarlet fever, typhoid fever.
[4] Excludes pneumonia of the newborn for the Province of Quebec.

Series B51–58. *Stillbirths and rate, infant deaths and rate by sex, neo-natal death rate and maternal mortality rate, Canada, 1921 to 1960*

(all rates are per thousand live births)

Year	Stillbirths[1] Number	Rate	Infant deaths (under one year of age) Number	Infant death rates Male[2]	Female[2]	Both sexes	Neo-natal death rate[3]	Maternal mortality
	51	52	53	54	55	56	57	58
1960	6,471	13.5	13,077	31	24	27	18	0.4
1959	6,560	13.7	13,595	32	25	28	18	0.5
1958	6,726	14.3	14,178	34	26	30	19	0.6
1957	6,837	14.6	14,517	34	27	31	20	0.5
1956	6,976	15.5	14,399	35	29	32	20	0.6
1955	6,918[1]	15.6[1]	13,884	35	27	31	19	0.8
1954	7,231	16.6	13,934	36	28	32	19	0.7
1953	6,991	16.7	14,859	40	31	36	21	0.8
1952	7,277	18.0	15,408	43	34	38	23	0.9
1951	7,023	18.4	14,673	43	34	39	23[3]	1.1
1950	7,192	19.3	15,441	46	37	42	24	1.1
1949	7,285	19.8	15,935	48	38	43	24	1.5
1948	7,071	19.6	15,965	49	39	44	26	1.5
1947	7,646	20.5	17,229	52	40	46	27	1.6
1946	7,368	21.4	16,407	53	42	48	27	1.8
1945	6,884	22.9	15,779	57	47	52	29	2.3
1944	6,895	23.5	16,541	62	50	56	30	2.8
1943	6,988	23.9	16,117	61	49	55	30	2.9
1942	7,319	26.0	15,585	61	49	55	28	3.1
1941	7,091	26.9	16,117	68	53	61	31	3.6
1940	6,810	27.0	14,542	64	51	58	30	4.0
1939	6,515	27.4	14,607	69	53	61	31	4.3
1938	6,595	27.8	15,233	71	57	64	32	4.3
1937	6,433	28.2	17,628	86	68	77	34	4.9
1936	6,531	28.6	15,442	75	60	68	34	5.6
1935	6,594	28.9	16,549	81	63	72	35	4.9
1934	6,613	29.0	16,603	81	64	73	36	5.3
1933	6,988	30.4	17,022	83	65	74	37	5.0
1932	7,396	30.5	18,098	83	66	75	38	5.0
1931	7,778	31.5	21,269	96	76	86	42	5.1
1930	7,847	31.3	22,677	100	81	91	43[3]	5.8
1929	7,720	31.9	22,501	103	82	93	44[3]	5.7
1928	7,673	31.5	21,979	100	80	90	44	5.6
1927	7,464	31.0	22,784	105	84	95	45	5.5
1926	7,245	30.2	24,377	113[2]	90[2]	102	48	5.6[4]
1925	8,176	32.8	23,128	87[2]	70[2]	93	41[3]	4.9[4]
1924	8,401	33.4	23,602	86	71	94	42	5.3[4]
1923	8,425	34.1	25,571[4]	98	77	103[4]	44	5.0[4]
1922	8,536	32.9	26,399[4]	97	76	102[4]	44	5.1[4]
1921	9,089	34.3	27,051[4]	98	77	102[4]	43	4.7[4]

[1] See note to B51–52 for definition of stillbirth. Beginning in 1959 some provinces reduced the gestation period to 20 weeks and broadened the definition of 'life' by giving specific criteria. Excludes Yukon and Northwest Territories in 1921 to 1926.
[2] Quebec is excluded for 1921 to 1925, Newfoundland for 1921 to 1926 and Eukon and Northwest Territories for 1921 to 1949.

[3] See note to B53–57 for definition. Quebec is excluded for 1921 to 1925, Newfoundland for 1921 to 1929 and Yukon and Northwest Territories for 1921 to 1949.
[4] Excludes Yukon and Northwest Territories.

Series B 59–64. *Average annual infant death rates for selected causes, Canada, for five-year periods, 1931 to 1960*

(average annual rates per 100,000 live births)

Period[1]	Immaturity[2]	Congenital malformations and birth injuries, 750–61*	Bronchitis and pneumonia, 490–3, 500–2, 763*	Diarrhoea and enteritis, 571.0, 572.2, 572.3, 573,764*	Asphyxia and atelectasis, 762*	Communicable diseases[3]
	59	60	61	62	63	64
1960	1,079	698	412	119	318	57
1959	1,107	740	406	129	320	64
1956–60	1,140	773	447	136	339	76
1951–5	1,159	865	522	211	332	143
1946–50[1]	1,163	989	628	433	Not comparable	245
1941–5	1,167	1,092	780	625	Not comparable	449
1936–40	1,436	980	826	793	Not comparable	681
1931–5	1,647	1,002	864	1,227	Not comparable	743

* Numbers refer to categories of the International Statistical Classification of Diseases, Injuries and Causes of Death (Seventh Revision), although these may not be strictly comparable over the period for some diseases.

[1] Newfoundland included for 1949 and following years. Yukon and Northwest Territories included for 1950 and following years.

[2] Due to changes in classification, not strictly comparable over the period; includes all deaths involving immaturity either as the underlying cause or as a complication.

[3] Includes measles, scarlet fever, whooping cough, diphtheria, influenza, erysipelas, acute poliomyelitis, cerebrospinal meningitis, tuberculosis and syphilis.

Series B 65–74. *Life expectancy by sex, at selected ages, Canada, census years, 1871 to 1956*

Year	At birth		At age 20		At age 40		At age 60		At age 80	
	Males	Females	Males	Females	Males	Females	Males	Females	Males	Females
	65	66	67	68	69	70	71	72	73	74
1956	67.61	72.92	51.19	55.80	32.74	36.69	16.54	19.34	5.89	6.75
1951	66.33	70.83	50.76	54.41	32.45	35.63	16.49	18.64	5.84	6.38
1941	62.96	66.30	49.57	51.76	31.87	33.99	16.06	17.62	5.54	6.03
1931	60.00	62.10	49.05	49.76	31.98	33.02	16.29	17.15	5.61	5.92
1921[1]	—	—	49.1	49.2	32.2	33.0	16.6	17.1	6.0	6.1
1881[2]	—	—	48.0	47.8	33.2	33.8	18.0	19.0	6.9	7.5
1871[2]	—	—	47.9	47.3	33.4	33.6	18.2	18.2	6.8	6.5

[1] All provinces except Quebec.

[2] Ontario, Quebec, Nova Scotia and New Brunswick.

Series B75–81. *Number of marriages and rate, average age at marriage for brides and bridegrooms, number of divorces and rate, net family formation, Canada, 1921 to 1960*

	Marriages		Average age at marriage (years)[1]		Divorces[2]		Net family formation[2] (thousands of families)
	Number	Rate per thousand population	Brides	Bridegrooms	Number	Rate per hundred thousand population	
Year							
	75	**76**	**77**	**78**	**79**	**80**	**81**
1960	130,338	7.3	24.7	27.7	6,980	39.1	58
1959	132,474	7.6	24.8	27.7	6,543	37.4	67
1958	131,525	7.7	24.8	27.8	6,279	36.8	71
1957	133,186	8.0	24.9	27.8	6,688	40.3	103
1956	132,713	8.3	25.0	27.9	6,002	37.4	84
1955	128,029	8.2	25.1	28.0	6,053	38.6	74
1954	128,629	8.4	25.2	28.1	5,923	38.8	86
1953	131,034	8.8	25.3	28.2	6,160	41.6	91
1952	128,474	8.9	25.3	28.3	5,650	39.1	90
1951	128,408	9.2	25.3	28.3	5,270	37.7	93
1950	125,083	9.1	25.3	28.5	5,386	39.3	71
1949	124,087	9.2	25.4	28.7	6,052	45.1	74
1948	126,118	9.6	25.4	28.6	6,978	54.5	79
1947	130,400	10.1	25.3	28.6	8,213	65.6	72
1946	137,398	10.9	25.3	28.6	7,757	63.2	104
1945	111,376	9.0	25.5	29.0	5,101	42.3	50
1944	104,656	8.5	25.6	29.2	3,827	32.1	48
1943	113,827	9.4	25.4	29.0	3,398	28.9	55
1942	130,786	10.9	25.2	29.0	3,091	26.6	72
1941	124,644	10.6	25.1	28.9	2,462	21.4	68
1940	125,797	10.8	25.2	28.9	2,416	21.3	70
1939	106,266	9.2	25.1	29.0	2,073	18.4	54
1938	90,709	7.9	25.3	29.3	2,228	20.0	39
1937	89,983	7.9	25.2	29.3	1,833	16.6	39
1936	82,941	7.4	25.0	29.1	1,570	14.4	32
1935	78,908	7.1	25.0	29.0	1,431	13.2	30
1934	75,034	6.8	24.9	29.1	1,123	10.5	28
1933	65,516	6.0	24.9	29.2	931	8.8	20
1932	64,141	5.9	24.9	29.2	1,007	9.6	19
1931	68,239	6.4	24.9	29.2	700	6.8	29
1930	73,341	7.0	25.0	29.2	875	8.6	39
1929	78,977	7.7	24.9	29.1	817	8.2	48
1928	76,009	7.5	25.0	29.3	790	8.0	47
1927	71,071	7.2	25.1	29.3	748	7.8	44
1926	68,378	7.0	25.1	29.3	608	6.4	38
1925	66,378	6.9	25.3	29.8	550	5.9	31
1924	66,573	7.1	25.2	29.7	540	5.9	29
1923	67,820[3]	7.3[3]	25.3	29.7	505	5.6	25
1922	65,861[3]	7.2[3]	25.4	29.9	543	6.1	20
1921	71,254[3]	7.9[3]	25.5	29.9	558	6.4	37

[1] Excluding the Province of Quebec for 1921 to 1925, Newfoundland for 1921 to 1948 and Yukon and Northwest Territories for 1921 to 1949.

[2] Excluding Newfoundland for 1921 to 1948. For the definition of net family formation, see the text.

[3] Excluding Yukon and Northwest Territories.

Series B82–91. *Estimated births, deaths, natural increase, marriages (number and rates), immigration, emigration, Canada,[1] 1900 to 1920*

(series B82–87 in thousands; series B88–91 in rates per thousand population)

	Number (thousands)						Rates per 1,000 population			
Year	Births	Deaths	Natural increase	Marriages	Immigrants	Emigrants[2]	Births	Deaths	Natural increase	Marriages
	82	**83**	**84**	**85**	**86**	**87**	**88**	**89**	**90**	**91**
1920	254	116	138	80	139	40	29.2	13.3	15.9	9.2
1919	234	116	118	70	108	15	27.7	13.7	14.0	8.3
1918	237	131	106	56	42	16	28.8	15.9	12.9	6.8
1917	236	103	133	61	73	131	29.1	12.7	16.4	7.5
1916	247	105	142	64	56	154	30.7	13.0	17.7	8.0
1915	255	100	155	63	37	139	31.9	12.5	19.4	7.9
1914	253	100	153	67	150	140	31.9	12.6	19.3	8.4
1913	247	102	145	71	401	301	31.7	13.1	18.6	9.1
1912	236	98	138	71	376	296	31.3	13.0	18.3	9.4
1911	220	98	122	63	331	256	30.1	13.4	16.7	8.6
1910	216	93	123	58	287	204	30.4	13.1	17.3	8.2
1909	209	89	120	53	174	111	30.2	12.8	17.4	7.7
1908	204	85	119	49	143	71	30.3	12.6	17.7	7.3
1907	193	84	109	49	272	125	29.5	12.8	16.7	7.5
1906	188	83	105	47	212	94	29.9	13.2	16.7	7.5
1905	188	79	109	45	141	122	31.0	13.0	18.0	7.4
1904	186	80	106	43	131	62	31.4	13.5	17.9	7.3
1903	180	76	104	42	139	75	31.3	13.2	18.1	7.3
1902	175	75	100	38	89	46	31.3	13.4	17.9	6.8
1901	170	77	93	38	56	62	31.2	14.1	17.1	7.0
1900	146	87	59	37	42	30	27.2	16.2	11.0	6.9

[1] Covers total present territory except Newfoundland.   [2] Residual.

Series B92–99. *Birth, death, marriage and infant mortality rates, death rates for selected causes for the Province of Quebec, death rate in the City of Montreal, 1867 to 1920*

	Province of Quebec							Montreal death rate per 1,000 population
	Rate per 1,000 population			Rate of infant mortality[1]	Death rate per 100,000 population			
Year	Births	Deaths	Marriages		Tuberculosis	Cancer and malignant tumours	Heart diseases	
	92	93	94	95	96	97	98	99
1920	37.6	17.7	9.4	163	143	55.1	83.0	17.2
1919	35.8	15.7	9.7	142	139	52.1	73.0	15.8
1918	38.6	22.3	5.9	138	154	49.6	85.5	22.0
1917	37.9	17.9	8.0	136	145	50.2	77.7	17.8
1916	38.0	18.1	7.9	165	152	46.0	71.9	17.7
1915	38.8	16.9	7.2	153	149	49.9	71.3	18.0
1914	37.6	16.8	7.5	161	160	46.7	70.7	19.8
1913	38.4	17.6	8.4	168	156	46.8	68.7	21.5
1912	38.0	16.4	8.0	161	158	46.4	63.4	20.0
1911	38.1	18.3	7.8	185	171	47.8	72.6	21.2
1910	38.6	18.6	7.5	174	166	40.9	65.8	22.4
1909	39.4	18.6	7.5	139	164	42.2	64.1	22.0
1908	34.6	19.4	6.4	209	158	38.8	67.9	23.0
1907	34.4	17.4	6.9	—	155	40.7	60.3	22.6
1906	35.7	18.7	7.0	130	159	38.2	64.3	22.9
1905	35.5	18.2	6.9	—	154	37.5	58.0	23.0
1904	36.1	18.4	7.1	110	160	32.2	72.5	23.4
1903	36.2	18.8	6.7	134	171	34.7	75.5	24.3
1902	34.0	17.5	6.8	136	168	37.7	75.6	22.6
1901	33.6	19.5	6.1	167	180	33.7	71.2	23.3
1900	33.0	20.1	6.2	187	184	36.2	71.3	25.5
1899	35.2	20.4	6.9	—	190	34.7	66.5	24.5
1898	37.9	20.0	6.8	—	181	34.2	68.8	20.7
1897	37.1	21.8	6.5	—	194	36.2	73.5	22.5
1896	38.2	19.9	6.4	—	180	30.1	80.2	21.9
1895	37.9	20.5	6.6	—	—	30.0	67.7	24.8
1894	34.9	21.0	6.1	—	—	29.0	67.4	27.3
1893	37.5	21.6	6.5	—	—	—	—	24.0
1892	37.1	21.4	6.5	—	—	—	—	24.5
1891	38.9	22.2	6.2	—	—	—	—	24.2
1890	37.8	22.3	6.3	—	—	—	—	24.8
1889	38.5	21.9	6.5	—	—	—	—	26.6
1888	39.1	21.6	7.0	—	—	—	—	28.9
1887	39.7	20.7	6.9	—	—	—	—	28.0
1886	40.2	23.1	6.8	—	—	—	—	25.4
1885	37.4	25.2	6.6	—	—	—	—	46.7
1884	38.5	19.4	6.6	—	—	—	—	26.7
1883	41.7	—	—	—	—	—	—	25.6
1882	41.7	—	—	—	—	—	—	27.1
1881	40.7	—	—	—	—	—	—	27.2
1880	42.4	—	—	—	—	—	—	26.9
1879	42.8	—	—	—	—	—	—	27.4
1878	44.4	—	—	—	—	—	—	30.5
1877	44.1	—	—	—	—	—	—	35.1
1876	45.2	—	—	—	—	—	—	34.3
1875	46.0	—	—	—	—	—	—	33.3
1874	44.0	—	—	—	—	—	—	36.2
1873	42.9	—	—	—	—	—	—	39.0
1872	42.7	—	—	—	—	—	—	37.4
1871	41.6	—	—	—	—	—	—	—
1870	41.6	—	—	—	—	—	—	—
1869	42.3	—	—	—	—	—	—	—
1868	42.8	—	—	—	—	—	—	—
1867	43.5	—	—	—	—	—	—	—

[1] Number of deaths of age 0 to 1 year per 1,000 live births.

Series B 100–107. *Number of births, deaths, immigrants and emigrants ; birth and death rates for intercensal periods ; number of children aged under 5 years per 1,000 women aged 15–44, Canada, 1851 to 1961*

Period[1]	Births	Deaths	Immigrants[2]	Emigrants (residual)	Population at the middle of the period[3]	Annual rates per 1,000 population[4]		Number of children under 5 per 1,000 women 15–44[5]
			(numbers in thousands)			Births	Deaths	
	100	**101**	**102**	**103**	**104**	**105**	**106**	**107**
1956–61	2,362	687	744	262	17,160	27.5	8.0	583
1951–6	2,106	633	780	181	15,045	28.0	8.4	555
1941–51	3,186	1,214[6]	548	379	12,577	25.3	9.7	397
1931–41	2,294	1,072	150	242	10,942	21.0	9.8	466
1921–31	2,415	1,055	1,203	974	9,583	25.2	11.0	546
1911–21	2,338	988[7]	1,612	1,381	7,998	29.2	12.4	567
1901–11	1,931	811	1,759	1,043	6,289	30.7	12.9	536
1891–1901	1,546	828	326	506	5,102	30.3	16.2	558
1881–91	1,538	824	903	1,109	4,579	33.6	18.0	614
1871–81	1,477	754	353	440	4,007	36.9	18.8	666
1861–71	1,369	718	187	379	3,460	39.6	20.8	775
1851–61	1,281	611	209	85	2,833	45.2	21.6	877

[1] Excluding Newfoundland except for 1951 to 1961.
[2] Immigration during census years divided into January–May, June–December in proportion of 5/12 and 7/12 to correspond to usual census date.
[3] Mean of the population at both ends of the period.
[4] Calculated by dividing one-tenth of the births or deaths for the decade by the population at the middle of the period; for 1951 to 1956 and 1956 to 1961 division by one-fifth of births and deaths.
[5] At the census year beginning the period.
[6] Allows for 36,000 deaths due to World War II.
[7] Allows for 120,000 deaths due to World War I and the influenza epidemic.

Series B 108–115. *Number of physicians, dentists and nurses, population per physician, dentist and nurse, number of graduates of medical and dental schools, Canada, 1871 to 1960*

Year	Physicians[1]		Graduates of Canadian medical schools[4]	Dentists[5]		Graduates of Canadian dental schools[7]	Nurses[8]	
	Number[2]	Population per physician[3]		Number[6]	Population per dentist[3]		Number[9]	Population per nurse[3]
	108	**109**	**110**	**111**	**112**	**113**	**114**	**115**
1960	—	—	863	5,780	3,018	215	68,502	255
1959	19,000[10]	918	859	5,753	2,963	193	64,666	264
1958	—	—	828	5,564	2,981	203	60,864	273
1957	—	—	893	5,481	2,934	186	59,419	271
1956	—	—	816	5,416	2,898	168	54,518	288
1955	—	—	894	5,354	2,855	174	50,131	305
1954	16,031[11]	954	896	5,298	2,802	172	47,775[12]	303[12]
1953	—	—	825	5,215	2,773	178	43,880	321
1952	—	—	783	5,071	2,763	215	43,924	311
1951	14,341[11]	977	858	4,912	2,792	295	41,088	325
1950	—	—	791	4,627	2,906	306	41,159	318
1949	13,873	969	679	4,549[12]	2,810[12]	180	38,292	335
1948	13,373[12]	950[12]	632	4,601	2,728	99	37,917	331
1947	13,263[13]	945[13]	567	4,602	2,671	149	34,929	352
1946	—	—	513			102	33,348	362
1945	—	—	769	—	—	116	31,389	381
1944	—	—	523			140	31,087	379
1943	11,620	1,014	496	—	—	166	29,595	394
1942	—	—	539			120	27,853	413
1941	11,873	968	562	4,210[13]	2,729[13]	97	25,826	441
1940	—	—	606	—	—	117	—	—
1939	—	—	—	—	—	115	—	—
1931	10,020	1,034	482	4,039	2,566	—	20,462[13]	506[13]
1921	8,706	1,008	406	3,158	2,779	—	21,385[14]	410[14]
1911	7,411	970	351	2,183	3,294	—	5,600	1,284
1901	5,442	978	—	1,310	4,064	—	280	19,014
1891	4,448	1,065	—	753	6,290	—	—	—
1881	3,507	1,217	—	510	8,369	—	—	—
1871[15]	2,792	1,249	—	319	10,928	—	—	—

[1] Active civilian; census figures for 1941 and earlier years.
[2] As of September for 1949, 1948, July for 1947, March for 1943, June for other years.
[3] Based on census data and Dominion Bureau of Statistics intercensal estimates of population; for dentists, 1947 to 1960, and nurses, 1941 to 1960, population is for June of previous year.
[4] Number of schools producing graduates increased from eight in 1911 to nine in 1925, ten in 1951, eleven in 1954 and twelve in 1957.
[5] Registered dentists for 1947 to 1960; census figures for 1941 and earlier years; includes Active Service personnel for 1941 and later years.
[6] As of January for 1947 to 1960, June for other years.
[7] Schools producing graduates have totalled five throughout; a sixth is expected to produce graduates in 1961.
[8] Registered nurses for 1941 to 1960; census figures for 1931 (graduate nurses) and earlier years ('nurses').
[9] As of January for 1941 to 1960, June for other years.
[10] Estimate.
[11] Excluding graduates of year.
[12] Excluding Newfoundland for this and earlier years.
[13] Excluding Yukon and Northwest Territories for this and earlier years.
[14] Includes nurses-in-training.
[15] Provinces of Nova Scotia, New Brunswick, Quebec and Ontario.

Series B116–124. *Annual rates of notifiable diseases, Canada, 1926 to 1960*

(rates per 100,000 population)

Year[1]	Chickenpox, 087*	Diphtheria, 055*	Measles, 085*	Mumps, 089*	Pertussis (whooping cough), 056*	Poliomyelitis (all types), 080*	Scarlet fever and streptococcal sore throat, 050, 051*	Tuberculosis, 001–019*	Typhoid and paratyphoid fever, 040, 041*
	116	117	118	119	120	121	122	123	124
1960	—	.3	—	—	33.6	5.1	119.1	35.5	1.9
1959	—	.2	—	—	41.5	10.8	133.9	37.6	3.1
1958	—	.4	—	—	40.7	1.9	65.2	42.3	1.8
1957	—	.9	—	—	45.0	1.6	52.5	46.2	1.7
1956	—	.8	336.1	—	53.0	3.8	72.7	52.3	2.8
1955	214.5	.9	363.3	173.5	87.3	6.5	59.7	58.6	2.4
1954	247.3	1.4	241.5	176.3	76.0	15.7	86.0	63.0	3.1
1953	320.2	.9	390.5	244.9	63.3	59.8	107.8	65.7	3.1
1952	317.9	1.3	389.2	266.3	59.0	33.0	145.4	70.0	3.5
1951	333.5	1.8	438.3	251.6	63.6	18.2	110.4	77.8	4.0
1950[1]	260.1	3.1	406.6	319.0	89.0	6.8	71.9	87.0	5.2
1949	346.2	6.1	447.4	187.8	60.7	18.6	71.2	94.8	5.8
1948	326.3	7.0	515.7	192.2	55.3	9.1	63.5	93.9	4.4
1947	258.9	12.4	315.0	257.5	82.4	18.3	63.2	105.7	5.6
1946	237.3	20.7	550.4	212.4	62.5	20.6	80.5	119.1	7.5
1945	262.5	23.1	223.8	169.2	101.1	3.2	105.5	113.9	7.3
1944	297.6	27.0	463.7	166.1	103.8	6.1	181.1	125.3	10.4
1943	258.6	23.8	513.5	410.1	162.0	2.8	163.4	104.5	9.8
1942	265.7	25.4	225.6	449.8	158.0	5.9	185.2	100.6	9.8
1941	242.5	24.9	705.4	199.6	144.9	16.4	153.9	88.0	13.5
1940	288.3	20.5	403.5	118.8	174.9	1.7	128.0	86.6	13.8
1939	225.1	25.8	395.3	51.9	159.8	3.2	140.5	88.4	11.7
1938	242.3	33.0	236.4	75.4	143.7	5.2	154.9	81.0	16.5
1937	220.1	26.7	520.5	130.9	157.7	35.4	156.5	77.4	20.5
1936	232.6	18.6	509.6	272.1	148.7	8.9	198.5	79.2	16.7
1935	255.2	18.5	767.6	209.1	166.1	3.4	167.3	81.0	18.2
1934	218.7	21.1	271.4	78.9	181.6	4.8	154.0	76.3	21.7
1933	219.8	22.4	127.8	108.9	137.7	2.4	97.1	79.6	22.0
1932	170.5	37.3	510.7	118.3	114.9	9.1	93.8	84.2	23.6
1931	185.8	57.1	247.6	107.7	88.5	12.9	125.8	69.4	28.4
1930[1]	199.7	78.8	211.9	92.8	115.2	10.1	173.1	64.4	22.1
1929	180.7	90.6	424.3	121.4	106.1	7.7	161.5	57.6	19.0
1928	165.3	90.2	284.9	245.8	68.3	8.1	151.3	56.9	23.1
1927	143.5	89.1	295.2	—	70.2	6.4	162.5	55.4	85.1
1926	139.5	76.7	421.6	—	74.5	1.2	152.3	59.7	19.6

* Numbers refer to categories of the International Statistical Classification of Diseases, Injuries and Causes of Death (Seventh Revision).

[1] Newfoundland is included since 1950 and Prince Edward Island since 1930.

Series B125–137. *Number of hospitals operating and reporting, rated bed capacity, number of beds per 1,000 population, by category of hospitals; number of bassinets in public and federal hospitals, Canada, 1932 to 1960*

	Number of hospitals					Number of beds and cribs (rated capacity) in hospitals reporting				Number of beds and cribs per 1,000 population			Number of bassinets (rated capacity) in public and federal hospitals
	Public general and special		Public tuberculosis[2]	Public and private mental[3]	Federal[4]	Public general and special	Tuberculosis[5]	Public and private mental[3]	Federal[4]	Public general and special	Tuberculosis	Mental	
Year[1]	Number operating	Number reporting movement of patients	(number reporting)										
	125	126	127	128	129	130	131	132	133	134	135	136	137
1960	936[8]	925	52	105	77	97,967	10,494	63,148	11,938	5.37	.59	3.53	15,507
1959	963	940	50	108	53	99,271	10,753	60,629	11,473	5.68	.62	3.47	15,110
1958	957	922	51	109	47	94,944	11,658	59,904	12,445	5.56	.68	3.52	14,434
1957	920	894	54	106	48	89,613	12,760	57,193	12,552	5.40	.77	3.45	14,073
1956	909	872	56	104	52	87,949	13,524	58,014	12,799	5.47	.84	3.62	13,785
1955	896	858	56	97	55	83,564	13,646	57,009	13,417	5.32	.87	3.64	13,318
1954	870	817	55	96	53	80,517	13,798	54,346	13,130	5.27	.90	3.56	12,546
1953	855	810	56	78	56	73,689	15,220	51,328	13,491	4.96	1.03	3.46	11,915
1952[1]	795	777	57	75	52	70,333	14,365	48,893	13,184	4.86	.99	3.39	11,074
1951	780	778	60	69	78	68,982	14,194	46,096	13,898	4.92	1.01	3.30	10,796
1950	770	763	59	67	81	66,423	13,739	45,081	13,513	4.84	1.00	3.29	10,287
1949	743	738	55	64	90	62,995	12,836	44,055	13,995	4.68	.95	3.28	9,638
1948	717	696	47	59	78	59,435	10,940	45,682	12,782	4.64	.85	3.57	9,111
1947	687	671	46	59	77	58,365[6]	10,862	45,180	13,379	4.65	.87	3.61	9,021
1946	638	615	44	60	20[7]	57,994[6]	10,141	45,443	1,626[7]	4.72	.83	3.70	8,605
1945	617	604	42	59	15[7]	56,144[6]	9,712	45,124	856[7]	4.65	.80	3.74	7,859
1944	608	602	40	59	13[7]	55,098	9,482	42,500	533[7]	4.61	.79	3.56	7,458
1943	613	611	39	59	13[7]	54,056	9,254	42,454	549[7]	4.58	.78	3.61	7,079
1942	614	611	41	59	13[7]	53,472	9,250	41,762	557[7]	4.59	.79	3.59	6,774
1941	614	608	39	60	18[7]	53,809	8,655	40,115	628[7]	4.68	.75	3.49	6,525
1940	613	604	39	60	194	52,611	8,850	39,441	10,337	4.62	.78	3.47	6,285
1939	607	606	39	59	84	51,488	8,733	39,277	3,881	4.57	.78	3.49	5,980
1938	610	610	38	57	32	50,074	7,696	38,671	3,398	4.49	.69	3.47	6,281
1937	584	584	—	57	—	48,345	—	37,798	—	4.38	—	3.43	5,854
1936	573	573	—	57	32	47,657	—	37,379	3,393	4.35	—	3.42	5,637
1935	572	572	—	56	—	46,876	—	35,987	—	4.32	—	3.32	5,497
1934	568	568	—	58	—	45,936	—	34,918	—	4.28	—	3.26	5,380
1933	564	564	—	60	—	45,027	—	32,781	—	4.23	—	3.09	5,854
1932	577	569	—	58	35	41,490	—	32,951	3,427	3.95	—	3.14	5,231

[1] Excludes Newfoundland, 1932 to 1952.
[2] Nonfederal tuberculosis sanatoria.
[3] Includes psychiatric units.
[4] Includes all federal hospitals for 1947 and later years except that certain hospitals of the Department of National Defence are believed to be unreported.
[5] Beds set up. Bed capacity available only from 1954: 1954, 14,120; 1955, 13,756; 1956, 13,596; 1957, 13,220; 1958, 12,031.

[6] Estimated.
[7] Includes only the Indian Health Services Hospitals of the Department of National Health and Welfare.
[8] Thirty-six hospitals were reclassified to related institutions (nursing stations, homes for the aged, etc.).

Series B138–148. *Public general and special allied hospitals : number of beds and cribs, movement of patients, expenditure per patient-day, full-time personnel, Canada, 1932 to 1960*

	Number of beds and cribs (capacity) in hospitals reporting			Movement of patients (excluding newborn)				Net expenditure per patient-day[3]	Personnel (full time)		
Year[1]	Public general	Public special	Percentage of general and special reporting to operating	Number of admissions[2]	Number of patient-days (thousands)	Average days' stay of separations	Percentage occupancy (based on capacity)		Number of beds (excluding bassinets) in hospitals reporting	Total personnel	Number of nurses (graduate and student)
	138	139	140	141	142	143	144	145	146	147	148
1960	85,427	11,167	—	2,580,780	28,980	11.1	82.2	21.32	96,533	155,992	51,970
1959	83,916	13,694	98.3	2,493,973	28,668	11.2	80.5	18.88	94,343	142,870	48,077
1958	80,123	13,148	98.2	2,402,827	27,270	10.9	80.1	17.24	93,271	131,920	44,269
1957	77,372	10,786	98.4	2,318,779	25,794	10.7	80.2	15.58	88,158	122,024	41,884
1956	75,384	10,634	97.8	2,218,692	24,855	11.0	78.9	14.31	85,920	112,838	38,611
1955	71,699	10,631	98.5	2,085,450	23,655	10.9	78.7	13.50	82,181	106,677	37,425
1954	66,081	9,397	93.7	1,914,993	21,978	11.1	79.8	12.85	75,478	95,471	34,066
1953	62,102	8,121	95.3	1,849,802	20,813	10.9	81.2	11.96	69,698	88,804	31,864
1952[1]	59,816	8,217	96.7	1,760,052	20,186	9.6	81.1	10.96	68,033	80,948	29,470
1951	57,360	11,314	99.6	1,681,487	19,798	10.5	79.0	10.25	68,674	83,405	31,250
1950	55,058	10,471	98.7	1,588,247	18,848	10.6	78.8	9.55	65,529	78,146	31,854
1949	51,855	9,821	97.9	1,527,751	17,849	10.3	79.1	8.30	61,676	72,579	27,860
1948	50,245	8,721	99.2	1,427,561	16,906	10.5	78.2	7.92	58,966	65,696	26,550
1947	48,507	8,363	97.7	1,350,185	16,198	10.6	77.9	7.35	56,870	62,195	24,857
1946	46,930	9,836	98.1	1,256,516	16,094	11.1	77.5	6.61	56,766	56,801	22,926
1945	45,523	9,368	97.9	1,144,928	15,024	11.4	74.9	4.78	54,891	50,495	21,424
1944	45,862	8,874	99.4	1,071,288	14,354	11.6	71.6	5.03	54,736	48,530	20,820
1943	44,096	9,842	99.0	1,008,843	13,931	12.0	70.6	5.89	53,938	45,676	20,093
1942	42,866	9,968	98.8	940,330	13,181	12.5	68.3	4.63	52,624	43,192	19,290
1941	43,199	10,106	99.1	899,873	12,926	12.7	66.4	—	53,085	42,090	18,743
1940	42,538	9,931	99.7	844,698	12,609	13.4	65.5	—	52,329	40,129	18,019
1939	41,509	9,979	99.9	787,493	11,487	13.4	62.8	—	51,380	37,383	17,050
1938	40,039	10,035	99.9	766,639	12,004	—	65.7	—	50,074	36,823	16,653
1937	38,754	9,591	99.9	741,421	11,773	—	66.7	—	48,345	34,465	15,530
1936	38,218	8,653	99.9	699,553	11,727	—	68.4	—	46,871	33,424	15,321
1935	38,044	8,832	99.9	642,066	11,253	—	65.8	—	46,876	31,350	14,308
1934	37,145	8,791	99.9	594,158	10,471	—	62.4	—	45,936	30,569	13,911
1933	36,731	8,296	99.9	549,144	9,790	—	60.0	—	46,314	29,330	13,375
1932	33,844	4,841	99.8	544,699	9,637	—	59.3	3.07	41,485	28,923	13,380

[1] Excludes Newfoundland, 1932 to 1952.
[2] Includes admissions in psychiatric units.

[3] Based on adult and child patient-days (excluding newborn days) and including out-patient expenditure, but excluding chronic hospitals. Yukon and Northwest Territories excluded throughout.

Series B149–158. *Mental institutions : movement of patients, cost per patient-day, full-time personnel, Canada, 1932 to 1960*

	First admissions[2]		Number of re-admissions[2]	Number of patient-days[2] (thousands)	Average number of patients[2]	Percentage occupancy	Turnover of patients[3] (per cent)	Cost per patient-day[4] (dollars)	Personnel (full time)[4]	
Year[1]	Number admitted in year	Number per 100,000 population							Total	Nurses (graduate and student)
	149	150	151	152	153	154	155	156	157	158
1960	26,935	151	16,186	25,084	68,535	106	63	4.31[5]	27,182	6,103
1959	28,066	161	15,118	24,732	67,759	109	64	5.31[5]	26,005	5,965
1958	26,536	156	13,760	24,857	68,102	114	59	4.08	24,773	5,477
1957	25,582	155	12,090	24,287	66,541	116	57	3.70	23,095	5,018
1956	25,097	156	11,341	24,189	66,090	114	55	3.34	20,598	4,777
1955	21,774	139	10,448	23,644	64,779	114	50	2.97	18,543	4,424
1954	20,627	135	8,724	23,006	63,031	116	47	2.92	18,561	4,414
1953	15,925	108	7,206	22,081	60,496	118	38	2.70	17,499	4,035
1952	15,056	104	5,901	21,060	57,541	118	36	2.53	15,756	4,212
1951	13,152	94	4,591	20,299	55,614	121	32	2.40	14,414	4,083
1950	11,912	87	4,499	19,797	54,240	120	30	2.23	13,461	3,943
1949	11,556	86	3,920	19,292	52,855	120	29	1.94	12,812	2,904
1948[1]	10,685	84	3,499	18,706	51,111	112	28	1.77	11,844	2,471
1947	9,745	78	3,335	18,286	50,099	111	26	1.46	11,368	2,241
1946	9,752	80	3,144	18,025	49,384	109	26	1.22	10,240	2,323
1945	9,489	79	2,779	17,642	48,334	107	25	1.08	9,834	2,060
1944	9,170	77	2,629	17,384	47,498	112	25	1.03	8,906	2,049
1943	8,556	73	2,390	17,044	46,697	110	23	.98	8,749	2,113
1942	8,410	72	2,282	16,865	46,205	111	23	.95	8,425	2,205
1941	7,902	69	2,401	16,525	45,273	113	23	.96	8,426	2,457
1940	7,736	68	2,087	16,104	44,000	112	22	.92	8,689	2,887
1939	8,301	74	2,250	15,786	43,250	110	24	.89	8,463	2,516
1938	8,581	77	2,384	15,758	43,173	112	25	.91	8,397	2,455
1937	8,703	79	2,258	15,036	41,195	109	27	.84	8,071	2,343
1936	9,002	82	2,121	14,362	39,240	105	28	.80	7,430	2,161
1935	8,604	80	2,166	13,889	38,052	106	28	.74	6,937	2,200
1934	8,096	75	1,965	13,250	36,300	104	28	.84	6,870	2,360
1933	7,518	71	1,683	—	—	—	—	.83	6,577	2,334
1932	7,628	73	1,828	—	—	—	—	.88	6,558	2,369

[1] Excludes Newfoundland, 1932 to 1948. Yukon and Northwest Territories excluded throughout.
[2] Includes psychiatric units.

[3] First admissions plus readmissions divided by average number of patients as a percentage.
[4] Excludes psychiatric units.
[5] Quebec financial data not available: therefore an increase in cost per patient-day.

Series B159–169. *Public and federal tuberculosis institutions : number of beds, movement of patients, cost per patient-day, full-time personnel, Canada, 1937 to 1960*

Year[1]	Number of beds set up 31 December[2]	Per-centage occu-pancy[3]	Movement of patients					Cost per patient-day (dollars)	Personnel (full time)[7]		
			Number of first admissions[4]	Number of re-admissions[5]	Number of dis-charges[6]	Number of patient-days (thousands)	Mean length of stay of tuberculous discharges		Number of beds in sanatoria reporting	Total personnel	Nurses (graduate and student)
	159	160	161	162	163	164	165	166	167	168	169
1960	13,011	77	10,048	3,842	14,682	3,725	264	10.41	10,494	7,789	1,111
1959	13,538	81	10,545	4,084	15,476	4,008	285	9.86	10,753	7,655	1,218
1958	14,655	82	11,500	4,241	16,128	4,361	300	9.22	11,658	7,985	1,264
1957	15,958	82	12,909	4,549	17,970	4,766	310	8.54	12,760	8,542	1,287
1956	16,678	86	11,880	4,488	16,949	5,251	327	7.55	13,524	8,717	1,499
1955	17,605	87	12,357	4,229	16,690	5,608	362	7.08	13,646	9,006	1,541
1954	17,683	92	11,520	4,339	16,424	5,947	372	6.84	13,798	9,451	1,577
1953	18,977	93	11,112	4,382	15,172	6,338	362	6.29	15,220	9,823	1,758
1952	18,501	91	10,867	4,393	13,991	6,145	337	6.18	14,365	9,167	1,645
1951	18,407	89	10,346	4,553	13,046	5,987	301	5.87	14,194	8,009	1,433
1950[1]	17,790	87	10,466	4,584	13,068	5,643	331	5.24	13,739	7,758	1,376
1949[1]	15,825	91	10,146	4,272	12,769	5,271	312	5.08	12,836	6,585	1,118
1948	14,512	91	9,541	4,231	12,304	4,784	290	4.85	10,940	6,070	1,073
1947	14,355	84	9,518	3,627	10,682	4,432	298	4.27	10,862	5,653	1,070
1946	13,594	87	10,416	3,441	10,624	4,261	287	3.49	10,141	5,269	956
1945	12,105	90	9,287	2,818	9,784	3,886	316	3.17	9,712	4,879	862
1944	11,576	90	8,597	2,708	9,045	3,814	320	2.85	9,482	4,335	873
1943	11,319	92	8,722	2,568	9,208	3,795	322	2.65	9,254	4,424	858
1942	11,245	92	8,525	2,479	9,002	3,760	317	2.60	9,250	4,286	930
1941	10,911	93	8,509	2,660	8,994	3,682	322	2.49	8,655	4,368	1,000
1940	10,459	92	8,232	2,641	8,578	3,590	326	2.22	8,850	4,462	1,039
1939	10,160	92	7,741	2,471	7,483	3,395	311	2.36	8,733	4,567	1,209
1938	8,825	91	7,253	2,301	7,567	2,868	361	—	7,696	3,631	—
1937	—	—	—	—	6,603	2,391	323	—	—	—	—

[1] Newfoundland included beginning in 1950 except for series B159 and B160 which begin in 1949. Northwest Territories included beginning in 1952. Yukon excluded throughout.
[2] Bed capacity available from 1954: 1954, 18,106; 1955, 18,105; 1956, 17,028; 1957, 16,634; 1958, 15,235.
[3] Average number of patients to beds set up at 31 December.
[4] Excludes newborn.
[5] Readmissions 'to continue treatment' excluded 1952 to 1958.
[6] Includes 'reviews out' 1938 to 1950.
[7] Excludes federal sanatoria.

Series B170–181. *Financial statistics of public health institutions, Canada, 1932 to 1960*

(all series except B170, B174 and B178 in thousands of dollars)

Year[1]	Public general and special hospitals				Public mental institutions				Public tuberculosis institutions			
	Number of beds (rated capacity) in hospitals reporting income and expenditure	Operating income		Total net expendi-tures	Number of beds (rated capacity) in hospitals reporting income and expenditure	Operating income		Operating expendi-tures	Number of beds set up as at 31 December in hospitals reporting income and expenditure	Operating income		Operating expendi-tures
		Total	Grants by govern-ments			Total	Grants by govern-ments			Total	Grants by govern-ments	
	170	171	172	173	174	175	176	177	178	179	180	181
1960	92,526	566,093	12,577	592,842	60,054	116,700	75,477	116,585	11,042	31,080	22,016	31,900
1959	91,083	490,862	10,579	509,846	41,071	90,645[2]	65,602[2]	89,923[2]	10,413	29,268	23,898	29,607
1958	89,203	418,506	26,894	444,161	59,904	96,449	87,097	96,327	11,658	30,446	23,882	30,410
1957	86,206	371,958	26,334	393,401	57,193	85,735	76,012	85,302	12,760	32,472	25,297	32,190
1956	83,694	329,390	21,644	347,356	58,014	77,845	67,187	76,942	13,524	32,191	25,315	32,003
1955	79,023	294,986	24,566	309,722	57,009	68,024	57,697	68,048	13,646	31,242	25,390	31,133
1954	73,374	261,622	24,347	273,004	54,346	62,984	52,035	64,087	13,949	31,174	26,533	31,180
1953[1]	65,475	225,590	22,609	235,512	51,328	57,703	46,868	57,229	15,220	30,883	25,602	32,439
1952[1]	—	198,537	18,545	204,041	48,893	59,983	50,858	59,925	14,365	28,586	24,878	29,184
1951	—	208,002	28,891	196,203	46,096	55,920	47,976	57,078	14,194	25,992	22,283	26,815
1950	—	175,982	23,360	162,714	45,081	48,124	41,254	48,453	14,377	22,293	19,807	22,893
1949	—	155,886	21,609	146,867	44,055	39,376	32,590	39,413	12,237	18,901	16,672	19,166
1948	—	130,109	22,274	125,005	45,682	35,059	28,766	34,879	10,964	16,918	14,738	17,043
1947	—	107,309	17,229	106,792	45,180	27,614	22,591	27,757	10,862	13,595	11,701	14,223
1946	—	85,602	14,735	84,503	45,443	26,978	22,203	27,316	10,141	11,302	9,234	11,573
1945	—	74,696	13,355	74,059	45,144	22,634	18,414	22,951	9,696	9,372	7,915	10,189
1944	—	68,264	12,230	68,940	42,500	21,864	17,469	21,878	9,471	8,605	7,356	8,935
1943	—	60,596	10,786	59,403	42,454	19,215	15,476	19,199	9,242	8,670	7,394	8,619
1942	—	53,386	11,557	53,381	41,762	18,537	15,070	18,465	9,234	8,146	6,879	8,115
1941	—	—	—	—	40,115	19,084	16,032	19,069	8,639	7,859	6,555	7,753
1940	—	—	—	—	39,441	19,546	14,039	19,543	8,834	7,028	6,419	6,965
1939	—	—	—	—	39,277	16,624	13,138	16,607	8,717	7,026	6,257	6,882
1938	—	—	—	—	38,671	15,787	12,672	16,054	—	—	—	—
1937	—	—	—	—	37,798	14,052	10,935	14,017	—	—	—	—
1936	—	—	—	—	37,379	14,301	10,064	14,222	—	—	—	—
1935	—	—	—	—	35,987	10,941	8,347	10,939	—	—	—	—
1934	—	—	—	—	34,918	13,721	10,081	13,691	—	—	—	—
1933	—	—	—	—	32,781	11,395	8,069	11,315	—	—	—	—
1932	—	—	—	—	32,951	12,131	9,121	12,041	—	—	—	—

[1] Excludes Newfoundland, 1932 to 1952, and Yukon and Northwest Territories throughout.
[2] Quebec data not available.

Series B182–194. *Public general hospitals:*[1] *number of hospitals and beds, beds per 1,000 population, patients treated, average days' stay per patient, operating costs and distribution of income, Ontario, quinquennial years, 1900 to 1935*

Year	Number of hospitals	Number of beds	Number of beds per 1,000 population	Patients treated Number	Patients treated Number per 1,000 population	Average days' stay per patient treated[2]	Operating costs Total (thousand dollars)	Operating costs Per patient-day (dollars)	Per cent distribution of income Patients	Per cent distribution of income Investments and property	Per cent distribution of income Donations and bequests	Per cent distribution of income Municipal grants	Per cent distribution of income Provincial grants
	182	183	184	185	186	187	188	189	190	191	192	193	194
1935	144	13,859	3.8	246,562	67	13.4	10,609	3.46	54.3	2.0	5.4	27.4	12.0
1930	139	12,886	3.8	218,753	65	13.7	10,937	3.94	67.0	2.1	7.1	15.6	8.2
1925	118	9,979	3.2	152,102	49	14.0	7,212	3.54	64.3	2.2	7.6	16.9	9.0
1920	90	8,149	2.8	130,382	46	14.9	5,849	3.16	64.8	2.1	9.5	17.6	6.1
1915	80	7,116	2.6	82,690	30	17.7	2,273	1.62	51.2	3.3	7.5	30.0	7.9
1910	70	5,523	2.2	52,321	21	19.2	1,265	1.30	51.7	4.2	13.4	20.1	10.6
1905	56	—	—	37,736	16	20.1	829	1.12	48.6	4.8	15.5	18.4	12.7
1900	51	—	—	29,572	14	24.5	549	0.77	35.3	3.6	26.4	16.4	18.3

[1] Excluding convalescent hospitals and homes for incurables.   [2] Based not on discharges but on total patients treated.

Series B195–215. *Miscellaneous statistics relating to hospitals in the Province of Quebec, quinquennial years, 1885 to 1930*

(series B200–203 and B210–215 in thousands of dollars)

Hospitals for insane

Year	Number of institutions	Staff	Patients admitted	Patients discharged[1]	Patients at 31 December	Revenue Total	Revenue Patients	Revenue Provincial government	Expenditures
	195	196	197	198	199	200	201	202	203
1930	7	1,552	2,243	1,743	8,438	2,563	355	1,428	2,565
1925	6	1,130	1,751	1,429	6,676	1,952	314	1,166	1,960
1920	6	963	1,290	1,290	5,443	1,416	285	974	1,468
1915	6	897	1,063	1,068	5,074	850	166	578	857
1910	—	—	1,030	848	4,114	—	—	449	—
1905	—	—	720	613	3,460	—	—	376	—
1900	—	—	618	580	3,025	—	—	322	—
1895	—	—	441	402	2,660	—	—	267	—
1890	—	—	713	663	2,327	—	—	249	—
1885	—	—	385	413	1,844	—	—	220	—

Maternity and foundling hospitals

Year	Number of institutions Hospitals	Number of institutions Maternity hospitals	Number of institutions Foundling hospitals	Number of nurses	Patients admitted	Patients at 31 December	Revenue Total	Revenue Patients	Revenue Provincial government	Revenue Municipalities	Revenue Private donations	Expenditures
	204	205	206	207	208	209	210	211	212	213	214	215
1930	58	4	5	3,474	97,905	7,207	8,071	3,458	1,594	524	752	8,071
1925	54	4	3	2,605	65,226	4,331	4,677	1,557	988	260	458	4,677
1920	50	4	2	1,819	51,389	4,159	3,529	1,620	42	194	517	3,561

[1] Including deceased.

Series B 216–219. *Number of institutions and of inmates in lunatic asylums and hospitals,*
Canada, 1871, 1881, 1891 and 1901

Year	Lunatic asylums		Hospitals	
	Number of hospitals	Number of inmates	Number of hospitals	Number of inmates
	216	**217**	**218**	**219**
1901	39[1]	11,679[1]	152[2]	7,007[2]
1891	17	7,029	124	4,781
1881	13	4,655	83	5,118
1871[3]	7	2,823	38	1,816

[1] Figures corresponding to what is called 'asylums' in the census.
[2] Includes isolation, maternity and not specified hospitals; excludes sanitariums and homes for convalescents and incurables.
[3] Nova Scotia, New Brunswick, Quebec and Ontario.

Series B 220–224. *Government expenditures on health, Canada, 1933 to 1960*

(series B 220–223 in millions of dollars, series B 224 in dollars)

Year[1,]	Federal	Provincial	Municipal	All governments	All government expenditures per capita	Year	Federal	Provincial	Municipal	All governments	All government expenditures per capita
	220	**221**	**222**	**223**	**224**		**220**	**221**	**222**	**223**	**224**
1960	323.7	553.8[5]	52.4[4]	929.9	52.04	1950	72.2	171.8	30.5	274.5	20.05
1959	279.5	470.9	68.4	818.8	46.83	1949	69.3	156.0	27.6	252.9	18.84
1958	185.8	362.7	75.0	623.5	36.50	1948[2]	59.9	114.2	25.2[3]	199.3	15.57
1957	118.3	331.6	81.0	530.9	31.96	1947	56.8	87.4	23.0[3]	167.2	13.35
1956	112.0	287.7	70.2	469.9	29.22	1943	1.7	34.7	15.4	51.9	—
1955	103.3	270.6	64.7	438.6	27.94	1941	1.3	30.2	15.5	47.0	—
1954	100.5	256.7	64.7	421.8	27.59	1939	1.2	30.4	15.6	47.1	—
1953	94.0	228.7	51.3	374.0	25.19	1937	1.0	26.3	15.4	42.7	—
1952	87.6	210.4	38.8	336.8	23.38	1933	0.7	18.6	15.2	34.5	—
1951	81.7	189.5	35.0	306.1	21.89						

[1] For 1947 to 1958, federal expenditures are for fiscal year ending 31 March of following year, provincial expenditures are for fiscal year ending in the following year, municipal expenditures are for the calendar year. For all years before 1947 data are for the fiscal year ending closest to 31 December of year given for the relevant government.

[2] Excluding Newfoundland for 1948 and before.
[3] Gross expenditures (see source, p. 36).
[4] Estimates.
[5] Preliminary.

Series B 225–227. *Estimated enrolment in nonprofit medical insurance plans, Canada, at 31 December,*
1937 to 1960

Year[1]	Total	Comprehensive plans	Limited plans	Year[1]	Total	Comprehensive plans	Limited plans
	225	**226**	**227**		**225**	**226**	**227**
1960[2]	5,129,636	3,371,124	1,758,512	1948	631,935	331,737	300,198
1959	4,861,079	3,146,019	1,715,060	1947	417,328	237,284	180,044
1958	4,446,331	2,729,580	1,716,751	1946	166,763	153,723	13,040
1957	4,153,933	2,353,387	1,800,546	1945	112,000	—	—
1956	3,600,752	2,005,549	1,595,203	1944	75,000	—	—
1955[1]	3,143,024	1,694,563	1,448,461	1943	50,000	—	—
1954	2,688,120	—	—	1942	41,000	—	—
1953	2,353,459	1,104,895	1,248,564	1941	35,000	—	—
1952	1,948,406	929,776	1,018,630	1940	25,000	—	—
1951	1,569,215	734,887	834,328	1939	13,100	—	—
1950	1,240,226	561,887	678,339	1938	4,020	—	—
1949	888,210	410,582	477,628	1937	733	—	—

[1] Includes Newfoundland beginning in 1955. Yukon and Northwest Territories excluded throughout.

[2] Data for 1960 are preliminary.

Series B228–242. *Family allowances, old age security and old age assistance, Canada, 1945 to 1960*

| | Family allowances | | | | | Old age security | | | | | | Old age assistance | | | |
| | | | Average monthly allowance in March | | Net total annual amount paid[2] (thousand dollars) | | Net total annual amount paid[2] (thousand dollars) | Revenue[3] (thousand dollars) | | | | | | Per cent of recipients to population aged 65–69 | Federal contribution[2] (thousand dollars) |
Year[1]	Number of families receiving allowance in March	Number of children for whom allowance was paid in March	Per family (dollars)	Per child (dollars)		Number of pensioners in March		Personal income tax	Corporation income tax	Sales tax	Grant or loan from federal government	Number of recipients in March	Average monthly amount of assistance (dollars)		
	228	**229**	**230**	**231**	**232**	**233**	**234**	**235**	**236**	**237**	**238**	**239**	**240**	**241**	**242**
1960	2,551,264	6,219,989	16.27	6.67	491,214	876,410	574,887	185,550	91,336	270,000	28,001	98,773	50.74	21.11	30,349
1959	2,492,581	6,035,256	16.15	6.67	474,787	854,284	559,280	146,350	55,328	173,623	183,979	97,836	50.97	20.91	30,207
1958	2,406,734	5,796,380	16.08	6.68	437,887	827,560	473,859	135,001	60,664	175,792	102,402	92,484	52.19	19.94	24,961
1957	2,326,891	5,571,436	14.49	6.05	397,518	797,486	379,111	124,999	67,336	179,270	7,506	89,907	37.03	19.81	20,291
1956	2,263,618	5,377,436	14.35	6.04	382,535	771,753	366,218	102,500	53,328	160,378	50,013	93,023	36.56	20.49	20,918
1955	2,195,027	5,169,042	14.20	6.03	366,466	745,620	353,205	100,900	46,000	143,054	63,252	94,625	36.56	21.01	20,869
1954	2,116,709	4,942,044	14.08	6.03	350,114	716,399	338,971	90,700	55,600	146,833	45,838	93,273	36.50	20.80	20,288
1953	2,041,341	4,729,172	13.94	6.02	334,198	686,127	323,142	45,250	36,850	141,558	99,483	87,675	36.57	19.74	19,129
1952	1,966,721	4,530,186	13.82	6.00	320,458	643,013	76,067[4]	100	2,000	24,298	49,669	41,601[5]	37.47[5]	9.45[5]	2,277[4]
1951	1,910,192	4,367,391	13.72	6.00	309,465	—	—	—	—	—	—	—	—	—	—
1950	1,852,269	4,202,263	13.64	6.01	297,514	—	—	—	—	—	—	—	—	—	—
1949[1]	1,729,150	3,888,653	13.25	5.89	270,910	—	—	—	—	—	—	—	—	—	—
1948	1,669,944	3,755,572	13.31	5.92	263,165	—	—	—	—	—	—	—	—	—	—
1947	1,588,456	3,633,062	13.62	5.95	245,141	—	—	—	—	—	—	—	—	—	—
1946	1,406,151	3,299,100	14.05	5.99	172,632	—	—	—	—	—	—	—	—	—	—
1945[6]	1,237,754	2,956,844	14.18	5.94	—	—	—	—	—	—	—	—	—	—	—

[1] Excluding Newfoundland for 1949 and before.
[2] During fiscal year ending 31 March.
[3] Total revenue is equal to total amount paid.
[4] Programme in effect for last three months only of the fiscal year.
[5] Excluding Newfoundland, Yukon and Northwest Territories.
[6] In July.

Series B243–250. *Old age pensions and pensions for the blind: average monthly pension, number of pensioners, per cent of pensioners to population and federal contribution, Canada, 1928 to 1960*

| | Old age pensions | | | | Pensions for the blind | | | |
Year[1]	Average monthly pension[2] in March (dollars)	Number of pensioners[3]	Per cent of pensioners to population aged 70 and over	Federal contribution[4] (thousand dollars)	Average pension[2] in March (dollars)	Number of pensioners[3]	Per cent of pensioners to population[5]	Federal contribution[4] (thousand dollars)
	243	**244**	**245**	**246**	**247**	**248**	**249**	**250**
1960	—	—	—	—	53.05	8,671	.092	4,917
1959	—	—	—	—	53.15	8,747	.094	4,235
1958	—	—	—	—	54.02	8,400	.092	3,576
1957	—	—	—	—	39.24	8,256	.094	2,959
1956	—	—	—	—	39.36	8,230	.093	2,918
1955	—	—	—	—	38.99	8,122	.094	2,886
1954	—	—	—	—	38.88	8,214	.096	2,914
1953	—	—	—	—	39.17	8,332	.099	2,985
1952	—	—	—	—	39.26	8,079	.098	721[6]
1951[7]	39.39	308,825	47.16	77,340	38.83	11,335	.081	2,996
1951	37.44	302,173	46.14	99,268	38.84	11,198	.086	3,901
1950	35.25	282,584	45.16	89,652	38.73	10,517	.078	3,537
1949[1]	29.22	251,865	43.27	64,232	29.59	9,567	.074	2,532
1948	29.41	229,158	41.27	56,978	29.73	8,476	.067	2,108
1947	24.03	209,029	39.39	43,830	24.63	7,311	.059	1,615
1946	23.98	196,941	38.58	41,291	24.62[8]	6,945[8]	.057[8]	1,527[8]
1945	23.86	187,512	37.54	39,503	24.63	6,663	.056	1,472
1944	22.20	181,384	37.44	32,196	23.84	6,374	.054	1,244
1943	17.82	183,601	39.11	28,861	19.55	6,374	.055	1,115
1942	—	—	—	28,770	—	6,374	—	1,108
1941	—	186,834	—	28,472	—	6,208	—	1,067
1940	—	188,099	—	29,142	—	5,828	—	984
1939	—	186,154	—	28,886	—	5,265	—	860
1938	—	181,512	—	28,082	—	4,290	—	673
1937	—	174,889	—	28,727	—	567[9]	—	16[9]
1936[10]	—	123,441	—	17,967	—	—	—	—
1935[11]	—	107,279	—	16,140	—	—	—	—
1934[11]	—	98,111	—	—	—	—	—	—
1933	—	—	—	—	—	—	—	—
1932[12]	—	70,516	—	12,039	—	—	—	—
1931[12]	—	65,951	—	7,051	—	—	—	—
1930[12]	—	55,416	—	5,658	—	—	—	—
1929[13]	—	13,294	—	—	—	—	—	—
1928[14]	—	9,002	—	—	—	—	—	—

[1] Excluding Newfoundland and Yukon in 1949 and before.
[2] This amount does not include supplements paid by some provinces since 1942.
[3] In March for 1943 to 1960; in December for 1928 to 1942.
[4] For fiscal year ending 31 March for 1943 to 1960; calendar years for 1930 to 1942.
[5] To population aged 20–69 years for 1952 to 1960; to total population for other years.
[6] Programme for the last three months only of the fiscal year, i.e. for January, February, March 1952.
[7] The figures for 1951 relate to the number of pensioners and the average pension in December, and the amount paid during the last nine months of 1951.
[8] Excluding Northwest Territories this year and before.
[9] Nova Scotia, New Brunswick, Quebec, Ontario and Manitoba only.
[10] Excluding Quebec.
[11] Excluding Quebec and New Brunswick.
[12] Excluding Quebec, New Brunswick, Nova Scotia and Prince Edward Island.
[13] At 30 September; Manitoba, Saskatchewan, Alberta, British Columbia and Northwest Territories only.
[14] Manitoba, Saskatchewan and British Columbia only.

Series B251–255. *Federal government annuities: contracts issued, money received and paid and number and value of contracts in force, Canada, 1909 to 1960*

Year[1]	Number of contracts issued	Purchase money received	Payments under vested annuity contracts	Value of contracts at 31 March (million dollars)	Number of contracts in force at 31 March	Year[1]	Number of contracts issued	Purchase money received	Payments under vested annuity contracts	Value of contracts at 31 March (million dollars)	Number of contracts in force at 31 March
		(thousand dollars)						(thousand dollars)			
	251	252	253	254	255		251	252	253	254	255
1960	15,942	56,041	43,286	1,156.9	428,709	1935	3,930	13,376	3,115	47.2	20,226
1959	23,349	63,017	41,177	1,105.8	422,943	1934	2,412	7,071	2,598	35.2	16,565
1958	17,937	62,149	39,056	1,047.6	403,857	1933	1,375	3,547	2,301	29.3	14,400
1957	18,413	64,421	36,964	989.3	380,335	1932	1,726	4,194	2,122	26.9	13,273
1956	22,471	69,945	34,498	930.2	372,520	1931	1,772	3,612	1,849	23.6	11,781
1955	24,542	68,594	31,943	864.5	349,661	1930	1,257	3,156	1,647	20.7	10,183
1954	18,466	64,380	29,749	798.5	325,682	1929	1,328	4,272	1,369	18.3	9,095
1953	18,433	62,787	27,694	736.5	307,962	1928	1,223	3,843	1,044	14.9	7,913
1952	17,038	57,549	25,820	675.9	289,693	1927	503	1,895	865	11.4	6,829
1951	21,775	59,648	23,965	620.4	275,813	1926	668	1,939	730	10.0	6,426
1950	21,078	63,133	22,032	563.2	258,679	1925	486	1,607	592	8.4	5,862
1949	36,332	64,311	20,120	501.7	242,292	1924	409	1,459	476	7.2	5,405
1948	40,945	75,068	17,588	429.5	210,935	1923	339	1,028	387	5.9	5,137
1947	43,585	72,010	14,952	357.2	173,254	1922	277	748	319	5.0	4,860
1946	25,538	46,955	12,938	287.5	133,387	1921	195	532	279	4.4	4,673
1945	15,796	33,076	11,725	243.5	112,184	1920	204	409	249	3.9	4,535
1944	19,354	26,600	10,850	213.6	99,430	1919	147	322	—	3.6	4,396
1943	9,608	20,415	10,148	190.3	81,627	1918	187	333	—	3.3	4,306
1942	8,593	19,631	9,445	172.9	73,347	1917	285	432	—	3.1	4,160
1941	11,994	18,804	8,708	156.1	65,780	1916	325	442	—	2.7	3,920
1940	9,014	20,002	7,929	140.4	55,300	1915	264	315	—	2.3	3,625
1939	8,518	18,189	7,057	122.8	46,970	1914	318	391	—	2.0	3,381
1938	5,724	13,550	6,369	107.6	39,015	1913	373	417	—	—	—
1937	7,806	23,615	5,556	88.2	33,685	1912	1,032	442	—	—	—
1936	6,357	21,282	4,097	67.0	26,249	1911	1,069	393	—	—	—
						1910	566	434	—	—	—
						1909[2]	66	50	—	—	—

[1] Fiscal year ending 31 March of year given. [2] Seven months.

Series B256–259. *Veterans expenditure: total expenditures, pensions, war allowances, hospital and medical services, Canada, 1934 to 1961*

(thousand dollars)

Year[1,2]	Total expenditures[3]	Pensions[4]	War allowances[4]	Hospital and medical services	Year[1,2]	Total expenditures[3]	Pensions[4]	War allowances[4]	Hospital and medical services
	256	257	258	259		256	257	258	259
1961	280,839	150,695	58,428	49,754	1948	158,908	77,093	12,438	48,031[6]
1960	276,189	149,656	57,338	48,581	1947	175,659	70,748	—	—
1959	276,626	150,726	54,871	50,882	1946	122,346	59,453	—	—
1958	264,200	145,583	47,990	51,230	1945	85,971	49,070	—	—
1957	236,620	130,308	41,259	47,340	1944	64,882	42,774	—	—
1956	230,164	130,662	39,074	43,403	1943	58,480	40,737	—	—
1955	217,902	128,773	28,246	43,880	1942	55,295	39,790	—	—
1954	213,843	127,579	26,846	42,828	1941	55,969	40,106	—	—
1953	212,260	127,027	27,160	41,313	1940	55,664	40,620	—	—
1952	185,896	103,677	25,752[5]	39,425[6]	1939	52,683	40,613	—	—
1951	173,693	95,550	22,923	37,903[6]	1938	52,902	—	—	—
1950	173,222	96,049	20,018	38,704[6]	1934	51,250	—	—	—
1949[2]	181,621	102,951	19,741	40,014[6]					

[1] Fiscal year ending 31 March of the year given.
[2] Excludes Newfoundland for 1949 and before.
[3] Excludes costs of administration for certain items.
[4] Excludes costs of administration.
[5] Includes $2,206,812 for assistance to unemployable veterans.
[6] Excludes amounts spent for funerals.

Series B260–265. *Provincial and municipal transfer payments for selected social welfare programmes, Canada, 1926 to 1960*
(millions of dollars)

Year[1]	Provincial				Municipal		Year[1]	Provincial				Municipal	
	Direct relief	Aid to aged persons[2]	Mothers' and dependents' allowances	Grants to private noncommercial institutions	Direct relief	Grants to private noncommercial institutions		Direct relief	Aid to aged persons[2]	Mothers' and dependents' allowances	Grants to private noncommercial institutions	Direct relief	Grants to private noncommercial institutions
	260	261	262	263	264	265		260	261	262	263	264	265
1960	25	67[3]	72	703	53	20	1942	7	—	9	27	1	10
1959	17	60	73	567	44	19	1941	15	10	9	27	3	9
1958	14	52	68	365	33	18							
1957	18	54	48	290	23	20	1940	30	—	10	26	6	9
1956	20	47	37	264	19	16	1939	57	10	10	25	10	9
							1938	58	—	9	24	14	8
1955	17	43	33	248	18	17	1937	70	10	8	22	13	8
1954	14	40	27	228	16	23	1936	71	—	7	20	20	8
1953	11	35	24	191	14	19							
1952	11	33	23	171	14	18	1935	79	—	6	19	21	8
1951	17	40	20	158	11	15	1934	82	—	5	20	22	8
							1933	57	3	5	17	17	8
1950	22	43	19	137	7	13	1932	38	—	5	18	12	8
1949	12	40	16	120	5	14	1931	21	—	5	18	5	8
1948[1]	11	31	14	92	4	13							
1947	6	24	12	59	4	12	1930	3	—	5	17	1	8
1946	5	—	12	39	2	11	1929	1	—	5	16	—	8
							1928	—	—	4	15	—	8
1945	4	—	11	30	1	11	1927	—	—	4	12	—	7
1944	6	—	10	31	1	10	1926	—	—	4	12	—	8
1943	6	15	10	30	1	10							

[1] Excluding Newfoundland, 1926 to 1948.
[2] For fiscal year ending nearest to 31 December of the year given. Includes only old age pensions for 1933 to 1943; includes net ordinary and capital expenditures, 1947 to 1960.
[3] Preliminary. Includes aid to blind persons.

Series B266–270. *Government expenditures on social welfare, by level of government and per capita, Canada, 1913 to 1960*
(series B266–269 in millions of dollars; series B270 in dollars)

Year[1,2]	Federal	Provincial	Municipal	All governments	All government expenditures per capita	Year[1,2]	Federal	Provincial	Municipal	All governments	All government expenditures per capita
	266	267	268	269	270		266	267	268	269	270
1960	2,036.2	335.0[4]	46.2[5]	2,417.4	135.28	1948[2]	584.4	104.1	24.8[3]	713.3	55.73
1959	1,882.7	291.2	38.0	2,211.9	126.52	1947	512.6	91.9	21.7[3]	626.3	50.00
1958	1,898.8	264.7	35.0	2,198.6	128.72						
1957	1,636.8	240.4	31.6	1,908.9	114.92	1943	132.4	65.7	25.0	223.1	18.94
1956	1,290.5	209.2	33.9	1,533.6	95.36	1941	103.1	59.4	24.0	186.5	16.23
						1939	113.7	86.2	35.2	235.2	20.91
1955	1,243.5	192.7	32.4	1,468.6	93.55	1937	126.4	101.5	39.0	266.9	24.20
1954	1,240.8	178.7	29.9	1,449.5	94.82	1933	96.7	57.4	41.9	196.0	18.46
1953	1,114.9	157.7	27.1	1,299.7	87.55						
1952	1,030.4	147.9	26.1	1,204.3	83.60	1930	73.0	52.2	31.5	156.8	15.38
1951	761.3	138.1	24.6	924.1	66.08	1926	49.7	28.6	20.7	99.0	10.49
						1921	58.6	22.8	18.8	100.2	11.42
1950	685.9	128.4	21.7	836.0	61.08	1913	2.7	4.3	8.2	15.2	—
1949	669.5	118.9	19.8	808.2	60.21						

[1] For 1947 to 1960, federal expenditures are for fiscal year ending 31 March of following year, provincial expenditures are for fiscal year ending in the following year, municipal expenditures are for the calendar year. For all years before 1947 data are for the fiscal year ending closest to 31 December of year given for the relevant government.
[2] Excluding Newfoundland, for 1949 and before.
[3] Gross expenditures (see source, p. 36).
[4] Preliminary.
[5] Estimate.

APPENDIX. EARLY VITAL STATISTICS FOR THE PROVINCE OF QUEBEC

Series B271–277. *Births, marriages and deaths for the Roman Catholic population of the Province of Quebec: numbers and average annual rates, by decades, 1608 to 1890*

Period	Population at the middle of the period	Numbers			Rates per 1,000 population		
		Births	Marriages	Deaths	Births	Marriages	Deaths
	271	272	273	274	275	276	277
1881–90	1,220,000	519,850	—	—	42.6	—	—
1871–80	1,070,000	502,684	83,789	266,061	47.0	7.8	24.8
1861–70	980,000	440,559	71,885	205,950	45.0	7.3	21.0
1851–60	840,000	379,744	61,352	163,068	45.2	7.3	19.4
1841–50	610,000	317,920	52,819	142,573	52.1	8.7	23.4
1831–40	450,000	248,182	40,872	125,490	55.1	9.1	27.9
1821–30	345,000	196,175	32,444	94,939	56.9	9.4	27.5
1811–20	265,000	146,106	25,230	71,796	55.1	9.5	27.1
1801–10	203,000	115,073	19,091	59,142	56.7	9.4	29.1
1791–1800	156,000	89,754	15,012	43,385	57.5	9.6	27.8
1781–90	119,000	68,321	10,930	35,617	57.4	9.2	29.9
1771–80	91,500	56,456	8,990	30,162	61.7	9.8	33.0
1761–70	70,700	45,606	7,916	23,663	64.5	11.2	33.5
1751–60	57,000	33,974	6,433	21,765	59.6	11.3	38.2
1741–50	47,500	26,554	4,957	15,284	55.9	10.4	28.7
1731–40	38,800	22,079	3,669	10,004	56.9	9.5	25.8
1721–30	28,300	15,721	2,899	6,907	55.5	10.2	24.4
1711–20	21,000	11,954	2,131	5,215	56.9	10.1	22.1
1701–10	16,300	9,306	1,462	3,901	57.1	9.0	23.9
1691–1700	13,800	6,890	1,352	2,212	49.9	9.8	16.0
1681–90	10,800	4,632	979	1,963	42.9	8.1	16.2
1671–80	7,400	4,093	558	700	55.3	7.5	9.4
1661–70	3,400	2,026	690	475	59.6	20.3	14.0
1651–60	—	737	243	230	—	—	—
1641–50	—	212	65	110	—	—	—
1631–40	—	66	23	52	—	—	—
1621–30	—	6	2	11	—	—	—
1611–20	—	1	1	10	—	—	—
1608–10	—	—	—	19	—	—	—

SECTION C: THE LABOUR FORCE

KENNETH BUCKLEY, *University of Saskatchewan*

This section presents the official statistics of the gainfully occupied and of the labour force from 1881 to 1960. In addition, private estimates of labour force participation are presented.

The published sources of the data are publications of the Dominion Bureau of Statistics or, in the case of the Census before 1921, the Census Office of the Department of Agriculture. Consequently, the following list of published sources, with the one exception noted, are all D.B.S. publications:

Census of Canada, decennial census, 1911 to 1951 (Ottawa, Queen's Printer) prepared by the Dominion Bureau of Statistics, 1921 to 1951, and by the Census Office, Department of Agriculture, 1911; *Children in Gainful Occupations* (Ottawa, King's Printer, 1929); *Canadian Labour Force Estimates, 1931–1945*, Reference Paper No. 23 (Revised) (Ottawa, Queen's Printer, 1957); *The Labour Force, November, 1945–January, 1955*, Reference Paper No. 58 (Ottawa, Queen's Printer, 1955); *The Labour Force, November, 1945–July, 1958*, Reference Paper No. 58 (1958 Revision) (Ottawa, Queen's Printer, 1958); *The Labour Force, September, 1960* (*Supplement*) (Ottawa, Queen's Printer, 1960). In addition unpublished data were obtained, firstly, from the files of two divisions of the Dominion Bureau of Statistics, the Census Division and the Special Surveys Division, and, secondly, from a private source.

General note

The primary data on which the statistics of this section are based were obtained in the decennial censuses, in which case they apply to census dates or years, and by the Labour Force Survey described more fully below, which was taken quarterly from November 1945 to November 1952 and monthly thereafter. The decennial censuses were based on complete coverage of the population of working ages, in so far as that was possible; the Labour Force Survey is a sample survey from which estimates for the whole of the population of working ages are made. Annual data before 1946, aside from the census benchmark years, are, in the main, estimated by interpolation. Other data on the unemployed, the material from the Unemployment Insurance Commission Offices, established in 1941, and from the Employment Offices, both of which are in the federal Department of Labour, have not been used, since their degree of representativeness of the whole population is not clear.

The first three tables of this section are from the Census of Canada. The census used the 'gainfully occupied' concept until 1951 when it was replaced by the 'labour force' concept. The latter concept has been used in labour force sample surveys by the Dominion Bureau of Statistics since November 1945. More recently the gainfully occupied reported in the censuses of 1921, 1931 and 1941 have been adjusted to the labour force concept so that annual interpolations of Canada's labour force and some of its major components could be extended from 1 June 1946 back to 1 June 1921.

A gainful occupation is defined as

...one by which the person who pursues it earns money or in which he assists in the production of marketable goods.... Older persons who because of physical disability or other reasons had given up their former occupations were enumerated as 'Retired', while only those young persons not attending school and regularly employed in some gainful occupation were included among the gainfully occupied. Children, 14 years and over, assisting parents in the work of the farm or in some family business in a 'No Pay' capacity were considered as gainfully occupied, but daughters assisting with household duties in their own homes without wages were not included....

Housewives and students were excluded by this definition. And under the definition young people who had never held a job were not included among the 'gainfully occupied' even if they were seeking work; unemployed persons who had held a job were included.

In 1941 all persons 14 years and over, and in earlier censuses those 10 years and over, were classified as 'gainfully occupied' or 'not gainfully occupied'. The former were further classified as employer, own-account, wage earner or unpaid family worker; the latter as homemaker, student, retired or other. The question was designed to establish the customary activity of the respondent, even if the respondent was not holding a job or seeking work at the actual date of the census. For a full discussion of the concept of gainfully occupied, see *Census, 1941*, vol. VII, pp. xii–xvii.

In addition, wage earners were asked in 1931 and 1941 whether they were employed or unemployed on the census date. If not employed, the reason was classified as no job, lay-off, holiday, illness, accident, strike or lockout, or other cause. (D.B.S., *Canadian Labour Force Estimates, 1945*, Reference Paper No. 23 (Revised), p. 8.) A question on unemployment was also asked in the 1891 census (see *Census, 1901*, vol. I, p. vii), but whatever material was obtained was not published and is not now available in any form.

By the labour force concept, the noninstitutional population 14 years and over is classified as 'in the labour force' or 'not in the labour force' during the survey week. The coverage of those in the labour force is defined by the statement that

...those who were at work during any part of the week, or had jobs from which they were temporarily absent, or were looking for work are included in the labour force (as either employers, own-accounts, paid workers, or unpaid family workers). Those who did not work for pay or profit during the survey week and had no job and were not looking for work, are classed as not in the labour force (as either permanently unable or too old to work, keeping house, going to school, retired or voluntarily idle, or other). (See Reference Paper No. 23 (Revised), p. 8.)

The figures of the labour force presented in section C exclude inmates of institutions, Indians living on reservations, residents of the Yukon and Northwest Territories and members of the military services (armed forces). The gainfully occupied excludes the first and third categories. The treatment of Indians varied from census to census and this is noted in footnotes to series C1 to series C46.

The labour force includes some classes not included in the gainfully occupied: persons such as pensioners, students, housewives who are not usually gainfully occupied but who worked during the survey week are included; young persons out of school seeking work for the first time are also included in the labour force although they are not and have not been gainfully occupied. Another class, the voluntarily idle in the survey week, is excluded from the labour force although some of them would be classed as gainfully occupied on the basis of their activity in the previous year. These differences in concept do not greatly affect the two totals of the working population apart from the difference in coverage of part-time workers and of those seeking work for the first time. (For a more detailed discussion, see *Census, 1951*, vol. X, pp. 245–6.) This explains why, in recent censuses, the historical tables may be entitled 'Labour Force' although the totals are of the gainfully occupied in 1941 and in all earlier census years (see, for example, *Census, 1951*, vol. IV, table I).

It should also be remarked that the 1951 census of the labour force was enumerated by the census field staff and its results, which appear in the first three tables of this section, do not agree precisely with the results for June 1951 obtained by the staff of the Labour Force Survey. For an analysis of differences in responses to these two types of enumeration, see the chapter 'Comparative Checks', *Census, 1951*, vol. XI, pp. 79–93. See, also, the general note on population statistics in section A.

The Labour Force Survey reaches about 35,000 households chosen by area sampling methods across the country. The survey was first made in November 1946 and continued on a quarterly basis until November 1952. Since that time the survey has been undertaken each month. The major results are published in a monthly bulletin of D.B.S. entitled *The Labour Force* (catalogue no. 71–001). Other data secured by the surveys but not published are listed in the bulletins and may be secured on request.

The major classifications of the labour force estimates presented in this volume were taken from the surveys nearest 1 June in each year (the second quarter survey from 1946 to 1952, the May survey since 1953) to maintain consistency with the projections of the labour force estimates from 1946 to 1921 and with census data. In addition to the major sources cited in the notes below, the user of labour force estimates should also consult *The Labour Force, September, 1960* (*Supplement*) which contains a convenient historical series of the labour force and its major components at each survey date from November 1945 to September 1960 in a revised form introduced in *The Labour Force* of the same date. In that issue some changes in terms and in concepts were introduced. The terms 'employed' and 'unemployed' replaced respectively the terms 'persons with jobs' and 'persons without jobs and seeking work'. Persons 'employed' in the new classification are equivalent to 'persons with jobs' minus 'persons not at work because of temporary layoff up to 30 days' in the old classification. The numbers in the last-named group are added to 'persons without jobs and seeking work' to yield the estimate of the 'unemployed'. The relevant estimates of 'persons not at work because of temporary layoff up to 30 days' required to adjust the labour force series to an 'employed' and 'unemployed' basis from 1946 to 1960 are given in the note to series C47–55. Current issues of *The Labour Force* publish the annual averages of the estimates of the labour force and its major components from 1946 to the year last ended. The bulletins also contain helpful commentaries upon changes in the current labour force statistics.

C1–7. Population and gainfully occupied 14 years of age and over, in nonagricultural and agricultural pursuits, census years, 1881 to 1941, and for the labour force in 1951

SOURCE: for series C1 and C3, 1911 to 1951, and series C2, 1901 to 1951, *Census, 1951*, vol. IV, table I; for series C1 and C3, 1881 to 1911, and series C2, 1881 to 1891, *Census, 1921*, vol. IV, table III,

p. xiii; for series C5, 1901 to 1941, *Census, 1951*, vol. IV, table II; for series C5 in 1951, *ibid.*, table IV; for series C5, 1881 to 1891, *Census, 1921*, vol. IV, table VI.

Total persons gainfully occupied in agricultural pursuits in 1881 and 1891 appear in the source cited in an occupational table based upon the classifications of 1881. However, since the figures for later years agree with figures for the same years appearing in the 1951 census, the series C5 is a consistent one. Series C4, persons in nonagricultural pursuits, was obtained by subtracting series C5 from series C2.

In this table, persons seeking work for the first time have been excluded from the labour force in 1951. They are excluded from the gainfully occupied by definition (see the general note to this section). As a result, series C2 in 1951 does not agree with series C36 in 1951, which includes 8,970 males and 4,502 females seeking work for the first time.

Figures for Newfoundland, included in 1951, are as follows: all occupations, 106,540, of whom 3,682 were in agricultural pursuits.

The absolute decline of persons in agricultural pursuits from 1891 to 1901 for Canada as a whole was the result of a decline in the numbers of unpaid family workers enumerated rather than in operators and wage earners. The differences in the changes which occurred in the three main components in this and in other decades from 1891 to 1951 are illustrated in George V. Haythorne, *Labour in Canadian Agriculture* (Cambridge, Harvard University Press, 1960), chart 6, p. 27.

See the general note for definitions of the gainfully occupied and of the labour force.

C8–35. Gainfully occupied 14 years of age and over, by occupations and by sex, census years, 1891 to 1941, and for the labour force in 1951

SOURCE: for 1891, *Census, 1931*, vol. VII, table 65; for 1901 to 1951, *Census, 1951*, vol. X, table 62.

In an occupational classification persons are assigned to the occupation in which they are working or usually work regardless of the industry in which they pursue the occupation.

Totals of all occupations are not shown in this table. In all years except 1891 and 1951, they add to the same totals shown in series C2. There is a discrepancy in 1951 because series C2 includes Newfoundland while series C8–35 do not. The relevant figures for Newfoundland in 1951 are 89,460 males and 17,080 females or a total provincial labour force of 106,540. Neither table includes persons seeking their first jobs in 1951. They therefore differ from series C36 in 1951, which does (see note to series C1–7).

The classifications in series C8–35 add to a total in 1891 which is 9,239 higher than series C2 in 1891. The difference of 9,239 is listed in the 1891 census as 'members of religious orders' in so-called 'non-productive pursuits'. They were also excluded from the gainfully occupied in the 1921 census table which was the source of the figure for 1891 in series C2.

An earlier series of the gainfully occupied by occupations from 1881 to 1921 based upon the classifications of 1881 may be found in *Census, 1921*, vol. IV, table VI, p. xv. A similar distribution, but without a sex breakdown, was also used in 1871. However, the source emphasizes (*Census, 1921*, vol. IV, p. xv) that the classification of occupation has changed materially from census to census. However, following the census of 1931, the occupational classifications from 1891 to 1921 were adjusted to conform with the classification of 1931. Later, the 1941 and 1951 classifications were rearranged on the basis of the 1931 classification, although some adjustment of the 1931 allocations was necessary. The principal changes in the 1931 classification were to move accountants from 'Professional' to 'Clerical' and to transfer female labourers, packers and wrappers, previously classified under 'Labourers' and 'Transportation', to 'Manufacturing and trade'. (See notes to source table in the 1951 census volume cited above.)

Figures for 1951 were enumerated on the 'labour force' concept. However, a check on 'usual occupation' versus 'occupation at census date' supports the conclusion that this change in concept does not appreciably affect the comparability of the statistics of occupations (see *Census, 1951*, vol. X, p. 245). For other notes on the occupational classification, see *Census, 1941*, vol. I, p. 328 and vol. VII, pp. xii–xvii.

It should be remarked that the occupational table, 1901 to 1951, in vol. IV of the 1951 census was corrected after publication. The revised version appears in the source (vol. X) cited above.

See the note to series C1–7 with respect to the absolute decline in the gainfully occupied in agriculture from 1891 to 1901.

See the general note for definitions of the gainfully occupied and of the labour force.

C36–46. Gainfully occupied, by age and sex, census years, 1911 to 1941, and for the labour force in 1951

SOURCE: *Census, 1911*, vol. VI, table IV; *Census, 1921*, vol. IV, table 4; D.B.S., *Children in Gainful Occupations*, for series C36 in 1921; *Census, 1931*, vol. VII, table 40; *Census, 1941*, vol. VII, table 3; *Census, 1951*, vol. IV, table 3.

The totals agree with those shown in series C2 with the exception of 1951 (see footnote 2, series C36–46). The distribution by age and sex in 1951 of persons seeking work for the first time, who are included in this table but not in series C1–7 and series C8–35, may be found in *Census, 1951*, vol. IV, table 3. The table differs from series C8–35 in one other respect in 1951; it includes Newfoundland and series C8–35 does not.

See the general note for definitions of the gainfully occupied and of the labour force.

C47–55. The labour force and its main components, the noninstitutional population, the armed services, the civilian noninstitutional population, 14 years of age and over, 1921 to 1960

SOURCE: for 1921 to 1930, D.B.S., Reference Paper No. 23 (Revised), appendix; for 1931 to 1945, *ibid.*, table 1; for series C49–51 and C54 and C55 from 1946 to 1958, D.B.S., Reference Paper No. 58 (1958 Revision), table 1; for series C52 and C53, *ibid.*, table 6; for series C48 from 1946 to 1960, correspondence with the Department of National Defence; for series C47–55 in 1959 and 1960, files of Special Surveys Division, Dominion Bureau of Statistics; series C47 from 1946 to 1958 is the sum of series C48 and series C49.

The estimates from 1946 to 1960 were obtained in labour force surveys. See the general note to this section for a description of the surveys and the definitions employed.

The estimates from 1921 to 1945 were made by the Labour Division of D.B.S. Series C49 from 1921 to 1945 was obtained from the intercensal estimates of population which are made annually and published, by age and sex, in D.B.S., Reference Paper No. 40, 1953. The census enumerations of the total gainfully occupied in 1921, 1931 and 1941 and of the unemployed in 1931 and 1941 were adjusted to conform to the labour force concepts. Appropriate data were available to interpolate the total civilian labour force and its main components in the two intercensal intervals from 1921 to 1941 with the exception of the component 'persons without jobs and seeking work' (series C54) which was extrapolated from 1931 to 1921. For the period 1942

to 1945, Canadian data were supplemented by United States experience with respect to the pattern of change in labour force participation. The procedures, which are too detailed to describe here, are described fully in Reference Paper No. 23 (Revised), pp. 8–13 and appendix. Estimates of the civilian labour force and its main components by sex and of paid workers by industry from 1931 to 1945 are published and described in the same source. Series C52, persons with jobs in nonagricultural industries, is also distributed into 'paid workers' and 'other classes of worker' from 1931 to 1945 in the source.

To adjust series C51 to the total 'employed', the concept now used in *The Labour Force*, 'persons on temporary lay-off up to 30 days' need to be subtracted. Adding 'persons on temporary lay-off up to 30 days' to series C54, persons without jobs and seeking work, yields the total 'unemployed'. The relevant series in thousands of 'persons on temporary lay-off up to 30 days' from 1 June 1946 to 1 June 1960 required to make these adjustments which is given in D.B.S., *The Labour Force, 1960 (Supplement)*, pp. 4–6, follows: 1946, 18; 1947, less than 10 (not statistically significant); 1948, 16; 1949, less than 10; 1950, 13 (excluding Manitoba); 1951, 13; 1952, 19; 1953, 12; 1954, 10; 1955, 11; 1956, less than 10; 1957, 13; 1958, 19; 1959, 21; 1960, 20.

C56–69. The civilian noninstitutional population, 14 years of age and over, the labour force and its main components, by sex, 1931 to 1960

SOURCE: for 1931 to 1945, D.B.S., Reference Paper No. 23 (Revised), table 2; for 1946 to 1958, D.B.S., Reference Paper No. 58 (1958 Revision), tables 1 and 6; for 1959 and 1960, files of the Special Surveys Division, Dominion Bureau of Statistics.

See general note to this section and the note to series C47–55.

C70–84. The labour force, by age and sex, 1946 to 1960

SOURCE: for 1946 to 1958, D.B.S., Reference Paper No. 58 (1958 Revision), table 4; for 1959 and 1960, files of the Special Surveys Division, Dominion Bureau of Statistics.

These estimates were obtained by labour force surveys. See the general note to this section for a description of the surveys and the definitions employed. Members of the armed services and persons in institutions are not included.

C85–97. The labour force, participation rates by age group and sex, selected years, 1921 to 1959

SOURCE: unpublished estimates by Sylvia Ostry and A. N. Polianski secured from the authors.

The authors interpolated the labour force survey estimates for the weeks ending 16 May and 20 June 1959, to obtain estimates for 1 June 1959. The underlying data for 1951 were obtained in *Census, 1951*, vol. X, table 61. The data on gainfully occupied in 1921, 1931 and 1941 were obtained in *Census, 1941*, vol. I, table 1 and *Census, 1921*, vol. IV, table IV. The following description was supplied by Mr Polianski:

Series prior to 1951 were adjusted to shift from a 'gainfully occupied' concept to a 'labour force' concept. For 1921, the female labour force was increased by 18.0 per cent, 60 per cent of the adjustment was allocated equally to age groups 14–19 years and 65 years and over, and 40 per cent equally to other age groups. This adjustment assumes that the discrepancies are most likely to occur in marginal age groups where labour force attachment is tenuous. The male labour force was adjusted by 2.0 per cent, equally distributed between those of 14–19 years and 65 and over.... The labour force for 1931 and 1941 was adjusted by 6 per cent, of which one-third was added to the male labour force and two-thirds to the female labour force, distributed as before. See *Census, 1951*, vol. X, pp. 245–7.

C98–109. Persons with jobs, class of worker, agricultural and nonagricultural, 1946 to 1960

SOURCE: for 1946 to 1958, D.B.S., Reference Paper No. 58 (1958 Revision), table 6; for 1959 and 1960, files of the Special Surveys Division, Dominion Bureau of Statistics.

All estimates were obtained by labour force surveys. See the general note to this section for a description of the surveys and the definitions used. Totals, not shown in this table, may be found in series C47–55 and series C56–69.

The armed services and persons in institutions are not included.

C110–125. Persons with jobs, class of worker, agricultural and nonagricultural, by sex, 1946 to 1960

Source and comment are the same as in series C98–109.

C126–129. Persons with jobs, class of worker, nonagricultural, by sex, 1931 to 1945

SOURCE: D.B.S., Reference Paper No. 23 (Revised), table 2.

Members of the armed services and persons in institutions are not included. See also series C47–55, series C56–69 and the notes on them.

C130–151. Persons with jobs, all classes, by industry and sex, 1946 to 1960

SOURCE: series C130 and C131 are a repetition of series C60 and C67; for series C132–151, for 1945 to 1951, D.B.S., Reference Paper No. 58, table 8, for 1952 to 1960, files of the Special Surveys Division, Dominion Bureau of Statistics.

C152–162. Paid workers with jobs in the labour force, by industry, 1931 to 1960

SOURCE: for 1931 to 1945, D.B.S., Reference Paper No. 23 (Revised), table 3; for 1946 to 1951, D.B.S., Reference Paper No. 58, table 8; for 1952 to 1960, files of the Special Surveys Division, Dominion Bureau of Statistics.

The estimates from 1946 to 1960 are from labour force surveys. For a description of the data and procedures used to establish comparability in the industrial classifications of the 1931 census, the 1941 census and the labour force estimates of 1946, and for the interpolations from 1932 to 1940 and 1942 to 1945, see Reference Paper No. 23 (Revised), pp. 13–14.

C163–190. Persons with jobs, all classes, by occupation and sex, 1948 to 1960

SOURCE: for 1948 to 1951, D.B.S., Reference Paper No. 58, table 9; for 1952 to 1960, files of the Special Surveys Branch, Dominion Bureau of Statistics.

All estimates were obtained by labour force surveys. See the general note to this section. In an occupational classification, persons with jobs are allocated to the occupation they pursue regardless of the industry in which they are employed.

C191–194. Marital status of females with jobs, 1946 to 1960

SOURCE: for 1946 to 1958, D.B.S., Reference Paper No. 58 (1958 Revision), table 9; for 1959 and 1960, files of the Special Surveys Division, Dominion Bureau of Statistics.

All estimates were obtained by labour force surveys. See the general note to this section.

Series C1–7. *Population and gainfully occupied 14 years of age and over, in nonagricultural and agricultural pursuits, census years, 1881 to 1941, and for the labour force in 1951*

	Population 14 years old and over	Number of persons engaged in				Per cent of total in	
		All occupations		Nonagricultural pursuits	Agricultural pursuits	Nonagricultural pursuits	Agricultural pursuits
Year[1]		Number	Per cent of population 14 and over				
	1	2	3	4	5	6	7
1951[1,2]	9,949,737	5,286,153	53.13	4,455,712	830,441	84.29	15.71
1941[3]	8,205,766	4,195,951	49.25	3,112,135	1,083,816	74.17	25.83
1941[4]	8,520,350	4,510,535	52.94	3,426,719	1,083,816	75.97	24.03
1931	7,298,447	3,921,833	53.74	2,794,151	1,127,682	71.25	28.75
1921[5]	5,928,687	3,164,348	53.37	2,129,065	1,035,283	67.28	32.72
1911[6]	4,955,585	2,723,634	54.96	1,789,899	933,735	65.72	34.28
1911[6]	5,514,388	2,723,634	49.39	—	—	—	—
1901[7]	4,063,943	1,782,832	43.86	1,065,972	716,860	59.79	40.21
1891[8]	3,611,882	1,606,369	44.47	871,162	735,207	54.23	45.77
1881[8]	3,162,122	1,377,585	43.56	715,319	662,266	51.93	48.07

[1] Excludes Yukon and Northwest Territories for all years. Includes Newfoundland for 1951 only.
[2] For gainfully occupied data Indians on reserves are excluded in labour force concept.
[3] Excludes persons on active service.
[4] Includes persons on active service.

[5] Gainfully occupied data excludes Indians on reserves engaged in fishing and trapping.
[6] Gainfully occupied data, series C2–7, are for persons 10 years of age and over in 1911 and all previous censuses. Population in 1911 is shown, first, for 14 years and over; second, for 10 years and over. Prior to 1911 population is for 10 years and over.
[7] Gainfully occupied data excludes Indians engaged in fishing and trapping.
[8] Gainfully occupied data excludes nomadic Indians.

Series C8–35. *Gainfully occupied 14 years of age and over, by occupations and by sex, census years, 1891 to 1941, and for the labour force in 1951*

| Year[1] | Agriculture | | Fishing and trapping | | Logging | | Mining and quarrying | | Manufacturing and mechanical | | Construction | | Transportation and communication | |
| | Males | Females | Males | Females | Males | Females | Males | Females | Males | Females | Males | Females | Males | Females |
	8	9	10	11	12	13	14	15	16	17	18	19	20	21
1951[3]	794,307	32,452	34,361	246	96,534	35	65,771	49	779,057	201,612	318,331	743	446,818	39,457
1941[1]	1,064,847	18,969	51,126	324	80,248	2	71,861	25	561,001	148,180	212,716	777	294,800	16,845
1931	1,103,638	24,044	47,208	496	43,982	—	58,584	6	394,788	101,054	202,960	96	271,086	17,944
1921	1,017,404	17,879	29,099[4]	49[4]	38,526	—	48,061	2	317,019	89,658	162,184	91	184,732	14,836
1911[6]	917,848	15,887	34,547	265[10]	42,658[7]	—	62,404[8]	3	275,439	96,795	150,520	47	153,586	5,340
1901[6]	707,924[9]	8,936	27,160[10]	24[10]	16,055	—	28,341	4	229,027	70,508	89,100	65	81,161	1,322
1891[6]	723,013	12,194	42,597[11,12]	204[11,12]	—[12]	—[12]	15,410	—	175,861	62,111	86,605	89	60,326	1,089

Year[1]	Trade and finance		Service						Clerical		Labourers[2]		Not stated	
			Total		Professional		Personal							
	Males	Females	Males	Females	Males	Females	Males	Females	Males	Females	Males	Females	Males	Females
	22	23	24	25	26	27	28	29	30	31	32	33	34	35
1951[3]	393,824	126,937	503,971	415,966	180,539	163,719	187,600	248,766	227,076	314,637	321,840	1,989	50,482	13,118
1941[1]	296,599	74,018	308,550	416,906	120,782	127,084	144,726	288,651	159,779	154,272	251,889	804	9,695	1,718
1931	295,975	56,439	270,511	346,442	103,723	117,219	128,119	228,406	141,187	117,497	425,255	987	1,357	297
1921	245,664	47,670	193,994	226,179	78,071	92,754	73,223	132,424	127,325[5]	90,612	305,774	441	5,508	1,641
1911[6]	193,154	28,651	139,054	183,841	53,720	45,402	68,996	137,221	72,595	33,756	317,008	236	—	—
1901[6]	91,795	7,757	100,623	135,582	39,521	34,679	47,788	100,306	46,220	12,569	126,726	1,141	751	41
1891[6]	81,130	6,934	87,533	116,259	34,442	25,092	35,108	90,373	21,029	3,092	115,546	1,052	—	—

[1] Excludes Yukon, Northwest Territories and Newfoundland in all years and in 1941 excludes persons on active service.
[2] Includes labourers in all industries except agriculture, fishing and trapping, logging, mining.
[3] Indians on reserves are excluded in labour force concept.
[4] Excludes Indians on reserves.
[5] Includes proof readers, shippers, weighmen and postmen classified elsewhere in other years. Addition of these in 1931 would have added 18% to males in this occupation group.

[6] 10 years and over in 1911, 1901, 1891.
[7] Includes pulp mill employees.
[8] Includes almost all mine and smelter employees except clerical.
[9] Includes all farmers' sons 14 years and over, whether or not reported in gainful occupation.
[10] Excludes Indians.
[11] Excludes nomadic Indians.
[12] Series C12–13 included with series C10–11 for 1891.

Series C36–46. *Gainfully occupied, by age and sex, census years, 1911 to 1941, and for the labour force in 1951*

Year[1]	Total 14 years and over	14 years	15–19 years	20–24 years	25–34 years	35–44 years	45–54 years	55–59 years	60–64 years	65–69 years	70 years and over
	36	37	38	39	40	41	42	43	44	45	46
Both sexes											
1951[1]	5,299,625[2]	10,179	509,735	753,307	1,292,975	1,116,088	825,650	307,099	245,005	154,493	85,094
1941[3]	4,195,951	12,394	429,897	571,022	1,017,437	792,471	681,850	280,544	205,248	124,895	80,193
1931	3,921,833	13,716	442,777	618,354	914,962	771,862	623,871	355,145		100,440	80,706
1921	3,164,348	20,745	390,258	450,328	775,547	926,690[4]		462,875[4]		137,905	
1911[5]	2,723,634	25,153[6]	800,964		1,787,919[7]					109,598	
Males											
1951[1]	4,130,802	7,896	310,878	495,245	1,024,753	915,888	686,992	261,810	214,941	136,965	75,434
1941[3]	3,363,111	10,683	287,048	356,064	796,667	681,117	607,067	254,089	186,033	112,627	71,716
1931	3,256,531	11,743	311,686	429,018	759,361	690,452	567,977	322,507		90,934	72,853
1921	2,675,290	16,827	278,339	324,102	663,919	845,278[4]		421,658[4]		125,167	
1911[5]	2,358,813	17,376[6]	620,972		1,619,885[7]					100,580	
Females											
1951[1]	1,168,823	2,283	198,857	258,062	268,222	200,200	138,658	45,289	30,064	17,528	9,660
1941[3]	832,840	1,711	142,849	214,958	220,770	111,354	74,783	26,455	19,215	12,268	8,477
1931	665,302	1,973	131,091	189,336	155,601	81,410	55,894	32,638		9,506	7,853
1921	489,058	3,918	111,919	126,226	111,628	81,412[4]		41,217[4]		12,738	
1911[5]	364,821	7,777[6]	179,992		168,034[7]					9,018	

[1] Excludes Yukon and Northwest Territories for all years. Includes Newfoundland for 1951 only.
[2] Difference between series C36 and series C2 for 1951 consists of persons seeking work for the first time (8,970 males and 4,502 females).
[3] Excludes persons on active service.

[4] Age groups are 35–49 years and 50–64 years.
[5] 10 years and over.
[6] 10–14 years.
[7] 25–64 years.

Series C 47–55. *The labour force and its main components, the noninstitutional population, the armed services, the civilian noninstitutional population, 14 years of age and over, 1921 to 1960*

(thousands)

Year[1, 2]	Non-institutional population[3]	Armed services	Civilian non-institutional[3]	Civilian labour force				Persons without jobs and seeking work	Persons not in the labour force
				Total	Persons with jobs				
					Total	In non-agricultural industries	In agriculture		
	47	48	49	50	51	52	53	54	55
1960	11,879	120	11,759	6,391	5,992	5,317	675	399	5,368
1959	11,651	120	11,531	6,186	5,852	5,128	724	334	5,345
1958	11,452	119	11,333	6,120	5,750	5,011	739	370	5,213
1957	11,183	117	11,066	5,970	5,774	5,002	772	196	5,096
1956	10,888	117	10,771	5,738	5,572	4,753	819	166	5,033
1955	10,689	118	10,571	5,585	5,371	4,498	873	214	4,986
1954	10,475	113	10,362	5,476	5,255	4,362	893	221	4,886
1953	10,231	104	10,127	5,386	5,271	4,373	898	115	4,741
1952	10,028	95	9,933	5,344	5,239	4,312	927	105	4,589
1951	9,764	68	9,696	5,236	5,155	4,164	991	81	4,460
1950[2, 4]	9,657	47	9,610	5,198	5,056	3,990	1,066	142	4,412
1949	9,296	42	9,254	5,092	4,991	3,877	1,114	101	4,162
1948	9,158	35	9,123	5,035	4,954	3,768	1,186	81	4,088
1947	9,030	37	8,993	4,954	4,862	3,690	1,172	92	4,039
1946[1]	8,981	213	8,768	4,862	4,738	3,467	1,271	124	3,906
1945	8,784	736	8,048	4,520	4,447	3,303	1,144	73	3,528
1944	8,699	779	7,920	4,548	4,485	3,349	1,136	63	3,372
1943	8,587	716	7,871	4,567	4,491	3,373	1,118	76	3,304
1942	8,477	392	8,085	4,569	4,434	3,295	1,139	135	3,516
1941	8,352	296	8,056	4,466	4,271	3,047	1,224	195	3,590
1940	8,247	107	8,140	4,607	4,184	2,840	1,344	423	3,533
1939	8,131	9	8,122	4,649	4,120	2,741	1,379	529	3,473
1938	8,004	7	7,997	4,588	4,066	2,707	1,359	522	3,409
1937	7,876	6	7,870	4,526	4,115	2,776	1,339	411	3,344
1936	7,754	6	7,748	4,466	3,895	2,576	1,319	571	3,282
1935	7,626	5	7,621	4,402	3,777	2,479	1,298	625	3,219
1934	7,496	5	7,491	4,338	3,707	2,430	1,277	631	3,153
1933	7,371	5	7,366	4,275	3,449	2,192	1,257	826	3,091
1932	7,245	5	7,240	4,211	3,470	2,233	1,237	741	3,029
1931	7,121	5	7,116	4,151	3,670	2,454	1,216	481	2,965
1930	6,978	6	6,972	4,060	3,689	2,451	1,238	371	2,912
1929	6,825	5	6,820	3,964	3,848	2,541	1,307	116	2,856
1928	6,660	5	6,655	3,861	3,796	2,491	1,305	65	2,794
1927	6,491	5	6,486	3,757	3,690	2,406	1,284	67	2,729
1926	6,331	5	6,326	3,658	3,550	2,299	1,251	108	2,668
1925	6,206	4	6,202	3,580	3,423	2,203	1,220	157	2,622
1924	6,082	4	6,078	3,502	3,344	2,138	1,206	158	2,576
1923	5,973	4	5,969	3,433	3,323	2,110	1,213	110	2,536
1922	5,893	5	5,888	3,380	3,230	2,038	1,192	150	2,508
1921	5,785	5	5,780	3,313	3,121	1,956	1,165	192	2,467

[1] From 1946 on, the figures apply to the survey week ending closest to 1 June. For 1931 to 1945, the figures apply to 1 June.
[2] Newfoundland included beginning in 1950.
[3] Excludes Indians living on reserves and residents of the Yukon and Northwest Territories.

[4] June 1950, no survey was made in Manitoba owing to flood conditions. The Manitoba component of these estimates was calculated using a straight line interpolation between June 1949 and June 1951.

Series C56–69. *The civilian noninstitutional population, 14 years of age and over, the labour force and its main components, by sex, 1931 to 1960*

(thousands)

Year[1,2]	Males							Females						
	Civilian noninstitutional population[3]	Labour force					Persons not in the labour force	Civilian noninstitutional population[3]	Labour force					Persons not in the labour force
		Total	Persons with jobs			Persons without jobs and seeking work			Total	Persons with jobs			Persons without jobs and seeking work	
			Total	In non-agricultural industries	In agriculture					Total	In non-agricultural industries	In agriculture		
	56	57	58	59	60	61	62	63	64	65	66	67	68	69
1960	5,861	4,752	4,402	3,773	629	350	1,109	5,898	1,639	1,590	1,544	46	49	4,259
1959	5,752	4,659	4,361	3,684	677	298	1,093	5,779	1,527	1,491	1,444	47	36	4,252
1958	5,660	4,640	4,316	3,633	683	324	1,020	5,673	1,480	1,434	1,378	56	46	4,193
1957	5,533	4,550	4,376	3,643	733	174	983	5,533	1,420	1,398	1,359	39	22	4,113
1956	5,380	4,415	4,271	3,494	777	144	965	5,391	1,323	1,301	1,259	42	22	4,068
1955	5,277	4,331	4,144	3,307	837	187	946	5,294	1,254	1,227	1,191	36	27	4,040
1954	5,173	4,270	4,074	3,216	858	196	903	5,189	1,206	1,181	1,146	35	25	3,983
1953	5,056	4,200	4,097	3,249	848	103	856	5,071	1,186	1,174	1,124	50	12	3,885
1952	4,959	4,147	4,059	3,218	841	88	812	4,974	1,197	1,180	1,094	86	17	3,777
1951	4,833	4,057	3,993	3,101	892	64	776	4,863	1,179	1,162	1,063	99	17	3,684
1950[2,4]	4,826	4,064	3,944	2,971	973	120	762	4,784	1,134	1,112	1,019	93	22	3,650
1949	4,656	3,978	3,892	2,910	982	86	678	4,598	1,114	1,099	967	132	15	3,484
1948	4,604	3,943	3,880	2,854	1,026	63	661	4,519	1,092	1,074	914	160	18	3,427
1947	4,542	3,869	3,793	2,792	1,001	76	673	4,451	1,085	1,069	898	171	16	3,366
1946[1]	4,398	3,756	3,649	2,578	1,071	107	642	4,370	1,106	1,089	889	200	17	3,264
1945	3,772	3,102	3,053	2,110	943	49	670	4,276	1,418	1,394	1,193	201	24	2,858
1944	3,711	3,137	3,008	2,150	948	39	574	4,209	1,411	1,387	1,199	188	24	2,798
1943	3,715	3,183	3,136	2,189	947	47	532	4,156	1,384	1,355	1,184	171	29	2,772
1942	3,969	3,465	3,364	2,421	943	101	504	4,116	1,104	1,070	874	196	34	3,012
1941	4,009	3,468	3,313	2,247	1,066	155	541	4,047	998	958	800	158	40	3,049
1940	4,151	3,628	3,273	2,107	1,166	355	523	3,989	979	911	733	178	68	3,010
1939	4,196	3,690	3,247	2,055	1,192	443	506	3,926	959	873	686	187	86	2,967
1938	4,140	3,652	3,209	2,030	1,179	443	488	3,857	936	857	677	180	79	2,921
1937	4,081	3,610	3,254	2,088	1,166	356	471	3,789	916	861	688	173	55	2,873
1936	4,025	3,571	3,073	1,920	1,153	498	454	3,723	895	822	656	166	73	2,828
1935	3,966	3,529	2,982	1,843	1,139	547	437	3,655	873	795	636	159	78	2,782
1934	3,906	3,487	2,932	1,806	1,126	555	419	3,585	851	775	624	151	76	2,734
1933	3,848	3,446	2,721	1,608	1,113	725	402	3,518	829	728	584	144	101	2,689
1932	3,787	3,401	2,747	1,647	1,100	654	386	3,453	810	723	586	137	87	2,643
1931	3,726	3,357	2,931	1,844	1,087	426	369	3,390	794	739	610	129	55	2,596

[1] From 1946 on, the figures apply to the survey week ending closest to 1 June. For 1931 to 1945, the figures apply to 1 June.
[2] Newfoundland included beginning in 1950.
[3] Excludes Indians living on reserves and residents of the Yukon and Northwest Territories.
[4] June 1950, no survey was made in Manitoba owing to flood conditions, though an estimate is included here. See footnote (4), series C47–55.

Series C70–84. *The labour force, by age and sex, 1946 to 1960*

(thousands)

Year[1,2]	14–19 years			20–24 years			25–44 years			45–64 years			65 and over		
	Total	Males	Females	Total	Males	Females	Total	Males	Females	Total	Males	Females	Total	Males	Females
	70	71	72	73	74	75	76	77	78	79	80	81	82	83	84
1960	589	344	245	813	520	293	2,943	2,274	669	1,818	1,425	393	228	189	39
1959	547	324	223	786	508	278	2,880	2,253	627	1,747	1,381	366	226	193	33
1958	560	334	226	785	510	275	2,851	2,232	619	1,688	1,359	329	236	205	31
1957	546	320	226	759	495	264	2,781	2,197	584	1,646	1,331	315	238	207	31
1956	512	303	209	743	482	261	2,683	2,137	546	1,566	1,285	281	234	208	26
1955	511	308	203	728	477	251	2,620	2,092	528	1,509	1,259	250	217	195	22
1954	524	317	207	737	478	259	2,546	2,050	496	1,452	1,229	223	217	196	21
1953	510	314	196	739	479	260	2,485	1,999	486	1,436	1,211	225	216	197	19
1952	520	320	200	733	474	259	2,459	1,960	499	1,408	1,188	220	224	205	19
1951	530	323	207	733	469	264	2,380	1,904	476	1,362	1,153	209	231	208	23
1950[2,3]	535	335	200	750	491	259	2,330	1,878	452	1,351	1,150	201	232	210	22
1949	558	347	211	742	484	258	2,243	1,803	440	1,309	1,127	182	240	217	23
1948	565	362	203	742	489	253	2,193	1,768	425	1,306	1,117	189	229	207	22
1947	575	359	216	731	475	256	2,154	1,736	418	1,265	1,095	170	229	204	25
1946	606	371	235	707	440	267	2,069	1,657	412	1,250	1,079	171	230	209	21

[1] Week ending closest to 1 June.
[2] Newfoundland included beginning in 1950. Yukon and Northwest Territories excluded throughout.
[3] June 1950, no survey was made in Manitoba owing to flood conditions, though an estimate is included here. See footnote (4), series C47–55.

Series C85–97. *The labour force, participation rates by age group and sex, selected years, 1921 to 1959*

(percentages)

Year	Males						Females						Total both sexes
	14–19 years	20–24 years	25–34 years	35–64 years	65 years and over	Total	14–19 years	20–24 years	25–34 years	35–64 years	65 years and over	Total	
	85	86	87	88	89	90	91	92	93	94	95	96	97
1959	42.1	93.2	98.2	95.1	32.0	82.0	29.4	47.7	26.4	26.5	5.0	26.9	54.0
1951[1]	48.8	92.3	96.4	93.2	38.6	82.2	31.4	46.8	24.2	19.6	5.1	23.6	53.1
1941[2]	55.4	91.5	97.9	95.2	58.9	85.9	30.1	46.5	27.5	15.2	19.9	24.5	56.1
1931	57.3	92.6	97.7	95.8	69.0	87.4	29.1	47.0	21.7	13.5	22.8	23.6	56.4
1921	65.4	92.3	96.2	94.3	71.0	88.3	29.5	38.3	19.9	11.8	19.0	20.5	55.8

[1] Excludes new seekers.   [2] Includes armed services.

Series C98–109. *Persons with jobs, class of worker, agricultural and nonagricultural, 1946 to 1960*

(thousands)

Year[1,2]	Total				Nonagricultural				Agricultural			
	Paid workers	Own account workers[3]	Employers[4]	Unpaid family workers[5]	Paid workers	Own account workers[3]	Employers[4]	Unpaid family workers[5]	Paid workers	Own account workers[3]	Employers[4]	Unpaid family workers[5]
	98	99	100	101	102	103	104	105	106	107	108	109
1960	4,887	608	333	164	4,775	229	266	47	112	379	67	117
1959	4,695	626	347	184	4,571	228	279	50	124	398	68	134
1958	4,595	630	327	198	4,493	216	257	45	102	414	70	153
1957	4,538	696	328	212	4,450	242	256	54	88	454	72	158
1956	4,326	707	323	216	4,219	238	248	48	107	469	75	168
1955	4,101	734	307	229	3,977	234	231	56	124	500	76	173
1954	3,950	759	312	234	3,825	258	226	53	125	501	86	181
1953	3,951	732	321	267	3,842	238	239	54	109	494	82	213
1952	3,900	731	307	301	3,795	235	231	51	105	496	76	250
1951	3,736	912	188	319	3,625	348	139	52	111	564	49	267
1950[2,6]	3,553	968	188	347	3,429	379	134	48	124	589	54	299
1949	3,479	932	230	350	3,326	350	152	49	153	582	78	301
1948	3,367	960	240	387	3,225	336	162	45	142	624	78	342
1947	3,262	952	231	417	3,139	346	158	47	123	606	73	370
1946	3,143	925	212	458	2,986	295	147	39	157	630	65	419

[1] Survey week ending closest to 1 June.
[2] Newfoundland included beginning in 1950. Yukon and Northwest Territories excluded throughout.
[3] Without paid employees.
[4] With own business, profession or farm.
[5] In a business or on a farm.
[6] June 1950, no survey was made in Manitoba owing to flood conditions, though an estimate is included here. See footnote (4), series C47–55.

Series C110–125. *Persons with jobs, class of worker, agricultural and nonagricultural, by sex, 1946 to 1960*

(thousands)

Year[1,2]	Nonagricultural								Agricultural							
	Paid workers		Own account workers[3]		Employers[4]		Unpaid family workers[5]		Paid workers		Own account workers[3]		Employers[4]		Unpaid family workers[5]	
	Males	Females	Males	Females	Males	Females	Males	Females	Males	Females	Males	Females	Males	Females	Males	Females
	110	111	112	113	114	115	116	117	118	119	120	121	122	123	124	125
1960	3,337	1,438	184	45	245	21	—[6]	40	106	—[6]	375	—[6]	65	—[6]	83	34
1959	3,228	1,343	186	42	261	18	—[6]	41	117	—[6]	392	—[6]	66	—[6]	102	32
1958	3,214	1,279	175	41	237	20	—[6]	38	93	—[6]	410	—[6]	68	—[6]	112	41
1957	3,186	1,264	205	37	239	17	13	41	83	—[6]	449	—[6]	70	—[6]	131	27
1956	3,049	1,170	200	38	233	15	12	36	101	—[6]	465	—[6]	75	—[6]	136	32
1955	2,880	1,097	197	37	213	18	17	39	116	—[6]	496	—[6]	74	—[6]	151	22
1954	2,768	1,057	220	38	213	13	15	38	116	—[6]	496	—[6]	85	—[6]	161	20
1953	2,803	1,039	203	35	224	15	19	35	102	—[6]	488	—[6]	81	—[6]	177	36
1952	2,789	1,006	200	35	214	17	15	36	99	—[6]	486	10	74	—[6]	182	68
1951	2,653	972	301	47	132	—[6]	15	37	102	—[6]	555	—[6]	48	—[6]	187	80
1950[2,7]	2,501	928	324	55	127	—[6]	19	29	118	—[6]	581	—[6]	53	—[6]	221	78
1949	2,446	880	304	46	144	—[6]	16	33	138	15	572	10	76	—[6]	196	105
1948	2,399	826	287	49	153	—[6]	15	30	131	11	610	14	77	—[6]	208	134
1947	2,332	807	295	51	151	—[6]	14	33	112	11	592	14	72	—[6]	225	145
1946	2,178	808	252	43	137	10	11	28	143	14	619	11	64	—[6]	245	174

[1] Survey week ending closest to 1 June.
[2] Newfoundland included beginning in 1950. Yukon and Northwest Territories excluded throughout.
[3] Without paid employees.
[4] With own business, profession or farm.
[5] In a business or on a farm.
[6] Less than 10,000.
[7] June 1950, no survey was made in Manitoba owing to flood conditions, though an estimate is included here. See footnote (4), series C47–55.

Series C126–129. *Persons with jobs, class of worker, nonagricultural, by sex, 1931 to 1945*

(thousands)

Year[1]	Paid workers		Other workers	
	Males	Females	Males	Females
	126	**127**	**128**	**129**
1945	2,014	923	96	270
1944	2,041	935	109	264
1943	2,085	849	104	335
1942	2,090	711	331	163
1941	1,883	683	364	117
1940	1,595	602	512	131
1939	1,504	575	551	111
1938	1,500	575	530	102
1937	1,531	577	557	111
1936	1,432	562	488	94
1935	1,380	561	463	75
1934	1,374	557	432	67
1933	1,182	535	426	49
1932	1,291	557	356	29
1931	1,512	516	332	94

[1] Figures apply to 1 June. Excludes Newfoundland, Yukon and Northwest Territories throughout.

Series C130–151. *Persons with jobs, all classes, by industry and sex, 1946 to 1960*

(thousands)

Year[1,2]	Agriculture		Forestry		Fishing and trapping		Mining, quarrying and oilwells[3]		Manufacturing		Construction	
	Males	Females	Males	Females	Males	Females	Males	Females	Males	Females	Males	Females
	130	**131**	**132**	**133**	**134**	**135**	**136**	**137**	**138**	**139**	**140**	**141**
1960	629	46	70	—[4]	23	—[4]	92	—[4]	1,195	293	418	12
1959	677	47	63	—[4]	17	—[4]	83	—[4]	1,214	297	438	11
1958	683	56	68	—[4]	17	—[4]	114	—[4]	1,179	289	447	12
1957	733	39	99	—[4]	30	—[4]	113	—[4]	1,190	303	447	10
1956	777	42	84	—[4]	29	—[4]	106	—[4]	1,131	288	420	—[4]
1955	837	36	83	—[4]	27	—[4]	106	—[4]	1,089	276	358	—[4]
1954	858	35	60	—[4]	34	—[4]	103[3]	—[4]	1,087	270	335	—[4]
1953	848	50	69	—[4]	29	—[4]	90	—[4]	1,125	276	349	—[4]
1952	841	86	76	—[4]	40	—[4]	94	—[4]	1,086	270	349	—[4]
1951	892	99	87	—[4]	37	—[4]	84	—[4]	1,082	274	347	—[4]
1950[2,5]	973	93	59	—[4]	50	—[4]	73	—[4]	1,047	274	335	—[4]
1949	982	132	57	—[4]	28	—[4]	82	—[4]	1,051	259	343	—[4]
1948	1,026	160	62	—[4]	24	—[4]	73	—[4]	1,026	237	290	—[4]
1947	1,001	171	59	—[4]	32	—[4]	75	—[4]	1,047	250	252	—[4]
1946	1,071	200	39	—[4]	28	—[4]	74	—[4]	994	245	238	—[4]

Year[1,2]	Transportation, storage and communication		Public utilities		Trade		Finance, insurance, real estate		Service	
	Males	Females	Males	Females	Males	Females	Males	Females	Males	Females
	142	**143**	**144**	**145**	**146**	**147**	**148**	**149**	**150**	**151**
1960	383	67	65	—[4]	655	311	123	103	749	745
1959	376	65	69	—[4]	631	285	122	94	671	680
1958	375	62	68	—[4]	630	279	113	94	622	629
1957	373	67	69	—[4]	610	281	109	91	603	595
1956	376	60	60	—[4]	606	256	106	87	576	549
1955	341	56	53	—[4]	592	247	101	77	557	518
1954	347	60	54	—[4]	564	244	99	72	533	484
1953	372	53	51	—[4]	568	238	88	69	508	474
1952	367	53	54	—[4]	528	249	92	69	532	436
1951	343	51	41	—[4]	478	227	87	70	515	427
1950[2,5]	327	49	40	—[4]	438	204	81	65	521	413
1949	325	45	41	—[4]	437	205	83	60	463	386
1948	332	38	36	—[4]	444	194	80	57	487	377
1947	333	39	36	—[4]	409	190	78	51	471	359
1946	300	39	30	—[4]	372	195	74	51	429	349

[1] Figures apply to survey week ending closest to 1 June.
[2] Newfoundland included beginning 1950. Yukon and Northwest Territories excluded throughout.
[3] The estimates are correct within the sampling variability. However, owing to a revision in the sample the estimates for 1954 and later are not comparable, for purposes of measuring change, with the estimates for 1953 and earlier.
[4] Less than 10,000.
[5] June 1950, no survey was made in Manitoba owing to flood conditions, though an estimate is included here. See footnote (4), series C47–55.

Series C152–162. *Paid workers with jobs in the labour force, by industry, 1931 to 1960*

(thousands)

Year[1,2]	Agri-culture	Forestry	Fishing and trapping	Mining, quarrying and oil wells[3]	Manu-facturing	Con-struction	Trans-portation, storage and communi-cation	Public utilities	Trade	Finance, insurance, real estate	Service
	152	153	154	155	156	157	158	159	160	161	162
1960	112	62	—[4]	93	1,414	364	417	74	783	209	1,352
1959	124	53	—[4]	84	1,437	375	407	77	723	200	1,211
1958	102	62	—[4]	114	1,401	393	407	76	725	191	1,116
1957	88	89	12	116	1,413	387	407	75	705	184	1,062
1956	107	71	11	109	1,347	355	403	67	682	176	998
1955	124	69	—[4]	107	1,297	302	368	59	649	165	952
1954	125	49	—[4]	104[3]	1,281	277	371	59	630	158	888
1953	109	61	—[4]	91	1,319	299	382	54	629	141	859
1952	105	63	13	95	1,282	289	385	59	607	149	853
1951	111	70	—[4]	85	1,270	279	356	46	538	144	828
1950[2,5]	124	47	11	74	1,222	267	343	44	479	134	808
1949	153	47	—[4]	83	1,212	271	329	45	470	130	733
1948	142	51	—[4]	73	1,166	226	329	39	469	122	743
1947	123	47	—[4]	74	1,199	182	333	39	436	115	707
1946[1]	157	31	—[4]	72	1,144	184	308	34	419	111	674
1945	—		58	52	1,196	113	305	29	389	102	693
1944	—		63	60	1,263	110	292	27	364	97	700
1943	—		62	68	1,250	149	276	26	337	92	674
1942	—		81	81	1,131	144	262	25	344	89	644
1941	—		87	89	904	170	247	26	346	80	617
1940	—		59	84	712	126	219	24	309	82	582
1939	—		56	82	627	127	206	22	302	82	575
1938	—		55	79	632	134	204	23	296	82	570
1937	—		65	80	657	139	212	21	289	82	563
1936	—		58	70	592	132	207	21	280	82	552
1935	—		60	64	579	125	194	21	262	82	554
1934	—		49	58	560	165	193	20	254	83	549
1933	—		31	52	481	81	190	21	237	83	541
1932	—		31	55	528	118	208	23	254	83	548
1931	—		40	60	605	154	246	24	269	83	547

[1] From 1946 on, figures apply to the survey week ending closest to 1 June. For 1931 to 1945 the figures apply to 1 June.

[2] Newfoundland included beginning in 1950. Yukon and Northwest Territories excluded throughout.

[3] The estimates are correct within the sampling variability. However, owing to a revision in the sample the estimates for 1954 and later are not comparable, for purposes of measuring change, with the estimates for 1953 and earlier.

[4] Less than 10,000.

[5] June 1950, no survey was made in Manitoba owing to flood conditions, though an estimate is included here. See footnote (4), series C47–55.

Series C163–190. *Persons with jobs, all classes, by occupation and sex, 1948 to 1960*
(thousands)

Year[1,2]	Managerial		Professional		Clerical		Transportation		Communication		Commercial		Financial	
	Males	Females	Males	Females	Males	Females	Males	Females	Males	Females	Males	Females	Males	Females
	163	164	165	166	167	168	169	170	171	172	173	174	175	176
1960	449	56	344	254	285	467	374	—[5]	55	38	258	174	56	—[5]
1959	478	56	334	228	276	446	356	—[5]	54	35	253	165	52	—[5]
1958	441	53	315	195	260	439	376	—[5]	49	36	241	154	50	—[5]
1957	460	49	298	192	271	424	358	—[5]	45	41	236	161	48	—[5]
1956	410	42	261	162	263	401	373	—[5]	41	36	226	140	45	—[5]
1955	397	46	256	160	253	366	352	—[5]	44	38	220	143	39	—[5]
1954	436	40	235	142	248	354	333	—[5]	45	37	202	138	37	—[5]
1953	454	42	229	157	239	330	343	—[5]	44	39	205	135	29	—[5]
1952	410	49	223	123	262	333	344	—[5]	41	34	200	149	35	—[5]
1951	376	46	222	121	250	327	333	—[5]	39	30	191	137	32	—[5]
1950[2,6]	359	51	223	117	249	305	328	—[5]	38	32	202	124	22	—[5]
1949	333	42	195	110	224	289	343	—[5]	39	27	195	138	27	—[5]
1948[7]	225	29	187	100	223	282	335	—[5]	39	24	269	128	32	—[5]

Year[1,2]	Service		Agricultural		Fishing, logging, trapping		Mining		Manufacturing and mechanical trades[3]		Construction		Labourers and unskilled workers[4]	
	Males	Females	Males	Females	Males	Females	Males	Females	Males	Females	Males	Females	Males	Females
	177	178	179	180	181	182	183	184	185	186	187	188	189	190
1960	271	348	637	45	77	—[5]	60	—[5]	871	179	328	—[5]	337	15
1959	251	313	684	45	68	—[5]	52	—[5]	833	181	337	—[5]	333	11
1958	247	305	690	56	75	—[5]	71	—[5]	831	174	336	—[5]	334	12
1957	234	285	743	39	105	—[5]	72	—[5]	830	188	345	—[5]	331	11
1956	232	271	788	42	96	—[5]	67	—[5]	781	182	343	—[5]	345	16
1955	217	253	844	36	94	—[5]	69	—[5]	758	163	304	—[5]	297	15[5]
1954	215	246	866	35	79	—[5]	66	—[5]	734	170	288	—[5]	290	—[5]
1953	207	223	853	50	79	—[5]	60	—[5]	746	175	315	—[5]	294	11[5]
1952	215	220	846	87	101	—[5]	63	—[5]	736	171	316	—[5]	267	—[5]
1951	196	204	899	99	109	—[5]	60	—[5]	725	186	323	—[5]	238	—[5]
1950[2,6]	214	202	978	93	101	—[5]	54	—[5]	725	184	343	—[5]	108	—[5]
1949	184	187	990	132	72	—[5]	61	—[5]	719	167	347	—[5]	163	—[5]
1948[7]	191	185	1,025	158	76	—[5]	60	—[5]	754	157	259	—[5]	205	—[5]

[1] Figures apply to the survey week ending closest to 1 June.
[2] Newfoundland included beginning in 1950. Yukon and Northwest Territories excluded throughout.
[3] Includes stationary enginemen and occupations associated with electric power production.
[4] Not including labourers in agriculture, fishing, logging, trapping and mining.
[5] Less than 10,000.
[6] June 1950, no survey was made in Manitoba owing to flood conditions, though an estimate is included here. See footnote (4), series C47–55.
[7] Figures are also available in the source for August 1947. No earlier figures are available.

Series C191–194. *Marital status of females with jobs, 1946 to 1960*
(thousands)

Year[1,2]	Total	Single	Married	Other[3]
	191	192	193	194
1960	1,590	703	716	171
1959	1,491	661	671	159
1958	1,434	661	616	157
1957	1,398	681	569	148
1956	1,301	657	509	135
1955	1,227	648	451	128
1954	1,181	640	426	115
1953	1,174	667	392	115
1952	1,180	684	385	111
1951	1,162	684	370	108
1950[2,4]	1,112	676	328	108
1949	1,099	672	321	106
1948	1,074	655	317	102
1947	1,069	670	299	100
1946	1,089	687	314	88

[1] Figures apply to the survey week ending closest to 1 June.
[2] Newfoundland included beginning in 1950. Yukon and Northwest Territories excluded throughout.
[3] Includes widowed, divorced and permanently separated.
[4] June 1950, no survey was made in Manitoba owing to flood conditions, though an estimate is included here. See footnote (4), series C47–55.

SECTION D: WAGES AND WORKING CONDITIONS

DOUGLAS C. HARTLE, *University of Toronto*

The statistics of this section fall into seven major divisions determined largely by conceptual distinctions but also by the agencies originating or processing the statistics. The first subsection, on indexes of wage rates, on wage rates and on piece-rate earnings (series D 1–165), presents a selection of the data published by the Economics and Statistics Branch of the Department of Labour on wages and piece rates in Canada in the period since 1900 as well as new estimates prepared for *Historical Statistics for Canada* by the author from the records of that Department. Series D 166–231, the second subsection, present miscellaneous statistics of wage rates, earnings and hours in the latter half of the nineteenth century compiled by the Bureau of Industry of Ontario and by federal immigration officers. The third subsection, series D 232–279, contains statistics of average annual earnings drawn from the decennial censuses and estimates of labour income prepared by the Dominion Bureau of Statistics as components of the *National Accounts*. Subsection four, series D 280–411, is a selection of the statistics of annual average earnings and hours of work prepared by the Dominion Bureau of Statistics with the exception of six series prepared by T. M. Brown. The fifth subsection, series D 412–433, is devoted to statistics of union membership and strikes and walkouts prepared by the Economics and Statistics Branch, Department of Labour. The sixth subsection, series D 434–447, presents the more important statistics in the field of Workmen's Compensation. The final subsection, series D 448–470, contains statistics generated by the operations of the National Employment Service and the Unemployment Insurance Commission.

The main sources for data for this section are federal government publications. The Department of Labour publications are listed first, Dominion Bureau of Statistics publications second and other publications third. The publication concerning wages and hours of labour, annual since 1920, published by the Department of Labour and printed by the Queen's Printer, has had various titles as follows:

Department of Labour, *Wages and Hours of Labour in Canada*, annual 1920 to 1941 (Ottawa, King's Printer); *Wage Rates and Hours of Labour in Canada*, annual 1943 to 1947; *Annual Report on Wage Rates and Hours of Labour in Canada*, 1948 to 1951; *Wage Rates, Salaries and Hours of Labour in Canada*, 1952; *Wage Rates and Hours of Labour in Canada*, 1953 to 1956; *Wage Rates and Hours of Labour*, 1957; *Wage Rates and Salaries*, 1958; *Wage Rates, Salaries and Hours of Labour*, 1959 and 1960.

Other publications of the Department of Labour are:

Department of Labour, *Labour Organization in Canada*, annual since 1911 (Ottawa, Queen's Printer); Department of Labour, *The Labour Gazette*, monthly since September 1900 (Ottawa, Queen's Printer), various issues; Department of Labour, *Strikes and Lockouts in Canada*, reviewed annually in *The Labour Gazette* until 1946, as a supplement to *The Labour Gazette*, 1947 to 1951, and as a separate document since 1952 (Ottawa, Queen's Printer).

The following publications of the Dominion Bureau of Statistics were used:

Dominion Bureau of Statistics, *Labour Income, 1926–1958* (Ottawa, Queen's Printer, 1960); *Estimates of Labour Income*, monthly (Ottawa, Queen's Printer), various issues; *General Review of the Manufacturing Industries of Canada, 1957 and 1958* (Ottawa, Queen's Printer, 1960 and 1961); *Earnings and Hours of Work in Manufacturing*, annual since 1946 (Ottawa, Queen's Printer); *Review of Man Hours and Hourly Earnings, 1945–1959* (Ottawa, Queen's Printer, 1960); *Employment, Payrolls and Weekly Earnings January 1949–June 1953 with Historical Series* (Ottawa, Queen's Printer, 1953); *Review of Employment and Payrolls*, annual since 1942 (Ottawa, Queen's Printer), issues for 1958 and 1959; *Canada Year Book*, annual since 1905 (Ottawa, Queen's Printer), issues for 1942 and 1943–44; *Annual Report on Benefit Periods Established and Terminated under the Unemployment Insurance Act*, monthly since 1942 (Ottawa, Queen's Printer).

Other publications used are:

Department of Health and Welfare, *Government Expenditures and Related Data on Health and Social Welfare, 1947 to 1953*, 2nd edition, and *1947 to 1959*, 3rd edition (Ottawa, Queen's Printer, 1955 and 1961); *Report of the Minister of Agriculture*, annual since 1867 (Ottawa, Queen's Printer; reports for early years were printed by private printers), reports 1871 to 1876 and 1881 to 1891; *Annual Report of the Department of the Interior*, 1873 to 1936 (Ottawa, King's Printer; reports for early years were printed by private printers), reports 1892 to 1904; *Annual Report of the Bureau of Industries for the Province of Ontario*, 1882 to 1919 (Toronto, King's Printer; reports for early years were printed by private printers), reports 1885 to 1890; A. H. Le Neveu, 'Comment' on 'Changes in the Industrial Distribution of Wages in the United States, 1939–1949', Conference on Research in Income and Wealth, *Studies in Income and Wealth*, vol. 23 (Princeton, Princeton University Press, 1958); Robert E. Olley, *Construction Wage Rates in Ontario, 1864–1903* (M.A. thesis deposited in the Douglas Library, Queen's University, Kingston, Ontario, 1961).

INDEX NUMBERS OF WAGE RATES, WAGE RATES AND PIECE-RATE EARNINGS
(Series D 1–165)

General note

All the published data in the tables contained in this division were taken from annual wage reports of the Department of Labour. For many years these reports have been prepared by the Economics and Research Branch of the Department. While the Department of Labour collected some data on wages and hours beginning in 1900, parts of which were published from time to time in *The Labour Gazette*, it was only in 1921 that publication of a series of regular annual reports on wages and hours began. Prior to 1950 these reports were published as supplements to *The Labour Gazette*; beginning with 1950 they have been published as separate documents. The latest report available for the preparation of these tables is entitled *Wage*

Rates, Salaries and Hours of Labour, 1960. The title of the report has undergone a number of changes, however, which are shown in the full list of sources given at the beginning of this section.

The reports on wage rates and hours of labour are numbered serially. The first report, issued in March 1921 and numbered as Report No. 1 in the series, contained all the data for the years 1901 to 1920 except those for coal mining, which appeared in Report No. 3, and the indexes for metal mining, steamships, laundries and telephones, which first appeared in Report No. 24. In addition to the annual reports a number of special reports were included in the series in the first few years after 1921 and there was no report issued for 1942. Consequently the number of each report did not correspond with either the number of years over which reports had been published or the number of years for which information on wage rates and hours was given.

The early wage reports were based on information obtained from trade unions, collective agreements, departmental field representatives and *The Labour Gazette* field representatives throughout Canada as well as from an annual mail survey of employers. With the expansion of the survey of employers over the years the information obtained from employers has supplanted information obtained from other sources. By 1959 all of the basic data were obtained from an annual mailed wage survey of employers except for: construction, obtained from the Industrial Relations Branch of the Department of Labour from field interviews; railways and stevedoring, obtained from collective agreements. The establishment is the unit for which data are obtained.

The wage information has always been collected on an occupational basis. Until 1947 selected employers were sent a blank form and asked to report, together with other data, the hourly or weekly wages and standard hours (hours per week beyond which an employee would be considered to be working overtime) of their employees in designated, selected occupations, together with a count of the number of employees at each wage rate, for the pay period covered by the survey. In recent years this pay period has been the last one before 1 October. Before 1947, because no descriptions of the occupations were provided with the questionnaires and because variations in the definitions of some occupations existed among establishments, this approach made it extremely difficult to aggregate the submitted wage data on a consistent basis. The editing of the wage schedules necessarily required important arbitrary decisions. The development of occupational definitions and their provision to employers from 1947 onward, the still later development in 1958 of wage-reporting schedules which incorporated these definitions in the schedules, and the introduction of standard editing procedures have undoubtedly improved the comparability of the published data.

The occupational reporting schedules in current use attempt to elicit wage data for a large number of occupations characteristic of an industry. Among the criteria used to select occupations to be surveyed are that the occupations should be of numerical importance in the industry or community, that they be important in the production process or processes, that they may be clearly defined and that they reflect the various levels of skill in the industry. However, it should be noted that because establishments in an industry vary widely in their characteristics, such as size and production process, the same occupations are not reported by each establishment, though the key occupations are usually reported by each establishment. Moreover, owing to occupational shifts within establishments, the same establishment may submit data for different occupations from survey to survey.

The industrial coverage of the survey has been gradually expanded over the years. In the earliest reports wage data were given for the building and printing trades, electric and steam railways, and certain 'metal' and manufacturing industries. Since 1921 new industries have been added, many industry subgroups have been dropped or added, and groupings have been changed. By 1958 the report covered 85 industries in provincial detail in eight major industry groups as well as special wage data for a large number of communities for male labourers, selected maintenance trades and office occupations in manufacturing. The industrial classification in 1959 'largely conforms' with the Standard Industrial Classification (of 1948) of the Dominion Bureau of Statistics; but exceptions were made in a few industries. The industrial classification has not remained the same over time.

The series reproduced in this volume are only a small selection from the published wage data. The selection was made from those series which covered the longest time span, involved relatively few classificatory changes, represented different types of industries, and illustrated geographic differentials at least in some cases. Occupations were selected which had relatively stable content, in so far as this could be estimated, and showed skilled–unskilled and male–female wage differentials.

Until 1958, except to indicate the total number of establishments which responded in a given year (13,500 in 1958, 23,000 in 1960) and, in recent years, the minimum coverage requirements for publication, the wage reports did not contain information with respect to coverage. The criteria for publication are outlined in Report No. 41 for 1958 on page 6. They ensure the confidentiality of the data provided for a particular establishment but do not appear to ensure that the published rates are representative. The 1958 report (p. 3) stated that the mailing list 'is designed to include the large or important establishments, the majority of the medium sized establishments, and comparatively few of the small establishments, except when the industry consists mostly of small establishments'. A response of 90 per cent was achieved which 'in all industries includes the major or large establishments'. In the 1959 report the coverage was given at 19,500 establishments, covering, as far as was known, all those having 15 or more employees in the industries and communities surveyed.

The number of establishments and total employment reported in each industry in the wage survey can be estimated, at least since 1956, from information given in the annual report *Working Conditions in Canada* which is also published by the Economics and Research Branch of the Department of Labour, Ottawa. This report is based on a survey which is carried out in April of each year using the same mailing list as the October wages survey. It is understood that the response rate has been approximately the same for the two surveys. The coverage of the wage survey for particular occupations cannot be determined because the total number of persons as specified for particular occupations is not known.

The wage rates reported are those paid for regular daytime work including cost-of-living payments but excluding overtime earnings, shift differentials, fringe benefits and the like (see Report, No. 42, p. 10). The rates are for fully qualified workers. The most common type of time rate obtained was the hourly rate. Consequently, in most cases where daily, weekly or monthly rates were reported these were converted to an hourly basis; they were converted to hourly rates by dividing by the appropriate standard hours of work. In some cases, however, daily, weekly or monthly rates were published when they were the common period of payment. For wages paid on piece work or production bonus systems, a calculation of how they worked out on a time basis, that is as straight-time earnings, was made and published.

The published data of series D1–165 may be divided into three periods, each distinguished from the other by the way in which the data were obtained, by the manner of processing or by the manner of presentation. For the first period, from 1901 to 1920, wage data were presented, by occupation, for 13 cities for building trades, metal trades, printing trades and street railways, for 10 cities for steam railways, and for Nova Scotia, Alberta and Vancouver Island for coal mining. Data for common factory labour, for miscellaneous factory trades and for occupations in logging and sawmilling were also given for 1911 to 1920 for a sample of employers. They were shown as reports, labelled 'samples', for individual employers. Wage indexes for the same period for metal mining, laundries and steamships were added in the 1940 report (No. 24) but the actual rates have not been published. At least part of these data had apparently been accumulated during the years since 1900 and some had been published in *The Labour Gazette*. The 'sample' data for 1911 to 1920 were collected from employers at one time in a single set of questionnaires covering all years from 1911 to 1920. The sample data for 1911 to 1920 were, with few exceptions, published as a single rate for each occupation reported for each region for each 'sample'. A single rate in each year was usually given also for each occupation in each region for the building trades, metal trades, printing trades, street railways, steam railways and (in Report No. 3) for coal mines. It is not clear how these single rates were obtained; the Economics and Research Branch of the Department of Labour feels it safe to assume they were 'predominant' rates.

The second period is from 1921 to 1942. The data for this period were obtained on a year to year basis by the methods previously mentioned. As increasing reliance was placed on surveys of employers, a growing part of the material was listed by localities by employer, the latter being designated by numbers. In both this material and some of that obtained by other means the data were commonly given by ranges. Averages, even by localities, were not given. The difficulties of using the data thus presented are discussed more fully in the notes on series D64–73.

In the third period, which begins in 1943, weighted average rates by occupations for various industries and regions were published as well as ranges of these rates. The publication of data by individual employers or establishments ceased. In the report for 1943 (No. 26) the indexes were recalculated back to 1939 using a detailed weighting scheme.

D1–11. Index numbers of average wage rates for selected main industries, 1901 to 1960

SOURCE: for 1959 and 1960, *Wage Rates, Salaries and Hours of Labour, 1960*, Report No. 43, p. 26; for 1910 to 1958, Report No. 42, p. 26.

For a description of the construction of the indexes and their coverage see especially Reports Nos. 1, 3, 19, 24, 26, 36, 42 and 43.

The method of constructing the indexes had one common element throughout the period. The first step was always to obtain a measure of the change in a rate for an occupation within an industry for each region. The occupational rate was in each case specific to the industry and the occupations were selected to be representative of all occupations in the industry. These measures of change of rate for an occupation within an industry were then averaged for all localities to give a countrywide average. The countrywide averages for all the occupations within an industry were then averaged to give a measure of the change for the industry as a whole on a countrywide basis.

Aside from this common element the method of constructing the indexes varied among three periods roughly coinciding with those noted in the general note for series D1–165. For 1900 to 1921 (Reports Nos. 1 and 3) the procedure appeared to be the following. An index of the wage rate for each occupation within each industry and for each locality was prepared with base 1913. For the sample data the occupational rates by industry and locality were presumably simple averages of the data from the relevant 'samples' (see general note to series D1–165). For the occupational data not obtained from the 'samples', unweighted averages or prevailing rates were probably used. For each occupation within each industry a simple (unweighted) average was taken among all localities to obtain a countrywide index of the rate for each occupation within each industry. The occupational indexes within each industry were then combined as a simple average to form the industry indexes which were published. In the earlier reports an unweighted average of industry indexes was calculated to give the general wage index. However, in the 1935 report (No. 19) the general index was recalculated by weighting the individual industry indexes in each case by an average of the numbers employed in 1921 and 1931 in the industry as reported for these years in the decennial censuses or censuses of industry of the Dominion Bureau of Statistics. Indexes for metal mining, laundries (later services) and steamships (later dropped) were published in the 1940 report (No. 24) for this period and a new general index was prepared combining the industry indexes, including those newly calculated, using as weights the averages of the numbers employed in 1921 and 1931 except for metal mining for which the averages are for 1921, 1931 and 1938. This general index, aside from the dropping of steamships, has not been revised further but has been mechanically linked to the later indexes. The individual indexes for each industry for this period have not been revised at any time after they were first prepared.

It is stated, apparently erroneously, in the 1943 and later reports that the method of link relatives was used from 1901 onward. This statement is in contradiction of statements of earlier reports about the way in which the indexes for 1901 to 1921 were made and it is also inconsistent with the way in which the index for coal mines for 1900 to 1921 was prepared and presented in Report No. 3 in which it is stated that the method used for coal mines was the same as that used for the other indexes. In that report, indexes for individual occupations in coal mining are presented by region, a simple average of occupations in each region is taken and then a simple average of the industry indexes for all regions is taken to give the countrywide index. In the use of simple averages to obtain industry indexes it makes no difference whether occupational indexes for localities are averaged before taking industry indexes or industry indexes for each locality are calculated before being combined for all localities.

From 1921 to 1939 the method of link relatives was used. Calculations were made for each year of the percentage change from the preceding year in occupations selected to be representative, in each industry by locality. A simple average of these percentage changes for all localities was taken for each occupation in each industry. Next a simple average of the percentage changes of the various occupations in an industry gave the percentage change for the industry. This percentage change was then 'linked' to the index for previous years. The general index for this period is the weighted average of industry indexes, the weights being the same as those described for the period 1901 to 1921.

It is not clear how a single wage rate was arrived at in the period 1921 to 1939 for each selected occupation within an industry and in the various localities. In some cases simple averaging of the occupational wage rates may have been done; in other cases a representative wage rate may have been chosen; or there may have been a combination of both methods. In view of the way in which much of the wage rate data, and particularly those on manufacturing, were published it appears likely that heavy reliance was placed on using a representative rate.

Since 1943 a different method of calculation of the index numbers has been followed and indexes were recalculated back to 1939 on the new basis. Weighted average wage rates are calculated for each of the selected occupations within an industry for each of the five regions in Canada—the Atlantic Provinces, Quebec, Ontario, the Prairie Provinces, and British Columbia. However, if any region contains less than 2 per cent of the industry's labour force in the most recent decennial census year, no average is calculated for that region. For any one occupation, to obtain the countrywide occupational index, the regional average wage rates are multiplied by a percentage corresponding to the proportion of the industry's labour force in each region as reported in the most recent decennial census. The sum of the products for any year, expressed as a percentage of a similar aggregate for the base year, is the index number for the occupation. These occupational indexes are then multiplied by their appropriate occupational weights, and the aggregate divided by the sum of the weights is the index number for the industry. Each occupational weight is determined by dividing the number of workers in that occupation reported by employers to the Annual Wage Rate Survey in the most recent decennial census year into the total number of workers reported in all the occupations selected for the index. The resulting proportion is the occupational weight. These weights are generally held constant from year to year except at the most primary level where the regional occupational rate within an industry is calculated by, in effect, dividing the total wage bill by the numbers covered.

To obtain an index number for a major group, such as foods and beverages or textile products, subgroup indexes computed by the above method are weighted by labour force data for such subgroup as reported in the most recent decennial census and the aggregate divided by the sum of the weights. Larger industrial groups are obtained by a similar procedure.

In the indexes presented herein the weights for the period 1939 to 1949 were based on numbers employed in 1941 as obtained from the 1941 decennial census. For the period 1949 to 1960 the weights are based on numbers employed in 1951 as reported in the decennial census that year and supplemented by information obtained in the wage rate survey itself in that year. The indexes using the different sets of weights were mechanically linked at 1949. Similarly, the new indexes were mechanically linked to the old at 1939. No recalculations of earlier data were made at the time the linkings were done.

The current wage indexes are computed on the base 1949 = 100. The previous base, 1939 = 100, was dropped in 1954. In the 1953 Report indexes on both bases were published. Changes in the base year have corresponded, generally speaking, with changes in census weights and changes in the occupations making up the occupational indexes, and in some cases have been accompanied by major changes in the methods of calculating the indexes. Changes in base were not accompanied by a reworking of the earlier series using the new weights but were achieved through mechanical linking.

The index numbers from 1939 onward, derived from the weighted averages of occupational wage rates reported for a selection of occupations in an industry, reflect changes in numbers employed in subcategories of an occupation, as well as changes in the structure of wage rates.

D12–39. Index numbers of average wage rates for industry groups and selected components in manufacturing, Canada, 1939 to 1960

SOURCE: Department of Labour, *Wage Rates and Hours of Labour*: annual reports as follows for indexes on the base 1949 = 100: 1960 and 1959, No. 43; 1958 to 1954 inclusive, No. 41; 1953, No. 40; 1952, No. 39; 1951, No. 37; 1950, No. 36; 1949, No. 38. Indexes on the base 1939 = 100 were taken from: 1953 and 1952, No. 36; 1951 and 1950, No. 35; 1949, No. 36; 1948, No. 33; 1947, No. 34; 1946 and 1945, No. 35; 1944, No. 31; 1943, No. 32; 1942, No. 31; 1941, No. 34; 1940, No. 29; 1939, No. 30.

See the discussion of series D1–11. Indexes for a much larger number of industry groups than hitherto were published for the period from 1939 onward.

D40–59. Hourly wage rates in selected building trades, by city, 1901 to 1960

SOURCE: Department of Labour, *Wage Rates and Hours of Labour* annual reports as follows: 1960, No. 43; 1959, No. 42; 1958 to 1947 inclusive, Nos. 41–30, inclusive; 1946 to 1942 inclusive, No. 29; 1941 to 1929, No. 25; 1928 and 1927, No. 14; 1926, No. 25; 1925 to 1921 inclusive, No. 14; 1920, No. 25; 1919 to 1901 inclusive, No. 1.

Rates are given here for four occupations in five major Canadian cities. Comparable data for other occupations and cities also have been published. It is believed that these series for the building trades are among the most consistent series which have been published in the annual wage reports. The occupational definitions in the building trades have changed less over the years than those of most occupations; and there probably has been substantially less variability in the hourly wage rates paid to a particular occupation in a particular city at a particular point in time than has generally been the case for other occupations. The published wage rates for each occupation represent the 'prevailing' rates in the particular city. In recent years these data have been obtained from a field survey conducted by the Industrial Relations Branch of the Department of Labour for the administration of the Fair Wages and Hours of Labour Act. The rates are 'deemed to be generally accepted as current for competent workmen in each trade or classification employed in the location indicated', and in nearly all cases are union rates.

The rates published for this and all other industries in the annual wage *Reports* do not include overtime earnings, shift differentials, non-production bonuses (except cost-of-living bonus payments), shares in company profits and the monetary value of such fringe benefits as group insurance, sick benefits, uniforms, etc. The rates are derived from the employee's wage before deductions are made for taxes, unemployment insurance contributions, pensions payments, etc. The rates are intended to apply to fully qualified workers in their occupations. Unless otherwise stated, the rates apply to male workers only. Where women and men are reported in an occupation, separate rates are shown for them. Rates for beginners, learners, apprentices, foremen and lead hands, are not included, although rates for helpers are sometimes shown separately. The rates for part-time employees working less than half the standard hours are not included.

D60–63. Standard hours worked per week in selected building trades, five cities, selected years, 1905 to 1955

SOURCE: same as series D40–59.

Standard hours of work per week are defined as the number of hours worked per week beyond which the worker is usually considered to be working overtime. Until 1943 standard hours were published for each occupation in each city. From 1944 to 1948 standard hours were omitted entirely from the annual reports. From 1949 to 1957 the standard hours for the group of all of the building trades in each city were published. Standard hours data for the building trades were dropped again from the 1958, 1959 and 1960 reports. Series D60–63 are consistent with series D40–59.

Hours data were published for most occupations in most industries up until 1943 and again from 1949 onward.

D64–73. Comparison of specially computed weighted average hourly wage rates, published weighted average wage rates, and medians and means computed from published 'sample rates' for selected occupations in the pulp and paper industry, Canada, selected years, 1917 to 1951

SOURCE: series D64–66 were developed in the summer of 1960 by the author for this volume; D67 from Department of Labour *Wage Rates and Hours of Labour in Canada*, Reports Nos. 34 and 29 for 1951 and 1946 data, respectively; D69, D70 and D72 computed from *Wages and Hours of Labour in Canada*, Nos. 25, 21, 16, 15, 14, and 1 for the data for the years 1941, 1936, 1931, 1926, 1921 and 1917, respectively.

Although the Department of Labour has published occupational wage data for each of the years back to 1901 for some industries, important changes were made by the Department in the methods of publication of the basis information collected by the annual surveys. With the exception of a few occupations, such as the building trades given in series D40–59, these changes in publication practice make it impossible to obtain completely consistent series for all of the years for which information has been published.

Up to and including Report No. 25, which covered the years 1929, 1940 and 1941, 'sample' wage rates were published each year for particular occupations. These sample rates consisted of a listing for each occupation of the 'predominant' wage rates selected by the editors of the material from the rates reported by establishments. These sample rates pose a number of serious problems for the derivation of meaningful time series. It should be noted, however, that there are a number of occupations for which wage rates were not given on a sample wage rate basis. These included metal trades, printing trades, electric street railways, civil employees, steam railways, local trucking, cartage and building trades.

The first difficulty in handling the sample wage rate data arises in attempting to decide from which published report the sample wage data for a particular year should be selected for a given occupation. Each published report includes sample rates for at least three (usually not consecutive) years; and there is thus a substantial amount of overlap among the reports. For example, for the occupation 'millwright' in the pulp and paper industry for the year 1929 sample wage rates appear in 11 separate reports. There are substantial differences among the reports in the sample rates given for this occupation for this year. Usually, a time series would be made up of the most recently published data for each year in the series. However, this procedure is not necessarily appropriate with respect to the sample wage data because the sample rates for various years given in an individual report are stated to be comparable, but apparently no attempt was made to maintain comparability among reports. As stated on page 12 in the introductory notes to the 25th *Wages and Hours of Labour in Canada* report:

The main object of these reports is to show the changes in wage rates and in hours of labour during the periods covered. The figures given in *each report afford a continuous record for the years included*, the data being from the same sources as far as possible. Whenever a new source of information comes available, the figures for previous years are secured if possible, and the record is revised accordingly. [Emphasis added.]

Just how important these changes have been for millwrights (an occupation selected at random) can be seen in the following table. The unweighted arithmetic means of the sample rates for 1929 have varied from 67.8 cents per hour (Report No. 14) to 59.8 cents per hour (Report No. 20). The change in wage rates from 1920 to 1929 was − 5.2 per cent if measured in terms of the sample rates given in Report No. 14, the most recent report which included comparable data for *both* dates; the change in wage rates from 1920 to 1929 was − 13.0 per cent if measured in terms of the most recently published data for *each* date (Report No. 14 for 1920 data and Report No. 25 for 1929 data). The significance of these discrepancies depends, of course, on the uses to which the data are put.

If the dictum quoted above is accepted (that changes should only be measured between the dates given in individual reports) it follows that the − 5.2 per cent change measured from data given in Report No. 14 is the better estimate and not the change based on the most recently published data. Furthermore, if this dictum is accepted, changes can only be measured between those years which happen to have been covered in a single report. For the years 1933 to 1941 for those industries and occupations which were published on the basis of sample rates it is only possible to measure the change between two contiguous years or between any one year in the period and the year 1929. A strictly consistent time series is clearly impossible.

It must be recognized that changes in the establishment composition of an industry, or in the occupations within those establishments, create an inherent problem for the derivation of consistent time series. The problem necessarily exists in all regular surveys in which the universe changes. It certainly is not confined to the sample wage data published by the Department prior to 1942. The unique feature of these data is not the existence of the problem but of the Department's approach to it in earlier years.

Even assuming that by taking the sample wage rate data from the last published source a *roughly* comparable series for the period 1920 to 1941 could be developed, other difficulties remain. The sample wage data for each year consist of listings of the 'predominant' rates. In order to convert these annual listings into an annual time series each listing must be somehow described by a single statistic—a measure of central tendency. Unfortunately, the most appropriate measure of central tendency cannot be derived. Since 1943 the Department of Labour has published each year weighted average wage rates for each occupation, by locality, instead of the listings of sample wage rates which were published for earlier years. The average wage rates are computed by weighting the wage rates reported for a particular occupation by the number of employees at each wage rate. This aggregation procedure is obviously superior to the sample listings; and it would be eminently desirable to be able to derive from the earlier sample listings weighted average wage rates which would be comparable with the more recently published data. Because the earlier published reports did not indicate the number of employees paid at each of the listed sample rates, and because no record of this information was kept by the Department, there is no way in which this aggregation procedure can be applied to the sample listings.

Furthermore, there is some reason to believe that the method of selecting 'predominant' wage rates for inclusion in the sample listings in earlier years may have destroyed the possibility of obtaining a measure of central tendency from the sample listings which would provide a reasonable estimate of the weighted average of the submitted wage data from which the listed wage rates were selected. In the introductory notes to Report No. 25 (p. 12) it is stated that:

Unweighted arithmetic means of the hourly wage rates for millwrights, pulp and paper industry, computed from the sample rates for this occupation provided in Wages and Hours of Labour in Canada *Reports, 1920 to 1941*[1]

Year	Report 11 No. of samples	Report 11 Mean wage rate	Report 12 No. of samples	Report 12 Mean wage rate	Report 13 No. of samples	Report 13 Mean wage rate	Report 14 No. of samples	Report 14 Mean wage rate	Report 15 No. of samples	Report 15 Mean wage rate	Report 16 No. of samples	Report 16 Mean wage rate	Report 17 No. of samples	Report 17 Mean wage rate	Report 18 No. of samples	Report 18 Mean wage rate
1941	—	—	—	—	—	—	—	—	—	—	—	—	—	—	—	—
1940	—	—	—	—	—	—	—	—	—	—	—	—	—	—	—	—
1939	—	—	—	—	—	—	—	—	—	—	—	—	—	—	—	—
1938	—	—	—	—	—	—	—	—	—	—	—	—	—	—	—	—
1937	—	—	—	—	—	—	—	—	—	—	—	—	—	—	—	—
1936	—	—	—	—	—	—	—	—	—	—	—	—	—	—	—	—
1935	—	—	—	—	—	—	—	—	—	—	—	—	—	—	—	—
1934	—	—	—	—	—	—	—	—	—	—	—	—	—	—	32	58.4
1933	—	—	—	—	—	—	—	—	—	—	—	—	27	51.4	33	53.4
1932	—	—	—	—	—	—	—	—	—	—	9	57.6	27	54.7	—	—
1931	—	—	—	—	—	—	9	64.2	9	64.2	9	64.7	—	—	—	—
1930	—	—	—	—	—	—	11	67.9	10	66.8	9	64.7	—	—	—	—
1929	—	—	—	—	11	67.0	13	67.8	—	—	—	—	24	60.8	26	64.8
1928	—	—	13	67.6	13	67.6	13	67.6	—	—	—	—	—	—	—	—
1927	13	68.0	13	67.6	13	67.6	13	67.6	—	—	—	—	—	—	—	—
1926	13	67.0	13	67.0	13	67.0	13	67.0	10	67.5	—	—	—	—	—	—
1925	13	65.3	13	65.3	13	65.3	13	65.3	—	—	—	—	—	—	—	—
1924	13	64.6	—	—	—	—	—	—	—	—	—	—	—	—	—	—
1923	13	64.5	13	64.5	13	64.5	—	—	—	—	—	—	—	—	—	—
1922	13	62.0	13	62.0	—	—	—	—	—	—	—	—	—	—	—	—
1921	12	62.4	12	62.4	12	62.4	12	62.4	—	—	—	—	—	—	—	—
1920	4	71.5	4	71.5	4	71.5	4	71.5	—	—	—	—	—	—	—	—

Year	Report 19 No. of samples	Report 19 Mean wage rate	Report 20 No. of samples	Report 20 Mean wage rate	Report 21 No. of samples	Report 21 Mean wage rate	Report 22 No. of samples	Report 22 Mean wage rate	Report 23 No. of samples	Report 23 Mean wage rate	Report 24 No. of samples	Report 24 Mean wage rate	Report 25 No. of samples	Report 25 Mean wage rate
1941	—	—	—	—	—	—	—	—	—	—	—	—	33	73.1
1940	—	—	—	—	—	—	—	—	—	—	31	71.6	33	69.6
1939	—	—	—	—	—	—	—	—	29	68.3	31	69.1	—	—
1938	—	—	—	—	—	—	28	67.9	29	68.0	—	—	—	—
1937	—	—	—	—	26	65.4	29	64.8	—	—	—	—	—	—
1936	—	—	34	59.5	26	58.8	—	—	—	—	—	—	—	—
1935	40	58.6	36	57.4	—	—	—	—	—	—	—	—	—	—
1934	40	57.0	—	—	—	—	—	—	—	—	—	—	—	—
1933	—	—	—	—	—	—	—	—	—	—	—	—	—	—
1932	—	—	—	—	—	—	—	—	—	—	—	—	—	—
1931	—	—	—	—	—	—	—	—	—	—	—	—	—	—
1930	—	—	—	—	—	—	—	—	—	—	—	—	—	—
1929	31	61.4	27	59.8	19	64.3	20	63.2	20	63.2	21	63.4	19	62.2
1928	—	—	—	—	—	—	—	—	—	—	—	—	—	—
1927	—	—	—	—	—	—	—	—	—	—	—	—	—	—
1926	—	—	—	—	—	—	—	—	—	—	—	—	—	—
1925	—	—	—	—	—	—	—	—	—	—	—	—	—	—
1924	—	—	—	—	—	—	—	—	—	—	—	—	—	—
1923	—	—	—	—	—	—	—	—	—	—	—	—	—	—
1922	—	—	—	—	—	—	—	—	—	—	—	—	—	—
1921	—	—	—	—	—	—	—	—	—	—	—	—	—	—
1920	—	—	—	—	—	—	—	—	—	—	—	—	—	—

[1] When the sample rate was published as a range the arithmetic mean of the range was computed. In the rare instances when *daily* wage rates and weekly hours were published these data were excluded from the sample list.

Wages in manufacturing are shown by samples numbered one, two, etc., each sample showing the predominant rate in a certain establishment; in some cases for large establishments two or three samples are given; in other cases where the same rate is paid by a number of firms a sample may represent several such firms in order to avoid repetition.

The practice of including several wage rates for the largest establishments in each listing would, of course, mean that the arithmetic mean of the wage rates given in any list would have some rough weighting in that a representation is given to more than one wage rate for the establishment. However, the practice of publishing only one wage rate to represent a number of establishments which had the same wage rate would destroy this 'natural' weighting scheme if there was relatively little wage dispersion among a significant number of the establishments with considerable numbers of employees.

In order to assess the comparability of the sample wage data with weighted average wage rates of the nature of those published since 1943 a limited but time-consuming test was conducted in the summer of 1960 for three occupations in the pulp and paper industry. The test consisted of the following steps. (1) The original wage returns for all establishments in the pulp and paper industry which reported to the wages survey since its inception were obtained in so far as possible from the files of the Department held in the Public Archives. (2) From these original returns weighted average wage rates were computed for three occupations (grindermen, digester cooks, and millwrights) for each of the years 1917, 1921, 1926, 1931, 1936, 1941, 1946 and 1951. (3) The medians and simple arithmetic means of the most recently published sample wage data were computed for each of the above years and for each of the three occupations. The occupations selected had not been involved in a regrouping of the wage data provided for the pulp and paper industry and appeared to be relatively stable in terms of content. The initial year 1917 was selected because the coverage was extremely limited prior to that date. The terminal date 1951 was selected because it permitted some overlap of the weighted average wage rates computed from the original returns for this volume with the published weighted average wage rates since June 1943. Every fifth year in the period 1917 to 1951 was selected because of the limited computational resources available.

Series D64 and series D65 indicate respectively the number of establishment returns from which wage rates were obtained and the number of employees in these establishments in each occupation. The wage rates given in series D66 were computed in the same way as the weighted average wage rates published by the Department since 1943. Each individual reported rate was multiplied by the number employed at that rate in the year for which the calculation is made, the products were added and the sum divided by the total number of employees.

It can be seen that for the years 1946 and 1951, when the computed rates (series D66) and the published weighted average rates (series D67) are both available, the differences between them were in every case not more than 2 per cent. These small differences could have arisen because of small differences in coverage (late reporting establishments might have been omitted from the computation of the published average wage rate) and in editing procedures. For most purposes it is reasonable to assume that, since 1946 at least, the computed weighted average wage rate provided a reasonable estimate of the published weighted average wage rate. It can be assumed, with a few qualifications that will be discussed later, that the computed average wage rates for the years prior to 1943 provide a reasonably reliable estimate of the weighted average wage rates that could have been published in those years had it been the Department's policy to compute them.

Series D70 and series D72 give the medians and unweighted arithmetic means of the sample rates published for the three occupations in the selected years. The sample data were taken in each case from the most recent wage report possible. Series D71 and series D73 provide a comparison of these measures with the computed weighted average wage rate given in series D66. In the rates shown for grindermen it can be seen that the median sample rates were closer to the computed weighted average rate more frequently than were the mean sample rates. However, the differences between the medians and means of the sample rates were generally small. The medians differed from the computed weighted average wage rates by no more than 8 per cent but the variation was from 8 per cent below in 1931 to 7 per cent above in 1921. The medians were usually below the computed rates, but not consistently so.

For digester cooks the median and mean sample rates were never below and almost invariably above the computed weighted average wage rates; and the mean sample rates were closer to the computed wage rates than were the median sample rates. A comparison of the same series for millwrights shows the same picture of variation.

The test which has just been discussed seems to suggest that the medians and means of the published sample wage rates do not provide reliable estimates of the weighted average wage rates which could have been computed from the wage data submitted to the Department of Labour. Because the differences in some years were substantial and not consistent with respect to direction a measurement of the changes in wage rate from year to year for one occupation could yield large differences between the changes based on the mean or median sample rate and the changes based on the computed weighted averages. There is no clear indication

as to whether the median or the mean of the published sample rates provides a better estimate of the computed weighted average wage rate. On the basis of this evidence it appears that time series based on the means or medians of the published sample wage rates would probably be misleading for many purposes.

This criticism must be qualified in four respects. The above test assumes that the computed wage rates provide a precise standard against which the median and mean wage rates computed from the sample rates may be compared. However, it should be borne in mind that although every effort was made to select from the material filed by the Department of Labour in the archives the original returns for each establishment which reported wage rates for any of the pulp and paper occupations in any year since 1908, it was impossible to ascertain the degree to which this attempt was successful. For the years 1946 to 1951 the small differences between the published weighted average wage rates and the computed weighted average wage rates suggest that there were few if any establishments omitted from the test; for earlier years, when fewer establishments were included in the survey, greater disparities may have existed between the establishments included in the computation and those included in the sample wage rates. As indicated above, the disparity may have been in either direction in specific years. Because no records were kept in the Department of Labour as to the establishments reporting in the years before 1943 for which data were published it is now impossible to ascertain with certainty which establishments should be included in the computations of the weighted average wage rates. In making the test all of the establishments listed in annual Dominion Bureau of Statistics publications on the pulp and paper industry (from the earliest of those publications) were taken from the Department of Labour files, if available, and the wage data for the specified occupations used in the computation of the weighted average wage rates.

The second qualification is similar to the first. Even had all of the establishment returns used to derive the sample wage rates been located, the computed weighted average wage rates could differ from the median or means of the sample rates because of differences in editing procedures. The early questionnaires returned for the wage survey did not include occupational descriptions. There is a multitude of ambiguities as to the comparability of occupational titles. The original editing procedures are unknown. In the development of the computed average wage rates conservative editing procedures were adopted in the sense that only wage rates reported for an occupation which had the same literal title were included.

Thirdly, the means and medians were derived from the most recently published sample listings for the appropriate years; and hence sample listings for each occupation were taken from a number of different reports. As previously mentioned, the listings for the same occupation are not strictly comparable unless taken from the same report. This is an intrinsic problem of the sample data which cannot be avoided.

Finally, although the lack of comparability of the sample listings among wage reports applies to virtually all industries and occupations, comparison of the medians and means of the published sample wage rates with the computed weighted average wage rates has been made for only three occupations in one industry. There is no way of knowing if the same results would be obtained if a similar test were applied to other industries and occupations.

Although these qualifications weaken the negative results indicated above, the lack of comparability of the sample listings among individual wage reports, the differences in the year-to-year changes in the sample data when measured in terms of medians or arithmetic means, and the disparities between either of these measures and the computed weighted averages in some years mean that judgements have to be made in deriving time series from the sample wage data which should be made by the user. It was therefore decided that potential users would be better served by this detailed discussion of the sample wage data than by the publication of wage series based upon them which might be misleading for some purposes.

From the table given earlier which shows the wage data available for millwrights in the annual *Wages and Hours of Labour in Canada* reports, the reader can ascertain the specific wage reports in which the sample wage data for specific years can be located.

It would be desirable that, when adequate resources are available, weighted average wage rates for the principal occupations in the principal industries be computed from the original questionnaires which fortunately are still available in the Public Archives.

D74-76. Specially computed weighted average hourly wage rates for selected occupations in the pulp and paper industry, by province, selected years, 1917 to 1951

SOURCE: worksheets developed under the author's direction in the summer of 1960 for this volume.

Series D74-76 were derived in precisely the same way and from the same basic data as series D66, except that the latter applies to Canada while the former apply to particular provinces. For series D74-76 it is possible to make the same comparisons with published data for the provinces for the years 1946 and 1951 as were made for Canada in series D64-73. The comparable published weighted average rates are given in series D82, D83 and D86 for the Maritimes; in series D91, D92 and D95 for Quebec; in series D96, D97 and D100 for Ontario; in series D101, D102 and D105 for British Columbia and Manitoba. Because the provincial–regional breakdowns altered over the years comparisons are not always possible.

For further interpretation of series D74-76 see the notes to series D64-73.

D77-105. Hourly wage rates in selected occupations in the pulp and paper industry, for Canada and by region, 1911 to 1920 and 1943 to 1960

SOURCE: Department of Labour, *Wage Rates and Hours of Labour in Canada*, Reports Nos. 26-43 inclusive, for the years 1943 to 1958, No. 1 for the years 1911 to 1920.

The wage rates from 1943 to 1960 are the weighted average rates prepared by the Department of Labour. The data in series D77, D78 and D81 are the same as the data given in series D67 for the relevant dates. See the notes to series D64-73 for the way in which these rates were calculated.

Sample rates have been provided for the years 1911 to 1920 for many of the series because all of the rates came from the same report (Report No. 1) and are comparable from year to year for the years 1911 to 1920. When two sample rates were published for the same occupation (and there were never more available on a consistent basis) the arithmetic mean of the two rates was computed for the derivation of the series. The sample wage data were published on a weekly wage basis in most instances. They were converted to an hourly wage basis using the hours per week data provided in the same report. See the notes to series D64-73 for a discussion of the problems involved in obtaining time series from the sample wage data.

A rough estimate of the current coverage of the wage survey can be obtained from the fact that establishments in this industry reporting to the survey of working conditions (the same mailing list as the annual wages survey) employed 61,348 workers in 1958, according to the machine runs of the former survey.

Some occupations in the pulp and paper industry are common to the whole industry; other occupations are particular to its divisions. The grinderman and digester cook operations are specific to the pulp operations of companies in the industry. However, the beaterman and machine tender occupations are found in the newsprint and in the 'papers other than newsprint' sectors of the industry. The wages paid in the two sectors of the paper operations are unequal. In this table the rates given are for beaterman and machine tenders engaged in the production of newsprint. The rates for millwright maintenance men apply to all sectors of the pulp and paper industry.

Sample wage rates for this industry for Canada were also published for the years 1920 to 1941 but are not presented here. The information given in the table for millwrights included in the notes to series D64-73 indicates the reports from which the sample wage data for particular years may be obtained. The difficulties involved in deriving consistent time series from these sample rates are also discussed in the notes to series D64-73.

D106-110. Hourly wage rates for selected occupations in the motor-vehicle industry, Ontario, 1943 to 1960

SOURCE: Department of Labour, *Wage Rates and Hours of Labour*, Reports Nos. 26-43 inclusive.

The wage rates are weighted average rates prepared by the Department of Labour. See the notes to series D64-73 for the way in which the Department obtained these rates.

The data are only for Ontario. Until 1958 all reporting establishments were located in Ontario. In 1959 and 1960, data for other provinces were given but this table includes only the Ontario rates to maintain comparability with earlier years.

Prior to 1945 the industry was called the automobile industry. It is now defined to include 'establishments primarily engaged in manufacturing or assembling complete vehicles' and includes automobiles, trucks, trailers, etc. (See Report No. 41, p. 175.)

The machine runs of the working conditions survey, which has approximately the same coverage as the wages survey, indicate that in 1958 the reporting establishments in this industry employed 29,479 workers.

Sample wage rates published for this industry for Canada for the years 1920 to 1941 are not given here. The information given in the table relating to millwrights included with the notes to series D64-73 indicates the reports from which the sample data for particular years in this period can be obtained. The difficulties involved in the derivation of consistent time series from these sample rates are also discussed in the notes to series D64-73.

D111-130. Hourly wage rates and piece-rate earnings for selected occupations in the cotton industry, for Canada and by region, 1911 to 1920 and 1943 to 1960

SOURCE: Department of Labour, *Wage Rates and Hours of Labour*, Reports Nos. 26-43 inclusive, for the years 1943 to 1960, No. 1 for the years 1911 to 1920.

Wage rates for 1943 to 1960 are weighted average rates; for 1911 to 1920 they are based on sample rates. See the notes to series D64-73 and D77-105. No sample rates for all Canada (series D111-113) for 1911 to 1920 are given here since they would have required unweighted averaging of regional sample rates. In the regional data for 1911 to 1920 only one sample rate was given in each occupation in each region.

Workers in the cotton industry, like those in a number of other important industries in Canada, are paid in two ways; some are paid an hourly wage, others are paid according to their output. Prior to 1955, the Department of Labour did not separate these two forms of payment in the published tables. Earnings from piece work or incentive work were converted to straight time earnings per hour and were averaged in with the reported hourly wage rates. It must be borne in mind, therefore, that the series break between the years 1954 and 1955 for the piece rates and incentive rates were separated from hourly rates in 1955 and thereafter.

From the working conditions survey machine runs it is estimated that the reporting establishments to the wages survey in the cotton industry employed about 16,230 workers in 1958.

Sample wage rates were also published for this industry for Canada for the years 1921 to 1942 but are not included here. The information given in the table relating to millwrights included with the notes to series D 64–73 indicates the reports from which the sample data for particular years in this period can be obtained. The difficulties involved in the derivation of consistent time series from these sample rates are also discussed in the notes to series D 64–73.

D 131–165. Hourly wage rates and piece-rate earnings for selected occupations in the meat-packing industry, for Canada and by region, 1911 to 1920 and 1943 to 1960

SOURCE: Department of Labour, *Wage Rates and Hours of Labour*, Reports Nos. 26–43 inclusive, for the years 1943 to 1960, No. 1 for the years 1911 to 1920.

The rates for 1943 to 1960 are weighted averages; those for 1911 to 1920 are from sample rates. These rates were obtained and processed in the same way as those of series D 77–105. See the notes to series D 77–105 and D 64–73.

The sample rates for 1911 to 1920 are for two occupations and for Ontario only. In all years two and in some years three sample rates were given for each of the occupations in the industry. The series provided are the arithmetic means of the two sample rates which were provided continuously for each occupation in each year and are therefore comparable from year to year.

The rates before and including 1954 were based on averages of hourly rates and hourly piece-rate or incentive-rate earnings. In 1955 and thereafter the data for hourly rates and hourly piece-rate earnings are given separately. See also the note to series D 111–130.

For 1958 it is estimated from the working conditions survey machine runs that the establishments in the meat-packing industry reporting to the wages survey employed about 22,836 workers.

Sample wage rates were also published for this industry for Canada for the years 1920 to 1941 but are not given here. The information given in the table relating to millwrights included with the notes to series D 64–73 indicates the reports from which the sample data for particular years in this period can be obtained. The difficulties involved in the derivation of consistent time series from these sample rates are also discussed in the notes to series D 64–73.

MISCELLANEOUS EARLY WAGE RATES, EARNINGS AND HOURS (Series D 166–231)

General note

The data in this division of section D are, in the main, for the period before 1900. They are based on material found in two sources, firstly, annual reports of the Bureau of Industries of Ontario for several years in the 1880's, found in Ontario *Sessional Papers* and secondly, annual reports of the Department of Agriculture of Canada until 1891 followed by annual reports of

the Department of the Interior of Canada from 1892 onward. The former presents material collected in a survey-type operation for Ontario, the latter material obtained through immigration offices in Canada for most parts of the country. The immigration office was in the Federal Department of Agriculture from Confederation until 1891 and thereafter in the Federal Department of the Interior.

D 166–187. Average weekly hours and wages for males over 16 years of age, selected occupations, Ontario, 1884 to 1889

SOURCE: Ontario *Sessional Papers, Annual Report(s) of the Bureau of Industries of the Province of Ontario* as follows: for 1889 in *Sessional Papers, 1890*, vol. XXII, part VII, pp. 81–5; for 1888 in *Sessional Papers, 1889*, vol. XXI, part IX, pp. 74–80; for 1887 in *Sessional Papers, 1888*, vol. XX, part VI, pp. 60–1; for 1884 to 1886 in *Sessional Papers, 1887*, vol. XIX, part VI, pp. 282–6. Page references are to pages in the reports of the Bureau of Industries.

The Bureau of Industry of the Province of Ontario conducted extensive annual surveys of wages, hours, earnings and working conditions in the province in the 1880's. Wage and hour information was obtained from both employers and employees in part by mailed questionnaires and in part through interviews. Copies of the questionnaires and instructions to the interviewers are reproduced in some of the annual reports of the Bureau which appear in the Sessional Papers cited above. The data given here are for the combined returns of employers and individual workers except for 1887 when returns were obtained only for individual workers.

The coverage of the annual surveys is outlined in the 1889 *Sessional Papers*, part VII, pp. 29–31. The wage data for 1888, for example, were obtained from 756 employers in Ontario who together employed 19,393 workers. Schedules were also obtained from 2,554 'workmen' who, presumably, worked on their own account. Only a few of the large numbers of occupations covered are represented here. Together with the qualitative discussion the wage and hour data provided in the Bureau's reports give an extremely useful account of wages and working conditions in Ontario during the period.

D 188–195. Average wages paid in selected occupations as reported by Toronto and Ottawa immigration agents, 1871 to 1876

SOURCE: *Annual Reports of the Department of Agriculture*, Ottawa, for the years to which the data apply, found in *Sessional Papers* of Canada.

From Confederation to 1891, immigration was the responsibility of the Federal Department of Agriculture; in 1892 it became the responsibility of the Federal Department of the Interior. The Departments had immigration agents located in a number of Canadian cities. In their annual reports to the Departments these immigration agents included, although not consistently, tables which indicated wages for some occupations and the prices of the principal items in the consumer budget. Series D 188–195 are based on data selected from the annual reports of the Ottawa and Toronto immigration agents, the first two agencies after Confederation to provide this type of information on a consistent basis.

The reports do not indicate clearly how the immigration agents obtained their estimates. However, it seems evident from the text in many of the reports for the years covered in this table and for later years that employers informed the agents of their employment needs and the wages they would pay. This employer information is the likely source of the immigration agent data, for in years in which it was reported there was little demand for labour, no rates were given. It should be noted, nevertheless, that the wage estimates provided by some agents changed little, if at all, from year to year.

D196–207. Range of wages paid in selected occupations as reported by immigration agents, selected areas, 1881 to 1904

SOURCE: *Annual Report(s) of the Department of Agriculture*, Ottawa, for the years to which the data apply from 1881 to 1891; *Annual Report(s) of the Department of the Interior*, Ottawa, for the years to which the data apply from 1892 to 1904, both found in *Sessional Papers* of Canada.

See the note to series D188–195.

During the 1880's the number of immigration agencies was increased and the wage data were reported both more frequently and more consistently. In 1892, however, many of the agencies were closed, those remaining being at points of arrival in Canada or in the west. Hence only two agencies are covered from 1891 to 1904.

D208–231. Annual earnings, hours per week and days employed in year for males over 16 years of age, selected occupations, Ontario, 1884 to 1889

SOURCE: Ontario *Sessional Papers, Annual Report of the Bureau of Industries*: for 1889 in vol. XXII, part VII, pp. 99–103; for 1888 in vol. XXI, part IX, p. 87; for 1887 in vol. XX, part VI, pp. 62–3; for 1886 in vol. XIX, part VI, pp. 287–91; for 1885 in vol. XVIII, part VI, pp. 48–52; for 1884 in vol. XVII, part VII, pp. 42–5. Page references are to the reports of the Bureau of Industries.

See the note to series D166–187.

These series, like series D166–187, were obtained from the annual reports of the Ontario Bureau of Industry. Unlike the wage data provided in the earlier series, the earnings data were obtained solely from returns made by individual workers. Earnings, hours and days employed are given for many additional occupations in the annual reports.

AVERAGE ANNUAL EARNINGS AND LABOUR INCOME (Series D232–279)

D232–237. Average annual earnings, average weeks employed and average weekly earnings, by occupation group, males, Canada, 1931, 1941 and 1951

SOURCE: Le Neveu, 'Comment' on 'Changes in the Industrial Distribution of Wages in the United States, 1939–1949', in *Studies in Income and Wealth*, vol. 23. The estimates for 1931 were made by Sylvia Ostry from 1931 census data using classifications provided by D.B.S.

The series are based on decennial census data. For 1931 the annual earnings and weeks employed data are arithmetic means of the raw data, while in 1941 and 1951 the estimates are based on medians of the data. Because the frequency distributions of the earnings of the individuals in each occupation group were probably skewed to the right, the arithmetic means no doubt overstate the earnings in 1931, relative to the median earnings given in the other years.

D238–253. Annual labour income including supplementary labour income, by industry, Canada, 1926 to 1960

SOURCE: for 1957 to 1960, D.B.S., *National Accounts, Income and Expenditure, 1961*, table 22, p. 32, less military pay and allowances, table 20, p. 30; for 1926 to 1956, D.B.S., *Labour Income, 1926–1958*, table 17, p. 31.

The labour income estimates are industrial and geographic breakdowns of the 'wages, salaries and supplementary labour income' estimates which form part of the gross national product estimates. The estimates for most industries are based on the data obtained in the census of industry surveys conducted annually by D.B.S. and other annual D.B.S. surveys. However, for some industries estimates are based on census income data projected by related series. As would be expected, the estimates are probably less reliable for such sectors as service, agriculture and trade. The estimates for pre-war years are probably less reliable than more recent estimates. The sources and methods are discussed in the source document and in D.B.S., *National Accounts: Income and Expenditures, 1926–1956*, pp. 139–43.

Supplementary labour income includes expenditures by employers on labour account that can be regarded as payment for labour services. It includes employers' contributions to pension funds, employee welfare funds, unemployment insurance and workmen's compensation. Employer contributions to medical aid and hospitalization are excluded.

D254–266. Annual labour income including supplementary labour income, by province and region, 1926 to 1960

SOURCE: for 1957 to 1960, D.B.S., *National Accounts, Income and Expenditure, 1961*, table 31, p. 39; for 1926 to 1956, D.B.S., *Labour Income, 1926–1958*, table 6, p. 15.

See note to series D238–253.

D267–279. Annual wages and salaries in manufacturing, by province and region, 1926 to 1960

SOURCE: for 1957 to 1960, D.B.S., *Estimates of Labour Income, April, 1962*, table 5, p. 10; for 1926 to 1956, D.B.S., *Labour Income, 1926–1958*, table 7, p. 15.

See the note to series D238–253.

These series provide a provincial–regional breakdown of series D243 except that supplementary labour income has been excluded.

EARNINGS AND HOURS OF WORK
(Series D 280–411)
General note

The Dominion Bureau of Statistics provides, on a continuing basis, a large number of series on earnings and hours of work. This basic information is classified in a wide variety of ways which include: industrial, regional, provincial, and city breakdowns; earnings data (annual, weekly and hourly) classified by sex, and by status of the worker. Although an attempt has been made to include the more important series from the variety of sources available at D.B.S., many series have been omitted because of space limitations.

There are three basic surveys conducted by the Bureau from which all of these series are derived. (1) Census of industry surveys have been conducted annually since 1917. Among these is the Census of Manufactures which is the responsibility of the Industry and Merchandising Division of D.B.S. (2) The monthly survey of employment and payrolls is the responsibility of the Employment Section of the Labour Division of D.B.S. Data from this survey are available since 1921; but payroll information was not elicited prior to 1941. Payroll information was subsequently made available back to 1939 on an annual basis. The monthly survey provides average annual and weekly earnings data for all employees of the covered establishments (this information appears in the D.B.S. monthly publication *Employment and Payrolls*); since 1945, data are obtained on man-hours and hourly earnings (this information appears in the D.B.S. publication *Man-Hours and Hourly Earnings*) for the group of employees in the responding establishments for whom the employers keep records of the actual hours worked. The monthly survey does not attempt to cover all industries and only those establishments which customarily employ 15 or more employees are included. (3) An annual survey is conducted of the manufacturing establishments included in the monthly survey described under (2). This survey was transferred to the Employment Section of the Labour Division in 1946, superseding a somewhat similar inquiry previously made by the Census of Manufactures discussed elsewhere in this volume. In 1946 and 1947, the survey related to the last week in November. Beginning in 1948 it has related to the final week in October. Previously, the record prepared by the Census of Manufactures had related to one week in the month of highest employment in the various establishments. The purpose of this October survey has been to obtain additional detail on hours and earnings. The information gathered is published in D.B.S., *Earnings and Hours of Work in Manufacturing*.

While the Census of Manufactures is discussed elsewhere in this volume a few general remarks concerning items (2) and (3), above, are in order. The basic limitation of the monthly employment surveys is the limited industrial and establishment coverage. Some industries are not covered at all, such as agriculture, fishing and trapping. Others, such as services, are covered only partially (government, health, education services are covered by other Divisions in D.B.S. for example). The coverage within the industries that come within the purview of the monthly survey is uneven, as described in the note to series D343–360. In industries where a large proportion of total employment is in a large number of small establishments (such as trade and services) the coverage is substantially less than in highly concentrated industries, such as mining. The employment and payrolls totals in the industries characterized by many small establishments may be distorted by the failure to take into the survey new establishments as they emerge, although a conscientious attempt is made to deal with this intractable problem.

No information is published on the response rate to the survey although it is understood to be over 95 per cent. The characteristics of the non-respondents are known for manufacturing, mining and a few other industry groups covered by census-type surveys carried out elsewhere in the Bureau.

D280–287. Annual earnings in manufacturing industries, production and other workers, by sex, Canada, 1905, 1910 and 1917 to 1959

SOURCE: for 1948 to 1959, D.B.S., *General Review of the Manufacturing Industries, 1959*, table 33, pp. 79 and 80; for 1905, 1910 and 1917 to 1947 inclusive the data were supplied directly by the Central Research and Development Staff, D.B.S. The last-mentioned data are revisions of the published data.

These series are derived from information obtained from the survey of manufacturers conducted annually by D.B.S. as part of its annual census of Industry and Merchandising. This census attempts to cover all Canadian manufacturing establishments.

Prior to 1925 the number of production workers was computed as the sum of the numbers recorded each month divided by twelve, whether the establishment was operating twelve months or not. Beginning with the statistics for 1925, in seasonal industries, the average was computed by dividing the sum of the production workers on the 15th of each month by the number of months in operation. This change in method increased the apparent number of employees in groups containing seasonal industries and in the over-all total. In 1931 the old method of computing the average number of production workers was again adopted.

In 1935 working proprietors were asked to report themselves

as salaried employees and to report their withdrawals for personal use with the earnings of supervisory and office employees. This practice has been continued in subsequent years. Prior to 1935 the number of working proprietors and their withdrawals were imputed on a rough basis by D.B.S.

Before 1949 there was no attempt made to cover the supervisory and office employees in head offices of companies if these were not in the same locality as an operating establishment of the company. This would result in an underestimate of the number and earnings of supervisory and office employees.

In 1937 and subsequent years travelling salesmen were specifically included with salaried employees. In 1930 the respondents were specifically asked to *exclude* salesmen as salaried employees. In other years the respondents were given no specific instruction with respect to their treatment of salesmen.

D288–296. Average annual, weekly and hourly earnings, male and female wage earners, manufacturing industries, Canada, 1934 to 1960

SOURCE: for 1960, D.B.S., *Earnings and Hours of Work in Manufacturing, 1960*, table 1, p. 17; for 1958 and 1959, D.B.S., *General Review of the Manufacturing Industries, 1959*, table 35, p. 84; for 1934 to 1957, D.B.S., *General Review of the Manufacturing Industries, 1958*, table 35, p. 82 except for series D296 for 1950 and 1951 found in D.B.S., *Earnings and Hours of Work in Manufacturing, 1958*, table 11, p. 44.

Series D288–296 provide a breakdown of series D287. However, the revisions in the latter series for the years prior to 1948 are not available for the former series. From 1934 to 1945, inclusive, all data refer to one week in the month of highest employment of all establishments covered by the annual D.B.S. census of manufactures. From 1946 to 1960 the weekly and hourly data are based on returns from the October survey of manufacturing establishments employing 15 or more. In 1946 and 1947 the weekly and hourly data apply to the last week in the month of November; since 1947 they refer to the last week in October. The annual average earnings for wage earners of both sexes continue to be derived directly from the D.B.S. census of manufactures and are based on the annual payrolls and the number of male and female wage earners of all reporting manufacturing establishments. The annual earnings are calculated on the basis of these figures, correlated with the weekly earnings of male and female wage earners as reported in the annual survey *Earnings and Hours of Work in Manufacturing* as compiled by the Employment Section of the Labour Division. For the method used in calculating annual earnings for males and females separately, see pages 84 and 85 of *General Review of the Manufacturing Industries of Canada, 1957*. The average annual earnings of males and females are estimated. The term 'wage earner' adopted in the table is used by the Employment Section of the Labour Division of D.B.S. and is roughly synonymous with the term 'production and related workers' adopted for series D284–287 which is used by the Industry and Merchandising Division of D.B.S. in the annual survey of manufacturers.

D297–305. Average annual, weekly and hourly earnings, male and female salaried employees, manufacturing industries, Canada, 1946 to 1960

SOURCE: for 1960 for all series and for D301 for 1958, D.B.S., *Earnings and Hours of Work in Manufacturing, 1960*, table 2, p. 20; for 1958 and 1959, D.B.S., *General Review of the Manufacturing Industries, 1959*, table 38, p. 89; for 1946 to 1957, D.B.S., *General Review of the Manufacturing Industries, 1958*, table 38, p. 87.

These series provide a breakdown of series D283. However, the revisions for the latter series for the years prior to 1948 are not available for the former series. As described in the note to series D 280–289, the annual data for salaried employees of both sexes, series D 297, are obtained from the annual census of manufacturing establishments. The weekly and hourly data are based on survey of manufacturing establishments employing 15 or more conducted in the last week of October each year, except in 1946 and 1947 when it was the last week in November. The average *annual* earnings of males and females are estimated. The term 'salaried employees' used in the table has been adopted by the Employment Section of the Labour Division of D.B.S., and is generally equivalent to the term 'supervisory and office employees' used in series D 280–283 which has been adopted by the Industry and Merchandising Division of D.B.S. in the annual census of manufactures.

See also the notes to series D 280–287 and series D 288–296.

A breakdown of the average weekly earnings of salaried employees in manufacturing into managerial and professional and office employees is given in the following table.

Average weekly earnings of managerial, professional and office employees, manufacturing, 1951, 1954 and 1957

(dollars)

	Managerial and professional employees			Office workers		
Year	Both sexes	Male	Female	Both sexes	Male	Female
1957	124.53	126.47	72.24	67.98	81.08	50.80
1954	109.67	111.14	64.89	59.29	70.94	44.16
1951	98.38	99.73	57.04	51.14	60.68	37.77

SOURCE: D.B.S., *General Review of the Manufacturing Industries, 1958*, table 41, pp. 92–3.

These figures provide a breakdown of series D 298, D 301 and D 304. The data in these three series, as described earlier in this note, are obtained from the annual October survey of manufacturing establishments employing 15 or more. The data used to obtain the breakdown between managerial and office workers are also obtained in the same annual October survey, but on a three-year-cycle basis only, until 1960.

D 306–318. Percentage distribution of employees in manufacturing industries, by classes of weekly earnings, selected years, 1934 to 1959

SOURCE: for 1959, D.B.S., *General Review of the Manufacturing Industries of Canada, 1959*, table 43, p. 97; for other years, D.B.S., *General Review of the Manufacturing Industries, 1957*, table 42, p. 98. The basic source document is D.B.S., *Earnings and Hours of Work in Manufacturing*, but changes in class intervals have made it impossible to obtain consistent series on the earlier basis.

These series provide frequency distributions of the same data for which averages are given in series D 292, D 295, D 301 and D 304. From 1934 to 1944 information on frequency distributions in a range of earnings was collected through the annual census of manufactures for one week in the year from virtually all establishments in the industry. In 1950 and triennially thereafter, data were collected in the October survey of establishments with 15 employees or more.

D 319–326. Annual averages of hourly earnings of hourly rated wage earners, selected industry groups, Canada, 1945 to 1960

SOURCE: for 1960, D.B.S., *Review of Man-Hours and Hourly Earnings, 1945–60*, table 1, pp. 10–11; for 1946 to 1959 from D.B.S., *Review of Man-Hours and Hourly Earnings, 1945–1959*, table 1, pp. 10–11; for 1945 data see table 9, pp. 27–30 of the same source.

The data for these series are obtained from the monthly survey of establishments employing 15 or more. The statistics relate, in the main, to hourly rated wage earners or production

and related workers employed full time and part time. Wage earners whose earnings do not *directly* depend upon the number of hours worked, such as route drivers and many piece-rate workers, are excluded where employers cannot furnish statistics of hours for such workers. The number of workers covered is therefore less than the number included in the October survey of establishments with 15 or more employees as reported in *Earnings and Hours of Work in Manufacturing*.

The annual averages are averages of the returns made for the last pay period in each month. Earnings include overtime work, incentive bonuses, and cost-of-living bonuses (if paid on a regular basis). Earnings are before deductions. The value of board and lodging, even if part of the remuneration of workers, is not included; nor are employer contributions made on behalf of the employee such as unemployment insurance and workmen's compensation. Series D 326 includes hotels, restaurants, laundries, dry cleaning and pressing plants and recreational services.

D 327–334. Annual averages of hours per week of hourly rated wage earners, selected industry groups, Canada, 1945 to 1960

SOURCE: for 1960, D.B.S., *Review of Man-Hours and Hourly Earnings, 1945–1960*, table 3, pp. 14–15; for 1946 to 1959, D.B.S., *Review of Man-Hours and Hourly Earnings, 1945–1959*, table 3, pp. 14–15; for 1945 see table 9, pp. 27–30 of the same source.

See the notes to series D 319–326 which are comparable with series D 327–334. All paid hours falling in the reported pay periods, such as paid sick leave and paid vacations and holidays, are included in these series. Overtime hours are included. The annual data are averages of the monthly returns for the last pay period in the months January to December. Series D 334 includes the same items as series D 326 (see above).

D 335–342. Averages of weekly wages of hourly rated wage earners, selected industry groups, Canada, 1945 to 1960

SOURCE: for 1960, D.B.S., *Review of Man-Hours and Hourly Earnings, 1945–60*, table 2, pp. 12–13; for 1946 to 1959 from D.B.S., *Review of Man-Hours and Hourly Earnings, 1945–1959*, table 2, pp. 12–13; for 1945 see table 9, pp. 27–30 of the same source.

See the notes to series D 319–326, which are comparable with series D 335–342.

D 343–360. Annual averages of weekly wages and salaries, selected industry groups and composite, Canada, 1939 to 1960

SOURCE: series D 345–346 and D 352–355 for 1939 to 1946 are from D.B.S., *Employment, Payrolls and Weekly Earnings, January 1949–June 1953 with Historical Series*, table 16, pp. 88–91; for 1948 and 1949 from D.B.S., *Review of Employment and Payrolls, 1957*, table 16, pp. 62–3; for 1950 to 1954 from D.B.S., *Review of Employment and Payrolls, 1958*, table 18, pp. 62–3; for 1955 to 1959, from D.B.S., *Review of Employment and Payrolls, 1959*, table 10, pp. 36–7; for 1960, D.B.S., *Review of Employment and Payrolls, 1960*, table 8, pp. 34–5. All other series are from the last-named source, table 13, p. 48.

The information given in these series is gathered through a monthly survey conducted by D.B.S. of establishments with 15 or more employees. The Employment Section of the Labour Division of D.B.S. which conducts the survey has estimated that the coverage of the Employment and Payrolls survey at 1 June 1951, in terms of the proportion of all paid workers, was as shown in the table on p. 79.

The respondents are asked to include all salaried and other employees excluding only owners and persons employed for less than one day or an equivalent number of hours in the reported

Coverage of employment on payrolls survey as a percentage of all paid workers, by industry, at 1 June 1951

Industry	Per cent of paid workers covered
Forestry (chiefly logging)	76
Mining (includes milling, quarrying and oil wells)	96
Manufacturing	92
Transportation, storage and communications	89
Construction	82
Public utilities	72
Trade	57
Finance, insurance and real estate	81
Services[1]	45
All industries included	79
All industries	62

SOURCE: Employment Section of Labour Division of D.B.S.

[1] Services includes mainly hotels, restaurants, laundries, dry-cleaning plants, recreational and business services.

pay period. Gross payrolls disbursed to these workers for their last pay periods in the month are reported (before deductions). These earnings therefore include overtime pay, bonuses, allowances and commissions (if paid on a regular basis) and amounts paid absent employees. Employees on strike or laid off because of an industrial dispute are not included unless they draw pay from their employer during the period. Earnings do not include board and lodging, employer contributions made on behalf of the employee or bonuses paid at irregular or infrequent intervals. In the years 1950 to 1959 the data are averages of the returns for the last pay period in the months January to December, inclusive. In earlier years the data for a given year are averages of the returns for the last pay period in December of the previous year to November of the given year, inclusive.

D 361–376. Percentage distribution of male and female wage earners in manufacturing, by hours worked per week, Canada, 1946 to 1958

SOURCE: D.B.S., *Earnings and Hours of Work in Manufacturing*, for the years to which the data apply.

These data are based on material obtained in the annual survey of manufacturing establishments employing 15 or more persons. In 1946 and 1947 data apply to the last week in November; in subsequent years data apply to the last week in October.

See also the notes on series D 288–296.

D 377–389. Percentage distribution of wage earners in manufacturing working specified number of hours in one week in the month of highest employment, by sex, Canada, 1938 to 1945

SOURCE: data for 1938, 1939 and 1942 to 1945 are from D.B.S., *General Review of the Manufacturing Industries, 1957*, table 29, p. 74 except for series D 389; data for 1940 and 1941 are from *Canada Year Book, 1943–1944*, p. 392, except for series D 389; series D 389 was supplied by the Employment Section, Labour Division, D.B.S.

These data are based on returns made by all manufacturing establishments to the annual census of manufactures. In this source the term 'production workers' is used. For consistency the term 'wage earners' has been used here.

Because overtime was excluded in 1938 and 1939, data for later years are not consistent. By month of highest employment is meant the month of highest employment of the reporting establishment. The weeks reported varied among establishments in any year and changed from year to year for the same establishment. Series D 389 does not agree with series D 284 and D 285 because the latter two series are based on annual averages while the former is based on month of highest employment.

D 390–402. Percentage distribution of wage earners in manufacturing working specified number of hours per week in the month of highest employment, Canada, 1932 to 1937

SOURCE: *Canada Year Book, 1942*, table 19, p. 386. The percentages have been calculated for these series from the actual numbers of wage earners given in the source.

These data are based on returns made by all manufacturing establishments to the annual census of manufactures. The hours worked exclude overtime.

See also the notes to series D 280–287.

D 403–405. Average weekly hours of all salaried employees in manufacturing, by sex, Canada, 1946 to 1960

SOURCE: D.B.S., *Earnings and Hours of Work in Manufacturing, 1957, 1959* and *1960*, pp. 38, 23 and 20 respectively.

The data of this table are based on the annual survey of manufacturing establishments employing 15 or more employees. The employees covered include office workers and managerial and professional employees. The average weekly hours are for the last week of October in 1948 to 1959; for 1946 and 1947 they are for the last week in November. Average weekly hours are published separately for office workers for 1951, 1954, 1957 and 1959 in the source publications for these years. They are so close to those for all salaried employees that they are not shown separately.

See also the notes to series D 297–305.

D 406–411. Average hours worked by persons with jobs, Canada, 1926 to 1955

SOURCE: based upon data prepared under the direction of T. M. Brown, formerly of the Department of Trade and Commerce, now at Queen's University, Kingston, in connection with his work on econometric models for Canada.

These data are given only to 1955. The Productivity Research Section of the Industry and Merchandising Division, Dominion Bureau of Statistics, is in the process of developing data on average hours worked per week and total annual hours for the commercial nonagricultural economy starting with 1947: the resulting estimates may revise the data given here. In particular, the hours worked per week, given in the labour force survey reports, are in class ranges of hours. In the preparation of the data given here, special tabulations of the results of each survey in 1949 were used to determine the distribution of numbers working various hours within each class range. These results were used to estimate average hours worked within each class range for the period 1946 to 1955. The work of D.B.S. will also use data on numbers within class ranges in some later year or years.

The estimates for the nonagricultural sector were prepared on two bases: the first method was used for the period 1926 to 1945; the second method was used for the later period when the labour force survey data became available. For the earlier period employment estimates were based on the decennial censuses interpolated by employment estimates taken from D.B.S., *Employment and Payrolls*. No attempt was made to take seasonal variations into account in estimating monthly employment in these years. Hours were estimated from the Department of Labour, *Wages and Hours of Labour in Canada* and *The Labour Gazette* and the hours data supplied by the annual census of manufactures and the Employment Section of the Labour Division, D.B.S. Because the wages survey only contains estimates of standard hours, and the census of manufactures is limited in coverage, and for many years in the period excluded overtime hours, these estimates of average hours worked per week and per year by paid workers are necessarily precarious. An attempt was made however to utilize all available information.

With the development of the labour force survey in late 1945, first on a quarterly and later on a monthly basis, it became possible to make much more refined estimates because both more reliable employment estimates were provided and respondents reported to the survey with respect to hours worked. The estimates have been based in part on special tabulations of the labour force survey data provided to the Economics Branch of Trade and Commerce by D.B.S. Seasonal variations are taken into account as are the statutory and conventional holidays.

The estimates of average hours worked per week and per year by persons with jobs in the agricultural sector prior to 1945 are extremely rough, and virtually no published data are available. The average man-hours per week in this earlier period were derived almost entirely from personal estimates of individuals intimately acquainted with agricultural practices in Canada. The estimates for the years since 1945 are, of course, based on the labour force survey and are much more reliable.

STATISTICS OF LABOUR UNIONS AND STRIKES AND LOCKOUTS (Series D 412–433)

General note

The statistics of union membership and strikes and lockouts have been collected by the federal Department of Labour established in 1900 under the Conciliation Act, 1900. Included in its chief duties were the administration of certain provisions of the Conciliation Act 'designed to aid in prevention and settlement of labour disputes' and 'the collection and classification of statistical and other information relative to the conditions of labour' (*Canada Year Book*, *1920*, p. 525). The Department collected data on strikes and lockouts from the beginning; it was only with 1911 that the information it gathered on union membership was sufficiently complete to permit publication of a total.

For a short description of the history of the labour movement in Canada see the *Canada Year Book*, *1957–58*, pp. 795–802.

D412–413. Union membership in Canada, showing those with international affiliation, 1911 to 1960

SOURCE: for series D412, years 1911 to 1958, federal Department of Labour, *Labour Organization in Canada*, *1958*; for 1959 and 1960 from the 1960 report; for series D413 from estimates prepared by Dr J. T. Montague of the Department of Labour from information contained in the annual reports.

Until 1959 no specific definition of a trade union had been adopted by the Department for statistical purposes so that the coverage probably was not entirely consistent from year to year. However, because the vast majority of union members belonged to trade organizations which posed no definitional problems, the marginal cases were not of great numerical importance and probably do not affect the trend significantly.

D414–425. Union membership by congress affiliation, 1942 to 1960

SOURCE: federal Department of Labour, *Labour Organization in Canada*, for the years to which the data apply.

The international affiliations of Canadian unions in the period covered were with either the American Federation of Labor (AFL) or with the Congress of Industrial Organizations (CIO), both having their membership mainly in the United States.

From 1942 to 1947 inclusive, the split in membership between 'other' unaffiliated international unions, series D423, and 'unaffiliated national, regional and local unions', series D425, was not given in the reports. In each of these years the total membership of the 'other' unaffiliated membership was determined from the data given in the table entitled 'International Unions; Number of Branches and Membership' in the annual reports, *Labour Organization in Canada*. This total was then subtracted from the item 'Unaffiliated National and International Unions'. This residual, together with the items giving the membership in national, regional or local unions, is given in the table as 'Unaffiliated National, Regional and Local Unions'.

Similarly, from 1942 to 1947, inclusive, the splits in membership between TLC only, series D415, and TLC/AFL, series D416, or CCL only, series D418, and CCL/CIO, series D419, were not given in the annual reports cited above. The membership of TLC only was determined by summing the membership of: international unions affiliated with TLC in Canada but unaffiliated in the United States; TLC national union affiliate; TLC local and federal unions. The same procedure was used to determine the membership of unions affiliated with CCL only.

This table possibly could be pushed back to earlier years using the data available in the annual reports, but the changing forms of the report make this procedure much more precarious for the years prior to 1942.

See the note to series D412–413 for a discussion of the basic data problem. The definitional problem is largely confined to the data included in series D425.

D426–433. Number of strikes and lockouts, employers and workers involved and time loss, Canada, 1901 to 1960

SOURCE: series D426, D427, D429, D430 and D433 for 1945 to 1960 are from federal Department of Labour, *Strikes and Lockouts in Canada*, *1960*, table 1, p. 5; all other data are from the 1956 issue of the same publication, table 1, p. 6.

In 1958 all strikes and lockouts involving six or more workers and lasting at least one working day, and strikes and lockouts involving more than six workers and lasting less than one day or for more than one day and involving fewer than six workers but exceeding a total of nine man-days, are included in the series, if they come to the attention of the Department. Most of the information is obtained from reports of the Unemployment Insurance Commission. In earlier years the basis for inclusion in the series was unspecified.

The total number of workers involved includes the reported total number on strike or locked out, even if those on strike did not belong to the union. Workers laid off as the result of a work stoppage are not included.

Since 1956 the number of employers (Series D428) has been deleted because in some cases, for example, the 'employer' is a builders' exchange that comprises a multitude of individual contractors. Series D431 and D432 have also been dropped because the former was unreliable and the latter was difficult to interpret.

See the 'Explanatory Notes', pp. 26–7 of *Strikes and Lockouts in Canada*, *1958*, for additional details on concepts.

WORKMEN'S COMPENSATION (Series D 434–447)

General note

Workmen's compensation is under provincial jurisdiction. The data, therefore, are obtained from reports of the various provincial workmen's compensation boards.

D434-444. Industrial accidents, fatal and nonfatal, reported by provincial workmen's compensation boards, by province, 1928 to 1960

SOURCE: federal Department of Labour, *The Labour Gazette*. The data were published first in the March issue, 1931, and annually in the issues for the same months until 1945, in the April issues of 1946 to 1952, in the June issue, 1953, and in May issues thereafter. The full series given here may be found in the monthly issues for May 1962, May 1960, May 1956, April 1952, April 1951, April 1948, March 1943, March 1938, March 1935 and March 1933.

The principal limitation of these series is that they do not include accidents of workers not covered by workmen's compensation. For a number of provinces accidents which required 'medical aid only' were not reported in the early years; only accidents which required compensation were included. The source document provides details on the number of fatal accidents and the number that involved permanent disabilities.

D445-447. Provincial expenditures for workmen's compensation, 1921 to 1958

SOURCE: data for series D447 for the years 1921 to 1943 are from an unpublished table supplied by the federal Department of National Health and Welfare, Research Division, and are based on information provided by the National Income Section, D.B.S. For years 1947 to 1952 the data are from federal Department of National Health and Welfare, Research Division, *Government Expenditures and Related Data on Health and Social Welfare, 1947-1953*, table 9, p. 21 (second edition). For the years 1953 to 1958 the data are from the third edition of this report which covers the years 1947 to 1959, appendix 10.

The data give totals for all provinces. Prior to 1947 only the 'total' expenditures, and then only for some years, were available.

EMPLOYMENT SERVICE AND UNEMPLOYMENT INSURANCE (Series D448-470)

General note

Various provinces had employment services prior to 1919. These provided facilities, through local offices, for the listing of vacancies by employers, and for the listing of applications for work by persons seeking jobs. The Employment Offices Coordination Act of 1918 made provision for the federal government participating in the employment service, the Department of Labour being charged with the responsibility. The employment service was a joint Dominion-provincial operation from 1919 until July 1941, with the federal government being largely a coordinating agency. With the establishment of national unemployment insurance in 1941 the employment service became in the main a national responsibility and has been nationally operated from 1 August 1941.

A federal unemployment insurance scheme went into effect on 1 July 1941 under the Unemployment Insurance Act of 1940. Until 1940, measures concerning unemployment, involving as they did civil rights, were the responsibility of the provinces. An amendment to the British North America Act in 1940 permitted the federal government to undertake an unemployment insurance operation.

D448-450. Monthly averages of applications, vacancies and placements by federal employment offices in regular and casual work, 1919 to 1960

SOURCE: prior to July 1941, data are from the Dominion-Provincial Employment Service published regularly in *The Labour Gazette* beginning with the issue for July 1919. From 1 July 1941 the data are from monthly issues of *The Labour Gazette* and are based on returns made by the Unemployment Insurance Commission on form 751.

These series should be interpreted with extreme caution, for they are a by-product of administrative procedures and may reflect changes in those procedures as well as in underlying conditions. In particular it should be borne in mind that the applications and vacancy statistics are probably affected by prevailing employment conditions. With persistent and widespread unemployment, employers have ample applicants for jobs and may not register their vacancies with an employment agency. Similarly, under these conditions workers who are not entitled to unemployment benefits may not apply for jobs with the employment agency after repeated disappointments.

Placements include casual as well as regular placements. From April 1943 to 27 March 1952 placements included 'transfers in' only. The definition of the placement was changed on 28 March 1952. Subsequent to that date placements included 'transfers out' (confirmed transfers between local National Employment Service Offices in which one office refers an applicant to a vacancy registered at another local office).

The substantial increases in the series in 1942 arose because of compulsory registrations of workers and vacancies during the war. See *The Labour Gazette*, May 1942, p. 551, June 1942, p. 675 and September 1942, p. 1018.

D451-464. Number of persons insured with unemployment insurance commission, by industry, at book renewal periods, 1942 to 1960

SOURCE: the basic source document is D.B.S., *Annual Reports on Benefit Periods Established and Terminated* for the years to which the data apply. However, the series reproduced were provided directly by the Unemployment Insurance Section, Labour Division, D.B.S., in August 1960.

There have been important changes in the industrial coverage of the Unemployment Insurance Act. The sharp changes in series D453 and D454 were the result of extensions of coverage. Consult the annual issues of the source cited above for a description of these changes and the *Supplement* to the *Statistical Report on the Operation of the Unemployment Insurance Act, 1954-1958*. The appendices to the *Supplement* describe the basic changes in the provisions and terms of the Unemployment Insurance Act.

The estimates of insured persons by industry are based on a 10 per cent sample of book renewals.

There are some discrepancies from the published data. The material given here is based on the original data.

D465-470. Unemployment insurance, insured population and beneficiary and claimant data, 1942 to 1960

SOURCE: The basic source document is D.B.S., *Statistical Report on the Operation of the Unemployment Insurance Act* monthly. However, the series given were supplied directly by the Unemployment Insurance Section, Labour Division, D.B.S., August 1960.

Like series D448-450, these series must be interpreted with extreme caution because they reflect changes in administrative procedures.

Series D465 does not equal series D451 because the latter is a count of the insured population at a particular date while the former is an average of the insured population counts each month. The insured population includes both contributors and claimants.

The number of initial and renewal claims, series D466, shows the number of new cases of recorded unemployment among insured persons during the year. However, to the extent that the initial claims include requests for re-establishment of a benefit period following an uninterrupted period on claim this series overstates the number of new cases of recorded unemployment.

The average number of claimants includes those claiming either regular, seasonal or fishing benefits and is a yearly average of the month-end count.

The number of beneficiaries, series D468, is an average of the weekly data and includes the number of persons who have received one or more benefit payments.

For further description of the meanings of terms consult the 'Glossary of Terms' included at the end of each monthly report.

APPENDIX TO SECTION D

WAGE RATES AND INDEXES OF WAGE RATES, SELECTED OCCUPATIONS IN THE CONSTRUCTION INDUSTRY IN ONTARIO, 1889 to 1903 (Series D471–488)

D471–484. Total number of days worked and average daily wage rates in selected occupations, Ottawa and Toronto areas, 1889 to 1903

SOURCE: Robert E. Olley, *Construction Wage Rates in Ontario, 1864–1903*; for the Ottawa area, table 1, pp. 13–14; for the Toronto area, table 2, pp. 16–17. The entries in series D482 for 1901 and 1902 are from table A-3, p. 93.

These data are derived from the Auditor General's Reports on public expenditure by the federal government. They therefore represent wage rates paid by the latter. The Auditor General throughout this period, J. L. McDougall, reported public expenditures in great detail, giving usually for each employee of the federal government the name, capacity, time worked, wage rate, and earnings. Those for whom such information was given included construction workers and labourers. The material prepared by Olley, presented in series D471–484, is based on the latter data.

While Olley obtained all relevant material from the reports on all departments of government the main body of entries was found in those sections of the reports applying to the Department of Public Works and the Department of Railways and Canals. The workers for whom the data were available were, in the main, employed on canal maintenance, building maintenance, harbour and wharf works and routine repair construction jobs. Larger projects, such as construction of new canals or public buildings, were let on contract and no relevant data are available for them.

The more well-settled parts of Ontario were divided into two areas called the Ottawa area and the Toronto area. The Ottawa area included Eastern Ontario. Its western boundaries were the Lennox and Addington county line (between Kingston and Belleville) as far north as it goes and then diagonally north to Mattawa on the Ottawa River (west of the City of Ottawa). The Toronto area is the remainder of Ontario except the north and northwest. Its northern boundary was a line from Mattawa northwest to Lake Nipissing and then west to the north end of Georgian Bay. There was more building work characteristic of large cities in the Ottawa area than in the Toronto area owing to the presence in Ottawa of the federal government and its major buildings. Construction in the Ottawa area also included a considerable amount of work on the St Lawrence and Rideau canals. Construction in the Toronto area was more frequently characterized by work on small dispersed projects. The largest of these was almost always work on the Welland Canal.

Average daily wage rates were calculated for six occupations:

carpenter, painter, mason and bricklayer, plasterer, stonecutter and labourer. However, owing to the limited amount of data for plasterers and stonecutters in the two areas and for masons and bricklayers in the Toronto area, Olley regarded the results for these occupational groups as uncertain and they are not presented here. The estimates for the class 'labourers' in both areas are probably the most reliable. Carpenters' wages are next in reliability. The rates for painters in the Toronto area are the least reliable. The entries for the Ottawa area for masons and bricklayers in 1889 and painters in 1889 and 1890 must be viewed with some scepticism.

Great care was given to making the wage rates as widely representative as possible. Workers for whom data are included were paid by the day. Civil employees, such as lockmen, who were employed on a yearly basis, were not included. The information in the Auditor General's reports was given in a way that made impossible an accurate separation of construction labourers from non-construction labourers. Hence, all labourers employed by the day were included, even though some, a relatively small proportion of the total, were employed on other than construction projects. Tradesmen, whose income appeared to include some payment for management, were excluded.

With few exceptions, the reports of the Auditor General gave only payments for work by the day. Consequently, the wage data prepared by Olley are average daily wage rates. Wage payments by the hour appeared too infrequently to permit estimation of hourly rates and material on the length of the working day was limited. Olley believes, however, that the length of the working day did not change greatly in this period. However, he does state that there may have been a moderate tendency toward some shortening of the work day, on the average, toward the end of the period which he studied.

A common procedure was used in the calculation of the average daily wage rate for each occupation. Usually the number of men employed, the number of days worked, and the rate per day were given. With these data, the total wage bill for each occupation was calculated. The total wage bill was then divided by the number of days worked, the result being the estimate of the average daily wage rate.

The first calculations made by Olley produced an anomaly for carpenters' wages in the Toronto area in 1901 and 1902. The cause of this anomaly was that the data on carpenters engaged on harbour work were unusable in these two years though usable in all other years. Carpenters on harbour work were paid less than other carpenters and their exclusion in 1901 and 1902 artificially raised the calculated wage rates in these years. Olley overcame this difficulty by adjusting the carpenters' wage rates in 1901 and 1902 on the basis of the movement of carpenters' rates in all construction activity other than that on harbour work. The adjustment took account of the movement of wage rates between 1900 and 1903 for which years the data on carpenters' rates on harbour work were quite usable. The adjusted rates for 1901 and 1902 are used in this volume.

D485–488. Combined indexes of wage rates of selected occupations in the construction industry, Ottawa and Toronto areas, 1889 to 1903

SOURCE: Olley, *Construction Wage Rates in Ontario, 1864–1903*; for series D485–486, table 17, p. 78; for series D487–488, table 20, p. 84. The entries in series D486 and D488 for 1901 and 1902 are from table A-5, pp. 94–5.

See the note to series D471–484 for the method of calculating the average daily wage rate for each occupation in each area and for the geographical extent of the two areas.

The combined indexes of average daily wage rates for each

occupation in each area were obtained by putting the wage-rate series in index form with base 1891 and then taking a weighted average of the indexes. The weights used to combine the several indexes were based on the relative numbers engaged in each occupation as recorded in the 1891 census for Ontario as a whole. This was the only feasible procedure since no occupational data for subdivisions of the province were available. The actual weights used were obtained for the Ottawa and Toronto areas separately by multiplying the numbers engaged in an occupation by the average wage rate for the occupation in each area in 1891, with the weights proportional to the hypothetical wage bill for each occupation in each area. This procedure is exactly analogous to weighting actual wage rates by numbers employed and then constructing a combined index.

The numbers engaged and the weights used for obtaining series D487-488 appear in the following table:

Numbers employed in Ontario and weights used in construction of combined indexes for four occupations

Occupation	Number in Ontario, 1891	Weight, Ottawa area	Weight, Toronto area
Mason and bricklayer	6,004	.1468	.1605
Carpenter	20,085	.3758	.3486
Painter	5,301	.0973	.0946
Labourer	31,930	.3801	.3963
Total	62,780	1.0000	1.0000

SOURCE: Olley, *Construction Wage Rates in Ontario, 1864–1903*, table 19a, p. 83.

The same weighting system, but with labourers excluded, was used for series D485-486.

Olley's adjusted figures for carpenters in the Toronto area for 1901 and 1902 were used in this volume (see the note to series D471–484).

Additional sources of historical data on wages and working conditions

In addition to the sources cited for series given in this section attention is directed to the following publications which include empirical data on wages and working conditions not given in this volume. The list does not attempt to be exhaustive. Province of Ontario, *Annual Reports of the Bureau of Labour*. The first report was for the year ending 31 December 1900. These reports gave detailed returns for each of a large number of manufacturing establishments in Ontario. The returns show the number of male and female employees, annual earnings, and average weekly wages for skilled and unskilled workers. Province of British Columbia, *Annual Reports of the Department of Labour*. The first report was for the year ending 31 December 1918. Frequency distribution of weekly wage rates and hours worked per week, by industry, for males and females, by age, were published for many years.

Report of the Committee Re Bill No. 21, *Journals of the House of Commons of the Dominion of Canada*, Session 1909–1910, appendix to vol. 45, part III. Discussion of procedures by which wage data were collected by the Department of Labour, Exhibit D, pp. 400–10 provides wages and hours per day for 14 building trades for 29 towns and cities.

Report on Phases of Employment Conditions in Canadian Industry, National Employment Commission (Purvis Commission), Ottawa 1937. Detailed information on working conditions at this time.

Series D1–11. *Index numbers of average wage rates for selected main industries, 1901 to 1960*

(1949 = 100)

| Year | General index | Logging | Coal mining | Metal mining | Manufacturing | | | Construction | Railways | Telephones | Personal service |
| | | | | | All manufacturing | Durable goods | Nondurable goods | | | | |
	1	2	3	4	5	6	7	8	9	10	11
1960¹	175.5	184.3	148.2	169.4	175.0	176.6	173.2	192.6	166.4	178.0	156.8
1959¹	168.9	176.2	147.3	164.3	168.9	170.8	167.0	180.7	165.7	—	146.1
1959²	169.5	176.5	147.8	165.5	169.9	172.1	167.7	180.7	165.7	178.7	144.9
1958	162.6	172.0	147.6	160.8	164.2	166.1	162.2	171.0	153.3	175.4	143.5
1957	156.5	168.4	137.4	156.2	158.6	160.7	156.3	160.7	153.3	165.9	138.9
1956	148.7	160.8	123.6	150.8	149.8	151.2	148.3	150.7	146.8	157.6	136.1
1955	141.7	138.2	122.8	140.3	142.2	143.7	140.7	145.4	137.8	152.8	132.3
1954	137.9	138.0	123.5	136.7	138.5	140.0	136.9	140.0	137.8	147.6	128.6
1953	133.6	135.5	124.0	132.3	134.6	136.3	132.8	136.2	137.2	136.6	123.3
1952	127.7	133.3	124.0	130.1	128.4	130.2	126.5	128.6	136.8	128.4	117.6
1951	119.1	109.6	111.1	121.6	120.3	121.7	118.8	118.6	121.9	115.7	110.6
1950	105.5	97.0	102.8	106.8	106.1	106.6	105.6	104.8	105.1	104.8	102.9
1949	100.0	100.0	100.0	100.0	100.0	100.0	100.0	100.0	100.0	100.0	100.0
1948	95.7	101.2	98.4	95.7	94.5	94.7	94.4	95.7	100.0	92.7	93.8
1947	84.9	90.2	85.0	87.2	84.1	84.9	83.5	84.1	83.6	87.3	87.4
1946	75.9	77.4	74.8	75.1	74.1	74.5	73.8	78.1	82.0	82.6	75.6
1945	69.3	70.9	74.6	70.9	67.2	68.2	66.5	71.2	73.7	82.9	69.4
1944	67.4	67.6	74.5	69.2	64.9	65.6	64.4	70.4	73.7	80.8	66.1
1943	65.3	66.2	63.6	68.1	62.8	63.6	62.1	69.3	73.7	80.5	65.3
1942	59.9	58.2	57.7	65.7	57.6	57.7	57.5	64.4	67.5	73.9	59.7
1941	55.3	52.7	55.8	62.1	52.9	52.0	53.6	60.6	64.3	70.2	56.7
1940	50.8	48.5	52.1	56.9	47.9	46.6	48.8	56.7	58.8	66.9	54.1
1939	48.9	46.3	51.0	55.3	45.9	45.1	46.5	54.3	58.8	66.0	51.3
1938	48.7	47.1	51.0	55.1	45.5	—	—	53.9	58.8	65.8	51.1
1937	47.3	43.4	48.8	54.8	44.1	—	—	52.6	56.4	65.0	50.4
1936	44.0	37.4	48.5	52.5	40.9	—	—	51.1	52.9	61.9	49.8
1935	43.2	33.8	48.4	51.2	39.9	—	—	50.8	52.9	61.4	49.5
1934	42.0	30.4	47.6	50.3	39.1	—	—	49.2	50.2	61.8	49.3
1933	41.6	26.5	47.3	49.0	38.0	—	—	50.2	51.7	58.0	49.7
1932	43.8	31.0	48.0	49.6	39.9	—	—	56.7	52.9	58.5	50.8
1931	47.2	37.7	49.5	51.2	42.7	—	—	62.3	57.3	62.7	52.1
1930	48.8	45.1	49.5	51.9	43.8	—	—	64.7	58.8	62.5	52.3
1929	48.5	45.7	49.4	51.9	43.8	—	—	62.9	58.8	62.2	52.2
1928	47.7	45.8	49.4	51.5	43.5	—	—	59.0	57.1	61.5	52.1
1927	47.1	45.2	49.1	51.6	43.2	—	—	57.0	57.1	60.3	51.7
1926	46.1	44.2	49.0	51.5	42.6	—	—	54.8	53.6	59.2	51.2
1925	45.8	44.0	49.0	51.6	42.4	—	—	54.2	53.6	58.8	50.8
1924	46.3	49.0	56.2	50.9	42.8	—	—	54.0	53.6	58.7	51.2
1923	45.7	43.2	57.8	50.8	42.5	—	—	52.9	53.6	58.5	51.1
1922	44.5	36.8	57.8	48.7	40.9	—	—	51.7	53.1	57.6	50.4
1921	47.7	47.3	60.9	52.7	43.8	—	—	54.2	56.3	60.6	49.9
1920	52.3	65.9	57.8	56.9	47.0	—	—	57.5	63.6	60.9	45.2
1919	44.0	58.9	49.9	48.9	39.0	—	—	47.1	52.9	—	38.5
1918	37.4	51.0	46.1	48.7	31.8	—	—	40.1	45.4	—	33.6
1917	31.9	44.3	38.2	44.9	27.7	—	—	35.0	35.8	—	29.1
1916	27.8	33.8	32.6	40.5	24.9	—	—	32.6	30.4	—	26.0
1915	26.0	28.3	29.9	36.6	23.0	—	—	32.2	29.3	—	24.4
1914	25.8	29.7	29.8	36.2	22.3	—	—	32.1	29.0	—	25.2
1913	25.5	31.8	29.2	36.1	21.7	—	—	31.8	28.8	—	24.1
1912	24.8	31.3	28.8	36.7	21.0	—	—	30.5	28.1	—	—
1911	24.0	30.3	28.5	34.9	20.7	—	—	28.7	27.6	—	—
1910	24.4	29.6	27.5	34.6	—	—	—	27.6	25.9	—	—
1909	23.6	28.6	27.8	35.0	—	—	—	26.4	24.9	—	—
1908	23.2	27.1	27.7	34.6	—	—	—	25.9	24.8	—	—
1907	22.6	27.9	27.3	34.1	—	—	—	25.5	23.3	—	—
1906	21.9	27.5	25.5	34.6	—	—	—	24.4	22.9	—	—
1905	21.1	26.4	25.2	32.5	—	—	—	23.2	21.4	—	—
1904	20.7	25.3	24.9	32.1	—	—	—	22.2	22.1	—	—
1903	20.2	24.9	24.9	32.9	—	—	—	21.4	21.6	—	—
1902	19.6	24.3	24.5	34.1	—	—	—	20.5	20.7	—	—
1901	18.6	23.8	24.2	33.8	—	—	—	19.2	19.8	—	—

¹ Expanded survey coverage. See general note to series D1–165.   ² 1958 survey coverage.

Series D12–39. *Index numbers of average wage rates for industry groups and selected components in manufacturing, Canada, 1939 to 1960*

Year	Food and beverages			Tobacco, cigars and cigarettes	Rubber products	Leather products	Textile products (except clothing)			Clothing (textile and fur)		
	All	Slaughtering and meat packing	Breweries				All	Cotton yarn and cloth	Synthetic and silk textiles	All	Men's and boys' suits and overcoats	Women's and misses' coats and suits
	12	13	14	15	16	17	18	19	20	21	22	23
Base 1949 = 100												
1960	176.4	181.6	207.8	198.0	164.3	164.0	157.6	160.2	151.1	156.2	161.3	149.5
1959[1]	170.5	176.5	198.1	193.3	159.7	159.4	150.3	150.3	145.1	152.5	155.2	150.8
1959[2]	170.8	178.8	198.1	193.3	160.2	161.6	151.3	151.0	145.4	153.4	155.8	148.7
1958	164.8	169.7	188.1	184.4	153.2	155.2	146.4	145.8	140.3	149.1	153.1	138.8
1957	156.7	161.4	181.3	174.6	150.4	151.5	141.6	143.0	133.8	144.0	148.3	135.6
1956	147.9	151.2	168.6	164.8	145.0	143.8	135.7	138.6	128.1	136.4	143.4	126.7
1955	140.3	144.2	157.9	160.3	139.6	134.5	131.0	131.5	125.3	129.7	133.3	125.2
1954	135.5	138.5	152.9	155.0	138.1	133.1	129.5	129.5	125.4	126.8	130.8	119.5
1953	131.2	136.3	148.1	152.0	134.9	129.9	128.1	128.7	124.3	124.9	130.0	110.9
1952	125.1	129.6	131.9	141.0	127.4	123.2	125.0	127.5	120.1	119.6	124.9	110.8
1951	117.5	125.4	117.7	135.1	124.3	115.3	117.6	117.1	115.7	112.8	116.9	101.1
1950	104.6	106.1	105.2	109.6	105.4	103.7	106.7	106.1	107.7	103.5	104.0	98.4
1949	100.0	100.0	100.0	100.0	100.0	100.0	100.0	100.0	100.0	100.0	100.0	100.0
Base 1939 = 100												
1952	—	299.0	267.4	351.0	277.0	279.0	—	312.4	305.7	—	257.3	226.9
1951	—	289.4	236.5	340.8	269.3	260.8	—	288.1	294.2	—	241.5	204.2
1950	—	245.2	210.4	281.8	228.8	235.4	—	262.0	256.2	—	216.0	203.8
1949	—	231.3	199.7	253.9	217.6	228.1	—	248.6	248.4	—	207.0	210.8
1948	—	217.0	182.9	232.2	213.7	219.3	—	230.6	218.2	—	214.8	206.3
1947	—	189.1	160.7	186.4	190.1	198.5	—	189.0	186.8	—	203.0	186.2
1946	—	165.4	148.4	156.9	167.7	167.5	—	161.6	164.7	—	182.1	176.2
1945	—	141.0	127.9	140.5	143.4	153.5	—	148.7	148.9	—	164.1	152.7
1944	—	137.3	123.5	140.3	139.8	145.4	—	139.1	147.0	—	151.9	137.5
1943	—	135.1	121.9	131.5	134.4	142.9	—	136.6	141.3	—	146.6	134.5
1942	—	119.0	117.1	120.4	127.1	134.8	—	128.1	129.0	—	129.8	131.8
1941	—	112.7	113.3	113.0	117.1	122.5	—	123.8	122.9	—	117.9	126.9
1940	—	103.2	103.9	102.8	102.1	105.9	—	109.6	106.8	—	107.2	101.7
1939	—	100.0	100.0	100.0	100.0	100.0	—	100.0	100.0	—	100.0	100.0

Year	Wood products	Paper products			Printing and publishing	Iron and steel products			Transportation equipment			Brass and copper products	Electrical apparatus and supplies	Clay products	Petroleum refining and products	Chemical products
		All	Newsprint	Boxes and containers		All	Agricultural implements	Heating and cooking apparatus	All	Motor-vehicles	Aircraft and parts					
	24	25	26	27	28	29	30	31	32	33	34	35	36	37	38	39
Base 1949 = 100																
1960	165.8	187.2	186.1	177.5	181.3	182.9	173.4	176.5	176.3	170.6	188.8	184.4	172.3	183.7	194.3	189.0
1959[1]	160.0	178.7	177.4	169.4	173.7	176.0	162.4	174.0	171.9	163.9	182.7	177.6	166.5	177.0	185.2	182.1
1959[2]	161.3	179.1	177.4	171.0	174.2	176.6	161.1	175.4	172.8	164.1	182.8	179.1	170.9	178.0	185.2	183.0
1958	155.6	175.4	173.4	167.3	166.3	170.9	162.1	172.2	165.1	156.6	178.4	175.3	166.2	173.5	178.4	177.3
1957	152.6	171.6	170.8	158.3	159.5	165.2	152.0	170.1	158.8	152.6	169.9	166.0	160.2	170.7	176.1	169.4
1956	142.9	162.7	162.7	149.3	152.5	156.4	143.5	161.4	149.9	142.7	163.6	153.7	149.9	161.0	164.0	160.2
1955	136.4	151.7	151.8	142.0	146.9	148.0	144.6	149.3	142.3	134.1	158.3	149.4	142.8	149.2	154.0	150.3
1954	132.6	145.5	144.4	138.2	142.8	143.3	142.5	145.2	140.0	130.0	154.2	145.4	139.5	144.7	147.5	146.2
1953	131.4	138.4	138.5	131.0	137.3	139.9	138.9	139.4	134.5	129.8	141.8	142.9	134.6	138.6	143.4	139.6
1952	128.4	129.9	128.8	126.2	130.0	133.7	137.3	132.0	128.3	125.7	133.9	132.2	130.1	126.1	137.6	133.1
1951	120.5	126.3	126.5	116.6	117.2	124.8	133.9	122.3	118.6	116.0	119.1	123.6	122.1	121.4	124.9	121.5
1950	107.1	105.6	105.3	102.3	108.1	107.3	110.8	107.7	104.9	105.2	105.8	109.9	106.1	105.7	107.2	107.9
1949	100.0	100.0	100.0	100.0	100.0	100.0	100.0	100.0	100.0	100.0	100.0	100.0	100.0	100.0	100.0	100.0
Base 1939 = 100																
1952	307.8	—	224.7	275.7	227.6	—	332.6	296.1	—	207.6	227.7	—	298.5	—	—	—
1951	293.2	—	220.4	259.7	204.9	—	321.0	276.1	—	191.9	212.1	—	281.6	—	—	—
1950	257.6	—	183.5	234.8	188.1	—	268.2	251.1	—	174.3	192.9	—	253.0	—	—	—
1949	238.8	—	175.6	223.4	173.9	—	242.5	234.2	—	165.9	181.8	—	239.6	—	—	—
1948	226.2	—	174.3	202.3	158.2	—	232.0	226.6	—	163.1	173.3	—	225.6	—	—	—
1947	205.2	—	158.4	175.8	138.9	—	207.3	192.0	—	151.1	162.9	—	195.5	—	—	—
1946	178.3	—	137.3	151.6	127.3	—	178.5	163.5	—	140.4	154.6	—	169.1	—	—	—
1945	156.1	—	120.9	138.5	118.5	—	157.5	155.4	—	130.3	148.7	—	156.8	—	—	—
1944	148.2	—	119.6	133.1	116.3	—	155.8	149.5	—	126.3	138.7	—	154.1	—	—	—
1943	142.9	—	115.4	128.9	113.7	—	151.9	143.5	—	122.7	134.0	—	149.2	—	—	—
1942	131.0	—	109.6	123.9	110.0	—	136.7	131.0	—	115.8	122.7	—	133.7	—	—	—
1941	117.7	—	107.7	115.5	105.8	—	117.6	115.6	—	108.6	109.5	—	123.2	—	—	—
1940	104.4	—	103.7	102.9	101.7	—	105.1	104.5	—	100.6	99.0	—	105.6	—	—	—
1939	100.0	—	100.0	100.0	100.0	—	100.0	100.0	—	100.0	100.0	—	100.0	—	—	—

[1] Expanded survey coverage. See general note to series D1–165.   [2] 1958 survey coverage.

Series D 40–59. *Hourly wage rates in selected building trades, by city, 1901 to 1960*

(dollars)

Year	Halifax				Montreal				Toronto			
	Carpenter	Electrician	Plumber	Labourer	Carpenter	Electrician	Plumber	Labourer	Carpenter	Electrician	Plumber	Labourer
	40	41	42	43	44	45	46	47	48	49	50	51
1960	2.02	2.27	2.21	1.45	2.35	2.45	2.62	1.75	2.90	3.40	3.41	2.00
1959	1.95	2.06	2.11	1.41	2.20	2.35	2.47	1.60	2.80	3.30	3.14	1.80
1958	1.905	2.01	2.02	1.37	2.10	2.20	2.32	1.50	2.50	3.00	2.79	1.70
1957	1.84	1.94	1.93	1.33	2.00	2.00	2.22	1.40	2.50	2.80	2.44	1.55
1956	1.77	1.87	1.86	1.26	1.90	2.00	2.12	1.30	2.40	2.65	2.44	1.45
1955	1.69	1.79	1.78	1.18	1.90	2.00	2.12	1.30	2.30	2.50	2.35	1.30
1954	1.61	1.71	1.70	1.10	1.80	1.90	2.00	1.25	2.25	2.43	2.35	1.25
1953	1.56	1.66	1.65	1.10	1.80	1.85	2.00	1.25	2.20	2.33	2.30	1.20
1952	1.48	1.58	1.55	1.06	1.70	1.80	1.794	1.15	2.10	2.20	2.15	1.10
1951	1.33	1.43	1.40	.91	1.55	1.65	1.70	1.00	2.00	2.15	2.00	1.10
1950	1.23	1.33	1.30	.81	1.40	1.50	1.58	.85	1.75	1.85	1.85	.95
1949	1.23	1.33	1.30	.81	1.25	1.35	1.55	.80	1.60	1.75	1.75	.95
1948	1.23	1.33	1.30	.75	1.25	1.35	1.45	.80	1.50	1.65	1.60	.85
1947	1.11	1.23	1.19	.64	1.06	1.11	1.15	.67	1.35	1.45	1.48	.78[1]
1946	1.05	1.17	1.13	.60	1.06	1.11	1.11	.67	1.20	1.35	1.30	.67
1945	.95	1.06	1.025	.52[1]	.96	1.01	1.01	.61	1.11	1.21	1.17	.67
1944	.95	1.06	1.025	.53[1]	.95	1.00	1.00	.60	1.07	1.17	1.17	.66
1943	.85	1.05	1.025	.53[1]	.95	1.00	1.00	.60	1.05	1.16[1]	1.16	.62
1942	.80	1.00	.95	.43[1]	.86	.92	1.00	.51	1.03	1.15	1.15	.62
1941	.80	1.00	.95	.38[1]	.81	.87	.90	.46	1.00	1.10	1.10	.45[1]
1940	.70	.95	.95	.35[1]	.77	.83	.85	.44	.95	1.10	1.00	.45[1]
1939	.70	.85	.85	.35[1]	.70	.75	.75	.40	.90	1.00	1.00	.43[1]
1938	.65	.85	.85	.35[1]	.70	.75	.75	.40	.95	1.00	1.00	.43[1]
1937	.60	.80	.75	.35[1]	.70	.75	.75	.40	.85	1.00	.90	.43[1]
1936	.60	.80	.75	.35[1]	.65[1]	.68[1]	.70[1]	.38[1]	.80	1.00	.90	.50
1935	.58[1]	.80	.75	.35[1]	.65[1]	.68[1]	.70[1]	.35[1]	.80	1.00	.90	.50
1934	.55	.80	.75	.35[1]	.45[1]	.58[1]	.63[1]	.28[1]	.70[1]	.93[1]	.85	.45[1]
1933	.55	.80	.78[1]	.35[1]	.48[1]	.65	.63[1]	.28[1]	.70[1]	1.00	.85	.43[1]
1932	.675	.85	.85	.38[1]	.68[1]	.75	.75	.35	.90	1.00	1.00	.40[1]
1931	.73	1.00	1.00	.38[1]	.70[1]	.83[1]	.90	.35	1.10	1.25	1.25	.50[1]
1930	.73	.90	.90	.40[1]	.80[1]	.83[1]	.90	.40[1]	1.10	1.25	1.25	.53[1]
1929	.73	.80	.85	.40	.83[1]	.75[1]	.85	.38[1]	1.00	1.15	1.25	.53[1]
1928	.66	.70	.70	.35	.73[1]	.70[1]	.85	.35[1]	1.00	1.00	1.125	.53[1]
1927	.60	.60	.65	.35	.70[1]	.70[1]	.73[1]	.35[1]	.90	.90	1.00	.50[1]
1926	.57	.60	.60	.30[1]	.70[1]	.65[1]	.75	.35[1]	.85[1]	.80	1.00	.50[1]
1925	.57	.60	.60	.33[1]	.70[1]	.65[1]	.73[1]	.35[1]	.85[1]	.80	1.00	.50[1]
1924	.57	.60	.60	.33[1]	.70[1]	.68[1]	.70[1]	.38[1]	.85[1]	.80	1.00	.53[1]
1923	.57	.60	.60	.33[1]	.66[1]	.68[1]	.70[1]	.40[1]	.88[1]	.80	.90	.53[1]
1922	.57	.60	.60	.33[1]	.58[1]	.58[1]	.70[1]	.33[1]	.80[1]	.80	.90	.53[1]
1921	.66	70	.70	.38[1]	.65[1]	.63[1]	.70[1]	.35[1]	.90	.875	.90	.55[1]
1920	.66	.70	.70	.43[1]	.675	.73[1]	.75[1]	.45	.90	.875	.90	.60[1]
1919	.66	.70	.70	.45	.60	.70	.55	.40	.73[1]	.75	.70[1]	.50
1918	.50	.50	.55	.40	.50	.45[1]	.425	.35	.63[1]	.675	.65	.45
1917	.40	.375	.40	.25	.50	.43[1]	.425	.30	.55	.55[1]	.50	.40
1916	.40	.375	.40	.25	.45	.40	.425	.30	.45	.48[1]	.475	.35
1915	.40	.375	.40	.25	.45	.40	.425	.30	.45	.40	.45	.30
1914	.35	.35	.385	.25	.45	.40	.425	.30	.45	.40	.45	.30
1913	.35	.35	.35	.25	.42	.35	.40	.30	.45	.40	.45	.30
1912	.34[1]	.30	.35	.2225	.40	.30	.375	.28	.40	.40	.40	.28
1911	.30	.26[1]	.30	.195	.35	.275	.35	.25	.37	.40	.40	.28
1910	.30	.26[1]	.30	.195	.30	.275	.35	.2225	.35	.35	.40	.28
1909	.27	.25	.25	.195	.29[1]	.28	.325	.2225	.33	.325	.40	.25
1908	.26[1]	.25	.25	.195	.275	.28	.32	.2225	.33	.325	.375	.25
1907	.26[1]	.20[1]	.25	.1667	.275	.25	.32	.20	.33	.325	.375	.25
1906	.25	.19[1]	.25	.1667	.275	.2225	.30	.20	.325	.325	.375	.25
1905	.25	.20[1]	.2225	.1667	.275	.2225	.25	.20	.325	.275	.35	.25
1904	.24[1]	.19[1]	.2225	.1667	.225	.2225	.25	.20	.30	.25	.325	.25
1903	.24[1]	.20	.2225	.15	.225	.20	.25	.175	.30	.25	.3225	.25
1902	.22	.185	.2225	.15	.20	.20	.25	.175	.30	.25	.30	.23
1901	.22	.15	.2225	.14	.175	.1667	.185	.15	.25	.23[1]	.275	.23

[1] A range of hourly wage rates for this occupation was published. To conserve space the arithmetic mean of the two items of the range was computed and rounded where applicable.

Series D40–59. *Hourly wage rates in selected building trades by city, 1901 to 1960 (continuation)*

(dollars)

Year	Winnipeg				Vancouver			
	Carpenter	Electrician	Plumber	Labourer	Carpenter	Electrician	Plumber	Labourer
	52	**53**	**54**	**55**	**56**	**57**	**58**	**59**
1960	2.50	2.75	2.80	1.65	2.92	3.26	3.14	2.19
1959	2.40	2.65	2.70	1.55	2.80	3.10	2.90	2.07
1958	2.30	2.55	2.60	1.45	2.68	3.10	2.90	1.95
1957	2.15	2.35	2.40	1.30	2.44	2.81	2.70	1.81
1956	2.05	2.20	2.25	1.20	2.25	2.42	2.55	1.66
1955	2.10	2.10	2.15	1.10	2.22	2.42	2.35	1.63
1954	1.90	1.90	2.00	1.05	2.22	2.38	2.35	1.60
1953	1.90	1.90	2.00	1.05	2.17	2.30	2.25	1.55
1952	1.80	1.90	1.90	.95	2.00	2.10	2.10	1.50
1951	1.65	1.65	1.75	.88	2.00	1.95	2.10	1.40
1950	1.50	1.50	1.65	.80	1.68	1.78	1.75	1.20
1949	1.40	1.40	1.55	.75	1.60	1.70	1.70	1.00
1948	1.35	1.35	1.50	.75	1.55	1.70	1.65	1.00
1947	1.25	1.25	1.35	.70	1.40	1.50	1.50	.90
1946	1.15	1.15	1.25	.63	1.25	1.35	1.35	.80
1945	1.05	1.05	1.15	.63[1]	1.12	1.19	1.19	.71[1]
1944	1.00	1.025	1.10	.59[1]	1.12	1.19	1.19	.73[1]
1943	1.00	1.025	1.10	.53[1]	1.12	1.17[1]	1.19	.68[1]
1942	1.00	.95	1.10	.48[1]	.99	1.09[1]	1.13	.59[1]
1941	.95	.95	1.05	.48[1]	.86[1]	.98[1]	1.125	.50[1]
1940	.85	.85	.95	.47[1]	.83[1]	.93[1]	1.00	.48[1]
1939	.85	.85	.95	.43[1]	.83[1]	.88[1]	1.00	.48[1]
1938	.85	.85	.95	.425	.83[1]	.88[1]	1.00	.48[1]
1937	.85	.85	.95	.425	.76[1]	.88[1]	1.00	.48[1]
1936	.75	.85	.90	.40[1]	.71[1]	.88[1]	1.00	.48[1]
1935	.75	.85	.90	.40[1]	.71[1]	.88[1]	1.00	.48[1]
1934	.75	.88[1]	.90	.40[1]	.75[1]	.88[1]	.88[1]	.43[1]
1933	.75	.95[1]	1.00	.38[1]	.76[1]	.88[1]	.95[1]	.43[1]
1932	1.00	1.00	1.15	.45[1]	.875	1.00	1.00	.45[1]
1931	1.00	1.00	1.15	.45[1]	1.00	1.09[1]	1.125	.50
1930	1.10	1.10	1.25	.46[1]	1.00	1.09[1]	1.25	.56[1]
1929	1.10	1.10	1.20	.46[1]	1.00	1.125	1.1875	.50
1928	1.05	1.00	1.125	.45[1]	1.00	1.00	1.125	.56[1]
1927	1.00	1.00	1.125	.45[1]	.9375	1.00	1.125	.56[1]
1926	1.00	1.00	1.125	.45[1]	.935	.95[1]	1.05	.51[1]
1925	.85	.85	1.00	.43[1]	.875	.88[1]	1.00	.51[1]
1924	.85	.85	1.00	.45[1]	.84[1]	.88[1]	1.00	.51[1]
1923	.85	.81[1]	.95[1]	.45[1]	.8125	.88[1]	1.00	.51[1]
1922	.85	.81[1]	.90	.45[1]	.8125	.83[1]	.95[1]	.48[1]
1921	.90	.90	1.00	.53[1]	.8125	.83[1]	.90	.56[1]
1920	1.00	.925	1.00	.58[1]	.89[1]	1.00	1.00	.63[1]
1919	.75	.75	.80	.50	.75	.75	.78	.55[1]
1918	.60	.70	.65	.38[1]	.70	.75	.75	.4725
1917	.55	.65	.59[1]	.35	.51[1]	.625	.625	.3125
1916	.50	.65	.55	.30	.45	.6225	.5625	.3125
1915	.48[1]	.65	.55	.275	.45	.625	.625	.3125
1914	.48[1]	.45	.55	.275	.5325	.625	.625	.375
1913	.48[1]	.45	.55	.275	.5325	.625	.625	.4375
1912	.48[1]	.45	.55	.275	.52[1]	.625	.625	.4375
1911	.45	.40	.50	.275	.50	.50	.625	.4375
1910	.45	.40	.50	.25	.50	.50	.625	.4375
1909	.45	.40	.50	.25	.4375	.50	.50	.375
1908	.38[1]	.35	.48[1]	.25	.4375	.50	.50	.345
1907	.38[1]	.35	.48[1]	.25	.4375	.4375	.50	.345
1906	.36[1]	.35[1]	.43[1]	.25	.4375	.4375	.50	.345
1905	.35	.30	.40	.25	.4375	.4375	.50	.345
1904	.35	.30	.40	.25	.40	.4375	.50	.345
1903	.35	.275	.40	.25	.40	.39	.50	.345
1902	.275	.225	.40	.22	.3333	.39	.40	.30
1901	.25	.225	.40	.20	.3333	.3333	.3366	.25

[1] A range of hourly wage rates for this occupation was published. To conserve space the arithmetic mean of the two items of the range was computed and rounded where applicable.

Series D 60–63. *Standard hours worked per week in selected building trades, five cities, selected years, 1905 to 1955*

Halifax

Year[1]	Carpenter 60	Electrician 61	Plumber 62	Labourer 63
1955		40[2,3]		
1950		40[2,3]		
1940	44	44	44	44–48
1935	44	44	44	44–48
1930	44	44	44	44–54
1925	44	44	44	44–54
1920	44–54	44	44	48–54
1915	54	48–54	50	54
1910	54	54	50	54
1905	54	54–60	50	54

Montreal

Year[1]	Carpenter 60	Electrician 61	Plumber 62	Labourer 63
1955		40[2,3]		
1950		40[2,3]		
1940	44	44	44	44–50
1935	40–48	40–48	40–44	40–48
1930	44–55	44–46.5	44	44–60
1925	44–60	44–46.5	44–49.5	50–60
1920	48	54	44	50
1915	54	54	54	54
1910	54	54	54	54
1905	54	60	54	60

Toronto

Year[1]	Carpenter 60	Electrician 61	Plumber 62	Labourer 63
1955		40[2,3]		
1950		40[2,3]		
1940	40	40	40	40–50
1935	40	40	40	40–48
1930	44	44	40–44	44–60
1925	44	44	44	44–60
1920	44	44	44	44–60
1915	44	44	44	44
1910	44	44	44	44
1905	44	44	44	44

Winnipeg

Year[1]	Carpenter 60	Electrician 61	Plumber 62	Labourer 63
1955		40–42.5[2]		
1950		40[2,3]		
1940	44	44	44	44–48
1935	44	44	44	44–48
1930	44	44	44	44–60
1925	44	44	44	50–60
1920	44	44	44	50–60
1915	50	44	44	60
1910	50–54	48–54	48	60
1905	53–54	54	48	60

Vancouver

Year[1]	Carpenter 60	Electrician 61	Plumber 62	Labourer 63
1955		40[2]		
1950		40[2]		
1940	40–44	40–44	40–44	40–48
1935	40–44	40–44	40–44	40–48
1930	44	40–44	40	40–44
1925	44	44	40–44	44
1920	44	44	44	44
1915	44	44	44	44
1910	44	44	44	44
1905	44	44	44	44

[1] No information is available for year 1945.
[2] Standard hours per week for all workers in the construction industry. Information was not available by trade.
[3] Labourers 40–50 hours per week.

Series D 64–73. *Comparison of specially computed weighted average hourly wage rates, published weighted average wage rates, and medians and means computed from published 'sample rates' for selected occupations in the pulp and paper industry, Canada, selected years, 1917 to 1951*

Year	Specially computed wage rates based on weighted averages of establishment data — Number of establishments 64	Number of employees for which rates reported by establishment 65	Wage rate (dollars) 66	Published wage rates — Wage rate (dollars) 67	As a percentage of computed rate 68	Sample wage rates — Number of sample rates 69	Median — Wage rate (dollars) 70	Median — As a percentage of computed rate 71	Unweighted mean — Wage rate (dollars) 72	Unweighted mean — As a percentage of computed rate 73
Grinderman (pulp)										
1951	48	657	1.35	1.34	99	—	—	—	—	—
1946	39	657	.82	.80	98	—	—	—	—	—
1941	34	573	.57	—	—	31	.56	98	.54	95
1936	31	706	.44	—	—	26	.44	100	.42	95
1931	19	495	.50	—	—	11	.46	92	.45	90
1926	18	437	.46	—	—	12	.45	98	.45	98
1921	15	484	.45	—	—	13	.48	107	.46	102
1917	3	77	.29	—	—	—	—	—	—	—
Digester cook (pulp)										
1951	49	165	1.79	1.76	98	—	—	—	—	—
1946	37	113	1.13	1.12	99	—	—	—	—	—
1941	37	117	.82	—	—	32	.92	112	.89	109
1936	35	106	.73	—	—	31	.74	101	73	100
1931	25	85	.71	—	—	8	.80	113	.71	101
1926	19	57	.71	—	—	8	.80	113	.72	101
1921	10	25	.64	—	—	9	.67	105	.64	100
1917	1	3	.62	—	—	—	—	—	—	—
Millwright (maintenance)										
1951	62	1,342	1.64	1.63	99	—	—	—	—	—
1946	55	934	.95	.96	101	—	—	—	—	—
1941	52	748	.71	—	—	33	.70	99	.73	103
1936	41	549	.53	—	—	26	.58	109	.59	111
1931	30	315	.68	—	—	9	.60	88	.64	94
1926	26	385	.64	—	—	10	.70	109	.68	106
1921	25	406	.60	—	—	12	.65	108	.62	103
1917	4	23	.34	—	—	—	—	—	—	—

Series D74–76. *Specially computed weighted average hourly wage rates for selected occupations in the pulp and paper industry, by province, selected years, 1917 to 1951*

(dollars)

Year	Grinderman (pulp)	Digester cook (pulp)	Millwright (maintenance)	Grinderman (pulp)	Digester cook (pulp)	Millwright (maintenance)	Grinderman (pulp)	Digester cook (pulp)	Millwright (maintenance)	Grinderman (pulp)	Digester cook (pulp)	Millwright (maintenance)
	74	75	76	74	75	76	74	75	76	74	75	76
	Nova Scotia and New Brunswick			Quebec			Ontario			British Columbia and Manitoba		
1951	1.24	1.85	1.67	1.23	1.70	1.56	1.39	1.81	1.71	1.49	1.86	1.74
1946	.70	1.12	.90	.77	1.09	.90	.82	1.13	1.04	.91	1.18	1.04
1941	.50	.84	.64	.49	.82	.66	.60	.80	.88	.64	.91	.80
1936	.37	.75	.46	.40	.75	.46	.47	.73	.76	.47	.60	.62
1931	.45	.69	.54	.43	.70	.54	.50	.75	.83	.53	.68	.69
1926	.46	.59	.49	.43	.77	.62	.50	.72	.72	.44	.68	.73
1921	.30	.67	.48	.44	.55	.54	.49	.67	.71	.27	—	.73
1917	—	—	—	.29	.62	.34	.30	—	.33	—	—	—

Series D77–105. *Hourly wage rates in selected occupations in the pulp and paper industry,[1] for Canada and by region, 1911 to 1920 and 1943 to 1960*

(dollars)

Year	Grinderman (pulp)	Digester cook (pulp)	Beaterman (newsprint)	Machine tender (newsprint)	Millwright (maintenance)	Grinderman (pulp)	Digester cook (pulp)	Beaterman (newsprint)	Machine tender (newsprint)	Millwright (maintenance)	Grinderman (pulp)	Digester cook (pulp)	Millwright (maintenance)	Grinderman (pulp)	Year	Grinderman (pulp)
	Canada					The Maritimes[2]					New Brunswick			Nova Scotia		Nova Scotia
	77	78	79	80	81	82	83	84	85	86	87	88	89	90		90
1960	1.96	2.58	2.18	3.73	2.44	—	—	—	—	—	1.81	2.34	2.31	1.29	1920	.36
1959	1.88	2.47	2.05	3.58	2.34	—	—	—	—	—	1.75	2.29	2.33	1.26	1919	.20
1958	1.83	2.43	1.90	3.52	2.33	—	—	—	—	—	1.73	2.26	2.28	1.22	1918	.18
1957	1.78	2.36	1.84	3.48	2.26	1.64	2.34	1.87	3.53	2.30	—	—	2.24	—	1917	.17
1956	1.69	2.25	1.73	3.31	2.15	1.58	2.23	1.80	3.38	2.20	—	—	2.15	—	1916	.17
1955	1.59	2.13	1.58	3.16	1.99	1.47	2.10	1.68	3.23	2.06	—	—	2.01	—	1915	.15
1954	1.52	2.03	1.52	2.99	1.92	1.41	2.02	1.56	3.04	1.97	—	—	1.92	—	1914	.15
1953	1.46	1.94	1.46	2.88	1.82	1.37	1.94	1.49	2.95	1.89	—	—	1.81	—	1913	.15
1952	1.38	1.82	1.35	2.69	1.67	—	—	1.35	2.95	—	1.30	1.72	1.64	1.01	1912	.15
1951	1.34	1.76	1.32	2.65	1.63	—	—	1.31	2.80	—	1.30	1.72	1.66	.94	1911	.15
1950	1.10	1.47	1.08	2.24	1.36	—	—	1.10	2.44	—	1.07	1.44	1.38	.85		
1949	1.04	1.40	1.02	2.16	1.26	—	—	1.01	2.38	—	1.00	1.35	1.26	.86		
1948	1.03	1.39	1.02	2.15	1.25	—	—	—	2.34	—	1.03	1.35	1.25	.82		
1947	.94	1.26	.91	1.99	1.10	—	—	—	2.20	—	.93	1.23	1.09	.79		
1946	.80	1.12	.75	1.79	.96	.70	1.09	—	2.01	.92	—	—	—	—		
1945	.66	1.00	.63	1.65	.82	.64	.96	—	1.85	.80	—	—	—	—		
1944	.65	.99	.63	1.63	.80	.65	.99	.62	1.86	.78	—	—	—	—		
1943	.61	.94	.62	1.63	.77	.59	.95	.57	1.80	.74	—	—	—	—		

Series D77–105. *Hourly wage rates for selected occupations in the pulp and paper industry,[1] for Canada and by region, 1911 to 1920 and 1943 to 1960 (continuation)*

(dollars)

Year	Quebec					Ontario					British Columbia				
	Grinder-man (pulp)	Digester cook (pulp)	Beater-man (news-print)	Machine tender (news-print)	Mill-wright (mainten-ance)	Grinder-man (pulp)	Digester cook (pulp)	Beater-man (news-print)	Machine tender (news-print)	Mill-wright (mainten-ance)	Grinder-man (pulp)	Digester cook (pulp)	Beater-man (news-print)	Machine tender (news-print)	Mill-wright (mainten-ance)
	91	92	93	94	95	96	97	98	99	100	101	102	103	104	105
1960	1.84	2.51	2.00	3.60	2.35	2.03	2.58	2.54	3.80	2.49	2.14	2.82	2.35	4.03	2.70
1959	1.79	2.43	1.97	3.49	2.26	1.92	2.45	—	3.62	2.35	2.05	2.72	2.28	3.76	2.56
1958	1.77	2.38	1.86	3.45	2.27	1.89	2.41	—	3.54	2.33	1.99	2.60	—	3.68	2.53
1957	1.75	2.35	1.76	3.48	2.22	1.85	2.37	1.98	3.46	2.30	1.82	2.34	1.90	3.38	2.24
1956	1.62	2.21	1.68	3.30	2.10	1.74	2.26	1.83	3.25	2.19	1.82	2.32	—	3.32	2.23
1955	1.51	2.10	1.53	3.16	1.90	1.63	2.12	1.69	3.11	2.05	1.75	2.21	—	3.16	2.17
1954	1.44	2.02	1.49	3.00	1.84	1.55	2.03	1.61	2.92	1.97	1.67	2.05	—	3.00	2.06
1953	1.37	1.91	1.41	2.84	1.74	1.50	1.92	1.50	2.85	1.87	1.62	2.00	1.55	2.97	1.93
1952	1.26	1.77	1.28	2.60	1.58	1.43	1.82	1.41	2.74	1.78	1.57	1.95	1.50	2.82	1.91
1951	1.25	1.77	1.29	2.58	1.57	1.38	1.73	1.35	2.70	1.69	1.49	1.86	1.41	2.75	1.81
1950	1.06	1.47	1.06	2.21	1.31	1.11	1.46	1.08	2.20	1.40	1.21	1.51	1.14	2.41	1.48
1949	.99	1.40	1.00	2.15	1.21	1.07	1.38	1.04	2.14	1.32	1.15	1.46	1.08	2.16	1.41
1948	.97	1.40	.99	2.14	1.18	1.06	1.37	1.05	2.08	1.32	1.15	1.42	1.15	2.32	1.42
1947	.88	1.26	.88	1.98	1.06	.96	1.24	.96	1.93	1.17	1.03	1.28	1.01	2.15	1.27
1946	.75	1.11	.72	1.79	.91	.82	1.12	.81	1.74	1.03	.91[3]	1.16[3]	.84[3]	1.93[3]	1.12[3]
1945	.62	1.01	.59	1.63	.77	.68	1.00	.68	1.63	.91	.76[4]	1.04[3]	.66[3]	1.75[3]	.96[3]
1944	.61	.98	.60	1.61	.76	.67	1.00	.68	1.59	.90	.74[4]	.98[4]	.66[4]	1.74[4]	.89[4]
1943	.55	.91	.54	1.58	.71	.67	.98	.66	1.62	.89	.74[4]	.98[4]	.67[4]	1.75[4]	.89[4]
1920	.38	—	.523	—	—	.58	—	—	.54	—	—	—	—	—	—
1919	.27	—	.415	—	—	.48	—	—	.45	—	—	—	—	—	—
1918	.24	—	.365	—	—	.405	—	—	.382	—	—	—	—	—	—
1917	.23	—	.295	—	—	.27	—	—	.255	—	—	—	—	—	—
1916	.18	—	.26	—	—	.225	—	—	.215	—	—	—	—	—	—
1915	.17	—	.235	—	—	.16	—	—	.16	—	—	—	—	—	—
1914	.17	—	.235	—	—	.19	—	—	.19	—	—	—	—	—	—
1913	.17	—	.235	—	—	.19	—	—	.19	—	—	—	—	—	—
1912	.17	—	.22	—	—	—	—	—	—	—	—	—	—	—	—
1911	.17	—	—	—	—	—	—	—	—	—	—	—	—	—	—

[1] See note, series D77–105 for the nature of the occupations.
[2] In 1953 and subsequent years Newfoundland included with Maritime Provinces.
[3] Figures are for Manitoba and British Columbia.
[4] Figures are for the Western provinces.

Series D106–110. *Hourly wage rates for selected occupations in the motor-vehicle industry, Ontario,[1] 1943 to 1960*

(dollars)

Year	Assemblers	Machine operators	Painters and enamellers	Body trimmers	Mill-wrights
	106	107	108	109	110
1960	2.14	2.11	2.20	2.19	2.45
1959	2.06	2.03	2.12	2.06	2.40
1958	1.98	1.95	2.03	2.03	2.20
1957	1.94	1.87	2.00	1.96	2.16
1956	1.80	1.74	1.88	1.86	2.08
1955	1.68	1.69	1.80	1.75	1.89
1954	1.63	1.66	1.73	1.70	1.85
1953	1.65	1.64	1.73	1.63	1.83
1952	1.60	1.61	1.66	1.61	1.79
1951	1.49	1.42	1.58	1.47	1.55
1950	1.35	1.34	1.37	1.35	1.38
1949	1.27	1.29	1.30	1.31	1.34
1948	1.26	1.28	1.27	1.27	1.35
1947	1.15	1.20	1.19	1.21	1.26
1946	1.07	1.10	1.11	1.12	1.15
1945	1.01	.97	1.06	.95	1.01
1944	.99	.96	1.00	.97	1.02
1943	.94	.95	.98	.96	.98

[1] Up to and including 1958 all of the reporting establishments were located in Ontario. Since that time establishments in Quebec, British Columbia and Manitoba supply some information to be found in the annual reports.

Series D 111–130. *Hourly wage rates and piece-rate earnings for selected occupations in the cotton industry, for Canada and by region, 1911 to 1920 and 1943 to 1960*

(dollars)

		Canada			
Year	Loom fixers (male)	Spinners (female)	Spinners (male)	Carders (male)	Twisters (female)
	111	112	113	114	115
Hourly wage rates					
1960	1.57	1.10	1.16	1.24	1.18
1959	1.49	1.12	1.19	1.21	1.10
1958	1.44	1.05	1.14	1.17	1.03
1957	1.37	1.02	—	1.13	1.13
1956	1.35	.92	—	1.07	.99
1955	1.30	.86	1.07	1.06	.97
Straight time earnings per hour, piece or incentive work					
1960	1.64	1.33	1.39	1.40	1.34
1959	1.55	1.24	1.29	1.33	1.27
1958	1.58	1.21	1.28	1.30	1.25
1957	1.59	1.20	1.28	1.29	1.25
1956	1.49	1.19	1.25	1.26	1.16
1955	1.42	1.10	1.17	1.22	1.19
Averages of hourly wage rates and hourly incentive earnings					
1954	1.35	1.05	1.16	1.14	1.09
1953	1.30	1.05	1.20	1.13	1.09
1952	1.30	1.04	1.19	1.08	1.05
1951	1.21	.95	1.00	1.00	.95
1950	1.10	.86	.96	.91	.86
1949	1.06	.81	.96	.88	.81
1948	1.00	.73	.92	.79	.72
1947	.87	.58	.77	.65	.59
1946	.76	.49	.57	.55	.48
1945	.71	.45	.51	.52	.44
1944	.667	.418	.491	.488	.428
1943	.662	.407	.460	.476	.412

	Nova Scotia and New Brunswick					Quebec					Ontario				
Year	Loom fixers (male)	Spinners (female)[1]	Spinners (male)[2]	Carders (male)	Twisters (female)	Loom fixers (male)	Spinners (female)[1]	Spinners (male)[3]	Carders (male)	Twisters (female)	Loom fixers (male)	Spinners (female)[1]	Spinners (male)	Carders (male)	Twisters (female)
	116	117	118	119	120	121	122	123	124	125	126	127	128	129	130
Hourly wage rates															
1960	—	—	—	—	—	1.59	1.08	1.14	1.17	—	1.59	1.26	—	1.34	1.19
1959	—	—	—	—	—	1.46	1.07	1.19	1.12	—	1.55	1.22	1.19	1.31	1.11
1958	—	—	—	—	—	1.41	1.00	1.03	1.13	1.01	1.52	—	—	1.30	1.13
1957	—	—	—	—	—	1.34	.97	—	1.10	1.00	1.46	—	—	1.27	1.18
1956	—	—	—	—	—	1.33	.85	—	1.05	.91	1.38	1.01	—	1.18	1.07
1955	—	—	—	—	—	1.24	.73	.96	1.03	.93	1.37	1.01	—	1.14	1.03
Straight time earnings per hour, piece or incentive work															
1960	—	—	—	—	—	1.63	1.36	1.40	1.41	1.45	1.75	1.29	1.33	1.44	1.31
1959	—	—	—	—	—	1.52	1.24	1.29	1.32	—	1.74	1.27	1.34	1.45	1.31
1958	—	—	—	—	—	1.55	1.25	1.27	1.28	1.21	1.69	1.18	1.29	1.35	1.28
1957	—	—	—	—	—	1.59	1.24	1.28	1.24	—	1.62	1.17	1.28	1.35	1.25
1956	—	—	—	—	—	1.49	1.24	1.25	1.24	1.22	1.57	1.12	1.19	1.31	1.16
1955	—	—	—	—	—	1.43	1.15	1.17	1.19	1.17	1.47	1.03	1.16	1.27	1.20
Averages of hourly wage rates and hourly incentive earnings															
1954	—	—	—	—	—	1.35	1.04	1.16	1.07	1.05	1.36	1.06	1.19	1.24	1.13
1953	1.27	.97	—	1.17	—	1.27	1.06	1.15	1.06	1.05	1.35	1.05	1.33	1.23	1.12
1952	1.37	1.00	—	1.22	—	1.28	1.04	1.12	1.02	1.05	1.35	1.05	1.57	1.19	1.07
1951	1.33	.93	—	1.09	—	1.17	.93	.93	.93	.92	1.28	.99	1.45	1.11	1.01
1950	1.12	.90	—	1.07	—	1.06	.84	.84	.85	.85	1.17	.89	1.25	.99	.87
1949	1.15	.84	—	1.09	—	1.00	.79	.83	.82	.80	1.13	.86	1.22	.93	.81
1948	.94	.66	—	.82	—	1.01	.74	.79	.76	.72	1.01	.74	1.14	.83	.73
1947	.91	.55	—	.66	.55	.83	.58	.66	.63	.61	.90	.59	.89	.69	.59
1946	.75	.45	—	.54	.41	.77	.50	.55	.55	.53	.73	.48	.67	.56	.48
1945	.70	.40	—	.48	.38	.71	.46	.52	.52	.47	.71	.43	—	.52	.44
1944	.675	.394	—	.472	.375	.677	.423	.485	.488	.442	.676	.410	—	.491	.424
1943	.679	.383	—	.444	.389	.659	.407	.458	.470	.412	.665	.413	—	.510	.423
1920	—	.304[4]	.455[4]	—	—	.449	.282	.461	—	—	.637	.324	—	—	—
1919	—	.272	.424	—	—	.399	.245	.401	—	—	.530	.245	—	—	—
1918	—	.235	.307	—	—	.363	.223	.364	—	—	.400	.185	—	—	—
1917	—	.180	.281	—	—	.273	.166	.274	—	—	.345	.185	—	—	—
1916	—	.139	.217	—	—	.252	.162	.254	—	—	.284	.153	—	—	—
1915	—	.126	.211	—	—	.239	.154	.240	—	—	.263	.145	—	—	—
1914	—	.121	.207	—	—	.239	.154	.240	—	—	.263	.145	—	—	—
1913	—	.111	.196	—	—	.237	.145	.223	—	—	.258	.130	—	—	—
1912	—	.103	.179	—	—	.225	.137	.211	—	—	.345	.125	—	—	—
1911	—	.091	.179	—	—	.209	.128	.196	—	—	.231	.117	—	—	—

[1] Ring spinners when specified.
[2] Mule spinners.
[3] Mule spinners 1911 to 1920; ring spinners 1943 to 1959.
[4] For 1911 to 1920 for New Brunswick only.

Series D131–165. *Hourly wage rates and piece-rate earnings for selected occupations in the meat-packing industry, for Canada and by region, 1911 to 1920 and 1943 to 1960*

(dollars)

Year	Canada Slaughterers, general butchers	Boners	Labourers	Truck drivers	Linkers (female)	Quebec Slaughterers, general butchers	Boners	Labourers	Truck drivers	Linkers (female)
	131	132	133	134	135	136	137	138	139	140
Hourly wage rates										
1960	2.00	2.02[3]	1.78	2.03[4]	1.53	1.92	1.95[3]	1.73	2.06[4]	1.42
1959	1.94	1.97[3]	1.74	2.02[4]	1.42	1.91	1.97[3]	1.67	2.06[4]	1.26
1958	1.88	1.90	1.63	1.90	1.37	1.93	1.92	1.55	1.96	1.23
1957	1.83	1.81	1.62	1.77	1.31	1.84	1.85	1.53	1.80	1.22
1956	1.69	1.70	1.53	1.67	1.23	1.70	1.72	1.41	1.66	1.16
1955	1.63	1.60	1.41	1.60	1.17	1.59	1.61	1.45	1.64	1.14
Straight time earnings per hour, piece or incentive work										
1960	2.24	2.28[3]	—	—	1.94	—	—	—	—	—
1959	2.21	2.22[3]	—	—	1.84	—	—	—	—	—
1958	2.14	2.21	—	2.22	1.79	—	—	—	—	—
1957	1.96	2.00	—	2.02	1.63	—	—	—	—	—
1956	1.81	1.87	—	1.84	1.48	—	—	—	—	—
1955	—	1.82	—	1.84	1.46	—	—	—	—	—
Averages of hourly wage rates and hourly incentive earnings[5]										
1954	1.58	1.60	1.38	1.54	1.21	1.53	1.56	1.43	1.60	1.11
1953	1.53	1.58	1.34	1.55	1.20	1.45	1.49	1.39	1.59	1.07
1952	1.46	1.50	1.28	1.48	1.18	1.40	1.41	1.29	1.52	1.03
1951	1.42	1.45	1.24	1.44	1.16	1.35	1.40	1.28	1.41	1.07
1950	1.21	1.24	1.06	1.20	.92	1.14	1.19	1.09	1.20	.86
1949	1.15	1.17	1.00	1.12	.87	1.10	1.13	1.01	1.12	.78
1948	1.09	1.11	—	1.06	—	1.06	1.03	—	1.04	—
1947	.95	.95	—	.94	—	.94	.94	—	.91	—
1946	.85	.84	—	.81	—	.81	.78	—	.77	—
1945	.71	.72	—	.68	—	.68	.66	—	.63[6]	—
1944	.70	.69	—	.64	—	.63	.60	—	.56	—
1943	.70	.67	—	.62	—	.62	.60	—	.56	—

Year	Ontario Slaughterers, general butchers[1]	Boners	Labourers	Truck drivers[2]	Linkers (female)	Manitoba Slaughterers, general butchers	Boners	Labourers	Truck drivers	Linkers (female)	Saskatchewan Slaughterers, general butchers	Boners	Labourers	Truck drivers	Linkers (females)
	141	142	143	144	145	146	147	148	149	150	151	152	153	154	155
Hourly wage rates															
1960	1.90	1.95[3]	1.74	1.99[4]	1.43	2.30	2.34[3]	1.90	2.09[4]	1.56	1.97	1.96[3]	1.80	—	1.68
1959	1.82	1.80[3]	1.77	1.99[4]	1.34	2.11	2.23[3]	1.79	—	1.41	1.94	1.89[3]	1.70	—	1.59
1958	1.71	1.68	1.65	1.79	1.26	2.03	2.13	1.69	1.91	1.38	—	—	1.54	1.83	1.41
1957	1.74	1.58	1.64	1.63	1.21	1.93	1.98	1.59	1.85	1.35	1.80	1.76	1.55	1.78	1.44
1956	1.52	1.53	1.57	1.63	1.18	1.78	1.82	1.48	1.73	1.17	1.63	—	1.41	1.67	—
1955	1.52	1.49	1.37	1.46	1.04	1.76	1.69	1.41	1.65	1.15	1.62	1.61	1.38	1.61	—
Straight time earnings per hour, piece or incentive work															
1960	2.26	2.66[3]	—	—	1.97	—	—	—	—	—	2.22	2.24[3]	—	—	1.93
1959	2.19	2.58[3]	—	—	1.88	—	—	—	—	—	2.18	2.17[3]	—	—	1.83
1958	2.22	2.74	—	—	1.93	—	—	—	—	—	2.05	2.15	—	—	1.78
1957	2.01	2.22	—	—	1.74	—	—	—	—	—	1.88	—	—	—	1.62
1956	1.83	—	—	—	1.58	—	—	—	—	—	—	—	—	—	1.50
1955	1.74	—	—	—	—	—	—	—	—	—	1.83	—	—	—	1.48
Averages of hourly wage rates and hourly incentive earnings[5]															
1954	1.51	1.53	1.35	1.45	1.09	1.64	1.65	1.34	1.55	1.19	1.57	1.62	1.38	1.52	1.34
1953	1.46	1.57	1.31	1.49	1.15	1.69	1.67	1.31	1.58	1.22	1.52	1.57	1.35	1.51	1.28
1952	1.38	1.51	1.23	1.39	1.10	1.57	1.61	1.30	1.60	1.23	1.49	1.58	1.34	1.44	1.25
1951	1.36	1.45	1.20	1.38	1.14	1.54	1.55	1.20	1.59	1.22	1.43	1.39	1.24	1.39	1.19
1950	1.16	1.28	1.03	1.16	.89	1.28	1.29	1.02	1.29	.93	1.23	1.19	1.03	1.17	.97
1949	1.11	1.22	.96	1.08	.82	1.18	1.20	1.04	1.16	.94	1.22	1.15	1.00	1.12	.95
1948	1.02	1.12	—	1.03	—	1.15	1.18	—	1.09	—	1.15	1.13	—	1.04	—
1947	.93	.95	—	.89	—	.97	.98	—	.99	—	.94	.98	—	.91	—
1946	.84	.85	—	.80	—	.88	.87	—	.84	—	.83	.77	—	.76	—
1945	.73	.73	—	.67	—	.71	.74	—	.70	—	.67	.72	—	.66	—
1944	.73	.72	—	.66	—	.71	.72	—	.69	—	.67	.73	—	—	—
1943	.73	.71	—	.65	—	.71	.70	—	.66	—	.66	.70	—	—	—
1920	.680	—	—	.495	—	—	—	—	—	—	—	—	—	—	—
1919	.558	—	—	.445	—	—	—	—	—	—	—	—	—	—	—
1918	.458	—	—	.306	—	—	—	—	—	—	—	—	—	—	—
1917	.375	—	—	.285	—	—	—	—	—	—	—	—	—	—	—
1916	.280	—	—	.268	—	—	—	—	—	—	—	—	—	—	—
1915	.258	—	—	.249	—	—	—	—	—	—	—	—	—	—	—
1914	.240	—	—	.236	—	—	—	—	—	—	—	—	—	—	—
1913	.236	—	—	.227	—	—	—	—	—	—	—	—	—	—	—
1912	.228	—	—	.222	—	—	—	—	—	—	—	—	—	—	—
1911	.208	—	—	.200	—	—	—	—	—	—	—	—	—	—	—

Series D131–165. *Hourly wage rates and piece-rate earnings for selected occupations in the meat-packing industry, for Canada and by region, 1911 to 1920 and 1943 to 1960 (continuation)*

(dollars)

Year	Alberta					British Columbia				
	Slaughterers, general butchers	Boners	Labourers	Truck drivers	Linkers (female)	Slaughterers, general butchers	Boners	Labourers	Truck drivers	Linkers (female)
	156	157	158	159	160	161	162	163	164	165
Hourly wage rates										
1960	2.07	2.07[3]	1.86	2.15[4]	1.76	2.15	2.19[3]	1.85	—	1.76
1959	2.05	2.10[3]	1.79	2.06[4]	1.68	2.08	2.15[3]	1.76	2.17[4]	1.68
1958	2.03	2.09	1.67	1.97	1.62	2.02	1.96	1.73	2.01	1.53
1957	1.93	1.97	1.63	1.84	1.47	2.01	1.91	1.66	1.92	1.48
1956	1.78	1.78	1.48	1.69	1.39	1.84	1.81	1.57	1.79	1.34
1955	1.70	1.67	1.46	1.63	1.28	1.75	1.71	1.48	1.74	1.31
Straight time earnings per hour, piece or incentive work										
1960	2.22	2.23[3]	—	—	1.85	—	2.21[3]	—	—	2.10
1959	2.25	2.23[3]	—	—	1.83	—	—	—	—	—
1958	2.10	2.11	—	2.03	1.71	—	—	—	—	—
1957	1.93	2.00	—	1.89	1.60	—	—	—	—	—
1956	1.77	1.76	—	1.74	1.46	—	—	—	—	—
1955	1.78	1.76	—	1.73	1.47	—	—	—	—	—
Averages of hourly wage rates and hourly incentive earnings[5]										
1954	1.69	1.69	1.45	1.59	1.33	1.68	1.63	1.41	1.65	1.24
1953	1.67	1.64	1.40	1.59	1.34	1.62	1.63	1.40	1.61	1.23
1952	1.59	1.53	1.32	1.50	1.27	1.62	1.56	1.35	1.57	1.22
1951	1.50	1.45	1.26	1.43	1.21	1.47	1.48	1.31	1.48	1.13
1950	1.26	1.21	1.05	1.22	.98	1.30	1.32	1.12	1.25	.93
1949	1.20	1.17	.99	1.14	.89	1.22	1.15	1.07	1.18	.89
1948	1.09	1.07	—	1.10	—	1.18	1.11	—	1.08	—
1947	.95	.92	—	.98	—	1.00	.93	—	.96	—
1946	.87	.83	—	.85	—	.90	.88	—	.86	—
1945	.72	.71	—	.73	—	.76	.74	—	.72	—
1944	.72	.70	—	.68	—	.77	.72	—	.73	—
1943	.71	.70	—	.66	—	.77	.70	—	.70	—

1 For the years 1911 to 1920 the occupation was specified as 'slaughterer'.
2 For the years 1911 to 1920 the occupation was specified as 'driver'.
3 Specified as 'beef boner'.
4 Truck drivers specified as 'heavy'.

5 From 1943 to 1954, inclusive, some hourly piece-rate and incentive-rate earnings may have been averaged in with the wage-rate data for Quebec, Manitoba and British Columbia.
6 For Montreal only.

Series D166–187. *Average weekly hours and wages for males over sixteen years of age, selected occupations, Ontario, 1884 to 1889*

Year[1]	Butcher		Carpenter		Cotton mill employees						Labourer[2]		Machinist		Millwright		Paper mill machine tender		Plumber		Printer	
					Carder		Loom fixer		Spinner													
	Hours	Dollars	Hours	Dollars	Hours	Dollars	Hours	Dollars	Hours	Dollars	Hours	Dollars	Hours	Dollars	Hours	Dollars	Hours	Dollars	Hours	Dollars	Hours	Dollars
	166	167	168	169	170	171	172	173	174	175	176	177	178	179	180	181	182	183	184	185	186	187
1889	65.81	9.03	56.88	10.37	60.00	13.48	60.74	10.67	60.28	9.71	59.49	7.25	58.17	10.80	59.22	12.14	62.28	10.07	60.89	11.84	56.74	9.09
1888	66.20	8.55	55.52	10.35	60.00	6.63	60.00	10.07	57.65	7.68	58.12	7.20	58.42	10.47	61.95	12.76	66.25	9.85	53.88	12.31	57.61	9.05[3]
1887	65.45	7.23	52.87	9.82	60.00	7.50	60.25	11.38	60.23	8.34	58.99	7.18	56.93	9.65	73.83	11.57	57.00	8.00	55.64	11.45[4]	54.97	10.03
1886	62.78	9.04	57.38	9.61	60.94	6.81	60.00	11.00	60.20	6.22	58.45	7.18	59.62	9.83	58.96	13.52	63.58	9.89	55.42	12.18	57.37	9.98
1885	63.62	9.00	58.98	9.97	58.75	6.30	61.03	8.57	54.94	6.19	60.81	7.05	59.14	10.16	60.81	11.30	60.00	10.46	59.95	10.91	55.95	8.51
1884	58.42	10.00	59.08	9.85	59.55	8.26	59.46	10.71	59.45	7.69	58.56	6.79	59.25	9.96	60.17	12.22	59.00	12.06	60.00	10.84	58.33	9.37

1 Returns obtained from employers and individual workers. In 1884 the respondents were asked to submit returns for the last full week of April and October, and an average was computed. In 1885 and 1886 the data apply to the last full week in October. In 1887 the data were based on the returns submitted for one full week in each of the months of October, November or December. In 1888 and 1889 the respondents were asked to submit returns for a representative week in the last six months of each year.
2 Specified as general labourer in 1888 and 1889.
3 Newspaper printer.
4 Combined plumber and gasfitter in 1887.

Series D188–195. *Average wages paid[1] in selected occupations as reported by Toronto and Ottawa immigration agents, 1871 to 1876*

(dollars)

Year	Agency	Butchers	Carpenters (house)	Farm labourers (skilled)	Millwrights	Plumbers	Cotton carders (male)	Cotton weavers (male)	Female domestics per month with board
		188	189	190	191	192	193	194	195
1876	Toronto	1.25	1.50	1.00	1.50	1.50	1.00	1.25	6.00–9.00
1875	Toronto	1.25	1.50	1.25	1.50	1.50	1.25	1.25	5.00–8.00
1874	Toronto	1.25	1.75	15.00–20.00[2]	1.50	1.50	1.25	1.25	5.00–7.00
	Ottawa	14.00–20.00[2]	1.50–2.25[3]	14.00–16.00[2]	2.25–3.50	2.00–2.25	—	—	5.00–8.00
1873	Toronto	1.25	1.50	1.25	1.50	1.75	1.25	1.25	5.00–7.00
	Ottawa	14.00[2]	1.50–2.00[3]	16.00[2]	—	—	—	—	6.00
1872	Toronto	1.00	1.50	1.00	1.50	1.50	1.00	1.00	4.00–6.00
	Ottawa	—	1.75[3]	15.00[2]	—	—	—	—	6.00
1871	Toronto	1.00	1.50	1.00	1.00	1.00	1.00	1.00	4.00–6.00
	Ottawa	—	1.75[3]	13.00[2]	2.00	—	—	—	5.00

[1] Unless otherwise specified wage rates are per diem without board. [3] Unspecified as to type.
[2] By month with board.

Series D196–207. *Range of wages paid in selected occupations as reported by immigration agents, selected areas, 1881 to 1904*

(dollars)

Year	Immigration agency district	Farm labourers per day without board From	To	Carpenters per day without board From	To	Female domestics per month with board From	To	Lumbermen per month with board From	To	General labourers per day without board From	To	Mill hands per day without board From	To
		196	197	198	199	200	201	202	203	204	205	206	207
1904	Montreal	10.00[1]	20.00[1]	2.00	2.25	8.00	15.00	25.00	30.00	1.25	1.75	1.25	1.75
1903	Montreal	10.00[1]	18.00[1]	1.75	2.25	8.00	18.00	16.00	30.00	1.25	1.50	2.00	3.00
1902	Montreal	10.00[1]	20.00[1]	1.50	2.00	8.00	15.00	18.00	30.00	1.25	1.50	1.25	1.75
1901	Montreal	10.00[1]	20.00[1]	2.00	2.50	8.00	15.00	18.00	30.00	1.25	1.75	1.25	1.75
1900	Montreal	10.00[1]	18.00[1]	1.50	2.00	6.00	12.00	15.00	25.00	1.00	1.50	1.00	1.50
1899	Montreal	10.00[1]	15.00[1]	1.50	2.00	6.00	12.00	20.00	30.00	1.00	1.50	1.00	1.50
1898	Montreal	10.00[1]	15.00[1]	1.50	2.00	6.00	10.00	15.00	20.00	1.00	1.50	1.00	1.50
1897	Montreal	1.00	1.25	1.50	2.00	6.00	10.00	15.00	20.00	1.00	1.50	1.00	1.50
1896	Montreal	1.00	1.25	1.50	2.00	6.00	12.00	15.00	22.00	1.00	1.50	1.00	1.50
1894	Montreal	1.00	1.25	1.50	2.00	6.00	12.00	18.00	22.00	1.00	1.25	1.00	1.50
	St. John, N.B.	1.00	1.50	2.00	2.50	6.00	10.00	15.00	20.00	1.00	1.50	1.50	2.00
1893	Montreal	1.00	1.25	1.50	2.00	6.00	12.00	20.00	25.00	1.00	1.50	1.00	1.50
	St. John, N.B.	1.00	1.50	2.00	2.50	6.00	10.00	15.00	20.00	1.00	1.50	1.50	2.00
	Halifax	1.00	1.25	1.25	2.00	5.00	10.00	1.00[2]	1.25[2]	1.00	1.25	1.00	1.25
1892	St. John, N.B.	1.00	1.50	2.00	2.50	6.00	10.00	18.00	25.00	1.25	1.50	1.50	2.00
	Montreal	1.00	1.25	1.75	2.25	6.00	12.00	15.00	20.00	1.00	1.50	1.00	1.50
	Halifax	1.00	1.25	1.50	2.50	6.00	12.00	1.00[2]	1.25[2]	1.00	1.25	1.00	1.50
1891	Halifax	1.00	1.25	1.50	2.50	6.00	12.00	1.00[2]	1.25[2]	1.00	1.25	1.00	1.50
	St. John, N.B.	1.00	1.50	2.00	2.50	6.00	10.00	18.00	25.00	1.25	1.50	1.50	2.00
	Quebec	1.00	—	1.50	2.00	6.00	9.00	20.00	25.00	—	—	—	—
	Sherbrooke	1.00	1.50	1.00	2.00	6.00	8.00	1.00[2]	1.55[2]	1.00	1.50	1.00	2.50
	Montreal	1.00	1.25	1.75	2.25	6.00	12.00	15.00	20.00	1.00	1.25	1.00	1.50
	Ottawa	12.00[1]	16.00[1]	1.25	2.25	7.00	10.00	1.50[2]	1.75[2]	1.25	1.50	—	—
	Kingston	1.00	1.30	1.50	2.00	6.00	9.00	1.00[2]	1.50[2]	1.00	1.25	1.00	1.50
	Toronto	1.00	1.25	2.00	2.25	6.00	9.00	12.00	15.00	1.25	1.50	—	—
	Hamilton	1.25	1.25	2.50	3.50	8.00[3]	12.00[3]	15.00	25.00	1.25	1.50	1.25[4]	1.50[4]
	London, Ont.	1.25	1.50	1.50	1.75	6.00	10.00	1.00[2]	—	1.25	1.50	1.50	2.00
	Port Arthur	1.25	1.50	2.50	3.00	10.00	15.00	1.50[2]	2.00[2]	1.25	1.75	1.75	2.50
	Winnipeg	1.25	—	2.50	—	12.50	—	1.50[2]	—	1.25	—	1.75	—
	Brandon	15.00[5]	35.00[5]	2.00	3.00	10.00	15.00	1.50[2]	2.00[2]	1.50	1.75	1.75	3.00
	Regina	1.75	2.00	2.50	3.50	6.00	14.00	—	—	1.50	2.00	—	—
	Calgary	1.75	—	2.75	—	14.00	—	2.00[2]	—	1.75	—	—	—
	Vancouver	1.25	2.50	2.25	3.50	12.00	25.00	1.50[2]	2.25[2]	1.75	2.50	1.25	2.25
1890	Halifax	1.00	1.10	1.75	2.50	7.00	12.00	1.00[2]	1.25[2]	1.00	1.25	1.00	1.50
	St. John, N.B.	1.20	1.50	1.80	2.00	6.00	12.00	20.00	25.00	1.50	1.75	1.50	2.25
	Quebec	1.00	—	1.50	2.00	5.00	9.00	20.00	25.00	—	—	—	—
	Sherbrooke	1.00	1.25	1.00	2.50	4.00	8.00	1.00[2]	1.50[2]	1.00	1.25	1.00	1.50
	Montreal	1.00	1.25	1.75	2.25	6.00	12.00	15.00	22.00	1.00	1.25	1.00	1.50
	Ottawa	144.00[6]	180.00[6]	1.25	2.25	7.00	9.00	1.50[2]	1.75[2]	1.25	1.40	—	—
	Kingston	1.00	1.30	1.50	2.25	6.00	9.00	1.00[2]	1.50[2]	1.00	1.40	1.25	1.50
	Toronto	1.00	1.25	2.00	2.25	6.00	9.00	12.00	15.00	1.25	1.40	—	—
	Hamilton	—	1.25	2.00	2.50	8.00	12.00	—	—	1.25	1.50	.50	3.00
	London, Ont.	1.25	1.50	1.50	1.75	7.00	9.00	—	1.00[2]	1.25	1.50	1.50	2.00
	Port Arthur	1.50	1.75	2.50	3.00	10.00	16.00	1.50[2]	2.00[2]	1.50	1.75	1.75	2.50
	Winnipeg	1.00	1.50	2.50	3.00	8.00	15.00	.70[2]	.90[2]	1.25	1.75	1.00	2.00
	Brandon	15.00[1]	30.00[1]	2.00	2.50	10.00	15.00	1.50[2]	—	1.50	1.75	1.75	3.00
	Regina	1.75	2.00	2.00	3.00	8.00	15.00	—	—	1.50	2.00	—	—
	Calgary	1.75	—	2.50	—	10.00	—	2.00[2]	—	1.75	—	—	—
	Vancouver	1.25	2.50	2.50	3.50	12.00	25.00	1.50[2]	2.25[2]	1.25	2.25	1.25	2.25

Series D 196–207. *Range of wages paid in selected occupations as reported by immigration agents, selected areas, 1881 to 1904*
(continued)
(dollars)

Year	Immigration agency district	Farm labourers per day without board		Carpenters per day without board		Female domestics per month with board		Lumbermen per month with board		General labourers per day without board		Mill hands per day without board	
		From	To	From	To	From	To	From	To	From	To	From	To
		196	**197**	**198**	**199**	**200**	**201**	**202**	**203**	**204**	**205**	**206**	**207**
1889	Halifax	1.00	1.10	1.90	2.20	5.00	10.00	1.00[2]	1.25[2]	1.00	1.10	1.00	1.50
	St. John, N.B.	1.20	1.50	2.00	2.50	6.00	9.00	20.00	24.00	1.50	—	1.80	2.25
	Quebec	—	—	1.25	1.75	5.00	8.00	18.00	25.00	—	—	—	—
	Sherbrooke	1.00	1.25	1.00	2.00	4.00	8.00	1.00[2]	1.25[2]	1.00	—	1.00	1.25
	Montreal	1.00	1.25	1.75	2.25	5.00	10.00	22.00	28.00	1.25	1.50	1.00	1.50
	Ottawa	144.00[6]	180.00[6]	1.25	2.25	6.00	8.00	1.75[2]	—	1.00	1.40	—	—
	Kingston	1.00	1.25	1.50	2.50	6.00	9.00	1.00[2]	1.50[2]	1.00	1.25	1.25	1.50
	Toronto	—	1.00	2.00	2.50	6.00	10.00	1.25[2]	2.00[2]	1.25	1.60		
	Hamilton	—	1.25	2.00	2.25	8.00	12.00	15.00	25.00	1.25	1.50	.50[7]	3.00[7]
	London, Ont.	1.25	1.50	1.75	2.00	—	8.00	—	—	—	1.25	—	18.00[1]
	Port Arthur	1.25	1.50	2.00	3.00	10.00	16.00	1.25[2]	1.75[2]	1.25	1.75	1.75	2.50
	Winnipeg	1.00	1.50	2.00	3.00	5.00	15.00	—	1.00[2]	1.00	1.75	1.25	1.50
	Brandon	1.25	1.50	2.00	3.00	8.00	15.00	20.00	30.00	1.25	2.00	1.75	3.75
	Regina	2.00	—	3.00	—	12.00	—	—	—	2.00	—	—	—
	Moose Jaw	1.50	1.75	2.50	3.00	8.00	12.00	—	—	1.25	1.75	—	—
	Calgary	1.50	—	2.25	—	12.00	—	1.50[2]	—	1.50	—	—	—
	Vancouver	1.25	2.50	2.50	3.50	12.00	25.00	1.25[2]	2.00[2]	1.25	2.00	1.25	2.00
	Victoria	20.00[1]	35.00[1]	2.50	3.50	12.00	20.00	40.00	75.00	1.75	2.00	1.50	2.50
1888	Halifax	1.00	1.25	1.90	2.16	4.00	8.00	1.00[2]	1.25[2]	1.00	1.30	1.00	1.50
	St. John, N.B.	1.00	1.50	1.50	2.00	6.00	9.00	15.00	18.00	1.30	1.50	1.25	2.00
	Quebec	10.00[8]	14.00[8]	1.50	—	5.00	8.00	15.00	25.00	—	—	—	—
	Sherbrooke	1.00	—	1.00	1.75	6.00	8.00	1.00[2]	1.25[2]	1.00	—	1.00	1.50
	Montreal	1.00	1.25	2.00	2.50	5.00	10.00	22.00	28.00	1.25	1.50	1.00	1.50
	Ottawa	144.00[6]	180.00[6]	1.25	2.00	6.00	8.00	1.75[2]	—	1.25	—	—	—
	Kingston	1.00	1.25	1.50	2.25	5.00	9.00	12.00	25.00	1.00	1.30	1.00	1.25
	Toronto	1.00	1.25	2.00	2.25	6.00	9.00	12.00	18.00	1.15	1.50	1.25	1.50[4]
	Hamilton	1.25	1.25	2.00	2.25	7.00	10.00	—	—	1.25	1.50	1.25[4]	1.50[4]
	London, Ont.	1.00	1.25	1.50	1.75	8.00	—	—	—	1.00	1.25	18.00[5]	—
	Port Arthur	1.50	1.75	2.00	3.00	10.00	16.00	1.50[2]	2.00[2]	1.50	2.00	1.75	2.50
	Winnipeg	5.00[1]	30.00[1]	1.50	3.00	5.00	15.00	15.00	35.00	1.00	1.75	—	—
	Qu'Appelle	20.00[1]	35.00[1]	2.00	3.00	10.00	20.00	—	—	—	—	—	—
	Medicine Hat	1.00	1.25	2.75	—	12.00	—	1.50[2]	2.00[2]	1.25	1.75	1.75	—
	Victoria	2.00	—	3.00	—	18.00	—	2.50[2]	—	1.75	—	2.25	—
1887	Halifax	1.25	—	9.00[9]	12.00[9]	4.00	8.00	16.00	24.00	—	1.25	16.00[5]	30.00[5]
	Montreal	1.00	1.25	2.00	2.50	5.00	10.00	22.00	28.00	1.25	1.50	1.00	1.50
	Ottawa	12.00[1]	16.00[1]	1.75	2.25	5.00	10.00	—	—	1.25	1.40	—	—
	Kingston	1.00	1.25	1.50	2.00	5.00	9.00	12.00	25.00	1.00	1.25	1.00	1.50
	Hamilton	1.25	1.25	2.00	2.25	7.00	10.00	15.00	25.00	1.12	1.50	1.25[4]	1.50[4]
	Medicine Hat	25.00[1]	35.00[1]	2.50	3.50	12.00	18.00	—	—	—	—	—	—
1886	Montreal	1.00	1.25	1.50	2.00	5.00	10.00	22.00	28.00	1.00	1.25	1.00	1.50
	Kingston	1.00	1.25	1.50	2.00	6.00	9.00	14.00	25.00	1.00	1.25	1.00	1.50
	Hamilton	1.00	1.25	1.50	2.00	7.00	10.00	15.00	25.00	1.00	1.25	1.25[4]	1.50[4]
	Winnipeg	1.00	1.50	2.25	—	5.00	12.00	1.00[2]	1.50[2]	1.00	1.50	1.00	1.25
	Port Arthur	1.50	1.75	2.50	3.00	12.00	18.00	18.00	30.00	1.50	2.00	1.75	2.50
1885	Halifax	1.00	1.25	10.00[10]	12.00[10]	5.00	8.00	15.00[11]	20.00[11]	1.00	1.25	16.00[5]	30.00[5]
	St. John, N.B.	1.20	1.50	1.50	2.00	6.00	10.00	15.00	25.00	1.30	1.50	1.25	2.00
	Montreal	1.00	1.25	1.50	2.00	5.00	10.00	22.00	28.00	1.00	1.25	1.00	1.50
	Ottawa	12.00[8]	15.00[8]	—	1.75	6.00	8.00	12.00	25.00	—	1.25	1.00	1.50
	Kingston	1.00	1.50	1.25	1.75	5.00	9.00	1.25[2]	1.50[2]	1.00	1.25	1.00	1.50
	Toronto	1.00	1.25	1.75	2.00	6.00	8.00	15.00	20.00	1.25	1.50	1.00	2.00
	Hamilton	1.00	1.25	1.50	2.00	7.00	10.00	15.00	25.00	1.00	1.25	1.25[4]	1.50[4]
	London, Ont.	1.00	1.50	1.25	1.75	7.00	9.00	—	—	1.00	1.37	—	—
	Port Arthur	1.50	—[12]	2.00	2.75	12.00	16.00	18.00[13]	30.00[13]	1.50	1.75	1.50	2.50
	Winnipeg	1.25	—	1.50	—	15.00	—	—	—	1.50	—	—	—
	Brandon	6.00[9]	12.00[9]	2.00	3.00	8.00	15.00	—	—	1.25	1.50	1.50	2.50
	Qu'Appelle	40.00[5]	50.00[5]	2.00	3.00	12.00	16.00	—	—	1.50	2.00	2.25	—[12]
1884	Montreal	1.00	1.50	1.50	2.25	6.00	10.00	25.00[5]	30.00[5]	1.00	1.25	1.00	1.50[4]
	Hamilton	1.00	1.25	1.75	2.00	6.00	8.00	20.00	30.00	1.15	1.25	1.25[4]	1.50[4]
	Port Arthur	2.00	—[12]	2.50	3.00	12.00	16.00	2.00[2]	2.25[2]	2.00	—[12]	2.00	2.25
1883	Montreal	1.00	1.50	1.50	2.25	6.00	10.00	25.00	30.00	1.00	1.25	1.00	1.50
	Hamilton	1.00	1.25	1.75	2.00	7.00	8.00	20.00	30.00	1.00	1.25	1.25[4]	1.50[4]
	Winnipeg	1.50	—	2.00	2.75	10.00	18.00	15.00[14]	30.00[14]	1.50	2.25	—	—
1882	Montreal	1.00	1.50	1.50	2.25	6.00	10.00	25.00	30.00	1.00	1.50	1.00	1.50
	Ottawa	14.00[1]	20.00[1]	1.50	1.75	6.00	10.00	—	—	1.50	—	—	—
	Hamilton	1.00	1.25	1.75	2.00	7.00	8.00	20.00	30.00[15]	1.25	1.35	1.25[4]	1.50[4]
	Winnipeg	30.00[1]	40.00[1]	3.50	4.00	15.00	20.00	—	30.00[15]	2.75	3.00	—	—
1881	Hamilton	1.25	1.50	1.50	2.00	6.00	8.00	—	—	—	—	.75[16]	2.50[16]

[1] Per month with board.
[2] Per day without board.
[3] General servants.
[4] Spinners (cotton).
[5] Per month without board.
[6] Per annum with board.
[7] Cotton mill hands.
[8] Per month with board by the year.
[9] Per week without board.
[10] 'Per week and found'.
[11] Probably per month with board but not clearly specified.
[12] Typographical error.
[13] Woodsmen.
[14] Cordwood choppers.
[15] Sawmill men.
[16] Factory operatives.

Series D208–231. *Annual earnings, hours per week and days employed in year for males over sixteen years of age, selected occupations, Ontario, 1884 to 1889*

Year[1]	Butcher			Carpenter			Cotton mill operative[2]			Labourer[3]		
	Hours per week	Days in year	Annual earnings (dollars)	Hours per week	Days in year	Annual earnings (dollars)	Hours per week	Days in year	Annual earnings (dollars)	Hours per week	Days in year	Annual earnings (dollars)
	208	209	210	211	212	213	214	215	216	217	218	219
1889	70.33	286.33	378.42	57.34	255.87	418.46	59.40	288.26	358.88	55.33	205.00	297.14
1888	66.40	284.90	395.00	54.88	267.16	452.69	59.13	247.75	321.72	53.21	217.15	320.22
1887	64.91	308.91	369.62	53.41	240.01	411.34	60.00	282.75	385.71	59.41	221.48	270.67
1886	61.00	308.00	374.89	56.35	263.58	395.70	60.00	250.00	370.83	55.32	224.94	295.64
1885	60.88	301.75	438.63	56.87	250.83	444.18	59.67	202.67	259.87	58.05	249.47	290.09
1884	58.29	262.86	426.14	57.45	249.72	396.28	60.00	233.75	399.50	59.63	253.93	300.24

Year[1]	Machinist			Millwright			Plumber			Printer[4]		
	Hours per week	Days in year	Annual earnings (dollars)	Hours per week	Days in year	Annual earnings (dollars)	Hours per week	Days in year	Annual earnings (dollars)	Hours per week	Days in year	Annual earnings (dollars)
	220	221	222	223	224	225	226	227	228	229	230	231
1889	57.08	276.60	467.86	59.50	292.75	485.08	55.95	276.53	484.87	58.52	285.52	437.24
1888	57.55	276.40	474.64	—	—	—	56.35	269.18	501.94	57.75	291.49	455.88
1887	57.24	267.61	432.64	73.83	228.67	420.79	56.26[5]	240.33[5]	458.38[5]	54.63	255.52	424.78
1886	58.63[6]	270.53[6]	449.77[6]	59.10	278.00	545.35	57.20	256.40	541.49	58.23	281.42	425.29
1885	57.11	259.82	419.16	60.80	276.00	578.40	57.75	274.58	428.27	55.64	272.51	439.90
1884	58.78	241.98	394.67	60.60	253.50	599.50	59.25	252.88	374.63	56.32	274.56	423.99

[1] Returns obtained from individual workers. In 1884 to 1886, inclusive, the data refer to a year ending 31 October. From 1887 to 1889 the data apply to the calendar year.

[2] In 1885 the data are for weavers; in 1884, 1886, 1887 and 1888 the data are for spinners; in 1889 the data are for all sub-occupations except beamer and weaver.

[3] In 1886 general labourers are specified; and in 1888 and 1889 builder's labourers are specified.

[4] Newspaper printers are specified for 1884 to 1886, inclusive.

[5] Plumber and gasfitter.

[6] Foundry machine-shop employees.

Series D232–237. *Average[1] annual earnings, average[1] weeks employed and average weekly earnings, by occupation group, males, Canada, 1931, 1941 and 1951*

Year	Labourers (non-primary)	Semi-skilled	Skilled	Clerical, commercial and financial	Professional	Managerial
	232	233	234	235	236	237
	Average annual earnings (dollars)					
1951	1,552	2,132	2,292	2,206	2,944	3,603
1941	566	933	1,052	1,139	1,553	2,082
1931	480	791	1,042	1,192	1,924	2,468
	Average weeks employed					
1951	50.04	50.94	50.88	51.18	51.25	51.41
1941	39.58	50.40	50.19	51.03	51.23	51.38
1931	32.5	38.5	40.1	47.2	48.7	50.1
	Average weekly earnings (dollars)					
1951	31.02	41.85	45.05	43.10	57.44	70.08
1941	14.30	18.51	20.96	22.32	30.31	40.52
1931	14.74	20.52	25.96	25.21	39.48	49.22

[1] Medians for the years 1941 and 1951; means for 1931.

Series D238–253. *Annual labour income including supplementary labour income, by industry, Canada, 1926 to 1960*
(millions of dollars)

Year	Total labour income[1]	Agriculture	Forestry	Fishing and trapping	Mining	Manufacturing	Construction	Transportation	Storage	Communications	Public utilities	Wholesale trade	Retail trade	Finance	Services	Government non-military
	238	239	240	241	242	243	244	245	246	247	248	249	250	251	252	253
1960	18,119	191	346	23	588	5,410	1,281	1,374	60	452	357	1,071	1,658	827	2,649	1,832
1959	17,463	182	307	23	587	5,303	1,309	1,384	61	427	345	1,019	1,592	772	2,448	1,704
1958	16,521	178	288	26	561	5,029	1,346	1,302	55	413	320	953	1,488	734	2,219	1,609
1957	16,018	172	354	21	569	5,034	1,341	1,306	53	385	288	919	1,420	698	2,006	1,452
1956	14,890	172	388	23	528	4,766	1,239	1,247	49	342	249	830	1,304	619	1,820	1,314
1955	13,223	161	342	20	457	4,299	936	1,123	44	303	212	739	1,187	554	1,650	1,196
1954	12,452	159	323	21	425	4,053	889	1,061	41	278	211	693	1,125	513	1,549	1,111
1953	12,125	171	311	20	417	4,100	908	1,088	39	249	202	658	1,056	470	1,431	1,005
1952	11,218	172	326	20	418	3,772	799	1,011	37	229	186	614	972	434	1,302	926
1951	10,104	158	395	21	364	3,396	655	919	32	210	166	542	894	393	1,165	794
1950	8,629	144	270	20	303	2,881	564	777	27	183	146	469	787	344	1,042	672
1949	8,000	134	199	17	279	2,688	523	763	26	167	133	436	719	313	978	625
1948	7,414	131	253	18	245	2,550	482	728	24	145	111	390	628	287	875	547
1947	6,399	130	248	14	201	2,205	383	619	22	127	85	342	527	256	769	471
1946	5,487	120	234	15	179	1,836	293	555	20	111	68	292	457	219	646	442
1945	5,037	109	177	14	163	1,933	189	518	20	91	54	248	392	180	552	397
1944	4,998	107	151	12	170	2,115	165	501	19	82	50	225	359	166	504	372
1943	4,812	103	134	11	168	2,074	225	457	16	74	48	203	329	154	466	350
1942	4,282	95	112	9	169	1,756	228	384	14	69	46	196	313	144	437	310
1941	3,608	86	98	7	165	1,315	194	336	13	64	42	185	305	132	408	258
1940	2,959	83	85	5	148	954	131	286	11	60	39	157	260	120	370	250
1939	2,601	78	62	4	139	765	104	267	10	59	39	141	228	119	352	234
1938	2,515	77	45	4	131	732	107	261	8	57	37	132	224	118	345	237
1937	2,538	76	73	4	132	749	108	259	9	56	36	137	231	116	334	218
1936	2,241	71	50	4	107	635	81	244	9	51	33	124	204	113	312	203
1935	2,079	67	40	4	90	580	68	229	8	50	33	115	188	106	304	197
1934	1,939	62	34	4	79	521	53	219	8	47	32	106	179	105	295	195
1933	1,788	59	25	3	63	451	51	213	8	47	32	103	161	109	288	175
1932	1,975	61	23	3	63	490	83	239	7	50	35	113	174	114	323	197
1931	2,408	78	31	4	77	608	155	290	7	58	38	129	211	126	379	217
1930	2,786	100	53	6	97	723	191	337	8	62	40	144	250	139	420	216
1929	2,940	113	69	7	107	804	232	362	8	60	36	139	247	142	417	197
1928	2,715	113	65	7	100	745	187	353	6	56	35	129	224	128	385	182
1927	2,506	112	61	7	88	683	158	338	6	53	35	121	203	112	359	170
1926	2,366	112	59	7	81	643	155	319	5	50	32	114	181	103	347	158

[1] Excludes the armed services.

Series D254–266. *Annual labour income including supplementary labour income, by province and region,[1] 1926 to 1960*
(millions of dollars)

Year	Total Canada[2]	Total Atlantic Region	Newfoundland	Prince Edward Island	Nova Scotia	New Brunswick	Quebec	Ontario	Total Prairie Region	Manitoba	Saskatchewan	Alberta	British Columbia
	254	255	256	257	258	259	260	261	262	263	264	265	266
1960	18,119	1,210	258	45	523	384	4,642	7,571	2,744	858	615	1,213	1,957
1959	17,463	1,139	236	42	499	362	4,449	7,352	2,641	829	603	1,168	1,873
1958	16,521	1,075	222	38	475	340	4,237	6,973	2,427	771	567	1,091	1,763
1957	16,018	1,061	226	38	465	332	4,103	6,741	2,301	738	534	1,029	1,765
1956	14,890	1,018	215	36	440	327	3,817	6,198	2,160	700	499	961	1,649
1955	13,223	922	191	33	405	293	3,377	5,546	1,919	635	445	839	1,426
1954	12,452	879	177	31	391	280	3,214	5,204	1,825	604	439	782	1,302
1953	12,125	857	170	29	385	273	3,126	5,075	1,764	600	410	754	1,279
1952	11,218	806	151	28	367	260	2,906	4,720	1,549	551	350	648	1,214
1951	10,104	744	137	25	331	251	2,636	4,258	1,375	499	314	562	1,072
1950	8,629	636	116	22	289	209	2,237	3,624	1,201	437	278	486	915
1949	8,000	607	106	21	281	199	2,007	3,346	1,111	410	263	438	825
1948	7,414	484	—	19	267	198	2,007	3,105	1,012	383	243	386	794
1947	6,399	462	—	18	266	178	1,756	2,658	872	330	219	323	641
1946	5,487	401	—	16	232	153	1,493	2,257	784	291	204	289	544
1945	5,037	373	—	15	223	135	1,406	2,082	676	256	176	244	495
1944	4,998	366	—	14	226	126	1,411	2,081	638	242	163	233	496
1943	4,812	339	—	12	210	117	1,369	2,028	570	218	144	208	499
1942	4,282	296	—	9	183	104	1,197	1,834	523	206	132	185	425
1941	3,608	245	—	9	147	89	980	1,569	482	187	124	171	327
1940	2,959	208	—	9	122	77	778	1,272	417	158	112	147	279
1939	2,601	186	—	9	107	70	683	1,103	377	143	101	133	248
1938	2,515	178	—	8	102	68	667	1,061	362	137	97	128	242
1937	2,538	177	—	8	101	68	673	1,064	379	145	103	131	241
1936	2,241	154	—	7	88	59	594	936	343	132	94	117	211
1935	2,079	142	—	7	80	55	550	865	326	126	90	110	194
1934	1,939	131	—	6	74	51	512	804	311	121	86	104	179
1933	1,788	120	—	6	67	47	472	739	292	114	81	97	163
1932	1,975	133	—	7	74	52	519	814	329	129	92	108	178
1931	2,408	162	—	8	90	64	632	989	406	160	114	132	216
1930	2,786	190	—	9	106	75	727	1,141	477	189	134	154	248
1929	2,940	205	—	10	114	81	762	1,202	508	201	143	164	260
1928	2,715	193	—	9	108	76	699	1,107	475	188	134	153	238
1927	2,506	182	—	8	102	72	640	1,021	441	175	124	142	219
1926	2,366	177	—	8	100	69	598	962	420	166	119	135	207

[1] Excludes the armed services.   [2] Includes Yukon, Northwest Territories, and Canadian residents abroad.

Series D 267–279. *Annual wages and salaries in manufacturing, by province and region, 1926 to 1960*

(millions of dollars)

Year	Total Canada[1]	Total Atlantic Region	New-found-land	Prince Edward Island	Nova Scotia	New Bruns-wick	Quebec	Ontario	Total Prairie Region	Manitoba	Saskat-chewan	Alberta	British Columbia
	267	268	269	270	271	272	273	274	275	276	277	278	279
1960	5,188	199	32	4	92	71	1,603	2,589	354	152	49	153	442
1959	5,096	187	31	4	87	65	1,545	2,583	357	155	48	154	424
1958	4,823	180	30	3	86	61	1,474	2,431	329	143	44	142	409
1957	4,838	188	33	3	91	61	1,475	2,447	320	141	41	138	407
1956	4,586	180	31	3	84	62	1,396	2,323	292	134	37	121	395
1955	4,148	166	29	3	76	58	1,267	2,096	263	121	35	107	355
1954	3,903	163	31	3	72	57	1,210	1,963	247	116	34	97	320
1953	3,954	167	27	3	76	61	1,220	2,019	247	121	33	93	301
1952	3,637	162	26	3	76	57	1,121	1,846	224	112	30	82	283
1951	3,270	143	23	2	64	54	1,003	1,664	195	100	26	69	265
1950	2,766	122	19	2	54	47	850	1,407	169	88	23	58	218
1949	2,584	119	18	2	54	45	808	1,298	162	86	22	54	197
1948	2,462	100	—	2	53	45	773	1,235	153	81	21	51	200
1947	2,132	89	—	2	47	40	680	1,058	134	71	20	43	171
1946	1,770	80	—	2	44	34	575	859	116	62	18	36	140
1945	1,869	87	—	2	52	33	615	894	111	61	17	33	162
1944	2,053	96	—	2	61	33	676	985	115	63	18	34	181
1943	2,013	88	—	1	56	31	667	968	102	55	17	30	188
1942	1,704	70	—	1	42	27	543	852	89	52	13	24	150
1941	1,281	51	—	1	28	22	399	669	72	41	10	21	90
1940	933	41	—	1	22	18	281	485	58	32	9	17	68
1939	747	32	—	1	17	14	227	382	51	29	7	15	55
1938	715	30	—	1	16	13	216	367	49	28	7	14	53
1937	732	33	—	1	17	15	220	377	49	28	7	14	53
1936	620	27	—	1	14	12	185	319	43	25	6	12	46
1935	567	25	—	1	13	11	167	292	42	24	6	12	41
1934	510	24	—	1	12	11	154	258	38	21	6	11	36
1933	442	20	—	1	10	9	136	223	34	19	5	10	29
1932	479	22	—	1	11	10	143	243	40	23	6	11	31
1931	595	27	—	1	14	12	178	299	50	29	7	14	41
1930	707	32	—	1	17	14	208	356	58	33	9	16	53
1929	787	33	—	1	17	15	228	412	56	32	9	15	58
1928	730	30	—	1	15	14	211	378	54	31	8	15	57
1927	669	28	—	1	13	14	197	342	48	28	7	13	54
1926	631	28	—	1	13	14	183	323	44	26	6	12	53

[1] Includes Yukon, Northwest Territories, and Canadian residents abroad.

Series D280–287. *Annual earnings in manufacturing industries, production and other workers, by sex, Canada, 1905, 1910 and 1917 to 1959*

Year	Supervisory and office employees				Production workers			
	Number of males (thousands)	Number of females (thousands)	Total earnings (millions of dollars)	Average annual earnings (dollars)	Number of males (thousands)	Number of females (thousands)	Total earnings (millions of dollars)	Average annual earnings (dollars)
	280	281	282	283	284	285	286	287
1959	220.9	85.2	1,529.6	4,998	786.0	211.9	3,543.5	3,551
1958	221.9	86.0	1,469.3	4,773	772.3	209.4	3,333.2	3,395
1957	226.3	87.6	1,403.4	4,471	827.3	217.8	3,416.2	3,269
1956	216.3	85.0	1,272.0	4,222	831.3	220.4	3,298.7	3,136
1955	206.9	80.6	1,147.1	3,990	796.7	214.3	2,995.3	2,963
1954	199.8	79.2	1,075.1	3,854	780.0	209.1	2,821.6	2,853
1953	195.8	78.4	1,016.7	3,707	828.4	224.9	2,940.3	2,792
1952	188.2	74.8	923.9	3,513	810.1	215.3	2,713.7	2,647
1951	176.9	70.9	816.7	3,296	792.4	218.2	2,459.6	2,434
1950	164.5	66.6	692.6	2,998	736.5	215.8	2,078.6	2,183
1949	157.5	64.0	628.4	2,836	732.5	217.2	1,963.5	2,067
1948	141.0	57.2	532.6	2,687	738.7	218.8	1,876.8	1,960
1947	135.2	55.9	474.4	2,482	721.4	219.2	1,610.6	1,712
1946	126.9	54.0	410.7	2,305	662.2	214.4	1,329.2	1,516
1945	128.3	62.0	416.9	2,192	679.8	248.0	1,426.9	1,538
1944	126.4	65.4	416.6	2,172	743.6	285.6	1,610.4	1,565
1943	128.3	64.3	387.6	2,013	761.8	285.0	1,597.4	1,526
1942	122.9	53.9	334.2	1,890	731.3	242.5	1,347.0	1,383
1941	117.1	41.6	285.9	1,801	626.2	175.4	977.9	1,220
1940	104.2	31.5	241.4	1,779	491.0	135.0	678.9	1,084
1939	98.1	26.6	217.6	1,746	415.2	117.8	519.7	975
1938	95.2	25.3	207.2	1,720	408.9	112.2	498.0	956
1937	91.0	24.7	195.8	1,692	426.9	117.3	525.4	965
1936	81.3	23.0	172.9	1,659	379.8	110.0	438.7	896
1935	76.1	21.7	160.2	1,638	353.7	104.9	398.9	870
1934	71.8	20.1	148.5	1,615	326.5	101.1	355.0	830
1933	67.7	18.7	139.0	1,608	287.2	94.7	296.9	777
1932	68.1	18.7	151.1	1,739	288.7	93.0	322.2	844
1931	71.0	20.2	171.9	1,884	337.5	99.5	415.2	950
1930	64.1	20.5	169.9	2,008	416.6	113.2	527.4	995
1929	67.7	21.1	175.4	1,976	454.5	122.9	601.5	1,041
1928	64.3	19.8	162.8	1,936	427.6	119.3	558.3	1,021
1927	60.4	18.0	151.3	1,930	400.0	114.2	511.1	994
1926	58.2	17.1	142.2	1,890	374.0	109.6	483.2	999
1925		71.3	133.4	1,872	451.4		436.4	967
1924		70.5	131.5	1,864	422.4		411.0	973
1923		73.8	137.2	1,857	437.3		420.2	961
1922		71.9	130.6	1,816	386.5		363.8	941
1921		70.5	130.8	1,854	371.3		370.9	999
1920		77.4	140.0	1,810	499.1		544.3	1,090
1919		75.6	113.1	1,497	496.3		456.9	920
1918		64.8	95.2	1,470	520.7		453.2	870
1917		62.5	82.2	1,317	523.5		397.8	760
1910		42.9	42.7	994	465.0		194.0	417
1905		35.0	29.6	846	347.7		130.4	375

Series D 288–296. *Average annual, weekly and hourly earnings, male and female wage earners, manufacturing industries, Canada, 1934 to 1960*

(dollars)

Year	Wage earners (both sexes)			Male wage earners			Female wage earners		
	Annual	Weekly	Hourly	Annual	Weekly	Hourly	Annual	Weekly	Hourly
	288	289	290	291	292	293	294	295	296
1960	—	72.39	1.77	—	80.34	1.93	—	43.96	1.14
1959	3,551	71.35	1.72	3,929	79.20	1.88	2,149	43.36	1.11
1958	3,396	67.85	1.65	3,749	75.03	1.80	2,092	41.90	1.08
1957	3,269	65.31	1.61	3,609	72.21	1.75	1,974	39.49	1.05
1956	3,136	63.97	1.53	3,458	70.67	1.66	1,923	39.29	1.00
1955	2,963	60.53	1.44	3,267	66.86	1.57	1,833	37.52	.95
1954	2,853	57.99	1.40	3,145	63.98	1.51	1,764	35.90	.93
1953	2,792	56.75	1.36	3,082	62.71	1.47	1,723	35.07	.91
1952	2,647	55.17	1.30	2,915	60.85	1.40	1,638	34.17	.86
1951	2,434	51.32	1.22	2,693	56.46	1.31	1,492	31.27	.82
1950	2,183	45.94	1.06	2,419	50.93	1.14	1,376	29.00	.72
1949	2,067	42.61	.98	2,291	47.33	1.07	1,315	27.18	.68
1948	1,960	41.25	.95	2,175	45.73	1.02	1,233	25.91	.65
1947	1,713	37.19	.85	1,909	41.35	.92	1,067	23.11	.58
1946	1,516	32.38	.74	1,702	36.23	.81	943	20.08	.50
1945	1,538	30.98	.67	1,739	35.04	.74	984	19.84	.47
1944	1,564	31.05	.65	1,761	34.95	.71	1,051	20.89	.48
1943	1,525	29.87	.61	1,726	33.80	.67	987	19.33	.43
1942	1,383	28.18	.56	1,558	31.75	.62	854	17.41	.37
1941	1,220	24.95	.49	1,355	27.72	.54	736	15.05	.32
1940	1,084	22.35	.45	1,202	24.82	.49	655	13.52	.27
1939	975	20.14	.43	1,076	22.23	.46	619	12.78	.28
1938	956	19.49	.42	1,055	21.49	.45	594	12.10	.27
1937	965	—	—	—	—	—	—	—	—
1936	896	18.96	.39	995	20.92	.42[1]	577	12.20	.26[1]
1935	870	18.50	.38	966	20.41	.41[1]	570	12.04	.26[1]
1934	830	18.30	.37	930	20.31	.41[1]	539	11.80	.25[1]

[1] Estimated on the basis of hours worked by female workers in 1938 and 1939 as compared with those worked by male workers in these years.

Series D 297–305. *Average annual, weekly and hourly earnings, male and female salaried employees, manufacturing industries, Canada, 1946 to 1960*

(dollars)

Year	Salaried employees (both sexes)			Male salaried employees			Female salaried employees		
	Annual	Weekly	Hourly	Annual	Weekly	Hourly	Annual	Weekly	Hourly
	297	298	299	300	301	302	303	304	305
1960	—	100.47	—	—	116.41	—	—	57.98	—
1959	4,998	97.10	2.52	5,817	112.78	2.90	2,874	55.73	1.48
1958	4,773	93.74	2.43	5,549	108.34	2.79	2,769	54.07	1.44
1957	4,471	89.92	2.33	5,205	104.63	2.68	2,576	51.84	1.38
1956	4,222	85.23	2.19	4,918	99.05	2.51	2,449	49.31	1.30
1955	3,990	80.57	2.06	4,636	93.50	2.36	2,332	47.02	1.24
1954	3,854	77.81	2.00	4,499	90.99	2.31	2,227	45.00	1.19
1953	3,707	73.87	1.89	4,327	86.43	2.19	2,159	43.13	1.14
1952	3,513	70.75	1.80	3,985	82.60	2.07	2,323	41.26	1.09
1951	3,296	65.98	1.67	3,852	77.55	1.94	1,907	38.42	1.01
1950	2,998	58.74	1.48	3,507	69.35	1.73	1,739	34.38	.90
1949	2,836	54.85	1.37	3,317	65.37	1.60	1,655	32.62	.85
1948	2,687	52.91	1.31	3,147	63.47	1.54	1,551	31.26	.81
1947	2,484	49.78	1.23	2,933	60.21	1.46	1,396	28.68	.74
1946	2,270	43.85	1.07	2,680	53.21	1.27	1,305	25.91	.66

Series D 306–318. *Percentage distribution of employees in manufacturing industries, by classes of weekly earnings, selected years, 1934 to 1959*

(dollars)

Year	Under $10.00	10.00 to 19.99	20.00 to 29.99	30.00 to 39.99	40.00 to 49.99	50.00 to 59.99	60.00 to 69.99	70.00 to 79.99	80.00 to 89.99	90.00 to 99.99	100.00 and over	Total	Average weekly earnings
	306	307	308	309	310	311	312	313	314	315	316	317	318
Male wage earners													
1959	—	1	1	3	6	9	14	20	18	11	17	100	79.20
1956	—	1	2	4	8	14	22	20	13	7	—	100	70.67
1953	1	2	2	5	12	21	27	16	7	3	4	100	62.71
1950	1	2	5	14	26	28	14	6	2	1	1	100	50.93
1944	3	9	25	31	20	9	2	1[1]	—	—	—	100	34.95
1940	6	29	37	19	6	3[1]	—	—	—	—	—	100	24.82
1936	10	40	35	11	3	1[1]	—	—	—	—	—	100	20.92
1934	12	43	32	10	2	1[1]	—	—	—	—	—	100	20.31
Female wage earners													
1959	2	5	16	23	22	15	10	5	2	—	—	100	43.36
1956	2	7	19	26	22	14	7	2	1	—	—	100	39.29
1953	3	9	26	28	20	10	3	1	—	—	—	100	35.07
1950	3	16	35	30	12	2	1	—	1	—	—	100	29.00
1944	10	45	33	10	2	—	—	—	—	—	—	100	20.89
1940	23	68	8	1[1]	—	—	—	—	—	—	—	100	13.52
1936	30	65	4	1[1]	—	—	—	—	—	—	—	100	12.20
1934	34	61	4	1	—	—	—	—	—	—	—	100	11.80
Male salaried employees													
1959	—	—	1	1	3	5	7	9	11	11	52	100	112.78
1956	—	—	1	2	5	7	10	12	13	12	38	100	99.05
1953	—	—	2	3	7	11	15	14	13	10	25	100	86.43
1950	—	1	5	8	13	19	17	12	8	5	12	100	69.35
1944	1	6	13	21	20	15	9	15[1]	—	—	—	100	46.24
1940	—	—	—	—	—	—	—	—	—	—	—	—	—
1936	—	—	—	—	—	—	—	—	—	—	—	—	—
1934	—	—	—	—	—	—	—	—	—	—	—	—	—
Female salaried employees													
1959	—	1	3	10	23	27	19	10	4	2	1	100	55.73
1956	—	1	4	18	31	25	12	5	2	1	1	100	49.31
1953	—	2	9	30	34	17	5	2	1	—	—	100	43.13
1950	—	4	27	43	19	5	1	1	—	—	—	100	34.38
1944	2	31	52	13	2	—	—	—	—	—	—	100	23.79
1940	—	—	—	—	—	—	—	—	—	—	—	—	—
1936	—	—	—	—	—	—	—	—	—	—	—	—	—
1934	—	—	—	—	—	—	—	—	—	—	—	—	—

[1] and over.

Series D 319–326. *Annual averages of hourly earnings of hourly rated wage earners, selected industry groups, Canada, 1945 to 1960*

(dollars)

Year	Mining			Manufacturing			Con-struction	Service
	All	Metal	Coal	All	Durable goods	Non-durable goods		
	319	320	321	322	323	324	325	326
1960	2.09	2.17	1.75	1.78	1.94	1.64	1.94	1.04
1959	2.04	2.13	1.74	1.72	1.87	1.58	1.84	1.00
1958	1.96	2.03	1.73	1.66	1.80	1.53	1.78	.97
1957	1.88	1.95	1.62	1.61	1.73	1.47	1.76	.94
1956	1.73	1.80	1.50	1.52	1.64	1.39	1.65	.89
1955	1.61	1.66	1.48	1.45	1.56	1.33	1.52	.86
1954	1.58	1.62	1.48	1.41	1.52	1.30	1.48	.83
1953	1.54	1.57	1.50	1.36	1.48	1.23	1.44	.79
1952	1.48	1.49	1.50	1.30	1.41	1.18	1.32	.74
1951	1.35	1.36	1.37	1.18	1.27	1.08	1.19	.70
1950	1.22	1.22	1.30	1.04	1.13	.96	1.06	.66
1949	1.18	1.16	1.28	.99	1.07	.91	1.01	.64
1948	1.12	1.11	1.25	.92	.99	.85	.94	.59
1947	.99	1.00	1.11	.81	.88	.74	.85	.53
1946	.88	.88	.97	.71	.77	.64	.77	.47
1945	.85	.85	.94	.69	.76	.61	.74	.43

Series D 327–334. *Annual averages of hours per week of hourly rated wage earners, selected industry groups, Canada, 1945 to 1960*

(hours)

| Year | Mining | | | Manufacturing | | | Con-struction | Service |
| | All | Metal | Coal | All | Durable goods | Non-durable goods | | |
	327	328	329	330	331	332	333	334
1960	41.7	41.9	39.7	40.4	40.7	40.1	40.4	39.1
1959	41.5	41.7	38.6	40.7	41.0	40.4	40.2	39.4
1958	41.5	41.8	39.0	40.2	40.3	40.1	40.7	39.5
1957	42.3	42.9	39.3	40.4	40.5	40.2	41.2	39.8
1956	42.8	43.0	40.8	41.0	41.1	40.7	41.1	40.2
1955	43.2	44.1	39.7	41.0	41.2	40.8	39.9	40.4
1954	42.6	44.1	38.5	40.7	40.9	40.4	40.3	40.9
1953	42.6	44.4	37.9	41.3	41.7	40.9	41.7	41.9
1952	42.7	44.4	38.6	41.5	41.6	41.3	41.5	42.6
1951	43.1	44.1	39.3	41.7	41.9	41.5	40.3	42.5
1950	43.0	45.1	38.1	42.3	42.4	42.3	39.9	42.5
1949	42.7	45.4	37.7	42.2	42.4	42.0	39.7	42.2
1948	42.8	44.9	38.3	42.3	42.5	42.1	39.2	42.3
1947	42.3	44.4	37.2	42.5	42.8	42.3	39.3	42.5
1946	42.7	44.9	39.2	42.7	42.8	41.8	38.4	43.1
1945	43.9	45.7	40.8	44.1	44.5	43.7	38.9	43.8

Series D 335–342. *Averages of weekly wages of hourly rated wage earners, selected industry groups, Canada, 1945 to 1960*

(dollars)

| Year | Mining | | | Manufacturing | | | Con-struction | Service |
| | All | Metal | Coal | All | Durable goods | Non-durable goods | | |
	335	336	337	338	339	340	341	342
1960	87.26	90.89	69.36	71.96	78.70	65.68	78.36	40.58
1959	84.80	88.73	67.00	70.16	76.66	63.90	74.20	39.29
1958	81.30	84.77	67.43	66.77	72.42	61.31	72.36	38.28
1957	79.35	83.70	63.51	64.96	70.15	59.17	72.55	37.37
1956	73.92	77.27	61.04	62.40	67.45	56.74	67.77	35.94
1955	69.68	73.07	58.88	59.45	64.35	54.30	60.49	34.62
1954	67.14	71.27	57.02	57.43	62.13	52.36	59.85	34.03
1953	65.69	69.75	56.93	56.25	61.55	50.51	60.26	32.93
1952	63.20	66.11	57.78	53.83	58.49	48.65	54.99	31.52
1951	58.06	60.02	54.04	49.29	53.38	45.03	47.86	29.62
1950	52.46	54.93	49.49	44.03	47.74	40.57	42.13	28.09
1949	50.22	52.75	48.37	41.74	45.28	38.18	40.18	26.92
1948	48.02	49.93	47.80	38.96	42.24	35.70	36.89	24.87
1947	41.83	44.49	41.37	34.47	37.71	31.39	33.25	22.70
1946	37.53	39.60	37.98	30.15	33.00	26.92	29.53	20.08
1945	37.40	38.85	38.23	30.47	34.04	26.57	28.59	18.92

Series D 343–360. *Annual averages of weekly wages and salaries, selected industry groups and composite, Canada, 1939 to 1960*
(dollars)

| Year | Forestry (chiefly logging) | Mining | | | Manufacturing | | | Con-struction | Transportation—storage—communication | | | Communication | | Public utility opera-tion | Trade | Finance, insurance and real estate | Service | In-dustrial com-posite |
| | | All | Metal | Coal | All | Durable goods | Non-durable goods | | All | Steam rail | Storage | All | Tele-phones | | | | | |
	343	344	345	346	347	348	349	350	351	352	353	354	355	356	357	358	359	360
1960	74.85	93.80	95.67	71.61	78.19	84.20	72.86	80.46	82.32	83.05	72.72	80.47	76.88	91.52	65.19	70.83	53.08	75.83
1959	71.63	90.76	92.89	69.07	75.84	81.67	70.52	76.55	79.65	81.19	68.87	76.09	72.61	88.08	63.12	68.82	50.27	73.47
1958	71.74	86.60	88.64	69.42	72.67	77.93	67.77	74.54	74.72	75.57	65.93	71.31	67.97	83.85	60.20	66.40	48.23	70.43
1957	69.38	83.89	86.69	65.57	69.94	74.81	65.08	73.63	71.20	72.98	63.19	65.50	63.88	78.99	57.51	63.36	45.77	67.93
1956	65.40	78.01	80.32	62.02	66.71	71.42	61.91	68.58	67.29	69.32	59.92	61.23	60.05	74.39	54.64	60.29	42.93	64.44
1955	60.62	73.53	76.28	60.20	63.48	68.01	59.04	62.11	64.56	66.59	57.18	59.58	58.68	70.80	52.42	56.79	40.71	61.05
1954	59.89	70.67	74.15	58.48	61.15	65.56	56.87	61.15	62.76	65.27	55.66	56.78	56.02	67.87	50.73	53.93	38.91	59.04
1953	58.26	68.91	72.43	58.35	59.29	63.93	54.52	60.88	61.24	64.51	55.34	53.92	53.27	65.45	48.51	51.86	37.12	57.53
1952	55.84	65.79	68.37	58.73	56.36	60.65	52.07	55.82	56.81	58.96	50.15	49.55	49.55	62.00	46.08	49.35	34.41	54.41
1951	49.13	60.33	62.74	54.71	51.68	55.31	48.14	48.79	54.14	58.03	47.73	45.78	45.29	56.48	43.08	46.48	31.81	50.04
1950	42.44	54.27	57.02	50.48	46.49	49.76	43.54	43.42	49.34	52.64	43.28	42.48	42.06	51.44	39.02	44.09	29.64	45.08
1949	40.62	51.49	54.41	48.92	43.97	47.14	41.18	41.28	48.39	52.37	42.01	39.59	39.39	48.14	36.97	42.22	28.05	42.96
1948	39.11	48.77	51.12	47.81	40.67	43.46	38.20	37.99	45.51	49.44	39.32	36.69	36.59	45.16	34.38	40.08	25.87	40.06
1947	35.42	43.03	46.25	41.61	36.34	38.96	34.08	34.85	41.23	44.63	35.55	33.73	33.63	41.05	31.29	38.34	23.48	36.19
1946	29.03	39.21	41.63	39.03	32.27	34.66	30.27	31.62	37.53	40.06	33.95	32.44	32.57	38.17	28.45	36.11	21.90	32.48
1945	26.90	38.61	41.03	38.20	32.46	35.58	29.24	30.66	36.05	38.45	32.95	31.53	31.62	36.91	26.85	34.77	20.71	32.04
1944	26.54	38.05	40.68	36.95	32.49	35.71	28.55	30.63	34.62	36.06	31.99	31.27	31.37	37.01	26.21	33.61	20.25	31.85
1943	24.78	36.09	39.70	33.18	31.39	34.44	27.28	30.83	33.15	34.55	32.10	29.59	29.64	35.70	25.24	32.48	19.42	30.79
1942	20.70	34.81	38.61	31.11	28.99	32.14	25.52	27.29	31.70	33.21	30.61	28.26	28.21	34.16	24.07	31.46	18.21	28.62
1941	19.18	32.64	36.58	27.68	26.73	29.28	24.31	23.78	30.34	31.64	29.92	27.96	27.85	31.88	22.81	30.00	17.43	26.65
1940	17.30	30.24	34.60	24.34	24.48	26.72	23.09	22.71	29.72	30.85	29.45	28.20	28.13	30.20	22.53	29.70	16.74	24.94
1939	17.37	28.69	33.50	22.16	22.79	24.28	21.82	18.83	28.68	30.17	26.64	28.55	28.53	29.53	21.83	29.59	16.33	23.44

Series D 361–376. *Percentage distribution of male and female wage earners in manufacturing, by hours worked per week, Canada, 1946 to 1958*

| Year | 30 or less | 31–34 | 35–39 | 40 | 41–43 | 44 | 45–47 | 48 | 49–50 | 51–53 | 54 | 55–64 | 65 or over | Total | Average hours per week | Employees reported |
	361	362	363	364	365	366	367	368	369	370	371	372	373	374	375	376
								Wage earners of both sexes								
1958	6.0	5.0	10.0	38.0	11.0	5.0	9.0	5.0	3.0	3.0	1.0	3.0	1.0	100	41.1	862,907
1955	6.0	4.0	8.0	32.0	11.0	6.0	12.0	7.0	4.0	3.0	1.0	5.0	1.0	100	42.0	905,562
1952	6.0	3.0	8.0	26.0	12.0	7.0	14.0	8.0	5.0	4.0	1.0	5.0	1.0	100	42.6	995,785
1949	6.3	3.1	8.5	15.3	11.1	8.6	18.8	10.7	5.7	3.9	1.2	5.9	.9	100	43.2	804,971
1948	6.1	3.0	8.4	13.2	10.9	9.3	18.9	11.8	6.1	4.0	1.3	6.0	1.0	100	43.6	821,827
1947	6.7	2.9[1]	7.8[1]	12.2	10.6	8.5	18.7	12.9	6.5	4.3	1.3	6.5	1.1	100	43.7	821,510
1946	6.7	—[1]	—[1]	9.9	11.5	10.3	18.2	13.7	6.6	5.4	1.6	4.4	.9	100	43.7	764,433
								Male wage earners								
1958	5.0	4.0	8.0	40.0	11.0	4.0	9.0	5.0	4.0	3.0	1.0	4.0	1.0	100	41.7	675,979
1955	4.0	4.0	7.0	34.0	11.0	6.0	11.0	7.0	4.0	4.0	1.0	6.0	1.0	100	42.7	710,117
1952	5.0	3.0	7.0	27.0	11.0	6.0	14.0	8.0	5.0	4.0	1.0	7.0	1.0	100	43.4	712,296
1949	4.3	2.3	6.7	15.5	10.4	8.8	19.1	12.6	6.3	4.4	1.3	7.1	1.2	100	44.4	618,508
1948	4.4	2.2	6.4	12.9	9.9	9.7	19.4	13.9	6.6	4.6	1.5	7.3	1.2	100	44.7	637,822
1947	4.6	2.1[2]	6.1[2]	11.9	9.2	8.7	19.7	15.0	7.0	4.9	1.6	7.8	1.4	100	44.9	634,998
1946	4.7	—[2]	—[2]	9.6	10.6	10.7	18.8	15.8	7.1	6.3	1.9	5.4	1.1	100	44.9	583,603
								Female wage earners								
1958	12.0	7.0	15.0	31.0	12.0	5.0	10.0	3.0	2.0	2.0	—	1.0	—	100	38.7	186,928
1955	12.0	6.0	14.0	25.0	13.0	6.0	12.0	4.0	3.0	2.0	1.0	2.0	—	100	39.4	195,445
1952	12.0	6.0	14.0	21.0	14.0	7.0	14.0	4.0	3.0	2.0	1.0	2.0	—	100	39.6	193,489
1949	12.8	5.8	14.6	14.8	13.2	7.9	17.6	4.5	3.9	2.3	.5	2.0	.1	100	39.5	186,463
1948	12.2	5.6	15.0	14.1	14.5	7.9	17.4	5.1	4.1	2.0	.5	1.5	.1	100	39.8	184,005
1947	13.7	5.5[3]	13.6[3]	13.4	15.0	7.8	15.9	5.7	4.9	2.0	.5	1.9	.1	100	39.7	186,512
1946	13.1	—[3]	—[3]	10.8	14.6	8.9	16.1	7.1	5.0	2.5	.9	1.2	.1	100	40.0	180,830

[1] In 1946, 10.8% of wage earners of both sexes worked 31–39 hours.
[2] In 1946, 8.0% of male wage earners worked 31–39 hours.
[3] In 1946, 19.7% of female wage earners worked 31–39 hours.

Series D 377–389. *Percentage distribution of wage earners in manufacturing working specified number of hours in one week in the month of highest employment, by sex, Canada, 1938 to 1945*

Year	30 or less	31–43	44	45–47	48	49–50	51–54	55	56–64	65 or over	Total	Average hours per week	Employees reported
	377	378	379	380	381	382	383	384	385	386	387	388	389
						Wage earners of both sexes							
1945	7.4	16.2	12.1	10.8	21.4	9.8	8.4	3.2	7.6	3.1	100.0	46.2	1,076,496
1944	7.4	12.7	9.5	9.1	20.6	9.8	10.8	4.4	11.8	3.9	100.0	47.5	1,188,905
1943	6.2	10.7	7.4	8.3	20.5	9.6	12.5	5.2	14.6	5.0	100.0	48.8	1,208,022
1942	4.3	8.6	7.7	7.0	21.4	9.2	12.9	5.6	16.9	6.4	100.0	50.2	1,143,727
1941[2]	3.7	7.9	8.7	7.1	19.4	9.5	12.3	5.7	19.1	6.5	100.0	50.5	979,220
1940[2]	3.8	9.4	9.1	7.9	19.3	10.3	10.4	4.9	18.7	6.1	100.0	50.1	773,318
1939	3.4	14.6	13.8	10.9	22.2	11.2	7.9	4.1	10.4	1.5	100.0	47.2	586,959
1938	4.1	16.9	14.3	11.3	20.7	10.6	6.7	3.5	10.4	1.5	100.0	46.7	586,829
						Male wage earners							
1945	5.4	13.1	11.7	9.8	22.9	10.0	9.5	3.8	9.7	4.1	100.0	47.6	765,751
1944	5.3	9.8	9.0	7.9	21.5	9.5	11.9	5.0	15.1	5.0	100.0	49.1	850,034
1943	4.6	7.9	6.2	7.2	21.5	8.8	13.2	5.7	18.3	6.6	100.0	50.4	866,094
1942	3.6	7.0	6.9	5.6	21.7	8.4	12.6	5.8	20.4	8.0	100.0	51.3	843,914
1941[2]	3.2	6.8	8.0	5.8	20.0	8.5	12.0	5.8	22.0	7.9	100.0	51.5	749,340
1940[2]	3.2	8.9	8.0	7.0	20.0	9.2	10.3	4.8	21.3	7.3	100.0	50.9	601,597
1939	2.8	14.2	12.7	10.0	22.8	10.6	8.2	4.4	12.5	1.8	100.0	48.1	455,110
1938	3.4	16.6	13.1	10.5	21.3	10.0	7.4	3.6	12.3	1.8	100.0	47.3	457,041
						Female wage earners							
1945	12.3	23.8	13.2	13.2	17.7	9.1	5.7	1.9	2.4	.7	100.0	42.7	310,745
1944	12.5	20.1	10.8	12.2	18.4	10.5	8.2	2.9	3.4	1.0	100.0	43.6	338,871
1943	10.0	17.6	10.3	11.2	18.2	11.6	10.7	4.0	5.3	1.1	100.0	44.8	341,908
1942	6.2	13.0	9.9	11.1	20.8	11.5	13.5	4.9	7.2	1.9	100.0	46.9	299,813
1941[2]	5.4	11.5	10.9	11.4	17.8	12.8	13.3	5.3	9.5	2.0	100.0	47.1	229,880
1940[2]	5.8	11.3	13.1	11.2	16.9	14.1	10.8	5.2	9.5	2.0	100.0	47.3	171,721
1939	5.3	15.8	17.8	13.9	20.4	13.2	6.6	3.5	3.2	.3	100.0	45.2	131,849
1938	6.7	17.9	18.3	14.2	18.8	12.6	4.5	3.1	3.5	.4	100.0	44.6	129,788

[1] For 1938 to 1939 hours worked do not include overtime, while for 1940 to 1945 overtime is included.   [2] Percentage distribution computed.

Series D 390–402. *Percentage distribution of wage earners in manufacturing working specified number of hours per week in the month of highest employment, Canada, 1932 to 1937*

Year	40 or less	41–43	44	45–47	48	49–50	51–54	55	56–59	60 or over	Total	Average hours per week	Total wage earners
	390	391	392	393	394	395	396	397	398	399	400	401	402
1937	11.8	1.7	14.5	9.1	22.1	11.4	8.2	7.4	3.7	10.2	100	48.8	671,544
1936	12.5	2.0	13.3	8.5	22.9	11.2	7.9	7.2	3.9	10.6	100	48.7	603,712
1935	12.8	2.0	13.8	7.9	23.0	11.0	7.9	7.4	3.7	10.5	100	48.7	568,446
1934	13.3	1.9	13.1	7.3	18.0	13.6	7.7	8.8	4.1	12.2	100	49.2	530,354
1933	16.8	1.9	12.9	6.7	15.3	13.4	9.0	9.0	2.9	12.0	100	48.7	493,273
1932	15.7	1.9	13.0	6.3	16.4	13.6	8.9	8.0	3.6	12.5	100	48.9	498,569

Series D 403–405. *Average weekly hours of all salaried employees in manufacturing, by sex, Canada, 1946 to 1960*

Year	Both sexes	Males	Females
	403	404	405
1960	38.5	38.8	37.6
1959	38.5	38.9	37.6
1958	38.5	38.8	37.6
1957	38.6	39.0	37.6
1956	38.9	39.4	37.9
1955	39.1	39.6	37.9
1954	39.0	39.4	37.9
1953	39.0	39.5	37.9
1952	39.4	39.9	38.0
1951	39.5	40.0	38.2
1950	39.7	40.2	38.4
1949	40.1	40.8	38.6
1948	40.3	41.1	38.8
1947	40.4	41.2	38.9
1946	41.1	42.0	39.5

Series D406–411. *Average hours worked by persons with jobs,[1] Canada, 1926 to 1955*

Year	Total economy		Nonagriculture		Agriculture[2]		Year	Total economy		Nonagriculture		Agriculture[2]	
	Per week	Per year	Per week	Per year	Per week	Per year		Per week	Per year	Per week	Per year	Per week	Per year
	406	407	408	409	410	411		406	407	408	409	410	411
1955	43.00	2,242	40.59	2,116	55.33	2,885	1940	52.29	2,734	47.86	2,502	60.53	3,165
1954	43.27	2,256	40.68	2,121	55.10	2,873	1939	51.68	2,695	47.21	2,461	59.45	3,100
1953	43.52	2,269	41.14	2,145	54.81	2,858	1938	51.28	2,674	47.18	2,460	(58.42)	(3,046)
1952	43.40	2,269	41.06	2,147	53.78	2,812	1937	51.34	2,677	47.11	2,456	(58.92)	(3,072)
1951	43.75	2,281	41.58	2,168	52.69	2,747	1936	50.51	2,641	45.43	2,375	(59.29)	(3,100)
1950	44.82	2,337	42.89	2,236	51.85	2,703	1935	50.25	2,620	44.58	2,324	(59.95)	(3,126)
1949	45.03	2,348	42.80	2,232	52.59	2,742	1934	49.77	2,595	43.45	2,266	(60.51)	(3,155)
1948	45.60	2,384	43.04	2,250	53.70	2,808	1933	48.69	2,539	41.05	2,140	(61.02)	(3,182)
1947	45.49	2,372	43.04	2,244	53.05	2,766	1932	49.29	2,577	42.01	2,197	(61.28)	(3,204)
1946	46.74	2,437	43.57	2,272	55.37	2,887	1931	50.88	2,653	44.87	2,340	(61.91)	(3,228)
1945	48.18	2,512	44.34	2,312	58.38	3,044	1930	53.03	2,765	48.13	2,510	(62.41)	(3,254)
1944	50.13	2,616	50.60	2,384	62.16	3,250	1929	53.89	2,810	49.23	2,567	(62.90)	(3,280)
1943	51.01	2,660	46.84	2,442	62.81	3,275	1928	54.16	2,832	49.28	2,576	(63.23)	(3,306)
1942	52.22	2,723	48.16	2,511	63.29	3,300	1927	54.58	2,846	49.42	2,577	(63.84)	(3,329)
1941	52.43	2,734	48.42	2,525	61.95	3,230	1926	54.98	2,867	49.64	2,588	64.38	3,357

[1] Hours in nonagriculture have been adjusted to take into account the effects of statutory and conventional holidays.

[2] The data for hours worked in agriculture for 1927 to 1938 were based largely on straight-line interpolation between 1926, for which some data were available, and 1939, for which estimates were made in connection with the war effort. For this reason they are placed in brackets.

Series D412–413. *Union membership in Canada, showing those with international affiliation, 1911 to 1960*

(thousands)

Year	Total union membership	Membership in unions with international affiliation	Year	Total union membership	Membership in unions with international affiliation
	412	413		412	413
1960	1,459.2	1,052.0	1935	280.6	143.6
1959	1,458.6[1]	1,055.7	1934	281.3	161.4
1958	1,454.0	1,062.3	1933	285.7	167.7
1957	1,386.2	990.5	1932	283.1	176.1
1956	1,351.7	947.5	1931	310.5	215.9
1955	1,268.2	893.8	1930	322.4	230.9
1954	1,267.9	904.7	1929	319.5	230.4
1953	1,219.7	850.5	1928	300.6	211.3
1952	1,146.1	796.0	1927	290.3	204.4
1951	1,028.5[2]	725.6	1926	274.6	202.5
1950	—	—	1925	271.1	199.8
1949	1,005.6[3]	712.6	1924	260.6	202.0
1948	977.6	675.0	1923	278.1	203.8
1947	912.1	620.5	1922	276.6	206.2
1946	831.7	573.3	1921	313.3	222.9
1945	711.1	471.0	1920	373.8	267.2
1944	724.2	468.0	1919	378.0	260.2
1943	664.5	425.4	1918	248.9	201.4
1942	578.4	379.0	1917	204.6	164.9
1941	461.7	288.0	1916	160.4	129.1
1940	362.2	227.0	1915	143.3	114.7
1939	359.0	216.7	1914	166.2	140.5
1938	381.6	230.5	1913	175.8	149.6
1937	383.5	217.5	1912	160.1	136.4
1936	322.7	174.8	1911	133.1	119.4

[1] Approximately 23,000 members added as a result of change in coverage.

[2] Data for 1949 and earlier years apply to 31 December. From 1951 the figures relate to 1 January.

[3] Includes Newfoundland for the first time.

Series D414–425. *Union membership by congress affiliation, 1942 to 1960*

Year	Canadian Labour Congress			Canadian Congress of Labour			American Federation of Labor only	Congress of Industrial Organizations only	Unaffiliated international unions		Canadian and Catholic Federation of Labour	Unaffiliated national, regional and local unions
	CLC total	CLC only	CLC/AFL-CIO	CCL total	CCL only	CCL/CIO			Railway brother-hoods	Other		
	414	415	416	417	418	419	420	421	422	423	424	425
1960	1,122,831	234,083	888,748	—	—	—	33,117		9,857	66,434	101,942	124,978
1959	1,153,756	256,646	897,110	—	—	—	18,699[4]		9,808	70,994	97,092	108,227
1958	1,144,120	237,054[2]	907,066[3,4]	—	—	—	18,432		9,608[3]	79,970	104,255	97,615[2]
1957[1]	1,070,129	203,643[5]	866,486[6]	—	—	—	1,184		33,594[4]	81,205	99,372	100,701
	Trades and Labour Congress											
	TLC	TLC	TLC/AFL									
1956	640,271	111,467	528,804[7]	377,926	86,836	291,090[7]	1,050[8]		43,877	81,122	101,169	106,237
1955	600,791	107,260	493,531	361,271	96,361	264,910	9,290	2,500	40,307	58,627	99,801	95,620
1954	596,004	100,212	495,792	360,782	92,590	268,192	9,748	2,430	40,922	62,127	100,312	95,586
1953	558,722	97,450	461,272	352,538	101,737	250,801	10,524	3,000	41,751	61,935	104,486	86,758
1952	522,965	91,999	430,966	330,778	102,256	228,522	9,555	2,000	41,385	62,592	89,013	87,833
1951	470,926	80,953	389,973	312,532	107,587	204,945	11,307	1,500[10]	40,459	50,205[10]	86,184	55,408
1950[9]	—	—	—	—	—	—	—	—	—	—	—	—
1949	459,068	104,265	354,803	301,729	98,461	203,268[10,11]	13,996	27,475[10]	41,363	25,303[11]	80,089	56,616
1948	439,029	105,782	333,247	338,627	93,771	244,856	9,367	3,777	41,126	2,351	93,370	49,947
1947	403,003	104,590	298,413	329,058	97,100	231,958	6,274	2,174	39,627	2,326	91,026	38,636
1946	356,121	93,582	262,539	314,025	92,912[12]	221,113	9,513	1,680	37,731	2,247	70,367	40,013
1945	312,391	87,687	224,704	244,750	93,268	151,482	6,227	163	37,273	2,669	68,205	39,439
1944	284,732	52,886	231,846	272,146	99,687	172,459	9,516	159	36,147	1,924	74,624	44,940
1943	249,450	39,324	210,126	245,812	105,514	140,298	11,459	3,877	34,590	1,330	68,576	49,439
1942	230,290	32,634	197,656	200,089	84,942	115,147	6,622	2,400	32,984	607	54,556	50,832

[1] On 1 May 1956 the TLC and CCL were merged to form CLC. One Big Union agreed to affiliate members gradually with CLC.

[2] Amalgamated Civil Servants of Canada (11,000 members) left CLC and joined with CSAO to form CSA of C (independent).

[3] Brotherhood of Railroad Trainmen joined CLC/AFL-CIO in 1957.

[4] Operating Engineers (15,000 members) and Technical Engineers (1,000 members) were expelled from CLC but retained affiliation with AFL-CIO.

[5] British Columbia Teachers Federation (8,000) left CLC and were dropped from survey.

[6] Brotherhood of Locomotive Firemen joined CLC and AFL-CIO in the United States.

[7] These figures represent TLC/AFL-CIO and CCL/AFL-CIO. The first convention of the merged AFL-CIO was held in December 1955.

[8] In 45th Report, *Labour Organization in Canada*, shown in table 2, p. 15, as affiliated with AFL only as of 1 January 1956. Because AFL had, at that time, merged with CIO, membership shifted to AFL-CIO affiliation.

[9] Data for 1950 not published because of change in dating. For 1949 and earlier years data refer to 31 December; subsequently to 1 January.

[10] The International Union of Mine, Mill and Smelter Workers, with about 25,000 members, were expelled from the CCL in 1949 and from the CIO in 1950.

[11] The United Electrical Radio and Machine Workers of America, with a membership of about 25,000, were expelled from the CIO in the United States and from the CCL in Canada in 1949.

[12] In December 1946 the United Mine Workers of America which had been unaffiliated with respect to its United States membership, and affiliated with the CCL with respect to its Canadian membership, became affiliated with the AFL. The union withdrew from the AFL in December 1947. The data do not take this change in United States affiliation into account.

Series D 426–433. *Number of strikes and lockouts, employers and workers involved and time loss, Canada, 1901 to 1960*

Year	Number beginning during the year	Number of strikes and lockouts	Number of employers	Number of workers involved	Strikes and lockouts in existence during year, all industries — Time loss — In man working days	Average days per nonagricultural paid worker	Average days per worker involved	Per cent of estimated working time
	426	427	428	429	430	431	432	433
1960	268	274	—	49,408	738,700	—	—	.06
1959	203	218	—	100,127	2,286,900	—	—	.19
1958	253	262	—	112,397	2,872,340	—	—	.24
1957	242	249	—	91,409	1,634,880	—	—	.14
1956	221	229	437	88,680	1,246,000	.29	14.05	.11
1955	149	159	386	60,090	1,875,400	.47	31.21	.18
1954	156	174	872	62,250	1,475,200	.39	23.70	.15
1953	167	174	384	55,988	1,324,720	.34	23.66	.13
1952	216	222	518	120,818	2,879,960	.77	23.84	.29
1951	257	259	646	102,870	901,740	.25	8.77	.08
1950	158	161	345	192,153	1,389,040	.40	7.23	.13
1949	132	137	542	51,437	1,063,670	.32	20.68	.11
1948	147	154	674	42,820	885,790	.27	20.68	.09
1947	232	236	1,173	104,120	2,397,340	.77	23.02	.26
1946	225	228	1,299	139,474	4,516,390	1.49	32.38	.50
1945	106	197	418	96,068	1,457,420	.49	15.17	.17
1944	195	199	400	75,290	490,139	.16	6.51	.06
1943	401	402	651	218,404	1,041,198	.35	4.77	.12
1942	352	354	492	113,916	450,202	.16	3.95	.05
1941	229	231	658	87,091	433,914	.17	4.98	.06
1940	166	168	894	60,619	266,318	.12	4.39	.04
1939	120	122	243	41,038	224,588	.11	5.47	.04
1938	142	147	614	20,395	148,678	.08	7.29	.02
1937	274	278	630	71,905	886,393	.44	12.33	.15
1936	155	156	709	34,812	276,997	.15	7.96	.05
1935	120	120	719	33,269	288,703	.16	8.68	.05
1934	189	191	1,100	45,800	574,519	.33	12.54	.11
1933	122	125	617	26,558	317,547	.20	11.96	.07
1932	111	116	497	23,390	255,000	.15	10.90	.05
1931	86	88	266	10,738	204,238	.10	19.02	.04
1930	67	67	338	13,768	91,797	.04	6.67	.01
1929	88	90	263	12,946	152,080	.07	11.75	.02
1928	96	98	548	17,581	224,212	.11	12.75	.04
1927	72	74	480	22,299	152,570	.08	6.84	.03
1926	75	77	512	23,834	266,601	.14	11.19	.05
1925	86	87	497	28,949	1,193,281	.69	41.22	.23
1924	64	70	435	34,310	1,295,054	.76	37.75	.26
1923	77	86	450	34,261	671,750	.39	19.61	.13
1922	89	104	732	43,775	1,528,661	.95	34.92	.32
1921	159	168	1,208	28,257	1,048,914	.66	37.12	.22
1920	310	322	1,374	60,327	799,524	.42	13.25	.14
1919	332	336	1,967	148,915	3,400,942	1.79	22.84	.60
1918	228	230	782	79,743	647,942	—	—	—
1917	158	160	758	50,255	1,123,515	—	—	—
1916	118	120	332	26,538	236,814	—	—	—
1915	62	63	120	11,395	95,042	—	—	—
1914	58	63	261	9,717	490,850	—	—	—
1913	143	152	1,077	40,519	1,036,254	—	—	—
1912	179	181	1,321	42,860	1,135,786	—	—	—
1911	99	100	533	29,285	1,821,084	—	—	—
1910	94	101	1,233	22,203	731,324	—	—	—
1909	88	90	372	18,114	880,663	—	—	—
1908	72	76	179	26,071	703,571	—	—	—
1907	183	188	950	34,060	520,142	—	—	—
1906	149	150	965	23,382	378,276	—	—	—
1905	95	96	332	12,513	246,138	—	—	—
1904	103	103	591	11,420	192,890	—	—	—
1903	171	175	1,124	38,408	858,959	—	—	—
1902	124	125	532	12,709	203,301	—	—	—
1901	97	99	285	24,089	737,808	—	—	—

Series D 434–444. *Industrial accidents, fatal and nonfatal, reported by provincial workmen's compensation boards, by province, 1928 to 1960*

(number)

Year	Total	Newfound-land	Prince Edward Island	Nova Scotia	New Brunswick	Quebec	Ontario	Manitoba	Saskat-chewan	Alberta	British Columbia[1]
	434	435	436	437	438	439	440	441	442	443	444
1960	542,657	10,498	1,791	17,879	19,311	100,704	240,469	22,071	22,032	46,471	61,431
1959	547,058	9,385	1,861	17,462	13,587	99,258	252,504	18,588	21,800	48,277	64,336
1958	511,544	8,179	1,468	15,797	13,385	95,868	228,539	18,588	20,699	45,912	63,109
1957	563,299	8,658	1,393	17,623	14,711	110,401	248,492	18,414	20,803	46,933	75,871
1956	553,387	10,855	1,469	18,890	16,482	106,004	232,291	18,342	20,195	49,594	79,265
1955	496,396	9,913	1,420	17,902	15,032	95,257	208,814	17,332	17,282	43,432	70,012
1954	463,943	9,233	1,151	17,287	12,946	87,011	193,588	16,827	18,363	40,452	67,085
1953	480,269	9,732	1,005	16,855	12,928	93,306	201,976	17,346	16,218	41,965	68,938
1952	476,313	9,675	882	17,724	14,267	97,177	195,206	17,246	14,579	39,520	70,037
1951	447,011	6,228[2]	860	17,573	15,177	95,930	176,563	17,212	13,676	35,804	67,988
1950	415,170	—	686	16,697	15,023	86,246	163,723	16,513	11,441	33,337	71,504
1949	412,343	—	219[3]	17,055	13,794	85,040	166,632	17,125	10,830	32,396	69,252
1948	417,396	—	—	17,519	15,115	93,028	161,733	16,753	10,627	28,557	74,064
1947	371,245	—	—	16,445	14,693	96,135	117,192	15,746	10,152	25,864	75,018
1946	351,524	—··	—	17,507	13,275	90,900	122,523	14,795	9,509	23,068	59,947
1945	310,141	—	—	16,537	11,193	82,724	103,693	13,477	7,509	19,154	55,854
1944	322,067	—	—	16,725	11,365	84,308	109,506	13,630	6,784	19,286	60,463
1943	349,291	—	—	16,931	11,355	90,564	121,237	13,948	6,921	19,700	68,635
1942	348,795	—	—	17,778	11,535	96,888	117,886	13,787	6,766	18,680	65,475
1941	295,582	—	—	15,804	11,295	82,568	102,290	13,378	6,823	16,928	46,496
1940	233,804	—	—	13,948	10,940	65,704	72,292	11,202	6,249	14,982	38,487
1939	180,979	—	—	11,823	8,126	53,651	53,110	9,401	5,260	11,832	27,776
1938	183,103	—	—	11,408	7,834	58,335	52,272	9,331	4,508	11,928	27,487
1937	212,022	—	—	11,953	11,521	70,081	62,042	9,153	4,296	11,313	31,663
1936	150,363	—	—	10,246	8,957	39,502	54,147	9,299	4,642	9,198	14,372
1935	140,451	—	—	8,971	7,251	35,163	52,128	8,237	3,597	11,058	14,046
1934	125,454	—	—	8,063	7,858	31,557	48,573	6,578	3,223	9,608	9,994
1933	95,966	—	—	5,168	6,683	26,723	33,163	5,505	2,390	8,160	8,174
1932	111,331	—	—	5,024	4,386	30,643	34,758	5,695	2,817	8,974	19,034
1931	117,625	—	—	6,349	5,841	25,921[4]	45,239	6,671	3,969	10,049	13,586
1930	134,098	—	—	8,812	5,624	19,850	58,343	8,310	2,639[5]	12,607	17,913
1929	155,086	—	—	9,474	7,507	21,377	71,291	10,449	—	14,899	20,089
1928	123,030	—	—	7,669	6,699	2,625[6]	65,468	9,591	—	13,400	17,578

[1] Cases of 'medical aid only' not included from 1928 to 1931 and in 1934, 1936.
[2] From 1 April 1951.
[3] From 1 July 1949.

[4] Cases of medical aid only included after 1 September 1931.
[5] From 1 July 1930.
[6] From 1 September 1928.

Series D 445–447. *Provincial expenditures for workmen's compensation, 1921 to 1958*[1]

(thousands of dollars)

Year	Total cash benefits and medical aid and hospitalization	Cash benefits	Medical aid and hospitalization
	445	446	447
1958	112,448	80,028	32,420
1957	106,225	76,632	29,593
1956	95,720	69,562	26,158
1955	85,867	62,157	23,710
1954	79,997	58,227	21,770
1953	76,550	57,285	19,265
1952	74,080	55,985	18,095
1951	64,268	48,640	15,628
1950	57,592	43,845	13,747
1949[2]	53,857	40,905	12,952
1948	57,117	45,260	11,857
1947	49,271	40,058	9,213
1946	—	—	—
1943	—	—	32,515
1941	—	—	25,579
1939	—	—	18,782
1937	—	—	20,155
1933	—	—	11,788
1930	—	—	17,544
1926	—	—	11,034
1921	—	—	10,400

[1] The data include provincial 'net ordinary and capital expenditures'.
[2] Newfoundland included 1949 and subsequent years.

Series D 448–450. *Monthly averages of applications, vacancies and placements by federal employment offices in regular and casual work, 1919 to 1960*

Year	Applications	Vacancies	Placements	Year	Applications	Vacancies	Placements
	448	**449**	**450**		**448**	**449**	**450**
1960	346,167	94,077	79,858	1940	74,050	42,656	39,592
1959	315,961	97,986	82,173	1939	65,664	33,533	32,073
1958	316,949	82,887	70,011	1938	65,222	33,437	31,858
1957	304,455	93,295	73,142	1937	59,352	34,866	32,461
1956	249,348	118,802	87,248	1936	56,671	29,615	27,621
1955	249,235	102,748	79,465	1935	54,702	31,381	29,483
1954	247,499	90,693	71,799	1934	60,364	35,049	33,841
1953	227,940	107,430	82,784	1933	56,185	30,807	29,341
1952	203,848	109,073	81,709	1932	54,369	30,502	29,351
1951	180,390	110,964	76,520	1931	68,846	40,532	39,292
1950	173,048	97,027	65,900	1930	51,082	32,169	30,723
1949	149,220	85,557	57,015	1929	45,894	35,669	33,197
1948	138,052	98,799	59,362	1928	49,791	42,202	39,194
1947	135,769	128,065	64,154	1927	46,156	37,798	34,564
1946	163,225	158,544	71,618	1926	45,206	38,078	34,180
1945	209,749	201,771	124,465	1925	46,420	37,254	34,402
1944	207,107	227,397	144,993	1924	43,281	34,339	30,511
1943	224,135	253,050	162,002	1923	49,098	45,082	38,546
1942	128,677	115,153	74,635	1922	45,690	39,157	32,793
1941	69,288	45,975	42,314	1921	45,369	35,966	29,646
				1920	48,501	47,413	37,320
				1919[1]	39,922	41,186	30,387

[1] Averages of final ten months of 1919.

Series D 451–464. *Number of persons insured with unemployment insurance commission, by industry, at book renewal periods, 1942 to 1960*

(thousands)

Year[1]	Total	Agriculture	Forestry and logging	Fishing, hunting and trapping	Mining, quarrying and oil wells	Manufacturing	Construction	Transportation, storage and communication	Public utility operation	Trade	Finance, insurance and real estate	Service	Unspecified	Claimants
	451	**452**	**453**	**454**	**455**	**456**	**457**	**458**	**459**	**460**	**461**	**462**	**463**	**464**
1960	4,109.6	9.9	59.9	7.6	102.6	1,286.6	275.5	371.6	47.0	703.8	161.8	548.9	16.4	518.1
1959	4,072.9	9.6	63.0	6.7	104.4	1,295.7	317.1	371.1	48.2	699.3	156.3	538.7	20.0	442.9
1958	4,055.1	7.4	69.2	8.0	109.7	1,288.4	325.1	390.4	47.1	681.7	153.2	525.7	11.2	438.0
1957	3,807.3	7.5	81.0	10.8	102.6	1,286.3	318.3	384.5	45.0	643.0	141.7	478.4	16.0	292.3
1956	3,726.3	6.4	125.5	.7	104.8	1,218.9	378.2	336.0	39.8	608.1	130.9	476.5	32.4	268.1
1955	3,256.9	4.1	76.3	.3	98.6	1,184.5	270.9	319.7	40.9	566.3	124.0	412.4	14.5	144.3
1954	3,231.1	2.7	55.2	.1	95.3	1,143.5	182.0	328.3	36.8	522.3	117.7	345.5	22.0	379.9
1953	3,150.7	2.2	73.2	.3	90.9	1,180.7	199.9	343.9	34.3	494.6	111.0	348.2	8.9	262.6
1952	3,090.2	2.1	97.1	.4	101.2	1,123.3	185.1	345.9	34.2	485.9	107.0	341.0	28.4	238.7
1951	3,007.9	2.2	107.8	.4	93.0	1,161.1	172.4	320.8	38.2	487.3	105.1	325.8	7.0	186.7
1950	2,618.6	1.7	39.5	.6	81.7	986.7	142.5	294.9	31.8	423.8	84.8	291.1	11.7	227.8
1949	2,610.2	1.4	11.9	.6	79.8	1,000.8	143.5	251.0	30.9	444.4	82.8	296.6	25.0	241.7
1948	2,298.3	1.9	14.8	.8	72.8	981.0	124.3	235.6	23.6	390.7	75.7	254.5	9.8	113.1
1947	2,280.2	1.5	13.4	.2[2]	72.3	996.7	117.4	218.3	23.8	392.5	70.2	256.2	5.7	112.0
1946	2,128.7	1.5	2.3[2]	—[2]	71.0	924.3	93.3	222.9	19.5	346.1	68.9	237.2	141.9	—
1945	2,198.8	1.5	1.0	—	68.2	1,143.1	69.5	200.4	20.3	332.8	65.4	266.1	30.6	—
1944	2,209.9	1.4	.5	—	78.0	1,191.3	67.1	178.2	19.2	313.4	63.9	253.9	43.0	—
1943	1,997.1	1.1	.2	—	70.4	1,064.4	104.9	167.7	14.1	274.5	59.3	219.4	21.8	—
1942	2,438.9	2.3	3.8	—	92.5	1,235.1	160.7	206.4	21.4	361.4	67.5	287.8	—	—

[1] The data for 1942 relate to 31 August. From 1943 to 1954, inclusive, the data apply to 1 April. With the exception of 1957, when the data relate to 1 May, for subsequent years the data apply to 1 June.

[2] From 1946 to 1942 forestry and logging, series D 453, includes fishing, hunting and trapping, series D 454.

Series D 465–470. *Unemployment insurance, insured population and beneficiary and claimant data, 1942 to 1960*

(thousands)

Year	Insured population (annual average)	Initial and renewal claims (yearly total)	Claimants (annual average)	Beneficiaries (annual average)	Weeks compensated (yearly total)	Benefits paid (yearly total) (dollars)
	465	**466**	**467**	**468**	**469**	**470**
1960	4,134	2,700	518.2	430.0	21,601	481,836
1959	4,114	2,428	454.2	384.8	19,170	406,097
1958	4,108	2,781	551.5	459.8	23,152	492,901
1957	3,987	2,373	380.2	295.0	14,572	305,076
1956	3,750	1,625	272.3	218.1	11,177	210,330
1955	3,436	1,930	319.1	261.0	12,389	229,124
1954	3,294	2,102	356.8	270.0	13,124	241,113
1953	3,197	1,680	251.7	168.6	8,718	157,779
1952	3,129	1,391	219.4	139.5	7,257	118,810
1951	3,046	1,144	167.3	100.1	5,222	76,669
1950[1]	2,743	1,150	188.0	127.9	6,988	99,057
1949	2,591	934	149.3	130.3	5,148	65,351
1948	2,436	649	94.7	92.2	3,390	40,268
1947	2,314	443	71.3	70.1	2,756	32,039
1946	2,168	489	97.8	101.3	4,245	51,085
1945	2,148	296	41.1	31.7	1,224	14,576
1944	—	91	10.5	8.6	283	3,277
1943	—	37	—	2.8	85	941
1942	—	27	—	1.4	30	353

[1] Claims data on supplementary (now called seasonal) benefit included as of March 1950. The period during which these benefits were paid varied. In the winter of 1957–8 these benefits were paid in the period 1 December 1957 to 30 June 1958. In subsequent years the dates were 1 December to mid-May.

APPENDIX. WAGE RATES AND INDEXES OF WAGE RATES, SELECTED OCCUPATIONS IN THE CONSTRUCTION INDUSTRY IN ONTARIO, 1889 TO 1903

Series D 471–484. *Total number of days worked and average daily wage rates in selected construction occupations, Ottawa and Toronto areas, 1889 to 1903*

Year[1]	Ottawa area					
	Labourers		Carpenters		Masons and bricklayers	
	Total days worked (number)	Average daily wage rate (dollars)	Total days worked (number)	Average daily wage rate (dollars)	Total days worked (number)	Average daily wage rate (dollars)
	471	**472**	**473**	**474**	**475**	**476**
1903	71,024	1.39	22,492	2.08	1,823	2.69
1902	64,402	1.39	20,617	2.04	2,126	2.70
1901	55,015	1.36	17,541	2.05	2,588	2.57
1900	50,228	1.31	19,824	2.01	3,513	2.48
1899	40,514	1.30	18,302	2.03	2,988	2.45
1898	44,228	1.27	19,202	2.02	2,620	2.49
1897	41,277	1.29	18,066	2.01	1,730	2.52
1896	44,799	1.27	17,917	2.05	2,432	2.52
1895	34,134	1.27	18,800	2.04	2,181	2.40
1894	36,890	1.28	18,507	2.02	2,569	2.43
1893	34,383	1.29	18,173	1.97	1,467	2.34
1892	31,686	1.30	18,662	1.99	1,704	2.50
1891	49,947	1.28	17,740	1.97	2,620	2.58
1890	49,001	1.28	15,935	2.02	2,197	2.51
1889	51,975	1.28	7,244	2.02	151	2.96

[1] Fiscal years ending 30 June of the year given.

Series D 471–484. *Total number of days worked and average daily wage rates in selected construction occupations, Ottawa and Toronto areas, 1889 to 1903 (continuation)*

| | Ottawa area | | Toronto area | | | | | |
| | Painters | | Labourers | | Carpenters | | Painters | |
Year[1]	Total days worked (number)	Average daily wage rate (dollars)	Total days worked (number)	Average daily wage rate (dollars)	Total days worked (number)	Average daily wage rate (dollars)	Total days worked (number)	Average daily wage rate (dollars)
	477	**478**	**479**	**480**	**481**	**482**	**483**	**484**
1903	6,326	2.03	50,944	1.42	16,972	1.92	772	1.85
1902	5,755	2.02	30,406	1.38	9,100	1.85	1,026	1.79
1901	7,395	2.01	35,771	1.30	10,119	1.86	448	1.82
1900	6,744	1.93	24,418	1.29	11,085	1.86	260	1.67
1899	4,562	1.93	19,783	1.32	8,991	1.86	150	1.82
1898	5,283	1.96	21,280	1.32	8,755	1.86	327	1.69
1897	5,515	1.98	21,730	1.28	8,030	1.83	311	1.70
1896	4,068	1.93	18,381	1.28	10,047	1.85	339	1.75
1895	3,112	1.90	15,958	1.30	9,294	1.81	165	1.86
1894	3,711	1.92	13,007	1.31	8,016	1.81	96	1.56
1893	2,575	1.94	20,528	1.36	8,081	1.84	304	1.92
1892	1,584	1.89	23,488	1.37	7,870	1.83	253	1.92
1891	1,710	1.93	23,068	1.37	7,991	1.84	747	1.92
1890	494	1.57	20,259	1.40	7,602	1.86	472	1.77
1889	1,580	2.19	26,719	1.36	9,655	1.93	589	1.77

[1] Fiscal years ending 30 June of the year given.

Series D 485–488. *Combined indexes of wage rates of selected occupations in the construction industry, Ottawa and Toronto areas, 1889 to 1903*

(1891 = 100)

| | Carpenters, masons and painters | | Carpenters, masons, labourers and painters | |
Year[1]	Ottawa area	Toronto area	Ottawa area	Toronto area
	485	**486**	**487**	**488**
1903	104.94	104.09	106.55	103.92
1902	103.82	100.97	105.63	100.73
1901	101.96	101.06	104.23	98.41
1900	100.27	94.68	101.05	94.24
1899	100.50	90.74	100.93	92.78
1898	100.80	98.60	100.35	97.80
1897	100.94	94.08	101.03	93.65
1896	101.80	99.25	100.84	96.81
1895	100.21	95.03	99.88	94.82
1894	99.95	95.93	100.19	95.84
1893	97.34	102.88	99.14	101.21
1892	99.48	101.55	100.41	100.83
1891	100.00	100.00	100.00	100.00
1890	97.87	97.62	98.86	99.44
1889	107.14	103.17	104.56	101.49

[1] Fiscal years ending 30 June of the year given.

SECTION E: NATIONAL INCOME AND THE CAPITAL STOCK

M. C. URQUHART, *Queen's University*

The statistical data of this section are in three subsections and an appendix. They contain data on national income and expenditure and related aggregates from 1926 to 1960 in series E 1–129; on income produced, by industry, from 1919 to 1926 and on gross capital formation from 1901 to 1930 in series E 130–159; on the stock of tangible capital from 1926 onwards in series E 160–201; and, in the appendix, on income produced, by industry, from 1911 to 1920 and on gross national product for census years from 1870 to 1920 in series E 201–224.

The arrangement of this section differs somewhat from that of most of the other sections in that the first two tables on national income and gross national product, on the one hand, and gross national expenditure, on the other, for the period 1926 to 1960, are not immediately followed by data on national income or income produced for the period preceding 1926. The reason for the different arrangement is that all the data in series E 1–129 are articulated in the sense that each set of series is consistent with or can be easily reconciled with the other data of the subsection: hence these data form a logical group.

The following official publications were used as sources of material:

Three publications of the Dominion Bureau of Statistics, *National Accounts, Income and Expenditure, 1926–1956* (Ottawa, Queen's Printer, 1958), *National Accounts, Income and Expenditure, 1962* (Ottawa, Queen's Printer, 1963), *Private and Public Investment in Canada, 1946–1957* (Ottawa, Queen's Printer, 1959); Department of Trade and Commerce, *Private and Public Investment in Canada, Outlook*, annual since 1946 (Ottawa, Queen's Printer), issues for 1960, 1961 and 1962; Department of Trade and Commerce, *Private and Public Investment in Canada, 1926–1951* (Ottawa, Department of Trade and Commerce, 1951); Wm. C. Hood and Anthony Scott, Royal Commission on Canada's Economic Prospects, *Output, Labour and Capital in the Canadian Economy* (Hull, Queen's Printer, 1957).

Three privately published sources were used:

J. J. Deutsch, 'War Finance and the Canadian Economy, 1914–1920', *The Canadian Journal of Economics and Political Science*, vol. VI, no. 4 (November 1940) (Toronto, University of Toronto Press); K. A. H. Buckley, *Capital Formation in Canada, 1896–1930* (Toronto, University of Toronto Press, 1951); O. J. Firestone, International Association for Research in Income and Wealth, *Canada's Economic Development, 1867–1953*, Income and Wealth, series VII (London, Bowes and Bowes, 1958); in addition some unpublished material was provided directly by the Dominion Bureau of Statistics and some data were obtained from an unpublished private memorandum by D. H. Jones of the Dominion Bureau of Statistics.

General note

In contrast with other sections of this volume, detailed descriptions of the concepts and methods of estimation of most of the data of this section are found in a small number of readily accessible sources. A lengthy description of such concepts and methods for the data of the national accounts for 1926 to 1960 is found in D.B.S., *National Accounts, Income and Expenditure, 1926–56*. Likewise, descriptions of concepts and methods used in the capital formation estimates for 1926 to 1960 can be found in D.B.S., *Private and Public Investment in Canada, 1946–57* (quite brief), and in Department of Trade and Commerce, *Private and Public Investment in Canada, 1926–51*; in addition, much of the comment on the development of estimates of construction expenditures, given in section R, 'Construction and Housing', in this volume, applies to all fixed capital formation. The material on the capital stock and the explanation of concepts and methods (with the exception of inventory stocks) come from Hood and Scott, *Output Labour and Employment in the Canadian Economy*. The remaining material, which is small in quantity, is found in four additional sources. Owing to the accessibility of this limited number of sources, to the general familiarity of users with the concepts of the national accounts, and to the amount of space that a thorough discussion of concepts would require, the general description of concepts is made relatively short. Descriptions of the content of the various individual series are given, however, in sufficient detail for general use of the material.

The source volumes are drawn on heavily for the descriptions given here without explicit acknowledgement in each instance except when a direct quotation is used. Substantial parts of this text are paraphrased from them.

Since national income estimation draws on nearly the whole range of economic statistics, substantial parts of the content of other sections of this volume are related closely to the data of this section. These data include: the distribution of labour income by industry and by province, series D 238–266; detail of the current account balance of payments which appears in series F 57–90; the implicit price deflators obtained in the conversion of gross national expenditure in current dollars to constant dollars, series J 153–164; income in agriculture, series L 67–77; capital formation in manufacturing by main groups, series Q 307–349; some of the detail of construction expenditure, in section R. Of the foregoing data, the industrial distribution of labour income and the implicit price deflators are taken from the *National Accounts* and hence are consistent with the totals of the national accounts: the remainder were modified slightly for national accounts purposes. There are also other data, in several sections, related to but not explicitly adjusted to concepts and methods used in preparing the national accounts.

The data of this section are, with one exception, national totals, whether the particular series is a component of some larger aggregate or a grand total of some kind itself. For example, each component of gross national product in series E 1–12, as well as each of the aggregates for national income and for gross national product, is a total for all Canada. The exception is found in series E 79–90 which gives personal income by province.

In all data of this section Newfoundland is included from 1949 onward.

NATIONAL INCOME AND EXPENDITURE AND RELATED AGGREGATES,
1926 to 1960 (Series E1–129)

General note

The first estimates of national income of Canada, prepared by scholars in Great Britain, predate the First World War. The history of the official preparation of national income estimates in Canada begins, however, in 1919 with the publication of estimates for 1911 and 1918, prepared by R. H. Coats, Dominion Statistician, even though they appeared in a private publication, the *Monetary Times Annual*, 3 January 1919. Thereafter at intervals, estimates of national income, with limited component detail, were published by the Dominion Bureau of Statistics until the Second World War. In the meantime, D. C. McGregor in 1934, the Bank of Nova Scotia in 1935 and later, and the research staff of the Rowell-Sirois Royal Commission of Dominion-Provincial Relations in 1939 and 1940 also published historical estimates.

The development of a comprehensive set of national accounts by the Dominion Bureau of Statistics, with all the now familiar detail, began, however, at the end of the Second World War. The estimates in elaborated form were eventually carried back to 1926 with the use of concepts, methods and additional raw material that rendered the earlier estimates obsolete. The earlier work was useful, however, in having resulted in the preparation and preservation of many data that were of great value for the revised estimates. (See Simon A. Goldberg, 'The Development of the National Accounts in Canada', *The Canadian Journal of Economics and Political Science*, vol. xv, no. 1 (February 1949) for a description of the historical development of the national accounts in Canada. See also Firestone, *Canada's Economic Development 1867–1953*, for the history and reproduction of all the earlier estimates.)

Gross national product is the '...value of the unduplicated total of goods and services produced in a given period...by Canadian residents' (*National Accounts, 1926–1956*, p. 107). From a different viewpoint, it can also be regarded as a money measure of the production, in some period, of final goods and services (plus changes in inventories of raw materials and intermediate goods) by factors of production owned by Canadian residents (see below the definition of a Canadian resident). It is gross because it is a measurement of output before any allowance is made for capital consumption, the using up of capital in the form of depreciation, obsolescence, fire loss and the like during the period for which output is measured. The basic measurement is made in terms of the prices at which these goods and services are valued in the market in the period in which they are produced, though for some purposes measurement is made in constant dollars, the dollars of some base period. The period of measurement for all the data given here is a year; the Dominion Bureau of Statistics also publishes quarterly data which are available for as far back as 1947.

National income is the total of all income paid to or accruing to Canadian residents for the services of factors of production owned by them. In it, property income is measured net after provision for making good capital consumption. The addition to national income of indirect taxes less subsidies and of capital consumption allowances and miscellaneous valuation adjustments yields a total containing all the charges against gross national product as defined. In conformity with common practice, gross national product in Canada is calculated as the sum of the three foregoing items.

Gross national expenditure at market prices is a measure of gross final user outlay by Canadian residents on currently produced goods and services (including net investment abroad) plus changes in inventories owned by Canadian residents. Conceptually it is exactly equal in size to gross national product.

Canadian residents are defined as 'both individuals and institutions such as government agencies, corporations, and non-profit institutions which are normally resident in Canada' (D.B.S., *National Accounts, 1926–1956*, p. 106). Canadian tourists and commercial travellers travelling abroad and members of the Canadian diplomatic service or official missions and of the armed forces abroad are treated as Canadian residents. Their counterparts from other countries, temporarily in Canada, are not treated as Canadian residents.

Measures of gross national product and gross national expenditure and their components are supplemented by a number of sector accounts, each sector being made up of those participants in economic life who have common characteristics. The sector accounts present the transactions among them. The Canadian sector accounts are limited to four: (1) a personal income and expenditure account; (2) a government revenue and expenditure account; (3) a business consolidated operating account; and (4) a receipts and expenditure account for the rest of the world covering international current account transactions. Each of the foregoing accounts concerns well-defined economic units with common characteristics. But together they do not take account of the expenditures on private capital formation and the provision of the saving that make the capital formation possible. Participants in all four of the above sectors contribute to saving and investment. A fifth account then deals with saving and investment. The components of the five accounts (in finer detail than given in this volume) include all the items that enter into the gross national product and the gross national expenditure and are articulated with one another. All but the business operating account and the foreign account are given here: the latter appears in nearly the same form as given in the national accounts in section F. For a fuller description of the logic of the sector accounts see D.B.S., *National Accounts, 1926–1956*, p. 117.

While national income includes only income earned for productive service rendered, and national expenditure includes only outlay for goods and services, the sector accounts include transfer payments from one sector to another or, in the case of government interest payments, within sectors. A transfer payment is a payment from one economic body to another without there being any offsetting consideration such as provision of goods or services or debt instruments. Payment of interest on the public debt, though not called a transfer payment in the national accounts, is treated like a transfer payment.

Attention is drawn to a few of the conventions followed in the construction of the national accounts.

First, the personal sector covers in addition to individuals and families—in their capacity as income receivers, consumers and savers—private noncommercial institutions and private pension funds. Private noncommercial institutions are bodies whose service charges are not expected to cover expenses: they include municipal, lay and religious hospitals, universities, labour unions, professional organizations, fraternal societies and charitable institutions. These institutions are, in effect, treated as associations of individuals. Their operating expenditures are included with personal expenditure; their investment income is included with investment income of persons; and gifts to them from government and business are treated as transfer payments to persons. In what follows the word 'persons' is to be interpreted as meaning the personal sector as described above.

Second, personal insurance with all insurance companies in their strictly insurance operations is regarded as having two aspects. One aspect is the transfer of a (major) part of the premium receipts from those paying premiums to claimants either in the same or in future periods. These transfers are regarded as any transfer payment: they are not treated as a part of national income or expenditure and are not reflected within the sector account itself. The other aspect is that insurance companies provide a service in administering these transfers. The administrative expenses of insurance relating to persons are regarded as personal expenditure on consumer goods and services.

Life insurance companies have an added characteristic. They also hold savings of individuals in connexion with both their life insurance reserves and in the purely investment features of some policies. In this regard, they also are treated as 'associations of individuals'. All investment income of the companies is regarded as a part of personal income. The investment expense of managing the portfolio is treated as a part of personal expenditure. Thus all administrative expenses of life insurance companies are included in personal consumer expenditure, part for their services of insurance management, part for their services of portfolio management. The treatment followed makes saving of life insurance companies a part of personal saving.

Third, banks and similar institutions render services to persons without specific charge. They recover the cost of these services from the excess of interest received on their own loans and investments over payments of deposit interest. An imputed amount equal to the value of these services is included in both personal and national income and expenditure. Deposit interest paid persons is also included as a part of personal and national income. Thus banks, in this aspect of their operations, are treated somewhat like associations of individuals.

Fourth, in common with the practice of nearly all countries which have a highly developed market economy, the measurement of gross national product and expenditures covers mainly provision of goods and services through transactions in markets. But there are exceptions. Income in kind of farmers and of employees in nonfarm sectors is included in both income and expenditure. Imputed income (and expenditure) on owner-occupied homes and government buildings and imputed capital consumption allowances on them are also included. The current operation of these owner-occupied buildings is regarded as taking place in the business sector, however, and all capital consumption allowances are allocated to it. While owner-occupied residential construction is included with business gross fixed capital formation, government building construction is included with government capital formation.

Fifth, the operations of extra-budgetary government funds, such as those of the Unemployment Insurance Commission, Workmen's Compensation and Old Age Security, are consolidated in the government account.

Finally, government enterprises that operate mainly on a commercial basis, meeting their operating expenditures from the sale of goods and services, are included with the business sector and only net profits and interest on advances or loans to them are credited to government receipts. Their capital expenditure is also classified as business gross fixed capital formation except for post-office buildings and equipment which are included with government gross fixed capital formation.

The raw material for constructing the national accounts is drawn from a major part of all economic statistics. Much of it appears in other sections of this volume. The source material becomes progressively better from earlier to later years, less improvisation in its use is needed and the final estimates become correspondingly more accurate.

Five main categories of estimating techniques are used, either separately or in combination. First, a substantial part of the final data is obtained more or less in the form required from annual surveys or reports covering, in many cases, the whole period, or, in other cases, only the later years: relatively little manipulation of the data is required to obtain the final estimates. Second, some of the data are available in fairly full coverage in the form desired for benchmark years: interpolation or extrapolation to other years is made by use of related but less complete data. Third, the estimates may be built up by combining data on quantities of goods and services with their prices in unit value or index form to obtain a value estimate: in some cases, the price and quantity data are those actually desired; in others, particularly for price series, data for as closely related items as possible are used. Fourth, some of the income data, particularly for unincorporated business, are estimated by construction of synthetic operating accounts, income being obtained by subtracting expenses from gross income. Fifth, certain incomes are obtained by their calculation as a percentage of some larger total.

A major part of the data for wages and salaries—it is estimated at 75 per cent in 1955—comes from annual surveys or reports. These include material collected by D.B.S. for the whole period in censuses of manufacturing, mining, forestry, and power laundries and dry-cleaning establishments, in annual surveys of steam and electric railways and local urban transport, electric utilities, telephones and telegraphs, and, beginning in 1938, air transport, in 1941, bus and motor-vehicle transport, in 1942, public general hospitals, in 1944, the storage industry, in 1949, oil pipelines, and in 1954, water transport. Data for all insurance companies are available throughout from annual reports of the Superintendent of Insurance, and from provincial registrars of loan and trust companies. Banking wages and salaries data throughout are provided by the Canadian Bankers Association from bank returns. Federal and provincial wages and salaries, including those connected with extra-budgetary funds, and teachers' salaries are obtained throughout from public accounts and departmental reports. Municipal expenditures are available in fairly full coverage beginning in 1942 and less fully for earlier years. In some instances, when the D.B.S. annual censuses or surveys did not cover all wages in an industry, they were adjusted upon the basis of the ratio of total revenues of all companies, which were usually known, to the revenues of covered companies. Head office employees were not covered before 1946 in mining and 1949 in manufacturing and an estimate to include them in earlier years was added.

Estimates of wages and salaries using benchmark data rely most heavily on reasonably complete information from the censuses for 1941 and 1951 and somewhat less complete data of the census of 1931 (which applied, in many cases, to 1930); in some instances, when a new annual survey was begun the results for the first year were used as the benchmark for earlier years, for example, in air transport. Estimates are based on census benchmark data for 1931 (or 1930), 1941 and 1951 for radio and lately television broadcasting (1931 required some manipulation), agriculture, fishing, wholesale and retail trade, miscellaneous finance, legal services, domestic service, and laundries, cleaning and dyeing establishments. Estimates are based on census benchmarks in 1941 and 1951 for hunting and trapping, water transport (1941 only), taxi service, grain elevators (storage), health services outside hospitals and hotels and restaurants.

The methods of interpolation and extrapolation varied. They were frequently considerably more satisfactory after 1941 than before. For the treatment of agriculture see section L. A sample of the methods used in other industries follows. In fisheries, the projectors are based on total value of fish caught and landed (see section M); in hunting and trapping, on the value of wild life fur production; in water transport, on payrolls indexes (see section D) since 1941 and on an index obtained by combining an index of numbers employed in shipping and stevedoring with an index of wage rates in water transport before 1941; in taxi service, on payrolls in transportation, communication and service after 1951, on an index combining number of passenger cars registered and average weekly earnings of truck drivers for 1941 to 1951 and on the number of registered taxis in Canada and wage rate indexes for 1926 to 1941; in grain elevators (storage) on methods like those used in water transport; in wholesale and retail trade, for each separately, on indexes of payrolls after 1941, on indexes of wholesale and retail sales from 1930 to 1940 and on indexes combining employment with the general average index of wage rates before 1930; and on like methods for other groups using benchmark data.

The above group, based on use of benchmark data and more or less closely associated projecting material, covered approximately 23 per cent of wages and salaries in 1955.

A final group, accounting for about 2 per cent of wages and salaries in 1955, was also based in part on benchmark data built up from the censuses of 1931, 1941 and 1951 but the projections to other years were made on rather remotely related data. For example, the indexes used in projecting wages and salaries of those in applied science, journalism, accounting, art and music are projected on a combined index of doctors' salaries, general employment and general average wage rates for 1926 to 1941, on a payroll index for service between 1941 and 1951, and on a combined index of paid workers in service and the consumer price index after 1951. Other groups in this category include religious service, recreational service, business service, barbering and hairdressing, undertaking and other personal service.

Income in kind is calculated, by industry, by projecting census or special survey benchmark data on the basis of movements in employment and living costs. In forestry, since 1944, it is estimated from annual surveys.

Supplementary labour income, namely, employers' contributions to pensions, social insurance and welfare funds, is estimated in a number of ways. For banks, railways, insurance companies and federal and provincial governments, the data are available for each year from annual surveys or published reports and through correspondence. For manufacturing, electric power, trade, mining and telephone, the data obtained in a survey made by D.B.S. in 1944 are projected to other years on the basis of the trend in total wages and salaries in each industry. Beginning in 1946 employer contributions to pension funds and in 1954 to group insurance are obtained from *Taxation Statistics* (see below). The Unemployment Insurance Commission and provincial workmen's compensation boards provide data on employer contributions to their funds.

Corporate profits are obtained from compilations made by the Department of National Revenue from tax returns. Beginning in 1944, they are published in the Department's *Taxation Statistics*. For 1926 to 1944 a special tabulation, by industry, was prepared by the Department of National Revenue from a sample of corporation tax returns of a list of about 1,000 companies including subsidiaries filed in consolidated returns. All large companies—largeness was determined by sales—were included and for smaller companies the proportion covered became progressively smaller as company size decreased. While the profits and taxes of banks and insurance companies are covered in *Taxation Statistics*, these institutions were not covered in the sample since the information was available in reports made to the Department of Finance and the Superintendent of Insurance.

As will be noted below, the corporation tax data are also very valuable for other financial information.

Rent, interest and miscellaneous investment income is divided between that received by or accruing to persons on one hand and governments on the other; income of this kind received by corporations is reflected in profits. Investment income of farm operators and most other unincorporated business from outside their own businesses is included with personal investment income. Dividends received from Canadian corporations are not included since corporate profits are calculated before dividend payments.

Basic sources of data for estimating investment income both received and paid by businesses and government are found, for all years, in *Taxation Statistics* and the corporate sample study (see above), in reports of the Superintendent of Insurance of Canada for federally registered insurance companies, for loan and trust companies and for fraternal and mutual benefit societies, in the reports required of provincially registered loan and trust companies and fraternal societies by provinces (particularly in Ontario and Quebec), in material on credit unions, assembled by the federal department of agriculture, in federal and provincial public accounts and departmental and agency reports. In addition the Central Mortgage and Housing Corporation, in operation since the end of the war, has collected much information on mortgages, housing and housing rentals and provides a good deal of information generated in its own operations. Benchmark data for investment income in industrial pension funds were obtained by special D.B.S. surveys for 1938, 1944 and 1953 and for municipal pension funds in 1945, 1946 and 1949. The decennial and prairie quinquennial census also provide benchmark data particularly for housing and agriculture. Consumer credit outstanding was assembled beginning in 1938 by the Bank of Canada and more recently by D.B.S. International payments of investment income are obtained from balance of payments data (see section F). D.B.S. estimates mortgage debt of farmers and interest paid by them from the census and farm surveys (see section L).

Personal investment income is in most cases calculated for each of its various categories as a residual. First, estimates of interest, nonresidential rental and like payments are made; where interest payments are not directly available they are calculated by multiplying the amount of debt outstanding by a representative rate of interest. Second, the total net rental for all housing and the distribution of ownership of housing between the personal and other sectors of the economy are estimated. Third, the portion of net rents and interest paid to business and government is calculated. The remainder is then assigned to the personal sector.

Bond interest received and paid in the nonpersonal sectors is fairly well covered in the sources of annual data referred to above. It is one of the stronger parts of the estimates.

Estimation of mortgage interest provides an example of the application of interest rates to total debt outstanding. Farm mortgages outstanding and farm mortgage interest paid are calculated by D.B.S. from agricultural benchmark data, from farm surveys and other sources. The amount of farm mortgage debt held by business and government is then calculated, the remainder being assigned to the personal sector. Farm mortgage interest paid is then divided between persons and others in proportion to their relative holdings. Personal holdings of nonfarm mortgages 'are assumed to be an arbitrary percentage of mortgage holdings by business and government' (*National Accounts, 1926–1956*, p. 144). Personal receipts of nonfarm mortgage interest are then calculated by multiplying personal mortgage holdings by an average rate of interest (obtained by the Central

Mortgage and Housing Corporation from reports of twelve leading life insurance companies). Personal mortgage interest receipts are fortunately (from a measurement viewpoint) relatively small since they are among the least satisfactory of the estimates.

Personal receipts of bank deposit interest require that total bank deposit interest paid be split between the personal and other sectors. This division has been done, beginning in 1943, by the Bank of Canada by subtracting interest paid corporations and paid abroad from total deposit interest as reported to the Department of Finance. Before 1943 it is projected on the basis of the levels of interest-bearing deposits and the interest rate paid on such deposits.

Nonfarm residential rents include paid net rents on rented homes and imputed net rents on owned homes. The basic data on distribution of residences between owned and rented homes are obtained in the decennial census. Central Mortgage and Housing Corporation adjusts and keeps these data up to date from data collected in its own operations and other sources. Average annual gross paid rents, were available in 1941. They were projected forward to 1948 and backward for earlier years on the rent component of the cost of living index. From 1949 they have been collected by a monthly survey of D.B.S. Cost of facilities included in reported rents, such as janitor services, use of furniture, stoves and refrigerators, light, heat and the like, are deducted to give a gross space rent: facility costs were obtained by a survey of landlords by D.B.S. in 1955 and projected, apparently rather arbitrarily, to other years. The total gross space rental value of all residences is then calculated by multiplying the number of residential units by average gross space rents—average imputed owner-occupied space rents differ from those of rented units only in proportion to differences in number of rooms between the two. Total net rents are then calculated from total gross rents by subtraction of costs of repair and maintenance, property taxes, fire insurance, mortgage interest, real estate transfer costs and depreciation. The part accruing to persons is then obtained by subtracting the net paid rents received by business and governments from the total net rent as calculated. The Central Mortgage and Housing Corporation and D.B.S. calculate much of the operating expenses from the relevant sources listed above.

Imputed returns for services provided without direct charge by banks and other financial institutions are made from their operating expenses.

All the above calculations are first made without differentiating between interest paid for use of land and capital on one hand and interest on the public debt and the transfer portion on consumer credit interest on the other. These latter are subtracted, in their entirety, from the total first obtained to yield the figures used for calculating national income.

Government investment income is calculated year by year from government public accounts and reports of departments and agencies.

The calculation of net farm income of unincorporated farmers from farm production is described in section L. Adjustments for national income purposes are noted in the notes to series E 5 of this section.

Net income of nonfarm unincorporated business, the earnings of working proprietors from their own businesses, makes substantial use of benchmark data and projections from them. Average income of independent professional practitioners is obtained from *Taxation Statistics* beginning in various years for different professions from 1946 onward. Total income for the years concerned for each profession is obtained by multiplying the average incomes by the numbers of practitioners. The latter

are available for various years from 1938 onward from decennial census data, from D.B.S. surveys, including after 1946 the labour force survey (see section C) and from professional associations. Average incomes of each of the various professions were also available in the 1941 census and in other years from special surveys of D.B.S.—doctors for 1939 and 1944 to 1946, dentists for 1941 to 1944, lawyers for 1946 to 1948, accountants in 1944. Various means of making estimates for intervening years were made. For 1931 to 1937 the estimated income for all professions together in 1938 is carried back on the basis of the movement in total net income of independent professional practitioners paying income tax. For 1926 to 1931 the projection was on the basis of data prepared for the Rowell-Sirois Commission.

The remaining unincorporated data are calculated, most commonly, from fewer benchmark years and interpolations are frequently made on less closely connected indexes than those for professional practice. Fishing and hunting and trapping are, however, calculated for all years by subtraction of operating expenses from gross revenue. Two examples of calculation of other nonfarm unincorporated business must suffice. Income in retail trade is calculated by applying 'a weighted average ratio of "net profits (before withdrawals) to net sales"' (*National Accounts, 1926–1956*, p. 151). The ratios are obtained from periodic surveys of operating results and financial structure from 1941 onward (see section T). Net sales are calculated by use of census benchmark data for 1931, 1941 and 1951 and projections are made on the basis of annual retail sales data obtained mainly from the annual (or monthly) surveys of retail trade (see section T). Unincorporated income in construction for 1953 and later years is calculated by multiplying number of proprietors, obtained from the labour force survey (see section C), by average net incomes reported in *Taxation Statistics*. A benchmark for 1946 is calculated similarly but by use of average net income obtained in the construction census. Interpolation between 1946 and 1953 is done by use of an index formed from the ratio between gross and net income, from *Taxation Statistics*, and the data on total new and repair expenditure on residential housing. Projection to 1942 is based on an estimate of number of proprietors and an index of wage rates in construction. For 1926 to 1941, decennial census benchmark data for 1931 and 1941 are projected by an index based on volume of construction and wage rates in construction.

Indirect taxes and subsidies are from the public accounts and department and agency reports, all available annually.

Depreciation allowances were obtained directly from annual data for private incorporated business and government enterprises and less directly for the remaining part. Depreciation of private incorporated business is from *Taxation Statistics* and the corporate sample (*supra*): adjustments for full coverage are sometimes needed and are made in the same way as for corporation profits. Depreciation of government enterprises comes from annual reports: for municipal enterprises some estimation is necessary.

Depreciation for unincorporated business is estimated in many ways. Retail trade and construction are used here to illustrate them. For retail stores, depreciation is calculated as a percentage of total sales of such stores. The percentage is determined from the surveys of operating results and financial structure of trade businesses, referred to above (see also section T). In construction a special tabulation of returns to the construction census in 1946 provided an estimation of gross value of work done by form of business organization. The ratio of depreciation to gross value of work done (from *Taxation Statistics*) was applied to gross revenue of those unincorporated concerns with paid employees, to estimate depreciation for them. For other years it was estimated that depreciation of the unincorporated group was a constant proportion (equal to that of 1946) of that for incorporated construction business. An allowance for the self-employed without employees is included in the final total for all industry in the estimation of capital outlay such as that on tools charged to current expense.

Depreciation on housing is calculated on a replacement cost basis from data provided by Central Mortgage and Housing on the stock of housing and its characteristics and on the estimated rates of replacements and on valuations.

The chief basic sources for the miscellaneous adjustments are *Taxation Statistics* and the corporate sample and government enterprise reports. Information from banks for the later years comes from bank returns to the Department of Finance and some data on unincorporated retail trade from surveys of trade.

Methods similar to those used in calculating incomes are used for the expenditures. Government expenditure comes from public accounts and department and agency reports. The estimation of private construction expenditure is dealt with in section R; gross expenditure on machinery and equipment, the other component of business gross fixed capital formation, is obtained by methods very similar to those used for construction. The estimation of exports and imports is described in section F.

The estimation of consumer expenditure on goods basically relies very heavily on census data for 1930, 1941 and 1951. Some use is also made of family expenditure surveys for 1948, 1953 and later years. In the decennial merchandising censuses, wholesale sales of retailers and retail sales of wholesalers, service groups and miscellaneous manufacturers were obtained. Totals of their retail sales could thus be calculated. For commodity groups in which retail sales to businesses were important, the personal share was estimated for 1931 from the census and for years in the neighbourhood of 1951 from the personal expenditure surveys. The data are projected to other years largely on the basis of estimates of sales of retailers (see section T). Retail sales of manufacturing bakeries and dairies, in house-to-house deliveries, are estimated from annual data collected in the census of manufactures and by the Agricultural Division of D.B.S. Estimates of new automobile purchases were prepared from data collected separately from automobile dealers (see series T 61–66); business purchases of automobiles, determined from the stock of business-owned vehicles in 1954 and an average turnover period obtained in 1954 from various surveys and projected to other years on the basis of sales of commercial vehicles, were deducted. Estimates of goods received in kind are those used in preparing the estimates of income. Some smaller items were obtained by other miscellaneous methods.

For personal expenditure on services, a substantial part comes from annual censuses or surveys, part is estimated from decennial census benchmarks, part has been calculated already in the estimation of income, and a small part comes from miscellaneous sources. The part estimated from annual data includes services of power laundries and cleaning and dyeing establishments, steam railways, electric railways and buses, air carriers, express companies, steamships, central electrical stations, telegraph and telephone companies, hospitals and universities. The personal proportion of purchase of these services is frequently obtained from the companies themselves (see, for example, series P 39–45). The part estimated from decennial census benchmark years includes repair services of most kinds including automobile repair and maintenance, funeral and burial expenses, recreation and hotel accommodation; these services are projected to other years by related series. A number of other items such

as taxi fares, barbering and hairdressing and expenses of charitable institutions are also estimated for benchmark years but projected on unrelated data. Service expenditures already calculated in the estimation of income include outlays on residential space rents and cost of rented furniture, domestic servants, board and lodging (service part only), outlay for professional service, services of financial intermediaries and the like. The business portion of professional services is obtained from various surveys of these professions noted above. Net personal expenditure abroad comes from balance of payments data (see section F).

The bulk of inventories is accounted for by farm inventories and grain in commercial channels, and by manufacturers' and trade inventories. Farm inventories have been obtained for all years by sample surveys (see section L). Grain in commercial channels is available annually from the Board of Grain Commissioners, *Grain Trade of Canada*, and from D.B.S., *Grain Statistics*. Manufacturers' inventories were obtained in the census of manufactures, 1926 to 1943, from the capital survey, 1944 to 1948, and by separate regular survey by D.B.S. since then. Wholesale trade inventories for 1926 to 1951 are based on the decennial census: for intercensal years they are projected on data from the corporate study and *Taxation Statistics*, supplemented by some other material. Since 1951, wholesale inventories are projected from data obtained in the monthly survey of wholesale establishments. Retail trade inventories are estimated much like those of wholesale trade.

The method of valuing the physical change in inventories is discussed in the notes to series E 28–45 and E 21–23.

E 1–12. National income and gross national product, by component, 1926 to 1960

SOURCE: for 1954 to 1960, D.B.S., *National Accounts, 1962*, table 1, p. 26, and directly from D.B.S.; for 1926 to 1954, D.B.S., *National Accounts, Income and Expenditure, 1926–1956*, table 1, pp. 32–3.

For methods of estimation see the general note to series E 1–129.

E 1. Wages, salaries and supplementary labour income include all payments for labour services to Canadian residents who are employed by businesses or by others. Wages and salaries of the members of the diplomatic services abroad and of others abroad who are classified as Canadian residents are included (see the general note to series E 1–129). This item measures wage and salary income before deduction of direct taxes or other levies. It includes income in kind, such as free board or lodging provided to employees, employee and employer contributions to pension funds, welfare funds, unemployment insurance and that part of workmen's compensation insurance that is to provide for working time lost or permanent loss of working capacity. It does not include that part of the workmen's compensation insurance contributions which is to cover hospital and medical expenses, and which is regarded as a cost of employment for the individual and hence does not form part of his income. Gratuities of the employed are included. Pay of members of the military services is not included as it is given separately in series E 2.

E 2. Military pay and allowances include payment for services to members of the armed forces in Canada and overseas, dependents' and subsistence allowances, clothing allowances, food and clothing issued in kind, and the rehabilitation grant of one month's pay and dependents' allowance, made at the time of discharge from the services. War-service gratuities and post-discharge rehabilitation benefits are not included but are treated as transfer payments.

E 3. Corporation profits before taxes are basically profits of private corporations as calculated for income tax purposes but some adjustments to the income tax data are made to give the profits reported here the following characteristics. First, while depreciation is allowed as an expense before profits are calculated, depletion is not treated as an expense for national income purposes: hence the profits given are before deduction of depletion allowances. Charitable donations of corporations are treated as a part of profits and are considered a distribution of earnings rather than an expense. Provincial direct mining and logging taxes are included as a part of profits. Bank profits are adjusted by substituting, in expenses, an estimate of bad debt losses for the banks' own provisions for bad debt losses and for additions to inner reserves. Interest income of non-Canadian non-life insurance companies retained in Canada and profits of co-operatives are included with corporation profits.

Dividends and profits remitted abroad to non-residents by Canadian corporations are not included as a part of profits as they do not accrue to Canadian residents. No deduction is made, however, for that part of undistributed profits that accrues to non-residents.

Corporation profits are measured net. First, losses of those companies who have losses are subtracted from profits of the profit-making companies. Second, dividends paid by one company to another are not counted as a part of income of the receiving company, and hence are reflected in profits only once. Third, profits refunded to the government through the negotiation of war contracts are not included.

Capital gains and losses are not included as a part of profits. Nor are net profits of government-owned enterprise which are included in E 4.

The profits of corporations as given in series E 3 reflect income from interest on their holdings of the public debt and from consumer financing. Since these payments are treated as transfer payments they must be eliminated in arriving at a total of national income. For the way in which the adjustment is made see the note to series E 4.

E 4. Rent, interest and miscellaneous investment income are calculated from: (1) investment or property income received by persons; (2) government investment income; and (3) adjustments, to remove from income interest payments on the public debt and the transfer portion of interest on consumer debt and to add withholding taxes to income.

Persons are defined to include individuals and private non-commercial institutions, such as charitable organizations, hospitals and universities (see the general note to series E 1–129 and the notes to series E 66–78). Personal receipts include net rents (actually received and imputed), bond, mortgage and deposit interest, originating in Canada, received by or accruing to Canadian persons, interest and dividends received by persons from abroad, and miscellaneous investment income. In the latter, interest received by life insurance companies on behalf of Canadian policy-holders is much the largest item; it also includes a number of quantitatively small items such as investment income of fraternal and mutual benefit societies, interest on private pension funds and on behalf of persons who have purchased federal government annuities, profits of mutual non-life insurance companies and finally net royalties.

Interest income includes, in addition to interest actually received, an amount equal to the services provided to persons without charge by certain financial intermediaries, such as chartered banks, savings banks, trust and loan companies and credit unions (see the general note to series E 1–129). Similarly, interest received by life insurance companies, before any deduction for the costs of operation of the life insurance companies that are incurred for the provision of services to policy-holders, is included.

Net rental income of persons includes paid and imputed rents

on both farm and nonfarm residential buildings (including garages), and paid rents on nonresidential buildings and on farms. Farm rents include both income paid in kind and cash rents. The rents are net after the payment out of actual gross rents of expenses such as cost of fuel, services, water, electricity, gas and hot water and amortization of furniture, stoves, refrigerators and washing machines where these services or facilities are provided, and of repair and maintenance expense, property tax, depreciation, fire insurance, real estate commissions on transfers of existing buildings and also after deduction of interest on mortgages on these properties. It should be noted that there is no imputation for nonresidential rents on owner-occupied farms: any such income is included in series E 5, 'accrued net income of farm operators from farm production'.

Net rents paid to nonfarm incorporated business for use of their property is included here and not with series E 6.

Government investment income includes profits (net of losses) of government business enterprises, interest on government loans and advances, interest receipts of public funds, and an imputed net rent on government-owned buildings.

Interest on government loans and advances consists of interest on loans to government corporations and agencies, interest on loans to other governments, and interest on loans to foreign governments.

Interest receipts of public funds include the receipts from investments of the Unemployment Insurance Commission, Workmen's Compensation Boards pension funds and like funds.

Finally there are the adjustments noted above. First, withholding taxes on interest and dividends paid abroad are added since they come from income produced and retained in Canada, and since they have not been included elsewhere (in the calculation of corporation profits, interest and dividends paid abroad, including that part which is withheld as a tax, were subtracted from corporation profits).

Conceptually, all the above interest income excludes receipts from interest on the Canadian public debt, though interest on debt of foreign governments is included. In fact, the above calculations are first made including interest from all public debt. Once a total has been calculated from the above items, the entire interest on the debt of Canadian governments, including that part paid abroad, is deducted. The part paid domestically is deducted since it is regarded as a transfer payment; the part paid abroad is deducted since it represents a transfer abroad of claims on goods produced in Canada and therefore the income created in producing these goods does not accrue to residents of Canada. But interest on some of the public debt is paid to corporations and is reflected in their profits. The subtraction of all interest on the public debt from rent, interest and miscellaneous investment income means that in effect this series is a residual, picking up investment income that is not included in any of the other series.

Similarly, interest on consumer debt, except that part which pays for the services provided in transferring consumer credit and in transferring interest thereon between lenders and borrowers, is regarded as a transfer payment and is treated exactly like the public debt. After first being included in the above calculations all that part of consumer debt which is treated as a transfer payment is subtracted from series E 4. Part of consumer debt interest has, like interest on the public debt, been paid to corporations and is reflected in their profits. The subtraction of all of it from this series has the same effect as subtracting all interest on the public debt.

E 5. Accrued net income of farm operators from farm products includes the net income that could properly be attributed to unincorporated farm operators for their own contribution of labour and entrepreneurial inputs, for labour provided by un-paid family workers and for the services of farm capital, land, structures and equipment owned by farm operators, excluding imputed income from owned farm houses.

This series differs somewhat from the figure of net income of farming operators from farming operations given in series L 67–72 in that the latter: (1) includes profits of corporations engaged in agriculture, imputed rents of owned farm residences, and receipts of farmers under the Prairie Farm Assistance Act and the Prairie Farm Income Plan (treated as transfer payments for the national accounts); (2) is based on a slightly different method of valuation of inventories; (3) excludes agricultural income in Newfoundland since 1949; and (4) uses paid rather than accrued profits of the Canadian Wheat Board and of Canadian Co-operative Wheat Producers. For a reconciliation of annual net income of farm operators as included in this series with the income of farm operators as measured in series L 67–72, see table 52 in the source volumes. See also the note to series L 67–72 on the calculation of farm income.

The estimates given here do not include profits of incorporated farms (which are treated like any corporation), wages and income in kind paid hired labour, rent paid others for farm lands, buildings, and other facilities and imputed rents on owner-occupied housing. Nor is any outside income such as property income from ownership of outside property or labour income for services provided to others outside the operator's own farm included.

The total given here, therefore, is much less than income originating on farms, series E 46, even after allowing for the fact that capital consumption allowances are included in the latter. Nor is it a measure of income available to farmers because it excludes imputed residential rents and receipts of outside income.

Fur farms are included.

E 6. Net income of nonfarm unincorporated business is essentially the same in the nature of its content as that of farm operators. It is made up of a mixture of a return to proprietors of unincorporated business for their own labour and entre-preneurial effort and that of unpaid family workers and a return on owned property actually used in these unincorporated businesses. It does not include outside income obtained from property lent or rented to others or outside income from labour services provided to other businesses than the proprietor's own.

Quantitatively, in terms of the amount of income generated, nonfarm unincorporated business income is most important in absolute amounts in service, retail trade, construction and manu-facturing, in that order in the later years of the period covered; but substantial incomes are received by unincorporated business proprietors in transportation, finance insurance and real estate, wholesale trade, fishing and trapping, and forestry. Very small amounts of income are received by unincorporated businesses in mining and practically none in public utilities. Unincor-porated businesses in the service category, referred to above, include those engaged in independent professional practice, such as doctors, dentists, lawyers, accountants, engineers, architects and similar independent professional pursuits.

The distribution of income of unincorporated enterprise among industries is given in the source in table 24 in both publications.

E 7. Inventory valuation adjustment is to correct for the fact that corporation profits and the net income of those nonfarm unincorporated businesses that deal in commodities include as a part of their gross income the change in the value of inventories as reflected in the books of these businesses. Since the book value of inventories may rise or fall owing to changes in the prices at which the physical inventories are valued, as well as to

changes in the physical stock of inventories, and since the former component does not reflect current production, but a capital gain or loss, it is not included as a part of national income. The inventory valuation adjustment removes the changes in inventory values caused by the price movements referred to above. The adjustment leaves, as a part of income arising from current production, the value of the physical change in inven-tories valued at current prices.

The inventory valuation adjustment in this series does not include any adjustment for the Canadian Wheat Board or the Canadian Co-operative Wheat Producers. In the calculation of their profits, in order to attribute the appropriate amount to farm income, inventory changes were already included as the value of the physical change.

A distribution among industries of the value of the physical change in inventories may be found in the source in table 26.

E 8. Net national income is the sum of all factor remunera-tions received by or accruing to Canadian residents from the contributions of services of the factors to production. It is the sum of the entries in series E 1–7.

E 9. Indirect taxes include: customs import duties, federal excise duties and excise (sales) taxes, and miscellaneous small other federal indirect taxes; provincial government amusement, corporation (not on profits), gasoline and retail sales taxes, revenue from licences, permits and fees, the business share of motor-vehicle licences and permits, from miscellaneous taxes on natural resources and from small amounts of other miscel-laneous indirect taxes; municipal real and personal property taxes, retail sales taxes, and miscellaneous other indirect taxes and licences, permits and fees.

Subsidies are contributed in the main by the federal govern-ment. They were largest in the wartime years, but grew rapidly again from 1955 onwards. Agricultural subsidies form one large class and include such items as wheat acreage reduction pay-ments, Canadian Wheat Board trading losses, agricultural prices support board losses, freight assistance on western feed grain and a number of other subsidies on agricultural products. Other subsidies include emergency gold-mine assistance, maritime freight rate subsidies, subsidies on movement of coal and like items. In the war, subsidies paid by the commodity prices stabilization corporations were important.

E 10. Capital consumption allowances and miscellaneous valuation adjustments include depreciation on structures and machinery and equipment, an amount equal to capital outlay charged to current expense, the claim portion of business and residential fire and other property damage insurance and of certain other financial insurance such as fidelity insurance, scrap and salvage allowances including the value of the sale to con-sumers of used motor-vehicles by businesses (other than used car dealers), a group of items consisting of amortization, de-velopment write-offs, deferred maintenance and miscellaneous charges to reserves, all of which are analogous to or in lieu of depreciation, and bad debt allowances less recoveries. No allow-ance is included for depletion of natural resources since depletion is not regarded as a part of capital consumption for national in-come purposes. The sum of the above items is reduced by a valuation adjustment for noncapital outlays (in the national account sense used here) charged to capital account. The latter are of three kinds. First, surface exploration costs in the mining and oil industry, such as geophysical surveys and the like, are not included as capital formation on the expenditure side of the national accounts, nor have they been charged as an operating expense in arriving at profits: they are deducted, therefore, in the computation of this series. Second, brokerage fees paid in the purchasing of stocks and bonds by businesses other than those who engaged in such activities as a part of their regular business are also deducted and for the same reason: they are not included as a part of capital formation on the expenditure side, nor have they been included as an expense in arriving at profits. Finally, in similar vein, real estate commissions on the transfer of existing (as distinct from new) nonresidential buildings and structures have not been entered as either an element of expenditure in gross national expenditure nor as a charge against receipts of the business of persons paying them: they are also deducted as a capital valuation adjustment. For the treatment of real estate fees on transferring existing housing, see the note to series E4.

Owing to lack of availability of data, no depreciation estimates are made for property of unincorporated companies in forestry, hunting and trapping, for property of religious, social and welfare organizations, or for universities before 1949.

Most depreciation, particularly that estimated from business accounts, is based upon book values and consequently is most likely on a basis of original cost. Depreciation on housing, however, is on the basis of current replacement cost.

A breakdown of capital consumption allowance and miscellaneous valuation adjustments by form of organization appears in table 51 of the source volumes.

E11. Residual error of estimate is an allowance for inaccuracies of the statistical estimates of series E1–10. Conceptually, gross national product and gross national expenditure should be exactly equal. In the calculations, owing to shortcomings in the accuracy of estimates of the components of gross national product and gross national expenditure, the components of each do not add to exactly the same totals. The totals are made equal by adding half the difference between the adjusted sums of the component estimates of each of gross national income and gross national expenditure to the lower unadjusted total and subtracting half the difference from the higher unadjusted total. Thus series E11 is equal in absolute value to series E26.

E12. Gross national product at market prices is the sum of series E8–11.

E13–27. Gross national expenditure by components, 1926 to 1960

SOURCE: for 1955 to 1960, D.B.S., *National Accounts, 1962*, table 2, p. 26, and directly from D.B.S.; for 1926 to 1954, D.B.S., *National Accounts, 1926–1956*, table 2, pp. 32–3.

The items of series E13–23 are components of total gross expenditure by Canadian residents on final goods and services and on inventories. Series E24, exports of goods and services, is the value of those goods and services sold to residents of other countries. Series E25, imports of goods and services, is a measure of the goods and services provided from abroad on which part of the expenditure of the items in series E13–24 is made. Gross national expenditure at market prices is the total of gross expenditure on goods and services measured at the prices that are actually paid in the market.

E13. Personal expenditure on consumer goods and services is final purchases of such commodities, valued at prices in the market, by those classified as persons (see the general note to series E1–129 for the definition of a person). Since the general concept of a consumer good or service is a familiar one a detailed listing is not given but attention is paid to only a few features of this item.

Purchases by persons of consumer durables such as automobiles, stoves, refrigerators, radio and television sets, furniture and the like (but excluding dwellings and permanent fixtures) are included as consumer expenditure. Purchases of both new and used durables are included but trade-in allowances are subtracted.

Hospitalization expenditure includes a number of different types of items. Expenditures on private noncommercial and municipal hospitalization are in general calculated on the basis of the operating expenditures of these institutions. When the expenses of the noncommercial institutions are included as a part of consumer expenditure, the fees for services paid to these institutions are not included as well: such a practice would mean double counting. The amounts paid to provincial and federal hospitals by paying patients are also included, but the uncovered expenditures of these hospitals are included with government purchases of goods and services. Other hospitalization expenses include revenues of private commercial hospitals and the operating costs of private sickness and accident insurance plans and of prepaid voluntary hospital insurance plans. The part of such hospitalization and medical costs paid for by business, of which Workmen's Compensation payments are the most important, is excluded.

Medical care is put in at the cost of the care in all cases; operating costs of medical care plans are included but the insurance premiums for those insured for such care are not included.

Other noncommercial institutions, such as religious, fraternal and charitable organizations, and universities (excluding university residences), are treated like the noncommercial hospitals and their operating expenditures included. Expenditures on services of university residences are entered at the fees paid for lodging and board.

Personal expenditure for private commercial and trade school instruction and for other private schools is also based on their expenditures. Publicly operated schools are, of course, included in government expenditure.

Expenditures on insurance of all kinds are based on the operating costs, including profits, of those parts of the businesses related to persons. The premiums paid and claims received are not included as they are regarded as interpersonal transfers, except the part that pays for the operating costs of insurance companies (see the general note to series E1–131 and the note to series E4). Similarly, the operating costs of those making and servicing consumer debt are included as consumer expenditure but the interest on the debt is regarded as a transfer payment and not included.

An imputation is made of the value of banking services provided to individuals but not paid for as an explicit charge (see the general note to series E1–129 and the note to series E4).

Income in kind which is included in the income side is also entered with expenditure. These include food and fuel used on farms from farm production, and the value of free lodging and board of non-farm employees such as those living in bunk houses, hotels, and aboard ship, meals and such perquisites of employees in other activities, and meals and clothing provided to those in the armed services. Hotel and meal expenses covered by expense accounts and which are a part of the cost of doing one's job are not included.

Expenditures abroad of Canadian tourists and of members of the armed forces and diplomatic service are included: they enter also as a part of imports, since the goods and services on which the expenditures are made are provided from abroad. Expenditures of tourists from abroad and of the diplomatic and military services of other countries in Canada are not included since they are not outlays by Canadian residents.

Private expenditure on motor-vehicle licences and operators' permits and like outlays are treated as a direct tax, and consequently are not treated as a part of personal expenditure on consumer goods and services.

E14–16. Government expenditures on goods and services consist of the outlays for currently produced goods and services by federal, provincial and municipal bodies including municipal schools, but excluding government enterprise that operates primarily on a commercial basis. The division between current expenditure, series E 15, and gross fixed capital formation, series E 16, corresponds approximately to the division between business operating expenditure and outlay on fixed capital goods. Gross fixed capital formation is the outlay for new publicly owned office buildings, nonrental housing, schools, provincial and federal hospitals, streets, roads, bridges, sidewalks, sewers, machinery and equipment and the like. Capital expenditure includes major alterations and improvements but not maintenance and repair expenditures of the ordinary kind necessary to keep the capital equipment in usable condition. Though capital outlays of government enterprises are, in general, excluded, the capital outlays on post-office buildings, facilities and equipment are included. Defence equipment and installations are not treated as a part of capital formation. In accordance with the usual practice, purchases of previously produced capital goods, unless imported, or of land are not included.

Current expenditure consists of the outlay for wages and salaries of the civil and military service, school teachers and other employees, all other military or defence outlay on goods and services, an imputed gross rent (gross of depreciation) on government buildings but not on other capital goods, costs of fuel, electricity, telephone service, travel of civil servants and like items. Military expenditures and the expenses of the diplomatic service abroad are included. Gifts abroad, whether financial or in kind, are also included with the exception of the transfer of military equipment produced in earlier years but transferred to other countries; the latter are not a draft on current production and since military goods are not treated as capital, it is not necessary to enter any transaction in the national accounts to record the transfer. While expenditures for capital facilities of the post office are included in government capital formation its current operations are not included: in the latter regard the post office is treated as a government enterprise. All interest on the public debt is treated like a transfer payment, but the part paid abroad is included in imports of goods and services (series E 25).

The current government expenditures include the administrative expenditures of the extra-budgetary funds and other nonbusiness activities such as those of the War Assets Corporation, Canadian Broadcasting Corporation and Workmen's Compensation Boards.

The net expenditures of certain government commodity holding agencies, such as those holding strategic materials, are placed under current expenditure and the change in inventories is not treated as a part of capital formation, either in series E 14–16 or series E 21–23.

E 17–20. Business gross fixed capital formation consists of gross expenditure on newly produced structures and machinery and equipment by private business, by government enterprises that operate mainly on a commercial basis and by persons for residential and institutional structures. Purchases of land and of used buildings and structures and second-hand machinery are not included since they are not the products of current production; imported used machinery and equipment are included, since they are 'new' to Canada and form an addition to the capital stock.

The content of capital formation in construction is dealt with at length in section R. It includes buildings of all kinds and engineering constructions such as railway road beds, dams, power transmission lines, oil pipelines, and the like (see section R, especially the general note). Machinery and equipment includes industrial machinery, generating turbines, transportation equipment, office and store equipment and furniture, small tools,

and like items. Expenditures on major improvements are included.

In the main, expenditure on gross fixed capital formation is defined similarly to that used for income tax calculation, but there are two exceptions. First, a small number of businesses, for example, the major railways before the Second World War, did not or do not use depreciation accounting but charge replacement of structures and equipment to operating account. Second, some businesses and tradesmen may not treat smaller tools or possibly furniture as a capital item but rather charge them as a current expenditure. In the estimates given here, these capital outlays charged to current expenditure are included.

The estimates are gross. No allowance for depreciation, fire loss, accidental damage or other destruction has been made.

The expenditures are, in the main, on an accrual basis. For example, if a structure is in process of construction for more than one year, the estimates are for the work actually put in place in each year. The amount done each year is largely estimated from progress payments.

For a reconciliation of the estimates given here with those in *Private and Public Investment in Canada*, see the source volumes, table 54, and D.B.S., *Private and Public Investment in Canada, 1946–1957*, table 15, p. 39.

E 21–23. Value of the physical change in inventories is the sum of the changes in physical stock (see page 122) multiplied in each case by average current prices for the year.

Nonfarm business inventories, series E 22, cover all private businesses (except those handling grain) and government enterprises. No allowance is made for stocks held directly by various government commodity agencies not organized as business enterprises either in series E 21–23 or in series E 14–16. These agencies include bodies holding defence stocks of strategic materials, certain agricultural agencies other than the Canadian Wheat Board and the like (see the note to series E 14–16).

Changes in inventory of grain in commercial channels include the holdings of the Canadian Wheat Board as well as the private trade. Change in farm inventories covers grain, livestock and poultry.

For a distribution among the industries of the value of the physical change in inventories see the source volumes, table 26.

E 24. Exports of goods and services are receipts for commodity exports, freight and shipping, tourist expenditures of foreigners in Canada and interest and dividends received from abroad. These items as set out in section F, series F 57–90, are adjusted for national accounts purposes as follows. Official contributions to other countries during the war and after and mutual aid to North Atlantic Treaty Organization countries are omitted from exports since they are included in the national accounts under government expenditure. Transmittal of inheritances and migrants' funds are left out as they are considered part of the capital account in the national accounts; and Newfoundland is excluded from the balance of payments in 1946 to 1948.

E 25. Imports of goods and services are the counterpart of exports given in series E 24. The current account payments given in series F 57–90 are adjusted in the same way as exports (see the note to series E 24).

A reconciliation of the balance of payments measurements of exports and imports of goods and services with those used for national accounting is given in the source volumes, table 55.

E 26. Residual error of estimate in an adjustment for inaccuracies of measurement of gross national product and gross national expenditure (see the note to series E 11).

E 28–45. Gross national expenditure in constant (1949) dollars, by components, 1926 to 1960

SOURCE: for 1955 to 1960, D.B.S., *National Accounts*, 1962, table 56, p. 64, and directly from D.B.S.; for 1926 to 1954, D.B.S., *National Accounts, 1926–1956*, table 5, pp. 36–7.

The data of series E 28–45 differ from those of series E 13–27 only in that these expenditures are measured in constant (1949) dollars rather than current dollars and that there are adjusting entries, described below, not present in series E 13–27. The content of each of the series given here is the same, therefore, as that given under the same heading in series E 13–27.

The estimation of constant dollar expenditure from current dollar expenditure was done in two steps, common to all the main categories given here with the exception of inventories. First, the individual subcomponents of the expenditure categories of series E 13–27 were deflated in rather fine detail by, for the most part, Laspeyres-type price indexes. For example, eighty items of personal expenditure on consumer goods and services were deflated separately; government and business gross capital formation were deflated in considerable but somewhat less detail. Exports and imports were deflated in fine detail largely by the use of price relatives. The deflated subcomponents in each group were then added to obtain the constant dollar components given here.

The values of the physical changes in nonfarm inventories and in farm inventories and grain in commercial channels were calculated in separate ways.

The value of the physical change in nonfarm inventories was obtained by deflating the year end stocks of inventories by price indexes which put them in constant prices of the base period. The value of the physical change in constant dollars was then obtained by subtracting year beginning from year end inventories. For farm inventories and grain in commercial channels, the changes in physical quantities were valued directly at base year prices. In both cases the subcomponents were added to give the two main components presented here.

The residual error of estimate, series E 43, was deflated by an implicit price index obtained by dividing, for each year, the sum of all the noninventory components of gross national expenditure measured in current dollars by the sum of the same components measured in constant dollars.

The grand total of gross national expenditure in constant dollars is the sum of all the components measured in constant dollars plus the adjusting entries.

The adjusting entries are necessary because the data were first deflated for three different periods using three different constant dollar valuations and because each component as well as gross national expenditure was linked at the year of overlap between the periods. Data for 1926 to 1947 were first put in 1935–39 dollars, data for 1947 to 1956 in 1949 dollars, and data for 1956 to 1960 in 1957 dollars. Each component as well as each subtotal and the grand total of gross national expenditure were then linked at 1947 and 1956 to put each series in 1949 dollars. Owing to divergences in price movements of components this procedure resulted in the components of subtotals not adding exactly to the gross national expenditure for the years 1926 to 1946 and 1957 to 1960. Accordingly, series E 36 must be added to the sum of series E 33–35 to yield series E 32. Similarly, series E 40 is added to series E 38 and E 39 to yield E 37. Adjusting entries for government expenditure, series E 28–31, are necessary only for 1957 to 1960, since it was not broken into components before 1949; to conserve space they have been given in a footnote. Finally, when the subtotals are added to the grand total a further adjusting entry, series E 44, is required.

Implicit price deflators may be obtained for each component, for each subtotal and for gross national expenditure by dividing each series in current dollars by the corresponding series in constant dollars. These implicit prices indexes are given in series J 153–164. It should be noted they are base weighted (Laspeyres) indexes used at the finest level of deflation combined into broader current weighted (Paasche) indexes through the derivation of the latter as implicit indexes.

E 46–65. Gross domestic product at factor cost, by industry, 1926 to 1960

SOURCE: for 1955 to 1960, D.B.S., *National Accounts*, 1962, table 21, p. 38, and table 4, p. 27, and directly from D.B.S.; for 1926 to 1954, D.B.S., *National Accounts, 1921–1956*, table 21, pp. 56–7, and table 4, pp. 34–5.

Gross domestic product at factor cost is the value of all goods and services produced in Canada without regard to whether the income generated in their production is paid to or accrues to Canadian residents or to residents of other countries. The reconciliation of gross domestic product at factor cost with gross national product at market prices appears in series E 61–65.

The gross product of each industry, the value added, is the sum of factor payments originating in the industry—wages, salaries, and supplementary labour income, corporation profits before taxes, rental and other investment income and net income of unincorporated enterprises—and the capital consumption allowances in the industry.

Attention need be drawn to only a few general features of the assignment of value added among industries. The basic unit for assigning labour income and the inventory valuation adjustment among industries has been the establishment. The establishment's operations have been assigned to the industry in which it does the largest part of its business. For example, a vertically integrated incorporated company engaged in both mining and smelting would have the mining establishment's activities assigned to mining and the smelting operations to manufacturing. Other items of companies' operations, such as corporation profits, rent, interest and miscellaneous investment income, the net income of unincorporated business and capital consumption allowances, cannot be assigned among establishments: in such cases the item is assigned to the industry that plays the largest role in the whole company's business.

Investment income originating in each industry is calculated by subtracting investment receipts from outside the industry, including interest and dividends received from abroad, from payments made by the industry, including payments of dividends and interest to residents of other countries. Thus dividends or interest received by a company in one industry from a subsidiary in another industry would be credited to the subsidiary's industry. Net rents are attributed to the industry which owns the property being rented: for example, net rent paid by the operator of a retail store would be credited to the finance, insurance and real estate industry.

Government activities are assigned in a number of ways. Government enterprises (or their establishment) are assigned to particular industries with which their activities are identifiable, just as private enterprises or establishments are assigned. The post office, treated as an enterprise, is assigned to communication. Public education and health, that is, schools, hospitals and like establishments, are assigned to the service industry. The entire net rent and capital consumption allowances on government buildings have been also assigned to the service industry since such a large part is connected with schools and hospitals (D.B.S. contemplates transferring these items to the real estate industry). Trading profits of government establishments are in the industry with which the trading profits are most closely connected.

Public administration and defence includes only those government activities for which there is no similar private type of operation in the other industrial groups. It includes the Department of National Defence and the armed services, and federal, provincial and municipal departments engaged in general administration. While public schools and hospitals are included in services, the departments administering them are included in public administration, and while provincial government establishments engaged in highway maintenance should probably have been assigned to transportation, it was not statistically feasible to do so and they are included with public administration.

The finance, insurance and real estate industry includes, in addition to the obvious activities its name implies, some less obvious ones. Net imputed rental income and capital consumption allowances on owned houses are included here, as is mortgage interest paid by persons on residential property. The value imputed to services provided to personal depositors by banks (see the general note to series E 1–129 and the note to series E 4) is included here also.

The service industry includes, in addition to the activities noted above, theatres and other entertainment, professional services, domestic services, barber shops, hotels, cleaning and laundering and the like.

The industrial distribution of wages, salaries and supplementary labour income is given in series D 238–253. In addition the industrial distribution of investment income and of income of unincorporated business, including farm income, may be found in tables 23 and 24, respectively, of the source volumes.

E 66–78. Personal income and its disposition, 1926 to 1960

SOURCE: for 1954 to 1960, D.B.S., *National Accounts, 1962*, table 3, p. 27, and table 47, p. 58, and directly from D.B.S.; for 1926 to 1954, D.B.S., *National Accounts, 1926–1956*, table 3, pp. 34–5, and table 47, pp. 88–9.

Persons include certain private nonprofit organizations which are treated as associations of individuals. For the definition of persons see the general note to series E 1–129.

Personal income may be derived from national income or its components in two ways. One way, given here, is to add to national income those payments to persons made on grounds other than their provision of productive services, the transfer payments and interest on the public debt, and to subtract from the resulting total the part of the national income not paid out to persons to yield personal income. Alternatively, personal income could be derived by adding to those several parts of national income paid out to persons the transfer payments and interest on the public debt. The latter is the procedure used in constructing the personal sector account proper: it is given in table 7 of the source volumes.

E 66. National income is described in the general note to series E 1–129 and in the notes to series E 1–8.

E 67. Transfer payments include family allowances, old age pensions, pensions to the blind, mothers' allowances, veterans' pensions and gratuities, unemployment insurance benefits, government grants to the non-profit institutions included with persons, such as operating and capital grants to hospitals, charitable organizations and universities, and like items. They do not include here charitable contributions of private business which are already included in national income.

E 68. Interest on the public debt includes the entire amount of interest paid by all levels of government. The part that does not go into the hands of or accrue to persons is offset by items in series E 70 and series E 77 (see the notes to these series and also to series E 4).

E 70. Earnings not paid out to persons include undistributed corporation profits, corporation profits taxes, withholding taxes, government investment income including that part that comes from holding its own interest-bearing securities, the undistributed earnings of the Canadian Wheat Board and the Canadian Co-operative Wheat Producers, inventory valuation adjustment and employer and employee contributions to social insurance and government pension funds.

E 71. Personal income is a mixed concept. It is conceptually that part of national income paid out to persons plus transfer payments from other sectors. However, it includes some income that is not received by persons in the accounting period in which it is entered: for example, it includes the interest earnings of life insurance companies (see the general note to series E 1–129). Personal income is measured before the payment of any direct taxes.

E 72. Personal direct taxes are made up of personal income taxes, including the part earmarked for the old age security fund, succession duties, the personal share of motor-vehicle licences and permits, directly collected hospital taxes and small miscellaneous items.

E 73. Personal disposable income is presumably that income at a person's discretionary disposal, but see the note to series E 71.

E 75. Personal expenditure on consumer durables includes outlay on house trailers, new and used automobiles, home furnishings and furniture, stoves and ranges, other appliances, radios and television sets, jewellery, watches, clocks, silverware, sporting goods, household tools and garden equipment and like items. The values of trade-ins are subtracted.

E 76. Non-durable consumer goods consist of food items, including the food content of income in kind and the food content only of meals bought in restaurants or served in university residences, tobacco products and alcoholic beverages including the beverage content of on-premise consumption, clothing and personal furnishings including armed forces issue, household fuel, soap and cleaning supplies and other household supplies, gasoline, oil and grease for automobiles and other use, drugs, cosmetics and toilet preparations, newspapers and magazines, local and provincial sales taxes not included in prices of goods, and miscellaneous other goods.

E 77. Consumer services consist of items clearly recognizable as services and components of other expenditures that are not so obvious. In the former category are such things as laundry and dry-cleaning service, dressmaking and tailoring, repair service of all kinds, gross space rent of tenants, imputed net residential rents of owner-occupied dwellings, plus imputed capital consumption allowances, real estate taxes, insurance and the like paid by owner-occupiers of dwellings, lodging expenses, electricity, gas, telephone, domestic service, moving expenses, water, janitor service, rental of furniture and appliances, household maintenance repair, automobile repair charges, bridge, tunnel and ferry tolls, fares for taxis, railway, electric railway and bus, steamship and plane travel, health outlay for medical, dental, osteopathic, chiropractic, nursing and hospital care, death expenses, expenditures on beauty parlours and barber shops, outlays for recreational, educational, religious and charitable activities, legal services, stock and bond commission, hotels, net expenditure abroad and miscellaneous others. Among the less obvious items there are two main types. First, expenditures on meals and alcoholic beverages bought on premises are divided into two parts, a food or beverage cost and a service cost for serving them: the latter is included among services. Second, only the administration costs of theft and personal property insurance, automobile insurance, prepaid medical care, accident and sickness insurance, life insurance, consumer credit, and union dues are included: the remaining part of insurance outlay and union dues is either considered as a transfer payment, as saving, or as a part of capital consumption allowances and miscellaneous valuation adjustments.

For a much more detailed breakdown of consumer expenditure, see the source volumes, table 47, and for a detailed listing of items included in expenditure categories see D.B.S., *National Accounts, 1926–1956*, pp. 175–6.

E78. Personal saving, the part of disposable income remaining in the hands of persons after their expenditures on consumer goods, includes the saving of life insurance companies. It does not make any allowance for inventory valuation adjustment of unincorporated business. Nor does it include the part of Canadian Wheat Board and Canadian Co-operative Wheat Producers profits credited to net farm income in national income.

E79–90. Personal income by province, 1926 to 1960

SOURCE: for 1955 to 1960, D.B.S., *National Accounts, 1962*, table 28, p. 44, and directly from D.B.S.; for 1926 to 1954, D.B.S., *National Accounts, 1926–1956*, table 28, pp. 64–5.

Personal income of each province and 'foreign countries' is that part of total personal income of Canadian residents, given in series E71, received by or accruing to persons in the province (see the general note to E1–129 for the definition of a person).

The part of personal income assigned to 'foreign countries', series E90, consists of the income of Canadians temporarily abroad, such as those in the diplomatic service and members of the armed forces abroad.

E91–101. Government revenue and expenditure, by component, all governments, 1926 to 1960

SOURCE: for 1955 to 1960, D.B.S., *National Accounts, 1962*, tables 9 and 10, p. 31, and directly from D.B.S.; for 1926 to 1954, D.B.S., *National Accounts, 1926–1956*, tables 9 and 10, pp. 42–3.

Consolidated government revenues and expenditures given here cover the non-commercial activities of all governments. They do not include the revenues and expenditures of government business enterprise: these commercial enterprises enter the accounts given here only in so far as the government receives profits from them or interest payments on loans made to them. Nor is the operation of government-owned buildings included here since it has been included in the business sector; however, a net imputed rental income is included in revenue, a gross rental expenditure in expenditures and the cost of construction of government buildings is in government capital formation. On the other hand, the receipts and expenditures of extra-budgetary funds and agencies not set up on a commercial basis are included in addition to those of general government departments. These extra-budgetary funds and agencies include bodies like the unemployment insurance commission, the old age security fund, the workmen's compensation boards, regulatory bodies, municipal schools, provincial and federal hospitals—municipal hospitals are included in the personal sector—and like bodies. However, when specific fees paid for certain government non-commercial services are already covered in personal expenditures, such as fees paid federal or provincial hospitals, or in the prices of commodities sold by businesses, such as inspection fees, they are not included in government revenue but are deducted from the corresponding government expenditure.

Some items ordinarily included in government revenues and expenditures in the official public accounts are excluded or adjusted in the government sector of the national accounts since they are not transactions relevant to the national accounts. Thus, sale of existing fixed capital assets, such as war assets, are not included in revenue, and purchases of existing capital goods or land are not included in expenditure. Similarly, write-downs of active assets to non-active accounts, provision of reserves for possible loss on active assets and for veterans' conditional benefits, the transfer of military equipment acquired in earlier years to NATO countries and a number of other items, some of which are mentioned in the notes to the individual series, are excluded.

The basic data on government revenues and expenditures are for fiscal years. The data for the federal government are adjusted to calendar years for 1938 to 1960 but are for the fiscal year ending 31 March of the following year for 1926 to 1937. Provincial government data are for calendar years from 1952 to 1960 but for fiscal years ending nearest the end of the calendar year for 1926 to 1951. Municipal data are nearly always on a calendar year basis to begin with.

A reconciliation of the federal government surplus or deficit given here with that of the public accounts is given in table 53 of the source volumes.

E91. Personal direct taxes are described in the note to series E72. More detail, by level of government, is given in table 38 of the source volumes.

E92. Corporation direct taxes are taxes on corporation income (profits) by the federal and provincial governments. They include the non-refundable part of federal excess profits taxes, the special provincial taxes on mining and logging profits and the part of the federal profits tax earmarked for the old age security fund but exclude, in addition to the refundable part of excess profits taxes, profits taxes later adjusted by renegotiation of war contracts. Corporation profits taxes are given on an accrual basis here. The source tables give the amounts actually collected and the adjustment for accruals separately and table 39 of the source volume gives further detail by level of government.

E93. Withholding taxes are taxes on dividends, interest, rent and royalties transmitted abroad. See also the note to series E4.

E94. Indirect taxes are described in the note to series E9.

E95. Investment income is described in the note to series E4. More detail by level of government is given in table 41 of the source volumes.

E96. Employee and employer contributions to social insurance and pension funds include contributions to the unemployment insurance fund, workmen's compensation, public service (civil and military) pensions funds of all levels of government and industrial employees' vacation funds of provinces. The parts of personal income tax, corporation income tax and general sales tax earmarked for the old age security fund are not included here; they appear as part of the tax receipts of each category from which they are taken. More detail by level of government is given in table 42 of the source volumes.

E97. Government revenue and expenditure is equal to the sum of the revenues of series E91–96 and also to the sum of expenditures, including the surplus or deficit, in series E98–101.

E98. Purchases of goods and services are described in the note to series E14–16.

E99. Transfer payments include interest on the public debt as well as other transfer payments. Interest on the public debt is measured gross including that part paid on debt held in government funds as well as intergovernment payments of interest. Transfer payments do not include grants from one level of government to others. See also the notes to series E67 and E68. More detail by level of government appears in table 44 of the source. Transfer payments among governments, although netted out in the consolidation of expenditures and revenues here, are given in some detail in table 46 of the source.

E100. Subsidies are described in the note to series E9. Intergovernment subsidies are not included. More detail by level of government may be found in table 45 of the source.

E 101. The surplus or deficit given here is the item that balances expenditure with revenue. See the beginning note to series E 91–101 for information relevant to the difference between the surplus as measured here and that in the public accounts.

E 102–111. National saving and investment, by components, 1926 to 1960

SOURCE: for 1955 to 1960, D.B.S., *National Accounts, 1962*, tables 17 and 18, pp. 34–5, and directly from D.B.S.; for 1926 to 1954, D.B.S., *National Accounts, 1926–1956*, tables 17 and 18, pp. 48–51.

E 102. Personal net saving is described in the note to series E 78.

E 103. Business gross saving includes undistributed corporation profits, all capital consumption allowances and miscellaneous valuation adjustments and the profits of the Canadian Wheat Board and Canadian Co-operative Wheat Producers accruing to farmers. The latter are included here since they are not included in undistributed corporation profits and were not included in the measure of farm income used in the calculation of personal savings (series E 66–78). See the notes to series E 3, E 5, E 10 and E 78.

E 104. Inventory valuation adjustment is included here since investment in inventories, series E 109, is the value of the physical change only, while the income data from which personal and business savings are calculated were based upon use of changes in book values of inventories for all but farm and grain inventories. See also the note to series E 7.

E 105. Government surplus or deficit is described in the note to series E 101.

E 106. Residual error of estimate is explained in the note to series E 11.

E 107. Gross national saving is the sum of series E 102–106 and also of series E 108–111.

E 108. Business gross fixed capital formation is described in the note to series E 17–20.

E 109. Value of the physical change in inventories is described in the note to series E 21–23.

E 110. Surplus or deficit on current account is obtained by subtracting imports, series E 25, from exports, series E 24. See the note to series E 24–25.

E 111. For the residual error of estimate, see the note to series E 11.

E 112–125. Total gross fixed capital formation in current and constant dollars and gross fixed capital formation by industry in current dollars, 1926 to 1960

SOURCE: for 1958 to 1960, Department of Trade and Commerce, *Private and Public Investment in Canada, Outlook, 1962* issue, table 1, p. 11, and unnumbered table on p. 24, *Outlook, 1961*, table 1, p. 11, *Outlook, 1960*, table 1, p. 11; for 1946 to 1957, D.B.S., *Private and Public Investment in Canada, 1946–1957*, table 3, pp. 13–16; for 1926 to 1945, series E 112 and E 125 from D.B.S., *Private and Public Investment in Canada, 1946–1957*, table 1, p. 11, series E 113–124 from the National Accounts and Balance of Payments Division of the Dominion Bureau of Statistics. The data for 1926 to 1949, in a form that permits the arrangement given here, appeared in Department of Trade and Commerce, *Private and Public Investment in Canada, 1926–1951*; there have been some revisions and reclassifications of the data among industries since it appeared.

Total gross fixed capital formation in current dollars, series E 112, is the sum of government outlay, series E 16, and business outlay, series E 17. This expenditure, including both government and business, is distributed by industry in series E 113–124.

For a description of the basis of estimation of the construction

component of gross fixed capital, see the general note to section R; the comments there on construction are also relevant, in the main, to the machinery and equipment components, which are added to construction here. See also the notes to series E 16 and E 17–20.

Public expenditures on resource development such as reforestation and restocking of fish are not included as capital formation; however, outlay on roads, protection fences and fire-watching towers are included. Expenditures on surface exploration for oil and minerals are not included.

For incorporated business, capital formation was allocated among industries on an establishment basis in so far as possible. See also the notes to series E 46–65; the same considerations that prevailed there in the allocation of business units among industries also apply here.

E 117. Utilities include electric power, gas distribution, railway transport and telegraphs, urban transit, water transport and services, motor transport, grain elevators, telephones, broadcasting, municipal waterworks, air transport, warehousing, oil and gas pipelines, and toll highways and bridges.

E 120. Wholesale and retail trade cover wholesale trade, chain stores, independent stores, department stores and automotive trade.

E 121. 'Finance, insurance and real estate' is given in the source in subcategories of banks, insurance, trust and loan, and other financial companies. The largest part of the latter is described as 'expenditures of real estate companies engaged in developing, owning and leasing properties' (D.B.S., *Private and Public Investment in Canada, 1946–1957*, p. 29, n. 1).

E 122. Commercial services cover laundries and dry cleaners, theatres, hotels, some commercial vehicles not already covered, professional services, independent restaurants, and recreation and amusement centres.

E 123. Institutional services include churches, universities, schools, hospitals and privately operated social and welfare institutions.

E 124. Government departments outlay is somewhat less than government gross fixed capital formation, given in series E 16, since the latter includes also a small amount of government non-rented housing (in series E 119 here) and expenditures for provincial hospitals and schools and for municipal schools (in series E 123 here).

See D.B.S., *National Accounts, 1926–1956* and *National Accounts, 1962*, table 54 in each volume, for a reconciliation of series E 112 with business gross fixed capital formation, series E 17. See also D.B.S., *Private and Public Investment in Canada, 1946–1957*, table 15, p. 39, and same title, *Outlook* for each year, table 9.

E 126–129. Total gross fixed capital formation, all governments, by type of investing body, 1926 to 1960

SOURCE: for 1958 to 1960, Department of Trade and Commerce, *Private and Public Investment in Canada, Outlook, 1962*, table 6, p. 16, *Outlook, 1961*, table 6, p. 16, *Outlook, 1960*, table 6, p. 16; for 1950 to 1957, all series, and for 1946 to 1949, series E 127–128, from D.B.S., *Private and Public Investment in Canada, 1946–1957*, table 11, p. 35; for 1926 to 1945, series E 127–128 and for 1926 to 1949, series E 129 from Department of Trade and Commerce, *Private and Public Investment in Canada, 1926–1951*, series E 127 obtained by adding federal, table 82, p. 186, provincial, table 90, p. 189, and municipal, table 108, p. 197; series E 128 obtained by adding federal public housing, table 70, p. 180, provincial institutional and housing expenditure, table 90, p. 189, and municipal institutional and housing expenditure, table 108, p. 197; series E 129 obtained by adding federal government institutions for 1941 to 1949 (calculated by subtracting federal government housing, table 70, p. 180, from federal public housing and institutions, table 82, p. 186), federal government departments, table

85, p. 187, provincial government departments, table 93, p. 191, and municipal government departments, table 111, p. 199; series E126 for 1926 to 1949 is obtained as the sum of series E127–129. The addition of government institutions to federal government departments for 1949 and earlier years is necessary in order to make the data consistent with the treatment from 1950 onwards (see the note to series R16–27).

E127. Government-owned enterprises are described in the notes to E4. See also the notes to series E16 and series E17–20. This outlay is included with business gross fixed capital formation in series E17–20.

E128. Government-owned institutions and housing include only federal non-rental housing, provincial hospitals, schools and universities and municipal hospitals and schools. The part of the outlay included here for provincial universities and municipal hospitals is included with business gross fixed capital formation in series E17–20; the remainder is included with government gross fixed capital formation, series E16.

E129. Government department capital formation is described in the note to series E16. Post-office buildings are included here in all years and very small amounts of housing in 1926 to 1940.

INCOME PRODUCED AND CAPITAL FORMATION BEFORE 1926
(Series E130–159)
General note

Many of the sources of data for national income used for the period from 1926 onward were also available for earlier years. For example, fairly comprehensive data on annual production in agriculture began in 1908. Fisheries production was available annually, in improved form, from 1911, the annual census of manufactures and of electrical stations began in 1917, mineral production was available from 1886 and the census of mining from 1920, collection of employment data began in 1921, and many of the data on banks, insurance and other financial companies, on railways, telegraphs and telephones and on governments were available annually as were the data on foreign trade. At the same times improved annual data on wage rates and prices were emerging. A census of manufacturing was taken with each decennial census until 1911 and 'postal' censuses for 1905 and 1915. An incomplete census of trade was taken for 1923.

In addition, some material was available for Ontario from an annual census of manufactures for 1900 to 1914.

These data form much of the basis for the estimates of national income for 1919 to 1926 and the estimates of capital formation for 1901 to 1930 given in this subsection.

E130–142. Net domestic income, by industry, 1919 to 1926

SOURCE: *Estimates of Net Domestic Income at Factor Cost and Labour Income by Industry, 1919–1926* (a private, unpublished, mimeographed memorandum prepared by D. H. Jones, of D.B.S.), table 1.

These estimates of net domestic income, 1919 to 1926, correspond to those appearing for gross domestic product, by industry, in series E46–65 for 1926 to 1960 with the exception that the latter measures product at factor costs plus capital consumption allowances and miscellaneous valuation adjustments while the former includes only factor incomes. The difference between the two totals in 1926, the year of overlap, is equal to the capital consumption allowances and adjustments.

The concepts of the two sets of series are identical but methods of measurement are quite different. Estimates of national income and related aggregates, prepared by D.B.S. before it began

its publication of the national accounts at the Second World War's end, had been 'derived for the most part by subtracting estimates of materials and services used and depreciation from the value of gross output, industry by industry, using for this purpose a fairly extensive body of economic statistics collected annually or decennially by the Dominion Bureau of Statistics' (source, p. 2). The worksheets underlying the earlier estimates provided the main basis for the estimates given here. Unpublished revisions of the original data were used, and in a few cases the data were traced back to the primary sources. The data were rearranged and adjusted to fit the later concepts and industry classification.

The levels of the estimates were adjusted, industry by industry, by linking them with the official series at 1926. As a check, estimates of net domestic income excluding agriculture and public administration and defence, prepared on the same basis of calculation as for 1919 to 1926, were extended to 1927, 1928 and 1929. The estimates of the projected series were 99.2 per cent of the sum of the same components of the official series in 1927, 99.2 per cent in 1928 and 99.6 per cent in 1929. Agriculture and public administration and defence were calculated by exactly the same methods for 1919 to 1926 as for the later official series and a check would have been meaningless.

The relation of the industry groups given here to those of series E46–65 is apparent from the headings. Two points need attention. No inventory valuation adjustment has been made for wholesale and retail trade. And the net imputed rent of government buildings is included with finance, insurance and real estate and not with service.

E143–155. Labour income, by industry, 1919 to 1926

SOURCE: same document as for series E132–144, table 2.

Wages and salaries were estimated for 1919 to 1925 by use, in so far as possible, of methods identical to those used from 1926 onward (see the general note to series E1–129). Wages in construction were based on the value of construction and its implied labour content from material in Buckley, *Capital Formation in Canada, 1896–1930.* The resulting estimates were then adjusted upwards to take account of supplementary labour income, industry by industry, in the proportion that it bore to wages and salaries in 1926.

A check made by comparing the change in labour income as derived from earnings of wage earners in the 1921 and 1931 censuses with that obtained from the national income data between the two periods suggested, on the basis of reasonable assumptions, that the estimating techniques were quite good.

E156–159. Gross domestic capital formation, by quinquennial periods, 1901 to 1930

SOURCE: Buckley, *Capital Formation in Canada, 1896–1930,* table H, p. 135.

Conceptually, Buckley's estimates cover the same items as in the national accounts from 1926 onward and in series E112–125. Government fixed capital formation is included as well as private capital formation. All commercial vehicles and 20 per cent of outlay on passenger automobiles are included as belonging to government or business capital formation. Housing is included but consumer durables are not. The estimate of inventory investment is the value of the physical change in inventories.

Buckley's estimates of fixed capital formation were built up, in the main, from annual flows of construction materials and machinery and equipment. Imports are added to production and exports are subtracted to estimate the flows. The derivation of the construction estimates is described in section R (see the note to series R151). The values of flows of machinery and equipment at producers' prices were adjusted for taxes, freight and mark-ups.

The main sources of the machinery and equipment data were annual reports of external trade, the federal censuses of manufactures for 1900, 1905, 1910, 1915 and annually from 1917 to 1930 and the Ontario census of manufactures for 1900 to 1914. In addition, annual direct estimates of outlay on railway rolling stock, for the whole period, were calculated from railway and government accounts, on shipbuilding from shipping reports of the Department of National Revenue and on motor-vehicle sales from registration of motor-vehicles for 1904 to 1916. Freight costs were estimated by data provided by D.B.S. as far back as 1913 or from estimates in Viner, *Canada's Balance* (see section F), before that. Sales and excise taxes were calculated by applying rates of tax to the values at producers' prices (import duties were already included) and mark-up margins from material provided by D.B.S. The data for 1926 to 1930 are mainly from estimates in *Public Investment and Capital Formation* (see section R) which was based on the same methods.

Investment in inventories was calculated from various official annual data for livestock on farms from 1907, grain on farms from 1909 and grain in commercial channels from 1910; for earlier years some data were obtained from censuses and some were estimated on the basis of production. Manufacturing inventories were obtained from D.B.S. for the postal census of 1915 and the annual census of manufactures: for 1900, 1905 and 1910 they were taken as 50 per cent of the working capital, the ratio being based on the 1915 data. Trade inventories were estimated as a constant proportion of the sum of exports and imports, the proportion being based on the same ratios that existed in 1925 to 1930. All trade inventory investment in 1901 to 1925 and manufacturing investment in 1901 to 1915 were estimated by the five-year periods given here. Price indexes used for deflating inventory investment in livestock and grain were mainly based on official sources; for manufacturing and trade, the wholesale price index of D.B.S., *Prices and Price Indexes* (see section J), was used.

The years 1926 to 1930 are given to provide an overlap with the official data.

The source also contains annual estimates of the flow of five categories of machinery and equipment at producers' prices and quinquennial estimates of capital formation for the same categories.

STOCK OF BUSINESS AND SOCIAL CAPITAL AT YEAR END, 1926 to 1955, AND INVENTORIES AT YEAR END, 1926 to 1960 (Series E160–201)

General note

The estimates of series E160–199 were prepared, under the direction of Wm. C. Hood and Anthony Scott, as a part of the staff work of the Royal Commission on Canada's Economic Prospects. The concept of capital used here corresponds very closely to that underlying the estimates of fixed capital formation given in earlier tables of this section. The estimates cover the fixed tangible capital stocks, with the capacity to produce services or utilities, that have themselves been produced. They do not include, therefore, the value of natural resources, land, forest stands, mineral and oil deposits and the like, or intangible assets such as goodwill and the accumulated training, skills and knowledge of people. Residential housing is included in capital but other consumer durables are not. Inventories in the usual sense of the term are not included.

Gross capital is valued at its monetary cost. Most of the estimates reproduced here are at cost in constant (1949) dollars, and in some sense are a measure of the gross physical stock of fixed capital. The estimates of 'industry' capital given here are also measured at original cost: in these estimates, each item of capital in the stock is measured in the prices that prevailed at the time it was actually produced.

The net capital stock is measured by subtraction from the gross stock of an estimate of that part of the service capacity of the gross stock which has been used up in depreciation, obsolescence and fire destruction and other damage. For the estimates of the net capital stock in constant dollars, depreciation and the like are measured in constant dollars, just as the gross stock was. For the estimates of the net capital stock at original cost, the depreciation and like items are valued in prices of the years in which the capital was produced.

Industry capital covers a slightly different part of the economy than that covered in the national accounts by business gross fixed capital formation in nonresidential construction and machinery and equipment. The latter includes churches, universities and private and municipal hospitals; in the capital stock, these institutions are covered in social capital. Government business enterprise, however, remains in the industry group.

In the calculation of the size of the capital stock, the 'perpetual inventory' method was used. The estimation of capital stock in any one year required a knowledge of the length of life of capital goods and the amount of gross capital formation in them for each year before the date for which the stock is being measured, as far back as the average length of life of the capital. The gross stock, at the required date, is then estimated as the sum of capital formation in these preceding years. For example, if the length of life of a capital item is ten years and if the gross stock at the end of 1939 were to be measured, it would be obtained by adding together gross capital formation for the item from 1930 to 1939. The estimation of the gross capital stock at the end of 1940 would be obtained, then, by subtracting from the 1939 year end stock the gross capital formation in 1930 and adding to it that in 1940.

The net capital stock is obtained by cumulating the annual capital consumption of the capital goods still covered in the gross stock and by subtracting this accumulative amount from the gross stock. The authors of the source study calculated depreciation and like costs on a straight line basis over the life of the capital good. A capital good with a 10-year life would be depreciated at 10 per cent per year.

When the capital formation, on which the stock estimates are based, was first estimated in current dollars (as it was in most cases either in the source volume itself or in the data prepared by others that were used) it was calculated in constant dollars by deflation of the current dollar estimates of capital formation by an index of the cost per unit of the capital formed. Similarly, for the constant dollar net capital formation estimates, it was necessary to adjust the depreciation on the capital item to the constant dollar basis.

The above methods of calculating the capital stock require estimates of capital formation (for as far back as 1870 for long-lived capital to obtain the 1926 stock estimate), of the length of life of capital goods and of the movements of prices (costs) of the capital goods.

Capital formation was obtained by somewhat different methods for 1926 to 1955 and for the period before 1926. For 1926 to 1945, the capital formation estimates were with slight modification taken from Department of Trade and Commerce, *Private and Public Investment in Canada, 1926–1951*; for 1945 to 1955 they are based on the reports of actual expenditure obtained in the preparation of the annual *Private and Public Investment in Canada, Outlook* (see section R for a discussion of the construction component obtained in these two sources). For the period prior to 1926, main reliance for capital formation estimates was placed on Buckley's estimates in *Capital Formation in Canada, 1896–1930* (see section R); some separate rather rough estimates were also made for this earlier period from other data. The capital formation estimates (and their cumulation) was in fairly fine detail for 1926 to 1955; they were in much broader aggregates for the preceding period.

Detail on the length of life of capital goods was obtained, in the main, from studies in Canada, the United States and the United Kingdom in the nineteen-thirties by engineers and accountants to determine appropriate depreciation allowances for income tax purposes. The results were available in bulletins published by internal revenue services. Greatest use was made of the United States bulletin. In most cases no provision was made for changing length of life of specific types of capital; an exception was in urban transport systems in which change from street cars to buses meant a shorter life for equipment.

Price indexes came from a variety of sources. Some were based on indexes used for deflating capital expenditure in the national accounts, from 1926 onward, some were from United States indexes, adjusted for duties, transportation and the like, and some were constructed from data on material prices and wages indexes. Before 1926, Buckley's implicit price index of construction costs and, for machinery, wholesale indexes of prices were used in some cases.

The data for the earlier years, on which capital formation and price indexes were based, were frequently sketchy. Fortunately, the seriousness of this shortcoming is mitigated by the fact that when capital formation is growing rapidly, the capital stock is largely made up from capital formed in the years most immediately preceding its date of measurement.

E160–171. 'Industry' gross and net capital stock, in 1949 prices and at original cost, by structures and machinery and equipment, year end, 1926 to 1955

SOURCE: Hood and Scott, *Output, Labour and Capital in the Canadian Economy*, table 6 B. 7, pp. 451–2.

See the general note to series E160–201 and the notes to series E14–16 and E17–20 for what is included in 'industry' and for concepts.

The data in this table were calculated on an aggregative basis. Other calculations of the data of Series E160–165, based on a cumulation of data prepared separately for each of several industries but availiable only for 1945 to 1955, show a considerably larger increase in the capital stock for the relevant years than those given here. See the source, pages 288, 434 and 444.

E172–185. Gross stock of social capital in 1949 dollars, public and private, by type, year end, 1926 to 1955

SOURCE: Hood and Scott, *Output, Labour and Capital in the Canadian Economy*, table 6 B. 5, pp. 447–8.

See the general note to series E160–201 and the notes to series E14–16 and E17–20 for the nature of social capital and for concepts.

E176. Other government engineering structures include canals, sewers, wharves and docks and like items when not operated on a commercial basis.

E182. Other private institutional includes municipal religious and lay hospitals, universities, welfare institutions and like structures.

E186–199. Net stock of social capital in 1949 dollars, public and private, by type, year end, 1926 to 1955

SOURCE: Hood and Scott, *Output, Labour and Capital in the Canadian Economy*, table 6 B. 6, pp. 449–50.

See the general note to series E160–201 and the notes to series E14–16 and E17–20 for the content of social capital and for concepts. See also the notes to series E172–185.

E200–201. Business inventories, book value, all industry and manufacturing industry, year end, 1926 to 1960

SOURCE: data provided by the National Income and Balance of Payments Division, D.B.S.

For the way in which data on inventories are obtained see the general note to series E1–129.

APPENDIX TO SECTION E

ESTIMATES OF GROSS NATIONAL PRODUCT AND GROSS INCOME PRODUCED, 1870 to 1920 (Series E202–224)

National income estimates for years before 1920 are necessarily on much less firm ground than for later years and they become progressively less firm the farther back they are carried. This is true, not only because fewer statistical data were collected in earlier years, but also because the standards of collection were less adequate and the amount of processing of individual parts of the data much less extensive. For these reasons these data must be regarded as on a different level of accuracy from the rest of the data of this section. For a comment on data available before 1920 see the general note to series E130–159.

E202–213. Gross income produced, by industry, and national income, 1911 to 1920

SOURCE: J. J. Deutsch, 'War Finance and the Canadian Economy, 1914–20', *Canadian Journal of Economics and Political Science*, vol. VI, no. 4 (November 1940), table 1, p. 538.

Series E156–165, on income produced, correspond conceptually to gross domestic product at factor cost since no deduction for depreciation has been made in the calculation of income produced. There are differences, however, between the content here and in series E46–65 and series E130–142. For one matter, income from housing is not included. Further, it appears that, apart from the underlying scarcities of data in the earlier period, assignment of activities to industry groups differ. For instance, farm income includes the part represented by paid farm rents which are assigned to the finance, insurance and real estate industry in series E46–65 and series E132–142. A part of the differences in individual industry incomes from those of series E130–142 must be attributed, however, to techniques of measurement.

It appears from the notes accompanying the table in the source that a substantial part of the estimation was done by subtracting expenses from receipts, for Deutsch explains in a general note that the 'net values shown here are after deductions for estimated values of materials and supplies used, for taxes and other expenses but not for depreciation' (source, p. 539). It is explicitly stated that agricultural income was calculated this way. Benchmark data were used in some cases to calculate ratios of expenses to income: for instance, manufacturing expenses were based on the census of industry for 1917 to 1921; this is also probably true of the electric power industry. It must also have been true of the fisheries for which only gross values of production of fish were available in all years. Similarly, in the period covered here, the gross values of mineral production and production of forest products were all that were available each year. Income in the fur industry was estimated from fur exports. Construction was estimated from contracts awarded. Service income was estimated from income produced by steam railways, electric railways, telephones and education, by the federal civil service and by provincial government salary earners for all years; it was stated that these groups represented about one-third of service income.

Primary industry excludes the processing of primary products which is included with manufacturing.

Deutsch states that 'Owing to the paucity of statistics for this period, the estimates...are necessarily rough. While the absolute figures may be very approximate, it is believed that the relative year-to-year changes are represented with a useful degree of accuracy' (source, p. 539).

E214–224. Gross national product by industry, decennially, 1870 to 1920

SOURCE: Firestone, *Canada's Economic Development, 1867–1953*, table 89, p. 281.

The estimates of series E214–221 are for income produced at factor cost gross of depreciation. In this respect, they correspond to the estimates of series E158–167.

The estimates are based largely on decennial census, or, in 1920, production census material. The characteristic method for calculating income in all the commodity-producing industries, except construction, was either to subtract reported costs of materials, fuels and the like from the gross values of goods produced, or to reduce gross value of production by some proportion to take account of costs of materials and fuels, the proportion being based on the experience of later periods. Sometimes combinations of both methods were used.

Data for agricultural production in the censuses of 1870 to 1890 contained only quantities of products and did not cover all of them. Valuations were obtained from other sources, one method

being to project prices backward from a later period by using wholesale prices of as nearly related products as possible. Forest products of farms are included in the forest products industry.

Construction was mainly calculated from estimates of the flow of construction materials obtained by adding imports to production and subtracting exports. The work of tradesmen covered in the census of manufactures remained in manufacturing and was eliminated from construction.

Income in service industries was calculated by estimating, from census data, income per person for a sample made up of those in professional service, and then by multiplying an average of this income and income produced per person in the commodity-producing industries by the total numbers employed in service.

Residential gross rents were estimated by multiplying the number of all occupied dwellings in each year, obtained from the census, by an estimate of shelter expenses per dwelling. The latter was obtained for 1930 from shelter expenses in the national accounts and the number of occupied dwellings from the census. It was projected to 1900 on cost-of-living indexes and to earlier years by an index of prices of selected building materials and construction labour, adjusted for quality of housing according to number of persons per dwelling. Rents for farm homes were subtracted from the total first obtained on the assumption that average farm home rents were half the national average. Four-fifths of the resulting estimate of gross nonfarm residential rents was used for the rent figure, the reduction being made to avoid duplication for values of shelter materials covered in other industries.

These estimates should be regarded as only giving a rough indication of trend. The estimate for 1920, after adjustment for conceptual differences by data given in the source—depreciation is given at 409 million dollars in 1920—is nearly 11 per cent above that given in series E132. These estimates must not be treated as extensions backward of the official data beginning in 1926. It should also be borne in mind that a great deal of estimation by inference from more or less related data has been used, particularly for earlier years.

Series E 1–12. *National income and gross national product, by components, 1926 to 1960*

(millions of dollars)

Year[1]	Wages, salaries and supplementary labour income	Military pay and allowances	Corporation profits before taxes	Rent, interest, and miscellaneous investment income	Accrued net income of farm operators from farm production	Net income of nonfarm unincorporated business	Inventory valuation adjustment	Net national income at factor cost	Indirect taxes less subsidies	Capital consumption allowances and miscellaneous valuation adjustments	Residual error of estimate	Gross national product at market prices
	1	2	3	4	5	6	7	8	9	10	11	12
1960	18,245	509	2,880	2,470	1,186	2,213	− 70	27,433	4,470	4,423	− 39	36,287
1959	17,459	496	3,003	2,315	1,121	2,210	− 122	26,482	4,259	4,204	− 30	34,915
1958	16,521	491	2,605	2,104	1,200	2,125	− 35	25,011	3,882	3,899	102	32,894
1957	16,018	476	2,581	1,980	1,026	2,008	− 78	24,011	3,861	4,009	28	31,909
1956	14,890	424	2,908	1,767	1,450	1,965	− 238	23,166	3,636	3,642	141	30,585
1955	13,223	394	2,570	1,684	1,264	1,791	− 189	20,737	3,237	3,266	− 108	27,132
1954	12,432	367	1,963	1,511	1,017	1,656	86	19,032	2,947	2,905	− 13	24,871
1953	12,110	309	2,294	1,329	1,575	1,688	− 11	19,294	2,911	2,673	142	25,020
1952	11,208	270	2,364	1,175	1,959	1,572	106	18,654	2,717	2,422	202	23,995
1951	10,103	201	2,455	1,020	1,933	1,519	− 643	16,588	2,469	2,203	− 90	21,170
1950	8,629	137	2,118	890	1,322	1,439	− 374	14,161	2,000	1,913	− 68	18,006
1949	8,000	115	1,562	703	1,248	1,389	− 112	12,905	1,808	1,673	− 43	16,343
1948	7,414	82	1,715	651	1,378	1,269	− 506	12,003	1,765	1,441	− 89	15,120
1947	6,399	83	1,566	591	1,120	1,173	− 571	10,361	1,608	1,223	− 27	13,165
1946	5,487	340	1,269	581	1,056	1,072	− 254	9,551	1,270	998	31	11,850
1945	5,037	1,117	1,106	618	906	918	− 37	9,665	1,004	968	198	11,835
1944	4,998	1,068	1,081	589	1,088	811	− 52	9,583	1,112	1,005	150	11,850
1943	4,812	910	1,125	571	720	747	− 83	8,802	1,118	1,037	131	11,088
1942	4,282	641	1,135	532	929	701	− 122	8,098	1,086	1,043	100	10,327
1941	3,608	386	951	416	463	637	− 156	6,305	1,055	893	75	8,328
1940	2,959	193	667	351	483	531	− 121	5,063	831	750	99	6,743
1939	2,601	32	521	301	362	475	− 56	4,236	734	637	29	5,636
1938	2,515	9	334	262	353	461	67	4,001	639	604	34	5,278
1937	2,538	9	432	270	280	445	− 87	3,887	705	594	71	5,257
1936	2,241	9	314	242	199	398	− 36	3,367	660	555	71	4,653
1935	2,079	9	237	219	218	357	− 20	3,099	585	531	100	4,315
1934	1,939	8	191	202	167	315	− 39	2,783	578	522	101	3,984
1933	1,788	8	73	173	66	282	− 22	2,368	537	528	77	3,510
1932	1,975	8	− 98	223	104	320	109	2,641	537	576	73	3,827
1931	2,408	8	13	269	94	418	172	3,382	557	646	114	4,699
1930	2,786	8	144	339	343	540	239	4,399	593	711	25	5,728
1929	2,940	8	396	369	392	618	− 15	4,708	681	717	28	6,134
1928	2,715	7	433	360	636	585	1	4,737	679	671	− 41	6,046
1927	2,506	7	368	314	600	532	29	4,356	634	611	− 52	5,549
1926	2,366	7	325	287	609	489	46	4,129	612	567	− 156	5,152

[1] Newfoundland included beginning in 1949 in all series in section E.

Series E 13–27. *Gross national expenditure, by components, 1926 to 1960*

(millions of dollars)

Year	Personal expenditure on consumer goods and services	Government expenditure on goods and services			Business gross fixed capital formation				Value of the physical change in inventories			Exports of goods and services	Imports of goods and services	Residual error of estimate	Gross national expenditure at market prices
		Total	Current expenditure	Gross fixed capital formation	Total	New residential (Construction)	New non-residential (Construction)	New machinery and equipment	Total	Nonfarm business	Farm and grain in commercial channels				
	13	14	15	16	17	18	19	20	21	22	23	24	25	26	27
1960	23,540	6,769	5,199	1,570	6,692	1,443	2,577	2,672	410	325	85	7,008	−8,172	40	36,287
1959	22,591	6,490	4,967	1,523	6,894	1,734	2,589	2,571	357	421	− 64	6,683	−8,131	31	34,915
1958	21,245	6,180	4,791	1,389	6,975	1,763	2,811	2,401	−322	−197	−125	6,340	−7,423	−101	32,894
1957	20,072	5,722	4,340	1,382	7,335	1,409	3,103	2,823	231	305	− 74	6,391	−7,813	− 29	31,909
1956	18,833	5,386	4,126	1,260	6,774	1,526	2,589	2,659	1,084	808	276	6,365	−7,715	−142	30,585
1955	17,389	4,792	3,758	1,034	5,210	1,378	1,848	1,984	311	133	178	5,764	−6,443	109	27,132
1954	16,175	4,461	3,519	942	4,779	1,227	1,671	1,881	−130	− 40	− 90	5,147	−5,574	13	24,871
1953	15,592	4,432	3,454	978	4,998	1,166	1,719	2,113	583	351	232	5,400	−5,843	−142	25,020
1952	14,781	4,279	3,239	1,040	4,451	933	1,566	1,952	512	90	422	5,573	−5,400	−201	23,995
1951	13,460	3,271	2,491	780	3,959	895	1,270	1,794	914	564	350	5,089	−5,613	90	21,170
1950	12,026	2,344	1,756	588	3,348	883	1,042	1,423	550	399	151	4,183	−4,513	68	18,006
1949	10,923	2,127	1,620	507	3,032	794	920	1,318	49	150	−101	4,021	−3,853	44	16,343
1948	10,085	1,797	—	—	2,619	609	816	1,194	113	85	28	4,050	−3,633	89	15,120
1947	9,090	1,541	—	—	2,085	494	597	994	403	437	− 34	3,640	−3,621	27	13,165
1946	8,031	1,796	—	—	1,388	368	435	585	333	360	− 27	3,210	−2,877	− 31	11,850
1945	6,969	3,656	—	—	1,031	318	253	460	−311	148	−459	3,597	−2,910	−197	11,835
1944	6,274	4,978	—	—	900	267	256	377	−145	− 10	−135	3,561	−3,569	−149	11,850
1943	5,808	4,177	—	—	887	220	364	303	−180	28	−208	3,444	−2,917	−131	11,088
1942	5,500	3,674	—	—	1,064	214	354	496	135	−202	337	2,361	−2,307	−100	10,327
1941	5,103	1,635	—	—	1,085	240	287	558	88	130	− 42	2,467	−1,976	− 74	8,328
1940	4,488	1,116	—	—	803	186	208	409	255	87	168	1,808	−1,629	− 98	6,743
1939	3,984	683	—	—	592	174	164	254	282	101	181	1,451	−1,328	− 28	5,636
1938	3,897	666	—	—	592	148	170	274	57	− 21	78	1,356	−1,257	− 33	5,278
1937	3,884	619	—	—	633	164	188	281	9	113	−104	1,591	−1,409	− 70	5,257
1936	3,549	544	—	—	458	131	148	179	− 72	68	−140	1,428	−1,183	− 71	4,653
1935	3,338	542	—	—	369	107	116	146	39	34	5	1,143	−1,017	− 99	4,315
1934	3,182	503	—	—	298	92	91	115	32	19	13	1,018	− 948	−101	3,984
1933	2,984	462	—	—	234	72	78	84	− 91	− 68	− 23	826	− 828	− 77	3,510
1932	3,194	584	—	—	319	90	121	108	−100	−127	27	804	− 901	− 73	3,827
1931	3,773	688	—	—	622	158	265	199	− 95	− 54	− 41	967	−1,142	−114	4,699
1930	4,367	721	—	—	926	191	384	351	77	41	36	1,286	−1,625	− 24	5,728
1929	4,621	640	—	—	1,161	230	490	441	52	146	− 94	1,632	−1,945	− 27	6,134
1928	4,314	560	—	—	1,007	220	413	374	159	126	33	1,773	−1,808	41	6,046
1927	3,893	531	—	—	830	204	299	327	253	163	90	1,618	−1,629	53	5,549
1926	3,542	488	—	—	702	201	240	261	135	154	− 19	1,650	−1,522	157	5,152

Series E28–45. *Gross national expenditure in constant (1949) dollars, by components, 1926 to 1960*
(millions of dollars)

Year	Personal expenditure on consumer goods and services	Government expenditures on goods and services			Business gross fixed capital formation				
		Total	Current expenditure	Gross fixed capital formation	Total	Construction		New machinery and equipment	Adjusting entry
						New residential	New non-residential		
	28	29	30	31	32	33	34	35	36
1960	17,945	4,197[1]	3,067	1,141	4,345	937	1,637	1,770	1
1959	17,392	4,155[1]	3,055	1,109	4,575	1,157	1,683	1,735	—
1958	16,585	4,093[1]	3,044	1,056	4,761	1,219	1,884	1,650	8
1957	16,083	3,833[1]	2,867	968	5,115	998	2,112	1,995	10
1956	15,603	3,794	2,869	925	4,891	1,110	1,816	1,965	—
1955	14,662	3,563	2,767	796	3,962	1,040	1,365	1,557	—
1954	13,650	3,415	2,676	739	3,723	946	1,272	1,505	—
1953	13,338	3,517	2,748	769	3,926	905	1,306	1,715	—
1952	12,633	3,516	2,670	846	3,588	737	1,235	1,616	—
1951	11,817	2,806	2,140	666	3,301	727	1,074	1,500	—
1950	11,642	2,242	1,680	562	3,167	833	988	1,346	—
1949	10,923	2,127	1,620	507	3,032	794	920	1,318	—
1948	10,451	1,902	—	—	2,758	638	850	1,270	—
1947	10,657	1,850	—	—	2,496	610	700	1,186	—
1946	10,323	2,294	—	—	1,846	512	569	777	—12
1945	9,267	4,542	—	—	1,420	472	352	618	—22
1944	8,444	6,499	—	—	1,235	401	355	496	—17
1943	7,902	5,714	—	—	1,234	343	513	389	—11
1942	7,692	5,189	—	—	1,567	356	524	682	5
1941	7,471	2,531	—	—	1,682	427	456	802	—3
1940	7,034	1,794	—	—	1,343	363	349	638	—7
1939	6,510	1,156	—	—	1,053	361	286	427	—21
1938	6,337	1,127	—	—	1,050	310	293	456	—9
1937	6,420	1,056	—	—	1,112	336	317	470	—11
1936	6,036	961	—	—	866	288	269	323	—14
1935	5,775	971	—	—	708	242	216	266	—16
1934	5,534	916	—	—	580	207	173	213	—13
1933	5,272	842	—	—	462	168	150	154	—10
1932	5,414	1,041	—	—	609	200	226	194	—11
1931	5,877	1,160	—	—	1,143	322	473	358	—10
1930	6,203	1,178	—	—	1,608	363	635	608	2
1929	6,490	1,027	—	—	1,948	426	779	734	9
1928	6,128	908	—	—	1,736	426	677	636	—3
1927	5,577	868	—	—	1,449	405	502	553	—11
1926	5,010	792	—	—	1,208	399	402	426	—19

Year	Value of the physical change in inventories				Exports of goods and services	Imports of goods and services	Residual error of estimate	Adjusting entry	Gross national expenditure in constant (1949) dollars
	Total	Nonfarm business	Farm and grain in commercial channels	Adjusting entry					
	37	38	39	40	41	42	43	44	45
1960	361	262	86	13	5,806	—6,743	28	—90	25,849
1959	308	334	—91	65	5,574	—6,776	22	—8	25,242
1958	—286	—158	—141	13	5,368	—6,150	—74	100	24,397
1957	210	246	—89	53	5,389	—6,571	—22	80	24,117
1956	955	648	307	—	5,340	—6,662	—110	—	23,811
1955	419	134	285	—	4,969	—5,742	87	—	21,920
1954	—216	—39	—177	—	4,616	—5,013	11	—	20,186
1953	590	320	270	—	4,809	—5,269	—117	—	20,794
1952	489	81	408	—	4,850	—4,882	—167	—	20,027
1951	849	493	356	—	4,380	—4,685	79	—	18,547
1950	561	398	163	—	3,999	—4,206	66	—	17,471
1949	49	150	—101	—	4,021	—3,853	44	—	16,343
1948	87	70	17	—	4,193	—3,749	93	—	15,735
1947	446	520	—74	—	4,141	—4,176	32	—	15,446
1946	536	562	—82	56	4,115	—3,717	—40	—106	15,251
1945	—462	211	—831	158	5,059	—3,986	—258	—30	15,552
1944	—204	5	—252	43	5,168	—5,020	—199	4	15,927
1943	—309	52	—439	78	5,340	—4,246	—181	—97	15,357
1942	336	—302	796	—158	3,852	—3,549	—142	—129	14,816
1941	68	216	—199	51	4,298	—3,310	—111	—143	12,486
1940	658	159	588	—89	3,281	—2,888	—157	—154	10,911
1939	699	191	595	—87	2,885	—2,599	—47	—121	9,536
1938	274	—36	377	—67	2,623	—2,436	—55	—49	8,871
1937	66	210	—194	50	2,903	—2,600	—117	—20	8,820
1936	—235	134	—456	87	2,845	—2,352	—123	24	8,022
1935	107	75	32	—	2,366	—2,076	—175	2	7,678
1934	45	34	10	1	2,152	—1,943	—181	24	7,127
1933	—242	—134	—119	11	1,903	—1,824	—140	86	6,359
1932	—171	—264	137	44	1,883	—1,925	—129	76	6,798
1931	—309	—109	—231	31	2,036	—2,248	—186	94	7,567
1930	255	54	238	—37	2,264	—2,811	—36	18	8,679
1929	109	256	—201	54	2,603	—3,092	—40	16	9,061
1928	332	195	147	—10	2,766	—2,838	61	—56	9,037
1927	448	281	176	—9	2,444	—2,530	79	—65	8,270
1926	253	260	—33	26	2,437	—2,296	231	—59	7,576

[1] Includes adjusting entries as follows: 1957, —2; 1958, —9; 1959, —7; 1960, —11.

Series E 46–65. *Gross domestic product at factor cost, by industry, 1926 to 1960*

(millions of dollars)

Year	Agriculture	Forestry	Fishing and trapping	Mining, quarrying and oil wells	Manufacturing	Construction	Transportation	Storage	Communication	Electric power, gas and water utilities
	46	47	48	49	50	51	52	53	54	55
1960	1,745	403	91	1,433	8,427	1,745	2,103	89	744	1,070
1959	1,660	380	95	1,340	8,286	1,872	2,133	88	686	998
1958	1,732	336	108	1,151	7,753	1,974	1,940	80	623	935
1957	1,551	413	88	1,222	7,904	1,935	2,032	77	581	879
1956	1,973	462	98	1,196	7,605	1,752	1,983	79	532	768
1955	1,767	438	85	1,071	6,779	1,385	1,719	68	473	664
1954	1,482	406	89	887	6,291	1,325	1,499	60	422	594
1953	2,048	370	81	782	6,453	1,356	1,554	66	373	545
1952	2,421	369	88	777	6,150	1,134	1,453	58	349	490
1951	2,382	445	103	794	5,474	921	1,362	48	311	441
1950	1,716	353	99	653	4,714	874	1,123	40	258	392
1949	1,600	252	80	547	4,303	796	1,019	37	222	341
1948	1,706	284	80	525	3,909	689	1,012	37	202	305
1947	1,422	279	64	446	3,310	557	918	22	187	275
1946	1,331	267	82	364	2,816	440	865	29	169	229
1945	1,160	208	77	325	2,960	311	877	31	151	221
1944	1,335	166	64	315	3,171	247	863	26	140	226
1943	961	155	59	362	3,198	302	—	—	1,214	—
1942	1,160	131	51	388	2,889	306	—	—	1,071	—
1941	680	114	42	391	2,220	263	—	—	902	—
1940	693	100	29	363	1,622	188	—	—	723	—
1939	570	76	25	335	1,260	156	—	—	647	—
1938	558	54	23	303	1,174	154	—	—	595	—
1937	485	82	25	328	1,170	154	—	—	594	—
1936	403	55	25	270	987	117	—	—	553	—
1935	425	44	23	213	882	99	—	—	508	—
1934	374	38	21	183	786	81	—	—	489	—
1933	276	30	17	133	648	73	—	—	437	—
1932	326	27	16	109	728	113	—	—	475	—
1931	343	40	20	142	966	205	—	—	569	—
1930	628	61	30	182	1,246	253	—	—	672	—
1929	698	78	39	218	1,341	292	—	—	733	—
1928	932	72	41	189	1,255	242	—	—	740	—
1927	883	69	39	168	1,148	210	—	—	663	—
1926	886	66	41	155	1,063	204	—	—	632	—

Year	Wholesale trade	Retail trade	Finance, insurance and real estate	Public administration and defence	Service	Gross domestic product at factor cost	Indirect taxes less subsidies	Net income paid to non-residents	Residual error of estimate	Gross national product at market prices
	56	57	58	59	60	61	62	63	64	65
1960	1,506	3,016	3,383	2,342	4,239	32,336	4,470	−480	39	36,287
1959	1,487	2,924	3,175	2,201	3,850	31,175	4,259	−489	− 30	34,915
1958	1,387	2,787	2,911	2,100	3,537	29,354	3,882	−444	102	32,894
1957	1,371	2,573	2,646	1,928	3,255	28,455	3,861	−435	28	31,909
1956	1,260	2,437	2,337	1,738	2,969	27,189	3,636	−381	141	30,585
1955	1,080	2,243	2,298	1,590	2,666	24,326	3,237	−323	− 108	27,132
1954	999	2,075	2,113	1,478	2,493	22,213	2,947	−276	− 13	24,871
1953	993	2,024	1,902	1,314	2,345	22,206	2,911	−239	142	25,020
1952	1,045	1,927	1,724	1,196	2,163	21,344	2,717	−268	202	23,995
1951	836	1,545	1,497	995	1,972	19,126	2,469	−335	− 90	21,170
1950	774	1,534	1,355	809	1,764	16,458	2,000	−384	− 68	18,006
1949	717	1,449	1,144	740	1,638	14,885	1,808	−307	− 43	16,343
1948	623	1,222	1,002	629	1,474	13,699	1,765	−255	− 89	15,120
1947	602	1,121	817	554	1,283	11,857	1,608	−273	− 27	13,165
1946	471	1,033	806	782	1,107	10,791	1,270	−242	31	11,850
1945	386	877	737	1,514	969	10,804	1,004	−171	198	11,835
1944	376	791	726	1,440	895	10,781	1,112	−193	150	11,850
1943	307	703	678	1,260	842	10,041	1,118	−202	131	11,088
1942	307	644	665	951	781	9,344	1,086	−203	100	10,327
1941	289	579	574	644	726	7,424	1,055	−226	75	8,328
1940	238	484	543	443	648	6,074	831	−261	99	6,743
1939	204	445	530	266	608	5,122	734	−249	29	5,636
1938	212	449	483	246	595	4,846	639	−241	34	5,278
1937	184	424	460	227	574	4,707	705	−226	71	5,257
1936	170	386	452	212	528	4,158	660	−236	71	4,653
1935	159	347	423	206	507	3,836	585	−206	100	4,315
1934	139	307	410	203	485	3,516	578	−211	101	3,984
1933	135	274	442	183	474	3,122	537	−226	77	3,510
1932	164	327	457	205	535	3,482	537	−265	73	3,827
1931	196	429	514	225	661	4,310	557	−282	114	4,699
1930	274	516	568	224	745	5,399	593	−289	25	5,728
1929	204	520	601	205	757	5,686	681	−261	28	6,134
1928	204	495	513	189	765	5,637	679	−229	− 41	6,046
1927	195	440	528	177	663	5,183	634	−216	− 52	5,549
1926	172	396	492	165	632	4,904	612	−208	− 156	5,152

Series E66–78. *Personal income and its disposition, 1926 to 1960*

(millions of dollars)

Year	Net national income at factor cost	Transfer payments	Interest on the public debt	Total 66+67+68	Earnings not paid out to persons	Personal income	Personal direct taxes	Personal disposable income	Personal expenditures on consumer goods and services				Personal net saving
									Total	Durables	Nondurables	Services	
	66	67	68	69	70	71	72	73	74	75	76	77	78
1960	27,433	3,120	1,095	31,648	−4,213	27,435	−2,360	25,075	−23,540	−2,664	−11,813	−9,063	1,535
1959	26,482	2,755	963	30,200	−4,164	26,036	−2,088	23,948	−22,591	−2,678	−11,373	−8,540	1,357
1958	25,011	2,637	782	28,430	−3,755	24,675	−1,795	22,880	−21,245	−2,499	−10,878	−7,868	1,635
1957	24,011	2,076	739	26,826	−3,635	23,191	−1,917	21,274	−20,072	−2,430	−10,402	−7,240	1,202
1956	23,166	1,766	714	25,646	3,761	21,885	−1,732	20,153	−18,833	−2,431	− 9,736	−6,666	1,320
1955	20,737	1,737	669	23,143	3,405	19,738	−1,499	18,239	−17,389	−2,245	− 9,065	−6,079	850
1954	19,032	1,634	669	21,335	2,914	18,421	−1,437	16,984	−16,175	−1,970	− 8,373	−5,832	809
1953	19,294	1,461	610	21,365	3,029	18,336	−1,432	16,904	−15,592	−2,001	− 8,199	−5,392	1,312
1952	18,654	1,359	580	20,593	3,198	17,395	−1,323	16,072	−14,781	−1,780	− 8,051	−4,950	1,291
1951	16,588	1,032	553	18,173	2,349	15,824	−1,030	14,794	−13,460	−1,490	− 7,610	−4,360	1,334
1950	14,161	1,030	545	15,736	2,308	13,428	− 740	12,688	−12,026	−1,451	− 6,711	−3,864	662
1949	12,905	948	572	14,425	1,787	12,638	− 789	11,849	−10,923	−1,146	− 6,288	−3,489	926
1948	12,003	862	558	13,423	1,522	11,901	− 822	11,079	−10,085	− 934	− 6,070	−3,081	994
1947	10,361	839	559	11,759	1,384	10,375	− 791	9,584	− 9,090	− 841	− 5,390	−2,859	494
1946	9,551	1,106	554	11,211	1,492	9,719	− 796	8,923	− 8,031	− 596	− 4,829	−2,606	892
1945	9,665	546	512	10,723	1,603	9,120	− 809	8,311	− 6,969	− 375	− 4,193	−2,401	1,342
1944	9,583	259	423	10,265	1,400	8,865	− 838	8,027	− 6,274	− 323	− 3,772	−2,179	1,753
1943	8,802	210	371	9,383	1,341	8,042	− 698	7,344	− 5,808	− 297	− 3,541	−1,970	1,536
1942	8,098	222	310	8,630	1,237	7,393	− 495	6,898	− 5,500	− 337	− 3,240	−1,923	1,398
1941	6,305	194	291	6,790	939	5,851	− 296	5,555	− 5,103	− 421	− 2,908	−1,774	452
1940	5,063	207	273	5,543	629	4,914	− 139	4,775	− 4,488	− 390	− 2,474	−1,624	287
1939	4,236	229	275	4,740	450	4,290	− 112	4,178	− 3,984	− 312	− 2,186	−1,486	194
1938	4,001	226	266	4,493	425	4,068	− 115	3,953	− 3,897	− 305	− 2,136	−1,456	56
1937	3,887	237	273	4,397	390	4,007	− 112	3,895	− 3,884	− 331	− 2,165	−1,388	11
1936	3,367	224	277	3,868	321	3,547	− 95	3,452	− 3,549	− 284	− 1,960	−1,305	− 97
1935	3,099	221	280	3,600	252	3,348	− 80	3,268	− 3,338	− 254	− 1,841	−1,243	− 70
1934	2,783	220	284	3,287	153	3,134	− 64	3,070	− 3,182	− 219	− 1,786	−1,177	− 112
1933	2,368	181	283	2,832	42	2,790	− 69	2,721	− 2,984	− 173	− 1,637	−1,174	− 263
1932	2,641	160	275	3,076	61	3,015	− 64	2,951	− 3,194	− 193	− 1,731	−1,270	− 243
1931	3,382	141	253	3,776	161	3,615	− 63	3,552	− 3,773	− 266	− 2,046	−1,461	− 221
1930	4,399	112	244	4,755	417	4,338	− 71	4,267	− 4,367	− 340	− 2,410	−1,617	− 100
1929	4,708	93	235	5,036	428	4,608	− 68	4,540	− 4,621	− 417	− 2,557	−1,647	− 81
1928	4,737	87	231	5,055	501	4,554	− 59	4,495	− 4,314	− 383	− 2,367	−1,564	181
1927	4,356	77	234	4,667	433	4,234	− 59	4,175	− 3,893	− 317	− 2,091	−1,485	282
1926	4,129	74	231	4,434	420	4,014	− 53	3,961	− 3,542	− 279	− 1,840	−1,423	419

Series E79–90. *Personal income, by province, 1926 to 1960*

(millions of dollars)

Year	Newfoundland	Prince Edward Island	Nova Scotia	New Brunswick	Quebec	Ontario	Manitoba	Saskatchewan	Alberta	British Columbia	Yukon and Northwest Territories	Foreign countries
	79	80	81	82	83	84	85	86	87	88	89	90
1960	395	102	848	617	6,736	11,023	1,398	1,351	2,006	2,850	50	59
1959	363	93	804	573	6,353	10,566	1,328	1,177	1,932	2,755	41	51
1958	343	85	757	541	6,071	9,978	1,262	1,107	1,850	2,608	39	34
1957	329	76	721	513	5,742	9,399	1,132	1,019	1,660	2,527	42	31
1956	311	78	675	497	5,318	8,617	1,126	1,226	1,635	2,332	43	27
1955	277	69	627	450	4,847	7,918	999	1,022	1,410	2,064	31	24
1954	258	69	607	435	4,647	7,397	927	809	1,309	1,911	27	25
1953	242	66	591	414	4,469	7,209	943	1,136	1,373	1,844	24	25
1952	219	71	553	406	4,152	6,749	934	1,209	1,328	1,728	23	23
1951	205	60	499	383	3,763	6,093	881	1,106	1,228	1,568	21	17
1950	177	53	463	348	3,317	5,285	755	707	919	1,398[1]	—	6
1949	163	51	438	328	3,062	4,904	725	796	892	1,273	—	6
1948	—	47	415	317	2,951	4,570	731	777	880	1,206	—	7
1947	—	44	421	291	2,606	4,017	612	634	729	1,016	—	5
1946	—	43	412	284	2,339	3,738	594	641	686	922	—	60
1945	—	42	378	250	2,172	3,656	516	531	559	832	—	184
1944	—	36	358	221	2,075	3,510	495	657	579	783	—	151
1943	—	33	330	204	1,975	3,303	453	428	447	754	—	115
1942	—	27	283	179	1,750	2,965	420	543	506	645	—	75
1941	—	23	228	148	1,470	2,494	343	272	323	511	—	39
1940	—	21	190	127	1,217	2,038	287	276	310	432	—	16
1939	—	19	162	111	1,085	1,751	250	266	262	384	—	—
1938	—	18	158	105	1,033	1,674	240	197	271	372	—	—
1937	—	19	158	106	1,032	1,657	272	148	255	360	—	—
1936	—	18	139	94	926	1,470	214	176	188	322	—	—
1935	—	16	127	85	856	1,401	198	181	187	297	—	—
1934	—	14	117	79	813	1,315	194	142	184	276	—	—
1933	—	12	106	73	731	1,182	173	115	145	253	—	—
1932	—	13	111	77	786	1,252	193	146	169	268	—	—
1931	—	16	135	94	953	1,533	222	143	199	320	—	—
1930	—	21	159	113	1,101	1,779	289	235	271	370	—	—
1929	—	24	169	121	1,163	1,873	303	271	290	394	—	—
1928	—	22	166	114	1,083	1,753	324	401	324	367	—	—
1927	—	22	150	109	993	1,628	270	375	350	337	—	—
1926	—	21	147	108	938	1,537	295	357	293	318	—	—

[1] Yukon and the Northwest Territories included with British Columbia before 1951.

Series E91–101. *Government revenue and expenditure, by component, all governments, 1926 to 1960*

(millions of dollars)

	Revenue							Expenditure			
	Direct taxes		With-holding taxes	Indirect taxes	Invest-ment income	Employee and employer contributions to social insurance and government pension funds	Total government revenue and expenditure	Purchases of goods and services	Transfer payments	Subsidies	Surplus (+) or deficit (−) on transactions relating to national accounts
Year	Persons	Corporations									
	91	92	93	94	95	96	97	98	99	100	101
1960	2,360	1,544	79	4,705	1,063	751	10,502	6,769	4,215	235	− 717
1959	2,088	1,581	74	4,464	998	652	9,857	6,490	3,718	205	− 556
1958	1,795	1,315	48	4,028	937	615	8,738	6,180	3,419	146	−1,007
1957	1,917	1,337	83	3,977	849	590	8,753	5,722	2,815	116	100
1956	1,732	1,413	69	3,759	834	532	8,339	5,386	2,480	123	350
1955	1,499	1,272	67	3,319	753	476	7,386	4,792	2,406	82	106
1954	1,437	1,082	58	3,033	687	422	6,719	4,461	2,303	86	− 131
1953	1,432	1,220	54	3,021	651	410	6,788	4,432	2,071	110	175
1952	1,323	1,384	55	2,817	617	375	6,571	4,279	1,939	100	253
1951	1,030	1,416	56	2,597	534	336	5,969	3,271	1,585	128	985
1950	740	983	54	2,063	471	256	4,567	2,344	1,575	63	585
1949	789	718	47	1,885	419	239	4,097	2,127	1,520	77	373
1948	822	687	41	1,840	386	224	4,000	1,797	1,420	75	708
1947	791	702	35	1,785	375	181	3,869	1,541	1,398	177	753
1946	796	654	29	1,506	404	149	3,538	1,796	1,660	236	− 154
1945	809	599	29	1,266	430	136	3,269	3,656	1,058	262	−1,707
1944	838	598	27	1,379	367	133	3,342	4,978	682	267	−2,585
1943	698	640	27	1,329	348	128	3,170	4,177	581	211	−1,799
1942	495	629	29	1,179	269	114	2,715	3,674	532	93	−1,584
1941	296	510	24	1,129	211	69	2,239	1,635	485	74	45
1940	139	327	13	884	165	39	1,567	1,116	480	53	− 82
1939	112	115	10	717	121	35	1,110	683	504	−17	− 60
1938	115	94	10	701	101	33	1,054	666	492	62	− 166
1937	112	101	10	715	116	34	1,088	619	510	10	− 51
1936	95	83	9	674	119	28	1,008	544	501	14	− 51
1935	80	65	7	608	93	26	879	542	501	23	− 187
1934	64	52	6	586	80	23	811	503	504	8	− 204
1933	69	37	5	545	65	21	742	462	464	8	− 192
1932	64	32	—	546	66	23	731	584	435	9	− 297
1931	63	33	—	575	72	26	769	688	394	18	− 331
1930	71	40	—	600	103	29	843	721	356	7	− 241
1929	68	48	—	686	136	27	965	640	328	5	− 8
1928	59	45	—	684	140	22	950	560	318	5	67
1927	59	38	—	637	122	20	876	531	311	3	31
1926	53	34	—	614	117	17	835	488	305	2	40

Series E102–111. *National saving and investment, 1926 to 1960*

(millions of dollars)

	Saving					Gross national saving and investment	Investment			
Year	Personal net saving	Business gross saving	Inventory valuation adjustment	Government surplus (+) or deficit (−)	Residual error of estimate		Business gross fixed capital formation	Value of the physical change in inventories	Surplus (+) or deficit (−) on current account with non-residents	Residual error of estimate
	102	103	104	105	106	107	108	109	110	111
1960	1,535	5,269	− 70	− 717	− 39	5,978	6,692	410	−1,164	40
1959	1,357	5,185	−122	− 556	− 30	5,834	6,894	357	−1,448	31
1958	1,635	4,774	− 35	−1,007	102	5,469	6,975	− 322	−1,083	−101
1957	1,202	4,863	− 78	100	28	6,115	7,335	231	−1,422	− 29
1956	1,320	4,793	−238	350	141	6,366	6,774	1,084	−1,350	−142
1955	850	4,292	−189	106	−108	4,951	5,210	311	− 679	109
1954	809	3,484	86	− 131	− 13	4,235	4,779	−130	− 427	13
1953	1,312	3,378	− 11	175	142	4,996	4,998	583	− 443	−142
1952	1,291	3,083	106	253	202	4,935	4,451	512	173	−201
1951	1,334	2,853	−643	985	− 90	4,439	3,959	914	− 524	90
1950	662	2,831	−374	585	− 68	3,636	3,348	550	− 330	68
1949	926	2,149	−112	373	− 43	3,293	3,032	49	168	44
1948	994	2,131	−506	708	− 89	3,238	2,619	113	417	89
1947	494	1,885	−571	753	− 27	2,534	2,085	403	19	27
1946	892	1,508	−254	− 154	31	2,023	1,388	333	333	− 31
1945	1,342	1,414	− 37	−1,707	198	1,210	1,031	−311	687	−197
1944	1,753	1,332	− 52	−2,585	150	598	900	−145	− 8	−149
1943	1,536	1,318	− 83	−1,799	131	1,103	887	−180	527	−131
1942	1,398	1,361	−122	−1,584	100	1,153	1,064	135	54	−100
1941	452	1,174	−156	45	75	1,590	1,085	88	491	− 74
1940	287	956	−121	− 82	99	1,139	803	255	179	− 98
1939	194	862	− 56	− 60	29	969	592	282	123	− 28
1938	56	724	67	− 166	34	715	592	57	99	− 33
1937	11	810	− 87	− 51	71	754	633	9	182	− 70
1936	− 97	673	− 36	− 51	71	560	458	− 72	245	− 71
1935	− 70	612	− 20	− 187	100	435	369	39	126	− 99
1934	−112	553	− 39	− 204	101	299	298	32	70	−101
1933	−263	464	− 22	− 192	77	64	234	− 91		− 77
1932	−243	407	109	− 297	73	49	319	−100	97	− 73
1931	−221	504	172	− 331	114	238	622	− 95	175	−114
1930	−100	717	239	− 241	25	640	926	77	− 339	− 24
1929	− 81	949	− 15	− 8	28	873	1,161	52	− 313	− 27
1928	181	964	1	67	− 41	1,172	1,007	159	− 35	41
1927	282	835	29	31	− 52	1,125	830	253	− 11	53
1926	419	773	46	40	−156	1,122	702	135	128	157

Series E 112–125. *Total gross fixed capital formation in current and constant dollars and gross fixed capital formation by industry in current dollars, 1926 to 1960*

(millions of dollars)

Year	Total capital expenditure, current dollars	Agriculture and fishing	Forestry	Mining, quarrying and oil wells	Manufacturing	Utilities[1]	Construction industry	Housing	Wholesale and retail trade	Finance, insurance and real estate	Commercial services	Institutional services	Government departments	Total capital expenditure, constant (1949) dollars
	112	113	114	115	116	117	118	119	120	121	122	123	124	125
1960	8,262	550	54	400	1,178	1,772	130	1,456	381	279	215	573	1,274	—
1959	8,417	539	48	342	1,144	1,842	145	1,752	363	267	203	536	1,236	5,587
1958	8,364	465	33	342	1,095	2,153	157	1,782	356	180	169	514	1,118	5,690
1957	8,717	434	48	606	1,479	2,308	158	1,430	370	136	184	454	1,110	6,051
1956	8,034	488	76	542	1,394	1,762	200	1,547	325	124	162	402	1,012	5,816
1955	6,244	426	63	336	947	1,136	174	1,397	329	102	130	408	796	4,758
1954	5,721	400	46	278	822	1,164	97	1,238	368	107	107	338	756	4,462
1953	5,976	557	34	253	969	1,254	91	1,189	330	78	118	303	800	4,695
1952	5,491	562	39	205	973	1,194	73	971	196	50	97	285	846	4,434
1951	4,739	525	58	164	793	939	66	947	234	69	108	242	594	3,967
1950	3,936	482	34	114	502	759	71	923	234	61	104	213	439	3,729
1949	3,539	443	26	96	536	689	55	822	193	32	68	195	384	3,539
1948	3,087	352	28	70	573	566	59	635	162	33	96	148	375	3,248
1947	2,440	278	32	42	528	410	52	526	119	21	62	91	279	2,919
1946	1,674	185	13	27	337	251	33	407	83	15	39	76	208	2,223
1945	1,320	127	12	16	280	194	30	330	42	10	34	46	198	1,818
1944	1,343	102	14	17	211	374	19	279	38	6	16	28	238	1,845
1943	1,521	60	6	16	277	416	23	250	13	3	14	19	422	2,118
1942	1,556	91	8	22	446	221	25	244	35	5	22	16	418	2,298
1941	1,465	111	7	32	430	159	17	251	32	6	43	17	360	2,264
1940	1,028	99	6	29	274	131	12	186	35	7	14	18	215	1,719
1939	746	77	5	31	98	120	11	174	30	8	24	30	138	1,318
1938	754	80	5	34	115	135	9	148	34	6	15	27	146	1,330
1937	809	77	5	33	140	141	12	164	28	6	18	22	164	1,414
1936	574	56	4	31	83	93	7	131	19	5	22	19	105	1,077
1935	491	44	3	31	67	73	7	107	15	5	11	14	114	935
1934	404	40	3	11	50	62	2	92	18	5	10	13	99	778
1933	319	23	2	9	42	55	2	72	10	5	7	15	76	627
1932	444	32	2	7	47	95	4	90	16	8	6	32	104	841
1931	804	40	4	22	95	221	11	158	25	11	12	52	153	1,468
1930	1,154	91	6	45	163	295	28	191	43	14	26	64	188	1,997
1929	1,344	127	7	46	225	344	33	230	68	20	44	54	148	2,244
1928	1,163	142	6	32	215	246	25	220	50	14	40	47	127	1,995
1927	965	114	6	18	179	204	15	204	27	14	32	45	108	1,675
1926	808	94	6	17	129	174	14	201	24	8	19	38	84	1,384

[1] Includes expenditure in 1942 to 1945 on Park Steamships, Canol Project and Alaska Highway and Northern Staging Route.

Series E 126–129. *Total gross fixed capital formation, all governments, by type of investing body, 1926 to 1960*

(millions of dollars)

Year	Total public investment	Government-owned enterprise	Government-owned institutions and housing	Government departments[1]	Year	Total public investment	Government-owned enterprise	Government-owned institutions and housing	Government departments[1]
	126	127	128	129		126	127	128	129
1960	2,569	931	365	1,274	1940	318	65	10	243
1959	2,569	987	346	1,236	1939	212	56	18	138
1958	2,679	1,237	324	1,118	1938	228	65	17	146
1957	2,617	1,199	309	1,109	1937	244	66	14	164
1956	2,229	947	270	1,012	1936	162	45	12	105
1955	1,660	604	260	796	1935	155	32	9	114
1954	1,613	646	211	756	1934	126	19	8	99
1953	1,650	635	215	800	1933	107	21	10	76
1952	1,635	556	233	846	1932	160	34	22	104
1951	1,286	488	204	594	1931	282	99	30	153
1950	1,026	409	178	439	1930	359	130	41	188
1949	931	372	168	391	1929	338	153	37	148
1948	784	272	130	382	1928	260	102	31	127
1947	532	175	72	285	1927	224	88	28	108
1946	382	95	75	212	1926	168	61	23	84
1945	355	118	33	204					
1944	486	220	23	243					
1943	639	140	41	458					
1942	595	76	38	481					
1941	522	60	18	444					

[1] The entries in series E 129 for 1940 to 1949 differ from those in series E 124 in that series E 129 includes U.K. plant expansion in 1940, 1941, 1942 and 1943 of 27, 82, 59 and 33 million dollars respectively, assigned to series E 116 in series E 112–125, and in that series E 129 also includes some federal government institutional expenditures for 1941 to 1949 not included in series E 124.

Series E130–142. *Net domestic income, by industry, 1919 to 1926*
(millions of dollars)

Year	Total net domestic income	Agri-culture	Forestry	Fishing, hunting and trapping	Mining, quarrying and oil wells	Manu-facturing	Con-struction	Trans-portation, communi-cation and public utilities	Whole-sale trade	Retail trade	Finance, insurance and real estate	Public admini-stration and defence	Service
	130	131	132	133	134	135	136	137	138	139	140	141	142
1926	4,337	795	64	33	139	929	201	551	155	358	381	165	566
1925	4,139	896	59	31	122	829	175	496	136	326	364	163	542
1924	3,641	574	64	29	104	769	165	477	122	297	355	155	530
1923	3,829	699	57	30	109	821	181	488	117	312	341	157	517
1922	3,589	643	48	32	108	725	187	460	114	299	322	156	495
1921	3,454	561	37	22	92	723	179	441	108	314	305	164	508
1920	4,541	924	69	38	135	1,142	245	468	146	360	277	175	562
1919	3,958	783	53	35	99	1,032	165	413	144	280	238	222	494

Series E143–155. *Labour income, by industry, 1919 to 1926*
(millions of dollars)

Year	Total labour income	Agri-culture	Forestry	Fishing, hunting and trapping	Mining, quarrying and oil wells	Manu-facturing	Con-struction	Trans-portation, communi-cation and public utilities	Whole-sale trade	Retail trade	Finance, insurance and real estate	Public admini-stration and defence	Service
	143	144	145	146	147	148	149	150	151	152	153	154	155
1926	2,373	112	59	7	81	643	155	406	114	181	103	165	347
1925	2,236	108	54	6	74	586	156	380	106	169	97	163	337
1924	2,194	104	59	5	72	559	156	390	104	161	92	155	337
1923	2,191	103	53	5	80	573	152	395	101	160	88	157	324
1922	2,028	94	44	6	66	508	137	383	95	154	84	156	301
1921	2,091	106	34	5	71	516	133	392	100	166	90	164	314
1920	2,602	132	64	6	78	704	197	436	133	225	91	175	361
1919	2,181	110	49	7	54	586	123	349	113	119	77	222	300

Series E156–159. *Gross domestic capital formation, by quinquennial periods, 1901 to 1930*
(millions of dollars)

Period	Gross domestic capital formation	Construction	Machinery and equipment	Inventories
	156	157	158	159
1926–30	5,831	3,109	2,097	625
1921–25	3,641	2,271	1,211	159
1916–20	4,033	2,122	1,322	589
1911–15	3,279	2,007	912	360
1906–10	2,287	1,439	586	262
1901–05	1,283	681	380	222

Series E160–171. *'Industry' gross and net capital stock, in 1949 prices and at original cost, by structures and machinery and equipment, year end, 1926 to 1955*

(millions of dollars)

	Gross and net stock in 1949 prices						Gross and net stock at original cost					
	Gross stock			Net stock			Gross stock			Net stock		
Year[1]	Total	Construction	Machinery and equipment	Total	Construction	Machinery and equipment	Total	Construction	Machinery and equipment	Total	Construction	Machinery and equipment
	160	161	162	163	164	165	166	167	168	169	170	171
1955	38,040.2	20,902.6	17,137.6	23,041.1	12,333.2	10,707.9	35,394.8	18,209.8	17,365.0	24,186.4	12,496.2	11,690.2
1954	36,498.2	20,297.3	16,200.9	21,897.9	11,652.4	10,245.5	32,551.6	16,639.6	15,912.0	22,211.2	11,311.2	10,900.0
1953	34,902.3	19,810.5	15,091.8	20,702.1	10,969.7	9,732.4	29,719.0	15,379.0	14,340.0	20,214.7	10,181.7	10,033.0
1952	33,206.8	19,384.2	13,822.6	19,194.6	10,256.9	8,937.7	26,654.4	14,096.5	12,558.0	17,772.3	8,958.1	8,814.2
1951	31,669.3	19,005.4	12,663.9	17,757.2	9,589.4	8,168.2	23,796.9	12,860.9	10,936.0	15,413.7	7,771.6	7,642.1
1950	30,317.4	18,821.8	11,495.6	16,522.1	9,067.6	7,454.5	21,330.6	11,966.6	9,364.0	13,413.4	6,897.8	6,515.6
1949[1]	29,045.0	18,583.6	10,461.4	15,500.6	8,638.2	6,862.4	19,402.7	11,256.7	8,146.0	11,944.9	6,249.2	5,695.7
1948	27,765.3	18,407.4	9,357.9	14,448.2	8,271.9	6,176.3	17,597.1	10,646.1	6,951.0	10,543.5	5,694.4	4,849.1
1947	26,374.7	18,159.0	8,215.7	13,375.4	7,939.5	5,435.9	15,886.3	10,069.3	5,817.0	9,214.0	5,193.1	4,020.9
1946	25,309.1	18,105.1	7,204.0	12,450.5	7,732.6	4,717.9	14,621.3	9,707.3	4,914.0	8,214.3	4,874.8	3,339.5
1945	24,888.8	18,119.7	6,769.1	12,034.5	7,641.1	4,393.4	13,996.9	9,466.9	4,530.0	7,761.0	4,697.5	3,063.5
1944	24,831.4	18,170.8	6,660.6	11,907.4	7,767.0	4,140.4	13,709.1	9,343.1	4,366.0	7,538.7	4,697.1	2,841.6
1943	24,936.8	18,298.9	6,637.9	11,830.3	7,980.5	3,849.8	13,520.2	9,267.2	4,253.0	7,320.9	4,747.8	2,573.1
1942	25,089.6	18,409.4	6,680.2	11,899.8	8,180.6	3,719.2	13,318.7	9,131.7	4,187.0	7,150.3	4,738.1	2,412.2
1941	24,830.5	18,292.7	6,537.8	11,699.0	8,222.5	3,476.5	12,925.7	8,906.7	4,019.0	6,842.9	4,656.8	2,186.1
1940	24,359.2	18,128.9	6,230.3	11,463.4	8,291.0	3,172.4	12,486.5	8,715.5	3,771.0	6,557.2	4,627.7	1,929.5
1939	24,060.8	18,017.5	6,043.3	11,402.2	8,432.7	2,969.5	12,229.3	8,580.3	3,649.0	6,432.0	4,657.2	1,774.8
1938	23,899.7	17,862.5	6,037.2	11,574.0	8,612.1	2,961.9	12,132.6	8,451.8	3,680.8	6,483.7	4,714.5	1,769.2
1937	23,721.0	17,688.1	6,032.9	11,692.8	8,775.7	2,917.1	12,042.4	8,312.4	3,730.0	6,504.2	4,760.3	1,743.9
1936	23,424.4	17,502.4	5,922.0	11,766.0	8,909.2	2,856.8	11,834.3	8,156.1	3,678.2	6,492.3	4,782.2	1,710.1
1935	23,639.4	17,603.5	6,035.9	12,034.9	9,087.5	2,947.4	11,890.5	8,047.8	3,842.7	6,626.7	4,839.4	1,787.3
1934	23,815.5	17,633.6	6,181.9	12,420.9	9,316.7	3,104.2	12,063.3	7,939.4	4,123.9	6,841.1	4,923.9	1,917.2
1933	24,063.1	17,708.1	6,355.0	12,913.6	9,592.2	3,321.4	12,199.8	7,858.0	4,341.8	7,125.1	5,033.4	2,091.7
1932	24,351.1	17,807.4	6,543.7	13,506.7	9,895.0	3,611.7	12,379.7	7,788.6	4,591.1	7,468.9	5,153.1	2,315.8
1931	24,514.3	17,837.9	6,676.4	13,999.9	10,129.7	3,870.2	12,472.9	7,682.2	4,790.7	7,762.4	5,233.2	2,529.2
1930	24,256.2	17,633.1	6,623.1	14,094.8	10,124.0	3,970.8	12,227.3	7,440.8	4,786.5	7,826.5	5,172.2	2,654.3
1929	23,536.5	17,244.4	6,292.1	13,751.8	9,950.0	3,801.8	11,639.3	7,081.8	4,557.5	7,594.3	4,985.2	2,609.1
1928	22,767.0	16,703.7	6,063.3	13,106.1	9,610.5	3,495.6	10,933.5	6,610.8	4,322.7	7,132.8	4,674.5	2,458.3
1927	22,395.9	16,259.3	6,136.6	12,642.7	9,356.2	3,286.5	10,465.3	6,215.8	4,249.5	6,797.5	4,429.9	2,367.6
1926	22,224.2	15,986.2	6,238.0	12,432.6	9,266.4	3,166.2	10,129.0	5,935.8	4,193.2	6,614.4	4,293.3	2,321.1

[1] Beginning in 1949, additions to the capital stock in Newfoundland (but not the initial stock) are included.

Series E172–185. *Gross stock of social capital in 1949 dollars, public and private, by type, year end, 1926 to 1955*

(millions of 1949 dollars)

	Government social capital						Privately owned social capital					Total social capital		
		Construction						Construction		Institutional machinery and equipment				
Year[1]	Total	Total	Roads	Buildings	Other engineering structures	Machinery and equipment	Total	Total	Housing	Institutional	Institutional machinery and equipment	Total	Construction	Machinery and equipment
	172	173	174	175	176	177	178	179	180	181	182	183	184	185
1955	10,942.4	9,608.2	3,569.5	3,310.3	2,728.4	1,334.2	25,812.8	25,546.5	21,742.1	3,804.4	266.3	36,762.0	35,161.5	1,600.5
1954	10,612.8	9,235.5	3,409.2	3,137.7	2,688.6	1,377.3	24,688.4	24,447.1	20,871.8	3,575.3	241.3	35,301.2	33,682.6	1,618.6
1953	10,343.0	8,989.5	3,290.4	2,983.0	2,716.1	1,353.5	23,789.6	23,576.2	20,184.9	3,391.3	213.4	34,132.6	32,565.7	1,566.9
1952	10,039.1	8,720.6	3,188.9	2,732.2	2,747.9	1,318.5	22,958.0	22,767.4	19,543.8	3,223.6	190.6	32,997.1	31,488.0	1,509.1
1951	9,649.2	8,369.6	3,024.0	2,597.7	2,747.9	1,279.6	22,268.1	22,101.7	19,044.8	3,056.9	166.4	31,917.3	30,471.3	1,446.0
1950	9,400.0	8,141.6	2,881.2	2,457.8	2,802.6	1,258.4	21,550.2	21,406.1	18,501.1	2,905.0	144.1	30,950.2	29,547.7	1,402.5
1949[1]	9,198.6	7,957.6	2,742.4	2,373.3	2,841.9	1,241.0	20,718.3	20,595.3	17,843.4	2,751.9	123.0	29,916.9	28,552.9	1,364.0
1948	8,979.7	7,761.4	2,579.7	2,302.2	2,879.5	1,218.3	19,889.4	19,785.8	17,185.1	2,600.7	103.6	28,869.1	27,547.2	1,321.9
1947	8,771.5	7,598.2	2,424.4	2,241.8	2,932.0	1,173.3	19,153.7	19,065.8	16,580.2	2,485.6	87.9	28,925.2	26,664.0	1,261.2
1946	8,606.0	7,460.4	2,289.3	2,199.5	2,971.6	1,145.6	18,508.7	18,424.4	16,016.7	2,407.7	84.3	27,114.7	25,884.8	1,229.9
1945	8,463.5	7,339.5	2,203.9	2,172.2	2,963.4	1,124.0	17,987.0	17,902.8	15,564.6	2,338.2	84.2	26,450.5	25,242.3	1,208.2
1944	—	—	2,188.2	—	2,965.9	1,085.7	—	—	—	—	86.6	—	—	1,172.3
1943	—	—	2,175.6	—	2,978.2	1,029.1	—	—	—	—	90.9	—	—	1,120.0
1942	—	—	2,177.8	—	2,917.0	866.1	—	—	—	—	96.1	—	—	962.2
1941	—	—	2,161.8	—	2,856.7	699.9	—	—	—	—	100.1	—	—	800.0
1940	—	—	2,104.8	—	2,799.6	513.5	—	—	—	—	103.5	—	—	617.0
1939	—	—	2,002.3	—	2,816.4	434.6	—	—	—	—	105.9	—	—	540.5
1938	—	—	1,884.3	—	2,807.1	412.4	—	—	—	—	105.8	—	—	518.2
1937	—	—	1,753.5	—	2,798.0	392.0	—	—	—	—	106.0	—	—	498.0
1936	—	—	1,627.9	—	2,770.1	372.4	—	—	—	—	106.2	—	—	478.6
1935	—	—	1,564.8	—	2,746.2	356.7	—	—	—	—	108.4	—	—	465.1
1934	—	—	1,497.6	—	—	338.3	—	—	—	—	110.0	—	—	448.3
1933	—	—	1,428.9	—	—	324.4	—	—	—	—	110.8	—	—	435.2
1932	—	—	1,390.6	—	—	311.1	—	—	—	—	110.9	—	—	422.0
1931	—	—	1,319.7	—	—	292.7	—	—	—	—	107.3	—	—	400.0
1930	—	—	1,214.9	—	—	270.8	—	—	—	—	101.5	—	—	372.3
1929	—	—	1,103.3	—	—	253.0	—	—	—	—	97.0	—	—	350.0
1928	—	—	1,018.4	—	—	252.2	—	—	—	—	97.7	—	—	349.9
1927	—	—	946.1	—	—	255.8	—	—	—	—	98.8	—	—	354.6
1926	—	—	885.0	—	—	258.1	—	—	—	—	99.2	—	—	357.3

[1] Beginning in 1949, additions to the capital stock in Newfoundland (but not the initial stock) are included.

Series E186–199. *Net stock of social capital in 1949 dollars, public and private, by type, year end, 1926 to 1955*

(millions of 1949 dollars)

	Government social capital						Privately owned social capital					Total social capital		
	Total	Construction				Machinery and equipment	Total	Construction			Machinery and equipment	Total	Construction	Machinery and equipment
Year[1]		Total	Roads	Buildings	Other engineering structures			Total	Housing	Institutional				
	186	187	188	189	190	191	192	193	194	195	196	197	198	199
1955	6,701.5	6,162.2	2,197.3	2,394.9	1,570.0	539.3	15,424.5	15,231.6	12,891.3	2,340.3	192.9	22,126.0	21,393.8	732.2
1954	6,406.1	5,829.3	2,088.5	2,273.0	1,467.8	576.8	14,486.4	14,309.4	12,171.9	2,137.5	177.0	20,892.5	20,138.7	753.8
1953	6,160.5	5,556.5	1,986.0	2,167.1	1,403.4	604.0	13,795.3	13,638.6	11,656.7	1,981.9	156.7	19,955.8	19,195.1	760.7
1952	5,866.4	5,247.0	1,890.4	2,036.4	1,320.2	619.4	13,182.2	13,041.0	11,197.4	1,843.6	141.2	19,048.6	18,288.0	760.6
1951	5,531.7	4,901.9	1,755.1	1,873.5	1,273.3	629.8	12,743.5	12,619.9	10,911.1	1,708.8	123.6	18,275.2	17,521.8	753.4
1950	5,348.1	4,685.2	1,651.6	1,774.4	1,259.2	662.9	12,296.6	12,189.3	10,598.1	1,591.2	107.3	17,644.7	16,874.5	770.2
1949[1]	5,243.8	4,543.9	1,557.2	1,731.5	1,255.1	700.0	11,716.1	11,625.1	10,153.0	1,472.1	91.0	16,959.9	16,168.9	791.0
1948	5,149.2	4,144.0	1,448.8	1,701.6	1,263.6	735.2	11,152.4	11,077.3	9,720.7	1,356.6	75.1	16,301.6	15,491.3	810.3
1947	5,038.2	4,289.4	1,339.8	1,681.8	1,267.8	748.8	10,676.7	10,618.7	9,342.2	1,276.5	58.0	15,714.9	14,908.1	806.8
1946	4,988.5	4,215.6	1,251.3	1,679.7	1,284.6	772.9	10,287.2	10,238.7	9,004.8	1,233.9	48.5	15,275.7	14,454.3	821.4
1945	4,983.4	4,190.6	1,195.0	1,691.5	1,304.1	792.8	9,993.5	9,952.6	8,756.7	1,195.9	40.9	14,976.9	14,143.2	833.7
1944	—	—	1,210.9	—	1,330.0	786.4	—	—	—	—	38.3	—	—	—
1943	—	—	1,238.7	—	1,371.1	766.0	—	—	—	—	39.2	—	—	—
1942	—	—	1,287.9	—	1,348.2	632.6	—	—	—	—	41.8	—	—	—
1941	—	—	1,329.9	—	1,325.6	488.4	—	—	—	—	45.4	—	—	—
1940	—	—	1,335.1	—	1,303.5	317.2	—	—	—	—	48.8	—	—	—
1939	—	—	1,290.7	—	1,366.0	248.8	—	—	—	—	51.7	—	—	—
1938	—	—	1,226.9	—	1,406.7	237.1	—	—	—	—	52.3	—	—	—
1937	—	—	1,134.6	—	1,449.9	225.7	—	—	—	—	53.2	—	—	—
1936	—	—	1,030.2	—	1,475.5	214.5	—	—	—	—	55.2	—	—	—
1935	—	—	988.7	—	1,502.2	208.7	—	—	—	—	58.2	—	—	—
1934	—	—	939.5	—	—	203.1	—	—	—	—	62.1	—	—	—
1933	—	—	806.6	—	—	201.4	—	—	—	—	66.1	—	—	—
1932	—	—	888.2	—	—	202.5	—	—	—	—	70.0	—	—	—
1931	—	—	848.9	—	—	197.4	—	—	—	—	69.8	—	—	—
1930	—	—	774.9	—	—	182.1	—	—	—	—	64.9	—	—	—
1929	—	—	690.2	—	—	158.5	—	—	—	—	58.2	—	—	—
1928	—	—	632.6	—	—	142.9	—	—	—	—	53.9	—	—	—
1927	—	—	587.7	—	—	131.9	—	—	—	—	51.0	—	—	—
1926	—	—	551.4	—	—	124.4	—	—	—	—	48.6	—	—	—

[1] Beginning in 1949, additions to the capital stock in Newfoundland (but not the initial stock) are included.

Series E200–201. *Business inventories, book value, all industry and manufacturing industry, year end, 1926 to 1960*

(millions of dollars)

Year	Total all industry	Manufacturing industry		Year	Total all industry	Manufacturing industry
	200	201			200	201
1960	—	—		1940	1,986	929
1959	9,095	4,259		1939	1,776	789
1958	8,601	4,061		1938	1,625	743
1957	8,883	4,283		1937	1,702	761
1956	8,508	4,149		1936	1,502	654
1955	7,463	3,615		1935	1,400	613
1954	7,167	3,487		1934	1,346	600
1953	7,293	3,641		1933	1,290	576
1952	6,926	3,468		1932	1,339	600
1951	6,937	3,492		1931	1,570	712
1950	5,734	2,788		1930	1,803	841
1949	4,962	2,449		1929	1,955	871
1948	4,698	2,384		1928	1,798	829
1947	4,098	2,147		1927	1,674	757
1946	3,106	1,632		1926	1,543	709
1945	2,488	1,388				
1944	2,313	1,265				
1943	2,263	1,222				
1942	2,179	1,069				
1941	2,276	1,095				

APPENDIX. ESTIMATES OF GROSS NATIONAL PRODUCT AND GROSS INCOME PRODUCED, 1870 TO 1920

Series E202–213. *Gross income produced, by industry, and national income, 1911 to 1920*

(millions of dollars)

Year	Income produced										Net interest and dividends paid abroad	National income
	Primary industry						Secondary industry					
	Agriculture	Forestry	Mining	Fisheries	Electric power	Trapping	Manufacturing	Construction	Services	Total		
	202	203	204	205	206	207	208	209	210	211	212	213
1920	1,230	177	135	28	53	21	1,275	145	1,510	4,574	−166	4,408
1919	1,470	123	105	33	48	19	1,120	95	1,370	4,383	−172	4,211
1918	1,260	123	130	36	44	18	1,085	60	1,140	3,896	−182	3,714
1917	1,060	103	110	33	35	17	1,030	60	1,030	3,478	−176	3,302
1916	930	109	100	24	29	17	625	60	950	2,844	−167	2,677
1915	870	108	75	22	23	16	425	105	840	2,484	−160	2,324
1914	750	112	75	19	21	15	390	205	830	2,417	−164	2,253
1913	660	110	80	20	18	15	440	275	870	2,488	−129	2,359
1912	600	109	75	20	15	14	435	260	790	2,318	−109	2,209
1911	670	100	55	21	13	14	410	225	670	2,178	− 93	2,085

Series E214–244. *Gross national product, by industry, decennially, 1870 to 1920*

(millions of dollars)

Year	Commodity-producing industries						Services	Rent	Net interest and dividends paid abroad	Indirect taxes less subsidies	Gross national product
	Agriculture	Fishing and trapping	Mining	Forest operations	Manufacturing	Construction					
	214	215	216	217	218	219	220	221	222	223	224
1920	1,073	47	140	212	1,335	306	1,953	361	−166	268	5,529
1910	509	21	59	86	508	113	752	182	− 82	87	2,235
1900	282	17	35	52	223	41	311	90	− 32	38	1,057
1890	217	13	11	53	189	37	214	69	− 30	30	803
1880	186	11	6	50	110	22	130	58	− 16	24	581
1870	153	5	4	44	87	14	96	43	− 4	17	459

SECTION F: THE BALANCE OF INTERNATIONAL PAYMENTS, INTERNATIONAL INDEBTEDNESS AND FOREIGN TRADE

HERBERT MARSHALL, *Dominion Statistician (Retired)*

The statistics presented in this section are in three major divisions. Series F1–163 present private and official estimates of the balance of payments on current and capital account from 1900 to 1960. This subsection is itself divided into three parts: series F1–56 contain the estimates of the balance of payments of Professors Jacob Viner and Frank Knox for the period 1900 to 1926; series F57–90 contain the official estimates of the balance of payments, current account, prepared by the Dominion Bureau of Statistics for the period 1926 to 1960; series F91–163 contain the official estimates of the balance of payments on capital account from 1926 to 1960. Series F164–241, the second major division, present the official and some private estimates of Canadian international indebtedness and of Canadian claims against foreign assets for the period 1900 to 1960. Series F242–399, the third major division, present statistics of foreign trade from 1867 to 1960.

The major sources are the following:

Jacob Viner, *Canada's Balance of International Indebtedness, 1900–1913* (Cambridge, Harvard University Press, 1924), hereafter referred to as *Canada's Balance*; Frank A. Knox, 'Canadian Capital Movements and the Canadian Balance of International Payments, 1900–1934' in Herbert Marshall, Frank A. Southard and Kenneth W. Taylor, *Canadian American Industry* (New Haven, Yale University Press and Toronto, Ryerson Press, 1936), hereafter referred to as 'Excursus'; Frank A. Knox, *Dominion Monetary Policy, 1929–1934*, a report prepared for The Royal Commission on Dominion–Provincial Relations (Ottawa, mimeographed, 1939), hereafter *Dominion Monetary Policy*; Dominion Bureau of Statistics, *The Canadian Balance of International Payments, A Study of Methods and Results* (Ottawa, King's Printer, 1939), hereafter *Red Book*; Dominion Bureau of Statistics, *The Canadian Balance of International Payments, 1926 to 1948* (Ottawa, King's Printer, 1949), hereafter *Blue Book*; Dominion Bureau of Statistics, *Canadian Balance of International Payments in the Post-War Years, 1946–1952* (Ottawa, Queen's Printer, 1953), hereafter, *Balance of Payments, 1946–1952*; Dominion Bureau of Statistics, *Canadian Balance of International Payments, 1959 and International Investment Position* (Ottawa, Queen's Printer, 1960); also the annual balance of payments reports of the same Dominion Bureau of Statistics series from 1953 to 1958; Dominion Bureau of Statistics, *Trade of Canada* (Ottawa, Queen's Printer, annual reports since 1958); K. W. Taylor, *Statistical Contributions to Canadian Economic History* (Toronto, Macmillan, 1931), vol. II; K. W. Taylor, 'Post-war Fluctuations in the Volume of Canadian Foreign Trade,' *Journal of the Canadian Bankers' Association*, vol. 34 (April 1927), pp. 301 ff.; Dominion Bureau of Statistics, *Review of Foreign Trade* (Ottawa, Queen's Printer, beginning 1954 and subsequent issues); Dominion Bureau of Statistics, *Prices and Price Indexes, 1913–1926*, and same report, *1913–1933* (Ottawa, King's Printer).

CANADIAN BALANCE OF INTERNATIONAL PAYMENT (Series F1–163)

General note

The tables setting forth the details of the balance of payments present a summary of the multiform receipts and payments connected with the 'visible' and 'invisible' exports and imports arising from Canada's commercial and financial transactions with other countries. The 'visible' item is the trade in commodities with gold placed in a separate category. All other items are classed as 'invisibles' and include receipts and payments connected with interest and dividends, tourist and travel, freight and shipping, immigrants' and emigrants' funds, inheritances, inward and outward capital movements and many others. The statements are divided into current and capital accounts, the latter purporting to show how surplus or deficit differences in the current account are balanced through capital movements both long and short term.

Balance of payments data in this subsection cover the period 1900 to date but they are presented in distinct periods because strict comparability cannot be maintained between the different periods and, indeed, there are elements of incomparability within a single period. In the earliest years for which balance of payments statements are available, lack of recorded data for many of the items made necessary extensive reliance on estimates. The extent to which Viner and Knox were obliged to rely upon estimates and indirect methods is indicated more fully in the individual notes which follow. For the period commencing with 1926 the foundations were laid in the Dominion Bureau of Statistics for a comprehensive collection of factual data on items for which no such recorded information had previously existed.

The Dominion Bureau of Statistics began about 1926 to develop balance of payments statistics giving particular attention at the start to foreign investments in Canada and Canadian investments abroad because of their basic importance. The Bureau's investigations were supplemented by special studies made for it by visiting economists from the universities. As the programme for Canadian statistics was developed (the Dominion Bureau of Statistics was established in 1918) more records became available to assist in covering the different aspects of Canada's international accounts. At first mere estimates of many groups of transactions were all that was possible, but, eventually, records based on compilations were established which extended the range of more accurate knowledge.

About the middle of the interwar period a permanent staff to work on the balance of payments data was established. Depression, exchange depreciation, and a growing awareness of the need for more accurate and specific detail led to an enlargement of the staff and a more rapid building up of recorded factual data.

During the nineteen-thirties information was obtained from thousands of commercial, industrial and financial firms in Canada for the period from 1926 on. As these records were not obtained for the years prior to 1926 the construction of comparable balance of payments statements before that period is not practicable. Many important groups of transactions can only be estimated by projecting backward the trends known to have existed from 1926 on. Consequently the estimates for the period prior to 1926 have not been compiled officially.

By the beginning of World War II most of the important types of transactions and channels through which Canada's international transactions flow had been carefully investigated and improved techniques and more complete records established. A description of the methods employed up to 1939 was given in the *Red Book*, published in 1939, which describes the progress in substituting direct primary statistical returns for estimates derived from secondary data.

Some important developments which arose at the beginning of the period commencing with 1939 were closely linked with the work done in the pre-war period. They came about as the result of an investigation by an interdepartmental committee set up for the purpose of finding means to improve certain important administrative records for balance of payments purposes. The recommendations of the committee resulted in improved import and export valuations for trade statistics and in a greatly improved system of collecting and tabulating information for tourist and travel statistics.

During World War II intergovernmental transactions assumed a dominating importance in the balance of payments and entirely new problems arose which required the development of new techniques. The Canadian exchange situation and the problems of financing Allied expenditures in Canada required a different framework for the presentation of Canada's international accounts. When sterling became inconvertible it was necessary to prepare two sets of balance of payments statements, one for countries with convertible exchange and one for the sterling area. The change required the introduction of some new statistical procedures.

Establishment of exchange control and the Foreign Exchange Control Board provided a new source of information for balance of payments purposes. The analysis of exchange transactions assisted in the preparation of the bilateral statements. This was useful in many ways but it became quite clear that conventional balance of payments statements could not be constructed exclusively from exchange data. The main reason is that gross data are required in many instances where exchange data are in net figures. Exchange data proved very valuable sources of information on many service transactions. The availability of these new data led to the development of new techniques in estimating many miscellaneous current transactions.

With the discontinuance of exchange control and the Foreign Exchange Control Board in 1951 this source of information ceased to exist. However, the experience gained in the analysis of exchange transactions suggested new lines of direct inquiries to supplement and improve the pre-war methods which came into use again.

In summary, institutional changes, the war and post-war growth of the Canadian economy, conceptual changes, war and post-war financial problems, improving sources of information and other factors gave rise to many changes in comparability over the 60-year period. It seemed best, therefore, to deal with the data by periods in each of which they are largely comparable as to method, range and concept and to explain the new developments in each period so that those who use them may make their own attempt at continuity according to the purpose in view.

Five stages can be distinguished in terms of major improvements in the quality of the estimates. Viner's estimates were the first stage. The revision of Viner's estimates and their extension to 1926 by Knox was the second of these stages. The introduction of the official estimates in 1926 by the Dominion Bureau of Statistics marks the third stage. The two major revisions, fully described in the *Red Book* and the *Blue Book*, which determined the character of the estimates from 1938 to 1945 and from 1946 to the present time, mark the fourth and fifth stages in the development of Canada's balance of payments statistics. More recently Penelope Hartland has made estimates of Canada's balance of payments back to 1867, but owing to the paucity of the records in this earlier period these estimates are not so firmly based as those of Viner and accordingly are subject to a more considerable margin of error. Hartland's estimates may be found in Penelope Hartland, 'Canadian Balance of Payments since 1868' in Conference on Research in Income and Wealth, *Trends in the American Economy in the Nineteenth Century*, Studies in Income and Wealth, vol. 24 (Princeton, Princeton University Press, 1960).

F1–17. Canadian balance of international payments, between Canada and all countries, current account, 1900 to 1913

SOURCE: Viner, *Canada's Balance*, table II, p. 31; table III, p. 32; table XXVI, p. 95; table XXIX, pp. 102–3; table XXX, p. 105; table XXXI, p. 106.

F1 and 9. Commodity trade. Viner obtained his statistics of commodity trade from official sources. Concerning these he states (*Canada's Balance*, p. 25):

Statistics of exports are published for 'total exports', for 'exports of Canadian produce', and for 'exports of foreign produce'.... Included in exports of 'foreign produce' are foreign goods exported from customs warehouses without having passed into the channels of Canadian trade, and foreign goods exported after having been 'entered for consumption in Canada'. The amount of exports of foreign produce is generally greater, therefore, than the difference between 'total imports' and 'imports entered for consumption'. To obtain the commodity balance of trade, the statistics of 'total imports' and 'total exports' must be used.

To the statement above Viner appended the following note (p. 25 n.):

Since 1916 a comprehensive reorganization of Canadian commerce statistics has been effected, and what is said here should be understood to be applicable to the period under study, but not necessarily to subsequent years. Statistics of 'total imports' are, since the fiscal year 1920, no longer published, and statistics of goods exported from warehouses are collected and published separately as 'transit trade'. The Customs Department has informed the writer that the difference between 'total imports' and 'imports entered for consumption' was due almost wholly to imports of wheat in bond from the United States, for reëxport overseas, when it appeared in the statistics of exports of foreign produce. Such wheat would now appear only in the statistics of transit trade.

For balance of payments purposes Viner made certain adjustments in the official figures to eliminate noncommercial items and to allow for certain omissions in the records. Imports and exports of settlers' effects were deducted. Other noncommercial items were ignored because of their relative unimportance. Goods ex-warehoused for ships' stores were deducted but allowed for in his estimates of the freight item.

An addition to imports was made for the estimated value of ships purchased by Canadian companies for use in foreign trade and ships of British registry and construction for use in the coastwise or internal traffic which were not recorded in import statistics.

F2 and 10. Gold transactions. Because of the unreliability of Canadian customs statistics of gold movements Viner devised his own method of estimating these movements, including unrecorded imports and exports. No distinction was made between monetary and nonmonetary gold. John Stovel has attempted this division for the period 1900 to 1926 (see *Canada in the World Economy* (Cambridge, Harvard University Press, 1959), p. 338).

F3 and 11. Tourist and travel. Viner stated (p. 83): 'No statistics are collected for tourists entering Canada from the United States. Their expenditures, which are unquestionably of considerable importance, can only be guessed at.' He used an estimate made by a Canadian newspaper of an expenditure of $50 million as a basis for his own annual estimates. For tourists from overseas, an estimate of $1,000 per cabin tourist for those travelling by sea, made by others, was accepted and for steerage passengers he estimated a *per capita* expenditure of $300. Numbers of tourists from overseas were derived from immigration records.

Expenditures of Canadian tourists who travelled overseas with first-class passages were estimated at $1,000 and $300 for steerage passengers. Numbers were obtained from official records of returning Canadians arriving by sea.

No statistics being available for the number of Canadian tourists to the United States nor of their expenditures, Viner concluded (p. 87) that 'The best guess possible in the absence of any statistical data is that Canadian tourists spend one half as much in the United States as is spent by American tourists in Canada.'

F4 and 12. Interest and dividends. Viner used various sources to compute an average rate of return on the total of British and foreign investment in Canada. (1) Municipal bonds: average interest yield at current market prices; source: C. H. Burgess, 'Review of the Municipal Bond Market, 1896–1913', *Monetary Times Annual* (January 1914), pp. 80–1. (2) Industrial, railway and financial stocks and bonds: interest yield at current market prices; source: R. H. Coats, *Report of the Board of Inquiry into the Cost of Living*, vol. II, p. 625 (55 common stocks, 5 preferred stocks, and 9 bonds). (3) Average rate of yield on securities and loans of all fire insurance companies in Canada; computed from statistics in *Canada Year Book* and annual reports of the Superintendent of Insurance. (4) Government of Canada average rate of interest paid on bonded debt; *Public Accounts of Canada*, 1914, p. 751, based on par value of bonded debt and exclusive of domestic loans.

In arriving at the average rates the several groups of indexes were not weighted but Viner stated (p. 98):

A crude allowance has been made for the greater relative importance of bonds in the foreign investments in Canada, and also for the magnifying influence on the index, of interest yields if computed in terms of actual current prices, by giving to the index for the yield of Canadian Government bonds on a par value basis equal weight with the seven other indexes combined.

Viner estimated on the basis of what information was available that the average return on all Canadian investments abroad was 4 per cent. He states (p. 91):

The bulk of the Canadian banking investments abroad consisted of call loans in New York, and on these the interest rate averaged 3.6 per cent throughout the period under study. The net income would, of course, be substantially less, as banking expenses would have to be deducted therefrom. The interest on other Canadian investments abroad should average higher, probably somewhere between 4 and 5 per cent. It will be estimated that the average return on all Canadian investments abroad was 4 per cent.

F5 and 13. Freight and shipping. The calculation of receipts and payments on transportation in connexion with imports and exports of goods is necessarily a complex undertaking. Viner on this subject states (p. 68): 'The method used in the present study to ascertain the freight on imports is admittedly inadequate, but appears to the writer to be the best available under the circumstances.'

His method was to collect for the year 1907 freight rates and import values by weight or measurement on a few representative commodities, including railroad rates and import values for goods purchased in the United States, and on ocean freights and import values for goods brought from the United Kingdom. Bulky and light articles were included in the sample. He secured these data for the iron and steel and cotton textile groups and computed the *ad valorem* percentage of freight charges to import values. It was assumed that the results obtained were representative of all light and bulky commodities. After taking into consideration a variety of factors such as the expenditure of vessels and ship's crew in ocean ports, the movement of freight rates and prices, he arrived at a percentage of freight charges to imports for each year.

For receipts by Canada for the services of her transport facilities he estimated that 2 per cent of the value of exports would cover the payment to be made to Canada.

F6 and 14. Insurance. These items include life insurance, fire insurance and miscellaneous insurance such as casualty, sickness, employers' liability and the like. Marine and other insurance on freight carried are not covered in these series but are included in freight and shipping.

Receipts (F6) are for income of Canadian life and fire insurance companies on their business abroad; the one Canadian company engaged in other types of insurance abroad was not covered since its foreign business was small. Receipts on life insurance are based on official data contained in Coats's *Cost of Living Report*, vol. II. On the basis of data for 1909 to 1913 the amount of 2 per cent of insurance in force outside Canada is taken as the excess of premium income over all expenditures abroad. This percentage was applied to life insurance in force outside Canada which was available in the *Cost of Living Report* for 1902 to 1913; figures for 1900 to 1901 are estimated from incomplete data. Receipts of Canadian fire insurance companies on business done abroad were estimated for the complete period from *Annual Report(s)* of the Superintendent of Insurance. It was estimated that the net income received by Canadian companies was 10 per cent of the excess of premiums over losses on foreign business.

Net payments to foreign countries for life and fire insurance were obtained from the excess of premium income of foreign companies operating in Canada over their expenditures in Canada. The data were obtained from the *Annual Reports* of the Superintendent of Insurance. Net payments for other insurance for 1900 to 1910 was calculated at 20 per cent of premium receipts of foreign companies in Canada, obtained mainly from the *Canada Year Book* or reports of the Superintendent of Insurance; for 1911 to 1913 they were obtained from the *Canada Year Book*. Interest income of foreign insurance companies from investments in Canada are included with interest and dividends (F12) and are excluded here.

F7 and 15. All other current items. In his group of non-commercial transactions in the current account Viner includes capital brought into Canada by immigrants and capital taken out of Canada by emigrants and also immigrant and emigrant remittances. For migrant capital he estimated the *per capita* amount brought in or taken out and multiplied it by the numbers of migrants.

As regards remittances he estimated that the total amount remitted to friends and relatives abroad exceeded by 50 per cent the amount of foreign postal money orders issued in Canada, including the amount remitted in settlement of small commercial transactions.

Remittances to Canada were estimated as the total of postal money orders received from abroad. It was assumed that non-commercial remittances to Canada by other methods than through the post office were offset by commercial remittances sent through the post office.

Viner also assumed that credits and debits for sundry other items such as payments for diplomatic and other services abroad were offset by receipts for the same.

F 18–33. Canadian balance of international payments, between Canada and all countries, capital account, 1900 to 1913

SOURCE: Viner, *Canada's Balance*, table XXV, p. 94; table XXXVIII, p. 126; table XLI, p. 134; table XLIII, p. 138; table XLIV, p. 139.

Viner reached his figures for the annual flow of capital into Canada by two methods. First, after estimating all the other items in the balance of payments he derived from them a residual item which he took for his preliminary estimate of the annual inflow. Secondly, he made the direct estimates shown here on the basis of available data, which showed considerable differences for individual years but were close for the period as a whole. He surmised that the yearly discrepancies were due to such causes as temporary loans and discrepancies between the official recording of the borrowing and their actual receipt.

From scanty data Viner estimated that total Canadian capital invested abroad at the end of 1899 amounted to $100 million. He estimated that from 1900 to 1913 miscellaneous investments abroad by Canadians in securities and by Canadian railways in lines and equipment in the United States amounted to $50 million. To these miscellaneous investments he added $87 million for holdings of foreign securities by Canadian banks and their net assets in foreign countries. His estimate of total investment by Canadians abroad for the period was, therefore, $137 million. Data for bank net assets abroad were based on monthly reports made by the commercial banks to the Department of Finance. He estimated that the foreign securities held by the banks were 60 per cent of the 'railway and other bonds, debentures and stocks' held by the banks in Canada at the end of each year. His estimates of $50 million of miscellaneous investments were assumed to have had a fairly equal distribution during the period.

F 34–46. Canadian balance of international payments, between Canada and all countries, current account, 1900 to 1926

SOURCE: for series F 34–45, Knox, *Monetary Policy*, Appendix; series F 46 was calculated by the author of this section from Knox's data; also see Knox, 'Excursus'.

F 34 and 40. Commodity trade. Knox in the 'Excursus' uses Viner's figures for commodity trade from 1900 to 1913 but in *Monetary Policy* (p. 84) he revised them 'to exclude previously recorded imports and re-exports of foreign products in transit across Canada; and to eliminate certain small types of exports and imports for which no receipts are obtained or payments made'. This, along with certain other revisions, provided him with data on a generally comparable basis from 1900 to the end of his period. For this reason his 1900 to 1913 figures are included in F 34–46.

F 35. Gold transactions. Knox also rejected the Customs

records for gold transactions and applied the Viner method in the calculation of the net balances for his period.

F 36 and 41. Tourist and travel. In the 'Excursus' Knox states (p. 321): 'Estimates for the years since 1914 were made by the use of the estimates obtained in recent years, with such adjustments as seemed appropriate. They become increasingly unreliable therefore for the earlier years and are little more than guesses for the war years.'

F 37 and 42. Interest and dividends. Estimates by Knox for interest payments were made on the basis of an issue by issue study of the interest due each year on the portion of the security owned abroad. Dividends payments made on capital invested directly in Canada were estimated as a percentage of the direct capital investment, the percentage being derived from the relationship between dividend disbursements and capital employed. This relationship was estimated from a sample group of companies for which balance sheets were available back to 1920 and a smaller group for which they were available back to 1914. In this connexion Knox stated ('Excursus', p. 311): 'The estimate is but a very rough approximation, both because of this method of calculating the rate per cent of dividend payments and because of the character of the estimate of the total direct investment itself....'

Rates of dividends on Canadian stocks owned abroad were calculated from various available sources.

Interest and dividend receipts by Canada included: (1) interest received by the Dominion Government from the Government of Great Britain and other countries and from bank balances abroad; (2) earnings of commercial banks on their net banking assets calculated at the rate which the total net profit of all commercial banks bore to their total assets each year. The yield of British Treasury issues held by the banks was calculated at $5\frac{1}{2}$ per cent and on foreign bonds at the annual yield of 60 high-grade United States bonds; (3) returns received by insurance companies on capital abroad calculated at the rate per cent which total earnings bore to the total assets outside Canada; (4) dividends received on miscellaneous Canadian investments abroad calculated by using the rates of interest and dividends paid on all capital invested in Canadian industrial enterprises.

In *Monetary Policy*, Knox mentions that small changes were made in the 'Excursus' estimates of interest and dividends payments because of changes in the estimates of capital inflows.

F 38 and 43. All other current. The figures given by Knox for other current items (sundry small items) differ in *Monetary Policy* from those in the 'Excursus'. The reason is that in the former he includes freight and insurance and in debits a new item, the cost of the Canadian Expeditionary Forces for the years 1914 to 1920. These were, in millions of dollars, respectively, for the period, 5, 30, 100, 175, 170, 95 and 20.

In the 'Excursus', p. 320, Knox states: 'The methods used in making the estimates for the years 1920–26 were similar to those used by the Dominion Bureau of Statistics; for the years 1914–19 transportation statistics do not permit anything but rough estimates. The differences between Viner's estimates for 1913 and those made by the writer for 1914 arise largely from the use of different methods of computation. Either method probably gives a rough idea of the yearly change within the years to which it applies.'

F 47–56. Canadian balance of international payments, between Canada and all countries, capital account, 1900 to 1926

SOURCE: Same as F 34–36.

In the 'Excursus', Knox uses Viner's data without change for the period 1900 to 1913. For the period 1914 to 1926 he made estimates directly from available data and used Dominion Bureau of Statistics estimates for the years he included beyond 1926. These were earlier estimates of the Bureau, later superseded. Concerning his tabulation in *Monetary Policy* Knox states (p. 85): 'The estimates for the years 1900 to 1926 have been recast from the form given in Marshall, Southard and Taylor to conform to the set-up now used by the Dominion Bureau of Statistics.' Because of this new form of presentation and because of better information which had become available since the 'Excursus' was written some of the latter data were revised. Capital movements arising from the international trade in securities were shown separately. For the years 1914 to 1926 complete data on new issues and retirements were not available but some small net amounts were included in the net total which explains some apparent arithmetic errors. For the period 1900 to 1913 Viner did not have detailed information on new issues and retirements, hence only net amounts are shown.

Owing to improved information obtained by the Bureau of Statistics on transactions between branch and subsidiary companies in Canada and their head offices abroad, Knox concluded that his earlier estimates of direct capital movements for the period 1914 to 1926 were probably much too high and substituted smaller estimates of direct capital inflow.

Another change was a complete revision of the estimates for net foreign assets of Canadian banks for the period 1900 to 1926. New information had made it possible (p. 88) 'to estimate with a fair degree of accuracy the probable amount of some foreign asset and liability items which could not formerly be segregated'.

For the Viner period 1900 to 1913, Knox uses the Viner direct estimation of net capital movement. He shows net long-term capital movement which is the sum of two items: the net amount of the international trade in securities and the net amount of all other forms of private investments in Canada and Canadian investments abroad. (This is obtained by deducting from Viner's miscellaneous British and foreign investments the Canadian miscellaneous investments abroad.) To these he adds capital movements arising from *net* changes in Canadian bank balances in other countries.

F 57–71. Canadian balance of international payments, all countries and by major areas, current account, 1926 to 1945

SOURCE: *Blue Book*, pp. 155–62.

The data for the period covered in this table are presented in two sub-periods owing to changes in data availability and in treatment of data between the period 1926 to 1937 and the period 1938 to 1945 (see the general note to series F 1–163).

F 57 and 64. Commodity trade. With respect to commodity trade in the period 1926 to 1937, the *Red Book*, p. 55, states:

Canadian import statistics include all goods 'entered for consumption,' that is, goods which have passed through the customs and into the hands of the importer. They do not include goods in transit, for example, goods passing from the United States via Windsor, through Southern Ontario to another United States point, nor do they include goods still held in bond. Export statistics include all commodities shipped out of Canada except goods ex-warehoused for ships' stores.

Goods shipped out of Canada include exports of domestic produce and the re-exports of foreign produce which has first been entered for consumption.

To adjust the commodity trade statistics for balance of payments purposes deductions were made by the Bureau of Statistics for settlers' effects, free advertising materials, cinematograph films later paid for on a more or less royalty basis and otherwise accounted for, donations of articles from abroad, and certain other minor items. As was done by Viner and Knox,

allowance was made for the unrecorded import of ships. Some adjustments were made also to correct overvaluation due to Canadian Customs policy regarding exchange disparities.

For the period up to 1936 declared merchandise imported by Canadian tourists returning to Canada duplicates the value of such purchases included in the estimate of Canadian tourist expenditures outside of Canada. However, no adjustment was made for this item because of lack of data. Commencing with 1936 an adjustment became possible because official provision was made to exempt from duty purchases up to $100. Such were recorded separately in customs statistics.

In the period 1938 to 1945 important adjustments to commodity trade figures were made and these were carried back to 1926 and are included in the tables for that period in this volume.

During the period 1921 to 1935 imports of distilled spirits from the United Kingdom were overvalued by the inclusion of internal taxes which the Canadian importer did not have to pay. These valuations were adjusted by substitution of the British export declared value. In 1929 alone the adjustment amounted to over $27 million.

A special investigation revealed the extent of overvaluation of imports due to the use of arbitrary powers vested in the Department of National Revenue under the dumping clause of the Customs Act. After the extent of the overvaluation had been studied over a period of years they were estimated and carried back to 1931.

War conditions gave rise to many situations which had important effects on the adjustments necessary for balance of payments purposes of the official trade statistics in the period. Taking the year 1947 as illustrative, the following table is of interest:

Adjustments to commodity import totals, 1947,
deductions from imports

(millions of dollars)

Newfoundland	– 9.4
Tourist imports	– 15.8
Property of foreign governments	– 4.7
Property of Canadian government	– 4.2
Rate spread on imports	– 11.6
Settlers' effects	– 10.9
All other net adjustments	– 7.4
	– 64.0
Net warehousing	+ 25.0
Net deductions	– 39.0

SOURCE: *Blue Book*, p. 106.

The adjustment for rate spreads reflected the difference between buying and selling rates of the Foreign Exchange Control Board.

During the war period there were abnormal movements of commodities on government account. By 1947 they were much less important. These included imports into Canada of military equipment, aircraft and other war materials which were not for the account of Canadian residents. There were also goods furnished under United States Lend Lease to the British and other governments for air training purposes in Canada and imports of components of equipment purchased by the United Kingdom from the United States for use in production or air training in Canada. It was also necessary to make adjustments in imports of war materials purchased in the United States by Canada to bring the timing of imports and payments into conformity and avoid related entries in the capital account.

Net warehousing reflects the change during the year in the value of goods in customs warehouses. For balance of payments purposes the time at which the goods are received into the warehouses seemed more indicative of the international transactions than the time when they were withdrawn by importers for consumption and included in import totals.

After 1940 trade with Newfoundland was deducted and dealt with otherwise. This was due to the special statistical treatment of Newfoundland which was more convenient for foreign exchange control arrangements. See the note on F62, 68 and 69 for the way in which transactions with Newfoundland were treated from 1940 to its confederation with Canada in 1949.

The special investigation mentioned in connexion with the adjustment in import values included exports. Though the prescribed value of exports in customs regulations was 'the actual cost or value at the time of exportation at the points in Canada where consigned for export', it was found that in actual practice there were numerous departures from the instruction. Inland and sometimes overseas freight had been included in an important proportion of export entries. From 1940 on, as a result of the discussions of the interdepartmental committee, exporters were instructed to report on the customs form an item showing 'the actual amount received or to be received in terms of Canadian dollars, exclusive of freight, insurance or other service charges'.

For the year 1947 the following adjustments were made to commodity export totals:

Adjustments to commodity export totals, 1947, deductions from exports

(millions of dollars)

Newfoundland	− 57.1
Private donations (excluding UNRRA)	− 7.6
Wheat adjustment	− 13.7
Settlers' effects	− 11.0
Other net deductions (noncommercial transactions, ships, and UNRRA)	− 12.6
Total deductions	− 102.0
Receipts by War Supplies Ltd	+ 13.0

SOURCE: *Blue Book*, p. 109.

Because of the inconvertibility of sterling during and after World War II, a division of the balance of payments into currency areas became necessary. This led to the study of prewar trade to provide a basis for a more accurate record of the destination of certain primary products, particularly wheat.

Up to 1938 the exports of wheat to the United Kingdom were often exaggerated, particularly in the late twenties, and those to European countries understated because of change in destination *en route*. There was also some understatement, at times in this period, of deliveries to the United States. An analysis of all available sources of information provided data which permitted adjustments to the export figures back to 1926. From 1938, data received from the Board of Grain Commissioners for Canada and the United States Department of Commerce were used to assist in keeping the record straight.

Other net deductions include some of a special character. The *Blue Book* states (p. 109):

Part of the item represents entries to cover unrecorded sales of used corvettes to South American governments and another part reflects a deduction from exports for the amount by which recorded exports of ships in 1947 to one purchaser exceeded receipts on the contracts for the ships during the year. Most of these receipts had been credited in earlier years in the balance of payments when the funds were received as this procedure comes closer to measuring the international transactions involved in the production and sale of ships.

During the war when much of Canadian production was exported under bulk contracts this device of substituting payments for the customs records of shipments was used for balance of payments purposes. This applied to British payments through official channels for war supplies and food, to payments by the United States government for war supplies and metals

exported under the Hyde Park Agreement, and to the expenditures on account of various countries from the Mutual Aid or other appropriations. This substitution of financial data on payments for the value of goods shipped was a major adjustment made necessary by the special conditions in the construction of balance of payments statements with the two currency areas for the years 1941 to 1946. Hence in the balance of payments statements the commodity item reflects international payments as contrasted with published figures of international trade which reflect movements of goods.

F58. Gold transactions. In the earliest balance of payments statistics compiled by the Dominion Bureau of Statistics, no distinction was made between monetary and nonmonetary movements. This earlier method was superseded by a more direct and simple procedure. In the revised tables for 1926 to 1937 which appear in the *Blue Book* as well as in the estimates for 1938 to 1945, the movements were shown separately and the data based on new methods.

Provision was made in the current account of the balance of payments for an item covering gold production which was available for export. This represents closely the value of production less Canadian consumption and is the international credit arising from the production of gold whether it is actually exported or is taken into the Canadian official reserves. Since these reserves include holdings of gold, a rise in the total due to an increase in the holdings of gold currently produced appears in the capital account as a debit reflecting the rise in Canadian foreign assets. This is offset by a credit entry in the current account in the item 'nonmonetary gold'.

Monetary gold movements may have different causes but they are usually significant in the balance of payments through changes in the holdings of gold in Canada's official liquid reserves. They represent monetary movements on Canadian account as, for example, when there are sales of gold from the reserves to settle liabilities abroad, or receipts of gold from other countries in settlement of debt. There have been gold transactions on account of other countries which have had no effect on the Canadian balance of payments. Foreign-owned gold has been held in Canada for safe-keeping and under earmark.

F59. Tourist and travel. Due to inadequacies in the method of estimating tourist and travel expenditures in the period 1926 to 1937, particularly as regards obtaining a representative sample of expenditures in total and by different types, new methods were developed early in the Second World War period. It was found that the expenditures of visitors to Canada had been greatly exaggerated in the Bureau's earlier estimates and, to a lesser extent, so had Canadian expenditures abroad. The data were revised on a new basis back to 1926 following an extensive reorganization of the methods of estimating tourist movements. The changes in the Second World War not only provided a huge increase in the sample information on expenditures but, in addition, provided for the centralized count and analysis of tourist movements in the Dominion Bureau of Statistics. This permitted an adequate classification of different types of tourist and travel movements and the application of appropriate average expenditures to each type.

Most of the data required were obtained directly but information on the expenditures of Americans visiting Canada by other means than automobiles was received through samples collected by the United States authorities and made available to Canada. Canada reciprocated by supplying information on the expenditures of Canadians in the United States and of Americans who visited Canada in automobiles.

F60 and 66. Interest and dividends. In the period 1926 to 1937 interest payments were calculated from the Bureau's issue by issue records of all Canadian bond issues held in whole or in part outside Canada. Original geographical distribution of ownership was adjusted by more recent information supplied for corporations by the corporations concerned, through the monthly returns made by Canadian investment dealers, stock exchanges, etc., and by information made available by financial institutions in the United Kingdom. An annual return was made to the Bureau on dividend payments by Canadian companies which had common or preferred stocks owned in other countries.

Certain payments which partake of the nature of interest or dividends were originally included in the capital rather than the current account. These arose principally through the operation of branch plants and the remittances of certain agencies such as trust companies, to their clients abroad. Later in revised statistics published for this period in the *Blue Book* and included herein, estimates of this group of income transfers were included in the 'miscellaneous income' component of the items 'all other current credits and debits'. The nature of these income transactions is described in the following statement from the *Red Book* (p. 99):

A considerable number of American branch plants located in Canada take out a licence to do business in Canada and do not become incorporated; therefore, they have no stock issue and do not declare dividends. Remittances to the United States, in such cases, are in the nature of profit remittances. Trust companies and other financial concerns may hold Canadian securities as nominees for nonresidents and remit the dividends abroad. The nature of the returns received from these companies is such that it is impossible to separate the profits, dividends, and interest from other capital movements. They are, therefore, included in the items dealing with branch plants, trust companies, etc., in the capital account of the balance of payments statement.

A discussion of the revisions, which were made back to 1926, may be found in the *Blue Book*, pp. 131–6.

Canada received interest and dividends from direct and miscellaneous investments abroad. Transfers by a branch or subsidiary to the Canadian head office were included in the current account. Some transactions were in the nature of profit remittances and difficult to separate from other movements of capital funds between the branch and the Canadian head office and consequently the capital account includes some amounts which are more akin to interest or dividends.

Miscellaneous portfolio investments in the United States by foreign countries were the subject in this period, i.e. 1926 to 1937, of an investigation by the Finance and Investment Division of the Bureau of Foreign and Domestic Commerce in Washington. A census of foreign portfolio investments and earnings, taken by that agency, collected very reliable information which was made available to Canada.

For miscellaneous investments in countries other than the United States a weighted index of interest rates, based on what information was available, was applied to these investments. As well as foreign securities, this group includes Canadian holdings of the stocks of Canadian companies located abroad, the dividends of which are a matter of record.

No interest or dividends on Canadian government credits abroad were received from 1931 until 1937.

No income receipts were included for the net assets of Canadian banks outside Canada since close relationships between gross earnings and periodic transfers of income to Canada did not seem to exist. It appeared that often profits earned abroad were held abroad.

In many cases the interest and dividends due on foreign securities held in Canada by Canadian insurance companies are lodged in centres outside Canada and owing to the nature of the accounts were indistinguishable from capital items. Known

remittances of interest and dividends to Canada were included in the current account item. The remainder form part of the insurance item in the capital account.

In the period 1938 to 1945, data on interest and dividend payments and receipts were improved and extended. The *Blue Book* states (p. 131):

Payments of interest to other countries on Canadian bonds and debentures are computed in detail from the records of bond issue originally sold out of Canada which are maintained in the International Payments Branch. These records of individual issues originally placed outside of Canada have been adjusted for subsequent retirements and refinancing. Important adjustments are also made according to the chief groups of issues to account for the effects of the trade in outstanding securities upon these records. Statistics on the net international trade in different groups of bonds, making these adjustments possible, have been available for the period since 1937. From 1932 through 1936 data were available only on the trade in total securities.... Sufficient data are available, however, to make satisfactory adjustments to the estimated interest payments computed on the basis of the original distribution of Canadian ownership bonds....The calculation of interest payments also takes account of defaults of interest and payments of arrears, information on these being supplied by a special schedule when not available in public sources.

The introduction of exchange control provided additional sources of information since an analysis of conversions of interest payments into United States dollars could be made. There was a large measure of agreement with computed totals. Another check on the accuracy of the basic records was provided by the requirement of the Foreign Exchange Control Board in 1939 for a declaration of Canadian holdings of securities payable in foreign currencies. Totals from these declarations were usually close to the Bureau's records.

The chief source of information on dividends paid by Canadian companies abroad remained the records collected by Dominion Bureau of Statistics questionnaires. From these reports total dividends payments could be calculated and also the distribution to three geographical areas: United Kingdom, United States and all other countries. These returns were received from 1932 for most Canadian companies with significant percentages of shares held abroad. For some groups of companies the dividend record was obtained back to 1926, but the coverage had become most comprehensive since about 1935.

Exchange control provided another source of information for this item. Companies paying dividends to nonresidents had to furnish to the Foreign Exchange Control Board information on the amounts paid abroad. Current payments to residents of the United States, United Kingdom and other countries were available from this source for the period of control.

Included in income payments by Canada were accruals of income such as revenue accruing during the war period to residents of enemy-occupied territories and proscribed territories from investments in Canada. Income of that nature was included as a debit in the interest and dividend item of the current account and offset by a credit in the capital account.

The interest and dividend item did not include reinvestment in Canada by externally owned and controlled companies. Only interest or dividends formally paid out were included. The *Blue Book* states (p. 131): 'While there may be theoretical reasons for preferring the inclusion of reinvested earnings in the income account the practical difficulties and delays in getting the information have led to the Canadian practice of limiting the account to actual cash payments.'

In 1938 to 1946 a change was made in the treatment of the profits of unincorporated branches remitted to head offices abroad. In earlier periods such were not included in the dividend item which was restricted to formal declarations of dividends. Previously they were in capital account as being indistinguishable from other capital movements. When more detailed information became available they were put first of all in miscellaneous income payments in revised statistics published in the *Blue Book* for years back to 1926, but for the 1938 to 1946 period they have been included among the figures of dividends.

Interest receipts from Canadian holdings of foreign bonds had been computed from estimates of holdings built up from information received from security dealers which was used along with other available information to adjust the original geographical distribution of the investment. A new and very helpful source of information became available in 1939 through the declaration of holdings of foreign securities by Canadians made to the Foreign Exchange Control Board. While some types of holdings were not required to be declared, the declarations were believed to have provided an improved basis of computing interest receipts. This source was supplemented by an analysis of receipts of United States dollars exchange which showed a large part of the interest received from bonds. While these records of exchange transactions are not complete they included the larger receipts and also revealed new kinds of interest receipts such as that collected by the Foreign Exchange Control Board on holdings of short-term United States securities.

Data on receipts of dividends by Canadian companies from direct investments abroad were more completely covered by this exchange analysis because they were usually large enough to be listed individually.

During the exchange control period the information on dividend receipts obtained from the analysis of exchange records could also be reconciled with the Bureau's corporate records. Information obtained from the International Economics Unit of the United States Department of Commerce also was used as a check.

Analysis of exchange receipts and payments furnished data which led to the exclusion from the interest and dividends item of some remittances of income. The *Blue Book* states (p. 135):

Data on these remittances first became available from the analysis of exchange receipts and payments developed in 1940. Estimates of miscellaneous income have been made for the prewar years on the basis of records obtained since 1940. Throughout the period commencing with 1926 the estimates of miscellaneous income are included among the miscellaneous current transactions because of their diverse character and the lack of precise information for a large part of the period. The miscellaneous remittances cover receipts and payments of the following types: interest on mortgages and loans, rents, crop share rentals, income received by Canadians from foreign estates and trusts, profits from speculation and certain types of business like the income of Canadian financial institutions from their branches abroad. Certain profits of unincorporated branches of industrial and commercial concerns are also included in the earlier part of the period covered in the balance of payments. A large part of the miscellaneous income is offsetting, there being substantial Canadian receipts as well as the larger Canadian payments.

F 61 and 67. Freight and shipping.

In the period 1926 to 1937 freight receipts and payments were estimated largely by indirect methods which were too detailed to be described here. They are presented very fully in the *Red Book*, pp. 70–96. Towards the end of the period indirect methods of estimation were replaced largely by direct data reported by railways and shipping operators.

The methods used in the period 1938 to 1945 were developed around 1936 and have prevailed since. During the war period some innovations had to be introduced to meet constantly changing situations.

Included in the freight and shipping item are the following:

Payments: payments by Canadian importers for services performed by foreign ships and railways and the expenditure of Canadian ships in foreign ports; payments for imports by pipeline, truck and air; payments to foreign owners of vessels covering the time charter of foreign ships.

Receipts: the earnings of Canadian ships and railways carrying exports and the expenditure of foreign ships and crews in Canadian ports; earnings of Canadian railways on in-transit traffic in Canada between foreign ports; receipts from the operation of non-resident owned railways in Canada; earnings of Canadian ships operating between foreign ports; shipping insurance is included in the freight and shipping series from 1926 to 1945 (see *Blue Book*, p. 117). For the treatment of life insurance, which is in the capital account, see *Blue Book*, p. 137.

These numerous items in the freight and shipping account are necessary because Canadian exports are entered in Customs documents f.o.b. the point of original shipment, and the valuation for imports is fair market value for consumption in the country from which the goods are purchased. That is, the valuations are exclusive of the cost of freight and other services.

From 1936 onward most of the information required was and still is obtained through questionnaires sent to railways and ship operators. It is supplemented for some inland freight by information reported in Customs export forms and the tonnage statistics and other information from official sources. Exchange control data were not of much use as a source for estimates of freight receipts and payments because of the many variations in the terms of payment in commercial trade. However, exchange data were used at times to check on the earnings of Canadian railways on in-transit traffic and for international transportation by truck and air.

F 62, 68 and 69. All other current.

From 1926 to 1937 a number of items were originally included in the 'all other current items group'. And in addition some other transactions were added to the revised figures for the period 1926 to 1937 which were published in the *Blue Book*. These additions included miscellaneous income and profits already referred to, service transactions associated with international direct investments, and supplements to the amounts originally used for personal and immigrant remittances.

No direct information was available for remittances of immigrants and emigrants. Ten million dollars was originally added in most years to the total of post office money order remittances to the United States and the United Kingdom to account for remittances through other channels than postal money orders. This was done to correct an underestimate made on the assumption that sums remitted by emigrants and immigrants through non-post office channels were equal to the amount of money order remittances for small purchases abroad. Subsequently in the revised figures supplements were added to provide for the higher levels of transfers indicated by data derived from exchange control.

Expenditures of other governments in Canada include consular and diplomatic services and receipts of pensions from abroad. The information was obtained from the government departments in other countries when possible and estimates made for the remainder. Education, charitable and missionary contributions were credits for grants received by Canadian institutions from British and United States endowments and contributions by parent bodies and others to Canadian religious organizations. On the debit side are the expenditures of Canadian churches on missionary effort abroad. As much information as possible was obtained from relevant sources and estimates made of the total.

Advertising receipts and expenditures were obtained by

annual questionnaire from newspapers, magazines and other periodicals, advertising agencies, railways, exhibitions, etc.

Estimates of earnings and payments on the use of motion picture films were made with the assistance of expert advice such as that given by the Motion Picture Distributors and Exhibitors of Canada. The geographical distribution was made on the basis of the percentage of feature films used in Canadian theatres.

The *per capita* amount of capital brought into or taken out of the country by migrants was estimated for various classes of migrants and multiplied by the number involved.

Earnings of residents of Canada employed in the United States and residents of the United States employed in Canada concern mainly the debits and credits arising from commuter traffic in the Detroit–Windsor area. It does not include the international exchange of professional services which are either offsetting or provided for elsewhere.

Since the developments in the treatment of 'all other current' items can best be handled for the periods 1938 to 1945 and 1946 to 1960 together, the following note deals with both periods.

In the period following 1938 and up to 1951 new data derived from exchange control were an important source in covering the diverse groups of transactions embraced in 'all other current' items. Following the termination of exchange control at the end of 1951, direct methods of reporting to the Dominion Bureau of Statistics had to be introduced or reinstated for many of the transactions covered.

In volume and composition this group changed considerably from 1938 onward. Foreign exchange control had made available a wealth of detail on widely scattered transactions. Those which were large enough to require an exchange form furnished a record which, when analysed, yielded much information on service items. Many transactions of the same type, too small to require separate forms, were reported in bulk as sundries. Samples were obtained from time to time of the composition of the sundry item as a basis for eliminating transactions which were included elsewhere in the current account and to classify the remainder into meaningful groups. The results were such that the combination of large items and sundry transactions was believed to have yielded 'a generally reliable measure of the broad groups shown and reasonably accurate for the aggregate'.

A second group of data emerged from the analysis of international business transactions carried on by permit holders of the Foreign Exchange Control Board. Certain firms were permitted to employ foreign currency accounts and inter-company accounts. Analysis of these accounts was on a broad functional basis because of their diversity, but it had to be sufficiently selective so that the data could be integrated with figures from other sources. The *Canadian Balance of International Payments in the Post-war Years, 1946–52* states (p. 83): 'It should be clear from the above that the exchange data, while yielding information on many items which are widely dispersed in origin and therefore difficult to collect otherwise, permitted only a very broad classification in most cases. It is particularly difficult to subdivide business services satisfactorily because of their variable and heterogeneous character.'

As distinct from prewar data, postwar figures include inheritances, Newfoundland transactions with other countries, and a segregation of what were believed to represent current transactions on insurance account as distinct from the capital account. Gross transactions of other items were substituted for the net transactions used in prewar statements.

Prewar statements did not include specific estimates for inheritances and other transactions connected with the settlement of estates and trusts. The data from exchange control indicated that debits and credits for these were offsetting to a considerable extent so their omission probably did not affect greatly the net balance.

Beginning with 1940 there were important changes in the treatment of transactions on Newfoundland account which continued until Newfoundland entered Confederation in 1949. Even before 1940 Newfoundland used Canadian currency and her banking was done by branches of Canadian banks. From 1940 onward, by an arrangement between Newfoundland and Canada, Newfoundland turned over its surpluses of United States dollars to Canada or was to receive her needs for United States dollars from Canada. The only item covering transactions entered in the current account in this period was the transfer of United States dollars. Newfoundland's net United States dollar receipts were included in the miscellaneous receipts from the United States as many of them originated in allied military expenditure in Newfoundland. Exports to and imports from Newfoundland, which were financed in Canadian dollars, were not included in the figures for commodity trade used for balance of payments purposes. Newfoundland's dealings in sterling were managed under a similar arrangement but the net balances were small in amount and are included in the capital account in series F125. Since its confederation in 1949, Newfoundland transactions with other countries have been included in the appropriate parts of the balance of payments along with other Canadian transactions.

During the war period government expenditures became exceedingly large. These included Canadian military operations abroad, Commonwealth Air Training in Canada, and the construction by the United States of airfields, highways and pipelines in Northern Canada. In 1945 and 1946 there were Canadian reimbursements to Western European countries for war expenditures by them during military operations on the continent. In 1944 there were debits due to special payments by the Canadian to the United States government to cover the purchase of airfields and telephone lines and other settlements.

In the nineteen-fifties United States defence expenditures in Canada became substantial with the construction of defence installations in the north and the expansion and maintenance of bases in Newfoundland.

Business services account for a large part of all the other current items group. They include such items as royalties, patents and copyrights, administrative, management and professional services, advertising and publicity services on imports, commissions and similar items. A large proportion of these are connected with direct investments. Since 1952 information on these transactions has largely been collected on questionnaires sent by the Bureau to companies with international operations or affiliations.

Official contributions by the Canadian Government from 1946 to 1948 represent contributions to UNRRA and post-UNRRA, military relief, and a small carryover of wartime mutual aid. These contributions were used mainly to finance exports which are included in commodity trade. The credit item is offset by the debit item for contributions.

Contributions to the International Refugee Organization, which first appeared in 1948, formed a significant part of the total until 1952. Included also in recent years are contributions to Palestine and Greece, United Nations and Korean Relief Agencies, The United Nations International Children's Emergency Fund and other organizations. In the nineteen-fifties expenditures under the Colombo Plan were dominant. Mutual aid to NATO countries is shown as a separate item from 1950 on. It is included in the current receipts to show the total of goods and services supplied to other countries and is offset in current payments because of its nature as a contribution.

In the period 1940 to 1945 'Canadian overseas expenditures'

related to the armed services are shown separately. War expenditures after 1945 are shown separately in the source only for 1946. They cover receipts and expenditures of the Canadian government related to World War II. A variety of expenditures is involved, ranging from pay and allowances and other expenses of Canadian personnel overseas to a special payment in 1946 of $21 million to the United States Treasury to cover the purchase of immovable assets left in Canada and certain military equipment. Defence expenditures in recent years are included in various parts of the accounts, mainly in 'all other current items' in the case of services, and in merchandise trade in the case of procurement of defence equipment and supplies.

F 72–90. Canadian balance of international payments, all countries and by major areas, current account, 1946 to 1960

SOURCE: D.B.S., *Balance of Payments, 1946–1952*, pp. 94–5, and subsequent annual reports; D.B.S., *Canadian Balance of International Payments, 1959 and International Investment Position*, pp. 55–8; data for 1959 and 1960 were provided by the National Income and Balance of Payments Division, D.B.S.

F 72 and 81. Commodity trade. No important changes in compilation methods were introduced in this period (see note for F 57 and 64). Exports of military equipment and other commodities to Canadian Armed Forces abroad were not included in Canadian export statistics after 1949. Likewise, equipment and supplies returned to Canada by the Canadian Armed Forces abroad were not included in imports. Prior to 1950 both were so recorded but were deducted from trade statistics for balance of payment purposes.

F 73 and 87. Mutual aid. For the treatment of mutual aid see note for F 57 and 64.

F 74. Gold transactions. There was no change in basic methods in the period 1946 to the present (see note for F 58). During the Second World War the Exchange Fund Account became the repository of the official reserves at the disposal of the Foreign Exchange Control Board. When the Board was discontinued in 1951 the Bank of Canada as administrator of the Exchange Fund Account became the repository agency.

F 75 and 82. Travel expenditures. See note for F 59 and F 68. The same methods have been in use during this period but there was some adjustment in compilation procedures. Owing to the very large numbers of returns, resort was had to sampling. *Balance of Payments, 1946–1952*, states (p. 75): 'For shorter visits (by motorists) it has been found that satisfactory data can be obtained without fully processing all permits. This principle has also been applied to other types...of traffic....'

F 76 and 83. Interest and dividends. With the discontinuance of the Foreign Exchange Control Board in 1951 and the end of exchange control, the alternative or supplementary information provided was no longer available. The methods used prior to exchange control, extended and elaborated by the knowledge gained in the control period, were resumed. Since the end of exchange control the Bureau's annual questionnaire to Canadian owners of direct investments abroad includes a question on receipts of dividends, profits and interest. To check on income from portfolio holdings, a new survey of Canadian holdings of United States stocks was made from information obtained directly from many of the principal corporations in the United States. In connexion with estimates of dividend payments to nonresidents, records are supplemented by an analysis of the withholding tax applicable to certain payments.

As previously, reinvestments in Canada by externally owned or controlled companies which are not actually paid out as interest or dividends are excluded. They are reflected in the statement of the balance of international indebtedness. Pay-

ments to nonresident owners which are held in Canada are included but are offset by a credit in the capital account. This also applies to dividends formally paid out but reinvested.

F 77 and 84. Freight and shipping. There was no change in concept or method. See note for F 61 and 67.

F 79, 85, 86, 87 and 88. All other current. The treatment of these series is dealt with in the note to F 62, 68 and 69.

F 72–90. 'Other sterling area' includes the countries of the Commonwealth, United Kingdom dependencies, and Ireland, Iraq and Iceland; in addition, Burma became a member of the sterling area in 1948, Jordan in 1950 and Libya in 1952. Other O.E.E.C. countries include all the countries participating in the Organization for European Economic Co-operation which are not also members of the sterling area, namely, Austria, Belgium, Luxembourg, Denmark, France, West Germany, Greece, Italy, Netherlands, Norway, Portugal, Sweden, Switzerland and Turkey, and their overseas territories up to 1956. These are the nonsterling area countries which participate in the European Recovery Programme. The figures for 1946 are given for the sake of comparability. The 'All other countries' group is made up primarily of Latin America, nonsterling area countries in Asia and Continental European countries other than those in the O.E.E.C. group, the International Bank for Reconstruction and Development, International Finance Corporation and International Monetary Fund and all other countries not specified above.

F 91–103. Canadian balance of international payments, all countries and by major areas, capital account, 1927 to 1937

SOURCE: D.B.S., *Blue Book*, pp. 163–6; and for discussion of concepts and method, see *Red Book*, chs. 5, 6 and 7; *Blue Book*, pt. 2, chs. 8 and 9; D.B.S., *Balance of Payments, 1946–52*, p. 85.

The three periods 1927 to 1937, 1938 to 1945 and 1946 to 1960 may be considered together because of the fact that the methods described in the *Red Book* still prevail in a general way. Where improvements have been made earlier figures in many cases have been revised. The introduction of foreign exchange control in 1939 made data available which tended to corroborate some important earlier estimates. It also had other important results in that it made possible the segregation of items from aggregates, clarified situations which led to the transfer of items from capital to current account, and furnished much additional information on short-term capital movements. When Foreign Exchange Control was discontinued in 1951, the prewar methods were resumed but they were amplified in the light of knowledge gained during exchange control.

Canadian statistical sources for recording international capital movements were built up in the nineteen-thirties along with the related earlier extensive records of international investments introduced in the nineteen-twenties. For example, regular monthly returns to the Dominion Bureau of Statistics on international transactions in outstanding securities were introduced in 1933 and, shortly thereafter, annual returns were obtained from direct investment companies with historical records going back to 1926. These statistics were the result of arrangements with security dealers, bankers, and brokers handling such security transactions, with branches and subsidiaries in Canada controlled abroad, and with Canadian companies with branches and subsidiaries abroad. In addition regular reporting arrangements were introduced in the nineteen-thirties covering international transactions of insurance companies and trust companies.

Records of the international investments entering into the Canadian balance of international indebtedness were built up in the Dominion Bureau of Statistics since 1926. Nonresident investments in Canada are of great importance because of their effects in the balance of payments. Extensive corporation records, including comprehensive data for direct investments in branch plants and subsidiary companies, were set up to cover investments in Canadian companies. From the information received, foreign investments in Canadian enterprises (incorporated in Canada or unincorporated) were classified by area of ownership and control and by kinds of business and industrial groups. While the ownership of most issues of stock can be secured from stock registers, in some cases, as in the instance of nominee holdings in Canada for owners abroad, much of this type of ownership is covered from other sources.

For nonresident holdings of bearer bonds and debentures the information is less exact, though many companies supply estimates of the distribution of ownership of such holdings. In the absence of this information, reference is made to the original sale of the issue. Subsequent changes in the original distribution of ownership can be estimated from data received on the international trade in securities reported by security dealers and others. Since 1937 these figures have been classified according to the chief groups of bonds and stocks.

There have been indirect indicators of the volume of Canadian bonds owned outside Canada which tend to corroborate these adjusted records. They include the sales of foreign exchange to service interest payments on Canadian bonded debt and the declaration of holdings of securities payable in foreign currencies required by the Foreign Exchange Control Board in 1939. The latter included Canadian issues payable in foreign currencies. Though small holdings were exempt, this did not appear to affect seriously the value of the check.

Equity investments of nonresidents are valued at book values, and bonds and debentures and preferred stocks at par in Canadian dollars.

Comprehensive data covering private investments of Canadian capital abroad are also of long standing. They are contained in records maintained in the Bureau of Statistics of Canadian companies with direct investments in branches, subsidiaries or controlled companies located outside Canada. Up-to-date information on the location of the investments and their value is collected by schedules. The general valuation plan followed is to take the book value as shown in the records of the company abroad.

For private holdings of foreign securities (portfolio investments), records have been built up from various sources. More comprehensive and detailed sources of information for this class of investment also became available in 1939 through the declarations of holdings of foreign securities to the Foreign Exchange Control Board. These data were considered by the Bureau to have covered the major part of Canadian holdings of foreign securities although a report on small holdings was not required.

It is difficult to adjust these records for subsequent changes in portfolio investments according to individual issues, but changes in the Canadian holdings of the principal groups of United States and foreign securities can be estimated from monthly reports on the international trade in securities. Data relating to the estimates for recent years are considered to be generally indicative of present holdings in the aggregate. They seemed reasonable in the light of receipts of income by Canadians from foreign securities which were revealed in the analysis of exchange transactions during the period of exchange control.

Records of Canadian holdings of the capital stock of the larger United States companies, moreover, have been brought up to date at the Bureau by obtaining from these companies statements of shares held in Canada in 1953 and 1960. The group of companies covered represents a large part of the total holdings.

Canadian holdings of foreign bonds obtained by the same method are valued at par or nominal value in Canadian dollars.

The external assets of Canadian banks and insurance companies are not included in Canadian investments abroad because such assets have to be considered in relation to external liabilities.

The *Blue Book* includes a number of changes from those published in the *Red Book*. Revised figures are shown for capital movements arising from the trade in outstanding securities in the years 1926 to 1932 which were prior to the introduction of the regular monthly statistics on this trade. Transactions for this earlier period were estimated to be the difference between all other recorded capital movements and the net balance on current account for the years 1927 to 1932. That is why no residual item appears in series F 103. The resulting figures are not widely different from estimates from a new study of capital movements in the period concerned although actual data available were often incomplete.

A second revision in the earlier capital account involves the transfer to the current account of items formerly consolidated in the item covering direct investments in the capital account (certain current service transactions reported between branches and subsidiaries abroad). These originally had been covered in the net inter-company transactions of the companies concerned, aggregated with capital transactions in a separate item of the capital account before the war.

Exchange control brought to light new information on short-term capital movements, for example, the working balances abroad of many Canadian companies with an export or import business. Among other short-term movements are the balances of nonresidents in Canadian dollars maintained in Canadian banks. Semi-annual returns were required by the Foreign Exchange Control Board for such balances. With the cessation of control this form of inquiry has been continued. In the recent period there have also been important balances maintained in Canada by the British and other governments for the purchase of commodities and other activities.

Other short-term movements arise from fluctuations in inter-company accounts and other commercial accounts payable or receivable connected with international trade. These were reported by permit holders during exchange control but not in complete detail. Where the record was not complete the unrecorded movement was reflected in the balancing item of errors and omissions. Annual returns from direct investment companies to the Bureau continue to cover many of these short-term changes, supplemented also by some quarterly returns.

An outstanding development in the 1938 to 1948 period was the making of large loans and credits to overseas governments by the Canadian government. Loans and export credits to the United Kingdom and other overseas countries rose from $31 million at the beginning of the period to $2,000 million at the end of 1949.

Variations in the level of official holdings of gold and foreign currencies by the Canadian government also had a marked effect upon the totals of Canadian external assets. From $459 million in Canadian dollar terms in 1939 they reached a year end peak of $1,667 million in 1945. By the end of 1947 they had declined to $511 million and by 1948 were up to $1,006 million and to $1,786 million by the end of 1959. Much the largest part of these holdings took the form of gold and United States dollars.

Holdings of gold are included as a foreign asset since they represent part of Canada's official reserves of convertible exchange, being a potential source of United States funds. In 1947 and in 1959 there were payments in gold valued at $74 million and $59 million, respectively, representing part of Canada's quota in the International Monetary Fund. Canada's total quota in that fund in Canadian notes and deposits as well as gold amounted in United States dollar terms to $550 million by the end of 1959, and the aid in subscriptions to the capital of the International Bank at the same date totalled $65 million. In both of these cases (IMF and IBRD), the quota payments and subscriptions are offsetting in the capital account. The increase in foreign assets are offset by corresponding increases in Canadian liabilities abroad as regards demand notes and deposits in Canadian currency, while the subscriptions in gold or convertible exchange result in a change in the form of Canadian assets abroad.

Data on loans and advances are obtained from official sources. Drawings on loans and advances made by the government of Canada include, in the case of nonsterling area countries, advances under the War Appropriation Act (interim advances) net of repayments, together with drawings under the Exports Credits Insurance Act.

Other capital movements 'comprise a variety of transactions including changes in accounts receivable and payable and in inter-company accounts, short and long-term loans between private unrelated parties, changes in private and chartered bank holdings of foreign exchange, and the net change in Canadian dollar short-term holdings of [IMF and IBRD]'. The statistical coverage of accounts receivable and payable and of inter-company accounts is limited to some types of company.

Also included in other capital movements is the balancing item covering the difference between the current account balance and recorded capital movements less the changes in official holdings of gold and foreign exchange. The difference has usually been small in proportion to gross international transactions. A study of this residual over a number of years suggests that it represents principally changes in receivables and payables not directly recorded.

F 104–145. Canadian balance of international payments, all countries and by major areas, capital account, 1938 to 1945

SOURCE: D.B.S., *Blue Book*, pp. 168–70.

For the description of methods see note for F 91–103.

F 146–163. Canadian balance of international payments, all countries and by major areas, capital account, 1946 to 1960

SOURCE: D.B.S., *Balance of Payments, 1946–52*, p. 94; subsequent annual reports, 1953 to 1958; *Canadian Balance of International Payments, 1959, and International Investment Position*, pp. 55–9; data for 1959 and 1960 were provided by the National Income and Balance of Payments Division, D.B.S.

A description of the methods used since 1946 is given in the note to F 91–103.

F 155. 'Loans by Government of Canada, drawings' includes, in the case of nonsterling area countries, advances under War Appropriation Act (interim advances) net of repayments, together with drawings under Export Credit Insurance Act loans.

F 160. Other capital movements include, in addition to the items described in the note to F 91–103, a balancing item representing unrecorded capital movements and errors and omissions.

Some capital transactions with overseas countries which cannot be segregated are included with the United States. All other countries include the IMF and the IBRD. For a description of countries in 'other sterling area' and O.E.E.C., see note for F 72–90.

F 162. Balance settled by exchange transfers. 'During the period of exchange control, multilateral settlements were calculated directly for the sterling area from banking and exchange control sources. Figures for "other O.E.E.C." and "other"

countries were residuals in those bilateral accounts. The sum of these was then applied against the United States account. In 1952 after allocation of the global residual item, the bilateral residuals were taken as the measure of multilateral settlements' (*Balance of Payments, 1946–52*, p. 86).

CANADIAN INTERNATIONAL INDEBTED-NESS AND CLAIMS (Series F 164–241)

General note

The international investment position reveals Canada's situation as both a creditor and debtor nation. Though there is a close relationship between capital movements as shown in the balance of payments and the international investment position the latter is affected by numerous additional factors. These include such items as the retention of corporate earnings, revaluation of assets and liabilities (including the writing off of exploration and development expense), the untransferred capital and inheritances of migrants, and numerous others. Hence the annual change in the investment position cannot be deduced from the balance of payments statement alone.

The inflow of capital into Canada plus the reinvestment of earnings thereon in Canada had created by the end of 1959 a long-term investment by outsiders in Canada of more than $20 billion. Including other liabilities the gross amount was more than $22 billion. At the same time Canada had foreign assets of over $8 billion, a large part of which consisted of assets owned by the Canadian government in the form of loans and advances and official reserves of gold and foreign exchange. In both cases, assets and liabilities are exclusive of short-term commercial indebtedness and blocked currencies.

Foreign capital has been a vital source of financing in most periods of Canadian development though there is less over-all dependence now on external sources than in earlier periods. The 1900 to 1913 period of Canada's history witnessed one of her most rapid developments. The opening of the Canadian West and the related growth in other parts of the country brought in large amounts of British capital, the investment mostly taking the form of bonds.

United States investment in Canada exceeded that of Britain early in the interwar period. It grew rapidly during World War I and participated in the expansion of Canadian industry and utilities. A considerable proportion was in branches and subsidiaries controlled by United States companies. However, Canadian capital resources had grown and a relatively smaller share of Canadian expansion was financed by nonresident capital than was the case in the 1900 to 1913 period. Moreover, Canadian capital was being invested abroad. Canadians in the nineteen-twenties were making principally portfolio investments abroad and in the nineteen-thirties they were financing withdrawals of such capital by Britain and the United States.

During the Second World War and the early postwar period there was a considerable reduction in Canadian net indebtedness to the United Kingdom because of the repatriation of Canadian government and railway bonds, and the war loan of 1942 and postwar loan of 1946 extended by the Canadian government to the United Kingdom.

A rapid growth in nonresident investment has occurred since 1948. This flow has been largely from the United States but there have been significant increases in British investments as well as from investors in Western Europe. At first the outstanding feature of these recent capital inflows was that they have been made directly in Canadian industries rather than in portfolio holdings of government and railway bonds characteristic of the early period. But following this aspect of Canadian expansion more of the capital inflows were connected with borrowings abroad by Canadian provinces and municipalities.

There have been considerable increases in the share of foreign ownership in Canadian manufacturing and mining industries. More than one half the capital invested since 1948 in these fields, including the petroleum industry, has been owned by nonresidents; the trend has resulted in a great increase in the number of Canadian firms controlled abroad, and in the place of nonresident capital in Canadian industry.

Concurrently with the growing importance of concerns controlled by non-residents, however, the Canadian economy has been expanding. There have been large investments of Canadian capital concentrated in spheres other than industry, such as in public utilities and other forms of assets owned by Canadian governments and municipalities, also in housing and agricultural and other forms of personal property and in Canadian commercial establishments. There have also been large increases in Canadian owned assets abroad. But the prominent place occupied by non-resident capital in Canadian industry is a special feature of Canada's international investment position (see C. D. Blyth, *Encyclopedia Canadiana*, vol. 5, p. 302).

F 164–192. Estimates of the Canadian balance of international indebtedness excluding short-term commercial indebtedness and blocked currency balances, selected year ends, 1926 to 1960

SOURCE: D.B.S., *Canadian Balance of International Payments, 1959 and International Investment Position*, p. 64; data for 1959 and 1960 were provided by the National Income and Balance of Payments Division, D.B.S.

In November 1959 the Dominion Bureau of Statistics issued a Reference Paper entitled *Canada's External Short-term Assets and Liabilities, 1945–1957* (catalogue no. 67–504, occasional). In this Reference Paper a more comprehensive estimate than ever given before of the Canadian balance of international indebtedness for the years 1945 to 1957 is presented. It pointed out that in the annual reports, *Canadian Balance of International Payments*, the effects of certain capital movements on Canada's balance of indebtedness had not been covered adequately. The tables had included an overall estimate of Canada's short-term assets abroad, other than short-term commercial indebtedness and blocked currencies, but no detailed analysis had been given. Moreover, neither totals nor an analysis of short-term receivables and payables had been available. The more comprehensive figures shown in the Reference Paper constituted an attempt to remedy these deficiencies. Page 2 of the document describes the results as follows:

The effect of these additions in 1956 is shown in Statement I [of the Reference Paper] when additional payables and receivables of $0.7 billion and $0.4 billion respectively are recorded. The figure of $0.5 billion for 'other Canadian short-term assets abroad' is also replaced by a more complete one which is better described as 'bank balances and other short-term funds abroad n.i.e.' The net effect is to increase the estimate of Canada's net international indebtedness at the end of 1956 from $9.7 billion to $10.0 billion. In 1957 the new material adds $0.7 billion to the estimate of net indebtedness. The estimates regularly published and the more comprehensive figures now available for the years 1945 to 1958 appear in Tables II and III. These reveal that over these years the payables outstanding at the year-ends ranged between $0.3 billion and $1.0 billion, and receivables between $0.1 billion and $0.4 billion. Bank balances and other short-term funds abroad n.i.e. varied between $0.1 billion and $0.9 billion.

F 193–207. Estimates of foreign capital invested in Canada, selected year ends, 1900 to 1960

SOURCE: D.B.S., *Canadian Balance of International Payments, 1959 and International Investment Position*, table XIII, p. 71, for years since 1926; for 1914 to 1925, based on Knox, 'Excursus', p. 299; for

1900 to 1913, based on Viner, *Canada's Balance*, p. 139; revised data for 1955 to 1959 and data for 1960 were provided by the National Income and Balance of Payments Division, D.B.S.

It may be noted that Viner estimated total Canadian claims against foreign assets of $100 million as of the end of 1899 and total Canadian indebtedness at the same date of $1,200 million of which $1,040 million was held in Britain, $150 million in the United States and the balance in other countries. The estimates for the years 1900 to 1924 included here were obtained by adding cumulated inflows to Viner's estimate for 1899.

F 208–230. British and foreign capital invested in Canada, all countries and by major areas, by type of investment and direct investment, selected year ends, 1930 to 1960

SOURCE: data were provided by the National Income and Balance of Payments Division, D.B.S., and contain many revisions from the last published source, D.B.S., *Canadian Balance of International Payments, 1959 and International Investment Position*, table IX, p. 68; table X, p. 69.

The following note is applicable to all statistics of foreign investment in Canada. Common and preference stocks are included at book (equity) values as shown in the balance sheets of the issuing companies, bonds and debentures are valued at par, liabilities in foreign currencies being converted into Canadian dollars at the original par exchange. Investments in Canadian companies have been classified according to principal activities in Canada. Investments by petroleum and natural gas companies in exploration and development of petroleum, in refining and production of petroleum products, in pipelines and tankers and in petroleum products mechandising are all included in the petroleum and natural gas group. Investments in Canada shown as owned by residents of the United States and the United Kingdom include some investments held for residents of other countries. Direct investment covers investment in branches, subsidiaries, and controlled companies.

F 231–241. Canadian long-term investments abroad, all countries and by major areas, by type, selected year ends, 1926 to 1960

SOURCE: data were provided by the National Income and Balance of Payments Division, D.B.S., and contain many revisions from the last published source, D.B.S., *Canadian Balance of International Payments, 1959 and International Investment Position*, table VII, p. 65.

FOREIGN TRADE (Series F 242–359)

General note

In *Statistical Contributions to Canadian Economic History*, p. 1, Taylor states:

Fragmentary statistics relating to the foreign trade of Canada exist back to the early days of French colonization, and in some decades of the seventeenth and eighteenth centuries were compiled with considerable care and completeness. Provincial statistics for British North America go back fairly regularly, but not consistently, to the early years of the nineteenth century. For the Dominion of Canada as a whole figures are available only since 1868. In the earlier years even of this modern period methods of compilation and classification left much to be desired; but there has been steady improvement in the quality of the statistics, and from about 1880 they are substantially satisfactory.

In his volume *Canada's Balance of International Indebtedness* (p. 27) Viner comments:

For the items they cover, with the exception of gold coin, the Canadian statistics of exports and imports are probably as close to accuracy as is reasonably to be expected of any comprehensive statistics. An exceptionally efficient Customs Department collects with great care the data for both import and export statistics, and no allowance need be made, with the exception noted, for inaccuracy in the published statistics. Until June 30, 1900, the statistics of exports were regarded by the Customs Department as inaccurate for shipments overland to the United States, and an addition of 5 per cent was made annually to the collected statistics of exports to the United States, to cover unrecorded exports. In 1900, however, the Customs installed a new system of collection of export statistics for overland shipments, and abandoned as unnecessary the allowance for unrecorded items.

After Confederation, Canadian annual trade statistics were published until 1906 for fiscal years ending 30 June and commencing with 1907 for fiscal years ending 31 March. From 1939 the annual data have been on a calendar year basis but supplementary reports made data available on a calendar year basis back to 1927. During World War II there was some curtailment in the amount of information published but after 1944 the publication of full details was resumed.

Earlier Canadian trade statistics were originally compiled on a general trade basis but totals were shown for both special and general trade for imports. In 1917 import statistics were restricted to goods entered for consumption. The adoption of the special trade principle did not affect the official figures for imports greatly because of the minor importance of the goods passing through warehouses but not entered for domestic consumption. In 1920 a similar change was introduced which excluded from exports goods re-exported from bonded warehouses. Re-exports of goods which had been entered for consumption continued to be included in total Canadian exports.

In the compilation of trade statistics the recording of movements of gold created problems. The unreliable records in trade statistics of these movements were pointed out by both Viner and Knox. The difficulties of valuing gold after the general abandonment of the gold standard in the early nineteen-thirties and other difficulties connected with differentiating between monetary and nonmonetary gold movements led to the decision to exclude all movements of gold from trade statistics except certain industrial gold products. The trade statistics since 1939 show separately a supplementary item 'net exports of nonmonetary gold'. Gold coins and gold in concentrates were excluded from the statistics at the same time as bullion.

Canada's system of valuing exports and imports has remained unchanged since Confederation. Imports are valued f.o.b. the inland point of purchase in the country from which the goods are shipped to Canada, and exports at the inland point of shipment in Canada for export. Thus, in theory, the value of Canadian imports and exports is exclusive of all costs connected with their movement such as freight, insurance and handling. However, as pointed out in the discussion of the commodity item in the balance of international payments, the valuations of imports and exports have not always been so clear-cut and have included instances where they were f.a.s. or c.i.f. and there were other instances of overvaluation.

The coverage of Canadian trade statistics was changed with the entry of Newfoundland into Confederation on 1 April 1949. From this date, of course, imports from Newfoundland and exports to Newfoundland are not shown since they have become an integral part of the Canadian nation.

In 1960 a change was made in the types of commodities included in totals of Canadian exports and imports. Various noncommercial and special transactions, which had previously been included, were excluded in the new compilations. Removed from exports are Canadian army, navy and airforce stores, n.o.p., settlers' effects and gifts and donations. Removed from imports are film imported for reproduction and then re-exported, be-

quests of personal effects or furniture, clothing and books sent for charitable purposes, articles for diplomats from abroad, arms, military stores and other goods belonging to NATO or Commonwealth countries, casual gifts from abroad, tourist purchases exempt of duty, settlers' effects and the like.

Figures prior to 1959 are on the old basis. Figures for 1959 are presented on both the new and old basis except for series F 298–315 and F 316–333; in the latter series, data for 1959 are given on the new basis only. All data for 1960 are on the new basis.

A statement of the changes that were made in 1960 may be found in D.B.S., *Trade of Canada, Imports, January 1960*, pp. i–viii. Data on the revised basis are given for 1946 to 1959 in that publication.

F 242–245. Foreign trade, domestic exports, total exports, total imports and balance of trade, declared values, Canada and all countries, 1868 to 1960

SOURCE: D.B.S., *Trade of Canada, 1958*, vol. 1, p. 19, and subsequent annual reports of the same series; data for 1959 and 1960, new basis, were provided by the External Trade Division, D.B.S. (see end of general note to series F 242–399).

F 246–269. Foreign trade, exports of domestic and foreign produce excluding coin and bullion, by main groups, declared values and values prevailing in 1900, 1869 to 1915

SOURCE: Taylor, *Statistical Contributions to Canadian Economic History*, vol. II, p. 12.

Taylor describes his method as follows (p. 2):

In the present study the method of eliminating (so far as that is possible) the effect of price fluctuations has been to revalue all the individual items in the trade of Canada in terms of their 1900 values. Wherever in the Customs Reports physical quantities (i.e., tons, bushels, gallons, yards, etc.) are given, each of these quantities has been multiplied by the average import or export price of that commodity as it was in the fiscal year ended June 30, 1900. Where quantities are not stated, prices are assumed to have moved in harmony with the most closely related commodities for which quantities are given. For instance, woollen clothing is assumed to have been subject to the same price fluctuations as the weighted average price of all wool items for which quantities are given. The effect of these simple, though laborious calculations, is to reduce all these trade statistics to a constant price basis or unit of value....

As a by-product of the process of expressing all imports and exports in '1900 dollars', index numbers of import and export prices were also obtained.

F 270–293. Foreign trade, imports excluding coin and bullion, by main groups, declared values and values at prices prevailing in 1900, 1869 to 1915

SOURCE: Taylor, *Statistical Contributions to Canadian Economic History*, vol. II, p. 10.

See note for F 246–269.

F 294–297. Foreign trade, exports of domestic and foreign produce and imports, declared values and estimated values at prices prevailing in fiscal year 1913, 1891 to 1926

SOURCE: Taylor, 'Post-War Fluctuations in the Volume of Canadian Foreign Trade', pp. 301 ff.

Series F 294–297 are also the work of Taylor. Taylor changed his base year from 1900 to 1913 and covers the period 1891 to 1926. On this basis, calculations were not made for main groups as they were for the 1900 base series.

The April 1927 issue of the *Journal of the Canadian Bankers'*

Association contains the following description of Taylor's method.

The method of study...is to take the actual quantities (bushels, yards, tons, etc.) of thirty-seven principal imports and thirty-one principal exports which passed in or out each year; value these quantities at fixed prices (in this case the average import or export price of each commodity in the fiscal year 1912–13); total these values; and, finally, assume that the prices of the residue of imports and exports not included in the selected lists, moved in harmony with the prices of the selected imports and exports respectively. The result is, in effect, a statement of what our imports and exports would have totalled had prices remained exactly as they were in 1912–13. It is a recalculation, as it were, of our trade in terms of '1913 dollars'.

Since this table includes the war years 1914 to 1918 the figures for those years are subject to influences which render them abnormal in some respects. They should be interpreted with this in mind.

See also series F360–379 and F380–399 for estimates by groups for 1914 and 1918 to 1929.

F298–315. Foreign trade, domestic exports, by main groups, declared values (adjusted) and values at 1948 prices, 1926 to 1960

SOURCE: D.B.S., *Review of Foreign Trade, First Half of Year, 1954*, pp. 26–30, and subsequent issues of the *Review*; data for 1959 and 1960 were provided by the External Trade Division, D.B.S.

These tables show the adjusted declared values and values at 1948 prices of Canada's domestic exports from 1926 to 1960. They differ from series F246–269 and F294–297 in several respects: (1) they cover domestic exports only; (2) they are for *adjusted* declared values; (3) the base is 1948.

In the D.B.S., *Review of Foreign Trade, First Half of the Year, 1954*, p. 23, there is the following description of methods:

Price indexes for exports and imports, designed to serve a dual purpose as deflators for the trade statistics as well as indicators of price change, have been published by the Bureau of Statistics on the present basis since 1949. These indexes are based on representative samples of the commodities entering Canada's exports and imports. Each commodity entering each sample is priced, if possible, by calculating a unit value from the trade statistics themselves. In cases where inadequate quantity reporting in the trade statistics prevents the calculation of a satisfactory unit value series use is made of alternative price sources, especially the wholesale and retail price records of Canada and the United States. The price relatives in the export and import samples are then averaged using weights representative of the base-period pattern of trade.

The adjustments made in the declared values are described as follows (p. 23):

The commodity classification used in compiling the price indexes, and to which the value series were adjusted, differs somewhat from that used in compiling the published trade statistics. These adjustments were made to simplify the pricing problem, and are not of major significance. The groups usually designated in the trade statistics as agricultural and vegetable products and animals and animal products have been combined into one group: agricultural and animal products. From this group the sub-group of rubber and its products has been transferred to the miscellaneous commodities group. Ships have been transferred from the miscellaneous commodities group to iron and steel and their products, phosphate rock from non-metallic minerals to chemicals and fertilizer, advertising matter from wood products and paper to miscellaneous commodities, and a few other changes designed to improve group classification by component material have been made. Imports of merchandise into Canada for use of the United Kingdom government or our NATO allies have been deducted from the total imports because of their special nature; otherwise the totals are the same as usually presented for Canadian trade.

Page 24 of the document quoted states:

The indexes here presented are believed to be reasonably accurate for the periods 1926–1940 and 1946–1953. For the period 1941–1945 their validity in the usual sense is dubious. The composition of Canada's trade was sharply different from its peacetime pattern in these years, but since no reliable price indicators could be obtained for the bulk of the war materials recorded in the trade statistics the price indexes could not be adjusted to reflect the change in the composition of trade. The meaning which should therefore be attached to the price indexes for the war years is that they reflect movements in prices of commodities important in Canada's peacetime trade, not that they reflect the course of prices actually used in valuing all the commodities entering Canada's trade. The difference between these two price index concepts would probably be especially pronounced in the case of the iron and steel and the non-ferrous metals groups in both exports and imports, the chemicals group in exports, and the miscellaneous products group and the total indexes for both exports and imports.

The statement continues on p. 25:

One further limitation should be mentioned which affects all price index comparisons over long periods of time. The sample of commodities and the weights used in the index are most applicable to the periods which served as the basis for their selection. As the time from the base period lengthens the universe which the sample represents will normally tend to change somewhat, and the relative importance of the various commodities in the sample will also tend to change. As a result, the index will become progressively less representative of its universe. Because the series here presented were calculated in two parts with different time and weighting bases (1935–39 and 1948), it is felt that the time distortion which would otherwise affect comparisons made with these series has been significantly reduced. However, some measure of time distortion will still apply to the series....

F316–333. Foreign trade, imports, by main groups, declared values (adjusted) and values at 1948 prices, 1926 to 1960

SOURCE: same as F298–315.

See note for F298–315.

F334–341. Foreign trade, exports excluding gold, by destination, major areas, 1886 to 1960

SOURCE: D.B.S., *Trade of Canada, 1958*, vol. 1, p. 26; data for 1959 and 1960 were provided by the External Trade Division, D.B.S.

Exports are exports of domestic and foreign produce.

F342–347. Foreign trade, imports excluding gold, by origin, major areas, 1886 to 1960

SOURCE: same as F334–341.

Imports are imports for consumption.

F348–356. Foreign trade, total exports, imports and trade balance with all countries, the United States and the United Kingdom, 1901 to 1960

SOURCE: D.B.S., *Review of Foreign Trade, 1959*, p. 53; data for 1959 and 1960, new basis, were provided by the External Trade Division, D.B.S. (see the end of the general note to series F242–399).

F357–359. Foreign trade, indexes of import and export prices and terms of trade, 1869 to 1960

SOURCE: for 1869 to 1915, Taylor, *Statistical Contributions to Canadian Economic History*, vol. 2, p. 6; for 1913 to 1926, D.B.S., *Prices and Price Indexes, 1913–1926*, p. 168, and same title, *1913–1933*, p. 191; for 1927 to 1956, D.B.S., *Review of Foreign Trade, First Half Year, 1954*, p. 26, and subsequent issues of the *Review*; for 1957 to 1960, data were provided by the External Trade Division, D.B.S.

For 1913 to 1926 the price indexes shown are those compiled in D.B.S. These were based on fifty export and sixty import items. The 1913–26 report states (p. 164):

...index numbers of export and import values are computed by the Prices' Division of the Bureau. These index numbers are so constructed as to eliminate the influence of changes in the quantities of exports and imports.... Fixed quantities of exports and imports are multiplied by the average values of each calendar year and the aggregate amounts turned into index numbers. The quantities selected refer to the year 1913, but if the quantity in that year was not considered sufficiently representative for the period investigated, it was amended by reference to later years.

For a description of the methods for 1926 to 1960, see note for F298–315.

APPENDIX TO SECTION F

F360–379. Foreign trade, exports of domestic produce, by main groups, declared values and values at prices prevailing in 1914, 1914 to 1929

SOURCE: for 1914, 1921, 1922 and 1926 to 1929, *Canada Year Book, 1930*, p. 583; for 1924 and 1925, *Canada Year Book, 1929*, p. 597; for 1923, *Canada Year Book, 1927 to 1928*, p. 608; for 1920, *Canada Year Book, 1922 to 1923*, p. 478; for 1919, *Canada Year Book, 1921*, p. 405; for 1918, *Canada Year Book, 1920*, p. 347. The trade data in declared values are given in the *Canada Year Book* of 1919 and earlier years on a different classification for the years omitted in this table.

These data were prepared at the Dominion Bureau of Statistics and are conceptually similar to Taylor's estimates (see the note to series F246–269). Although the group classifications are not the same, these series bridge in an approximate way the earlier Taylor and later D.B.S. series of exports and imports, by main groups, in current and constant prices.

F380–399. Foreign trade, imports, by main groups, declared values and values at prices prevailing in 1914, 1914 to 1929

SOURCE: same as for series F360–379, sometimes on adjacent pages.

See the note to series F360–379.

Series F1–17. *Canadian balance of international payments, between Canada and all countries, current account, 1900 to 1913*
(millions of dollars)

	Current receipts								Current payments								Current account balance
Year	Merchandise exports (adjusted)	Exports of gold coin and bullion	Tourist and travel receipts	Interest and dividends	Freight and shipping	Insurance receipts	All other current receipts[1]	Total receipts	Merchandise imports (adjusted)	Imports of gold coin and bullion	Tourist and travel payments	Interest and dividends	Freight and shipping	Insurance payments[2]	All other current payments[1]	Total current payments	
	1	2	3	4	5	6	7	8	9	10	11	12	13	14	15	16	17
1913	458.8	12.6	30.5	8.7	9.2	4.0	51.9	575.7	664.1	30.1	37.2	137.2	28.6	6.4	86.3	990.0	−414.3
1912	361.9	13.8	29.4	8.7	7.3	3.6	54.2	479.0	640.2	11.0	33.0	117.5	28.5	6.4	77.6	914.2	−435.2
1911	295.9	5.7	26.2	8.6	5.9	3.3	56.7	402.3	501.6	32.6	28.6	101.5	23.1	4.9	64.7	757.0	−354.7
1910	294.6	2.0	24.7	9.6	5.9	3.0	54.2	394.2	436.7	13.7	25.0	92.1	18.8	3.9	54.6	644.8	−250.6
1909	287.3	1.4	19.6	8.3	5.8	2.8	46.5	371.6	353.7	8.2	19.6	83.9	15.4	4.2	46.6	531.5	−159.9
1908	264.0	4.1	19.2	4.6	5.3	2.5	38.2	337.9	286.8	25.8	18.1	75.9	14.1	3.1	45.8	469.6	−131.7
1907	252.6	18.7	16.2	5.5	5.1	2.3	41.3	341.7	369.6	22.9	15.8	56.6	15.5	3.2	40.8	524.5	−182.8
1906	252.3	15.4	16.8	6.0	5.1	2.0	36.7	334.3	309.1	20.5	15.4	51.7	14.6	4.7	30.0	445.9	−111.6
1905	221.6	7.5	13.3	5.3	4.5	2.0	31.5	285.7	262.1	7.1	11.4	47.4	12.6	4.7	23.4	368.7	− 83.0
1904	195.6	2.5	12.8	4.5	3.9	1.6	23.9	244.8	246.4	10.4	8.9	43.0	11.4	+3.2	18.9	335.8	− 91.0
1903	226.5	.3	10.5	5.2	4.5	1.5	24.7	273.2	253.9	11.4	7.4	40.7	10.8	3.1	15.1	342.4	− 69.2
1902	215.3	.6	11.0	5.0	4.3	1.2	20.9	258.4	206.8	6.0	7.5	39.4	9.9	4.3	11.9	285.8	− 27.4
1901	199.5	5.7	8.0	3.9	4.0	.9	12.1	234.1	187.8	4.9	6.4	37.4	9.6	.7	8.7	255.4	− 21.3
1900	181.2	3.7	7.1	4.0	3.6	.7	10.2	210.5	181.6	7.7	5.9	36.0	9.2	.5	7.1	247.0	− 36.5

[1] Includes capital of immigrants and emigrants and noncommercial remittances.   [2] Excess of claims receipts over premium payments shown as a plus sign.

Series F18–33. *Canadian balance of international payments, between Canada and all countries, capital account, 1900 to 1913*
(millions of dollars)

	Investments by Canadian banks in		Miscellaneous Canadian investments abroad	Total Canadian capital moving abroad	British and foreign capital investments in Canada										Totals net	
					Securities			Miscellaneous			Total					
Year	Foreign securities	Banking abroad			By Britain	By United States	By other countries	By Britain	By United States	By other countries	By Britain	By United States	By other countries	All countries	Net capital movement	Errors and omissions
	18	19	20	21	22	23	24	25	26	27	28	29	30	31	32	33
1913	1.5	12.3	5.0	18.8	359.9	85.1	18.3	15.8	49.9	17.7	375.7	135.0	36.0	546.7	+527.9	+113.6
1912	2.6	7.8[1]	5.0	.2[1]	194.6	34.6	5.0	20.2	47.1	19.6	214.8	81.7	24.6	321.1	+321.3	−113.9
1911	3.6	5.1[1]	5.0	3.5	222.1	21.1	.4	22.3	55.1	27.4	244.4	76.1	27.8	348.4	+344.9	− 9.8
1910	6.3	37.2[1]	5.0	25.9[1]	188.5	6.1	6.8	30.0	66.5	15.3	218.4	72.7	22.1	313.2	+339.1	+ 88.5
1909	3.9	25.7	4.0	33.6	187.5	20.4	1.1	25.2	15.8	3.4	212.7	36.2	4.5	253.4	+219.8	+ 59.9
1908	1.5	87.0	4.0	92.5	156.5	12.3	4.5	24.9	20.5	3.4	181.4	32.7	8.0	222.1	+129.6	− 2.1
1907	.3	26.2[1]	4.0	21.8[1]	41.0	10.3	.4	24.2	15.7	3.4	65.3	26.0	3.8	95.1	+116.9	− 65.9
1906	1.2	16.7[1]	3.0	12.5[1]	46.7	12.1	3.8	21.8	17.5	3.4	68.5	29.5	7.3	105.3	+117.8	+ 6.2
1905	.6	12.2	3.0	15.8	54.5	14.8	.3	21.9	17.7	3.4	76.4	32.4	3.7	112.5	+ 96.7	+ 13.7
1904	.3	17.9[1]	3.0	21.2	23.9	6.5	3.2	5.6	19.3	3.4	29.5	25.8	6.6	61.9	+ 40.7	− 50.3
1903	1.0	20.7[1]	3.0	16.7[1]	23.7	3.5	.3	5.2	18.6	3.4	28.9	22.1	3.7	54.7	+ 71.4	+ 2.2
1902	3.3	2.0[1]	2.0	3.3	6.6	5.6	3.6	5.3	17.8	3.4	11.9	23.3	7.1	42.3	+ 39.0	+ 11.6
1901	4.3	22.4	2.0	28.7	10.0	1.0	.3	5.0	17.3	3.4	15.1	18.3	3.7	37.1	+ 8.4	− 12.9
1900	7.2	12.1[1]	2.0	2.9[1]	5.1	1.0	.3	5.0	16.9	3.4	10.1	17.9	3.7	31.7	+ 34.6	− 1.9
1899[2]	—	—	—	100.0	—	—	—	—	—	—	1,040.0	150.0	10.0	1,200.0	—	—

[1] Capital withdrawals from abroad.   [2] Total outstanding at end of 1899.

Series F 34–46. *Canadian balance of international payments, between Canada and all countries, current account, 1900 to 1926*
(millions of dollars)

Year	Current receipts						Current payments					Net balance	
	Merchandise exports (adjusted)	Gold trade balance	Tourist and travel receipts	Interest and dividends	All other current receipts	Total receipts (excluding gold)	Merchandise imports (adjusted)	Tourist and travel expenditures	Interest and dividend payments	All other current payments	Total current payments	Net balance including all gold	Net balance excluding all gold
	34	35	36	37	38	39	40	41	42	43	44	45	46
1926	1,266.5	+38.0	182.2	45.3	167.5	1,661.5	989.1	79.1	263.4	156.7	1,488.3	+211.2	+173.2
1925	1,241.1	+19.9	170.4	40.2	140.2	1,591.9	872.4	69.7	250.7	145.8	1,338.6	+273.2	+253.3
1924	1,032.6	+ 7.0	149.4	40.3	131.3	1,353.6	789.9	68.3	242.3	122.6	1,223.1	+137.5	+130.5
1923	1,003.9	+80.3	130.7	40.5	135.3	1,310.4	885.1	61.8	254.0	139.7	1,340.6	+ 50.1	− 30.2
1922	884.1	−46.0	110.5	39.9	116.9	1,151.4	744.6	56.8	230.3	121.1	1,152.8	− 47.4	− 1.4
1921	800.4	+42.0	98.2	47.3	124.7	1,070.6	827.8	57.5	234.3	150.2	1,269.8	−157.2	−199.2
1920	1,267.1	+35.0	91.4	46.8	159.9	1,565.2	1,428.7	62.5	212.9	219.5	1,923.6	−323.4	−358.4
1919	1,261.7	+13.9	75.9	39.6	122.0	1,499.2	951.4	52.4	211.5	247.5	1,462.8	+ 50.3	+ 36.4
1918	1,209.4	+16.0	66.8	32.4	108.6	1,417.2	922.4	34.7	214.0	343.9	1,515.0	− 81.8	− 97.8
1917	1,555.2	− .9	55.1	28.3	110.7	1,749.3	996.5	31.5	204.1	340.3	1,572.4	+176.0	+176.9
1916	1,072.4	+11.6	45.8	23.6	114.5	1,256.3	762.4	29.3	190.5	262.8	1,245.0	+ 22.9	+ 11.3
1915	613.9	−14.6	37.2	13.1	91.0	755.2	447.2	29.2	173.3	148.2	797.9	− 57.3	− 42.7
1914	369.1	+23.0	34.8	16.6	73.2	493.7	470.8	41.8	180.9	111.4	804.9	−288.2	−311.2
1913	442.9	− 4.8	30.5	8.7	65.1	547.2	654.9	37.2	137.2	121.3	950.6	−408.2	−403.4
1912	351.7	+12.8	29.4	8.7	65.1	454.9	626.0	33.0	117.5	112.5	889.0	−421.3	−434.1
1911	284.1	−19.4	26.2	8.6	65.9	384.8	506.3	28.6	101.5	92.7	729.1	−363.7	−344.3
1910	280.8	− 6.1	24.7	9.6	63.1	378.2	429.0	25.0	92.1	77.3	623.4	−251.3	−245.2
1909	269.0	− 1.1	19.6	8.3	55.2	352.1	339.6	19.6	83.9	66.2	509.3	−158.3	−157.2
1908	249.3	−13.9	19.2	4.6	46.0	319.1	282.6	18.1	75.9	63.0	439.6	−134.4	−120.5
1907	253.8	+ 3.8	16.2	5.5	48.7	324.2	363.0	15.8	56.6	59.5	494.9	−166.9	−170.7
1906	254.0	+ 6.1	16.8	6.0	43.8	320.6	312.3	15.4	51.7	49.3	428.7	−102.0	−108.1
1905	205.2	+14.0	13.3	5.3	38.0	261.8	263.6	11.4	47.4	40.7	363.1	− 87.3	−101.3
1904	176.1	+ 7.9	12.8	4.5	29.4	222.8	249.2	8.9	43.0	27.1	328.2	− 97.5	−105.4
1903	201.9	+ 6.5	10.5	5.2	30.7	248.3	251.8	7.4	40.7	29.0	328.9	− 74.1	− 80.6
1902	190.4	+11.6	11.0	5.0	26.4	232.8	203.4	7.5	39.4	26.1	276.4	− 32.0	− 43.6
1901	170.2	+23.2	8.0	3.9	17.0	199.1	182.6	6.4	37.4	19.0	245.4	− 23.1	− 46.3
1900	156.0	+16.0	7.1	4.0	14.5	181.6	176.5	5.9	36.0	15.8	234.2	− 36.6	− 52.6

Series F 47–56. *Canadian balance of international payments, between Canada and all countries, capital account, 1900 to 1926*
(millions of dollars)

Year	New issues Canadian securities	Retirement of Canadian securities	Net movement (+) inward net retirement (−)[1]	Net sales of outstanding securities (estimated)	Dominion Government dealing with other governments, war finance	Net change in external assets of Canadian banks	Other capital movements net	Total net movement of capital	Balance on current account	Balancing item; errors or omissions
	47	48	49	50	51	52	53	54	55	56
1926	326.2	165.9	+161.0	−135.0	+ 2.3	− 51.8	+ 26.3	+ 2.8	+211.2	−214.0
1925	239.8	231.4	+ 13.0	− 80.0	+ 1.9	− 92.8	+ 14.6	−143.3	+273.2	−129.9
1924	280.6	146.2	+143.0	− 50.0	+ 20.7	− 15.7	− .4	+ 97.6	+137.5	−235.1
1923	156.3	51.0	+109.6	− 40.0	+ 63.8	− 12.7	+ 9.0	+129.7	+ 50.1	−179.8
1922	292.6	80.4	+210.3	− 20.0	+ 46.8	+ 27.0	− .01	+264.1	− 47.4	−216.7
1921	246.3	113.9	+123.6	− 40.0	+ 27.9	+144.4	+ 26.1	+282.0	−157.2	−124.8
1920	221.5	61.0	+153.7	− 55.0	+ 31.0	+ 42.4	+ 13.5	+185.6	−323.4	+137.8
1919	239.4	216.2	+ 25.1	− 40.0	− 25.6	− 21.7	+ 30.9	− 31.3	+ 50.3	− 19.0
1918	56.4	66.5	− 12.8	− 10.0	−119.3	− 28.5	+ 6.3	−164.3	− 81.8	+246.1
1917	196.2	68.7	+126.9	− 10.0	−113.1	+ 10.8	+ 12.4	+ 27.0	+176.0	−203.0
1916	315.0	56.3	+254.2	− 8.0	− 52.6	−129.4	+ 8.2	+ 72.4	+ 22.9	− 95.3
1915	236.7	54.0	+179.0	− 5.0	+ 60.4	−113.4	+ .4	+121.4	− 57.3	− 64.1
1914	197.1	4.5	+298.1	− 3.0	+ 24.3	+ 21.2	+ 1.2	+341.8	−288.2	− 53.6
1913	—	—	+463.2	—	—	− 15.9	+ 78.5	+525.8	−408.2	−117.6
1912	—	—	+236.1	—	—	+ 8.4	+ 80.0	+324.5	−421.3	+ 96.8
1911	—	—	+255.5	—	—	+ 8.7	+ 87.9	+352.1	−363.7	+ 11.6
1910	—	—	+202.0	—	—	+ 33.5	+106.2	+341.7	−251.3	− 90.4
1909	—	—	+209.0	—	—	− 31.8	+ 40.4	+217.6	−158.3	− 59.3
1908	—	—	+173.3	—	—	− 99.0	+ 44.8	+119.1	−134.4	+ 15.3
1907	—	—	+ 51.7	—	—	+ 25.9	+ 39.4	+117.0	−166.9	+ 49.9
1906	—	—	+ 62.6	—	—	+ 13.3	+ 39.7	+115.6	−102.0	− 13.6
1905	—	—	+ 69.5	—	—	− 10.4	+ 40.0	+ 99.1	− 87.3	− 11.8
1904	—	—	+ 33.6	—	—	− 23.4	+ 25.3	+ 35.5	− 97.5	+ 62.0
1903	—	—	+ 27.5	—	—	+ 20.4	+ 24.2	+ 72.1	− 74.1	+ 2.0
1902	—	—	+ 15.8	—	—	− 2.0	+ 24.5	+ 38.3	− 32.0	− 6.3
1901	—	—	+ 11.3	—	—	− 24.5	+ 23.8	+ 10.6	− 23.1	+ 12.5
1900	—	—	+ 6.4	—	—	+ 12.1	+ 23.4	+ 41.9	− 36.6	− 5.3

[1] For the years 1914 to 1926, complete new issues and retirement figures are not available; some small net amounts are included in series F 49 thus explaining the apparent arithmetical errors in these columns during those years.

Series F 57–71. *Canadian balance of international payments, all countries and by major areas, current account, 1926 to 1945*

(millions of dollars)

| | Current receipts | | | | | | | Current payments | | | | | | | |
Year	Merchandise exports	Net exports of non-monetary gold[1]	Tourist and travel expenditures	Interest and dividends	Freight and shipping	All other current credits[2]	All current receipts	Merchandise imports	Tourist and travel expenditures	Interest and dividends	Freight and shipping	Canadian overseas expenditures	All other current debits	All current payments	Net balance[3]
	57	58	59	60	61	62	63	64	65	66	67	68	69	70	71
1938 to 1945 basis							All countries								
1945	3,474	96	165	80	340	301	4,456	1,442	83	251	222	721	191	2,910	+ 1,546
1944	3,590	110	119	71	322	345	4,557	1,398	58	264	252	1,085	482	3,539	+ 1,018
1943	3,050	142	88	59	288	437	4,064	1,579	36	261	294	499	189	2,858	+ 1,206
1942	2,515	184	81	67	221	308	3,376	1,406	26	270	228	191	154	2,275	+ 1,101
1941	1,732	204	111	60	185	166	2,458	1,264	21	286	167	97	132	1,967	+ 491
1940	1,202	203	104	52	138	77	1,776	1,006	43	313	132	29	104	1,627	+ 149
1939	906	184	149	57	102	59	1,457	713	81	306	119	—	112	1,331	+ 126
1938	844	161	149	66	95	46	1,361	649	86	307	105	—	114	1,261	+ 100
1926 to 1937 basis															
1937	1,041	145	166	76	112	53	1,593	776	87	302	137	—	111	1,413	+ 180
1936	954	132	142	75	80	47	1,430	612	75	311	97	—	91	1,186	+ 244
1935	732	119	117	64	68	45	1,145	526	64	270	82	—	78	1,020	+ 125
1934	648	114	106	57	52	43	1,020	484	50	268	79	—	71	952	+ 68
1933	532	82	89	38	44	44	829	368	44	264	66	—	89	831	— 2
1932	495	70	114	37	38	54	808	398	49	302	66	—	89	904	— 96
1931	601	57	153	48	54	59	972	580	71	330	79	—	86	1,146	— 174
1930	880	39	180	59	70	69	1,297	973	92	348	103	—	118	1,634	— 337
1929	1,178	37	198	61	92	80	1,646	1,272	108	322	130	—	125	1,957	— 311
1928	1,341	40	177	46	96	88	1,788	1,209	98	275	116	—	122	1,820	— 32
1927	1,215	32	163	41	97	85	1,633	1,057	100	257	109	—	120	1,643	— 10
1926	1,272	30	152	32	96	83	1,665	973	99	240	105	—	121	1,538	+ 127
1938 to 1945 basis							United Kingdom								
1945	1,422	0	2	4	145	100	1,673	100	2	53	30	696	45	926	+ 747
1944	1,796	0	2	8	139	118	2,063	94	2	55	28	1,085	53	1,317	+ 746
1943	1,636	0	1	4	128	120	1,889	100	2	51	40	499	48	740	+ 1,149
1942	1,424	0	2	5	114	112	1,657	116	2	50	41	191	34	434	+ 1,223
1941	914	0	2	4	110	63	1,093	137	2	66	28	97	29	359	+ 734
1940	542	0	5	2	60	27	636	133	2	74	32	29	23	293	+ 343
1939	332	0	7	2	34	9	384	106	11	78	36	—	16	247	+ 137
1938	337	0	8	2	34	8	389	119	15	81	30	—	17	262	+ 127
1926 to 1937 basis															
1937	385	0	11	2	38	8	444	148	16	85	43	—	17	309	+ 135
1936	342	0	8	2	23	7	382	120	15	84	26	—	15	260	+ 122
1935	258	0	7	2	21	7	295	110	12	76	21	—	14	233	+ 62
1934	234	0	7	2	11	7	261	103	10	75	14	—	13	215	+ 46
1933	188	0	5	2	8	11	214	80	10	72	12	—	14	188	+ 26
1932	149	0	7	1	5	14	176	61	14	91	11	—	13	190	— 14
1931	139	0	8	1	9	13	170	85	14	102	12	—	14	224	— 54
1930	174	0	8	2	7	12	203	147	18	115	12	—	17	309	— 106
1929	224	0	9	2	8	13	256	188	20	113	12	—	22	355	— 99
1928	288	0	9	2	11	13	323	194	19	100	10	—	21	344	— 21
1927	271	0	10	2	10	12	305	171	20	101	11	—	21	324	— 19
1926	315	0	8	2	15	12	352	148	21	97	8	—	20	294	+ 58
1938 to 1945 basis							Other sterling area[4]								
1945	354	0	—[5]	4	38	19	415	113	—[5]	1	4	—	2	120	+ 295
1944	174	0	—[5]	1	30	39	244	102	—[5]	1	5	—	3	111	+ 133
1943	127	0	—[5]	1	20	29	177	100	—[5]	1	7	—	2	110	+ 67
1942	117	0	—[5]	2	13	37	169	110	—[5]	1	8	—	4	123	+ 46
1941	184	0	1	1	9	33	228	142	1	2	8	—	4	157	+ 71
1940	157	0	1	1	16	11	186	103	1	2	4	—	—[5]	110	+ 76
1939	104	0	2	3	9	—[5]	118	71	2	2	3	—	1	79	+ 39
1938	105	0	2	3	9	—[5]	119	65	2	2	4	—	2	75	+ 44

Series F 57–71. *Canadian balance of international payments, all countries and by major areas, current account, 1926 to 1945*
(continued)

(millions of dollars)

Year	Current receipts							Current payments							Net balance[3]
	Merchandise exports	Net exports of nonmonetary gold[1]	Tourist and travel expenditures	Interest and dividends	Freight and shipping	All other current credits[2]	All current receipts	Merchandise imports	Tourist and travel expenditures	Interest and dividends	Freight and shipping	Canadian overseas expenditures	All other current debits	All current payments	
	57	58	59	60	61	62	63	64	65	66	67	68	69	70	71
United States															
1938 to 1945 basis															
1945	1,134	96	163	48	134	169	1,744	1,119	81	192	188	—	128	1,708	+ 36
1944	1,444	110	117	42	146	176	2,035	1,113	56	203	219	—	413[6]	2,004	+ 31
1943	1,224	142	87	34	137	274	1,898	1,311	34	205	247	—	120	1,917	− 19
1942	911	184	79	43	92	152	1,461	1,116	24	215	179	—	107	1,641	− 180
1941	566	204	107	39	64	65	1,045	910	18	214	131	—	90	1,363	− 318
1940	424	203	98	29	49	31	834	702	40	233	78	—	73	1,126	− 292
1939	344	184	137	27	46	42	780	472	67	220	61	—	76	896	− 116
1938	268	161	134	25	39	36	663	400	66	218	55	—	73	812	− 149
1926 to 1937 basis															
1937	391	145	149	31	45	42	803	463	65	211	68	—	73	880	− 77
1936	369	132	129	31	41	36	738	352	54	222	53	—	58	739	− 1
1935	285	119	107	24	33	35	603	299	48	190	47	—	48	632	− 29
1934	226	114	96	20	32	33	521	278	36	189	55	—	43	601	− 80
1933	177	82	81	17	28	30	415	205	30	188	45	—	60	528	− 113
1932	169	70	103	18	25	37	422	246	30	205	48	—	61	590	− 168
1931	254	57	141	25	38	41	556	372	52	221	61	—	55	761	− 205
1930	397	39	167	30	52	51	736	634	67	225	80	—	74	1,080	− 344
1929	519	37	184	30	68	61	899	875	81	202	103	—	75	1,336	− 437
1928	507	40	163	20	68	69	867	810	72	169	92	—	73	1,216	− 349
1927	489	32	148	16	69	67	821	690	72	151	84	—	72	1,069	− 248
1926	476	30	140	12	64	65	787	652	70	138	85	—	73	1,018	− 231
Other countries															
1938 to 1945 basis															
1945	564	0	—[5]	24	23	13	624	110	—[5]	5	—[7]	—	41	156	+ 468
1944	176	0	—[5]	20	7	12	215	89	—[5]	5	—[7]	—	13	107	+ 108
1943	63	0	—[5]	20	3	14	100	68	—[5]	4	—[7]	—	19	91	+ 9
1942	63	0	—[5]	17	2	7	89	64	—[5]	4	—[7]	—	9	77	+ 12
1941	68	0	1	16	2	5	92	75	—[5]	4	—[7]	—	9	88	+ 4
1940	79	0	—[5]	20	13	8	120	68	—[5]	4	18	—	8	98	+ 22
1939	126	0	3	25	13	8	175	64	1	6	19	—	19	109	+ 66
1938	134	0	5	36	13	2	190	65	3	6	16	—	22	112	+ 78
1926 to 1937 basis															
1937	265	0	6	43	29	3	346	165	6	6	26	—	21	224	+ 122
1936	243	0	5	42	16	4	310	140	6	5	18	—	18	187	+ 123
1935	189	0	3	38	14	3	247	117	4	4	14	—	16	155	+ 92
1934	188	0	3	35	9	3	238	103	4	4	10	—	15	136	+ 102
1933	167	0	3	19	8	3	200	83	4	4	9	—	15	115	+ 85
1932	177	0	4	18	8	3	210	91	5	6	7	—	15	124	+ 86
1931	208	0	4	22	7	5	246	123	5	7	9	—	17	161	+ 85
1930	309	0	5	27	11	6	358	192	7	8	11	—	27	245	+ 113
1929	435	0	5	29	16	6	491	209	7	7	15	—	28	266	+ 225
1928	546	0	5	24	17	6	598	205	7	6	14	—	28	260	+ 338
1927	455	0	5	23	18	6	507	196	8	5	14	—	27	250	+ 257
1926	481	0	4	18	17	6	526	173	8	5	12	—	28	226	+ 300

[1] All exports of nonmonetary gold are included in the account with the United States.

[2] In millions of dollars, 10, 45, 96, 104, 96 and 95 of war services to the United Kingdom are included in 'all other current credits' in the years from 1940 to 1945, respectively.

[3] Including Mutual Aid and other contributions as shown in the capital accounts. See series F 104–163.

[4] Includes only 'other Commonwealth' in 1938 and 1939. Both 'other Commonwealth countries' and 'other sterling area' are included in the final panel of the table from 1926 to 1937, that is, in countries other than the United Kingdom and the United States.

[5] Less than $500,000.

[6] Includes $280 million special payments to United States Treasury.

[7] Included in the amount shown for the United States.

Series F72–90. *Canadian balance of international payments, all countries and by major areas, current account, 1946 to 1960*

(millions of dollars)

Year	72 Merchandise exports (adjusted)	73 Mutual aid to NATO countries	74 Gold production available for export	75 Travel expenditures	76 Interest and dividends	77 Freight and shipping	78 Inheritances and immigrants' funds	79 All other current receipts[1]	80 Total current receipts	81 Merchandise imports (adjusted)	82 Travel expenditures	83 Interest and dividends	84 Freight and shipping	85 Inheritances and immigrants' funds	86 Official contributions	87 Mutual aid to NATO countries	88 All other current payments	89 Total current payments[2]	90 Current account balance
All countries																			
1960	5,392	43	162	420	173	442	102	419	7,153	5,540	627	653	533	181	61	43	758	8,396	−1,243
1959	5,150	63	148	391	182	420	109	392	6,855	5,572	598	671	525	165	72	63	693	8,359	−1,504
1958	4,887	142	160	349	168	401	97	375	6,579	5,066	542	612	460	145	53	142	690	7,710	−1,131
1957	4,894	107	147	363	154	445	124	388	6,622	5,488	525	589	515	157	40	107	656	8,077	−1,455
1956	4,837	157	150	337	142	457	99	442	6,621	5,565	498	523	502	115	30	157	597	7,987	−1,366
1955	4,332	222	155	328	160	398	86	391	6,072	4,543	449	483	415	105	24	222	529	6,770	−698
1954	3,929	284	155	305	147	313	89	208	5,520	3,916	389	423	356	94	11	284	479	5,952	−432
1953	4,152	246	144	302	165	318	91	281	5,737	4,210	365	404	374	91	25	246	465	6,180	−443
1952	4,339	200	150	275	145	383	85	281	5,858	3,850	341	413	375	94	16	200	405	5,694	+164
1951	3,950	145	150	274	115	351	77	249	5,311	4,097	286	450	354	70	9	145	423	5,828	−517
1950	3,139	57	163	275	91	284	57	231	4,297	3,129	226	475	301	61	5	57	377	4,631	−334
1949	2,989	—	139	285	83	303	68	222	4,089	2,696	193	390	253	59	6	—	315	3,912	+177
1948	3,030[3]	—	119	279	70	336	84	229	4,147	2,598	134	325	279	50	23	—	287	3,696	+451
1947	2,723[3]	—	99	251	64	322	69	220	3,748	2,535	167	337	278	49	38	—	295	3,699	+49
1946	2,393[3]	—	96	221	70	311	65	209	3,365	1,822	135	312	219	35	97	—	382	3,002	+363
United Kingdom																			
1960	924	—	—	20	32	93	26	50	1,145	611	70	83	89	25	3	0	98	979	+166
1959	781	—	—	18	35	80	26	43	983	618	62	90	85	26	0	0	89	970	+13
1958	766	—	—	18	32	84	17	43	960	537	52	76	70	26	0	0	95	856	+104
1957	734	—	—	18	10	95	40	41	938	520	47	78	69	20	0	0	86	820	+118
1956	818	—	—	14	14	98	24	47	1,015	493	46	73	59	14	0	0	78	763	+252
1955	772	—	—	13	41	97	20	39	982	406	40	75	49	16	0	0	66	652	+330
1954	660	—	—	13	35	73	19	36	836	391	35	62	39	13	0	0	67	607	+229
1953	656	—	—	12	28	79	18	37	830	463	31	57	42	12	0	0	92	697	+133
1952	727	—	—	10	29	105	20	34	925	350	27	56	43	12	0	0	50	537	+388
1951	636	—	—	8	30	91	14	42	821	417	20	57	43	10	0	0	51	598	+223
1950	469	—	—	7	6	61	12	35	590	399	19	54	36	10	0	0	48	566	+24
1949	701	—	—	11	9	89	38	49	897	300	17	55	32	10	0	0	37	451	+446
1948	703	—	—	9	9	105	52	44	922	287	12	50	34	7	0	0	46	436	+486
1947	749	—	—	7	8	114	47	42	967	182	9	53	32	8	0	0	50	334	+633
1946	626	—	—	3	7	107	45	52	840	138	3	54	32	3	0	0	110	340	+500
Other sterling area																			
1960	340	—	—	6	18	31	6	8	409	284	14	1	4	2	42	0	19	366	+43
1959	288	—	—	6	28	26	7	8	363	263	13	1	3	3	64	0	17	364	−2
1958	299	—	—	6	13	24	13	8	363	212	11	1	3	2	49	0	16	294	+69
1957	246	—	—	5	22	27	8	7	315	239	11	1	2	2	38	0	18	311	+4
1956	256	—	—	4	21	29	5	9	324	222	8	1	3	1	28	0	13	276	+48
1955	254	—	—	4	21	27	4	8	318	211	8	1	3	1	22	0	12	258	+60
1954	206	—	—	3	17	18	4	7	255	183	7	—	3	1	8	0	9	211	+44
1953	251	—	—	3	13	18	4	7	296	172	6	—	6	1	18	0	10	213	+83
1952	293	—	—	3	7	20	3	5	331	185	5	—	5	1	15	0	6	217	+114
1951	265	—	—	3	4	23	3	3	301	310	5	—	5	1	—	0	4	325	−24
1950	201	—	—	3	8	18	1	3	234	244	5	—	3	1	—	0	6	257	−23
1949	300	—	—	2	4	30	1	3	340	187	4	—	5	2	—	0	4	205	+135
1948	293	—	—	1	4	34	2	4	338	192	4	—	7	1	—	0	4	209	+129
1947	366	—	—	1	6	39	1	3	416	160	3	—	5	1	—	0	5	174	+242
1946	269	—	—	1	2	34	—	3	309	129	1	—	6	—	5	0	3	145	+164

Series F 72–90. *Canadian balance of international payments, all countries and by major areas, current account, 1946 to 1960 (continued)*

(millions of dollars)

Year	72 Merchandise exports (adjusted)	73 Mutual aid to NATO countries	74 Gold production available for export	75 Travel expenditures	76 Interest and dividends	77 Freight and shipping	78 Inheritances and immigrants' funds	79 All other current receipts[1]	80 Total current receipts	81 Merchandise imports (adjusted)	82 Travel expenditures	83 Interest and dividends	84 Freight and shipping	85 Inheritances and immigrants' funds	86 Official contributions	87 Mutual aid to NATO countries	88 All other current payments	89 Total current payments[2]	90 Current account balance
United States																			
1960	3,040	—	162	375	102	220	50	330	4,279	3,713	462	531	324	141	0	0	469	5,640	−1,361
1959	3,101	—	148	351	99	228	52	311	4,380	3,727	448	547	326	123	0	0	439	5,610	−1,230
1958	2,908	—	160	309	100	206	47	280	4,010	3,443	413	500	294	104	0	0	432	5,186	−1,176
1957	2,931	—	147	325	95	222	47	303	4,070	3,878	403	480	351	124	0	0	413	5,649	−1,579
1956	2,854	—	150	309	80	223	45	354	4,015	4,021	391	427	351	94	0	0	370	5,654	−1,639
1955	2,508	—	155	303	78	203	45	318	3,700	3,283	363	388	287	82	0	0	332	4,735	−1,035
1954	2,355	—	155	283	69	169	42	233	3,306	2,800	320	345	261	75	0	0	312	4,113	−807
1953	2,458	—	144	282	101	164	41	253	3,443	3,046	307	334	296	74	0	0	290	4,347	−904
1952	2,346	—	150	257	85	174	38	224	3,274	2,817	294	344	302	77	0	0	289	4,123	−849
1951	2,326	—	150	258	57	164	32	191	3,178	2,842	246	382	276	55	0	0	328	4,129	−951
1950	2,046	—	163	260	50	157	31	170	2,877	2,093	193	411	240	47	0	0	293	3,277	−400
1949	1,521	—	139	267	40	126	18	158	2,259	1,809	165	325	193	44	0	0	244	2,870	−601
1948	1,508	—	119	267	37	131	18	167	2,247	1,797	113	267	213	37	0	0	213	2,640	−393
1947	1,061	—	99	241	36	104	18	153	1,712	1,951	152	274	221	37	0	0	211	2,846	−1,134
1946	948	—	96	216	47	101	19	140	1,507	1,378	130	250	169	31	0	0	216	2,174	−607
O.E.E.C. countries other than Commonwealth																			
1960	591	—	—	13	12	57	15	19	707	371	65	36	99	11	4	—	135	721	−14
1959	449	—	—	11	11	49	16	20	556	364	60	31	95	11	1	—	114	676	−120
1958	522	—	—	11	13	46	14	29	635	302	52	33	70	14	1	—	116	594	+41
1957	502	—	—	10	12	54	22	24	624	286	48	28	80	10	1	—	104	557	+67
1956	470	—	—	6	12	61	18	18	585	320	41	20	75	4	1	—	107	568	+17
1955	379	—	—	5	13	39	13	15	464	229	32	17	64	4	1	—	93	440	+24
1954	351	—	—	4	12	29	20	12	428	188	23	14	42	4	1	—	63	335	+93
1953	371	—	—	4	13	30	22	10	450	173	18	11	23	3	1	—	48	277	+173
1952	473	—	—	4	13	43	20	9	562	149	13	11	19	3	—	—	34	230	+332
1951	366	—	—	4	14	40	22	5	451	173	8	9	21	3	—	—	14	228	+223
1950	200	—	—	4	14	24	11	12	265	113	8	8	14	2	2	—	10	157	+108
1949	246	—	—	4	14	28	8	4	304	79	6	7	16	2	1	—	8	119	+185
1948	296	—	—	2	6	32	8	4	348	75	4	5	15	2	13	—	9	122	+226
1947	333	—	—	1	2	38	2	7	383	64	2	7	14	1	7	—	11	107	+276
1946	321	—	—	1	2	45	1	4	374	38	1	5	9	1	34	—	38	126	+248
Countries other than sterling, O.E.E.C. and United States[4]																			
1960	497	—	—	6	9	41	5	12	570	561	16	2	17	2	12	—	37	647	−77
1959	441	—	—	5	9	37	8	11	511	600	15	2	16	2	7	—	34	676	−165
1958	392	—	—	5	10	41	6	15	469	572	14	2	14	2	3	—	31	638	−169
1957	481	—	—	5	15	47	7	13	568	565	16	2	13	1	1	—	35	633	−65
1956	439	—	—	4	15	46	7	14	525	509	12	2	14	2	1	—	29	569	−44
1955	329	—	—	3	7	32	4	11	386	414	6	2	12	2	1	—	26	463	−77
1954	357	—	—	2	14	24	4	10	411	354	4	2	11	1	2	—	28	402	+9
1953	416	—	—	1	10	27	6	12	472	356	3	2	7	1	6	—	25	400	+72
1952	500	—	—	1	11	41	4	9	566	349	1	2	7	1	—	—	26	387	+179
1951	357	—	—	1	10	33	6	8	415	355	1	2	9	1	9	—	26	403	+12
1950	223	—	—	1	13	24	2	11	274	280	1	2	8	1	1	—	22	317	−43
1949	221	—	—	—	16	30	4	8	279	231	1	2	7	1	5	—	20	267	+12
1948	230	—	—	—	14	34	3	10	292	247	1	2	10	4	10	—	15	289	+3
1947	214	—	—	1	12	27	1	15	270	178	1	2	6	2	31	—	18	238	+32
1946	229	—	—	—	12	24	—	10	275	139	—	2	3	—	58	—	15	217	+58

[1] Includes war services in 1946 of $24 million.

[2] Military receipts and expenditures are included in F 88 in 1946, and thereafter in trade figures, in Mutual Aid to NATO countries, and in 'all other receipts and payments'.

[3] Includes receipts by War Supplies, Ltd, from sale of war material and equipment to the United States of $55 million and $13 million in 1946 and 1947, respectively.

[4] Includes O.E.E.C. dependencies, 1957 to 1960.

Series F 91–103. *Canadian balance of international payments, all countries and by major areas, capital account, 1927 to 1937*
(millions of dollars)

Year	New issues of Canadian securities	Retirement of Canadian securities	Net new issues (+) or net retirements (−)	Net sales (+) or net purchases (−) of outstanding securities		Direct investment transactions	Insurance transactions	Net change in the external assets of Canadian banks	Monetary gold movement (net)	Other capital movements[1]	Net capital movement[2]	Net balance on current account	Balancing item
				Estimated	Recorded								
	91	**92**	**93**	**94**	**95**	**96**	**97**	**98**	**99**	**100**	**101**	**102**	**103**
					All countries								
1937	+ 90	−170	− 80	—	− 5	−64	−10	−13	—	—	−172	+180	− 8
1936	+106	−270	−164	—	+ 8	−62	−26	+ 3	—	—	−241	+244	− 3
1935	+117	−256	−139	—	+51	−44	−18	—	− 2	—	−152	+125	+27
1934	+111	−169	− 58	—	+ 9	−45	+ 3	−19	− 4	—	−114	+ 68	+46
1933	+134	−166	− 32	—	+51	−59	− 1	+24	+ 6	—	− 11	− 2	+13
1932	+104	−105	− 1	+ 85	—	−28	− 1	+38	+ 3	—	+ 96	− 96	—
1931	+200	−202	− 2	+ 45	—	+10	+34	+28	+33	+26	+174	−174	—
1930	+400	−110	+290	+ 56	—	+37	+ 9	—	−36	−19	+337	−337	—
1929	+297	−150	+147	− 2	—	+18	+19	+88	+37	+ 4	+311	−311	—
1928	+207	−200	+ 7	−126	—	+21	−12	+87	+49	+ 6	+ 32	− 32	—
1927	+301	−160	+141	−171	—	+35	−15	+16	− 7	+11	+ 10	− 10	—
					United Kingdom								
1937	+ 4	− 29	− 25	—	+20	− 3	—	− 16	—	—	− 24	+135	—
1936	+ 1	− 33	− 32	—	+12	− 6	− 6	+ 3	—	—	− 29	+122	—
1935	+ 5	− 29	− 24	—	−13	− 2	− 9	+ 5	—	—	− 43	+ 62	—
1934	+ 57	− 47	+ 10	—	+78	− 1	+11	+ 1	—	—	+ 99	+ 46	—
1933	+ 73	− 35	+ 38	—	+53	− 3	+10	− 4	—	—	+ 94	+ 26	—
1932	+ 17	− 30	− 13	− 5	—	− 8	+ 4	+ 5	—	—	− 17	− 14	—
1931	+ 1	− 22	− 21	− 20	—	− 2	+ 3	+17	—	—	− 23	− 54	—
1930	+ 18	− 36	− 18	+ 4	—	− 9	+ 3	−10	—	+ 2	− 28	−106	—
1929	+ 28	− 43	− 15	—	—	—	+ 4	+ 3	—	—	− 8	− 99	—
1928	+ 21	− 64	− 43	− 5	—	+ 2	− 4	+ 9	—	—	− 41	− 21	—
1927	+ 45	− 60	− 15	− 5	—	+10	− 5	− 1	—	—	− 16	− 19	—
					United States								
1937	+ 86	−140	− 54	—	−36	−58	−12	+ 3	—	—	−157	− 77	—
1936	+105	−236	−131	—	− 8	−50	−21	− 3	—	—	−213	− 1	—
1935	+112	−227	−115	—	+68	−40	−10	−20	− 2	—	−119	− 29	—
1934	+ 53	−119	− 66	—	−68	−40	− 9	−24	− 4	—	−211	− 80	—
1933	+ 60	−129	− 69	—	+ 3	−53	−12	+31	+ 6	—	− 94	−113	—
1932	+ 87	− 74	+ 13	+ 65	—	−16	− 5	+ 8	+ 3	—	+ 68	−168	—
1931	+199	−178	+ 21	+ 35	—	+14	+30	+38²	+33	—	+171	−205	—
1930	+381	− 72	+309	+ 18	—	+51	+ 5	−23²	−36	—	+324	−344	—
1929	+268	−105	+163	− 11	—	+22	+15	+92	+37	—	+318	−437	—
1928	+185	−135	+ 50	− 82	—	+26	− 8	+63	+49	—	+ 98	−349	—
1927	+255	− 99	+156	−131	—	+28	−10	+16	− 7	—	+ 52	−248	—
					Other countries								
1937	—	− 1	− 1	—	+11	− 3	+ 2	—	—	—	+ 9	+122	—
1936	—	− 1	− 1	—	+ 4	− 6	+ 1	+ 3	—	—	+ 1	+123	—
1935	—	—	—	—	− 3	− 3	+ 1	+15	—	—	+ 10	+ 92	—
1934	+ 1	− 3	− 2	—	− 1	− 4	+ 1	+ 4	—	—	− 2	+102	—
1933	+ 1	− 2	− 1	—	− 5	− 3	+ 1	− 3	—	—	− 11	+ 85	—
1932	—	− 1	− 1	+ 25	—	− 4	—	+25	—	—	+ 45	+ 86	—
1931	—	− 2	− 2	+ 30	—	− 2	+ 1	− 2	—	+ 1	+ 26	+ 85	—
1930	+ 1	− 2	− 1	+ 34	—	− 5	+ 1	+ 8	—	+ 4	+ 41	+113	—
1929	+ 1	− 2	− 1	+ 9	—	− 4	—	− 7	—	+ 4	+ 1	+225	—
1928	+ 1	− 1	—	− 39	—	− 7	—	+15	—	+ 6	− 25	+338	—
1927	+ 1	− 1	—	− 35	—	− 3	—	+ 1	—	+11	− 26	+257	—

[1] F 100 includes net loans and advances to other countries, by Canadian government, of 6 million in 1930 and 1 million in 1931.

[2] The 1930 figure contains a special entry for a government of Canada deposit in New York originating from a new issue in 1930. The 1931 figure reflects the liquidation of that asset by the Canadian government.

Series F104–145. *Canadian balance of international payments, all countries and by major areas, capital account, 1938 to 1945*
(millions of dollars)

Year	New issues of Canadian securities	Retirement of Canadian securities	Net new issues or net retirements	Net sales of outstanding securities	Canadian government loans to other countries[1] — War loans	Canadian government loans — Postwar loans	Change in reserves of gold and United States dollars increase (−)	Change in sterling balances increase (−)	Other capital movements	Net movement of capital	Mutual aid and 1942 contributions	UNRRA, military and other official relief	Current account balance	Balancing item
	104	105	106	107	108	109	110	111	112	113	114	115	116	117
							All countries							
1945	+ 91	−211	−120	+351	+ 64	−105	−667	− 1	−215[1]	−693	− 748	−110	+1,546	+ 5
1944	+ 92	−200	−108	+198	+ 57	—	−278	+ 4	+ 79	− 48	− 936	− 24	+1,018	−10
1943	+146	−322	−176	+272	+ 18	—	−364	—	−427	−677	− 512	− 6	+1,206	−11
1942	—	−351	−351	+148	−700	—	−144	+818	+123	−106	−1,000	− 2	+1,101	+ 7
1941	—	−229	−229	+ 38	—	—	+160	−728	+262	−497	—	—	+ 491	+ 6
1940	—	−191	−191	+ 5	—	—	+ 79	− 82	+ 1	−188	—	—	+ 149	+39
1939	+155	−251	− 96	+ 82	—	—	[2]	[2]	−122	−136	—	—	+ 126	+10
1938	+ 89	−151	− 62	+ 29	—	—	[2]	[2]	− 73	−106	—	—	+ 100	+ 6

Year	Redemption of securities	Net purchase of securities	Other capital (net)	Repatriation of securities	War loan to United Kingdom	Investment in fixed production assets	Change in sterling balances decrease (+)	Special payments and adjustments	Net capital movements	Mutual aid and 1942 contributions	Special receipts of convertible exchange[4]	Balancing item[5]	Total
	Private transactions			Capital debit or credits (+) official transactions									
	118	119	120	121	122	123	124	125	126	127	128	129	130
				United Kingdom and other Commonwealth countries[3]									
1945	−31	−41	−16	− 1	+ 64	—	− 1	−324[6]	−350	− 660	− 33	+ 1	−1,042
1944	−32	−27	+61	− 2	+ 57	− 2	+ 4	− 57	+ 2	− 834	− 55	+ 8	− 879
1943	−10	−26	−33	− 4	+ 18	−205	—	−306[7]	−566	− 503	−143	− 4	−1,216
1942	−30	− 8	−13	−296	−700	+ 58	+818	− 74	−245	−1,000	− 23	− 1	−1,269
1941	−10	−36	− 4	−188	—	+157	−728	—	−809	—	—	+ 4	− 805
1940	−13	−28	−54	−137	—	+100	− 82	—	−214	—	−248	+43[5]	− 419
1939	−45	− 5	+42	− 75	—	—	—	—	− 83	—	− 2	[5]	—
1938	−21	−12	−26	—	—	—	—	—	− 59	—	—	[5]	—

Year	New issues of Canadian securities	Retirement of Canadian securities	Net new issues (+) or net retirements (−)	Net sales (+) or net purchases (−) of outstanding securities — Canadian securities	United States and foreign securities	Net change in reserves of gold and United States dollars decline (+) or increase (−)	Export credits and interim advances	Other capital movements and adjusting entries (net)	Net capital movements above	Mutual aid	Contribution to UNRRA and post-UNRRA	Military and other relief	Special receipts of convertible exchange[4]	Balancing item[5]	Total
	131	132	133	134	135	136	137	138	139	140	141	142	143	144	145
						Non-Commonwealth countries									
1945	+ 91	−179	− 88	+296	+96	−667	−105	+125	−343	− 88	−34	−76	+ 33	+ 4	−504
1944	+ 92	−166	− 74	+183	+42	−278	—	+ 77	− 50	−102	−11	−13	+ 55	−18	−139
1943	+146	−308	−162	+254	+44	−364	—	+117	−111	− 9	—	− 6	+143	− 7	+ 10
1942	—	− 25	− 25[8]	+132	+24	−144	—	+152	+139	—	—	− 2	+ 23	+ 8	+168
1941	—	− 31	− 31[8]	+ 46	+28	+160	—	+109	+312	—	—	—	—	+ 2	+314
1940	—	− 41	− 41	+ 15	+18	+ 79[9]	—	− 45	+ 26	—	—	—	+248	− 4[5]	+270
1939	+155	−131	+ 24	+ 69	+18	[9]	—	−164	− 53	—	—	—	+ 2	[5]	—
1938	+ 38	− 79	− 41	+ 48	− 7	—	—	− 47	− 47	—	—	—	—	[5]	—

[1] Excluding interim advances to sterling area in 1945 of 209 million which is included in 'Other capital movements'.
[2] Not available.
[3] Transactions with the sterling area are covered from 1940 to 1945.
[4] This represents gold and United States dollars received from the United Kingdom in part settlement of her deficiency with Canada, and used in turn to settle part of Canada's deficiency with the United States.
[5] Reflecting multilateral settlements up to the introduction of exchange control, and thereafter, errors and omissions.
[6] Includes 209 million interim advances most of which were cancelled in the 1946 financial settlement with the United Kingdom.
[7] Including 190 million repayment of working capital.
[8] Excluding refunding issues.
[9] Available data included in other capital movements.

Series F 146–163. *Canadian balance of international payments, all countries and by major areas, capital account, 1946 to 1960*

(millions of dollars)

Column key:
146 = Direct investments in Canada[1]; 147 = Direct investments abroad[1]; Canadian securities: 148 = Trade in outstanding bonds and debentures, 149 = Trade in outstanding common and preferred stocks, 150 = New issues, 151 = Retirements; Foreign securities: 152 = Trade in outstanding issues, 153 = New issues, 154 = Retirements; Loans by government of Canada: 155 = Drawings, 156 = Repayment of postwar loans, 157 = Repayment of war loans; 158 = Change in Canadian dollar holdings of foreigners; 159 = Change in official holdings of gold and foreign exchange; 160 = Other capital movements[2]; 161 = Net capital movements; 162 = Balance settled by exchange transfers; 163 = Total financing of current account balance.

All countries

Year	146	147	148	149	150	151	152	153	154	155	156	157	158	159	160	161	162	163
1960	+645	−85	+3	+49	+447	−253	−20	−18	+18	—	+32	—	+120	+39	+266	+1,243	0	+1,243
1959	+550	−80	+91	+110	+707	−258	−32	−13	+12	—	+34	—	+13	+70	+301	+1,504	0	+1,504
1958	+420	−48	—	+88	+677	−158	+13	−17	+7	−1	+34	+30	+106	−109	+122	+1,131	0	+1,131
1957	+514	−68	−45	+137	+798	−133	+24	−24	+6	−34	+20	+30	−35	+105	+126	+1,455	0	+1,455
1956	+583	−104	+11	+188	+667	−141	+20	−18	—	—	+39	+30	−24	−33	+148	+1,366	0	+1,366
1955	+417	−74	−165	+138	+166	−184	+25	−48	+17	—	+39	+30	+89	+44	+204	+698	0	+698
1954	+392	−81	−66	+129	+331	−203	+7	−33	+1	—	+42	+30	+34	−124	−28	+432	0	+432
1953	+426	−63	−52	+21	+335	−146	+22	−23	+1	—	+37	+50	+18	+38	−185	+443	0	+443
1952	+346	−77	−166	+72	+316	−89	+12	−20	—	—	+33	+23	−66	+37	−511	+164	0	−164
1951	+309	−20	+38		+411	−184	+15	−3	+3	—	+34	+34	−192	−56	+128	+517	0	+517
1950	+222	+36	+329		+210	−284	+70	−2	+8	−50	+23	+51	+233	−722	+210	+334	0	+334
1949	+94	+13	+8		+105	−147	+22	−4	+5	−120	+13	+5	+40	−128	+80	+177	0	+177
1948	+71	+15	+3		+150	−114	+7	−3	+7	−142	+16	+64	+21	−492	+7	+451	0	+451
1947	+61	+6	−13		+95	−364	+1	−3	+7	−565	+2	+109	+26	+742	−101	−49	0	−49
1946	+40	+14	+194		+218	−539	+25	−4	+13	−750	—	+94	+70	+267	+23	−363	0	−363

United Kingdom and other sterling area

Year	146	147	148	149	150	151	152	153	154	155	156	157	158	159	160	161	162	163
1960	+124	−19	−13	+16	+26	−27	−3	−1	+1	—	+17	—	+6	—	−37	−58	+267	−209
1959	+86	−52	+7	+7	+45	−30	+2	—	+2	—	+16	+30	+19	+3	−6	−57	+68	−11
1958	+91	−16	+3	+4	+41	−16	+2	—	+1	—	+16	+30	+9	+1	+39	+91	+264	+173
1957	+68	−11	—	+87	+59	−21	+4	—	—	−34	—	—	+20	+1	+33	+228	+350	+122
1956	+98	−27	+11	+72	+36	−2	+4	−1	—	—	+15	+30	+14	+1	+9	+261	+561	+300
1955	+68	−9	−2	+28	+15	−11	−9	−21	+1	—	+15	+30	+11	+2	+60	+177	+567	+390
1954	+75	−23	+20	+21	+20	−17	+3	−1	+1	—	+15	+30	+6	+4	+32	+94	+367	+273
1953	+45	−22	+3	+7	+7	−7	+3	—	—	—	+14	+50	+17	+3	+37	+129	+345	+216
1952	+15	−19	—	+6	+1	−9	+3	—	—	—	+14	+23	+22	+43	+62	+16	+486	+502
1951	+30	−6	−16		+7	−24	—	—	+1	—	+14	+34	−128	−17	+82	+23	+176	+199
1950	+19	−4	+35		+26	−19	+1	−1	+1	−50	—	+51	+116	−28	−39	+13	+14	+1
1949	+13	−3	+16		+45	−10	+2	−2	+1	−120	—	+5	+62	+6	+27	+87	+494	+581
1948	+10	−3	+4		+41	−14	+2	−4	+1	−52	—	+64	+20	+4	+18	+7	+622	+615
1947	+3	−3	+11		+59	−42	+3	−3	+1	−423	—	+104	+4	+1	+16	+357	+518	+875
1946	+2	−10	+48		+36	−77	+1	−4	+5	−540	—	+89	+32	+16	+39	+491	+173	+664

United States

Year	146	147	148	149	150	151	152	153	154	155	156	157	158	159	160	161	162	163
1960	+437	−48	−9	+54	+381	−200	+4	−13	+12	0	0	0	+60	+39	+288	+1,005	+356	+1,361
1959	+424	−7	−19	+75	+622	−211	−34	−8	+6	0	0	0	+8	+67	+388	+1,349	+119	+1,230
1958	+303	−16	−10	+70	+600	−132	+11	−13	+4	0	0	0	+83	−108	+147	+952	+224	+1,176
1957	+390	−35	−70	+5	+722	−105	+20	−15	+4	0	0	0	+10	+104	+58	+1,068	+511	+1,579
1956	+406	−70	−35	+69	+601	−133	+10	−13	—	0	0	0	−48	−34	+103	+856	+783	+1,639
1955	+306	−56	−159	+92	+127	−169	+31	−8	+2	0	0	0	+66	+42	+151	+425	+610	+1,035
1954	+288	−46	−87	+87	+299	−184	+6	−3	+1	0	0	0	+19	−121	+18	+277	+530	+807
1953	+346	−33	−85	+8	+322	−132	+20	−1	+1	0	0	0	+1	+42	−223	+244	+660	+904
1952	+319	−42	−170	+66	+315	−75	+9	−5	—	0	0	0	−37	+80	−458	+158	+1,007	+849
1951	+270	−4	+20		+404	−159	+18	−3	+2	0	0	0	−53	−39	+59	+515	+436	+951
1950	+200	+41	+362		+210	−263	+68	−2	+7	0	0	0	+89	−694	+249	+267	+133	+400
1949	+84	+16	+25		+105	−136	+19	−4	+1	0	0	0	+8	−134	+38	+70	+671	+601
1948	+61	+15	+5		+150	−96	+9	−3	+1	0	0	0	+14	−490	+1	+385	+778	+393
1947	+58	+6	+3		+95	−313	−2	−3	+3	0	0	0	+3	+743	—	+505	+629	+1,134
1946	+38	+7	+241		+218	−460	+21	−4	+6	0	0	0	+27	+251	−76	+331	+276	+607

Series F146–163. Canadian balance of international payments, all countries and by major areas, capital account, 1946 to 1960 *(continued)*

(millions of dollars)

Column key (groups): **Direct investment** — 146 Direct investments in Canada[1], 147 Direct investments abroad[1]; **Canadian securities** — 148 Trade in outstanding bonds and debentures, 149 Trade in outstanding common and preferred stocks, 150 New issues, 151 Retirements; **Foreign securities** — 152 Trade in outstanding issues, 153 New issues, 154 Retirements; **Loans by government of Canada** — 155 Drawings, 156 Repayment of postwar loans, 157 Repayment of war loans; 158 Change in Canadian dollar holdings of foreigners; 159 Change in official holdings of gold and foreign exchange; 160 Other capital movements[2]; 161 Net capital movements; 162 Balance settled by exchange transfers; 163 Total financing of current account balance.

O.E.E.C. countries other than Commonwealth

Year	146	147	148	149	150	151	152	153	154	155	156	157	158	159	160	161	162	163
1960	+83	-15	+25	+11	+39	-25	-1	—	—	—	+15	—	+7	—	+23	+162	-148	+14
1959	+40	-5	+64	+28	+40	-16	—	—	—	—	+18	—	+10	—	-74	+105	+15	+120
1958	+28	-5	+17	+14	+26	-10	—	—	—	—	+18	—	+4	—	+12	+104	-145	-41
1957	+56	-3	+30	+45	+16	-7	+2	-5	—	—	+18	—	+3	—	+27	+176	-243	-67
1956	+77	—	+38	+47	+30	-4	+6	—	—	—	+18	—	+3	—	+35	+250	-267	-17
1955	+43	-2	+16		+21	-3	+3	—	—	—	+15	—	+12	—	+6	+113	-137	-24
1954	+29	-1	+14		+12	-1	-1	—	—	—	+20	—	+4	—	+3	+78	-171	-93
1953	+34	-2	+25		+3	-1	—	—	—	—	+18	—	+4	—	+10	+92	-265	-173
1952	+10	-5	+9		—	-5	—	—	—	—	+16	—	+5	—	+23	+46	-378	-332
1951	+9	—	+34		—	—	—	—	—	—	+13	—	-11	—	-2	+37	-260	-223
1950	+3	-2	+2	—	—	-2	—	—	—	—	+16	—	+21	—	-2	+36	-144	-108
1949	-3	-2	-1	—	—	-1	—	—	—	—	+11	—	+12	—	-5	-13	-172	-185
1948	—	—	-1	—	—	-4	—	—	—	-67	+16	—	+10	—	-5	-51	-175	-226
1947	—	—	—	—	—	-9	—	—	—	-118	+2	—	-20	—	-9	-154	-122	-276
1946	—	—	+1	—	—	-2	—	—	—	-188	—	—	+13	—	-1	-177	-71	-248

Countries other than sterling, O.E.E.C. and United States[3]

Year	146	147	148	149	150	151	152	153	154	155	156	157	158	159	160	161	162	163
1960	+1	-3	—	—	+1	-1	-20	—	—	—	—	—	+47	—	+8	+18	+59	+77
1959	—	-16	+4	—	—	-1	—	—	—	—	—	—	+14	—	+7	-7	+172	+165
1958	-2	-24	-10	—	+10	—	—	—	—	—	—	—	+10	—	+8	-16	+185	+169
1957	—	-19	-5	—	+1	—	—	—	—	—	+2	—	-2	—	—	-17	+82	+65
1956	+2	-7	-3	—	—	-2	—	—	—	—	+6	—	+7	—	+1	-1	+45	+44
1955	—	-9	-2		+3	-1	—	-19	+15	—	—	—	-5	—	-13	-17	+94	+77
1954	—	-10	+28		—	-1	-1	-29	—	—	—	—	+5	—	-17	+1	+8	+9
1953	+1	-7	-3		+3	-2	—	—	—	—	—	—	+4	—	-9	-22	-50	-72
1952	+2	-14	+4		—	—	-1	-15	—	—	+2	—	-2	—	-14	-36	-143	-179
1951	—	-5	—		—	—	-3	—	—	—	+6	—	—	—	-11	-12	—	-12
1950	—	+1	—	—	—	—	+1	—	—	—	+7	—	+7	—	+2	+18	+25	+43
1949	—	+2	—	—	—	—	+1	—	—	—	+2	—	-2	—	-10	+7	+5	+12
1948	—	+2	+3	—	—	—	—	—	—	-23	—	—	+3	—	-7	-16	+19	+3
1947	—	+3	+1	—	—	—	+3	—	+3	-24	—	+5	+1	—	-32	+21	+11	+32
1946	—	+3	—	—	—	—	—	—	+2	-22	—	+5	-2	—	-15	+26	+32	+58

[1] Exclusive of undistributed profits.

[2] 'Other capital movements' include subscriptions in gold or foreign exchange to IMF and IBRD in 1946, 1947, 1959 and 1960 respectively of -8, -74, -59, and -1 million, subscription of -4 to IFC in 1956, subscription of -4 to IDA in 1960, refunding loan proceeds set aside for retirement of -18 in 1949 and its use for retirement (+18) in 1950, all attributed to United States account, and British financial settlement and interim advances net of +38 in 1946 in the United Kingdom account.

[3] Includes O.E.E.C. dependencies, 1957 to 1960.

Series F 164–192. *Estimates of the Canadian balance of international indebtedness excluding short-term commercial indebtedness and blocked currency balances, selected year ends, 1926 to 1960*

(billions of dollars)

| | Canadian liabilities, foreign capital invested in Canada | | | | | | | | Gross liabilities | | | |
| | | | | | | | | | | | | |
Year	Direct invest-ments	Govern-ment and municipal bonds	Other portfolio invest-ments[1]	Miscel-laneous invest-ments	Total non-resident long-term invest-ments in Canada	Equity of nonresi-dents in Canadian assets abroad	Canadian dollar holdings of non-residents	Canadian short-term assets of inter-national financial agencies	Total	To United States	To United Kingdom	To other countries, IBRD and IMF
	164	165	166	167	168	169	170	171	172	173	174	175
1960	12.9	3.3	4.6	1.4	22.2	1.1	.6	.4	24.3	18.2	3.5	2.7
1959	11.9	3.1	4.4	1.3	20.8	1.0	.5	.4	22.7	16.9	3.4	2.4
1958	10.9	2.6	4.4	1.0	19.0	.9	.5	.2	20.6	15.5	3.2	1.9
1957	10.1	2.3	4.2	.9	17.5	.8	.4	.2	18.9	14.2	3.1	1.7
1956	8.9	2.1	3.7	.8	15.6	.8	.4	.2	17.0	12.6	2.8	1.5
1955	7.7	1.9	3.3	.6	13.5	.7	.4	.2	14.8	11.1	2.5	1.2
1954	6.8	2.1	3.2	.6	12.5	.6	.3	.2	13.7	10.3	2.3	1.0
1953	6.0	2.1	2.9	.5[3]	11.5	.6	.3	.3	12.6	9.5	2.2	1.0
1952	5.2	2.0	2.7	.4[3]	10.4	.4	.3	.3	11.4	8.5	2.0	.9
1951	4.5	2.1	2.5	.3	9.5	.4	.4	.3	10.6	7.9	1.9	.8
1950	4.0	2.0	2.4	.3	8.7	.3	.6	.3	9.9	7.1	2.0	.8
1949	3.6	1.8	2.3	.3	8.0	.3	.4	.3	8.9	6.4	1.8	.7
1948	3.3	1.6	2.3	.3	7.5	.3	.3	.3	8.4	6.0	1.7	.7
1947	3.0	1.5	2.4	.3	7.2	.3	.3	.3	8.1	5.7	1.7	.7
1946	2.8	1.6	2.5	.3	7.2	.3	.4	—	7.8	5.7	1.7	.4
1945	2.7	1.7	2.4	.3	7.1	.2	.3	—	7.6	5.4	1.8	.4
1939	2.3	1.7	2.6	.3	6.9	.2[4]	.3[4]	—	7.4	4.5	2.6	.3
1933	2.4	1.7	3.0	.3	7.4	—[4]	—[4]	—	7.7	4.7	2.8	.2
1930	2.4	1.7	3.2	.3	7.6	—[4]	—[4]	—	8.0	4.9	2.9	.2
1926	1.8	1.4	2.5	.3	6.0	—[4]	—[4]	—	6.4	3.5	2.7	.2

| | Canadian assets, Canadian capital invested abroad | | | | | | | Gross assets | | | | |
| | | | | | | | | | | | | |
Year	Direct invest-ments	Port-folio invest-ments	Govern-ment of Canada loans and advances	Govern-ment of Canada subscrip-tions to inter-national financial agencies	Total Canadian long-term invest-ments abroad	Govern-ment of Canada holdings of gold and foreign exchange	Other Canadian short-term assets abroad	Total	Govern-ment of Canada holdings of gold and foreign exchange	Assets in United States[2]	Assets in United Kingdom[2]	Assets in other countries, IBRD, IFC and IMF
	176	177	178	179	180	181	182	183	184	185	186	187
1960	2.5	1.3	1.4	.6	5.7	1.8	1.2	8.8	1.8	3.6	1.5	1.9
1959	2.3	1.1	1.5	.6	5.5	1.8	1.0	8.3	1.8	3.3	1.4	1.9
1958	2.1	1.1	1.5	.4	5.1	1.9	1.0	7.9	1.9	3.1	1.4	1.6
1957	2.1	1.1	1.5	.4	5.0	1.8	.9	7.7	1.8	3.0	1.4	1.5
1956	1.9	1.0	1.6	.4	4.8	1.9	.6	7.3	1.9	2.6	1.4	1.4
1955	1.7	1.0	1.6	.4	4.7	1.9	.3	7.0	1.9	2.2	1.4	1.4
1954	1.6	.9	1.7	.4	4.6	1.9	.4	6.9	1.9	2.1	1.5	1.4
1953	1.5	.9	1.8	.4	4.5	1.8	.3	6.6	1.8	2.0	1.5	1.4
1952	1.3	.8[3]	1.9	.4	4.4	1.8	.3	6.4	1.8	1.7	1.5	1.4
1951	1.2	.6	1.9	.4	4.1	1.8	.1	6.0	1.8	1.4	1.5	1.3
1950	1.0	.6	2.0	.4	4.0	1.9	.1	5.9	1.9	1.1	1.6	1.3
1949	.9	.6	2.0	.4	4.0	1.2	.1	5.2	1.2	1.1	1.6	1.3
1948	.8	.6	1.9	.4	3.6	1.0	—	4.7	1.0	.8	1.5	1.4
1947	.8	.6	1.8	.4	3.6	.5	—	4.1	.5	.8	1.5	1.3
1946	.8	.6	1.4	—	2.7	1.3	—	4.0	1.3	.8	1.2	.7
1945	.7	.6	.7	—	2.0	1.7	.1	3.8	1.7	.9	.7	.5
1939	.7	.7	—	—	1.4	.5	—[5]	1.9	.5	.9	.1	.4
1933	.4	.9	—	—	1.3	—[4]	—[5]	1.4	—	.8	—	.6
1930	.4	.8	—	—	1.3	—[4]	—[5]	1.5	—	.9	.1	.5
1926	.4	.5	—	—	.9	—[4]	—[5]	1.3	—	.7	.1	.5

Series F 164–192. *Estimates of the Canadian balance of international indebtedness excluding short-term commercial indebtedness and blocked currency balances, selected year ends, 1926 to 1960 (continuation)*

(billions of dollars)

| | | Canadian net international indebtedness | | | | |
	Year	Net liabilities	Government of Canada holdings of gold and foreign exchange	Net liabilities in United States[2]	Net liabilities in United Kingdom[2]	Net liabilities in other countries, IBRD, IFC, IDA, and IMF
		188	189	190	191	192
	1960	15.5	−1.8	14.6	2.0	.8
	1959	14.4	−1.8	13.7	2.0	.6
	1958	12.7	−1.9	12.4	1.9	.3
	1957	11.2	−1.8	11.2	1.7	.1
	1956	9.7	−1.9	10.0	1.4	—
	1955	7.8	−1.9	8.8	1.1	−.2
	1954	6.8	−1.9	8.2	.9	−.4
	1953	6.0	−1.8	7.5	.7	−.4
	1952	5.0	−1.8	6.8	.5	−.5
	1951	4.6	−1.8	6.5	.4	−.5
	1950	4.0	−1.9	6.0	.4	−.5
	1949	3.7	−1.2	5.3	.2	−.6
	1948	3.7	−1.0	5.2	.2	−.7
	1947	4.0	−.5	4.9	.2	−.6
	1946	3.8	−1.3	4.9	.5	−.3
	1945	3.9	−1.7	4.6	1.1	−.1
	1939	5.5	−.5	3.6	2.5	−.1
	1933	6.3	—	3.9	2.8	−.4
	1930	6.5	—	4.0	2.8	−.3
	1926	5.1	—	2.8	2.6	−.3

[1] Includes income-accumulating investment funds.
[2] Excludes Government of Canada holdings of gold and foreign exchange.
[3] New series not strictly comparable with earlier years.

[4] Not available.
[5] Not available; net external assets of Chartered Banks of Canada amounted to $370 million in 1926, $180 million in 1930, and $91 million in 1933.

Series F 193–207. *Estimates of foreign capital invested in Canada, selected year ends, 1900 to 1960*

(millions of dollars)

Year	Total nonresident investment			Percentage of total nonresident investment			Investment by residents of the United States			Investment by residents of the United Kingdom			Investment by residents of other countries		
	Direct	Port-folio[1]	Total	United States	United Kingdom	Other countries	Direct	Port-folio[1]	Total	Direct	Port-folio[1]	Total	Direct	Port-folio[1]	Total
	193	194	195	196	197	198	199	200	201	202	203	204	205	206	207
1960	12,872	9,328	22,200	75	15	10	10,549	6,169	16,718	1,535	1,824	3,359	788	1,335	2,123
1959	11,906	8,951	20,857	76	15	9	9,912	5,914	15,826	1,384	1,815	3,199	610	1,222	1,832
1958	10,880	8,130	19,010	76	16	8	9,045	5,396	14,441	1,296	1,792	3,088	539	942	1,481
1957	10,129	7,335	17,464	75	17	7	8,472	4,792	13,264	1,163	1,754	2,917	494	789	1,283
1956	8,868	6,701	15,569	76	17	7	7,392	4,397	11,789	1,048	1,620	2,668	428	684	1,112
1955	7,728	5,745	13,473	76	18	6	6,513	3,762	10,275	890	1,466	2,356	325	517	842
1954	6,764	5,780	12,544	77	17	6	5,787	3,877	9,664	759	1,418	2,177	218	485	703
1953	6,003	5,458	11,461	77	18	5	5,206	3,664	8,870	612	1,396	2,008	185	398	583
1952	5,218	5,167	10,385	77	18	5	4,530	3,467	7,997	544	1,342	1,886	144	358	502
1951	4,520	4,957	9,477	76	19	5	3,896	3,363	7,259	497	1,281	1,778	127	313	440
1950	3,975	4,689	8,664	76	20	4	3,426	3,123	6,549	468	1,282	1,750	81	284	365
1949	3,586	4,377	7,963	74	22	4	3,095	2,811	5,906	428	1,289	1,717	63	277	340
1948	3,270	4,239	7,509	74	22	4	2,807	2,760	5,567	400	1,210	1,610	63	269	332
1947	2,986	4,205	7,191	72	23	5	2,548	2,653	5,201	372	1,275	1,647	66	277	343
1946	2,826	4,355	7,181	72	23	5	2,428	2,730	5,158	335	1,335	1,670	63	290	353
1945	2,713	4,379	7,092	70	25	5	2,304	2,686	4,990	348	1,402	1,750	61	291	352
1939	2,296	4,617	6,913	60	36	4	1,881	2,270	4,151	366	2,110	2,476	49	237	286
1933	2,352	5,013	7,365	61	36	3	1,933	2,559	4,492	376	2,307	2,683	43	147	190
1930	2,427	5,187	7,614	61	36	3	1,993	2,667	4,660	392	2,374	2,766	42	146	188
1926	1,782	4,221	6,003	53	44	3	1,403	1,793	3,196	336	2,301	2,637	43	127	170
1924[3]	—	—	5,616	55	42	3	—	—	3,094	—	—	2,372	—	—	150
1922[3]	—	—	5,207	50	47	3	—	—	2,593	—	—	2,464	—	—	150
1920[3]	—	—	4,870	44	53	3	—	—	2,128	—	—	2,577	—	—	165
1918[3]	—	—	4,536	36	60	4	—	—	1,630	—	—	2,729	—	—	177
1916[3]	—	—	4,323	30	66	4	—	—	1,307	—	—	2,840	—	—	176
1914[3]	—	—	3,837	23	72	5	—	—	881	—	—	2,778	—	—	178
1913[2]	—	—	3,746	21	75	5	—	—	780	—	—	2,793	—	—	173
1910[2]	—	—	2,529	19	77	4	—	—	487	—	—	1,958	—	—	84
1905[2]	—	—	1,540	19	79	2	—	—	290	—	—	1,212	—	—	39
1900[2]	—	—	1,232	14	85	1	—	—	168	—	—	1,050	—	—	14

[1] Including miscellaneous investments.
[2] Estimated by Jacob Viner, *Canada's Balance of International Indebtedness, 1900 to 1913.*

[3] Estimated by F. A. Knox, 'Excursus', appearing in *Canadian-American Industry*, Marshall, Southard and Taylor. Statistics for 1926 and subsequent years are official data collected by the Dominion Bureau of Statistics.

Series F 208–230. *British and foreign capital invested in Canada, all countries and by major areas, by type of investment and direct investment, selected year ends, 1930 to 1960*

(millions of dollars)

	Total long-term investments														
	Government				Manu-facturing (excluding petroleum and refining)	Petroleum and natural gas	Other mining and smelting	Public utilities							Total long-term invest-ment
Year	Dominion	Pro-vincial	Muni-cipal	Total govern-ment				Rail-ways	Other (excluding pipelines and public enter-prise)	Total public utilities (excluding pipelines)	Merchan-dising	Financial	Other enter-prises	Miscel-laneous invest-ments	
	208	**209**	**210**	**211**	**212**	**213**	**214**	**215**	**216**	**217**	**218**	**219**	**220**	**221**	**222**
						All countries									
1960	611	1,632	1,026	3,269	6,115	3,727	1,977	1,406	743	2,149	872	2,380	297	1,414	22,200
1959	612	1,585	915	3,112	5,726	3,455	1,783	1,405	739	2,144	878	2,190	284	1,285	20,857
1958	564	1,276	781	2,621	5,381	3,187	1,657	1,413	712	2,125	784	1,938	254	1,063	19,010
1957	501	1,165	660	2,326	5,051	2,849	1,570	1,396	661	2,057	715	1,782	235	879	17,464
1956	502	1,081	552	2,135	4,579	2,275	1,330	1,426	628	2,054	683	1,488	207	818	15,569
1955	529	888	452	1,869	4,025	1,854	1,121	1,364	574	1,938	616	1,231	178	641	13,473
1954	659	964	433	2,056	3,721	1,488	981	1,428	570	1,998	571	1,014	154	561	12,544
1951	1,013	771	319	2,103	2,715	693	586	1,436	524	1,960	377	595	120	328	9,477
1945	726	624	312	1,662	1,723	157	359	1,599	493	2,092	220	525	70	284	7,092
1930	682	592	432	1,706	1,459	150	311	2,244	634	2,878	190	543	82	295	7,614
						United States									
1960	382	1,544	977	2,903	4,818	3,184	1,701	479	551	1,030	608	1,587	234	653	16,718
1959	383	1,509	872	2,764	4,530	3,108	1,513	472	544	1,016	612	1,471	225	587	15,826
1958	396	1,207	741	2,344	4,234	2,866	1,386	489	523	1,012	549	1,314	200	536	14,441
1957	342	1,099	620	2,061	3,982	2,570	1,307	489	471	960	508	1,202	185	489	13,264
1956	340	1,021	511	1,872	3,606	2,063	1,129	536	460	996	496	983	170	474	11,789
1955	393	836	411	1,640	3,173	1,716	975	560	433	994	448	816	147	367	10,275
1954	515	914	393	1,822	2,961	1,426	867	627	470	1,097	412	649	128	302	9,664
1951	887	732	279	1,898	2,173	682	497	656	439	1,095	260	353	106	195	7,259
1945	682	574	194	1,450	1,382	152	280	720	374	1,094	158	285	62	130	4,990
1930	440	517	248	1,205	1,174	147	234	832	522	1,354	125	251	76	94	4,660
						United Kingdom									
1960	48	47	32	127	985	270	152	755	125	880	214	469	51	211	3,359
1959	60	48	33	141	945	162	160	783	125	908	225	413	45	200	3,199
1958	65	47	33	145	933	134	171	794	115	909	197	360	41	198	3,088
1957	64	47	34	145	887	108	162	784	112	896	174	332	36	177	2,917
1956	72	45	35	152	824	72	118	765	97	862	159	284	29	168	2,668
1955	67	39	35	141	746	31	86	698	86	784	145	241	25	157	2,356
1954	71	38	35	144	676	17	68	699	65	764	136	213	22	137	2,177
1951	70	38	38	146	488	7	58	704	56	760	102	142	10	65	1,778
1945	—	45	112	157	296	7	60	806	90	896	57	186	6	85	1,750
1930	235	69	182	486	273	3	72	1,352	100	1,452	61	243	5	171	2,766
						All other countries									
1960	181	41	17	239	312	273	124	172	67	239	50	324	12	550	2,123
1959	169	28	10	207	251	185	110	150	70	220	41	306	14	498	1,832
1958	103	22	7	132	214	187	100	130	74	204	38	264	13	329	1,481
1957	95	19	6	120	182	171	101	123	78	201	33	248	14	213	1,283
1956	90	15	6	111	149	140	83	125	71	196	28	221	8	176	1,112
1955	69	13	6	88	106	107	60	106	55	161	23	174	6	117	842
1954	73	12	5	90	84	45	46	102	35	137	23	152	4	122	703
1951	56	1	2	59	54	4	31	76	29	105	15	100	4	68	440
1945	44	5	6	55	45	1	19	73	29	102	5	54	2	69	352
1930	7	6	2	15	12	—	5	60	12	72	4	49	1	30	188

Series F 208–230. *British and foreign capital invested in Canada, all countries and by major areas, by type of investment and direct investment, selected year ends, 1930 to 1960 (continuation)*

(millions of dollars)

Year	Manufacturing (excluding petroleum refining)	Petroleum and natural gas	Other mining and smelting	Utilities (excluding pipelines)	Merchandising	Financial	Other enterprises	Total direct investment
	223	224	225	226	227	228	229	230
All countries								
1960	5,342	3,313	1,439	285	757	1,464	272	12,872
1959	5,011	3,082	1,223	282	761	1,289	258	11,906
1958	4,668	2,816	1,116	287	684	1,073	236	10,880
1957	4,376	2,559	1,044	286	621	1,026	217	10,129
1956	3,906	2,144	908	292	605	818	195	8,868
1955	3,434	1,754	811	320	538	706	165	7,728
1954	3,156	1,384	671	319	501	590	143	6,764
1951	2,248	641	419	361	361	378	112	4,520
1945	1,359	141	237	375	202	339	60	2,713
1930	1,090	142	217	450	160	304	64	2,427
United States								
1960	4,348	2,885[1]	1,348	224	501	1,028	215	10,549
1959	4,097	2,836	1,146	217	505	904	207	9,912
1958	3,806	2,598	1,030	216	458	750	187	9,045
1957	3,590	2,380	971	215	423	719	174	8,472
1956	3,195	1,978	857	223	428	551	160	7,392
1955	2,835	1,637	781	270	377	475	138	6,513
1954	2,633	1,344	650	298	348	396	118	5,787
1951	1,921	636	397	341	249	253	99	3,896
1945	1,191	141	215	358	147	198	54	2,304
1930	932	141	191	423	109	136	61	1,993
United Kingdom								
1960	768	208[1]	66	40	208	198	47	1,535
1959	732	116	68	40	219	168	41	1,384
1958	716	90	77	41	191	142	39	1,296
1957	663	64	68	37	167	131	33	1,163
1956	611	56	48	39	151	115	28	1,048
1955	537	23	26	33	139	109	23	890
1954	477	7	17	16	131	90	21	759
1951	305	4	18	16	97	48	9	497
1945	156	—	22	16	51	98	5	348
1930	155	1	25	27	48	133	3	392
All other countries								
1960	226	220[1]	25[1]	21	48	238	10	788
1959	182	130	9	25	37	217	10	610
1958	146	128	9	30	35	181	10	539
1957	123	115	5	34	31	176	10	494
1956	100	110	3	30	26	152	7	428
1955	62	94	4	17	22	122	4	325
1954	46	33	4	5	22	104	4	218
1951	22	1	4	4	15	77	4	127
1945	12	—	—	1	4	43	1	61
1930	3	—	1	—	3	35	—	42

[1] New series not strictly comparable with earlier series.

Series F 231–241. *Canadian long-term investments abroad,[1] all countries and by major areas, by type, selected year ends, 1926 to 1960*

(millions of dollars)

Year	Direct investment in branches, subsidiaries and controlled companies					Portfolio investments in foreign securities			Total private long-term investments abroad	Government of Canada credits	Total
	Railways and utilities	Industrial and commercial	Mining and petroleum	Other concerns	Total direct investment	Stocks	Bonds	Total portfolio investment			
	231	232	233	234	235	236	237	238	239	240	241
All countries											
1960	451	1,472	459	113	2,495	1,013	267	1,280	3,775	1,418	5,193
1959	457	1,343	417	78	2,295	916	249	1,165	3,460	1,451	4,911
1958	429	1,250	427	43	2,149	856	250	1,106	3,255	1,484	4,739
1957	425	1,198	410	40	2,073	805	257	1,062	3,135	1,515	4,650
1956	418	1,106	340	27	1,891	785	221	1,006	2,897	1,565	4,462
1955	438	993	291	20	1,742	767	224	991	2,733	1,635	4,368
1954	427	935	245	12	1,619	723	203	926	2,545	1,705	4,250
1953	402	851	215	9	1,477	690	179	869	2,346	1,778	4,124
1952	326	765	163	11	1,265	669[2]	161	830	2,095	1,866	3,961
1951	320	723	117	6	1,166	467	142	609	1,775	1,922	3,697
1949	276	553	91	6	926	477	161	638	1,564	2,000	3,564
1947	246	414	155	7	822	426	153	579	1,401	1,816	3,217
1945	239	337	138	6	720	454	167	621	1,341	707	2,048
1939	249	289	123	10	671[2]	511	208	719[2]	1,390	31	1,421
1930	—	—	—	—	443	—	—	789	1,232	31	1,263
1926	—	—	—	—	397	—	—	493	890	36	926

Series F231–241. *Canadian long-term investments abroad,*[1] *all countries and by major areas, by type, selected year ends, 1926 to 1960 (continued)*

(millions of dollars)

| Year | Direct investment in branches, subsidiaries and controlled companies | | | | | Portfolio investments in foreign securities | | | Total private long-term investments abroad | Government of Canada credits | Total |
| | Railways and utilities | Industrial and commercial | Mining and petroleum | Other concerns | Total direct investment | Stocks | Bonds | Total portfolio investment | | | |
	231	232	233	234	235	236	237	238	239	240	241
United States											
1960	369	938	223	94	1,624	803	122	925	2,549	—	2,549
1959	382	862	191	63	1,498	716	111	827	2,325	—	2,325
1958	379	833	197	31	1,440	647	111	758	2,198	—	2,198
1957	380	833	206	32	1,451	587	118	705	2,156	—	2,156
1956	378	804	190	22	1,394	569	84	653	2,047	—	2,047
1955	393	710	175	15	1,293	539	89	628	1,921	—	1,921
1954	390	686	145	10	1,231	490	89	579	1,810	—	1,810
1953	365	624	123	7	1,119	469	95	564	1,683	—	1,683
1952	293	566	95	8	962	450[2]	86	536	1,498	—	1,498
1951	288	549	71	4	912	289	87	376	1,288	—	1,288
1949	247	413	58	3	721	345	98	443	1,164	—	1,164
1947	217	272	37	5	531	283	83	366	897	—	897
1945	212	214	25	4	455[2]	317	92	409	864	—	864
1939	211	176	21	4	412[2]	380	121	501[2]	913	—	913
1930	—	—	—	—	260	—	—	459	719	—	719
1926	—	—	—	—	250	—	—	195	445	—	445
United Kingdom											
1960	14	239	—	2	255	26	16	42	297	1,047[3]	1,344
1959	10	224	—	1	235	25	12	37	272	1,064[3]	1,336
1958	3	196	—	1	200	27	14	41	241	1,080[3]	1,321
1957	3	168	—	1	172	33	15	48	220	1,127[3]	1,347
1956	3	135	—	1	139	30	16	46	185	1,157[3]	1,342
1955	2	128	—	1	131	29	17	46	177	1,202	1,379
1954	1	118	—	—	119	17	14	31	150	1,247	1,397
1953	1	103	—	—	104	16	13	29	133	1,292	1,425
1952	1	80	—	—	81	17	14	31	112	1,357	1,469
1951	1	73	—	—	74	17	17	34	108	1,394	1,502
1949	—	58	—	1	59	21	19	40	99	1,434	1,533
1947	—	64	—	—	64	26	26	52	116	1,331	1,447
1945	—	53	—	1	54[2]	26	27	53[2]	107	561	668
1939	—	53	—	6	59[2]	22	21	43[2]	102	—	102
1930	—	—	—	—	14	—	—	45	59	—	59
1926	—	—	—	—	17	—	—	45	52	—	52
Other Commonwealth countries[4]											
1960	10	126	156	10	302	9	19	28	330	35	365
1959	8	120	153	10	291	8	19	27	318	35	353
1958	7	102	150	7	266	8	21	29	295	34	329
1957	8	93	131	3	235	7	21	28	263	—	263
1956	8	85	98	—	191	7	21	28	219	—	219
1955	4	83	72	—	159	7	21	28	187	—	187
1954	4	74	60	—	138	6	7	13	151	—	151
1953	6	73	54	—	133	6	8	14	147	—	147
1952	7	70	35	—	112	6	8	14	126	—	126
1951	7	61	20	—	88	6	8	14	102	—	102
1949	6	51	19	—	76	6	8	14	90	—	90
1947	8	47	30	—	85	7	11	18	103	—	103
1945	7	34	28	—	69	7	12	19	88	—	88
1939	7	30	17	—	54	7	15	22	76	—	76
Other foreign countries											
1960	58	169	80	7	314	175	110	285	599	336	935
1959	57	137	73	4	271	167	107	274	545	352	897
1958	40	119	80	4	243	174	104	278	521	370	891
1957	34	104	73	4	215	178	103	281	496	388	884
1956	29	82	52	4	167	179	100	279	446	408	854
1955	39	72	44	4	159	192	97	289	448	433	881
1954	32	57	40	2	131	210	93	303	434	458	892
1953	30	51	38	2	121	199	63	262	383	486	869
1952	25	49	33	3	110	196	53	249	359	509	868
1951	25	39	26	2	92	155	30	185	277	528	805
1949	23	31	14	2	70	105	36	141	211	566	777
1947	21	31	88	2	142	110	33	143	285	485	770
1945	20	36	85	1	142[2]	104	36	140[2]	282	146	428
1939	31	30	85	—	146[2]	102	51	153[2]	299	31	330
1930	—	—	—	—	160[5]	105	180	285[5]	454[5]	31	485[5]
1926	—	—	—	—	140[5]	—	—	253[5]	393[5]	36	429[5]

[1] Figures include investments of insurance companies and banks which are held mainly against liabilities to nonresidents, and subscriptions by the Government of Canada to the International Bank for Reconstruction and Development, the International Finance Corporation, the International Development Association, and the International Monetary Fund, which are partly offset by short-term assets in Canada of these institutions. Figures include the equity of nonresidents in assets abroad of Canadian companies.

[2] New series not strictly comparable with earlier years.

[3] Excludes deferred interest amounting to $22 million at the end of 1956 and to $44 million at the end of subsequent years.

[4] Includes investments in Newfoundland prior to 1949.

[5] Includes investments in 'other Commonwealth countries'.

Series F242–245. *Foreign trade, domestic exports, total exports, total imports and balance of trade, declared values, Canada and all countries, 1868 to 1960*

(thousands of dollars)

Year[1]	Domestic exports	Total exports[2]	Total imports	Balance of trade	Year[1]	Domestic exports	Total exports[2]	Total imports	Balance of trade
	242	243	244	245		242	243	244	245
1960	5,255,575	5,386,792	5,482,695	− 95,903	1915	409,419	461,443	455,956	+ 5,487
1959[3]	5,021,672	5,140,300	5,508,920	− 368,620	1914	431,588	455,437	619,194	− 163,757
1959[4]	5,060,710	5,179,378	5,654,423	− 475,045	1913	355,755	377,068	671,207	− 294,139
1958	4,825,439	4,926,289	5,192,351	− 266,062	1912	290,224	307,716	522,405	− 214,689
1957	4,839,094	4,919,519	5,623,410	− 703,891	1911	274,316	290,000	452,725	− 162,725
1956	4,789,746	4,863,143	5,705,449	− 842,306					
1955	4,281,784	4,351,284	4,712,370	− 361,086	1910	279,247	298,764	370,318	− 71,554
1954	3,881,272	3,946,917	4,093,196	− 146,280	1909	242,603	259,922	288,594	− 28,672
1953	4,117,406	4,172,601	4,382,830	− 210,229	1908	246,961	263,369	352,541	− 89,172
1952	4,301,081	4,355,960	4,030,468	+ 325,492	1907[1]	180,545	192,087	250,226	− 58,139
1951	3,914,460	3,963,384	4,084,856	− 121,472	1906	235,484	246,658	283,740	− 37,082
1950	3,118,386	3,157,073	3,174,253	− 17,180	1905	190,855	201,472	251,964	− 50,492
1949	2,992,961	3,022,453	2,761,207	+ 261,245	1904	198,414	211,056	243,909	− 32,853
1948	3,075,438	3,110,029	2,636,945	+ 473,083	1903	214,402	225,230	225,095	+ 135
1947	2,774,902	2,811,790	2,573,944	+ 237,846	1902	196,020	209,971	196,738	+ 13,233
1946	2,312,215	2,339,166	1,927,279	+ 411,886	1901	177,431	194,509	177,931	+ 16,578
1945	3,218,330	3,267,424	1,585,775	+1,681,649	1900	168,972	183,238	172,652	+ 10,586
1944	3,439,953	3,483,099	1,758,898	+1,724,200	1899	137,361	154,881	149,422	+ 5,459
1943	2,971,475	3,001,352	1,735,077	+1,266,275	1898	144,549	159,530	126,307	+ 33,223
1942	2,363,773	2,385,466	1,644,242	+ 741,224	1897	123,632	134,458	106,618	+ 27,840
1941	1,621,003	1,640,454	1,448,792	+ 191,663	1896	109,708	116,315	105,361	+ 10,954
1940	1,178,954	1,193,217	1,081,951	+ 111,267	1895	102,828	109,313	100,676	+ 8,637
1939	924,926	935,922	751,055	+ 184,866	1894	103,852	115,686	109,071	+ 6,615
1938	837,584	848,684	677,451	+ 171,233	1893	105,489	114,431	115,171	− 740
1937	997,367	1,012,122	808,896	+ 203,225	1892	99,032	112,154	115,160	− 3,006
1936	937,825	950,509	635,191	+ 315,318	1891	88,672	97,470	111,534	− 14,064
1935	724,977	737,936	550,314	+ 187,621	1890	85,257	94,309	111,682	− 17,373
1934	649,314	656,306	513,469	+ 142,837	1889	80,272	87,211	109,098	− 21,887
1933	529,449	535,484	401,214	+ 134,269	1888	81,382	90,185	100,672	− 10,487
1932	489,883	497,913	452,614	+ 45,299	1887	80,961	89,510	105,107	− 15,597
1931	587,653	599,560	628,098	− 28,538	1886	77,757	85,195	95,992	− 10,797
1930	863,684	883,148	1,008,479	− 125,332	1885	79,132	87,211	99,756	− 12,545
1929	1,152,416	1,178,342	1,298,993	− 120,650	1884	79,833	89,222	105,973	− 16,751
1928	1,339,409	1,363,788	1,222,318	+ 141,470	1883	87,702	97,454	121,861	− 24,407
1927	1,210,597	1,231,042	1,087,118	+ 143,924	1882	94,138	101,766	111,145	− 9,379
1926	1,261,241	1,276,599	1,008,342	+ 268,257	1881	83,945	97,320	90,488	+ 6,832
1925	1,239,554	1,251,666	890,193	+ 361,473	1880	72,900	86,140	69,900	+ 16,240
1924	1,029,699	1,042,253	808,144	+ 234,108	1879	62,431	70,787	78,702	− 7,915
1923	1,002,401	1,015,986	903,030	+ 112,956	1878	67,990	79,155	90,396	− 11,241
1922	880,409	894,224	762,409	+ 131,815	1877	68,030	75,142	94,126	− 18,984
1921	800,149	814,144	799,478	+ 14,665	1876	72,491	79,726	92,513	− 12,787
1920	1,268,014	1,298,162	1,336,921	− 38,759	1875	69,710	76,847	117,408	− 40,561
1919[1]	1,235,958	1,289,792	941,014	+ 348,778	1874	76,742	87,356	123,181	− 35,825
1919[1]	1,216,444	1,268,765	919,712	+ 349,053	1873	76,538	85,944	124,509	− 38,565
1918	1,540,028	1,586,170	963,532	+ 622,638	1872	65,831	78,629	104,955	− 26,326
1917	1,151,376	1,179,211	846,451	+ 332,760	1871	57,630	67,483	84,214	− 16,731
1916	741,611	779,300	508,201	+ 271,099					
					1870	59,043	65,571	66,902	− 1,331
					1869	52,401	56,257	63,155	− 6,898
					1868	48,505	52,702	67,090	− 14,388

[1] The data are for calendar years since 1919, for fiscal years ending 31 March of the year given from 1908 to 1919 and for fiscal years ending 30 June of the year given from 1868 to 1906. Both calendar and fiscal totals are shown for 1919. The totals for 1907 are for the nine months ending 31 March 1907.

[2] Includes exports of foreign produce.
[3] New basis. See end of general note to series F242–399.
[4] Old basis.

Series F 246–269. *Foreign trade, exports of domestic and foreign produce excluding coin and bullion, by main groups, declared values and values at prices prevailing in 1900, 1869 to 1915*

(thousands of dollars)

Year[1]	Agricultural products A. mainly foods		Agricultural products B. not foods		Agricultural products total A and B		Animal products		Fibres and textiles		Wood, wood products and paper	
	Declared values	Valued at 1900 prices	Declared values	Valued at 1900 prices	Declared values	Valued at 1900 prices	Declared values	Valued at 1900 prices	Declared values	Valued at 1900 prices	Declared values	Valued at 1900 prices
	246	247	248	249	250	251	252	253	254	255	256	257
1915	160,435	115,392	13,195	13,189	173,630	128,581	105,852	74,813	13,743	13,388	68,933	51,079
1914	179,177	138,388	31,056	34,533	210,233	172,921	77,768	63,571	3,298	3,780	63,525	45,744
1913	141,921	109,224	20,533	17,238	162,454	126,462	63,254	47,954	4,465	3,982	56,557	39,967
1912	111,882	86,659	6,480	4,717	118,362	91,376	67,413	53,246	3,713	4,913	51,137	36,227
1911	82,114	61,756	10,073	6,248	92,187	68,004	70,672	56,770	3,315	3,505	56,295	38,516
1910	97,999	70,879	6,704	5,111	104,703	75,990	71,200	58,052	3,498	3,552	57,045	39,612
1909	81,447	62,795	3,900	3,485	85,347	66,280	67,463	54,509	3,372	3,283	48,572	33,716
1908[1]	73,105	58,338	5,110	4,598	78,215	62,936	71,289	58,051	3,548	2,976	53,150	36,196
1907[1]	44,321	39,308	6,456	6,533	50,777	45,841	78,285	62,963	2,829	2,162	49,617	40,194
1906	57,966	50,559	4,339	3,527	62,305	54,086	85,319	73,769	3,422	4,379	45,679	37,986
1905	34,744	30,631	3,682	3,591	38,426	34,222	77,080	73,901	3,088	3,496	39,687	35,477
1904	41,993	38,377	4,232	3,509	46,225	41,886	77,246	71,934	2,427	2,099	38,215	31,946
1903	49,805	48,261	3,552	2,910	53,357	51,171	84,208	76,051	1,753	1,676	41,879	36,797
1902	45,283	43,469	3,406	2,930	48,690	46,399	76,035	72,197	2,250	2,372	35,455	31,821
1901	37,839	37,986	2,164	1,787	40,003	39,773	69,286	65,885	2,147	2,188	33,323	33,039
1900	37,111	37,111	2,414	2,414	39,525	39,525	71,946	71,946	1,783	1,783	32,680	32,680
1899	35,890	34,958	2,378	2,870	38,268	37,828	59,722	66,420	856	1,089	30,931	32,303
1898	43,343	39,325	1,439	1,645	44,782	40,970	58,600	66,131	1,193	1,306	29,481	29,806
1897	24,983	29,643	1,825	1,673	26,808	31,316	51,104	57,852	3,146	3,158	33,129	35,366
1896	17,357	18,993	1,278	1,344	18,635	20,337	49,817	54,209	2,237	2,002	28,854	31,580
1895	18,269	20,241	1,625	1,825	19,894	22,066	46,875	47,165	2,121	2,047	25,498	27,281
1894	26,047	25,427	1,348	1,222	27,395	26,649	46,196	46,310	1,137	831	27,995	28,884
1893	27,215	25,637	986	760	28,201	26,397	42,515	42,823	1,009	1,329	29,078	30,013
1892	30,541	26,263	951	918	31,492	27,181	40,946	40,628	1,106	1,567	24,783	26,237
1891	17,860	15,137	2,143	964	20,003	16,101	37,308	37,471	873	755	27,122	28,865
1890	16,964	16,194	855	966	17,819	17,160	35,455	33,862	898	755	28,326	29,045
1889	16,910	14,340	592	879	17,502	15,219	32,378	34,030	791	728	25,152	26,080
1888	20,689	16,989	1,402	1,362	22,091	18,351	33,934	36,384	655	550	23,655	24,583
1887	23,391	21,304	615	860	24,006	22,164	30,940	35,473	553	474	22,808	23,719
1886	21,123	17,978	603	714	21,726	18,692	29,706	34,897	498	463	23,514	25,079
1885	19,046	15,517	361	505	19,407	16,022	34,515	37,739	467	432	23,069	24,380
1884	18,145	13,339	331	527	18,476	13,866	32,669	31,864	529	446	27,949	29,831
1883	29,318	20,748	613	896	29,931	21,644	30,190	29,837	514	452	27,204	27,737
1882	34,669	21,961	1,225	1,458	35,894	23,419	29,399	31,953	451	351	25,484	27,907
1881	31,104	23,549	477	728	31,581	24,277	29,631	34,837	613	403	26,321	30,435
1880	31,908	23,979	842	1,627	32,750	25,606	24,812	31,288	1,214	912	18,006	24,268
1879	25,894	19,587	495	1,005	26,389	20,592	21,586	28,350	898	746	14,106	18,973
1878	26,737	17,497	705	781	27,442	18,278	21,657	25,099	925	639	20,371	25,449
1877	18,862	13,483	844	1,538	19,706	15,021	21,270	23,593	1,013	749	23,967	28,194
1876	25,916	17,514	522	585	26,438	18,099	19,829	21,069	1,175	773	20,739	23,215
1875	17,000	10,502	403	564	17,403	11,066	17,666	19,881	1,119	649	25,179	26,361
1874	19,474	11,064	310	519	19,784	11,583	19,266	21,714	1,142	623	27,309	33,620
1873	14,917	9,234	363	515	15,280	9,749	17,901	22,003	1,610	681	29,395	33,476
1872	13,163	8,835	456	570	13,619	9,405	15,506	17,049	1,543	918	24,391	30,422
1871	9,253	6,422	834	735	10,087	7,157	15,929	17,989	987	647	22,959	27,509
1870	13,475	9,432	411	547	13,886	9,979	15,117	18,561	926	997	21,388	28,104
1869	12,022	6,894	313	347	12,335	7,241	10,307	12,508	550	352	19,699	27,617

Series F 246–269. *Foreign trade, exports of domestic and foreign produce excluding coin and bullion, by main groups, declared values and values at prices prevailing in 1900, 1869 to 1915 (continuation)*

(thousands of dollars)

Year[1]	Iron and its products		Nonferrous metals		Nonmetallic minerals		Chemicals and allied products		Miscellaneous		Total exports	
	Declared values	Valued at 1900 prices	Declared values	Valued at 1900 prices	Declared values	Valued at 1900 prices	Declared values	Valued at 1900 prices	Declared values	Valued at 1900 prices	Declared values	Valued at 1900 prices
	258	259	260	261	262	263	264	265	266	267	268	269
1915	20,418	34,791	46,913	47,469	9,287	7,923	4,937	4,267	17,730	14,501	461,443	376,812
1914	18,121	25,025	54,087	53,160	8,873	8,620	5,404	4,790	14,128	12,085	455,437	389,696
1913	14,577	18,424	49,945	47,644	9,928	9,523	5,614	5,334	10,274	8,391	377,068	307,681
1912	11,704	14,030	35,285	37,086	8,112	7,485	4,562	4,356	7,429	6,124	307,716	254,843
1911	9,826	10,246	34,217	36,217	10,045	9,800	4,180	4,054	9,262	7,505	290,000	234,617
1910	7,949	7,775	33,343	35,601	8,655	8,247	3,388	3,364	8,984	7,238	298,764	239,431
1909	6,880	6,852	30,682	30,082	7,708	7,102	2,793	2,752	7,105	5,799	259,922	210,375
1908[1]	6,191	6,584	33,555	29,374	8,056	7,971	2,767	2,637	6,598	5,357	263,369	212,082
1907[1]	6,074	6,601	28,234	23,418	7,570	7,101	2,526	2,344	19,070	16,133	244,982	206,757
1906	5,733	6,966	28,503	25,318	7,825	7,879	2,194	2,127	5,677	5,030	246,658	217,540
1905	5,313	5,745	26,312	25,665	6,721	6,866	1,721	1,637	4,513	4,298	201,472	191,307
1904	6,238	7,242	27,512	27,598	6,534	6,446	1,669	1,511	3,989	3,688	211,056	194,350
1903	7,156	7,553	23,174	23,371	7,656	7,280	1,614	1,426	4,343	4,060	225,230	209,385
1902	6,538	8,061	27,061	26,878	7,213	6,877	1,391	1,367	5,338	5,155	209,971	201,127
1901	4,192	4,070	33,457	32,917	7,249	6,846	1,033	1,084	4,148	4,043	194,509	189,845
1900	3,764	3,764	18,845	18,845	6,182	6,182	553	553	7,960	7,960	183,238	183,238
1899	3,124	2,648	8,835	9,133	4,935	4,477	523	483	7,687	8,054	154,881	162,435
1898	1,336	1,036	10,043	11,324	4,848	4,547	663	579	8,584	8,836	159,530	164,535
1897	1,807	1,292	7,053	7,567	4,704	4,214	340	297	6,367	6,939	134,458	148,001
1896	1,348	1,265	3,942	4,336	4,631	3,992	441	411	6,410	6,837	116,315	124,969
1895	1,221	1,070	2,484	2,927	4,904	4,188	383	481	5,933	6,113	109,313	113,338
1894	994	857	1,760	1,642	4,640	3,873	268	242	5,301	5,215	115,686	114,503
1893	962	900	1,199	1,752	4,666	3,730	300	276	6,501	6,388	114,431	113,608
1892	777	740	1,396	1,944	4,831	3,986	314	269	6,509	6,294	112,154	108,846
1891	660	538	1,619	1,464	4,616	3,609	426	280	4,843	4,625	97,470	93,708
1890	785	624	1,221	972	4,238	3,380	131	42	5,436	5,217	94,309	91,057
1889	751	573	1,026	687	3,618	2,859	—	—	5,993	5,843	87,211	86,019
1888	697	586	1,146	847	3,179	2,782	—	—	4,828	4,684	90,185	88,767
1887	561	528	1,296	1,129	2,846	2,763	—	—	6,500	6,707	89,510	92,957
1886	453	411	1,611	1,341	2,598	2,473	—	—	5,089	5,253	85,195	88,609
1885	515	467	1,309	1,042	2,481	2,380	—	—	5,448	5,464	87,211	87,926
1884	747	730	1,200	995	2,275	2,313	—	—	5,377	5,108	89,222	85,153
1883	862	1,036	1,117	1,006	1,949	2,006	—	—	5,687	5,175	97,454	88,893
1882	1,148	1,832	1,127	1,678	1,972	1,982	—	—	6,291	5,845	101,766	94,967
1881	1,201	1,644	1,000	1,157	1,834	1,793	—	—	5,139	5,259	97,320	99,805
1880	1,401	1,713	1,415	1,355	1,581	1,469	—	—	4,961	5,272	86,140	91,883
1879	608	1,158	1,620	1,590	1,640	1,564	—	—	3,940	4,281	70,787	77,254
1878	732	1,458	1,276	1,170	1,678	1,309	—	—	5,074	5,014	79,155	78,416
1877	654	1,411	1,590	1,223	2,220	1,605	—	—	4,722	4,814	75,142	76,610
1876	761	913	2,421	1,514	1,444	1,121	—	—	6,919	6,338	79,726	73,042
1875	817	1,013	2,206	2,108	1,451	1,227	—	—	11,007	10,315	76,847	72,620
1874	1,027	1,078	1,639	1,142	2,168	1,762	—	—	15,021	14,952	87,356	86,474
1873	1,630	1,187	2,598	2,315	3,268	2,945	—	—	14,262	14,392	85,944	86,748
1872	1,167	1,434	2,456	2,392	2,400	2,378	—	—	17,547	18,380	78,629	82,378
1871	849	766	888	817	2,039	2,684	—	—	13,745	14,715	67,483	72,284
1870	627	744	445	506	1,878	2,504	—	—	11,304	12,786	65,571	74,181
1869	421	543	703	416	1,239	1,956	—	—	11,003	12,305	56,257	62,938

[1] The data are for fiscal years ending 31 March of the year given from 1908 to 1915 and for fiscal years ending 30 June of the year given from 1869 to 1907. The figures for 1907 are for twelve months ending 30 June 1907, and for 1908 they are for the twelve months ending 31 March 1908.

Series F 270–293. *Foreign trade, imports excluding coin and bullion, by main groups, declared values and values at prices prevailing in 1900, 1869 to 1915*

(thousands of dollars)

Year[1]	Agricultural products A. mainly foods		Agricultural products B. not foods		Agricultural products total A and B		Animal products		Fibres and textiles		Wood, wood products and paper	
	Declared values	Valued at 1900 prices	Declared values	Valued at 1900 prices	Declared values	Valued at 1900 prices	Declared values	Valued at 1900 prices	Declared values	Valued at 1900 prices	Declared values	Valued at 1900 prices
	270	271	272	273	274	275	276	277	278	279	280	281
1915	65,748	55,746	30,028	26,393	95,776	82,067	34,429	35,181	83,487	68,835	26,757	27,250
1914	62,899	55,688	34,719	26,519	97,618	82,207	41,093	39,302	109,154	84,644	37,397	34,627
1913	66,731	55,264	38,784	28,429	105,515	83,693	53,744	54,573	111,513	90,029	44,504	44,027
1912	62,990	51,388	30,585	21,932	93,575	73,320	38,513	39,013	88,744	73,550	33,197	35,719
1911	52,004	45,259	27,210	18,946	79,214	64,205	30,672	29,985	87,916	70,549	26,852	24,780
1910	43,035	38,324	22,320	16,641	65,355	54,965	29,172	27,670	78,427	64,661	19,898	17,086
1909	39,483	34,614	18,158	15,153	57,641	49,767	21,457	20,839	56,481	49,223	15,912	14,358
1908[1]	42,303	37,250	19,221	15,875	61,524	53,125	22,981	19,785	71,655	59,651	20,748	16,169
1907[1]	35,978	34,154	20,480	18,460	56,458	52,614	23,670	20,068	70,384	58,281	19,010	14,532
1906	33,381	32,161	16,926	15,911	50,307	48,072	23,617	23,425	59,293	50,360	14,342	12,855
1905	30,622	29,538	13,898	13,484	44,520	43,022	18,578	20,310	51,884	46,916	13,609	13,141
1904	29,293	29,012	12,949	13,485	42,242	42,497	17,992	21,629	51,272	45,387	13,936	13,599
1903	25,093	26,761	13,158	13,679	38,251	40,440	18,236	21,344	48,239	46,025	10,773	11,278
1902	24,658	25,750	11,224	11,678	35,882	37,428	16,407	17,170	42,636	42,473	9,285	11,111
1901	26,974	26,167	11,062	11,580	38,036	37,747	14,023	13,705	37,285	36,927	8,197	9,318
1900	26,488	26,488	10,947	10,947	37,435	37,435	13,759	13,759	36,377	36,377	7,766	7,766
1899	26,040	27,540	9,588	11,520	35,628	39,060	11,933	12,320	33,521	36,583	6,617	7,355
1898	21,191	23,777	6,574	7,187	27,765	30,964	10,139	11,771	29,132	33,253	5,829	7,173
1897	16,727	18,628	8,590	11,295	25,317	29,923	7,649	9,777	23,851	30,218	4,909	6,204
1896	16,161	17,613	6,581	8,961	22,742	26,574	7,600	9,318	27,422	30,673	4,787	5,854
1895	18,933	20,571	5,403	8,007	24,336	28,578	7,474	9,564	25,497	29,605	4,308	4,796
1894	18,585	17,796	7,257	9,663	25,842	27,459	7,860	9,376	26,466	28,118	4,889	4,991
1893	17,066	15,608	7,347	9,742	24,413	25,350	8,095	10,130	31,083	31,583	4,436	4,449
1892	19,205	17,253	8,181	11,110	27,386	28,363	7,994	9,004	29,299	30,593	4,500	4,299
1891	17,135	15,360	7,077	8,511	24,212	23,871	8,081	8,301	28,670	26,856	5,203	5,521
1890	17,710	15,568	7,398	9,388	25,108	24,956	8,886	9,760	29,476	27,034	5,454	5,912
1889	17,217	15,509	6,494	7,643	23,711	23,152	10,129	10,108	28,415	27,683	4,978	5,071
1888	15,494	14,074	6,455	8,725	21,949	22,799	9,373	9,192	25,825	25,383	4,733	4,616
1887	15,570	14,579	5,081	6,755	20,651	21,334	9,182	8,568	30,580	31,470	6,630	5,626
1886	14,548	12,923	5,141	6,771	19,689	19,694	8,822	8,322	26,942	27,296	6,453	5,789
1885	17,488	15,697	4,886	5,980	22,374	21,677	9,990	9,088	26,165	24,450	6,139	5,464
1884	18,713	14,764	5,379	6,499	24,092	21,263	10,128	8,836	25,864	23,179	7,093	6,078
1883	17,323	12,670	5,170	6,003	22,493	18,673	10,650	8,953	34,242	29,332	7,071	6,712
1882	16,120	11,790	4,902	6,053	21,022	17,843	9,228	8,583	33,724	27,867	5,382	4,344
1881	14,574	10,485	3,691	5,040	18,265	15,525	7,998	7,510	29,336	26,417	3,664	3,783
1880	11,053	8,470	3,707	5,185	14,760	13,655	6,432	6,554	22,233	19,506	2,848	2,540
1879	20,986	15,522	4,028	6,014	25,014	21,536	5,081	5,739	21,035	23,175	3,367	2,967
1878	25,840	16,418	3,904	5,703	29,744	22,121	6,047	6,854	22,176	22,984	4,220	3,528
1877	26,091	16,684	3,922	5,618	30,013	22,302	7,072	7,547	25,261	23,263	4,205	3,587
1876	23,762	14,202	4,319	5,661	28,081	19,863	6,640	6,021	20,798	17,567	3,408	2,515
1875	24,575	13,215	4,757	6,700	29,332	19,915	9,312	9,136	31,650	26,833	—	—
1874	27,732	15,444	5,594	8,144	33,326	23,588	7,664	7,386	31,409	25,590	—	—
1873	30,529	16,794	4,583	6,286	35,112	23,080	6,345	5,858	30,749	20,046	—	—
1872	20,583	12,578	4,228	6,028	24,811	18,606	7,791	6,772	31,335	17,645	—	—
1871	18,504	10,834	3,455	5,314	21,959	16,148	6,262	4,863	17,111	10,989	—	—
1870	19,267	12,495	3,373	5,404	22,640	17,899	4,751	3,555	19,683	18,417	—	—
1869	17,584	10,523	3,093	4,115	20,677	14,638	2,659	1,928	18,978	14,145	—	—

Series F 270–293. *Foreign trade, imports excluding coin and bullion, by main groups, declared values and values at prices prevailing in 1900, 1869 to 1915 (continuation)*

(thousands of dollars)

Year[1]	Iron and its products		Nonferrous metals		Nonmetallic minerals		Chemicals and allied products		Miscellaneous		Total imports	
	Declared values	Valued at 1900 prices	Declared values	Valued at 1900 prices	Declared values	Valued at 1900 prices	Declared values	Valued at 1900 prices	Declared values	Valued at 1900 prices	Declared values	Valued at 1900 prices
	282	283	284	285	286	287	288	289	290	291	292	293
1915	77,844	90,083	23,191	24,284	64,234	66,682	14,343	12,846	35,895	34,825	455,956	442,053
1914	143,865	133,418	35,574	33,793	85,289	79,281	17,073	14,571	52,131	46,171	619,194	548,014
1913	164,017	158,791	39,289	34,611	82,471	80,284	17,612	16,220	52,542	47,805	671,207	610,033
1912	111,142	114,518	31,867	33,795	66,727	63,202	13,913	12,484	44,727	41,759	522,405	487,360
1911	91,968	92,840	27,580	30,316	53,430	47,529	12,472	10,822	42,621	38,618	452,725	409,824
1910	65,893	68,360	21,125	23,367	45,715	42,505	10,759	9,144	33,974	31,070	370,318	338,828
1909	44,614	44,422	14,865	15,236	41,970	37,175	9,415	8,153	26,239	23,935	288,594	263,108
1908[1]	67,274	62,201	18,957	14,548	47,023	39,706	9,897	8,225	32,482	27,746	352,541	301,156
1907[1]	60,751	59,602	20,520	15,171	45,166	40,002	11,319	9,771	38,502	33,831	345,780	303,871
1906	49,437	50,602	17,533	14,658	33,757	30,425	8,269	7,881	27,185	25,250	283,740	263,528
1905	45,864	48,543	13,537	13,629	33,142	29,527	7,656	7,446	23,174	22,543	251,964	245,077
1904	45,529	43,484	11,336	14,587	31,957	26,701	7,108	6,816	22,537	21,840	243,909	236,540
1903	45,477	45,060	10,036	11,139	26,677	21,317	6,977	6,825	20,429	20,316	225,005	223,744
1902	36,333	35,978	8,592	10,948	22,538	20,314	6,239	6,250	18,826	19,251	196,738	200,923
1901	29,956	29,018	7,167	8,332	21,255	19,755	5,685	5,277	16,327	16,126	177,931	176,205
1900	33,476	33,476	5,820	5,820	18,538	18,538	5,422	5,422	14,059	14,059	172,652	172,652
1899	22,608	27,213	5,114	7,329	16,358	17,629	4,971	5,256	12,672	14,150	149,422	166,895
1898	19,445	22,402	4,533	5,288	14,328	14,844	4,502	4,579	10,634	11,955	126,307	142,227
1897	13,982	16,294	3,275	5,332	13,754	13,700	3,802	3,842	10,079	12,021	106,618	127,311
1896	13,394	14,297	2,972	4,956	13,737	14,143	3,838	3,915	8,869	10,066	105,361	119,796
1895	10,756	13,307	2,783	5,221	12,930	12,794	3,467	3,577	9,126	10,684	100,676	118,126
1894	12,910	13,924	3,064	4,759	14,313	13,290	3,621	3,775	10,106	10,782	109,071	116,474
1893	14,727	15,635	3,733	4,960	15,050	13,546	4,102	4,019	9,531	9,874	115,171	119,546
1892	14,550	13,890	3,704	4,962	14,658	13,593	3,899	3,869	9,170	9,345	115,160	117,918
1891	15,143	13,140	3,811	4,651	14,139	12,885	3,698	3,620	8,577	8,162	111,534	107,007
1890	14,433	13,831	2,310	2,949	12,151	10,982	3,737	3,805	10,128	9,802	111,683	109,031
1889	13,298	13,693	2,044	2,487	12,425	11,116	3,541	3,312	10,557	10,299	109,008	106,921
1888	11,743	12,742	1,948	2,319	12,929	15,611	3,516	3,370	8,656	9,013	100,672	105,045
1887	14,445	17,054	2,606	3,823	11,347	9,859	3,546	3,526	6,120	6,283	105,107	107,543
1886	11,211	11,305	1,732	2,482	10,215	8,971	3,242	3,139	7,687	7,563	95,992	94,561
1885	11,548	11,216	1,574	2,047	10,411	8,327	3,275	2,897	8,281	7,701	99,756	92,867
1884	14,463	12,715	1,873	2,415	11,390	8,773	3,234	2,649	7,836	6,852	105,973	92,760
1883	19,524	16,617	2,043	2,847	10,198	7,897	3,010	1,751	12,630	10,673	121,861	103,455
1882	17,991	15,454	1,496	2,349	8,457	6,870	2,564	1,722	11,281	9,631	111,145	94,663
1881	13,837	11,081	1,242	1,979	6,643	5,614	2,023	1,417	7,480	6,545	90,488	79,871
1880	9,594	7,988	995	1,392	4,733	4,997	2,348	1,810	5,958	5,443	69,901	63,885
1879	8,053	7,099	980	1,040	5,196	4,619	2,306	1,796	7,671	7,398	78,703	75,369
1878	9,103	7,274	810	886	5,458	5,183	2,532	1,718	10,306	9,086	90,396	79,634
1877	9,613	6,981	816	782	5,793	5,114	2,145	1,630	9,208	7,717	94,126	78,923
1876	14,703	8,634	839	729	5,982	4,574	1,993	2,067	10,069	7,601	92,513	69,571
1875	18,207	8,953	1,310	1,225	6,299	4,241	2,321	2,372	18,978	14,012	117,409	86,687
1874	19,958	14,068	1,277	1,028	7,310	4,811	1,887	935	20,350	15,318	123,181	92,724
1873	14,809	13,160	1,276	1,187	5,391	3,680	2,263	1,514	28,564	20,399	124,509	88,924
1872	14,605	11,032	1,549	1,259	3,922	2,195	1,697	1,292	19,245	13,205	104,955	72,006
1871	10,552	7,633	558	534	3,757	3,407	1,863	1,657	22,154	16,141	84,214	61,372
1870	7,279	5,932	475	501	3,547	3,335	1,611	1,597	6,916	5,608	66,902	56,844
1869	7,178	5,375	320	319	3,453	3,045	1,514	1,689	8,376	6,328	63,155	47,467

[1] The data are for fiscal years ending 31 March of the year given from 1908 to 1915, and for fiscal years ending 30 June of the year given from 1869 to 1907. The figures for 1907 are for twelve months ending 30 June 1907 and for 1908 they are for the twelve months ending 31 March 1908.

Series F 294–297. *Foreign trade, exports of domestic and foreign produce and imports, declared values and estimated values at prices prevailing in fiscal year 1913, 1891 to 1926*

(thousands of dollars)

Year[1]	Exports		Imports		Year[1]	Exports		Imports	
	Declared values	Valued at 1913 prices	Declared values	Valued at 1913 prices		Declared values	Valued at 1913 prices	Declared values	Valued at 1913 prices
	294	**295**	**296**	**297**		**294**	**295**	**296**	**297**
1926	1,328,700	896,956	927,329	718,787	1905	201,472	236,579	251,964	299,145
					1904	211,056	248,118	243,909	282,134
1925	1,081,362	769,597	796,932	581,516	1903	225,230	267,840	225,094	273,457
1924	1,058,763	820,438	893,367	605,613	1902	209,971	253,989	196,738	251,600
1923	945,296	692,218	802,579	582,271	1901	194,509	236,864	177,931	222,328
1922	753,927	493,858	747,804	512,909					
1921	1,210,428	504,864	1,240,159	559,423	1900	183,237	237,103	172,652	222,312
					1899	154,881	214,659	149,422	216,050
1920	1,286,659	614,995	1,064,528	579,339	1898	159,529	212,902	126,307	185,919
1919	1,268,765	655,244	919,712	564,288	1897	134,458	198,683	106,618	156,293
1918	1,586,170	816,366	963,532	649,610	1896	116,314	164,467	105,361	147,386
1917	1,179,211	899,697	846,451	711,910					
1916	779,300	689,002	508,201	530,060	1895	109,313	147,321	100,676	159,230
					1894	115,685	149,152	109,071	147,100
1915	461,442	442,968	455,956	480,014	1893	114,431	150,186	115,171	150,530
1914	455,437	473,471	619,194	611,971	1892	112,154	138,934	115,160	148,119
1913	377,068	377,068	671,207	671,207	1891	97,470	123,100	111,534	141,394
1912	307,716	315,343	522,405	511,692					
1911	290,000	292,483	452,725	453,846					
1910	298,764	297,761	370,318	388,171					
1909	259,922	264,918	288,594	324,565					
1908[1]	263,369	271,468	352,541	371,973					
1907[1]	244,982	254,418	345,780	385,873					
1906	246,658	275,217	283,740	322,166					

[1] The data are for fiscal years ending 31 March of the year given from 1908 to 1915, and for fiscal years ending 30 June of the year given from 1869 to 1907. The figures for 1907 are for twelve months ending 30 June 1907 and for 1908 they are for the twelve months ending 31 March 1908.

Series F 298–315. *Foreign trade, domestic exports, by main groups, declared values (adjusted) and values at 1948 prices, 1926 to 1960*

(thousands of dollars)

Year	Agricultural and animal products		Fibres, textiles and products		Wood, wood products and paper		Iron and steel products		Nonferrous metals and products	
	Declared values (adjusted)	Values at 1948 prices	Declared values (adjusted)	Values at 1948 prices	Declared values (adjusted)	Values at 1948 prices	Declared values (adjusted)	Values at 1948 prices	Declared values (adjusted)	Values at 1948 prices
	298	**299**	**300**	**301**	**302**	**303**	**304**	**305**	**306**	**307**
1960	1,142,428	1,147,016	40,518	36,668	1,591,919	1,343,392	605,960	372,211	1,213,999	815,860
1959[1]	1,212,381	1,214,811	26,803	24,864	1,515,962	1,261,200	574,453	355,259	1,114,784	765,648
1958	1,275,150	1,320,031	20,660	19,129	1,413,989	1,185,238	450,572	286,805	1,023,607	712,818
1957	1,124,543	1,175,071	27,162	24,165	1,456,125	1,214,449	549,641	362,799	981,742	637,909
1956	1,225,876	1,278,285	22,568	20,761	1,514,458	1,260,997	465,712	325,445	952,330	577,169
1955	1,006,146	1,042,638	22,816	21,443	1,520,921	1,288,916	402,957	298,929	847,499	567,268
1954	1,062,206	1,097,320	20,969	19,308	1,378,354	1,185,171	307,537	232,454	709,017	526,758
1953	1,339,348	1,294,056	24,333	213,326	1,295,396	1,095,009	376,891	280,842	682,183	505,320
1952	1,403,747	1,304,597	27,697	230,808	1,366,787	1,116,656	417,538	317,761	706,732	495,604
1951	1,213,176	1,056,773	36,858	263,648	1,399,076	1,143,035	350,369	277,629	569,870	413,248
1950	990,520	937,992	29,573	26,217	1,112,945	1,059,947	273,242	240,318	457,262	397,273
1949	1,085,648	1,049,949	25,217	24,387	875,318	894,094	334,023	299,841	426,608	403,221
1948	1,045,471	1,045,471	45,554	45,555	953,674	953,674	362,913	362,913	395,948	395,948
1947	982,017	1,029,424	49,347	58,398	886,192	963,252	297,121	336,490	303,937	349,754
1946	914,484	1,079,674	53,760	81,331•	625,591	865,505	245,329	298,091	247,810	325,637
1945	1,185,864	1,504,903	56,881	84,019	488,041	763,757	567,556	713,906	352,546	609,941
1944	1,088,306	1,466,719	59,742	90,108	440,901	715,748	792,210	101,305	339,908	642,548
1943	767,018	1,194,732	30,620	48,220	391,070	698,339	799,529	115,205	332,705	643,529
1942	502,823	946,035	28,932	45,562	389,805	762,827	563,475	858,955	308,903	596,357
1941	472,715	980,736	30,820	50,032	387,113	788,417	241,820	395,130	244,012	469,253
1940	369,871	780,318	22,696	40,028	348,006	758,183	127,694	222,463	194,712	395,756
1939	335,807	809,173	14,428	31,709	242,541	591,563	63,475	123,732	182,890	305,049
1938	293,903	643,113	13,055	29,536	211,613	558,345	60,357	116,294	179,664	345,507
1937	371,166	606,480	14,400	28,235	262,968	693,846	66,603	132,675	194,876	318,424
1936	457,257	916,346	12,227	25,849	210,207	611,066	52,332	108,572	134,437	267,802
1935	314,374	680,463	9,640	21,186	175,871	524,988	50,170	111,488	115,673	245,069
1934	299,856	660,475	7,335	15,186	161,137	485,352	37,625	84,172	89,678	196,662
1933	257,899	682,272	7,046	15,657	131,359	386,350	22,500	49,342	67,041	149,979
1932	252,869	714,319	4,815	10,771	133,982	333,288	16,599	34,798	44,204	110,510
1931	266,986	667,465	5,394	10,875	185,493	402,237	19,665	41,663	56,159	125,635
1930	382,306	692,583	7,302	12,969	249,690	492,485	48,192	100,000	93,454	175,996
1929	538,173	782,228	9,472	14,869	292,601	552,077	90,636	174,972	118,167	153,663
1928	783,442	1,117,606	9,731	14,721	289,126	522,831	70,873	138,966	92,953	123,937
1927	682,556	921,128	10,927	16,993	280,959	500,818	68,353	128,725	79,176	103,228
1926	730,580	956,256	7,112	10,332	286,306	502,291	75,798	143,015	74,669	88,891

Series F 298–315. *Foreign trade, domestic exports, by main groups, declared values (adjusted) and values at 1948 prices, 1926 to 1960 (continuation)*

(thousands of dollars)

Year	Nonmetallic minerals and products		Chemicals and fertilizers		Miscellaneous products		All commodities	
	Declared values (adjusted)	Values at 1948 prices	Declared values (adjusted)	Values at 1948 prices	Declared values (adjusted)	Values at 1948 prices	Declared values (adjusted)	Values at 1948 prices
	308	**309**	**310**	**311**	**312**	**313**	**314**	**315**
1960	339,569	205,426	237,687	206,147	83,495	62,356	5,255,575	4,272,825
1959[1]	294,235	178,324	201,729	175,722	81,324	63,091	5,021,672	4,089,309
1958	250,351	151,452	197,051	172,096	191,967	149,042	4,823,347	3,999,458
1957	357,287	223,864	195,303	172,376	132,430	102,738	4,824,233	3,986,969
1956	299,241	191,698	182,854	160,539	126,707	100,084	4,789,746	3,945,425
1955	211,624	141,176	183,507	159,849	86,314	68,940	4,281,784	3,637,879
1954	145,573	96,919	161,293	140,254	96,323	77,994	3,881,272	3,372,086
1953	147,393	98,590	137,885	117,749	113,977	92,139	4,117,406	3,480,478
1952	143,474	100,261	124,565	104,413	110,540	85,227	4,301,080	3,531,264
1951	131,529	99,870	131,690	112,844	81,892	61,898	3,914,460	3,074,988
1950	103,655	86,092	100,525	96,473	50,665	45,236	3,118,387	2,879,397
1949	73,710	65,578	70,698	67,395	101,739	98,108	2,992,961	2,897,348
1948	94,915	94,915	79,840	79,840	97,123	97,123	3,075,438	3,075,438
1947	74,614	84,596	83,804	93,322	97,870	108,744	2,774,902	3,029,360
1946	57,360	74,300	67,589	80,271	100,292	119,111	2,312,215	2,893,880
1945	59,555	78,672	111,318	123,549	396,253	446,733	3,218,014	4,679,850
1944	58,398	76,940	100,688	110,282	559,582	626,631	3,439,735	5,088,365
1943	62,192	82,155	86,390	92,593	501,897	605,424	2,971,421	4,871,181
1942	56,580	73,960	77,333	82,975	435,873	526,416	2,363,724	4,297,680
1941	45,172	68,442	58,676	63,502	140,529	178,790	1,620,857	3,123,038
1940	33,754	49,275	31,223	37,348	50,831	68,783	1,178,787	2,362,298
1939	29,332	44,987	24,263	31,674	31,842	48,318	924,578	2,050,062
1938	25,013	38,508	19,496	25,059	34,258	52,222	837,359	1,777,832
1937	30,896	53,360	21,667	27,957	34,607	52,754	997,183	1,867,383
1936	23,974	41,621	17,750	23,202	29,437	46,651	937,621	2,047,207
1935	17,900	32,310	16,372	20,593	24,827	39,345	724,827	1,670,108
1934	15,758	29,509	14,350	18,373	23,471	39,118	649,210	1,523,967
1933	13,309	23,597	12,004	17,195	17,636	28,958	529,394	1,326,802
1932	9,658	16,397	11,033	14,403	16,619	26,421	489,779	1,215,332
1931	14,977	27,632	10,849	13,477	27,879	42,759	587,402	1,311,165
1930	22,862	38,683	16,320	18,482	43,295	60,467	863,421	1,598,927
1929	29,720	46,437	21,828	23,751	51,532	71,373	1,152,129	1,789,020
1928	26,583	41,862	18,357	18,827	47,950	64,104	1,339,015	2,047,423
1927	27,074	43,738	17,266	17,546	43,845	56,941	1,210,156	1,790,171
1926	27,095	45,309	16,488	16,023	42,832	49,746	1,260,880	1,796,125

[1] New basis. See end of general note to series F 242–399.

12-2

Series F 316–333. *Foreign trade, imports, by main groups, declared values (adjusted) and values at 1948 prices, 1926 to 1960*

(thousands of dollars)

Year	Agricultural and animal products		Fibres, textiles and products		Wood, wood products and paper		Iron and steel products		Nonferrous metals and products	
	Declared values (adjusted)	Values at 1948 prices	Declared values (adjusted)	Values at 1948 prices	Declared values (adjusted)	Values at 1948 prices	Declared values (adjusted)	Values at 1948 prices	Declared values (adjusted)	Values at 1948 prices
	316	317	318	319	320	321	322	323	324	325
1960[1]	737,710	809,780	431,975	508,206	256,701	180,521	2,046,258	1,396,763	476,633	344,637
1959[1]	733,062	802,916	425,470	516,974	263,203	188,406	2,086,064	1,446,660	479,231	354,723
1958	716,373	714,230	387,297	447,225	226,912	163,599	1,844,480	1,288,944	442,795	333,429
1957	705,432	678,300	408,651	453,049	217,722	172,795	2,122,967	1,537,267	495,540	377,410
1956	673,870	675,220	416,390	466,804	220,279	177,931	2,221,640	1,667,897	503,327	379,011
1955	600,292	601,494	381,613	399,594	188,431	157,814	1,597,472	1,275,936	411,512	329,737
1954	579,962	569,644	333,324	343,308	158,912	138,007	1,312,976	1,094,513	368,638	308,479
1953	526,025	540,066	387,115	385,572	154,445	131,891	1,521,044	1,266,481	376,170	314,260
1952	522,597	510,847	359,440	331,281	129,411	112,238	1,402,232	1,195,423	304,218	252,463
1951	583,679	476,857	483,520	304,867	132,383	111,809	1,328,055	1,084,126	297,353	245,340
1950	522,763	483,145	364,509	333,494	95,859	85,895	977,582	842,017	219,730	205,547
1949	422,469	428,033	333,032	332,035	82,461	78,014	889,398	831,213	177,861	168,748
1948	403,014	403,014	350,619	350,619	70,549	70,549	783,401	783,401	156,419	156,419
1947	414,457	447,094	390,589	447,407	87,236	94,718	758,132	858,586	167,840	180,279
1946	354,911	432,291	264,121	376,240	67,736	80,255	487,674	632,521	124,369	150,750
1945	267,085	361,414	196,761	297,222	48,322	60,782	387,083	517,490	99,766	138,371
1944	234,375	328,716	190,575	273,030	42,652	53,921	428,927	581,990	106,702	150,073
1943	189,627	275,620	195,283	291,032	39,376	51,404	420,411	571,210	115,578	166,538
1942	159,348	273,793	189,066	347,547	37,186	51,149	377,829	513,354	82,426	118,258
1941	167,311	359,036	161,139	335,008	35,471	51,782	431,860	611,699	94,810	139,017
1940	157,276	389,297	147,329	336,367	36,599	57,185	299,917	441,703	71,670	108,590
1939	144,195	389,716	100,866	291,520	32,154	56,410	182,927	291,285	42,521	69,821
1938	138,395	362,290	87,443	254,194	30,538	55,422	162,750	261,655	38,529	65,749
1937	159,569	349,166	115,273	281,841	32,330	57,939	211,118	346,663	47,148	74,957
1936	139,658	349,145	98,915	265,900	25,683	49,485	135,540	243,339	35,125	63,517
1935	122,521	303,269	85,191	234,685	21,414	41,339	112,562	202,086	33,658	61,644
1934	118,995	271,678	83,873	226,683	20,855	37,918	93,776	169,884	25,994	48,586
1933	100,046	246,418	70,275	212,954	18,783	33,843	60,749	108,286	18,045	32,928
1932	109,910	260,450	68,949	229,066	22,837	39,855	67,418	111,990	22,016	39,174
1931	154,564	336,008	90,152	279,108	34,947	59,840	115,494	198,784	39,470	68,524
1930	237,196	402,027	149,150	350,941	49,998	87,104	222,651	372,949	69,826	111,721
1929	278,641	434,020	198,929	306,989	62,821	102,816	336,576	534,247	97,268	138,756
1928	281,013	399,166	201,743	302,917	57,319	93,353	323,460	528,529	69,018	102,552
1927	264,979	376,390	183,492	296,432	50,413	80,275	248,687	405,027	59,267	87,029
1926	232,670	354,679	184,237	276,632	46,445	72,119	221,843	348,809	50,808	71,966

Year	Nonmetallic minerals and products		Chemicals and fertilizers		Miscellaneous products		All commodities	
	Declared values (adjusted)	Values at 1948 prices	Declared values (adjusted)	Values at 1948 prices	Declared values (adjusted)	Values at 1948 prices	Declared values (adjusted)	Values at 1948 prices
	326	327	328	329	330	331	332	333
1960[1]	660,749	670,131	346,972	310,073	525,698	418,216	5,482,695	4,746,922
1959[1]	698,138	685,794	334,455	301,583	489,299	420,721	5,508,920	4,815,490
1958	676,000	634,741	297,212	263,719	574,180	537,118	5,165,249	4,433,690
1957	771,763	711,302	299,718	270,259	573,182	506,341	5,594,976	4,798,430
1956	760,785	745,867	293,772	263,000	566,081	478,513	5,656,144	5,005,437
1955	659,171	655,239	205,012	241,139	563,504	470,763	4,667,007	4,223,535
1954	594,638	575,265	224,984	207,711	494,755	485,840	4,068,190	3,722,837
1953	654,524	624,545	225,785	206,884	507,986	457,645	4,353,094	3,979,062
1952	638,754	628,076	190,843	175,085	464,059	375,756	4,011,555	3,633,654
1951	681,356	626,246	194,992	166,375	375,749	225,539	4,077,083	3,230,652
1950	608,445	582,801	161,517	157,117	222,819	183,390	3,173,224	2,876,902
1949	531,449	523,079	134,540	134,540	188,061	192,685	2,759,271	2,689,347
1948	603,271	603,271	121,291	121,291	145,998	145,998	2,634,562	2,634,562
1947	449,340	507,348	115,943	118,794	187,382	196,623	2,570,920	2,921,500
1946	330,446	487,383	95,039	113,819	197,991	212,436	1,922,287	2,512,793
1945	263,954	417,648	81,210	103,058	206,022	184,773	1,550,203	2,114,874
1944	269,304	433,661	82,553	107,072	377,763	337,589	1,732,851	2,380,289
1943	249,858	414,358	71,633	94,878	406,472	422,967	1,688,238	2,418,690
1942	220,300	391,992	67,877	86,688	372,103	442,453	1,506,135	2,375,607
1941	189,090	356,773	66,246	89,886	130,955	174,374	1,276,882	2,216,809
1940	160,534	337,256	52,488	75,631	102,077	143,973	1,027,890	1,939,415
1939	132,347	297,408	44,183	81,368	69,210	112,171	748,403	1,585,599
1938	121,265	263,047	35,662	66,782	60,400	103,071	674,982	1,430,046
1937	136,019	291,886	37,868	69,228	67,659	103,771	806,984	1,588,551
1936	115,199	257,715	32,269	59,646	49,776	86,869	632,165	1,365,367
1935	103,602	240,934	29,993	55,749	38,355	73,336	547,296	1,202,848
1934	101,829	236,811	28,314	52,433	36,994	71,972	510,630	1,100,495
1933	78,063	209,846	24,142	42,578	27,919	63,308	398,022	910,805
1932	94,994	221,431	28,209	48,303	34,004	76,758	448,337	983,195
1931	105,469	261,061	31,956	54,439	51,717	104,268	623,769	1,338,560
1930	164,552	317,055	37,082	59,809	72,701	120,966	1,003,156	1,820,609
1929	185,807	332,987	40,246	68,679	92,606	128,798	1,292,894	2,052,212
1928	162,104	292,079	37,032	62,030	86,260	110,874	1,217,949	1,882,455
1927	155,310	266,855	33,408	52,860	84,022	88,912	1,079,578	1,643,193
1926	152,622	231,596	31,424	51,179	83,341	70,687	1,003,390	1,456,298

[1] New basis. See end of general note to series F 242–399.

Series F 334–341. *Foreign trade, exports excluding gold, by destination, major areas, 1886 to 1960*
(thousands of dollars)

Year[1]	Exports of Canadian produce						Exports of foreign produce	
	United Kingdom	United States	Other Commonwealth countries	Other foreign countries	Total Commonwealth countries	Total foreign countries	Total Commonwealth countries	Total foreign countries
	334	335	336	337	338	339	340	341
1960	915,290	2,932,171	326,108	1,082,006	1,241,398	4,014,177	13,691	117,526
1959[2]	785,802	3,083,151	273,305	879,414	1,059,107	3,962,565	10,912	107,716
1959[3]	788,618	3,107,846	274,960	889,286	1,063,578	3,997,132	10,926	107,742
1958	773,804	2,827,417	282,771	939,355	1,056,575	3,766,772	7,796	95,146
1957	722,669	2,867,608	233,117	1,000,838	955,786	3,868,447	8,689	86,597
1956	812,706	2,818,655	243,216	915,169	1,055,922	3,733,824	7,680	65,717
1955	769,313	2,559,343	237,125	716,004	1,006,437	3,275,347	6,194	63,306
1954	653,408	2,317,153	195,053	715,657	848,461	3,032,810	6,429	59,215
1953	665,232	2,418,915	232,353	800,906	897,585	3,219,821	5,752	49,443
1952	745,845	2,306,955	261,687	986,593	1,007,533	3,293,548	8,069	46,810
1951	631,461	2,297,674	240,946	744,379	872,407	3,042,053	6,689	42,235
1950	469,910	2,020,988	185,179	442,309	655,089	2,463,297	3,969	34,716
1949	704,956	1,503,459	310,067	474,479	1,015,022	1,977,938	5,835	23,657
1948	686,914	1,500,987	345,477	542,060	1,032,391	2,043,047	4,884	29,706
1947	751,198	1,034,226	417,303	572,175	1,168,501	1,606,401	6,897	29,991
1946	597,506	887,941	307,195	519,574	904,701	1,407,514	3,393	23,557
1945	963,238	1,196,977	523,610	534,506	1,486,848	1,731,482	14,053	35,040
1944	1,235,030	1,301,322	385,421	518,179	1,620,451	1,819,502	8,829	34,316
1943	1,032,047	1,149,232	369,015	420,581	1,401,662	1,569,814	11,566	18,311
1942	741,717	885,523	412,100	324,433	1,153,817	1,209,956	9,315	12,378
1941	658,228	599,713	220,413	142,649	878,641	742,362	6,119	13,332
1940	508,096	442,984	147,861	80,013	655,957	522,997	5,201	9,062
1939	328,099	380,392	102,707	113,727	430,806	494,119	1,427	9,569
1938	339,689	270,461	103,214	124,220	442,902	394,681	2,428	8,672
1937	402,062	360,012	104,159	131,133	506,221	491,146	1,988	12,767
1936	395,352	333,917	84,294	124,262	479,646	458,179	1,494	11,190
1935	303,501	261,685	74,143	85,648	377,644	347,333	1,183	11,776
1934	270,492	218,597	64,926	95,299	335,418	313,896	1,241	5,751
1933	210,697	168,243	44,483	106,026	255,181	274,269	960	5,074
1932	178,172	158,705	38,985	114,021	217,157	272,726	1,302	6,728
1931	170,597	240,197	49,184	127,675	219,781	367,872	1,713	10,194
1930	235,214	373,424	81,129	173,917	316,342	547,341	2,149	17,315
1929	290,294	492,686	105,006	264,429	395,301	757,115	2,372	23,554
1928	446,129	481,531	99,228	312,522	545,356	794,053	2,541	21,838
1927	409,546	466,887	90,209	243,954	499,755	710,841	2,768	17,677
1926[1]	459,223	457,877	95,701	248,439	554,924	706,317	2,001	13,356
1921	312,845	542,323	90,607	243,388	403,452	785,711	2,302	18,962
1916	451,852	201,106	30,677	57,974	482,529	259,081	12,056	25,633
1911[1]	132,157	104,116	16,811	21,233	148,967	125,349	5,169	10,514
1906	127,456	83,546	10,965	13,516	138,421	97,063	5,884	5,289
1901	92,857	67,984	7,891	8,699	100,748	76,683	12,632	4,446
1896	62,718	37,789	4,048	5,152	66,766	42,942	4,343	2,263
1891	43,244	37,743	3,893	3,791	47,137	41,534	6,221	2,578
1886[1]	36,694	34,284	3,263	3,515	39,957	37,799	5,109	2,329

[1] Figures from 1926 to 1960 are for calendar years, from 1911 to 1921 they are for fiscal years ending 31 March of the year given and prior to 1907 they are for fiscal years ending 30 June of the year given.

[2] New basis. See end of general note to series F 242–399.
[3] Old basis.

Series F 342–347. *Foreign trade, imports excluding gold, by origin, major areas, 1886 to 1960*

(thousands of dollars)

	Imports for consumption from								Imports for consumption from					
Year[1]	United Kingdom	United States	Other Common-wealth countries	Other foreign countries	Total Common-wealth countries	Total foreign countries		Year[1]	United Kingdom	United States	Other Common-wealth countries	Other foreign countries	Total Common-wealth countries	Total foreign countries
	342	**343**	**344**	**345**	**346**	**347**			**342**	**343**	**344**	**345**	**346**	**347**
1960	588,932	3,686,625	279,069	928,069	868,001	4,614,694		1935	116,670	312,417	57,218	64,009	173,889	376,426
								1934	113,416	293,780	43,651	62,623	157,061	356,403
1959[2]	588,573	3,709,065	239,240	972,043	827,813	4,681,108		1933	97,878	217,291	34,806	51,238	132,685	268,529
1959[3]	596,561	3,829,438	240,893	987,531	837,454	4,816,969		1932	93,508	263,549	34,549	61,007	128,058	324,557
1958	526,650	3,572,379	209,862	883,460	736,512	4,455,839		1931	109,468	393,775	42,532	82,323	152,000	476,098
1957	521,958	3,998,549	238,861	864,042	760,819	4,862,591								
1956	484,679	4,161,667	221,232	837,871	705,911	4,999,538		1930	162,632	653,676	65,183	126,987	227,816	780,664
								1929	194,778	893,585	62,287	148,343	257,064	1,041,928
1955	400,531	3,452,178	209,772	649,889	610,302	4,102,067		1928	190,757	825,651	63,333	142,576	254,090	968,228
1954	392,471	2,961,379	181,759	557,586	574,231	3,518,965		1927	182,620	706,684	58,333	139,481	240,953	846,165
1953	453,391	3,221,214	170,571	537,654	623,962	3,758,868		1926[1]	164,707	668,747	49,907	124,980	214,614	793,727
1952	359,757	2,976,962	184,704	509,044	544,461	3,486,006								
1951	420,984	2,812,927	306,104	544,840	727,089	3,357,767		1921	213,973	856,177	52,029	117,979	266,003	974,156
								1916	77,404	370,880	27,826	32,091	105,230	402,971
1950	404,213	2,130,476	241,411	398,153	645,624	2,528,629		1911[1]	109,935	275,824	19,533	47,433	129,468	323,257
1949	307,450	1,951,860	186,779	315,118	494,229	2,266,978		1906	69,184	169,256	14,605	30,694	83,789	199,951
1948	299,502	1,805,763	204,612	327,069	504,114	2,132,831								
1947	189,370	1,974,679	165,024	244,871	354,394	2,219,550		1901	42,820	107,378	3,833	23,900	46,653	131,278
1946	201,433	1,405,297	139,067	181,482	340,501	1,586,779		1896	32,824	53,529	2,389	16,619	35,213	70,148
								1891	42,019	52,033	2,318	15,163	44,337	67,197
1945	140,517	1,202,418	131,151	111,689	271,668	1,314,107		1886[1]	39,033	42,819	2,383	11,757	41,416	54,575
1944	110,598	1,447,226	109,755	91,318	220,354	1,538,544								
1943	134,965	1,423,672	103,666	72,773	238,631	1,496,445								
1942	161,113	1,304,680	112,664	65,786	273,776	1,370,465								
1941	219,419	1,004,498	140,523	84,351	359,942	1,088,849								
1940	161,216	744,231	106,167	70,336	267,383	814,567								
1939	114,007	496,898	74,893	65,257	188,900	562,155								
1938	119,292	424,730	66,806	66,622	186,099	491,353								
1937	147,291	490,505	89,304	81,795	236,596	572,300								
1936	122,971	369,141	66,348	76,730	189,319	445,872								

[1] Figures from 1926 to 1960 are for calendar years, from 1911 to 1921 they are for fiscal years ending 31 March of the year given and prior to 1907 they are for fiscal years ending 30 June of the year given.

[2] New basis. See end of general note to series F 242–399.
[3] Old basis.

Series F 348–356. *Foreign trade, total exports, imports and trade balance with all countries, the United States and the United Kingdom, 1901 to 1960*

(thousands of dollars)

Year	Total exports			Imports			Trade balance		
	All countries	United States	United Kingdom	All countries	United States	United Kingdom	All countries	United States	United Kingdom
	348	349	350	351	352	353	354	355	356
1960	5,386,792	3,036,416	924,941	5,482,695	3,686,625	588,932	− 95,903	− 650,209	+ 336,009
1959[1]	5,140,300	3,181,903	794,271	5,508,920	3,709,065	588,573	− 368,620	− 527,162	+ 205,698
1959[2]	5,179,378	3,206,543	797,098	5,654,423	3,829,438	596,562	− 475,045	− 622,895	+ 200,536
1958	4,926,289	2,914,705	778,901	5,192,351	3,572,379	526,650	− 266,062	− 657,614	+ 252,251
1957	4,919,519	2,941,675	727,825	5,623,410	3,998,549	521,958	− 703,891	−1,056,874	+ 205,867
1956	4,863,143	2,879,014	818,432	5,705,449	4,161,667	484,679	− 842,306	−1,282,653	+ 333,753
1955	4,351,284	2,612,182	773,994	4,712,370	3,452,178	400,531	− 361,086	− 839,997	+ 373,463
1954	3,946,917	2,367,439	658,315	4,093,196	2,961,380	392,472	− 146,280	− 593,941	+ 265,843
1953	4,172,601	2,463,051	668,874	4,382,830	3,221,214	453,391	− 210,229	− 758,163	+ 215,482
1952	4,355,960	2,349,044	751,049	4,030,468	2,976,962	359,757	+ 325,492	− 627,918	+ 391,292
1951	3,963,384	2,333,912	635,721	4,084,856	2,812,927	420,985	− 121,472	− 479,015	+ 214,736
1950	3,157,073	2,050,460	472,536	3,174,253	2,130,476	404,213	− 17,180	− 80,016	+ 68,323
1949	3,022,453	1,524,024	709,261	2,761,207	1,951,860	307,450	+ 261,246	− 427,836	+ 401,811
1948	3,110,029	1,522,185	688,697	2,636,945	1,805,763	299,502	+ 473,083	− 283,578	+ 389,195
1947	2,811,790	1,056,598	753,664	2,573,944	1,974,679	189,370	+ 237,846	− 918,082	+ 504,294
1946	2,339,166	908,577	598,799	1,864,564[3]	1,405,297	141,341[3]	+ 471,601[3]	− 496,720	+ 457,458[3]
1945	3,267,424	1,227,439	971,455	1,555,600[3]	1,202,418	121,693[3]	+1,711,824[3]	+ 25,022	+ 849,763[3]
1944	3,483,099	1,334,554	1,238,078	1,758,898	1,447,226	110,599	+1,724,200	− 112,671	+1,127,479
1943	3,001,352	1,166,655	1,037,224	1,735,077	1,423,672	134,965	+1,266,275	− 257,018	+ 902,258
1942	2,385,466	896,621	747,891	1,644,242	1,304,680	161,113	+ 741,224	− 408,059	+ 586,778
1941	1,640,455	609,690	661,238	1,448,792	1,004,498	219,419	+ 191,663	− 394,808	+ 441,819
1940	1,193,218	451,944	512,317	1,081,951	744,231	161,216	+ 111,267	− 292,287	+ 351,101
1939	935,922	389,754	323,886	751,056	496,898	114,007	+ 184,866	− 107,145	+ 214,879
1938	848,684	278,758	341,424	677,451	424,731	119,292	+ 171,233	− 145,973	+ 222,132
1937	1,012,122	372,221	403,359	808,896	490,505	147,292	+ 203,225	− 118,284	+ 256,067
1936	950,509	344,787	396,270	635,191	369,142	122,971	+ 315,318	− 24,355	+ 273,299
1935	737,936	273,120	304,318	550,315	312,417	116,670	+ 187,621	− 39,297	+ 187,648
1934	656,306	224,023	271,370	513,469	293,780	113,416	+ 142,837	− 69,757	+ 157,954
1933	535,484	172,955	211,314	401,214	217,291	97,878	+ 134,269	− 44,337	+ 113,436
1932	497,914	165,022	179,095	452,614	263,549	93,508	+ 45,299	− 98,528	+ 85,586
1931	599,560	249,801	171,660	628,098	393,775	109,468	− 28,538	− 143,975	+ 62,192
1930	883,148	389,912	236,527	1,008,479	653,676	162,632	− 125,332	− 263,764	+ 73,895
1929	1,178,342	515,338	291,829	1,298,993	893,585	194,778	− 120,650	− 378,248	+ 97,052
1928	1,363,788	502,690	447,868	1,222,318	825,652	190,757	+ 141,470	− 322,962	+ 257,111
1927	1,231,042	483,851	411,527	1,087,118	706,684	182,620	+ 143,924	− 222,833	+ 228,907
1926	1,276,599	470,564	464,444	1,008,342	668,747	164,707	+ 268,257	− 197,183	+ 295,737
1925	1,251,666	450,859	493,170	890,193	578,575	162,119	+ 361,473	− 127,716	+ 331,052
1924	1,042,253	394,624	388,434	808,145	524,473	148,892	+ 234,109	− 129,849	+ 239,542
1923	1,015,986	420,328	361,888	903,031	610,354	154,479	+ 112,956	− 190,026	+ 207,409
1922	894,224	347,617	375,627	762,409	509,909	136,859	+ 131,815	− 162,292	+ 238,768
1921	814,144	334,973	309,842	799,478	555,091	123,150	+ 14,665	− 220,118	+ 186,692
1920	1,298,162	581,408	343,217	1,336,921	921,235	231,488	− 38,759	− 339,827	+ 111,729
1919	1,289,792	487,618	538,974	941,014	739,598	87,659	+ 348,778	− 251,979	+ 451,315
1918	1,233,689	441,273	586,558	910,171	741,339	72,906	+ 323,518	− 300,066	+ 513,652
1917	1,577,567	405,385	801,863	1,006,056	827,401	76,516	+ 571,511	− 422,016	+ 815,347
1916	1,094,062	251,599	718,724	767,410	595,369	117,637	+ 326,652	− 343,770	+ 601,087
1915	629,841	181,061	361,486	450,960	316,934	74,364	+ 178,881	− 135,873	+ 287,123
1914	413,067	169,318	184,115	482,076	308,634	98,754	− 69,009	− 139,316	+ 85,361
1913	447,699	167,974	224,515	659,993	427,974	139,900	− 212,294	− 260,000	+ 84,615
1912	352,948	129,251	176,646	636,790	410,242	133,429	− 283,842	− 280,992	+ 43,217
1911	289,055	100,770	147,182	503,542	319,942	113,352	− 214,487	− 219,172	+ 33,831
1910	289,844	108,198	140,500	435,251	262,142	107,722	− 145,407	− 153,944	+ 32,778
1909	282,887	100,869	145,783	347,067	202,479	89,565	− 64,180	− 101,611	+ 56,219
1908	257,318	80,233	141,120	282,707	166,062	71,057	− 25,388	− 85,829	+ 70,062
1907	245,954	90,430	126,110	366,575	216,769	96,252	− 120,621	− 126,339	+ 29,858
1906	241,768	79,743	135,051	312,114	187,757	77,664	− 70,346	− 108,014	+ 57,387
1905	209,176	64,014	120,519	262,765	155,495	64,825	− 53,589	− 91,481	+ 55,693
1904	180,727	55,069	103,844	245,418	149,356	58,493	− 64,691	− 94,287	+ 45,351
1903	207,858	54,102	129,161	243,451	140,177	63,579	− 35,592	− 86,075	+ 65,582
1902	201,654	52,137	127,544	204,396	116,679	53,598	− 2,742	− 64,542	+ 73,946
1901	177,502	48,705	107,412	184,740	110,863	42,840	− 7,237	− 62,157	+ 64,572

[1] New basis. See end of general note to series F 242–399.
[2] Old basis.

[3] Adjusted for Canadian-owned military equipment returned to Canada.

Series F 357–359. *Foreign trade, indexes of import and export prices and the terms of trade, 1869 to 1960*

Year[1,2]	Price indexes		Export price as a percentage of import price (terms of trade)	Year[1,2]	Price indexes		Export price as a percentage of import price (terms of trade)
	Import	Export			Import	Export	
	357	358	359		357	358	359
(base 1948 = 100)				(base 1900 = 100)			
1960	115.5	123.0	106.5	1915	103.1	122.5	118.8
1959	114.4	122.8	107.3	1914	112.9	116.9	103.5
1958	116.5	120.6	103.5	1913	110.0	122.5	111.4
1957	116.4	121.0	104.0	1912	107.2	120.7	112.6
1956	113.0	121.4	107.4	1911	110.5	123.7	111.9
1955	110.5	117.7	106.5	1910	109.3	124.8	114.2
1954	109.5	115.1	105.1	1909	108.6	123.5	113.7
1953	109.4	118.3	108.1	1908	117.0	124.2	106.2
1952	110.4	121.8	110.3	1907	113.8	118.5	104.1
1951	126.2	123.0	97.5	1906	107.7	113.4	105.3
1950	110.3	108.3	98.2	1905	102.7	105.3	102.5
1949	102.6	103.3	100.7	1904	103.1	108.7	105.3
1948	100.0	100.0	100.0	1903	100.7	107.6	106.8
1947	88.0	91.6	104.1	1902	98.0	104.3	106.4
1946	76.5	79.9	104.4	1901	101.0	102.5	101.5
1945	73.3[2]	70.9[2]	96.7[2]	1900	100.0	100.0	100.0
1944	72.8[2]	67.8[2]	92.9[2]	1899	89.6	95.4	106.5
1943	69.8[2]	61.0[2]	87.4[2]	1898	88.8	97.0	109.2
1942	63.4[2]	55.0[2]	86.8[2]	1897	83.8	90.9	108.5
1941	57.6[2]	51.9[2]	90.1[2]	1896	87.9	93.1	105.9
1940	53.0	49.9	94.2	1895	85.3	96.5	113.1
1939	47.2	45.1	95.6	1894	93.7	101.0	107.8
1938	47.2	47.1	99.8	1893	96.3	100.7	104.6
1937	50.8	53.4	105.1	1892	97.8	103.0	105.3
1936	46.3	45.8	98.9	1891	104.2	104.0	99.8
1935	45.5	43.4	95.4	1890	102.4	103.5	101.1
1934	46.4	42.6	91.8	1889	102.1	101.3	99.2
1933	43.7	39.9	91.3	1888	95.9	101.6	106.0
1932	45.6	40.3	88.4	1887	97.7	96.3	98.6
1931	46.6	44.8	96.1	1886	101.5	96.1	94.7
1930	55.1	54.0	98.0	1885	107.3	99.2	92.5
1929	63.0	64.4	102.2	1884	114.3	104.8	91.7
1928	64.7	65.4	101.1	1883	117.8	109.6	93.1
1927	65.7	67.6	102.9	1882	117.4	107.2	91.3
1926	68.9	70.2	101.9	1881	113.3	97.5	86.1
(base 1913 = 100)				1880	109.4	93.8	85.7
1926	131.2	147.0	112.0	1879	104.4	91.6	87.8
				1878	113.5	100.9	88.9
1925	139.2	151.7	109.0	1877	119.3	98.1	82.3
1924	141.7	139.6	98.5	1876	132.9	109.1	82.1
1923	147.6	136.8	92.7				
1922	135.3	137.8	101.8	1875	135.4	105.8	78.2
1921	160.6	164.8	102.6	1874	132.9	101.0	76.1
				1873	140.1	99.1	71.7
1920	220.2	229.7	104.3	1872	145.7	95.5	65.6
1919	179.9	205.1	114.0	1871	137.2	93.4	68.1
1918	166.4	195.9	117.7				
1917	143.3	178.1	124.3	1870	117.6	88.4	75.2
1916	114.7	125.4	109.3	1869	133.0	89.4	67.2
1915	92.7	111.2	120.0				
1914	92.7	103.4	111.5				
1913	100.0	100.0	100.0				

[1] The indexes are for calendar years for 1913 to 1960 for the data of base 1948 = 100 and base 1913 = 100; for data of base 1900 = 100 they are for fiscal years ending 31 March of the year given from 1908 to 1915 and for fiscal years ending 30 June of the year given from 1869 to 1907.

[2] Price indexes and terms of trade for war years are not subject to the usual interpretation. See text.

APPENDIX TO SECTION F

Series F 360–379. *Foreign trade, exports of domestic produce, by main groups, declared values and values at prices prevailing in 1914, 1914 to 1929*

(thousands of dollars)

Year[1]	Agricultural and vegetable products		Animals and their products		Fibres and textiles		Wood and paper		Iron and its products		Nonferrous metals	
	Declared values	Valued at 1914 prices	Declared values	Valued at 1914 prices	Declared values	Valued at 1914 prices	Declared values	Valued at 1914 prices	Declared values	Valued at 1914 prices	Declared values	Valued at 1914 prices
	360	361	362	363	364	365	366	367	368	369	370	371
1929	646,514	560,734	158,757	90,410	9,678	6,005	288,622	181,143	82,257	91,135	112,778	106,478
1928	555,111	419,364	165,845	104,429	10,904	8,932	284,543	176,846	62,754	53,936	90,841	81,477
1927	574,994	409,401	167,292	109,378	7,666	5,904	284,120	172,453	74,285	75,457	80,639	68,876
1926	606,059	409,995	190,976	121,871	8,940	5,445	278,675	163,740	74,735	81,322	97,476	84,505
1925	443,299	315,741	163,031	116,877	9,711	5,787	253,610	146,049	57,406	59,242	90,371	82,254
1924	430,932	371,386	140,423	99,408	8,055	5,911	273,355	151,477	66,976	72,153	65,911	63,974
1923	407,760	328,635	135,841	100,367	7,851	6,287	228,756	134,037	51,138	48,465	44,358	42,096
1922	317,579	226,892	135,799	97,149	4,586	3,441	179,926	91,257	28,312	24,197	27,886	28,361
1921	482,140	197,391	188,360	92,153	18,784	11,695	284,561	108,168	76,501	54,910	45,939	34,760
1920	415,820	—	314,018	—	34,028	—	213,914	—	81,786	—	54,976	—
1919	288,893	—	244,991	—	28,030	—	154,569	—	81,911	—	79,261	—
1918	587,432	—	209,497	—	30,805	—	116,385	—	64,837	—	90,072	—
1914	201,190	201,190	76,591	76,591	1,934	1,934	63,202	63,202	15,483	15,483	53,304	53,304

Year[1]	Nonmetallic minerals		Chemicals and allied products		Miscellaneous		Total exports	
	Declared values	Valued at 1914 prices	Declared values	Valued at 1914 prices	Declared values	Valued at 1914 prices	Declared values	Valued at 1914 prices
	372	373	374	375	376	377	378	379
1929	27,402	16,529	19,438	18,392	18,264	14,395	1,363,710	1,085,221
1928	25,808	14,870	17,366	15,747	15,036	10,513	1,228,208	886,114
1927	28,881	17,534	16,204	14,031	18,077	12,466	1,252,158	885,500
1926	24,713	14,308	17,354	14,033	16,428	11,034	1,315,356	906,253
1925	20,729	15,300	16,210	11,163	14,700	10,528	1,069,067	762,941
1924	26,776	13,462	15,560	10,357	17,363	13,324	1,045,351	801,452
1923	27,647	13,857	14,047	8,743	14,053	10,384	931,451	692,871
1922	22,699	10,777	9,423	6,244	14,030	9,228	740,241	497,546
1921	40,345	15,995	20,143	13,110	32,390	15,042	1,189,164	543,224
1920	30,343	—	22,884	—	71,723	—	1,239,492	—
1919	26,662	—	56,800	—	255,326	—	1,216,444	—
1918	19,984	—	48,582	—	372,434	—	1,540,028	—
1914	9,323	9,323	4,831	4,831	5,731	5,731	431,589	431,589

[1] For fiscal years ending 31 March of the year shown.

Series F 380–399. *Foreign trade, imports, by main groups, declared values and values at prices prevailing in 1914, 1914 to 1929*

(thousands of dollars)

Year[1]	Agricultural and vegetable products		Animals and their products		Fibres and textiles		Wood and paper		Iron and products		Nonferrous metals	
	Declared values	Valued at 1914 prices	Declared values	Valued at 1914 prices	Declared values	Valued at 1914 prices	Declared values	Valued at 1914 prices	Declared values	Valued at 1914 prices	Declared values	Valued at 1914 prices
	380	**381**	**382**	**383**	**384**	**385**	**386**	**387**	**388**	**389**	**390**	**391**
1929	233,130	205,346	71,662	49,541	206,444	141,484	59,215	35,168	346,311	372,700	75,438	73,713
1928	238,185	174,776	65,790	47,780	186,996	127,307	51,751	31,346	259,574	285,073	60,190	56,319
1927	213,098	163,557	53,214	44,693	183,584	125,705	47,962	27,433	229,430	227,499	52,748	47,004
1926	203,417	143,725	49,186	41,395	184,762	109,209	40,403	25,076	181,197	168,258	47,693	45,292
1925	173,586	131,129	41,492	48,154	165,441	93,240	38,185	24,067	134,684	112,405	41,112	41,415
1924	186,469	128,384	45,027	53,437	173,796	97,358	40,977	23,577	173,474	140,504	43,433	41,960
1923	161,670	131,257	46,737	48,819	170,147	101,401	35,846	22,059	138,724	122,951	37,493	36,617
1922	172,666	121,445	46,646	46,723	139,997	82,785	35,791	20,566	110,211	76,805	29,773	28,058
1921	259,431	112,892	61,722	35,122	243,608	85,402	57,449	27,238	245,626	155,893	55,651	48,321
1920	241,846	—	95,099	—	231,560	—	43,183	—	186,320	—	52,176	—
1919	157,507	—	41,505	—	178,190	—	35,400	—	192,527	—	41,649	—
1918	148,959	—	60,570	—	152,311	—	28,471	—	195,249	—	46,203	—
1914	97,618	97,618	41,093	41,093	109,154	109,154	37,397	37,397	143,865	143,865	35,574	35,574

Year[1]	Nonmetallic minerals		Chemical and allied products		Miscellaneous		Total imports	
	Declared values	Valued at 1914 prices	Declared values	Valued at 1914 prices	Declared values	Valued at 1914 prices	Declared values	Valued at 1914 prices
	392	**393**	**394**	**395**	**396**	**397**	**398**	**399**
1929	166,964	140,749	37,723	29,029	68,492	59,941	1,265,679	1,107,671
1928	153,049	124,529	33,572	24,158	59,849	49,709	1,108,956	920,997
1927	156,785	113,349	31,845	22,310	62,227	49,570	1,030,892	821,210
1926	139,034	99,798	28,404	20,449	53,233	39,780	927,329	692,982
1925	131,013	93,926	24,760	17,954	46,660	35,008	796,933	597,298
1924	155,899	101,148	26,088	17,145	48,204	34,380	893,367	637,893
1923	139,989	78,993	25,793	16,705	46,180	34,150	802,579	592,952
1922	137,604	81,822	24,630	12,766	50,486	34,098	747,804	505,128
1921	206,095	93,882	37,887	16,731	72,690	35,805	1,240,159	611,286
1920	121,956	—	30,043	—	62,345	—	1,064,528	—
1919	135,250	—	34,283	—	103,400	—	919,712	—
1918	129,789	—	27,841	—	174,141	—	963,533	—
1914	85,289	85,289	17,073	17,073	52,131	52,131	619,194	619,194

[1] For fiscal years ending 31 March of the year shown.

SECTION G: GOVERNMENT FINANCE

J. HARVEY PERRY, *Canadian Tax Foundation*

This section contains data on revenues, expenditures and debt of federal, provincial and municipal governments. It falls into three main parts, the finances of the federal government from Confederation to 1960 in series G1–61, the finances of all governments for 1933, 1937, 1939, 1941, 1943 and 1945 to 1960 in series G62–309 and miscellaneous provincial and municipal statistics for earlier years in series G310–410. The second part, which presents data classified on a consistent basis for all levels of government, is further subdivided into consolidated government finance, all governments, in series G62–110, federal government finance in series G111–156, provincial government finance consolidated for Canada in series G157–207, municipal government finance consolidated for Canada in series G208–243, provincial government totals, by province, in series 244–276 and municipal government totals for each province in series G277–309.

The sources of data for the material of this section are: Government of Canada, *Public Accounts of Canada*, annual since Confederation (Ottawa, Queen's Printer); Dominion Bureau of Statistics, *Comparative Statistics of Public Finance, 1945 and 1951 to 1959* (Ottawa, Queen's Printer, 1959); Dominion Bureau of Statistics, *Comparative Statistics of Public Finance 1956 to 1960* (Ottawa, Queen's Printer, 1960); Dominion Bureau of Statistics, *A Consolidation of Public Finance Statistics, Municipalities, Provinces and the Government of Canada, 1959 and 1960, Actual* (Ottawa, Queen's Printer); Dominion Bureau of Statistics, *Financial Statistics of Provincial Governments, 1960, Direct and Indirect Debt, Actual* (Ottawa, Queen's Printer, 1962); Royal Commission on Dominion–Provincial Relations, Public Accounts Inquiry, Appendix 1, *Dominion of Canada and Canadian National Railways and Provincial Governments, Comparative Statistics of Public Finance 1913, 1921, 1925 to 1939* (Ottawa, 1939); Wilfrid Eggleston and C. T. Kraft, Royal Commission on Dominion–Provincial Relations, *Dominion–Provincial Subsidies and Grants* (Ottawa mimeographed, 1939); Canadian Tax Foundation, *Canadian Fiscal Facts, 1957* (Toronto, Canadian Tax Foundation, 1957) and *Canadian Fiscal Facts, 1958 Supplement* (Toronto, Canadian Tax Foundation, 1958).

In addition to the data obtained from the foregoing sources a good deal of material was prepared in the Office of the Comptroller of The Treasury, Department of Finance, Ottawa, and in the Public Finance Section of the Dominion Bureau of Statistics. Other sources of statistics on government finance in Canada include the *Public Accounts* of the various provinces, *Budget Speeches* and *Estimates* of both the federal and provincial governments, D.B.S., *Canada Year Book*, D.B.S., *Canadian Statistical Review*, monthly with periodic *Supplements*, Bank of Canada, *Statistical Summary*, monthly with periodic *Supplements* and Canadian Tax Foundation, *National Finances*.

Special mention should be made of the *Report of the Auditor General to the House of Commons*, annual (Ottawa, Queen's Printer). From the fiscal year 1885–6 until the fiscal year 1941–2 the details of federal expenditure (and, as time progressed, also income to some extent) were given in the *Report of the Auditor General*, and the *Public Accounts* contained largely summary statements. From the fiscal year 1941–2 to 1960–1 and for the fiscal years 1884–5 and earlier the detail appears in the *Public Accounts*. The *Public Accounts* have been prepared by the Department of Finance from 1878 onwards; prior to

that year they were prepared by a Board of Audit. See Public Accounts of Canada for the fiscal year ending 31 March 1943, p. xii, for a brief history of the preparation of the *Public Accounts* and *Auditor General's Report* until that time.

General note

The data presented herein are based on reports for fiscal years. Over the period since Confederation the fiscal years of the various governments have changed. Those of the federal and provincial governments have been as follows:

Canada (federal governments): 30 June, Confederation to 1906; 31 March, 1907 (nine months) and subsequent years.

Newfoundland since its Confederation with Canada: 31 March, 1950 and subsequent years.

Prince Edward Island: 31 December, 1873 to 1905; 30 September, 1906 (nine months) to 1911; 31 December, 1912 (fifteen months) to 1942; 31 March, 1944 (fifteen months) and subsequently.

Nova Scotia: 31 December, Confederation to 1892; 30 September, 1893 (nine months) to 1934; 30 November, 1935 (fourteen months) to 1949; 31 March, 1951 (sixteen months) and subsequently.

New Brunswick: 31 October, Confederation to 1882; 31 December, 1883 (fourteen months) to 1893; 31 October, 1894 (ten months) to 1950; 31 March, 1951 (five months) and subsequently.

Quebec: 31 December, 1868 (eighteen months); 30 June, 1870 (eighteen months) to 1940; 31 March, 1941 (nine months) and subsequently.

Ontario: 31 December, Confederation to 1908; 31 October, 1909 (ten months) to 1934; 31 March, 1935 (five months) and subsequently.

Manitoba: 30 June, 1871 to 1875; 31 December, 1876 (eighteen months) to 1884; 30 June, 1885 (six months) to 1887; 31 December, 1888 (eighteen months) to 1910; 30 November, 1911 (eleven months) to 1921; 31 August, 1922 (nine months) to 1924; 30 April, 1925 (eight months) to 1946; 31 March, 1947 (eleven months) and subsequently.

Saskatchewan: 31 December, 1905 (four months); 28 February, 1907 (fourteen months) to 1913; 30 April, 1914 (fourteen months) to 1946; 31 March, 1947 (eleven months) and subsequently.

Alberta: 31 December, 1905 (four months) to 1927; 31 March, 1928 (fifteen months) and subsequently.

British Columbia: 31 December, 1871 to 1878; 30 June, 1879 (six months) to 1908; 31 March, 1909 (nine months) and subsequently.

Municipalities for the most part have operated on a calendar year.

From Confederation there have been transfers of funds among governments. By the terms of the British North America Act, the provincial sources of tax revenue were limited to direct taxes. This provision meant that, in particular, they gave up revenue from customs duties, which in all but Upper Canada (Ontario) was the main source of income. Even though the Dominion assumed much expenditure previously made by the provinces, provincial subsidies were deemed a necessity. Originally the major part of provincial revenues came from Dominion unconditional subsidies. These, though they have become relatively unimportant, continue throughout the period. Conditional grants to the provinces were made from 1912 onward. Special grants and grants for old age pensions were introduced in 1927 and grants for other social services were begun in various later years. Contributions to unemployment and farm relief were important from 1931 to 1940. (See Eggleston and Kraft, *Dominion-Provincial Subsidies and Grants*.)

With the outbreak of the Second World War, wartime tax agreements were made between the federal and provincial governments whereby the provinces gave up, for the war's duration, the levying of personal income and corporation taxes in return for payments by the federal government to the provinces. These transfers of tax sources, with the addition of succession duties, by many of the provincial governments, under temporary tax rental agreements renewed each five years approximately, continued from 1946 to 1961. These various arrangements have meant, quite apart from other trends, that federal tax revenues have been increased relatively and provincial tax revenues reduced. The offsetting payments by the federal government to the provinces form unconditional receipts for the latter. Details of the tax arrangements that have been in effect over these two decades may be found in several official and unofficial sources and especially in the reports of the Dominion–Provincial Conferences of 1951 and 1956.

The jurisdiction assigned to the Dominion and the provinces by the British North America Act and its amendments and court decisions about these jurisdictions have had important effects on transfers from the federal to provincial governments. By the interpretation of the clauses of the B.N.A. Act on property and civil rights on which jurisdiction was assigned to the provinces, by the assignment of education and hospitals to the provinces and on other grounds, the federal government has been constrained or felt itself constrained from participating directly in activities in which payments were made to individuals with any but the most rudimentary conditions attached to them. Thus unemployment insurance was ruled *ultra vires* for the federal government in 1937, and it was not until a constitutional amendment was passed in 1940 that the federally administered plan was introduced. Similarly, any welfare payment that involves a means test or is based on a condition of prior performance by the individual concerned has been regarded as a matter of provincial jurisdiction. Consequently, federal expenditure in partial payment of old age assistance, based on a means test to those aged 65 to 69, in effect in most provinces, takes the form of payments to the provinces who administer the schemes and make the payments to individuals. On the other hand the federal government administers and pays directly the old age pensions to all 70 years of age and over and the family allowances for all children under 16 years of age in which cases the tests are simply a matter of age. The federal government payments for old age assistance, unemployment assistance (as distinct from unemployment insurance), education and the like therefore go through the provinces. Similarly, federal government payments for hospital insurance and care are made through the provinces.

FEDERAL GOVERNMENT FINANCE
(Series G 1–61)
General note

Revenue and debt are presented in the original categories of the *Public Accounts*; expenditures have been grouped under functional headings rather than by departments.

In order to match the years for which finances are designated in series G 62–309 the data for the year designated in the stub of each table are those of the fiscal year ending in the year following. Consequently, until 1905 the data for each designated year are for the fiscal year ending 30 June of the year following; from 1906 to 1960 they are for the fiscal year ending 31 March of the year following.

See Canadian Tax Foundation, *Canadian Fiscal Facts*, for data on a wide range of federal tax rates from their inception to 1956.

The data of series G 1–61 include revenues and expenditures on both current and capital account where such distinctions were made.

G 1–25. Federal government, budgetary revenue by major source, 1867 to 1960

SOURCE: prepared in the office of the Comptroller of the Treasury of Canada, Department of Finance, from *Public Accounts of Canada*.

The data of series G 1–21 exclude all revenues earmarked for special funds outside the budget such as unemployment insurance, federal old age security fund (old age pensions) and the like. They exclude also cash flows relating either to new debt or redemption of existing debt. Tax receipts credited to the old age security fund are shown separately in series G 22–25.

Tax revenues are divided between direct and indirect; the former (series G 1–6) includes those levied on income and capital and the latter (series G 7–12) those on sales, purchases or the performance of a service.

G 1. Income taxes on the profits of corporations, from fiscal year 1952 exclude revenue from the old age security portion of the tax. See also the note to series G 23.

G 2. Income taxes at graduated rates on personal incomes include revenue from various special taxes levied during World War II (e.g. national defence tax) but not revenue from forced savings tax equal to the estimated refundable portion for the fiscal years 1942–3 to 1946–7. Series G 2 also excludes revenue from old age security tax levied since 1952. It includes revenue from federal gift tax levied under the Income Tax Act. See also the note to series G 24.

G 3. Nonresident taxes were withheld at rates from 5 to 15 per cent on certain interest, dividends and similar forms of payment going abroad.

G 4. The federal succession duty was converted to an estate tax from 1 January 1959. Succession duties were not levied by the federal government prior to the fiscal year 1941–2 at which time they were introduced in connection with the wartime tax agreements with the provinces. See the general note to section G.

G 5. Excess profits taxes were levied during and after World Wars I and II. For the fiscal years 1942–3 to 1946–7 series G 5 excludes revenues equal to the estimated refundable (forced saving) portion of the tax.

G 7. Net sales tax is revenue from the sales tax on manufactures, less refunds of revenue from this source. Series G 7 excludes revenue from old age security tax on sales.

G 8. Other excise taxes include revenue from a group of taxes on sales of commodities which has varied greatly over the period. Typical subjects taxed have been automobiles, radios, television sets, jewellery, cigarettes (in addition to excise duties) and miscellaneous luxury goods. (See special War Revenue Act and Excise Tax Act.)

G 9. Excise duties are levied solely on liquor and tobacco products.

G 11. Miscellaneous indirect taxes include Chinese head tax prior to World War I, taxes on insurance premiums and on export of electricity.

G14. Post office revenues are gross receipts from services provided by the Post Office Department less certain amounts charged directly against revenue for salaries and rent allowances at semi-staff and revenue offices, commissions at sub-offices and transit charges on Canadian mail forwarded through or delivered in foreign countries.

G15. Return on investment in crown corporations is a special compilation to show separately this item as distinct from that of series G16 with which it is grouped in the *Public Accounts*. Series G15 is mainly profits from or interest on loans to the Bank of Canada, Canadian National Railways, Central Mortgage and Housing Corporation, Polymer Corporation, and other entities defined as crown corporations under the Financial Administration Act.

G16. Other return on investments is profits from and interest on all loans, advances and investments other than those made to or in crown corporations. For example, it includes return on loans to foreign governments.

G17. Miscellaneous nontax revenue includes revenue from bullion and coinage, from privileges, licences and permits, from proceeds from sales, from receipts for services or service fees, from refunds of expenditure and sundry small items.

G20. Special receipts and credits are nonrecurring revenue items. Included are capital refunds, special receipts under war appropriation acts and other such items. Since 1955 they are not shown separately.

G22. Old age security tax on corporation income was levied at 2 per cent from 1 January 1952 and at 3 per cent from 1 January 1959.

G23. Old age security tax on personal income was levied at 2 per cent from 1 July 1952 up to a maximum of $60 on the taxpayer, and at 3 per cent from 1 July 1959 up to a maximum of $90 on the tax-payer.

G24. Old age security tax on manufacturers' sales was levied at 2 per cent from 1 January 1952; at 3 per cent from 10 April 1959. It is in addition to the tax covered in series G7.

G26–44. Federal government, budgetary expenditures classified by function, 1867 to 1960

SOURCE: prepared in the office of the Comptroller of the Treasury of Canada, Department of Finance, from *Public Accounts of Canada*.

The data of series G26–42 exclude all expenditures from funds outside the budget such as unemployment insurance, old age security, and national defence equipment account. They include both current and capital expenditures, but not debt retirement. The functional classification is one prepared by the Department of Finance. It differs both as to number of headings and classifications of individual expenditures between headings from that prepared by the Dominion Bureau of Statistics which appears in series G128–142.

G26. Defence and mutual aid include Department of National Defence, Defence Production and defence aid to other countries. It excludes the national defence equipment account given in series G44.

G27. Veterans' benefits include payments for veterans' pensions and assistance, and hospitalization.

G28. Health expenditures are mainly grants to provinces to assist provincial health services, for capital outlays on hospitals and, beginning in July 1958, the federal contribution to hospital insurance.

G29. Family allowances are monthly allowances paid for each child under the age of sixteen, beginning in July 1945.

G30. Unemployment assistance and relief projects include the federal share of payments for relief of unemployed made through the provinces as well as contributions to provincial and municipal relief projects.

G31. Old age assistance, blind and disabled persons' allowances are the federal share of means test pensions, administered by the provinces, for persons aged 65 to 69 and for disabled and blind persons 18 years of age and over.

G32. Old age security fund deficit is the payment charged to budgetary expenditure of the deficit of the old age security fund when in some years the receipts of earmarked taxes fell short of payments. See also the note to series G43.

G33. Other welfare and security expenditures are mainly welfare expenditures on Indians and budgetary expenditures under the Annuities Act and the Unemployment Insurance Act.

G34. Education is mainly grants to universities and to the provinces for vocational training.

G35. Transportation and communication are mainly outlays of the Department of Transport, Department of Public Works and the Post Office Department.

G36. Resource development includes a wide range of expenditures, but mainly Atomic Energy of Canada, National Research Council and the Departments of Agriculture, Fisheries, Mines and Technical Surveys, Northern Affairs, Trade and Commerce on resource development.

G37. Public debt charges are gross interest and carrying charges on public debt.

G38. General government includes general administration, law and order and justice.

G39. International cooperation includes contributions to international agencies of all kinds of which Canada is a member, aid in postwar rehabilitation, Colombo Plan aid and the like.

G40. Payments to provincial and municipal governments are principally made up of payments under wartime tax agreements and tax rental agreements, statutory subsidies and payment in lieu of taxes. See also the general note to section G.

G43. Old age security fund pension payments are given for information only, since payments for old age security are made from the O.A.S. fund and not from budgetary expenditure.

G44. National defence equipment account was credited with the value of defence materials and supplies transferred to members of the North Atlantic Treaty Organization, which credits could be used in subsequent years to purchase equipment and supplies for the Canadian forces. For a more detailed statement see *Public Accounts of Canada*.

G45–61. Federal government, total direct and indirect debt less sinking funds, by type, 1867 to 1960

SOURCE: prepared in the office of the Comptroller of the Treasury of Canada, Department of Finance, from *Public Accounts of Canada*.

The debt shown in this table is in a sense gross debt (except for the sinking fund allowance). Considerable amounts of this debt may be held by public corporations such as the Bank of Canada. In addition the federal government has substantial investments in foreign exchange balances, in cash balances, in loans to other countries, in crown companies and agencies and the like.

G45. Bonded debt given in this series is a direct liability of the federal government and includes Canada Savings Bonds. It is the total of bonds outstanding regardless of whether part is held by government corporations, agencies or funds.

G46. Sinking fund includes only assets (bonds) held specifically to meet retirements of maturing issues.

G48. Treasury bills include one month to one year maturities.

G49. Notes are the liability for the Dominion of Canada note issue. With the establishment of the Bank of Canada this liability was transferred to the Bank in March 1935.

G50. Species reserves were transferred to the Bank of Canada in March 1935.

G51. Loans to chartered banks were advances of Dominion of Canada notes to the chartered banks under the Finance Act, first passed in 1914.

G53. Savings deposits and certificates were mainly deposits with the Post Office Savings Branch.

G54. Annuity, insurance, pension accounts are federal government liabilities under annuity contracts issued by the Annuities Branch, Department of Labour, under insurance issued to veterans, civil servants and others and for pensions to public servants.

G55. Other direct debt is mainly outstanding cheques and accounts payable.

G57. Guaranteed bonds and debentures are mainly bonds of the Canadian National Railways and its predecessors. Small amounts at times for the National Harbours Board, Canadian National Steamships Ltd and the like are included.

G58. Other guarantees include guarantees of loans made under the National Housing Act, of bank loans to the Canadian Wheat Board and under the Farm Improvement Loans Act; of credits under the Export Credits Insurance Act and sundry other small items.

G61. Security investment account is given for information only, since it is an asset comprised of government bonds held directly by the government. It is used for temporary transactions in government bond issues.

FINANCES OF ALL GOVERNMENTS, SELECTED YEARS, 1933 TO 1943 AND ALL YEARS 1945 TO 1960 (Series G62–309)

General note

These data were compiled by the Dominion Bureau of Statistics. It has almost from its beginning (continuing the practice of the authors of the *Canada Year Book* before the establishment of the Bureau) published data on government finance in Canada based on official data. In its preparation the material was adjusted to achieve comparability among levels of government and to eliminate double counting of intergovernment transfers. Over the years, however, both the underlying concepts and the availability of information have changed with the result that a historical series compiled from periodic reports issued in the past would not be consistent from year to year. Nor would they be consistent with special compilations covering some periods of years prepared for various Royal Commissions and for fiscal conferences among governments. Two of these compilations were particularly important. The Royal Commission on Dominion–Provincial Relations had prepared data, for the federal government and the provinces, for 1913, 1921 and 1925 to 1939. For the Dominion–Provincial Conference on Reconstruction in 1945 a compilation covering all governments for the years 1933, 1937, 1939, 1941 and 1943 was prepared. These studies represented important pioneering efforts on which most subsequent developments have been based though they failed to produce, between themselves, consistent historical series because of differences of concepts. Further, the way in which material was prepared by the various governments made it difficult to establish a consistent series.

Only recently has the Dominion Bureau of Statistics issued series on a consistent basis for a number of years. These compilations were prepared primarily for the Federal–Provincial Conferences of 1955 and 1959–60 but were issued for public use under the title *Comparative Statistics of Public Finance: Federal, Provincial and Municipal Governments*. Publications for

each level of government and all governments combined then became a regular matter. The concepts employed are those agreed upon after discussion extending over many years between officials of the Dominion Bureau of Statistics and officials of provincial and municipal governments. These discussions have also led to material coming to the Dominion Bureau of Statistics from provincial and municipal governments in a form that permits the consistent application of the agreed concepts.

The data of series G62–309 are an amplification of the series given in the latter publications. Where those series gave only one immediate post-war year (1945), with a gap to 1951, the present series has been completed for all years 1945 to 1960. A breakdown of debt figures for individual provinces and municipalities for the years 1946 to 1950 inclusive is not available so that only the totals given in the *Canada Year Book* are shown. For the years 1933, 1937, 1939, 1941 and 1943, the figures prepared for the Dominion–Provincial Conference on Reconstruction (1945) were used with some adjustments to make them more consistent with the post-war figures. Comparable data for still earlier years are fragmentary and will probably remain so for lack of detailed information in certain areas, as for example, municipal capital expenditures. However, data on current account revenues and expenditures for the provinces for certain earlier years, prepared for the Royal Commission on Dominion–Provincial Relations, are given in later tables (series G310–410). Where less detailed information is required the government finance data prepared for the National Accounts are also of assistance. They are available for all calendar years from 1926 onward (see section E). More detailed statistics on federal tax collections are available in Department of National Revenue, *Taxation Statistics*, and in annual reports of the Department. In the municipal field, additional sources of information are the statistics issued by the departments of municipal affairs and the financial statements published by the larger municipalities. Later tables also give some ancillary information on selected items of provincial and municipal revenue.

For a detailed explanation of the great number of individual adjustments made to published official figures of federal, provincial and municipal finance and a reconciliation of the adjusted figures with the original official presentation, see the text of D.B.S., *Comparative Statistics of Public Finance, 1956 to 1960*, and of annual D.B.S. reports entitled *Financial Statistics of the Government of Canada, Financial Statistics of Provincial Governments* and *Financial Statistics of Municipal Governments*.

The following comments explain the principal differences between the form of presentation followed by the Dominion Bureau of Statistics and that usually found in the official publications of the federal, provincial and municipal governments:

1. Revenues are presented by D.B.S. by 'source' and expenditures by 'function'. The main effect on revenues is the segregation of 'tax' and 'nontax' sources. Tax sources are then distributed under the main and in general familiar tax headings, and nontax sources are grouped under such headings as 'privileges, licences and permits', 'government enterprises', and the like. The main effect on expenditure is to rearrange published data, which usually appear as departmental expenditures, into groupings which bring together under a common heading all outlays for a similar purpose or function.

2. Revenues include receipts of funds and expenditures include outlays of some funds which are frequently outside the normal scope of the published budgetary accounts. For example the earmarked receipts of the old age security fund of the federal government are included as federal revenues and the outlays as federal expenditures. Similarly, at the provincial level there are many funds or bodies, such as commissions, loan and development boards and the like, whose ordinary operating revenues and

expenditures are treated as part of the general fund. A complete list of provincial funds and trust accounts included with the general accounts in 1959 may be found in D.B.S., *Financial Statistics of Provincial Governments' Revenue and Expenditure, Actual, 1959*, pp. 12–13. Where there is an appropriation from the general budget to a fund, the actual outlay of the fund for the year is substituted for the budgetary appropriation.

In contrast, for publicly owned enterprises, as distinct from special funds, only the net profit or the net deficit incurred by these enterprises and taken into the government accounts is reflected in these statistics, with the exception that the full annual profits of liquor commissions are included as provincial revenues whether remitted or retained.

3. Expenditures are inclusive of capital outlays frequently not treated as part of the general budget in published official accounts. Expenditures out of capital funds of municipalities in Quebec were not available in some years. See also footnotes 2 and 3 on page 214.

4. In tables of consolidated statements for all levels of government, intergovernmental transfers and debts are adjusted to eliminate duplication. General grants—those not earmarked for a designated purpose—are eliminated as an expenditure of the grantor government and as a revenue of the receiving government; specific grants—those made to be applied for a designated expenditure—are included under that expenditure heading (for example, transportation and communication) for the grantor government and are deducted from the revenue and the corresponding expenditure of the receiving government. In the tables for separate levels of government, the amount of general intergovernmental subsidies that has been eliminated is given in a separate column and an all-inclusive expenditure total including these grants is also given. In the consolidated statements all intergovernment transfer payments, including grants or subsidies for general purposes, are excluded.

5. In some cases expenditures and revenues related to the same service are 'netted' and only the balance shown. For all governments, interest receipts are subtracted from interest payments with the result that interest receipts do not appear in revenue and only net interest payments in expenditures. Revenue of government institutions is subtracted from their expenditure and only net expenditure given. Capital account receipts are deducted from the corresponding category of capital expenditures. The netting of grants-in-aid and share-cost contributions against gross expenditures has been discussed in the fourth point above. This treatment is not always followed; for example, post office revenues and expenditures are 'gross'.

Consequently, the revenues shown are net revenues and their total makes up net general revenue. Correspondingly, expenditures are net expenditures and their total makes up net general expenditure.

1. ALL GOVERNMENTS CONSOLIDATED
(Series G 62–110)

G 62–82. All governments, net general revenue by major source, selected years, 1933 to 1960

SOURCE: for 1945 and 1951 to 1960, D.B.S., *Comparative Statistics of Public Finance, 1945 and 1951 to 1959*, D.B.S., *Comparative Statistics of Public Finance, 1956 to 1960*, D.B.S., *A Consolidation of Public Finance Statistics, Municipalities, Provinces and The Government of Canada, 1959 and 1960, Actual*; for 1946 to 1950 special compilation by D.B.S., Public Finance Section; for 1933, 1937, 1939, 1941 and 1943 from Dominion–Provincial Conference on Reconstruction, *Comparative Statistics of Public Finance*, adjusted by the Public Finance Section, D.B.S., to make them more comparable with the later years.

G 62–74. Tax revenue brings together tax revenues of all three levels of government. For the federal government revenues included in this series, the explanations previously given for series G 1–25 are generally applicable except for the inclusion of revenue from the old age security taxes in the various main series G 62, G 63 and G 66. Provincial revenues are receipts from corporate and individual income taxes (in some years), from retail sales taxes (G 66), gasoline taxes (G 67), miscellaneous taxes on liquor, tobacco, meals, amusements, etc. (G 68), and revenue from provincial succession duties (G 72). The main municipal taxes are on real and personal property (G 71) and general sales (G 66). See also the individual tables for each of the federal government, provincial governments and municipal governments in series G 111–127, G 157–179, and G 208–221 respectively.

G 75–79. Privileges, licences and permits bring together certain nontax revenues for all three levels of government. Revenues from privileges, licences and permits are receipts from charges made for direct benefits conferred or privileges granted as distinct from levies in the form of taxes to support general government functions, although the distinction is difficult to make consistently (for example, revenues from the earmarked old age security taxes are treated as tax revenues). The bulk of these nontax revenues is received by the provinces, with minor amounts going to the federal government and the municipalities.

G 75. Liquor control includes licences for the purchase or sale of alcoholic products. It does not include profits on sales by provincial liquor control boards which are in series G 80.

G 76. Motor-vehicles are licences for the ownership or operation of motor-vehicles.

G 77. Natural resources include various dues, fees, royalties and licences in respect of fish and game, forests, mines, water resources, and the like.

G 78. 'Other' includes various other licences: for example, building permits, trade and occupation licences, dog licences, etc.

G 80. Government enterprises are as follows: the main federal government enterprises have been mentioned previously in the note to series G 15; provincial enterprises include liquor control boards, hydro-electric and telephone commissions or companies, railways, and like operations; municipal enterprises include water works, street railway commissions, hydro-electric or gas distributing systems, telephone companies and like operations. Only profits are included; interest on loans to government enterprises is netted out against debt charges, series G 90.

G 81. Other revenue is that from sales and services (documents, publications, bridge tolls, and so forth), from fines and penalties, and all miscellaneous revenues not given under previous headings.

G 83–95. All governments, net general expenditure by major function, selected years, 1933 to 1960

SOURCE: same as for series G 62–82.

In these series, expenditures of all three levels of government are brought together. The main differences between the concepts employed by the Department of Finance for series G 25–44 and those used by D.B.S. in the functional analysis of federal expenditures are that the Department of Finance excludes and D.B.S. includes transactions related to old age security and the national defence equipment account in the main compilation, that D.B.S. does some netting of revenues against expenditures and that the Department of Finance has a larger number of categories of expenditure. The remaining variations arise from the allocation of the federal expenditure to a different heading in the two analyses. Some of these variations are given below (G 128–142). In the present series under some headings the bulk of the expenditures are provincial or municipal. This applies particularly to health, education, transportation and communication, natural resources and protection of persons and property.

See also the notes to series G 128–142, G 180–191 and G 222–230.

G96–110. All governments, direct and indirect debt, selected years, 1933 to 1960

SOURCE: same as for series G 62–82.

The data of this table do not include allowances for surpluses, reserves, unexpended balances and deferred revenue. All intergovernmental debt has been eliminated.

G 96. Funded debt includes unmatured bonded debt and treasury bills having a term of two or more years.

G 99. Short-term treasury bills include treasury bills, treasury notes and deposit certificates having a term of less than two years.

G 100. Savings deposits and certificates are mainly deposits in the Post Office Savings Branch.

G 102. Other liabilities include accounts and other payables (in the form of trust funds and other deposits, in bonds and debentures due and bond or debenture interest due) and sundry other liabilities.

G 104. Guaranteed bonds and debentures are mainly guarantees made by governments of the debt of their public enterprises. Most municipal debt is shown as direct debt regardless of its being for general purposes, for education or for utilities.

G 109. Other guarantees are very largely those made by the Government of Canada. See the note to series G 58.

2. FEDERAL GOVERNMENT (Series G111–156)

G111–127. Federal government, net general revenue by major source, selected years, 1933 to 1960

SOURCE: same as for series G 62–82.

See the notes to series G 1–25.

G 111. Corporate income tax includes revenue from the excess profits tax and the part of the corporate income tax earmarked for the old age security fund. See series G 1, G 5 and G 22.

G 112. Individual income tax includes the portion earmarked for the old age security fund shown separately in series G 23.

G 115. General sales tax includes that portion earmarked for the old age security fund shown separately in series G 24.

G 116. Motor fuel tax was a gasoline tax levied by the federal government during and immediately after World War II.

G 117. Excise duties and taxes include the items shown separately in series G 8 and G 9.

G 126. Other revenue includes post office gross receipts and miscellaneous revenues from sales and services, several of which are shown separately in series G 1–25. Interest on investments is not included (see the note to series G 135).

G128–142. Federal government net general expenditure by major function, selected years, 1933 to 1960

SOURCE: same as for series G 62–82.

See the general note to series G 62–309 and the note to series G 83–95.

G 128. Defence and mutual aid include the national defence equipment account shown separately in series G 44.

G 130. Health is made up in large part of grants to provinces. See the note to series G 28.

G 131. Social welfare includes payments of old age pensions from the old age security fund to all aged 70 and over, family allowances, national employment services, contributions to provincial governments towards old age assistance to persons

aged 65 to 69 years, towards blind persons' allowances and towards aid to unemployed and unemployables and relatively small other payments.

G 132. Education includes grants to universities, grants for vocational training and outlays for Indian and Eskimo schools. In 1957 the $50 million grant to the Canada Council for a University Capital Grants fund is included.

G 133. Transportation and communication include highways, roads and bridges, air services, canal services, maritime services, railway and steamship services, Board of Transport commissioners, harbours and rivers, trans-Canada highway and the like. Freight subsidies on other than agricultural products are included. The post office which appears under this heading in series G 35 is not included here but appears in series G 139. The Canadian Broadcasting Corporation and payments of deficits of the Canadian National Railways appear in series G 139, 'other', of which government enterprises is a part.

G 134. Natural resources and primary industries include fish and game, forests, minerals and mines, water resources, lands settlement and agriculture. Included in the latter with other expenditures are the various payments made directly or indirectly to farmers and the like. Expenditures on such entities as the National Research Council and Atomic Energy of Canada Limited are not included here but appear in series G 139, 'other', of which government enterprises is a part.

G 135. Debt charges are net after subtraction of revenue from interest on government investments from gross debt charges. See also series G 37, G 15 and G 16.

G 136. General government in this series differs from series G 38 in that the latter includes protection of persons and property, shown separately in this table in series G 137, and also includes recreational and cultural services and trade and industrial development, both of which are given in 'other' series G 139, in this table.

G 137. Protection of persons and property includes expenditures of the Royal Canadian Mounted Police, judges' salaries and travelling allowances, and costs of penitentiaries.

G 138. International cooperation and assistance include assistance to other countries, contributions to international organizations and costs of representation abroad of the Department of External Affairs. General administration of the Department of External Affairs is included in series G 139.

G 139. 'Other' includes payments to own government enterprise (for example, the deficit of the C.N.R. and the payments to the Canadian Broadcasting Corporation), recreational and cultural services (including $50 million Endowment Fund of Canada Council in 1957), post office, trade and industrial development, local planning and development, civil defence, immigration, external affairs, and sundry other items. Some of these items are shown separately in the source.

G 141. Intergovernment transfers include payments under the Dominion–Provincial tax-rental or tax-sharing agreements, provincial share of income tax on power utilities, statutory subsidies and special grants to Newfoundland and grants in lieu of taxes on federal property. These are all unconditional payments. Grants-in-aid and shared-cost contributions are included in the appropriate federal government functional expenditures.

G143–156. Federal government, direct and indirect debt, selected years, 1933 to 1960

SOURCE: same as for series G 62–82.

See the general note to series G 62–309 and the notes to series G 45–61.

3. PROVINCIAL GOVERNMENTS CONSOLIDATED (Series G157–207)

See the general note to section G and the general note to series G62–309.

G157–179. Provincial governments, net general revenue by major source, selected years, 1933 to 1960

SOURCE: same as for series G62–82.

The headings on this table are largely like those of series G62–82 and series G111–127. Additional comments are made only when points of difference arise.

See the general note to section G and the general note to series G62–309.

G157. Corporate income tax for years from 1947 to 1960 was levied by Quebec, which did not participate in tax-rental and tax-sharing agreements after the wartime tax agreements expired, and by Ontario, from 1947 to 1951 and 1957 to 1960; in 1952 to 1956 Ontario had tax-rental agreements on corporation income taxes with the federal government. The figures for 1949 to 1951 also include the 5 per cent provincial corporation tax levied by the eight other provinces under terms of the 1947 tax-rental agreements.

G158. Individual income tax for the years 1954 to 1960 is revenue from a tax levied only by Quebec.

G160. General sales taxes are general retail sales taxes.

G161. Motor fuel tax is the tax on petroleum products used for transportation purposes. It is net of rebates for motor fuel sold for uses which are tax-exempt.

G162. Other sales taxes include those on amusements and admission in all provinces, tobacco and alcoholic beverages in some provinces, hospital tax on meals in Quebec and long-distance telephone tax in Nova Scotia.

G163. Real and personal property tax has been levied by only a few of the provinces in the period covered.

G164. Succession duties were levied only by Ontario and Quebec in the period 1947 to 1960; for other provinces in this period, succession duties were rented to the federal government from 1 April 1947 under the tax-rental and tax-sharing agreements.

G165. Other taxes include hospital insurance premiums, taxes on fire insurance premiums, fire prevention taxes, public utilities taxes, property and security transfers taxes and corporation taxes other than on income.

G167. Liquor control privileges, licences and permits include the sale of individual liquor permits to buy liquor, and sale of licences for premises, banquet licences and the like. They do not include profits of liquor control boards which are in government enterprises (series G172).

G168. Motor-vehicle licences include operators' and vehicle licences.

G169. Natural resources privileges, licences and permits include: fish and game royalties; fishing, hunting and trapping licences; timber royalties, grazing fees, hay and wood cutting privileges; mining (including oil and gas) royalties, dues or bonuses; beach, sand and water lot leases and water power or storage leases, licences or permit fees; income taxes on mining and logging operations.

G170. Other privileges, licences and permits includes registration and search fees and a miscellaneous group mostly of small items.

G172. Government enterprises are almost entirely profits from sales of liquor by liquor control boards.

G173. Other revenue includes sales and services, which is the largest item, fines and penalties and a small amount of miscellaneous other revenue.

G175–176. Federal-provincial tax-sharing and tax rentals are payments from the federal government under federal provincial tax agreements.

G177. Subsidies, etc., are mainly statutory subsidies to the provinces, Atlantic Provinces equalization grants, special payments to Newfoundland and a share of income tax on power utilities.

G180–191. Provincial governments, net general expenditure by major function, selected years, 1933 to 1960

SOURCE: same as for series G62–82.

In each case provincial expenditure on a specific function excludes any grants received from another government specifically for that function but includes a grant made to another government in aid of that function. Thus trans-Canada highway grants from the federal government are not included under provincial expenditure on transportation and communication, whereas provincial road and street grants to municipalities are included under this provincial heading.

G180. Health includes provincial expenditures under the federal-provincial hospital insurance plans (which in the main relate to general hospitals), mental care hospitals, tuberculosis sanitaria, public health, and like health expenditures.

G181. Social welfare includes aid to aged and blind persons, unemployment assistance, mothers' allowances, child welfare and sundry other social welfare.

G182. Education is grants to schools operated by local authorities, grants to universities, colleges and other schools, expenditures on technical schools and teachers' colleges, education of the handicapped, superannuation and pensions and small other educational expenses.

G183. Transportation and communication are mainly expenditure on highways, roads and bridges (including grants for this purpose to municipalities). Small amounts for railways, waterways, telephone, telegraph and wireless are included.

G184. Natural resources and primary industries include fish and game, forest, land settlement and agriculture, minerals and mines, water resources and sundry other.

G185. Debt charges are mainly net interest payments (gross payments less interest earned on loans and investments), amortization of premium or discount and certain management charges.

G186. General government includes expenditure on executive, administrative and legislative functions and small amounts for research, planning and statistics.

G187. Protection of persons and property includes law enforcement, provincial jails and reformatories, police protection and sundry other.

G188. Other includes archives, art galleries, libraries, museums, parks, beaches and other recreational areas, trade and industrial development, local planning and development, contributions to government enterprises, housing, rural electrification, aid to municipal winter works and the like.

G190. Subsidies to municipalities are unconditional subsidies not tied to any specific function.

G192–207. Provincial governments, direct and indirect debt, selected years, 1933 to 1960

SOURCE: same as for series G62–82; and in addition D.B.S., *Financial Statistics of Provincial Governments, 1959, Direct and Indirect Debt, Actual* and same title but for 1960.

Direct debt includes debts of those funds treated as a part of the 'general fund' in these statistics, namely, liabilities of capital and loan funds, current accounts, working capital funds and special funds. Liabilities of government enterprises, trust funds and provincial universities are not included. Most provinces set up sinking funds for the retirement of their funded debt.

In the indirect debt only that part of the direct debt of another entity which is specifically guaranteed by a provincial government is included.

The notes to series G96–110 generally apply to the relevant headings here except as noted below.

G192. Funded debt is the gross amount outstanding.

G202. Guaranteed bonds and debentures are largely the debt of provincial government enterprises, of which power and telephone systems are the most important. They include also guaranteed debt of universities, municipalities and school corporations.

G205. Other indirect debt is, in the main, guarantees of liabilities of provincial government enterprises other than in the form of bonds and debentures.

4. MUNICIPAL GOVERNMENTS CONSOLIDATED (Series G208–243)

The statistics of municipal governments cover revenue and expenditure of incorporated municipalities, other unincorporated local government areas and some joint boards set up separately but which carry on through ordinary municipal account in most areas. They exclude, except where it is impossible to separate items, the revenue and expenditure of municipal enterprises, of hospitals, of libraries and of certain special areas except for surpluses, deficits or levies of these bodies actually taken into the accounts. For education, only the local school taxes and their expenditure to school boards, capital expenditures on schools and servicing of school debt are included. Actual operating cost of schools is not included though capital expenditures on them are included.

Owing to differences among provinces and within them and the complexity of types of arrangement the notes given below can cover only the main features of the data. For more detail of municipal government finances see D.B.S., *Financial Statistics of Municipal Governments, 1959, Revenue and Expenditure, Assets and Liabilities, Actual.*

G208–221. Municipal governments, net general revenue by major source, selected years, 1933 to 1960

SOURCE: same as for series G62–82.

G211. General sales tax is principally a retail sales tax levied by Quebec municipalities.

G213. Real and personal property tax includes special assessments as well as the general municipal tax, business tax, and tax for education. It is mainly a tax on real property but some personal property has been taxed in the Maritime Provinces over the years and vestiges remain in the Prairie Provinces and British Columbia.

G214. Other tax revenue includes poll taxes and sundry other.

G217. Government enterprises include profits of the municipalities' own enterprises and payments in lieu of taxes by federal and provincial enterprises.

G218. Other revenue includes income from tax penalties and miscellaneous other revenue.

G220. Subsidies from other governments include unconditional subsidies only and grants in lieu of municipal taxes from other governments. Municipal grants for specific purposes

are included in the relevant expenditures for those purposes by the granting government.

See also the notes to series G62–82 and the general note to series G62–309.

G222–230. Municipal governments, net general expenditure by major function, selected years, 1933 to 1960

SOURCE: same as for series G62–82.

G222. Health includes hospital care, public health, medical, dental and allied services and small other general health expenditures.

G223. Social welfare includes aid to unemployed and unemployables, child care and sundry other items.

G224. Education is mainly expenditures of local school boards or boards of education from school taxes collected by the municipality and passed along. It includes the direct cost to the municipality only and includes capital expenditure financed from borrowed funds.

G225. Transportation and communication includes expenditure for roads, streets and bridges.

G226. Debt charges do not include those on debentures issued by, or on behalf of, municipal enterprise. The item is net of interest earned or sinking funds. See the note to series G208–243.

G229. Other includes sanitation and waste removal, recreation and community services, payments to own government enterprise and sundry other.

G231–243. Municipal governments, direct and indirect debt, selected years, 1933 to 1959

SOURCE: same as for series G62–82.

G231 and G237. Funded direct debt and guaranteed bonds and debentures are the gross amounts outstanding. Guaranteed bonds and debentures are mainly guarantees of bonds of municipal enterprises.

See also the notes to series G208–243 and to series G96–110.

5. PROVINCIAL GOVERNMENT TOTALS, BY PROVINCE (Series G244–276)

Previous explanations of concepts of revenue, expenditure and debt are applicable to these data; for reconciliations with official data appearing in provincial public accounts and other official sources see the sources cited for G62–82 and D.B.S., *Financial Statistics of Provincial Governments*, published annually. Newfoundland is included only from its Confederation with Canada in 1949.

G244–254. Provincial governments, total net general revenue, by province, selected years, 1933 to 1960

SOURCE: for 1959 and 1960, *Financial Statistics of Provincial Governments, Revenue and Expenditure, Actual*, for the relevant years; for 1954 to 1958, same as for G62–82; for 1933 to 1953 data provided directly by Public Finance Section, D.B.S.

G255–265. Provincial governments, total net general expenditure, by province, selected years, 1933 to 1960

SOURCE: same as for series G244–254.

G266–276. Provincial governments, direct and indirect debt, by province, selected years, 1933 to 1960

SOURCE: for 1959 and 1960, *Financial Statistics of Provincial Governments, Direct and Indirect Debt, Actual*, for the relevant years; for 1933 to 1958, same as for series G244–254. The total of all provinces for 1946 to 1950 is from the Canada Year Book.

6. MUNICIPAL GOVERNMENT TOTALS FOR EACH PROVINCE (Series G277–309)

See the note to series G244–276.

Breakdowns by province for all series are not available for 1946 to 1960.

G277–287. Municipal governments, total net general revenue, by province, selected years, 1933 to 1960

SOURCE: for 1933 to 1958, same as for series G244–254; for 1959 and 1960, D.B.S., *Financial Statistics of Municipal Governments, 1959 and 1960, Revenue and Expenditure, Assets and Liabilities, Actual.*

G288–298. Municipal governments, total net general expenditure, by province, selected years, 1933 to 1960

SOURCE: same as for series G277–287.

G299–309. Municipal governments, direct and indirect debt, by province, selected years, 1933 to 1960

SOURCE: same as for series G277–287.

MISCELLANEOUS PROVINCIAL AND MUNICIPAL STATISTICS (Series G310–410)

As explained previously, series adjusted to the basis of presentation now followed by the Dominion Bureau of Statistics are only available from 1933 on. However, adjusted data for earlier years are available from studies of the Royal Commission on Dominion–Provincial Relations for provincial revenue and expenditure on current account and debt. While these differ in some important respects from the D.B.S. basis they are consistent within themselves and give a reliable indication of trends from 1913 to 1937. Statutory and other subsidies paid by the Dominion to the provinces in the years 1868 to 1938 were also presented in a publication prepared for the same commission and in the next following source cited. Also available are annual figures of selected provincial tax revenues from the beginning of the century to recent years. These were compiled directly from provincial public accounts by the Canadian Tax Foundation, and appear in *Canadian Fiscal Facts*, published by that organization. Finally, also from the latter source, there is reproduced a table of annual taxes levied by a selected group of Canadian municipalities in the period 1916 to 1957.

The data prepared for the Royal Commission on Dominion–Provincial Relations followed much the same practices regarding netting of revenue against expenditure as those used by D.B.S. (see the general note to series G62–309). For a statement of the adjustments made to data as ordinarily presented in public accounts see the source cited for series G310–317, pp. 2–4.

G310–317. Total provincial revenues, current account, by major category, 1913, 1921, 1925 to 1937

SOURCE: Royal Commission on Dominion–Provincial Relations, Public Accounts Inquiry, appendix 1, *Dominion of Canada and Canadian National Railways and Provincial Governments, Comparative Statistics of Public Finance, 1913, 1921, 1925 to 1939*, statement 27, p. 54.

These statistics include current revenue only as compared with D.B.S. adjusted data given in series G62–309, which includes capital revenue. Tax revenues are classified, but other revenues are not classified as nontax as they are in D.B.S. data.

A detailed schedule appears in the source giving a code of the classification of revenue to the main groups of revenue.

Revenue from two sources, Public Domain and Liquor Control, are shown separately, whereas in the D.B.S. classification these would appear under several headings, depending on the nature of the revenue.

G311. Federal subsidies include general subsidies only; subsidies for specific functions are deducted from gross expenditure on that function.

G312. Taxes include corporation taxes of all kinds, income taxes on persons, succession duties, taxes on real and personal property, gasoline taxes, amusement, sales and miscellaneous taxes.

G313. Licences, permits and fees include revenue from automobile licences to the extent of about three-quarters of the total in later years.

G314. Public domain is mainly royalties and stumpage charges, but also includes income from agricultural and grazing lands, fish and game and the like.

G315. Liquor control is mainly profits from sales.

G316. All other current revenues include revenues from sale of commodities and services, fines and penalties, interest on school lands and common school funds, refunds of expenditures and other.

G317. Federal subventions and grants-in-aid are largely grants for old age pensions and unemployment relief.

G318–329. Total provincial expenditures, current account, by major category, 1913, 1921, 1925 to 1937

SOURCE: same as for series G310–317, statement 36, p. 84.

These statistics include current expenditure only as compared to D.B.S. adjusted data given in series G180–191 which include capital outlays. The division by functions is generally similar with the exception of there not being a category for government enterprise.

See the source for a detailed schedule showing the way in which individual expenditure items are coded to expenditure categories.

G319. Net debt charges include, in addition to charges on direct debt, small amounts on indirect debt when not paid by the borrower. Interest revenue received by the provinces has been deducted.

G320. Relief is provincial expenditure only and does not include the amounts contributed by the federal government.

G321. Other public welfare includes public health, provincial institutions net of institutional revenue, hospital grants, child welfare, mothers' and deserted wives' allowances, the provincial share of old age pensions, employment bureaus, inspection of factories and buildings, vital statistics and small amounts of sundry other.

G322. Education is grants to schools and universities, agricultural and veterinary colleges, normal schools, technical schools, school inspection and like expenditures. Institutional revenue is netted against expenditure where relevant.

G323. Administration of justice includes expenditures on courts, police magistrates, police, jails, reformatories and sundry other.

G324. Legislation includes the lieutenant-governors' offices and government houses, elections and legislatures.

G325. General government is administrative costs not assigned to other particular functions, ministers' salaries and expenses, land titles offices, civil service superannuation and the like.

G326. Agriculture includes experimental stations and extension services, the provincial share of agricultural relief and sundry other.

G327. Public domain is expenditure on resources and lands.

G328. Highways, bridges and ferries are that part of construction charged to current account and maintenance. Highway grants to municipalities and expenditures on docks and wharves are included.

G329. All other is grants to municipalities in lieu of taxes, revenue collected by the province and paid to municipalities, commissions and fees paid to municipalities and refunds and remissions.

G330–339. Total provincial revenue, current account, by province, 1913, 1921, 1925 to 1937

SOURCE: same as for series G310–317, statement 28, p. 68.

G340–349. Selected provincial revenues by province, succession duties, 1901 to 1957

SOURCE: Canadian Tax Foundation, *Canadian Fiscal Facts, 1957*, pp. 78–105.

Most provinces enacted succession duties in the 1890's and gave them up in 1947 under the tax-rental agreements. The Ontario and Quebec levies have remained in effect throughout.

G350–358. Selected provincial revenues by province, corporation taxes, 1901 to 1957

SOURCE: same as for series G340–349.

Most provinces enacted specific taxes on corporations in the eighteen-nineties and, mainly during the nineteen-twenties and nineteen-thirties, taxes on corporation profits. In all provinces these taxes were suspended in 1941 under the Wartime Tax Agreements. Corporation profits taxes were revived only by Ontario and Quebec in 1947, though Ontario entered tax-sharing agreements on corporate profits with the federal government again for the period 1952 to 1956. Nova Scotia continued to collect a tax on long-distance telephone calls.

G359–368. Selected provincial revenues by province, motor-vehicle licences and gasoline taxes, 1904 to 1957

SOURCE: same as for series G340–349.

Motor-vehicle and operator licences appeared before World War I and gasoline taxes during the nineteen-twenties.

G369–377. Selected provincial revenues by province, from natural resources, 1901 to 1957

SOURCE: same as for series G340–349.

This item includes various charges, fees, licences, royalties, rentals, stumpages and similar charges from natural resources.

G378–388. Federal government statutory subsidies, by province, and special grants and conditional subsidies, total all provinces, 1868 to 1938

SOURCE: for series G378–387, Wilfrid Eggleston and C. T. Kraft, Royal Commission on Dominion–Provincial Relations, *Dominion–Provincial Subsidies and Grants* (Ottawa, mimeographed, 1939), pp. 187–9; for series G388, Canadian Tax Foundation, *Canadian Fiscal Facts, 1957*, p. 66.

G378–387. Statutory subsidies only are given in these series.

G388. Other grants and subsidies include special grants, grants for relief, for old age pensions, for pensions for the blind.

See also the general note to section G.

G389–398. Provincial governments, outstanding debt, direct and indirect, by province, 1913, 1921, 1925 to 1937

SOURCE: same as for series G310–317, statement 10, pp. 28–9.

The indirect debt includes guaranteed bonds, guaranteed bank loans and other contingent liabilities.

G399–410. Taxes levied (including local improvement) for selected municipalities, 1906 to 1957

SOURCE: Canadian Tax Foundation, *Canadian Fiscal Facts, 1957*, pp. 214–15.

These are taxes on real and personal property only. Figures are for taxes levied as distinct from taxes collected.

Series G1–25. *Federal government, budgetary revenue by major source, 1867 to 1960*

(millions of dollars)

| | Direct taxes | | | | | | Indirect taxes | | | | | | Total tax revenue |
| | Income tax | | | Estate tax[2] | Excess profits tax | Total direct taxes | Net sales tax | Other excise taxes | Excise duties | Customs import duties | Miscellaneous indirect taxes | Total indirect taxes | |
Year[1]	Corporation	Individual	Nonresident										
	1	**2**	**3**	**4**	**5**	**6**	**7**	**8**	**9**	**10**	**11**	**12**	**13**
1960	1,276.6	1,711.2	88.2	84.9	—	3,160.9	720.6	290.7	344.9	498.7	—	1,854.9	5,015.8
1959	1,142.9	1,566.6	73.3	88.4	—	2,871.2	732.7	286.6	335.2	525.7	.9	1,881.1	4,752.3
1958	1,020.6	1,353.5	61.2	72.6	—	2,507.9	694.5	240.6	316.7	486.5	1.2	1,739.5	4,247.4
1957	1,234.8	1,499.8	64.3	71.6	—	2,870.5	703.2	249.4	300.1	498.1	1.5	1,752.3	4,622.8
1956	1,268.3	1,400.5	76.4	79.7	—	2,824.9	717.1	267.1	271.4	549.1	18.3	1,823.0	4,647.9
1955	1,027.7	1,185.6	66.2	66.6	—	2,346.1	641.5	260.7	249.4	481.2	16.8	1,649.6	3,995.7
1954	1,020.6	1,183.4	61.3	44.8	—	2,310.1	572.2	252.0	226.5	397.2	15.5	1,463.4	3,773.5
1953	1,191.2	1,187.7	53.8	39.1	—	2,471.8	587.3	296.0	226.7	407.3	14.5	1,531.8	4,003.6
1952	1,240.1	1,180.0	53.7	38.1	—	2,511.9	566.2	275.7	241.4	389.4	13.0	1,485.7	3,997.6
1951	1,130.7	975.7	55.0	38.2	2.3	2,201.9	573.5	312.4	217.9	346.4	5.7	1,455.9	3,657.8
1950	799.2	652.3	61.6	33.6	10.1	1,556.8	460.1	226.7	241.1	295.7	4.9	1,228.5	2,785.3
1949	603.2	622.0	47.5	29.9	−1.8	1,300.8	403.4	168.0	220.6	225.9	4.4	1,022.3	2,323.1
1948	492.0	762.6	43.4	25.5	44.8	1,368.3	377.3	258.8	204.6	223.0	4.1	1,067.8	2,436.1
1947	364.2	659.8	35.9	30.8	227.0	1,317.7	372.3	268.5	196.8	293.0	3.8	1,134.4	2,452.1
1946	238.8	670.5	30.1	23.6	442.5	1,405.5	298.2	280.8	196.0	237.4	9.7	1,022.1	2,427.6
1945	217.8	686.6	28.3	21.5	426.7	1,380.9	212.2	284.7	186.7	128.9	9.0	821.5	2,202.4
1944	276.4	672.8	28.5	17.3	341.3	1,336.3	209.4	333.7	151.9	115.1	8.2	818.3	2,154.6
1943	311.4	698.4	26.9	15.1	428.7	1,480.5	304.9	333.8	142.1	167.8	7.7	956.3	2,436.8
1942	348.0	484.2	28.0	13.3	434.6	1,308.1	232.9	255.8	138.7	119.0	12.2	758.6	2,066.7
1941	185.8	296.2	28.2	7.0	135.2	652.4	236.2	217.2	110.1	142.4	2.6	708.5	1,360.9
1940	131.6	103.5	13.0	—	24.0	272.1	179.7	104.4	88.6	130.8	2.5	506.0	778.1
1939	77.9	45.4	11.1	—	—	134.4	137.4	28.6	61.1	104.3	2.4	333.8	468.2
1938	85.2	46.9	9.9	—	—	142.0	122.1	39.6	51.3	78.8	2.4	294.2	436.2
1937	69.8	40.4	10.2	—	—	120.4	138.0	42.8	52.0	93.5	2.5	328.8	449.2
1936	58.0	35.5	8.9	—	—	102.4	112.8	39.7	45.9	83.8	2.4	284.6	387.0
1935	42.5	33.0	7.2	—	—	82.7	77.6	35.1	44.4	74.0	3.8	234.9	317.6
1934	35.8	25.2	5.8	—	—	66.8	72.4	39.8	43.2	76.6	6.1	238.1	304.9
1933	27.4	29.2	4.8	—	—	61.4	61.4	45.2	35.5	66.3	2.3	210.7	272.1
1932	36.0	26.0	—	—	—	62.0	56.8	25.4	37.8	70.1	2.4	192.5	254.5
1931	36.5	24.8	—	—	—	61.3	41.7	17.9	48.7	104.1	1.7	214.1	275.4
1930	44.4	26.6	—	—	—	71.0	20.2	14.5	57.7	131.2	2.1	225.7	296.7
1929	41.8	27.2	—	—	.2	69.2	44.1	19.3	65.0	179.4	1.8	309.6	378.8
1928	34.6	24.8	—	—	.5	59.9	62.6	20.4	63.7	187.2	2.4	336.3	396.2
1927	33.4	23.2	—	—	.9	57.5	70.6	19.6	57.4	157.0	2.9	307.5	365.0
1926	29.3	18.1	—	—	.7	48.1	81.2	24.4	48.5	141.9	2.9	298.9	347.0
1925	31.7	23.9	—	—	1.2	56.8	72.9	25.2	42.9	127.3	2.8	271.1	327.9
1924	31.0	25.2	—	—	2.7	58.9	63.2	22.6	38.6	108.1	2.5	235.0	293.9
1923	28.5	25.7	—	—	4.7	58.9	98.0	22.7	38.2	121.5	2.4	282.8	341.7
1922	28.0	31.7	—	—	13.0	72.7	89.8	16.7	35.8	118.0	2.4	262.7	335.4
1921	38.9	39.8	—	—	22.8	101.5	61.3	12.4	36.7	105.7	2.3	218.4	319.9
1920	13.9	32.5	—	—	40.8	87.2	37.6	41.2	37.1	163.3	2.4	281.6	368.8
1919	7.1	13.2	—	—	44.1	64.4	—	15.6	42.7	168.8	2.1	229.2	293.6
1918	1.4	8.0	—	—	32.9	42.3	—	11.8	30.3	147.1	2.2	191.4	233.7
1917	—	—	—	—	21.2	21.2	—	2.2	27.2	144.2	1.9	175.5	196.7
1916	—	—	—	—	12.5	12.5	—	2.1	24.4	134.1	1.7	162.3	174.8

Series G1–25. *Federal government, budgetary revenue by major source, 1867 to 1960 (continued)*

(millions of dollars)

| | Direct taxes | | | | | | Indirect taxes | | | | | | |
| | Income tax | | | | | | | | | | | | |
Year[1]	Cor-poration	Individual	Non-resident	Estate tax[2]	Excess profits tax	Total direct taxes	Net sales tax	Other excise taxes	Excise duties	Customs import duties	Miscel-laneous indirect taxes	Total indirect taxes	Total tax revenue
	1	**2**	**3**	**4**	**5**	**6**	**7**	**8**	**9**	**10**	**11**	**12**	**13**
1915	—	—	—	—	—	—	—	1.6	22.4	98.6	2.1	124.7	124.7
1914	—	—	—	—	—	—	—	.1	21.5	75.9	—	97.5	97.5
1913	—	—	—	—	—	—	—	—	21.4	104.7	—	126.1	126.1
1912	—	—	—	—	—	—	—	—	21.4	111.8	—	133.2	133.2
1911	—	—	—	—	—	—	—	—	19.3	85.0	—	104.3	104.3
1910	—	—	—	—	—	—	—	—	16.9	71.8	—	88.7	88.7
1909	—	—	—	—	—	—	—	—	15.2	59.8	—	75.0	75.0
1908	—	—	—	—	—	—	—	—	14.9	47.1	—	62.0	62.0
1907	—	—	—	—	—	—	—	—	15.8	57.2	—	73.0	73.0
1906[1]	—	—	—	—	—	—	—	—	11.8	39.7	—	51.5	51.5
1905	—	—	—	—	—	—	—	—	14.0	46.1	—	60.1	60.1
1904	—	—	—	—	—	—	—	—	12.6	41.5	—	54.1	54.1
1903	—	—	—	—	—	—	—	—	12.9	40.5	—	53.4	53.4
1902	—	—	—	—	—	—	—	—	12.0	36.7	—	48.7	48.7
1901	—	—	—	—	—	—	—	—	11.2	31.9	—	43.1	43.1
1900	—	—	—	—	—	—	—	—	10.3	28.3	—	38.6	38.6
1899	—	—	—	—	—	—	—	—	9.9	28.2	—	38.1	38.1
1898	—	—	—	—	—	—	—	—	9.6	25.2	—	34.8	34.8
1897	—	—	—	—	—	—	—	—	7.9	21.6	—	29.5	29.5
1896	—	—	—	—	—	—	—	—	9.2	19.4	—	28.6	28.6
1895	—	—	—	—	—	—	—	—	7.9	19.8	—	27.7	27.7
1894	—	—	—	—	—	—	—	—	7.8	17.6	—	25.4	25.4
1893	—	—	—	—	—	—	—	—	8.4	19.1	—	27.5	27.5
1892	—	—	—	—	—	—	—	—	8.4	20.9	—	29.3	29.3
1891	—	—	—	—	—	—	—	—	7.9	20.5	—	28.4	28.4
1890	—	—	—	—	—	—	—	—	6.9	23.4	—	30.3	30.3
1889	—	—	—	—	—	—	—	—	7.6	23.9	—	31.5	31.5
1888	—	—	—	—	—	—	—	—	6.9	23.7	—	30.6	30.6
1887	—	—	—	—	—	—	—	—	6.1	22.1	—	28.2	28.2
1886	—	—	—	—	—	—	—	—	6.3	22.4	—	28.7	28.7
1885	—	—	—	—	—	—	—	—	5.8	19.4	—	25.2	25.2
1884	—	—	—	—	—	—	—	—	6.5	18.9	—	25.4	25.4
1883	—	—	—	—	—	—	—	—	5.5	20.0	—	25.5	25.5
1882	—	—	—	—	—	—	—	—	6.3	23.0	—	29.3	29.3
1881	—	—	—	—	—	—	—	—	5.9	21.6	—	27.5	27.5
1880	—	—	—	—	—	—	—	—	5.3	18.4	—	23.7	23.7
1879	—	—	—	—	—	—	—	—	4.2	14.1	—	18.3	18.3
1878	—	—	—	—	—	—	—	—	5.4	12.9	—	18.3	18.3
1877	—	—	—	—	—	—	—	—	4.8	12.8	—	17.6	17.6
1876	—	—	—	—	—	—	—	—	4.9	12.6	—	17.5	17.5
1875	—	—	—	—	—	—	—	—	5.6	12.8	—	18.4	18.4
1874	—	—	—	—	—	—	—	—	5.1	15.3	—	20.4	20.4
1873	—	—	—	—	—	—	—	—	5.6	14.3	—	19.9	19.9
1872	—	—	—	—	—	—	—	—	4.5	12.9	—	17.4	17.4
1871	—	—	—	—	—	—	—	—	4.7	12.8	—	17.5	17.5
1870	—	—	—	—	—	—	—	—	4.3	11.8	—	16.1	16.1
1869	—	—	—	—	—	—	—	—	3.6	9.3	—	12.9	12.9
1868	—	—	—	—	—	—	—	—	2.7	8.4	—	11.1	11.1
1867	—	—	—	—	—	—	—	—	3.0	8.6	—	11.6	11.6

[1] Figures are for fiscal year ending nearest to 31 December of year named. Federal fiscal year end was changed from 30 June to 31 March in 1907 so 1906 figures are for nine months only.

[2] Includes duties levied under the Dominion Succession Duty Act.

Series G 1–25. *Federal government, budgetary revenue by major source, 1867 to 1960 (continuation)*

(millions of dollars)

Year[1]	Post office	Nontax revenue — Return on investments — Crown corporations	Other	Miscellaneous	Total	Total ordinary revenue	Special receipts and credits	Total budgetary revenue	Tax credits to old age security fund — Income tax — Corporation	Individual	Sales tax	Total
	14	15	16	17	18	19	20	21	22	23	24	25
1960	173.6	194.6	89.2	144.5	601.9	5,617.7	—	5,617.7	103.5	229.4	270.2	603.1
1959	167.6	152.8	86.9	130.2	537.5	5,289.8	—	5,289.8	91.3	185.6	270.0	546.9
1958	157.5	146.5	74.7	128.6	507.3	4,754.7	—	4,754.7	55.3	146.4	173.6	375.3
1957	152.9	114.5	54.9	103.7	426.0	5,048.8	—	5,048.8	60.7	135.0	175.8	371.5
1956	145.8	153.2	53.4	106.2	458.6	5,106.5	—	5,106.5	67.3	125.0	179.3	371.6
1955	137.4	85.0	64.3	117.6	404.3	4,400.0	—	4,400.0	53.3	102.5	160.4	316.2
1954	131.3	77.6	55.9	56.4	321.2	4,094.7	28.8	4,123.5	46.0	100.9	143.1	290.0
1953	111.0	103.5	48.4	55.3	318.2	4,321.8	74.5	4,396.3	55.6	90.7	146.8	293.1
1952	111.9	71.9	45.0	51.3	280.1	4,277.7	83.1	4,360.8	36.8	45.3	141.6	223.7
1951	104.6	73.2	44.4	59.7	281.9	3,939.7	41.2	3,980.9	2.0	.1	24.3	26.4
1950	90.5	67.6	21.9	53.4	233.4	3,018.7	93.8	3,112.5	—	—	—	—
1949	84.5	64.6	26.9	29.6	205.6	2,528.7	51.4	2,580.1	—	—	—	—
1948	80.6	57.4	50.5	24.5	213.0	2,649.1	122.3	2,771.4	—	—	—	—
1947	77.8	57.5	18.3	24.1	177.7	2,629.8	241.9	2,871.7	—	—	—	—
1946	73.0	58.1	11.3	18.5	160.9	2,588.5	419.4	3,007.9	—	—	—	—
1945	68.6	56.0	14.9	21.3	160.8	2,363.2	650.0	3,013.2	—	—	—	—
1944	66.1	49.5	11.3	18.6	145.5	2,300.1	387.2	2,687.3	—	—	—	—
1943	61.0	41.5	6.9	23.9	133.3	2,570.1	194.9	2,765.0	—	—	—	—
1942	48.9	31.3	9.9	26.0	116.1	2,182.8	66.7	2,249.5	—	—	—	—
1941	46.0	15.8	5.9	35.2	102.9	1,463.8	24.7	1,488.5	—	—	—	—
1940	40.4	8.7	6.2	26.3	81.6	859.7	12.4	872.1	—	—	—	—
1939	36.7	5.2	8.1	23.4	73.4	541.6	20.5	562.1	—	—	—	—
1938	35.5	5.2	7.9	13.2	61.8	498.0	4.1	502.1	—	—	—	—
1937	35.6	5.3	7.8	12.4	61.1	510.3	6.4	516.7	—	—	—	—
1936	34.3	3.1	8.1	12.5	58.0	445.0	9.1	454.1	—	—	—	—
1935	32.5	3.8	6.8	11.5	54.6	372.2	.4	372.6	—	—	—	—
1934	31.2	2.7	8.2	11.5	53.6	358.5	3.4	361.9	—	—	—	—
1933	30.9	4.1	7.0	9.9	51.9	324.0	.6	324.6	—	—	—	—
1932	31.0	3.7	7.5	9.9	52.1	306.6	5.1	311.7	—	—	—	—
1931	32.2	3.8	5.6	9.8	51.4	326.8	7.7	334.5	—	—	—	—
1930	30.2	4.7	5.7	12.3	52.9	349.6	8.1	357.7	—	—	—	—
1929	33.3	4.4	9.1	15.7	62.5	441.3	11.7	453.0	—	—	—	—
1928	30.6	3.9	8.3	16.4	59.2	455.4	6.2	461.6	—	—	—	—
1927	31.6	3.5	7.4	15.2	57.7	422.7	8.1	430.8	—	—	—	—
1926	29.1	1.6	7.0	14.0	51.7	398.7	2.4	401.1	—	—	—	—
1925	30.3	2.3	6.2	14.0	52.8	380.7	2.6	383.3	—	—	—	—
1924	28.8	1.8	9.5	12.8	52.9	346.8	5.7	352.5	—	—	—	—
1923	28.9	1.5	10.4	14.3	55.1	396.8	10.9	407.8	—	—	—	—
1922	29.0	1.8	14.7	13.7	59.2	394.6	15.0	409.6	—	—	—	—
1921	26.4	2.3	19.6	13.7	62.0	381.9	13.0	395.0	—	—	—	—
1920	26.7	2.1	22.7	14.1	65.6	434.4	2.5	436.9	—	—	—	—
1919	24.5	3.3	13.8	14.5	56.1	349.7	—	349.7	—	—	—	—
1918	21.6	2.6	4.8	51.2	79.2	312.9	—	312.9	—	—	—	—
1917	21.3	2.5	2.0	38.3	64.1	260.8	—	260.8	—	—	—	—
1916	20.9	2.3	.8	33.9	57.9	232.7	—	232.7	—	—	—	—
1915	18.9	2.7	.6	25.2	47.4	172.1	—	172.1	—	—	—	—
1914	13.0	2.2	.8	19.5	35.5	133.0	—	133.0	—	—	—	—
1913	13.0	1.4	.6	22.1	37.1	163.2	—	163.2	—	—	—	—
1912	12.1	.9	.5	22.0	35.5	168.7	—	168.7	—	—	—	—
1911	10.5	.8	.5	20.0	31.8	136.1	—	136.1	—	—	—	—
1910	9.1	.7	1.0	18.3	29.1	117.8	.1	117.9	—	—	—	—
1909	8.0	1.1	1.7	15.7	26.5	101.5	.1	101.6	—	—	—	—
1908	7.4	.4	1.8	13.5	23.1	85.1	.4	85.5	—	—	—	—
1907	7.1	.2	1.7	14.0	23.0	96.0	—	96.0	—	—	—	—
1906[1]	5.1	.1	1.1	10.2	16.5	68.0	—	68.0	—	—	—	—
1905	5.9	.3	1.8	12.0	20.0	80.1	—	80.1	—	—	—	—
1904	5.1	.3	1.8	9.9	17.1	71.2	—	71.2	—	—	—	—
1903	4.7	.2	2.0	10.4	17.3	70.7	—	70.7	—	—	—	—
1902	4.4	.2	1.8	10.9	17.3	66.0	3.3	69.3	—	—	—	—
1901	3.9	.2	1.7	9.1	14.9	58.0	—	58.0	—	—	—	—
1900	3.4	.2	1.6	8.7	13.9	52.5	—	52.5	—	—	—	—
1899	3.2	.1	1.6	8.0	12.9	51.0	—	51.0	—	—	—	—
1898	3.2	.1	1.5	7.1	11.9	46.7	—	46.7	—	—	—	—
1897	3.5	.1	1.4	6.0	11.0	40.5	—	40.5	—	—	—	—
1896	3.2	.1	1.3	4.6	9.2	37.8	—	37.8	—	—	—	—
1895	2.9	—	1.4	4.6	8.9	36.6	—	36.6	—	—	—	—
1894	2.8	—	1.3	4.5	8.6	34.0	—	34.0	—	—	—	—
1893	2.8	—	1.2	4.9	8.9	36.4	—	36.4	—	—	—	—
1892	2.8	—	1.1	5.0	8.9	38.2	—	38.2	—	—	—	—
1891	2.6	—	1.1	4.8	8.5	36.9	—	36.9	—	—	—	—
1890	2.5	—	1.1	4.7	8.3	38.6	—	38.6	—	—	—	—
1889	2.4	—	1.1	4.9	8.4	39.9	—	39.9	—	—	—	—
1888	2.2	.2	1.1	4.7	8.2	38.8	—	38.8	—	—	—	—
1887	2.4	.1	.8	4.4	7.7	35.9	—	35.9	—	—	—	—
1886	2.0	.2	.8	4.1	7.1	35.8	—	35.8	—	—	—	—

Series G1–25. *Federal government, budgetary revenue by major source, 1867 to 1960 (continued)*
(millions of dollars)

Year	Nontax revenue					Total ordinary revenue	Special receipts and credits	Total budgetary revenue	Tax credits to old age security fund			
	Post office	Return on investments			Total				Income tax		Sales tax	Total
		Crown corporations	Other	Miscellaneous					Corporation	Individual		
	14	15	16	17	18	19	20	21	22	23	24	25
1885	1.9	.2	2.1	3.8	8.0	33.2	.3	33.5	—	—	—	—
1884	1.8	.1	1.9	3.6	7.4	32.8	.6	33.4	—	—	—	—
1883	1.7	.1	.9	3.7	6.4	31.9	.9	32.8	—	—	—	—
1882	1.8	.2	.8	3.7	6.5	35.8	1.0	36.8	—	—	—	—
1881	1.6	.2	.7	3.4	5.9	33.4	1.8	35.2	—	—	—	—
1880	1.4	.1	.6	3.8	5.9	29.6	—	29.6	—	—	—	—
1879	1.3	.1	.7	3.0	5.1	23.4	—	23.4	—	—	—	—
1878	1.2	.1	.5	2.4	4.2	22.5	4.5	27.0	—	—	—	—
1877	1.2	—	.6	3.0	4.8	22.4	—	22.4	—	—	—	—
1876	1.1	—	.7	2.7	4.5	22.0	.9	22.9	—	—	—	—
1875	1.1	.1	.7	2.3	4.2	22.6	—	22.6	—	—	—	—
1874	1.2	—	.8	2.2	4.2	24.6	—	24.6	—	—	—	—
1873	1.2	—	.6	2.5	4.3	24.2	.3	24.5	—	—	—	—
1872	.9	—	.4	2.1	3.4	20.8	.2	21.0	—	—	—	—
1871	.7	—	.5	2.0	3.2	20.7	—	20.7	—	—	—	—
1870	.6	—	.6	2.1	3.3	19.4	—	19.4	—	—	—	—
1869	.6	—	.4	1.6	2.6	15.5	—	15.5	—	—	—	—
1868	.6	—	.8	.9	3.3	14.4	—	14.4	—	—	—	—
1867	.5	—	.2	1.4	2.1	13.7	—	13.7	—	—	—	—

See p. 198 for footnotes.

Series G26–44. *Federal government, budgetary expenditure classified by function, 1867 to 1960*
(millions of dollars)

Year[1]	Defence and mutual aid	Veterans' benefits	Health	Welfare and social security					Education	Transportation and communication
				Family allowances	Unemployment assistance and relief projects	Old age assistance, blind and disabled persons' allowances	Old age security fund deficit	Other		
	26	27	28	29	30	31	32	33	34	35
1960	1,537.9	292.3	269.8	506.2	51.5	51.3	—	166.0	29.3	681.2
1959	1,536.8	288.3	227.2	491.2	40.2	50.6	—	138.0	35.8	633.1
1958	1,442.4	288.8	132.1	474.8	23.9	49.7	184.0	122.5	34.4	607.8
1957	1,687.4	277.2	64.6	437.9	8.2	39.8	103.9	107.9	72.4	498.5
1956	1,783.8	251.5	62.0	397.5	7.9	30.5	56.0	96.0	21.4	408.2
1955	1,768.6	248.5	56.4	382.5	—	29.5	63.3	86.5	10.4	340.7
1954	1,687.9	240.1	53.1	366.5	—	24.3	45.8	84.0	10.4	358.9
1953	1,857.8	238.7	49.5	350.1	—	23.2	—	82.8	9.6	299.4
1952	1,972.9	241.4	44.9	334.2	—	22.1	—	84.7	10.5	260.0
1951	1,446.5	216.1	41.0	320.5	—	83.2	49.7	78.4	11.7	244.4
1950	787.3	216.5	33.1	309.5	2.9	103.2	—	85.8	4.8	219.0
1949	387.2	246.6	29.5	297.5	3.6	93.2	—	66.6	4.2	243.3
1948	268.8	277.0	19.1	270.9	—	66.8	—	67.5	4.5	200.2
1947	196.0	341.3	8.4	263.2	—	59.1	—	88.9	9.7	159.2
1946	387.6	604.8	6.0	245.1	—	45.4	—	89.2	15.6	133.2
1945	2,942.1	401.7	2.3	172.6	—	42.8	—	67.6	13.7	128.7
1944	3,999.9	114.1	1.1	—	—	41.0	—	48.4	2.8	142.8
1943	4,241.6	69.5	.7	—	—	33.5	—	41.4	5.6	189.9
1942	2,563.3	61.5	1.1	—	—	31.0	—	35.8	6.8	116.3
1941	1,267.7	58.3	1.1	—	2.0	29.6	—	19.2	6.5	71.4
1940	730.1	59.9	1.0	—	19.7	29.9	—	9.8	1.0	85.6
1939	125.7	60.4	.9	—	39.7	30.0	—	7.5	.8	119.7
1938	34.8	57.4	.9	—	42.8	29.1	—	6.3	1.0	122.5
1937	32.7	56.2	.1	—	68.5	28.7	—	6.1	.1	105.4
1936	22.9	56.8	.1	—	78.0	21.1	—	6.5	.1	108.2
1935	17.2	55.1	.6	—	79.4	16.7	—	6.0	.1	98.4
1934	13.9	54.6	.5	—	61.0	14.9	—	5.2	.1	101.5
1933	13.2	55.1	.5	—	36.0	12.3	—	5.1	.1	110.9
1932	13.5	55.9	.6	—	36.7	11.5	—	5.2	.2	160.7
1931	17.9	61.1	.9	—	38.3	10.1	—	5.7	.3	80.7

Series G 26–44. *Federal government, budgetary expenditure classified by function, 1867 to 1960 (continued)*

(millions of dollars)

Year[1]	Defence and mutual aid	Veterans' benefits	Health	Welfare and social security					Education	Transportation and communication
				Family allowances	Unemployment assistance and relief projects	Old age assistance, blind and disabled persons' allowances	Old age security fund deficit	Other		
	26	27	28	29	30	31	32	33	34	35
1930	23.4	57.0	.9	—	4.4	5.6	—	7.2	.4	115.0
1929	21.8	50.1	1.0	—	—	1.5	—	6.2	.4	107.8
1928	19.6	63.2	.9	—	—	.8	—	5.5	1.2	86.2
1927	17.6	61.9	.8	—	2.0	.2	—	5.5	.9	82.1
1926	14.8	46.0	.7	—	—	.1	—	4.9	1.1	79.8
1925	14.1	46.1	.6	—	—	—	—	5.4	.9	74.2
1924	13.2	45.1	.6	—	—	—	—	5.1	.8	73.8
1923	13.4	45.1	.6	—	—	—	—	5.8	.9	84.4
1922	14.2	48.0	.7	—	.9	—	—	5.7	.6	149.8
1921	17.5	56.1	.7	—	.5	—	—	5.6	.7	160.5
1920	30.2	76.1	.7	—	—	—	—	4.7	.6	164.4
1919	346.6	74.6	.5	—	1.5	—	—	3.4	.2	61.4
1918	438.7	30.3	.4	—	—	—	—	3.6	—	86.2
1917	343.8	8.2	.4	—	—	—	—	3.8	—	93.9
1916	312.0	2.8	.4	—	—	—	—	2.8	—	68.5
1915	172.5	.8	.3	—	—	—	—	3.0	—	84.5
1914	72.4	.7	.4	—	—	—	—	3.1	—	78.5
1913	13.5	.1	.2	—	—	—	—	3.5	—	90.7
1912	11.4	.1	.1	—	—	—	—	4.9	—	68.9
1911	9.7	.1	.1	—	—	—	—	3.4	—	62.6
1910	9.2	.1	.1	—	—	—	—	2.1	—	61.0
1909	6.1	.1	—	—	—	—	—	1.9	—	53.6
1908	6.5	.1	—	—	—	—	—	1.8	—	72.7
1907	6.9	.1	—	—	—	—	—	1.8	—	58.2
1906[1]	4.4	—	—	—	—	—	—	1.6	—	29.7
1905	5.7	—	—	—	—	—	—	2.2	—	36.0
1904	4.2	—	—	—	—	—	—	2.0	—	34.3
1903	3.7	—	—	—	—	—	—	1.6	—	26.3
1902	2.6	—	—	—	—	—	—	1.7	—	23.1
1901	2.8	—	—	—	—	—	—	1.8	—	25.2
1900	3.2	—	—	—	—	—	—	1.6	—	23.8
1899	3.6	—	—	—	—	—	—	1.6	—	19.0
1898	2.6	—	—	—	—	—	—	1.4	—	19.5
1897	1.8	—	—	—	—	—	—	1.3	—	15.8
1896	2.6	—	—	—	—	—	—	1.2	—	13.5
1895	2.2	—	—	—	—	—	—	1.2	—	16.0
1894	1.7	—	—	—	—	—	—	1.2	—	14.3
1893	1.4	—	—	—	—	—	—	1.3	—	15.1
1892	1.5	—	—	—	—	—	—	1.2	—	13.7
1891	1.4	—	—	—	—	—	—	1.2	—	13.7
1890	1.4	—	—	—	—	—	—	1.3	—	14.7
1889	1.4	—	—	—	—	—	—	1.4	—	15.5
1888	1.4	—	—	—	—	—	—	1.3	—	15.0
1887	1.9	—	—	—	—	—	—	1.4	—	13.5
1886	1.6	—	—	—	—	—	—	1.5	—	15.4
1885	4.5	—	—	—	—	—	—	1.9	—	19.2
1884	2.8	—	—	—	—	—	—	1.8	—	22.2
1883	1.1	—	—	—	—	—	—	1.9	—	23.3
1882	.8	—	—	—	—	—	—	1.8	—	19.9
1881	9	—	—	—	—	—	—	1.7	—	12.3
1880	.8	—	—	—	—	—	—	1.3	—	14.0
1879	.8	—	—	—	—	—	—	1.1	—	14.0
1878	.8	—	—	—	—	—	—	1.0	—	11.6
1877	.6	—	—	—	—	—	—	.9	—	12.3
1876	.6	—	—	—	—	—	—	1.0	—	13.5
1875	1.1	—	—	—	—	—	—	1.0	—	13.1
1874	1.1	—	—	—	—	—	—	.8	—	10.8
1873	1.3	—	—	—	—	—	—	.6	—	9.6
1872	1.3	—	—	—	—	—	—	.5	—	9.0
1871	1.7	—	—	—	—	—	—	.3	—	8.8
1870	.9	—	—	—	—	—	—	.3	—	5.8
1869	1.2	—	—	—	—	—	—	.2	—	4.0
1868	.9	—	—	—	—	—	—	.3	—	1.7
1867	.8	—	—	—	—	—	—	.3	—	1.8

[1] Figures are for fiscal year ending nearest to 31 December of year named. Federal fiscal year end was changed from 30 June to 31 March in 1907 so 1906 figures are for nine months only.

Series G26–44. *Federal government, budgetary expenditure classified by function, 1867 to 1960 (continuation)*
(millions of dollars)

Year[1]	Resources and development	Public debt charges	General government	International cooperation	Payments to provincial and municipal governments	Unclassified	Total budgetary expenditure	Old age security fund pension payments	National defence equipment account
	36	37	38	39	40	41	42	43	44
1960	532.2	797.6	386.9	85.3	563.4	7.2	5,958.1	592.4	—
1959	477.8	783.5	368.0	83.0	542.5	6.9	5,702.9	574.9	—
1958	420.5	648.0	378.4	61.2	490.0	5.5	5,364.0	559.3	211.7
1957	313.7	567.4	405.8	47.6	401.2	53.9	5,087.4	473.9	24.3
1956	283.2	534.1	410.6	46.8	405.7	53.8	4,849.0	379.1	45.9
1955	244.1	514.3	291.9	33.2	358.5	4.7	4,433.1	366.2	51.3
1954	212.8	502.3	286.5	34.8	362.6	5.3	4,275.3	353.3	74.3
1953	227.5	495.7	279.5	36.6	344.6	55.6	4,350.5	339.0	32.9
1952	214.3	464.9	236.9	31.6	341.7	77.2	4,337.3	323.1	−14.2
1951	171.9	531.0	299.6	29.1	129.5	80.3	3,732.9	76.1	—
1950	244.9	439.0	221.8	15.0	125.5	92.9	2,901.2	—	—
1949	191.2	450.8	170.0	11.4	104.6	148.9	2,448.6	—	—
1948	179.5	475.2	150.3	15.0	101.7	79.4	2,175.9	—	—
1947	136.8	466.7	156.4	26.3	155.9	127.7	2,195.6	—	—
1946	131.7	477.2	165.1	4.2	108.8	220.3	2,634.2	—	—
1945	138.3	437.6	129.9	3.6	112.7	542.6	5,136.2	—	—
1944	132.2	339.8	138.6	1.3	108.2	175.4	5,245.6	—	—
1943	147.5	262.1	66.7	1.9	109.8	152.0	5,322.2	—	—
1942	80.8	202.5	69.5	2.7	109.1	1,106.7	4,387.1	—	—
1941	98.0	171.6	90.0	.7	35.5	33.4	1,885.0	—	—
1940	47.5	145.7	66.7	.6	19.4	32.7	1,249.6	—	—
1939	78.7	134.6	38.3	1.3	19.4	23.8	680.8	—	—
1938	53.5	133.1	45.1	1.9	21.4	3.3	553.1	—	—
1937	29.2	132.1	41.7	1.5	21.3	11.0	534.4	—	—
1936	26.2	137.4	37.3	1.4	16.9	19.1	532.0	—	—
1935	36.2	134.5	36.5	.8	17.8	33.3	532.6	—	—
1934	29.8	138.5	26.0	1.5	15.4	15.2	478.1	—	—
1933	22.2	139.7	30.4	.8	15.3	16.6	458.2	—	—
1932	56.5	135.0	33.1	.8	15.3	7.4	532.4	—	—
1931	37.6	121.1	33.5	1.1	14.0	26.4	448.7	—	—
1930	34.8	121.3	29.3	1.2	19.2	21.9	441.6	—	—
1929	35.9	121.6	28.9	1.2	14.4	14.5	405.3	—	—
1928	38.6	125.0	28.4	1.2	14.2	9.3	394.1	—	—
1927	31.9	128.9	22.7	.6	14.4	10.3	379.8	—	—
1926	31.7	129.7	20.7	.3	12.7	16.7	359.2	—	—
1925	36.2	130.7	19.5	.3	12.7	14.9	355.6	—	—
1924	37.2	134.8	16.6	.3	12.6	12.1	352.2	—	—
1923	39.3	136.2	18.8	.6	12.7	14.0	371.8	—	—
1922	34.8	137.9	19.5	.4	12.2	16.5	441.2	—	—
1921	45.6	135.2	23.4	.4	12.2	17.9	476.3	—	—
1920	58.8	139.5	20.2	.5	11.5	21.7	528.9	—	—
1919	62.3	125.4	23.2	.5	11.5	29.0	740.1	—	—
1918	23.9	77.4	8.0	.3	11.3	15.5	695.6	—	—
1917	31.7	47.8	16.3	—	11.3	16.3	573.5	—	—
1916	30.2	35.8	14.4	—	11.5	18.3	496.7	—	—
1915	26.0	21.4	9.5	—	11.5	8.4	337.9	—	—
1914	42.5	15.7	13.2	—	11.5	8.4	246.4	—	—
1913	34.6	12.9	14.6	—	11.4	3.4	184.9	—	—
1912	17.7	12.6	9.8	—	13.2	4.4	143.1	—	—
1911	19.2	12.3	7.5	—	10.3	10.8	136.0	—	—
1910	15.6	12.5	8.2	—	9.1	3.7	121.6	—	—
1909	17.5	13.1	8.1	—	9.4	4.1	113.9	—	—
1908	18.5	11.6	7.1	—	9.1	4.1	131.5	—	—
1907	13.9	11.0	6.0	—	9.1	3.3	110.3	—	—
1906[1]	8.7	6.7	4.1	—	6.7	2.7	64.6	—	—
1905	12.3	10.8	5.3	—	6.7	2.0	81.0	—	—
1904	11.7	10.6	5.6	—	4.5	3.6	76.5	—	—
1903	8.5	11.1	5.1	—	9.8	3.8	69.9	—	—
1902	8.4	11.1	4.3	—	4.4	3.5	59.1	—	—
1901	9.1	11.0	4.2	—	4.4	2.9	61.4	—	—
1900	5.0	10.8	4.1	—	4.3	2.7	55.5	—	—
1899	4.9	10.7	4.2	—	4.3	1.9	50.2	—	—
1898	4.6	10.8	4.1	—	4.2	1.8	49.0	—	—
1897	3.2	10.5	4.2	—	4.2	2.0	43.0	—	—
1896	2.2	10.6	4.3	—	4.2	2.3	40.9	—	—
1895	2.1	10.5	4.4	—	4.2	1.4	42.0	—	—
1894	2.7	10.5	4.5	—	4.2	1.8	40.9	—	—
1893	3.3	10.2	4.1	—	4.2	1.3	40.9	—	—
1892	3.2	9.8	4.0	—	3.9	1.4	38.7	—	—
1891	2.7	9.8	3.9	—	3.9	3.6	40.2	—	—
1890	3.0	9.6	3.9	—	3.9	1.1	38.9	—	—
1889	3.0	9.7	3.5	—	3.9	1.5	39.9	—	—
1888	3.6	10.1	3.7	—	4.1	2.6	41.8	—	—
1887	4.7	9.8	3.5	—	4.2	4.1	43.1	—	—
1886	3.8	9.7	2.3	—	4.2	1.4	39.9	—	—

Series G26–44. *Federal government, budgetary expenditure classified by function, 1867 to 1960 (continued)*

(millions of dollars)

Year[1]	Resources and development	Public debt charges	General government	International cooperation	Payments to provincial and municipal governments	Unclassified	Total budgetary expenditure	Old age security fund pension payments	National defence equipment account
	36	37	38	39	40	41	42	43	44
1885	6.5	10.1	4.4	—	4.2	9.4	60.2	—	—
1884	2.8	9.4	2.8	—	4.0	1.8	47.6	—	—
1883	4.6	7.7	3.0	—	3.6	11.3	56.5	—	—
1882	3.9	7.7	2.8	—	3.6	1.1	41.6	—	—
1881	3.5	7.7	2.6	—	3.5	1.2	33.4	—	—
1880	1.6	7.6	2.6	—	3.5	1.2	32.6	—	—
1879	1.4	7.8	2.3	—	3.4	2.0	32.8	—	—
1878	1.3	7.2	2.4	—	3.4	1.9	29.6	—	—
1877	1.4	7.0	2.5	—	3.5	1.3	29.5	—	—
1876	1.5	6.8	2.3	—	3.6	2.3	31.6	—	—
1875	1.9	6.4	2.4	—	3.7	1.5	31.1	—	—
1874	3.5	6.6	2.5	—	3.8	3.2	32.3	—	—
1873	3.4	5.7	2.5	—	3.8	6.1	33.0	—	—
1872	2.3	5.2	2.6	—	2.9	14.8	38.6	—	—
1871	1.9	5.2	1.6	—	2.9	2.8	25.2	—	—
1870	1.9	5.1	1.4	—	2.6	.9	18.9	—	—
1869	2.7	5.0	1.4	—	2.6	.8	17.9	—	—
1868	1.6	4.9	1.6	—	2.6	.9	14.5	—	—
1867	1.5	4.1	1.5	—	2.6	1.1	13.7	—	—

See p. 201 for footnote 1.

Series G45–61. *Federal government, total direct and indirect debt less sinking funds, by type, 1867 to 1960*

(millions of dollars)

	Direct debt												Indirect debt				
	Unmatured debt less sinking fund				Dominion of Canada notes												
Year[1]	Bonded debt	Sinking fund	Net	Treasury bills	Notes	Less specie reserve	Less loans to chartered banks	Net	Savings deposits and certificates	Annuity, insurance, pension accounts	Other direct debt	Total net direct debt	Guaranteed bonds and debentures	Other guarantees	Total indirect debt	Total direct and indirect debt	Security investment account
	45	46	47	48	49	50	51	52	53	54	55	56	57	58	59	60	61
1960	14,132.9	17.0	14,115.9	1,935.0	—	—	—	—	28.5	3,955.5	1,337.4	21,372.3	1,672.7	3,343.6	5,016.3	26,388.6	101.5
1959	13,765.1	85.3	13,679.8	2,125.0	—	—	—	—	29.4	3,565.4	1,290.3	20,689.9	1,430.1	2,945.0	4,375.1	25,065.0	77.9
1958	13,979.1	83.2	13,895.9	1,595.0	—	—	—	—	34.1	3,301.9	1,151.1	19,978.0	987.9	2,253.7	3,241.6	23,219.6	98.0
1957	12,720.1	211.7	12,508.4	1,525.0	—	—	—	—	34.9	2,712.8	1,041.0	17,822.1	1,028.4	1,632.1	2,660.5	20,482.6	79.8
1956	12,743.4	210.8	12,532.6	1,625.0	—	—	—	—	35.9	2,427.2	1,148.5	17,769.2	792.5	1,253.4	2,045.9	19,815.1	204.3
1955	13,307.6	210.8	13,096.8	2,100.0	—	—	—	—	36.2	2,185.6	1,121.4	18,540.0	792.5	711.2	1,503.7	20,043.7	721.6
1954	12,906.4	190.9	12,715.5	1,590.0	—	—	—	—	36.8	1,977.4	1,097.5	17,417.2	908.4	353.1	1,261.5	18,678.7	45.6
1953	13,176.2	101.8	13,074.4	1,400.0	—	—	—	—	37.8	1,772.9	1,211.5	17,496.6	670.8	120.1	790.9	18,287.5	18.0
1952	13,260.5	27.6	13,232.9	1,550.0	—	—	—	—	39.3	1,567.1	1,218.4	17,607.7	527.8	46.4	574.2	18,181.9	59.5
1951	13,295.4	25.9	13,269.5	1,400.0	—	—	—	—	38.0	1,416.3	858.8	16,982.6	528.5	69.2	597.7	17,580.3	58.9
1950	13,602.4	22.7	13,579.7	1,400.0	—	—	—	—	37.7	979.3	693.6	16,690.3	576.5	38.4	614.9	17,305.2	9.6
1949	13,772.5	8.0	13,764.5	1,300.0	—	—	—	—	38.7	810.9	800.8	16,714.9	570.5	70.1	640.6	17,355.5	18.7
1948	14,114.6	—	14,114.6	1,300.0	—	—	—	—	37.7	718.0	766.2	16,936.5	554.6	28.6	583.2	17,519.7	455.8
1947	14,198.2	—	14,198.2	1,300.0	—	—	—	—	36.2	610.7	1,044.6	17,189.7	521.9	20.5	542.4	17,732.1	686.4
1946	14,718.4	—	14,718.4	1,280.0	—	—	—	—	35.8	526.8	1,134.0	17,695.0	566.9	14.7	581.6	18,276.6	276.4
1945	14,595.5	—	14,595.5	1,696.0	—	—	—	—	35.5	458.0	1,107.6	17,892.6	541.1	9.2	550.3	18,442.9	151.5
1944	11,653.5	—	11,653.5	1,886.0	—	—	—	—	33.5	406.5	933.9	14,913.4	666.7	84.7	691.4	15,604.8	335.9
1943	9,311.8	—	9,311.8	1,400.0	—	—	—	—	28.3	366.6	695.9	11,802.6	699.4	53.5	752.9	12,555.5	184.6
1942	6,523.5	—	6,523.5	1,370.0	—	—	—	—	24.4	424.9	472.5	8,815.3	716.8	90.3	807.1	9,622.4	34.2
1941	5,345.3	—	5,345.3	520.0	—	—	—	—	21.7	330.8	412.6	6,630.4	818.8	136.1	954.9	7,585.3	41.8
1940	3,892.0	5.2	3,886.8	480.0	—	—	—	—	22.2	264.0	350.2	5,003.2	984.0	121.8	1,105.8	6,109.0	30.1
1939	3,540.7	67.2	3,473.5	155.0	—	—	—	—	23.1	243.1	66.8	3,961.5	1,084.5	68.4	1,152.9	5,114.4	6.7
1938	3,230.7	70.0	3,160.7	155.0	—	—	—	—	23.0	221.2	55.7	3,615.6	1,085.5	87.6	1,173.1	4,788.7	.3
1937	3,164.6	65.7	3,098.9	150.0	—	—	—	—	22.6	201.3	50.6	3,540.2	1,050.6	18.4	1,069.0	4,609.2	.3
1936	3,187.3	61.8	3,125.5	150.0	—	—	—	—	21.9	177.0	68.1	3,542.5	1,003.3	14.8	1,018.1	4,560.6	.3
1935	3,145.3	58.2	3,087.1	120.0	—	—	—	—	22.0	150.6	52.2	3,431.9	994.6	96.0	1,090.6	4,522.5	.6
1934	2,869.3	54.5	2,814.8	192.6	—	—	—	—	22.5	126.2	49.8	3,205.9	987.3	104.4	1,091.7	4,297.6	3.9
1933	2,733.6	69.4	2,664.2	125.0	172.6	71.4	40.1	61.1	23.1	109.5	46.6	3,029.5	993.2	93.2	1,086.4	4,115.9	—
1932	2,606.0	66.0	2,540.0	110.0	180.9	69.9	48.4	62.6	23.9	98.5	43.0	2,878.0	996.2	28.2	1,024.4	3,902.4	9.7
1931	2,564.3	62.4	2,501.9	15.0	157.4	64.7	32.0	60.7	23.9	90.1	43.4	2,735.0	1,000.5	—	1,000.5	3,735.5	4.4
1930	2,379.0	59.9	2,319.1	—	141.1	81.5	6.5	53.1	24.8	80.3	44.9	2,522.2	954.9	—	954.9	3,477.1	1.0
1929	2,283.6	56.2	2,227.4	—	174.3	65.9	50.2	58.2	26.1	70.4	46.4	2,428.5	837.0	—	837.0	3,265.5	—
1928	2,357.6	52.5	2,305.1	—	204.5	60.8	83.5	60.2	28.4	61.4	47.6	2,502.7	714.2	—	714.2	3,216.9	—
1927	2,409.2	49.0	2,360.2	—	188.6	95.3	36.0	57.3	31.1	51.6	45.6	2,545.8	666.7	—	666.7	3,212.5	—
1926	2,480.9	45.5	2,435.4	—	172.2	100.9	12.5	58.8	31.9	42.7	44.1	2,612.9	618.0	—	618.0	3,230.9	—

Series G45–61. *Federal government, total direct and indirect debt less sinking funds, by type, 1867 to 1960 (continued)*
(millions of dollars)

Year[1]	Direct debt — Unmatured debt less sinking fund — Bonded debt	Sinking fund	Net	Treasury bills	Dominion of Canada notes — Notes	Less specie reserve	Less loans to chartered banks	Net	Savings deposits and certificates	Annuity, insurance, pension accounts	Other direct debt	Total net direct debt	Indirect debt — Guaranteed bonds and debentures	Other guar-antees	Total indirect debt	Total direct and indirect debt	Security investment account
	45	46	47	48	49	50	51	52	53	54	55	56	57	58	59	60	61
1925	2,444.1	42.1	2,402.1	70.0	182.6	99.1	10.0	73.5	32.8	36.2	45.2	2,659.7	580.6	—	580.6	3,240.3	—
1924	2,415.7	39.2	2,376.5	122.3	206.7	124.0	14.7	68.0	33.6	30.2	48.8	2,679.4	582.1	—	582.1	3,261.5	
1923	2,444.2	36.2	2,408.0	91.3	216.6	103.4	23.0	90.2	34.2	25.5	44.0	2,693.2	525.8	—	525.8	3,219.0	—
1922	2,486.5	33.1	2,453.4	94.7	242.7	130.2	13.9	98.6	31.8	20.7	45.5	2,744.7	454.0	—	454.0	3,198.7	—
1921	2,451.6	30.1	2,421.5	143.8	241.5	85.7	47.2	108.6	34.7	16.8	44.0	2,769.4	249.0	—	249.0	3,018.4	
1920	2,476.8	27.0	2,449.8	75.8	277.9	83.9	86.6	107.4	39.2	14.3	45.5	2,732.0	222.9	—	222.9	2,954.9	—
1919	2,553.8	22.3	2,531.5	73.8	311.9	105.1	109.7	97.1	42.3	12.4	47.3	2,804.4	174.4	—	174.4	2,978.4	.1
1918	2,203.6	18.7	2,184.9	73.8	289.3	122.2	71.8	95.3	53.1	10.7	46.1	2,463.9	174.3	—	174.3	2,638.2	.2
1917	1,428.3	17.2	1,411.1	75.1	250.8	120.4	28.8	101.6	53.4	9.6	46.1	1,696.9	174.0	—	174.0	1,870.9	.2
1916	979.2	14.0	965.2	100.0	183.3	118.8	13.0	51.5	56.2	8.5	54.8	1,236.2	173.5	—	173.5	1,409.7	.2
1915	621.0	12.6	608.4	25.0	178.0	121.3	1.1	55.6	53.5	7.3	52.1	801.9	172.0	—	172.0	973.9	.2
1914	400.5	10.8	389.7	19.6	157.1	94.9	5.4	56.8	54.0	6.1	63.2	589.4	160.3	—	160.3	749.7	.2
1913	303.5	9.1	294.4	8.3	117.9	101.3	—	16.6	55.6	5.1	54.0	434.0	116.0	—	116.0	550.0	.2
1912	260.9	13.7	247.2	—	112.1	98.7	—	13.4	57.2	4.3	48.7	370.8	89.2	—	89.2	460.0	.2
1911	286.8	12.4	274.4	—	113.4	99.2	—	14.2	58.2	3.3	46.6	396.7	65.8	—	65.8	462.5	.2
1910	275.9	11.2	264.7	—	90.0	74.5	—	15.5	58.1	2.5	48.4	389.2	—	—	—	389.2	.2
1909	262.3	14.8	247.5	17.0	87.2	70.1	—	17.1	58.3	1.8	44.1	385.8	—	—	—	385.8	.2
1908	282.6	38.5	244.1	13.6	79.4	61.8	—	17.6	59.9	1.1	41.9	378.2	—	—	—	378.2	7.1
1907	229.0	42.2	186.8	9.3	60.5	41.7	—	18.8	62.6	.8	46.0	324.3	—	—	—	324.3	6.9
1906	215.0	46.0	169.0	1.2	54.8	37.6	—	17.2	62.6	.7	45.7	296.4	—	—	—	296.4	1.2
1905	212.6	48.0	164.6	2.9	50.0	35.0	—	15.0	61.9	.6	64.3	309.3	—	—	—	309.3	1.5
1904	217.0	47.0	170.0	2.9	47.4	35.3	—	12.1	62.0	.5	47.9	295.4	—	—	—	295.4	2.5
1903	217.0	44.8	172.2	4.9	41.6	29.4	—	12.2	62.2	.3	39.0	290.8	—	—	—	290.8	4.7
1902	236.8	53.5	183.3	—	39.0	25.9	—	13.1	60.8	.2	24.5	281.9	—	—	—	281.9	.2
1901	236.9	50.9	186.0	—	32.8	18.9	—	13.9	58.4	.2	38.0	296.5	—	—	—	296.5	.2
1900	236.5	48.3	188.2	—	27.7	14.6	—	13.1	56.0	.1	34.4	291.8	—	—	—	291.8	.2
1899	236.6	45.8	190.8	—	26.1	12.5	—	13.6	53.1	.1	30.3	287.9	—	—	—	287.9	.2
1898	236.8	43.4	193.4	3.9	24.3	13.1	—	11.2	50.2	.1	29.8	288.6	—	—	—	288.6	.2
1897	237.0	40.9	196.1	—	22.2	10.8	—	11.4	50.1	—	29.1	286.7	—	—	—	286.7	.2
1896	227.4	38.5	188.9	4.9	22.4	10.7	—	11.7	48.9	—	28.9	283.3	—	—	—	283.3	.2
1895	228.0	36.4	191.6	1.9	20.4	8.8	—	11.6	46.8	—	28.6	280.5	—	—	—	280.5	.2
1894	225.3	34.4	190.9	—	19.5	7.8	—	11.7	44.5	—	28.7	275.8	—	—	—	275.8	.7
1893	214.5	32.4	182.1	2.4	20.1	8.3	—	11.8	43.0	—	28.3	267.6	—	—	—	267.6	.5
1892	209.8	30.7	179.1	1.5	18.5	6.4	—	12.1	41.8	—	28.4	262.9	—	—	—	262.9	.5
1891	209.2	28.6	180.6	—	17.3	5.0	—	12.3	39.5	—	29.3	261.7	—	—	—	261.7	.5
1890	199.9	26.5	173.4	7.8	16.2	3.9	—	12.3	39.4	—	26.6	259.5	—	—	—	259.5	.6
1889	201.3	24.6	176.7	1.9	15.4	3.3	—	12.1	41.0	—	26.5	258.2	—	—	—	258.2	.6
1888	203.8	22.7	181.1	—	15.5	3.3	—	12.2	42.9	—	25.5	261.7	—	—	—	261.7	.6
1887	194.2	21.0	173.2	5.6	16.3	3.9	—	12.4	41.4	—	27.0	259.6	—	—	—	259.6	.7
1886	190.5	19.1	171.4	1.2	15.1	2.8	—	12.3	40.8	—	25.6	251.3	—	—	—	251.3	1.0
1885	192.6	17.5	175.1	1.3	16.3	3.9	—	12.4	37.2	—	25.8	251.8	—	—	—	251.8	1.0
1884	174.0	15.8	158.2	19.0	15.7	2.5	—	13.2	33.0	—	23.0	246.4	—	—	—	246.4	1.1
1883	175.2	14.3	160.9	—	15.4	2.4	—	13.0	29.2	—	22.7	225.8	—	—	—	225.8	1.1
1882	138.8	12.9	125.9	—	16.0	2.6	—	13.4	26.2	—	21.1	186.6	—	—	—	186.6	1.1
1881	145.6	12.2	133.4	—	15.8	3.7	—	12.1	21.8	—	22.2	189.5	—	—	—	189.5	1.1
1880	147.2	11.0	136.2	—	14.6	3.0	—	11.6	15.8	—	22.3	185.9	—	—	—	185.9	1.1
1879	148.6	9.7	138.9	—	13.6	2.8	—	10.8	11.1	—	21.3	182.1	—	—	—	182.1	1.1
1878	138.3	8.5	129.8	—	10.8	2.9	—	7.9	9.2	—	21.2	168.1	—	—	—	168.1	1.1
1877	130.2	7.4	122.8	—	10.5	2.5	—	8.0	8.5	—	25.7	165.0	—	—	—	165.0	1.1
1876	130.8	6.4	124.4	—	10.7	2.7	—	8.0	7.5	—	25.7	165.6	—	—	—	165.6	1.3
1875	120.3	5.5	114.8	—	11.6	3.0	—	8.6	7.0	—	22.3	152.7	—	—	—	152.7	1.3
1874	108.4	5.7	102.7	—	10.8	2.8	—	8.0	7.2	—	25.3	143.2	—	—	—	143.2	1.3
1873	94.7	4.1	90.6	—	12.2	3.3	—	8.9	7.2	—	27.0	133.7	—	—	—	133.7	1.5
1872	84.3	3.6	80.7	—	11.3	2.5	—	8.8	6.1	—	28.0	123.6	—	—	—	123.6	1.7
1871	84.5	3.5	81.0	—	10.6	2.5	—	8.1	5.2	—	22.1	116.4	—	—	—	116.4	2.1
1870	83.6	2.5	81.1	—	7.5	1.6	—	5.9	4.5	—	19.9	111.4	—	—	—	111.4	2.9
1869	85.8	2.1	83.7	—	7.8	1.7	—	6.1	3.4	—	19.0	112.2	—	—	—	112.2	.6
1868	89.4	2.0	87.4	—	5.3	1.0	—	4.3	2.5	—	15.2	109.4	—	—	—	109.4	1.0
1867	72.8	2.2	70.6	—	4.3	.8	—	3.5	1.7	—	18.1	93.9	—	—	—	93.9	1.0

[1] Figures are for close of fiscal year ending nearest to 31 December of year named.

Series G62–82. *All governments, net general revenue by major source,[1] selected years, 1933 to 1960*

(millions of dollars)

	Taxes												
	Income tax							Excise duties and taxes	Customs duties	Real and personal property	Succession duties	Other	Total taxes
Year[2]	Corporate	Individual	Non-resident	Total	General sales	Motor fuel	Other sales						
	62	63	64	65	66	67	68	69	70	71	72	73	74
1960	1,649	2,002	88	3,739	1,283	403	60	633	499	1,340	145	188	8,290
1959	1,483	1,807	73	3,363	1,285	383	57	621	526	1,205	145	163	7,748
1958	1,302	1,548	61	2,911	1,113	364	57	557	487	1,069	128	78	6,764
1957	1,510	1,676	64	3,250	1,115	347	52	549	498	982	124	69	6,986
1956	1,398	1,562	76	3,036	1,125	301	48	538	549	868	144	67	6,676
1955	1,135	1,318	66	2,519	994	270	46	510	481	771	139	75	5,805
1954	1,116	1,309	61	2,486	881	241	45	478	397	716	85	64	5,393
1953	1,296	1,278	54	2,628	875	224	46	524	407	657	70	72	5,503
1952	1,342	1,225	54	2,621	836	200	41	508	390	607	71	80	5,354
1951	1,304	977	55	2,336	716	182	38	517	347	538	72	81	4,827
1950	961	652	62	1,675	561	157	34	455	296	407	65	116	3,766
1949	707	622	48	1,377	481	139	35	378	226	375	59	104	3,174
1948	625	763	43	1,431	440	125	31	448	223	343	55	96	3,192
1947	653	660	36	1,349	416	114	19	446	293	311	62	80	3,090
1946	682	671	30	1,383	335	110	18	423	237	282	58	62	2,908
1945	645	687	28	1,360	242	89	17	425	129	284	46	33	2,625
1943	741	700	27	1,468	331	71	8	331	288	266	39	36	2,838
1941	353	311	28	692	259	85	6	201	245	256	34	48	1,826
1939	89	61	11	161	145	53	3	87	107	249	28	49	882
1937	79	55	10	144	144	39	3	76	113	241	37	47	844
1933	31	38	5	74	61	26	3	67	81	235	13	39	599

	Privileges, licences and permits					Government enterprises	Other revenue	Total net revenue
Year[2]	Liquor control	Motor-vehicles	Natural resources	Other	Total			
	75	76	77	78	79	80	81	82
1960	47	172	281	72	572	342	511	9,715
1959	45	165	309	72	591	321	478	9,138
1958	38	146	270	66	520	325	460	8,069
1957	41	140	282	59	522	283	426	8,217
1956	33	128	293	56	510	318	391	7,895
1955	33	114	261	52	460	235	373	6,873
1954	31	94	188	47	360	218	324	6,295
1953	32	88	198[4]	43	361	222	368	6,454
1952	31	81	—[4]	201	313	207	362	6,236
1951	28	73	—[4]	168	269	187	262	5,545
1950	27	67	101	42	237	183	254	4,440
1949	26	58	83	39	206	163	247	3,790
1948	25	50	62	33	170	155	303	3,820
1947	24	46	44	30	144	149	410	3,793
1946	21	38	44	28	131	168	542	3,749
1945	20[3]	32	—[4]	64	116	187[3]	696	3,624
1943	—[3]	30	34	22	—	—[3]	249	3,173
1941	—[3]	32	35	20	—	—[3]	160	2,073
1939	—[3]	28	25	18	—	—[3]	124	1,077
1937	—[3]	26	26	18	—	—[3]	113	1,027
1933	—[3]	21	13	16	—	—[3]	93	742

[1] After elimination of intergovernmental transfers. Yukon and Northwest Territories are included from 1954 in provincial portion and from 1957 in municipal portion.

[2] Figures are for fiscal year ending nearest 31 December of year named.

[3] Included in 'other revenue'.

[4] Included in 'other privileges, licences and permits'.

Series G83–95. *All governments, net general expenditure by major function,*[1] *selected years, 1933 to 1960*
(millions of dollars)

Year[2]	Defence and mutual aid	Veterans' pensions and benefits	Health	Social welfare	Education	Transportation and communication	Natural resources and primary industries	Debt charges	General government	Protection of persons and property	International cooperation and assistance	Other	Total net expenditure
	83	84	85	86	87	88	89	90	91	92	93	94	95
1960	1,534	296	841	1,629	1,579	1,452	567	817	532	448	82	1,007	10,784
1959	1,542	293	732	1,506	1,330	1,402	460	830	492	414	80	895	9,976
1958	1,664	295	535	1,427	1,108	1,259	421	702	478	380	63	827	9,159
1957	1,706	288	445	1,247	1,043	1,166	330	640	491	345	53	783	8,537
1956	1,819	261	394	1,073	841	1,004	288	593	487	309	35	705	7,809
1955	1,759	245	369	1,020	746	843	281	543	362	282	33	543	7,026
1954	1,724	233	354	970	680	711	275	539	334	261	27	572	6,680
1953	1,817	232	310	912	632	675	276	520	333	235	29	506	6,477
1952	1,917	234	290	869	571	657	259	497	277	215	12	483	6,281
1951	1,417	209	256	662	498	544	204	526	340	204	30	469	5,359
1950	607	210	232	638	442	474	192	464	236	83	17	544	4,139
1949	385	229	209	596	392	461	186	472	156	73	11	612	3,782
1948	269	270	154	506	342	429	173	475	138	60	9	514	3,339
1947	195	335	113	466	273	345	163	499	110	50	25	523	3,097
1946	466	602	84	416	225	255	174	512	95	42	2	484	3,357
1945	2,517	406	68	307	186	172	176	489	124	98	159	981	5,683
1943	4,016	65	52	125	151	293	118	323	—[3]	—[3]	—	429	5,572
1941	1,253	56	47	104	138	128	139	256	—[3]	—[3]	—	255	2,376
1939	127	55	47	161	129	163	98	266	—[3]	—[3]	—	231	1,277
1937	33	53	42	194	117	160	63	273	—[3]	—[3]	—	208	1,143
1933	15	51	35	133	107	89	34	299	—[3]	—[3]	—	187	950

[1] After elimination of intergovernmental transfers. Yukon and Northwest Territories are included from 1954 in provincial portion and from 1957 in municipal portion.

[2] Figures are for fiscal year ending nearest 31 December of year named.

[3] Included in 'other' expenditure.

Series G96–110. *All governments, direct and indirect debt,*[1] *selected years, 1933 to 1960*
(millions of dollars)

Year[2]	Direct debt								Indirect debt						Total direct and indirect debt
	Funded debt	Less sinking funds	Net funded debt	Short-term treasury bills	Savings deposits and certificates	Temporary loans and overdrafts	Other liabilities	Total direct debt	Guaranteed bonds and debentures	Less sinking funds	Net total	Guaranteed bank loans	Other	Total indirect debt	
	96	97	98	99	100	101	102	103	104	105	106	107	108	109	110
1960	22,012	825	21,187	1,998	29	295	6,056	29,565	4,866	82	4,784	231	3,263	8,279	37,844
1959	20,868	836	20,032	2,172	29	273	5,517	28,023	4,313	68	4,245	192	2,902	7,339	35,362
1958	20,637	870	19,767	1,622	34	231	5,040	26,694	3,427	48	3,379	157	2,245	5,781	32,475
1957	18,528	937	17,591	1,565	37	232	4,264	23,689	3,271	37	3,234	235	1,516	4,985	28,674
1956	18,107	859	17,248	1,654	39	188	4,140	23,269	2,551	23	2,528	202	1,184	3,914	27,183
1955	18,241	774	17,467	2,115	38	145	3,730	23,495	2,316	14	2,302	178	609	3,089	26,584
1954	17,487	709	16,778	1,595	39	146	3,442	22,000	2,354	10	2,344	164	248	2,756	24,756
1953	17,525	640	16,885	1,413	40	97	3,268	21,703	1,934	12	1,922	127	36	2,085	23,788
1952	17,217	554	16,663	1,593	41	108	2,994	21,399	1,652	9	1,643	50	36	1,729	23,128
1951	16,919	508	16,411	1,468	39	88	2,517	20,523	1,518	10	1,508	49	37	1,594	22,117
1950	16,760	476	16,284	1,463	39	89	1,893	19,768	1,482	22	1,460	51	—	1,511	21,279
1949	16,821	511	16,310	1,339	108	88	1,728	19,573	1,371	19	1,352	77	1	1,430	21,003
1948	16,865	409	16,456	1,340	105	71	1,617	19,589	1,161	21	1,140	36	—	1,177	20,766
1947	16,763	381	16,382	1,340	102	68	1,824	19,716	1,035	14	1,021	23	—	1,044	20,760
1946	17,358	384	16,974	1,315	100	30	1,788	20,207	803	5	798	14	—	812	21,019
1945	17,238	379	16,859	1,720	38	50	1,711	20,378	733	8	725	8	—	733	21,111
1943	—	—	11,888	1,212	70[3]	65	1,237	14,472	—	—	933	49	16	998	15,470
1941	—	—	8,093	381	60[3]	108	670	9,312	—	—	1,120	133	31	1,284	10,596
1939	—	—	6,060	263	66[3]	154	474	7,017	—	—	1,480	56	33	1,569	8,586
1937	—	—	5,581	254	70[3]	129	422	6,456	—	—	1,488	16	29	1,533	7,989
1933	—	—	5,075	219[4]	54[3]	149	250	5,747	—	—	1,420	96	27	1,543	7,290

[1] After eliminating intergovernmental debt. Yukon and Northwest Territories are included from 1954 in provincial portion and from 1957 in municipal portion.

[2] Figures are as at fiscal year end nearest 31 December of year named.

[3] Savings deposits only, certificates included in 'short-term treasury bills'.

[4] Includes Dominion notes outstanding of 64 million.

Series G 111–127. *Federal government, net general revenue by major source, selected years, 1933 to 1960*

(millions of dollars)

	Taxes										
	Income tax				General sales	Motor fuel	Excise duties and taxes	Customs duties	Succession duties	Other	Total tax revenue
Year[1]	Corporate	Individual	Nonresident	Total							
	111	112	113	114	115	116	117	118	119	120	121
1960	1,380	1,941	88	3,409	991	—	633	499	85	1	5,618
1959	1,234	1,752	74	3,060	1,003	—	621	526	88	1	5,299
1958	1,076	1,500	61	2,637	868	—	557	487	72	1	4,622
1957	1,296	1,635	64	2,995	879	—	549	498	71	2	4,994
1956	1,336	1,526	76	2,938	896	—	538	549	80	18	5,019
1955	1,081	1,288	66	2,435	802	—	510	481	67	17	4,312
1954	1,067	1,284	61	2,412	715	—	478	397	45	16	4,063
1953	1,247	1,278	54	2,579	733	—	524	407	39	15	4,297
1952	1,277	1,225	54	2,556	705	—	508	390	38	24	4,221
1951	1,141[2]	977	55	2,173	598	—	517	347	38	18	3,691
1950	834[2]	652	62	1,548	460	—	455	296	34	17	2,810
1949	601[2]	622	48	1,271	403	—	378	226	30	15	2,323
1948	537[2]	763	43	1,343	377	—	448	223	26	19	2,436
1947	591[2]	660	36	1,287	372	2	446	293	31	21	2,452
1946	681[2]	671	30	1,382	298	36	423	237	24	27	2,427
1945	645[2]	687	28	1,360	212	30	425	129	21	25	2,202
1943	740[2]	698	27	1,465	305	25	331	288	15	7	2,436
1941	321[2]	296	28	645	236	25	201	245	7	2	1,361
1939	78	46	11	135	137	—	87	107	—	2	468
1937	70	40	10	120	138	—	76	113	—	2	449
1933	27	29	5	61	61	—	67	81	—	2	272

	Privileges, licences and permits			Government enterprises	Other revenue	Total net revenue		Privileges, licences and permits			Government enterprises	Other revenue	Total net revenue
Year[1]	Natural resources	Other	Total				Year[1]	Natural resources	Other	Total			
	122	123	124	125	126	127		122	123	124	125	126	127
1960	4	19	23	108	354	6,102	1950	2	14	16	44	182	3,052
1959	6	20	26	88	323	5,736	1949	1	14	15	28	179	2,545
1958	11	19	30	100	314	5,066	1948	3	10	13	28	238	2,715
1957	4	17	21	78	302	5,395	1947	2	9	11	27	350	2,840
1956	5	16	21	125	276	5,441	1946	2	9	11	48	487	2,973
1955	4	15	19	60	277	4,668	1945	—[3]	11	11	90	654	2,957
1954	3	13	16	51	234	4,364	1943	1	5	6	50	91	2,583
1953	3[3]	11	14	61	278	4,650	1941	1	3	4	8	68	1,441
1952	—[3]	17	17	47	290	4,575	1939	1	2	3	1	52	524
1951	—[3]	16	16	40	189	3,936	1937	—	3	3	1	49	502
							1933	—	3	3	—	40	315

[1] Figures are for fiscal year ending nearest 31 December of year named.
[2] Includes excess profits tax.
[3] Included in 'other privileges, licences and permits'.

Series G 128–142. *Federal government, net general expenditure by major function, selected years, 1933 to 1960*

(millions of dollars)

Year[1]	Defence and mutual aid	Veterans' pensions and benefits	Health	Social welfare	Education	Transportation and communication	Natural resources and primary industries	Debt charges	General government	Protection of persons and property	International cooperation assistance	Other	Sub-total	Inter-government transfers	Total net expenditure
	128	129	130	131	132	133	134	135	136	137	138	139	140	141	142
1960	1,534	296	267	1,328	65	377	366	654	266	79	82	556	5,870	565	6,435
1959	1,542	293	227	1,262	69	376	286	657	252	76	80	524	5,644	544	6,188
1958	1,665	295	130	1,202	65	329	263	546	262	73	63	509	5,402	490	5,892
1957	1,706	288	62	1,047	97	282	183	500	299	65	53	475	5,057	401	5,458
1956	1,820	261	62	896	39	216	156	471	316	61	35	430	4,763	406	5,169
1955	1,760	245	57	853	25	174	159	438	208	52	33	311	4,315	359	4,674
1954	1,724	233	54	817	22	164	168	432	200	55	27	313	4,209	363	4,572
1953	1,817	232	49	782	20	153	172	422	208	47	29	306	4,237	345	4,582
1952	1,917	234	46	747	19	141	162	400	167	45	12	301	4,191	341	4,532
1951	1,417	209	42	545	19	120	117	432	240	41	30	308	3,520	129	3,649
1950	607	210	34	477	13	114	120	377	199	32	17	332	2,532	125	2,657
1949	385	229	29	445	12	105	126	388	123	27	11	421	2,301	104	2,405
1948	269	270	19	386	12	84	98	395	104	25	9	338	2,009	102	2,111
1947	195	335	9	365	14	66	103	420	82	21	25	367	2,002	156	2,158
1946	466	602	6	333	19	53	128	429	74	18	2	358	2,488	109	2,597
1945	2,517	406	5	250	8	46	139	404	62	34	159	933	4,963	113	5,076
1943	4,016	65	2	67	7	205	88	222	217	14	—	67	4,970	110	5,080
1941	1,253	56	1	47	9	27	107	146	57	13	—	56	1,772	35	1,807
1939	127	55	1	58	4	46	68	153	46	11	—	48	617	19	636
1937	33	53	1	73	3	31	34	166	38	10	—	45	487	21	508
1933	15	51	1	45	2	28	17	189	31	10	—	40	429	15	444

[1] Figures are for fiscal year ending nearest 31 December of year named.

Series G143–156. *Federal government, direct and indirect debt, selected years, 1933 to 1960*

(millions of dollars)

Year [1]	Direct debt							Indirect debt						Total direct and indirect debt
	Funded debt	Less sinking funds	Net funded debt	Short-term treasury bills	Savings deposits and certificates	Other liabilities	Total direct debt	Guaranteed bonds and debentures	Less sinking funds	Net total	Guaranteed bank loans	Other	Total indirect debt	
	143	144	145	146	147	148	149	150	151	152	153	154	155	156
1960	14,133	17	14,116	1,935	28	5,290	21,369	1,673	—	1,673	209	3,135	5,017	26,386
1959	13,765	85	13,680	2,125	29	4,851	20,685	1,430	—	1,430	169	2,776	4,375	25,060
1958	13,979	83	13,896	1,595	34	4,438	19,963	988	—	988	140	2,114	3,242	23,205
1957	12,720	212	12,508	1,525	35	3,727	17,795	1,028	—	1,028	166	1,467	2,661	20,456
1956	12,744	211	12,533	1,625	36	3,579	17,773	793	—	793	101	1,152	2,046	19,819
1955	13,308	211	13,097	2,100	36	3,323	18,556	793	—	793	130	581	1,504	20,060
1954	12,906	191	12,715	1,590	37	3,058	17,400	908	—	908	133	221	1,262	18,662
1953	13,176	102	13,074	1,400	38	2,907	17,419	741	4	737	110	10	857	18,276
1952	13,261	28	13,233	1,550	39	2,721	17,543	610	5	605	35	12	652	18,195
1951	13,295	26	13,269	1,400	38	2,274	16,981	620	7	613	33	13	659	17,640
1950	13,603	23	13,580	1,400	37	1,659	16,676	679	16	663	38	—	701	17,377
1949	13,772	17	13,755	1,300	39	1,583	16,677	677	17	660	70[2]	—	730	17,407
1948	14,114	—	14,114	1,300	38	1,450	16,902	646	20	626	29[2]	—	655	17,557
1947	14,198	—	14,198	1,300	36	1,620	17,154	596	13	583	20[2]	—	603	17,757
1946	14,718	—	14,718	1,280	36	1,626	17,660	610	4	606	15[2]	—	621	18,281
1945	14,595	—	14,595	1,696[3]	36	1,520	17,847	586	5	581	6	4	591	18,438
1943	9,539	—	9,539	1,150[3]	28	1,068	11,785	758	5	753	42	28	823	12,608
1941	5,595	—	5,595	270	22	513	6,400	941	5	936	118	38	1,092	7,492
1939	3,540	67	3,473	155	23	299	3,950	1,290	5	1,285	51	37	1,373	5,323
1937	3,165	66	3,099	150	23	259	3,531	1,304	6	1,298	4	37	1,339	4,870
1933	2,793	69	2,724	129[4]	23	146	3,022	1,287	28	1,259	76	25	1,360	4,382

[1] Figures are as at fiscal year end nearest to 31 December of year named.
[2] May include other guaranteed debts.
[3] Includes deposit certificates for 1943 and prior years.
[4] Includes Dominion notes.

Series G157–179. *Provincial governments, net general revenue by major source, selected years, 1933 to 1960*

(millions of dollars)

Year [1]	Taxes									
	Income tax			General sales	Motor fuel	Other sales	Real and personal property	Succession duties	Other	Total taxes
	Corporate	Individual	Total							
	157	158	159	160	161	162	163	164	165	166
1960[2]	269	61	330	212	402	57	8	60	177	1,246
1959	249	54	303	209	382	55	8	56	155	1,168
1958	226	48	274	187	364	53	9	56	67	1,010
1957	214	41	255	183	347	49	8	53	60	955
1956	62	36	98	178	300	45	8	64	39	732
1955	54	30	84	149	269	43	7	72	40	664
1954	49	25	74	129	240	43	7	40	33	566
1953	49	—	49	108	224	44	6	31	44	506
1952	65	—	65	101	200	39	7	33	42	487
1951	163	—	163	91	182	36	7	34	53	566
1950	127	—	127	76	157	34	7	31	46	478
1949	106	—	106	62	139	35	6	29	41	418
1948	88	—	88	48	125	31	6	29	36	363
1947	62	—	62	31	112	19	7	31	25	287
1946	1	—	1	25	74	18	7	34	6	165
1945	—	—	—	21	59	16	6	25	4	131
1943	—	1	1	18	46	8	7	24	4	108
1941	31	11	42	16	60	6	5	27	22	178
1939	11	12	23	3	53	3	6	28	23	139
1937	9	12	21	2	39	3	4	37	23	129
1933	3	5	8	—	26	3	4	13	19	73

Series G 157–179. *Provincial governments, net general revenue by major source, selected years, 1933 to 1960 (continuation)*

(millions of dollars)

| Year[1] | Privileges, licences and permits | | | | | Government enterprises | Other revenue | Sub-total | Transfers from other governments | | | | Total net revenue |
| | Liquor control | Motor vehicles | Natural resources | Other | Total | | | | Federal-provincial tax sharing | Federal-provincial tax rentals | Subsidies etc. | Sub-total | |
	167	168	169	170	171	172	173	174	175	176	177	178	179
1960	47	172	277	28	524	191	53	2,014	480	—	58	538	2,552
1959	45	164	303	27	539	186	52	1,945	460	—	58	518	2,463
1958	38	146	259	23	466	180	53	1,709	398	—	69	467	2,176
1957	40	140	278	20	478	167	40	1,640	353	—	29	382	2,022
1956	33	128	288	20	469	157	37	1,395	—	366	29	395	1,790
1955	33	114	257	18	422	141	32	1,259	—	320	32	352	1,611
1954	31	94	185	17	327	130	30	1,053	—	327	32	359	1,412
1953	32	88	195[2]	16	331	128	28	993	—	309	32	341	1,334
1952	31	81	—[2]	170	282	130	25	924	—	303	31	334	1,258
1951	28	73	—[2]	139	240	118	25	949	—	96	31	127	1,076
1950	27	67	99	14	207	115	28	828	—	93	30	123	951
1949	26	58	82	12	178	111	26	733	—	80	28	108	841
1948	25	50	59	11	145	107	27	642	—	84	19	103	745
1947	24	46	42	11	123	103	27	540	—	131	19	150	690
1946	21	38	42	10	111	104	21	401	—	84	17	101	502
1945	20	32	—[2]	47	99	80	12	322	—	88	19	107	429
1943	—[3]	30	33	10	—	—[3]	70	251	—	93	17	110	361
1941	—[3]	32	34	9	—	—[3]	49	302	—	20	17	37	339
1939	—[3]	28	24	9	—	—[3]	36	236	—	—	22	22	258
1937	—[3]	26	25	9	—	—[3]	32	221	—	—	24	24	245
1933	—[3]	20	13	8	—	—[3]	19	133	—	—	19	19	152

[1] Figures are for fiscal year ending nearest 31 December of year named.
[2] Included in 'other privileges, licences and permits'.
[3] Included in 'other revenue'.

Series G 180–191. *Provincial governments, net general expenditure by major function, selected years, 1933 to 1960*

(millions of dollars)

| Year[1] | Health | Social welfare | Education | Transportation and communication | Natural resources and primary industries | Debt charges | General | Protection of persons and property | Other | Sub-total | Subsidies to municipalities | Total net expenditure |
	180	181	182	183	184	185	186	187	188	189	190	191
1960	508	257	698	713	201	67	125	136	93	2,798	70	2,868
1959	436	206	602	680	174	57	110	126	86	2,477	66	2,543
1958	330	191	521	622	158	55	95	116	76	2,164	61	2,225
1957	301	168	452	587	147	55	83	108	78	1,979	54	2,033
1956	261	143	362	561	132	55	70	92	54	1,730	41	1,771
1955	246	134	333	447	122	55	65	82	53	1,537	36	1,573
1954	234	124	274	371	107	57	55	78	47	1,347	37	1,384
1953	209	103	234	353	102	53	52	77	44	1,227	30	1,257
1952	192	95	221	367	94	57	48	67	39	1,180	27	1,207
1951	174	92	196	299	85	57	45	61	41	1,050	23	1,073
1950	158	87	183	250	72	52	37	51	35	925	16	941
1949	143	80	160	254	60	53	33	46	33	862	14	876
1948	102	62	142	255	75	52	34	35	28	785	13	798
1947	78	54	124	207	60	49	28	29	19	648	8	656
1946	57	44	88	135	46	51	21	24	12	478	9	487
1945	42	41	70	78	37	56	22[2]	21[2]	9	376	9	385
1943	35	33	50	55	30	60	—[2]	—[2]	38	301	3	304
1941	30	34	43	71	32	63	—[2]	—[2]	38	311	3	314
1939	30	68	38	89	30	61	—[2]	—[2]	39	355	5	360
1937	26	82	33	101	29	54	—[2]	—[2]	35	360	3	363
1933	19	46	28	34	17	50	—[2]	—[2]	25	219	—	219

[1] Figures are for fiscal year ending nearest to 31 December of year named.
[2] Included in 'other expenditure'.

Series G192–207. *Provincial governments, direct and indirect debt, selected years, 1933 to 1960*

(millions of dollars)

	Direct debt								Indirect debt							Total direct and indirect debt
Year[1]	Funded debt	Less sinking funds	Net funded debt	Short-term treasury bills	Savings deposits and certificates	Temporary loans and overdrafts	Other liabilities	Total direct debt	Guaranteed bonds and debentures	Less sinking funds	Net debt	Guaranteed bank loans	M.I.A.[2] act loans	Other	Total indirect debt	
	192	193	194	195	196	197	198	199	200	201	202	203	204	205	206	207
1960	3,806	671	3,135	62	—[3]	32	437	3,666	3,362	83	3,279	26	2	129	3,436	7,102
1959	3,514	634	2,880	47	—[3]	26	370	3,323	2,996	67	2,929	25	2	126	3,082	6,405
1958	3,454	668	2,786	27	—[3]	26	336	3,175	2,577	50	2,527	21	2	131	2,681	5,856
1957	3,029	619	2,410	40	2	25	304	2,781	2,344	39	2,305	70	2	49	2,426	5,207
1956	2,939	550	2,389	29	3	21	270	2,712	1,840	25	1,815	103	3	32	1,953	4,665
1955	2,714	470	2,244	15	2	17	240	2,518	1,589	16	1,573	49	3	29	1,654	4,172
1954	2,629	429	2,200	5	2	30	219	2,456	1,459	11	1,448	32	3	28	1,511	3,967
1953	2,638	446	2,192	13	2	1	205	2,413	1,201	8	1,193	21	3	27	1,244	3,657
1952	2,451	423	2,028	43	2	9	199	2,281	1,049	5	1,044	19	3	26	1,092	3,373
1951	2,297	365	1,932	68	1	1	196	2,198	901	5	896	22	3	25	946	3,144
1950	2,036	308	1,728	63	2	5	207	2,005	787	5	782	23	4	—	809	2,814
1949	2,049	344	1,705	39	69	10	119	1,942	682	4	678	16	4	1	699	2,641
1948	1,864	264	1,600	40	67	7	106	1,820	502	3	499	16	5	1	521	2,341
1947	1,744	231	1,513	40	66	20	108	1,747	424	3	421	11	5	—	437	2,184
1946	1,848	223	1,625	35	64	3	91	1,818	179	3	176	8	5	—	189	2,007
1945	1,832	203	1,629	24[4]	2	24	123	1,802	134	4	130	6	5[5]	—	141	1,943
1943	—	—	1,502	62[4]	42	1	94	1,701	—	—	134	6	—[5]	12	152	1,853[6]
1941	—	—	1,557	111	38	8	84	1,798	—	—	135	14	—[5]	18	167	1,965[6]
1939	—	—	1,569	108	43	11	87	1,818	—	—	145	10	—[5]	20	175	1,993[6]
1937	—	—	1,385	103	47	14	76	1,625	—	—	139	12	—	18	169	1,794[6]
1933	—	—	1,177	89	31	10	47	1,354	—	—	102	17	—	17	136	1,490[6]

[1] Figures are as at fiscal year end nearest to 31 December of year named.
[2] Municipal Improvements Assistance Act.
[3] Included in other liabilities.
[4] Deposit certificates included for years 1943 and prior.
[5] Included in other guaranteed debt.

[6] These totals differ from those on the table showing provincial debt by province (series G266–276). The breakdown of debt by type was only available after elimination of intergovernment debt as follows: 1933, 83; 1937, 172; 1939, 202; 1941, 203; 1943, 198.

Series G208–221. *Municipal governments, net general revenue by major source, selected years, 1933 to 1960*

(millions of dollars)

	Taxes								Nontax revenue			Total tax and nontax revenue	Subsidies from other governments	Total net revenue
	Income tax			General sales	Other sales	Real and personal property	Other	Total taxes	Privileges, licences and permits	Government enterprises	Other revenue			
Year[1]	Corporate	Individual	Total											
	208	209	210	211	212	213	214	215	216	217	218	219	220	221
1960	—	—	—	82	4	1,331	7	1,424	25	41	104	1,594	99	1,693
1959	—	—	—	74	3	1,196	8	1,281	25	45	103	1,454	91	1,545
1958	—	—	—	58	4	1,060	10	1,132	24	45	93	1,294	85	1,379
1957	—	—	—	53	3	974	7	1,037	22	37	84	1,180	74	1,254
1956	—	—	—	51	3	860	10	924	20	35	78	1,057	52	1,109
1955	—	—	—	43	3	764	18	828	19	32	64	943	45	988
1954	—	—	—	37	2	709	15	763	17	36	60	876	42	918
1953	—	—	—	34	2	651	13	700	16	33	62	811	30	841
1952	—	—	—	30	2	600	14	646	14	30	47	737	29	766
1951	—	—	—	27	2	531	10	570	13	29	48	660	24	684
1950	—	—	—	25	—	400	53	478	14	24	44	560	15	575
1949	—	—	—	16	—	369	48	433	13	24	42	512	9	521
1948	—	—	—	15	—	337	41	393	12	20	38	463	8	471
1947	—	—	—	13	—	304	34	351	10	19	33	413	6	419
1946	—	—	—	12	—	275	29	316	9	16	34	375	7	382
1945	—	—	—	9	1	278	4	292	6	17	30	345	6	351
1943	—	—	—	8	—	260	25	293	8	14	26	341	7	348
1941	—	4	4	7	—	251	24	286	8	12	25	331	3	334
1939	1	3	4	5	—	243	23	275	7	10	25	317	5	322
1937	1	3	4	4	—	237	21	266	6	9	23	304	5	307
1933	—	4	4	—	—	231	18	253	5	6	30	294	—	294

[1] Figures are for fiscal year ending nearest 31 December of year named.

Series G222–230. *Municipal governments, net general expenditure by major function, selected years, 1933 to 1960*
(millions of dollars)

Year[1]	Health	Social welfare	Education[2]	Transportation and communication	Debt charges[2]	General government	Protection of persons and property	Other	Total net expenditure
	222	223	224	225	226	227	228	229	230
1960	66	44	814[2]	361	96[2]	141	232	357	2,111
1959	68	38	658	346	118	129	212	284	1,853
1958	75	34	522	309	101	121	191	241	1,594
1957	81	32	494	296	85	109	172	229	1,498
1956	70	34	440	226	67	101	156	221	1,315
1955	65	33	388	221	50	89	148	179	1,173
1954	65	29	384	176	50	78	128	212	1,122
1953	52	27	378	167	45	73	111	157	1,010
1952	52	27	331	147	39	62	103	146	907
1951	41	25	283	123	36	55	102	122	787
1950	40	74	246	110	35	—[3]	—[3]	177	682
1949	37	71	220	102	31	—[3]	—[3]	158	619
1948	33	58	188	90	28	—[3]	—[3]	148	545
1947	26	47	135	72	30	—[3]	—[3]	137	447
1946	21	39	118	67	32	—[3]	—[3]	114	391
1945	21	16	108	48	29	40	43	39	344
1943	15	25	94	33	41	—[3]	—[3]	94	302
1941	16	23	86	30	47	—[3]	—[3]	92	294
1939	16	35	87	28	52	—[3]	—[3]	88	306
1937	15	39	81	28	53	—[3]	—[3]	82	298
1933	15	42	77	27	60	—[3]	—[3]	82	303

[1] Figures are for fiscal year ending nearest 31 December of year named.
[2] From 1933 to 1959 school debenture debt charges are included in series G226; in 1960 these charges are included in series G224.
[3] Included in 'other expenditure'.

Series G231–243. *Municipal governments, direct and indirect debt, selected years, 1933 to 1960*
(millions of dollars)

	Direct debt						Indirect debt						Total direct and indirect debt
Year[1]	Funded debt	Less sinking funds	Net funded debt	Temporary loans and overdrafts	Other liabilities	Total direct debt	Guaranteed bonds and debentures	Less sinking funds	Net debt	Guaranteed bank loans	Other	Total indirect debt	
	231	232	233	234	235	236	237	238	239	240	241	242	243
1960	4,277	152	4,125	264	381	4,770	74	2	72	—	—	72	4,842
1959	3,803	133	3,670	246	339	4,255	80	2	78	—	—	78	4,333
1958	3,399	118	3,281	185	343	3,809	14	—	14	—	—	14	3,823
1957	2,994	106	2,888	207	277	3,372	15	—	15	—	—	15	3,387
1956	2,645	98	2,547	167	327	3,041	14	—	14	—	—	14	3,055
1955	2,408	93	2,315	128	204	2,647	15	—	15	—	—	15	2,662
1954	2,113	89	2,024	116	200	2,340	16	1	15	1	—	16	2,356
1953	1,845	92	1,753	96	192	2,041	17	1	16	1	—	17	2,058
1952	1,612	103	1,509	99	158	1,766	18	1	17	1	—	18	1,784
1951	1,433	117	1,316	87	164	1,567	17	1	16	1	—	17	1,584
1950	1,224	145	1,079	84	138	1,301	23	1	22	—	—	22	1,323
1949	1,103	150	953	78	122	1,153	23	1	22	—	—	22	1,175
1948	995	145	850	64	119	1,033	24	1	23	—	—	23	1,056
1947	939	150	789	48	114	951	25	—	25	—	—	25	976
1946	982	161	821	27	111	959	24	—	24	—	—	24	983
1945	1,003	176	827	26	116	969	23	1	22	1	—	23	992
1943	—	—	846	64	76	986	—	—	46	1	2	49	1,035[2]
1941	—	—	941	100	73	1,114	—	—	49	2	2	53	1,167[2]
1939	—	—	1,017	143	89	1,249	—	—	50	2	3	55	1,304[2]
1937	—	—	1,097	115	89	1,301	—	—	50	3	2	55	1,356[2]
1933	—	—	1,173	140	58	1,371	—	—	59	3	2	64	1,435[2]

[1] Figures are as at 31 December of year named.
[2] These totals differ from those on table showing municipal debt by province (series G299–309). The breakdown of debt by type was only available after elimination of intergovernment debt as follows: 1933, 26; 1937, 30; 1939, 37; 1941, 47; 1943, 41.

Series G244–254. *Provincial governments, total net general revenue, by province, selected years, 1933 to 1960*
(millions of dollars)

Year[1]	New-found-land	Prince Edward Island	Nova Scotia	New Brunswick	Quebec	Ontario	Manitoba	Saskat-chewan	Alberta	British Columbia	Total[2]
	244	245	246	247	248	249	250	251	252	253	254
1960	64	16	92	87	641	833	104	149	246	320	2,552
1959	60	14	90	77	605	778	100	146	279	314	2,463
1958	62	13	76	71	557	647	77	141	236	296	2,176
1957	39	9	64	62	515	595	74	136	246	282	2,022
1956	37	8	58	57	446	482	66	122	241	273	1,790
1955	33	8	54	53	413	432	59	103	225	231	1,611
1954	33	8	51	51	339	399	57	99	175	200	1,412
1953	32	8	49	49	299	371	56	98	186	186	1,334
1952	32	7	47	47	285	365	55	91	144	185	1,258
1951	25	6	39	41	277	304	46	75	106	157	1,076
1950	21	5	36	32	239	266	41	67	105	139	951
1949	18	5	34	30	207	236	38	61	88	124	841
1948	—	5	33	28	203	220	36	56	63	101	745
1947	—	5	32	29	194	223	34	53	48	72	690
1946	—	4	22	20	151	151	23	37	36	58	502
1945	—	3	19	16	119	134	22	35	34	47	429
1943	—	2	17	12	97	117	19	31	27	39	361
1941	—	2	14	11	94	111	19	25	25	38	339
1939	—	2	12	8	60	87	16	21	20	32	258
1937	—	2	10	7	57	87	15	17	19	31	245
1933	—	1	7	5	31	52	13	12	12	19	152

[1] Figures are for fiscal year ending nearest 31 December of year named.   [2] Includes unconditional transfers from Government of Canada. Agrees with series G179.

Series G255–265. *Provincial governments, total net general expenditure, by province, selected years, 1933 to 1960*
(millions of dollars)

Year[1]	New-found-land	Prince Edward Island	Nova Scotia	New Brunswick	Quebec	Ontario	Manitoba	Saskat-chewan	Alberta	British Columbia	Total[2]
	255	256	257	258	259	260	261	262	263	264	265
1960	75	15	112	95	749	937	137	150	266	332	2,868
1959	65	20	92	80	601	808	128	142	234	283	2,543
1958	62	14	86	71	533	742	98	137	215	267	2,225
1957	48	11	74	63	493	657	76	124	199	288	2,033
1956	44	10	71	59	434	552	63	110	170	258	1,771
1955	42	10	58	54	400	489	52	101	159	208	1,573
1954	39	9	53	51	350	421	49	96	138	178	1,384
1953	33	7	51	48	311	384	47	86	118	172	1,257
1952	29	7	46	45	313	372	42	80	104	169	1,207
1951	30	8	49	40	261	336	43	72	82	152	1,073
1950	27	7	52	41	224	279	35	62	73	141	941
1949	26	6	51	37	193	261	35	58	58	151	876
1948	—	6	43	40	230	235	33	55	55	101	798
1947	—	6	34	33	186	198	25	52	42	80	656
1946	—	4	24	25	140	156	18	35	31	54	487
1945	—	4	19	17	111	127	16	28	23	40	385
1943	—	2	13	10	91	102	14	20	22	30	304
1941	—	2	13	10	88	113	15	21	20	32	314
1939	—	3	15	17	108	116	17	29	22	33	360
1937	—	2	19	17	88	120	17	45	21	34	363
1933	—	1	11	6	50	73	16	22	18	22	219

[1] Figures are for fiscal year ended nearest 31 December of year named.   [2] Includes unconditional subsidies paid to municipalities. Agrees with series G191.

Series G 266–276. *Provincial governments, direct and indirect debt, by province, selected years, 1933 to 1960*

(millions of dollars)

Year[1]	Newfoundland	Prince Edward Island	Nova Scotia	New Brunswick	Quebec	Ontario	Manitoba	Saskatchewan	Alberta	British Columbia	Total
	266	**267**	**268**	**269**	**270**	**271**	**272**	**273**	**274**	**275**	**276**
1960	122	36	281	263	1,308	3,281	488	450	222	651	7,102
1959	109	35	260	241	1,101	3,128	401	372	173	585	6,405
1958	103	28	251	229	990	2,943	312	355	71	574	5,856
1957	99	26	233	229	930	2,585	250	290	47	518	5,207
1956	86	23	220	217	880	2,283	214	243	96	403	4,665
1955	83	21	202	194	816	2,014	192	231	96	323	4,172
1954	68	19	194	183	793	1,939	186	192	100	293	3,967
1953	51	18	190	182	727	1,755	167	184	103	280	3,657
1952	48	18	185	181	676	1,565	155	175	106	264	3,373
1951	37	18	180	176	660	1,376	141	165	111	280	3,144
1950	10	16	166	164	627	1,177	118	163	120	253	2,814
1949	10	15	143	151	636	1,076	98	152	138	222	2,641
1948	—	14	121	136	628	884	82	152	136	188	2,341
1947	—	12	112	115	596	810	77	157	139	166	2,184
1946	—	11	99	105	416	763	95	202	158	158	2,007
1945	—	11	96	95	377	757	92	196	164	155	1,943
1943	—	9	92	96	401	789	110	213	179	162	2,051
1941	—	10	102	100	419	848	115	229	176	169	2,168
1939	—	9	101	100	405	869	124	234	174	179	2,195
1937	—	6	93	82	286	806	122	216	175	180	1,966
1933	—	4	67	62	171	692	118	153	158	148	1,573

[1] Figures are as at fiscal year end nearest to 31 December of year named.

Series G 277–287. *Municipal governments, total net general revenue, by province, selected years, 1933 to 1960*

(millions of dollars)

Year[1]	Newfoundland	Prince Edward Island	Nova Scotia	New Brunswick	Quebec	Ontario	Manitoba	Saskatchewan	Alberta	British Columbia	Total[2]
	277	**278**	**279**	**280**	**281**	**282**	**283**	**284**	**285**	**286**	**287**
1960	6	3	43	40	412	694	79	96	153	167	1,693
1959	6	3	39	36	383	628	73	88	138	151	1,545
1958	5	3	36	33	326	562	68	83	127	136	1,379
1957	4	2	34	30	293	519	64	78	112	118	1,254
1956	4	2	30	26	267	453	59	71	97	100	1,109
1955	3	2	27	24	239	400	53	66	87	87	988
1954	3	2	25	22	226	360	49	62	85	84	918
1953	2	2	24	21	217	319	46	57	76	77	841
1952	2	2	23	19	193	293	45	51	68	70	766
1951	2	1	20	16	182	254	42	46	58	63	684
1950	—	—	—	—	—	—	—	—	—	—	575
1949	—	—	—	—	—	—	—	—	—	—	521
1948	—	—	—	—	—	—	—	—	—	—	471
1947	—	—	—	—	—	—	—	—	—	—	419
1946	—	—	—	—	—	—	—	—	—	—	382
1945	—	1	12	9	100	125	23	27	26	28	351
1943	—	1	11	8	94	128	22	30	27	27	348
1941	—	—	10	8	92	133	21	22	23	25	334
1939	—	—	10	7	84	131	21	22	23	24	322
1937	—	—	9	6	81	133	20	15	21	22	307
1933	—	—	9	5	73	128	19	17	20	23	294

[1] Figures are for fiscal year ending nearest to 31 December of year named.

[2] Includes unconditional transfers from provincial governments. Agrees with series G 221.

Series G 288–298. *Municipal governments, total net general expenditure, by province, selected years, 1933 to 1960*
(millions of dollars)

Year[1]	New-found-land	Prince Edward Island	Nova Scotia	New Brunswick	Quebec	Ontario	Manitoba	Saskat-chewan	Alberta	British Columbia	Total
	288	289	290	291	292	293	294	295	296	297	298
1960	7	5	53	41	469[2]	930	102	114	191	199	2,110
1959	6	3	47	41	377[2]	820	85	108	180	186	1,853
1958	6	4	43	39	278[3]	727	76	96	158	167	1,594
1957	7	3	39	34	248[3]	699	71	89	155	153	1,498
1956	5	3	33	33	229[3]	602	66	82	138	124	1,315
1955	3	3	28	29	202[3]	540	64	74	120	110	1,173
1954	3	3	29	27	197[3]	505	58	69	114	117	1,122
1953	3	2	27	26	251	379	53	61	113	95	1,010
1952	2	2	27	24	237	339	48	54	91	83	907
1951	1	2	25	20	201	294	46	47	76	75	787
1950	—	—	—	—	—	—	—	—	—	—	682
1949	—	—	—	—	—	—	—	—	—	—	619
1948	—	—	—	—	—	—	—	—	—	—	545
1947	—	—	—	—	—	—	—	—	—	—	447
1946	—	—	—	—	—	—	—	—	—	—	391
1945	—	1	11	9	92	126	24	27	26	28	344
1943	—	1	10	7	83	110	20	24	23	24	302
1941	—	1	10	6	86	106	20	21	21	23	294
1939	—	1	10	7	91	112	21	20	21	23	306
1937	—	1	10	7	85	114	21	18	20	22	298
1933	—	1	9	6	85	123	20	18	19	22	303

[1] After elimination of intergovernmental transfers.
[2] Includes $56 million capital expenditure for schools; does not include other capital expenditures out of capital fund.
[3] Does not include capital expenditure out of capital fund.

Series G 299–309. *Municipal governments, direct and indirect debt, by province, selected years, 1933 to 1960*
(millions of dollars)

Year[1]	New-found-land	Prince Edward Island	Nova Scotia	New Brunswick	Quebec	Ontario	Manitoba	Saskat-chewan	Alberta	British Columbia	Total
	299	300	301	302	303	304	305	306	307	308	309
1960	20	8	109	101	1,593	1,750	175	165	482	439	4,842
1959	19	7	100	95	1,422	1,570	148	144	445	383	4,333
1958	16	6	88	89	1,198	1,440	125	124	393	344	3,823
1957	17	7	78	82	1,028	1,266	118	111	364	316	3,387
1956	14	6	73	74	969	1,110	105	99	317	288	3,055
1955	11	6	62	69	855	945	94	86	261	273	2,662
1954	7	5	61	64	772	854	84	73	227	209	2,356
1953	6	4	56	58	681	746	73	57	181	196	2,058
1952	5	4	52	54	602	623	69	49	145	181	1,784
1951	4	4	45	47	549	546	66	47	125	151	1,584
1950	—	—	—	—	—	—	—	—	—	—	1,323
1949	—	—	—	—	—	—	—	—	—	—	1,175
1948	—	—	—	—	—	—	—	—	—	—	1,056
1947	—	—	—	—	—	—	—	—	—	—	976
1946	—	—	—	—	—	—	—	—	—	—	983
1945	—	—	—	—	—	—	—	—	—	—	992
1943	—	2	22	19	472	282	60	76	50	93	1,076
1941	—	3	25	22	503	342	72	87	57	103	1,214
1939	—	3	27	22	523	413	82	98	62	111	1,341
1937	—	3	27	23	507	404	96	87	67	112	1,386
1933	—	2	29	22	508	540	100	68	74	118	1,461

[1] Figures are as at 31 December of year named.

Series G310–317. *Total provincial revenues, current account, by major category, 1913, 1921, 1925 to 1937*

(millions of dollars)

Year[1]	Total current revenues	Federal subsidies	Taxes	Licences, permits and fees	Public domain	Liquor control	All other current revenues	Federal subventions and grants-in-aid[2]
	310	311	312	313	314	315	316	317
1937	247.0	21.2	134.2	34.2	21.1	29.8	6.6	82.4
1936	221.6	16.9	113.6	35.3	18.7	26.7	10.3	72.6
1935	194.7	17.1	97.8	30.5	17.6	22.8	9.0	57.7
1934	164.9	16.1	79.2	29.1	14.4	17.5	8.7	57.5
1933	154.3	15.3	76.8	27.8	11.3	14.8	8.1	40.4
1932	158.4	15.4	75.0	27.6	12.2	19.8	8.4	45.2
1931	162.0	15.0	70.0	26.3	15.6	26.4	8.8	42.6
1930	178.3	14.3	77.7	28.7	17.0	31.0	9.7	9.2
1929	180.3	14.1	71.4	32.0	19.0	36.1	7.8	2.6
1928	164.2	14.2	57.5	30.0	20.0	32.9	9.5	2.3
1927	152.5	14.5	58.5	27.4	20.3	24.7	7.2	1.5
1926	136.2	12.5	55.3	23.8	19.7	17.6	7.2	1.4
1925	122.8	12.4	47.5	21.7	18.2	15.8	7.2	1.7
1921	91.1	11.9	35.3	15.4	14.8	7.9	5.9	1.5
1913	46.4	12.9	9.3	6.9	11.0	2.2	4.1	.1

[1] Fiscal years ending nearest the end of the year given: for fiscal years and fiscal year changes of the provinces see the general note to this section.

[2] Not included in total current revenues.

Series G318–329. *Total provincial expenditures, current account, by major category, 1913, 1921, 1925 to 1937*

(millions of dollars)

Year[1]	Total current expenditures	Debt charges[2]	Public welfare Relief	Public welfare Other	Education	Administration of justice	Legislation	General government	Agriculture	Public domain	Highways, bridges and ferries	All other
	318	319	320	321	322	323	324	325	326	327	328	329
1937	261.1	50.9	42.9	45.8	32.5	11.7	3.2	19.3	6.2	14.5	25.3	8.7
1936	237.5	50.4	41.9	41.1	29.3	10.1	2.6	16.4	5.4	16.6	19.9	4.8
1935	243.3	54.4	52.7	36.1	28.0	10.5	2.4	15.6	5.0	15.4	20.8	2.6
1934	235.4	52.9	55.4	34.7	28.2	10.2	3.0	14.9	5.0	11.2	17.6	2.3
1933	202.9	50.2	33.3	31.0	28.8	9.6	2.4	14.4	4.9	9.9	15.9	2.8
1932	207.0	49.0	25.1	32.5	30.3	10.3	2.4	14.8	6.0	13.1	17.8	5.6
1931	210.5	39.2	25.8	34.3	34.2	11.5	2.4	15.4	6.4	14.2	22.7	4.4
1930	187.9	29.5	4.1	33.4	33.8	11.6	3.2	15.6	6.3	15.3	28.7	6.5
1929	163.2	27.8	.9	26.2	31.2	10.2	2.6	14.7	5.5	12.3	25.6	6.1
1928	150.1	25.9	.1	23.5	29.3	9.9	2.6	14.1	4.9	10.7	23.3	5.8
1927	142.2	26.2	.1	20.8	27.8	9.1	3.2	13.0	4.6	9.8	20.7	6.9
1926	127.0	25.0	.1	18.5	25.7	8.5	2.4	12.1	4.2	8.9	15.8	5.8
1925	120.9	23.1	.2	17.6	25.6	8.7	2.7	12.1	3.9	7.5	13.5	6.1
1921	91.4	14.4	.4	12.1	20.9	7.5	2.5	12.0	3.8	5.5	8.3	4.0
1913	48.9	3.3	—	4.3	9.6	4.9	1.9	6.5	2.3	5.3	8.7	2.2

[1] Fiscal years ending nearest the end of the year given: for fiscal years and fiscal year changes of the provinces see the general note to this section.

[2] Excluding sinking funds.

Series G330–339. *Total provincial revenue, current account, by province, 1913, 1921, 1925 to 1937*

(millions of dollars)

Year[1]	Total current revenues	Prince Edward Island	Nova Scotia	New Brunswick	Quebec	Ontario	Manitoba	Saskatchewan	Alberta	British Columbia
	330	331	332	333	334	335	336	337	338	339
1937	247.0	1.6	10.1	7.5	57.5	87.6	15.3	17.1	18.9	31.3
1936	221.6	1.5	9.5	6.6	43.5	87.0	14.0	14.0	17.0	28.4
1935	194.7	1.3	9.3[2]	6.0	41.5	70.0	12.9	13.5	14.3	25.9
1934	164.9	1.2	7.0	5.3	35.8	54.6	12.6	11.4	13.9	23.1
1933	154.3	1.2	6.2	5.0	30.7	54.8	12.1	11.7	12.6	19.8
1932	158.4	1.2	7.1	5.4	33.4	55.1	10.6	12.0	12.9	20.7
1931	162.0	1.1	7.6	5.8	36.8	57.2	9.6	10.1	11.7	22.1
1930	178.3	1.2	6.9	6.3	43.1	58.4	11.2	13.3	13.8	24.1
1929	180.3	1.1	6.3	6.4	46.1	54.8	11.8	14.0	14.5	25.4
1928	164.2	1.0	5.8	5.7	41.1	47.5	10.3	15.7	14.1	23.1
1927	152.5	.9	5.6	5.2	35.8	45.0	9.4	13.3	14.6[3]	22.8
1926	136.2	.9	4.0	4.1	31.3	39.9	10.3	12.8	11.1	21.9
1925	122.8	.8	3.5	3.4	26.8	34.5	9.6	12.4	10.7	21.2
1921	91.1	.8	3.3	2.7	21.0	21.9	7.4	9.5[2]	8.0	16.6
1913	46.4	.5	1.7	1.4	8.7	9.4	4.1	6.1[2]	4.4	10.2

[1] Fiscal years ending nearest the end of the year given: for fiscal years and fiscal year changes of the provinces see the general note to this section.

[2] Fourteen-month period.

[3] Fifteen-month period.

Series G 340–349. *Selected provincial revenues by province,[1] succession duties, 1901 to 1957*

(thousands of dollars)

Year[2]	Total nine provinces	Prince Edward Island	Nova Scotia	New Brunswick	Quebec	Ontario	Manitoba	Saskat-chewan	Alberta	British Columbia
	340	341	342	343	344	345	346	347	348	349
1957	64,555	—	2	4	35,372	29,161	6	6	4	—
1956	72,046	—	5	—	46,558	25,462	5	10	6	—
1955	40,663	—	2	—	14,798	25,819	12	25	7	—
1954	31,133	—	5	6	10,913	20,164	5	23	17	—
1953	32,726	1	12	1	12,833	19,821	8	13	37	—
1952	34,190	12	25	1	12,429	21,652	15	30	26	—
1951	31,121	3	26[7]	1[8]	13,007	17,828	28	127	101	—
1950	28,628	6	—	5	13,325	14,978	32	23	98	161
1949	28,709	21	73	46	11,834	15,995	92	101	149	398
1948	29,932	63	208	53	9,085	17,944	403	475[13]	652	1,049
1947	32,842	93	513	432	11,353	15,227	809[13]	641[13]	855	2,919
1946	24,904	109	661	1,072	6,299	12,525	767	618	1,130	1,723
1945	23,707	82	879	677	5,382	12,783	667	463	903	1,871
1944	23,682	46[5]	511	365	6,505	13,321	344	454	686	1,450
1943	21,907	—	662	600	6,796	11,636	543	393	459	818
1942	27,220	57	688	222	12,076	11,676	737	330	673	761
1941	19,192	43	410	383	5,015[9]	11,172	603	262	415	889
1940	27,808	44	550	526	12,404	11,500	875	352	395	1,162
1939	30,458	75	557	177	12,277	15,315	605	376	372	704
1938	36,417	68	746	319	11,838	20,214	404	241	1,326	1,261
1937	26,620	45	606	398	7,637	15,991	464	311	343	825
1936	19,949	43	567	619	4,698	11,985	375	324	271	1,067
1935	9,604	20	463[6]	415	3,402	3,469[8]	340	223	293	979
1934	10,923	50	298	150	2,698	6,515	423	149	257	383
1933	13,155	31	263	259	3,070	8,081	267	177	471	536
1932	11,893	35	515	192	3,799	6,137	347	199	258	411
1931	18,624	12	256	294	6,675	9,505	452	318	553	559
1930	20,265	26	312	199	5,268	11,229	1,034	463	897	837
1929	13,690	29	290	320	4,184	6,610	733	405	383	736
1928	11,376	17	222	414	3,741	4,667	607	363	587[5]	758
1927	15,530	9	188	461	3,054	9,469	757	290	—	702
1926	13,744	19	537	595	2,257	8,762	422	333	254	565
1925	10,826	15	258	299	2,423	5,787	592[12]	283	460	709
1924	9,362	6	136	164	2,978	4,175	456	484	190	773
1923	8,258	9	223	134	2,620	3,858	291	276	164	683
1922	11,102	21	121	262	3,005	6,523	169[11]	309	128	564
1921	8,385	11	159	151	2,100	4,822	299	324	177	342
1920	7,491	8	196	90	1,787	4,014	478	271	273	374
1919	6,030	4	181	75	1,459	3,527	193	145	174	272
1918	8,871	4	117	95	4,737	3,158	198	116	205	241
1917	5,935	4	131	30	1,741	3,228	306	70	147	278
1916	4,709	10	161	78	1,376	2,452	296	44	152	140
1915	4,398	6	107	155	1,661	1,721	412	64	110	162
1914	3,651	8	53	20	1,604	1,288	283	74[15]	72	249
1913	2,942	6	53	98	1,064	1,146	268	46	67	194
1912	2,810	2[4]	78	45	1,227	874	344	34	54	152
1911	2,611	3	42	6	1,072	1,051	166[10]	40	31	200
1910	1,902	5	54	33	838	758	73	28	5	108
1909	1,546	4	71	12	634	682	52	3	10	78[9]
1908	1,978	7	79	32	621	1,155	43	4	2	35
1907	1,552	5[3]	65	15	568	834	13	2[14]	—	50
1906	1,621	7[3]	63	12	421	1,016	71	—	1	30
1905	1,009	7	50	42	183	684	12	—	—	31
1904	1,022	4	41	25	450	459	13	—	—	30
1903	619	3	35	23	154	387	5	—	—	12
1902	606	4	55	17	223	236	7	—	—	64
1901	583	1	46	12	164	336	3	—	—	21

[1] No revenues for Newfoundland were given in the source.
[2] Fiscal years ending within the year given: for fiscal years and fiscal year changes of the provinces see the general note to this section.
[3] 9 months ending 30 September.
[4] 15 months ending 31 December.
[5] 15 months ending 31 March.
[6] 14 months ending 30 November.
[7] 16 months ending 31 March.
[8] 5 months ending 31 March.
[9] 9 months ending 31 March.
[10] 11 months ending 30 November.
[11] 9 months ending 31 August.
[12] 8 months ending 30 April.
[13] 11 months ending 31 March.
[14] 14 months ending 28 February.
[15] 14 months ending 30 April.

Series G350–358. *Selected provincial revenues by province,[1] corporation taxes, 1901 to 1957*

(thousands of dollars)

Year[2]	Total eight provinces	Prince Edward Island	Nova Scotia	New Brunswick	Quebec	Ontario	Manitoba	Saskatchewan	Alberta
	350	351	352	353	354	355	356	357	358
1957	81,045	—	241	—	80,421	383	—	—	—
1956	72,264	—	216	—	70,460	1,588	—	—	—
1955	64,227	—	196	—	63,763	268	—	—	—
1954	65,199	—	185	—	64,075	939	—	—	—
1953	78,592	—	171	—	63,865	14,556	—	—	—
1952	162,581	—	113	—	68,146	94,322	—	—	—
1951	130,988	—	82[6]	—	54,445	76,461	—	—	—
1950	109,282	—	—	—	44,916	64,366	—	—	—
1949	105,515	—	54	—	44,548	60,912	—	1	—
1948	75,710	—	50	—	30,996	44,664	—	—	—
1947	684	—	47	—	67	534	34[13]	—	2
1946	845	—	46	—	79	650	69	—	1
1945	580	—	40	—	99	361	79	—	1
1944	338	—	36	—	110	96	94	—	2
1943	321	—	55	—	573	−481[17]	166	2	6
1942	40,662	—	222	—	16,185	22,247	378	222	1,408
1941	40,552	120	1,543	1,147	10,537[8]	21,960	2,828	902	1,515
1940	24,670	172	1,364	1,039	6,593	10,500	2,306	1,139	1,557
1939	28,460	172	1,169	869	12,163	9,505	2,118	898	1,566
1938	23,291	166	1,108	869	8,430	8,511	1,854	923	1,430
1937	21,971	164	1,015	522	7,337	9,057	1,827	975	1,074
1936	19,148	161	987	516	6,182	7,132	1,705	1,423	1,042
1935	9,040	147	1,115[5]	495	4,063	137[7]	1,497	588	998
1934	15,429	133	963	495	3,967	6,151	1,602	1,109	1,009
1933	16,052	125	802	517	3,961	6,410	1,693	1,370	1,174
1932	14,941	117	830	548	3,488	6,889	1,376	711	982
1931	12,574	102	787	443	3,425	4,670	1,183	987	977
1930	10,754	85	772	437	3,444	3,070	1,014	986	946
1929	10,024	84	745	416	3,066	2,869	973	1,050	821
1928	9,685	81	692	401	3,113	2,746	952	857	843[16]
1927	8,270	78	731	393	2,524	2,630	1,049	865	—
1926	9,129	116	731	590	2,455	2,502	1,053	837	845
1925	7,654	34	593	244	2,461	2,421	489[12]	722	690
1924	8,217	33	695	245	2,323	2,728	757	665	771
1923	7,361	30	549	248	2,213	2,025	793	778	725
1922	7,234	40	559	249	2,010	2,509	613[11]	603	651
1921	6,781	53	541	255	1,641	2,204	1,111	524	452
1920	5,995	35	314	222	1,582	2,131	714	578	419
1919	4,993	22	276	135	1,530	1,674	651	326	379
1918	4,535	22	117	131	1,289	1,755	540	319	362
1917	4,108	16	93	121	1,102	1,632	520	304	320
1916	3,850	17	68	109	1,035	1,658	417	254	292
1915	3,855	18	66	53	983	1,765	415	347	208
1914	3,197	17	60	51	925	1,319	362	258[15]	205
1913	2,610	17	43	50	941	878	349	161	171
1912	2,236	23[4]	—	47	777	842	262	127	158
1911	2,088	16	—	48	712	825	238[10]	115	134
1910	1,922	15	—	37	688	752	228	185[14]	17
1909	1,790	17	—	34	653	719[9]	223	35	109
1908	1,649	17	—	34	566	695	190	28	119
1907	1,517	16	—	31	464	672	182	—	152
1906	1,164	9[3]	—	37	315	664	159	—	—
1905	917	12	—	32	304	446	123	—	—
1904	837	13	—	30	261	421	112	—	—
1903	630	13	—	29	226	254	108	—	—
1902	581	13	—	26	232	246	64	—	—
1901	550	9	—	25	214	238	64	—	—

[1] No revenues for Newfoundland were given in the source. Corporation taxes for British Columbia were not given separately in the source.
[2] Fiscal years ending within the year given: for fiscal years and fiscal year changes of the provinces see the general note to this subsection.
[3] 9 months ending 30 September.
[4] 15 months ending 31 December.
[5] 14 months ending 30 November.
[6] 16 months ending 31 March.
[7] 5 months ending 31 March.
[8] 9 months ending 31 March.
[9] 10 months ending 31 October.
[10] 11 months ending 30 November.
[11] 9 months ending 31 August.
[12] 8 months ending 30 April.
[13] 11 months ending 31 March.
[14] 3 years' revenue.
[15] 14 months ending 30 April.
[16] 15 months ending 31 March.
[17] Refunds exceeded collections.

Series G 359–368. *Selected provincial revenues by province,[1] motor-vehicle licences and gasoline taxes, 1904 to 1957*

(thousands of dollars)

Year[2]	Total nine provinces	Prince Edward Island	Nova Scotia	New Brunswick	Quebec	Ontario	Manitoba	Saskatchewan	Alberta	British Columbia
	359	360	361	362	363	364	365	366	367	368
1957	416,389	2,004	18,034	14,584	108,612	162,689	17,628	21,739	32,838	38,261
1956	373,401	1,900	16,933	13,653	95,445	146,164	14,884	20,408	30,207	33,807
1955	326,161	1,786	14,401	12,246	84,421	122,659	13,484[12]	20,199	27,853	29,112
1954	304,701	1,676	13,493	10,632	79,167	113,689	13,262	19,482	25,971	27,329
1953	275,123	1,613	12,484	9,848	70,934	103,542	11,488	16,520	23,043	25,051
1952	248,847	1,411	11,321	9,170	66,335	92,983	10,706	13,987	19,393	23,541
1951	217,192	1,327	12,554[5]	2,210[6]	53,722	85,857	9,187	12,133	18,152	22,050
1950	185,825	1,148	—	8,422	45,644	76,088	8,327	11,402	16,108	18,686
1949	176,605	1,047	9,189	7,960	42,870	67,971	7,357	9,985	13,488	16,738
1948	159,487	928	8,602	7,512	37,060	61,953	6,804	9,483	11,904	15,241
1947	115,697	674	7,664	6,217	26,020	44,434	4,694	6,362[14]	9,094	10,538
1946	91,872	542	5,617	4,378	21,123	33,891	4,469	6,307	7,728	7,817
1945	78,772	460	4,475	3,489	18,869	28,312	4,016	5,754	6,928	6,469
1944	76,382	433[3]	3,957	3,151	17,087	28,488	4,071	6,057	6,704	6,434
1943	73,136	—	3,843	2,825	17,082	28,230	3,817	4,369	6,435	6,535
1942	90,217	375	4,109	3,048	19,442	37,704	4,502	6,479	7,081	7,477
1941	78,810	440	4,786	3,525	11,596[7]	35,841	4,253	5,275	5,849	7,245
1940	81,809	460	4,490	3,518	17,936	33,719	4,257	5,142	5,575	6,712
1939	67,426	475	4,094	3,070	14,761	26,337	3,802	3,567	5,185	6,135
1938	65,930	441	3,846	2,976	14,531	26,325	3,646	3,576	4,555	6,034
1937	62,036	415	3,398	2,531	13,049	26,586	3,150	3,993	3,567	5,347
1936	55,671	313	2,975	2,057	11,711	24,086	2,768	3,291	3,646	4,824
1935	41,505	283	3,080[4]	1,856	10,618	11,917[6]	2,948	2,883	3,563	4,357
1934	47,973	276	2,189	1,644	10,027	20,943	2,511	2,993	3,392	3,998
1933	46,146	259	1,976	1,561	9,947	19,981	2,398	3,024	3,070	3,930
1932	45,329	253	2,207	1,630	10,382	19,647	2,223	2,278	2,975	3,734
1931	43,747	245	2,004	1,556	9,815	16,472	2,281	3,806	3,626	3,942
1930	41,145	270	1,807	1,523	9,288	16,206	1,910	3,000	3,816	3,325
1929	38,929	223	1,446	1,319	7,992	16,251	1,620	3,734	3,432[3]	2,912
1928	28,134	162	1,231	1,021	5,571	10,994	1,426	2,266	2,907[3]	2,556
1927	21,411	118	920	845	4,589	9,950	1,185	1,510	—	2,294
1926	21,403	100	759	700	3,752	9,747	1,100	1,718	1,577	1,950
1925	16,556	81	576	501	3,145	7,568	520[11]	1,297	1,265	1,603
1924	12,486	69	535	451	2,158	4,780	910	1,342	1,142	1,099
1923	11,044	53	480	374	2,145	4,293	737[10]	1,003	984	975
1922	9,086	47	418	301	1,983	3,477	455[10]	701	901	803
1921	7,802	38	372	274	1,387	2,945	539	946	719	582
1920	5,738	31	256	197	1,134	1,991	400	693	682	354
1919	4,720	16	148	116	880	1,580	379	744	611	246
1918	3,649	14	92	90	650	1,214	236	625	535	193
1917	2,356	5	35	62	489	931	178	252	270	134
1916	1,409	1	42	38	241	640	111	111	130	95
1915	929	—	26	23	180	335	83	66	106	110
1914	548	1	12	15	123	149	40	49[13]	60	99
1913	315	—	11	11	71	106	35	35	46	—
1912	201	—	7	8	49	73	20	13	31	—
1911	105	—	—	4	27	51	14[9]	5	4	—
1910	46	—	—	—	11	24	9	1	1	—
1909	29	—	—	—	9	12[8]	3	—	5	—
1908	19	—	—	—	5	10	2	1	1	—
1907	13	—	—	—	3	8	—	—	2	—
1906	9	—	—	—	2	6	—	—	1	—
1905	3	—	—	—	—	3	—	—	—	—
1904	1	—	—	—	—	1	—	—	—	—

[1] Revenues in Newfoundland from these sources were, in order, in thousands of dollars, from 1950 to 1957: 1,383; 1,760; 2,154; 2,611; 3,107; 3,698; 4,606; 5,345.

[2] Fiscal years ending within the year given: for fiscal years and fiscal year changes of the provinces see the general note to this section.

[3] 15 months ending 31 March.

[4] 14 months ending 30 November.

[5] 16 months ending 31 March.

[6] 5 months ending 31 March.

[7] 9 months ending 31 March.

[8] 10 months ending 31 October.

[9] 11 months ending 30 November.

[10] 9 months ending 31 August.

[11] 8 months ending 30 April.

[12] Revised in 1958 supplement to exclude revenue of Municipal and Public Utility Board. This figure used.

[13] 14 months ending 30 April.

[14] 11 months ending 31 March.

Series G 369–377. *Selected provincial revenues by province,[1] from natural resources, 1901 to 1957*

(thousands of dollars)

Year[2]	Total eight provinces	Nova Scotia	New Brunswick	Quebec	Ontario	Manitoba	Saskatchewan	Alberta	British Columbia
	369	370	371	372	373	374	375	376	377
1957	191,843	926	3,610	29,881	20,349	3,268	23,151	68,705	41,953
1956	154,478	941	2,796	26,970	18,279	2,823	12,460	56,213	33,996
1955	115,526	870	2,450	20,328	15,343	1,876[11]	8,317	42,226	24,116
1954	116,766	845	2,817	19,311	14,180	1,432	10,380[12]	44,305	23,496
1953	107,632	786	2,848	20,454	18,095	1,592	4,680	34,994	24,183
1952	89,857	638	2,769	22,422	13,548	1,623	3,622	27,865	17,370
1951	60,517	932[4]	348[6]	15,840	9,094	1,338	2,488	17,528	12,949
1950	47,858	—	1,522	11,278	8,868	927	2,359	11,289	11,614
1949	47,611	750	1,840	15,842	9,580	1,166	2,189	6,808	9,436
1948	40,432	727	1,910	12,910	8,513	713	2,062	3,904	9,693
1947	37,740	446	1,724	16,244	7,075	480[10]	1,649[10]	2,853	7,269
1946	29,708	582	1,271	10,603	6,769	443	1,472	2,523	6,045
1945	25,872	576	1,142	9,603	5,026	507	933	2,600	5,485
1944	24,686	629	1,124	8,282	5,925	396	916	2,057	5,357
1943	26,358	681	1,106	9,202	6,712	350	857	2,089	5,361
1942	25,481	783	1,086	8,932	6,086	319	639	1,880	5,756
1941	20,668	795	1,015	5,818[7]	5,408	332	484	1,605	5,211
1940	17,956	839	933	5,099	4,207	264	359	1,458	4,797
1939	22,368	728	531	8,806	6,079	246	285	1,379	4,314
1938	19,197	700	732	6,309	4,730	316	374	1,179	4,857
1937	16,582	723	841	5,287	3,745	307	289	1,091	4,299
1936	14,892	670	449	4,970	3,472	249	292	853	3,937
1935	9,662	722[3]	513	3,596	359[9]	273	205	714	3,280
1934	9,256	615	540	2,312	2,185	195	158	640	2,611
1933	8,072	401	191	2,468	1,641	162	166	517	2,526
1932	10,832	448	353	3,543	2,275	141	225	626	3,221
1931	13,628	570	335	4,804	3,129	128	158	498	4,006
1930	14,499	661	736	5,467	2,730	—	—	7	4,898
1929	16,944	755	874	6,238	4,252	—	—	14	4,811
1928	16,976	711	911	6,420	4,005	—	—	48[13]	4,881
1927	17,032	780	856	6,408	3,987	—	—	—	5,001
1926	16,376	682	735	5,717	4,126	—	—	300	4,816
1925	15,350	348	953	4,767	4,522	—	—	271	4,489
1924	14,335	728	1,111	4,101	3,819	—	—	205	4,371
1923	12,054	712	820	3,477	2,336	—	—	254	4,455
1922	13,091	530	455	3,989	3,923	—	—	292	3,902
1921	13,739	606	1,066	3,771	3,661	—	—	280	4,355
1920	11,633	656	1,353	2,970	3,028	—	—	286	3,340
1919	9,143	607	639	2,281	2,089	—	—	217	3,310
1918	8,321	641	549	1,516	2,338	—	—	145	3,132
1917	8,500	724	373	1,568	2,977	—	—	19	2,839
1916	6,613	805	372	1,684	1,383	—	—	7	2,362
1915	7,655	716	438	1,737	1,576	—	—	18	3,170
1914	8,846	748	399	1,589	1,640	—	—	—	4,470
1913	10,527	839	320	1,510	2,043	—	—	—	5,815
1912	9,664	774	345	1,533	2,037	—	—	—	4,975
1911	9,600	633	375	1,127	1,776	—	—	—	5,689
1910	9,354	596	335	1,034	1,836	—	—	—	5,553
1909	5,479	605	250	906	844[8]	—	—	—	2,874[7]
1908	6,959	661	134	978	1,820	—	—	—	3,366
1907	5,459	602	180	1,018	1,178	—	—	—	2,481
1906	5,186	613	171	1,266	1,831	—	—	—	1,305
1905	5,231	614[5]	134	1,380	2,001	—	—	—	1,102
1904	5,362	585[5]	176	1,167	2,584	—	—	—	850
1903	5,028	610[5]	123	1,242	2,307	—	—	—	737
1902	3,585	487[5]	108	1,055	1,331	—	—	—	604
1901	3,780	437[5]	101	1,234	1,480	—	—	—	528

[1] Revenues in Newfoundland from this source were, in order, in thousands of dollars, from 1950 to 1957: 606; 372; 654; 787; 533; 339; 422; 814. No revenues from this source were given for Prince Edward Island.

[2] Fiscal years ending within the year given: for fiscal year and fiscal year changes of the provinces see the general note to this section.

[3] 14 months ending 30 November.

[4] 16 months ending 31 March.

[5] Includes licences, fees and other miscellaneous revenue.

[6] 5 months ending 31 March.

[7] 9 months ending 31 March.

[8] 10 months ending 31 October.

[9] 5 months ending 31 March.

[10] 11 months ending 31 March.

[11] 1955 and subsequent years include mining and timbering revenues from school lands. Timber revenues consist of permits, sales, berths, dues and rentals and timber seizures.

[12] 1954 and subsequent years include revenue from school lands.

[13] 15 months ending 31 March.

Series G 378–388. *Federal government statutory subsidies, by province, and special grants and conditional subsidies, total all provinces, 1868 to 1938*

(millions of dollars)

Year[1]	Total statutory subsidies	Prince Edward Island	Nova Scotia	New Brunswick	Quebec	Ontario	Manitoba	Saskatchewan	Alberta	British Columbia	Other grants and subsidies
	378	379	380	381	382	383	384	385	386	387	388
1938	13.7	.4	.7	.7	2.6	2.9	1.7	2.1	1.8	.9	90.6
1937	13.7	.4	.7	.7	2.6	2.9	1.7	2.1	1.8	.9	76.1
1936	13.8	.4	.7	.7	2.6	2.9	1.7	2.1	1.8	.9	61.8
1935	13.8	.4	.7	.7	2.6	2.9	1.7	2.1	1.8	.9	60.2
1934	13.7	.4	.7	.7	2.6	2.9	1.7	2.1	1.8	.9	42.2
1933	13.7	.4	.6	.7	2.6	2.9	1.7	2.1	1.7	.9	47.3
1932	13.7	.4	.7	.7	2.6	2.9	1.7	2.1	1.7	.9	45.7
1931	17.4	.4	.7	.7	2.3	2.6	6.5	1.9	1.7	.7	11.1
1930	12.5	.4	.7	.7	2.3	2.6	1.5	2.1	1.6	.7	3.8
1929	12.6	.4	.7	.7	2.3	2.6	1.5	2.0	1.7	.7	3.9
1928	12.5	.4	.7	.7	2.3	2.6	1.5	2.0	1.6	.7	4.2
1927	12.5	.4	.7	.7	2.3	2.6	1.5	2.0	1.6	.7	2.4
1926	12.4	.4	.7	.7	2.3	2.6	1.5	1.9	1.7	.7	2.9
1925	12.3	.4	.7	.7	2.3	2.6	1.5	1.8	1.7	.7	4.1
1924	12.4	.4	.7	.7	2.3	2.6	1.5	1.9	1.7	.7	6.2
1923	12.2	.4	.7	.7	2.3	2.6	1.5	1.8	1.6	.7	9.0
1922	12.2	.4	.7	.7	2.3	2.6	1.5	1.8	1.6	.7	6.1
1921	11.5	.4	.6	.6	2.0	2.4	1.5	1.8	1.6	.6	2.9
1920	11.5	.4	.6	.6	2.0	2.4	1.5	1.8	1.6	.6	1.7
1919	11.3	.4	.6	.6	2.0	2.4	1.4	1.7	1.6	.6	1.0
1918	11.4	.4	.6	.6	2.0	2.4	1.4	1.7	1.6	.6	1.1
1917	11.5	.4	.6	.6	2.0	2.4	1.4	1.7	1.6	.7	1.0
1916	11.5	.4	.6	.6	2.0	2.4	1.4	1.7	1.6	.7	.9
1915	11.5	.4	.6	.6	2.0	2.4	1.4	1.7	1.6	.7	.8
1914	11.3	.4	.6	.6	2.0	2.4	1.5	1.7	1.4	.7	.7
1913	13.2	.4	.6	.6	2.0	2.4	3.6	1.6	1.3	.7	.5
1912	10.3	.3	.6	.6	2.0	2.4	.8	1.5	1.3	.7	—
1911	9.1	.3	.6	.6	1.7	2.1	.8	1.2	1.2	.7	—
1910	9.4	.3	.6	.6	1.7	2.1	.9	1.4	1.3	.5	—
1909	9.1	.3	.6	.6	1.7	2.1	.8	1.3	1.3	.5	—
1908	9.0	.3	.6	.6	1.7	2.1	.8	1.2	1.2	.5	—
1907	6.7	.2	.4	.5	1.1	1.3	.6	1.1	1.1	.3	—
1906	6.7	.2	.4	.5	1.1	1.3	.6	1.1	1.1	.3	—
1905	4.5	.2	.4	.5	1.1	1.3	.6	—	—	.3	—
1904	4.4	.2	.4	.5	1.1	1.3	.5	—	—	.3	—
1903	4.4	.2	.4	.5	1.1	1.3	.5	—	—	.3	—
1902	4.4	.2	.4	.5	1.1	1.3	.5	—	—	.3	—
1901	4.3	.2	.4	.5	1.1	1.3	.5	—	—	.2	—
1900	4.3	.2	.4	.5	1.1	1.3	.5	—	—	.2	—
1899	4.3	.2	.4	.5	1.1	1.3	.5	—	—	.2	—
1898	4.2	.2	.4	.5	1.1	1.3	.5	—	—	.2	—
1897	4.2	.2	.4	.5	1.1	1.3	.5	—	—	.2	—
1896	4.2	.2	.4	.5	1.1	1.3	.5	—	—	.2	—
1895	4.3	.2	.4	.5	1.1	1.3	.5	—	—	.2	—
1894	4.2	.2	.4	.5	1.1	1.3	.4	—	—	.2	—
1893	3.9	.2	.4	.5	1.0	1.2	.4	—	—	.2	—
1892	3.9	.2	.4	.5	1.0	1.2	.4	—	—	.2	—
1891	3.9	.2	.4	.5	1.0	1.2	.4	—	—	.2	—
1890	3.9	.2	.4	.5	1.0	1.2	.4	—	—	.2	—
1889	4.1	.2	.4	.5	1.0	1.3	.4	—	—	.2	—
1888	4.2	.2	.4	.5	1.0	1.3	.4	—	—	.2	—
1887	4.2	.2	.4	.5	1.0	1.3	.4	—	—	.2	—
1886	4.2	.2	.4	.5	1.0	1.3	.4	—	—	.2	—
1885	4.0	.2	.4	.5	1.0	1.3	.2	—	—	.2	—
1884	3.6	.2	.4	.5	1.0	1.2	.2	—	—	.2	—
1883	3.6	.2	.4	.5	1.0	1.2	.2	—	—	.2	—
1882	3.5	.2	.4	.5	1.0	1.2	.2	—	—	.2	—
1881	3.5	.2	.4	.4	1.0	1.2	.1	—	—	.2	—
1880	3.4	.2	.4	.4	1.0	1.2	.1	—	—	.2	—
1879	3.4	.2	.4	.4	1.0	1.2	.1	—	—	.2	—
1878	3.5	.2	.4	.4	1.0	1.2	.1	—	—	.2	—
1877	3.7	.2	.5	.5	1.0	1.2	.1	—	—	.2	—
1876	3.7	.2	.5	.5	1.0	1.2	.1	—	—	.2	—
1875	3.8	.2	.5	.5	1.0	1.2	.1	—	—	.2	—
1874	3.8	.3	.5	.5	1.0	1.2	.1	—	—	.2	—
1873	2.9	—	.5	.3	.8	1.0	.1	—	—	.2	—
1872	2.9	—	.5	.3	.8	1.0	.1	—	—	.2	—
1871	2.6	—	.4	.3	.8	1.0	.1	—	—	—	—
1870	2.6	—	.4	.3	.9	1.0	—	—	—	—	—
1869	2.6	—	.5	.3	.9	.8	—	—	—	—	—
1868	2.2	—	.3	.3	.9	.7	—	—	—	—	—

[1] Fiscal year ending in the year given.

Series G389–398. *Provincial governments, outstanding debt, direct and indirect, by province, 1913, 1921, 1925 to 1937*

(millions of dollars)

Year[1]	Total nine provinces	Prince Edward Island	Nova Scotia	New Brunswick	Quebec	Ontario	Manitoba	Saskatchewan	Alberta	British Columbia
	389	390	391	392	393	394	395	396	397	398
1937	1,960.3	5.9	93.1	82.0	285.6	807.0	122.4	215.9	169.7[2]	178.7
1936	1,836.2	5.6	84.5	72.8	235.6	783.8	125.0	180.5	170.5[3]	177.9
1935	1,806.6	5.4	78.5	67.2	209.9	795.4	121.7	186.0	171.8	170.7
1934	1,697.9	4.3	71.6	62.8	188.2	750.5	121.0	173.4	164.9	161.2
1933	1,580.4	3.9	67.5	61.4	170.4	692.5	118.5	153.7	158.3	154.3
1932	1,494.7	3.7	60.7	59.6	145.8	652.0	117.1	146.0	159.3	150.7
1931	1,400.5	3.4	59.7	58.3	125.4	598.2	116.1	137.6	154.6	147.4
1930	1,246.1	2.8	55.4	52.5	104.9	552.7	107.7	99.6	138.2	132.2
1929	1,103.8	2.6	51.0	46.1	96.9	486.8	101.1	76.4	126.9	116.1
1928	1,041.0	2.4	44.5	43.2	96.2	454.3	96.4	63.8	134.5	105.6
1927	985.7	2.2	41.7	39.7	98.5	422.6	91.9	59.9	130.3	98.8
1926	951.5	2.1	38.6	37.8	98.4	407.0	90.1	58.8	122.8	95.9
1925	913.0	2.1	36.6	36.2	96.8	384.5	87.7	58.1	116.1	94.9
1921	633.3	1.2	21.8	28.6	61.3	219.0	72.2	53.1	95.8	80.3
1913	285.0	1.0	11.7	11.5	31.8	41.5	45.6	39.2	52.1	50.6

[1] Fiscal year end nearest 31 December of the year given.
[2] Excludes unpaid interest 6.1 (estimated).
[3] Excludes unpaid interest 2.7.

Series G399–410. *Taxes levied (including local improvement) for selected municipalities, 1906 to 1957*

(millions of dollars)

Year[5]	Halifax	Saint John	Montreal[1]	Quebec[1]	Toronto	Hamilton	Winnipeg[2]	Regina	Edmonton	Calgary[3]	Vancouver[3]	Victoria
	399	400	401	402	403	404	405	406	407	408	409	410
1957	8.2	4.7	64.1	7.4	82.7	24.8	22.0	8.0	19.4	14.8	30.3	3.9
1956	7.4	4.0	63.5	7.1	74.0	21.7	21.2	6.1	17.0	11.8	26.6	3.7
1955	7.0	3.9	54.1	7.0	68.3	20.0	19.1	5.4	14.8	10.7	25.8	3.4
1954	6.7	3.7	50.2	6.9	64.7	18.6	17.8	4.5	13.7	10.5	23.4	3.2
1953	6.3	3.4	48.5	6.7	60.3	17.7	17.4	3.9	12.2	8.6	20.2	3.1
1952	6.3	3.1	46.5	6.6	59.3	16.4	17.1	3.5	11.6	7.6	19.0	3.0
1951	5.1	2.7	43.5	5.2	54.6	13.0	15.9	3.3	9.3	6.2	17.3	2.8
1950	4.1	2.7	35.0	5.1	45.1	10.4	14.5	2.9	7.4	5.4	15.8	2.5
1949	4.0	2.5	34.0	4.9	41.5	9.3	13.5	2.8	6.0	5.1	15.4	2.4
1948	3.7	2.2	32.2	4.9	36.6	8.7	11.6	2.6	5.4	4.4	14.5	2.0
1947	3.6	2.0	29.2	4.5	35.7	7.2	10.0	2.3	5.0	3.8	13.5	1.9
1946	3.0	2.0	27.4	4.4	31.4	6.4	9.4	2.2	4.7	3.3	12.6	1.7
1945	2.8	1.9	27.2	4.3	28.8	6.0	8.5	2.1	4.4	3.0	11.7	1.7
1944	2.8	1.8	27.1	4.2	30.6	6.4	8.4	2.1	4.2	2.9	11.5	1.5
1943	2.6	1.6	26.9	4.3	29.5	6.5	8.4	2.1	3.7	2.8	11.4	1.4
1942	2.4	1.7	26.6	4.3	30.5	6.1	8.3	2.2	3.7	2.9	11.3	1.4
1941	2.3	2.1	27.1	4.3	32.3	6.3	8.3	2.2	3.7	2.8	10.8	1.4
1940	2.3	2.0	27.1	4.2	33.6	6.7	8.4	2.2	3.6	2.9	10.8	1.5
1939	2.2	2.0	24.7	4.2	33.8	6.4	8.4	2.3	3.6	3.0	10.9	1.5
1938	2.2	2.0	24.7	4.2	35.3	6.6	8.9	2.3	3.7	3.2	11.0	1.6
1937	2.1	2.1	24.7	4.3	35.2	6.8	9.0	2.4	3.7	3.4	10.4	1.7
1936	2.1	1.9	25.5	4.2	34.6	7.0	9.2	2.4	3.8	3.7	10.1	1.8
1935	2.1	1.9	25.7	4.2	35.5	7.1	9.5	2.4	3.7	3.6	11.1	1.7
1934	2.0	1.8	25.0	4.1	34.9	6.7	9.9	2.4	4.4	3.7	12.0	1.7
1933	2.0	1.7	24.8	4.1	36.3	6.9	10.1	2.4	4.1	3.8	12.6	1.9
1932	2.0	1.9	24.8	4.1	37.4	6.9	10.9	2.5	4.4	4.3	12.8	1.9
1931	2.0	1.8	24.4	3.9	36.7	6.5	11.0	2.6	4.3	4.0	12.7	1.8
1930	2.0	1.6	24.8	3.8	33.5	6.1	10.8	2.2	4.1	3.8	12.0	1.7
1929	1.9	1.6	22.7	3.4	31.4	5.9	10.5	2.0	3.9	3.5	10.9	1.7
1928	1.9	1.6	21.8	3.2	30.0	5.7	9.9	1.9	3.7	3.4	6.6	1.7
1927	1.9	1.7	20.0	3.0	29.4	5.6	9.6	1.9	3.6	3.4	5.9	1.6
1926	1.8	1.8	19.5	2.9	27.2	5.6	9.2	1.9	3.5	3.1	5.6	1.6
1925	1.8	1.8	18.9	2.7	27.3	5.4	9.3	1.8	3.6	3.2	5.6	1.8
1924	1.8	1.7	18.6	2.7	26.7	5.1	9.4	1.7	3.3	3.4	5.6	1.8
1923	2.0	1.7	17.9	2.5	26.4	4.9	9.8	1.8	3.3	3.6	5.6	1.8
1922	1.9	1.7	16.6	2.3	26.0	5.0	10.1	2.0	3.4	3.8	5.8	1.6
1921	2.0	1.7	16.6	2.0	25.0	4.4	9.8	2.1	4.1	4.2	5.8	1.4
1920	1.5	1.6	15.4	2.0	21.2	3.5	7.6	1.7	4.5	4.0	5.8	1.3
1919	1.2	1.3	14.1	1.6	19.3	2.9	7.5	1.6	3.7	3.5	4.9	1.3
1918	.9	1.0	13.6	1.6	20.1	2.6	7.2	1.5	3.7	3.0	4.7	1.2
1917	.9	1.1	9.3	1.4	16.9	2.1	6.0	1.2	3.2	2.7	4.3	1.3
1916	.7	.8	8.5	1.3	15.0	2.0	6.1	1.3	3.3	1.0	4.0	1.3
1915	.7	.8	8.3	1.1	14.5	1.9	5.9	1.6	3.4	2.7	4.2	1.6
1914	.7	.7	8.4	1.0	11.2	1.7	5.8	1.0	3.8	3.3	4.2	1.9
1913	.6	.7	8.3	.9	9.6	1.5	4.9	1.0	3.5	—	3.4	1.7
1912	—	.7	6.8	.8	7.4	1.2	3.8	.8	1.5	—	3.2	1.4
1911	—	.6	5.2	.8	6.4	1.0[4]	3.4	.4	.7	—	2.3	1.0
1910	—	.6	4.3	.7	—	1.0[4]	2.7	.3	.6	—	1.8	.8[4]
1909	—	.6	3.6	.7	—	.8[4]	2.5	.2	.5	—	1.3	.6[4]
1908	—	.6	3.1	.7	—	.7[4]	2.4	.2	.4	—	1.1	.5[4]
1907	—	.6	2.9	.7	—	.7[4]	2.3	.2	.3	—	1.0	.4[4]
1906	—	.5	2.7	.6	—	.6[4]	1.9	.1	.2	—	.7	.4[4]

[1] Real property taxes. Montreal figures do not include business tax and special assessments for local improvements. Quebec figures include general, special, school and water taxes.
[2] Includes levy for Greater Water Districts for 1918 and subsequent years.
[3] Excludes business taxes.
[4] Estimated.
[5] Fiscal year ending nearest the end of the year given.

SECTION H: BANKING AND FINANCE

E. P. NEUFELD, *University of Toronto*

The data of this section are presented in eleven groups or subsections: the supply of money, series H 1–35; central banking, series H 36–54; chartered banking, series H 55–301; various savings institutions, series H 302–344; life insurance statistics, series H 345–423; fire and casualty insurance statistics, series H 424–465; loan companies in Canada, series H 466–502; trust companies in Canada, series H 503–548; instalment finance and small loan companies, series H 549–568; federal government lending agencies, series H 569–587; and miscellaneous financial statistics, series H 588–683.

Sources of the material given here draw fairly heavily on private as well as official publications. The official publications are:

Bank of Canada, *Statistical Summary*, monthly, and *Statistical Summary Supplement*, annual in recent years; *Returns of the Chartered Banks* to the Department of Finance, monthly, published in the *Canada Gazette*, as well as separately; the *Canada Gazette* (Ottawa, Queen's Printer); *Memoranda and Tables Respecting the Bank of Canada*, material prepared for submission to parliament at the revision of the Bank Act in 1954; *Annual Report of the Superintendent of Insurance for Canada*, annual since 1875 (Ottawa, Queen's Printer); Department of Agriculture of Canada, *Credit Unions in Canada*, annual (Ottawa, Queen's Printer); Industrial Development Bank, *Annual Report*; Dominion Bureau of Statistics, *Canada Year Book* (Ottawa, Queen's Printer); Province of Ontario, *Public Accounts* (Toronto, Queen's Printer); *Annual Reports* of the provinces of Ontario and Quebec by registrars of trust and loan companies.

The following private publications were used:

C. A. Curtis, *Statistical Contributions to Canadian Economic History*, vol. 1 (Toronto, The Macmillan Company of Canada, 1931); R. M. Breckenridge, *The History of Banking in Canada* (Washington, Government Printing Office, 1910); B. H. Beckhart, *The Banking System of Canada* (New York, H. Holt and Company, 1910); *Monetary Times*; Montreal and Canadian Stock Exchanges, *Monthly Review*. In addition material was obtained directly from: The Canadian Bankers Association; Central Mortgage and Housing Corporation; Canadian Farm Loan Board; Wood, Gundy and Company, Limited; McLeod, Young, Weir and Company, Limited; and Moss, Lawson and Company, Limited.

General note

This section includes statistics of the Canadian capital market. A capital market may be thought of as being concerned with accumulating and distributing funds and with effecting changes in ownership of outstanding securities created by that activity. Accordingly, statistics of the capital market should, ideally, include a comprehensive record of such accumulation, distribution and change of ownership as well as the terms (e.g. interest rates and exchange rates) on which such transactions take place.

Funds are gathered and distributed by banks, by nonbank financial intermediaries, and in a limited way by the nonfinancial corporate sector and the personal sector as well. The emphasis in this section is on the financial institutions, primarily because relevant statistics of the other sectors are not available.

In Canada the important financial intermediaries which accumulate and distribute funds are the chartered banks, the Quebec savings banks, the Bank of Canada and Industrial Development Bank, the various government savings institutions (see series H 322–332), the trust and loan companies, the various government boards dispensing credit including Central Mortgage and Housing Corporation, the life, fire, and casualty insurance companies and societies, the instalment finance and small personal loan companies, the credit unions, and the investment trusts. Each one, as later comments will show, is slightly different from the others and makes a unique contribution to the development of the capital market.

The extent to which these various financial institutions are engaged in accumulating funds is broadly indicated by the change in their total liabilities, while the source and character of such funds is to some extent indicated by the nature of those liabilities (e.g. capital, deposits, or debentures). The way in which such institutions distribute their funds is indicated by the character of their assets (e.g. mortgages, loans, bonds). This makes it necessary to compile statistics of the assets and liabilities of financial intermediaries.

This section includes some information at least on all of the aforementioned institutions except certain government credit boards and investment trusts. Statistics of these latter-mentioned intermediaries are not yet available. The principal limitations of the statistics included are that they do not span the whole life of the institutions, and in some cases do not include all the individual companies. Nor are their assets and liabilities always shown in totally adequate detail, or in consistent classifications over the years. In addition, it was not possible to record the financial assets and liabilities of nonfinancial corporations and of individuals.

The changes in the size and character of currency or 'money' is of special interest to financial institutions, particularly banks whose liabilities serve as a medium of exchange, and to the student of monetary theory and practice. Series H 1–35 include data of this general area. They are perhaps as complete as the raw statistics permit.

Control of the currency in Canada is effected through the central bank, the Bank of Canada, and comprehensive series of its assets and liabilities have been included. Growth of the assets of the Bank of Canada normally implies that an increase in the chartered banks' cash has occurred; this in turn makes possible an increase in chartered bank deposits or, by our definition, an increase in the supply of money.

Trading in stocks in Canada is undertaken by firms which have purchased memberships in the various stock exchanges—particularly the Toronto and Montreal exchanges. Trading in bonds is largely confined to over-the-telephone transactions between investment dealers (who usually also possess memberships in the stock exchanges) and the larger financial institutions. These investment dealers also underwrite new stock and bond issues and advise investors and borrowers on financial matters in general.

Of these investment dealers about a dozen of the largest are also referred to as 'money market dealers' because of their transactions in very short-term securities and loans. They enjoy temporary borrowing privileges at the central bank. The principal short-term securities in which they deal are commercial paper, finance company paper, and Government of Canada treasury bills and bonds. No statistics of the assets and liabilities of investment dealers and stock brokers have been made public.

Information on the volume of business they do is also not complete. The value of shares traded on the larger stock exchanges is known and has been included in this section, but there is no public information on the volume of transactions in bonds and other securities.

One way of indicating in a general way the size and the character of the demand for capital market funds is to compile series of new securities issues and retirements by type of issue. Unfortunately, reliable statistics of this type are not available prior to the year 1936 (see series H661–683) and series H651–660, which are of more limited usefulness but which span a much longer period, have therefore been included.

Statistics of interest rates and stock prices reflect changing conditions in the capital market and are usually based on the changing terms on which outstanding securities are being traded. Series H631–650 include statistics of the prices of various types of stocks, and series H588–618 show yields on various bonds and stocks.

The cost of exchanging Canadian currency into foreign currency is indicated by the statistics of exchange rates, and these are included in series H619–630. It may be noted that transactions in Canada's foreign exchange market are largely effected by the chartered banks through several brokers who are employees of the Canadian Bankers' Association.

Generally speaking the series included in this section are most reliable and most consistent for the years 1946 to 1959, the period on which the Bank of Canada has concentrated in its compilation of monetary and financial statistics.

Prior to that period the series frequently are subject to important limitations of quality and consistency and great care must be exercised in using them. In a number of instances they have been included only because on balance it appeared that they would be useful for certain limited purposes, and would serve as a guide to future researchers wishing to improve and expand on them.

SUPPLY OF MONEY (Series H1–35)

General note

These series are the result of an attempt to compile information on the supply of money and on Canada's coinage. Any definition of 'money' involves a degree of arbitrary judgement, because deposits of many nonbank financial intermediaries may to a limited extent be used as a medium of exchange, and because liabilities of such intermediaries may serve as close substitutes for bank deposits in the role of liquid assets of the general public.

Here, however, it has been decided to confine the concept of money to chartered bank deposit liabilities and bank notes and coin held outside the chartered banks. Series H1–10 represent the most consistent series of the components of this concept of supply of money which it appears practicable to compile. Series H11–20 are much less satisfactory and have been included because they are available for a longer period of time.

H1–10. Currency and chartered bank deposits, 1913 to 1960

SOURCE: Curtis, *Statistical Contributions*, vol. 1; *Returns of the Chartered Banks*; Bank of Canada, *Statistical Summary* and *Supplements*. Some of the data were adjusted for purposes of this table.

Before 1935 series H1 includes both Dominion and chartered bank notes held by the general public; it excludes notes held by the chartered banks and Dominion notes deposited by them in the central gold reserves. The Bank of Canada began to issue notes in March 1935 and it assumed the liability of Dominion notes outstanding at that time as well. Gradual curtailment of the note issue privileges of the chartered banks began with the revision of the Bank Act, 1934. Very few chartered bank notes were outstanding by 1950, at which time (January) the liability for them was assumed by the Bank of Canada.

The only break in the consistency of series H1 occurs in 1923, prior to which statistics of notes held by the chartered banks include foreign notes. However, the series has been adjusted for this by applying the ratio of chartered bank notes held by the chartered banks to total chartered bank notes, for subsequent years, to the figures of total chartered bank notes for the years 1913 to 1922. In this way an estimate of chartered bank holdings of chartered bank notes was obtained, which was then subtracted from total chartered bank notes outstanding to obtain an estimate of chartered bank notes held by the public. The estimate of Dominion notes held by the general public prior to 1935 was obtained by subtracting from the figure of total Dominion notes outstanding (as published in the *Canada Gazette*) the amount of such notes held by the chartered banks—the latter computed by subtracting from the figure of gold and Dominion notes deposited in the central gold reserves as it appears on the banks' returns, the amount of gold so held as shown in a footnote to the return.

Series H2 for the years 1913 to 1928 was compiled after making a rough estimate of coin held by the chartered banks. Since 1929 chartered bank holdings of coin have been reported to the Department of Finance, and since March 1935 they have appeared on the banks' monthly return. Bank of Canada holdings are not published.

From 1913 to 1934 series H7 includes foreign currency deposits in Canada but excludes Canadian dollar deposits owned by foreign banks. These constitute offsetting errors in the basic concept of Canadian dollar deposits, but of course it is not likely that they offset each other exactly. In addition the float which has been deducted contained some foreign currency cheques and drafts. From 1935 to 1938 the banks reported their total deposits in Canada to the Bank of Canada, and series H7 is based on this information; in order that the component series H4–6 add to series H7, series H6 has for the years 1935 to 1938 been treated as the residual. The chartered banks reported both total and component Canadian dollar deposits in Canada to the Bank of Canada for the years 1939 to 1945 and these form the basis for series H4–7 for that period.

Further statistical refinements in the treatment of float and in reporting foreign currency deposits were made in 1954. Series H4–7 and series H10 for the years 1945 to 1960 reflect these changes and, as far as estimates permit, are consistent over those years. The exception to this is series H4 which was revised in 1957 to exclude certain business and institutional deposits which, amounting to $140 million, were transferred to series H6 at that time. It was in 1938 that the figure for 'personal savings deposits' as such became available, prior to which time series H4 was one of 'public notice deposits'. The change had the effect at that time of reducing series H4 by $185 million and increasing series H6 by a like amount.

H11–20. Notes and coin held by banks and general public and chartered bank Canadian deposit liabilities, 1867 to 1960

SOURCE: *Memoranda and Tables Respecting the Bank of Canada*; Bank of Canada, *Statistical Summary* and *Supplements*; monthly *Returns of the Chartered Banks*.

These series are included because they provide information on the supply of money for a longer period than do series H 1–10. They are however inferior to the latter-mentioned series and great care must be exercised in using them. While estimates of notes held by the chartered banks can be made for the period 1913 to 1923, by the technique referred to when discussing series H 1–10, this becomes more difficult prior to 1913 when the banks reported notes of and cheques on other banks as one item.

Series H 14–16 reflect the Government of Canada's long-standing authority to issue notes for general circulation. The Province of Canada under an Act of 1866 issued notes in limited amounts, secured by specie reserve and government debentures, and this authority was retained and frequently enlarged after Confederation. The issue of such notes was encouraged by the Bank Act of 1871 which provided that the banks should not issue notes of a smaller denomination than $4 (changed to $5 in 1881) and should hold at least one-third (raised in 1881 to 40 per cent) of their reserves in Dominion notes. In 1935 the Bank of Canada assumed the liability for all Dominion notes outstanding, and these were eventually replaced with Bank of Canada notes.

The authority of the chartered banks to issue notes existed, within prescribed limits, until 1934. At that time this authority was sharply curtailed and its eventual withdrawal provided for in the Bank Act of 1944. In 1950 the Bank of Canada assumed the liability for any outstanding chartered bank notes in return for a payment of a like sum from the banks, and for this reason series H 17–19 end in that year.

H 21–26. Canadian coin minted, 1870 to 1960

SOURCE: Royal Canadian Mint.

These series of the production of Canadian coinage were supplied directly by the Royal Canadian Mint. At first Canadian coinage was struck by the Royal Mint at London and The Mint, Birmingham, Ltd, England. The Ottawa Branch of the Royal Mint opened on 2 January 1908. By 21–22 Geo. V, c. 48, it was constituted a branch of the Department of Finance, and by the Proclamation of 14 November 1931, issued under section 3 of that Act, it has, since 1 December 1931, operated as the Royal Canadian Mint.

All 10 cent, 25 cent, 50 cent and 1 dollar coins are of silver. All 5 cent coins dated prior to 1922 are of silver. Five cent coins dated subsequent to 1922 are of nickel, tombac or steel. All 1 cent pieces are of bronze. The 1 cent pieces were reduced in size during 1920. In that year 6,901,626 large and 15,472,153 small cents were minted. The 5 cent pieces were increased in size in 1922.

H 27–35. Gold received and coinage issued by the mint, 1901 to 1960

SOURCE: *Canada Year Book*; Royal Canadian Mint.

Since its foundation in 1908 the Mint at Ottawa has received gold bullion for treatment and subsequently has issued the treated gold. Series H 27 shows the amount of such gold received and series H 28 and H 29 show the amounts of gold issued in the form of bullion and of coin. No gold coin has been struck since 1919.

Over the years the Mint has issued most of its gold to the Government of Canada. At present the Mint purchases the fine gold produced from the rough bullion it receives and issues it in bullion form to the Bank of Canada for the account of the Minister of Finance. Official reserves of gold are held in the Exchange Fund Account of the Government of Canada. In the case of gold-mining companies authorized to sell gold in the open market, the Mint will deliver their gold to various domestic and foreign processors. Most of the gold produced in Canada is received by the Mint. For example, in 1958 Canada produced 4,571,137 ounces of gold and the Mint received 3,958,459 ounces.

CENTRAL BANKING (Series H 36–54)

H 36–54. Bank of Canada, assets and liabilities, 1935 to 1960

SOURCE: Bank of Canada, *Statistical Summary*.

The Bank of Canada began operations in March 1935. It began by assuming the liability for Dominion Notes outstanding in return for which it received the gold and silver holdings of the Government of Canada as well as securities of that government. At the same time the banks transferred their holdings of gold to the Bank of Canada in exchange for deposits with the Bank of Canada. These deposits (series H 51) together with Bank of Canada notes held by the Bank of Canada (series H 47) constitute the bank cash of the chartered banks.

In May 1940 official reserves of foreign exchange and gold were sold by the Bank of Canada (for government securities) to the Government of Canada's Foreign Exchange Control Board and held in the Exchange Fund Account. While the F.E.C.B. has been abolished, official reserves have not been retransferred to the Bank of Canada, and are still held in the government's Exchange Fund Account. The Bank of Canada does hold foreign exchange for its own account as is indicated in series H 43; and it acts as the government's agent for managing the Exchange Fund Account.

Bank of Canada holdings of Government of Canada direct and guaranteed securities at par value are given in that Bank's *Statistical Summary*, as are its holdings of the same securities for the year 1954 and after, classified into Treasury Bills, two years to maturity and under, over two years to maturity to five years, over five years to ten years, and over ten years to maturity. That same publication carries both weekly and monthly statistics of the Bank's balance sheet, while its *Annual Report* contains a statement of the Bank's yearly profits.

CHARTERED BANKING (Series H 55–301)

General note

The statistical record of chartered banking in Canada has been shaped materially by the decennial revision of the Bank Act. This periodic revision permitted the authorities to request statistical information of the banks on specific areas of interest at various times in banking history; it permitted the trend toward more detailed banking statistics to proceed relatively smoothly; and it permitted banking statistics to be classified in a way which improved their usefulness in economic analysis. But as a consequence of these frequent changes it is difficult to construct consistent series of banking statistics over a long period of time. This is particularly the case with statistics of bank assets, and somewhat less so with those of bank liabilities, and explains the decision made to show bank assets in a number of tables, each table reflecting changes in certain asset components from the table which preceded it.

Most of the statistics for the period preceding 1929 were compiled from C. A. Curtis, *Statistical Contribution to Canadian Economic History*, vol. 1, 'Statistics of Banking', which volume remains the most comprehensive and convenient source of detailed banking statistics for that period. Readers are also referred to that volume for detailed discussion of historical banking statistics in general, and of particular series as well, full details of which cannot be given here. In addition the monthly return of the banks to the Department of Finance, appearing in the *Canada Gazette*, was frequently resorted to; it constitutes the primary source of statistics for the Curtis volume. Since 1935 the Bank of Canada, *Statistical Summary* and *Supplements*, have proved most helpful for this study; in addition, they show weekly and monthly statistics of chartered bank assets and liabilities.

The banks of Lower Canada were required to submit annual returns to the Provincial Parliament even before the provinces of Upper and Lower Canada were united in 1841. The first monthly returns appeared in 1851 and applied to all banks incorporated under 'The Free Banking Act', while the 1855 amendment of the charter of the Bank of Montreal required such returns from that bank. All chartered banks formed thereafter were required to submit monthly returns to government. Consolidated monthly statements of the banks of the Province of Canada began in August 1856, were continued under an Act of 1867 which extended Ontario and Quebec charters to 1870, and were retained in the Bank Act of 1871—in reality the first Bank Act of the Dominion of Canada. (See Curtis, p. 2.)

Before 1900, banking statistics concentrated on the Canadian business of the banks. They were intended primarily to provide information on the solvency of banks and in that way afford some protection against mismanagement, to the depositors and note holders of the banks, as well as to the shareholders. It was not until 1890 that all banks regularly made returns to the Department of Finance although most of them did, and it appears that the general trend of the growth of banking is not seriously distorted by this statistical deficiency. (See Curtis, p. 4.)

The foreign business of the banks expanded as years went by and after 1900 some distinction between foreign business and Canadian business is made in the statistics. This foreign business arose both from the purchase of foreign securities by the banks in Canada and from the establishment of branches abroad. The assets and liabilities of the banks' foreign branches after 1900 began to appear as loans 'elsewhere than in Canada' and deposits 'elsewhere than in Canada', not as 'foreign currency' loans and deposits, as was later the case.

But beginning with the special returns made to the Bank of Canada in 1935 the statistics of banking have been shaped so as to more adequately serve the dual purpose of assuring sound banking practice and of permitting more satisfactory economic analysis: hence shift in deposit classification from 'deposits in Canada' and 'elsewhere than in Canada' to 'Canadian dollar deposits' and 'foreign currency deposits', as well as improvement in the statistics of 'float'. Classification of loans by type of loan and the compilation of statistics on loan authorization (not included here because of their recent origin, but which can be found in the Bank of Canada's *Statistical Summary*) have also appeared in recent years.

H 55–225. Chartered bank assets, 1867 to 1960

SOURCE: Curtis, *Statistical Contributions*, vol. 1; *Returns of the Chartered Banks*; Bank of Canada, *Statistical Summary* and *Supplement*.

Apart from the general comments already made, an understanding of the statistics of chartered bank assets will require the user of this volume to pay attention to the changes in headings from one table to another, to the footnotes which apply to the tables and to the additional comments given here. By and large, changes in headings indicate the nature of the changes which have taken place in particular series from one table to another, while footnotes frequently indicate changes which have taken place within the period covered by a table. The order of the series is maintained as much as appears technically possible from

one table to another, so it is not difficult to join particular series where no fundamental change in the series has taken place.

Footnotes to these tables may be found at the end of series H 225 and should be consulted when using any of the series H 55–225.

H 55–86. Chartered bank assets, 1945 to 1960

SOURCE: see source for series H 55–225.

Bank assets in this table show Canadian securities whether payable in Canadian currency or not, loans in Canadian currency, and foreign currency assets, as well as certain other items. It differs from the table covering the years 1934 to 1944 in a number of ways. Loans are classified to show the emergence of Canada Savings Bond financing in the post-war period (series H 71), the growth of instalment finance company borrowing (series H 72), and the participation of banks in house financing after they became approved lenders under the National Housing Act in 1954 (series H 75). Further information on bank loans by type of borrower or loan can be found in Bank of Canada, *Statistical Summary*.

Call and short-term loans are shown as one item (series H 66–67), whereas previously only call loans were shown.

Canadian corporation securities are shown separately instead of being combined with nongovernment foreign securities, as was previously the case, and the latter is combined with foreign government securities to give one figure for foreign securities (series H 81). Government of Canada and provincial securities are now shown separately, and Government of Canada treasury bills are shown as a separate item.

Day-to-day loans which can be and are called at very short notice appear for the first time reflecting the development of the money market since 1954, while gold and coin in Canada and balances with other banks in Canada being of negligible importance are not shown. It should be remembered that 'call loans' which have appeared on the banks' statements since 1891 have in practice not been treated as such. The item 'notes of other banks' and also the item 'deposits with government against notes' have disappeared with the loss of the banks' note issuing privileges.

For this period it has been possible to give a figure of total Canadian assets (series H 79) as well as total assets (series H 86).

H 87–112. Chartered bank assets, 1934 to 1944

SOURCE: see source for series H 55–225.

The principal changes in this table from the one showing assets for 1923 to 1933 (series H 113–136) arise from formation of the Bank of Canada. Notes of and deposits with the Bank of Canada (series H 87) generally took the place of Dominion Notes (series H 114) and central gold reserve deposits (series H 115), and series H 88 became of negligible importance as the banks transferred their gold to the Bank of Canada in exchange for deposits with the Bank of Canada.

In addition Government of Canada and Provincial Securities are now classified into those maturing in two years or less and those maturing in over two years. Canadian municipal securities and foreign government securities are now shown separately, but other foreign and other nongovernment Canadian securities are not.

H 113–136. Chartered bank assets, 1923 to 1933

SOURCE: see source for series H 55–225.

These series differ only slightly from those covering the period 1913 to 1922 (series H 137–160). Series H 128 now includes only chartered bank notes whereas previously (series H 152) it included foreign notes as well. Series H132 is composed of the former series H156 and the foreign notes previously included in series H152.

H137–160. Chartered bank assets, 1913 to 1922

SOURCE: see source for series H55–225.

For the first time gold and subsidiary coin held in Canada (series H137) and that held abroad (series H156) are shown separately. Previously they were shown as one item, headed 'specie' (series H161). The arrangement, outlined in the 1913 revision of the Bank Act, whereby the banks could exceed their hitherto defined limits of their note circulation provided they deposited gold or Dominion notes in the central gold reserves, led to the new item 'Central Gold Reserve Deposits' (series H139).

Municipal loans are also shown separately in this period and separate series (series H152, 153) for notes of and for cheques on other banks appear for the first time.

H161–179. Chartered bank assets, 1900 to 1912

SOURCE: see source for series H55–225.

These series reflect the first important attempt to show the banks' foreign business in their returns to the Department of Finance. Foreign call loans and current loans (series H176, 177) now appear as separate items whereas previously they were combined with equivalent Canadian dollar items, or were not reported at all. Actually the result of reporting on foreign business seems to have increased total assets in the return by about 40 million dollars.

Provincial securities were apparently shifted from the general security series (series H185) to series H165 with the result that Government of Canada security holdings are not shown separately as they were from 1880 to 1891.

H180–196. Chartered bank assets, 1891 to 1899

SOURCE: see source for series H55–225.

In this period assets are shown in less, rather than greater, detail than is the case in the period which precedes it, although not all the minute loan and security classifications available for the period 1880 to 1890 are shown in the table for that period (series H197–213). The reader is referred to the Curtis volume where further classifications are given.

Series H182 appears for the first time reflecting legislation requiring the banks to deposit funds in a Bank Circulation Redemption Fund, a fund held by the Minister of Finance and intended to redeem notes of failed banks where the liquidator was not in a position to do so after sixty days of the bank's suspension.

H197–213. Chartered bank assets, 1880 to 1890

SOURCE: see source for series H55–225.

In this period Government of Canada securities are shown separately (series H200) and a new series including provincial municipal and foreign public securities is included (series H201). Loans to Government of Canada and provincial governments are shown separately (series H203, 204) and a series (series H205) for municipal loans appears for the first time.

H214–225. Chartered bank assets, 1867 to 1879

SOURCE: see source for series H55–225.

The character of these series is obvious from the preceding comments and from the footnotes which apply to it. The numerous footnotes and the gaps in statistics from 1867 to 1870 reflect the changes introduced by the Bank Act of 1871.

H226–245. Chartered bank liabilities and cash ratio, 1867 to 1960

SOURCE: Curtis, *Statistical Contributions*, vol. 1; *Returns of the Chartered Banks*; Bank of Canada, *Statistical Summary* and *Supplements*.

Some explanatory comments on bank liabilities were given in discussing series H1–20 and others are included in the footnotes to series H226–245. However, the former-mentioned series differ in some respects from the equivalent item in this table because they are intended to conform to a concept of supply of money, whereas these series are a record of balance sheet information.

For the years 1945 to 1960 series H234 is a consistent series of Canadian dollar deposits. Before that period it conforms more to the concept of deposits in Canada since it includes foreign deposits in Canada, although it excludes Canadian dollar deposits payable to foreign banks which are included in series H235. As indicated earlier, prior to 1900 no figures for the banks' foreign deposit liabilities were reported to the Department of Finance.

It will be noted that until 1945 total liabilities are shown as being slightly smaller than total assets. This apparently is because all liabilities to shareholders were not shown in the returns. There was no item for 'undivided profits'.

Series H243–245 showing statistics of the Canadian cash ratio are included because of the importance of that ratio for monetary management. The concept however loses its force in earlier years because the banks held large sums of liquid assets abroad as a reserve against Canadian note and deposit liabilities.

H246–265. Assets and liabilities of banks of Ontario and Quebec, 1856 to 1879

SOURCE: Curtis, *Statistical Contributions*, vol. 1, pp. 80–90.

These statistics are included because they include years prior to Confederation whereas the total chartered bank statistics do not; and also because the latter-mentioned statistics suffer in the early post-Confederation period through the failure of some Maritime banks to submit returns whereas the record of Ontario and Quebec banks is virtually complete.

H266–288. Chartered banks, earnings, expenses and additions to shareholders equity and inner reserves, 1929 to 1960

SOURCE: The Canadian Bankers' Association; Bank of Canada, *Statistical Summary* and *Supplements*.

While most of these series are self-explanatory, it should be explained that inner reserves are the unpublished and tax-free reserves which the banks are permitted to hold as a provision against possible losses on certain of their loans and securities.

H289–294. Number of chartered banks and branches, amalgamations and insolvencies, 1867 to 1960

SOURCE: compiled from data supplied by the Inspector-General of Banks, Ottawa; and *Canada Year Book*, 1931, pp. 909–10 and recent issues. Other data can be found in Curtis, *Statistical Contributions*, vol. 1, pp. 3–4; Breckenridge, *The History of Banking in Canada*, appendix v; Beckhart, *The Banking System of Canada*, p. 362.

H295–301. Cheques cashed at individual clearing-house centres, by location, 1924 to 1959

SOURCE: *Canada Year Book*.

These statistics of cheques paid through the banks located in various clearing-house centres and charged to deposit accounts should not be confused with clearing-house statistics. While statistics of the latter are also available and for a long period of time, they have not been included because of their serious statistical limitations.

VARIOUS SAVINGS INSTITUTIONS
(Series H302–344)

H302–322. Statistics of Quebec savings banks, 1875 to 1960

SOURCE: *Canada Gazette*; Bank of Canada, *Statistical Summary*.

These series constitute assets and liabilities of the two banks operating under the Quebec Savings Banks Act, the Montreal City and District Savings Bank and La Banque d'Economie de Québec.

These banks have always been savings banks in character, and not commercial banks. They were not permitted to issue notes for circulation, and their investments have been confined largely to specified securities and collateral loans.

H323–332. Deposits with government savings institutions, 1868 to 1960

SOURCE: *Canada Year Book*; Province of Ontario, *Public Accounts*; Province of Alberta, *Public Accounts*; Bank of Canada, *Statistical Summary, Supplement, 1960*.

Both the federal and certain of the provincial governments have at various times sponsored savings banks. The Post Office Savings Bank was introduced as part of a general measure for a uniform postal system in 1867. Its operations for a number of years were confined to Ontario and Quebec.

The Dominion Government Savings Bank arose from the terms of the British North America Act. These required the federal government to assume the liabilities of the savings banks which the governments of Nova Scotia and New Brunswick had sponsored for many years. The federal government also became responsible for managing them, and this it did through the Department of Finance.

The resulting Dominion Government Savings Bank was eventually and gradually absorbed by the Post Office Savings Bank, disappearing entirely in 1929.

The Manitoba Provincial Savings Office, which began operations in 1920, ceased operations in 1932.

H333–344. Credit unions, assets and liabilities, 1947 to 1959

SOURCE: Federal Department of Agriculture, *Credit Unions in Canada*; Bank of Canada, *Statistical Summary, Financial Supplement, 1959*.

Credit unions are cooperatives for accumulating savings and for lending them to members by making loans and mortgages, and by buying securities. The first such cooperative in Canada, and in North America, was established at Lévis in the Province of Quebec in 1900. Ontario introduced legislation for their incorporation in 1922, Nova Scotia in 1935, and the other provinces between 1935 and 1939.

LIFE INSURANCE STATISTICS
(Series H345–423)

General note

Life insurance in Canada is written largely by life insurance companies, but to a minor extent by fraternal benefit societies as well. Both companies and societies may operate under either federal or provincial legislation, but all foreign companies must register with and comply with the provisions of the federal

government. Federally registered companies have always predominated in the industry, and these have been composed of British and United States companies as well as Canadian companies.

While even the first Canadian life insurance company, The Canada Life Assurance Company, formed in 1847, was required to submit returns to Parliament, supervision of life companies in Canada really began with the appointment of a federal Superintendent of Insurance in 1875. Almost all life insurance statistics in Canada arise from the returns the companies are required to make to the Superintendent, and to the various provincial supervisory authorities.

H345–372. Life insurance premiums, claims, net new policies effected and insurance in force, 1869 to 1959

SOURCE: *Reports of the Superintendent of Insurance for Canada*; *Canada Year Book*.

H373–408. Total assets of Canadian life insurance companies under federal registration and assets in Canada of British and foreign companies under federal registration, 1910 to 1959

SOURCE: *Reports of the Superintendent of Insurance for Canada*; *Canada Year Book*; Bank of Canada, *Statistical Summary*.

Some Canadian life insurance companies are very active in other countries and foreign companies, as indicated above, write substantial amounts of insurance in Canada. This led the Superintendent of Insurance to require returns from individual companies on the amount of assets actually held in Canada—that is, assets which could be presumed to be available for meeting liabilities in Canada. Hence series H363, H364, H375, H385, H386. Series H363, H364 have not yet been extended back beyond 1954.

H409–423. Percentage distribution of mortgage loans, average interest rates and average term of loans of twelve insurance companies, 1926 to 1955

SOURCE: Central Mortgage and Housing Corporation.

The sample of companies from which these series are compiled included twelve federally registered companies all of which were active from 1918 onwards and whose mortgage holdings in 1956 comprised 76.8 per cent of the mortgages held by all federally registered companies in that year.

FIRE AND CASUALTY INSURANCE
STATISTICS (Series H424–465)

H424–451. Fire insurance statistics, 1869 to 1959

SOURCE: *Reports of the Superintendent of Insurance for Canada*; *Canada Year Book*.

Fire insurance companies in Canada, like life companies, may operate under provincial or federal legislation with foreign companies being required to operate under the latter. Administrative supervision of fire insurance companies, as of life companies, began in 1875 with the appointment of a federal superintendent of insurance. Provincial supervision of a similar nature soon followed.

H452–465. Casualty insurance statistics, 1875 to 1959

SOURCE: *Reports of the Superintendent of Insurance for Canada*; *Canada Year Book*.

In casualty insurance is included a wide variety of insurance other than fire and life. For example, it includes automobile, personal accident, aviation, bail, burglary, fraud, and a number of other types of insurance.

LOAN COMPANIES IN CANADA
(Series H466–502)

General note

Canadian loan companies began as building societies in the 1840's. At about the same time, English loan companies first began to operate in Canada. Canadian loan companies have always been able to operate under either federal or provincial legislation and, in contrast to provincial life and fire insurance companies, the provincial loan companies constitute a significant proportion of all loan companies in Canada. Compilation and completeness of statistics is identical to that of trust companies discussed with reference to series H503–529.

The outstanding characteristics of the loan companies have been the high proportion of mortgage loans in their total assets and the large proportion of their liabilities in the form of debentures.

H466–486. Operations of loan companies in Canada, 1914 to 1959

SOURCE: *Reports of the Superintendent of Insurance for Canada*; *Canada Year Book*.

H487–502. Certain mortgage loan companies, assets and liabilities, 1946 to 1960

SOURCE: Bank of Canada, *Statistical Summary, Supplement 1960*; Superintendent of Insurance for Canada; Provinces of Ontario and Quebec, Annual Reports on Loan and Trust Companies.

These series, while covering a relatively short period of time, are included because they show assets and liabilities in greater detail than do series H466–486. They include the assets of Investors Syndicate of Canada Limited and subsidiary companies, which are not included in series H466–486, and the assets of almost all of the companies included in series H466–486.

TRUST COMPANIES IN CANADA
(Series H503–548)

H503–529. Operations of trust companies in Canada, 1914 to 1959

SOURCE: *Canada Year Book*; *Reports of the Superintendent of Insurance for Canada*.

As in the case of the insurance and loan companies, trust companies may be incorporated under either federal or provincial legislation. The first trust company to begin operations was the Toronto General Trusts Corporation, in 1881.

While the statistics of federal companies are complete, being based on returns required to be made to the Superintendent of Insurance, those of provincial companies are based on summary information made available to the federal Superintendent of Insurance and include more than 95 per cent of the business of such companies.

Trust companies on the one hand invest their shareholders' funds and guaranteed funds obtained by taking interest-bearing deposits and by selling trust certificates; they retain the profits derived from such investments. On the other hand they manage estates, trusts and agency funds on commission.

The companies act as executors, trustees, and administrators under wills or by appointment; as trustees under various settlements, and for bond issues and bankruptcies; as managers of estates of the living, financial agents for municipalities and companies and transfer agents and registrars for stocks and bond issues; and as guardians of minors or incapable persons.

H530–548. Certain trust companies, assets and liabilities, 1946 to 1959

SOURCE: Bank of Canada, *Statistical Summary, Financial Supplement, 1959*; Superintendent of Insurance for Canada; Provinces of Ontario and Quebec, Annual Reports on Loan and Trust Companies.

These series, like series H487–502, are included because they show assets and liabilities in greater detail than do series H503–529, which however cover a much longer period of time.

INSTALMENT FINANCE AND SMALL LOAN COMPANIES (Series H549–568)

H549–558. Instalment and other finance companies, estimates of major assets and liabilities, 1947 to 1960

SOURCE: Dominion Bureau of Statistics; Superintendent of Insurance for Canada; Bank of Canada, *Statistical Summary, Supplement, 1960*.

These series include the assets and liabilities of sales finance companies, and of companies licensed under the federal Small Loans Act and affiliates engaged in making personal loans.

The principal business of the sales finance companies is to finance purchases of new and used cars, but financing of household durable goods and of commercial and industrial items such as vehicles is also important to them.

H559–568. Small loan companies chartered by the Dominion Government, assets and liabilities, 1928 to 1959

SOURCE: *Canada Year Book*; *Report of the Superintendent of Insurance of Canada on Small Loan Companies and Money Lenders*.

Licensed small loan companies operate under the federal Small Loans Act. Their principal business is to make personal loans on the security of promissory notes, and frequently the additional security of endorsements and chattel mortgages. There are four such companies, the first one of which appeared in 1928.

FEDERAL GOVERNMENT LENDING AGENCIES (Series H569–587)

H569–576. Canadian Farm Loan Board, loans approved and paid out, 1930 to 1959

SOURCE: *Canada Year Book*; Canadian Farm Loan Board.

The Canadian Farm Loan Board began operations in 1929, and was appointed by the Governor in Council under provisions of the Canadian Farm Loan Act of 1927. It became the Farm Credit Corporation in 1959. Its purpose is to make loans to farmers to enable them to buy farm land, livestock and farm equipment, to improve their farms, and to pay debts and operating expenses.

The loans are secured by mortgages, have a term of up to 30 years and are repayable in annual instalments. The funds are obtained by the Board from the federal Minister of Finance at current interest rates and are lent to farmers at a slightly higher rate so as to cover expenses.

H577–587. Industrial Development Bank, assets, liabilities and loan transactions, 1945 to 1960

SOURCE: Industrial Development Bank, *Annual Reports*; Bank of Canada, *Statistical Summary, Supplement, 1960*.

The Industrial Development Bank began operations in 1945 as a wholly owned subsidiary of the Bank of Canada. Its purpose has been to provide medium- and long-term loans to a wide range of small and medium-sized businesses who are not able to obtain satisfactory accommodation from other sources. In the Budget Speech of 20 June 1961, the Minister of Finance announced that legislation would be introduced permitting the Bank to make loans to all types of business enterprises, providing loans on reasonable terms are not available to them from other sources; and he expressed the government's desire to see the Bank increase its activity in assisting a change of ownership of small businesses. The Bank has the authority to purchase a portion of the equity of a business for subsequent resale.

In addition to providing term loans the Bank also provides technical engineering, accounting, and managerial advice where needed.

MISCELLANEOUS FINANCIAL STATISTICS
(Series H 588–683)

H 588–603.   Bond and stock yields, in the month of December, 1900 to 1959

SOURCE: Series H 588, 596, 597, 598, 599, Bank of Canada, *Statistical Summary*; series H 589, Dominion Bureau of Statistics from data issued by A. E. Ames & Co. Ltd; Dominion Bureau of Statistics from data issued by Wood, Gundy & Co. Ltd; series H 591 direct from Wood, Gundy & Co. Ltd; series H 592–595 McLeod, Young, Weir & Co. Ltd; series H 600–603 Moss, Lawson & Co. Ltd.

Historical statistics of interest rates in Canada are woefully incomplete, as can be seen from the table showing series H 588–603. These series have been compiled by various institutions, at various times, using various criteria, and so must be interpreted cautiously. They do indicate the general trend of interest rates, and something of the pattern of rates, but serve more to illustrate the serious gaps which exist in our information on interest rates.

H 588. This series begins in 1934 because the system of tendering for Government of Canada treasury bills was introduced at that time.

H 589. In 1919, three issues were used, viz. 5 % 1931, 5½ % 1933 and 5½ % 1937. In 1920, 5½ % 1934 was added. In 1923, 5 % 1943 was substituted for 5 % 1931 while in 1926, 5½ % 1933, 5½ % 1934 and 5½ % 1937 were dropped and 4½ % 1940, 4½ % 1944 and 4½ % 1936 were added. In 1932, 4½ % 1948, 4½ % 1949 and 4 % 1947 were added, and 4½ % 1940 was dropped. In 1936, 4½ % 1947 and 3 % 1950 were substituted for 5 % 1943 and 4½ % 1944.

H 591. From 1905 to 1920, six issues are included, four industrials and two utilities. From 1921 to 1945 nine issues are included, six industrials and three utilities. From 1946 to 1954 twelve issues are included, eight industrials and four utilities.

H 592–595. Each series is an average of ten issues. The issues included have, of course, changed over the years, but are broadly representative of their group.

H 596–599. The theoretical yields are derived from a yield curve drawn through a scatter diagram of actual yields of issues of various maturities on a particular date. These series were discontinued after 1958 because of the arbitrary nature of the

yield curve based on points which were becoming widely scattered.

H 600–603. These statistics of stock yields are compiled each week by the firm of Moss, Lawson & Co.

H 604–618.   Bond and stock yields, annual averages, 1900 to 1959

SOURCE: see source for series H 588–603.

Series H 604–618 differ from series H 588–603 only in that they are annual average statistics whereas the latter are December figures.

H 619–630.   Foreign exchange rates, 1910 to 1960

SOURCE: Bank of Canada, *Statistical Summary* and *Financial Supplements*; Dominion Bureau of Statistics; *Monetary Times*; Bank of Montreal.

Series H 619–624 differ from series H 625–630 only in that the former are December figures whereas the latter are annual average figures.

H 631–650.   Stock exchange statistics, 1914 to 1959

SOURCE: Dominion Bureau of Statistics; Montreal and Canadian Stock Exchanges, *Monthly Review*; Toronto Stock Exchange, *Monthly Review*; Bank of Canada, *Statistical Summary*.

Series H 631–636 differ from series H 637–642 only in that they are yearly averages of monthly statistics whereas the latter are December statistics.

H 651–660.   Sales of Canadian bonds, by class of bond and country of sale, 1904 to 1959

SOURCE: *Canada Year Book*; *Monetary Times*.

These series are subject to a number of limitations. They are gross, not net, figures, and almost certainly do not include all issues, particularly in earlier years. It is not known whether the division among the various categories was based on consistent criteria over the years. Statistics of sales by country (series H 658–660) can only be approximations particularly in earlier years when gold standard arrangements made it easy to sell even new and outstanding currency issues to foreign buyers.

H 661–683.   Net new security issues, 1936 to 1960

SOURCE: Bank of Canada, *Statistical Summary*, November 1961, pp. 677–80.

These series of net new security issues were compiled by the Bank of Canada, and were computed by subtracting retirements from gross new issues. They constitute the most reliable measure available of the total amount of funds supplied to borrowers in exchange for securities. Borrowers included are the Government of Canada, provinces, municipalities and corporations. The series also show the net amount of securities payable in foreign currencies which were issued by each type of borrower. Statistics of retirements of issues and of gross new issues on which these series are based may be found in the Bank of Canada's *Statistical Summary*.

Series H1–10. *Currency and chartered bank deposits, 1913 to 1960*
(millions of dollars)

| Year end | Currency outside banks | | | Chartered bank deposits (less float) | | | | Total | | Float |
| | Notes | Coin | Total | Personal savings | Government of Canada | Other (less float) | Total (less float) | Including Government of Canada | Excluding Government of Canada | |
	1	2	3	4	5	6	7	8	9	10
1960	1,732	144	1,876	7,215	510	4,313	12,037	13,914	13,404	884
1959	1,705	128	1,832	6,900	404	4,057	11,360	13,193	12,789	919
1958	1,660	121	1,781	6,844	319	4,303	11,466	13,247	12,927	1,224
1957	1,555	112	1,667	6,108[1]	423	3,725[1]	10,256	11,923	11,500	1,151
1956	1,498	108	1,605	6,007	246	3,580	9,833	11,438	11,192	1,330
1955	1,449	101	1,550	5,633	517	3,697	9,847	11,397	10,880	1,002
1954	1,362	96	1,458	5,218	176	3,462	8,856	10,314	10,137	827
1953	1,335	94	1,430	4,756	473	3,130	8,359	9,789	9,316	752
1952	1,289	88	1,377	4,600	49	3,281	7,930	9,307	9,258	706
1951	1,191	84	1,275	4,296	88	3,100	7,484	8,759	8,671	489
1950	1,136	78	1,214	4,176	257	3,116	7,549	8,763	8,506	430
1949	1,110	74	1,184	4,086	164	2,776	7,026	8,210	8,046	291
1948	1,115	70	1,185	3,752	236	2,725	6,713	7,898	7,662	359
1947	1,046	66	1,112	3,453	216	2,455	6,124	7,236	7,020	322
1946	1,031	65	1,096	3,179	281	2,482	5,942	7,038	6,757	298
1945	992	63	1,055	2,635	846[1]	2,185[1]	5,666[1]	6,721[1]	5,875[1]	275[1]
1944	930	60	990	2,173	707	2,022	4,902	5,892	5,185	243
1943	794	55	849	1,698	577	1,815	4,090	4,939	4,362	266
1942	633	49	681	1,423	314	1,661	3,398	4,079	3,765	210
1941	450	42	492	1,474	74	1,362	2,910	3,402	3,328	198
1940	341	38	379	1,451	21	1,161	2,633	3,012	2,991	172
1939	247	34	281	1,551	99	1,064	2,714	2,995	2,896	136
1938	207	31	238	1,475	62	887	2,424	2,662	2,600	116
1937	207	30	237	1,583[1]	13[1]	661[1]	2,257[1]	2,494[1]	2,481[1]	130
1936	191	29	220	1,548	25	622	2,195	2,415	2,390	128
1935	170	28	198	1,486	12	590[1]	2,088[1]	2,286[1]	2,274[1]	120
1934	157	27	184	1,407	24	517	1,948	2,132	2,108	102
1933	151	26	177	1,357	33	457	1,847	2,024	1,991	86
1932	144	27	171	1,378	53	417	1,848	2,019	1,966	80
1931	160	27	187	1,360	111	496	1,967	2,154	2,043	102
1930	163	25	188	1,426	27	548	2,001	2,189	2,162	127
1929	187	26	213	1,434	60	624	2,118	2,331	2,271	152
1928	193	25	218	1,520	46	582	2,148	2,366	2,320	167
1927	192	24	216	1,445	43	580	2,068	2,284	2,241	136
1926	190	23	213	1,373	16	512	1,901	2,114	2,098	124
1925	176	23	199	1,319	22	502	1,843	2,042	2,020	130
1924	177	23	200	1,238	25	498	1,761	1,961	1,936	151
1923	187	23	210	1,180	38	484	1,702	1,912	1,874	133
1922	184	23	207	1,185	19	464	1,668	1,875	1,856	117
1921	191	23	214	1,241	34	471	1,746	1,960	1,926	109
1920	235	23	258	1,293	10	540	1,843	2,101	2,091	150
1919	237	22	259	1,138	121	590	1,849	2,108	1,987	146
1918	229	21	250	958	148	620	1,726	1,976	1,828	116
1917	200	19	219	996	18	501	1,515	1,734	1,716	96
1916	157	17	174	845	18	408	1,271	1,445	1,427	77
1915	131	16	147	721	26	397	1,144	1,291	1,265	64
1914	113	16	129	663	11	329	1,003	1,132	1,121	49
1913	117	15	132	625	9	351	985	1,117	1,108	61

[1] Change in definition. See note to series H1–10.

Series H11–20. *Notes and coin held by banks and general public and chartered bank Canadian deposit liabilities, 1867 to 1960*
(millions of dollars)

| Year end | Subsidiary coin issue | | | Dominion or Bank of Canada note issue | | | Chartered bank note issue | | | Canadian deposits of the chartered banks |
| | Held by banks | Held by others | Total | Held by banks | Held by others | Total | Held by banks | Held by others | Total | |
	11	12	13	14	15	16	17	18	19	20
1960	—	144	—	330	1,732	2,062	—	—	—	12,921
1959	—	128	153	316	1,705	2,021	—	—	—	12,279
1958	23	121	144	338	1,660	1,998	—	—	—	12,690
1957	23	112	135	349	1,555	1,904	—	—	—	11,407
1956	19	108	127	371	1,498	1,869	—	—	—	11,162
1955	20	101	121	289	1,449	1,739	—	—	—	10,848
1954	20	96	116	262	1,362	1,624	—	—	—	9,683
1953	19	94	113	264	1,335	1,599	—	—	—	9,111
1952	18	88	106	273	1,289	1,561	—	—	—	8,636
1951	16	84	100	273	1,191	1,464	—	—	—	7,973
1950	15	78	93	231	1,136	1,367	—	—	—	7,979
1949	12	74	86	212	1,096	1,307	—	—	—	7,317
1948	11	70	81	191	1,098	1,289	—	14	14	7,072
1947	11	66	77	184	1,028	1,211	—	16	16	6,446
1946	11	65	76	177	1,009	1,186	—	21	21	6,240

Series H11–20. *Notes and coin held by banks and general public and chartered bank Canadian deposit liabilities, 1867 to 1960*
(*continued*)

(millions of dollars)

Year end	Subsidiary coin issue			Dominion or Bank of Canada note issue			Chartered bank note issue			Canadian deposits of the chartered banks
	Held by banks	Held by others	Total	Held by banks	Held by others	Total	Held by banks	Held by others	Total	
	11	12	13	14	15	16	17	18	19	20
1945	11	63	74	163	966	1,129	1	25	26	5,942
1944	9	60	69	139	897	1,036	1	33	34	5,145
1943	9	55	64	123	752	874	1	42	43	4,356
1942	5	49	54	121	573	694	2	60	62	3,608
1941	7	42	49	116	380	496	3	71	73	3,108
1940	7	38	45	98	262	360	4	80	84	2,805
1939	5	34	39	71	162	233	5	85	90	2,850
1938	5.2	30.6	35.8	56.8	118.4	175.3	6.2	88.3	94.5	2,498.1
1937	4.8	29.7	34.5	53.9	111.4	165.3	5.7	96.0	101.7	2,386.8
1936	5.0	29.0	34.0	47.9	87.9	135.7	5.9	103.2	109.1	2,322.9
1935	5.4	28.3	33.7	40.6	59.1	99.7	7.9	111.0	118.9	2,208.4
1934	6.6	27.1	33.7	183.2	33.8	217.0	13.0	123.4	136.4	2,050.4
1933	7.0	26.3	33.3	152.3	30.3	182.6	11.4	120.7	132.1	1,933.0
1932	6.6	26.8	33.4	162.0	29.2	191.2	12.1	115.0	127.1	1,928.0
1931	5.7	27.1	32.8	143.9	30.5	174.4	11.9	129.1	141.0	2,068.8
1930	7.0	25.4	32.4	145.8	29.6	175.4	15.0	133.0	148.0	2,127.8
1929	6.2	26.1	32.3	172.3	31.6	203.9	20.0	155.5	175.5	2,270.3
1928	6.3[1]	24.7[1]	31.0	191.9	30.0	221.9	22.9	163.2	186.1	2,314.9
1927	5.9[1]	24.1[1]	30.0	191.6	29.2	220.8	19.6	163.1	182.7	2,204.4
1926	7.0[1]	23.0[1]	30.0	179.6	30.8	210.4	15.7	159.4	175.1	2,024.8
1925	—	—	30.1	208.9	18.3	227.2	16.2	157.7	173.9	1,972.8
1924	—	—	30.1	233.4	28.3	261.7	16.8	148.9	165.7	1,911.7
1923	—	—	30.2	220.5	28.2	248.7	21.1	159.1	180.2	1,834.9
1922	—	—	30.2	229.9	27.4	257.3	—	—	176.2	1,784.1
1921	—	—	30.3	253.7	27.2	280.9	—	—	184.6	1,855.3
1920	—	—	30.3	279.3	32.4	311.7	—	—	228.8	1,993.4
1919	—	—	28.8	288.3	30.4	318.7	—	—	232.5	1,994.7
1918	—	—	25.5	298.1	29.3	327.4	—	—	224.5	1,842.2
1917	—	—	23.0	245.1	27.8	272.9	—	—	192.9	1,610.6
1916	—	—	21.1	156.5	24.5	181.0	—	—	148.8	1,348.3
1915	—	—	19.8	156.7	22.1	178.8	—	—	122.2	1,207.7
1914	—	—	19.7	143.2	19.2	162.4	—	—	106.0	1,052.3
1913	—	—	19.0	111.2	20.0	131.2	—	—	108.6	1,046.2
1912	—	—	18.0	94.6	21.2	115.8	—	—	110.0	1,058.6
1911	—	—	16.7	97.7	17.5	115.2	—	—	102.0	966.1
1910	—	—	15.3	76.0	14.7	90.7	—	—	87.7	860.6
1909	—	—	14.1	73.2	13.8	87.0	—	—	81.3	797.3
1908	—	—	13.4	66.1	13.3	79.4	—	—	73.1	663.8
1907	—	—	13.4	50.0	12.6	62.6	—	—	77.5	585.3
1906	—	—	12.1	44.3	12.2	56.5	—	—	78.4	611.7
1905	—	—	11.3	38.1	10.9	49.0	—	—	70.0	529.5
1904	—	—	10.8	38.4	9.4	47.8	—	—	64.5	471.8
1903	—	—	10.4	30.9	10.2	41.1	—	—	62.5	411.9
1902	—	—	9.8	24.7	9.7	34.4	—	—	60.6	382.9
1901	—	—	9.0	21.4	8.9	30.3	—	—	54.4	347.6
1900	—	—	—	19.8	8.6	28.4	—	—	50.8	308.2
1899	—	—	—	17.9	8.5	26.4	—	—	46.0	283.3
1898	—	—	—	17.1	7.5	24.6	—	—	40.3	257.0
1897	—	—	—	17.7	6.9	24.6	—	—	38.0	232.5
1896	—	—	—	15.2	6.5	21.7	—	—	33.1	204.7
1895	—	—	—	16.0	6.4	22.4	—	—	32.6	197.3
1894	—	—	—	15.2	6.0	21.2	—	—	32.4	192.3
1893	—	—	—	13.3	6.5	19.8	—	—	34.4	179.3
1892	—	—	—	12.4	6.4	18.8	—	—	36.2	180.4
1891	—	—	—	10.1	6.1	16.2	—	—	35.6	161.5
1890	—	—	—	9.7	5.9	15.6	—	—	35.0	133.9
1889	—	—	—	9.1	6.0	15.1	—	—	33.6	126.2
1888	—	—	—	10.7	5.9	16.6	—	—	34.8	121.9
1887	—	—	—	10.0	5.7	15.7	—	—	34.4	105.6
1886	—	—	—	9.4	5.9	15.3	—	—	29.8	99.8
1885	—	—	—	12.4	5.4	17.8	—	—	32.4	101.9
1884	—	—	—	11.0	5.4	16.4	—	—	31.9	92.3
1883	—	—	—	11.2	5.6	16.8	—	—	33.6	96.6
1882	—	—	—	10.5	5.6	16.1	—	—	36.5	96.9
1881	—	—	—	9.9	5.1	15.0	—	—	32.4	89.6
1880	—	—	—	10.5	3.7	14.2	—	—	27.3	79.2
1879	—	—	—	9.1	3.2	12.3	—	—	22.3	68.5
1878	—	—	—	8.1	2.0	10.1	—	—	21.5	66.4
1877	—	—	—	8.9	2.7	11.6	—	—	21.8	63.8
1876	—	—	—	8.3	2.8	11.1	—	—	22.3	63.6
1875	—	—	—	8.5	2.8	11.3	—	—	23.3	60.1
1874	—	—	—	9.6	2.5	12.1	—	—	28.5	70.1
1873	—	—	—	9.1	3.0	12.1	—	—	29.0	57.9
1872	—	—	—	8.2	3.4	11.6	—	—	27.9	53.2
1871	—	—	—	6.9	4.1	11.0	—	—	24.5	50.3
1870	—	—	—	—	—	7.4	—	—	18.5	52.1
1869	—	—	—	—	—	5.8	—	—	12.5	47.6
1868	—	—	—	—	—	4.3	—	—	10.7	41.1
1867	—	—	—	—	—	4.3	—	—	9.8	32.6

[1] Estimated.

Series H21-26. *Canadian coin minted, 1870 to 1960*

Year	One cent pieces	Five cent pieces[1]	Ten cent pieces	Twenty-five cent pieces	Fifty cent pieces	Silver dollars
	21	22	23	24	25	26
1960	75,772,775	37,157,433 (N)	45,446,835	22,835,327	3,488,897	1,420,486
1959	83,615,343	11,552,523 (N)	19,691,433	13,503,461	3,095,535	1,443,502
1958	57,827,413	7,592,320 (N)	10,908,306	9,743,033	2,957,200	3,039,564
1957	100,422,054	7,329,862 (N)	15,631,952	12,364,001	2,171,689	496,389
1956	78,685,535	9,399,854 (N)	16,732,844	11,269,353	1,379,499	209,092
1955	56,686,307	5,356,020 (N)	12,294,649	9,552,505	753,511	274,810
1954	21,898,646	6,998,662 (St)	4,435,795	2,318,891	506,305	242,815
1953	72,293,723	16,638,218 (St)	18,467,020	11,141,851	1,781,191	1,087,265
1952	67,633,553	10,892,877 (St)	10,476,340	8,861,657	2,598,337	408,835
1951	80,431,912	13,343,991[2]	15,080,983	8,292,816	2,423,692	420,620
1950	60,444,992	11,970,520 (N)	17,823,075	9,673,335	2,384,179	261,002
1949	33,128,933	13,037,090 (N)	11,336,172	7,988,830	858,991	572,298
1948	69,623,227	11,405,913 (N)	10,061,534	6,958,362	76,217	39,915
1947	31,093,901	7,603,724 (N)	4,431,926	1,524,554	424,885	65,595
1946	56,662,071	6,952,684 (N)	6,300,066	2,210,810	950,235	93,055
1945	77,268,591	18,893,216 (St)	10,979,570	5,296,495	1,959,528	38,391
1944	44,131,216	11,532,784 (St)	9,383,582	7,216,237	2,460,205	—
1943	89,111,969	24,760,256 (T)	21,143,229	13,559,575	3,109,583	—
1942	76,113,708	10,243,778[3]	10,214,011	6,935,871	1,974,165	—
1941	56,336,011	8,681,785 (N)	8,716,386	6,654,672	1,714,874	—
1940	85,740,532	13,920,197 (N)	16,526,470	9,583,650	1,996,566	—
1939	21,600,319	5,661,123 (N)	5,501,748	3,532,495	287,976	1,363,816
1938	18,365,608	3,898,974 (N)	4,197,323	3,149,245	192,018	90,304
1937	10,719,054	4,593,263 (N)	2,691,332	2,843,498	192,016	241,002
1936	8,768,769	4,400,450 (N)	2,460,871	972,094	38,550	306,100
1935	7,529,233	3,891,151 (N)	384,592	537,997	—	428,120
1934	7,062,539	3,832,483 (N)	384,656	384,505	—	—
1933	12,079,310	2,597,867 (N)	672,368	421,282	38,435	—
1932	21,316,190	3,198,566 (N)	1,154,317	537,994	19,213	—
1931	3,842,776	5,100,830 (N)	2,067,421	537,815	57,581	—
1930	2,513,041	3,685,991 (N)	1,827,071	961,174	—	—
1929	12,164,474	5,562,262 (N)	3,259,645	2,691,485	228,021	—
1928	9,121,744	4,558,725 (N)	2,451,969	2,089,539	—	—
1927	3,553,928	5,285,627 (N)	—	468,096	—	—
1926	2,145,920	933,577 (N)	—	—	—	—
1925	1,000,360	200,050 (N)	—	—	—	—
1924	1,596,388	3,066,658 (N)	—	—	—	—
1923	1,019,160	2,475,201 (N)	—	—	—	—
1922	1,243,903	4,763,186 (N)	—	—	—	—
1921	7,555,964	2,501,238[4]	2,458,064	575,268	176,793[4]	—
1920	22,373,779	10,660,964	6,295,574	1,937,299	559,521	—
1919	11,201,347	8,105,052	7,868,308	5,844,569	1,085,305	—
1918	12,905,708	5,790,276	5,109,450	4,167,533	832,805	—
1917	11,917,993	5,625,038	4,995,002	3,202,234	739,715	—
1916	11,110,142	2,404,399	4,231,223	1,454,129	454,853	—
1915	4,836,966	1,153,486	672,408	238,378	—	—
1914	3,403,937	4,190,669	2,543,616	1,202,322	157,537	—
1913	5,733,372	5,581,883	3,591,552	2,186,588	263,290	—
1912	5,109,599	5,849,562	3,237,096	2,504,085	283,248	—
1911	4,659,947	3,683,686	2,727,557	1,704,004	204,475	—
1910	5,161,925	5,939,133	4,648,577	3,590,745	640,141	—
1909	3,944,168	1,890,865	1,514,129	1,311,052	198,648	—
1908	2,329,095	1,197,780	761,631	466,625	121,260	—
1907	3,200,000	5,200,000	2,620,000	2,088,000	300,000	—
1906	4,100,000	3,100,000	1,700,000	1,237,843	350,000	—
1905	2,000,000	2,600,000	1,000,000	800,000	40,000	—
1904	2,500,000	2,400,000	1,000,000	400,000	60,000	—
1903	4,000,000	3,640,000	1,820,000	846,150	140,000	—
1902	3,000,000	4,320,000	1,820,000	1,264,000	120,000	—
1901	4,100,000	2,000,000	1,200,000	640,000	80,000	—
1900	3,600,000	1,800,000	1,100,000	1,320,000	118,000	—
1899	2,400,000	3,000,000	1,200,000	415,580	50,000	—
1898	1,000,000	580,717	720,000	—	100,000	—
1897	1,500,000	1,319,283	—	—	—	—
1896	2,000,000	1,500,000	650,000	—	—	—
1895	1,200,000	—	—	—	—	—
1894	1,000,000	500,000	500,000	220,000	29,036	—
1893	2,000,000	1,700,000	500,000	100,000	—	—
1892	1,200,000	860,000	520,000	510,000	151,000	—
1891	1,452,500	1,800,000	800,000	120,000	—	—
1890	1,000,000	1,000,000	450,000	200,000	20,000	—
1889	—	1,200,000	600,000	66,340	—	—
1888	4,000,000	1,000,000	500,000	400,000	60,000	—
1887	1,500,000	500,000	350,000	100,000	—	—
1886	1,500,000	1,700,000	800,000	540,000	—	—
1885	—	1,100,000	400,000	192,000	—	—
1884	2,500,000	200,000	150,000	—	—	—
1883	—	600,000	300,000	960,000	—	—
1882	4,000,000	1,000,000	1,000,000	600,000	—	—
1881	2,000,000	1,500,000	950,000	820,000	150,000	—

Series H21–26. *Canadian coin minted, 1870 to 1960 (continued)*

Year	One cent pieces	Five cent pieces¹	Ten cent pieces	Twenty-five cent pieces	Fifty cent pieces	Silver dollars
	21	22	23	24	25	26
1880	—	3,000,000	1,500,000	400,000	—	—
1879	—	—	—	—	—	—
1878	—	—	—	—	—	—
1877	—	—	—	—	—	—
1876	4,000,000	—	—	—	—	—
1875	—	1,000,000	1,000,000	1,000,000	—	—
1874	—	800,000	600,000	1,600,000	—	—
1873	—	—	—	—	—	—
1872	—	2,000,000	1,000,000	2,240,000	80,000	—
1871	—	1,400,000	800,000	400,000	200,000	—
1870	—	2,800,000	1,600,000	900,000	450,000	—

¹ N = Nickel; T = Tombac; St = Steel.
² 9,029,048 (N); 4,314,943 (St).
³ 6,847,544 (N); 3,396,234 (T).
⁴ Struck and later remelted.

Series H27–35. *Gold received and coinage issued by the mint, 1901 to 1960*

Year	Gold received (fine ounces)	Gold bullion issued (fine ounces)	Coinage issued (dollars)						
			Gold	Silver	Nickel	Steel	Tombac	Bronze	Total issued
	27	28	29	30	31	32	33	34	35
1960	4,024,626	4,014,771	—	13,432,252	1,735,707	—	—	748,101	15,916,060
1959	3,908,640	3,836,680	—	8,273,564	576,680	—	—	829,116	9,679,360
1958	3,958,459	4,088,706	—	8,044,753	379,616	—	—	578,274	9,002,643
1957	3,896,084	3,776,711	—	6,236,429	366,491	—	—	1,004,221	7,607,143
1956	3,801,789	3,774,599	—	5,389,464	469,993	—	—	786,855	6,646,312
1955	3,947,637	3,952,764	—	4,269,157	267,801	—	—	566,863	5,103,821
1954	3,829,431	3,998,836	—	1,864,968	27	350,230	—	263,897	2,479,122
1953	3,684,074	3,626,497	—	6,138,686	234	831,915	—	655,130	7,625,964
1952	3,953,158	4,031,068	—	4,869,552	598	576,965	—	683,821	6,130,936
1951	4,169,480	4,167,486	—	5,213,677	423,003	182,829	—	783,329	6,602,838
1950	4,422,968	4,347,962	—	5,641,805	640,510	—	—	607,003	6,889,319
1949	3,925,618	3,865,296	—	4,148,842	637,500	—	—	321,901	5,108,243
1948	3,401,991	3,405,073	—	2,829,956	615,500	—	—	708,300	4,153,756
1947	2,868,469	2,859,084	—	1,186,000	391,000	—	—	360,300	1,937,300
1946	2,652,245	2,665,965	—	1,701,000	291,500	—	—	528,500	2,521,000
1945	2,503,416	2,499,163	—	3,416,300	—	950,300	—	748,500	5,115,100
1944	2,862,048	2,829,755	—	4,006,000	571,000	—	400	454,600	5,032,000
1943	3,616,959	3,645,740	—	7,044,000	—	—	1,238,000	881,300	9,163,300
1942	4,611,982	4,611,892	—	3,764,000	361,576	—	169,424	783,500	5,078,500
1941	5,092,609	5,134,348	—	3,534,000	454,000	—	—	575,300	4,563,300
1940	4,999,847	5,026,793	—	4,845,000	660,500	—	—	822,800	6,328,300
1939	4,869,239	4,834,214	—	2,794,032	321,000	—	—	214,600	3,329,632
1938	4,398,258	4,308,067	—	1,376,000	153,500	—	—	184,300	1,713,800
1937	3,933,453	3,937,911	—	1,322,200	251,100	—	—	105,400	1,678,700
1936	3,603,335	3,625,549	—	809,200	202,600	—	—	87,200	1,099,000
1935	3,158,780	3,177,497	—	601,020	194,000	—	—	75,100	870,120
1934	3,008,977	3,038,019	—	172,300	193,000	—	—	69,900	435,200
1933	2,568,838	2,589,649	—	155,000	125,000	—	—	120,800	400,800
1932	2,829,529	2,873,221	—	287,000	165,000	—	—	213,200	665,200
1931	1,721,237	1,735,112	—	475,400	281,000	—	—	51,400	807,800
1930	862,075	722,469	—	326,000	164,500	—	—	13,400	503,900
1929	438,351	468,384	—	1,081,000	267,000	—	—	123,300	1,471,300
1928	1,325,113	1,305,200	—	867,000	250,000	—	—	92,100	1,209,100
1927	1,448,180	1,451,907	—	574,000	240,000	—	—	37,500	860,500
1926	1,375,502	1,347,668	—	50,000	168,500	—	—	28,200	246,700
1925	120,570	122,375	—	14,000	126,000	—	—	22,100	162,100
1924	111,193	107,597	—	—	74,500	—	—	11,900	86,400
1923	613,738	639,507	—	28,000	127,000	—	—	19,300	174,300
1922	1,087,206	1,086,131	—	24,000	69,000	—	—	12,400	105,400
1921	818,265	802,966	—	128,000	—	—	—	60,700	188,700
1920	557,784	567,421	—	1,356,000	—	—	—	209,085	1,565,085
1919	520,378	491,602	661,326	3,258,044	—	—	—	115,100	4,034,470
1918	239,072	167,442	518,378	2,402,000	—	—	—	131,817	3,052,195
1917	40,369	88,852	286,379	1,862,000	—	—	—	116,900	2,205,479
1916			29,740	1,179,516	—	—	—	110,646	1,319,902
1915			—	61,344	—	—	—	50,354	111,698
1914			1,572,044	626,198	—	—	—	35,057	2,233,299
1913			1,908,700	927,131	—	—	—	55,572	2,891,403
1912	506,178	141,088	1,477,710	1,303,237	—	—	—	49,977	2,830,924
1911			1,250,470	1,343,001	—	—	—	54,275	2,647,746
1910			136,325	1,151,186	—	—	—	42,020	1,329,531
1909			79,195	648,700	—	—	—	39,300	767,195
1908			3,095	38,541	—	—	—	21,604	63,240
1907	—	—	—	1,194,000	—	—	—	32,000	1,226,000
1906	—	—	—	807,461	—	—	—	41,000	848,461
1905	—	—	—	450,000	—	—	—	20,000	470,000
1904	—	—	—	350,000	—	—	—	25,000	375,000
1903	—	—	—	633,850	—	—	—	40,000	673,850
1902	—	—	—	774,000	—	—	—	30,000	804,000
1901	—	—	—	420,000	—	—	—	41,000	461,000

Series H36–54. *Bank of Canada, assets and liabilities, 1935 to 1960*

(millions of dollars)

Year end	Treasury bills[1]	Government of Canada direct and guaranteed securities			Total[1]	Provincial government securities	Advances	Foreign currency assets[2]	Investment in I.D.B.[3]	All other accounts[4]	Total assets or liabilities
		Other maturities[1]									
		2 years and under	Over 2 years	Total							
	36	37	38	39	40	41	42	43	44	45	46
1960	404.4	353.4	1,932.0	2,285.4	2,689.7	—	—	78.8	89.4	186.5	3,044.4
1959	305.9	514.5	1,800.3	2,314.8	2,620.6	—	—	59.7	83.6	204.2	2,968.1
1958	35.9	245.2	2,340.7	2,585.8	2,621.8	—	2.0[7]	93.8	77.9	148.9	2,944.4
1957	467.1	779.2	1,181.3	1,960.4	2,427.5	—	—	80.3	61.2	89.7	2,658.7
1956	505.2	519.7[1]	1,368.9[1]	1,888.7[1]	2,393.9[1]	—	—	77.7	48.0	28.1	2,547.7
1955	262.6	1,021.2	1,083.6	2,104.9	2,367.5	—	2.0[7]	114.7	35.1	100.9	2,620.2
1954	168.5	1,193.0	860.6	2,053.6	2,222.0	—	—	66.4	35.6	76.9	2,400.8
1953	374.5	1,002.1	893.7	1,895.7	2,270.2	—	—	67.2	36.3	63.5	2,437.2
1952	282.9	1,176.9	767.2	1,944.1	2,227.0	—	—	84.5	30.8	39.2	2,381.4
1951	186.4	955.3	1,049.3	2,004.7	2,191.1	—	—	204.2	27.8	21.0	2,444.1
1950	262.7	966.6	712.5	1,679.1	1,941.8	—	—	359.6	25.0	24.0	2,350.3
1949	243.6	1,537.8	227.8	1,765.6	2,009.2	—	—	79.7	25.0	12.0	2,125.9
1948	249.5	984.2	779.1	1,763.3	2,012.7	—	—	0.5	25.0	20.4	2,058.6
1947	253.8	768.2	858.5	1,626.7	1,880.6	—	—	2.0	25.0	18.7	1,926.2
1946	233.4	962.0	708.2	1,670.2	1,903.6	2.0	—	1.0	15.0	27.1	1,948.6
1945	181.1	973.3	687.7	1,661.0	1,842.1	3.5	—	156.8	10.0	19.5	2,031.9
1944	95.7	808.7	573.0	1,381.7	1,477.4	3.4	—	172.3	10.0	24.3	1,687.4
1943	84.3	699.4	472.7	1,172.1	1,256.4	4.0	—	0.6	—	47.3	1,308.3
1942	111.7	691.6	209.1	900.7	1,012.4	4.0	1.3[7]	0.5	—	30.1	1,048.2
1941	61.0	327.1	216.6	543.7	604.7	3.8	—	200.9	—	33.5	842.9
1940	109.7	335.1	127.3	462.4	572.1	3.7	—	38.4	—	12.4	626.6
1939	89.3	89.1	49.9	139.0	228.2	3.5	—	290.0	—	5.5	527.2
1938	65.2	76.1	40.9	117.0	182.2	3.3	—	214.3	—	5.2	404.9
1937	67.2	12.1	91.3	103.4	170.6	3.3	—	209.9	—	6.5	390.3
1936	43.7	14.6	99.0	113.6	157.3	3.0	—	190.8	—	5.9	357.0
1935	2.6	28.3	83.4	111.7	114.3	—	3.5[8]	186.4	—	3.5	307.7

Year end	Liabilities							
	Notes in circulation			Canadian dollar deposits			Foreign currency liabilities	All other accounts[5, 6]
	Held by							
	Chartered banks	Others	Total	Government of Canada	Chartered banks	Other		
	47	48	49	50	51	52	53	54
1960	329.8	1,731.9	2,061.7	35.7	662.6	33.3	68.6	182.5
1959	315.7	1,704.8	2,020.5	45.6	637.0	34.8	50.0	180.2
1958	338.2	1,659.9	1,998.0	34.9	662.7	25.0	83.9	139.9
1957	348.6	1,555.1	1,903.7	35.4	517.6	31.2	70.0	100.8
1956	370.9	1,497.8	1,868.7	38.8	511.5	31.2	62.2	35.4
1955	289.4	1,449.0	1,738.5	89.2	551.0	34.0	98.0	109.5
1954	261.6	1,361.9	1,623.5	56.3	529.6	30.5	63.1	97.9
1953	263.8	1,335.3	1,599.1	51.5	623.9	29.5	63.8	69.3
1952	272.5	1,288.7	1,561.2	16.2	626.6	44.5	82.9	50.0
1951	273.1	1,191.1	1,464.2	94.9	619.0	66.1	155.6	44.4
1950	231.3	1,136.1	1,367.4	24.7	578.6	207.1	133.6	39.0
1949	211.8	1,095.6	1,307.4	30.7	541.7	126.9	79.6	39.5
1948	190.8	1,098.3	1,289.1	98.1	547.3	81.0	0.4	42.7
1947	183.9	1,027.5	1,211.4	68.8	536.2	67.5	2.0	40.4
1946	176.9	1,009.3	1,186.2	60.5	565.5	93.8	1.0	41.7
1945	162.9	966.2	1,129.1	153.3	521.2	29.8	156.8	41.7
1944	139.4	896.6	1,036.0	12.9	401.7	27.7	172.3	36.8
1943	122.9	751.5	874.4	20.5	340.2	17.8	—	55.4
1942	121.1	572.5	693.6	51.6	259.9	19.1	—	24.0
1941	116.3	379.6	496.0	73.8	232.0	6.0	—	35.1
1940	98.3	261.6	359.9	10.9	217.7	9.5	—	28.5
1939	70.6	162.2	232.8	46.3	217.0	17.9	—	13.3
1938	56.8	118.4	175.3	16.7	200.6	3.1	—	9.3
1937	53.9	111.4	165.3	11.1	196.0	3.5	—	14.4
1936	47.9	87.9	135.7	18.8	187.0	2.1	—	13.4
1935	40.6	59.1	99.7	17.9	181.6	0.8	—	7.7

[1] From 31 December 1956 on, the basis for the valuation of securities held by the Bank of Canada was changed to amortized values, whereas previously the basis was 'not exceeding market values'; for this reason, dates prior to 1956 are not directly comparable with those after.
[2] Foreign exchange and foreign securities. Includes gold for following year ends: 1935, 180.5; 1936, 179.4; 1937, 179.9; 1938, 185.9; 1939, 225.7.
[3] Industrial Development Bank capital stock, bonds and debentures.

[4] Bank premises and all other assets.
[5] For all year end dates prior to 31 December 1956, Government of Canada deposits are shown before the transfer of Bank of Canada profits for these years from 'All other accounts' to Government of Canada deposits.
[6] Capital, rest fund and all other liabilities.
[7] To chartered and savings banks.
[8] To Government of Canada.

Series H55–86. *Chartered bank assets, 1945 to 1960*
(millions of dollars)

Year end	Notes of and deposits with Bank of Canada	Canadian day-to-day loans	Deposits with government against notes[1]	Treasury bills	Other Government of Canada direct and guaranteed securities[2] 2 years and under	Over 2 years	Total	Other Canadian securities Provincial[2]	Municipal	Corporate	Total[2]
	55	56	57	58	59	60	61	62	63	64	65
1960	992	172	—	967	615	1,472	2,088	324	208	473	1,005
1959	953	101	—	974	657	1,169	1,827	346	204	512	1,063
1958	1,001	123	—	950	826	1,736	2,562	415	195	554	1,164
1957	866	210	—	805	410	1,425	1,835	285	168	509	962
1956	882	74	—	740	406	1,269	1,675	269	185	510	964
1955	840	81	—	427	475	2,157	2,632	322	218	482	1,022
1954	791	68	—	360	636	2,318	2,953	264	177	353	794
1953	888	—	—	244	482	2,034	2,516	280	152	341	773
1952	899	—	—	138	869	1,777	2,647	304	159	370	834
1951	892	—	—	236	499	2,019	2,518	321	167	393	881
1950	810	—	—	129	694	2,256	2,950	385	194	402	981
1949	753	—	1	126	763	2,224	2,986	408	161	382	951
1948	738	—	1	129	656	2,173	2,830	408	140	450	998
1947	720	—	1	139	482	2,028	2,509	448	133	352	933
1946	742	—	1	147	1,052	2,118	3,170	312	115	205	632
1945	684	—	2	170	1,119	1,983	3,102	297	91	117	505

Year end	Loans in Canadian currency — Call and short: To stock brokers	To others	Provincial	Municipal	Grain dealers	Canada Savings Bonds	Instalment finance companies	General loans[3,4]	Total loans	Insured residential mortgages	Canadian dollar items in transit (net)	Customers' liabilities under acceptances, guarantees and letters of credit	All other Canadian assets
	66	67	68	69	70	71	72	73	74	75	76	77	78
1960	65	73	128	217	463	186	371	5,031	6,535	971	884	257	321
1959	72	67	39	231	434	188	409	4,701	6,142	968	919	207	290
1958	54	62	69	217	351	169	352	4,138	5,411	790	1,224	197	253
1957	58	133	89	193	412	176	281	4,063	5,405	586	1,151	224	230
1956	89	68[2]	95	177	372	169	394	3,998	5,363[2]	493	1,330	210	211
1955	112	67	83	124	361	163	310	3,670	4,891	294	1,002	203	183
1954	68	75	61	103	404	147	181	3,056	4,096[3]	74	827[3]	155	172
1953	61	93	65	96	391	165	256	2,979	4,105	—	751	155	160
1952	73	82	79	97	257	146	236	2,550	3,519	—	752	199	160
1951	78	30	68	94	177	137	83	2,504	3,171	—	512	225	154
1950	134		72	84	160	124	127	2,241	2,941	—	431	258	135
1949	133		62	72	170	116	91	1,798	2,442	—	306	164	124
1948	101		83	56	179	97	74	1,728	2,317	—	374	206	113
1947	105		57	41	138	92	76	1,616	2,125	—	336	201	104
1946	135		33	25	113	92	1,250		1,649	—	273	213	96
1945	251		44	21	105	—	1,124		1,546	—	272	141	95

Year end	Total Canadian assets	Foreign currency assets — Cash items[5]	Foreign securities	Call loans	Current loans	Total foreign assets	Total assets	Total foreign and Canadian securities
	79	80	81	82	83	84	85	86
1960	14,192	540	557	814	814	2,725	16,917	4,617
1959	13,442	361	526	711	794	2,392	15,835	4,390
1958	13,676	393	494	613	666	2,167	15,840	5,170
1957	12,274	444	431	576[2]	520[2]	1,971[1]	14,245	4,033
1956	11,942	356	375	345[2]	375[2]	1,451	13,393	3,754
1955	11,575	327	282	177	341	1,127	12,702	4,363
1954	10,291	332	322	196	293	1,143	11,433	4,429
1953	9,592	280	244	272	268	1,064	10,656	3,777
1952	9,148	283	262	170	264	979	10,128	3,881
1951	8,589	254	206	131	278	869	9,458	3,841
1950	8,636	264	196	100	247	807	9,443	4,256
1949	7,853	276	244	70	211	801	8,653	4,307
1948	7,705	250	244	78	240	812	8,517	4,201
1947	7,067	281	273	56	234	844	7,911	3,854
1946	6,924	251	278	77	178	784	7,708	4,227
1945	6,517	282	244	120	151	797	7,311	4,021

See p. 239 for footnotes.

Series H87–112. *Chartered bank assets, continuation, 1934 to 1944*
(millions of dollars)

| | | | | | Holdings of securities | | | | | | | | Loans in Canada | | | | | |
| | | | | | Government of Canada and provincial securities | | | | Other Canadian and non-government foreign securities | Foreign government securities | | | | | | | |
Year end	Notes of and deposits with Bank of Canada	Gold and coin in Canada	Deposits with government against notes	Balances with other chartered banks in Canada	2 years and under	Over 2 years	Total	Canadian municipal securities			Total	Call	Provincial	Municipal	Other banks in Canada	Other current loans	Total loans in Canada
	87	88	89	90	91	92	93	94	95	96	97	98	99	100	101	102	103
1944	541	8	2	2	1,941	1,288	3,229	77	96	210	3,611	92	12	17	—	1,182	1,303
1943	463	8	3	2	1,664	963	2,627	63	72	177	2,940	48	8	45	—	1,104	1,205
1942	381	6	4	3	1,262	739	2,001	69	83	140	2,293	31	6	62	—	1,100	1,199
1941	348	7	4	3	793	723	1,516	79	89	75	1,759	32	15	71	—	1,084	1,202
1940	316	7	5	3	691	597	1,288	92	99	51	1,530	40	17	92	—	999	1,148
1939	288	4	5	4	671	682	1,353	99	122	72	1,646	53	16	112	—	960	1,141
1938	257	5	5	4	469	693	1,162	101	127	73	1,463	65	22	112	—	806	1,005
1937	250	5	6	5	427	684	1,111	112	130	59	1,411	76	23	90	—	749	938
1936	235	5	7	3	469	647	1,116	110	112	47	1,384	114	20	96	—	675	905
1935	222	5	7	5	431	525	956	99	53	46	1,155	83	19	106	—	820	1,028
1934	189	39	7	5	404	376	781	93	40	54	966	103	30	108	—	839	1,080

| Year end | Notes of other chartered banks | Cheques on other banks | Customers' liabilities under acceptances and letters of credit | Balances due from banks and agencies abroad | Certain foreign assets | | | All other assets | Total assets |
					Other cash items[6]	Call loans	Current loans		
	104	105	106	107	108	109	110	111	112
1944		243	121	213	104	96	130	85	6,459
1943	1	266	112	237	89	96	100	87	5,609
1942	2	210	113	225	51	74	113	93	4,767
1941	3	198	124	174	34	48	136	97	4,137
1940	4	172	68	171	33	42	131	101	3,731
1939	5	136	53	199	40	49	147	105	3,822
1938	6	116	53	170	37	51	152	107	3,431
1937	6	130	64	102	30	60	166	108	3,281
1936	6	128	67	125	30	75	162	110	3,242
1935	8	119	58	112	35	65	145	115	3,079
1934	13	102	51	86	31	99	134	78	2,919

Series 113–136. *Chartered bank assets, continuation, 1923 to 1933*
(millions of dollars)

| | | | | | | Holdings of securities | | | | Loans in Canada | | | | | |
| | | | | | | Government of Canada and provincial securities | Other Canadian and foreign securities | | | Government of Canada | | | | | |
Year end	Gold and subsidiary coin in Canada	Dominion notes	Central gold reserve deposits	Deposits with government against notes	Balances with other banks in Canada			Total	Call		Provincial	Municipal	Other banks in Canada	Other current loans	Total loans in Canada
	113	114	115	116	117	118	119	120	121	122	123	124	125	126	127
1933	39	140	18	7	3	651	210	861	106	—	29	109	—	898	1,142
1932	38	153	20	7	4	562	216	778	103	—	28	112	—	964	1,207
1931	46	129	26	7	4	478	216	694	135	—	46	126	—	1,082	1,389
1930	47	127	33	7	5	409	196	604	205	—	30	96	—	1,149	1,480
1929	47	131	56	6	6	297	151	448	262	—	25	97	—	1,403	1,787
1928	47	134	79	6	5	371	154	525	266	—	23	73	—	1,231	1,593
1927	48	139	74	6	6	326	204	529	242	—	25	55	—	1,083	1,405
1926	45	138	69	6	6	304	180	484	151	—	25	61	—	970	1,206
1925	50	157	71	6	6	352	198	550	136	—	24	53	—	903	1,116
1924	44	182	61	8	11	324	211	536	128	—	22	50	—	939	1,139
1923	44	164	66	11	4	259	168	427	116	—	23	66	—	1,012	1,277

See p. 239 for footnotes.

Series H113–136. *Chartered bank assets, continuation, 1923 to 1933*

(millions of dollars)

Year end	Notes of other chartered banks	Cheques on other banks	Customers' liabilities under letters of credit	Certain foreign assets		Call loans	Current loans	All other assets	Total assets
				Balances due from banks and agencies abroad	Other cash items[7]				
	128	129	130	131	132	133	134	135	136
1933	11	86	49	83	29	90	138	120	2,816
1932	12	80	43	113	33	91	152	121	2,852
1931	12	102	55	110	35	83	188	118	2,998
1930	15	127	78	90	59	146	214	111	3,144
1929	20	152	113	102	50	245	251	107	3,521
1928	23	167	99	78	56	293	262	103	3,470
1927	20	136	83	74	58	291	265	97	3,232
1926	16	124	75	76	54	273	270	98	2,940
1925	16	130	70	74	50	259	238	103	2,896
1924	17	151	61	79	42	187	185	104	2,807
1923	21	133	51	64	42	176	171	109	2,700

Series H137–160. *Chartered bank assets, continuation, 1913 to 1922*

(millions of dollars)

Year end	Gold and subsidiary coin in Canada	Dominion notes	Central gold reserve deposits	Deposits with government against notes	Balances with other banks in Canada	Holdings of securities			Loans in Canada						
						Government of Canada and provincial securities	Other Canadian and foreign securities	Total	Call	Government of Canada	Provincial	Municipal	Other banks in Canada	Other current loans	Total
	137	138	139	140	141	142	143	144	145	146	147	148	149	150	151
1922	79	183	61	6	5	202	139	341	98	—	19	57	—	1,065	1,240
1921	60	196	68	7	6	214	153	368	113	—	8	65	—	1,174	1,360
1920	63	177	113	6	7	120	238	358	115	—	13	56	—	1,302	1,485
1919	63	173	126	6	6	150	310	460	126	—	15	43	—	1,207	1,391
1918	61	176	131	6	6	207	307	514	89	—	8	31	—	1,076	1,204
1917	55	167	97	6	7	189	280	468	72	—	10	36	—	859	976
1916	45	125	44	7	6	31	232	263	83	4	2	24	—	820	933
1915	43	146	17	7	15	16	107	122	84	14	5	31	—	776	910
1914	39	138	10	7	8	11	94	106	69	5	14	38	—	786	912
1913	26	105	8	7	5	11	93	104	73	—	4	31	—	822	930

Year end	Notes of other banks[8]	Cheques on other banks	Liabilities of customers under letters of credit	Certain foreign assets		Call loan	Current loans	All other assets	Total assets
				Balances due from banks and agencies abroad	Gold and subsidiary coin abroad				
	152	153	154	155	156	157	158	159	160
1922	44	117	20	71	15	186	158	94	2,619
1921	51	109	23	76	19	170	145	89	2,747
1920	54	150	44	106	20	211	185	76	3,057
1919	36	146	51	79	18	172	169	71	2,967
1918	31	116	34	57	18	150	119	67	2,690
1917	24	96	22	65	27	134	112	66	2,323
1916	20	77	9	76	27	174	76	102	1,984
1915	15	64	9	103	25	137	58	67	1,738
1914	13	49	12	46	24	85	43	64	1,556
1913	15	61	9	35	19	116	58	53	1,551

See p. 239 for footnotes.

Series H 161–179. *Chartered bank assets, continuation, 1900 to 1912*
(millions of dollars)

Year end	Specie	Dominion notes	Deposits with government against notes	Balances with other banks in Canada	Holdings of securities			Loans in Canada					
					Government of Canada and provincial securities	Other Canadian and foreign securities	Total	Call	Government of Canada	Provincial	Other banks in Canada[9]	Other current	Total
	161	162	163	164	165	166	167	168	169	170	171	172	173
1912	33.8	94.6	6.4	9.2	9.9	92.3	102.1	70.7	—	5.1	.1	881.3	957.1
1911	37.5	97.7	5.8	8.9	9.1	85.8	94.9	72.6	—	2.5	.6	774.9	850.6
1910	33.4	76.0	5.0	8.2	13.1	84.2	97.3	64.0	—	2.1	3.8	677.1	747.0
1909	27.5	73.2	4.6	8.7	12.8	73.0	85.8	63.6	—	3.1	4.3	592.7	663.7
1908	27.1	66.1	4.1	12.4	10.5	63.8	74.3	43.8	—	3.9	6.3	511.8	565.9
1907	25.1	50.0	4.3	10.4	9.2	61.9	71.1	44.5	4.9	.4	1.3	556.6	607.7
1906	23.8	44.3	4.3	9.8	9.5	62.8	72.4	57.5	—	1.4	5.7	548.7	613.3
1905	19.7	38.1	3.4	8.6	9.2	59.8	69.0	49.7	—	2.1	.7	458.4	510.8
1904	17.6	38.4	3.3	8.2	9.6	56.0	65.5	39.0	—	2.9	.8	413.8	466.5
1903	16.1	30.9	3.1	6.4	10.7	52.9	63.6	39.0	—	2.7	.9	384.5	427.1
1902	12.9	24.7	3.3	4.9	9.5	51.8	61.3	51.4	—	4.2	.7	322.9	379.2
1901	11.6	21.4	2.6	5.8	9.8	46.5	56.3	37.7	—	2.8	.7	289.2	330.3
1900	11.8	19.8	2.4	4.4	12.5	37.8	50.3	34.0	—	3.1	1.6	275.6	314.4

Year end	Certain foreign assets					
	Notes of and cheques on other banks	Balances due from banks and agencies abroad	Call loans	Current loans	All other assets	Total assets
	174	175	176	177	178	179
1912	81.7	33.6	106.0	41.0	60.6	1,526.1
1911	62.1	46.4	92.1	38.0	56.1	1,390.1
1910	48.0	38.3	90.7	40.4	45.5	1,229.8
1909	45.8	31.4	138.5	40.1	38.5	1,157.8
1908	36.4	49.6	97.1	30.4	38.1	1,001.4
1907	33.9	22.4	43.5	22.9	30.1	921.3
1906	38.9	23.4	59.0	36.5	28.6	954.2
1905	28.3	22.7	61.0	30.9	23.0	815.5
1904	23.8	29.9	48.8	17.3	20.6	729.9
1903	21.7	22.0	35.0	18.6	18.6	663.1
1902	20.5	22.7	43.7	34.1	18.1	625.4
1901	17.0	18.3	45.3	32.2	21.2	562.1
1900	16.4	16.9	27.2	20.1	17.9	501.5

Series H 180–196. *Chartered bank assets, continuation, 1891 to 1899*
(millions of dollars)

Year end	Specie	Dominion notes	Deposits with government against notes	Balances with other banks in Canada	Holdings of securities			Loans in Canada and abroad						Notes of and cheques on other banks	Balances due from banks and agencies abroad	All other assets	Total assets
					Government of Canada	Provincial, other Canadian and foreign public	Total[10]	Call	Government of Canada	Provincial	Other banks in Canada[11]	Current	Total				
	180	181	182	183	184	185	186	187	188	189	190	191	192	193	194	195	196
1899	9.6	17.9	2.1	4.8	4.8	31.4	36.2	32.4	—	2.4	.4	266.7	301.8	12.4	34.4	12.4	431.7
1898	9.0	17.1	2.0	4.0	5.1	34.4	39.5	26.5	—	2.8	—	229.9	259.2	10.8	35.4	13.5	390.5
1897	8.3	17.7	1.9	4.3	4.7	30.7	35.5	19.9	—	1.8	—	205.9	227.6	11.8	39.1	13.9	360.1
1896	8.6	15.2	1.8	3.4	2.8	22.5	25.3	14.0	—	.9	.2	210.5	225.6	9.0	26.3	14.5	329.7
1895	8.2	16.0	1.8	3.7	2.8	20.6	23.5	17.1	—	.7	—	202.1	219.9	9.1	26.1	14.0	322.2
1894	8.0	15.2	1.8	3.1	3.1	18.4	21.5	17.8	—	1.4	—	195.8	215.0	8.6	28.4	12.3	313.9
1893	7.7	13.3	1.8	3.6	3.2	16.7	19.9	14.2	—	2.3	—	200.4	216.9	8.3	21.8	10.9	304.2
1892	6.7	12.4	1.8	3.6	3.3	14.9	18.2	20.0	—	2.4	.2	198.5	221.1	8.7	22.7	10.5	305.7
1891	5.8	10.1	.8	3.3	3.1	11.3	14.3	14.4	—	.6	—	186.6	201.6	9.1	24.8	10.9	280.8

See p. 239 for footnotes.

Series H197–213. *Chartered bank assets, continuation, 1880 to 1890*

(millions of dollars)

			Holdings of certain securities				Certain loans in Canada and abroad										
Year end	Specie	Dominion notes	Balances with other banks in Canada	Government of Canada	Provincial, municipal and foreign public	Total	Government of Canada	Provincial	Municipal	Collateral loans	Loans to or deposits made in other banks	Other current	Total	Notes of and cheques on other banks	Balances due from banks and agencies abroad	All other assets	Total assets
	197	198	199	200	201	202	203	204	205	206	207	208	209	210	211	212	213
1890	6.7	9.7	3.3	2.5	6.1	8.6	.9	1.7	2.7	13.4	.5	180.5	199.8	7.7	13.2	11.1	260.1
1889	6.0	9.1	3.2	2.6	5.6	8.2	1.0	.9	1.7	13.5	.5	173.6	191.3	7.8	14.7	11.9	252.2
1888	7.4	10.7	3.6	2.0	4.5	6.5	1.2	.6	3.7	11.7	.7	165.0	183.0	8.3	22.7	13.1	255.3
1887	6.0	10.0	3.9	2.7	3.7	6.4	1.0	2.1	2.1	10.5	.4	154.3	171.0	6.5	16.4	12.4	232.6
1886	6.0	9.4	3.0	4.4	3.0	7.5	1.1	1.6	2.1	13.2	.6	140.1	158.7	7.1	18.0	13.3	222.9
1885	6.7	12.4	3.2	4.3	3.4	7.7	1.2	1.3	1.6	12.6	.9	139.6	157.1	7.9	20.0	12.9	227.9
1884	7.5	11.0	2.3	1.4	1.6	3.0	1.5	.9	1.3	11.9	.7	138.0	154.3	6.1	17.5	14.1	215.8
1883	7.2	11.2	3.3	.9	1.3	2.2	.8	1.7	1.3	10.4	.6	148.6	163.4	7.3	22.3	11.3	228.2
1882	6.6	10.5	3.3	1.0	1.3	2.3	.7	.9	2.0	16.9	.4	156.6	177.4	6.8	13.0	10.8	230.7
1881	6.6	9.9	2.6	1.1	1.8	2.9	.9	.8	.6	14.0	.9	131.5	148.7	5.8	25.6	11.5	213.6
1880	6.0	10.5	4.3	1.1	1.6	2.7	.6	.6	.7	8.0	.7	109.9	120.5	4.6	31.8	12.1	192.5

Series H214–225. *Chartered bank assets, continuation, 1867 to 1879*

(millions of dollars)

					Certain loans in Canada and abroad							
Year end	Specie	Dominion notes	Balances due from other banks in Canada[12]	Government of Canada and provincial securities	Government of Canada and provincial	Collateral loans	Other[13]	Total	Notes of and cheques on other banks	Balances due from banks and agencies abroad	Other assets	Total assets
	214	215	216	217	218	219	220	221	222	223	224	225
1879	6.8	9.1	4.7	2.1	.7	5.9	103.3	109.8	4.6	24.6	16.6	178.3
1878	5.6	8.1	4.5	2.2	1.9	5.8	123.9	131.6	4.4	7.1	14.6	178.1
1877	6.1	8.9	3.5	2.7	1.0	5.5	122.1	128.7	4.4	8.0	14.1	176.4
1876	6.2	8.3	3.6	1.3	.4	6.8	130.1	137.3	4.2	8.2	12.8	181.9
1875	6.9	8.5	3.5	1.2	.2	3.5	130.6	134.3	4.6	9.8	14.5	183.3
1874	7.5	9.6	3.8	1.7	.2	5.6	148.2	153.9	5.6	10.3	8.5	200.9
1873	7.2	9.1	2.7	1.4	.3	2.5	126.4	129.2	4.6	9.8	8.8	172.8
1872	6.3	8.2[14]	2.0	1.5	.5	—	116.1	116.7	4.0	10.8	8.1	157.6
1871	8.8	6.9[14]	2.0	1.4	1.3	—	91.9	93.2	3.0	14.4	6.3	136.0
1870	14.0	—	9.9[15]	4.8[16]	—	—	—	75.7	2.4	—	4.2	111.0
1869	15.1	—	6.0[15]	6.0[16]	—	—	—	62.9	2.3	—	6.9	99.2
1868	12.4	—	8.7[15]	3.7[16]	—	—	—	56.1	2.1	—	6.1	89.1
1867	9.9	—	5.2[15]	5.6[16]	—	—	—	56.7	2.0	—	4.7	84.1

[1] More fully 'Deposits with the government for the security of note circulation'.

[2] Figures for Government of Canada and provincial security holdings for 1957 and after are based on 'amortized values'. Before that year they are based on 'not exceeding market value'. The reallocation of inner reserves which this change in valuation entailed was applied against other asset items, mainly general loans, foreign currency loans and corporate securities. Therefore 1957 and later figures for these asset items are not strictly comparable with those for earlier years.

[3] From 1956 foreign currency loans made by Canadian branches were all excluded from the categories 'Loans in Canadian currency' and included in the 'Foreign currency assets' category.

[4] Figures for 1954 and later are not adjusted for items in transit. This transit item amounted to +37 at the end of June 1954.

[5] Includes 'Gold and coin outside of Canada', 'Government and bank notes other than Canadian', 'Deposits with other banks in currencies other than Canadian', and 'Foreign currency items in transit (net)'.

[6] Includes 'Gold and subsidiary coin held elsewhere than in Canada', and 'Government and bank notes other than Canadian'.

[7] Includes 'Gold and subsidiary coin held elsewhere than in Canada' and 'United States and other foreign currencies'. The latter item was previously included in the item 'Notes of other banks'.

[8] Prior to 1923 includes notes of foreign banks.

[9] Secured loans and bills rediscounted.

[10] Excludes corporate securities other than railway securities.

[11] Secured loans and bills rediscounted.

[12] From 1867 to 1879 presumably includes loans to other banks.

[13] Includes loans against stocks of other banks.

[14] Includes provincial notes.

[15] Includes balances due from banks outside Canada.

[16] Apparently includes loans to government.

Series H226–245. *Chartered bank liabilities and cash ratio, 1867 to 1960*

(millions of dollars)

Year end	Notes in circulation	Advances from Bank of Canada[2]	Canadian deposits[1]							Canadian and foreign interbank deposits	Foreign deposits[5]
			Government of Canada	Provincial governments	Personal savings[3]	Other notice[3]	Public demand[4]	Other banks	Total		
	226	227	228	229	230	231	232	233	234	235	236
1960	—	—	510	119	7,215	576	4,301	201	12,921	—	—
1959	—	—	404	136	6,900	558	4,144	138	12,279	—	2,372
1958	—	2	319	136	6,844	618	4,636	137	12,690	—	2,077
1957	—	—	423	125	6,108	548	4,095	108	11,407	—	1,827
1956	—	—	246	169	6,007	444	4,180	116	11,162	—	1,369
1955	—	2	517	181	5,633	464	3,915	139	10,848	—	1,056
1954	—	—	176	190	5,218	397	3,597	104	9,683	—	1,030
1953	—	—	473	166	4,756	278	3,368	69	9,111	—	963
1952	—	—	49	214	4,600	325	3,373	75	8,636	—	905
1951	—	—	88	185	4,296	316	2,993	95	7,973	—	878
1950	—	—	257	158	4,176	383	2,874	132	7,979	—	835
1949	14	—	164	167	4,086	347	2,483	70	7,317	—	795
1948	16	—	236	149	3,752	305	2,550	80	7,072	—	868
1947	18	—	216	113	3,453	287	2,295	81	6,446	—	898
1946	21	—	281	119	3,179	290	2,293	78	6,240	—	892
1945	26	—	846	86	2,635	230	2,084	60	5,942	—	901
1944	34	—	763	88	2,423		1,862	—	5,136	114	746
1943	43	—	662	88	1,948		1,697	—	4,395	100	655
1942	62	—	417	68	1,673		1,499	—	3,657	85	545
1941	73	—	114	53	1,669		1,268	—	3,104	68	462
1940	84	—	66	67	1,641		1,031	—	2,805	67	405
1939	90	—	130	50	1,741		853	—	2,774	129	474
1938	95	—	64	43	1,660		734	—	2,501	67	420
1937	102	—	13	39	1,583		699	—	2,334	76	409
1936	109	—	25	47	1,548		682	—	2,302	53	418
1935	119	—	12	41	1,486		641	—	2,180	50	379
1934	136	35	24	28	1,407		575	—	2,034	45	325
1933	132	50	33	28	1,357		502	—	1,920	51	322
1932	127	57	53	19	1,378		466	—	1,916	61	329
1931	141	47	111	20	1,360		567	—	2,058	59	310
1930	148	21	27	21	1,426		642	—	2,116	78	372
1929	175	82	60	32	1,434		729	—	2,255	123	442
1928	186	73	46	17	1,520		715	—	2,298	135	383
1927	183	33	43	19	1,445		684	—	2,191	87	374
1926	175	12	16	16	1,373		609	—	2,014	62	334
1925	174	15	22	22	1,319		597	—	1,960	51	354
1924	166	30	25	31	1,238		595	—	1,889	58	334
1923	180	31	38	44	1,180		560	—	1,822	47	300
1922	176	29	19	31	1,185		538	—	1,773	51	288
1921	185	87	34	29	1,241		541	—	1,845	49	271
1920	229	109	10	19	1,293		657	—	1,979	47	357
1919	232	104	121	19	1,138		703	—	1,981	53	275
1918	225	107	148	15	958		711	—	1,832	38	207
1917	193	48	18	17	996		569	—	1,600	33	175
1916	149	7	18	18	845		458	—	1,339	30	163
1915	122	2	26	19	721		424	—	1,190	33	135
1914	106	11	11	20	663		350	—	1,044	33	99
1913	109	—	9	23	625		381	—	1,038	29	103
1912	110.0	—	15.4	24.3	632.6		379.8	—	1,052.1	22.9	87.1
1911	102.0	—	8.1	25.0	591.1		335.0	—	959.2	16.7	80.6
1910	87.7	—	6.0	24.7	544.2		280.9	—	855.8	10.7	70.6
1909	81.3	—	8.2	24.6	499.1		261.3	—	793.2	9.8	75.1
1908	73.1	—	4.3	11.6	429.7		210.2	—	655.8	13.1	66.9
1907	77.5	—	11.3	7.5	402.6		157.2	—	578.6	21.7	53.4
1906	78.4	—	4.7	9.7	398.8		192.1	—	605.3	16.3	64.2

Series H226-245. *Chartered bank liabilities and cash ratio, 1867 to 1905 (continued)*
(millions of dollars)

Year end	Notes in circulation	Advances from Bank of Canada[2]	Canadian deposits[1]								Canadian and foreign interbank deposits	Foreign deposits[5]
			Govern-ment of Canada	Provincial govern-ments	Personal savings[3]	Other notice[3]	Public demand[4]	Other banks	Total			
	226	**227**	**228**	**229**	**230**	**231**	**232**	**233**	**234**		**235**	**236**
1905	70.0	—	5.2	6.3	356.9		155.3	—	523.7		11.3	44.1
1904	64.5	—	5.5	7.1	319.1		134.3	—	466.0		9.4	38.8
1903	62.5	—	3.9	4.0	279.3		120.5	—	407.7		8.9	34.5
1902	60.6	—	6.5	3.1	254.2		115.9	—	379.7		10.0	37.2
1901	54.4	—	4.9	2.8	233.4		102.3	—	343.4		9.0	31.4
1900	50.8	—	4.6	2.9	188.5		109.4	—	305.4		7.5	20.4
1899	46.0	—	4.6	2.5	173.8		99.5	—	280.4		8.5	—
1898	40.3	—	3.5	2.0	157.8		90.7	—	254.0		5.8	—
1897	38.0	—	5.1	2.3	140.1		81.9	—	229.4		4.5	—
1896	33.1	—	3.2	2.3	126.1		70.5	—	202.1		5.9	—
1895	32.6	—	4.9	2.3	119.7		67.5	—	194.4		7.7	—
1894	32.4	—	5.4	2.2	113.2		68.9	—	189.7		6.4	—
1893	34.4	—	3.4	3.0	107.9		62.6	—	176.9		6.9	—
1892	36.2	—	4.4	3.0	101.5		68.7	—	177.6		7.1	—
1891	35.6	—	3.2	2.6	90.2		62.6	—	158.6		4.6	—
1890	35.0	—	3.5	2.1	80.3		53.7	—	139.6		3.8	—
1889	33.6	—	4.8	2.7	71.0		55.2	—	133.7		3.7	—
1888	34.8	—	11.8	2.6	66.2		55.7	—	136.3		4.6	—
1887	34.4	—	5.3	2.0	56.6		49.0	—	112.9		5.1	—
1886	29.8	—	5.5	1.3	50.6		49.2	—	106.6		3.4	—
1885	32.4	—	6.2	2.5	49.7		52.1	—	110.5		3.5	—
1884	31.9	—	4.8	2.6	49.4		42.9	—	99.7		2.9	—
1883	33.6	—	7.0	3.2	52.0		44.6	—	106.8		4.0	—
1882	36.5	—	8.5	2.2	49.4		47.5	—	107.6		4.2	—
1881	32.4	—	11.6	2.1	43.6		46.0	—	103.3		3.6	—
1880	27.3	—	7.6	2.3	37.1		42.2	—	89.2		3.5	—
1879	22.3	—	10.3	.6	30.6		37.9	—	79.4		3.8	—
1878	21.5	—	4.9	.8	31.3		35.1	—	72.1		3.4	—
1877	21.8	—	6.3	1.2	28.4		35.4	—	71.3		3.5	—
1876	22.3	—	6.2	4.5	28.6		35.1	—	74.4		4.4	—
1875	23.3	—	5.9	4.6	26.1		34.0	—	70.6		4.1	—
1874	28.5	—	11.6	4.9	33.5		36.6	—	86.6		12.1	—
1873	29.0	—	6.9	3.1	27.0		31.0	—	68.0		7.2	—
1872	27.9	—	7.9	—	23.4		29.8	—	61.1		3.2	—
1871	24.5	—	9.3	—	21.1		29.2	—	59.5		2.2	—
1870	18.5	—	—	—	32.9		19.2	—	52.1		1.9	—
1869	12.5	—	—	—	28.8		18.8	—	47.6		1.4	—
1868	10.7	—	—	—	23.5		17.6	—	41.1		1.4	—
1867	9.8	—	—	—	17.2		15.3	—	32.5		3.7	—

Series H226–245. *Chartered bank liabilities and cash ratios, 1906 to 1960 (continuation)*

(millions of dollars)

Year end	Acceptances, guarantees and letters of credit[6]	Capital and rest fund			Total Canadian liabilities	Total liabilities[7]	Daily average data (annual)[8]		
		Capital paid up	Rest fund	Total			Chartered bank cash in Canada	Canadian deposits of the chartered banks	Per cent of cash to Canadian deposits
	237	238	239	240	241	242	243	244	245
1960	257	266	730	996	14,263	16,917	985	12,052	8.2
1959	207	254	661	915	13,463	15,835	999	12,187	8.2
1958	197	226	581	807	13,764	15,840	943	11,452	8.2
1957	224	212	512	724	12,417	14,244	870	10,601	8.2
1956	210	195	452	647	12,059	13,428	873	10,527	8.3
1955	203	181	374	555	11,646	12,702	834	9,915	8.4
1954	155	168	344	512	10,403	11,433	853	8,959	9.5
1953	155	153	260	413	9,693	10,656	883	8,624	10.2
1952	199	149	220	369	9,223	10,128	844	8,110	10.4
1951	225	148	209	357	8,580	9,458	792	7,759	10.2
1950	258	146	198	344	8,608	9,443	755	7,487	10.1
1949	164	146	191	337	7,858	8,653	746	7,178	10.4
1948	206	146	186	332	7,649	8,517	711	6,547	10.9
1947	201	146	182	328	7,013	7,911	670	6,209	10.8
1946	213	146	177	323	—	7,708	672	5,916	11.4
1945	141	146	137	283	—	7,311	603	5,284	11.4
1944	121	146	137	283	—	6,441	538	4,575	11.8
1943	112	146	137	283	—	5,594	423	3,895	10.9
1942	113	146	137	283	—	4,752	342	3,263	10.5
1941	124	146	135	281	—	4,121	313	2,975	10.5
1940	68	146	134	280	—	3,715	289	2,722	10.6
1939	53	146	134	280	—	3,807	269	2,582	10.4
1938	53	146	134	280	—	3,419	254	2,412	10.5
1937	64	146	134	280	—	3,269	240	2,357	10.2
1936	67	146	134	280	—	3,233	225	2,213	10.2
1935	58	146	133	279	—	3,070	216	2,080	10.3
1934	51	146	133	279	—	2,910	201	1,966	10.2
1933	49	145	133	278	—	2,806	189	1,941	9.8
1932	43	145	162	307	—	2,843	172	1,955	8.8
1931	55	145	162	307	—	2,983	169	2,103	8.1
1930	78	145	162	307	—	3,129	176	2,141	8.2
1929	113	143	158	301	—	3,504	191	2,293	8.3
1928	99	124	137	261	—	3,456	193	2,254	8.5
1927	83	123	134	257	—	3,217	187	2,085	9.0
1926	75	117	125	242	—	2,926	192	1,958	9.8
1925	70	116	125	241	—	2,884	—	—	—
1924	61	122	123	245	—	2,795	—	—	—
1923	51	123	124	247	—	2,686	—	—	—
1922	20	125	131	256	—	2,603	—	—	—
1921	23	129	128	258	—	2,730	—	—	—
1920	44	128	133	261	—	3,039	—	—	—
1919	51	119	125	244	—	2,951	—	—	—
1918	34	109	116	225	—	2,673	—	—	—
1917	22	112	114	226	—	2,308	—	—	—
1916	9	113	113	226	—	1,933	—	—	—
1915	9	114	112	226	—	1,725	—	—	—
1914	12	114	113	227	—	1,542	—	—	—
1913	9	115	112	227	—	1,536	—	—	—
1912	—	114.9	106.8	221.7	—	1,514.2	—	—	—
1911	—	108.0	96.9	204.9	—	1,379.2	—	—	—
1910	—	99.7	84.0	183.7	—	1,219.8	—	—	—
1909	—	97.8	77.8	175.6	—	1,146.6	—	—	—
1908	—	96.5	74.4	170.9	—	991.8	—	—	—
1907	—	96.0	70.9	166.9	—	910.6	—	—	—
1906	—	95.5	69.3	164.8	—	947.5	—	—	—

Series H226–245. *Chartered bank liabilities and cash ratio, 1867 to 1905 (continued)*

(millions of dollars)

							Daily average data (annual)[8]		
Year end	Acceptances, guarantees and letters of credit[6]	Capital and rest fund			Total Canadian liabilities	Total liabilities[7]	Chartered bank cash in Canada	Canadian deposits of the chartered banks	Per cent of cash to Canadian deposits
		Capital paid up	Rest fund	Total					
	237	**238**	**239**	**240**	**241**	**242**	**243**	**244**	**245**
1905	—	85.3	59.9	145.2	—	807.4	—	—	—
1904	—	80.1	54.1	134.2	—	722.1	—	—	—
1903	—	78.6	50.6	129.2	—	655.1	—	—	—
1902	—	72.8	44.5	117.3	—	616.8	—	—	—
1901	—	67.6	37.4	105.0	—	554.1	—	—	—
1900	—	67.1	34.5	101.6	—	493.8	—	—	—
1899	—	63.6	30.0	93.6	—	429.6	—	—	—
1898	—	63.2	28.0	91.2	—	392.0	—	—	—
1897	—	62.3	27.5	89.8	—	362.2	—	—	—
1896	—	61.7	26.7	88.4	—	330.2	—	—	—
1895	—	62.2	27.7	89.9	—	325.1	—	—	—
1894	—	61.7	27.5	89.2	—	318.1	—	—	—
1893	—	62.1	26.5	88.6	—	307.3	—	—	—
1892	—	61.9	25.1	87.0	—	308.6	—	—	—
1891	—	61.3	23.7	85.0	—	284.5	—	—	—
1890	—	60.1	21.9	82.0	—	260.8	—	—	—
1889	—	60.3	20.4	80.7	—	252.4	—	—	—
1888	—	60.2	19.1	79.3	—	255.7	—	—	—
1887	—	60.4	17.8	78.2	—	231.4	—	—	—
1886	—	61.2	17.9	79.1	—	229.6	—	—	—
1885	—	61.8	17.8	79.6	—	227.0	—	—	—
1884	—	61.6	18.3	79.9	—	215.3	—	—	—
1883	—	61.5	17.5	79.0	—	224.8	—	—	—
1882	—	61.0	—	—	—	149.8	—	—	—
1881	—	59.7	—	—	—	140.3	—	—	—
1880	—	59.8	—	—	—	121.5	—	—	—
1879	—	60.4	—	—	—	105.8	—	—	—
1878	—	64.3	—	—	—	97.3	—	—	—
1877	—	63.8	—	—	—	97.0	—	—	—
1876	—	66.1	—	—	—	101.2	—	—	—
1875	—	66.8	—	—	—	97.4	—	—	—
1874	—	63.6	—	—	—	126.1	—	—	—
1873	—	58.1	—	—	—	104.6	—	—	—
1872	—	51.0	—	—	—	93.4	—	—	—
1871	—	40.5	—	—	—	86.5	—	—	—
1870	—	34.2	—	—	—	72.5	—	—	—
1869	—	33.8	—	—	—	61.5	—	—	—
1868	—	31.7	—	—	—	53.2	—	—	—
1867	—	33.4	—	—	—	46.1	—	—	—

[1] Figures for 1945 to 1960 are on a new basis and therefore are not strictly comparable with those of earlier years. See explanatory notes.
[2] From 1914 to 1934, 'Advances under the Finance Act'.
[3] Prior to 1944 'Public notice deposits', except 1867 to 1870, when it was 'Cash deposits bearing interest'.
[4] 1867 to 1870 'Cash deposits not bearing interest'.
[5] Includes foreign interbank deposits from 1945 to 1960.
[6] From 1923 to 1934 'Letters of credit outstanding'; from 1913 to 1922, 'Acceptances under letters of credit'.

[7] Prior to 1883 excludes paid up capital and rest.
[8] Averages of juridical days except that from July 1954 in accordance with section 71 of the Bank Act of 1954, Bank of Canada notes and Canadian dollar deposit liabilities are averages of the four consecutive Wednesdays ending the second last Wednesday in the previous month. Prior to 1935 bank cash is composed of gold and coin in Canada, Dominion notes, and 'free' central gold reserve deposits; from 1935 to 1959 it is composed of chartered bank holdings of Bank of Canada notes, and chartered bank deposits with the Bank of Canada.

Series H246–265. *Assets and liabilities of banks of Ontario and Quebec, 1856 to 1879*

(millions of dollars)

		Certain cash items									
Year end	Coin, bullion and provincial notes	Specie	Dominion notes	Balances due from other banks in Canada	Balances due from banks and agencies abroad	Dominion and provincial securities	Loans to Dominion government	Loans to provincial governments	Other loans, discounts and advances	Notes of and cheques on other banks	Total assets
	246	247	248	249	250	251	252	253	254	255	256
1879	—	6.3	8.5	4.1	23.7	1.9	—	.5	97.7	4.2	160.5
1878	—	5.1	7.5	4.0	6.2	1.9	—	1.6	117.9	4.0	160.5
1877	—	5.6	7.7	3.1	6.4	2.5	—	.7	117.6	4.1	160.1
1876	—	5.9	8.0	3.4	7.8	1.2	—	.1	128.1	4.0	170.1
1875	—	6.3	7.9	3.0	9.2	1.2	—	.1	122.6	4.3	167.2
1874	—	6.8	9.0	3.5	10.0	1.2	—	—	141.4	5.3	184.3
1873	—	6.4	8.6	2.2	8.5	1.2	.2	—	118.4	4.2	156.8
1872	—	5.8	7.7	1.7	10.1	1.3	.5		107.3	3.7	144.6
1871	—	6.5	6.7	1.9	14.2	1.4	1.2		86.9	2.9	128.9
1870	13.6	—	—		9.7	4.8			72.4	2.4	106.8
1869	13.4	—	—		6.4	5.9			57.4	2.2	89.4
1868	11.3	—	—		8.1	3.5			50.7	2.0	80.7
1867	9.1	—	—		4.7	5.5			50.7	1.8	75.8
1866	8.5	—	—		6.5	6.8			43.1	1.7	70.5
1865	7.6	—	—		6.6	7.8			43.0	1.4	73.0
1864	5.6	—	—		1.6	6.0			44.7	1.2	65.0
1863	6.5	—	—		3.1	5.4			41.7	1.4	63.1
1862	6.2	—	—		2.4	4.6			41.6	1.1	60.5
1861	7.0	—	—		4.4	3.5			40.2	1.1	60.9
1860	4.3	—	—		3.8	2.8			40.1	1.2	57.7
1859	3.4	—	—		2.9	3.3			40.4	1.1	52.4
1858	2.5	—	—		2.7	2.1			31.7	.8	40.8
1857	2.3	—	—		1.5	2.0			30.6	.7	37.9
1856	2.4	—	—		1.7	2.5			32.8	1.2	41.2

		Certain deposits (Canadian and foreign)							
Year end	Notes	Dominion government	Provincial governments	Cash deposits bearing interest	Cash deposits not bearing interest	Total	Canadian and foreign interbank deposits	Capital paid up	Total liabilities
	257	258	259	260	261	262	263	264	265
1879	19.9	9.4	.6	26.1[1]	36.3[2]	72.4	3.5	54.0	96.0
1878	19.2	4.1	.8	26.7	33.4	64.9	3.0	58.1	87.2
1877	19.6	5.4	1.2	24.2	33.4	64.2	2.8	58.7	86.7
1876	20.7	5.8	4.5	25.5	33.8	69.5	3.8	62.1	94.1
1875	20.8	5.4	4.5	22.1	32.5	64.6	3.8	61.3	89.3
1874	25.4	10.7	4.9	29.5	34.1	79.2	10.9	58.5	115.6
1873	25.7	6.1	3.1	23.4	29.2	61.8	6.9	53.2	94.5
1872	24.9	7.4	—	20.4	29.0	56.8	3.0	47.3	84.8
1871	22.9	9.0	—	19.3[1]	28.1[2]	56.4	1.9	38.5	81.3
1870	17.6	—	—	31.8	18.4	50.2	1.8	32.4	69.6
1869	10.6	—	—	26.3	16.9	43.1	1.3	30.7	55.0
1868	9.6	—	—	21.4	16.0	37.5	1.2	29.3	48.0
1867	8.1	—	—	15.4	14.3	29.7	3.5	30.4	41.3
1866	9.9	—	—	12.4	14.3	26.7	3.1	28.4	39.0
1865	12.1	—	—	14.7	15.3	29.9	1.0	30.7	43.0
1864	8.6	—	—	14.5	9.5	24.0	1.4	29.8	34.0
1863	10.5	—	—	10.9	11.7	22.5	.5	27.0	33.6
1862	9.7	—	—	9.6	10.2	19.8	.8	26.4	30.4
1861	13.7	—	—	9.5	9.7	19.2	.3	26.9	33.1
1860	12.5	—	—	7.7	8.3	16.0	1.2	25.7	29.8
1859	10.7	—	—	5.3	8.0	13.3	1.8	23.9	25.7
1858	9.4	—	—	2.4	6.7	9.1	1.4	18.1	19.9
1857	8.8	—	—	2.3	5.8	8.1	.9	17.2	17.8
1856	12.6	—	—	3.0	6.3	9.3	1.1	15.6	23.0

[1] From 1871 to 1879 the heading was 'Other deposits, payable after notice or on a fixed day'.

[2] From 1871 to 1879 the heading was 'Other deposits, payable on demand'.

Series H266–288. *Chartered banks, earnings, expenses and additions to shareholders' equity and inner reserves, 1929 to 1960*

(millions of dollars)

Financial years ending in	Current operating earnings				Current operating expenses						Net income	
	Interest and discount on loans	Interest, dividends, and trading profits on securities	Exchange, commission, service charges and other current operating earnings	Total	Interest on deposits	Remuneration to employees	Contributions to pension funds	Provision for depreciation of bank premises	Other current operating expenses	Total	Net current operating earnings	Capital profits and non-recurring income
	266	**267**	**268**	**269**	**270**	**271**	**272**	**273**	**274**	**275**	**276**	**277**
1960	525.5	182.3	134.6	842.4	270.9	229.7	13.2	18.4	113.7	645.9	196.5	3.7
1959	455.1	169.4	122.3	746.8	241.2	211.6	13.1	16.4	102.5	584.8	162.0	3.3
1958	386.9	160.5	126.0	673.4	203.4	198.0	12.3	14.3	91.9	519.9	153.5	1.5
1957	380.6	118.4	109.5	608.5	183.4	188.3	13.8	12.7	86.0	484.2	124.3	.4
1956	314.2	102.8	96.5	513.5	129.1	167.8	14.0	11.4	77.5	399.8	113.7	3.1
1955	236.3	128.4	89.0	453.7	105.2	153.1	13.6	10.1	70.1	352.1	101.6	− .6
1954	219.3	124.3	81.9	425.5	91.5	143.6	13.6	9.0	63.5	321.2	104.3	1.8
1953	191.6	111.4	75.5	378.5	65.7	133.4	13.0	7.1	56.6	275.8	102.8	− .4
1952	166.3	100.8	70.0	337.1	61.5	125.3	12.6	7.0	53.4	259.8	77.3	− .3
1951	155.7	91.6	68.5	315.8	58.3	117.2	12.3	7.5	51.3	246.5	69.3	.9
1950	125.0	101.3	55.8	282.1	57.9	102.2	11.6	6.7	44.6	223.0	59.1	− 1.4
1949	115.7	99.6	52.7	268.0	55.0	95.2	11.1	4.2	43.3	208.8	59.3	− 1.2
1948	106.5	89.7	47.2	243.4	50.9	87.2	10.6	3.6	40.5	192.9	50.6	− .8
1947	90.1	92.8	46.4	229.3	46.6	78.9	9.5	3.5	35.4	173.9	55.4	− .2
1946	70.7	89.1	43.5	203.3	41.1	65.4	8.0	3.4	30.0	147.8	55.5	.3
1945	60.2	70.9	40.6	171.7	34.8	56.4	3.8	3.2	26.8	125.0	46.7	− .5
1944	57.3	60.0	36.7	154.0	28.7	51.8	3.6	2.3	26.3[2]	112.7[2]	41.3[2]	.4
1943	60.0	51.2	35.2	146.4	24.5	49.1	2.1	2.7	22.5[2]	100.9[2]	45.5[2]	.4
1942	63.5	45.0	30.1	138.6	22.2	48.4	2.1	2.1	19.7	94.7	43.9	.2
1941	64.0	41.7	28.6	134.3	21.8	44.9	2.1	2.2	18.9	89.9	44.4	− .2
1940	61.7	41.0	26.2	128.9	22.4	41.8	2.0	2.2	18.8	87.2	41.7	− .2
1939	57.1	38.4	26.7	122.2	23.6	40.3	1.9	1.8	17.8	85.4	36.8	− .3
1938	58.2	39.2	22.4	119.8	23.9	39.1	1.8	1.8	17.6	84.2	35.6	.0
1937	57.7	39.6	23.3	120.6	24.0	38.6	1.8	1.7	18.5	84.6	36.0	.2
1936	57.5	42.9	22.1	122.5	27.5	37.5	1.5	1.8	17.8	86.1	36.4	− .5
1935	67.2	38.9	30.1	136.2	33.1	37.5	1.4	1.1	19.0	92.1	44.1	− .2
1934	75.5	36.8	21.6	133.9	40.2	37.6	1.3	.9	19.4	99.4	34.5	− .3
1933	79.9	37.7	29.5	147.1	45.4	38.7	1.3	.9	19.5	105.8	41.3	.3
1932	97.7	33.2	27.8	158.7	50.7	41.5	1.3	1.2	20.3	115.0	43.7	.0
1931	108.4	28.8	26.2	163.4	55.1	45.0	1.3	1.6	21.8	124.8	38.6	− .1
1930	131.5	22.0	26.5	180.0	58.7	48.0	1.3	2.9	26.3	137.2	42.8	.1
1929	150.5	22.8	31.0	204.3	65.0	47.0	1.1	3.1	28.1	144.3	60.0	1.8

Financial years ending in	Distribution of net income					Undivided profits from operating earnings, net after transfers to rest account	Additions to shareholders' equity				
	Provision for losses and addition to inner reserves	Provision for income taxes	To dividends and share-holders' equity	To dividends	To share-holders' equity		Rest account			Capital paid up from issue of new shares	Net addition to share-holders' equity
							From operating earnings and undivided profits	From retransfers from inner reserves	From premium on new shares		
	278	**279**	**280**	**281**	**282**	**283**	**284**	**285**	**286**	**287**	**288**
1960	25.2[1]	90.7	84.3	54.0	30.3	− 2.2	16.8	15.7	36.2	11.5	78.0
1959	32.3[1]	65.2	67.8	47.6	20.2	2.7	9.0	8.5	72.7	31.7	124.7
1958	16.0[1]	69.6	69.4	40.0	29.4	− 1.5	14.2	16.8	28.6	10.5	68.6
1957	2.8[1]	56.6	65.3	35.4	29.9	3.2	8.0	18.7	33.3	16.5	79.7
1956	14.1[1]	41.7	61.0	31.9	29.1	− 5.7	15.9	19.0	42.1	14.2	85.5
1955	22.5[1]	37.2	41.3	26.2	15.1	2.4	8.7	4.0	19.8	13.7	48.6
1954	− 32.9[1]	58.0	81.0	21.5	59.5	2.5	9.0	48.0	29.9	16.2	105.7
1953	24.9[1]	30.1	47.4	20.4	27.0	− 6.1	16.1	17.0	1.9	2.3	31.2
1952	27.0	25.5	24.5	18.6	5.9	− 4.6		10.5	.5	− .4	6.7
1951	27.9	19.7	22.6	17.3	5.3	− .7		6.0	5.6	2.8	13.7
1950	20.6	13.9	23.2	15.6	7.6	.6	7.0		—	—	7.6
1949	20.2	15.3	22.6	15.1	7.5	2.7	4.8		—	—	7.6
1948	15.5	13.4	20.8	14.9	5.9	1.9	4.0		—	—	5.9
1947	17.2	16.5	21.5	14.2	7.3	2.3	5.0		—	—	7.3
1946	− 6.9	16.2	46.5	12.6	33.9	− 6.1	40.0		—	—	33.9
1945	21.6	12.0	12.6	9.6	3.0	3.0			—	—	3.0
1944	18.2	12.1	11.4	9.4	2.0	2.0			—	—	2.0
1943	17.0	17.3[3]	11.6	9.6	2.0	2.0			—	—	2.0
1942	17.9[4]	14.6	—	11.6	—	—			—	—	—
1941	16.2	15.7	—	12.3	—	—			—	—	—
1940	17.1	12.1	—	12.3	—	—			—	—	—
1939	15.1	9.2	—	12.2	—	—			—	—	—
1938	14.6	8.9	—	12.1	—	—			—	—	—
1937	15.5	8.4	—	12.3	—	—			—	—	—
1936	15.2	8.4	—	12.3	—	—			—	—	—
1935	23.3	8.3	—	12.3	—	—			—	—	—
1934	13.7	8.1	—	12.4	—	—			—	—	—
1933	20.8	7.8	—	13.0	—	—			—	—	—
1932	19.2	8.3	—	16.2	—	—			—	—	—
1931	12.6	8.4	—	17.5	—	—			—	—	—
1930	15.5	8.1	—	19.3	—	—			—	—	—
1929	35.4	8.3	—	18.1	—	—			—	—	—

[1] After deduction of retransfers from inner reserves to undivided profits and rest account.

[2] For years 1943 to 1929 excludes taxes; for years 1944 to 1959 includes taxes other than income taxes.

[3] For years 1943 to 1929 includes all taxes.

[4] For years 1942 to 1929 includes additions to shareholders' equity.

Series H289–294. *Number of chartered banks and branches, amalgamations and insolvencies, 1820 to 1960*

Year	Number of banks active at year end	New banks: active	New banks: charters not used	Amalga-mations	Insol-vencies	Number of branches in Canada
	289	290	291	292	293	294
1960	9	—	—	—	—	5,051
1959	9	—	—	—	—	4,879
1958	9	—	—	—	—	4,677
1957	9	—	—	—	—	4,529
1956	9	—	—	1	—	4,416
1955	10	—	—	1	—	4,246
1954	11	—	—	—	—	4,088
1953	11	1	—	—	—	3,932
1952	10	—	—	—	—	3,848
1951	10	—	—	—	—	3,776
1950	10	—	—	—	—	3,679
1949	10	—	—	—	—	3,562
1948	10	—	—	—	—	3,410
1947	10	—	—	—	—	3,323
1946	10	—	—	—	—	3,219
1945	10	—	—	—	—	3,106
1944	10	—	—	—	—	3,087
1943	10	—	—	—	—	3,084
1942	10	—	—	—	—	3,129
1941	10	—	—	—	—	3,300
1940	10	—	—	—	—	3,311
1939	10	—	—	—	—	3,319
1938	10	—	—	—	—	3,332
1937	10	—	—	—	—	3,336
1936	10	—	—	—	—	3,398
1935	10	—	—	—	—	3,431
1934	10	—	—	—	—	3,527
1933	10	—	—	—	—	3,637
1932	10	—	—	—	—	3,772
1931	10	—	—	1	—	3,970
1930	11	—	—	—	—	4,083
1929	11	1	—	—	—	4,069
1928	10	—	1	1	—	3,966
1927	11	—	—	—	—	3,870
1926	11	—	—	—	—	3,770
1925	11	—	—	2	—	3,840
1924	13	—	—	2	—	4,040
1923	15	—	1	1	1	4,227
1922	17	—	—	1	—	4,451
1921	18	—	—	—	—	4,659
1920	18	—	1	—	—	4,676
1919	18	—	—	1	—	4,337
1918	19	—	—	2	—	3,440
1917	21	—	—	1	—	3,306
1916	22	—	—	—	—	3,198
1915	22	—	1	—	—	3,159
1914	22	—	1	1	1	3,049
1913	24	—	—	2	—	2,962
1912	26	—	1	2	—	2,813
1911	28	1	—	1	—	2,554
1910	28	1	—	1	2	2,367
1909	30	—	—	1	—	2,164
1908	31	1	2	1	3	1,927
1907	34	—	—	1	—	1,886
1906	35	—	1	1	1	1,745
1905	37	1	1	1	1	1,454
1904	38	1	—	—	—	1,145
1903	37	3	5	2	—	1,049
1902	36	2	1	1	—	904
1901	35	1	—	1	—	750
1900	35	—	1	1	—	708
1899	36	—	—	—	1	663
1898	37	—	1	—	—	622
1897	37	—	—	—	—	555
1896	37	—	—	—	—	533
1895	37	—	—	—	1	530
1894	38	—	—	—	2¹	513
1893	40	—	—	—	1	502
1892	41	—	—	—	—	479
1891	41	—	—	—	—	468
1890	41	—	1	—	—	426
1889	41	—	—	—	—	402
1888	41	—	—	—	—	—
1887	41	—	—	—	—	—
1886	46	—	—	—	5	—

Year	Number of banks active at year end	New banks: active	New banks: charters not used	Amalga-mations	Insol-vencies	Number of branches in Canada
	289	290	291	292	293	294
1885	46	—	—	—	—	—
1884	46	2	2	—	—	335
1883	44	2	1	1	1	—
1882	44	1	3	—	—	—
1881	43	—	—	—	1	—
1880	44	—	—	—	—	—
1879	44	—	—	—	4	295
1878	48	—	—	—	—	—
1877	48	—	—	—	1	—
1876	49	1	1	2	—	—
1875	50	—	1	1	—	—
1874	51	1	1	—	—	230
1873	50	6	3	—	1	—
1872	45	8	2	—	—	—
1871	37	3	2	—	—	—
1870	34	—	—	1	—	—
1869	35	2	—	—	—	—
1868	33	—	1	1	1	123
1867	35	2	—	—	—	—
1866	33	1	—	—	2	—
1865	34	3	8	—	1	—
1864	32	3	1	—	—	—
1863	29	—	1	—	2²	—
1862	31	1	—	—	3	—
1861	33	2	—	—	—	—
1860	31	1	—	—	—	—
1859	30	3	1	—	3	—
1858	30	1	1	—	—	—
1857	29	3	1	—	—	—
1856	26	3	2	—	—	—
1855	23	7	1	—	—	—
1854	16	1	—	—	—	—
1853	15	—	—	—	—	—
1852	15	—	—	—	—	—
1851	15	—	—	—	—	—
1850	15	—	—	—	—	—
1849	15	—	1	—	1	—
1848	16	—	—	—	—	—
1847	16	—	2	—	—	—
1846	16	—	—	—	—	—
1845	16	—	—	—	—	—
1844	16	—	—	—	—	—
1843	16	1	—	—	—	—
1842	15	—	—	—	1	—
1841	16	—	2	—	—	—
1840	16	—	—	—	1	—
1839	17	—	—	1	—	—
1838	18	1	—	1	1	—
1837	19	1	—	—	3	—
1836	21	7	—	—	—	—
1835	14	3	—	—	—	—
1834	11	3	—	—	—	—
1833	8	1	—	—	—	—
1832	7	1	—	—	—	—
1831	6	1	—	—	1	—
1830	6	—	—	—	—	—
1829	6	—	—	—	—	—
1828	6	—	—	—	—	—
1827	6	—	—	—	—	—
1826	6	—	—	—	—	—
1825	6	1	—	—	—	—
1824	5	—	—	—	—	—
1823	5	—	—	—	—	—
1822	5	3	—	—	—	—
1821	2	1	—	—	—	—
1820	1	1	—	—	—	—

¹ Both Newfoundland.

² Charters repealed.

Series H 295–301. *Cheques cashed at individual clearing-house centres, by location, 1924 to 1959*

(millions of dollars)

Year	Toronto	Montreal	Winnipeg	Calgary	Vancouver	Other centres	Total[1]
	295	296	297	298	299	300	301
1959	94,286	64,371	16,911	8,529	14,230	50,543	248,869
1958	82,218	57,779	15,632	7,646	13,144	44,871	221,290
1957	73,498	54,938	13,419	8,319	13,523	41,862	205,558
1956	66,301	52,524	13,753	7,280	12,580	39,852	192,290
1955	55,629	43,262	11,294	5,416	10,398	35,352	161,351
1954	50,647	38,498	11,417	4,985	9,753	32,763	148,063
1953	42,579	34,179	12,073	5,021	9,791	33,775	137,417
1952	36,607	31,720	11,508	4,453	9,194	31,715	125,197
1951	32,272	29,185	10,374	3,349	8,213	28,792	112,185
1950	30,276	26,099	8,960	2,871	6,902	25,528	100,635
1949	24,712	22,037	9,186	2,508	6,157	22,954	87,554
1948	22,655	20,979	8,376	2,073	5,765	20,839	80,687
1947	20,211	20,611	7,381	1,779	5,321	19,194	74,498
1946	19,907	18,828	6,366	1,602	4,354	18,190	69,248
1945	18,761	17,487	6,936	1,524	3,615	20,063	68,385
1944	14,446	15,441	6,986	1,498	3,059	19,246	60,677
1943	13,091	13,762	5,592	1,201	2,636	17,514	53,797
1942	11,541	11,392	3,873	948	2,222	15,551	45,526
1941	11,355	9,905	4,011	924	1,905	11,143	39,243
1940	10,511	8,714	3,847	764	1,673	8,927	34,437
1939	10,174	8,759	3,440	662	1,587	6,995	31,617
1938	10,428	9,006	2,656	651	1,546	6,637	30,924
1937	12,227	10,596	2,989	659	1,693	7,003	35,166
1936	12,169	10,150	4,661	636	1,683	6,630	35,929
1935	10,643	8,307	4,633	617	1,350	5,997	31,546
1934	11,389	8,835	4,682	527	1,321	6,114	32,867
1933	10,222	7,944	4,798	558	1,207	5,253	29,981
1932	8,066	7,136	3,138	514	1,190	5,800	25,844
1931	9,512	9,757	3,280	648	1,416	6,973	31,586
1930	10,655	12,271	3,712	898	1,813	8,142	37,491
1929	13,714	15,558	4,789	1,254	2,366	8,990	46,670
1928	12,673	13,962	5,188	1,097	1,984	8,573	43,477
1927	10,537	11,780	4,005	734	1,596	7,442	36,094
1926	8,210	9,133	3,877	718	1,553	6,867	30,358
1925	7,588	7,766	4,183	622	1,475	6,493	28,126
1924	7,659	7,502	3,793	638	1,410	6,156	27,157

[1] 1924, 31 centres; 1925 to 1947, 33 centres; 1948 to 1959, 35 centres.

Series H302–322. *Statistics of Quebec savings banks,[1] 1875 to 1960*
(millions of dollars)

		Canadian securities						Mortgages and loans					
Year end	Bank of Canada notes plus deposits with Bank of Canada and the chartered banks[2]	Government of Canada[3,4]	Provincial[3,4]	Municipal[4]	Other	Total	Insured NHA mortgages	Other mortgages	Loans otherwise secured	Unsecured loans	Total[7]	All other assets[5]	Total assets
	302	303	304	305	306	307	308	309	310	311	312	313	314
1960	25.6	38.7	86.7	40.7	25.2	191.3	10.4	50.6	8.0	6.4	75.4	19.0	311.4
1959	26.4	28.2	89.7	46.5	21.2	185.6	10.7	47.1	7.1	6.2	71.0	14.9	298.0
1958	24.7	28.2	102.1	53.3	18.1	201.7	10.7	40.0	6.5	5.6	62.8	13.7	302.9
1957	26.3	38.8	85.6	52.2	16.8	193.4	10.1	30.7	8.8	4.0	53.6	12.5	285.7
1956	20.3	44.9	83.2	56.0	15.4	199.4	9.2	20.4	7.8	3.2	40.6	12.4	272.7
1955	18.5	54.9	80.0	56.7	16.2	207.8	5.6	14.1	5.9	2.3	27.9	10.9	265.1
1954	19.5	64.7	68.0	46.9	15.6	195.2	2.7	10.0	5.0	2.4	20.2	8.1	242.9
1953	14.7	91.6	49.0	37.3	10.5	188.4	—	6.7	4.6	3.0	14.3	8.6	225.9
1952	13.6	95.5	48.1	33.1	8.1	184.7	—	4.4	4.4	1.7	10.5	9.3	218.1
1951	16.7	89.6	48.6	27.8	9.2	175.3	—	1.7	4.3	.5	6.5	6.6	205.1
1950	13.0	93.0	51.5	25.2	9.5	179.1	—	.5	4.1	.3	4.9	6.6	203.7
1949	13.8	96.5	46.4	22.5	8.6	174.0	—	.2	4.1	.1	4.4	5.8	198.0
1948	11.3	95.4	41.6	19.4	8.0	164.5	—	—	4.0	.1	4.1	4.9	184.8
1947	11.2		126.1	18.9	6.5	151.5	—	—	—	—	4.4	5.9	172.9
1946	9.9		112.3	22.7	5.5	140.5	—	—	—	—	4.1	4.9	159.4
1945	8.7		97.2	20.8	6.8	124.7	—	—	—	—	5.0	4.6	143.1
1944	7.9		83.6	20.9	5.7	110.2	—	—	—	—	3.4	4.9	126.4
1943	10.7		62.1	21.0	5.9	89.0	—	—	—	—	3.1	1.8	104.6
1942	8.3		49.0	21.7	5.8	76.5	—	—	—	—	3.3	1.8	89.8
1941	9.0		44.6	22.4	5.6	72.6	—	—	—	—	3.2	1.8	86.6
1940	9.0		42.7	23.3	5.4	71.4	—	—	—	—	3.6	1.7	85.7
1939	10.7		45.6	24.9	6.0	76.5	—	—	—	—	3.9	1.8	92.8
1938	9.7		43.3	25.3	5.7	74.3	—	—	—	—	4.6	1.7	90.3
1937	9.3		38.6	24.9	4.8	68.3	—	—	—	—	5.1	1.8	84.6
1936	9.3		34.5	24.8	5.1	64.4	—	—	—	—	5.3	1.9	80.9
1935	7.9		31.9	26.6	3.4	61.9	—	—	—	—	5.3	1.9	76.9
1934	8.3		28.2	27.0	4.1	59.2	—	—	—	—	5.8	1.9	75.4
1933	7.1		27.2	28.4	4.1	59.8	—	—	—	—	7.1	2.5	76.4
1932	8.3		25.6	28.4	4.5	58.6	—	—	—	—	7.8	2.5	77.1
1931	7.9		25.9	29.4	5.0	60.3	—	—	—	—	9.5	2.5	80.1
1930	8.3		23.9	26.7	4.3	54.9	—	—	—	—	11.9	2.5	77.6
1929	8.3		22.1	25.0	3.2	50.2	—	—	—	—	16.6	2.4	77.6
1928	8.5		23.7	26.0	3.2	52.9	—	—	—	—	16.2	2.3	79.8
1927	9.6		23.2	26.2	3.4	52.8	—	—	—	—	14.3	2.3	79.0
1926	9.7		23.2	27.3	3.1	53.6	—	—	—	—	10.6	2.3	76.2
1925	9.4		21.7	27.2	2.9	51.7	—	—	—	—	9.6	2.5	73.1
1924	10.4		20.2	25.5	2.6	48.3	—	—	—	—	10.2	2.3	71.2
1923	9.8		19.6	23.3	2.3	45.2	—	—	—	—	10.8	2.3	68.1
1922	9.7		17.1	21.0	2.3	40.4	—	—	—	—	11.8	2.2	64.1
1921	9.5		16.2	20.5	3.0	39.6	—	—	—	—	11.9	2.8	63.8
1920	9.8		14.2	19.6	3.2	37.9	—	—	—	—	13.6	2.5	62.8
1919	8.5		12.4	19.5	3.2	35.1	—	—	—	—	12.2	2.5	58.3
1918	10.5		8.5	18.8	3.1	30.5	—	—	—	—	9.8	2.3	53.2
1917	7.2		6.9	19.3	3.2	29.3	—	—	—	—	10.4	1.5	48.5
1916	6.5		5.8	19.1	3.3	28.2	—	—	—	—	11.6	1.4	47.8
1915	6.9		2.0	19.2	3.4	24.6	—	—	—	—	11.5	1.4	44.4
1914	5.5		1.7	19.0	3.4	24.0	—	—	—	—	11.2	1.4	42.1
1913	5.4		1.6	19.9	3.6	25.0	—	—	—	—	11.8	1.4	43.6
1912	3.9		4.1	20.2	4.0	28.3	—	—	—	—	11.9	1.4	45.5
1911	4.8		4.1	17.5	3.1	24.6	—	—	—	—	11.3	1.4	42.2
1910	3.2		4.0	15.1	3.1	22.2	—	—	—	—	10.4	1.3	37.1
1909	3.2		4.0	13.8	3.0	20.7	—	—	—	—	9.1	1.4	34.4
1908	3.1		4.0	12.6	2.7	19.3	—	—	—	—	8.7	1.3	32.4
1907	2.3		4.0	11.6	2.5	18.1	—	—	—	—	9.8	1.3	31.4
1906	1.7		4.0	11.8	2.4	18.2	—	—	—	—	9.5	1.3	30.8
1905	2.2		3.5	11.4	2.2	17.1	—	—	—	—	8.7	1.2	29.1
1904	2.3		3.3	9.2	1.6	14.1	—	—	—	—	9.1	1.2	26.7
1903	1.9		3.3	7.4	1.5	12.2	—	—	—	—	9.8	1.2	25.1
1902	1.6		3.3	7.4	1.3	12.0	—	—	—	—	8.6	1.1	23.4
1901	1.8		3.2	7.1	1.1	11.4	—	—	—	—	7.9	1.1	22.2
1900	2.0		2.3	6.2	.7	9.3	—	—	—	—	8.4	1.1	20.8
1895	2.1		6.3		—	6.3	—	—	—	—	7.1	.9	16.4
1890	1.5		5.1		—	5.1	—	—	—	—	5.3	.9	12.8
1885	1.4		3.9		—	3.9	—	—	—	—	4.3	1.1	10.7
1880	2.5		1.6		—	1.6	—	—	—	—	3.8	1.0	8.9
1875	1.8		1.2		—	1.3	—	—	—	—	4.2	1.1	8.3

Series H302–322. *Statistics of Quebec savings banks,*[1] *1875 to 1960 (continuation)*
(millions of dollars)

Year end	Secured advances from — Bank of Canada	Secured advances from — Chartered banks[6]	Deposits — Government of Canada	Deposits — Provincial governments	Deposits — Public	Deposits — Total	All other liabilities[8]	Shareholders' equity[9]
	315	316	317	318	319	320	321	322
1960	—	1.6	5.6	3.8	285.3	294.7	1.4	13.7
1959	—	2.0	12.2	2.1	267.7	282.0	.7	13.3
1958	—	4.1	6.7	4.1	274.1	284.9	1.1	12.9
1957	—	4.7	9.9	2.8	255.1	267.8	.8	12.5
1956	—	7.7	.3	.9	251.0	252.3	.5	12.2
1955	—	5.3	.4	.1	246.8	247.3	.6	11.9
1954	—	3.0	.3	.1	227.3	227.8	.5	11.6
1953	—	2.5	.3	.1	211.8	212.2	.4	10.9
1952	—	1.9	—	.1	205.1	205.3	.3	10.7
1951	—	.8	.1	.1	193.3	193.5	.3	10.5
1950	—	2.3	.3	.1	190.3	190.7	.5	10.2
1949	—	1.4	1.0	.1	185.2	186.3	.4	10.0
1948	—	2.4	.8	.1	171.4	172.3	.4	9.8
1947	—	1.0	.6	.1	160.4	161.1	.6	10.2
1946	—	1.7	.5	.1	146.0	146.6	.8	10.3
1945	—	1.6	.7	.1	129.5	130.3	1.5	9.7
1944	—	1.2	.9	.1	112.7	113.7	2.0	9.4
1943	—	—	.7	.1	93.2	93.9	1.6	3.0
1942	—	—	.9	.1	77.3	78.3	2.8	3.0
1941	—	—	1.4	.1	74.8	76.3	1.6	3.0
1940	—	—	.6	.1	73.8	74.5	2.6	3.0
1939	—	—	—	.1	82.7	82.8	1.6	3.0
1938	—	—	—	.1	80.3	80.4	1.6	3.0
1937	—	—	—	.1	75.2	75.2	1.3	3.0
1936	—	—	—	.1	71.4	71.5	1.5	3.0
1935	—	—	—	—	—	67.8	6.4	3.0
1934	—	—	—	.1	65.4	65.5	2.3	3.0
1933	—	—	—	.2	65.5	65.7	3.4	3.0
1932	—	—	—	.2	66.7	66.9	3.0	3.0
1931	—	—	—	.2	68.3	68.4	4.6	3.0
1930	—	—	.1	.2	67.5	67.8	2.9	3.0
1929	—	—	.1	.2	67.2	67.5	3.3	3.0
1928	—	—	.1	.1	71.2	71.4	1.9	3.0
1927	—	—	.1	.1	70.8	71.0	1.8	2.9
1926	—	—	.1	.1	68.7	69.0	1.6	2.5
1925	—	—	.1	.1	66.0	66.1	1.4	2.5
1924	—	—	.1	.1	64.4	64.5	1.3	2.5
1923	—	—	.1	—	61.4	61.5	1.2	2.5
1922	—	—	.1	—	57.6	57.7	1.2	2.5
1921	—	—	.1	—	57.0	57.1	1.5	2.5
1920	—	—	.1	—	56.0	56.1	1.6	2.5
1919	—	—	1.8	—	50.4	52.2	1.1	2.5
1918	—	—	.9	—	43.1	44.0	4.4	2.5
1917	—	—	.3	—	42.6	42.9	1.1	2.2
1916	—	—	.2	—	42.5	42.7	1.0	1.3
1915	—	—	.3	—	39.2	39.5	1.0	1.3
1914	—	—	.2	—	37.1	37.4	1.0	1.3
1913	—	—	.1	—	38.9	39.0	.9	1.3
1912	—	—	.1	—	41.0	41.1	.9	1.3
1911	—	—	.1	—	37.8	37.9	.9	1.3
1910	—	—	.1	—	33.2	33.3	.6	1.3
1909	—	—	.1	—	30.9	31.0	.5	1.0
1908	—	—	.1	—	29.1	29.2	.5	.9
1907	—	—	.1	—	28.4	28.5	.6	.9
1906	—	—	.1	—	27.9	28.0	.5	.9
1905	—	—	.1	—	26.3	26.4	.6	.9
1904	—	—	.1	—	24.0	24.1	.6	.9
1903	—	—	.1	—	22.4	22.6	.6	.9
1902	—	—	.1	—	20.7	20.9	.6	.9
1901	—	—	.1	—	19.7	19.8	.6	.9
1900	—	—	.1	—	18.4	18.5	.5	.9
1895	—	—	.1	—	14.3	14.4	.4	.9
1890	—	—	.1	—	10.9	11.0	.4	.9
1885	—	—	.1	—	9.0	9.1	.4	.9
1880	—	—	.2	—	7.4	7.6	.4	.9
1875	—	—	.4	—	6.4	6.8	.5	.8

[1] Operating under the federal Quebec Savings Banks Act.
[2] Beginning in 1957 excludes deposits in foreign currencies with chartered banks. Prior to 1935 the item included cash in hand and on deposit with the chartered banks.
[3] Beginning in 1957 figures for holdings of Government of Canada and provincial government securities are based on 'amortized value' and are therefore not directly comparable with preceding figures which are based on 'not exceeding market value'.
[4] Includes guaranteed bonds.
[5] Includes bank premises, poor fund and charity fund investments, deposits with and balances due from other banks (not included elsewhere) and other assets.
[6] Prior to 1954, includes balances due to chartered banks.
[7] Prior to 1948 mostly secured loans.
[8] Includes poor fund and charity fund trust and other liabilities.
[9] Capital, rest account and undivided profits at latest year end, from 1944 to 1959; before that, paid up capital only.

Series H323–332. *Deposits with government savings institutions, 1868 to 1960*
(millions of dollars)

Year	Post Office Savings Bank[1]	Dominion Government Savings Bank[1,2]	Newfoundland Savings Bank[1]	Province of Ontario Savings Office[1]	Alberta treasury branches[1]				Manitoba Provincial Savings Office[4]	Total deposits
					Public deposits		Provincial Government deposits	Total		
					Not bearing interest	Bearing interest				
	323	324	325	326	327	328	329	330	331	332
1960	29	—	28	74	22	30	7	58	—	189
1959	34	—	28	81	23	30	5	58	—	201
1958	34	—	28	80	21	26	6	53	—	195
1957	35	—	28	79	19	23	7	50	—	192
1956	36	—	29	80	15	21	7	43	—	188
1955	37	—	28	72	15	22	6	43	—	180
1954	38	—	27	59	17	20	6	43	—	167
1953	39	—	26	62	18	19	5	41	—	168
1952	38	—	25	59	16	18	3	36	—	158
1951	37	—	25	64	13	16	3	32	—	158
1950	39	—	23	66	15	16	3	34	—	162
1949	38	—	22	64	15	15	3	32	—	156
1948	36	—	—	63	13	13	4	30	—	129
1947	35.8	—	—	61.6	12.8	11.5	1.6	25.9	—	123.2
1946	35.5	—	—	47.4	12.6	10.0	1.9	24.5	—	107.4
1945	33.5	—	—	42.6	12.0	7.4	1.5	20.9	—	97.0
1944	28.3	—	—	38.0	7.3	2.6	2.0	11.9	—	78.2
1943	24.4	—	—	35.7	3.7	1.1	1.8	6.6	—	66.7
1942	21.7	—	—	33.8	2.3	.6	1.3	4.2	—	59.7
1941	22.2	—	—	36.9	1.7	.4	.6	2.7	—	61.8
1940	23.1	—	—	37.1	1.0	.3	.4	1.7	—	60.9
1939	23.0	—	—	40.1	.5	.1	.2	.8	—	63.9
1938	22.6	—	—	40.3	—	—	—	—	—	62.9
1937	21.9	—	—	37.7	—	—	—	—	—	59.6
1936	22.0	—	—	32.0	—	—	—	—	—	54.0
1935	22.5	—	—	22.3	—	—	—	—	—	44.8
1934	23.2	—	—	21.4[3]	—	—	—	—	—	44.6
1933	23.9	—	—	21.5	—	—	—	—	—	45.4
1932	23.9	—	—	23.7	—	—	—	—	—	47.6
1931	24.8	—	—	26.9	—	—	—	—	1.5	53.2
1930	26.1	—	—	23.3	—	—	—	—	2.2	51.6
1929	28.4	—	—	22.8	—	—	—	—	2.2	53.4
1928	23.5	7.6	—	19.8	—	—	—	—	2.1	53.0
1927	23.4	8.5	—	18.8	—	—	—	—	2.2	52.9
1926	24.0	8.8	—	18.4	—	—	—	—	2.4	53.6
1925	24.7	8.9	—	19.2	—	—	—	—	2.6	55.4
1924	25.2	9.1	—	21.3	—	—	—	—	2.4	58.0
1923	22.4	9.4	—	10.6	—	—	—	—	2.1	44.5
1922	24.8	9.8	—	2.5	—	—	—	—	1.2	38.3
1921	29.0	10.2	—	—	—	—	—	—	1.6	40.8
1920	31.6	10.7	—	—	—	—	—	—	.9	43.2
1919	41.7	11.4	—	—	—	—	—	—	—	—
1918	41.3	12.2	—	—	—	—	—	—	—	—
1917	42.6	13.6	—	—	—	—	—	—	—	—
1916	40.0	13.5	—	—	—	—	—	—	—	—
1915	40.0	14.0	—	—	—	—	—	—	—	—
1914	41.6	14.0	—	—	—	—	—	—	—	—
1913	42.7	14.4	—	—	—	—	—	—	—	—
1912	43.6	14.7	—	—	—	—	—	—	—	—
1911	43.3	14.7	—	—	—	—	—	—	—	—
1910	43.6	14.7	—	—	—	—	—	—	—	—
1909	45.2	14.7	—	—	—	—	—	—	—	—
1908	47.6	15.0	—	—	—	—	—	—	—	—
1907	47.5	15.1	—	—	—	—	—	—	—	—
1906	45.7[5]	16.2[5]	—	—	—	—	—	—	—	—
1905	45.4	16.6	—	—	—	—	—	—	—	—
1904	45.4	16.7	—	—	—	—	—	—	—	—
1903	44.3	16.5	—	—	—	—	—	—	—	—
1902	42.3	16.1	—	—	—	—	—	—	—	—
1901	40.0	16.1	—	—	—	—	—	—	—	—
1900	37.5	15.6	—	—	—	—	—	—	—	—
1899	34.8	15.5	—	—	—	—	—	—	—	—
1898	34.5	15.6	—	—	—	—	—	—	—	—
1897	32.4	16.6	—	—	—	—	—	—	—	—
1896	28.9	17.9	—	—	—	—	—	—	—	—
1895	26.8	17.6	—	—	—	—	—	—	—	—
1894	25.3	17.8	—	—	—	—	—	—	—	—
1893	24.2	17.7	—	—	—	—	—	—	—	—
1892	22.3	17.2	—	—	—	—	—	—	—	—
1891	21.7	17.7	—	—	—	—	—	—	—	—

Series H 323–332. *Deposits with government savings institutions, 1868 to 1960 (continued)*

(millions of dollars)

Year	Post Office Savings Bank[1]	Dominion Government Savings Bank[1,2]	Newfoundland Savings Bank[1]	Province of Ontario Savings Office[1]	Alberta treasury branches[1] Public deposits Not bearing interest	Bearing interest	Provincial Government deposits	Total	Manitoba Provincial Savings Office[4]	Total deposits
	323	**324**	**325**	**326**	**327**	**328**	**329**	**330**	**331**	**332**
1890	22.0	19.0	—	—	—	—	—	—	—	—
1889	23.0	20.0	—	—	—	—	—	—	—	—
1888	20.7	20.7	—	—	—	—	—	—	—	—
1887	19.5	21.3	—	—	—	—	—	—	—	—
1886	17.2	20.0	—	—	—	—	—	—	—	—
1885	15.1	17.9	—	—	—	—	—	—	—	—
1884	13.2	16.0	—	—	—	—	—	—	—	—
1883	12.0	14.2	—	—	—	—	—	—	—	—
1882	9.5	12.3	—	—	—	—	—	—	—	—
1881	6.2	9.6	—	—	—	—	—	—	—	—
1880	3.9	7.1	—	—	—	—	—	—	—	—
1879	3.1	6.1	—	—	—	—	—	—	—	—
1878	2.8	5.7	—	—	—	—	—	—	—	—
1877	2.6	4.8	—	—	—	—	—	—	—	—
1876	2.7	4.3	—	—	—	—	—	—	—	—
1875	2.9	4.2	—	—	—	—	—	—	—	—
1874	3.2	4.0	—	—	—	—	—	—	—	—
1873	3.2	3.0	—	—	—	—	—	—	—	—
1872	3.1	2.2	—	—	—	—	—	—	—	—
1871	2.5	2.1	—	—	—	—	—	—	—	—
1870	1.6	1.8	—	—	—	—	—	—	—	—
1869	.9	1.6	—	—	—	—	—	—	—	—
1868	.2	1.5	—	—	—	—	—	—	—	—

[1] As at 31 March.
[2] The Government Savings Bank was amalgamated with the Post Office Savings Bank in 1929.
[3] From 1922 to 1934, as at 31 October.
[4] 1920 and 1921 as at 30 November, 1922 to 1924 as at 31 August, 1925 to 1931 as at 30 April.
[5] 1868 to 1906 as at 30 June.

Series H 333–344. *Credit unions, assets and liabilities, 1947 to 1959*

(millions of dollars)

Year end[1]	Assets Loans[2]	Mortgages[2]	Investments[3]	Cash	Other assets	Total assets or liabilities	Liabilities Shares	Deposits	Other liabilities	Surplus funds	Supplementary information Number of credit unions	Number of members (thousands)
	333	**334**	**335**	**336**	**337**	**338**	**339**	**340**	**341**	**342**	**343**	**344**
1959	394	338	257	131	34	1,155	399	657	29	69	4,566	2,347
1958[4]	320	295	238	127	30	1,009	341	594	18	56	4,485	2,187
1957	258	262	200	108	24	852	272	515	18	47	4,349	2,060
1956	226	236	183	94	22	761	232	468	16	45	4,258	1,870
1955	174	211	163	87	18	653	194	409	11	39	4,100	1,731
1954	151	171	144	71	15	552	161	350	15	26	3,920	1,561
1953	129	155	133	51	21	489	133	320	27	9	3,606	1,434
1952	94	131	120	56	23	424	102	294	8	20	3,333	1,260
1951	76	113	100	51	18	359	81	253	7	18	3,121	1,138
1950	72	98	92	36	14	312	68	221	8	15	2,965	1,036
1949[1]	63	87	92	34	6	282	58	206	4	14	2,819	940
1948	54	75	85	36	4	254	45	194	13	2	2,608	851
1947	41	67	77	30	3	218	32	174	3	9	2,516	779

[1] Includes Newfoundland credit unions from 1949.
[2] For 1947 to 1955 the division of total loans between mortgage loans and other loans has been estimated by the Research Department, Bank of Canada.
[3] A breakdown of investments by type is not available.
[4] Includes estimates for Ontario.

Series H345–372. *Life insurance premiums, claims, net new policies effected and insurance in force, 1869 to 1959*
(millions of dollars)

	Registered by federal government											
	Companies				Societies				Total			
Year	Insurance premiums[1]	Claims[1,2]	Net new policies effected	Insurance in force 31 December	Insurance premiums	Claims	Net new policies effected	Insurance in force 31 December	Insurance premiums	Claims	Net new policies effected	Insurance in force 31 December
	345	346	347	348	349	350	351	352	353	354	355	356
1959	698	223	5,622	40,874	11	4	129	639	708	228	5,751	41,513
1958	649	212	5,130	36,496	10	4	118	581	658	216	5,248	37,077
1957	607	201	4,936	33,087	8	4	79	441	615	205	5,016	33,528
1956	565	181	4,120	29,087	7	4	68	399	572	185	4,187	29,487
1955	520	162	3,155	25,452	7	4	59	366	527	166	3,213	25,817
1954	486	154	2,657	23,135	6	4	49	348	493	159	2,705	23,482
1953	455	137	2,555	21,227	6	4	48	327	461	141	2,603	21,554
1952	423	130	2,287	19,091	6	5	44	307	429	135	2,331	19,397
1951	394	128	1,991	17,236	5	4	40	289	399	132	2,030	17,525
1950	370	122	1,799	15,746	5	4	37	275	375	126	1,836	16,020
1949	350	118	1,636	14,409	5	4	34	259	355	122	1,671	14,668
1948	327	109	1,504	13,105	5	4	31	241	331	113	1,535	13,347
1947	304	102	1,453	11,900	5	4	39	286	310	106	1,493	12,187
1946	284	99	1,394	10,812	5	4	37	268	289	103	1,431	11,081
1945	261	98	1,003	9,751	5	4	29	246	266	102	1,031	9,997
1944	244	93	901	9,139	4	4	27	226	249	97	928	9,365
1943	229	82	888	8,534	4	4	25	213	233	86	913	8,747
1942	216	79	819	7,876	4	4	25	196	219	83	844	8,071
1941	203	75	688	7,349	3	4	19	183	207	79	707	7,531
1940	200	76	590	6,975	4	4	15	178	204	80	606	7,153
1939	198	74	589	6,776	3	4	17	177	202	78	605	6,954
1938	199	67	627	6,630	3	4	21	180	202	71	648	6,810
1937	199	63	672	6,542	3	4	17	174	202	66	689	6,716
1936	201	60	618	6,403	3	4	13	169	204	64	631	6,572
1935	200	57	588	6,259	3	3	13	158	203	60	602	6,147
1934	203	56	595	6,221	3	4	13	167	206	60	608	6,388
1933	207	59	579	6,248	3	3	11	171	210	62	590	6,418
1932	216	60	653	6,472	4	4	12	176	220	64	665	6,648
1931	225	57	783	6,622	4	4	15	184	229	60	789	6,806
1930	221	55	885	6,492	4	4	16	185	225	59	901	6,678
1929	211	51	978	6,157	4	4	20	188	215	55	999	6,345
1928	195	42	1,045	5,608	4	4	22	186	199	46	1,067	5,794
1927	175	38	954	5,044	4	4	21	192	179	42	975	5,236
1926	161	35	909	4,610	4	4	17	193	165	39	926	4,803
1925	147	33	807	4,159	4	3	22	187	150	36	829	4,345
1924	130	31	699	3,764	4	3	17	184	134	34	716	3,948
1923	118	29	631	3,433	4	4	17	188	122	33	648	3,622
1922	107	27	579	3,173	4	4	15	186	111	31	594	3,358
1921	99	24	577	2,935	4	3	16	203	103	28	594	3,137
1920	90	26	699	2,657	4	4	17	203	94	30	716	2,860
1919	75	21	573	2,188	3	2	10	134	78	23	583	2,322
1918	62	28	307	1,785	3	3	5	129	65	31	313	1,914
1917	55	21	282	1,585	6	2	6	110	61	24	288	1,695
1916	48	19	231	1,422	2	2	3	99	50	21	234	1,514
1915	45.1	17.2	221.1	1,311.6	—	—	—	—	—	—	—	—
1914	41.1	14.3	217.0	1,242.2	—	—	—	—	—	—	—	—
1913	38.6	13.5	231.6	1,168.6	—	—	—	—	—	—	—	—
1912	35.7	12.8	219.2	1,070.3	—	—	—	—	—	—	—	—
1911	31.6	11.1	176.9	950.2	—	—	—	—	—	—	—	—

Series H345–372. *Life insurance premiums, claims, net new policies effected and insurance in force, 1869 to 1959 (continued)*
(millions of dollars)

	Registered by federal government											
	Companies				Societies				Total			
Year	Insurance premiums[1]	Claims[1,2]	Net new policies effected	Insurance in force 31 December	Insurance premiums	Claims	Net new policies effected	Insurance in force 31 December	Insurance premiums	Claims	Net new policies effected	Insurance in force 31 December
	345	346	347	348	349	350	351	352	353	354	355	356
1910	29.8	10.9	152.8	856.1	—	—	—	—	—	—	—	—
1909	26.5	10.0	131.7	780.4	—	—	—	—	—	—	—	—
1908	24.7	9.7	99.9	719.5	—	—	—	—	—	—	—	—
1907	23.1	9.9	90.4	685.5	—	—	—	—	—	—	—	—
1906	22.4	8.9	95.0	656.3	—	—	—	—	—	—	—	—
1905	22.1	8.8	105.9	630.3	—	—	—	—	—	—	—	—
1904	20.0	8.5	98.3	587.9	—	—	—	—	—	—	—	—
1903	18.2	7.5	91.6	548.4	—	—	—	—	—	—	—	—
1902	17.1	7.0	80.6	508.8	—	—	—	—	—	—	—	—
1901	15.2	6.8	73.9	463.8	—	—	—	—	—	—	—	—
1900	15.0	6.4	68.9	431.1	—	—	—	—	—	—	—	—
1899	13.0	5.7	67.4	404.2	—	—	—	—	—	—	—	—
1898	12.0	4.9	54.8	368.5	—	—	—	—	—	—	—	—
1897	11.2	5.1	48.3	344.0	—	—	—	—	—	—	—	—
1896	10.6	4.7	42.7	327.8	—	—	—	—	—	—	—	—
1895	10.3	3.8	44.3	319.3	—	—	—	—	—	—	—	—
1894	9.9	4.1	49.5	308.2	—	—	—	—	—	—	—	—
1893	9.6	3.8	45.2	295.6	—	—	—	—	—	—	—	—
1892	9.1	4.0	44.6	279.1	—	—	—	—	—	—	—	—
1891	8.4	3.7	37.9	261.5	—	—	—	—	—	—	—	—
1890	8.0	3.1	40.5	248.4	—	—	—	—	—	—	—	—
1889	8.2[3]	2.9[3]	44.6[3]	232.0[3]	—	—	—	—	—	—	—	—
1888	6.6	2.5	41.2	211.8	—	—	—	—	—	—	—	—
1887	6.0	2.2	38.0	191.7	—	—	—	—	—	—	—	—
1886	5.2	2.0	35.2	171.3	—	—	—	—	—	—	—	—
1885	4.6	2.0	27.2	150.0	—	—	—	—	—	—	—	—
1884	4.1	1.5	23.4	135.5	—	—	—	—	—	—	—	—
1883	3.8	1.6	21.6	124.2	—	—	—	—	—	—	—	—
1882	3.5	1.3	20.1	115.0	—	—	—	—	—	—	—	—
1881	3.1	1.4	17.6	103.3	—	—	—	—	—	—	—	—
1880	2.7	1.1	13.9	91.3	—	—	—	—	—	—	—	—
1879	2.6	1.0	11.4	86.3	—	—	—	—	—	—	—	—
1878	2.6	1.0	12.2	84.8	—	—	—	—	—	—	—	—
1877	2.6	1.0	13.5	85.7	—	—	—	—	—	—	—	—
1876	2.8	.9	13.9	84.3	—	—	—	—	—	—	—	—
1875	2.9	.7	15.1	85.0	—	—	—	—	—	—	—	—
1874	2.8	—	19.1	85.7	—	—	—	—	—	—	—	—
1873	2.6	—	21.1	77.5	—	—	—	—	—	—	—	—
1872	2.3	—	21.0	67.2	—	—	—	—	—	—	—	—
1871	} 4.6[4]	—	13.3	45.8	—	—	—	—	—	—	—	—
1870		—	12.2	42.7	—	—	—	—	—	—	—	—
1869	}	—	12.9	35.7	—	—	—	—	—	—	—	—

Series H345–372. *Life insurance premiums, claims, net new policies effected and insurance in force, 1869 to 1959 (continuation)*
(millions of dollars)

	Provincial licensees												Totals			
	Companies				Societies				Total							
Year	Insurance premiums	Claims	Net new policies effected	Insurance in force 31 December	Insurance premiums	Claims	Net new policies effected	Insurance in force 31 December	Insurance premiums	Claims	Net new policies effected	Insurance in force 31 December	Insurance premiums	Claims	Net new policies effected	Insurance in force 31 December
	357	358	359	360	361	362	363	364	365	366	367	368	369	370	371	372
1959	39	11	418	1,998	6	3	36	275	45	14	454	2,273	753	242	6,205	43,786
1958	36	11	416	2,114	5	3	40	241	41	14	457	2,355	699	230	5,705	39,433
1957	31	9	342	1,733	8	4	68	373	38	13	410	2,106	653	217	5,426	35,634
1956	26	7	295	1,431	7	4	56	348	33	10	352	1,780	605	195	4,539	31,266
1955	22	5	299	1,173	7	4	53	325	29	9	352	1,498	556	174	3,565	27,315
1954	19	5	217	906	8	4	64	385	28	9	281	1,290	521	168	2,986	24,772
1953	17	4	169	775	6	5	55	319	24	8	224	1,094	485	149	2,827	22,648
1952	16	5	142	648	7	4	45	289	23	8	187	937	451	143	2,517	20,335
1951	12	3	108	491	5	3	26	217	17	7	134	709	416	139	2,164	18,234
1950	12	4	101	483	5	3	34	226	17	7	135	709	393	133	1,971	16,730
1949	10	2	81	414	4	3	32	187	14	5	113	601	369	127	1,784	15,269
1948	9	2	81	381	3	2	21	167	12	5	102	548	344	118	1,638	13,895
1947	8	2	84	332	3	2	20	157	11	4	104	489	321	110	1,596	12,676
1946	7	2	76	281	4	2	25	148	10	4	101	429	299	107	1,532	11,510
1945	6	1	55	213	3	2	20	133	8	3	75	346	274	105	1,106	10,343
1944	5	1	38	171	2	2	12	93	7	3	50	265	256	100	978	9,630
1943	3.6	1.1	35.4	138.4	1.9	1.8	13.5	87.9	5.5	2.9	48.9	226.3	238	89	962	8,973
1942	2.7	.9	31.5	108.2	1.8	1.7	10.2	79.3	4.5	2.6	41.7	187.4	224	85	885	8,259
1941	2.2	.9	21.8	85.2	1.8	1.7	11.1	79.3	4.0	2.6	32.9	164.5	211	81	740	7,696
1940	2.0	.8	14.1	66.1	1.5	1.6	8.3	62.6	3.5	2.5	22.5	128.8	207	82	628	7,282
1939	2.1	.9	11.8	64.8	1.4	2.3	7.1	69.8	3.5	3.2	18.9	135.0	205	81	624	7,088
1938	1.9	.8	14.2	64.2	1.4	1.6	7.8	69.7	3.2	2.4	22.0	133.9	205	73	670	6,944
1937	1.7	.5	11.7	55.8	1.4	1.5	7.9	70.2	3.3	2.1	19.6	126.0	206	68	708	6,842
1936	1.4	.4	11.1	53.5	1.6	1.7	6.5	76.5	3.0	2.2	17.6	130.0	207	66	649	6,702
1935	2.5	1.4	13.7	88.1	1.6	1.6	4.1	74.4	4.1	2.9	17.8	162.4	207	63	619	6,579
1934	2.5	1.3	12.5	87.3	1.7	1.6	5.0	76.8	4.3	2.9	17.6	164.1	210	62	626	6,552
1933	2.6	1.5	11.2	90.5	1.9	1.7	4.8	80.3	4.5	3.2	16.0	170.8	215	65	606	6,589
1932	2.8	1.4	11.6	94.9	2.0	1.6	5.0	83.2	4.7	3.0	16.5	178.1	225	67	682	6,826
1931	2.9	1.0	18.1	104.5	2.3	1.6	5.8	97.6	5.2	2.6	23.9	202.1	234	63	822	7,008
1930	2.7	1.0	19.5	95.5	2.4	1.8	6.4	94.9	5.0	2.8	26.0	190.6	230	61	927	6,868
1929	2.7	.7	31.6	104.1	2.5	1.8	5.5	98.9	5.3	2.5	37.1	203.0	220	57	1,036	6,548
1928	2.1	.4	19.8	78.1	2.9	2.1	9.0	121.1	5.1	2.5	28.8	199.1	204	48	1,096	5,993
1927	2.0	.4	15.2	66.1	2.9	1.9	8.9	118.9	4.9	2.3	24.1	185.0	184	44	999	5,421
1926	1.8	.2	17.2	61.0	2.2	1.5	5.3	86.8	4.0	1.7	22.6	147.8	169	40	949	4,951
1925	1.6	.2	16.2	52.8	3.2	2.0	5.1	115.9	4.8	2.3	21.3	168.7	155	38	850	4,514
1924	1.2	.2	11.1	48.7	4.0	2.0	5.1	123.8	5.2	2.2	16.3	172.5	139	36	732	4,120
1923	.8	.9	16.0	39.5	2.6	2.6	6.0	150.2	3.4	2.6	22.0	189.7	126	35	670	3,811
1922	.9	.1	16.8	32.4	3.4	2.5	4.7	142.9	4.3	2.6	21.5	175.4	116	33	616	3,534
1921	.8	.1	13.1	30.1	3.5	2.7	9.4	192.8	4.4	2.8	22.6	222.9	107	30	616	3,360
1920	.5	.1	5.7	18.0	2.7	2.5	7.3	156.8	3.3	2.5	13.1	174.7	97	32	729	3,035
1919	.5	.1	5.7	16.4	3.9	3.5	11.2	207.4	4.4	3.6	16.9	223.9	82	26	600	2,546
1918	.4	.1	4.3	13.0	4.4	4.3	5.2	226.1	4.8	4.5	9.4	239.1	70	36	322	2,153
1917	.5	.1	5.5	17.2	6.9	5.6	14.2	398.7	7.4	5.7	19.7	415.9	68	30	308	2,111
1916	.4	.1	3.2	13.0	4.9	4.5	18.4	335.8	5.3	4.6	21.6	348.1	55	25	256	1,862
1915	—	—	—	—	—	—	—	—	—	—	—	—	—	—	—	—
1914	—	—	—	—	—	—	—	—	—	—	—	—	—	—	—	—
1913	—	—	—	—	—	—	—	—	—	—	—	—	—	—	—	—
1912	—	—	—	—	—	—	—	—	—	—	—	—	—	—	—	—
1911	—	—	—	—	—	—	—	—	—	—	—	—	—	—	—	—

[1] Entries for the years 1875 to 1953 are on the cash basis; entries for subsequent years are on the revenue basis.
[2] Death claims, matured endowments and disability claims.
[3] Including 20 months' business of the Canada Life.
[4] Figure is for years 1869 to 1871 inclusive.

Series H373–408. *Total assets of Canadian life insurance companies under federal registration and assets in Canada of British and foreign companies under federal registration, 1888 to 1959*

(millions of dollars)

Year end	Canadian companies (book values)[1]												Assets held abroad[3]	Assets held in Canada[4]
	Bonds	Stocks	Mortgage loans on real estate	Agreements of sale of real estate	Real estate	Collateral loans	Policy loans	Cash	Investment income due and accrued	Outstanding insurance premiums and annuity considerations	Other assets[2]	Total assets		
	373	374	375	376	377	378	379	380	381	382	383	384	385	386
1959	3,868.5	406.7	2,863.6	5.5	265.3	n.a.	394.6	68.7	78.6	69.4	74.4	8,095.3	2,736.9	5,358.4
1958	3,700.9	367.6	2,609.0	5.1	254.7	n.a.	370.0	79.7	71.2	64.5	60.5	7,583.2	2,574.8	5,008.4
1957	3,528.4	354.6	2,432.2	5.4	227.7	.1	352.1	66.7	65.1	61.9	9.9	7,103.9	2,430.9	4,673.0
1956	3,382.8	355.4	2,228.9	5.7	185.8	.1	320.1	64.0	59.6	56.4	10.4	6,669.6	2,309.1	4,360.5
1955	3,399.2	331.1	1,907.8	6.3	157.3	—	299.0	60.3	56.1	53.3	8.0	6,278.4	2,232.1	4,046.3
1954[6]	3,371.7	331.8	1,575.4	4.6	135.8	—	286.8	52.4	52.6	52.9	8.4	5,872.4	2,131.4	3,741.0
1953	3,352.2	301.6	1,311.9	4.7	109.6	—	269.0	60.6	49.8	101.1	6.8	5,568.2	—	—
1952	3,218.5	295.1	1,131.1	5.5	97.7	.8	251.4	64.5	44.9	92.6	4.9	5,207.0	—	—
1951	3,376.1		995.0	6.7	78.9	1.2	231.4	68.7	41.2	84.8	4.6	4,888.6	—	—
1950	3,332.6		836.4	6.3	56.4	1.8	207.7	48.1	37.7	79.7	5.0	4,611.7	—	—
1949	3,239.3		689.6	7.6	43.1	2.2	192.1	46.5	35.7	72.8	4.8	4,333.7	—	—
1948	3,205.1		548.7	10.4	34.5	3.0	183.5	52.9	34.9	69.0	4.6	4,146.5	—	—
1947	3,139.8		395.3	13.5	32.9	4.6	176.1	58.2	32.5	61.8	4.4	3,919.1	—	—
1946	3,001.7		302.1	19.7	33.3	3.6	171.5	36.7	30.5	56.3	3.8	3,659.3	—	—
1945	2,823.8		266.8	23.7	36.2	.1	176.6	36.3	29.3	53.0	4.0	3,449.8	—	—
1944	2,517.9		256.0	28.2	41.3	—	183.5	29.7	28.7	51.1	3.5	3,140.1	—	—
1943	2,251.0		275.0	30.9	52.2	—	200.1	32.4	29.1	48.0	3.4	2,922.0	—	—
1942	2,013.1		293.6	32.3	59.7	.1	220.7	30.6	30.6	46.3	3.3	2,730.3	—	—
1941	1,828.2		303.6	30.6	67.4	—	234.6	40.5	30.0	45.3	3.3	2,583.6	—	—
1940	1,671.8		306.3	25.8	74.4	.1	245.0	53.2	30.8	45.3	3.1	2,455.8	—	—
1939	1,561.8		304.9	23.1	77.7	.2	246.9	59.0	30.0	43.6	2.9	2,350.0	—	—
1938	1,477.3		300.7	21.5	78.1	.2	255.6	42.4	30.1	42.6	2.5	2,251.0	—	—
1937	1,366.5		298.1	20.2	77.0	.7	259.6	39.9	30.0	42.5	2.3	2,137.0	—	—
1936	1,251.0		298.0	17.7	80.5	.2	261.2	31.3	29.4	40.9	3.1	2,013.2	—	—
1935	1,100.0		300.7	15.1	75.5	.8	272.2	40.2	31.1	41.5	3.6	1,880.7	—	—
1934	993.0		310.8	14.5	69.4	.1	284.5	32.2	31.6	42.5	2.6	1,781.3	—	—
1933	885.2		323.1	13.9	63.1	.1	294.3	31.4	31.8	44.6	3.5	1,691.0	—	—
1932	853.6		335.6	13.0	58.3	.1	295.1	17.1	31.7	47.4	3.1	1,655.1	—	—
1931	860.5		345.4	11.7	53.8	.3	267.6	13.3	29.5	49.4	3.0	1,634.5	—	—
1930	785.9		338.1	14.3	47.2	.8	229.1	18.8	25.8	46.3	3.6	1,509.9	—	—
1929	733.1		327.2	—	34.9	5.1	195.6	6.3	21.9	38.8	3.3	1,366.3	—	—
1928	655.7		294.8	—	29.9	.4	162.8	7.5	19.5	33.6	2.2	1,206.4	—	—
1927	559.2		253.1	—	27.4	.3	141.3	7.2	18.3	28.0	1.7	1,036.5	—	—
1926	494.3		217.8	—	27.5	1.6	128.1	6.8	17.3	24.4	1.2	919.0	—	—
1925	430.5		193.3	—	26.2	1.3	113.8	7.8	16.5	21.5	1.3	812.2	—	—
1924	377.2		175.9	—	26.0	2.4	107.9	6.4	16.7	20.2	1.1	733.6	—	—
1923	313.5		158.4	—	21.9	2.1	91.4	6.1	15.3	17.4	.3	626.5	—	—
1922	277.2		139.6	—	19.5	2.5	77.8	5.3	13.8	15.6	.6	551.8	—	—
1921	243.1		119.9	—	18.1	1.4	60.2	4.5	11.3	13.8	.6	472.9	—	—
1920	227.8		103.9	—	17.2	1.6	49.3	2.9	9.3	11.1	.1	423.3	—	—
1919	204.6		91.3	—	16.8	1.8	44.6	2.4	8.1	9.0	.3	378.9	—	—
1918	179.7		90.7	—	16.3	1.2	43.9	3.9	7.4	7.8	.2	351.1	—	—
1917	149.6		92.7	—	17.4	1.3	42.7	4.2	7.3	7.2	.3	322.7	—	—
1916	125.7		95.9	—	15.1	2.5	41.1	3.7	7.2	6.6	.3	298.1	—	—
1915	104.4		96.1	—	14.1	1.7	39.3	5.2	6.7	6.6	.3	274.2	—	—
1914	94.9		94.8	—	12.8	2.1	36.2	4.2	5.8	6.8	.3	257.8	—	—
1913	87.8		87.2	—	11.5	1.5	30.9	3.4	4.8	6.0	.2	233.2	—	—
1912	86.0		75.2	—	9.0	2.9	25.9	2.9	4.0	5.3	.3	211.6	—	—
1911	82.8		63.6	—	8.0	2.4	23.0	2.5	3.4	4.8	.3	190.7	—	—
1910	79.3		53.2	—	6.7	1.9	20.4	2.3	2.7	4.3	.3	170.8	—	—
1909	72.7		45.3	—	6.2	1.8	18.4	2.6	2.4	4.1	.3	153.8	—	—
1908	64.9		39.8	—	5.5	1.3	16.8	3.7	2.1	4.1	.3	138.5	—	—
1907	59.1		36.7	—	5.2	2.5	14.1	1.6	2.0	3.7	.3	125.2	—	—
1906	55.3		31.8	—	4.8	4.0	11.1	2.0	1.7	3.5	.4	114.6	—	—
1905	49.9		26.7	—	4.8	3.4	9.7	2.7	1.4	3.4	.4	102.4	—	—
1904	44.3		23.6	—	4.9	2.9	8.8	1.9	1.3	3.2	.4	91.2	—	—
1903	38.8		21.1	—	4.8	3.2	7.9	1.6	1.2	2.8	.3	81.6	—	—
1902	33.1		19.6	—	5.0	3.6	7.0	1.5	1.0	2.4	.2	73.5	—	—
1901	27.1		19.1	—	5.1	3.9	6.4	1.1	1.0	2.3	.2	66.2	—	—
1900	22.0		18.3	—	4.9	3.9	6.0	1.0	.9	2.2	.2	59.5	—	—
1899	17.3		17.4	—	4.5	4.8	5.4	1.0	.9	2.0	.2	53.8	—	—
1898	15.2		16.3	—	4.2	3.8	4.9	1.3	.8	1.8	.2	48.5	—	—
1897	12.9		15.8	—	3.9	3.0	4.5	1.0	.8	1.6	.1	43.6	—	—
1896	10.5		14.6	—	3.7	2.8	4.1	1.0	.8	1.5	.1	39.0	—	—
1895	9.5		13.1	—	3.2	2.9	3.6	1.0	.7	1.4	.1	35.3	—	—
1894	8.3		12.0	—	2.7	3.2	3.1	1.0	.7	1.3	—	32.4	—	—
1893	7.1		11.7	—	2.4	3.1	2.7	.3	.6	1.2	.1	29.2	—	—
1892	6.3		11.2	—	2.1	2.2	2.3	.3	.5	1.0	—	26.0	—	—
1891	5.1		9.9	—	1.9	2.5	2.0	.4	.5	.8	.1	23.2	—	—
1890	5.0		9.4	—	1.5	1.4	1.7	.3	.4	.8	.2	20.7	—	—
1889	4.7		8.9	—	1.1	.8	1.6	.4	.4	.7	.1	18.7	—	—
1888	4.4		6.7	—	.6	1.1	1.3	.6	.3	.9	.1	16.0	—	—

Series H373–408. *Total assets of Canadian life insurance companies under federal registration and assets in Canada of British and foreign companies under federal registration, 1888 to 1959 (continuation)*

(millions of dollars)

	British companies (market values)										
Year end	Bonds	Stocks	Mortgage loans on real estate	Real estate	Collateral loans	Policy loans	Cash	Investment income due and accrued	Outstanding insurance premiums and annuity considerations	Other assets	Assets held in Canada
	387	388	389	390	391	392	393	394	395	396	397
1959	222.7	63.9	90.3	12.5	—	8.3	3.3	1.5	2.1	1.6	406.2
1958	211.6	60.0	80.0	6.0	—	7.3	2.7	1.3	2.0	3.4	374.3
1957	182.1	46.0	71.8	5.2	—	6.7	2.9	1.1	1.7	.1	317.5
1956	161.1	49.7	59.1	3.8	—	5.6	2.8	.9	1.3	.1	284.3
1955	159.8	44.7	45.6	3.8	—	4.8	3.1	.8	1.1	.1	263.9
1954[6]	153.0	34.9	33.8	3.0	—	4.4	4.4	.8	1.1	.1	235.5
1953	124.1	27.1	31.8	3.0	—	3.9	2.7	.8	1.9	.3	195.6
1952	113.4	24.0	22.0	2.6	—	3.6	2.5	.6	1.0	—	169.8
1951		131.0	14.8	2.4	—	3.2	1.9	.6	1.1	—	155.0
1950		126.3	9.2	2.2	—	2.8	2.8	.5	.9	—	144.6
1949		111.2	7.5	2.2	—	2.5	3.6	.5	.8	.1	128.3
1948		102.8	7.0	2.1	—	2.3	3.7	.4	.8	.1	119.1
1947		82.7	5.0	1.4	—	2.1	2.7	.3	.8	.1	95.0
1946		61.1	5.1	.5	—	2.1	1.7	.3	.7	—	71.6
1945		58.5	5.0	.4	—	2.1	1.3	.4	.6	—	68.3
1944		53.9	5.3	.5	—	2.3	1.3	.4	.5	—	64.3
1943		51.7	6.1	.8	—	2.6	1.0	.4	.5	—	63.2
1942		46.9	6.6	.8	—	2.9	1.1	.5	.5	—	59.2
1941		48.3	7.3	.9	—	3.1	1.4	.5	.5	—	62.0
1940		44.7	7.7	1.2	—	3.5	1.2	.5	.5	.1	59.4
1939		52.8	8.2	1.1	—	3.7	1.3	.5	.5	—	68.1
1938		55.2	8.9	1.1	—	3.8	.9	.5	.5	.1	71.1
1937		52.6	9.6	1.1	—	4.0	.9	.5	.5	—	69.1
1936		53.9	10.2	1.0	—	4.0	.8	.6	.5	.1	71.1
1935		51.2	10.9	.9	—	4.3	1.0	.6	.5	.1	69.4
1934		52.9	11.3	.9	—	4.6	1.2	.6	.5	.1	72.1
1933		42.8	11.7	.8	—	4.7	.8	.6	.5	.1	62.0
1932		40.8	12.1	.8	—	4.8	.8	.6	.5	.1	60.6
1931		38.6	12.3	.7	—	4.7	.7	.6	.6	.3	58.4
1930		36.9	12.5	.7	—	4.1	.9	.6	.5	.2	56.5
1929		32.1	13.0	.8	—	4.0	.8	.5	.5	.1	51.9
1928		32.7	13.5	.9	—	3.8	.6	.5	.5	.1	52.5
1927		32.2	13.3	.9	—	3.6	.7	.4	.5	—	51.7
1926		32.2	13.2	1.0	—	3.5	.4	.4	.6	—	51.3
1925		30.6	12.8	.8	—	3.4	.6	.4	.6	—	49.3
1924		30.2	11.2	.9	—	3.3	.6	.4	.6	—	47.1
1923		29.2	10.8	.8	—	3.2	.4	.4	.5	—	45.3
1922		25.3	10.1	.8	—	3.2	.8	.4	.5	—	41.1
1921		21.5	10.7	.9	—	3.0	.8	.4	.4	.1	37.8
1920		19.6	12.7	.9	—	2.6	.8	.4	.4	.1	37.5
1919		20.0	13.0	1.3	—	2.4	.8	.4	.4	.1	38.4
1918		17.8	14.2	1.1	.2	2.5	.7	.5	.4	.4	37.7
1917		16.0	15.7	1.0	.2	2.5	.7	.4	.3	—	36.9
1916		16.0	16.9	1.0	.2	2.7	.8	.4	.3	—	38.3
1915		14.7	17.8	1.0	.2	2.7	.7	.4	.3	—	37.8
1914		15.3	18.4	.9	.1	2.6	.9	.4	.4	—	38.9
1913		15.1	17.9	.9	.1	2.4	.4	.3	.4	—	37.6
1912		16.4	12.4	.9	.1	2.0	.4	.2	.3	—	32.7
1911		16.3	10.1	.6	.1	1.9	.1	.2	.3	—	29.7
1910		15.3	9.1	.7	.1	1.8	.3	.2	.3	—	27.7
1909		14.7	8.9	.7	.1	1.7	.3	.2	.3	—	26.9
1908		14.1	7.9	.7	.1	1.7	.5	.1	.3	—	25.5
1907		13.5	7.6	.8	.4	1.5	.2	.1	.3	—	24.5
1906		13.3	7.3	.8	.4	1.3	.3	.1	.3	—	23.7
1905		15.2	7.3	.9	.2	1.2	.4	.1	.3	—	25.6
1904		14.3	7.3	.9	.6	1.1	.2	.1	.3	—	24.7
1903		13.8	7.3	.9	.7	1.0	.2	.1	.3	—	24.3
1902		13.3	7.7	1.1	.5	1.0	.6	.1	.3	—	24.6
1901		13.0	8.2	1.1	.4	1.0	.5	.1	.3	—	24.5
1900		12.7	8.5	1.0	—	.9	.3	.1	.3	—	23.9
1899		12.7	8.2	.9	.1	.9	.3	.1	.3	—	23.5
1898		12.7	8.2	.9	—	.8	.3	.1	.2	—	23.3
1897		12.2	7.8	.7	.2	.7	.6	.1	.2	—	22.5
1896		11.4	7.7	.6	—	.8	.4	.1	.2	—	21.3
1895		11.2	7.3	.6	—	.8	.3	.1	.2	—	20.5
1894		11.0	6.5	.5	—	.7	.3	.1	.2	—	19.3
1893		9.6	5.8	.5	—	.6	.3	.1	.2	—	17.1
1892		8.6	5.3	.5	—	.5	.3	.1	.2	—	15.6
1891		6.9	4.5	.5	—	.4	.2	.1	.2	—	12.7
1890		6.1	3.6	.4	—	.4	.1	.1	.2	—	11.1
1889		5.3	2.9	.5	—	.4	.1	—	.2	—	9.5
1888		—	—	—	—	—	—	—	—	—	—

Series H373–408. *Total assets of Canadian life insurance companies under federal registration and assets in Canada of British and foreign companies under federal registration, 1888 to 1959 (continuation)*

(millions of dollars)

Year end	Foreign companies (market values)										
	Bonds	Stocks	Mortgage loans on real estate	Real estate	Policy loans	Cash	Investment income due and accrued	Outstanding insurance premiums and annuity considerations	Other assets	Assets held in Canada	Total assets held in Canada[5]
	398	399	400	401	402	403	404	405	406	407	408
1959	1,026.7	1.7	349.2	6.9	70.0	14.6	17.6	7.3	.3	1,494.3	7,258.9
1958	1,008.3	1.8	311.5	6.1	66.6	15.3	16.2	6.9	.2	1,432.9	6,815.6
1957	990.2	1.7	298.2	4.4	64.8	10.9	15.0	6.3	.3	1,391.8	6,382.3
1956	919.1	1.9	232.3	3.0	61.8	10.8	13.4	5.7	.1	1,248.1	5,892.9
1955	977.0	2.0	191.9	2.4	58.6	11.9	12.0	4.9	.1	1,260.8	5,571.0
1954[6]	967.7	.8	164.3	1.1	57.0	9.4	12.4	5.4	—	1,218.2	5,194.7
1953	883.4	.8	147.6	1.4	53.7	20.4	11.8	22.3	—	1,141.3	—
1952	841.2	—	122.1	1.4	51.5	22.2	11.0	20.5	.1	1,070.0	—
1951	821.8		92.9	1.4	49.1	20.1	10.1	19.9	.1	1,015.4	—
1950	853.6		36.6	1.5	45.1	24.5	9.4	18.2	.1	989.0	—
1949	843.0		7.4	1.5	43.3	23.3	8.1	16.6	—	943.7	—
1948	786.7		4.9	1.5	41.6	14.7	8.1	15.5	—	873.0	—
1947	762.3		5.1	1.5	41.1	19.5	8.2	14.6	—	852.2	—
1946	729.5		7.2	1.5	40.7	25.0	7.9	13.5	.1	825.3	—
1945	680.4		7.6	1.5	41.7	18.2	7.4	12.9	.1	769.8	—
1944	618.3		12.8	2.5	43.8	15.2	7.4	11.9	.1	711.9	—
1943	572.4		18.0	2.6	47.1	15.8	6.9	11.1	—	674.0	—
1942	507.5		18.4	2.8	50.5	19.7	7.1	10.1	—	616.2	—
1941	474.3		19.1	4.8	53.0	14.4	6.8	9.4	—	581.7	—
1940	440.1		19.8	5.2	54.7	11.6	6.8	8.8	—	547.0	—
1939	416.5		17.5	5.5	58.6	15.8	6.4	8.5	—	528.9	—
1938	399.7		21.7	5.7	60.2	10.0	6.1	8.2	—	511.7	—
1937	383.7		22.1	6.6	60.5	9.9	6.1	8.2	—	497.1	—
1936	391.1		25.0	5.7	60.3	9.9	6.2	8.3	—	506.5	—
1935	376.6		26.6	5.3	60.7	8.4	6.2	8.5	—	492.3	—
1934	372.1		28.0	2.6	61.2	8.1	6.3	8.7	—	486.9	—
1933	340.8		29.6	2.6	60.5	6.6	6.2	8.5	—	454.8	—
1932	340.8		30.3	2.6	58.0	6.0	6.0	8.8	—	452.5	—
1931	331.4		31.2	2.4	50.8	7.2	5.7	8.9	—	437.6	—
1930	311.8		30.5	2.4	43.3	5.8	5.3	8.4	—	407.5	—
1929	267.5		23.4	2.4	37.0	4.7	4.5	7.2	.8	348.5	—
1928	242.2		23.5	2.5	31.0	4.4	4.0	6.8	—	314.4	—
1927	220.0		23.8	2.8	26.9	3.9	3.5	5.6	—	286.5	—
1926	190.8		19.1	3.8	24.1	3.1	3.2	5.1	.1	249.4	—
1925	173.2		12.4	1.8	21.7	2.8	2.9	4.5	—	219.2	—
1924	163.1		10.2	1.2	19.5	4.3	2.6	4.1	—	204.9	—
1923	148.7		9.5	.6	17.6	3.1	2.4	3.8	—	185.6	—
1922	132.7		8.8	.5	16.0	2.6	2.2	3.4	—	166.2	—
1921	114.1		9.0	.5	14.0	4.3	1.7	3.1	—	147.0	—
1920	99.4		9.1	.2	12.0	3.9	1.5	2.8	—	129.1	—
1919	86.1		10.1	.2	11.3	2.1	1.4	2.3	—	113.5	—
1918	71.5		10.6	.1	11.2	2.0	1.3	1.8	—	98.6	—
1917	62.4		10.8	.1	11.0	4.2	1.3	1.5	—	91.3	—
1916	55.1		11.1	.1	10.8	2.5	1.2	1.4	—	82.1	—
1915	49.7		12.0	.1	10.9	2.4	1.2	1.3	—	77.5	—
1914	50.8		9.2	.1	10.0	.8	1.0	1.2	—	73.1	—
1913	46.7		11.4	.2	8.7	.7	.9	1.1	—	69.7	—
1912	46.0		5.8	.1	7.0	.4	.8	1.0	—	60.9	—
1911	43.1		3.1	.1	6.6	.5	.6	.8	—	54.8	—
1910	39.9		3.0	.1	6.0	.9	.5	.7	—	51.2	—
1909	38.0		.8	.1	6.1	.8	.5	.7	—	47.0	—
1908	38.4		.8	.4	5.5	.6	.5	.6	—	46.8	—
1907	35.0		.9	.4	4.7	.4	.2	.6	—	42.3	—
1906	35.6		1.0	.4	3.7	.6	.2	.6	—	42.2	—
1905	34.5		1.0	.4	3.0	.7	.2	.7	—	40.5	—
1904	33.1		.7	.4	2.7	.6	.1	.6	.4	38.8	—
1903	30.2		.6	.4	2.4	1.0	.1	.6	—	35.3	—
1902	27.8		.7	.4	1.9	.6	.2	.5	—	32.2	—
1901	25.9		.7	.4	1.6	.5	.1	.5	—	29.8	—
1900	24.4		.8	.4	1.3	.5	.1	.5	—	27.9	—
1899	23.8		.8	.4	1.0	.3	.1	.4	—	26.7	—
1898	20.6		.6	.4	.7	.9	.1	.3	—	23.6	—
1897	19.6		.5	.5	.6	.7	.1	.3	—	22.3	—
1896	18.3		.4	.5	.6	.6	—	.3	—	20.8	—
1895	15.5		.3	.5	.5	.2	.1	.3	—	17.4	—
1894	14.3		.6	.5	.4	.2	—	.4	—	16.4	—
1893	13.2		.6	.5	.4	.3	—	.4	—	15.3	—
1892	12.3		.3	.5	.2	.3	—	.4	—	14.1	—
1891	10.7		.3	.5	.3	.2	—	.3	—	12.3	—
1890	9.6		.2	.8	.3	.2	—	.3	—	11.3	—
1889	7.1		—	.7	.2	.2	—	.3	—	8.7	—
1888	—		—	—	—	—	—	—	—	—	—

¹ Prior to 1910 at market values mostly.

² From 1958 on, includes shares purchased under mutualization plan, which in that year was an innovation. Figure for 1958, 46.7; for 1959, 59.3. From 1888 to 1909 includes the item 'agents' balances and bills receivable'.

³ A residual, series 384 minus series 386. No allowance made for exchange valuation adjustment in series 384 (see footnote 4).

⁴ Consists of assets physically held in Canada. Foreign pay securities are converted into Canadian dollars at the rate £1 = $2.80 U.S. = $2.80 Canadian.

⁵ Use of this figure deserves caution. Note that it is composed of essentially dissimilar items: in the case of Canadian companies, book values; British and foreign, market values. Total assets held in Canada at book values as reported by the Bank of Canada: 1954, $5,226; 1955, $5,586; 1956, $6,009; 1957, $6,511; 1958, $6,933; 1959, $7,474 (millions of dollars).

⁶ Owing to changes in actuarial practice these figures are not strictly comparable with those for earlier years.

Series H409–423. *Percentage distribution of mortgage loans, average interest rates and average term of loans of twelve insurance companies, 1926 to 1955*

Year end	Value of mortgage loans, by type of property (in per cents)					Average interest rates[1] (in per cents)					Average term of loans (in years)				
	Nonfarm					Nonfarm					Nonfarm				
	Residential	Other	Total	Farm	Total	Residential	Other	Total	Farm	Total	Residential	Other	Total	Farm	Total
	409	**410**	**411**	**412**	**413**	**414**	**415**	**416**	**417**	**418**	**419**	**420**	**421**	**422**	**423**
1955	62.4	37.5	99.9	—	100.0	5.91	5.68	5.82	6.11	5.82	5.2	6.9	5.4	—	5.4
1954	61.9	38.0	99.9	—	100.0	6.06	5.86	5.99	6.00	5.99	6.7	9.4	7.1	—	7.1
1953	63.7	36.2	99.9	—	100.0	6.03	5.92	5.99	6.15	5.99	5.4	8.6	5.9	6.7	5.9
1952	73.3	26.4	99.7	—	100.0	5.81	5.54	5.74	6.24	5.74	5.2	6.7	5.3	4.0	5.3
1951	72.4	27.3	99.7	—	100.0	5.36	4.89	5.24	6.04	5.24	5.3	12.2	6.1	6.9	6.1
1950	71.1	28.4	99.5	.5	100.0	5.03	4.59	4.91	5.66	4.91	5.7	6.4	5.7		5.6
1949	74.5	24.7	99.2	.8	100.0	5.01	4.70	4.93	5.67	4.94	6.2	11.2	7.5	6.6	7.5
1948	69.2	29.8	99.0	1.0	100.0	4.98	4.56	4.85	5.53	4.86	5.9	12.9	7.9	6.4	7.9
1947	69.7	29.2	98.9	1.1	100.0	4.97	4.59	4.85	5.49	4.86	7.2	8.9	7.6	7.0	7.6
1946	65.9	33.2	99.1	.9	100.0	5.01	4.68	4.90	5.64	4.91	7.3	9.3	8.0	7.0	8.0
1945	72.0	27.5	99.5	.5	100.0	5.02	4.77	4.95	5.63	4.95	6.6	9.1	7.4	6.9	7.4
1944	76.5	22.4	98.9	1.1	100.0	5.07	4.96	5.05	5.65	5.05	6.8	6.6	6.7	7.7	6.7
1943	76.5	22.6	99.1	.9	100.0	5.12	4.90	5.07	5.11	5.07	6.6	8.4	7.0	8.4	7.0
1942	81.0	18.6	99.6	—	100.0	5.11	4.86	5.06	5.62	5.06	6.4	7.2	6.5	11.1	6.5
1941	65.9	33.9	99.8	—	100.0	5.11	4.96	5.06	5.26	5.06	7.2	8.7	7.7	9.6	7.7
1940	52.3	47.2	99.5	.5	100.0	5.09	4.76	4.93	5.78	4.94	7.5	11.1	9.2	8.2	9.2
1939	54.1	45.2	99.3	.7	100.0	5.08	4.98	5.03	5.54	5.03	7.4	10.0	8.6	6.1	8.6
1938	49.4	48.2	97.6	2.4	100.0	5.17	5.01	5.09	5.69	5.11	6.4	7.3	6.9	6.7	6.9
1937	60.8	38.7	99.5	.5	100.0	5.29	5.14	5.23	5.49	5.23	6.5	8.7	7.4	6.8	7.3
1936	63.7	35.7	99.4	.6	100.0	5.47	5.13	5.35	5.61	5.35	6.4	6.9	6.6	5.5	6.6
1935	68.6	28.0	96.6	3.4	100.0	5.62	5.62	5.65	5.91	5.63	5.8	6.8	6.1	8.6	6.5
1934	74.8	24.4	99.2	.8	100.0	6.08	6.12	6.09	6.48	6.09	5.7	9.5	6.6	5.3	6.6
1933	76.7	20.9	97.6	2.4	100.0	6.51	5.51	6.30	5.58	6.28	5.4	11.7	6.8	10.0	6.8
1932	53.9	44.1	98.0	2.0	100.0	6.51	6.34	6.43	6.66	6.44	6.6	12.4	9.2	7.2	9.2
1931	66.6	31.8	98.4	1.6	100.0	6.34	6.27	6.32	7.61	6.34	7.1	8.3	7.4	6.1	7.4
1930	58.5	31.2	89.7	10.3	100.0	6.50	6.29	6.43	7.70	6.56	6.5	7.8	7.0	7.0	7.0
1929	51.8	34.7	86.5	13.5	100.0	6.47	6.14	6.34	7.23	6.46	6.4	9.2	7.5	9.7	7.8
1928	53.4	30.4	83.8	16.2	100.0	6.38	6.04	6.25	7.28	6.42	6.5	8.2	7.1	8.2	7.3
1927	57.0	29.3	86.3	13.7	100.0	6.45	6.17	6.36	7.31	6.49	6.6	7.9	7.0	7.8	7.1
1926	59.8	29.4	89.2	10.8	100.0	6.50	6.23	6.41	7.47	6.53	7.2	8.1	7.5	8.6	7.6

Average weight by amount.

Series H424–451. *Fire insurance statistics, 1869 to 1959*

(millions of dollars)

	Registered by the federal government															
Year	Canadian companies				British companies				Foreign companies				Total			
	Net premiums	Amount of policies taken during year	Amount of risk at date of statement	Net claims	Net premiums	Amount of policies taken during year	Amount of risk at date of statement	Net claims	Net premiums	Amount of policies taken during year	Amount of risk at date of statement	Net claims	Net premiums	Amount of policies taken during year	Amount of risk at date of statement	Net claims
	424	425	426	427	428	429	430	431	432	433	434	435	436	437	438	439
1959	52	—	—	26	74	—	—	38	71	—	—	33	197	—	—	96
1958	49	—	—	24	68	—	—	33	60	—	—	31	177	—	—	88
1957	44	—	—	25	59	—	—	44	53	—	—	41	156	—	—	110
1956	42	—	—	21	57	—	—	31	56	—	—	34	156	—	—	86
1955	41	—	—	19	53	—	—	30	53	—	—	29	146	—	—	78
1954	39	12,068	10,812	18	55	17,265	16,519	26	54	15,394	18,275	26	148	44,728	45,606	70
1953	38	10,493	9,645	15	54	16,158	15,170	27	54	14,560	16,773	25	146	41,211	41,703	67
1952	34	9,108	8,389	13	52	13,457	13,678	24	54	12,807	15,251	24	140	35,372	37,317	61
1951	29	7,513	7,120	12	51	13,021	12,684	21	54	12,369	13,687	19	134	32,904	33,491	52
1950	25	6,441	6,249	13	46	11,177	11,016	24	45	9,894	11,692	22	116	27,512	28,957	59
1949	24	5,684	5,496	10	41	9,578	9,945	18	39	9,042	10,530	18	104	24,304	25,971	47
1948	21	5,182	4,827	10	38	9,244	8,708	17	39	10,913	9,486	18	98	25,339	23,021	45
1947	19	4,574	4,204	8	31	7,602	7,213	14	37	9,972	8,510	18	87	22,149	19,927	40
1946	16	3,581	3,677	7	23	6,124	6,377	13	30	7,078	7,323	15	69	16,783	17,376	35
1945	14	3,224	3,288	6	20	5,310	5,444	11	24	6,000	6,323	13	58	14,534	15,055	31
1944	13	3,200	3,105	6	19	5,243	5,073	10	22	6,130	5,997	13	55	14,573	14,174	29
1943	12	2,806	2,960	5	16	4,536	4,903	8	19	5,497	5,524	9	47	12,839	13,387	22
1942	12	2,756	2,844	5	16	4,784	4,641	7	19	5,220	5,081	9	47	12,759	12,566	20
1941	12	2,927	2,532	4	18	5,247	4,270	6	20	5,172	4,585	7	49	13,346	11,387	18
1940	10	2,535	2,308	3	15	4,859	4,179	5	17	4,678	4,251	7	42	12,072	10,738	15
1939	9	2,157	2,144	3	15	4,839	4,042	6	16	4,121	4,014	7	41	11,117	10,200	16
1938	9	2,120	2,060	3	16	4,444	3,982	7	17	3,859	3,912	7	42	10,423	9,954	17
1937	9	2,055	1,968	3	17	4,049	4,026	6	17	3,729	3,779	6	42	10,432	9,773	15
1936	8	1,733	1,686	3	16	4,292	3,980	6	16	3,557	3,583	6	40	9,582	9,248	14
1935	8	1,774	1,660	3	17	4,522	4,079	6	16	3,346	3,043	6	41	9,642	8,783	15
1934	8	1,820	1,647	3	18	4,523	4,201	7	15	3,163	2,957	6	41	9,507	8,805	17
1933	8	1,861	1,682	4	19	5,267	4,286	10	15	3,516	3,039	8	42	10,644	9,008	22
1932	8	1,978	1,689	5	20	4,547	4,365	12	18	3,184	3,248	13	47	9,710	9,302	30
1931	9	2,011	1,713	5	22	4,481	4,488	13	20	4,297	3,344	12	50	10,790	9,545	30
1930	9	1,924	1,704	5	24	4,518	4,690	14	20	3,870	3,243	12	53	10,311	9,637	30
1929	9	2,125	1,599	5	26	4,882	4,709	14	21	3,826	3,126	11	56	10,833	9,434	30
1928	9	1,671	1,478	4	26	4,187	4,412	12	20	3,229	2,979	10	55	9,087	8,870	26
1927	7	1,561	1,233	3	25	3,816	4,175	10	19	3,154	2,880	8	51	8,531	8,288	21
1926	7	1,630	1,217	3	25	3,832	4,032	12	20	3,254	2,802	10	53	8,716	8,051	26
1925	7	1,324	1,092	3	24	3,245	3,722	12	20	3,077	2,770	12	51	7,646	7,583	27
1924	7	1,194	1,054	4	24	3,069	3,065	14	20	2,725	2,563	12	50	6,988	7,222	29
1923	6	1,447	980	4	25	3,073	3,366	15	20	2,792	2,461	13	51	7,312	6,807	32
1922	7	1,363	1,613	5	24	2,842	3,197	17	18	2,667	2,139	11	48	6,871	6,949	33
1921	7	1,248	1,039	4	23	2,734	3,039	13	17	3,157	1,942	10	47	7,139	6,021	28
1920	8	1,500	1,102	3	25	2,992	3,005	11	17	2,299	1,862	8	51	6,791	5,970	22
1919	6	1,171	864	3	20	2,433	2,570	8	13	1,820	1,489	6	40	5,424	4,923	17
1918	6	903	757	3	19	2,148	2,415	10	12	1,555	1,352	7	36	4,606	4,524	19
1917	5	819	689	2	16	1,915	2,158	8	10	1,315	1,139	6	31	4,049	3,986	16
1916	5	743	662	3	14	1,606	1,959	8	9	1,069	1,099	5	28	3,418	3,720	15
1915	5	673	683	3	14	1,438	1,828	7	8	1,000	1,021	5	26	3,111	3,532	14
1914	5	664	700	3	14	1,398	1,736	8	9	1,042	1,020	5	27	3,104	3,456	15
1913	5	722	685	3	13	1,319	1,596	7	8	894	872	4	26	2,934	3,152	14
1912	5	654	644	3	12	1,149	1,430	6	6	572	609	3	23	2,374	2,683	12
1911	5	572	550	3	11	998	1,270	6	5	417	461	2	21	1,988	2,280	11
1910	4	528	503	3	10	936	1,144	5	4	353	388	2	19	1,817	2,034	10
1909	4	455	474	2	10	832	1,059	5	4	292	330	2	17	1,580	1,863	9
1908	4	424	444	3	10	789	977	6	3	253	290	2	17	1,466	1,711	10
1907	4	375	412	2	9	749	937	5	3	239	265	2	16	1,363	1,615	8
1906	3	324	355	2	9	672	855	4	3	214	234	1	15	1,210	1,444	7

Series H424-451. *Fire insurance statistics, 1869 to 1959 (continued)*

(millions of dollars)

	Canadian companies				British companies				Foreign companies				Total			
Year	Net pre-miums	Amount of policies taken during year	Amount of risk at date of state-ment	Net claims	Net pre-miums	Amount of policies taken during year	Amount of risk at date of state-ment	Net claims	Net pre-miums	Amount of policies taken during year	Amount of risk at date of state-ment	Net claims	Net pre-miums	Amount of policies taken during year	Amount of risk at date of state-ment	Net claims
	424	425	426	427	428	429	430	431	432	433	434	435	436	437	438	439
1905	3	302	328	1	9	650	785	4	3	189	205	1	14	1,140	1,318	6
1904	3	239	297	3	8	607	745	9	2	153	173	2	13	999	1,215	14
1903	2	217	261	1	7	581	727	4	2	136	152	1	11	933	1,140	6
1902	2	215	246	1	7	557	695	3	2	120	134	1	11	892	1,075	4
1901	2	171	222	1	7	542	694	5	1	108	122	1	10	822	1,039	7
1900	1.3	154.9	190.6	1.0	5.8	540.4	618.8	5.5	1.2	108.1	120.0	1.2	8.3	803.4	929.3	7.8
1899	1.2	130.0	169.8	.6	5.7	525.0	654.9	3.9	1.1	100.8	112.2	.7	7.9	755.8	936.9	5.2
1898	1.1	111.0	159.9	.6	5.2	481.4	629.8	3.6	1.0	88.8	105.7	.6	7.4	681.2	895.4	4.8
1897	1.0	107.3	154.2	.7	5.2	470.5	611.8	3.3	1.0	86.0	102.4	.6	7.2	663.7	868.5	4.7
1896	1.1	114.4	141.3	.7	5.0	460.0	591.7	2.8	1.0	94.9	112.7	.6	7.1	669.3	845.6	4.2
1895	1.2	130.6	143.7	.8	4.8	436.8	575.7	3.4	1.0	100.3	118.4	.8	6.9	667.6	837.8	5.0
1894	1.1	121.6	150.2	.8	4.6	435.2	567.9	3.1	1.0	96.8	117.9	.7	6.7	653.6	836.1	4.6
1893	1.1	123.8	154.6	.8	4.6	458.3	563.0	3.5	1.0	105.6	124.0	.8	6.8	687.6	841.7	5.1
1892	1.1	112.6	148.6	.8	4.5	366.9	549.2	2.9	1.0	107.7	123.6	.7	6.5	587.2	821.4	4.4
1891	1.3	135.9	177.8	.9	4.2	411.7	497.6	2.6	.7	75.7	84.3	.4	6.2	623.4	759.6	3.9
1890	1.2	135.1	178.7	.7	4.1	427.9	374.9	2.2	.5	57.6	67.1	.3	5.8	620.7	620.7	3.3
1889	1.2	123.0	158.9	.7	4.0	403.3	468.4	2.0	.4	46.5	57.3	.2	5.6	572.8	684.5	2.9
1888	1.1	120.2	159.1	.8	3.9	376.5	434.9	2.1	.4	44.9	56.7	.2	5.4	541.6	650.7	3.1
1887	1.1	109.2	154.2	.8	3.7	378.0	422.3	2.3	.4	35.9	56.3	.3	5.2	523.1	632.8	3.4
1886	1.1	114.5	142.7	.7	3.4	349.1	339.2	2.3	.4	42.1	50.9	.2	4.9	505.8	532.8	3.3
1885	1.1	111.2	143.8	.6	3.4	337.2	421.2	1.9	.4	37.6	47.8	.2	4.9	486.0	612.8	2.7
1884	1.1	118.7	148.0	.8	3.5	354.5	413.4	2.3	.4	40.8	44.1	.2	5.0	514.0	605.5	3.2
1883	1.1	122.3	149.9	.8	3.2	351.0	380.6	2.0	.4	40.3	41.7	.2	4.6	513.6	572.3	2.9
1882	1.0	124.1	152.6	.7	2.9	321.4	339.5	1.8	.3	32.5	34.7	.2	4.2	478.0	526.8	2.7
1881	1.2	140.3	153.4	1.3	2.4	271.0	277.7	1.7	.3	30.0	31.0	.2	3.8	441.4	462.2	3.1
1880	1.2	131.1	154.4	.7	2.0	227.5	229.7	.9	.2	25.4	27.4	.1	3.5	384.0	411.6	1.7
1879	1.1	124.7	158.8	.7	1.9	213.1	208.3	1.3	.2	22.9	20.3	.2	3.2	360.7	387.4	2.1
1878	1.2	127.3	171.4	.8	2.0	213.1	202.7	.9	.2	19.4	35.8	.1	3.4	359.8	409.9	1.8
1877	1.6	168.9	217.7	2.2	1.9	206.7	184.3	5.7	.2	21.0	19.3	.6	3.8	396.6	421.3	8.5
1876	1.9	198.5	231.8	1.6	1.6	178.7	153.9	1.2	.2	23.9	18.9	.1	3.7	401.1	404.6	2.9
1875	1.6	168.9	190.3	1.0	1.7	167.0	154.8	1.3	.3	17.4	19.3	.2	3.6	353.2	364.4	2.6
1874	1.5	126.6	126.7	.7	1.8	177.3	155.1	1.1	.3	25.2	25.1	.1	3.5	329.2	306.8	1.9
1873	.8	71.8	91.0	.5	1.8	172.5	147.6	1.0	.4	26.8	40.1	.2	3.0	271.0	278.8	1.7
1872	.8	76.5	72.2	.5	1.5	174.4	145.7	1.1	.3	26.5	33.8	.3	2.6	277.4	251.7	1.9
1871	.7	68.9	68.5	.4	1.3	148.1	132.7	1.0	.3	27.3	27.3	.2	2.3	244.3	228.5	1.6
1870	.5	54.6	59.5	.5	1.2	131.6	120.9	1.0	.2	12.9	11.2	.1	1.9	199.1	191.5	1.2
1869	.5	41.1	59.3	.3	1.1	120.7	115.2	.6	.2	9.7	13.8	.2	1.8	171.5	188.4	1.4

Series H424–451. *Fire insurance statistics, 1869 to 1959 (continuation)*
(millions of dollars)

	Provincial licensees				Lloyd's, London				Total			
Year	Net premiums	Amount of policies taken during year	Amount of risk at date of statement	Net claims incurred	Net premiums	Amount of policies taken during year	Amount of risk at date of statement	Net claims incurred	Net premiums	Amount of policies taken during year	Amount of risk at date of statement	Net claims incurred
	440	**441**	**442**	**443**	**444**	**445**	**446**	**447**	**448**	**449**	**450**	**451**
1959	27	—	—	15	9	—	—	8	233	—	—	119
1958	24	—	—	13	9	—	—	7	210	—	—	109
1957	20	—	—	12	8	—	—	8	184	—	—	130
1956	16	—	—	10	8	—	—	7	180	—	—	103
1955	15	—	—	9	6	—	—	8	168	—	—	95
1954	13	2,251	3,064	7	7	973	949	3	169	47,951	49,619	80
1953	14	2,710	3,394	7	7	1,086	1,112	4	167	44,888	46,209	78
1952	12	2,177	2,869	6	6	708	908	3	158	38,257	41,095	70
1951	12	2,119	2,888	6	6	832	904	3	152	35,854	37,283	61
1950	11	1,846	2,519	6	5	650	756	4	131	30,008	32,232	68
1949	10	1,661	2,378	6	5	542	627	2	119	26,513	28,974	55
1948	9	1,474	2,098	5	4	517	497	3	111	27,330	25,615	53
1947	8	1,379	1,970	4	3	371	365	1	98	23,898	22,262	45
1946	7	1,014	1,700	4	2	222	248	1	78	18,019	19,324	40
1945	6	922	1,492	3	1	188	210	1	66	15,644	16,757	35
1944	6	751	1,453	3	1	176	205	1	62	15,500	15,832	33
1943	4.6	761.7	1,273.3	2.1	1.1	173.9	222.0	1.0	53	13,775	14,882	25
1942	4.7	679.2	1,250.0	2.2	1.7	258.9	278.4	1.5	54	13,698	14,094	24
1941	4.0	682.8	1,120.2	2.2	1.9	286.7	287.1	1.2	55	14,315	12,794	21
1940	4.4	775.5[1]	1,123.9	2.0	1.6	304.5	255.4	1.1	48	13,052	12,117	19
1939	5.8[1]	803.9[1]	1,285.0[1]	3.2[1]	—	—	—	—	47	11,921	11,485	19
1938	5.3	803.3	1,214.4	3.1	—	—	—	—	48	11,226	11,168	20
1937	3.6	539.3	976.2	1.8	—	—	—	—	46	10,972	10,750	17
1936	5.0	731.0	1,184.9	2.2	—	—	—	—	45	10,373	10,433	16
1935	5.3	924.9	1,644.0	2.4	—	—	—	—	46	10,567	10,427	17
1934	5.6	625.5	1,240.4	2.9	—	—	—	—	47	10,132	10,045	20
1933	5.3	451.5	1,190.2	3.6	—	—	—	—	47	11,096	10,198	25
1932	5.7	534.2	1,284.1	4.2	—	—	—	—	53	10,874	10,586	34
1931	7.2	566.5	1,341.2	5.0	—	—	—	—	58	11,356	10,886	35
1930	5.9	535.6	1,345.2	4.3	—	—	—	—	59	10,847	11,018	35
1929	5.6	559.8	1,324.8	3.8	—	—	—	—	62	11,351	10,756	34
1928	5.6	544.3	1,297.8	2.8	—	—	—	—	60	9,732	10,167	28
1927	5.9	508.4	1,225.0	2.8	—	—	—	—	57	9,040	9,513	24
1926	6.1	501.8	1,286.3	3.1	—	—	—	—	59	9,218	9,338	29
1925	5.7	465.7	1,215.1	3.2	—	—	—	—	57	8,112	8,798	30
1924	4.8	379.8	1,037.6	3.4	—	—	—	—	55	7,360	8,258	33
1923	4.9	400.3	975.8	3.4	—	—	—	—	55	7,573	7,690	35
1922	4.9	393.0	1,036.2	3.6	—	—	—	—	53	6,864	7,385	36
1921	5.5	464.6	1,269.8	3.5	—	—	—	—	53	6,604	7,290	31
1920	5.2	471.5	1,054.1	2.3	—	—	—	—	56	7,262	7,024	24
1919	4.3	435.6	1,004.9	2.1	—	—	—	—	44	5,859	5,928	19
1918	4.2	404.0	1,000.5	2.4	—	—	—	—	40	5,010	5,524	22
1917	4.1	365.3	891.3	2.3	—	—	—	—	35	4,414	4,877	19
1916	3.9	368.3	849.9	2.2	—	—	—	—	32	3,787	4,570	17
1915	—	—	—	—	—	—	—	—	—	—	—	—
1914	—	—	—	—	—	—	—	—	—	—	—	—
1913	—	—	—	—	—	—	—	—	—	—	—	—
1912	—	—	—	—	—	—	—	—	—	—	—	—
1911	—	—	—	—	—	—	—	—	—	—	—	—
1910	—	—	—	—	—	—	—	—	—	—	—	—
1909	—	—	—	—	—	—	—	—	—	—	—	—
1908	—	—	—	—	—	—	—	—	—	—	—	—
1907	—	—	—	—	—	—	—	—	—	—	—	—
1906	—	—	—	—	—	—	—	—	—	—	—	—

[1] Prior to 1940, Lloyd's figures included in provincial.

Series H452–465. *Casualty insurance statistics,*[1] *1875 to 1959*

(millions of dollars)

	Registered by the federal government								Provincial licensees		Lloyd's, London		Total	
	Canadian companies		British companies		Foreign companies		Total							
Year	Net premiums written	Net claims incurred	Net premiums written	Net claims incurred	Net premiums written	Net claims incurred	Net premiums written	Net claims incurred	Net premiums written	Net claims incurred	Net premiums written	Net claims incurred	Net premiums written	Net claims incurred
	452	453	454	455	456	457	458	459	460	461	462	463	464	465
1959	220	132	105	57	231	135	556	325	57	32	32	17	645	373
1958	207	130	104	61	222	137	532	328	53	28	30	22	615	378
1957	180	123	93	65	201	140	475	328	40	25	23	23	538	376
1956	157	100	81	50	177	117	415	267	24	14	19	15	459	296
1955	143	83	72	38	156	93	371	214	24	14	18	12	413	240
1954	131	76	67	35	139	81	337	192	22	12	18	14	378	218
1953	121	68	63	32	132	76	316	176	15	9	18	9	348	194
1952	101	57	54	29	118	65	272	151	10	5	15	10	297	165
1951	80	47	45	25	98	58	222	130	8	4	12	6	241	140
1950	66	35	40	19	82	41	188	95	8	3	10	5	205	104
1949	57	29	34	16	66	32	157	77	7	3	9	4	173	85
1948	45	22	32	16	56	27	133	65	6	3	8	4	147	72
1947	36	18	26	13	49	25	112	55	6	3	7	4	125	62
1946	28	13	20	9	40	18	88	41	4	2	5	3	97	45
1945	22	10	16	7	31	15	69	33	4	1	4	2	77	36
1944	19	9	14	6	28	16	62	31	3.2	1.3	3.5	1.4	68	33
1943	17	8	13	5	22	13	52	26	2.6	1.1	3.3	2.1	58	29
1942	16	6	13	5	20	10	49	22	2.5	1.0	4.3	2.7	56	26
1941	16	7	13	5	20	10	48	22	2.3	.9	5.5	3.3	56	26
1940	14	6	12	5	17	8	43	19	2.0	.9	4.8	2.4	50	22
1939	13	5	11	5	16	7	40	17	6.3[2]	3.6[2]	—	—	46	20
1938	12	6	11	5	14	8	38	19	5.5	3.5	—	—	43	22
1937	12	5	10	5	13	6	35	17	1.4	.9	—	—	36	18
1936	9	4	9	4	11	5	29	14	2.1	1.2	—	—	31	15
1935	9	4	8	4	10	5	27	13	2.5	1.3	—	—	29	14
1934	9	4	8	4	9	4	26	12	2.0	1.1	—	—	28	13
1933	9	4	8	3	8	4	25	11	2.2	1.0	—	—	27	12
1932	10	5	9	4	10	5	29	14	2.2	1.2	—	—	31	15
1931	11	6	11	6	13	7	35	19	2.4	1.4	—	—	37	20
1930	13	6	13	7	16	10	41	23	3.9	2.2	—	—	45	25
1929	12	6	14	7	16	8	42	22	1.2	.7	—	—	43	22
1928	11	6	13	8	14	9	39	24	2.2	1.1	—	—	41	25
1927	11	6	11	7	11	8	33	21	1.4	.8	—	—	34	22
1926	9	4	9	5	10	6	28	14	2.3	1.9	—	—	30	16
1925	9	4	8	4	10	5	26	13	1.3	.6	—	—	28	13
1924	8	4	7	4	9	4	23	11	.8	.4	—	—	24	12
1923	8	4	7	5	9	6	25	15	1.2	.7	—	—	26	16
1922	8	3	7	3	8	3	22	10	2.2	1.2	—	—	24	11
1921	8	4	8	5	7	5	23	14	3.8	2.4	—	—	27	17
1920	8	4	8	4	8	3	23	10	3.0	1.7	—	—	26	12
1919	6	3	5	3	5	3	16	8	2.9	1.6	—	—	19	10
1918	5	3	4	2	5	2	14	6	2.6	1.6	—	—	17	8
1917	5	2	4	2	5	2	13	6	2.8	1.5	—	—	16	7
1916	4	2	2	1	3	2	9	5	1.8	1.6	—	—	11	7
1915	3.3	1.7	2.4	1.3	2.4	1.2	8.1	4.1	—	—	—	—	—	—
1914	3.7	2.0	3.2	1.6	2.3	1.0	9.3	4.6	—	—	—	—	—	—
1913	3.9	1.8	3.2	1.4	2.2	1.1	9.3	4.3	—	—	—	—	—	—
1912	3.2	1.6	2.7	1.1	2.0	.8	7.8	3.5	—	—	—	—	—	—
1911	2.9	1.3	2.0	.8	1.5	.6	6.4	2.7	—	—	—	—	—	—

Series H452–465. *Casualty insurance statistics,*[1] *1875 to 1959 (continued)*
(millions of dollars)

	Registered by the federal government								Provincial licensees		Lloyd's, London		Total	
	Canadian companies		British companies		Foreign companies		Total							
Year	Net premiums written	Net claims incurred	Net premiums written	Net claims incurred	Net premiums written	Net claims incurred	Net premiums written	Net claims incurred	Net premiums written	Net claims incurred	Net premiums written	Net claims incurred	Net premiums written	Net claims incurred
	452	453	454	455	456	457	458	459	460	461	462	463	464	465
1910	2.6	1.1	1.7	.7	1.0	.3	5.3	2.2	—	—	—	—	—	—
1909	2.1	1.0	1.3	.5	.7	.2	4.1	1.7	—	—	—	—	—	—
1908	1.7	.9	1.2	.5	.6	.2	3.5	1.6	—	—	—	—	—	—
1907	1.9	1.0	1.0	.4	.5	.2	3.3	1.5	—	—	—	—	—	—
1906	1.6	.8	.8	.4	.4	.1	2.9	1.4	—	—	—	—	—	—
1905	1.3	.6	.8	.3	.3	.1	2.4	1.1	—	—	—	—	—	—
1904	1.1	.6	.7	.3	.3	.1	2.0	1.0	—	—	—	—	—	—
1903	1.0	.5	.6	.3	.2	.1	1.8	.9	—	—	—	—	—	—
1902	.8	.4	.5	.2	.1	—	1.5	.7	—	—	—	—	—	—
1901	.7	.4	.5	.2	.1	.1	1.3	.7	—	—	—	—	—	—
1900	.6	.3	.4	.3	.1	.1	1.1	.6	—	—	—	—	—	—
1899	.5	.2	.4	.2	.1	.1	1.0	.5	—	—	—	—	—	—
1898	.4	.2	.3	.2	.1	.1	.9	.4	—	—	—	—	—	—
1897	.4	.2	.3	.1	.1	.1	.8	.4	—	—	—	—	—	—
1896	.4	.2	.2	.1	.1	.1	.7	.4	—	—	—	—	—	—
1895	.3	.1	.1	.1	.1	.1	.5	.2	—	—	—	—	—	—
1894	.3	.1	.1	—	.1	.1	.5	.2	—	—	—	—	—	—
1893	.2	.1	.1	.1	.1	—	.5	.2	—	—	—	—	—	—
1892	.2	.1	.1	—	.1	—	.4	.2	—	—	—	—	—	—
1891	.2	.1	.1	—	.1	—	.4	.2	—	—	—	—	—	—
1890	.2	.1	.1	—	.1	—	.4	.1	—	—	—	—	—	—
1889	.2	.1	.1	—	.1	—	.4	.2	—	—	—	—	—	—
1888	.2	.1	—	—	.1	.1	.4	.1	—	—	—	—	—	—
1887	.2	.1	—	—	.1	—	.3	.1	—	—	—	—	—	—
1886	.2	.1	—	—	.1	—	.3	.1	—	—	—	—	—	—
1885	.1	—	—	—	—	—	.2	.1	—	—	—	—	—	—
1884	.1	—	—	—	—	—	.2	.1	—	—	—	—	—	—
1883	.1	.1	—	—	—	—	.2	.1	—	—	—	—	—	—
1882	.1	—	—	—	—	—	.2	.1	—	—	—	—	—	—
1881	.2	.1	—	—	—	—	.3	.1	—	—	—	—	—	—
1880	.1	.1	—	—	—	—	.1	.1	—	—	—	—	—	—
1879	.1	—	—	—	—	—	.1	—	—	—	—	—	—	—
1878	.1	—	—	—	—	—	.2	.1	—	—	—	—	—	—
1877	.1	—	—	—	—	—	.1	.1	—	—	—	—	—	—
1876	.1	—	—	—	—	—	.1	.1	—	—	—	—	—	—
1875	.1	—	—	—	.1	—	.1	—	—	—	—	—	—	—

[1] For the years 1875 to 1920 inclusive, premiums and claims were shown on the cash basis; for 1921 and subsequent years, premiums are on the written, and claims on the incurred basis.

[2] Prior to 1940, Lloyd's included in provincial total.

Series H466–486. *Operations of loan companies in Canada, 1914 to 1959*
(millions of dollars)

Year end	Companies supervised by the federal government[1]							Companies not supervised by the federal government[2]						
	Assets (book value)	Liabilities to the public	Capital stock			Reserve and contingency funds	Total liabilities to shareholders	Assets (book value)	Liabilities to the public	Capital stock			Reserve and contingency funds	Total liabilities to shareholders
			Authorized	Subscribed	Paid up					Authorized	Subscribed	Paid up		
	466	467	468	469	470	471	472	473	474	475	476	477	478	479
1959	409	364	—	—	19	26	45	263	192	—	—	21	49	70
1958	359	315	—	—	19	25	44	247	178	—	—	20	48	68
1957	320	280	53	18	18	21	39	229	160	38	26	21	39	68
1956	297	258	53	16	18	19	38	140	106	27	15	11	18	35
1955	281	246	53	15	17	17	35	130	98	24	14	10	17	32
1954	255	222	51	19	16	17	34	118	88	22	14	10	15	30
1953	217	184	51	19	16	15	32	107	78	23	14	10	14	28
1952	207	175	51	19	16	15	32	96	70	23	14	10	11	26
1951	203	166	56	22	18	17	37	89	64	24	14	10	10	25
1950	191	153	56	24	21	16	38	90	60	31	19	16	10	30
1949	180	144	56	21	18	16	35	80	52	26	17	14	10	29
1948	165	131	56	21	18	15	35	78	49	29	17	16	10	30
1947	155	121	56	22	18	15	34	76	47	21	17	15	10	29
1946	145	114	56	21	18	13	31	70	44	27	16	15	9	26
1945	134	103	56	21	18	12	31	64	38	27	16	15	9	25
1944	131	98	59	25	19	13	33	59	34	28	17	15	8	25
1943	127	94	59	25	19	13	33	59	32	30	18	16	9	27
1942	127	93	59	25	19	13	34	58	30	29	19	17	9	28
1941	131	97	59	25	19	14	34	58	30	30	19	17	9	28
1940	134	99	59	26	19	14	35	59	31	32	20	18	10	29
1939	136	101	59	26	19	15	35	59	30	37	20	18	10	29
1938	136	101	59	26	19	15	35	58	28	37	20	18	10	30
1937	136	100	59	26	19	15	36	57	28	42	20	18	11	29
1936	137	101	59	26	19	15	36	59	29	43	20	18	11	29
1935	138	102	59	27	19	16	36	64	29	50	25	22	12	35
1934	140	104	59	27	19	16	37	67	31	57	26	23	12	36
1933	139	101	61	28	20	15	37	67	30	51	27	23	12	35
1932	144	108	60	27	20	15	36	68	32	54	25	22	13	38
1931	148	111	65	29	21	15	36	66	32	43	20	18	13	35
1930	143	106	65	28	20	15	36	63	31	40	18	16	13	30
1929	135	99	65	28	20	14	36	71	44	34	14	13	11	26
1928	135	98	65	28	20	14	36	80	49	42	21	18	12	31
1927	135	96	71	30	21	15	39	77	46	42	16	15	12	30
1926	120	80	84	34	23	15	39	84	49	51	22	20	14	37
1925	111	71	89	34	24	15	38	83	47	57	23	21	17	40
1924	102	64	89	34	23	14	37	87	45	59	23	23	17	41
1923	105	64	94	37	25	15	41	83	42	56	23	22	16	40
1922	102	60	97	37	25	14	39	86	44	61	25	24	17	44
1921	97	55	—	—	26	14	40	—	—	—	—	—	—	—
1920	90	53	—	—	24	13	38	—	—	—	—	—	—	—
1919	75	42	—	—	20	12	32	—	—	—	—	—	—	—
1918	70	39	—	—	20	11	31	—	—	—	—	—	—	—
1917	70	39	—	—	20	11	31	—	—	—	—	—	—	—
1916	71	41	—	—	20	10	30	—	—	—	—	—	—	—
1915	72	42	—	—	19	10	30	—	—	—	—	—	—	—
1914	71	41	—	—	19	9	29	—	—	—	—	—	—	—

Series H 466–486. *Operations of loan companies in Canada, 1914 to 1959 (continuation)*

(millions of dollars)

Year end	Assets (book value)	Liabilities to the public	Authorized	Subscribed	Paid up	Reserve and contingency funds	Total liabilities to shareholders
			Capital stock				
	480	481	482	483	484	485	486
1959	672	556	—	—	40	76	115
1958	605	493	—	—	39	73	112
1957	549	441	91	44	39	59	108
1956	437	364	80	32	29	37	73
1955	411	344	77	30	26	34	67
1954	373	310	73	33	26	32	63
1953	324	263	74	33	26	29	61
1952	303	246	74	33	26	26	58
1951	292	229	80	35	29	28	62
1950	280	213	87	43	37	26	67
1949	260	196	82	38	32	27	64
1948	244	179	85	39	33	25	64
1947	231	168	77	38	33	25	63
1946	215	158	83	37	32	22	57
1945	197	141	83	38	32	21	56
1944	190	132	87	42	34	21	58
1943	186	126	89	43	35	22	60
1942	185	123	88	44	36	23	62
1941	189	127	89	44	36	23	62
1940	193	130	92	46	37	24	64
1939	195	130	96	46	37	25	64
1938	194	129	96	46	38	25	65
1937	193	129	101	46	37	26	65
1936	196	131	102	47	37	26	65
1935	202	131	109	52	41	27	71
1934	207	134	116	53	42	28	72
1933	206	131	112	54	43	27	72
1932	211	140	114	52	42	27	74
1931	214	142	109	49	39	28	71
1930	206	137	105	46	37	27	66
1929	207	143	98	43	34	25	61
1928	215	147	107	49	38	27	67
1927	212	142	113	46	36	27	69
1926	205	130	135	56	44	29	76
1925	194	118	146	57	45	31	79
1924	189	109	148	57	46	30	78
1923	188	106	150	59	47	31	82
1922	189	104	158	62	49	31	83
1921	—	—	—	—	—	—	—
1920	—	—	—	—	—	—	—
1919	—	—	—	—	—	—	—
1918	—	—	—	—	—	—	—
1917	—	—	—	—	—	—	—
1916	—	—	—	—	—	—	—
1915	—	—	—	—	—	—	—
1914	—	—	—	—	—	—	—

[1] Includes companies chartered by the governments of Nova Scotia (from 1925), New Brunswick (from 1934), and Manitoba (from 1938) which by arrangement are inspected by the federal Department of Insurance.

[2] The data for 1957 include for the first time the figures of one loan company incorporated under the laws of Quebec, the capital stock of which has been issued largely outside of Canada but whose debentures for the greater part are now held in Canada.

Series H487–502. *Certain mortgage loan companies, assets and liabilities, 1946 to 1960*

(millions of dollars)

Year end	Assets[1]										Liabilities[1]					
	Securities					Mortgage loans and sale agreements	Real estate	Cash	Other assets	Total assets or liabilities	Deposits	Debentures	Other liabilities	Capital	Reserves	Earned surplus
	Government of Canada[2]	Provincial bonds[2]	Municipal bonds[2]	Corporate and other bonds[3]	Preferred and common stocks											
	487	488	489	490	491	492	493	494	495	496	497	498	499	500	501	502
1960[4]	58	23	7	16	44	657	12	21	22	860	134	599	23	32	58	14
1959	54	21	7	15	41	589	12	24	20	784	123	539	12	35	56	18
1958	57	19	7	15	38	533	11	18	16	714	137	457	12	36	55	17
1957	46	11	6	12	29	488	11	22	16	641	118	413	11	34	50	14
1956	46	9	6	10	28	467	9	14	10	600	120	374	12	34	47	12
1955	54	12	7	12	24	418	8	18	6	559	126	337	10	32	43	11
1954	57	7	7	13	16	375	8	14	5	502	107	304	10	32	41	8
1953	45	6	4	9	13	331	8	14	6	436	91	259	12	31	36	7
1952	44	5	5	8	15	299	8	13	6	404	90	231	11	30	36	6
1951	43	5	4	6	14	276	8	16	6	378	85	212	10	30	36	5
1950	43	7	3	8	14	250	7	14	4	350	88	186	9	29	34	4
1949	41	8	3	8	13	196	7	11	3	290	81	142	7	26	31	2
1948	48	6	2	7	14	170	7	11	3	269	76	125	9	27	29	3
1947	64	5	2	7	13	145	7	12	2	257	69	120	9	27	29	2
1946	64	7	2	6	11	126	7	10	2	234	62	107	10	27	27	2

[1] Book values of assets and liabilities of the six largest companies registered with the Government of Canada or the province of Ontario or Quebec (representing approximately 97 per cent of the assets of all companies so registered in 1958) and of Investors Syndicate of Canada Limited and subsidiary companies (incorporated by special act of Manitoba).

[2] Includes guaranteed bonds.
[3] Includes small amounts of foreign bonds.
[4] Estimated.

Series H503–529. *Operations of trust companies in Canada, 1914 to 1959*

(millions of dollars)

	Companies supervised by the federal government[1]									Companies not supervised by the federal government								
	Assets (book value)			Estates, trusts and agency funds	Capital			Reserve and contingency funds	Unappropriated surpluses	Assets (book value)			Estates, trusts and agency funds	Capital			Reserve and contingency funds	Unappropriated surpluses
Year end	Company funds	Guaranteed funds	Total		Authorized	Subscribed	Paid up			Company funds	Guaranteed funds	Total		Authorized	Subscribed	Paid up		
	503	504	505	506	507	580	509	510	511	512	513	514	515	516	517	518	519	520
1959	40	262	301	1,128	—	—	17	21	1	117	661	778	5,775	—	—	32	76	9
1958	37	239	275	990	—	—	17	18	2	107	588	695	5,329	—	—	32	66	9
1957	39	177	216	887	36	19	18	13	3	97	473	570	4,696	57	32	32	39	8
1956	37	170	207	815	33	18	17	12	2	92	446	538	4,319	57	31	31	37	8
1955	32	159	191	735	32	16	15	12	2	88	437	526	3,986	54	32	31	35	6
1954	29	141	170	664	32	15	15	11	2	83	384	467	3,735	60	30	30	32	6
1953	30	110	140	631	33	15	15	9	2	82	268	350	3,471	55	30	29	30	6
1952	29	107	136	589	33	15	15	9	2	75	265	340	3,384	53	29	29	27	6
1951	28	94	122	544	35	15	15	9	2	74	258	333	3,283	53	29	29	26	5
1950	28	93	121	495	35	15	15	10	2	72	247	320	3,126	53	29	29	25	5
1949	26	90	116	560	35	15	15	8	2	68	210	278	2,828	47	26	26	26	5
1948	26	82	108	521	32	15	14	8	1	68	191	259	2,792	47	26	24	25	5
1947	23	72	95	481	30	14	13	8	1	66	172	238	2,736	47	26	24	24	5
1946	24	62	86	392	28	14	14	7	1	65	154	219	2,758	49	25	24	22	5
1945	22	53	76	363	25	13	13	7	1	67	136	203	2,754	57	26	25	21	4
1944	21	48	69	339	25	13	12	7	1	62	124	186	2,594	51	25	25	18	5
1943	21	42	62	313	25	13	12	6	1	60	112	172	2,529	52	25	24	16	5
1942	20	38	58	291	25	13	12	6	1	61	107	168	2,445	52	24	24	16	4
1941	21	39	59	269	25	13	12	6	1	58	109	167	2,419	52	25	24	15	4
1940	20	35	56	257	25	13	12	6	1	58	108	166	2,417	52	25	24	16	4
1939	20	36	56	242	25	13	12	6	1	61	115	176	2,422	54	27	25	16	4
1938	20	37	57	236	25	13	12	6	—	61	115	176	2,346	54	27	25	16	4
1937	17	36	53	228	21	11	10	5	—	64	123	188	2,331	65	30	28	17	4
1936	16	35	52	226	19	11	10	5	1	64	122	186	2,312	67	30	28	19	3
1935	16	35	51	243	20	12	11	4	1	65	114	179	2,254	67	30	28	19	2
1934	16	32	48	230	21	12	11	4	1	63	118	181	2,206	67	30	28	18	3
1933	15	27	43	225	22	12	11	4	—	63	119	182	2,103	74	32	28	19	3
1932	15	25	41	216	22	12	11	3	—	66	119	185	2,062	73	32	29	20	2
1931	15	26	41	216	23	12	10	3	1	66	126	192	1,962	73	32	28	21	2
1930	15	26	41	205	23	12	10	3	1	71	138	209	1,872	72	33	28	22	3
1929	15	24	39	210	21	12	11	3	—	67	118	185	1,626	67	32	28	21	2
1928	15	24	39	203	20	12	10	3	—	41	74	115	875	34	21	19	14	1
1927	14	22	36	161	20	12	10	3	—	39	59	99	805	35	20	18	11	2
1926	13	18	31	140	19	12	10	2	—	33	52	85	733	35	19	17	10	2
1925	12	16	28	131	18	11	10	2	—	30	46	76	699	31	18	15	10	2
1924	12	14	26	123	17	11	9	2	—	30	42	72	674	31	18	15	10	1
1923	11	11	21	103	16	10	8	2	—	32	40	73	648	33	20	17	10	1
1922	10	9	19	92	16	10	8	2	—	31	33	64	630	39	20	25	10	1
1921	10	9	19	79	—	—	8	2	—	—	—	—	—	—	—	—	—	—
1920	10	9	20	57	—	—	7	2	—	—	—	—	—	—	—	—	—	—
1919	10	13	23	52	—	—	7	2	—	—	—	—	—	—	—	—	—	—
1918	9	13	22	56	—	—	6	1	—	—	—	—	—	—	—	—	—	—
1917	8	11	19	38	—	—	5	1	—	—	—	—	—	—	—	—	—	—
1916	8	10	18	37	—	—	6	1	—	—	—	—	—	—	—	—	—	—
1915	7	10	17	31	—	—	5	1	—	—	—	—	—	—	—	—	—	—
1914	11	9	19	30	—	—	6	3	—	—	—	—	—	—	—	—	—	—

Series H503–529. *Operations of trust companies in Canada, 1914 to 1959 (continuation)*

(millions of dollars)

Year end	Totals								
	Assets (book value)			Estates, trusts and agency funds	Capital			Reserve and contingency funds	Unappropriated surpluses
	Company funds	Guaranteed funds	Total		Authorized	Subscribed	Paid up		
	521	522	523	524	525	526	527	528	529
1959	157	922	1,079	6,903	—	—	49	97	11
1958	143	827	970	6,319	—	—	48	85	11
1957	136	650	786	5,582	93	51	50	52	11
1956	128	617	745	5,134	90	49	48	49	10
1955	120	596	717	4,720	86	47	46	48	9
1954	113	524	637	4,398	92	45	45	42	8
1953	111	379	490	4,102	88	45	45	39	8
1952	104	373	477	3,972	86	44	44	37	7
1951	103	352	455	3,827	88	44	44	35	7
1950	100	341	441	3,621	88	44	43	34	7
1949	94	300	394	3,388	82	41	40	34	7
1948	94	273	367	3,312	79	41	39	33	7
1947	90	243	333	3,217	77	40	38	32	6
1946	89	216	305	3,151	76	40	38	30	6
1945	90	189	279	3,118	82	40	38	28	6
1944	83	171	255	2,933	76	38	37	25	6
1943	81	154	234	2,842	77	38	36	22	6
1942	81	145	226	2,736	77	37	36	21	5
1941	79	147	226	2,688	77	39	36	21	5
1940	78	144	222	2,674	77	39	36	22	5
1939	81	151	232	2,665	79	40	37	22	5
1938	81	152	234	2,583	79	40	37	22	4
1937	82	159	241	2,559	85	41	38	23	4
1936	80	157	238	2,538	86	41	38	24	4
1935	81	149	229	2,497	87	42	39	23	3
1934	79	149	228	2,436	88	42	38	22	3
1933	79	146	225	2,329	96	44	38	22	3
1932	81	144	225	2,278	96	44	40	24	3
1931	82	152	233	2,178	95	44	39	24	3
1930	86	164	250	2,077	95	45	38	25	3
1929	81	143	224	1,836	88	44	39	24	2
1928	56	99	154	1,078	54	34	30	17	2
1927	53	82	135	967	55	32	28	14	2
1926	46	70	117	873	54	31	26	13	2
1925	43	62	104	830	49	29	25	12	2
1924	42	57	98	797	48	29	24	12	1
1923	43	51	94	751	49	29	25	12	1
1922	42	42	83	722	55	29	32	12	1
1921	—	—	—	—	—	—	—	—	—
1920	—	—	—	—	—	—	—	—	—
1919	—	—	—	—	—	—	—	—	—
1918	—	—	—	—	—	—	—	—	—
1917	—	—	—	—	—	—	—	—	—
1916	—	—	—	—	—	—	—	—	—
1915	—	—	—	—	—	—	—	—	—
1914	—	—	—	—	—	—	—	—	—

[1] Includes companies chartered by the Governments of Nova Scotia (from 1925), New Brunswick (from 1934) and Manitoba (from 1938) which, by arrangement, are inspected by the federal Department of Insurance.

Series H530–548. *Certain trust companies, assets and liabilities, 1946 to 1959*

(millions of dollars)

	Assets[1]										
		Securities									
Year end	Government of Canada[2]	Provincial bonds[2]	Municipal bonds[2]	Corporate and other bonds[3]	Preferred and common stocks	Mortgage loans and sale agreements	Real estate	Other loans	Cash	All other assets	Total assets or liabilities
	530	531	532	533	534	535	536	537	538	539	540
1959	182	96	43	142	33	385	11	48	39	19	999
1958	167	111	44	111	29	323	10	54	35	17	902
1957	131	75	38	99	28	257	10	39	35	15	728
1956	127	70	39	84	25	252	10	32	41	13	692
1955	147	88	43	69	19	213	9	34	30	14	666
1954	161	67	37	61	18	165	9	31	29	10	588
1953	121	44	28	35	17	137	9	18	23	8	440
1952	123	41	27	34	16	125	8	20	29	8	432
1951	133	39	25	31	15	117	8	20	19	8	414
1950	146	38	22	27	14	100	8	17	20	7	399
1949	139	33	20	21	15	86	8	16	16	7	362
1948	131	24	16	21	15	76	7	17	16	5	329
1947	129	17	13	18	15	68	6	15	13	6	300
1946	121	14	11	13	15	65	7	18	14	5	283

Year end	Liabilities[1]							Estates, trusts and agency funds and safe custody accounts
	Trust deposits	Investment certificates	Loans	Capital	Reserves	Earned surplus	Other liabilities	
	541	542	543	544	545	546	547	548
1959	336	552	6	34	54	7	11	6,403
1958	349	449	7	33	49	7	9	5,835
1957	280	346	7	35	45	7	8	5,130
1956	282	311	8	34	42	7	7	4,679
1955	267	307	7	32	40	6	7	4,324
1954	240	263	7	31	35	5	7	4,056
1953	180	177	8	32	33	6	6	3,785
1952	175	177	7	31	32	5	5	3,628
1951	163	170	8	31	32	5	4	3,496
1950	158	163	8	30	30	5	4	3,330
1949	135	153	7	30	28	4	4	3,159
1948	128	130	8	28	27	4	4	3,067
1947	112	118	7	28	27	4	4	2,980
1946	101	110	7	30	27	4	5	2,977

[1] Book values of assets and liabilities of the 17 largest companies registered with the Government of Canada or the province of Quebec or Ontario (representing approximately 94 per cent of the assets of all companies so registered in 1958).

[2] Includes guaranteed bonds.
[3] Includes small amounts of foreign bonds.

Series H549–558. *Instalment and other finance companies,*[1] *estimates of major assets and liabilities, 1947 to 1960*
(millions of dollars)

Year end		Assets					Liabilities			
	Cash and marketable securities	Notes receivable				Total of foregoing assets	Chartered bank loans[2]	Short-term notes[3]	Other notes and debentures	All other net[4]
		Retail paper		Wholesale paper	Cash loans					
		Consumer's goods	Other goods							
	549	550	551	552	553	554	555	556	557	558
1960	112	871	379	234	503	2,099	371	389	721	618
1959	131	844	344	197	446	1,962	409	380	623	547
1958	58	787	257	191	382	1,675	352	244	572	507
1957	52	795	288	202	347	1,684	281	355	580	468
1956	39	769	279	182	343	1,612	394	307	490	421
1955	29	605	192	145	273	1,244	310	213	374	347
1954	35	497	164	93	209	998	181	154	350	313
1953	34	519	184	115	173	1,025	256	193	302	274
1952	27	373	167	98	148	813	236	137	200	240
1951	30	185	128	108	114	565	83	118	196	168
1950	11	202	91	71	93	468	127	41	163	137
1949	10	116	68	37	77	308	91	16	103	98
1948	9	70	60	29	64	232	74	14	71	73
1947	10	48	58	29	54	199	76	14	46	63

[1] Instalment finance companies, companies licensed under the Small Loans Act and affiliates engaged in making personal loans. Excludes subsidiaries of merchandisers who finance sales of their parent companies only.

[2] Chartered bank loans as published in the banking statistics. Items in float and any other differences between these figures and those carried in the books of the finance companies would affect 'all other net'.

[3] Notes with original maturity of one year or less. Does not include paper issued by some of the smaller companies for which no information is available.

[4] Balancing item. Includes capital, reserves and 'other' liabilities; fixed and 'other' assets are netted out.

Series H 559–568. *Small loan companies chartered by the Dominion government, assets and liabilities, 1928 to 1959*
(millions of dollars)

Year end	Assets					Liabilities				
	Small loan balances	Balances, large loans and other contracts	Cash	Other	Total	Borrowed money	Reserves for losses	Paid-up capital	Other	Total
	559	560	561	562	563	564	565	566	567	568
1959	255.3	17.5	3.1	2.6	278.5	238.7	5.7	14.3	9.8	278.5
1958	230.7	14.0	3.3	2.8	250.8	211.1	5.4	5.3	29.0	250.8
1957	165.6	26.4	3.3	2.9	198.3	162.9	4.4	5.3	25.7	198.3
1956	70.8	68.5	4.3	3.2	146.8	108.6	3.4	5.3	29.5	146.8
1955	74.5	44.4	3.0	2.9	124.8	90.7	3.2	5.3	25.6	124.8
1954	76.9	29.4	2.8	2.2	111.4	80.7	2.9	5.3	22.5	111.4
1953	71.8	23.1	3.1	1.7	99.7	71.2	2.6	4.6	21.3[1]	99.7
1952	67.6	14.6	3.7	1.6	87.6	73.6	2.2	4.6	7.2	87.6
1951	61.1	8.9	2.5	1.4	74.0	60.3	2.1	4.6	7.0	74.0
1950	51.9	5.2	1.8	2.4	61.2	49.0	2.0	4.6	5.6	61.2
1949	43.7	2.6	1.8	.8	48.9	37.7	1.5	4.6	5.1	48.9
1948	36.5	1.6	3.8	.7	42.7	31.9	1.3	4.6	4.9	42.7
1947	24.4	6.8	1.1	.4	32.6	22.0	1.1	4.6	4.9	32.6
1946	20.3	4.0	.4	.2	24.9	15.0	.9	4.2	4.8	24.9
1945	13.4	1.5	.7	.4	16.0	7.1	.6	4.0	4.3	16.0
1944	11.5	—	.5	.5	12.6	4.8	.6	3.8	3.4	12.6
1943	9.8	—	.4	.4	10.6	3.6	.6	3.7	2.7	10.6
1942	8.5	—	.2	.3	9.1	2.6	.6	3.7	2.2	9.1
1941	7.6	—	.3	.1	7.9	4.3	.5	1.2	1.9	7.9
1940	6.3	.1	.4	.1	6.8	3.7	.4	1.2	1.5	6.8
1939	5.1	—	.3	—	5.5	2.3	.4	1.2	1.6	5.5
1938	4.8	—	.4	—	5.2	2.7	.3	1.0	1.2	5.2
1937	4.9	—	.3	—	5.2	2.9	.2	1.0	1.0	5.1
1936	4.1	—	.2	—	4.4	2.6	.1	1.0	.7	4.4
1935	3.0	—	.2	—	3.2	1.7	.1	1.0	.4	3.2
1934	2.4	—	.3	—	2.7	1.3	.1	1.0	.2	2.6
1933	1.2	—	.3	—	1.6	.4	—	1.0	.2	1.6
1932	.6	—	—	—	.7	.3	—	.3	.1	.7
1931	.8	—	—	—	.8	.5	—	.3	—	.8
1930	.6	—	—	—	.7	.5	—	.1	—	.6
1929	.4	—	—	—	.5	.3	—	.1	.1	.5
1928	.1	—	—	—	.2	—	—	.1	.1	.2

[1] Surplus paid in by shareholders amounted to $10.0 million in 1953.

Series H 569–576. *Canadian farm loan board, loans approved and paid out, 1930 to 1959*

(series H 569 and 571 in numbers: series H 570 and 572–576 in thousands of dollars)

Year[1]	Loans approved					Loans paid out		
	First mortgage		Second mortgage		Total amount	First mortgage	Second mortgage	Total
	Number	Amount	Number	Amount				
	569	**570**	**571**	**572**	**573**	**574**	**575**	**576**
1959	4,805	30,145	—	—	30,145	28,368	—	28,368
1958	3,702	21,278	—	—	21,278	19,344	—	19,344
1957	2,921	13,979	—	—	13,979	13,154	30	13,184
1956	2,057	8,127	204	183	8,310	8,039	215	8,254
1955	2,145	7,902	395	323	8,226	7,850	357	8,207
1954	2,091	7,367	591	450	7,817	6,606	394	7,001
1953	1,685	5,459	559	394	5,852	4,766	342	5,109
1952	1,437	3,930	494	309	4,238	4,131	338	4,469
1951	1,796	4,312	680	410	4,722	4,289	404	4,693
1950	1,949	4,716	801	474	5,189	4,481	462	4,943
1949	1,821	4,450	756	469	4,919	4,169	426	4,595
1948	1,301	3,145	517	315	3,461	2,911	274	3,185
1947	1,312	3,165	404	254	3,419	3,031	243	3,274
1946	918	2,161	258	163	2,324	1,978	143	2,121
1945	728	1,623	176	101	1,724	1,561	100	1,661
1944	603	1,316	162	91	1,407	1,252	84	1,336
1943	601	1,156	135	59	1,215	1,260	60	1,320
1942	1,024	1,891	155	76	1,967	2,054	80	2,134
1941	1,459	2,655	228	104	2,759	2,619	108	2,728
1940	2,380	4,149	464	200	4,349	4,131	212	4,343
1939	2,267	4,077	560	269	4,346	4,041	297	4,339
1938	1,913	3,473	776	369	3,842	4,652	612	5,264
1937	5,099	9,005	2,835	1,504	10,509	9,269	1,805	11,074
1936	5,100	8,907	3,236	2,052	10,958	6,192	1,232	7,424
1935	532	881	72	45	926	538	9	547
1934	287	491	—	—	491	559	—	559
1933	536	983	—	—	983	1,276	—	1,276
1932	1,049	2,025	—	—	2,025	1,996	—	1,996
1931	1,458	3,212	—	—	3,212	3,517	—	3,517
1930	1,787	3,981	—	—	3,981	2,630	—	2,630

[1] Fiscal year ending 31 March of the year given.

Series H 577–587.　*Industrial development bank, assets, liabilities and loan transactions, 1945 to 1960*

(millions of dollars)

Year[3]	Assets			Total assets or liabilities	Liabilities			Loan transactions		Loans outstanding plus undisbursed authorizations	
	Loans out-standing[1,2]	Govern-ment of Canada securities	All other assets		Capital and reserves	Bonds and deben-tures out-standing	All other liabilities	Disburse-ments (during period)[2]	Repay-ments (during period)[2]	Amount[1]	Number of customers on books
	577	578	579	580	581	582	583	584	585	586	587
1960	103.1	—	3.7	106.8	41.8	63.6	1.4	29.7	23.5	120.0	1,967
1959	96.9	—	1.8	98.7	39.4	57.7	1.6	29.3	20.5	109.3	1,609
1958	88.8	—	1.6	90.4	37.9	51.0	1.5	31.2	14.2	104.3	1,322
1957	71.9	—	1.9	73.8	36.1	35.5	2.2	32.6	12.9	88.3	1,022
1956	52.2	—	.9	53.1	34.6	17.7	.8	20.1	12.0	76.9	820
1955	44.0	—	2.0	46.0	33.0	9.5	3.5	12.7	10.7	52.3	693
1954	42.1	—	1.0	43.1	31.9	10.7	.5	11.5	8.0	48.1	661
1953	38.9	—	.9	39.8	29.5	8.9	1.4	11.3	5.8	45.9	633
1952	33.4	—	.7	34.1	28.7	3.9	1.5	8.9	4.7	40.5	584
1951	29.2	—	.7	29.9	27.9	1.3	.7	12.3	5.1	38.1	551
1950	21.9	5.1	4.1	31.1	27.2	—	3.9	6.4	4.7	26.0	490
1949	20.3	6.2	3.7	30.2	26.5	—	3.7	8.1	5.3	24.2	438
1948	17.5	8.2	3.5	29.2	25.8	—	3.4	9.8	3.8	23.8	404
1947	11.5	14.1	2.2	27.8	25.7	—	2.1	8.2	1.9	17.0	322
1946	5.1	10.2	.2	15.5	15.4	—	.1	4.6	.5	9.4	205
1945	.9	8.9	.3	10.1	10.1	—	—	1.0	—	3.2	80

[1] Includes small amount of investments.
[2] The change in loans outstanding does not equal the difference between disbursements and repayments because of financial year end accounting adjustments.

[3] As at 30 September of the year given.

Series H588–603. *Bond and stock yields, in the month of December, 1900 to 1959*
(yield in per cent)

Year	Treasury bills (3 months)[1]	Long term Canadas[2]	Province of Ontario[2]	Bonds Corporation[3]	Municipal[3]	Provincial[3]	Public utilities[3]	Industrial[3]	Theoretical Government of Canada[4] 2 years	5 years	10 years	15 years	Stocks[5] Banks	Preferred and 'A'	Common	Mines
	588	589	590	591	592	593	594	595	596	597	598	599	600	601	602	603
1959	5.016	—	—	—	6.60	6.12	6.04	6.14	5.24	5.81	5.25	5.32	3.22	5.12	3.96	5.43
1958	3.456	—	—	—	5.38	5.14	5.14	5.22	4.62	4.52	4.48	4.78	3.14	4.80	3.81	4.96
1957	3.65	—	—	—	5.12	4.60	5.03	5.04	3.88	3.92	3.71	3.75	3.83	5.39	5.03	7.11
1956	3.607	—	—	—	5.45	5.03	4.98	5.22	4.48	4.51	4.08	3.97	3.28	5.02	4.51	6.64
1955	2.592	—	—	—	4.04	3.82	3.98	4.15	3.34	3.45	3.42	3.41	3.37	4.34	4.14	5.64
1954	1.084	—	—	3.82	3.75	3.34	3.75	4.00	1.87	2.57	2.90	3.05	3.17	4.53	4.47	5.52
1953	1.884	—	—	4.17	4.50	4.07	4.31	4.48	3.20	3.61	3.64	3.61	4.00	5.19	5.57	6.76
1952	1.299	—	—	4.20	4.60	4.15	4.33	4.43	3.07	3.52	3.67	3.62	4.17	5.46	5.32	5.81
1951	.900	—	—	4.09	4.75	4.21	4.31	4.44	2.26	2.82	3.41	3.50	4.34	5.60	5.44	5.87
1950	.625	—	—	3.40	3.51	3.26	3.44	3.58	2.17	2.55	2.97	2.99	3.75	5.43	5.83	6.66
1949	.5115	—	—	3.30	3.50	3.02	3.26	3.51	1.65	2.17	2.63	2.75	3.77	6.08	6.35	5.80
1948	.412	—	—	3.50	3.54	3.17	3.47	3.61	1.58	2.27	2.71	2.93	3.97	5.73	6.01	6.43
1947	.4095	—	—	3.28	3.13	2.82	3.34	3.42	1.42	1.76	2.24	2.56	3.79	5.29	5.63	4.41
1946	.398	—	—	3.31	—	—	—	—	1.40	1.70	2.31	2.60	3.36	4.51	4.69	4.52
1945	.363	—	—	3.96	—	—	—	—	1.38	1.77	2.48	2.83	3.25	4.60	4.19	3.77
1944	.374	—	—	4.05	—	—	—	—	1.44	2.08	2.67	2.99	3.86	5.37	5.08	5.74
1943	.412	—	—	4.38	—	—	—	—	1.55	2.24	2.76	3.00	4.43	5.82	5.76	7.15
1942	.519	—	—	4.68	—	—	—	—	1.48	2.22	3.00	3.06	4.68	6.64	6.53	12.82
1941	.547	—	—	4.54	—	—	—	—	1.46	2.17	2.99	3.06	4.72	6.57	6.51	12.92
1940	.637	—	—	4.39	—	—	—	—	1.34	2.12	2.83	3.11	4.63	6.58	5.96	9.96
1939	.808	—	—	4.59	—	—	—	—	1.72	2.40	3.27	3.50	4.24	5.85	5.52	8.15
1938	.676	—	—	4.23	—	—	—	—	1.15	1.79	2.64	3.03	4.35	5.80	5.64	7.93
1937	.763	3.53	3.76	4.53	—	—	—	—	1.68	2.34	3.04	3.21	4.37	5.90	5.75	7.32
1936	.753	3.11	3.34	4.61	—	—	—	—	1.22	1.63	2.48	2.94	4.06	5.16	4.20	5.58
1935	1.249	3.67	3.96	5.29	—	—	—	—	—	—	—	—	4.73	5.71	4.53	6.42
1934	2.83	3.46	3.65	5.50	—	—	—	—	—	—	—	—	4.57	6.51	4.82	6.55
1933	—	4.62	4.72	7.96	—	—	—	—	—	—	—	—	—	—	—	—
1932	—	4.83	4.92	9.60	—	—	—	—	—	—	—	—	—	—	—	—
1931	—	5.42	5.20	7.73	—	—	—	—	—	—	—	—	—	—	—	—
1930	—	4.56	4.50	5.85	—	—	—	—	—	—	—	—	—	—	—	—
1929	—	4.92	4.90	5.85	—	—	—	—	—	—	—	—	—	—	—	—
1928	—	4.71	4.60	5.50	—	—	—	—	—	—	—	—	—	—	—	—
1927	—	4.38	4.35	5.41	—	—	—	—	—	—	—	—	—	—	—	—
1926	—	4.82	4.75	5.67	—	—	—	—	—	—	—	—	—	—	—	—
1925	—	4.86	4.80	5.74	—	—	—	—	—	—	—	—	—	—	—	—
1924	—	4.88	4.75	5.95	—	—	—	—	—	—	—	—	—	—	—	—
1923	—	5.11	5.14	6.13	—	—	—	—	—	—	—	—	—	—	—	—
1922	—	5.32	5.42	6.17	—	—	—	—	—	—	—	—	—	—	—	—
1921	—	5.65	5.72	6.52	—	—	—	—	—	—	—	—	—	—	—	—
1920	—	6.35	6.15	6.67	—	—	—	—	—	—	—	—	—	—	—	—
1919	—	5.60	5.75	6.31	—	—	—	—	—	—	—	—	—	—	—	—
1918	—	—	6.00	6.33	—	—	—	—	—	—	—	—	—	—	—	—
1917	—	—	6.00	6.37	—	—	—	—	—	—	—	—	—	—	—	—
1916	—	—	4.90	6.04	—	—	—	—	—	—	—	—	—	—	—	—
1915	—	—	5.25	6.15	—	—	—	—	—	—	—	—	—	—	—	—
1914	—	—	4.25	5.70	—	—	—	—	—	—	—	—	—	—	—	—
1913	—	—	4.40	5.77	—	—	—	—	—	—	—	—	—	—	—	—
1912	—	—	4.25	5.34	—	—	—	—	—	—	—	—	—	—	—	—
1911	—	—	4.00	5.12	—	—	—	—	—	—	—	—	—	—	—	—
1910	—	—	4.00	5.14	—	—	—	—	—	—	—	—	—	—	—	—
1909	—	—	3.90	5.11	—	—	—	—	—	—	—	—	—	—	—	—
1908	—	—	4.00	5.41	—	—	—	—	—	—	—	—	—	—	—	—
1907	—	—	4.25	6.00	—	—	—	—	—	—	—	—	—	—	—	—
1906	—	—	3.70	5.36	—	—	—	—	—	—	—	—	—	—	—	—
1905	—	—	3.65	5.22	—	—	—	—	—	—	—	—	—	—	—	—
1904	—	—	3.75	—	—	—	—	—	—	—	—	—	—	—	—	—
1903	—	—	3.76	—	—	—	—	—	—	—	—	—	—	—	—	—
1902	—	—	3.76	—	—	—	—	—	—	—	—	—	—	—	—	—
1901	—	—	3.80	—	—	—	—	—	—	—	—	—	—	—	—	—
1900	—	—	3.72	—	—	—	—	—	—	—	—	—	—	—	—	—

[1] December weighted average of weekly tenders. 1935 figure is for 11 December. 1934 figure is for 1 March.

[2] December average. 1937 figure is for March.

[3] Year end.

[4] Actual yields for 1959 and 1958. Issues used in 1959: 3% October 1/59–63; 3¾% Sept. 1/65; 3½% May 1/70; 3¼% June 1/74–76. Issues used in 1958: 3% December 15/60; 3% October 1/59–63; 2¾% June 15/67–68; 4¼% September 1/72.

Theoretical yields 1936 to 1957. Column 598 changes to 9 years in years 1936 to 1949. Date of quotation: 1959, 16 December; 1958, 17 December; 1957, 13 December; 1956, 14 December; 1955, 13 December; 1940 to 1954, 15 December; theoretical 15 year bonds: 1 December for 1936–37 inclusive, monthly average for 1938–40 inclusive. Theoretical 9 year, 5 year and 2 year bonds; 1 December for 1936–39 inclusive. Generally a mid-December quotation. 1958–59 closing yield.

[5] December average.

Series H604–618. *Bond and stock yields, annual averages, 1900 to 1959*

(yield in per cent)

Year	Treasury bills (3 months)[1]	Long term Canadas[2]	Province of Ontario[2,3]	Municipal[4]	Provincial[4]	Public utilities[4]	Industrial[4]	Theoretical Government of Canada[5] 2 years	5 years	10 years	15 years	Stocks[6] Banks	Preferred and 'A'	Common	Mines
	604	605	606	607	608	609	610	611	612	613	614	615	616	617	618
1959	4.82	—	—	5.94	5.60	5.55	5.59	4.95	5.40	5.01	4.99	3.01	4.86	3.70	4.95
1958	2.31	—	—	5.13	4.70	4.90	4.98	3.38	3.49	3.73	4.50	3.46	4.96	4.13	5.60
1957	3.78	—	—	5.52	5.02	5.21	5.38	4.52	4.56	4.30	4.19	3.51	5.28	4.68	6.79
1956	2.90	—	—	4.57	4.16	4.28	4.53	3.61	3.75	3.61	3.60	3.19	4.67	4.12	5.95
1955	1.57	—	—	3.71	3.38	3.73	3.98	2.18	2.66	2.94	3.07	3.04	4.26	4.09	5.34
1954	1.44	—	—	3.98	3.55	3.94	4.14	2.21	2.81	3.03	3.14	3.50	4.82	4.99	5.97
1953	1.71	—	—	4.66	4.15	4.36	4.49	3.25	3.55	3.69	3.68	3.92	5.22	5.41	6.20
1952	1.06	—	—	4.65	4.13	4.24	4.29	2.68	3.22	3.58	3.59	4.28	5.61	5.35	5.71
1951	.79	—	—	4.07	3.65	3.82	3.89	2.37	2.69	3.18	3.24	4.00	5.37	5.22	5.98
1950	.55	—	—	3.46	3.12	3.30	3.50	1.81	2.22	2.67	2.78	3.65	5.64	5.96	6.10
1949	.49	—	—	3.56	3.16	3.39	3.57	1.66	2.24	2.64	2.83	3.92	6.26	6.54	6.27
1948	.41	—	—	3.43	3.13	3.44	3.51	1.44	2.27	2.72	2.93	3.96	5.59	5.84	5.50
1947	.41	—	—	—	—	—	—	1.43	1.75	2.25	2.57	3.52	4.92	5.04	4.30
1946	.39	—	—	—	—	—	—	1.39	1.69	2.32	2.61	3.24	4.39	4.06	4.31
1945	.37	—	—	—	—	—	—	1.39	1.92	2.54	2.93	3.60	5.02	4.62	4.62
1944	.39	—	—	—	—	—	—	1.46	2.13	2.68	2.99	4.25	5.45	5.33	6.27
1943	.48	—	—	—	—	—	—	1.52	2.23	2.81	3.01	4.34	5.89	5.82	8.60
1942	.54	—	—	—	—	—	—	1.48	2.18	3.03	3.06	4.87	6.96	7.19	15.02
1941	.58	—	—	—	—	—	—	1.40	2.11	2.92	3.10	4.77	6.63	6.42	11.33
1940	.70	—	—	—	—	—	—	1.48	2.16	2.96	3.28	4.62	6.31	5.88	10.84
1939	.71	—	—	—	—	—	—	1.51	2.11	2.88	3.16	4.35	5.96	5.57	8.17
1938	.59	—	—	—	—	—	—	1.14	1.93	2.76	3.09	4.36	5.98	5.82	7.37
1937	.72	—	—	—	—	—	—	1.37	2.07	2.93	3.17	4.05	5.29	4.72	6.81
1936	.85	3.26	3.59	—	—	—	—	1.28	1.72	2.46	2.97	4.42	5.44	4.28	5.66
1935	1.50	3.58	3.88	—	—	—	—	—	—	—	—	4.88	6.20	4.66	7.21
1934	2.50	3.97	4.11	—	—	—	—	—	—	—	—	4.98	6.82	4.84	6.39
1933	—	4.60	4.68	—	—	—	—	—	—	—	—	—	—	—	—
1932	—	5.12	5.21	—	—	—	—	—	—	—	—	—	—	—	—
1931	—	4.55	4.63	—	—	—	—	—	—	—	—	—	—	—	—
1930	—	4.73	4.71	—	—	—	—	—	—	—	—	—	—	—	—
1929	—	4.94	4.90	—	—	—	—	—	—	—	—	—	—	—	—
1928	—	4.52	4.43	—	—	—	—	—	—	—	—	—	—	—	—
1927	—	4.62	4.54	—	—	—	—	—	—	—	—	—	—	—	—
1926	—	4.86	4.79	—	—	—	—	—	—	—	—	—	—	—	—
1925	—	4.86	4.78	—	—	—	—	—	—	—	—	—	—	—	—
1924	—	5.00	4.94	—	—	—	—	—	—	—	—	—	—	—	—
1923	—	5.09	5.19	—	—	—	—	—	—	—	—	—	—	—	—
1922	—	5.41	5.42	—	—	—	—	—	—	—	—	—	—	—	—
1921	—	5.99	6.00	—	—	—	—	—	—	—	—	—	—	—	—
1920	—	6.09	5.95	—	—	—	—	—	—	—	—	—	—	—	—
1919	—	5.50	5.63	—	—	—	—	—	—	—	—	—	—	—	—
1918	—	—	6.01	—	—	—	—	—	—	—	—	—	—	—	—
1917	—	—	5.51	—	—	—	—	—	—	—	—	—	—	—	—
1916	—	—	5.14	—	—	—	—	—	—	—	—	—	—	—	—
1915	—	—	4.68	—	—	—	—	—	—	—	—	—	—	—	—
1914	—	—	4.30	—	—	—	—	—	—	—	—	—	—	—	—
1913	—	—	4.34	—	—	—	—	—	—	—	—	—	—	—	—
1912	—	—	4.14	—	—	—	—	—	—	—	—	—	—	—	—
1911	—	—	3.93	—	—	—	—	—	—	—	—	—	—	—	—
1910	—	—	3.95	—	—	—	—	—	—	—	—	—	—	—	—
1909	—	—	3.89	—	—	—	—	—	—	—	—	—	—	—	—
1908	—	—	4.14	—	—	—	—	—	—	—	—	—	—	—	—
1907	—	—	4.04	—	—	—	—	—	—	—	—	—	—	—	—
1906	—	—	3.67	—	—	—	—	—	—	—	—	—	—	—	—
1905	—	—	3.63	—	—	—	—	—	—	—	—	—	—	—	—
1904	—	—	3.77	—	—	—	—	—	—	—	—	—	—	—	—
1903	—	—	3.76	—	—	—	—	—	—	—	—	—	—	—	—
1902	—	—	3.79	—	—	—	—	—	—	—	—	—	—	—	—
1901	—	—	3.77	—	—	—	—	—	—	—	—	—	—	—	—
1900	—	—	3.61	—	—	—	—	—	—	—	—	—	—	—	—

[1] Average of weekly weighted averages of successful tenders. 1945 figure excludes special issue of varying maturity authorized by PC4501 of 70 million. 1940 figure excludes special issue of varying maturity to the Bank of Canada of 75 million. 1935 figure includes one 9 month issue. 1934 figure includes all issues.

[2] Average of monthly averages.

[3] From 1900 to 1919 inclusive, an average of month end yields of January, April, June, October and December.

[4] Average of month end yields.

[5] Generally mid month quotations in order to make columns 611–614 consistent. Actual yields for 1959 and 1958. Issues used in 1959: 3% 1 October 1959–63;

3¾% 1 September 1965; 3½% 1 May 1970; 3¼% 1 June 1974–76. Issues used in 1958: 3% 15 December 1960; 3% 1 October 1959–63; 2¾% 15 June 1967–68; 4¼% 1 September 1972. Theoretical yields 1936 to 1957 inclusive. Date of quotation: theoretical 15 year bonds; 1st of month for 1936 to 1937 inclusive, monthly average for 1938 to 1940 inclusive, 15th of month for 1941 and thereafter. Theoretical 9 year, 5 year and 2 year bonds, 1st of month for 1936 to 1939 inclusive, 15th of month for 1940 and thereafter. The 10 year bond 1953 to 1959 becomes 9 year from 1936 to 1952.

[6] Average of weekly average yields.

Series H619–630. *Foreign exchange rates, 1910 to 1960*

Year	December U.S. dollar in Canadian funds			December Sterling in Canadian funds			Annual U.S. dollar in Canadian funds			Annual Sterling in Canadian funds		
	High	Low	Average[1]	High	Low	Average[2]	High	Low	Average[1]	High	Low	Average[2]
	619	620	621	622	623	624	625	626	627	628	629	630
1960	99.81	97.50	98.24	279.97	273.95	275.83	99.81	94.94	96.97	279.97	266.10	272.28
1959	95.34	94.88	95.12	266.89	265.50	266.21	98.19	94.56	95.90	275.81	265.17	269.39
1958	96.69	96.31	96.46	271.03	269.78	270.50	99.16	95.75	97.06	278.91	268.19	272.76
1957	98.63	96.91	97.74	276.81	271.97	274.29	98.63	94.22	95.88	276.81	262.34	267.88
1956	96.47	95.78	96.05	268.63	266.81	267.54	99.97	95.66	98.41	280.69	266.19	275.16
1955	100.03	99.88	99.91	280.44	279.88	280.15	100.06	96.47	98.63	280.44	268.75	275.35
1954	97.03	96.59	96.80	270.50	269.00	269.88	98.75	96.34	97.32	278.31	269.00	273.39
1953	97.63	97.00	97.31	274.44	272.63	273.52	99.78	96.75	98.34	280.94	272.38	276.66
1952	97.53	96.56	97.06	273.56	270.69	272.40	101.13	95.88	97.89	281.25	266.75	273.40
1951	103.88	101.19	102.56	290.75	281.38	286.49	107.31	101.19	105.28	300.50	281.38	294.68
1950	106.00	104.59	105.31	296.75	293.00	294.86	110.50[3]	103.25[3]	108.92[3]	308.75[3]	289.25[3]	304.44[3]
1949	110.50[4]	110.00[4]	—	308.75	307.25	—	110.50	100.00	103.08	308.75	307.25	376.13
1948	100.50	100.00	—	404.00	402.00	—	100.50	100.00	100.25	404.00	402.00	403.00
1947	100.50	100.00	—	404.00	402.00	—	100.50	100.00	100.25	404.00	402.00	403.00
1946	100.50	100.00	—	404.00	402.00	—	100.50	100.00	105.75	404.00	402.00	425.54
1945	110.50	110.00	—	445.00	443.00	—	110.50	110.00	110.45	445.00	443.00	444.78
1944	111.00	110.00	—	447.00	443.00	—	111.00	110.00	110.50	447.00	443.00	445.00
1943	111.00	110.00	—	447.00	443.00	—	111.00	110.00	110.50	447.00	443.00	445.00
1942	111.00	110.00	—	447.00	443.00	—	111.00	110.00	110.50	447.00	443.00	445.00
1941	111.00	110.00	—	447.00	443.00	—	111.00	110.00	110.50	447.00	443.00	445.00
1940	111.00	110.00	—	447.00	443.00	—	111.00	110.00	110.50	447.00	443.00	445.00
1939	111.00	110.00	—	447.00	443.00	—	111.00	110.00	103.70	447.00	443.00	461.05
1938	101.11	100.66	100.93	—	—	471.33	103.50	99.92	100.56	—	—	491.62
1937	100.17	99.94	100.04	—	—	499.85	100.31	99.73	99.99	—	—	494.32
1936	100.05	99.84	99.92	—	—	490.42	100.69	99.50	100.06	—	—	497.45
1935	101.19	100.56	100.93	—	—	497.55	102.63	99.00	100.51	—	—	492.68
1934	99.69	97.66	98.78	—	—	488.65	101.63	96.88	99.00	—	—	498.91
1933	100.50	98.25	99.54	—	—	509.57	123.00	95.50	108.74	—	—	460.73
1932	118.50	112.50	115.44	—	—	378.66	119.50	106.63	113.52	—	—	398.01
1931	124.88	115.25	121.05	—	—	409.23	124.88	99.97	103.81	—	—	470.78
1930	100.19	99.95	100.23	—	—	485.97	101.28	99.84	100.16	—	—	486.98
1929	101.38	100.56	100.78	—	—	492.12	103.00	100.13	100.76	—	—	489.38
1928	100.28	100.03	100.27	—	—	485.74	100.44	99.75	100.09	—	—	487.06
1927	100.17	99.98	100.09	—	—	488.26	100.19	99.81	100.00	—	—	485.73
1926	100.13	99.92	100.07	—	—	484.96	100.63	99.80	99.98	—	—	485.50
1925	100.11	99.97	100.05	—	—	485.15	100.47	99.91	100.02	—	—	483.05
1924	100.66	100.03	100.00	—	—	468.75	103.59	99.94	101.27	—	—	446.71
1923	102.66	102.06	102.41	—	—	445.88	103.00	100.34	101.96	—	—	465.96
1922	101.28	99.98	100.50	—	—	461.25	106.63	99.86	101.54	—	—	452.54
1921	109.66	104.88	107.59	—	—	448.38	117.75	104.88	111.64	—	—	429.04
1920	119.00	113.88	116.38	—	—	407.57	119.00	108.00	112.47	—	—	408.36
1919	111.00	104.78	107.59	—	—	408.33	105.25	101.88	103.57	—	—	454.80
1918	101.69	101.38	101.50	—	—	482.08	102.44	100.47	101.59	—	—	482.24
1917	100.55	100.02	100.25	—	—	476.39	100.94	99.00	100.18	—	—	475.34
1916	100.06	99.97	99.98	—	—	474.72	100.81	99.92	100.18	—	—	475.86
1915	100.06	99.94	100.00	—	—	471.25	101.00	99.92	100.39	—	—	474.93
1914	100.88	100.02	100.50	—	—	489.42	99.98	98.00	99.92	—	—	490.19
1913	100.03	99.97	100.00	—	—	485.30	100.00	99.92	100.01	—	—	486.39
1912	100.06	100.02	100.04	—	—	485.35	99.97	99.94	100.00	—	—	
1911	—	—	—	—	—	—	—	—	—	—	—	—
1910	100.02	99.92	99.97	—	—	485.35	100.05	99.91	99.98	—	—	486.32

[1] Figures for 1928 to 1960 are averages of noon rates of business days; 1914 to 1927, averages of daily high and low quotations; 1910, 1912, 1913, averages of monthly high and low quotations.

[2] Figures for 1925 to 1960 are averages of noon rates of business days; 1910 to 1924 averages of monthly high and low quotations.

[3] Official rates were withdrawn on 30 September and the exchange market reopened. The average noon rates for 1950 are a simple average of the mid-rates for the first nine months plus the market rates for the last three months.

[4] The rate of exchange was officially fixed from 16 September 1939 to 30 September 1950. Figures shown for those years are official buying and selling rates.

Series H631–650. *Stock exchange statistics, 1914 to 1959*

Year	Index of common stock prices (monthly average) (1935–39 = 100)					Preferred stock prices (1935–39 = 100)	Index of common stock prices (December) (1935–39 = 100)					Preferred stock prices (1935–39 = 100)
	Banks	In-dustrials	Mines	Utilities	Total[1]		Banks	In-dustrials	Mines	Utilities	Total[1]	
	631	632	633	634	635	636	637	638	639	640	641	642
1959	355.8	272.2	118.7	197.3	265.4	157.2	347.2	269.3	112.8	190.6	261.5	149.9
1958	273.2	247.6	103.8	189.1	239.4	160.6	328.0	266.8	116.1	195.8	259.1	159.8
1957	263.8	271.0	114.0	199.8	258.2	151.3	234.9	224.0	89.4	173.9	216.2	151.1
1956	275.8	282.7	134.4	206.3	269.0	166.2	276.2	281.7	129.4	203.6	267.8	154.4
1955	246.3	239.6	116.9	197.0	232.7	177.2	253.4	257.0	121.4	204.2	247.6	173.9
1954	208.0	182.3	91.3	165.0	181.2	170.2	227.0	210.5	100.9	181.8	206.8	175.4
1953	168.9	160.1	92.1	157.2	160.3	162.3	180.2	152.7	79.9	146.4	153.6	161.7
1952	148.4	176.6	103.6	168.3	173.1	160.1	155.4	169.9	103.4	167.4	168.4	160.7
1951	144.6	172.0	99.2	162.3	168.3	164.5	144.2	180.6	103.4	177.0	177.3	159.5
1950	147.4	127.6	89.9	132.5	131.6	156.7	152.6	144.4	88.2	141.2	146.3	160.2
1949	134.4	103.1	87.4	117.4	109.4	143.0	140.6	112.5	92.4	122.5	117.9	150.7
1948	129.3	107.2	82.0	120.2	112.5	144.6	132.4	111.1	84.0	120.2	115.8	144.6
1947	130.8	99.3	86.7	117.3	106.0	154.0	133.6	100.3	86.6	112.1	106.2	148.1
1946	130.0	108.6	97.8	132.5	115.7	155.9	133.5	99.3	83.7	118.3	106.4	156.0
1945	95.7	93.7	95.2	120.2	99.6	137.0	107.5	105.8	108.2	135.9	112.5	146.6
1944	82.0	78.8	81.3	100.8	83.8	123.1	88.1	80.7	80.6	105.4	86.6	129.8
1943	80.5	78.6	70.1	101.3	83.5	112.4	78.9	75.8	74.9	96.6	80.5	115.8
1942	81.2	60.4	52.3	70.4	64.2	96.6	74.4	67.2	54.7	83.8	71.3	100.4
1941	90.5	63.9	72.4	70.7	67.5	99.7	90.5	63.9	63.2	68.7	67.2	100.7
1940	95.6	74.2	81.2	80.9	77.4	100.8	94.6	65.9	80.2	76.4	70.3	101.7
1939	102.5	91.2	104.5	86.1	91.5	101.6	103.1	90.9	99.3	90.7	92.2	110.1
1938	101.6	94.6	103.1	90.4	94.9	100.6	102.5	98.7	110.9	87.3	97.3	104.8
1937	109.3	113.6	102.1	122.4	115.8	114.8	99.7	92.2	93.7	98.2	94.5	97.7
1936	98.0	109.6	107.7	110.7	108.8	97.6	107.2	117.0	117.0	124.6	117.7	113.3
1935	89.6	79.9	85.9	92.7	83.6	85.5	91.6	98.5	92.9	99.0	98.0	89.0
1934	92.1	68.1	—	104.9	78.1	82.2	96.5	69.1	—	94.2	78.6	86.1
1933	84.7	51.8	—	97.3	62.5	67.4	79.1	61.3	—	94.8	68.6	72.6
1932	92.0	34.8	—	97.6	50.6	63.7	82.6	32.4	—	90.7	47.6	60.6
1931	123.1	53.7	—	167.8	77.7	87.9	113.5	40.9	—	117.6	59.1	76.0
1930	141.1	94.5	—	248.2	124.1	114.9	132.2	66.2	—	207.7	94.0	99.5
1929	164.8	146.8	—	293.4	173.8	126.1	143.5	115.5	—	261.1	142.6	121.1
1928	170.9	102.3	—	281.3	145.4	131.7	180.1	130.5	—	297.0	167.3	130.2
1927	140.7	72.4	—	243.7	112.5	126.3	154.4	88.9	—	269.4	131.2	134.9
1926	122.2	53.9	—	200.6	90.7	120.7	124.6	58.9	—	212.5	95.2	122.3
1925	115.0	41.7	—	173.0	73.5	—	121.3	47.8	—	179.3	80.8	—
1924	105.4	33.6	—	169.1	64.3	—	110.8	34.9	—	168.6	65.9	—
1923	107.6	33.0	—	158.6	62.4	—	104.0	32.6	—	161.7	62.2	—
1922	103.5	29.6	—	142.5	57.1	—	105.3	32.2	—	146.0	60.2	—
1921	103.9	26.8	—	130.2	52.7	—	104.2	26.1	—	132.3	52.3	—
1920	105.7	34.2	—	137.2	60.9	—	101.5	29.3	—	133.3	55.3	—
1919	110.6	29.7	—	157.6	59.8	—	109.4	33.9	—	143.8	61.9	—
1918	104.9	24.0	—	151.6	53.1	—	106.9	25.5	—	162.3	56.1	—
1917	106.6	23.9	—	166.6	55.2	—	104.1	22.0	—	159.5	52.1	—
1916	111.0	26.1	—	171.2	58.3	—	107.9	27.7	—	166.4	59.0	—
1915	114.0	20.4	—	160.8	51.6	—	114.1	24.2	—	177.5	57.6	—
1914[3]	115.7	20.1	—	191.8	55.7	—	—	—	—	—	—	—

Series H631–650. *Stock exchange statistics, 1914 to 1959 (continuation)*

Year	Montreal and Canadian Stock Exchanges (monthly average)				Toronto Stock Exchange (monthly average)			
	Brokers' loans (millions of dollars)	Industrial shares traded (thousand shares)	Quoted market values (billions of dollars)[2]	Value of all shares traded (millions of dollars)	Brokers' loans (millions of dollars)	Shares traded (million shares)	Quoted market value (billions of dollars)[2]	Value of all shares traded (millions of dollars)
	643	644	645	646	647	648	649	650
1959	24.48	2,188	48.08	75.2	42.8	63.6	50.58	155.0
1958	21.68	1,597	41.42	61.7	38.8	69.1	43.14	125.5
1957	29.81	1,688	43.90	62.2	62.4	78.0	45.23	155.5
1956	36.42	1,952	42.49	96.6	86.8	112.6	45.26	209.2
1955	27.93	1,867	35.35	96.8	65.2	126.6	40.12	224.9
1954	19.28	1,465	24.09	63.8	45.7	64.7	27.38	112.5
1953	26.94	1,055	18.07	42.5	48.7	71.1	20.36	95.3
1952	34.67	1,037	15.31	49.5	51.3	50.0	16.42	92.5
1951	27.64	1,676	11.46	67.1	40.0	46.8	11.79	97.9
1950	20.63	1,752	8.97	55.2	36.3	42.2	8.88	75.2
1949	17.16	899	8.26	24.9	29.8	20.8	7.24	37.7
1948	18.50	962	8.87	27.8	29.9	20.9	7.31	36.6
1947	19.03	967	9.08	24.4	31.0	26.6	7.14	38.7
1946	22.48	1,308	9.30	39.2	31.5	31.2	7.52	62.4
1945	16.90	1,072	7.89	23.7	28.2	39.4	6.36	51.5
1944	10.25	532	7.16	10.9	17.6	14.4	5.00	22.2
1943	7.55	485	7.10	9.2	9.2	9.6	4.46	15.2
1942	5.46	180	6.22	3.7	7.8	3.2	3.36	4.9
1941	5.71	196	6.81	4.5	8.6	4.4	3.66	6.9
1940	8.78	395	7.20	7.9	11.7	6.2	3.92	11.0
1939	12.08	707	7.01	18.0	16.8	10.1	4.77	24.4
1938	15.04	684	7.48	22.9	23.7	17.7	5.06	37.0
1937	33.16	1,303	6.83	48.6	37.9	23.0	4.65	54.2
1936	22.93	1,207	8.50	—	—	37.6	6.45	58.3
1935	18.01	—	7.33	—	—	14.4	4.55	28.7
1934	19.61	—	—	—	—	28.4	3.76	34.6
1933	15.25	—	—	—	—	—	—	—
1932	—	—	—	—	—	—	—	—
1931	—	—	—	—	—	—	—	—
1930	—	—	—	—	—	—	—	—
1929	—	—	—	—	—	—	—	—
1928	—	—	—	—	—	—	—	—
1927	—	—	—	—	—	—	—	—
1926	—	—	—	—	—	—	—	—
1925	—	—	—	—	—	—	—	—
1924	—	—	—	—	—	—	—	—
1923	—	—	—	—	—	—	—	—
1922	—	—	—	—	—	—	—	—
1921	—	—	—	—	—	—	—	—
1920	—	—	—	—	—	—	—	—
1919	—	—	—	—	—	—	—	—
1918	—	—	—	—	—	—	—	—
1917	—	—	—	—	—	—	—	—
1916	—	—	—	—	—	—	—	—
1915	—	—	—	—	—	—	—	—
1914[3]	—	—	—	—	—	—	—	—

[1] Excluding mining stock index.
[2] End of month averages.

[3] Exchanges closed August to December 1914. Average is for first seven months of the year.

Series H651–660. *Sales of Canadian bonds, by class of bond and country of sale, 1904 to 1959*

(millions of dollars)

Year	Dominion[1]	Provincial	Municipal	Railway	Parochial and mis-cellaneous	Corporation	Total	Sold in Canada	Sold in United States	Sold in Great Britain
	651	652	653	654	655	656	657	658	659	660
1959	2,775	653	351	—	74	369	4,222	3,749	473	—
1958	2,625	791	401	—	62	729	4,609	4,122	487	—
1957	2,469	646	306	—	50	1,025	4,495	3,888	607	—
1956	1,357	558	266	—	53	860	3,094	2,623	471	—
1955	1,349	434	227	—	66	586	2,662	2,507	155	—
1954	3,201	401	210	—	51	607	4,469	4,295	174	—
1953	1,951	437	187	—	35	336	2,945	2,639	307	—
1952	831	427	148	—	49	574	2,028	1,744	285	—
1951	595	370	196	—	38	452	1,650	1,266	384	—
1950	2,168	374	150	—	30	431	3,153	2,981	173	—
1949	790	449	135	—	24	285	1,683	1,543	140	—
1948	445	313	84	—	21	311	1,174	1,024	150	—
1947	293	230	239	—	15	380	1,156	1,068	88	—
1946	985	114	141	—	43	581	1,865	1,801	64	—
1945	3,578	162	30	—	11	154	3,935	3,855	80	—
1944	3,401	67	113	—	11	92	3,684	3,629	55[2]	—
1943	3,670	98	14	—	20	53	3,855	3,729	126	—
1942	2,431	97	24	—	—	14	2,565	2,550	16	—
1941	1,037	70	15	—	—	16	1,138	1,127	11	—
1940	1,181	169	25	—	—	26	1,400	1,400	—	—
1939	405	154	27	7[3]	—	236	828[4]	697	128	—
1938	283	119	35	19	—	56	513	424	40	49
1937	334	174	52	30	—	90	680	592	88	—
1936	258	119	34	133	—	220	764	677	86	1
1935	428	123	45	48	—	61	706	543	162	1
1934	291	140	25	33	—	41	529	421	50	58
1933	440	83	41	1	—	4	570	435	60	75
1932	226	128	96	13	—	11	473	378	81	14
1931	858	126	85	122	—	59	1,251	1,091	156	4
1930	140	160	110	137	—	220	767	369	394	5
1929	—	120	99	199	—	243	661	378	264	19
1928	—	93	27	48	—	285	454	278	160	16
1927	45	115	73	80	—	290	602	374	224	5
1926	105	77	65	35	—	251	532	264	259	9
1925	169	107	46	41	—	120	484	271	182	30
1924	175	90	89	157	—	69	580	337	240	4
1923	200	106	84	28	—	97	515	428	85	2
1922	200	115	87	14	—	77	492	250	242	—
1921	—	161	85	97	—	61	404	213	178	12
1920	—	126	56	97	—	46	325	102	223	—
1919	753	52	26	35	—	43	910	705	199	5
1918	689	19	44	20	—	5	775	727	33	15
1917	650	15	24	18	—	19	726	546	175	5
1916	175	33	94	22	—	32	357	103	207	47
1915	170	48	67	34	—	16	335	115	179	41
1914	49	56	79	60	—	29	273	33	54	186
1913	34	37	111	66	—	126	374	46	51	277
1912	25	26	47	45	—	130	273	38	31	204
1911	—	11	30	86	—	140	267	45	18	204
1910	45	10	49	41	—	86	231	39	4	188
1909	63	9	32	101	—	61	265	60	10	194
1908	48	1	45	—	—	103	196	25	6	165
1907	—	9	14	—	—	59	83	15	5	63
1906	—	10	8	—	—	36	54	23	4	27
1905	—	—	9	—	—	126	135	40	9	—
1904	—	11	15	—	—	9	35	24	8	3

[1] Excludes treasury bills, deposit certificates and other financing for a term of less than one year and the Canada Conversion Loan of 1958.
[2] Not including bonds purchased by Canadian dealers and later sold in the United States.
[3] From 1936 on C.N.R. financing included in Dominion (column 651). From 1940 on C.P.R. issues included in Corporation (column 656).
[4] Includes $4,000,000 distributed elsewhere.

Series H661–683. *Net new security issues, 1936 to 1960*
(par values in millions of Canadian dollars)

	Total bonds, treasury bills and short term paper											Total corporate stocks			
	Government of Canada			Nongovernment											
Year	Bonds	Treasury bills and notes and deposit certificates	Total	Pro-vincial bonds	Muni-cipal bonds	Cor-porate bonds	'Other' bonds	Total bonds	Finance company paper	Total	Total	Pre-ferred	Com-mon	Total	Total
	661	**662**	**663**	**664**	**665**	**666**	**667**	**668**	**669**	**670**	**671**	**672**	**673**	**674**	**675**
1960	704	−92	612	477	319	302	21	1,119	10	1,129	1,741	52	182	234	1,975
1959	141	582	723	568	326	108	18	1,020	135	1,155	1,878	73	331	404	2,281
1958	1,382	−130	1,252	614	323	662	4	1,603	−111	1,492	2,744	25	287	312	3,056
1957	−120	50	−70	549	278	954	4	1,785	48	1,833	1,764	89	426	516	2,279
1956	−616	−150	−766	540	224	794	6	1,564	94	1,658	892	175	514	689	1,581
1955	340	195	535	210	234	324	26	794	59	853	1,387	95	367	462	1,849
1954	−301	130	−171	293	240	445	31	1,009	−39	969	799	25	147	173	972
1953	451	—	451	272	182	394	−3	845	56	900	1,351	51	186	237	1,588
1952	−148	—	−148	306	152	378	28	864	20	884	735	16	229	245	980
1951	−458	−100	−558	250	176	293	—	719	77	796	238	−15	207	192	430
1950	−157	300	143₂	159	136	383	—	67	25	703	846	5	111	116	962
1949	−680[2]	−100	−780[2]	331	105	170	—	60	2	608	−172	—	56	56	−116
1948	−329	100	−229	199	78	260	—	537	—	537	308	18	33	51	359
1947	−260	−346	−606	263[3,4]	−31[4]	151	—	383	11	394	−212	59	−61[3]	−2[3]	−214
1946	137	−250	−113	−2	−5	−8	—	−15	3	−12	−125	−14	81	67	−58
1945	3,710	−695	3,015	−16	−43	−1	—	−60	—	−60	2,955	−7	32	25	2,980
1944	2,776	248	3,024	−44	−27	−43	—	−114	—	−114	2,910	—	—	—	2,910
1943	2,564	535	3,099	−2	−53	−66	—	−121	—	−121	2,978	—	—	—	2,978
1942	1,648	633	2,281	−54	−61	−166	—	−281	—	−281	2,000	—	—	−3	1,997
1941	537	290	827	−21	−46	−70	—	−137	—	−137	690	—	—	—	690
1940	329	315	644	73	−30	−71	—	−28	—	−28	616	—	—	19	635
1939	14	200	214	55	−41	−25	—	−11	—	−11	203	—	—	14	217
1938	75	5	80	52	−34	13	—	31	—	31	111	—	—	9	120
1937	−5	—	−5	66	−25	2	—	43	—	43	38	—	—	32	70
1936	150	12	162	53	−27	18	—	44	—	44	206	—	—	44	250

	Of which payable in currencies other than Canadian							
Year	Government of Canada bonds	Nongovernment bonds				Total bonds	Corporate preferred and common stocks[5]	Total bonds and stocks
		Provincial	Municipal[1]	Corporate	Total			
	676	**677**	**678**	**679**	**680**	**681**	**682**	**683**
1960	− 1	17	85	1	104	103	5	108
1959	−149	239	113	15	367	219	2	220
1958	− 2	144	115	184	443	441	2	444
1957	− 68	44	97	382	523	455	−31	425
1956	−116	191	84	208	483	367	3	370
1955	− 60	−50	17	− 39	− 72	−132	41	− 90
1954	− 3	47	18	83	147	145	1	146
1953	− 6	111	56	112	280	273	28	301
1952	− 2	58	41	135	234	232	—	232
1951	− 53	221	68[1]	− 9	280	227	—	227
1950	− 73₂	− 9	4	39	34	− 39	—	− 39
1949	12[2]	−30	− 6	− 11	− 47	− 35	—	− 35
1948	148	−33	− 9	− 9	− 51	97	—	97
1947	− 30	−61	−72	−165	−298	−328	−13	−341
1946	−153	−32	− 8	−134	−174	−327	− 8	−335
1945	− 46	−10	− 8	− 54	− 72	−118	—	−118
1944	− 65	−21	− 5	− 21	− 47	−112	—	−112
1943	−139	−24	− 11	− 36	− 71	−210	—	−210
1942	−172	−70	− 12	−149	−231	−403	—	−403
1941	−206	−31	− 14	− 30	− 75	−281	—	−281
1940	−128	−10	−16	− 37	− 63	−191	—	−191
1939	− 56	− 1	−15	−138	−154	−210	—	−210
1938	− 9	−13	−21	− 36	− 70	− 79	—	− 79
1937	− 10	−22	−16	− 90	−128	−138	—	−138
1936	− 29	−23	−14	−164	−201	−230	—	−230

[1] For 1936 to 1951, estimates only.
[2] Excludes Newfoundland sterling issue assumed by Government of Canada in June 1949 (net $62 millions).
[3] Includes retirement of $112 millions Montreal Light, Heat and Power stock and issue of $112 millions Quebec Hydro bonds.

[4] Includes the issue of $62 millions Quebec Municipal Commission bonds (guaranteed by Province of Quebec) of which $2 million of bonds are payable in other currencies and the retirement from municipal bonds of the debt of certain school corporations.
[5] Canadian stock issues with dividends payable in U.S. dollars.

SECTION J: PRICE INDEXES

A. ASIMAKOPULOS, *McGill University*

The price indexes presented here have been grouped into four subsections: wholesale price indexes, series J1–83, including the earlier estimates of wholesale price indexes by H. Michell, R. H. Coats and the Department of Labour, series J1–33, and the Dominion Bureau of Statistics estimates of wholesale price indexes in series J34–83; export and import prices indexes in series J84–127; retail price indexes in series J128–152; and implicit price indexes of gross national expenditure and its components in series J153–164. In addition there is an appendix which provides index numbers of fifteen foodstuffs for the years 1848 to 1913 prepared by Michell. Index numbers are given only for all commodities and other broad groups. Price series for some individual commodities will be found in other sections where the commodity is a very important part of the area covered; for example, the price series for wheat is found in Section L, Agriculture. A list of price series in other sections appears in the index.

Sources: The following is a list of references which proved useful in compiling the tables shown here:

R. H. Coats, *Wholesale Prices in Canada, 1890–1909* (Ottawa, Government Printing Bureau, 1910); Department of Labour, *Wholesale Prices, Canada*, annual 1910 to 1917 (Ottawa, Government Printing Bureau and King's Printer); R. H. Coats, *Report of the Board of Inquiry into Cost of Living*, vol. II (Ottawa, Department of Labour, 1915); *Prices in Canada and Other Countries, 1924*, Labour Gazette Supplement, January 1925; K. W. Taylor and H. Michell, *Statistical Contributions to Canadian Economic History*, vol. II (Toronto, Macmillan, 1931); Dominion Bureau of Statistics, *Prices and Price Indexes* (Ottawa, Queen's Printer, various years since 1923). The first report of *Prices and Price Indexes*, published in 1923, covered the period 1918 to 1922. Subsequent reports were 1913 to 1923, 1913 to 1924 and so on annually to the report for 1913 to 1940. Publication was suspended during the war and resumed in 1945, with an issue covering 1913 to 1943, followed three years later with a report for 1944 to 1947. The 22nd and 23rd in the series were published for 1948 and 1949 to 1952, and the publications were continued on a monthly basis from 1954. In addition to these reports the following publications of the Dominion Bureau of Statistics were used: *Wholesale Price Index Numbers of Canadian Farm Products, 1890–1933, 1913 = 100* (Ottawa, King's Printer, 1934); *Wholesale Price Index Numbers of Canadian Farm Products, 1935–39 = 100* (Ottawa, King's Printer, 1947); *Wholesale Price Indexes, 1913–1950*, Reference Paper No. 24 (Ottawa, King's Printer, 1951); *Canadian Index Numbers of Industrial Material Prices* (Ottawa, King's Printer, 1939); *Price Index Numbers of Residential Building Materials 1926 to 1948* (Ottawa, King's Printer, 1949); *Non-Residential Building Materials Price Index, 1935–1952*, Reference Paper No. 43 (Ottawa, Queen's Printer, 1953); *Export and Import Price Indexes, 1926–1948*, Reference Paper No. 5 (Ottawa, King's Printer, 1949); *Export and Import Price Indexes by Months, July 1945–June 1950, 1948 = 100*, Reference Paper No. 8 (Ottawa, King's Printer, 1950); *An Official Cost of Living Index for Canada* (Ottawa, King's Printer, 1940); *The Consumer Price Index, January 1949–August 1952* (Ottawa, Queen's Printer, 1952); *National Accounts Income and Expenditure, 1926–1956* (Ottawa, Queen's Printer, 1958); *National Accounts Income and Expenditure, 1960* (Ottawa, Queen's Printer, 1961); and *Canadian Statistical Review, Supplements*. The last-mentioned publications, issued biennially since 1953, contain the annual record of the statistical series carried in the monthly issues of the *Canadian Statistical Review* back to 1926.

General note

A price index number is a device for measuring price change in a group of commodities with reference to a base period for which the index is made equal to 100. It is an average of the price relatives of the individual commodities within the group of commodities, where a price relative is the ratio of the price of a commodity in a given period to its price in a base period. There are various kinds of averages which can be used to obtain the price index numbers, arithmetic mean, geometric mean and the like. In the calculation of these averages the price relatives may or may not be weighted according to measures of the relative importance of the commodities in some period. The most commonly used type of index number in the series presented here is the Laspeyres index whose formula is $\Sigma q_0 p_1 / \Sigma q_0 p_0$, where the p's stand for prices and the q's for quantities, the '0' subscript for the base period and the '1' subscript for the given period. It can be derived, as shown in the formula, by dividing the sum of the products of the base year quantities and given year prices by the sum of the products of the base year quantities and prices, and this was the actual procedure used by the Dominion Bureau of Statistics in its early years. It can also be derived by taking a weighted arithmetic average of the price relatives, with the weights being base period expenditure on the commodities, and this procedure is now used by D.B.S. in its calculations. The index numbers obtained by each procedure are identical. In what follows, whenever a Laspeyres index is being considered, statements that the weights are quantities of commodities in a base period mean that the first method of calculation was used, while statements that the weights are values or base period expenditures mean that the second method of calculation was used.

WHOLESALE PRICE INDEXES
(Series J1–83)

General note

The term wholesale price indexes is here taken to include index numbers obtained from price series which are at various points in distributive channels below the retail level. The term 'wholesale' as used here is thus not an exact description.

Wholesale price indexes in Canada for the period before 1913 are found in three distinct and separate sets of estimates. The first index numbers of Canadian prices were contained in Coats's special report prepared while he was with the Department of Labour, *Wholesale Prices, Canada, 1890–1909*. The Department of Labour carried forward Coats's estimates from 1910 to 1924. Two sets of index numbers, prepared by Michell and by the Dominion Bureau of Statistics, go back as far as 1867. Michell's estimates were carried through to 1925 and those of D.B.S. to the present, though the origins of its data changed substantially after 1913. The main sources of price data for the Michell and

Coats–Department of Labour estimates throughout and D.B.S. estimates until 1913 were newspapers and trade journals, and it was difficult to obtain many continuous series of prices for well-defined commodity specifications. In addition it was difficult to weight properly the price series which could be put together. For these reasons index numbers of earlier periods and particularly before 1913 should be treated as providing approximations only to price behaviour during the period. The three sets of price indexes do in fact exhibit differences in certain years both in level and direction of change in their measurements of similar price indexes.

The Dominion Bureau of Statistics, from the time it began publishing wholesale prices in 1923, became virtually the only body preparing current data.

The first report on prices of the Dominion Bureau of Statistics, *Prices and Price Indexes, 1918–1922*, contained a continuation and revision of the official index numbers of wholesale prices for Canada previously published by the Department of Labour. Three main classification schemes were used to group the 238 commodities for which prices were collected, namely, according to chief component material, to purpose, and to origin and degree of manufacture. The base period was 1913 = 100. A Laspeyres type base-weighted index number formula was used, based on the quantities of the commodities marketed in 1913. The concept of 'net weights' was used, with one exception noted below, to avoid duplication as much as possible. For example, since some wheat appears again as flour and flour as bread, a deduction was therefore made from wheat for the amount that went into the manufacture of flour and from flour for the amount made into bread to obtain the net weights for wheat and flour respectively. The individual commodity weights were used to obtain the group indexes. The group indexes subsequently were combined using group weights designed to reflect the relative value of each group in the total value of trade of the country. The exception to the use of net weights lies in the use of gross weights to obtain the indexes for the raw and partly manufactured groups of the origin and degree of manufacture classification. These were the total marketings of the commodity, that is, the net weights plus an amount to represent the quantities incorporated in items in the fully and chiefly manufactured series. For example, the weight for wheat included the quantity of wheat used in the manufacture of flour as well as the net weight for wheat.

Prices and Price Indexes, 1913–1928, contained a revision of the index numbers with 1926 as the base. The number of price series used was increased to 502. The weights were based on quantities marketed in 1926. These quantities were adjusted to a net basis as in 1913 to avoid duplication, where possible, when the commodity is included more than once as in the case of wheat and flour. Again the sole exception to this procedure was the use of gross weights to calculate the index numbers for the raw and partly manufactured groups of the origin and degree of manufacture classification. For all classifications a threefold system of weights was used rather than the previous twofold system. Quantity weights were used for combining individual commodity prices into sub-group indexes. Value weights, designed to give representation to sub-groups in proportion to the value of all commodities belonging to them and to eliminate, where necessary, the counting of commodity quantities twice when they appeared in different forms in two or more sub-groups, were used to combine sub-group indexes into group indexes. Value weights based on total marketings were used to arrive at index numbers for all commodities. The new weights were used for the years from 1926 on, and this new series of index numbers was linked with the series obtained for the period 1913 to 1925 which used 1913 weights. A consideration of the method of linking is given below.

Index numbers of commodities classified according to chief component material for the period 1890 to 1912 were published by the Bureau from the time of the first *Prices and Price Indexes*. The index numbers were unweighted arithmetic means of price relatives. In *Prices and Price Indexes, 1913–1927*, the annual index for the general wholesale composite was carried back to 1867. It was based on the prices of 89 commodities.

A revised set of weighted index numbers for the period 1890 to 1912 was published in *Prices and Price Indexes, 1913–1934*. Commodity weights only were used. For the chief component material and for the purpose classifications the weights seem to have been based on quantities marketed not later than 1900; for example, Ontario wheat had a larger weight than Western wheat. But the commodity weights used for the origin and degree of manufacture classification were the weights used for the index numbers 1913 to 1925 and therefore were based on quantities marketed in 1913. Of the two sets of weights the one used for the chief component material and the purpose classifications would appear to be the more reasonable since it is based on quantities which more nearly represent the situation in the period 1890 to 1912. This is one of the reasons why the index numbers for the origin and degree of manufacture classification for the period 1890 to 1912 were recalculated for this study on the basis of the weights of around 1900 referred to above.

The principle of using net weights was maintained for the period 1890 to 1912 with the exception noted above of the raw and partly manufactured series. The adjustment of the net weights used in the general wholesale index for the amount incorporated in items in the fully and chiefly manufactured category was carried out incorrectly in this period. To net weights full 'gross' weights, representing total marketings, were added, instead of the difference between the two. This fact made it necessary to recalculate also the raw and partly manufactured series for the period 1890 to 1912, making the adjustments required to give full weight to the commodities in the raw and fully manufactured category.

The general wholesale index number from 1867 to 1889 was revised and published in *Prices and Price Indexes, 1913–1943*. The index number formula employed was an unweighted geometric mean of the price relatives in place of the arithmetic mean previously used. It was calculated with 1890 as base year and linked at that date with the weighted index numbers for the later years. Index numbers were also computed for the eight groups but have been hitherto available only in D.B.S. files. They are published here for the first time. Since prices for only 89 commodities were available, mainly in the vegetable and animal product groups, the commodities included in the groups are too few to give other than an approximate indication of price changes in each group during that period.

The latest series of wholesale price index numbers on the base 1935–1939 were presented in 1951 in *Wholesale Price Indexes, 1913–1950*. The weighting concept used for this series differed from the weighting concepts of the earlier series. Full values rather than net weights were used. That is, the weights for each item depend on quantities marketed, with no adjustment for the quantities incorporated in more fully manufactured items. Weights for individual commodities, for sub-groups and for groups were used. The number of price series included for the indexes was increased to 604 and specifications were improved for many commodities. The index numbers on the 1926 base up to 1934 were linked to the 1935–1939 based series from 1935 onward at December 1934 (see below for discussion of linking method).

The price quotations used in the Bureau's index numbers were obtained from newspapers and trade journals for the period

1867 to 1890. A major source of price data for the period 1890 to 1913 was the Department of Labour's collection obtained mainly from journals. But in subsequent periods the Bureau depended to a lesser extent upon newspapers and trade journals for its prices as direct reference was made to wholesale dealers and manufacturers. The present procedure was described as follows in *Wholesale Price Indexes, 1913–1950*: 'The principal sources of basic price material are industrial firms and government agencies with direct market contacts. In only two instances are trade journals utilized. The majority of prices are collected by mail. The pricing date specified on most forms is the 15th of the month.'

The following table gives a summary of the number of commodity price series, weighting systems and index number formulas used for the D.B.S. general wholesale price index.

Number of price series, weighting factors and index number formulas used in D.B.S. general wholesale price index, 1867 to 1960

Period	Number of price series	Weights used	Index number formula
1935–1960	604	Average of quantities marketed in period 1935–1939	Laspeyres
1934	567⎱	Net quantities marketed in 1926 (deductions made for materials used in domestic production)	Laspeyres
1926–1933	502⎰		
1913–1925	236	Net quantities marketed in 1913	Laspeyres
1900–1912	203⎱	Net quantities marketed around 1900	Laspeyres
1890–1899	247⎰		
1867–1889	89	None	Unweighted geometric means of price relatives

The general wholesale price index, on the base 1935–1939 as published here, is the result of linking together five different segments, 1867 to 1890, 1890 to 1913, 1913 to 1926, 1926 to 1934, 1935 to 1960. The linking was accomplished by calculating the ratio of the index number on the new base to the index number on the old base for some year or month, when both index numbers were available, and then multiplying the index numbers on the old basis by this ratio to bring them to a level comparable with the new index numbers.

Given the year or month at which the linking is done the above procedure adjusts entirely for the difference of base on which the two indexes were originally calculated. It remains, however, that the whole level of the index series that is converted to the new base may be affected by the actual month or year chosen for the linking. For there may be differences in the way the two indexes move relative to one another during a period in which they overlap for two reasons. Firstly, there may be some differences in the number or kinds of commodities included in the two index series. Secondly, the weights given to the commodities may vary between the two series. If the two series actually do move differently during a period from which the date of linking is to be chosen the date selected will affect the general level of the converted series. Thus, there is no unique answer to the question of what adjustment should be made to convert the old index number to the level of the new. But this lack of uniqueness is not too serious a problem if the linking period is one of fairly stable prices, because then the ratio of the two index numbers varies only slightly from month to month. The link ratios used by D.B.S. were obtained in periods of relatively stable prices and therefore unlikely to be much different from other ratios which could have been used. The ratios of annual index numbers were used in 1890, 1913 and 1926, and the ratio for the month of December 1934 was used to link the 1926 and 1935–1939 based indexes.

The procedures used by D.B.S. to calculate series J72–83 differ somewhat from those described above for the remainder

of the D.B.S. wholesale prices included here. General comments on series J72–83 appear in the notes to series J70–74 and series J75–83 below.

Since all the series of this subsection and, indeed, a vast majority of the series throughout this section were prepared by D.B.S., the practice adopted has been to acknowledge only authors and agencies other than D.B.S. in the titles of the tables in these notes and in the statistical tables which follow.

J1–14. Wholesale price indexes (Michell), 1868 to 1925

SOURCE: Taylor and Michell, *Statistical Contributions*, vol. II, pp. 47–88.

Professor Michell's index numbers were calculated from the prices of 70 commodities using an unweighted geometric mean of price relatives. The 70 commodities were split into 13 groups classified according to chief component material and the group indexes shown in the table were calculated from their prices. The number of commodities in each of these groups is, as a consequence, small, and not necessarily representative of all the items which would fall in the group. Monthly indexes were also computed for the period August 1868 to December 1918, using monthly prices of 35 of the 70 commodities. The price quotations used by Michell were obtained mainly from the *Monetary Times* (Toronto) and the *Toronto Globe*. For the most part the prices represent Toronto market quotations, with a few from Montreal. The prices are those ruling at the last market day of each month. When two quotations, a high and a low, were given, the high was invariably taken.

J15–33. Wholesale price indexes (Department of Labour), 1890 to 1924

SOURCE: Coats, *Wholesale Prices in Canada, 1890–1909*, p. 11; series continued in the annual reports *Wholesale Prices, Canada, 1910* to *1917*; and full series published in *Prices in Canada and Other Countries, 1924*, though with some errors.

Mr Coats's index numbers were based on price quotations for over 200 commodities. The original series for 1890 to 1909 was based on 230 commodities, and the number was increased to 272 for subsequent years. For most of the commodities these price quotations, in a primary or representative wholesale market, were obtained for the opening week day of each month in each year back to 1890 and an annual average calculated. Monthly quotations were not in all cases considered necessary, as in the case of articles of which the prices are fixed at considerable intervals, and in other cases were not available. For the latter, annual averages, based in each instance upon expert opinion, were secured. Most of the quotations were for Toronto or Montreal markets, with newspapers and trade journals the main source of information, but the books of manufacturers and wholesalers were also consulted for some of the commodities. The commodities were grouped according to a mixed component material and purpose classification, and index numbers were obtained for the groups as well as for the total. The index numbers are unweighted arithmetic means of the price relatives. The index numbers were also calculated monthly from September 1910 to December 1924 and they were published in this form in the regular issues of the *Labour Gazette*.

J34–44. Wholesale price indexes, chief component material classification, 1867 to 1960

SOURCE: for series J34, 1867 to 1934, *Prices and Price Indexes, 1949–1952*, pp. 14–16, and for the years 1935 to 1960 from D.B.S. files; series J35 was specially calculated for the present volume; series J36–40 and J43–44 for the period 1867 to 1912 are from unpublished D.B.S. files, for 1913 to 1952 they are from *Prices and Price Indexes, 1942–1952*, pp. 20–47, and for 1953 to 1960 from monthly *Prices and Price Index* reports; series J41 for 1867 to 1912 and 1935 to 1952 is from unpublished D.B.S. files, for 1913 to 1934 from *Prices and Price Indexes, 1949–1952,* p. 36, and for the years 1953 to 1960 from the monthly reports of *Prices and Price Indexes*; series J42 was specially calculated for this volume for the years 1867 to 1934, and for 1935 to 1960 is from *Prices and Price Indexes, 1949–1952,* p. 36, and, thereafter, from monthly *Prices and Price Indexes.*

J34. General wholesale price index (excluding gold). Gold prices were not included in the general wholesale index numbers calculated on the base years 1913 and 1926, but were included from 1935 on when the index numbers were revised in 1951 and placed on the base 1935–1939. Gold prices are thus included in D.B.S. publications for the years 1935 to the present. The general wholesale price index published by D.B.S. on the base 1935–1939 from 1867 to date excludes gold from 1867 to 1934 and includes it from 1935 on. This series was not presented here in this form for two reasons. First, because, in linking the 1926 series with the 1935–1939 series, the index numbers used for December 1934 on the 1935–1939 base to form the linking ratio excluded gold, and therefore the adjustment of the level of the 1926 based series to that of the 1935–1939 based series was incomplete. Second, since the price of gold was stable over long periods of time, and its weight on the 1935–1939 basis was not insignificant (4.44 per cent of the total), comparisons of rates of price change would be affected by the inclusion or exclusion of gold. It was therefore decided to present two series, J34 and J35, in which the treatment of gold would be consistent throughout, gold being excluded in one case and included in the other.

The general wholesale price index numbers (excluding gold) are available monthly, on the 1935–1939 basis from 1891 to 1934, in *Prices and Price Indexes, 1949–1952,* pp. 14–16.

J35. General wholesale price index (including gold). In the special calculation for this volume, gold prices were treated in the same way as the prices of the other commodities in the period 1867 to 1934. The index for 1867 to 1890 includes unweighted price relatives of gold in taking geometric means. Three sets of net weights were applied to gold during the period 1890 to 1934, with the segments linked, following D.B.S. procedure, to the 1935–1939 based series. See also the note to series J34.

This general wholesale price index (including gold) is also available monthly back to January 1935 in *Prices and Price Indexes, 1949–1952,* and in subsequent monthly issues of the same report.

J36–40. The weighting systems and the method of linking these several series have already been discussed above in the general note to this section. The number of commodities available in the earlier years does not allow for too detailed a breakdown into component groups and the caution expressed when presenting Michell's group indexes in series J1–14 above should also be kept in mind here, although there are more commodities in the Bureau's series even in the years 1867 to 1889. The number of commodities in each of the groups from 1890 to 1934 is given in *Prices and Price Indexes, 1913–1934,* p. 16.

Monthly indexes on the 1935–1939 base are available from 1890. They have been published in *Wholesale Price Indexes, 1913–1950,* from 1935 to 1950 and they are continued from that date in the monthly *Prices and Price Indexes.*

J41. Non-ferrous metals and their products (excluding gold). The reasons for publishing two series for this group, J41 excluding gold and J42 including gold, are the same as those stated for the general wholesale price index (see series J34). The need for a consistent treatment is even greater here because of

the much greater weight of gold in this group, the 1935–1939 weight being 44.4 per cent.

Monthly indexes are available from 1890. They are published in the monthly *Prices and Price Indexes* reports.

J42. Nonferrous metals and their products (including gold). Gold prices were treated like those of other commodities in the group for this period. See also the note to series J41.

Monthly indexes of nonferrous metals and their products (including gold) are contained in *Wholesale Price Indexes, 1913–1950,* pp. 38–43, for the period 1935 to 1950 and are continued in monthly *Prices and Price Indexes.*

J43–44. See note for series J36–40.

J45–61. Wholesale price indexes, classified according to origin and degree of manufacture, 1890 to 1948

SOURCE: 1890 to 1912, specially calculated for this study; 1913 to 1943, *Prices and Price Indexes, 1913–1943,* pp. 45–6. Series J45–46 are continued to 1948 in *Prices and Price Indexes, 1948,* p. 13.

The commodities contained in the general wholesale index have been grouped according to their origin and degree of manufacture and different weighting principles have been applied. As explained in the general note to series J1–83, the system of net weights used for the general index previous to the 1935–1939 base was modified for the commodities in the raw and partly manufactured group of this classification to allow for the quantities of the commodities incorporated in the items in the fully and chiefly manufactured group. For the period 1890 to 1912, the index numbers presented here differ from the numbers published by D.B.S. The weights used in the calculations for this study are based on the net weights used for the general wholesale index for the period 1890 to 1912, instead of the weights for 1913 to 1925 which were also used for the earlier period by D.B.S. In addition an error in adjusting the net weights for items in the raw and partly manufactured categories is here corrected. For the period 1913 to 1925 the weights used for these index numbers were based on 1913 quantities marketed. The 1913 and 1926 based series were linked using the ratio of the two indexes for 1926. The number of commodities included in each of the groups for the whole period is shown in *Prices and Price Indexes, 1913–1934,* p. 52, *Prices and Price Indexes, 1913–1943,* p. 45 and *Prices and Price Indexes, 1948,* p. 13.

Monthly index numbers are available for all the components shown from 1919 to 1943 in the annual *Prices and Price Indexes,* starting with the first one for 1918 to 1922. Monthly index numbers for total raw and partly manufactured and for total fully and chiefly manufactured are available from 1913 to 1948. For the period 1913 to 1945 they are contained in *Wholesale Prices, Annual Supplement, 1946,* for 1946 and 1947 in *Prices and Price Indexes, 1944–1947,* and for 1948 in *Prices and Price Indexes, 1948.*

J62–69. Wholesale price indexes, classified according to purpose, 1890 to 1948

SOURCE: 1890 to 1943, *Prices and Price Indexes, 1913–1943,* p. 38. Series J62, 63, 68 were published for the period 1944 to 1948 in *Prices and Price Indexes, 1948,* p. 13.

These index numbers are the result of combining commodities in the general wholesale index according to the purpose they are expected to serve. The weights and linking procedures used were the same as for the general wholesale index. These index numbers were discontinued in this form when the general wholesale index was revised and put on the 1935–1939 base. The number of commodities included in each of the groups for the period covered is shown in *Prices and Price Indexes,*

1913–1940, p. 34, *Prices and Price Indexes, 1913–1943*, p. 38, and *Prices and Price Indexes, 1948*, p. 13.

Monthly index numbers for all the components shown are available from 1922 to 1943 in annual *Prices and Price Indexes*, starting with the report for 1913 to 1923. For the total Consumer goods and Producer goods categories, they are available from 1913 to 1948 in *Wholesale Prices, Annual Supplement, 1946*, *Prices and Price Indexes, 1944–1947*, and *Prices and Price Indexes, 1948*.

J70–74. Wholesale price index numbers, classified according to degree of manufacture, 1890 to 1959, industrial materials, residential and nonresidential building materials, 1926 to 1960

SOURCE: Series J70 was specially calculated for this volume for the period 1890 to 1934 to include gold in the same way as the prices of other commodities (see note to series J34); for the period 1935 to 1952 series J70 is from *Prices and Price Indexes, 1949–1952*, p. 18; and for 1953 to 1960 it is from monthly *Prices and Price Indexes*. Series J71 was recalculated for this study from material in D.B.S. worksheets for the period 1890 to 1934; for the period 1935 to 1960 it is from the same source as series J70. Series J72 and J73 are from *Prices and Price Indexes, 1949–1952*, pp. 18 and 84 for the period 1926 to 1952, and for 1953 to 1959 are from monthly *Prices and Price Indexes*. Series J74 is from *Canadian Statistical Review, 1959 Supplement*, p. 65, for the period 1935 to 1958, and for 1959–60 from monthly *Prices and Price Indexes*.

J70. The index numbers for the raw and partly manufactured group for the period 1913 to 1934, which are published in *Prices and Price Indexes, 1949–1952*, have not been used here because of the way in which gold prices were included. The 1926 based indexes, which excluded gold, were linked to the new indexes using the ratio of the 1935–1939 based index number for January 1935, excluding gold, to the 1926 index number for that date. To the index number thus obtained, the gold price index was directly added. The weight given to the gold index (13.07 per cent) was the weight of gold in the 1935–1939 index. This older published index number series for raw and partly manufactured from 1913 to 1934 thus treated gold prices in a different manner than the prices of other commodities and it was decided to construct a more consistent series here, treating gold in the same way as other commodities.

The list of items included in the raw and partly manufactured category from 1935 to date is shown in *Wholesale Price Indexes, 1913–1950*, pp. 87–9.

Monthly indexes have been calculated for the period from January 1935. They have not been published in revised form for the years 1935 to 1949 and are available only in D.B.S. files. The indexes for 1950 to 1952 are in *Prices and Price Indexes, 1949–1952*, p. 19 and the data for subsequent years are to be found in the monthly *Prices and Price Indexes*.

J71. The index numbers for fully and chiefly manufactured commodities for the period 1890 to 1934 were recalculated because of an error in the published series for 1913 to 1934 which was introduced when the 1926 based series was linked to the 1935–1939 based series using data for January 1935 to form the link ratio. The figures published for 1913 to 1934 were approximately 2.4 per cent too high.

The items included in the fully and chiefly manufactured category from 1935 to 1960 are listed in *Wholesale Price Indexes, 1913–1950*, pp. 89–95. Monthly indexes are available from January 1935. They are published for 1948 to 1950 in *Wholesale Price Indexes, 1913–1950*, p. 44, for 1950 to 1952 in *Prices and Price Indexes, 1949–1952*, p. 19, and since that time in the monthly *Prices and Price Indexes*.

J72. The index numbers of industrial materials prices are obtained from the unweighted geometric means of the price relatives of 30 commodities. The commodities were considered to fall into two groups, eighteen commodities whose prices were very sensitive to changes in economic conditions and twelve commodities with more stable prices. The purpose of the index was to provide a statistical measurement specially suited to a week-by-week examination of price behaviour in the markets which provide the basic materials required by industry. The 25 manufacturing materials and five food products included in the index are shown in *Canadian Index Numbers of Industrial Material Prices*, p. 21. The method of construction is described in the same source.

The index numbers are available monthly from 1926 to 1948 in *Prices and Price Indexes, 1948*, p. 45. For 1949 they are in the monthly *Price Movements* publication for that year, and for 1950 to 1952 in *Prices and Price Indexes, 1949–1952*, p. 19. They have been continued up to the present in the monthly *Prices and Price Indexes* publications.

Weekly index numbers have been published in *Canadian Index Numbers of Industrial Material Prices*, p. 12, for 1938; they are in *Prices and Price Indexes, 1913–1939*, p. 10, for 1939; and they are in the monthly D.B.S. publication *Price Movements* for the period 1940 to 1960.

J73. The residential building materials price index was developed to give a more precise measurement of this important part of housing cost than the older building and construction materials index (series J68). The importance of individual residential material items and groups of items has been determined from on-the-site survey data and National Housing Administration experience. The weights have been based upon units of material requirements valued at 1946 prices for the national housing target for that year. There are 90 price series in the residential building materials index classified into nine groups. Value percentage weights have been applied to individual commodity price relatives to obtain the group index numbers and these, in turn, have been combined using value percentage weights to obtain the total index. The attempt is made to obtain the selling prices, f.o.b. site, to large contractors for the commodities included but in many cases wholesale prices of building materials are used. To provide regional coverage in pricing, the commodity weights within groups were subdivided in accordance with regional production weights, obtained from Census of Industry records of the D.B.S., and regional prices used. For a fuller description of method see D.B.S., *Price Index Numbers of Residential Building Materials, 1926 to 1948*.

Index numbers for the nine component groups are available annually for the whole period in the sources mentioned above. Monthly index numbers for both total and components are available from January 1946: 1946 to 1948 in *Price Index Numbers of Residential Building Materials, 1926 to 1948*, pp. 6–7; 1949 to 1952 in *Prices and Price Indexes, 1949–1952*, pp. 84–5; 1953 to 1960 in monthly *Prices and Price Indexes*. This index is also available back to 1913 in D.B.S. files. It was extended back to that date on the basis of movements in the general building materials index (series J68).

J74. The nonresidential building materials price index was constructed to measure the price change of building materials used in the construction of new nonresidential buildings. Along with the residential materials index, it replaced the old building and construction materials index (series J68). The weights for the index were calculated from the results of a survey of large general contractors conducted in late 1950. Data were obtained on the construction of 99 nonresidential buildings with a contract value of over thirty million dollars built in Canada during the years 1948 to 1950. The materials were divided into twelve groups which in turn were composed of sub-groups of individual commodities. A Laspeyres type index number formula was used and commodity, sub-group and group weights were applied. The prices used are, wherever possible, the prices paid by contractors f.o.b. site. Where this is not possible manufacturers' or wholesale distributors' prices are used. Where regional price differences are important, regional prices are combined using weights to represent the estimated value of nonresidential building construction in the regions from which the prices were obtained. For a fuller description of method, see *Non-Residential Building Materials Price Index, 1935–1952*.

Monthly index numbers for the composite and the twelve groups are available from January 1949: 1949 to 1952 in *Prices and Price Indexes, 1949–1952*, pp. 86–7, 1953 to 1960 in monthly *Prices and Price Indexes*. This index is also available back to 1913 in D.B.S. files but has not been published for the period before 1935. It was extended back to that date in two steps. For 1926 to 1935, annual indexes were developed from the residential building materials series; for 1913 to 1925, movements in the general building materials index (series J 68) were used.

J75–83. Wholesale price index numbers of Canadian farm products, 1890 to 1960

SOURCE: for the years 1890 to 1934, *Prices and Price Indexes, 1913–1934*, p. 54; for 1935 to 1952, *Prices and Price Indexes, 1949–1952*, p. 104; for 1953 to 1960, monthly *Prices and Price Indexes* for Canada figures, and D.B.S. files for regional index numbers.

The wholesale price index numbers of Canadian farm products measure the prices of these products at terminal markets. Prices are obtained from market sources for clearly specified commodities in the same way as other wholesale prices. This series of index numbers differs from the index numbers of prices received by farmers (see series L 88) in that the latter measure prices at the farm and are based on more broadly defined items. The wholesale price index numbers of Canadian farm products are published here in two time segments, the first from 1890 to 1934 with base 1913 and the second from 1926 to 1960 with base 1935–1939. The overlap of nine years will provide an indication of the relationship between the two series.

The series from 1890 to 1934 contains three sets of implicit weights. From 1890 to 1913 quantity weights were used. These are based upon an average of the production figures for the commodities included in the index as reported in the decennial censuses of production for 1890, 1900 and 1910. From 1913 to 1926 the commodity weights were based on the total quantities marketed in 1913. From 1926 to 1934 the weights were based on quantities marketed in 1926 and sub-group and group weights were used as well as individual commodity weights. The three segments were linked in 1913 and 1926 by means of the overlaps between the periods using the three sets of weights. The index with base 1913 was published up to 1940 in *Prices and Price Indexes, 1913–1940*, p. 41. The Canadian farm products index was also published with 1926 = 100 in the *Prices and Price Indexes* reports for the period 1890 to 1948. For each of the field and the animal products groups the implicit weights used were as for the 1913 based index, but the total, for the complete period, was obtained by combining the groups using the 1926 weights.

The index numbers from 1926 to 1960, on base 1935–1939, use a system of three sets of weights: individual commodity, sub-group and group weights. The average values of quantities marketed during the five-year period 1935 to 1939 were used to establish the weights which were employed in a Laspeyres type index number formula. Indexes are also shown separately for Eastern and Western Canada.

The commodities included in the index numbers are shown in *Wholesale Price Index Numbers of Canadian Farm Products, 1890–1933*, pp. 11–12, and *Wholesale Price Index Numbers of Canadian Farm Products, 1935–1939 = 100*, pp. 3–5. The same two sources provide a full description of the methodology employed in estimating the index prices of farm products. Monthly indexes are available from January 1926 for Canada and the eastern and western regions: 1926 to 1944 in *Wholesale Price Index Numbers of Canadian Farm Products, 1935–1939 = 100*, pp. 9–15; 1945 to 1952 in *Prices and Price Indexes, 1949–1952*, pp. 104–5. From 1953 to 1960 they are available for Canada in the monthly *Prices and Price Indexes* and regional indexes are available in D.B.S. files.

EXPORT AND IMPORT PRICE INDEXES
(Series J 84–127)

J84–95. Export price indexes (Taylor), 1869 to 1915

SOURCE: Taylor and Michell, *Statistical Contributions to Canadian Economic History*, vol. II, pp. 18–19.

The use of the term 'price' indexes is perhaps inappropriate here because the price used in each case is not for a clearly defined and consistent grade, but is the average price of all grades of the particular commodity bought or sold. The prices used are obtained by dividing the total value of sales of a particular commodity by the total quantity sold. The 'unit valuations' thus obtained would vary because of changes in the quality of the commodity sold even though there were no change in any price. The index numbers were obtained as a by-product of constructing constant dollar value series of exports and imports. All the individual items in the trade of Canada were revalued in terms of their values in the fiscal year ending 30 June 1900. The aggregate value figures thus obtained for the totals and the component groups were divided into the corresponding aggregates in current dollars to obtain a Paasche type index number with current year weights. It should be noted that the data relate to fiscal, not calendar, years. For a fuller description of method see the source, pp. 1–7.

J96–107. Import price indexes (Taylor), 1869 to 1915

SOURCE: Taylor and Michell, *Statistical Contributions*, vol. II, pp. 16–17. For the relevant commentary, see note to series J 84–95.

J108–117. Export price indexes, 1913 to 1960
J118–127. Import price indexes, 1913 to 1960

SOURCE: for 1913 to 1934 (panel B), *Prices and Price Indexes, 1913–1934*, p. 158; for 1926 to 1953 (panel A), with the exceptions noted below, *Review of Foreign Trade, First Half Year, 1954*, pp. 23–31; for 1954 to 1960, the monthly reports, *Trade of Canada, Exports and Imports*.

A full description of method may be found in *Prices and Price Indexes, 1913–1926*, pp. 163–70, with respect to panel B of both export and import series, and in *Export and Import Price Indexes, 1926–1948* and *Export and Import Price Indexes by Months, July 1945–June 1950*, with respect to the method underlying the estimates of section A of both export and import series. The statistics are presented in two panels because of a difference in methods: panel A covers the years 1926 to 1960, panel B the years 1913 to 1934. The following note on the table is accordingly subdivided into two parts.

Panel A. The index numbers are based mainly on unit valuation series obtained from trade statistics (see note for series J 84–95) but some price series, obtained from wholesale and retail price records in Canada and the United States, have also been used. The index numbers presented here are the result of linking two sections, one from 1926 to 1945 calculated with base 1935–1939 = 100, the other from 1946 to the present calculated with 1948 as base. For 1926 to 1945 the individual price relatives were weighted by the percentage of their 1935–1939 value to the 1935–1939 group value to obtain the group indexes. The group indexes were in turn weighted by their percentage share in the 1935–1939 total to obtain the total indexes. A similar weighting procedure was employed for the years 1946 to 1960 but the individual commodity and group weights were from 1948 value data. The series for 1926 to 1945 were adjusted to the level of the 1948 based series by using the ratio of the new and old indexes for 1948 as the link ratio. The validity of the indexes is questionable for the war years 1941 to 1945. They reflect movements in prices of commodities important in Canada's peacetime trade which were, of course, not the prices actually used in valuing all commodities entering Canada's trade during that period.

The index numbers presented here differ from the previously published figures in certain cases where errors have been corrected in the original calculations or corrections made in the prices used. The main changes, however, are in the import price indexes, series J118–127, total and agricultural and other primary products for the period 1926 to 1935, and of chemicals and allied products, 1926 to 1945.

Panel B. The index numbers are based on unit valuation series for 50 export commodities and 60 import commodities. A Laspeyres type index number formula was used with the commodity and group weights obtained from 1913 export and import values. The caution expressed in panel *A* above about the validity of these indexes for the war years should be repeated here.

D.B.S. also published index numbers for wholesale prices of exports and imports for the period 1913 to 1940 (1926 = 100). The method used is outlined in *Prices and Price Indexes, 1913–1933,* pp. 194–8, and the figures for the full period are in *Prices and Price Indexes, 1913–1940,* p. 52. The movements of the two sets of index numbers—the unit valuation and wholesale prices—are very similar in the period of overlap.

J118–127. Import price indexes, 1913 to 1960

SOURCE: See source for series J108–117 and series J118–127.

For the commentary, see note to series J108–117 and series J118–127.

RETAIL PRICE INDEXES
(Series J128–152)

General note

Retail price indexes measure the changing cost to the consumer of selected goods and services. They are based on average prices paid by consumers in retail stores. The Department of Labour and the Dominion Bureau of Statistics have constructed retail price indexes for Canada. The first set of retail price indexes was constructed by Mr R. H. Coats, at that time with the Department of Labour, and presented in volume II of the *Report of the Board of Inquiry into Cost of Living.* A hypothetical family budget was constructed to represent the weekly consumption of food and fuel and lighting items of an urban working class family of five. Prices for the items were obtained by local correspondents of the *Labour Gazette* in approximately 60 cities. Dominion average prices of the 29 food items and the five fuel and lighting items were obtained by taking simple averages of the prices in each city. Index numbers with base 1900 = 100 were constructed for Canada and the provinces. Index numbers of rents and some services were also presented. The calculation of

expenditures on this family budget (with rent for a six-roomed dwelling) were continued until August 1940.

In addition to the calculated expenditures on this weekly budget, the Department of Labour published a cost-of-living index with base 1913 (see *Prices in Canada and Other Countries, 1926, issued as a Supplement to the Labour Gazette, January, 1927,* pp. 8–10). It was given only for June and December from 1914 to 1917; figures for April and September were also available for 1918 to 1926; from 1927 onward the indexes were given monthly in the *Labour Gazette.* Group indexes for food, fuel and lighting, rent, clothing and sundries were given. An attempt was made to weight the items according to their relative importance in the wage-earners' family budgets but no extensive family budget survey was carried out.

The first D.B.S. index numbers of retail prices were presented in *Prices and Price Indexes, 1913–1926,* pp. 92–5, with 1913 = 100. The object of this index was stated as 'the measurement of the general movement of retail prices and living costs in the Dominion as a whole'. The weights used for the index were based on the total consumption of each commodity in 1913. The Bureau made use of the Department of Labour collection of prices in the earlier years, and also obtained prices directly from retailers. The D.B.S. index was presented in a revised form with base 1926 = 100 in *Prices and Price Indexes, 1913–1928,* pp. 181–7. The number of commodities was greatly increased and a system of sub-group and group weights, as well as individual item weights, was used. The whole weighting system was again based on estimated aggregate consumption in Canada. The 1913 based index was linked to the 1926 based index using the 1926 ratio of the new and old index numbers as the link.

The index was revised in 1940 and placed on the base 1935–1939 (see *An Official Cost of Living Index for Canada*). The weights were obtained from a family budget survey conducted in 1938 of urban wage-earner families with annual earnings between $450 and $2500. This change in the method of arriving at the weights represented a shift in the Bureau's thinking towards the view of the Department of Labour that a retail price index should measure the cost of living of a well-defined group. This change of view at D.B.S. was one reason why the Department of Labour's index was discontinued.

The next revision (*The Consumer Price Index January 1949–August 1952*) also made use of data obtained from a family budget survey, *Canadian Non-Farm Family Expenditures, 1947–48,* Reference Paper No. 42. The title was changed from 'Cost of Living Index' to avoid any implication that the index is a measure of all changes in living costs. The index was defined on page 9 as follows: 'the Consumer Price Index measures the percentage change through time in the cost of purchasing a constant "basket" of goods and services representing the consumption of a particular population group during a given period of time.'

J128–131. Index numbers of a family budget (Department of Labour), 1900 to 1939

SOURCE: for 1900, 1905, 1910 to 1917, *Wholesale Prices, Canada, 1917,* pp. 93–120; 1918 to 1928, *Prices and Price Indexes, 1913–1928,* pp. 196–7; 1929 to 1938, *Prices and Price Indexes, 1913–1938,* pp. 65–6; 1939, *Labour Gazette,* monthly issues for 1940. The dollar expenditure figures given in these sources were converted into the index numbers shown by dividing through by the relevant 1913 figure.

The commodity prices used in this index were weighted according to a 'theoretical weekly budget for a working man's family of 5'. The list of quantities was 'based on estimates by various official bodies in the United States and Great Britain and on limited inquiries in Canada which may be regarded as fairly typical of ordinary household expenses per week.' Only individual item—not group—weights were used. The prices were collected by local correspondents of the *Labour Gazette* in approximately 60 cities. The Canada average prices used were obtained by averaging the city prices for each commodity. Returns were also obtained for the 'prevailing rental for a representative workingman's dwelling of the better class, with and without sanitary conveniences' but, for the family budget, only the weekly rental of a dwelling with sanitary conveniences was used.

These indexes can be calculated on a monthly basis from 1910 using prices published in the *Labour Gazette* from 1910 to August 1940. Provincial and city cost-of-living indexes can also be constructed on an annual and monthly base from 1910 to August 1940 from prices in these sources.

J132–138. Price indexes of selected retail services (D.B.S. and Coats), 1900 to 1938

SOURCE: Coats, *Report of the Board of Inquiry into the Cost of Living*, vol. II, pp. 317–67, for the period 1900 to 1913 (arithmetically converted by the author of this section from base 1900 = 100 to base 1913 = 100); for the period 1913 to 1938, *Prices and Price Indexes*, annual reports from 1913–1925 to 1913–1938. The latter series is given in the source with base 1926 = 100 as well as the base 1913 = 100 used here.

In each of the notes on the four series J132 to 135 the D.B.S. estimates from 1913 on are dealt with first followed by the notes on Coats's series for the period before 1913.

J132. *Domestic electric light* (*D.B.S.*). Because of the numerous and varied methods of charging for electricity and with the most generally used method a sliding scale in which the unit price decreases with increased consumption and a fixed service charge, it was impossible to compute index numbers directly from rates. The average monthly bills for five standard levels of consumption were used. A set of index numbers was available for each municipality, one for each of the standard consumption levels used. The 1913 bills were divided into the corresponding bills for other years to obtain municipal index numbers. A weighted index number was constructed for each province and for Canada by weighting each municipal index number with the number of customers in the municipality concerned in 1913. Only one of the sets of index numbers computed for each municipality was used, and the one selected was for the consumption quantity which was closest to the actual average consumption for that municipality (see *Prices and Price Indexes, 1913–1928*, pp. 262–4).

The index numbers are also available for the provinces in the reports cited above.

Electric lighting (*Coats*). The index numbers are based on the survey of rates in 68 localities. 'Some difficulties in compilation were imposed by the differences in the methods of levying charges which prevail, these including flat rates, meter rates, rates based on the number and power of lamps used, rates based on house valuation, rates reflecting cost of installation, etc., with varying sliding scales and discounts. It is thought however that the table will show the general tendency of costs with a fair degree of accuracy' (Coats, *op. cit.* p. 317).

Provincial index numbers are also available in the same source.

J133–134. *Manufactured fuel gas and Natural fuel gas* (*D.B.S.*). In the construction of the index numbers the rates for each locality were weighted by the average domestic consumption in that locality in the base year. The weights were obtained from the firms reporting.

Index numbers are also available for the provinces and certain cities.

Illuminating gas and Fuel gas (*Coats*). The index numbers are based on rates obtained from a survey of 38 localities. Provincial index numbers are also available in Coats, *op. cit.* pp. 327–9.

J135. *Public ward hospital charges* (*D.B.S.*). The index numbers shown were obtained from average rates for this service calculated from returns obtained from about 200 hospitals. The rates for Canada were obtained by averaging individual hospital rates.

Hospital charges for public ward patients (*Coats*). Data were obtained from completed circulars sent to hospitals requesting information as to the tariff charged in each year from 1900 to 1913 for public ward and other hospital services. Some 274 circulars were sent out, and 131 completed forms were used to arrive at the published figures.

J136. *Street-car fares.* From 1913 to 1925 the index numbers were based on average fares calculated from returns made by municipal electric railways showing the total number of passengers carried and the total revenue received for fares. Returns were received from 35 municipal railways. The average Canada rates were obtained by dividing the total revenue by the total number of passengers carried. From 1926 forward the index numbers were based on movements in actual tariffs in effect.

Index numbers for provinces are available in the same source.

J137–138. *Domestic telephone rates and business telephone rates.* Average rates were calculated for 74 localities. The rates in each locality were weighted by the number of telephones in the base year to obtain the Canada and provincial figures used for index numbers.

J139–146. Cost-of-living index, 1913 to 1952

SOURCE: for the period 1913 to 1934, the indexes were recalculated by the Prices Division, D.B.S., to correct for a linking error in the published figures; for 1935 to 1941, *Prices and Price Indexes, 1949–1952*, p. 135; for 1942 to 1952 the figures, which are inclusive of all taxes, were obtained from D.B.S. files.

For a more detailed description of the methods of derivation of the index numbers than can be given in the following note, see *Prices and Price Indexes, 1913–1926*, pp. 92–5; *Prices and Price Indexes, 1913–1928*, pp. 181–7; and *An Official Cost of Living Index of Canada*.

The cost-of-living index numbers presented here have been derived using three sets of implicit weights which have been used in Laspeyres type index number formulas. For 1913 to 1925, 1913 weights, for 1926 to 1934, 1926 weights, and for 1935 to 1952, 1935–39 weights were employed. The principles used to arrive at weights were not the same throughout. The 1913 and 1926 weights were based on total consumption of the commodities included in these years, and the object was to measure the general movements of prices and costs. The 1935–39 weights were based on the consumption patterns of a group of urban wage earning families, obtained from the budget study of 1938, and the object was changed to measure, in the first instance, the average cost of living of a particular, although important, group. The group weights in 1913, 1926 and 1935–39 based indexes are shown in the following table.

Group weights in 1913, 1926, and 1935–39 based retail price indexes

Group	1913	1926	1935–39
Food	35	30	31
Rent	18	20	19
Fuel and Light	7	6	6
Clothing	20	18	12
Miscellaneous and homefurnishing	20	26	32

The index numbers presented here were obtained by the usual D.B.S. linking procedure. The 1913 based indexes were linked to the 1926 based indexes using the year 1926 to form the link ratio, while the 1926 and 1935–39 based indexes were linked using the indexes for January 1935 to obtain the link ratio.

The monthly indexes were adjusted first and then averaged to obtain the annual indexes shown.

These index numbers differ from those published by D.B.S. (e.g. in *Prices and Price Indexes, 1949–1952*, p. 135). It has not been possible to reconstruct the method of linking the group indexes to obtain the figures published, but presumably some slight variant of the usual method was employed because the difference between the two sets of figures is slight. The index numbers for the total category, shown in the D.B.S. publication *Prices and Price Indexes, 1949–1952* for the period 1913 to 1934 on base 1935–39, were obtained by combining the linked group indexes using the 1935–39 base weights. This procedure is inappropriate because the consumption patterns in the periods 1913 to 1925 and 1926 to 1934 are better represented by the 1913 and 1926 group weights than by the 1935–39 group weights. The importance of food and clothing, in particular, is underestimated in the period 1913 to 1925 by this procedure. These two groups showed the greatest price increases as a result of World War I, and thus the total index published by D.B.S. in *Prices and Price Indexes, 1949–1952*, is lower than the one shown here which linked the total in the same way as the group indexes. The difference between the two indexes is over 3 per cent for 1920. The index numbers presented here include all taxes and thus there is also a slight difference between these figures and those published by D.B.S. for the years 1942 to 1952. The latter index numbers did not include taxes. It was considered undesirable in a period of price control, when wages were adjusted by the cost-of-living index, to include taxes in the calculation of the index.

Monthly index numbers are available for total and components from 1914: 1914 to 1947 in *Prices and Price Indexes, 1944–1947*, pp. 60–6 (the total figures however suffer from the linking procedure used for 1913 to 1934); 1948 in *Prices and Price Indexes, 1948*, p. 60; 1949 to 1952 in *Prices and Price Indexes, 1949–1952*, p. 136; 1953 to 1960 in monthly issues of *Prices and Price Indexes*.

J147–152. Consumer price index, 1913 to 1960

SOURCE: the Total index for 1913 to 1934 was recalculated by the Prices Division D.B.S. (see below); the Total, 1934 to 1958 and groups, 1926 to 1958, *Canadian Statistical Review, 1959, Supplement*, p. 58; the Total and groups, 1959 and 1960, monthly *Prices and Price Indexes, January 1961*.

These indexes for 1949 to 1960 have been prepared using weights obtained from the 1948 family budget study. Beginning with January 1961, a new weighting system based on expenditure patterns of 1957 and giving somewhat more detail was begun. The indexes for the years 1957 to 1960 inclusive were recalculated using the 1957 weights but are not given here.

For a detailed description of the method of constructing the consumer price index from January 1949 onward see *The Consumer Price Index, January 1949–August 1952*. See also D.B.S., *The Consumer Price Index for Canada (1949 = 100) — Revision based on 1957 Expenditure*, D.B.S. Catalogue No. 62–518.

The prices entering into the index number calculations from 1949 onward were collected from retail outlets at intervals ranging from every month to once a year depending upon price sensitivity. Where it was possible to collect accurate prices by mail, coverage extended to 33 cities. Where this was difficult because of the necessity of taking account of quality changes, collection was restricted to eight cities where full time pricing agents are located. Within each city, prices for each item were collected from a representative sample of retail outlets. Weights were used in averaging prices, for each city, from different types of stores, such as independent and chain food stores and department and special clothing stores, to reflect the relative importance

of these retail outlets in the sales of the commodities considered. Similarly a Dominion average price is obtained by weighting city average prices.

The prices were combined with a set of individual item, sub-group and group weights in a Laspeyres type index number formula. The weights were obtained from detailed budget information provided by a sample of urban families with annual incomes from $1,650 to $4,050 in the budget study of 1948 (see general note for series J128–152) and relate to the year ending 31 August 1948 with the exception of food items for which weights relate to the year ending September 1949. Information was obtained from 1,157 families. The average size of the families included was 3.0 members.

This consumer price index was linked with the 1935–39 based cost-of-living index using the ratio of the two indexes for January 1949. The index numbers for the total category of the C.P.I. shown here from 1913 to 1934 differ from the figures published by D.B.S. (e.g. in *Prices and Price Indexes, 1949–1952*, pp. 110–11) because of the revision of the 1935–39 based indexes mentioned above (see note to series J139–146).

Monthly indexes for Canada are available from 1949 in the sources mentioned above. Indexes are also available for 10 regional cities on an annual and monthly basis.

IMPLICIT PRICE INDEXES OF GROSS NATIONAL EXPENDITURES
(Series J153–164)

J153–164. Implicit price indexes of gross national expenditures, 1926 to 1960

SOURCE: 1926 to 1954, *National Accounts, Income and Expenditure, 1926–1956*, pp. 36–7; 1955 to 1960, *National Accounts, Income and Expenditure, 1962*, p. 64, and *1963*, p. 60.

For a discussion of the method of obtaining these implicit price indexes, see *National Accounts, Income and Expenditure, 1926–1956*, pp. 176–85.

The implicit price indexes shown in this table were obtained as a by-product of the attempt to measure year-to-year changes in real gross national expenditure and its components. An indirect procedure was used in obtaining them. The first step was to deflate sub-categories of gross national expenditure by base weighted price indexes, the latter being selected or constructed to represent the commodity content and base weights of the items within the sub-category as closely as possible. A fine breakdown of sub-categories was used. For instance, there were 70 sub-categories of consumer expenditure; men's clothing is an example of such a sub-category. The constant dollar series of sub-categories are added together to obtain the constant dollar values of group categories and of the various categories of totals. Each implicit price index is then obtained by dividing current dollar expenditures for each group or total by the corresponding constant dollar expenditures.

The implicit price indexes thus obtained are equivalent to price indexes in which base year weights are used to combine prices of individual commodities into sub-category price indexes and current weights are used to combine indexes for sub-categories into group categories and totals. Therefore the year-to-year changes in these indexes result not only from changes in prices, but also from changes in expenditure patterns. To the extent that expenditure patterns have changed these implicit price indexes are not comparable from year to year, although each one of them is comparable with the base period.

The period 1926 to 1960 has been deflated in three time segments, 1926 to 1947, 1947 to 1956 and 1956 to 1960. The first time segment, 1926 to 1947, was deflated at a fine level of detail with price indexes based on the average of 1935–39 prices; the second time segment, 1947 to 1956, was deflated at a similar level of detail with price indexes based on 1949 prices; the third time segment was deflated also at a similar level of detail with price indexes based on 1957 prices. The three series were then linked together at the published detail, major component levels, and at the total gross national expenditure level by using the relation between the three implicit price indexes at the years of overlap, 1947 and 1956.

It should be pointed out that series J160, J161 and J162 are not truly final product price indexes. They are weighted combinations of input prices and, therefore, do not reflect the influence of productivity changes in on site construction or in putting machinery into place upon final output prices.

Implicit price indexes for gross national expenditure for the years 1867, 1870, 1880, 1890, 1900, 1910, 1920, are given in

O. J. Firestone, *Canada's Economic Development 1867–1953*, Income and Wealth, Series VII, International Association for Research in Income and Wealth (London, Bowes and Bowes, 1958), p. 66.

APPENDIX TO SECTION J

INDEX NUMBERS OF FIFTEEN FOODSTUFFS
(Series J165–167)

J165–167. Wholesale price indexes of 15 foodstuffs (Michell), 1848 to 1913

SOURCE: Taylor and Michell, *Statistical Contributions*, vol. II, p. 55.

The prices from which these index numbers were calculated were obtained from Toronto newspapers as outlined in the note to series J1–14, above. The indexes are unweighted geometric means of price relatives.

Series J1–14. *Wholesale price indexes by commodity groups (Michell), 1868 to 1925*
(1900 = 100)

Year	All commodities	Vegetable products		Animals and their products						Iron and its products	Non-ferrous metals and their products	Non-metallic minerals and their products	Chemicals and allied products	Imported foods
		All	Grains and flour	All	Animals and meats	Fish	Furs	Hides and leather	Dairy products					
	1	**2**	**3**	**4**	**5**	**6**	**7**	**8**	**9**	**10**	**11**	**12**	**13**	**14**
1925	187.9	193.2	217.6	206.5	206.9	195.8	—	144.9	241.1	143.1	149.8	182.5	174.8	163.9
1924	181.6	191.5	185.7	186.0	175.9	204.9	—	135.6	222.4	150.1	136.9	197.9	178.0	164.8
1923	181.9	180.4	163.4	193.8	187.4	171.1	—	139.0	241.6	154.7	129.1	206.4	184.6	163.7
1922	182.3	179.7	178.4	197.5	199.2	178.7	—	143.6	226.9	141.8	109.2	224.8	202.3	151.9
1921	197.7	195.1	216.9	206.0	209.0	184.5	—	150.7	269.7	175.4	110.2	246.2	228.3	167.4
1920	287.5	311.5	354.5	314.1	302.6	231.6	—	264.1	336.4	233.9	162.2	247.3	273.7	278.2
1919	269.2	278.7	298.6	333.0	325.4	241.2	—	304.9	314.9	198.5	143.2	192.2	238.6	239.0
1918	256.5	239.6	333.0	290.2	317.2	229.2	429.6	230.5	266.4	231.6	221.4	192.2	303.6	213.9
1917	236.7	227.3	301.9	255.0	264.0	193.9	300.6	246.3	240.5	230.9	206.6	172.2	294.3	180.8
1916	176.6	175.1	191.3	191.9	191.3	187.8	202.1	190.4	193.5	130.5	165.9	134.1	245.1	154.6
1915	142.3	152.5	181.4	149.4	155.8	151.5	106.3	153.6	167.3	90.8	119.4	125.1	178.7	131.3
1914	131.3	133.1	152.4	152.3	158.1	158.7	159.7	146.8	151.5	85.5	102.2	115.1	133.7	113.8
1913	129.3	126.0	133.3	155.1	156.0	147.4	221.7	143.4	137.1	85.8	113.4	110.1	122.4	115.0
1912	130.9	143.6	159.9	146.2	140.3	144.4	230.7	132.6	149.2	81.2	115.3	107.4	120.3	121.3
1911	121.8	137.4	141.9	130.2	126.2	139.8	187.7	119.1	124.7	81.0	93.3	105.9	116.4	114.8
1910	118.5	120.5	136.6	137.1	145.0	140.5	175.0	116.7	130.4	80.9	86.6	110.4	110.3	101.7
1909	114.9	120.7	153.1	129.5	128.1	119.6	178.3	118.4	130.2	79.5	83.1	101.9	109.7	97.9
1908	116.3	123.5	154.3	118.0	117.6	103.9	182.4	103.2	128.1	83.5	84.2	102.1	112.6	104.1
1907	117.4	124.1	141.4	124.3	121.5	120.0	175.6	110.1	127.0	87.0	122.8	101.5	113.9	104.3
1906	111.8	112.7	123.0	121.8	118.4	111.5	164.6	115.2	114.0	82.8	112.9	104.8	110.3	94.0
1905	106.1	112.1	133.6	111.6	105.9	102.9	148.9	107.9	108.6	78.2	90.6	105.5	105.6	96.4
1904	101.1	108.0	125.5	102.3	94.7	108.4	124.1	102.9	45.4	79.4	78.3	110.6	105.1	93.5
1903	102.6	105.6	109.8	105.3	105.9	104.7	119.5	103.3	100.6	84.9	79.9	116.9	103.4	93.6
1902	101.3	107.1	115.2	104.0	112.2	93.8	102.4	102.9	97.9	86.0	76.6	105.9	97.2	94.1
1901	99.8	104.2	108.7	100.4	106.5	98.5	98.6	99.8	90.4	87.8	93.0	101.0	97.3	106.4
1900	100.0	100.0	100.0	100.0	100.0	100.0	100.0	100.0	100.0	100.0	100.0	100.0	100.0	100.0
1899	91.9	101.4	103.2	83.9	87.5	101.6	82.4	95.8	95.1	87.2	93.9	98.3	94.2	93.6
1898	91.1	100.4	112.1	89.2	86.5	88.6	87.1	63.0	83.7	73.3	66.3	99.6	98.1	95.2
1897	85.6	87.5	88.9	83.6	80.6	85.4	66.9	91.7	84.4	75.5	60.4	104.7	106.0	91.0
1896	83.1	86.2	89.4	77.0	73.6	98.8	58.2	80.4	80.6	81.5	61.2	105.2	102.9	88.1
1895	88.3	94.8	110.9	84.0	86.8	97.5	57.9	84.9	84.9	82.0	56.5	98.6	108.1	88.6
1894	92.1	97.0	98.4	87.2	93.9	94.2	81.3	73.9	96.1	83.4	67.7	103.4	119.9	93.9
1893	99.2	102.2	102.1	98.1	111.7	96.0	90.6	81.9	101.4	88.5	72.2	110.3	117.2	103.2
1892	96.5	102.6	115.8	88.3	97.0	85.0	70.2	80.7	95.4	89.2	74.6	116.8	125.7	105.4
1891	104.7	124.5	142.2	91.0	97.3	94.9	72.5	84.4	96.4	91.7	78.3	114.7	131.8	130.3
1890	103.4	118.8	125.5	89.7	100.0	94.0	64.8	80.9	93.3	97.5	83.4	119.3	125.9	133.3
1889	104.7	111.1	126.2	93.3	99.2	107.3	76.0	82.8	101.2	107.6	94.1	116.0	137.9	124.6
1888	105.8	114.5	147.8	94.0	107.8	101.6	55.0	87.6	102.8	104.4	101.1	111.0	137.9	109.8
1887	102.5	109.7	119.1	92.7	96.4	78.8	58.7	95.9	110.6	102.7	87.4	113.3	128.5	114.0
1886	97.3	98.3	110.8	91.2	92.6	73.6	55.4	104.9	100.3	96.5	80.7	114.3	126.7	102.8
1885	101.0	106.4	134.6	91.6	97.6	84.5	46.1	105.7	99.3	102.8	80.4	120.1	127.8	106.7
1884	110.5	110.4	138.0	105.8	116.5	98.4	66.7	104.2	114.9	107.1	93.2	123.0	145.1	108.9
1883	114.4	119.4	148.0	107.0	122.8	104.1	58.3	105.7	117.1	113.1	99.7	128.7	132.5	114.9
1882	120.3	127.9	161.2	110.7	134.9	100.4	57.1	106.9	117.6	117.7	104.8	128.1	150.4	120.5
1881	115.1	124.8	164.3	100.9	110.1	73.1	58.7	109.8	114.3	113.6	95.7	130.2	162.8	128.8
1880	114.1	121.7	151.2	98.1	100.7	75.6	57.4	113.9	106.9	128.8	103.0	122.6	160.3	129.3
1879	105.1	114.9	147.2	87.9	91.5	70.7	58.9	97.0	92.3	116.3	98.6	113.2	153.3	114.9
1878	103.2	108.9	131.2	88.4	90.6	67.4	67.5	96.9	87.7	111.4	94.9	116.9	157.0	116.7
1877	114.2	122.7	164.3	100.4	105.4	74.8	72.0	103.1	112.4	120.1	100.4	115.7	163.2	125.6
1876	117.2	116.1	144.3	104.5	112.3	85.2	88.0	97.1	109.2	133.5	110.7	133.1	172.5	126.7
1875	124.9	121.8	154.2	111.7	127.3	80.0	92.8	99.7	114.1	148.0	115.1	147.6	180.5	126.8
1874	130.3	133.8	166.3	112.2	118.9	82.0	92.3	106.3	127.2	152.9	122.3	145.2	194.0	140.9
1873	129.7	122.4	165.9	108.7	110.2	78.5	91.9	108.4	115.6	189.6	136.5	158.3	201.5	126.7
1872	132.5	130.0	158.7	109.2	105.7	80.2	106.1	110.4	109.7	187.0	141.2	160.7	201.0	135.2
1871	123.1	126.4	111.5	105.7	109.9	85.4	82.6	106.0	107.5	131.0	122.9	161.0	174.0	131.5
1870	122.5	116.5	141.2	113.0	130.6	80.6	98.6	102.3	106.1	127.2	124.0	154.2	179.6	126.7
1869	117.3	116.0	153.4	102.0	111.9	76.1	88.4	89.4	112.9	128.5	121.6	149.5	177.0	120.3
1868	120.1	122.0	192.3	102.2	109.3	74.1	89.7	92.9	115.3	130.9	115.4	164.5	176.8	120.4

Series J 15–33. *Wholesale price indexes by commodity groups (Department of Labour), 1890 to 1924*

(1890–99 = 100)

Year	Total	Grains and fodder	Animals and meats	Dairy produce	Fish	Other foods	Textiles	Hides, leather, boots	Metals	Implements	Fuel and lighting	Lumber	Building materials Miscellaneous	Paints, oil, glass	House furnishings	Drugs and chemicals	Furs, raw	Liquors and tobaccos	Sundries
	15	16	17	18	19	20	21	22	23	24	25	26	27	28	29	30	31	32	33
1924	223.2	190.6	215.8	206.7	171.4	192.6	253.4	154.6	185.1	225.8	233.8	338.2	224.2	270.7	264.7	175.3	567.9	268.4	158.2
1923	224.1	175.6	224.2	215.2	178.5	189.3	244.7	159.6	184.4	226.5	246.3	343.0	221.4	276.3	270.4	178.7	601.1	264.4	159.0
1922	224.3	187.4	244.0	204.7	182.7	190.6	234.3	163.7	168.0	229.0	263.2	322.1	207.9	272.0	283.7	183.7	651.3	265.7	158.9
1921	246.1	205.7	263.7	241.3	204.5	207.2	247.5	179.9	179.1	253.1	258.1	383.4	240.1	310.1	344.7	200.3	521.1	275.9	184.0
1920	333.6	360.6	357.4	314.7	247.4	295.1	396.9	313.6	241.5	258.3	310.0	486.5	258.7	444.2	381.0	231.5	1132.1	312.1	215.2
1919	293.2	310.9	357.8	296.5	236.6	251.5	373.1	349.5	206.0	240.4	237.1	310.8	224.5	379.0	321.2	232.0	1009.2	275.8	211.6
1918	278.3	316.2	354.5	259.4	247.0	250.5	356.9	279.7	273.1	225.0	221.8	267.1	226.4	310.8	256.8	283.4	602.2	216.6	219.5
1917	237.0	281.5	288.1	230.5	205.8	220.6	263.4	275.1	259.1	181.6	193.0	214.5	203.5	222.4	203.7	267.9	411.6	167.8	186.8
1916	182.0	195.2	217.7	183.5	184.8	156.2	193.4	233.4	198.9	135.2	132.6	182.1	154.9	200.5	157.1	252.2	299.8	142.4	143.0
1915	148.0	186.9	187.2	161.4	149.7	125.5	149.2	180.5	152.4	112.1	108.8	175.7	115.9	157.1	136.5	181.3	161.9	135.6	116.6
1914	136.1	156.5	192.3	154.4	156.0	118.8	133.5	171.8	113.9	106.8	110.9	182.1	111.4	140.7	129.5	121.6	205.4	136.9	108.5
1913	135.5	136.8	180.8	154.7	158.0	117.4	130.8	163.9	119.1	105.6	118.2	181.3	112.7	144.8	126.2	113.3	307.9	134.7	113.1
1912	134.4	167.3	160.8	159.0	155.7	126.0	120.7	152.4	117.4	104.7	113.3	166.5	105.4	148.6	114.5	115.5	297.3	155.2	104.3
1911	127.4	148.4	146.6	136.2	143.6	118.7	119.2	139.6	108.3	104.5	100.5	165.4	102.6	154.5	110.4	112.1	252.9	151.2	110.3
1910	124.2	140.7	163.6	135.7	145.1	111.3	114.6	135.4	97.6	104.5	103.0	158.5	109.2	145.6	110.6	109.5	234.5	132.9	118.0
1909	121.2	149.9	148.6	133.6	134.0	107.6	108.3	135.4	101.9	102.4	103.8	154.6	105.7	135.2	110.4	103.9	227.2	117.5	121.6
1908	120.8	148.3	129.6	136.3	120.5	110.3	111.0	120.0	106.3	104.2	102.2	162.6	107.5	136.8	112.8	107.1	231.8	118.0	117.6
1907	126.2	140.2	133.8	131.5	129.5	112.5	126.1	125.5	134.8	107.1	108.8	165.2	108.7	141.2	112.7	108.5	239.4	125.5	123.0
1906	120.0	118.5	130.1	120.2	121.8	103.1	123.4	128.1	118.6	106.0	106.4	152.7	104.7	135.3	113.0	106.3	229.2	108.1	120.9
1905	113.8	116.4	120.7	115.1	115.7	100.7	114.6	119.6	108.4	106.1	104.1	134.1	106.8	125.3	107.3	106.4	217.4	108.1	121.1
1904	111.4	115.5	111.3	107.2	119.5	101.8	110.4	113.6	99.7	106.2	103.0	131.3	107.2	122.4	112.7	109.0	171.3	107.8	119.1
1903	110.5	106.5	117.9	108.9	116.2	98.1	105.9	115.7	105.5	105.7	111.0	128.8	107.7	126.3	109.6	105.5	168.1	107.0	115.9
1902	109.0	116.1	122.2	106.9	110.2	98.4	101.0	118.2	102.8	104.7	104.9	122.0	104.6	128.1	109.2	102.2	145.2	103.7	116.8
1901	107.0	107.3	111.3	120.5	113.2	98.6	103.6	112.8	110.4	102.2	98.1	114.6	106.0	121.9	107.9	99.8	140.9	103.3	110.9
1900	108.2	99.9	103.4	109.0	106.4	96.4	100.0	113.8	121.2	100.1	100.8	114.0	111.8	125.9	110.2	101.5	147.3	103.3	113.0
1899	100.1	96.7	95.1	101.4	110.0	93.6	99.8	109.4	111.9	98.0	96.9	95.8	97.2	107.6	100.2	93.3	111.8	102.3	109.5
1898	96.1	98.8	97.9	92.9	99.6	94.3	95.2	105.0	87.6	94.3	93.5	90.8	87.4	100.0	99.6	96.8	111.1	103.9	103.3
1897	92.2	80.6	90.4	90.1	98.6	86.0	98.0	100.1	85.7	93.1	96.4	93.9	87.7	95.5	99.8	96.5	88.0	103.9	91.2
1896	92.5	85.2	82.4	90.1	102.6	87.1	96.9	92.9	87.5	98.5	98.9	97.1	93.9	96.2	97.5	99.8	80.7	98.0	92.6
1895	95.6	98.8	92.2	94.8	101.4	95.2	93.6	98.6	87.0	101.0	97.0	102.8	95.2	96.1	97.9	100.3	80.5	99.4	91.3
1894	97.2	94.3	98.7	104.6	96.4	95.0	97.3	89.9	91.1	102.2	97.5	104.6	98.7	95.5	101.3	103.1	113.5	98.7	93.7
1893	102.5	99.1	117.7	110.4	99.7	102.1	101.2	101.8	102.1	102.6	102.9	103.7	103.7	98.6	101.1	104.4	123.6	99.4	100.3
1892	102.8	106.7	108.5	105.8	90.6	104.7	102.2	99.8	107.6	102.9	106.6	104.4	106.8	98.2	100.9	104.4	103.7	99.7	98.9
1891	108.5	123.9	104.7	106.2	97.3	121.3	104.2	102.6	114.4	103.2	106.7	102.7	110.4	103.8	100.5	101.3	99.7	99.0	106.7
1890	110.3	116.7	111.2	103.0	103.3	120.3	111.4	100.6	125.4	103.8	107.4	103.5	117.6	109.5	100.2	110.5	86.5	94.9	112.0

Series J34–44. *Wholesale price indexes, chief component material classification, 1867 to 1960*

(1935–39 = 100)

Year	General index (excluding gold)	General index (including gold)	Vegetable products	Animals and their products	Fibres, textiles and textile products	Wood, wood products, paper	Iron and its products	Nonferrous metals and their products (excluding gold)	Nonferrous metals and their products (including gold)	Nonmetallic minerals and their products	Chemicals and allied products
	34	35	36	37	38	39	40	41	42	43	44
1960	—	230.9	203.0	247.6	229.8	303.8	256.2	—	177.8	185.6	188.2
1959	237.0	230.6	199.5	254.3	228.0	304.0	255.7	238.0	174.6	186.5	187.0
1958	233.5	227.8	198.1	250.7	229.0	298.5	252.6	224.1	167.3	188.5	183.0
1957	233.8	227.4	197.0	238.4	236.0	299.4	252.7	240.7	176.0	189.3	182.3
1956	233.7	225.6	197.3	227.7	230.2	303.7	239.8	280.2	199.2	180.8	180.1
1955	226.0	218.9	195.1	226.0	226.2	295.7	221.4	259.3	187.6	175.2	177.0
1954	222.7	217.0	196.8	236.0	231.1	286.8	213.4	224.1	167.5	177.0	176.4
1953	226.3	220.7	199.0	241.7	239.0	288.6	221.4	225.3	168.6	176.9	175.7
1952	232.0	226.0	210.3	248.2	251.5	291.0	219.0	233.5	172.9	173.9	180.1
1951	246.3	240.2	218.6	297.7	295.9	295.5	208.7	241.6	180.6	169.8	187.3
1950	215.4	211.2	202.0	251.3	246.7	258.3	183.6	200.8	159.5	164.8	157.8
1949	201.7	198.3	190.5	237.5	222.5	241.6	175.5	179.9	145.2	158.3	155.2
1948	197.2	193.4	185.7	236.7	216.3	238.3	161.4	185.1	146.9	150.8	152.2
1947	165.8	163.3	157.3	183.0	179.5	208.8	140.7	155.1	130.2	129.1	136.7
1946	139.2	138.9	134.2	160.2	137.9	172.1	127.4	111.1	108.0	114.5	120.3
1945	132.0	132.1	131.6	150.0	130.8	154.9	117.9	106.4	107.6	113.5	124.0
1944	130.5	130.6	129.1	146.6	130.7	151.6	117.8	106.8	107.8	114.3	124.9
1943	127.8	127.9	123.5	146.9	130.8	142.2	116.8	106.8	107.8	115.6	125.3
1942	122.8	123.0	114.9	137.1	131.2	132.3	116.0	105.8	107.2	114.5	127.9
1941	116.2	116.4	106.1	123.8	128.4	127.0	112.8	105.7	107.2	111.1	118.6
1940	107.8	108.0	98.1	106.1	118.1	119.0	108.7	105.2	106.9	106.7	108.5
1939	99.0	99.2	89.1	100.6	98.9	107.5	104.8	98.1	100.0	99.7	100.3
1938	101.9	102.0	100.5	102.6	95.5	106.9	105.8	98.3	98.9	101.5	100.4
1937	108.4	107.7	118.6	105.6	105.4	102.5	105.4	114.6	107.7	100.6	101.1
1936	96.7	96.8	98.8	96.0	101.4	93.6	92.6	96.3	97.6	98.2	98.4
1935	94.1	94.4	92.9	94.9	99.6	89.9	91.7	92.5	95.7	99.7	99.9
1934	93.4	92.0	91.5	89.5	102.2	90.7	91.2	87.5	92.1	100.9	102.3
1933	87.4	87.4	81.4	79.1	97.8	87.2	89.5	87.5	85.7	99.1	102.4
1932	86.9	85.7	75.3	79.5	97.8	95.9	90.5	80.2	75.7	100.3	105.7
1931	94.0	93.2	78.1	98.4	103.0	109.7	91.6	87.9	77.1	101.5	109.2
1930	112.9	111.5	106.6	132.0	114.8	123.1	95.5	109.7	91.0	107.2	116.9
1929	124.6	122.8	125.7	145.2	128.1	130.3	98.2	134.9	106.8	109.0	120.2
1928	125.6	123.9	127.6	144.0	132.6	137.0	97.7	125.1	100.7	108.6	120.1
1927	127.3	125.5	135.0	135.8	131.5	136.7	100.9	124.4	100.3	113.2	123.9
1926	130.3	128.5	137.3	133.2	140.3	138.7	104.8	136.0	107.5	117.3	126.0
1925	133.8	131.1	138.1	133.6	157.8	141.0	109.6	141.3	108.7	117.7	125.5
1924	129.5	126.9	122.5	122.3	165.4	147.0	116.4	129.0	104.4	122.2	129.2
1923	127.7	125.3	114.9	126.6	164.0	156.8	121.4	129.6	104.6	122.5	131.6
1922	126.8	124.5	118.4	127.8	142.7	147.5	109.7	132.4	105.6	125.6	132.8
1921	143.4	140.4	142.1	146.0	134.6	179.5	134.2	132.0	105.5	136.8	147.4
1920	203.2	198.2	229.2	193.2	247.6	214.2	176.5	184.3	123.5	131.6	178.3
1919	174.7	170.6	186.8	187.5	229.8	152.0	145.8	181.6	122.6	109.9	148.0
1918	166.0	162.3	175.6	169.3	220.4	123.7	164.5	193.0	126.5	96.6	149.5
1917	148.9	145.8	171.0	147.1	160.8	110.8	159.2	195.7	127.5	84.1	123.6
1916	109.8	108.1	119.5	113.2	108.9	88.8	109.7	183.8	123.3	68.0	98.3
1915	91.8	90.6	103.8	98.6	81.8	78.4	77.4	145.4	110.0	61.9	85.9
1914	85.4	84.5	88.9	96.7	79.8	83.7	70.6	128.8	104.3	63.0	82.2
1913	83.4	82.6	79.8	94.4	81.6	88.7	72.3	133.9	106.1	66.7	79.8
1912	85.2	84.5	93.4	90.1	73.6	86.3	67.1	136.0	107.1	66.6	78.0
1911	81.1	80.3	85.8	81.2	76.2	86.1	66.3	118.4	99.4	62.5	74.4

Series J34-44. *Wholesale price indexes, chief component material classification, 1867 to 1960 (continued)*

(1935–39 = 100)

Year	General index (excluding gold)	General index (including gold)	Vegetable products	Animals and their products	Fibres, textiles and textile products	Wood, wood products, paper	Iron and its products	Nonferrous metals and their products (excluding gold)	Nonferrous metals and their products (including gold)	Nonmetallic minerals and their products	Chemicals and allied products
	34	35	36	37	38	39	40	41	42	43	44
1910	78.5	77.8	81.0	84.0	78.3	81.2	65.3	119.5	100.0	63.5	69.0
1909	77.6	76.9	85.1	80.3	73.6	73.9	66.4	115.1	106.4	64.2	67.3
1908	76.3	75.6	84.7	75.2	71.3	75.5	69.9	118.2	99.4	65.2	72.4
1907	76.4	75.8	81.1	76.0	78.7	76.7	72.3	156.8	115.9	63.6	73.4
1906	70.7	70.2	71.7	70.9	76.3	73.0	69.0	147.4	111.9	61.2	64.0
1905	70.4	70.0	75.9	69.8	71.1	68.4	65.0	127.6	103.5	62.4	65.5
1904	68.3	67.8	75.0	64.2	71.6	66.6	66.0	115.8	98.4	64.2	65.1
1903	67.5	67.1	70.9	65.9	65.9	66.4	70.6	112.5	97.0	65.1	63.3
1902	66.6	66.2	68.7	68.2	65.4	59.1	71.0	114.7	97.8	62.9	62.9
1901	63.7	63.5	64.6	64.3	65.1	55.9	71.2	136.3	107.2	60.7	64.4
1900	62.4	62.1	58.9	64.6	67.9	56.3	78.7	139.3	108.5	57.0	61.8
1899	60.6	60.4	63.7	61.1	60.9	51.5	67.5	129.6	104.3	53.7	58.4
1898	59.4	59.3	66.6	58.1	60.3	50.0	58.9	99.2	91.3	53.5	58.7
1897	56.8	56.7	59.7	56.2	61.3	49.6	59.1	95.7	89.8	54.0	59.0
1896	55.9	55.9	58.0	53.1	62.5	49.8	64.6	102.6	92.7	55.0	60.4
1895	57.9	57.8	60.8	56.4	61.3	51.8	64.0	97.9	90.8	55.1	60.0
1894	59.1	58.9	60.7	58.1	61.6	54.9	66.3	99.4	91.4	56.2	60.8
1893	63.2	63.0	66.3	63.4	65.5	53.6	71.2	117.0	98.9	57.5	61.3
1892	62.3	62.1	65.7	60.3	65.7	53.8	72.9	126.2	102.8	58.0	61.6
1891	67.1	66.8	80.7	60.3	69.0	53.0	75.0	138.6	108.1	57.2	62.8
1890	67.1	66.8	76.2	60.6	75.5	53.4	81.6	148.9	112.5	58.7	62.5
1889	66.1	65.8	77.0	64.7	73.3	52.2	76.8	144.6	109.7	55.5	62.6
1888	66.2	65.7	79.8	63.3	70.7	50.8	76.5	156.6	117.6	53.5	63.4
1887	63.7	63.6	71.4	63.6	75.3	49.7	74.3	131.3	101.0	53.4	62.4
1886	62.3	62.2	70.3	62.5	68.6	47.1	73.0	128.2	99.0	55.1	62.5
1885	63.3	63.1	72.2	62.8	67.0	48.1	75.2	131.2	100.9	57.2	62.7
1884	67.0	66.8	74.6	71.5	68.3	48.9	79.6	141.5	107.7	62.1	66.1
1883	70.2	69.8	82.0	73.5	72.2	51.1	80.5	152.8	115.0	66.3	65.8
1882	72.5	72.0	90.6	74.5	79.6	48.4	83.3	160.8	120.2	63.9	68.4
1881	72.4	71.9	91.8	72.5	85.6	43.0	83.6	161.3	120.5	63.8	71.9
1880	71.8	71.3	88.5	68.1	95.1	34.7	99.1	167.4	124.4	57.1	75.8
1879	65.5	65.2	79.3	60.0	74.2	37.8	84.2	154.9	116.4	54.0	73.4
1878	68.0	67.6	81.0	60.4	78.5	41.2	83.9	163.6	121.3	57.4	74.6
1877	73.4	72.9	90.5	67.4	90.8	42.7	90.7	169.2	125.2	62.3	75.6
1876	77.6	76.9	86.6	71.9	91.1	44.0	100.4	177.5	129.5	75.7	78.6
1875	82.8	82.0	91.7	73.8	104.9	48.1	113.2	183.3	134.0	77.1	81.4
1874	86.4	85.4	96.6	74.5	116.0	49.0	128.3	189.9	137.9	76.2	82.9
1873	90.9	89.6	91.4	74.7	129.9	46.8	147.0	205.9	147.6	88.5	83.9
1872	90.6	89.3	92.6	72.7	155.7	41.1	142.1	207.1	148.3	87.9	81.9
1871	81.3	80.3	92.4	71.8	112.5	40.6	104.6	195.8	141.5	81.3	76.7
1870	79.8	78.7	88.2	74.8	105.0	35.5	105.8	203.1	145.9	79.9	78.4
1869	80.7	79.6	89.1	73.7	117.4	33.9	106.7	203.8	146.9	81.0	78.6
1868	80.0	79.0	96.4	70.8	108.4	31.7	106.8	197.6	143.2	87.3	78.4
1867	80.2	79.1	94.0	71.2	107.7	30.5	114.8	—	—	—	—

Series J45–61. *Wholesale price indexes, classified according to origin and degree of manufacture, 1890 to 1948*

(1926 = 100)

Year	Total raw and partly manufactured[1]	Total fully and chiefly manufactured	Articles of farm origin (domestic and foreign)						Articles of marine origin			Articles of forest origin			Articles of mineral origin		
			Field (grains, fruits, cotton, etc.)			Animal											
			Raw and partly manufactured	Fully and chiefly manufactured	Total	Raw and partly manufactured	Fully and chiefly manufactured	Total	Raw and partly manufactured	Fully and chiefly manufactured	Total	Raw and partly manufactured	Fully and chiefly manufactured	Total	Raw and partly manufactured	Fully and chiefly manufactured	Total
	45	46	47	48	49	50	51	52	53	54	55	56	57	58	59	60	61
1948	156.2	140.3	—	—	—	—	—	—	—	—	—	—	—	—	—	—	—
1947	130.7	117.4	—	—	—	—	—	—	—	—	—	—	—	—	—	—	—
1946	109.5	98.8	—	—	—	—	—	—	—	—	—	—	—	—	—	—	—
1945	105.6	94.0	—	—	—	—	—	—	—	—	—	—	—	—	—	—	—
1944	104.0	93.6	—	—	—	—	—	—	—	—	—	—	—	—	—	—	—
1943	99.1	93.1	84.9	89.1	87.1	111.2	94.2	101.6	119.3	133.4	129.6	138.1	83.6	109.0	96.7	101.3	99.2
1942	90.1	91.9	73.1	88.6	81.4	102.9	94.3	98.0	98.6	118.3	113.0	128.5	77.6	101.3	94.8	101.0	98.2
1941	81.8	88.8	63.2	86.8	75.9	95.0	89.0	91.6	79.6	96.8	92.1	117.1	76.9	95.6	92.5	98.0	95.5
1940	75.3	81.5	59.4	79.2	70.1	84.1	78.6	81.0	74.6	81.3	79.5	103.4	75.5	88.5	88.9	92.0	90.6
1939	67.5	75.3	50.7	71.4	61.8	80.1	72.0	75.5	67.2	72.7	71.2	88.0	70.9	78.9	82.3	88.6	85.8
1938	72.7	78.2	63.0	76.5	70.3	79.8	74.3	76.7	65.4	72.0	70.2	85.5	69.9	77.2	81.5	90.5	86.5
1937	84.3	80.5	82.8	83.4	83.1	82.7	76.2	79.0	72.1	71.7	71.8	94.0	61.1	76.4	85.2	91.6	88.8
1936	70.8	73.6	63.8	73.8	69.2	73.6	71.4	72.4	67.1	70.1	69.3	80.8	57.5	68.4	79.9	85.2	82.8
1935	66.0	72.8	56.2	72.8	65.1	71.6	69.9	70.6	61.8	72.0	69.2	74.5	56.1	64.7	79.6	85.3	82.8
1934	63.5	74.1	54.2	73.9	64.8	66.0	69.8	68.2	60.3	75.1	71.1	76.3	56.1	65.5	77.5	86.0	82.2
1933	56.6	70.2	45.3	71.2	59.3	59.0	62.5	61.0	56.2	65.4	62.9	69.7	57.2	63.0	75.6	84.6	80.6
1932	55.0	69.8	41.0	67.1	55.1	59.0	61.1	60.6	56.2	66.6	63.8	69.6	68.9	69.2	77.0	84.9	81.4
1931	61.9	74.8	44.0	69.5	57.7	76.8	71.6	73.9	70.3	77.6	75.6	79.4	78.7	79.0	77.9	85.1	81.9
1930	82.2	87.3	67.4	84.0	76.3	103.7	89.4	95.6	86.9	98.4	95.3	90.9	86.4	88.5	86.1	90.3	88.4
1929	97.5	93.0	89.5	90.7	90.1	114.7	98.5	105.5	96.8	108.5	105.3	100.5	87.8	93.7	92.7	92.8	92.8
1928	97.4	95.0	90.2	93.9	92.2	114.7	97.7	105.1	91.5	104.0	100.6	99.4	97.9	98.6	91.2	91.8	91.5
1927	99.9	96.5	99.0	96.9	97.9	106.6	95.8	100.5	96.7	101.5	100.2	97.0	99.5	98.3	94.6	94.6	94.6
1926	100.0	100.0	100.0	100.0	100.0	100.0	100.0	100.0	100.0	100.0	100.0	100.0	100.0	100.0	100.0	100.0	100.0
1925	100.8	103.8	100.6	106.9	104.0	100.4	100.5	100.5	94.4	99.1	97.8	100.3	105.9	103.3	101.9	101.5	101.7
1924	94.8	101.9	89.4	102.7	96.6	91.5	90.4	90.9	95.9	91.8	92.9	104.7	110.2	107.6	101.8	106.9	104.6
1923	91.1	103.1	83.6	101.2	93.1	90.8	99.4	95.7	99.6	80.1	85.4	113.1	112.6	112.8	105.6	107.4	106.6
1922	94.7	100.4	86.3	95.3	91.2	95.3	96.3	95.9	90.3	92.2	91.7	106.0	107.5	106.8	103.5	108.8	106.4
1921	107.2	116.1	101.8	110.7	106.6	104.7	111.0	108.2	90.2	91.6	91.2	123.4	148.7	136.9	111.1	123.2	117.8
1920	154.1	156.5	176.9	175.9	176.4	146.8	145.4	146.0	133.7	106.9	114.1	156.9	146.4	151.3	124.9	142.5	134.6
1919	130.3	132.1	144.8	140.5	142.5	146.4	139.7	142.6	127.8	111.3	115.8	112.1	104.3	107.9	105.2	121.7	114.3
1918	120.8	127.7	132.7	136.5	134.7	133.2	125.7	129.0	120.0	108.6	111.7	90.8	88.7	89.7	104.9	123.6	115.2
1917	113.6	113.5	131.2	118.8	124.5	113.3	111.8	112.5	100.4	82.3	87.2	82.1	72.4	76.9	98.7	115.0	107.7
1916	86.4	84.6	90.2	85.4	87.6	86.4	85.8	86.1	81.0	65.7	69.8	68.0	56.4	61.8	83.1	87.4	85.5
1915	72.5	71.1	77.8	73.7	75.6	75.0	72.7	73.7	73.7	61.8	65.0	57.4	54.9	56.1	68.4	69.3	68.9
1914	66.2	65.6	65.9	64.6	65.2	75.6	67.0	70.7	72.5	60.7	63.9	61.8	55.5	58.4	61.5	67.7	64.9
1913	63.8	64.8	58.4	59.9	59.2	73.0	67.8	70.1	78.7	61.2	65.9	67.0	54.0	60.1	64.1	70.9	67.9
1912	66.6	64.5	70.5	64.2	67.6	67.5	66.0	66.6	80.6	60.0	64.9	65.2	52.6	58.5	62.9	67.5	65.2
1911	62.0	62.2	62.8	61.8	62.4	61.1	60.5	60.6	72.9	56.5	60.9	65.2	51.0	58.4	59.7	66.9	63.9
1910	60.3	62.3	57.3	62.0	59.7	64.6	64.7	64.5	78.2	51.4	56.3	61.2	51.6	55.0	59.4	65.3	62.6
1909	61.4	62.5	62.4	62.4	62.8	61.5	60.1	60.7	67.4	50.5	54.6	56.0	51.1	50.5	59.6	67.1	64.0
1908	59.0	63.8	60.6	64.0	62.3	55.6	59.6	57.6	70.1	42.9	47.4	56.7	51.4	51.1	62.2	70.7	67.2
1907	58.5	60.9	58.9	60.2	59.6	56.5	60.3	58.4	71.1	46.3	52.5	56.5	50.8	50.8	63.8	72.7	69.0
1906	56.1	60.2	52.7	54.3	53.6	54.0	58.9	56.5	63.7	46.3	50.1	55.0	50.4	49.6	60.6	69.9	66.2
1905	53.5	61.0	51.6	60.8	56.1	52.0	53.7	52.8	57.1	44.8	48.2	51.2	50.4	46.3	58.1	69.1	64.9
1904	52.8	59.4	52.6	58.2	55.4	49.2	48.3	48.6	61.5	45.1	47.1	49.9	50.6	45.2	59.4	70.0	65.9
1903	52.3	59.1	51.6	51.8	51.7	49.4	53.6	51.5	58.1	43.6	47.1	49.8	48.9	45.0	60.8	72.3	67.9
1902	50.6	58.6	49.6	52.4	51.0	51.2	53.1	52.2	54.6	41.3	44.6	43.7	48.4	39.7	58.8	71.0	66.5
1901	48.7	57.7	44.7	51.7	48.1	49.3	50.6	49.9	53.7	43.5	45.1	41.7	45.6	37.9	59.3	70.5	66.3
1900	47.2	58.8	41.4	51.0	46.0	48.2	51.7	50.0	54.7	41.1	44.5	42.3	46.8	38.5	57.4	73.6	67.8
1899	45.2	56.2	43.4	50.4	46.8	44.0	47.9	46.0	55.5	41.0	44.4	37.9	41.4	34.4	53.4	69.3	63.7
1898	45.4	55.6	43.4	54.1	48.6	43.9	45.0	44.4	46.1	38.9	41.6	37.0	41.1	33.6	49.7	66.4	60.6
1897	42.3	54.0	37.7	50.1	43.6	42.4	45.0	43.7	48.1	37.9	40.7	36.9	41.4	33.5	50.4	65.9	60.4
1896	40.4	54.4	37.1	48.0	42.4	39.0	42.6	40.9	51.2	40.0	43.0	38.0	40.4	34.4	51.5	69.6	63.3
1895	42.2	55.7	40.6	49.7	45.0	42.0	44.9	43.5	50.2	38.9	41.8	38.7	40.5	35.1	51.0	70.5	63.8
1894	42.1	57.3	40.9	48.9	44.8	41.5	49.0	45.4	47.8	36.9	39.7	41.1	40.4	37.1	50.8	73.4	65.8
1893	45.4	60.3	44.8	53.2	48.9	47.0	52.1	49.6	49.2	38.4	41.4	40.1	40.1	36.3	53.8	75.4	68.0
1892	44.9	60.7	42.6	55.3	48.7	45.0	48.7	46.9	47.9	32.7	35.8	40.6	40.0	36.7	54.7	76.8	69.3
1891	49.4	64.3	52.8	64.9	58.6	44.5	48.1	46.3	48.5	37.9	40.7	39.8	39.6	36.0	55.6	77.5	70.0
1890	48.3	66.3	48.2	66.1	56.8	45.7	47.1	46.3	47.9	39.7	42.5	39.9	38.7	36.0	57.2	82.0	73.5

[1] Excludes gold.

Series J62–69. *Wholesale price indexes, classified according to purpose, 1890 to 1948*

(1926 = 100)

Year	Consumer goods			Producers goods				
	All	Foods, beverages, and tobacco	Other	All	Producers equipment	Producer materials		
						All	Building and construction	Manufacturers
	62	63	64	65	66	67	68	69
1948	140.8	152.3	—	—	—	—	195.7	—
1947	117.3	122.4	—	—	—	—	166.4	—
1946	101.1	107.5	—	—	—	—	134.8	—
1945	98.1	103.4	—	—	—	—	127.3	—
1944	97.4	101.4	—	—	—	—	127.3	—
1943	97.0	102.4	93.4	95.1	113.7	93.0	121.2	88.2
1942	95.6	98.1	94.0	88.3	109.4	86.0	115.2	81.1
1941	91.1	89.5	92.2	83.6	105.7	81.1	107.3	76.6
1940	83.4	79.4	86.1	78.7	100.0	76.3	95.6	73.0
1939	75.9	73.9	77.2	70.4	95.4	67.6	89.7	63.9
1938	77.2	77.1	77.2	75.8	95.1	73.7	89.1	71.1
1937	79.5	81.2	78.4	86.1	93.8	85.2	94.4	83.6
1936	74.7	73.4	75.5	72.4	90.0	70.4	85.3	67.9
1935	73.6	70.4	75.7	69.5	89.8	67.2	81.2	64.8
1934	74.1	69.7	77.0	67.8	88.9	65.5	82.5	62.6
1933	71.1	63.8	76.0	63.1	86.0	60.5	78.3	57.5
1932	71.3	61.5	77.8	62.4	88.7	59.5	77.2	56.5
1931	76.2	70.4	80.0	67.1	90.0	64.6	81.9	61.7
1930	89.3	93.1	86.8	82.5	92.9	81.3	90.8	79.7
1929	94.7	100.0	91.1	96.1	94.6	96.3	99.0	95.9
1928	95.6	99.6	92.9	96.7	93.7	97.0	97.4	96.9
1927	95.7	99.4	93.3	98.5	101.1	98.2	96.1	98.6
1926	100.0	100.0	100.0	100.0	100.0	100.0	100.0	100.0
1925	97.0	97.7	96.5	104.9	99.2	105.5	102.9	106.2
1924	94.2	90.4	96.8	99.4	102.7	99.0	106.6	97.5
1923	94.7	91.2	97.0	97.6	102.5	97.1	111.9	93.7
1922	96.9	90.2	101.4	98.8	104.1	98.2	108.7	95.8
1921	108.9	105.1	111.5	113.3	113.8	113.3	122.7	110.8
1920	136.1	150.8	126.3	164.3	108.6	171.0	144.0	177.3
1919	115.2	127.9	106.7	139.8	90.7	145.2	117.8	151.6
1918	102.7	119.0	91.9	133.3	81.9	139.0	100.7	148.1
1917	90.5	109.1	78.1	120.6	65.3	127.7	87.4	136.0
1916	72.2	81.2	66.2	89.7	55.7	93.5	69.5	99.1
1915	62.8	68.7	58.8	77.1	51.2	80.0	60.5	84.6
1914	62.1	65.0	60.1	70.1	52.4	72.1	62.8	74.2
1913	62.0	61.8	62.2	67.7	55.1	69.1	67.0	69.5
1912	62.4	65.8	60.1	66.7	53.9	68.1	64.9	68.7
1911	59.5	60.8	58.7	61.9	52.1	63.0	65.1	62.7
1910	58.8	59.0	58.7	63.9	52.2	65.2	62.0	65.7
1909	58.7	58.9	58.6	63.9	53.2	65.1	63.5	65.4
1908	59.9	59.4	60.2	61.1	54.1	61.9	65.0	61.4
1907	58.1	57.6	58.5	59.8	52.1	60.6	60.1	60.7
1906	55.0	53.5	56.0	56.1	50.1	56.8	58.0	56.6
1905	55.5	54.0	56.5	56.4	50.9	57.0	55.2	57.3
1904	55.8	52.4	58.0	55.3	53.6	55.5	55.7	55.5
1903	56.1	52.3	58.6	53.3	54.9	53.1	54.1	52.9
1902	54.2	49.9	57.1	53.8	53.0	53.9	50.2	54.5
1901	52.2	47.2	55.5	51.6	51.1	51.7	48.6	52.2
1900	50.0	46.8	52.1	50.9	46.8	51.3	50.2	51.5
1899	47.9	46.5	48.9	47.2	44.1	47.5	44.8	48.0
1898	47.9	46.3	49.0	48.3	44.2	48.7	42.3	49.8
1897	47.5	43.7	50.0	45.5	45.1	45.5	41.5	46.2
1896	46.9	41.6	50.4	43.0	45.5	42.7	44.6	42.4
1895	48.2	45.3	50.2	46.2	45.6	46.3	44.8	46.6
1894	49.5	47.0	51.1	45.5	46.1	45.4	46.8	45.2
1893	51.4	49.4	52.8	50.3	48.0	50.5	46.9	51.1
1892	50.9	48.3	52.6	50.9	47.8	51.2	47.5	51.8
1891	52.4	52.2	52.5	54.6	47.1	55.4	46.9	56.8
1890	52.0	51.4	52.4	54.3	47.2	55.1	49.1	56.1

Series J70–74. *Wholesale price indexes, classified according to degree of manufacture, industrial materials, residential and nonresidential building materials, 1890 to 1960*

Year	1935–39 = 100				1949 = 100	Year	1935–39 = 100	
	Raw and partly manufactured[1]	Fully and chiefly manufactured	Industrial materials	Residential building materials	Nonresidential building materials		Raw and partly manufactured[1]	Fully and chiefly manufactured
	70	71	72	73	74		70	71
1960	209.6	242.2	240.4	294.5	132.3	1925	128.8	134.8
1959	210.9	241.6	240.2	296.3	131.7	1924	121.3	132.4
1958	209.3	238.3	229.8	290.2	129.8	1923	116.7	133.9
1957	209.4	237.9	240.3	292.8	130.0	1922	121.2	130.4
1956	215.8	231.5	248.2	292.9	128.0	1921	136.7	150.8
1955	209.7	224.5	236.0	283.4	123.4	1920	194.7	203.3
1954	204.8	224.2	223.7	277.5	121.8	1919	165.2	171.6
1953	207.0	228.8	232.3	282.6	124.4	1918	153.4	165.9
1952	218.7	230.7	252.6	284.8	123.2	1917	144.5	147.4
1951	237.9	242.4	296.1	286.2	118.6	1916	111.0	109.9
1950	212.8	211.0	244.6	242.7	105.0	1915	93.7	92.4
1949	197.1	199.2	218.0	228.0	100.0	1914	86.0	85.2
1948	196.3	192.4	222.7	217.5	95.9	1913	83.0	84.2
1947	164.3	162.4	187.0	180.4	84.5	1912	86.5	83.8
1946	140.1	138.0	148.6	154.5	75.0	1911	80.7	80.8
1945	136.2	129.8	143.2	148.3	71.4	1910	78.5	80.9
1944	134.4	129.1	143.1	146.6	70.9	1909	79.9	81.2
1943	131.1	126.9	140.0	139.1	70.2	1908	76.9	82.9
1942	123.0	123.7	135.1	130.9	69.2	1907	76.3	82.6
1941	114.4	118.8	125.2	122.6	66.1	1906	73.2	78.2
1940	103.1	109.9	113.3	110.3	62.2	1905	69.9	79.2
1939	94.9	101.9	99.0	102.3	60.3	1904	69.0	77.2
1938	99.4	103.5	95.8	101.4	61.4	1903	68.4	76.8
1937	113.7	104.4	116.3	106.9	63.0	1902	66.3	76.1
1936	98.2	96.1	96.9	96.6	58.4	1901	63.8	74.9
1935	93.8	94.7	90.3	92.6	58.0	1900	61.9	76.4
1934	90.0	95.3	86.8	95.5	—	1899	59.3	73.0
1933	79.3	91.2	78.3	89.0	—	1898	59.7	72.2
1932	75.3	90.7	74.2	87.5	—	1897	55.7	70.1
1931	82.7	97.2	86.8	95.1	—	1896	53.4	70.7
1930	106.5	113.4	110.3	104.9	—	1895	55.5	72.3
1929	124.7	120.8	132.8	112.4	—	1894	55.4	74.4
1928	124.6	123.4	134.4	108.8	—	1893	59.7	78.3
1927	127.5	125.3	139.6	107.2	—	1892	59.0	78.8
1926	127.7	129.9	144.3	109.6	—	1891	64.6	83.5
						1890	63.3	86.1

[1] Includes gold prices.

Series J75–83. *Wholesale price indexes of Canadian farm products, 1890 to 1960*[1]

	1935–39 = 100										1913 = 100		
	Canada			Eastern			Western				Canada		
Year	Field	Animal	Total	Field	Animal	Total	Field	Animal	Total	Year	Field	Animal	Total
	75	76	77	78	79	80	81	82	83		75	76	77
1960	189.1	264.1	226.6	—	—	—	—	—	—				
1959	176.1	271.6	223.9	—	—	—	—	—	—				
1958	171.4	274.5	222.9	181.3	260.9	237.6	163.2	302.1	209.0	1934	95.4	87.9	92.6
1957	169.2	258.0	213.6	179.2	247.6	224.9	164.2	279.0	199.4	1933	81.2	77.5	79.8
1956	181.6	246.9	214.2	210.0	237.5	228.5	167.6	265.9	200.0	1932	72.9	78.8	75.1
										1931	77.3	100.7	86.1
1955	180.1	245.1	212.6	199.3	235.6	223.6	170.7	264.2	201.6				
1954	170.9	256.2	213.6	179.6	248.0	224.8	166.6	274.7	202.2	1930	124.2	133.6	127.7
1953	179.4	263.8	221.6	182.0	255.4	231.2	178.2	280.9	212.1	1929	166.4	146.0	158.8
1952	223.0	277.5	250.2	281.2	262.6	268.8	194.3	307.7	231.7	1928	164.3	148.4	158.4
1951	200.4	336.9	268.6	210.0	315.1	280.4	195.6	381.1	256.8	1927	177.2	137.2	162.2
										1926	177.4	129.8	159.6
1950	191.9	281.4	236.7	186.7	263.6	238.2	194.5	317.5	235.1				
1949	191.9	265.4	228.7	190.5	252.7	232.2	192.6	291.2	225.1	1925	174.1	137.2	160.5
1948	200.6	263.7	232.1	211.0	253.5	239.5	195.5	284.2	224.8	1924	146.6	126.2	139.1
1947	184.1	200.2	192.2	169.6	194.3	186.2	191.3	212.3	198.1	1923	130.0	123.5	127.6
1946	177.9	181.2	179.5	159.6	176.7	171.0	186.9	190.5	187.9	1922	144.3	128.6	138.5
										1921	177.8	142.2	164.8
1945	162.5	170.2	166.4	160.9	165.1	163.7	163.3	180.7	169.0				
1944	144.5	166.1	155.3	145.8	161.1	156.1	143.9	176.3	154.6	1920	295.3	195.8	258.8
1943	129.0	161.8	145.4	149.6	157.3	154.8	118.9	170.9	136.1	1919	252.8	199.3	233.1
1942	109.7	144.6	127.1	136.2	141.8	140.0	96.6	150.2	114.3	1918	234.0	173.5	211.9
1941	88.9	124.4	106.6	101.0	123.0	115.7	82.9	127.2	97.5	1917	238.4	153.8	207.5
										1916	157.4	118.7	143.3
1940	85.4	106.7	96.1	94.6	105.8	102.1	80.9	108.6	90.0				
1939	83.7	101.5	92.6	95.2	100.6	98.8	78.0	103.2	86.3	1915	136.4	103.2	124.3
1938	100.9	104.8	102.9	90.7	104.7	100.1	105.9	105.1	105.6	1914	116.0	101.7	110.8
1937	128.9	106.0	117.4	117.8	105.8	109.8	134.3	106.3	125.1	1913	100.0	100.0	100.0
1936	102.2	93.7	97.9	110.3	94.4	99.6	98.2	92.2	96.2	1912	123.7	92.9	116.0
										1911	105.8	84.6	100.5
1935	84.4	94.1	89.2	85.6	94.5	91.6	83.8	93.2	86.9				
1934	80.5	86.5	83.5	89.1	87.8	88.2	76.3	83.8	78.8	1910	98.9	89.2	96.5
1933	69.3	69.2	69.3	82.8	70.1	74.3	62.6	67.5	64.2	1909	119.4	86.2	111.1
1932	60.4	70.5	65.5	68.6	71.2	70.3	56.4	69.2	60.6	1908	108.0	79.9	101.0
1931	65.0	92.7	78.9	78.4	93.3	88.4	58.4	91.5	69.3	1907	105.3	79.0	98.7
										1906	85.0	74.3	82.3
1930	105.8	133.3	119.5	126.0	131.7	129.8	95.8	136.6	109.3				
1929	137.2	144.4	140.8	136.5	142.4	140.5	137.5	148.6	141.2	1905	88.1	72.4	84.2
1928	134.3	138.2	136.3	131.4	136.5	134.8	135.8	141.6	137.7	1904	91.4	69.8	86.0
1927	149.4	127.8	138.6	152.7	127.9	136.1	147.8	127.7	141.2	1903	87.7	69.4	83.1
1926	158.5	130.2	144.4	180.9	131.4	147.7	147.4	127.9	141.0	1902	83.3	71.4	80.3
										1901	79.7	69.3	77.1
										1900	73.2	67.8	71.9
										1899	72.2	61.8	69.6
										1898	81.0	61.6	76.2
										1897	67.6	59.6	65.6
										1896	70.0	56.3	66.6
										1895	73.0	59.2	69.6
										1894	67.2	58.8	65.1
										1893	77.8	64.8	74.6
										1892	78.3	62.2	74.3
										1891	90.4	62.3	83.4
										1890	84.9	63.3	79.5

[1] The index numbers of farm prices of agricultural products are shown in Section L, Agriculture.

Series J84–95. *Export price indexes (Taylor), 1869 to 1915*

(1900 = 100)

Year[1]	Total	Agricultural products			Animal products	Fibres and textiles	Wood, wood products and paper	Iron and steel	Non-ferrous metals	Non-metallic minerals	Chemicals and allied products	Miscellaneous
		Mainly foods	Not foods	Total foods and not foods								
	84	85	86	87	88	89	90	91	92	93	94	95
1915	122.5	139.0	100.1	135.0	141.4	102.7	134.9	58.7	98.9	117.2	115.7	122.2
1914	116.9	129.5	89.9	121.6	122.3	87.3	138.8	72.4	101.8	102.9	112.8	116.9
1913	122.5	129.9	119.2	128.5	131.9	112.1	141.5	79.1	104.8	104.2	105.2	122.5
1912	120.7	129.1	137.4	129.6	126.6	75.6	141.1	83.5	95.2	108.4	104.7	121.3
1911	123.7	133.0	161.2	135.5	124.5	94.6	146.2	95.9	94.5	102.5	103.1	123.4
1910	124.8	138.2	131.2	137.8	122.6	98.5	144.0	102.2	93.7	104.9	100.7	124.1
1909	123.5	129.7	111.9	128.7	123.8	102.7	144.1	100.3	102.0	108.5	101.5	122.5
1908[1]	124.2	125.3	111.2	124.3	122.8	119.2	146.8	94.0	114.2	101.0	104.9	123.2
1907[1]	118.5	112.7	98.8	110.7	124.3	130.8	123.4	92.0	120.5	106.6	107.7	118.2
1906	113.4	114.7	123.0	115.2	115.7	78.2	120.2	82.3	112.6	99.3	103.2	112.8
1905	105.3	113.4	102.5	112.2	104.3	88.4	111.9	92.5	102.6	97.9	105.2	105.0
1904	108.7	109.4	120.6	110.3	107.4	115.7	119.6	86.1	99.7	101.3	110.5	108.2
1903	107.6	103.2	122.1	104.2	110.8	104.6	113.7	94.7	99.2	105.2	113.1	107.0
1902	104.3	104.2	116.2	104.9	105.3	94.9	111.4	81.1	100.7	104.8	101.8	103.5
1901	102.5	99.7	121.1	100.6	105.2	98.1	100.8	103.0	101.6	105.9	95.4	102.6
1900	100.0	100.0	100.0	100.0	100.0	100.0	100.0	100.0	100.0	100.0	100.0	100.0
1899	95.4	102.9	82.9	101.2	89.9	78.6	95.8	118.0	96.7	110.2	108.2	95.5
1898	97.0	110.2	87.5	109.3	88.6	91.4	98.9	129.0	88.7	106.6	114.5	97.2
1897	90.9	84.3	109.1	85.6	88.4	99.6	93.7	139.8	93.2	111.6	114.5	91.8
1896	93.1	91.5	95.1	91.7	91.9	111.7	91.4	106.5	90.9	115.9	107.3	93.8
1895	96.5	90.3	89.1	90.2	99.4	103.6	93.5	114.2	84.9	117.1	79.6	97.1
1894	101.0	102.4	110.3	102.8	99.7	136.8	97.0	115.9	107.2	119.8	110.7	101.7
1893	100.7	106.2	129.7	106.8	99.3	76.0	96.9	106.9	68.5	125.1	108.7	101.8
1892	103.0	116.3	103.6	115.9	100.8	70.6	94.5	105.0	71.9	121.2	116.7	103.4
1891	104.0	118.0	222.4	124.2	99.6	115.6	94.0	122.6	110.6	127.9	152.1	104.7
1890	103.5	105.4	88.5	103.8	104.7	118.9	97.5	125.7	125.7	125.3	311.9	104.2
1889	101.3	117.9	67.4	115.0	95.2	108.7	96.5	131.0	149.3	126.6	—	102.5
1888	101.6	121.7	102.9	120.3	93.3	119.0	96.3	118.9	135.3	114.2	—	103.0
1887	96.3	109.7	71.5	108.4	87.3	116.7	96.2	106.2	114.8	103.0	—	96.9
1886	96.1	117.5	84.5	116.2	85.2	107.6	93.8	110.2	120.2	105.0	—	96.9
1885	99.2	122.7	71.5	121.1	91.5	108.1	94.6	110.2	125.6	104.2	—	99.7
1884	104.8	136.0	62.8	133.3	102.5	118.6	93.7	102.3	120.7	98.4	—	105.2
1883	109.6	141.3	68.4	138.3	101.2	113.7	98.1	83.2	111.0	97.2	—	109.8
1882	107.2	157.8	84.0	153.3	92.0	128.4	91.3	62.7	67.2	99.5	—	107.6
1881	97.5	132.1	65.6	130.1	85.1	152.1	86.5	73.1	86.5	102.2	—	97.7
1880	93.8	133.1	51.7	127.8	79.3	133.1	74.2	81.8	104.4	107.7	—	94.1
1879	91.6	132.2	49.3	128.1	76.1	120.3	74.4	52.5	101.8	104.9	—	92.1
1878	100.9	152.8	90.2	150.2	86.3	144.7	80.1	50.2	109.1	128.2	—	101.2
1877	98.1	139.8	54.9	131.2	90.2	135.2	85.1	46.3	130.0	138.3	—	98.1
1876	109.1	148.0	89.3	146.1	94.2	152.0	89.4	83.4	159.9	128.8	—	109.1
1875	105.8	161.8	71.5	157.3	88.9	172.4	95.5	80.7	104.6	118.3	—	106.7
1874	101.0	176.0	59.8	170.7	88.7	180.4	81.2	95.3	143.5	123.1	—	100.4
1873	99.1	161.6	70.5	156.8	81.4	236.5	87.8	137.4	112.2	110.9	—	99.2
1872	95.5	149.0	80.0	144.8	91.0	168.1	80.2	81.4	102.7	100.9	—	95.5
1871	93.4	144.1	113.4	141.0	88.6	152.5	83.5	110.8	108.7	75.9	—	93.5
1870	88.4	142.9	75.2	139.2	81.5	92.9	76.1	84.3	88.0	75.0	—	88.4
1869	89.4	174.4	90.2	170.3	82.4	156.2	71.3	77.6	169.0	63.4	—	89.4

[1] From 1869 to 1907 the data are for fiscal years ending 30 June of the year given, from 1908 to 1915 the data are for fiscal years ending 31 March of the year given

Series J96–107. *Import price indexes (Taylor), 1869 to 1915*

(1900 = 100)

Year[1]	Total	Agricultural products			Animal products	Fibres and textiles	Wood, wood products and paper	Iron and steel	Non-ferrous metals	Non-metallic minerals	Chemicals and allied products	Miscel-laneous
		Mainly foods	Not foods	Total foods and not foods								
	96	**97**	**98**	**99**	**100**	**101**	**102**	**103**	**104**	**105**	**106**	**107**
1915	103.1	118.0	113.8	116.7	97.9	121.2	98.7	86.5	95.5	96.4	111.7	103.0
1914	112.9	112.9	130.9	118.7	104.5	128.9	108.0	107.9	105.3	107.6	117.2	112.9
1913	110.0	120.7	136.4	126.1	98.5	123.8	101.1	103.3	113.5	102.7	108.6	109.8
1912	107.2	122.6	139.4	127.6	98.7	120.7	92.9	97.1	94.3	105.6	111.5	107.1
1911	110.5	114.9	143.7	123.4	102.3	124.6	108.4	99.0	91.0	112.4	115.3	110.3
1910	109.3	112.3	134.2	118.8	105.5	121.3	116.5	96.4	90.4	107.5	117.7	109.3
1909	108.6	114.0	119.8	115.8	102.9	114.8	110.0	100.4	97.6	112.9	115.4	109.6
1908[1]	117.0	113.6	121.1	115.8	116.2	120.1	128.3	108.1	130.3	118.4	119.9	117.1
1907[1]	113.8	105.3	110.9	107.2	117.9	120.7	130.9	101.8	135.3	112.9	115.9	113.8
1906	107.7	103.8	106.4	104.6	100.8	117.7	111.6	97.7	119.5	110.9	104.9	107.7
1905	102.7	103.7	103.1	103.4	91.5	110.6	103.6	94.5	99.3	112.2	102.7	102.8
1904	103.1	100.9	96.0	99.5	83.2	113.0	102.5	104.7	77.7	119.6	104.3	103.2
1903	100.7	93.8	96.3	94.6	85.4	104.8	95.6	100.9	90.1	125.1	102.2	100.5
1902	98.0	95.8	96.2	95.9	95.6	100.3	83.5	101.0	78.5	110.9	99.8	97.8
1901	101.0	103.1	95.5	100.8	102.3	100.9	87.9	103.2	86.1	107.6	107.7	101.2
1900	100.0	100.0	100.0	100.0	100.0	100.0	100.0	100.0	100.0	100.0	100.0	100.0
1899	89.6	94.6	83.2	91.3	96.9	91.7	90.0	83.1	69.8	91.9	94.6	89.6
1898	88.8	89.1	91.5	89.7	86.1	87.6	81.3	86.8	85.7	96.6	98.3	88.9
1897	83.8	89.8	76.1	84.6	78.3	78.9	79.1	85.9	61.5	100.3	99.0	83.9
1896	87.9	91.8	73.5	85.6	81.5	89.5	81.8	93.7	60.0	97.2	98.1	88.1
1895	85.3	92.1	67.5	85.2	78.1	86.1	89.8	80.8	53.3	101.1	97.0	85.4
1894	93.7	104.4	75.1	94.2	83.9	94.1	97.9	92.7	64.4	107.7	96.0	93.8
1893	96.3	110.0	75.3	96.4	79.9	98.5	99.7	94.3	75.3	111.1	102.0	96.5
1892	97.8	111.3	73.7	96.6	88.8	95.8	104.7	104.8	74.7	107.8	100.8	98.1
1891	104.2	111.5	83.1	101.5	97.4	106.8	94.3	115.2	82.0	109.7	102.2	105.0
1890	102.4	113.7	78.8	100.7	91.1	109.0	92.3	104.4	78.3	110.7	98.2	103.3
1889	102.1	111.0	84.9	102.4	100.2	102.7	98.2	97.2	82.2	111.8	106.9	102.5
1888	95.9	110.1	74.0	96.3	101.9	101.8	102.6	92.2	84.1	82.8	104.3	96.1
1887	97.7	106.8	75.3	96.8	107.2	97.2	117.8	84.7	68.2	115.1	100.6	97.4
1886	101.5	112.5	76.0	100.0	106.0	98.8	111.4	99.2	69.8	113.9	103.3	101.6
1885	107.3	111.4	81.7	103.2	109.9	107.0	112.3	102.9	76.9	125.1	113.1	107.5
1884	114.3	126.7	82.8	113.3	114.7	111.6	116.7	113.8	77.6	129.8	122.2	114.3
1883	117.8	136.7	84.5	120.4	119.0	116.7	105.3	117.5	71.8	129.2	171.5	118.3
1882	117.4	136.7	81.0	117.8	107.6	121.0	123.8	116.3	63.7	123.0	148.9	117.2
1881	113.3	138.9	73.3	117.7	106.5	111.0	96.9	124.8	62.8	118.3	142.7	114.2
1880	109.4	130.5	71.5	107.3	98.2	113.9	112.1	120.0	71.5	94.8	129.7	109.3
1879	104.4	135.2	67.0	116.1	88.5	90.8	113.5	113.4	94.3	112.5	128.4	103.7
1878	113.5	157.4	68.5	134.5	88.3	96.6	119.6	125.2	91.4	105.2	147.4	113.4
1877	119.2	156.3	69.8	134.6	93.7	108.6	117.2	137.6	104.3	113.3	131.6	119.3
1876	132.9	167.3	76.3	141.3	110.2	118.3	135.5	170.4	115.1	130.7	96.5	132.5
1875	135.4	186.0	71.0	147.3	101.9	118.0	—	203.4	106.9	148.5	97.9	135.5
1874	132.9	179.6	68.7	141.3	103.7	122.8	—	141.9	124.2	151.9	201.9	132.9
1873	140.1	181.8	72.9	152.2	108.3	153.4	—	112.6	107.6	146.4	149.5	140.1
1872	145.7	163.6	70.1	133.3	115.1	177.7	—	132.3	123.0	178.6	131.3	145.7
1871	137.2	170.8	65.0	136.0	128.8	155.8	—	138.3	104.5	110.2	112.4	137.2
1870	117.6	154.2	62.4	126.6	133.7	106.9	—	122.7	94.8	106.3	100.8	123.2
1869	133.0	167.1	75.2	141.3	137.8	134.2	—	133.5	100.3	113.4	89.7	132.3

[1] From 1869 to 1907 the data are for fiscal years ending 30 June of the year given, from 1908 to 1915 the data are for fiscal years ending 31 March of the year given.

Series J108–117. *Export price indexes, 1913 to 1960*

Year	Total	Agricultural and animal products — Vegetables and their products	Agricultural and animal products — Animals and their products	Fibres, textiles and textiles products	Wood, wood products and paper	Iron and steel and their products	Nonferrous metals and their products	Nonmetallic minerals and their products	Chemicals and allied products	Miscellaneous products
	108	109	110	111	112	113	114	115	116	117
Panel A 1948 = 100										
1960	123.2	99.6		110.5	118.5	162.8	150.6	165.3	115.3	133.9
1959	122.8	99.8		107.8	120.2	161.7	145.6	165.0	114.8	128.9
1958	120.6	96.6		108.0	119.3	157.1	143.8	165.3	114.5	128.8
1957	121.3	95.7		112.4	119.9	151.5	156.3	159.6	113.3	128.9
1956	121.4	95.9		108.7	120.1	143.1	165.0	156.1	113.9	126.6
1955	117.7	96.5		106.4	118.0	134.8	149.4	149.9	114.8	125.2
1954	115.1	96.8		108.6	116.3	132.3	134.6	150.2	115.0	123.5
1953	118.3	103.5		114.1	118.3	134.2	135.0	149.5	117.1	123.6
1952	121.8	107.6		120.0	122.4	131.4	142.6	143.1	119.3	129.7
1951	123.0	114.8		139.8	122.4	126.2	137.9	131.7	116.7	132.3
1950	108.3	105.6		112.8	105.0	113.7	115.1	120.4	104.2	112.0
1949	103.3	103.4		103.4	97.9	111.4	105.8	112.4	104.9	103.7
1948	100.0	100.0		100.0	100.0	100.0	100.0	100.0	100.0	100.0
1947	91.6	95.4		84.5	92.0	88.3	86.9	88.2	89.8	90.0
1946	79.9	84.7		66.1	75.4	82.3	76.1	77.2	84.2	84.2
1945	70.9	78.8		67.7	63.9	79.5	57.8	75.7	90.1	88.7
1944	67.6	74.2		66.3	61.6	78.2	52.9	75.9	91.3	89.3
1943	61.0	64.2		63.5	56.0	69.4	51.7	75.7	93.3	82.9
1942	55.0	53.1		63.5	51.1	65.6	51.8	76.5	93.2	82.8
1941	51.9	48.2		61.6	49.1	61.2	52.0	66.0	92.4	78.6
1940	49.9	47.4		56.7	45.9	57.4	50.8	68.5	83.6	73.9
1939	45.1	41.5		45.5	41.0	51.3	50.1	65.2	76.6	65.9
1938	47.1	45.7		44.2	41.2	51.9	52.0	64.9	77.8	65.6
1937	53.4	61.2		51.0	37.9	50.2	61.2	57.9	77.5	65.7
1936	45.8	49.9		47.3	34.4	48.2	50.2	57.6	76.5	63.1
1935	43.4	46.2		45.5	33.5	45.0	47.2	55.4	79.5	63.5
1934	42.6	45.4		48.3	33.2	44.7	45.6	53.4	78.1	60.0
1933	39.9	37.8		45.0	34.0	45.6	44.7	56.4	73.3	60.9
1932	40.3	35.4		44.7	40.2	47.7	40.0	58.9	76.6	62.9
1931	44.8	40.0		49.6	46.1	47.2	44.7	54.2	80.5	65.2
1930	54.0	55.2		56.3	50.7	48.2	53.1	59.1	88.3	71.6
1929	64.4	68.8		63.7	53.0	51.8	76.9	64.0	91.9	72.2
1928	65.4	70.1		66.1	55.3	51.0	75.0	63.5	97.5	74.8
1927	67.6	74.1		64.3	56.1	53.1	76.7	61.9	98.4	77.0
1926	70.2	76.4		68.9	57.0	53.0	84.0	59.8	102.9	86.1
Panel B 1913 = 100										
1934	96.1	91.2	110.5	68.4	98.5	75.3	95.3	143.7	59.3	—
1933	86.1	74.4	97.2	68.0	96.1	78.8	91.6	146.2	58.1	—
1932	85.1	69.3	98.9	47.8	109.4	79.1	78.1	140.7	70.5	—
1931	95.2	73.6	118.3	68.0	125.7	79.3	88.5	155.9	76.6	—
1930	116.8	99.0	145.9	89.4	142.2	80.5	109.4	164.0	83.7	—
1929	136.9	130.1	155.7	126.0	153.9	82.9	126.6	177.0	85.5	—
1928	137.6	132.1	155.7	143.7	156.4	81.0	121.1	172.8	87.4	—
1927	144.0	143.5	145.7	126.7	158.5	92.0	120.0	173.3	97.0	—
1926	147.0	150.9	148.0	140.3	162.4	82.9	129.4	172.8	107.6	—
1925	151.7	155.2	155.1	165.8	167.9	83.8	132.9	169.9	109.6	—
1924	139.6	133.1	136.3	161.1	173.3	88.3	123.3	181.1	109.0	—
1923	136.8	122.2	142.0	134.2	178.0	90.8	121.2	190.1	118.2	—
1922	137.8	129.3	136.2	117.1	168.3	107.9	123.6	189.2	117.0	—
1921	164.8	159.3	150.4	139.0	216.3	93.8	130.8	256.3	125.7	—
1920	229.7	256.1	209.1	190.1	250.5	131.4	167.3	275.9	138.8	—
1919	205.1	235.0	211.3	263.1	177.8	106.1	173.9	208.7	138.2	—
1918	195.9	238.1	191.5	283.4	153.6	90.7	158.1	203.8	132.2	—
1917	178.1	221.0	164.6	229.7	137.6	85.9	156.7	147.4	88.3	—
1916	125.4	131.5	131.8	153.4	106.2	90.2	139.2	139.5	102.3	—
1915	111.2	119.8	116.3	129.6	98.5	92.4	99.3	118.1	104.1	—
1914	103.4	104.1	107.0	102.8	99.7	109.6	99.7	99.7	104.2	101.7
1913	100.0	100.0	100.0	100.0	100.0	100.0	100.0	100.0	100.0	—

Series J118–127. *Import price indexes, 1913 to 1960*

Year	Total	Agricultural and animal products		Fibres, textiles and their products	Wood, wood products and paper	Iron and steel and their products	Nonferrous metals and their products	Nonmetallic minerals and their products	Chemicals and fertilizer	Miscellaneous products
		Vegetables and their products	Animals and their products							
	118	119	120	121	122	123	124	125	126	127
				Panel A 1948 = 100						
1960	116.1	91.1		88.0	142.2	146.5	138.3	99.1	111.9	125.7
1959	114.4	91.3		82.3	139.7	144.2	135.1	101.8	110.9	116.3
1958	116.5	100.3		86.6	138.7	143.1	132.8	106.5	112.7	106.9
1957	116.4	104.0		90.2	126.0	138.1	131.3	108.5	110.9	113.2
1956	113.0	99.8		89.2	123.8	133.2	132.8	102.0	111.7	118.3
1955	110.5	99.8		95.5	119.4	125.2	124.8	100.6	109.9	119.7
1954	109.5	104.4		99.8	117.5	120.4	120.4	102.1	108.1	105.3
1953	109.4	97.4		100.4	117.1	120.1	119.7	104.8	109.4	111.0
1952	110.4	102.3		108.5	115.3	117.3	120.5	101.7	109.0	123.5
1951	126.2	122.4		158.6	118.4	122.5	121.2	108.8	117.2	166.6
1950	110.3	108.2		109.3	111.6	116.1	106.9	104.4	102.8	121.5
1949	102.6	98.7		100.3	105.7	107.0	105.4	101.6	100.0	97.6
1948	100.0	100.0		100.0	100.0	100.0	100.0	100.0	100.0	100.0
1947	88.0	92.7		87.3	92.1	88.3	93.1	79.2	97.6	95.3
1946	76.9	82.1		70.2	84.4	77.1	82.5	67.8	83.5	93.2
1945	73.5	73.9		66.2	79.5	74.8	72.1	63.2	84.0	111.5
1944	73.1	71.3		69.8	79.1	73.7	71.1	62.1	82.1	111.9
1943	70.0	68.8		67.1	76.6	73.6	69.4	60.3	80.5	96.1
1942	63.6	58.2		54.4	72.7	73.6	69.7	56.2	83.5	84.1
1941	57.8	46.6		48.1	68.5	70.6	68.2	53.0	78.6	75.1
1940	53.2	40.4		43.8	64.0	67.9	66.0	47.6	74.0	70.9
1939	47.3	37.0		34.6	57.0	62.8	60.9	44.5	57.9	61.7
1938	47.3	38.2		34.4	55.1	62.2	58.6	46.1	56.9	58.6
1937	50.9	45.7		40.9	55.8	60.9	62.9	46.6	58.3	65.2
1936	46.4	40.0		37.2	51.9	55.7	55.3	44.7	57.6	57.3
1935	45.5	39.7		36.3	51.8	55.7	54.6	43.0	57.2	52.3
1934	45.3	38.5		37.0	55.0	55.2	53.5	43.0	57.6	51.4
1933	42.5	35.2		33.0	55.5	56.1	54.8	37.2	60.4	44.1
1932	44.4	36.8		30.1	57.3	60.2	56.2	42.9	62.2	44.3
1931	45.4	40.7		32.3	58.4	58.1	57.6	40.4	62.6	49.6
1930	54.0	53.7		42.5	57.4	59.7	62.5	51.9	66.1	60.1
1929	61.9	59.0		64.8	61.1	63.0	70.1	55.8	62.4	71.9
1928	63.4	65.2		66.6	61.4	61.2	67.3	55.5	63.6	77.8
1927	64.6	65.1		61.9	62.8	61.4	68.1	58.2	67.4	94.5
1926	67.9	60.4		66.6	64.4	63.6	70.6	65.9	65.5	117.9
				Panel B 1913 = 100						
1934	95.9	95.5	53.4	95.3	112.8	85.4	134.6	96.7	163.5	—
1933	88.9	87.2	51.6	81.0	116.2	83.0	130.0	87.4	155.3	—
1932	90.4	87.2	36.6	74.6	114.8	94.1	123.5	97.5	164.0	—
1931	95.9	100.9	58.0	86.0	117.9	92.6	107.0	100.6	151.7	—
1930	116.0	117.0	75.1	123.0	144.8	99.4	148.2	117.2	154.5	—
1929	123.0	130.6	94.9	147.1	150.9	95.7	117.9	123.6	134.3	—
1928	127.1	144.4	119.2	153.8	142.1	93.6	99.9	124.8	138.6	—
1927	126.4	153.3	95.0	143.7	141.7	95.0	97.4	130.1	148.2	—
1926	131.2	149.6	86.9	158.0	164.7	95.0	98.0	141.7	148.7	—
1925	139.2	154.8	93.6	184.0	175.6	98.6	94.0	143.9	140.3	—
1924	141.7	167.2	78.9	181.7	167.0	107.4	87.1	145.4	146.9	—
1923	147.6	174.4	87.3	182.4	178.2	108.8	92.0	162.2	143.7	—
1922	135.3	131.8	85.3	156.5	161.3	103.5	93.7	181.6	164.3	—
1921	160.6	200.3	91.4	165.0	174.8	137.6	90.7	179.3	215.2	—
1920	220.2	264.2	203.3	285.4	298.6	146.4	103.5	207.1	230.6	—
1919	179.9	190.6	224.1	264.6	142.2	127.4	118.0	144.3	218.3	—
1918	166.4	159.9	152.3	241.9	130.2	131.3	123.6	149.6	246.8	—
1917	143.3	149.0	166.9	167.1	102.6	119.8	139.9	134.3	205.9	—
1916	114.7	130.0	119.1	121.5	92.3	94.2	143.6	92.9	210.3	—
1915	92.7	109.3	104.1	92.6	87.7	79.2	110.9	74.0	128.4	—
1914	92.7	96.7	102.4	96.0	92.3	87.5	92.6	93.0	93.8	—
1913	100.0	100.0	100.0	100.0	100.0	100.0	100.0	100.0	100.0	—

Series J128–131. Price index numbers of a family budget (Department of Labour), 1900 to 1939

(1913 = 100)

Year	Total	Food	Fuel and light	Rent	Year	Total	Food	Fuel and light	Rent
	128	129	130	131		128	129	130	131
1939	122.6	113.1	147.5	125.3	1925	150.2	147.3	174.6	142.5
1938	124.2	116.7	147.5	124.4	1924	147.6	140.5	178.3	143.8
1937	123.4	117.5	147.0	121.1	1923	150.2	143.5	186.2	144.2
1936	118.7	110.3	148.0	117.8	1922	148.9	141.7	184.0	143.6
					1921	161.9	164.9	199.0	140.2
1935	115.2	104.9	149.1	115.5					
1934	114.2	103.0	150.1	114.7	1920	184.7	217.9	192.1	128.4
1933	112.0	95.8	150.7	119.3	1919	158.1	189.2	160.6	107.7
1932	118.4	96.8	159.1	133.3	1918	147.2	177.3	149.6	97.7
1931	133.1	115.7	166.9	143.9	1917	129.4	155.6	124.1	89.4
					1916	105.4	119.8	100.9	83.5
1930	151.8	149.4	170.6	145.8					
1929	154.1	154.6	171.7	144.5	1915	98.7	107.2	95.7	85.3
1928	151.7	150.4	171.9	143.2	1914	102.0	105.4	99.5	98.3
1927	151.2	149.9	173.3	142.0	1913	100.0	100.0	100.0	100.0
1926	153.1	152.8	176.5	142.0	1912	98.3	100.0	95.4	98.3
					1911	92.7	97.3	93.6	95.2
					1910	91.2	94.8	92.2[1]	83.9
					1905	78.2[1]	81.2[1]	85.5[1]	69.4[1]
					1900	69.7[1]	74.7[1]	78.6[1]	57.5[1]

[1] Data for the month of December only.

Series J132–138. Price indexes of selected retail services, 1900 to 1938

(1913 = 100)

Year	Domestic electric light	Manu-factured fuel gas	Natural fuel gas	Public ward hospital charges	Street car fares	Domestic telephone rates	Business telephone rates
	132	133	134	135	136	137	138
	Dominion Bureau of Statistics						
1938	55.6	123.8	159.1	205.4	150.8	129.1	148.0
1937	55.9	123.9	159.1	204.8	150.8	129.1	147.1
1936	58.7	122.7	159.1	200.1	148.6	129.1	146.9
1935	59.3	122.8	160.7	199.5	149.3	129.1	146.9
1934	60.4	123.2	161.0	199.1	151.2	129.1	146.9
1933	60.2	123.4	161.9	200.6	151.8	129.1	146.9
1932	60.1	123.6	162.6	204.1	152.0	128.8	146.8
1931	60.2	125.2	161.9	204.1	151.6	128.8	146.8
1930	61.5	127.7	159.5	204.5	148.9	128.8	146.8
1929	63.8	128.1	160.7	203.9	146.3	128.8	146.7
1928	66.5	128.6	160.8	196.9	144.5	128.8	146.7
1927	68.0	129.0	166.9	185.2	142.9	128.8	146.8
1926	68.7	131.1	172.4	183.2	142.9	120.2	124.0
1925	69.9	131.6	179.3	181.2	142.9	119.4	123.6
1924	72.2	134.6	162.2	180.4	142.9	—	—
1923	74.4	135.7	163.0	177.1	140.5	—	—
1922	—	140.6	163.2	175.0	140.5	—	—
1921	—	143.6	137.6	170.5	121.4	—	—
1920	—	125.4	125.1	156.9	119.0	—	—
1919	—	111.1	116.1	149.1	111.9	—	—
1918	—	107.4	114.0	134.4	100.0	—	—
1917	—	100.7	113.9	119.4	100.0	—	—
1916	—	96.3	112.5	110.0	100.0	—	—
1915	—	98.1	112.5	109.0	102.4	—	—
1914	—	98.3	107.0	104.0	104.8	—	—

Year	Domestic electric light	Manu-factured fuel gas	Natural fuel gas	Public ward hospital charges	Street car fares	Domestic telephone rates	Business telephone rates
	132	133	134	135	136	137	138
	Coats						
1913	100.0	100.0	100.0	100.0	100.0	100.0	100.0
1912	109.1	101.3	100.0	94.2	—	—	—
1911	113.4	100.0	98.8	89.7	—	—	—
1910	118.1	105.2	102.4	88.1	—	—	—
1909	125.3	106.5	104.9	85.5	—	—	—
1908	128.0	109.1	104.9	82.3	—	—	—
1907	130.3	110.4	107.3	79.6	—	—	—
1906	132.8	109.1	106.1	76.7	—	—	—
1905	135.6	122.1	118.3	72.3	—	—	—
1904	137.5	128.6	119.5	71.6	—	—	—
1903	137.9	122.9	120.7	68.6	—	—	—
1902	137.8	129.9	122.0	67.7	—	—	—
1901	139.3	129.9	122.0	67.6	—	—	—
1900	141.4	129.9	122.0	67.6	—	—	—

Series J139–146. *Cost-of-living index, 1913 to 1952*

(1935–39 = 100)

Year	Total	Food	Fuel and light	Rent	Clothing	Home furnishings	Miscellaneous	Retail prices (commodities only)
	139	140	141	142	143	144	145	146
1952	188.4	237.4	151.1	147.4	209.4	197.8	151.5	216.6
1951	185.4	241.1	147.1	140.0	203.1	194.4	145.0	216.0
1950	167.3	210.9	138.3	132.9	182.3	169.2	136.0	191.3
1949	161.6	203.0	131.1	123.0	183.1	167.6	132.2	186.2
1948	155.7	195.5	124.8	120.7	174.4	162.6	126.8	178.7
1947	136.3	159.5	115.9	116.7	143.9	141.6	120.4	150.2
1946	124.5	140.4	107.4	112.7	126.3	124.5	116.5	133.4
1945	120.4	133.0	107.0	112.1	122.1	119.0	113.5	127.6
1944	119.8	131.3	110.6	111.9	121.5	118.4	113.1	126.6
1943	119.2	130.7	112.9	111.5	120.5	118.0	111.5	125.6
1942	117.2	127.2	112.8	111.3	120.0	117.9	107.8	122.6
1941	111.7	116.1	110.3	109.4	116.1	113.8	105.1	114.9
1940	105.6	105.6	107.1	106.3	109.2	107.2	102.3	106.6
1939	101.5	100.6	101.2	103.8	100.7	101.4	101.4	101.0
1938	102.2	103.8	97.7	103.1	100.9	102.4	101.2	102.8
1937	101.2	103.2	98.9	99.7	101.4	101.5	100.1	102.0
1936	98.1	97.8	101.5	96.1	99.3	97.2	99.1	98.1
1935	96.2	94.6	100.9	94.0	97.6	95.4	98.7	95.9
1934	95.6	93.0	101.8	93.4	97.2		97.9	—
1933	94.3	85.3	101.7	99.3	93.6		98.4	—
1932	98.9	86.2	106.2	110.6	100.9		100.6	—
1931	109.0	103.7	109.2	120.2	114.6		103.5	—
1930	120.8	132.3	111.0	123.6	131.0	105.8		—
1929	121.6	135.4	111.8	120.5	135.2	105.3		—
1928	120.2	132.2	112.4	118.1	135.8	104.9		—
1927	119.7	131.6	113.6	115.3	135.9	105.4		—
1926	121.7	134.2	116.0	116.7	139.7	106.3		—
1925	120.4	126.9	115.7	118.2	141.7	107.7		—
1924	119.3	121.1	118.0	118.2	142.1	109.8		—
1923	121.5	123.7	121.3	117.8	145.2	112.0		—
1922	121.1	122.8	121.5	114.8	147.1	112.7		—
1921	132.3	145.0	127.0	110.1	173.7	112.7		—
1920	150.4	188.8	119.0	100.7	213.8	110.6		—
1919	129.8	164.1	99.6	87.9	175.2	101.2		—
1918	118.1	153.6	91.8	80.6	152.5	91.3		—
1917	104.3	133.7	83.1	76.3	130.3	81.6		—
1916	88.1	103.5	74.7	71.1	110.8	74.9		—
1915	81.4	93.3	73.3	70.4	97.4	70.8		—
1914	80.0	92.0	74.5	72.6	89.2	70.4		—
1913	79.5	88.7	76.3	74.8	88.3	70.4		—

Series J147–152. *Consumer price index, 1926 to 1960*

(1949 = 100)

Year	Total	Food	Shelter	Clothing	Household operation	Other commodities and services
	147	148	149	150	151	152
1960	128.0	122.2	143.7	110.9	123.3	137.6
1959	126.5	121.1	141.4	109.9	122.7	134.9
1958	125.1	122.1	138.4	109.7	121.0	130.9
1957	121.9	118.6	134.9	108.5	119.6	126.1
1956	118.1	113.4	132.5	108.6	117.1	120.9
1955	116.4	112.1	129.4	108.0	116.4	118.1
1954	116.2	112.2	126.5	109.4	117.4	117.4
1953	115.5	112.6	123.6	110.1	117.0	115.8
1952	116.5	116.8	120.2	111.8	116.2	116.0
1951	113.7	117.0	114.4	109.8	113.1	111.5
1950	102.9	102.6	106.2	99.7	102.4	103.1
1949	100.0	100.0	100.0	100.0	100.0	100.0
1948	97.0	97.5	98.3	95.6	96.8	96.5
1947	84.8	79.5	95.1	78.9	86.2	91.6
1946	77.5	70.0	91.8	69.2	77.2	88.7
1945	75.0	66.3	91.4	66.9	74.9	86.4
1944	74.6	65.5	91.2	66.6	75.7	86.1
1943	74.2	65.2	90.9	66.1	76.1	84.8
1942	72.9	63.4	90.7	65.8	76.0	82.0
1941	69.6	57.9	89.2	63.6	73.8	80.0
1940	65.7	52.6	86.6	59.9	70.3	77.9
1939	63.2	50.2	84.6	54.9	66.5	77.2
1938	63.7	51.7	84.1	55.4	66.0	77.0
1937	63.0	51.4	81.3	55.4	65.9	76.2
1936	61.1	48.8	78.3	54.2	64.9	75.5
1935	59.9	47.2	76.6	53.6	64.1	75.2
1934	59.5	46.3	76.2	53.2	64.1	75.1
1933	58.7	42.5	81.0	51.3	63.8	75.9
1932	61.6	43.0	90.1	55.3	66.2	77.4
1931	67.8	51.7	98.0	62.8	68.3	79.4
1930	75.2	65.9	100.7	71.8	70.2	80.8
1929	75.7	67.5	98.2	74.1	70.8	80.1
1928	74.8	65.9	96.3	74.4	71.0	79.8
1927	74.5	65.7	94.0	74.5	71.6	80.0
1926	75.8	66.9	95.1	76.6	72.3	80.9
1925	75.0	—	—	—	—	—
1924	74.3	—	—	—	—	—
1923	75.6	—	—	—	—	—
1922	75.4	—	—	—	—	—
1921	82.4	—	—	—	—	—
1920	93.6	—	—	—	—	—
1919	80.8	—	—	—	—	—
1918	73.5	—	—	—	—	—
1917	65.0	—	—	—	—	—
1916	54.9	—	—	—	—	—
1915	50.7	—	—	—	—	—
1914	49.8	—	—	—	—	—
1913	49.5	—	—	—	—	—

Series J153–164. *Implicit price indexes of gross national expenditures, 1926 to 1960*

(1949 = 100)

| Year | Gross national expenditure at market prices | Gross national expenditure at market prices (excluding inventories) | Personal expenditure on consumer goods and services | Government expenditure on goods and services | | | Business gross fixed capital formation | | | | Exports of goods and services | Imports of goods and services |
| | | | | Total | Current expenditure | Gross fixed capital formation | Total | New residential construction | New non-residential construction | New machinery and equipment | | |
	153	154	155	156	157	158	159	160	161	162	163	164
1960	140.4	141.2	131.2	161.3	169.5	137.6	154.0	154.0	157.4	151.0	120.7	121.2
1959	138.3	139.1	129.9	156.2	162.6	137.3	150.7	149.9	153.8	148.2	119.9	120.0
1958	134.8	135.6	128.1	151.0	157.4	131.5	146.5	144.6	149.2	145.5	118.1	120.7
1957	132.3	133.1	124.8	149.3	151.4	142.8	143.4	141.2	146.9	141.5	118.6	118.9
1956	128.5	129.1	120.7	142.0	143.8	136.2	138.5	137.5	142.6	135.3	119.2	115.8
1955	123.8	124.7	118.6	134.5	135.8	129.9	131.5	132.5	135.4	127.4	116.0	112.2
1954	123.2	122.5	118.5	130.6	131.5	127.5	128.4	129.7	131.4	125.0	111.5	111.2
1953	120.3	121.0	116.9	126.0	125.7	127.2	127.3	128.8	131.6	123.2	112.3	110.9
1952	119.8	120.2	117.0	121.7	121.3	122.9	124.1	126.6	126.8	120.8	114.9	110.6
1951	114.1	114.5	113.9	116.6	116.4	117.1	119.9	123.1	118.2	119.6	116.2	119.8
1950	103.1	103.2	103.3	104.5	104.5	104.6	105.7	106.0	105.5	105.7	104.6	107.3
1949	100.0	100.0	100.0	100.0	100.0	100.0	100.0	100.0	100.0	100.0	100.0	100.0
1948	96.1	95.9	96.5	94.5	—	—	95.0	95.5	96.0	94.0	96.6	96.9
1947	85.2	85.1	85.3	83.3	—	—	83.5	81.0	85.3	83.8	87.9	86.7
1946	77.7	77.9	77.8	78.3	—	—	75.2	71.9	76.5	75.3	78.0	77.4
1945	76.1	76.4	75.2	80.5	—	—	72.6	67.4	71.9	74.4	71.1	73.0
1944	74.4	74.7	74.3	76.6	—	—	72.9	66.6	72.1	76.0	68.9	71.1
1943	72.2	72.3	73.5	73.1	—	—	71.9	64.1	71.0	77.8	64.5	68.7
1942	69.7	70.2	71.5	70.8	—	—	67.9	60.1	67.6	72.7	61.3	65.0
1941	66.7	66.4	68.3	64.6	—	—	64.5	56.2	62.9	69.6	57.4	59.7
1940	61.8	62.6	63.8	62.2	—	—	59.8	51.3	59.6	64.1	55.1	56.4
1939	59.1	59.8	61.2	59.1	—	—	56.2	48.2	57.4	59.5	50.3	51.1
1938	59.5	60.4	61.5	59.1	—	—	56.4	47.8	58.0	60.1	51.7	51.6
1937	59.6	60.0	60.5	58.6	—	—	56.9	48.8	59.3	59.8	54.8	54.2
1936	58.0	57.6	58.8	56.6	—	—	52.9	45.5	55.1	55.4	50.2	50.3
1935	56.2	56.5	57.8	55.8	—	—	52.1	44.3	53.8	54.9	48.3	49.0
1934	55.9	55.8	57.5	54.9	—	—	51.4	44.4	52.7	54.1	47.3	48.8
1933	55.2	55.0	56.6	54.9	—	—	50.7	42.9	52.1	54.6	43.4	45.4
1932	56.3	56.7	59.0	56.1	—	—	52.4	44.9	53.5	55.8	42.7	46.8
1931	62.1	61.4	64.2	59.3	—	—	54.4	49.0	56.0	55.6	47.5	50.8
1930	66.0	66.8	70.4	61.2	—	—	57.6	52.6	60.5	57.7	56.8	57.8
1929	67.7	67.8	71.2	62.3	—	—	59.6	54.0	62.9	60.1	62.7	62.9
1928	66.9	67.3	70.4	61.7	—	—	58.0	51.7	61.0	58.8	64.1	63.7
1927	67.1	67.2	69.8	61.2	—	—	57.3	50.4	59.6	59.1	66.2	64.4
1926	68.0	68.1	70.7	61.6	—	—	58.1	50.4	59.7	61.2	67.7	66.3

APPENDIX. INDEX NUMBERS OF FIFTEEN FOODSTUFFS

Series J165–167. *Wholesale price indexes of 15 foodstuffs (Michell), 1848 to 1913*

(1900 = 100)

| Year | All | Vegetable products | Animal products | Year | All | Vegetable products | Animal products | Year | All | Vegetable products | Animal products |
	165	166	167		165	166	167		165	166	167
				1890	106	121	94	1865	124	144	109
				1889	109	122	99	1864	108	130	92
1913	146	138	153	1888	121	143	104	1863	101	130	84
1912	155	164	147	1887	107	116	99	1862	94	128	71
1911	135	142	130	1886	104	116	94	1861	98	115	92
1910	141	136	146	1885	110	133	94	1860	112	138	93
1909	143	152	135	1884	121	135	109	1859	124	165	96
1908	135	153	121	1883	127	146	113	1858	108	129	94
1907	130	141	122	1882	137	157	121	1857	154	168	134
1906	120	124	116	1881	128	158	106	1856	150	185	125
1905	117	131	106	1880	117	146	96	1855	155	223	111
1904	107	123	96	1879	106	137	85	1854	134	200	95
1903	107	110	104	1878	100	128	81	1853	108	142	85
1902	104	107	102	1877	125	159	101	1852	91	99	84
1901	107	109	104	1876	122	141	107	1851	85	106	70
1900	100	100	100	1875	132	157	116	1850	87	107	73
1899	96	104	90	1874	135	160	116	1849	80	98	67
1898	94	106	86	1873	123	157	100	1848	91	120	71
1897	85	86	85	1872	117	152	92				
1896	82	88	78	1871	126	159	99				
1895	94	105	85	1870	122	142	110				
1894	95	97	93	1869	126	148	109				
1893	104	101	106	1868	139	189	109				
1892	102	113	94	1867	124	175	90				
1891	112	139	93	1866	122	143	106				

SECTION K: LANDS AND FORESTS

G. K. GOUNDREY, *University of Alberta*

The data in this section are divided into two parts. Series K1–106 contain statistics on lands, including total areas, public parks, sales, grants and alienation of public lands, and receipts from sales and for use of public lands. Series K107–223 contain statistics on forests, including data on production and exports of primary and secondary products, forest fires, and forestry revenues and expenditure of provinces.

The following sources were used in preparing the data of this section for series K1–106, on lands.

For the federal government: Department of the Interior, *Annual Report* (Ottawa, King's Printer), reports for 1875 to 1936; Department of Indian Affairs, *Annual Report* (Ottawa, King's Printer), reports for 1880 to 1936; Department of Mines and Resources, *Annual Report* (Ottawa, King's Printer) reports, for 1937 to 1949; Department of Resources and Development, *Annual Report* (Ottawa, Queen's Printer), reports for 1950 to 1954; Department of Northern Affairs and National Resources, *Annual Report* (Ottawa, Queen's Printer), reports for 1955 to 1959; Dominion Bureau of Statistics, *Census of Canada*, volumes concerning agriculture (Ottawa, Queen's Printer); Dominion Bureau of Statistics, *Canada Year Book* (Ottawa, Queen's Printer), various years; Dominion Bureau of Statistics, *Canadian Forestry Statistics, Revised 1959* (Ottawa, Queen's Printer, 1960); Department of Mines and Technical Surveys, Geographical Branch, *Atlas of Canada* (Ottawa, Queen's Printer, 1957); Norman L. Nicholson, Department of Mines and Technical Surveys, Geographical Branch, Memoir 2, *The Boundaries of Canada, Its Provinces and Territories* (Ottawa, Queen's Printer, 1954); *Canada Gazette* (Ottawa, Queen's Printer), various years; *Statutes of Canada* (Ottawa, Queen's Printer), various years; Archives of Canada, Manuscript Division, Post-Confederation Collection R.G. 15, B. 7, unpublished data presented to the Royal Commission on the Natural Resources of Alberta and the Royal Commission on the Natural Resources of Saskatchewan. Provincial government reports used for series K1–106 were: Nova Scotia, Department of Lands and Forests, *Annual Report* (Halifax, Queen's Printer), various years to 1959, and Nova Scotia, Department of Crown Lands, *Annual Report* (Halifax, King's Printer), earlier years; New Brunswick, Department of Lands and Mines, *Annual Report* (Fredericton, Queen's Printer), various years to 1959, and New Brunswick, Department of Crown Lands, *Annual Report* (Fredericton, King's Printer), earlier years; Quebec, Department of Lands and Forests, *Annual Report* (Quebec, King's Printer) various years prior to 1943; Quebec, Department of Colonization, *Annual Report* (Quebec, Queen's Printer), reports of 1940 to 1959; Ontario, Department of Lands, Forests and Mines, *Annual Report* (Toronto, King's Printer), reports for 1917 to 1920; Ontario, Department of Lands and Forests, *Annual Report* (Toronto, Queen's Printer), reports for 1921 to 1959; Manitoba, Department of Mines and Natural Resources, *Annual Report* (Winnipeg, Queen's Printer), reports for 1931 to 1960; Saskatchewan, Department of Natural Resources, *Annual Report* (Regina, King's Printer), reports for 1931 to 1947; Saskatchewan, Department of Agriculture, *Annual Report* (Regina, Queen's Printer), reports for 1947 to 1960; Alberta, Department of Lands and Mines, *Annual Report* (Edmonton, King's Printer), reports for 1931 to 1950; Alberta, Department of Lands and Forests, *Annual Report* (Edmonton, Queen's Printer), reports for 1951 to 1960; British Columbia, Department of Public Works and Lands, *Annual Report* (Victoria, King's Printer), reports for 1874 to 1907; British Columbia, Department of Lands, *Annual Report* (Victoria, King's Printer), reports for 1908 to 1945; British Columbia, Department of Lands and Forests, *Annual Report* (Victoria, Queen's Printer),

reports for 1946 to 1959. In most cases these annual reports have been printed in the *Sessional Papers* of the provinces concerned. Nongovernment publications used for series K1–106 were: Arthur S. Morton and Chester Martin, *History of Prairie Settlement and 'Dominion Lands' Policy* (Toronto, The Macmillan Company of Canada, 1938), vol. II in the series *Canadian Frontiers of Settlement*, edited by W. A. Mackintosh and W. L. G. Joerg; Canadian Pacific Railway Company, *Annual Report*, for 1927 to 1960.

The following sources were used in preparing the data of this section for series K107–223, on forests.

For the federal government: Dominion Bureau of Statistics, *Canadian Forestry Statistics, Revised, 1959* (Ottawa, Queen's Printer, 1960); *Report of Royal Commission on Pulpwood*, Sessional Paper 310 of 1924 (Ottawa, King's Printer, 1924). The administration of forest lands by the Dominion Government has been under the supervision of various departments: the Department of the Interior until 1936, the Department of Mines and Resources 1937 to 1949, the Department of Resources and Development 1950 to 1952 and the Department of Northern Affairs and National Resources 1953 to 1960. Thus, the publications by the forestry branch, mentioned below, are printed by the department concerned: Forestry Branch, *Forest Fire Losses in Canada* (Ottawa, King's Printer), reports for 1948 to 1950; Director of Forestry, *Annual Report* (Ottawa, King's Printer), reports for 1937 to 1947; Lands, Parks and Forestry Branch, *Annual Report* (Ottawa, King's Printer), reports for 1918 to 1936; Forestry Branch, *Forest Fires in Canada 1917*, Bulletin 69 (Ottawa, King's Printer, 1918); Forestry Branch, *Forest Fires in Canada, 1914-15-16*, Bulletin 64 (Ottawa, King's Printer, 1917); Forestry Branch, *Forest Fires in Canada, 1909*, Bulletin 9 (Ottawa, King's Printer, 1910); Forestry Branch, *Forest Fires in Canada, 1908*, Bulletin 7 (Ottawa, King's Printer, 1909). Nongovernment publications used for series K107–223 were: K. W. Taylor, 'Statistics of Foreign Trade' *Statistical Contributions to Canadian Economic History, Volume II* (Toronto, The Macmillan Company of Canada, 1931); A. Milton Moore, Canadian Tax Foundation, *Forestry Tenures and Taxes in Canada*, Tax Paper No. 11 (Toronto, Canadian Tax Foundation, 1957); Newsprint Association of Canada, *Newsprint Data*, 1958; Newsprint Association of Canada, *Annual Newsprint Supplement, 1961* (April 1962).

In addition to the data obtained from published sources some material and a good deal of help were obtained from federal agencies, notably: the Forestry Branch and the National Parks Branch of the Department of Northern Affairs and National Resources; the Indian Affairs Branch of the Department of Citizenship and Immigration; the Department of Mines and Technical Surveys; the Archives of Canada; the National Library; the Parliamentary Library; and especially the Dominion Bureau of Statistics.

General note

The task of assembling statistical series on lands and forests (as well as other natural resources) in Canada is complicated by diffusion of control and irregularity in records. Canadian natural resources are vested in the crown and since Confederation the rights of the crown have been vested in separate agencies, the Dominion government and the provinces. There have been Dominion lands and provincial lands since 1870. This has meant that no single agency publishes information concerning resources, and the classifications, definitions and basic content of the reports vary widely. Even at the present time, when the Dominion Bureau of Statistics is collecting and publishing information about resources, it is frequently impossible to reconcile the published statistics of D.B.S. with those of the provincial departments responsible for the administration of the natural resource concerned.

The search for records of land grants, patents, leases and timber rights presupposes a knowledge of the constitutional disposition of crown lands and of changes in such disposition from time to time. Before Confederation, Canadian natural resources were vested in the crown in the right of the provinces. The British North America Act of 1867 specified the continuance of provincial control in the originally federated provinces by section 109 of the Act:

All Lands, Mines, Minerals, and Royalties belonging to the several Provinces of Canada, Nova Scotia, and New Brunswick at the Union, and all Sums then due or payable for such Lands, Mines, Minerals or Royalties, shall belong to the several Provinces of Ontario, Quebec, Nova Scotia, and New Brunswick in which the same are situate or arise, subject to any Trusts existing in respect thereof, and to any Interest other than that of the Province in the same.

In 1870 the Dominion government secured massive territories not included in provincial boundaries by the purchase of Rupert's Land (the drainage basin of Hudson and James Bays) from the Hudson's Bay Company. At the same time the Imperial government transferred the 'North-Western Territory' to the Dominion. The Red River settlers demanded provincial status including local control of public lands but the Manitoba Act which created the new province (*Statutes of Canada*, 33 Vic. (1870), c. 3, s. 30) provided that 'All ungranted or waste lands in the Province shall be...vested in the Crown, and administered by the Government of Canada for the purposes of the Dominion...'. When the Manitoba bill was being considered in the Dominion legislature the Prime Minister, the Hon. Sir John A. Macdonald, summarized the main purpose of this section in the following words: 'They [the residents of the Red River colony] wished Rupert's Land made into one Province, and to have all the lands within the boundary as in other Provinces...[but] the land could not be handed over to them, as it was of the greatest importance to the Dominion to have possession of it, for the Pacific Railway must be built by means of the land through which it had to pass.' Doubts concerning the constitutional validity of section 30 of the Manitoba Act were removed retroactively by an amendment to the British North America Act in 1871 which confirmed the Manitoba Act 'for all purposes whatsoever'.

When British Columbia entered the Dominion in 1871 it was on the same conditions regarding crown lands as applied to the original four provinces: that is, British Columbia was assumed to have control of the lands and other natural resources within its boundaries. However, the construction of a Pacific railway within ten years was one of the terms of union and in return for an annual payment of $100,000 from the Dominion government the province agreed to convey 'in trust...in furtherance of the construction of the said Railway, a similar extent of Public Lands along the line of Railway throughout its entire length in British Columbia, not to exceed however Twenty (20) Miles on each side of said line, as may be appropriated for the same purpose by the Dominion Government from the Public Lands in the North West Territories and the Province of Manitoba'. In 1883 the province of British Columbia transferred lands in the 'Peace River Block' to the Dominion in lieu of those unfit for settlement, in the railway belt. The total transferred to the Dominion in the railway belt and the Peace River Block was 14,181,000 acres. (A. S. Morton and Chester Martin, *History of Prairie Settlement and 'Dominion Lands' Policy*, pp. 269–70.) Of this amount only 1,300 acres were accepted as land grant by the Canadian Pacific Railway Company and 12,832,400 acres were returned to the province in 1930. (The dates of the transfers and a discussion of the agreements are given in the *Annual Report of the Department of the Interior, 1930–31*, p. 34.) The Dominion government continued to pay the annual indemnity of $100,000.

Outside provincial boundaries the territories were Dominion lands without any special constitutional proviso. In the lower portions of the central plains including the province of Manitoba the Dominion government pursued after 1870 a land grant policy to encourage railway construction and a free homestead policy to hasten settlement. When Saskatchewan and Alberta were accorded provincial status in 1905 (effective 1 September), the Dominion retained their natural resources as had been done in Manitoba 'for the purposes of the Dominion'. The resources were returned to all the prairie provinces in 1930.

Restoration of the natural resources to the respective provinces necessitated the settlement of claims entered by the provincial governments against the government of Canada with respect to the disposition and administration of the resources while in Dominion hands. Royal commissions were appointed to recommend terms of settlement for each of the provinces. The exhibits and counter-exhibits presented to these commissions contain a wealth of information about the disposition and administration of Dominion lands along with summaries and discussions of the administration of resources in other provinces. In some cases the exhibits correct figures published in the annual reports of the Department of the Interior for Canada and provide detail not otherwise available.

The exhibits presented by the provincial governments to the royal commissions dealing with the question of compensation for Alberta and Saskatchewan, the exhibits of the federal government, and the evidence and proceedings of these commissions are to be found in the Public Archives of Canada, Manuscript Division, Post-Confederation Collection R.G. 15, B. 7 (information for the use of Dominion Counsel). A summary of the evidence before the royal commission on Manitoba's claims is available in the library of the University of Manitoba. In the notes to the tables which follow, the collection in the Public Archives is referred to as the Saskatchewan Resources Commission or the Alberta Resources Commission, depending on the section of the collection to which reference is made. The volumes of exhibits and papers relating to the Saskatchewan Commission are numbered: those relating to Alberta are lettered.

A great deal of information, based upon the material of the Resources Commissions and on data in the Annual Report of the Department of the Interior, may be found in Chester Martin's part on Dominion Lands Policy in Morton and Martin, *History of Prairie Settlement and 'Dominion Lands' Policy*.

Provincial sources must be consulted for information on the resources of the four original provinces of the Dominion and on British Columbia. After 1930 provincial sources must be searched for all provinces. In the notes on this section the departmental reports cited as source materials are either of the government of Canada or of the province concerned depending on the heading under which the source is given.

Lack of uniformity in available statistics concerning natural resources is particularly noticeable in data on forest resources. Even the collection and publication of data by the Dominion Bureau of Statistics as at present does not resolve the difficulty. Log scales (the factors used to convert logs into feet board measure) vary from province to province making it extremely difficult to arrive at estimates of depletion and primary forest production. Provincial reports concerning the number of sawmill licences issued and the lumber sawn (on which provincial charges may be based) frequently do not agree with the returns to the Dominion Bureau of Statistics. Forest products are reported in different units involving conversion factors: e.g. lineal feet, cubic feet, number, feet board measure, etc. At many stages in the collation of material, variations in the provincial forests—differences in species, sizes of logs, etc.—render uniform conversion factors inapplicable and introduce questions of judgement and evaluation.

A concerted effort is being made to improve and expand Canada's forestry statistics at the present time. Officers of the Dominion Bureau of Statistics and of the Forestry Branch of the Department of Northern Affairs and National Resources (now the Department of Forestry) are working on this problem. It did not seem appropriate at this time to attempt to produce series on forests the reliability of which would necessarily fall short of those already produced by the joint efforts of these agencies and published by the Dominion Bureau of Statistics.

The earlier reference volume, *Forest and Forest Product Statistics—Canada*, Forestry Branch Bulletin No. 106, produced by the Department of Northern Affairs and National Resources, has been replaced by a publication of the Dominion Bureau of Statistics which incorporates revisions of data in the earlier publication, based on the work of a joint committee on forest statistics. The newer publication, *Canadian Forestry Statistics (Revised 1959)*, has been used throughout as a source of forest statistics.

LANDS (Series K 1–106)

K 1–2. Area of Canada and provinces, 1867 to 1959

SOURCE: for latest areas, D.B.S., *Canadian Forestry Statistics, Revised 1959*, p. 7, table 1; for earlier areas, special calculations of the Department of Mines and Technical Surveys. Apart from present areas, given in the first cited source, the entries in this table were derived from planimetric map measurement done by the Department of Mines and Technical Surveys for the author of this section. For this measurement the legal descriptions of boundaries and the changes in them with the dates of change were obtained from Nicholson, *The Boundaries of Canada*. From this information, measurement of areas within the described boundaries was done on current maps. The error of these planimetric measurements is considered to be ±5 per cent. The area of that portion of Labrador assumed to belong to Newfoundland prior to the 1927 Privy Council Decision, which defined the present boundary, was derived by subtracting from the present area of Quebec and Labrador the area given for Quebec prior to the decision (*Canada Year Book, 1915*, p. 63, and *1926*, p. 5). This procedure yielded an estimate of 852 square miles for Labrador before 1927.

It is important to note that these estimates for the period before 1949 have been obtained by measurement in 1960 on current base maps. They will therefore not necessarily correspond

Land and water areas, by province, 1959

(thousands of square miles)

Province	Land area	Water area	Total area
Newfoundland			
Labrador	101.9	10.9	112.8
Island	41.2	2.2	43.4
Prince Edward Island	2.2	—	2.2
Nova Scotia	20.4	1.0	21.4
New Brunswick	27.8	.5	28.4
Quebec	523.9	71.0	594.9
Ontario	344.1	68.5	412.6
Manitoba	211.8	39.2	251.0
Saskatchewan	220.2	31.5	251.7
Alberta	248.8	6.5	255.3
British Columbia	359.3	7.0	366.3
Northwest Territories	1,253.4	51.5	1,304.9
Yukon	205.3	1.7	207.1
Total Canada	3,560.0	291.6	3,851.8

SOURCE: D.B.S., *Canadian Forestry Statistics, Revised, 1959*, table 1, p. 7.

to areas given in various issues of the *Canada Year Book*, which reflect both changes in boundaries and in accuracy of measurement at the time of publication. For the same reasons the breakdown of area into land and water is not reliable as given in official sources for earlier years.

The land and water areas of the provinces, in 1959, were compiled by the Forestry Branch, Department of Northern Affairs and National Resources as shown in the table above.

K 3–4. Area of National and Historic parks and of provincial parks, 1885 to 1959

SOURCE: *Canada Gazette*; *Statutes of Canada*; D.B.S., *Canada Year Book, 1954*, pp. 26–30, and *1959*, pp. 15 and 19–21. National and Historic parks, series K 3, was calculated by building up figures from the beginning using data from the first two sources, which in statutes and orders-in-council give establishment of parks, changes in boundaries, and descriptions of federal parks. Provincial figures come from the last-named source.

Federal parks include National parks, which are generally scenic and recreational, and Historic parks, which contain sites of historic interest. The method of assembly of federal park areas results in legal areas being given which do not agree with the areas of national parks given in *Canadian Forestry Statistics, 1959*, table 2, p. 9. The latter gives areas within park boundaries: for example, the areas may include road allowances in the western provinces which are vested in provinces and are not within the legally defined areas of the park. Occasionally also townsites, or parts thereof, and railway sidings and right of way are privately owned and therefore not in the legally defined area of the parks.

The areas of provincial parks, unlike those of the federal parks, take no account of changes in park boundaries, between the date when the park was established and 1959. The series accumulates present park areas according to the date at which the parks were created.

In both series K 3 and K 4 the absence of an entry for a year indicates no change whatsoever in boundaries. In one or two cases where identical figures for successive years appear, changes have occurred but they were either compensating or too small to affect the rounded figures.

K 5–13. Land acreage patented in Canada, by province, 1871 to 1959

SOURCE: for all Dominion lands: for 1955 to 1959, Department of Northern Affairs and National Resources, *Annual Report*; for 1950 to 1954, Department of Resources and Development, *Annual Report*; for 1937 to 1949, Department of Mines and Resources, *Annual Report*; for 1901 to 1936, *Annual Report of the Department of the Interior*; for 1873 to 1900, *Annual Report of the Department of the Interior, 1914*, table H, p. 174; for provincial lands: series K 5, British Columbia: for 1946 to 1959, Department of Lands and Forests, *Annual Report*; for 1911 to 1945, Minister of Lands, *Annual Report*; for 1908 to 1910, Department of Public Works, *Annual Report*; for 1874 to 1907, Department of Lands and Public Works, *Annual Report*, various years throughout; series K 6, Alberta: for 1951 to 1959, Department of Lands and Forests, *Annual Report*; for 1931 to 1950, Department of Lands and Mines, *Annual Report*; series K 7, Saskatchewan: for 1948 to 1959, Department of Agriculture, *Annual Report*; for 1931 to 1947, Department of Natural Resources, *Annual Report*; series K 8, Manitoba: for 1931 to 1959, Department of Mines and Natural Resources; series K 9, Ontario: for 1921 to 1959, Department of Lands and Forests, *Annual Report*; for 1917 to 1920, Department of Lands, Forests and Mines, *Annual Report*; series K 10, Quebec: for 1940 to 1957, Department of Colonization, *Annual Report*; prior to 1943, Department of Lands and Forests, *Annual Report*; series K 11, New Brunswick: for 1879 to 1959, Department of Lands and Mines, *Annual Report*; also Saskatchewan Resources Commission, vol. 5, *Administration in the Older Provinces*; series K 12, Nova Scotia: for 1926 to 1959, Department of Lands and Forests, *Annual Report*;

for 1871 to 1925, Department of Crown Lands, *Annual Report*; also found in Saskatchewan Resources Commission, vol. 5, p. 23; series K13, Canada: see source for Dominion Lands above.

The term 'patented' is used to mean that a deed bearing title to land has been drawn up by the crown agency concerned, that is, the federal or a provincial government, for crown land that had not previously transferred into private hands and that this deed is then transferred to a private party. Acreage patented therefore is a measure of the amount of crown land that is alienated from the crown for the first time. As measured here the area includes all surface rights and might include part or all of subsoil rights. The disposition by governments of land once in private hands but reacquired by the crown is not included: the transfer of the land from a private party to government and back to a private party would ordinarily be achieved by the transfer of a deed that had been issued at the first alienation of the land.

It has been noted already that there were Dominion lands and provincial lands (see the general note to Section K). Until 1936 the areas patented by the Dominion government have been distributed here among the provinces, when possible, according to the location of the land. (Very small amounts of land in the Yukon and present Northwest Territories prior to 1936 are not included in this table.) In Alberta, Saskatchewan and Manitoba nearly all land, until 1930, was patented by the Dominion government: with the transfer of the natural resources to these provinces in 1930 (effective 15 July for Manitoba and 1 October for Saskatchewan and Alberta) the responsibility was transferred to the provinces, though the federal government continued to issue a small number of deeds, already in process at the time of transfer, for several years. In British Columbia after 1882 the case was the same as for the Prairie Provinces for the railway belt and the Peace River Block: that is, the federal government controlled resources and issued patents until most of these lands were transferred back to the province effective 1 August 1930. At the same time the British Columbia government issued the patents for all other lands in its boundaries. The remaining provinces controlled their resources from the beginning and patenting was purely a provincial matter.

The data of this table do not include figures for Newfoundland or Prince Edward Island because the necessary information was not readily available. Newfoundland recognizes squatters' rights and has a number of ways of proving ownership. Not all land in fact alienated from the crown is recorded. All of Prince Edward Island had been alienated by royal grant by 1767 (Martin, '"Dominion Lands" Policy', p. 473). By 1873, on Prince Edward Island's entrance into Confederation, 457,000 acres (one third of the total area) had been repurchased by the province and most of it transferred to smallholders in fee simple.

Some data are available for the amount of land previously patented at the time these series begin. In New Brunswick prior to Confederation 7.6 million acres were patented; in Quebec prior to 1880, the Minister of Lands and Forests reports 6.2 million acres patented. In material prepared for the Saskatchewan Resources Commission the federal government estimated that before 1905 it had patented 12.5 million acres in Manitoba, 15.0 million acres in Saskatchewan and 14.6 million acres in Alberta.

A general picture of the extent of land alienated or in process of alienation, in Canada at the end of the period covered here, is given in the *Canada Year Book, 1960*, as a percentage of total land area as follows: British Columbia, 5.3; Alberta, 37.5; Saskatchewan, 47.4; Manitoba, 21.7; Ontario, 12.0; Quebec, 8.3; New Brunswick, 59.2; Nova Scotia, 80.5; Prince Edward Island, 94.2; Canada, 10.2 per cent.

The acreages given here include patents issued for all transfers from the crown including those for homesteads, preemptions, military scrip and soldier settlement, transfers to the Métis, land sales, land grants to railways, Hudson's Bay land and the like. Railway companies receiving land grants and the Hudson's Bay Company received their patents when the land was surveyed. In the case of the former the title was passed by notification (selection of the land by the railway). In the latter case certain sections were set aside in each township in the fertile belt and notification after survey was again the method. The Hudson's Bay Company and railway lands are included here at the time the titles passed to the companies or their nominees. See Martin, '"Dominion Lands" Policy', pp. 220–43 on Hudson's Bay Company lands and pp. 245–98 on railway land grants.

K5. Acreage patented in British Columbia for 1873 to 1908 and for 1937 to 1959 is that patented by the province only; for 1909 to 1936, the acreage patented is that for both the Dominion and the province. Acreage patented by the Dominion prior to 1909 is included with the data of series K7. The year of record for the province was the calendar year throughout: the year of record of the Dominion is that described in the note to series K6–8.

Not included in the acreage deeded by the province are the following special alienations done by notification: in 1883, a wagon road grant of 60,000 acres; in 1892, a grant to the Vancouver Island Development Company of 500,000 acres; railway subsidies in 1896 of 30,000 acres, in 1897 of 2,168,327 acres, and in 1898 of 2,719,087 acres; in 1907, a university endowment grant of 2,000,000 acres.

K6–8. Acreage patented in Alberta, Saskatchewan and Manitoba is that patented by the Dominion only for 1873 to 1930, by the Dominion and the provinces for 1931 to 1936, and by the provinces only, beginning in 1937. Patents on Manitoba swamp lands, certain of which belonged to the province before the transfer of resources in 1930, are not included (see Martin, '"Dominion Lands" Policy', pp. 435–8). The year of record for the Dominion was: the year ending 31 October of the year given from 1876 to 1894; the calendar year for 1895 to 1899; the fiscal year ending 30 June of the year given, for 1900 to 1906; and the fiscal year ending 31 March, of the year given for 1907 to 1936. Data for the Dominion are for 6 months in 1900 and for 9 months in 1907. The year of record of the prairie provinces is their fiscal year: see the general note to Section G for their fiscal years.

K9–12. Acreages patented for Ontario, Quebec, New Brunswick and Nova Scotia are those patented by the provinces only. The year of record was the fiscal year of the province concerned. See the general note to Section G for fiscal years of the provinces.

K13. Acreages patented by Canada after the return of the resources to the provinces include those in the Yukon and Northwest Territories, in Indian Lands and in certain other small areas held by the Dominion. A handful of patents in the former Dominion lands in the provinces, which had already been put in process at the time of transfer of the resources, is included here in the years after 1936.

K 14–29. Total acreage patented and average area patented by type of entry, by province, western provinces, 1881 to 1960

SOURCE: for 1872 to 1900, *Annual Report of the Department of the Interior*; for all other years the sources for Dominion lands and for the provinces of Alberta, Saskatchewan, and Manitoba are the same as those given for series K5–13 for the provinces included.

Data for 1881 to the first entry for 1931 are for land patented by the Dominion; data for the second entry for 1931 to 1960 for land patented by the provinces.

The data of these series are given for two reasons. First, land was disposed of in a number of ways in the settlement of the west and these data show, for three methods of land disposition, the actual acreage for which a deed was transferred: the methods of land acquisition referred to are by homestead, by preemption and by purchased homestead. Second, the data of series K 30–45 give homestead and other types of entries by number of entries. An entry was the formal arrangement by which an individual agreed or contracted to take up land. The area of a homestead was a quarter section (one quarter of a square mile) in most cases, which supposedly approximated 160 acres but in fact usually fell somewhat short of that size. In addition homesteads in British Columbia were on the average considerably smaller than the quarter section size.

The issue of a patent lagged behind the entry by varying periods depending on the form of land disposal and the dispatch with which a farmer met the conditions necessary to secure title. The data on average acreage patented per patent issued will give an indication of the sizes of farms on which entries were made a few years earlier.

In the period of Dominion control of resources, the distinctions between homesteads, preemptions and purchased homesteads were the following. In general, homesteads were free, involving only payment of a small fee and the performance of certain residence and improvement requirements, over a minimum time of three years, before title was issued. Preemption allowed an individual homesteader to take up an adjoining quarter section at a lower price than the regular price on government land after the patent was issued on the original homestead. Purchased homesteads were government land purchased at a government set price by regular homesteaders, and could be at some distance from the original 'free' homestead. The regulations and prices on preemptions and purchased homesteads were changed from time to time. As with homesteads, the title was issued for the preemptions or purchased homesteads only after all the cultivation and improvement requirements were met and the purchase price paid.

The act establishing 'free' homesteads in the prairie region was passed in 1872: it changed somewhat and made statutory the provisions of an order-in-council of 1871. The free homestead remained a basic part of Dominion land policy until the transfer of the resources in 1930. Provisions were made for purchased homesteads of up to 640 acres in the same act; and preemption of an adjoining quarter section was introduced in 1874. The right of acquiring purchased homesteads was withdrawn in 1881 and preemptions rights were withdrawn at 1 January 1890. Both preemptions and purchased homesteads were reintroduced on a restricted basis in 1908; they were discontinued in 1918 to make way for soldiers' settlement legislation.

The amount of homesteading was limited until after 1881. A new Dominion Land Act of 1879 in conjunction with new arrangements about railway land led to designation of even numbered sections in each township as homestead land in 1882. Odd numbered sections, outside the railway belt and apart from those elsewhere transferred to the railways in land exchanges, were for sale. With these arrangements made, the pace of homestead settlement increased substantially.

After the transfer of the resources to the provinces, there was no further homesteading in British Columbia where it had always been on Dominion lands. Manitoba discontinued granting of homesteads in 1931, and Saskatchewan in 1940. Alberta discontinued homestead grants in 1939 but began in their stead a system of agricultural leases (known from 1949 as homestead leases) in designated parts of the province. These leases were made the basis for transfer of title not earlier than ten years after the lease was first taken.

Since the patenting of land and the transfer of title under all the foregoing arrangements took place only after the settlement and other requirements were met, patents continued to be issued after the right of entry ceased.

See Martin, '"Dominion Lands" Policy', for an extended treatment of arrangements about disposition of land in the west.

K 30–33. Land grants, entries and cancellations, number and acreage, by type of grant, Alberta, 1931 to 1960

SOURCE: the same departmental reports for Alberta given in the source for series K 5–13.

The data for entries are for agricultural and homestead leases for 1941 to 1960 and for homestead and soldiers' grants for earlier years. (See the note to series K 14–29.) The agricultural and homestead leases were on the average for larger areas than the traditional quarter section: the average civilian lease in 1946 was 196 acres, in 1950 was 230 acres, in 1955 was 259 acres and in 1960 was 341 acres.

The number of cancellations in Panel A for 1943 to 1951 is given for agricultural leases and homestead and soldier grants. The acreage figures, however, are given for cancellations of the civilian leases only. See footnote (3) to series K 30–33 for the numbers which the acreage figures represent.

K 34–41. Land grants, number of entries and cancellations by province and type of grant, western provinces, 1872 to 1931

SOURCE: *Annual Report of the Department of the Interior*, 1875 to 1931; material prepared for the Alberta Resources Commission and Saskatchewan Resources Commission.

The data of series K 34–41 are for entries on Dominion lands, while the resources of the prairie provinces were held in the right of the Dominion, and in the case of British Columbia, while the Dominion held land in the railway belt and Peace River Block. An entry indicates that an individual has filed an application for a specific parcel of land and has been found eligible for the particular category of grant for which he has filed.

The number of entries only is given in the source for each year and not the acreage; in certain cases tables giving acreages for entries appear but these were always calculated by assuming an area of 160 acres for a homestead entry. An exact calculation of acreage entered for in any year cannot be obtained from the data but an approximation can be made if the number of entries in any one year are related to the average acreage per patent a few years later, given in series K 14–29. For homesteads the patent was issued three years after the entry was made if all requirements had been met; the patent would be delayed longer if the requirements had not been met and was issued only on their fulfilment. Homesteads and soldiers' grants in the prairies were for a quarter section of land; South African Veterans' grants were each one half section of land.

A breakdown of entries by province is available in the source only as far back as 1906. Prior to 1906, to as far back as 1887, the entries were given for the local land offices at which they were made. For presentation here the entries of land offices within the boundaries of each of the provinces as later established were added to yield provincial totals. This procedure would not give an exact allocation by province since some of the land offices near the boundaries of the provinces, as they were later created, served areas that crossed provincial borders; however, a fairly good approximation of entries by province is probably obtained by the procedure.

See the note to series K 14–29 for a description of the homestead.

Provision for second homesteads was first made in the Dominion Land Act of 1883 but it was abolished in 1886. From 1923, second homesteads were allowed to those in drought areas to permit them to move north. In 1928 the provision was made more general for those who had proved their first homestead prior to 1925.

South African Veterans' grants, authorized by the Military Bounty Act of 1908, were provided as a bounty for volunteers, including female nurses, in the South African war. These grants were for adjoining quarter sections, without fee but with the prevailing homestead duties: the grant was in the form of transferable scrip.

Soldier grants were authorized in 1917 by the Soldier Settlement Act for veterans of the First World War. They too required the usual homestead duties but no fee was required.

Entries were cancelled for non-fulfilment of the homestead requirements, sometimes voluntarily, sometimes on the initiative of the Dominion. In the latter case, while the homestead requirements were supposed to be met within three years, a good deal of leeway in time was granted. The *Annual Report of the Department of the Interior* gives a distribution of cancellations in a particular year by the time at which the original entry was made. While cancellation was most common in the first few years after the entry, they sometimes came more than twenty years later. Partly because the South African Veterans' grants were in transferable scrip more than 95 per cent of the acreage located was ultimately patented. See Martin, '"Dominion Lands" Policy', for a fuller discussion of cancelled entries and estimates of total cancellations by various types of entry until 1930.

K 42–45. Preemptions and purchased homesteads, number of entries and cancellations, by province, Alberta and Saskatchewan, 1874 to 1931

SOURCE: same as for series K 34–41.

See the notes to series K 14–29 and series K 34–41.

K 46–56. Land sales and cancellations, school lands and other provincial lands, by province, prairie provinces, 1931 to 1960

SOURCE: the sources are those given for the provinces of Alberta, Saskatchewan and Manitoba in the source list for series K 5–13.

The Dominion Lands Act of 1872 set aside sections 11 and 29 of each township in Dominion lands for school lands. The revenues from the sale or lease of these lands were to be used for building up a fund for providing school services. When the resources were transferred to the provinces in 1930, the unsold school lands were used for the same purpose by the provinces. Other provincial lands were also put up for sale from year to year.

The public or provincial land sales, series K 46, K 50 and K 53, do not include the school land sales. The data for cancelled sales include cancellations on all lands disposed of by sale. Some of these cancellations were for land sold while the resources of the prairie provinces were still under the control of the Dominion.

K 57–64. Land sales, school land and miscellaneous, by province, prairie provinces, and school land cancellations, Alberta, 1905 to 1931

SOURCE: *Annual Report of the Department of the Interior*, supplemented by data from the Alberta and Saskatchewan Resources Commissions.

These sales were made by the Dominion before the resources were transferred to the provinces.

See the note to series K 46–56.

K 65–72. Land grants and sales, by province, Ontario and Quebec, 1867 to 1959

SOURCE: for Ontario: for 1881 to 1920, Department of Lands, Forests and Mines, *Annual Report*; for 1921 to 1959, Department of Lands and Forests, *Annual Report*; for Quebec: for 1867 to 1943, Department of Lands and Forests, *Annual Report*, various years; for sales and reversion to the crown prior to 1930, *Saskatchewan Resources Commission*, vol. 5, p. 71.

Both Ontario and Quebec had systems of land grants, somewhat similar to the homestead system, and of land sales, of which parts were to support particular purposes and parts used for general revenue. Acres located, free grant townships, in Ontario, series K 65 and K 66, and free grants in Quebec, series K 70, belong in the former category; the remaining series are in the latter category. University land sales in Ontario began in 1897: after 1940, all lands were treated as common crown lands and all sales included in series K 67. The data for Quebec are not available after 1943.

K 73–74. Sales of Indian lands, acreage and value, Canada, 1874 to 1956

SOURCE: for 1880 to 1936, Department of Indian Affairs, *Annual Report*; for all other years, reports of Indian Affairs Branch, contained in the *Annual Report* of various departments: for 1950 to 1956, Department of Citizenship and Immigration; for 1937 to 1949, Department of Mines and Resources; for 1873 to 1880, Department of the Interior.

These lands, originally granted to the Indians, were surrendered by the Indians for sale and the sums so raised were credited to the Indians concerned. Sales of land to individual members of the band were not separated from sales to people outside the reserve.

K 75–90. Land sales by railway companies having Dominion land grants, and the Hudson's Bay Company, 1893 to 1930

SOURCE: Alberta Resources Commission, vol. T(1), Exhibit 28 A. These data are also given in *Annual Report of the Department of the Interior*.

These data give total sales and do not allow for cancellations. They do not include, however, lands returned to the government to extinguish various claims.

See the general note to Section K for a general background of Dominion land policy.

For the encouragement of railway building, large amounts of Dominion lands, that is, those in the Prairie Provinces and lands transferred to the Dominion in British Columbia, were given to railways. Railway grants of Dominion lands totalled 38,657,088 acres of which 32,928,896 went to the Canadian Pacific Railway and its present subsidiaries and 5,728,192 went to the Canadian Northern (later integrated into the Canadian National Railways system) and its subsidiaries. The government received some of these lands back, however, as repayment of a government loan to the C.P.R., for indemnity on coal lands when special charges for coal land had not been met, and in payment of survey fees. The net grant of Dominion lands totalled 31,783,654 acres of which 26,055,463 went to the C.P.R. and its subsidiaries.

The practice of granting land to railways ended formally in 1894. In fact commitments already made to railway companies had yet to be met, depending on whether the lines had been built or not, and large amounts of land were reserved to aid in railway building until 1908. Even then some lands were to be sold by the Crown itself to aid in construction of a railway to Hudson Bay.

Considerable parts of the sales of railway land were cancelled when the purchasers could not meet the terms of their contracts. Prior to 1931, cancelled C.P.R. sales amounted to 22 per cent of sales. The values per acre on land for which sales were cancelled averaged considerably higher than those where the sales were completed.

The railways of series K 77–84 were or became a part of the C.P.R. system. Those of series K 85–88 were or became part of the Canadian Northern and later the Canadian National Railway system.

As part of terms of purchase of Rupert's Land from the Hudson's Bay Company, one-twentieth of the fertile belt in Alberta, Saskatchewan and Manitoba remained in the hands of the Hudson's Bay Company. The original acreage of Hudson's Bay lands was 7,031,257 acres (*Annual Report of the Department of the Interior, 1930*, p. 26). This acreage was reduced to 6,639,059 acres by a compromise concerning Hudson's Bay Company sections in Indian reserves, national parks, and forest reserves (evidence before the Alberta Resources Commission).

See Martin, '"Dominion Lands" Policy', for a detailed description and much data on the railway and Hudson's Bay lands.

K 91–96. Land sales by the Hudson's Bay Company, Canadian Northern Land Department and Canadian Pacific Railway Company, 1925 to 1960

SOURCE: for series K 91–92, the Land Department, Hudson's Bay Company, Winnipeg, Manitoba; for series K 93–94, the Real Estate Department, Canadian National Railways, Montreal, P.Q.; for series K 95–96, Canadian Pacific Railway Company, *Annual Report*, report for each year.

Hudson's Bay sales are for the year ending 31 January of the year given. These sales are for farm lands only.

See the notes to series K 75–90.

K 97–106. Government receipts on account of Dominion lands, 1873 to 1931

SOURCE: *Annual Report of the Department of the Interior, 1931*, pp. 28–31.

The Dominion government collected revenue in a variety of ways from its ownership of resources. The headings to the various series indicate the nature of the different types of receipts; only revenue from scrip needs elaboration. Scrip, exchangeable for land, grazing rights, mineral rights, etc., was issued by the government of Canada to: half-breeds in settlement of their rights in Rupert's Land and the Northwest Territories; discharged soldiers and members of the Royal North West Mounted Police; and to settlers who were in Rupert's Land prior to the government of Canada taking over these lands.

FORESTS (Series K 107–223)

K 107–118. Primary forest production and exports of primary products, by type of product (excluding fuelwood), 1908 to 1960

SOURCE: for 1958 to 1960, D.B.S., *Canadian Forestry Statistics, 1961*, table 7, p. 14, and table 9, p. 15; for 1922 to 1957, D.B.S., *Canadian Forestry Statistics, Revised, 1959*, table 7, pp. 20–1, and table 9, p. 25; for 1908 to 1921, Report of the *Royal Commission on Pulpwood*, Sessional Paper 310 of 1924, pp. 94 and 96.

Fuelwood, given in the source, is excluded here because the quality of the estimates for it is far below that of the items included here.

It appears doubtful if consistent estimates for many of the items of primary forest production before 1922 can be obtained. However, data are available for volume of pulpwood production back to 1913 and pulpwood exports back to 1908 in the *Report of the Royal Commission on Pulpwood*. For the Commission, production was calculated from mill consumption plus exports.

K 119–123. Principal statistics of woods operations, 1926 to 1959

SOURCE: for 1958 and 1959, D.B.S., *Canadian Forestry Statistics, 1961*, table 6, p. 14; for 1926 to 1957, D.B.S., *Canadian Forestry Statistics, Revised 1959*, table 6, p. 19.

These data in the source were derived from D.B.S., *Operations in the Woods*, published annually, but were revised from previously published data.

For 1926 to 1957 in the calculation of employee man-years, series K 119, workers employed in transporting products from the woods to the manufacturing plant or user are included; for 1958 and 1959, they are excluded.

K 124–138. Lumber production, by species, external trade and estimated consumption, 1908 to 1960

SOURCE: for 1958 to 1960, D.B.S., *Canadian Forestry Statistics, 1961*, table 12, p. 16, table 14, p. 17, table 16 and table 17, p. 18; for 1908 to 1957, D.B.S., *Canadian Forestry Statistics, Revised 1959*, table 12, pp. 30–1, table 14, p. 35, table 16, p. 39, table 17, p. 41.

It is extremely difficult to produce accurate figures for lumber production. The industry is composed of a large number of units, many very small and keeping a minimum of records. In a large number of cases returns to the Dominion Bureau of Statistics cannot be reconciled with returns to provincial departments. It is generally felt that the figures for lumber production prior to 1908 are unreliable. They would have to be derived largely from provincial returns, and in many cases these returns cover only crown lands. There is also a problem of units of measurement. Many returns to provincial departments did not specify units, failing to differentiate between superficial feet, feet board measure, cubic feet and lineal feet.

Total volume of production, series K 127, exceeds the sum of total softwood production and total hardwood production in some years owing to a small unspecified category.

More information on the lumber industry is included in the source. Production by province, more detail of production by species and the like are available.

K 139–145. Principal statistics of the lumber industry, 1917 to 1959

SOURCE: for 1958 and 1959, D.B.S., *Canadian Forestry Statistics, 1961*, table 10, p. 15; for 1917 to 1957, D.B.S., *Canadian Forestry Statistics, Revised, 1959*, table 10, p. 27.

K 146–155. Wood pulp, production and exports, 1908 to 1960

SOURCE: for 1958 to 1960, D.B.S., *Canadian Forestry Statistics, 1961*, table 20, p. 19, tables 21 and 22, p. 20; for 1908 to 1957, D.B.S., *Canadian Forestry Statistics, Revised, 1959*, table 20, pp. 46–7, table 21, pp. 48–9 and table 22, pp. 52–3.

Other detail is given in the source.

K 156–168. Manufactured paper, capacity, production and exports, 1916 to 1960

SOURCE: series K 156: Newsprint Association of Canada, *Annual Newsprint Supplement, 1961*, table 1, p. 2; series K 157–158: for 1958 to 1960, D.B.S., *Canadian Forestry Statistics, 1961*, table 23 and table 24, p. 21, table 25, p. 22; for 1916 to 1957, D.B.S., *Canadian Forestry Statistics, Revised, 1959*, table 23, pp. 54–5, table 24, pp. 56–7, table 25, pp. 60–1.

Additional detail is available in the source.

K 169–175. Principal statistics of the pulp and paper industry, 1919 to 1959

SOURCE: for 1958 and 1959, D.B.S., *Canadian Forestry Statistics, 1961*, table 18, p. 18; for 1919 to 1957, D.B.S., *Canadian Forestry Statistics, Revised, 1959*, table 18, p. 43.

See the general note to series Q 1–137 for a discussion of the meaning of the series and changes in them.

K 176–183. Value of exports, wood, wood products and paper, by type of product, 1869 to 1915

SOURCE: K. W. Taylor, 'Statistics of Foreign Trade' in K. W. Taylor and H. Michell, *Statistical Contributions to Canadian Economic History*, vol. II.

The classification of exports used in more recent publications of D.B.S., *Trade of Canada*, is not directly comparable with the Taylor classification given here. However, some of the series of this table overlap with series given earlier in this section: for other series, the user could bridge the gap between the series of this table and series given earlier in this section by using annual D.B.S., *Trade of Canada*, and its predecessors.

K 184–188. Forest fires, Canada (excluding the Yukon and Northwest Territories), 1908 to 1960

SOURCE: for 1951 to 1960, Department of Forestry, Forest Research Branch; for 1950, Department of Resources and Development, Forestry Branch, *Forest Fire Losses in Canada, 1950*; for 1937 to 1949, Department of Mines and Resources, Forestry Branch, *Forest Fire Losses in Canada, 1948* and *1949*, and *Annual Report of the Director of Forestry* from 1937 to 1947; from 1918 to 1936, Department of the Interior, *Annual Report, Report of the Director of Forestry* for each year; for 1908 to 1917, Department of the Interior, Forestry Branch, Bulletin 69, *Forest Fires in Canada, 1917*, Bulletin 64, *Forest Fires in Canada, 1914–15–16*, Bulletin 9, *Forest Fires in Canada, 1909*, and Bulletin 7, *Forest Fires in Canada, 1908*. For 1918 to 1926, the published data have been supplemented by material from the records of the Forestry Branch. The data for 1908 do not cover Ontario; those for 1909 do not cover Ontario and Quebec; the data for 1914 to 1917 cover only the four western provinces.

The major source of consistent data on forest fires in Canada is the Forestry Research Branch latterly of the Department of Forestry (Canada). Information on forest fires is reported by the provincial services, the federal forest service, protective associations, etc. Prior to 1908 only fragmentary data are available, although there are reports concerning fires in national parks, forest reserves, and in some provinces, particularly in protected areas. The general consensus of opinion, expressed frequently in the *Annual Report of the Director of Forestry*, for example in 1938, is that early figures seriously underestimate both the number of fires and the acreage burned. Recent figures, since 1938, are considered quite accurate with respect to areas burned, although there are indications that the number of fires may have been overstated in more recent years.

The data for 1951 to 1960 are revised and differ from those published in *Forest Fire Losses in Canada*, annual issues. There are two reasons for the changes. (1) The Province of British Columbia has revised its method of reporting forest fires caused by railroads and no longer counts as forest fires, fires that do not leave the roadbeds. This has resulted in the removal of 6,309 fires from the statistics since 1951. (2) Double counting of statistics on some fires occurring on Indian Reserves has been eliminated. Both the Indian Affairs Branch and the provinces involved had been reporting figures for the same fires.

There is a significant amount of information concerning fires in the period before 1908 in the reports of geological field parties, published in the *Report of the Geological Survey of Canada*, the reports of survey parties, and the annual reports of the relevant provincial departments. To date, however, these bits of information have not been collected and consolidated.

K 189–199. Principal forestry revenues, Canada and each province, selected years 1933 to 1943 and 1945 to 1955

SOURCE: A. M. Moore, *Forestry Tenures and Taxes in Canada*, pp. 260–83.

Each province in Canada has its own system for collecting revenues from its forest industries. The major problem of assessing and comparing these charges is one of definition. Forest lands are disposed of in many ways, by licences, permits, leases, concessions, and the like, and various methods such as annual lease payments, licence fees, stumpage charges, fire protection charges and the like are used to levy charges. The latter are referred to in different ways, and are not comparable among provinces. The classification work has been done by Moore and is explained in the study. In general, the revenues refer specifically to forest industries, but they include revenues from closely related activities.

K 200–223. Gross ordinary and capital forestry expenditures, selected years 1933 to 1943 and 1945 to 1955

SOURCE: same as for series K 189–199.

In his study, Moore carefully reclassified expenditures on forestry for selected years by provincial governments and the federal government by purpose. Unless carefully reclassified, the expenditures in one province can rarely be compared directly with those in another province. In series K 200–223, two general classes of expenditures are totalled from Moore's classification. In many cases, outlays closely related to forestry are included.

The following consolidation of Moore's classes of expenditures were made: Alberta, 'forest protection and timber operations', and 'forest and prairie fire suppression'; Saskatchewan, 'fire suppression' and 'fire prevention'; Manitoba, 'fire prevention' and 'fire patrol'; Ontario, normal fire protection, detection and suppression are included with 'Basic Organization'—only 'Extra fire fighting' is reported separately; Quebec, 'protection of forests' and 'extinction of fires' in fire protection and suppression, 'forest research' and 'entomology service' under Research; New Brunswick, 'fire prevention and control', 'forest fire protection—improvements' and 'forest fire prevention'; Nova Scotia, 'fire fighting and prevention', 'purchase of fire-fighting equipment', 'maintenance of fire equipment' and 'fire towers'; Newfoundland, 'protection against forest fires', 'grant to fire protection association' and 'forest fire patrol—Whitbourne'.

Series K 1-2. *Area of Canada and provinces, 1867 to 1959*

(square miles)

Year	Total area of Canada	Area within provincial boundaries
	1	**2**
1949–59	3,851,809	2,339,830 Newfoundland entered Confederation, 1949
Land	3,560,238	2,101,454
Fresh water	291,571	238,376
1927–48	3,695,624	2,183,645 Privy Council Award of Labrador to Newfoundland, 1927
1912–26	3,807,450	2,295,471 Quebec, Ontario and Manitoba enlarged, 1912
1905–11	3,807,450	1,563,403 Alberta and Saskatchewan formed, 1905
1898–1904	3,807,450	1,056,417 Quebec enlarged, 1898
1889–97	3,807,450	942,272 Ontario enlarged and defined; Manitoba enlarged, 1889
1880–88	3,807,450	899,692 Northern Islands to Canada, 1880
1874–79	3,357,348	840,300 Temporary Ontario boundary, 1874
1873	3,357,348	767,377 Prince Edward Island entered Confederation, 1873
1871–72	3,355,164	765,193 British Columbia entered Confederation, 1871
1870	2,988,909	398,938 Rupert's Land and Northwest Territories to Canada, Manitoba formed, 1870
1867–69	384,598	384,598 Original Confederation of Ontario, Quebec, Nova Scotia and New Brunswick, 1867

Series K 3-4. *Area of National and Historic parks and provincial parks, 1885 to 1959*

(square miles)

Year	National and Historic parks	Provincial parks		Year	National and Historic parks	Provincial parks
	3	**4**			**3**	**4**
1959	—	57,925		1915	—	—
1958	29,280	57,465		1914	7,921	—
1957	29,289	57,463		1913	4,016	11,076
1956	29,133	59,516		1912	—	—
				1911	4,028	8,413
1955	29,146	42,294				
1954	—	43,864		1910	—	—
1953	—	41,156		1909	10,744	—
1952	29,148	35,956		1908	10,743	—
1951	29,148	—		1907	10,573	—
				1906	—	—
1950	—	35,863				
1949	—	34,862		1905	—	—
1948	29,148	34,548		1904	—	—
1947	29,070	—		1903	5,678	—
1946	29,640	34,534		1902	5,312	—
				1901	1,172	—
1945	29,705	31,134				
1944	—	31,134		1900	—	—
1943	—	30,530		1899	—	—
1942	—	—		1898	—	—
1941	29,727	30,522		1897	—	—
				1896	—	—
1940	—	26,442				
1939	—	26,401		1895	353	7,585
1938	29,726	18,652		1894	—	2,749
1937	29,826	13,236		1893	—	2,741
1936	29,819	12,722		1892	—	—
				1891	—	—
1935	—	12,707				
1934	—	12,707		1890	—	—
1933	—	12,455		1889	—	—
1932	—	12,454		1888	299	—
1931	—	12,161		1887	290	—
				1886	420	—
1930	29,360	12,159				
1929	30,175	—		1885	10	—
1928	28,905	—				
1927	28,905	12,153				
1926	26,548	—				
1925	26,245	11,196				
1924	26,209	—				
1923	—	—				
1922	26,206	11,196				
1921	9,092	11,076				
1920	9,385	—				
1919	—	—				
1918	8,878	—				
1917	8,872	—				
1916	—	—				

Series K5–13. *Land acreage patented in Canada, by province, 1871 to 1959*

(thousands of acres)

Year[1]	British Columbia	Alberta	Saskatchewan	Manitoba	Ontario	Quebec	New Brunswick	Nova Scotia	Canada
	5	6	7	8	9	10	11	12	13
1959	91.3	320.1	40.9	35.2	20.5	N/A	7.2	3.2	.1
1958	58.8	166.3	41.3	31.9	29.2	N/A	6.2	4.0	.1
1957	89.9	125.2	37.1	29.7	27.6	54.2	10.8	3.1	.2
1956	80.3	117.1	—	19.7	35.4	79.1	9.1	3.2	.6
1955	65.9	87.8	55.2	31.6	40.0	76.9	13.3	3.6	1.0
1954	73.4	70.9	55.5	34.7	55.2	93.4	10.6	4.5	.3
1953	99.0	58.5	69.8	43.3	54.7	95.5	15.8	3.1	.4
1952	98.6	41.6	223.7	36.1	58.6	86.5	24.3	4.1	.1
1951	77.5	157.8	40.4	13.1	55.8	87.7	3.2	2.9	—
1950	75.7	58.2	55.8	23.8	118.0	72.1	16.5	—	1.3
1949	219.7	136.6	88.7	21.3	56.0	82.3	16.6	2.0	2.4
1948	85.1	129.4	82.8	18.5	—	70.6	68.0[5]	2.0	1.6
1947	111.6	169.9	—	27.0	89.1	91.9	31.6	.2	3.0
1946	110.2	183.4	125.9	21.9	74.2	85.4	21.0	.4	1.0
1945	85.0	296.4	290.4	36.8	78.7	87.6	48.0[5]	.6	2.8
1944	65.3	249.4	265.4	35.2	77.0	65.8	13.7	.4	3.1
1943	65.5	229.7	256.3	21.6	41.7	57.1	11.8	.6	.9
1942	64.3	229.6	352.6	14.1	33.3	179.8	15.5	3.1	1.6
1941	64.5	295.6	454.9	4.5	36.9	107.9	23.2	.2	2.8
1940	59.6	301.4	505.0	9.8	36.3	148.1	11.9	.1	4.0
1939	59.9	517.4	204.1	15.1	40.8	95.2	7.8	1.5	5.5
1938	66.3	382.4	284.4	28.4	48.5	97.1	6.9	1.1	3.7
1937	93.7	325.6	335.2	39.9	27.5	41.4	4.9	.6	5.7[2]
1936	69.1	435.7	312.5	68.5	44.8	31.7	2.2	.9	—
1935	77.5	328.7	367.2	85.1	13.3	24.7	6.0	.7	—
1934	62.8	170.5	—[3]	42.3	42.8	135.7	3.6	.3	—
1933	59.2	191.8	291.9	23.4	36.4	19.3	5.2	1.3	—
1932	61.6	142.0	261.7	75.5	60.1	34.4	10.3	.7	—
1931	86.2	151.6	166.4	77.6	77.3	46.2	6.3	1.3	—
1930	87.4	349.2	376.8	81.9	84.8	44.2	12.7	2.8	—
1929	135.8	308.7	537.6	72.5	71.6	187.4	9.8	1.7	—
1928	101.2	461.7	382.6	66.5	67.3	47.1	12.8	2.2	—
1927	94.0	356.4	363.6	58.0	74.6	70.6	8.3	1.0	—
1926	106.8	243.6	402.0	135.3	94.8	57.9	11.7	7.0	—
1925	103.8	232.4	269.5	97.7	91.4	402.9[4]	12.9	.9	—
1924	195.6	257.8	389.8	112.2	102.0	87.6	12.3	2.8	—
1923	99.3	336.3	1,237.7	177.2	111.4	89.8	10.2	.8	—
1922	155.7	739.8	883.0	362.2	108.1	136.3	14.9	2.5	—
1921	201.1	979.7	1,338.3	397.4	91.8	306.1[6]	15.8	3.3	—
1920	238.7	903.1	1,541.7	317.0	101.3	388.9[6]	19.5	5.0	—
1919	548.5	1,176.8	1,616.0	233.8	104.8	227.8	39.1	9.1	—
1918	292.8	1,420.3	2,053.6	215.0	84.6	134.9	19.5	5.3	—
1917	218.8	1,157.0	1,636.6	192.7	111.0	139.6	12.2	5.3	—
1916	129.6	1,209.0	1,686.5	160.0	—	83.4	15.4	11.4	—
1915	106.1	1,554.0	2,205.6	204.2	—	74.4	10.6	7.0	—
1914	273.7	1,901.1	3,036.2	225.5	—	557.7[6]	17.9	14.5	—
1913	404.8	1,567.7	2,392.0	223.5	—	338.7[6]	12.8	6.4	—
1912	286.3[7]	1,189.5	1,786.5	143.8	—	739.1[6]	12.2	5.3	—
1911	543.7	1,253.9	2,268.6	163.6	—	145.7	15.7	9.9	—
1910	318.8	1,196.5	2,279.9	165.8	—		12.8	11.9	—
1909	342.8	1,315.1	2,499.3	382.1	—	395.3 {	16.3	13.2	—
1908	253.5[10]	—[10]	6,139.0[10]	—[10]	—		14.6	10.4	—
1907	599.4[9]	—	2,361.3[8]	—	—	126.2	19.3	9.9	—
1906	336.1	—	4,181.3	—	—	156.2	15.1	12.8	—
1905	133.2	—	6,196.3	—	—	128.0	15.3	24.3	—
1904	107.4	—	2,979.5	—	—		18.6	18.8	—
1903	83.7	—	3,263.8	—	—	287.7 {	21.5	32.6	—
1902	87.9	—	4,709.6	—	—		22.7	21.7	—
1901	4,632.8	—	6,846.3	—	—	100.6	17.7	31.4	—
1900	104.7	—	310.5[8]	—	—	79.7	18.8	17.6	—
1899	672.1	—	714.7	—	—	75.1	18.1	40.8	—
1898	371.4[9]	—	646.7	—	—	93.1	16.9	187.1[15]	—
1897	609.6[9]	—	499.9	—	—	79.9	15.2	42.9	—
1896	36.8[9]	—	531.9	—	—	62.2	17.3	188.0	—
1895	95.5	—	349.0	—	—	70.6	11.5	62.6	—
1894	47.2	—	420.2[11]	—	—	73.5	10.6	53.6	—
1893	124.6	—	502.6	—	—	108.5	16.2	27.4	—
1892	309.9[9]	—	549.3	—	—	65.8	17.1	43.0	—
1891	143.5	—	411.1	—	—	159.4	23.5	35.9	—
1890	99.3	—	626.0	—	—	101.5	35.4	36.8	—
1889	134.2	—	661.6	—	—	81.1	30.2	42.4	—
1888	94.3	—	647.6	—	—	64.2	26.6	27.8	—
1887	74.0	—	1,071.4	—	—		26.7	26.0	—
1886	50.5	—	942.1	—	—	146.2 {	29.2	37.0	—

Series K 5–13. *Land acreage patented in Canada, by province, 1871 to 1959 (continued)*

(thousands of acres)

Year[1]	British Columbia	Alberta	Saskatchewan	Manitoba	Ontario	Quebec	New Brunswick	Nova Scotia	Canada
	5	6	7	8	9	10	11	12	13
1885	128.8	—	898.5	—	—	83.6	40.6	25.5	—
1884	146.2	—	909.6	—	—	91.8	43.7	57.0	—
1883	54.6[9]	—	831.3	—	—	61.9	59.7	48.5	—
1882	23.6	—	506.8	—	—	86.7	59.7	38.5	—
1881	23.1	—	400.9	—	—	44.7	56.7	66.4	—
1880	24.1	—	173.4	—	—	6,203.2[12]	37.2	63.4	—
1879	46.8	—	426.1	—	—	—	35.9	45.1	—
1878	31.2	—	462.9	—	—	—	1,832.3[13]	12.6	—
1877	10.0	—	478.8	—	—	—	—	25.8	—
1876	18.0	—	50.9	—	—	—	—	35.0	—
1875	18.0	—	74.2[14]	—	—	—	—	46.5	—
1874	26.2	—	92.3[14]	—	—	—	—	107.3	—
1873	—	—	67.2[14]	—	—	—	—	116.0	—
1872	—	—	—	—	—	—	—	136.7	—
1871	—	—	—	—	—	—	—	134.7	—

[1] See the notes to series K 5–13 for year endings.
[2] The acreage patented by the government of Canada prior to 1937 is distributed by the provinces.
[3] The government of Canada patented 8,585 acres; the provincial figure is not available.
[4] Includes a grant of 306,760 acres to Inter-provincial and James Bay Railroad Company.
[5] Includes grants to the Dominion of Canada, Acadian Forest Experimental Station, 1945, 22,500 acres and National Park, 1948, 50,880 acres.
[6] Includes railway grants: 1921, 64,500 acres; 1920, 48,400 acres; 1914, 424,300 acres; 1913, 147,400 acres; 1912, 547,100 acres.
[7] Area of 4,000,000 acres repurchased by the crown not included.

[8] For 1907, 9 months ending 31 March 1907; for 1906, 6 months ending 30 June 1906.
[9] See note to series K 5 for special grants not included.
[10] For 1873 to 1908 series K 7 includes land acreage patented for Alberta, Saskatchewan, Manitoba, Yukon and Northwest Territories and Dominion lands in British Columbia.
[11] Year ended 31 October 1894: 66,102 acres patented in November and December 1894.
[12] Acreage patented for the period 1867 to 1880.
[13] Acreage patented for the period 1867 to 1878.
[14] For 1875, 1 January 1875 to 31 October 1875; for 1874, calendar year; for 1873, May 1873 to 31 December 1873.
[15] Includes 150,000 acre railway land grant.

Series K 14–29. *Total acreage patented and average area patented by type of entry, by province, western provinces, 1881 to 1960*

Year[1, 2]	Homesteads							
	Total acreage patented (thousands of acres)				Average acreage patented per patent issued (acres)			
	British Columbia	Alberta	Saskatchewan	Manitoba	British Columbia	Alberta	Saskatchewan	Manitoba
	14	15	16	17	18	19	20	21
1960	—	76.9	—	—	—	230.1	—	—
1959	—	76.7	—	—	—	231.1	—	—
1958	—	114.6	—	—	—	235.4	—	—
1957	—	61.1	—	—	—	227.2	—	—
1956	—	1.5	—	—	—	150.9	—	—
1955	—	1.1	—	—	—	158.4	—	—
1954	—	.8	—	—	—	159.2	34.3	—
1953	—	.6	3.5	—	—	157.8	159.8	—
1952	—	1.3	3.1	—	—	159.9	156.4	—
1951	—	5.9	3.5	—	—	144.8	159.3	—
1950	—	15.1	8.2	—	—	152.2	156.8	—
1949	—	42.4	14.5	—	—	155.4	157.1	—
1948	—	74.9	16.0	—	—	154.5	156.6	—
1947	—	111.3	—	—	—	154.4	—	—
1946	—	129.8	37.9	—	—	154.3	156.1	—
1945	—	160.4	49.2	.1	—	153.4	155.3	81.0
1944	—	184.3	95.6	—	—	154.1	157.2	—
1943	—	171.6	79.5	.3	—	153.8	156.8	160.0
1942	—	204.9	128.8	.3	—	154.8	157.1	136.5
1941	—	266.3	151.1	.2	—	151.1	156.9	158.3
1940	—	273.9	54.4	5.3	—	154.8	155.0	154.4
1939	—	443.6	175.7	10.0	—	195.1	155.4	150.9
1938	—	306.2	256.6	21.7	—	155.6	155.3	150.8
1937	—	292.1	296.6	33.4	—	156.7	156.1	152.6
1936	—	401.5	281.0	61.6	—	156.8	156.2	147.8

Series K 14–29. *Total acreage patented and average area patented by type of entry, by province, western provinces, 1881 to 1960 (continued)*

Year[1,2]	Homesteads							
	Total acreage patented (thousands of acres)				Average acreage patented per patent issued (acres)			
	British Columbia	Alberta	Saskatchewan	Manitoba	British Columbia	Alberta	Saskatchewan	Manitoba
	14	**15**	**16**	**17**	**18**	**19**	**20**	**21**
1935	—	261.8	—	76.0	—	157.6	—	151.3
1934	—	148.2	251.7	32.4	—	156.8	154.8	150.5
1933	—	159.8	—	17.3	—	157.6	—	148.9
1932	—	99.3	161.1	19.4	—	157.1	155.9	146.2
1931[2]	—	1.8	—	—	—	159.6	—	—
1931[3]	5.6	72.2	108.8	13.4	100.2	156.3	156.1	150.2
1930	10.2	109.5	180.5	30.3	104.0	155.6	155.8	149.1
1929	15.6	108.0	169.3	40.7	105.6	156.7	154.4	149.2
1928	20.0	120.9	141.1	45.5	116.1	156.0	154.9	149.8
1927	16.1	118.4	118.0	30.3	124.8	156.0	155.5	150.2
1926	13.8	102.2	124.7	43.4	119.7	155.4	156.2	152.3
1925	15.4	121.2	109.3	54.8	126.1	156.4	157.4	155.4
1924	16.1	174.8	166.3	76.4	123.2	155.6	157.0	153.5
1923	27.6	277.2	292.2	149.2	127.8	156.2	156.7	153.9
1922	35.8	572.4	570.9	321.3	123.8	156.3	156.9	155.7
1921	35.3	723.3	823.9	352.5	133.5	157.6	157.6	156.7
1920	22.3	610.6	740.8	264.1	125.4	161.6	157.1	156.9
1919	33.2	548.4	729.3	167.7	139.7	159.5	160.1	156.4
1918	31.8	866.4	1,251.7	183.2	141.4	160.9	160.6	161.0
1917	30.9	812.5	1,109.4	145.1	136.1	163.7	163.4	157.9
1916	22.0	1,023.7	1,346.1	109.0	131.9	168.4	165.7	157.5
1915	27.1	1,340.9	1,987.6	188.4	136.6	173.2	169.0	157.1
1914	26.5	1,753.1	2,791.7	198.5	141.1	173.9	170.6	155.4
1913	13.3	1,380.1	2,161.9	145.0	136.1	169.9	166.5	155.5
1912	15.1	961.5	1,611.8	106.4	142.1	158.6	158.7	153.7
1911	12.4	1,049.4	1,860.3	92.3	148.0	158.5	158.5	153.8
1910	14.8	1,066.1	2,049.4	90.2	142.2	159.0	158.4	153.1
1909	14.9	930.5	2,072.7	156.6	144.7	158.7	158.5	154.6
1908	14.8	—[4]	2,300.7[4]	—[4]	144.9	—[4]	158.6[4]	—[4]
1907	3.8	—	1,417.5	—	153.2	—	159.4	—
1906	8.4	—	1,366.5	—	147.3	—	158.8	—
1905	9.2	—	928.4	—	151.2	—	158.2	—
1904	8.1	—	647.4	—	139.6	—	158.5	—
1903	13.4	—	504.7	—	142.4	—	158.0	—
1902	32.2	—	687.9	—	147.8	—	158.2	—
1901	36.0	—	299.9	—	152.4	—	159.0	—
1900	1.8	—	183.1	—	137.8	—	155.7	—
1899	4.8	—	401.6	—	144.6	—	156.0	—
1898	3.9	—	282.4	—	133.9	—	158.3	—
1897	4.4	—	296.1	—	132.6	—	151.1	—
1896	6.8	—	273.4	—	170.7	—	164.4	—
1895	9.5	—	195.5	—	155.4	—	157.8	—
1894	15.3	—	223.1	—	157.8	—	156.6	—
1893	29.9	—	290.6	—	155.0	—	158.1	—
1892	22.1	—	260.7	—	146.1	—	159.5	—
1891	9.2	—	179.1	—	146.0	—	155.9	—
1890	6.5	—	212.4	—	157.8	—	153.4	—
1889	8.5	—	246.4	—	149.0	—	155.3	—
1888	—	—	269.5	—	—	—	155.7	—
1887	—	—	373.6	—	—	—	160.0	—
1886	—	—	466.9	—	—	—	160.3	—
1885	—	—	272.6	—	—	—	159.2	—
1884	—	—	288.4	—	—	—	159.1	—
1883	—	—	292.7	—	—	—	161.0	—
1882	—	—	64.0	—	—	—	158.4	—
1881	—	—	38.5	—	—	—	154.1	—

[1] For 1881 to 1894, departmental years ending 31 October of year given; for 1895 to 1899, calendar years; for 1900, 6 months ending 30 June; for 1901 to 1906, fiscal years ending 30 June of year given; for 1907, 9 months ending 31 March; for 1908 to 1931, fiscal years ending 31 March of year given; for Alberta, 1931 to 1960, fiscal years ending 31 March of year given; for Saskatchewan, 1931 to 1946, fiscal years ending 30 April of year given; for Saskatchewan, 1948 to 1954, fiscal years ending 31 March of year given; for Manitoba, 1932 to 1945, fiscal years ending 30 April of year given.

[2] For 1931 to 1960, data are from the provinces, see the notes.

[3] Data are for land patented by the Dominion for this and prior years. Data for 1931 are for 6 months, 1 April 1930 to 30 September 1930 for British Columbia, Alberta and Saskatchewan; for the period 1 April 1930 to 15 July 1930 for Manitoba.

[4] For 1881 to 1908, series K 16 and K 20 include Alberta, Saskatchewan, Manitoba and Yukon.

Series K 14–29. *Total acreage patented and average area patented by type of entry, by province, western provinces, 1881 to 1960 (continuation)*

Year[1,2]	Preemptions				Purchased homesteads			
	Total acreage patented (thousands of acres)		Average area of preemptions patented (acres)		Total acreage patented (thousands of acres)		Average area of purchased homesteads patented (acres)	
	Alberta	Saskatchewan	Alberta	Saskatchewan	Alberta	Saskatchewan	Alberta	Saskatchewan
	22	23	24	25	26	27	28	29
1960	—	1.7	—	158.7	.2	.2	160.0	160.0
1959	—	1.0	—	160.0	.2	.2	160.0	161.0
1958	—	2.2	—	155.1	.3	—	326.0	—
1957	—	4.1	—	158.5	18.7	.3	242.6	159.5
1956	—	2.9	—	159.3	80.8	.3	231.4	160.0
1955	—	5.1	—	159.3	58.9	.2	211.7	161.0
1954	—	11.6	—	159.0	43.8	.6	216.7	154.5
1953	—	10.5	—	158.7	34.9	.3	215.3	160.5
1952	—	7.1	—	158.1	17.2	.5	186.6	160.3
1951	—	4.6	—	159.9	19.0	.3	191.7	159.5
1950	—	3.4	—	159.7	13.2	.3	191.4	160.0
1949	.2	13.1	160.0	159.2	.3	.6	160.0	158.5
1948	—	12.1	—	159.2	—	.9	—	151.3
1947	—	—	—	—	—	—	—	—
1946	—	10.0	—	158.9	—	.6	—	156.3
1945	.3	39.0	160.0	159.0	.2	1.8	157.6	152.4
1944	.3	31.7	160.0	159.3	—	1.7	—	156.8
1943	—	11.7	—	157.5	—	.8	—	159.4
1942	.3	4.5	159.0	156.8	—	.9	—	149.7
1941	—	4.4	—	158.0	.3	.6	159.5	160.0
1940	—	3.5	—	158.4	.2	.3	160.0	160.0
1939	.3	1.8	158.5	148.9	—	.2	—	161.0
1938	.5	.6	160.3	157.3	.1	.3	132.9	160.0
1937	.5	2.1	158.4	160.0	—	.2	—	160.0
1936	1.0	1.9	159.8	159.5	.2	.2	160.0	160.0
1935	.9	—	154.5	—	.5	—	152.6	—
1934	.5	.6	160.0	158.8	.1	.2	111.1	160.0
1933	1.1	—	160.0	—	.3	—	158.5	—
1932	.5	—	160.0	—	—	—	—	—
1931[2]	—	—	—	—	—	—	—	—
1931[3]	2.1	9.9	159.8	156.4	.2	.3	160.0	158.5
1930	10.6	58.2	159.8	158.9	1.4	3.9	158.8	146.1
1929	19.9	92.5	158.8	158.1	1.1	7.2	161.0	157.0
1928	16.3	90.6	158.4	158.7	2.1	8.7	159.6	157.9
1927	11.6	75.4	156.2	158.0	1.3	6.5	157.1	157.3
1926	12.0	61.7	157.7	157.9	1.6	7.7	158.0	154.4
1925	10.8	56.3	158.1	158.5	1.8	6.5	159.6	155.0
1924	15.4	60.4	157.6	158.0	2.1	8.6	149.2	153.3
1923	16.3	71.9	156.7	157.6	3.2	10.7	145.6	151.3
1922	83.4	150.7	158.3	158.3	8.3	17.8	150.0	154.5
1921	169.1	361.6	158.4	158.6	18.1	44.2	154.7	155.6
1920	191.1	584.6	158.7	159.0	23.5	56.8	156.6	155.5
1919	215.4	452.3	158.3	158.8	27.0	64.8	154.5	155.1
1918	384.5	591.6	159.3	159.0	44.5	92.8	157.7	156.4
1917	207.8	359.1	159.0	159.0	39.7	78.0	159.3	156.3
1916	84.7	141.1	158.4	158.5	28.7	56.2	157.6	156.6
1915	43.6	85.0	159.7	158.4	21.4	56.1	158.6	156.7
1914	10.5	39.7	159.4	159.3	16.5	57.3	157.5	158.7

Series K 30–33. *Land grants, entries and cancellations, number and acreage, by type of grant,*
Alberta, 1931 to 1960

Year[1]	Entries		Cancellations		Year[1]	Entries		Cancellations	
	Number	Acres	Number	Acres		Number	Acres	Number	Acres
	30	**31**	**32**	**33**		**30**	**31**	**32**	**33**
Panel A. Homestead and agricultural leases, civilian					*Panel B.* Soldier grants and veterans' agricultural leases				
1960	439	149,757	578	149,229	1960	23	6,405	88	24,632
1959	233	58,115	441	149,821	1959	20	6,335	57	16,521
1958	333	84,267	473	123,756	1958	33	9,054	127	38,930
1957	564	144,138	509	127,923	1957	50	14,035	87	23,973
1956	783	197,114	674	165,308	1956	91	24,987	119	35,597
1955	791	204,700	673	168,004	1955	111	30,201	88	24,476
1954	747	193,146	505	129,172	1954	112	32,271	101	28,083
1953	869	222,770	413	106,778	1953	130	37,505	105	29,950
1952	1,037	261,314	518	125,676	1952	194	54,943	100	27,438
1951	1,156	286,056	364[2]	83,633[3]	1951	334	93,712	211	59,311
1950	992	228,044	273[2]	54,041[3]	1950	252	71,147	100	24,686
1949	754	166,817	290[2]	49,276[3]	1949	202	54,037	85	21,147
1948	985	219,595	413[2]	53,965[3]	1948	561	138,473	114	26,021
1947	283	50,227	417[2]	29,691[3]	1947	906	242,615	35	8,278
1946	330	64,522	567[2]	22,344[3]	1946	40	9,144	2	480
1945	312	59,742	625[2]	14,284[3]	1945	—	—	—	—
1944	208	37,714	990[2]	17,435[3]	1944	—	—	—	—
1943	170	29,982	931[2]	9,568[3]	1943	—	—	—	—
1942	200	—	928[4]	—	1942	—	—	—	—
1941	224	—	1,119[4]	—	1941	—	—	—	—
1940	25[5]	—	1,648[4]	—	1940	—	—	—	—
1939	1,350	—	2,345[4]	—	1939	3	—	—	—
1938	1,590	—	2,663[4]	—	1938	10	—	—	—
1937	1,425	—	1,914[4]	—	1937	7	—	—	—
1936	1,515	—	1,816[4]	—	1936	13	—	—	—
1935	2,750	—	—	—	1935	30	—	—	—
1934	3,680	—	—	—	1934	26	—	—	—
1933	2,300	—	1,633[4]	—	1933	23	—	—	—
1932	2,547	—	1,302[4]	—	1932	19	—	—	—
1931	2,229	—	—	—	1931	81	—	—	—

[1] For fiscal year ending 31 March of the year given.
[2] For 1943 to 1951 includes homestead and soldier grant cancellations.
[3] Acreage for cancellation of agricultural leases only. The figures given are for 359 cancellations in 1951, 252 in 1950, 229 in 1949, 225 in 1948, 155 in 1947, 118 in 1946, 83 in 1945, 100 in 1944 and 58 in 1943.

[4] For 1932 to 1942 the data are for total entries cancelled.
[5] Includes some soldier grants. Homestead grants were discontinued in 1939. See the note to series K 14–29.

Series K 34–41. *Land grants, number of entries and cancellations by province and type of grant, western provinces, 1872 to 1931*

Year[1]	British Columbia		Alberta		Saskatchewan		Manitoba	
	Entries	Cancellations	Entries	Cancellations	Entries	Cancellations	Entries	Cancellations
	34	35	36	37	38	39	40	41
Panel A. Homesteads								
1931	574	111	7,122	2,428	2,834	1,219	454	381
1930	893	202	9,795	3,823	6,089	2,261	727	552
1929	773	161	8,933	2,741	5,808	1,717	643	654
1928	173	262	3,411	2,203	2,961	1,522	688	1,034
1927	116	153	2,145	1,489	2,702	1,330	797	547
1926	150	131	1,556	1,211	2,363	1,312	616	746
1925	193	119	1,192	1,552	1,804	1,475	464	1,025
1924	186	207	1,326	1,722	1,699	1,499	632	759
1923	153	236	2,207	2,652	2,104	2,278	879	1,895
1922	200	207	2,928	3,383	2,733	2,370	1,488	1,846
1921	120	208	2,874	3,365	1,670	2,360	725	1,403
1920	134	166	3,448	3,673	1,918	2,389	1,232	1,663
1919	54	140	2,169	1,946	1,191	1,100	813	929
1918	177	180	3,808	2,813	2,741	2,193	1,593	1,128
1917	268	333	4,550	4,101	4,105	3,558	2,276	1,578
1916	413	267	6,410	5,149	6,247	5,722	3,960	1,593
1915	802	435	10,076	5,432	8,790	4,953	4,420	1,694
1914	1,931	350	12,208	6,615	14,504	7,662	3,186	1,370
1913	375	292	12,942	6,694	17,556	8,288	2,826	2,006
1912	325	—[2]	15,184	—[2]	20,484	—[2]	3,158	18,608[2]
1911	206	—	15,964	—	25,227	—	3,082	22,122
1910	277	—	17,187	—	21,575	—	2,529	16,832
1909	429	—	13,771	—	21,120	—	3,761	14,677
1908	237	—	9,614	—	18,825	—	1,748	15,668
1907	72	—	6,843	—	13,501	—	1,231	14,110
1906	108	—	12,263	—	27,692	—	1,806	11,637
1905[3]	187	—	9,138	—	19,787	—	1,707	11,296
1904	208	—	8,201	—	15,659	—	2,005	8,702
1903	120	—	8,069	—	19,941	—	3,253	5,208
1902	117	—	5,681	—	6,612	—	2,263	3,296
1901	86	—	3,806	—	2,332	—	1,933	1,682
1900	80	—	2,470	—	2,703	—	2,154	1,096
1899	17	—	1,745	—	2,159	—	2,124	1,746
1898	41	—	1,049	—	960	—	1,426	1,546
1897	17	—	230	—	301	—	609	1,090
1896	91	—	411	—	362	—	993	1,165
1895	67	—	1,000	—	461	—	866	1,222
1894	—	—	—	—	—	—	3,209[4]	1,558
1893	119	—	1,513	—	1,159	—	1,276	—
1892	97	—	1,257	—	1,797	—	1,687	—
1891	160	—	784	—	930	—	1,651	—
1890	272	—	524	—	758	—	1,401	—
1889	431	—	504	—	1,242	—	2,225	1,337
1888	295	—	230	—	425	—	1,665	935
1887	356	—	271[5]	—	356[6]	—	1,053[7]	633
1886	—	—	—	—	—	—	2,657[4,8]	1,033
1885	—	—	—	—	—	—	1,858[4]	—
1884	—	—	—	—	—	—	3,753[4]	1,334
1883	—	—	—	—	—	—	6,063[4]	—
1882	—	—	—	—	1,121	—	6,262	—
1881	—	—	—	—	23	—	2,730	—
1880	—	—	—	—	—	—	2,074[4]	—
1879	—	—	—	—	—	—	4,068[4]	—
1878	—	—	—	—	—	—	1,788[4]	—
1877	—	—	—	—	—	—	845[4]	—
1876	—	—	—	—	—	—	347[4]	—
1875	—	—	—	—	—	—	499[4]	—
1874	—	—	—	—	—	—	1,376[4]	—
1873	—	—	—	—	—	—	878[9]	—
1872	—	—	—	—	—	—	283[9]	—
Panel B. Soldier grants								
1931	49	23	339	203	108	106	10	173
1930	55	29	422	365	224	199	19	153
1929	52	11	413	285	249	204	28	124
1928	27	23	216	383	226	201	35	212
1927	21	16	184	190	217	238	46	130
1926	27	8	183	182	296	209	70	111
1925	29	7	195	253	280	220	80	135
1924	32	13	187	230	349	242	142	145
1923	46	—	328	—	370	—	468	—
1922	68	—	614	—	590	—	383	—
1921	58	—	1,171	—	1,188	—	475	—
1920	117	—	2,739	—	1,996	—	1,129	—
1919	—	—	501	—	—	—	—	—

Series K 34–41. *Land grants, number of entries and cancellations by province and type of grant, western provinces, 1872 to 1931 (continued)*

Year[1]	British Columbia Entries	British Columbia Cancellations	Alberta Entries	Alberta Cancellations	Saskatchewan Entries	Saskatchewan Cancellations	Manitoba Entries	Manitoba Cancellations
	34	35	36	37	38	39	40	41

Panel C. South African Veterans' grants

Year[1]	BC Entries	BC Cancel.	Alta. Entries	Alta. Cancel.	Sask. Entries	Sask. Cancel.	Man. Entries	Man. Cancel.
1914	—	—	61	—	48	—	1	—
1913	—	—	97	—	79	—		—
1912	—	—	857	—	920	—	6	—
1911	—	—	778	—	1,185	—	10	—
1910	—	—	1,300	—	1,530	—	22	—
1909	—	—	179	—	166	—	—	—

[1] For 1872 to 1894, departmental years ending 31 October of year given; for 1895 to 1899, calendar years; for 1900, 6 months ending 30 June; for 1901 to 1906, fiscal years ending 30 June of year given; for 1907, 9 months ending 31 March; for 1908 to 1931, fiscal years ending 31 March of year given.
[2] Total homestead entries cancelled entered under Manitoba where available, 1884 to 1912.
[3] See note for the division of entries by province prior to 1906.

[4] Total homestead entries for provinces and territories.
[5] Including 2 military bounty warrants.
[6] Including 22 military bounty warrants.
[7] Including 21 military bounty warrants.
[8] Including 561 military homesteads of 320 acres each.
[9] Including certain entries from the territories.

Series K 42–45. *Preemptions and purchased homesteads, number of entries and cancellations by province, Alberta and Saskatchewan, 1874 to 1931*

Year[1]	Alberta Entries (42)	Alberta Cancellations (43)	Saskatchewan Entries (44)	Saskatchewan Cancellations (45)
		Panel A. Preemptions		
1931	—	75	—	47
1930	—	177	—	177
1929	—	246	—	402
1928	—	546	—	740
1927	—	518	—	914
1926	—	613	—	863
1925	—	1,199	—	1,103
1924	—	301	—	823
1923	—	218	—	673
1922	—	149	—	490
1921	—	232	—	557
1920	—	297	—	521
1919	—	199	—	301
1918	220	482	547	708
1917	452	655	1,008	1,092
1916	578	775	1,662	1,313
1915	737	937	2,108	1,517
1914	1,604	1,440	4,560	2,509
1913	2,935	2,336	5,642	3,074
1912	3,682	—[2]	6,929	6,103[2]
1911	5,680	—	9,938	7,095
1910	7,759	—	9,533	3,463
1909	4,560	—	9,501	260
1908	—	—	—	32
1907	—	—	—	8
1906	—	—	—	38
1905	—	—	—	48
1904	—	—	—	96
1903	—	—	—	174
1902	—	—	—	242
1901	—	—	—	202
1900	—	—	—	155
1899	—	—	—	299
1898	—	—	—	382
1897	—	—	—	245
1896	—	—	—	255
1895	—	—	—	263
1894	—	—	—	411
1893	—	—	—	—
1892	—	—	—	—
1891	—	—	—	—
1890	—[3]	—	371[3]	—
1889	—	—	1,355	829
1888	—	—	454	1,892
1887	—	—	585	497
1886	—	—	1,046	637
1885	—	—	653	—
1884	—	—	2,762	972
1883	—	—	4,120	—
1882	—	—	5,654	—
1881	—	—	1,649	—
1880	—	—	1,004	—
1879	—	—	1,729	—
1878	—	—	1,580	—
1877	—	—	594	—
1876	—	—	263	—
1875	—	—	391	—
1874	—	—	643	—
		Panel B. Purchased homesteads		
1931	—	7	—	6
1930	—	10	—	19
1929	—	13	—	25
1928	—	27	—	49
1927	—	28	—	73
1926	—	24	—	56
1925	—	49	—	63
1924	—	18	—	75
1923	—	8	—	35
1922	—	9	—	29
1921	—	16	—	24
1920	—	11	—	4
1919	—	2	—	13
1918	67	12	124	46
1917	106	33	156	65
1916	92	31	210	50
1915	117	49	233	73
1914	239	61	517	97
1913	340	60	740	104
1912	365	—[4]	1,043	175[4]
1911	487	—	1,273	163
1910	359	—	897	49
1909	208	—	623	21

[1] For 1874 to 1894, year ending 31 October of year given; for 1895 to 1899, calendar year; for 1900, 6 months ending 30 June; for 1901 to 1906, fiscal year ending 30 June of year given; for 1907, 9 months ending 31 March; for 1908 to 1931, fiscal year ending 31 March of year given.
[2] Preemption cancellations 1874 to 1912, for Alberta and Saskatchewan included in series K 45.

[3] Preemption entries 1874 to 1890, for Alberta and Saskatchewan included in series K 44.
[4] Purchased homestead cancellations, 1909 to 1912, for Alberta and Saskatchewan included in series K 45.

Series K 46–56. *Land sales and cancellations, school lands and other provincial lands, by province, prairie provinces, 1931 to 1960*

	Alberta				Saskatchewan			Manitoba			
	Public land sales (acres)	School land sales		Total cancelled sales (acres)	Provincial land sales (acres)	School land sales (acres)	Total cancelled sales (acres)	Provincial land sales (acres)	School land sales		Total cancelled sales (acres)
Year[1]		Number of acres	Value (dollars)						Number of acres	Value (dollars)	
	46	**47**	**48**	**49**	**50**	**51**	**52**	**53**	**54**	**55**	**56**
1960	13,800	13,592	—	7,284	1,371	221	639	5,645	—	—	—
1959	7,765	22,423	97,296	9,609	2,150	196	1,120	9,319	—	—	—
1958	12,967	16,740	—	26,204	1,005	156	1,710	7,521	—	—	—
1957	14,288	18,177	—	8,416	1,246	555	3,186	7,121	—	—	2,840
1956	20,291	18,170	—	3,364	3,846[2]	2,483[2]	18,515[2]	6,008	165	1,651	1,963
1955	31,414	24,667	—	4,936	6,197	4,352	14,061	15,341	1,354	17,766	—
1954	38,017	28,759	—	1,620	19,552[3]	122,165[3]	46,596	37,298	13,574	97,483	—
1953	20,871	31,941	—	2,622	38,723[4]	2,228	11,434[2]	86,038	15,581	150,598	—
1952	85,339	98,664	—	937	9,903	4,664	7,015	98,347	53,521	451,797	—
1951	14,551	58,185	—	633	19,644	9,423	9,974	62,995	29,913	261,888	162
1950	32,619	61,456	—	—	30,588	29,625	6,211	93,629	14,359	119,878	320
1949	7,031	34,212	378,286	860	30,111	74,295[2]	7,353	52,562	7,863	60,123	1,235
1948	5,338	—	5,431	381[5]	164,641[2,6]	280	15,162	36,248	18,933	147,183	720
1947	8,816	—	16,275	622[5]	—	—	—	27,953	21,417	226,307	573
1946	7,088	—	17,692	216[5]	1,295	269	13,872	579	170	1,467	851
1945	8,970	—	31,357	127[5]	2,380	170	12,449	776	59	634	2,887
1944	—	—	2,985	—	2,371	73	—	2,197	3	6	3,316
1943	—	872	8,770	—	2,088	129	5,426	6,364	42	359	4,314
1942	—	845	—	—	3,071	84	15,219	17,963	29	293	5,672
1941	—	—	—	—	8,094	91	—	21,198	54	537	4,636
1940	—	2,604	—	—	19,389	118	31,298	27,182	657	5,323	4,573
1939	—	—	—	—	23,612	48	22,425	32,185	4,590	31,534	2,825
1938	—	120	—	—	20,081	38	22,907	32,885	11,065	92,726	3,791
1937	—	5,591	—	—	14,231	24	45,290	13,431	336	2,960	5,527
1936	—	338[8]	—	—	31,163	122	44,747	11,483	488	3,288	6,006
1935	—	—	—	—	—	—	—	37,810	2,029	12,908	14,619
1934	—	—	—	—	6,211	1,066	80,987	20,125	1,109	7,613	38,896
1933	—	—	—	—	—	—	—	14,738	21	211	16,309
1932	—	—	—	—	—	—	—[7]	17,558	135	1,544	18,595
1931	—	—	—	—	—	—	—	5,360	—	—	9,305

[1] For Alberta, 1931 to 1960, fiscal years ending 31 March of year given; for Saskatchewan, 1931 to 1946, fiscal years ending 30 April of year given; for Saskatchewan, 1948 to 1960, fiscal years ending 31 March of year given; for Manitoba, 1931 to 1946, fiscal years ending 30 April of year given; for Manitoba, 1947, 11 months ending 31 March; for Manitoba, 1948 to 1960, fiscal years ending 31 March of year given.

[2] For 1948 to 1956, series K 50–51 include Veterans' cultivation leases; for 1953 to 1956, series K 52 includes terminations of such leases.

[3] Includes lands added to existing Veterans' cultivation leases and changes in acreage from unbroken to cultivated lands.

[4] Includes 29,127 acres held in individual Veterans' cultivation leases but farmed cooperatively, existing before fiscal 1953 but not accounted for in previous reports.

[5] Public land sales cancellations only.

[6] Includes Veterans' cultivation leases of school lands.

[7] 545 sales cancelled, no acreage given.

[8] Total area sold since the transfer of resources, 30 September 1930.

Series K 57–64. *Land sales, school land and miscellaneous, by province, prairie provinces, and school land cancellations, Alberta, 1905 to 1931*

Year[1]	Alberta				Saskatchewan		Manitoba	
	Cash, time, drainage, irrigation, etc. (acres)	School lands			School lands		School lands	
		Number of acres	Value (dollars)	Cancelled sales (acres)	Number of acres	Value (dollars)	Number of acres	Value (dollars)
	57	58	59	60	61	62	63	64
1931[2]	7,056	14,674	166,887	5,804	293	2,241	6,318	75,147
1930	5,825	28,677	345,992	16,918	372,011	5,435,354	4,231	50,403
1929	11,221	299,393	4,266,713	26,052	357,412	4,608,151	12	97
1928	7,059	210,933	3,556,164	27,105	276,800	5,446,630	41	296
1927	6,600	69	877	33,583	482	6,611	451	3,444
1926	9,243	271	4,606	40,387	563	7,293	32	245
1925	6,204	50	1,129	38,378	222	2,951	117	753
1924	4,575	422	6,974	33,807	356	3,998	458	1,629
1923	4,727	145	2,391	28,285	4,155	54,601	332	4,274
1922	13,164	4,985	75,997	23,988	35,341	475,031	4,065	41,566
1921	5,897	122,536	2,165,850	19,381	84,405	1,234,058	10,463	130,975
1920	8,430	12	128	13,144	83	948	86	864
1919	84,533	90,310	1,570,557	6,888	535,066	12,060,096	132	1,212
1918	23,501	96,860	1,906,282	3,576	214,743	4,154,276	16,073	182,982
1917	38,502	144,993	2,039,037	4,568	116,695	1,664,234	37,370	352,539
1916	19,481	146	2,246	3,067	1,174	17,222	142	1,676
1915	26,227	73	2,153	3,820	359	5,802	14	190
1914	53,723	375	10,711	1,593	701	15,155	40	285
1913	106,591	2,375	111,240	320	103,593	2,003,528	64,539	711,147
1912	105,271	373	5,403	365	1,517	48,421	203	4,209
1911	295,306	182,384	2,216,912	366	304,581	4,568,722	670	15,438
1910	143,539	235,013	2,571,430	160	14,777	235,811	80,291	773,471
1909	79,901	723	10,381	160	540	6,320	121	1,545
1908	91,695	10,239	99,485	160	1,388	26,325	103,092	1,066,860
1907[1]	80,116	—	—	320	11,801	173,155	125,087	1,526,546
1906[1]	83,867	127,706	1,491,821	—	26,663	381,714	692	8,570
1905[3]	—	1,791	49,940	300	145,906	1,423,087	271,384	2,181,067

[1] Fiscal years ending 31 March of year given, 1908 to 1931, 9 months ending 31 March 1907, and fiscal year ending 30 June 1906.

[2] For 6 months, 1 April 1930 to 30 September 1930 for Alberta and Saskatchewan, series K 57–62; for Manitoba, series K 63–64, 1 April 1930 to 15 July 1930.

[3] Cumulative sales prior to 1 September 1905.

Series K65–72. *Land grants and sales, by province, Ontario and Quebec, 1867 to 1959*

(acres granted or sold)

Year[1]	Ontario					Quebec		
	Grants		Sales					
	Acres located, free grant townships	Locations by returned soldiers	Agricultural and townsite lands	University lands	School lands	Free grants	Crown and clergy lands sold	Cancellations of sales
	65	66	67	68	69	70	71	72
1959	462	—	14,894	—	—	—	—	—
1958	—	797	16,772	—	—	—	—	—
1957	261	617	11,827	—	—	—	—	—
1956	2,709[2]	—[2]	21,341	—	—	—	—	—
1955	1,823	—	21,866	—	—	—	—	—
1954	2,757	—	20,918	—	—	—	—	—
1953	4,656	—	29,751	—	—	—	—	—
1952	3,411	—	32,809	—	—	—	—	—
1951	3,608	—	26,056	—	—	—	—	—
1950	6,193	—	58,903	—	—	—	—	—
1949	5,873	—	51,688	—	—	—	—	—
1948	—	—	—	—	—	—	—	—
1947	8,244	—	46,030	—	—	—	—	—
1946	5,737	—	45,173	—	—	—	—	—
1945	2,309[2]	—[2]	65,660	—	—	—	—	—
1944	2,694	—	38,812	—	—	—	—	—
1943	2,069	471	22,113	—	—	1,894	203,413	185,956
1942	5,921	501	17,570	—	—	607	216,849	186,253
1941	15,883	726	28,838	—	—	378	197,397	140,212
1940	22,640	1,158	38,009	396	—	1,529	290,976	206,797
1939	33,638	1,296	38,000	323	—	2,630	459,846	290,903
1938	36,763	2,846	38,811	355	—	664	390,359	369,527
1937	37,514	4,604	45,387	1,049	—	31	401,882	226,551
1936	58,965	5,449	61,070	719	—	1,352	275,593	358,827
1935	21,071	3,784	39,824	520	50	1,972	362,593	165,300
1934	48,152	10,897	82,857	1,746	—	4,202	556,606	253,679
1933	75,274	13,114	78,825	570	100	4,943	201,876	140,410
1932	70,269	11,586	83,029	1,261	375	3,387	211,981	153,661
1931	58,460	6,247	92,278	642	349	2,944	197,442	116,325
1930	62,891	—	113,129	—	573	1,882	162,814	121,461
1929	56,577	—	66,922	314	—	2,028	145,371	107,130
1928	43,279	—	83,772	499	—	1,451	156,897	97,278
1927	57,297	—	110,542	639	—	1,502	167,864	49,812
1926	65,733	—	86,220	657	—	3,781	175,511	100,360
1925	69,643	—	117,488	1,798	—	2,702	183,896	77,683
1924	98,487	—	173,643	3,710	—	3,289	174,291	89,751
1923	90,143	—	113,032	3,063	—	5,146	212,615	66,328
1922	135,656	—	132,188	2,155	369	5,229	216,133	65,818
1921	118,638	—	139,027	836	58	1,313	177,313	100,301
1920	88,814	—	72,591	721	297	184	197,226	207,977
1919	72,421	—	49,704	120	72	94	186,085	175,362
1918	54,183	—	51,401	1,288	339	59	297,409	75,646
1917	78,193	—	109,304	2,075	—	263	256,477	96,396
1916	85,139	—	98,209	2,968	50	150	207,380	103,658
1915	185,021	—	146,307	5,230	20	350	206,565	80,490
1914	258,371	—	137,666	6,047	25	689	202,587	97,466
1913	221,255	—	202,088	10,485	121	1,280	194,091	62,307
1912	237,152	—	349,319	11,891	3	1,205	179,130	68,095
1911	224,042	—	118,573	5,627	—	1,984	119,465	67,340
1910	194,760	—	92,560	4,020	37	775	124,849	91,315
1909	196,603	—	78,658	3,740	151	615	220,645	41,842
1908	297,543	—	74,912	3,110	157	650	292,479	86,431
1907	180,864	—	79,419	1,740	104	916	227,031	110,726
1906	126,085	—	69,861	1,412	107	322	195,736	112,053
1905	143,716	—	72,432	1,978	397	9,350	189,883	58,853
1904	152,699	—	72,781	2,731	624	11,038	135,752	43,481
1903	201,042	—	30,466	3,741	100	8,026	150,638	46,506
1902	193,070	—	66,868	5,722	421	10,200	190,231	40,779
1901	148,312	—	43,617	5,787	59	12,600	186,090	35,545
1900	132,665	—	65,996[3]	4,336	255	9,599	163,528	31,572
1899	85,194	—	69,279	3,953	273	11,450	149,971	72,053
1898	102,947	—	50,231	6,885	215	10,631	190,195	73,578
1897	91,910	—	60,148	6,010[4]	331	12,346	184,667	40,584
1896	95,476	—	49,471	793[4]	205	31,869	129,604	37,044
1895	100,040	—	35,209	969	1,119	26,814	167,708	39,912
1894	99,435	—	28,048	2,047	558	31,650	149,667	46,751
1893	57,440	—	28,136	889	413	37,646	156,925	40,534
1892	59,733	—	30,436	974	682	15,898	102,252	25,674
1891	79,948	—	71,855	7,740	356	2,117	137,829	38,203

Series K 65–72. *Land grants and sales, by province, Ontario and Quebec, 1867 to 1959 (continued)*

(acres granted or sold)

	Ontario					Quebec		
	Grants		Sales					
Year[1]	Acres located, free grant townships	Locations by returned soldiers	Agricultural and townsite lands	University lands	School lands	Free grants	Crown and clergy lands sold	Cancellations of sales
	65	66	67	68	69	70	71	72
1890	83,273	—	50,045	9,407	755	200	129,014	31,710
1889	114,050	—	53,640	2,874[4]	505	3,281	120,178	41,910
1888	109,002	—	52,962	—	737	2,093	107,260	27,779
1887	122,772	—	67,315	—	898	3,444	100,862	55,168
1886	162,734	—	55,641	—	940	3,474	101,788	25,504
1885	176,351	—	99,919	—	1,639	3,045	119,894	34,734
1884	161,964	—	61,189	—	1,067	6,099	135,241	77,365
1883	134,594	—	69,357	—	1,312	8,232	207,526	60,302
1882	129,535	—	98,814	—	2,514	7,901	219,368	36,226
1881	153,764	—	88,543	—	2,587	7,041	179,562	32,260
1880	—	—	621,162[5]	—	1,002[6]	9,027	129,768	69,761
1879	—	—	—	—	1,463	17,424	180,886	74,008
1878	—	—	—	—	2,300	7,962	139,134	63,766
1877	—	—	—	—	3,551	5,790	83,123	—
1876	—	—	—	—	2,238	3,606	73,185	—
1875	—	—	—	—	1,944	4,015	91,179	—
1874	—	—	—	—	3,584	4,271	109,609	—
1873	—	—	—	—	4,909	7,130	131,496	—
1872	—	—	—	—	2,068	11,212	174,592	—
1871	—	—	—	—	3,702[6]	21,302	169,155	—
1870	—	—	105,704[3, 7]	—	3,256[8]	8,051[1]	159,849[1]	—
1869	—	—	—	—	6,183	—	—	—
1868	—	—	—	—	4,323	10,502[1]	220,687[1]	—
1867	—	—	—	—	5,581[8]	—	—	—

[1] For Ontario: for 1867 to 1908, calendar years; for 1909, 10 months ending 31 October; for 1910 to 1934, fiscal years ending 31 October of the year given; for 1935, 5 months ending 31 March; for 1936 to 1960, fiscal years ending 31 March of the year given. For Quebec: for 1868, 18 months ending 31 December 1868; for 1870, 18 months, 1 January 1869 to 30 June 1870; for 1871 to 1940, fiscal years ending 30 June of the year given; for 1941, 9 months ending 31 March 1941; for 1942 and 1943, fiscal years ending 31 March of the year given.

[2] For 1945 to 1956, 'Locations by returned soldiers' are included in series K 65, 'Acres located, free grant townships'.

[3] For 1867 to 1900, series K 67 includes mining lands.

[4] For 1897, includes 97 acres of railway lands. For 1889 to 1896, series K 68 designated railway lands.

[5] Total for 1871 to 1880.

[6] For 1871 to 1880, common school lands only; total grammar school lands sold comprised 47,303 acres.

[7] Total for 1867 to 1870.

[8] For 1867 to 1870, common school lands only; total grammar school lands sold comprised 7,155 acres.

Series K73–74. *Sales of Indian lands, acreage and value, Canada, 1874 to 1956*
(series K73 in acres; series K74 in dollars)

Year[2]	Acreage	Value		Year[2]	Acreage	Value
	73	74			73	74
1956	—[1]	809,946		1915	15,268	142,969
				1914	4,510	218,411
1955		211,032		1913	7,835	132,513
1954	—	714,109		1912	83,496	1,219,474
1953	—	42,576		1911	52,331	678,568
1952	—	666,415				
1951	—	49,597		1910	81,603	952,043
				1909	64,924	462,682
1950	—	38,174		1908	40,163	167,777
1949	—	—		1907	80,358	422,086
1948	—	709,362		1906	38,033	365,684
1947	—	249,001				
1946	—	65,238		1905	33,840	56,981
				1904	67,965	62,943
1945	—	172,812		1903	109,350	279,294
1944	—	45,068		1902	103,461	160,520
1943	—[1]	72,028		1901	40,720	45,135
1942	—[1]	45,441				
1941	11,782	71,295		1900	52,455	51,115
				1899	65,632	41,971
1940	5,472	39,934		1898	14,168	27,318
1939	—	—		1897	14,451	12,521
1938	—	44,611		1896	17,759	21,052
1937	—	78,665				
1936	14,650	134,233		1895	32,206	72,423
				1894	41,297	76,419
1935	7,422	58,382		1893	25,693	72,215
1934	6,535	37,790		1892	22,817	45,185
1933	3,559	49,986		1891	18,951	26,477
1932	2,948	54,594				
1931	3,508	22,285		1890	6,731	22,951
				1889	15,322	22,345
1930	29,222	452,664		1888	21,345	30,345
1929	19,740	204,388		1887	28,806	39,347
1928	11,480	113,957		1886	10,132	12,862
1927	50,959	206,946				
1926	24,571	224,713		1885	9,629	13,183
				1884	24,177	44,610
1925	21,623	36,710		1883	32,412	31,557
1924	16,480	72,651		1882	48,903	54,192
1923	6,898	64,955		1881	33,294	52,787
1922	5,804	58,207				
1921	32,492	127,592		1880	96,239	67,157
				1879	61,997	45,115
1920	114,819	1,088,899		1878	73,364	54,555
1919	19,010	104,657		1877	43,813	75,244
1918	34,545	136,231		1876	37,357	86,799
1917	35,121	76,387				
1916	29,348	66,741		1875	33,650	38,065
				1874	29,074	—

[1] For 1942 to 1956, acreage not given.
[2] For 1874 to 1906, fiscal years ending 30 June of the year given; for 1907, 9 months ending 31 March 1907; for 1908 to 1956, fiscal years ending 31 March of the year given.

Series K 75–90. *Land sales by railway companies having Dominion land grants, and the Hudson's Bay Company,*
1893 to 1930

(areas in thousands of acres, values in thousands of dollars)

Year[1]	Hudson's Bay Company		Canadian Pacific Railway Company		Manitoba South Western Colonization Railway Company		Calgary and Edmonton Railway Company		Great North West Central Railway Company		Canadian Northern Railway Company		Qu'Appelle, Long Lake and Saskatchewan Railroad and Steamboat Company		Total	
	Area	Value	Area	Value	Area	Value	Area	Value	Area	Value	Area	Value	Area	Value	Area	Value
	75	76	77	78	79	80	81	82	83	84	85	86	87	88	89	90
1930	216.0	2,090.5	255.2	3,145.5	6.9	49.5	6.0	68.4	3.8	39.0	67.5	934.9	7.7	32.9	563.1	6,360.6
1929	289.9	3,349.6	447.6	4,902.6	8.3	61.1	17.6	200.0	7.5	82.4	83.5	1,189.8	5.4	73.2	859.8	9,858.7
1928	289.7	3,546.6	387.0	4,349.8	4.9	46.3	17.2	205.7	9.2	93.6	67.7	924.0	7.9	93.8	783.6	9,259.8
1927	282.7	3,414.5	249.5	2,980.0	3.7	27.0	8.7	96.8	4.5	47.5	107.5	1,586.9	10.0	143.0	666.5	8,295.7
1926	184.6	2,276.1	169.0	2,263.9	3.7	31.0	10.1	93.6	3.7	45.9	79.1	1,128.0	7.6	115.6	457.8	5,954.2
1925	84.8	1,117.6	91.3	1,602.5	1.7	13.9	8.5	132.5	2.2	35.2	57.0	770.7	1.9	28.6	247.4	3,700.9
1924	33.4	456.4	45.9	775.2	.6	3.8	1.3	14.1	.8	14.9	71.5	1,103.4	6.2	92.1	159.8	2,460.1
1923	25.0	366.3	83.5	1,249.0	.4	5.1	1.0	15.6	1.1	21.6	11.2	190.1	1.1	17.0	123.3	1,864.6
1922	33.6	545.6	101.5	1,732.4	1.5	15.5	3.0	51.6	.2	4.0	14.2	263.2	1.3	22.3	155.2	2,633.6
1921	178.3	3,037.4	275.6	5,899.0	1.5	20.1	11.7	191.9	5.1	96.6	69.9	1,455.3	11.4	160.5	553.6	10,860.8
1920	276.6	4,724.9	571.6	11,356.1	4.6	56.8	27.0	425.7	28.0	464.6	86.3	1,685.2	32.1	474.9	1,026.2	19,188.2
1919	285.6	4,979.0	602.6	10,580.7	5.3	67.2	31.8	479.5	14.5	252.8	65.1	1,262.0	33.8	527.7	1,038.7	18,148.7
1918	386.4	6,914.9	545.3	11,044.9	25.9	321.0	53.3	815.6	16.0	275.7	39.5	732.4	49.7	783.1	1,116.2	20,887.6
1917	254.9	4,234.2	405.8	6,612.4	12.5	165.2	33.8	573.9	8.8	141.4	17.8	298.9	21.5	331.6	755.2	12,357.4
1916	79.3	1,273.1	242.2	3,670.4	4.8	58.8	11.7	172.0	4.6	81.2	—	—	12.2	180.4	354.9	5,435.9
1915	16.4	306.6	151.3	2,496.9	.5	5.5	23.0	444.0	.3	7.0	—	—	1.3	19.1	192.8	3,279.0
1914	26.3	572.8	264.0	4,242.1	7.6	91.9	19.6	460.1	—	—	182.5	2,009.6	1.6	21.5	501.6	7,398.2
1913	53.6	1,128.9	447.2	6,348.4	2.8	48.6	4.2	44.2	1.6	32.1	182.5	2,009.6	15.4	255.4	707.1	9,867.2
1912	42.6	808.9	855.3	12,420.5	18.9	117.5	10.9	154.4	.6	11.4	365.9	4,216.6	35.2	495.1	1,329.4	18,224.4
1911	267.0	3,747.8	715.1	10,372.7	20.3	284.9	11.8	116.2	1.4	27.4	277.4	3,336.8	113.5	1,237.2	1,406.7	19,122.9
1910	104.4	1,297.5	655.6	10,473.4	14.5	127.0	18.3	182.9	.6	6.9	285.4	2,783.0	106.0	964.6	1,184.8	15,835.2
1909	25.4	288.8	29.3	383.4	10.4	84.8	6.4	66.5	.2	7.9	—	—	27.7	380.4	99.4	1,211.9
1908	21.2	267.2	81.1	727.4	32.0	153.0	8.6	75.6	1.3	13.9	196.9	1,746.5	5.6	68.9	346.7	3,052.5
1907[1]	69.2	742.2	851.1	4,817.7	3.1	22.6	59.5	346.1	4.0	41.5	289.6	1,711.1	1.4	16.8	1,277.8	7,698.0
1906	236.2	1,863.4	1,012.3	6,015.1	83.4	360.9	85.8	480.1	20.0	137.5	205.0	1,014.4	—	—	1,642.7	9,871.2
1905	139.7	865.9	411.5	2,045.8	80.3	296.9	109.2	512.9	17.6	103.6	231.7	1,221.5	—	—	990.0	5,046.6
1904	144.9	879.9	857.5	3,516.9	29.5	113.3	129.0	563.5	41.9	177.1	64.5	313.6	—	—	1,267.2	5,504.2
1903	330.0	1,939.8	2,260.7	8,472.3	250.4	699.2	231.8	909.6	128.4	522.5	183.7	631.5	843.9	1,476.9	4,229.0	14,651.8
1902	269.6	1,412.3	1,362.5	4,440.5	206.4	713.4	323.5	1,033.4	—	—	—	—	39.8	147.4	2,201.8	7,747.0
1901	82.3	399.8	340.0	1,046.7	59.7	215.0	116.7	352.0	—	—	—	—	22.3	74.8	621.0	2,088.3
1900	70.2	352.6	379.1	1,152.8	133.5	437.4	46.7	128.3	—	—	—	—	18.9	54.0	648.4	2,125.1
1899	56.9	274.6	261.8	814.9	58.0	199.6	24.7	53.3	—	—	—	—	61.0	178.5	462.5	1,520.9
1898	62.0	310.0	242.1	757.8	106.5	364.0	15.5	—	—	—	—	—	22.5	—	448.6	—
1897	10.8	53.3	135.7	431.1	63.8	634.6	9.4	—	—	—	—	—	2.5	—	222.2	—
1896	9.3	52.4	66.6	220.4	21.3	88.6	10.6	—	—	—	—	—	.3	—	108.0	—
1895	4.3	23.2	55.5	177.0	5.6	22.3	46.8	—	—	—	—	—	2.4	—	114.6	—
1894	7.5	48.2	43.2	131.6	6.3	280.0	11.0	—	—	—	—	—	.6	—	68.7	—
1893	—	—	93.2	295.3	14.2	57.6	11.3	—	—	—	—	—	1.6	—	120.2	—

[1] For 1893 to 1899, calendar years; for 1900 to 1906, fiscal years ending 30 June of the year given; for 1907, 9 months ending 31 March 1907; for 1908 to 1930, fiscal years ending 31 March of the year given.

Series K 91–96. *Land sales by Hudson's Bay Company, Canadian Northern Land Department and Canadian Pacific Railway Company, 1925 to 1960*

(series K 91, 93, 95 in acres; series K 92, 94, 96 in dollars)

| Year[1] | Hudson's Bay Company | | Canadian Northern Land Department | | Canadian Pacific Railway Company | |
| | Acreage | Value | Acreage | Value | Acreage | Value[2] |
	91	92	93	94	95	96
1960	2,244	9,856	—	—	—[3]	1,600,000[2]
1959	636	3,450	8,531	88,378	—[3]	3,400,000
1958	3,482	16,514	7,171	44,891	14,072	4,700,000
1957	5,218	35,015	10,857	64,488	57,876	7,600,000
1956	3,991	26,391	6,978	55,875	34,559	6,500,000
1955	10,500	43,260	7,689	43,061	42,950	5,000,000
1954	56,052	269,731	16,198	116,321	57,326	3,600,000
1953	131,425	511,629	43,321	267,296	25,629[4]	2,800,000
1952	81,370	376,965	21,818	202,478	23,945[5]	2,900,000
1951	96,344	356,478	10,439	66,655	104,417	6,600,000
1950	87,662	468,774	12,786	81,652	65,285	2,200,000
1949	120,847	494,249	39,044	259,195	87,748	3,000,000[2]
1948	120,412	654,572	28,050	226,015	178,469	3,336,041
1947	161,853	863,164	45,883	398,137	133,118	650,274
1946	241,135	1,413,693	85,036	935,413	212,170	1,141,102
1945	277,998	1,726,941	70,335	708,364	278,932	1,603,044
1944	159,914	993,307	70,661	742,366	232,371	1,373,018
1943	111,366	517,510	25,485	274,128	135,352	702,470
1942	86,568	431,621	9,664	72,205	94,233	488,239
1941	47,519	306,899	11,273	103,332	89,449	569,717
1940	51,596	395,817	14,553	125,137	99,933	807,678
1939	40,649	269,712	13,444	125,064	106,148	762,315
1938	47,663	331,358	12,577	129,266	116,085	996,214
1937	47,208	334,030	13,356	124,111	129,751	1,330,149
1936	32,913	245,855	16,869	176,680	92,210	955,520
1935	36,512	240,782	6,257	60,944	124,354	1,217,890
1934	21,931	107,336	6,712	71,991	120,355	1,334,343
1933	15,755	101,614	4,953	39,122	67,100	716,925
1932	11,659	92,245	8,121	68,646	59,581	803,664
1931	54,522	543,607	8,350	97,361	87,687	1,254,101
1930	235,773	2,334,760	30,402	398,883	199,312	3,137,109
1929	283,611	3,165,196	—	—	408,506	5,058,675
1928	263,646	3,229,903	—	—	664,411	7,743,847
1927	271,282	3,259,820	—	—	430,368	5,111,798
1926	163,966	2,031,291	—	—	—	—
1925	68,979	928,551	—	—	—	—

[1] For series K 91–92, years ending 31 January of year given; for series K 93–96, calendar years.

[2] For 1949 to 1960, values are rounded to nearest $100,000.

[3] No acreage given.

[4] Agricultural lands only, sold for $194,780.

[5] Agricultural lands only, sold for $177,193.

Series K 97–106. *Government receipts on account of Dominion lands, 1873 to 1931*

(dollars)

Year[1]	Homestead fees	Preemption fees	Sales Cash	Sales Scrip	Timber dues	Grazing lands Cash	Grazing lands Scrip	Hay, coal-mining fees, stone quarries, export tax on gold, etc., cash	National parks	Gross revenue
	97	98	99	100	101	102	103	104	105	106
1931	109,890	—	84,288	—	486,424	67,495	—	640,082	218,844	1,832,173
1930	175,080	—	428,124	27	1,131,024	162,688	—	1,816,955	245,930	4,249,893
1929	161,890	—	785,661	—	1,395,726	171,012	—	1,197,890	234,613	4,152,279
1928	72,551	—	732,324	—	1,388,140	161,045	—	963,644[2]	275,343	3,763,409
1927	57,700	—	544,874	—	1,190,975	162,097	—	1,084,695	238,239	3,418,554
1926	46,900	—	467,601	—	1,098,692	166,388	—	793,358	180,886	2,880,197
1925	36,590	—	410,222	612	981,400	149,070	—	639,749	176,650	2,493,867
1924	38,640	—	404,952	160	847,773	141,871	—	723,763	115,163	2,353,847
1923	53,460	—	414,279	900	825,465	153,697	—	823,184	75,305	2,431,767
1922	73,540	—	761,850	—	683,491	144,345	—	1,071,396	74,303	2,918,530
1921	53,880	—	1,721,172	—	705,314	183,757	—	1,234,558	76,850	4,086,076
1920	67,460	—	2,799,605	80	589,780	183,662	—	896,413	76,742	4,738,921
1919	42,190	—	2,192,861	323	408,728	148,180	—	630,976	55,007	3,616,282
1918	83,180	7,870	3,046,092	131	482,006	125,301	240	630,428	52,161	4,557,810
1917	112,110	14,690	2,707,204	333	429,403	128,342	—	600,934	45,851	4,190,238
1916	170,350	22,760	1,090,842	—	378,961	118,955	160	476,409	37,494	2,443,640
1915	238,295	28,720	696,672	80	310,934	101,711	400	1,594,905	37,896	3,177,867
1914	317,412	61,660	1,303,587	240	378,365	84,926	320	865,499	48,800	3,313,820
1913	337,055	85,940	1,650,492	6,157	463,739	79,413	—	781,283[2]	37,449	3,655,202
1912	391,703	102,070	1,967,183	3,257	400,669	69,519	1,520	729,127	56,498	3,978,037
1911	445,135	156,485	1,193,756	1,438	387,055	60,703	2,356	774,569	69,055	3,306,073
1910	415,232	174,250	1,239,037	9,974	377,856	67,807	5,081	459,870	43,698	3,022,446
1909	389,039	141,550	951,442	20,136	269,837	53,313	3,258	253,339	31,321	2,277,678
1908[1]	301,694	—	656,303	92,311	473,609	43,212	4,048	266,415	27,233	2,094,579
1907[1]	215,450	—	503,202	11,350	379,476	43,712	400	214,257	15,887[2]	1,490,503
1906	417,834	—	442,589	7,655	292,685	51,584	80	297,302	18,884	1,709,315
1905	304,806	—	154,128	19,645	266,951	36,145	5,237	364,928	14,060[2]	1,339,382
1904	255,772	—	196,750	189,705	397,344	19,790	13,921	495,583	9,498[2]	1,681,825
1903	320,410	—	155,537	158,453	470,917	13,912	15,041	607,724	5,064[2]	1,890,887
1902	144,425	—	66,950	169,767	207,791	7,292	8,409	737,882[2]	2,861[2]	1,432,679
1901	79,910	—	40,361	326,270	209,399	4,726	14,672	1,102,147[2]	4,047	1,874,159
1900	72,690	—	103,248	88,756	126,346	8,383	4,083	1,038,383[2]	2,728	1,503,743
1899	58,235	—	116,594	21,308	155,361	5,246	—	1,130,706	2,994	1,584,328
1898	34,780	—	80,179	28,918	119,314	4,729	510	699,383	3,046	1,009,741
1897	21,179	—	49,336	16,929	68,993	4,715	2,500	8,634	2,132	198,676
1896	18,278	—	46,374	46,930	61,923	7,072	6,256	5,814	2,735	227,095
1895	29,665	—	37,294	23,270	74,079	5,354	8,628	5,230	2,322	202,983
1894	36,462	—	53,255	27,841	81,291	5,741	7,688	6,243	2,524	250,069
1893	37,690	—	96,171	77,231	105,865	6,381	11,542	6,266	4,983	394,826
1892	46,994	—	111,651	97,822	106,461	3,727	17,223	5,617	3,648	459,761
1891	29,164	—	91,665	171,425	102,903	3,080	16,194	8,788[2]	2,397	463,068
1890	35,920	8,580	54,897	228,744	84,643	1,306	9,022	9,242	1,094	464,019
1889	39,460	10,550	57,513	318,239	90,290	2,208	16,803	3,947	2,529	594,088
1888	23,691	4,830	52,238	313,523	94,965	5,922	23,023	2,354[2]	2,952	569,987
1887	19,614	6,888	48,176	337,640	65,112	14,243	39,488	1,650[2]	—	588,533
1886	26,110	14,371	76,140	214,658	64,820	29,563	3,131	1,285	—	457,974
1885	25,645	17,100	199,275	45,876	87,475	17,090	—	816	—	451,565
1884	41,580	28,810	424,863	40,920	147,983	11,371	—	641	—	1,001,777[3]
1883	73,015	54,725	516,092	33,638	90,066	22,844	—	914	—	1,051,404[3]
1882	54,155	39,844	1,240,328	50,591	58,753	2,245	—	40	—	1,805,735[3]
1881	20,450	10,802	71,170	70,828	32,028	—	—	—	—	206,991
1880	41,255	10,241	45,709	81,686	25,121	—	—	—	—	206,801
1879	17,690	—	4,998	210,905	325	—	—	—	—	234,733
1878	14,540	—	2,795	120,160	1,620	—	—	—	—	139,584
1877	2,250	—	1,086	136,955	320	—	—	—	—	140,755
1876	4,680	—	3,479	320	387	—	—	—	—	8,866
1875	11,510	—	13,667	—	2,335	—	—	—	—	27,641
1874	7,310	—	19,835	—	2,711	—	—	—	—	29,981
1873	6,960	—	19,170	—	109	—	—	—	—	26,239

[1] For 1873 to 1906, fiscal years ending 30 June of the year given; for 1907, 9 months ending 31 March 1907; for 1909 to 1931, fiscal years ending 31 March of the year given.
[2] Includes some scrip.

[3] Includes sales of colonization lands amounting to $354,036 in 1882, $248,492 in 1883 and $253,713 in 1884. These were the only years in which there were substantial sales of colonization lands.

Series K 107–118. *Primary forest production and exports of primary products, by type of product (excluding fuel wood), 1908 to 1960*

(logs and bolts, volume in billions of feet board measure; pulpwood, volume in thousands of cords; all values in thousands of dollars)

	Production						Exports					
	Logs and bolts		Pulpwood		Other value	Total value	Logs and bolts		Pulpwood		Other value	Total value
Year	Volume	Value	Volume	Value			Volume	Value	Volume	Value		
	107	108	109	110	111	112	113	114	115	116	117	118
1960	—	—	—	—	—	—	29	3,091	1,152	25,840	13,164	42,095
1959	8,573	344,424	14,069	320,244	24,528	689,196	21	2,250	1,107	25,706	12,684	40,640
1958	7,606	311,746	12,764	275,154	22,605	609,505	24	2,340	1,286	29,944	12,098	44,382
1957	8,131	409,227	14,968	340,235	36,937	786,398	35	3,167	1,800	42,332	15,170	60,669
1956	8,055	443,888	17,469	419,471	38,685	902,045	30	3,265	1,953	44,206	13,904	61,375
1955	8,194	393,861	16,088	369,476	31,874	795,211	39	3,532	1,883	43,274	13,338	60,144
1954	7,862	345,068	14,740	323,800	23,426	692,294	52	3,976	1,826	41,900	11,644	57,520
1953	7,947	331,296	13,545	309,011	25,674	665,981	51	4,539	1,784	42,704	13,978	61,221
1952	7,778	344,932	14,755	346,802	38,177	729,912	54	4,892	2,529	61,837	25,715	92,444
1951	7,502	339,423	18,152	416,196	24,795	780,415	46	4,831	2,894	66,077	9,853	80,761
1950	7,388	279,745	13,424	280,838	18,514	579,097	59	4,378	1,782	33,590	7,171	45,139
1949	6,712	229,450	10,309	202,544	24,418	456,412	73	4,094	1,644	30,384	12,649	47,128
1948	7,120	250,649	13,815	271,560	22,949	545,158	84	4,785	2,353	43,573	14,236	62,594
1947	7,116	251,990	13,657	249,912	22,566	524,469	55	3,055	2,001	34,529	14,074	51,658
1946	6,026	181,476	12,111	196,243	20,336	398,055	51	1,955	1,868	28,731	14,488	45,173
1945	5,654	152,312	10,973	159,270	13,903	325,485	59	2,238	1,684	23,882	7,643	33,764
1944	5,667	152,179	9,643	126,851	11,321	290,351	90	3,468	1,509	20,012	6,618	30,099
1943	5,769	126,983	8,987	104,184	9,092	240,259	66	2,683	1,546	18,565	3,368	24,616
1942	5,716	117,762	8,723	86,947	8,450	213,159	116	2,981	1,994	20,314	2,894	26,188
1941	6,384	108,927	8,397	74,879	9,604	193,410	220	4,018	1,856	15,929	3,241	23,188
1940	6,123	90,535	8,717	74,731	9,285	174,551	182	3,689	1,552	12,522	6,108	22,320
1939	4,558	55,685	6,900	58,303	10,701	124,689	331	5,478	1,539	11,901	3,570	20,950
1938	4,209	52,760	6,438	53,762	9,004	115,525	266	4,093	1,752	13,642	2,005	19,740
1937	4,593	58,004	8,298	63,057	9,731	130,792	278	5,012	1,705	12,088	2,411	19,512
1936	3,997	44,828	7,002	48,680	9,129	102,637	291	3,676	1,236	8,276	1,756	13,709
1935	3,349	34,078	6,095	41,196	8,323	83,597	334	3,351	1,110	7,041	1,601	11,993
1934	3,041	29,116	5,774	38,303	6,632	74,050	258	2,637	1,021	6,680	1,430	10,747
1933	2,451	23,158	4,746	33,214	6,260	62,632	283	2,691	719	4,696	1,178	8,566
1932	2,166	18,030	4,222	36,751	6,698	61,479	204	1,897	620	4,831	1,421	8,148
1931	2,675	32,889	5,200	51,973	12,024	96,886	59	701	957	9,360	2,670	12,731
1930	5,379	75,563	5,977	67,530	19,975	163,067	233	2,799	1,330	13,612	7,552	23,962
1929	5,317	79,279	6,536	76,120	22,407	177,806	306	4,345	1,295	13,315	9,451	27,111
1928	5,053	76,431	6,296	74,588	20,507	171,526	330	4,607	1,532	15,270	8,496	28,373
1927	4,695	74,270	5,929	70,285	19,802	164,357	370	5,055	1,542	15,703	8,786	29,543
1926	4,747	75,792	5,621	68,263	20,511	164,566	323	4,809	1,392	14,067	9,086	27,962
1925	4,541	76,633	5,092	62,182	30,946	169,761	292	4,778	1,424	14,169	9,778	28,725
1924	4,891	87,997	4,647	57,778	28,035	173,810	344	5,861	1,330	13,536	8,854	28,251
1923	4,358	74,448	4,655	57,120	27,168	158,736	260	5,095	1,384	13,525	8,198	26,818
1922	3,594	58,337	3,924	50,735	23,549	132,621	185	3,271	1,011	10,360	5,477	19,107
1921	—	—	3,273	—	—	—	—	—	1,093	—	—	—
1920	—	—	4,025	—	—	—	—	—	1,247	—	—	—
1919	—	—	3,499	—	—	—	—	—	1,070	—	—	—
1918	—	—	3,560	—	—	—	—	—	1,350	—	—	—
1917	—	—	3,122	—	—	—	—	—	1,018	—	—	—
1916	—	—	2,833	—	—	—	—	—	1,068	—	—	—
1915	—	—	2,356	—	—	—	—	—	950	—	—	—
1914	—	—	2,197	—	—	—	—	—	973	—	—	—
1913	—	—	2,144	—	—	—	—	—	1,035	—	—	—
1912	—	—	—	—	—	—	—	—	981	—	—	—
1911	—	—	—	—	—	—	—	—	848	—	—	—
1910	—	—	—	—	—	—	—	—	943	—	—	—
1909	—	—	—	—	—	—	—	—	936	—	—	—
1908	—	—	—	—	—	—	—	—	842	—	—	—

Series K 119–123. *Principal statistics of woods operations, 1926 to 1959*
(values in thousands of dollars)

Year	Employees (number of man-years)[1]	Salaries and wages	Cost of materials	Net value of production	Gross value of production
	119	120	121	122	123
1959	82,551	347,406	57,004	658,712	715,716
1958	67,327	338,284	68,595	570,016	638,611
1957	119,944	430,805	89,942	733,113	823,054
1956	132,015	472,035	97,808	841,334	939,143
1955	149,000	506,000	100,459	729,114	829,573
1954	127,000	428,000	84,396	643,974	728,370
1953	136,000	439,000	81,993	622,546	704,539
1952	150,000	466,000	91,815	671,373	763,189
1951	163,000	428,000	90,814	730,208	821,022
1950	141,000	343,000	72,884	540,162	613,046
1949	137,000	313,000	67,574	424,414	491,987
1948	156,000	360,000	68,760	510,255	579,015
1947	160,000	331,000	65,643	494,178	559,821
1946	149,000	248,000	44,443	391,263	435,706
1945	145,000	228,000	40,282	323,955	364,237
1944	140,000	208,000	37,039	293,781	330,820
1943	126,000	159,000	32,859	246,969	279,828
1942	140,000	151,000	31,445	218,064	249,510
1941	108,000	97,000	21,195	204,421	225,616
1940	126,000	109,000	33,243	168,840	202,083
1939	75,333	79,000	34,000	123,747	157,747
1938	71,000	74,000	32,000	116,266	148,266
1937	100,000	60,000	31,486	131,764	163,250
1936	90,000	54,000	26,000	108,804	134,804
1935	79,000	60,000	25,629	89,832	115,462
1934	74,000	47,000	23,427	82,113	105,540
1933	65,000	46,800	14,067	79,706	83,773
1932	60,000	43,200	13,817	78,289	92,106
1931	52,000	37,000	21,170	119,954	141,124
1930	90,000	67,000	31,030	175,823	206,853
1929	97,000	80,000	32,938	186,632	219,570
1928	103,000	80,000	31,945	181,006	212,951
1927	86,000	74,000	30,741	174,197	204,938
1926	81,000	72,000	30,668	173,769	204,436

[1] Man-year in British Columbia is 260 days; in other provinces 300 days.

Series K 124–138. *Lumber production, by species, external trade and estimated consumption, 1908 to 1960*

(volume in millions of feet board measure; value in thousands of dollars)

Year	Softwood production — Douglas fir volume	Spruce and balsam fir volume	Red and white pines volume	Total softwoods volume	Total hardwood production volume	Total production — Volume	Value	Exports — To United Kingdom volume	To United States volume	To other countries volume	Total exports — Volume	Value	Imports volume	Stocks on hand[1] volume	Estimated consumption volume[2]
	124	125	126	127	128	129	130	131	132	133	134	135	136	137	138
1960	—	—	—	—	—	8,012	—	671	3,486	417	4,574	346,300	243	1,244	3,496
1959	2,045	2,750	370	7,196	395	7,591	490,540	349	3,524	308	4,180	323,717	310	1,059	3,651
1958	2,110	2,376	347	6,800	379	7,179	459,901	437	3,125	380	3,942	293,600	268	989	3,631
1957	1,871	2,468	430	6,653	446	7,100	466,228	509	2,704	433	3,647	282,690	237	1,114	3,610
1956	2,085	2,695	468	7,279	460	7,740	539,262	486	3,067	399	3,951	328,099	285	1,034	3,905
1955	2,270	2,774	459	7,547	374	7,920	541,563	844	3,281	489	4,614	386,298	226	866	3,618
1954	2,124	2,398	462	6,817	427	7,244	482,912	870	2,796	383	4,049	326,027	172	951	3,429
1953	1,971	2,611	480	6,781	524	7,306	494,386	601	2,452	324	3,377	283,115	159	1,013	3,898
1952	1,743	2,511	483	6,298	510	6,808	483,195	857	2,252	231	3,340	297,205	152	823	3,613
1951	1,778	2,448	534	6,430	518	6,949	507,650	896	2,168	375	3,439	312,623	133	816	3,549
1950	1,782	2,231	520	6,107	447	6,554	422,481	276	3,024	279	3,579	291,121	86	723	3,083
1949	1,594	2,050	459	5,442	493	5,915	334,790	477	1,404	308	2,189	160,986	81	744	3,755
1948	1,514	2,120	445	5,399	509	5,909	340,851	566	1,615	287	2,468	196,575	43	693	3,294
1947	1,410	2,154	453	5,298	579	5,878	322,048	1,121	1,065	549	2,735	209,215	115	503	3,258
1946	1,128	1,912	414	4,565	517	5,083	230,190	710	965	409	2,083	126,193	59	—	3,059
1945	1,151	1,724	339	4,116	398	4,514	181,046	879	929	193	2,001	99,995	51	—	2,564
1944	1,141	1,685	364	4,091	421	4,512	170,351	852	879	152	1,883	90,950	36	—	2,666
1943	1,234	1,629	361	3,992	371	4,364	151,900	903	730	108	1,741	74,739	34	—	2,657
1942	1,534	1,759	387	4,526	404	4,935	149,855	647	1,432	100	2,180	80,692	41	—	2,796
1941	1,525	1,947	398	4,623	318	4,941	129,288	827	1,232	242	2,301	74,813	60	—	2,700
1940	1,692	1,557	410	4,339	291	4,629	105,991	1,617	651	280	2,549	69,803	82	—	2,162
1939	1,595	1,106	346	3,747	230	3,977	78,332	1,224	627	361	2,212	50,548	77	—	1,842
1938	1,402	1,132	319	3,521	247	3,768	72,633	985	450	318	1,753	37,412	80	—	2,096
1937	1,407	1,256	386	3,718	288	4,006	82,777	1,057	539	370	1,966	47,589	120	—	2,159
1936	1,422	908	299	3,197	215	3,412	61,966	958	531	369	1,858	38,669	89	—	1,644
1935	1,115	919	259	2,769	202	2,973	47,911	734	351	345	1,431	27,514	71	—	1,613
1934	1,032	774	229	2,426	151	2,578	40,510	861	234	396	1,491	27,842	57	—	1,144
1933	818	583	186	1,845	113	1,958	27,709	487	297	357	1,141	18,980	57	—	875
1932	642	592	180	1,684	124	1,810	26,882	195	327	269	791	14,159	43	—	1,062
1931	936	686	317	2,313	179	2,498	45,978	132	665	262	1,060	22,053	94	—	1,532
1930	1,254	1,313	500	3,711	275	3,989	87,711	194	1,121	327	1,642	39,689	135	—	2,482
1929	1,605	1,471	627	4,472	266	4,742	113,350	190	1,403	360	1,953	53,533	240	—	3,029
1928	1,517	1,277	593	4,081	255	4,337	103,590	208	1,358	336	1,902	51,471	263	—	2,699
1927	1,437	1,197	540	3,877	217	4,098	97,509	229	1,636	328	2,193	59,832	195	—	2,100
1926	1,294	1,318	609	3,967	217	4,185	101,071	177	1,777	295	2,249	64,586	171	—	2,107
1925	1,103	1,226	659	3,684	205	3,889	99,726	—	—	—	2,202	—	90	—	1,777
1924	1,000	1,331	739	3,679	198	3,879	104,445	—	—	—	2,087	—	132	—	1,924
1923	1,040	1,240	724	3,543	184	3,728	108,291	—	—	—	2,408	—	169	—	1,489
1922	821	1,116	643	2,992	143	3,139	84,554	—	—	—	2,007	—	148	—	1,279
1921	681	946	566	2,648	216	2,869	82,449	—	—	—	1,038	—	124	—	1,955
1920	902	1,622	738	4,015	251	4,299	168,172	—	—	—	1,936	—	168	—	2,531
1919	818	1,475	569	3,294	186	3,820	122,031	—	—	—	—	—	—	—	—
1918	716	1,238	910	3,441	202	3,887	103,701	—	—	—	—	—	—	—	—
1917	704	1,572	894	3,792	147	4,152	83,655	—	—	—	—	—	—	—	—
1916	575	1,521	781	3,316	174	3,491	58,365	—	—	—	—	—	—	—	—
1915	454	1,798	972	3,633	210	3,843	61,920	—	—	—	—	—	—	—	—
1914	602	1,698	775	3,678	268	3,946	60,363	—	—	—	—	—	—	—	—
1913	793	1,339	823	3,553	264	3,817	65,796	—	—	—	—	—	—	—	—
1912	890	1,488	1,054	4,080	310	4,390	69,476	—	—	—	—	—	—	—	—
1911	846	1,680	1,189	4,628	291	4,918	75,831	—	—	—	—	—	—	—	—
1910	636	1,379	1,180	4,125	279	4,452	70,609	—	—	—	—	—	—	—	—
1909	470	1,216	1,213	3,514	220	3,815	62,819	—	—	—	—	—	—	—	—
1908	372	1,076	1,088	3,013	147	3,348	54,351	—	—	—	—	—	—	—	—

[1] Stocks on hand, 31 December.

[2] Estimated consumption = production − exports + imports + opening inventories − closing inventories.

Series K 139–145. *Principal statistics of the lumber industry, 1917 to 1959*

(series K 139–140 in numbers; series K 141–145 in thousands of dollars)

Year	Establishments	Employees	Salaries and wages	Cost of fuel and electricity	Cost of materials	Net value of production	Gross value of production
	139	140	141	142	143	144	145
1959	5,678	48,659	144,759	9,841	313,399	248,582	571,822
1958	5,769	47,763	142,700	9,204	300,343	236,753	546,299
1957	6,276	50,664	143,166	8,407	309,581	237,700	555,688
1956	6,629	57,078	153,809	8,958	350,746	279,711	639,414
1955	7,333	58,586	152,557	8,673	338,870	296,940	644,483
1954	7,696	57,010	139,572	7,439	301,118	263,629	572,186
1953	8,194	60,933	142,131	7,043	304,585	269,066	580,694
1952	8,283	60,931	135,541	7,191	299,507	261,326	568,023
1951	7,934	62,415	132,059	6,512	313,175	271,866	591,552
1950	7,551	58,722	111,492	5,402	252,322	239,225	496,948
1949	7,460	55,032	97,449	4,359	205,935	186,121	396,415
1948	7,035	56,756	95,066	3,763	208,568	196,936	409,267
1947	6,481	55,426	83,360	3,075	208,544	190,515	402,133
1946	6,001	49,352	63,811	2,394	156,108	129,408	287,910
1945	5,295	44,040	54,018	1,948	126,007	103,154	231,108
1944	5,506	43,516	51,516	1,861	118,167	96,529	216,557
1943	5,140	43,954	49,564	3,150	101,022	91,714	195,885
1942	5,277	47,765	49,562	2,938	98,774	91,207	192,919
1941	4,655	45,104	41,465	2,317	84,435	76,660	163,412
1940	4,675	39,501	34,022	1,257	70,949	61,700	133,905
1939	3,941	32,399	26,396	833	54,448	44,852	100,133
1938	3,873	31,182	25,345	803	52,788	39,265	92,856
1937	3,836	33,917	27,174	842	57,280	46,727	104,850
1936	3,638	28,760	21,357	762	43,599	35,983	80,343
1935	3,698	25,727	17,712	652	35,928	29,325	65,905
1934	3,572	22,605	14,118	560	29,487	24,772	54,819
1933	3,517	17,779	10,040	475	22,871	16,092	39,438
1932	3,595	18,285	10,761	411	23,406	14,691	38,507
1931	3,562	22,361	16,410	568	37,379	24,822	62,769
1930	3,531	43,457	28,513	597	72,957	47,590	121,143
1929	3,161	46,466	36,158	734	83,744	62,511	146,990
1928	2,967	44,862	34,722	812	80,452	58,161	139,425
1927	2,720	44,598	34,422	842	77,439	55,340	133,621
1926	2,780	35,078	34,925	811	78,921	55,450	135,183
1925	2,700	35,457	34,097	815	78,220	55,379	134,414
1924	2,761	35,494	34,784	898	83,142	57,890	141,929
1923	2,883	35,070	33,491	—	73,326	—	139,895
1922	2,922	31,891	27,622	—	60,812	—	114,325
1921	3,126	30,336	26,708	—	57,243	—	116,891
1920	3,481	41,158	44,729	1,046	103,078	103,040	207,164
1919	3,410	39,121	35,494	1,203	72,691	70,506	144,401
1918	3,095	33,917	29,885	727	45,877	99,730	146,333
1917	2,879	32,078	24,582	—	40,725	—	115,885

Series K146–155. *Wood pulp, production and exports, 1908 to 1960*
(volumes in thousands of tons; values in thousands of dollars)

Year	Production				Exports					
	Groundwood		Total pulp		Groundwood		Total pulp		To United States	
	Volume	Value	Volume	Value	Volume	Value	Volume	Value	Volume	Value
	146	147	148	149	150	151	152	153	154	155
1960	—	—	—	—	235	16,348	2,601	325,122	2,000	256,170
1959	5,656	229,656	10,832	744,940	240	16,661	2,450	311,253	1,966	254,049
1958	5,375	222,296	10,137	703,366	233	16,195	2,219	285,449	1,832	239,874
1957	5,574	227,668	10,425	706,195	248	17,567	2,283	292,406	1,847	235,258
1956	5,723	231,236	10,734	706,233	275	19,594	2,374	304,536	1,920	245,081
1955	5,467	218,558	10,151	693,403	262	18,188	2,366	297,304	1,869	233,797
1954	5,338	214,102	9,673	655,917	232	16,502	2,180	271,418	1,670	206,435
1953	5,123	209,900	9,077	624,866	228	15,828	1,950	248,675	1,599	202,248
1952	5,175	217,352	8,968	650,021	255	20,413	1,941	291,863	1,589	225,082
1951	5,172	213,953	9,315	727,880	323	26,742	2,243	365,133	1,831	276,761
1950	4,911	173,035	8,473	502,584	248	14,038	1,846	208,556	1,694	191,006
1949	4,719	166,592	7,853	445,138	207	11,921	1,557	171,504	1,305	141,641
1948	4,414	168,343	7,675	485,966	297	19,257	1,798	211,564	1,591	184,973
1947	4,275	147,424	7,254	403,853	319	19,099	1,699	177,803	1,499	156,122
1946	3,998	111,514	6,615	287,624	268	12,571	1,419	114,021	1,253	99,973
1945	3,342	86,375	5,601	231,873	274	12,101	1,435	106,055	1,094	79,589
1944	3,076	71,669	5,271	211,041	237	10,134	1,408	101,563	1,078	77,082
1943	2,999	63,427	5,273	194,519	273	10,069	1,556	100,013	1,269	80,970
1942	3,260	64,802	5,606	192,145	278	10,507	1,511	95,267	1,197	76,088
1941	3,495	61,327	5,721	175,440	271	8,836	1,412	85,898	1,109	68,161
1940	3,305	55,505	5,291	149,005	204	6,265	1,069	60,930	825	46,577
1939	2,738	43,062	4,166	97,132	169	4,090	706	31,001	607	26,837
1938	2,462	39,228	3,668	87,897	124	2,914	554	27,731	454	21,562
1937	3,309	46,144	5,142	116,729	167	4,146	871	41,816	698	32,765
1936	2,910	38,251	4,485	92,337	134	2,841	754	31,247	641	26,504
1935	2,505	32,035	3,868	79,722	124	2,632	662	27,626	531	22,290
1934	2,340	30,557	3,636	75,727	120	2,728	606	25,445	479	20,053
1933	1,825	25,151	2,980	64,114	132	2,688	609	23,355	487	18,815
1932	1,696	28,018	2,663	64,412	116	2,562	452	18,930	363	15,051
1931	2,016	37,097	3,168	84,781	165	4,606	623	30,057	492	23,646
1930	2,283	48,317	3,619	112,356	209	5,967	760	39,060	647	32,141
1929	2,421	51,617	4,021	129,033	209	5,907	831	43,368	711	36,285
1928	2,128	47,549	3,608	121,184	204	5,546	864	45,615	724	37,633
1927	1,922	44,175	3,279	114,443	261	7,761	879	46,996	711	37,942
1926	1,901	44,800	3,230	115,154	382	11,506	1,006	52,077	818	43,220
1925	1,622	39,130	2,773	100,216	360	10,573	961	47,932	824	41,587
1924	1,428	36,166	2,465	90,324	254	7,916	782	40,243	691	36,348
1923	1,420	37,587	2,476	99,073	341	11,599	875	47,027	678	38,797
1922	1,241	31,079	2,150	84,948	315	9,400	818	41,038	610	33,083
1921	932	32,314	1,549	78,338	223	9,272	527	33,134	391	23,762
1920	1,090	49,890	1,960	141,553	304	17,575	820	76,384	625	61,633
1919	991	23,317	1,716	73,320	312	7,182	709	37,185	493	27,970
1918	880	19,113	1,557	64,356	181	4,786	584	33,360	544	30,157
1917	924	25,919	1,464	65,515	250	7,082	512	26,193	474	23,049
1916	827	—	1,296	—	330	5,649	559	17,344	467	14,275
1915	744	—	1,075	—	—	—	364	9,279	—	—
1914	645	—	935	—	—	—	425	8,865	—	—
1913	600	—	855	—	—	—	298	5,914	—	—
1912	499	—	683	—	—	—	348	5,952	—	—
1911	362	—	497	—	—	—	260	4,903	—	—
1910	370	—	475	—	—	—	329	5,695	—	—
1909	326	—	445	—	—	—	281	4,899	—	—
1908	279	—	363	—	—	—	240	4,071	—	—

Series K 156–168. *Manufactured paper, capacity, production and exports, 1916 to 1960*
(volumes are in thousands of tons; values in thousands of dollars)

Year	Newsprint capacity	Production				Exports							
		Newsprint production		Total paper products		Newsprint exports		Total exports of paper		Newsprint exports to U.S.		Total paper exports to U.S.	
		Volume	Value	Volume	Value	Volume	Value	Volume[1]	Value[1]	Volume	Value	Volume[1]	Value[1]
	156	157	158	159	160	161	162	163	164	165	166	167	168
1960	7,611	—	—	—	—	6,190	757,930	6,490	798,702	5,230	631,230	5,360	647,412
1959	7,521	6,351	730,455	8,550	1,106,071	5,910	722,271	6,202	762,232	5,092	614,706	5,245	633,802
1958	7,239	6,031	699,906	8,081	1,044,640	5,683	690,209	5,929	724,699	4,881	590,167	5,009	606,361
1957	6,756	6,362	729,009	8,300	1,056,371	5,901	715,490	6,154	751,153	5,058	610,290	5,199	627,402
1956	6,243	6,445	735,644	8,467	1,070,492	5,967	708,385	6,203	741,292	5,219	615,942	5,359	632,804
1955	6,064	6,196	688,338	8,000	981,439	5,763	665,877	5,990	694,239	5,028	578,322	5,192	595,513
1954	5,920	6,001	657,487	7,650	925,591	5,522	635,670	5,675	655,938	4,867	558,634	4,976	570,823
1953	5,723	5,755	633,408	7,377	887,858	5,375	619,033	5,541	639,077	4,917	564,464	5,055	578,456
1952	5,510	5,707	600,516	7,202	838,105	5,327	591,790	5,526	622,136	4,851	534,373	4,990	549,318
1951	5,360	5,561	564,361	7,225	824,030	5,112	536,372	5,359	574,106	4,775	496,852	4,950	517,584
1950	5,227	5,319	506,968	6,812	710,154	4,938	485,746	5,118	505,314	4,725	463,156	4,878	477,089
1949	5,113	5,187	467,976	6,540	641,460	4,789	440,054	4,952	459,050	4,346	395,260	4,457	404,808
1948	4,883	4,640	402,100	6,064	582,347	4,328	383,123	4,588	416,682	3,917	340,334	4,068	354,177
1947	4,729	4,474	355,541	5,775	507,101	4,221	342,293	4,452	373,070	3,675	291,893	3,777	300,482
1946	4,641	4,162	280,810	5,347	396,956	3,858	265,865	4,046	287,438	3,323	224,782	3,396	229,644
1945	4,672	3,324	189,024	4,360	282,838	3,059	179,451	3,286	203,012	2,534	146,508	2,594	152,542
1944	4,726	3,040	165,655	4,044	255,546	2,806	157,191	3,013	177,290	2,409	133,399	2,471	138,729
1943	4,678	3,046	152,963	3,966	234,036	2,810	144,707	2,984	160,825	2,545	129,787	2,607	135,023
1942	4,763	3,257	147,074	4,232	230,269	3,005	141,066	3,242	157,838	2,792	130,519	2,897	137,952
1941	4,703	3,520	158,925	4,525	241,450	3,262	154,357	3,587	176,184	2,762	129,162	2,921	139,107
1940	4,716	3,504	158,447	4,319	225,837	3,243	151,360	3,490	170,880	2,586	119,362	2,609	121,312
1939	4,633	2,927	120,859	3,601	170,776	2,659	115,687	2,796	124,127	2,206	97,058	2,231	98,425
1938	4,535	2,669	107,051	3,249	151,650	2,425	104,615	2,545	112,873	1,938	85,191	1,959	86,161
1937	4,211	3,674	126,424	4,345	175,885	3,455	126,466	3,532	136,164	2,899	105,699	2,928	107,084
1936	4,218	3,225	105,215	3,807	146,355	2,993	103,640	3,061	110,861	2,399	83,546	2,430	84,832
1935	4,263	2,765	88,436	3,281	125,753	2,575	87,924	2,618	94,042	2,052	70,957	2,067	71,615
1934	4,182	2,605	86,811	3,070	120,892	2,414	82,504	2,454	87,634	1,960	68,092	1,972	68,676
1933	4,149	2,022	66,960	2,419	96,690	1,838	69,201	1,871	72,396	1,520	58,315	1,534	58,874
1932	4,142	1,919	85,540	2,291	113,873	1,777	82,966	2,042	86,324	1,520	72,007	1,530	72,605
1931	4,127	2,227	111,420	2,611	143,630	2,008	107,233	2,042	111,114	1,753	94,355	1,766	95,163
1930	3,902	2,498	136,182	2,927	173,306	2,333	133,371	2,373	138,530	2,008	115,259	2,024	116,664
1929	3,512	2,725	150,800	3,197	192,989	2,515	148,866	2,564	154,919	2,173	129,022	2,195	130,899
1928	3,262	2,414	144,147	2,849	184,305	2,207	141,104	2,253	147,157	1,935	123,507	1,954	125,199
1927	2,716	2,083	132,287	2,469	168,231	1,882	123,222	1,925	129,638	1,748	114,042	1,765	115,827
1926	2,121	1,889	121,065	2,266	158,182	1,732	114,091	1,770	121,414	1,628	106,759	1,643	108,799
1925	1,823	1,537	106,269	1,885	140,161	1,402	98,945	1,442	106,624	1,321	93,104	1,337	95,461
1924	1,638	1,388	100,277	1,719	133,319	1,219	90,991	1,263	99,248	1,193	88,994	1,213	91,707
1923	1,465	1,252	93,213	1,589	127,184	1,138	85,611	1,179	93,771	1,115	83,827	1,133	86,625
1922	1,277	1,081	75,971	1,367	106,260	959	68,363	995	74,826	888	62,860	905	65,000
1921	1,151	805	78,785	1,019	106,554	709	69,786	734	75,511	655	63,542	669	64,994
1920	1,016	876	80,865	1,215	132,023	762	72,920	781	86,744	—	—	—	—
1919	905	795	54,428	1,090	87,753	708	49,811	727	59,983	—	—	—	—
1918	837	735	46,231	968	73,124	636	37,301	650	42,951	—	—	—	—
1917	—	690	38,868	856	59,250	596	32,561	607	35,622	—	—	—	—
1916	—	—[2]	—	—	—	526	21,099	533	23,466	—	—	—	—

[1] Represents the weight of items of export classification for which tonnage figures are available: for example, exports of paper products are not recorded by weight, and exports of paper boards for 1927 to 1937 were not recorded by weight. Value of exports, however, covers all exports of paper and paper products.

[2] Annual average production: for 1913 to 1914, 436,000 tons; 1915 to 1919, 710,000 tons (*Newsprint Data, 1958*).

Series K 169–175. *Principal statistics of the pulp and paper industry, 1919 to 1959*

(series K 169–170 in numbers; series K 171–175 in thousands of dollars)

Year	Establishments	Employees	Salaries and wages	Cost of fuel and electricity	Cost of materials	Net value of production	Gross value of production
	169	170	171	172	173	174	175
1959	127	65,028	322,311	108,859	628,269	761,036	1,498,164
1958	128	64,084	307,416	105,797	597,805	702,951	1,406,553
1957	128	69,940	307,628	108,637	617,176	693,476	1,419,288
1956	126	65,985	297,572	103,506	625,205	736,346	1,465,058
1955	125	62,205	265,298	91,041	546,079	689,818	1,326,938
1954	125	60,837	252,598	84,891	515,258	641,517	1,241,665
1953	127	58,194	235,742	80,380	499,351	599,935	1,179,665
1952	128	57,803	225,353	76,740	497,047	584,101	1,157,888
1951	126	57,291	213,170	75,626	483,014	679,258	1,237,897
1950	123	52,343	169,247	69,112	373,883	511,143	954,138
1949	123	52,050	157,704	64,110	348,663	423,376	836,148
1948	117	51,924	151,663	63,843	349,244	412,770	825,858
1947	115	49,946	129,478	55,442	295,444	356,085	706,972
1946	113	44,967	101,365	46,202	223,448	258,165	527,815
1945	109	39,996	80,463	39,033	179,369	180,402	398,805
1944	104	37,896	75,833	37,359	157,995	174,492	369,846
1943	106	37,020	71,199	36,211	143,956	164,244	344,412
1942	105	38,002	69,656	36,226	135,970	164,500	336,697
1941	106	37,154	63,678	34,437	125,437	174,852	334,726
1940	103	34,719	56,074	31,045	108,759	158,231	298,035
1939	100	31,016	44,737	25,095	79,934	103,124	208,152
1938	99	30,943	42,619	23,801	71,063	89,034	183,898
1937	98	33,205	48,758	29,121	91,122	106,002	226,245
1936	93	29,478	39,440	25,691	72,203	85,739	183,633
1935	95	27,836	35,893	22,683	57,995	78,648	159,326
1934	95	26,993	33,307	21,978	53,427	77,243	152,648
1933	95	24,037	26,658	18,902	47,633	56,881	123,415
1932	98	24,561	28,348	19,822	48,971	66,856	135,649
1931	103	26,669	34,792	22,928	63,948	87,858	174,734
1930	109	33,027	45,775	26,158	81,992	107,524	215,674
1929	108	34,202	50,214	25,356	96,875	121,740	243,971
1928	110	33,614	47,323	24,547	88,490	120,040	233,077
1927	114	32,876	45,674	24,024	84,813	110,492	219,330
1926	115	31,279	44,176	20,424	85,365	109,580	215,370
1925	114	28,031	38,561	17,507	76,515	99,071	193,093
1924	115	27,627	37,650	17,396	72,234	89,629	179,260
1923	110	29,234	38,383	18,422	71,323	95,077	184,822
1922	104	25,830	32,919	16,982	64,693	77,276	158,951
1921	100	24,619	34,199	14,962	62,276	73,765	151,003
1920	100	31,298	45,254	16,989	84,209	135,222	236,420
1919	99	26,647	32,264	12,503	54,085	71,325	137,913

Series K 176–183. *Value of exports, wood, wood products and paper, by type of product, 1869 to 1915*

(thousands of dollars)

Year[1]	Total wood, wood products and paper	Ashes	Logs	Lumber	Square timber	Paper	Wood pulp	Other
	176	177	178	179	180	181	182	183
1915	68,933	51	1,259	33,240	1,240	15,588	9,266	8,289
1914	63,525	49	818	33,286	1,365	12,753	6,365	8,589
1913	56,557	62	1,028	33,439	1,976	6,351	5,510	8,221
1912	51,137	75	767	32,383	1,696	3,915	5,094	7,207
1911	56,295	95	1,193	36,166	1,528	3,953	5,716	7,644
1910	57,045	90	1,002	38,495	1,521	3,185	5,205	7,547
1909	48,572	92	928	32,395	1,682	3,524	4,307	5,644
1908[1]	53,150	88	699	35,911	2,488	3,554	4,038	6,372
1907[1]	49,617	96	552	36,268	2,160	2,436	3,893	4,212
1906	45,679	105	557	32,940	2,185	2,028	3,478	4,386
1905	39,687	98	480	27,949	1,808	1,811	3,400	4,141
1904	38,215	101	419	28,085	2,572	1,147	2,409	3,482
1903	41,879	117	434	30,983	2,783	894	3,151	3,517
1902	35,455	133	565	27,522	1,953	27	2,046	3,209
1901	33,323	120	1,055	24,969	2,274	42	1,938	2,925
1900	33,168	138	761	25,059	2,485	31	1,816	2,878
1899	30,931	111	1,570	22,749	2,566	—	—	3,945
1898	29,481	112	1,800	20,737	3,110	—	—	3,722
1897	33,129	102	2,126	25,436	2,576	—	—	2,889
1896	28,854	110	1,731	21,299	2,966	—	—	2,748
1895	25,498	123	2,233	18,714	2,071	—	—	2,357
1894	27,995	110	2,862	19,899	2,782	—	—	2,342
1893	29,078	121	1,518	22,134	2,880	—	—	2,425
1892	24,783	115	1,116	18,370	3,012	—	—	2,170
1891	27,122	123	730	20,667	3,626	—	—	1,976
1890	28,326	106	683	21,160	4,710	—	—	1,667
1889	25,152	132	567	19,230	3,726	—	—	1,497
1888	23,655	159	405	18,509	3,069	—	—	1,513
1887	22,808	168	301	18,213	2,726	—	—	1,400
1886	23,514	162	278	17,733	3,951	—	—	1,390
1885	23,069	181	213	17,403	3,712	—	—	1,560
1884	27,949	246	237	20,177	5,658	—	—	1,631
1883	27,204	318	263	19,648	5,673	—	—	1,302
1882	25,484	346	283	18,749	4,746	—	—	1,360
1881	26,321	302	371	18,025	6,356	—	—	1,267
1880	18,006	319	134	13,609	2,761	—	—	1,183
1879	14,106	255	95	10,674	2,235	—	—	847
1878	20,371	301	85	13,831	5,137	—	—	1,017
1877	23,967	472	84	15,024	7,322	—	—	1,065
1876	20,739	424	34	14,121	5,179	—	—	961
1875	25,179	546	24	16,936	6,867	—	—	806
1874	27,309	539	50	19,657	6,001	—	—	1,062
1873	29,395	690	87	20,442	6,646	—	—	1,530
1872	24,391	638	64	15,925	6,580	—	—	1,184
1871	22,959	636	84	15,001	5,928	—	—	1,310
1870	21,388	576	112	14,803	4,697	—	—	1,200
1869	19,699	724	96	13,371	4,497	—	—	1,011

[1] For 1869 to 1907, years ending 30 June of the year given; for 1908 to 1915, years ending 31 March of the year given.

Series K 184–188. *Forest fires, Canada (excluding Yukon and Northwest Territories), 1908 to 1960*

Year	Number of fires			Acres burned		Year	Number of fires			Acres burned	
	Under 10 acres	Over 10 acres	Total	Total	Merchantable		Under 10 acres	Over 10 acres	Total	Total	Merchantable
	184	185	186	187	188		184	185	186	187	188
1960	5,988	1,217	7,205	1,470,676	416,684	1935	3,277[1]	1,678[1]	4,955	856,183	172,592
1959	3,846	890	4,736	537,819	65,276	1934	4,014[1]	1,897[1]	5,911	1,475,117	321,414
1958	5,336	1,311	6,647	3,291,541	541,221	1933	3,999[1]	2,299[1]	6,298	1,008,558	204,405
1957	4,559	1,039	5,598	452,416	71,470	1932	3,777[1]	2,521[1]	6,298	2,463,923	708,085
1956	3,656	884	4,540	2,016,428	645,608	1931	—	—	6,965	2,093,922	394,824
1955	5,048	1,144	6,192	1,375,199	344,548	1930	—	—	6,805	2,670,188	746,129
1954	2,506	446	2,952	264,295	72,136	1929	—	—	6,712	6,028,551	663,574
1953	4,994	1,448	6,442	1,358,129	203,116	1928	—	—	4,243	1,346,026	217,350
1952	3,844	1,042	4,886	975,249	182,900	1927	2,838	767	3,605	471,878	114,708
1951	3,453	1,049	4,502	896,015	135,091	1926	4,154	1,536	5,690	1,824,015	575,732
1950	3,769	1,541	5,310	2,226,765	259,205	1925	3,876	1,614	5,490	1,316,321	217,293
1949	5,334	1,712	7,046	2,599,272	395,497	1924	3,995	1,629	5,624	1,984,786	377,146
1948	3,863	1,505	5,368	3,184,983	949,530	1923	3,705	2,484	6,189	6,190,817	1,853,079
1947	3,893	1,124	5,017	613,007	105,098	1922	5,425	2,774	8,199	3,323,401	609,132
1946	4,372	1,531	5,903	1,016,706	109,478	1921	3,905	2,168	6,073	2,142,446	408,455
1945	3,681	1,080	4,761	741,531	159,909	1920	3,315	1,943	5,258	1,708,368	363,142
1944	3,943	1,877	5,820	2,403,061	503,764	1919	3,438	1,785	5,223	7,589,669	2,159,995
1943	2,355	1,015	3,370	827,830	87,809	1918	3,064	1,079	4,143	562,752	75,527
1942	3,437	1,354	4,791	1,838,471	318,435	1917[2]	1,437	680	2,117	857,714[3]	135,382[3]
1941	3,833	2,118	5,951	4,252,651	1,498,128	1916[2]	1,324	444	1,768	277,598[3]	21,645[3]
1940	4,477	1,807	6,284	2,691,135	462,454	1915[2]	1,849	913	2,762	2,207,361[3]	705,039[3]
1939	3,990	1,623	5,613	1,115,179	199,288	1914[2]	2,898	939	3,837	1,023,431[3]	205,991[3]
1938	4,476	2,171	6,647	3,125,768	722,199						
1937	3,886	2,063	5,949	4,271,431	662,792	1909[2]	—	—	1,134	435,000	—
1936	4,031	1,915	5,946	3,026,646	919,764	1908[2]	—	—	835	188,390	—

1 Estimated by the Forestry Branch from incomplete reports.
2 See the notes to series K 184–188 for the provinces covered by these data.
3 Acres reported cover only fires over 10 acres in extent.

Series K 189–199. *Principal forestry revenues, Canada and each province, selected years 1933 to 1943 and 1945 to 1955*
(thousands of dollars)

Year[1]	Government of Canada	British Columbia	Alberta	Saskatchewan	Manitoba	Ontario	Quebec	New Brunswick	Nova Scotia	Prince Edward Island	Newfoundland
	189	190	191	192	193	194	195	196	197	198	199
1955	149	30,739	4,151	682	1,039	15,011	19,640	3,345	451	39	136
1954	133	24,900	3,720	650	1,000	14,110	14,737	2,923	370	37	99
1953	163	21,705	3,357	699	1,056	15,286	11,719	3,703	263	28	122
1952	123	20,940	3,667	640	1,034	19,069	13,340	3,265	307	19	131
1951	132	16,220	2,498	749	1,061	14,099	16,569	2,939	318	15	127
1950	81	12,428	2,235	615	674	13,213	11,304	2,015[2]	275[3]	6	107
1949	71	10,064	1,717	575	518	7,523	7,692	1,971	191	—	80
1948	72	9,521	1,802	671	567	7,718	13,043	2,084	170	—	81
1947	82	8,108	1,599	632	587	6,929	10,677	1,889	164	—	99
1946	77	5,687	1,307	504[4]	386[4]	7,020	13,703	1,425	129	—	90
1945	78	5,061	1,047	582	367	5,730	8,175	1,288	124	—	73
1943	162	4,344	877	726	342	4,744	5,010	1,241	129	—	—
1941	86	4,740	790	550	288	4,306	6,250	1,130	125	—	—
1939	49	3,984	389	306	232	3,035	3,585[5]	652	127	—	—
1937	44	3,876	383	278	264	3,756	4,427[5]	966	136	—	—
1933	38	2,160[6]	162	104	145	1,698	1,777[5]	331	120	—	—

1 Fiscal years ending nearest 31 December of the year given.
2 17 months ended 31 March 1951.
3 16 months ended 31 March 1951.
4 11 months ended 31 March 1947.
5 Fiscal years beginning 1 July, within the year.
6 Calendar year.

Series K 200–223. *Gross ordinary and capital forestry expenditures, selected years 1933 to 1943 and 1945 to 1955*

(thousands of dollars)

Year[1]	Government of Canada		British Columbia			Alberta		Saskatchewan		Manitoba	
	Forest research[2]	Total	Fire protection, prevention and suppression	Forest research	Total	Fire protection, prevention and suppression	Total	Fire protection, prevention and suppression	Total	Fire prevention, and protection	Total
	200	201	202	203	204	205	206	207	208	209	210
1955	4,533	6,925	2,345	56	10,064	1,350	2,390	308	494	252	1,438
1954	3,902	6,970	2,126	59	9,557	1,134	2,078	285	473	122	1,125
1953	3,553	7,469	2,081	60	8,905	993	2,093	304	476	134	1,153
1952	3,250	6,237	2,911	82	9,563	709	1,806	261	405	160	1,084
1951	2,626	5,164	4,157	74	8,570	590	1,665	198	327	102	869
1950	2,892	4,433	2,482	30	5,796	744	1,705	199	307	103	855
1949	2,782	5,068	1,905	32	4,834	686[3]	1,337	320	438	157	1,011
1948	1,824	2,955	1,491	28	4,024	87	671	191	377	211	991
1947	1,700	2,170	1,362	16	3,324	18	467	74	511	69	589
1946	1,152	1,499	1,224	23	2,639	49	430	198[4]	—	64[4]	421[4]
1945	438	681[5]	1,073	13	2,151	59	380	95	—	45	233
1943	300	725[5]	579	11	1,338	19	318	43	—	46	197
1941	304	399[5]	687	11	1,447	162	386	127	—	57	231
1939	350	407	803	14	1,475[6]	137	307	34	—	80	200[6]
1937	268	318	465	14	1,107[6]	53	213	458	—	74	223[6]
1933	249	297	—	—	495[6]	32	187	78	—	38	143

Year[1]	Ontario			Quebec			New Brunswick		Nova Scotia		Prince Edward Island	Newfoundland	
	Extra fire fighting	Forest research	Total	Fire protection and suppression	Forest research	Total	Forest fire prevention and protection	Total	Fire protection	Total	Total	Fire protection	Total
	211	212	213	214	215	216	217	218	219	220	221	222	223
1955	4,152	—	15,996	3,490[7]	N/A	8,357	346	2,486	252	1,182	86	52	354
1954	704	141	11,102	2,289[7]	N/A	6,736	204	2,113	177	843	76	62	409
1953	980	284	12,704	3,060	53	7,807	258	2,647	173	691	55	66	297
1952	281	267	12,323	1,893	48	6,447	344	1,964	210	652	48	87	316
1951	533	244	12,022	1,880	48	6,006	279	1,261	167	651	32	60	328
1950	301	227	11,755	1,854	50	5,555	493[8]	1,910[8]	258[9]	860[9]	25	56	334
1949	1,501	210	13,402	1,794	52	6,317	249[10]	1,102	212	505	22	48	387
1948	1,724	197	10,445	1,466	46	4,778	1,027	1,526	328	619	11	49	473
1947	444	222	6,760	1,146	90	4,498	750	1,226	282	498	2	78	448
1946	302	230	5,708	1,047	115	3,830	549	1,009	142	304	—	64	301
1945	234	234	3,972	954	77	3,213	323	512	43	176	—	—	—
1943	74	12	2,667	575	65	2,559	212	314	24	176	—	—	—
1941	—	—	2,482	1,096	56	2,766[11]	156	247	16	107	—	—	—
1939	—	—	2,417	735[12]	51[12]	2,132[11, 12]	147	240	34	110	—	—	—
1937	—	—	2,364	625[12]	10[12]	1,966[12]	126	222	35	118	—	—	—
1933	—	—	1,683	527[12]	6[12]	1,634[12]	82	148	41	181	—	—	—

[1] Fiscal years ending nearest 31 December of the year given.
[2] For 1933 to 1947 administrative services are included; for 1949 and 1950 outlays for forest insect control board are included; for 1946 to 1951 forest entomology is included; for 1952 to 1955 forest biology is included.
[3] The classification of expenditure was changed in 1949; from 1949 to 1955 forest protection and timber operations are included.
[4] 11 months ending 31 March 1947.
[5] Excludes expenditures for internment and prisoner of war operations charged to the Dominion Forest Service.
[6] Excludes expenditures made from unemployment relief funds.
[7] Includes entomology service. For 1933 to 1953 entomology service is included in forest research, series K 215.
[8] 17 months ending 31 March 1951.
[9] 16 months ending 31 March 1951.
[10] Classification changed in 1949.
[11] Excludes expenditures for National Forestry Programme–Youth Aid.
[12] Fiscal year beginning 1 July, within the year.

SECTION L: AGRICULTURE

DAVID L. MacFARLANE, *Macdonald College, McGill University*

The statistics of agriculture presented here are in six sub-sections. Series L1–124 are the general statistics of the industry. Series L125–166 are crop statistics. Series L167–264, the third subsection, cover the major statistics of livestock and livestock products. Series L265–317 cover exports of major agricultural products and the domestic disappearance of food products in Canada. Series L318–350 contain miscellaneous agricultural statistics including data on farm tractors, farm implements, grain elevator capacity and early farm wage rates. With the exception of some data from the censuses of 1851 and 1861, which appear in the first two tables of the first subsection, all of these sub-sections are confined to the years since Confederation in 1867. An appendix is devoted to the major statistics of agriculture generated by the many colonial censuses taken since the beginning of European settlement in 1608. This subsection on earlier colonial statistics, series L351–375, is the fifth subsection.

The major official sources of the statistics are the following: the *Census of Canada*, 1870–71 to 1956; *Census of Canada* (the province), 1851–52, 1861; *Statistical Year Book* (Ottawa, King's Printer); and the following publications of the Dominion Bureau of Statistics, all of them published in Ottawa by the Queen's (King's) Printer: *Quarterly Bulletin of Agricultural Statistics*; *Monthly Bulletin of Agricultural Statistics*; *Canada Year Book*; *The Labour Force, November, 1945–January, 1955*, Reference Paper No. 58 (1958 Revision); *Farm Net Income* (1959); *Handbook of Agricultural Statistics, Part II, Farm Income, 1926–57*; *Prices and Price Indexes* (various years); *Index of Farm Prices of Agricultural Products, 1956, No. 1*; *Livestock Market Review, 1953 Supplement*; *Canadian Statistical Review, 1953 Supplement*; *Canadian Statistical Review, 1959 Supplement*; *Livestock and Animal Product Statistics, 1960*; *Handbook of Agricultural Statistics, Part I, Field Crops, 1908–1958*; *Numbers and Values of Livestock, 1906 to 1943*; *Production and Value of Shorn Lamb, 1920 to 1943*; *Dairy Statistics*, successive issues; *Grain Trade of Canada*, annual; *Handbook of Agricultural Statistics, Part IV, Food Consumption in Canada, 1926–55*, Reference Paper No. 25.

The *Eleventh Census of Newfoundland, 1945*, and the *Quebec Statistical Yearbook, 1914* were also used.

In addition to the foregoing published sources some of the data were secured from the files of the Agriculture Division, Dominion Bureau of Statistics, and the Market Information Service of the Department of Agriculture in Ottawa, and it is to be noted particularly that even when published sources are given here some of the entries may differ from those in the published sources. The Agriculture Division of Dominion Bureau of Statistics checked nearly all tables and in some cases provided more accurate entries than those given in the sources: these entries are used in this section. See also the supplementary note on page 350.

General note

Section A, dealing with population, details the history of the censuses in Canada including the pre-Confederation period. As noted there, the censuses of population and agriculture have traditionally been a joint operation. In fact, from Confederation until 1912, the census was the responsibility of the Ministry of Agriculture. The early censuses typically had less than ten enumeration items. The first comprehensive census, that of 1870–1, had two agricultural schedules comprising 65 columns. By 1951 the agricultural schedule had 21 sections and 194 questions. Some of the questions required entries in as many as seven columns.

Over the years, there have been adjustments of census techniques as well as an evolution of definitions. This is, of course, a natural and necessary process but renders some historical comparisons of doubtful validity. For example the 1880–1 census explained for the first time the acreage and state of lands occupied, and from this evolved the definition of 'a farm' adopted in the 1921 Census of Canada: a farm consisted of a tract of land of one acre or more in extent, and producing in 1920 agricultural products to the value of $50 or more. Beginning in 1951, a farm was defined as a holding on which agricultural operations were carried out: the holding could consist of a single tract of land or of a number of separate tracts held under the same or different tenures; it had to be three acres or more in size or from one to three acres in size with agricultural production valued at $250 or more during the previous year. (A farm has been redefined for the forthcoming 1961 census. It will then consist of a holding of 1 acre or more with the sales of agricultural products during the past 12 months valued at $50 or more.)

As noted in Section A of this volume, the completeness of the census enumeration and the accuracy of replies to questions has long been debated. Previous to the 1956 Census of Agriculture, no effort had been made by means of a field check to measure the extent of the difficulties encountered in making a complete and accurate enumeration. These difficulties included definitional problems, the inability of some census enumerators to perform a thorough job, and difficulties experienced by some farmers in answering questions concerning their farms.

'As part of the 1956 Census of Agriculture, a Quality Check Sample Survey was undertaken to provide estimates of the completeness of coverage of the census and to provide checks on the quality of selected items.' (This and the immediately following quotations were taken from *Census of Canada, 1956, Agriculture*, Bulletin 2–11, pp. xii–xiv.) This quality check was undertaken in all provinces except Newfoundland and entailed a post-census re-enumeration of 4771 farms in 601 stratified sampling areas. This represented 0.8 per cent of the universe of Canadian farms.

The re-enumeration was performed by approximately 200 enumerators selected from the regular census enumerators on the basis of their competence in completing the regular census enumeration. They were given additional training and assigned to areas in which they had not previously enumerated....The questionnaire used for re-enumeration contained similar questions and referred to the same time period as the census for acreages sown to individual crops and respecting numbers of livestock on farms at 1 June. Additional explanations for particular questions and additional questions were included to facilitate complete coverage of farms, to encourage accuracy in response to individual questions and to compensate, as in the case of pigs, for the later interview date. With respect to acreages sown or to be sown to individual crops for harvest in 1956, it was recognized that the data reported in the re-enumeration could differ from that reported in the regular census, if there were elements of intention to seed in the census reports and those intentions were not realized or were changed by the time the re-enumeration took place.

The effectiveness of the Quality Check Sample in detecting error in the Census totals is limited by the sampling error associated with the sample estimates. Where the sampling error is large, errors in Census totals can also be large and may even remain undetected. Given the variability that exists in the farm universe, the design and size of the Quality Check Sample determine the sampling errors of resulting estimates.

It was observed that for most of the items selected, the sample estimate differs from the census total by an amount which could be attributed to sampling error. For example, the sample estimate for total acreage in farms differed from the census total by 3.8 per cent. The probability of this positive difference occurring because of sampling error alone is approximately 0.29 and the observed difference was not judged as unusually large. However, the sample estimate of number of farms differs from the census total by 7.6 per cent and the probability of a positive difference this large or larger is less than 0.01. In this case, the observed difference could not safely be attributed solely to sampling error and it would appear that the hypothesis that the census enumeration was a complete and accurate coverage of the number of farms would have to be rejected. Considering that there is no significant under-enumeration of farm acreage, much of the apparent under-enumeration in the number of farms is probably due to the application of the definition of what constitutes a farm between the Census enumeration and the Quality Check enumeration. On the other hand, a rejection of the hypothesis that the census enumeration was complete and accurate would be appropriate with respect to the number of pigs on farms where the same definitional problem is not present.

Similar interpretations can be made for other individual items.

The estimates of the differences contain components due to sampling, definitional difficulties, changes in intentions, memory recall and the actual under-enumeration. These estimates, though providing a measure of under-enumeration, do not provide a means of adjusting census statistics. However, by indicating the relative stability of estimate by item, they should condition the use of the census statistics in any particular study.

In addition to the Census Division of the Dominion Bureau of Statistics, there are three other important agencies collecting agricultural statistics. Most important is the Agricultural Division of the Dominion Bureau of Statistics. This Division publishes a wider range of annual, quarterly, weekly and daily agricultural statistics. The Statistics Branch of the Board of Grain Commissioners has a major responsibility for the collection of grain marketing statistics most of which are released in cooperation with the Agriculture Division of the Dominion Bureau of Statistics. The last of these four agencies is the Market Information Section of the Canada Department of Agriculture. It tabulates data from the daily counts of livestock tradings and slaughterings, supervised by departmental inspection officers who are principally concerned with inspection and market controls in the livestock industry. It also collects and publishes a fairly wide range of data on fruit and vegetable marketings and prices, secured in a similar manner to the livestock statistics.

We now consider the scope of the estimates provided by the Agriculture Division of the Dominion Bureau of Statistics and the methods employed in collecting them. This description is based largely on published reports and internal memoranda of the Agriculture Division of the Dominion Bureau of Statistics. Agricultural statistics collected in Canada can be classified conveniently into the three categories: those pertaining to the farm level; those relating to distributive trades; and finally those dealing with the processing industries.

Statistics at the farm level are nearly all collected by the Dominion Bureau of Statistics and for certain of these co-operative arrangements are made with provinces for collection. The Census of Agriculture provides data on the basic structure and other characteristics of the farm universe. Distributive and processing statistics form an important part of the statistical system, not only as statistics in themselves, but also for use in constructing balance sheets of production and utilization of agricultural commodities. The balance sheet provides a check on current estimates. In some instances processing plants provide the acreages and production estimates.

The Decennial Census of Agriculture for Canada and the Quinquennial Census of Agriculture for the Prairie Provinces (from 1916 onward) and for Canada in 1956 provide the basic count of producing units, crop acreages and livestock numbers. They also provide information on the value of farm capital, use of land, tenure, machinery on farms and many other facts which are made available on a county or census division basis. The census in particular provides the beginning and ending 'benchmarks' for intercensal sample surveys and the list of farmers' names which constitutes the frame for such sampling. The Agriculture Division provides current estimates of crop acreages, livestock numbers, production and volume of farm commodities, output of food processing plants, indexes of farm prices and production, wage rates, farm income and expenditures and domestic disappearance of foods.

Most of the surveys of the Agricultural Division are of the mailed questionnaire type. The advantages of mail questionnaires are cheapness and relative rapidity in making estimates. The disadvantages are lack of control of the sample in non-random general surveys and, to a lesser extent, in special surveys. Being voluntary, the sample in these surveys is not necessarily random and it is thus not possible to determine the error of estimate from the data secured.

In the special surveys, the Division attempts to simulate a random sample. Selection of correspondents is made according to area representations, with due regard to size of farm. Respondents are given a subscription to a farm newspaper of their choice and also an illustrated annual D.B.S. publication. A response of 65 to 70 per cent is received from such correspondents and fairly accurate estimates are being produced at a relatively low cost. The sampling rate is usually small.

The various surveys undertaken by the Agriculture Division may be summarized as follows:

Complete coverage: *Monthly*—dairy factory production; stocks of meats, dairy products, eggs and fruits and vegetables; production of flour, oilseed crushings, sugar. *Annual*—fur farm and nursery production; greenhouse industries. *Quarterly*—uninspected livestock slaughter.

Partial coverage: *Non-random general surveys*—June and December surveys of livestock and crops and the like; surveys of maple products, honey and fruit and vegetables in those provinces where they are important. *Special surveys*—selected correspondents report on field crops, dairying, poultry, hogs and farm prices.

The semi-annual June and December surveys of crops and livestock are general farm surveys. In both, data are collected only for the respondent's own farm. The June survey, comprising 62 questions, includes inquiries on acreage sown to individual crops and farm inventories of livestock. Similar information is collected for livestock and poultry in the December survey, and in addition the questionnaire includes total wages paid to hired help and abandonment or diversion of acreages for four principal crops.

For seven of the provinces the mailing list or frame is a set of addressograph plates made up from names reported in the Census of Agriculture and regular mailing facilities are used.

For Ontario, questionnaires are distributed by Rural Postal Route system under special arrangement with the Post Office, and in Quebec through local schools. Census addressograph lists for all provinces will be available from the 1961 census returns. For Newfoundland no comprehensive agricultural estimates are yet provided, but an annual fall survey is conducted to obtain information for a few items of production. An attempt is made in both June and December surveys to place a questionnaire in the hands of every farmer in the country. Approximately a 25 per cent return is received. A systematic edit of the schedules is undertaken and the large and unusual types of farms are segregated. Tabulations are made of the 'paired' farms, that is, the farms for which reports were received in a previous survey, and for all farms. Separate tabulations are made for large farms and for unusual farms.

The paired farm ratio is the basis on which most current estimates have been made. This method requires a starting-point or 'benchmark' which is generally provided by the census. Thus for cattle in June 1951 the number reported in the census in Quebec might be 1,000,000. The paired farm ratio in June 1952 might indicate a 3 per cent increase and, therefore, the estimate for that date would be 1,030,000.

Since its inception, the Bureau in its agricultural work has, as noted, maintained close cooperation with provincial and federal government departments and with such agencies as the Board of Grain Commissioners, the Canadian Wheat Board and provincial milk control boards and similar organizations. Each province excepting the Atlantic Provinces and British Columbia employs an agricultural statistician who works closely with the Agriculture Division of the Dominion Bureau of Statistics. The Division maintains a regional agricultural office in the Atlantic region. The provincial agricultural statistics offices are autonomous units. There is no federal financial support and no federal statistical officers are attached to the provincial Departments. While having no formal control over the provincial statistical offices, the Bureau attempts through periodic conferences to co-ordinate the work of these offices so as to insure comparability of agricultural statistics through the country.

The interesting historical features of agricultural development are reflected in some of the tables of these series. Indeed this collection of agricultural statistics is designed primarily to bring together for the convenience of the user the historical series of wide general interest; and secondly, through brief descriptive texts and source notes, it provides a guide to the historical statistical sources on Canadian agriculture.

The statistics of a nation are an important and even indispensable tool in an accurate portrayal of the life of that nation. The extent to which statistical data are cited or taken account of in historical writings is obviously dependent upon the ready availability of data to the writer. An understandable lack of knowledge as to the existence of historical statistics on agriculture and the relative inaccessibility of the volumes in which many of them may be found have combined to prevent their more widespread and effective use.

The present work underlines the importance of further research in this field-work which could not be undertaken within the scope of the present project. Such studies would assuredly afford rich materials for inclusion in future revisions of the present volume.

GENERAL STATISTICS (Series L1–124)

L1–6. General statistics, farm population, farm holdings and tenure, Canada and by region, census dates, 1861 to 1956

SOURCE: for 1901 to 1956, *Census of Canada, 1956, Agriculture: Canada*, Bulletin 2-11, pp. 1-1, 1-2, 9-1, 9-10; *Newfoundland*, Bulletin 2-1, pp. 1-1, 2-1, 3-1; *Prince Edward Island*, Bulletin 2-2, pp. 1-1, 8-1; *Nova Scotia*, Bulletin 2-3, pp. 1-1, 9-1, 10-1; *New Brunswick*, Bulletin 2-4, pp. 1-1, 9-1, 10-1; *Quebec*, Bulletin 2-5, pp. 1-1, 9-1, 10-1; *Ontario*, Bulletin 2-6, pp. 1-1, 9-1, 10-1; *Manitoba*, Bulletin 2-7, pp. 1-1, 9-1, 10-1; *Saskatchewan*, Bulletin 2-8, pp. 1-1, 9-1, 10-1; *Alberta*, Bulletin 2-9, pp. 1-1, 9-1, 10-1; *British Columbia*, Bulletin 2-10, pp. 1-1, 9-1, 10-1; *Census of the Prairie Provinces, 1946 Agriculture*, pp. 4 and 5: for 1851 to 1891, *Census of Canada, 1941*, vol. VIII, *Agriculture, Part I* and *Part II*, table 1 for each province; *Census of Canada, 1931*, vol. VIII, *Agriculture*, pp. xxvii–xxviii; *Census of Canada, 1891*, vol. 4, p. 15; *Census of Canada, 1871*, vol. 4, pp. 254–403.

See Section A of this volume for the dates of censuses.

The data presented in this table represent farm population, numbers of farms and tenure of farms for Canada and regions. For the last two census years, 1951 and 1956, the figures for the Maritimes include Newfoundland. With respect to the numbers of farms, deductions were made for plots under one acre in the census years 1891, 1901 and 1911, when possible, in order to render numbers of farms data comparable with the later censuses. The numbers of plots deducted in this adjustment are as in the following table. Apparently, the data were not available to make the adjustment for Quebec in 1891 and no adjustment for it is made in that year, nor for the very small numbers in the Territories in that year.

Deductions of plots under 1 acre, Canada and by province, census years, 1891 to 1911

(numbers of plots)

	1911	1901	1891
Canada	30,141	33,615	78,275
Prince Edward Island	256	266	558
Nova Scotia	1,143	1,555	4,521
New Brunswick	455	577	2,259
Quebec	9,990	10,489	—
Ontario	14,693	20,073	69,413
Manitoba	1,278	243	563
Saskatchewan	317	167	—
Alberta	500	7	—
British Columbia	1,509	238	961

SOURCE: *Census of Canada, 1941*, Agriculture, vols. VII and VIII, table 1 and footnotes.

The data for 1861 relate to Lower Canada and Upper Canada respectively as Quebec and Ontario were known at that time.

Since 1931, but not including 1936 or 1946, the Census of the Prairie Provinces has included the Yukon and Northwest Territories. Farms on Indian Reserves were not included in 1911, 1921 and 1926. In the 1871 and 1881 censuses, statistics were collected for the Province of Manitoba and for the territories of Alberta, Saskatchewan and Assiniboia. In 1891 and 1901, the data for the Prairie Provinces refer to the province of Manitoba and the territories of Alberta and Saskatchewan. The latter territories became provinces of Canada in 1905 and thus, from the 1911 census onwards, the data represent the Provinces of Manitoba, Saskatchewan and Alberta.

There were no farm population data for Canada before the 1931 census. In this series, the farm population refers to all persons living on a farm regardless of occupation. There has been a gradual decline in the farm population since 1931, though not for all provinces, e.g. Quebec, Alberta and British Columbia.

For the definition of a farm see the General Note. Until 1956 the term 'occupied farm' was used. By that time the numbers of commuting farmers—those living in a nearby town and commuting to their farms—had risen to such an extent in some Prairie areas that the term 'occupied farm' no longer described all operating units. It is interesting that in the 1941 and 1951 censuses the numbers of 'non-resident' farms were counted.

The number of farms increased until 1941; however, there has been a significant decline since the Second World War. The most striking trend in land tenure is reflected in the significant increase in 'owner-tenant' operations in the Prairie Provinces.

L7–14. General statistics, use of land in farms, Canada and by region, census dates, 1851 to 1956

SOURCE: for 1901 to 1956, the same source bulletins as for series L1–6, the material being found on p. 1–1 and 1–2 in each bulletin; *Census of the Prairie Provinces, 1946, Agriculture,* pp. 4–5; for 1861 to 1891, *Census of Canada, 1890–91,* vol. 2, pp. 245–349 and vol. IV; *Census of Canada, 1880–81,* vol. 3, table XXII; *Census of Canada, 1870–71,* vol. 4.

The most significant series in the table is that concerned with the area of improved land under crops. It reflects the periods of most rapid growth of Canadian agriculture and the slow expansion of crop acreage since 1941.

Prior to 1881, the data are primarily for Quebec and Ontario, or rather for Lower and Upper Canada respectively. It will also be noted that the data for Quebec for the 1861 census are expressed not in thousands of acres but rather in thousands of arpents, where 1 acre = 1.183 arpents.

In the 1891 census in Quebec, the areas reported in arpents were not corrected to acres as was done in the other censuses. The areas for Quebec are thus a combination of arpents for that part of the province using the arpent as the unit of measurement and acres for the remainder of the province. The *Census of Canada, 1901,* vol. II, p. x, table 3, gives an estimate of the area under crops corrected to acres as 4,064,716 acres.

The 1891, 1881 and 1871 definitions are probably not entirely comparable to those used later. For example, it seems likely that some land classified as improved pasture in the earlier years was classified as woodlands or other unimproved land in later years.

Previous to the 1911 census, the data for the Prairie Provinces relate to the province of Manitoba and the territories of Alberta, Assiniboia and Saskatchewan. The data indicate that for this region there was a rapid increase in the area in farms through the 1920's and that since then the area has tended to become fairly stable. Land in crops has increased relatively slowly while there has been a fairly rapid increase in summer-fallow acreage. These data thus reflect an important change in agricultural practice. Regionally there are differences; for example the area in farms in the Prairie Provinces increased by about 1,500,000 from 1951 to 1956, whereas in the Eastern Canadian regions there have been small reductions.

L15–38. General statistics, current values of farm capital, Canada and by regions, 1901 to 1960

SOURCE: for 1901, 1911 and 1921, *Census of Canada, 1921,* vol. v, table 5, pp. 5–6; for 1917 to 1920, *Canada Year Book, 1920,* pp. 188–267; for 1922 to 1927, *Canada Year Book, 1929,* pp. 35–6, 212–84; for 1928 to 1934, Dominion Bureau of Statistics, *Monthly Bulletin of Agricultural Statistics,* issues for 1929 to 1939; for 1935 to 1940, Dominion Bureau of Statistics, the files of the Agriculture Division; for 1941 to 1956, *Quarterly Bulletin of Agricultural Statistics, January–March, 1959,* pp. 23–6; for 1957 to 1960, Dominion Bureau of Statistics, files of the Agriculture Division. Material was also provided by the Agriculture Division, D.B.S. to adjust the values given for livestock and poultry in the source for 1921 to 1934 to make them comparable with the data from 1935 onward. This meant adding the value of poultry in some years in which they were excluded and the value of fur farm animals. The changes in the poultry series meant that the totals of farm capital for the period concerned were also adjusted.

These annual values are estimated from reports on transactions reported by selected correspondents over the country.

The methods employed are essentially the same as those detailed later in considering farm income statistics. It is apparent that the annual estimates have used the census as a general benchmark in 1931, 1941 and 1951, and equally apparent that this was not done in 1921. While the census represents a satisfactory way to describe the universe (numbers of farms, acreages, of various machines, of livestock and buildings), values such as capital cannot likely be secured with a desired degree of accuracy by census enumeration.

L39–42. General statistics, current values of farm capital, Ontario, 1883 to 1900

SOURCE: *Statistical Yearbook, 1894,* p. 361; *1895,* p. 303; *1898,* p. 74; *1904,* p. 106.

These data are for Ontario only and were collected by provincial agencies, but published in various numbers of the *Statistical Yearbook* (Ottawa). Data on a provincial and national basis appear first in the 1901 census and decennially thereafter.

L43–66. General statistics, farm labour, employment and wages, males aged 14 and over, Canada and by region, 1891 to 1960

SOURCE: series L43–45, for 1946 to 1960, Dominion Bureau of Statistics, *The Labour Force, September, 1960,* pp. 4–12, and *The Labour Force, June, 1962,* p. 4; employment data by regions for 1946 to 1960 from unpublished material provided by D.B.S.; wage rates from D.B.S., *Quarterly Bulletin of Agricultural Statistics,* issues for July–September of each year 1948 to 1961; for decennial census data, 1891 to 1951 material provided by George Haythorne, federal Department of Labour, from decennial census volumes. The latter are the data on which are based the charts in George V. Haythorne, *Labour in Canadian Agriculture,* Harvard Studies in Labor and Agriculture (Cambridge, Massachusetts, distributed by the Harvard University Press, 1960). Haythorne's sources were: *Census of Canada, 1951,* vol. IV, table 3; *Census of Canada, 1941,* vol. VII, tables 3 and 4; *Census of Canada, 1931,* vol. VII, table 40; *Census of Canada, 1921,* vol. IV, tables 1 and 4; *Census of Canada, 1911,* vol. VI, tables 1 and 5; *Occupation and Industry Trends in Canada,* SP-8, 1954, table 7.

In 1901 classification by occupations was not made for the provinces in the census. Haythorne made estimates based on national totals distributed in relation to the number of farms in each province in the case of farm operators; in relation to the number of weeks of hired labour in the case of paid workers; and with the residual in each case taken as the number of unpaid family workers. Provincial totals of all agricultural workers are given in *Occupation and Industry Trends in Canada,* SP-8, 1954, table 5. The census date was near 1 April in 1891 and 1901 and near 1 June from 1911 to 1951.

In Haythorne's data for 1951, farm operators (not given here) and total farm employment are from table 7 of *Occupation and Industry Trends in Canada,* which is based on an occupational rather than an industrial classification. Wage earners and unpaid family workers data are from *Census of Canada, 1951,* vol. IV, p. xii, table 3, which is based on an industry classification. Haythorne assumed that the number of paid workers would be approximately the same in the two classifications but adjusted the number of unpaid family workers upward to make the components add to the total. (For an explanation of the differences between the two classifications see *Census of Canada, 1951,* vol. IV, p. xii.)

Since 1945 D.B.S. has conducted quarterly surveys of all industry groups in the Canadian labour force to obtain data on employment characteristics. Since November 1952 these surveys have been conducted each month. On questions of method and reliability of these surveys, the reader is referred to the general note of the labour force section, Section C. See

Section C for the distinction also between labour force survey and decennial census concepts.

The regional data for numbers of unpaid family workers and of paid workers, obtained in the labour force survey for 1946 to 1960, are of a lower order of reliability than total male farm employment by regions or all employment series for Canada, owing to the relative smallness of the numbers of unpaid family workers or paid workers in the sample in each region.

The D.B.S. estimates wage rates of paid farm labourers three times per year based on mail questionnaire sample surveys of selected farmer correspondents. Separate estimates are made for (a) with board and (b) without board for each of (1) hired by the hour, (2) hired by the day, (3) hired by the month and (4) hired by the year. The total wages paid during the calendar year to farm labourers is estimated annually from mail questionnaire sample surveys of farmers, but is used only for annual projection of the Census of Agriculture enumeration of the farm wage bill. This in turn is used in estimating this category of costs in deriving estimates of net farm income.

L67–72. General statistics, income from farming operations, Canada, 1926 to 1960

SOURCE: for 1926 to 1955, D.B.S., *Handbook of Agricultural Statistics, Part II, Farm Income*, revised edition, p. 26; for 1956 to 1960, data provided by the Agriculture Division, D.B.S. These data are published regularly in D.B.S., *Farm Net Income* (annual) and D.B.S., *Quarterly Bulletin of Agricultural Statistics*.

The estimates in this and the following three tables measure that income accruing to farm operators and their unpaid family help as a result of their farming operations, that is, returns for management and labour services to farmers and their unpaid family help, and returns on their equity in the capital invested in the farm enterprise. These estimates do not include income obtained by farmers from sources other than the farms they operate, nor do they cover all income originating in agriculture. Three types of income originating in agriculture which are excluded from these estimates are: (1) net farm rent, (2) interest payments on farm mortgages and agreements of sale, and (3) wages paid to hired farm help.

Realized gross income, series L70, is obtained by summing the cash income obtained from the sale of farm products, income in kind and supplementary payments. Cash income from the sale of farm products includes Canadian Wheat Board participation payments, subsidies, net cash advances on farm stored grains in Western Canada and deficiency payments. Income in kind is made up of all farm produce grown on farms and consumed in farm homes and the imputed rental value of the farm home. It also includes the value of those products obtained from the farm woodlot and used in either the farm home or the farm business.

Supplementary payments are payments made under the provisions of such legislation as the Prairie Farm Assistance Act, the Western Grain Producers' Acreage Payment Plan and the Federal Provincial Emergency Unthreshed Grain Assistance Act.

In the preparation of farm net income estimates, two separate series were developed: (1) realized net income of farm operators from farming operations, series L71, and (2) total net income of farm operators from farming operations, series L72. Realized net farm income is the difference between realized gross farm income and the sum of operating expenses and depreciation charges. One drawback in the estimates of realized net farm income is that the gross income measure on which it is based omits inventory changes; thus realized net farm income fails to reflect total production in any year for which operating expenses

and depreciation charges have been incurred. To provide an estimate of net income arising from production in any given calendar year an inventory adjustment is made and the resultant estimate is termed total net income, series L72.

The methods employed in preparing estimates of cash farm income naturally vary with the organization of marketing facilities for various products. The sources of information used in the calculation of the principal components of cash farm income estimates are considered next. Data required to estimate the physical quantities of farm products sold off farms and information about the various payments associated with farm production are obtained from government agencies such as the Canadian Wheat Board, the Board of Grain Commissioners, Departments of Agriculture, the Census of Agriculture, and are used in conjunction with periodic D.B.S. surveys of production and disposition of crops, livestock and animal products and from marketing boards and processors of agricultural products. Most of the prices used in the valuation of farm product sales are obtained by means of a monthly mail-questionnaire survey of several thousand farmers situated across Canada. Some prices are obtained from processors of farm products and some from the federal and provincial Departments of Agriculture.

The sources of information for income in kind are the Census of Agriculture, together with periodic Bureau surveys of production and disposition of crops, livestock and animal products. The home consumed produce is valued at the price the farmer would have received had it been sold. House rent is imputed on the basis of the actual cost of maintaining the farm home and was calculated by making an allowance for repairs, depreciation, returns on investment and taxes.

Estimates of supplementary payments are obtained from the various government agencies administering the legislation under which these payments are made. Livestock inventories are based on the Census of Agriculture projected according to the information obtained from the December survey of livestock numbers (see the general note to this section). Grain inventories are obtained by means of a mail-questionnaire survey of a selected list of farmers. Prices used to value the change in inventories of grain are those prices collected through the monthly mail-questionnaire surveys of farm prices. Changes in inventories of livestock are valued by means of information obtained from the June and December surveys of values per head of livestock and poultry.

The sources of information used to estimate operating expenses and depreciation charges include: Census of Agriculture; annual census of those industries serving agriculture, such as the feeds industry and the farm machinery manufacturers and distributors; farm management surveys; Departments of Agriculture; mail-questionnaire surveys; Prices Division and the Public Finance and Transportation Division of the D.B.S.

Considering the many opportunities that exist for checking quantity and price data from more than one source, as well as the basic methods employed, it is considered that Canadian farm income data possess a good degree of reliability.

The data are usually revised somewhat after they first appear.

L73–77. General statistics, cash income from the sale of farm products by commodity groups, Canada, 1926 to 1960

SOURCE: for 1926 to 1955, D.B.S., *Handbook of Agricultural Statistics, Part II, Farm Income*, revised edition, pp. 37–57; for 1956 to 1960, revised data provided by the Agriculture Division, D.B.S. These data regularly appear in D.B.S., *Farm Cash Income* (quarterly and annual) and *Quarterly Bulletin of Agricultural Statistics*.

See the note to series L67–72.

L 78–82. General statistics, cash income from the sale of farm products, by region, 1926 to 1960

SOURCE: for 1926 to 1955, D.B.S., *Handbook of Agricultural Statistics, Part II, Farm Income*, revised edition, pp. 37–57; for 1956 to 1960, revised data provided by the Agriculture Division, D.B.S. These data appear regularly in the current sources given for series L 73–77.

See the note to series L 67–72.

L 83–87. General statistics, realized net income of farm operators from farming operations, by region, 1926 to 1960

SOURCE: for 1926 to 1957, D.B.S., *Handbook of Agricultural Statistics, Part II, Farm Income*, revised edition, pp. 26–35; for 1958 to 1960, revised data provided by the Agriculture Division, D.B.S. These data appear regularly in D.B.S., *Farm Net Income* (annual) and *Quarterly Bulletin of Agricultural Statistics*.

See the note to series L 67–72.

L 88–97. General statistics, indexes of farm prices and costs, Canada, 1913 to 1960

SOURCE: for 1913 to 1959, the following publications of the Dominion Bureau of Statistics: *Prices and Price Indexes, 1949–1952*, p. 93; for years 1913 to 1952, *Livestock Market Review, 1953 Supplement*, p. 34; *Canadian Statistical Review, 1953 Supplement*, p. 104; *Indexes of Farm Prices of Agricultural Products*, issues for 1956, No. 1 and October 1960; *Livestock Market Review 1960*, p. 34; *Canadian Statistical Review, July 1959*, pp. 32, 52, *December 1961*, pp. 25, 47; for 1960, revised data provided by the Agriculture Division, D.B.S.

The index of commodities and services used by farmers is designed to measure the percentage change through time in the cost of purchasing a constant or equivalent 'basket' of goods and services representing the commodities and services used by Canadian farm families for purposes of operating their farms and for family living. It is a 'price' index and expresses current prices as a percentage of prices in 1935-1939. The 'basket' of goods and services included in the index was originally based on purchases reported in a national survey of Canadian farmers in 1938 but has been modified over the years by introduction of items which have become important in farm production and farm living since that time. However, a total revision of the weighting system is called for, and is now projected on the basis of a comprehensive 1958 survey.

The general index is expressed as a composite index inclusive of equipment and materials, tax and interest rates, farm wage rates, farm family living costs and farm machinery. The index is also published exclusive of living costs.

Each item in the index is weighted by its relative importance in farm operating and family living costs in the base period, 1938, measured at retail prices. The indexes are published three times a year, January, April and August. Exceptions to the thrice yearly price collection are groceries, meats and livestock feeds which are priced monthly, and taxes and interest rates which are priced annually. Wage rates are provided by surveys of correspondents who report to the Agricultural Division of D.B.S. Mortgage interest rates and taxes are obtained from the same source. Farm implement and machinery prices are received from implement manufacturers who supply a large part of the farm market. Fertilizer, seed and binder twine prices are obtained from the large firms or organizations supplying these items. Prices for a large number of clothing, household equipment and sundry items are obtained from mail order catalogues. All other items not specifically mentioned above are priced at selected retail outlets serving farm communities.

This is one of the most widely used indexes in the entire field of agricultural statistics.

L 98–113. General statistics, wholesale market prices of major agricultural products, by selected markets, 1855 to 1960

SOURCE: Taylor and Michell, *Statistical Contributions to Canadian Economic History*, vol. II, pp. 47–88; and the following publications of the Dominion Bureau of Statistics: *Prices and Price Indexes*, successive issues; *Livestock and Animal Product Statistics, 1960*, pp. 23, 24, 43, 44, 58, 66, 73; and unpublished data from the Dominion Bureau of Statistics and the Market Information Section of the Canada Department of Agriculture.

This table contains estimates of wholesale market prices for important farm products. While the table stub reads in terms of calendar years, from 1868 data for crops are on a crop year basis. Thus, opposite 1960, the prices for crops relate to the 1960–1 crop years. From 1858 to 1867 the estimates are average prices of fall wheat at Toronto. From 1868 to 1888 the estimates are average prices of Winter No. 2 white at Toronto and for 1889 to 1904 the prices here are for No. 1 Northern at Winnipeg. From 1905 the prices refer to the Winnipeg cash closing No. 1 Northern, basis in store, Fort William. For oats, the data from 1858 to 1904 refer to Ontario No. 2 white in Toronto, whereas from 1905 the grade refers to Winnipeg cash closing price No. 2 C.W., basis in store, Fort William. For barley, from 1858 to 1888 the prices are based on Toronto. No grade is specified. From 1889 to 1904 they are Western Malting barley at Winnipeg. From 1905 the prices refer to Winnipeg cash closing No. 3 C.W., basis in store, Fort William. The prices of rye from 1858 to 1919 refer to Ontario No. 2 at Toronto; and from 1920 onwards refer to the Winnipeg cash closing No. 2 C.W., basis in store, Fort William. Prices for flax are recorded from 1920 and refer to the Winnipeg cash closing No. 1 C.W.

The prices of steers recorded in this table are for different grades over the years. From 1890 to 1918 they refer to choice butcher steers; from 1919 to 1929 to good steers, 1000–1200 pounds; from 1930 to 1935 to good and choice steers over 1050 pounds; from 1935 to 1945 to good steers over 1050 pounds; from 1949 to 1957 to good steers over 1000 pounds; and from 1958 to 1960 to good steers, all weights.

For the years 1890 to 1912 hog prices refer to choice selects; 1913 to 1922 to selects; 1923 to 1929 to thick smooth; 1930 to 1939 to bacon grade; 1940 to August 1959 B1, dressed; and September 1959 to 1960 to grade B dressed. From 1890 to 1939 prices are on a live basis and from 1940 to 1960 on a dressed basis. Until 1934 all hogs were graded alive; in that year carcass grading was inaugurated and in October 1940 live grading was discontinued. The conversion rate is .75 pounds of dressed hogs to one pound, live weight. The prices of sheep from 1871 to 1911 refer to export ewes; for 1912 to light ewes; from 1913 to 1921 to choice sheep; 1922 to 1948 to good handy-weight sheep; and since 1949 to good sheep. The prices for steers, hogs and sheep from 1890 to 1910 were taken from the *Toronto Globe*, as reported in Taylor and Michell, *op. cit.*; from 1890 to 1910 they are averages of quotations on the first market day of each month; and from 1911 to 1918, averages of quotations on the first market day of each week. From 1919 to 1960 the prices are weighted averages compiled by the Canada Department of Agriculture.

The wholesale prices tabulated for eggs record the values of a dozen grade A large in the Montreal market. Data for butter are a record of the prices of the 1st grade creamery prints in the Montreal market. Data for these were recorded as far back as 1914.

The prices of potatoes, series L 111–113, are from unpublished data of the Market Information Service, Canada Department of Agriculture, and relate to average seasonal wholesale prices in these markets.

L114–118. General statistics, index numbers of wholesale prices of selected farm products, 1913 to 1960

SOURCE: for 1913 to 1952, D.B.S., *Prices and Price Indexes, 1949–1952*, grains, p. 20; livestock, p. 24; fresh meats, milk and its products and eggs, p. 26; for 1953, D.B.S., *Prices and Price Indexes, December 1954*, grains, p. 9; livestock, fresh meats, milk and its products and eggs, p. 10; for 1954, D.B.S., *Prices and Price Indexes, December 1955*, grains, p. 9; livestock, fresh meats, milk and its products and eggs, p. 10; for 1955, D.B.S., *Prices and Price Indexes, August 1956*, grains, p. 9; livestock, fresh meats, milk and its products and eggs, p. 10; for 1956, D.B.S., *Prices and Price Indexes, November 1957*, grains, p. 8; livestock, fresh meats, milk and its products and eggs, p. 9; for 1957, D.B.S., *Prices and Price Indexes, July 1958*, grains, p. 7; livestock, fresh meats, milk and its products and eggs, p. 8; for 1958 to 1960, D.B.S., *Prices and Price Indexes, April 1961*, grains, livestock, milk and its products, fresh meats and eggs, p. 13.

This table presents indexes of five components of the general wholesale price index for agricultural products presented in series J77. The principal use for the wholesale price index of Canadian Farm Products is as a measurement of pure price change for prices received by farmers at terminal markets. The movement of this series may be compared through time with the nonagricultural components of the general index of wholesale prices.

The collection of prices for these items hinges on a heterogeneous list of sources. Fundamental to this was the establishment of a schedule in which the items included were set out in precise terms, that is, grade, terms of sale, unit of sale, size of shipment, geographical point of sale, etc. Since these indexes are components of the general index of wholesale prices, readers are referred to Section J for consideration of methodology and to series J75–83 for the general index of wholesale prices of farm products and for field products and animal products components of it.

L119–124. General statistics, indexes of physical volume of agricultural production, Canada and by region, 1935 to 1960

SOURCE: for 1935 to 1944, D.B.S., *Index of Farm Production, 1956*, p. 2; for 1945 to 1958, D.B.S., *Index of Farm Production, 1960*, p. 3; for 1959 and 1960 revised data from the Agriculture Division, D.B.S.

The index numbers of physical volume of agricultural production have been prepared regionally since 1935. In constructing the index no consideration is given to changes occurring in the quality of production from year to year; it is generally assumed that the influence of this factor is negligible. This would not appear to be true when an item as important in the index as the Western wheat crop is of low quality. Consequently, when adverse weather conditions in 1950, wet weather and frost in 1951, and the worst rust epidemic on record plus unfavourable weather conditions in 1954 significantly reduced the quality of the wheat crop in those years, the index was adjusted for these factors.

In constructing the index, provision is made to avoid double counting of farm production. Within a province such double counting would occur when feed grains credited to field crop production are fed to livestock and appear later as livestock and livestock products. Interprovincially, this duplication could appear when feed grains produced in one province are fed in another and when feeder cattle raised in one section of the country are shipped to another for finishing.

The base period used is the five-year period 1935–1939. The index is based on a fixed base weighted aggregative formula. The

commodities included in the index are the major items of agricultural production which are sold through commercial channels and/or consumed in farm homes. Omitted, for the most part, are commodities which are used almost entirely as feed for livestock and those relatively insignificant products for which there is little reliable information regarding production and prices.

CROP STATISTICS (Series L125–166)

L125–138. Crop statistics, grain and hay, acreage and production, Canada, crop years, 1852 to 1960

SOURCE: *Statistical Year Book, 1904*, pp. 1–104; D.B.S., *Handbook of Agricultural Statistics, Part I, Field Crops, 1908–1958*, pp. 1, 18, 30, 42, 60, 102; D.B.S., *Quarterly Bulletin of Agricultural Statistics*, January–March 1959, pp. 29, 30, and 1960, pp. 28, 29. See also the supplementary note on p. 350.

The figures recorded are taken mainly from the Handbook of Agricultural Statistics as the latter goes back to 1908–9. Prior to 1908 there are no annual data for these crops, other than wheat; thus for this earlier period data are for census years only. There are some other earlier statistics on a provincial basis.

L139–146. Crop statistics, wheat, production, imports, exports and home consumption, Canada, crop years, 1869 to 1961

SOURCE: for 1868 to 1955, D.B.S., *Monthly Bulletin of Agricultural Statistics*, September 1937, p. 275; D.B.S., *Handbook of Agricultural Statistics, Part I, Field Crops*, p. 1; *Report of the Canadian Wheat Board Crop Year, 1954–55*, pp. 1–6; D.B.S., *Grain Trade of Canada, 1959–1960*, pp. 11, 88, 104; for 1956 to 1961, revised data from the Agriculture Division D.B.S., including intercensal revisions. The Agriculture Division also supplied revised data for apparent home consumption, series L146 for 1922 to 1937 and for a few other individual entries for all series L139–146 for the period before 1956. See also the supplementary note on page 350.

These series were originally published in the September 1937 issues of the Monthly Bulletin of Agricultural Statistics. There were no contemporary production estimates available for the years 1868–9 to 1878–9 exclusive of 1870–1. Production data for these years were derived by allowing a *per capita* disappearance of 6½ bushels per year for domestic human consumption, seed, and other requirements. For the years 1880–1 to 1907–8 the wheat estimates were compiled by using data from the provincial Departments of Agriculture and census data when available and making allowances for the remaining provinces where no crop-reporting systems had been established. These were established as follows: Ontario 1882, Manitoba 1883, New Brunswick 1897, Saskatchewan and Alberta 1898, Prince Edward Island 1907, Nova Scotia and Quebec 1908, British Columbia 1911.

Commencing with 1908, the annual estimates are those of the Census and Statistics Office and later the Dominion Bureau of Statistics in cooperation with the provincial Departments of Agriculture.

In calculating the apparent home consumption of wheat for the years prior to 1930, total account was not taken of changes in the annual carry-over stocks of wheat and wheat flour. Carry-over data on wheat stocks became available in 1921, and on wheat flour stocks in 1926. Net changes in these stocks have been allowed for in the years for which they are available. The low figures for apparent home consumption for the years 1924 and 1925 are probably due to under-estimates of the 1924 and 1925 crops. No long-term revision of the official estimates of production for the years 1908 to 1930 has yet been made.

L147–166. Crop statistics, special crops, production and farm value, Canada, crop years, selected years 1720 to 1901 and 1909 to 1960

SOURCE: for 1909 to 1960, D.B.S., *Handbook of Agricultural Statistics*, Part I, *Field Crops*, pp. 1, 18, 30, 42, 60, 102; D.B.S., *Quarterly Bulletin of Agricultural Statistics, January–March 1960*, pp. 28, 29, *January–March 1959*, pp. 29, 30; for decennial census years, 1871 to 1901, *Census of Canada* (Agriculture), decennially, 1871 to 1911; for years before 1871, *Census of Canada, 1871*, vol. 4, pp. 254–367. The Agriculture Division, D.B.S., provided revised data for various entries from 1957 onward. See also the supplementary note on page 350.

LIVESTOCK AND LIVESTOCK PRODUCT STATISTICS (Series L167–264)

L167–232. Livestock statistics, number on farms and farm values at 1 June, Canada and by region, 1871 to 1960

SOURCE: D.B.S., *Livestock and Animal Product Statistics, Numbers and Values of Livestock, 1906–43*, pp. 75–106; D.B.S., *Production and Value of Shorn Wool, 1920–43*; D.B.S., *Livestock and Animal Products Statistics, 1960*, pp. 10, 11, 35, 50, 64. Data on number of hens and chickens were prepared by the Agriculture Division, D.B.S., from the *Quarterly Bulletin of Agricultural Statistics, 1947*, p. 179, for years up to and including 1940 and from *Production of Poultry and Eggs* (annual) and especially the 1958 issue. The Agriculture Division also provided the data on the value of horses, of hogs and of sheep and lambs for the regions of Canada for 1940 to 1951, as well as assembling corrected figures in many instances in these series from 1951 to 1960. See also the supplementary note on p. 350.

The numbers of livestock on farms are compiled in the census years. The estimates of the intercensal years are based on survey questionnaires distributed to all farmers on 1 June each year and from which a return of approximately 20 per cent is received. For consideration of the methods employed in these surveys see the General note to this section. The census, 1871 to 1901, unlike the censuses since 1911, was conducted in early April; thus the data before and after 1911, being for different dates, are not comparable.

Total values of the various classes of livestock were revised by applying the values per head to the revised estimates of numbers on farms. Values per head are based on crop correspondents estimates, except in the census years.

L233–242. Livestock product statistics, estimated number slaughtered and weight of meat produced, Canada, 1871 to 1960

SOURCE: for 1871, *Census of Canada, 1870–71*, vol. 4, *Agriculture*, pp. 70–1, 254, 403; for 1881, *Census of Canada, 1880–81*, vol. 3; for 1891, *Census of Canada, 1890–91*, vol. 4; for 1920 to 1934, D.B.S., *Livestock and Animal Product Statistics, 1940*, cattle and calves, beef, p. 17, hogs and pork, p. 44, sheep and lambs, mutton and lamb, p. 65; for 1935 to 1940, D.B.S., *Livestock and Animal Product Statistics, 1954*, cattle and calves, p. 13, hogs, p. 36, pork, p. 36, sheep and lambs, mutton and lamb, p. 53; for 1941 to 1950, D.B.S., *Livestock and Animal Product Statistics, 1956*, cattle, calves and beef, p. 14, hogs and pork, p. 37, sheep and lambs, mutton and lambs, p. 54; for 1951 to 1958, D.B.S., *Livestock and Animal Product Statistics, 1959*, cattle and calves, beef, p. 15, hogs and pork, p. 37, sheep and lambs, mutton and lamb, p. 53; for 1959 and 1960, D.B.S., *Livestock and Animal Product Statistics, 1960*, cattle and calves, beef, p. 16, hogs and pork, p. 38, sheep and lambs, mutton and lamb, p. 53. Chicken meat is from D.B.S., *Production of Poultry and Eggs*, annual. Chicken meat was given for cold dressed weight until 1955; beginning in 1956, it was given as eviscerated weight. To make the series on chicken meat consistent throughout the data for 1940 to 1955 in the source were converted to eviscerated by using the factor eviscerated weight equals

77 per cent of cold dressed weight. See also the supplementary note on page 350.

Farm output of meat animals is estimated by a balance sheet approach: (beginning inventory plus births) minus (ending inventory plus death loss) equals farm output. This is corrected for duplication of feeder cattle movements. Farm output minus live exports plus direct imports for slaughter equals total slaughter in Canada. Total slaughter minus inspected slaughter equals uninspected slaughter. Surveys of uninspected slaughtering plants are also made.

L243–252. Livestock product statistics, milk production and disposition of milk, Canada, 1920 to 1960

SOURCE: series L243, 249, 251, and 252, for 1920 to 1939, *Dairy Statistics of Canada, 1946*, p. 6; for 1940 to 1949, *ibid. 1955*, p. 28; for 1950 to 1951, *ibid. 1953*, p. 11; for 1952 to 1956, *ibid. 1957*, p. 9; for 1957, *ibid. 1960*, p. 7; for 1958 to 1960, *ibid. 1961*, p. 7; series L244–247, for 1920 to 1944, D.B.S., unpublished; for 1945 to 1947, *ibid. 1948*, p. 6; for 1952 to 1956, *ibid. 1957*, p. 11; for 1957, *ibid. 1960*, p. 8; for 1958 to 1960, *ibid. 1961*, p. 8. Series 248, for 1920 to 1956, D.B.S., unpublished; for 1957 to 1960, same as series L244–247. Series L250, for 1920 to 1939, D.B.S., unpublished; for 1940 to 1949, *Dairy Statistics, 1955*, p. 28; for 1950 to 1951, *ibid.* p. 11; for 1952 to 1956, *ibid. 1957*, p. 9; for 1957, *ibid. 1960*, p. 7; for 1958 to 1960, *ibid. 1961*, p. 7. See also the supplementary note on page 350.

Milk production estimates are made monthly for all provinces of Canada except Newfoundland for five different utilization classifications as follows: (1) milk equivalent of dairy factory products; (2) fluid milk and cream sold to consumers; (3) milk equivalent of farm-made butter; (4) milk used in farm homes (on farms that have milk cows); and (5) whole milk fed to livestock. The provincial estimate for milk production is taken to be the sum of milk used in these five classifications. This procedure, rather than an estimate based on total number of milk cows and production per cow, has been followed because it is possible to achieve virtually full coverage in monthly reports for all dairy factory products and from a preponderant proportion of fluid milk distributing plants. Since factory production utilizes almost 60 per cent of the total milk produced, and fluid sales another 30 per cent, the proportion of production subject to estimate by sampling procedures is small. Farm use components, namely, farm butter made, milk used in farm homes and milk fed to livestock are estimated monthly from reports submitted by a corps of some 5,500 farm correspondents. The estimate is made by calculating direction and extent of change in each succeeding month from an established benchmark month. The fluid sales component is estimated similarly from plant reports covering all controlled and numerous other market areas. The benchmarks are derived from census and market data.

L253–260. Livestock product statistics, milk products, production, Canada, selected years 1850 to 1915 and 1916 to 1960

SOURCE: series L253, for 1900 to 1919, D.B.S., *Dairy Products Industries, 1958*, p. 32; for 1920 to 1945, D.B.S., *Dairy Statistics, 1946*, p. 8; for 1946 to 1949, *ibid. 1950*, p. 6; for 1950 to 1951, *ibid. 1953*, p. 14; for 1952 to 1956, *ibid. 1957*, p. 12; for 1957, *ibid. 1960*, p. 15; for 1958 to 1960, *ibid. 1961*, p. 15; series L254, for 1850 to 1910, decennial censuses; for 1920 to 1960, same as series 253; series L255, for 1850 to 1910, same as L254; for 1920 to 1946, same as series L253; for 1946 to 1948, *Dairy Statistics, 1948*, p. 2; for 1949, D.B.S., unpublished; series L256, for 1920 to 1938, *Dairy Statistics, 1946*, p. 8; for 1939 to 1944, D.B.S., unpublished; for 1945 to 1948, *Dairy Statistics, 1949*, p. 7; for 1949 to 1951, *ibid. 1952*, p. 8; for 1952 to 1956, *ibid. 1957*, p. 13; for 1957, *ibid. 1960*, p. 15; for 1958 to 1960, *ibid. 1961*, p. 15; series L257, for 1920 to 1945, *ibid. 1946*, p. 14;

for 1946 to 1949, *ibid. 1950*, p. 6; for 1950 to 1951, *ibid. 1953*, p. 14; for 1952 to 1956, *ibid. 1957*, p. 12; for 1957, *ibid. 1960*, p. 19; for 1958 to 1960, *ibid. 1961*, p. 19; series L 258–260, for 1920 to 1945, *ibid. 1946*, p. 12; for 1946 to 1949, *ibid. 1950*, p. 12; for 1950 to 1951, *ibid. 1953*, p. 16; for 1952 to 1956, *ibid. 1957*, p. 14; for 1957, *ibid. 1960*, p. 17; for 1958 to 1960, *ibid. 1961*, p. 17. See also the supplementary note on page 350.

See the note to series L 243–252.

L 261–264. Livestock product statistics, butter and cheese, homemade production, selected years, 1847 to 1910

SOURCE: *Census of Canada, 1870–71*, vol. 4; *1880–81*, vol. 3; *1890–91*, vol. 4; *1901*, vol. II; *1911*, vol. IV.

See the note to series L 243–252.

EXPORTS AND DOMESTIC DISAPPEARANCE
(Series L 265–317)

L 265–271. Exports of major agricultural products, grains (except wheat), quantity and value, Canada, crop years, 1868 to 1960

SOURCE: for 1960, D.B.S., *Grain Trade of Canada, 1960*, pp. 95–7; for 1909 to 1959, D.B.S., *Handbook of Agricultural Statistics*, Part I, pp. 171–3; for earlier years, *Canada Year Book, 1910*, pp. 94–115; *The Statistical Year Book of Canada, 1904*, pp. 106–33; *The Statistical Year Book of Canada, 1901*, pp. 94–115.

Oats in these tables includes the oat equivalent of rolled oats and oatmeal.

The data provided for barley must be carefully observed as its method of collection has changed over the years. Those from 1908–9 onwards refer to barley and the barley equivalent of malt, whereas the previous records refer to barley only. The conversion factor is 1 bu. (36 lb.) of malt equals 1 bu. of barley. The figures in and after 1948 include both pot and pearl barley, the latter having been previously omitted. It must be particularly noted that the figures given under barley from the years 1868 to 1876 include rye. Thus there are no corresponding data for rye for these years. Rye includes the rye equivalent of rye flour since the year 1918 until this was discontinued in 1950.

L 272–293. Exports of major agricultural products, animals and animal products, quantity and value, Canada, 1868 to 1960

SOURCE: D.B.S., *Livestock and Animal Products Statistics, 1960*, pp. 30, 47, 62, 65, 71; D.B.S., *Livestock and Animal Products Statistics, 1959*, pp. 30, 31, 46, 61, 65, 74; *Canada Year Book, 1910*, pp. 58–137; *The Statistical Year Book of Canada, 1904*, pp. 106–33; *The Statistical Year Book of Canada, 1901*, pp. 94–115.

Beef includes fresh, chilled, frozen, pickled in barrels and the beef content of sausage and bolognas.

L 294–299. Exports of bacon, hams and lard, quantity and value, Canada, 1868 to 1910

SOURCE: *Canada Year Book, 1910*, pp. 58–137; *The Statistical Year Book of Canada, 1904*, pp. 106–33; *The Statistical Year Book of Canada, 1901*, pp. 94–113.

L 300–317. Domestic disappearance of food products, per capita, Canada, 1919 to 1960

SOURCE: for 1956 to 1960, D.B.S., *Quarterly Bulletin of Agricultural Statistics, October–December, 1961*, pp. 223–6, 252, *April–June 1961*, p. 125, *April–June 1960*, p. 119, *April–June 1959*, p. 123, *January–March 1958*, p. 51; for 1926 to 1955, D.B.S., *Handbook of Agricultural Statistics*, Part IV, *Food Consumption in Canada, 1926–1955* (Reference Paper No. 25), pp. 1–31; for 1924 and earlier, and for some series prior to 1935, data are from D.B.S., *Livestock and*

Animal Products, 1940: a considerable amount of revised data for years throughout the whole period were provided by the Agriculture Division, D.B.S. See also the supplementary note on page 350.

It should be noted, especially, that many of the entries for the whole period given in the sources were revised by the Agriculture Division, D.B.S., after the sources were published and the data were provided directly by the Agriculture Division, D.B.S. In particular, the entire series on fluid milk consumption, which represents fluid milk sales and farm-home consumed milk and cream, on a milk equivalent basis (series L 306), has been revised to make it consistent for the whole period: the revision does away with a wastage factor which had been in effect from 1920 to 1954 and makes other corrections. Some of the entries for evaporated whole milk (series L 307) have been revised. The revisions for cheese consumption were mainly for 1940 to 1945. The entire series of ice cream consumption, which represents gallons of ice cream converted to a poundage basis (series L 309), has been changed by use of a conversion factor of 5.5 pounds per gallon of ice cream instead of 5 pounds per gallon as had been used previously. Butter consumption has been revised in a large number of years throughout the period and potato consumption from 1941 to 1954. A smaller number of revisions were made in some of the other series.

The general procedure in this compilation was to start with an estimate of production at either the farm or processor level. Adjustments are made for beginning and year end inventories and for imports and exports to obtain total supplies. To obtain an estimate of apparent domestic disappearance, that portion of total supplies which is not used as human food was subtracted.

Apparent domestic disappearance figures calculated in this way (without allowance for waste in trade channels) represent what might be called 'the product weight' of each category of food moving into trade channels.

Much of the accuracy of disappearance data presented in this report depends upon the accuracy of the production estimates. This varies for different products. Production estimates of most foodstuffs are made up in part from the results of mail-questionnaire sample surveys of producers (farmers) and, in part, from statistics reported by firms handling the product at some stage of its journey from producer to consumer. One technique provides a check against the other.

For some foods, particularly vegetables and potatoes, almost complete reliance has to be placed upon the results of producer surveys since no other data exist for many of these products. With other foods, such as meats and dairy products, reports from handlers and processors, etc., can be used to check production estimates. One of the weaker links in the production estimates probably is that of self-supplied foods, that is, the quantities of garden produce, eggs and poultry, dairy products and other livestock products produced on farms and on nonfarm-properties and consumed by the producers.

MISCELLANEOUS AGRICULTURAL
STATISTICS (Series L 318–350)

L 318–329. Farm tractors, number on farms and estimated annual sales, 1921 to 1960

SOURCE: provided by the Agriculture Division, Dominion Bureau of Statistics. The Agriculture Division used the trade journal *Canadian Farm Implements* as the source of the data for tractor sales from 1921 to 1959. The sales data for 1960 are the figures prepared by the Division. The Dominion Bureau of Statistics has published data on tractor sales since 1937 but continued to use trade data until 1956 in estimating numbers of tractors on farms as the latter gave more complete regional coverage. From 1957 onward the Bureau has published sales with a provincial and regional breakdown regularly. The differences between the trade data and those prepared by the Bureau were usually not great enough to affect seriously the validity of the estimates of tractor numbers on farms for which they were used.

The basic counts of tractors on farms were obtained in the census of 1921, 1931, 1941, 1951 and 1956 (as at 1 June) for all provinces; in addition the quinquennial census of the Prairie Provinces provided counts for them at 1 June in 1926, 1936 and 1946. These are the data given for the census years.

The estimates of numbers on farms for intervening years are based in each case on adding sales to the previous year's number on farms and subtracting an estimate of the number of tractors retired. Estimates of the latter are made mainly by using data of the census counts and sales between census years.

The data for numbers on farms are revised after each new census is taken, for the intervening years since the last previous census, to make them consistent with census data. Revisions were not yet available for 1957 onward on the basis of the 1961 census data.

The data do not include either sales or numbers on farms of Newfoundland (except for 1960) or the Northwest Territories. Sales data are for calendar years.

L330–336. Number of implements on farms and number of farms reporting electric power, Canada and the Prairie Provinces, census dates 1871 and 1921 to 1956

SOURCE: for Canada, for 1921 to 1951, series L331 and L335, *Census of Canada, 1951*, vol. VI, *Agriculture*, part I, table 13, p. 131; for 1921 to 1956 for all other series, *Census of Canada, 1956*, Bulletin 2–11, table 1, pp. 1–1 and 1–2 except for series L330 for 1921, *Census of Canada, 1921*, vol. V, *Agriculture*, table 38, p. 58; for 1871, *Census of Canada, 1870–71*, vol. 3, table XXII, p. 118; for Prairie Provinces, for decennial census years, 1921 to 1951, series L331 and L335, *Census of Canada, 1951*, vol. VI, *Agriculture*, part II, table 13 for each province; for 1921 to 1956 for all other series, *Census of Canada, 1956*, Bulletins 2–7, 2–8 and 2–9, table 1 for each province except for series L330 for 1921, *Census of Canada, 1921*, vol. V, *Agriculture*, table 38, p. 58; for 1926, 1936 and 1946, *Census of the Prairie Provinces, 1946*, vol. IV, *Agriculture*, table 21, p. 18.

Data on farm machines and implements on farms were collected in the Census of 1871 and then not again until 1931, with the exception of automobiles and trucks and tractors for which a count began in 1921. In addition to the items included in the table, the 1871 census recorded 573,648 ploughs, harrows and cultivators, 68,003 horse rakes and 167,964 fanning mills. Other implements are also given in the censuses from 1931 onward.

L337–346. Grain elevator storage capacities, by type of elevator and by region, 1911 to 1960

SOURCE: Board of Grain Commissioners for Canada, *Grain Elevators in Canada*, annual, and predecessor issues under different titles.

These data are collected by the Board of Grain Commissioners as part of their administration of the regulations of the grain trade.

All grain elevators doing general business with the public must be licensed. The main reason for capacity being unlicensed is that it is not in use in the particular licence period. The amount of unlicensed capacity is ordinarily small but in a few years has been significant.

Country elevators receive grain from individual farmers; terminal elevators deal only with businesses or public bodies engaged in the grain trade.

L347–350. Four wage series for farm labour, Ontario, 1882 to 1908

SOURCE: *Annual Report of the Bureau of Industries for the Province of Ontario*, issue for each year.

The Ontario Bureau of Industries carried out an annual survey of farm wages in which annual and monthly wage rates with and without board were recorded. A large number of Bureau of Industries rural reporters collected data directly from farmers, markets, workers and local research groups in all parts of Ontario.

The report for 1886 included information concerning the size of sample used: for annual wages with and without board, 3,779 and 1,851 respectively; for monthly rates with and without board, 5,596 and 2,245 respectively. (See *Annual Report of the Bureau of Industries, 1886*, p. 170, footnote.) There is no indication of alteration in sample size here or in other reports and no indication of whether rates apply to summer or winter.

APPENDIX

EARLY COLONIAL AGRICULTURAL STATISTICS (Series L351–375)

General note

The following series, L351–375, are extensions backward of series L1–124, generally on a provincial basis. Extending back to 1667 they provide data about land use and acreages of specific crops and numbers of livestock in the early days of Canada's development. Most of these data were derived from the Census of 1871. Neither that volume nor other publications concerned with this period provide useful guides respecting the reliability of the data.

Data relating to the agriculture of Newfoundland extend back to 1845. It is interesting that the acreage of improved land in 1891 exceeded that of 1945. Later censuses carried out by D.B.S. show a further very sharp decline from the 1945 level. The 1956 Census also shows livestock numbers in 1956 to be only a fraction of those enumerated in 1945. Information on change in definitions or in enumeration methods which might account for these large declines could be secured from neither the D.B.S. nor the Newfoundland government. It is suggested that users of this series should not make comparisons between statistics gathered by the colonial administration of Newfoundland and those of the D.B.S.

L351–354. Land utilization in the colonial period

SOURCE: *Census of Canada, 1871*, vol. 4, pp. 10, 32, 66, 67, 100, 101, 102, 114, 116, 118, 119, 120, 124, 126, 128, 130, 131, 138; *Eleventh Census of Newfoundland, 1945* (1857–1945), pp. 1–20; *Quebec Statistical Yearbook, 1914*, pp. 100–8; *Census of Canada, 1911*, Bulletin IV, pp. 1–145.

L355–369. Agricultural production in the colonial period

SOURCE: same as series L351–354.

L370–375. Livestock on farms in the colonial period

SOURCE: same as series L351–354.

Series L372, other cattle, includes the numbers of oxen. Only for Upper Canada are the figures for oxen given separately for the years 1826 to 1841, 1861 and 1871, as seen in the following table.

The number of oxen included in other cattle for other provinces in isolated years are: for Nova Scotia, 32,214 in 1871; for New Brunswick, 11,132 in 1871 and 19,111 in 1861; for Quebec, 48,348 in 1871; for Assiniboia, 3,152 in 1857.

Number of oxen in Upper Canada, 1826 to 1841,
1861 and 1871

Year	Number of oxen
1871	47,941
1861	99,605
1841	49,940
1840	48,990
1839	47,491
1838	47,703
1837	48,453
1836	48,938
1835	46,080
1834	42,455
1833	41,870
1832	39,054
1831	36,131
1830	33,517
1829	33,332
1828	29,814
1827	29,081
1826	26,302

Supplementary note

Between the time of the original preparation of the data of this section and their appearance in the first page proof, the data for 1956 to 1960 of series L125–260 and of series L300–317 had been revised by the Agriculture Division, D.B.S., on the basis of data obtained in the 1961 census. The type has been reset and the revised data appear in this section. Most of the revised data had appeared in D.B.S. publications such as: *Handbook of Agricultural Statistics, Part I, Field Crops, 1908–63*; *Quarterly Bulletin of Agricultural Statistics, April–June, 1963*; *Livestock and Animal Product Statistics, 1962*; and *Production of Poultry and Eggs, 1962*. Some of the revised data, however, were not yet published and were obtained directly from the Agriculture Division, D.B.S. There may be revisions of data for other series than those listed above, particularly the data on farm income, series L67–87, for 1956 to 1960 as a result of the 1961 census information, but these revisions were not complete at the time the page proof was being checked.

Series L1–6. *General statistics, farm population, farm holdings and tenure, Canada and by region,*
census dates, 1861 to 1956

Year	Farm popu-lation	Number of occupied farms	Owner	Tenant	Owner and tenant	Manager	Year	Farm popu-lation	Number of occupied farms	Owner	Tenant	Owner and tenant	Manager
	1	2	3	4	5	6		1	2	3	4	5	6
		Canada							**Ontario**				
1956[1,2]	2,746,755	575,015	442,488	35,521	90,764	6,242	1956	683,148	140,602	117,013	6,368	14,784	2,437
1951[1,2]	2,911,996	623,091	481,447	44,983	89,226	7,435	1951	702,778	149,920	122,531	8,852	15,909	2,628
1941	3,152,449	732,832	548,821	94,287	84,896	4,828	1941	704,420	178,204	139,750	21,543	15,282	1,629
1931	3,289,140	728,623	583,706	74,382	67,942	2,593	1931	800,960	192,174	156,678	21,514	13,233	749
1921	—	711,090[4]	609,572	55,948	39,962	5,608	1921	—	198,053	167,188	20,199	9,128	1,538
1911	—	682,329[3,4]	603,971	54,013	24,345	—	1911	—	212,108[3]	174,102	29,102	8,904	—
1901	—	511,073[3,4]	444,680	43,890	22,503	—	1901	—	204,054[3]	162,780	29,298	11,976	—
1891	—	542,181[3]	474,784	64,425	—	2,972[5]	1891	—	216,195[3]	180,178	34,926	—	1,091[5]
1881	—	464,025	403,491	57,245	—	3,289[5]	1881	—	206,989	169,140	36,690	—	1,159[5]
1871[6]	—	367,862	326,160	39,583	—	2,119[5]	1871	—	172,258[3]	144,212	27,340	—	706[5]
		Maritimes					1861	—	131,883[8]	—	—	—	—
1956[2]	284,273	55,010	51,005	584	2,624	797			**Prairie Provinces**				
1951[2]	332,160	63,709	58,675	749	2,769	1,516	1956[1]	901,207	232,038	136,476	26,290	67,441	1,831
1941	358,482	77,096	71,162	2,103	3,259	572	1951[1]	963,975	248,720	151,216	31,292	64,638	1,574
1931	413,382	86,334	80,927	2,217	2,917	273	1946	994,548	269,601	166,820	44,329	57,395	1,057
1921	—	97,788	93,098	2,096	1,809	785	1941[1]	1,148,282	296,469	173,613	62,111	59,156	1,589
1911	—	104,359[3]	99,203	3,960	1,196	—	1936	1,235,451	300,523	191,815	57,157	50,263	1,288
1901	—	105,232[3]	100,217	2,950	2,065	—	1931[1]	1,195,488	288,079	198,770	42,709	45,646	954
1891	—	113,248	106,979	5,956	—	313[5]	1926	—	248,162[4]	169,331	40,261	36,133	2,437
1881	—	106,339	98,347	7,557	—	435[5]	1921	—	255,657[4]	200,656	27,067	25,643	2,291
1871[10]	—	77,518	72,889	4,348	—	281[5]	1916	—	218,563	179,721	16,156	20,356	2,330
		Quebec					1911	—	199,203[3,4]	178,182	10,354	10,667	—
1956	765,459	122,617	116,668	1,269	3,890	790	1901	—	55,176[3,4]	50,663	2,037	2,476	—
1951	792,756	134,336	126,697	2,566	3,791	1,282	1891[9]	—	31,252[3]	28,536	2,547	—	169[5]
1941	838,861	154,669	143,312	5,610	4,970	777	1881[9]	—	10,091	9,662	341	—	88[5]
1931	777,017	135,957	126,120	5,089	4,305	443			**British Columbia**				
1921	—	137,619	130,036	4,537	2,416	630	1956	112,668	24,748	21,326	1,010	2,025	387
1911	—	149,701[3]	137,972	8,695	3,034	—	1951	120,292	26,406	22,328	1,524	2,119	435
1901	—	140,110[3]	125,808	8,612	5,690	—	1941	102,446	26,394	20,984	2,920	2,229	261
1891	—	174,996	154,227	19,479	—	1,290[5]	1931	102,367	26,079	21,211	2,853	1,841	174
1881	—	137,863	123,932	12,344	—	1,587[5]	1921	—	21,973	18,594	2,049	966	364
1871	—	118,086	109,059	7,895	—	1,132[5]	1911	—	16,958[3]	14,512	1,902	544	—
1861	—	105,671[7]	—	—	—	—	1901	—	6,501[3]	5,212	993	296	—
							1891	—	6,490[3]	4,864	1,517	—	109[5]
							1881	—	2,743	2,410	313	—	20[5]

[1] Includes Yukon and Northwest Territories.
[2] Includes Newfoundland.
[3] See the note to series L 1–6 for deductions made from census tables for small plots.
[4] In 1926, 1921 and 1911, farms on Indian Reserves were not included in the Prairie Provinces and in the totals for Canada.
[5] Employees.
[6] Four provinces: Nova Scotia, New Brunswick, Quebec and Ontario.
[7] Lower Canada.
[8] Upper Canada.
[9] Includes Assiniboia, Manitoba, Saskatchewan and Alberta.
[10] Includes only Nova Scotia and New Brunswick.

Series L7–14. *General statistics, use of land in farms, Canada and by region, census dates, 1851 to 1956*
(thousands of acres)

Year	Area in farms	Under crops	Pasture	Summer fallow	Other	Total	Woodland	Total unimproved
	7	8	9	10	11	12	13	14
Canada								
1956[1,2]	173,924	62,944[3]	10,058	24,620	2,705	100,327	19,540	73,597
1951[1,2]	174,047	62,212[4]	10,005	22,032	2,604	96,853	22,780	77,194
1941	173,563	56,280[4]	8,503	23,535	3,318	91,636	22,266	81,927
1931	163,114	58,340[4]	8,012	17,007	2,373	85,732	26,645	77,382
1921	140,888	50,034[4]	7,602	12,001	1,133	70,770	23,770	70,118
1911	108,969	35,898[4]	—	2,538	—	48,734	17,478	60,235
1901[12]	63,422	21,242[4]	—	—	—	30,166	16,792	33,256
1891[12]	60,288	19,905	15,285	—	464[5]	28,537	24,634	—
1881	45,358	15,112	6,386	—	401[5]	21,899	23,492	—
1871[6]	36,046	11,820	5,241	—	275[5]	17,336	—	—
Maritimes								
1956[2]	6,894	1,469[3]	621	19	142	2,251	3,631	4,644
1951[2]	7,824	1,636[4]	603	11	93	2,343	4,273	5,482
1941	8,950	1,912[4]	709	16	148	2,785	4,612	6,164
1931	9,645	2,080[4]	703	34	114	2,940	5,275	6,703
1921	10,210	2,055[4]	825	75	173	3,128	5,539	7,082
1911	11,001	2,265[4]	—	2	—	3,471	5,676	7,529
1901	10,719	2,134[4]	—	—	—	3,394	5,757	7,325
1891	11,766	2,524	1,652	—	45[5]	4,222	—	7,544
1881	10,333	2,259	1,436	—	36[5]	3,731	—	6,635
1871[7]	8,859	1,569	1,208	—	21[5]	2,798	—	6,061
1861[7]	—	—	—	—	—	1,780	—	—
1851[7]	—	—	—	—	—	1,443	—	—
Quebec								
1956	15,910	5,550[3]	2,643	67	370	8,630	4,878	7,280
1951	16,786	5,790[4]	2,685	47	306	8,829	5,874	7,957
1941	18,063	6,138[4]	2,519	7	399	9,063	5,963	9,000
1931	17,304	6,140[4]	2,601	28	225	8,994	6,036	8,310
1921	17,257	6,001[4]	2,858	74[8]	132	9,065	6,335	8,192
1911	15,613	5,575	—	4	—	8,162	5,099	7,451
1901	14,444	4,768[4]	—	—	—	7,440	5,442	7,004
1891[12]	15,962	4,611	—	—	74[5]	8,671	—	7,291
1881	12,626	4,148	2,207	—	55[5]	6,410	—	6,216
1871	11,026	3,714	1,943	—	46[5]	5,704	—	5,322
1861	10,375	2,928	1,843	—	33[5]	4,804	5,571	—
1851[9]	8,113	2,072	1,503	—	30[5]	3,605	4,508	—
Ontario								
1956	19,880	8,219[3]	3,471	334	548	12,572	3,339	7,307
1951	20,880	8,645[4]	3,235	334	479	12,693	3,853	8,187
1941	22,388	9,262[4]	3,238	321	543	13,363	3,865	9,025
1931	22,841	9,591[4]	2,943	345	394	13,273	4,702	9,568
1921	22,629	9,381[4]	3,042	526[8]	221	13,169	4,515	9,460
1911	22,172	10,048[4]	—	248	—	13,653	3,936	8,519
1901	21,350	9,550[4]	—	—	—	13,266	4,823	8,083
1891	21,092	10,366	3,462	—	330[5]	14,158	—	6,934
1881	19,260	8,370	2,619	—	305[5]	11,294	—	7,966
1871	16,163	6,537	2,089	—	207[5]	8,834	—	7,328
1861	13,355	4,102	1,861	—	89[5]	6,052	7,303	—
1851	9,826	2,283	1,361	—	58[5]	3,703	6,123	—
Prairie Provinces								
1956[1]	126,701	47,017[3]	3,003	24,112	1,574	75,707	6,537	50,990
1951[1]	123,854	45,468[4]	3,138	21,570	1,663	71,840	7,023	52,014
1946	117,539	41,696	2,068	20,399	1,232	65,395	5,416	52,143
1941	120,132	38,379[4]	1,865	23,116	2,171	65,533	6,823	54,598
1936	113,112	40,194	1,579	16,854	2,221	60,850	11,906	52,263
1931	109,738	40,014[4]	1,649	16,558	1,598	59,820	9,421	49,963
1926	88,930	34,987	919	12,853	505	49,265	6,456	39,665
1921	87,932	32,205[4]	790	11,275[8]	594	44,863	6,306	43,069
1916	73,300	24,629	—	—	9,701	34,330	6,765	38,970
1911	57,643[10]	17,726[4]	—	2,278	—	22,970	1,222	34,673
1901	15,412	3,608[4]	—	—	—	5,593	378	9,820
1891[11]	6,312	1,261	4,799	—	6[5]	1,267	246	6,169
1881[11]	2,698	251	24	—	3[5]	279	—	2,419
British Columbia								
1956	4,539	690[3]	320	87	69	1,167	855	3,372
1951	4,702	672[4]	343	70	62	1,148	1,156	3,554
1941	4,034	589[4]	172	75	57	893	1,014	3,140
1931	3,542	505[4]	115	42	42	705	1,212	2,837
1921	2,860	392[4]	87	52	13	544	1,076	2,316
1911	2,540	284[4]	—	5	—	478	1,544	2,062
1901	1,497	182[4]	—	—	—	474	391	1,024
1891	3,330	50	713	—	8[5]	58	2,558	—
1881	441	84	98	—	3	185	—	256

[1] Includes data for Yukon and Northwest Territories.
[2] Includes Newfoundland.
[3] Includes field, vegetable, fruit and nursery crop land but excludes home gardens.
[4] Includes field, garden, orchard and nursery crop land.
[5] Gardens and orchards. In later censuses these were included with the area under crops (series L8).
[6] Four provinces: Nova Scotia, New Brunswick, Quebec and Ontario.
[7] Nova Scotia and New Brunswick.
[8] Includes idle land.
[9] Thousands of arpents.
[10] Area in farms includes only improved acreage of Indian Reserves.
[11] Includes Assiniboia, Manitoba, Saskatchewan and Alberta.
[12] See the notes to series L7–14 for unit of measurement in Quebec, 1891.

Series L15–38. *General statistics, current values of farm capital, Canada and by region, 1901 to 1960*
(thousands of dollars)

Year	Canada				Maritimes				Quebec			
	Lands and buildings	Implements and machinery	Livestock and poultry[1]	Total[1]	Lands and buildings	Implements and machinery	Livestock and poultry[1]	Total[1]	Lands and buildings	Implements and machinery	Livestock and poultry[1]	Total[1]
	15	16	17	18	19	20	21	22	23	24	25	26
1960	7,409,115	2,247,879	1,921,766	11,578,760	289,693	88,234	67,944	445,871	1,087,513	305,408	340,290	1,733,211
1959	7,163,792	2,188,671	1,988,861	11,341,324	293,368	86,883	69,761	450,012	1,052,787	292,950	335,733	1,681,470
1958	6,869,391	2,178,334	1,879,366	10,927,091	274,950	86,270	65,247	426,467	1,018,908	280,291	317,397	1,616,596
1957	6,527,584	2,197,775	1,517,552	10,242,911	258,234	86,228	58,709	403,171	984,183	270,124	263,240	1,517,547
1956	6,456,456	2,193,297	1,422,720	10,072,473	256,358	83,561	61,700	401,619	984,183	259,870	257,156	1,501,209
1955	6,236,094	2,210,000	1,462,663	9,908,757	245,686	81,346	65,386	392,418	938,446	250,957	250,456	1,439,859
1954	5,983,724	2,240,868	1,424,076	9,648,668	238,533	80,928	63,898	383,359	927,435	247,629	258,127	1,433,191
1953	6,034,349	2,152,463	1,556,502	9,743,314	243,910	77,694	71,553	393,157	881,699	239,272	284,580	1,405,551
1952	5,622,186	2,037,947	1,790,874	9,451,007	238,283	71,919	82,528	392,730	869,841	226,145	328,942	1,424,928
1951	5,512,519	1,931,880	2,014,153	9,458,552	241,047	68,456	88,878	398,381	846,973	211,937	340,543	1,399,453
1950	5,022,642	1,681,075	1,467,581	8,171,298	233,011	62,133	71,447	366,591	752,753	189,607	269,538	1,211,898
1949	4,716,823	1,415,546	1,370,793	7,503,162	216,936	56,092	65,569	338,597	670,357	169,413	263,290	1,103,060
1948	4,665,126	1,194,947	1,244,981	7,105,054	215,697	49,674	63,336	328,707	712,878	150,561	245,199	1,108,638
1947	4,214,119	1,026,573	1,148,853	6,389,545	212,357	44,477	61,644	318,478	687,219	135,505	233,754	1,056,478
1946	3,897,005	905,491	1,075,332	5,877,828	194,372	39,733	60,062	294,167	661,520	123,153	223,389	1,008,062
1945	3,711,473	826,632	1,042,301	5,580,406	199,553	36,309	56,387	292,249	635,819	114,031	204,570	954,420
1944	3,649,477	758,083	1,081,967	5,489,527	202,396	33,685	57,134	293,215	643,324	106,189	212,548	962,061
1943	3,454,480	722,277	1,097,966	5,274,723	176,688	32,103	57,081	265,872	639,359	100,801	216,491	956,651
1942	3,238,024	660,492	782,648	4,681,164	171,173	29,913	37,569	238,655	602,177	93,786	137,398	833,361
1941	3,029,846	596,046	621,285	4,247,177	158,143	27,587	31,239	216,969	543,358	85,203	112,417	740,978
1940	2,963,226	568,349	682,522	4,214,097	151,740	27,159	36,796	215,695	500,577	84,413	132,429	717,419
1939	3,106,885	547,393	644,485	4,298,763	182,751	27,181	37,242	247,174	523,906	84,937	122,011	730,854
1938	3,083,056	543,781	587,077	4,213,914	174,594	27,426	36,061	238,081	498,396	85,550	116,007	699,953
1937	3,253,346	526,876	603,672	4,383,894	181,704	27,067	37,456	246,227	521,470	84,525	117,408	723,403
1936	3,292,258	524,429	573,632	4,390,319	195,888	27,249	34,896	258,033	518,246	85,297	101,560	705,103
1935	3,449,255	533,546	540,507	4,523,308	182,721	27,872	32,608	243,201	585,005	86,886	95,715	767,606
1934	3,467,808	538,685	457,654	4,464,147	190,932	27,318	29,693	247,943	581,254	83,649	82,525	747,428
1933	3,425,200	573,867	444,092	4,443,159	185,573	28,869	30,906	245,348	615,735	88,403	77,540	781,678
1932	3,666,088	650,664	415,886	4,732,638	195,685	31,923	30,419	258,027	650,166	97,270	81,339	828,775
1931[2]	4,053,282	650,664	552,289	5,256,235	202,495	31,923	35,453	269,871	684,131	97,270	97,713	879,114
1930	4,440,476	650,664	758,224	5,849,364	210,188	31,923	52,244	294,355	759,808	97,270	148,964	1,006,143
1929	4,698,745	665,172	949,241	6,313,158	252,363	30,561	61,090	344,014	832,196	111,940	195,147	1,139,283
1928	4,698,745	665,172	935,944	6,299,861	252,363	30,561	60,360	343,284	832,196	111,940	174,838	1,118,974
1927	4,698,745	665,172	865,654	6,229,571	252,363	30,561	54,044	336,968	832,196	111,940	153,902	1,008,038
1926	4,698,745	665,172	786,638	6,150,555	252,363	30,561	52,621	335,545	832,196	111,940	141,648	1,085,784
1925	4,698,745	665,172	761,258	6,125,175	252,363	30,561	50,853	333,787	832,196	111,940	137,740	1,081,876
1924	4,698,745	665,172	691,868	6,055,785	252,363	30,561	46,315	329,239	832,196	111,940	122,459	1,066,595
1923	4,698,745	665,172	659,313	6,023,230	252,363	30,561	44,677	327,601	832,196	111,940	117,209	1,061,345
1922	4,232,588	665,180	728,870	5,626,638	229,149	30,561	56,376	316,086	765,852	111,949	130,963	1,008,764
1921[2]	5,053,216	665,180	842,313	6,560,709	244,685	30,561	52,562	327,808	850,021	111,949	123,695	1,085,665
1920	4,232,588	391,669[3]	1,041,246	5,665,503	—	—	—	—	—	—	—	—
1919	3,719,777	387,079[3]	1,296,602	5,403,458	—	—	—	—	—	—	—	—
1917	3,719,777	387,079[3]	1,102,261	5,209,117	—	—	—	—	—	—	—	—
1911[2]	3,343,730	257,008	631,103	4,231,841	190,958	14,265	37,833	243,056	638,210	51,955	97,590	787,755
1901[2]	1,403,270	108,666	275,168	1,787,104	120,580	9,500	24,449	154,529	350,550	27,038	58,488	436,076

U & B

Series L15-38. *General statistics, current values of farm capital, Canada and by region, 1901 to 1960 (continuation)*

(thousands of dollars)

Year	Ontario Lands and buildings	Implements and machinery	Livestock and poultry[1]	Total[1]	Prairie Provinces Lands and buildings	Implements and machinery	Livestock and poultry[1]	Total[1]	British Columbia Lands and buildings	Implements and machinery	Livestock and poultry[1]	Total[1]
	27	28	29	30	31	32	33	34	35	36	37	38
1960	2,082,207	612,719	599,818	3,294,744	3,547,616	1,171,404	840,003	5,559,023	402,086	70,114	73,711	545,911
1959	2,097,820	592,496	611,543	3,301,859	3,329,966	1,148,281	893,887	5,372,134	389,851	68,061	77,937	535,849
1958	1,940,271	580,630	587,890	3,108,791	3,272,661	1,163,396	839,450	5,275,507	362,601	67,747	69,382	499,730
1957	1,813,947	572,965	466,084	2,852,996	3,123,635	1,200,601	673,990	4,998,226	347,585	67,857	55,529	470,971
1956	1,750,076	559,834	430,056	2,739,966	3,136,328	1,223,746	618,743	4,978,817	329,511	66,286	55,065	450,862
1955	1,687,624	544,512	459,295	2,691,431	3,040,945	1,268,710	630,269	4,939,924	323,393	64,475	57,257	445,125
1954	1,592,526	533,884	454,733	2,581,143	2,916,853	1,134,626	591,439	4,822,918	308,377	63,801	55,879	428,057
1953	1,545,687	514,480	490,068	2,550,235	3,063,852	1,258,327	651,149	4,973,328	299,201	62,690	59,152	421,043
1952	1,450,590	485,739	561,148	2,497,477	2,782,345	1,193,320	754,836	4,730,501	281,127	60,824	63,420	405,371
1951	1,419,364	445,278	681,728	2,546,370	2,727,067	1,147,449	830,387	4,704,903	278,068	56,760	72,617	409,445
1950	1,194,178	389,352	485,067	2,068,597	2,586,270	986,337	588,808	4,161,415	256,430	53,646	52,721	362,797
1949	1,142,096	335,569	449,679	1,927,344	2,446,660	808,210	545,381	3,800,251	240,774	46,262	46,874	333,910
1948	1,106,022	290,879	413,595	1,810,496	2,410,958	664,714	478,443	3,554,115	219,571	39,119	44,408	303,098
1947	1,054,186	257,402	374,225	1,685,813	2,059,045	555,696	438,414	3,053,155	201,312	33,493	40,816	275,621
1946	985,659	232,517	362,179	1,580,355	1,874,696	481,167	390,803	2,746,666	180,758	28,921	38,899	248,578
1945	967,838	213,717	333,099	1,514,654	1,742,720	436,913	410,654	2,590,287	165,543	25,662	37,591	228,796
1944	1,002,519	196,931	322,299	1,521,749	1,650,905	398,449	453,148	2,502,502	150,333	22,829	36,838	210,000
1943	987,758	187,294	335,242	1,510,294	1,513,408	381,468	454,237	2,349,113	137,207	20,611	34,915	192,793
1942	867,636	169,443	242,136	1,279,215	1,468,893	349,521	340,037	2,158,451	128,145	17,829	25,508	171,482
1941	836,148	150,359	203,888	1,190,395	1,377,908	317,769	252,803	1,948,480	114,289	15,128	20,938	150,355
1940	877,186	145,253	220,868	1,243,307	1,322,893	296,927	269,596	1,889,416	110,830	14,597	22,833	148,260
1939	899,302	144,023	217,858	1,261,183	1,386,734	276,785	247,077	1,910,596	114,192	14,467	20,297	148,956
1938	901,080	142,582	197,490	1,241,152	1,393,666	273,914	217,400	1,884,980	115,320	14,309	20,119	149,748
1937	943,301	138,883	198,942	1,281,126	1,495,090	262,704	229,769	1,987,563	111,781	13,697	20,097	145,575
1936	922,617	137,514	193,656	1,253,787	1,539,585	261,193	224,602	2,025,380	115,922	13,176	18,918	148,016
1935	900,990	157,118	178,289	1,216,397	1,668,197	268,797	216,738	2,153,732	112,342	12,873	17,157	142,372
1934	956,180	129,208	145,706	1,231,094	1,622,339	287,227	182,819	2,092,385	117,103	11,283	16,911	145,297
1933	886,172	136,692	144,201	1,167,065	1,614,713	308,064	175,080	2,097,857	123,007	11,839	16,365	151,211
1932[2]	968,509	151,928	130,030	1,250,467	1,719,542	356,658	158,331	2,234,536	132,181	12,885	15,767	160,833
1931[2]	1,072,847	151,928	174,764	1,399,539	1,949,228	356,658	226,478	2,532,364	144,581	12,885	17,880	175,346
1930	1,136,874	151,928	244,566	1,533,368	2,188,256	356,658	280,386	2,825,300	145,350	12,885	31,963	190,198
1929	1,299,454	169,954	306,870	1,776,278	2,166,676	343,338	348,058	2,858,072	148,056	9,379	38,075	195,510
1928	1,299,454	169,954	307,243	1,776,651	2,166,676	343,338	358,215	2,868,229	148,056	9,379	35,287	192,722
1927	1,299,454	169,954	286,341	1,755,749	2,166,676	343,338	343,090	2,853,104	148,056	9,379	28,278	185,713
1926	1,299,454	169,954	258,288	1,727,696	2,166,676	343,338	309,988	2,820,002	148,056	9,379	24,093	181,528
1925	1,299,454	169,954	249,875	1,719,283	2,166,676	343,338	301,949	2,811,963	148,056	9,379	20,831	178,266
1924	1,299,454	169,954	227,540	1,696,948	2,166,676	343,338	277,932	2,787,946	148,056	9,379	17,622	175,057
1923	1,299,454	169,954	227,851	1,697,259	2,166,676	343,338	251,844	2,761,858	148,056	9,379	17,731	175,166
1922	1,111,361	169,953	234,828	1,516,143	1,921,145	343,338	288,862	2,553,345	205,081	9,379	17,841	232,301
1921[2]	1,283,950	169,953	235,379	1,689,282	2,503,012	343,338	410,155	3,256,505	171,548	9,379	20,522	201,449
1920	—	—	—	—	—	—	—	—	—	—	—	—
1919	—	—	—	—	—	—	—	—	—	—	—	—
1917	—	—	—	—	—	—	—	—	—	—	—	—
1911[2]	926,134	77,734	219,833	1,223,701	1,417,527	109,505	261,661	1,788,693	170,901	3,549	14,186	188,636
1901[2]	747,963	52,698	131,828	932,489	158,087	18,231	54,198	230,516	26,090	1,198	6,204	33,492

[1] Includes value of bees only in census years. Includes poultry except for years 1917, 1919 and 1920. Includes fur animals on farms except for years 1901, 1911, 1917, 1919 and 1920.

[2] Census data.

[3] Implements only.

Series L39-42. *General statistics, current values of farm capital, Ontario, 1883 to 1900*

(thousands of dollars)

Year	Lands and buildings	Implements	Livestock and poultry	Total	Year	Lands and buildings	Implements	Livestock and poultry	Total
	39	40	41	42		39	40	41	42
1900	794,216	57,324	123,275	974,815	1890	816,325	50,516	104,087	970,927
1899	776,712	54,995	115,806	947,513	1889	—	—	—	—
1898	766,301	52,977	103,744	923,022	1888	—	—	—	—
1897	760,145	51,299	93,650	905,094	1887	—	—	—	—
1896	762,704	50,730	96,858	910,292	1886	831,758	50,531	107,209	989,498
1895	777,087	50,944	103,958	931,990	1885	—	—	—	—
1894	791,318	51,530	111,548	954,396	1884	798,866	47,831	103,107	949,803
1893	802,854	51,436	116,071	970,361	1883	817,824	43,522	99,882	961,228
1892	811,472	51,003	117,501	979,977					
1891	812,513	50,651	108,721	971,886					

Series L43–66. *General statistics, farm labour, employment and wages,[1] males aged 14 and over, Canada and by region, 1891 to 1960*

Year	Canada[2] Total farm employment (thousands)	Unpaid family workers (thousands)	Paid workers (thousands)	Wages, by month with board (dollars)	Atlantic[2] Total farm employment (thousands)	Unpaid family workers (thousands)	Paid workers (thousands)	Wages, by month with board (dollars)	Quebec Total farm employment (thousands)	Unpaid family workers (thousands)	Paid workers (thousands)	Wages, by month with board (dollars)
	43	44	45	46	47	48	49	50	51	52	53	54
					Labour force surveys							
1960	623	76	100	129	51	—[4]	—[4]	102	120	29	19	120
1959	670	94	119	128	56	—[4]	13	104	166	44	25	117
1958	675	110	95	120	51	—[4]	—[4]	98	162	50	17	115
1957	721	127	89	118	41	10	—[4]	103	171	53	13	113
1956	758	132	96	115	45	—[4]	—[4]	102	167	58	13	108
1955	831	147	117	103	49	—[4]	10	98	181	63	11	96
1954	864	164	118	106	51	10	—[4]	92	212	67	23	94
1953	851	181	117	107	57	10	—[4]	85	203	72	21	97
1952	841	182	99	105	58	14	—[4]	91	203	70	14	101
1951	892	187	102	101	63	13	—[4]	89	228	78	18	100
1950	973[5]	221	118	88	84	23	11	78	249	92	21	80
1949	982	196	138	85	79	19	11	—	235	75	23	85
1948	1,026	208	131	87	84	19	12	—	249	76	22	—
1947	1,001	225	112	83	81	16	—[4]	—	237	87	16	—
1946	1,071	245	143	75	97	24	13	—	276	99	27	—
					Decennial Census data							
1951	798	134	125	—	65	10	12	—	188	58	22	—
1941	1,065	255	179	—	94	23	15	—	252	93	27	—
1931	1,103	277	200	—	106	29	14	—	224	86	24	—
1921[6]	1,017	207	169	—	112	23	16	—	214	67	26	—
1911	918	103	152	—	111	13	14	—	202	34	23	—
1901[7]	708	184	85	—	122	24	8	—	194	57	17	—
1891	723	241	79	—	133	44	15	—	205	72	15	—

Year	Ontario Total farm employment (thousands)	Unpaid family workers (thousands)	Paid workers (thousands)	Wages, by month with board (dollars)	Prairie Provinces Total farm employment (thousands)	Unpaid family workers (thousands)	Paid workers (thousands)	Wages, by month with board[3] (dollars)	British Columbia Total farm employment (thousands)	Unpaid family workers (thousands)	Paid workers (thousands)	Wages, by month with board (dollars)
	55	56	57	58	59	60	61	62	63	64	65	66
					Labour force surveys							
1960	155	14	32	116	270	26	32	147	27	—[4]	—[4]	146
1959	164	15	42	116	259	26	31	142	25	—[4]	—[4]	139
1958	156	16	35	105	278	34	27	137	28	—[4]	—[4]	130
1957	192	21	34	105	296	41	29	135	21	—[4]	—[4]	121
1956	204	24	38	104	319	42	32	127	23	—[4]	—[4]	120
1955	231	28	49	90	343	45	42	118	27	—[4]	—[4]	115
1954	239	30	48	88	345	55	35	120	17	—[4]	—[4]	120
1953	222	36	38	93	351	62	45	124	18	—[4]	—[4]	110
1952	210	35	37	91	351	61	38	119	19	—[4]	—[4]	112
1951	219	29	38	89	359	66	32	109	23	—[4]	—[4]	112
1950	240	33	38	81	375	69	43	96	25	—[4]	—[4]	98
1949	251	35	46	75	384	65	49	93	33	—[4]	—[4]	86
1948	255	39	42	—	403	72	47	92	35	—[4]	—[4]	94
1947	263	40	45	—	388	79	34	89	32	—[4]	—[4]	79
1946	279	41	52	—	390	81	40	83	29	—	11	83
1945	—	—	—	—	—	—	—	—	—	—	—	—
					Decennial Census data							
1951	194	24	38	—	324	40	46	—	27	2	7	—
1941	265	51	58	—	414	84	66	—	40	4	13	—
1931	298	66	65	—	434	92	84	—	41	4	13	—
1921[6]	289	58	54	—	368	56	65	—	34	3	8	—
1911	301	33	58	—	280	22	49	—	24	1	8	—
1901[7]	303	82	45	—	79	20	12	—	10	1	3	—
1891	331	113	41	—	46	11	6	—	8	1	2	—

[1] Number of workers as of June of the year given; wages as of 15 August of the year given.

[2] Newfoundland included only from 1950 for number of workers but not for wages.

[3] Saskatchewan only.

[4] Less than 10,000.

[5] Includes an estimate for Manitoba which was not covered in the June 1950 survey because of flood conditions.

[6] Data for 1891 to 1921 include males 10 years and over: subsequently 14 years and over.

[7] Estimated. See the notes to series L43–66.

Series L67–72. *General statistics, income from farming operations, Canada, 1926 to 1960*

(thousands of dollars)

Year	Cash income from farm products	Income in kind	Supplementary payments	Realized gross income	Realized net income	Total net income	Year	Cash income from farm products	Income in kind	Supplementary payments	Realized gross income	Realized net income	Total net income
	67	68	69	70	71	72		67	68	69	70	71	72
1960	2,781,538	352,043	77,204	3,210,785	1,303,065	1,319,604	1940	735,381	175,715	9,691	920,787	392,243	469,896
1959	2,791,190	344,464	22,087	3,157,741	1,273,163	1,199,363	1939	712,076	176,992	1,686	890,754	377,206	430,804
1958	2,794,615	340,665	60,128	3,195,408	1,402,218	1,337,599	1938	649,658	174,369	—	824,027	329,154	364,201
1957	2,573,341	328,069	1,987	2,903,397	1,196,958	1,058,268	1937	638,456	177,223	—	815,679	317,844	307,024
1956	2,641,873	328,312	5,004	2,975,189	1,238,093	1,458,135	1936	587,282	174,897	—	762,179	287,559	245,037
1955	2,350,198	328,435	33,338	2,711,971	1,078,111	1,289,964	1935	532,583	166,109	—	698,692	233,910	237,636
1954	2,375,427	324,569	2,427	2,702,423	1,123,248	1,025,272	1934	503,234	160,656	—	663,890	210,271	202,967
1953	2,786,223	334,744	1,572	3,122,539	1,559,847	1,644,382	1933	419,643	153,633	—	573,276	142,364	108,947
1952	2,859,143	345,888	5,131	3,210,162	1,629,362	1,919,439	1932	409,045	149,327	—	558,372	109,833	130,192
1951	2,782,750	334,567	10,356	3,127,673	1,645,579	1,936,990	1931	471,913	182,360	—	654,273	155,359	135,909
1950	2,143,786	295,920	13,806	2,453,512	1,121,812	1,219,757	1930	641,925	226,074	—	867,999	277,233	361,061
1949	2,412,709	299,179	17,628	2,729,516	1,513,860	1,415,787	1929	931,765	246,069	—	1,177,834	544,801	417,098
1948	2,394,673	315,907	20,748	2,731,328	1,566,698	1,554,080	1928	1,064,246	241,128	—	1,305,374	665,638	641,526
1947	1,936,744	285,037	11,577	2,233,358	1,181,070	1,130,293	1927	940,399	240,410	—	1,180,809	568,914	631,920
1946	1,692,543	269,978	16,950	1,979,471	1,064,478	1,077,980	1926	961,194	239,574	—	1,200,768	615,926	618,058
1945	1,664,809	259,191	6,440	1,930,440	1,107,466	868,175							
1944	1,814,596	247,687	17,872	2,080,155	1,271,424	1,143,041							
1943	1,400,243	243,174	31,414	1,674,831	909,634	792,854							
1942	1,107,615	223,767	55,362	1,386,744	702,256	1,029,509							
1941	880,849	191,871	29,477	1,102,197	541,325	488,736							

Series L73–77. *General statistics, cash income from the sale of farm products, by commodity groups,*
Canada, 1926 to 1960

(thousands of dollars)

Year	Crops	Livestock	Dairy	Poultry and eggs	Other sources	Year	Crops	Livestock	Dairy	Poultry and eggs	Other sources
	73	74	75	76	77		73	74	75	76	77
1960	1,061,451	851,836	517,752	271,934	155,769	1940	303,205	220,917	120,466	52,443	48,041
1959	1,019,981	907,391	514,208	277,583	94,114	1939	343,931	177,461	113,384	48,311	30,675
1958	997,544	931,086	495,565	298,511	132,037	1938	296,540	155,290	121,378	46,953	29,497
1957	970,947	783,960	459,824	276,772	83,825	1937	262,431	182,914	112,820	48,358	31,933
1956	1,065,840	760,453	432,536	293,707	94,341	1936	255,832	146,252	107,197	47,593	30,408
1955	817,505	732,679	438,392	283,073	111,887	1935	234,482	129,960	98,690	43,429	26,022
1954	889,588	723,484	426,538	261,799	76,445	1934	231,658	110,613	95,518	41,594	23,851
1953	1,321,866	702,999	415,905	270,573	76,452	1933	190,696	83,175	89,506	35,789	20,477
1952	1,390,522	742,738	398,996	245,815	86,203	1932	186,115	79,275	88,489	35,696	19,470
1951	1,164,131	899,704	387,899	248,194	93,178	1931	177,720	110,517	107,346	51,613	24,717
1950	778,582	788,385	342,965	167,174	80,486	1930	271,119	156,172	110,360	72,304	31,970
1949	1,087,582	714,874	364,573	182,065	81,243	1929	484,178	212,420	118,190	79,373	37,604
1948	1,033,623	710,252	397,414	184,633	89,499	1928	618,412	208,639	121,001	79,377	36,817
1947	863,775	492,963	335,948	168,609	87,026	1927	523,798	193,010	118,998	71,245	33,348
1946	729,234	463,455	296,844	146,013	73,947	1926	555,731	191,609	118,055	64,331	31,468
1945	688,834	488,585	279,662	152,781	61,387						
1944	851,738	498,717	276,404	132,269	73,340						
1943	535,388	437,426	255,003	120,138	83,702						
1942	364,358	374,008	225,052	97,411	102,148						
1941	326,591	291,479	159,919	63,632	68,705						

Series L78–82. *General statistics, cash income from the sale of farm products, by region,*[1] *1926 to 1960*

(thousands of dollars)

Year	Maritimes	Quebec	Ontario	Prairie Provinces	British Columbia	Year	Maritimes	Quebec	Ontario	Prairie Provinces	British Columbia
	78	79	80	81	82		78	79	80	81	82
1960	121,293	415,265	869,329	1,248,600	127,051	1940	37,932	114,421	215,774	336,497	30,757
1959	114,832	420,276	855,542	1,276,092	124,448	1939	34,556	98,829	208,974	339,479	30,238
1958	115,214	420,989	854,807	1,281,179	122,426	1938	36,185	91,397	201,156	291,250	29,670
1957	110,329	383,341	790,199	1,173,395	116,077	1937	38,042	88,813	201,912	280,723	28,966
1956	118,366	385,296	780,551	1,244,406	113,254	1936	34,824	80,388	176,532	270,348	25,190
1955	106,832	398,855	766,237	972,588	105,686	1935	31,600	71,479	160,897	245,563	23,044
1954	108,335	382,953	726,397	1,050,656	107,086	1934	27,857	67,508	149,922	235,939	22,008
1953	101,284	371,103	749,106	1,458,476	106,254	1933	24,889	57,109	135,901	182,621	19,123
1952	117,736	395,026	770,675	1,471,894	103,812	1932	21,400	58,651	131,472	179,448	18,074
1951	107,192	394,941	800,666	1,375,552	104,399	1931	28,078	74,064	171,004	176,925	21,842
1950	97,469	335,262	650,083	969,608	91,364	1930	38,526	91,622	213,471	268,072	30,234
1949	93,105	320,877	652,269	1,256,412	90,046	1929	39,809	109,334	256,832	491,847	33,943
1948	97,559	332,673	650,290	1,220,481	93,670	1928	40,449	110,574	259,610	620,439	33,174
1947	85,404	272,717	535,194	958,605	84,824	1927	39,644	101,083	246,443	524,336	28,893
1946	83,278	233,760	461,733	838,507	75,265	1926	40,159	101,324	245,868	547,237	26,606
1945	76,390	225,821	442,625	847,504	72,469						
1944	74,404	213,791	410,710	1,048,103	67,588						
1943	69,917	192,246	389,083	691,805	57,192						
1942	57,210	172,351	357,848	475,180	45,026						
1941	43,268	138,220	274,503	388,959	35,899						

[1] For cash income from the sale of farm products for Canada see series L67.

Series L83–87. *General statistics, realized net income of farm operators from farming operations, by region,*[1] *1926 to 1960*

(thousands of dollars)

Year	Maritimes	Quebec	Ontario	Prairie Provinces	British Columbia	Year	Maritimes	Quebec	Ontario	Prairie Provinces	British Columbia
	83	84	85	86	87		83	84	85	86	87
1960	50,575	182,238	337,788	676,505	55,959	1940	27,556	86,772	109,625	149,855	18,435
1959	45,410	187,671	315,070	671,677	53,335	1939	24,807	73,870	111,298	149,026	18,205
1958	50,322	198,011	350,994	744,953	57,938	1938	26,717	66,266	106,933	111,230	18,008
1957	49,715	186,848	312,873	592,976	54,546	1937	28,523	60,373	104,247	107,200	17,501
1956	54,736	185,834	300,962	644,799	51,762	1936	27,648	59,159	93,304	92,026	15,422
1955	47,831	223,153	327,818	431,032	48,277	1935	24,817	49,828	79,621	66,130	13,514
1954	51,639	212,716	303,323	503,899	51,671	1934	20,792	45,994	72,496	58,347	12,642
1953	46,146	220,706	351,119	886,819	55,057	1933	18,792	38,173	61,557	13,130	10,712
1952	64,591	239,247	374,655	896,733	54,136	1932	14,164	37,157	52,756	−3,154	8,910
1951	59,957	251,601	429,460	846,603	57,958	1931	18,975	51,295	84,588	−10,728	11,229
1950	55,784	208,211	315,127	494,552	48,138	1930	29,659	69,251	115,149	44,897	18,277
1949	55,364	206,216	357,215	843,959	51,106	1929	32,426	85,306	155,167	250,366	21,536
1948	62,559	229,709	370,302	848,835	55,293	1928	34,695	87,557	159,809	363,020	20,557
1947	52,629	172,401	284,821	621,193	50,026	1927	35,733	80,793	154,782	280,094	17,512
1946	57,076	158,235	253,125	549,750	46,292	1926	37,155	84,632	160,479	317,554	16,106
1945	52,937	164,854	264,730	577,068	47,877						
1944	52,647	154,453	240,423	779,719	44,182						
1943	49,879	133,273	219,450	469,857	37,175						
1942	42,939	132,878	215,833	281,289	29,317						
1941	30,256	105,060	159,790	223,513	22,706						

[1] For realized net income of farm operators from farming operations for Canada see series L71.

Series L88–97. *General statistics, indexes of farm prices and costs, Canada, 1913 to 1960*

(1935–39 = 100)

| Year | Index of farm prices of agricultural production[1] | Index numbers of commodities and services used by farmers | | | | | | | | |
| | | Composite index inclusive of living costs | Composite index exclusive of living costs | Equipment and material | Farm machinery[2] | Tax and interest rates | Farm wage rates | Farm family living costs | Hog/barley ratio Winnipeg | Hog/feed ratio Toronto |
	88	89	90	91	92	93	94	95	96	97
1960	239.4	254.8	276.7	222.7	254.2	214.5	555.3	221.7	18.7	—
1959	242.9	249.8	269.5	219.1	248.4	204.7	538.2	220.1	18.6	7.3
1958	245.5	242.7	259.9	213.0	236.7	196.7	513.2	217.0	23.5	9.2
1957	234.2	238.7	255.9	211.3	223.8	191.9	501.4	212.7	25.5	9.8
1956	234.6	230.3	247.6	208.8	209.4	184.7	470.3	204.5	18.4	7.5
1955	232.7	224.5	238.3	204.6	198.8	177.2	439.7	203.8	17.2	7.4
1954	236.8	224.2	237.2	203.3	—	174.6	441.2	204.5	23.1	9.0
1953	250.4	225.3	239.8	207.4	—	168.2	449.1	203.6	20.6	8.9
1952	274.4	229.8	243.1	215.8	195.4	161.4	445.5	210.0	15.7	6.6
1951	296.8	217.5	230.0	206.0	186.8	151.8	416.6	198.6	19.1	8.4
1950	260.8	197.3	210.4	189.9	165.1	144.3	368.7	177.6	16.6	7.8
1949	255.4	191.7	204.1	180.3	158.3	138.7	373.3	173.2	19.1	9.1
1948	255.8	183.7	197.6	173.1	141.6	131.3	371.2	162.8	20.3	8.6
1947	215.8	157.5	170.4	139.5	126.3	125.0	341.4	138.3	17.9	8.6
1946	204.1	145.0	157.0	128.0	118.8	117.2	314.6	127.1	18.7	8.8
1945	185.7	140.6	152.1	125.9	115.1	113.4	298.1	123.2	18.1	8.2
1944	172.4	137.9	148.0	126.0	118.2	111.2	275.3	122.8	18.2	7.9
1943	157.8	134.7	143.4	122.4	117.1	106.3	267.8	121.6	19.0	7.1
1942	133.1	126.6	131.6	119.2	114.4	104.3	211.6	119.0	20.6	6.8
1941	110.2	115.2	116.1	107.8	109.1	102.9	163.4	114.0	21.3	6.7
1940	96.8	107.5	106.8	101.8	105.8	102.1	131.8	108.5	24.1	7.2
1939	91.8	99.4	99.3	95.7	103.6	101.1	110.3	99.5	27.0	7.3
1938	105.0	101.8	101.7	101.2	104.1	100.6	105.0	101.9	22.8	7.0
1937	119.7	104.3	105.3	108.4	97.2	98.2	102.6	102.9	13.6	5.1
1936	96.9	98.2	98.1	98.7	97.8	99.2	94.7	98.3	19.2	5.8
1935	88.0	96.4	95.4	95.6	95.5	101.0	87.6	97.9	24.2	6.8
1934	—	96.5	95.5	96.8	94.6	102.3	82.3	97.9	19.3	6.9
1933	—	92.2	89.8	88.8	92.1	102.9	77.7	95.8	17.8	5.4
1932	—	95.1	93.3	89.3	94.1	113.2	83.4	97.8	14.1	5.0
1931	—	102.1	100.9	92.2	94.9	119.5	110.7	103.9	27.0	7.4
1930	—	115.7	117.0	105.6	97.0	128.4	145.6	113.7	37.3	8.9
1929	—	123.7	127.9	117.6	97.5	130.3	163.8	117.3	17.3	6.9
1928	—	125.0	129.3	118.3	97.6	130.8	168.3	118.5	13.2	5.5
1927	—	126.7	131.2	119.9	97.5	134.7	169.5	119.8	13.2	5.9
1926	—	126.8	130.6	119.9	97.6	135.5	164.5	121.1	22.7	8.3
1925	—	128.6	131.8	123.2	97.9	135.2	159.4	123.9	15.9	7.4
1924	—	129.3	131.9	122.3	102.4	137.3	160.0	125.5	11.5	5.6
1923	—	129.6	130.6	118.3	92.9	138.6	166.5	128.3	18.9	6.2
1922	—	131.7	134.1	124.6	89.9	141.1	161.0	127.9	21.4	8.4
1921	—	147.4	152.5	147.4	111.4	143.2	184.4	139.9	17.9	6.8
1920	—	180.3	186.5	190.1	92.2	136.7	238.6	171.3	12.8	5.6
1919	—	157.5	167.9	169.1	86.9	127.2	216.4	143.0	16.6	6.7
1918	—	148.2	160.2	164.1	82.1	125.9	190.8	131.1	14.8	6.6
1917	—	128.6	140.5	140.7	62.0	110.5	171.4	111.5	14.0	6.9
1916	—	97.8	100.5	101.7	55.1	102.5[3]	97.6	93.7	14.7	6.6
1915	—	89.6	91.6	96.9	54.4	86.0[3]	82.7	86.5	13.0	—
1914	—	84.1	85.3	90.2	55.0	79.7[3]	78.0	82.3	16.4	—
1913	—	—	—	85.4	54.6	—	—	80.1	21.0	—

[1] Excluding Newfoundland.
[2] Including motor trucks from 1935.
[3] Tax rates only.

Series L98–113. *General statistics, wholesale market prices of major agricultural products, by selected markets, 1855 to 1960*
(series L98–102 in cents per bushel, series L107 in cents per dozen, all other series in cents per pound)

| Year[1] | Fort William[2] | | | | | Toronto | | | | Montreal | | | | Prince Edward Island | New Brunswick | Quebec |
| | Wheat No. 1 Northern | Oats No. 2, CW | Barley No. 3, CW | Rye No. 2, CW | Flax seed No. 1, CW | Steers, good, all weights | Hogs, B1 dressed[3] | Sheep, good | Poultry | Eggs, grade A large | Butter, 1st grade, creamery prints | Cheese, new large coloured No. 1 | Wool | Potatoes | Potatoes | Potatoes |
	98	99	100	101	102	103	104	105	106	107	108	109	110	111	112	113
1960	167/4	81/2	107/5	105	311/4	22.65	23.75	9.12	—	49.3	64.8	—	—	—	—	—
1959	165/7	82/4	108/1	109/7	334/2	25.10	23.80	9.11	—	48.9	65.0	—	—	4.24	3.72	3.17
1958	166/2	77/6	109/7	108	302	22.90	28.13	8.36	—	53.1	64.5	—	40.0	2.60	2.35	1.93
1957	162/3	76/3	111	106	303	18.82	30.05	8.49	—	51.5	60.7	—	52.0	2.59	2.37	1.99
1956	168/1	80/6	116	119/7	298/4	19.07	26.50	8.62	—	58.0	58.6	—	49.0	2.74	2.39	2.06
1955	174	83/5	114/3	110/1	360/1	19.60	25.05	8.18	—	58.5	59.7	—	49.0	3.16	2.89	2.30
1954	173	90/4	122/4	112/2	309/1	19.34	30.90	9.03	—	52.1	59.9	—	51.0	3.70	3.24	2.86
1953	186/2	73/2	109/7	99/1	283/6	20.11	30.40	9.52	—	64.8	61.0	—	51.0	1.57	1.55	1.17
1952	185/6	80/3	136/5	158/2	329	25.85	25.70	14.80	—	54.2	62.4	—	48.0	3.06	2.92	2.79
1951	188/2	91/1	133/5	193/5	428/1	33.49	32.85	19.77	—	66.2	65.0	—	95.0	5.83	5.11	4.59
1950	191/2	96/1	149/6	184/5	441/4	26.72	28.98	14.32	—	51.5	57.9	—	63.0	1.86	1.72	1.39
1949	205/7	91	157/2	146	371/6	21.29	30.20	10.87	—	56.5	61.9	—	41.0	1.96	1.81	1.57
1948	205	78/1	119/3	140	403/1	19.40	29.96	9.33	—	56.0	69.8	35.4	39.0	2.01	1.89	1.71
1947	158/4	84/1	126	374/5	500	14.63	22.04	8.33	—	46.8	52.6	30.8	33.0	3.46	3.37	3.04
1946	138/4	56/4	75/2	287/6	300	13.05	19.85	8.55	—	44.3	40.8	20.6	31.0	2.05	1.95	1.89
1945	125	51/4	64/6	224	275	12.20	17.90	7.35	—	43.3	36.9	20.6	31.0	2.57	2.57	2.55
1944	125	51/4	64/6	126/1	275	11.99	17.25	5.06	—	40.6	36.5	20.6	31.0	2.36	2.34	2.10
1943	123/2	51/4	64/6	115/4	250	11.99	16.87	8.41	—	44.8	36.1	20.4	31.0	2.32	2.26	2.13
1942	94/4	49/2	61/1	68/4	225	10.39	15.69	8.14	—	40.6	36.5	19.0	31.0	2.35	2.36	2.30
1941	76/5	49/1	59/2	60/1	158/1	8.90	13.26	6.03	—	34.6	34.8	15.3	31.0	2.16	2.01	1.90
1940	74	34/6	44/3	49/6	144/3	7.83	11.42[2]	5.33	—	31.9	27.5	16.5	30.3	1.08	.99	.85
1939	76/4	35/5	43/4	59/7	172/3	6.89	8.91[2]	4.49	—	30.9	25.0	14.6	19.3	1.63	1.57	1.37
1938	62	29	36	40/5	143/4	6.27	9.45	4.16	—	33.6	28.4	14.8	16.8	1.61	1.54	1.25
1937	131/4	50/3	57/5	72/3	164/2	7.40	8.92	4.22	—	31.6	28.0	14.8	29.2	.94	.85	.73
1936	122/5	53	70/6	98/5	171/3	—	8.43	3.98	—	33.3	25.3	13.1	20.8	1.63	1.51	1.43
1935	84/5	34/5	36	42/7	147/5	6.46	8.94	3.27	—	31.1	24.9	11.5	15.3	1.76	1.67	1.47
1934	81/6	42/6	48/2	52/7	138/7	5.54	8.60	2.87	—	31.6	24.3	10.4	18.1	.65	.62	.56
1933	68	33/7	39	47/4	148	4.63	5.54	2.63	—	28.0	23.3	10.4	13.7	1.25	1.11	1.01
1932	54/2	26/3	32/2	37/6	90/4	5.56	4.66	2.48	24.2	30.4	22.6	11.2	10.3	1.08	1.00	.93
1931	59/7	31/3	37/3	40	93/6	6.22	7.39	3.77	35.5	34.3	26.7	14.0	14.3	.69	.64	.62
1930	64/2	29/7	28/3	34/6	114/1	8.78	12.32	5.38	36.1	45.5	34.5	18.7	17.9	1.04	1.05	.98
1929	124/2	58/5	56/3	80/2	247/4	10.16	12.38	6.52	40.6	48.1	41.9	21.5	28.8	2.28	2.25	2.09
1928	124	58/6	71/3	100/6	202/2	10.48	10.51	6.51	39.5	49.3	40.8	23.3	34.5	1.12	.97	.92
1927	146/3	65/1	85/2	108/2	189/7	8.20	10.35	6.39	36.6	49.9	40.6	20.8	26.1	—	—	—
1926	146/2	58/6	72/6	99/6	195	7.33	13.32	6.82	36.3	46.5	39.7	21.4	30.6	—	—	—
1925	151/2	49/5	63/7	89/6	213/6	7.35	12.85	6.95	35.9	43.8	39.2	23.2	40.0	—	—	—
1924	168/4	59/5	88/4	121	241/1	6.75	9.10	6.88	34.6	42.8	38.0	19.6	35.8	—	—	—
1923	107	41/4	63/2	69/1	215/1	6.95	9.76	6.60	33.1	47.4	40.7	23.1	31.2	—	—	—
1922	110/4	47/2	54/2	75/1	227/2	7.36	12.63	6.30	36.6	45.1	38.2	19.9	21.7	—	—	—
1921	129/7	47/4	61/6	92/3	210/2	7.58	11.72	6.84	37.7	51.1	44.6	20.0	20.0	—	—	—
1920	199/4	53/5	90	160/5	209/5	12.89	18.98	9.36	38.5	66.8	60.6	30.7	40.0	—	—	—
1919	217/4	100/2	161/4	179.9	4.84	13.06	19.59	10.37	41.4	63.3	57.4	25.6	60.0	—	—	—
1918	224/1	78/6	108/6	149.8	3.89	12.89	18.17	13.71	38.2	59.5	46.6	23.2	71.0	—	—	—
1917	221	82/7	137	194.7	3.48	11.15	15.55	11.88	26.8	51.8	42.2	22.8	65.0	—	—	—
1916	205/5	63/2	109/2	—	2.58	8.42	10.54	8.36	20.0	39.5	35.1	19.8	30.0	—	—	—
1915	113/2	43/2	64/7	—	1.76	7.99	8.47	6.34	19.4	32.6	31.1	16.4	23.0	—	—	—
1914	132/1	57/4	69/3	—	1.52	8.29	8.29	6.14	21.1	33.8	27.1	14.2	16.0	—	—	—
1913	89/3	36/1	46/6	—	1.30	6.99	9.03	5.54	—	—	—	—	16.5	—	—	—
1912	89/3	34/6	48	—	—	6.76	7.69	4.89	—	—	—	—	13.5	—	—	—
1911	100/6	41/6	61/1	—	—	5.91	6.62	4.16	—	—	—	—	13.8	—	—	—
1910	94/2	33/7	54/4	—	—	6.15	8.48	4.74	—	—	—	—	13.2	—	—	—
1909	100/6	35/1	46/3	—	—	5.64	7.30	4.02	—	—	—	12.1	11.9	—	—	—
1908	110/3	41/7	53	74.2	—	4.95	5.95	4.22	—	—	—	12.6	8.7	—	—	—
1907	105/3	42	51/4	80.7	—	4.85	6.44	4.71	—	—	—	12.6	13.6	—	—	—
1906	79/5	36/1	43/6	66.6	—	4.52	6.81	4.63	—	—	—	12.6	16.5	—	—	—
1905	77/4	34	39/2	65.7	—	4.57	6.22	3.89	—	—	—	11.2	15.1	—	—	—
1904	91.6	36.2	39.6	67.9	—	4.50	5.09	3.45	—	—	—	9.3	11.1	—	—	—
1903	78.8	31.4	31.9	54.2	—	4.47	5.83	3.33	—	—	—	11.6	9.0	—	—	—
1902	72.9	36.8	37.8	50.2	—	4.90	6.55	3.58	—	—	—	10.7	7.2	—	—	—
1901	75.2	40.3	39.5	53.7	—	4.36	6.69	3.34	—	—	—	9.6	8.5	—	—	—
1900	74.6	34.3	35.9	48.9	—	4.23	5.76	3.64	—	—	—	11.2	10.5	—	—	—
1899	70.9	32.2	32.6	51.4	—	3.88	4.62	3.44	—	—	—	10.5	9.0	—	—	—
1898	93.2	38.3	39.7	51.3	—	3.80	4.87	3.35	—	—	—	8.3	10.8	—	—	—
1897	78.7	27.1	28.0	46.6	—	3.39	5.05	3.19	—	—	—	9.5	11.7	—	—	—
1896	65.5	20.3	21.8	34.0	—	3.02	3.87	2.92	—	—	—	8.5	11.3	—	—	—

Series L 98–113. *General statistics, wholesale market prices of major agricultural products, by selected market, 1855 to 1960 (continued)*

(series L 98–102 in cents per bushel, series L 107 in cents per dozen, all other series in cents per pound)

Year[1]	Fort William					Toronto				Montreal				Prince Edward Island	New Brunswick	Quebec
	Wheat No. 1 Northern	Oats No. 2, CW	Barley No. 3, CW	Rye No. 2, CW	Flax seed No. 1, CW	Steers, good, all weights	Hogs, B 1[2] dressed	Sheep, good	Poultry	Eggs, grade A large	Butter, 1st grade, creamery prints	Cheese, new large coloured No. 1	Wool	Potatoes	Potatoes	Potatoes
	98	99	100	101	102	103	104	105	106	107	108	109	110	111	112	113
1895	71.8	27.2	30.8	45.3	—	3.71	4.28	3.33	—	—	—	8.9	12.9	—	—	—
1894	61.2	30.2	27.0	47.0	—	3.96	4.60	3.65	—	—	—	10.5	10.6	—	—	—
1893	73.3	27.8	29.5	45.0	—	4.45	6.21	4.93	—	—	—	10.5	10.6	—	—	—
1892	80.1	22.2	30.2	51.7	—	3.87	4.98	4.81	—	—	—	10.5	10.3	—	—	—
1891	93.1	34.6	33.0	78.6	—	3.96	4.82	4.99	—	—	—	10.0	11.2	—	—	—
1890	90	46	44.4	63.0	—	4.18	4.63	5.50	—	—	—	9.8	12.4	—	—	—
1889	99	32.7	56.2	47.5	—	3.95	4.74	4.85	—	—	—	—	—	—	—	—
1888	105	35.4	62.7	62.1	—	4.36	5.84	5.20	—	—	—	—	—	—	—	—
1887	83	42.4	71.2	67.4	—	4.30	5.54	5.35	—	—	—	—	—	—	—	—
1886	83	32.2	59.3	51.8	—	4.36	4.80	4.78	—	—	—	—	—	—	—	—
1885	84	33.8	79.6	59.2	—	4.75	4.75	4.33	—	—	—	—	—	—	—	—
1884	86	35.2	69.9	60.2	—	5.50	5.80	4.57	—	—	—	—	—	—	—	—
1883	113	37.9	72.2	60.5	—	5.75	6.10	5.34	—	—	—	—	—	—	—	—
1882	108	44.2	74.7	62.7	—	5.35	7.25	8.07	—	—	—	—	—	—	—	—
1881	134	43.8	89.2	84.7	—	4.98	6.73	6.50	—	—	—	—	—	—	—	—
1880	118	36.0	86.4	82.7	—	4.82	5.43	6.25	—	—	—	—	—	—	—	—
1879	122	36.3	70.7	74.0	—	4.61	4.88	6.00	—	—	—	—	—	—	—	—
1878	96	33.3	90.6	51.6	—	5.80	4.28	6.41	—	—	—	—	—	—	—	—
1877	110	34.1	62.4	—	—	5.16	5.71	5.46	—	—	—	—	—	—	—	—
1876	136	44.5	77.8	63.0	—	4.86	6.53	5.80	—	—	—	—	—	—	—	—
1875	105	35.3	83.8	61.4	—	5.16	7.27	6.08	—	—	—	—	—	—	—	—
1874	100	45.8	96.1	71.7	—	5.80	6.73	6.33	—	—	—	—	—	—	—	—
1873	121	45.3	112.2	72.4	—	7.21	5.23	5.92	—	—	—	—	—	—	—	—
1872	125	41.0	66.7	67.1	—	7.48	4.74	6.38	—	—	—	—	—	—	—	—
1871	125	40.8	64.5	70.5	—	7.48	5.35	5.75	—	—	—	—	—	—	—	—
1870	127	47.5	67.4	73.3	—	6.80	—	—	—	—	—	—	—	—	—	—
1869	85	37.5	64.3	52.4	—	6.00	—	—	—	—	—	—	—	—	—	—
1868	109	45	82.2	44.4	—	5.50	—	—	—	—	—	—	—	—	—	—
1867	180	47	67	80	—	—	—	—	—	—	—	—	—	—	—	—
1866	160	32	60	58	—	—	—	—	—	—	—	—	—	—	—	—
1865	120	40	69	56	—	—	—	—	—	—	—	—	—	—	—	—
1864	96	43	76	59	—	5.92	—	—	—	—	—	—	—	—	—	—
1863	95	43	80	59	—	5.39	—	—	—	—	—	—	—	—	—	—
1862	100	41	69	60	—	5.14	—	—	—	—	—	—	—	—	—	—
1861	115	28	48	60	—	5.23	—	—	—	—	—	—	—	—	—	—
1860	131	3	63	72	—	5.72	—	—	—	—	—	—	—	—	—	—
1859	140	—	79	70	—	5.77	—	—	—	—	—	—	—	—	—	—
1858	106	—	59	62	—	5.64	—	—	—	—	—	—	—	—	—	—
1857	—	—	—	—	—	7.08	—	—	—	—	—	—	—	—	—	—
1856	—	—	—	—	—	7.56	—	—	—	—	—	—	—	—	—	—
1855	—	—	—	—	—	6.58	—	—	—	—	—	—	—	—	—	—

[1] Data for series L 98–102 are for crop years ending in the following year. Data for all other series are for calendar years.

[2] The fractions given for grain prices, except those given in decimals, are in eighths of a cent.

[3] See the note to series L 98–113 for a change in method of pricing, between 1939 and 1940.

Series L114–118. *General statistics, index numbers of wholesale prices of selected farm products, 1913 to 1960*

(1935–39 = 100)

Year	Grains	Livestock	Meats, fresh	Milk and its products	Eggs	Year	Grains	Livestock	Meats, fresh	Milk and its products	Eggs
	114	115	116	117	118		114	115	116	117	118
1960	179.8	292.4	300.4	246.3	143.2	1935	89.2	95.7	92.1	93.5	95.5
1959	179.1	307.1	315.7	247.3	143.7	1934	82.6	84.2	83.0	88.2	99.3
1958	174.0	310.0	314.8	243.6	154.2	1933	66.6	67.1	70.6	81.7	87.8
1957	174.9	282.1	278.7	236.0	150.8	1932	59.1	74.3	77.1	80.3	100.0
1956	188.4	265.6	262.6	227.1	174.6	1931	61.1	92.2	96.8	99.7	115.6
1955	188.0	263.2	271.2	224.9	172.0	1930	99.2	135.2	141.8	128.4	165.3
1954	187.2	283.3	283.9	226.2	157.3	1929	142.6	150.8	159.4	145.0	173.1
1953	201.0	288.1	292.5	228.0	194.2	1928	141.1	149.3	151.4	144.4	171.6
1952	206.2	316.4	343.5	232.5	169.4	1927	151.7	124.4	130.3	140.6	179.2
1951	217.3	407.8	423.1	235.8	217.0	1926	150.4	121.4	127.1	135.7	165.0
1950	219.4	334.1	337.7	214.2	168.9	1925	165.9	123.7	119.4	137.2	185.8
1949	218.6	296.9	297.6	217.6	184.9	1924	132.5	113.1	106.7	132.2	173.7
1948	200.7	281.1	274.9	233.6	181.6	1923	114.9	114.6	109.0	139.9	155.1
1947	167.7	204.7	185.1	185.2	152.4	1922	127.4	120.1	114.9	131.2	159.5
1946	135.7	183.9	170.8	146.0	146.6	1921	163.6	131.1	124.9	161.9	190.4
1945	134.9	170.4	163.8	133.9	141.9	1920	258.2	215.0	180.6	195.8	254.1
1944	134.0	165.4	162.8	133.5	134.3	1919	241.1	200.6	174.0	185.9	235.6
1943	118.5	166.3	160.7	133.2	147.0	1918	232.6	223.4	173.2	159.2	207.9
1942	97.1	150.3	145.8	131.8	134.9	1917	225.3	188.7	138.8	143.8	185.0
1941	85.7	126.9	131.1	126.3	110.1	1916	141.5	141.5	103.3	115.2	143.0
1940	84.0	109.9	112.6	104.8	98.8	1915	133.4	133.3	90.9	105.0	115.0
1939	70.5	104.1	107.8	97.6	94.8	1914	105.4	136.2	94.6	96.5	124.4
1938	102.5	102.6	105.2	106.4	104.8	1913	92.0	117.4	87.5	96.5	119.3
1937	138.9	106.6	105.2	105.7	99.7						
1936	99.6	90.9	89.8	96.6	104.4						

Series L119–124. *General statistics, indexes of physical volume of agricultural production, Canada and by region, 1935 to 1960*

(1935–39 = 100)

Year	Canada	Maritimes	Quebec	Ontario	Prairie Provinces	British Columbia	Year	Canada	Maritimes	Quebec	Ontario	Prairie Provinces	British Columbia
	119	120	121	122	123	124		119	120	121	122	123	124
1960	154.4	116.2	142.5	150.3	164.4	150.6	1945	110.9	99.3	100.7	107.6	115.0	131.1
1959	144.6	111.3	139.0	145.7	148.9	146.9	1944	140.4	121.4	131.1	114.0	159.9	140.0
1958	145.3	113.9	139.0	158.5	142.9	145.1	1943	113.7	109.5	112.3	89.4	128.2	114.7
1957	133.9	120.7	132.9	142.7	129.9	143.7	1942	164.2	101.5	121.7	125.0	209.9	99.9
1956	169.5	116.8	138.4	137.5	205.1	127.8	1941	109.1	95.3	108.2	107.9	111.2	113.4
1955	150.4	121.8	143.8	129.6	168.8	131.2	1940	130.1	100.1	111.8	103.8	154.4	115.5
1954	119.7	111.4	129.8	129.1	111.5	131.4	1939	128.7	100.7	111.9	108.0	149.6	110.4
1953	157.9	109.6	132.9	129.5	187.7	136.3	1938	107.4	98.5	97.6	101.1	114.9	102.5
1952	166.2	104.7	124.7	119.6	213.1	133.3	1937	83.7	103.8	97.6	102.1	65.9	101.1
1951	154.7	103.2	139.0	128.6	181.5	126.9	1936	85.1	101.8	99.3	90.2	75.8	94.8
1950	137.8	127.9	136.3	128.1	145.1	134.2	1935	95.2	95.2	93.6	98.7	93.9	91.2
1949	122.3	132.2	126.4	124.9	116.4	148.7							
1948	125.1	113.2	121.6	119.0	129.1	143.7							
1947	116.0	108.1	102.6	107.7	122.4	146.4							
1946	125.6	112.7	112.2	117.6	132.8	151.9							

Series L125–138. *Crop statistics, grain and hay, acreage and production, Canada, crop years, 1851 to 1960*
(seeded acres in thousands of acres; production in thousands of bushels except for Tame hay, series L136, in tons)

Year[1]	All wheat		Oats for grain		Barley		Rye		Flaxseed		Tame hay		Mixed grains	
	Seeded acres	Production	Seeded acres	Production	Seeded acres	Production	Seeded acres	Production	Seeded acres	Production	Acres	Production (tons)	Seeded acres	Production
	125	126	127	128	129	130	131	132	133	134	135	136	137	138
1960	24,500	445,077	9,089	344,209	7,886	215,644	534	8,436	2,052	17,191	11,735	20,102	1,467	62,627
1959	22,149	398,077	9,234	345,731	9,286	237,811	514	7,712	2,551	22,342	11,471	17,924	1,398	63,835
1958	21,561	392,719	8,829	316,912	9,404	216,007	544	8,387	3,486	19,205	11,484	19,193	1,440	62,788
1957	22,781	573,040	10,471	467,517	8,390	269,065	547	8,434	3,041	34,991	10,922	19,655	1,561	66,618
1956	22,600	519,178	10,958	399,451	9,887	251,102	746	13,840	1,836	18,990	10,842	20,186	1,701	66,266
1955	25,539	331,981	10,052	306,401	7,842	175,196	787	12,812	1,178	10,998	10,737	20,118	1,670	63,649
1954	26,384	634,040	9,873	413,971	8,908	262,121	1,505	28,845	956	9,748	10,564	20,015	1,550	67,738
1953	26,164	701,973	11,057	471,117	8,478	291,572	1,236	24,025	1,110	11,660	10,629	19,720	1,572	64,054
1952	25,254	553,678	11,897	493,886	7,840	245,435	1,127	17,616	1,158	9,478	10,538	20,190	1,524	69,433
1951	27,311	466,490	11,184	401,768	6,510	167,495	1,138	13,005	584	4,959	10,228	14,834	1,421	62,838
1950	27,387	366,028	10,988	304,595	5,923	118,044	1,206	10,193	312	2,242	10,346	13,480	1,449	48,312
1949	23,705	381,413	10,854	345,305	6,400	152,281	2,352	27,521	1,958	18,449	10,405	17,598	1,327	53,678
1948	24,122	338,506	10,733	270,190	7,391	139,886	1,202	13,630	1,791	13,822	10,671	17,404	981	30,220
1947	24,756	411,601	11,782	360,860	6,186	146,852	711	8,716	886	6,774	10,500	15,879	1,164	47,629
1946	23,198	316,320	13,210	351,234	6,944	148,792	492	5,849	873	6,225	10,752	19,282	1,208	40,392
1945	22,677	414,859	13,412	474,044	7,008	187,326	649	8,480	1,217	8,882	10,786	16,921	1,274	48,948
1944	16,734	282,377	14,735	461,567	8,138	208,365	515	6,401	2,984	18,432	10,504	19,189	1,254	30,065
1943	21,560	556,067	13,532	641,488	6,879	256,037	1,308	24,187	1,536	15,470	10,474	18,327	1,481	61,565
1942	21,949	314,710	12,278	306,052	5,312	110,401	929	11,140	1,043	6,780	10,365	14,448	1,435	45,620
1941	28,726	540,190	12,298	380,526	4,342	104,256	1,035	13,994	382	3,049	9,843	16,658	1,220	43,133
1940	26,756	520,623	12,790	384,407	4,347	103,147	1,102	15,307	298	2,044	9,784	15,544	1,218	44,072
1939	25,930	360,010	13,010	371,382	4,454	102,242	741	10,988	210	1,259	9,679	15,859	1,160	39,161
1938	25,570	180,210	13,048	268,442	4,331	83,124	894	5,771	241	775	9,542	15,137	1,128	36,129
1937	25,605	219,218	13,288	271,778	4,438	71,922	625	4,281	477	1,795	9,638	15,769	1,172	33,639
1936	24,116	281,935	14,006	394,348	3,887	83,975	720	9,606	307	1,667	9,460	16,019	1,152	39,535
1935	23,985	275,849	13,731	321,120	3,612	63,742	685	4,706	227	910	9,560	12,502	1,159	37,926
1934	25,991	281,892	13,529	307,478	3,658	63,359	583	4,177	244	632	9,598	13,095	1,167	33,009
1933	27,182	443,061	13,148	391,561	3,758	80,773	774	8,470	462	2,719	9,478	15,323	1,196	39,036
1932	26,355	321,325	12,838	328,278	3,791	67,383	799	5,322	648	2,465	9,682	15,928	1,196	39,431
1931	24,898	420,672	13,259	423,148	5,559	135,160	1,448	22,018	582	5,069	11,362	18,037	1,201	44,276
1930	25,155	302,192	12,480	282,838	5,926	102,313	992	13,160	382	2,060	11,359	17,668	1,119	35,754
1929	24,119	566,726	13,136	452,153	4,881	136,391	840	14,618	378	3,614	11,175	18,525	1,107	39,130
1928	22,460	479,665	13,240	439,713	3,506	96,938	743	15,571	476	4,885	11,137	19,527	1,004	37,622
1927	22,896	407,136	12,741	383,416	3,648	99,987	754	12,179	738	5,995	10,353	16,119	956	33,875
1926	20,790	395,475	12,556	402,296	3,524	87,118	643	9,158	842	6,237	10,200	16,544	860	33,106
1925	22,056	262,097	14,491	405,976	3,407	88,807	891	13,751	1,277	9,695	10,348	16,217	848	31,995
1924	21,886	474,199	14,388	563,998	2,785	76,998	1,448	23,232	630	7,140	10,117	15,874	844	29,750
1923	22,423	399,786	14,541	491,239	2,600	71,865	2,105	32,373	566	5,008	10,308	15,294	780	27,708
1922	23,261	300,858	16,994	426,233	2,796	59,790	1,842	21,455	533	4,112	10,879	12,028	861	22,272
1921	18,232	263,189	15,850	530,710	2,552	63,311	650	11,306	1,428	7,998	10,618	13,923	812	32,421
1920	19,126	193,260	14,952	394,387	2,646	56,389	753	10,207	1,093	5,473	10,822	16,842	902	27,852
1919	17,354	189,075	14,790	426,312	3,154	77,287	555	8,504	1,068	6,055	10,740	15,217	922	35,662
1918	14,756	233,743	13,313	403,010	2,392	55,058	212	3,857	920	5,935	8,335	13,947	497	16,157
1917	15,370	262,781	10,996	410,211	1,803	42,770	148	2,876	658	8,260	7,921	14,814	413	10,585
1916	15,109	393,543	11,556	464,954	1,718	54,017	122	2,486	463	6,114	7,876	10,873	467	17,518
1915	10,294	161,280	10,062	313,078	1,496	36,201	111	2,017	1,084	7,175	8,087	10,477	463	16,382
1914	11,015	231,717	10,434	404,669	1,613	48,319	119	2,300	1,553	17,539	8,262	11,096	474	15,792
1913	10,997	224,159	9,966	391,629	1,581	49,398	127	2,428	2,022	26,130	8,376	12,402	496	17,198
1912	11,006	231,237	9,641	365,694	1,522	44,451	132	2,500	1,351	15,443	8,786	14,347	526	15,707
1911	8,864	132,078	8,656	245,393	1,283	28,848	115	1,542	582	4,245	8,344	10,521	427	13,086
1910	7,750	166,744	9,303	353,466	1,865	55,398	91	1,715	138	2,213	8,210	11,877	582	19,391
1909	6,610	112,434	7,911	250,377	1,746	46,762	100	1,711	139	1,499	8,211	11,450	582	19,049
1901	4,224	55,572	5,368	151,497	872	22,224	117	2,317	23	172	6,453	7,853	273	7,268
1891	2,704	42,223	3,961	83,428	868	17,223	—	1,341	—	138	6,010	7,694	—	—
1881	2,342	32,350	—	70,493	—	16,845	—	2,097	—	109	4,458	5,053	—	—
1871	1,647	16,724	—	42,489	—	11,496	—	1,064	—	118	3,650	3,819	—	—
1861	1,631	27,275	1,634	38,772	258	5,104	154	1,817	—	—	—	1,552	—	—
1851	1,208	15,756	1,004	20,369	73	1,120	92	644	—	—	—	1,469	—	—

[1] Crop year ending in the year given: data actually apply to the preceding calendar year.

Series L139–146. *Crop statistics, wheat, production, imports, exports and home consumption, Canada, crop years, 1869 to 1961*

(thousands of bushels)

Year[1]	Production	Imports			Exports			Apparent home consumption
		Wheat	Wheat flour	Wheat and flour	Wheat	Wheat flour	Wheat and flour	
	139	140	141	142	143	144	145	146
1961	518,395	3	4	7	317,568	35,682	353,249	156,900
1960	445,077	4	3	7	240,321	36,970	277,291	156,206
1959	398,077	2	2	4	257,421	37,125	294,546	163,988
1958	392,719	—2	1	1	279,912	40,381	320,293	157,519
1957	573,040	132	15	148	230,856	33,540	264,396	154,820
1956	519,178	3	17	20	272,260	40,000	312,260	164,113
1955	331,981	172	6	178	211,288	40,622	251,909	162,176
1954	634,040	452	4	457	208,835	46,246	255,081	143,926
1953	701,973	7	10	17	329,026	56,501	385,527	150,456
1952	553,678	3	14	18	304,722	51,103	355,825	169,895
1951	466,490	6	6	12	185,039	55,921	240,961	148,538
1950	366,028	1	3	4	179,457	45,680	225,137	131,107
1949	381,413	288	1	289	184,235	48,094	232,329	124,672
1948	338,506	771	54	825	133,505	61,477	194,982	152,779
1947	411,601	16	—2	16	163,388	76,033	239,421	159,655
1946	316,320	—2	74	75	278,070	65,116	343,186	157,682
1945	414,859	2	402	405	280,288	62,657	342,946	170,776
1944	282,377	8	425	433	283,165	60,590	343,755	177,150
1943	556,067	—2	3	3	158,112	56,588	214,701	170,495
1942	314,710	—2	29	29	179,902	45,926	225,828	145,288
1941	540,190	—2	122	123	184,907	46,300	231,206	129,451
1940	520,623	16	428	444	162,158	30,516	192,674	130,830
1939	360,010	1,559	333	1,891	139,315	20,719	160,034	123,492
1938	180,210	5,744	395	6,139	79,342	16,243	95,586	103,276
1937	219,218	147	256	403	189,407	20,365	209,773	100,163
1936	281,935	15	276	292	232,020	22,405	254,425	114,291
1935	275,849	3	894	897	144,375	21,376	165,751	100,044
1934	281,892	11	402	413	170,234	24,546	194,780	102,280
1933	443,061	51	122	173	240,137	24,168	264,304	97,214
1932	321,325	124	93	216	182,803	24,226	207,030	117,168
1931	420,672	132	113	244	228,536	30,157	258,694	150,207
1930	302,192	1,004	382	1,386	155,766	30,501	186,267	117,968
1929	566,726	995	351	1,346	354,425	53,139	407,564	124,425
1928	479,665	149	326	473	288,567	44,396	332,963	111,640
1927	407,136	139	268	407	251,266	41,615	292,881	99,180
1926	395,475	155	224	379	275,557	49,035	324,592	61,864
1925	262,097	353	277	630	146,958	45,764	192,722	87,381
1924	474,199	41	400	441	292,425	54,096	346,522	92,175
1923	399,786	94	304	398	229,849	49,516	279,365	130,794
1922	300,858	193	180	373	150,935	34,834	185,770	107,441
1921	263,189	305	150	455	136,969	30,247	167,215	59,747
1920	193,260	115	87	202	63,450	29,049	92,500	100,962
1919	189,075	291	31	322	55,921	41,039	96,960	92,436
1918	233,743	184	97	281	118,580	50,661	169,240	64,784
1917	262,781	86	218	304	140,224	34,341	174,565	88,520
1916	393,543	131	174	305	235,739	33,419	269,158	124,690
1915	161,280	1,964	216	2,180	63,902	22,848	86,750	76,710
1914	231,717	130	228	358	114,902	20,685	135,587	96,487
1913	224,159	619	270	889	95,511	20,233	115,744	109,304
1912	231,237	141	234	375	78,787	18,814	97,601	134,012
1911	132,078	108	300	408	48,443	13,955	62,398	70,088
1910	166,744	73	136	209	52,624	15,184	67,808	99,145
1909	112,434	28	151	179	47,624	9,037	56,662	55,951
1908	93,131	104	199	303	40,078	7,506	47,584	45,851
1907	135,602	35	199	234	39,435	7,031	46,466	89,370
1906	107,033	65	189	254	40,399	6,894	47,293	59,993
1905	71,838	92	191	283	14,700	5,947	20,647	51,474
1904	81,888	37	184	221	16,779	7,144	23,923	58,186
1903	97,073	85	159	244	32,986	5,795	38,781	58,536
1902	88,337	148	212	360	26,118	4,889	31,007	57,690
1901	55,572	105	210	315	9,740	5,034	14,774	41,113
1900	59,912	27	228	255	16,845	3,456	20,301	39,866
1899	66,495	36	259	295	10,305	3,567	13,872	52,919
1898	54,418	58	160	218	18,963	5,623	24,586	30,051
1897	39,570	84	118	202	7,855	1,808	9,753	30,019
1896	55,703	142	187	329	9,920	840	10,760	45,272

Series L 139–146. *Crop statistics, wheat, production, imports, exports and home consumption, Canada, crop years, 1869 to 1961* (continued)

(thousands of bushels)

Year[1]	Production	Imports			Exports			Apparent home consumption
		Wheat	Wheat flour	Wheat and flour	Wheat	Wheat flour	Wheat and flour	
	139	**140**	**141**	**142**	**143**	**144**	**145**	**146**
1895	43,221	500	215	715	8,826	1,003	9,829	34,107
1894	41,347	61	146	207	9,272	1,929	11,201	30,353
1893	48,182	9	155	164	9,272	1,846	11,118	37,229
1892	60,721	66	165	231	8,714	1,715	10,429	50,523
1891	42,223	148	258	406	2,108	1,336	3,444	39,185
1890	30,792	189	764	953	422	518	940	30,805
1889	32,965	15	1,165	1,180	491	590	1,081	33,064
1888	38,954	12	281	293	2,164	1,575	3,739	35,508
1887	38,225	23	763	786	5,632	2,341	7,973	31,038
1886	42,736	66	906	972	3,419	1,738	5,157	38,551
1885	45,363	373	2,431	2,804	2,341	557	2,898	45,269
1884	30,841	299	2,390	2,689	746	888	1,634	31,896
1883	47,752	44	1,192	1,236	5,867	2,201	8,068	40,920
1882	38,000	346	776	1,122	3,845	2,114	5,959	33,163
1881	32,350	77	889	966	2,524	1,978	4,502	28,813
1880	34,276	10	458	468	5,091	2,450	7,541	27,203
1879	30,359	4,210	1,409	5,619	6,611	2,587	9,198	26,780
1878	25,903	5,635	1,416	7,051	4,394	2,143	6,537	26,416
1877	22,601	4,589	2,471	7,060	2,393	1,209	3,602	26,059
1876	26,093	5,856	1,692	7,548	6,070	1,870	7,940	25,701
1875	23,853	5,105	2,105	7,210	4,383	1,363	5,746	25,318
1874	24,180	8,406	1,296	9,702	6,581	2,432	9,013	24,869
1873	23,838	5,821	1,255	7,076	4,380	2,134	6,514	24,401
1872	23,149	4,168	1,694	5,862	2,993	2,039	5,032	23,979
1871	16,724	4,202	1,767	5,969	1,749	1,379	3,128	23,563
1870	22,578	4,403	1,469	5,872	3,557	1,720	5,277	23,173
1869	22,156	3,592	1,572	5,164	2,809	1,689	4,498	22,822

[1] For the crop year ending in the year given: production data actually apply to the preceding calendar year.

[2] Less than 500 bushels.

Series L147–166. *Crop statistics, special crops, production and farm value, Canada, crop years, selected years 1720 to 1901 and 1909 to 1960*

(values in thousands of dollars; quantities in thousands of units)

Year[1]	Corn for grain Quantity (thousands of bushels)	Corn for grain Value (thousands of dollars)	Buckwheat Quantity (thousands of bushels)	Buckwheat Value (thousands of dollars)	Peas, dry Quantity (thousands of bushels)	Peas, dry Value (thousands of dollars)	Beans, dry Quantity (thousands of bushels)	Beans, dry Value (thousands of dollars)	Soy beans Quantity (thousands of bushels)	Soy beans Value (thousands of dollars)
	147	148	149	150	151	152	153	154	155	156
1960	30,906	35,820	1,431	1,520	1,016	2,203	1,155	4,403	6,783	12,684
1959	29,785	36,031	2,001	2,093	1,119	2,439	1,223	4,476	6,579	12,368
1958	29,525	34,844	2,212	2,363	1,351	2,747	1,094	3,735	6,476	12,628
1957	27,814	33,377	3,177	3,665	1,817	3,618	1,146	4,383	5,269	11,328
1956	35,558	37,699	2,418	2,908	1,019	2,598	1,215	5,105	5,993	12,525
1955	24,891	36,011	2,465	2,692	1,096	2,690	1,012	5,060	4,778	11,467
1954	23,088	31,238	3,572	3,747	1,313	2,682	1,180	4,872	5,013	12,282
1953	21,192	30,535	2,858	3,713	956	2,616	1,296	5,714	4,128	10,526
1952	15,900	28,500	3,022	4,077	752	2,116	1,229	5,151	3,844	10,571
1951	14,103	22,585	2,938	3,884	652	1,824	1,185	5,685	3,323	8,474
1950	13,964	17,960	2,646	3,265	772	1,967	1,598	5,329	2,610	5,899
1949	12,697	16,739	3,120	3,823	1,167	3,235	1,434	5,906	1,824	4,195
1948	6,887	12,893	4,180	4,857	1,558	4,319	1,287	7,017	1,110	3,397
1947	11,007	11,635	3,956	3,853	2,045	5,881	1,364	4,082	1,072	2,369
1946	10,635	11,054	4,310	3,680	1,335	3,655	1,099	2,788	844	1,604
1945	11,976	11,830	4,720	3,920	990	2,454	1,211	3,067	681	1,362
1944	7,994	6,926	5,339	4,251	1,341	2,908	1,208	2,648	570	1,026
1943	14,689	11,646	4,454	3,178	1,393	2,908	1,316	2,072	872	1,509
1942	13,672	9,868	4,139	2,819	1,182	2,354	1,651	2,808	217	—
1941	6,956	3,826	6,692	3,838	1,355	2,652	1,477	2,721	—	—
1940	8,097	4,453	6,848	4,103	1,307	2,350	1,527	3,138	—	—
1939	7,690	3,614	7,079	4,098	1,365	2,113	1,557	1,725	—	—
1938	5,415	3,466	7,745	5,592	1,200	2,012	1,296	1,597	—	—
1937	6,083	4,258	8,596	6,088	1,229	1,991	876	1,790	—	—
1936	7,765	3,494	7,949	4,017	1,616	1,767	1,161	1,693	—	—
1935	6,798	4,419	8,635	4,572	1,588	1,660	814	1,079	—	—
1934	5,054	2,982	8,483	4,233	1,377	1,371	891	878	—	—
1933	5,057	2,276	8,424	3,585	1,518	1,288	1,141	629	—	—
1932	5,449	2,274	6,917	3,454	1,369	1,160	1,304	941	—	—
1931	5,826	5,054	10,903	7,124	2,371	3,487	1,439	3,261	—	—
1930	5,183	5,469	10,470	9,867	1,980	4,079	1,491	4,920	—	—
1929	5,241	5,860	10,899	10,128	2,588	4,786	1,170	4,184	—	—
1928	4,262	4,212	10,800	9,727	2,795	4,959	1,037	2,408	—	—
1927	7,813	7,780	9,882	8,598	2,635	4,610	1,160	3,060	—	—
1926	10,564	9,939	10,546	8,965	3,411	5,616	1,501	3,877	—	—
1925	11,998	14,227	11,412	10,149	3,240	5,676	1,194	3,307	—	—
1924	13,608	12,466	9,744	8,192	2,898	4,987	1,042	2,773	—	—
1923	13,798	11,510	9,701	8,141	3,429	6,141	1,303	3,714	—	—
1922	14,904	12,317	8,230	7,285	2,770	5,439	1,090	3,156	—	—
1921	14,335	16,593	8,995	11,512	3,528	8,534	1,265	4,918	—	—
1920	16,940	22,080	10,551	15,831	3,406	9,739	1,389	6,215	—	—
1919	14,205	24,903	11,376	18,018	4,313	12,899	3,563	19,284	—	—
1918	7,763	14,307	7,149	10,443	3,026	10,724	1,274	9,493	—	—
1917	6,282	6,747	5,976	6,375	2,218	4,919	413	2,228	—	—
1916	14,368	10,243	7,866	5,913	3,472	5,724	723	2,207	—	—
1915	13,924	9,808	8,626	6,213	3,362	4,895	798	1,844	—	—
1914	16,768	10,781	8,372	5,320	3,952	4,382	801	1,505	—	—
1913	16,942	10,534	10,517	6,544	3,913	4,944	920	2,008	—	—
1912	19,182	12,360	8,466	5,443	4,669	4,770	1,016	1,956	—	—
1911	14,318	7,664	7,200	4,095	4,789	4,196	826	1,417	—	—
1910	19,258	12,760	7,806	4,554	8,145	7,124	1,325	1,881	—	—
1909	22,868	11,834	7,153	4,269	7,060	5,970	1,245	1,988	—	—
1901	—	—	4,547	—	12,349	—	861	—	—	—
1891	—	—	4,995	—	14,823	—	800	—	—	—
1881	—	—	4,901	—	13,750[3]	—	—	—	—	—
1871	—	—	3,726	—	9,906	—	220	—	—	—
1852	—	—	—	—	—	—	—	—	—	—
1734	—	—	—	—	—	—	—	—	—	—
1720	—	—	—	—	—	—	—	—	—	—

Series L 147–166. *Crop statistics, special crops, production and farm value, Canada, crop years, selected years 1720 to 1901 and 1909 to 1960 (continuation)*

(values in thousands of dollars; quantities in thousands of units)

Year[1]	Potatoes Quantity (thousands of cwt.)	Potatoes Value (thousands of dollars)	Fodder corn Quantity (thousands of tons)	Field roots Quantity (thousands of tons)	Sugar beets Quantity (thousands of tons)	Sugar beets Value (thousands of dollars)	Tobacco Quantity (thousands of pounds)	Tobacco Value (thousands of dollars)	Maple syrup[1] Quantity (thousands of gallons)	Maple syrup[1] Value (thousands of dollars)
	157	158	159	160	161	162	163	164	165	166
1960	35,614	98,317	3,943	335	1,240	15,842	169,904	90,403	2,716	10,898
1959	39,610	68,221	3,753	398	1,325	19,177	197,302	89,603	2,358	9,460
1958	43,744	75,675	3,605	351	1,054	13,948	164,865	78,589	2,485	8,440
1957	42,325	74,274	3,450	425	893	15,470	161,940	72,059	3,134	10,342
1956	40,191	71,032	3,436	447	981	13,170	134,840	57,685	2,677	9,936
1955	32,163	77,951	3,046	453	1,004	12,108	184,763	77,788	2,231	10,882
1954	41,803	55,004	3,621	489	900	12,061	139,190	59,617	2,422	11,038
1953	36,959	103,795	3,881	502	1,023	15,493	139,719	56,797	1,948	7,306
1952	29,928	101,189	3,661	526	965	14,440	153,792	66,213	3,470	12,175
1951	43,825	54,329	4,717	618	1,116	18,299	120,298	51,292	2,309	8,555
1950	42,480	64,292	4,149	545	859	11,749	139,820	55,453	2,983	10,636
1949	44,395	72,749	3,933	674	629	9,202	126,629	50,272	2,485	9,126
1948	38,017	83,103	3,094	658	606	8,685	106,688	37,460	2,394	8,541
1947	41,756	71,133	3,323	884	736	9,196	141,384	49,472	3,923	14,139
1946	31,870	71,333	3,064	866	619	6,567	92,345	30,620	2,144	6,282
1945	44,187	67,198	3,801	1,154	566	6,283	105,416	31,001	1,530	4,497
1944	39,949	71,412	3,605	1,316	474	4,980	69,104	19,646	3,090	9,057
1943	39,711	60,143	3,930	1,271	716	6,053	89,699	21,539	2,299	5,750
1942	37,039	46,234	3,783	1,262	712	5,405	94,182	19,338	3,251	6,716
1941	42,300	35,394	4,155	1,951	825	5,612	64,020	11,086	2,276	3,562
1940	36,390	41,065	4,514	1,884	586	4,430	107,703	19,444	3,048	4,210
1939	35,938	33,093	4,413	1,908	498	3,286	101,395	20,270	2,593	3,444
1938	42,547	26,650	3,928	1,814	422	2,492	72,093	17,140	3,300	3,849
1937	39,614	45,125	3,128	1,910	556	3,233	46,116	9,374	1,674	2,245
1936	38,670	30,854	4,078	1,755	459	2,501	55,470	10,870	2,946	3,714
1935	48,095	23,822	3,815	2,026	413	2,328	38,735	7,218	2,907	3,523
1934	42,745	33,092	3,123	1,731	442	2,784	44,904	6,524	2,333	3,040
1933	39,416	24,920	2,858	1,889	506	3,097	53,987	6,178	1,842	2,060
1932	52,305	22,359	2,884	1,469	436	2,663	50,848	7,085	2,436	2,706
1931	48,241	39,858	3,476	2,054	467	3,209	36,539	7,142	1,832	3,457
1930	39,930	63,372	3,322	1,812	366	2,458	29,590	6,081	3,007	5,251
1929	50,195	40,874	3,666	2,179	418	3,018	41,757	6,788	3,344	6,118
1928	46,458	54,341	3,548	1,863	370	2,881	43,829	8,978	3,067	5,584
1927	46,937	69,204	4,490	1,711	508	3,350	28,824	7,380	3,138	4,935
1926	40,217	82,860	4,692	1,814	459	2,794	29,141	6,976	2,460	4,898
1925	56,648	47,956	5,741	2,030	334	2,268	18,711	4,358	2,721	5,288
1924	55,497	56,418	5,321	1,906	216	1,401	21,297	3,518	2,911	5,991
1923	55,745	50,320	5,879	2,202	190	1,500	25,948	4,548	—	—
1922	64,406	82,148	6,362	1,979	268	1,742	13,249	2,393	—	—
1921	80,299	129,803	5,642	2,909	412	5,279	48,088	5,893	—	—
1920	75,344	118,894	4,943	2,806	240	2,606	33,770	15,548	—	—
1919	62,610	102,235	4,788	3,067	180	1,845	14,232	4,967	—	—
1918	47,936	80,804	2,690	1,587	118	794	8,495	2,786	—	—
1917	37,978	50,982	1,908	922	71	440	5,943	1,082	—	—
1916	36,211	36,460	3,383	1,505	141	776	9,000	1,224	—	—
1915	51,404	41,598	3,251	1,724	109	651	10,000	1,020	—	—
1914	47,125	38,418	2,616	1,671	148	906	12,500	1,275	—	—
1913	50,931	37,329	3,038	2,000	201	1,005	6,500	819	—	—
1912	42,853	42,478	2,681	1,905	175	1,154	—	—	—	—
1911	33,277	27,427	2,705	2,174	188	1,096	17,632	2,422	—	—
1910	59,453	36,399	2,780	2,693	86	500	—	—	—	—
1909	44,273	34,819	2,938	2,532	109	578	—	—	—	—
1901	55,363[2]	—	—	76,076[2]	—	—	11,267	—	—	—
1891	53,491[2]	—	—	49,680[2]	—	—	4,278	—	—	—
1881	55,369[2]	—	—	48,251[2]	—	—	2,528	—	—	—
1871	47,330[2]	—	—	27,893[2]	—	—	1,596	—	—	—
1852	—	—	—	—	—	—	1,210	—	—	—
1734	—	—	—	—	—	—	166	—	—	—
1720	—	—	—	—	—	—	48	—	—	—

[1] Crop year ending in the year given: data actually apply to the preceding calendar year except for maple syrup which applies to the current calendar year.

[2] In thousands of bushels.
[3] Peas and beans.

Series L 167–232. *Livestock statistics, number on farms and farm values at 1 June,*
Canada and by region, 1871 to 1960

(number of animals in thousands; value of animals in thousands of dollars)

| | Milk cows | | Other cattle and calves | | Horses | | Hogs | | Sheep and lambs | | Hens and chickens |
Year	Number	Value	Number	Value	Number	Value	Number	Value	Number	Value	Number
	167	168	169	170	171	172	173	174	175	176	177
1960	2,965	589,756	8,372	961,845	552	72,324	5,070	127,851	1,607	25,408	67,261
1959	2,955	594,822	8,103	991,241	598	72,700	6,519	169,661	1,608	26,075	71,611
1958	3,028	554,614	7,962	895,021	661	73,084	5,931	207,805	1,630	29,226	72,343
1957	3,098	445,326	8,167	719,649	722	73,381	4,758	154,515	1,628	27,133	71,636
1956	3,160	447,057	7,851	668,119	782	74,384	4,731	115,064	1,620	25,983	67,535
1955	3,151	460,980	7,452	674,436	832	75,867	4,800	132,915	1,634	27,726	65,019
1954	3,120	450,340	7,050	615,755	917	72,929	4,440	159,783	1,636	28,950	69,441
1953	3,084	521,130	6,722	697,576	1,055	85,126	3,970	124,425	1,592	31,202	64,918
1952	3,006	633,027	6,147	789,597	1,179	94,820	5,428	147,829	1,534	33,920	59,010
1951	2,973	741,356	5,390	852,585	1,304	94,130	4,914	185,773	1,461	38,439	64,541
1950	3,119	547,020	5,224	560,498	1,496	102,932	4,372	147,507	1,579	27,937	55,779
1949	3,237	502,139	5,404	476,588	1,642	122,644	4,452	152,648	1,773	25,594	63,628
1948	3,357	454,114	5,627	422,716	1,789	137,168	3,946	122,766	2,050	25,954	62,561
1947	3,411	397,021	5,674	351,058	1,937	148,757	4,957	119,636	2,465	27,250	78,143
1946	3,485	382,985	5,689	314,772	2,136	157,975	4,277	95,590	2,792	27,895	73,183
1945	3,631	354,615	6,001	304,898	2,374	165,747	4,964	98,996	3,032	28,711	74,477
1944	3,668	357,805	5,876	287,648	2,568	194,739	6,790	123,706	3,213	32,087	77,229
1943	3,623	368,976	5,499	281,758	2,667	215,204	7,413	121,943	3,107	34,059	68,824
1942	3,614	252,725	5,098	173,793	2,759	189,224	6,808	72,738	2,972	20,621	66,334
1941	3,626	191,128	4,891	138,389	2,789	184,461	6,081	54,912	2,840	17,039	58,994
1940	3,650	184,706	4,730	173,694	2,780	175,697	6,002	70,807	2,887	19,902	57,014
1939	3,681	170,804	4,693	154,961	2,761	185,783	4,364	60,104	2,911	19,458	55,749
1938	3,730	148,772	4,761	126,960	2,770	195,631	3,527	46,569	3,047	17,605	51,665
1937	3,844	152,161	5,071	128,029	2,845	204,310	4,016	49,382	3,071	17,172	52,235
1936	3,805	139,916	5,024	114,126	2,878	206,990	4,136	45,344	3,159	17,064	54,396
1935	3,841	132,994	5,132	110,676	2,911	188,181	3,651	42,843	3,224	16,145	52,538
1934	3,861	110,102	5,209	86,718	2,918	167,370	3,736	36,739	3,291	13,743	55,040
1933	3,690	112,704	5,264	89,841	2,973	153,687	3,854	34,213	3,307	13,221	54,710
1932	3,592	114,600	4,956	85,194	3,084	141,512	4,670	22,067	3,604	11,933	59,700
1931	3,372	160,655	4,601	94,952	3,114	205,087	4,700	33,288	3,627	19,680	61,277
1930	3,233	192,347	4,453	154,302	3,191	193,074	3,735	55,282	3,438	23,352	60,484
1929	3,213	239,553	4,305	200,749	3,264	226,047	4,048	65,867	3,350	33,283	59,778
1928	3,295	237,563	4,163	192,883	3,265	245,792	4,217	62,522	3,128	32,661	54,221
1927	3,366	205,647	4,238	165,593	3,297	250,593	4,302	59,777	2,968	29,177	50,862
1926	3,373	176,937	4,445	139,110	3,361	241,288	4,037	64,969	2,830	28,387	49,741
1925	3,273	166,503	4,703	145,241	3,348	232,529	4,009	63,285	2,628	25,652	48,678
1924	3,195	146,798	4,940	133,944	3,384	217,590	4,594	56,692	2,499	22,572	48,319
1923	3,179	151,028	4,796	124,058	3,341	212,210	3,986	47,227	2,601	20,180	47,092
1922	3,168	152,662	5,099	134,587	3,401	246,631	3,493	51,176	3,045	23,268	45,514
1921	3,087	188,518	5,283	146,567	3,452	414,808	3,324	35,869	3,200	20,675	41,125
1920	2,986	238,497	5,167	247,683	3,404	359,248	3,152	72,430	3,179	32,044	35,575
1919	2,997	278,876	5,488	323,989	3,445	407,189	3,623	91,866	2,949	43,618	37,629
1918	2,901	253,792	5,350	331,111	3,346	425,124	3,677	96,887	2,636	42,140	35,796
1917	2,927	250,236	4,862	282,293	3,210	404,941	3,292	84,330	2,422	36,940	34,936
1916	2,881	200,764	4,618	256,630	3,167	408,651	3,562	61,990	2,334	24,441	34,075
1915	2,834	174,985	4,387	199,089	3,115	392,393	3,464	48,343	2,359	18,910	—
1914	2,786	160,943	4,125	177,804	2,992	379,965	3,640	45,065	2,310	16,426	—
1913	2,766	—	4,089	—	2,827	—	3,683	—	2,333	—	—
1912	2,692	—	3,994	—	2,694	—	3,684	—	2,172	—	—
1911	2,645	111,833	3,881	84,021	2,599	381,916	3,635	26,987	2,174	10,702	29,773
1910	2,592	110,454	3,923	121,215	2,478	328,282	3,304	37,335	2,246	13,474	—
1909	2,593	94,212	4,058	116,905	2,327	304,199	3,287	38,782	2,327	13,460	—
1908	2,659	90,142	4,338	114,319	2,248	280,403	3,546	32,906	2,380	12,153	—
1907	2,686	—	4,467	—	2,106	—	3,701	—	2,350	—	—
1906	2,703	—	4,499	—	1,963	—	3,379	—	2,543	—	—
1901	2,199	—	3,377	—	1,578	—	2,354	—	2,510	—	16,651
1891	1,820	—	2,301	—	1,471	—	1,734	—	2,564	—	—
1881	1,592	—	1,923	—	1,059	—	1,208	—	3,049	—	—
1871	1,251	—	1,373	—	837	—	1,366	—	3,156	—	—

Series L167–232. *Livestock statistics, number on farms and farm values at 1 June, Canada and by region, 1871 to 1960 (continuation)*

(number of animals in thousands; value of animals in thousands of dollars)

	Maritimes										
	Milk cows		Other cattle and calves		Horses		Hogs		Sheep and lambs		Hens and chickens
Year	Number	Value	Number	Value	Number	Value	Number	Value	Number	Value	Number
	178	**179**	**180**	**181**	**182**	**183**	**184**	**185**	**186**	**187**	**188**
1960	176	29,672	262	21,363	29	4,179	147	3,812	161	2,316	3,679
1959	181	30,350	253	20,935	34	4,616	173	4,643	171	2,529	3,885
1958	191	27,998	254	18,747	41	4,750	139	4,830	174	2,592	3,755
1957	204	24,795	281	16,575	47	5,191	126	3,979	180	2,562	3,683
1956	213	27,133	283	16,968	52	5,756	134	3,417	180	2,709	3,846
1955	212	29,366	276	17,037	55	5,923	148	4,402	188	2,940	3,685
1954	214	27,444	266	14,709	62	6,459	164	5,938	195	2,946	3,915
1953	212	32,784	260	17,751	69	7,738	143	4,229	188	3,184	3,590
1952	206	38,325	238	20,368	72	8,894	203	5,492	180	2,649	3,620
1951	204	40,140	222	21,722	78	8,534	199	8,052	185	3,702	3,839
1950	211	31,841	218	15,593	84	9,766	191	5,998	189	2,745	3,632
1949	214	27,777	217	12,718	88	10,656	182	6,308	186	2,150	4,041
1948	219	27,457	218	11,390	92	11,467	168	5,393	203	2,292	3,697
1947	229	24,718	228	10,347	95	12,455	176	4,887	235	2,283	4,833
1946	244	23,002	247	9,856	100	14,061	154	3,859	260	2,399	4,371
1945	258	20,867	260	8,633	104	14,193	170	3,579	284	2,631	4,216
1944	261	20,429	275	8,723	108	14,495	208	4,177	295	2,691	4,322
1943	257	21,007	258	9,038	109	14,601	205	3,935	300	2,849	3,760
1942	260	12,922	242	5,229	110	12,220	189	2,166	278	1,509	3,637
1941	269	10,015	237	4,089	109	11,487	161	1,505	275	1,301	3,022
1940	271	11,528	248	6,624	110	10,937	184	2,371	276	1,644	2,899
1939	278	11,090	265	6,755	111	11,825	164	2,423	282	1,659	2,953
1938	273	10,507	264	6,373	110	11,494	158	2,222	291	1,514	2,977
1937	272	10,531	258	6,325	112	11,691	177	2,443	283	1,495	3,036
1936	269	9,871	226	5,176	108	10,845	158	2,264	283	1,377	3,152
1935	277	8,804	242	4,715	113	10,558	150	2,054	287	1,325	2,955
1934	284	7,700	277	4,272	115	9,528	139	1,553	308	1,196	3,031
1933	276	8,217	308	5,673	120	9,505	146	1,391	329	1,289	3,180
1932	267	8,788	294	5,248	124	9,217	189	1,483	353	1,249	3,406
1931	253	10,416	282	4,794	124	12,615	170	1,476	418	1,936	3,401
1930	250	12,742	280	8,746	128	12,526	154	2,653	428	2,652	3,301
1929	253	14,908	267	9,480	129	13,630	158	3,028	425	3,309	3,167
1928	256	15,003	251	8,533	131	14,756	174	3,356	435	3,549	3,026
1927	264	12,861	258	7,423	132	14,135	173	3,100	418	3,176	2,822
1926	271	12,972	273	7,322	137	13,641	160	3,109	443	3,382	2,707
1925	260	12,059	269	7,902	134	12,740	150	2,694	440	3,322	2,937
1924	252	10,098	277	7,017	134	12,939	167	2,570	440	2,905	3,098
1923	247	10,699	281	7,201	133	12,412	148	2,189	445	2,682	2,855
1922	261	11,429	326	8,371	144	14,451	142	2,579	533	3,254	3,023
1921	272	13,665	334	7,180	149	20,034	162	2,138	565	3,119	2,755
1920	293	19,144	378	15,174	163	20,402	180	4,180	595	4,820	2,782
1919	291	21,576	400	19,767	170	21,888	204	6,032	506	5,972	2,775
1918	278	18,376	382	16,407	162	19,887	183	5,247	457	5,272	2,576
1917	279	17,650	289	12,127	157	17,566	158	4,338	402	4,098	2,400
1916	273	13,997	286	10,157	159	17,518	163	2,932	395	2,766	2,412
1915	268	11,318	289	8,617	159	19,647	167	2,758	398	2,248	—
1914	265	10,557	293	8,058	159	19,975	169	2,764	405	2,001	—
1913	268	—	304	—	160	—	176	—	424	—	—
1912	290	—	328	—	161	—	197	—	446	—	—
1911	304	9,479	319	4,712	163	19,439	207	1,536	471	1,697	2,525
1910	303	10,476	322	—	163	—	208	—	504	—	—
1909	303	9,429	330	—	163	—	209	—	531	2,251	—
1908	309	9,100	352	—	165	—	219	—	574	2,263	—
1907	310	—	370	—	159	—	208	—	617	—	—
1906	311	—	370	—	156	—	192	—	584	—	—
1901	290	—	366	—	158	—	145	—	593	—	1,906
1891	294	—	327	—	162	—	142	—	662	—	—
1881	287	—	342	—	141	—	141	—	765	—	—
1871	206	—	232	—	94	—	120	—	633	—	—

Series L 167–232. *Livestock statistics, number on farms and farm values at 1 June, Canada and by region, 1871 to 1960 (continuation)*

(number of animals in thousands; value of animals in thousands of dollars)

	Quebec										
	Milk cows		Other cattle and calves		Horses		Hogs		Sheep and lambs		Hens and chickens
Year	Number	Value	Number	Value	Number	Value	Number	Value	Number	Value	Number
	189	190	191	192	193	194	195	196	197	198	199
1960	1,009	177,584	902	69,945	108	21,492	895	22,375	238	3,094	11,485
1959	1,007	174,211	884	67,719	121	21,538	1,158	30,108	265	3,710	11,520
1958	1,033	165,280	887	62,194	135	21,870	978	32,274	305	4,575	11,978
1957	1,054	135,966	939	52,639	148	22,511	837	25,110	325	4,551	11,269
1956	1,054	137,059	948	52,492	164	24,198	887	22,178	339	4,740	10,882
1955	1,035	128,340	940	49,672	174	25,230	1,005	27,459	338	4,901	9,989
1954	1,000	128,000	900	49,015	188	26,132	905	31,280	352	5,628	11,624
1953	965	147,645	900	59,305	215	20,315	800	33,374	354	6,016	10,090
1952	925	173,900	835	67,140	220	31,240	1,264	25,000	332	6,642	9,888
1951	904	182,628	737	66,014	233	29,110	1,108	39,670	316	6,641	10,090
1950	936	139,494	720	48,090	247	28,899	977	35,040	350	4,907	7,900
1949	959	134,274	740	44,832	265	31,800	880	29,284	391	5,891	10,160
1948	986	123,213	782	41,317	287	35,875	772	23,260	464	5,590	9,430
1947	1,013	113,467	798	34,887	281	36,811	882	22,697	548	6,356	12,260
1946	1,013	112,454	778	32,893	282	37,788	744	17,768	594	6,284	11,130
1945	1,031	97,907	817	31,466	298	39,932	745	13,821	644	6,125	11,130
1944	1,018	97,766	889	32,508	325	44,525	907	16,192	620	6,251	11,690
1943	987	103,614	840	32,937	319	44,022	915	16,416	573	6,072	9,270
1942	994	64,597	760	15,196	326	37,164	834	9,424	547	3,391	9,190
1941	1,001	47,038	756	12,104	333	37,149	808	7,603	526	2,788	8,063
1940	1,008	46,368	767	21,465	328	38,388	958	13,415	528	3,362	7,987
1939	984	42,333	813	21,962	317	34,597	759	11,384	541	3,270	7,517
1938	967	39,651	826	19,826	307	34,987	656	9,845	575	3,210	6,946
1937	949	40,824	801	19,224	294	34,421	786	11,000	579	3,224	7,112
1936	928	35,264	757	16,658	282	31,629	713	7,632	590	3,090	7,246
1935	928	31,542	726	11,608	276	33,096	617	8,641	615	3,074	6,537
1934	940	27,266	779	10,130	272	29,051	556	7,224	576	2,305	6,631
1933	948	27,483	808	9,700	272	26,150	484	5,326	640	2,562	6,669
1932	930	27,915	944	12,273	300	27,000	669	4,685	737	2,212	8,063
1931	892	39,864	816	10,723	301	31,367	728	5,359	734	3,604	7,862
1930	824	44,534	853	25,389	312	29,500	744	11,896	723	4,655	8,202
1929	847	59,318	810	30,959	321	34,015	781	14,790	720	6,482	7,964
1928	898	57,655	750	25,777	324	35,105	778	14,033	722	6,916	7,886
1927	882	47,983	716	20,749	324	34,473	785	13,205	722	6,437	7,282
1926	862	42,350	708	18,459	322	32,614	749	13,413	716	6,690	6,852
1925	827	41,964	712	18,967	321	31,365	715	12,727	711	6,379	6,504
1924	805	34,619	720	16,560	321	31,487	716	11,458	702	5,617	6,174
1923	792	33,058	736	16,438	318	31,019	705	10,632	708	4,969	5,913
1922	810	36,351	760	17,541	322	32,362	634	11,891	842	6,451	5,910
1921	811	46,039	784	13,338	333	47,091	691	6,996	856	5,230	5,252
1920	815	61,140	834	31,688	362	46,500	689	17,904	836	8,359	4,800
1919	818	68,670	887	36,854	379	50,759	778	18,665	790	10,265	5,223
1818	808	63,832	880	39,614	362	47,396	663	17,230	745	10,436	6,000
1917	805	65,591	800	36,600	352	46,235	595	16,946	677	10,157	6,079
1916	752	46,642	735	37,118	353	40,572	622	10,567	658	6,914	6,114
1915	743	37,506	699	28,326	355	39,783	736	10,678	720	5,403	—
1914	750	35,348	692	27,399	360	48,421	734	10,515	727	4,801	—
1913	774	—	742	—	362	—	761	—	752	—	—
1912	763	—	708	—	365	—	752	—	635	—	—
1911	754	29,376	699	8,727	372	48,714	794	5,399	637	2,710	4,833
1910	740	28,852	691	—	371	—	736	—	656	—	—
1909	740	24,427	717	—	365	—	752	—	681	3,726	—
1908	765	24,471	770	—	364	—	776	—	718	3,567	—
1907	770	—	791	—	353	—	785	—	680	—	—
1906	789	—	794	—	341	—	790	—	787	—	—
1901	734	—	632	—	321	—	404	—	654	—	3,112
1891	550	—	146	—	344	—	370	—	730	—	—
1881	491	—	539	—	274	—	329	—	890	—	—
1871	406	—	378	—	253	—	371	—	1,008	—	—

Series L167–232. *Livestock statistics, number on farms and farm values at 1 June,*
Canada and by region, 1871 to 1960 (continuation)

(number of animals in thousands; value of animals in thousands of dollars)

	Ontario										
	Milk cows		Other cattle and calves		Horses		Hogs		Sheep and lambs		Hens and chickens
Year	Number	Value	Number	Value	Number	Value	Number	Value	Number	Value	Number
	200	**201**	**202**	**203**	**204**	**205**	**206**	**207**	**208**	**209**	**210**
1960	975	224,250	1,997	243,546	95	15,010	1,726	50,054	353	6,707	24,808
1959	967	225,311	1,948	249,532	102	14,484	2,056	61,680	364	6,916	26,457
1958	982	210,148	1,924	233,235	115	14,950	1,764	72,324	380	7,980	27,028
1957	996	163,344	1,955	189,344	130	15,600	1,529	56,573	381	7,620	28,175
1956	1,026	159,015	1,876	174,390	140	15,216	1,548	40,256	394	7,482	24,934
1955	1,025	167,075	1,900	187,683	151	17,214	1,440	45,200	400	8,195	25,190
1954	1,020	165,240	1,870	175,998	172	15,308	1,315	54,195	402	8,629	27,400
1953	1,015	181,685	1,825	198,478	200	18,200	1,260	41,720	407	9,753	25,445
1952	980	223,440	1,695	222,698	219	21,462	1,700	49,760	385	10,783	21,600
1951	957	283,302	1,509	256,750	261	22,518	1,756	70,006	360	12,413	23,767
1950	1,008	202,608	1,364	153,156	327	27,141	1,800	62,690	398	9,159	20,739
1949	1,043	181,482	1,419	129,266	356	32,396	1,820	67,487	420	6,970	21,964
1948	1,077	169,089	1,441	117,713	384	36,480	1,532	52,399	493	7,656	22,934
1947	1,096	143,576	1,475	96,612	420	41,580	1,900	47,630	578	7,526	27,789
1946	1,119	143,232	1,495	92,417	445	43,610	1,550	38,781	629	7,687	27,091
1945	1,147	130,758	1,553	83,484	470	44,650	1,560	35,140	665	7,881	26,176
1944	1,136	126,096	1,513	77,835	491	50,082	1,700	32,470	697	8,202	25,496
1943	1,131	130,065	1,492	82,932	512	55,808	1,800	29,425	709	9,610	24,824
1942	1,125	91,125	1,466	61,572	522	45,936	1,829	22,497	677	6,364	23,063
1941	1,156	71,666	1,484	49,116	532	45,644	1,882	19,495	662	5,018	21,764
1940	1,139	67,189	1,442	60,577	538	43,080	1,986	22,198	695	5,703	21,381
1939	1,133	63,453	1,409	56,376	540	49,698	1,536	21,542	736	5,980	21,324
1938	1,131	53,162	1,410	43,695	544	55,488	1,422	18,699	762	5,654	20,936
1937	1,138	54,619	1,357	43,411	544	56,022	1,480	18,351	793	5,519	21,097
1936	1,149	52,859	1,359	40,770	551	57,855	1,403	16,316	819	5,734	21,546
1935	1,156	48,543	1,340	38,860	554	50,941	1,222	14,842	890	5,392	21,598
1934	1,158	37,053	1,356	29,836	557	45,109	1,175	11,752	920	4,823	21,471
1933	1,170	39,777	1,367	28,713	570	42,728	1,256	12,141	973	4,359	21,679
1932	1,168	39,729	1,369	27,372	576	36,275	1,373	7,209	1,025	4,020	21,640
1931	1,098	59,270	1,416	32,881	577	50,529	1,359	11,987	1,045	6,653	22,524
1930	1,136	75,192	1,350	52,642	587	47,537	1,380	18,983	1,040	8,061	22,217
1929	1,147	97,455	1,330	70,556	586	55,380	1,407	21,652	1,035	12,219	22,160
1928	1,167	98,206	1,314	71,196	589	58,344	1,545	21,012	928	11,269	20,180
1927	1,200	88,322	1,306	62,688	596	60,216	1,599	20,783	873	10,254	19,982
1926	1,180	74,745	1,361	53,651	608	57,978	1,484	22,123	808	9,806	19,120
1925	1,132	67,785	1,448	57,150	622	55,136	1,446	21,639	790	9,141	19,902
1924	1,104	60,108	1,572	54,847	641	51,408	1,568	18,222	791	8,518	19,441
1923	1,158	67,309	1,439	47,862	649	54,777	1,515	17,509	823	7,765	18,636
1922	1,128	64,990	1,462	50,005	661	59,310	1,367	19,723	894	8,062	17,946
1921	1,097	75,819	1,536	43,942	669	82,624	1,386	14,542	979	6,897	15,526
1920	1,071	98,088	1,567	89,624	690	74,562	1,466	34,196	1,001	11,833	14,626
1919	1,051	112,005	1,645	111,679	714	78,584	1,576	39,390	956	17,204	15,044
1918	1,016	97,719	1,640	110,008	738	81,682	1,573	41,695	825	16,778	15,399
1917	1,048	96,912	1,585	99,440	782	88,310	1,198	30,247	794	14,689	15,604
1916	1,062	80,735	1,498	97,338	802	100,262	1,390	25,013	737	9,208	15,681
1915	1,083	75,269	1,436	68,191	816	97,932	1,483	20,759	719	7,189	—
1914	1,083	69,628	1,384	62,704	822	95,765	1,596	20,146	712	6,198	—
1913	1,099	—	1,406	—	808	—	1,728	—	750	—	—
1912	1,077	—	1,440	—	808	—	1,802	—	749	—	—
1911	1,106	52,134	1,396	29,351	812	113,541	1,887	13,578	742	4,428	13,414
1910	1,072	51,461	1,404	—	794	—	1,682	—	740	—	—
1909	1,071	42,844	1,505	—	794	—	1,662	—	766	5,079	—
1908	1,103	39,712	1,624	—	789	—	1,941	—	757	4,476	—
1907	1,159	—	1,668	—	764	—	2,176	—	717	—	—
1906	1,188	—	1,675	—	740	—	1,921	—	831	—	—
1901	1,018	—	1,470	—	721	—	1,563	—	1,046	—	9,662
1891	876	—	1,065	—	772	—	1,121	—	1,022	—	—
1881	782	—	920	—	590	—	701	—	1,359	—	—
1871	639	—	764	—	489	—	875	—	1,515	—	—

Series L 167–232. *Livestock statistics, number of farms and farm values at 1 June,*
Canada and by region, 1871 to 1960 (continuation)

(number of animals in thousands; value of animals in thousands of dollars)

	Prairie Provinces										
	Milk cows		Other cattle and calves		Horses		Hogs		Sheep and lambs		Hens and chickens
Year	Number	Value	Number	Value	Number	Value	Number	Value	Number	Value	Number
	211	**212**	**213**	**214**	**215**	**216**	**217**	**218**	**219**	**220**	**221**
1960	714	139,808	4,870	587,449	297	29,123	2,256	49,457	755	11,249	22,280
1959	712	146,294	4,684	610,730	317	29,601	3,069	71,090	712	11,219	24,745
1958	733	134,100	4,577	543,073	346	29,782	3,000	95,946	676	12,012	25,114
1957	758	108,667	4,678	432,600	372	28,027	2,226	68,464	653	10,874	24,229
1956	777	111,317	4,413	395,644	401	27,148	2,115	47,126	621	9,572	23,653
1955	788	122,609	4,023	390,408	424	25,428	2,151	54,244	628	10,184	22,355
1954	798	115,416	3,716	348,808	465	22,810	2,010	66,616	608	10,044	22,707
1953	805	142,660	3,472	392,394	541	26,443	1,725	52,105	568	10,567	22,238
1952	810	179,937	3,137	447,429	633	30,368	2,200	57,232	566	11,030	20,587
1951	823	215,743	2,686	469,369	696	31,105	1,802	65,962	532	13,901	23,393
1950	871	159,142	2,677	318,809	798	33,248	1,351	41,889	575	9,849	20,280
1949	927	145,714	2,794	269,254	888	43,480	1,522	47,998	708	9,459	24,017
1948	979	122,330	2,944	232,857	980	48,624	1,418	40,176	811	9,263	23,163
1947	972	104,207	2,925	193,049	1,092	53,060	1,934	42,791	1,019	10,051	29,436
1946	1,002	94,305	2,898	164,007	1,254	57,146	1,771	33,989	1,207	10,381	26,766
1945	1,085	95,082	3,092	166,031	1,444	61,443	2,428	45,276	1,324	10,874	29,401
1944	1,149	104,353	2,933	153,967	1,584	79,607	3,887	69,284	1,471	13,517	32,140
1943	1,148	105,750	2,645	143,052	1,666	94,500	4,409	70,810	1,399	14,147	27,687
1942	1,141	76,926	2,387	81,343	1,740	90,097	3,877	37,750	1,346	8,474	27,541
1941	1,108	56,853	2,181	65,083	1,752	86,497	3,152	25,574	1,251	7,083	23,432
1940	1,143	54,783	2,074	77,439	1,742	78,618	2,800	31,750	1,258	8,254	21,659
1939	1,196	49,384	2,014	63,730	1,732	85,171	1,859	24,095	1,223	7,684	20,717
1938	1,268	40,922	2,058	50,792	1,749	89,304	1,248	15,234	1,275	6,377	17,948
1937	1,391	41,439	2,443	52,718	1,838	98,249	1,522	16,932	1,265	5,991	18,021
1936	1,365	37,128	2,472	45,656	1,880	103,028	1,814	18,531	1,316	5,970	19,425
1935	1,393	39,695	2,619	50,168	1,913	90,367	1,616	16,776	1,279	5,457	18,647
1934	1,392	33,974	2,603	37,628	1,920	80,591	1,821	15,715	1,330	4,634	20,784
1933	1,214	33,276	2,592	40,488	1,955	72,191	1,922	14,903	1,226	4,310	20,414
1932	1,145	34,042	2,178	35,076	2,028	65,958	2,388	8,284	1,342	3,717	23,380
1931	1,046	45,614	1,936	41,379	2,054	107,420	2,391	13,956	1,284	6,492	23,212
1930	950	54,320	1,802	60,486	2,105	99,241	1,403	20,778	1,102	6,685	22,352
1929	895	61,975	1,715	80,222	2,165	118,218	1,649	25,380	1,018	9,443	21,789
1928	910	61,222	1,665	78,054	2,160	132,950	1,674	23,244	914	9,377	18,716
1927	960	51,929	1,787	67,384	2,182	136,863	1,701	21,861	854	8,002	17,101
1926	1,003	42,960	1,936	53,858	2,230	132,047	1,603	25,551	779	7,518	17,944
1925	997	40,960	2,129	56,002	2,209	128,630	1,661	25,575	635	6,135	16,704
1924	981	38,522	2,235	51,032	2,226	117,362	2,104	23,885	517	5,000	17,248
1923	929	36,238	2,197	48,674	2,177	109,233	1,578	16,324	574	4,258	17,424
1922	921	36,683	2,396	53,535	2,211	135,625	1,309	16,330	724	5,032	16,708
1921	860	48,960	2,465	74,386	2,240	259,127	1,043	11,522	739	4,910	15,623
1920	764	54,825	2,234	100,116	2,130	210,224	772	15,222	692	6,426	11,656
1919	798	71,905	2,405	145,018	2,123	248,373	1,020	26,513	644	9,325	13,178
1918	760	69,774	2,299	155,173	2,027	268,951	1,218	31,753	555	8,855	10,690
1917	759	66,334	2,046	124,890	1,854	245,148	1,304	32,001	497	7,289	9,504
1916	758	56,128	1,972	105,015	1,788	243,257	1,350	22,782	496	5,051	8,498
1915	706	47,770	1,844	88,040	1,721	228,494	1,040	13,572	474	3,688	—
1914	653	42,366	1,644	72,973	1,589	208,292	1,102	11,176	420	3,043	—
1913	590	—	1,527	—	1,435	—	983	—	361	—	—
1912	527	—	1,413	—	1,300	—	900	—	301	—	—
1911	447	18,839	1,362	38,223	1,195	192,388	712	6,112	285	1,604	8,033
1910	444	17,750	1,401	—	1,095	—	645	—	306	—	—
1909	446	15,849	1,404	—	956	—	628	—	309	2,138	—
1908	449	15,280	1,489	—	884	—	574	—	294	1,626	—
1907	415	—	1,537	—	784	—	496	—	299	—	—
1906	384	—	1,560	—	683	—	439	—	305	—	—
1901	134	—	216	—	340	—	126	—	183	—	1,623
1891	83	—	148	—	148	—	54	—	36	—	—
1881	20	—	40	—	28	—	17	—	6	—	—

Series L167–232. *Livestock statistics, number on farms and farm values at 1 June, Canada and by region, 1871 to 1960 (continuation)*

(number of animals in thousands; value of animals in thousands of dollars)

	Milk cows		Other cattle and calves		Horses		Hogs		Sheep and lambs		Hens and chickens
Year	Number	Value	Number	Value	Number	Value	Number	Value	Number	Value	Number
	222	223	224	225	226	227	228	229	230	231	232
1960	91	18,473	342	39,542	23	2,520	46	1,196	100	1,800	5,009
1959	88	18,656	335	42,325	23	2,461	63	1,764	97	1,843	5,004
1958	89	17,088	320	37,772	24	2,280	50	1,750	95	1,995	4,468
1957	86	12,556	315	28,591	25	2,083	40	1,240	90	1,620	4,280
1956	90	12,538	333	28,625	27	2,064	48	1,307	86	1,464	4,221
1955	90	13,590	314	29,636	28	2,072	56	1,610	81	1,506	3,800
1954	89	14,240	297	27,225	30	2,220	46	1,754	79	1,703	3,795
1953	87	16,356	266	29,648	30	2,430	42	1,371	76	1,682	3,555
1952	85	17,425	242	31,962	34	2,856	60	1,971	71	1,798	3,315
1951	85	19,543	237	38,730	36	2,865	49	2,083	68	1,782	3,452
1950	93	13,935	244	24,850	40	3,878	53	1,890	67	1,276	3,228
1949	94	12,892	234	20,518	44	4,312	48	1,569	67	1,123	3,446
1948	96	12,025	244	19,439	46	4,723	56	1,537	79	1,153	3,337
1947	101	11,053	248	16,163	50	4,851	64	1,631	85	1,034	3,825
1946	106	9,992	271	15,599	54	5,370	58	1,192	101	1,145	3,825
1945	110	10,001	278	15,284	58	5,530	60	1,180	114	1,200	3,554
1944	104	9,161	265	14,615	60	6,030	89	1,583	130	1,426	3,581
1943	99	8,540	264	13,799	61	6,273	84	1,357	126	1,382	3,283
1942	95	7,155	243	10,453	61	3,807	79	901	124	883	2,903
1941	92	5,556	233	7,997	63	3,684	78	735	126	849	2,713
1940	90	4,838	200	7,589	62	4,674	74	1,073	130	939	3,088
1939	89	4,544	192	6,138	60	4,492	45	660	130	865	3,238
1938	91	4,530	202	6,274	60	4,358	43	569	144	850	2,858
1937	93	4,748	212	6,351	56	3,927	51	656	151	943	2,969
1936	94	4,794	210	5,866	56	3,633	47	601	151	893	3,027
1935	88	4,410	205	5,325	56	3,219	46	530	154	897	2,801
1934	86	4,109	194	4,852	55	3,091	44	495	157	785	3,123
1933	82	3,951	188	5,267	57	3,113	46	452	139	701	2,768
1932	81	4,126	171	4,625	57	3,062	51	406	147	735	3,211
1931	83	5,491	151	5,175	57	3,156	52	510	147	995	4,278
1930	72	5,559	168	7,039	59	4,270	54	972	144	1,299	4,412
1929	70	5,897	183	9,532	62	4,804	54	1,017	152	1,830	4,698
1928	65	5,477	183	9,323	61	4,637	46	877	129	1,550	4,413
1927	61	4,552	171	7,349	63	4,906	44	828	102	1,218	3,616
1926	58	3,910	166	5,820	64	5,008	41	773	83	991	3,117
1925	57	3,735	145	5,220	62	4,658	38	650	52	675	2,632
1924	53	3,451	136	4,488	62	4,394	40	557	48	532	2,358
1923	53	3,724	144	3,883	64	4,769	41	573	51	506	2,265
1922	46	3,209	156	5,135	63	4,883	41	653	52	469	1,926
1921	46	4,035	163	7,721	61	5,932	42	671	61	519	1,968
1920	42	5,300	154	11,081	60	7,560	44	928	55	606	1,711
1919	40	4,720	150	10,671	59	7,585	45	1,266	53	852	1,409
1918	39	4,091	148	9,909	59	7,208	40	962	53	799	1,131
1917	36	3,749	142	9,236	65	7,682	38	798	51	707	1,349
1916	35	3,262	127	7,002	65	7,042	38	696	48	502	1,361
1915	34	3,122	120	5,915	64	6,537	38	576	48	382	—
1914	34	3,044	112	6,670	63	7,512	39	464	46	383	—
1913	34	—	110	—	62	—	34	—	46	—	—
1912	34	—	105	—	60	—	32	—	41	—	—
1911	34	2,005	105	3,008	57	7,834	34	362	39	263	969
1910	34	1,915	105	—	54	—	34	—	41	—	—
1909	33	1,663	102	—	49	—	36	—	40	266	—
1908	33	1,579	104	—	46	—	37	—	37	221	—
1907	32	—	101	—	45	—	36	—	37	—	—
1906	30	—	100	—	44	—	36	—	36	—	—
1901	22	—	103	—	37	—	41	—	33	—	347
1891	18	—	109	—	44	—	31	—	49	—	—
1881	11	—	69	—	26	—	17	—	28	—	—

Series L233–242. *Livestock product statistics, estimated number slaughtered and weight of meat produced, Canada, 1871 to 1960*

(animals slaughtered in thousands of head; meat produced in thousands of pounds)

Year	Number of cattle	Beef, cold dressed weight	Number of calves	Veal, cold dressed weight	Number of hogs	Pork, cold trimmed weight	Number of sheep and lambs	Mutton and lamb, cold dressed weight	Number of chickens	Chicken meat, eviscerated weight[1]
	233	234	235	236	237	238	239	240	241	242
1960	2,471	1,266,280	1,082	125,155	7,804	988,035	737	31,561	114,922	357,939
1959	2,261	1,153,037	1,094	120,505	9,662	1,237,682	726	31,784	116,948	365,198
1958	2,438	1,220,239	1,191	125,544	7,466	973,599	716	31,297	113,516	356,012
1957	2,514	1,244,584	1,358	148,058	6,295	818,403	763	33,180	96,763	315,336
1956	2,421	1,172,603	1,333	139,805	6,858	881,964	771	32,688	89,064	308,912
1955	2,271	1,102,619	1,295	134,551	6,932	887,708	755	32,385	80,362	225,093
1954	2,222	1,078,927	1,254	131,723	6,144	795,609	721	30,702	67,730	246,676
1953	2,005	994,081	1,165	123,765	6,198	796,482	693	29,708	66,831	238,232
1952	1,719	864,000	969	100,638	8,057	1,039,405	674	29,743	66,075	251,032
1951	1,592	785,553	1,040	108,004	6,753	876,513	584	26,581	60,914	218,863
1950	1,674	787,741	1,282	127,577	6,793	875,455	742	32,130	48,420	178,474
1949	1,843	863,364	1,285	133,729	6,466	845,268	877	38,828	51,865	189,034
1948	1,939	910,363	1,362	137,565	6,694	863,288	1,031	44,131	43,946	166,255
1947	1,944	926,321	1,287	129,626	7,394	976,728	1,326	59,653	52,563	196,974
1946	2,216	1,059,644	1,334	136,287	6,856	890,798	1,413	63,456	50,219	182,963
1945	2,401	1,142,540	1,419	146,992	8,709	1,130,388	1,477	64,228	50,175	192,073
1944	1,872	920,371	1,250	127,062	11,512	1,515,361	1,266	53,674	51,905	199,834
1943	1,586	789,605	1,199	128,400	10,426	1,407,557	1,226	52,550	46,375	178,544
1942	1,526	751,434	1,328	130,671	9,695	1,250,889	1,186	50,977	44,607	171,737
1941	1,516	723,739	1,308	123,985	9,116	1,114,758	1,170	50,850	39,766	151,897
1940	1,402	643,459	1,419	122,734	7,237	864,535	1,280	52,461	—	—
1939	1,337	615,620	1,348	116,775	5,122	624,965	1,477	60,304	—	—
1938	1,389	639,170	1,389	115,896	4,853	587,249	1,519	60,671	—	—
1937	1,398	623,122	1,478	129,639	5,745	678,686	1,534	60,289	—	—
1936	1,336	619,472	1,248	113,467	5,405	647,968	1,576	62,733	—	—
1935	1,275	595,395	1,206	106,083	4,700	563,745	1,610	63,087	—	—
1934	1,136	561,135	995	113,396	4,625	635,530	1,536	66,044	—	—
1933	997	498,300	910	97,370	4,694	626,649	1,547	63,431	—	—
1932	936	476,679	817	89,075	4,699	624,080	1,459	59,835	—	—
1931	970	497,661	799	87,080	4,181	561,522	1,511	61,951	—	—
1930	943	484,805	809	96,295	3,974	530,860	1,438	60,409	—	—
1929	1,065	534,429	774	82,829	4,376	595,587	1,387	56,871	—	—
1928	1,082	533,180	784	80,731	4,572	609,488	1,290	52,906	—	—
1927	1,124	573,342	776	73,797	4,471	601,336	1,260	54,171	—	—
1926	1,075	552,396	709	75,196	4,449	607,733	1,145	46,937	—	—
1925	1,051	542,264	705	76,162	4,611	608,612	1,139	48,977	—	—
1924	977	513,135	670	68,299	4,712	617,246	1,151	49,476	—	—
1923	979	529,855	609	62,098	3,973	518,529	1,217	65,707	—	—
1922	991	543,949	634	65,957	3,618	485,495	1,183	55,601	—	—
1921	933	476,814	511	56,243	3,157	420,801	1,293	55,612	—	—
1920	1,091	530,420	554	57,052	3,301	437,079	1,171	50,336	—	—
1891[2]	958	—	—	—	1,791	—	1,464	—	—	—
1881[2]	658	—	—	—	1,303	—	1,496	—	—	—
1871[2]	508	—	—	—	1,216	—	1,557	—	—	—

[1] Chicken meat (series L242) given on cold dressed basis from 1941 to 1955 in the source is converted here to eviscerated weight by use of conversion factor of 77 per cent to make it consistent with the data presented for 1956 onward.

[2] Decennial census data: animals killed or sold.

Series L243–252. *Livestock product statistics, milk, production and disposition of milk, Canada, 1920 to 1960*
(thousands of pounds)

Year	Total milk production[1]	Used in factories					Fluid sales[2]	Used on farms		
		Creamery butter	Cheddar cheese	Concentrated products	Ice cream	Other		Dairy butter	Farm home consumed	Fed to livestock
	243	**244**	**245**	**246**	**247**	**248**	**249**	**250**	**251**	**252**
1960	17,746,475	7,497,430	1,214,092	1,169,725	696,320	133,232	5,018,391	233,906	1,007,134	761,237
1959	17,614,706	7,618,525	1,184,216	931,163	680,289	123,501	5,050,808	256,441	1,016,226	739,222
1958	17,672,982	7,862,166	1,004,531	924,432	621,622	111,792	5,111,397	282,049	1,055,025	685,277
1957	17,035,204	7,098,881	1,089,396	989,288	596,989	108,474	5,116,669	296,338	1,065,371	659,810
1956	16,966,242	7,097,548	932,217	944,618	564,961	109,870	5,233,999	326,218	1,112,333	644,478
1955	16,946,447	7,454,701	879,780	913,997	550,970	85,788	4,961,774	348,158	1,098,716	652,563
1954	16,527,800	7,329,582	938,828	863,710	486,965	83,858	4,713,598	388,020	1,068,449	654,790
1953	16,035,920	7,085,122	844,184	848,543	489,753	73,600	4,548,102	445,369	1,048,818	652,429
1952	15,308,657	6,569,456	745,998	897,123	477,085	72,264	4,326,392	528,409	1,051,372	640,558
1951	15,309,971	6,025,376	989,054	857,180	456,588	69,510	4,618,510	628,626	1,055,990	609,137
1950	15,322,350	6,126,102	1,087,866	741,771	428,796	59,797	4,545,490	640,839	1,090,114	601,575
1949	15,917,504	6,555,831	1,302,433	678,365	433,369	50,331	4,468,125	740,024	1,069,676	619,350
1948	15,781,705	6,692,287	991,738	781,446	360,194	57,147	4,407,140	816,801	1,032,552	642,400
1947	16,343,889	6,817,005	1,358,545	666,954	334,972	33,342	4,579,132	780,601	1,119,818	653,520
1946	16,130,451	6,361,034	1,627,543	624,546	226,196	32,466	4,682,363	775,101	1,132,062	669,140
1945	16,842,602	6,883,992	2,080,473	630,445	233,670	23,044	4,422,038	748,239	1,117,851	702,850
1944	16,847,203	7,000,345	2,006,102	607,802	252,461	20,932	4,320,797	814,882	1,117,452	706,430
1943	16,732,299	7,303,342	1,833,120	578,110	246,402	19,590	4,093,680	840,153	1,114,822	703,080
1942	16,737,236	6,667,907	2,297,235	554,210	217,580	13,851	3,735,675	1,459,762	1,085,736	705,220
1941	16,668,037	6,697,419	1,684,502	491,335	202,504	17,774	3,434,201	1,766,302	1,064,230	709,770
1940	15,448,494	6,202,483	1,611,791	388,900	157,747	13,247	3,323,254	1,853,303	1,185,829	711,940
1939	15,781,104	6,264,810	1,405,324	334,749	142,225	—	3,011,515	2,047,416	1,790,754	774,720
1938	15,819,707	6,258,600	1,388,479	311,598	140,529	—	3,013,270	2,130,545	1,789,911	776,320
1937	15,125,223	5,783,598	1,463,009	275,010	146,027	—	2,774,427	2,194,079	1,676,374	801,480
1936	15,122,426	5,874,313	1,334,183	200,254	129,642	—	2,828,751	2,233,432	1,697,646	812,320
1935	14,572,026	5,639,909	1,124,787	186,705	103,492	—	2,773,175	2,281,233	1,655,861	794,600
1934	14,452,262	5,497,908	1,112,682	165,822	94,067	—	2,786,248	2,315,837	1,646,452	821,640
1933	14,083,977	5,132,234	1,244,841	152,786	89,916	—	2,688,035	2,321,032	1,594,318	849,840
1932	13,997,328	5,009,790	1,349,871	146,865	97,008	—	2,699,411	2,313,495	1,569,252	801,360
1931	14,339,686	5,289,612	1,276,314	157,949	129,360	—	2,759,321	2,307,993	1,593,545	816,000
1930	13,071,421	4,348,432	1,333,978	201,406	152,516	—	2,524,288	2,283,157	1,444,538	774,000
1929	12,410,443	3,998,668	1,329,958	195,949	153,918	—	1,760,806	2,272,128	1,894,330	796,002
1928	12,708,158	3,933,513	1,619,348	197,004	133,921	—	1,814,454	2,326,954	1,910,517	764,234
1927	12,914,586	4,143,077	1,546,238	204,694	117,296	—	1,839,013	2,384,215	1,945,823	720,408
1926	13,475,614	4,148,469	1,923,394	180,703	108,365	—	1,896,115	2,430,379	2,044,898	735,770
1925	13,420,984	3,967,877	1,983,958	187,792	92,621	—	1,889,198	2,485,378	2,033,754	773,102
1924	13,183,714	4,187,907	1,676,724	176,895	86,324	—	1,860,444	2,540,804	1,855,362	792,090
1923	12,807,618	3,811,958	1,698,193	173,233	88,183	—	1,825,885	2,589,380	1,796,988	816,891
1922	12,107,683	3,570,070	1,521,196	130,968	75,273	—	1,728,274	2,510,067	1,697,101	868,061
1921	11,897,545	3,013,911	1,815,716	170,920	85,638	—	1,700,257	2,513,742	1,662,319	928,693
1920	10,976,236	2,614,703	1,671,061	203,412	90,739	—	1,565,035	2,422,643	1,539,213	863,454

[1] 'Total milk production' includes milk for farm-made cheese, 1920 to 1939, inclusive, and so is not the sum of series L244–252.

[2] 'Fluid sales' include fluid milk and fluid cream in terms of whole milk.

Series L253–260. *Livestock product statistics, milk products, production, Canada, selected years 1850 to 1915 and 1916 to 1960*

(series L257 in thousands of gallons; all other series in thousands of pounds)

Year	Creamery butter	Farm butter (dairy)	Farm cheese	Cheddar cheese	Ice cream	Evaporated milk	Condensed milk	Skim milk powder
	253	254	255	256	257	258	259	260
1960	320,403	9,996	—	110,372	41,228	316,950	14,420	171,969
1959	325,578	10,959	—	107,656	40,017	302,697	14,553	176,437
1958	335,990	12,079	—	91,321	36,566	305,267	14,194	185,625
1957	303,371	12,664	—	99,036	35,117	316,824	14,730	120,710
1956	303,314	13,939	—	84,747	33,233	305,152	17,172	79,005
1955	318,577	14,878	—	79,980	32,410	294,938	13,237	87,115
1954	313,320	16,582	—	85,348	28,645	280,350	13,648	83,332
1953	302,783	19,033	—	76,744	28,809	272,009	18,462	82,914
1952	280,746	22,583	—	67,818	27,262	305,715	16,539	88,229
1951	257,165	26,830	—	88,784	25,366	290,443	19,541	52,748
1950	261,464	27,352	—	97,654	23,822	256,484	14,541	53,263
1949	279,805	31,625	—	116,915	24,790	231,306	23,543	64,312
1948	285,629	34,906	730	89,025	25,206	250,058	35,102	64,021
1947	290,952	33,359	740	121,952	23,441	211,829	29,357	54,503
1946	271,491	33,124	740	146,099	15,829	191,586	31,026	42,580
1945	293,811	31,976	744	186,757	16,352	200,529	28,582	37,111
1944	298,777	34,824	753	180,081	17,667	184,344	31,021	29,703
1943	311,709	35,904	761	164,553	17,243	178,368	26,915	22,352
1942	284,591	62,383	787	206,215	15,226	185,762	23,076	26,670
1941	285,848	75,483	798	151,212	14,171	165,964	24,605	26,524
1940	264,724	79,201	815	144,685	11,039	135,877	14,429	26,392
1939	267,613	87,459	856	125,059	9,053	116,885	7,571	25,339
1938	267,347	91,010	933	123,971	8,945	105,720	9,231	25,545
1937	247,057	93,724	1,002	130,626	9,295	91,331	11,396	18,492
1936	250,932	95,405	1,061	119,123	8,252	71,074	7,987	18,530
1935	240,919	97,447	1,095	100,427	6,588	66,218	9,149	18,890
1934	234,853	98,925	1,036	99,347	5,988	56,465	9,127	16,868
1933	219,233	99,147	980	111,146	5,723	53,421	9,899	13,307
1932	214,002	98,825	917	120,524	6,175	47,916	14,825	11,485
1931	225,955	98,590	856	113,957	8,234	45,954	15,486	12,978
1930	185,751	97,529	813	119,105	9,708	57,631	23,360	14,307
1929	170,810	97,058	775	118,746	9,797	53,995	25,482	12,788
1928	168,027	99,400	733	144,585	8,525	51,654	27,729	12,509
1927	176,979	101,846	698	138,057	7,466	51,855	30,910	12,752
1926	177,209	103,818	671	171,732	6,898	44,183	27,703	11,454
1925	169,495	106,167	652	177,139	5,896	44,550	29,833	10,635
1924	178,894	108,535	640	149,708	5,495	42,433	30,875	10,868
1923	162,835	110,610	617	151,624	5,613	45,825	27,119	9,797
1922	152,502	107,222	596	135,821	4,791	32,393	21,241	5,922
1921	128,745	107,379	567	162,117	5,451	31,203	38,998	5,749
1920	111,692	103,488	534	149,202	5,776	30,470	53,663	5,843
1919	103,891	—	—	166,422	—	16,108	62,216	5,237
1918	93,298	—	—	174,878	—	38,612	40,700	4,267
1917	87,527	—	—	194,904	—	29,415	32,106	3,070
1916	82,564	—	—	192,969	—	—	—	—
1915	83,991	—	—	183,887	—	—	—	—
1910	64,489	137,110	1,371	199,904	—	—	—	—
1907	45,930	—	—	204,789	—	—	—	—
1900	36,067	105,343	—	220,833	—	—	—	—
1890	—	111,577	6,267	—	—	—	—	—
1880	—	102,545	3,185	—	—	—	—	—
1870	—	75,173	5,140	—	—	—	—	—
1860	—	51,565	4,602	—	—	—	—	—
1850	—	32,336	3,629	—	—	—	—	—

Series L261–264. *Livestock product statistics, butter and cheese, homemade production, selected years, 1847 to 1910*

(thousands of pounds)

Year	Maritimes	Quebec[1]	Ontario[1]	Prairie Provinces and British Columbia[2]	Year	Maritimes	Quebec[1]	Ontario[1]	Prairie Provinces and British Columbia[2]
	261	262	263	264		261	262	263	264
		Butter					Cheese		
1910	22,342	19,586	63,254	31,928	1910	212	359	296	504
1900	18,301	18,357	55,379	13,306	1890	753	4,201	1,066	187
1890	18,778	30,113	55,565	7,121	1880	870	559	1,702	54
1880	15,681	30,631	54,862	1,371	1870	1,195	512	3,433	—
1870	13,260	24,289	37,624	—	1860	1,228	687	2,687	—
1860	9,836	15,907	25,822	—	1850	652[3]	764	2,213	—
1850	6,665[3]	9,610	16,061	—	1847	—	—	668	—
1847	—	—	3,380	—					

[1] Prior to 1867 Quebec and Ontario were known as Lower Canada and Upper Canada respectively.

[2] Prior to 1905 series L264 included Manitoba, Northwest Territories and British Columbia.

[3] Nova Scotia and New Brunswick.

Series L265–271. *Exports of major agricultural products, grains (except wheat), quantity and value, Canada, crop years, 1868 to 1960*

(values in thousands of dollars; quantities as designated individually)

Year[1]	Oats Quantity (thousands of bushels)	Oats Value (thousands of dollars)	Barley Quantity (thousands of bushels)	Barley Value (thousands of dollars)	Rye Quantity (thousands of bushels)	Rye Value (thousands of dollars)	Flax seed Quantity (thousands of bushels)
	265	266	267	268	269	270	271
1960	6,076	—	63,759	—	4,515	—	12,494
1959	7,513	—	70,444	—	3,222	—	14,276
1958	26,184	—	80,298	—	5,446	—	13,650
1957	18,681	—	81,537	—	5,448	—	21,582
1956	4,142	—	68,700	—	12,918	—	11,583
1955	22,247	—	80,876	—	9,311	—	6,345
1954	70,700	—	93,742	—	16,835	—	5,172
1953	65,371	—	122,077	—	8,993	—	4,060
1952	70,646	—	73,472	—	6,820	—	2,882
1951	35,397	—	27,403	—	9,367	—	4,131
1950	20,547	—	20,848	—	9,954	—	3,034
1949	23,220	—	24,605	—	10,239	—	4,413
1948	10,202	—	4,327	—	10,226	—	1,788
1947	29,759	—	7,658	—	5,274	—	61
1946	43,861	—	5,088	—	3,003	—	346
1945	85,798	—	39,968	—	6,340	—	4,327
1944	74,735	—	37,200	—	8,175	—	10,050
1943	63,323	—	34,862	—	2,114	—	5,202
1942	11,861	—	3,009	—	2,845	—	865
1941	13,651	—	4,594	—	2,043	—	76
1940	23,591	—	12,829	—	2,824	—	18
1939	12,934	—	16,811	—	788	—	14
1938	8,228	—	16,166	—	650	—	16
1937	9,501	—	19,617	—	3,634	—	178
1936	15,515	—	10,115	—	2,459	—	19
1935	17,863	—	17,443	—	1,189	—	12
1934	9,141	—	5,470	—	2,582	—	187
1933	14,419	—	7,470	—	2,868	—	794
1932	18,010	—	15,369	—	9,048	—	251
1931	11,477	—	19,976	—	2,090	—	1,998
1930	4,169	—	2,653	—	348	—	415
1929	16,310	—	40,191	—	5,751	—	1,935
1928	14,865	—	26,517	—	11,265	—	2,386
1927	8,701	—	38,927	—	8,303	—	3,278
1926	36,827	—	34,181	—	6,223	—	2,953
1925	38,460	—	27,772	—	6,338	—	4,966
1924	43,302	—	15,396	—	7,579	—	3,482
1923	25,883	—	13,842	—	10,177	—	2,322
1922	30,117	—	12,422	—	4,525	—	2,631
1921	32,015	—	10,816	—	3,226	—	2,834
1920	19,077	—	10,891	—	2,504	—	861
1919	13,679	—	8,272	—	940	—	1,198
1918	32,548	—	6,553	—	1,037	—	3,855
1917	68,204	—	7,873	—	1,022	—	6,451
1916	56,286	—	8,855	—	818	—	3,447
1915	13,651	—	2,886	—	280	—	4,633
1914	36,521	—	12,299	—	127	—	18,052
1913	15,066	—	9,431	—	26	—	13,632
1912	11,541	—	2,643	—	1	—	3,714
1911	7,819	—	1,155	—	83	—	2,106
1910	7,820	—	2,080	—	53	—	2,365
1909	7,294	—	2,933	—	264	—	760
1908	—	—	1,990	1,223	—	—	11
1907	—	—	1,198	638	—	—	122
1906	—	—	880	469	—	—	3
1904[2]	7,124	2,360	1,058	489	102	55	—
1903	9,314	3,120	947	457	470	270	—
1902	6,119	2,396	457	231	399	240	—
1901	9,959	2,958	2,386	1,123	687	425	—
1900	8,662	2,618	2,156	1,010	474	279	—
1899	11,738	3,664	239	110	327	196	—
1898	11,977	3,597	444	159	1,140	616	—
1897	8,353	2,118	1,831	566	216	93	—
1896	2,278	639	841	316	0	0	—
1895	1,881	596	1,708	721	63	33	—
1894	3,866	1,385	597	264	63	33	—
1893	9,132	3,180	2,041	944	59	39	—
1892	7,623	2,650	5,203	2,613	221	190	—
1891	400	175	4,893	2,930	340	226	—
1890	1,592	511	9,976	4,600	437	221	—
1889	893	319	9,948	6,464	—	—	—
1888	731	238	9,370	6,494	0	0	—
1887	2,619	843	9,457	5,258	124	67	—
1886	5,052	1,764	8,554	5,725	171	99	—
1885	3,138	1,144	9,067	5,504	287	180	—
1884	2,011	732	7,780	5,105	873	566	—
1883	1,809	737	8,817	6,293	1,048	713	—
1882	4,737	1,937	11,588	10,114	1,282	1,191	—
1881	3,565	1,426	8,800	6,260	870	784	—
1880	5,916	2,145	7,240	4,482	958	703	—
1879	3,562	1,205	5,384	4,789	641	364	—
1878	4,413	1,714	7,267	4,316	416	252	—
1877	7,783	1,308	6,346	4,567	95	65	—
1876	2,644	1,139	10,168	7,430	—	—	—
1875	2,990	1,447	5,419	5,363	—	—	—
1874	998	456	3,748	4,077	—	—	—
1873	629	217	4,347	2,956	—	—	—
1872	486	180	5,606	3,475	—	—	—
1871	542	231	4,833	3,426	—	—	—
1870	2,188	720	6,664	4,753	—	—	—
1869	763	362	4,630	5,004	—	—	—
1868	1,738	754	4,056	3,186	—	—	—

[1] For 1909 to 1960 the crop year for grains is from 1 August to 31 July of the year given; for 1908 the crop year was 9 months ending 31 March; for 1867 to 1907 the year ending 30 June of the year given.

[2] No entries are available for 1905.

Series L272–293. *Exports of major agricultural products, animal and animal products, quantity and value, Canada, 1868 to 1960*

(values in thousands of dollars; quantities as designated individually)

Year[1]	Cattle and calves[2] Quantity (number of head)	Value (thousands of dollars)	Beef Quantity (thousands of pounds)	Value (thousands of dollars)	Hogs[2] Quantity (number of head)	Value (thousands of dollars)	Pork Quantity (thousands of pounds)	Value (thousands of dollars)	Sheep and lambs[2] Quantity (number of head)	Value (thousands of dollars)	Mutton and lamb Quantity (thousands of pounds)	Value (thousands of dollars)
	272	273	274	275	276	277	278	279	280	281	282	283
1960	272,800	—	25,942	—	6,781	—	73,090	—	3,154	—	109	—
1959	342,698	—	29,959	—	4,530	—	76,066	—	29,878	—	749	—
1958	670,484	—	63,924	—	8,069	—	69,405	—	41,318	—	1,377	—
1957	387,532	—	55,312	—	1,865	—	43,513	—	17,788	—	472	—
1956	56,517	—	18,634	—	1,655	—	67,870	—	5,090	—	45	—
1955	67,613	—	12,787	—	8,930	—	80,100	—	8,874	—	273	—
1954	89,194	16,602	22,580	—	26,508	—	76,136	—	2,402	—	53	—
1953	69,505	15,096	28,819	—	21,124	—	78,122	—	2,347	—	52	—
1952	15,446	4,278	68,054	—	703	—	32,095	—	661	—	46	—
1951	239,113	63,065	96,910	—	4,321	—	33,014	—	31,727	—	2,737	—
1950	458,756	79,126	90,740	—	1,646	—	85,099	—	87,658	—	2,761	—
1949	420,655	61,449	106,903	—	2,334	—	77,909	—	40,539	—	3,956	—
1948	457,352	73,900	133,822	—	7,363	—	229,496	—	51,909	—	5,056	—
1947	83,223	14,972	50,952	—	11,160	—	251,178	—	6,048	—	4,569	—
1946	104,618	18,015	138,191	—	7,590	—	300,777	—	4,653	—	11,268	—
1945	79,507	12,257	194,754	—	9,218	—	462,049	—	100,911	—	7,951	—
1944	59,173	9,055	107,411	—	9,739	—	717,714	—	137,808	—	1,589	—
1943	62,725	9,592	13,549	—	9,326	—	587,475	—	3,431	—	891	—
1942	215,778	17,584	15,961	—	5,999	—	537,431	—	6,049	—	628	—
1941	254,127	16,810	7,905	—	37,210	—	482,040	—	4,173	—	349	—
1940	233,781	12,443	—	—	7,203	—	353,015	—	3,991	—	183	—
1939	293,425	15,353	4,352	—	5,808	—	194,992	—	3,340	—	205	—
1938	179,224	9,181	5,692	569	5,500	30	178,494	31,879	3,073	64	202	39
1937	321,760	15,677	17,265	1,339	82,863	1,349	219,142	36,732	2,924	54	284	53
1936	285,414	12,497	12,416	830	76,488	1,256	174,493	28,097	3,533	64	232	39
1935	134,358	6,862	13,513	1,248	19,424	303	132,435	20,902	3,621	52	316	45
1934	64,975	4,031	15,092	944	4,602	22	123,750	19,267	2,090	33	370	50
1933	60,134	3,669	10,010	583	6,031	22	79,303	8,907	1,872	27	406	48
1932	33,285	2,130	4,466	384	5,593	25	46,061	4,705	1,633	25	348	48
1931	56,286	3,617	3,757	435	3,911	29	17,538	2,624	2,042	37	333	58
1930	63,322	3,398	8,087	1,263	2,324	24	20,475	4,610	2,876	66	242	48
1929	253,505	13,960	31,231	5,031	3,942	71	38,957	8,725	11,143	184	573	132
1928	245,428	—	—	—	23,263	—	52,354	—	11,506	—	—	—
1927	295,274	—	—	—	197,106	—	82,582	—	20,138	—	—	—
1926	241,968	—	—	—	85,972	—	109,983	—	21,754	—	—	—
1925	267,292	—	26,541	2,318	89,323	—	149,809	—	40,383	—	1,167	234
1924	218,601	—	20,557	2,327	28,197	—	128,171	—	20,719	—	1,716	404
1923	184,990	—	29,146	2,942	1,554	—	103,647	—	30,603	—	3,610	847
1922	240,327	—	28,405	3,330	2,338	—	100,822	—	91,864	—	7,897	1,342
1921	232,247	—	53,507	8,504	3,154	—	105,093	—	100,663	—	6,406	1,627
1920	315,179	—	—	—	1,399	—	109,364	—	184,002	—	—	—
1919	311,596	30,069	127,113	—	29,542	—	254,160	—	120,131	1,610	1,933	—
1918	191,356	14,137	86,565	—	8,184	—	157,425	—	134,705	1,706	856	—
1917	166,182	7,884	45,546	—	14,894	—	231,533	—	59,224	495	168	—
1916	241,560	12,626	47,422	—	1,527	—	211,388	—	94,478	594	100	—
1915	185,903	9,268	18,828	—	62,763	—	155,440	—	42,832	287	1,065	—
1914	219,729	7,907	13,133	—	214,989	—	78,531	—	20,543	128	65	—
1913	44,296	2,237	1,571	—	3,694	—	28,390	—	13,760	81	46	—
1912	61,517	4,098	949	—	689	—	43,949	—	21,418	122	49	—
1911	124,923	8,537	974	—	1,714	—	70,381	—	46,597	287	18	1,627
1910	157,386	10,792	1,318	110	3,011	9	51,247	—	111,107	608	70	8
1909	162,945	10,771	1,572	128	366	4	574	52	118,896	569	39	4
1908	150,993	9,301	2,253	148	942	14	770	63	227,001	1,197	342	42
1907	162,141	10,932	1,455	102	454	12	480	47	254,665	1,203	64	6
1906	176,030	11,657	2,888	201	783	13	776	58	244,262	1,172	105	8
1905	167,102	11,361	1,332	92	2,806	41	2,236	188	288,313	780	161	10
1904	157,417	10,425	2,963	255	1,351	26	4,289	446	364,053	1,545	90	9
1903	176,780	11,343	2,378	206	23,986	—	1,331	123	401,443	1,656	84	8
1902	184,473	10,664	4,327	414	5,778	—	623	54	348,443	1,484	83	6
1901	169,279	9,064	9,710	813	944	—	742	51	394,681	1,626	77	6
1900	205,524	9,081	2,847	220	1,634	—	1,110	45	459,944	1,894	43	3
1899	218,847	8,523	364	25	814	—	2,155	57	405,322	1,541	140	11
1898	213,010	8,723	898	54	814	—	1,602	52	351,789	1,272	138	9
1897	161,369	7,159	1,660	73	988	—	772	28	313,410	1,002	202	11
1896	104,451	7,082	411	21	8,333	—	1,343	65	391,490	2,151	150	7
1895	93,802	7,121	5,674	438	805	—	520	32	291,751	1,624	112	6
1894	86,057	6,500	2,277	147	1,009	—	756	38	233,361	833	82	9
1893	107,224	7,745	356	21	14,800	—	903	82	360,509	1,248	90	8
1892	107,179	7,749	146	6	284	—	142	8	329,427	1,385	383	14
1891	117,761	8,772	310	16	334	—	68	4	299,347	1,146	292	24
1890	81,454	6,949	252	15	670	—	239	14	315,931	1,274	62	4
1889	102,919	5,708	449	28	1,297	—	285	18	360,131	1,263	119	8
1888	100,747	5,013	551	24	1,583	—	294	20	395,074	1,276	493	28
1887	116,274	6,487	451	22	1,442	—	617	36	443,495	1,592	415	21
1886	91,866	5,825	533	29	2,994	—	346	19	359,407	1,182	422	22
1885	143,003	7,378	542	34	1,652	—	555	35	335,043	1,261	330	19
1884	89,263	5,681	424	27	3,883	—	631	44	304,403	1,545	177	11
1883	66,396	3,898	629	41	3,858	—	807	70	308,474	1,388	397	23
1882	62,106	3,256	750	50	3,263	—	1,225	94	311,669	1,229	334	19
1881	62,277	3,465	1,373	84	2,819	12	1,578	114	354,155	1,372	174	9
1880	54,944	2,764	693	42	6,229	—	1,281	67	398,746	1,423	101	5
1879	46,569	2,097	2,051	148	6,803	—	498	25	308,093	988	301	18
1878	29,925	1,152	5,134	452	3,201	—	914	59	242,989	699	411	36
1877	22,656	716	5,421[3]	376	2,063	—	2,976	220	209,899	583	—[3]	—
1876	25,357	601	1,762[3]	140	3,886	—	2,934	243	141,187	508	—[3]	—
1875	38,968	823	2,066[3]	134	16,779	—	3,041	248	242,438	638	—[3]	—
1874	39,623	951	6,610[3]	270	6,983	—	11,232	315	252,081	702	—[3]	—
1873	25,637	—	1,610[3]	113	5,335	—	4,988	268	315,832	—	—[3]	—
1872	22,438	—	2,130[3]	161	2,878	—	2,126	138	353,178	—	—[3]	—
1871	79,613	—	4,578[3]	241	11,187	47	6,215	502	313,619	829	—[3]	—
1870	107,731	—	3,106[3]	198	107,155	—	6,544	274	147,375	—	—[3]	—
1869	65,251	—	2,370[3]	154	32,271	—	2,677	203	195,682	—	—[3]	—
1868	44,442	—	3,491[3]	203	10,902	—	3,506	239	102,433	—	—[3]	—

Series L272–293. *Exports of major agricultural products, animal and animal products, quantity and value, Canada, 1868 to 1960 (continuation)*

(values in thousands of dollars; quantities as designated individually)

	Horses		Wool		Butter		Cheese		Eggs	
Year[1]	Quantity (number of head)	Value (thousands of dollars)	Quantity (thousands of pounds)	Value (thousands of dollars)	Quantity (thousands of pounds)	Value (thousands of dollars)	Quantity (thousands of pounds)	Value (thousands of dollars)	Quantity (thousands of dozen)	Value (thousands of dollars)
	284	285	286	287	288	289	290	291	292	293
1960	10,214	—	3,678	—	—	—	—	—	—	—
1959	16,218	—	5,002	—	10,504	—	20,009	—	—	—
1958	21,821	—	4,002	—	5	—	15,701	—	19,386	—
1957	15,050	—	3,917	—	4	—	8,456	—	9,628	—
1956	8,698	698	3,594	—	2,115	824	12,217	4,178	3,939	1,910
1955	12,652	797	2,883	—	7,403	2,838	13,749	4,045	4,040	1,851
1954	17,775	912	2,865	—	143	91	5,006	1,544	7,274	3,365
1953	12,563	—	3,756	—	191	—	16,429	4,518	7,718	—
1952	6,996	—	3,039	—	866	—	2,095	880	13,420	—
1951	11,072	—	2,656	—	544	—	30,653	10,232	7,103	—
1950	26,858	—	4,328	—	1,629	—	63,110	16,552	14,792	—
1949	12,989	—	3,920	—	1,069	—	52,695	16,257	42,504	—
1948	21,599	—	4,929	—	882	—	39,827	12,042	81,238	—
1947	15,662	—	5,103	—	3,107	—	55,531	14,162	86,150	—
1946	40,120	—	6,409	—	4,509	—	106,495	21,948	61,347	—
1945	19,059	—	11,927	—	5,598	—	135,409	27,909	114,623	—
1944	22,196	—	15,520	—	4,727	—	131,429	27,062	62,201	—
1943	17,697	—	2,316	—	9,409	—	129,741	26,811	41,111	—
1942	4,764	—	384	—	1,601	—	141,504	26,904	28,489	—
1941	2,659	—	3,025	—	1,482	—	92,331	13,555	16,276	—
1940	5,416	—	2,681	—	1,338	—	106,631	15,723	10,980	—
1939	5,953	—	4,664	—	12,399	—	90,945	12,249	1,274	—
1938	5,914	—	4,260	693	3,893	872	80,089	11,874	1,842	498
1937	11,243	—	4,813	1,396	4,096	1,147	88,955	13,062	1,602	424
1936	18,107	—	9,103	2,171	5,128	1,179	81,890	11,347	1,204	326
1935	6,025	—	8,363	1,418	7,697	1,796	55,719	6,427	1,301	333
1934	4,479	—	4,260	639	428	101	61,168	6,572	2,001	454
1933	6,470	—	11,258	1,912	4,437	827	74,167	8,077	1,987	423
1932	5,077	—	3,712	322	3,506	656	86,940	8,915	273	68
1931	7,961	—	4,770	524	10,680	2,330	84,788	10,595	634	156
1930	4,429	—	4,382	632	1,180	410	80,164	13,207	189	71
1929	—	—	6,090	1,670	1,400	583	92,946	18,504	1,148	424
1928	—	—	—	—	—	—	—	—	—	—
1927	—	—	—	—	—	—	—	—	—	—
1926	—	—	—	—	—	—	—	—	—	—
1925	—	—	5,625	2,434	24,502	8,716	126,963	24,112	2,691	1,001
1924	—	—	6,009	1,947	13,649	5,071	116,777	23,426	2,890	1,027
1923	—	—	8,667	2,304	21,994	8,243	114,549	20,828	3,614	1,410
1922	—	—	1,034	242	8,430	3,224	133,850	25,440	4,400	2,039
1921	—	—	7,288	2,168	9,739	5,129	133,620	37,147	6,580	4,428
1920	—	—	9,085	5,472	17,613	9,844	126,396	36,337	6,000	3,497
1919	—	—	4,882	3,303	13,659	6,141	152,207	35,224	733	382
1918	—	—	10,577	—	4,926	—	169,531	—	4,897	—
1917	—	—	5,837	—	7,990	—	180,733	—	5,167	—
1916	—	—	4,546	—	3,441	—	168,962	—	7,898	—
1915	—	—	5,660	—	2,725	—	137,602	—	3,593	—
1914	—	—	2,841	—	1,229	—	144,478	—	124	—
1913	—	—	977	—	828	—	155,216	—	147	—
1912	—	—	747	—	8,844	—	163,451	—	203	—
1911	—	—	1,197	258	3,143	744	181,896	20,740	92	—
1910	2,762	554	2,321	538	4,615	1,010	180,960	21,608	160	42
1909	2,028	367	1,081	202	6,326	1,521	164,907	20,385	553	124
1908	2,270	516	1,848	456	4,787	1,069	189,710	22,887	1,366	302
1907	2,115	440	1,229	331	18,078	4,012	178,142	22,006	2,592	556
1906	2,794	525	1,425	353	34,032	7,076	215,834	24,433	2,922	495
1905	2,659	451	1,972	418	31,764	5,930	215,733	20,300	3,601	713
1904	2,395	402	1,775	306	24,588	4,724	233,981	24,184	5,780	1,053
1903	3,878	590	—	—	34,129	6,955	229,100	24,713	7,404	1,436
1902	12,687	1,457	—	—	27,856	5,660	200,946	19,686	11,635	1,733
1901	7,609	910	1,044	186	16,336	3,296	195,926	20,697	11,363	1,692
1900	10,053	1,167	2,181	418	25,260	5,122	185,984	19,856	10,188	1,458
1899	12,384	898	90	14	20,139	3,701	189,828	16,777	9,652	1,267
1898	14,349	1,497	1,014	177	11,254	2,047	196,703	17,573	10,370	1,255
1897	17,993	1,711	7,740	1,428	11,453	2,089	164,221	14,676	7,477	978
1896	21,852	2,113	3,916	824	5,889	1,052	164,689	13,956	6,521	907
1895	14,744	1,313	5,463	1,049	3,650	697	146,005	14,253	6,501	808
1894	8,734	946	80	16	5,535	1,096	154,977	15,488	5,142	714
1893	13,219	1,461	1,169	228	7,036	1,297	133,946	13,407	6,805	868
1892	11,063	1,354	916	201	5,737	1,056	118,270	11,652	7,931	1,090
1891	11,658	1,417	1,108	246	3,768	602	106,202	9,509	8,023	1,160
1890	16,550	1,936	1,048	236	1,951	340	94,260	9,372	12,840	1,795
1889	17,767	2,171	1,015	218	1,781	332	88,535	8,916	14,029	2,160
1888	20,397	2,458	995	223	4,415	799	84,173	8,928	14,171	2,122
1887	18,779	2,269	1,416	317	5,486	979	73,604	7,109	12,945	1,826
1886	16,525	2,148	1,524	317	4,669	832	78,113	6,755	12,758	1,728
1885	11,978	1,555	990	196	7,331	1,431	79,655	8,265	11,543	1,831
1884	11,595	1,618	1,501	310	8,076	1,612	69,755	7,252	11,491	1,960
1883	13,019	1,633	1,376	280	8,106	1,706	58,041	6,452	13,451	2,256
1882	20,920	2,327	1,053	247	15,162	2,936	50,807	5,501	10,499	1,644
1881	21,993	2,094	1,405	410	17,649	3,573	49,256	5,510	9,090	1,104
1880	21,393	1,880	3,619	921	18,535	3,058	40,369	3,893	6,452	741
1879	16,629	1,377	3,014	692	14,308	2,102	46,414	3,790	5,441	574
1878	14,179	1,274	2,446	707	13,007	2,382	38,054	3,998	5,263	646
1877	8,306	779	2,476	699	14,692	3,073	35,930	3,748	5,026	535
1876	4,299	442	2,907	934	12,250	2,541	35,024	3,751	3,881	508
1875	4,382	461	2,647	920	9,268	2,337	32,342	3,886	3,521	434
1874	5,339	570	2,765	984	12,233	2,620	24,051	3,523	4,408	588
1873	—	—	3,126	1,451	15,209	2,809	19,483	2,280	3,754	509
1872	—	—	3,196	1,365	19,068	3,613	16,424	1,840	3,725	454
1871	—	—	2,892	839	15,439	3,065	8,271	1,110	3,312	424
1870	—	—	2,444	770	12,261	2,354	5,828	674	2,461	315
1869	—	—	2,820	817	10,853	2,342	4,503	550	1,539	188
1868	—	—	1,606	444	10,650	1,698	6,142	620	1,893	206

[1] For most series 1868 to 1906 data are for years ending 30 June of the year given; for 1907 9 months ending 31 March 1907; for 1908 to 1960, fiscal years ending 31 March of the year given. See footnote (2) for series given on a different basis.

[2] Calendar years: for cattle and calves, 1925 to 1960; for hogs, 1910 to 1960; for sheep and lambs, 1920 to 1960. Years ending 31 March of the year given: for cattle and calves, 1907 to 1924; for hogs, 1907 to 1909; for sheep and lambs, 1907 to 1919. Years ending 30 June of the year given, 1868 to 1906.

[3] Series L274 includes mutton for these years.

Series L 294–299. *Exports of bacon, hams and lard, quantity and value, Canada, 1868 to 1910*
(values in thousands of dollars; quantities as designated individually)

Year[1]	Bacon		Hams		Lard	
	Quantity (thousands of pounds)	Value (thousands of dollars)	Quantity (thousands of pounds)	Value (thousands of dollars)	Quantity (thousands of pounds)	Value (thousands of dollars)
	294	295	296	297	298	299
1910	45,577	6,431	3,261	417	1,483	133
1909	72,173	8,414	3,288	421	357	35
1908	92,001	10,790	3,174	371	1,305	131
1907	75,379	9,018	1,831	204	196	20
1906	99,125	11,667	3,783	420	130	13
1905	116,835	12,194	2,866	322	1,284	110
1904	124,060	12,603	3,884	419	494	46
1903	137,954	15,455	4,002	451	2,414	236
1902	105,841	12,163	2,137	241	319	22
1901	103,021	11,494	2,529	284	847	59
1900	132,176	12,472	2,856	286	197	11
1899	111,869	9,954	4,784	463	1,656	68
1898	76,845	7,291	8,464	749	253	19
1897	59,546	5,060	9,582	783	228	17
1896	47,058	3,802	6,678	580	174	13
1895	37,526	3,546	2,608	261	1,276	104
1894	26,827	2,754	1,682	184	803	77
1893	17,288	1,830	1,216	140	710	67
1892	11,544	1,094	598	58	32	2
1891	7,151	591	403	38	48	3
1890	7,235	607	257	24	82	6
1889	3,880	361	187	20	92	8
1888	6,702	629	318	31	75	7
1887	11,031	871	395	35	159	12
1886	8,144	621	423	33	96	7
1885	7,189	631	963	87	64	5
1884	7,547	732	571	62	215	21
1883	3,737	437	518	62	51	6
1882	9,214	1,007	616	64	135	14
1881	9,785	718	570	41	210	20
1880	8,617	468	956	66	499	31
1879	3,977	243	670	46	312	18
1878	4,519	367	1,169	111	265	28
1877	15,781[2]	1,252[2]	—	—	540	63
1876	9,026[2]	839[2]	—	—	638	52
1875	9,964[2]	827[2]	—	—	339	40
1874	20,238[2]	1,587[2]	—	—	2,137	218
1873	39,982[2]	2,323[2]	—	—	2,393	204
1872	14,049[2]	999[2]	—	—	1,114	106
1871	11,586[2]	1,019[2]	—	—	1,291	149
1870	19,627[2]	1,553[2]	—	—	1,369	200
1869	8,799[2]	870[2]	—	—	465	58
1868	10,580[2]	783[2]	—	—	—	—

[1] For 1908 to 1910 data are for fiscal years ending 31 March of the year given; for 1907, 9 months ending 31 March 1907; for 1868 to 1906, fiscal years ending 30 June of the year given.

[2] Includes ham.

Series L 300–317. *Domestic disappearance of food products, per capita, Canada, 1919 to 1960*
(series L 304 in dozens, all other series in pounds)

Year[1]	Wheat flour[1]	Beef[2]	Pork[3]	Hens and chickens[4]	Eggs	Fish[5]	Milk	Whole milk evapor- ated[6]	Cheese	Ice cream	Total butter	Lard[7]	Mar- garine	Pota- toes, white fresh[1,8]	Apples[1,9]	Re- fined sugar	Coffee	Tea
	300	301	302	303	304	305	306	307	308	309	310	311	312	313	314	315	316	317
1960	135.2[10]	70.0	52.6	20.8	23.0	7.7	345.9	17.7	7.2	12.7	17.0	7.2	9.4	143.6	21.5	96.6	9.0	2.4
1959	136.0[10]	65.6	56.7	22.0	23.3	7.6	356.0	17.3	7.0	12.6	18.1	10.3	8.7	126.3	29.0	98.3	9.4	2.6
1958	142.8[10]	68.0	49.4	21.1	24.2	7.5	320.4	17.7	6.9	11.8	19.1	7.0	8.5	130.8	24.6	97.6	8.6	2.6
1957	138.8[10]	72.0	44.4	19.4	25.0	6.9	381.9	18.2	6.8	11.6	20.3	7.4	7.8	161.1	23.7	93.6	8.4	2.8
1956	145.1[10]	71.4	49.2	23.6	24.3	7.2	405.1	18.6	6.4	11.3	20.5	8.8	7.7	153.3	—	99.3	8.1	2.8
1955	147.8	69.1	49.2	23.4	24.0	7.3	396.3	18.4	6.7	11.3	20.3	8.6	8.1	148.5	45.5	97.1	6.6	2.7
1954	148.5	70.2	45.4	22.4	23.9	7.1	388.3	18.1	6.4	10.3	20.4	8.3	7.6	146.3	34.3	94.2	6.2	2.9
1953	131.8	65.1	48.7	21.5	22.9	6.9	387.0	18.5	6.2	10.6	20.7	8.3	7.5	155.9	30.4	94.8	7.2	3.1
1952	153.1	54.4	56.0	24.0	22.2	6.8	381.8	18.3	5.8	10.3	20.7	10.0	7.7	146.8	31.9	96.2	6.7	3.2
1951	157.0	49.3	58.6	19.5	20.0	6.9	415.8	17.9	5.7	10.0	21.2	9.5	7.4	143.3	35.4	95.4	6.3	3.0
1950	158.3	50.6	54.9	17.1	19.7	6.8	421.8	17.5	5.6	9.5	22.3	9.5	6.8	177.5	37.3	101.0	6.0	4.0
1949	149.2	56.7	55.0	16.7	19.3	6.3	422.7	14.8	5.3	10.2	22.1	9.9	5.5	158.8	38.6	100.6	7.3	3.2
1948	139.2	59.2	48.0	14.9	20.8	6.0	424.2	15.5	4.8	10.8	26.7	8.5	—	163.7	34.6	100.5	6.8	2.7
1947	164.1	64.8	52.4	19.5	22.0	5.4	454.1	14.5	6.2	10.3	26.2	9.9	—	142.1	47.5	90.6	4.1	3.6
1946	183.9	68.8	43.5	21.8	21.8	5.5	474.6	11.9	5.1	7.1	24.1	8.4	—	178.5	40.9	75.1	6.9	2.2
1945	197.2	67.0	52.7	21.3	21.6	6.8	475.5	12.6	5.9	7.7	28.1	11.3	—	156.8	25.6	74.3	4.5	4.2
1944	183.7	65.7	62.6	21.1	22.0	5.9	470.9	11.3	5.5	8.4	29.2	12.4	—	172.8	46.1	86.6	8.2	3.2
1943	183.2	62.8	62.3	19.9	22.2	6.7	453.2	13.5	5.6	8.3	27.6	13.8	—	189.2	39.4	77.5	4.9	3.1
1942	188.3	60.7	58.9	19.7	21.7	6.0	420.9	12.5	4.5	7.3	32.3	13.3	—	182.0	41.1	76.6	3.8	2.5
1941	165.5	58.5	51.6	16.9	20.2	6.6	394.1	9.8	5.0	6.8	30.9	10.8	—	194.4	34.3	101.0	4.7	3.2
1940	164.2	54.5	44.7	16.7	20.1	6.1	396.2	9.0	4.0	5.3	31.0	7.0	—	213.0	37.2	96.5	3.5	3.6
1939	191.1	53.2	38.4	16.0	21.4	—	426.2	8.4	4.0	4.4	30.9	4.8	—	166.1	40.1	99.3	4.1	3.8
1938	183.3	57.2	37.7	15.6	20.9	—	430.7	6.7	4.0	4.4	30.9	3.7	—	173.2	26.8	92.6	3.8	3.3
1937	168.0	54.6	42.5	15.8	21.6	—	403.0	6.0	3.8	4.6	31.4	3.5	—	211.7	30.2	91.4	3.4	3.6
1936	174.1	55.1	41.4	16.2	21.8	—	413.4	5.1	3.8	4.1	30.9	3.8	—	197.5	—	85.7	3.6	3.6
1935	179.2	53.6	39.3	16.0	22.6	—	408.4	4.3	3.8	3.4	30.6	3.9	—	198.6	—	87.5	3.2	3.2
1934	173.6	50.6	47.4	14.0	22.3	—	412.7	3.6	3.8	3.0	30.5	6.4	—	265.4	—	83.2	3.2	3.5
1933	175.4	45.8	52.0	11.1	22.8	—	402.7	3.3	3.6	3.0	29.7	6.9	—	219.0	—	78.7	3.2	3.7
1932	179.5	45.5	55.3	9.6	24.0	—	406.2	3.2	3.4	3.3	29.8	8.2	—	210.8	—	87.2	2.9	3.8
1931	173.9	48.5	51.9	7.7	24.9	—	419.5	4.0	3.7	4.4	30.4	8.2	—	293.8	—	89.9	3.1	3.1
1930	175.9	49.1	52.8	7.9	24.4	—	388.8	4.5	3.9	5.2	30.7	8.4	—	235.9	—	92.9	3.0	4.9
1929	168.9	51.1	58.0	7.4	24.8	—	364.5	4.5	3.9	5.3	30.3	8.6	—	180.0	—	90.1	2.8	3.8
1928	180.4	50.5	58.4	6.8	24.8	—	378.8	4.3	4.0	4.8	29.7	8.3	—	284.2	—	92.6	2.8	3.9
1927	185.4	54.5	54.5	6.6	24.1	—	392.7	4.1	3.7	4.2	29.2	7.8	—	243.0	—	85.4	2.7	3.9
1926	177.1	55.2	53.5	6.3	23.4	—	417.0	3.9	4.5	4.0	29.4	7.9	—	239.7	—	92.4	2.6	3.9
1925	—	56.0	53.3	6.3	26.8	—	422.1	—	4.0	3.5	28.4	8.0	—	—	—	—	—	—
1924	—	53.0	54.8	6.4	26.1	—	406.4	—	3.6	3.3	28.5	8.2	—	—	—	—	—	—
1923	—	57.2	50.5	6.4	25.4	—	402.1	—	—	3.4	29.1	9.1	—	—	—	—	—	—
1922	—	58.2	48.6	6.2	25.0	—	384.1	—	—	3.0	27.2	8.2	—	—	—	—	—	—
1921	—	51.2	41.7	6.4	22.1	—	382.6	—	—	3.4	26.8	9.6	—	—	—	—	—	—
1920	—	57.4	42.1	—	—	—	362.8	—	—	3.7	24.0	9.3	—	—	—	—	—	—
1919	—	58.4	58.2	—	—	—	—	—	—	—	—	—	—	—	—	—	—	—

[1] Data are for calendar years except for: wheat, series L 300 for 1926 to 1955 data are for crop years 1 August to 31 July ending in the following year; potatoes and apples, series L 313 and L 314, for 1955 and earlier years data are for crop years 1 July to 30 June ending in the following year.
[2] Data for beef are cold dressed carcass weight.
[3] Data for pork are cold trimmed carcass weight.
[4] Hens and chickens for 1921 to 1955, data are for dressed weight; for 1956 to 1960 data are for eviscerated weight. The conversion factor is .77.

[5] Fish and shellfish, fresh and frozen.
[6] Includes substantial quantities of powdered skim milk used in the feeds industry.
[7] Prior to 1949 includes certain quantities of lard used in manufacture of shortening.
[8] For 1950 and prior years potatoes includes the amount dumped or fed to livestock.
[9] Data for apples are on a fresh equivalent basis.
[10] Includes rye flour.

Series L318–329. *Farm tractors, numbers on farms and estimated annual sales, 1921 to 1960*

Year[3]	Canada[1] Number on farms	Canada[1] Number sold	Maritimes Number on farms	Maritimes Number sold	Quebec Number on farms	Quebec Number sold	Ontario Number on farms	Ontario Number sold	Prairie Provinces Number on farms	Prairie Provinces Number sold	British Columbia Number on farms	British Columbia Number sold
	318	319	320	321	322	323	324	325	326	327	328	329
1960	565,051[2]	26,165[2]	22,780[2]	1,474[2]	71,300	4,971	155,184	7,044	298,368	11,864	17,419	812
1959	549,061	26,101	21,807	1,249	67,472	4,891	150,605	7,150	292,286	11,871	16,891	940
1958	533,170	22,922	20,999	1,093	63,696	4,908	145,950	6,187	286,235	10,039	16,290	695
1957	518,431	21,730	20,246	1,214	59,660	4,801	141,795	5,626	280,956	9,451	15,774	638
1956	499,498	27,317	19,023	1,786	54,322	5,379	136,062	8,406	274,809	10,220	15,282	1,526
1955	483,215	28,321	18,037	1,606	50,189	5,804	130,596	8,978	269,543	10,318	14,850	1,615
1954	466,087	27,310	16,987	1,420	45,737	4,962	124,758	8,006	264,223	11,709	14,382	1,213
1953	449,855	40,719	16,112	2,638	41,931	6,279	119,552	9,815	258,230	20,536	14,030	1,451
1952	426,081	44,954	14,336	2,976	37,115	6,706	113,170	12,253	247,851	21,430	13,609	1,589
1951	399,557	50,898	12,304	2,663	31,971	7,699	105,204	16,806	236,930	22,194	13,148	1,536
1950	362,929	55,420	10,858	2,245	25,967	6,325	92,966	17,488	221,487	27,962	11,651	1,400
1949	322,946	61,863	9,341	2,022	21,046	5,826	80,200	17,125	202,071	35,082	10,288	1,808
1948	278,408	44,469	7,908	2,243	16,513	4,378	67,699	11,958	177,760	23,696	8,528	2,194
1947	246,001	32,940	6,191	1,277	13,107	2,922	58,970	8,582	161,341	19,045	6,392	1,114
1946	225,233	22,762	5,226	932	10,834	1,930	52,705	6,300	151,161	12,695	5,307	905
1945	205,769	18,666	4,515	642	9,332	1,268	48,106	4,819	139,390	11,360	4,426	517
1944	192,423	20,836	4,032	604	8,346	1,454	44,588	5,725	131,534	12,407	3,923	646
1943	177,414	7,462	3,556	184	7,215	499	40,409	1,771	122,940	4,812	3,294	196
1942	172,124	17,162	3,462	440	6,827	1,231	39,116	5,008	119,616	10,065	3,103	418
1941	159,752	20,422	3,103	565	5,869	1,703	35,460	6,408	112,624	11,359	2,696	387
1940	146,263	20,968	2,372	542	4,623	1,485	30,619	5,760	106,271	12,782	2,378	399
1939	131,549	13,420	1,671	333	3,580	626	26,268	3,514	97,988	8,755	2,042	192
1938	122,610	13,633	1,240	147	3,078	485	23,613	3,289	92,790	9,582	1,889	130
1937	112,989	7,385	1,049	—	2,723	—	21,128	—	86,299	7,154	1,790	231
1936	105,548	3,720	889	—	2,417	—	18,993	—	81,657	3,584	1,592	136
1935	103,911	2,206	889	—	2,417	—	18,993	—	80,132	2,157	1,480	49
1934	103,554	1,518	889	—	2,417	—	18,993	—	79,806	1,455	1,449	63
1933	103,771	777	889	—	2,417	—	18,993	—	80,068	762	1,404	15
1932	104,653	892	889	—	2,417	—	18,993	—	80,949	878	1,405	14
1931	105,360	842	889	—	2,417	—	18,993	—	81,659	787	1,402	55
1930	110,019	9,108	928	—	2,565	—	19,978	—	85,076	8,991	1,472	117
1929	105,214	14,557	895	—	2,495	—	19,347	—	81,052	14,557	1,425	—
1928	92,802	17,143	800	—	2,232	—	17,296	—	71,200	17,143	1,274	—
1927	75,482	10,026	658	—	1,832	—	14,214	—	57,730	10,026	1,048	—
1926	65,480	6,513	568	—	1,585	—	12,286	—	50,136	6,513	905	—
1925	60,015	4,053	504	—	1,419	—	10,944	—	46,343	4,053	805	—
1924	57,428	2,112	460	—	1,315	—	10,569	—	44,344	2,112	740	—
1923	55,914	4,166	435	—	1,267	—	9,600	—	43,907	4,166	705	—
1922	51,832	4,222	379	—	1,127	—	8,453	—	41,253	4,222	620	—
1921	47,455	3,428	317	—	968	—	7,161	—	38,485	3,428	524	—

[1] Excludes Yukon and Northwest Territories throughout.
[2] Includes Newfoundland for 1960 only.
[3] Number on farms are at 1 June; numbers sold are for calendar years.

Series L330–336. *Number of implements on farms and number of farms reporting electric power, Canada and Prairie Provinces, census dates, 1871 and 1921 to 1956*

Year	Number of implements on farms Automobiles	Binders	Combines	Gasoline engines	Motor trucks	Threshing machines	Number of farms reporting electric power
	330	331	332	333	334	335	336
Panel A. Canada							
1956[1]	352,018	—	136,927	249,779	277,183	—	422,604
1951	329,667	303,374	90,500	183,051	196,122	96,691	319,383
1941	315,461	—	19,013	168,225	377,480	93,001	—
1931	321,284	431,403	8,917	179,765	48,401	105,544	73,351[2]
1921	157,022[3]	—	—	—	—[3]	—	26,842[2]
1871[4]	—	44,204[5]	—	—	—	30,735	—
Panel B. Prairie Provinces							
1956	145,274	—	116,817	188,499	161,803	—	126,179
1951	141,337	159,924	79,117	119,136	113,512	43,414	64,130
1946	127,900	196,518	38,870	98,907	56,177	42,691	—
1941	128,257	—	18,081	80,745	43,363	44,218	—
1936	116,676	238,983	9,827	86,152	21,293	46,701	—
1931	133,499	248,547	8,897	83,044	21,517	49,610	8,786[2]
1926	101,529	—	—	—	5,640	—	—
1921	73,359[3]	—	—	—	—[3]	—	4,354[2]

[1] Includes data for Yukon and Northwest Territories.
[2] Includes some farms reporting gas.
[3] Series L330 includes motor trucks for 1921.
[4] Includes Nova Scotia, New Brunswick, Quebec and Ontario only.
[5] Reapers and mowers.

Series L 337–346. *Grain elevator capacities, 1911 to 1960*
(millions of bushels of wheat)

Year[1]	Total country, terminal and mill elevators	Country elevators[2]				Terminal and mill elevators				
		Total	Manitoba[3]	Saskatchewan	Alberta[4]	Total	British Columbia	Prairie Provinces[5]	Lakehead	Eastern other than Lakehead
	337	338	339	340	341	342	343	344	345	346
Licensed capacity										
1960[1]	639.0	369.1	49.2	192.3	127.6	270.0	25.9	40.3	93.3	110.4
1959	648.2	391.2	51.2	205.5	134.5	257.0	25.8	40.3	93.1	97.8
1958	639.1	386.6	50.5	202.2	133.8	252.5	24.9	40.3	93.1	94.2
1957	632.2	380.0	49.9	198.4	131.7	252.2	24.8	40.1	93.1	94.1
1956	622.2	371.7	48.8	193.5	129.4	250.5	23.2	40.1	93.1	94.1
1955	599.3	352.8	47.4	182.8	122.6	246.5	21.2	40.0	93.1	92.2
1954	581.0	338.2	45.9	177.0	115.3	242.8	21.4	37.5	93.1	90.8
1953	561.5	323.0	44.1	167.9	110.9	238.5	23.0	37.4	93.1	84.9
1952	539.3	306.8	40.4	159.2	107.2	232.5	23.0	37.9	86.6	84.9
1951	526.9	290.9	37.8	150.7	102.3	236.0	22.9	37.4	93.1	82.5
1950	506.2	278.7	35.4	143.9	99.4	227.5	22.9	37.5	84.6	82.5
1949	489.9	264.2	34.5	133.7	96.0	225.7	21.2	37.3	84.6	82.5
1948	486.2	265.2	33.9	135.4	95.8	221.1	18.4	37.5	82.7	82.5
1947	482.4	264.7	33.8	137.4	93.4	217.8	18.4	37.0	78.9	83.5
1946	495.2	268.3	34.8	139.6	93.9	226.9	18.3	36.9	88.2	83.5
1945	566.7	288.0	39.0	151.2	97.8	278.7	22.8	35.3	129.7	90.9
1944	596.4	304.7	43.4	159.9	101.5	291.7	22.8	35.7	143.6	89.6
1943	602.8	306.8	43.8	161.4	101.6	296.0	22.8	35.6	146.1	91.4
1942	602.0	307.3	44.1	161.0	102.2	294.6	22.7	35.4	146.6	89.9
1941	599.4	305.3	44.1	159.8	101.4	294.1	22.8	36.7	144.5	90.1
1940	508.8	272.4	34.7	150.2	87.5	236.3	22.8	36.3	93.0	84.3
1939	423.0	189.5	23.4	99.9	66.2	233.5	22.8	35.2	92.8	82.7
1938	401.5	181.5	22.3	94.4	64.9	220.0	20.8	35.2	82.9	81.1
1937	349.2	152.3	21.4	72.9	58.0	196.9	15.1	30.3	70.5	81.1
1936	394.1	174.9	21.0	91.7	62.2	219.2	20.8	36.0	81.2	81.2
1935	412.0	183.6	21.6	97.4	64.6	228.3	20.8	35.8	91.8	79.9
1934	400.4	176.2	20.3	91.6	64.4	224.2	21.8	35.9	89.3	77.2
1933	411.2	184.9	21.6	96.9	66.3	226.2	21.9	35.2	92.8	76.3
1932	415.8	190.4	22.2	101.3	66.9	225.5	21.7	35.3	92.9	75.6
1931	391.5	172.4	21.3	87.2	63.9	219.1	20.2	31.7	91.6	75.6
Licensed and unlicensed capacity										
1930	414.7	193.3	23.8	103.9	65.7	221.3	20.2	32.0	92.9	76.1
1929	394.6	192.9	24.2	104.0	64.7	201.7	18.4	27.9	86.9	68.5
1928	358.3	178.6	24.2	96.2	58.2	179.6	14.4	25.8	86.9	52.5
1927	310.8	155.1	21.7	87.8	45.6	155.7	9.6	25.8	72.7	47.6
1926	284.8	146.6	20.6	85.0	41.0	138.2	8.3	24.3	64.3	41.3
1925	281.7	141.3	20.0	82.9	38.4	140.4	8.3	24.1	64.9	43.1
1924	269.9	138.3	20.4	81.0	36.9	131.6	4.5	22.6	64.4	40.1
1923	251.2	132.3	20.5	76.2	35.6	118.9	1.7	19.7	63.3	34.2
1922	238.1	132.3	23.2	72.5	36.6	105.8	1.3	13.6	56.8	34.2
1921	231.6	129.2	23.2	70.2	35.8	102.4	1.3	13.7	53.3	34.2
1920	231.2	129.0	23.9	68.9	36.2	102.2	1.3	12.1	54.7	34.2
1919	226.3	126.9	24.9	68.1	34.0	99.3	1.3	12.0	52.3	33.8
1918	221.3	124.9	24.8	67.3	32.8	96.4	1.3	12.0	51.4	31.8
1917	211.6	117.3	23.6	64.4	29.4	94.3	1.3	12.0	49.4	31.6
1916	193.8	103.5	21.3	58.6	23.6	90.3	1.3	13.0	45.3	30.7
1915	181.0	94.3	22.2	52.9	19.3	86.6	1.3	13.0	43.1	29.3
1914	168.6	86.7	22.1	48.1	16.5	81.9	—	10.5	42.2	29.3
1913	154.8	81.8	23.4	43.0	15.3	73.0	—	1.7	41.5	29.9
1912	127.2	70.9	22.3	36.5	12.1	56.3	—	1.7	29.4	25.2
1911	108.6	62.1	22.5	29.3	10.3	46.5	—	1.7	25.7	19.1

[1] For 1960 data as at 1 August 1960; for 1911 to 1959 data as at 1 December of the year given.
[2] Includes warehouses in earlier years.
[3] Includes Ontario country elevators.
[4] Includes British Columbia country elevators.
[5] Includes Kenora-Keewatin terminal and mill.

Series L 347–350. *Four wage series for farm labour, Ontario, 1882 to 1908*
(dollars)

Year	Rate per year with board	Rate per year without board	Rate per month with board	Rate per month without board	Year	Rate per year with board	Rate per year without board	Rate per month with board	Rate per month without board
	347	348	349	350		347	348	349	350
1908	190	295	21.57	31.07	1895	150	246	15.38	25.45
1907	—	—	—	—	1894	156	247	16.55	25.61
1906	196	298	22.19	31.90	1893	160	255	17.13	25.97
					1892	156	253	16.52	25.92
1905	192	296	21.61	31.32	1891	158	257	16.66	25.81
1904	190	291	21.49	31.02					
1903	183	274	19.44	28.04	1890	157	253	16.88	26.56
1902	165	268	18.52	27.51	1889	162	249	17.59	26.01
1901	165	263	17.78	27.05	1888	157	251	16.99	26.50
					1887	159	250	16.91	26.04
1900	155	248	16.57	25.73	1886	158	251	17.06	26.64
1899	149	243	15.38	24.93					
1898	148	246	15.31	25.44	1885	160	253	17.32	27.18
1897	144	236	14.29	24.47	1884	167	257	19.44	29.11
1896	144	243	14.57	24.11	1883	173	264	20.37	30.21
					1882	166	249	17.00	25.00

APPENDIX. EARLY COLONIAL AGRICULTURAL STATISTICS

Series L 351–354. *Land utilization in the colonial period*

Year	Land occupied	Land improved	Land in pasture	Land under culture	Year	Land occupied	Land improved	Land in pasture	Land under culture
	351	352	353	354		351	352	353	354
		Newfoundland			1719	—	—	8,018	63,032
1869	—	—	—	41,715	1718	—	—	8,378	61,176
1857	—	42,609	—		1716	—	—	7,397	57,240
1845	83,428	—	—	29,645	1713	—	—	7,468	53,161
					1712	—	—	7,636	52,965
		Prince Edward Island							
1871	1,028,240	445,103	—	445,103	1707	—	—	5,743	43,501
1861	996,185	368,127	—	368,127	1706	—	—	5,533	43,671
					1698	—	—	5,159	32,524
		Nova Scotia			1695	—	—	3,595	28,110
1871	—	1,627,091[1]	823,322	790,155[3]	1692	—	—	3,642	26,669
1861	—	—	—	971,816					
1851	—	799,310	—		1688	—	—	—	28,663
1827	—	—	—	292,009	1685	—	—	—	24,390
1762	—	—	—	14,340	1681	—	—	—	24,827
					1679	—	—	—	21,900
		New Brunswick			1668	—	—	—	15,642
1871	—	1,171,157[1]	385,105	778,461[3]					
1861	—	885,108	—		1667	—	—	—	11,488
1851	—	—	—	643,954					
1840	—	—	—	435,861			Upper Canada		
					1871	16,162,676	8,833,626[1]	2,089,177	6,537,438[3]
		Lower Canada[2]			1861	13,354,896	6,051,609	—	
1871	11,025,786	5,703,944[1]	1,943,182	3,714,304[3]	1851	9,828,655	—	—	3,705,523
1861	10,375,418	—	—	4,804,235	1848	8,413,591	—	766,768	1,780,157
1851	8,113,408	3,605,167	—	—	1842	6,212,726	—	—	1,751,528
1844	6,710,289	2,671,768	—	—					
1831	4,981,823	—	—	2,066,213	1841	6,868,504	—	—	1,811,431
					1840	7,011,706	—	—	1,713,163
1827	—	—	1,944,397	1,002,198	1839	6,670,083	—	—	1,556,677
1784	—	—	—	1,569,818	1838	6,769,050	—	—	1,469,737
1765	—	—	—	941,342	1837	6,280,611	—	—	1,440,505
1739	—	—	25,596	188,105					
1736	—	—	23,763	164,741	1836	6,089,694	—	—	1,283,709
					1835	5,703,219	—	—	1,309,785
1734	—	—	17,657	163,111	1834	5,127,064	—	—	1,004,779
1732	—	—	18,800	133,263	1833	5,154,211	—	—	988,956
1730	—	—	18,102	130,791	1832	4,716,372	—	—	916,357
1727	—	—	14,833	102,100					
1726	—	—	13,454	96,202	1831	4,387,777	—	—	818,416
					1830	4,018,385	—	—	773,727
1724	—	—	11,282	83,419	1829	3,726,330	—	—	717,553
1723	—	—	11,019	82,245	1828	3,632,540	—	—	668,326
1722	—	—	13,018	62,734	1827	3,579,554	—	—	645,792
1721	—	—	12,203	62,145					
1720	—	—	10,132	61,357	1826	3,353,453	—	—	599,744

[1] Includes small acreages for gardens and orchards.

[2] For 1667 to 1831, areas are given in arpents.

[3] Land under crops specified.

Series L 355–369. *Agricultural production statistics of the colonial period*
(all series in bushels except as noted for Quebec in footnotes)

Year	Wheat	Barley	Rye	Oats	Peas	Buckwheat	Indian corn
	355	356	357	358	359	360	361
				Newfoundland			
1869	747	—	—	11,150	—	—	—
1857	1,932[1]	—	—	9,038	—	—	—
1845	—	—	—	11,695	—	—	—
				Prince Edward Island			
1871	269,392	176,441	—	3,128,576	—	75,109	2,411
1861	346,125	223,195	—	2,218,578	—	50,127	
				Nova Scotia			
1871	227,497	296,050	33,987	2,190,099	19,740	234,157	23,349
1861	312,081	269,578	59,706	1,978,137	21,333	195,340	15,529
1851	297,157	196,097	61,438	1,384,437	21,638[3]	170,301	37,475
1827	152,861	448,627[4]	—	—	—	—	
				New Brunswick			
1871	204,911	70,547	23,792	3,044,134	26,850	1,231,091	27,658
1861	279,775	94,679	57,504	2,656,883	25,449	904,321	17,420
1851	206,635	74,300	—	1,411,164	42,663	689,004	62,225
				Lower Canada			
1871	2,058,076	1,668,208	458,970	15,116,262	2,205,585	1,676,078	603,356
1861	2,654,354[6]	2,281,674[6]	844,192[6]	17,551,296[6]	2,648,777[6]	1,250,025[6]	334,861[6]
1851	3,073,943	495,766	325,422	8,977,400	1,415,136	532,412	401,284
1844	942,829	1,195,447	333,440	7,238,744	1,219,413	374,801	141,000
1831	3,407,756	1,074,866[4]	—	3,202,274	984,758	—	—
1827	2,921,240	363,117	—	2,441,529	823,318	862,649[4]	—
1739[6]	634,605	—	—	162,207	100,596[4]	—	5,931
1736[6]	669,744	—	—	162,681	74,294[4]	—	5,215
1734[6]	737,892	3,462	—	163,988	63,549	—	5,223
1732[6]	468,219	—	—	118,290	114,985[4]	—	11,174
1730[6]	458,722	—	—	105,510	106,053[4]	—	9,463
1727[6]	440,739	—	—	105,189	98,909[4]	—	14,070
1726[6]	411,070	—	—	95,470	88,045[4]	—	11,678
1724[6]	300,024	—	—	75,583	68,555[4]	—	6,815
1723[6]	295,522	—	—	73,111	67,441[4]	—	6,675
1722[6]	341,205	—	—	79,426	86,285[4]	—	11,277
1721[6]	282,700	4,585	—	64,035	57,400	—	7,205
1720[6]	134,439	—	—	62,053	55,331	—	4,159
1719[6]	234,566	—	—	50,416	46,408	—	6,487
1718[6]	249,549	—	—	48,880	38,520[4]	—	4,493
1716[6]	252,304	—	—	41,549	39,074[4]	—	11,910
1713[6]	236,049	—	—	43,540	38,408[4]	—	3,871
1712[6]	292,415	—	—	52,191	45,893[4]	—	5,353
1707[6]	179,855	—	—	30,004	34,850[4]	—	4,618
1706[6]	211,634	—	—	38,158	42,639[4]	—	4,295
1696[6]	160,978	—	—	21,797	23,301[4]	—	10,251
1695[6]	129,154	—	—	13,955	20,710[4]	—	6,490
1692[6]	89,711	—	—	13,810	12,300[4]	—	4,597
1688[6]	100,971	28,554[2]	—	—	—	—	—
1667[6]	130,978[1]	—	—	—	—	—	—
				Upper Canada			
1871	14,233,389	9,461,233	547,609	22,138,958	7,653,545	585,158	3,148,467
1861	24,620,425	2,821,962	973,181	21,220,874	9,601,396	1,248,637	2,256,290
1851	12,682,550	625,452	472,429	11,395,467	3,027,681	679,635	1,688,805
1848	7,558,776	515,727	446,293	7,055,730	1,752,834	432,573	1,137,555
1842	3,221,989	1,031,334	292,969	4,788,167	1,191,550	352,786	691,359

Series L 355–369. *Agricultural production statistics of the colonial period (continuation)*

Year	Hay (tons)	Potatoes (bushels)	Turnips (bushels)	Other roots (bushels)	Butter (pounds)	Cheese (pounds)	Beef (barrels of 20 pounds)	Pork (barrels of 20 pounds)
	362	363	364	365	366	367	368	369
			Newfoundland					
1869	20,458	308,357	17,100	9,847	162,508	—	—	—
1857	16,299	228,571	5,132	1,801	135,568	158	—	—
1845	11,008	341,160	—	—	—	—	—	—
			Prince Edward Island					
1871	66,349	3,375,726	395,358	2,991	981,939	155,524	—	—
1861	31,088	2,972,333	350,784	—	711,487	109,133	—	—
			Nova Scotia					
1871	443,732	5,560,975	468,139	150,839[2]	7,161,867	884,853	—	—
1861	334,287	3,824,814	554,318	87,727	4,532,711	901,296	—	—
1851	287,837	1,986,789	467,127	32,325	3,613,890	652,069	—	—
1827	163,212	3,278,280	—	—	—	—	—	—
			New Brunswick					
1871	344,793	6,562,355	603,721	98,358[2]	5,115,947	154,758	—	—
1861	324,160	4,041,339	634,364	50,590	4,591,477	218,067	—	9,692,169[5]
1851	225,093	2,792,394	539,803	47,880	3,050,939	—	—	—
			Lower Canada					
1871	1,225,640	18,068,323	812,073	597,160[2]	24,289,127	512,435	—	—
1861	689,977	12,770,471[6]	892,434[6]	500,323[2, 6]	15,906,949	686,297	67,054	196,598
1851	755,579	4,429,016	354,250	—	9,670,036	764,304	43,031	172,157
1844	—	9,918,863	—	—	—	—	—	—
1831	—	7,357,416	—	—	—	—	—	—
1827	—	6,796,310	—	—	—	—	—	—
			Upper Canada					
1871	1,804,476	17,138,534	22,455,543	2,706,903[2]	37,623,643	3,432,797	—	—
1861	861,844	15,325,920	18,206,959	2,452,569[2]	26,828,264	2,687,172	67,508	336,744
1851	693,727	4,973,285	3,097,818	—	16,061,532	3,418,346	113,445	317,010
1848	—	4,751,346	—	—	3,380,406	668,357	99,231	—
1842	—	8,080,402	—	—	—	—	—	—

[1] Designated as grains.
[2] Carrots and mangels.
[3] Peas and beans.
[4] Other grains.
[5] Pounds of pork slaughtered
[6] Minots.

Series L370–375. *Livestock on farms in the colonial period*

Year	Horses	Milk cows	Other cattle[1]	Calves and heifers	Pigs	Sheep
	370	**371**	**372**	**373**	**374**	**375**
			Newfoundland			
1869	3,764	6,446	7,275[2]	—	19,081	23,044
1857	3,509	6,924	12,962	—	17,551	10,737
1845	4,171	—	13,309	—	—	—
			Prince Edward Island			
1871	25,329	—	62,984[2]	—	52,514	147,364
1861	18,765	—	60,012[2]	—	38,553	107,245
			Nova Scotia			
1871	49,579	122,688	151,279	—	54,162	398,377
1861	41,927	110,504	151,793[2]	—	53,217	332,653
1851	28,789	86,856	156,857[2]	—	51,533	282,180
1827	12,951	—	110,818	—	71,482	173,731
			New Brunswick			
1871	44,786	83,220	80,467	—	65,805	234,418
1861	35,347	69,437	92,025[2]	—	73,995	214,092
1851	22,044	50,955	106,263	—	47,932	168,038
1840	18,282	—	90,260	—	71,915	141,053
			Lower Canada			
1871	253,377	406,542	376,920	—	371,452	1,007,800
1861	248,515	328,370	200,992	287,611	286,400	682,229
1851	148,620	295,552	112,028	183,972	256,794	648,665
1844	146,726		469,851	—	197,935	602,821
1831	116,686		388,706	—	295,137	543,343
1827	142,432	260,015	145,012	—	241,735	829,122
1784	30,146	44,291	22,094	32,206	70,465	84,696
1765	13,488	22,748	12,533	14,732	28,562	28,022
1734	5,056		33,179	—	23,646	19,815
1721	5,603		23,388	—	16,250	13,823
1720	5,270		24,866	—	17,944	12,175
1719	4,024		18,241	—	14,418	8,435
1706	1,872		14,191	—	—	1,820
1698	684		10,209	—	5,147	994
1695	580		9,181	—	5,333	918
1692	400		7,456	—	3,045	903
1688	218		7,719	—	3,701	1,061
1685	156		7,474	—	—	787
1681	94		6,948	—	—	572
1679	145		6,983	—	—	719
1667	—		3,107	—	—	85
			Upper Canada			
1871	489,001	638,759	764,415	—	874,664	1,514,914
1861	377,681	451,640	99,605	464,083	776,001	1,170,225
1851	201,670	296,875	192,140	225,249	571,496	967,168
1848	151,389		565,845	—	484,241	833,807
1842	113,647		504,963	—	394,366	575,730
1841	75,316	157,411	106,696	—	—	—
1840	72,696	148,483	98,555	—	—	—
1839	66,220	136,171	95,098	—	—	—
1838	63,396	129,711	98,352	—	—	—
1837	57,250	120,110	97,563	—	—	—
1836	55,064	121,024	93,644	—	—	—
1835	48,118	110,051	85,451	—	—	—
1834	43,217	99,823	79,250	—	—	—
1833	40,254	95,042	77,630	—	—	—
1832	36,822	92,274	74,226	—	—	—
1831	33,428	84,373	71,293	—	—	—
1830	30,776	80,892	66,054	—	—	—
1829	28,388	75,071	68,097	—	—	—
1828	25,701	67,188	67,118	—	—	—
1827	25,228	66,878	56,752	—	—	—
1826	23,866	62,198	49,971	—	—	—
			Assiniboia			
1856	2,681	3,679	5,936	—	1,929	2,245

[1] Includes oxen. For number of oxen see the note to series L370–375.   [2] Neat cattle.

SECTION M: FISHERIES

H. SCOTT GORDON, *Carleton University*

The statistics of Canada's production and trade in fish are presented in four parts: primary operations in the fisheries (series M1–68), processing (series M69–102), value of exports and imports (series M103–133), and miscellaneous fisheries statistics (series M134–146).

The great bulk of the data of this section is derived from two sources: Dominion Bureau of Statistics, *Fisheries Statistics of Canada* for the period 1917 to 1960; Department of Marine and Fisheries, *Annual Report, Fisheries* for the period from Confederation to 1917. The following is a complete list of published sources used. The source publications of the Dominion Bureau of Statistics are: Dominion Bureau of Statistics, *Fisheries Statistics of Canada*, annual since 1917 (Ottawa, Queen's Printer) in 1960 presented in eleven publications, a *Canada Summary* and a report for each province; *Ninth Census of Canada, 1951*, vol. IX, *Fisheries* (Ottawa, Queen's Printer, 1953); *Wholesale Price Indexes, 1913–1950*, Reference Paper No. 24 (Ottawa, King's Printer, 1951); *Prices and Price Indexes* (Ottawa, Queen's Printer) reports of 1950 to 1960. Other federal department publications used for this section include: Department of Marine and Fisheries, *Annual Report, Fisheries*, annual 1868 to 1917 (Ottawa, King's Printer) sometimes called *Fisheries Report*, various issues; Department of Trade and Commerce, *Trade of Canada*, annual (Ottawa, King's Printer) issues 1911 to 1929; Department of Trade and Commerce, *Canada Year Book*, annual (Ottawa, King's Printer) issues 1905 to 1910; Department of Customs, *Trade and Navigation*, annual (Ottawa, Queen's Printer) issues 1867 to 1914; Department of Customs, *Report*, annual (Ottawa, King's Printer) issues 1911 to 1913; *Public Accounts of Canada, Part II*, annual (Ottawa, Queen's Printer) reports 1943 to 1960; *Report of the Auditor General to the House of Commons*, annual (Ottawa, King's Printer) reports 1932 to 1942. Other sources for data in this section are: Oscar E. Sette, U.S. Department of Commerce, Bureau of Fisheries, *Statistics of the Catch of Cod off the East Coast of North America to 1926*, appendix IX to the Report of the U.S. Commission of Fisheries for 1927 (Washington, U.S. Government Printing Office, 1928); A. W. H. Needler, U.S. Department of Commerce, *Statistics of the Haddock Fishery in North American Waters* (Washington, U.S. Government Printing Office, 1930); F. H. Bell, H. A. Dunlop, N. L. Freeman, *Pacific Coast Halibut Landings 1888 to 1950 and Catch According to Area of Origin* (Seattle, Washington, International Fisheries Commission, 1952); Newfoundland, Department of Natural Resources, *Report of the Newfoundland Fisheries Board and General Review of the Fisheries with Statistical Survey*, annual from 1941 to 1948, two earlier reports for the years 1937 to 1940 (St. John's, various printers); Newfoundland, *Annual Report of the Department of Marine and Fisheries*, annual 1928 to 1930 (St. John's, Newfoundland, 1929 to 1931).

In addition to the statistics obtained from the above published sources, data were also obtained directly from the Economics Service, Department of Fisheries, Ottawa and the International Fisheries Commission, Seattle, Washington.

The series included here contain the most generally useful data now being compiled. However, a great deal more information is currently available. Much of it may be found in the D.B.S. comprehensive annual volumes *Fisheries Statistics of Canada*. In addition the reader is referred to the following: (*a*) the Federal Department of Fisheries basebooks on fisheries statistics: No. 1, *Landings in the Inshore Fishery of the Maritime Provinces, 1919–1950* (Ottawa, mimeographed, 1953); No. 2, *The Canadian Commercial Fisheries of the Great Lakes* (Ottawa, mimeographed, 1955); No. 3, *The Commercial Salmon Fisheries of British Columbia* (Ottawa, mimeographed, 1958); (*b*) The Department of Fisheries, *British Columbia Catch Statistics*, monthly and annual (Ottawa, Queen's Printer); (*c*) *Canadian Fisheries Statistics* published as a supplement to the *Canadian Fisheries Annual* (Gardenvale, Quebec); and (*d*) Dominion Bureau of Statistics, *Monthly Review of Canadian Fisheries Statistics*, monthly (Ottawa, Queen's Printer).

Reference should also be made to the monograph published by the Royal Commission on Canada's Economic Prospects, *The Commercial Fisheries of Canada* (Ottawa, Queen's Printer, 1957).

Various statistics on fish landings, production, numbers of fishermen, etc., are to be found in the numerous provincial and federal Royal Commission reports that have been made since Confederation and in other official documents. However, examination of these statistics reveals that they are almost invariably derived from the Department's *Annual Report* in the early years.

General note

Under the power given to it by the British North America Act the federal government has full legislative jurisdiction over both the coastal and inland fisheries of Canada. Consequently all the regulations governing fishing are made by the federal government. Some of these regulations concerning the inland fisheries are made on the recommendation of the provinces. Initially full administrative control also lay with the federal government. As a result of various court awards and agreements with the provinces through the years, administration of the fisheries has become divided between the federal and provincial governments. The result is that the federal government administers all tidal and sea fisheries except those of Quebec, the inland fisheries of the Atlantic Provinces, excepting possibly ponds and lakes in Newfoundland, and the fisheries of the Yukon and Northwest Territories. Quebec administers all its fisheries including those in salt waters. Ontario, the Prairie Provinces and British Columbia administer their freshwater species though the last does not collect any statistics.

The processing industries are under the legislative and administrative control of the provinces, though inspection for sanitary purposes and for export are under federal control. In the case of the inland fisheries the inspection is largely limited to whitefish for exportation.

Until the fiscal year ending 31 March 1917, the statistics of the fisheries were assembled by the Fisheries Branch of the Department of Marine and Fisheries (established shortly after Confederation) through its widespread organization of fisheries officers. Starting with 1917 the data have been assembled at the Dominion Bureau of Statistics though the fisheries officers of the Department of Fisheries (established as a self-contained department in 1930) continue to play an important part in gathering the data (see below).

The quality of the data contained in the *Annual Report* for the period before 1917 is not high. Methods of reporting differed from area to area, the quality of the personnel engaged in statistical collection left much to be desired, and apparently the supervisory procedures were not sufficiently well developed to permit the early discovery and correction of errors in reporting and in methods of collection. On examination, the *Annual Reports* leave many questions unanswered concerning the bases on which the various compilations were made. The user of these series will find it useful to refer to the comments made by Ruth Fulton Grant in *Canadian Atlantic Fishery* (Toronto, Ryerson Press, 1934), appendix A. The quality of the statistics is undoubtedly much higher for the period since 1917.

PRIMARY OPERATIONS (Series M1–68)

General note

Primary operations include the catching and landing of all products of the coastal and inland waters.

In most of the fisheries under federal administration, including all fisheries of the Maritime Provinces, the commercial waters of British Columbia and in the Yukon and Northwest Territories, the primary data on landings are obtained from purchase slips made out by the buyer at the time of landing and first sale, a procedure begun in the nineteen-fifties. These slips are sent to offices of the Department of Fisheries where they are tabulated and the tabulations forwarded to the Dominion Bureau of Statistics for assembling. They include data on the species sold, quantity, prices, location of purchase and sometimes the size of fish and type of gear used.

Supplementary purchase slips are prepared by fisheries officers, representing estimates of landed weight equivalents of fish processed by fishermen, direct sales to local users, bait used and fish consumed by fishermen's families.

In Newfoundland, marketing facilities and practices are such that the foregoing procedures cannot be used. For instance, especially in the more remote parts, a considerable amount of processing on shore may be done by the fishermen themselves. In these parts the data are assembled by fisheries officers visiting these parts and obtaining the information from local contacts who can provide estimates of landings and of what is in storage. These contacts are often retired fishermen who frequent the waterfront. Other data come from reports of buyers. Checks on the catch landed are made from data on the amount of salt sold by local storekeepers, from data on fish marketings obtained from local storekeepers and from the quantities inspected as the product goes through warehouses for export.

In the remaining areas of Canada the data are collected through provincial administrative officers, tabulated in provincial offices and assembled in the Dominion Bureau of Statistics. In Quebec the province collects data from buyers who report weekly purchases, or, in the remote areas, by the procedure used in the remote areas of Newfoundland. In Ontario data are collected from fishermen who are required to report as a condition of obtaining licenses. In Manitoba the data are based on reports from fish buyers. In Alberta and Saskatchewan data come from fish buyers and fishermen.

Before the recent procedures were introduced, in the nineteen-fifties, heavy reliance was placed on working back from data on processed fish and fish products, with the use of conversion factors to estimate the landings in primary form from the processed form data. Information on the processed forms was obtained from fish processing and handling plants and from fisheries inspectors for exported fish. Procedures like those described above for recent practice in the more remote parts of Newfoundland were also used. (See also the general note to series M69–102.)

Prior to 1917 the data were obtained by officers of the Fisheries Branch of the Department of Marine and Fisheries probably in much the same way they are now collected in the remoter parts of Newfoundland and also by using information on processed fish products as was the custom later. A revision of procedures in the fiscal year 1910–11 improved the quality of the data collected by the Department. Prior to that year the reports covered marketings and included values of forms after processing on land. The Department's *Annual Reports* suggest these might also have some duplication owing to the nature of the reporting forms provided to the officers. For instance it was suspected herring used as bait was reported separately as bait but also added in with other totals. Beginning with 1910–11 the officers were provided with two forms of improved design, one for recording data on landings and the other to give marketing of primary or processed products (excluding sales of primary products to processors) as they moved into channels of trade.

Fish are landed in primary forms varying from 'fresh round', that is as taken from the water, to split and salted or even further processed form. The value of landings is the actual value received on landing whatever the form.

The basis of measuring weight on landing is given in D.B.S., *Fisheries Statistics of Canada, Canadian Summary, 1960*, p. 4 as follows for the Atlantic Provinces:

Fish and shellfish in the Atlantic Coast Provinces are reported as follows: cod, haddock, pollock, hake, cusk, catfish and skate as 'gutted head on', halibut, swordfish and tuna as 'gutted head off' except in Newfoundland which reports halibut as 'gutted head on'. All other sea fish and freshwater fish are shown as 'round' [that is, as taken from the water]. Molluscs and crustaceans are reported as 'in shell' except scallops which are 'shucked' and squid which are in the 'round'.

Some species of fish are landed in various forms and are converted to the forms mentioned above by multiplying the landed weight by the following conversion factors....

The conversion factors for the Atlantic fisheries are given in this reference.

The same source reports that: in British Columbia and Manitoba the species as landed are not converted to a common form and are the sum of fish in the round, gutted head on and gutted head off; in Ontario landings are reported in the round form except that it is possible the figures include some dressed fish in the 'Northern Inland Waters'; in Saskatchewan landings are reported as gutted head on; in Alberta landings are reported as round weight with a factor of 12 to 16 per cent being used to convert dressed fish landed to round form; in the Northwest Territories fish are measured in the round, those landings made in dressed form being converted to the round by a suitable conversion factor.

In *Fisheries Statistics of Canada, 1930* it is stated that fresh fish (i.e. weight landed) is gutted head on for cod, haddock, hake and cusk and pollock, that it is gutted head and tail off for albacore and that in all other cases it means fish as it comes from the water, that is, in the round. It is probable the reporting was on a reasonably uniform basis from year to year, at least for major species, in the east, but the west coast measures may contain considerable variation in the mixture of different forms on landing.

M1-11. Value of fish landed, by province, 1911 to 1960

SOURCE: for 1917 to 1960, D.B.S., *Fisheries Statistics of Canada*; for 1910 to 1917, Department of Marine and Fisheries (hereafter D.M.F.), *Annual Report, Fisheries*.

Figures for Newfoundland in *Fisheries Statistics of Canada* begin in 1952. Prior to 1919 no landed values were reported in Ontario, Manitoba, Saskatchewan, Alberta and the Yukon. Value of fish landed is value at the vessel's or boat's side on landing, based on sale to the first buyer. The values given cover fish of all kinds, molluscs and crustaceans, livers, tongues and scales, seaweed, seal pelts, bait worms and other aquatic life from both sea and inland fisheries.

For values landed by main species see series M25–37. See also the general note to series M1–68.

M12–24. Quantities of fish landed, by region and by major species, 1869 to 1960

SOURCE: for 1917 to 1960, D.B.S., *Fisheries Statistics of Canada*; 1910 to 1917, D.M.F., *Annual Report, Fisheries*, except as noted below.

M12. Cod, for 1869 to 1917, is from Sette, *Statistics of the Catch of Cod off the East Coast of North America, to 1926*, table 7, p. 3. Sette's primary data prior to 1917 were drawn from the Department *Annual Report*. For 1910 to 1916 (fiscal years 1911 to 1917) Sette took the catch landed as reported. For years prior to 1910 he converted marketings, which were given in Departmental reports and were solely for dried cod before 1903, to a landed basis, using conversion factors which are given in the document cited. These conversion factors were designed to give estimates on a fresh round basis. In an appended note to the document he states that he had mistakenly assumed landings were reported (presumably from 1910 onward) on a round basis but that they were in fact on a fresh gutted basis.

M13. Haddock, 1880 to 1910, is from Needler, *Statistics of the Haddock Fishery in North American Waters*, table 2, pp. 30–1. Statistics contained in Needler are calculated from the weights of products marketed as reported in the Department *Annual Report* with the use of conversion factors to yield weight on a fresh gutted basis as given here. These factors are given in the document referred to. Needler also makes the following comment (p. 31):

Doubt is cast on the accuracy of catches before 1888, when 'hake and haddock' are given together in the detailed statistics, when the total for haddock is perhaps only an estimate, and when certain discrepancies occur in the compilation of the provincial totals to make the Canadian totals. The extreme catch in 1897 is due entirely to one county, Digby, which showed an increase of 400 per cent in the catch with no increase in the fishing equipment. This record is considered doubtful in the 1897 report itself, and we place no reliance on it here.

By using a figure for the Digby catch of the average in the two adjacent years Needler arrives at an estimate for the total catch of 52,400 thousand pounds for 1897. There is a period of nine years from 1910–11 to 1918 during which haddock-landing statistics are available from the Department *Annual Reports*. The statistics available from this source differ from Needler's by varying amounts. Needler's figures are invariably larger than those contained in the *Reports*, in most years the difference being of the order of 5 to 7 million pounds. But in two years, 1910–11 and 1918, the difference approached 15 million pounds.

East coast cod and herring totals presented in M12 and M16 are aggregates of the provincial data recorded in the official statistics.

M18. Scallop figures were reported in the official statistics in barrels for the period 1915–16 to 1934. These have been con-

verted to pounds using the conversion factor 1 barrel = 20 pounds shucked. Scallop figures were reported in the official statistics in gallons for the period 1934 to 1950. These have been converted to pounds using the conversion factor 1 gallon = 10 pounds shucked.

M24. The west coast halibut statistics contained here are drawn exclusively from the records of the Dominion Bureau of Statistics and the Department *Annual Reports*. Prior to 1934 the total landings for British Columbia halibut include landings by United States vessels at British Columbia ports.

The International Fisheries Commission constructed a revised series of Pacific halibut landings dating from 1888 in which they attempted, in so far as possible, to make corrections for duplications and errors in the official statistics. The International Fisheries Commission Statistics of landings differ markedly from those recorded here for the period 1918 to 1933. The full series of Canadian Pacific halibut landings compiled by the International Fisheries Commission is reprinted in this volume as series M145. The reader is referred to the note on M145 and to Bell, Dunlop and Freeman, *Pacific Coast Halibut Landings 1888 to 1950 and Catch According to Area of Origin* for a full description of the Commission's procedures in construction of their series.

M25–37. Value of fish landed, by region and by major species, 1911 to 1960

SOURCE: for 1917 to 1960, D.B.S., *Fisheries Statistics of Canada*; for 1911 to 1917, D.M.F., *Annual Report, Fisheries*.

See the general note to series M1–68.

M38–48. Number of persons engaged in primary fishing operations, by province, 1878 to 1960

SOURCE: for 1917 to 1960, D.B.S., *Fisheries Statistics of Canada*; for 1878 to 1917, D.M.F., *Annual Report, Fisheries*.

The basis on which the number of fishermen is calculated differs from province to province.

M39. In Newfoundland the count represents the number of persons who were employed in the fishery for two weeks or more during the year.

M40–43. In Nova Scotia, New Brunswick, Prince Edward Island and Quebec the data are based on one count for the year without reference to the amount of time the person was engaged in the fishery.

M44. In Ontario the count is based on the number of commercial fishing licences issued but adjustment is made to correct for the issuance of more than one licence to a person and for the fact that certain licensees may fail to engage in fishing.

M45–47. In Manitoba, Saskatchewan, Alberta and the Northwest Territories the data given are the total of all commercial licences issued with no adjustment for duplication or failure of licensees to engage in the fishery. In view of the fact that different licences are necessary for different lakes and different seasons of the year, the data given here for these provinces undoubtedly contain a substantial amount of duplication and must be regarded as a considerable overestimate of the number of persons engaged in the fishery.

M48. In British Columbia the count is based chiefly on the number of commercial licences issued with corrections for duplication. Estimates are made of the number of fishermen working as crews on fish packers and carrying smacks and these are included in the data given here. The data do not include men employed to operate salmon traps.

Estimates of the numbers of fishermen are also available in certain other official documents: (1) *Ninth Census of Canada, 1951*, vol. IV, *Labour Force*, table 3. The data contained there record as fishermen all those for whom fishing was their main occupation for the week preceding the census. (2) *Ninth Census of Canada, 1951*, vol. IX, *Fisheries*, table 1. The data contained there record as fishermen all those who spent fifteen days or more fishing or earned $100.00 or more from fishing during 1951. (3) D.B.S., *The Labour Force*, monthly, various issues. The data contained there record as fishermen those for whom fishing was the main occupation during the week preceding the survey.

M 49-59. Aggregate value of capital equipment employed in primary fishing operations, by province, 1878 to 1960

SOURCE: prepared by the Economics Service, Department of Fisheries from: for 1917 to 1960, D.B.S., *Fisheries Statistics of Canada*; for 1878 to 1916-17, D.M.F., *Annual Report, Fisheries*.

The total value of capital equipment covered in this table consists of the value of boats, vessels (including fishing smacks) and the value of fishing gear such as nets of all kinds, lines, lobster traps and the like used in the primary industry. The values of wharves, fish houses and ice houses are not included. The valuation basis employed differs from province to province and in a number of cases the valuation concept employed is far from clear. In the Maritime Provinces, Newfoundland, British Columbia and the Northwest Territories the data represent the market value of capital equipment as estimated by fisheries officers. In Saskatchewan and Alberta the data represent fisheries officers' estimates but it is not clear whether these are estimates of market value or some other valuation concept. In Ontario the data are derived from the fishermen's own valuation of their capital equipment. The basis on which this valuation should be made is not specified in the forms sent to the fishermen. In Quebec, since 1952, the value reported for draggers and long-liners is the depreciated book value; prior to 1952 it was an estimated market value: other fishing craft have been valued at estimated market value throughout: the value of fishing gear represents replacement value throughout. In Manitoba fishing gear is valued at the depreciated book value: the value of fishing craft is based on fishery officers' estimates of the average value of craft used in their district, but it is unclear whether market value, depreciated value, replacement value, or some other concept is the basis for the estimation.

M 60-68. Capital equipment employed in primary fishing operations, by province and by type of equipment, 1951

SOURCE: D.B.S., *Ninth Census of Canada, 1951*, vol. IX, *Fisheries*.

The figures given here are estimated from a sample taken by regular census procedures. The Canada total is not equal to the aggregate of the provincial totals as some small values in the provincial statistics could not be published in the source. The data given in this table do not correspond exactly with those given in series M 49-59 due to different methods of compilation.

A breakdown of the value of capital equipment into the categories shown is also given in D.B.S., *Fisheries Statistics of Canada* and D.M.F., *Annual Report, Fisheries*.

FISH PROCESSING (Series M 69-102)

General note

Data on fish processing plants were obtained, like those of other sections of the Census of Industry, by questionnaire sent to the processing establishments. The fisheries officers of the Department of Fisheries assist in obtaining accurate returns expeditiously.

Prior to the collection of the data by the Dominion Bureau of

Statistics, more limited data were collected by the fisheries officers of the Fisheries Branch, Department of Marine and Fisheries. These data were limited to the value of products marketed, the numbers employed in processing and handling plants and capital invested in processing and handling plants. They were obtained by the fisheries officers going to the plants and obtaining the information directly.

Particularly in the earlier years a considerable amount of processing was done by the fishermen themselves after landing. Data on the value of products thus prepared were estimated by fisheries officers from information obtained in much the same way as those on landings in the remote areas of Newfoundland even in 1960 (see the general note to series M 1-68). A major part of the information is obtained from local merchants and in the warehouses where fish for export are inspected. By 1960 this type of small local processing was confined largely to Newfoundland.

No information is collected on processing in Ontario and the Prairie Provinces.

The data for series M 69-102 cover fish processors, whose main business is cutting, freezing, drying, salting, smoking, pickling, canning, etc., and fish packers and handlers, whose main business is handling, who buy and sell fresh fish only, or who buy processed fish or fish products and sell without further processing.

M 69-78. Market value of fisheries products, by major process forms, Canada, 1870 to 1960

SOURCE: prepared by the Economics Service, Department of Fisheries from: for 1917 to 1960, D.B.S., *Fisheries Statistics of Canada*; for 1870 to 1917, D.M.F., *Annual Report, Fisheries*.

The values given in the table represent the sales value f.o.b. the processing plant, except for items sold directly to the consumer by fishermen or exported directly by fishermen, in which cases the values given represent the amounts received by fishermen.

The process categories listed in the table include the following specific product forms contained in the original statistics.

M 70. Fresh whole includes fresh round or dressed fish, molluscs and crustaceans in the shell, and fresh roe, livers and caviar. Frozen whole (series M 72), not given as a separate category prior to 1945, is included with series M 70 prior to that year. Prior to the fiscal year ending 31 March 1910 the sources of information did not always list in detail the marketed form of the minor species. It is assumed that this fish was sold in the fresh state and therefore has been included under the category fresh whole.

M 71. Fresh filleted includes fresh fillets, lobster meat, shelled scallops, shucked meats. Frozen filleted (series M 73), not given as a separate category prior to 1945, is included with series M 71 prior to that year.

M 72. Frozen whole includes the same items as series M 70. The values, however, of molluscs and crustaceans marketed in frozen form are small. This item is included in series M 70 prior to 1945.

M 73. Frozen filleted includes frozen fillets, frozen blocks and sticks, fresh and frozen steaks and frozen shucked molluscs or crustaceans. This item is included in series M 71 prior to 1945.

M 74. Canned includes all species canned and also canned and salted.

M 75. Smoked includes smoked round or dressed and smoked fillets.

M 76. Salted and pickled include salted, dried, boneless, mild cured, green salted, pickled, vinegar cured, dry salted and salted and smoked.

M77. Oil includes all types of marine oils used for vitamin and industrial purposes.

M78. Meal includes fish meal, whale meal, liver meal, offal meal.

M79–84. Fish processing plant inputs, 1917 to 1960

SOURCE: D.B.S., *Fisheries Statistics of Canada.*

M79 and 82. Wages and salaries includes payments made for contract or piece work.

M80 and 83. Materials used includes fish, which is by far the largest item, salt, containers, process supplies and other materials.

M81 and 84. Fuel and electricity includes coal, fuel oil, other petroleum products, wood, etc., as well as electricity.

M85–88. Number of persons employed in fish processing plants, by area and by sex, 1895 to 1960

SOURCE: prepared by the Economics Service, Department of Fisheries from: for 1917 to 1960, D.B.S., *Fisheries Statistics of Canada*; for 1895 to 1917, D.M.F., *Annual Report, Fisheries.*

The number of persons employed in processing plants is calculated on the following basis: (1) salaried employees are counted once for the year in question; (2) the number of wage employees is calculated on the basis of the average number of workers employed. This average is calculated from counts of employees made monthly. Until 1953 this average was based on the number of months the plant in question actually operated. Since 1953 the average has been calculated on the basis of twelve months whether the plant operated for the whole of that period or not. The present method of calculation is therefore closer to a concept of person-years-worked than to a count of number of persons employed. The present method of calculation would clearly be a considerable underestimate of the number of persons who were employed in fish processing plants for some period during the year.

Prior to 1917 the figures are total number of persons employed, the breakdown by sex not being available before that date.

M89–102. Number of fish processing establishments, by area and by value of output, 1919 to 1960

SOURCE: for 1939 to 1958 the statistics were directly provided by the Dominion Bureau of Statistics; for 1959 and 1960 and for 1919 to 1938, D.B.S., *Fisheries Statistics of Canada.*

VALUE OF EXPORTS AND IMPORTS
(Series M103–133)

M103–109. Value of exports of fish and fish products, by region, 1867 to 1960

SOURCE: prepared by the Economics Service, Department of Fisheries from: for 1930 to 1960, D.B.S., *Fisheries Statistics of Canada*; for 1914 to 1929, Department of Trade and Commerce, *Trade of Canada*; for 1911 to 1913, Department of Customs, *Report*; for 1867 to 1912, Department of Customs, *Trade and Navigation.*

M105. Other Europe include Austria, Azores and Madeira, Belgium and Luxemburg, Denmark, France, Germany, Greece, Greenland, Ireland, Italy, Netherlands, Norway, Portugal, Spain, Sweden, Switzerland, Rumania, Poland, U.S.S.R., Yugoslavia, Hungary, Albania, Bulgaria, Malta.

M106. Continental South America include Argentina, British Guiana, Bolivia, Brazil, Chile, Colombia, Ecuador, Peru, Surinam, Uruguay and Venezuela.

M107. Central America and Caribbean include Bahamas, Barbados, Bermuda, British Honduras, Costa Rica, Cuba, Danish West Indies, Dominican Republic, El Salvador, French West Indies, Guatemala, Haiti, Honduras, Jamaica, Leeward and Windward Islands, Mexico, Netherland Antilles, Nicaragua, Panama, and Tobago and Trinidad.

M108. United States and possessions include Alaska, Hawaii, Puerto Rico and United States.

M110–120. Value of exports of fish and fish products, by major species, 1871 to 1960

SOURCE: prepared by the Economics Service, Department of Fisheries from: for 1917 to 1960, D.B.S., *Fisheries Statistics of Canada*; for 1911 to 1917, Department of Trade and Commerce, *Trade of Canada*; for 1905 to 1910, Department of Trade and Commerce, *Canada Year Book*; for 1867 to 1904, Department of Customs, *Trade and Navigation.*

The species classification includes all products derived from the species in question except reduction products which are included under M119.

M110. Groundfish includes the following sea fish: cod, catfish, cusk, flounders and soles, haddock, hake, pollock, redfish, turbot and small amounts of related species of seafish. The distinction between groundfish and pelagic fish is that the former species are found on the bottom while the latter are found nearer the surface of the water. Halibut, which are groundfish, are shown separately in series M111.

M118. All other shellfish include clams, oysters, scallops, squid, crabs and shrimps and prawns.

M119. Oil and meal include these products from all species.

M120. All other includes a large variety of seafish and inland fish, not already covered, and sealskins.

M121–133. Value of imports of fish and fish products, by major species, 1873 to 1960

SOURCE: prepared by the Economics Service, Department of Fisheries from: for 1918 to 1960, D.B.S., *Fisheries Statistics of Canada*; for 1914 to 1917, Department of Trade and Commerce, *Trade of Canada*; for 1873 to 1914, Department of Customs, *Trade and Navigation.*

The species classification includes all products derived from the species in question except reduction products which are included under series M132.

M122. Groundfish include cod, haddock, pollock and ling.

M131. All other shellfish include shrimps and prawns, squid.

M132. Oil and meal include all meal and oil products from all species including whale oil.

M133. All other includes all other species of seafish or inland fish, fur skins of marine animals, fish livers, sponges and turtles.

MISCELLANEOUS FISHERIES STATISTICS
(Series M134–146)

M134–138. Index of prices received by fishermen and index of wholesale prices of fish products, 1913 to 1960

SOURCE: data for series M134–137 supplied by Economics Service, Department of Fisheries; series M138 is from D.B.S., *Wholesale Price Indexes, 1913–1950*, from annual issues from 1950 to 1960 of D.B.S., *Prices and Price Indexes*, and from D.B.S., *Fisheries Statistics of Canada*, 1918 to 1960.

M139–144. Expenditures of the federal Department of Fisheries, 1932 to 1960

SOURCE: prepared by the Economics Service, Department of Fisheries from: for 1943 to 1960, *Public Accounts, Part II*; for 1932 to 1942, Auditor General's *Reports.*

The data shown in this table record the expenditures for the fiscal year in which they were actually made. The data published in *Public Accounts* record the amounts for the recouping of the working fund of the Prices Support Board and of the indemnity funds as of the year in which that fund was replenished by a general vote. Consequently, the totals recorded in this table do not correspond in all cases with those published in the *Public Accounts*.

This table records only the expenditures under the jurisdiction of the federal Department of Fisheries. Expenditures by other federal departments and agencies (for example, expenditures by the Department of Public Works on the construction and maintenance of wharves and harbours) are not included.

Data on expenditures of the federal Department of Fisheries are available for years prior to 1932 in the Auditor General's *Reports*.

M140. Administration includes all departmental administration expenditure that might be found in any government department.

M141. Resource development includes expenditure for Fisheries Research Board, Protection Branch, Fish Culture Branch, the Development of the Deep Sea Fisheries and the Destruction of all Predators.

M142. Price support and deficiency payments include the Fishing Bounty, first instituted to encourage fishing in 1882, and payments made under the Fisheries Prices Support Board.

M143. Other subsidies include payments made to assist the fishery through the Fishermen's Indemnity Plan and for the construction of vessels and bait facilities.

M144. Other expenditures include expenditures for international commissions, Inspection Branch, Consumer Branch, contributions to fishery exhibitions, wartime damage compensation, etc.

M145. Pacific halibut landings, according to the International Fisheries Commission, Canada, 1890 to 1958

SOURCE: data for 1951 to 1958 were obtained directly from the International Fisheries Commission; for 1890 to 1950, Bell, Dunlop and Freeman, *Pacific Coast Halibut Landings 1888 to 1950 and Catch According to Area of Origin*, table 1, pp. 10 and 11.

The source states that 'all figures are for salable halibut with

heads off and viscera removed. Inquiry of older members of the industry indicated that in general such net weights have been used in this fishery since early times...' (p. 19).

For 1929 to 1958 the data were collected directly by the International Fisheries Commission. For years prior to 1929 the estimates are based upon data for British Columbia obtained from Department of Marine and Fisheries annual reports and publications of the Dominion Bureau of Statistics, amended by information obtained from records of fish exchanges, by material from the *Pacific Fisherman*, a trade journal published in Seattle, and by logs and other records obtained from shipowners and captains.

The figures are landings by Canadian registered vessels. Apparently landings by United States vessels in British Columbia were shipped in bond to the United States. There was little landing by Canadian vessels in United States ports.

Although it is stated that the data are for calendar years it appears that for 1907 to 1917 they are for the fiscal year ending 31 March of the following year.

It appears that there may have been an error in recording the figure for 1907 in the source and that the figure given and reproduced here is for the total of Canadian and United States landings in British Columbia. In the detail in the source the figure for landings by Canadian vessels in British Columbia is 5,093 thousand pounds; the figure of 12,915 thousand pounds is the total of landings by both Canadian and United States vessels in British Columbia.

M146. Exports of dried cod, Newfoundland, 1806 to 1948

SOURCE: for 1930 to 1948, *Report of the Newfoundland Fisheries Board*; for 1927 to 1929, *Newfoundland Fisheries Reports*; for 1806 to 1926, Sette, *Statistics of the Catch of Cod off the East Coast of North America to 1926*, table 2, pp. 738 and 739. Sette gave the source of his data as: for 1804 to 1904, William MacGregor, *Report on the Trade and Commerce of Newfoundland for the Four Years ending June 30, 1906*; for 1905 to 1924, annual reports of the Department of Marine and Fisheries in Newfoundland; for 1925 and 1926 the United States Consul, St. John's, Newfoundland.

The information appearing in this table was reported in quintals in the source. It has been converted to thousand pounds using the conversion factor 1 quintal = 112 pounds.

Series M1-11. *Value of fish landed, by province, 1911 to 1960*

(thousands of dollars)

Year[1]	Canada[2]	Newfound-land	Nova Scotia	Prince Edward Island	New Brunswick	Quebec	Ontario	Manitoba	Saskat-chewan	Alberta	British Columbia
	1	2	3	4	5	6	7	8	9	10	11
1960	100,490.7	15,856.1	26,094.4	4,639.6	9,357.6	4,504.0	4,983.0	3,866.7	1,367.2	1,158.6	27,961.6
1959	105,533.8	14,529.1	27,111.5	4,286.5	8,763.3	4,316.2	4,866.4	3,756.8	1,190.3	1,015.7	34,995.3
1958	116,529.5	11,311.9	24,954.5	3,754.4	7,498.6	4,194.7	7,271.2	3,540.4	1,090.6	878.7	51,352.5
1957	94,247.1	13,671.6	23,083.8	3,549.8	7,013.8	4,067.9	7,046.6	3,279.4	938.9	853.9	30,021.2
1956	105,956.6	15,089.5	25,038.4	3,948.7	8,146.3	4,440.3	7,927.3	2,947.0	783.9	790.2	36,057.6
1955	91,390.4	14,160.8	23,582.0	3,279.1	6,753.3	3,452.6	6,782.9	3,476.6	763.0	687.5	27,710.6
1954	97,542.0	14,704.4	23,046.0	2,948.4	7,310.5	2,930.9	7,012.6	3,087.9	740.7	666.8	34,457.6
1953	89,832.3	12,014.6	21,928.4	2,869.9	6,910.4	3,394.7	7,027.1	2,716.5	553.2	666.7	31,280.5
1952	92,746.4[2]	12,927.7	22,679.3	2,660.2	7,825.0	3,572.2	7,406.6	3,438.8	679.4	653.9	30,157.9
1951	88,527.0	—	21,398.0	2,239.7	7,588.3	3,375.4	7,035.3	4,263.2	909.5	544.1	40,637.
1950	82,187.0	—	21,399.5	2,556.0	6,791.6	3,200.3	6,252.0	3,879.8	718.1	436.8	36,345.2
1949	67,452.9	—	18,690.9	2,055.2	6,437.2	3,294.9	5,496.8	2,820.5	520.8	341.9	27,250.7
1948	75,374.5	—	19,070.9	2,201.1	7,884.8	3,434.9	5,683.2	3,181.3	512.6	375.0	32,643.6
1947	57,515.5	—	15,155.6	1,880.1	5,995.6	2,767.3	4,803.3	3,476.6	483.6	449.1	22,354.4
1946	67,161.5	—	20,559.6	3,085.5	7,145.4	4,475.3	5,597.0	3,303.7	729.2	600.3	21,372.0
1945	64,838.7	—	19,223.4	2,309.1	5,477.5	4,987.9	6,483.7	3,418.2	881.6	741.9	21,200.6
1944	52,078.4	—	14,850.8	1,797.2	5,403.6	3,973.9	4,389.3	2,830.1	1,032.1	464.8	17,333.5
1943	48,712.8	—	12,827.8	1,869.3	5,192.5	3,879.2	4,703.7	3,427.6	773.2	393.2	15,643.9
1942	41,734.7	—	8,874.8	1,148.4	3,649.3	2,747.0	3,573.8	2,727.0	383.5	212.8	18,415.0
1941	34,377.9	—	6,930.1	758.5	2,827.6	2,080.4	3,031.2	2,448.2	261.5	197.3	15,836.4
1940	23,630.4	—	5,800.2	553.6	2,028.4	1,611.3	2,560.4	1,554.5	227.7	221.8	9,067.5
1939	21,931.4	—	5,307.8	683.1	2,186.4	1,690.6	2,514.6	1,228.3	229.4	195.7	7,891.0
1938	22,829.5	—	5,323.6	649.1	1,799.5	1,714.0	2,850.6	1,307.1	250.3	261.5	8,668.6
1937	23,193.1	—	6,015.2	713.6	1,910.6	1,642.8	3,140.4	1,372.5	283.4	267.9	7,837.9
1936	22,083.6	—	5,491.6	725.4	2,099.8	1,877.6	2,713.8	1,262.0	182.6	213.9	7,503.7
1935	20,755.8	—	4,762.1	640.8	1,882.4	1,789.6	2,371.9	920.3	146.4	139.2	8,082.4
1934	19,714.9	—	4,619.4	695.1	1,915.7	2,070.9	1,832.5	965.8	115.8	155.1	7,330.1
1933	16,213.8	—	3,405.9	519.2	1,618.8	1,764.2	1,677.0	725.2	97.6	92.3	6,320.5
1932	15,060.6	—	3,856.3	713.6	1,505.2	1,451.8	1,708.2	858.4	112.9	102.5	4,731.8
1931	18,382.8	—	4,833.9	765.0	2,006.8	1,636.6	2,041.0	907.7	178.0	110.1	5,881.0
1930	29,762.7	—	6,843.0	843.6	2,520.2	2,199.3	2,692.7	1,377.2	124.8	266.1	12,873.3
1929	33,699.5	—	7,342.8	933.6	3,002.2	2,467.3	3,050.6	2,038.9	375.2	400.1	14,070.2
1928	33,748.5	—	7,396.0	849.0	2,618.0	2,319.6	3,477.1	1,621.0	370.5	422.3	14,633.6
1927	32,518.3	—	7,148.8	963.7	2,461.4	2,146.4	2,804.4	1,422.7	284.2	434.9	14,842.4
1926	35,327.0	—	8,669.9	924.3	2,876.8	2,470.2	2,521.7	1,744.6	267.8	506.0	15,332.5
1925	30,014.9	—	7,191.0	1,008.2	2,915.6	2,195.2	2,654.7	1,061.3	300.8	293.8	12,382.6
1924	27,365.4	—	6,269.5	879.2	3,315.4	1,725.9	2,803.3	886.4	298.9	218.3	10,954.3
1923	26,441.4	—	5,779.0	1,105.8	2,824.4	1,596.5	2,477.4	739.3	180.8	263.2	11,466.9
1922	27,593.2	—	7,443.3	904.7	2,706.3	1,551.2	2,211.7	658.0	150.1	159.2	11,801.5
1921	23,173.6	—	7,018.1	468.8	2,218.4	1,261.8	2,295.8	759.7	150.9	192.5	8,787.5
1920	31,265.7	—	9,277.0	954.2	2,480.0	1,881.5	2,727.4	879.4	176.1	231.6	12,625.4
1919	37,760.1	—	11,411.7	874.5	2,988.4	3,174.7	2,742.0	1,011.9	271.3	171.0	15,205.8
1918[3]	32,478.8	—	10,492.7	822.2	4,245.9	3,285.2	—	—	—	—	13,632.8
1917	31,302.6	—	9,833.9	963.2	3,896.4	2,169.2	—	—	—	—	12,546.4
1917[1, 4]	20,856.7	—	7,411.8	819.7	3,754.4	1,873.2	—	—	—	—	6,997.4
1916[4]	19,572.3	—	6,663.5	497.2	3,244.8	1,468.4	—	—	—	—	7,698.3
1915[4]	19,015.7	—	6,010.8	801.1	3,443.1	1,114.2	—	—	—	—	7,624.9
1914[4]	21,385.2	—	6,584.9	1,016.8	2,945.6	1,190.5	—	—	—	—	9,647.3
1913[4]	16,766.4	—	5,247.8	895.1	2,909.2	857.1	—	—	—	—	6,857.2
1912[4]	17,810.0	—	6,302.8	705.8	3,307.0	944.5	—	—	—	—	6,550.0
1911[4]	15,753.3	—	7,133.2	743.6	3,192.5	923.1	—	—	—	—	3,760.8

[1] For 1911 to 1917, fiscal years ending 31 March of the year given; 1917 to 1960, calendar years.

[2] The figures shown under provinces do not add to those shown for Canada (series M1) owing to the inclusion of data for the Yukon and Northwest Territories in series M1 and to discrepancies in some years in the official statistics. Newfoundland is included beginning in 1952.

[3] New Brunswick and Quebec figures include sea fish only. Inland fish landings not reported for this year.

[4] Figures apply to sea fisheries only.

Series M 12–24. *Quantities of fish landed, by region and by major species, 1869 to 1960*
(thousands of pounds)

	East coast[2]							Inland			West coast		
Year[1]	Cod	Haddock	Lobsters	Swordfish	Herring and sardines	Redfish	Scallops	Whitefish	Blue pickerel	Yellow pickerel	Salmon	Herring	Halibut
	12	13	14	15	16	17	18	19	20	21	22	23	24
1960	604,621	95,126	51,517	3,890	246,329	46,859	7,716	27,068	5	13,890	75,153	187,675	27,161
1959	639,138	111,997	45,714	6,703	238,916	40,618	4,909	24,796	50	12,996	105,680	444,032	23,799
1958	530,932	103,366	42,950	5,376	233,044	61,371	3,332	24,023	834	15,475	181,318	405,123	23,708
1957	641,834	131,638	44,438	5,180	222,314	46,361	3,329	24,444	6,398	19,215	131,897	295,376	22,542
1956	654,124	155,390	51,960	4,612	196,200	59,646	2,606	22,884	12,020	20,922	113,530	491,396	23,315
1955	579,562	135,573	48,569	4,546	201,090	43,980	1,684	21,990	12,070	19,739	131,008	305,692	19,679
1954	639,341	117,989	46,675	4,304	217,913	48,739	1,780	24,577	8,210	16,759	178,862	360,962	25,199
1953	530,599	72,969	46,397	3,324	224,719	46,543	1,780	25,571	10,399	15,974	186,914	298,241	24,882
1952[2]	622,009	63,975	47,857	3,158	292,905	38,561	1,261	27,895	7,447	16,599	146,965	189,497	23,488
1951	227,172	55,990	45,573	2,544	208,256	4,054	599	26,505	4,102	17,073	197,594	365,432	20,214
1950	250,080	47,319	44,685	2,156	230,761	2,070	784	24,776	8,665	13,877	184,699	397,566	18,882
1949	246,284	46,580	38,205	2,237	185,803	2,046	436	22,509	9,831	13,535	147,368	344,527	17,997
1948	256,075	56,789	35,647	2,363	226,173	1,139	871	19,909	5,868	15,980	145,168	416,967	18,753
1947	231,275	31,558	31,884	1,792	239,367	429	932	16,023	1,753	14,463	162,800	256,331	24,119
1946	323,123	34,738	38,309	2,776	249,853	301	879	19,200	1,972	13,754	149,676	212,365	17,991
1945	291,075	32,221	37,180	2,717	195,727	25	963	18,871	6,582	14,801	170,965	257,654	14,905
1944	235,104	25,965	33,350	1,989	213,565	28	603	17,700	9,413	14,984	107,572	187,104	13,167
1943	213,938	30,745	30,109	3,021	215,541	32	574	16,781	9,661	13,503	121,421	182,794	12,687
1942	193,557	26,206	28,025	1,934	189,781	127	700	16,706	4,438	12,804	162,198	232,483	11,028
1941	194,754	28,777	27,802	1,346	191,990	38	784	17,866	1,621	12,630	190,035	168,852	12,929
1940	191,633	35,557	26,799	2,290	169,566	281	665	16,818	2,118	10,580	143,190	339,501	12,694
1939	161,918	38,516	31,466	1,788	177,256	589	496	16,462	6,158	12,051	147,637	216,481	13,397
1938	168,338	39,359	31,438	1,093	151,796	478	957	15,424	7,317	12,881	173,466	132,891	12,025
1937	150,932	38,882	30,995	1,502	139,643	97	1,838	17,368	9,450	14,302	169,174	192,980	11,721
1936	169,188	40,301	28,327	1,785	167,531	211	1,708	14,460	6,900	14,564	199,550	162,062	10,592
1935	152,246	36,843	31,997	2,234	139,261	—	1,332	14,746	5,123	10,955	178,943	100,851	10,193
1934	170,125	35,607	36,199	1,409	142,662	—	899	14,462	2,432	12,251	165,990	82,036	9,768
1933	155,648	26,888	37,492	1,714	120,612	—	863	15,214	4,216	10,627	141,050	107,737	17,081
1932	142,619	36,018	48,349	1,036	95,630	—	468	13,848	4,061	8,950	129,149	100,320	16,885
1931	146,200	36,385	43,549	1,263	104,948	—	236	15,622	5,405	9,235	128,704	148,108	18,200
1930	166,147	48,634	40,726	1,193	116,262	—	373	16,975	5,928	10,315	229,621	122,196	25,480
1929	197,883	54,541	37,282	634	144,596	—	358	19,639	2,583	12,850	151,404	131,567	30,392
1928	214,982	48,171	32,244	809	137,292	—	526	18,070	2,150	14,261	225,746	153,512	30,282
1927	197,864	42,171	31,683	730	128,606	—	773	18,566	3,117	14,002	149,040	172,425	30,053
1926	269,476	49,680	33,958	1,294	141,591	—	464	19,064	3,038	12,609	212,556	130,127	31,510
1925	227,736	34,439	34,084	455	124,049	—	354	18,665	3,445	8,688	187,338	143,788	31,824
1924	184,779	33,786	27,221	558	138,459	—	207	16,771	3,060	10,161	196,516	115,762	33,138
1923	177,251	30,456	38,163	1,434	96,189	—	278	15,779	3,255	10,387	151,476	103,582	33,467
1922	232,021	30,773	36,392	1,116	125,996	—	216	15,878	6,358	8,315	150,908	100,252	29,318
1921	200,424	26,922	39,362	685	94,210	—	98	18,407	6,406	6,485	84,203	94,487	32,587
1920	194,860	44,174	39,998	335	132,842	—	84	18,176	3,380	6,188	126,286	100,136	23,877
1919	255,945	56,457	34,581	741	131,676	—	274	19,740	2,392	6,173	166,835	56,787	21,078
1918	216,239	55,437	26,410	364	171,884	—	250	20,504	—	—	149,350	63,692	18,623
1917	221,546	71,242	47,487	434	106,240	—	132	—	—	—	160,152	48,724	11,353
1917[1]	196,286	58,203	48,090	928	177,689	—	189	—	—	—	119,643	49,603	12,306
1916	211,689	58,252	44,528	1,853	198,354	—	137	—	—	—	136,939	46,745	19,490
1915	177,286	56,600	40,882	498	206,035	—	—	—	—	—	136,974	56,341	21,444
1914	163,538	40,563	51,465	1,332	198,631	—	—	—	—	—	150,935	64,906	22,346
1913	170,049	50,382	55,514	656	213,403	—	—	—	—	—	122,106	72,957	25,328
1912	207,220	53,022	58,914	794	240,067	—	—	—	—	—	110,367	54,544	19,649
1911	312,651	45,672	57,910	272	212,022	—	—	—	—	—	93,783	27,519	21,906
1910[1]	248,990	—	—	—	—	—	—	—	—	—	—	—	—
1909	—	60,000	—	—	—	—	—	—	—	—	—	—	—
1908	217,170	49,000	—	—	—	—	—	—	—	—	—	—	—
1907	—	47,000	—	—	—	—	—	—	—	—	—	—	—
1906	203,364	48,100	—	—	—	—	—	—	—	—	—	—	—
1905	223,355	55,900	—	—	—	—	—	—	—	—	—	—	—
1904	238,610	46,900	—	—	—	—	—	—	—	—	—	—	—
1903	248,163	41,400	—	—	—	—	—	—	—	—	—	—	—
1902	299,173	45,200	—	—	—	—	—	—	—	—	—	—	—
1901	299,900	60,500	—	—	—	—	—	—	—	—	—	—	—
1900	267,684	50,200	—	—	—	—	—	—	—	—	—	—	—
1899	278,155	62,700	—	—	—	—	—	—	—	—	—	—	—
1898	212,837	59,200	—	—	—	—	—	—	—	—	—	—	—
1897	237,534	96,000[3]	—	—	—	—	—	—	—	—	—	—	—
1896	239,021	52,000	—	—	—	—	—	—	—	—	—	—	—
1895	241,078	48,700	—	—	—	—	—	—	—	—	—	—	—
1894	280,454	54,900	—	—	—	—	—	—	—	—	—	—	—
1893	266,507	53,300	—	—	—	—	—	—	—	—	—	—	—
1892	269,464	67,000	—	—	—	—	—	—	—	—	—	—	—
1891	254,691	60,000	—	—	—	—	—	—	—	—	—	—	—
1890	257,320	53,200	—	—	—	—	—	—	—	—	—	—	—
1889	271,368	50,300	—	—	—	—	—	—	—	—	—	—	—
1888	315,254	94,900	—	—	—	—	—	—	—	—	—	—	—
1887	323,476	86,400	—	—	—	—	—	—	—	—	—	—	—
1886	324,215	85,400	—	—	—	—	—	—	—	—	—	—	—
1885	323,218	74,400	—	—	—	—	—	—	—	—	—	—	—
1884	306,717	86,800	—	—	—	—	—	—	—	—	—	—	—
1883	322,536	69,200	—	—	—	—	—	—	—	—	—	—	—
1882	270,909	71,500	—	—	—	—	—	—	—	—	—	—	—
1881	322,675	47,100	—	—	—	—	—	—	—	—	—	—	—

Series M12–24. *Quantities of fish landed, by region and by major species, 1869 to 1960 (continued)*

(thousands of pounds)

	East coast[2]							Inland			West coast		
Year[1]	Cod	Haddock	Lobsters	Swordfish	Herring and sardines	Redfish	Scallops	Whitefish	Blue pickerel	Yellow pickerel	Salmon	Herring	Halibut
	12	13	14	15	16	17	18	19	20	21	22	23	24
1880	327,754	43,600	—	—	—	—	—	—	—	—	—	—	—
1879	320,245	—	—	—	—	—	—	—	—	—	—	—	—
1878	270,749	—	—	—	—	—	—	—	—	—	—	—	—
1877	244,520	—	—	—	—	—	—	—	—	—	—	—	—
1876	249,258	—	—	—	—	—	—	—	—	—	—	—	—
1875	224,636	—	—	—	—	—	—	—	—	—	—	—	—
1874	239,367	—	—	—	—	—	—	—	—	—	—	—	—
1873	264,253	—	—	—	—	—	—	—	—	—	—	—	—
1872	247,331	—	—	—	—	—	—	—	—	—	—	—	—
1871	202,381	—	—	—	—	—	—	—	—	—	—	—	—
1870	173,527	—	—	—	—	—	—	—	—	—	—	—	—
1869	154,007	—	—	—	—	—	—	—	—	—	—	—	—

[1] For 1869 to 1909 and for 1917 to 1960, calendar years; for 1910 to 1917, fiscal years ending 31 March of the year given.

[2] Newfoundland is included in series M12–18 for 1952 to 1960 only.

[3] See note to series M13 for unusual size of this figure.

Series M25–37. *Value of fish landed, by region and by major species, 1911 to 1960*

(thousands of dollars)

	East coast[2]							Inland			West coast		
Year[1]	Cod	Haddock	Lobsters	Swordfish	Herring and sardines	Redfish	Scallops	Whitefish	Blue pickerel	Yellow pickerel	Salmon	Herring	Halibut
	25	26	27	28	29	30	31	32	33	34	35	36	37
1960	16,537.5	3,685.0	18,031.4	1,341.6	3,682.1	1,172.4	2,020.8	3,494.0	1.5	3,020.4	18,401.0	2,178.0	4,379.0
1959	17,023.2	4,969.9	17,387.4	1,383.1	3,278.9	977.3	1,871.9	3,548.5	15.2	2,993.8	20,503.0	7,355.0	4,398.0
1958	13,228.3	4,092.3	15,375.5	1,439.3	2,825.7	1,488.2	1,268.8	3,496.4	215.7	3,387.0	37,129.0	6,712.0	4,902.0
1957	15,057.0	4,209.9	14,501.4	1,340.9	2,514.7	1,032.2	1,285.4	3,611.3	1,151.3	3,603.0	18,885.0	4,892.0	3,673.0
1956	16,395.7	4,881.9	18,023.3	1,295.2	2,390.8	1,273.6	1,117.7	3,635.9	1,802.3	3,160.8	21,356.0	7,077.0	5,067.0
1955	14,366.7	4,325.2	16,470.0	1,090.4	2,045.9	1,015.4	730.5	3,726.3	1,448.5	3,092.8	18,481.0	4,187.0	2,555.0
1954	15,990.2	4,243.5	15,558.0	1,139.0	2,730.8	1,105.8	632.6	4,424.8	1,231.4	2,667.1	23,578.8	4,564.9	3,983.6
1953	12,587.6	3,000.8	15,718.3	1,105.2	2,457.6	1,054.7	693.7	4,352.1	1,041.3	2,539.6	21,848.4	3,677.8	3,661.3
1952	16,119.7	2,972.3	14,051.8	888.3	3,349.0	975.5	604.1	4,748.9	1,049.8	2,907.9	19,555.2	3,201.0	3,955.2
1951	6,816.9	2,668.6	12,206.0	997.6	2,889.2	120.0	226.8	4,529.6	816.6	3,280.7	28,396.1	5,653.6	3,428.8
1950	7,140.2	2,365.7	12,137.0	705.5	2,061.9	56.9	346.9	4,020.8	1,385.4	2,496.0	24,335.9	5,149.2	3,837.3
1949	7,398.9	2,123.0	10,201.3	725.8	2,560.1	61.9	171.3	3,510.4	887.1	1,851.6	15,655.8	4,173.5	2,785.1
1948	8,533.9	2,643.5	9,507.8	861.3	3,580.9	37.2	417.1	3,173.8	880.5	2,471.6	19,952.6	5,184.9	2,725.6
1947	6,414.8	1,369.3	8,274.5	701.8	3,034.6	12.4	440.7	2,318.7	346.3	2,521.1	12,576.7	2,461.7	3,884.4
1946	11,041.5	1,592.1	11,365.0	981.4	3,377.7	6.7	521.4	2,728.6	353.8	2,254.7	12,812.0	1,853.2	2,908.1
1945	10,590.1	1,452.1	9,783.0	1,030.2	2,554.1	.2	508.7	3,087.6	1,316.1	2,185.3	11,267.9	1,939.0	2,600.6
1944	8,365.5	1,137.9	7,329.5	616.5	2,727.8	.2	276.9	2,607.1	848.2	1,757.2	7,255.5	1,392.0	2,231.8
1943	7,517.0	1,282.3	5,844.0	819.9	2,570.8	.3	278.6	2,663.4	1,256.9	1,654.1	7,201.5	1,370.8	2,398.1
1942	5,570.4	961.3	3,888.7	446.0	1,836.3	1.1	235.8	2,336.6	497.1	1,113.8	12,794.5	1,252.8	1,593.1
1941	4,037.2	745.7	2,911.9	217.8	1,502.3	.3	168.5	1,908.9	168.6	972.8	11,424.6	655.5	1,242.0
1940	3,035.6	754.8	2,471.6	253.5	931.2	2.0	128.7	1,463.1	182.2	787.4	5,503.7	1,203.1	1,103.3
1939	2,026.6	658.6	2,934.2	185.7	1,128.2	1.6	62.3	1,212.5	369.4	640.3	5,827.8	507.7	970.0
1938	2,089.9	635.5	2,864.1	101.5	898.8	3.1	124.0	1,182.0	453.7	713.2	6,331.4	316.2	840.7
1937	2,044.3	637.4	3,749.6	170.2	700.9	.8	279.0	1,421.5	718.2	795.9	5,275.7	440.3	927.1
1936	2,151.1	668.8	3,452.1	150.3	868.8	1.4	313.2	1,184.3	503.7	867.5	5,154.8	383.3	802.3
1935	1,821.7	574.8	3,171.0	148.4	797.9	—	207.0	1,069.1	256.2	616.6	6,172.2	287.4	657.0
1934	2,199.8	514.1	3,210.0	117.6	756.9	—	166.8	1,013.4	102.1	559.3	5,792.8	201.2	575.6
1933	1,695.3	331.3	2,296.1	117.6	547.5	—	161.3	817.1	223.5	436.7	4,463.9	468.8	867.8
1932	1,437.5	507.4	3,106.9	39.4	458.3	—	73.2	832.7	146.2	547.5	3,443.4	183.4	677.3
1931	2,040.5	603.4	3,255.2	140.0	581.9	—	39.0	1,034.5	140.5	607.4	3,291.4	633.1	1,156.2
1930	3,243.4	1,006.1	3,677.7	139.1	742.6	—	90.2	1,409.3	361.6	740.4	8,178.1	717.2	2,402.6
1929	4,038.2	1,052.6	3,847.6	69.6	1,103.1	—	104.5	1,785.4	155.0	1,148.3	7,310.0	961.5	3,555.6
1928	4,102.1	983.3	3,612.0	112.2	899.6	—	140.8	1,653.2	258.0	1,289.3	8,153.8	1,412.7	2,964.3
1927	3,447.6	727.2	3,962.1	88.1	888.7	—	207.2	1,484.7	124.7	1,065.8	8,194.6	1,342.0	3,343.1
1926	5,121.8	903.9	4,155.9	146.4	1,033.2	—	147.8	1,537.2	121.5	1,142.9	8,562.6	1,006.5	4,068.9
1925	4,516.7	656.8	3,813.3	67.8	901.9	—	93.7	1,425.9	206.7	833.0	7,141.8	992.2	3,121.8
1924	4,016.5	614.0	2,824.1	66.6	1,237.9	—	64.8	1,290.7	122.4	792.3	5,315.3	764.3	3,884.2
1923	2,744.0	500.9	4,378.0	94.7	903.0	—	81.0	1,226.9	130.2	700.5	5,470.7	902.9	4,234.6
1922	4,104.8	543.9	3,624.8	81.1	782.4	—	50.1	1,036.2	190.8	573.8	7,610.3	806.7	2,773.6
1921	3,526.4	474.1	3,068.0	74.0	635.2	—	29.7	1,363.8	128.1	501.9	4,482.6	635.9	3,170.0
1920	5,000.1	878.9	4,557.1	41.2	1,073.2	—	23.6	1,315.9	202.8	469.2	7,819.3	868.0	3,185.7
1919	8,100.2	1,363.1	3,307.0	96.0	1,093.5	—	71.3	1,354.6	143.5	490.4	10,602.8	695.7	2,639.8
1918	7,653.4	1,851.1	2,123.4	49.4	2,761.8	—	66.4	—	—	—	8,892.2	1,012.9	2,633.7
1917	5,994.0	1,610.2	3,284.5	22.6	1,929.8	—	26.8	—	—	—	9,678.1	677.3	1,290.4
1917[1]	4,041.9	1,219.6	3,476.7	44.7	1,924.8	—	37.8	—	—	—	4,827.3	579.8	943.2
1916	3,552.8	776.3	2,943.5	81.6	1,633.5	—	15.4	—	—	—	5,743.7	517.1	991.2
1915	2,727.4	907.6	2,990.4	23.0	1,909.6	—	—	—	—	—	5,308.4	609.3	1,070.3
1914	2,577.8	779.9	3,498.2	46.7	1,482.5	—	—	—	—	—	7,166.5	708.1	1,187.6
1913	1,744.1	771.8	3,307.5	32.5	1,331.6	—	—	—	—	—	3,647.9	823.2	953.2
1912	2,757.3	699.6	2,978.8	37.8	2,007.6	—	—	—	—	—	4,132.0	565.3	953.2
1911	4,327.6	694.7	2,690.3	18.3	1,605.0	—	—	—	—	—	2,109.4	363.1	707.6

[1] For 1911 to 1917, fiscal years ending 31 March of the year given; 1917 to 1960, calendar years.

[2] Newfoundland is included in series M25–31 beginning in 1952.

Series M 38–48. Number of persons engaged in primary fishing operations, by province, 1878 to 1960

Year[1]	Canada[2]	Newfound-land	Nova Scotia	Prince Edward Island	New Brunswick	Quebec	Ontario	Manitoba[3]	Saskat-chewan	Alberta	British Columbia[4]
	38	39	40	41	42	43	44	45	46	47	48
1960	78,171	18,291	12,780	3,274	6,175	6,004	3,409	5,289	1,700	5,730	15,159
1959	80,045	18,430	13,012	3,260	6,382	6,424	3,527	5,312	1,650	6,089	15,456
1958	82,930	18,364	13,747	3,209	6,220	7,277	3,224	5,682	1,600	7,846	15,263
1957	79,044	16,469	15,265	3,000	8,167	6,712	3,066	5,395	1,500	5,941	12,999
1956	74,623	14,956	14,379	2,967	9,785	6,312	3,135	5,389	997	4,277	11,851
1955	62,511	—	14,221	2,863	10,066	6,383	3,483	5,775	921	5,247	12,836
1954	63,262	—	14,864	2,794	9,703	6,272	3,567	5,970	1,066	5,324	13,038
1953	63,675	—	14,614	2,763	10,636	6,868	3,807	5,441	1,840	4,809	12,449
1952	64,342	—	15,248	2,665	10,536	6,054	3,878	6,410	2,368	5,105	13,066
1951	65,391	—	15,607	2,660	11,201	6,982	3,833	6,578	1,280	3,325	13,213
1950	65,037	—	15,723	2,895	11,621	8,031	3,886	5,904	1,322	2,825	12,159
1949	64,799	—	14,896	2,909	11,040	8,663	3,930	5,313	1,713	3,182	12,242
1948	66,115	—	14,915	3,046	10,973	9,042	3,736	6,700	1,370	3,659	12,226
1947	65,419	—	14,475	3,307	11,073	8,094	4,026	6,465	1,659	3,606	12,491
1946	73,514	—	15,860	2,960	11,074	9,980	4,244	7,293	2,173	5,588	13,665
1945	67,711	—	14,413	2,410	10,768	8,949	3,982	6,150	2,030	5,689	13,292
1944	64,208	—	13,863	2,269	10,392	8,820	3,809	6,169	2,381	4,004	12,463
1943	61,459	—	13,370	2,172	10,180	9,688	3,610	6,185	1,919	2,398	11,903
1942	61,307	—	13,452	2,267	10,481	10,566	3,336	5,557	1,581	1,897	12,199
1941	63,745	—	15,149	2,445	11,212	10,849	3,608	6,618	1,305	2,312	10,217
1940	68,817	—	17,590	2,874	12,425	13,270	4,020	4,205	1,284	2,676	10,444
1939	68,941	—	17,548	3,454	13,795	12,917	4,206	3,707	1,341	2,334	9,609
1938	71,510	—	18,548	3,309	14,130	12,684	4,170	3,819	1,547	2,954	10,314
1937	69,981	—	18,088	3,310	13,920	11,385	4,440	3,824	1,388	2,405	11,184
1936	71,735	—	18,359	3,093	14,207	13,778	4,280	3,586	973	2,035	11,393
1935	68,557	—	17,907	3,365	12,988	14,093	3,988	3,241	710	1,265	10,965
1934	68,634	—	18,448	2,973	13,062	13,981	4,125	3,031	530	767	11,700
1933	65,506	—	17,133	3,194	12,289	13,627	3,984	2,822	614	743	11,066
1932	64,484	—	16,258	3,018	13,411	13,618	3,816	2,868	686	676	10,116
1931	61,811	—	15,527	2,431	12,764	12,743	3,865	3,437	623	911	9,495
1930	63,836	—	15,265	2,281	12,047	11,226	4,074	4,781	945	1,179	12,000
1929	64,083	—	15,747	2,202	11,920	9,944	4,043	4,687	1,313	1,516	12,675
1928	62,785	—	15,857	2,396	11,040	10,847	4,128	4,172	1,084	1,401	11,818
1927	63,415	—	16,131	2,675	10,198	10,916	4,156	4,095	970	1,161	13,076
1926	61,371	—	16,315	2,916	9,024	10,892	4,145	3,809	864	1,212	12,162
1925	58,273	—	16,266	3,017	8,939	10,711	4,263	3,390	794	914	9,944
1924	53,914	—	15,805	2,537	8,743	8,824	4,267	2,828	908	675	9,274
1923	53,517	—	16,742	2,503	9,228	8,837	3,742	2,530	572	595	8,734
1922	57,880	—	19,495	2,201	9,394	10,089	4,003	2,113	423	615	9,495
1921	55,230	—	19,292	2,075	8,152	8,494	3,600	1,889	494	538	10,623
1920	57,197	—	18,965	2,793	8,218	8,894	3,693	1,688	577	631	11,669
1919	67,804	—	22,083	3,391	10,847	10,767	4,156	2,332	733	545	12,865
1918	68,516	—	21,598	3,684	13,212	10,876	3,918	2,235	846	733	11,239
1917	72,390	—	21,767	3,450	15,726	9,657	3,705	2,192	1,661	1,032	12,967
1917	69,624[1]	—	22,126	3,465	15,672	9,115	3,592	1,728	1,477	675	11,557
1916	74,862	—	22,765	3,093	16,702	8,851	4,114	1,165	927	5,711[5]	11,310
1915	69,954	—	22,606	3,360	15,945	9,194	4,076	1,555	813	947	11,232
1914	71,776	—	22,312	3,764	15,540	9,177	3,511	1,162	645	4,130	11,316
1913	65,081	—	21,443	3,308	14,944	9,417	3,604	1,420	484	1,589	8,747
1912	65,926	—	21,661	3,206	15,239	11,080	3,196	1,919	559	320	8,608
1911	68,610	—	21,580	4,466	16,158	10,998	3,611	1,909	717	464	8,583
1910	68,663	—	23,158	3,403	14,825	10,795	3,601	639	563	732	10,811[4]
1909	71,070	—	24,521	3,499	15,600	10,893	3,263	560	476	420	11,768
1908	71,254	—	23,543	3,594	14,319	11,235	3,180	854	425	1,270	12,834
1906	76,104	—	24,206	3,577	14,477	11,893	3,085	1,460	813	1,658	15,535
1905	82,871	—	25,362	3,437	14,273	13,367	3,185	2,659	1,098	1,270	18,220
1904	77,345	—	24,454	3,889	13,265	12,817	3,125	4,559[3]	—[3]	—[3]	15,236
1903	79,134	—	23,398	3,706	12,442	14,875	3,003	2,573	—	—	19,137
1902	77,801	—	23,327	4,324	13,067	12,123	2,885	3,512	—	—	18,563
1901	79,370	—	23,974	4,313	12,702	12,311	2,802	2,914	—	—	20,354
1900	81,064	—	25,212	4,994	12,639	13,097	2,502	1,326	—	—	21,294
1899	79,893	—	25,171	4,753	12,974	13,250	2,430	1,039	—	—	20,246
1898	81,534	—	26,235	4,404	12,273	12,332	2,847	1,329	—	—	22,114
1897	78,959	—	25,373	4,459	11,571	12,044	3,009	1,667	—	—	20,936
1896	75,237	—	24,975	4,754	11,270	13,415	3,298	1,600	—	—	15,925
1895	71,334	—	25,615	3,758	10,389	12,243	3,259	1,585	—	—	14,485
1894	70,719	—	25,478	3,329	11,650	12,081	4,155	1,376	—	—	12,650
1893	67,753	—	23,847	3,522	11,305	11,565	2,629	953	—	—	13,932
1892	63,678	—	24,070	5,020	12,265	10,694	2,709	750	—	—	8,170
1891	65,575	—	24,376	4,026	12,222	12,530	2,920	835	—	—	8,666
1890	66,256	—	27,684	4,798	11,139	11,367	3,045	—	—	—	8,223
1889	65,003	—	27,334	4,245	10,527	11,583	3,528	—	—	—	7,786
1888	62,683	—	28,107	4,379	9,840	11,114	3,303	—	—	—	5,940
1887	64,158	—	27,991	4,059	11,087	12,105	2,762	—	—	—	6,154
1886	62,000	—	27,485	3,496	9,359	12,652	2,797	—	—	—	6,211
1885	62,821	—	29,905	3,535	10,185	13,660	2,716	—	—	—	2,820
1884	61,822	—	29,997	4,020	8,676	12,983	2,865	—	—	—	3,281
1883[6]	62,225	—	—	—	—	—	—	—	—	—	—
1882	61,283	—	28,500	4,482	9,952	12,959	2,603	—	—	—	2,787
1881	59,056	—	27,526	3,635	8,737	13,657	2,608	—	—	—	2,893
1880	60,657	—	29,276	4,031	8,566	14,771	2,130	—	—	—	1,883
1879	61,395	—	27,610	5,198	8,053	15,055	3,358	—	—	—	2,121
1878	61,337	—	26,527	5,206	8,712	14,706	3,382	—	—	—	2,804

[1] For 1878 to 1906 and for 1917 to 1958 calendar years; for 1908 to 1917 fiscal years ending 31 March of the year given.

[2] The figures shown under the provinces do not add to that shown for Canada (series M38) owing to the inclusion of data for Yukon and Northwest Territories in series M38 and to discrepancies in some years in the official statistics. Newfoundland is included beginning in 1956.

[3] From 1891 to 1904 data for Manitoba include the Northwest Territories (Alberta and Saskatchewan).

[4] For 1888 to 1910 a number of cannery employees are included.

[5] Includes anglers.

[6] Breakdown by provinces not available.

Series M49–59. *Aggregate value of capital equipment employed in primary fishing operations, by province, 1878 to 1960*
(thousands of dollars)

Year[1]	Canada[2]	Newfoundland	Nova Scotia	Prince Edward Island	New Brunswick	Quebec	Ontario	Manitoba[3]	Saskatchewan	Alberta	British Columbia
	49	50	51	52	53	54	55	56	57	58	59
1960	129,281.9	17,148.7	23,052.7	3,855.8	10,268.4	6,843.1	7,996.7	2,541.1	1,114.5	—	56,240.0
1959	121,200.4	15,996.5	21,110.8	3,599.2	9,542.2	5,820.7	8,416.5	2,457.6	1,232.9	—	52,839.0
1958	114,531.9	15,044.1	20,880.7	2,709.1	8,010.6	5,160.1	7,204.3	2,409.3	784.9	—	51,461.0
1957	120,850.0	14,676.0	25,303.6	3,046.5	9,588.0	4,778.8	7,191.6	2,489.4	695.9	684.4	51,815.0
1956	114,005.3	13,720.0	23,126.6	3,235.2	8,767.6	4,781.0	7,096.3	2,568.0	553.5	434.2	49,266.0
1955	98,962.5	—	22,193.2	3,176.4	8,939.7	3,906.2	7,412.0	2,664.9	516.5	591.7	49,024.0
1954	112,846.6	14,755.6	21,935.8	3,017.2	7,981.3	3,662.0	7,397.2	2,730.1	879.4	603.8	49,421.3
1953	97,715.9	—	20,867.6	2,987.6	7,977.1	3,688.6	7,063.7	2,583.2	663.9	459.9	51,066.6
1952	95,204.0	—	21,550.9	2,785.9	7,938.3	3,263.2	6,717.7	3,148.1	663.6	416.6	48,330.4
1951	86,915.9	—	19,731.3	2,644.9	7,297.1	3,296.8	6,125.3	3,309.0	559.5	221.0	43,399.8
1950	75,100.1	—	17,364.2	2,451.1	6,679.7	3,349.1	5,732.7	2,737.3	278.5	187.9	35,894.0
1949	65,189.0	—	15,501.7	2,256.9	6,229.2	3,216.6	5,267.8	1,812.0	315.3	162.2	30,069.9
1948	63,643.7	—	14,233.6	1,966.1	5,793.5	2,964.3	4,982.4	2,146.4	526.9	285.3	30,530.1
1947	53,373.9	—	11,885.8	1,792.9	4,740.7	2,817.8	4,528.2	2,095.9	451.6	264.9	24,622.9
1946	44,702.9	—	8,773.3	1,140.4	4,082.4	2,610.3	4,123.2	1,844.7	—	457.0	21,664.9
1945	38,388.1	—	7,617.5	875.1	3,607.4	2,317.9	3,590.0	1,614.3	264.8	445.5	18,051.0
1944	32,848.4	—	6,575.2	826.6	3,396.8	2,000.6	3,154.8	1,670.5	355.5	324.0	14,539.1
1943	29,091.4	—	5,842.2	690.3	2,811.6	1,872.2	2,968.7	1,610.2	242.0	350.4	12,698.5
1942	26,997.5	—	5,490.1	649.5	2,688.4	1,975.2	2,715.7	1,431.6	180.0	213.9	11,647.5
1941	25,377.9	—	5,396.5	707.4	2,612.9	1,832.6	2,845.6	1,195.1	133.0	275.0	10,375.1
1940	24,187.0	—	5,365.7	778.1	2,889.6	1,853.0	2,833.0	957.7	142.3	276.8	9,085.9
1939	23,780.7	—	5,588.5	902.0	3,013.8	2,050.5	2,880.8	839.6	140.8	303.5	8,056.4
1938	24,444.5	—	5,682.8	860.3	2,869.4	1,976.6	2,868.9	865.6	162.2	241.4	8,912.0
1937	24,604.9	—	5,788.7	893.9	2,818.0	1,892.7	2,908.8	785.7	162.1	230.7	9,117.0
1936	25,016.2	—	5,460.4	907.0	2,853.9	2,210.4	2,740.7	790.4	102.8	185.0	9,758.0
1935	24,156.9	—	5,218.8	850.6	2,852.9	2,240.5	2,583.0	750.0	68.0	156.0	9,426.9
1934	23,913.3	—	5,110.5	841.5	2,845.8	2,184.8	2,506.2	676.5	55.8	133.3	9,548.1
1933	23,063.8	—	5,074.3	860.4	2,757.3	2,114.6	2,532.2	650.3	56.3	142.1	8,863.3
1932	22,186.4	—	5,328.7	837.6	2,932.6	2,116.1	2,591.0	636.6	68.7	144.2	7,514.7
1931	23,489.6	—	5,924.6	660.9	3,173.4	2,071.5	2,803.6	797.2	88.7	279.6	7,674.2
1930	30,300.6	—	6,429.2	686.2	3,320.9	2,116.3	3,026.5	1,035.0	84.1	372.5	13,213.7
1929	30,583.1	—	6,537.3	676.0	3,392.0	2,070.3	3,073.1	1,047.6	119.7	379.3	13,275.7
1928	28,237.2	—	6,278.0	677.4	3,269.5	1,820.7	3,018.3	853.6	116.4	302.2	11,889.0
1927	28,737.1	—	6,890.6	771.6	3,067.2	1,795.3	2,887.4	842.4	84.7	214.9	12,176.8
1926	25,873.7	—	6,687.6	810.5	3,010.2	1,841.6	2,941.6	786.5	82.9	183.8	9,523.3
1925	22,707.2	—	6,600.6	881.1	2,860.1	1,820.8	2,897.4	694.3	73.4	128.5	6,746.2
1924	20,320.9	—	6,069.7	840.1	2,837.4	1,577.7	2,641.1	650.7	81.4	126.6	5,490.4
1923	20,623.4	—	6,729.8	827.0	2,700.6	1,462.4	2,481.4	606.2	45.3	118.2	5,648.7
1922	22,396.9	—	7,254.5	678.7	2,656.7	1,502.3	2,979.1	529.3	30.6	116.0	6,646.4
1921	22,707.6	—	7,068.5	579.9	2,574.0	1,775.0	2,828.7	502.6	37.4	127.0	7,208.8
1920	26,221.3	—	7,731.9	825.5	2,984.2	2,063.8	2,948.6	609.8	50.4	134.5	8,864.9
1919	25,082.9	—	7,827.8	896.6	3,401.8	2,472.3	2,659.8	617.4	54.1	115.6	7,034.6
1918	23,513.1	—	6,969.3	771.0	3,533.6	1,919.6	2,380.8	580.0	58.0	125.1	7,170.3
1917	20,600.3	—	6,168.1	884.5	3,335.4	1,324.4	2,095.9	361.1	69.3	67.6	6,287.1
1917[1]	17,189.4	—	5,917.5	742.9	2,755.8	994.2	1,768.2	317.7	64.4	31.3	4,590.9
1916	14,795.3	—	5,077.0	596.0	2,435.4	961.4	1,662.6	249.9	49.2	40.3	3,716.9
1915	14,038.4	—	4,799.5	693.2	2,366.6	941.1	1,570.7	217.6	43.6	16.7	3,382.7
1914	13,827.0	—	4,529.2	613.9	2,181.9	909.8	1,347.7	203.4	30.0	13.5	3,991.0
1913	13,315.6	—	4,522.5	565.8	2,126.3	786.2	1,583.7	184.1	12.1	8.4	3,518.7
1912	11,233.1	—	3,595.9	419.1	1,872.0	851.6	1,048.9	321.1	9.3	14.5	3,091.8
1911	10,605.8	—	3,511.0	430.4	1,844.9	710.9	1,011.4	320.4[3]	27.4	17.1	2,727.2
1910	10,229.2	—	3,330.1	397.2	1,732.4	731.1	1,037.1	220.2	21.0	9.9	2,742.6
1909	9,839.3	—	3,488.0	407.8	1,694.5	684.5	1,029.4	168.3	17.0	4.0	2,344.6
1908	9,385.4	—	3,090.4	358.6	1,645.8	763.7	963.9	267.5	14.6	9.6	2,271.3
1906[1]	9,542.9	—	3,164.6	343.7	1,522.0	813.7	862.4	365.1	29.9	9.6	2,431.9
1905	9,343.5	—	3,308.4	298.9	1,549.2	780.0	860.1	424.5[3]	52.9		2,059.6
1904	8,375.6	—	3,036.6	319.7	1,501.5	733.1	840.6	505.7	—	—	1,438.4
1903	8,470.0	—	3,028.7	276.8	1,435.9	751.1	763.0	445.9	—	—	1,768.6
1902	7,829.2	—	2,768.1	268.4	1,377.7	656.1	745.1	335.6	—	—	1,678.2
1901	7,871.1	—	2,609.1	287.2	1,658.0	669.6	667.6	296.0	—	—	1,683.6
1900	7,555.0	—	2,577.8	298.0	1,738.7	588.2	739.4	172.3	—	—	1,440.6
1899	6,829.4	—	2,453.7	279.9	1,578.7	591.9	643.3	66.6	—	—	1,215.3
1898	6,670.9	—	2,371.2	270.4	1,424.6	627.8	526.3	162.4	—	—	1,288.2
1897	6,440.0	—	2,522.7	244.1	1,198.1	495.2	641.0	172.2	—	—	1,166.7
1896	6,781.8	—	2,441.2	237.9	1,328.6	547.2	711.3	152.0	—	—	1,363.6
1895	6,556.8	—	2,662.5	260.3	1,174.0	535.7	725.3	141.6	—	—	1,057.4
1894	6,780.0	—	2,863.2	228.3	1,167.5	659.0	702.8	138.2[3]	—	—	1,020.5
1893	6,309.8	—	2,705.7	321.0	1,004.8	523.5	663.9	120.6	—	—	970.3
1892	5,709.4	—	2,275.1	271.9	957.8	444.6	712.8	59.8	—	—	987.4
1891	5,690.2	—	2,441.0	276.3	1,034.5	451.0	584.2	44.7	—	—	858.5
1890	5,761.6	—	2,910.7	269.9	770.8	493.5	563.4	—	—	—	753.3
1889	5,310.8	—	2,676.4	228.6	795.7	485.8	551.6	—	—	—	572.7
1888	5,543.1	—	2,865.9	254.0	837.0	610.5	558.6	—	—	—	417.1
1887	5,253.3	—	2,666.5	189.1	884.4	680.9	469.9	—	—	—	362.5
1886	5,020.1	—	2,645.1	183.2	824.1	701.1	336.7	—	—	—	329.9
1885	5,240.8	—	2,786.6	271.0	752.1	818.5	378.3	—	—	—	234.3
1884	4,903.1	—	2,670.9	137.0	720.7	767.0	361.2	—	—	—	246.3
1883[4]	1,900.4	—	710.9	37.8	457.3	252.7	188.5	—	—	—	253.2
1882	4,448.5	—	2,127.6	117.0	869.4	783.0	321.8	—	—	—	229.7
1881	3,672.8	—	1,959.3	74.3	552.1	756.5	210.6	—	—	—	120.0
1880	3,797.4	—	2,225.5	106.0	490.7	719.7	177.5	—	—	—	78.0
1879	3,825.0	—	2,188.1	154.1	505.1	750.9	151.7	—	—	—	75.1
1878	4,000.7	—	2,309.2	144.8	552.4	743.7	160.0	—	—	—	90.6

[1] For 1878 to 1906 and for 1917 to 1960, calendar years; for 1908 to 1917, fiscal years ending 31 March of the year given.
[2] The data shown under provinces do not add to that shown for Canada (series M49) owing to the inclusion of data for the Yukon and Northwest Territories in series M49 and to discrepancies in some years in the official statistics. Newfoundland is included beginning in 1952.

[3] Prior to 1894 these data are for Manitoba only; from 1894 to 1904 they include the Northwest Territories (Alberta and Saskatchewan); from 1905 to 1911 series M56 includes Keewatin.
[4] Data for this year include nets and weirs only; vessels and boats, included in other years, are not recorded for 1883.

Series M60–68. *Capital equipment employed in primary fishing operations, by province and by type of equipment, 1951*
(estimated market value in thousands of dollars)

Equipment	Canada	Newfound-land	Nova Scotia	Prince Edward Island	New Brunswick	Quebec	Ontario	Prairie Provinces and Northwest Territories	British Columbia
	60	**61**	**62**	**63**	**64**	**65**	**66**	**67**	**68**
Fishing craft	57,949	7,597	12,758	870	2,856	1,301	3,553	835	29,695
Gear	31,970	4,765	5,213	1,132	5,972	2,114	4,417	1,955	6,076
Shore equipment	13,881	2,767	1,817	457	903	609	2,533	1,887	2,702
Total	103,800	15,129	19,788	2,459	9,731	4,024	10,503	4,677	38,473

Series M69–78. *Market value of fisheries products, by major process forms, Canada, 1870 to 1960*
(thousands of dollars)

Year[1]	Total all forms	Fresh[3] Whole	Fresh[3] Filleted	Frozen[3] Whole	Frozen[3] Filleted	Canned	Cured Smoked	Cured Salted and pickled	Reduction products Oil	Reduction products Meal
	69	**70**	**71**	**72**	**73**	**74**	**75**	**76**	**77**	**78**
1960	198,005.1	51,267.4	11,444.4	15,478.1	42,080.8	41,750.3	1,811.6	23,190.7	2,561.8	4,323.4
1959	203,039.9	46,513.3	12,536.2	12,478.5	40,667.1	50,512.9	1,896.4	20,037.1	5,120.0	9,573.3
1958	231,540.6	50,064.2	12,656.9	16,373.2	37,228.6	71,596.9	2,090.1	22,284.3	5,881.2	9,895.3
1957	188,017.7	43,813.0	12,396.2	10,291.2	32,871.6	49,695.4	2,080.9	22,772.3	3,988.7	7,355.1
1956	196,577.1	47,695.3	12,310.9	15,286.4	30,947.3	45,554.1	2,053.5	22,190.5	6,218.3	11,077.5
1955[2]	184,166.8	43,325.7	12,839.2	10,699.8	30,379.7	41,494.3	2,909.6	24,670.0	4,806.1	8,771.8
1954	162,507.6	42,744.7	10,625.7	11,221.1	16,790.1	51,119.0	3,275.5	12,494.8	3,862.3	7,489.8
1953	149,332.4	40,017.9	11,384.6	12,515.5	12,561.4	46,297.9	2,779.8	12,477.8	3,176.2	6,006.1
1952	149,820.7	42,699.1	10,648.5	12,064.2	14,668.2	40,580.3	4,429.1	14,261.2	2,584.6	5,653.1
1951	175,893.5	42,361.8	10,216.4	14,674.3	12,541.1	61,133.2	4,217.1	13,343.5	6,899.6	7,451.9
1950	153,119.3	43,707.5	9,457.0	15,714.2	8,528.8	43,062.7	3,946.1	13,619.9	5,495.5	6,534.3
1949	132,306.5	31,841.2	7,702.1	12,106.2	6,407.7	37,228.1	3,616.4	16,249.2	6,561.4	7,621.5
1948	139,826.1	34,092.7	7,592.8	12,905.1	7,380.3	42,269.0	3,365.9	16,067.8	7,891.4	5,493.4
1947	123,900.2	28,804.2	6,027.6	12,497.7	4,547.2	47,038.6	3,088.1	11,697.3	4,799.8	2,766.7
1946	121,124.7	30,894.7	7,810.3	8,862.2	8,972.3	39,128.5	4,556.0	12,632.0	3,934.5	1,446.5
1945	113,871.1	34,702.7	8,463.1	6,730.8[3]	6,596.4	34,481.4	3,648.3	9,445.2	6,025.6	1,976.2
1944	89,439.5	29,585.1[3]	10,605.1[3]	—[3]	—[3]	26,049.7	2,409.1	10,017.5	7,419.2	1,921.0
1943	85,594.5	29,816.5	7,900.5	—	—	27,292.5	2,670.6	8,887.0	5,557.6	2,145.3
1942	75,116.9	21,368.3	5,543.1	—	—	31,948.6	1,918.4	6,630.2	4,326.0	2,286.4
1941	62,259.0	18,480.3	3,795.5	—	—	26,829.7	1,753.7	5,213.1	3,211.8	1,919.9
1940	45,118.9	15,685.6	3,237.5	—	—	17,873.4	1,279.3	3,021.3	1,199.3	1,980.8
1939	40,075.9	15,366.1	1,871.3	—	—	15,479.0	1,021.8	3,548.4	725.7	1,230.3
1938	40,493.0	14,971.2	1,983.2	—	—	16,297.6	1,038.3	3,375.9	849.6	1,151.4
1937	38,976.3	15,888.4	1,928.0	—	—	13,619.6	1,018.2	3,470.6	1,182.7	1,151.2
1936	39,165.1	14,787.0	1,896.7	—	—	15,564.5	997.9	3,451.3	816.5	1,026.0
1935	34,427.9	13,507.8	1,221.5	—	—	13,638.1	918.6	3,261.1	651.6	689.3
1934	34,022.3	11,755.7	1,134.9	—	—	14,208.1	882.8	4,234.3	504.0	662.6
1933	27,496.9	11,303.1	890.1	—	—	10,193.7	549.4	3,353.0	275.6	426.0
1932	25,957.1	11,021.0	778.9	—	—	9,789.3	633.2	2,447.9	259.6	565.8
1931	30,517.3	13,619.0	847.0	—	—	9,048.7	766.0	4,375.1	425.5	895.0
1930	47,804.2	18,106.6	1,256.0	—	—	18,444.1	1,240.9	5,847.9	1,108.2	1,093.8
1929	53,518.5	22,059.3	1,077.3	—	—	17,047.4	1,870.7	7,755.1	1,844.9	1,013.0
1928	55,051.0	21,192.7	894.2	—	—	18,445.0	1,708.8	8,689.3	2,121.3	1,236.8
1927	49,497.0	20,468.2	593.0	—	—	16,616.4	1,606.6	6,841.4	1,595.3	1,051.4
1926	56,360.6	21,401.9	220.8	—	—	21,641.7	2,280.1	8,188.3	1,215.4	607.1
1925	47,942.1	18,463.5	165.6	—	—	17,411.8	1,569.4	8,626.7	728.4	246.3
1924	44,534.2	19,908.0	83.5	—	—	14,154.4	1,242.7	7,987.0	470.7	91.5
1923	42,565.5	19,516.3	83.7	—	—	14,832.2	1,194.6	5,819.2	367.2	43.7
1922	41,800.2	16,718.0	61.2	—	—	15,418.1	1,079.0	7,628.5	236.0	49.3
1921	34,931.9	17,399.1	35.4	—	—	9,886.4	953.6	6,020.9	65.7	27.3
1920	49,241.3	17,725.2	28.8	—	—	19,755.1	1,901.7	8,503.7	645.5	15.1
1919	56,513.8	20,209.0	75.4	—	—	19,734.1	1,350.4	13,517.1	979.2	10.3
1918	60,250.5	22,074.4	67.3	—	—	18,779.8	1,556.4	15,424.1	1,698.7	24.6
1917	52,312.0	18,438.3	26.0	—	—	19,564.9	1,236.5	11,663.8	823.5	10.2
1917[1]	39,208.4	15,911.7	38.5	—	—	12,455.3	1,016.7	8,630.4	510.3	15.7
1916	35,860.7	15,222.3	18.0	—	—	11,380.1	847.4	7,514.7	371.4	5.8
1915	31,264.6	13,533.5	—	—	—	9,363.3	954.8	6,335.7	404.7	
1914	33,207.7	13,386.1	—	—	—	11,586.6	747.6	6,350.5	445.2	4.4
1913	33,389.5	13,274.2	—	—	—	11,039.8	675.2	7,084.2	632.5	16.0
1912	34,667.9	12,445.8	—	—	—	11,502.1	932.6	8,120.2	789.2	—
1911	29,965.4	10,170.8	—	—	—	8,154.8	747.6	9,378.3	326.6	—
1910	29,629.2	10,411.7	—	—	—	9,356.3	510.9	7,854.9	200.0	—
1909	25,451.1	8,819.1	—	—	—	7,003.7	387.0	7,726.1	252.2	—
1908	25,499.3	9,525.7	—	—	—	6,763.9	432.2	7,346.8	539.1	—
1906	26,279.5	10,208.3	—	—	—	6,464.3	610.5	7,589.2	253.5	—

Series M 69–78. *Market value of fisheries products, by major process forms, Canada, 1870 to 1960 (continued)*
(thousands of dollars)

Year[1]	Total all forms	Fresh Whole	Fresh Filleted	Frozen Whole	Frozen Filleted	Canned	Cured Smoked	Cured Salted and pickled	Reduction products Oil	Reduction products Meal
	69	70	71	72	73	74	75	76	77	78
1905	29,479.6	10,317.0	—	—	—	9,431.6	588.5	7,683.5	259.5	—
1904	23,516.4	9,032.4	—	—	—	5,076.7	562.6	7,404.4	209.3	—
1903	23,101.9	8,690.5	—	—	—	5,162.5	447.7	7,269.0	225.6	—
1902	21,959.4	8,331.4	—	—	—	4,979.9	455.2	6,750.0	230.4	—
1901	25,737.2	8,131.7	—	—	—	8,099.7	512.8	7,405.1	226.7	—
1900	21,557.6	7,141.6	—	—	—	5,139.8	320.6	7,225.5	208.8	—
1899	21,891.7	7,375.2	—	—	—	5,808.5	417.0	6,705.3	235.0	—
1898	19,667.1	7,670.2	—	—	—	4,621.4	377.3	5,685.7	199.8	—
1897	22,783.5	7,368.5	—	—	—	7,196.0	266.3	6,689.3	162.5	—
1896	20,407.4	6,731.2	—	—	—	4,544.0	305.4	7,287.1	224.6	—
1895	20,199.3	6,395.0	—	—	—	4,599.1	234.2	7,262.5	248.2	—
1894	20,719.6	6,765.0	—	—	—	4,180.0	192.3	7,628.7	298.3	—
1893	20,686.7	6,838.3	—	—	—	4,853.5	119.5	7,024.8	321.9	—
1892	18,941.2	6,865.9	—	—	—	3,136.0	329.7	6,895.8	359.9	—
1891	18,977.9	5,618.4	—	—	—	3,542.3	623.2	7,392.2	358.7	—
1890	17,714.9	5,745.2	—	—	—	3,811.9	353.0	6,305.3	315.0	—
1889	17,655.3	5,817.3	—	—	—	3,717.5	672.6	6,005.6	407.8	—
1888	17,418.5	6,345.3	—	—	—	2,325.8	379.4	7,129.4	390.7	—
1887	18,386.1	6,302.9	—	—	—	2,662.9	405.4	7,777.2	405.2	—
1886	18,679.3	5,621.4	—	—	—	3,281.4	291.4	7,961.6	507.6	—
1885	17,723.6	4,521.5	—	—	—	3,077.5	410.6	8,498.5	491.5	—
1884	17,766.4	4,452.9	—	—	—	3,071.3	542.4	8,509.6	477.4	—
1883	16,958.2	4,338.4	—	—	—	3,072.4	375.9	7,904.3	665.8	—
1882	16,824.1	4,089.9	—	—	—	4,280.4	324.6	6,976.7	630.1	—
1881	15,817.2	2,742.5	—	—	—	4,064.0	296.7	7,463.4	669.5	—
1880	14,500.0	—	—	—	—	—	—	—	—	—
1879	13,529.3	—	—	—	—	—	—	—	—	—
1878	13,215.7	—	—	—	—	—	—	—	—	—
1877	12,005.9	—	—	—	—	—	—	—	—	—
1876	11,117.0	—	—	—	—	—	—	—	—	—
1875	10,350.4	—	—	—	—	—	—	—	—	—
1874	11,681.9	—	—	—	—	—	—	—	—	—
1873	10,755.0	—	—	—	—	—	—	—	—	—
1872	9,570.1	—	—	—	—	—	—	—	—	—
1871	7,573.2	—	—	—	—	—	—	—	—	—
1870	6,577.4	—	—	—	—	—	—	—	—	—

[1] For 1870 to 1906 and for 1917 to 1960, calendar years; for 1908 to 1917, fiscal years ending 31 March of the year given.
[2] Newfoundland included beginning in 1955.
[3] For 1944 and previous frozen whole and frozen filleted, series M72 and M73 are included with fresh whole and fresh filleted, series M70 and M71 respectively.

Series M 79–84. *Fish processing plant inputs, 1917 to 1960*
(thousands of dollars)

Year[1]	East coast[1] Salaries and wages paid	East coast[1] Materials used	East coast[1] Fuel and electricity used	West coast Salaries and wages paid	West coast Materials used	West coast Fuel and electricity used	Year[1]	East coast[1] Salaries and wages paid	East coast[1] Materials used	East coast[1] Fuel and electricity used	West coast Salaries and wages paid	West coast Materials used	West coast Fuel and electricity used
	79	80	81	82	83	84		79	80	81	82	83	84
1960	22,226.3	85,756.8	2,211.7	9,619.6	38,340.7	706.3	1935	1,463.9	5,832.0	154.6	2,090.0	8,940.7	190.4
1959	19,672.7	82,053.1	2,072.4	10,420.7	47,729.2	1,093.5	1934	1,420.7	5,979.3	134.1	2,134.4	9,587.9	189.5
1958	18,879.1	73,694.6	1,941.5	11,406.5	68,281.6	1,124.0	1933	1,198.5	4,252.0	120.5	1,825.6	6,708.3	143.7
1957	18,392.2	71,690.7	2,170.5	10,817.2	43,425.2	962.6	1932	1,312.4	4,989.3	133.9	1,509.5	5,274.3	140.8
1956	18,476.1	70,955.0	2,053.6	10,458.4	49,535.4	959.8	1931	1,608.1	6,387.4	163.5	1,574.8	5,533.4	149.6
1955	16,527.0	61,215.4	1,832.7	9,793.4	40,705.7	830.4	1930	1,854.1	7,928.9	168.2	3,472.3	13,152.6	281.0
1954	15,138.8	52,969.3	1,669.0	10,862.3	42,663.4	935.6	1929	1,923.3	8,675.9	201.4	3,488.6	12,820.9	270.2
1953	13,772.5	46,426.0	1,574.7	9,319.9	39,481.7	835.8	1928	1,772.7	7,670.6	208.1	3,488.4	12,908.2	286.8
1952	14,360.2	51,294.7	1,697.0	10,066.1	35,163.2	835.7	1927	1,648.6	6,995.5	186.9	3,725.3	11,369.4	278.4
1951[1]	13,395.7	49,974.8	1,792.2	11,348.5	51,646.3	931.9	1926	1,748.9	7,829.7	185.9	3,873.9	14,204.4	290.8
1950	9,277.7	40,662.4	968.4	9,444.5	39,296.8	804.6	1925	1,619.6	7,044.4	172.6	3,351.5	11,636.3	239.4
1949	8,684.6	36,489.6	968.7	8,285.2	32,600.4	762.4	1924	1,443.1	5,938.9	141.3	2,791.6	10,150.4	259.1
1948	9,021.2	39,343.5	1,100.3	8,020.2	35,244.2	681.9	1923	1,448.1	6,560.0	168.5	2,321.8	8,771.2	197.7
1947	7,949.3	32,087.7	823.2	7,911.5	30,692.7	588.1	1922	1,489.0	6,843.7	193.7	2,152.7	8,734.9	227.4
1946	7,996.1	40,179.9	642.6	6,748.9	27,832.9	461.1	1921	1,330.5	5,279.6	197.9	1,639.4	6,409.9	214.1
1945	6,332.2	34,443.3	538.0	5,634.9	27,621.0	435.8	1920	1,866.0	8,906.1	227.9	2,988.1	10,441.7	353.2
1944	5,406.4	24,504.5	481.7	5,664.4	21,402.0	427.8	1919	1,658.3	8,423.9	184.9	2,597.3	10,895.6	299.1
1943	4,604.5	22,367.2	403.8	5,435.2	20,999.6	446.3	1918	1,676.2	9,424.7	166.0	2,952.7	12,082.6	391.1
1942	3,483.6	14,261.2	297.5	4,907.1	23,485.2	463.2	1917	1,876.2	—	177.3	1,746.9	—	202.1
1941	2,729.3	10,176.4	262.0	4,008.4	19,936.4	378.2							
1940	2,233.1	8,184.2	201.0	3,173.7	13,277.6	284.1							
1939	1,916.1	7,092.2	168.1	2,431.3	11,022.5	222.4							
1938	1,762.2	6,632.9	177.3	2,465.8	10,449.2	230.3							
1937	1,774.4	6,858.9	157.9	2,268.2	9,459.8	239.4							
1936	1,601.1	6,665.9	138.6	2,402.7	9,794.0	248.6							

[1] Newfoundland included beginning in 1951.

Series M 85–88. *Number of persons employed in fish processing plants, by area and by sex, 1895 to 1960*

Year[1]	East coast[2]		West coast		Year[1]	East coast[2]		West coast	
	Male	Female	Male	Female		Male	Female	Male	Female
	85	86	87	88		85	86	87	88
1960	8,609	3,187	1,718	954	1925	4,681	4,153	4,910	2,528
1959	8,183	2,965	2,007	1,006	1924	4,579	4,051	4,956	1,950
1958	8,205	3,007	1,989	1,071	1923	4,845	4,479	4,173	1,950
1957	8,006	2,943	2,194	1,064	1922	5,621	4,638	4,194	2,124
1956	8,618	3,215	2,346	1,072	1921	4,905	4,141	3,232	1,819
1955	7,926	3,285	2,357	1,058	1920	6,637	4,645	5,073	2,139
1954	7,377	2,879	2,848	1,098	1919	6,171	4,242	5,379	2,559
1953	7,560	2,779	2,275	1,127	1918	5,717	3,857	6,149	2,769
1952	9,027	4,475	2,579	1,470	1917	6,442	3,916	5,971	1,653
1951	9,295[2]	4,807[2]	3,051	1,553	1917[1]	18,496		6,798	
					1916	20,464		6,510	
1950	7,010	3,944	2,812	1,095					
1949	7,388	4,479	3,029	1,191	1915	17,137		7,096	
1948	7,511	4,806	2,818	1,362	1914	17,199		9,391	
1947	7,218	4,191	3,283	1,766	1913	16,190		6,881	
1946	8,191	5,126	3,263	2,816	1912	17,809		6,559	
					1911	16,053		8,525	
1945	6,850	4,613	3,110	2,928					
1944	6,366	4,756	3,462	2,688	1910	12,805		8,689	
1943	5,775	4,113	3,190	2,821	1909	13,353		—	
1942	5,183	3,578	3,410	3,546	1908[1]	11,441[3]		—	
1941	4,751	3,177	3,997	3,917	1906	12,317		—	
1940	4,450	3,151	4,332	3,111	1905	14,037		—	
1939	4,520	4,023	3,824	2,447	1904	13,981		—	
1938	4,451	3,930	3,445	2,658	1903	14,018		—	
1937	4,545	3,916	3,229	2,354	1902	13,563		—	
1936	4,714	3,928	3,859	2,737	1901	15,315		—	
1935	4,365	3,931	3,566	2,499	1900	18,205		—	
1934	4,634	3,942	3,714	2,512	1899	18,708		—	
1933	4,331	3,921	3,523	2,267	1898	16,548		—	
1932	4,644	4,374	2,789	1,917	1897	15,165		—	
1931	4,679	3,947	2,828	1,617	1896	14,175		—	
1930	4,584	3,791	4,729	2,618	1895	13,030		—	
1929	4,701	3,906	5,375	2,385					
1928	4,540	3,718	5,090	2,086					
1927	4,605	3,846	5,725	2,521					
1926	4,854	4,118	5,908	2,528					

[1] For 1895 to 1906 and for 1917 to 1960 calendar years; for 1908 to 1917 fiscal years ending 31 March of the year given.

[2] Newfoundland included in series M 85 and M 86 beginning in 1951.

[3] Only those employed in lobster canneries included from 1895 to 1908.

Series M89–102. *Number of fish processing establishments by area and by value of output, 1919 to 1960*

Year[1]	East coast							West coast						
	Establishments having production valued at							Establishments having production valued at						
	Under $10,000	$10,000–$19,999	$20,000–$49,999	$50,000–$199,999	$200,000–$999,999	$1,000,000 and under $5,000,000	$5,000,000 and over	Under $10,000	$10,000–$19,999	$20,000–$49,999	$50,000–$199,999–	$200,000–$999,999	$1,000,000 and under $5,000,000	$5,000,000 and over
	89	90	91	92	93	94	95	96	97	98	99	100	101	102
1960	60	45	77	161	111	24	—	1	3	5	7	24	12	3
1959	71	32	81	173	104	20	1	1	3	3	8	19	17	4[3]
1958	88	26	84	174	96	23	—	1	4	4	10	18	15	5
1957	86	27	66	172	95	21	—	2	2	6	8	21	15	2
1956	105	41	69	199	90	21	—	2	5	6	6	27	13	4
1955	107	53	89	157	66	20	—	8	5	9	9	21	18	2
1954	119	58	96	158	62	19	—	5	5	16	16	19	19	2
1953	111	68	102	155	70	12	—	3	6	17	13	22	14	3
1952	106	67	134	164	73	12	—	2	7	11	21	22	14	1
1951[1]	130	65	142	153	65	16	—	9	—	7	12	18	20	3
1950	118	58	129	161	45	11	—	3	2	7	13	23	17	3
1949	116	70	140	151	45	9	—	3	1	7	8	29	17	1
1948	114	67	150	151	45	10	—	1	2	5	9	28	16	1
1947	109	94	142	128	42	9	—	3	4	3	14	28	17	1
1946	86	75	145	149	50	8	—	2	2	7	19	31	11	1
1945	84	73	122	146	36	8	—	2	2	5	15	39	9	—
1944	104	81	140	112	18	7	—	2	—	4	20	37	9	—
1943	102	92	131	104	20	5	—	1	—	3	20	38	7	—
1942	146	93	105	69	10	4	—	1	1	5	15	33	9	1
1941	179	89	78	34	8	4	—	2	1	7	18	35	8	—
1940	225	64	56	25	8	2	—	6	—	—	24	34	3	—
1939	293	86	51	17	7	2	—	6	3	—	20	25	4	—
1938	326	92	45		23[2]			6	4	7		58[2]		
1937	347	81	61		23			9	12	10		54		
1936	363	91	53		26			9	9	16		57		
1935	377	95	48		19			12	7	14		58		
1934	392	99	55		20			14	6	17		62		
1933	399	68	41		16			19	6	18		53		
1932	360	102	57		21			14	9	17		49		
1931	372	105	53		33			7	10	29		53		
1930	344	118	69		40			10	10	20		88		
1929	339	128	79		45			9	6	31		93		
1928	350	116	74		37			6	10	17		103		
1927	396	109	81		38			11	10	24		104		
1926	431	138	65		39			25	6	31		96		
1925	457	151	64		29			27	9	22		87		
1924	519	108	44		31			23	13	21		73		
1923	550	161	71		27			23	21	12		73		
1922	513	160	79		32			38	21	21		69		
1921	552	90	61		33			21	8	14		60		
1920	515	161	116		39			11	14	10		72		
1919	509	162	98		53			9	5	11		79		

[1] Newfoundland plants included beginning in 1951.
[2] Establishments having production valued at $50,000 or over.
[3] Includes one head office with no value.

Series M103–109. *Value of exports of fish and fish products, by region, 1868 to 1960*

(thousands of dollars)

Year[1,2]	Total exports	United Kingdom	Other Europe	Continental South America	Central America and Caribbean	United States and possessions	Other
	103	104	105	106	107	108	109
1960	138,130.3	11,524.7	6,481.8	1,295.4	12,214.6	102,472.4	4,123.4
1959	147,815.6	22,363.1	6,345.2	1,677.7	13,053.8	101,467.6	2,908.2
1958	154,468.5	25,452.5	6,170.9	1,418.9	11,425.4	106,825.8	3,175.0
1957	132,453.7	7,731.3	5,610.3	1,456.6	12,743.9	100,925.7	3,985.9
1956	133,706.8	8,799.5	6,500.5	1,003.0	13,309.4	99,991.2	4,103.2
1955	128,843.8	5,783.4	9,062.2	1,201.8	11,666.4	96,444.9	4,685.1
1954[2]	132,641.9	12,005.2	9,246.7	2,768.2	12,273.9	93,031.1	3,316.8
1953	114,375.5	5,249.0	8,442.7	791.1	11,085.9	87,140.6	1,666.2
1952	116,754.1	1,311.7	7,782.3	1,118.3	11,762.2	92,265.8	2,513.8
1951	123,044.9	8,077.5	10,828.2	1,601.9	10,127.1	89,530.4	2,879.8
1950	117,784.9	5,050.5	14,490.1	1,247.4	9,647.3	85,363.2	1,986.4
1949	99,530.2	8,081.4	8,185.2	2,051.4	9,950.9	69,048.4	2,212.9
1948	89,697.0	1,829.6	9,824.5	1,299.2	6,942.2	62,784.9	7,016.6
1947	83,811.2	6,760.1	10,718.8	1,517.9	6,187.0	46,691.7	11,935.7
1946	88,679.1	13,321.2	12,633.8	879.1	4,036.0	53,739.5	4,069.5
1945	84,800.6	13,794.4	4,537.9	574.5	3,669.6	54,098.0	8,126.2
1944	68,642.6	18,331.5	310.0	497.4	3,638.8	42,829.9	3,035.0
1943	60,313.1	17,677.7	198.6	365.4	2,543.8	37,466.8	2,060.8
1942	51,907.3	19,855.2	2.8	561.4	2,302.2	27,652.0	1,533.7
1941	42,963.5	15,348.9	47.3	622.0	2,727.3	21,655.2	2,562.8
1940	32,662.0	9,883.7	302.1	284.2	1,474.0	16,963.2	3,754.8
1939	29,641.2	8,718.2	1,524.3	267.2	1,387.1	13,964.1	3,780.3
1938	27,543.7	6,880.7	2,000.9	352.4	1,420.4	12,917.1	3,972.2
1937	28,902.2	6,721.8	1,962.3	336.9	1,463.4	14,229.3	4,188.5
1936	25,398.1	5,781.7	1,589.0	208.8	1,184.1	13,035.6	3,598.9
1935	24,859.5	6,759.5	1,725.5	217.1	1,389.0	10,656.9	4,111.5
1934	22,497.1	5,542.3	2,646.4	161.3	1,508.2	9,538.6	3,100.3
1933	20,223.6	4,384.0	2,878.2	165.6	1,087.5	9,037.5	2,670.8
1932	18,752.1	4,220.6	1,821.9	159.7	1,207.3	8,942.5	2,400.1
1931[1]	25,848.6	5,707.9	2,753.8	259.2	1,710.1	11,919.8	3,497.8
1931[1]	29,694.0	5,181.4	3,805.1	516.0	2,368.1	14,249.7	3,573.7
1930	37,185.2	4,178.0	5,254.1	952.3	3,241.5	17,101.7	6,457.6
1929	37,962.9	3,780.5	5,831.7	1,037.4	3,011.8	17,845.0	6,456.5
1928	35,660.3	5,448.2	4,691.8	1,055.6	2,981.9	15,742.7	5,740.1
1927	36,365.5	5,613.2	4,428.3	894.2	2,992.8	16,386.0	6,051.0
1926	37,487.5	7,264.5	4,750.4	1,069.7	3,112.2	14,929.3	6,361.4
1925	33,967.0	6,709.9	4,496.8	831.5	2,875.0	14,541.6	4,512.2
1924	30,925.8	5,801.1	4,041.3	701.4	2,187.3	14,195.0	3,999.7
1923	27,816.9	3,757.4	4,153.5	964.6	2,286.9	14,169.1	2,485.4
1922	29,578.4	5,593.2	3,941.8	1,109.2	2,712.1	13,816.3	2,405.8
1921	33,615.1	7,703.4	1,613.9	1,782.9	3,122.9	16,928.9	2,463.1
1920	42,228.0	9,890.8	3,455.2	2,277.3	4,285.9	19,871.0	2,447.8
1919	37,137.1	8,634.3	1,790.0	1,009.2	3,890.3	19,571.8	2,241.5
1918	32,602.2	6,746.0	4,001.4	768.4	2,767.5	16,853.3	1,465.6
1917	24,889.3	7,316.8	1,671.3	969.6	2,289.1	11,400.6	1,241.9
1916	22,378.0	6,731.8	1,695.5	1,206.4	1,857.3	9,503.1	1,383.9
1915	19,687.1	5,448.9	1,600.2	604.7	1,579.4	8,993.8	1,460.1
1914	20,623.6	7,008.9	2,054.0	848.8	1,818.3	7,392.3	1,501.3
1913	16,336.7	3,946.5	1,808.9	1,041.3	1,875.7	6,325.8	1,338.5
1912	16,704.7	5,132.0	1,593.7	917.2	1,950.5	6,030.9	1,080.4
1911	15,675.5	4,435.9	1,525.6	1,171.2	2,048.1	5,484.0	1,010.7
1910	15,663.2	5,136.2	1,629.2	1,009.0	1,666.4	5,096.3	1,126.1
1909	13,319.7	3,579.6	1,513.3	797.5	1,657.0	4,740.2	1,032.1
1908	13,867.4	3,502.6	1,459.2	1,099.8	1,742.3	5,211.7	851.8
1907[1]	10,362.1	2,411.1	1,089.8	860.6	1,396.9	3,868.7	735.0
1906[1]	16,025.8	6,139.6	1,362.3	917.8	1,739.0	5,318.7	548.4
1905	11,114.3	2,524.5	1,031.3	606.6	1,408.4	4,954.9	588.6
1904	10,759.0	3,084.9	1,053.3	513.6	1,186.0	4,600.8	320.4
1903	11,800.2	3,904.8	1,194.4	880.0	1,333.8	4,164.2	323.0
1902	14,143.3	6,374.9	756.2	724.1	1,246.7	4,606.1	435.3
1901	10,720.4	3,113.3	860.0	665.7	1,263.2	4,497.9	320.3
1900	11,169.1	4,071.1	798.0	675.3	1,317.2	4,049.8	257.7
1899	9,009.7	3,611.0	734.2	557.2	1,705.4	3,183.7	118.2
1898	10,841.7	4,822.7	535.5	628.3	1,685.5	2,979.6	190.1
1897	10,314.3	4,366.1	462.2	517.9	1,886.6	2,999.3	82.2
1896	11,077.8	4,462.0	344.3	772.9	2,134.7	3,303.2	60.7
1895	10,692.2	4,144.0	209.6	796.0	2,423.6	3,027.0	92.0
1894	11,102.7	4,586.7	323.9	681.9	2,096.9	3,260.7	152.6
1893	8,743.0	2,347.1	278.7	568.9	1,997.2	3,504.2	46.9
1892	9,675.4	3,006.8	366.2	482.2	2,268.9	3,452.0	99.3
1891	9,715.4	2,747.9	284.7	542.6	2,082.2	3,807.8	250.2
1890	8,461.9	2,707.4	327.1	481.2	2,000.9	2,850.5	94.8
1889	7,212.2	1,249.9	352.5	488.2	2,093.4	2,840.0	188.2
1888	7,793.2	1,544.9	375.2	456.2	2,116.1	3,123.9	176.9
1887	6,875.8	1,704.2	301.7	539.3	1,527.4	2,717.5	85.7
1886	6,843.4	1,586.8	531.7	442.1	1,645.1	2,587.5	50.2
1885	7,960.0	1,543.0	300.1	393.1	2,040.3	3,560.7	122.8
1884	8,591.7	1,621.8	393.1	462.2	2,454.4	3,598.2	62.0
1883	8,809.1	2,337.1	297.4	547.2	2,361.7	3,189.7	76.0
1882	7,682.1	2,130.0	265.3	568.9	2,222.5	2,441.2	54.2
1881	6,867.7	1,562.8	217.7	577.1	2,257.1	2,241.6	11.4
1880	6,579.7	1,154.2	279.0	588.1	2,759.4	1,738.9	60.1
1879	6,928.9	1,494.8	302.2	515.4	2,644.7	1,899.2	72.6
1878	6,854.0	1,043.5	235.9	507.3	2,555.8	2,367.0	144.5
1877	5,874.4	808.3	310.6	506.7	2,827.1	1,317.9	103.8
1876	5,501.0	687.1	196.9	488.3	2,557.6	1,475.3	95.8
1875	5,380.5	652.9	196.4	210.4	2,615.3	1,644.8	60.7
1874	5,292.4	700.8	316.2	437.7	2,159.3	1,616.7	61.7
1873	4,779.3	483.2	—	—	—	—	—
1872	4,386.2	379.9	—	—	—	—	—
1871	3,994.3	348.6	—	—	—	—	—
1870	3,608.5	321.0	—	—	—	—	—
1869	3,242.7	236.2	—	—	—	—	—
1868	3,357.5	226.9	—	—	—	—	—

[1] From 1868 to 1906 fiscal years ending 30 June of the year given; nine months ending 31 March 1907; for 1908 to 1931 fiscal years ending 31 March of the year given; for 1931 to 1960 calendar years.

[2] Newfoundland exports included beginning 1954.

Series M 110–120. *Value of exports of fish and fish products, by major species, 1871 to 1960*

(thousands of dollars)

Year[1]	Groundfish	Halibut	Herring and pilchards	Sardines and anchovies	Salmon	Whitefish	Lobster Fresh	Lobster Canned	All other shellfish	Oil and meal[2]	All other
	110	111	112	113	114	115	116	117	118	119	120
1960	45,189.8	6,536.1	4,049.5	3,523.2	20,348.4	7,083.2	17,702.3	2,453.0	3,112.3	5,846.5	22,286.0
1959	44,074.8	6,114.9	3,892.9	2,952.7	30,950.4	6,317.5	17,258.8	1,925.2	2,046.6	9,051.9	23,229.9
1958	45,848.5	6,253.9	3,661.7	2,797.7	41,322.7	6,471.7	15,589.9	1,821.5	1,807.7	5,167.9	23,725.3
1957	45,442.4	5,329.7	3,854.0	2,275.9	18,047.2	6,235.9	16,413.8	2,062.6	1,935.6	7,120.7	23,735.9
1956	42,420.4	4,594.6	3,633.6	2,117.1	21,444.4	5,927.6	16,845.7	2,072.9	1,629.8	9,834.2	23,186.5
1955	42,440.7	3,579.9	3,352.7	1,666.4	23,006.8	5,835.8	16,713.5	1,842.9	1,686.2	7,878.9	20,840.0
1954[3]	39,867.4	4,703.5	3,989.8	1,585.2	32,493.4	5,973.1	13,696.7	1,920.7	1,700.7	6,379.5	20,331.9
1953	35,360.8	3,886.1	3,937.4	1,404.7	23,177.5	6,209.2	13,769.1	1,966.7	1,849.6	4,283.7	18,530.7
1952	37,084.3	4,197.5	4,876.9	3,069.5	17,678.6	6,428.5	14,104.1	2,352.2	1,048.0	7,132.4	18,782.1
1951	38,515.0	4,228.3	5,304.3	1,766.8	20,802.0	6,357.4	11,798.1	2,214.2	1,196.1	11,085.3	19,777.4
1950	34,173.5	5,024.7	4,642.2	1,544.7	22,920.9	5,672.1	11,533.1	2,906.0	1,267.8	9,561.2	18,538.7
1949	26,413.6	2,994.9	4,696.1	1,959.4	18,314.4	4,985.1	10,115.6	2,353.2	1,001.1	10,915.8	15,781.0
1948	16,834.6	3,148.1	10,985.3	2,828.0	17,245.2	3,983.1	9,182.0	2,381.6	808.2	7,829.3	14,471.6
1947	12,964.9	3,464.4	17,193.8	3,869.8	16,835.0	2,904.0	7,627.1	2,437.9	907.0	1,451.9	14,155.4
1946	18,080.8	1,055.5	17,397.9	1,038.5	16,432.9	3,584.8	9,572.4	3,781.1	808.8	2,192.0	14,734.4
1945	18,196.4	1,606.7	12,303.6	361.9	13,639.8	3,587.2	9,518.0	2,689.6	804.3	4,652.7	17,440.4
1944	13,815.8	807.2	10,004.7	268.6	12,901.2	3,496.3	5,786.8	3,146.9	502.1	5,272.9	12,640.1
1943	8,954.2	1,584.8	9,574.1	50.9	13,924.1	3,403.9	4,331.1	2,242.7	349.7	3,191.5	12,706.1
1942	8,215.0	592.0	7,950.2	529.6	15,658.4	2,680.2	3,004.6	929.0	348.8	3,697.3	8,302.2
1941	5,848.2	729.6	6,266.9	1,114.2	13,377.8	2,215.5	2,463.4	739.3	273.3	3,114.9	6,820.4
1940	5,039.2	680.0	2,796.7	953.5	9,953.8	2,031.9	2,016.6	715.4	130.9	2,480.3	5,863.8
1939	3,288.9	1,203.1	1,916.6	724.6	10,772.4	1,444.3	2,011.2	1,431.3	100.0	1,543.3	5,205.5
1938	2,673.3	910.2	1,214.8	629.0	9,477.8	1,514.9	1,952.7	1,898.8	175.7	1,774.2	5,322.3
1937	2,865.0	679.7	1,168.4	693.9	9,945.8	1,605.9	2,438.4	1,984.2	307.6	1,729.8	5,483.5
1936	2,862.0	595.3	1,204.5	471.8	8,406.5	1,458.8	2,100.8	2,080.0	304.5	1,040.1	4,873.8
1935	2,834.5	486.0	1,261.0	448.2	9,460.5	1,260.4	1,641.3	2,274.8	238.4	601.0	4,353.4
1934	3,130.6	393.0	1,065.0	383.1	7,747.4	977.1	1,550.4	2,499.4	154.3	820.8	3,775.7
1933	2,719.9	338.9	1,071.6	226.8	6,871.0	988.4	1,605.9	2,450.9	166.6	444.1	3,339.5
1932	2,455.2	111.2	852.8	182.8	5,675.2	854.1	1,854.4	2,469.5	129.9	758.0	3,409.0
1931	3,742.6	391.6	1,834.2	291.7	7,994.7	1,003.8	1,875.8	3,113.4	159.2	1,074.9	4,366.7
1930	5,695.4	464.9	2,508.2	412.8	8,819.0	1,215.1	2,279.2	3,234.9	264.8	1,678.4	5,296.7
1929	6,519.4	667.5	3,059.3	578.0	10,848.6	1,518.7	2,266.0	3,113.6	345.3	2,294.8	6,335.2
1928	6,637.4	508.3	3,342.8	536.8	11,566.4	1,401.8	1,514.7	3,107.3	325.3	2,663.1	6,492.3
1927	5,626.7	445.3	3,640.2	396.3	10,805.1	1,332.3	1,485.4	3,236.3	320.1	938.0[2]	6,588.7
1926	6,715.3	581.2	3,776.2	—	11,568.3	1,455.5	1,349.7	3,607.1	316.0	1,052.6	6,667.6
1926[1]	6,843.7	430.9	3,972.7	—	12,808.8	1,374.9	1,255.9	4,037.3	248.2	609.4	5,905.7
1925	6,033.1	592.8	3,375.4	—	12,598.3	1,170.5	1,269.7	2,820.3	250.0	599.4	5,257.5
1924	5,002.1	520.2	3,334.6	—	9,500.0	1,147.4	1,320.7	4,467.6	189.8	319.5	5,123.9
1923	6,196.4	753.7	2,262.3	—	6,248.5	1,111.1	1,041.7	4,807.7	135.3	234.7	5,025.5
1922	7,247.2	855.0	2,221.6	—	7,886.9	1,150.5	1,403.3	3,756.4	120.3	140.9	4,796.3
1921	7,504.3	913.1	3,478.9	—	8,665.7	1,330.7	1,033.7	5,179.6	115.3	251.0	5,142.8
1920	11,502.4	476.1	3,748.4	—	13,769.6	1,060.4	848.4	4,083.7	109.9	1,240.4	5,388.7
1919	11,397.5	629.2	3,799.1	—	11,538.0	1,078.0	789.0	2,230.1	5.4	712.1	4,958.7
1918	9,266.0	628.3	2,974.3	—	9,684.7	—	855.5	3,325.1	10.4	800.3	5,057.6
1917	6,856.1	441.5	1,707.6	—	7,118.9	—	1,037.8	3,639.3	3.5	454.1	3,630.5
1916	6,122.2	549.7	1,381.1	—	7,137.1	—	934.5	2,672.2	3.4	375.9	3,201.9
1915	4,661.6	454.2	1,523.1	—	5,696.7	—	849.4	3,013.8	6.9	348.6	3,132.8
1914	4,742.1	282.3	1,028.3	—	7,417.3	—	707.5	2,984.0	4.1	447.8	3,010.2
1913	4,416.6	147.3	908.5	—	4,028.0	—	629.0	3,048.8	6.5	628.1	2,523.9
1912	4,270.7	130.0	858.2	—	4,312.5	—	566.9	3,080.6	5.8	1,076.3	2,403.7
1911	4,389.2	139.1	682.5	—	4,091.9	—	529.4	2,735.9	2.3	455.7	2,649.5
1910	3,619.9	84.2	1,073.5	—	4,887.6	—	528.3	2,619.2	2.8	386.4	2,461.3
1909	3,348.2	136.7	988.0	—	3,002.3	—	463.4	2,755.0	1.8	441.4	2,182.9
1908	3,714.7	107.2	652.6	—	3,438.1	—	480.7	2,651.5	3.8	259.4	2,559.4
1907	3,101.6	58.1	624.2	—	2,550.6	—	163.5	1,368.9	3.5	152.5	2,339.2
1906[1]	3,548.0	35.4	615.6	—	5,707.3	—	497.5	3,010.2	2.1	111.9	2,497.8
1905	2,955.0	75.2	571.8	—	2,111.2	—	376.3	2,754.6	1.8	43.3	2,225.1
1904	2,793.7	77.1	517.7	—	2,031.4	—	384.5	2,519.8	1.4	46.6	2,386.4
1903	3,389.7	32.9	445.6	—	2,984.7	—	398.3	2,591.6	2.3	53.6	1,901.5
1902	3,201.5	55.6	528.9	—	5,397.3	—	365.2	2,149.4	2.9	80.6	2,361.9
1901	2,807.3	34.1	411.8	—	3,151.1	—	301.4	2,283.9	4.0	49.7	1,677.1
1900	2,311.4	42.5	344.0	—	3,057.6	—	305.5	2,372.9	1.8	51.0	2,682.4
1899	2,724.1	39.0	312.0	—	2,584.2	—	367.6	2,320.1	1.6	46.9	1,514.2
1898	2,595.0	63.3	356.3	—	3,624.2	—	336.7	2,290.9	2.2	35.1	1,538.0
1897	2,706.8	104.1	365.6	—	3,107.9	—	330.8	2,075.2	2.0	49.9	1,572.0
1896	3,082.4	84.7	438.2	—	2,802.1	—	340.9	2,146.3	2.3	32.9	2,148.0
1895	3,332.8	102.7	474.7	—	2,181.8	—	306.8	1,829.0	1.6	41.0	2,421.8
1894	3,162.8	60.9	481.9	—	2,597.8	—	258.3	2,073.3	1.6	24.0	2,442.1
1893	3,024.9	33.0	503.2	—	1,037.9	—	291.0	1,780.3	1.5	65.5	2,005.7
1892	3,180.7	34.0	489.1	—	1,414.6	—	254.7	1,655.1	1.9	53.6	2,591.7
1891	3,131.1	22.6	547.6	—	1,919.8	—	179.4	1,750.8	1.2	18.3	2,144.6
1890	3,028.5	14.9	472.1	—	2,230.6	—	140.6	997.7	1.2	41.2	1,535.1
1889	3,104.7	14.4	541.0	—	931.3	—	110.8	1,095.8	1.4	55.4	1,357.4
1888	3,132.8	11.1	615.3	—	1,154.6	—	109.0	1,220.5	1.6	41.2	1,507.1
1887	2,550.5	11.4	440.5	—	793.2	—	80.8	1,379.2	1.5	27.0	1,591.7
1886	2,741.6	13.3	306.9	—	682.8	—	81.8	1,663.0	6.3	63.7	1,284.0

Series M110–120. *Value of exports of fish and fish products, by major species, 1871 to 1960 (continued)*

(thousands of dollars)

Year[1]	Groundfish	Halibut	Herring and pilchards	Sardines and anchovies	Salmon	Whitefish	Lobster Fresh	Lobster Canned	All other shellfish	Oil and meal[2]	All other
	110	111	112	113	114	115	116	117	118	119	120
1885	3,158.6	7.6	630.4	—	808.9	—	52.5	1,653.2	1.8	117.2	1,529.8
1884	3,839.0	12.8	712.5	—	1,023.9	—	40.9	1,145.6	1.1	153.6	1,661.4
1883	3,788.9	12.3	702.0	—	1,421.8	—	31.4	1,478.9	.9	157.2	1,215.7
1882	3,427.6	7.0	567.7	—	1,113.4	—	14.4	1,431.7	1.1	161.3	957.9
1881	3,180.0	4.1	463.8	—	470.5	—	1.3	1,347.9	1.0	120.5	1,278.6
1880	3,564.0	1.0	456.0	—	547.0	—	.8	918.0	.6	118.5	973.8
1879	3,197.1	.1	447.0	—	926.5	—	.6	1,104.0	2.6	131.3	1,119.7
1878	3,192.2	.1	486.3	—	759.9	—	.7	926.6	1.1	131.6	1,355.5
1877	3,390.0	.7	606.8	—	271.4	—	—	669.5	.9	120.8	814.3
1876	3,040.8	.9	596.2	—	222.2	—	—	571.9	.7	131.4	936.9
1875	2,725.0	.5	532.2	—	382.9	—	1.8	592.7	.3	88.9	1,056.2
1874	2,884.2	24.5	391.2	—	399.6	—	.4	523.5	.5	129.7	938.8
1873	2,754.9	—	380.5	—	215.4	—	5.7	277.7	46.8	126.6	971.7
1872	—	—	—	—	203.0	—	—	—	—	75.1	—
1871	—	—	—	—	258.4	—	—	—	—	79.6	—

[1] For years 1871 to 1906, fiscal years ending 30 June of the year given; nine months ending 31 March 1907; for 1908 to 1926, fiscal years ending 31 March of the year given; for 1926 to 1960, calendar years.

[2] Oil only is included for 1871 to 1927.

[3] Newfoundland exports included beginning in 1954.

Series M121–133. *Value of imports of fish and fish products, by major species, 1873 to 1960*

(thousands of dollars)

Year[1]	Total	Ground-fish[2]	Halibut	Herring and pilchards	Sardines and anchovies	Salmon	Tuna	Lobster Fresh	Lobster Canned	Oyster	All other shellfish	Oil and meal[3]	All other[4]
	121	122	123	124	125	126	127	128	129	130	131	132	133
1960	17,213.3	166.2	269.6	871.2	1,216.7	1,214.8	1,472.4	217.3	21.6	960.9	5,164.3	1,251.2	4,387.1
1959	16,352.0	196.5	281.8	830.4	1,363.8	483.4	1,493.9	375.9	37.3	959.4	2,583.1	991.8	6,754.7
1958	17,481.7	119.7	220.0	997.5	1,388.5	2,574.0	1,027.9	155.5	30.9	932.8	2,481.7	1,744.7	5,808.5
1957	16,541.5	166.5	390.2	791.1	1,372.1	3,647.5	819.3	215.4	42.5	886.0	2,054.6	824.4	5,331.9
1956	17,490.4	195.8	393.9	764.5	1,188.8	5,206.7	815.4	217.5	73.0	840.6	2,422.8	901.5	4,469.9
1955	12,611.7	126.8	308.1	740.8	1,376.5	288.6	467.5	224.8	74.4	660.0	2,081.0	2,521.2	3,742.0
1954[5]	10,848.4	102.2	256.4	612.4	1,071.3	346.4	645.4	222.9	67.9	638.9	1,346.8	1,836.8	3,701.0
1953	9,114.5	67.3	180.6	481.4	1,100.8	150.1	123.1	196.3	125.2	669.0	1,560.4	1,204.4	3,255.9
1952	7,109.2	69.4	47.2	488.8	873.3	28.1	344.2	240.9	31.5	668.8	1,195.5	501.0	2,620.5
1951	7,485.1	61.0	235.8	481.3	1,281.6	190.0	268.9	188.4	60.6	617.2	827.6	778.6	2,494.1
1950	5,142.7	41.5	75.4	425.8	699.4	10.0	126.9	138.7	105.2	574.2	577.9	402.2	1,965.5
1949	6,397.8	306.1	92.7	287.3	760.4	519.0	94.3	61.7	42.1	680.9	1,038.3	761.4	1,753.6
1948	11,600.6	1,403.3	71.7	458.3	869.8	580.7	138.1	497.5	53.6	21.9	2.1	5,847.2	1,656.4
1947	12,952.3	874.4	29.5	350.0	720.2	500.3	248.3	412.3	41.4	355.7	224.7	7,417.9	1,777.6
1946	7,242.4	1,509.8	19.3	276.4	172.8	606.8	63.6	328.4	46.6	498.7	21.4	2,270.9	1,427.7
1945	5,695.8	1,227.2	21.1	134.9	20.9	313.2	.3	290.1	3.9	436.5	1.4	2,208.4	1,037.9
1944	4,649.1	1,139.0	29.5	193.9	38.0	467.8	—	183.6	4.4	226.6	—	1,405.5	960.8
1943	4,261.8	917.3	36.6	148.1	38.3	368.1	—	187.7	20.4	2.6	—	1,742.1	800.6
1942	3,463.7	653.3	24.6	150.3	12.2	294.0	11.6	169.0	1.9	2.3	.1	1,334.7	809.7
1941	3,444.2	422.7	32.0	85.4	37.5	457.0	121.1	42.7	9.5	49.4	58.4	1,215.0	913.5
1940	3,501.6	392.9	39.3	110.1	193.5	320.1	314.7	25.7	10.0	242.3	263.2	890.4	699.4
1939	3,438.6	95.1	17.1	142.1	357.5	333.1	377.1	66.7	38.1	239.1	392.4	672.5	707.8
1938	3,036.2	92.1	51.7	192.5	358.0	475.2	230.9	59.3	80.6	245.3	204.4	470.3	575.9
1937	2,877.1	54.8	38.6	176.0	319.2	199.6	171.5	137.3	68.5	275.3	225.0	627.8	583.5
1936	2,918.3	92.1	49.7	205.8	368.6	229.9	188.9	21.5	200.1	241.6	248.7	539.5	531.9
1935	2,597.9	61.3	63.4	181.5	360.0	118.6	116.3	1.9	91.0	212.3	146.8	733.7	511.1
1934	2,122.7	170.1	48.3	125.9	286.9	266.0	—	1.2	75.3	191.1	125.1	310.4	522.4
1933	1,694.3	34.5	21.3	145.7	250.7	138.0	—	1.4	80.1	183.0	137.2	231.7	470.7
1932	1,862.3	81.5	39.9	201.6	294.4	121.2	—	1.4	40.7	220.5	52.1	180.8	628.2
1931	2,653.9	177.8	78.3	223.6	452.8	161.1	—	1.4	95.0	301.7	38.2	241.1	882.9
1930	3,446.6	326.9	118.4	350.3	525.3	194.2	—	2.7	79.8	383.0	—	264.5	1,201.5
1929	4,233.9	404.1	163.9	401.9	788.5	232.7	—	5.7	107.7	482.1	—	243.4	1,403.9
1928	4,068.1	434.0	153.8	469.9	677.4	201.5	—	5.3	54.2	443.1	—	316.5	1,312.4
1927	3,768.9	563.7	194.6	415.4	650.1	170.2	—	2.2	2.0	385.1	—	288.2	1,097.4
1926	3,045.8	247.3	121.6	402.3	483.1	155.9	—	1.8	.1	369.3	—	286.7	977.7
1926	2,590.5	174.7	141.6	371.7	414.1	102.1	—	.7	.5	361.3	—	171.2	852.6
1925	3,061.3	458.9	102.5	324.1	546.6	111.9	—	2.5	6.1	340.8	—	284.0	883.9
1924	2,527.0	276.1	71.7	247.1	467.3	140.8	—	2.2	14.0	386.5	—	150.9	770.4
1923	2,965.8	437.0	225.9	375.7	427.5	297.3	—	3.0	41.1	374.8	—	108.7	674.8
1922	3,169.6	509.5	195.4	342.8	471.4	501.5	—	3.5	34.8	376.9	—	71.8	662.0
1921	4,292.5	964.0	247.8	462.1	709.2	238.5	—	8.9	104.0	455.1	—	278.3	824.6

Series M 121–133. *Value of imports of fish and fish products, by major species, 1873 to 1960 (continued)*

(thousands of dollars)

Year[1]	Total	Ground-fish[2]	Halibut	Herring and pilchards	Sardines and anchovies	Salmon	Tuna	Lobster Fresh	Lobster Canned	Oyster	All other shellfish	Oil and meal[3]	All other[4]
	121	122	123	124	125	126	127	128	129	130	131	132	133
1920	4,051.9	503.3	205.8	598.6	526.2	463.7	—	9.7	99.4	496.9	—	262.1	886.2
1919	3,183.8	600.5	74.0	712.5	70.4	211.0	—	2.5	74.9	321.1	—	541.9	575.0
1918	2,923.6[6]	523.7	52.4	559.6	150.4	270.7	—	2.3	40.4	260.4	—	524.6	539.1[6]
1917	2,476.3[6]	467.5	43.8	351.5	346.6	198.1	—	6.3	17.5	337.0	—	243.7	464.3[6]
1916	1,591.1[6]	152.8	38.9	338.7	224.8	55.2	—	4.7	37.9	285.2	—	153.5	299.4[6]
1915	1,856.3[6]	368.0	80.0	259.0	317.7	46.8	—	2.7	9.3	266.2	—	96.5[3]	410.1[4,6]
1914	2,331.8	442.1	127.1	238.9	418.4	112.6	—	3.3	22.8	390.4	—	100.0	476.2
1913	2,674.8	691.6	131.9	234.8	434.8	157.1	—	3.2	.4	406.8	—	134.2	480.0
1912	2,409.6	786.0	115.7	248.6	288.7	61.8	—	6.7	39.3	406.0	—	137.0	319.8
1911	1,995.1	495.8	84.0	197.5	316.4	44.6	—	3.7	49.1	379.5	—	120.9	303.6
1910	1,772.7	557.5	57.7	183.3	231.2	58.3	—	.7	30.1	364.0	—	84.2	205.7
1909	1,709.3	690.4	46.5	141.2	201.0	37.8	—	1.9	39.9	301.6	—	112.6	136.4
1908	1,941.7	851.9	53.7	243.4	172.0	37.2	—	.7	4.7	349.6	—	85.5	143.0
1907	1,659.1	684.7	36.7	179.3	116.4	91.1	—	.1	29.5	325.7	—	71.7	123.9
1906	2,049.1	892.6	54.0	243.9	137.0	62.0	—	.2	58.9	350.7	—	84.6	165.3
1905	1,504.0	384.1	40.6	184.2	135.2	55.5	—	.1	86.2	359.0	—	126.9	132.2
1904	1,585.7	515.4	38.6	164.1	109.5	54.6	—	1.4	48.3	360.2	—	132.0	161.6
1903	1,403.4	396.6	38.5	201.1	90.0	88.6	—	1.5	53.4	315.1	—	91.8	126.8
1902	1,145.2	213.6	21.0	176.2	98.3	140.4	—	2.4	57.2	252.9	—	58.8	124.4
1901	981.6	130.0	18.5	138.0	95.2	85.1	—	2.0	85.3	242.4	—	57.8	127.3
1900	1,213.4	307.0	14.5	135.6	87.3	136.6	—	3.0	87.1	254.1	—	61.0	127.2
1899	955.4	235.6	20.0	83.7	86.0	57.7	—	3.7	106.4	231.1	—	50.3	80.9
1898	1,009.1	357.1	5.9	63.8	81.7	122.4	—	4.3	8.6	187.4	—	76.2	101.7
1897	1,036.7	359.3	4.0	34.8	61.2	159.5	—	2.8	3.2	191.9	—	113.7	106.3
1896	1,067.9	481.1	2.8	62.0	59.9	58.6	—	3.2	.9	203.4	—	76.8	119.2
1895	1,243.2	549.5	1.5	112.1	52.5	39.9	—	2.8	65.3	210.8	—	57.8	151.0
1894	1,515.0	756.0	4.0	123.7	80.0	42.4	—	7.9	65.7	238.2	—	46.1	151.2
1893	1,225.2	401.7	5.1	160.7	77.2	33.3	—	7.5	53.1	261.6	—	106.3	118.7
1892	1,422.7	644.4	5.0	162.4	62.3	41.6	—	7.4	48.8	275.4	—	74.2	101.2
1891	1,415.1	551.4	4.4	217.7	63.8	42.0	—	5.7	7.8	283.9	—	131.3	107.1
1890	1,076.7	236.9	5.1	247.6	70.9	32.1	—	5.2	1.3	309.7	—	62.1	105.8
1889	1,076.4	248.7	4.3	281.2	66.2	35.9	—	4.8	.3	285.6	—	67.6	81.8
1888	1,020.2	220.9	6.0	227.3	63.8	39.8	—	4.3	8.0	312.5	—	45.0	92.6
1887	982.2	194.9	3.9	195.4	70.0	39.5	—	3.9	1.1	300.9	—	85.3	87.3
1886	902.2	128.0	3.0	213.0	59.5	34.0	—	2.6	3.8	273.0	—	92.4	92.9
1885	1,117.7	224.9	1.5	19.2	—	11.6	—	2.4	2.0	284.0	—	162.3	409.8
1884	1,586.6	235.7	2.2	28.4	—	27.7	—	3.7	2.0	300.3	—	168.4	818.2
1883	1,653.3	264.4	2.0	23.4	—	36.0	—	4.0	3.1	309.8	—	239.2	771.4
1882	1,232.0	217.9	.9	20.0	—	37.9	—	4.2	2.6	264.7	—	130.9	552.9
1881	1,266.5	180.0	1.1	38.1	—	46.6	—	3.9	2.9	213.7	—	273.5	506.7
1880	1,112.9	188.6	.7	38.0	—	30.1	—	2.4	3.2	189.5	—	133.1	527.3
1879	1,192.9	214.5	.5	18.3	—	34.1	—	3.0	9.1	191.0	—	137.8	584.6
1878	1,300.4	255.4	1.1	36.8	—	25.7	—	2.7	11.2	206.8	—	166.4	594.3
1877	1,371.4	291.2	1.2	52.4	—	17.5	—	2.2	15.2	236.5	—	108.4	646.8
1876	1,609.1	315.9	.6	53.7	—	6.4	—	4.0	13.6	233.1	—	47.0	934.8
1875	1,600.3	206.8	.5	45.9	—	21.7	—	5.2	15.3	283.5	—	109.9	911.5
1874	1,832.9	158.5	.3	20.0	—	1.8	—	8.0	2.8	182.5	—	42.3	1,416.7
1873	1,001.7	92.5	.5	5.4	—	.2	—	5.1	.3	167.3	—	14.2	716.2

[1] From 1873 to 1906 fiscal years ending 30 June of the year given; nine months ending 31 March 1907; for 1908 to 1926 fiscal years ending 31 March of the year given; for 1926 to 1960 calendar years.
[2] Groundfish includes codfish, haddock, pollock and ling.
[3] Oil only is included 1873 to 1915.

[4] Fish meal not reported separately 1873 to 1915, presumably included in series M 133 for those years.
[5] Newfoundland included beginning in 1954.
[6] Sponges of marine production not included 1915 to 1918.

Series M134–138. *Index of prices received by fishermen and index of wholesale prices of fish products, 1913 to 1960*

(1935–39 = 100)

	Index of prices received by fishermen				Fisheries wholesale price index		Index of prices received by fishermen				Fisheries wholesale price index
Year	Canada[1]	British Columbia	Maritimes, Quebec	Fresh water fisheries		Year	Canada[1]	British Columbia	Maritimes, Quebec	Fresh water fisheries	
	134	**135**	**136**	**137**	**138**		**134**	**135**	**136**	**137**	**138**
1960	411	630	316	252	339.6	1935	98	103	96	94	97.9
1959	382	527	330	256	326.4	1934	94	102	93	85	99.4
1958	382	554	313	250	312.0	1933	83	97	73	79	88.1
1957	308	402	279	220	302.6	1932	79	79	75	86	89.5
1956	349	507	292	213	296.9	1931	90	85	95	91	105.1
1955	304	388	284	214	274.1	1930	120	119	124	113	133.3
1954	299	369	286	218	262.4	1929	140	156	135	124	147.5
1953	283	331	282	212	259.4	1928	132	128	135	134	140.5
1952	308	384	287	232	278.8	1927	140	170	133	108	140.3
1951	311	405	263	256	283.7	1926	132	140	134	115	140.0
1950	294	377	253	242	260.7	1925	126	128	132	112	137.7
1949	258	307	254	193	257.3	1924	117	104	136	101	129.6
1948	296	379	270	217	254.1	1923	122	131	129	99	117.2
1947	240	235	248	232	231.6	1922	128	159	125	86	128.8
1946	258	254	282	220	212.7	1921	132	163	126	93	128.3
1945	238	208	266	232	194.7	1920	162	195	163	109	156.5
1944	221	211	249	186	177.8	1919	168	205	170	110	160.1
1943	214	194	232	200	174.4	1918	—	206	189	—	155.6
1942	189	227	176	155	148.0	1917	—	—	—	—	123.4
1941	144	169	131	128	125.6	1916	—	—	—	—	96.6
1940	111	116	107	111	115.6	1915	—	—	—	—	90.5
1939	102	115	97	93	102.2	1914	—	—	—	—	89.1
1938	101	107	96	102	99.6	1913	—	—	—	—	90.2
1937	104	97	108	107	100.0						
1936	98	84	106	104	98.6						

[1] Excluding Newfoundland.

Series M139–144. *Expenditures of the federal Department of Fisheries, 1932 to 1960*

(thousands of dollars)

Year[1,2]	Total expenditure	Administration	Resource development	Price support and deficiency payments	Other subsidies	Other expenditures	Year[1,2]	Total expenditure	Administration	Resource development	Price support and deficiency payments	Other subsidies	Other expenditures
	139	**140**	**141**	**142**	**143**	**144**		**139**	**140**	**141**	**142**	**143**	**144**
1960	19,810.2	2,990.1	12,309.8	760.0	1,091.0	2,659.3	1945	2,620.5	179.6	1,422.8	158.2	176.6	683.3
1959	17,577.3	2,502.0	10,744.5	895.4	1,052.7	2,382.7	1944	1,978.4	163.9	1,250.6	159.4	145.3	259.2
1958	16,395.1	2,610.8	9,943.9	754.7	667.6	2,418.1	1943	1,913.4	150.7	1,221.0	159.9	61.5	320.3
1957	13,689.1	2,563.6	8,043.4	741.9	635.3	1,704.9	1942	1,704.4	146.8	1,211.1	160.0	—	186.5
1956	11,822.4	2,261.3	6,842.1	647.3	560.6	1,511.1	1941	2,005.4	148.9	1,169.6	159.9	—	526.9
1955	10,315.6	2,011.8	6,384.7	159.2	450.1	1,309.8	1940	3,023.5	124.7	1,453.2	160.0	—	1,285.7
1954	10,701.4	1,497.3	5,908.8	1,548.0	514.9	1,232.4	1939	2,568.4	127.7	1,682.9	160.0	—	597.9
1953	9,594.3	1,158.8	6,014.0	195.7	473.2	1,752.6	1938	2,151.0	140.5	1,471.3	160.0	—	379.4
1952	9,863.7	1,004.9	5,131.0	1,379.3	402.2	1,946.3	1937	2,033.4	135.0	1,370.2	160.0	—	368.2
1951	8,183.2	583.1	5,968.1	248.5	361.7	1,021.8	1936	1,710.3	120.3	1,384.5	160.0	—	45.6
1950[2]	7,917.2	767.7	4,810.4	1,029.0	79.3	1,230.8	1935	1,640.6	110.2	1,334.4	160.0	—	36.0
1949	5,864.1	406.2	3,867.9	697.2	82.6	810.2	1934	1,596.5	111.3	1,287.8	159.3	—	38.0
1948	4,315.0	254.7	2,977.5	160.0	97.8	825.0	1933	1,786.9	142.8	1,400.3	159.8	—	84.0
1947	3,839.2	195.8	2,585.4	160.0	87.8	810.1	1932	2,045.9	177.1	1,647.2	159.4	—	62.1
1946	3,628.4	187.2	2,077.8	159.9	123.3	1,080.3							

[1] Fiscal years ending 31 March of the year given.   [2] Newfoundland included beginning in 1950.

Series M 145. *Pacific halibut landings, according to the International Fisheries Commission, Canada, 1890 to 1958*

(thousands of pounds)

Year	Quantity 145	Year	Quantity 145	Year	Quantity 145	Year	Quantity 145	Year	Quantity 145	Year	Quantity 145	Year	Quantity 145
1958	29,194												
1957	24,754												
1956	25,597												
1955	22,148	1945	15,121	1935	10,208	1925	7,353	1915	18,609	1905	—	1895	2,537
1954	27,526	1944	13,371	1934	9,718	1924	9,628	1914	—	1904	—	1894	1,730
1953	25,853	1943	12,940	1933	8,286	1923	9,121	1913	—	1903	—	1893	1,369
1952	24,779	1942	11,244	1932	6,412	1922	9,227	1912	—	1902	—	1892	1,358
1951	21,045	1941	13,109	1931	7,783	1921	10,157	1911	—	1901	—	1891	1,136
1950	18,999	1940	12,900	1930	7,633	1920	8,616	1910	—	1900	—	1890	633
1949	18,921	1939	13,688	1929	9,040	1919	7,466	1909	—	1899	—		
1948	18,782	1938	12,350	1928	10,209	1918	6,328	1908	8,072	1898	—		
1947	24,159	1937	11,917	1927	8,466	1917	9,901	1907	12,915	1897	1,968		
1946	18,637	1936	10,741	1926	7,891	1916	12,185	1906	—	1896	2,281		

Series M 146. *Exports of dried cod, Newfoundland, 1806 to 1948*

(thousands of pounds)

Year[1]	Quantity 146	Year	Quantity 146	Year	Quantity 146	Year	Quantity 146	Year	Quantity 146	Year	Quantity 146	Year	Quantity 146
1948	119,760												
1947	84,502												
1946	114,343												
1945	111,845	1925	138,615	1905	165,875	1885	143,888	1865	107,670	1845	112,026	1825	109,028
1944	86,652	1924[1]	130,491	1904	134,043	1884	163,255	1864	113,825	1844	95,442	1824	97,824
1943	85,737	1923	141,643	1903	152,362	1883	171,587	1863	111,898	1843	104,855	1823	96,851
1942	85,266	1922	166,162	1902	160,079	1882	155,804	1862	142,222	1842	112,804	1822	98,725
1941	76,735	1921	178,309	1901	144,363	1881	171,984	1861	138,698	1841	113,089	1821	100,503
1940	128,137	1920	152,745	1900	138,108	1880	154,955	1860	149,879	1840	102,569	1820	100,930
1939	102,104	1919	200,258	1899	145,670	1879	155,430	1859	136,891	1839	96,922	1819	103,515
1938	117,111	1918	188,358	1898	137,350	1878	115,921	1858	116,266	1838	81,146	1818	112,968
1937	102,651	1917	203,975	1897	128,300	1877	115,819	1857	155,940	1837	88,138	1817	114,628
1936	122,732	1916	175,618	1896[1]	127,212	1876	119,669	1856	142,053	1836	95,363	1816	117,222
1935	116,453	1915	159,194	1895	147,012	1875	128,150	1855	124,027	1835	79,810	1815	121,662
1934	114,309	1914	122,555	1894	124,062	1874	178,733	1854	86,701	1834	90,302	1814	106,149
1933	125,597	1913	139,699	1893	118,758	1873	147,480	1853	103,344	1833	76,556	1813	99,832
1932	117,543	1912	157,761	1892	117,523	1872	125,086	1852	108,971	1832	69,348	1812	79,639
1931	114,936	1911	155,476	1891	139,421	1871	130,759	1851	113,921	1831	84,635	1811	103,436
1930	129,381	1910	132,465	1890	116,583	1870	131,060	1850	121,988	1830	106,222	1810	99,061
1929[1]	140,278	1909	168,254	1889	120,569	1869	123,660	1849	131,619	1829	103,515	1809	90,745
1928[1]	144,872	1908	194,027	1888	131,681	1868	99,463	1848	103,081	1828	100,800	1808	64,527
1927[1]	176,260	1907	169,038	1887	120,963	1867	112,570	1847	93,853	1827	100,800	1807	75,579
1926	161,151	1906	159,314	1886	150,548	1866	99,309	1846	98,449	1826	107,962	1806	86,555

[1] From 1896 to 1924 and from 1927 to 1929 data are for years ending 30 June of the following year. All other years are calendar years.

SECTION N: MINERALS AND FUEL

JOHN DAVIS, *British Columbia Electric Company, Ltd*

The statistics of minerals and fuels are presented in three sub-sections: metallic minerals in series N1–88, nonmetallic minerals including structural materials in series N89–169, and fuels in series N170–198. Each subsection begins with Canadian production and progresses to imports, then to exports and ends with the principal statistics of the industry. In addition, the apparent domestic consumption of the principal fuels is included in the final subsection.

The sources of the mineral statistics presented in this section and other sources that were consulted include the following publications of the Dominion Bureau of Statistics:

Canadian Mineral Statistics, 1886–1956, Reference Paper No. 68 (Ottawa, Queen's Printer, 1957); *General Review of the Mining Industry*, Catalogue No. 26–201 (Ottawa, Queen's Printer), annual; *Canada Year Book* (Ottawa, Queen's Printer), annual; *Preliminary Estimates of Mineral Production*, Catalogue Nos. 26–202 and 26–203; annual bulletins on individual mining industries: *Silver, Lead, Zinc Mining Industry*, Catalogue No. 26–216 (Ottawa, Queen's Printer), annual; *Asbestos Mining Industry*, Catalogue No. 26–205 (Ottawa, Queen's Printer), annual; *Coal Mining Industry*, Catalogue No. 26–206 (Ottawa, Queen's Printer), annual; *Crude Petroleum and Natural Gas Industry*, Catalogue No. 26–213 (Ottawa, Queen's Printer), annual; *Refined Petroleum Products*, Catalogue No. 45–204 (Ottawa, Queen's Printer), annual; *Petroleum Products Industry*, Catalogue No. 45–205 (Ottawa, Queen's Printer), annual; *Trade of Canada* (Ottawa, Queen's Printer), annual from 1926 to 1960.

In addition to the foregoing publications of the Bureau the following were also used: Department of Trade and Commerce, *Annual Reports*, in Canada, *Sessional Papers*; Dominion Coal Board, *Annual Report* (Ottawa, Queen's Printer); John Davis, *Canadian Energy Prospects*, published by Royal Commission on Canada's Economic Prospects (Ottawa, Queen's Printer, 1957); submissions to hearings of the National Energy Board and the Royal Commission on Energy.

Data from the files of the Mineral Statistics Section, Industry and Merchandising Division of the Dominion Bureau of Statistics and of the Mineral Resources Division of the Department of Mines and Technical Surveys were used. Also unpublished materials on the fuel industry in Canada were supplied by the Co-ordination and Economics Department of Imperial Oil Limited, Toronto, the Canadian Petroleum Association, Calgary, and the private gas utilities in Alberta and Ontario.

A summary of the methods currently used to compute the mineral production of Canada was supplied by the Mineral Statistics Section of the Dominion Bureau of Statistics. See also D.B.S., *General Review of the Mining Industry, 1960*, pp. A-42 to A-46.

In cases of conflict between data published by the Dominion Bureau of Statistics and provided by the Department of Mines and Technical Surveys, particularly for the early years, the latter, which were carefully checked in the Department, were used.

General note

The first systematic annual survey of the production, exports and imports of minerals and fuel was undertaken in 1886 by the Geological Survey of Canada, a branch of the Department of the Interior (*Sessional Papers*, vol. 21, no. 12, 1888, part III, pp. 27–8). The statistical report was based upon the returns of 665 schedules of some 2,000 mailed out and 185 replies to 400 letters supplemented by information provided by the Department of Mines in British Columbia and the Chief Inspector of Mines in Nova Scotia. Field-work was begun in the same year and continued in subsequent years to improve knowledge of individual mining operations in various parts of the country. By 1890 the number of 'circulars' mailed, including 'reminders', had increased to 5,500, and 650 letters were written to mining establishments. Meanwhile the mailing list of establishments was continuously revised and improved (*Sessional Papers*, vol. 24, no. 14, 1891, pp. 42–4).

The Survey Branch of Interior became the Department of the Geological Survey in May 1890. In June 1907, the Division of Mineral Resources and Statistics of this Department was transferred to the Mines Branch of the newly organized Department of Mines. The files of mineral production of the Mines Branch for the years 1917 to 1919 were turned over to the Dominion Bureau of Statistics following the Statistics Act of 1918 which shifted the responsibility for the future collection of mining statistics to the new Bureau. The report on production in 1920 was completed by the Mines Branch. The Bureau assumed the full task in 1921.

There have been minor and some major changes in the methods of estimating mineral production. An early statement of the method appears in *Sessional Papers*, vol. XLII, no. 13, 1907–8, paper no. 26b, pp. 5–6. Quantities of production of the metallic metals secured by mailed schedules were valued by the average New York prices for the year. Spot prices, that is, the prices received by producers on shipments, were applied to the quantities of other mineral products. The schedules returned by operators were also checked against 'railway shipments, exports, and all other sources of information available'. In the same year an historical series extending back to 1895 was published, '... the earlier years being corrected and revised to make the method of statement conform with that adopted for recent years' (S.P. no. 26b, inside cover). The practice of consulting other federal departments and departments or mining bureaus of the provinces was continued. By 1916 the correspondence list included 3,500 smelter, mine and quarry operators.

The general methods of the Mines Branch were employed by the Dominion Bureau of Statistics until 1925–26. The following description of method appears in *Mineral Production of Canada, 1922*, pp. 11–12:

For statistical and comparative purposes, it has always been customary to determine the value of the metals, copper, gold, silver, lead, nickel and zinc as far as possible on the basis of the quantities of metals recovered from Canadian ores smelted during the year, either in Canada or abroad, and to compute the value of this production in each refined metal in a recognized market. The value of the non-metallics, and of the structural materials, was determined as the value received by the producer at point of shipment. In this report, no departure has been made from the practice previously followed. The New York market was used in the case of the principal metals since most sales of Canadian products are made on that market.

Some major changes were introduced in 1926. The price of zinc, formerly basis the St. Louis market, was based upon the London market. The price of lead, formerly based upon the Montreal price, was also shifted to London. See *Mineral Production in Canada, 1926*, p. 13. Later these (as well as the price of silver) were shifted again to the averages of Montreal prices for the year. See the notes to series N 9, N 10, N 19, N 20, N 25 and N 26. The method of computing nickel and copper production was changed substantially beginning in 1926 (see *Mineral Production in Canada, 1928*, pp. 317–18 and notes to series N 3, N 4, N 13 and N 14).

As a result of these and other minor changes the series 'are not strictly comparable throughout the whole period.... Earlier methods resulted in a somewhat higher value than those now in use would have shown. However the changes do not interfere with the general usefulness of the figures in showing the broad trends in the mineral industry' (*Canada Year Book, 1955*, p. 510).

The data given in this section cover the economically important minerals and fuels. Data on other minerals are given in the source but these minerals are either unimportant or available only for limited time periods.

METALLIC MINERALS (Series N 1–88)

N 1–26. Canadian production of principal metallic minerals, 1886 to 1960

SOURCE: for the years 1886 to 1955, Dominion Bureau of Statistics, *Canadian Mineral Statistics, 1886–1956*; for the years 1956 to 1960, Dominion Bureau of Statistics, *General Review of the Mining Industry*, successive annual issues; for series N 24, 1933 to 1941, the files of the Mineral Statistics Section, Dominion Bureau of Statistics.

N 1 and N 2. The quantity of cobalt is the cobalt metal produced at Canadian smelters, plus the Canadian-produced cobalt content of salts and oxides made at these smelters, plus the cobalt content of ores and concentrates exported. The value of the former is the total sales value as reported by the smelters; the value of the latter is the gross value received by the exporters.

N 3 and N 4. Copper production includes: (1) recoverable copper in ores and concentrates for export valued at the average Montreal price for the year. Recoverable copper is total copper content less smelter losses estimated as ten pounds of copper per ton of concentrates; (2) copper content of blister copper made at Canadian smelters valued at the average Montreal price for the year; (3) copper content of nickel-copper matte exported by Canadian smelters which is valued at a price agreed upon by the Ontario Department of Mines and the Dominion Bureau of Statistics and which usually runs about three cents below the Canadian price to allow for a refinery margin for treatment of the matte.

A major change in estimating both the quantity and value of copper production was made beginning in 1926 which had the effect of reducing the valuation put on copper production. See D.B.S., *Mineral Production of Canada, 1928*, pp. 317–18.

N 5 and N 6. Gold is all gold in bullion produced plus the recoverable gold in all other Canadian mine products. The price is the average price set by the United States expressed in Canadian funds.

N 7 and N 8. Beginning in 1939 iron production represents mine shipments at the values reported by the shippers. Earlier, when it was of less importance, it was export tonnage and sales value.

N 9 and N 10. Production includes lead in base bullion produced at Trail, British Columbia plus recoverable lead in ores and concentrates exported. The allowance for smelter losses is 5 per cent. The value is the average Montreal price for the year.

There was a major change in this series beginning in 1926 when an annual average of London price quotations was substituted for the Montreal price for all production outside of Ontario. The London price was used to the end of 1939; for each year from 1940 to 1946, prices were the averages of those agreed upon by Canadian producers and the Government of the United Kingdom; from 1947 to 1950, average New York prices were used; from 1951 to 1960, average Montreal prices were used. The change in 1926 reduced the value of production below 1925 although the quantity produced increased by 12 per cent (see *Mineral Production of Canada, 1926*, p. 13).

N 11 and N 12. Magnesium is production of magnesium metal plus magnesium content of alloys valued as reported by shipper.

N 13 and N 14. Nickel production includes: (1) refined and electrolytic nickel produced at Canadian refineries valued at the average price obtained from sales during the year; (2) nickel in nickel oxides and nickel salts at the total selling value of these products; (3) nickel in matte exported, valued at a price set by the Ontario Department of Mines and the Dominion Bureau of Statistics which allows a few cents for refinery treatment of the matte; (4) recoverable nickel in concentrates shipped internally to Ontario and Saskatchewan valued at an arbitrary price.

This general method of estimating nickel production was introduced in 1926. Consequently, there is an inconsistency in the series before and since that year. For the older method see D.B.S., *Mineral Production in Canada, 1928*, p. 318.

N 17 and N 18. Since 1946 the production of platinum is the assay content of concentrates and refinery residues exported plus the platinum content of the matte shipped for export and platinum recovered from placer workings valued at the average New York price. Prior to 1946 production was defined as recoverable metals in smelter products at their sales value to the producer and placer platinum at the average New York price for the year.

N 19 and N 20. Silver includes silver bullion produced and the recoverable silver in other smelter products and in Canadian ores exported, valued at the average Montreal price for the year. Before 1951 the average New York price was used.

N 23 and N 24. Uranium is based upon reports of producers of the U_3O_8 content of uranium precipitates or concentrates and of the value received by the shipper.

N 25 and N 26. Zinc production includes recoverable zinc in ores exported, with an allowance of 160 pounds per ton of concentrates for smelter losses, and zinc refined at Trail and Flin Flon. The total quantity is valued at the average Montreal price for the year.

There was a shift in the pricing base beginning in 1926. Formerly, prices quoted on the St. Louis market were used. In 1926 an average of London price quotations was introduced. Following 1926, the markets on which prices were based were the same as for lead (see the note to series N 9 and N 10).

N 27–49. Canadian imports of principal metallic minerals, 1880 to 1960

SOURCE: for the years 1880 to 1925, the files of the Mineral Resources Division, Department of Mines and Technical Surveys; for 1926 to 1960, Dominion Bureau of Statistics, *Trade of Canada*.

N 27 and N 28. These figures include only the imports of the raw materials alumina, bauxite and cryolite for 1928 to 1960; alumina and cryolite for 1923 to 1927; alumina for 1905 to 1922; alumina and cryolite for 1903 and 1904 and cryolite for 1895 to 1902. Canada does not produce any aluminium ores.

N 29 and N 30. Aluminium imports include: aluminium pigs, ingots, blocks and scrap for 1949 to 1960; aluminium notch bars, slabs, billets, blooms, pigs, ingots, blocks and scrap for 1932 to

1948; aluminium ingots and blocks only, for 1928 to 1931; aluminium ingots, blocks, sheets, strips or plates for 1910 to 1928; aluminium pigs, ingots, blocks, notch bars, slabs, billets and blooms for 1905 to 1909.

N 33–34. Copper imports include: (1) copper in blocks, pigs or ingots; (2) copper scrap, cathode plates or electrolytic copper for melting; (3) copper-covered steel wire and rods and copper in bars or rods for the manufacture of trolley, telegraph and telephone wires, electric wires, electric cables and electrical conductors; (4) copper in bars or rods.

Minor changes in import classifications took place in 1895, 1918, 1919, 1920, 1923, 1930, 1936, 1943 and 1949 but these appear to have little significance for the consistency of the series.

N 37 and N 38. These figures include lead imports in semi-processed and processed forms (that is, lead in pigs, blocks, bars and sheets) and also old and scrap lead. For 1916 to 1920 the classification was 'imports of lead'.

N 39 and N 40. Prior to 1956 this category was called manganese oxide rather than manganese ore.

N 41 and N 42. Nickel imports include: (1) rods containing 90 per cent or more of nickel for wire; (2) nickel in ingots, blocks and shot; (3) nickel bars, rods, strips and sheets; (4) nickel-silver in ingots and blocks; (5) nickel-chromium in bars and rods.

Changes in import classifications occurred in 1921, 1928, 1936 and 1949.

N 43. Platinum imports include for 1926 to 1960: (1) platinum wire and bars, strips, sheets or plates; (2) platinum, palladium, iridium, osmium, ruthenium and rhodium in lumps, ingots, powder, sponge and scrap; for 1919 to 1925 platinum wire and bars, strips, sheets or plates; for 1915 to 1918 platinum as crucibles, wire, bars, etc.; for 1885 to 1914 platinum.

N 44 and N 45. Silver imports include silver in bars, blocks, ingots, drops, sheets or plates, unmanufactured.

N 46 and N 47. Tin imports include tin in blocks, pigs, bars or granular form.

N 48 and N 49. Zinc imports include zinc and zinc alloys in pigs, slabs, blocks and anodes. Prior to 1945 considerable quantities of spelter from the United States are included. Imports of manufactures of zinc are included for 1917, 1918 and 1919: their values are $79, $85 and $43 thousand respectively.

N 50–81. Canadian exports of principal metallic minerals, 1868 to 1960

SOURCE: for 1868 to 1925, the files of the Mineral Resources Division, Department of Mines and Technical Surveys; for 1926 to 1960, Dominion Bureau of Statistics, *Trade of Canada*.

N 82–88. Principal statistics of the Canadian metallic mining industries, 1923 to 1960

SOURCE: for 1923 to 1944, the files of the Mineral Statistics Section, Dominion Bureau of Statistics; for 1945 to 1960, Dominion Bureau of Statistics, *General Review of the Mining Industry*, successive annual issues.

N 85 and N 86. For the years up to and including 1949 a general category 'cost of materials' included all supplies, fuels and electricity. Fuels and electricity have been obtained separately since 1950.

NONMETALLIC MINERALS (Series N 89–169)

N 89–119. Canadian production of principal nonmetallic minerals, 1886 to 1960

SOURCE: for 1886 to 1955, Dominion Bureau of Statistics, *Canadian Mineral Statistics, 1886–1956*; for 1956 to 1960, Dominion Bureau of Statistics, *General Review of the Mining Industry*, successive annual issues.

Owing to the fact that it is difficult to obtain the figures of the actual production of nonmetallic minerals, and because the first actual measurement is made when the product is sold, plant shipments are taken to represent the quantities of production of the nonmetallic minerals. Values are f.o.b. shipping points of the producers or values of shipments as reported by the producers. An exception to this latter rule is in the valuation of sulphur (see note to series N 105 and N 106 below).

N 95 and N 96. Prior to 1941 the Dominion Bureau of Statistics included peat moss as a product of manufacturing rather than as a non-processed mineral product. The series given here include some duplication resulting from the resale of peat moss purchased from other producers.

N 105 and N 106. Sulphur includes pyrites, and, beginning in 1927, sulphur in smelter gas, and, beginning in 1958, elemental sulphur. Elemental sulphur had been previously treated as a manufacture. Pyrite is a by-product of the milling of sulphide ores. It is valued by applying the average price of the sulphur content of pyrite in Eastern Canada. The quantity of sulphur in smelter gas used chiefly to produce sulphuric acid is estimated as the sulphur in sulphuric acid and sulphur dioxide marketed. The value is arbitrary. Another sulphur in acid made by roasting zinc sulphide concentrates is valued at the average price of the sulphur content of pyrite concentrates. Elemental sulphur production and values are based upon quantities of shipments and their values.

From 1886 to 1890 the sulphur content of pyrite shipped was assumed to be 40 per cent. It was calculated at 41 per cent from 1891 to 1910.

N 111 and N 112. Sand and gravel production are shipments by operators of sand and gravel pits or dredges. Special forms are utilized in the collection of data for sands produced by provincial, municipal and federal governments for use in construction projects.

N 120–142. Canadian imports of principal nonmetallic minerals, 1885 to 1960

SOURCE: for 1885 to 1925, the files of the Mineral Resources Division, Department of Mines and Technical Surveys; for 1926 to 1960, Dominion Bureau of Statistics, *Trade of Canada*.

N 143–162. Canadian exports of principal nonmetallic minerals, 1875 to 1960

SOURCE: for 1875 to 1925, the files of the Mineral Resources Division, Department of Mines and Technical Surveys; for 1926 to 1960, Dominion Bureau of Statistics, *Trade of Canada*.

N 163–169. Principal statistics of the Canadian nonmetallic mining industries, 1925 to 1960

SOURCE: for 1925 to 1944, the files of the Mineral Statistics Section, Dominion Bureau of Statistics; for 1945 to 1960, Dominion Bureau of Statistics, *General Review of the Mining Industry*, successive annual issues.

This table does not include the principal statistics for the production of total clay products and other structural materials.

FUELS (Series N 170–198)

N 170–175. Canadian production of fuels, 1867 to 1960

SOURCE: for all series, 1886 to 1955, Dominion Bureau of Statistics, *Canadian Mineral Statistics, 1886–1956*; for 1956 to 1960, Dominion Bureau of Statistics, *General Review of the Mining Industry*, successive annual issues; for 1867 to 1885, the files of the Mineral Statistics Section, Dominion Bureau of Statistics.

N 170 and N 171. See note 1 to the table for the change in definition of quantity produced or output after 1918. The output tonnage is valued at the average realization from sales.

N172 and N173. Production is the natural gas output minus the gas which is wasted or flared. Deductions are made for gas withdrawn from storage. Data are supplied to the Dominion Bureau of Statistics by the Oil and Gas Conservation Boards of the western provinces. British Columbia and Saskatchewan report an average price for natural gas. For Alberta the price is the average of prices shown on the producers' reports. Firms in New Brunswick and the Northwest Territories report their prices. Ontario natural gas is valued at an arbitrary wholesale price.

N174 and N175. The production of crude petroleum is obtained on a provincial basis. The average prices received for the oil sold is applied to the quantities produced. Production in the Northwest Territories is valued by the gross realization of sales. Firms in New Brunswick report the quantities and values of production there.

N176–181. Canadian imports of principal fuels, 1880 to 1960

SOURCE: for 1880 to 1925, the files of Mineral Statistics Section, Dominion Bureau of Statistics and of the Mineral Resources Division, Department of Mines and Technical Surveys; for 1926 to 1960, Dominion Bureau of Statistics, *Trade of Canada*, successive annual issues. Many of these import data (and the export data in series N182–187) have not hitherto been compiled for publication in a single table, particularly for petroleum and natural gas. The data have been checked by several agencies with the result that the time series are extensive and accurate. Private gas utilities in Alberta and Ontario and the major oil companies were consulted. Through their detailed records of import and export data, some gaps in the previously published data have been eliminated.

N176 and N177. Tonnages of coal shown are 'imported coal entered for consumption' including coal for ships stores. They are the amounts cleared from customs ports duty paid. Figures shown under this heading differ from 'landed coal'. The latter is the total amount that enters the country. The amounts at customs ports awaiting clearance are usually quite large.

N178 and N179. It should be noted that considerable volumes of 'natural gas' imported by pipeline in pre-war years were in fact a mixed gas containing both manufactured and natural gas.

N180 and N181. These import data relate solely to crude petroleum used by Canadian refineries. They include import item 7,153, crude petroleum for refining, and item 7,158, crude petroleum n.o.p. Difficulty was experienced in obtaining comparable statistics prior to 1949 because the import classifications changed from time to time. For 1880 to 1898 the data include imports of crude and refined petroleum.

N182–187. Canadian exports of principal fuels, 1868 to 1960

SOURCE: see the source note to series N176–181 which also applies to series N182–187. In addition *Canada Year Book, 1911* (p. 421) was used for coal exports, 1868 to 1885.

N184 and N185. There were no exports of natural gas from Canada from 1900 until the early nineteen-fifties. Natural gas was exported to Buffalo and Detroit before 1900 but the quantities are no longer available. It is also reported that Ontario rescinded a permit to build a pipeline in the Detroit River bed in 1901, and in 1907 Ontario passed a law prohibiting the export of natural gas and electricity.

N186 and N187. These data are for crude petroleum exported principally for use in foreign refineries. In the early years, particularly before 1900, there was no clear-cut classification of crude petroleum. It is therefore questionable whether the figures in this series are entirely comparable back to 1881.

N188–191. Apparent consumption of principal fuels in Canada, 1907 to 1960

SOURCE: compiled for this publication by the author of the section. The data were obtained from a combination of sources, principally the Dominion Bureau of Statistics and the private fuel companies.

Only quantity figures are given. Value figures are misleading because, first, they might be interpreted to mean cost to the consumer, and secondly, in the case of petroleum products, they are a mixture of very differently priced products.

N188. Consumption of coal was calculated from total output (including use for power purposes, for employees, for briquettes, put on waste heap, put on bank less lifted from waste heap and bank, and including all shipments) plus total imports less total exports.

N189. Consumption of natural gas was calculated as production plus imports only where appreciable and minus exports only where appreciable.

N190. Consumption of crude petroleum was calculated as production plus imports minus exports solely of crude oil.

N191. Consumption of petroleum products was calculated as total refinery shipments of all petroleum products in Canada plus imports minus exports of petroleum products. These figures are included here to emphasize that the domestic consumption volume of the end product is quite different from the apparent consumption of crude petroleum by Canadian refineries. Much of the difference is due to the balance of imports and exports of petroleum products to and from Canada.

N192–198. Principal statistics of the Canadian fuels industries, 1922 to 1960

SOURCE: for 1922 to 1944, the files of the Mineral Statistic Section, Dominion Bureau of Statistics and of the Mineral Resources Division, Department of Mines and Technical Surveys; for 1945 to 1960, Dominion Bureau of Statistics, *General Review of the Mining Industry*, successive annual issues.

In the published sources for 1960 the numbers of establishments, N192, declines in 1960 as a result of a change in the method of reporting. In the oil industry, reports were previously available for individual wells. A single report is now made for each province in which the firm is operating. The number of establishments in 1960 was obtained from the Mineral Statistics Section of the Dominion Bureau of Statistics.

N196. The term 'processing' used here means extraction, sorting, washing, drying, pumping and other similar minehead or wellhead costs. It does not refer to any manufacturing of the raw material into a semi-finished product.

N198. The meaning of 'net value' was changed radically after the Imperial Statistical Conference of 1935. Prior to 1935, 'net value of production', called 'net sales', was the gross value of production less only freight and treatment charges in the case of mines and less only the value of ores in the case of smelters. From 1935 to 1960, 'net value added by processing' is the gross value of production minus freight and treatment charges, the value of ores, and the full cost of all fuel, electricity and consumable supplies.

Series N 1–26. *Canadian production of principal metallic minerals, 1886 to 1960*
(all values in thousands of dollars; quantities as designated individually)

Year	Cobalt		Copper		Gold		Iron ore	
	Quantity (thousands of pounds)	Value (thousands of dollars)	Quantity (thousands of pounds)	Value (thousands of dollars)	Quantity (thousands of troy ounces)	Value (thousands of dollars)	Quantity (thousands of tons)	Value (thousands of dollars)
	1	2	3	4	5	6	7	8
1960	3,569	6,763	878,524	264,847	4,629	157,152	21,551	175,083
1959	3,150	5,955	790,539	233,103	4,483	150,508	24,488	192,666
1958	2,710	5,308	690,227	174,431	4,571	155,334	15,726	126,131
1957	3,923	7,784	718,219	206,898	4,434	148,757	22,272	167,221
1956	3,517	9,065	709,721	292,958	4,384	151,024	22,348	160,362
1955	3,319	8,564	651,987	239,756	4,542	156,789	16,283	110,436
1954	2,253	5,913	605,464	175,713	4,366	148,765	7,362	49,667
1953	1,603	4,013	506,504	150,954	4,056	139,598	6,510	44,103
1952	1,422	3,227	516,075	146,679	4,472	153,246	5,272	33,744
1951	952	2,000	539,942	149,026	4,393	161,873	4,681	31,141
1950	584	964	528,418	123,211	4,441	168,989	3,605	23,414
1949	619	952	526,914	104,719	4,124	148,447	3,675	21,204
1948	1,545	2,029	481,464	107,160	3,530	123,536	1,337	7,488
1947	573	876	451,723	91,542	3,070	107,458	1,919	9,313
1946	74	70	367,937	46,632	2,833	104,096	1,550	6,823
1945	109	90	474,914	59,322	2,697	103,824	1,135	3,635
1944	36	34	547,070	65,257	2,923	112,532	553	1,910
1943	176	191	575,190	67,171	3,651	140,575	641	2,032
1942	84	88	603,662	60,417	4,841	186,390	545	1,517
1941	263	256	643,317	64,407	5,345	205,789	516	1,426
1940	794	1,235	655,593	65,773	5,311	204,479	415	1,211
1939	733	1,213	608,826	60,935	5,094	184,116	124	342
1938	459	791	571,250	56,554	4,725	166,206	—	—
1937	507	848	530,029	68,917	4,096	143,326	—	—
1936	888	805	421,028	39,514	3,748	131,293	—	—
1935	681	513	418,998	32,312	3,285	115,595	—	—
1934	595	592	364,761	26,671	2,972	102,537	—	—
1933	467	598	299,982	21,635	2,949	84,350	—	—
1932	491	588	247,679	15,294	3,044	71,479	—	—
1931	521	651	292,304	24,114	2,694	58,093	—	—
1930	694	1,144	303,478	37,948	2,102	43,454	—	—
1929	929	1,802	248,121	43,415	1,928	39,862	—	—
1928	957	1,672	202,696	28,598	1,891	39,082	—	—
1927	881	1,765	140,147	17,195	1,853	38,300	—	—
1926	665	1,136	133,095	17,490	1,754	36,263	—	—
1925	1,116	2,329	111,451	15,650	1,736	35,881	—	—
1924	949	1,682	104,457	13,605	1,525	31,532	—	—
1923	888	2,531	86,882	12,529	1,233	25,495	31	115
1922	570	1,852	42,880	5,738	1,263	26,116	18	57
1921	252	756	47,621	5,954	926	19,149	60	230
1920	566	1,605	81,601	14,244	765	15,814	129	518
1919	596	1,019	75,054	14,028	767	15,850	197	693
1918	760	1,640	118,769	29,251	700	14,464	212	886
1917	674	1,138	109,227	29,688	739	15,273	215	759
1916	800	805	117,150	31,867	930	19,235	275	715
1915	412	383	100,785	17,411	918	18,978	398	774
1914	702	590	75,736	10,302	773	15,983	245	542
1913	1,642	420	76,977	11,754	803	16,599	308	630
1912	1,868	314	77,832	12,719	612	12,649	216	523
1911	1,704	171	55,648	6,887	473	9,781	210	522
1910	2,196	55	55,692	7,094	494	10,206	259	574
1909	3,066	95	52,494	6,815	454	9,382	268	659
1908	2,448	111	63,703	8,414	476	9,842	238	568
1907	1,478	104	56,979	11,398	406	8,383	313	667
1906	642	81	55,610	10,720	556	11,502	249	522
1905	236	100	48,093	7,498	685	14,159	291	—
1904	32	20	41,384	5,307	796	16,463	219	—
1903	—	—	42,684	5,649	912	18,844	264	—
1902	—	—	38,804	4,511	1,032	21,337	404	—
1901	—	—	37,827	6,097	1,167	24,129	314	—
1900	—	—	18,937	3,066	1,350	27,908	122	—
1899	—	—	15,078	2,655	1,029	21,262	75	241
1898	—	—	17,747	2,135	666	13,775	58	153
1897	—	—	13,301	1,502	292	6,027	51	130
1896	—	—	9,393	1,022	133	2,755	92	192
1895	—	—	7,772	836	101	2,084	103	238
1894	—	—	7,709	737	55	1,129	110	227
1893	—	—	8,110	872	47	977	126	299
1892	—	—	7,087	819	44	908	103	269
1891	—	—	9,529	1,227	45	931	69	142
1890	—	—	6,014	947	56	1,150	77	155
1889	—	—	6,810	936	63	1,295	84	152
1888	—	—	5,563	927	53	1,099	79	152
1887	—	—	3,260	367	57	1,188	76	146
1886	—	—	3,505	386	71	1,463	64	—

Series N1–26. *Canadian production of principal metallic minerals, 1886 to 1960 (continuation)*
(all values in thousands of dollars; quantities as designated individually)

Year	Lead Quantity (thousands of pounds)	Lead Value (thousands of dollars)	Magnesium Quantity (thousands of pounds)	Magnesium Value (thousands of dollars)	Nickel Quantity (thousands of pounds)	Nickel Value (thousands of dollars)	Palladium, iridium and other precious metals Quantity (thousands of troy ounces)	Palladium, iridium and other precious metals Value (thousands of dollars)
	9	10	11	12	13	14	15	16
1960	411,300	43,927	14,577	4,314	429,013	295,640	—[2]	—[2]
1959	373,391	39,617	12,204	3,180	373,110	257,009	178	5,917
1958	373,361	42,414	13,592	4,065	279,117	194,142	154	4,840
1957	362,969	50,670	16,770	5,255	375,917	258,977	217	7,896
1956	377,709	58,583	19,212	6,080	357,030	222,205	163	6,681
1955	405,525	58,315	—	6,585[4]	349,857	215,866	214	8,322
1954	436,990	58,251	—	6,587[4]	322,558	180,173	189	7,956
1953	387,412	50,077	—	6,336[4]	287,386	160,430	166	7,495
1952	337,684	54,671	—	5,366[4]	281,117	151,349	157	7,559
1951	316,463	58,229	—	3,907[4]	275,806	151,270	165	7,950
1950	331,394	47,886	—	1,545[4]	247,318	112,105	149	7,578
1949	319,550	50,489	—	1,041	257,379	99,173	182	8,290
1948	334,502	60,344	—	1,860	263,479	86,904	148	6,295
1947	323,337	44,200	—	725	237,251	70,651	110	4,388
1946	353,974	23,893	321	76	192,125	45,385	118	5,163
1945	346,994	17,350	7,359	1,607	245,131	61,982	459	18,671
1944	304,582	13,706	10,580	2,576	274,599	69,204	43	1,960
1943	444,061	16,670	7,154	2,075	288,019	71,675	126	5,233
1942	512,143	17,218	809	356	285,212	69,998	223	8,279
1941	460,167	15,471	11	3	282,258	68,657	97	3,396
1940	471,850	15,864	—	—	245,558	59,823	92	3,521
1939	388,570	12,314	—	—	226,106	50,920	135	4,200
1938	418,928	14,009	—	—	210,573	53,914	131	3,677
1937	411,999	21,053	—	—	224,905	59,507	120	3,180
1936	383,181	14,994	—	—	169,739	43,877	104	2,483
1935	339,105	10,625	—	—	138,516	35,345	85	1,963
1934	346,277	8,437	—	—	128,687	32,139	84	1,699
1933	266,475	6,373	—	—	83,265	20,130	31	645
1932	255,947	5,410	—	—	30,328	7,180	38	902
1931	267,342	7,260	—	—	65,666	15,267	47	1,218
1930	332,894	13,103	—	—	103,769	24,455	34	896
1929	326,523	16,544	—	—	110,276	27,115	17	809
1928	337,947	15,553	—	—	96,756	22,319	14	628
1927	311,423	16,477	—	—	66,799	15,262	12	554
1926	283,801	19,241	—	—	65,714	14,374	10	640
1925	253,591	23,127	—	—	73,857	15,947	8	649
1924	175,485	14,221	—	—	69,536	19,470	10	863
1923	111,234	7,986	—	—	62,454	18,332	2	184
1922	93,307	5,818	—	—	17,597	6,159	1	—
1921	66,680	3,829	—	—	19,293	6,753	1	—
1920	35,954	3,214	—	—	61,336	24,534	1	—
1919	43,828	3,053	—	—	44,545	17,818	1	—
1918	51,398	4,754	—	—	92,507	37,003	1	—
1917	32,576	3,628	—	—	84,330	33,732	2	—
1916	41,498	3,533	—	—	82,959	29,035	2	—
1915	46,316	2,594	—	—	68,309	20,493	1	—
1914	36,338	1,628	—	—	45,518	13,055	1	—
1913	37,663	1,755	—	—	49,677	14,903	—	—
1912	35,763	1,598	—	—	44,842	13,452	1	—
1911	23,785	828	—	—	34,099	10,230	1	—
1910	32,988	1,216	—	—	37,271	11,181	1	—
1909	45,857	1,692	—	—	26,283	9,462	1	—
1908	43,196	1,814	—	—	19,143	8,232	—	—
1907	47,739	2,542	—	—	21,190	9,535	1	—
1906	54,608	3,089	—	—	21,491	8,949	—	3
1905	56,865	2,677	—	—	18,876	7,551	1	17
1904	37,531	1,617	—	—	10,548	4,219	1	19
1903	18,139	769	—	—	12,506	5,002	3	62
1902	22,956	934	—	—	10,693	5,026	4	86
1901	51,901	2,249	—	—	9,189	4,595	—	—
1900	63,170	2,761	—	—	7,080	3,328	—	—
1899	21,862	977	—	—	5,744	2,068	—	—
1898	31,915	1,206	—	—	5,518	1,821	—	—
1897	39,018	1,397	—	—	3,998	1,399	—	—
1896	24,200	721	—	—	3,397	1,189	—	—
1895	16,462	532	—	—	3,889	1,361	—	—
1894	5,703	188	—	—	4,907	1,871	—	—
1893	2,135	80	—	—	3,983	2,071	—	—
1892	808	33	—	—	2,414	1,400	—	—
1891	89	4	—	—	4,035	2,421	—	—
1890	105	5	—	—	1,436	933	—	—
1889	165	6	—	—	830	498	—	—
1888	675	30	—	—	—	—	—	—
1887	205	9	—	—	—	—	—	—
1886	—	—	—	—	—	—	—	—

Series N1-26. *Canadian production of principal metallic minerals, 1886 to 1960 (continuation)*

(all values in thousands of dollars; quantities as designated individually)

Year	Platinum Quantity (thousands of troy ounces)	Platinum Value (thousands of dollars)	Silver Quantity (thousands of troy ounces)	Silver Value (thousands of dollars)	Tungsten Quantity (thousands of pounds)	Tungsten Value (thousands of dollars)	Uranium Quantity (thousands of pounds)	Uranium Value (thousands of dollars)	Zinc[1] Quantity (thousands of pounds)[1]	Zinc Value (thousands of dollars)
	17	18	19	20	21	22	23	24	25	26
1960	484[2]	28,874[2]	34,017	30,244	—[3]	—[3]	25,495	269,938	813,745	108,635
1959	150	11,015	31,924	28,023	—[3]	—[3]	31,784	331,143	792,015	96,943
1958	146	9,481	31,163	27,053	691	1,898	26,805	279,538	850,198	92,501
1957	200	17,835	28,823	25,183	1,921	5,279	13,271	136,304	827,482	100,043
1956	151	15,726	28,432	25,498	2,271	6,351	4,581	45,732	845,265	125,437
1955	170	14,748	27,984	24,676	1,943	5,508	—	26,032	866,714	118,306
1954	154	12,950	31,118	25,908	2,171	5,796	—	26,373	752,982	90,207
1953	138	12,551	28,299	23,774	2,446	5,689	—	—	803,523	96,101
1952	122	10,917	25,222	21,066	1,493	4,488	—	—	743,604	129,833
1951	153	14,543	23,126	21,865	3	7	—	—	682,224	135,763
1950	125	10,256	23,221	18,768	284	160	—	—	626,455	98,040
1949	154	11,603	17,641	13,099	252	252	—	—	576,524	76,372
1948	121	10,623	16,110	12,082	1,046	1,046	—	—	468,327	65,238
1947	95	5,582	12,504	9,003	496	681	—	—	415,726	46,686
1946	122	7,673	12,544	10,493	—	—	—	—	470,620	36,755
1945	208	8,017	12,943	6,083	1	1	—	—	517,214	33,309
1944	158	6,065	13,627	5,860	887	246	—	—	550,823	23,685
1943	220	8,459	17,345	7,849	1,509	1,084	—	—	610,754	24,430
1942	258	10,899	20,695	8,728	521	406	—	—	580,257	19,793
1941	124	4,750	21,754	8,323	83	39	—	925	512,382	17,477
1940	108	4,240	23,834	9,116	12	7	—	410	424,029	14,464
1939	149	5,223	23,164	9,378	9	5	—	1,122	394,554	12,108
1938	161	5,197	22,219	9,660	—	—	—	1,045	381,507	11,724
1937	139	6,753	22,978	10,313	—	—	—	877	370,338	18,154
1936	132	5,321	18,334	8,274	—	—	—	606	333,183	11,045
1935	105	3,446	16,619	10,767	—	—	—	414	320,650	9,937
1934	116	4,491	16,415	7,791	—	—	—	159	298,580	9,088
1933	25	858	15,188	5,746	—	—	—	248	199,132	6,393
1932	27	1,099	18,348	5,811	—	—	—	—	172,284	4,144
1931	45	1,597	20,562	6,142	—	—	—	—	237,245	6,059
1930	34	1,543	26,444	10,089	—	—	—	—	267,644	9,635
1929	13	847	23,143	12,264	—	—	—	—	197,267	10,627
1928	11	709	21,936	12,762	—	—	—	—	184,647	10,143
1927	11	718	22,737	12,817	—	—	—	—	165,496	10,251
1926	10	924	22,372	13,895	—	—	—	—	149,938	11,110
1925	9	1,028	20,229	13,971	—	—	—	—	109,269	8,328
1924	9	1,091	19,736	13,180	—	—	—	—	98,909	6,275
1923	1	142	18,602	12,068	—	—	—	—	60,416	3,992
1922	—	46	18,626	12,577	—	—	—	—	56,290	3,218
1921	—	23	13,543	8,485	—	—	—	—	53,089	2,471
1920	1	38	13,330	13,450	—	—	—	—	39,864	3,058
1919	1	74	16,021	17,802	—	—	—	—	32,195	2,362
1918	1	71	21,384	20,604	27	12	—	—	35,083	2,862
1917	1	104	22,221	18,092	1	—	—	—	29,669	2,641
1916	1	85	25,460	16,717	—	—	—	—	23,365	2,992
1915	—	22	26,626	13,229	—	—	—	—	15[1]	555
1914	1	34	28,450	15,594	—	—	—	—	11	263
1913	—	9	31,846	19,041	—	—	—	—	8	187
1912	—	23	31,956	19,440	28	—	—	—	6	212
1911	1	29	32,559	17,355	—	—	—	—	3	101
1910	—	8	32,869	17,580	—	—	—	—	5	120
1909	1	14	27,529	14,179	—	—	—	—	18	243
1908	—	3	22,106	11,686	—	—	—	—	—	3
1907	—	7	12,780	8,349	—	—	—	—	2	49
1906	—	3	8,473	5,659	—	—	—	—	1	24
1905	1	12	6,000	3,621	—	—	—	—	9	139
1904	1	11	3,578	2,047	—	—	—	—	478[1]	24
1903	2	33	3,199	1,710	—	—	—	—	900	49
1902	2	47	4,291	2,238	—	—	—	—	142	7
1901	—	—	5,539	3,265	—	—	—	—	—	—
1900	—	—	4,468	2,740	—	—	—	—	213	9
1899	—	1	3,412	2,033	—	—	—	—	814	47
1898	—	2	4,452	2,594	—	—	—	—	788	36
1897	—	2	5,558	3,323	—	—	—	—	—	—
1896	—	1	3,205	2,150	—	—	—	—	—	—
1895	—	4	1,578	1,030	—	—	—	—	—	—
1894	—	1	848	534	—	—	—	—	—	—
1893	—	2	429	330	—	—	—	—	—	—
1892	—	4	311	272	—	—	—	—	—	—
1891	—	10	415	410	—	—	—	—	—	—
1890	—	5	401	419	—	—	—	—	—	—
1889	—	4	383	359	—	—	—	—	—	—
1888	—	6	437	411	—	—	—	—	—	—
1887	—	6	355	347	—	—	—	—	—	—

[1] From 1898 to 1904 the figures represent thousands of pounds of zinc contained in ores shipped; from 1905 to 1915 thousands of tons of ore concentrates shipped from mines; from 1916 to 1960 thousands of pounds of recoverable zinc in ores exported plus refined zinc made in Canada.

[2] Palladium, iridium and other precious metals included with platinum, series N17 and N18, for 1960 in order not to disclose individual company data.

[3] There was no tungsten production in 1959 and 1960.

[4] Includes the value of calcium production.

Series N 27–49. *Canadian imports of principal metallic minerals, 1880 to 1960*[1]
(all values in thousands of dollars; quantities as designated individually)

Year	Alumina, bauxite, cryolite Quantity (thousands of cwt)	Value (thousands of dollars)	Aluminium[2] Quantity (thousands of cwt)	Value (thousands of dollars)	Cobalt ore Quantity (thousands of pounds)	Value (thousands of dollars)	Copper[3] Quantity (thousands of cwt)	Value (thousands of dollars)
	27	28	29	30	31	32	33	34
1960	59,824	46,428	30	645	—	—	94	2,878
1959	45,270	36,975	29	628	—	—	115	3,437
1958	46,482	35,088	230	5,440	—	—	85	2,358
1957	51,121	48,275	48	1,186	—	1	200	5,655
1956	52,159	33,393	54	1,401	2	1	229	9,047
1955	61,906	25,967	5	99	38	11	70	2,544
1954	59,331	21,216	4	74	10	1	71	1,896
1953	53,777	16,720	3	108	4,288	628	318	8,278
1952	49,149	13,417	11	147	14,943	2,318	321	9,431
1951	48,171	16,574	6	185	3,688	761	86	1,712
1950	37,312	10,569	10	133	3,913	436	45	1,035
1949	35,887	10,378	2	21	81	2	38	776
1948	40,307	10,962	5	32	848	65	42	844
1947	28,003	9,760	15	139	—	—	39	782
1946	25,724	9,074	17	193	1,170	451	28	472
1945	18,880	7,787	7	67	2,390	869	28	436
1944	26,613	10,272	6	60	3,676	1,328	8	132
1943	60,662	23,168	2	18	2,236	786	17	283
1942	26,680	13,310	—	1	4,336	1,485	11	184
1941	23,233	9,333	1	18	4,600	1,543	21	362
1940	13,963	6,410	4	148	3,921	1,165	17	311
1939	10,211	3,708	6	108	592	148	15	221
1938	7,495	2,920	12	140	—	—	14	189
1937	6,219	4,398	13	218	—	—	14	223
1936	3,489	2,937	7	132	—	—	11	146
1935	2,551	2,927	7	107	—	—	8	98
1934	1,643	2,211	4	64	—	—	8	91
1933	1,099	1,963	2	49	—	—	4	53
1932	1,035	2,060	3	40	—	—	9	96
1931	1,963	3,316	3	66	—	—	114	1,184
1930	2,185	3,284	2	41	—	—	418	5,870
1929	2,902	3,422	3	76	—	—	726	13,161
1928	3,344	4,634	14	416	—	—	501	7,602
1927	2,557	6,200	11	331	—	—	367	5,095
1926	1,515	3,488	10	271	—	—	294	4,343
1925	1,290	2,722	7	218	—	—	390	5,654
1924	1,298	2,446	7	183	—	—	290	3,965
1923	1,336	2,326	8	194	—	—	402	6,287
1922	426	938	12	251	—	—	265	3,781
1921	300	638	7	213	—	—	185	2,593
1920	1,148	1,889	19	623	—	—	456	8,597
1919	586	1,565	8	248	—	—	280	5,769
1918	1,864	2,071	3	109	—	—	223	5,879
1917	1,743	1,866	7	317	—	—	267	8,078
1916	538	1,114	14	524	—	—	220	5,988
1915	350	893	27	631	—	—	168	2,868
1914	286	571	38	746	—	—	221	3,213
1913	307	615	35	605	—	—	363[3]	6,034[3]
1912	224	448	24	410	—	—	325	4,258
1911	186	372	25	531	—	—	264	3,487
1910	195	403	32	675	—	—	198	2,670
1909	118	235	6[2]	167[2]	—	—	137	1,906
1908	15	30	4	132	—	—	120	2,400
1907	127	269	9[2]	218[2]	—	—	26[3]	521[3]
1906	90	239	7	168	—	—	139	2,364
1905	54	139	6	155	—	—	106	1,498
1904	—	123	—	—	—	—	77	1,020
1903	—	45	—	—	—	—	83	1,066
1902	—	9	—	—	—	—	73	993
1901	—	2	—	—	—	—	41	674
1900	—	3	—	—	—	—	43	736
1899	—	2	—	—	—	—	37	525
1898	—	2	—	—	—	—	49	520
1897	—	2	—	—	—	—	18	166
1896	—	3	—	—	—	—	15	178
1895	—	—	—	—	—	—	14	147
1894	—	—	—	—	—	—	1	7
1893	—	—	—	—	—	—	2	16
1892	—	—	—	—	—	—	3	15
1891	—	—	—	—	—	—	1	10
1890	—	—	—	—	—	—	1	12
1889	—	—	—	—	—	—	—	3
1888	—	—	—	—	—	—	—	2
1887	—	—	—	—	—	—	—	3
1886	—	—	—	—	—	—	1	7

Series N 27–49. *Canadian imports of principal metallic minerals, 1880 to 1960 (continuation)*
(all values in thousands of dollars; quantities as designated individually)

Year	Iron ore		Lead[2]		Manganese ore[4]		Nickel[5]	
	Quantity (thousands of tons)	Value (thousands of dollars)	Quantity (thousands of pounds)	Value (thousands of dollars)	Quantity (thousands of cwt)	Value (thousands of dollars)	Quantity (thousands of pounds)	Value (thousands of dollars)
	35	36	37	38	39	40	41	42
1960	5,056	48,370	1,635	175	1,127	2,544	3,524	3,951
1959	2,801	27,129	4,377	386	2,369	5,017	3,715	3,541
1958	3,413	28,932	3,678	325	841	1,723	4,309	3,894
1957	4,539	36,387	3,251	400	2,626	7,520	4,183	3,842
1956	5,069	38,722	483	74	4,160	9,137	5,108	4,804
1955	4,539	31,563	438	58	3,506	7,338	4,205	3,544
1954	3,035	20,416	381	51	979	2,277	3,167	2,673
1953	4,168	28,194	624	83	1,334	2,720	6,166	4,498
1952	4,268	26,519	974	175	3,888	8,274	3,298	2,741
1951	3,831	22,671	1,469	360	4,442	9,078	2,612	2,369
1950	3,071	16,802	3,014	350	2,714	4,994	2,674	2,082
1949	2,517	12,057	5,206	658	2,757	4,476	2,896	2,017
1948	4,300	15,507	161	25	4,606	6,450	2,727	1,570
1947	3,945	12,717	33	8	4,470	6,146	2,753	1,416
1946	2,282	6,467	95	6	2,880	2,485	3,204	1,581
1945	3,740	8,596	84	8	3,966	4,572	1,525	801
1944	3,127	7,394	36	5	1,716	2,370	849	461
1943	3,906	9,056	31	5	1,025	1,445	1,090	595
1942	2,702	6,230	31	3	1,148	860	997	473
1941	3,255	7,135	594	42	2,089	1,171	2,021	918
1940	2,418	5,513	347	19	1,409	777	1,188	525
1939	1,765	4,179	105	7	596	622	1,394	529
1938	1,302	2,830	111	6	421	464	981	401
1937	2,125	4,721	125	10	1,545	802	983	403
1936	1,317	2,634	97	6	1,285	684	933	382
1935	1,510	2,960	179	8	736	353	572	253
1934	977	1,827	162	6	619	234	691	257
1933	206	401	104	5	687	294	993	352
1932	68	184	187	8	30	88	539	234
1931	808	1,718	797	33	—	—	782	305
1930	1,485	3,324	2,286	128	1,976	992	1,382	471
1929	2,448	5,026	1,434	85	1,983	991	1,605	564
1928	2,223	4,325	693	42	2,129	1,059	1,167	429
1927	1,487	2,876	517	42	1,398	1,451	2,453	807
1926	1,466	2,854	884	80	767	779	1,118	243
1925	1,037	2,016	610	61	293[4]	428[4]	1,060	212
1924	913	2,345	809	64	30	65	875	180
1923	1,942	5,765	3,159	176	26	56	826	248
1922	887	2,259	2,266	123	6	20	1,367	258
1921	661	2,109	2,018	103	28	97	372	148
1920	1,984	5,716	27,771	2,274	26	73	736	257
1919	1,683	4,706	14,088	1,022	—	—	644[5]	225[5]
1918	2,201	5,896	15,706	1,351	—	—	671	294
1917	2,251	5,125	16,980	1,732	—	—	1,020	403
1916	2,340	4,419	27,450	2,078	—	—	785	230
1915	1,504	2,332	43,528	2,066	—	—	675	172
1914	1,147	2,387	16,406	632	—	—	551	144
1913	1,942	3,878	12,694	527	—	—	713	194
1912	2,048[6]	3,932[6]	30,100	1,034	—	—	581	135
1911	—	—	23,062	551	—	—	557	137
1910	—	—	13,830	392	—	—	398	98
1909	—	—	6,386[2]	197[2]	—	—	249	67
1908	—	—	8,117	360	—	—	310	94
1907	—	—	9,329[2]	334[2]	—	—	—	—
1906	—	—	9,884	328	—	—	—	—
1905	—	—	7,487	186	—	—	—	—
1904	—	—	10,870	161	—	—	—	—
1903	—	—	11,007	103	—	—	—	—
1902	—	—	14,088	154	—	—	—	—
1901	—	—	10,162	175	—	—	—	—
1900	—	—	7,785	261	—	—	—	—
1899	—	—	15,946	323	—	—	—	—
1898	—	—	11,063	300	—	—	—	—
1897	—	—	7,580	188	—	—	—	—
1896	—	—	8,101	196	—	—	—	—
1895	—	—	7,400	156	—	—	—	—
1894	—	—	7,871	170	—	—	—	—
1893	—	—	10,689	248	—	—	—	—
1892	—	—	10,867	287	—	—	—	—
1891	—	—	10,203	291	—	—	—	—
1890	—	—	12,028	343	—	—	—	—
1889	—	—	8,840	257	—	—	—	—
1888	—	—	8,364	243	—	—	—	—
1887	—	—	7,531	215	—	—	—	—
1886	—	—	4,974	194	—	—	—	—
1885	—	—	4,547	111	—	—	—	—
1884	—	—	4,911	132	—	—	—	—
1883	—	—	5,737	178	—	—	—	—
1882	—	—	4,720	157	—	—	—	—
1881	—	—	3,446	128	—	—	—	—
1880	—	—	3,030	124	—	—	—	—

Series N 27–49. *Canadian imports of principal metallic minerals, 1880 to 1960 (continuation)*

(all values in thousands of dollars; quantities as designated individually)

Year	Platinum[2] Value (thousands of dollars)	Silver Quantity (thousands of ounces)	Silver Value (thousands of dollars)	Tin[2] Quantity (thousands of cwt)	Tin[2] Value (thousands of dollars)	Zinc[2] Quantity (thousands of cwt)	Zinc[2] Value (thousands of dollars)
	43	44	45	46	47	48	49
1960	12,951	3,849	3,473	84	8,258	1	22
1959	6,466	2,808	2,484	94	9,182	17	158
1958	8,641	3	2	78	7,060	12	122
1957	15,431	1,859	1,633	93	8,539	1	18
1956	19,580	1,010	902	85	8,194	2	43
1955	15,723	87	75	97	8,814	1	28
1954	17,784	60	50	86	7,442	2	32
1953	16,517	287	231	83	8,264	1	16
1952	17,373	146	128	88	10,595	10	194
1951	17,078	1,050	848	137	19,577	32	665
1950	21,340	342	274	108	10,337	1	21
1949	10,737	1,333	973	82	7,862	1	23
1948	10,738	718	528	81	7,898	—	7
1947	7,532	71	57	89	6,677	1	24
1946	8,613	1,928	1,586	84	5,977	—	6
1945	4,061	2	1	72	4,983	2	31
1944	62	—	—	27	1,768	90	822
1943	426	—	—	26	1,504	272	2,456
1942	628	31	13	72	4,167	118	1,064
1941	1,745	264	101	174	9,652	1	15
1940	5,560	1,355	519	118	6,235	—	5
1939	221	3,851	1,533	58	2,833	—	3
1938	238	2,011	850	53	2,205	—	1
1937	296	1,987	870	59	3,116	—	3
1936	141	—	2,390	48	2,182	—	1
1935	56	—	5,585	47	2,323	1	6
1934	52	—	2,193	40	2,054	—	1
1933	49	—	676	28	1,149	2	6
1932	30	—	586	31	809	2	5
1931	46	—	467	41	1,067	4	14
1930	87	—	611	53	1,757	44	214
1929	158	—	958	57	2,671	27	166
1928	139	—	985	54	2,822	18	108
1927	95	—	897	48	3,066	14	90
1926	138	—	1,011	51	3,264	12	95
1925	158	—	1,025	44	2,460	56	508
1924	167	—	665	40	1,971	43	344
1923	118	—	723	42	1,747	39	343
1922	91	—	658	37	1,166	50	368
1921	84	—	582	26	840	39	304
1920	106	—	2,453	48	3,030	50	534
1919	145	—	3,590	37	2,105	238	1,866
1918	31	—	437	35	2,492	313	2,804
1917	114	—	1,063	37	1,786	371	3,641
1916	89	—	875	35	1,372	148	2,141
1915	84	—	337	29	1,010	159	2,011
1914	80	—	629	34	1,191	140	741
1913	146	—	840	51	2,252	173	953
1912	232	—	1,100	49	2,134	218	1,304
1911	176	—	848	40	1,624	151	861
1910	102	—	975	32	1,059	141	752
1909	46[2]	—	—	34[2]	981[2]	82[2]	452[2]
1908	60	—	—	35[2]	1,282	96	505[2]
1907	113[2]	—	—	22[2]	892[2]	61[2]	395[2]
1906	54	—	—	33	1,172	75	449
1905	62	—	—	29	819	63	348
1904	28	—	—	27	720	60	303
1903	21	—	—	25	729	50	254
1902	19	—	—	32	599	53	222
1901	20	—	—	29	698	35	162
1900	58	—	—	22	581	35	186
1899	10	—	—	29	306	24	137
1898	10	—	—	25	292	38	126
1897	9	—	—	19	250	20	91
1896	6	—	—	21	210	31	121
1895	4	—	—	25	214	24	94
1894	7	—	—	—	—	29	126
1893	14	—	—	—	—	37	174
1892	2	—	—	—	—	36	190
1891	4	—	—	—	—	24	136
1890	5	—	—	—	—	33	164
1889	3	—	—	—	—	29	121
1888	13	—	—	—	—	24	96
1887	1	—	—	—	—	33	124
1886	1	—	—	—	—	29	104
1885	1	—	—	—	—	24	81

[1] See the notes to series N 27–49 for the content and changes in content of the various series.

[2] For aluminium, lead, platinum, tin and zinc, for 1908 and 1909 data are for fiscal years ending 31 March of the year given; for 1907 data are for 9 months ending 31 March 1907; for 1906 and earlier years data are for fiscal years ending 30 June of the year given.

[3] For copper, for 1908 to 1913 data are for fiscal years ending 31 March of the

year given; for 1907 data are for 9 months ending 31 March 1907; for 1906 and earlier years data are for fiscal years ending 30 June of the year given.

[4] For manganese ore, for 1920 to 1925 data are for fiscal years ending 31 March of the year given.

[5] For nickel, for 1908 to 1919 data are for fiscal years ending 31 March of the year given.

[6] For 9 months ending 31 December 1912.

Series N50–81. *Canadian exports of principal metallic minerals, 1868 to 1960*
(all values in thousands of dollars; quantities as designated individually)

	Aluminium				Copper			
	Primary forms and scrap		Semi-fabricated		Copper blister, ore matte, etc., and scrap		Ingots, bars, cakes, slabs, etc.	
Year	Quantity (thousands of cwt)	Value (thousands of dollars)	Quantity (thousands of cwt)	Value (thousands of dollars)	Quantity (thousands of cwt)	Value (thousands of dollars)	Quantity (thousands of cwt)	Value (thousands of dollars)
	50	51	52	53	54	55	56	57
1960	11,594	252,083	602	16,071	1,183	31,616	5,561	170,153
1959	10,469	217,971	464	12,713	766	20,027	4,449	130,247
1958	9,941	212,780	318	9,662	828	17,927	4,493	109,904
1957	9,821	220,777	252	8,609	1,177	30,524	3,976	110,080
1956	10,360	230,021	142	4,786	1,112	42,483	3,497	141,767
1955	10,475	203,356	258	7,615	1,197	40,657	3,064	109,650
1954	9,648	173,351	349	9,041	1,167	30,719	3,123	91,356
1953	9,463	164,372	348	9,007	1,236	32,677	2,640	80,940
1952	8,322	143,395	472	11,710	723	15,963	2,274	71,406
1951	7,167	113,267	296	7,586	757	15,290	2,037	59,023
1950	6,807	97,713	229	5,493	771	15,814	2,685	59,666
1949	6,026	85,878	212	5,155	811	15,967	2,543	53,715
1948	6,999	89,333	123	3,404	676	11,020	2,323	50,683
1947	4,490	54,545	78	2,068	696	11,114	1,750	33,486
1946	3,876	50,083	49	1,307	377	2,651	2,028	27,463
1945	7,776	122,549	38	1,070	415	2,933	2,587	32,098
1944	5,941	93,708	62	2,310	579	4,035	2,705	29,049
1943	7,510	124,479	—	—	821	5,965	1,287	12,731
1942	6,290	112,155	—	—	824	6,127	1,972	19,491
1941	3,855	75,798	—	—	1,225	9,334	2,528	25,352
1940	1,744	33,119	—	—	1,417	10,754	3,090	31,369
1939	1,433	25,950	—	—	1,595	12,164	3,316	33,730
1938	1,315	23,329	—	—	1,438	10,899	3,635	35,858
1937	997	17,968	—	—	903	9,292	2,961	38,705
1936	597	11,114	—	—	536	3,507	3,109	27,461
1935	626	10,370	—	—	1,184	7,820	2,435	18,061
1934	445	7,561	—	—	660	3,992	1,876	13,944
1933	354	6,156	—	—	554	3,239	1,533	10,347
1932	197	2,933	—	—	658	3,417	1,191[1]	6,796[1]
1931	253	3,987	—	—	916	7,786	—	—
1930	461	8,135	—	—	2,291	30,405	—	—
1929	764	13,665	—	—	2,468	37,232	—	—
1928	424	8,298	—	—	1,893	23,269	—	—
1927	524	10,611	—	—	1,330	14,641	—	—
1926	255	5,951	—	—	1,183	14,492	—	—
1925	273	6,559	—	—	1,147	14,176	—	—
1924	181	3,991	—	—	997	11,582	—	—
1923	176	3,380	—	—	761	9,351	—	—
1922	96	1,637	—	—	544	6,269	—	—
1921	54	1,260	—	—	452	6,359	—	—
1920	197	6,095	—	—	863	14,733	—	—
1919	146	4,455	—	—	639	9,601	—	—
1918	216	7,224	—	—	743	9,394	—	—
1917	223	7,621	—	—	1,024	18,480	—	—
1916	184	5,201	—	—	1,308	22,061	—	—

Series N 50–81. *Canadian exports of principal metallic minerals, 1868 to 1960 (continued)*
(all values in thousands of dollars; quantities as designated individually)

| | Aluminium | | | | Copper | | | |
| | Primary forms and scrap | | Semi-fabricated | | Copper blister, ore matte, etc., and scrap | | Ingots, bars, cakes, slabs, etc. | |
Year	Quantity (thousands of cwt)	Value (thousands of dollars)	Quantity (thousands of cwt)	Value (thousands of dollars)	Quantity (thousands of cwt)	Value (thousands of dollars)	Quantity (thousands of cwt)	Value (thousands of dollars)
	50	51	52	53	54	55	56	57
1915	187	3,334	—	—	856	9,288	—	—
1914	145	2,365	—	—	708	7,362	—	—
1913	130	1,762	—	—	844	9,804	—	—
1912	183	2,002	—	—	765	8,800	—	—
1911	50	748	—	—	552	5,460	—	—
1910	77	1,160	—	—	570	5,841	—	—
1909	61	918	—	—	544	5,832	—	—
1908	17	400	—	—	511	5,935	—	—
1907	55	1,109	—	—	547	8,742	—	—
1906	45	899	—	—	424	7,303	—	—
1905	25	508	—	—	407	5,444	—	—
1904	13	278	—	—	386	4,216	—	—
1903	—	—	—	—	384	3,874	—	—
1902	—	—	—	—	261	2,477	—	—
1901	—	—	—	—	325	3,405	—	—
1900	—	—	—	—	236	1,742	—	—
1899	—	—	—	—	114	1,200	—	—
1898	—	—	—	—	116	840	—	—
1897	—	—	—	—	140	850	—	—
1896	—	—	—	—	55	281	—	—
1895	—	—	—	—	37	237	—	—
1894	—	—	—	—	16	92	—	—
1893	—	—	—	—	48	269	—	—
1892	—	—	—	—	—	278	—	—
1891	—	—	—	—	—	348	—	—
1890	—	—	—	—	—	398	—	—
1889	—	—	—	—	—	168	—	—
1888	—	—	—	—	—	257	—	—
1887	—	—	—	—	26	138	—	—
1886	—	—	—	—	29	249	—	—
1885	—	—	—	—	26	263	—	—
1884	—	—	—	—	27	273	—	—
1883	—	—	—	—	14	149	—	—
1882	—	—	—	—	19	183	—	—
1881	—	—	—	—	12	126	—	—
1880	—	—	—	—	14	193	—	—
1879	—	—	—	—	4	48	—	—
1878	—	—	—	—	4	36	—	—
1877	—	—	—	—	19	245	—	—
1876	—	—	—	—	19	250	—	—
1875	—	—	—	—	18	241	—	—
1874	—	—	—	—	9	112	—	—
1873	—	—	—	—	10	121	—	—

Series N 50–81. *Canadian exports of principal metallic minerals, 1868 to 1960 (continuation)*
(all values in thousands of dollars; quantities as designated individually)

| | Cobalt | | | | Iron ore | | Lead | | | |
| | Contained in ore | | Metals and alloys | | | | Ore and scrap[3] | | Pig lead | |
Year	Quantity (thousands of pounds)	Value (thousands of dollars)	Quantity (thousands of pounds)	Value (thousands of dollars)	Quantity (thousands of tons)	Value (thousands of dollars)	Quantity (thousands of cwt)	Value (thousands of dollars)	Quantity (thousands of cwt)	Value (thousands of dollars)
	58	59	60	61	62	63	64	65	66	67
1960	—	—	846	1,376	18,975	155,472	1,160	10,085	1,929	15,958
1959	—	—	684	1,220	20,779	157,814	1,135	10,286	1,845	15,183
1958	—	—	1,034	1,918	13,878	107,674	1,090	10,722	1,847	15,377
1957	15	16	2,168	4,156	20,130	152,281	890	10,534	1,691	18,862
1956	16	15	1,444	3,586	20,265	144,443	1,003	13,573	1,593	21,452
1955	—	—	1,555	3,518	14,569	99,814	1,176	15,115	1,854	22,078
1954	3	6	1,144	3,801	6,127	39,719	1,213	14,727	2,328	25,803
1953	37	60	781	2,487	4,820	30,843	1,244	14,859	2,058	22,976
1952	—	—	336	773	3,847	22,333	584	8,061	2,595	41,615
1951	35	47	193	383	3,226	18,596	421	7,167	2,115	38,123
1950	17	15	1[2]	10[2]	2,227	13,310	421	5,863	2,303	32,241
1949	49	37	46	230	2,550	14,117	436[3]	5,161[3]	2,271	36,725
1948	871	641	120	528	1,070	5,301	112	1,563	2,075	32,759
1947	89	69	100	389	1,750	6,023	135	1,602	2,499	29,099
1946	48	41	622	1,199	1,145	4,353	120	737	2,082	15,978
1945	65	57	904	2,202	771	2,553	157	574	2,146	8,603
1944	26	24	1,186	2,455	308	1,153	190	650	2,058	6,395
1943	163	189	1,125	2,529	375	1,451	115	425	3,087	9,222
1942	93	97	1,171	2,724	296	1,056	119	409	4,216	15,243
1941	280	281	1,187	2,388	282	1,040	132	441	3,686	13,085
1940	478	388	528	1,053	252	924	183	462	3,031	9,028
1939	204	178	136	268	11	43	82	400	3,615	9,450
1938	66	41	133	201	—	1	72	345	3,099	8,638
1937	92	59	60	95	5	14	165	863	3,531	16,978
1936	526	213	46	73	3	9	94	288	3,214	10,113
1935	419	125	28	47	3	10	113	290	2,829	6,871
1934	219	85	70	94	3	12	236	510	2,832	5,238
1933	54	19	76	103	2	2	76	268	2,843	4,923
1932	125	58	79	141	1	2	37	149	2,140	3,269
1931	273	166	75	152	2	5	44	177	2,164	4,483
1930	400	442	79	245	.1	3	263	1,258	2,054	7,015
1929	379	484	372	851	4	19	160	1,047	2,284	10,053
1928	—	531	259	553	3	13	150	894	2,554	10,172
1927	1,366	243	368	767	2	12	130	845	2,394	11,981
1926	746	192	191	377	1	7	136	796	2,025	12,984
1925	—	—	310	702	4	20	375	2,342	1,601	11,809
1924	—	—	173	394	5	22	132	785	1,087	6,866
1923	—	—	240	574	8	29	79	536	471	2,496
1922	—	—	116	310	2	14	109	550	415	1,877
1921	—	593	69	188	4	13	63	257	238	992
1920	—	537	315	537	20	99	75	386	—	2
1919	—	1,006	110	275	14	78	131	616	113	773
1918	—	1,901	366	1,047	130	651	227	1,322	75	669
1917	—	1,543	334	1,075	164	661	134	925	10	62
1916	—	—	—	—	161	542	90	558	1	8

Series N 50–81. *Canadian exports of principal metallic minerals, 1868 to 1960 (continued)*
(all values in thousands of dollars; quantities as designated individually)

	Cobalt				Iron ore		Lead			
	Contained in ore		Metals and alloys				Ore and scrap[3]		Pig lead	
Year	Quantity (thousands of pounds)	Value (thousands of dollars)	Quantity (thousands of pounds)	Value (thousands of dollars)	Quantity (thousands of tons)	Value (thousands of dollars)	Quantity (thousands of cwt)	Value (thousands of dollars)	Quantity (thousands of cwt)	Value (thousands of dollars)
	58	59	60	61	62	63	64	65	66	67
1915	—	—	—	—	80	207	18	40	21	79
1914	—	—	—	—	135	361	2	3	5	20
1913	—	—	—	—	126	427	3	9	—	—
1912	—	—	—	—	118	382	3	8	—	—
1911	—	—	—	—	38	133	1	2	1	3
1910	—	—	—	—	114	324	—	1	77	248
1909	—	—	—	—	22	62	62	133	113	361
1908	—	—	—	—	4	72	45	153	139	469
1907	—	—	—	—	26	46	220	866	36	164
1906	—	—	—	—	75	149	181	622	33	114
1905	—	—	—	—	—	—	—	1,047	—	—
1904	—	—	—	—	—	—	—	559	—	—
1903	—	—	—	—	—	—	—	426	—	—
1902	—	—	—	—	—	—	—	457	—	—
1901	—	—	—	—	—	—	—	1,805	—	—
1900	—	—	—	—	6	14	—	1,918	—	—
1899	—	—	—	—	4	10	—	467	—	—
1898	—	—	—	—	—	—	—	885	—	—
1897	—	—	—	—	—	1	—	925	—	—
1896	—	—	—	—	1	2	—	462	—	—
1895	—	—	—	—	2	4	—	435	—	—
1894	—	—	—	—	—	21	—	145	—	—
1893	—	—	—	—	8	26	—	3	—	—
1892	—	—	—	—	8	37	—	3	—	—
1891	—	—	—	—	15	33	—	5	—	—
1890	—	—	—	—	14	31	—	—	—	—
1889	—	—	—	—	25	60	—	—	—	—
1888	—	—	—	—	14	40	—	—	—	—
1887	—	—	—	—	23	72	—	1	—	—
1886	—	—	—	—	8	23	—	—	—	—
1885	—	—	—	—	54	132	—	—	—	—
1884	—	—	—	—	25	67	—	—	—	—
1883	—	—	—	—	45	139	—	—	—	—
1882	—	—	—	—	44	135	—	—	—	—
1881	—	—	—	—	45	115	—	—	—	—
1880	—	—	—	—	31	76	—	—	—	—
1879	—	—	—	—	4	8	—	—	—	—
1878	—	—	—	—	5	13	—	—	—	—
1877	—	—	—	—	8	15	—	1	—	—
1876	—	—	—	—	14	31	—	—	—	—
1875	—	—	—	—	32	76	4	8	—	—
1874	—	—	—	—	44	98	—	—	—	—
1873	—	—	—	—	47	112	—	—	—	—
1872	—	—	—	—	26	65	—	—	—	—
1871	—	—	—	—	27	58	—	—	—	—
1870	—	—	—	—	15	35	—	—	—	—
1869	—	—	—	—	28	60	—	—	—	—
1868	—	—	—	—	25	55	—	—	—	—

Series N 50–81. *Canadian exports of principal metallic minerals, 1868 to 1960 (continuation)*
(all values in thousands of dollars; quantities as designated individually)

Year	Nickel				Platinum, including palladium, rhodium, iridium, etc.	
	Contained in matte, speiss and oxide		Nickel fine			
	Quantity (thousands of cwt)	Value (thousands of dollars)	Quantity (thousands of cwt)	Value (thousands of dollars)	Quantity (thousands of ounces)	Value (thousands of dollars)
	68	69	70	71	72	73
1960	1,743	115,781	2,167	142,549	403	16,069
1959	1,396	93,629	2,042	133,227	358	12,497
1958	1,381	93,794	1,703	118,786	—	15,014
1957	1,508	100,393	2,065	147,860	—	27,720
1956	1,450	87,864	2,087	135,045	—	35,386
1955	1,348	80,403	2,129	134,766	—	26,303
1954	1,346	74,326	1,828	107,829	—	27,630
1953	1,304	71,642	1,598	90,901	—	26,279
1952	1,299	71,310	1,541	79,672	—	30,529
1951	1,177	61,089	1,447	75,601	—	30,340
1950	1,095	47,731	1,338	57,569	—	21,201
1949	1,161	42,449	1,382	49,874	—	18,016
1948	1,212	29,341	1,425	44,461	—	16,777
1947	926	21,368	1,415	39,075	—	11,659
1946	623	11,255	1,616	43,949	—	15,409
1945	601	10,995	1,563	43,783	—	13,298
1944	702	12,760	1,950	55,640	—	6,769
1943	806	14,908	1,905	53,438	—	7,717
1942	1,010	19,113	1,766	49,295	—	9,831
1941	997	18,678	1,755	49,002	—	6,424
1940	847	15,650	1,643	45,513	—	5,899
1939	990	18,351	1,358	39,582	—	6,137
1938	923	17,156	1,054	35,340	—	9,320
1937	859	16,037	1,369	42,877	—	8,375
1936	669	12,694	1,067	31,900	—	6,842
1935	611	11,386	816	24,900	—	5,056
1934	634	12,555	547	16,358	133	5,186
1933	460	9,623	421	13,173	29	1,169
1932	169	3,261	152	4,023	15	1,156
1931	364	7,041	271	7,140	14	1,135
1930	486	9,243	431	11,263	20	1,611
1929	412	7,991	684	17,545	3	220
1928	460	8,462	512	13,320	1	78
1927	417	7,386	290	7,896	1	53
1926	392	6,074	247	6,386	1	55
1925	402	6,694	301	5,981	—	42
1924	367	5,177	260	5,090	—	48
1923	290	4,077	229	4,649	—	34
1922	168	2,536	144	4,288	—	4
1921	81	1,418	48	1,684	1	63
1920	517	9,006	85	2,983	—	54
1919	304	4,785	106	3,292	—	29
1918	858	10,556	17	707	—	1
1917	813	8,709	—	—	—	11
1916	804	8,662	—	—	1	42
1915	664	7,394	—	—	—	11
1914	465	5,149	—	—	—	2
1913	495	5,196	—	—	—	8
1912	442	4,662	—	—	—	4
1911	326	3,676	—	—	—	2
1910	360	4,039	—	—	2	63
1909	256	2,676	—	—	—	2
1908	194	1,867	—	—	—	1
1907	194	2,280	—	—	—	5
1906	207	2,043	—	—	—	15
1905	173	1,570	—	—	—	—
1904	112	1,091	—	—	—	—
1903	127	1,116	—	—	—	—
1902	—	1,007	—	—	—	—
1901	—	751	—	—	—	1
1900	—	1,031	—	—	—	—
1899	—	940	—	—	—	—
1898	—	1,019	—	—	—	—
1897	—	723	—	—	—	—
1896	—	658	—	—	—	—
1895	—	522	—	—	—	—
1894	—	559	—	—	—	—
1893	—	630	—	—	—	—
1892	—	293	—	—	—	—
1891	—	667	—	—	—	—
1890	—	90	—	—	—	—

Series N 50–81. *Canadian exports of principal metallic minerals, 1868 to 1960 (continuation)*
(all values in thousands of dollars; quantities as designated individually)

	Silver				Zinc			
	Ore and concentrates		Bullion		Ore and scrap		Spelter	
Year	Quantity (thousands of ounces)	Value (thousands of dollars)	Quantity (thousands of ounces)	Value (thousands of dollars)	Quantity (thousands of cwt)	Value (thousands of dollars)	Quantity (thousands of cwt)	Value (thousands of dollars)
	74	75	76	77	78	79	80	81
1960	8,897	8,255	12,761	11,315	3,505	17,179	4,142	46,355
1959	6,815	6,210	15,141	13,511	3,815	21,556	3,591	33,732
1958	5,099	4,274	16,027	14,280	4,468	21,957	3,914	33,428
1957	5,979	4,943	12,800	11,691	3,850	21,440	4,040	43,481
1956	6,924	5,871	14,342	12,821	4,096	26,997	3,675	47,013
1955	5,874	4,858	16,599	14,485	3,921	23,451	4,277	47,107
1954	8,672	6,961	14,467	11,992	3,706	19,204	4,121	39,188
1953	5,687	4,613	14,633	12,232	3,937	23,279	3,168	34,293
1952	3,546	2,830	14,929	12,618	3,708	34,973	3,337	61,310
1951	2,413	2,060	15,381	14,420	3,182	28,245	2,923	55,424
1950	3,494	2,743	8,355	6,679	2,693	18,116	2,938	40,594
1949	4,055	3,005	6,212	4,568	2,254	13,217	3,366	42,483
1948	3,295	2,434	5,434	4,026	1,229	5,651	2,898	36,686
1947	2,722	1,998	7,514	5,429	906	3,359	2,745	26,661
1946	1,864	1,429	2,317	2,061	1,239	3,485	2,898	24,175
1945	2,232	1,153	2,724	1,444	1,973	6,118	2,439	14,123
1944	2,390	1,170	3,577	1,763	2,358	7,349	1,920	7,667
1943	2,253	1,040	9,199	4,518	2,268	6,256	2,586	10,260
1942	3,535	1,487	10,646	4,466	1,593	4,273	3,043	10,783
1941	4,069	1,513	13,166	5,072	1,166	2,402	2,822	9,877
1940	5,633	2,052	13,613	5,113	724	905	3,341	11,134
1939	6,828	2,801	14,203	5,724	452	579	3,120	9,344
1938	5,869	2,541	22,683	9,838	482	1,189	2,644	8,627
1937	5,769	2,567	14,620	6,556	721	2,752	2,684	12,739
1936	3,347	1,494	12,784	5,789	441	791	2,804	8,524
1935	1,364	882	16,963	10,953	259	401	2,709	7,810
1934	1,745	714	10,664	4,934	433	703	2,379	6,991
1933	3,302	1,093	10,739	3,759	146	182	1,735	4,991
1932	3,488	983	13,504	3,978	8[4]	10[4]	1,753	3,852
1931	4,017	1,168	14,649	4,231	11[4]	10[4]	2,380	5,555
1930	8,473	3,401	15,779	6,180	518	1,108	1,510	5,146
1929	7,058	3,736	14,880	8,023	334	1,678	1,351	7,032
1928	6,816	3,824	14,806	8,580	295	1,643	1,272	6,603
1927	5,445	2,894	15,971	8,995	563	1,041	1,124	6,827
1926	5,890	3,547	15,242	9,560	870	1,507	960	7,108
1925	4,755	3,021	14,317	9,861	967	1,778	498	3,781
1924	4,822	3,014	13,656	9,069	1,279	1,626	400	2,520
1923	4,861	3,091	12,324	8,046	11	5	385	2,514
1922	6,471	4,281	10,931	7,403	1	1	570	3,055
1921	2,782	1,655	10,385	6,544	1	1	257	1,336
1920	1,903	2,008	9,931	10,231	63	122	70	512
1919	2,855	2,851	12,550	13,560	133	296	77	701
1918	4,225	3,736	15,132	14,647	211	477	—	—
1917	21,719	17,621	—	—	—	—	—	—
1916	25,279	15,638	—	—	—	—	—	—

Series N50–81. *Canadian exports of principal metallic minerals, 1868 to 1960 (continued)*
(all values in thousands of dollars; quantities as designated individually)

| | Silver | | | | Zinc | | | |
| | Ore and concentrates | | Bullion | | Ore and scrap | | Spelter | |
Year	Quantity (thousands of ounces)	Value (thousands of dollars)	Quantity (thousands of ounces)	Value (thousands of dollars)	Quantity (thousands of cwt)	Value (thousands of dollars)	Quantity (thousands of cwt)	Value (thousands of dollars)
	74	75	76	77	78	79	80	81
1915	27,672	13,812	—	—	—	—	—	—
1914	28,020	15,585	—	—	—	—	—	—
1913	37,372	21,441	—	—	—	—	—	—
1912	34,912	19,494	—	—	—	—	—	—
1911	31,217	15,807	—	—	—	—	—	—
1910	30,700	15,650	—	—	—	—	—	—
1909	31,127	15,720	—	—	—	—	—	—
1908	20,884	12,403	—	—	—	—	—	—
1907	14,814	9,942	—	—	—	—	—	—
1906	—	5,686	—	—	—	—	—	—
1905	—	2,777	—	—	—	—	—	—
1904	—	1,904	—	—	—	—	—	—
1903	—	1,989	—	—	—	—	—	—
1902	—	1,820	—	—	—	—	—	—
1901	—	2,027	—	—	—	—	—	—
1900	—	2,342	—	—	—	—	—	—
1899	—	1,624	—	—	—	—	—	—
1898	—	2,902	—	—	—	—	—	—
1897	—	3,576	—	—	—	—	—	—
1896	—	2,272	—	—	—	—	—	—
1895	—	994	—	—	—	—	—	—
1894	—	360	—	—	—	—	—	—
1893	—	214	—	—	—	—	—	—
1892	—	57	—	—	—	—	—	—
1891	—	225	—	—	—	—	—	—
1890	—	204	—	—	—	—	—	—
1889	—	212	—	—	—	—	—	—
1888	—	219	—	—	—	—	—	—
1887	—	206	—	—	—	—	—	—
1886	—	26	—	—	—	—	—	—
1885	—	29	—	—	—	—	—	—
1884	—	13	—	—	—	—	—	—
1883	—	9	—	—	—	—	—	—
1882	—	7	—	—	—	—	—	—
1881	—	15	—	—	—	—	—	—
1880	—	68	—	—	—	—	—	—
1879	—	154	—	—	—	—	—	—
1878	—	666	—	—	—	—	—	—
1877	—	43	—	—	—	—	—	—
1876	—	354	—	—	—	—	—	—
1875	—	473	—	—	—	—	—	—

[1] Nine months, 1 April to 31 December 1932.
[2] Alloys only.
[3] Lead scrap included for 1949 to 1960.
[4] Zinc in ore excluded in 1931 and 1932.

Series N 82–88. *Principal statistics of the Canadian metallic industries, 1923 to 1960*

(all values in thousands of dollars)

Year	Number of establishments	Number of employees	Salaries and wages	Cost of fuel and electricity	Cost of process supplies and containers	Gross value of production	Net value added by processing
	82	83	84	85	86	87	88
1960	678	61,882	308,043	38,161	129,454	1,003,696	706,059
1959	822	63,871	306,931	34,551	123,941	1,023,962	726,631
1958	754	61,999	289,630	32,110	114,352	864,084	601,244
1957	844	62,554	278,533	31,588	99,380	791,257	532,031
1956	886	57,564	242,947	28,410	79,309	743,722	509,210
1955	794	53,364	211,249	22,525	72,523	669,762	465,927
1954	693	51,599	195,197	20,651	67,571	555,989	389,227
1953	556	51,711	191,395	19,470	62,075	486,048	333,413
1952	618	55,338	197,683	19,201	63,415	535,126	377,127
1951	572	52,271	170,853	16,567	58,064	549,498	406,829
1950	553	47,697	142,030	15,144	51,140	473,291	344,925
1949	497	46,181	132,275		111,271	414,629	303,358
1948	508	41,890	114,744		84,118	394,360	310,242
1947	712	39,314	96,768		75,871	311,445	235,574
1946	840	35,445	77,464		57,118	340,726	183,608
1945	854	32,913	68,817		54,072	231,671	177,600
1944	402	34,559	71,891		59,000	248,680	189,680
1943	343	37,575	79,992		67,809	292,497	224,688
1942	468	43,013	89,545		78,417	327,063	248,646
1941	620	48,277	93,305		80,387	325,301	244,914
1940	759	46,885	83,759		69,687	300,824	231,137
1939	772	45,594	79,198		66,908	273,746	206,838
1938	870	43,703	74,917		60,213	251,489	191,276
1937	987	43,476	72,808		52,044	227,121	175,077
1936	853	36,440	57,671		29,911	170,079	140,168
1935	605	29,659	46,841		—	—	114,147
1934	622	25,845	39,759		—	115,175	—
1933	788	19,083	29,535		—	92,827	—
1932	317	16,588	26,205		—	81,068	—
1931	313	17,574	28,584		—	82,153	—
1930	339	21,997	35,055		—	81,359	—
1929	518	23,006	36,507		—	94,612	—
1928	538	21,056	32,458		—	79,690	—
1927	507	18,672	28,165		—	75,583	—
1926	1,495	17,516	26,449		—	82,323	—
1925	318	15,560	24,164		—	76,396	—
1924	389	14,288	21,557		—	65,065	—
1923	331	11,504	17,864		—	48,198	—

Series N 89–119. *Canadian production of principal nonmetallic minerals, 1886 to 1960*

(all values in thousands of dollars; quantities in thousands of tons)

Year	Asbestos		Gypsum		Magnesitic dolomite		Peat moss	
	Quantity (thousands of tons)	Value (thousands of dollars)	Quantity (thousands of tons)	Value (thousands of dollars)	Quantity (thousands of tons)	Value[1] (thousands of dollars)	Quantity (thousands of tons)	Value (thousands of dollars)
	89	**90**	**91**	**92**	**93**	**94**	**95**	**96**
1960	1,118	121,400	5,206	9,499	—	3,279	186	6,088
1959	1,050	107,433	5,879	8,394	—	3,051	184	6,227
1958	925	92,277	3,964	5,189	—	2,529	149	4,779
1957	1,046	104,489	4,577	7,745	—	3,046	138	4,735
1956	1,014	99,860	4,896	7,260	—	2,783	128	4,241
1955	1,064	96,191	4,668	8,037	—	2,152	118	3,485
1954	924	86,409	3,950	7,095	—	1,909	99	3,019
1953	911	86,053	3,841	7,400	—	2,017	82	2,643
1952	929	89,255	3,591	6,538	—	2,161	75	2,474
1951	973	81,584	3,803	5,881	—	2,149	77	2,433
1950	875	65,855	3,666	6,708	—	1,718	75	2,257
1949	575	39,746	3,014	5,424	—	1,536	80	2,377
1948	717	42,231	3,217	5,548	—	1,588	90	2,768
1947	662	33,006	2,497	4,735	—	1,167	80	2,280
1946	558	25,241	1,811	3,672	—	1,226	97	2,396
1945	467	22,805	840	1,783	—	1,279	84	2,011
1944	419	20,620	596	1,512	—	1,139	80	1,870
1943	467	23,170	447	1,381	—	1,260	64	1,461
1942	439	22,663	566	1,254	—	1,059[1]	54	1,069
1941	478	21,469	1,593	2,248	—	831	28	644
1940	347	15,620	1,449	2,066	—	897	—	—
1939	364	15,859	1,422	1,935	—	474	—	—
1938	290	12,890	1,009	1,502	—	420	—	—
1937	410	14,506	1,047	1,540	—	677	—	—
1936	301	9,958	834	1,279	—	769	—	—
1935	210	7,055	542	932	—	486	—	—
1934	156	4,936	461	864	—	383	—	—
1933	158	5,211	383	676	—	360	—	—
1932	123	3,040	439	1,080	—	263	—	—
1931	164	4,813	864	2,112	11	296	—	—
1930	242	8,390	1,071	2,819	13	336	—	—
1929	306	13,173	1,212	3,346	19	491	—	—
1928	273	11,238	1,246	3,744	13	347	—	—
1927	275	10,621	1,063	3,251	7	230	—	—
1926	279	10,099	884	2,771	5	137	—	—
1925	274	8,978	740	2,390	6	122	—	—
1924	226	6,711	646	2,208	4	101	—	—
1923	231	7,523	578	2,243	5	134	—	—
1922	164	5,553	559	2,161	3	76	—	—
1921	93	4,906	387	1,786	4	81	—	—
1920	200	14,792	429	1,894	18	513	—	—
1919	159	10,975	299	1,215	11	328	—	—
1918	158	8,971	152	823	39	1,017	—	—
1917	154	7,230	336	882	58	728	—	—
1916	154	5,229	343	739	55	564	—	—
1915	137	3,575	475	855	15	127	—	—
1914	118	2,910	517	1,156	—	2	—	—
1913	161	3,850	636	1,448	1	3	—	—
1912	136	3,137	578	1,325	2	10	—	—
1911	127	2,943	518	993	1	6	—	—
1910	102	2,574	525	934	—	2	—	—
1909	87	2,302	473	810	—	3	—	—
1908	91	2,573	341	576	—	1	—	—
1907	90	2,505	486	647	—	—	—	—
1906	82	2,060	469	634	—	—	—	—
1905	68	1,503	442	536	—	—	—	—
1904	48	1,226	346	373	—	—	—	—
1903	42	930	314	388	—	—	—	—
1902	40	1,148	334	379	—	—	—	—
1901	40	1,260	294	340	—	—	—	—
1900	29	748	252	259	—	—	—	—
1899	26	486	245	257	—	—	—	—
1898	24	491	219	233	—	—	—	—
1897	30	445	240	245	—	—	—	—
1896	12	430	207	178	—	—	—	—
1895	9	368	226	203	—	—	—	—
1894	8	421	224	202	—	—	—	—
1893	6	310	193	196	—	—	—	—
1892	6	390	241	241	—	—	—	—
1891	9	1,000	204	206	—	—	—	—
1890	10	1,260	227	194	—	—	—	—
1889	6	427	213	205	—	—	—	—
1888	4	255	176	179	—	—	—	—
1887	5	227	154	157	—	—	—	—
1886	3	206	162	179	—	—	—	—

Series N 89–119. *Canadian production of principal nonmetallic minerals, 1886 to 1960 (continuation)*
(all values in thousands of dollars; quantities in thousands of tons)

Year	Quartz[2] Quantity (thousands of tons)	Quartz[2] Value (thousands of dollars)	Salt Quantity (thousands of tons)	Salt Value (thousands of dollars)	Sodium sulphate Quantity (thousands of tons)	Sodium sulphate Value (thousands of dollars)	Titanium dioxide Quantity (thousands of tons)	Titanium dioxide Value (thousands of dollars)
	97	98	99	100	101	102	103	104
1960	2,261	3,267	3,315	19,356	214	3,449	—	12,947
1959	2,164	3,437	3,290	18,035	180	2,882	—	8,507
1958	1,454	2,538	2,375	14,990	173	2,863	—	6,575
1957	2,139	3,185	1,772	13,990	158	2,569	186	9,741
1956	2,142	3,037	1,591	12,144	181	2,838	157	7,683
1955	1,870	2,040	1,245	10,122	179	2,800	117	5,193
1954	1,716	1,575	970	8,340	158	2,386	88	3,841
1953	1,786	2,071	955	6,975	116	1,681	101	4,206
1952	1,783	2,254	972	7,775	123	1,709	31	1,238
1951	1,905	2,258	965	7,906	192	2,384	14	739
1950	1,731	1,740	859	7,011	131	1,616	2	150
1949	1,722	1,589	749	5,567	120	1,615	—	—
1948	2,017	2,083	741	4,836	154	2,136	—	—
1947	1,836	1,797	729	4,437	103	1,793	—	—
1946	1,413	1,555	538	3,626	106	1,118	—	—
1945	1,514	1,535	673	4,055	93	884	—	—
1944	1,740	1,658	695	4,074	102	988	—	—
1943	1,777	1,608	688	4,379	107	1,025	—	—
1942	1,738	1,538	654	3,844	131	1,080	—	—
1941	2,053	1,366	561	3,196	116	932	—	—
1940	1,858	1,204	465	2,823	94	830	—	—
1939	1,583	1,100	425	2,487	71	628	—	—
1938	1,380	962	440	1,913	63	553	—	—
1937	1,377	1,129	459	1,799	80	618	—	—
1936	1,047[2]	598[2]	391	1,773	76	553	—	—
1935	233	425	360	1,881	45	344	—	—
1934	273	482	322	1,955	67	588	—	—
1933	186	298	280	1,940	50	485	—	—
1932	189	276	264	1,948	22	272	—	—
1931	196	303	259	1,904	45	421	—	—
1930	226	418	272	1,695	32	294	—	—
1929	266	562	330	1,578	5	64	—	—
1928	283	524	299	1,496	6	69	—	—
1927	234	496	269	1,615	6	11	—	—
1926	232	553	263	1,480	7	14	—	—
1925	197	364	234	1,411	4	19	—	—
1924	151	323	208	1,375	1	6	—	—
1923	264	599	202	1,714	1	10	—	—
1922	110	209	182	1,628	1	12	—	—
1921	100	313	165	1,674	1	19	—	—
1920	128	468	210	1,545	1	19	—	—
1919	95	528	148	1,398	—	—	—	—
1918	268	630	132	1,285	—	—	—	—
1917	216	496	139	1,048	—	—	—	—
1916	137	251	133	718	—	—	—	—
1915	127	205	120	600	—	—	—	—
1914	54	85	107	494	—	—	—	—
1913	78	170	101	491	—	—	—	—
1912	100	195	95	460	—	—	—	—
1911	61	84	92	443	—	—	—	—
1910	88	92	84	410	—	—	—	—
1909	57	71	84	415	—	—	—	—
1908	45	53	80	379	—	—	—	—
1907	57	124	73	342	—	—	—	—
1906	48	66	77	329	—	—	—	—
1905	—	—	67	321	—	—	—	—
1904	—	—	69	322	—	—	—	—
1903	—	—	62	298	—	—	—	—
1902	—	—	64	293	—	—	—	—
1901	—	—	59	262	—	—	—	—
1900	—	—	62	279	—	—	—	—
1899	1	1	59	254	—	—	—	—
1898	—	1	57	249	—	—	—	—
1897	—	—	51	226	—	—	—	—
1896	—	—	44	170	—	—	—	—
1895	—	—	52	160	—	—	—	—
1894	—	—	57	171	—	—	—	—
1893	—	1	62	196	—	—	—	—
1892	—	—	45	162	—	—	—	—
1891	—	—	45	161	—	—	—	—
1890	—	1	44	199	—	—	—	—
1889	—	—	33	130	—	—	—	—
1888	—	—	59	185	—	—	—	—
1887	—	—	60	166	—	—	—	—
1886	—	—	62	227	—	—	—	—

Series N 89–119. *Canadian production of principal nonmetallic minerals, 1886 to 1960 (continuation)*
(all values in thousands of dollars; quantities in thousands of tons)

Year	Sulphur		Cement		Lime		Sand and gravel	
	Quantity (thousands of tons)	Value (thousands of dollars)	Quantity (thousands of tons)	Value (thousands of dollars)	Quantity (thousands of tons)	Value (thousands of dollars)	Quantity (thousands of tons)	Value (thousands of dollars)
	105	106	107	108	109	110	111	112
1960	1,002	10,470	5,787	93,261	1,530	19,302	192,074	111,164
1959	888	8,770	6,284	95,148	1,686	21,304	185,124	104,651
1958	848	8,483	6,153	96,414	1,596	19,466	160,211	96,282
1957	750	7,130	6,049	93,167	1,379	16,679	159,830	91,939
1956	710	6,862	5,022	75,233	1,296	15,668	148,801	81,957
1955	628	5,985	4,404	65,650	1,331	15,811	127,524	67,775
1954	532	4,876	3,927	59,036	1,215	14,742	110,961	57,988
1953	359	3,173	3,892	58,842	1,229	14,484	101,034	53,485
1952	424	3,851	3,241	48,059	1,176	13,613	102,896	51,339
1951	372	3,121	2,976	40,446	1,241	14,083	92,973	44,628
1950	301	2,190	2,930	35,894	1,124	12,281	73,095	36,435
1949	262	2,039	2,785	32,902	1,019	11,310	63,356	31,182
1948	229	1,836	2,472	28,265	1,054	10,655	68,671	30,630
1947	222	1,823	2,089	21,969	977	8,543	56,790	23,114
1946	235	1,785	2,023	20,123	841	7,075	39,950	15,530
1945	250	1,881	1,483	14,246	832	6,525	29,751	10,568
1944	248	1,756	1,258	11,621	885	6,927	28,400	10,280
1943	258	1,753	1,278	11,599	908	6,833	25,744	9,006
1942	304	1,995	1,597	14,365	885	6,531	26,350	9,005
1941	260	1,703	1,465	13,064	861	6,358	31,605	10,376
1940	171	1,298	1,323	11,775	717	5,195	31,375	11,759
1939	211	1,668	1,003	8,511	552	4,004	31,294	11,241
1938	112	1,045	966	8,241	487	3,543	32,224	12,003
1937	131	1,155	1,080	9,096	549	3,825	27,001	10,493
1936	122	1,033	789	6,908	468	3,336	22,124	6,921
1935	67	634	638	5,580	405	2,926	21,213	6,389
1934	52	516	662	5,668	368	2,746	14,854	4,035
1933	57	510	526	4,537	324	2,432	11,739	4,464
1932	53	470	787	6,931	321	2,395	14,470	4,481
1931	50	429	1,778	15,826	345	2,764	21,749	6,651
1930	38	315	1,931	17,713	491	4,039	28,548	8,345
1929	43	351	2,150	19,337	674	5,909	27,847	7,318
1928	39	321	1,929	16,739	507	4,535	28,103	5,809
1927	25	198	1,762	14,392	445	3,923	22,953	6,056
1926	9	64	1,524	13,013	414	3,781	17,113	4,941
1925	8	59	1,420	14,047	359	3,388	11,019	3,220
1924	10	96	1,312	13,398	320	3,179	11,604	3,181
1923	11	113	1,320	15,065	351	3,267	12,753	3,017
1922	7	74	1,215	15,438	314	3,165	11,666	3,503
1921	12	116	1,007	14,195	241	2,781	11,575	2,537
1920	68	719	1,164	14,798	330	3,819	11,531	4,201
1919	66	523	874	9,802	250	2,311	10,364	2,680
1918	154	1,705	629	7,077	223	1,876	11,262	2,367
1917	155	1,611	834	7,724	230	1,558	9,182	2,326
1916	117	1,084	940	6,548	192	1,091	8,156	1,838
1915	116	985	994	6,977	177	1,016	6,446	1,625
1914	94	745	1,255	9,188	246	1,361	—	2,505
1913	65	521	1,515	11,019	265	1,609	—	2,259
1912	33	314	1,248	9,107	297	1,845	—	1,512
1911	34	366	996	7,645	264	1,518	573	408
1910	22	187	832	6,412	205	1,137	625	408
1909	27	223	712	5,346	196	1,133	482	256
1908	19	225	467	3,710	126	713	299	161
1907	19	212	427	3,781	166	975	298	120
1906	18	170	372	3,171	183	1,009	337	139
1905	14	125	238	1,924	—	750	307	153
1904	15	134	169	1,338	—	780	400	190
1903	14	128	126	1,225	—	900	356	124
1902	15	139	126	1,128	—	892	160	119
1901	14	131	79	660	—	830	197	117
1900	16	155	73	663	—	800	198	102
1899	11	111	69	633	—	800	242	102
1898	13	129	44	398	—	650	166	90
1897	16	117	36	275	—	650	153	77
1896	14	101	26	202	—	650	225	80
1895	14	103	22	174	—	700	277	118
1894	17	122	19	145	—	900	325	87
1893	22	176	28	194	—	900	329	122
1892	26	179	21	148	—	411	298	85
1891	26	203	16	109	—	251	244	60
1890	20	123	18	92	—	412	342	66
1889	29	307	16	70	—	363	283	53
1888	25	286	9	36	—	340	261	38
1887	15	171	1	82	—	395	181	30
1886	17	193	—	—	—	284	125	24

Series N89–119. *Canadian production of principal nonmetallic minerals, 1886 to 1960 (continuation)*
(all values in thousands of dollars; quantities in thousands of tons)

Year	Limestone[3] Quantity (thousands of tons)	Limestone[3] Value (thousands of dollars)	Sandstone[3] Quantity (thousands of tons)	Sandstone[3] Value (thousands of dollars)	Granite Quantity (thousands of tons)	Granite Value (thousands of dollars)	Clay products Value (thousands of dollars)
	113	114	115	116	117	118	119
1960	36,406	44,763	3,421	3,079	5,237	11,886	38,227
1959	36,583	45,322	4,769	4,681	4,848	10,093	42,515
1958	30,271	38,683	2,908	3,597	4,800	12,525	41,710
1957	32,619	41,281	2,539	4,247	4,958	12,758	35,922
1956	29,106	39,306	1,579	1,992	2,431	6,575	37,785
1955	24,108	32,322	623	873	5,619	9,667	35,260
1954	18,830	25,144	830	824	12,835	13,042	32,360
1953	17,462	23,783	974	686	1,351	5,555	29,778
1952	15,958	22,319	219	649	2,490	7,327	24,962
1951	15,532	20,902	1,125	1,174	1,951	6,014	23,528
1950	12,267	15,965	3,685	4,418	2,071	4,971	21,791
1949	10,951	13,877	597	1,014	2,321	5,110	17,982
1948	10,003	12,523	578	1,066	1,043	3,779	17,629
1947	9,498	11,967	793	975	552	3,175	14,486
1946	7,218	8,179	496	778	319	2,006	12,207
1945	5,677	6,284	291	466	222	1,285	8,913
1944	5,565	5,528	147	223	270	1,304	6,996
1943	6,265	6,106	164	251	780	1,522	6,608
1942	6,443	6,469	154	227	1,366	1,946	7,082
1941	7,151	6,058	170	306	601	1,499	7,575
1940	6,109	5,126	176	306	1,148	1,884	6,345
1939	4,150	3,818	176	332	1,102	2,120	5,151
1938	4,289	3,865	102	218	705	1,379	4,536
1937	5,543	4,674	235	344	1,135	1,827	4,517
1936	3,732	3,144	286	496	942	1,319	3,471
1935	3,632	3,254	343	838	326	1,126	3,013
1934	3,748	3,158	115	143	200	782	2,680
1933	2,573	2,143	99	109	257	680	2,263
1932	3,687	3,228	500	349	491	1,111	3,650
1931	6,262	6,306	924	1,333	1,191	2,763	7,841
1930	7,733	8,076	385	769	1,851	3,380	10,594
1929	7,721	8,173	159	399	1,728	3,081	13,905
1928	6,949	7,267	101	223	1,196	2,367	12,382
1927	6,438	7,146	133	233	730	1,384	11,173
1926	5,284	5,657	44	112	1,064	1,575	10,357
1925	4,644	5,050	88	146	972	2,015	9,530
1924	4,249	4,832	95	240	420	1,013	9,215
1923	3,688	4,476	23	67	398	1,159	10,483
1922	3,152	4,176	25	81	458	1,486	11,438
1921	3,322	5,155	28	78	319	938	8,858
1920	—	5,666	—	165	—	1,509	10,665
1919	—	3,075	—	87	—	851	7,906
1918	—	2,342	—	103	—	591	4,583
1917	—	2,284	—	261	—	639	4,779
1916	—	2,224	—	146	—	1,247	4,121
1915	—	2,312	—	249	—	1,526	3,914
1914	—	2,673	—	487	—	2,177	6,872
1913	—	3,204	—	397	—	1,654	9,504
1912	—	2,763	—	329	—	1,373	10,576
1911	—	2,595	—	451	—	1,120	8,360
1910	—	2,250	—	502	—	740	7,630
1909	—	2,140	—	374[4]	—	455	6,451
1908	—	1,681[3]	—	—[3]	—	282	4,501
1907	—	1,833	—	—	15	195	5,772
1906	—	2,084	—	—	—	278	5,073
1905	—	2,073	—	—	—	226	4,710
1904	—	2,114	—	—	—	150	3,842
1903	—	2,231	—	—	—	200	4,034
1902	—	2,127	—	—	—	210	3,625
1901	—	1,838	—	—	—	155	3,383
1900	—	1,565	—	—	—	80	3,195
1899	—	1,552	—	—	13	91	2,988
1898	—	1,335	—	—	24	81	2,691
1897	—	1,037	—	—	10	62	2,326
1896	—	1,043	—	—	19	107	2,228
1895	—	1,137	—	—	19	85	2,487
1894	—	1,270	—	—	16	110	2,560
1893	—	1,131	—	—	23	94	2,620
1892	—	633	—	—	24	89	2,178
1891	—	723	—	—	14	70	1,803
1890	—	985	—	—	13	66	2,041
1889	—	937	—	—	10	80	1,652
1888	—	665	—	—	21	147	1,495
1887	—	581	—	—	21	143	1,399
1886	—	650	—	—	6	63	1,126

[1] For 1942 to 1960 the figures include the value of brucite granules.
[2] For 1936 to 1960 low grade fluxing sand figures are included.
[3] Prior to 1909 the value of production of sandstone is included in series N 114, the value of production of limestone.

Series N 120–142. *Canadian imports of principal nonmetallic minerals, 1885 to 1960*
(all values in thousands of dollars; quantities as designated individually)

Year[1]	Granite[2] Value (thousands of dollars)	Gypsum, crude and ground Quantity (thousands of tons)	Value (thousands of dollars)	Phosphate rock Quantity (thousands of cwt)	Value (thousands of dollars)	Silex or crystallized quartz Quantity (thousands of cwt)	Value (thousands of dollars)
	120	121	122	123	124	125	126
1960	427	60	495	18,840	8,320	210	161
1959	409	118	347	15,941	7,468	276	184
1958	467	108	609	14,883	6,854	240	151
1957	408	92	360	14,464	5,898	274	187
1956	356	70	303	12,553	5,186	538	327
1955	322	16	124	11,764	4,513	490	252
1954	313	5	51	12,897	4,578	568	275
1953	279	1	17	11,530	3,951	611	1,733
1952	188	1	19	9,418	3,130	523	1,980
1951	188	2	24	9,994	3,179	608	2,870
1950	186	1	24	9,821	3,296	495	408
1949	201	1	20	12,416	3,880	459	239
1948	197	1	22	9,640	2,911	349	169
1947	212	9	76	9,708	2,858	300	165
1946	203	4	23	7,474	2,165	214	114
1945	66	1	22	6,354	1,451	145	247
1944	69	1	17	7,765	1,710	175	530
1943	64	5	29	5,217	1,085	228	946
1942	62	1	23	5,427	1,053	196	442
1941	69	1	22	4,741	864	102	130
1940	57	1	16	3,317	664	83	57
1939	77	1	18	2,498	477	55	61
1938	73	—	14	2,568	456	61	78
1937	91	—	13	2,279	454	86	104
1936	78	—	10	1,669	298	81	84
1935	74	—	8	1,270	235	67	76
1934	71	—	5	635	165	46	53
1933	54	—	5	367	75	87	83
1932	56	—	5	1,311	347	124	168
1931	54	1	18	2,834	619	105	130
1930	87	1	31	944	298	101	111
1929	88	1	24	364	115	80	80
1928	55	1	48	208	68	57	74
1927	5	1	46	350	95	64	75
1926	6	1	39	285	66	51	60
1925	2	5	70	280	62	44	39
1924	2	3	65	234	57	39	50
1923	13	4	43	317	86	46	58
1922	6	3	27	230	56	21	25
1921	5	3	34	274	87	24	36
1920	5	2	29	270	114	23	26
1919	5	1	25	—	30	13	14
1918	4	—	4	—	90	12	12
1917	3	—	6	—	63	17	13
1916	5	3	18	—	16	34	18
1915	2	2	10	—	14	8	6
1914	5	4	21	—	20	17	16
1913	15	7	34	—	14	14	16
1912	21	11	36	—	25	13	11
1911	4	4	15	—	46	8	8
1910	3	19	34	—	73	13	12
1909	2	15	29	—	39	11	9
1908	3	14	44	—	35	10	8
1907	9	12	40	—	32	26	22
1906	38	9	27	—	31	11	12
1905	28	6	20	—	18	8	6
1904[1]	8	—	1	—	8	6	4
1903	1	1	2	—	19	4	3
1902	—	1	2	—	15	4	4
1901	1	—	2	—	20	4	2
1900	—	—	1	—	6	4	3
1899	—	—	1	—	6	4	3
1898	—	1	2	—	—	3	3
1897	—	—	1	—	—	3	3
1896	—	1	1	—	—	3	2
1895	—	1	1	—	—	3	2
1894	—	—	2	—	—	2	2
1893	—	1	1	—	—	2	1
1892	—	1	3	—	—	1	1
1891	—	—	1	—	—	4	2
1890	—	1	4	—	—	2	3
1889	—	1	3	—	—	5	1
1888	—	1	3	—	—	5	2
1887	—	2	3	—	—	15	5
1886	—	2	3	—	—	3	1

Series N 120–142. *Canadian imports of principal nonmetallic minerals, 1885 to 1960 (continuation)*
(all values in thousands of dollars; quantities as designated individually)

Year[1]	Salt Quantity (thousands of cwt) 127	Salt Value (thousands of dollars) 128	Sulphur Quantity (thousands of cwt) 129	Sulphur Value (thousands of dollars) 130	Cement Quantity (thousands of cwt) 131	Cement Value (thousands of dollars) 132	Clay Quantity (thousands of cwt) 133	Clay Value (thousands of dollars) 134
1960	3,839	841	6,575	6,629	450	728	4,090	3,322
1959	7,399	1,578	6,649	6,925	585	859	4,370	3,411
1958	6,818	1,503	7,507	8,324	831	1,003	4,095	3,215
1957	7,350	1,649	8,339	9,752	1,848	1,870	4,331	3,112
1956	6,382	1,606	9,482	11,858	11,992	8,078	4,639	3,141
1955	7,305	1,884	7,467	9,387	10,358	8,443	3,829	2,803
1954	7,408	2,151	6,203	7,816	8,023	6,317	3,322	2,370
1953	6,147	2,017	7,182	8,527	8,690	7,403	3,820	2,640
1952	5,762	2,060	8,304	8,377	10,199	9,068	3,571	2,310
1951	5,176	1,954	7,919	8,960	8,146	7,448	4,068	2,630
1950	4,765	1,734	7,807	7,730	4,852	3,789	3,428	2,273
1949	4,734	1,568	5,611	5,214	7,994	6,878	3,444	1,958
1948	3,721	1,079	7,092	5,529	3,922	3,995	3,672	2,090
1947	4,398	1,247	7,228	5,466	4,370	3,844	3,374	1,784
1946	4,566	1,367	5,470	4,271	1,225	1,099	2,769	1,286
1945	2,743	805	4,977	4,063	114	142	2,876	1,183
1944	2,946	847	4,719	3,876	49	77	2,774	1,111
1943	1,686	589	4,371	3,524	65	84	2,555	926
1942	1,387	441	5,802	4,681	92	116	3,026	1,074
1941	1,629	450	4,705	3,920	42	59	2,944	1,087
1940	2,250	558	4,312	3,628	46	70	2,630	974
1939	2,353	507	3,044	2,454	58	58	2,009	740
1938	2,163	454	1,874	1,472	170	105	1,842	718
1937	2,329	466	4,514	3,669	214	134	2,694	925
1936	2,178	461	3,375	2,802	140	107	2,233	776
1935	2,565	527	2,733	2,298	62	60	1,703	709
1934	2,776	586	3,154	2,589	50	46	1,565	586
1933	2,712	651	2,816	2,530	67	38	1,103	506
1932	2,041	596	2,100	2,023	75	58	732	456
1931	2,618	752	2,484	2,282	134	143	1,254	529
1930	2,568	661	3,595	3,177	502	570	1,610	684
1929	3,531	937	4,699	3,789	196	189	2,019	767
1928	3,781	1,123	3,655	2,963	119	146	1,682	623
1927	3,535	1,082	3,554	2,918	68	88	1,405	548
1926	3,768	1,037	3,683	2,946	74	78	1,298	477
1925	3,873	1,077	2,932	1,983	76	63	1,189	428
1924	3,658	1,134	2,631	1,777	97	69	1,277	494
1923	3,437	1,068	2,715	1,804	62	75	1,413	567
1922	3,917	1,274	2,463	1,701	108	83	874	381
1921	2,594	1,025	1,575	1,273	42	76	788	360
1920	3,113	1,435	2,895	2,114	115	112	1,281	651
1919	2,948	1,310	1,121	1,015	49	51	788	362
1918	3,310	1,267	1,841	2,059	21	20	211	554
1917	3,416	1,088	1,649	1,515	30	20	232	416
1916	3,024	695	1,469	1,187	72	32	381	325
1915	2,750	518	604	480	99	40	439	237
1914	2,853	541	839	871	343	147	—	288
1913	2,889	565	609	633	889	109	—	324
1912	2,693	468	773	807	5,020	1,970	—	288
1911	2,416	421	439	446	2,343	841	—	270
1910	2,528	448	457	475	1,223	468	—	293
1909	2,326	431	458	459	498	167	—	216
1908	2,529	444	425	411	1,644	532	—	197
1907	2,438	442	520	522	2,371	844	—	271
1906	2,322	422	420	435	2,038	690	—	226
1905	2,274	432	351	364	2,955	1,053	—	197
1904[1]	2,284	412	194	205	2,488	1,000	—	145
1903	2,473	403	244	259	2,331	874	—	176
1902	2,525	425	246	325	2,001	851	—	141
1901	2,279	374	239	271	1,630	661	—	141
1900	2,046	325	211	215	1,312	503	—	123
1899	1,948	300	245	266	1,302	469	—	—
1898	2,137	326	380	374	1,089	362	—	—
1897	2,278	346	87	88	747	257	—	—
1896	2,127	363	69	64	735	251	—	—
1895	2,102	363	49	57	706	250	—	—
1894	2,125	382	58	62	788	282	—	—
1893	2,130	361	64	77	820	324	—	—
1892	2,205	381	48	67	663	284	—	—
1891	2,106	381	36	46	655	311	—	—
1890	1,736	310	44	44	692	323	—	—
1889	1,920	292	24	34	448	187	—	—
1888	1,947	253	20	25	448	185	—	—
1887	2,135	321	31	39	381	157	—	—
1886	1,925	295	29	44	—	126	—	—

Series N 120–142. *Canadian imports of principal nonmetallic minerals, 1885 to 1960* (continuation)

(all values in thousands of dollars; quantities as designated individually)

Year[1]	Lime Quantity (thousands of cwt)	Lime Value (thousands of dollars)	Sand and gravel Quantity (thousands of tons)	Sand and gravel Value (thousands of dollars)	Sand silica Quantity (thousands of cwt)	Sand silica Value (thousands of dollars)	Titanium oxide, white pigments and antimony oxide Quantity (thousands of pounds)	Titanium oxide, white pigments and antimony oxide Value (thousands of dollars)
	135	136	137	138	139	140	141	142
1960	676	430	886	444	14,417	2,405	54,230	7,745
1959	628	388	1,097	571	15,843	2,525	61,707	8,988
1958	313	203	234	247	12,067	2,115	59,201	8,535
1957	564	343	263	350	14,897	2,408	68,836	10,870
1956	946	551	319	370	16,807	2,597	76,007	12,661
1955	500	283	259	275	14,709	2,146	71,884	10,573
1954	531	289	284	287	13,117	1,884	64,492	9,198
1953	430	233	187	190	14,064	1,928	63,929	8,500
1952	334	170	183	175	12,858	1,772	48,584	6,514
1951	294	159	261	214	13,859	1,991	59,397	8,505
1950	281	160	201	209	11,467	1,565	54,250	7,054
1949	330	176	171	155	10,222	1,362	41,587	5,158
1948	478	219	135	113	11,680	1,447	39,293	4,610
1947	261	115	94	83	10,669	1,148	27,312	2,966
1946	152	50	71	71	7,800	914	23,931	2,194
1945	127	36	104	78	8,209	927	21,359	2,046
1944	134	35	84	58	9,152	914	20,175	1,871
1943	182	64	83	53	10,181	1,011	16,890	1,533
1942	125	44	132	90	10,818	1,011	14,643	1,423
1941	89	27	119	107	8,423	783	13,220	1,321
1940	83	23	160	98	5,575	557	8,770	783
1939	121	33	148	69	3,354	349	9,004	803
1938	133	36	87	62	3,441	339	4,710	512
1937	100	32	132	98	4,257	374	5,630	527
1936	19	12	122	78	2,872	271	4,198	424
1935	13	9	98	81	2,472	283	2,870	310
1934	7	5	61	57	1,923	226	984[3]	131[3]
1933	5	4	89	72	1,282	160	—	—
1932	6	6	36	49	1,184	163	—	—
1931	11	11	155	140	2,154	235	—	—
1930	42	28	185	168	3,287	353	—	—
1929	89	49	269	217	4,679	491	—	—
1928	108	65	588	275	3,088	332	—	—
1927	116	70	290	200	2,977	346	—	—
1926	77	43	255	212	3,102	372	—	—
1925	94	48	282	184	2,870	353	—	—
1924	88	47	151	118	2,636	324	—	—
1923	100	56	355	247	3,351	317	—	—
1922	51	28	351	176	2,157	224	—	—
1921	24	20	165	115	929	136	—	—
1920	55	49	219	268	2,267	332	—	—
1919	80	53	201	200	792	111	—	—
1918	100	54	311	436	—	—	—	—
1917	243	78	329	312	—	—	—	—
1916	424	96	234	184	—	—	—	—
1915	380	98	200	121	—	—	—	—
1914	682	211	274	225	—	—	—	—
1913	773	238	440	440	—	—	—	—
1912	660	207	533	446	—	—	—	—
1911	457	162	241	247	—	—	—	—
1910	425	139	196	197	—	—	—	—
1909	337	118	151	154	—	—	—	—
1908	287	99	134	135	—	—	—	—
1907	253	99	266	224	—	—	—	—
1906	294	108	196	226	—	—	—	—
1905	228	82	105	142	—	—	—	—
1904[1]	109	40	111	108	—	—	—	—
1903	62	22	92	96	—	—	—	—
1902	49	18	47	59	—	—	—	—
1901	39	15	36	43	—	—	—	—
1900	26	11	36	41	—	—	—	—
1899	31	11	30	42	—	—	—	—
1898	26	9	32	43	—	—	—	—
1897	32	11	21	25	—	—	—	—
1896	20	7	19	25	—	—	—	—
1895	24	6	20	25	—	—	—	—
1894	14	5	42	34	—	—	—	—
1893	14	5	26	32	—	—	—	—
1892	12	4	—	28	—	—	—	—
1891	13	4	—	24	—	—	—	—
1890	16	5	—	37	—	—	—	—
1889	26	9	—	34	—	—	—	—
1888	20	8	—	32	—	—	—	—
1887	22	9	—	31	—	—	—	—
1886	22	9	—	26	—	—	—	—
1885	—	—	—	23	—	—	—	—

[1] For all series for 1904 and earlier years, data are for fiscal years ending 30 June of the year given.

[2] This series includes: for 1929 to 1960, sawn and rough granite; for 1928, sawn granite, 1 January to 31 December and rough granite, 1 April to 31 December; for 1898 to 1927, sawn granite only.

[3] For 9 months ending 31 December 1934.

Series N 143–162. *Canadian exports of principal nonmetallic minerals, 1875 to 1960*

(all values in thousands of dollars; quantities as designated individually)

	Asbestos[1]						Gypsum or plaster		Cement	
	Crude[2]		Milled fibres[2]		Waste, refuse or shorts					
Year	Quantity (thousands of tons)	Value (thousands of dollars)	Quantity (thousands of tons)	Value (thousands of dollars)	Quantity (thousands of tons)	Value (thousands of dollars)	Quantity (thousands of tons)	Value (thousands of dollars)	Quantity (thousands of cwt)	Value (thousands of dollars)
	143	144	145	146	147	148	149	150	151	152
1960	—	247	458	85,803	610	34,064	4,274	7,054	3,622	2,821
1959	—	426	402	76,376	612	33,629	4,849	9,845	6,063	5,003
1958	—	479	318	61,330	548	28,936	2,898	4,871	2,825	2,467
1957	1	568	393	73,949	637	32,542	3,411	5,905	6,766	6,052
1956	1	526	377	69,028	586	30,341	3,841	6,988	2,491	1,985
1955	1	481	366	63,435	635	30,888	3,039	4,931	3,378	3,139
1954	1	578	313	53,876	574	28,112	2,831	4,205	433	496
1953	1	720	317	55,183	561	28,070	2,770	3,794	52	78
1952	1	705	340	56,647	562	29,158	2,763	2,847	15	21
1951	1	548	325	48,855	617	30,930	3,028	3,128	9	12
1950	1	544	290	39,114	539	23,094	2,970	3,061	84	111
1949	1	416	182	22,769	353	13,749	2,545	2,637	67	52
1948	1	557	237	25,552	452	15,290	2,617	2,703	255	201
1947	1	445	224	20,276	412	11,571	1,937	2,043	308	198
1946	1	294	215	16,216	304	7,330	1,489	1,599	400	236
1945	1	367	210	15,858	230	5,618	559	582	987	535
1944	2	650	182	13,635	213	5,361	387	434	737	377
1943	2	860	211	15,674	230	5,848	185	213	604	344
1942	3	1,191	198	15,057	226	5,667	490	544	959	476
1941	3	935	217	13,616	234	4,860	1,166	1,186	1,088	518
1940	2	728	180[2]	11,654[2]	155	3,143	1,312	1,347	1,050	414
1939	186[2]	12,463[2]	—[2]	—[2]	160	2,902	1,260	1,390	548	160
1938	166	10,872	—	—	123	2,238	810	933	313	101
1937	197	10,973	—	—	195	3,242	841	961	254	83
1936	137	7,392	—	—	158	2,567	650	756	241	57
1935	100	5,300	—	—	100	1,585	439	508	195	44
1934	83	4,029	—	—	75	1,100	355	414	245	55
1933	79	3,998	—	—	70	991	287	344	184	47
1932	43	2,115	—	—	70	986	372	470	187	39
1931	71	3,929	—	—	89	1,245	619	741	399	124
1930	104	6,442	—	—	131	2,011	719	872	696	212
1929	144	10,127	—	—	148	2,507	893	1,087	819	253
1928	129	8,803	—	—	136	2,178	825	1,241	936	341
1927	133	8,697	—	—	130	2,038	589	960	874	308
1926	142	8,670	—	—	136	1,992	668	1,069	1,001	358
1925	137	8,090	—	—	121	1,592	534	861	3,493	1,498
1924	110	6,298	—	—	95	1,220	472	748	537	214
1923	138	7,629	—	—	78	931	397	579	1,728	825
1922	105	5,994	—	—	57	562	325	505	1,488	700
1921	63	5,465	—	—	22	216	230	418	848	651
1920	153	11,522	—	—	36	366	244	414	—	466
1919	119	9,626	—	—	25	261	148	200	—	2,194
1918	119	7,787	—	—	22	228	68	81	—	14
1917	94	4,903[1]	—	—	52[1]	431[1]	224	245	—	17
1916	97[1]	3,872[1]	—	—	34[1]	241[1]	221	252	—	2
1915	85	2,735	—	—	25	157	292	336	—	5
1914	81	2,299	—	—	19	109	346	404	—	2
1913	104	2,848	—	—	25	139	418	504	—	2
1912	88	2,349	—	—	—	—	365	423	—	2
1911	75	2,067	—	—	—	—	362	425	—	4
1910	71	2,109	—	—	—	—	346	417	—	13
1909	57	1,730	—	—	—	—	315	372	—	113
1908	61	1,843	—	—	—	—	280	325	—	35
1907	57	1,669	—	—	—	—	375	425	—	10
1906	60	1,689	—	—	—	—	404	463	—	8
1905	47	1,386	—	—	—	—	—	—	—	3
1904	37	1,161	—	—	—	—	—	—	—	5
1903	32	891	—	—	—	—	—	—	—	3
1902	31	995	—	—	—	—	—	—	—	2
1901	32	1,070	—	—	—	—	—	—	—	2
1900	17	693	—	—	—	—	—	—	—	3
1899	18	473	—	—	—	—	—	—	—	3
1898	15	494	—	—	—	—	—	—	—	2
1897	16	473	—	—	—	—	—	—	—	1
1896	12	568	—	—	—	—	—	—	—	1
1895	7	422	—	—	—	—	—	—	—	1
1894	8	478	—	—	—	—	—	—	—	—
1893	6	339	—	—	—	—	—	—	—	1
1892	5	373	—	—	—	—	—	—	—	1
1891	8	562	—	—	—	—	—	—	—	3
1890	7	529	—	—	—	—	—	—	—	—
1889	6	360	—	—	—	—	—	—	—	—
1888	4	278	—	—	—	—	—	—	—	—
1887	3	159	—	—	—	—	—	—	—	—
1886	3	206	—	—	—	—	—	—	—	—

Series N 143-162. *Canadian exports of principal nonmetallic minerals, 1875 to 1960 (continuation)*

(all values in thousands of dollars; quantities as designated individually)

Year	Clay		Lime		Sand and gravel		Salt		Sulphur (contained in pyrites)	
	Quantity (thousands of cwt)	Value (thousands of dollars)	Quantity (thousands of cwt)	Value (thousands of dollars)	Quantity (thousands of tons)	Value (thousands of dollars)	Quantity (thousands of cwt)	Value (thousands of dollars)	Quantity (thousands of tons)	Value (thousands of dollars)
	153	154	155	156	157	158	159	160	161	162
1960	139	268	433	426	418	540	—	3,461	—	1,259
1959	110	243	493	430	486	537	25,482	4,640	—	1,019
1958	130	307	344	362	353	409	8,134	2,917	—	1,879
1957	105	280	724	742	321	392	9,158	3,241	—	2,853
1956	94	149	638	623	420	426	6,679	2,287	—	2,649
1955	147	95	581	538	336	383	2,929	1,001	—	2,002
1954	113	35	616	551	306	325	24	26	189	1,567
1953	84	25	666	543	368	348	47	32	130	1,034
1952	184	39	464	374	350	330	57	45	198	1,643
1951	162	35	710	534	370	359	91	63	178	1,177
1950	55	15	661	509	349	328	82	53	112	473
1949	97	18	604	499	337	315	69	63	91	382
1948	89	19	661	471	384	347	113	127	50	196
1947	81	17	572	298	377	295	224	244	56	282
1946	78	16	498	284	353	234	117	116	68	286
1945	23	6	420	237	317	193	106	105	75	315
1944	49	14	309	137	292	183	64	81	91	353
1943	2	4	308	133	382	213	161	118	105	410
1942	2	5	169	75	509	219	187	129	166	701
1941	1	2	260	114	454	159	251	122	130	585
1940	1	2	472	121	373	111	127	62	48	231
1939	1	2	184	75	242	79	213	76	110	793
1938	1	3	128	51	609	146	237	68	22	145
1937	1	3	203	85	364	78	187	62	46	252
1936	3	3	233	98	333	74	111	47	52	285
1935	6	3	105	50	100	21	181	51	8	48
1934	8	2	213	152	88	17	132	48	10	95
1933	10	2	208	192	102	16	107	43	15	121
1932	3	1	187	188	178	34	113	36	17	90
1931	8	4	289	283	486	146	123	55	27	140
1930	10	6	447	445	2,589	468	175	74	27	160
1929	16	7	485	428	1,903	442	187	71	32	247
1928	20	21	401	357	797	232	59	36	32	250
1927	15	3	421	368	638	178	24	23	14	106
1926	15	4	374	345	908	278	23	19	—	—
1925	7	8	326	312	865	198	46	27	—	—
1924	1	1	455	411	1,036	210	19	11	—	1
1923	—	—	487	428	765	183	17	10	10	47
1922	3	2	287	271	684	116	15	10	—	—
1921	2	1	254	247	1,397	202	7	8	8	32
1920	5	2	460	382	1,492	194	6	9	119	458
1919	—	—	193	129	1,074	131	12	15	89	389
1918	—	—	150	71	903	230	18	17	240	949
1917	—	—	—	75	1,075	291	173	94	280	974
1916	—	—	—	66	1,115	388	3	2	157	557

Series N 143–162. *Canadian exports of principal nonmetallic minerals, 1875 to 1960 (continued)*
(all values in thousands of dollars; quantities as designated individually)

Year	Clay		Lime		Sand and gravel		Salt		Sulphur (contained in pyrites)	
	Quantity (thousands of cwt)	Value (thousands of dollars)	Quantity (thousands of cwt)	Value (thousands of dollars)	Quantity (thousands of tons)	Value (thousands of dollars)	Quantity (thousands of cwt)	Value (thousands of dollars)	Quantity (thousands of tons)	Value (thousands of dollars)
	153	154	155	156	157	158	159	160	161	162
1915	—	—	—	16	808	381	9	6	138	527
1914	—	—	—	17	952	802	10	5	90	378
1913	—	—	—	29	645	441	5	3	46	212
1912	—	—	—	35	660	460	3	4	6	12
1911	—	—	—	40	573	408	5	5	32	121
1910	—	—	—	45	625	408	3	3	31	110
1909	—	—	—	49	482	256	3	2	35	157
1908	—	—	—	43	299	161	5	4	17	97
1907	—	—	—	56	298	120	22	8	25	80
1906	—	—	—	57	337	140	6	3	26	65
1905	—	—	—	86	307	153	14	6	20	56
1904	—	—	—	74	400	130	10	4	18	50
1903	—	—	—	131	356	124	19	6	21	60
1902	—	—	—	116	160	119	7	4	19	50
1901	—	—	—	99	197	117	27	7	25	57
1900	—	—	—	81	198	102	26	9	18	41
1899	—	—	—	74	242	102	8	3	16	34
1898	—	—	—	50	166	90	4	1	10	26
1897	—	—	—	53	153	77	4	1	15	31
1896	—	—	—	71	225	80	3	1	15	34
1895	—	—	—	72	277	118	3	1	8	38
1894	—	—	—	84	325	87	3	1	9	33
1893	—	—	—	87	329	122	3	1	—	—
1892	—	—	—	122	298	85	1	1	—	—
1891	—	—	—	120	244	60	4	1	—	—
1890	—	—	—	—	342	66	5	1	—	—
1889	—	—	—	—	283	53	6	2	—	—
1888	—	—	—	—	261	38	11	4	—	—
1887	—	—	—	—	181	30	108	12	—	—
1886	—	—	—	—	125	24	157	17	—	—
1885	—	—	—	—	111	23	173	19	—	—
1884	—	—	—	—	74	20	117	15	—	—
1883	—	—	—	—	55	14	140	19	—	—
1882	—	—	—	—	60	16	127	18	—	—
1881	—	—	—	—	59	15	240	45	—	—
1880	—	—	—	—	54	11	327	46	—	—
1879	—	—	—	—	47	9	414	49	—	—
1878	—	—	—	—	50	8	285	37	—	—
1877	—	—	—	—	12	2	493	61	—	—
1876	—	—	—	—	—	—	637	84	—	—
1875	—	—	—	—	—	—	380	67	—	—

[1] For 1888 to 1916 the export figures were defined as 'The Produce of the Mine'.

[2] For 1939 and earlier years data for asbestos milled fibres are included with crude asbestos, series N 143–144.

Series N 163–169. *Principal statistics of the Canadian nonmetallic mining industries, 1925 to 1960*

(all values in thousands of dollars)

Year	Number of establishments	Number of employees	Salaries and wages	Cost of fuel and electricity	Cost of process supplies and containers	Gross value of production	Net value added by processing
	163	164	165	166	167	168	169
1960	205	11,206	49,546	10,256	22,321	182,022	148,972
1959	186	11,719	48,879	10,214	21,993	168,929	136,428
1958	193	11,660	46,895	9,542	19,651	141,827	112,405
1957	192	12,310	48,361	10,148	22,057	159,092	126,561
1956	209	12,548	47,128	9,631	20,295	152,572	122,414
1955	243	11,722	42,391	8,616	18,422	140,368	112,872
1954	207	10,892	37,878	7,075	16,247	122,102	98,627
1953	210	11,099	36,892	6,811	16,187	119,980	96,772
1952	196	11,247	36,002	6,414	16,237	121,843	98,920
1951	197	10,611	31,035	6,326	15,560	113,712	91,493
1950	200	10,116	25,334	5,307	12,022	94,198	76,700
1949	199	8,606	19,745	12,621		64,342	51,722
1948	203	9,604	21,297	15,347		67,190	51,844
1947	207	9,593	17,342	12,901		54,471	41,570
1946	192	9,108	14,308	10,012		43,416	33,404
1945	203	8,318	12,712	8,962		40,341	31,379
1944	248	8,233	12,164	8,105		37,737	29,632
1943	257	7,989	11,056	8,410		39,243	30,833
1942	290	8,117	10,793	7,822		35,678	27,856
1941	250	7,370	9,088	7,056		33,342	26,286
1940	206	6,471	7,618	5,906		25,217	19,312
1939	199	6,175	6,850	5,170		23,870	18,699
1938	167	5,933	6,322	4,365		19,025	14,660
1937	172	6,294	6,729	5,393		21,343	15,950
1936	152	4,723	4,652	3,594		15,714	12,121
1935	150	3,808	3,576	2,829		11,876	9,046
1934	170	3,737	3,238	—		9,994	—
1933	133	3,072	2,360	—		9,819	—
1932	117	2,688	2,506	—		7,748	—
1931	126	3,314	3,522	—		10,900	—
1930	153	5,373	5,723	—		15,229	—
1929	140	6,167	7,202	—		21,087	—
1928	137	6,052	6,746	—		18,827	—
1927	159	6,054	6,662	—		17,560	—
1926	155	5,910	6,800	—		16,496	—
1925	168	5,210	5,308	—		14,506	—

Series N 170–175. *Canadian production of fuels, 1867 to 1960*

(all values in thousands of dollars; quantities as designated individually)

Year	Coal[1] Quantity (thousands of tons)	Coal[1] Value (thousands of dollars)	Natural gas[2] Quantity (billions of cubic feet)	Natural gas[2] Value (thousands of dollars)	Crude petroleum Quantity (thousands of barrels)	Crude petroleum Value (thousands of dollars)
	170	171	172	173	174	175
1960	11,011	74,676	522,972	52,197	189,534	422,926
1959	10,627	73,876	417,335	39,609	184,778	422,093
1958	11,687	79,963	337,804	32,058	165,496	398,748
1957	13,189	90,221	220,007	20,963	181,848	453,594
1956	14,916	95,350	169,153	16,850	171,981	406,562
1955	14,819	93,579	150,772	15,099	129,440	305,640
1954	14,914	96,600	120,735	12,482	96,080	243,877
1953	15,901	102,722	100,986	10,877	80,810	200,582
1952	17,579	111,026	88,686	9,518	61,237	143,038
1951	18,587	109,039	79,461	7,159	47,616	116,655
1950	19,139	110,140	67,822	6,433[2]	29,044	84,620
1949	19,120	110,915	60,457	11,620	21,305	61,118
1948	18,450	106,684	58,603	15,633	12,287	37,419
1947	15,869	77,475	52,657	13,430	7,692	19,576
1946	17,812	75,820	47,900	12,165	7,586	14,989
1945	16,507	67,588	48,412	12,310	8,483	13,632
1944	17,026	70,433	45,067	11,423	10,099	15,430
1943	17,859	62,878	44,276	13,159	10,052	16,470
1942	18,865	62,898	45,697	13,302	10,365	15,969
1941	18,226	58,060	43,495	12,665	10,134	14,415
1940	17,567	54,676	41,232	13,001	8,591	11,160
1939	15,693	48,677	35,185	12,507	7,826	9,846
1938	14,295	43,982	33,445	11,587	6,966	9,230
1937	15,836	48,752	32,381	11,675	2,944	5,399
1936	15,229	45,792	28,113	10,762	1,500	3,422
1935	13,888	41,963	24,911	9,363	1,447	3,492
1934	13,810	42,046	23,162	8,760	1,411	3,449
1933	11,903	35,924	23,138	8,712	1,145	3,139
1932	11,739	37,118	23,420	8,899	1,044	3,023
1931	12,243	41,208	25,875	9,027	1,543	4,212
1930	14,881	52,850	29,377	10,290	1,522	5,034
1929	17,497	63,065	28,378	9,977	1,117	3,732
1928	17,564	63,758	22,583	8,614	624	2,035
1927	17,427	61,867	21,377	8,043	477	1,516
1926	16,478	59,875	19,208	7,557	364	1,312
1925	13,135	49,262	16,903	6,833	332	1,251
1924	13,638	53,594	14,881	5,709	161	467
1923	16,991	72,059	15,961	5,885	170	522
1922	15,157	65,518	14,683	5,847	179	611
1921	15,057	72,452	14,078	4,594	188	642
1920	16,947[1]	82,497[1]	16,846	4,233	196	822
1919	13,919[1]	55,623[1]	19,938	4,176	240	736
1918	14,978	55,193	20,140	4,351	305	885
1917	14,047	43,200	27,409	5,045	214	542
1916	14,483	38,817	25,467	3,958	198	392
1915	13,267	32,111	20,124	3,706	215	301
1914	13,638	33,472	21,693	3,485	215	343
1913	15,012	37,335	20,478	3,309	228	406
1912	14,513	36,019	15,287	2,363	243	345
1911	11,323	26,468	11,644	1,918	291	357
1910	12,909	30,910	—	1,346	316	389
1909	10,501	24,781	—	1,207	421	560
1908	10,886	25,195	—	1,013	528	747
1907	10,511	24,382	—	815	789	1,057
1906	9,763	19,732	—	584	570	762
1905	8,668	17,520	—	380	634	856
1904	8,255	16,592	—	328	503	936
1903	7,960	15,943	—	202	487	1,049
1902	7,467	15,211	—	196	531	951
1901	6,486	12,699	—	339	622	1,008
1900	5,777	13,742	—	417	710	1,151
1899	4,925	10,283	—	387	809	1,202
1898	4,173	8,224	—	322	758	1,062
1897	3,786	7,304	—	326	710	1,012
1896	3,746	7,226	—	276	727	1,156
1895	3,478	6,739	—	423	726	1,087
1894	3,847	7,429	—	314	829	835
1893	3,783	7,359	—	376	798	874
1892	3,288	6,364	—	150	780	984
1891	3,578	7,019	—	—	755	1,010
1890	3,085	5,676	—	—	795	903
1889	2,658	4,894	—	—	705	654
1888	2,603	4,674	—	—	695	714
1887	2,429	4,388	—	—	714	557
1886	2,117	3,740	—	—	584	526

Series N170–175. *Canadian production of fuels, 1867 to 1960 (continued)*

(all values in thousands of dollars; quantities as designated individually)

Year	Coal[1]		Natural gas[2]		Crude petroleum	
	Quantity (thousands of tons)	Value (thousands of dollars)	Quantity (billions of cubic feet)	Value (thousands of dollars)	Quantity (thousands of barrels)	Value (thousands of dollars)
	170	171	172	173	174	175
1885	1,921	3,418	—	—	588	—
1884	1,985	3,594	—	—	571	—
1883	1,819	3,110	—	—	473	—
1882	1,848	3,248	—	—	390	—
1881	1,537	2,689	—	—	369	—
1880	1,483	2,657	—	—	350	—
1879	1,126	2,051	—	—	575	—
1878	1,090	1,941	—	—	312	—
1877	1,037	1,794	—	—	312	—
1876	995	1,730	—	—	312	—
1875	1,030	1,747	—	—	220	—
1874	1,064	1,763	—	—	169	—
1873	} 3,033	} 5,073	—	—	365	—
1872			—	—	308	—
1871			—	—	270	—
1870	753	1,243	—	—	250	—
1869	688	1,155	—	—	220	—
1868	623	1,073	—	—	200	—
1867	631	1,057	—	—	190	—

[1] For 1919 to 1960 the figures represent total output including use at the mine by the company and stockpile and waste charges and the like. For the years prior to 1919 the figures include only sales, colliery consumption and coal used by operators.

[2] For 1950 and prior years the value data include natural gasoline. Western provinces natural gas is valued at wellhead price, Ontario natural gas at wholesale price.

Series N176–181. *Canadian imports of principal fuels, 1880 to 1960*

(all values in thousands of dollars; quantities as designated individually)

Year	Coal[1,2]		Natural gas		Crude petroleum[3,4]	
	Quantity (thousands of tons)	Value (thousands of dollars)	Quantity (billions of cubic feet)	Value (thousands of dollars)	Quantity (thousands of barrels)	Value (thousands of dollars)
	176	177	178	179	180	181
1960	13,565	76,961	5,571	1,634	—	283,172
1959	14,236	84,488	11,963	3,797	115,289	277,495
1958	14,491	88,016	34,716	7,775	104,039	273,948
1957	19,480	117,714	30,551	7,240	111,905	305,557
1956	22,613	128,737	15,695	3,480	106,470	270,882
1955	19,743	106,551	11,116	2,698	86,678	229,480
1954	18,580	104,795	6,236	2,029	78,772	212,497
1953	23,266	136,567	6,097	1,991	79,478	207,987
1952	24,933	150,670	5,982	1,901	81,200	206,840
1951	26,801	168,089	3,699	1,286	83,284	231,039
1950	26,955	174,764	3,254	1,163	78,660	200,538
1949	22,195	141,149	1,263	488	73,947	189,396
1948	30,874	186,388	404	239	75,559	192,027
1947	28,892	138,950	433	253	68,447	127,472
1946	26,107	120,354	368	239	63,407	89,483
1945	25,062	102,432	346	233	56,806	72,321
1944	28,724[1]	113,138[1]	271	182	57,048	71,943
1943	28,109	101,245	232	158	49,754	66,384
1942	24,937	81,851	197	135	44,120	57,454
1941	20,388	61,588	172	117	46,791	56,442
1940	17,427	49,630	130	92	42,623	48,320
1939	14,999	41,579	114	75	37,095	39,650
1938	13,012	35,826	133	87	34,245	41,067
1937	14,671	38,159	114	75	38,915	46,678
1936	13,123	34,955	118	76	35,833	39,538
1935	12,079	33,331	106	70	33,052	33,818
1934	12,975	35,065	107	70	30,643	31,917
1933	11,204	28,122	101	73	27,270	20,294
1932	11,959	31,338	121	91	25,432	26,324
1931	13,121	36,829	109	75	29,070	22,673

Series N176–181. *Canadian imports of principal fuels, 1880 to 1960 (continued)*

(all values in thousands of dollars; quantities as designated individually)

Year	Coal[1,2]		Natural gas		Crude petroleum[3,4]	
	Quantity (thousands of tons)	Value (thousands of dollars)	Quantity (billions of cubic feet)	Value (thousands of dollars)	Quantity (thousands of barrels)	Value (thousands of dollars)
	176	177	178	179	180	181
1930	18,773	56,694	152	97	28,931	38,300
1929	18,204	56,013	133	85	30,291	46,174
1928	17,206	54,333	128	83	24,404	35,258
1927	18,687	61,785	104	66	19,562	31,073
1926	16,579	59,760	119	75	16,298	31,345
1925	16,350	59,159	64	41	12,584	33,642
1924	16,725	67,028	—	—	13,317	20,271
1923	20,990	96,370	—	—	11,219	17,488
1922	13,024	61,182	—	—	12,014	21,679
1921	18,302	88,925	—	—	10,158	20,029
1920	18,844	98,034	—	—	8,312	20,844
1919	17,293	61,161	—	—	11,585	19,831
1918	21,679	71,651	—	—	10,789	21,723
1917	20,857	70,562	—	—	9,328	14,436
1916	17,581	38,290	—	—	7,231	8,460
1915	12,466	28,346	—	—	5,503	3,678
1914	14,721	39,801	—	—	5,577	5,751
1913	18,202	47,949	—	—	4,630	5,251
1912	14,596	39,478	—	—	3,431	3,997
1911	14,559	39,293	—	—	2,047	2,189
1910	10,598	28,450	—	—	1,532[3]	1,639[3]
1909	9,873	26,832	—	—	903[3]	1,322[3]
1908	10,297	28,351	—	—	712[3]	895
1907	10,651	28,861	—	—	379[3]	471[3]
1906	7,444[2]	19,154[2]	—	—	566	668
1905	7,431	20,440	—	—	643	901
1904	6,937	20,113	—	—	123	276
1903	5,519	15,226	—	—	61	136
1902	5,189	12,999	—	—	17	41
1901	4,864	13,156	—	—	10	27
1900	4,424	11,012	—	—	10	23
1899	4,193	10,227	—	—	8	12
1898	3,374	9,100	—	—	259[4]	725[4]
1897	3,226	9,009	—	—	240	697
1896	3,323	9,020	—	—	229	740
1895	3,031	8,724	—	—	217	525
1894	3,008	9,719	—	—	188	440
1893	3,213	10,368	—	—	171	446
1892	3,176	9,779	—	—	161	476
1891	3,058	9,321	—	—	145	498
1890	2,664	8,155	—	—	145	516
1889	2,580	8,502	—	—	133	484
1888	3,399	8,778	—	—	129	408
1887	2,281	7,582	—	—	123	467
1886	1,963	6,657	—	—	109	422
1885	1,942	7,128	—	—	108	415
1884	1,999	7,459	—	—	90	380
1883	1,675	6,351	—	—	88	359
1882	1,275	4,659	—	—	86	398
1881	1,159	4,068	—	—	41	262
1880	977	2,740	—	—	20	131

[1] For 1944 and earlier years the figures include imports of briquettes. In the years 1945 to 1960 when these were shown separately in *Trade of Canada* the amounts were very small.

[2] For coal, for 1906 and earlier years the figures are for fiscal years ending 30 June of the year given.

[3] For crude petroleum 1908 and 1909 data are for fiscal years ending 31 March of the year given; for 1907 data are for 9 months ending 31 March 1907; for 1880 to 1906 data are for fiscal years ending 30 June of the year given.

[4] See the note to series N176–181 for the change in content of these series.

Series N 182–187. *Canadian exports of principal fuels, 1868 to 1960*

(all values in thousands of dollars; quantities as designated individually)

Year	Coal[1] Quantity (thousands of tons)	Coal[1] Value (thousands of dollars)	Natural gas Quantity (billions of cubic feet)	Natural gas Value (thousands of dollars)	Crude petroleum Quantity (thousands of barrels)	Crude petroleum Value (thousands of dollars)
	182	183	184	185	186	187
1960	853	6,789	91,046	18,051	42,235	94,450
1959	474	3,582	84,764	16,953	33,362	74,541
1958	339	2,908	86,972	17,984	31,679	73,044
1957	396	3,358	15,731	2,322	55,674	140,975
1956	594	4,710	9,642	1,118	42,908	103,923
1955	593	4,871	11,360	—	14,834	36,253
1954	219	1,716	7,148	—	2,345	6,318
1953	255	2,000	9,629	—	2,507	6,228
1952	389	3,204	8,145	—	1,424	3,452
1951	435	3,496	—	—	342	807
1950	395	3,198	—	—	—	—
1949	432	3,564	—	—	—	—
1948	1,273	11,556	—	—	1	3
1947	715	5,441	—	—	—	1
1946	862	5,946	—	—	—	—
1945	841	5,304	—	—	—	—
1944	1,010	5,985	—	—	—	—
1943	1,110	5,428	—	—	—	—
1942	816	4,278	—	—	1	3
1941	531	2,597	—	—	—	2
1940	505	2,362	—	—	—	—
1939	376	1,667	—	—	—	—
1938	353	1,541	—	—	—	—
1937	355	1,442	—	—	—	—
1936	412	1,793	—	—	—	—
1935	418	1,907	—	—	—	—
1934	306	1,401	—	—	—	—
1933	259	1,188	—	—	305	395
1932	285	1,433	—	—	208	245
1931	360	1,910	—	—	465	677
1930	625	3,346	—	—	550	881
1929	843	4,375	—	—	805	1,548
1928	864	4,470	—	—	615	1,099
1927	1,113	5,890	—	—	537	924
1926	1,028	5,739	—	—	601	852
1925	786	4,329	—	—	211	347
1924	773	4,837	—	—	522	529
1923	1,654	10,661	—	—	68	138
1922	1,819	11,159	—	—	201	289
1921	1,987	13,896	—	—	154	376
1920	2,558	18,015	—	—	77	293
1919	2,070	12,439	—	—	17	11
1918	1,817	9,405	—	—	8	28
1917	1,733	7,387	—	—	—	—
1916	2,135	7,099	—	—	4	11
1915	1,767	5,406	—	—	1	2
1914	1,423	3,880	—	—	—	—
1913	1,562	3,961	—	—	—	—
1912	2,127	5,822	—	—	1	4
1911	1,501	4,357	—	—	—	—
1910	2,377	6,077	—	—	—	—
1909	1,588	4,456	—	—	—	—
1908	1,730	4,661	—	—	—	—
1907	1,894	4,880	—	—	—	—
1906	1,835	4,738	—	—	—	—
1905	1,635	4,029	—	—	—	—
1904	1,557	4,036	—	—	—	—
1903	1,955	5,220	—	—	—	—
1902	2,090	5,402	—	—	—	—
1901	1,574	4,829	—	—	—	1
1900	1,788	4,840	—	—	—	—
1899	1,293	3,864	—	—	—	—
1898	1,150	3,619	—	—	—	—
1897	986	2,964	—	—	—	—
1896	1,107	2,389	—	—	—	—
1895	1,011	3,318	—	—	1	1
1894	1,104	3,542	—	—	2	3
1893	960	3,270	—	—	3	4
1892	824	2,807	—	—	9	13
1891	971	3,394	—	—	13	18
1890	724	2,437	—	—	12	18
1889	665	2,335	—	—	7	11
1888	589	1,975	—	—	6	75
1887	581	1,696	—	—	14	14
1886	521	1,426	—	—	7	10

Series N 182–187. *Canadian exports of principal fuels, 1868 to 1960 (continued)*

(all values in thousands of dollars; quantities as designated individually)

| | Coal[1] | | Natural gas | | Crude petroleum | |
| | Quantity (thousands of tons) | Value (thousands of dollars) | Quantity (billions of cubic feet) | Value (thousands of dollars) | Quantity (thousands of barrels) | Value (thousands of dollars) |
Year						
	182	183	184	185	186	187
1885	480[1]	1,468[1]	—	—	10	11
1884	452	1,201	—	—	31	30
1883	444	1,159	—	—	—	1
1882	421	1,079	—	—	—	—
1881	420	1,123	—	—	—	—
1880	345	1,014	—	—	—	—
1879	316	937	—	—	—	—
1878	340	1,211	—	—	—	—
1877	250	856	—	—	—	—
1876	278	977	—	—	—	—
1875	288	938	—	—	—	—
1874	418	1,344	—	—	—	—
1873	405	952	—	—	—	—
1872	296	579	—	—	—	—
1871	318	662	—	—	—	—
1870	287	589	—	—	—	—
1869	440	763	—	—	—	—
1868	265	641	—	—	—	—

[1] For 1868 to 1885 data are for fiscal years ending 30 June of the year given.

Series N 188–191. *Apparent consumption of principal fuels in Canada, 1907 to 1960*

Year	Coal (thousands of tons)	Natural gas (billions of cubic feet)	Crude petroleum (thousands of barrels)	Petroleum products (thousands of barrels)	Year	Coal (thousands of tons)	Natural gas (billions of cubic feet)	Crude petroleum (thousands of barrels)	Petroleum products (thousands of barrels)
	188	189	190	191		188	189	190	191
1960	23,723	437,497	272,859	—	1930	33,030	29,528	29,736	39,553
1959	24,389	344,534	266,705	302,303	1929	34,858	28,511	25,144	39,991
1958	25,840	285,548	237,856	279,106	1928	33,906	22,711	20,454	33,258
1957	32,273	234,827	238,079	272,461	1927	35,001	21,481	16,787	27,512
1956	36,935	175,205	235,543	263,311	1926	32,029	19,327	13,673	22,509
1955	33,969	150,372	201,285	235,398	1925	28,699	16,967	12,705	19,341
1954	33,274	119,823	172,508	204,056	1924	29,590	—	12,099	18,729
1953	38,911	97,454	157,869	187,268	1923	36,326	—	11,397	16,641
1952	42,123	86,523	141,013	171,113	1922	26,362	—	11,153	14,814
1951	44,953	83,160	130,558	153,271	1921	31,372	—	9,030	14,057
1950	45,699	71,076	107,704	133,752	1920	33,232	—	8,689	12,889
1949	40,883	61,720	95,252	116,290	1919	29,142	—	7,694	—
1948	48,050	59,007	87,845	105,319	1918	34,839	—	5,797	—
1947	44,046	53,090	76,139	97,366	1917	33,171	—	4,086	—
1946	43,056	48,268	70,993	81,185	1916	29,929	—	5,533	—
1945	40,728	48,758	65,289	70,898	1915	23,966	—	5,821	—
1944	44,740	45,338	67,147	68,443	1914	26,935	—	5,297	—
1943	44,858	44,508	59,806	63,051	1913	31,652	—	—	—
1942	42,987	45,894	54,484	62,636	1912	26,982	—	—	—
1941	38,083	43,667	56,924	64,939	1911	24,382	—	—	—
1940	34,489	41,362	51,214	57,787	1910	21,130	—	—	—
1939	30,315	35,299	44,921	52,545	1909	18,786	—	—	—
1938	26,954	33,578	42,068	48,130	1908	19,454	—	—	—
1937	30,151	32,495	41,858	46,321	1907	19,269	—	—	—
1936	27,941	28,231	31,102	41,548					
1935	25,548	25,018	34,529	39,149					
1934	26,479	23,269	32,100	36,974					
1933	22,848	23,239	28,111	34,707					
1932	23,412	23,541	26,269	34,499					
1931	25,004	25,984	30,148	37,762					

Series N 192–198. *Principal statistics of the Canadian fuels industries, 1922 to 1960*
(all values in thousands of dollars)

Year	Number of establishments	Number of employees	Salaries and wages	Cost of fuel and electricity	Cost of process supplies and containers	Gross value of production	Net value added by processing
	192	193	194	195	196	197	198
1960	23,224	17,627	70,507	11,957	23,636	591,138	530,879
1959	21,690	18,206	70,825	11,702	20,367	529,393	497,323
1958	20,012	20,226	75,566	11,371	21,054	503,740	471,315
1957	19,055	22,390	83,524	10,833	22,141	555,546	522,571
1956	16,811	24,187	85,821	9,948	20,263	512,916	482,704
1955	14,329	23,458	76,344	8,584	16,337	413,440	388,519
1954	12,357	24,807	78,271	8,068	14,864	352,741	329,810
1953	11,437	26,766	83,854	8,708	15,244	314,059	290,108
1952	10,236	28,029	87,935	7,413	16,297	256,477	232,767
1951	9,061	28,490	81,138	5,916	14,017	232,096	212,163
1950	8,203	28,453	74,491	5,154	11,212	201,181	184,815
1949	7,421	28,595	72,222		16,546	189,589	173,043
1948	6,765	27,791	65,814		18,346	153,929	135,583
1947	6,445	25,307	52,425		12,818	105,196	92,378
1946	6,504	28,705	54,096		13,910	97,557	83,648
1945	6,343	29,159	56,324		12,716	89,230	76,513
1944	6,279	29,953	63,721		14,157	92,648	78,491
1943	6,168	30,754	55,351		12,654	88,340	75,687
1942	6,238	30,117	48,567		12,278	88,671	76,393
1941	6,205	30,335	44,246		10,593	81,696	71,103
1940	6,325	30,364	39,627		10,559	75,238	64,680
1939	6,251	30,242	35,825		9,734	67,742	58,008
1938	6,223	30,934	33,862		9,151	62,093	52,942
1937	6,099	30,850	36,470		9,927	61,019	51,092
1936	6,072	30,045	32,629		8,677	56,032	47,355
1935	6,031	28,857	29,574		13,876	50,569	36,693
1934	5,435	28,458	28,525	3,684	—	50,587	—
1933	5,190	27,460	24,803	3,405	—	45,093	—
1932	5,121	28,966	27,558	3,220	—	46,093	—
1931	5,242	30,761	32,509	3,391	—	50,729	—
1930	5,034	32,982	42,130	3,993	—	64,835	—
1929	5,346	33,913	48,400	3,992	—	72,509	—
1928	5,263	33,034	47,343	3,919	—	70,486	—
1927	5,461	31,895	41,612	3,683	—	67,646	—
1926	5,534	30,256	37,579	4,750	—	68,744	—
1925	5,632	26,350	34,725	4,104	—	57,346	—
1924	5,024	28,581	36,592	4,381	—	59,770	—
1923	5,261	33,064	47,384	4,776	—	78,466	—
1922	5,263	32,919	40,657	3,184	—	71,976	—

SECTION P: ELECTRIC POWER

JOHN DAVIS, *British Columbia Electric Company, Ltd*

This section contains the major statistics of the electric power industry in Canada.

The published sources are the following publications of the Dominion Bureau of Statistics: *Electric Power Statistics*, annual 1956 to 1960 (Ottawa, Queen's Printer), various years; *Central Electric Stations*, annual 1917 to 1955 (Ottawa, Queen's Printer); *Canada Year Book*, annual (Ottawa, Queen's Printer). In addition to these publications, data from the files of the Water Resources Branch of the Department of Northern Affairs and Natural Resources and of the Public Utilities Section of the Dominion Bureau of Statistics were used. The latter frequently contained revisions of published data.

General note

The generation of electric power and its distribution and sale to the final consumer are almost entirely handled by the electric utility industry in Canada. In addition, substantial quantities of electricity are produced by manufacturing and mining companies for use in their own industrial operations. A very small part of this power is also sold to the public in special circumstances where this is more economic than supply by a distant utility.

Statistics covering the main aspects of utility operations have been published by the Dominion Bureau of Statistics annually since 1917. It was not until the mid-thirties, however, that complete data covering the use of electricity, by type of customer or type of industry, were collected. Furthermore, until 1956 the only information available about power generation by industrial companies was their total output. It should be noted, however, that when industrial producers had organized their power production in separate corporations, these corporations would be treated as central electrical stations (see below). Since 1956, when the Dominion Bureau of Statistics undertook a complete revision of its electric power statistics, the coverage of industrial power producers has been almost as extensive as that of electric utilities.

Series P 1–62 are based upon the series of annual reports published by the Dominion Bureau of Statistics, *Central Electric Stations* for the years 1917 to 1955 and *Electric Power Statistics* for 1956 and later years though for some years unpublished revisions and unpublished data have been incorporated. Apart from annual reports of the utilities themselves, there is little other published statistical data about the electric power industry in Canada. The progressive development of the country's hydroelectric resources is well described in regular reports issued by the (federal) Water Resources Branch and its predecessor the Dominion Water Power Branch. This branch under slightly changing name has been under various departments: for 1912 to 1936, Department of the Interior; for 1937 to 1949, Department of Mines and Resources; for 1950 to 1952, Department of Resources and Development; for 1953 to 1960, Department of Northern Affairs and National Resources. These reports are the source of series P 75–77. In each year since 1921 the *Canada Year Book* has included a section dealing with electric power. For individual provinces some data are normally available from the provincial statistical department or from the department responsible for water resources. This information, however, is unlikely to be any more extensive than that contained in Dominion Bureau of Statistics reports although it may be rather more detailed.

A relatively new report issued by the Dominion Bureau of Statistics, *Electric Power Survey of Capability and Load*, annual, gives data about generating capability, peak loads, and energy output. These statistics, which cover both utilities and industrial power producers, are available only for 1950 and later years.

Five detailed surveys of power plant and equipment have been made at irregular intervals since 1918: (1) *Electric Generation and Distribution in Canada* by Leo G. Denis, published in 1918 by the Commission of Conservation, Canada; (2) *Central Electric Stations in Canada (Part II)*, Water Resources Paper No. 27, published in 1919 by the Dominion Water Power Branch; (3) *Central Electric Stations in Canada (Part II)*, Water Resources Paper No. 33, published in 1923 by the Dominion Water Power Branch; (4) *Central Electric Stations in Canada (Part II)*, Water Resources Paper No. 55, published in 1928 by the Dominion Water Power Branch; (5) *Inventory of Prime Mover and Electric Generating Equipment as at December 31, 1958*, made by the Dominion Bureau of Statistics.

A considerable amount of information is available about electric rates in reports issued by the Dominion Bureau of Statistics. A report on the cost of electricity to residential customers entitled *Index Numbers of Rates for Electricity for Residential Lighting and Table of Monthly Bills*, issued in 1926, provided historic monthly bills and index numbers for 1913 and 1923 to 1925 with index base 1913. This report was extended to cover commercial and small power customers in 1927 when the second of an annual series of publications was issued. Originally entitled *Index Numbers of Rates for Electricity for Residence Lighting and Tables of Monthly Bills for Domestic Service, Commercial Lighting and Small Power*, this series continues at present as *Electricity Bills for Domestic, Commercial, and Small Power Service*. Unfortunately the detailed nature of these reports makes it impossible to prevent a useful summary of rates in this section on electric power statistics.

In many of the historical series that follow, two figures appear for the year 1956. One is based on the old *Central Electric Station* series and the other on the new *Electric Power Statistics*. The difference between the two figures indicates the significance of the break in historical continuity. This break is caused by the reclassification of power producers which occurred in 1956. The earlier statistical series were limited to organizations selling power to the public and these organizations were called central electric stations. Most were electric utilities although a few were industrial establishments which sold a limited amount of power, to their own employees or to a nearby municipality. Statistics relating to these establishments were limited to the utility aspect of their power production.

In the revised electric power statistics issued after 1956 all producers of electricity are included, and each producer is classified as either an electric utility or an industrial establishment. Organizations whose primary function is to sell the electricity they generate or purchase are classified as utilities. Those generating power primarily for use in their own industrial operations, principally manufacturing or mining, are classified as industrial establishments. The major difference between the old series and the new is that several blocks of power previously treated as sales by a central electric station to an industrial customer are now treated as energy produced by an industrial establishment for its own use. The effect of this change is particularly marked in series P11–12, P29 and P32, and P39, P41 and P44.

In general the distinction between the two classifications, utility and industry, is quite clear cut. Some anomalies do, however, arise from the corporate structure of individual industrial concerns. For example, in otherwise similar situations the production of power may be treated by one firm as an internal departmental operation while another may create a separate corporate entity to handle it. In the first case the power producer would be classified as an industrial establishment and in the second as a utility.

These two terms cover organizations which vary widely in size. Utilities range from huge multi-plant systems with annual kilowatt-hour generation and sales measured in billions to small village distribution systems selling only a few thousand kilowatt-hours a year. A similar variation exists in the size of industrial power producers. In organization and function, utilities also show considerable differences. A utility may be a private company, a provincial crown corporation, or a municipally owned electric system. It may not even generate power as it may purchase all or a part of the power it sells, usually from another utility but sometimes from an industrial establishment.

All energy sales and transfers between power producers have been allowed for in the statistics so that duplications are excluded. Output figures are the sum total of kilowatt-hours produced in Canada, adjusted in series P20–26 to show the amount of energy imported and exported. Similarly, sales and revenue figures, series P29–33 and 41–45, record transactions with the final consumer in Canada.

In several of the series, a distinction is made between publicly and privately operated utilities (or central stations). This is based upon utility status at the end of each year. In probably all instances where a decrease has occurred in annual figures for privately operated utilities, this indicates a change of ownership rather than any real reduction in overall operations.

P1–6. Installed power generating capacity, by type of prime mover and class of ownership, 1917 to 1960

SOURCE: for 1917 to 1955 D.B.S., *Central Electric Stations*, successive annual issues; for 1956 to 1960, D.B.S., *Electric Power Statistics*, successive annual issues. Some figures were provided or revised and brought up to date by the Public Utilities Section, Public Finance and Transportation Division of the Dominion Bureau of Statistics.

These series present the total installed capacity of generating plants in service at the end of each year. This capacity is the design capacity under specified conditions and is not necessarily the maximum output that can be produced. Moreover, in the case of hydro-electric stations the amount of water available at any time may limit the output.

In 1956, both the basis of reporting and the unit of measure were changed. Until 1955 series P1–5 present for central electric stations the installed capacity of the prime mover, the hydraulic or steam turbine, measured in horsepower. Series P6 shows the

capacity of the electrical generating equipment driven by the prime movers: this is shown in kilovolt-amperes, which may approximately be converted to kilowatts by multiplying by .83. For 1956 and subsequent years the nameplate rating of the generating equipment in kilowatts is shown. If allowance is made for the reclassification of power producers and the changed unit of measure, the kilowatt capacity of electric utilities, series P4–6, may be considered as the continuation of series P6 while series P1–3 gives generator capacity for both electric utilities and industrial establishments. The generator capacity of the industrial establishments is the difference between series P1 and P6. A generator capacity of approximately 1,500,000 kilowatts was added by the inclusion in 1956 of industrial plants not covered previously.

P7–13. Net generation of electrical energy, by type of prime mover and class of ownership, 1919 to 1960

SOURCE: same source as for series P1–6. The data for 1949 to 1956 are presented on both the old and the new basis; the revised data on the new basis were provided by the Public Utilities Section of the Dominion Bureau of Statistics.

Data on generation are for 'net' generation or generating station output. This means that electricity used in the generating station for the operation of station auxiliary equipment is not included.

The total net output of the generating equipment recorded in series P1–6 is presented in series P7–13. Although two sets of figures appear for 1949 to 1956 the totals in series P13 are almost the same on both bases for corresponding years; the slight differences are explained by revisions made when the new data for 1949 to 1956 were prepared. After 1927 when industrial generation figures are first available, the net output shown is virtually the total electric production in Canada. The only kilowatt-hours excluded would be those produced by small isolated plants in nonmanufacturing commercial establishments for their own use and emergency or stand-by generating equipment.

P14–19. Net generation of electrical energy of electric utilities and industrial establishments, by type of prime mover, 1947 to 1960

SOURCE: data provided by the Public Utilities Branch, D.B.S.

Series P14–19 are the same total kilowatt-hour figures in P13 rearranged to new electric utility and industrial establishment basis. Series P14 and P17 are the same as series P11 and P12 on the new basis. While the total generation by industrial establishments recorded in series P17 for the years 1947 to 1955 can be regarded as accurate, the distribution between hydro and thermal in series P18 and P19 contains a substantial element of estimation. See also the note to series P7–13.

P20–28. Exports, imports and consumption of electrical energy in Canada, 1921 to 1960

SOURCE: same source as for series P1–6.

Series P25 and series P13 are identical. As they are total generation, the 1956 reclassification of power producers does not affect them, nor does it affect the components of series P20–27. (See also the note to series P7–13.)

The total amount of electricity consumed in Canada is the kilowatt-hours generated in the country less net exports to the United States. This is given in series P26 and broken down by end use in series P63–74. Another, and more significant measure of electricity consumption is the apparent primary consumption, series P28. The difference between series P26 and P28, series P27, is sales of surplus or secondary hydro-electric energy. These sales fluctuate considerably from year to year as they depend upon the availability of plant and of water at generating stations and the existence of markets for the power. It is mostly sold, on an interruptible basis and as a substitute fuel, for use in electric boilers. By far the largest consumer of this secondary energy is the pulp and paper industry.

Series P 28 is the best electric power indicator of economic activity in Canada as the disturbing effect of annual variations in net exports and electric boiler sales has been removed. It includes all utility sales, industrial establishment consumption, and transmission and distribution loss.

Electricity has been exported from Canada to the United States since the turn of the century but no official records exist of the quantities before 1907. Since that year, when the Electricity and Fluid Exportation Act came into force, licensing of exports has been required. As a result, administrative records of the number of kilowatt-hours produced for export for fiscal years ending 31 March are available after 1907. Consistent calendar year figures cannot, however, be traced back further than 1921. The export licences have always classified exports as firm or surplus, depending on the contractual arrangements between the supplier and the purchaser, but the earliest calendar year for which this breakdown is available is 1939. The figures in series P 20–22 were obtained from Dominion Bureau of Statistics records. The most complete source, on a fiscal year basis, is the annual reports of the Standards Branch of the Department of Trade and Commerce.

The earliest official records of imports are for 1926, but it is probable that imports occurred before that year. In 1927, when industrial generation, series P 13, is first available, all the various components of the total electricity supply are available for Canada and series P 28 begins.

P 29–33. Sales of power to ultimate customers, by type, Canada, 1930 to 1960

SOURCE: same source as for series P 1–6.

These series present final sales of electricity to the public under the usual customer classifications—residential and farm service, commercial, industrial, and street lighting. The statistics are derived from utility billing records and, therefore, reflect each utility's own customer classification for rate purposes. Although the series are consistent from year to year, they are not consistent internally. The principal inconsistency is between the commercial and industrial categories, for certain customers might be classified one way by one utility and the other way by another utility. This is particularly true of some of the larger nonmanufacturing commercial customers.

The only significant difference between the two sets of figures for 1956 is in the industrial category. The substantial reduction there is a measure of the blocks of power formerly treated as sales by a central electric station to an industrial customer and now treated as industrial generation.

Except for some small discrepancies mentioned in the footnotes to the three tables, series P 29–33, P 34–38, and P 41–45 correspond as they show kilowatt-hour sales, number of customers, and revenues received from the sale of electricity. Sales figures contain some elements of estimation as flat-rate water-heaters are not metered and some other services such as street lighting are often not metered.

Data for 1930 to 1956 cover central electric stations only; data for 1956 to 1960 cover, in addition, sales to the public by industrial establishments.

P 34–38. Numbers of ultimate customers of power, by type, 1920 to 1960

SOURCE: same source as for series P 1–6.

Customer numbers are derived from utility billing records. Utilities are asked to report the number of customers served in December each year. A customer may normally be regarded as a single service or account, for many firms will be customers of more than one utility or receive service from one utility at several locations. Commercial and industrial customers are reported together until 1923 and street lighting customers not at all until 1929.

Also see the note to series P 29–33.

P 39–45. Revenue from the sale of electricity, 1917 to 1960

SOURCE: same source as for series P 1–6.

Revenue categories were not established on the present basis until 1929. Previously revenues were classified as from lighting and from all other purposes. Revenues arising from inter-utility sales in Canada have been eliminated, although, as a footnote points out, proper allowance was not made in a few years. All revenues shown in series P 41–45 are from sales to the final consumer. Export revenues are shown for 1937 and succeeding years on a calendar year basis; for 1927 to 1936 on a fiscal year basis. (See note (1) to series P 39–45.)

Data for 1917 to 1956 cover central electric stations only; from 1956 to 1960 they cover industrial establishments as well.

P 46–49. Capital invested in fixed assets in the power industry, selected years, 1891 to 1943 and 1956 to 1960

SOURCE: for 1891, 1900, 1905, 1910 and 1915, *Canada Year Book*, *1905*, pp. 132 and 138, *1911*, p. 33, *1913*, p. 222 and *1916–17*, p. 292 respectively; for other years, same source as for series P 1–6.

Some data about capital invested were collected by the Dominion Bureau of Statistics continuously from 1917 until 1943. Collection was discontinued in the same year that the Bureau gave up collecting equivalent information from manufacturing industries. In 1956 collection of investment data from electric utilities were resumed. Despite the gap between 1944 and 1955, the data from 1917 on are comparable. Fixed assets are reported at original cost and include generating equipment, transmission and distribution facilities, and other property and equipment but not nonelectric utility assets. The data prior to 1917 probably correspond broadly with the data for years 1917 to 1943.

P 50–51. Number of employees and earnings in the power industry, 1917 to 1960

SOURCE: same source as for series P 1–6.

At least for years since 1945, these series represent only employees employed on administration, operation, and maintenance. Engineering staffs and construction forces employed directly by utilities have been excluded. This has required some estimation as employees may be engaged on both maintenance and construction work and administrative employees may have part of their time charged to capital work. In addition to their own employees, utilities may have large engineering and construction staffs of contractors engaged on the construction of new facilities. During the years 1946 to 1953 there were important reporting inconsistencies. Earnings estimates have since been revised but the number of employees in these years has been omitted because it was not possible to adjust the original figures.

It is not entirely clear from the pre-war reports just which construction employees were included. The early reports excluded salaried construction workers but appear to have included wage-earners. However, construction employees would not have been as significant as in postwar years, either in total or proportionately.

P 52–56. Cost of fuel to generate electricity, 1919 to 1960

SOURCE: same source as for series P 1–6.

This table shows expenditures on fuel for the generation of electricity. Under coal is included all types, bituminous, sub-bituminous and lignite. Other fuels, series P 56, are principally gasoline, kerosene and wood. The energy generated with this fuel is reported as series P 8.

P 57–62. Number of power plants and pole line mileage, 1917 to 1960

SOURCE: same source as for series P 1–6.

The number of power plants in operation was one of the earliest central electric station statistics collected. It had more significance as a measure of the industry's size before the development of extensive transmission networks joining all plants into a single integrated system. In 1954 collection of these figures was discontinued.

Similarly, less significance attaches to the figure for pole line mileage today than in earlier years. With the construction of higher voltage and multicircuit lines, the mileage figure includes without distinction one mile of transmission line with a carrying capacity of several hundred thousand kilowatts and a mile of low voltage distribution line of limited capacity. The figures show the total route mileage of all types of line, steel tower, wood pole and underground cable.

P 63–74. Energy consumption in Canada by end uses, 1935 to 1960

SOURCE: for 1935 to 1946: for series P 64 and series P 66–72, Davis, *Canadian Energy Prospects*, table 10, p. 376; for series P 65, D.B.S. *Central Electric Stations*, annual issues; for other series, Dominion Bureau of Statistics, Public Finance and Transportation Division, Public Utilities Section; for 1947 and 1948, *Electric Power Statistics, 1960*, table 17, pp. 50–1; for 1949 to 1960, the Public Utilities Section, D.B.S.

The total electricity consumption in Canada shown in series P 26 is broken down into its principal end uses in series P 63–74. These series combine sales by central stations or electric utilities and the consumption of electricity by industrial establishments as reported by the Dominion Bureau of Statistics in the annual census of industry. Although there is some difficulty in exactly reconciling the figures from these two sources, the series can be regarded as substantially correct. Series P 64–70 and P 72 are based upon reported figures while series P 71 and P 73–74 are residuals.

Total consumption and residential and farm consumption shown in series P 63 and P 64 correspond to series P 26 and P 30 and commercial and street-lighting in series P 65 corresponds to the sum of series P 31 and series P 33. Consumption by manufacturing and mining industries is the sum of reported figures, either their purchases from electric utilities or energy they generated for their own use. Taken together series P 66–73

correspond approximately to industrial sales by central stations/electric utilities (series P 32) plus energy generated by industrial establishments (series P 12). The difference arises from sales of energy by industrial producers to their own customers.

The consumption shown for other industries (series P 73) is merely a residual, sales by central stations or electric utilities to their industrial customers who are not classified by the Dominion Bureau of Statistics for census of industry in the manufacturing or mining industries. It is not possible to define what sorts of use the series covers as this depends upon individual utility rate structures for industrial customers and their interpretation. Manufacturing and mining are specifically excluded, and most sales to wholesale and retail trade and the services would be supplied under commercial rates. Some of these latter sales, however, which are for power rather than lighting uses would be included in series P 73. Also included would be some sales to nonelectric utilities, transportation, the construction industry, and defence establishments.

Series P 74 is simply the difference between the total supply (series P 26, energy generated less net exports) and reported consumption. This is usually called 'energy lost and unaccounted for' which consists of energy losses in transmission and distribution lines and in substations. Line losses are limited to losses on electricity produced by central stations/electric utilities. Losses incurred by industrial establishments in the generation of power for their own use are included with consumption in series P 66–72 as they cannot be separated.

P 75–77. Hydraulic turbine installations, 1890 to 1960

SOURCE: for series P 77, 1890 to 1899, files of the Water Resources Branch, Department of Northern Affairs and Natural Resources; for 1900 to 1936, *Canada Year Book, 1937*, p. 390; for 1937 to 1945, *Canada Year Book, 1946*, p. 362; for 1946 to 1949, *Canada Year Book, 1954*, pp. 556–7; for 1950 to 1960, *Canada Year Book, 1961*, p. 570; for series P 75 and P 76 from 1928 to 1960, successive issues of *Canada Year Book*.

These series are included because they go back almost thirty years beyond the earliest central stations report. They come from the records of the Water Resources Branch and differ from the Dominion Bureau of Statistics figures. The Branch maintains a record of water power installations and includes mechanical power facilities as well as hydro-electric. Moreover, the Branch figures record plant expected to be in service at the end of the year whereas the Bureau records show plant actually in service at the end of each year. In addition, industrial establishments are classified somewhat differently by the Branch. Therefore, although series P 77 shows central station installations separately for the years 1928 to 1960, there are considerable differences from series P 2 which is central station installations as reported by the Bureau. Each series can be regarded as consistent in itself, but it is series P 2 which is consistent with all the other power series except for these three, P 75–77.

Series P1-6. *Installed power generating capacity, by type of prime mover and class of ownership, 1917 to 1960*

Year	Total[1]	Hydro[1]	Thermal[1]	Publicly[2] operated	Privately[2] operated	Generator capacity of utilities
	1	2	3	4	5	6
	Utilities and industrial generator capacity (thousands of kilowatts)			Electric utilities generator capacity (thousands of kilowatts)		
1960	23,048.7	18,656.9	4,391.8	12,532.7	5,899.8	18,432.4
1959	21,128.4	17,550.0	3,578.4	11,213.4	5,723.9	16,937.3
1958	18,669.4	15,687.2	2,982.2	9,567.3	5,301.9	14,869.2
1957	16,728.2	14,112.8	2,615.4	8,019.6	5,020.0	13,039.6
1956	15,496.2	13,070.0	2,426.1	7,334.1	4,724.6	12,058.6
	Central electric stations (series P1-5, prime mover capacity in thousands of horsepower; series P6, generator capacity in thousands of kilovolt-amperes)					
1955	17,985.6	15,538.7	2,446.9	9,497.2	8,488.5	14,914.6
1954	16,721.8	14,461.5	2,226.3	8,710.3	8,011.5	13,916.8
1953	15,661.0	13,423.4	2,237.7	7,382.9	8,278.1	13,083.9
1952	14,221.8	12,550.8	1,671.0	6,542.3	7,679.5	11,854.3
1951	13,030.6	11,786.0	1,243.6	5,804.7	7,225.9	10,780.1
1950	11,976.2	11,029.8	946.4	5,171.7	6,804.5	9,960.2
1949	10,883.3	9,973.4	909.9	4,359.0	6,524.2	9,103.7
1948	10,219.6	9,470.3	749.3	4,085.1	6,134.5	8,514.5
1947	9,786.1	9,131.9	654.2	3,760.8	6,025.3	8,138.7
1946	10,001.7	9,378.9	622.8	3,612.5	6,389.2	8,312.4
1945	9,840.3	9,216.6	623.7	3,460.3	6,380.0	8,182.3
1944	9,898.9	9,268.0	630.9	3,424.7	6,474.2	8,231.7
1943	9,797.6	9,205.2	592.4	2,426.5	7,371.1	8,148.0
1942	8,808.7	8,234.3	574.4	2,408.3	6,400.3	7,432.2
1941	8,352.2	7,784.4	567.8	2,304.4	6,047.8	7,017.8
1940	8,130.8	7,567.1	563.7	2,291.1	5,839.7	6,857.6
1939	7,801.3	7,241.0	560.3	2,285.3	5,516.0	6,601.2
1938	7,672.6	7,155.6	517.0	2,240.9	5,431.7	6,494.5
1937	7,539.4	7,023.2	516.2	2,202.6	5,336.8	6,374.3
1936	7,319.9	6,810.7	509.2	2,173.0	5,146.9	6,198.3
1935	7,311.0	6,808.0	503.0	2,037.8	5,274.2	6,070.9
1934	7,061.6	6,560.7	500.9	1,964.0	5,097.6	5,877.2
1933	6,809.6	6,306.0	503.6	1,966.9	4,842.7	5,656.4
1932	6,528.5	6,036.3	492.3	1,824.0	4,704.5	5,435.3
1931	5,890.8	5,422.3	468.5	1,719.5	4,171.3	4,884.6
1930	5,572.6	5,144.1	428.5	1,658.1	3,914.5	4,620.5
1929	5,097.4	4,718.9	378.5	1,426.2	3,671.3	4,194.3
1928	4,786.9	4,445.5	341.4	1,387.7	3,399.2	3,899.8
1927	4,318.4	3,975.0	343.4	1,406.7	2,911.7	3,507.1
1926	3,946.2	3,609.4	336.8	1,400.7	2,545.5	3,141.2
1925	3,742.7	3,416.0	326.7	1,380.2	2,362.5	2,987.1
1924	3,017.6	2,708.0	309.6	1,199.1	1,818.5	2,418.8
1923	2,573.4	2,282.5	290.9	1,006.6	1,566.8	1,983.7
1922	2,408.7	2,112.3	296.4	727.5	1,681.1	1,846.4
1921	2,111.4	1,826.4	285.1	539.7	1,571.7	1,583.1
1920	2,033.6	1,754.1	279.5	481.5[2]	1,415.5[2]	1,558.3
1919	2,024.9	1,737.0	287.9	478.2	1,428.9	1,576.2
1918	1,958.6	1,682.2	276.5	406.9	1,434.2	1,525.5
1917	1,844.6	1,652.7	191.9	400.3	1,444.3	1,387.5

[1] Series P1-3 include main plant and auxiliary equipment throughout; industrial plant is included from 1956 on.

[2] Series P4-5 do not include industrial equipment in any year; and for 1917 to 1920 auxiliary equipment is excluded. The auxiliaries excluded totalled 90.4 thousand horsepower in 1917 and 136.6 thousand horsepower in 1920. Main plant in 1921 was 534.3 thousand horsepower for publicly owned plants and 1,443.5 thousand horsepower for privately owned.

Series P7–13. *Net generation of electrical energy, by type of prime mover and class of ownership, 1919 to 1960*
(millions of kilowatt-hours)

Year	Hydro plants[1]	Thermal plants[1]	Publicly operated	Privately operated	Total utilities	Industrial establishments[2]	Total generation
	7	8	9	10	11	12	13
Electric utilities							
1960	83,202	5,954	57,850	31,306	89,156	25,301	114,457
1959	77,768	5,281	53,395	29,654	83,049	21,622	104,671
1958	71,171	4,782	46,829	29,124	75,953	21,572	97,526
1957	66,040	5,483	45,117	26,406	71,523	19,592	91,115
1956[3]	64,242	4,404	42,873	25,773	68,646	19,809	88,455
1955	59,774	3,340	—	—	63,114	19,107	82,221
1954	53,010	3,282	—	—	56,292	18,247	74,540
1953	49,409	3,836	—	—	53,245	17,056	70,301
1952	49,578	2,293	—	—	51,871	14,625	66,497
1951	46,096	1,776	—	—	47,872	13,904	61,776
1950	39,713	1,693	—	—	41,406	13,976	55,382
1949	35,992	1,445	—	—	37,437	13,454	50,890
Central electric stations							
1956	73,525	4,480	42,868	35,136	78,004	10,400	88,404
1955	69,478	3,433	38,279	34,632	72,911	8,825	81,735
1954	62,572	3,364	32,553	33,383	65,936	8,040	73,977
1953	58,926	3,934	28,448	34,413	62,861	7,127	69,988
1952	57,024	2,386	26,526	32,883	59,409	6,695	66,104
1951	52,955	1,897	24,381	30,471	54,852	6,595	61,447
1950	46,624	1,870	20,061	28,432	48,494	6,544	55,037
1949	42,779	1,639	17,687	26,732	44,419	6,174	50,593
1948	41,070	1,320	16,692	25,697	42,390	4,872	47,262
1947	42,273	1,152	15,759	27,666	43,425	3,750	47,174
1946	40,692	1,045	14,739	26,998	41,737	2,926	44,663
1945	39,131	999	14,599	25,531	40,130	2,590	42,720
1944	39,553	1,045	14,910	25,689	40,599	2,972	43,571
1943	39,660	819	9,937	31,082	40,480	3,471	43,950
1942	36,583	772	9,178	28,177	37,355	3,652	41,007
1941	32,629	689	8,524	24,794	33,318	3,161	36,479
1940	29,524	585	7,822	22,287	30,109	2,953	33,062
1939	27,829	509	7,047	21,291	28,338	2,641	30,979
1938	25,688	467	6,666	19,488	26,154	2,449	28,603
1937	27,176	512	7,372	20,316	27,688	2,538	30,225
1936	24,933	470	6,887	18,515	25,402	1,696	27,099
1935	22,884	399	5,515	17,765	23,283	1,644	24,927
1934	20,817	380	5,136	16,061	21,197	1,552	22,749
1933	17,006	333	3,673	13,666	17,339	1,358	18,697
1932	15,724	328	3,714	12,338	16,052	1,401	17,453
1931	16,025	306	4,140	12,191	16,331	1,289	17,620
1930	17,749	345	5,157	12,937	18,094	1,374	19,468
1929	17,604	359	5,188	12,774	17,963	1,343	19,306
1928	16,106[1]	232[1]	4,877	11,461	16,338	1,173	17,509
1927	14,346	203	4,605	9,444	14,549	828	15,377
1926	11,911	182	4,296	7,797	12,093	—	—
1925	9,942	169	3,583	6,527	10,110	—	—
1924	9,159	156	3,291	6,024	9,315	—	—
1923	7,936	163	3,025	5,074	8,099	—	—
1922	6,570	171	1,621	5,120	6,741	—	—
1921	5,448	167	1,298	4,316	5,614	—	—
1920	5,730	165	1,438	4,456	5,895	—	—
1919	5,353	144	1,221	4,132	5,497	—	—

[1] For 1919 to 1928 generation by hydro and thermal not strictly comparable with later years. For these years energy generated by auxiliary (thermal) plants at hydro stations was included with hydro. The change in reporting these plants as thermal probably accounts for only a small part of the increased thermal generation in 1929.

[2] Includes manufacturing, mining and electric railways.
[3] Some central stations were reclassified as industrial establishments.

Series P 14–19. *Net generation of electrical energy of electric utilities and industrial establishments, by type of prime mover, 1947 to 1960*

(millions of kilowatt-hours)

Year	Electric utilities			Industrial establishments		
	Total	Hydro	Thermal	Total	Hydro	Thermal
	14	15	16	17	18	19
1960[1]	89,156	83,202	5,954	25,301	22,680	2,621
1959	83,049	77,768	5,281	21,622	19,272	2,350
1958	75,953	71,171	4,782	21,572	19,338	2,235
1957	71,523	66,040	5,483	19,592	17,333	2,259
1956	68,646	64,242	4,404	19,809	17,614	2,195
1955	63,114	59,774	3,340	19,107	16,964	2,143
1954	56,292	53,010	3,282	18,247	16,321	1,927
1953	53,245	49,409	3,836	17,056	15,113	1,943
1952	51,871	49,578	2,293	14,625	12,784	1,842
1951	47,872	46,096	1,776	13,904	12,158	1,746
1950	41,406	39,713	1,693	13,976	12,422	1,554
1949	37,437	35,992	1,445	13,454	12,000	1,454
1948	35,889	34,712	1,177	11,373	9,952	1,421
1947	36,181	35,132	1,049	10,994	9,711	1,283

Series P 20–28. *Exports, imports and consumption of electrical energy in Canada, 1921 to 1960*

(millions of kilowatt-hours)

Year	Energy exported to U.S.A.			Energy imported from U.S.A.	Net exports to U.S.A.	Energy generated (net)	Energy consumed in Canada	Consumption in electric boilers	Apparent primary consumption
	Firm	Surplus	Total						
	20	21	22	23	24	25	26	27	28
1960	1,040.1	4,471.8	5,511.9	356.9	5,155.0	114,457.2	109,302.2	7,357.7	101,944.5
1959	1,075.7	3,517.3	4,593.0	512.0	4,081.0	104,670.6	100,589.5	6,289.8	94,299.7
1958	1,173.0	2,912.9	4,085.9	245.1	3,840.8	97,525.6	93,684.7	5,969.3	87,715.4
1957	1,311.3	3,521.2	4,832.5	833.0	3,999.5	91,114.8	87,115.2	2,583.8	84,531.4
1956	1,383.5	3,720.2	5,103.7	239.2	4,864.5	88,454.6	83,590.1	2,962.0	80,628.1
1955	1,516.3	2,917.2	4,433.5	158.6	4,274.9	82,221.3	77,946.4	2,957.6	74,988.8
1954	1,506.8	1,211.5	2,718.3	119.0	2,599.3	74,539.6	71,940.3	3,575.1	68,365.2
1953	1,701.8	722.2	2,424.0	180.6	2,243.4	70,300.9	68,057.5	3,375.8	64,681.6
1952	1,638.5	854.7	2,493.2	20.0	2,473.2	66,496.5	64,023.3	3,724.7	60,298.6
1951	1,618.1	757.5	2,375.5	9.0	2,366.6	61,775.7	59,409.1	3,129.0	56,280.1
1950	1,539.4	386.5	1,925.9	2.6	1,923.3	55,382.0	53,458.7	2,892.0	50,566.7
1949	1,378.6	378.2	1,756.8	31.2	1,725.5	50,890.2	49,164.6	2,813.9	46,350.8
1948	1,436.8	306.3	1,743.1	86.4	1,656.7	47,262.1	45,605.3	2,219.0	43,386.3
1947	1,429.0	637.5	2,066.5	53.0	2,013.5	47,174.4	45,160.9	5,544.4	39,616.6
1946	1,407.3	1,074.3	2,481.6	9.5	2,472.1	44,662.9	42,190.8	8,058.8	34,132.0
1945	1,426.3	1,220.1	2,646.4	15.9	2,630.5	42,720.4	40,089.9	5,541.4	34,548.4
1944	1,412.2	1,173.1	2,585.3	14.1	2,571.2	43,571.3	41,000.1	2,729.7	38,270.4
1943	1,429.5	1,115.6	2,545.0	.6	2,544.4	43,950.2	41,405.8	2,113.8	39,291.9
1942	1,435.0	1,018.8	2,453.7	.6	2,453.1	41,007.5	38,554.3	2,239.1	36,315.2
1941	1,443.9	915.6	2,359.5	.7	2,358.9	36,479.1	34,120.3	3,381.4	30,738.8
1940	1,408.1	727.4	2,135.6	.7	2,134.9	33,062.5	30,927.6	4,837.9	26,089.7
1939	1,424.7	487.9	1,912.6	.7	1,912.0	30,978.6	29,066.7	6,590.4	22,476.3
1938	—	—	1,826.5	.6	1,825.9	28,602.7	26,776.8	5,751.4	21,025.5
1937	—	—	1,847.1	1.3	1,845.8	30,225.4	28,379.6	7,313.0	21,066.6
1936	—	—	1,578.1	.8	1,577.3	27,098.6	25,521.3	6,942.8	18,578.5
1935	—	—	1,364.6	.7	1,363.9	24,926.7	23,562.7	6,244.6	17,318.1
1934	—	—	1,248.8	.6	1,248.2	22,748.8	21,500.6	5,337.1	16,163.5
1933	—	—	989.4	.6	988.8	18,696.9	17,708.1	3,741.2	13,966.9
1932	—	—	667.9	.6	667.3	17,453.1	16,785.8	2,902.7	13,883.1
1931	—	—	1,235.3	5.4	1,229.9	17,620.3	16,390.5	1,938.6	14,451.8
1930	—	—	1,619.6	5.8	1,613.8	19,467.9	17,854.0	2,104.8	15,749.2
1929	—	—	1,444.5	6.1	1,438.4	19,305.7	17,867.3	2,162.5	15,704.8
1928	—	—	1,587.8	5.2	1,582.5	17,509.0	15,926.5	1,808.5	14,118.0
1927	—	—	1,632.6	5.0	1,627.6	15,377.5	13,749.9	1,713.8	12,036.1
1926	—	—	1,506.0	5.4	1,500.6	—	—	982.2	—
1925	—	—	1,285.5	—	1,285.5	—	—	507.0	—
1924	—	—	1,302.3	—	1,302.3	—	—	260.5	—
1923	—	—	1,343.5	—	1,343.5	—	—	—	—
1922	—	—	976.5	—	976.5	—	—	—	—
1921	—	—	885.3	—	885.3	—	—	—	—

Series P 29–33. *Sales of power to ultimate customers, by type, Canada, 1930 to 1960*

(millions of kilowatt-hours)

Year	Total domestic sales	Residential and farm service	Commercial	Industrial	Street lighting	Year	Total domestic sales	Residential and farm service	Commercial	Industrial	Street lighting
	29	30	31	32	33		29	30	31	32	33
	Electric utilities¹					1945	33,929	3,365	1,614	28,724	226
1960	76,863	20,397	7,489	48,320	657	1944	34,446	3,047	1,418	29,783	198
1959	71,888	19,007	8,058	44,220	603	1943	34,416	2,844	1,261	30,119	193
1958	65,324	17,291	7,225	40,253	555	1942	31,341	2,717	1,313	27,112	199
1957	60,544	15,858	6,113	38,062	511	1941	27,566	2,582	1,309	23,459	215
1956	56,383	14,339	5,323	36,247	474						
	Central electric stations					1940	24,891	2,437	1,207	21,042	206
1956	66,131	14,332	5,322	46,003	474	1939	23,420	2,311	1,109	19,796	204
						1938	21,336	2,173	1,032	17,934	197
1955	61,341	12,760	4,704	43,416	462	1937	23,464	2,007	959	20,305	192
1954	56,537	11,281	4,210	40,640	407	1936	21,295	1,887	871	18,347	190
1953	54,184	9,878	3,881	40,045	380						
1952	50,927	8,741	3,489	38,348	348	1935	19,277	1,770	872	16,448	188
1951	46,707	7,726	3,153	35,507	321	1934	17,175	1,717	808	14,462	188
						1933	12,746	1,650	747	10,164	185
1950	41,570	6,750	2,809	31,707	303	1932	—	1,639	767	—	—
1949	38,037	5,679	2,409	29,664	285	1931	—	1,564	763	—	—
1948	36,207	4,984	2,155	28,804	264						
1947	37,601	4,383	2,061	30,912	245	1930	—	1,490	744	—	—
1946	35,394	3,882	1,840	29,449	223						

¹ Includes sales to the public by industrial establishments.

Series P 34–38. *Number of ultimate customers of power, by type, 1920 to 1960*

(thousands)

Year	Total	Residential¹	Commercial	Industrial²	Street lighting	Year	Total	Residential¹	Commercial	Industrial²	Street lighting
	34	35	36	37	38		34	35	36	37	38
	Electric utilities³					1940	2,006.5	1,686.4	265.2	52.6	2.3
1960	5,188.3	4,542.8	534.7	105.4	5.4	1939	1,941.7	1,623.7	262.6	53.2	2.2
1959	5,018.7	4,381.6	528.6	103.5	5.0	1938	1,873.6	1,559.4	259.9	52.2	2.2
1958	4,809.6	4,188.9	516.0	99.8	4.9	1937	1,806.0	1,500.1	252.3	51.5	2.1
1957	4,611.2	4,004.2	506.5	95.7	4.7	1936	1,740.8	1,443.1	245.1	50.6	2.0
1956	4,427.7	3,835.0	491.2	97.0	4.5						
	Central electric stations					1935	1,694.7	1,402.0	240.5	50.3	2.0
1956	4,424.6	3,832.2	490.9	97.0	4.5	1934	1,660.1	1,379.2	229.2	49.8	2.0
						1933	1,666.9	1,371.8	244.3	48.8	2.0
1955	4,224.9	3,645.3	481.9	93.3	4.4	1932	1,657.5	1,357.5	248.5	49.5	2.0
1954	4,001.6	3,449.0	451.6	88.9²	4.2	1931	1,632.8	1,336.7	244.6	49.5	1.9
1953	3,817.5	3,283.6	444.0	85.9	4.1						
1952	3,620.6	3,112.3	422.4	82.0	3.9	1930	1,607.9	1,317.3	238.8	50.0	1.7
1951	3,439.8	2,952.0	405.3	78.8	3.7	1929	1,555.9	1,292.5	233.9⁴	28.0⁴	1.5
						1928	1,464.0	1,207.5	215.7	40.8	—
1950	3,269.8	2,797.4	392.5	76.4	3.5	1927	1,382.0	1,142.5	199.4	40.0	—
1949	3,076.4	2,619.8	379.5	73.8	3.2	1926	1,337.6	1,110.6	188.6	38.4	—
1948	2,822.0	2,398.8	349.7	70.4	3.1						
1947	2,643.3	2,246.3	327.0	67.6	2.8	1925	1,279.7	1,063.5	181.0	35.2	—
1946	2,476.8	2,104.5	306.6	63.0	2.7	1924	1,201.0	988.5	176.4	36.0	—
						1923	1,112.5	920.2	159.9	32.4	—
1945	2,333.2	1,987.4	285.4	57.9	2.6	1922	1,053.5	889.3		164.2	—
1944	2,238.0	1,906.5	273.5	55.7	2.5	1921	973.2	830.1		143.2	—
1943	2,164.9	1,848.1	259.6	54.7	2.4						
1942	2,125.3	1,803.7	264.7	54.5	2.4	1920	894.2	764.9		129.3	—
1941	2,081.3	1,755.9	269.0	54.0	2.4						

¹ Includes farm service.
² Until 1954, customers buying electricity for resale (other central stations) were recorded as industrial customers. In 1955 and later years this type of customer was excluded; in 1955 such customers numbered 624.

³ Includes sales to the public by industrial establishments.
⁴ In 1929, small industrial customers included in commercial, series P 36.

Series P 39–45. *Revenue from the sale of electricity, 1917 to 1960*

(thousands of dollars)

Year	Total revenue	Export revenue[1]	Revenue from sales in Canada[1, 2]	Residential[3]	Commercial	Industrial[1]	Street lighting
	39	40	41	42	43	44	45
			Electric utilities[4]				
1960	821,048	14,351	806,697	326,543	147,318	316,650	16,186
1959	769,667	13,895	755,772	305,662	141,518	293,787	14,805
1958	705,082	13,379	691,703	278,531	131,844	268,121	13,207
1957	657,780	17,782	639,998	257,038	119,501	251,553	11,906
1956	608,898	16,852	592,046	235,497	107,487	237,818	11,244
			Central electric stations				
1956	634,125	16,852	617,273	235,344	108,526	262,166	11,237
1955	560,383	11,726	548,657	211,533	97,095	229,619	10,410
1954	505,526	7,420	498,106	190,693	88,911	208,851	9,651
1953	469,047	8,343	460,704	168,271	80,686	202,803	8,944
1952	415,494	9,174	406,320	144,650	71,535	182,256	7,879
1951	374,643	7,938	366,705	127,660	64,351	167,394	7,300
1950	323,833	6,102	317,731	109,015	57,367	144,536	6,813
1949	280,312	4,844	275,468	90,303	49,075	129,995	6,095
1948	257,377	4,376	253,001	79,920	42,869	124,549	5,663
1947	243,706	5,611	238,095	70,259	40,790	121,679	5,367
1946	226,096	7,070	219,026	62,820	37,205	113,740	5,261
1945	215,105	7,574	207,531	55,736	32,911	113,855	5,029
1944	215,246	7,842	207,404	53,311	30,505	119,014	4,574
1943	204,802	7,715	197,087	51,308	28,147	112,904	4,728
1942	203,835	7,864	195,971	50,707	29,422	110,825	5,017
1941	186,080	6,420	179,660	48,683	29,414	96,494	5,069
1940	166,229	4,892	161,337	46,444	27,482	82,466	4,945
1939	151,881	4,317	147,564	43,794	25,741	73,114	4,915
1938	144,332	4,183	140,149	41,302	24,284	69,715	4,848
1937	143,547	3,979	139,568	39,253	23,109	72,454	4,752
1936	—	3,596	135,865	38,399	22,225	70,467	4,774
1935	—	3,129	127,178	36,774	20,974	64,666	4,764
1934	—	2,948	124,464	36,508	20,078	63,182	4,696
1933	—	2,282	117,532	35,954	19,497	57,374	4,707
1932	—	1,788	121,213	36,422	20,432	59,506	4,853
1931	—	3,374	122,311	35,259	20,656	61,622	4,774
1930	—	4,244	126,038	34,115	20,619	66,717	4,587
1929	—	4,075	122,883	33,628	23,304[5]	61,559[5]	4,392
1928	—	2,964	112,327	50,301[6]		62,026[6]	—
1927	—	4,798	104,033	45,833		58,200	—
1926	—	—	88,934	42,046		46,888	—
1925	—	—	79,342	38,829		40,513	—
1924	—	—	74,617	36,011		38,606	—
1923	—	—	67,497	33,187		34,310	—
1922	—	—	62,173	31,699		30,474	—
1921	—	—	58,272	28,797		29,475	—
1920	—	—	—	25,382		—	—
1919	—	—	—	20,210		—	—
1918	—	—	—	16,953		—	—
1917	—	—	—	18,404		—	—

[1] For 1936 and earlier years, export revenue is included with industrial, series P44, and thus in series P41. Export revenues, series P40, for 1927 to 1936 are for fiscal years ending 31 March of the year given.

[2] Until 1956, when industrial revenues from ultimate customers were reported separately, sales to other utilities for resale were reported as industrial sales. Revenue duplications were then removed by subtracting reported costs of power purchased. In making this adjustment for the years 1926 to 1931, proper allowance was not made for interprovincial sales. Industrial and total revenues are, therefore, understated for these six years by amounts which grow from about $250,000 in 1926 to perhaps $5 million in 1931.

[3] Includes farm service.

[4] Includes sales to the public by industrial establishments.

[5] In 1929 revenues from small industrial customers included with commercial.

[6] From 1921 to 1928 reported revenues were classified as from lighting and from all other purposes. These are shown above as residential, commercial and industrial respectively. Before 1921 only lighting revenue was reported.

Series P46–49. *Capital invested in fixed assets in the power industry, selected years, 1891 to 1943 and 1956 to 1960*

(millions of dollars)

Year	Total	Publicly operated utilities	Privately operated utilities	Generating plant assets (public and private)	Year	Total	Publicly operated utilities	Privately operated utilities	Generating plant assets (public and private)
	46	47	48	49		46	47	48	49
					1930	1,138.2	413.3	723.9	684.9
	Electric utilities				1929	1,055.7	370.0	685.8	636.5
1960	7,083.9	5,104.3	1,979.6	3,802.0	1928	956.9	342.0	614.9	585.2
1959	6,570.7	4,657.0	1,913.7	3,468.4	1927	866.8	338.8	528.1	524.1
1958	6,076.7	4,282.0	1,794.7	3,117.8	1926	756.2	325.4	430.8	449.1
1957	5,595.8	3,924.2	1,671.7	2,856.7					
1956	4,891.9	3,423.3	1,468.6	2,471.0	1925	726.7	316.9	409.9	436.8
					1924	628.7	302.0	326.6	362.0
	Central electric stations				1923	581.8	274.7	307.0	330.2
1943	1,778.2	629.0	1,149.2	1,055.3	1922	568.1	241.6	326.4	—
1942	1,747.9	619.9	1,128.0	1,036.3	1921	484.7	157.2	327.4	—
1941	1,641.5	586.7	1,054.7	951.4					
					1920	448.3	137.1	311.2	—
1940	1,615.4	565.9	1,049.5	950.7	1919	416.5	129.0	287.6	—
1939	1,564.6	549.9	1,014.7	930.5	1918	401.9	113.8	288.2	—
1938	1,545.4	542.5	1,002.9	919.2	1917	356.0	73.2	282.8	—
1937	1,497.3	517.4	980.0	899.5					
1936	1,483.1	525.7	957.5	894.6	1915	248.6	—	—	—
					1910	110.8	—	—	—
1935	1,459.8	497.6	962.3	898.8	1905	80.4	—	—	—
1934	1,430.9	474.5	956.4	890.2	1900	11.9	—	—	—
1933	1,386.5	472.6	913.9	866.6	1891	4.1	—	—	—
1932	1,335.9	455.9	880.0	831.3					
1931	1,230.0	444.1	785.9	736.1					

Series P50–51. *Number of employees and earnings in the power industry, 1917 to 1960*

Year	Number of employees	Wages and salaries (thousands of dollars)	Year	Number of employees	Wages and salaries (thousands of dollars)
	50	51		50	51
	Electric utilities		1940	19,054	28,896
1960	41,034	190,204	1939	18,848	28,223
1959	39,440	182,789	1938	17,929	27,149
1958	39,394	170,211	1937	17,018	25,624
1957	37,817	153,952	1936	16,087	23,367
1956	36,118	137,967			
			1935	15,342	22,520
	Central electric stations		1934	14,974	21,829
1956	36,602	139,819	1933	14,717	21,432
			1932	15,395	23,261
1955	35,178	128,370	1931	17,014	26,307
1954	33,762	120,322			
1953	—	115,652	1930	17,857	27,287
1952	—	102,166	1929	16,164	24,832
1951	—	89,130	1928	15,855	24,087
			1927	14,708	22,946
1950	—	71,774	1926	13,406	19,943
1949	—	70,552			
1948	—	62,975	1925	13,263	18,756
1947	—	54,111	1924	12,956	17,947
1946	—	46,423	1923	11,094	14,784
			1922	10,684	14,495
1945	21,283	39,521	1921	10,714	15,235
1944	19,770	36,945			
1943	19,120	35,786	1920	10,693	14,627
1942	19,764	34,286	1919	9,656	11,487
1941	19,880	31,648	1918	9,696	10,354
			1917	8,847	7,778

Series P 52–56. *Cost of fuel to generate electricity, 1919 to 1960*
(thousands of dollars)

Year	Total	Coal[1]	Fuel oil and diesel oil	Natural gas	Other fuels	Year	Total	Coal[1]	Fuel oil and diesel oil	Natural gas	Other fuels
	52	53	54	55	56		52	53	54	55	56
						1940	2,448	1,639	701	8	100
		Electric utilities				1939	2,017	1,340	555	10	112
1960	21,679	10,114	6,397	5,168	—	1938	2,011	1,405	462	9	135
1959	19,285	9,087	5,240	4,958	—	1937	2,583	1,551	504	15	513
1958	19,645	10,638	4,389	4,618	—	1936	2,304	1,424	406	18	456
1957	23,733	14,394	6,177	3,162	—						
1956	20,347	11,434	6,477	2,466	—	1935	2,055	1,279	368	11	397
						1934	2,002	1,318	294	10	380
		Central electric stations				1933	1,846	1,309	291	9	237
1955	17,078	9,449	5,833	1,729	67	1932	1,834	1,389	304	12	129
1954	16,970	10,985	4,564	1,124	297	1931	1,892	1,453	351	9	79
1953	19,727	14,304	4,310	810	303						
1952	13,421	8,698	3,827	596	300	1930	2,595	1,988	484	22	101
1951	11,000	6,430	3,438	815	317	1929	3,016	2,070	764	58	124
						1928	2,280	1,759	314	32	175
1950	10,486	6,241	3,180	637	428	1927	2,303	1,818	245	38	202
1949	10,185	6,253	3,282	225	425	1926	2,137	1,722	209	31	175
1948	8,414	4,862	3,025	138	389						
1947	6,684	3,993	2,300	118	273	1925	2,266	1,797	269	38	162
1946	5,708	3,400	1,786	123	399	1924	2,388	1,918	192	33	245
						1923	2,639	2,207	271	8	153
1945	5,099	3,426	1,317	138	218	1922	2,677	2,295	186	18	178
1944	5,488	3,278	1,907	109	194	1921	3,025	2,697	145	4	179
1943	3,968	2,830	889	93	156						
1942	3,490	2,570	722	83	115	1920	3,190	2,899	133	14	144
1941	2,934	2,050	750	47	87	1919	2,621	2,336	90	35	160

[1] Includes bituminous, sub-bituminous and lignite coal.

Series P 57–62. *Number of power plants and pole line mileage, 1917 to 1960*

Year	Number of power plants					Pole line mileage	Year	Number of power plants					Pole line mileage
	Total	Hydro	Thermal	Publicly owned	Privately owned			Total	Hydro	Thermal	Publicly owned	Privately owned	
	57	58	59	60	61	62		57	58	59	60	61	62
							1940	602	313	289	181	421	75,050
		Electric utilities					1939	611	313	298	184	427	72,132
1960	—	—	—	—	—	320,618	1938	589	313	276	183	406	66,977
1959	—	—	—	—	—	310,840	1937	568	314	254	179	389	63,035
1958	—	—	—	—	—	311,511	1936	561	312	249	171	390	59,436
1957	—	—	—	—	—	285,306							
1956	—	—	—	—	—	271,556	1935	566	316	250	169	397	57,602
							1934	573	314	259	171	402	56,214
		Central electric stations					1933	575	314	261	172	403	56,570
1956	—	—	—	—	—	272,609	1932	572	312	260	170	402	53,845
							1931	559	307	252	163	396	52,399
1955	—	—	—	—	—	243,773							
1954	—	—	—	—	—	222,158	1930	587	311	276	166	421	48,814
1953	524	340	184	221	303	213,176	1929	585	300	285	165	420	42,913
1952	562	344	218	225	337	190,316	1928	601	300	301	173	428	37,333
1951	647	357	290	270	377	170,582	1927	629	302	327	197	432	33,573
							1926	595	294	301	202	393	29,695
1950	665	348	317	270	395	151,726							
1949	650	341	309	259	391	135,329	1925	563	284	279	198	365	27,653
1948	635	309	326	242	393	113,411	1924	532	273	259	199	333	26,654
1947	607	310	297	230	377	98,530	1923	532	269	263	197	335	23,560
1946	600	305	295	203	397	89,231	1922	522	269	253	196	326	22,669
							1921	510	259	251	193	317	21,714
1945	600	302	298	208	392	83,178							
1944	626	320	306	202	424	80,073	1920	506	258	248	185	321	20,879
1943	622	322	300	197	425	78,063	1919	493	272	221	187	306	18,911
1942	616	320	296	188	428	77,909	1918	515	280	235	183	332	—
1941	607	313	294	183	424	77,253	1917	529	259	270	192	337	—

Series P63–74. *Energy consumption in Canada by end uses, 1935 to 1960*

(millions of kilowatt-hours)

Year	Total consumption	Residential and farm	Commercial and street lighting	Manufacturing industries — Pulp and paper	Primary iron and steel	Abrasives	Chemicals and allied products	Smelting and refining	Other	Mining	Other industries	Line losses, free service and unaccounted for
	63	64	65	66	67	68	69	70	71	72	73	74
1960	109,302	20,397	8,146	20,917	2,512	1,163	6,411	19,735	10,686	4,928	4,487	9,920
1959	100,589	19,007	7,459	19,371	2,303	1,071	5,947	15,902	10,332	4,810	4,557	9,830
1958	93,696	17,291	6,970	18,288	1,818	902	5,766	16,372	9,081	4,649	3,604	8,955
1957	87,118	15,858	6,486	16,050	2,554	1,202	4,832	14,955	8,682	4,339	3,718	8,443
1956	83,590	14,339	5,665	15,232	2,677	1,127	4,482	15,376	8,225	4,075	4,155	8,237
1955	77,946	12,713	5,127	15,177	2,212	1,034	4,247	15,196	7,339	3,428	4,152	7,320
1954	71,940	11,281	4,617	15,376	1,579	790	4,196	13,676	6,776	3,130	3,720	6,780
1953	68,057	9,878	4,261	14,701	1,927	1,030	3,896	13,312	6,405	2,915	3,300	6,434
1952	64,023	8,741	3,837	13,972	2,600	934	3,709	12,045	5,806	2,942	3,426	6,009
1951	59,409	7,726	3,473	13,143	2,363	1,121	3,905	10,801	5,544	2,813	2,740	5,779
1950	53,459	6,750	3,113	12,390	1,836	726	3,444	9,919	4,930	2,530	2,822	5,000
1949	49,165	5,679	2,703	11,730	1,877	719	3,092	9,228	4,463	2,294	2,723	4,656
1948	45,605	4,984	2,418	10,350	1,834	821	3,113	8,861	4,519	2,180	1,999	4,526
1947	45,161	4,383	2,306	12,289	1,708	832	2,815	8,056	4,496	2,121	2,345	3,810
1946	42,172	3,882	2,063	13,361	1,200	741	2,681	6,109	3,873	1,940	2,514	3,808
1945	40,090	3,365	1,840	10,855	1,628	712	2,306	6,756	4,092	1,869	3,135	3,532
1944	41,000	3,047	1,616	8,168	1,604	805	3,054	10,686	4,212	1,884	2,437	3,487
1943	41,406	2,844	1,454	8,039	2,018	917	2,808	11,280	4,550	1,895	2,140	3,461
1942	38,554	2,717	1,512	8,696	1,769	772	2,868	8,548	4,343	2,011	2,030	3,288
1941	34,226	2,582	1,525	9,209	1,493	587	2,433	5,942	3,466	2,081	1,689	3,220
1940	30,931	2,437	1,413	10,258	1,100	421	1,979	4,029	2,809	1,954	1,500	3,031
1939	29,071	2,311	1,313	11,084	529	280	1,547	3,493	2,497	1,761	1,237	3,019
1938	26,781	2,173	1,229	9,959	399	288	1,389	3,250	2,208	1,756	1,130	3,000
1937	28,383	2,007	1,151	12,037	573	419	1,507	2,604	2,281	1,503	1,922	2,379
1936	25,525	1,887	1,061	11,368	355	352	1,279	970	2,430	1,036	2,598	2,191
1935	23,558	1,770	1,059	10,592	321	286	1,199	1,073	1,919	1,025	1,986	2,328

Series P75–77. *Hydraulic turbine installations, 1890 to 1960*

(thousands of horsepower)

Year	Total	Industrial establishments	Central electric stations[1]
	75	76	77
1960	26,375.4	6,020.9	20,354.5
1959	24,888.4	5,665.4	19,223.0
1958	22,379.6	5,015.4	17,364.2
1957	19,891.0	2,756.8	17,134.2
1956	18,356.0	2,327.7	16,028.4
1955	17,511.1	2,177.7	15,334.4
1954	16,684.1	2,191.9	14,492.3
1953	14,929.1	1,475.3	13,435.8
1952	14,305.9	1,445.9	12,860.0
1951	13,342.5	1,466.8	11,875.7
1950	12,562.8	1,492.0	11,070.7
1949	11,613.3	1,164.9	10,448.4
1948	10,870.7	934.2	9,936.5
1947	10,490.9	987.5	9,503.4
1946	10,312.1	962.2	9,349.9
1945	10,283.6	968.3	9,315.4
1944	10,283.2	992.9	9,290.3
1943	10,214.5	992.9	9,221.6
1942	9,225.8	1,001.4	8,224.4
1941	8,845.0	1,001.4	7,843.6
1940	8,584.4	997.7	7,587.7
1939	8,289.2	997.7	7,292.5
1938	8,190.8	988.5	7,202.3
1937	8,112.8	1,038.1	7,074.6
1936	7,945.6	963.0	6,982.5
1935	7,909.1	962.9	6,946.2
1934	7,547.0	957.1	6,589.9
1933	7,332.1	951.4	6,380.7
1932	7,045.3	933.6	6,111.6
1931	6,666.3	931.8	5,734.5
1930	6,125.0	910.7	5,214.3
1929	5,727.2	909.7	4,817.5
1928	5,349.2	903.5	4,445.7
1927	4,798.9	—	—
1926	4,549.4	—	—
1925	4,338.3		
1924	3,590.6		
1923	3,191.9		
1922	3,008.3		
1921	2,754.2		
1920	2,515.6		
1919	2,470.1		
1918	2,378.7		
1917	2,287.4		
1916	2,222.2		
1915	2,105.5		
1914	1,951.2		
1913	1,688.9		
1912	1,481.5		
1911	1,363.1		
1910	977.2		
1909	890.5		
1908	820.6		
1907	727.6		
1906	608.0		
1905	454.2		
1904	355.2		
1903	298.5		
1902	272.6		
1901	238.9		
1900	173.3		
1899	143.2		
1898	128.2		
1897	99.6		
1896	94.5		
1895	87.9		
1894	85.3		
1893	79.0		
1892	73.1		
1891	71.9		
1890	71.5		

[1] Series P77 differs from series P2. See note to series P75–77.

SECTION Q: MANUFACTURES

ARTHUR J. R. SMITH, *Private Planning Association of Canada*

The statistics in the tables of this section fall into five main groups. Series Q1–137 contain data on general statistics for manufacturing industries, series Q138–195 on manufacturing production indexes by industry groups, series Q196–306 on value and volume of manufacturing output by commodities, series Q307–349 on new gross fixed capital formation and series Q350–375 on size of manufacturing establishments. In addition, an appendix, series Q376–407, contains data on primary and secondary manufacturing industry by industry groups.

The basic raw data on which all the series in this section are based were collected officially. For the most part, since 1917, the raw data were collected by the Dominion Bureau of Statistics in its annual census of manufactures; before 1917 they came from the census of manufactures taken with the decennial census or in special postal censuses. The data on fixed capital formation for 1926 to 1945 were obtained from tabulations prepared by the Department of National Revenue from income tax returns and those for 1946 to 1959 are based on returns to questionnaires obtained by the Dominion Bureau of Statistics on capital formation. In general, since the inception of the annual census of manufactures in 1917, the quality of the basic material has improved as experience was gained in the formulation of questionnaires, as better coverage of establishments was obtained and as the performance of respondents improved.

The basic tabulation and other preparation of the data were also done officially, mostly by the Dominion Bureau of Statistics and the predecessor official bodies responsible for the decennial census, but also by some other government agencies. Not only are these data mainly taken from Bureau material; the Dominion Bureau of Statistics gave a great deal of help in preparation of material of series Q1–375 in the specific form it is presented in this volume, though final responsibility for the presentation here lies with the Historical Statistics project. The tabulations of series Q376–407 were privately prepared, though also with the co-operation of the Bureau.

The published sources of data given in this section are entirely publications of the Dominion Bureau of Statistics, decennial Census Offices, or the Department of Trade and Commerce. Publications of the Dominion Bureau of Statistics are: Dominion Bureau of Statistics, *Canada Year Book*, annual since 1905 (Ottawa, Queen's Printer), various issues; *General Review of the Manufacturing Industries of Canada*, annual since 1949 (Ottawa, Queen's Printer), formerly called *The Manufacturing Industries of Canada*, annual 1930 to 1948, and the material before 1930 published in the *Canada Year Book*; *The Quantity of Manufacturing Production in Canada, 1923–1929* (Ottawa, King's Printer, 1932); *Revised Index of Industrial Production, 1935–1957*, Reference Paper No. 34 (Ottawa, Queen's Printer, 1959); *Canadian Statistical Review*, monthly since January, 1948 (Ottawa, Queen's Printer), formerly *Monthly Review of Business Statistics*, monthly, 1926 to December 1947; *Private and Public Investment in Canada, 1946–1957* (Ottawa, Queen's Printer, 1959). Publications of the Census Office are: Department of Agriculture, Census Branch, *Census of Canada, 1870–71*, vol. III (Ottawa, I. B. Taylor, 1875); Department of Agriculture, Census Branch, *Census of Canada, 1880–81*, vol. III (Ottawa, Maclean, Roger and Co.,

1883); Department of Agriculture, Census Branch, *Census of Canada, 1890–91*, vol. III (Ottawa, Queen's Printer, 1894); The Census Office, *Fourth Census of Canada, 1901*, vol. III, *Manufactures* (Ottawa, King's Printer, 1905); Department of Agriculture, Census and Statistics Office, *Postal Census of Manufactures, 1906* (Ottawa, King's Printer, 1907); Department of Trade and Commerce, The Census Office, *Fifth Census of Canada*, vol. III (Ottawa, King's Printer, 1913); Department of Trade and Commerce, Census and Statistics Office, *Postal Census of Manufacturers, 1916* (Ottawa, King's Printer, 1917). Publications of the Department of Trade and Commerce are: Department of Trade and Commerce, *Private and Public Investment in Canada, 1926–1951* (Ottawa, 1951); *Private and Public Investment in Canada Outlook 1961*, annual since 1946 (Ottawa, Queen's Printer, 1961).

In addition to the published data a large number of the statistics in this section were obtained from the Industry and Merchandising Division of D.B.S. These last-mentioned data will frequently differ from those given in published sources owing to revisions, reclassification of data and the inclusion of data that cannot be given separately in the more fine classifications of the source owing to the requirements of the Statistics Act concerning the confidentiality of individual returns. For finer industry detail than that given in *General Review of the Manufacturing Industries of Canada* see the individual industry publications listed at the end of the *General Review*.

GENERAL STATISTICS
FOR MANUFACTURING INDUSTRIES
(Series Q1–137)

General note

In the course of the preparation of the tables on general statistics for manufacturing, efforts were made to review and revise earlier figures to make all data from 1870 to 1959 as conceptually consistent and comparable as feasible. Especially significant adjustments have been made in previously published census data for 1870 to 1910 and in the annual data from 1917 to 1925 to bring the conceptual content of these earlier figures as closely as possible in line with that in the latest annual census of manufactures used. A new standard industrial classification, the Standard Industrial Classification of 1948, was introduced in 1949 and published figures since then have been classified on that basis. The Central Research and Development Staff and the Industry and Merchandising Division of D.B.S. have reclassified the data for all years before 1949 on the basis of the 1948 Standard Industrial Classification and all the data in series Q1–137 are based, therefore, on that classification. Consequently, much of the data for years preceding 1949 will not be found in published sources in the form presented herein.

In the reclassification of the data from the censuses before 1917 additional adjustments were also made. A number of categories of operations, included in the censuses, notably those connected with construction and some repair work, were omitted. In addition the censuses of 1900 and 1910 did not cover very small manufacturing establishments and the data given in this section are based on estimates, prepared by D.B.S., of all manufacturing activity including small establishments. These estimates therefore provide data which are consistent with those for 1870, 1880, 1890 and 1905 and for 1917 to 1959 which are based on full coverage of establishments of all sizes.

Some rather small industries, such as motion picture making, production of flax fibre and the blue printing industry, which had been dropped from the census of manufactures at various times between 1917 and 1948, have also been excluded for all years from the data given here.

The censuses of 1870, 1880, 1890, 1900 and 1910 were obtained by enumerators who called on the manufacturing concerns. The Postal Census of 1906 covering manufacturing in 1905 and the annual census of manufactures taken by D.B.S. since 1917 have collected data by mailed questionnaire. D.B.S. engages in a good deal of follow-up correspondence after each census to clear up ambiguities in returns and to assure the material is on a consistent basis.

The reporting units in each census have been establishments and not legal entities or companies. An establishment is defined as an operating unit which is primarily engaged in only one type of manufacturing activity. Actually, however, an establishment may straddle a number of different stages and types of production or fabrication, and may be involved not merely in manufacturing activities but also in various nonmanufacturing activities such as retail or wholesale merchandising, repair work, or on-site construction with its own employees. The result is that considerable skill is required to identify, enumerate, and classify by industry, establishments that are primarily engaged in manufacturing, and to compile relevant manufacturing data for such establishments. No data for the number of establishments are shown for 1900 and 1910, since the Censuses of 1901 and 1911 enumerated only establishments employing 'five hands and over'. But full coverage estimates have been made for persons engaged in manufacturing, salaries and wages, and value of production data and these provide the data given in series Q1–137. The exceptionally large figures for the number of establishments in 1870, 1880 and 1890 appear to be attributable in part to the inclusion of blacksmith shops as iron foundries, to the inclusion of a large number of repair establishments which cannot be satisfactorily eliminated from manufacturing establishments, and to the generally diffuse pattern of early manufacturing activity prior to spreading development of factory units. The 1906 *Postal Census of Manufactures* is strongly suspected of underenumeration.

A *Postal Census of Manufactures* in 1916, covering the year 1915, involved limitations in its coverage of manufacturing establishments and their operations, and the data could not be satisfactorily converted to a full coverage basis. No manufacturing data for 1915 have therefore been included in series Q1–137.

Regarding the number of persons engaged in manufacturing some conceptual differences exist between the statistics for 1949 to 1959 and those for earlier years. In the current series persons engaged in manufacturing represent an average for the year and exclude nonmanufacturing personnel, such as those in new construction work, those in retail or wholesale operations or repair work, those on outside piece work, etc. Supervisory and office employees include all executives and supervisory officials, working proprietors and partners, professional and technical employees, clerical employees, and superintendents and factory supervisors above the working foreman level. Production and related workers include all other factory workmen, working foremen doing work similar to that of the employees they supervise, and maintenance, warehousing and delivery staffs.

The main differences in treatment in the earlier figures have been as follows:

(1) Prior to 1949 no special effort was made to survey head offices if these were located in a separate locality and not attached to any operating establishment. In 1949 such offices began to be covered with a separate questionnaire.

(2) For the years prior to 1935, imputations were made for the number of working proprietors in each industry, along with an imputation of the amount of proprietors' withdrawals. For 1931 to 1935 the estimated number of proprietors and their withdrawals were included with salaried personnel; before 1930 they were included with wage-earners. It is uncertain whether such imputations were made for all years back to 1917. In 1935 questionnaires were amended to instruct working proprietors to include themselves and their withdrawals with salaried staff. The increase in supervisory and office employees between 1930 and 1931 was probably due to a change in classification of working proprietors rather than an increase in employment.

(3) From 1937 establishments were instructed to include travelling salesmen with salaried employees. There is little knowledge as to their treatment by reporting firms prior to this time. In 1930 firms were asked to exclude salesmen in reporting salaried employees. No specific mention was made of the appropriate treatment during the other years, although the instructions were changed in 1931 in such a way that firms may have begun to include salesmen at that time.

(4) Prior to 1925 the number of wage-earners was computed as the sum of the number recorded each month divided by 12, whether the establishment was operating twelve months or not. For 1925 to 1930 inclusive, in seasonal industries, the averages were computed by dividing the sum of the wage-earners reported on the 15th of each month by the number of months in operation. This change of method increased the apparent number of employees in groups containing seasonal industries and in the over-all total. In 1931 the old method of computing the average number of wage-earners was readopted.

Salaries and wages represent gross earnings of the employees described above, including salaries, wages, commissions, bonuses, the value of room and board where provided, deductions for income tax and social services, as well as any other allowances forming part of the employees' wages. Payments for overtime are included. Withdrawals by working owners or partners for normal living expenses for self and family are included but not their withdrawals for income tax. Series Q6 and Q7 represent the distribution of earnings between the two groups described above. The data of both are subject to biases similar to those suggested above.

Until 1952, gross value of production represents the total reported selling value of products produced by all manufacturing establishments, whether sold, transferred to other plants, or in stock. Since 1952, the figures on gross value of production are basically derived from the gross value of manufacturing shipments, adjusted for the difference between year-beginning and year-end inventories of finished products and goods in process. It should be noted that figures since 1952 in most D.B.S. manufacturing reports are actually the value of manufacturing shipments, unadjusted for changes in inventories, and are therefore different from the figures shown here for gross value of production.

Owing to the different channels of distribution of products (for example, to a central warehouse perhaps with no mark-up over cost of production, or to an affiliated establishment with only a nominal mark-up, or to wholesale, retail or ultimate customer trade channels with varying mark-ups) there does not exist a completely uniform basis for measuring gross value of production. The Dominion Bureau of Statistics seeks to have its respondents report the value of shipments, as far as possible, on the assumption that the goods were sold to an independent wholesaler. See also the general note under series Q196–306.

The gross value of production data also contain considerable duplication, since the products of one establishment frequently become the materials used by, and thus eventually part of the gross value of production of, other establishments. The aggregate gross value figures therefore reflect an exaggerated picture of manufacturing output, and these are not always a satisfactory measure of the importance of individual industries. For the purpose of measuring an industry's contribution to total output, a more meaningful and useful indicator of the output of manufacturing industries is 'census value added by manufacture' which is described below.

Cost of materials used is the laid-down cost at the works, including freight, duty, and the like, of materials and supplies actually used during the year, whether purchased or received as transfers from other establishments. Included are amounts paid to other establishments for work done on materials owned by the reporting establishment, and maintenance and repair supplies not chargeable to capital account. Excluded are returnable containers or any other items not charged to capital account, fuels, and goods bought from others or received as transfers for resale without further processing.

Cost of fuel and electricity includes laid-down costs at the works, including freight, duty, etc., of all fuels actually used during the year including fuel used in cars and trucks. When rental paid includes heat and light, the value of fuel and electricity used is not included. This item was not collected in the censuses before 1917.

Census value added by manufacture, as already noted above, is a more meaningful indicator than gross value of production of the contribution to total output and the relative importance of an industry or a group of industries. It is derived by subtracting the cost of materials and fuel and electricity from the gross value of production, and represents the values added to the materials used in manufacturing activity. Census value added can be taken as the amount available for the payment of salaries and wages, depreciation and interest, rent, taxes, repairs and all other overhead charges that must ordinarily be met, as well as profits. Census values added for all manufacturing establishments therefore add to a virtually non-duplicating estimate of the contribution made to total output by manufacturing establishments. Some element of duplication exists, however, since census value added includes the value of intermediate business service inputs used in manufacturing activity. For the years prior to 1917, no reliable information on fuel and electricity used was available and thus census value added for those years is defined as gross value of production less value of materials used. The possibility exists that the value of materials used for these years may have included the value of some fuels used.

As a concluding comment, it should be emphasized that it is difficult to evaluate the earlier data, especially the census data prior to 1917, in the light of subsequent changes in concepts, reporting schedules, and so forth. Despite a careful review and revision of the figures, some questions still remain about the comparability of data. The more recent data may have an upward bias if coverage of manufacturing establishments has been improved over the years, but any such bias that may exist is probably not very significant. More important is the fact that as better information has been developed on industrial detail and the nature of activities in establishments, a downward bias has

been introduced through extended ability to eliminate data pertaining to establishments engaged in repair, merchandising and other nonmanufacturing activities. At the same time, it should be noted that the data do not cover manufacturing activity carried out in the home, which was particularly important for early years, with a consequent tendency for upward bias over time in the manufacturing activity indicated in the data.

In these general statistics for manufacturing, data for Newfoundland are included beginning 1949.

Q1–11.   General statistics for all manufacturing industries, 1870 to 1959

SOURCE: for 1870, *Census of Canada, 1870–71*, vol. III; for 1880, *Census of Canada, 1880–81*, vol. III; for 1890, *Census of Canada, 1890–91*, vol. III; for 1900, *Census of Canada 1901*, vol. III; for 1905, *Postal Census of Manufactures 1906;* for 1910 *Census of Canada, 1911*, vol. III, for 1917 to 1959, *Annual Census of Manufactures*, as reported in various issues of the *Canada Year Book*, *The Manufacturing Industries of Canada* and *General Review of the Manufacturing Industries of Canada*. Data before 1949 were reclassified by D.B.S.

See the general note to series Q1–137 for comments on the data and its reclassification.

Q12–29.   General statistics for all manufacturing industries, by region, 1926 to 1959

SOURCE: annual census of manufactures, as reported in various issues of the *Canada Year Book* and *General Review of the Manufacturing Industries of Canada*. Data before 1949 were revised by D.B.S.

Regional manufacturing data do exist for the many years from 1927 to 1947 for which no data are shown in series Q12–29, as well as for the early census years and for 1917 to 1925. But these data are not consistent with the figures for total manufacturing shown in series Q1–11, and have therefore not been included here. It may be possible, however, at some later date to develop consistent regional data for all the years shown in series Q1–11.

Q30–137.   General statistics for manufacturing industries by major groups, 1870 to 1959

SOURCE: the same as those listed above for series Q1–11.

The eighteen major industry groups covered in series Q30–137 represent the seventeen major groups according to the Standard Industrial Classification of 1948 concepts used by the Dominion Bureau of Statistics, with the Clothing and Knitting Mills group of that classification shown as two groups instead of one for the period 1917 to 1959. Details on classification are described in D.B.S., *Standard Industrial Classification Manual, 1948*. Reporting establishments are classified or allotted to industries on the basis of the principal products produced or shipped.

Many types of adjustments have been involved in developing consistent figures for various industry groups. For example, previously published figures for the tobacco and tobacco products group included excise taxes in the gross value of production for the years 1917 to 1931; such taxes for these years have now been deducted from the gross value figures to provide for greater consistency. Another illustration is that in the nonferrous metals group, smelting was not classified as a manufacturing activity for the years 1920 to 1924 in previously published figures of this industry; the principal statistics for smelting have now been included for these years.

See also the general note to series Q1–137.

INDEXES OF
MANUFACTURING PRODUCTION
(Series Q138–195)

Q138. Index of total manufacturing production, 1923 to 1935

SOURCE: D.B.S., *The Quantity of Manufacturing Production in Canada, 1923–1929; General Review of the Manufacturing Industries of Canada, 1957, p. 27.*

This index, and nine components based upon a principal material classification (vegetable, animal, textiles, wood and paper, iron, nonferrous metals, nonmetallic minerals, chemicals and miscellaneous), were compiled for the years 1923 through 1946. They were superseded by the technically improved and more detailed indexes of manufacturing production shown in series Q139–195 from 1935 to date. But the earlier figures provide a good basis for evaluating changes in the volume of total manufacturing production during the 12 years prior to 1935. Technical details on the compilation of series Q138 are available in the first of the sources mentioned above. The detail by industry groups may be found in the source documents.

Q139–195. Manufacturing production indexes by groups, 1935 to 1959

SOURCE: D.B.S., *Revised Index of Industrial Production, 1935–1957; Canadian Statistical Review.*

The Canadian index of industrial production covers mining, manufacturing, electricity and gas, which together account for about one third of Canada's Gross Domestic Product at factor cost, a measure of the output of goods and services of industries located in Canada. The total manufacturing component alone, series Q139, accounts for over one quarter of Gross Domestic Product.

The indexes of manufacturing production, available on both annual and monthly bases, measure the physical volume of output in relation to the level in a given base period. For series Q139–195, the base period is 1949. The annual figures for more recent years are averages of monthly figures which are published currently in the *Canadian Statistical Review*, and which are available on a seasonally adjusted basis, as well as on an unadjusted basis. In the most recent revision of the production indexes, emphasis has been placed on constructing annual benchmark indexes for all industries from comprehensive data derived from the annual census of manufactures. The D.B.S. reference paper entitled *Revised Index of Industrial Production, 1935–1957* provides a comprehensive description of concepts and methods used in the preparation of the indexes, together with an analysis and appraisal of results.

The benchmark indexes are based, for as many industries as possible, on the *volume of net output* which is census value added in constant dollars derived by deducting materials, fuel and electricity in constant dollars from gross output in constant dollars. A little more than half the manufacturing universe, however, is represented by benchmark measures of the volume of gross output, or of materials used. In the monthly series, approximately 40 per cent of manufacturing output is based on man-hours data, adjusted to reflect as closely as possible physical output levels. These adjustments are based on observed historical trends of output per man-hour. The remaining monthly series are based on currently reported data of actual volume of production. As a result, while the manufacturing production indexes are adequate for measuring trends and cyclical changes in the volume of manufacturing output, these indexes are not suffici-

ently precise, particularly for recent years, to be used in conjunction with employment or man-hour data, for compiling productivity measures to show changes in output per employee or per man-hour.

In the series shown here, the index of total manufacturing production, series Q139, has two major components—the index of total durables manufacturing, series Q140, and the index of total nondurables manufacturing, series Q164. The eighteen industry groups shown are the seventeen major industry groups described in the 1948 D.B.S., *Standard Industrial Classification Manual*, with the foods and beverages group divided into separate parts. The commodity series shown within some of the major industry groups are intended to provide a basis for measuring changes in the volume of output of a number of the more important groups of commodities.

VALUE AND VOLUME OF OUTPUT OF
SELECTED MANUFACTURED PRODUCTS
(Series Q196–306)

General note

Figures are available on the value and volume of production or shipments of many hundreds of manufactured commodities. Only a relatively small number of more important types of products are included in the series shown here. The data are derived from the annual census of manufactures. Earlier data shown for a few commodities in the supplementary table are derived from the earlier decennial and postal censuses, and from early D.B.S. records. While a major part of the detail on which these series are based may be found in D.B.S., *General Review of the Manufacturing Industries of Canada*, unpublished detail was also used. The material was prepared by the Industry and Merchandising Division of D.B.S.

The values and volumes of commodities shown in series Q196–306 relate to goods made from own materials either in reporting plants or made by other manufacturers on the basis of a charge to reporting plants for work done. These figures cover total production, whether made for export or domestic use, including production for governments and institutions. Transfer shipments to sales outlets, distributing warehouses or to other manufacturing units of the reporting firms are included. Goods bought or received as transfers and resold without further processing are not included.

Values are computed on f.o.b. plant or plant warehouse basis and do not include sales tax or excise duties. Values of containers not returnable are included.

Prior to 1952 the values shown relate to the value of products made, while the values for 1952 and subsequent years relate to the shipments made during the year. The change from a production to a shipments basis, however, has not been applied to all industries; there are still a number of industries reporting on a production basis particularly in cases in which inventory changes tend to be relatively large. For most industries the change in concept does not materially affect the comparability of the production statistics, since in most cases inventory changes from year to year are only of a minor nature. But it should be noted that the shipments figures after 1952 are not strictly comparable with the earlier data.

For the purpose of calculating value of output correctly, all manufacturers should report the value of shipments or of products made on a standard basis. In practice, however, such standardization is impossible without resorting to difficult and arbitrary methods of valuation, especially since firms use different channels of distribution. Some firms sell direct to wholesalers while others sell direct to retailers or industrial users, and in some cases even sell direct to householders or ultimate consumers. Firms also distribute their products in a number of ways. For example, some ship through a central warehouse or sales branch which is charged only with the cost of production, the selling outlet being credited with all the profits made. In other cases some of the profits are credited to the manufacturing operation. The value of an identical unit of product reported to the annual census of manufactures thus varies in accordance with the methods of distribution used. To illustrate, let us assume that it costs one dollar to produce a unit of a given commodity. Its value as reported could perhaps be any one of the following:

	$
Shipped to wholesaler	1.10
Shipped to a retail store	1.20
Shipped to an ultimate consumer	1.50
Shipped to a central warehouse or sales branch at cost of production	1.00
Shipped to a central warehouse where profits are apportioned between manufacturing and selling	1.15

The values of shipments or products made as shown in series Q196–252 therefore actually represent various selling values, although D.B.S. seeks to obtain reporting, as widely as possible, on the basis of values of sales to independent wholesalers.

The figures in the historical series on values of production do not always relate to calendar years. In submitting their annual returns to the census of manufactures, firms are asked to submit figures for the calendar year if at all possible. Most report on that basis, but financial year reports are accepted in cases in which firms find it impossible to supply from their accounting records calendar year data on shipments or production. Two of the notable exceptions to calendar year reporting, for example, are cotton textiles and flour milling. In the case of flour mills, most of the reports submitted cover the crop year which ends 31 July. In the case of cotton textiles, some of the larger producers report on a financial year basis, ending in March or April.

Q196–252. Value of output of selected manufactured commodities, 1917 to 1959

SOURCE: D.B.S., *General Review of the Manufacturing Industries of Canada* (various issues); unpublished data compiled by the Industry and Merchandising Division of the Dominion Bureau of Statistics. See also individual industry reports on manufactures.

The user's attention is drawn to the last of the data given for series Q196–306, which carry a small number of the series back beyond 1917.

Q196. Wheat flour includes whole wheat and graham flour, as well as durum semolina and flour.

Q198. Refined sugar includes granulated, yellow or brown, pulverized icing and loaf sugar made from cane or beets.

Q199. Confectionery includes all sugar and chocolate confectionery in bulk, bars or packages. Penny goods, lozenges, toffee and chocolate or candy-coated nuts are also included, but not chewing gum.

Q203. Meats, fresh and frozen, includes meats sold fresh or fresh-frozen. Also includes fresh meats of animals slaughtered on a commission basis for firms or individuals not reporting under the Slaughtering and Meat Packing Industry.

Q204. Poultry, fresh and frozen, includes only poultry sold fresh or fresh-frozen by establishments classified to the Slaughtering and Meat Packing Industry.

Q205. Carbonated beverages include beverages bottled, canned or sold in bulk but do not include natural mineral waters.

Q206. Beer, etc., includes bottled, canned and draught beer, ale, stout, and porter produced. The values include excise taxes and duties.

Q207. Beverage spirits sold represent net sales outside the industry and do not include inter-company transfers. The values do not include excise taxes and duties.

During the years 1916 and 1917, as a war policy, legislation prohibiting the sale of alcoholic liquors, except for medicinal and scientific purposes, was passed in all the provinces except Quebec, where similar legislation was passed in 1919. The prohibition extended to the sale of beer and wine except in Quebec. Native wine could be sold, however, in Quebec.

After World War I, the provinces continued under prohibition for varying periods. Plebiscites were taken, from time to time, to ascertain the will of the electorate as to whether the policy of prohibition, adopted as an emergency measure, should be continued. During 1921, Quebec, British Columbia, and Yukon Territory discarded the existing prohibition laws and adopted policies of liquor sale under government control. The same course was followed by Manitoba in 1923, Alberta in 1924, Saskatchewan in 1925, Ontario and New Brunswick in 1927, Nova Scotia in 1930, and Prince Edward Island in 1948.

Q212. Rubber tires include pneumatic and solid tires for passenger cars, trucks, aeroplanes, tractors, implements, motor cycles and bicycles.

Q213. Leather footwear includes boots and shoes with leather or fabric uppers. It does not include felt footwear, slippers, moccasins or rubber footwear produced in the Rubber Footwear Industry.

Q219. Furniture includes furniture made of all types of materials, such as wood, metal, plastics, etc. It includes furniture for use in homes, offices, stores, restaurants, schools, churches, camps, lawns, etc. It does not, however, include mattresses and springs.

Q223. Paper bags include the following types of paper bags: (*a*) glassine, waxed paper, grease-proof paper, etc.; (*b*) millinery, garment and laundry; (*c*) self-opening; (*d*) wedge, including notion and novelty bags; and (*e*) paper bags, not specified, including multiwall.

Q225. Paper boards include container board, box board, building board and wet machine board.

Q227. Pig-iron produced includes basic, foundry and malleable pig-iron made for sale and own use. Since 1950 silvery pig-iron is also included. Values of pig-iron for own use are based on the average selling price of pig-iron sold.

Q228. Hot rolled iron and steel bars include light structurals prior to 1951. Values of products for own use are based on the average selling price of hot rolled iron and steel bars sold.

Q229. Structural steel shapes made in primary mills include light structurals since 1951, which were previously included with 'hot rolled iron and steel bars'. Also include sheet piling since 1949. Values of products for own use are based on the average selling price of structural steel shapes sold.

Q231. Steel pipes and tubing include welded and seamless steel pipes and tubing. Do not include rivetted pipes or sheet metal culverts.

Q232. Metal cans include metal cans made for food as well as nonfood products.

Q233. Farm implements. From 1870 to 1939 the gross value of production of the farm implement industry is taken as the value of farm implements produced. In this value are included items which are not classed as farm implements, but on the other hand, some farm machinery is produced as secondary products by establishments classified to other industrial groups. It is estimated that these values more or less counterbalance each other so that the value of production of the farm implements industry represents the value of farm implements produced. Had this method been used for 1958 the value of farm implements produced would have been overstated by 3 per cent. The gross value of production for the industry was $133.2 millions while the value of farm implements produced was only $129.1 millions. The data from 1940 to 1959 are for farm implements produced.

This series is continued back to 1870 for census years in the last part of the tables for series Q196–306.

Q234. Passenger automobiles include all types of cars, such as permanent closed cars, convertible cars and station wagons but do not include chassis sold without bodies. Selling values represent the wholesale value or the amount of money received by manufacturers from their dealers or distributors; taxes, dealers' commissions, etc., are not included.

Q235. Commercial auto vehicles include all wheeled vehicles for military use. Not included are universal carriers and scout cars or chassis sold without bodies. Selling values represent the wholesale value or the amount of money received by manufacturers from dealers, distributors and government. Taxes, dealers' commissions, etc., are not included.

Q237. Locomotives do not include railway electric cars.

Q239. Stoves and ranges include stoves and ranges for cooking and heating, but do not include stoves and ranges for restaurants. Stoves and ranges using all types of fuels, such as wood, coal, gas, electricity, gasoline and fuel oil, as well as some combination of fuels, are included.

Q240. Household mechanical refrigerators include electric, gas, and all other types.

Q241. Washing machines include only domestic washing machines powered by electricity or other power. Hand, automatic and conventional washing machines are included.

Q245. Clay bricks data are carried back to 1886 at the end of series Q196–306.

Q246. Cement data are carried back to 1887 at the end of series Q196–306.

Q247. Gasoline includes motor, aviation and tractor gasoline made for sale and own use.

Q248. Fuel oil includes 'heavy' and 'light' fuel oil made for sale and own use. It does not include 'aviation' or 'aviation turbine' fuel oil.

Q249. Coke includes beehive, by-product and gas retort coke. Petroleum coke is not included.

Q250. Soaps and synthetic detergents include laundry and household soaps, toilet soaps, soap powders, shaving and liquid soaps.

Q252. Medicinal and pharmaceutical preparations include patent medicines, antibiotics, vitamins, ethical specialties for human use as well as all other medicines for human and animal use.

Q253–306. Physical output of selected manufactured commodities, 1917 to 1959

SOURCE: D.B.S., *General Review of the Manufacturing Industries of Canada* (various issues); unpublished data compiled by the Industry and Merchandising Division of the Dominion Bureau of Statistics. See also individual industry reports.

The user's attention is drawn to the data at the end of series Q196–306 which carry a few of the series back beyond 1917.

Q253. See note to Q196.
Q255. See note to Q198.
Q256. See note to Q199.
Q260. See note to Q203.

Q261. See note to Q204.
Q262. See note to Q205.
Q263. See note to Q206.
Q264. See note to Q207.
Q269. See note to Q212.
Q270. See note to Q213.

Q271. Yarns produced include all yarns produced for own use, for sale, or on a commission or custom basis. It includes yarns made of cotton, wool and synthetic fibres and their mixtures. This series is carried back to 1887 at the end of series Q196–306.

Q277. Wood pulp includes both mechanical and chemical pulp. Since 1917 the figures also include mechanical and chemical screenings, and since 1946 defibrated and exploded wood, semi-chemical pulp, as well as other grades of pulp not specified as mechanical or chemical. This series is carried back to 1908 at the end of series Q196–306.

Q281. See note to Q225.
Q282. See note to Q227.

Q283. Steel ingots and castings produced include all types of steel ingots and castings as well as alloys. This series is carried back to 1894 at the end of series Q196–306.

Q284. See note to Q228.
Q285. See note to Q229.

Q286. Steel rails data are carried back to 1894 at the end of series Q196–306.

Q287. See note to Q231.

Q288. Plain steel wire produced includes the quantity made and used in subsequent processes in the same plant as in the manufacture of nails, galvanized wire, etc.

Q289. See note to Q234.
Q290. See note to Q235.
Q291. See note to Q237.

Q293. Aluminium produced is carried back to 1901 at the end of series Q196–306.

Q294. See note to Q239.
Q295. See note to Q240.
Q296. See note to Q241.

Q298. Clay bricks produced is carried back to 1905 at the end of series Q196–306.

Q299. Cement production is carried back to 1887 at the end of series Q196–306.

Q300. See note to Q247.
Q301. See note to Q248.
Q302. See note to Q249.
Q303. See note to Q250.

Q305. Sulphuric acid includes acid made for sale and own use. The reporting unit (66Be) was converted to 100 per cent acid by multiplying by .9319.

Q306. Fertilizer sold. SOURCE: *Fertilizer Trade in Canada* published by the Dominion Bureau of Statistics. Formerly published in D.B.S., *Quarterly Bulletin of Agricultural Statistics.*

NEW GROSS FIXED CAPITAL FORMATION

(Series Q307–349)

Q307–349. New gross fixed capital investment in manufacturing, 1926 to 1960

SOURCE: D.T.C., *Private and Public Investment in Canada Outlook, 1961*; D.B.S., *Private and Public Investment in Canada, 1946–1957*; D.T.C., *Private and Public Investment in Canada, 1926–1951.*

New gross fixed capital investment in manufacturing comprises expenditures made by manufacturing establishments on durable physical assets including structures, engineering works, land improvements, machinery and equipment created or acquired for the purpose of producing goods or services. These assets are considered to be durable when they are intended for use in their original form for more than one year. Included in the aggregates shown for total new gross fixed capital investment, series Q307, and for total new machinery and equipment expenditures, series Q309, are expenditures on certain types of equipment which are considered as capital expenditures, but which are charged to current or operating account by respondent establishments. Such expenditures are shown separately in series Q349.

Only those assets erected in Canada or acquired for use within the country are included.

The value of new construction work includes both contract work and work done by the firms' own employees, and the expenditures shown for each year represent as far as possible the value of construction work put in place in that year irrespective of the time payment is made.

New machinery and equipment investment includes the installed cost of machinery, motors, etc., and the delivered cost of office furniture and fixtures, motor vehicles and other equipment. An item is classified to the machinery and equipment category if it is of such a nature that it can be moved from the structure in which it is housed without materially altering the structure. Expenditures on new machinery and equipment are included in the year in which such machinery and equipment is paid for by the end user, so that progress payments on heavy machinery are included in the year in which the payments are made. The estimates reflect gross expenditures including replacement costs before deduction for scrap or trade-in values. Machinery includes both that for use by the owner and that for rent to others.

For further details on concepts, definitions, sources and estimating techniques, see appendix B to *Private and Public Investment in Canada, 1946–1957*, and for a recent description of coverage, see *Private and Public Investment in Canada, Outlook, 1961*. For a description of the preparation of the data from 1926 to 1947 see *Private and Public Investment in Canada, 1926–1951*.

Limitations in the sources of the industrial distribution figures for the years 1926 to 1945 made it necessary to combine some of the seventeen major groups delineated in the D.B.S. 1948 Standard Industrial Classification, and this practice was followed for the subsequent years for the sake of consistency. Thus, tobacco and tobacco products, rubber products, and leather products are grouped, electrical apparatus and supplies are included in nonferrous metal products, and products of petroleum and coal are shown in the nonmetallic mineral products.

The estimates for 1926 to 1945 are based upon a sample of corporation returns to the Department of National Revenue. They appear to provide a reasonably accurate indication of gross fixed capital investment during these two decades. But the data from 1946 to date are of distinctly superior technical quality and are based on comprehensive reporting by all manufacturing industries.

SIZE OF MANUFACTURING ESTABLISHMENTS

(Series Q350–375)

Q350–361. Number of establishments and gross value of production by size of establishment measured by gross value of production, selected years, 1900 to 1959

SOURCE: D.B.S., *General Review of the Manufacturing Industries of Canada* (various issues); *The Manufacturing Industries of Canada*, the

issues of 1945, 1941, 1936 and 1930 respectively, for the data for 1945, 1940, 1936 and 1930; *Canada Year Book*, the 1927 issue for 1925 data, 1925 issue for 1922 data, and 1906 issue for 1905 Postal Census data; *Postal Census of Manufactures, 1916* for 1915 and 1910 data; *Census of Canada, 1901*, vol. III, for 1900 data.

The figures shown from 1900 to 1945 are not comparable with those in subsequent years because of differences in coverage and changes in the definition of 'manufacturing'. It should be noted that the data on the number of establishments and gross value of production from 1900 through 1945 in series Q360 and Q361 do not correspond with the figures shown earlier in series Q1 and Q8. As noted above extensive revisions have been undertaken to develop more conceptually consistent and comparable figures for manufacturing in series Q1–137. But essential basic information is not available for similar revisions in the series relating to the size of manufacturing establishments.

The information collected for 1900 and 1910 pertains only to manufacturing establishments having five or more employees, with certain exceptions, and neither of the two postal censuses covered *all* of Canada's manufacturing establishments. In addition, electric light plants, gas plants, plumbing and tinsmithing, blacksmithing, dyeing and cleaning, bicycle repairing, and lock and gunsmithing, were included in the census of manufacturing in 1900, 1905, 1910 and 1915, painting and glazing are covered in all these years except 1910, and housebuilding is in the 1910 and 1915 totals. The figures shown for 1922 to 1945 include some establishments in the public utilities and service categories that cannot be eliminated in these data on size of establishments.

Q362–375. Number of establishments and number of employees by size of establishment measured by number of employees, selected years, 1915 to 1959

SOURCE: same as series Q350–361.

Data on the number of establishments and number of employees from 1915 to 1945 in series Q374 and Q375 do not correspond with the figures shown earlier in series Q1 and Q2. See note to series Q350–361.

There is also a small difference in the classifications of manufacturing establishments by number of employees. The grouping given for the years prior to 1940 varies slightly from that available for subsequent years. In addition to the class for under 5 employees the actual classes shown for these earlier years were 5 to 50 employees, 51 to 100 employees, 101 to 200 employees, 201 to 500 employees, and over 500 employees, instead of 5 to 49 employees, 50 to 99 employees, 100 to 199 employees, 200 to 499 employees, and 500 employees and over.

APPENDIX TO SECTION Q PRIMARY AND SECONDARY MANUFACTURING IN CANADA

(Series Q376–407)

Q376–407. Selected general statistics for all manufacturing industries, primary and secondary manufacturing, by industrial groups, selected years, 1870 to 1957

SOURCE: all data are from material prepared by Gordon K. Bertram of Los Angeles State College. Bertram's data for years 1926 to 1946 inclusive were obtained from D.B.S. worksheets prepared for the Royal Commission on Canada's Economic Prospects, some of the material from which is included in D. H. Fullerton and H. A. Hampson, *Canadian Secondary Manufacturing Industry*, Royal Commission on Canada's Economic Prospects (Hull, Queen's Printer, 1957); for 1957, the data were prepared from *General Review of the Manufacturing*

Industries of Canada, 1957 by Bertram; for 1919 the classification into the Standard Industrial Classification of 1948 was obtained from a special study of D.B.S. and the division into primary and secondary classifications was done by Bertram using the proportions of 1915; for 1870, 1880, 1890, 1900, 1910 and 1915 the classifications were prepared by Bertram from information in the censuses of manufactures for those years in the manner described below.

The basis of classification into primary and secondary, which is that used for the Royal Commision on Canada's Economic Prospects, is described in Fullerton and Hampson, *Canadian Secondary Manufacturing Industry*, pp. 3–4 as follows: primary manufacturing '...involve[s] either relatively minor processing of domestic resources, i.e. in which the value added by manufactures is relatively low, or those highly-intensive and often extremely complex industries which produce industrial materials from our basic natural resources for sale in mainly export markets. Flour milling, cheese factories and saw and planing mills are examples of the first type, while pulp and paper production (excluding finished paper goods) and smelting and refining are examples of the second...'; secondary manufacturing industries '...are characterized by a rather higher degree of processing and by a much greater dependence on the domestic market. They tend to be located close to the centre of that market, while the primary industries are usually found at or near the resource on which they are based...secondary manufacturing industries generally produce end products rather than industrial materials...(they) tend to be more labour-intensive than the basic resource industries. Examples...are textiles, clothing, transportation equipment and electrical apparatus and supplies'.

See *Canadian Secondary Manufacturing Industry*, appendix A, pp. 270–2 for the classification of manufacturing subgroups into primary and secondary groups.

The totals for Canada and for each industry in these series differ slightly from those given in the relevant individual series of series Q1–11 and series Q30–137 for the years before 1933. While Bertram's work was done in close communication with D.B.S. and the division into industries was based on the Standard Industrial Classification of 1948, slight differences in allocation by industry occurred. The differences are usually so small as to be negligible for most purposes.

For the censuses of 1900, 1910 and 1915, the reclassification of industries into the 1948 Standard Industrial Classification was complicated by the fact that, aside from the number of establishments, data were not given separately for industries in which there were less than three establishments in order to prevent disclosure of information for individual establishments. These data were given in subgroups classified 'all other industries' within the fourteen major groups into which manufacturing industry was classified at the time. In the absence of such industry detail the 'all other' in each of these fourteen groups was assigned to one of the seventeen groups of the 1948 classification to which the earlier group most closely corresponded. This procedure most likely led to somewhat too much being assigned to 'miscellaneous industries'. However, these quantities involved were not such as to make these problems cause serious shortcomings in the data provided in these series.

For a further description of the data of these series, see also the general note to series Q1–137.

Series Q1–11. *General statistics for all manufacturing industries, selected years, 1870 to 1910 and 1917 to 1959*

Year	Number of establishments	Persons engaged in manufacturing			Salaries and wages (thousands of dollars)			Cost and value (thousands of dollars)			
		Total	Supervisory and office employees	Production workers	Total	Supervisory and office employees	Production workers	Gross value of production	Cost of materials used	Cost of fuel and electricity	Census value added by manufacturing
	1	2	3	4	5	6	7	8	9	10	11
1959	36,193	1,303,956	306,049	997,907	5,073,074	1,529,618	3,543,456	—	12,552,201	568,880	—
1958	36,741	1,289,602	307,867	981,735	4,802,496	1,469,324	3,333,172	22,134,269[1]	11,821,567	549,307	9,763,391[1]
1957	37,875	1,359,061	313,884	1,045,177	4,819,628	1,403,402	3,416,226	22,283,019[1]	11,900,752	555,311	9,826,956[1]
1956	37,428	1,353,020	301,297	1,051,723	4,570,692	1,272,026	3,298,666	21,857,696[1]	11,721,537	523,941	9,612,220[1]
1955	38,182	1,298,461	287,469	1,010,992	4,142,410	1,147,142	2,995,267	19,625,723[1]	10,338,202	457,789	8,829,733[1]
1954[2]	38,028	1,267,966	278,936	989,030	3,896,688	1,075,101	2,821,586	17,546,279[1,2]	9,241,858	424,433	7,879,987[1,2]
1953	38,107	1,327,451	274,225	1,053,226	3,957,018	1,016,679	2,940,339	17,873,161[1]	9,380,559	411,788	8,080,813[1]
1952	37,929	1,288,382	263,027	1,025,355	3,637,620	923,905	2,713,715	17,016,695[1]	9,146,172	392,981	7,477,539[1]
1951	37,021	1,258,375	247,787	1,010,588	3,276,281	816,715	2,459,566	16,392,187	9,074,526	376,714	6,940,947
1950	35,942	1,183,297	231,053	952,244	2,771,267	692,633	2,078,634	13,817,526	7,538,535	336,933	5,942,058
1949	35,792	1,171,207	221,551	949,656	2,591,891	628,428	1,963,463	12,479,593	6,843,231	305,796	5,330,566
1948	33,420	1,155,721	198,230	957,491	2,409,368	532,595	1,876,773	11,875,170	6,632,882	303,500	4,938,787
1947	32,673	1,131,125	190,972	940,153	2,084,985	474,401	1,610,583	10,078,452	5,534,011	254,627	4,289,814
1946	31,188	1,057,460	180,894	876,566	1,739,802	410,652	1,329,151	8,033,099	4,357,992	210,382	3,464,725
1945	28,979	1,118,015	190,243	927,772	1,843,883	416,948	1,426,934	8,245,186	4,472,362	212,289	3,560,533
1944	28,413	1,221,081	191,838	1,029,243	2,027,028	416,615	1,610,413	9,066,846	4,831,129	225,473	4,010,244
1943	27,581	1,239,327	192,579	1,046,748	1,984,998	387,624	1,597,374	8,725,350	4,689,345	225,879	3,810,129
1942	27,791	1,150,616	176,798	973,818	1,681,150	334,150	1,347,000	7,548,215	4,036,068	206,650	3,305,495
1941	26,241	960,295	158,764	801,531	1,263,821	285,915	977,906	6,072,067	3,295,629	174,599	2,601,840
1940	25,471	761,639	135,646	625,993	920,267	241,364	678,903	4,526,618	2,448,383	136,952	1,941,282
1939	24,772	657,673	124,661	533,012	737,316	217,625	519,691	3,472,828	1,835,069	107,548	1,530,210
1938	25,166	641,573	120,473	521,100	705,185	207,160	498,025	3,335,985	1,806,551	101,898	1,427,538
1937	24,800	659,952	115,712	544,240	721,225	195,803	525,422	3,623,426	2,005,990	109,588	1,507,846
1936	24,170	593,970	104,231	489,739	611,613	172,901	438,712	3,000,721	1,623,394	88,582	1,288,747
1935	24,000	556,363	97,766	458,597	559,146	160,197	398,949	2,652,520	1,418,447	81,266	1,152,806
1934	24,177	519,542	91,939	427,603	503,539	148,511	355,028	2,392,388	1,228,786	76,864	1,086,736
1933	23,747	468,366	86,453	381,913	435,908	139,040	296,868	1,952,904	967,312	66,671	918,923
1932	23,071	468,570	86,802	381,708	473,253	151,058	322,195	1,979,012	953,905	70,116	954,990
1931	23,049	528,307	91,266	437,041	587,148	171,949	415,197	2,516,057	1,221,375	81,181	1,213,500
1930	22,586	614,348	84,608	529,740	697,214	169,858	527,356	3,236,606	1,664,265	92,698	1,479,642
1929	22,184	666,181	88,757	577,424	776,925	175,408	601,515	3,840,871	2,029,173	98,373	1,713,326
1928	21,937	631,060	84,076	546,984	721,131	162,815	558,314	3,543,551	1,893,516	90,415	1,559,621
1927	21,464	594,631	78,730	515,901	662,327	151,260	511,067	3,223,012	1,740,646	88,423	1,393,943
1926	21,269	558,861	75,273	483,588	625,416	142,240	483,176	3,090,179	1,726,252	82,904	1,281,021
1925	20,956	522,661	71,255	451,406	569,791	133,373	436,418	2,808,485	1,584,991	77,799	1,145,695
1924	20,693	492,939	70,526	422,413	542,504	131,500	411,004	2,606,650	1,456,494	77,272	1,072,884
1923	21,077	511,108	73,849	437,259	557,395	137,173	420,222	2,690,344	1,483,108	71,077	1,136,159
1922	21,017	458,400	71,933	386,467	494,394	130,633	363,761	2,389,216	1,289,187	67,704	1,032,325
1921	20,836	441,788	70,535	371,253	501,720	130,786	370,934	2,491,280	1,373,498	71,121	1,046,661
1920	22,376	576,417	77,354	499,063	684,288	140,014	544,724	3,667,579	2,081,255	93,602	1,492,722
1919	22,578	571,866	75,558	496,308	569,986	113,091	456,895	3,152,237	1,788,958	75,902	1,287,377
1918	22,007	585,530	64,789	520,741	548,454	95,239	453,215	3,165,139	1,796,882	98,227	1,270,030
1917	22,043	585,945	62,454	523,491	479,998	82,248	397,750	2,768,046	1,524,674	72,584	1,170,788
1910	—	509,977	42,948	465,029	236,680	42,698	193,982	1,151,722	601,647	—	550,075
1905	15,197	382,702	35,030	347,672	159,969	29,618	130,351	698,594	—	—	—
1900	—	422,824	—	—	133,452	—	—	555,876	310,488	—	245,388
1890	69,716	351,139	—	—	94,382	—	—	449,982	245,993	—	203,989
1880	47,079	248,042	—	—	57,720	—	—	304,663	177,681	—	126,982
1870	38,898	181,679	—	—	39,547	—	—	217,176	123,272	—	93,904

[1] From 1952 to 1959, most D.B.S. reports on manufacturing show value of shipments (unadjusted for inventory change) and are therefore different from the figures shown here for gross value of production. The figures for value added by manufacture also differ from those shown in most D.B.S. reports on manufacturing for the years 1952 to 1959 for the same reason.

[2] Owing to a change in the method of valuation in the petroleum industry, a slight discontinuity exists from 1954 onwards. See footnote (2) to series Q123 and Q125.

Series Q 12–29. *General statistics for manufacturing industries, by region, 1926 to 1959*

(values in thousands of dollars)

Year	Atlantic Provinces[1]			Quebec			Ontario		
	Total employees	Salaries and wages	Census value added by manufacture[2]	Total employees	Salaries and wages	Census value added by manufacture[2]	Total employees	Salaries and wages	Census value added by manufacture[2]
	12	13	14	15	16	17	18	19	20
Number of employees and values of salaries and wages and of value added									
1959	60,484	185,904	360,533	431,237	1,546,933	2,998,776	615,746	2,564,684	5,332,082
1958	60,990	179,706	372,977	429,358	1,476,606	2,970,775	606,362	2,412,655	4,914,074
1957	64,651	187,183	362,354	449,383	1,477,828	2,947,898	644,245	2,430,676	5,047,711
1956	65,774	178,708	353,904	446,137	1,396,415	2,888,149	641,190	2,310,634	4,868,570
1955	64,782	164,917	327,473	429,575	1,271,078	2,622,333	613,872	2,088,906	4,426,655
1954	63,384	157,451	313,323	424,095	1,214,661	2,448,028	598,914	1,954,767	3,930,730
1953	68,895	165,845	312,198	441,555	1,225,573	2,424,647	634,554	2,017,982	4,130,126
1952	69,720	159,263	310,618	429,698	1,125,945	2,288,643	609,696	1,844,186	3,811,107
1951	66,374	142,663	298,818	417,182	1,005,602	2,083,934	599,433	1,669,387	3,569,400
1950	60,810	119,862	244,981	390,163	851,335	1,798,320	566,513	1,412,999	3,068,142
1949	61,438	116,527	230,738	390,275	809,579	1,651,630	557,190	1,305,544	2,708,554
1948	56,432	98,546	191,396	383,835	756,079	1,533,798	551,556	1,210,438	2,486,008
1945	57,775	85,789	150,913	383,314	606,586	1,146,941	517,522	881,621	1,719,951
1942	54,759	68,661	119,497	398,336	535,582	1,057,448	542,217	839,932	1,669,191
1939	33,214	30,927	64,167	220,024	223,422	469,908	318,765	378,252	791,117
1936	30,649	26,192	52,623	194,685	182,098	376,995	288,883	314,759	686,279
1933	24,535	19,439	39,275	157,345	134,525	287,999	224,693	220,392	464,935
1929	40,009	32,757	63,740	206,468	225,081	500,426	328,340	406,452	912,445
1926	35,525	27,096	55,458	174,931	182,809	378,447	270,476	321,863	664,546
Percentage of national totals									
1959	4.6	3.7	3.5	33.1	30.5	29.1	47.2	50.6	51.7
1958	4.7	3.7	3.8	33.3	30.8	30.4	47.0	50.2	50.2
1957	4.8	3.9	3.7	33.1	30.7	30.0	47.4	50.4	51.4
1956	4.9	3.9	3.7	33.0	30.5	30.1	47.4	50.6	50.7
1955	5.0	4.0	3.7	33.1	30.7	30.0	47.3	50.4	50.6
1954	5.0	4.1	4.0	33.4	31.2	31.0	47.2	50.2	49.7
1953	5.2	4.2	3.9	33.3	31.0	30.3	47.8	51.0	51.7
1952	5.4	4.4	4.2	33.4	30.9	30.7	47.3	50.7	51.2
1951	5.3	4.3	4.3	33.2	30.7	30.0	47.6	51.0	51.4
1950	5.1	4.3	4.1	33.0	30.7	30.3	47.9	51.0	51.6
1949	5.2	4.5	4.3	33.3	31.2	31.0	47.6	50.4	50.8
1948	4.9	4.1	3.9	33.2	31.4	31.1	47.7	50.3	50.3
1945	5.1	4.7	4.3	34.3	32.9	32.2	46.3	47.8	48.3
1942	4.8	4.1	3.6	34.6	31.9	32.0	47.1	50.0	50.5
1939	5.0	4.2	4.2	33.5	30.3	30.7	48.5	51.3	51.7
1936	5.2	4.3	4.1	32.8	29.8	29.3	48.6	51.4	53.2
1933	5.2	4.4	4.3	33.6	30.9	31.3	48.0	50.6	50.6
1929	6.0	4.2	3.7	31.0	29.0	29.2	49.3	52.3	53.3
1926	6.4	4.3	4.3	31.3	29.2	29.5	48.4	51.5	51.9

Series Q 12–29. *General statistics for manufacturing industries, by region, 1926 to 1959 (continuation)*

(values in thousands of dollars)

Year	Prairie Provinces			British Columbia[3]			Yukon and Northwest Territories[3, 4]		
	Total employees	Salaries and wages	Census value added by manufacture[2]	Total employees	Salaries and wages	Census value added by manufacture[2]	Total employees	Salaries and wages	Census value added by manufacture[2]
	21	22	23	24	25	26	27	28	29
Number of employees and values of salaries and wages and of value added									
1959	95,206	353,537	780,518	101,168	421,405	848,404	115	610	650
1958	92,525	326,223	747,201	100,222	406,628	786,620	145	678	859
1957	94,985	318,153	694,799	105,631	405,130	767,914	166	658	1,410
1956	91,149	290,384	669,477	108,595	393,869	824,249	175	681	1,076
1955	87,654	263,094	624,380	102,408	353,811	750,878	170	605	1,733
1954	85,515	246,875	556,376	95,867	319,803	651,813	191	630	1,856
1953	88,426	246,127	509,398	93,844	300,921	615,686	177	570	1,012
1952	86,437	224,165	475,969	92,667	283,531	556,172	164	530	1,023
1951	81,587	195,596	395,586	93,647	262,626	592,449	152	406	759
1950	78,313	170,128	350,439	87,375	216,657	479,606	123	286	569
1949	79,222	163,478	329,373	82,934	196,404	409,665	148	359	605
1948	77,162	150,005	309,004	86,599	192,954	417,601	137	346	380
1945	71,426	109,427	234,492	87,914	160,333	307,719	64	127	518
1942	65,697	88,123	186,234	89,539	148,746	272,862	68	106	263
1939	43,083	50,758	101,692	42,532	53,859	103,234	55[3]	98[3]	92[3]
1936	40,035	42,824	85,189	39,718	45,740	87,661	—	—	—
1933	33,399	33,103	67,722	28,394	28,447	58,990	—	—	—
1929	43,217	54,893	123,704	48,127	57,741	113,011	—	—	—
1926	33,024	41,976	89,861	44,915	51,673	92,711	—	—	—
Percentage of national totals									
1959	7.3	7.0	7.6	7.8	8.3	8.2	—[4]	—[4]	—[4]
1958	7.2	6.8	7.6	7.8	8.5	8.0	—[4]	—[4]	—[4]
1957	7.0	6.6	7.1	7.7	8.4	7.8	—	—	—
1956	6.7	6.4	6.9	8.0	8.6	8.6	—	—	—
1955	6.7	6.4	7.1	7.9	8.5	8.6	—	—	—
1954	6.8	6.3	7.0	7.6	8.2	8.3	—	—	—
1953	6.6	6.2	6.4	7.1	7.6	7.7	—	—	—
1952	6.7	6.2	6.4	7.2	7.8	7.5	—	—	—
1951	6.5	6.0	5.7	7.4	8.0	8.6	—	—	—
1950	6.6	6.2	5.9	7.4	7.8	8.1	—	—	—
1949	6.8	6.3	6.2	7.1	7.6	7.7	—	—	—
1948	6.7	6.2	6.3	7.5	8.0	8.4	—	—	—
1945	6.4	5.9	6.6	7.9	8.7	8.6	—	—	—
1942	5.7	5.2	5.6	7.8	8.8	8.3	—	—	—
1939	6.5	6.9	6.6	6.5	7.3	6.8	—	—	—
1936	6.7	7.0	6.6	6.7	7.5	6.8	—	—	—
1933	7.1	7.6	7.4	6.1	6.5	6.4	—	—	—
1929	6.5	7.1	7.2	7.2	7.4	6.6	—	—	—
1926	5.9	6.7	7.0	8.0	8.3	7.3	—	—	—

[1] Newfoundland is included with the Atlantic Provinces from 1949 onwards, except that figures for the Newfoundland fish processing industry are not available, and are not included, for the years 1949 and 1950.

[2] From 1952 to 1959, the data for census value added shown here are not comparable with the national totals shown in series Q11, since revisions for inventory data are not available on a regional basis.

[3] Figures for the Yukon and the Northwest Territories are included with British Columbia prior to 1939.

[4] Less than .05 per cent of the national total for all years 1926 to 1958.

Series Q30–137. *General statistics for manufacturing industries by major groups, 1870 to 1959*
(thousands of dollars, except series Q30, Q31, Q36 and Q37)

Year	Foods and beverages						Tobacco and tobacco products					
	Number of establish-ments	Number of employees	Wages and salaries	Gross value of production	Cost of materials	Value added by manufacture	Number of establish-ments	Number of employees	Wages and salaries	Gross value of pro-duction	Cost of materials	Value added by manufacture
	30	31	32	33	34	35	36	37	38	39	40	41
1959	8,165	192,092	662,539	—	2,967,680	1,613,441[1]	40	10,287	38,078	—	212,771	111,694[1]
1958	8,417	190,445	623,290	4,542,573[1]	2,939,312	1,536,379[1]	40	10,319	37,144	305,863[1]	206,044	98,918[1]
1957	8,536	192,177	590,025	4,208,780[1]	2,704,377	1,437,423[1]	49	9,905	33,323	249,839[1]	160,710	88,284[1]
1956	8,023	183,008	531,634	3,832,198[1]	2,474,174	1,299,493[1]	51	9,613	30,309	239,166[1]	150,111	88,299[1]
1955	8,134	180,085	498,787	3,635,342[1]	2,319,783	1,262,080[1]	56	9,529	29,447	251,973[1]	163,027	88,214[1]
1954	8,090	177,883	477,059	3,578,626[1]	2,334,167	1,193,266[1]	53	9,469	27,869	224,825[1]	144,961	79,175[1]
1953	8,129	176,649	455,281	3,458,514[1]	2,296,740	1,113,026[1]	55	9,494	26,766	213,322[1]	138,491	74,191[1]
1952	8,263	175,552	429,650	3,457,272[1]	2,333,089	1,076,699[1]	61	9,277	25,405	218,271[1]	144,538	73,134[1]
1951	8,388	172,493	392,859	3,450,031	2,419,207	985,241	62	9,826	24,438	179,177	119,590	59,033
1950	8,401	167,664	346,715	3,029,811	2,102,438	885,322	68	10,322	22,629	188,331	122,611	65,176
1949	8,558	170,024	332,536	2,882,582	2,009,246	834,018	72	10,686	21,897	172,420	113,357	58,529
1948	8,686	168,893	311,236	2,839,531	2,034,844	766,435	79	10,459	19,550	153,993	95,851	57,667
1947	8,869	167,865	276,245	2,383,976	1,656,529	695,093	91	10,880	16,235	146,793	97,121	49,221
1946	8,862	160,821	241,770	2,040,709	1,408,819	604,120	95	10,849	14,411	119,634	79,225	39,982
1945	8,863	155,672	223,580	1,916,910	1,335,867	555,006	86	12,164	15,738	122,544	79,177	42,986
1944	8,979	152,823	212,092	1,880,304	1,328,807	526,450	82	11,780	14,541	98,973	60,110	38,513
1943	8,974	138,418	185,198	1,609,637	1,141,015	445,858	85	12,475	13,981	88,419	52,500	35,582
1942	9,063	135,085	168,365	1,436,012	976,822	437,892	96	12,987	13,079	83,027	48,602	34,103
1941	8,999	129,636	149,025	1,263,837	876,028	368,178	100	11,374	10,739	68,243	37,216	30,745
1940	8,958	118,630	128,896	1,007,846	676,765	314,671	102	11,052	10,170	68,996	39,593	29,131
1939	9,078	112,131	118,452	876,334	559,170	303,619	99	10,794	9,761	69,593	41,235	28,111
1938	9,314	109,264	114,034	870,977	571,669	286,274	105	10,438	9,471	67,304	41,445	25,626
1937	9,246	108,003	109,589	884,880	592,984	279,267	109	9,840	8,813	57,745	33,994	23,540
1936	9,127	99,814	97,562	787,540	507,836	267,644	111	9,315	8,363	53,212	30,906	22,099
1935	9,091	92,988	89,198	686,362	438,761	236,176	137	9,634	8,163	47,340	26,509	20,630
1934	9,393	89,551	84,049	641,097	404,636	225,346	149	9,508	7,807	43,054	22,785	20,075
1933	9,271	83,356	78,055	545,305	330,780	204,082	149	9,967	7,750	43,894	23,435	20,269
1932	9,045	81,006	80,610	555,473	321,798	223,142	134	9,675	8,043	46,062	25,540	20,325
1931	9,115	85,517	90,195	660,753	396,545	253,132	105	9,091	8,097	37,126	21,449	15,529
1930	8,837	95,613	95,584	846,727	537,575	297,492	103	8,905	7,838	43,282	24,287	18,853
1929	8,856	104,253	101,194	962,023	638,194	311,573	109	9,333	8,355	43,788	25,656	17,977
1928	8,683	99,060	95,963	944,791	643,480	289,284	115	8,664	8,086	39,386	24,754	14,473
1927	8,750	96,792	91,931	889,822	614,937	263,020	115	8,165	7,604	38,146	24,040	13,948
1926	8,699	93,845	86,856	846,885	603,931	230,896	122	8,455	7,623	41,331	22,588	18,580
1925	8,666	90,956	83,257	829,312	600,908	216,522	128	8,223	7,405	38,776	23,532	15,091
1924	8,412	80,681	81,152	753,262	536,995	205,133	130	8,378	7,338	40,449	17,873	22,421
1923	8,587	82,317	75,830	717,389	510,393	196,013	148	8,689	7,565	40,648	17,951	22,529
1922	8,584	70,108	73,669	709,069	503,610	194,537	142	8,551	7,415	43,092	20,149	22,766
1921	8,201	66,974	73,544	755,423	539,327	205,124	119	9,806	7,599	45,785	23,439	22,159
1920	8,627	77,158	83,186	1,035,877	775,911	246,521	125	9,276	8,619	53,892	28,388	25,323
1919	8,443	76,181	71,648	991,008	757,377	223,457	144	10,683	7,740	46,931	27,652	18,588
1918	8,375	70,021	58,559	875,389	655,013	210,180	153	10,143	6,500	35,931	19,040	16,722
1917	8,458	64,862	51,663	790,017	581,710	200,053	176	10,236	5,992	33,759	19,093	14,496
1910	—	65,459	23,503	280,749	187,260	93,489	—	9,557	4,301	25,484	12,207	13,277
1905	5,301	55,632	18,299	190,897	—	—	155	7,633	2,844	15,275	—	—
1900	—	59,231	15,811	153,854	116,975	36,879	—	7,077	2,653	11,959	3,774	8,185
1890	12,615	56,959	10,581	118,911	85,046	33,865	149	5,325	1,461	5,743	2,502	3,241
1880	5,383	25,802	5,803	82,409	63,516	18,893	96	3,757	729	3,060	1,572	1,488
1870	4,124	12,413	2,978	63,383	48,205	15,178	77	2,216	407	2,435	1,198	1,237

[1] See footnote (1) to series Q1–11.

Series Q30–137. *General statistics for manufacturing industries by major groups, 1870 to 1959 (continuation)*

(thousands of dollars, except series Q42, Q43, Q48 and Q49)

	Rubber products						Leather products					
Year	Number of establishments	Number of employees	Wages and salaries	Gross value of production	Cost of materials	Value added by manufacture	Number of establishments	Number of employees	Wages and salaries	Gross value of production	Cost of materials	Value added by manufacture
	42	43	44	45	46	47	48	49	50	51	52	53
1959	89	21,093	86,859	—	160,397	188,179[1]	586	31,012	82,735	—	143,766	129,812[1]
1958	89	19,943	76,445	308,430[1]	128,573	174,828[1]	598	30,151	78,684	246,027[1]	124,664	119,088[1]
1957	88	22,178	83,190	325,664[1]	144,247	176,456[1]	624	31,099	77,769	241,013[1]	122,530	116,139[1]
1956	91	23,136	82,155	364,173[1]	160,687	198,602[1]	646	31,384	74,970	238,946[1]	123,791	112,857[1]
1955	82	21,913	73,775	329,946[1]	137,075	188,698[1]	646	30,575	68,971	219,722[1]	108,962	108,644[1]
1954	73	20,894	67,477	259,937[1]	106,502	149,435[1]	673	30,748	67,161	202,511[1]	101,251	99,194[1]
1953	72	22,600	70,995	290,441[1]	114,337	172,380[1]	695	33,068	70,965	223,927[1]	116,416	105,454[1]
1952	70	21,582	65,477	285,650[1]	120,799	161,488[1]	701	32,103	66,153	215,846[1]	115,714	98,156[1]
1951	67	23,054	64,358	311,678	146,951	161,185	711	31,578	59,669	221,883	135,114	84,885
1950	61	21,812	54,263	239,185	101,774	134,062	747	32,990	57,810	210,563	121,218	87,419
1949	62	20,729	48,172	178,504	73,896	101,706	747	34,900	59,700	210,804	117,869	91,158
1948	56	21,703	48,273	194,112	84,223	107,000	757	34,291	55,123	203,759	114,819	86,948
1947	60	23,475	46,614	196,308	82,935	110,673	792	35,724	52,629	212,430	123,894	86,646
1946	60	22,055	37,813	159,408	62,136	93,451	776	37,290	49,713	192,749	108,703	82,319
1945	55	23,490	39,111	181,413	78,501	98,836	706	34,123	43,269	167,888	95,005	71,298
1944	56	21,421	35,979	169,511	81,188	82,813	650	31,925	40,050	155,424	88,757	65,172
1943	51	15,913	25,343	130,158	68,298	59,952	646	31,821	38,053	152,915	88,393	63,050
1942	49	15,497	23,413	122,231	61,576	58,896	645	32,698	35,323	140,954	85,068	54,529
1941	56	17,191	22,792	119,138	59,340	58,089	598	31,827	31,217	117,744	70,577	45,961
1940	52	14,297	16,835	83,021	38,228	43,404	591	27,898	24,692	93,825	53,880	38,884
1939	54	14,160	15,604	69,945	28,813	39,800	606	26,859	22,978	81,537	46,420	34,140
1938	53	12,879	14,062	61,031	24,301	35,492	598	25,160	20,946	69,961	38,011	31,056
1937	50	13,035	14,041	74,264	31,127	41,797	618	26,852	22,244	82,645	49,087	32,600
1936	50	11,881	11,954	62,055	23,599	37,199	610	25,477	19,937	72,462	41,691	29,824
1935	45	11,023	11,017	55,950	20,259	34,502	597	24,691	19,372	68,629	38,856	28,854
1934	51	11,079	10,859	55,230	18,440	35,598	604	23,000	17,451	61,367	33,611	26,890
1933	45	9,758	8,910	41,512	12,915	27,521	597	21,726	16,549	57,536	30,455	26,309
1932	47	10,325	9,341	40,747	11,907	27,756	556	20,428	17,230	54,516	27,653	26,099
1931	48	12,158	11,708	52,691	17,630	33,893	579	21,009	18,982	62,136	31,908	29,474
1930	47	15,163	15,895	73,753	28,822	43,608	562	21,041	20,098	72,807	40,001	31,987
1929	44	17,796	20,135	96,935	42,941	52,537	603	23,500	23,416	90,976	52,409	37,670
1928	45	17,095	18,944	97,209	45,119	50,791	636	24,518	24,332	103,624	62,688	39,960
1927	44	15,065	16,622	91,414	44,725	45,460	648	24,299	24,098	97,386	55,971	40,308
1926	39	13,587	14,708	86,508	49,902	35,408	661	23,520	23,490	90,191	51,933	37,143
1925	40	12,962	14,144	78,230	38,389	38,773	682	21,874	21,286	80,776	46,333	33,477
1924	38	10,778	11,413	57,412	24,468	31,861	700	22,361	22,219	81,515	45,652	34,758
1923	40	11,646	12,329	56,513	26,336	29,030	761	22,578	22,602	84,942	47,892	35,985
1922	62	10,369	10,623	46,487	19,295	26,080	748	21,824	21,964	84,034	44,722	38,237
1921	44	9,908	9,868	39,989	17,104	21,804	757	20,525	19,858	82,751	46,272	35,383
1920	35	15,238	16,199	80,717	41,838	37,500	471	21,807	23,448	129,788	84,039	44,605
1919	32	12,676	11,546	56,004	27,535	27,633	932	23,063	20,928	126,738	84,012	41,813
1918	30	10,842	8,501	46,280	21,508	23,778	922	20,714	15,420	93,118	58,293	33,854
1917	28	10,258	7,270	43,639	19,760	23,150	863	20,670	15,238	103,952	61,002	42,072
1910	—	1,869	937	7,046	3,608	3,438	—	25,108	11,908	64,068	35,045	29,023
1905	21	1,179	619	3,061	—	—	533	19,836	7,892	42,132	—	—
1900	—	762	336	1,589	977	612		35,135	12,056	52,435	32,808	19,627
1890	19	1,388	359	2,060	1,422	638	7,774	25,677	7,553	35,209	18,700	16,509
1880	4	525	177	771	478	293	6,809	27,457	6,701	36,456	21,871	14,585
1870	4	494	83	503	358	145	6,381	25,646	5,884	27,911	14,845	13,066

[1] See footnote (1) to series Q1–11.

Series Q30–137. *General statistics for manufacturing industries by major groups, 1870 to 1959 (continuation)*
(thousands of dollars, except series Q54, Q55, Q60 and Q61)

| Year | Textile products (excluding clothing) | | | | | | Knitting mills | | | | | |
| | Number of establishments | Number of employees | Wages and salaries | Gross value of production | Cost of materials | Value added by manufacture | Number of establishments | Number of employees | Wages and salaries | Gross value of production | Cost of materials | Value added by manufacture |
	54	55	56	57	58	59	60	61	62	63	64	65
1959	879	63,579	202,904	—	429,641	363,536[1]	319	20,992	52,187	—	98,659	—
1958	903	63,472	193,328	732,095[1]	394,621	322,533[1]	321	20,936	49,829	174,448[1]	88,610	83,975
1957	929	68,512	201,579	758,814[1]	412,434	330,985[1]	310	21,661	50,217	174,896[1]	88,782	84,148
1956	965	70,873	199,328	769,250[1]	430,420	323,821[1]	286	21,913	49,638	166,998[1]	83,926	81,159
1955	977	69,144	187,805	742,257[1]	408,891	319,549[1]	296	21,658	47,208	155,044[1]	75,706	77,466
1954	975	64,581	170,196	631,529[1]	350,114	269,169[1]	297	21,622	47,578	147,723[1]	70,119	75,755
1953	959	73,190	184,605	711,005[1]	388,325	309,546[1]	294	24,413	52,421	160,792[1]	77,704	81,264
1952	918	72,739	178,689	737,155[1]	418,523	305,640[1]	288	23,234	48,961	162,821[1]	80,374	80,619
1951	892	81,710	185,030	846,477	495,304	337,936	295	25,188	49,000	169,720	84,403	83,523
1950	846	80,328	169,175	741,263	412,683	315,557	293	25,255	44,141	146,226	68,718	75,853
1949	847	77,773	156,167	636,824	339,645	285,641	290	26,442	43,949	143,020	64,704	76,672
1948	722	75,816	141,002	604,946	331,943	261,775	271	27,034	42,807	148,556	69,115	77,807
1947	714	73,618	115,714	513,326	289,987	213,700	262	26,511	35,647	127,838	59,558	66,851
1946	684	66,889	95,074	401,231	215,853	177,176	247	24,941	30,211	105,209	47,272	56,681
1945	622	65,295	87,616	389,146	217,290	163,723	216	23,654	26,640	88,035	40,424	46,369
1944	593	64,017	84,666	387,470	217,165	162,040	200	22,939	25,535	84,218	39,133	43,882
1943	584	65,947	83,214	397,293	233,164	156,130	191	22,344	23,850	80,209	38,532	40,505
1942	577	69,032	81,471	409,171	230,430	170,826	186	23,462	23,423	80,134	38,550	40,485
1941	509	66,511	70,853	345,016	187,356	150,451	181	24,362	22,424	77,122	39,128	36,977
1940	488	58,585	59,685	283,971	150,816	126,419	172	23,225	20,696	69,427	35,755	32,755
1939	440	47,849	44,258	183,716	93,363	84,820	174	21,312	17,778	57,670	27,384	29,458
1938	433	45,640	40,237	155,050	80,344	69,984	174	20,031	16,154	49,505	23,049	25,713
1937	444	49,839	44,736	192,792	106,769	81,032	171	20,250	16,229	52,856	26,447	25,654
1936	443	47,669	40,791	175,412	93,695	76,938	168	19,429	15,120	49,469	24,361	24,338
1935	434	46,539	37,875	161,928	84,724	72,616	163	18,511	14,253	46,390	22,948	22,689
1934	428	44,631	36,410	156,644	80,458	71,739	167	17,978	13,566	44,957	21,831	22,377
1933	414	40,036	31,827	133,162	64,975	64,258	170	17,159	12,610	40,997	19,473	20,803
1932	384	36,979	30,854	110,820	52,790	54,516	169	17,055	13,475	43,253	19,350	23,198
1931	378	36,771	32,322	121,715	59,411	58,888	161	17,698	13,949	47,758	22,052	25,034
1930	347	36,479	31,464	137,340	75,371	58,596	167	18,570	15,057	54,118	25,510	27,949
1929	339	39,347	34,889	173,377	98,157	71,693	168	19,609	16,294	61,098	31,194	29,172
1928	335	40,045	35,229	171,041	100,923	66,562	165	17,974	15,057	58,552	31,252	26,608
1927	319	38,365	32,751	160,306	89,566	67,445	168	17,217	14,177	55,222	28,270	26,234
1926	289	35,922	29,233	157,126	94,888	59,207	167	16,474	13,312	53,676	29,213	23,770
1925	292	34,710	27,240	147,494	94,668	49,682	162	14,698	11,858	48,555	27,120	20,791
1924	295	32,818	25,233	140,948	88,593	49,667	158	13,917	11,090	44,506	24,758	19,140
1923	312	34,351	28,191	151,322	85,525	62,921	153	14,755	11,262	47,522	24,344	22,509
1922	288	32,883	26,422	135,016	69,231	62,769	141	14,179	10,572	44,963	22,544	21,719
1921	343	28,359	24,282	131,018	71,272	56,433	127	10,446	8,399	36,690	18,960	17,131
1920	335	33,743	29,593	197,191	120,264	73,543	128	14,024	11,072	56,737	34,238	21,729
1919	296	30,488	22,212	173,345	104,187	66,570	114	12,384	8,404	45,207	26,636	18,030
1918	280	29,684	18,840	155,195	93,798	58,901	108	12,627	7,231	45,755	26,527	18,616
1917	276	28,605	16,179	105,650	59,640	44,240	102	11,662	6,496	33,771	19,443	13,886
1910[2]	—	25,919	9,721	51,674	29,454	22,220	—	—	—	—	—	—
1905[2]	334	21,229	7,045	33,061	—	—	—	—	—	—	—	—
1900[2]	—	27,392	7,919	33,010	17,644	15,366	—	—	—	—	—	—
1890[2]	3,996	25,491	5,848	26,043	13,537	12,506	—	—	—	—	—	—
1880[2]	1,835	13,418	2,595	15,376	9,077	6,299	—	—	—	—	—	—
1870[2]	996	7,466	1,374	9,666	6,231	3,435	—	—	—	—	—	—

[1] See footnote (1) to series Q1–11.   [2] Knitting mills included with Clothing (textile and fur), series Q66–71.

Series Q 30–137. *General statistics for manufacturing industries by major groups, 1870 to 1959 (continuation)*

(thousands of dollars, except series Q 66, Q 67, Q 72 and Q 73)

Year	Clothing (textile and fur)						Wood products					
	Number of establishments	Number of employees	Wages and salaries	Gross value of production	Cost of materials	Value added by manufacture	Number of establishments	Number of employees	Wages and salaries	Gross value of production	Cost of materials	Value added by manufacture
	66	67	68	69	70	71	72	73	74	75	76	77
1959	2,359	87,678	227,513	—	401,132	—	9,808	123,791	387,862	—	761,354	644,856[1]
1958	2,460	87,740	217,973	747,460[1]	389,244	355,057[1]	9,848	120,922	369,582	1,343,975[1]	717,463	605,678[1]
1957	2,550	91,114	218,959	754,389[1]	398,406	352,614[1]	10,796	126,839	368,660	1,336,016[1]	730,076	585,783[1]
1956	2,525	89,799	208,216	739,733[1]	399,249	337,266[1]	11,103	135,583	376,349	1,454,957[1]	788,465	646,223[1]
1955	2,648	89,686	196,437	689,192[1]	359,883	326,308[1]	11,804	133,673	354,440	1,376,128[1]	723,815	633,395[1]
1954	2,733	89,693	191,495	648,351[1]	339,959	305,510[1]	12,165	128,931	323,122	1,193,672[1]	623,757	553,407[1]
1953	2,788	95,658	202,005	705,008[1]	361,558	341,058[1]	12,462	134,310	325,620	1,248,022[1]	649,731	583,389[1]
1952	2,753	94,434	191,579	684,415[1]	363,583	318,557[1]	12,467	130,468	299,431	1,170,551[1]	618,980	537,076[1]
1951	2,788	90,545	173,365	610,292	320,944	287,149	11,975	131,278	283,062	1,153,377	610,808	529,300
1950	2,758	90,993	167,082	587,988	308,833	277,037	11,301	126,169	246,325	985,859	510,564	463,854
1949	2,768	91,310	162,564	584,479	306,425	276,069	11,191	121,632	224,903	840,356	436,638	393,929
1948	2,829	87,471	149,060	561,133	292,102	267,222	10,495	124,306	214,742	839,045	428,914	401,402
1947	2,859	83,818	131,305	486,757	251,461	233,676	9,744	120,434	186,468	771,403	398,879	365,050
1946	2,741	80,927	116,055	446,123	238,298	206,337	8,846	105,472	142,339	560,341	297,924	256,437
1945	2,460	76,305	104,838	388,719	211,477	175,938	7,710	96,048	124,435	474,298	251,592	217,538
1944	2,190	71,975	95,020	357,533	196,596	159,690	7,590	93,385	117,966	442,096	231,469	205,775
1943	2,088	75,367	93,204	358,095	206,062	150,771	7,118	90,860	109,493	395,295	202,195	186,947
1942	2,078	78,396	88,753	340,857	198,087	141,519	7,219	93,180	103,060	379,504	194,896	178,856
1941	1,822	71,473	73,335	273,399	160,234	112,054	6,505	88,794	88,503	327,011	169,172	153,113
1940	1,690	62,422	59,403	220,312	127,934	91,421	6,401	76,744	70,791	259,324	134,487	120,664
1939	1,706	56,704	50,853	172,038	94,790	76,372	5,681	65,794	57,433	198,899	102,561	93,749
1938	1,705	54,468	47,848	159,700	87,149	71,716	5,638	62,831	53,825	180,168	95,884	81,819
1937	1,695	55,978	48,720	173,039	97,687	74,495	5,526	66,511	55,712	200,028	104,479	93,088
1936	1,620	51,916	43,394	157,922	89,039	68,055	5,284	57,354	44,975	158,234	82,200	73,776
1935	1,586	48,709	40,030	146,851	83,019	63,055	5,296	52,185	38,578	133,106	69,057	61,980
1934	1,566	46,433	36,639	139,344	79,195	59,410	5,184	47,566	33,245	114,954	58,082	54,948
1933	1,494	42,036	31,907	118,412	65,937	51,745	5,197	41,118	27,550	94,103	48,478	43,857
1932	1,327	39,585	33,003	115,372	62,516	52,234	5,217	42,906	31,479	100,124	51,737	46,594
1931	1,289	42,911	39,895	142,686	78,700	63,312	5,193	51,529	45,104	150,835	78,995	69,725
1930	1,220	45,981	44,381	164,936	91,208	73,115	5,213	77,426	63,912	238,064	127,721	108,085
1929	1,250	48,582	48,531	189,466	101,424	87,451	4,823	83,778	76,806	289,931	154,095	133,359
1928	1,251	48,643	48,165	188,340	103,421	84,221	4,660	80,042	71,766	273,061	146,719	123,967
1927	1,206	46,497	45,214	171,693	92,641	78,364	4,281	76,341	67,759	252,073	134,819	114,907
1926	1,111	42,728	42,094	159,490	89,029	69,834	4,280	64,246	65,532	242,425	128,953	111,133
1925	1,060	39,916	38,485	141,099	78,247	62,265	4,258	63,165	62,734	233,502	126,920	104,191
1924	1,026	38,266	37,288	133,606	71,454	61,597	4,424	63,822	64,268	239,341	131,415	105,623
1923	992	38,596	37,994	133,118	71,628	60,957	4,542	63,484	63,476	244,258	124,369	117,697
1922	894	36,824	36,141	127,584	67,266	59,667	4,546	57,840	55,411	207,894	104,804	100,898
1921	850	33,547	35,709	137,501	80,256	56,650	4,716	53,205	53,514	208,093	98,910	106,999
1920	980	41,222	45,228	182,615	105,617	76,390	5,122	73,032	78,224	335,592	167,300	165,626
1919	912	41,248	36,835	160,218	88,503	71,317	4,923	102,325	87,058	322,211	121,876	198,154
1918	834	38,509	27,970	125,328	68,171	56,595	4,556	86,766	69,504	224,335	85,003	137,352
1917	794	38,753	25,248	114,800	58,644	55,736	4,427	93,187	63,532	202,138	80,760	119,473
1910[2]	—	58,239	24,501	95,151	48,242	46,909	—	117,130	45,251	182,352	93,182	89,170
1905[2]	1,811	44,483	15,631	59,699	—	—	3,054	84,595	33,724	109,721	—	—
1900[2]	—	68,321	16,987	54,191	27,177	27,014	—	98,386	26,261	90,470	44,837	45,633
1890[2]	11,589	48,540	10,127	43,851	22,204	21,647	11,553	79,982	21,405	84,544	42,661	41,883
1880[2]	4,469	32,163	5,347	26,697	15,521	11,176	9,636	59,930	12,560	54,922	28,264	26,658
1870[2]	2,594	17,123	2,754	15,019	8,620	6,399	9,751	50,551	9,191	40,862	21,380	19,482

[1] See footnote (1) to series Q 1–11.   [2] Series 66–71 includes knitting mills.

Series Q30–137. *General statistics for manufacturing industries by major groups, 1870 to 1959 (continuation)*

(thousands of dollars, except series Q78, Q79, Q84 and Q85)

Year	Paper products						Printing and publishing industries					
	Number of establishments	Number of employees	Wages and salaries	Gross value of production	Cost of materials	Value added by manufacture	Number of establishments	Number of employees	Wages and salaries	Gross value of production	Cost of materials	Value added by manufacture
	78	79	80	81	82	83	84	85	86	87	88	89
1959	559	94,231	430,365	—	935,329	980,578[1]	4,359	73,926	308,264	—	267,305	552,888[1]
1958	562	92,935	409,578	1,904,217[1]	883,156	910,693[1]	4,433	72,221	287,971	763,128[1]	248,244	509,065[1]
1957	582	94,283	403,286	1,874,483[1]	883,395	877,986[1]	4,584	74,559	274,455	732,684[1]	245,024	481,737[1]
1956	568	93,705	386,887	1,901,271[1]	885,056	908,727[1]	4,585	72,361	254,373	689,954[1]	225,202	459,224[1]
1955	580	89,750	349,777	1,754,932[1]	793,008	867,149[1]	4,494	69,602	234,580	620,464[1]	199,162	416,305[1]
1954	569	87,370	331,556	1,633,725[1]	742,032	803,412[1]	4,227	68,614	220,276	579,283[1]	188,726	385,944[1]
1953	555	84,436	310,107	1,566,543[1]	717,460	765,566[1]	4,157	66,530	205,626	545,415[1]	175,222	366,027[1]
1952	543	82,965	292,682	1,516,240[1]	694,190	742,308[1]	4,124	64,485	186,251	489,073[1]	160,394	324,800[1]
1951	547	82,889	276,521	1,589,842	683,488	827,925	4,019	64,694	170,829	452,143	152,753	295,643
1950	528	77,519	225,197	1,251,144	541,261	638,111	3,869	63,125	154,370	413,012	135,510	274,099
1949	524	76,471	208,349	1,093,060	494,300	532,289	3,866	61,834	141,490	377,908	124,684	250,163
1948	522	75,980	197,398	1,061,360	485,238	509,993	2,496	54,541	119,088	307,346	96,385	208,208
1947	502	73,445	168,632	911,239	410,457	443,374	2,430	51,832	101,185	262,577	82,317	177,895
1946	486	67,442	134,320	695,080	313,411	333,820	2,379	48,731	86,113	221,689	65,258	154,349
1945	475	60,819	109,627	536,860	255,266	241,121	2,288	43,374	73,994	186,204	52,455	131,858
1944	456	56,823	101,618	495,189	226,018	230,482	2,272	40,389	66,594	167,155	47,151	118,220
1943	452	54,995	94,847	461,403	207,420	216,494	2,281	39,097	62,497	155,727	44,655	109,309
1942	446	55,199	92,150	448,577	197,423	213,670	2,349	39,083	59,150	145,541	43,384	100,416
1941	432	53,186	83,830	437,382	183,775	217,991	2,338	39,716	57,929	141,198	42,526	96,952
1940	419	47,954	71,978	375,797	151,882	191,868	2,297	37,737	53,049	125,815	36,019	88,194
1939	405	42,707	58,092	269,632	114,698	129,022	2,291	37,594	51,377	119,543	33,922	84,127
1938	405	42,604	55,853	242,077	103,029	114,436	2,273	37,459	50,565	117,593	32,768	83,354
1937	393	44,757	61,717	286,690	123,696	133,044	2,198	36,789	49,249	117,546	32,753	83,331
1936	369	40,101	50,862	233,221	97,500	109,271	2,184	35,346	46,354	110,345	29,325	79,592
1935	362	36,949	45,612	205,142	79,996	101,868	2,140	34,207	44,159	105,133	27,857	75,894
1934	360	35,830	42,517	192,585	73,375	96,672	2,126	32,980	41,846	99,010	25,741	71,924
1933	339	32,287	34,925	157,509	64,895	73,226	2,057	31,951	40,382	92,589	23,319	67,974
1932	329	32,256	36,560	169,368	65,500	83,570	1,966	32,515	44,525	101,316	26,402	73,611
1931	351	35,913	45,292	217,250	85,053	108,783	1,881	33,826	49,919	117,400	29,992	86,113
1930	346	42,626	55,918	261,621	104,975	129,991	1,831	34,877	52,722	133,040	34,975	96,746
1929	324	43,530	60,622	290,950	121,401	143,720	1,828	35,417	52,788	140,471	36,901	102,256
1928	322	42,218	56,732	277,346	111,373	140,999	1,811	33,633	48,882	129,285	35,009	93,070
1927	308	40,978	54,489	259,205	105,275	129,485	1,720	31,397	44,154	115,903	31,502	83,232
1926	290	38,610	51,994	248,831	102,066	125,973	1,647	29,415	41,501	105,756	29,302	75,359
1925	283	34,889	45,431	222,615	91,815	112,624	1,575	28,541	39,124	100,428	28,428	70,977
1924	276	34,388	44,772	207,790	86,861	103,153	1,625	27,707	38,177	98,483	27,868	69,449
1923	262	36,104	45,825	216,176	86,795	110,727	1,491	27,550	37,149	96,355	26,471	68,780
1922	249	32,253	39,736	188,074	78,055	93,846	1,520	26,853	35,610	93,780	24,560	68,196
1921	236	30,751	40,746	179,167	75,382	88,421	1,556	25,739	35,245	97,393	29,194	67,229
1920	277	39,163	53,559	278,728	106,074	155,840	1,779	29,088	37,337	104,521	33,415	70,064
1919	306	34,408	38,841	169,840	68,412	89,052	1,591	26,063	28,151	75,633	22,813	52,028
1918	302	32,903	32,079	143,880	56,920	74,574	1,556	24,000	21,922	60,258	19,454	40,000
1917	290	30,485	25,450	120,370	45,707	66,011	1,617	24,267	20,403	57,355	15,616	41,077
1910	—	15,180	7,626	32,999	15,477	17,522	—	17,939	10,957	26,486	7,813	18,673
1905	136	11,099	4,685	18,761	—	—	812	15,736	8,660	20,041	—	—
1900	—	9,221	3,347	12,420	5,416	7,004	—	13,359	6,243	14,200	3,990	10,210
1890	155	4,689	1,455	6,206	3,160	3,046	719	9,814	3,853	10,456	3,721	6,735
1880	83	2,186	576	2,976	1,628	1,348	489	6,915	2,256	6,785	2,605	4,180
1870	.29	1,464	295	1,725	874	851	372	4,298	1,405	4,128	1,492	2,636

[1] See footnote (1) to series Q1–11.

Series Q30–137. *General statistics for manufacturing industries by major groups, 1870 to 1959 (continuation)*
(thousands of dollars, except series Q90, Q91, Q96 and Q97)

	Iron and steel products						Transportation equipment					
Year	Number of establishments	Number of employees	Wages and salaries	Gross value of production	Cost of materials	Value added by manufacture	Number of establishments	Number of employees	Wages and salaries	Gross value of production	Cost of materials	Value added by manufacture
	90	91	92	93	94	95	96	97	98	99	100	101
1959	3,246	192,969	861,446	—	1,486,322	—	645	113,606	531,588	—	1,120,283	910,947[1]
1958	3,254	179,440	757,173	2,670,092[1]	1,270,710	1,342,827[1]	626	125,976	553,426	2,057,826[1]	1,153,569	883,507[1]
1957	3,073	198,555	807,093	2,924,476[1]	1,386,921	1,472,278[1]	623	144,639	591,461	2,266,600[1]	1,288,243	956,076[1]
1956	2,963	196,918	766,376	2,825,690[1]	1,315,814	1,444,536[1]	591	141,257	553,572	2,213,798[1]	1,286,297	906,155[1]
1955	2,895	181,700	667,657	2,258,717[1]	1,005,247	1,198,726[1]	594	131,789	490,435	1,971,630[1]	1,117,769	834,785[1]
1954	2,801	173,698	605,526	1,962,256[1]	829,238	1,087,283[1]	602	133,432	479,080	1,681,292[1]	986,721	677,116[1]
1953	2,698	188,236	643,474	2,116,534[1]	906,165	1,158,915[1]	621	156,059	555,411	2,098,469[1]	1,110,954	969,736[1]
1952	2,625	189,191	617,011	2,188,026[1]	947,993	1,187,037[1]	617	146,360	473,118	1,785,773[1]	1,009,471	760,421[1]
1951	2,435	183,323	547,315	1,904,650	860,565	991,335	599	122,517	368,106	1,541,590	870,179	657,424
1950	2,390	164,528	438,245	1,524,384	662,332	817,060	601	104,176	290,436	1,239,580	674,834	552,171
1949	2,347	163,622	413,228	1,419,146	619,500	760,934	596	104,750	270,852	1,063,211	584,064	466,529
1948	2,263	170,071	400,878	1,320,527	570,290	709,347	578	101,816	255,505	941,484	509,911	419,134
1947	2,200	162,399	334,044	1,064,654	451,267	580,342	550	103,558	229,584	798,285	423,897	363,537
1946	2,086	151,373	279,568	824,766	337,982	461,502	530	100,163	199,202	587,237	299,870	277,804
1945	1,921	169,653	314,534	953,782	396,102	528,280	495	154,221	325,831	1,029,226	494,541	522,194
1944	1,913	192,145	363,713	1,130,769	467,437	631,753	461	221,549	457,143	1,416,543	639,309	762,517
1943	1,778	213,601	394,657	1,204,947	525,441	705,833	435	223,688	440,743	1,317,039	609,180	694,086
1942	1,674	188,291	321,063	1,051,647	432,030	588,404	452	173,986	319,938	1,065,832	556,052	498,479
1941	1,530	138,737	218,306	767,653	315,022	428,708	416	116,439	191,297	719,760	402,350	309,198
1940	1,230	95,224	134,125	483,141	211,142	255,320	404	70,292	109,770	426,147	244,576	176,029
1939	1,199	73,560	93,117	321,282	130,797	179,017	407	48,632	66,481	234,856	132,605	98,265
1938	1,201	73,722	90,291	295,083	122,881	161,532	413	48,710	65,233	256,555	150,800	101,750
1937	1,166	77,975	96,203	336,183	147,799	175,927	414	50,522	68,208	291,648	181,575	105,908
1936	1,141	65,350	74,459	249,043	105,092	133,509	486	43,109	53,029	206,764	123,690	79,532
1935	1,115	58,594	65,186	208,802	88,586	110,674	501	41,308	49,757	191,838	118,595	69,842
1934	1,118	50,701	53,952	172,688	71,506	92,974	526	35,278	39,285	144,961	84,996	56,968
1933	1,153	42,778	42,631	125,968	49,213	70,570	521	31,712	30,458	92,731	50,157	39,855
1932	1,099	45,914	49,489	137,102	54,004	77,061	533	32,447	37,350	97,984	51,071	44,072
1931	1,112	62,585	75,994	234,362	92,300	133,799	545	40,020	51,659	156,739	83,735	69,820
1930	1,093	77,694	103,513	343,788	142,824	190,223	607	50,770	72,890	254,358	148,331	101,814
1929	1,069	90,334	123,601	435,291	185,354	236,857	623	56,118	84,385	369,592	227,277	137,776
1928	1,051	80,273	108,128	378,194	159,031	207,323	694	51,497	77,399	282,848	170,945	108,164
1927	1,038	74,003	95,788	326,224	135,869	179,769	691	43,531	62,793	245,197	144,654	96,959
1926	1,034	69,285	87,966	300,546	131,014	160,027	727	45,072	63,676	244,185	144,049	96,279
1925	966	59,185	73,921	245,176	104,867	131,285	724	40,737	54,642	196,366	113,694	79,220
1924	915	57,388	70,604	230,133	100,515	119,298	746	30,323	40,706	169,672	106,676	60,485
1923	914	62,460	78,987	283,207	133,031	140,903	772	34,051	46,574	207,310	131,850	71,502
1922	941	55,115	64,847	206,519	93,007	105,324	853	26,602	33,949	144,706	82,028	59,991
1921	1,048	61,858	77,761	267,405	121,802	135,986	827	26,318	36,034	158,050	89,605	65,521
1920	1,347	85,365	115,374	449,221	205,706	225,598	1,055	55,084	77,289	285,230	152,142	128,076
1919	1,269	78,589	92,740	351,103	143,959	182,456	922	51,344	65,605	251,739	129,413	120,251
1918	1,214	90,085	104,460	496,305	247,970	212,430	985	48,521	55,746	240,871	120,987	116,640
1917	1,184	91,915	92,057	448,576	226,982	197,996	1,046	49,395	47,734	197,795	100,675	92,870
1910	—	66,816	38,761	143,240	66,750	76,490	—	43,213	25,119	78,400	37,553	40,847
1905	972	43,475	22,018	69,514	—	—	538	26,193	13,108	40,305	—	—
1900	—	41,802	17,697	51,983	22,181	29,802	—	24,825	9,937	27,164	13,894	13,270
1890	12,727	45,600	16,186	55,871	23,543	32,328	4,009	18,529	6,561	23,345	10,157	13,188
1880	10,478	35,206	10,238	34,183	14,446	19,737	3,603	16,742	4,797	14,267	6,408	7,859
1870	8,091	28,260	7,883	24,914	9,217	15,697	3,039	14,316	3,455	9,889	3,480	6,409

[1] See footnote (1) to series Q1–11.

Series Q30–137. *General statistics for manufacturing industries by major groups, 1870 to 1959 (continuation)*
(thousands of dollars, except series Q102, Q103, Q108 and Q109)

| | Nonferrous metal products | | | | | | Electrical apparatus and supplies | | | | | |
| Year | Number of establishments | Number of employees | Wages and salaries | Gross value of production | Cost of materials | Value added by manufacture | Number of establishments | Number of employees | Wages and salaries | Gross value of production | Cost of materials | Value added by manufacture |
	102	103	104	105	106	107	108	109	110	111	112	113
1959	580	52,025	236,728	—	1,076,051	—	496	73,883	316,857	—	501,800	566,293[1]
1958	593	51,301	226,614	1,527,623[1]	930,931	526,932[1]	492	74,944	316,358	1,006,922[1]	473,903	523,827[1]
1957	592	54,581	228,268	1,691,622[1]	1,014,416	611,975[1]	486	81,432	320,417	1,076,355[1]	498,243	568,587[1]
1956	581	56,071	220,370	1,871,846[1]	1,128,962	672,097[1]	473	83,296	310,523	1,144,826[1]	558,250	577,412[1]
1955	581	53,311	201,110	1,634,631[1]	974,792	597,439[1]	468	76,244	264,031	981,932[1]	477,656	496,401 1
1954	573	50,494	182,191	1,263,124[1]	717,966	484,867[1]	457	75,075	258,510	872,183[1]	396,583	468,176[1]
1953	551	52,058	178,710	1,241,712[1]	726,128	457,881[1]	422	76,856	250,647	892,153[1]	383,744	501,453[1]
1952	552	50,938	167,045	1,218,686[1]	744,596	418,488[1]	401	69,200	217,565	731,398[1]	313,713	411,459[1]
1951	536	50,114	150,734	1,253,599	797,412	406,617	373	67,626	194,749	676,009	316,561	353,603
1950	536	44,680	119,536	960,752	606,692	311,539	382	60,262	155,334	580,578	260,305	315,137
1949	532	44,698	114,591	867,043	537,218	289,125	365	55,916	137,279	486,286	212,460	269,342
1948	503	46,048	108,779	844,598	556,238	248,226	314	53,873	122,114	425,725	180,345	241,334
1947	503	43,344	91,047	668,075	434,518	201,163	296	52,736	103,891	366,506	162,131	200,859
1946	474	40,855	75,856	484,619	311,084	148,492	266	43,998	74,510	234,573	101,940	129,969
1945	436	44,221	81,890	548,853	337,872	180,653	247	44,129	76,469	230,532	92,041	135,920
1944	401	55,480	100,605	709,275	428,904	239,329	234	48,834	82,305	283,071	120,413	160,170
1943	374	62,594	109,967	788,620	506,003	234,957	223	46,928	76,907	245,771	109,282	134,049
1942	371	51,261	84,891	692,697	412,325	241,181	225	39,676	61,799	208,873	92,799	113,824
1941	368	40,364	61,684	548,445	328,666	190,390	211	33,086	47,211	177,904	77,467	98,433
1940	351	29,197	42,409	410,780	249,437	140,344	194	25,120	33,247	130,001	58,371	70,009
1939	336	24,302	33,974	327,000	202,731	107,347	190	20,261	25,711	89,061	39,333	48,462
1938	333	24,087	33,033	344,571	216,709	111,679	188	20,353	24,978	90,129	35,916	53,014
1937	335	22,908	31,431	383,599	240,837	127,153	191	21,706	26,291	98,842	41,696	55,815
1936	326	19,898	25,589	278,876	182,299	91,808	186	17,037	19,502	72,289	30,435	40,616
1935	323	18,064	22,721	227,370	149,497	73,226	182	15,549	17,595	61,153	25,410	34,672
1934	314	16,520	19,878	186,999	98,405	84,215	174	13,057	15,220	50,235	21,308	27,940
1933	304	13,506	15,671	127,753	57,487	66,771	174	11,767	12,429	37,013	14,504	21,657
1932	283	12,399	16,493	98,846	47,519	46,278	169	14,305	16,262	53,265	20,415	31,874
1931	292	16,207	23,637	130,284	62,959	60,539	163	18,207	22,474	81,579	32,386	48,242
1930	280	18,188	26,059	145,881	68,627	69,937	149	20,568	26,260	104,578	43,112	60,383
1929	269	18,996	27,778	169,749	75,276	87,341	139	20,871	26,725	113,796	49,623	63,074
1928	269	17,375	24,742	144,295	59,961	78,284	137	18,193	22,756	93,672	38,784	53,929
1927	271	16,630	23,542	121,811	54,879	59,719	130	16,813	20,614	78,559	32,735	44,927
1926	271	14,849	20,575	113,734	60,417	46,487	132	15,246	18,627	69,767	30,196	38,506
1925	256	13,623	19,242	99,611	48,633	44,233	122	14,112	16,472	60,159	25,435	33,770
1924	239	13,521	18,165	78,888	38,279	34,923	109	13,670	16,090	56,490	24,371	31,235
1923	233	13,109	17,955	72,093	31,362	34,592	108	13,268	14,991	51,360	26,257	24,238
1922	232	10,976	14,332	53,285	20,487	30,326	101	10,630	12,162	41,208	17,547	22,790
1921	249	10,310	13,255	49,371	20,058	24,927	100	10,640	13,556	45,093	19,439	24,777
1920	240	14,699	21,962	97,548	43,766	45,086	99	14,115	16,587	55,966	27,221	27,748
1919	956	15,493	18,745	93,503	47,628	40,533	111	9,709	9,865	35,552	16,067	18,896
1918	642	15,770	18,627	114,924	64,084	42,113	83	8,994	8,599	31,416	14,686	16,063
1917	621	16,827	17,251	125,702	66,962	52,737	90	9,896	8,163	41,165	20,752	20,034
1910	—	12,810	8,471	59,845	26,811	33,034	—	6,427	3,548	15,235	6,384	8,851
1905	151	14,896	9,144	37,893	—	—	34	4,806	2,499	8,997	—	
1900	—	6,202	3,200	12,785	4,136	8,649	—	2,120	1,000	3,275	1,222	2,053
1890	741	4,771	2,027	7,400	3,357	4,043	24	428	168	866	336	530
1880	524	3,276	1,170	4,000	1,770	2,230	Industry nonexistent					
1870	274	1,618	476	1,594	673	921						

[1] See footnote (1) to series Q1–11.

Series Q30–137. *General statistics for manufacturing industries by major groups, 1870 to 1959 (continuation)*
(thousands of dollars, except series Q114, Q115, Q120 and Q121)

| | Nonmetallic mineral products | | | | | | Products of petroleum and coal | | | | | |
| | Number of establishments | Number of employees | Wages and salaries | Gross value of production | Cost of materials | Value added by manufacture | Number of establishments | Number of employees | Wages and salaries | Gross value of production | Cost of materials | Value added by manufacture |
Year	114	115	116	117	118	119	120	121	122	123	124	125
1959	1,251	43,349	178,654	—	240,923	405,957[1]	112	16,775	93,896	—	936,188	—
1958	1,248	40,858	161,812	640,731[1]	218,684	369,873[1]	115	17,427	89,491	1,465,619[1]	894,458	514,760[1]
1957	1,231	40,120	150,313	602,573[1]	209,982	340,621[1]	106	17,757	88,688	1,492,072[1]	898,830	534,157[1]
1956	1,183	40,165	143,223	575,993[1]	206,872	322,821[1]	107	17,685	81,680	1,377,485[1]	837,827	489,298[1]
1955	1,171	38,949	131,007	517,555[1]	174,489	302,996[1]	106	17,486	72,436	1,161,198[1,2]	704,385	417,821[1]
1954	1,160	35,229	114,849	437,931[1]	145,121	256,572[1]	104	17,559	69,682	1,024,437[1,2]	625,411	361,631[1,2]
1953	1,094	34,352	107,275	411,109[1]	134,119	242,016[1]	100	17,112	66,565	823,927[1]	576,311	212,390[1]
1952	1,057	31,422	92,819	352,454[1]	115,218	206,095[1]	101	16,905	63,573	780,855[1]	519,629	226,245[1]
1951	1,042	31,522	86,079	334,875	109,011	195,349	82	15,598	51,948	709,550	497,982	179,873
1950	1,045	29,603	72,380	286,541	91,168	168,378	76	15,177	44,425	616,126	442,418	144,489
1949	1,020	28,139	64,594	246,458	78,401	143,873	77	14,552	39,784	533,731	391,036	117,819
1948	934	27,278	58,816	232,148	72,577	134,898	75	13,678	34,766	491,962	369,035	97,064
1947	863	26,443	50,456	201,787	66,267	115,278	80	12,769	28,690	361,333	257,421	84,074
1946	833	24,387	39,651	160,475	49,957	94,591	77	12,106	24,198	286,008	190,528	79,047
1945	709	20,993	34,289	135,569	42,441	79,560	80	11,532	22,905	270,167	188,900	65,637
1944	666	20,034	32,872	136,146	43,347	79,251	82	11,556	23,259	280,123	191,368	73,274
1943	662	20,528	32,578	140,707	44,544	82,368	85	10,466	20,704	248,007	170,594	64,093
1942	699	20,386	29,914	138,570	41,925	82,883	83	10,321	18,789	219,505	149,219	58,334
1941	693	19,133	25,518	116,836	33,251	71,692	80	9,696	16,859	207,454	149,890	45,734
1940	724	16,164	19,712	86,738	23,415	54,425	80	9,251	15,185	168,886	115,898	43,268
1939	723	14,197	16,326	64,558	16,786	41,105	86	8,829	13,742	143,609	91,193	44,407
1938	764	14,194	16,103	60,896	15,551	38,791	92	8,605	13,673	136,725	93,023	36,176
1937	733	14,673	16,433	68,048	18,319	42,486	90	9,164	13,956	140,157	97,620	35,181
1936	698	12,839	13,378	52,097	13,393	32,888	105	9,135	13,024	125,674	83,141	35,819
1935	685	11,509	11,738	43,908	10,970	28,010	102	8,963	12,781	118,425	74,103	38,043
1934	683	10,370	10,387	40,588	9,303	26,523	95	9,235	12,028	114,610	72,206	36,396
1933	681	8,821	8,534	31,120	7,160	20,273	89	8,154	10,748	100,205	61,917	32,544
1932	711	10,285	10,920	35,189	7,120	23,277	73	7,755	10,879	101,510	64,479	31,462
1931	797	14,327	17,380	60,959	11,133	42,084	73	8,128	11,832	107,408	64,512	37,555
1930	780	18,324	22,142	74,882	14,656	50,507	69	9,104	14,055	128,380	88,883	33,244
1929	775	20,377	24,866	90,455	17,193	61,510	68	8,880	14,093	139,319	95,378	37,557
1928	761	18,450	22,198	77,574	14,430	53,250	70	8,233	12,532	117,831	74,548	37,761
1927	778	16,858	19,848	68,460	13,177	45,772	71	8,002	12,057	98,574	69,675	23,293
1926	820	16,308	18,318	62,028	12,098	40,952	73	8,046	11,790	104,723	67,143	32,343
1925	807	12,714	16,326	57,715	10,650	38,988	86	10,260	11,993	82,279	52,971	23,548
1924	724	14,796	16,269	55,269	9,013	38,256	89	8,055	11,764	79,589	51,883	20,284
1923	726	15,378	17,143	57,781	9,353	45,442	84	8,115	10,628	82,953	58,660	19,834
1922	743	13,740	15,219	51,230	7,548	35,895	76	7,254	10,262	84,255	53,392	26,148
1921	683	14,777	15,230	47,852	7,086	32,372	75	7,567	11,516	87,309	57,507	25,245
1920	696	16,656	19,788	57,430	8,956	39,576	82	8,286	12,146	94,623	60,788	28,464
1919	594	12,105	12,900	38,782	9,210	24,656	74	7,609	9,926	77,514	51,167	23,081
1918	831	11,781	10,874	36,417	9,857	21,991	83	6,790	7,676	67,483	42,846	20,264
1917	942	13,261	11,199	33,593	5,986	23,601	92	6,657	6,460	59,057	30,485	24,553
1910	—	20,838	9,643	28,155	4,420	23,735	—	3,473	2,156	13,608	6,212	7,396
1905	788	16,873	6,668	16,272	—	—	70	2,211	1,153	8,204	—	—
1900	—	14,019	3,684	9,460	1,491	7,969	—	1,811	944	6,589	3,612	2,977
1890	2,160	12,695	3,041	8,198	2,011	6,187	74	1,495	656	4,952	2,254	2,698
1880	2,364	11,016	2,216	6,179	1,913	4,266	80	1,002	433	5,223	2,560	2,663
1870	1,809	8,532	1,506	3,874	858	3,016	73	793	333	3,845	1,706	2,139

[1] See footnote (1) to series Q1–11.
[2] The method of valuation of the petroleum refining industry products was changed in 1954. Had the old method been used in 1954, it is estimated that the gross value of production for the 'Products of Petroleum and Coal' group in that year would have been 885 million dollars instead of 1,024 million dollars.

Series Q30–137. *General statistics for manufacturing industries by major groups, 1870 to 1959 (continuation)*
(thousands of dollars, except series Q126, Q127, Q132 and Q133)

	Chemicals and allied industries						Miscellaneous industries					
Year	Number of establishments	Number of employees	Wages and salaries	Gross value of production	Cost of materials	Value added by manufacture	Number of establishments	Number of employees	Wages and salaries	Gross value of production	Cost of materials	Value added by manufacture
	126	127	128	129	130	131	132	133	134	135	136	137
1959	1,137	54,782	243,218	—	627,366	701,480[1]	1,563	37,886	131,382	—	185,235	246,239[1]
1958	1,143	54,570	233,819	1,302,006[1]	589,316	664,853[1]	1,599	36,002	119,981	395,234[1]	170,066	220,598[1]
1957	1,137	54,708	222,045	1,213,122[1]	565,746	605,274[1]	1,579	34,942	109,881	359,621[1]	148,660	206,433[1]
1956	1,131	52,821	200,743	1,120,444[1]	527,564	556,241[1]	1,556	33,432	100,348	330,968[1]	138,870	187,989[1]
1955	1,126	51,856	185,268	1,038,837[1]	480,104	525,648[1]	1,524	31,511	89,240	286,223[1]	114,448	168,109[1]
1954	1,116	51,603	177,312	950,518[1]	437,051	481,253[1]	1,360	31,071	85,479	254,356[1]	102,179	148,822[1]
1953	1,105	50,207	164,591	898,139[1]	403,686	464,912[1]	1,350	32,223	85,954	268,129[1]	103,468	171,609[1]
1952	1,075	47,694	148,076	798,419[1]	357,819	415,945[1]	1,313	29,833	74,134	223,790[1]	87,550	133,372[1]
1951	1,037	45,664	131,310	776,489	366,957	384,026	1,173	28,756	66,909	210,805	87,292	120,900
1950	1,033	41,475	106,794	646,871	307,706	317,167	1,007	27,219	56,410	169,313	67,469	99,629
1949	1,037	41,328	100,690	587,398	280,008	288,172	893	26,401	51,147	156,363	59,778	94,600
1948	1,026	39,548	89,326	579,828	293,042	268,818	814	22,315	40,906	125,116	48,007	75,511
1947	1,046	39,237	78,994	488,307	238,307	234,057	812	23,037	37,606	116,859	47,068	68,323
1946	1,031	38,012	67,842	401,742	179,750	208,399	715	21,149	31,158	111,498	49,955	60,247
1945	992	61,366	107,074	498,739	228,922	252,985	618	20,956	32,043	126,299	74,489	50,631
1944	997	82,347	138,204	746,935	371,146	357,756	591	21,659	34,868	126,112	51,812	73,157
1943	961	92,736	147,327	774,876	375,812	381,295	593	21,549	32,436	116,233	66,253	48,850
1942	943	93,445	134,870	511,353	241,113	254,251	576	18,631	21,697	73,730	35,709	36,947
1941	866	54,388	76,091	312,654	141,165	159,216	537	14,382	16,210	51,271	22,465	27,958
1940	820	27,983	38,990	199,686	87,179	105,200	498	9,864	10,636	32,901	13,002	19,276
1939	817	22,834	31,841	163,694	68,332	90,041	480	9,154	9,537	29,862	10,938	18,348
1938	996	22,346	29,860	149,921	63,578	81,372	481	8,782	9,019	28,740	10,443	17,754
1937	960	22,425	28,953	154,124	68,546	80,292	461	8,725	8,697	28,341	10,578	17,236
1936	823	20,222	25,513	131,035	55,791	70,649	439	8,078	7,808	25,072	9,350	15,190
1935	813	19,221	23,973	121,694	50,707	66,677	428	7,719	7,138	22,502	8,597	13,398
1934	819	17,425	21,181	110,744	44,018	62,835	420	7,800	7,223	23,321	8,892	13,906
1933	706	15,598	18,962	94,907	35,813	55,885	386	6,636	6,011	18,186	6,395	11,324
1932	648	15,268	19,995	96,850	36,703	56,586	381	6,867	6,748	21,216	7,403	13,335
1931	604	15,206	20,901	108,020	42,967	61,375	363	7,204	7,808	26,355	9,648	16,203
1930	575	15,498	21,057	125,836	53,749	68,023	360	7,521	8,369	33,215	13,638	19,089
1929	539	16,606	22,531	143,237	59,749	78,859	358	8,854	9,917	40,418	16,950	22,944
1928	580	16,365	20,613	129,959	56,449	69,574	352	8,782	9,607	36,542	14,626	21,401
1927	569	14,798	18,965	117,287	52,605	61,203	357	8,970	9,921	35,731	15,307	19,898
1926	564	14,576	18,592	129,076	65,488	59,777	343	8,677	9,529	33,901	14,045	19,346
1925	503	13,974	17,475	116,290	59,757	53,277	346	8,122	8,756	30,102	12,624	16,981
1924	451	13,805	17,027	111,491	58,025	50,082	336	8,265	8,929	27,806	11,795	15,519
1923	469	15,159	18,399	113,840	57,953	52,410	483	9,498	10,495	33,557	12,938	20,090
1922	464	13,593	16,257	96,567	49,388	43,830	433	8,806	9,803	31,453	11,554	19,306
1921	446	12,138	15,667	89,755	44,953	41,363	459	8,920	9,937	32,635	12,932	19,137
1920	437	16,414	21,520	130,425	66,618	58,743	541	12,047	13,157	43,296	18,974	23,625
1919	403	14,750	15,428	94,095	44,167	46,205	556	12,748	11,511	43,354	18,344	24,657
1918	498	54,907	66,120	334,952	177,760	148,043	555	12,473	8,826	37,302	14,965	21,914
1917	523	55,422	50,934	227,512	98,602	122,406	514	9,587	8,729	29,195	12,855	15,947
1910	—	10,726	5,471	30,987	14,750	16,237		9,274	4,804	16,242	6,481	9,761
1905	245	4,988	2,303	14,855	—	—	242	7,838	3,478	10,087		
1900	—	5,971	2,539	12,591	7,029	5,562	—	7,190	2,830	7,902	3,325	4,577
1890	761	4,615	1,400	10,135	5,703	4,432	651	5,141	1,699	6,191	2,679	3,512
1880	633	3,768	989	7,058	4,145	2,913	593	4,879	1,143	4,301	1,907	2,394
1870	919	3,555	625	5,022	3,049	1,973	365	2,934	629	2,408	1,088	1,320

[1] See footnote (1) to series Q1–11.

Series Q 138. *Index of total manufacturing production, 1923 to 1935*
(1935–1939 = 100)

Year	Total manufacturing
	138
1935	86.5
1934	78.7
1933	66.9
1932	66.8
1931	79.0
1930	90.9
1929	100.2
1928	94.7
1927	86.9
1926	81.6
1925	71.7
1924	65.5
1923	66.7

Series Q 139–195. *Manufacturing production indexes by groups, 1935 to 1960*
(1949 = 100)

		Durables manufacturing								
			Wood products			Iron and steel products				
Year	Total manufacturing	Total durables	Total	Saw and planing mills	Furniture	Total	Machinery	Primary iron and steel	Sheet metal products	Iron castings
	139	**140**	**141**	**142**	**143**	**144**	**145**	**146**	**147**	**148**
1960	149.3	146.4	136.0	141.2	141.3	137.3	135.1	162.1	143.5	147.8
1959	149.8	149.5	136.6	140.5	146.3	147.2	135.9	167.7	149.6	157.5
1958	140.7	139.9	132.0	135.6	143.4	128.3	122.6	121.8	136.8	141.4
1957	142.9	146.7	127.3	128.4	141.0	139.6	146.3	149.0	126.2	129.4
1956	145.1	153.3	138.3	143.6	140.6	145.3	144.7	158.3	137.0	155.4
1955	134.7	139.7	136.4	143.9	133.7	123.8	120.3	133.0	125.6	122.6
1954	122.9	124.8	124.2	128.7	128.5	106.2	113.0	94.6	113.8	88.1
1953	126.4	133.6	125.4	129.6	126.5	115.3	111.6	120.8	114.1	94.2
1952	118.5	124.8	115.8	118.8	113.7	118.9	116.8	127.9	106.9	99.9
1951	115.0	119.9	114.8	119.3	109.1	117.0	117.7	129.0	108.2	104.7
1950	106.2	106.5	108.2	111.4	107.3	102.5	98.8	109.4	102.7	102.7
1949	100.0	100.0	100.0	100.0	100.0	100.0	100.0	100.0	100.0	100.0
1948	97.3	98.4	100.6	100.9	98.2	101.5	104.5	99.1	102.9	98.1
1947	93.2	93.3	98.2	96.4	99.9	93.6	103.0	93.9	95.3	87.6
1946	85.2	79.9	86.8	82.9	93.0	80.8	89.3	71.7	90.1	78.6
1945	92.9	99.8	77.2	72.8	77.8	96.3	92.2	96.7	95.9	80.9
1944	106.1	128.3	76.1	71.9	73.1	118.4	103.1	104.3	103.3	81.5
1943	104.0	128.2	73.6	68.6	71.7	131.6	114.9	117.9	106.4	92.4
1942	96.1	112.1	77.4	76.0	67.1	114.7	103.3	121.6	106.1	95.7
1941	78.7	85.8	74.5	72.1	69.9	86.4	91.4	88.0	83.8	90.6
1940	60.4	59.3	65.5	64.8	60.2	58.9	62.1	65.0	62.3	62.2
1939	48.7	42.7	54.0	52.8	49.7	39.1	35.1	43.8	52.3	41.3
1938	45.3	40.9	50.7	49.9	48.0	36.6	33.2	36.8	44.5	43.9
1937	49.2	44.9	53.6	52.3	51.5	42.9	39.4	44.9	55.6	53.4
1936	43.0	36.9	47.5	46.8	46.4	33.8	30.4	32.8	46.4	41.7
1935	39.0	32.7	42.3	41.0	40.3	29.2	26.3	27.6	36.8	38.8

Series Q 139–195. *Manufacturing production indexes by groups, 1935 to 1960 (continuation)*

(1949 = 100)

Durables manufacturing

	Transportation equipment					Nonferrous metal products			Electrical apparatus and supplies			Nonmetallic mineral products			
Year	Total	Aircraft and parts	Motor vehicles	Motor vehicles parts	Railway rolling stock	Total	Brass and copper products	Nonferrous metal smelting and refining	Total	Heavy electrical equipment	Telecommunication equipment	Total	Cement	Concrete products	Clay products
	149	150	151	152	153	154	155	156	157	158	159	160	161	162	163
1960	130.0	238.4	159.0	121.1	51.2	148.3	115.2	168.7	180.2	135.3	398.6	210.9	203.8	511.9	152.8
1959	131.5	249.4	148.8	132.9	61.5	134.7	119.3	145.7	184.8	142.5	420.7	223.2	221.8	534.2	170.2
1958	132.5	331.2	138.6	113.5	71.9	126.7	111.8	138.9	176.2	148.4	413.1	205.9	223.3	474.2	161.3
1957	151.2	350.4	162.0	121.5	92.3	127.6	105.5	141.8	183.6	163.4	377.8	191.3	221.1	356.9	145.5
1956	157.9	313.1	184.1	135.1	89.7	133.0	119.4	145.9	191.3	157.0	460.3	191.5	183.3	376.5	160.0
1955	145.1	308.8	167.7	130.1	75.7	127.5	111.1	140.1	176.2	126.2	543.4	171.1	156.1	317.6	146.6
1954	137.3	355.4	130.7	114.2	88.3	117.0	96.9	127.4	151.7	119.5	388.8	146.1	140.2	231.9	136.7
1953	165.2	398.4	164.4	146.1	101.9	120.5	106.5	126.0	150.9	132.3	351.1	139.2	139.5	182.4	130.8
1952	149.1	320.3	146.4	136.0	105.6	112.2	116.5	114.5	124.5	130.5	208.1	122.8	114.6	168.1	116.0
1951	131.3	194.6	143.5	135.1	102.6	114.1	116.7	114.0	120.7	130.4	139.5	119.8	106.6	130.7	120.7
1950	108.3	98.7	129.1	130.9	74.0	104.0	98.4	105.5	112.5	105.5	126.5	111.0	104.1	115.0	114.9
1949	100.0	100.0	100.0	100.0	100.0	100.0	100.0	100.0	100.0	100.0	100.0	100.0	100.0	100.0	100.0
1948	97.2	76.3	89.7	90.0	101.9	99.2	101.3	98.7	91.5	99.2	88.3	92.2	87.2	79.7	102.8
1947	95.3	87.8	90.3	91.5	79.5	89.6	97.3	87.7	89.6	86.5	108.5	86.3	76.0	62.0	91.2
1946	80.6	105.0	59.8	72.4	83.4	81.8	96.2	76.4	67.7	70.3	80.0	72.0	66.5	51.4	86.9
1945	157.0	444.7	77.3	92.0	89.5	98.8	159.8	94.3	70.7	—	—	63.7	48.7	35.0	65.5
1944	235.7	804.5	108.2	109.9	88.9	130.9	244.5	127.0	85.5	—	—	66.8	47.3	24.8	57.4
1943	198.4	452.4	123.3	123.8	93.0	145.6	292.9	138.9	85.0	—	—	68.8	50.0	21.5	55.0
1942	157.1	295.6	119.9	123.8	97.0	130.4	267.5	120.9	74.9	—	—	68.2	53.8	26.9	61.2
1941	106.1	144.0	100.2	92.4	81.7	98.9	145.4	100.3	61.8	—	—	60.1	52.8	23.9	68.0
1940	61.1	48.0	73.3	50.3	58.2	70.5	71.7	79.5	41.9	—	—	45.0	43.3	22.9	60.3
1939	37.7	23.4	44.6	38.0	44.7	58.4	43.0	71.3	28.4	—	—	35.7	35.6	16.3	51.1
1938	38.1	10.7	47.7	37.4	50.2	55.8	38.8	68.0	28.0	—	—	34.3	34.8	14.0	44.9
1937	43.4	3.9	60.5	41.7	56.2	54.4	40.6	65.8	32.5	—	—	38.2	38.3	14.5	45.7
1936	35.5	2.7	47.6	35.7	48.4	46.7	38.3	55.6	25.0	—	—	29.8	30.7	7.0	36.2
1935	34.2	1.8	48.9	32.6	43.8	40.1	31.8	47.5	22.9	—	—	24.6	21.7	4.2	31.0

Nondurables manufacturing

		Foods							Beverages				Tobacco and tobacco products	Rubber products	Leather products		
Year	Total non-durables	Total	Meat products	Dairy products	Canning and preserving	Grain mill products	Bakery products	Miscellaneous foods	Total	Carbonated beverages	Breweries	Distilleries			Total	Boots and shoes	Tanneries
	164	165	166	167	168	169	170	171	172	173	174	175	176	177	178	179	180
1960	151.8	147.1	156.5	152.8	149.5	132.5	144.1	142.9	160.2	158.7	146.4	194.8	182.0	143.3	111.8	—	—
1959	150.1	145.0	168.1	146.7	142.4	132.4	142.0	135.0	155.8	155.9	141.9	190.3	179.9	161.1	120.3	131.6	105.7
1958	141.3	140.1	151.7	143.0	146.1	130.6	137.8	130.3	147.7	145.9	135.2	179.0	173.2	137.2	114.4	122.7	109.1
1957	139.7	133.2	144.4	136.4	143.8	116.6	129.6	125.1	143.2	129.7	139.5	169.7	161.0	147.8	115.6	120.7	109.7
1956	138.1	131.4	144.7	130.5	134.4	116.9	135.4	122.0	138.4	122.6	131.4	174.6	145.9	154.0	115.6	119.4	111.1
1955	130.4	125.6	137.7	127.3	135.5	107.2	126.7	115.2	130.6	119.4	127.7	151.9	135.5	141.0	106.9	108.7	107.7
1954	121.2	120.2	126.5	120.4	129.1	108.1	122.4	112.2	121.7	104.5	120.5	145.4	124.7	119.2	100.2	103.9	93.8
1953	120.2	115.1	119.7	111.5	119.0	108.9	121.8	108.0	124.6	108.5	122.3	151.5	120.3	130.3	106.4	111.0	99.4
1952	113.2	112.8	122.6	103.2	119.8	108.6	114.8	106.3	115.5	102.0	116.3	131.2	108.0	118.9	101.0	106.4	83.7
1951	110.8	107.0	102.8	104.6	121.8	109.8	109.1	97.6	106.2	94.8	102.3	129.4	95.0	124.9	90.4	93.2	82.2
1950	106.0	104.4	104.3	97.8	112.0	99.6	103.0	107.5	102.1	102.1	99.5	107.4	103.4	116.8	95.6	94.0	102.6
1949	100.0	100.0	100.0	100.0	100.0	100.0	100.0	100.0	100.0	100.0	100.0	100.0	100.0	100.0	100.0	100.0	100.0
1948	96.3	99.5	100.4	101.7	102.7	97.9	99.0	96.0	95.3	87.2	98.5	97.4	93.4	116.4	95.5	91.4	106.3
1947	93.2	100.4	119.9	87.7	95.5	111.2	100.7	82.3	87.3	69.5	90.2	99.1	93.4	127.4	109.1	100.8	134.1
1946	89.8	103.0	134.1	83.1	105.5	113.3	103.9	82.2	82.2	55.7	77.9	120.0	90.6	89.5	124.0	118.4	144.2
1945	88.2	98.7	148.4	84.2	86.9	98.1	—	83.3	71.8	52.9	66.5	103.2	103.2	102.1	114.5	106.9	129.3
1944	89.5	97.7	153.4	79.2	85.8	97.8	—	83.7	66.7	64.0	58.5	77.4	89.6	84.4	110.5	100.2	125.6
1943	85.9	89.9	141.2	77.7	65.4	93.5	—	75.7	56.6	55.1	48.6	67.4	82.3	83.3	111.6	100.9	130.3
1942	84.3	83.4	126.2	72.9	71.1	71.6	—	74.7	60.8	56.0	54.9	66.5	76.0	85.3	110.8	99.1	125.5
1941	73.7	79.5	107.9	63.9	78.4	73.2	—	74.3	52.9	54.0	44.1	61.1	61.1	87.5	104.2	94.2	110.2
1940	61.6	68.5	91.8	55.2	63.1	64.7	—	63.7	45.5	48.9	33.8	61.8	53.1	66.0	85.7	77.7	101.8
1939	53.7	63.0	81.9	50.5	56.4	61.0	—	58.6	38.7	40.5	28.8	54.8	49.2	60.4	80.3	75.0	101.8
1938	49.0	59.0	70.7	48.7	52.3	57.9	—	53.7	37.1	34.8	28.5	57.8	45.9	55.0	68.9	66.1	81.7
1937	52.8	58.7	67.5	48.3	53.8	59.3	—	55.2	37.8	28.0	28.6	75.7	41.4	63.6	78.1	73.2	98.1
1936	48.1	56.6	66.6	46.0	51.7	59.9	—	52.9	32.1	23.9	25.1	61.0	35.7	54.5	71.1	65.5	95.9
1935	44.1	51.2	54.7	41.3	43.0	56.1	—	49.0	27.1	19.9	24.6	38.3	31.1	49.8	70.8	67.1	95.2

Series Q 139–195. *Manufacturing production indexes by groups, 1935 to 1960 (continuation)*

(1949 = 100)

	Nondurables manufacturing														
	Textile products				Clothing (textile and fur)			Paper products		Printing, publishing and allied trades	Products of petroleum and coal			Chemical and allied products	Miscellaneous manufacturing industries
Year	Total	Cotton goods	Wool goods	Synthetic textiles and silk	Total	Men's, women's and children's clothing	Knitting mills	Total	Pulp and paper		Total	Coke products	Petroleum products		
	181	182	183	184	185	186	187	188	189	190	191	192	193	194	195
1960	122.5	89.6	78.5	187.6	107.9	109.4	103.1	148.4	148.2	146.5	250.6	—	269.8	219.7	191.6
1959	124.4	94.2	84.8	181.1	113.1	109.9	116.6	144.7	141.8	143.2	241.5	104.8	259.1	208.4	183.2
1958	109.9	90.2	74.2	151.5	114.4	110.6	126.4	135.6	131.5	134.4	216.8	93.2	232.7	198.0	166.3
1957	117.6	100.0	86.9	156.6	116.8	112.6	130.8	135.5	133.6	138.2	223.5	120.2	236.8	183.4	153.3
1956	117.3	101.3	93.0	149.2	117.6	114.1	131.2	137.8	137.4	137.3	216.1	122.8	228.1	174.8	147.0
1955	114.0	102.7	89.2	143.3	112.8	111.0	121.3	131.0	131.1	127.1	188.3	114.3	197.8	165.5	136.4
1954	94.3	86.7	72.0	108.7	108.9	110.7	110.5	124.1	124.0	121.6	165.0	95.5	174.0	152.1	134.3
1953	107.9	97.3	89.6	127.5	115.0	117.0	113.7	118.1	117.5	114.7	153.5	113.1	158.7	139.9	141.1
1952	102.9	93.9	80.4	122.6	111.4	115.4	104.8	113.4	113.5	107.5	140.1	112.9	143.6	122.3	121.8
1951	113.1	109.5	95.7	134.0	101.2	101.0	104.7	117.5	117.5	105.1	128.5	107.4	131.2	120.0	119.0
1950	112.5	115.8	103.9	119.9	101.3	101.7	100.7	109.3	108.4	101.5	111.9	105.6	112.7	107.7	104.8
1949	100.0	100.0	100.0	100.0	100.0	100.0	100.0	100.0	100.0	100.0	100.0	100.0	100.0	100.0	100.0
1948	97.3	103.3	106.4	86.2	97.6	96.5	99.6	94.9	95.1	92.6	89.9	99.2	88.7	95.7	81.4
1947	94.0	96.4	111.0	77.2	92.2	92.5	86.7	89.1	89.1	83.6	79.8	83.9	79.3	90.8	84.1
1946	88.7	87.6	108.0	70.9	95.3	96.9	82.2	81.0	80.5	76.9	74.3	82.4	73.3	87.0	80.2
1945	87.5	91.4	99.0	65.1	91.4	96.8	73.6	69.1	67.7	67.3	71.9	101.7	67.4	107.1	98.3
1944	87.9	94.0	96.5	63.9	91.7	98.4	74.4	63.9	63.1	61.4	73.6	104.0	69.0	142.8	113.0
1943	93.8	108.3	102.4	61.9	97.7	106.9	75.7	60.0	59.5	59.7	65.1	84.3	62.3	135.1	112.1
1942	102.0	128.2	111.3	59.8	100.9	110.2	80.2	61.5	62.1	61.2	59.4	82.0	56.0	126.5	88.5
1941	91.7	121.6	94.4	51.8	88.4	90.3	80.9	61.6	63.5	60.6	61.1	78.3	58.5	77.2	60.8
1940	81.1	108.6	93.5	40.2	78.2	74.9	81.5	54.3	58.1	54.6	53.6	75.0	50.4	49.8	42.6
1939	59.5	78.5	64.9	35.7	67.3	61.7	78.5	45.2	47.6	54.7	48.1	57.2	46.8	40.7	38.6
1938	48.1	59.1	51.2	33.3	61.3	58.2	66.1	39.3	41.2	52.9	44.4	59.9	42.1	37.9	36.9
1937	59.8	76.4	67.0	37.4	65.3	63.9	67.1	48.9	54.0	56.5	44.9	64.0	42.0	39.3	37.1
1936	55.5	71.5	63.2	35.3	60.5	59.8	60.2	42.4	47.4	53.2	40.8	60.1	37.9	33.7	34.3
1935	49.7	57.2	59.3	36.1	57.2	57.9	53.8	38.6	43.6	50.2	37.8	52.8	35.6	31.4	31.4

Series Q 196–252. *Value of output of selected manufactured commodities, 1917 to 1959*
(thousands of dollars)

Year	Wheat flour	Bread	Refined sugar	Confectionery	Jams, jellies and marmalades	Canned fruits	Canned vegetables	Meats, fresh and frozen	Poultry, fresh and frozen	Carbonated beverages	Beer, ale, stout and porter[1]	Beverage spirits sold[2]	Cigarettes[3]	Cigars[3]
	196	197	198	199	200	201	202	203	204	205	206	207	208	209
1959	176,581	206,588	117,920	94,087	23,325	23,968	62,227	626,656	26,920	142,736	388,131	132,958	493,911	23,014
1958	169,642	203,659	133,374	96,964	21,716	22,216	60,178	593,092	27,923	133,879	361,610	125,563	439,367	22,518
1957	157,493	198,515	151,025	92,997	20,930	23,335	61,245	549,017	19,617	123,272	364,993	110,532	407,237	20,442
1956	167,911	186,061	121,727	81,226	19,985	23,290	59,605	500,242	27,493	107,715	339,474	107,076	366,114	19,723
1955	168,304	175,097	120,727	74,110	18,532	22,175	57,047	474,037	21,260	103,652	331,117	91,212	332,012	19,360
1954	180,178	173,166	111,362	75,543	19,301	23,482	51,578	457,065	17,215	92,771	317,726	91,408	303,682	17,926
1953	208,609	171,795	110,386	72,132	18,118	19,016	50,467	465,571	16,940	94,077	324,204	97,716	289,425	18,233
1952[8]	209,448	161,553	128,638	71,618	16,432	14,676	60,110	474,180	13,636	89,810	300,475	86,142	290,948	15,487
1951	213,638	149,482	133,896	65,223	15,275	20,916	53,010	495,838	13,141	77,286	271,555	84,454	261,910	13,897
1950	189,721	130,883	140,117	78,509	16,647	18,546	39,273	405,078	10,982	74,115	238,704	68,968	266,821	14,467
1949	188,615	121,716	113,238	76,031	13,515	18,451	39,521	370,908	9,180	73,144	228,334	60,761	255,714	15,539
1948	188,908	110,960	110,031	74,002	16,394	14,886	48,088	336,912	9,884	57,349	213,316	54,400	240,838	14,453
1947	211,156	92,140	77,429	56,621	18,000	17,213	35,160	203,545	7,640	48,116	194,312	50,671	220,649	14,082
1946	164,264	79,751	58,913	40,349	12,348	12,000	31,178	223,339	6,482	37,057	182,641	59,133	208,028	14,691
1945	139,811	73,769	59,991	41,276	11,018	5,709	22,643	231,875	7,757	34,598	157,568	46,863	207,613	11,715
1944	132,607	70,259	62,061	43,380	12,931	6,549	26,939	207,998	10,667	40,738	136,673	30,620	171,002	10,471
1943	112,345	68,904	49,830	40,203	10,678	4,226	15,288	168,593	6,333	36,785	114,759	25,207	155,931	9,666
1942	86,043	63,349	44,031	39,022	8,889	6,057	22,980	144,622	7,001	36,646	120,212	26,660	115,125	7,906
1941	79,270	58,322	60,757	38,233	8,114	7,501	23,331	118,721	4,369	37,155	96,421	18,636	86,653	7,300
1940	66,925	54,805	56,035	29,950	5,044	6,739	16,755	92,730	4,902	30,881	74,116	15,481	70,472	6,276
1939	54,322	51,665	49,016	26,725	4,975	7,769	14,446	81,972	3,162	26,278	59,130	17,918	57,277	5,411
1938	75,420	55,502	40,726	25,193	4,513	4,556	14,481	76,867	2,819	24,115	56,841	20,927	53,225	5,690
1937	80,597	55,253	40,254	24,861	4,822	5,252	17,084	76,961	2,972	20,576	57,438	27,360	52,138	5,857
1936	66,000	47,659	39,449	22,405	4,934	5,319	14,044	67,088	2,654	15,793	43,345	24,009	43,763	5,283
1935	57,169	44,491	35,816	20,420	4,231	4,757	12,058	59,046	2,100	12,782	40,071	18,213	41,526	5,159
1934	57,120	42,826	35,452	20,126	4,448	3,509	10,841	54,477	1,936	10,978	35,501	12,506	38,183	4,558
1933	49,284	39,125	36,794	16,895	4,598	2,895	8,221	43,610	1,472	9,900	30,099	10,399	34,878	4,731
1932	49,373	40,376	40,544	18,448	4,171	3,445	8,296	48,158	1,554	10,496	37,415	12,391	36,074	5,976
1931	56,597	46,930	43,339	23,545	5,357	2,445	10,943	62,330	1,851	12,533	47,965	12,958	42,865	7,247
1930	90,714	55,379	42,150	28,708	5,406	3,520	19,503	84,322	2,184	12,899	56,176	23,258	49,835	10,024
1929	114,553	59,635	46,160	32,514	7,069	3,827	15,224	94,196	2,102	11,827	60,834	41,437	49,259	9,997
1928	124,774	55,305	51,303	31,313	—	3,284	13,780	86,656	1,891	9,730	59,592	36,046	41,706	9,322
1927	125,111	54,386	59,718	29,765	—	2,256	11,635	77,547	2,204	7,676	50,511	23,963	36,282	9,415
1926	131,188	50,767	63,207	27,594	—	3,059	12,663	68,706	1,921	7,205	42,734	10,160	31,456	8,959
1925	131,858	49,268	66,983	27,072	—	—	—	64,354	—	6,714	38,058	8,488	27,869	8,717
1924	121,787	43,770	65,922	26,079	—	—	—	56,610	—	5,974	32,685	9,288	26,456	9,740
1923	102,571	41,319	76,145	27,448	—	—	—	53,561	—	6,240	28,490	3,080	23,964	10,442
1922	112,446	39,165	69,667	25,957	—	—	—	55,206	—	6,316	25,227	2,334	25,989	10,130
1921	136,257	42,662	68,627	27,142	—	—	—	62,672	—	8,906	30,020	2,626	31,114	11,365
1920	157,807	52,194	117,346	33,350	—	—	—	93,896	—	9,046	28,589	4,218	31,625	14,110
1919	185,982	42,948	100,712	33,263	—	—	—	81,455	—	4,537	19,123	4,467	25,457	12,811
1918	189,096	40,159	57,080	21,280	—	—	—	88,204	—	—	14,915	2,782	19,941	11,694
1917	170,382	42,452	60,223	12,977	—	—	—	79,576	—	—	15,426	2,658	12,474	10,148

Series Q 196–252. *Value of output of selected manufactured commodities, 1917 to 1959 (continuation)*
(thousands of dollars)

Year	Smoking tobacco[3]	Chewing tobacco and snuff[3]	Rubber tires	Boots and shoes with leather or fabric uppers (except felt)	Broad-woven cotton fabrics (unbleached or grey)	Broad-woven wool fabrics (all wool—woollen and worsted fabrics only)	Broad-woven synthetic fabrics (including silk)	Women's and misses' dresses (including house dresses)	Men's and youths' suits (excluding uniform suits)	Furniture	Newsprint paper	Book and writing paper	Wrapping paper	Paper bags
	210	211	212	213	214	215	216	217	218	219	220	221	222	223
1959	58,733	2,565	172,466	143,460	48,941	33,778	71,903	90,929	57,212	237,506	730,455	101,928	71,318	62,351
1958	55,771	4,832	153,463	136,073	47,023	27,295	57,122	85,084	58,316	220,237	699,906	91,079	64,650	57,876
1957	51,790	4,675	157,802	130,334	49,910	34,350	58,587	84,211	59,109	220,817	729,009	86,990	60,402	52,641
1956	53,655	4,760	175,569	124,536	56,059	36,920	62,757	80,926	61,768	223,469	735,644	86,524	61,098	52,238
1955	59,999	5,236	164,444	114,135	54,145	39,794	64,079	76,715	57,616	181,589	688,338	74,904	53,999	48,588
1954	62,604	5,471	130,771	112,210	45,379	34,527	58,032	73,781	57,637	166,814	657,487	68,614	51,341	45,274
1953	65,716	5,415	143,232	119,755	53,082	41,279	72,507	75,600	63,997	165,656	633,408	61,451	49,029	49,104
1952[8]	77,789	5,531	143,020	117,420	54,095	49,890	80,644	75,069	55,376	147,158	600,516	57,464	45,357	41,298
1951	65,327	5,485	162,297	109,401	68,796	64,038	92,551	69,497	55,628	138,302	564,361	63,790	49,664	43,166
1950	50,864	5,050	122,402	100,277	60,657	49,901	87,757	67,352	55,587	124,880	506,968	47,356	37,776	30,881
1949	47,313	5,357	86,342	106,656	47,963	51,121	83,805	70,892	53,990	113,441	467,976	40,599	30,033	25,898
1948	46,607	5,293	96,074	96,660	46,421	55,229	69,358	68,399	56,760	100,623	402,100	45,179	31,037	23,607
1947	42,968	5,679	101,730	94,870	36,122	50,550	52,522	57,362	46,489	87,059	355,541	39,727	26,010	19,603
1946	40,912	5,620	64,945	84,543	25,385	43,198	42,980	55,675	35,103	73,726	280,810	29,995	20,797	15,182
1945	39,123	5,602	76,674	75,512	26,637	39,220	38,534	47,578	28,221	51,964	189,024	24,468	17,559	12,268
1944	36,008	5,567	64,210	70,505	29,341	35,253	36,459	43,375	25,542	42,576	165,655	23,700	16,700	11,251
1943	35,536	5,456	59,147	70,298	33,371	40,950	37,051	39,851	23,128	40,528	152,963	19,047	15,614	9,820
1942	31,702	4,565	60,462	62,775	35,307	42,560	39,040	39,849	27,008	46,319	147,074	19,182	17,222	9,141
1941	29,251	3,710	57,336	52,975	30,928	29,150	37,006	32,789	25,093	44,260	158,925	18,476	16,745	7,884
1940	27,984	3,578	37,288	42,383	24,518	22,111	25,434	24,466	20,632	32,346	158,447	15,519	14,457	6,088
1939	24,498	3,334	27,889	38,233	15,647	14,239	21,354	22,215	21,352	24,688	120,859	12,774	10,712	5,276
1938	22,844	3,286	25,596	34,800	12,698	11,829	19,622	22,455	19,783	19,802	107,051	11,099	9,069	4,714
1937	22,608	3,490	31,887	38,120	17,178	15,373	20,865	24,440	22,324	24,616	126,424	12,620	10,238	4,610
1936	20,582	3,516	25,516	33,039	15,842	13,955	21,200	22,620	19,802	20,302	105,215	10,866	8,761	3,840
1935	19,546	3,473	24,101	35,720	13,406	12,752	21,996	21,946	18,169	17,158	88,436	10,441	7,957	3,266
1934	19,814	3,706	23,993	30,309	13,419	12,095	20,856	22,749	16,074	15,123	86,811	9,682	7,741	3,183
1933	20,834	3,779	15,962	30,281	13,496	11,838	16,127	20,069	12,499	13,377	66,960	8,927	6,442	2,685
1932	19,968	3,852	14,099	30,556	9,586	8,423	13,816	13,536	13,536	15,791	85,540	8,688	6,289	2,740
1931	19,951	4,593	22,900	34,905	10,503	7,579	11,949	25,903	16,243	25,377	111,420	10,154	7,480	3,226
1930	20,238	5,211	31,577	38,284	8,672	5,958	11,538	—	22,429	34,779	136,182	12,262	7,880	3,491
1929	18,521	5,582	44,393	45,613	12,073	—	7,309	—	27,075	33,506	150,800	13,637	9,726	—
1928	18,193	5,997	42,053	46,628	14,880	—	4,089	—	26,303	32,085	144,147	14,008	10,424	—
1927	17,463	6,242	42,004	44,579	20,268	—	2,746	—	23,229	27,699	132,287	12,916	9,608	—
1926	16,933	6,002	39,718	43,259	15,985	—	1,961	—	—	—	121,065	14,766	8,552	—
1925	16,547	5,890	34,887	37,511	21,228	—	1,466	—	—	—	106,269	13,145	8,130	—
1924	16,341	6,516	23,966	38,236	—	—	—	—	—	—	100,277	12,606	8,028	—
1923	17,008	6,957	24,600	41,915	—	—	—	—	—	—	93,213	13,582	7,666	—
1922	18,021	7,466	20,367	42,139	—	—	—	—	—	—	75,971	12,561	8,220	—
1921	16,188	7,586	16,067	39,722	—	—	—	—	—	—	78,785	12,551	6,634	—
1920	19,517	9,048	36,489	60,474	—	—	—	—	—	—	80,865	21,869	12,161	—
1919	16,298	8,661	—	58,599	—	—	—	—	—	—	54,428	12,571	7,979	—
1918	12,382	9,783	—	39,003	—	—	—	—	—	—	46,231	10,733	7,341	—
1917	8,200	10,142	—	—	—	—	—	—	—	—	38,868	9,333	5,892	—

Series Q 196–252. *Value of output of selected manufactured commodities, 1917 to 1959 (continuation)*
(thousands of dollars)

Year	Paper boxes	Paper boards	Printed periodicals (gross revenue from advertising)[4]	Pig-iron produced	Hot rolled iron and steel bars produced	Structural steel shapes made in primary mills	Steel rails produced	Steel pipes and tubing	Metal cans	Farm implements and parts produced[5]	Passenger automobiles	Commercial auto vehicles (including buses)	Automobile parts and accessories (except tires and auto fabrics)[6]	Locomotives, steam and diesel
	224	225	226	227	228	229	230	231	232	233	234	235	236	237
1959	221,544	163,152	282,953	229,132	139,735	34,968	31,700	106,004	114,450	151,974	611,318	170,506	360,066	66,824
1958	197,940	152,811	261,023	177,150	103,907	28,087	41,586	117,805	107,270	129,088	582,489	135,491	334,389	75,230
1957	188,921	143,079	249,575	207,372	129,302	43,538	39,979	132,178	97,844	117,896	638,063	149,522	355,121	94,830
1956	180,213	147,967	240,097	189,614	133,769	36,413	33,027	85,570	90,576	117,656	643,286	190,088	390,534	78,220
1955	161,008	130,366	212,474	160,993	95,336	25,833	22,353	57,573	88,559	109,701	605,760	143,070	350,702	59,693
1954	147,624	117,173	194,622	107,456	67,053	20,591	21,422	36,260	77,842	113,089	431,993	121,070	275,927	41,105
1953	143,506	114,978	180,824	151,487	92,779	29,733	26,466	41,943	74,309	159,851	531,848	198,625	382,317	42,259
1952[8]	127,934	106,067	157,049	135,313	106,351	24,084	21,224	56,040	78,991	194,688	409,071	253,074	348,577	38,306
1951	126,067	113,470	140,733	129,661	94,994	24,300	19,911	47,925	73,394	162,349	428,855	212,667	334,222	41,893
1950	105,965	92,532	127,491	100,053	70,350	13,504	21,305	33,405	63,162	141,674	436,850	163,881	272,864	22,285
1949	91,056	80,632	117,853	90,273	61,525	15,331	24,581	30,185	56,592	169,617	271,392	146,697	216,595	38,144
1948	80,474	80,865	100,035	80,310	59,860	12,910	21,887	19,785	53,159	139,079	201,024	137,222	177,560	20,048
1947	70,518	66,126	71,443	60,691	50,165	11,298	13,237	19,930	47,742	83,930	174,213	116,357	162,992	14,431
1946	57,957	50,214	56,277	35,480	37,166	7,697	10,716	15,931	47,348	53,991	79,041	81,204	113,533	25,966
1945	46,268	40,101	47,360	39,488	41,492	10,490	14,230	17,971	36,325	38,701	1,637	167,103	159,284	29,499
1944	42,908	39,092	43,379	40,017	37,479	9,185	15,922	15,819	33,078	26,297	Nil	213,260	210,341	18,916
1943	39,871	37,528	38,974	37,820	52,783	8,528	12,310	15,573	22,557	18,930	Nil	222,393	222,203	10,803
1942	38,770	38,642	35,526	42,581	46,734	10,175	8,216	18,118	34,678	19,638	10,217	229,103	198,018	8,604
1941	37,370	40,215	36,164	31,997	36,347	9,428	5,575	19,737	34,878	22,411	79,306	163,414	131,761	163
1940	28,493	31,079	34,261	27,701	28,656	8,834	7,840	13,217	25,673	18,285	81,316	91,192	74,055	6,616
1939	23,524	21,360	33,480	16,513	17,785	4,499	5,182	7,918	23,277	16,035	66,030	28,073	47,054	17
1938	23,008	19,288	34,353	16,126	15,825	3,479	5,003	6,861	20,578	21,299	76,587	26,497	52,167	5,635
1937	24,217	21,720	34,964	20,494	21,839	4,548	3,423	8,754	20,842	18,961	88,002	30,389	59,949	4,863
1936	20,729	17,531	32,869	13,429	13,571	1,869	4,885	6,448	18,049	15,957	72,108	19,141	43,268	2,367
1935	18,283	15,052	31,471	12,069	12,242	1,883	4,485	6,247	15,133	13,692	73,273	19,804	—	112
1934	16,876	13,351	29,975	7,715	9,246	1,095	3,660	5,233	14,706	8,818	53,930	12,770	—	Nil
1933	14,237	10,598	28,638	4,169	4,646	799	2,900	3,341	11,662	5,326	30,606	6,062	—	Nil
1932	13,853	9,621	32,059	2,829	4,698	744	2,123	4,025	10,134	5,510	31,533	6,071	—	61
1931	14,182	10,226	39,639	7,863	10,865	1,722	—	6,655	11,747	11,175	42,312	10,331	—	1,897
1930	15,066	12,194	44,633	14,308	8,713	1,631	—	10,066	15,367	26,902	73,335	10,212	—	6,773
1929	17,039	13,540	49,047	21,765	12,930	1,563	—	12,803	14,121	40,650	128,496	25,762	—	8,390
1928	16,059	10,656	43,075	20,412	—	—	—	10,593	13,216	41,200	119,022	11,058	—	3,086
1927	13,941	8,986	38,743	14,875	—	—	—	6,577	—	42,996	97,255	13,712	—	4,418
1926	12,341	8,826	34,857	16,532	—	—	—	5,950	—	38,269	101,870	14,247	—	3,316
1925	10,588	8,379	32,244	12,466	—	—	—	—	—	24,770	81,248	12,234	—	342
1924	10,043	8,229	32,335	13,427	—	—	—	—	—	26,447	65,508	8,125	—	5,679
1923	10,166	8,480	28,219	—	—	—	—	—	—	26,026	69,904	8,941	—	7,667
1922	9,051	7,000	28,864	—	—	—	—	—	—	18,240	60,464	5,232	—	1,987
1921	8,079	6,226	29,993	—	—	—	—	—	—	38,948	51,995	3,843	—	4,069
1920	14,442	12,905	30,729	—	—	—	—	—	—	50,301	78,151	8,154	—	1,384
1919	—	8,892	21,364	—	—	—	—	—	—	41,063	58,756	5,120	—	1,800
1918	—	5,551	—	—	—	—	—	—	—	38,305	54,111	5,855	—	7,312
1917	—	3,543	—	—	—	—	—	—	—	36,568	—	—	—	296

Series Q196–252. *Value of output of selected manufactured commodities, 1917 to 1959 (continuation)*

(thousands of dollars)

Year	Railroad cars (freight and passenger)	Stoves and ranges	House-hold mechanical refrigerators	Washing machines	Radios, all types (except combinations)	Electric wire and cable	Telephones and telephone equipment	Clay bricks[5]	Cement[5]	Gasoline[7]	Fuel oil[7]	Coke	Soaps and synthetic detergents	Paints and enamels, ready mixed	Medicinal and pharmaceutical preparations
	238	**239**	**240**	**241**	**242**	**243**	**244**	**245**	**246**	**247**	**248**	**249**	**250**	**251**	**252**
1959	40,370	52,857	44,549	36,565	24,485	150,574	78,116	27,618	95,148	512,300	302,950	65,149	97,931	95,787	154,334
1958	64,126	49,755	39,759	34,418	25,511	136,812	74,102	27,482	94,158	635,420	324,879	52,642	91,062	92,447	139,621
1957	98,666	47,280	42,430	31,011	25,642	153,846	85,408	22,590	93,167	610,611	356,577	63,442	82,947	85,768	126,297
1956	70,981	50,935	47,443	33,481	23,878	186,519	70,725	24,006	75,233	561,464	341,299	65,378	77,098	81,701	110,002
1955	27,822	47,186	49,558	30,525	19,177	150,732	55,447	22,158	65,650	506,622	256,309	58,241	70,633	77,457	100,878
1954	88,395	39,953	44,064	24,942	16,509	122,660	53,854	20,752	59,036	446,869[7]	218,374[7]	50,538	68,312	69,073	90,799
1953	85,879	45,198	50,944	28,062	28,021	123,299	43,975	18,353	58,842	355,808	156,504	64,172	65,333	72,757	87,098
1952[8]	92,259	41,609	46,047	27,547	22,179	121,828	40,229	14,851	48,059	329,532	155,592	58,701	61,057	67,852	81,432
1951	75,429	40,581	54,525	26,446	29,635	123,769	40,255	14,042	40,446	300,360	140,948	59,849	50,991	69,853	82,131
1950	33,214	45,092	66,226	29,162	33,498	90,858	29,721	12,714	35,894	269,252	111,563	56,984	47,757	61,557	69,325
1949	60,685	43,359	36,736	32,501	29,412	85,775	33,154	10,524	32,902	234,153	91,993	53,367	46,021	55,648	64,817
1948	71,208	37,291	25,164	31,254	25,411	85,234	32,256	9,597	28,265	192,763	89,116	54,663	51,783	55,528	55,942
1947	30,838	27,814	18,585	19,108	33,063	78,127	22,157	7,931	21,969	143,342	66,821	39,340	39,772	47,986	55,754
1946	31,832	18,537	8,597	8,247	15,760	39,975	10,746	6,628	20,123	117,837	44,671	32,676	28,203	37,330	54,324
1945	47,571	12,457	355	3,537	979	36,681	6,411	4,566	14,246	110,786	38,904	37,672	29,337	31,750	46,249
1944	35,935	9,460	71	1,679	Nil	32,150	9,782	3,155	11,621	122,793	38,414	37,780	26,963	29,081	43,359
1943	24,706	8,486	33	438	18	35,475	8,915	2,809	11,599	110,044	37,741	31,340	25,289	25,008	39,250
1942	11,001	10,147	4,586	3,718	4,682	34,790	8,436	3,018	14,365	91,958	34,667	27,712	25,632	25,494	33,200
1941	9,751	13,737	7,627	6,457	9,215	34,827	9,634	3,765	13,064	90,281	33,442	24,888	20,609	22,321	28,104
1940	18,525	12,638	6,249	5,841	11,268	26,784	5,981	3,277	11,775	71,336	25,240	21,938	16,827	16,809	21,119
1939	9,746	10,343	6,810	4,986	8,678	15,958	4,717	2,677	8,511	64,491	18,235	16,764	16,405	14,657	19,132
1938	25,593	9,262	6,341	5,059	8,802	14,267	5,830	2,341	8,241	58,649	17,769	16,895	14,715	13,914	17,315
1937	28,827	10,896	5,794	5,956	11,697	15,654	6,260	2,375	9,096	58,568	18,820	18,466	16,149	11,674	17,946
1936	9,530	9,457	5,055	5,601	11,388	10,638	3,022	1,749	6,908	50,587	18,704	16,710	13,538	12,255	16,134
1935	2,018	7,492	2,835	3,849	9,493	9,125	2,552	1,555	5,580	45,183	17,578	15,861	13,446	10,731	15,494
1934	150	6,469	3,502	3,821	8,196	8,467	2,057	1,384	5,668	42,458	17,833	15,862	11,520	9,544	14,413
1933	1,726	4,543	1,896	2,844	4,401	5,908	1,811	1,125	4,537	39,853	15,968	12,466	12,328	7,358	12,891
1932	358	4,525	2,219	3,317	6,809	7,965	4,416	1,779	6,931	45,113	13,050	12,095	12,318	7,267	12,853
1931	19,783	6,879	1,708	6,918	18,556	11,299	7,397	4,289	15,826	50,109	14,040	12,420	14,151	9,686	13,677
1930	34,533	8,884	1,608	9,392	19,197	17,605	11,034	5,582	17,713	60,790	16,429	15,852	15,063	11,771	7,291
1929	53,934	11,603	1,548	10,076	15,604	27,674	8,785	8,003	19,337	63,502	17,895	17,948	15,232	11,440	7,853
1928	11,286	11,007	781	8,311	7,486	19,777	7,162	7,282	16,739	52,229	14,451	14,536	14,034	11,440	7,355
1927	14,640	9,853	227	5,096	3,749	15,598	7,926	6,941	14,392	35,173	13,584	12,964	12,337	10,692	6,990
1926	17,438	—	—	3,371	2,253	12,933	7,509	6,526	13,013	40,468	12,007	13,306	—	—	—
1925	3,415	—	—	3,056	2,278	10,963	7,772	5,944	14,047	27,639	9,652	10,483	—	—	—
1924	15,944	—	—	2,113	—	9,850	6,463	5,723	13,398	—	9,077	10,433	—	—	—
1923	29,967	—	—	1,725	—	12,413	4,648	5,346	15,065	—	7,974	13,932	—	—	—
1922	4,843	—	—	1,222	—	9,040	3,149	6,554	15,438	—	6,143	9,052	—	—	—
1921	23,151	—	—	965	—	6,677	2,270	5,306	14,195	—	6,611	14,111	—	—	—
1920	21,804	—	—	—	—	9,976	2,424	6,841	14,798	—	10,342	15,399	—	—	—
1919	32,984	—	—	—	—	8,536	1,836	5,154	9,802	—	—	12,074	—	—	—
1918	34,933	—	—	—	—	5,155	1,449	2,519	7,077	—	—	9,915	—	—	—
1917	24,823	—	—	—	—	8,506	1,675	2,652	7,724	—	—	—	—	—	—

[1] Includes excise taxes and duties.

[2] Does not include excise taxes and duties.

[3] Figures include excise duties and sales tax for all years, except 1917, 1918 and 1919. For these three years excise duties and sales tax are not included.

[4] Composition of the printing and publishing industry was changed in 1948 by including publishers of periodicals who did no printing.

[5] For years prior to 1917 see supplement to series Q196–252 and Q253–306, p. 486.

[6] Includes batteries.

[7] A change in the method of valuation of the petroleum refining industry products for 1954 and subsequent years resulted in a larger increase compared with 1953 and earlier years, for gross value of production and value added, than would have occurred had the 1953 method been continued. See footnote 2 to series Q123 and Q125.

[8] Beginning in 1952, data are for shipments (see the general note to series Q196–306).

Series Q253–306. *Physical output of selected manufactured commodities, 1917 to 1959*

Year	Wheat flour (thousand cwt)	Bread (million pounds)	Refined sugar (million pounds)	Confectionery (thousand pounds)	Jams, jellies and marmalades (thousand pounds)	Canned fruits (thousand pounds)	Canned vegetables (thousand pounds)	Meats, fresh and frozen (tons)	Poultry, fresh and frozen (tons)	Carbonated beverages (thousand gallons)	Beer, ale, stout and porter (thousand gallons)	Beverage spirits sold (thousand proof gallons)	Cigarettes (millions)	Cigars (thousands)
	253	254	255	256	257	258	259	260	261	262	263	264	265	266
1959	40,897	1,653	1,629	222,167	113,012	147,846	486,185	916,362	34,541	157,463	235,184	16,173	34,273	313,472
1958	41,146	1,650	1,645	213,211	104,085	140,785	477,509	874,316	31,497	147,196	219,848	15,777	32,778	319,595
1957	37,359	1,653	1,533	222,849	102,481	148,851	489,804	831,109	22,344	137,151	224,783	13,830	30,395	283,706
1956	40,053	1,607	1,553	199,089	105,850	141,976	474,924	798,677	28,672	123,192	214,979	13,733	27,344	260,900
1955	40,295	1,530	1,578	150,570	104,987	149,585	489,597	749,604	22,222	118,442	211,102	11,848	24,864	257,233
1954	41,354	1,526	1,441	147,544	107,688	147,596	434,515	700,111	19,397	105,931	200,459	11,946	22,426	240,520
1953[2]	46,196	1,558	1,349	146,528	99,827	122,188	436,717	655,647	16,692	110,175	206,908	12,445	21,156	236,248
1952[2]	46,046	1,524	1,421	145,058	92,531	100,468	508,543	591,113	15,484	103,473	193,830	11,172	18,037	201,517
1951	45,821	1,418	1,310	134,487	84,832	134,322	439,421	514,571	12,207	94,803	177,658	10,801	15,816	169,408
1950	40,331	1,383	1,528	156,393	98,939	125,403	368,227	516,690	12,163	102,709	171,056	9,132	17,311	198,987
1949	39,792	1,350	1,386	157,008	86,344	127,165	401,822	550,407	10,321	101,188	173,294	8,842	17,053	207,213
1948	45,292	1,371	1,358	142,315	105,110	101,288	497,909	553,394	11,514	85,669	169,703	8,259	16,072	210,335
1947	56,093	1,385	1,085	121,449	120,224	127,976	359,727	446,617	10,553	69,413	160,875	8,854	15,687	214,745
1946	53,218	1,376	960	92,922	93,830	108,354	410,371	537,440	9,961	55,729	151,310	11,125	15,264	219,985
1945	49,230	1,292	981	97,412	87,132	56,650	320,363	597,455	12,366	51,335	128,910	9,151	17,685	207,861
1944	47,962	1,249	1,018	113,157	104,707	70,003	393,115	541,482	16,776	64,226	113,396	5,237	15,485	198,512
1943	47,014	1,244	871	105,640	92,613	42,217	226,484	443,716	10,067	58,020	95,691	4,738	13,591	200,370
1942	39,435	1,154	801	113,527	78,477	60,696	331,453	435,195	12,269	58,274	109,018	5,692	11,966	206,486
1941	40,904	1,068	1,227	134,698	75,196	85,432	369,530	427,601	8,424	59,804	90,247	4,994	9,548	196,724
1940	34,136	1,033	1,157	114,500	52,585	102,431	284,638	389,636	9,009	52,938	72,388	4,300	7,831	165,455
1939	30,873	999	1,157	108,309	52,977	116,500	250,422	366,190	7,488	43,956	62,780	5,151	7,163	135,825
1938	26,173	1,010	1,043	102,254	46,171	64,373	287,160	366,697	6,391	39,499	62,468	5,422	6,900	132,715
1937	27,849	963	1,026	102,097	48,081	69,142	324,794	390,621	7,342	31,699	63,467	7,482	6,724	129,873
1936	29,268	909	1,093	96,791	49,791	65,620	253,166	378,030	6,390	27,596	56,917	6,757	5,607	119,827
1935	27,710	904	969	91,100	44,141	58,441	221,215	324,243	5,341	22,432	54,657	4,356	5,325	120,508
1934	29,023	911	889	88,856	44,889	41,179	213,125	326,671	5,964	20,050	46,390	3,414	4,843	116,858
1933	29,845	878	872	87,958	45,943	38,578	159,323	289,035	4,791	16,970	37,910	3,061	4,310	112,030
1932	29,138	890	944	96,701	44,380	44,273	159,054	284,089	4,399	16,150	43,318	3,783	3,885	131,392
1931	29,180	943	998	104,891	53,043	22,298	160,584	290,198	3,774	17,487	52,089	3,504	4,432	155,412
1930	30,624	941	943	122,124	48,633	30,450	234,860	275,385	4,097	13,550	58,384	8,425	5,086	197,398
1929	38,723	936	932	126,013	61,944	31,467	150,947	289,662	3,132	12,249	62,087	15,712	4,967	191,041
1928	39,964	879	928	119,163	—	29,156	147,747	287,875	2,965	10,678	61,766	12,256	4,226	184,284
1927	36,823	786	979	111,091	—	17,083	119,461	291,707	3,410	8,712	54,912	9,025	3,613	171,161
1926	37,350	792	1,139	105,145	—	23,950	130,853	270,291	2,947	7,407	48,943	4,179	3,097	166,770
1925	34,827	760	1,171	103,743	—	—	—	278,757	—	6,878	48,399	3,945	2,705	148,811
1924	41,310	714	872	95,921	—	—	—	254,536	—	6,354	42,989	4,631	2,450	159,875
1923	37,389	670	842	97,769	—	—	—	234,056	—	6,409	39,200	2,029	2,079	174,286
1922	35,388	664	1,148	103,879	—	—	—	225,448	—	6,595	35,607	2,732	2,171	152,958
1921	30,031	619	784	89,486	—	—	—	200,387	—	9,177	41,796	2,680	2,604	163,075
1920	26,771	635	782	101,413	—	—	—	226,530	—	9,355	38,366	3,800	2,936	194,361
1919	34,972	596	1,017	111,755	—	—	—	207,421	—	10,322	34,891	4,803	2,964	200,517
1918	35,047	648	652	70,315	—	—	—	215,231	—	—	28,010	3,702	2,854	203,016
1917	34,667	707	778	43,257	—	—	—	245,635	—	—	26,792	3,535	—	—

Series Q253–306. *Physical output of selected manufactured commodities, 1917 to 1959 (continuation)*

Year	Smoking tobacco (thousand pounds)	Chewing tobacco and snuff (thousand pounds)	Rubber tires (thousands)	Boots and shoes with leather or fabric uppers (except felt) (thousand pairs)	Yarns produced (thousand pounds)	Broad-woven cotton fabrics (unbleached or grey) (thousand lineal yards)	Broad-woven wool fabrics (all wool—woollen and worsted fabrics only) (thousand lineal yards)	Broad-woven synthetic fabrics (including silk) (thousand lineal yards)	Women's and misses' dresses (including house dresses) (thousands)	Men's and youth's suits (excluding uniform suits) (thousands)	Wood pulp (thousand tons)[1]	Newsprint paper (thousand tons)	Book and writing paper (tons)	Wrapping paper (tons)
	267	268	269	270	271	272	273	274	275	276	277	278	279	280
1959	22,134	1,077	9,408	36,790	293,472	194,957	22,014	94,875	12,633	1,676	10,832	6,351	382,000	330,000
1958	21,609	1,892	8,415	36,374	252,338	191,880	16,044	85,243	12,217	1,675	10,137	6,031	344,622	292,727
1957	20,737	1,849	8,321	35,086	287,477	200,079	19,378	84,079	12,194	1,693	10,425	6,362	335,037	277,208
1956	21,588	1,868	8,596	34,390	307,106	214,923	21,862	95,986	11,704	1,891	10,734	6,445	341,580	288,146
1955	24,150	2,145	7,845	31,067	276,084	229,168	25,973	97,512	12,688	1,710	10,151	6,196	301,352	263,915
1954	25,125	2,160	6,596	30,684	238,706	182,362	19,296	83,184	12,725	1,647	9,673	6,001	269,353	250,408
1953	26,659	2,282	6,664	32,265	261,093	195,519	22,905	99,648	12,652	1,827	9,077	5,755	246,513	238,111
1952[2]	31,635	2,315	5,582	31,203	262,667	158,521	20,370	102,702	13,822	1,584	8,968	5,707	224,683	222,529
1951	28,095	2,473	6,050	27,480	313,630	207,079	24,709	117,171	12,684	1,560	9,315	5,561	253,081	257,332
1950	26,795	2,710	6,038	27,361	316,915	224,055	18,071	120,060	12,992	1,682	8,473	5,319	214,097	222,840
1949	26,203	2,987	5,033	29,564	276,293	182,631	20,097	116,034	13,461	1,721	7,853	5,187	199,317	195,585
1948	26,337	3,037	5,606	27,178	277,399	161,485	22,127	99,220	12,252	1,877	7,675	4,640	231,608	207,128
1947	25,404	3,360	6,191	29,400	265,580	152,945	23,768	82,941	10,486	1,752	7,254	4,474	210,762	188,742
1946	25,983	3,559	4,007	34,113	255,036	157,717	23,291	78,946	12,377	1,598	6,615	4,162	189,318	175,369
1945	26,235	3,782	3,490	30,979	251,669	167,070	22,056	82,116	12,005	1,344	5,601	3,324	162,198	162,175
1944	24,263	3,766	2,680	29,278	254,113	182,515	20,062	80,124	12,043	1,268	5,271	3,040	155,498	156,721
1943	24,809	3,869	1,988	28,506	—	189,409	21,339	83,301	12,813	1,192	5,273	3,046	122,174	145,545
1942	25,743	3,831	1,962	27,828	—	230,958	22,174	92,107	14,318	1,433	5,666	3,257	121,419	165,991
1941	26,020	3,348	3,831	26,708	—	239,331	18,135	92,548	12,682	1,429	5,721	3,520	117,444	162,581
1940	26,156	3,430	3,275	21,818	—	204,628	13,804	65,589	11,013	1,201	5,291	3,504	102,696	139,716
1939	24,710	3,415	3,039	21,342	—	171,130	11,655	57,210	10,020	1,306	4,166	2,927	90,135	109,907
1938	22,535	3,403	2,759	19,005	—	139,672	10,258	49,628	10,240	1,309	3,668	2,669	73,834	90,879
1937	22,439	3,636	3,353	20,748	—	166,294	12,554	53,990	10,160	1,433	5,142	3,674	84,168	108,734
1936	20,080	3,676	2,913	18,675	—	150,218	12,044	53,094	10,342	1,318	4,485	3,225	74,940	95,916
1935	19,128	3,670	2,788	19,274	—	132,899	11,443	54,112	7,448	1,281	3,868	2,765	70,350	82,517
1934	19,240	3,907	3,016	17,183	—	135,621	10,313	48,919	8,978	1,107	3,636	2,605	64,991	79,779
1933	19,921	3,819	2,223	17,019	—	145,588	10,604	30,623	8,294	902	2,980	2,022	60,683	67,780
1932	18,607	4,113	1,960	16,029	—	115,398	7,607	23,642	6,987	928	2,663	1,919	56,781	69,018
1931	17,756	4,754	2,896	16,214	—	108,039	5,347	16,478	8,849	988	3,168	2,227	73,572	79,403
1930	17,426	5,296	3,720	15,635	—	81,179	3,674	11,288	—	—	3,619	2,498	90,287	79,720
1929	15,931	5,757	4,766	17,975	—	90,988	—	5,966	—	—	4,021	2,725	70,213	92,014
1928	15,830	6,229	4,579	18,008	—	112,570	—	3,314	—	—	3,608	2,414	65,077	50,791
1927	15,313	6,582	4,076	18,212	—	157,429	—	2,050	—	—	3,279	2,083	60,696	51,269
1926	14,543	6,545	3,251	17,564	—	106,996	—	1,206	—	—	3,230	1,889	—	—
1925	14,675	6,650	3,242	15,332	—	132,125	—	792	—	—	2,773	1,536	—	—
1924	14,097	6,515	2,391	15,222	—	—	—	—	—	—	2,465	1,388	—	—
1923	14,395	6,789	2,425	15,551	—	—	—	—	—	—	2,476	1,251	—	—
1922	14,533	6,977	1,692	15,099	—	—	—	—	—	—	2,150	1,081	—	—
1921	12,528	6,906	963	12,229	—	—	—	—	—	—	1,549	805	—	—
1920	14,205	6,752	1,840	14,566	—	—	—	—	—	—	1,960	876	—	—
1919	14,762	8,028	—	16,635	—	—	—	—	—	—	1,716	795	—	—
1918	11,699	9,334	—	12,379	—	—	—	—	—	—	1,557	735	—	—
1917	—	—	—	—	—	—	—	—	—	—	1,464	690	—	—

Series Q253-306. *Physical output of selected manufactured commodities, 1917 to 1959 (continuation)*

Year	Paper boards (tons)	Pig-iron produced (long tons)[1]	Steel ingots and steel castings produced (short tons)[1]	Hot rolled iron and steel bars produced (short tons)	Structural steel shapes made in primary mills (short tons)	Steel rails produced (short tons)[1]	Steel pipes and tubing (short tons)	Plain steel wire produced (short tons)	Passenger automobiles (number)	Commercial auto vehicles (including buses) (number)	Locomotives steam and diesel (number)	Railroad cars (freight and passenger) (number)	Aluminium produced (short tons)[1]
	281	282	283	284	285	286	287	288	289	290	291	292	293
1959	1,256,000	4,182,775	5,901,487	949,865	268,573	286,989	488,900	360,874	296,943	67,262	380	3,585	593,630
1958	1,188,650	3,059,579	4,359,466	705,073	217,137	365,429	537,900	305,733	293,633	61,299	417	5,313	634,102
1957	1,114,726	3,718,350	5,068,149	865,533	347,693	393,926	612,400	290,881	334,112	71,798	530	10,475	556,715
1956	1,173,087	3,568,203	5,301,202	947,979	316,000	336,662	434,800	366,486	364,387	93,429	488	9,221	620,321
1955	1,027,441	3,215,367	4,534,672	742,494	241,698	228,991	331,300	316,593	361,683	78,345	362	3,736	612,543
1954	940,196	2,211,029	3,195,030	528,521	193,673	241,922	219,500	254,922	274,901	69,681	244	8,287	557,897
1953	948,955	3,012,268	4,116,068	732,275	283,203	303,318	220,800	252,026	344,281	120,312	260	8,464	548,445
1952[2]	874,582	2,681,585	3,703,111	786,972	231,091	253,675	258,700	286,761	269,017	150,094	226	11,954	499,758
1951	960,493	2,552,893	3,568,720	763,005	250,362	257,244	239,100	294,373	267,768	132,645	267	10,613	447,095
1950	876,894	2,317,121	3,383,575	684,934	153,144	286,672	233,100	262,966	268,720	105,997	146	4,762	396,882
1949	797,023	2,154,485	3,190,377	662,488	191,018	329,749	197,400	251,553	183,999	99,028	319	10,798	369,466
1948	817,432	2,125,739	3,200,480	634,315	175,031	337,244	138,900	246,461	150,671	96,931	176	11,524	367,079
1947	744,377	1,962,848	2,945,952	609,763	180,226	250,049	141,400	238,301	153,334	90,758	125	5,765	299,066
1946	683,643	1,406,252	2,327,285	492,853	131,894	206,374	120,900	184,392	83,709	79,657	271	10,092	194,117
1945	595,131	1,777,949	2,877,927	574,446	191,907	291,651	160,200	214,475	1,866	130,777	378	13,480	215,712
1944	588,348	1,852,628	3,016,162	534,196	155,908	325,486	138,200	200,203	Nil	158,038	190	9,251	462,065
1943	568,101	1,758,269	3,004,124	598,113	146,965	263,920	132,600	191,210	Nil	178,064	99	6,248	495,749
1942	609,175	1,975,014	3,109,851	592,016	184,701	183,430	153,800	202,116	11,966	216,057	71	1,501	340,596
1941	649,840	1,528,053	2,712,151	542,575	189,783	137,298	175,200	220,285	91,331	173,588	3	2,711	213,873
1940	500,094	1,309,099	2,253,769	453,788	183,728	199,998	143,000	222,727	102,664	113,102	55	5,328	109,144
1939	413,687	755,731	1,551,054	314,050	90,810	123,023	90,000	176,262	90,148	47,057	1	2,423	82,840
1938	356,891	705,427	1,293,812	277,783	65,633	126,479	73,500	144,513	105,392	42,325	49	5,385	71,204
1937	422,710	808,855	1,571,227	388,662	93,279	86,932	99,100	171,230	132,835	54,417	46	7,504	46,906
1936	363,778	678,231	1,249,672	283,146	41,537	130,135	79,300	151,106	108,340	33,790	23	2,116	29,640
1935	314,849	599,875	1,054,509	243,574	42,529	122,302	70,100	146,434	111,782	37,315	4	550	23,171
1934	280,724	404,995	848,716	185,212	25,838	108,292	59,700	117,708	80,118	24,205	0	31	17,433
1933	232,190	227,317	459,176	94,088	18,091	75,975	37,700	87,225	47,510	12,003	0	589	17,766
1932	209,938	144,130	380,067	100,662	16,005	50,501	45,300	86,931	48,332	10,095	3	282	19,793
1931	202,854	420,038	752,762	234,978	37,931	156,962	71,200	110,866	64,629	17,487	26	5,288	34,052
1930	233,217	747,178	1,130,808	184,286	35,997	261,444	110,800	148,505	115,535	16,742	108	8,348	38,109
1929	250,061	1,080,160	1,543,427	273,944	35,060	428,962	140,100	155,680	188,721	50,293	98	13,242	31,715
1928	193,061	1,037,727	1,382,976	302,923	—	391,092	118,000	148,815	176,096	17,527	48	3,058	41,399
1927	161,497	709,697	1,016,898	220,866	—	263,965	79,300	118,784	137,290	29,603	57	5,005	41,368
1926	155,469	757,317	869,413	218,344	—	186,838	72,300	123,542	154,061	30,440	57	3,335	19,455
1925	144,646	570,766	842,803	244,029	—	216,695	—	94,018	120,205	26,397	8	1,435	15,553
1924	135,252	593,049	738,939	191,055	—	224,795	—	84,731	98,365	18,043	84	4,544	13,622
1923	130,582	879,822	987,306	239,468	—	231,684	—	123,148	106,226	19,226	138	7,856	12,128
1922	113,200	382,692	537,742	152,768	—	140,970	—	136,900	79,094	8,169	46	847	6,439
1921	89,120	593,829	747,582	134,079	—	298,110	—	72,722	57,401	5,148	81	6,099	3,168
1920	158,041	973,568	1,232,717	386,740	—	255,323	—	107,129	79,369	10,174	21	5,084	11,192
1919	137,678	819,447	1,030,342	—	—	316,305	—	—	68,408	7,899	—	—	10,791
1918	87,749	1,067,456	1,873,749	—	—	162,746	—	—	69,801	7,319	—	—	11,768
1917	54,080	1,045,071	1,745,744	—	—	46,311	—	—	—	—	—	—	11,044

Series Q253–306. *Physical output of selected manufactured commodities, 1917 to 1959 (continuation)*

Year	Stoves and ranges (number)	Household mechanical refrigerators (number)	Washing machines (number)	Radios, all types (except combinations) (number)	Clay bricks (thousands)[1]	Cement (thousand barrels)[1]	Gasoline (thousand gallons)	Fuel oil (thousand gallons)	Coke (short tons)	Soaps and synthetic detergents (short tons)	Paints and enamels, ready mixed (thousand gallons)	Sulphuric acid produced (short tons of 100% acid)	Fertiliser sold for consumption in Canada (short tons)
	294	295	296	297	298	299	300	301	302	303	304	305	306
1959	537,011	256,778	326,883	713,309	551,114	35,910	3,436,195	3,259,658	4,089,833	174,528	21,987	1,739,000	908,214
1958	499,103	226,523	300,068	745,318	547,673	35,161	3,215,554	2,923,172	3,483,105	167,500	21,270	1,586,000	870,539
1957	484,719	235,539	276,747	732,827	473,728	34,565	3,061,716	3,004,082	4,119,200	159,329	20,585	1,290,000	808,251
1956	522,151	269,213	305,922	740,656	510,101	28,694	3,063,284	3,062,815	4,331,216	154,866	20,134	1,052,000	800,680
1955	482,375	271,582	279,802	621,957	489,240	25,168	2,761,318	2,406,707	4,004,624	147,448	19,809	950,277	790,774
1954	391,428	230,092	226,238	487,620	467,738	22,437	2,438,654	2,097,550	3,424,218	143,515	17,301	923,800	811,641
1953[2]	437,945	275,415	247,824	737,457	426,446	22,238	2,260,426	1,848,142	4,252,833	148,156	18,070	822,608	819,803
1952[2]	457,017	244,433	253,538	567,738	369,605	18,521	2,063,057	1,672,155	4,056,655	141,417	16,856	816,270	768,545
1951	525,061	277,836	236,730	628,395	379,434	17,008	1,845,847	1,505,830	3,931,626	133,576	17,423	820,867	770,507
1950	533,682	341,596	301,110	820,772	375,247	16,742	1,600,096	1,300,224	3,964,676	141,824	16,212	756,110	764,581
1949	643,786	346,254	334,473	791,051	330,867	15,917	1,440,467	1,126,485	3,864,603	125,929	14,735	707,717	741,726
1948	610,624	138,714	334,473	639,493	320,693	14,127	1,219,291	998,918	3,945,776	137,671	15,114	679,448	672,171
1947	600,331	108,106	220,039	984,276	295,446	11,936	1,074,550	916,016	3,514,151	122,646	14,455	668,802	660,721
1946	438,291	56,786	115,190	603,199	272,389	11,560	1,017,621	835,135	3,363,109	117,332	13,500	593,577	632,943
1945	443,484	2,418	59,908	50,317	200,241	8,472	953,017	771,188	3,912,320	136,646	12,593	664,302	575,107
1944	331,582	237	33,858	Nil	154,785	7,191	970,941	780,685	4,017,696	120,548	11,929	639,884	535,108
1943	287,274	358	13,200	979	138,678	7,302	869,288	752,304	3,551,773	118,512	10,086	522,607	489,861
1942	346,100	37,792	67,251	177,149	169,317	9,126	749,365	755,964	3,205,549	116,921	10,490	464,503	419,547
1941	408,470	64,093	128,262	386,372	208,871	8,369	857,924	732,494	3,145,715	112,087	9,105	334,566	324,201
1940	379,362	53,165	117,511	485,010	191,213	7,560	780,819	516,006	3,015,394	102,394	6,912	301,444	346,721
1939	329,635	57,460	103,882	348,507	165,024	5,731	740,564	510,467	2,410,095	100,815	6,112	237,927	334,003
1938	276,789	52,934	105,850	242,721	148,807	5,519	654,029	475,669	2,352,003	88,009	5,914	250,065	323,376
1937	330,262	52,068	133,475	289,247	153,770	6,169	640,300	484,592	2,570,335	94,518	5,126	263,463	298,276
1936	302,475	40,688	102,638	253,896	115,732	4,509	567,659	498,318	2,404,793	91,294	5,150	224,658	233,840
1935	217,982	22,452	84,676	191,293	100,538	3,648	513,717	469,968	2,257,604	90,674	4,461	209,128	212,479
1934	184,232	27,897	84,079	188,710	86,072	3,783	461,753	455,995	2,243,420	91,872	3,885	191,342	194,851
1933	127,351	15,059	58,931	112,272	67,700	3,007	422,937	430,314	1,772,164	83,132	3,032	138,054	166,407
1932	120,998	19,454	58,486	121,468	100,477	4,499	399,937	366,278	1,637,701	87,200	2,907	127,527	179,983
1931	176,062	9,879	76,693	291,711	237,143	10,162	469,925	428,753	1,832,700	85,049	3,889	111,401	284,217
1930	239,035	6,302	86,058	170,082	319,838	11,033	445,599	434,564	2,385,994	82,211	4,474	100,020	321,207
1929	309,184	4,252	100,224	150,050	458,630	12,284	436,621	448,700	2,677,581	79,192	5,490	103,207	323,750
1928	319,571	3,158	86,397	81,032	421,301	11,024	344,130	361,392	2,314,127	72,464	4,761	89,721	—
1927	278,183	1,590	62,136	47,500	398,439	10,066	258,550	286,526	2,026,438	69,390	4,252	91,764	169,564
1926	—	—	51,109	42,430	358,348	8,707	222,147	228,474	2,027,058	—	—	100,860	—
1925	—	—	48,060	48,531	351,186	8,117	164,850	172,387	1,546,739	—	—	77,700	—
1924	—	—	36,925	—	317,473	7,499	160,046	177,123	1,436,912	—	—	67,088	—
1923	—	—	28,937	—	323,965	7,544	124,156	139,683	1,668,298	—	—	81,215	—
1922	—	—	28,758	—	385,497	6,944	143,960	106,976	1,232,646	—	—	57,148	—
1921	—	—	24,892	—	301,385	5,753	119,888	129,716	1,463,999	—	—	43,981	—
1920	—	—	—	—	388,480	6,652	86,194	96,463	1,708,203	—	—	67,901	—
1919	—	—	—	—	365,894	4,995	—	—	1,675,032	—	—	45,485	—
1918	—	—	—	—	205,117	3,591	72,170	—	1,250,744	—	—	—	—
1917	—	—	—	—	257,040	4,768	—	—	1,245,862	—	—	—	—

[1] For years prior to 1917 see supplement to series Q196–252 and Q253–306, page 486.

[2] Data for 1952 to 1959 are for shipments (see the general note to series Q196–306).

Supplement to series Q 196–252 and Q 253–306. *Value and output of selected manufactured commodities, 1870 to 1916*

Year	Farm implements and parts produced (thousand dollars)	Clay bricks (thousand dollars)	Cement (thousand dollars)	Wood pulp (thousand tons)	Pig-iron produced (long tons)	Steel ingots and steel castings produced (short tons)	Steel rails produced (short tons)	Aluminium produced (short tons)	Clay bricks (thousands)	Cement (thousand barrels)
	233	245	246	277	282	283	286	293	298	299
1916	—	2,319	6,548	1,296	1,043,979	1,428,269	91,277	10,592	281,982	5,370
1915	14,596	2,248	6,977	1,075	815,871	1,020,784	234,922	9,184	284,550	5,681
1914	—	4,769	9,188	935	699,254	828,641	428,225	7,275	551,149	7,172
1913	—	7,376	11,019	855	1,008,006	1,169,034	567,514	7,033	785,229	8,659
1912	—	8,620	9,107	683	905,881	957,680	474,751	6,015	894,372	7,133
1911	—	6,515	7,645	497	819,228	882,396	403,813	4,840	732,902	5,693
1910	22,976	5,913	6,412	475	714,997	822,284	410,441	4,824	695,610	4,754
1909	—	4,843	5,346	445	676,037	754,719	386,210	3,042	596,494	4,068
1908	—	3,129	3,710	363	563,245	588,763	300,935	486	406,742	2,666
1907	—	4,250	3,781	—	582,110	706,982	348,836	2,961	517,938	2,442
1906	—	4,103	3,171	—	534,295	639,407	350,422	2,348	523,390	2,128
1905	13,668	3,934	1,924	—	469,023	451,863	200,351	1,295	523,820	1,361
1904	—	2,893	1,338	—	270,941	166,380	40,562	1,151	—	967
1903	—	2,832	1,225	—	265,969	203,296	1,392	875	—	720
1902	—	2,593	1,128	—	319,555	203,880	38,024	992	—	723
1901	—	2,400	660	—	244,979	29,214	998	142	—	450
1900	10,330	2,275	663	—	86,228	26,406	784	—	—	418
1899	—	2,195	633	—	91,913	24,640	935	—	—	397
1898	—	1,900	398	—	68,763	24,125	672	—	—	250
1897	—	1,600	275	—	51,792	20,608	560	—	—	205
1896	—	1,600	202	—	60,061	17,920	672	—	—	149
1895	—	1,670	174	—	37,905	19,040	—	—	—	128
1894	—	1,800	145	—	44,613	28,767	—	—	—	108
1893	—	1,800	194	—	49,953	—	—	—	—	159
1892	—	1,252	148	—	37,895	—	—	—	—	117
1891	—	1,062	109	—	21,331	—	—	—	—	93
1890	8,095	1,267	92	—	19,439	—	—	—	—	102
1889	—	1,274	70	—	23,144	—	—	—	—	90
1888	—	1,037	36	—	19,463	—	—	—	—	51
1887	—	987	82	—	22,167	—	—	—	—	70
1886	—	874	—	—	—	—	—	—	—	—
1880	4,783	—	—	—	—	—	—	—	—	—
1870	2,877	—	—	—	—	—	—	—	—	—

Series Q307–349. *New gross fixed capital investment in manufacturing, 1926 to 1960*
(millions of dollars)

Year	All manufacturing			Food and beverages			Rubber, leather, and tobacco and their products			Primary textiles and their products		
	Total new investment	New construction	New machinery and equipment	Total new investment	New construction	New machinery and equipment	Total new investment	New construction	New machinery and equipment	Total new investment	New construction	New machinery and equipment
	307	308	309	310	311	312	313	314	315	316	317	318
1960	1,200.7	354.6	846.1	150.4	52.2	98.2	34.7	9.8	24.9	27.1	6.0	21.1
1959	1,143.8	373.9	769.9	132.8	45.4	87.4	24.4	7.6	16.8	22.8	4.7	18.1
1958	1,095.0	397.6	697.4	126.2	40.5	85.7	22.4	6.6	15.8	23.3	2.6	20.7
1957	1,478.9	519.9	959.0	117.1	36.3	80.8	29.7	9.3	20.4	39.3	7.9	31.4
1956	1,393.8	487.7	906.1	109.1	32.6	76.5	26.4	8.2	18.2	38.3	10.3	28.0
1955	946.5	344.7	601.8	103.7	38.5	65.2	21.8	5.1	16.7	28.0	7.6	20.4
1954	822.1	287.6	534.5	104.3	38.6	65.7	21.1	5.7	15.4	28.5	7.5	21.0
1953	969.0	324.7	644.3	85.0	26.0	59.0	21.5	6.0	15.5	27.9	7.9	20.0
1952	972.6	343.6	629.0	77.3	26.6	50.7	14.6	3.8	10.8	31.5	7.0	24.5
1951	793.0	267.8	525.2	79.1	28.0	51.1	12.9	3.4	9.5	39.1	9.9	29.2
1950	502.5	135.4	367.1	75.2	26.0	49.2	9.8	2.3	7.5	27.4	6.6	20.8
1949	535.8	156.6	379.2	78.7	27.7	51.0	11.1	2.6	8.5	32.1	7.0	25.1
1948	573.0	180.8	392.2	88.4	31.9	56.5	12.1	3.5	8.6	35.6	6.5	29.1
1947	528.0	184.8	343.2	82.8	33.0	49.8	16.5	4.6	11.9	36.6	10.9	25.7
1946	337.2	132.2	205.0	53.1	24.7	28.4	12.8	6.7	6.1	24.6	8.4	16.2
1945	280.1	75.9	204.2	34.4	18.2	16.2	10.3	5.9	4.4	9.0	1.3	7.7
1944	211.4	61.3	150.1	22.1	10.7	11.4	5.0	2.3	2.7	6.7	1.8	4.9
1943	244.3[1]	84.6	159.7	14.1	6.1	8.0	3.9	2.2	1.7	2.6	.8	1.8
1942	386.5[1]	137.3	249.2	19.4	8.5	10.9	4.2	2.4	1.8	6.4	1.5	4.9
1941	347.5[1]	95.2	252.3	23.7	9.7	14.0	5.1	2.4	2.7	11.7	3.1	8.6
1940	247.1[1]	66.7	180.4	23.1	10.7	12.4	5.0	2.7	2.3	13.6	3.4	10.2
1939	98.4	33.4	65.0	18.5	7.5	11.0	3.1	1.1	2.0	5.6	.6	5.0
1938	115.2	44.8	70.4	19.6	7.8	11.8	3.3	.8	2.5	6.4	1.4	5.0
1937	140.4	64.1	76.3	19.0	8.5	10.5	4.2	1.8	2.4	8.8	2.6	6.2
1936	83.0	37.6	45.4	10.8	5.3	5.5	21.7	16.4	5.3	6.6	1.3	5.3
1935	66.6	21.1	45.5	8.9	3.5	5.4	2.0	.1	1.9	9.9	2.8	7.1
1934	49.9	19.5	30.4	5.3	1.6	3.7	1.9	.4	1.5	5.4	.6	4.8
1933	42.0	18.1	23.9	2.8	.8	2.0	4.4	2.9	1.5	4.5	.9	3.6
1932	47.2	19.3	27.9	8.0	4.9	3.1	1.5	.4	1.1	3.7	1.0	2.7
1931	95.3	40.9	54.4	12.6	7.2	5.4	2.2	.9	1.3	12.3	1.7	10.6
1930	163.0	75.5	87.5	17.4	7.4	10.0	4.3	2.1	2.2	9.9	6.8	3.1
1929	224.5	131.0	93.5	26.6	13.5	13.1	6.1	2.5	3.6	6.0	1.4	4.6
1928	214.5	121.7	92.8	19.3	9.6	9.7	5.8	2.9	2.9	8.5	.6	7.9
1927	179.0	86.9	92.1	13.4	4.4	9.0	4.5	1.1	3.4	13.5	6.2	7.3
1926	129.3	55.7	73.6	10.8	2.7	8.1	2.2	.8	1.4	7.2	4.7	2.5

Year	Clothing			Wood and its products			Pulp and paper and their products			Printing, publishing and allied products		
	Total new investment	New construction	New machinery and equipment	Total new investment	New construction	New machinery and equipment	Total new investment	New construction	New machinery and equipment	Total new investment	New construction	New machinery and equipment
	319	320	321	322	323	324	325	326	327	328	329	330
1960	12.2	2.3	9.9	49.5	16.1	33.4	164.3	34.1	130.2	29.2	7.4	21.8
1959	12.5	1.6	10.9	50.7	15.3	35.4	126.6	24.2	102.4	40.2	11.8	28.4
1958	8.2	.7	7.5	30.9	8.8	22.1	127.2	25.5	101.7	33.5	13.4	20.1
1957	10.8	1.2	9.6	39.0	10.3	28.7	266.3	66.3	200.0	40.1	17.3	22.8
1956	9.7	1.3	8.4	50.8	14.0	36.8	257.4	85.1	172.3	25.5	5.3	20.2
1955	9.2	1.4	7.8	43.0	12.1	30.9	138.9	33.1	105.8	24.1	6.4	17.7
1954	9.8	2.2	7.6	32.9	8.4	24.5	87.3	21.6	65.7	31.4	11.7	19.7
1953	14.4	3.8	10.6	34.6	10.4	24.2	104.1	22.5	81.6	16.4	3.8	12.6
1952	12.7	1.6	11.1	31.8	9.3	22.5	129.5	33.6	95.9	14.3	3.3	11.0
1951	13.2	4.1	9.1	38.6	11.2	27.4	125.3	41.9	83.4	24.3	6.3	18.0
1950	11.9	2.5	9.4	29.4	8.1	21.3	78.5	21.1	57.4	19.4	5.0	14.4
1949	13.7	3.0	10.7	26.7	7.5	19.2	81.5	26.8	54.7	20.1	6.3	13.8
1948	12.3	2.1	10.2	26.4	7.9	18.5	89.5	29.1	60.4	19.4	7.0	12.4
1947	14.0	3.7	10.3	32.1	11.4	20.7	81.0	31.2	49.8	13.8	5.4	8.4
1946	8.4	2.6	5.8	20.4	10.9	9.5	55.0	27.2	27.8	7.3	2.9	4.4
1945	13.6	9.2	4.4	5.2	1.6	3.6	16.6	5.8	10.8	6.0	3.9	2.1
1944	3.9	2.8	1.1	5.3	2.9	2.4	14.7	8.0	6.7	2.4	.2	2.2
1943	2.8	1.6	1.2	20.4	16.8	3.6	6.8	1.7	5.1	1.4	.2	1.2
1942	4.1	3.0	1.1	15.4	11.3	4.1	13.4	3.8	9.6	2.3	.3	2.0
1941	13.0	10.9	2.1	17.1	10.8	6.3	14.4	8.8	5.6	2.6	—	2.6
1940	4.1	2.4	1.7	11.1	8.0	3.1	14.9	5.1	9.8	4.8	.6	4.2
1939	3.3	1.4	1.9	6.7	4.9	1.8	6.1	3.9	2.2	6.0	.3	5.7
1938	1.4	.4	1.0	3.8	1.2	2.6	7.2	2.6	4.6	3.8	.6	3.2
1937	3.4	1.8	1.6	17.7	14.1	3.6	10.6	4.2	6.4	3.9	1.2	2.7
1936	1.9	.8	1.1	4.3	2.8	1.5	5.1	1.5	3.6	1.7	—	1.7
1935	.8	.1	.7	3.2	1.0	2.2	4.6	2.2	2.4	6.1	.6	5.5
1934	1.2	.4	.8	5.6	4.4	1.2	3.5	.8	2.7	.9	—	.9
1933	1.7	1.1	.6	8.5	7.0	1.5	.8	.1	.7	1.2	.3	.9
1932	1.8	1.3	.5	5.9	4.4	1.5	3.3	2.1	1.2	2.8	.7	2.1
1931	2.2	1.6	.6	3.2	1.0	2.2	13.2	11.3	1.9	3.1	.3	2.8
1930	1.8	.8	1.0	10.1	5.9	4.2	25.2	4.4	20.8	4.7	.2	4.5
1929	15.5	13.3	2.2	13.0	10.2	2.8	25.6	16.0	9.6	15.7	7.5	8.2
1928	12.3	10.8	1.5	11.1	7.4	3.7	49.0	31.8	17.2	16.2	9.4	6.8
1927	9.2	7.5	1.7	27.7	21.5	6.2	47.4	23.7	23.7	3.8	.5	3.3
1926	3.5	2.0	1.5	7.7	3.3	4.4	43.9	21.4	22.5	4.9	.8	4.1

Series Q 307–349. *New gross fixed capital investment in manufacturing, 1926 to 1960 (continuation)*
(millions of dollars)

Year	Iron and steel and their products			Transportation equipment			Non-ferrous metals and products including electrical apparatus and supplies			Non-metallic minerals and products including products of petroleum and coal		
	Total new investment	New construction	New machinery and equipment	Total new investment	New construction	New machinery and equipment	Total new investment	New construction	New machinery and equipment	Total new investment	New construction	New machinery and equipment
	331	332	333	334	335	336	337	338	339	340	341	342
1960	196.8	47.2	149.6	48.7	16.4	32.3	101.1	32.5	68.6	130.9	88.0	42.9
1959	165.7	40.9	124.8	65.7	20.5	45.2	90.7	36.3	54.4	195.4	135.1	60.3
1958	126.4	35.7	90.7	54.3	16.6	37.7	125.0	51.0	74.0	183.6	150.4	33.2
1957	179.6	54.5	125.1	62.4	18.1	44.3	188.7	105.0	83.7	208.6	142.8	65.8
1956	162.5	40.3	122.2	60.3	16.7	43.6	158.9	77.1	81.8	213.0	135.3	77.7
1955	95.2	27.0	68.2	54.3	20.2	34.1	112.2	45.4	66.8	156.7	122.6	34.1
1954	88.4	22.0	66.4	65.2	20.9	44.3	85.3	32.0	53.3	136.8	99.2	37.6
1953	114.0	35.6	78.4	97.3	46.9	50.4	115.3	53.4	61.9	113.9	72.7	41.2
1952	135.9	46.2	89.7	62.1	37.1	25.0	111.1	56.9	54.2	111.8	52.3	59.5
1951	97.2	47.1	50.1	48.9	21.8	27.1	80.3	38.7	41.6	89.4	33.2	56.2
1950	44.2	13.5	30.7	27.3	9.9	17.4	36.1	12.0	24.1	49.2	18.7	30.5
1949	52.3	14.6	37.7	22.0	6.7	15.3	45.5	15.2	30.3	47.5	25.0	22.5
1948	56.3	19.6	36.7	15.4	5.4	10.0	36.4	9.7	26.7	70.8	40.4	30.4
1947	54.9	16.0	38.9	14.1	5.2	8.9	31.1	12.0	19.1	55.7	34.7	21.0
1946	36.9	14.9	22.0	15.7	5.4	10.3	19.3	5.3	14.0	17.5	8.7	8.8
1945	31.3	12.8	18.5	10.8	2.2	8.6	10.7	1.5	9.2	12.2	7.8	4.4
1944	32.3	10.1	22.2	6.3	1.6	4.7	21.0	14.7	6.3	6.0	3.5	2.5
1943	28.3	4.3	24.0	20.1	6.6	13.5	42.7	36.2	6.5	7.1	3.7	3.4
1942	44.7	7.2	37.5	45.5	27.9	17.6	76.0	59.2	16.8	7.1	3.9	3.2
1941	41.9	9.9	32.0	11.9	3.0	8.9	46.6	26.0	20.6	8.5	5.3	3.2
1940	20.0	4.9	15.1	11.4	3.4	8.0	24.3	15.7	8.6	9.1	6.4	2.7
1939	9.4	4.3	5.1	7.4	2.9	4.5	7.6	.4	7.2	6.7	4.4	2.3
1938	10.2	5.0	5.2	20.8	14.5	6.3	9.1	1.3	7.8	7.3	5.3	2.0
1937	18.3	10.0	8.3	10.4	5.2	5.2	10.1	.8	9.3	8.8	7.0	1.8
1936	5.9	3.1	2.8	3.3	.9	2.4	3.6	.7	2.9	4.9	3.6	1.3
1935	5.0	2.4	2.6	5.2	2.4	2.8	2.6	.8	1.8	5.0	3.6	1.4
1934	4.9	2.5	2.4	3.4	2.1	1.3	2.1	.6	1.5	4.8	3.3	1.5
1933	1.8	.6	1.2	2.2	.6	1.6	1.4	.4	1.0	3.3	2.0	1.3
1932	2.1	.5	1.6	2.3	.2	2.1	3.8	.6	3.2	3.8	2.1	1.7
1931	9.7	4.7	5.0	2.8	.3	2.5	5.7	1.0	4.7	11.7	8.2	3.5
1930	17.5	12.5	5.0	5.1	1.8	3.3	9.3	1.8	7.5	30.9	27.2	3.7
1929	18.1	8.3	9.8	13.9	8.3	5.6	8.4	3.5	4.9	36.7	32.7	4.0
1928	12.1	4.8	7.3	13.2	7.0	6.2	5.5	1.5	4.0	35.2	32.0	3.2
1927	9.5	5.0	4.5	7.6	4.8	2.8	5.8	1.9	3.9	9.2	6.0	3.2
1926	8.4	4.3	4.1	1.9	.8	1.1	7.4	2.6	4.8	8.7	6.7	2.0

Year	Chemicals and their products			Miscellaneous manufacturing			Capital items charged to operating expenses
	Total new investment	New construction	New machinery and equipment	Total new investment	New construction	New machinery and equipment	New machinery and equipment
	343	344	345	346	347	348	349
1960	110.3	36.2	74.1	18.6	6.4	12.2	126.9
1959	81.0	24.5	56.5	16.5	6.0	10.5	118.8
1958	116.6	43.1	73.5	12.0	2.7	9.3	105.4
1957	149.7	65.6	84.1	15.1	6.6	8.5	132.5
1956	144.9	57.9	87.0	12.3	3.6	8.7	124.7
1955	56.3	21.6	34.7	10.8	3.7	7.1	92.3
1954	39.8	15.1	24.7	7.2	2.7	4.5	84.1
1953	122.3	32.0	90.3	8.7	3.6	5.0	93.6
1952	141.0	61.2	79.8	8.8	4.7	4.1	90.2
1951	57.7	19.2	38.5	7.4	3.0	4.4	79.6
1950	26.3	7.3	19.0	6.0	2.4	3.6	61.8
1949	37.8	11.9	25.9	5.9	2.3	3.6	60.9
1948	41.9	15.0	26.9	6.5	2.7	3.8	62.0
1947	33.7	14.4	19.3	5.7	2.3	3.4	56.0
1946	19.6	11.6	8.0	5.6	2.9	2.7	41.0
1945	7.6	4.0	3.6	3.3	1.7	1.6	109.1
1944	3.0	1.4	1.6	2.5	1.3	1.2	80.2
1943	5.6	2.5	3.1	3.1	1.9	1.2	85.4
1942	10.0	5.3	4.7	4.9	3.0	1.9	133.1
1941	12.1	3.2	8.9	4.0	2.1	1.9	134.9
1940	6.4	1.9	4.5	2.9	1.5	1.4	96.4
1939	3.4	1.0	2.4	1.6	.7	.9	13.0
1938	6.3	2.9	3.4	1.9	1.0	.9	14.1
1937	7.5	5.5	2.0	2.4	1.4	1.0	15.3
1936	2.7	.4	2.3	1.4	.8	.6	9.1
1935	3.1	1.1	2.0	1.1	.5	.6	9.1
1934	4.0	2.4	1.6	.8	.4	.4	6.1
1933	3.9	1.0	2.9	.7	.4	.3	4.8
1932	1.8	.7	1.1	.8	.4	.4	5.6
1931	4.1	1.8	2.3	1.6	.9	.7	10.9
1930	6.4	2.9	3.5	2.9	1.7	1.2	17.5
1929	16.1	10.9	5.2	4.1	2.9	1.2	18.7
1928	3.8	1.2	2.6	3.9	2.7	1.2	18.6
1927	5.9	2.4	3.5	3.1	1.9	1.2	18.4
1926	5.8	4.4	1.4	2.2	1.2	1.0	14.7

1 Excluding outlay by the United Kingdom government for wartime plant expansion, amounting to $28 million in 1940, $61 million in 1941, $84 million in 1942 and $28 million in 1943.

Series Q350–361. *Number of establishments and gross value of production by size of establishment measured by gross value of production, selected years, 1900 to 1959*

(establishments in thousands; total value of production in thousands of dollars)

Year	Under $25,000		$25,000 to $199,999		$200,000 to $499,999		$500,000 to $999,999		$1,000,000 and over		Total number of establishments	Total production
	Establishments	Total value of production	Establishments	Total value of production	Establishments	Total value of production	Establishments	Total value of production	Establishments	Total value of production		
	350	351	352	353	354	355	356	357	358	359	360	361
1959[1]	12.0	118,492	14.1	1,150,005	4.5	1,424,683	2.3	1,645,987	3.4	18,972,435	36.2	23,311,601
1958[1]	12.5	124,234	14.4	1,163,412	4.4	1,393,009	2.2	1,570,427	3.2	17,912,104	36.7	22,163,186
1957[1]	13.8	132,484	14.5	1,168,597	4.3	1,375,175	2.2	1,555,091	3.1	17,952,247	37.9	22,183,594
1955[1]	15.3	143,481	14.2	1,136,774	4.0	1,261,917	2.0	1,411,585	2.7	15,560,177	38.2	19,513,934
1950	16.1	145,592	12.9	1,007,383	3.3	1,029,829	1.6	1,112,819	2.0	10,521,903	35.9	13,817,526
1945	13.7	128,803	10.6	795,194	2.4	742,817	1.0	709,213	1.4	5,874,341	29.1	8,250,368
1940	15.5	130,757	7.0	516,017	1.5	473,213	.7	484,350	.8	2,924,836	25.5	4,529,173
1936	15.8	119,767	6.1	436,722	1.3	391,284	.5	358,346	.5	1,696,284	24.5	3,002,403
1930[2]	14.9	96,355	6.5	481,874	1.4	451,251	.6	392,124	.6	2,046,162	22.5	3,467,766
1925[2]	13.8	128,137	6.3	460,597	1.2	381,157	.5	344,834	.5	1,633,820	22.6	2,948,545
1922[2]	15.0	111,053	5.5	397,882	1.1	325,015	.5	355,702	.4	1,250,191	22.2	2,439,846
1915[3]	—	—	20.2[5]	383,652[5]	.6	198,835	.3	201,054	.2	623,596	21.3	1,407,137
1910[4]	—	—	18.1[5]	431,337[5]	.7	219,099	.2	156,519	.1	359,020	19.2	1,165,974
1905[3]	—	—	15.1[5]	—	.5	—	.1	—	.1	—	15.8	718,353
1900[4]	—	—	14.2[5]	—	.3	—	.1	—	.04	—	14.6	481,053

[1] Figures for 1955, 1957 to 1959 are for 'Value of factory shipments' and not 'Value of production'.
[2] Includes 'Central electric stations' and 'Dyeing, cleaning and laundry work' establishments.
[3] Postal census; incomplete coverage.
[4] Decennial census of establishments with five employees and over.
[5] Includes all establishments with value of production under $200,000.

Series Q362–375. *Number of establishments and number of employees by size of establishment measured by number of employees, selected years, 1915 to 1959*

(establishments in thousands, employees in actual numbers)

Year	Under 5 employees		5 to 49		50 to 99		100 to 199		200 to 499		500 and over		Total number of establishments	Total employees
	Establishments	Employees	Establishments	Employees	Establishments	Employees	Establishments	Employees	Establishments	Employees	Establishments	Employees		
	362	363	364	365	366	367	368	369	370	371	372	373	374	375
1959	14.6	31,710	16.2	255,064	2.3	156,127	1.3	173,220	.8	241,597	.4	429,551	36.2[1]	1,289,602[2]
1958	15.1	33,747	16.2	254,259	2.1	149,195	1.2	168,145	.7	238,246	.4	429,296	36.7[1]	1,303,956[2]
1957	16.0	35,020	16.5	257,445	2.1	148,329	1.2	168,810	.7	233,636	.4	498,196	37.9[1]	1,359,061[2]
1955	16.8	36,340	16.2	251,046	2.1	144,411	1.2	163,091	.7	227,667	.4	459,973	38.2[1]	1,298,461[2]
1950	16.7	34,719	15.1	235,546	1.9	133,374	1.1	156,489	.7	216,593	.3	395,304	35.9[1]	1,183,297[2]
1945	12.9	30,052	12.5	195,796	1.7	116,422	1.0	136,961	.6	193,122	.4	447,019	29.1	1,119,372
1940	13.1	31,788	9.7	150,497	1.2	87,028	.8	105,607	.5	157,021	.2	230,303	25.5	762,244
1936	13.4	26,659	8.6	131,315	1.0	72,902	.7	91,966	.4	126,368	.1	145,149	24.2	594,359
1930[3]	12.6	24,186	8.9	144,700	1.2	86,077	.7	102,626	.4	124,548	.2	167,075	24.0	649,212
1925[3]	12.3	25,025	7.8	127,934	1.1	75,866	.6	86,287	.4	112,315	.1	133,405	22.3	560,832
1922[3]	14.8	26,407	5.6	101,076	.9	67,619	.5	71,338	.4	103,232	.1	91,714	22.3	461,386
1915[4]	8.3	—	5.2	—	.7	—	.4	—	.2	—	.1	—	21.3	462,200

[1] Includes 'Not classifiable' establishments numbering approximately 725 in 1959, 1,000 in 1957 and 1958, 800 in 1955, and 200 in 1950.
[2] Includes employees in head offices located away from the plant, not counted in the size breakdowns.
[3] Includes 'Central electric stations' and 'Dyeing, cleaning and laundry work' establishments.
[4] Based on wage-earners only.

APPENDIX. PRIMARY AND SECONDARY MANUFACTURING IN CANADA

Series Q376–407. *Selected general statistics for all manufacturing industries, primary and secondary manufacturing, by industrial groups, selected years, 1870 to 1957*

(values in millions of dollars)

Year	Totals for Canada			Food and beverage			Tobacco and tobacco products, secondary	Rubber products, secondary	Leather products, secondary	Textile products, secondary	Clothing (textile and fur), secondary
	Total	Primary	Secondary	Total	Primary	Secondary					
	376	377	378	379	380	381	382	383	384	385	386
Number of firms											
1957	36,959	12,547	24,412	8,461	4,627	3,834	49	88	619	1,239	2,547
1946	31,188	12,282	18,906	8,862	4,860	4,002	95	60	776	931	2,741
1939	24,772	9,800	14,972	9,078	4,913	4,165	99	54	606	614	1,706
1933	23,747	9,598	14,149	9,271	5,218	4,053	149	45	597	584	1,494
1929	21,989	9,374	12,615	8,856	5,301	3,555	109	44	408	507	1,250
1926	21,023	9,253	11,770	8,699	5,555	3,144	122	39	415	456	1,111
1919	—						—		—	—	—
1915	12,367	8,291	4,076	7,436	5,601	1,835	166	15	525	248	2,489
1910	—			—			—	—	—	—	—
1900	—			—			—	—	—	—	—
1890	70,123	17,674	52,449	12,571	9,984	2,587	149	18	7,775	3,996	11,589
1880	47,046	10,495	36,551	5,388	3,751	1,637	96	4	6,809	1,835	4,469
1870	38,402	9,790	28,612	4,124	2,889	1,235	77	4	6,381	996	2,094
Gross value of production											
1957	21,969.3	6,572.2	15,397.0	4,138.5	2,569.3	1,569.2	249.7	326.1	141.4	919.8	749.1
1946	8,033.1	2,773.1	5,260.0	2,040.7	1,370.5	670.2	119.6	159.4	192.7	506.4	446.1
1939	3,472.8	1,192.0	2,280.8	876.3	539.2	337.1	69.6	69.9	81.5	241.4	172.0
1933	1,952.9	627.6	1,325.3	545.3	324.6	220.7	43.9	41.5	57.5	1,741.2	118.4
1929	3,878.9	1,202.3	2,676.6	962.0	586.3	375.7	85.2	96.9	87.6	234.5	189.5
1926	3,108.7	1,070.7	2,038.0	846.9	559.2	297.7	65.2	86.5	84.9	210.8	159.5
1919	3,162.6	1,142.2	2,020.4	991.0	687.8	303.2	64.3	56.0	126.7	218.6	160.2
1915	1,330.7	488.5	842.2	428.9	297.6	131.4	29.0	14.4	71.0	55.2	94.0
1910	1,147.7	408.8	739.0	280.8	191.4	89.4	25.5	7.1	64.1	51.7	95.2
1900	575.8	215.9	359.9	179.0	126.9	52.1	12.0	1.7	53.0	30.8	50.4
1890	452.6	156.5	296.1	118.9	79.9	39.1	5.7	2.1	35.2	26.0	43.9
1880	303.5	103.0	200.5	82.4	54.7	27.8	3.1	.8	36.5	15.4	26.7
1870	216.4	80.4	136.0	63.4	45.0	18.4	2.4	.5	27.9	9.7	15.0
Value added											
1957	9,765.5	2,324.7	7,440.9	1,422.5	601.7	820.7	88.3	176.5	116.0	415.1	352.4
1946	3,464.7	870.6	2,594.1	604.1	272.6	331.5	40.0	93.5	82.3	233.9	206.3
1939	1,530.2	409.1	1,121.1	303.6	137.3	166.4	28.1	39.8	34.1	114.3	76.4
1933	918.9	242.9	676.0	204.1	93.4	110.7	20.3	27.5	26.3	85.1	51.7
1929	1,753.3	437.8	1,315.5	311.6	127.3	184.3	59.4	52.5	36.3	100.9	87.5
1926	1,302.8	345.2	957.6	230.9	108.0	122.9	42.4	35.4	35.0	83.0	69.8
1919	1,406.0	405.4	1,000.7	233.6	121.0	112.6	36.6	28.5	42.7	87.7	71.7
1915	557.1	154.9	402.3	113.2	58.6	54.6	13.0	7.3	25.8	22.2	43.2
1910	547.3	157.6	389.7	93.7	50.5	43.2	13.3	3.5	29.0	22.2	46.9
1900	245.2	67.1	178.1	42.7	23.5	19.2	8.2	.6	19.8	14.3	25.1
1890	208.3	56.8	151.5	33.9	20.1	13.8	3.2	.6	16.6	12.5	21.6
1880	126.1	33.1	93.0	18.9	10.9	8.0	1.5	.3	14.6	6.3	11.2
1870	93.4	24.2	69.2	15.2	8.1	7.1	1.2	.1	13.1	3.4	6.4

Series Q376–407. *Selected general statistics for all manufacturing industries, primary and secondary manufacturing, by industrial groups, selected years, 1870 to 1957 (continuation)*

(values in millions of dollars)

Year	Wood products			Paper products			Printing, publishing and allied industries, secondary	Iron and steel products, secondary	Transportation equipment, secondary	Non-ferrous metal products		
	Total	Primary	Secondary	Total	Primary	Secondary				Total	Primary	Secondary
	387	**388**	**389**	**390**	**391**	**392**	**393**	**394**	**395**	**396**	**397**	**398**
Number of firms												
1957	10,045	7,643	2,402	580	127	453	4,543	3,063	618	592	23	569
1946	8,903	7,135	1,768	486	113	373	2,379	2,100	530	474	15	459
1939	5,681	4,697	984	405	100	305	2,291	1,199	407	336	14	322
1933	5,197	4,209	988	339	95	244	2,057	1,153	521	304	15	289
1929	4,823	3,905	918	324	108	216	1,828	1,069	623	269	10	259
1926	4,280	3,507	773	290	115	175	1,647	1,034	727	271	29	262
1919	—	—	—	—	—	—	—	—	—	—	—	—
1915	3,170	2,556	614	252	80	172	1,130	1,589	707	222	18	204
1910	—	—	—	—	—	—	—	—	—	—	—	—
1900	—	—	—	—	—	—	—	—	—	—	—	—
1890	11,553	7,580	3,973	154	58	96	719	12,727	4,009	741	16	725
1880	9,636	6,680	2,956	83	41	42	489	10,478	3,603	524	—	524
1870	9,751	6,840	2,911	29	21	8	372	8,091	3,039	274	—	274
Gross value of production												
1957	1,328.3	912.2	416.1	1,802.4	1,364.0	438.4	728.2	2,909.8	2,267.8	1,683.4	1,280.1	403.2
1946	585.6	404.4	181.2	695.1	527.8	167.3	221.7	826.7	587.2	484.6	304.7	179.9
1939	198.9	128.1	70.8	269.6	208.2	61.5	119.5	321.3	234.9	327.0	262.6	64.4
1933	94.1	54.0	40.1	157.5	123.4	34.1	92.6	126.0	92.7	127.8	100.6	27.2
1929	289.9	203.6	86.3	291.0	244.0	47.0	140.5	435.3	369.6	169.8	109.9	59.9
1926	242.4	178.6	63.8	248.8	215.4	33.5	105.8	300.5	244.2	113.7	72.9	40.9
1919	322.2	245.5	76.7	170.1	129.6	40.5	75.6	343.3	251.7	93.5	66.8	26.6
1915	115.6	88.1	27.5	53.0	40.3	12.6	33.6	144.8	86.8	74.2	53.1	21.2
1910	182.7	152.3	30.4	33.0	23.2	9.8	26.5	143.2	78.1	59.8	35.3	24.5
1900	91.1	72.0	19.2	12.4	8.7	3.8	14.2	51.9	29.3	12.8	7.1	5.6
1890	84.5	69.4	15.1	6.2	3.6	2.6	10.5	56.6	23.3	7.4	3.1	4.4
1880	54.9	45.6	9.3	3.0	2.5	.5	6.8	34.2	14.3	4.0	—	4.0
1870	40.9	34.2	6.7	1.7	1.1	.7	4.1	24.9	9.9	1.6	—	1.6
Value added												
1957	582.8	377.7	205.1	847.4	669.3	178.1	479.5	1,475.0	955.1	603.1	450.7	152.4
1946	267.3	179.9	87.4	333.8	258.2	75.7	154.3	462.7	277.8	148.5	69.6	78.9
1939	93.7	58.1	35.7	129.0	103.1	25.9	84.1	179.0	98.3	107.3	80.1	27.3
1933	43.9	22.8	21.0	73.2	56.9	16.3	68.0	70.6	39.9	66.8	54.5	12.2
1929	133.6	86.8	46.6	143.7	121.7	22.0	102.3	236.9	137.8	87.3	62.2	25.1
1926	111.1	75.5	35.7	126.0	109.6	16.4	75.4	160.0	96.3	46.5	27.5	18.9
1919	200.3	147.2	53.1	101.5	74.7	26.8	52.8	203.5	122.3	74.3	55.0	19.2
1915	61.5	45.2	16.3	26.3	19.4	6.9	24.2	75.3	40.7	36.7	27.2	9.5
1910	89.5	72.0	17.5	17.5	12.4	5.2	18.7	76.5	40.6	33.1	17.0	16.1
1900	46.2	35.1	11.1	7.0	5.0	2.0	10.2	29.8	14.3	5.7	2.6	3.1
1890	41.9	32.9	9.0	3.0	1.9	1.1	6.7	33.1	13.2	4.0	1.6	2.5
1880	26.7	20.9	5.7	1.3	1.1	.3	4.2	19.7	7.9	2.2	—	2.2
1870	19.5	15.5	4.0	.9	.6	.3	2.6	15.7	6.4	.9	—	.9

Series Q376–407. *Selected general statistics for all manufacturing industries, primary and secondary manufacturing, by industrial groups, selected years, 1870 to 1957 (continuation)*

(values in millions of dollars)

Year	Electrical apparatus and supplies, secondary	Nonmetallic mineral products			Products of coal and petroleum, secondary	Chemicals and allied products			Miscellaneous industries, secondary
		Total	Primary	Secondary		Total	Primary	Secondary	
	399	400	401	402	403	404	405	406	407
				Number of firms					
1957	486	1,220	31	1,189	106	1,132	96	1,036	1,571
1946	266	833	23	810	77	1,037	136	901	638
1939	190	723	24	699	86	817	52	765	480
1933	174	681	26	655	89	706	35	671	386
1929	139	775	23	752	68	539	27	512	358
1926	132	820	12	808	73	564	55	509	343
1919	—	—	—	—	—	—	—	—	—
1915	59	827	27	800	39	460	9	451	322
1910	—	—	—	—	—	—	—	—	—
1900	—	—	—	—	—	—	—	—	—
1890	24	2,660	21	2,639	26	762	15	747	650
1880	—	2,364	20	2,344	44	633	3	630	591
1870	—	1,836	40	1,796	50	919	—	919	365
				Gross value of production					
1957	1,078.2	599.2	147.4	451.8	1,491.9	1,201.9	299.1	902.8	353.5
1946	234.6	160.5	47.2	113.3	286.0	401.8	118.5	283.3	84.3
1939	89.1	64.6	17.8	46.8	143.6	163.7	36.2	127.5	29.9
1933	37.0	31.1	8.1	23.0	100.2	94.9	17.0	77.9	18.2
1929	113.8	90.5	28.3	62.2	139.3	143.2	30.3	113.0	40.4
1926	69.8	62.0	13.0	49.0	104.7	129.1	31.7	97.4	33.9
1919	35.6	38.8	10.5	28.3	77.5	94.1	2.0	92.1	43.4
1915	18.6	30.9	8.3	22.5	16.3	49.4	1.0	48.4	15.0
1910	15.2	28.2	5.9	22.3	9.6	30.9	.6	30.3	16.3
1900	3.3	8.9	1.1	7.8	4.3	12.7	.1	12.5	8.1
1890	.9	13.3	.3	13.0	2.2	10.2	.3	9.9	5.6
1880	—	6.2	.1	6.0	4.1	7.1	.1	7.0	4.3
1870	—	3.9	.1	3.7	3.1	5.0	—	5.0	2.4
				Value added					
1957	568.6	339.0	85.7	253.3	534.1	604.5	139.6	465.0	205.7
1946	130.0	94.6	27.8	66.7	79.0	208.4	62.6	145.9	48.2
1939	48.5	41.1	11.8	29.3	44.4	90.0	18.8	71.2	18.3
1933	21.7	20.3	5.3	15.0	32.5	55.9	10.0	45.9	11.3
1929	63.1	61.5	20.2	41.3	37.6	78.9	19.6	59.3	22.9
1926	38.5	41.0	9.6	31.4	32.3	59.8	15.0	44.8	19.3
1919	19.5	29.6	6.4	23.2	26.3	49.9	.9	49.0	25.0
1915	9.2	18.7	4.0	14.6	6.0	25.4	.5	24.9	8.6
1910	8.9	23.7	5.3	18.4	4.3	16.2	.4	15.8	9.8
1900	2.1	7.5	.9	6.6	1.4	5.6	—	5.5	4.7
1890	.5	8.9	.2	8.7	.7	4.5	.1	4.4	3.4
1880	—	4.3	.1	4.2	1.8	2.9	—	2.9	2.4
1870	—	3.0	.1	2.9	1.7	2.0	—	2.0	1.3

SECTION R: CONSTRUCTION AND HOUSING

KENNETH BUCKLEY, *University of Saskatchewan*

The construction and housing statistics presented in this section are in four subsections. Series R1–117 are official estimates of total construction, public and private, and by major types. These series cover the period 1926 to 1960. Series R118–139, the second subsection, are official estimates of the value of residential construction and of the physical stocks and flows of dwelling units. The value series R118–128 are for the period 1926 to 1960; the dwelling units series R129–139 are for the period 1921 to 1960. The third subsection, series R140–167, presents private estimates of total construction and of some major components of total construction. Some of these estimates cover the period since 1896 to 1930, others begin with Confederation. One series, net investment in railway transport and telegraph, covers the period 1850 to 1930. The final subsection, series R168–179, contains records of building permits issued and construction contracts awarded. With two exceptions, these series cover the period since 1911. One permit series begins with 1867, another with 1886.

The official construction and housing estimates and data on permits and contracts awarded were obtained from the following sources:

six publications of the Dominion Bureau of Statistics, including *New Residential Construction* (Ottawa, Queen's Printer), annual, *Private and Public Investment in Canada, 1946–1957* (Ottawa, Queen's Printer, 1959), catalogue no. 61–504, *National Accounts Income and Expenditure, 1926–1956* (Ottawa, Queen's Printer, 1958), *Canada Year Book* for the years 1958 and 1959; and *Annual Report of Building Permits in Canada, 1946* (Ottawa, King's Printer, 1947); Department of Trade and Commerce, *Private and Public Investment in Canada, 1926–1951* (Ottawa, 1951); Central Mortgage and Housing Corporation, *Canadian Housing Statistics* (Ottawa), first and second quarterly issues, 1955, and fourth quarter, 1959; and O. J. Firestone, *Residential Real Estate in Canada* (Toronto, University of Toronto Press, 1951). In addition the files of the Planning and Development Section, Business Finance Division of the Dominion Bureau of Statistics and the ledgers of the Economic Research Department, Central Mortgage and Housing Corporation were consulted for unpublished data.

Private sources included James Pickett 'Residential Capital Formation in Canada, 1871–1921', an unpublished paper which is a part of a doctoral dissertation in preparation in the Department of Social and Economic Research, University of Glasgow, and the following studies by the author of this section: *Capital Formation in Canada, 1896–1930* (Toronto, University of Toronto Press, 1955); 'Historical Estimates of Migration and Investment in Canada', Canadian Political Science Association, Conference on Statistics, 1960 (mimeograph); 'Capital Formation in Railway Transport and Telegraph in Canada, 1850 to 1930', Canadian Political Science Association, Conference on Statistics, 1962 (mimeograph). In addition, data on contracts awarded were obtained from *MacLean Building Review*, a monthly publication of Hugh C. MacLean (now Southam-MacLean) Publications Limited, Toronto.

General note

The primary source of the current statistics of construction and housing is the annual capital survey of the Dominion Bureau of Statistics. This survey was started on a limited basis in 1941

and extended after 1945, when a companion survey of investment intentions was undertaken. The questionnaire is sent to about 16,000 business establishments and is designed to determine the current level of new investment and repair and maintenance expenditures on structures and machinery and equipment by types, by industry, by province and for 'greater cities'. Surveys are also made of institutions, government departments and agencies and of housing. The primary source of information on housebuilding activity is a nationwide survey of starts and completions conducted jointly by the Dominion Bureau of Statistics and Central Mortgage and Housing Corporation. The direct surveys typically account for somewhat more than 70 per cent of the final estimates and, after adjustment to full coverage for the sectors surveyed, for about 85 per cent of the total. The remaining industrial sectors, including agriculture, fishing, independent retailers, and several service industries in which the typical production unit is small, are estimated by indirect methods.

New construction investment is defined as gross capital expenditures on new buildings, engineering structures and land improvements plus expenditures on major improvements. Building construction covers buildings of all kinds, residential, commercial, industrial and institutional. Engineering construction covers products such as highways and bridges, dams, railway road and track, docks, transmission lines, oil pipelines, etc. A major improvement is any project that alters the structural design or increases the value of an existing structure. For instance, adding a storey to an office building or a new wing to a hospital or school would constitute a major improvement.

Repair expenditures are defined as outlays made to maintain existing structures in 'a state of normal working efficiency'. While they are charged to current expenses in normal accounting practice, they may be postponable and they draw upon the same supply of construction labour and materials as new investment in structures. Routine maintenance, such as snow removal, janitorial services and minor repairs of roads, is excluded.

New and repair construction, taken together, are the total construction product of the country and include the value of so-called force account construction, which is construction work performed by employees of firms, as well as contract construction. 'Own account construction', as, for example, new construction and repair work performed by farmers, is also included.

The value of new construction and repair assigned to each year reflects as closely as possible the value of structures put in place or the value of work performed during that year.

A description of the procedures and concepts employed in the annual capital survey may be found in *Private and Public Investment in Canada, 1946–1957*, pp. 7–10. For a full discussion of the concepts underlying the official estimates one must turn to the two earlier studies; *Public Investment and Capital Formation, A Study of Public and Private Investment Outlay, Canada, 1926–1941* (Ottawa, 1945), hereafter referred to as *P.I.C.F.*, and *Private and Public Investment in Canada, 1926–1951* (Ottawa, 1951), hereafter referred to as *P.P.I.*

P.I.C.F. was a pioneering study of public and private investment in Canada prepared for the Dominion–Provincial Conference on Reconstruction in 1945. The estimates of direct government investment and repair and of housing investment and repair were prepared under the direction of O. J. Firestone. The estimates of private investment and repair, including publicly owned public utilities, were prepared under the direction of M. C. Urquhart. This study established the conceptual framework that has been followed, with minor modifications which are indicated in the notes to individual series, in estimating new investment and repair expenditures on structures and machinery and equipment.

Direct estimates of new and repair construction, with a breakdown between building and engineering construction, were made for most of the major user categories from 1926 to 1941 in *P.I.C.F.* Virtually all engineering construction was covered by this direct method. Construction outlays of the remaining categories were estimated by deducting in each year the direct estimates of building construction from an estimate of total building construction. The remaining categories covered by this indirect or residual method included fishing, manufacturing, construction, trade, finance, commercial services, churches, universities and private hospitals.

Total building construction was estimated by applying an index of the annual flow of building construction materials, excluding those used on farms, to the value of materials used in nonfarm building construction in 1941 to secure the value of materials used in each year from 1926 to 1941. These values were raised to full totals by applying ratios of the value of materials used to the value of building construction work performed. The ratios were obtained from the census of construction, which is described below. Total building construction was distributed to new and repair with ratios from the same source. The benchmark estimate for 1941 was made by adding estimates for types of building construction not covered by the 1941 construction census to the value of building construction covered by that census.

The Economics Branch Division of the Department of Reconstruction and Supply, later transferred to the Department of Trade and Commerce, with the co-operation of the Dominion Bureau of Statistics, developed methods to obtain direct estimates for the categories which had been treated as a residual in *P.I.C.F.* The revision of the estimates of *P.I.C.F.* was directed by O. J. Firestone. The estimates were published in *P.P.I.*, where they are linked with the current estimates from the capital surveys of the Dominion Bureau of Statistics.

With the exception of the housing estimates, which were thoroughly revised, the direct estimates of *P.I.C.F.* appeared unchanged or with minor revisions. Direct estimates of new and repair expenditures were prepared for the categories treated as a residual in *P.I.C.F.* Accordingly, the final totals of new and repair expenditures, 1926 to 1951, were sums of direct estimates and the earlier estimates of total building construction were dropped.

Two general methods were used in *P.P.I.* to obtain direct estimates for the residual categories of *P.I.C.F.* A sample study of manufacturing, construction, trade, finance (excluding banks) and commercial services provided the bulk of the new direct estimates. The sample was drawn from the income tax returns of corporations to the Department of National Revenue from 1926 to 1946. For a description of the sample and of estimating procedures, see *P.P.I.* p. 223. New and repair expenditures for fishing, the minor utilities, and private institutions were derived by applying more or less satisfactory indexes of trend to capital survey benchmark estimates, usually for one component of

investment in a postwar year and obtaining a breakdown of new and repair by applying ratios taken from postwar estimates.

P.P.I. followed and more fully realized the conceptual objectives established by *P.I.C.F.* In *P.P.I.*, for example, labour costs were added to the estimates of farm construction which were limited in the earlier study to the costs of materials used, and provision was made for full coverage of labour costs in the repair estimates. The relation between the estimates in *P.P.I.* and *P.I.C.F.* has been examined in another study and the conclusion of that study may be summarized here: the *P.P.I.* estimates of total construction exceed the *P.I.C.F.* by 16.5 per cent from 1926 to 1930, 13.6 per cent from 1931 to 1935 and 16.1 per cent from 1936 to 1940. The difference in 1941 was $186 million. Most of this was the result of the revision in the housing estimates. Since the figure for urban housing in 1941 was about the same in both studies, the difference was largely the result of housing repair, new rural nonfarm dwellings, major alterations and the addition of a small allowance for farm labour in *P.P.I.* In the earlier years the relative difference in the two series was roughly the same, but the pattern was different. In 1941 the *P.I.C.F.* estimate for the residual group was somewhat higher than the *P.P.I.* estimates for the same sectors. In the earlier years this relationship is reversed because of the greater weight given to urban housing in *P.I.C.F.* (See Buckley, 'Capital Formation in Canada', *Studies in Income and Wealth*, vol. 19, pp. 91–145.) The housing estimates of *P.P.I.* were taken from O. J. Firestone, *Residential Real Estate in Canada*. The methods and problems relating to the methods of estimating housing investment are discussed in the notes to series R 118–126 below.

The official estimates of total new and repair construction shown in series R 1–15 include both public and private expenditures. In this context public new and repair construction is made up of three major components: (1) construction expenditures by government enterprises, that is, publicly owned public utilities (series R 31–33), (2) federal expenditures on non-rental and rental housing (series R 121–123) and what is called public institutional construction (series R 94–96), namely provincial construction expenditures on hospitals, schools and universities, and municipal construction expenditures on hospitals and schools, and (3) construction expenditures by government departments (series R 16–27). Total public new and repair construction may be obtained by summing the series cited in the last sentence.

The National Accounts include only new construction and deduct from total public and private new construction direct government construction outlays. The latter category consists of government built, non-rental housing, construction outlays for provincial hospitals, provincial and municipal schools and all construction expenditures by government departments. These expenditures are included in the Gross National Expenditure with government expenditures on goods and services. For the reconciliation of total new construction with new construction as in the National Accounts, see *Private and Public Investment in Canada, 1946–1957*, p. 39.

Series R 127–128 gives total new housing construction in current and constant dollars from 1926 to 1960 on the national accounting definition, that is, total public and private residential capital formation less federal outlays on new non-rental housing.

The third subsection of the tables contains estimates of construction and housing made by individuals. These unofficial estimates were designed to project official series back to earlier dates. The sources and methods are described in the notes to the individual tables.

The statistics of the final subsection, permits issued and contracts awarded, although they originated in individual cities and in *MacLean Building Review* (later *Building Reporter*), a monthly publication of Hugh C. MacLean (now Southam-MacLean) Publications Ltd., Toronto, have been regularly assembled and published by the Dominion Bureau of Statistics.

Another source of valuable information on the construction industry and its products, which should be consulted by students of the industry, is the census of construction. When the annual census of industry was introduced by the Dominion Bureau of Statistics in 1917, an attempt was made to cover all establishments engaged in contract construction. Coverage improved in 1918 and 1919 and was maintained at approximately the 1919 level for four years. In 1923 general construction was dropped from the census of industry. In 1934 the census of construction was resumed and extended to cover force account construction by governments and some private firms as well as contract construction. It has been continued to the present time and although the coverage has greatly improved, it has varied and, consequently, the census does not provide a reliable historical index of year-to-year changes in the level of construction.

OFFICIAL CONSTRUCTION ESTIMATES
(Series R1–117)

R1–6. New and repair construction expenditures, private and public, in current and in constant dollar values, 1926 to 1960

SOURCE: for 1926 to 1957, *Private and Public Investment in Canada, 1946–1957*, pp. 11–12; for the estimates in current dollars, 1958 to 1960, the files of the Planning and Development Section, Business Finance Division, Dominion Bureau of Statistics.

For the concepts and procedures underlying series R1–3, see the general note to this section. Estimates for the period 1926 to 1949 were published in *Private and Public Investment in Canada, 1926–1951* (*P.P.I.*), and for years since 1950 in the annual outlook publications entitled *Private and Public Investment in Canada, Outlook*. The series presented here incorporate minor revisions of the originally published series. The changes in industrial classifications which were made did not affect the totals shown here. However, several changes did. The housing estimates were revised on conceptual grounds to include several supplementary building costs, for example, legal fees, architectural fees and the cost of landscaping. The housing estimates were also revised when the 1951 and, later, the 1956 census indicated more dwellings in Canada than had been reported by the annual housing surveys through the pre-census years. Revisions in the annual estimates of the existing housing stock also raised the estimate of housing repair, an estimate derived by applying a unit cost figure to the existing stock of dwellings. A further upward revision in housing repair was the result of an increase in the estimates of the annual repair cost per unit. For a more detailed treatment of the housing estimates, see the note to series R118–126.

The *P.P.I.* estimates for agriculture were also revised on the basis of data from the 1951 census. A more accurate method of inflating mining construction had the effect of reducing the *P.P.I.* estimates for that sector. (See *Private and Public Investment, 1946–1957*, p. 8.)

The price indexes used to deflate the construction series are weighted averages of indexes of wholesale prices of construction materials and of wage rates in the construction industry. Indexes on the base 1935–1939 were used to deflate the series from 1926 to 1947. Indexes on the base 1949 were used to deflate the series from 1948 to 1957. The two series were then linked by individual sub-components and by totals at 1947. This process

produced residual differences and consequently the total of individual series do not equal the published totals in all cases. For further discussion of the deflation procedures, see *National Accounts, Income and Expenditure, 1926–1956*, Sources and Methods, paragraphs 598–606, pp. 178–9 and paragraphs 631–3, pp. 182–3.

R7–15. New and repair construction expenditures, by type, 1926 to 1960

SOURCE: the files of the Planning and Development Section, Business Finance Division, Dominion Bureau of Statistics.

See the general note to this section for a description of the concepts and procedures underlying these estimates, and the note to series R1–6 for the revisions that have been made to the series since their original publication. Also see series R118–126 for the concepts and procedures used to estimate housing construction.

R16–27. New and repair construction by government departments, by level of government, 1926 to 1960

SOURCE: for 1926 to 1949, *Private and Public Investment in Canada, 1926–1951*, for federal government departments, table 85, p. 187, for provincial government departments, table 94, p. 192, and for municipal government departments, table 111, p. 199; for the period 1950 to 1957, *Private and Public Investment in Canada, 1946–1957*, item 3 in tables 11–14, pp. 35–8; for 1958 to 1960, the files of the Planning and Development Section, Business Finance Division, Dominion Bureau of Statistics.

In *P.P.I.* federal government outlays on hospitals for Indians, Eskimoes and veterans were not classified as department outlays from 1941 to 1949. They were included in the category of public housing and institutions. The amounts have been determined by deducting 'federal public housing' (*P.P.I.*, table 70, p. 180) from 'federal public housing and institutions' (*P.P.I.*, table 82, p. 186). These amounts were added to the *P.P.I.* totals for federal government departments from 1941 to 1949 and are consistent with the totals from *Private and Public Investment in Canada, 1946–1957* for the period 1950 to 1957. However, the figures in the latter source are in error for the years from 1946 to 1949 because the federal outlays on institutions were overlooked. This also affects the reconciliation of new public and private construction with new construction as shown in the National Accounts. (See *Private and Public Investment in Canada, 1946–1957*, table 15, p. 39.) However, the amounts are small. 'Other construction' is overstated in the National Accounts in the four years from 1946 to 1949 by $4.3, $5.2, $6.8 and $6.5 millions.

Conceptually, investment by government departments is a residual obtained by deducting from total public investment, investment by government enterprises and by government-owned institutions and public housing. The category therefore includes, in addition to government departments, federal agencies, for example, the Atomic Energy Control Board, not classified as a government enterprise. A government enterprise is the equivalent and more precise designation of what is termed a publicly owned public utility in *P.I.C.F.*, and in the present volume (see series R28–36). The estimates of construction by government departments from 1926 to 1941 were developed for *P.I.C.F.* and adjusted in *P.P.I.* for the transfer of Canadian Government Elevators and the National Harbours Board to the government enterprises sector and of provincial hospitals to provincial institutions. This practice has been continued in the classifications of the D.B.S. capital surveys (see general note).

Prior to 1949 for federal construction and prior to 1947 for provincial and municipal construction, the same general approach was used to estimate construction by each level of government.

Direct estimates were made for years at cyclical turning points using the best available records. Intervening years were interpolated on indexes considered representative of year to year changes in total construction. In subsequent years preliminary current estimates were generated by the annual capital survey of intentions. They were revised on the basis of each following survey, which provided the accomplished construction in the previous year, and also, in the case of the federal government, on the basis of internal records and published reports. The schedules employed in the capital survey followed the definitions established in *P.I.C.F.* and *P.P.I.* In spite of the change in the general approach after the war, the series are considered to be consistent from 1926 to 1960.

R 16–18. Direct estimates of federal nonwar new and repair construction were made for the selected years 1926, 1929, 1930, 1933, 1937 and, annually, from 1941 to 1948 on the basis of a detailed reclassification of items of expenditure contained in *Report of the Auditor-General* in each year and in the *Public Accounts*, 1942–3 to 1948–9. In this way items were picked up whether charged to capital or current account and assigned individually to new or repair construction. War outlays were compiled from records of the Department of Munitions and Supply. As a result of revision in this latter component of total construction, the *P.I.C.F.* estimates for 1939 to 1941 were lowered.

Indexes based upon a variety of federal data from published and unpublished sources were developed as interpolators for the three periods 1926 to 1929, 1930 to 1937, 1937 to 1941. The index in each period was applied to a single year base. Comparisons of the estimates yielded by the indexes with direct estimates in years other than the base years supported a conclusion that 'the likely margin of error in interpolation was found to be less than 10 per cent'. The initial interpolations were not adjusted to eliminate the bias of up to 10 per cent in these indexes. (See *P.I.C.F.*, p. 114.)

R 19–21. The direct estimates of new and repair construction by the provincial governments for 1926, 1929, 1930, 1933, 1937, 1941, 1944 and 1946 were based upon a detailed reclassification of itemized expenditures published in the provincial public accounts. The indexes for interpolations from 1926 to 1937 were based upon provincial public works expenditures and related investment activity drawn from the reports of the Royal Commission on Dominion–Provincial Relations, Public Accounts Inquiry. From 1937 to 1941 the indexes were based upon public works expenditures reported in the census of construction. The index for the period 1941 to 1944 was based upon capital expenditures on highways and public works by the provinces, and for the period 1944 to 1946 upon total provincial government expenditures. These indexes were applied to total construction and the interpolated totals were distributed to new and repair on a series of ratios derived by straight-line interpolation of the ratios available in the direct estimates of new and repair in the selected years.

Single bases were used in each interpolation, 1930 in the first period, 1937 in the second, 1942 in the third, and 1944 in the fourth. For the other selected years, the indexes yielded estimates differing from the direct estimates by less than 4 per cent in 1926, 1929, 1933 and 1937, by 3 per cent in 1941, 1 per cent in 1942 and less than 2 per cent in 1946. The initial interpolations were not adjusted for these differences.

R 22–24. Direct estimates for 1933, 1937, 1941 and 1944 were based upon published reports of municipalities, of Departments of Education and of Municipal Affairs in the provinces, of school corporations and other public institutions and, in some instances, upon information from individual municipalities and provincial government departments. These data were supplemented by bond issues of large municipalities and by municipal reports to the Construction Census Branch of the Dominion Bureau of Statistics.

An index of current expenditures by sixteen municipalities, from Reports of the Citizens Research Institute of Toronto, and an index of the bond issues of twenty-seven major cities, obtained from 'The Financial Post Record of Prospectuses' were used to extrapolate the current and the capital components, respectively, of the 1933 estimate back to 1926. This procedure yielded estimates of total new and repair construction, 1926 to 1933, which were then broken down into new and repair. Ratios of new to total new and repair in the peak year in the thirties were assigned to the year of the peak estimate of the twenties on the assumption that the cyclical variation in the ratios would be fairly uniform. The ratios were extrapolated backward to 1926 on the same assumption.

Interpolations in the intervals 1934 to 1936 and 1938 to 1940, on a 1937 base, and the breakdown of total construction into new and repair was made on the basis of a sample of sixteen municipalities reporting to the Construction Census Branch of the Dominion Bureau of Statistics.

The indexes used for interpolation in the intervals 1942 to 1943 and 1945 to 1946 on a 1944 base were based upon a selection of municipal government expenditures available in the Bank of Canada, *Statistical Supplement*, for years 1941 to 1947.

The annual capital survey is the basis of the estimates from 1947 to 1960. The extrapolation of the 1944 estimate to 1947 indicated a bias in the index used of up to 4 per cent. Bias in the earlier intervals was lower. The initial estimates were not adjusted to eliminate the apparent bias in the interpolations.

R 28–36. New and repair construction by privately and publicly owned public utilities, 1926 to 1960

SOURCE: for the period 1926 to 1945, *Private and Public Investment in Canada, 1926–1951*, tables 41–3, pp. 165–6; for the period 1946 to 1960, the files of the Planning and Development Section, Business Finance Division, Dominion Bureau of Statistics.

Publicly owned public utilities are commonly called government-owned business enterprises. In general, they are government-owned establishments whose principal source of revenue is through the sale of goods and services to the public. The terminology used here is consistent with the objective of the table, which is to show the relative spending by the private and the public sectors of the utilities industry.

Estimates for all the major utilities for the period 1926 to 1941 were made for *P.I.C.F.* That publication also provides descriptions of the sources and methods used (*P.I.C.F.* pp. 109–12). These utilities have been covered by the annual capital surveys since 1941. The estimates, 1926 to 1951, were included in *P.P.I.* In *P.P.I.* (p. 226), gross investment in telephones from 1926 to 1948 was distributed to construction and equipment from a 1948 benchmark on the basis of an index of telephone wire mileage adjusted for replacement costs and price changes. Estimates for some minor utilities were added, usually by projecting a benchmark in the forties from the capital survey back to 1926 on some index of trend. Certain additions were made which implied a shift of expenditures which had been included under government departments in the earlier study.

Totals for steam railways from 1926 to 1941 as published by *P.P.I.* contain a large error. The item replacements or renewals was introduced twice. Since the totals for all utilities and the totals of all construction were arrived at in *P.P.I.* by summing the individual direct estimates, the error also appears in these larger aggregates in *P.P.I.* and in total repair and total capital and repair in *Private and Public Investment, 1946–1957*. This point should be borne in mind in using these sources. The correct series were published in *P.I.C.F.*, but only for selected years; so it is not a simple matter to correct the annual series 1926 to 1941 without consulting the *P.I.C.F.* worksheets which, unfortunately, have been destroyed. The source and size of the error in selected years are treated in the note to series R 37–54.

The methods of estimating investment by public utilities, which are described in the note to series R 37–54, made it a simple matter to segregate the private and public sectors. The types of enterprises classified as public utilities are also listed in the note to series R 37–54.

R 37–54. New and repair construction, all public utilities, by type of utility, 1926 to 1960

SOURCE: for the period 1926 to 1946 *Private and Public Investment in Canada, 1926–1951*, for series R 37–39, table 47, p. 168, for series R 40–42, table 52, p. 170, for series R 43–45, table 55, p. 172, for series R 46–48, table 58, p. 173, for series R 49–51, table 61, p. 175, and for series R 52–54, table 62, p. 175; for the period 1947 to 1957, *Private and Public Investment in Canada, 1946–1957*, for series R 37–39, sum of item nos. 1 and 2, table 5, p. 23, for series R 40–42, item no. 3, table 5, p. 23, for series R 43–45, item no. 4, table 5, p. 24, for series R 46–48, item no. 8, table 5, p. 25, for series R 49–51, item no. 10, table 5, p. 26, for series R 52–54, the sum of item nos. 5, 6, 7, 9 and 11, table 5, pp. 24–6; for the period 1958 to 1960, for series R 37–54, the files of the Planning and Development Section, Business Finance Division, Dominion Bureau of Statistics. See series R 34–36 for annual totals of series R 37–54.

The methods of estimating construction outlays of public utilities are best illustrated by considering the utilities by major types. The major sources were correspondence with many of the larger companies, published company reports and various reports and unpublished data of the Dominion Bureau of Statistics. The basic estimates from 1926 to 1941 are from *P.I.C.F.* The description of sources and estimating procedures may be found in *P.I.C.F.* pp. 109–12. Annual series for the major types of utilities and for minor utilities as well as sources and procedures used to obtain the revised and additional minor series for the period 1926 to 1951 may be found in *P.P.I.* (pp. 226–8). The estimates for the major utility sectors from 1941 to 1960 and for all utilities 1951 to 1960 are from the annual capital surveys.

R 37–39. Electric power and gas distribution. The estimates of new construction from 1926 to 1941 are based upon either published reports of, or direct correspondence with, all the large companies in both the private and public sectors of the industry. Full coverage was achieved in each sector by raising the sample on the basis of the revenue of companies in the sample to total revenue as reported in D.B.S., *Central Electric Stations in Canada*. A large part of the outlays by private gas companies is included in the expenditures of the electric utilities.

Benchmark estimate of repair and maintenance expenditures in 1941 obtained from the capital survey for that year was run back to 1926 on a series relating annual repair outlays and revenues of the Ontario Hydro municipalities and total annual revenue in the industry. Estimates since 1941 are from the annual capital surveys.

R 40–42. Railway transport and telegraphs. About 90 per cent of the railway industry is represented by the Canadian National Railways and the Canadian Pacific Railways. New construction outlays in all years by the C.N.R., which is publicly owned, were obtained by correspondence. Outlays by the C.P.R. in 1926, 1929, 1930, 1933, 1937 and 1941 were obtained by correspondence and interpolated on the basis of series derived from the company's annual reports and supplementary data.

Estimates for other public and other private railways were based largely upon reports made directly to the Transportation and Public Utilities Branch of the Dominion Bureau of Statistics.

Construction repair and maintenance expenditures of the railways are included in the 'Maintenance of Way and Structures' accounts which are published in detail in D.B.S., *Annual Report on the Steam Railways of Canada*. The account also includes items, such as snow removal, which are not repair. These were deducted. Until 1940 this account also included capital retirement or renewal charges. Since replacement construction was added to what the railways call 'net investment' in structures to obtain estimates of new construction, it was also necessary to deduct from the maintenance account from 1926 to 1939, the offsetting renewal or retirement charges to avoid double counting. (The same adjustment was necessary in the maintenance of equipment account from 1926 to 1941.) In 1940 the railways changed their accounting procedures with respect to road and other structures. They began to use a system of depreciation accounts that was independent of the maintenance accounts for ways and structures. (They did the same for equipment in 1942.) For a discussion of the implications of these accounting practices for the estimating procedure, see *P.I.C.F.* pp. 109–10.

The authors of *P.P.I.* apparently missed the last step in the process of adjusting the maintenance accounts. Replacements are included in *P.P.I.* in new investment, where they belong; and charges for replacements or retirements are *also* included in the repair series of *P.P.I.* For total new and repair investment in 1926, 1929 and 1937, the amounts involved were $28.9 million, $36.6 million and $12.9 million, respectively.

R 43–45. Urban transit. Prior to 1946 this sector was called electric railways. The earlier estimates were not altered with the change in the name. In later years, however, 'the few remaining interurban Electric Railways have been included with Railway Transport and Telegraph'. (See *Private and Public Investment, 1947–1957*, p. 8.)

From 1941 to 1946 the estimates are derived from the annual capital surveys. From 1926 to 1940 the estimates are from the files of *P.I.C.F.* Electric railways were combined with steam railways in the published tables of *P.I.C.F.*

P.I.C.F. coverage of both the public and private sectors of urban transit by correspondence was very high. Annual data in the required detail were obtained by correspondence for the largest of the publicly owned systems and for the two largest privately owned systems. For other large systems similar data were obtained for the selected years 1926, 1929, 1930, 1933, 1937 and 1941. The data for the private and public sectors were raised to full coverage on the basis of the ratio of the revenue of all companies to the revenue of the companies covered.

R 46–48. Telephone companies. The estimates of total new investment and repair expenditures were obtained from *P.I.C.F.* for years prior to 1941 and of new construction and of repair and maintenance construction from the annual capital survey for the years following. New investment outlays from 1926 to 1940 in the public and private sectors were secured from annual company reports, company accounts and the public accounts of provincial governments for the large samples represented by the four largest private companies and all companies owned by provincial governments. The blow up was made on the ratios of total revenues of all companies to the revenues of the companies in the samples for the private and public sectors.

See the note to series R 28–36 for the method used to distribute new investment to construction and to machinery equipment.

Estimates of repair outlays from 1933 to 1941 were based upon reports received by the Transportation and Public Utilities Branch of the Dominion Bureau of Statistics. These were extrapolated from 1932 to 1926 with an index of operating expenses from a 1937 base.

R49–51. Municipal water works. The estimates are from *P.P.I.* Prior to 1949 they are based upon the pattern of new and repair expenditures of a sample of larger cities in 1933, 1937, 1941 and 1944. The expenditures of these cities were raised to full coverage by the ratio of total municipal new and repair expenditures to the new and repair expenditures of the cities covered. These ratios were interpolated for the years in the intervals between the selected years and extrapolated to 1926 and then applied to total municipal new and repair expenditures to secure estimates for other years.

Beginning in 1949 the estimates are based upon the annual capital surveys.

R52–54. Other utilities. These include water transport, motor carriers, air transportation, broadcasting, grain elevators, warehousing and oil pipelines. Federal grain elevators and the National Harbours Board, which were included in government departments in *P.I.C.F.*, are now treated as public utilities. Since about the mid-forties the expenditures by members of this group are from the annual capital surveys with supplementary data from published records. For the most part expenditures in earlier years were obtained by extrapolating a benchmark estimate from the capital survey back to 1926 on an appropriate index of trend. The nature of these indexes is described in *P.P.I.* pp. 226–8.

R55–93. New and repair construction in manufacturing, by industry, 1926 to 1960

SOURCE: for the period 1926 to 1945, *Private and Public Investment in Canada, 1926–1951*, tables 27–39, pp. 158–64; for the period 1946 to 1957, *Private and Public Investment in Canada, 1946–1957*, table 4, pp. 17–22; for the period 1958 to 1960, the files of the Planning and Development Section, Business Finance Division, Dominion Bureau of Statistics.

For the period prior to 1946 the estimates are based upon a sample of corporations reporting for income taxation to the Department of National Revenue. The following quotation from *P.P.I.* (p. 223) illustrates the coverage and the method:

the estimates are based on the tax records of 358 companies engaged in manufacturing in 1946 and active during the preceding 20-year period. To ensure comparability throughout the period the records of the same companies have been used irrespective of change in legal status. For example, if one company which had been formed as the result of a merger in 1938 was operating in 1946, the records of this company formed the basis for the years 1939 to 1946 and the records of the predecessor companies would be used for the period 1926 to 1938.... The 358 companies reported gross sales of $3,016 million in 1946...38 per cent of the gross value of production by manufacturing industry amounting to $8,036 million.

The 358 firms, selected on the basis of the industrial classification... were arranged in size groups, usually three or four within each industrial group, according to the size of the gross sales of the companies in 1945 or 1946. The corporate universe from which the sample was drawn was similarly grouped, and the ratio of universe sales calculated separately for each size group in each of the industrial classifications involved. These ratios were applied as blow-up factors to the sample data on capital and repair and maintenance expenditures for the years 1926 to 1946 inclusive. The resulting absolutes for each industrial group were then converted into a series of index numbers with 1946 as the base year. This index was applied to capital and repair and maintenance expenditure estimated for 1946....

The estimates from 1946 to 1960 are from the annual capital surveys with some groups combined as follows.

R58–60. Rubber, leather and tobacco products industries combine three groups in the source, viz., tobacco and tobacco products, rubber products and leather products.

R82–84. Nonferrous metals and electrical products industries combine two groups in the source, viz., nonferrous metal products and electrical apparatus and supplies.

R85–87. Nonmetallic minerals and petroleum and coal products combine two groups in the source, viz., nonmetallic mineral products and products of petroleum and coal.

R94–102. Institutional construction, new and repair, public and private, 1926 to 1960

SOURCE: for the years 1926 to 1945, *Private and Public Investment in Canada, 1926–1951*, tables 73–5, pp. 181–2; for the years 1946 to 1960, the files of the Planning and Development Section, Business Finance Division, Dominion Bureau of Statistics.

The estimates for the period 1926 to 1946 are from *P.P.I.* and from 1947 to 1960 they are from the annual capital surveys (see general note). The methods used to make the estimates permitted the allocation of the various institutions to the public and private sectors. The sources and methods of estimation for each major type of institution are described in the note to series R103–117.

R103–117. Institutional construction, new and repair, by type of institution, 1926 to 1960

SOURCE: for the period 1926 to 1945, *Private and Public Investment in Canada, 1926–1951*, tables 73, 76–9, pp. 181, 183–4; for the period 1946 to 1957, *Private and Public Investment in Canada, 1946–1957*, table 9, pp. 32–3; for the period 1958 to 1960, the files of the Planning and Development Section, Business Finance Division, Dominion Bureau of Statistics.

See series R100–102 for annual totals of series R103–117.

R103–105. Churches. Estimates from 1947 to 1960 are from the annual capital surveys (see general note). The 1947 estimate of new construction was projected to 1926 with an index based on the value of work performed on churches as reported in D.B.S., *The Construction Industry in Canada* from 1934 to 1947 and, for the earlier years, on the value of contracts awarded for church construction in *MacLean Building Review*.

A repair index, 1926 to 1947, was derived from the new construction series on the assumption that repair outlays would vary cyclically to one-half the extent of new construction.

The same sources and general method were used to devise indexes of trend for new and repair outlays for private hospitals.

R106–108. Universities. Estimates for 1947 to 1960 are from the annual capital surveys. The 1947 estimate was extrapolated on an index combining the annual net change in the value of university plant and equipment, which is published in D.B.S., *Higher Education in Canada*, and an estimate of annual depreciation of the stock. The ratio of repair to the value of plant and equipment in 1947, 2 per cent, was applied to stock series to obtain an annual repair series.

R109–111. Schools. Again the 1947 estimate was run back to 1926 on an index of trend. The index for four years in the period 1939 to 1947 was based upon data in *Comparative Statistics of Public Finance*, Dominion–Provincial Conference on Reconstruction (Ottawa, King's Printer, 1945) and in the capital survey for 1947. Intervening years were obtained by straight-line interpolation. A sample of annual expenditures by five provinces provided the basis for the index from 1926 to 1939.

R112–114. Hospitals. The estimates for private hospitals were obtained by the same general method and with the same sources described above for series R103–105.

The indexes to project the 1947 estimates of new and repair construction were based upon outlays reported in the public accounts of the provinces. Estimates of new construction of municipal hospitals in 1933, 1937, 1939, 1941 and 1943 were made on the basis of data in *Comparative Statistics of Public Finance* (Ottawa, 1945) and on the ratios of these new outlays in the selected years and in 1947 to total municipal new construction in the same years. Intervening years were interpolated. The 1933 ratio was applied to all years from 1926 to 1933. The series of ratios was then applied to total municipal new construction to obtain the required estimate.

Repair construction outlays on municipal hospitals were assumed to be a constant fraction of all municipal repair expenditures. The fraction was an average of this relationship in the period 1947 to 1950.

OFFICIAL HOUSING ESTIMATES
(Series R118–139)

R118–126. Value of residential construction, new and repair, private and public, 1926 to 1960

SOURCE: for 1926 to 1958, ledgers of the Economic Research Department, Central Mortgage and Housing Corporation; for 1959 and 1960, files of the Planning and Development Section, Business Finance Division, Dominion Bureau of Statistics.

The general method used to estimate annual residential capital formation in Canada is to estimate the amount of work put in place each year, measured in physical units and by types of unit. Then average prices, excluding supplementary costs, for each type of unit are applied to the unit series to obtain a value estimate. Supplementary building costs, such as architectural fees, are added to obtain the total value of the investment in new and converted units brought or being brought to completion during the year. An estimate of outlays to improve the existing housing stock is then added to obtain the estimate of gross residential capital formation or what is called the value of new residential construction, public and private. An estimate of repair construction is made by applying an estimated unit cost figure to the number of dwelling units in existence.

Public construction expenditures by government departments, government enterprises, crown corporations and agencies are estimated directly to distinguish the private and public components of new residential construction and repair which are shown in series R118–123.

The physical volume series underlying the estimates from 1921 to 1940 are from O. J. Firestone, *Residential Real Estate in Canada* (see notes to series R129–132 and series R133–139). The volume series from 1941 to 1960 and the valuation series from 1921 to 1960 were estimated by the Economic Research Department, Central Mortgage and Housing Corporation in Ottawa.

In his pioneering study, Firestone established the general procedures for the historical estimates. In 1945 these procedures were replaced by direct statistical observation. Nevertheless census results are still used to revise the data and improve the quality of the surveys. These periodic revisions have been necessary because the cumulated totals of the estimated annual dwelling unit completions since 1941 have fallen short of the intercensal changes from 1941 to 1951 and 1951 to 1956 that can be reliably inferred from the censuses of 1941, 1951 and 1956. Central Mortgage and Housing Corporation are developing revised methods of estimation that will come into effect when the data of the 1961 census are processed. These new methods will most probably result in revisions of the estimates for the nineteen-fifties.

Since 1921 there have been changes in the census definitions of a dwelling unit. Accordingly, the first step in the procedure is to establish uniformity in the census series. This requires adjusting each adjacent pair of census records to a uniform concept. For the

purpose of estimating housebuilding activity in the 1921 to 1941 period, the 1921 census results were increased by 7.1 per cent and the 1931 census data by 4.2 per cent; no adjustment was made to the 1941 census data. The second step is to determine the net change in available dwelling units, *in toto* and by major types and by areas, by subtraction of the earlier from the later census figures. These net changes are then raised to gross changes or intercensal dwelling unit completions by adding an estimate of the number of dwelling units that have disappeared from use through destruction or abandonment. This step is an important one in years of low construction activity because destroyed and abandoned units may then run as high as 25 per cent of annual completions. In years of high activity, destroyed and abandoned units, as estimated, run somewhat under 10 per cent of annual completions. Thus, a large error in the estimate of, say, 25 per cent would be less than 2.5 per cent of total annual completions.

The first of two fundamental problems in the general estimation procedure arises with the fourth step, that is, with the choice of the method of allocating the gross intercensal changes to the individual years in the intercensal interval. In the period 1921 to 1930, the annual distribution was made on the basis of an index of the domestic disappearance of brick, nails, glass, cement, lumber, paint, sanitary ware and furnaces. For the period 1931 to 1939, structural tile, steel pipe and soil pipe were added to the other materials. Some materials were dropped to obtain the 1940 index owing to an evident expansion of their use in non-residential construction. (See Firestone, *Residential Real Estate in Canada*, pp. 385–6.)

Following the 1951 census, and after adjustment of the census figures in 1941 and 1951 to a uniform definition, revised estimates of housing completions from June 1941 to June 1951 were prepared to raise the decade total from 653,935 units to 760,945. Estimates of housing completions by area were available from an annual survey by the Dominion Bureau of Statistics which began in 1945. These series were projected to 1941: the two urban series, centres of over and under 5,000 respectively, by an index of completions in 25 cities provided by the Bureau; the rural nonfarm and farm series, by an index of the domestic disappearance of selected building materials developed by Firestone. The indexes were then used to distribute annually the gross decennial changes in the stocks of dwellings.

Some revision in the volume series was made following the 1956 census. The annual completions since 1954 are based upon the estimates of the starts and completions surveys (see above).

To shift from completions during the year to value of work put in place, it is necessary to establish the annual physical volume of work put in place measured in physical units. To obtain this series it was assumed that, on the average, work equivalent to one third of the value of units under construction at the beginning of a year had been performed the year before and two thirds during the year in question. This two thirds of units under construction plus one third of the units started during the year but still under construction at the end of the year plus all completions during the year that were also started in the same year yields the required volume series measured in physical units. This is the equivalent of one third of starts plus two thirds of completions during the year.

Individual unit costs in 1955 for farm single and multiple and nonfarm single and nonfarm multiple dwelling units were determined by a study of approximately 90 per cent of all dwelling units built under N.H.A. in that year. The costs of the single and multiple units were average weight by type.

In May 1956 a study of units not under N.H.A. was undertaken to establish their distribution by types. This distribution provided weights which were applied to average prices basis N.H.A. units in 1955. The N.H.A. and non N.H.A. unit costs were then weighted and averaged to yield an average national unit price for nonfarm single units ($10,839) and multiple units ($7,084) in 1955.

The unit cost of farm dwelling units was set at $8,000 for 1955 on the basis of an examination of farm mortgage application forms.

The unit cost of conversions for 1955 was based upon a study of building permit data by the Dominion Bureau of Statistics. The estimate, $2,731 per unit, includes an allowance for understatement of 10 per cent.

The unit costs for each type of unit were projected back to 1926. An index of construction costs of single units under N.H.A. was used to project the 1955 unit costs of nonfarm single and multiple back to 1947. The series were carried from 1947 back to 1941 on a revised index combining wholesale building material prices and hourly wage rates in building trades and extended from 1941 to 1926 with a similar index of input prices with fixed weights.

The unit cost of farm dwellings in 1955 was projected to 1921 on an index of wholesale prices of building materials and average wages of farm workers weighted 74 : 26. The index applied to the unit cost of conversions combined material prices and hourly wage rates in trades weighted 55.3:44.7, respectively.

Several questions arise with respect to the adequacy of these procedures. The first is whether or not the indexes of the domestic disappearance of building materials will accurately reflect the year-to-year changes in housing construction from 1921 to 1941. Most of the materials in the indexes are also used in commercial, industrial and institutional construction which may have cyclical patterns unlike those of residential construction.

In the revision after the 1951 census, conversions were increased by only 56 per cent on an arbitrary basis. An increase was warranted because it is known that permit data do not include inexpensive conversions. Saskatoon was one of the cities in the sample used to estimate conversions. In a thorough study of permit data and residential construction in that city undertaken by the author of this section, it was discovered that permits covered from 20 to 25 per cent of the converted units in the period 1941 to 1951. This suggests that the number of conversions may be underestimated in the national series. If this were true it means that many conversions cheap enough to avoid permit regulations are treated as new single or multiple units and therefore valued at a much higher level than the average unit cost of conversions covered by permits. In turn the unit cost of conversions would itself be unduly high because it reflects only the most expensive conversions.

It is also my own impression that the series based upon the 1955 price of farm units is less representative of farm dwelling prices from 1926 to 1960 than the lower price series, derived from V.L.A. experience, which was formerly used.

Another question arises with respect to the implicit treatment of overhead and profit as a fixed proportion in the estimates for the 1926 to 1945 period. And, of course, the cost indexes based upon input prices make no allowance for possible productivity changes from 1926 to 1947.

While the current estimates are much more satisfactory, one must question the method of pricing units not in the N.H.A. component of the total on the base provided by the 1956 study cited above.

R 127–128. Value of new residential construction, as in the national accounts, in current dollars, 1926 to 1960, and in constant dollars, 1926 to 1958

SOURCE: for series R 127, 1926 to 1956, *National Accounts, Income and Expenditure, 1926–1956*, section 6, table 2, p. 32; for series R 128,

1926 to 1956, *National Accounts, Income and Expenditure, 1926–1956*, section 6, table 5, p. 36; for series R 127, 1957 to 1960, and series R 128, 1957 and 1958, the files of the Planning and Development Section, Business Finance Division, Dominion Bureau of Statistics.

See the general note and the note to series R 118–126 for the discussion of sources and procedures. For the purpose of the national accounts only government department expenditures on nonrental housing are deducted from the total of public and private new residential capital formation. This explains the difference between series R 124, which is the value of new public and private residential construction, and series R 127 which is the value of residential construction treated as 'private' in the national accounts.

For the method of deflating new residential construction as well as other construction components, see the note to series R 1–7.

R 129–132. Dwelling units completed, destroyed and abandoned, net increase and stock of dwelling units at year end, 1921 to 1960

SOURCE: 1921 to 1941, Firestone, *Residential Real Estate in Canada*, pp. 267 and 271; from 1941 to 1960, ledgers of the Economic Research Department, Central Mortgage and Housing Corporation.

For the method of estimating annual completions from 1921 to 1960, see the note to series R 118–126.

The estimates of destroyed and abandoned dwellings are based upon municipal reports of a sample of cities, records of farm fires reported to the Federal Government Fire Commissioner, and census data on abandoned farms. (See Firestone, *Residential Real Estate in Canada*, pp. 382–3.)

Stocks of dwellings in 1921, 1931 and 1941 are the adjusted census totals for 1921, 1931 and 1941 plus the estimated number of units completed from 1 June to 31 December in each census year. (See Firestone, *Residential Real Estate in Canada*, p. 378 ff.) The stocks in intercensal years are obtained by adding to the stocks in the census years the annual completions minus destroyed and abandoned units, that is, series R 129 minus series R 130, or series R 131.

The series from 1941 to 1951 and subsequently are derived in the same way, but the 1941 census was adjusted to conform with the 1951 census definition of dwelling units. In 1941 a dwelling was defined as a 'structurally separate set of self-contained living premises having its own entrance from outside the building containing it or from a common passage or stairway inside'. In 1951 the term 'self-contained' was omitted from the definition. It was estimated that the 1941 total of units would have been increased by 103,181 dwelling units by the application of the 1951 definition.

R 133–139. Number of dwelling units completed by area and by type, 1921 to 1960

SOURCE: for series R 133–134, 1921 to 1941, Firestone, *Residential Real Estate in Canada*, table XI, p. 389; for series R 135, 1921 to 1941, *Residential Real Estate in Canada*, table 67, p. 267; for series R 133–135, 1942 to 1951, *Canadian Housing Statistics*, 1st and 2nd quarter, 1955, table 8, p. 8; for 1952 to 1959, *Canadian Housing Statistics*, 4th quarter, 1959, table 2, p. 11, and, for 1960, the files of the Planning and Development Section, Business Finance Division, Dominion Bureau of Statistics; for series R 136–139, *Residential Real Estate in Canada*, tables 67, 68, pp. 267–8.

The distributions by area and by type from 1921 to 1941 are interpolations of census data adjusted to uniform definitions and classifications. (See Firestone, *Residential Real Estate in Canada*, pp. 382–3, 387, 391–4.) Similar interpolations were made by the Economic Research Department of C.M.H.C. on the basis of their revision of the volume series, 1941 to 1956 (see note to series R118–126). The D.B.S.-C.M.H.C. survey of starts and completions provides the distributions by area and type after 1954.

UNOFFICIAL ESTIMATES (Series R140–167)

R140–148. Estimates of the housing stock at the end of census years, 1871 to 1921

SOURCE: Pickett, 'Residential Capital Formation in Canada, 1871–1921', p. 5. This is an unpublished paper to be incorporated in a doctoral dissertation undertaken in the Department of Social and Economic Research, University of Glasgow.

These estimates were developed by Pickett as a preliminary stage in the estimation of annual housing completions from 1871 to 1921. Pickett followed the same general procedures used to obtain the official Canadian estimates from 1921 to 1941 (see note to series R118–126). The data reported in the decennial census from 1871 to 1921 had to be adjusted to a uniform classification and for consistent coverage.

Estimates for areas not enumerated in 1871, that is, for Prince Edward Island, the four western provinces, the Yukon and the Northwest Territories, were made on the assumption that persons per dwelling would be the same as in 1881. Temporary dwelling units were not reported in 1901, 1911 and 1921 and were estimated on the basis of one-roomed houses reported. Units in apartment buildings in 1911 and 1921 were estimated but considered of negligible importance in prior census years.

R149–150. Number and value of dwelling units completed, 1872 to 1921

SOURCE: see the source note to series R140–148. Original estimates appearing in the paper were revised by Mr. Pickett for inclusion in the present volume.

For the general method see the note to series R118–126. The estimates of gross decennial completions were made with a farm: nonfarm breakdown and excluded temporary dwelling units. It was assumed that destroyed and abandoned units in each decade were 3 per cent of the initial stock of permanent units.

Imports valued in constant prices were taken as a basis to estimate the decennial domestic disappearance of window glass. This index was adjusted for an obvious trend in the decade ratios of imported glass per dwelling unit. The adjusted index was then used to distribute gross decennial completions to the individual years. Unit costs in 1921 were obtained from Firestone, *Residential Real Estate in Canada* and projected to 1872 on a combined index of wholesale prices of construction materials and construction wage rates with constant weights. This index, admittedly crude owing to the paucity of official wage data prior to 1900, was developed in connection with a study of capital stock in the Dominion Bureau of Statistics.

The problem of an accurate valuation of dwelling units has been pointed out in the discussion of the official estimates, note to series R118–126. This is obviously a much more acute problem in these historical estimates. What is needed is a city by city search for firm data in historical records that must exist but which have not been investigated, at least, in the recent past.

Examining the level of the physical unit series, two observations may be made. The level in the eighteen-seventies, while much lower than Firestone's reported average (*Residential Real Estate in Canada*, p. 478), appears still to be too high. It is improbable that the 1873 peak was not exceeded until well after the turn of the century. The series from 1901 to 1921 conforms much more closely to what one familiar with existing permit records would expect than the Firestone estimates (*Canada's Economic Development, 1867–1953*, p. 299). However, the weak-

ness of a building materials index (see note to series R118–126), while much less pronounced in this adjusted index of window glass, is still present. Window glass is also used in non-residential construction which may move inversely to residential construction. Again from permit data and contracts awarded, one would expect to see a rise from 1920 to 1921. The wartime rise in 1917 may also be questioned. However, these estimates come much closer to one's impression of plausible behaviour than any others hitherto developed for these years.

R151. Estimates of total new and repair construction, 1896 to 1930

SOURCE: Buckley, *Capital Formation in Canada, 1896–1930*, p. 128.

The year 1921 was the only year in this period when both a decennial census and a construction census were taken. The decennial census data on the construction labour force and records of unemployment among union members in construction work were used to inflate the value of construction reported to the construction census to full coverage.

The annual flow of construction materials to construction uses was applied to the value of materials used in the benchmark year to estimate the value of the material component in each year from 1896 to 1930. The flow of construction materials is the annual domestic disappearance of such materials at producers' prices adjusted for the flow to non-construction uses and for freight charges and sales taxes.

The value of total construction in each year was estimated on the basis of available data on the relations between the material component, the labour component and overhead and profit included in the total cost of construction. For a full description of the sources of estimation, see *Capital Formation in Canada, 1896–1930*, pp. 72–89.

R152–154. New and repair construction, quinquennially, 1896 to 1930

SOURCE: Buckley, *Capital Formation in Canada, 1896–1930*, p. 129.

The annual values of total construction, series R151, were summed for each quinquennium. The breakdown to new and repair in 1926–1930 was made by applying the percentage distribution for this period in *P.I.C.F.* A series of repair expenditures, 1896 to 1930, was estimated directly for the major components of total construction. This series was inflated to full coverage on the basis of its relation to repair totals in the period 1926–30. The coverage, base 1926–30, was two thirds for the period 1911–30 and just over one half for the period 1896 to 1911. For a description of the direct estimates of the major components of total construction, see *Capital Formation in Canada, 1896–1930*, pp. 110–23.

R155. Imports of construction materials, 1868 to 1895

SOURCE: Buckley, 'Historical Estimates of Migration and Investment in Canada', table 5, p. 13.

The classification of construction materials from *P.I.C.F.*, with some adjustments, was used to transcribe the values and duties paid for imports of these materials from the annual trade reports. The commodity classifications in the trade records are reasonably detailed. Since there are no reliable estimates of total construction in the period 1867 to 1896, this import series is the best available index of the year-to-year changes in total construction in that period. Imports of materials accounted for one third of the flow to construction in the period 1900 to 1904. There was a very high conformity in imports, domestic production, and domestic disappearance of construction materials from 1900 to 1936. The three series moved in the same direction in every year but one in that period (see *Capital Formation in Canada, 1896–1930*, pp. 126–7).

R156. Net capital formation in railway transport and telegraphs, 1850 to 1930

SOURCE: Buckley, 'Capital Formation in Railway Transport and Telegraphs in Canada, 1850 to 1930', pp. 24–6.

The series covers new investment charged to capital. In other words it is net capital formation as the railways defined 'net'. Annual reports of privately and government owned railways provided the required information for a large sample of roads. Investment by the companies in the sample was raised to full coverage in two steps. Lines outside the sample and their dates of construction were identified and the annual outlays on new road construction, including new equipment costs, were estimated by applying an appropriate cost per mile. Improvement outlays by lines outside the sample were made on the basis of their total mileage and the average improvement expenditure per mile by selected lines in the sample. The source cited above provides a full description of the sources and procedures underlying the estimates and also describes their conceptual relation to the official estimates from 1926 to the present.

R157–161. New construction and repair, nonrailway transport structures, 1901 to 1930

SOURCE: Buckley, *Capital Formation in Canada, 1896–1930*, p. 137.

Other major transportation structures were products of direct government investment. See the note to series R162–167.

R162–167. New construction, federal government, 1868 to 1930, provincial governments, 1901 to 1930

SOURCE: for 1868 to 1899, Buckley, 'Historical Estimates of Net Migration and Investment in Canada', table 7, p. 16; for 1901 to 1930, Buckley, *Capital Formation in Canada, 1896–1930*, p. 138.

The major sources are the federal *Auditor General's Reports* and the *Public Accounts* of the provinces. The concepts of *P.I.C.F.* were closely followed so that the series could be linked to the official estimates from 1926 to the present. New construction includes all outlays whether charged to capital or current account. Railway rolling stock purchased for federally owned railways is the only non-construction expenditure included. For a full discussion, see *Capital Formation in Canada, 1896–1930*, pp. 112–13, 118–20.

BUILDING PERMITS AND CONTRACTS AWARDED
(Series R168–179)

R168–176. Value of construction contracts awarded, 1911 to 1960, and by type and by area, 1918 to 1960

SOURCE: for series R168, 1911 to 1933 and series R169–176, 1919 to 1933, successive January issues of *MacLean Building Review*, Hugh C. MacLean (now Southam-MacLean) Publications Ltd., Toronto; for 1934 to 1960, the files of the Economic Research Department, Central Mortgage and Housing Corporation.

While these series probably suffer from variations in relative coverage, they are a useful historical series on construction by type and by province back to 1918. Much greater detail may be obtained in the original reports. The title of the reports was changed in May 1945 from *MacLean Building Review* to 'Building Reporter', a removable section of *MacLean Building Guide*, published monthly by Southam-MacLean Publications Limited.

R177. Value of building permits issued, 1910 to 1960

SOURCE: for 1910 to 1920, *Canada Year Book, 1940*, p. 479; for 1920 to 1946, *Annual Report of Building Permits in Canada, 1946*, table 16, p. 36, table 17, pp. 37–40; for 1947 to 1957, *Canada Year Book* of 1958 and 1959; for 1958 to 1960, the files of the Planning and Development Section, Business Finance Division, Dominion Bureau of Statistics.

R178–179. Index of the number of building permits for new buildings *per capita*, Toronto, 1886 to 1910 and the number of permits for new buildings, Montreal, 1867 to 1910

SOURCE: Buckley, *Capital Formation in Canada, 1896–1930*, pp. 140–2.

These two series are given here because, with the exception of a series for Hamilton beginning in 1890, they are the only available permit series for the period before 1900. The existence of the Montreal Archives is responsible for the Montreal series. For the sources and method of deriving the Toronto index, see *Capital Formation in Canada, 1896–1930*, pp. 122–3.

Series R1–6. *New and repair construction expenditures, private and public, in current and in constant dollar values, 1926 to 1960*
(series R1–3 in millions of current dollars; series R4–6 in millions of constant (1949) dollars)

Year	Current dollar estimates			Constant dollar estimates		
	New construction	Repair construction	New and repair construction	New construction	Repair construction	New and repair construction
	1	2	3	4	5	6
1960	5,453	1,431	6,884	—	—	—
1959	5,709	1,367	7,076	3,774	—	—
1958	5,830	1,262	7,092	3,956	—	—
1957	5,784	1,237	7,021	3,993	830	4,823
1956	5,273	1,181	6,454	3,775	821	4,596
1955	4,169	1,136	5,305	3,129	838	3,967
1954	3,737	1,105	4,842	2,876	831	3,707
1953	3,756	1,070	4,826	2,893	811	3,704
1952	3,434	1,010	4,444	2,731	796	3,527
1951	2,871	987	3,858	2,405	830	3,235
1950	2,453	827	3,280	2,325	785	3,110
1949	2,166	765	2,931	2,166	765	2,931
1948	1,824	714	2,538	1,905	747	2,652
1947	1,397	613	2,010	1,671	728	2,399
1946	1,044	555	1,599	1,390	736	2,124
1945	745	513	1,258	1,045	726	1,772
1944	745	474	1,219	1,063	669	1,732
1943	1,021	397	1,418	1,504	571	2,073
1942	943	357	1,300	1,464	547	2,009
1941	809	330	1,139	1,322	548	1,870
1940	563	293	856	993	516	1,510
1939	467	283	750	855	521	1,379
1938	455	277	732	835	507	1,343
1937	505	269	774	910	482	1,395
1936	377	251	628	726	484	1,210
1935	328	238	566	644	469	1,114
1934	275	233	508	547	478	1,022
1933	224	215	439	459	440	899
1932	320	241	561	627	478	1,107
1931	583	287	870	1,085	537	1,624
1930	775	305	1,080	1,350	529	1,878
1929	880	328	1,208	1,481	552	2,034
1928	769	319	1,088	1,337	558	1,892
1927	620	296	916	1,099	534	1,633
1926	533	272	805	943	487	1,430

Series R7–15. *New and repair construction expenditures, by type, 1926 to 1960*
(millions of dollars)

Year	New construction					Repair and maintenance			New, repair and maintenance construction
	Building construction			Engineering	Building and engineering construction	Housing	Other construction	Housing and other construction	
	Housing	Other building	Total building						
	7	8	9	10	11	12	13	14	15
1960	1,456	1,729	3,185	2,268	5,453	457	974	1,431	6,884
1959	1,752	1,662	3,414	2,297	5,711	431	936	1,367	7,077
1958	1,782	1,554	3,336	2,494	5,830	407	855	1,262	7,092
1957	1,430	1,720	3,150	2,634	5,784	383	854	1,237	7,021
1956	1,547	1,630	3,177	2,096	5,273	355	826	1,181	6,454
1955	1,397	1,314	2,711	1,458	4,169	338	798	1,136	5,305
1954	1,238	1,177	2,415	1,322	3,737	316	789	1,105	4,842
1953	1,189	1,186	2,375	1,381	3,756	304	766	1,070	4,826
1952	971	1,100	2,071	1,363	3,434	287	723	1,010	4,444
1951	947	959	1,906	965	2,871	270	717	987	3,858
1950	923	770	1,693	760	2,453	226	601	827	3,280
1949	822	703	1,525	641	2,166	206	559	765	2,931
1948	635	612	1,247	577	1,824	189	525	714	2,538
1947	526	469	995	402	1,397	155	458	613	2,010
1946	407	332	739	305	1,044	133	422	555	1,599
1945	330	246	576	169	745	121	392	513	1,258
1944	279	251	530	215	745	115	359	474	1,219
1943	250	405	655	366	1,021	108	289	397	1,418
1942	244	471	715	228	943	97	260	357	1,300
1941	251	357	608	201	809	88	242	330	1,139
1940	186	232	418	145	563	80	213	293	856
1939	174	130	304	163	467	75	208	283	750
1938	148	128	276	179	455	74	203	277	732
1937	164	140	304	201	505	76	193	269	774
1936	131	103	234	143	377	71	180	251	628
1935	107	72	179	149	328	69	169	238	566
1934	92	65	159	118	275	70	163	233	508
1933	72	57	129	95	224	67	148	215	439
1932	90	87	177	143	320	70	171	241	561
1931	158	169	327	256	583	77	210	287	870
1930	191	260	451	324	775	78	227	305	1,080
1929	230	342	572	308	880	84	244	328	1,208
1928	220	295	515	254	769	81	238	319	1,088
1927	204	220	424	196	620	79	217	296	916
1926	201	165	366	167	533	78	194	272	805

Series R 16–27. *New and repair construction by government departments, by level of government, 1926 to 1960*

(millions of dollars)

Year	Federal government			Provincial governments			Municipal governments			All government departments		
	New con-struction	Repair con-struction	New and repair con-struction	New con-struction	Repair con-struction	New and repair con-struction	New con-struction	Repair con-struction	New and repair con-struction	New con-struction	Repair con-struction	New and repair con-struction
	16	17	18	19	20	21	22	23	24	25	26	27
1960	303	74	377	530	150	680	338	104	441	1,171	328	1,498
1959	330	63	393	486	133	619	313	88	401	1,129	284	1,413
1958	289	63	352	438	122	560	287	81	368	1,014	266	1,280
1957	306	62	368	461	113	574	258	72	330	1,025	247	1,272
1956	320	61	381	391	119	510	221	67	288	932	247	1,179
1955	243	65	308	289	124	413	196	51	247	728	240	968
1954	236	48	284	258	110	368	182	74	256	676	232	908
1953	315	50	365	228	93	321	167	57	224	710	200	910
1952	335	38	373	252	93	345	171	54	225	758	185	943
1951	204	57	261	189	87	276	141	48	189	534	192	726
1950	111	39	150	160	76	236	120	46	166	391	161	552
1949	118	24	142	141	61	202	85	42	127	344	127	471
1948	76	24	100	171	57	228	73	43	116	320	124	444
1947	39	21	60	134	54	188	67	42	109	240	117	357
1946	28	9	37	81	51	132	64	44	108	173	104	277
1945	65	9	74	45	40	85	36	40	76	146	89	235
1944	133	7	140	22	32	54	22	37	58	177	76	252
1943	260	6	266	30	21	51	22	29	51	312	56	368
1942	290	5	295	33	20	53	19	26	45	342	51	393
1941	234	5	239	48	25	73	18	25	43	300	55	355
1940	121	9	129	43	21	64	15	23	37	179	53	230
1939	30	11	41	65	30	95	19	24	43	114	65	179
1938	29	13	41	73	30	103	21	23	44	123	66	188
1937	20	10	30	103	27	130	19	20	39	142	57	199
1936	19	9	28	52	20	72	18	19	36	89	48	136
1935	27	9	36	52	24	76	19	17	36	98	50	148
1934	24	8	31	47	26	73	16	16	32	87	50	136
1933	22	6	29	24	13	37	19	20	38	65	39	104
1932	31	8	39	39	22	61	21	26	47	91	56	147
1931	51	13	64	60	28	87	23	30	53	134	71	204
1930	68	13	81	68	25	93	28	27	55	164	65	229
1929	49	14	64	51	23	74	28	26	53	128	63	191
1928	43	11	54	42	21	63	24	24	48	109	56	165
1927	39	9	48	32	18	50	22	23	45	93	50	143
1926	29	6	35	25	16	41	19	20	38	73	42	114

Series R28–36. *New and repair construction by privately and publicly owned public utilities, 1926 to 1960*

(millions of dollars)

Year	Privately owned public utilities			Publicly owned public utilities			All privately and publicly owned public utilities		
	New construction	Repair construction	New and repair construction	New construction	Repair construction	New and repair construction	New construction	Repair construction	New and repair construction
	28	29	30	31	32	33	34	35	36
1960	476	117	593	598	152	750	1,074	269	1,343
1959	463	121	584	655	154	809	1,118	275	1,393
1958	562	116	678	843	134	977	1,405	250	1,655
1957	653	121	774	822	148	970	1,475	269	1,744
1956	469	114	583	617	134	751	1,086	248	1,334
1955	247	111	358	402	146	548	649	257	906
1954	252	109	361	358	152	510	610	261	871
1953	352	127	479	340	146	486	692	273	965
1952	404	120	524	297	138	435	701	258	959
1951	256	117	373	241	126	367	497	243	740
1950	187	107	294	250	106	356	437	213	650
1949	140	106	246	236	95	331	376	201	577
1948	129	94	223	153	94	247	282	188	470
1947	82	78	160	92	84	176	174	162	336
1946	69	79	148	64	75	139	133	154	287
1945	33.4	83.3	116.7	39.9	65.2	105.1	73.3	148.5	221.8
1944	18.6	73.2	91.8	32.6	64.4	97.0	51.2	137.6	188.8
1943	28.6	58.3	86.9	79.0	52.2	131.2	107.6	110.5	218.1
1942	51.3	48.3	99.6	53.4	45.8	99.2	104.7	94.1	198.8
1941	47.2	42.1	89.3	36.1	51.1	87.2	83.3	93.2	176.5
1940	30.8	35.2	66.0	29.2	44.1	73.3	60.0	79.3	139.3
1939	24.8	31.0	55.8	29.9	41.1	71.0	54.7	72.1	126.8
1938	23.2	30.9	54.1	31.3	38.3	69.6	54.5	69.2	123.7
1937	25.7	32.5	58.2	30.5	39.4	69.9	56.2	71.9	128.1
1936	21.0	30.9	51.9	26.6	40.6	67.2	47.6	71.5	119.1
1935	17.7	29.6	47.3	22.0	36.2	58.2	39.7	65.8	105.5
1934	20.7	28.3	49.0	14.5	35.3	49.8	35.2	63.6	98.8
1933	17.1	26.2	43.3	13.4	32.6	46.0	30.5	58.8	89.3
1932	36.7	29.6	66.3	25.0	33.9	58.9	61.7	63.5	125.2
1931	79.9	34.8	114.7	64.6	45.1	109.7	144.5	79.9	224.4
1930	94.0	42.0	136.0	88.7	50.5	139.2	182.7	92.5	275.2
1929	102.0	50.7	152.7	103.5	56.5	160.0	205.5	107.2	312.7
1928	86.7	53.0	139.7	74.8	56.9	131.7	161.5	109.9	271.4
1927	64.4	46.6	111.0	53.9	51.4	105.3	118.3	98.0	216.3
1926	62.7	42.7	105.4	47.0	47.1	94.1	109.7	89.8	199.5

Series R 37–54. *New and repair construction, all public utilities, by type of utility, 1926 to 1960*

(millions of dollars)

Year	Electric power and gas distribution			Railway transport and telegraphs			Urban transit		
	New construction	Repair construction	New and repair construction	New construction	Repair construction	New and repair construction	New construction	Repair construction	New and repair construction
	37	38	39	40	41	42	43	44	45
1960	428.0	50.0	478.0	231.5	147.0	378.5	19.8	4.2	24.0
1959	464.3	49.8	514.1	234.8	160.0	394.8	4.9	4.3	9.2
1958	570.4	44.0	614.4	182.6	145.5	328.1	3.4	4.5	7.9
1957	624.6	44.9	669.5	188.4	162.7	351.1	9.3	5.4	14.7
1956	492.6	40.7	533.3	155.2	151.7	306.9	7.4	5.8	13.2
1955	325.0	36.2	361.2	88.6	171.1	259.7	4.8	5.5	10.3
1954	301.8	32.3	334.1	70.3	178.9	249.2	8.3	6.1	14.4
1953	354.6	33.1	387.7	106.6	196.0	302.6	12.9	5.7	18.6
1952	398.0	26.9	424.9	92.2	192.6	284.8	17.9	5.8	23.7
1951	314.8	28.2	343.0	58.7	180.1	238.8	16.1	5.8	21.9
1950	259.2	23.1	282.3	36.6	160.1	196.7	11.4	4.6	16.0
1949	228.1	20.1	248.2	53.9	153.8	207.7	5.8	5.1	10.9
1948	164.9	16.5	181.4	38.4	143.9	182.3	6.9	6.5	13.4
1947	82.0	15.8	97.8	27.3	116.8	144.1	6.0	6.8	12.8
1946	57.0	15.1	72.1	34.0	114.7	148.7	2.4	4.7	7.1
1945	26.4	14.4	40.8	23.6	112.3	135.9	1.4	4.6	6.0
1944	11.5	12.8	24.3	25.0	104.0	129.0	1.4	3.9	5.3
1943	23.8	9.9	33.7	22.3	84.0	106.3	1.3	3.6	4.9
1942	50.3	8.6	58.9	24.8	69.9	94.7	.9	2.9	3.8
1941	40.1	8.0	48.1	29.2	71.0	100.2	.8	2.5	3.3
1940	20.8	7.0	27.8	22.8	59.8	82.6	1.1	2.0	3.1
1939	19.1	6.8	25.9	21.0	53.9	74.9	1.0	1.9	2.9
1938	20.7	6.5	27.2	19.5	51.8	71.3	2.1	1.9	4.0
1937	16.2	6.4	22.6	23.6	55.0	78.6	2.3	1.8	4.1
1936	10.7	6.0	16.7	22.3	55.9	78.2	2.1	1.8	3.9
1935	14.9	6.0	20.9	19.2	51.6	70.8	1.3	1.7	3.0
1934	12.8	6.4	19.2	15.9	49.3	65.2	2.6	1.6	4.2
1933	11.1	6.2	17.3	12.4	44.7	57.1	1.1	1.6	2.7
1932	30.2	6.4	36.6	21.6	47.5	69.1	1.6	1.9	3.5
1931	59.7	6.3	66.0	66.9	62.7	129.6	3.9	2.4	6.3
1930	64.3	6.5	70.8	92.2	74.3	166.5	3.5	3.0	6.5
1929	48.4	6.2	54.6	122.7	89.4	212.1	5.6	3.3	8.9
1928	36.5	5.3	41.8	97.8	93.4	191.2	5.7	3.3	9.0
1927	24.8	5.1	29.9	72.9	82.2	155.1	5.1	3.1	8.2
1926	25.9	4.4	30.3	61.7	76.2	137.9	6.0	3.1	9.1

Year	Telephone companies			Municipal water works			Other utilities		
	New construction	Repair construction	New and repair construction	New construction	Repair construction	New and repair construction	New construction	Repair construction	New and repair construction
	46	47	48	49	50	51	52	53	54
1960	132.5	28.3	160.8	79.1	18.7	97.8	183.3	21.0	204.3
1959	126.9	26.1	153.0	87.4	15.4	102.8	200.1	19.4	219.5
1958	126.7	26.1	152.8	75.9	14.7	90.6	513.8	1.9	515.7
1957	112.7	25.1	137.8	62.2	14.9	77.1	478.2	16.2	494.4
1956	98.7	22.7	121.4	66.4	12.3	78.7	265.3	14.3	279.6
1955	90.8	19.3	110.1	48.2	12.2	60.4	91.5	13.1	104.6
1954	76.0	17.5	93.5	57.0	12.2	69.2	96.8	13.9	110.7
1953	70.9	16.3	87.2	44.4	9.3	53.7	102.5	12.5	115.0
1952	58.3	14.8	73.1	41.2	8.5	49.7	93.0	9.4	102.4
1951	53.2	13.7	66.9	28.6	6.9	35.5	25.2	8.4	33.6
1950	44.7	12.7	57.4	20.9	5.9	26.8	64.6	6.6	71.2
1949	51.3	11.7	63.0	13.1	4.0	17.1	24.3	6.2	30.5
1948	46.0	10.2	56.2	9.5	2.8	12.3	15.9	8.3	24.2
1947	35.3	10.2	45.5	6.8	3.1	9.9	16.1	9.8	25.9
1946	25.8	9.0	34.8	5.7	2.8	8.5	8.0	7.8	15.8
1945	12.0	6.3	18.3	3.2	2.6	5.8	6.8	8.2	15.0
1944	2.3	5.6	7.9	1.9	2.5	4.4	9.1	8.8	17.9
1943	1.2	5.1	6.3	2.1	2.1	4.2	56.9	5.9	62.8
1942	1.6	5.1	6.7	1.9	1.9	3.8	25.2	5.5	30.7
1941	1.6	4.9	6.5	2.0	2.0	4.0	10.6	4.8	15.4
1940	7.4	4.5	11.9	1.8	1.8	3.6	6.2	4.1	10.3
1939	5.7	4.2	9.9	2.7	2.0	4.7	5.2	3.3	8.5
1938	4.6	4.1	8.7	2.5	1.8	4.3	5.1	3.3	8.4
1937	5.4	4.0	9.4	2.3	1.6	3.9	6.5	3.0	9.5
1936	3.5	3.6	7.1	2.3	1.4	3.7	6.6	2.9	9.5
1935	.4	3.4	3.8	2.2	1.3	3.5	1.7	1.8	3.5
1934	.8	3.4	4.2	1.8	1.3	3.1	1.4	1.6	3.0
1933	2.3	3.3	5.6	2.3	1.6	3.9	1.3	1.4	2.7
1932	4.3	4.0	8.3	2.5	2.1	4.6	1.5	1.6	3.1
1931	7.3	4.4	11.7	2.7	2.4	5.1	4.0	1.7	5.7
1930	11.5	4.5	16.0	3.3	2.2	5.5	8.0	2.0	10.0
1929	18.5	4.1	22.6	3.3	2.1	5.4	7.1	2.0	9.1
1928	14.2	3.7	17.9	2.8	2.0	4.8	4.5	2.2	6.7
1927	11.0	3.5	14.5	2.5	1.9	4.4	2.0	2.1	4.1
1926	10.3	2.8	13.1	2.2	1.6	3.8	3.4	1.8	5.2

Series R 55–93. *New and repair construction in manufacturing, by industry, 1926 to 1960*

(millions of dollars)

Year	Food and beverage industries			Rubber, leather and tobacco and their products industries			Primary textiles and their products industries		
	New construction	Repair construction	New and repair construction	New construction	Repair construction	New and repair construction	New construction	Repair construction	New and repair construction
	55	56	57	58	59	60	61	62	63
1960	52.2	14.2	66.4	9.8	2.6	12.4	6.0	3.4	9.4
1959	45.4	14.7	60.1	7.6	3.1	10.7	4.7	3.1	7.8
1958	40.5	13.9	54.4	6.6	2.7	9.3	2.6	2.8	5.4
1957	36.3	13.0	49.3	9.3	2.9	12.2	7.9	3.1	11.0
1956	32.6	12.2	44.8	8.2	2.7	10.9	10.3	3.4	13.7
1955	38.5	12.7	51.2	5.1	2.4	7.5	7.6	2.9	10.5
1954	38.6	13.2	51.8	5.7	2.3	8.0	7.5	2.7	10.2
1953	26.0	12.8	38.8	6.0	2.6	8.6	7.9	2.8	10.7
1952	26.6	12.5	39.1	3.8	2.0	5.8	7.0	3.8	10.8
1951	28.0	11.8	39.8	3.4	1.9	5.3	9.9	4.0	13.9
1950	26.0	10.0	36.0	2.3	1.7	4.0	6.6	3.5	10.1
1949	27.7	10.4	38.1	2.6	1.7	4.3	7.0	3.6	10.6
1948	31.9	13.2	45.1	3.5	2.4	5.9	6.5	3.9	10.4
1947	33.0	10.8	43.8	4.6	2.7	7.3	10.9	2.8	13.7
1946	24.7	12.3	37.0	6.7	2.7	9.4	8.4	3.3	11.7
1945	18.2	11.6	29.8	5.9	9.2	15.1	1.3	2.9	4.2
1944	10.7	8.5	19.2	2.3	6.6	8.9	1.8	2.8	4.6
1943	6.1	8.1	14.2	2.2	2.5	4.7	.8	1.4	2.2
1942	8.5	11.8	20.3	2.4	2.7	5.1	1.5	1.1	2.6
1941	9.7	6.3	16.0	2.4	1.8	4.2	3.1	.9	4.0
1940	10.7	7.8	18.5	2.7	1.6	4.3	3.4	.6	4.0
1939	7.5	6.2	13.7	1.1	1.1	2.2	.6	.7	1.3
1938	7.8	7.3	15.1	.8	.3	1.1	1.4	.6	2.0
1937	8.5	6.9	15.4	1.8	.7	2.5	2.6	.4	3.0
1936	5.3	6.0	11.3	16.4	.5	16.9	1.3	.4	1.7
1935	3.5	2.5	6.0	.1	.5	.6	2.8	.3	3.1
1934	1.6	1.7	3.3	.4	.6	1.0	.6	.5	1.1
1933	.8	1.5	2.3	2.9	.6	3.5	.9	.3	1.2
1932	4.9	1.8	6.7	.4	.4	.8	1.0	.1	1.1
1931	7.2	2.3	9.5	.9	1.0	1.9	1.7	.1	1.8
1930	7.4	5.4	12.8	2.1	.4	2.5	6.8	.2	7.0
1929	13.5	3.4	16.9	2.5	2.9	5.4	1.4	.2	1.6
1928	9.6	3.2	12.8	2.9	1.7	4.6	.6	.3	.9
1927	4.4	6.1	10.5	1.1	1.7	2.8	6.2	.2	6.4
1926	2.7	4.9	7.6	.8	.5	1.3	4.7	.3	5.0

Year	Clothing industry			Wood and its products industries			Pulp and paper and their products industries		
	New construction	Repair construction	New and repair construction	New construction	Repair construction	New and repair construction	New construction	Repair construction	New and repair construction
	64	65	66	67	68	69	70	71	72
1960	2.3	1.2	3.5	16.1	6.5	22.6	34.1	9.2	43.3
1959	1.6	1.3	2.9	15.3	6.8	22.1	24.2	9.9	34.1
1958	.7	1.1	1.8	8.8	5.9	14.7	25.5	7.2	32.7
1957	1.2	1.1	2.3	10.3	6.5	16.8	66.3	8.1	74.4
1956	1.3	1.2	2.5	14.0	7.4	21.4	85.1	10.3	95.4
1955	1.4	1.2	2.6	12.1	7.6	19.7	33.1	8.9	42.0
1954	2.2	1.3	3.5	8.4	6.5	14.9	21.6	8.2	29.8
1953	3.8	1.5	5.3	10.4	7.8	18.2	22.5	7.0	29.5
1952	1.6	1.3	2.9	9.3	6.1	15.4	33.6	8.3	41.9
1951	4.1	1.4	5.5	11.2	7.7	18.9	41.9	9.7	51.6
1950	2.5	1.4	3.9	8.1	5.4	13.5	21.1	8.0	29.1
1949	3.0	1.9	4.9	7.5	5.7	13.2	26.8	8.7	35.5
1948	2.1	2.2	4.3	7.9	7.1	15.0	29.1	7.0	36.1
1947	3.7	1.9	5.6	11.4	6.5	17.9	31.2	6.4	37.6
1946	2.6	2.2	4.8	10.9	5.7	16.6	27.2	5.3	32.5
1945	9.2	2.1	11.3	1.6	5.3	6.9	5.8	1.9	7.7
1944	2.8	3.8	6.6	2.9	4.6	7.5	8.0	1.9	9.9
1943	1.6	.7	2.3	16.8	3.6	20.4	1.7	1.5	3.2
1942	3.0	.3	3.3	11.3	5.6	16.9	3.8	1.7	5.5
1941	10.9	.6	11.5	10.8	3.6	14.4	8.8	1.3	10.1
1940	2.4	.4	2.8	8.0	3.5	11.5	5.1	1.4	6.5
1939	1.4	.4	1.8	4.9	2.7	7.6	3.9	.9	4.8
1938	.4	.1	.5	1.2	1.8	3.0	2.6	.5	3.1
1937	1.8	.1	1.9	14.1	1.3	15.4	4.2	1.2	5.4
1936	.8	.2	1.0	2.8	.8	3.6	1.5	.6	2.1
1935	.1	.1	.2	1.0	.9	1.9	2.2	.4	2.6
1934	.4	—	.4	4.4	.7	5.1	.8	.2	1.0
1933	1.1	—	1.1	7.0	.5	7.5	.1	.1	.2
1932	1.3	.1	1.4	4.4	1.1	5.5	2.1	.1	2.2
1931	1.6	.1	1.7	1.0	1.1	2.1	11.3	.1	11.4
1930	.8	.1	.9	5.9	2.4	8.3	4.4	1.2	5.6
1929	13.3	.1	13.4	10.2	2.3	12.5	16.0	.2	16.2
1928	10.8	.1	10.9	7.4	1.0	8.4	34.8	1.5	36.3
1927	7.5	.1	7.6	21.5	.3	21.8	23.7	1.1	24.8
1926	2.0	.1	2.1	3.3	.4	3.7	21.4	.3	21.7

Series R 55–93. *New and repair construction in manufacturing, by industry, 1926 to 1960 (continuation)*
(millions of dollars)

Year	Printing, publishing and allied industries			Iron and steel and their products industries			Transportation equipment industries		
	New construction	Repair construction	New and repair construction	New construction	Repair construction	New and repair construction	New construction	Repair construction	New and repair construction
	73	74	75	76	77	78	79	80	81
1960	7.4	2.3	9.7	47.2	15.0	62.2	16.4	10.4	26.8
1959	11.8	2.0	13.8	40.9	16.0	56.9	20.5	10.2	30.7
1958	13.4	2.0	15.4	35.7	14.4	50.1	16.6	10.4	27.0
1957	17.3	2.0	19.3	54.5	16.6	71.1	18.1	11.6	29.7
1956	5.3	1.6	6.9	40.3	15.4	55.7	16.7	10.6	27.3
1955	6.4	2.2	8.6	27.0	12.6	39.6	20.2	10.6	30.8
1954	11.7	2.4	14.1	22.0	12.6	34.6	20.9	10.9	31.8
1953	3.8	2.0	5.8	35.6	15.6	51.2	46.9	11.9	58.8
1952	3.3	1.5	4.8	46.2	16.1	62.3	37.1	11.6	48.7
1951	6.3	1.7	8.0	47.1	13.0	60.1	21.8	6.9	28.7
1950	5.0	1.7	6.7	13.5	12.7	26.2	9.9	5.7	15.6
1949	6.3	1.4	7.7	14.6	12.4	27.0	6.7	5.3	12.0
1948	7.0	1.6	8.6	19.6	12.0	31.6	5.4	5.3	10.7
1947	5.4	1.6	7.0	16.0	10.1	26.1	5.2	3.1	8.3
1946	2.9	1.3	4.2	14.9	8.4	23.3	5.4	3.7	9.1
1945	3.9	.8	4.7	12.8	7.7	20.5	2.2	8.1	10.3
1944	.2	.6	.8	10.1	6.5	16.6	1.6	11.0	12.6
1943	.2	.6	.8	4.3	6.4	10.7	6.6	7.6	14.2
1942	.3	.4	.7	7.2	5.3	12.5	27.9	5.1	33.0
1941	—	.5	.5	9.9	4.0	13.9	3.0	3.9	6.9
1940	.6	.4	1.0	4.9	1.3	6.2	3.4	2.5	5.9
1939	.3	.4	.7	4.3	.7	5.0	2.9	2.2	5.1
1938	.6	.3	.9	5.0	.7	5.7	14.5	2.1	16.6
1937	1.2	.3	1.5	10.0	1.0	11.0	5.2	2.3	7.5
1936	—	.3	.3	3.1	.9	4.0	.9	2.2	3.1
1935	.6	.2	.8	2.4	.6	3.0	2.4	.7	3.1
1934	—	.3	.3	2.5	.6	3.1	2.1	.3	2.4
1933	.3	.2	.5	.6	.5	1.1	.6	.3	.9
1932	.7	.1	.8	.5	.2	.7	.2	.3	.5
1931	.3	.2	.5	4.7	.4	5.1	.3	1.5	1.8
1930	.2	.1	.3	12.5	.8	13.3	1.8	1.5	3.3
1929	7.5	.1	7.6	8.3	1.1	9.4	8.3	1.9	10.2
1928	9.4	.1	9.5	4.8	1.2	6.0	7.0	1.7	8.7
1927	.5	.2	.7	5.0	.6	5.6	4.8	1.1	5.9
1926	.8	.2	1.0	4.3	.6	4.9	.8	1.1	1.9

Year	Nonferrous metals and electrical products industries			Nonmetallic minerals and petroleum and coal products			Chemicals and their products industries			Miscellaneous manufacturing industries		
	New construction	Repair construction	New and repair construction	New construction	Repair construction	New and repair construction	New construction	Repair construction	New and repair construction	New construction	Repair construction	New and repair construction
	82	83	84	85	86	87	88	89	90	91	92	93
1960	32.5	16.8	49.3	88.0	32.5	120.5	36.2	10.8	47.0	6.4	1.9	8.3
1959	36.3	15.6	51.9	135.1	30.9	166.0	24.5	10.1	34.6	6.0	1.5	7.5
1958	51.0	12.5	63.5	88.0	32.5	120.5	43.1	9.2	52.3	2.7	1.4	4.1
1957	83.7	11.8	95.5	142.8	29.1	171.9	65.6	8.1	73.7	6.6	1.5	8.1
1956	77.1	15.2	92.3	140.9	20.5	161.4	57.9	6.2	64.1	3.6	1.4	5.0
1955	45.4	10.9	56.3	122.6	22.1	144.7	21.6	4.7	26.3	3.7	1.3	5.0
1954	32.0	11.8	43.8	99.2	18.5	117.7	15.1	6.2	21.3	2.7	1.0	3.7
1953	53.4	11.4	64.8	67.1	13.5	80.6	32.0	4.3	36.3	3.7	.9	4.6
1952	56.9	11.3	68.2	52.3	15.1	67.4	61.2	4.5	65.7	4.7	1.1	5.8
1951	38.7	9.1	47.8	33.2	13.0	46.2	19.2	4.0	23.2	3.7	.8	3.8
1950	12.0	6.0	18.0	18.7	6.4	25.1	7.3	4.3	11.6	2.4	.8	3.2
1949	15.2	9.4	24.6	25.0	4.5	29.5	11.9	3.9	15.8	2.3	.8	3.1
1948	9.7	7.2	16.9	40.4	8.9	49.3	15.0	4.3	19.3	2.7	1.0	3.7
1947	12.0	6.7	18.7	34.7	5.0	39.7	14.4	4.0	18.4	2.3	.8	3.1
1946	5.3	4.3	9.6	8.7	3.8	12.5	11.6	2.9	14.5	2.9	.9	3.8
1945	1.5	5.3	6.8	7.8	3.0	10.8	4.0	4.2	8.2	1.7	1.0	2.7
1944	14.7	6.9	21.6	3.5	2.8	6.3	1.4	3.7	5.1	1.3	1.0	2.3
1943	36.2	4.7	40.9	3.7	2.3	6.0	2.5	5.7	8.2	1.9	.7	2.6
1942	59.2	4.8	64.0	3.9	2.3	6.2	5.3	3.7	9.0	3.0	.7	3.7
1941	26.0	2.3	28.3	5.3	2.1	7.4	3.2	3.4	6.6	2.1	.5	2.6
1940	15.7	1.9	17.6	6.4	1.7	8.1	1.9	2.1	4.0	1.5	.4	1.9
1939	.4	.7	1.1	4.4	.7	5.1	1.0	.9	1.9	.7	.3	1.0
1938	1.3	.7	2.0	5.3	.7	6.0	2.9	1.0	3.9	1.0	.3	1.3
1937	.8	.3	1.1	7.0	.7	7.7	5.5	1.6	7.1	1.4	.3	1.7
1936	.7	.3	1.0	3.6	1.2	4.8	.4	1.5	1.9	.8	.2	1.0
1935	.8	.3	1.1	3.6	.9	4.5	1.1	.2	1.3	.5	.1	.6
1934	.6	.3	.9	3.3	.8	4.1	2.4	.4	2.8	.4	.1	.5
1933	.4	.1	.5	2.0	.8	2.8	1.0	1.4	2.4	.4	.1	.5
1932	.6	—	.6	2.1	.6	2.7	.7	1.5	2.2	.4	.1	.5
1931	1.0	.1	1.1	8.2	.9	9.1	1.8	1.3	3.1	.9	.1	1.0
1930	1.8	.1	1.9	27.2	.5	27.7	2.9	.8	3.7	1.7	.2	1.9
1929	3.5	.2	3.7	32.7	1.5	34.2	10.9	1.1	12.0	2.9	.2	3.1
1928	1.5	.2	1.7	32.0	1.7	33.7	1.2	1.1	2.3	2.7	.2	2.9
1927	1.9	.2	2.1	6.0	1.8	7.8	2.4	1.0	3.4	1.9	.2	2.1
1926	2.6	.1	2.7	6.7	1.5	8.2	4.4	.8	5.2	1.2	.2	1.4

Series R94–102. *Institutional construction, new and repair, public and private, 1926 to 1960*

(millions of dollars)

Year	Public			Private			Public and private		
	New construction	Repair construction	New and repair construction	New construction	Repair construction	New and repair construction	New construction	Repair construction	New and repair construction
	94	95	96	97	98	99	100	101	102
1960	297	36	333	203	23	226	500	59	559
1959	283	16	299	196	33	229	479	49	528
1958	254	29	283	203	20	223	457	49	506
1957	243	28	271	164	20	184	407	48	455
1956	219	26	245	140	19	159	359	45	404
1955	212	24	236	155	18	173	367	42	409
1954	169	20	189	128	15	143	297	35	332
1953	158	20	178	112	14	126	270	34	304
1952	160	19	179	92	14	106	252	33	285
1951	131	19	150	81	14	95	212	33	245
1950	109	12	121	78	16	94	187	28	215
1949	88	11	99	84	17	101	172	28	200
1948	56	7	63	70	22	92	126	29	155
1947	35	7	42	43	11	54	78	18	96
1946	32	6	38	34	11	45	66	17	83
1945	22.8	6.8	29.6	17.3	7.3	24.6	40.1	14.1	54.2
1944	15.5	6.1	21.6	9.0	6.9	15.9	24.5	13.0	37.5
1943	10.7	5.0	15.7	6.0	6.4	12.4	16.7	11.4	28.1
1942	8.7	4.2	12.9	5.2	6.5	11.7	13.9	10.7	24.6
1941	7.3	4.0	11.3	7.5	6.7	14.2	14.8	10.7	25.5
1940	8.5	3.5	12.0	7.4	6.6	14.0	15.9	10.1	26.0
1939	16.1	3.6	19.7	10.2	6.9	17.1	26.3	10.5	36.8
1938	15.1	3.5	18.6	8.5	7.0	15.5	23.6	10.5	34.1
1937	12.1	3.1	15.2	7.3	6.6	13.9	19.4	9.7	29.1
1936	10.5	2.9	13.4	6.0	6.3	12.3	16.5	9.2	25.7
1935	8.3	2.7	11.0	3.9	6.3	10.2	12.2	9.0	21.2
1934	6.9	2.6	9.5	4.1	6.3	10.4	11.0	8.9	19.9
1933	8.9	3.0	11.9	4.0	6.3	10.3	12.9	9.3	22.2
1932	19.1	3.9	23.0	9.3	7.1	16.4	28.4	11.0	39.4
1931	26.7	4.4	31.1	18.8	7.7	26.5	45.5	12.1	57.6
1930	36.6	4.0	40.6	19.5	7.6	27.1	56.1	11.6	67.7
1929	33.1	3.8	36.9	14.6	7.6	22.2	47.7	11.4	59.1
1928	27.9	3.7	31.6	13.9	7.8	21.7	41.8	11.5	53.3
1927	24.9	3.6	28.5	15.2	7.9	23.1	40.1	11.5	51.6
1926	20.1	3.1	23.2	13.2	7.3	20.5	33.3	10.4	43.7

Series R103–117. *Institutional construction, new and repair, by type of institution, 1926 to 1960*

(millions of dollars)

Year	Churches			Universities			Schools			Hospitals			Other		
	New construction	Repair construction	New and repair construction	New construction	Repair construction	New and repair construction	New construction	Repair construction	New and repair construction	New construction	Repair construction	New and repair construction	New construction	Repair construction	New and repair construction
	103	104	105	106	107	108	109	110	111	112	113	114	115	116	117
1960	59.3	9.2	68.5	74.7	4.3	79.0	229.6	29.4	259.0	125.2	14.7	139.9	11.3	.7	12.0
1959	54.6	7.9	62.5	73.2	4.3	77.5	213.5	18.8	232.3	128.1	17.3	145.4	9.5	.9	10.4
1958	55.0	7.9	62.9	55.7	5.0	60.7	201.9	21.6	223.5	136.1	13.8	149.9	8.6	.2	8.8
1957	52.8	8.3	61.1	38.0	4.0	42.0	197.6	20.4	218.0	111.7	14.0	125.7	7.3	1.2	8.5
1956	43.8	6.5	50.3	22.3	3.6	25.9	173.1	18.7	191.8	110.0	15.2	125.2	9.6	.8	10.4
1955	33.9	8.0	41.9	22.0	3.1	25.1	171.4	18.2	189.6	130.0	11.7	141.7	9.6	1.1	10.7
1954	30.6	6.0	36.6	16.6	2.7	19.3	136.1	15.8	151.9	106.4	9.3	115.7	7.6	.8	8.4
1953	24.8	5.9	30.7	14.5	2.2	16.7	122.2	15.2	137.4	103.1	10.1	113.2	5.0	.8	5.8
1952	25.2	5.2	30.4	9.4	2.4	11.8	130.7	14.1	144.8	81.4	10.5	91.9	5.1	1.0	6.1
1951	28.3	7.0	35.3	11.5	2.3	13.8	102.3	14.3	116.6	65.5	8.9	74.4	4.1	.9	5.0
1950	28.0	7.5	35.5	12.4	1.6	14.0	80.6	9.2	89.8	62.3	8.7	71.0	3.9	.8	4.7
1949	30.2	7.8	38.0	9.8	2.1	11.9	67.2	9.2	76.4	61.3	8.5	69.8	3.9	.8	4.7
1948	21.0	8.0	29.0	11.0	2.6	13.6	47.6	5.6	53.2	44.0	11.3	55.3	2.8	1.1	3.9
1947	9.8	4.8	14.6	11.9	2.3	14.2	27.6	5.0	32.6	27.0	5.3	32.3	1.7	.5	2.2
1946	5.6	3.8	9.4	10.8	2.1	12.9	24.5	5.0	29.5	23.8	5.3	29.1	1.5	.5	2.0
1945	2.2	2.9	5.1	6.1	2.0	8.1	12.9	4.5	17.4	18.9	4.7	23.6	—	—	—
1944	1.6	2.8	4.4	1.4	2.0	3.4	7.3	4.1	11.4	14.2	4.1	18.3	—	—	—
1943	1.0	2.6	3.6	1.8	2.0	3.8	6.9	3.3	10.2	7.0	3.5	10.5	—	—	—
1942	1.3	2.7	4.0	.9	2.0	2.9	5.6	2.9	8.5	6.1	3.1	9.2	—	—	—
1941	1.9	2.9	4.8	2.8	2.0	4.8	5.0	2.8	7.8	5.1	3.0	8.1	—	—	—
1940	2.1	2.9	5.0	2.0	1.9	3.9	6.4	2.5	8.9	5.4	2.8	8.2	—	—	—
1939	2.6	3.1	5.7	4.2	1.9	6.1	11.2	2.7	13.9	8.3	2.8	11.1	—	—	—
1938	3.2	3.2	6.4	1.4	1.9	3.3	7.2	2.6	9.8	11.8	2.8	14.6	—	—	—
1937	2.7	3.1	5.8	2.6	1.8	4.4	7.4	2.3	9.7	6.7	2.5	9.2	—	—	—
1936	1.8	2.8	4.6	1.4	1.8	3.2	8.4	2.1	10.5	4.9	2.5	7.4	—	—	—
1935	1.5	2.8	4.3	.9	1.8	2.7	6.0	1.9	7.9	3.8	2.5	6.3	—	—	—
1934	1.6	2.8	4.4	1.2	1.8	3.0	5.2	1.8	7.0	3.0	2.5	5.5	—	—	—
1933	2.0	2.9	4.9	.9	1.8	2.7	6.7	2.2	8.9	3.3	2.4	5.7	—	—	—
1932	4.4	3.5	7.9	1.8	1.8	3.6	15.8	2.9	18.7	6.4	2.8	9.2	—	—	—
1931	6.3	4.0	10.3	7.4	1.7	9.1	21.5	3.4	24.9	10.3	3.0	13.3	—	—	—
1930	6.8	4.1	10.9	8.2	1.5	9.7	31.3	3.0	34.3	9.8	3.0	12.8	—	—	—
1929	7.2	4.2	11.4	3.9	1.5	5.4	26.4	2.9	29.3	10.2	2.8	13.0	—	—	—
1928	8.6	4.5	13.1	1.8	1.4	3.2	24.8	2.7	27.5	6.6	2.9	9.5	—	—	—
1927	9.3	4.7	14.0	3.0	1.4	4.4	22.7	2.6	25.3	5.1	2.8	7.9	—	—	—
1926	7.9	4.3	12.2	3.1	1.3	4.4	17.6	2.2	19.8	4.7	2.6	7.3	—	—	—

Series R118–126. *Value of residential construction, new and repair, private and public, 1926 to 1960*

(millions of dollars)

Year	Private construction			Public construction			Private and public construction		
	New	Repair	Total	New	Repair	Total	New	Repair	Total
	118	119	120	121	122	123	124	125	126
1960	1,428	457	1,885	28	—	28	1,456	457	1,913
1959	1,720	431	2,151	32	—	32	1,752	431	2,183
1958	1,742	407	2,149	40	—	40	1,782	407	2,189
1957	1,391	383	1,774	39	—	39	1,430	383	1,813
1956	1,519	355	1,874	28	—	28	1,547	355	1,902
1955	1,373	338	1,711	24	—	24	1,397	338	1,735
1954	1,220	316	1,536	18	—	18	1,238	316	1,554
1953	1,149	304	1,453	40	—	40	1,189	304	1,493
1952	919	284	1,203	52	3	55	971	287	1,258
1951	890	267	1,157	57	3	60	947	270	1,217
1950	867	223	1,090	56	3	59	923	226	1,149
1949	751	204	955	71	2	73	822	206	1,028
1948	568	186	754	67	3	70	635	189	824
1947	494	153	647	32	2	34	526	155	681
1946	368	129	497	39	4	43	407	133	540
1945	318	121	439	12	0	12	330	121	451
1944	267	115	382	12	0	12	279	115	394
1943	220	108	326	30	0	30	250	108	358
1942	214	97	311	30	0	30	244	97	341
1941	240	88	328	11	0	11	251	88	339
1940	186	80	266	—	—	—	186	80	266
1939	174	75	249	—	—	—	174	75	249
1938	148	74	222	—	—	—	148	74	222
1937	164	76	240	—	—	—	164	76	240
1936	131	71	202	—	—	—	131	71	202
1935	107	69	176	—	—	—	107	69	176
1934	92	70	162	—	—	—	92	70	162
1933	72	67	139	—	—	—	72	67	139
1932	90	70	160	—	—	—	90	70	160
1931	158	77	235	—	—	—	158	77	235
1930	191	78	269	—	—	—	191	78	269
1929	230	84	314	—	—	—	230	84	314
1928	220	81	301	—	—	—	220	81	301
1927	204	79	283	—	—	—	204	79	283
1926	201	78	279	—	—	—	201	78	279

Series R127–128. *Value of new residential construction, as in the national accounts, in current dollars, 1926 to 1960, and in constant dollars, 1926 to 1958*

(millions of dollars)

Year	Current dollar values	Constant (1949) dollar values	Year	Current dollar values	Constant (1949) dollar values
	127	128		127	128
1960	1,443	—	1940	186	363
1959	1,734	—	1939	174	361
1958	1,763	1,220	1938	148	310
1957	1,409	997	1937	164	336
1956	1,526	1,110	1936	131	288
1955	1,378	1,040	1935	107	242
1954	1,227	946	1934	92	207
1953	1,166	905	1933	72	168
1952	933	737	1932	90	200
1951	895	727	1931	158	322
1950	883	833	1930	191	363
1949	794	794	1929	230	426
1948	609	638	1928	220	426
1947	494	610	1927	204	405
1946	368	512	1926	201	399
1945	318	472			
1944	267	401			
1943	220	343			
1942	214	356			
1941	240	427			

Series R 129–132. *Dwelling units completed, destroyed and abandoned, net increase and stock of dwelling units at year end,*
1921 to 1960

(thousands of units)

Year[1]	Dwelling units completed	Dwelling units destroyed and abandoned	Net increase	Stock of dwelling units	Year[1]	Dwelling units completed	Dwelling units destroyed and abandoned	Net increase	Stock of dwelling units
	129	130	131	132		129	130	131	132
1960	126.8	8.8	118.0	4,620.2			Old series		
1959	149.5	9.8	139.7	4,502.2					
1958	151.2	10.3	140.7	4,362.5	1941	56.8	7.5	49.5	2,692.9
1957	121.3	9.9	111.3	4,221.8	1940	52.5	6.9	45.6	2,643.4
1956	139.3	10.0	130.3	4,110.5	1939	51.7	7.5	44.2	2,597.8
					1938	44.0	7.0	37.0	2,553.6
1955	132.3	9.3	125.1	3,980.2	1937	48.6	8.1	40.5	2,516.6
1954	106.3	8.3	115.7	3,855.1	1936	39.3	7.0	32.3	2,476.1
1953	100.7	7.8	110.3	3,739.4					
1952	76.3	7.1	86.0	3,629.1	1935	32.9	6.3	26.6	2,443.8
1951	84.8	11.0	89.9	3,543.1	1934	27.7	5.9	21.8	2,417.2
					1933	21.9	5.5	16.4	2,395.4
1950	91.8	10.2	93.3	3,453.2	1932	28.1	6.6	21.5	2,379.0
1949[1]	91.7	8.8	95.0	3,359.9[1]	1931	47.8	7.9	39.9	2,357.5
1948	81.2	8.5	86.1	3,191.3					
1947	79.3	8.4	77.9	3,105.2	1930	53.0	6.6	46.4	2,317.6
1946	67.2	8.4	67.9	3,027.3	1929	64.7	7.0	57.7	2,271.2
					1928	62.9	6.1	58.6	2,213.5
1945	48.5	7.4	54.5	2,959.4	1927	56.8	6.2	50.6	2,156.7
1944	42.8	7.1	45.5	2,904.9	1926	55.2	6.0	49.2	2,106.1
1943	36.8	6.8	40.2	2,859.4					
1942	47.2	6.7	47.3	2,819.2	1925	44.7	5.6	39.1	2,056.9
1941	56.8	7.5	—	2,771.9	1924	38.7	4.9	33.8	2,017.8
					1923	43.4	5.3	38.1	1,984.0
					1922	42.3	5.2	37.1	1,945.9
					1921	34.1	4.4	29.7	1,908.8

[1] Newfoundland is included beginning in 1949; accordingly, the stock of dwelling units increases by more than the net increase (series R 131) in that year.

Series R 133–139. *Number of dwelling units completed by area and by type, 1921 to 1960*

(thousands of units)

Year	New structures			New structures			Converted structures
	Urban	Rural nonfarm	Farm	Single	Multiple	Total	
	133	134	135	136	137	138	139
1960	100,562	21,305	1,890	78,166	45,591	123,757	3,051
1959	118,930	23,553	3,188	95,455	50,216	145,671	3,837
1958	116,512	25,978	4,196	96,830	49,856	146,686	4,530
1957	89,323	23,617	4,343	81,096	36,187	117,283	3,982
1956	106,207	25,480	4,013	95,656	40,044	135,700	3,566
1955	102,025	21,726	4,178	90,553	37,376	127,929	4,340
1954	86,669	12,169	3,127	71,760	30,205	101,965	4,373
1953	80,226	13,056	3,557	68,916	27,923	96,839	3,824
1952	58,918	9,623	4,546	55,967	17,120	73,087	3,215
1951	65,387	12,254	3,669	60,366	20,944	81,310	3,500
1950	70,522	14,448	4,045	68,685	20,330	89,015	2,739
1949	68,873	14,133	5,227	68,966	19,267	88,233	3,422
1948	58,035	14,204	3,858	61,787	14,310	76,097	5,146
1947	51,900	16,200	4,100	58,800	13,500	72,300	7,000
1946	44,300	11,900	4,100	51,400	8,900	60,300	6,900
1945	29,400	9,500	3,600	33,400	9,100	42,500	6,000
1944	23,200	9,800	3,500	28,700	7,800	36,500	6,300
1943	19,100	10,200	3,400	24,900	7,800	32,700	4,100
1942	24,700	13,800	4,300	26,500	16,300	42,800	4,400
1941	30,000	18,000	5,200	29,300	23,900	53,200	3,600
1940	26,200	17,200	5,600	23,600	25,400	49,000	3,500
1939	25,300	17,400	6,100	26,700	22,100	48,800	2,900
1938	20,900	14,800	5,700	21,800	19,600	41,400	2,600
1937	24,600	16,000	6,300	25,000	21,900	46,900	1,700
1936	20,200	12,700	5,100	20,700	17,300	38,000	1,300
1935	17,100	10,400	4,300	17,600	14,200	31,800	1,100
1934	14,500	8,400	3,600	15,100	11,400	26,500	1,200
1933	12,100	6,200	2,700	11,800	9,200	21,000	900
1932	16,800	6,800	3,300	14,500	12,400	26,900	1,200
1931	30,800	9,700	5,200	24,000	21,700	45,700	2,100
1930	37,500	7,400	5,300	24,800	25,400	50,200	2,800
1929	47,400	7,500	6,200	30,000	31,100	61,100	3,600
1928	45,100	7,600	6,300	31,000	28,000	59,000	3,900
1927	39,500	7,100	5,900	29,700	22,800	52,500	4,300
1926	39,300	7,200	5,900	31,200	21,200	52,400	2,800
1925	30,900	6,100	5,000	26,500	15,500	42,000	2,700
1924	25,500	5,400	4,500	23,700	11,700	35,400	3,300
1923	30,000	6,300	5,200	28,800	12,700	41,500	1,900
1922	28,800	6,300	5,200	29,100	11,200	40,300	2,000
1921	22,700	5,300	4,300	24,400	7,900	32,300	1,800

Series R 140–148. *Estimates of the housing stock at the end of census years, 1871 to 1921*

(thousands of units)

Year	Occupied dwelling units at census dates			Vacant units at census dates	Available permanent units at census dates	Available dwellings at census dates	Units in institutions	Units completed in balance of census years	Stock at 31 December
	Temporary	Permanent	Total						
	140	**141**	**142**	**143**	**144**	**145**	**146**	**147**	**148**
1921	48	1,810	1,858	77[1]	1,887	1,935	1.3[2]	17[3]	1,951
1911	66	1,382	1,448	62	1,444	1,510	1.2[2]	20	1,529
1901	45	981	1,026	30	1,011	1,056	1.0	9	1,064
1891	22	856	878	54	910	932	.9	11	942
1881	15	738	753	47	785	800	.7	10	809
1871	12	594	606	28	622	634	.5	10	644

[1] Estimated by applying the 1911 ratio of vacancies to occupied dwellings to the 1921 number of occupied dwellings.
[2] Estimated by assuming a constant rate of increase between 1901 and 1931.

[3] Estimated as 50 per cent of Firestone's estimate of completions in 1921 (O. J. Firestone, *Canada's Economic Development, 1867–1953*, table 90).

Series R 149–150. *Number and value of dwelling units completed, 1872 to 1921*

(units in thousands; values in millions of dollars)

Year	Units completed	Value of completions	Year	Units completed	Value of completions
	149	**150**		**149**	**150**
1921	27.5	112.8	1895	11.1	16.0
			1894	12.4	18.4
1920	52.4	244.2	1893	14.0	20.9
1919	37.6	144.8	1892	17.6	26.6
1918	41.1	135.2	1891	12.4	16.9
1917	50.8	144.3			
1916	40.2	95.3	1890	14.2	20.1
			1889	15.2	22.0
1915	41.3	89.2	1888	16.2	23.3
1914	69.4	154.8	1887	20.3	28.0
1913	82.6	190.8	1886	20.0	26.5
1912	85.2	190.8			
1911	70.2	146.4	1885	18.0	24.0
			1884	14.0	20.2
1910	58.1	115.5	1883	12.9	18.7
1909	45.9	90.8	1882	16.1	24.4
1908	39.9	79.3	1881	17.7	28.3
1907	43.1	80.5			
1906	48.3	87.0	1880	14.5	24.4
			1879	15.1	23.1
1905	37.8	65.1	1878	15.4	23.6
1904	31.0	52.6	1877	17.7	28.6
1903	30.6	51.1	1876	19.9	34.8
1902	25.5	39.6			
1901	18.0	27.9	1875	23.1	42.9
			1874	29.8	63.7
1900	17.7	27.8	1873	38.5	90.0
1899	15.5	22.5	1872	27.7	63.8
1898	12.9	18.1			
1897	11.2	15.5			
1896	10.5	15.1			

Series R 151. *Estimates of total new and repair construction, 1896 to 1930*

(millions of dollars)

Year	Total construction	Year	Total construction
	151		**151**
1930	928	1910	453
1929	1,046	1909	396
1928	940	1908	322
1927	783	1907	360
1926	703	1906	316
1925	697	1905	253
1924	692	1904	220
1923	697	1903	194
1922	624	1902	150
1921	631	1901	118
1920	986	1900	119
1919	618	1899	87
1918	558	1898	75
1917	464	1897	67
1916	336	1896	78
1915	344		
1914	480		
1913	583		
1912	597		
1911	535		

Series R152–154. *New and repair construction, quinquennially, 1896 to 1930*

(millions of dollars)

Period	New construction	Repair construction	Gross new and repair construction
	152	153	154
1926–1930	3,109	1,290	4,399
1921–1925	2,271	1,070	3,341
1916–1920	2,122	841	2,963
1911–1915	2,007	531	2,538
1906–1910	1,439	408	1,847
1901–1905	681	254	935
1896–1900	269	156	425

Series R155. *Imports of construction materials, 1868 to 1895*

(thousands of dollars)

Year[1]	Total all construction materials	Year[1]	Total all construction materials
	155		155
1895	5,813	1880	5,440
1894	7,736	1879	4,333
1893	8,225	1878	5,252
1892	7,760	1877	5,920
1891	9,665	1876	7,795
1890	8,264	1875	10,272
1889	7,567	1874	7,242
1888	6,827	1873	9,526
1887	7,179	1872	5,460
1886	6,293	1871	2,923
1885	6,853	1870	2,128
1884	8,638	1869	1,784
1883	10,201	1868	1,471
1882	8,902		
1881	7,092		

[1] Fiscal year ending 30 June of year given.

Series R156. *Net capital formation in railway transport and telegraphs, 1850 to 1930*

(millions of dollars)

Year	Net capital formation	Year	Net capital formation	Year	Net capital formation
	156		156		156
1930	93.6	1900	18.4	1870	9.1
1929	143.4	1899	15.0	1869	5.0
1928	71.7	1898	17.9	1868	5.3
1927	75.4	1897	9.9	1867	3.7
1926	49.3	1896	5.5	1866	2.0
1925	31.0	1895	7.5	1865	1.5
1924	58.7	1894	10.5	1864	1.9
1923	73.6	1893	14.2	1863	.9
1922	25.7	1892	12.9	1862	1.5
1921	75.3	1891	20.6	1861	1.8
1920	86.1	1890	23.7	1860	5.2
1919	66.1	1889	25.9	1859	4.5
1918	66.1	1888	20.4	1858	10.3
1917	60.5	1887	19.8	1857	7.3
1916	42.0	1886	22.6	1856	9.2
1915	91.1	1885	32.6	1855	16.7
1914	126.5	1884	40.2	1854	13.3
1913	176.6	1883	35.6	1853	13.7
1912	153.5	1882	29.8	1852	6.2
1911	121.7	1881	13.4	1851	2.5
1910	105.1	1880	13.0	1850	1.3
1909	89.3	1879	12.2		
1908	97.2	1878	12.7		
1907	103.6	1877	14.8		
1906	57.6	1876	18.0		
1905	43.9	1875	13.2		
1904	33.8	1874	14.4		
1903	32.0	1873	23.7		
1902	20.7	1872	21.0		
1901	19.0	1871	15.8		

Series R 157–161. *New construction and repair, nonrailway transport structures, 1901 to 1930*

(millions of dollars)

| Year | Gross investment | | | | | Year | Gross investment | | | | |
| | Provincial highways and bridges | Canals | Harbour and river work | Repair | Gross investment and repair | | Provincial highways and bridges | Canals | Harbour and river work | Repair | Gross investment and repair |
	157	**158**	**159**	**160**	**161**		**157**	**158**	**159**	**160**	**161**
1930	54.3	—	51.7[1]	—	106.0	1915	6.9	6.2	13.7	4.9	31.7
1929	40.8	—	56.5[1]	—	97.3	1914	8.8	5.4	18.6	6.3	39.1
1928	—	—	—	—	—	1913	9.9	2.6	18.2	6.7	37.4
1927	—	—	—	—	—	1912	8.1	2.4	12.7	5.3	28.5
1926	19.1	13.5	9.3	13.8	55.7	1911	4.8	2.7	11.2	4.9	23.6
1925	18.7	12.3	14.6	14.0	59.6	1910	3.8	2.4	9.2	4.4	19.8
1924	15.6	10.2	15.9	12.8	54.5	1909	2.7	1.8	7.6	3.8	15.9
1923	24.6	8.0	14.9	12.3	59.8	1908	2.6	2.1	9.1	4.5	18.3
1922	21.2	7.2	10.7	10.1	49.2	1907	1.8	1.9	8.1	3.7	15.5
1921	20.3	6.2	9.8	8.9	45.2	1906	.8	1.0	4.8	2.6	9.2
1920	16.5	6.1	9.8	8.7	41.1	1905	.4	1.7	6.1	2.6	10.8
1919	10.0	4.9	6.9	6.8	28.6	1904	.4	2.2	5.3	2.3	10.2
1918	4.5	2.4	4.4	4.9	16.2	1903	.9	2.0	4.6	2.0	9.5
1917	4.2	1.9	8.3	4.4	18.8	1902	1.0	2.0	3.5	1.8	8.3
1916	4.2	4.5	10.5	4.7	23.9	1901	.6	2.2	2.5	1.6	6.9

[1] These totals include canals, harbour and river work, new and repair, and highway repair.

Series R 162–167. *New construction, federal government, 1868 to 1930, provincial governments, 1901 to 1930*

(millions of dollars)

| Year[1] | Federal government | | | | Provincial government | Total federal and provincial | Year[1] | Federal government | | | | Provincial government | Total federal and provincial |
| | Railway | Other transportation | Buildings and other | Total | | | | Railway | Other transportation | Buildings and other | Total | | |
	162	**163**	**164**	**165**	**166**	**167**		**162**	**163**	**164**	**165**	**166**	**167**
1930	—	—	—	63.2	67.7	130.9	1895	.3	5.2	.2	3.7	—	—
1929	—	—	—	45.9	51.5	97.4	1894	.5	3.7	.4	4.6	—	—
1928	—	—	—	40.2	41.2	81.4	1893	.2	2.8	.3	3.3	—	—
1927	—	—	—	36.9	31.6	68.5	1892	.4	2.2	.2	2.8	—	—
1926	2.7	22.8	3.1	28.6	24.1	52.7	1891	1.2	2.4	.4	3.9	—	—
1925	—	26.9	4.9	31.7	26.6	58.3	1890	2.1	2.2	.5	4.8	—	—
1924	—	26.1	5.0	31.1	24.8	55.9	1889	2.6	2.5	.6	5.7	—	—
1923	—	22.9	2.5	25.4	34.8	60.2	1888	1.8	1.8	.6	4.1	—	—
1922	1.0	17.9	2.0	20.8	30.2	51.0	1887	1.4	3.2	.6	5.2	—	—
1921	1.5	16.0	3.8	21.3	32.3	53.6	1886	1.4	2.7	.6	4.7	—	—
1920	1.7	15.9	5.4	23.0	25.0	48.0	1885	4.1	2.3	.6	6.9	—	—
1919	3.8	11.8	9.6	25.3	15.8	41.1	1884	5.0	2.8	.7	8.4	—	—
1918	6.4	6.8	8.1	21.3	8.6	29.9	1883	6.2	2.8	.4	9.3	—	—
1917	9.1	10.2	3.4	22.7	6.9	29.6	1882	4.0	2.2	.3	6.6	—	—
1916	15.3	15.0	3.8	34.1	9.4	43.5	1881	5.4	2.6	.5	8.6	—	—
1915	17.6	19.9	5.7	43.1	14.5	57.6	1880	4.0	2.7	.3	7.0	—	—
1914	19.6	24.0	10.4	54.0	17.3	71.3	1879	2.3	3.7	.2	6.2	—	—
1913	20.7	20.8	9.2	50.6	19.5	70.1	1878	2.6	4.3	.3	7.2	—	—
1912	17.6	15.1	4.8	37.5	15.7	53.2	1877	3.1	4.6	.5	8.3	—	—
1911	22.4	13.9	3.1	39.3	11.2	50.5	1876	4.8	3.2	.8	8.8	—	—
1910	23.6	11.6	2.1	37.3	9.1	46.4	1875	5.3	2.5	.7	8.5	—	—
1909	21.0	9.4	2.7	33.2	5.8	39.0	1874	4.4	2.7	.8	7.9	—	—
1908	27.5	11.2	4.6	43.3	5.0	48.3	1873	7.3	.8	.5	8.6	—	—
1907	21.0	10.0	3.3	34.4	3.0	37.4	1872	6.6	.5	.7	7.8	—	—
1906	6.2	5.8	2.1	14.1	1.3	15.4	1871	3.0	.2	.4	3.6	—	—
1905	3.9	7.8	3.5	15.2	.6	15.8	1870	.8	.1	.2	1.1	—	—
1904	3.6	7.5	2.5	13.6	.7	14.3	1869	.3	.1	.1	.5	—	—
1903	1.8	6.6	1.4	9.7	1.1	10.8	1868	.4	.1	.1	.7	—	—
1902	2.7	5.5	1.3	9.4	1.2	10.6							
1901	3.2	4.7	1.7	9.6	.8	10.4							
1900	—	—	—	—	—	—							
1899	1.1	4.9	.3	6.3	—	—							
1898	.3	4.1	.4	4.8	—	—							
1897	.2	3.1	.2	3.5	—	—							
1896	.3	2.9	.2	3.3	—	—							

[1] For 1901 to 1930, calendar years; for 1868 to 1899, fiscal year ending 30 June of year given.

Series R 168–176. *Value of construction contracts awarded, 1911 to 1960 and by type and by area, 1918 to 1960*
(millions of dollars)

| Year | Construction by type | | | | | Construction by area | | | |
| | Total | Residential | Business | Industrial | Engineering | Maritimes | Quebec | Ontario | Western Provinces |
	168	169	170	171	172	173	174	175	176
1960	3,053.7	769.8	1,118.6	286.3	879.0	267.6	722.9	1,325.9	737.3
1959	3,219.1	1,112.7	1,068.8	261.0	776.6	252.0	913.6	1,262.3	791.2
1958	3,593.7	1,413.2	1,125.4	248.8	806.3	291.8	1,042.9	1,489.6	769.5
1957	2,894.2	877.7	795.7	398.4	822.4	150.4	703.7	1,312.4	727.6
1956	3,426.9	1,077.4	828.9	455.6	1,065.0	160.7	988.1	1,427.8	850.2
1955	3,183.6	1,216.4	761.2	386.4	819.6	197.7	779.8	1,300.3	906.8
1954	2,155.0	900.0	695.0	169.7	390.3	134.2	538.1	939.7	542.9
1953	2,017.1	732.8	613.8	230.9	439.6	97.3	539.8	849.8	534.7
1952	1,812.3	511.3	526.4	245.9	528.6	129.2	397.9	732.8	552.3
1951	2,295.5	437.1	547.7	451.8	859.0	102.6	480.1	1,017.4	695.4
1950	1,525.8	541.7	440.4	141.0	402.6	83.0	534.0	597.2	311.7
1949	1,143.5	466.1	324.3	104.0	249.2	61.4	355.4	421.1	305.6
1948	954.1	373.1	315.3	74.9	190.9	68.0	327.1	350.6	208.3
1947	718.1	197.2	239.5	131.5	167.9	59.9	255.2	258.7	144.4
1946	663.4	213.1	186.8	138.3	125.2	40.8	226.8	252.8	142.9
1945	409.0	196.0	86.3	75.5	51.2	26.3	121.9	151.9	108.9
1944	292.0	131.2	68.6	58.7	33.4	19.7	89.9	111.7	706.2
1943	206.1	79.1	61.0	32.9	33.1	14.9	61.8	83.0	46.4
1942	281.6	79.3	98.2	74.1	30.1	26.3	92.2	108.7	54.4
1941	394.0	92.4	100.6	92.8	108.2	36.7	154.5	145.6	57.1
1940	346.0	67.7	104.6	121.8	52.0	21.1	96.3	146.8	81.7
1939	187.2	67.5	55.0	22.8	42.0	16.1	62.8	82.6	25.6
1938	187.3	55.0	63.3	16.0	52.9	19.5	65.8	73.1	28.9
1937	224.1	56.2	55.3	33.8	78.8	21.6	71.9	97.8	32.8
1936	162.6	42.9	37.8	15.0	67.0	17.9	45.7	72.4	26.5
1935	160.3	36.4	48.4	10.3	65.1	14.4	44.5	70.9	30.6
1934	125.8	30.6	37.5	8.0	49.7	10.0	34.1	63.4	18.3
1933	97.3	23.9	26.3	9.1	38.0	7.2	32.5	42.6	15.0
1932	132.9	28.9	39.4	7.8	56.8	9.3	52.5	49.3	21.7
1931	315.5	81.7	81.2	14.8	137.8	16.9	106.1	125.5	67.0
1930	457.0	93.3	151.1	31.5	181.1	19.4	154.7	175.5	107.4
1929	576.7	128.9	190.2	63.0	194.6	20.2	187.8	215.8	152.9
1928	472.0	139.2	170.2	63.3	99.3	36.2	144.2	188.4	103.3
1927	419.0	124.9	163.4	40.0	90.6	—	133.2	196.2	—
1926	372.9	109.6	112.4	79.7	71.3	8.4	151.9	141.9	70.7
1925	298.0	96.5	73.1	40.0	88.4	8.9	124.5	121.3	43.3
1924	276.3	91.2	73.7	21.8	89.6	8.6	89.5	136.0	42.1
1923	314.3	97.7	80.4	27.0	109.2	8.8	102.6	156.2	46.8
1922	331.8	104.2	81.4	25.8	120.5	11.2	103.3	166.6	50.8
1921	240.1	76.7	84.7	16.5	62.3	9.3	61.3	113.9	55.6
1920	255.6	54.9	86.1	64.6	50.0	21.4	54.9	108.1	71.2
1919	190.0	47.0	59.6	57.1	26.3	18.8	55.3	87.4	28.6
1918	99.8	14.7	26.2	39.0	20.0	23.2	23.6	33.4	19.6
1917	84.8	—	—	—	—	—	—	—	—
1916	99.3	—	—	—	—	—	—	—	—
1915	83.9	—	—	—	—	—	—	—	—
1914	242.0	—	—	—	—	—	—	—	—
1913	384.2	—	—	—	—	—	—	—	—
1912	463.1	—	—	—	—	—	—	—	—
1911	345.4	—	—	—	—	—	—	—	—

Series R177. *Value of building permits issued, 1910 to 1960*

(thousands of dollars)

Year	Building permits issued	Year	Building permits issued
	177		**177**
204 cities		1935	46,561
1960	1,382,147	1934	27,458
1959	1,636,995	1933	21,776
1958	1,621,636	1932	42,319
1957	1,307,151	1931	112,223
1956	1,318,927		
		1930	166,379
1955	1,309,024	1929	234,945
1954	1,151,087	1928	219,106
1953	1,088,880	1927	184,614
1952	802,738	1926	156,387
1951	681,162		
		1925	125,029
1950	801,765	1924	126,583
1949	616,161	1923	133,522
1948	536,058	1922	148,215
1947	373,231	1921	116,794
1946	383,597		
		1920	117,020
1945	197,187		
1944	128,728	**35 cities**	
1943	80,190	1920	106,054
1942	104,236	1919	77,113
1941	135,302	1918	36,838
		1917	33,936
1940	133,005	1916	39,724
58 cities		1915	33,567
		1914	96,781
1940	80,274	1913	153,663
1939	60,272	1912	185,233
1938	60,817	1911	138,170
1937	55,845		
1936	41,326	1910	100,358

Series R178–179. *Index of the number of permits for new buildings per capita, Toronto, 1886 to 1910,*
and the number of permits for new buildings, Montreal, 1867 to 1910

Year	Montreal, number of permits for new buildings	Toronto, index of permits for new buildings (1900 = 100)	Year	Montreal, number of permits for new buildings	Toronto, index of permits for new buildings (1900 = 100)
	178	**179**		**178**	**179**
1910	2,726	548.1	1885	429	—
1909	1,702	472.1	1884	317	—
1908	1,283	425.3	1883	260	—
1907	1,472	438.9	1882	231	—
1906	1,484	418.0	1881	248	—
1905	1,145	379.4	1880	209	—
1904	799	322.7	1879	240	—
1903	581	271.0	1878	241	—
1902	467	210.6	1877	349	—
1901	443	139.8	1876	463	—
1900	331	100.0	1875	732	—
1899	357	108.0	1874	850	—
1898	351	88.4	1873	724	—
1897	408	55.1	1872	728	—
1896	315	67.5	1871	1,060	—
1895	277	61.6	1870	603	—
1894	382	67.3	1869	490	—
1893	561	77.7	1868	551	—
1892	640	86.8	1867	281	—
1891	778	111.8			
1890	937	122.8			
1889	1,032	142.3			
1888	933	114.9			
1887	1,076	80.3			
1886	699	89.3			

SECTION S: TRANSPORTATION AND COMMUNICATION

J. L. McDOUGALL,[1] *Queen's University*

The data of this section are in subsections as follows: rail transport (series S1–163); water transport and canal statistics (series S164–214); roads and road transport (series S215–235); civil aviation (series S236–287); inter-city freight carried (series S288–293); the post office (series S294–322); telephone industry (series S323–349); telegraphs (series S350–359).

The published sources of data are mainly federal government publications.

For the following list of government publications, given in the order in which they appear, the title of the Dominion Bureau of Statistics has been shortened to D.B.S. and the place of publication and printer are omitted unless they are other than Ottawa and the Queen's Printer.

Annual Report of the Department of Railways and Canals, mainly the part on *Railway Statistics,* reports of 1875 to 1918; Dominion Bureau of Statistics, *Railway Statistics of Canada,* annual 1919 to 1921, *Statistics of Steam Railways of Canada,* annual 1922 to 1951, *Railway Transport,* latterly in six parts, annual 1952 to 1960, all reports; D.B.S., *Canada Year Book,* annual since 1918, and predecessor annual publications of the Department of Agriculture from 1886 to 1911 and the Department of Trade and Commerce from 1912 to 1917 under the titles, *Statistical Abstract and Record* for 1886 and 1887, *The Statistical Year Book of Canada* for 1888 to 1904, and *Canada Year Book* for 1905 to 1917; D.B.S., *Canal Statistics,* annual since 1919, and predecessor reports on *Canal Statistics,* a supplement to the *Annual Report of the Department of Railways and Canals,* for 1886 to 1918; D.B.S., *Road and Street Mileage and Expenditure,* annual 1952 to 1960, and predecessor reports, *Highway Statistics,* annual 1945 to 1951, and *The Highway and the Motor Vehicle,* annual 1925 to 1944; D.B.S., *The Motor Vehicle,* annual 1952 to 1960, in the latter year in four parts; D.B.S., *Civil Aviation,* annual since 1936; D.B.S., *Daily Bulletin, February 10, 1961* (Ottawa Dominion Bureau of Statistics, 1961); D.B.S., *Motor Transport Traffic Statistics: National Estimates,* annual; D.B.S., *Oil Pipe Line Transport,* annual, and predecessor reports *Pipe Line (Oil) Statistics;* Post Office Department, *Report of the Postmaster General,* annual since 1867; D.B.S., *Telephone Statistics,* annual since 1919, and predecessor reports, *Telephone Statistics,* an appendix to *Annual Report of the Department of Railways and Canals* for 1911 to 1918; Department of Trade and Commerce, *Private and Public Investment in Canada, Outlook,* annual since 1946; D.B.S., *Private and Public Investment in Canada, 1946–1957;* Department of Trade and Commerce, *Private and Public Investment in Canada, 1926–1951* (Ottawa, Department of Trade and Commerce, 1951); D.B.S., *Telegraph Statistics,* annual 1919 to 1936 and *Telegraph and Cable Statistics,* annual since 1937, and predecessor reports, *Telegraph Statistics,* a supplement to the *Annual Report of the Department of Railways and Canals* for 1912 to 1918.

Privately published sources of data are: W. A. Mackintosh *et al., Economic Problems of the Prairie Provinces* (Toronto, The Macmillan Company of Canada, 1935); K. Studnicki-Gizbert, 'Structure and Growth of Canadian Air Transport Industry' in Canadian Political Science Association, Conference on Statistics, 1960, *Papers* (Toronto, University of Toronto Press, 1962); Trans-Canada Air Lines, *Initial Submission to the Air Transport Board in the Matter of Trans-Con-*

tinental Air Services, Exhibits T.C.A.–411 and T.C.A.–414; Trans-Canada Air Lines, *Annual Report.*

Some unpublished data as noted in the text were also used.

RAIL TRANSPORT (Series S1–163)

General note

Systematic collection of railway statistics began in Canada for the year ending 30 June 1875, following the enactment of the Railway Statistics Act in 1875 which required all railways to furnish annual statements to the Department of Railways and Canals. Annual collection of data has continued to the present. A change to a calendar year basis was made at 1919 and two reports, one for the year to 30 June, the other for the year to 31 December, are available for that year. With the passing of time, the material published has improved in both quality and quantity.

The major change in these statistics comes at 1 July 1906 and only limited comparisons are possible between the statistics for the earlier years and those which have been collected since that time. There were substantially no changes in the forms between the fiscal years 1875 to 1906. Since then, there have been changes made from time to time, but in most cases it is possible to bridge the gaps. The present forms are modelled after those prescribed by the Interstate Commerce Commission for the railways of the United States.

The statistics of the early years should be received with gratitude because data for that period are so scarce, but they should also be treated with caution. For at least the first seven or eight years most railway companies were resistant to providing statistics and many refused altogether. Indications of heroic improvisations to overcome these difficulties appear in the text of the annual reports and are supported by the discrepancies between the reported totals and the details by companies.

The sources from which these data are drawn are *Railway Statistics of Canada* which appeared as part of the report of the Department of Railways and Canals until 1918. The issue for the year ending 30 June 1919 was initiated by the Statistical Branch of that department and completed by the Dominion Bureau of Statistics. With the issue for the year ending 31 December 1922 the title became *Statistics of Steam Railways of Canada* and so remained until 1951. In 1952 it became *Railway Transport* and was issued in parts, initially in five parts and now in six. This source gives data by company as well as the totals.

D.B.S., *Railway Freight Traffic* (catalogue numbers 52-001 and 52-205) gives monthly and annual freight carried by province, and by region for the Maritime and the Western provinces. It is available from 1923.

Since 1949 the Board of Transport Commissioners has published a *Waybill Analysis* (except for 1950) which gives informa-

[1] The material on air transport was prepared by K. Studnicki-Gizbert of the federal Department of Transport. The material on the telephone industry was prepared by C. S. Carter of The Bell Telephone Company of Canada. The material on the post office was prepared by W. M. Griffiths of the Post Office Department of Canada.

tion on carload all-rail traffic originating and terminating in Canada which is far more detailed than that available in any other source. Since 1954 it has been based on a continuous one per cent sample; previously it was based on all the traffic of four supposedly representative days in each year.

Railways have always been a major interest of the Canadian people and that interest has been expressed in subsidies and/or bond guarantees to private companies, in order to encourage construction, and in outright ownership. Where subsidies and bond guarantees were not sufficient to encourage private railway companies to build, the federal government undertook the construction and in some cases the operation of rail lines. The Intercolonial Railway and the Prince Edward Island Railways were owned and operated by the Dominion Government from the beginning. The National Transcontinental (from Winnipeg to Moncton) was built by the Dominion, beginning shortly after the turn of the century, under an agreement to lease to the Grand Trunk Pacific Railway on completion. The Hudson Bay Railway was also built by the Dominion.

The second great cycle of acquisitions by the Dominion began in 1917 when the Canadian Northern Railway was taken over because it was no longer able to sustain itself in the circumstances of the time. The Grand Trunk Pacific Railway followed in 1919. And since the Dominion would not excuse the Grand Trunk Railway from its liabilities in the Grand Trunk Pacific Railway, it was taken over in 1922. The Canadian National Railways Company was formed to consolidate control of Dominion lines and to operate them under unified management from October 1922. At the end of that year, it had a route mileage of 20,880 miles.

Only three of the provinces have owned railways and two, Ontario and British Columbia still do. Ontario built the Temiskaming and Northern Ontario (now known as the Ontario Northland) from North Bay to Cochrane in the early years of the present century and extended it to James Bay at the end of the nineteen-twenties. Alberta took over the Edmonton, Dunvegan and British Columbia from Edmonton to the Peace River country during the First World War when it was unable to pay interest on bonds guaranteed by the Province. It also had the Alberta and Great Waterways which ran from Edmonton to Fort McMurray. These Alberta lines were sold to the Canadian National and Canadian Pacific, jointly, in 1930 and have been operated jointly by them since then. British Columbia took over the Pacific Great Eastern also in the First War on account of default of bond interest on bonds guaranteed by the Province. At that time it ran from Squamish to Quesnel. Since the Second World War it has been extended to North Vancouver on the south and to Prince George and then the Peace River country on the north.

S1-17. Railroads before 1906, nominal capital, railroads completed and under construction, 1875 to 1906

SOURCE: *Annual Report of the Department of Railways and Canals,* individual reports for 1875 to 1906.

These returns cover the capital of all railways, including the direct investment of the Dominion in the Intercolonial Railway, Prince Edward Island Railway and in lines given to private railways and provincial government direct investment. Securities are entered at their par value, not at the price at which they were sold. Dominion aid includes outright grants to private railway companies, construction bonuses, lines built by the government and given to private companies, direct investment in government lines and the like. Government aid does not include any value for land grants made to railways.

Provincial government aid is similar in nature.

S18-23. Railroads before 1906, municipal aid by province and total aid all governments, paid and/or promised to railroads completed and under construction, 1875 to 1906

SOURCE: same as for series S1-17.

Series 18 differs from the sum of aid from governments calculable from series S6-15 in that aid promised is also included. Series S19-23 also include aid promised. No aid was given by Prince Edward Island municipalities as the railways there were owned by the federal government. Only in 1906 did aid from municipalities in British Columbia (0.2 million in that year) become large enough to be recorded after rounding of figures: municipalities in Alberta and Saskatchewan did not provide aid to amount to as much as $50,000 at any time in the period.

S24-38. Railroads before 1906, miles of first main track and rolling stock owned and hired, 1875 to 1906

SOURCE: same as for series S1-17.

The data in series S24-28 should be used with some reserve. The exact date at which track ceased to be designated as under construction may have been determined by financial rather than by physical tests. Bond interest of a line under construction can be capitalized; that of a line in operation can not. Therefore there is a strong tendency to defer the declaration that it is operational until it is earning a net profit. Once the rail is laid, service may be offered by the contractor so that the miles of line available to the public are more nearly represented by the miles completed (rails laid) than by the miles in operation.

Series S29-38 show the number of units of equipment under the control of Canadian railways whether owned or leased. No data were kept on their capacity.

S39-52. Railroads before 1906, train mileage, freight and passengers carried, 1875 to 1906

SOURCE: same as for series S1-17.

Series S39-42 cover revenue train mileage in road service. Series S43 covers all locomotive mileage including switching engine mileage and work train mileage whether in maintenance or in construction service. Series S44 is a record of revenue passengers carried by each railway. Duplications are therefore included whenever a passenger moves from one railway to another in making a through journey. Series S45-52 show the tons carried by classes in detail as presented in the source except that the heading of series S50 is 'firewood' in the years 1875 to 1904. Thereafter it becomes 'coal and other fuel' and series S52 'all other articles' shrinks accordingly. Interline hauls produce duplications in these series since tonnage recorded would be repeated by each railway by which it was carried.

S53-63. Railroads before 1906, gross earnings, operating expenses and net earnings, 1875 to 1906

SOURCE: same as for series S1-17.

These series are on the basis of classification used before 1907. Not too much violence is done to the facts, however, if one takes series S54, S55 and S59 as backward projections of series S132, S131 and S138 respectively, and the totals of earnings, series S53 and S130 are also roughly comparable as are total expenses series S58 and S137.

S64-68. Railroads before 1906, fatal accidents and injuries, 1875 to 1906

SOURCE: same as for series S1-17.

Series S64-67, fatal accidents, are probably a reasonable statement of the number of fatal accidents over the years, but one should not expect homogeneity in series S68, injuries. The definition of an injury must certainly have shifted in this period.

S69–76. Railroads, capital liability, aid to railroads, dominion, provincial and municipal, 1907 to 1960

SOURCE: for 1956 to 1960, series S69–72, D.B.S., *Railway Transport, 1960, Part I* (*Comparative Summary Statistics 1956 to 1960*), table 4, p. 8, series S73–76, no change in data since 1933; for 1952 to 1955, D.B.S., *Railway Transport, Part I* and *Part II*, individual issues for each year; for 1922 to 1951, D.B.S., *Statistics of Steam Railways*, each annual issue; for 1919 to 1921, D.B.S., *Railway Statistics of Canada*, each issue; for 1907 to 1918 *Annual Report of the Department of Railways and Canals*, each issue in the part on *Railway Statistics*.

The breaks in series S69 and S72 between 1922 and 1923 are due to the inclusion of the Intercolonial and of the National Transcontinental in the Accounts of the Canadian National Railways for the first time (see the general note to series S1–163). They were entered at $447,643,526 in 1923. At the same time government loans previously classified as current were included in both series S69 and S73. The breaks in series S69, S70 and S72 are due to the recapitalization of Canadian National Railways in 1937. At the time some of the debt was assumed as a direct obligation of the federal government and some was replaced by stock. The exchange of bonds of the C.N.R. for stock explains the break in series S70 and S72 between 1951 and 1952.

Series S74, in contrast to series S6, does not include the direct investment of the Canadian government in railways before they were transferred to the Canadian National Railways in 1923, nor direct investment by provincial governments in railways (see the general note to series S1–163).

Series S73–76 show by their stability the fact that other methods of giving aid have become more prominent. There is, effectively, no change in these series after 1915.

S77–90. Railroads, miles of line in operation, rolling stock, locomotives and passenger cars in service, 1907 to 1960

SOURCE: for 1956 to 1960, D.B.S., *Railway Transport, 1960, Part I*, series S77–80, table 1, p. 7, series S81–84, table 14, p. 20, series S85–90, table 13, p. 20; for years before 1956, same as for series S69–76.

S77–80. Iron rails were of minor importance by the opening of this period. They constituted only 39 miles of approximately 24,000 miles of first main track and 100 miles out of a total of 30,230 miles of all track at 1909. See also the note to series S24–38 regarding the measurement of miles in operation.

S83. Diesel electric locomotives are counted in number of units though most frequently operated in groups of two or three.

S90. Number of cars in company service is the total of cars not in revenue service. In 1960, of the total, 3,051 were cabooses and the balance were used in work train service.

S91–99. Railroads, rolling stock, freight cars in service, 1907 to 1960

SOURCE: for 1956 to 1960, D.B.S., *Railway Transport, 1960, Part I*, table 12, pp. 18–19; for years before 1956, same as for series S69–76.

In 1952 freight cars were reclassified, the number of classes was enlarged, and the new classification was extended back to 1948. The old classes 'flat', 'stock', 'tank' and 'refrigerator' remained unchanged. 'Box' cars were separated into 'automobile' and 'box'. 'Coal' cars were separated into 'ballast', 'gondola', 'hopper' and 'ore' cars and most of the 'other' cars were distributed over the same four classes.

To economize in space here, the old classes were continued after 1948, though there remain few cars in the 'other' group; but the numbers in the new classes are shown below. From the

data of the new classification, series S93 was obtained by adding box and automobile cars together and series S96 by adding ballast, gondola, hopper and ore cars. The new figure published for box cars can be found by subtracting the number of automobile cars from the box car total as shown in series S93.

Number of freight cars in service in new classes, on 31 December, 1948 to 1960

Year	Ballast	Gondola	Hopper	Ore	Automobile
1960	3,128	20,310	15,578	5,930	7,249
1959	3,140	20,428	15,601	5,964	7,270
1958	2,708	20,522	15,493	6,004	6,722
1957	2,646	19,904	13,788	5,967	6,733
1956	2,156	19,052	12,840	5,465	6,370
1955	2,378	18,592	12,247	2,559	7,406
1954	2,245	18,469	12,129	2,555	7,439
1953	1,940	17,603	11,598	1,960	7,560
1952	1,847	16,552	10,083	1,878	7,330
1951	1,803	14,098	8,897	1,902	6,396
1950	1,862	13,922	8,903	1,954	6,087
1949	1,772	14,135	9,100	1,902	6,075
1948	1,705	13,114	7,996	1,923	5,057

SOURCE: D.B.S., *Railway Transport, 1960, Part I*, table 12, pp. 18–19 and similar tables in *Railway Transport* for earlier years.

S100–111. Railroads, revenue train mileage, engine mileage and freight car mileage, 1907 to 1960

SOURCE: for 1956 to 1960, D.B.S., *Railway Transport, 1960, Part I*, table 9, pp. 10–13; for years before 1956, same as for series S69–76.

S100–105 and S109–111. Revenue train mileage and freight car mileage do not include work train service.

A mixed train as reported in the years to 1935 was one in which both freight cars and passenger train cars normally were carried. In and after 1936 such train miles were distributed on the basis of the number of car miles produced by the train. This tends to throw most of these train miles into the freight train class.

Motor unit cars are those cars which have space for the carrying of any one or all of passengers, baggage, express and mail and which also carry their own power unit. Previous to 1937 this mileage was not reported as train mileage but as passenger car mileage in such form that the series here cannot be projected backward.

S106–108. Gross total engine mileage (series S106) includes switching and work train mileage by steam and diesel locomotives and small amounts of both road revenue and switching mileage by other locomotives (mainly electric) in addition to the revenue road mileage given in series S107–108.

S112–119. Railroads, freight tonnage and mileage, passenger traffic and passenger mileage, 1907 to 1960

SOURCE: for 1956 to 1960, D.B.S., *Railway Transport, 1960, Part I*, table 9, pp. 10–13; for years before 1956 same as for series S69–76.

S112. Tons carried revenue freight is comparable with series S45 for the period 1875 to 1906 because it includes duplication arising from interline hauls in Canada. It is the sum of series S126–128.

S113. Revenue freight ton mileage is the product of tons carried times distance hauled; for example, 1000 tons hauled 1,000 miles or 10,000 tons hauled 100 miles each produce a million ton miles.

S114. Revenue and nonrevenue freight ton mileage differs from series S113 only in that it includes freight hauled on company service as well as revenue freight.

S115. Average load per loaded car mile shows increasing values over the years partly because of a rise in the carrying capacity of the equipment, partly because of a change in the nature of the traffic handled. A loss of less than carload freight or a gain in ore traffic would tend to raise it even if there were no change in a uniformly weighted series.

S 116. Average length of freight haul is affected by changes in the nature of the traffic carried (see the note to series S 115).

S 119. The rise in the average passenger journey is probably due to the loss of short haul traffic rather than to the gain of very long hauls.

S 120–128. Railroads, freight carried, by kind and by origin, 1907 to 1960

SOURCE: for 1956 to 1960, D.B.S., *Railway Transport, 1960, Part I*, series S 120–125 from table 11, pp. 13–18, series S 126–128 from table 9, pp. 10–13; for years before 1956 same as for series S 69–76.

In 1921 and later years, series S 120–125 include the carriage of a ton of freight only once even if it is carried on more than one Canadian line. Before 1921, if freight was carried by more than one railway company, it was included once for each Canadian carrier.

S 120–123. Products of agriculture, animals, mines and forests cover carload movements only.

S 124. Manufactures and miscellaneous freight carried include all manufactures and miscellaneous freight carried in carload or less than carload lots in the years 1907 to 30 June 1919. Thereafter it includes the carload movement only. In and after the year ending 31 December 1919, less than carload movements are the difference between series S 125 and the sum of series S 120–124.

S 126–127. Freight originating in Canada and freight received from U.S. roads are not homogeneous series. The heading of S 127 in the source is 'received from U.S. roads' in 1923 to 1927 and 1956 to 1960. It is 'received from foreign connections' in 1928 to 1955. The result is that traffic received at Canadian ports for furtherance by rail appears in series S 126 in 1923 to 1927 and 1956 to 1960; it is in series S 127 in the years 1928 to 1955 inclusive. See footnote 2 for treatment of foreign grain.

S 129–144. Railroads, gross earnings by source and operating expenses by function, 1907 to 1960

SOURCE: for 1956 to 1960, D.B.S., *Railway Transport, 1960*, table 8, p. 10; for years before 1956 same as for series S 69–76.

S 129. Total gross earnings include all rail line, water line and incidental earnings. See the notes to series S 130, S 135 and S 136.

S 130. Total rail line revenue includes, in addition to the items in series S 131–134, revenue from baggage, sleeping, parlour and chair cars, milk hauling, switching, water transfers and a small other passenger train item.

S 131. Freight receipts are for road haul service only. They do not include switching or water transfers.

S 132. Passenger revenue is revenue from road transportation of passengers only. It does not include revenue from the sale of space or any other auxiliary activity.

S 134. Express revenue is not a homogeneous series. From 1923 to 1955 the Canadian National Railway reported its gross express revenues; other roads reported only the rail portion of express revenues. In and after 1956, all roads conformed to the latter practice.

S 135. Water line revenue is a grab bag item. Until 1955 it included the operations of the Canadian Pacific Railway on the Upper Great Lakes which were mainly complementary to the rail operation; thereafter they are excluded from the railway report. The other component is the revenues of the Algoma Central and Hudson Bay Railway from the operations of bulk freighters. In 1955 the two were approximately equal in amount.

S 136. Incidental revenue is a sum of a number of minor items such as revenue from dining and buffet cars, news and restaurant service, demurrage, grain elevators, rent of buildings and sundry other. The drop in this item after 1955 is the result of a re-classification in the source of 'telegraphs and telephones', later described as 'commercial communications', from series S 136, 'incidental' to 'other income, rail and not rail'. The latter is, in the main, income from outside interests of railways and is not included in series S 129.

S 137–144. Operating expenses are given by the familiar functional groups. The growth in general expenses, series S 144, is due largely to the rise of the custom of paying pensions to all retired employees and to the custom of funding the accrued liability by annual charges to expense during the working life of the employee. In 1926 the charge to expenses for pensions was $1.5 million; in 1938, $6.6 million; in 1948, $18.9 million; in 1959, $59.5 million.

S 145–149. Railroads, freight and passenger receipts per unit of traffic, 1907 to 1960

SOURCE: series S 145 and S 147–149: for 1959 and 1960, D.B.S., *Railway Transport, 1960, Part I*, table 9, pp. 10–13; for 1955 to 1958, *Canada Year Book, 1960*, pp. 814–15; for 1944 to 1954, *Canada Year Book, 1956*, pp. 797–8; for 1936 to 1943, *Canada Year Book, 1948–49*, pp. 689–90; for 1915 to 1935, *Canada Year Book, 1937*, pp. 652–3; for 1910 to 1914, *Canada Year Book, 1921*, pp. 536–7; for 1907 to 1909, *Annual Report of the Department of Railways and Canals, 1909, Railway Statistics*, pp. 19–20; series S 146: for 1960, D.B.S., *Railway Transport, 1960, Part II*, table 2, p. 10; for 1952 to 1959, annual issues of *Railway Transport*; for 1949 to 1951 annual issues of *Steam Railways in Canada*; for 1885 to 1948, *Submission of Canadian Pacific Railway to the Royal Commission for Transportation appendix to Part I* (Montreal, 1949), p. 5.

The official statistics reported ton miles and passenger miles beginning in 1907. Therefore it is not possible to produce these unit revenues for earlier years. However, freight revenue per revenue freight ton mile is available for Canadian Pacific Railway back to 1885 and that series is given in series S 146.

S 150–153. Railroads, number of employees, hours worked and compensation paid, 1926 to 1960

SOURCE: for 1960, D.B.S., *Railway Transport, 1960, Part VI (Employment Statistics)*, table 6, p. 14; for years before 1960, annual issues of D.B.S., *Railway Transport* and its predecessor *Statistics of Steam Railways in Canada*.

S 150. The number of railway employees was first collected annually. From 1917 to 1925 it was on the basis of a quarterly count; from 1926 it has been based on an average of monthly counts. It does not include express, communications and other outside operations employees.

S 151 and 152. Hours worked and total compensation exclude express, communications and outside operations employees. In that way one comes closer to getting figures relating to railway operation as such rather than to the operation of the railways and all associated businesses.

Where figures of days worked are given in the source for daily rated employees they are converted on the basis of one day equals 8 hours.

The figures for earlier years are not comparable since they include all employees. Consequently they are not given here.

S 153. Total compensation charged to operating expenses is available from 1926 only. It is supposed to show the amount paid for labour used in all railway operations including express, communication and the like. It has the virtue of excluding wages paid to employees on new capital construction; but it is not exactly what it purports to be. The wages of storesmen, for example, are charged as part of the cost of material rather than to this account. The qualification of this series on such grounds is minor only.

S154–163. Railroads, fatal accidents and injuries, 1907 to 1960

SOURCE: for 1956 to 1960, D.B.S., *Transport Statistics, 1960, Part I*, tables 25 and 26, pp. 24–5; for years before 1956, same as for series S69–76.

See the note to series S64–68.

The number killed is probably a homogeneous series, but the number injured reported is affected by institutional factors. There is probably a stronger pressure to report injuries to employees recently because of the existence of Workmen's Compensation. Others killed, series S157, and injured, series S161, include postal, express, and pullman employees, trespassers and 'all other' among whom automobile accident victims are probably important.

WATER TRANSPORT AND CANAL STATISTICS
(Series S164–214)
General note

The movements through each of the canals of the St. Lawrence River system are so various that the published aggregate data can be taken as indicative only of broad trends. The limitations are still greater for totals through all the canals. A further difficulty is that the classifications in the canal statistics are not the same as in the railway statistics so that only occasionally can one make meaningful cross comparisons.

The major water movements have always been of bulk cargo carrying the freight of one consignor to one destination, with mechanical loading and unloading. The contract of carriage may be for a single cargo or for the movement of an agreed tonnage within the navigation season at the convenience of the carrier. The freight to be paid is negotiated as between shipper and the carrier.

The carriage of general merchandise upon the Lakes, in which the carrier holds itself out to accept the goods of many shippers, is usually done at differentials under the rail rates. This has normally been a minor part of the total tonnage handled, but a more important part of the total revenue earned.

The rise of import and export traffic through the lake ports in the ten years ending in 1960, and especially from 1959 onward with the opening of the St. Lawrence Seaway, has added a new dimension to what had been, until then, a relatively simple operation.

The basic source of data on canals and canal traffic is *Canal Statistics* which appeared as a supplement to the report of the Department of Railways and Canals from 1886 to 1918 and which has been published by the Dominion Bureau of Statistics thereafter. The D.B.S. *Shipping Report*, which begins with 1938, continues statistics of foreign shipping formerly published by the Department of National Revenue. In this form it was of limited value; but beginning with the year 1952 the report was greatly expanded to cover a wider list of countries of origin and destination in foreign trade, and the coasting trade was reported fully for the first time. The list of commodities was also revised to follow more closely the Standard Industrial Classification of 1948.

S164–170. Shipping, seagoing and inland vessels arrived at and departed from Canadian ports, 1868 to 1959

SOURCE: for 1936 to 1959, data supplied by the Transportation Section, Public Finance and Transportation Division of D.B.S.; for

1911 to 1935, *Canada Year Book, 1936*, p. 708; for 1868 to 1910, *Canada Year Book, 1911*, p. 380.

S171–177. Canals, total traffic through Canadian canals by nationality of vessel and origin of freight, navigation seasons, 1886 to 1960

SOURCE: for 1959 and 1960, D.B.S., *Canal Statistics, 1960*, table 1, pp. 14–15; for 1949 to 1958, *Canada Year Book, 1960*, p. 849; for 1941 to 1948, *Canada Year Book, 1951*, p. 760; for 1935 to 1940, *Canada Year Book, 1941*, p. 602; for 1911 to 1934, *Canada Year Book, 1936*, p. 702; for 1900 to 1910, *Canada Year Book, 1933*, p. 697; for 1886 to 1899, *Statistical Year Book of Canada, 1902*, p. 398.

S171–172. Number and registered tonnage of Canadian and British vessels are mainly Canadian registered vessels. The British vessels were unimportant until the opening of the St. Lawrence Seaway in 1959. In 1960 there were 1,303 British vessels with registered tonnage of 3,971,587 tons.

S173–174. Number and registered tonnage of United States and other foreign vessels were mainly United States vessels to 1950. Thereafter other foreign shipping increased steadily though still much less than United States shipping until 1959. In 1959 to 1960 other foreign tonnage was much greater than United States tonnage.

S177. The heavy concentration of freight originating in the U.S. in the years to 1914 is due to the movement of iron ore from the Minnesota-Michigan ranges through the Canadian Sault canal whose opening coincided with the coming into production of the Mesabi range and which was the preferred passage from Lake Superior until the opening of a deeper lock on the American side for the 1915 season.

S178–188. Canals, cargo tonnage through St. Lawrence Canals, 1900 to 1960

SOURCE: for 1919 to 1960, D.B.S., *Canal Statistics*, each individual issue; for 1900 to 1918, *Annual Report of the Department of Railways and Canals*, part on *Canal Statistics*, various years.

The data are also available before 1900 in annual reports of the Department of Railways and Canals.

These statistics are, of necessity, condensed. Series S178–184 cover tonnage of the named class in both directions. Series S187 covers traffic which originates and terminates on the St. Lawrence between Montreal and Brockville, both included, or which moves between Montreal and the Ottawa or Richelieu systems. Practically all the sheds for such traffic were and are located along the Lachine Canal.

S189–199. Canals, tonnage through Welland Canal, 1867 to 1960

SOURCE: D.B.S., *Canal Statistics*, each year, 1919 to 1960; *Annual Report of the Department of Railways and Canals*, part on *Canal Statistics*, each year 1869 to 1918; *Canada Year Book*, most years from 1912 to 1961.

The Welland and the Sault canals are both parts of an international waterway and therefore movements between U.S. ports will be contained in their figures. Way traffic, series S198, is traffic which enters at one end and fails to make the full transit (and conceivably, traffic which originates and terminates within the canal).

S200–205. Canals, expenditures and revenues, 1868 to 1959

SOURCE: Department of Transport, *Canal Services, Investment Operation and Maintenance Expenditures and Revenues as at March 31*, issue for 1959, 1954 and 1950, various tables throughout each issue.

With the opening of the seaway in 1959, all canals on the seaway were transferred to the St. Lawrence Seaway Authority. The canals then administered directly by the Department of Transport were relatively small and data for later years would not be comparable with those given here.

S 206–211. Water freight charges for wheat, Great Lakes system, 1917 to 1960

SOURCE: for 1939 to 1960, D.B.S., *Canal Statistics*, various years; for 1922 to 1938, D.B.S., *Canal Statistics, 1938*, p. 29; for 1917 to 1921, D.B.S., *Canal Statistics, 1922*, p. 23.

Water freights on grain from Fort William–Port Arthur are the result of a bargain between the shipper and the vessel owner for each movement. The series given herein are weighted annual averages of such bargains. These prices include all costs of loading, unloading, handling and other charges. At midsummer, 1955, these charges for movement from the Head of the Lakes to the Georgian Bay ports and Goderich totalled $11.15 per 1,000 bushels, which equalled 37.2 cents per ton, or about 28 per cent of the nominal charge of 4 cents per bushel. This gives a net revenue to the ship of .178 cents per ton mile for a weighted average distance of 537 miles.

At May 1955 the rate on grain from the St. Lawrence to U.K. ports was reported as 74 shillings and sixpence per long ton. Out of this amount the ship was reported as bearing a cost of $2.10 per long ton. This left a net revenue to the ship of .211 cents per short ton on an average distance of 3,450 miles.

Until 1959 the freight to Montreal normally included a transfer from a large vessel at Port Colborne up to 1932, and at some port between Port Colborne and Prescott thereafter, to a canal-sized vessel.

S 212–214. Wheat freight charges, Regina to Liverpool, 1861 to 1932

SOURCE: W. A. Mackintosh *et al.*, *Economic Problems of the Prairie Provinces*, table v, p. 284.

The data in the source were obtained from the Board of Grain Commissioners of Canada for rates from Regina to Fort William and Port Arthur, and from the *Canada Year Book* for Montreal to Liverpool. The data for Regina to Liverpool were built up from rates on the various parts of the route.

The charges do not include elevator handling charges.

ROADS AND ROAD TRANSPORT
(Series S 215–235)

General note

Road Transport has had the most vigorous growth and the poorest statistics of all major forms of transportation. The reason for the latter is obvious. Development has been in the hands of a larger number of entrepreneurs who have been able to get into the business with a limited initial capital and to grow without appealing to the capital market. It is only in the last few years that the industry has settled down enough to make the collection of statistics possible. Those who are interested in the recent statistics should consult D.B.S. reports numbers 53-205 to 53-215 which give the motor transport statistics for the Dominion as well as for the provinces.

S 215–221. Roads, summary of nonurban road mileage, by type of surface, 1925 to 1960

SOURCE: for 1952 to 1960, D.B.S., *Road and Street Mileage and Expenditure 1960*, table 8, p. 15, and same title 1959, p. 15; for 1945 to 1951, D.B.S., *Highway Statistics*, each year; for 1925 to 1944, D.B.S., *The Highway and The Motor Vehicle*, for each year.

The classifications used here are too coarse to permit a meaningful classification of road mileage other than to give a broad indication of the development of roads.

S 217. Concrete, bituminous pavement and bituminous surface, include all watertight surfaces regardless of the quality of construction.

S 220. Unimproved earth road mileage is included only because it was covered at one time. It is not a trustworthy figure because it includes surveyed road allowances which may or may not be passable.

S 222–235. Motor vehicles, registration, by use and by province, 1904 to 1960

SOURCE: All series, for 1912 to 1960, D.B.S., *The Motor Vehicle, 1960, Part III, Registrations*, table 1, pp. 8–13; series 222–225, for 1904 to 1911, D.B.S., *The Highway and the Motor Vehicle, 1939*, p. 5; series S 226–235, for 1904 to 1911, *Canada Year Book, 1937*, p. 668.

In *The Motor Vehicle, 1960, Part III*, the data of series S 223–224 were revised from earlier published data for the year 1930 onward. In previous reports, station wagons in Ontario had been included with commercial vehicles. In the 1960 report, they are included with passenger vehicles and it was possible to revise data for earlier years to transfer station wagons to the passenger vehicle group. In British Columbia, before 1960, station wagons were divided between passenger and commercial vehicles depending on the kinds of licences issued for them; in 1960 all station wagons are with passenger cars. It was not possible to revise the British Columbia data for earlier years. The revision of the Ontario data, for years before 1960, changed the divisions between passenger and commercial vehicles in the Canada totals. The revised data are given here.

The distinction between passenger and commercial vehicles is based more on the nature of the vehicle than the uses to which it is put. Thus livery and taxi cabs are included with passenger vehicles. All trucks, ambulances, buses, road tractors and the like are included in commercial vehicles whether in use for hire or in some other way.

CIVIL AVIATION (Series S 236–287)

General note

Data on Canadian civil aviation are not fully comparable over the years, partly because of the tremendous changes in structure, function and technology in the air transport industry, and partly because of changes in licensing, and in reporting and collating statistics.

In the following tables, the term 'goods' encompasses freight, express and excess baggage. Until 1937 'mail' refers to that carried under Canadian postal contract only. From then until about 1945, mail carried under contract from any government, and that carried for mines is included. Thereafter, such unofficial mail is classed as freight.

The table, series S 236–239, especially should be considered as a rough measure of growth pattern rather than as precise information. In keeping with the all-inclusive nature of the earlier reports, the data have been kept as broadly based as possible. Reported nonrevenue traffic has been included throughout. This includes data from provincial governments and certain large mines and other non-aviation companies until 1946. Prior to 1938, when control of aviation was vested in the Board of Transport Commissioners for Canada, coverage of the noncommercial element was somewhat broader, including private and contract carriers. From 1947 on, transoceanic services are included. To 1944, 'hours' include only those flown over Canadian territory; from 1945, data for Canadian carriers were computed to cover their entire route, while that for foreign carriers continued on an 'in Canada only' basis.

The tables of series S240–270 report revenue loads and mileages. Revenue data reported by non-aviation companies are included until 1946. Because classification of data as 'domestic' and 'international' (transborder) was along company lines until 1941, series S240–246 and series S247–253 each contain data which properly belong in the other. For 1936, all transborder is included in series S240–246. Trans-Canada Air Lines figures appear in series S247–253 in 1938, and in series S240–246 in 1937, 1939 and 1940.

From 1951 onward transborder traffic has been traffic between Canada and the United States. It should be noted that, until 1949, Canada-Newfoundland traffic was transborder traffic. From 1947 to 1950, series S247–253 include a small volume of transoceanic traffic, not reported separately until 1951. From 1951 only unit toll traffic is included.

From 1941 to 1952 inclusive, transborder traffic via Canadian carriers was not published separately, but has been inferred from data in the *Civil Aviation* annual and *Preliminary* annual reports.

Mileage in series S254–260 are on an 'in Canada' basis until 1944; beginning with 1945, mileages for Canadian carriers cover the entire route. Mileages of United States carriers in transborder traffic which are included with Canadian carriers in series S247–253 are on an 'in Canada' basis throughout.

As far as possible Dominion Bureau of Statistics, *Civil Aviation* was used as the main source of data. For prewar years D.B.S. figures were checked against and supplemented by the statistics compiled by: Harold G. Brandreth (*The History and Economics of Canadian Commercial Aviation*) unpublished; Department of Reconstruction, Directorate of Air Development, *Development of Commercial Air Services in Canada, 1919–1944*, unpublished; and Trans-Canada Air Lines, *Annual Reports*. For the postwar period (1947 to 1960) the official compilations were checked against air carrier reports to Air Transport Board. Some additional estimates and calculations of derived statistics were made by Statistics Section, Department of Transport and were previously published in K. Studnicki-Gizbert, 'Structure and Growth of Canadian Air Transport Industry'. Fleet and airport data were obtained from Financial Services Division and Civil Aviation Branch of the Department of Transport.

Unless otherwise specified the source of the data is D.B.S. *Civil Aviation* checked against the supplementary sources, as noted above.

S236–239. Canadian civil aviation activity, 1920 to 1960

SOURCE: prepared by K. Studnicki-Gizbert, Chief, Economics Division, Air Transport Board, Ottawa: see the general note to series S236–287 for the sources and methods used.

S236. Passengers carried are revenue and nonrevenue passengers on all services.

S237. Goods carried include revenue and nonrevenue freight cargo, express and excess baggage.

S238. Mail carried, until 1937 and again since 1946, includes that under postal contract only. It excludes mail carried by air on private charter or contract to the nearest post office. Such private air carriage of mail was quite common in mining areas in the nineteen-thirties. The latter mail is included with 'goods'.

S239. Hours flown includes revenue and nonrevenue hours.

S240–246. Civil aviation, domestic revenue traffic, 1936 to 1960

SOURCE: same as for series S236–239.

See the general note to series S236–287 for the meaning of the series headings.

S247–253. Civil aviation, transborder traffic, 1937 to 1959

SOURCE: same as for series S236–239.

Transborder traffic is traffic between Canada and the United States.

See the general note to series S236–287 for the meaning of the series headings.

S254–260. Civil aviation, transborder traffic via Canadian carriers, scheduled revenue traffic, 1941 to 1960

SOURCE: same as for series S236–239.

See the note to series S247–253 and the general note to series S236–287.

S261–267. Civil aviation, Atlantic and Pacific scheduled revenue traffic via Trans-Canada Airlines and Canadian Pacific Airlines, 1947 to 1960

SOURCE: same as for series S236–239.

Atlantic services are services between Canada and Europe. Pacific services are those between Canada and points in the Pacific or Orient.

See the general note to series S236–287 for the meaning of series headings.

S268–270. Civil aviation, contract and charter traffic, Canadian carriers, 1946 to 1960

SOURCE: same as for series S236–239.

S271–281. Civil aviation, operating revenues, operating costs per unit of capacity, passenger fares per unit of traffic and employment, Canadian carriers, 1936 to 1960

SOURCE: same as for series S236–239. See also below.

Between the war years of 1939 to 1945 and the postwar years beginning in 1946, there is a definite break in continuity in the development of air carriers operations. Therefore, quite apart from the different reliabilities of the statistical sources, the postwar and pre-1946 parts of the series are not strictly comparable.

S271. Total operating revenues for 1938 to 1945, compiled by the Directorate of Air Development, Department of Reconstruction, are in their unpublished work *Development of Commercial Air Services in Canada, 1919–1944*. This compilation was based on original reports to D.B.S.

S276. Other flying revenues includes in 1942 to 1944 nontransportation defence work of the Canadian Pacific Air Lines and Trans-Canada Air Lines. For 1946 to 1960, the main sources of nontransportation revenue 'other flying revenues' were flying training, aerial survey and crop spraying.

S277. Unit operating costs, T.C.A., are from: for 1938 to 1944, Department of Reconstruction, Directorate of Air Development, *Development of Commercial Air Services in Canada, 1919–1944*; for 1948 to 1957, Trans-Canada Air Lines, *Initial Submission to the Air Transport Board in the Matter of Trans-Continental Air Services*, exhibits T.C.A.–411 and T.C.A.–414 (Testimony of W. S. Harvey); for 1958 to 1960, Trans-Canada Air Lines, *Annual Report* and Economic and Accounting Branch, Air Transport Board.

S278. Unit operating costs, large independents, are from K. Studnicki-Gizbert, *Structure and Growth of Canadian Air Transport Industry*. The companies included for the prewar period are Canadian Airways, Dominion General Aviation, MacKenzie Air Transport, Starrat, H. Wings, St. Martin; for the postwar period the companies included are the scheduled carriers other than T.C.A. and Austin Airways.

S279–280. Average level of fares per passenger mile are derived from air carrier reports to the Air Transport Board. These series are relatively uniform and provide a good measure of the fare level.

S280. Number of employees is from D.B.S., *Civil Aviation*.

S282–287. Civil aviation, aircraft, airports and airport investment expenditures, 1946 to 1960

SOURCE: same as for series S236–239. The data are from the Department of Transport records.

S286. The expenditures are defined as 'expenditures on construction services…construction or acquisition of buildings, works, and/or new equipment'.

S287. Grants and contributions for airport development are mainly made to municipalities on a cost sharing basis. In addition the Department of Northern Affairs and National Resources has incurred, in certain years, some airport development expenditures.

INTERCITY FREIGHT CARRIED
(Series S288–293)

S288–293. Intercity ton miles performed, by type of carrier, 1938 to 1959

SOURCE: D.B.S., *Daily Bulletin, February 10, 1961*, p. 3.

These estimates were made by G. A. Wagdin, Director, Public Finance and Transportation Division, Dominion Bureau of Statistics from D.B.S., *Railway Transport, Part IV (Operating and Traffic Statistics)* and predecessor volumes, *Statistics of Steam Railways of Canada*; D.B.S., *Motor Transport Traffic Statistics, National Estimates*; D.B.S., *Shipping Report, Part III: Coastwise Shipping*; D.B.S., *Oil Pipe Line Transport* (previously *Pipe Line (Oil) Statistics*); D.B.S., *Civil Aviation*.

S290. Road ton mileage prior to 1957 was 'estimated by using the trend of Canadian registrations, U.S. Bureau of Public Roads average loads and average miles travelled with 1957 *Motor Transport Traffic Statistics* as the base' (source, p. 3). Data for 1957 to 1959 are from *Motor Transport Traffic Statistics*.

S291. Water ton mileage was 'estimated by using cargo data in "Shipping Statistics" together with assumed average distances for major water lanes. The ton-mile figures were then adjusted according to fluctuations of canal traffic in previous years' (source, p. 3).

S292. Air ton mileage 'Includes an estimate for bulk transportation ton-miles' (source, p. 3) in addition to unit toll goods carried.

S283. Oil ton mileage includes that of trunk and gathering lines.

THE POST OFFICE (Series S294–322)

S294–306. Post Office, number of post offices in Canada, by province, 1867 to 1960

SOURCE: provided by W. M. Griffith, Director, Comptroller's Branch, Post Office Department based upon material collected in the Department and presented in the *Report of the Postmaster General*, published annually.

These data include sub post offices as well as post offices. In the fiscal year ending 31 March 1960 there were 1,637 such sub post offices in the total for Canada.

S307–312. Post Office, transportation statistics, operations, 1867 to 1960

SOURCE: same as for series S294–306.

S307. Total number of land mail services is a total of the number of non-rail land services. It is a sum of the number of rural routes, series S310, and of other land mail services, series S312.

S308. Railway mail services (miles) are the number of miles of railway over which service was given.

S309. Rural route services (miles) are the total route mileage of all rural routes.

S310. Number of rural routes is the number of separate routes.

S311. Average rural route mileage is obtained by dividing series S309 by series S310.

S312. Number of other land services includes stage services (post office to post office by land), side services (railway or ship depot to post office), parcel post delivery in cities, street letter box pick-up service, conveyance of letter carriers, local services (general post office to postal stations) and the like. This series does not include rail services.

S313–316. Post Office, transportation statistics, operations (five year basis), 1868 to 1913

SOURCE: same as for series S294–306.

S313–314. Stage service is post office to post office by land (non-rail).

S315. Mileage of rail service performed is not available after 1893. However, the increasing use of rail service may be partly evident from miles of rail service in use, which rose from 5,130 miles in 1878 to 15,325 miles in 1898 and 28,791 miles in 1913.

S316. Number of water services is the number of regularly maintained movements of mail by water.

S317–320. Post Office, transportation statistics, cost of services, 1868 to 1960

SOURCE: same as for series S294–306.

S320. Non-rail land services include rural route services and other land services. See the notes to series S309–312.

S321–322. Post Office, gross postal revenues and pieces of first-class mail, 1868 to 1960

SOURCE: same as for series S294–306.

S321. Gross postal revenues are total receipts for post office services before any charges are made against them. Receipts include postage stamps and other postage revenue (by far the largest item), commissions on money orders and postal notes, transit charges on mail from other countries and the like. The figures here exceed those in series G14 since there was some netting of expenditure against receipts in obtaining that series (see series G14 and the note to it). The data in these series are dependable since they are based on a complete accounting as a part of the administrative control of operations.

S322. Pieces of first-class mail handled are based on estimates. The level of accuracy before the First World War was probably lower than that which can now be obtained.

THE TELEPHONE INDUSTRY
(Series S323–349)

General note

Telephone service in Canada is provided by some 2,600 separate telephone systems. They range in size from small co-operatives, municipal and privately owned concerns to the major province-wide systems.

The major systems are linked together in the Trans-Canada

Telephone System, which was established in 1931 to provide long-distance service on a nationwide scale. It is comprised of the following systems: The Avalon Telephone Company (joined in 1957); Maritime Telegraph and Telephone Co. Ltd; The New Brunswick Telephone Co. Ltd; The Bell Telephone Company of Canada; Manitoba Telephone System; Saskatchewan Government Telephones; Alberta Government Telephones; British Columbia Telephone Company. The Canadian Overseas Telecommunication Corporation (owned by the federal government) which provides overseas telephone facilities, became an associate member in 1956. The Manitoba, Saskatchewan and Alberta systems are owned by the respective provincial governments; the five other systems are shareholder-owned.

The 2,619 telephone systems in Canada at the end of 1958 were composed of 2,184 cooperative systems, 318 shareholder-owned companies, 86 systems owned by individuals or partnerships, and 31 government systems.

The largest system was The Bell Telephone Company of Canada, which operates throughout most of Ontario and Quebec and served 61 per cent of all the telephones in Canada. Recently its operations have been extended to include three locations in Newfoundland (Labrador Coast) and Frobisher Bay in the Northwest Territories. The eight members of The Trans-Canada Telephone System serve 89 per cent of all the telephones in Canada.

The cooperative systems are generally located in rural districts. They are composed of individuals who joined together to provide themselves with telephone service. They usually do not provide their own switching facilities and, therefore, contract with larger adjacent systems to provide such facilities and means of connections with other telephone systems.

The sources used appear in the individual source notes. See especially D.B.S., *Canada Year Book, 1934–35*, p. 781 for a historical sketch of the development of the industry.

S 323–331. Telephone industry, telephones and telephone conversations, 1886 to 1960

SOURCE: series S 323: for 1919 to 1960, *Canada Year Book*; for 1911 to 1918, records of The Bell Telephone Company of Canada; for 1901 to 1904 and for 1909 and 1910, *Canada Year Book*; for 1888 to 1893 and 1898 to 1900, *Statistical Year Book of Canada*; for 1886 and 1887 *Statistical Abstract and Record*; series S 324–331: D.B.S., *Telephone Statistics*, issues for all years.

S 323. Total telephones for 1911 to 1918 are not taken from official sources since in them the data for these years are as of 30 June. The data as of 31 December of these years were compiled by The Bell Telephone Company of Canada.

S 324–325. Numbers of business and residence telephones from 1934 onward were published in the source. Prior to 1934 the reported data were subdivided into business, residence and rural, with no further subdivision of rural. Inspection of available data indicated that it would be reasonable to break down the rural figures for 1921 to 1933 on the basis of 3 per cent business and 97 per cent residence: this procedure was adopted in the preparation of the data given here and makes it possible to extend the series back to 1920.

Business telephones, series S 324, includes public pay telephones. Residence telephones, series S 325, include throughout, residence extensions given separately in series S 326.

S 326. Residence extensions are additional telephones which are connected to the same circuit as the main residence telephone.

S 327. Telephones on automatic switchboards are commonly referred to as dial telephones.

S 329–331. Telephone conversations are defined as completed calls. Local conversations are estimated from counts of calls made on representative days throughout the year. Long-distance conversations are generally based on actual counts.

The meaning of the division between local and long distance calls has changed somewhat through the years. Historically, all calls have been separated into these two classes. Basically, a local call was one originated and completed in the same exchange area; a long distance call was one which went beyond the limits of a single exchange. Changes in telephone service, however, have made these definitions outdated, especially with the introduction of extended area service. Under extended area service, customers in one exchange area can call neighbouring exchange areas directly without incurring long-distance charges, and the call is classified as a local call. Consequently, neither the local nor the long-distance series is exactly comparable through time. Splits and combinations of local exchange areas resulted in changes in classifications of certain calls from local to long distance or the reverse. The effects of such changes were relatively unimportant until the introduction of the extended area service, mainly over the last ten years of the period covered; the widening of the extended area service has shifted a significant number of calls from long distance to local.

S 332–334. Telephone industry, gross capital expenditures on construction and new machinery and equipment, 1926 to 1960

SOURCE: for 1958 to 1960, Department of Trade and Commerce, *Private and Public Investment in Canada, Outlook*, individual issues for each year from 1960 to 1962; for 1946 to 1953, D.B.S., *Private and Public Investment in Canada, 1946–1957*, p. 25; for 1926 to 1945, Department of Trade and Commerce, *Private and Public Investment in Canada, 1926–1951*, p. 173.

These data include capital expenditures for new construction, new machinery and equipment and major alterations and improvements; they do not include outlay on land purchase or on purchase from others of structures or machinery put in place in earlier years (see the note to series E 118–131).

Beginning in 1946, the breakdown of the total between construction and machinery and equipment has been obtained from the telephone companies in their reports of such expenditure. Prior to 1946, the total was obtained from published company reports, which covered all the major companies, with an estimate for other companies based on the relationship of their revenue to the revenue of the major companies. The division between construction and machinery and equipment for 1926 to 1945 is described in *Private and Public Investment in Canada, 1926–1951*, p. 226, as follows: 'Construction outlays were estimated by applying an index to the 1948 construction figures. The index was established on the basis of change in telephone wire mileage adjusted for estimated replacement costs and price changes. This method yielded figures that were within 10 per cent of the actual figure reported by private telephone companies in the postwar years. The machinery and equipment figures are the differences between total capital outlays and outlays on construction.'

S 335–343. Telephone industry, property, revenues, expenses, taxes, interest, employees and wages, 1911 to 1960

SOURCE: series S 335–341: for 1919 to 1960, D.B.S., *Telephone Statistics*, various issues; for 1911 to 1918, series S 335 from *Canada Year Book, 1934–35*, p. 782, series S 336–341 from the *Annual Report of the Department of Railways and Canals*, appendix on *Telephone Statistics*, report for each year; series S 342–343: for all years, *Canada Year Book*, 1918 to 1961 inclusive.

S 335. Cost of property and equipment is gross property in use valued at cost. It includes land as well as structures and equipment.

S336–337. Total revenues include revenues from all sources, including local service, long-distance service, directory advertising and sales, rents and income from investments.

S344–349. Telephone industry, long-distance rates between Montreal and selected cities, 1918 to 1960

SOURCE: records of The Bell Telephone Company of Canada.

TELEGRAPH STATISTICS
(Series S350–359)

General note

The telegraph industry has been evolving rapidly in the last fifteen years. It began as a transmitter of messages. It is in the process of becoming a provider of leased wire and other services in which its advantages as against the telephone industry are much greater.

Telegraph statistics were first collected for the year ended 30 June 1912 and were then claimed to be the first such set of national telegraph statistics available.

The data of series S350–359 do not give statistics for numbers employed and salaries and wages. Canadian telegraph systems are, in the main, operated by the railways. The statistics given here are for commercial operations but the commercial operations are intrinsically intermingled with the railway communications function. Cost can be allocated but man-hours and pay cannot be easily or accurately allocated in the same way. Further, agents at small railway stations accept and receive commercial messages and are paid commissions which are in addition to their regular remuneration. Such agents are excluded from numbers employed but their remuneration has not been treated consistently over the years.

S350–359. Telegraph industry, telegraph statistics, 1912 to 1960

SOURCE: for 1937 to 1960, D.B.S., *Telegraph and Cable Statistics*; for 1919 to 1936, D.B.S., *Telegraph Statistics*; for 1912 to 1919 (fiscal years ending 30 June of year given), *Annual Report of the Department of Railways and Canals*, supplement on *Telegraph Statistics*. Data were taken from several issues of each of the foregoing reports.

S350. Operating revenue includes both transmission and nontransmission revenue.

S351. Operating expenses are after deduction of the proportion applicable to unit operations and to other departments. Details are given in *Telegraph and Cable Statistics*.

S352. Nontransmission revenues are part of operating revenues, series S350. For 1958 these nontransmission revenues were:

Leased circuit	$14,574,835
Other leased plant	3,828,870
Money order charges	231,259
Other nontransmission	809,900
	$19,444,864

In the same year transmission revenue from public and government messages was $17,601,609. The number of telegrams sent fell to the lowest point since 1945.

S353. Cost of property and equipment is the cost of the fixed assets in use before the deduction of accrued depreciation.

S354. Total telegrams transmitted includes those originating in Canada and received from the United States.

S357. Total cablegrams excluding duplications is a net figure to exclude the counting of the same cablegram twice: thus a cablegram transmitted through Canada is counted as it is received but not again as it is transmitted on to other countries. Some cablegrams originating and terminating abroad, but passing through Canada, included in this series, are not included in series S358 and S359.

Series S1–17. *Railroads before 1906, nominal capital, railroads completed and under construction, 1875 to 1906*
(millions of dollars)

Year[8]	Total capital	Share capital Total	Share capital Ordinary	Share capital Preference	Bonded debt	Aid from governments[1] Dominion[2]	Provincial Ontario	Provincial Quebec	Provincial New Brunswick	Provincial Nova Scotia	Provincial Manitoba	Provincial British Columbia	Form of government aid Bonuses	Form of government aid Loans	Aid from municipalities	Less included in paid up securities	Capital from other sources
	1	2	3	4	5	6	7	8	9	10	11	12	13	14	15	16	17
1906	1,332.5	561.7	385.1	176.6	504.2	194.2	16.5	16.8	4.2	3.8	1.9	.1	216.9	20.6	17.1	—	12.0
1905	1,248.7	526.4	371.0	155.4	465.5	188.7	14.3	16.7	4.2	3.3	1.9	—	208.2	20.6	17.2	—	10.4
1904	1,186.5	492.8	347.2	145.6	449.1	182.2	8.5	16.6	4.6	2.8	1.9	—	195.8	20.6	17.2	—	10.8
1903	1,146.6	483.8	346.9	136.8	424.1	177.7	8.4	16.4	4.5	2.1	1.2	—	189.9	20.6	16.6	—	11.6
1902	1,098.9	460.4	328.1	132.2	404.8	173.0	8.4	16.4	4.5	1.9	1.8	—	185.2	20.6	16.5	—	11.1
1901	1,042.8	424.4	291.3	133.1	391.7	166.2	7.8	16.3	4.5	1.8	1.8	—	177.6	20.6	16.3	—	11.8
1900	998.3	410.3	279.4	131.0	373.7	159.6	7.3	15.8	4.5	1.6	2.1	—	169.7	20.9	15.9	—	7.5
1899	964.7	391.3	270.3	121.0	362.1	155.6	7.3	15.6	4.5	1.6	1.6	—	165.5	20.5	15.7	—	9.3
1898	941.3	378.2	266.7	111.5	354.9	151.5	7.2	15.6	4.4	1.7	2.6	—	161.1	21.6	15.7	—	9.5
1897	921.9	367.6	260.4	107.2	348.8	149.9	7.1	15.4	4.5	1.5	2.6	—	159.2	21.6	15.6	—	8.7
1896	899.8	361.1	255.8	105.3	336.1	149.4	6.9	14.5	4.5	1.5	2.6	—	157.6	21.6	14.5	—	8.6
1895	894.6	361.4	255.8	105.7	330.8	150.8	6.7	14.4	4.5	1.4	2.6	—	158.6	21.6	14.2	—	7.7
1894	888.0	361.8	256.0	105.8	327.0	149.2	6.5	13.7	4.4	2.1	2.6	—	156.7	21.6	14.2	—	6.5
1893	872.2	371.9	253.0	118.8	307.2	147.2	6.4	12.6	4.4	2.1	2.6	—	153.5	21.6	14.0	—	3.6
1892	845.0	344.4	244.8	99.6	305.1	144.2	6.2	12.0	4.4	2.0	2.4	—	149.2	21.7	14.0	—	10.3
1891	816.6	339.8	238.8	101.0	292.3	142.9	6.0	10.9	4.3	2.0	2.5	—	147.2	21.2	13.8	—	2.1
1890	786.4	338.2	238.2	100.0	266.9	139.7	6.0	10.6	4.3	2.0	2.2	—	143.3	21.2	13.7	—	2.8
1889	760.6	332.6	236.7	95.9	251.7	135.9	5.9	10.0	4.2	1.9	2.0	—	138.4	21.2	13.5	—	2.9
1888	727.2	327.5	231.6	95.9	228.6	132.2	5.9	9.6	4.1	1.7	1.9	—	134.3	20.9	13.1	—	2.4
1887	683.8	324.1	227.3	96.8	194.8	129.5	5.9	7.7	4.0	1.7	1.9	—	129.8	20.6	12.8	—	1.3
1886	653.4	317.1	220.7	96.5	169.4	125.0	5.9	7.0	3.3	2.7	.4	—	124.7	19.3	12.6	—	10.0
1885	625.8	312.2	216.4	95.8	141.4	140.1[3]	5.9	6.9	3.6	2.7	—	—	119.6	39.6[3]	12.5	—	.5
1884	557.6	285.1	212.3	72.8	109.3	124.4	3.5	12.6	3.2	1.6	—	—	105.2	39.6	9.6	—	8.4
1883	500.7	267.4	193.9	73.5	102.1	94.2	3.3	12.5	2.8	1.5	—	—	91.9	21.3	9.2	—	7.8
1882	415.6	216.5	142.9	71.5	92.5	80.8[4]	3.2	11.4	1.6	.8	—	—	76.1	21.3	8.8	—	2.0
1881	389.3	199.5	128.1	71.5	84.9	80.1	2.7	11.6	1.6[5]	.8	—	—	75.5	21.3	7.5	—	.6
1880	371.1	190.0	119.5	70.5	80.7	74.2	3.0	11.1	2.7	.8	—	—	70.3	21.3	8.3	—	.2
1879	362.1	192.7	123.6[6]	69.1	81.1	66.2	2.5	8.5	2.7	.8	—	—	65.3	15.1	7.5	—	—
1878	360.6	191.3	122.2[6]	69.2	83.7	65.9	2.2	8.5	2.7	.8	—	—	64.8	15.1	7.2	1.9	—
1877	346.0	184.5	115.7[6]	68.9	79.9	55.3[7]	1.7	.4	2.2	—	—	—	46.7	15.1	6.6	1.3	—
1876	333.9	184.0	114.2[6]	69.7	76.9	51.9[7]	1.9	.2	2.1	—	—	—	39.6	17.5	6.5	.9	—
1875	318.6	180.9	112.4[6]	68.4	72.9	43.3	1.2	.2	.8	—	—	—	27.9	17.5	3.8	.5	—

[1] Including subscriptions to shares or bonds.
[2] See text for detailed notes on Dominion aid.
[3] Includes a loan of $29,880,912 to the Canadian Pacific Railway, not reported after this year.
[4] Not including $4,516,494 which appeared in former years as expenditures upon preliminary surveys, telegraph lines, and the like, Georgian Bay Branch, Dawson Route and Fort Frances Locks.
[5] This decrease is largely accounted for by the fact that $1,180,000 of paid up sum from New Brunswick granted to the European and North American Railway was in and after 1881 included in the share capital of the St John and Maine Railroad, when it was purchased by the latter.
[6] The capital statement included $10,653,763 as paid up capital of railways in American Territory, owned and operated by the Grand Trunk.
[7] Includes a loan of $2,311,667 to the Northern Railway not reported after this year.
[8] Year ending 30 June of year given.

Series S 18–23. *Railroads before 1906, municipal aid by province and total aid all governments, paid and/or promised to railroads completed and under construction, 1875 to 1906*

(millions of dollars)

| Year[3] | Total all governments | Province in which municipal governments located | | | | |
| | | Ontario | Quebec | New Brunswick | Nova Scotia | Manitoba |
	18	**19**	**20**	**21**	**22**	**23**
1906[1]	262.1	12.9	4.6	.3	.3	.6
1905	255.6	12.9	4.9	.3	.3	.6
1904	243.9	12.9	4.9	.3	.3	.6
1903	237.5	12.3	4.9	.4	.5	.6
1902	233.2	12.3	4.9	.4	.5	.6
1901	228.5	12.2	4.9	.4	.5	.6
1900	218.3	12.3	4.6	.4	.5	.6
1899	213.3	12.6	4.3	.4	.3	.6
1898	212.4	12.6	4.4	.4	.3	.6
1897	207.1	12.4	4.4	.4	.3	.6
1896	204.0	11.3	4.3	.4	.3	.6
1895	203.5	10.8	4.3	.4	.3	.6
1894	203.2	10.5	4.3	.4	.3	.6
1893	199.5	10.5	4.3	.3	.3	.6
1892	195.0	10.4	4.3	.3	.3	.6
1891	192.5	10.3	4.3	.3	.3	.6
1890	189.7	10.3	4.3	.3	.3	.6
1889	184.8	10.2	4.2	.3	.3	.6
1888	177.2	10.0	4.2	.3	.3	.6
1887	172.3	9.5	4.2	.3	.3	.6
1886	164.9	9.5	4.1	.3	.3	.6
1885	191.2	9.6	4.1	.3	.3	.5
1884	187.7	8.3	4.3	.3	.3	.5
1883	154.1	8.4	4.2	.3	.3	.5
1882	150.9	8.1	4.2	.3	.3	.3
1881	152.7	8.0	3.6	.3	.3	.2
1880	149.3[2]	8.2	3.8	.3	.3	—
1879	98.9	8.2	4.0	.3	.3	—
1878	98.7	8.1	4.0	.3	.3	—
1877	92.8	7.0	3.7	.3	.3	—
1876	83.9	6.7	3.5	.3	.2	—
1875	78.1	5.5	3.7	.2	.2	—

[1] For British Columbia the amount of municipal aid in 1906 would round to .2 million dollars. For years prior to 1906, for British Columbia, and for all years for Alberta and Saskatchewan (Northwest Territories) the municipal aid in each case was less than the minimum presented in this table.

[2] The appreciable increase here is largely due to expenditure on the Canadian Pacific Railway and to the purchase of the Rivière du Loup Section of the Intercolonial Railway.

[3] Year ending 30 June of year given.

Series S24–38. *Railroads before 1906, miles of first main track and rolling stock owned and hired, 1875 to 1906[1]*

Year[3]	Miles of first main track					Year[3]	Miles in operation	Year[3]	Miles in operation
	Completed (rails laid)	Under construction	Iron rails	Steel rails	Miles in operation				
	24	25	26	27	28		28		28
1906	21,518	2,141	74	21,444	21,353	1874	3,832	1840	16
						1873	3,613	1839	16
1905	20,601	1,067	68	20,532	20,487	1872	2,899	1838	16
1904	19,611	1,015	66	19,545	19,431	1871	2,695	1837	16
1903	19,078	1,357	101	19,133	18,988			1836	16
1902	18,868	766	107	18,761	18,714	1870	2,617		
1901	18,294	852	110	18,185	18,140	1869	2,524		
						1868	2,278		
1900	17,824	759	130	17,694	17,657	1867	2,278		
1899	17,359	799	177	17,210	17,250	1866	2,278		
1898	16,870	706	248	16,622	16,870				
1897	16,687	394	210	16,477	16,550	1865	2,240		
1896	16,387	242	250	16,137	16,270	1864	2,189		
						1863	2,189		
1895	16,091	225	346	15,745	15,977	1862	2,189		
1894	15,768	358	400	15,368	15,627	1861	2,146		
1893	15,320	150	437	14,883	15,005				
1892	14,870	210	607	14,262	14,564	1860	2,065		
1891	14,634	218	764	13,870	13,838	1859	1,994		
						1858	1,863		
1890	14,004	427	665	13,339	13,151	1857	1,444		
1889	13,325	416	786	12,539	12,585	1856	1,414		
1888	12,702	540	1,038	11,664	12,184				
1887	12,332	660	1,175	11,157	11,793	1855	877		
1886	11,524	751	1,220	10,303	10,773	1854	764		
						1853	506		
1885	10,773	812	1,228	9,545	10,273	1852	205		
1884	9,950	1,565	1,601	8,348	9,577	1851	159		
1883	9,066	2,299	1,725	7,341	8,697				
1882	8,069	3,189	1,984	6,086	7,331	1850	66		
1881	7,596	2,910	2,661	4,935	7,194	1849	54		
						1848	54		
1880	7,230[2]	1,078	3,157	4,050	6,858	1847	54		
1879	7,044[2]	945	3,177	3,814	6,226	1846	16		
1878	6,865[2]	1,041	3,258	3,583	5,782				
1877	5,574[2]	1,997	2,784	2,765	5,218	1845	16		
1876	5,157[2]	2,142	2,758	2,374	4,804	1844	16		
						1843	16		
1875	4,827[2]	2,276	2,746	2,055	4,331	1842	16		
						1841	16		

Year[3]	Number of units of rolling stock, owned and hired									
	Engines	Sleeping cars	Parlour or drawing room cars	First class cars	Second class and immigrant cars	Baggage, mail and express cars	Cattle and box cars	Refrigerator cars	Platform cars	Coal and dump cars
	29	30	31	32	33	34	35	36	37	38
1906	2,931	235	96	1,289	716	842	61,929	1,655	18,525	8,295
1905	2,906	194	48	1,285	683	796	57,229	1,511	18,669	8,787
1904	2,768	171	50	1,231	595	860	54,877	1,565	18,644	8,476
1903	2,587	157	147	1,148	590	818	53,107	1,221	18,285	7,639
1902	2,444	136	145	1,166	573	681	48,790	1,057	15,834	7,736
1901	2,433	135	123	1,159	649	815	45,904	1,001	16,348	6,775
1900	2,282	134	104	1,287	641	662	42,538	943	15,626	5,872
1899	2,217	168	100	1,239	640	668	41,151	787	15,811	5,582
1898	2,112	146	80	1,214	628	668	38,820	520	16,306	5,181
1897	2,096	132	94	1,085	688	674	37,471	—	15,352	4,931
1896	2,046	135	71	1,042	648	650	36,791	—	15,593	4,812
1895	2,023	174	42	1,076	702	664	36,360	—	15,758	4,845
1894	2,002	181	18	992	670	636	35,852	—	14,904	4,699
1893	1,954	146	15	977	664	610	35,741	—	15,719	3,455
1892	1,961	142	13	909	634	591	35,668	—	15,400	3,584
1891	1,850	141	1	849	624	560	34,365	—	14,614	3,559
1890	1,771	73	10	806	604	525	32,383	—	13,737	3,236
1889	1,761	103	2	795	581	517	31,025	—	13,925	3,235
1888	1,657	75	4	759	568	506	27,870	—	12,992	3,147
1887	1,633	77	2	764	514	463	24,770	—	12,865	2,957
1886	1,567	73	4	735	497	419	23,645	—	13,128	2,533
1885	1,524	43	4	704	501	403	22,166	—	13,761	2,391
1884	1,481	—	—	694	458	406	21,477	—	13,989	1,941
1883	1,383	—	—	671	397	368	21,399	—	12,731	1,895
1882	1,331	—	—	665	363	388	20,302	—	9,621	2,050
1881	1,211	—	—	640	353	344	17,916	—	8,209	1,716
1880	1,157	—	—	569	310	291	15,614	—	6,689	1,776
1879	1,106	—	—	548	327	274	14,983	—	6,618	1,731
1878	1,050	—	—	530	308	275	14,957	—	6,703	1,317
1877	995	—	—	497	294	241	13,712	—	6,917	1,050
1876	1,000	—	—	493	280	264	13,647	—	7,088	1,050
1875	980	—	—	488	277	235	12,843	—	6,404	1,050

[1] See note on series S 24–38.

[2] Includes wooden rails laid of the Quebec and St. John Railroad in the amounts of 25.5 miles in 1875 to 1877 and 23.5 miles from 1878 to 1880.

[3] Year ending 30 June of year given.

Series S 39–52. *Railroads before 1906, train mileage, freight and passengers carried, 1875 to 1906*

(all series in thousands of units)

Year[3]	Train mileage				Engine mileage	Passengers carried	Tons of freight							
	Total	Passengers	Freight	Mixed			Total freight carried[1]	Flour	Grain	Live-stock	Lumber (all kinds except firewood)	Fire-wood	Manu-factured goods	All other articles
	39	40	41	42	43	44	45	46	47	48	49	50	51	52
1906	72,723	28,072	39,045	5,607	94,181	27,990	57,967	1,770	6,442	1,453	7,516	14,026[2]	11,174	15,585[2]
1905	65,934	25,428	34,373	6,133	84,336	25,289	50,894	1,597	4,832	1,400	6,733	12,875[2]	9,913	13,543[2]
1904	61,312	23,503	28,278	9,531	80,508	23,641	48,098	1,667	4,621	1,587	6,354	13,002[2]	8,703	12,164[2]
1903	60,383	22,096	28,840	9,447	77,178	22,149	47,373	1,926	5,762	1,345	6,042	2,083	7,256	22,959
1902	55,730	21,104	24,892	9,734	70,276	20,680	42,377	1,818	5,174	909	5,414	1,578	6,168	21,314
1901	53,349	19,115	23,888	10,346	68,621	18,386	36,999	1,486	4,695	839	5,302	1,597	5,643	17,438
1900	55,178	20,922	24,663	9,593	67,712	21,500	35,946	1,618	4,864	861	5,653	1,277	5,384	16,289
1899	52,215	20,093	26,922	5,199	64,583	19,133	31,212	1,602	4,122	870	5,256	1,248	4,741	13,374
1898	50,688	19,306	26,868	4,514	60,104	18,444	28,786	1,423	3,933	1,001	4,548	1,036	4,333	12,512
1897	45,781	17,238	23,595	4,948	54,729	16,171	25,300	1,192	3,184	950	4,644	932	3,471	10,928
1896	44,501	15,847	23,300	5,354	55,787	14,810	24,267	1,186	3,157	913	3,820	858	3,419	10,915
1895	40,662	15,332	19,940	5,390	51,340	13,988	21,524	1,116	2,657	875	3,576	904	2,965	9,429
1894	43,770	16,543	21,423	5,804	57,402	14,462	20,721	1,113	2,568	840	3,609	1,011	2,921	8,659
1893	44,386	15,860	23,221	5,305	57,587	13,618	22,004	1,593	2,675	1,097	3,417	1,065	3,054	9,102
1892	44,448	15,237	24,399	4,812	56,994	13,533	22,190	1,284	3,646	1,171	3,339	896	2,709	9,145
1891	43,399	14,988	23,592	4,819	56,950	13,223	21,753	1,169	2,592	1,096	3,192	946	3,071	9,687
1890	41,849	14,363	22,428	5,058	49,513	12,821	20,787	1,137	3,083	872	3,179	807	3,781	7,807
1889	38,819	12,900	20,739	5,180	47,708	12,151	17,929	955	2,532	601	2,588	1,078	2,627	7,199
1888	37,391	11,860	20,652	4,763	46,489	11,417	17,173	1,123	2,147	529	2,361	653	2,483	7,870
1887	33,639	10,839	17,998	4,540	43,276	10,699	16,356	1,127	2,308	617	2,549	541	2,277	6,937
1886	30,481	9,214	15,914	5,183	37,359	9,861	15,670	1,112	2,533	605	2,302	498	2,266	6,304
1885	30,624	9,511	16,383	4,730	38,749	9,673	14,659	1,187	2,144	577	2,351	490	1,493	6,418
1884	29,759	9,316	15,711	4,255	37,391	9,982	13,712	839	1,831	298	2,575	468	1,076	5,004
1883	37,416	9,651	16,123	10,951	47,689	9,580	13,266	404	904	173	1,187	560	959	2,404
1882	27,846	8,795	15,638	2,375	33,375	9,352	13,576	300	893	150	1,391	297	837	2,259
1881	27,301	8,299	15,164	2,099	34,265	6,944	12,065	565	1,602	257	1,197	266	1,847	1,862
1880	22,427	7,312	10,775	4,157	26,576	6,463	9,939	526	1,396	154	895	170	489	2,732
1879	20,732	6,988	6,511	7,068	24,736	6,524	8,349	489	1,245	163	986	172	328	2,052
1878	19,669	6,225	9,982	3,462	24,092	6,444	7,883	457	1,161	172	882	168	326	1,832
1877	19,451	6,272	11,404	1,775	22,232	6,073	6,860	278	731	182	834	145	148	4,563
1876	18,104	5,837	9,616	2,650	21,001	5,545	6,332	293	826	171	724	113	145	4,060
1875	17,680	5,206	10,910	1,564	19,633	5,190	5,671	228	464	157	676	140	202	969

[1] Owing to some railways not classifying freight carried in some years the total may exceed the sum of the individual categories.

[2] Until 1903, coal was reported with 'all other articles' (series S 52) and series S 50 included firewood only. Beginning in 1904 coal and firewood were presented as a combined total and appear in series S 50; in the same period coal was not included in series S 52.

[3] Year ending 30 June of year given.

Series S53–63. *Railroads before 1906, gross earnings, operating expenses and net earnings, 1875 to 1906*
(millions of dollars)

Year[1]	Gross earnings					Operating expenses					Net earnings
	Total	Passenger	Freight	Mail and express	Other sources	Total	Maintenance of line, buildings, etc.	Working and repair of engines	Working and repair of cars	General operating expenses	
	53	54	55	56	57	58	59	60	61	62	63
1906	125.3	33.4	81.4	4.5	6.0	87.1	18.8	29.9	8.9	29.6	38.2
1905	106.5	29.0	68.2	4.0	5.3	80.0	17.8	26.9	7.8	27.5	26.5
1904	100.2	26.9	64.7	4.0	4.6	74.6	15.6	25.9	7.0	26.2	25.7
1903	96.1	24.9	63.1	3.4	4.7	67.5	15.5	22.8	6.0	23.1	28.6
1902	83.7	22.6	54.0	3.3	3.8	57.3	13.0	18.9	5.2	20.3	26.3
1901	72.9	19.4	46.7	3.1	3.7	50.4	11.2	16.5	4.4	18.3	22.5
1900	70.7	18.6	45.6	3.0	3.5	47.7	10.3	15.1	4.5	17.8	23.0
1899	62.2	15.9	40.1	2.8	3.4	40.7	9.0	12.6	3.3	15.8	21.5
1898	59.7	15.6	38.5	2.7	2.9	39.1	8.6	12.0	3.2	15.4	20.6
1897	52.4	13.9	33.5	2.6	2.3	35.2	7.6	10.9	3.1	13.6	17.2
1896	50.5	13.7	32.4	2.4	2.0	35.0	7.4	11.2	3.1	13.4	15.5
1895	46.8	13.3	29.5	2.2	1.7	32.7	7.0	10.4	2.7	12.6	14.0
1894	49.6	15.5	30.0	2.2	1.9	35.2	7.3	11.4	3.1	13.4	14.3
1893	52.0	15.1	32.9	2.2	1.9	36.6	7.6	12.1	3.4	13.5	15.4
1892	51.7	14.8	33.2	2.0	1.7	36.5	7.7	12.2	3.5	13.1	15.2
1891	48.2	14.3	30.5	1.9	1.5	35.0	7.5	11.8	3.2	12.5	13.2
1890	46.8	13.7	29.9	1.8	1.4	32.8	7.2	11.0	3.1	11.5	13.9
1889	42.1	13.2	26.7	1.7	.6	31.0	7.0	10.2	2.8	11.1	11.1
1888	42.2	12.7	26.4	1.6	1.4	30.6	6.8	10.3	3.0	10.5	11.5
1887	38.8	11.9	24.6	1.6	.8	27.6	6.4	9.1	2.8	9.3	11.2
1886	33.4	10.3	21.2	1.4	.5	24.1	5.2	8.0	2.4	8.5	9.3
1885	32.2	10.6	20.0	1.3	.4	23.0	5.1	7.9	2.3	8.7	8.2
1884	33.4	11.2	20.8	1.2	.3	25.5	5.2	8.8	2.3	9.2	7.8
1883	33.2	10.5	21.3	1.1	.3	24.7	5.0	8.2	2.2	9.2	8.6
1882	29.0	10.0	17.7	1.0	.2	22.3	4.6	6.8	2.2	8.6	6.6
1881	28.0	8.2	18.7	.9	.1	19.9	4.1	6.0	2.1	7.7	7.9
1880	23.6	7.1	15.5	.9	.1	16.7	3.7	5.2	1.6	6.3	6.7
1879	19.9	6.5	12.5	.8	.2	16.1	3.8	4.8	1.4	6.0	3.7
1878	20.5	6.4	13.1	.8	.2	16.1	3.6	4.9	1.6	6.0	4.4
1877	18.7	6.5	11.4	.7	.2	15.3	3.2	4.8	1.5	5.7	3.5
1876	19.4	6.3	12.2	.7	.2	15.8	3.8	4.8	1.6	5.6	3.6
1875	19.5	6.4	12.1	.7	.3	15.4	3.5	4.7	1.5	5.7	3.7

[1] Year ending 30 June of the year given.

Series S64–68. *Railroads before 1906, fatal accidents and injuries, 1875 to 1906*

Year[1]	Fatal accidents				Total injured	Year[1]	Fatal accidents				Total injured
	Total	Passengers	Employees	Others			Total	Passengers	Employees	Others	
	64	65	66	67	68		64	65	66	67	68
1906	361	16	139	206	1,365	1890	218	11	83	124	838
						1889	210	37	89	84	875
1905	468	35	206	227	1,357	1888	231	20	107	104	775
1904	395	25	192	178	1,405	1887	178	10	84	84	633
1903	420	53	186	181	1,453	1886	144	8	66	70	571
1902	330	19	146	165	1,328						
1901	317	16	118	183	1,317	1885	157	7	67	83	684
						1884	227	49	78	100	796
1900	325	7	123	195	1,317	1883	167	9	66	92	550
1899	284	20	119	145	1,185	1882	146	13	56	77	184
1898	270	5	98	167	1,097	1881	99	7	35	57	147
1897	213	7	76	130	807						
1896	161	11	46	104	619	1880	87	10	27	50	102
						1879	107	9	37	61	66
1895	187	9	51	127	658	1878	97	11	45	41	361
1894	211	12	67	132	694	1877	111	5	45	61	317
1893	216	11	72	133	708	1876	109	5	48	56	304
1892	233	14	110	109	879						
1891	196	13	65	118	818	1875	92	11	40	41	279

[1] Year ending 30 June of the year given.

Series S69–76. *Railroads, capital liability, aid to railroads, dominion, provincial and municipal, 1907 to 1960*

(millions of dollars)

Year[1]	Total[2]	Stocks	Debenture stock	Funded debt[2]	Total	Dominion[3]	Provincial[3]	Municipal
	69	70	71	72	73	74	75	76
1960	4,970.4	2,433.3	292.5	2,244.6	—	—	—	—
1959	4,791.7	2,376.4	292.6	2,122.7	—	—	—	—
1958	4,599.8	2,354.0	292.6	1,953.1	218.9	172.2	33.4	13.3
1957	4,330.2	2,272.9	292.6	1,764.7	218.9	172.2	33.4	13.3
1956	4,185.2	2,279.8	292.6	1,612.7	218.9	172.2	33.4	13.3
1955	4,108.6	2,250.7	292.7	1,565.1	218.9	172.2	33.4	13.3
1954	3,975.6	2,207.0	292.8	1,475.8	218.9	172.2	33.4	13.3
1953	3,861.8	2,122.2	300.4	1,439.1	218.9	172.2	33.4	13.3
1952	3,715.2	2,101.1	305.2	1,308.9	218.9	172.2	33.4	13.3
1951	3,571.7	1,341.0	305.2	1,925.5	218.9	172.2	33.4	13.3
1950	3,475.8	1,341.4	308.1	1,826.3	218.9	172.2	33.4	13.3
1949	3,269.6	1,268.7	308.1	1,629.9	218.9	172.2	33.4	13.3
1948	3,250.3	1,270.0	308.1	1,672.3	218.9	172.2	33.4	13.3
1947	3,308.6	1,314.2	309.4	1,685.0	218.9	172.2	33.4	13.3
1946	3,290.6	1,315.4	309.4	1,665.8	218.9	172.2	33.4	13.3
1945	3,490.7	1,363.4	309.6	1,817.7	218.9	172.2	33.4	13.3
1944	3,343.9	1,326.1	309.9	1,707.8	218.9	172.2	33.4	13.3
1943	3,356.6	1,303.7	311.2	1,741.7	218.9	172.2	33.4	13.3
1942	3,371.8	1,265.6	312.7	1,793.6	218.9	172.2	33.4	13.3
1941	3,397.5	1,294.8	402.7	1,699.9	218.9	172.2	33.4	13.3
1940	3,380.0	1,300.1	462.3	1,617.6	218.9	172.2	33.4	13.3
1939	3,367.7	1,320.3	514.1	1,533.4	218.9	172.2	33.4	13.3
1938	3,405.2	1,322.8	514.1	1,568.3	218.9	172.2	33.4	13.3
1937	3,374.1	1,325.6	514.1	1,534.5	218.9	172.2	33.4	13.3
1936	4,487.6	915.2	510.0	3,062.4	218.9	172.2	33.4	13.3
1935	4,460.3	923.8	510.0	3,026.4	218.9	172.2	33.4	13.3
1934	4,403.8	927.3	510.0	2,966.5	218.9	172.2	33.4	13.3
1933	4,390.5	928.8	510.0	2,951.7	218.9	172.2	33.4	13.3
1932	4,371.7	927.5	510.0	2,934.2	218.8	172.2	33.3	13.3
1931	4,232.0	928.0	510.0	2,794.0	218.7	172.2	33.3	13.2
1930	4,026.5	921.3	510.0	2,595.1	218.6	172.2	33.2	13.2
1929	3,902.7	910.5	495.1	2,497.1	218.6	172.2	33.2	13.2
1928	3,663.6	861.9	495.1	2,306.6	218.5	172.2	33.1	13.2
1927	3,582.5	823.3	506.9	2,252.3	218.5	172.2	33.1	13.2
1926	3,506.8	820.0	541.8	2,145.0	218.5	172.2	33.1	13.2
1925	3,471.1	836.9	541.8	2,092.4	218.5	172.2	33.1	13.2
1924	3,413.9	859.5	541.8	2,012.6	218.5	172.2	33.1	13.2
1923	3,264.7[2]	853.3	531.8	1,879.6[2]	217.8	172.2	32.5	13.0
1922	2,159.3	884.8	530.8	743.7	217.8	172.2	32.5	13.0
1921	2,164.7	880.5	492.1	792.1	217.8	172.2	32.5	13.0
1920	2,170.0	888.4	435.3	846.3	217.7	172.2	32.5	13.0
1919[1]	2,036.2	888.1	216.3	931.8	217.4	171.9	32.5	13.0
1919[1]	2,015.1	884.0	216.3	914.8	221.8	176.4	32.5	13.0
1918	1,999.9	877.6	216.3	906.0	221.6	176.3	32.4	12.9
1917	1,985.1	872.8	216.3	896.0	220.7	175.4	32.4	12.9
1916	1,893.9	848.3	176.3	869.3	219.7	174.5	32.4	12.9
1915	1,875.8	847.8	176.3	851.7	217.8	173.1	31.8	12.9
1914	1,808.8	853.1	173.3	782.4	212.2	167.9	31.4	12.9
1913	1,531.8	755.3	163.3[4]	613.3[4]	193.1	148.8	31.4	12.9
1912	1,588.9	770.5	—	818.5	187.6	143.9	30.8	12.9
1911	1,528.7	749.2	—	779.5	181.8	138.0	30.9	12.9
1910	1,410.3	687.6	—	722.7	182.0	136.5	32.8	12.7
1909	1,308.5	647.5	—	660.9	189.0	135.5	35.6	17.8
1908	1,239.8	607.9	—	631.9	185.9	133.0	35.2	17.6
1907	1,171.9	588.6	—	583.4	181.6	128.8	35.1	17.6

[1] From 1907 to 1919 the data are for the year ending 30 June of the year given. The year 1919 is also given on a calendar year basis as are all subsequent years.

[2] Beginning in 1923 total railway capital includes government loans previously classified under current liabilities.

[3] Excludes expenditures on government-owned railways.

[4] In 1913 perpetual consolidated debenture stock of the Canadian Pacific Railway is reported separately from funded debt into which it was originally classified.

34-2

Series S77–90. *Railroads, miles of line in operation, rolling stock, locomotives and passenger cars in service, 1907 to 1960*

	Miles in operation				Number of locomotives[3]				Number of passenger train cars[3]					
Year[1]	All tracks (iron and steel)[2]	Single track (iron and steel)[2]	Second track (steel)	Yard track, industrial track and sidings (iron and steel)	Total	Steam	Diesel electric	Electric	Total[4]	Dining, parlour and sleeping[4]	First and second class, immigrant and combination	Baggage, express, postal and other	Motor passenger cars	Number of cars in company service
	77	78	79	80	81	82	83	84	85	86	87	88	89	90
1960	59,193	44,029	2,288	12,876	3,752	403	3,308	41	5,119	1,147	1,602	2,259	111	19,165
1959	59,394	44,209	2,350	12,835	4,720	1,514	3,155	51	5,456	1,221	1,687	2,420	128	19,421
1958	59,319	44,125	2,444	12,750	4,823	1,960	2,799	64	5,733	1,236	1,938	2,420	139	19,547
1957	59,097	43,890	2,471	12,736	4,821	2,394	2,372	55	5,942[5]	1,229	2,076	2,508	129	19,586
1956	59,830	43,652	2,476	13,702	4,790	2,849	1,895	46	6,220[5]	1,284	2,317	2,516	90	19,389
1955	59,315	43,444	2,486	13,385	4,714	3,225	1,455	33	6,574	1,342	2,609	2,548	75	19,194
1954	58,760	43,132	2,485	13,143	4,771	3,586	1,152	33	6,648	1,326	2,710	2,549	63	19,023
1953	58,695	43,163	2,485	13,047	4,818	3,829	956	33	6,456	1,142	2,686	2,569	59	18,725
1952	58,291	42,953	2,488	12,850	4,810	4,014	763	33	6,328	1,150	2,729	2,394	55	18,170
1951	58,150	42,956	2,487	12,707	4,715	4,108	574	33	6,366	1,152	2,823	2,342	49	17,643
1950[6]	57,997	42,979	2,498	12,520	4,655	4,272	350	33	6,338	1,167	2,881	2,238	52	17,274
1949[6]	57,834	42,978	2,494	12,362	4,627	4,351	246	30	6,224	1,145	2,857	2,168	54	17,080
1948	57,005	42,248	2,495	12,262	4,521	4,340	148[7]	33	6,099	1,122	2,822	2,095	60	16,700
1947	57,051	42,322	2,489	12,240	4,451	4,364	54	33	6,030	1,120	2,822	2,024	64	16,654
1946	57,005	42,335	2,486	12,184	4,450	4,387	29	34	6,141	1,127	2,909	2,041	64	16,386
1945	56,937	42,352	2,487	12,098	4,431	4,382	15	34	6,211	1,125	2,963	2,055	68	16,217
1944	56,889	42,336	2,489	12,064	4,416	4,369	13	34	6,263	1,127	2,996	2,069	71	16,047
1943	56,825	42,346	2,491	11,988	4,364	4,320	10	34	6,319	1,131	3,041	2,074	73	15,660
1942	56,584	42,338	2,487	11,759	4,315	4,274	—	41	6,342	1,277	2,954	2,009	75	15,224
1941	56,701	42,441	2,499	11,761	4,199	4,159	—	40	6,235	1,305	2,864	1,989	77	14,547
1940	56,533	42,565	2,502	11,466	4,308	4,272	—	36	6,267	1,344	2,830	2,010	83	14,107
1939	56,601	42,637	2,499	11,465	4,373	4,337	—	36	6,387	1,424	2,850	2,028	85	14,044
1938	56,760	42,742	2,498	11,520	4,557	4,522	—	35	6,381	1,473	2,855	1,964	89	14,678
1937	56,835	42,727	2,500	11,608	4,667	4,632	—	35	6,395	1,547	2,850	1,910	88	15,202
1936	56,692	42,552	2,500	11,640	4,747	4,713	—	34	6,443	1,619	2,821	1,911	92	15,444
1935	57,171	42,916	2,507	11,748	4,795	4,761	—	34	6,669	1,685	2,968	1,917	99	15,329
1934	56,519	42,270	2,525	11,724	5,087	5,053	—	34	7,286	1,725	3,346	2,119	96	20,775
1933	56,679	42,336	2,531	11,812	5,187	5,148	—	39	7,354	1,739	3,376	2,142	97	18,128
1932	57,004	42,409	2,682	11,913	5,266	5,227	—	39	7,459	1,768	3,400	2,186	105	18,137
1931	56,851	42,280	2,688	11,883	5,377	5,337	—	40	7,611	1,809	3,473	2,225	104	18,588
1930	56,585	42,047	2,688	11,900	5,451	5,414	—	37	7,346	1,773	3,547	1,953	73	18,460
1929	55,813	41,380	2,658	11,775	5,531	5,495	—	36	7,250	1,703	3,627	1,852	68	18,748
1928	55,455	41,022	2,639	11,792	5,669	5,634	—	35	7,184	1,603	3,662	1,850	69	18,865
1927	54,717	40,507	2,647	11,498	5,660	5,628	—	32	6,922	1,425	3,587	1,845	65	18,461
1926	54,279	40,350	2,620	11,307	5,679	5,650	—	29	6,848	1,346	3,443	1,999	60	17,832
1925	54,100	40,350	2,614	11,134	5,752	5,723	—	29	6,839	1,269	3,520	1,993	57	17,942
1924	52,692	40,059	2,619	10,012	5,857	5,828	—	29	6,849	1,258	3,529	2,020	42	17,918
1923	51,936	39,654	2,591	9,680	5,897	5,871	—	26	6,785	1,092	3,525	2,140	28	17,539
1922	51,860	39,358	2,608	9,892	5,955	5,929	—	26	6,800	1,043	3,616	2,113	28	17,865
1921	51,747	39,191	2,629	9,755	6,027	6,017	—	10	6,767	1,041	3,797	1,929	—	17,306
1920	51,174	38,805	2,590	9,608	6,030	6,014	—	16	6,557	967	3,829	1,761	—	17,198
1919[1]	50,691	38,495	2,547	9,481	5,947	5,947	—	—	6,538	914	3,854	1,770	—	17,293
1919[1]	50,616	38,329	2,543	9,177	5,879	5,879	—	—	6,512	917	3,887	1,708	—	17,753
1918	50,640	38,252	2,523	9,238	5,756	5,756	—	—	6,376	917	3,741	1,718	—	18,890
1917	50,253	38,369	2,481	9,169	5,626	5,626	—	—	6,377	933	3,807	1,637	—	18,641
1916	48,319	36,985	2,489	8,396	5,490	5,490	—	—	6,326	909	3,821	1,596	—	17,708
1915	45,833	34,882	2,451	7,800	5,486	5,486	—	—	6,326	891	3,840	1,595	—	17,026
1914	40,605	30,795	2,293	7,518	5,447	5,447	—	—	6,002	834	3,751	1,417	—	16,353
1913	38,223	29,304	1,984	6,935	5,119	5,119	—	—	5,696	733	3,614	1,349	—	15,526
1912	34,629	26,840	1,752	6,148	4,484	4,484	—	—	4,946	601	3,180	1,165	—	10,466
1911	32,559	25,400	1,610	5,549	4,219	4,309	—	—	4,513	523	2,909	1,081	—	9,578
1910	31,429	24,730	1,543	5,154	4,079	4,079	—	—	4,320	475	2,829	1,016	—	8,648
1909	30,330	24,104	1,464	4,761	3,969	3,979	—	—	4,192	448	2,904	967	—	7,859
1908	28,695	22,967	1,211	4,546	3,872	3,872	—	—	4,026	413	1,326	908	—	7,180
1907	27,611	22,446	1,067	4,092	3,504	3,504	—	—	3,642	380	2,449	813	—	6,107

[1] From 1907 to 1919 the data are for the year ending 30 June of the year given. The year 1919 is also given on a calendar year basis as are all subsequent years.

[2] Beginning in 1913 small mileages in the United States, operated as part of the Canadian systems, are included.

[3] From 1917 onward leased locomotives and passenger cars are included. In 1907 and 1909 to 1912 leased equipment is excluded. In 1908 and 1913 to 1916 it was not specified.

[4] Includes pullman cars in Canadian service from 1928 onward but not before 1928.

[5] Includes 13 cars not specified by type.

[6] Newfoundland equipment included from 1949 onward.

[7] Includes 84 diesel locomotives formerly listed as switching and included under steam in 1947.

Series S91–99. *Railroads, rolling stock, freight cars in service, 1907 to 1960*

(capacity in thousands of tons)

| Year[1] | Total | | Box (number) | Flat (number) | Stock (number) | Coal[2] (number) | Tank (number) | Refrigerator (number) | Other[2] (number) |
	Number	Capacity							
	91	92	93	94	95	96	97	98	99
1960	191,553	9,841	118,466	12,645	4,917	44,946	472	10,076	31
1959	194,512	9,935	121,451	12,270	5,025	45,133	455	10,155	23
1958	196,893	9,998	124,326	12,058	5,195	44,727	382	10,184	21
1957	197,907	9,947	128,079	11,975	5,141	42,305	384	10,022	1
1956	191,974[3]	9,531	124,723	11,876	5,501	39,543	389	9,906	16
1955	185,956	9,031	122,220	12,037	5,776	35,776	378	9,735	34
1954	189,351	9,106	126,209	11,782	5,972	35,398	363	9,583	44
1953	187,980	8,934	127,313	11,690	6,057	33,110	328	9,438	44
1952	186,557	8,735	129,158	11,748	6,284	30,360	268	8,691	48
1951	180,725	8,315	127,714	11,062	6,509	26,700	460	8,231	49
1950	175,597	8,000	122,419	11,263	6,655	26,641	469	8,050	100
1949[4]	177,614	8,052	124,651	10,951	6,648	26,909	454	7,921	80
1948	172,406	7,755	123,539	10,326	6,115	24,738[2]	353	7,240	95[2]
1947	166,451	7,389	119,589	10,453	6,277	21,618	354	6,673	1,487
1946	163,345	7,194	116,809	10,868	6,382	20,938	358	6,467	1,523
1945	164,769	7,234	117,886	10,892	6,437	21,340	343	6,372	1,499
1944	164,067	7,159	117,068	10,953	6,471	21,104	348	6,587	1,536
1943	158,390	6,877	112,815	10,870	6,510	19,900	348	6,424	1,523
1942	155,311	6,706	110,916	11,998	6,029	18,106	362	6,372	1,528
1941	155,240	6,667	112,134	11,897	5,753	17,505	366	6,191	1,394
1940	160,697	6,879	116,629	12,049	5,866	17,453	389	6,534	1,777
1939	160,018	6,798	115,492	11,692	5,985	17,770	402	6,713	1,964
1938	168,329	7,042	121,954	12,462	6,436	18,115	405	7,005	1,952
1937	172,773	7,214	125,421	12,548	7,077	18,066	421	7,164	2,076
1936	172,008	7,121	124,448	12,991	7,219	17,463	432	7,331	2,124
1935	176,760	7,256	128,816	13,501	7,467	17,566	425	6,682	2,303
1934	195,052	7,830	141,768	15,124	8,744	18,115	468	7,904	2,929
1933	204,662	8,190	146,207	15,837	8,522	22,472	476	8,160	2,988
1932	210,996	8,377	150,979	16,370	9,048	22,722	480	8,341	3,056
1931	214,765	8,494	152,841	17,266	9,281	23,091	512	8,464	3,310
1930	215,027	8,445	151,500	17,728	9,479	22,251	516	8,151	5,402
1929	217,756	8,310	151,565	19,601	10,408	22,676	495	7,579	5,432
1928	217,028	8,085	148,717	20,335	11,312	23,278	466	6,950	5,970
1927	220,783	8,180	151,232	21,018	11,656	23,551	462	6,802	6,062
1926	221,255	8,145	150,499	21,631	11,746	23,663	456	6,616	6,644
1925	224,227	8,228	154,527	22,308	12,025	23,445	466	6,286	5,170
1924	226,163	8,283	155,656	22,748	12,335	23,486	453	6,329	5,156
1923	229,614	8,349	159,276	23,321	12,204	22,854	438	6,504	5,017
1922	228,575	8,188	158,622	24,186	11,542	20,557	405	6,463	6,800
1921	231,563	8,260	161,259	24,391	12,585	20,079	413	7,012	5,824
1920	224,489	7,889	155,964	24,939	11,164	20,249	414	6,204	5,555
1919[1]	219,795	7,588	154,044	25,657	11,023	17,908	414	5,591	5,158
1919[1]	217,258	7,499	153,520	24,768	9,189	18,375	419	6,022	4,965
1918	209,035	7,167	150,074	23,414	8,556	16,949	485	5,893	3,664
1917	203,499	6,804	145,290	25,322	7,883	15,649	731	5,234	3,390
1916	201,614	6,762	144,696	25,541	7,678	15,598	420	4,740	2,941
1915	201,690	6,731	145,307	25,290	7,553	15,703	560	4,713	2,556
1914	204,190	6,773	146,607	26,151	7,589	15,955	496	4,716	2,676
1913	182,221	5,857	128,511	25,177	6,745	14,746	479	3,911	2,712
1912	140,918	4,362	89,982	22,000	6,322	14,715	390	3,082	4,427
1911	127,158	3,806	79,412	21,069	5,809	13,768	277	2,807	4,016
1910	119,713	3,514	75,983	20,769	5,528	12,680	195	2,539	2,019
1909	117,779	3,385	74,477	21,188	5,518	11,721	197	2,466	2,212
1908	115,709	3,277	72,863	21,759	5,047	11,616	197	2,423	1,804
1907	107,407	2,909	68,149	20,477	4,817	10,358	132	1,917	1,557

[1] From 1907 to 1919 the data are for the year ending 30 June of the year given. The year 1919 is also given on a calendar year basis as are all subsequent years.

[2] Due to a revision in the system of classification some ballast and gondola cars included in series S99 prior to 1948 have been included in series S96 from 1948 onward.

[3] Includes 20 cars not specified by type.

[4] Newfoundland equipment included from 1949 onward.

Series S100–111. *Railroads, revenue train mileage, engine mileage and freight car mileage, 1907 to 1960*

(millions of miles)

	Revenue train mileage[2]						Engine mileage			Freight car mileage		
	Total		Passenger		Freight locomotive drawn train	Mixed[3]	Gross total	Revenue road		Loaded	Empty	Caboose
Year[1]	Grand total	Locomotive drawn train	Locomotive drawn train	Motor unit train				Steam	Diesel			
	100	**101**	**102**	**103**	**104**	**105**	**106**	**107**	**108**	**109**	**110**	**111**
1960	98.4	91.8	27.9	6.6	63.9	—	126.6	1.0	92.3	2,028.8	1,156.6	64.4
1959	106.6	99.8	31.5	6.7	68.4	—	138.1	9.6	92.8	2,105.3	1,148.3	68.5
1958	109.2	102.7	34.0	6.5	68.7	—	142.7	21.6	84.7	2,127.1	1,128.3	69.1
1957	119.6	115.2	37.2	4.5	78.0	—	159.6	45.8	73.9	2,261.8	1,200.7	77.6
1956	130.9	127.7	40.6	3.2	87.1	—	178.6	74.1	61.4	2,505.9	1,297.4	87.5
1955	123.6	121.7	42.6	2.0	79.1	—	168.0	76.8	52.1	2,222.4	1,113.4	79.1
1954	121.1	119.6	44.2	1.5	75.3	—	163.6	91.2	34.8	2,020.0	993.6	75.0
1953	132.0	130.8	45.8	1.2	85.0	—	181.1	112.9	27.4	2,258.0	1,105.9	84.6
1952	136.9	135.7	46.5	1.2	89.2	—	189.3	127.5	18.6	2,334.5	1,128.8	88.5
1951	133.4	132.2	45.0	1.2	87.2	—	185.8	131.0	11.8	2,276.5	1,021.2	86.6
1950[4]	125.1	123.9	42.5	1.3	81.4	—	172.8	127.5	5.4	2,102.5	910.6	80.8
1949	127.3	126.0	44.3	1.3	81.6	—	174.4	132.4	—	2,076.1	934.2	81.3
1948	129.5	128.0	44.6	1.5	83.4	—	179.4	136.3	—	2,136.3	901.3	83.2
1947	127.7	126.3	43.9	1.4	82.4	—	176.9	135.1	—	2,158.3	936.4	82.0
1946	123.5	122.0	44.2	1.5	77.8	—	168.8	130.4	—	2,006.6	889.3	77.5
1945	127.8	126.1	45.4	1.7	80.7	—	173.5	135.2	—	2,100.4	1,008.7	80.2
1944	130.1	128.5	44.9	1.7	83.6	—	175.6	137.7	—	2,161.6	1,053.2	82.7
1943	127.2	125.5	44.0	1.7	81.4	—	173.9	135.5	—	2,084.6	967.4	80.5
1942	120.4	118.3	41.3	2.0	77.1	—	162.5	127.6	—	1,976.3	916.0	76.3
1941	112.8	110.6	37.7	2.2	72.8	—	149.6	118.3	—	1,845.3	930.6	72.1
1940	96.7	94.3	34.8	2.4	59.4	—	125.9	99.7	—	1,476.6	737.9	58.1
1939	88.8	86.3	34.1	2.5	52.2	—	114.1	90.7	—	1,278.9	614.5	51.1
1938	85.7	83.5	34.1	2.2	49.4	—	109.4	87.4	—	1,159.6	562.2	48.0
1937	88.9	86.8	34.5	2.1	52.3	—	115.1	91.0	—	1,259.8	571.3	50.6
1936	83.4	83.4	33.2	—	50.2[3]	—	111.3	87.2	—	1,195.2	551.7	48.4
1935	79.5	79.5	32.0	—	39.9	7.5[3]	104.3	82.7	—	1,103.9	518.0	44.9
1934	77.9	77.9	31.7	—	38.8	7.4	102.8	81.2	—	1,059.3	525.6	43.9
1933	73.9	73.9	31.9	—	34.6	7.3	95.8	76.6	—	940.1	476.9	39.2
1932	81.3	81.3	35.0	—	38.8	7.5	104.9	84.1	—	994.9	515.7	42.8
1931	93.4	93.4	42.0	—	44.3	7.1	121.6	96.9	—	1,158.0	580.3	48.4
1930	107.5	107.6	47.9	—	52.5	7.1	141.5	111.7	—	1,366.3	654.8	56.4
1929	117.6	117.6	49.1	—	61.3	7.2	158.7	123.3	—	1,623.1	733.2	66.3
1928	124.9	125.0	48.9	—	68.9	7.1	167.5	131.5	—	1,786.0	902.1	74.4
1927	116.9	116.9	47.6	—	62.1	7.2	156.0	122.4	—	1,552.8	790.9	67.4
1926	113.5	113.5	46.3	—	60.2	7.0	151.3	119.1	—	1,527.6	760.2	64.9
1925	109.2	109.3	46.2	—	56.1	6.9	143.9	113.9	—	1,417.2	715.4	61.5
1924	109.9	110.0	46.8	—	56.3	6.8	143.8	112.6	—	1,339.9	639.6	59.2
1923	113.8	113.9	45.9	—	61.3	6.6	153.7	119.9	—	1,454.4	740.5	65.9
1922	107.5	107.6	44.4	—	56.5	6.6	141.1	112.6	—	1,318.5	629.2	60.1
1921	104.6	104.7	45.0	—	52.5	7.1	137.0	109.3	—	1,203.7	620.3	58.7
1920	117.2	117.4	47.4	—	62.2	7.6	157.5	124.1	—	1,384.0	515.3	66.8
1919[1]	107.0	107.1	44.9	—	54.5	7.6	145.1	113.5	—	1,213.5	465.5	60.1
1919[1]	103.7	103.8	41.0	—	55.0	7.7	136.9	110.4	—	1,181.8	497.9	59.5
1918	109.8	109.9	41.9	—	60.1	7.8	146.8	118.1	—	1,343.3	494.4	64.4
1917	115.7	115.8	44.1	—	62.9	8.7	150.3	—	—	1,402.6	561.1	66.7
1916	110.9	111.1	42.4	—	60.0	8.5	145.0	—	—	1,348.2	576.3	63.3
1915	93.0	93.2	41.6	—	43.7	7.7	116.4	—	—	958.4	387.2	45.7
1914	107.6	107.9	45.2	—	55.3	7.1	137.1	—	—	1,147.5	413.5	57.6
1913	113.0	113.4	45.7	—	60.3	7.0	145.1	—	—	1,211.7	381.0	63.7
1912	100.6	100.9	40.4	—	53.7	6.5	127.4	—	—	1,102.7	311.0	55.7
1911	89.5	89.7	37.0	—	46.2	6.3	112.0	—	—	946.9	312.0	47.8
1910	85.1	85.4	35.0	—	43.7	6.4	106.0	—	—	910.9	280.3	45.4
1909	79.7	79.7	32.3	—	40.3	7.1	97.9	—	—	775.5	281.2	37.6
1908	78.7	78.6	32.0	—	40.5	6.2	100.6	—	—	748.9	284.9	—
1907	75.1	75.1	30.2	—	38.9	6.0	100.2	—	—	—	—	—

[1] From 1907 to 1919 the data are for the year ending 30 June of the year given. The year 1919 is also given on a calendar year basis as are all subsequent years.
[2] Data pertain only to trains drawn by locomotives until 1937.

[3] From 1936 onward 'mixed train mileage' is included with 'freight locomotive drawn mileage'.
[4] Newfoundland traffic included from 1950 onward.

Series S112–119. *Railroads, freight tonnage and mileage, passenger traffic and passenger mileage, 1907 to 1960*

Year[1]	Tons carried revenue freight (millions of tons)	Revenue freight ton miles (millions of tons)	Revenue and nonrevenue freight ton miles (millions of tons)	Average load per loaded car mile (tons)	Average length of freight haul (miles)	Revenue passengers carried (millions)	Revenue passengers carried one mile (millions)	Average revenue passenger journey (miles)
	112	113	114	115	116	117	118	119
1960	178.8	65,444.8	67,325.8	33.11	413	19.5	2,264	116
1959	186.2	67,956.5	70,259.6	33.31	409	20.9	2,446	117
1958	174.2	66,356.8	68,914.3	32.35	432	21.4	2,486	116
1957	196.9	71,047.2	74,452.5	32.86	408	23.0	2,925	127
1956	214.1	78,820.0	83,105.0	33.12	416	26.1	2,908	112
1955	188.5	66,176.1	69,664.8	31.30	394	27.2	2,892	106
1954	162.5	57,547.3	61,397.0	30.34	402	28.4	2,863	101
1953	176.8	65,267.0	70,350.4	31.16	418	28.7	2,986	104
1952	185.1	68,430.4	73,961.1	31.68	422	30.2	3,151	104
1951	184.4	64,300.4	69,690.7	30.61	399	31.0	3,110	100
1950[2]	164.4	55,537.9	60,789.1	28.91	385	31.1	2,816	90
1949	162.3	56,338.2	61,660.2	29.65	395	34.9	3,913	92
1948	176.7	59,080.3	64,427.8	30.16	381	38.3	3,477	91
1947	175.6	60,143.0	65,234.6	30.23	393	40.9	3,733	91
1946	160.6	55,310.3	60,096.5	29.95	397	43.4	4,649	107
1945	167.8	63,349.1	68,406.2	32.57	430	53.4	6,380	120
1944	177.4	65,928.1	70,800.3	32.70	424	60.3	6,873	114
1943	177.3	63,915.1	68,389.0	32.75	417	57.2	6,525	114
1942	155.6	56,154.0	60,691.5	30.71	417	47.6	4,989	105
1941	134.1	49,982.5	54,823.1	29.71	428	30.0	3,206	108
1940	110.4	37,898.2	41,919.8	28.39	387	22.0	2,177	99
1939	94.6	31,465.0	34,883.5	27.28	372	20.5	1,752	86
1938	84.7	26,834.7	29,663.8	25.59	352	20.9	1,783	85
1937	92.5	26,926.1	30,103.2	23.90	327	22.0	1,929	88
1936	84.7	26,414.1	29,557.8	24.73	348	20.5	1,726	84
1935	77.1	24,325.2	27,158.4	24.60	351	20.0	1,585	79
1934	75.7	23,320.5	26,156.8	24.69	343	20.5	1,531	75
1933	63.6	21,092.6	23,426.2	24.92	368	19.2	1,393	73
1932	67.7	23,136.7	25,453.2	23.57	380	21.1	1,436	68
1931	86.0	25,707.4	28,579.3	24.68	347	26.4	1,748	66
1930	115.2	29,604.5	33,259.3	24.34	308	34.7	2,423	70
1929	137.9	35,025.9	39,790.5	24.52	304	39.1	2,897	74
1928	141.2	41,610.7	46,363.8	25.96	351	40.6	3,141	77
1927	126.0	34,901.7	39,284.8	25.30	329	41.8	3,052	73
1926	122.5	34,153.5	38,300.6	25.07	325	42.7	2,999	70
1925	109.9	31,965.2	35,584.4	25.11	338	41.5	2,911	70
1924	106.4	30,513.8	34,100.2	25.45	337	42.9	2,872	67
1923	118.3	34,067.7	38,448.8	26.44	333	44.8	3,076	69
1922	108.5	30,367.9	—	23.03	348	44.4	2,814	63
1921	103.1	26,621.6	—	22.12	318	46.8	2,961	63
1920	127.4	31,894.4	—	23.05	319	51.3	3,523	68
1919[1]	111.5	26,950.6	—	22.21	295	47.9	3,659	76
1919[1]	116.7	27,724.4	—	23.46	291	43.8	3,075	70
1918	127.5	31,029.1	—	23.10	303	44.9	3,161	70
1917	121.9	31,186.7	—	22.24	317	48.1	3,150	59
1916	109.7	28,195.4	—	20.91	316	49.0	2,727	55
1915	87.2	17,661.3	—	18.43	247	46.3	2,439	54
1914	101.4	22,063.3	—	19.18	217	46.7	3,089	66
1913	107.0	23,033.0	—	19.01	216	46.2	3,266	71
1912	89.4	19,558.2	—	17.87	—	41.1	2,910	71
1911	79.9	16,048.5	—	16.91	—	37.1	2,606	70
1910	74.5	15,712.1	—	17.13	—	35.9	2,467	69
1909	66.8	13,160.6	—	—	—	32.7	—	—
1908	63.1	12,961.5	—	—	—	34.0	—	—
1907	63.9	11,687.7	—	—	—	32.1	—	—

[1] From 1907 to 1919 the data are for the year ending 30 June of the year given. The year 1919 is also given on a calendar year basis as are all subsequent years.

[2] Newfoundland included from 1950 onward.

Series S 120–128. *Railroads, freight carried, by kind and by origin, 1907 to 1960*

(thousands of tons)

Year[1]	Products of agriculture	Animals and products	Products of mines	Products of forest	Manufactures and miscellaneous	Total[2]	Originating in Canada[2]	Received from U.S. roads[2]	Received from connecting roads in Canada[2]
	120	121	122	123	124	125	126	127	128
1960	26,666	1,695	65,541	14,960	48,286	158,462	133,855	24,607	20,375
1959	27,989	1,571	71,178	14,736	49,163	166,095	140,505	25,591	20,107
1958	29,309	1,635	59,896	14,557	46,535	153,442	129,238	24,203	20,758
1957	28,376	1,940	73,323	16,646	51,690	174,044	143,349	30,695	22,847
1956	34,771	2,085	78,397	18,958	53,113	189,608	156,518	33,090	24,470
1955	27,275	2,066	69,996	17,717	48,581	167,862	131,409	36,453	20,668
1954[3]	28,494	1,992	51,808	16,029	42,656	143,195	109,855	33,340	19,275
1953	36,306	1,868	53,082	16,194	48,799	156,249	119,986	36,263	20,502
1952	37,403	1,694	54,822	19,330	48,927	162,175	125,336	36,839	22,882
1951	31,739	2,196	56,055	20,836	50,434	161,261	121,836	39,425	23,103
1950	24,376	2,302	55,748	15,830	45,961	144,218	108,147	36,071	20,141
1949	28,290	2,539	51,741	15,596	44,552	142,719	108,560	34,159	19,573
1948	27,656	2,889	56,733	19,442	48,212	154,933	112,768	42,165	21,807
1947	32,080	2,894	51,225	18,837	47,820	152,856	108,931	43,925	22,710
1946	30,872	3,257	45,732	16,850	42,546	139,256	98,777	40,479	21,361
1945	37,826	3,728	43,490	14,771	47,533	147,349	104,149	43,199	20,409
1944	37,276	3,962	47,230	14,556	52,302	155,326	106,444	48,883	22,054
1943	30,977	3,478	54,313	13,439	51,108	153,314	100,477	52,837	23,952
1942	24,137	3,182	49,054	13,698	44,604	134,675	92,137	42,537	20,972
1941	25,705	2,721	41,429	12,504	34,449	116,808	86,124	30,684	17,246
1940	19,870	2,357	36,822	10,876	28,024	97,948	73,174	24,773	12,406
1939	20,300	2,255	31,305	8,447	22,324	84,631	63,064	21,567	9,946
1938	17,533	2,125	28,235	8,496	19,787	76,175	56,829	19,346	8,489
1937	13,733	2,441	31,211	9,665	25,171	82,220	59,349	22,872	10,258
1936	16,996	2,431	26,783	8,301	21,336	75,847	54,828	21,018	8,819
1935	15,716	2,211	24,093	8,262	18,859	69,141	50,526	18,615	7,940
1934	16,630	2,446	23,660	7,891	17,410	68,037	50,353	17,684	7,710
1933	16,159	2,319	18,382	6,265	14,239	57,364	41,983	15,381	6,271
1932	18,901	2,180	19,503	5,721	14,502	60,807	44,632	16,176	6,915
1931	18,187	2,428	25,623	7,921	19,970	74,130	53,099	21,030	11,864
1930	19,664	2,520	35,695	12,379	25,936	96,194	67,928	28,266	19,035
1929	22,140	2,999	42,273	15,304	32,471	115,187	79,907	35,190	22,668
1928	30,177	2,972	38,488	16,613	30,403	118,653	84,750	33,903	22,577
1927	23,590	3,066	36,413	15,942	27,000	106,011	74,764	31,248	19,956
1926	23,549	3,132	36,746	15,266	26,529	105,222	72,276	32,946	17,255
1925	22,775	3,215	30,030	14,152	24,400	94,625[4]	65,693	28,934	15,226
1924	22,054	3,289	30,150	13,965	22,101	91,600[4]	63,518	28,081	14,831
1923	23,236	3,231	36,361	14,842	24,541	102,259[4]	67,888	34,372	16,032
1922	22,887	3,022	27,355	12,697	21,307	87,309[4]	61,048	26,262	21,221
1921[2]	19,205	2,802	30,275	12,314	19,108	83,731[4]	55,325	28,408	19,400
1920	23,306	3,801	45,077	22,280	32,925	127,429[4]	65,097	34,954	27,379
1919[1]	21,335	5,279	36,471	20,580	27,825	111,489	61,024	30,328	20,138
1919[1]	20,135	5,274	41,410	21,254	28,265	116,701	63,558	31,645	21,497
1918	23,879	4,249	47,189	20,851	31,365	127,545[4]	68,387	34,041	25,118
1917	25,127	3,982	42,536	19,092	31,144	121,916[4]	67,134	31,332	23,453
1916	27,107	3,906	37,850	16,560	34,239	109,659	62,950	26,287	20,423
1915	16,387	3,358	33,129	13,978	20,251	87,206[4]	49,259	22,134	15,708
1914	18,370	3,345	38,260	16,012	25,348	101,396[4]	57,875	23,555	19,904
1913[2]	17,198	3,175	40,232	16,609	28,222	106,994[4]	56,829	27,317	21,286
1912	17,302	3,159	31,469	14,154	23,366	89,444	63,188	—	26,259
1911	13,811	3,192	28,652	13,238	20,994	79,884	55,152	—	24,733
1910	12,891	2,765	26,152	13,070	19,605	74,484	42,281	—	32,203
1909	11,963	2,807	23,931	11,595	16,531	66,827	36,075	—	30,756
1908	9,398	2,472	22,636	12,912	15,603	63,021	38,821	—	24,198
1907	9,523	2,469	18,460	10,231	15,818	56,499	42,383	—	13,848

[1] From 1907 to 1919 the data are for the year ending 30 June of the year given. The year 1919 is also given on a calendar year basis as are all subsequent years.

[2] From 1907 to 1912 no separate record was kept of tonnage received from U.S. roads: accordingly up to 1912, series S 128 might be labelled more accurately 'received from connecting roads and other carriers' and series S 126 'originating on the road'. For 1913 to 1920, the freight carried classified by kind of product included tonnage of freight originating in Canada, received from U.S. roads and received from connecting roads in Canada: consequently the total freight carried, series S 125, is the sum of series S 126–128. From 1921 onward, the tonnage carried classified by kind of product is for that originating in Canada and received from U.S. roads: consequently total freight carried, series S 125, is the sum of series S 126 and S 127. These changes cause discontinuities in the data at 1913 and again at 1921. Foreign grain received at Canadian ports and shipped by rail in Canada is included in series S 127: to make the series consistent throughout, the original published figures for 1932 to 1955 were adjusted to move foreign grain from series S 126 to series S 127.

[3] A new classification was adopted in 1954, which accounts for minor irregularities in the series.

[4] For 1913 to 1925, series S 125 includes small amounts of unclassified tonnage not included in series S 120–124.

Series S129–144. *Railroads, gross earnings by source and operating expenses by function, 1907 to 1960*
(millions of dollars)

		Gross earnings						
			Rail line					
Year[2]	Total gross[3]	Total (including other)[4]	Freight revenue[5]	Passenger revenue[6]	Mail revenue[6]	Express revenue[6]	Water line	Incidental
	129	130	131	132	133	134	135	136
1960	1,151.7	1,121.5	992.7	69.2	17.4	21.8	—	30.0
1959	1,224.6	1,193.8	1,058.0	73.6	17.7	23.1	—	30.6
1958	1,163.7	1,131.5	995.9	77.3	15.2	22.3	—	32.0
1957	1,263.1	1,228.2	1,080.1	86.9	15.4	22.4	—	34.9
1956	1,300.6	1,260.3	1,110.1	85.3	14.0	26.1	3.3	36.6
1955	1,198.4	1,137.1	965.9	83.0	14.5	50.1	4.4	56.6
1954	1,095.4	1,039.4	872.4	82.1	14.9	47.9	4.1	51.7
1953	1,205.9	1,148.6	971.8	86.0	15.3	51.8	4.9	52.2
1952	1,172.2	1,120.3	941.9	90.7	13.4	49.7	4.4	47.2
1951	1,088.6	1,040.6	876.0	89.0	12.5	42.0	4.1	43.7
1950[8]	959.0	916.7	769.2	78.6	14.7	36.0	3.4	37.8
1949	894.4	856.5	707.4	85.1	9.4	35.9	3.5	33.2
1948	875.8	840.5	698.7	83.5	9.2	32.5	3.5	31.0
1947	785.2	750.9	607.8	87.8	8.9	30.2	3.1	30.3
1946	718.5	684.6	531.8	100.0	8.6	27.7	2.7	30.4
1945	775.0	738.7	558.6	125.1	8.3	27.9	2.8	32.6
1944	796.6	762.2	577.7	131.6	8.3	26.0	2.7	30.9
1943	778.9	744.2	568.8	123.7	8.0	25.8	2.5	31.5
1942	663.6	635.9	503.1	91.4	7.8	19.4	2.7	24.5
1941	538.3	516.2	421.4	59.7	7.5	16.8	2.6	18.9
1940	429.1	412.0	334.4	42.6	7.2	19.4	2.1	14.6
1939	367.2	350.6	286.1	36.1	7.2	13.8	1.8	14.4
1938	336.8	320.0	255.9	37.0	7.1	12.4	1.5	14.9
1937	355.1	337.9	270.5	38.9	7.1	13.2	1.4	15.5
1936	334.8	319.0	256.1	35.9	7.0	12.7	1.2	14.2
1935	310.1	296.4	235.5	34.5	6.8	12.5	1.2	12.1
1934	300.8	287.6	227.3	34.3	6.7	12.3	1.0	11.7
1933	270.3	257.8	201.5	31.9	6.7	11.4	1.0	11.0
1932	293.4	280.2	216.7	36.5	7.0	12.6	1.3	11.5
1931	358.5	340.5	260.5	47.5	7.4	15.5	1.3	16.3
1930	454.2	430.4	322.7	66.8	7.8	20.5	2.0	21.0
1929	534.1	510.0	384.9	80.4	8.0	23.2	2.5	21.1
1928	563.7	540.8	413.6	83.8	7.8	22.9	2.6	19.9
1927	499.1	483.0	359.3	82.2	7.6	21.8	2.5	13.4
1926	493.6	477.9	356.3	81.2	7.4	21.6	2.6	13.2
1925	455.3	440.3	323.6	78.2	7.4	20.0	2.7	12.4
1924	445.9	428.7	310.8	80.2	7.4	19.6	2.5	14.8
1923	478.3	459.7	336.3	85.0	7.4	20.3	2.9	15.7
1922	440.7	425.8	315.6	79.3	7.6	13.6	2.8	11.9
1921	458.0	442.3	319.5	89.9	7.2	15.8	3.0	12.7
1920[2]	492.1	475.0	341.4	102.7	3.9	15.5	3.1	13.9
1919[2]	408.6	392.0	270.5	96.3	3.5	12.3	3.3	13.2
1919[2]	383.0	367.7	266.8	78.6	3.4	10.7	2.9	12.3
1918	330.2	316.1	228.2	67.1	3.3	9.8	2.6	11.1
1917	310.8	295.6	215.2	61.3	3.2	9.0	4.4	10.4
1916	261.9	252.8	184.1	53.1	3.1	6.8	.4	8.7
1915	199.8	—	132.5	50.2	3.0	6.1	—	—
1914	243.1	—	163.7	62.0	2.5	6.4	—	—
1913	256.7	—	174.7	64.4	2.1	6.4	—	—
1912	219.4	—	148.0	56.5	1.9	5.3	—	—
1911	188.7	—	124.7	50.6	1.9	4.7	—	—
1910	174.0	—	115.9	46.0	1.8	4.1	—	—
1909	145.1	—	95.4	39.1	1.7	3.6	—	—
1908	146.9	—	93.7	40.0	1.7	3.5	—	—
1907	146.7	—	95.2	39.2	1.6	3.3	—	—

Series S 129–144. *Railroads, gross earnings by source and operating expenses by function, 1907 to 1960 (continuation)*
(millions of dollars)

Year[2]	Total	Ways and structures	Equipment	Traffic[1]	Transportation Rail line	Water line	Miscellaneous operations	General expenses
	137	138	139	140	141	142	143	144
1960	1,050.6[7]	244.0	249.5	28.9	424.9	—	14.5	88.9
1959	1,103.1[7]	260.0	256.8	29.1	443.3	—	14.8	99.2
1958	1,080.3[7]	248.6	253.7	27.2	440.1	—	14.8	95.9
1957	1,136.9[7]	265.1	256.7	27.3	478.4	—	16.6	92.8
1956	1,127.9[7]	249.6	251.3	25.3	492.7	1.5	18.8	88.6
1955	1,048.6	212.4	227.9	23.8	483.3	2.2	17.7	81.3
1954	1,019.5	206.7	227.2	22.8	474.9	2.2	16.2	69.5
1953	1,100.4	227.1	254.0	22.8	513.7	2.4	16.4	64.0
1952	1,057.2	215.4	243.3	21.3	501.9	2.2	16.0	57.1
1951	977.2	202.5	224.2	20.0	466.7	2.0	15.6	46.7
1950[8]	833.7	164.0	189.5	18.6	402.3	1.7	14.3	43.3
1949	831.5	164.9	186.1	17.6	404.1	2.0	15.0	41.8
1948	808.1	160.0	174.5	16.8	401.9	1.9	14.6	38.5
1947	690.8	134.1	145.6	15.1	345.9	1.7	13.1	35.3
1946	623.5	122.1	135.9	13.8	303.1	1.5	14.0	33.2
1945	631.5	132.5	144.5	11.2	296.5	1.3	15.8	29.7
1944	634.8	138.3	146.7	11.1	294.6	1.2	14.5	28.4
1943	560.6	120.6	130.0	10.5	260.4	1.3	12.6	25.2
1942	485.8	100.0	119.3	10.3	225.2	1.4	9.8	19.8
1941	403.7	80.4	98.0	10.3	189.3	1.3	7.0	17.8
1940	335.3	63.9	82.7	10.2	156.2	1.1	4.9	16.7
1939	304.4	57.6	70.0	12.4	143.2	1.0	4.1	15.7
1938	295.7	55.2	69.2	12.6	139.4	.9	4.0	14.9
1937	300.7	58.3	73.2	12.3	138.4	.7	4.1	14.4
1936	283.3	60.4	63.8	12.1	130.1	.7	3.4	13.7
1935	263.9	55.3	57.4	11.8	123.7	.7	2.5	13.1
1934	252.0	53.5	54.0	11.5	118.0	.6	2.4	12.4
1933	233.1	48.2	48.0	11.8	111.7	.7	2.4	10.7
1932	256.7	50.5	49.6	13.2	128.3	.9	3.0	11.7
1931	321.0	66.1	65.1	17.6	155.6	.9	4.3	13.2
1930	380.7	78.0	82.1	18.9	182.6	1.2	5.6	13.7
1929	433.1	94.0	100.1	18.4	201.7	1.3	6.3	13.2
1928	442.7	97.8	101.9	18.0	206.7	1.3	5.9	12.8
1927	407.6	86.4	93.8	17.7	190.9	1.4	5.6	12.8
1926	389.5	81.1	91.8	16.1	182.7	1.4	5.2	12.3
1925	372.2	74.0	86.1	15.4	179.5	1.4	5.0	11.6
1924	382.5	78.1	85.1	15.2	186.5	1.3	5.0	12.0
1923	413.9	83.5	92.3	14.2	203.8	1.5	6.9	12.5
1922	393.9	79.9	93.8	12.9	189.4	1.6	5.3	11.9
1921	422.6	88.3	97.4	11.3	207.9	1.7	6.0	12.1
1920	478.2	100.2	115.6	9.6	231.6	1.9	7.8	12.2
1919[2]	376.8	82.3	85.6	7.2	182.0	2.2	7.1	10.4
1919[2]	341.9	69.0	78.4	6.5	170.4	2.2	5.6	9.7
1918	274.0	51.6	57.3	6.3	145.1	1.6	4.4	7.6
1917	222.9	41.2	46.4	6.2	114.3	3.3	4.0	7.6
1916	180.5	30.0	35.8	5.6	92.9	.2	3.3	6.8
1915	147.7	28.8	28.2	5.9	78.0	—	—	7.0
1914	179.0	35.3	36.4	6.5	94.1	—	—	6.6
1913	182.0	35.9	37.3	6.1	96.7	—	—	6.0
1912	150.7	31.5	29.8	5.3	79.0	—	—	5.1
1911	131.0	29.2	26.1	4.8	66.3	—	—	4.5
1910	120.4	27.0	26.0	4.4	58.9	—	—	4.1
1909	104.6	21.2	21.5	3.8	54.3	—	—	3.9
1908	107.3	20.8	20.3	—	62.5	—	—	3.8
1907	103.7	20.9	21.7	—	57.3	—	—	3.9

[1] The classification traffic, series S 140, was separated out of transportation, series S 141, in 1909.

[2] From 1907 to 1919 the data are for the year ending 30 June of the year given. The year 1919 is also given on a calendar year basis as are all subsequent years.

[3] Series S 129 includes small amounts for receipts from 'Joint Facilities'.

[4] Series S 130 is not the sum of series S 131–134. Small additional earnings from passenger train service and freight service are included. See footnotes (5) and (6) for this table.

[5] Freight revenue is the major source of gross earnings from freight service. Small additional earnings from freight service are realized from switching revenue, special service and the like.

[6] Gross earnings from passenger train service includes the major categories, passenger, mail and express revenue (as shown in series S 132–134); and minor categories, baggage, parlour car and the like which have not been included in this table.

[7] In 1956, three additional items were added to the usual categories under operating expenses; these items were equipment rents, joint facility rental and railway tax accruals. The total operating expenses including these items were: $1,132,278 in 1958; $1,203,530 in 1957; and $1,171,339 in 1956.

[8] Newfoundland is included beginning in 1950.

Series S145–149. *Railroads, freight and passenger receipts per unit of traffic, 1907 to 1960*

Year[1]	Freight receipts per ton mile (cents)	Freight revenue per ton mile, C.P.R.[2] (cents)	Freight receipts per ton originated[3] (dollars)	Average receipts per passenger mile (cents)	Average receipts per passenger (dollars)	Year	Freight revenue per ton mile, C.P.R.[2] (cents)
	145	146	147	148	149		146
1960	1.517	1.52	6.26	3.05	3.55		
1959	1.557	1.57	6.37	3.01	3.51		
1958	1.501	1.47	6.49	3.11	3.62		
1957	1.520	1.50	6.21	2.97	3.78		
1956	1.489	1.39	5.85	2.93	3.27	1906	.74
1955	1.460	1.43	5.75	2.87	3.05	1905	.77
1954	1.516	1.46	6.09	2.87	2.89	1904	.77
1953	1.489	1.42	6.22	2.88	2.99	1903	.74
1952	1.377	1.30	5.81	2.88	3.01	1902	.75
1951	1.362	1.31	5.43	2.86	2.87	1901	.75
1950	1.385	1.33	5.33	2.79	2.52	1900	.79
1949	1.256	1.20	4.96	2.66	2.44	1899	.74
1948	1.183	1.13	4.51	2.40	2.18	1898	.76
1947	1.009	.95	3.98	2.35	2.14	1897	.78
1946	.961	.93	3.82	2.15	2.30	1896	.75
1945	.882	.83	3.79	1.96	2.34	1895	.80
1944	.876	.85	3.72	1.92	2.18	1894	.87
1943	.890	.87	3.71	1.90	2.16	1893	.87
1942	.896	.86	3.74	1.83	1.92	1892	.84
1941	.843	.79	3.61	1.86	2.01	1891	.91
1940	.882	.84	3.41	1.96	1.94	1890	.84
1939	.909	.85	3.38	2.06	1.76	1889	.92
1938	.954	.90	3.36	2.07	1.77	1888	1.02
1937	1.005	.95	3.29	2.02	1.76	1887	1.01
1936	.969	.92	3.38	2.08	1.75	1886	1.10
1935	.972	.93	3.06	2.18	1.72	1885	1.20
1934	.975	.95	3.00	2.24	1.67		
1933	.955	.91	3.17	2.29	1.66		
1932	.937	.91	3.20	2.54	1.73		
1931	1.013	.96	3.03	2.72	1.79		
1930	1.090	1.04	2.80	2.76	1.92		
1929	1.099	1.04	2.79	2.77	2.06		
1928	.994	.94	2.93	2.67	2.06		
1927	1.029	.98	2.85	2.69	1.96		
1926	1.043	1.01	2.91	2.71	1.90		
1925	1.012	.97	2.95	2.69	1.89		
1924	1.019	.98	2.92	2.79	1.87		
1923	.987	.93	2.84	2.76	1.90		
1922	1.039	1.00	2.91	2.82	1.79		
1921	1.200	1.20	3.10	3.04	1.92		
1920	1.071	1.04	2.68	2.92	2.00		
1919[1]	1.003	1.00	2.43	2.63	2.01		
1919[1]	.962	—[1]	2.29[3]	2.56	1.80		
1918	.736	.85	1.79	2.12	1.49		
1917	.690	.70	1.77	1.95	1.14		
1916	.653	.64	1.68	1.95	1.08		
1915	.751	.77	1.52	2.02	1.08		
1914	.742	.75	1.61	2.01	1.33		
1913	.758	.78	1.64	1.97	1.39		
1912	.757	.77	1.66	1.94	1.38		
1911	.777	.82	1.56	1.94	1.36		
1910	.739	.78	1.56	1.87	1.28		
1909	.727	.76	1.43	1.92	1.20		
1908	.723	.75	1.49	1.92	1.17		
1907	.815	.78	1.49	1.91	1.22		

[1] From 1907 to 1919 the data are for the year ending 30 June of the year given. The year 1919 is also given on a calendar year basis as are all subsequent years.
[2] Figures in series S146 are for the calendar year throughout the period.

[3] In 1919 and prior years series S147 gives average receipts per ton hauled; from the second figure for 1919 onward it is for tons originated.

Series S 150–153. *Railroads, number of employees, hours worked and compensation paid, 1926 to 1960*

Year	Number of railway employees (thousands)	Hours worked (millions)	Total compensation (millions of dollars)	Total compensation charged to operating expenses (millions of dollars)
	150	**151**	**152**	**153**
1960	145.1	290.1	632.3	659.3
1959	156.3	315.6	668.8	689.2
1958	159.9	323.8	646.4	669.6
1957	177.2	357.1	678.0	702.2
1956	181.6	375.1	677.4	707.3
1955	171.8	369.3	595.9	601.7
1954	172.9	366.6	594.3	594.8
1953	188.6	404.6	655.5	644.5
1952	191.9	421.2	609.7	610.2
1951	183.5	425.9	570.7	566.6
1950	171.2	410.8	477.3	477.2
1949	173.1	419.6	478.2	473.3
1948	170.9	424.1	468.6	464.5
1947	166.3	409.7	393.5	391.6
1946	162.7	403.7	364.1	360.4
1945	163.7	406.4	343.3	339.0
1944	158.8	401.0	344.8	341.8
1943	154.0	394.2	299.4	294.1
1942	143.0	359.6	269.0	263.0
1941	134.1	333.6	231.7	226.2
1940	122.3	296.2	196.8	192.9
1939	116.0	274.7	183.0	184.6
1938	114.4	267.6	177.8	178.0
1937	121.5	288.5	179.1	176.7
1936	121.4	283.8	169.4	167.2
1935	116.3	267.8	160.0	158.7
1934	116.1	265.7	150.8	150.2
1933	110.9	248.4	145.6	145.6
1932	120.0	271.6	166.5	165.6
1931	140.0	326.2	211.7	209.8
1930	158.5	389.7	249.2	251.5
1929	171.3	434.9	270.5	260.9
1928	172.9	440.8	270.1	264.7
1927	164.7	418.6	253.8	240.1
1926	162.4	408.2	240.2	225.8

Series S154–163. *Railroads, fatal accidents and injuries, 1907 to 1960*
(number)

	Resulting from movement of trains								Other causes	
	Killed				Injured				Killed	Injured
Year[1]	Total	Passengers	Employees[2]	Others[2]	Total	Passengers	Employees	Others	Total	Total
	154	**155**	**156**	**157**	**158**	**159**	**160**	**161**	**162**	**163**
1960	262	2	24	236	1,586	151	895	540	10	1,903
1959	303	9	30	264	1,818	151	1,092	575	13	2,258
1958	304	1	33	270	1,462	83	1,016	363	23	2,422
1957	310	2	27	281	2,018	143	1,343	527	15	2,837
1956	359	7	55	297	2,311	84	1,637	590	20	2,842
1955	292	1	39	252	2,262	188	1,582	492	15	2,992
1954	281	4	37	240	2,359	215	1,646	498	16	3,132
1953	290	3	30	257	2,781	133	2,017	631	15	4,044
1952	375	2	61	312	3,156	125	2,430	601	18	4,753
1951	362	4	69	289	3,127	191	2,341	595	28	5,468
1950	299	18	54	227	3,098	262	2,244	592	18	6,051
1949	302	1	52	249	3,325	268	2,418	639	27	6,609
1948	352	15	76	261	3,841	284	2,906	651	33	7,315
1947	369	34	77	258	3,984	355	2,963	666	31	7,855
1946	304	2	90	212	3,780	349	2,844	587	23	8,858
1945	312	10	71	231	3,610	360	2,665	585	42	10,741
1944	320	8	81	231	3,548	416	2,637	495	33	10,831
1943	318	9	112	197	3,945	417	2,942	586	23	9,974
1942	411	43	103	265	3,430	639	2,163	628	32	8,100
1941	376	10	88	278	2,756	485	1,556	715	27	6,790
1940	275	5	49	221	2,070	277	1,278	515	25	5,145
1939	283	1	43	239	1,742	322	879	541	16	4,373
1938	284	4	45	235	1,741	314	898	529	11	4,139
1937	327	5	59	263	2,119	378	1,082	659	20	4,810
1936	362	6	83	273	2,572	657	1,293	622	19	5,160
1935	322	10	43	269	2,063	432	1,026	605	29	4,223
1934	295	16	43	236	2,106	417	1,119	570	20	4,094
1933	260	8	41	211	1,851	306	985	560	20	3,522
1932	304	7	57	240	1,855	339	957	559	22	3,716
1931	246	3	42	201	2,243	369	1,131	743	14	4,952
1930	425	15	81	329	2,692	488	1,477	727	38	8,371
1929	412	20	104	288	3,144	406	2,028	710	19	10,699
1928	479	15	114	350	3,257	326	2,214	717	28	10,548
1927	368	14	106	248	2,942	438	1,915	589	34	9,379
1926	424	20	102	302	3,068	375	2,141	552	35	8,638
1925	285	5	82	198	3,095	374	2,158	563	24	6,204
1924	334	19	105	210	3,197	401	2,350	446	28	6,611
1923	321	15	144	162	3,645	406	2,763	476	26	6,713
1922	323	11	107	205	3,256	336	2,440	480	18	5,991
1921	322	5	127	191	2,592	227	2,024	341	31	4,644
1920	360	28	145	187	3,402	456	2,513	433	33	5,278
1919[1]	399	33	162	204	2,712	372	1,904	436	41	4,505
1919[1]	359	34	151	174	2,546	296	1,860	390	27	3,616
1918	383	32	154	197	2,549	322	1,868	359	27	3,540
1917	419	24	177	218	2,682	410	1,909	363	33	2,747
1916	437	20	149	268	2,058	291	1,468	299	31	2,920
1915	366	17	108	241	1,578	304	1,578	328	19	1,583
1914	565	25	200	340	2,287	402	1,475	410	35	1,752
1913	710	38	298	374	2,966	650	1,834	482	32	1,606
1912	545	47	215	283	2,437	485	1,606	346	23	1,343
1911	465	28	202	235	1,906	288	1,314	304	28	1,423
1910	524	60	214	250	1,441	270	926	245	91	698
1909	478	36	182	260	1,404	281	897	226	27	782
1908	449	28	202	197	2,347	345	1,111	209	22	682
1907	598	70	249	268	2,152	352	1,126	220	11	454

[1] From 1907 to 1919 the data are for the year ending 30 June of the year given. The year 1919 is also given on a calendar year basis as are all subsequent years.

[2] Newfoundland included from 1 April 1949.

Series S164–170. *Shipping, seagoing and inland vessels[1] arrived at and departed from Canadian ports, 1868 to 1959*

(tonnage figures in thousands of tons)

Year[2]	Total tonnage	British[3] Number	British[3] Tons register	Canadian[3] Number	Canadian[3] Tons register	Foreign Number	Foreign Tons register
	164	165	166	167	168	169	170
1959	138,110	5,287	23,643	25,792	27,201	36,900	87,266
1958	117,816	5,355	22,125	27,407	27,930	30,093	67,761
1957	134,994	5,242	21,524	34,377	40,505	33,016	72,964
1956	130,520	4,752	19,775	34,599	37,813	33,237	72,933
1955	118,325	4,665	18,841	33,734	34,398	31,459	65,086
1954	114,346	4,605	19,050	35,162	32,280	30,539	63,016
1953	118,552	4,603	18,876	37,258	38,347	29,685	61,329
1952	105,180	4,490	18,241	35,173	31,454	28,028	55,485
1951	105,954	5,258	20,793	37,389	35,343	26,112	49,818
1950	95,659	4,843	18,762	37,606	35,297	24,270	41,600
1949[4]	88,533	4,230	16,724	36,665	33,032	23,655	38,777
1948	83,772	8,639	13,574	36,987	37,595	19,023	32,603
1947	76,711	7,566	13,528	34,007	35,138	16,071	28,045
1946	64,512	7,741	12,781	32,983	31,246	13,741	20,485
1945	63,168	7,336	11,365	31,335	32,833	12,134	18,969
1944	59,210	6,531	7,299	29,436	31,477	12,711	20,434
1943	54,851	6,646	7,381	27,038	30,494	12,747	16,975
1942	53,453	6,775	6,829	28,648	33,238	13,764	13,387
1941[5]	40,332	3,696	4,849	20,028	23,880	9,696	11,603
1940	95,363	10,782	30,385	48,317	34,201	34,142	30,777
1939	91,827	9,958	26,563	46,496	35,646	32,660	29,618
1938	—						
1937	94,587	9,581	27,300	44,101	33,421	61,185	33,866
1936	87,524	8,095	24,594	39,043	30,616	57,998	32,314
1935	86,435	7,678	23,676	33,579	28,622	55,763	34,136
1934	82,625	6,831	22,480	31,869	25,847	57,693	34,298
1933	76,272	6,323	20,865	28,725	24,318	64,388	31,089
1932	83,436	5,754	19,025	30,978	27,684	72,577	36,727
1931	90,912	5,826	20,008	33,877	29,542	83,383	41,362
1930	89,439	5,634	20,171	40,251	29,138	107,925	40,130
1929	93,735	6,400	21,626	39,038	29,792	75,745	42,317
1928	83,804	6,253	18,738	38,497	28,454	67,771	36,612
1927	77,332	6,448	18,118	34,015	25,693	62,344	33,522
1926	75,247	6,515	17,749	34,010	23,149	55,109	34,349
1925	77,939	5,763	16,463	44,432	26,621	84,084	34,855
1924	74,947	5,187	15,159	53,945	28,217	80,700	31,572
1923	72,403	4,869	13,869	59,364	26,423	87,199	32,111
1922	56,665	4,239	10,471	36,679	20,030	61,114	26,164
1921	54,649	4,526	10,546	39,877	22,237	50,370	21,866
1920	49,494	5,511	12,321	37,388	16,870	52,827	20,303
1919	53,229	6,099	14,054	37,023	17,567	52,273	21,608
1918	66,802	7,337	16,960	34,786	19,890	70,781	29,952
1917	65,713	7,387	16,145	39,978	20,290	74,850	29,277
1916	57,721	6,817	12,418	37,900	17,373	75,411	27,930
1915	53,604	6,949	13,931	29,359	17,505	48,635	22,168
1914	61,919	7,418	15,712	30,234	17,026	55,835	29,182
1913	57,849	7,307	13,896	42,624	20,678	47,303	23,275
1912	52,973	6,766	13,343	27,949	18,070	45,399	21,560
1911	47,430	6,870	12,712	29,670	16,380	40,892	18,337
1910	44,568	5,780	11,039	28,635	15,681	41,650	17,849
1909	40,702	5,795	10,405	29,247	13,806	38,677	16,490
1908	39,575	6,356	10,330	28,795	11,718	40,461	17,528
1907[6]	30,596	4,408	7,577	30,654	11,582	25,263	11,437
1906	34,732	5,104	9,059	32,239	11,242	37,644	14,431
1905	32,278	4,614	8,035	29,729	11,047	35,647	13,196
1904	31,202	4,997	8,046	30,934	9,955	35,739	13,201
1903	33,655	4,647	7,754	31,534	10,483	53,545	15,418
1902	30,025	4,363	6,866	33,202	9,655	40,148	13,505
1901	26,030	4,319	6,694	30,211	8,540	33,302	10,796
1900	26,914	4,707	6,729	32,516	9,517	34,317	10,668
1899	25,420	4,855	6,626	31,454	9,309	30,508	9,485
1898	24,746	4,121	5,777	28,116	8,235	31,810	10,734
1897	23,374	3,835	5,393	25,294	6,801	31,260	11,179
1896	21,870	3,226	4,385	31,597	7,465	30,161	10,021
1895	19,101	3,206	3,994	29,784	7,251	27,299	7,856
1894	20,353	3,381	4,147	34,719	8,251	27,906	7,955
1893	18,540	3,271	3,781	33,034	7,298	26,876	7,460
1892	18,692	3,402	3,586	32,944	7,631	28,997	7,475
1891	18,804	3,483	3,523	35,667	7,517	30,179	7,764
1890	18,446	3,671	3,617	38,222	7,709	30,532	7,120
1889	16,054	3,305	3,333	34,564	6,636	27,188	6,085
1888	15,217	3,316	3,326	33,395	6,183	27,592	5,708
1887	14,091	2,679	2,658	30,960	6,246	24,296	5,188
1886	13,969	2,960	3,101	30,011	5,943	19,357	4,925
1885	14,085	3,219	3,007	29,438	6,439	18,494	4,639
1884	14,359	3,327	3,257	31,260	5,940	20,569	5,162
1883	13,771	3,403	3,001	31,332	5,837	20,095	4,933
1882	13,380	3,335	3,165	33,607	5,722	18,678	4,493
1881	13,802	3,707	3,526	31,595	5,895	18,149	4,382
1880	13,578	2,990	2,643	33,077	6,780	16,809	4,155
1879	11,647	2,618	2,155	27,418	5,051	17,805	4,440
1878	12,055	2,954	2,295	26,850	4,884	18,223	4,876
1877	11,091	2,963	2,217	24,386	4,105	19,364	4,770
1876	9,911	26,641	5,716	—	—	16,806	4,195
1875	9,527	26,400	5,808	—	—	16,412	3,720
1874	11,400	31,470	6,760	—	—	18,295	4,639
1873	11,749	39,361	7,450	—	—	18,688	4,299
1872	12,808	37,656	8,155	—	—	16,269	4,653
1871	13,126	43,120	8,985	—	—	18,517	4,141
1870	11,416	40,421	7,973	—	—	14,764	3,443
1869	10,461	39,278	7,388	—	—	14,022	3,073
1868	12,982	40,593	8,284	—	—	15,537	4,699

[1] Exclusive of coastal vessels and ferriage.

[2] Figures for 1868 to 1906 inclusive are given for fiscal years ending 30 June of the year given. From 1907 to 1940 inclusive the data are for fiscal years ending 31 March of the year given. From 1941 to 1959 inclusive the data are given for calendar years.

[3] Canadian vessels were not separated from British in the years 1868 to 1876 inclusive.

[4] Newfoundland included with Canada from 1 April 1949.

[5] Nine months only as time period was changed from fiscal year ending 31 March 1940 to a calendar year ending 31 December 1941.

[6] Nine months only as fiscal year ending was changed from 30 June 1906 to 31 March 1907.

Series S171–177. *Canals, total traffic through Canadian canals by nationality of vessel and origin of freight, navigation seasons, 1886 to 1960[1]*

(tonnage figures in thousands of tons)

Year	Canadian and British vessels — Number	Registered tonnage	United States and other foreign vessels — Number	Registered tonnage	Tons of freight carried[2] — Total	Originating in Canada	Originating in United States
	171	172	173	174	175	176	177
1960	21,119	32,935	8,510	13,117	52,947	—	—
1959	22,488	31,837	8,071	11,555	51,076	30,830	20,246
1958	22,065	26,834	5,386	4,823	35,097	21,833	13,264
1957	24,523	27,948	4,913	5,167	37,230	21,460	15,771
1956	27,740	31,206	5,125	4,817	40,017	24,698	15,319
1955	22,958	27,842	5,214	4,843	34,874	20,003	14,872
1954	21,066	25,303	4,226	4,139	30,071	17,238	12,833
1953	23,378	27,845	4,185	4,697	33,373	18,464	14,909
1952	22,565	25,608	3,757	4,201	31,354	17,245	14,109
1951	22,141	22,951	3,407	4,298	29,325	16,004	13,321
1950	21,179	21,989	3,241	3,514	27,439	15,138	12,301
1949	21,724	20,774	2,495	3,260	24,374	14,801	9,573
1948	19,859	19,724	2,784	4,220	23,559	11,170	12,390
1947	18,542	18,614	2,332	3,796	21,514	10,288	11,225
1946	17,199	16,206	1,794	3,221	18,655	8,905	9,750
1945	21,064	19,068	1,553	3,426	22,320	10,491	11,829
1944	20,780	18,192	1,911	4,542	20,616	8,003	12,613
1943	20,855	18,273	2,617	5,687	21,476	7,838	13,638
1942	22,150	18,953	3,751	8,404	20,900	7,765	13,135
1941	24,418	20,211	3,456	5,421	23,453	10,334	13,119
1940	23,646	18,513	3,194	4,056	22,871	12,257	10,613
1939	24,768	18,241	2,757	3,096	23,391	14,150	9,241
1938	23,365	19,803	2,373	2,933	24,636	12,988	11,648
1937	24,669	17,905	2,869	3,527	23,351	11,911	11,440
1936	25,251	17,086	2,708	3,209	21,469	13,465	8,003
1935	23,822	15,291	2,035	2,578	18,206	11,187	7,019
1934	22,217	14,767	2,044	2,970	18,069	10,814	7,255
1933	21,364	15,225	2,200	3,046	18,780	12,725	6,056
1932	19,854	15,256	2,061	2,681	17,961	13,243	4,718
1931	25,830	15,870	1,821	1,749	16,189	11,434	4,755
1930	24,100	14,489	2,063	1,685	14,803	10,955	3,848
1929	25,917	13,741	2,400	2,323	13,700	9,690	4,010
1928	30,575	17,435	3,973	3,271	18,720	13,883	4,838
1927	36,162	17,473	4,013	3,364	17,488	11,864	5,624
1926	27,965	14,542	3,543	3,145	13,478	9,656	3,821
1925	28,361	14,965	3,587	3,825	14,131	9,570	4,560
1924	27,467	13,989	3,233	2,821	12,869	8,857	4,012
1923	27,112	13,014	3,399	3,326	11,199	7,637	3,562
1922	26,217	11,059	3,735	3,165	10,026	6,273	3,753
1921	25,720	10,079	2,969	2,330	9,407	4,562	4,845
1920	23,038	8,522	3,826	3,839	8,735	4,094	4,641
1919	20,682	8,736	4,092	5,259	9,995	4,866	5,129
1918	18,909	7,801	6,791	9,616	18,884	3,369	15,514
1917	21,588	9,832	6,594	10,260	22,239	5,904	16,275
1916	23,002	9,839	6,800	10,661	23,583	7,487	16,097
1915	21,575	9,398	6,415	7,385	15,199	6,789	8,409
1914	26,125	12,051	7,742	15,636	37,023	9,382	27,641
1913	28,654	12,078	10,739	24,239	52,054	11,131	40,923
1912	27,371	10,237	11,785	24,636	47,587	9,377	38,211
1911	25,585	9,172	10,370	18,232	38,030	7,793	30,237
1910	25,337	8,932	11,462	21,777	42,991	7,884	35,107
1909	22,507	7,812	9,996	16,459	33,721	7,378	26,343
1908	29,040	6,781	7,489	8,521	17,503	5,012	12,491
1907	28,833	6,329	9,328	11,605	20,544	—[2]	—[2]
1906	25,498	5,526	7,319	5,685	10,523	—	—
1905	23,726	5,191	7,085	5,096	9,372	—	—
1904	21,851	4,772	6,253	3,656	8,256	—	—
1903	23,767	5,213	6,695	4,236	9,214	—	—
1902	22,198	4,486	6,433	4,086	7,513	—	—
1901	20,860	3,980	5,634	2,482	5,665	—	—
1900	21,755	4,129	5,502	2,409	5,014	—	—
1899	23,579	4,309	6,101	3,286	6,226	—	—
1898	23,320	4,202	6,128	3,624	6,618	—	—
1897	23,375	4,046	7,024	4,702	8,501	—	—
1896	23,042	4,039	7,716	5,034	7,991	—	—
1895	17,745	3,110	5,010	1,510	3,336	—	—
1894	19,027	3,049	4,131	1,012	2,943	—	—
1893	20,857	3,434	4,585	1,286	3,547	—	—
1892	21,177	3,402	3,928	872	3,032	—	—
1891	19,246	3,135	3,602	838	2,903	—	—
1890	20,655	3,139	3,364	721	2,913	—	—
1889	19,393	2,996	4,542	831	3,166	—	—
1888	17,661	2,640	3,921	632	2,762	—	—
1887	18,991	2,848	3,883	567	2,821	—	—
1886	19,844	2,946	4,147	668	2,969	—	—

[1] Figures include duplications where two or more canals are used.

[2] Tons of freight carried not separated by origin prior to 1908.

Series S178–188. *Canals, cargo tonnage through St. Lawrence canals, 1900 to 1960*

(thousands of short tons)

Year	Wheat	Total agricultural products	Manufactures and miscellaneous	Forest products	Total coal	Total mine	Total all freight	Total up	Total down	Total way[1]	Total through[1]
	178	179	180	181	182	183	184	185	186	187	188
1960	3,874	8,039	5,644	306	1,021	6,349	20,338	8,810	11,538	—	—
1959	3,587	7,512	4,597	357	1,137	8,516	21,221	11,155	10,066	—	—
1958	2,784	4,868	3,012	488	1,039	3,378	11,762	4,670	7,092	—	—
1957	2,085	3,523	3,237	523	1,643	4,893	12,191	5,089	7,103	—	—
1956	2,587	4,524	3,132	524	1,774	5,299	13,500	5,778	7,721	—	—
1955	2,027	3,763	2,934	474	1,602	4,253	11,447	4,782	6,665	—	—
1954	2,372	4,176	2,815	525	1,474	2,116	9,367	2,794	6,663	904	8,733
1953	2,081	4,366	3,152	530	1,567	2,032	10,082	2,997	7,085	1,012	9,070
1952	1,942	3,840	2,941	606	1,973	2,449	9,386	3,238	6,599	919	8,917
1951	1,847	2,693	3,392	794	2,379	3,036	9,917	4,047	5,870	1,100	8,817
1950	1,892	2,798	3,433	710	2,315	3,023	9,969	4,158	5,811	1,100	8,860
1949	2,223	3,129	2,481	455	1,333	1,890	7,960	2,832	5,128	904	7,056
1948	888	1,343	2,232	627	2,671	3,171	7,378	2,727	4,651	989	6,389
1947	940	1,199	1,964	591	2,956	3,420	7,180	2,329	4,851	877	6,302
1946	666	1,068	1,391	440	2,462	2,847	5,751	1,644	4,106	780	4,951
1945	1,982	2,135	1,002	472	7,874	3,333	6,948	1,098	5,850	677	6,271
1944	499	651	1,150	323	3,088	3,733	5,883	1,067	4,796	673	5,190
1943	192	228	1,382	328	3,502	4,224	8,148	986	5,162	651	5,497
1942	155	273	1,701	545	3,035	3,655	6,163	1,234	4,908	681	5,281
1941	809	1,275	1,936	672	2,675	3,041	6,930	1,931	4,948	1,076	5,859
1940	1,253	2,015	2,014	808	2,438	2,842	7,480	2,684	4,796	1,076	6,404
1939	2,155	3,014	2,206	580	2,038	2,445	8,340	3,493	4,847	926	7,415
1938	2,166	4,755	2,222	616	1,234	1,661	9,238	3,290	5,968	951	8,265
1937	1,853	3,359	2,808	737	1,792	2,386	9,195	4,780	4,415	1,035	8,160
1936	1,376	3,195	1,700	758	1,427	2,629	8,289	4,195	4,093	948	7,340
1935	1,475	2,349	2,131	651	1,319	1,726	6,874	3,897	2,977	1,007	5,866
1934	1,593	2,330	2,011	752	1,333	1,559	6,660	3,595	3,065	899	5,761
1933	2,680	3,189	1,967	550	1,010	1,235	6,951	2,945	4,006	751	6,200
1932	2,711	3,676	1,539	413	885	1,054	6,694	2,199	4,495	650	6,044
1931	1,942	2,940	1,216	421	951	1,451	6,037	1,792	4,245	834	5,203
1930	2,400	2,879	974	727	1,028	1,591	6,179	1,841	4,338	1,016	5,163
1929	1,601	2,293	1,012	733	979	1,670	5,719	1,857	3,862	1,126	4,592
1928	3,837	5,135	948	764	890	1,555	8,412	1,785	6,627	1,090	7,321
1927	3,584	5,015	867	835	643	1,188	7,913	1,784	6,129	1,050	6,863
1926	2,351	3,350	724	745	890	1,297	6,124	1,474	4,649	892	5,232
1925	2,250	3,530	502	756	1,108	1,412	6,206	1,316	4,891	747	5,460
1924	2,994	3,593	380	586	770	971	5,536	943	4,594	593	4,943
1923	1,900	2,513	370	493	943	1,160	4,542	845	3,696	625	3,917
1922	1,767	2,576	373	432	753	934	4,320	993	3,327	723	3,597
1921	853	1,897	296	363	993	1,173	3,734	620	3,114	380	3,354
1920	385	480	208	531	1,687	1,845	3,068	609	2,459	401	2,667
1919	553	793	232	450	1,315	1,412	2,892	509	2,383	402	2,489
1918	198	330	235	398	1,975	2,061	3,031	452	2,580	289	2,742
1917	427	564	236	469	1,988	2,116	3,391	561	2,830	365	3,026
1916	334	661	212	651	1,748	1,841	3,368	699	2,670	394	2,974
1915	948	1,205	277	601	1,190	1,322	3,409	825	2,585	544	2,865
1914	1,543	2,020	297	669	1,247	1,399	4,391	986	3,406	699	3,693
1913	994	1,546	460	660	1,430	1,628	4,302	1,104	3,198	816	3,487
1912	794	1,120	464	579	1,103	1,305	3,477	959	2,518	824	2,653
1911	564	1,003	558	551	977	984	3,106	959	2,147	779	2,327
1910	582	931	497	564	754	759	2,761	844	1,917	801	1,960
1909	574	774	473	509	640	642	2,411	780	1,630	683	1,728
1908	708	860	233	180	656	728	2,009	584	1,425	436	1,573
1907	502	817	243	360	588	673	2,100	784	1,316	493	1,607
1906	336	612	215	271	451	523	1,036	602	1,034	436	1,200
1905	403	735	207	247	455	552	1,753	486	1,267	673	1,080
1904	275	502	148	211	467	559	1,427	432	996	586	842
1903	431	794	203	192	416	483	1,681	459	1,223	713	968
1902	444	575	141	102	213	268	1,093	290	803	611	482
1901	360	584	103	69	403	445	1,208	196	1,012	623	585
1900	276	694	96	96	375	416	1,309	194	1,115	641	668

[1] Way and through freight not separated from 1955 on.

Series S 189–199. *Canals, tonnage through Welland canal, 1867 to 1960*

(thousands of short tons)

Year[1]	Wheat	Total agricultural products[5]	Manufactures and miscellaneous[2]	Forest products	Total coal	Total mine	Total all freight	Total up	Total down	Total way[3]	Total through[3]
	189	190	191	192	193	194	195	196	197	198	199
1960	4,524	9,526	5,464	315	4,362	13,976	29,281	8,400	20,881	—	—
1959	3,956	8,706	5,078	364	4,785	13,357	27,506	9,597	17,909	—	—
1958	3,630	6,653	4,183	524	4,411	9,915	21,274	5,006	16,269	—	—
1957	2,764	5,054	4,296	561	5,503	12,462	22,373	5,141	17,232	—	—
1956	3,195	6,085	3,880	530	5,626	12,572	23,060	5,069	17,997	—	—
1955	2,733	5,336	3,470	510	5,422	9,515	20,894	4,260	16,634	—	—
1954	2,858	5,339	3,172	516	4,988	7,618	17,514	2,396	15,118	1,677	15,838
1953	2,795	5,607	4,138	500	5,966	9,297	19,542	2,582	16,960	1,692	17,850
1952	2,598	4,960	4,316	580	5,364	8,054	17,911	2,289	15,622	1,886	16,025
1951	2,808	4,118	4,076	614	4,842	7,390	16,198	2,752	13,445	1,789	14,409
1950	2,025	3,672	3,588	532	4,687	6,949	14,741	2,732	12,009	1,654	13,087
1949	2,890	4,476	3,501	504	3,391	5,211	13,692	2,141	11,552	1,468	12,224
1948	1,536	2,470	3,233	523	4,724	7,148	13,373	2,135	11,239	1,455	11,918
1947	1,528	2,405	3,228	501	3,877	5,671	11,806	1,945	9,861	1,475	10,330
1946	1,263	2,084	3,038	376	3,584	5,082	10,580	1,416	9,164	1,187	9,393
1945	2,726	3,475	2,897	453	4,014	6,138	12,962	1,127	11,835	1,280	11,683
1944	1,130	1,478	2,966	280	4,951	6,593	11,316	982	10,334	1,055	10,261
1943	643	810	2,855	287	4,512	6,164	10,116	811	9,305	1,071	9,045
1942	428	717	3,264	422	4,828	6,705	11,108	928	10,180	1,368	9,740
1941	1,577	2,274	3,724	512	5,002	6,719	13,230	1,511	11,719	1,877	11,354
1940	1,824	2,789	3,675	446	4,584	5,997	12,906	1,803	11,104	1,395	11,511
1939	2,697	3,849	2,745	449	3,687	4,685	11,728	2,252	9,475	1,065	10,663
1938	2,653	5,987	1,754	433	3,127	4,459	12,633	1,956	10,677	911	11,718
1937	1,872	3,583	1,901	497	3,880	5,767	11,748	3,103	8,645	1,029	10,719
1936	2,327	3,183	1,859	538	3,179	4,857	10,437	2,706	7,731	954	9,483
1935	1,880	2,715	2,292	367	2,708	3,576	8,951	2,322	6,629	—	—
1934	1,787	2,769	2,032	501	2,890	3,979	9,280	2,204	7,076	—	—
1933	2,833	3,683	2,085	340	2,500	3,087	9,194	1,818	7,377	—	—
1932	2,927	4,123	1,722	313	1,990	2,379	8,537	1,354	7,184	—	—
1931	2,146	3,161	1,194	350	2,008	2,570	7,274	987	6,288	—	—
1930	2,546	3,095	1,105	367	1,328	1,521	6,088	951	5,137	—	—
1929	1,685	2,439	944	332	747	1,055	4,770	868	3,902	—	—
1928	3,946	5,294	912	334	482	899	7,440	970	6,470	—	—
1927	3,615	5,047	787	356	567	1,058	7,247	915	6,333	—	—
1926	2,349	3,344	616	293	664	964	5,215	680	4,535	—	—
1925	2,261	3,500	519	288	1,059	1,274	5,640	594	5,046	—	—
1924	2,994	3,645	421	213	580	759	5,037	395	4,642	—	—
1923	1,915	2,562	254	170	596	770	3,756	339	3,417	—	—
1922	1,752	2,572	280	157	292	382	3,391	329	3,062	—	—
1921	859	1,874	205	155	773	843	3,075	276	2,800		
1920	357	438	205	170	1,383	1,462	2,276	201	2,075	—	—
1919	547	779	239	92	986	1,061	2,171	188	1,982	—	—
1918	162	288	230	124	1,403	1,533	2,174	182	1,992	197	1,977
1917	435	563	184	244	1,301	1,500	2,491	313	2,177	288	2,203
1916	336	694	185	266	1,180	1,401	2,545	500	2,045	230	2,315
1915	955	1,307	320	309	936	1,125	3,061	756	2,305	220	2,841
1914	1,560	2,116	361	360	949	1,023	3,861	856	3,005	136	3,725
1913	1,005	1,685	549	338	946	999	3,571	1,005	2,566	86	3,485
1912	796	1,206	626	228	709	792	2,852	826	2,026	65	2,787
1911	562	1,090	540	250	619	657	2,538	843	1,695	28	2,510

Series S189–199. *Canals, tonnage through Welland canal, 1867 to 1960 (continued)*

(thousands of short tons)

Year[1]	Wheat	Total agricultural products[5]	Manufactures and miscellaneous[2]	Forest products	Total coal	Total mine	Total all freight	Total up	Total down	Total way[3]	Total through[3]
	189	190	191	192	193	194	195	196	197	198	199
1910	587	1,035	58	622	577	611	2,326	724	1,601	—	—
1909	590	898	87	630	378	411	2,026	642	1,384	50	1,976
1908	732	976	36	356	317	335	1,703	411	1,292	8	1,695
1907	489	895	25	402	267	292	1,614	390	1,224	10	1,604
1906	327	650	28	370	148	154	1,202	223	979	11	1,191
1905	254	577	18	302	173	195	1,092	232	860	16	1,076
1904	165	374	26	257	114	154	811	185	626	9	802
1903	259	537	54	246	148	166	1,003	270	733	23	980
1902	225	351	22	206	64	86	665	85	581	—	—
1901	152	291	15	166	49	148	620	106	514	15	605
1900	138	376	14	224	47	105	719	118	601	31	689
1899	198	460	9	197	98	124	790	153	637	—	—
1898	208	720	14	231	162	175	1,140	—	—	—	—
1897	325	817	25	256	176	176	1,274	224	1,050	30	1,245
1896	321	789	10	257	223	224	1,280	291	989	36	1,244
1895	203	486	9	215	159	160	970	234	636	18	852
1894	271	591	4	209	204	204	1,008	249	759	19	990
1893	258	805	10	247	233	233	1,295	282	1,013	25	1,269
1892	232	527	7	210	212	212	956	270	685	26	930
1891	199	367	13	367	225	228	975	—	—	—	—
1890	118	519	30	237	202	230	1,016	299	717	37	979
1889	127	542	23	250	268	270	1,085	327	759	43	1,042
1888	161	420	17	201	224	241	879	297	582	—	—
1887	222	395	14	210	145	159	778	242	536	85	693
1886	154	415	18	249	271	298	980	327	653	—	—
1885	124	274	17	221	248	273	785	—	—	—	—
1884	145	306	5	200	274	327	838	354	484	92	746
1883	153	373	26	267	307	339	1,005	368	637	125	880
1882	215	306	22	211	238	252	791	282	508	—	—
1881	128	269	43	228	128	147	687	220	466	124	563
1880	242	442	32	202	110	144	820	—	—	—	—
1879	275	439	34	181	193	212	866	216	650	—	—
1878	192	403	29	227	295	310	969	268	701	—	—
1877	254	464	33	311	324	367	1,175	312	863	—	—
1876	202	410	58	262	288	370	1,100	329	771	—	—
1875	254	418	34	222	321	364	1,038	340	698	—	—
1874	413	647	51	310	324	381	1,389	405	984	—	—
1873	356	580	80	382	339	458	1,506	456	1,050	—	—
1872	240	538	138	371	187	286	1,333	410	923	—	—
1871[4]	435	699	139	322	125	279	1,478	396	1,082	—	—
1870[4]	432	622	114	285	98	254	1,312	365	947	—	—
1869	314	504	192	374	103	162	1,232	386	857	—	—
1868[4]	275	536	89	281	103	230	1,162	332	850	—	—
1867	—	—	—	—	—	—	933	245	689	—	—

[1] From 1867 to 1871 inclusive the data are for fiscal years ending 30 June of the year given. For all other years the data are for the navigation season.
[2] Includes animal products.
[3] Way and through freight not separated from 1955 on.

[4] Some merchandise on which tolls were not paid was not classified but is included in the total, series S195. These amounts are as follows: 39 thousand tons in 1871; 37 thousand tons in 1870; 27 thousand tons in 1868.
[5] Excludes animal products, which are small in volume.

Series S200–205. *Canals, expenditures and revenues, 1868 to 1959*
(thousands of dollars)

Year[1]	Total	Total capital	Invest-ment	Improve-ment	Operation and maintenance	Operating revenue	Year[1]	Total	Total capital	Invest-ment	Improve-ment	Operation and maintenance	Operating revenue
	200	201	202	203	204	205		200	201	202	203	204	205
1959	9,648	2,577	78 cr	2,655	7,070	1,552	1910	3,167	2,140	1,651	489	1,027	183
1958	8,603	1,515	17 cr	1,532	7,088	1,948	1909	3,551	2,602	1,874	728	949	200
1957	8,157	1,688	32 cr	1,720	6,470	1,731	1908	3,160	2,231	1,723	508	929	145
1956	7,529	1,543	783 cr	2,326	5,986	1,736	1907	1,795	1,152	888	264	643	107
							1906	2,709	1,872	1,552	320	837	108
1955	7,723	1,706	71 cr	1,777	6,017	1,477	1905	3,273	2,426	2,072	354	847	78
1954	8,966	2,738	30 cr	2,768	6,229	1,563	1904	2,927	2,183	1,881	302	744	80
1953	9,516	3,919	463 cr	4,382	5,597	1,518	1903	2,796	2,101	1,823	278	695	237
1952	7,932	3,200	58 cr	3,259	4,732	1,466	1902	2,926	2,331	2,115	217	595	302
1951	8,216	3,738	73 cr	3,811	4,478	1,329	1901	3,104	2,514	2,361	154	590	316
1950	6,184	2,179	14 cr	2,193	4,005	1,293	1900	3,305	2,772	2,640	133	533	323
1949	4,629	796	64 cr	860	3,833	1,727	1899	4,489	3,983	3,900	84	505	371
1948	3,686	394	27	367	3,292	1,015	1898	3,789	3,291	3,207	84	498	410
1947	3,001	115	87 cr	202	2,886	863	1897	2,931	2,453	2,349	104	478	386
1946	2,800	133	22 cr	155	2,667	859	1896	2,900	2,381	2,259	122	519	342
1945	2,654	97	21 cr	118	2,557	839	1895	3,153	2,698	2,452	246	455	341
1944	2,824	173	4 cr	177	2,651	900	1894	3,641	3,158	3,027	130	484	390
1943	2,415	27	42 cr	69	2,389	913	1893	2,809	2,303	2,070	233	506	398
1942	2,373	113	8 cr	122	2,260	908	1892	2,173	1,638	1,437	201	535	379
1941	2,485	—	162	142	2,181	845	1891	2,005	1,501	1,318	183	504	375
1940	2,676	431	1 cr	432	2,245	763	1890	1,658	1,190	1,026	163	468	403
1939	2,542	359	33 cr	392	2,183	724	1889	1,688	1,145	973	172	543	376
1938	2,332	211	21 cr	232	2,121	1,867	1888	1,688	1,188	1,033	155	500	348
1937	2,197	108	129 cr	237	2,089[2]	516	1887	2,358	1,873	1,784	89	485	353
1936	3,454	1,294	546	748	2,160	484	1886	1,867	1,386	1,333	52	481	364
1935	1,119[3]	1,696[3] cr	1,892[3] cr	196	2,814	474	1885	2,063	1,580	1,505	75	483	336
1934	3,512	1,421	1,975	554	2,091	650	1884	2,121	1,646	1,577	68	475	380
1933	5,664	3,357	3,122	235	2,307	590	1883	2,285	1,837	1,763	74	448	370
1932	6,726	4,197	3,904	293	2,529	718	1882	2,061	1,649	1,593	56	412	325
1931	13,328	10,606	10,307	300	2,722	537	1881	2,438	2,085	2,076	10	352	358
1930	11,952	9,651	9,324	327	2,301	639	1880	2,468	2,126	2,123	3	343	339
1929	15,581	13,441	13,165	277	2,139	649	1879	3,371	3,064	3,064	—	307	334
1928	16,486	14,170	13,763	407	2,316	741	1878	4,154	3,843	3,843	—	310	378
1927	16,289	14,298	13,846	452	1,992	467	1877	4,450	4,131	4,131	—	318	388
1926	14,541	12,526	12,024	501	2,015	533	1876	2,759	2,390	2,389	1	369	388
1925	12,893	11,079	10,620	459	1,814	550	1875	2,087	1,715	1,715	—	372	411
1924	9,113	7,227	6,747	480	1,886	545	1874	1,622	1,241	1,190	51	382	506
1923	7,355	5,559	4,995	564	1,795	386	1873	619	384	257	127	235	480
1922	7,377	5,319	4,483	837	2,058	510	1872	565	289	256	33	276	458
1921	8,397	6,643	5,450	1,193	1,754	341	1871	392	116	—	116	276	481
1920	6,828	5,378	4,580	798	1,450	318	1870	368	90	—	90	277	430
1919	3,798	2,376	2,212	164	1,422	258	1869	280	46	45	—	235	392
1918	3,137	1,894	1,782	112	1,243	252	1868	404	189	94	95	215	389
1917	5,852	4,704	4,305	399	1,148	286							
1916	7,730	6,540	6,142	398	1,190	281							
1915	7,157	5,935	5,491	444	1,223	235							
1914	4,447	3,219	2,830	389	1,228	279							
1913	3,749	2,591	2,259	332	1,157	247							
1912	4,163	3,003	2,561	442	1,160	218							
1911	3,796	2,790	2,349	440	1,006	201							

[1] Figures for 1868 to 1906 inclusive are for fiscal years ending 30 June of the year given; for 1907, nine months ending 31 March 1907; for 1908 to 1959 fiscal year ending 31 March of the year given.

[2] Adjustments totalling $2,747 thousand are not included.
[3] Heavy equipment sold back to the contractor in connection with the Prior Welland Canal of $2,359 thousand is included as a credit.

Series S206–211. *Water freight charges for wheat, Great Lakes system, 1917 to 1960*

Year	Fort William to Georgian Bay ports			Fort William to Montreal			Year	Fort William to Georgian Bay ports			Fort William to Montreal		
	Average charge per bushel (cents)	Average charge per ton (dollars)	Average charge per ton mile (cents)	Average charge per bushel (cents)	Average charge per ton (dollars)	Average charge per ton mile (cents)		Average charge per bushel (cents)	Average charge per ton (dollars)	Average charge per ton mile (cents)	Average charge per bushel (cents)	Average charge per ton (dollars)	Average charge per ton mile (cents)
	206	207	208	209	210	211		206	207	208	209	210	211
1960	5.05	1.68	.312	13.00	4.33	.353	1935	1.83	.61	.114	4.49	1.50	.122
1959	4.72	1.57	.292	13.32	4.44	.361	1934	2.22	.74	.138	5.80	1.93	.157
1958	6.04	2.01	.374	16.00	5.33	.434	1933	1.73	.58	.108	3.79	1.26	.103
1957	5.90	1.97	.367	16.00	5.33	.434	1932	2.07	.69	.128	5.09	1.69	.138
1956	5.51	1.83	.341	16.00	5.33	.434	1931	1.91	.64	.119	6.46	2.15	.175
1955	4.21	1.40	.261	13.50	4.50	.366	1930	2.00	.67	.124	7.95	2.65	.216
1954	4.26	1.42	.264	14.17	4.72	.384	1929	2.13	.71	.132	7.72	2.57	.209
1953	5.51	1.84	.343	15.90	5.30	.432	1928	2.80	.93	.173	8.39	2.79	.227
1952	5.53	1.84	.343	16.00	5.33	.434	1927	2.81	.94	.175	8.53	2.84	.231
1951	5.53	1.84	.343	16.00	5.33	.434	1926	3.01	1.00	.186	9.60	3.20	.260
1950	4.50	1.50	.279	12.50	4.17	.340	1925	3.21	1.07	.199	9.03	3.01	.245
1949	4.50	1.50	.279	12.50	4.17	.340	1924	3.62	1.21	.225	8.99	3.00	.244
1948	4.27	1.42	.264	11.17	3.72	.303	1923	4.07	1.35	.251	10.91	3.64	.296
1947	4.02	1.34	.250	10.00	3.33	.271	1922	4.13	1.38	.257	10.60	3.53	.287
1946	3.57	1.19	.222	8.00	2.67	.217	1921	2.96	.99	.184	10.86	3.62	.295
1945	3.50	1.17	.218	7.95	2.65	.216	1920	4.17	1.39	.259	11.64	3.87	.316
1944	3.56	1.19	.222	8.00	2.67	.217	1919	3.15	1.05	.203	10.76	3.58	.292
1943	3.52	1.17	.218	8.00	2.67	.217	1918	4.32	1.44	.277	11.39	3.80	.309
1942	3.50	1.17	.218	7.98	2.66	.217	1917	4.25	1.42	.270	8.78	3.26	.205
1941	3.30	1.10	.205	7.03	2.34	.191							
1940	2.34	.78	.145	6.77	2.26	.184							
1939	2.66	.89	.166	4.57	1.52	.124							
1938	2.27	.76	.142	5.57	1.86	.151							
1937	2.15	.72	.134	3.96	1.32	.107							
1936	2.01	.67	.125	4.40	1.47	.120							

Series S212–214. *Wheat freight charges, Regina to Liverpool, 1861 to 1932*

(cents per bushel)

Year	Regina to Fort William-Port Arthur	Montreal to Liverpool	Regina to Liverpool	Year	Regina to Fort William-Port Arthur	Montreal to Liverpool	Regina to Liverpool
	212	213	214		212	213	214
1932	12.0	5.8	28.5	1895	13.8	5.4	27.9
1931	12.0	6.0	29.1	1894	13.8	4.0	27.9
				1893	13.8	5.1	27.9
1930	12.0	5.0	27.6	1892	17.4	5.3	31.5
1929	12.0	5.5	28.2	1891	17.4	6.2	31.5
1928	12.0	7.0	30.3				
1927	12.0	9.0	32.3	1890	18.0	5.2	33.4
1926	12.0	9.5	33.1	1889	18.0	8.2	33.4
				1888	18.0	5.4	33.4
1925	12.0	8.0	31.8	1887	18.0	5.3	33.4
1924	12.0	9.0	33.1	1886	19.8	7.0	35.2
1923	12.0	9.0	33.6				
1922	12.0	10.0	34.6	1885	—	6.7	—
1921	18.0	16.0	45.6	1884	—	7.5	—
				1883	—	9.9	—
1920	19.5	32.0	67.5	1882	—	8.2	—
1919	14.4	32.0	58.2	1881	—	8.7	—
1918	14.4	138.0	165.9				
1917	10.8	106.0	128.3	1880	—	14.1	—
1916	10.8	42.0	62.4	1879	—	15.3	—
				1878	—	15.9	—
1915	10.8	26.4	44.7	1877	—	17.4	—
1914	10.8	7.0	24.3	1876	—	16.5	—
1913	10.8	8.0	26.0				
1912	10.8	7.7	25.7	1875	—	18.3	—
1911	10.8	4.2	21.2	1874	—	17.9	—
				1873	—	29.2	—
1910	10.8	3.8	21.1	1872	—	19.9	—
1909	10.8	4.3	20.8	1871	—	21.7	—
1908	10.8	5.5	20.8				
1907	10.8	4.4	20.8	1870	—	16.7	—
1906	10.8	5.3	20.8	1869	—	19.6	—
				1868	—	17.4	—
1905	10.8	4.5	20.4	1867	—	22.6	—
1904	10.8	1.9	20.4	1866	—	17.9	—
1903	10.8	3.4	20.4				
1902	12.0	3.8	21.6	1865	—	14.7	—
1901	12.0	3.4	21.6	1864	—	17.7	—
				1863	—	20.8	—
1900	12.0	7.6	26.7	1862	—	31.4	—
1899	12.0	5.2	26.7	1861	—	23.8	—
1898	12.9	7.3	26.7				
1897	13.8	6.5	26.7				
1896	13.8	5.9	26.7				

Series S215–221. *Roads, summary of nonurban road mileage, by type of surface, 1925 to 1960*

(thousands of miles)

Year[1]	Grand total[2]	Surfaced	Concrete, bituminous pavement and bituminous surface	Gravel, crushed stone and other surfaces	Earth		
		Total			Total[2]	Unimproved[2]	Improved
	215	216	217	218	219	220	221
1960	—	275.9	50.6	225.3	—	—	145.6
1959	—	268.7	46.0	222.8	—	—	154.3
1958	—	247.5	42.0	205.5	—	—	149.9
1957	—	231.0[5]	39.1	191.9	—	—	—
1956	—	209.3	37.0	172.3	—	—	—
1955	—	200.1	34.2	165.9	—	—	—
1954	524.1	192.6	33.3	159.3	331.4	—	—
1953	517.8	191.0	30.7	160.3	326.8	—	—
1952	512.8	181.3	28.6	152.7	331.5	—	—
1951	568.8	175.4	26.3	149.0	395.6	245.0[3]	150.6
1950	567.2	169.5	24.8	144.7	397.6	250.0[3]	147.6
1949	561.3	161.8	22.7	139.1	399.6	252.5[3]	147.1
1948	556.3	150.5	20.7	129.7	405.8	257.5[3]	148.3
1947	493.9	145.8	19.0	126.8	408.7	271.2[4]	137.5
1946	553.0	140.0	18.1	121.8	412.9	276.0[4]	136.9
1945	552.0	131.5	17.3	114.1	420.5	298.3[4]	122.2
1944	553.3	127.4	16.8	110.6	425.9	235.9[4]	190.0
1943	552.8	125.1	16.4	108.6	427.7	235.1[4]	192.6
1942	564.5	122.7	16.3	106.4	441.8	236.8[4]	205.0
1941	561.5	121.0	16.2	104.7	440.5	235.9[4]	204.6
1940	560.1	116.2	15.6	100.6	443.9	238.3[4]	205.6
1939	497.7	114.3	15.1	99.1	383.5	163.4[4]	220.1
1938	495.7	110.6	11.6	99.0	385.1	89.5	295.6
1937	559.0	114.0	10.0	104.1	445.0	148.7	296.3
1936	410.4	99.4	10.7	88.6	311.2	—	—
1935	410.8	96.4	10.2	86.2	314.4	—	—
1934	409.3	93.6	8.6	85.0	315.6	143.0	172.6
1933	409.1	94.7	8.0	86.7	314.4	138.6	175.8
1932	398.3	91.3	11.0	80.3	307.0	131.3	175.7
1931	378.1	87.4	6.7	80.7	290.7	133.0	157.7
1930	394.3	80.5	9.2	71.3	313.8	158.6	155.2
1929	390.1	72.2	8.6	63.6	317.8	179.3	138.5
1928	382.0	64.1	7.7	56.4	317.9	157.6	160.3
1927	—	—	—	—	—	—	—
1926	—	—	—	—	—	—	—
1925	—	47.4	6.1	41.4	—	—	—

[1] The date within the year to which the mileage applies varies.
[2] No data are available for these columns for 1955 to 1959 as the classification of unimproved earth roads was dropped in 1955.
[3] Includes unimproved road allowances not in use.
[4] Includes all road allowances.
[5] Includes 8,301 miles of surfaced road under the jurisdiction of the federal Department of Citizenship and Immigration and the Quebec Department of Colonization, not reported previously.

Series S222–235. *Motor vehicles, registration, by use and by province, 1904 to 1960*

(series S 222–225 in thousands; series S 226–235 in units)

Year	Total[1,2]	Passenger[3] automobiles	Commercial[4] vehicles	Other[5]	Newfoundland	Prince Edward Island	Nova Scotia	New Brunswick	Quebec	Ontario	Manitoba	Saskatchewan	Alberta	British Columbia
	222	223	224	225	226	227	228	229	230	231	232	233	234	235
1960	5,256.3	4,104.4	1,117.5	34.5	61,952	30,147	187,065	138,469	1,096,053	2,062,484	285,689	335,148	486,370	564,351
1959	5,017.7	3,886.4	1,097.1	24.2	51,145	27,502	180,435	129,629	1,404,366	1,973,737	269,974	326,690	456,458	545,491
1958	4,723.8	3,631.4	1,058.6	33.9	51,575	25,504	164,954	121,715	968,058	1,868,922	256,064	314,423	430,081	515,244
1957	4,497.1	3,428.4	1,033.8	34.9	47,982	23,725	164,286	116,712	901,065	1,793,499	246,188	300,326	405,229	491,884
1956	4,265.4	3,222.5	1,007.4	35.6	45,997	23,373	157,544	111,315	844,827	1,710,240	240,008	291,265	381,153	454,217
1955	3,948.7	2,960.9	951.5	36.3	39,766	22,145	149,841	106,648	743,682	1,617,853	222,474	274,950	356,839	409,343
1954	3,644.6	2,706.0	900.9	37.7	34,423	20,848	133,087	99,058	674,114	1,489,980	210,471	267,373	338,541	371,711
1953	3,430.7	2,527.5	863.0	40.2	29,576	20,286	129,564	93,914	617,855	1,406,119	203,652	257,504	318,812	348,830
1952	3,155.8	2,306.4	807.4	41.2	23,630	18,717	114,982	89,839	574,974	1,291,753	187,881	237,014	291,469	321,482
1951	2,872.4	2,105.9	723.4	43.2	20,058	16,896	105,262	83,023	500,729	1,205,098	171,265	215,540	259,841	291,417
1950	2,600.5	1,913.4	643.2	43.7	16,375	15,383	94,743	74,415	433,701	1,104,080	157,788	199,866	230,624	270,312
1949	2,290.6	1,673.4	577.2	40.0	13,981	13,211	83,443	67,280	384,733	970,137	139,836	185,027	200,428	230,008
1948	2,034.9	1,498.0	503.0	33.9	—	11,290	76,319	62,366	335,953	874,933	128,000	167,515	173,950	202,126
1947	1,836.0	1,371.5	438.4	26.1	—	9,948	70,300	51,589	296,547	800,058	112,149	158,512	155,386	179,684
1946	1,622.5	1,235.3	370.0	17.2	—	9,192	62,660	44,054	255,172	711,106	101,090	148,206	138,868	150,234
1945	1,497.1	1,161.3	321.6	14.2	—	8,835	56,699	41,577	228,681	662,719	92,758	140,257	130,153	134,788
1944	1,502.6	1,178.9	308.6	15.0	—	8,412	57,933	39,570	224,042	675,057	93,297	140,992	127,416	135,090
1943	1,511.8	1,195.3	300.2	16.4	—	8,032	59,194	40,205	222,676	691,615	93,494	133,839	127,559	134,691
1942	1,524.2	1,218.5	289.8	15.8	—	7,537	58,872	37,758	222,622	715,380	93,147	130,040	125,482	132,893
1941	1,572.8	1,281.2	277.1	14.5	—	8,015	62,805	41,450	232,149	739,194	96,573	131,545	126,127	134,499
1940	1,500.8	1,236.5	251.0	13.4	—	8,070	57,873	39,000	225,152	703,872	90,932	126,970	120,514	128,044
1939	1,439.2	1,191.9	235.0	12.3	—	8,040	53,008	38,116	213,148	682,891	88,864	119,018	113,702	122,087
1938	1,394.9	1,161.5	221.3	12.1	—	7,992	51,214	37,110	205,463	669,088	88,219	109,014	107,191	119,220
1937	1,319.7	1,104.9	203.7	11.1	—	8,011	50,048	36,780	197,917	623,918	80,860	105,064	100,434	116,341
1936	1,240.1	1,041.5	187.8	10.8	—	7,632	46,179	33,402	181,628	590,226	74,940	102,270	97,468	106,079
1935	1,176.1	992.1	173.5	10.5	—	8,231	43,952	31,217	170,644	564,076	70,660	94,792	93,870	98,411
1934	1,129.5	955.2	164.1	10.3	—	7,206	41,932	29,094	165,526	542,245	70,430	91,461	89,369	92,021
1933	1,083.2	919.9	153.3	10.0	—	6,940	40,648	26,867	160,012	520,353	68,590	84,944	86,041	88,554
1932	1,113.5	948.3	155.8	9.4	—	6,982	41,013	28,041	165,730	531,597	70,840	91,275	86,781	91,042
1931	1,200.7	1,028.1	162.9	9.6	—	7,744	43,758	33,627	177,485	562,216	75,210	107,830	94,642	97,932
1930	1,232.5	1,061.5	161.6	9.4	—	7,376	43,029	34,699	178,548	562,506	78,850	127,193	101,119	98,938
1929	1,187.3	1,030.9	147.6	8.9	—	6,116	39,972	31,736	169,105	540,207	77,259	128,426	98,720	95,571
1928	1,069.3	930.6	130.8	7.9	—	5,404	35,194	27,970	148,090	487,337	70,578	119,972	88,398	86,203
1927	939.7	830.0	102.1	7.6	—	4,371	29,914	24,457	128,104	433,504	63,412	105,088	73,306	77,327
1926	832.3	736.7	88.0	7.5	—	3,448	25,746	21,421	107,994	386,349	58,292	95,967	65,101	67,810
1925	724.0	641.2	74.9	7.9	—	2,947	22,745	18,863	97,418	342,174	50,884	77,940	54,538	56,427
1924	645.3	573.2	64.0	8.1	—	2,571	20,606	19,840	84,949	306,770	43,875	69,895	48,238	48,407
1923	576.0	513.1	54.6	8.3	—	2,440	18,232	16,662	71,320	278,752	42,083	63,224	42,323	40,854
1922	509.4	368.5	37.6	9.4	—	2,154	16,029	13,611	60,940	239,296	41,870	60,645	40,366	34,385
1921	464.8	333.6	29.3	7.8	—	1,750	14,050	13,460	54,670	206,521	40,336	61,184	39,852	32,900
1920	408.8	251.9	22.3	8.2	—	1,418	12,450	11,121	41,562	177,561	38,257	60,325	38,015	28,000
1919	342.4	196.4	14.4	8.0	—	1,250	10,030	8,252	33,525	144,804	31,208	56,855	34,000	22,420
1918	276.9	157.1	9.6	6.9	—	620	8,150	6,511	26,931	114,376	25,062	50,531	29,250	15,370
1917	203.5	115.6	6.1	6.8	—	303	5,100	4,889	21,213	88,970	18,169	32,505	20,624	11,645
1916	128.3	78.0	3.5	5.7	—	50	3,050	2,986	15,348	58,662	13,111	15,900	9,707	9,457
1915	95.3	60.7	.5	5.4	—	34	2,300	1,900	10,112	46,520	9,937	10,225	5,832	8,360
1914	74.2	45.7	.4	4.8	—	31	1,710	1,260	7,413	35,357	8,056	8,020	4,728	7,628
1913	54.3	29.3	—	3.7	—	26	511	824	5,452	26,600	6,397	4,659	3,773	6,138
1912	36.4	20.4	—	2.3	—	—	456	700	3,535	18,022	4,636	2,286	2,505	4,289
1911	21.8	13.8	—	.3	—	—	228	483	1,878	11,339	2,700	1,304	1,631	2,220
1910	9.2	5.9	—	—	—	—	148	299	786	4,230	1,715	531	423	1,026
1909	4.8	3.2	—	—	—	—	69	167	485	2,452	708	149	275	504
1908	3.1	2.2	—	—	—	—	—	104	396	1,754	418	74	45	263
1907	2.1	1.5	—	—	—	—	—	79	254	1,530	—	—	55	175
1906	1.4	1.2	—	—	—	—	—	41	167	1,176	—	22	41	1,447
1905	0.6	0.6	—	—	—	—	—	—	12	—	553	—	—	—	565
1904	0.5	0.5	—	—	—	—	—	—	—	535	—	—	—	535

[1] Includes registrations in the Yukon and Northwest Territories.
[2] From 1906 to 1922 inclusive series S 222 includes vehicles for which a description is not available.
[3] Includes livery and taxi-cabs.
[4] Includes buses, convertible trucks, road tractors, ambulances.
[5] Includes motorcycles.

Series S236–239. *Canadian civil aviation activity, 1920 to 1960*

Year	Passengers carried (number)	Goods carried[1] (pounds)	Mail carried (pounds)	Hours flown (number)	Year	Passengers carried (number)	Goods carried[1] (pounds)	Mail carried (pounds)	Hours flown (number)
	236	237	238	239		236	237	238	239
1960	5,451,716[4]	254,800,361[4]	37,579,496	736,655	1940	149,025	14,436,571	2,710,995	151,828
1959	5,348,032	223,532,796	35,558,226	830,238	1939	161,503	21,253,364	1,900,347	145,638
1958	4,578,568	206,850,920	33,628,013	744,795	1938	139,806	21,704,587	1,901,711	133,168
1957	4,355,474	271,891,417	31,413,504	782,816	1937	141,158	26,279,156	1,450,473	126,896
1956	3,923,539	326,899,918	27,914,288	772,389	1936	118,660	25,387,719	1,161,060[2]	101,953
1955	3,303,175	240,683,662	26,616,505	637,219	1935	157,472	26,439,224	1,126,084[2]	88,451
1954	2,865,547	115,013,477	24,228,571	494,333	1934	80,806	14,441,179	625,040[2]	75,871
1953	2,795,837	182,719,719	20,319,952	524,935	1933	69,126	4,205,901	539,358[2]	53,299
1952	2,360,847	140,734,542	18,328,310	491,722	1932	76,800[3]	3,129,974	413,687[2]	56,170
1951	1,947,980	63,786,417	16,824,652	582,707	1931	100,128[3]	2,372,467	470,461[2]	73,645
1950	1,553,346	48,486,243	14,501,110	329,514	1930	124,875[3]	1,759,259	474,199	92,993
1949	1,308,297	38,760,812	13,752,434	300,416	1929	96,375[3]	2,489,189	576,831	51,571
1948	1,136,208	38,385,146	10,340,024	322,987	1928	54,913[3]	1,641,250	316,631	28,719
1947	956,701	34,832,307	7,118,074	294,934	1927	16,664[3]	380,433	14,684	4,209
1946	836,548	25,226,986	5,930,338	211,588	1926	4,800[3]	65,308	3,960	2,321
1945	525,407	14,462,400	6,418,944	152,570	1925	3,683[3]	38,580	1,080	1,351
1944	403,938	12,430,645	7,296,265	122,422	1924	4,313[3]	77,385	—	1,893
1943	314,642	13,853,503	7,586,809	116,662	1923	2,328[2]	11,600	—	2,830
1942	229,047	12,651,939	5,470,209	117,876	1922	4,282[2]	11,481	—	2,541
1941	208,059	16,559,611	3,411,971	132,823	1921	9,153[2]	79,850	—	4,347
					1920	15,265[2]	6,740	—	6,505

[1] Freight, express and excess baggage.
[2] Carried under Canadian postal contracts only. See notes on series S236–239.
[3] Includes crew other than pilots.
[4] Do not contain nonrevenue passengers and nonrevenue goods.

Series S240–246. *Civil aviation, domestic revenue traffic, unit toll services, 1936 to 1960*

Year	Passengers carried (thousands)	Passenger miles (thousands)	Mail carried (thousands of pounds)	Mail carried (thousands of ton miles)	Goods carried (thousands of pounds)	Goods (thousands of ton miles)	Miles flown (thousands)
	240	241	242	243	244	245	246
1960	3,098.7	1,649,894	34,633[1]	10,418.5	65,687	23,295.5	54,704
1959	3,098.3	1,449,151	29,422	9,844.1	59,392	19,393.1	52,234
1958	2,651.1	1,224,057	27,868	9,186.4	48,453	17,775.1	46,335
1957	2,393.9	1,073,192	26,114	8,770.9	46,457	15,091.4	44,689
1956	2,115.6	946,463	23,414	7,950.3	47,977	13,102.4	39,795
1955	1,797.2	794,797	22,669	7,293.3	35,603	11,071.5	36,384
1954	1,559.6	707,404	20,647	6,604.3	27,454	8,358.4	32,394
1953	1,419.6	628,098	15,971	5,265.3	23,889	6,373.4	31,146
1952	1,248.8	542,162	14,320	4,689.0	22,396	5,393.4	28,838
1951	1,053.7	451,051	13,408	4,369.3	19,278	4,547.9	30,933
1950	864.8	374,781	12,630	4,043.6	16,520	4,122.9	22,674
1949	709.3	313,265	11,788	3,783.4	13,322	3,021.0	20,090
1948	600.8	253,721	8,535	2,603.3	12,244	2,357.3	18,429
1947	462.3	179,383	5,587	1,527.5	10,035	1,607.5	17,122
1946	445.8	156,389	4,652	1,428.4	9,270	1,108.0	16,520
1945	320.5	115,825	4,853	1,717.6	11,549	1,187.5	15,369
1944	274.4	99,985	5,361	1,993.2	9,980	1,323.9	14,562
1943	186.3	91,914	5,947	2,015.6	10,548	1,344.0	13,764
1942	149.0	64,779	4,349	1,395.7	10,841	1,088.4	11,985
1941	138.4	49,930	2,992	864.1	14,661	946.1	11,040
1940	115.6	36,779	2,563	601.3	12,848	738.3	9,895
1939	95.4	20,806	1,779	426.6	19,360	966.8	—
1938	88.7	8,602	1,305	139.4	19,594	953.7	—
1937	101.1	10,757	1,261	93.9	24,305	1,873.6	—
1936	97.9	8,654	1,161	89.6	22,947	1,066.0	—

[1] Includes international service by Canadian carriers.

Series S247–253. *Civil aviation, transborder traffic, 1937 to 1959*

Year	Passengers (thousands)	Passenger miles (thousands)	Mail (thousands of pounds)	Mail (thousands of ton miles)	Goods (thousands of pounds)	Goods (thousands of ton miles)	Miles flown (thousands)
	247	248	249	250	251	252	253
1959	1,366.3	317,847	3,541	420.6	20,200	2,440.7	11,398
1958	1,193.8	276,996	3,463	432.7	18,127	2,308.4	10,128
1957	1,179.3	255,686	3,323	394.7	18,677	2,123.8	9,263
1956	1,040.6	215,056	2,844	273.5	19,569	2,438.3	8,436
1955	915.8	172,898	2,521	192.0	18,273	2,325.0	7,544
1954	780.6	140,140	2,269	181.4	15,083	2,056.8	5,646
1953	718.9	137,452	1,925	146.7	14,091	1,952.5	5,628
1952	579.2	116,825	1,743	197.3	11,582	2,039.8	5,316
1951	536.9	112,819	1,830	367.2	7,995	2,007.6	5,289
1950	421.1	83,941	1,318	249.8	5,780	1,073.7	4,405
1949	364.1	62,828	1,293	314.2	3,963	767.2	3,728
1948	310.7	55,911	1,228	257.5	3,220	583.3	3,985
1947	311.4	49,808	1,108	118.6	2,214	201.5	4,747
1946	319.8	43,390	1,063	106.6	1,341	117.4	3,926
1945	187.9	26,265	1,401	147.4	862	112.1	2,532
1944	134.1	11,142	1,477	78.9	842	82.7	1,006
1943	95.6	8,587	1,269	78.8	763	95.1	763
1942	49.2	5,775	536	88.6	214	37.5	797
1941	42.8	3,962	269	30.5	58	10.3	771
1940	19.7	1,270	148	8.8	35	2.5	321
1939	15.5	1,013	121	6.8	20	.3	283
1938	13.4	2,291	597	142.2	30	7.1	2,750
1937	9.4	1,875	189	18.6	13	1.1	762

Series S254–260. *Civil aviation, transborder traffic via Canadian carriers, scheduled revenue traffic, 1941 to 1960*

Year	Passengers (thousands)	Passenger miles (thousands)	Mail (thousands of pounds)	Mail (thousands of ton miles)	Goods (thousands of pounds)	Goods (thousands of ton miles)	Miles flown (thousands)
	254	255	256	257	258	259	260
1960	—[1]	340,545	—[1]	401.2	—[1]	2,415.7	11,349
1959	848.0	284,278	1,917	348.9	12,553	2,130.2	9,220
1958	750.4	250,020	2,069	376.1	11,707	2,034.7	8,303
1957	665.0	225,938	1,864	342.3	11,821	1,875.5	7,387
1956	556.5	189,331	1,182	219.5	11,965	2,140.8	6,721
1955	429.7	144,263	746	141.2	11,315	2,014.7	5,542
1954	351.3	118,201	698	128.6	10,334	1,898.4	4,324
1953	340.7	116,416	550	99.9	9,820	1,768.3	4,328
1952	286.3	96,687	551	97.8	8,311	1,466.4	3,814
1951	254.1	80,826	532	85.4	4,725	768.9	3,293
1950	202.6	67,001	483	78.1	3,096	507.4	3,056
1949	151.1	47,767	350	59.1	1,748	287.0	2,365
1948	136.4	42,170	359	57.0	1,532	241.4	2,713
1947	122.0	35,215	322	53.0	659	99.2	3,290
1946	81.6	30,299	264	57.5	344	69.3	2,873
1945	34.1	15,705	317	73.1	205	50.7	1,658
1944	14.8	893	352	3.9	36	3.6	94
1943	11.0	683	349	3.7	40	3.2	76
1942	24.7	461	224	3.2	153	1.4	66
1941	3.3	237	2	1.0	8	.3	37

[1] Figures not available.

Series S261–267. *Civil aviation, Atlantic and Pacific scheduled revenue traffic via Trans-Canada Airlines and Canadian Pacific Airlines, 1947 to 1960*

Year	Passengers (thousands)	Passenger miles (thousands)	Mail (thousands of pounds)	Mail (thousands of ton miles)	Goods (thousands of pounds)	Goods (thousands of ton miles)	Miles flown (thousands)
	261	262	263	264	265	266	267
1960	—[1]	565,744	—[1]	2,634.8	—[1]	8,593.7	10,652
1959	230.2	623,958	1,556	2,922.5	4,520	7,982.0	15,952
1958	197.8	562,086	1,450	2,663.1	3,601	6,605.4	14,800
1957	158.3	438,452	1,285	2,300.3	3,415	6,431.6	12,396
1956	124.7	344,846	975	1,724.3	3,176	6,089.4	9,551
1955	84.2	236,283	852	1,503.0	2,588	4,409.8	6,667
1954	75.2	197,530	816	1,405.2	2,247	3,356.7	5,846
1953	62.4	151,084	564	942.3	1,918	2,587.1	5,410
1952	56.2	126,506	451	771.9	1,876	2,412.8	4,849
1951	54.4	156,053	339	569.6	1,618	1,987.2	6,325
1950	37.5	99,904	260	439.2	1,345	1,687.0	4,568
1949	37.4	100,913	250	415.8	1,256	1,581.3	4,578
1948	32.8	100,536	230	369.6	750	984.2	4,597
1947	15.8	50,370	152	251.6	408	531.0	2,387

[1] Figures not available.

Series S268–270. *Civil aviation, contract and charter traffic, Canadian carriers, 1946 to 1960*

Year	Passengers carried (thousands)	Goods carried (thousands of pounds)	Revenue miles flown (thousands)
	268	269	270
1960	509	123,200	23,939
1959	505	126,524	28,702
1958	424	128,006	26,372
1957	509	194,456	36,743
1956	524	246,886	42,370
1955	406	175,789	32,266
1954	320	63,141	15,456
1953	379	132,730	19,532
1952	295	94,694	17,447
1951	193	26,269	9,986
1950	165	19,813	8,286
1949	137	15,565	7,166
1948	143	18,169	7,905
1947	109	19,384	6,616
1946	83	13,046	5,399

Series S271–281. *Civil aviation, operating revenues, operating costs per unit of capacity, passenger fares per unit of traffic and employment, Canadian carriers, 1936 to 1960*

(series S271–276 in thousands of dollars; series S277–280 in cents per unit)

Year	Operating revenues, Canadian air service						Unit operating costs (per ton mile of capacity)		Average level of fares (per passenger mile)		Employment in air transport (number)
	Total operating revenues	Passenger[1]	Mail[1]	Goods[1]	Bulk transport revenues[1]	Other flying revenues	T.C.A.	Large independents	T.C.A.	Large independents	
	271	272	273	274	275	276	277	278	279	280	281
1960	231,226.8	168,718.9	13,794.1	16,177.7	27,199.8	5,336.3	36.72	—[4]	6.25	—[4]	17,106
1959	215,798.7	152,317.2	13,437.8	14,549.2	29,003.3	6,491.2	37.08	—	6.31	6.75	16,565
1958	196,615.8	131,167.0	12,981.6	12,440.9	29,896.6	10,129.8	38.03	65	6.28	6.89	15,990
1957	185,138.6	112,295.3	12,661.8	11,594.9	40,719.2	7,867.4	37.85	55	6.26	7.05	16,014
1956	178,569.8	96,180.5	11,532.9	10,296.7	53,435.6	7,124.1	37.81	45	6.27	7.30	14,848
1955	148,583.3	77,598.1	10,904.7	8,815.2	44,543.3	6,722.0	37.97	45	6.34	7.59	13,271
1954	105,461.8	66,748.5	10,873.2	6,705.7	15,149.5	5,984.9	42.84	90	6.26	7.56	11,690
1953	101,021.5	59,566.0	10,089.1	5,985.6	19,664.1	5,716.7	41.19	77	6.37	7.98	10,703
1952	88,133.2	51,681.7	9,830.7	5,370.4	16,952.0	4,298.4	39.60	80	6.44	8.41	9,398
1951	71,283.3	46,059.5	9,186.1	4,235.3	10,202.7	1,599.7	39.87	96	6.78[2]	5.98[2]	6,942
1950	55,935.9	37,255.9	8,405.4	3,595.7	5,231.3	1,447.6	43.24	101	6.69	7.40	6,337
1949	48,352.8	31,600.8	8,261.2	2,915.0	4,286.0	1,289.8	47.84	101	6.77	8.36	6,513
1948	43,004.0	25,604.4	7,384.2	2,335.9	5,826.5	1,853.0	50.32	117	6.68	7.70	5,983
1947	30,521.0	17,483.1	6,097.4	1,799.7	3,848.4	1,292.5	—	147	6.41	8.38	5,725
1946	20,925.7	11,385.4	5,278.5	1,157.4	2,442.2	662.3	—	163	5.18	9.75	5,413
1945	15,852.9	8,607.6[1]	5,556.4[1]	1,428.1[1]	—[1]	260.8	—	—	—	—	4,340
1944	17,119.3	7,878.1	5,081.0	1,571.8	—	2,588.4[3]	110.54	—	5.3	—	4,095
1943	16,387.0	7,647.3	4,758.3	1,878.7	—	2,102.7[3]	108.72	—	5.4	—	3,383
1942	12,133.0	5,020.7	4,047.4	1,451.5	—	1,613.4[3]	92.42	—	5.4	—	2,292
1941	8,948.4	3,626.2	3,615.3	979.7	—	727.2	83.83	160	5.4	—	1,590
1940	7,429.2	2,770.3	3,470.2	770.6	—	418.1	80.83	163	5.4	—	1,228
1939	5,310.5	2,009.1	1,985.6	973.1	—	342.7	93.72	146	4.0	—	1,050
1938	3,451.1	1,412.4	873.4	833.8	—	331.5	69.02	157	6.0	—	868
1937	—	—	—	—	—	—	—	102	—	—	617
1936	—	—	—	—	—	—	—	129	—	—	548

[1] No clear-cut distinction was observed between Unit Toll and Bulk Transportation (charter and contract carriage) traffic prior to 1946. Therefore from 1938 to 1945 inclusive, Bulk Transportation revenues were reported under 'Passenger', 'Mail' and 'Goods' Traffic revenues.

[2] This figure is distorted by specially priced defence transportation.

[3] Nontransportation defence work of Canadian Pacific and Trans-Canada Air Lines is included.

[4] Figures not available.

Series S282–287. *Civil aviation, aircraft, airports and airport investment expenditures, 1946 to 1960*

(series S282–285 in units; series S286 and 287 in thousands of dollars)

		Number of aircraft			Airport investment expenditures, federal government[1]	
					Department of Transport direct investment	Grants and contributions for airport development
Year	Total all aircraft	Commercial and state aircraft	Private aircraft	Licensed airports		
	282	**283**	**284**	**285**	**286**	**287**
1960	4,914	2,045	2,869	460	52,907	1,112
1959	4,547	2,034	2,513	483	52,542	802
1958	4,509	2,071	2,438	452	53,538	740
1957	4,005	2,001	2,004	550	35,499	704
1956	3,330	1,764	1,566	519	26,927	555
1955	3,148	1,682	1,466	495	20,543	521
1954	2,800	1,513	1,287	430	10,307	562
1953	2,654	1,503	1,151	433	8,336	585
1952	2,411	1,425	986	415	7,085	541
1951	2,306	1,454	852	403	6,099	533
1950	1,960	1,222	738	415	6,609	618
1949	2,001	1,334	667	361	—	—
1948	2,021	1,477	544	354	—	—
1947	1,873	1,574	299	273	—	—
1946	911	866	45	161	—	—

[1] Data relate to fiscal years ending 31 March of the next year.

Series S288–293. *Intercity ton miles performed, by type of carrier, 1938 to 1959*

(millions of ton miles)

Year	Total	Rail	Road	Water	Air	Oil pipe line
	288	**289**	**290**	**291**	**292**	**293**
1959	133,556	67,957	14,397	33,720	38	17,444
1958	126,878	66,357	14,080	29,457	35	16,951
1957	132,205	71,047	10,679	31,251	38	19,190
1956	141,208	78,820	10,614	33,594	39	18,141
1955	118,665	66,176	10,248	29,282	31	12,982
1954	102,099	57,547	10,012	25,250	20	9,270
1953	110,059	65,267	9,778	28,001	21	6,992
1952	108,456	68,430	8,903	26,313	17	4,793
1951	100,725	64,300	8,238	24,625	11	3,551
1950	87,673	55,538	7,597	23,032	10	1,496
1949	82,735	56,338	5,920	20,469	8	—
1948	84,062	59,080	5,193	19,782	7	—
1947	82,520	60,143	4,310	18,063	4	—
1946	74,471	55,310	3,501	15,657	3	—
1945	85,097	63,349	2,995	18,750	3	—
1944	85,912	65,928	2,668	17,313	3	—
1943	84,408	63,915	2,458	18,032	3	—
1942	76,112	56,154	2,424	17,532	2	—
1941	71,909	49,982	2,237	19,688	2	—
1940	58,934	37,898	1,847	19,188	1	—
1939	52,761	31,465	1,670	19,625	1	—
1938	49,039	26,835	1,515	20,688	1	—

Series S294–306. *Post Office, number of post offices in Canada, by province, 1867 to 1960*

Year[1]	Total for Canada	New-foundland	Prince Edward Island	Nova Scotia	New Brunswick	Quebec	Ontario	Manitoba	Saskatchewan	Alberta	British Columbia	Yukon	Northwest Territories
	294	295	296	297	298	299	300	301	302	303	304	305	306
1960	11,497	649	104	964	597	2,403	2,629	809	1,279	1,082	922	20	39
1959	11,634	647	104	1,031	634	2,405	2,624	814	1,298	1,089	932	19	37
1958	11,768	641	105	1,096	676	2,413	2,616	810	1,310	1,112	937	16	36
1957	11,879	640	105	1,117	703	2,435	2,627	817	1,318	1,124	940	16	37
1956	11,996	636	105	1,124	736	2,463	2,644	815	1,332	1,141	947	16	37
1955	12,138	626	105	1,148	789	2,487	2,654	822	1,347	1,156	955	16	33
1954	12,202	613	106	1,179	817	2,507	2,630	824	1,364	1,152	963	15	32
1953	12,259	606	105	1,215	834	2,516	2,613	831	1,384	1,156	955	13	31
1952	12,305	592	105	1,245	837	2,530	2,598	823	1,397	1,179	955	13	31
1951	12,390	573	105	1,278	874	2,545	2,602	823	1,407	1,179	958	15	31
1950	12,415	550	105	1,315	909	2,560	2,586	809	1,404	1,184	952	15	26
1949	11,930	—	105	1,362	922	2,567	2,590	806	1,418	1,186	933	15	26
1948	11,982	—	108	1,396	949	2,582	2,578	802	1,420	1,188	920	15	24
1947	12,033	—	109	1,441	968	2,577	2,562	791	1,429	1,195	923	15	23
1946	12,105	—	115	1,465	983	2,586	2,557	794	1,443	1,209	914	16	23
1945	12,169	—	114	1,475	991	2,594	2,566	795	1,466	1,216	914	16	22
1944	12,234	—	114	1,475	996	2,601	2,579	797	1,484	1,229	921	15	23
1943	12,313	—	115	1,487	1,001	2,604	2,597	799	1,499	1,244	928	16	23
1942	12,410	—	115	1,497	1,015	2,620	2,620	807	1,517	1,255	927	15	22
1941	12,477	—	115	1,508	1,020	2,627	2,639	810	1,528	1,262	932	15	21
1940	12,557	—	115	1,530	1,024	2,646	2,655	813	1,530	1,267	938	16	23
1939	12,514	—	115	1,540	1,026	2,625	2,640	806	1,515	1,266	940	18	23
1938	12,421	—	115	1,543	1,023	2,592	2,623	798	1,501	1,259	929	18	20
1937	12,272	—	114	1,551	1,009	2,542	2,589	794	1,482	1,246	908	18	19
1936	12,156	—	114	1,565	1,002	2,494	2,559	788	1,460	1,243	895	18	18
1935	12,069	—	114	1,571	1,000	2,466	2,540	788	1,433	1,228	892	18	19
1934	12,035	—	115	1,600	1,004	2,450	2,523	778	1,426	1,213	889	18	19
1933	12,074	—	114	1,629	1,016	2,446	2,524	778	1,423	1,215	892	19	18
1932	12,133	—	116	1,673	1,025	2,451	2,522	781	1,424	1,200	905	19	17
1931	12,427	—	125	1,751	1,041	2,516	2,576	818	1,448	1,224	890	21	17
1930	12,409	—	126	1,762	1,062	2,519	2,575	815	1,430	1,191	892	20	17
1929	12,430	—	127	1,770	1,079	2,528	2,586	816	1,423	1,189	876	20	16
1928	12,478	—	128	1,771	1,114	2,514	2,604	817	1,428	1,200	866	20	16
1927	12,440	—	130	1,778	1,113	2,463	2,614	817	1,428	1,195	867	20	15
1926	12,439	—	131	1,791	1,119	2,429	2,613	818	1,433	1,203	868	20	14
1925	12,376	—	130	1,793	1,126	2,396	2,588	813	1,414	1,211	871	19	15
1924	12,370	—	131	1,819	1,131	2,366	2,597	816	1,408	1,215	855	19	13
1923	12,288	—	133	1,836	1,139	2,325	2,577	803	1,403	1,194	849	20	9
1922	12,247	—	133	1,834	1,133	2,301	2,577	802	1,406	1,188	846	21	6
1921	12,252	—	136	1,844	1,134	2,293	2,582	798	1,416	1,187	834	23	5
1920	12,251	—	137	1,845	1,145	2,288	2,572	794	1,430	1,191	826	23	—
1919[2]	12,290	—	—	—	—	—	—	—	—	—	—	—	—
1918[2]	12,622	—	—	—	—	—	—	—	—	—	—	—	—
1917[2]	12,772	—	—	—	—	—	—	—	—	—	—	—	—
1916[2]	13,057	—	—	—	—	—	—	—	—	—	—	—	—
1915[2]	13,348	—	—	—	—	—	—	—	—	—	—	—	—
1914	13,811	—	292	2,008	1,386	2,587	3,345	799	1,452	1,151	763	—	28[3]
1913	14,178	—	442	2,032	1,440	2,600	3,775	773	1,342	1,017	733	24	
1912	13,859	—	470	2,003	1,452	2,508	3,845	737	1,229	919	672	24	
1911	13,324	—	468	1,968	1,421	2,398	3,788	721	1,097	828	613	22	
1910	12,887	—	467	1,953	1,410	2,341	3,748	700	983	695	570	20	
1909	12,479	—	465	1,938	1,397	2,269	3,694	687	861	600	547	21	
1908	11,823	—	452	1,913	1,333	2,175	3,594	651	707	478	501	19	
1907[1]	11,377	—	445	1,897	1,310	2,121	3,532	633	575	387	458	19	
1906[1]	11,141	—	441	1,892	1,305	2,090	3,506	621	513	326	429	18	

Series S294–306. *Post Office, number of post offices in Canada, by province, 1867 to 1960 (continued)*

Year[1]	Total for Canada	New-foundland	Prince Edward Island	Nova Scotia	New Brunswick	Quebec	Ontario	Manitoba	Saskatchewan	Alberta	British Columbia	Yukon	Northwest Territories
	294	295	296	297	298	299	300	301	302	303	304	305	306
1905	10,879	—	437	1,876	1,295	2,059	3,461	1,314[4]	—[4]	—[4]	437	—[4]	—[4]
1904	10,460	—	426	1,836	1,272	1,989	3,392	1,139[4]	—	—	406	—	—
1903	10,150	—	419	1,789	1,253	1,932	3,359	1,008[4]	—	—	390	—	—
1902	9,958	—	416	1,777	1,241	1,873	3,321	962[4]	—	—	368	—	—
1901	9,834	—	414	1,754	1,217	1,830	3,311	933[4]	—	—	375		
1900	9,627	—	412	1,723	1,196	1,781	3,282	869[4]	—	—	364	—	—
1899	9,420	—	409	1,686	1,180	1,744	3,228	830[4]	—	—	343	—	—
1898	9,282	—	409	1,673	1,182	1,698	3,213	796[4]	—	—	311	—	—
1897	9,191	—	406	1,657	1,183	1,664	3,198	790[4]	—	—	293	—	—
1896	9,103	—	389	1,648	1,181	1,640	3,185	786[4]	—	—	274	—	—
1895	8,832	—	368	1,589	1,162	1,600	3,138	729[4]	—	—	246	—	—
1894	8,664	—	358	1,562	1,146	1,575	3,102	692[4]	—	—	229	—	—
1893	8,406	—	347	1,534	1,140	1,533	3,058	414	232[5]	—	219	—[5]	—[5]
1892	8,288	—	339	1,481	1,123	1,486	3,060	406	206[5]	—	187	—	—
1891	8,061	—	324	1,431	1,101	1,441	3,026	389	182[5]	—	167	—	—
1890	7,913	—	320	1,404	1,089	1,429	2,997	359	164[5]	—	151	—	—
1889	7,838	—	315	1,399	1,085	1,423	2,971	346	155[5]	—	144	—	—
1888	7,671	—	304	1,372	1,070	1,385	2,927	339	145[5]	—	129	—	—
1887	7,534	—	298	1,345	1,048	1,372	2,891	332	131[5]	—	117	—	—
1886	7,295	—	292	1,300	1,019	1,320	2,835	311	113[5]	—	105	—	—
1885	7,084	—	280	1,255	997	1,289	2,762	303	101[5]	—	97	—	—
1884	6,837	—	271	1,203	932	1,252	2,713	291	92[5]	—	83	—	—
1883	6,395	—	252	1,131	883	1,210	2,617	207	29[5]	—	66	—	—
1882	6,171	—	244	1,091	828	1,177	2,571	183	16[5]	—	61	—	—
1881	5,935	—	237	1,037	802	1,147	2,493	150	10[5]	—	59	—	—
1880	5,773	—	234	1,008	784	1,123	2,427	113	34[5]	—	50	—	—
1879	5,606	—	228	994	762	1,102	2,353	98	21[5]	—	48	—	—
1878	5,378	—	224	960	731	1,052	2,298	59	7[5]	—	47	—	—
1877	5,161	—	213	938	680	1,025	2,203	49	7[5]	—	46	—	—
1876	5,015	—	208	915	663	999	2,130	46	5[5]	—	49	—	—
1875	4,892	—	197	901	651	3,054[6]		40	—		49	—	—
1874	4,706	—	179	868	633	2,943[6]		36	—		47	—	—
1873	4,518	—	180	833	611	2,814[6]		34	—		46	—	—
1872	4,135	—	—	768	586	2,716[6]		27	—		38	—	—
1871	3,943	—	—	742	564	2,637[6]		—	—		—	—	—
1870[2]	3,820	—	—	—	—	—		—	—		—	—	—
1869[2]	3,756	—	—	—	—	—		—	—		—	—	—
1868[2]	3,638	—	—	—	—	—		—	—		—	—	—
1867[2]	2,333	—	—	—	—	—		—	—		—	—	—

[1] Data are for the numbers at the end of the fiscal year ending in the year given. From 1867 to 1906 the fiscal year ended 30 June and from 1907 to 1960 the fiscal year ended 31 March.
[2] Not available by province.
[3] From 1906 to 1914 data are for Yukon and Northwest Territories.
[4] From 1893 to 1905 data in series S301 are for Manitoba and the Northwest Territories which included Alberta, Saskatchewan, Northern Manitoba, the present Northwest Territories and Yukon.
[5] From 1876 to 1892 data in series S302–303 are for the Northwest Territories as described in footnote (3).
[6] From 1871 to 1875 data are for Ontario and Quebec.

Series S307–312. *Post Office, transportation statistics, operations, 1868 to 1960*

Year[1]	Total number of land mail services	Railway mail services (miles)	Rural route services (miles)	Number of rural routes	Average rural route (miles)	Number of other land mail services	Year[1]	Total number of land mail services	Railway mail services (miles)	Rural route services (miles)	Number of rural routes	Average rural route (miles)	Number of other land mail services
	307	308	309	310	311	312		307	308	309	310	311	312
1960	11,262	—	136,173	5,516	24.7	5,746	1935	—	39,542	89,933	4,343	20.7	—
1959	11,674	—	133,062	5,464	24.4	6,210	1934	—	39,650	90,638	4,329	20.9	—
1958	12,083	—	130,889	5,424	24.1	7,379	1933	—	39,796	88,487	4,315	20.5	—
1957	12,489	—	128,610	5,396	23.8	7,093	1932	12,599	39,729	88,562	4,283	20.7	8,316
1956	—	—	126,881	5,356	23.7	—	1931	—	39,844	86,340	4,215	20.5	—
1955	12,908	—	124,593	5,319	23.4	7,589	1930	—	39,006	84,158	4,097	20.5	—
1954	13,282	—	122,344	5,278	23.2	8,004	1929	12,805	38,530	79,861	3,972	20.1	8,833
1953	13,353	—	120,750	5,236	23.1	8,117	1928	—	38,066	77,561	3,838	20.2	—
1952	13,442	—	119,326	5,199	23.0	8,243	1927	—	37,547	76,093	3,799	20.0	—
1951	13,485	—	116,517	5,170	22.5	8,315	1926	12,361	37,295	76,567	3,787	20.2	8,574
1950	13,402	37,036	112,672	5,087	22.1	8,315	1925	—	31,141	—	—	—	—
1949	12,858	38,866	110,448	4,976	22.2	7,882	1924	—	—	—	—	—	—
1948	12,903	39,070	108,573	4,912	22.1	7,991	1923	—	36,422	72,868	—	—	—
1947	12,899	39,064	107,180	4,887	21.9	8,012	1918	—	35,221	—	—	—	—
1946	12,913	39,169	106,436	4,850	21.9	8,063	1913	11,274	28,791	—	1,865	—	9,409
							1908[1]	8,098	21,475	—	—	—	—
1945	12,928	38,887	105,409	4,844	21.8	8,084	1903[1]	6,522	17,441	—	—	—	—
1944	13,105	38,910	105,338	4,844	21.7	8,261	1898	5,947	15,325	—	—	—	—
1943	—	38,877	104,917	4,846	21.7	—	1893	5,361	13,703	—	—	—	—
1942	—	38,843	104,489	4,845	21.6	—	1888	4,542	11,252	—	—	—	—
1941	—	39,000	103,669	4,841	21.4	—	1883	3,479	8,115	—	—	—	—
1940	—	39,164	100,662	4,815	20.9	—	1878	2,808	5,130	—	—	—	—
1939	13,140	39,446	96,971	4,712	20.4	8,428	1873	2,183	—	—	—	—	—
1938	12,809	39,641	94,717	4,540	20.9	8,269	1868	1,751	—	—	—	—	—
1937	12,890	39,631	93,223	4,436	21.0	8,454							
1936	12,577	39,731	91,370	4,379	20.9	8,198							

[1] Data are for the numbers at the end of the fiscal year, ending in the year given. From 1868 to 1903 the fiscal year ended 30 June and from 1908 to 1960 the fiscal year ended 31 March.

Series S313–316. *Post Office, transportation statistics, operations (five year basis), 1868 to 1913*

Year[1]	Stage route mileage[1] (miles)	Mileage travelled (stage) (thousands of miles)	Mileage of rail service performed (thousands of miles)	Water services[1] (number)
	313	314	315	316
1913	—	19,406	—	86
1908[1]	—	17,102	—	76
1903[1]	—	15,812	—	62
1898	—	—	—	60
1893	61,832	30,496	15,580	—
1888	56,264	24,749	11,532	51
1883	44,643	19,465	7,815	44
1878	38,730	15,427	5,708	41
1873	35,588	13,267	—	32
1868	27,764	10,622	—	30

[1] Data are for numbers at the end of the fiscal year, ending in the year given. From 1868 to 1903 the fiscal year ended 30 June and in 1908 and 1913 the fiscal year ended 31 March.

Series S317–320. *Post Office, transportation statistics, cost of services, 1868 to 1960*

(thousands of dollars)

Year[1]	Railway mail services	Water services	Air mail services	Non-rail land services	Year[1]	Railway mail services	Water services	Air mail services	Non-rail land services
	317	318	319	320		317	318	319	320
1960	16,635	2,790	13,276	26,579	1935	6,581	275	223	5,921
1959	15,057	2,515	13,056	24,960	1934	6,658	271	215	6,098
1958	14,958	2,399	12,700	23,316	1933	6,697	248	204	6,271
1957	13,902	2,311	11,635	21,085	1932	7,161	257	1,003	6,532
1956	14,255	2,207	11,052	18,518	1931	7,714	468	1,404	6,679
1955	14,487	2,318	10,882	17,783	1930	7,805	533	634	6,554
1954	15,111	2,406	10,070	16,975	1929	7,503	534	272	6,413
1953	12,944	2,559	9,835	15,589	1928	7,438	434	763	6,291
1952	11,831	2,377	9,356	14,476	1927	7,325	490	—	6,194
1951	13,986	2,181	8,491	13,673	1926	7,317	524	—	6,119
1950	8,867	2,117	8,298	12,903	1925	7,283	582	—	6,157
1949	8,682	2,512	7,772	11,859	1924	—	—	—	6,187
1948	8,545	2,915	6,497	10,599	1923	7,477	558	—	6,187
1947	8,324	2,362	7,147	9,592	1918	3,488	174	—	4,468
1946	8,113	2,320	8,657	8,905	1913	2,114	248	—	2,494
					1908[1]	1,677	219	—	1,342
1945	8,167	2,708	8,015	8,424					
1944	7,961	2,251	5,372	7,756	1903[1]	1,414	88	—	857
1943	7,617	1,920	4,305	7,120	1898	1,352	85	—	766
1942	7,346	1,636	3,700	6,727	1893	1,218	68	—	796
1941	7,061	1,002	3,838	6,389	1888	849	87	—	736
					1883	586	59	—	575
1940	6,981	283	2,326	6,313					
1939	6,944	281	1,313	6,244	1878	451	59	—	515
1938	6,897	277	375	6,088	1873	322	54	—	416
1937	6,809	273	287	5,992	1868	196	49	—	294
1936	6,721	266	276	5,945					

[1] Data are for fiscal years ending in the year given. From 1868 to 1903 the fiscal year ended 30 June and from 1908 to 1960 the fiscal year ended 31 March.

Series S 321–322. *Post Office, gross postal revenues and pieces of first-class mail, 1868 to 1960*

Year[1]	Gross postal revenues (thousands of dollars)	Pieces of first-class mail (millions)	Year[1]	Gross postal revenues (thousands of dollars)	Pieces of first-class mail (millions)
	321	322		321	322
1960	193,593	2,096.2	1910	11,069	501.2
1959	183,291	1,983.9	1909	9,928	456.5
1958	177,433	1,956.5	1908	9,483	436.7
1957	167,829	1,828.7	1907[1]	6,535	301.3
1956	158,286	1,727.0	1906[1]	7,708	357.3
1955	151,682	1,849.7	1905	6,786	315.5
1954	129,735	1,582.0	1904	6,306	286.4
1953	129,267	1,576.4	1903	5,683	262.4
1952	122,267	1,462.2	1902	5,158	220.6
1951	105,534	1,453.2	1901	4,642	218.5
1950	101,277	1,362.3	1900	4,367	205.4
1949	95,957	1,333.3	1899	4,336	177.8
1948	91,614	1,210.3	1898	4,687	163.1
1947	86,401	1,151.8	1897	4,311	150.0
1946	83,763	—	1896	4,006	140.8
1945	79,554	—	1895	3,815	131.6
1944	73,004	—	1894	3,734	130.8
1943	59,175	—	1893	3,696	129.1
1942	55,477	—	1892	3,543	123.7
1941	48,143	—	1891	3,375	118.3
1940	44,208	—	1890	3,224	113.6
1939	42,896	—	1889	2,984	112.0
1938	42,998	—	1888	2,966	96.8
1937	41,182	—	1887	2,603	90.7
1936	39,204	—	1886	2,469	86.1
1935	37,577	—	1885	2,400	82.2
1934	36,352	—	1884	2,331	79.7
1933	36,892	—	1883	2,264	75.7
1932	39,276	—	1882	2,022	67.5
1931	37,468	—	1881	1,767	57.8
1930	39,984	—	1880	1,648	53.6
1929	37,899	—	1879	1,534	50.8
1928	36,578	—	1878	1,620	50.5
1927	35,385	—	1877	1,501	47.0
1926	37,129	—	1876	1,485	46.4
1925	34,583	—	1875	1,537	42.0
1924	35,052	—	1874	1,476	39.4
1923	35,052	—	1873	1,407	34.6
1922	32,279	—	1872	1,193	30.6
1921	32,330	—	1871	1,080	27.1
1920	29,673	—	1870	1,011	24.5
1919	27,591	—	1869	973	21.9
1918	26,847	—	1868	1,025	18.1
1917	25,187	—			
1916	22,740	—			
1915	16,835	749.4			
1914	16,865	737.6			
1913	15,672	694.1			
1912	13,772	620.9			
1911	12,213	553.5			

[1] Data are for fiscal years ending in the year given. From 1868 to 1906 the fiscal year ended 30 June. Data for 1907 are for nine months ending 31 March, the fiscal year ending of all subsequent years.

Series S323–331. *Telephone industry, telephones and telephone conversations, 1886 to 1960*

Year	Number of telephones at 31 December (thousands)						Number of telephone conversations (millions)			Year	Total number of telephones at 31 December (thousands)
	Total[1]	Business	Residence[2]	Residence extension[2]	On automatic switchboards	On manual switchboards	Total	Local	Long distance		Total
	323	324	325	326	327	328	329	330	331		323
1960	5,728	1,674	4,054	462	5,018	710	9,579.9	9,364.6	215.3		
1959	5,439	1,569	3,870	409	4,598	841	9,250.2	9,044.8	205.4		
1958	5,118	1,486	3,632	348	4,192	926	8,707.6	8,513.4	194.2	1915	553
1957	4,827	1,409	3,418	308	3,855	972	8,255.7	8,077.1	178.6	1914	542
1956	4,499	1,334	3,165	266	3,478	1,021	7,764.8	7,593.5	171.3	1913	500
										1912	432
1955	4,152	1,237	2,915	224	3,070	1,082	6,961.5	6,808.4	153.1	1911	354
1954	3,860	1,154	2,706	188	2,764	1,096	6,347.5	6,209.8	137.7		
1953	3,606	1,085	2,521	170	2,486	1,120	6,084.7	5,952.8	131.9	1910	284
1952	3,352	1,017	2,335	155	2,240	1,112	5,609.7	5,483.0	126.7	1909	239
1951	3,114	957	2,157	141	2,005	1,109	5,273.6	5,146.2	127.4	1908	—
										1907	—
1950	2,917	902	2,015	128	1,811	1,106	5,012.6	4,894.7	117.9	1906	—
1949	2,700	846	1,854	115	1,627	1,073	4,559.3	4,454.0	105.3		
1948	2,452	778	1,674	95	1,399	1,053	4,117.2	4,025.3	91.9	1905	—
1947	2,231	712	1,519	81	1,256	975	3,843.3	3,760.6	82.7	1904	95[3]
1946	2,026	647	1,379	62	1,123	903	3,559.0	3,484.2	74.8	1903	82[3]
										1902	71[3]
1945	1,849	587	1,262	50	1,037	812	3,210.3	3,145.5	64.8	1901	63[3]
1944	1,752	558	1,194	49	989	763	3,012.7	2,956.0	56.7		
1943	1,692	534	1,158	49	961	731	2,979.8	2,929.4	50.4	1900	52[4]
1942	1,628	512	1,116	50	931	697	2,998.9	2,954.7	44.2	1899	44[4]
1941	1,562	494	1,068	55	861	701	3,011.5	2,971.8	39.7	1898	44[4]
										1897	—
1940	1,461	465	996	52	767	694	2,899.1	2,864.2	34.9	1896	—
1939	1,397	448	949	50	690	707	2,774.4	2,742.8	31.6		
1938	1,359	437	922	49	639	720	2,623.1	2,592.8	30.3	1895	—
1937	1,323	424	899	48	613	710	2,613.8	2,583.0	30.8	1894	34[4]
1936	1,266	407	859	47	563	703	2,472.5	2,444.5	28.0	1893	32[4]
										1892	—
1935	1,209	386	823	44	530	679	2,320.6	2,294.6	26.0	1891	25[4]
1934	1,197	383	814	43	508	689	2,304.3	2,278.9	25.4		
1933	1,192	371	821	—	489	703	2,271.6	2,247.2	24.4	1890	21[4]
1932	1,261	383	878	—	473	788	2,346.6	2,319.4	27.2	1889	18[4]
1931	1,364	402	962	—	475	889	2,454.3	2,421.1	33.2	1888	16[4]
										1887	15[4]
1930	1,403	406	997	—	432	971	2,512.8	2,475.3	37.5	1886	13[4]
1929	1,383	398	985	—	358	1,025	2,462.9	2,425.0	37.9		
1928	1,335	377	958	—	—	—	2,220.9	2,184.7	36.2		
1927	1,260	355	905	—	—	—	—	—	—		
1926	1,201	341	860	—	—	—	—	—	—		
1925	1,143	325	818	—	—	—	—	—	—		
1924	1,072	305	767	—	—	—	—	—	—		
1923	1,009	311	698	—	—	—	—	—	—		
1922	944	289	655	—	—	—	—	—	—		
1921	902	280	622	—	—	—	—	—	—		
1920	856	266	590	—	—	—	—	—	—		
1919	779	—	—	—	—	—	—	—	—		
1918	698	—	—	—	—	—	—	—	—		
1917	657	—	—	—	—	—	—	—	—		
1916	600	—	—	—	—	—	—	—	—		

[1] Series S323 is the sum of series S324 and S325; it is also the sum of series S327 and S328.
[2] Series S326 is included in series S325.
[3] Data as of 30 June.

[4] These data may be incomplete. The source records do indicate that data for British Columbia, New Brunswick, Nova Scotia, and Prince Edward Island are not included in the years 1888 to 1892.

Series S332–334. *Telephone industry, gross capital expenditures on new construction and machinery and equipment, 1926 to 1960*
(millions of dollars)

Year	Total expenditure	Construction	Machinery and equipment	Year	Total expenditure	Construction	Machinery and equipment
	332	333	334		332	333	334
1960	356.5	161.3	195.2	1940	20.7	7.4	13.3
1959	314.1	126.9	187.2	1939	23.3	5.7	17.6
1958	329.6	126.7	202.9	1938	20.2	4.6	15.6
1957	305.2	112.7	192.5	1937	20.8	5.4	15.4
1956	248.2	98.7	149.5	1936	15.4	3.5	11.9
1955	211.9	90.8	121.1	1935	14.6	.4	14.2
1954	181.0	76.0	105.0	1934	12.9	.8	12.1
1953	161.7	70.9	90.8	1933	13.6	2.3	11.3
1952	141.3	58.3	83.0	1932	18.1	4.3	13.8
1951	125.4	53.2	72.2	1931	30.9	7.3	23.6
1950	113.0	47.3	65.7	1930	42.8	11.5	31.3
1949	114.7	51.3	63.4	1929	44.6	18.5	26.1
1948	103.6	46.0	57.6	1928	33.8	14.2	19.6
1947	81.3	35.3	46.0	1927	27.5	11.0	16.5
1946	44.6	25.8	18.8	1926	25.7	10.3	15.4
1945	23.0	12.0	11.0				
1944	12.9	2.3	10.6				
1943	10.4	1.2	9.2				
1942	19.8	1.6	18.2				
1941	22.4	1.6	20.8				

Series S335–343.　*Telephone industry, property, revenues, expenses, taxes, interest, employees and wages, 1911 to 1960*
(thousands of dollars, except series S342)

Year[1]	Cost of property and equipment	Revenues — Total	Revenues — Long distance	Expenses, taxes and interest — Total	Operating expenses	Taxes	Interest	Employees — Number	Salaries and wages
	335	336	337	338	339	340	341	342	343
1960	2,692,484	627,983	216,963	549,043	419,764	83,721	45,558	57,670	247,128
1959	2,444,577	582,263	200,080	509,727	396,720	75,528	37,479	58,826	240,691
1958	2,202,747	507,690	172,828	451,673	367,689	52,965	31,019	61,400	234,298
1957	1,941,592	467,702	159,542	412,158	334,427	51,262	26,469	64,074	219,693
1956	1,672,364	422,370	145,285	366,118	296,633	47,682	21,803	60,121	193,993
1955	1,470,679	376,717	127,228	328,881	265,200	43,902	19,779	55,673	173,923
1954	1,301,546	340,623	110,955	296,384	236,222	40,664	19,498	51,929	159,329
1953	1,152,310	310,834	100,694	269,818	214,498	38,172	17,148	50,540	145,110
1952	1,027,528	279,002	91,316	244,506	193,248	37,069	14,189	48,207	131,371
1951	909,581	240,763	81,275	213,824	173,069	28,130	12,625	47,387	117,678
1950	806,826	198,823	69,583	178,194	151,158	15,542	11,494	45,396	102,093
1949	716,520	169,113	58,700	153,066	131,672	11,358	10,036	42,326	90,634
1948	615,942	150,533	51,676	131,570	111,272	11,667	8,631	38,851	77,498
1947	521,184	134,667	46,021	116,623	96,763	12,417	7,443	35,578	66,624
1946	454,215	120,675	41,487	105,751	83,638	14,770	7,343	33,170	54,147
1945	418,434	109,900	37,009	96,418	71,010	18,175	7,233	25,599	41,830
1944	401,863	101,082	31,978	87,739	64,889	15,592	7,258	21,978	37,261
1943	393,230	94,407	28,550	81,894	59,263	15,287	7,344	20,694	33,582
1942	386,164	87,057	24,057	75,222	55,507	12,403	7,312	20,360	31,580
1941	372,640	79,369	20,795	68,692	51,224	10,184	7,284	20,103	29,004
1940	359,454	72,008	17,648	62,267	47,688	7,140	7,439	18,696	27,147
1939	350,160	67,438	15,636	57,384	44,985	4,210	8,189	17,636	26,525
1938	342,227	64,749	14,734	55,231	43,628	4,050	7,553	17,925	26,020
1937	335,811	63,289	15,148	54,512	42,979	4,026	7,507	18,413	25,580
1936	330,048	59,771	13,667	51,938	40,507	3,643	7,788	17,775	23,366
1935	327,754	57,030	12,270	50,890	39,263	3,208	8,419	17,414	22,283
1934	331,187	57,380	12,540	50,989	38,678	3,640	8,671	17,291	21,168
1933	330,491	55,662	11,343	50,022	37,812	2,848	9,362	18,796	21,276
1932	333,169	60,685	12,356	55,344	43,295	2,882	9,167	21,354	24,116
1931	333,055	66,807	14,933	60,067	48,919	2,609	8,539	23,825	28,493
1930	319,101	69,420	16,501	61,886	51,848	2,258	7,780	26,575	32,086
1929	291,589	65,241	16,516	56,560	47,635	2,096	6,829	27,459	31,672
1928	263,202	61,791	15,019	51,543	—	—	—	24,373	28,501
1927	243,999	56,907	13,232	48,562	—	—	—	23,437	26,255
1926	227,156	50,523	11,789	38,141	—	—	—	23,083	25,219
1925	210,536	47,234	10,928	35,567	—	—	—	21,831	19,106
1924	193,884	44,323	10,183	33,616	—	—	—	21,685	18,293
1923	179,002	42,133	10,230	32,390	—	—	—	21,002	18,182
1922	167,333	39,559	9,650	29,966	—	—	—	19,321	17,306
1921	158,678	36,987	9,376	30,080	—	—	—	19,943	19,000
1920	144,561	33,474	8,655	28,044	—	—	—	21,187	17,294
1919[1]	125,017	29,401	7,386	20,081	—	—	—	20,491	15,775
1918[1]	104,369	22,753	5,655	13,645	—	—	—	17,336	10,411
1917	94,470	20,122	4,566	12,095	—	—	—	16,490	8,883
1916	88,520	18,594	4,024	11,147	—	—	—	15,247	7,853
1915	83,793	17,602	—	12,837	—	—	—	15,072	8,357
1914	80,258	17,297	—	12,882	—	—	—	16,799	8,250
1913	69,215	14,879	—	11,176	—	—	—	12,867	6,839
1912	56,888	12,274	—	9,095	—	—	—	12,783	2,660
1911	34,738	10,068	—	6,979	—	—	—	10,425	916

[1] Data as of 30 June or for years ending 30 June of the year given for 1911 to 1918; data as of 31 December or for years ending 31 December in 1919 and subsequent years.

Series S344–349.　*Telephone industry, long-distance rates between Montreal and selected cities, 1918 to 1960*
(rate for station-to-station, daytime, 3 minute call, in dollars)

Effective date	Between Montreal and — Ottawa	Toronto	Windsor	Halifax	Winnipeg	Vancouver
	344	345	346	347	348	349
6 November 1960	.80	1.70	2.10	2.00	2.75	3.50
1 June 1959	.80	1.70	2.10	2.00	2.85	3.65
1 December 1958	.80	1.70	2.10	2.00	2.95	4.40
15 May 1953	.80	1.75	2.30	2.00	2.95	4.40
22 July 1950	.80	1.75	2.30	1.75	3.00	4.70
1 September 1945	.65	1.75	2.30	1.75	3.00	4.70
10 July 1941	.65	1.75	2.30	1.75	3.25	5.75
1 April 1937	.65	1.75	2.30	1.80	3.75	6.75
1 September 1936	.65	1.90	2.85	1.80	3.75	6.75
1 January 1930	.65	1.90	2.85	2.05	4.00	8.00
1 February 1929	.70	1.95	3.05	2.05	4.00	8.00
21 April 1921	.70	2.05	3.25	3.20	7.05	14.50
20 November 1918	.70	2.05	3.25	3.20	7.10	14.60

Series S350–359. *Telegraph industry, telegraph statistics, 1912 to 1960*

(series S350–353 in thousands of dollars; series S354–359 in thousands of units)

Year[1]	Operating revenue	Operating expense	Non-transmission revenues	Cost of property and equipment	Total telegrams transmitted	Telegrams sent	Telegrams received from U.S.	Total cablegrams excluding duplication[2]	Cablegrams sent	Cablegrams received
	350	351	352	353	354	355	356	357	358	359
1960	58,546	45,538	28,523	267,379	16,257	13,726	1,820	2,663	1,199	933
1959	52,963	43,512	24,036	226,914	16,391	14,437	1,954	2,603	1,203	909
1958	47,634	39,909	19,445	199,289	17,296	15,375	1,921	2,500	1,154	909
1957	44,797	39,272	17,408	169,258	19,164	17,037	2,127	2,581	1,232	964
1956	40,720	33,689	14,067	149,954	20,381	18,150	2,231	2,430	1,151	939
1955	39,321	32,502	16,627	124,301	20,068	17,887	2,181	2,238	1,086	873
1954	38,204	33,204	6,453	118,272	19,806	17,763	2,143	2,106	1,000	831
1953	36,920	33,953	14,308	110,831	21,222	19,041	2,181	2,043	955	813
1952	33,094	31,617	11,462	100,221	21,614	19,513	2,101	1,934	887	777
1951	29,128	27,808	9,749	90,506	21,816	19,693	2,123	1,786	816	722
1950	23,922	22,546	7,722	82,296	20,478	18,520	1,958	1,688	748	663
1949	22,257	22,063	6,692	76,249	20,063	18,100	1,963	1,642	742	678
1948	19,423	20,292	5,627	71,121	19,013	16,970	2,043	1,580	743	702
1947	18,515	17,360	5,032	67,111	17,988	15,596	2,392	1,614	745	710
1946	17,998	16,029	4,826	63,910	18,442	16,222	2,220	1,846	845	812
1945	18,016	15,062	4,675	55,067	17,667	15,758	1,909	2,192	984	1,057
1944	16,986	14,405	4,403	53,674	16,445	14,805	1,640	2,325	982	1,225
1943	16,955	12,942	3,847	52,553	16,469	14,766	1,703	3,014	1,196	1,517
1942	14,826	11,925	3,059	49,193	15,422	13,661	1,761	2,832	1,150	1,327
1941	12,778	10,878	2,418	48,382	14,281	12,689	1,592	2,252	1,037	951
1940	10,923	9,625	2,118	47,476	12,732	11,261	1,471	1,657	832	662
1939	10,474	9,298	2,037	46,881	12,463	10,783	1,680	1,492	802	632
1938	10,611	9,400	2,039	46,366	12,814	11,220	1,594	1,404	699	612
1937	11,410	9,467	2,090	45,375	13,456	11,644	1,812	1,489	767	657
1936	10,379	8,710	1,797	43,709	12,735	11,002	1,733	1,392	730	631
1935	9,741	8,416	1,727	43,640	11,139	9,566	1,573	1,297	684	613
1934	9,973	8,436	2,515	41,950	10,546	8,992	1,554	1,691	891	819
1933	9,268	8,123	2,195	41,226	10,113	8,526	1,587	1,597	904	711
1932	9,381	9,020	1,949	41,082	10,496	9,096	1,400	1,514	853	653
1931	11,642	10,721	2,557	40,878	13,177	11,116	2,061	1,785	990	783
1930	14,265	11,791	3,181	50,520	15,527	12,991	2,536	2,053	1,143	893
1929	16,256	12,590	3,425	37,747	17,982	14,673	3,309	2,087	1,151	899
1928	14,741	11,647	2,647	31,953	16,857	13,619	3,238	2,242	1,286	957
1927	12,991	10,600	2,139	29,064	15,631	12,665	2,966	1,931	1,132	798
1926	12,143	10,166	1,899	26,444	14,935	12,199	2,736	1,733	1,019	714
1925	11,520	9,681	1,734	19,838	14,184	11,437	2,747	1,557	924	—
1924	10,930	9,604	1,556	19,537	15,461	10,813	4,648	1,507	866	—
1923	11,417	9,305	1,305	19,794	16,150	—[2]	—[2]	1,302	—[2]	—[2]
1922	11,019	9,846	1,802	—	15,271	—	—	1,182	—	—
1921	11,311	9,734	1,901	—	15,013	—	—	1,155	—	—
1920	11,337	9,590	1,853	—	15,590	—	—	1,162	—	—
1919[1]	9,499	7,813	1,486	—	14,200	—	—	935	—	—
1919[1]	8,812	6,901	1,204	—	13,096	—	—	869	—	—
1918	7,771	5,820	1,465	—	12,378	—	—	1,022	—	—
1917	7,273	4,940	998	—	11,818	—	—	1,085	—	—
1916	6,256	4,205	827	—	10,836	—	—	1,135	—	—
1915	5,536	4,129	817	—	9,952	—	—	977	—	—
1914	5,983	4,243	811	—	11,891	—	—	983	—	—
1913	6,095	4,034	589	—	11,177	—	—	878	—	—
1912	5,359	3,527	480	—	9,253	—	—	769	—	—

[1] From 1912 to 1919 data are for the year ending 30 June of the year given. Data for the year 1919 are also given on a calendar year basis as are all subsequent years.

[2] Totals only available prior to 1924.

SECTION T: INTERNAL TRADE AND SERVICE

M. C. URQUHART, *Queen's University*

The data of this section are in three parts. Series T1–96 contain statistics on retail trade, series T97–176 on wholesale trade and series T177–226 on service establishments. Data on external trade may be found in section F of this volume.

The published sources of data in this section are all publications of the Dominion Bureau of Statistics. Accordingly, in the following listing of published sources the name of the author, the Dominion Bureau of Statistics, is not repeated with each publication. Another shortcut in the listing is also followed. Until sometime in 1952, all the publications on trade and service used for this section, with the exception of those of the decennial census, were published in mimeographed form or by photo-offset process by the Dominion Bureau of Statistics and do not bear the imprint of the Queen's (King's) printer; beginning sometime in 1952, a large number of the publications, and shortly thereafter all of them, bear the imprint of the Queen's Printer. The name of the printer, therefore, has also been omitted except on decennial census publications. The list of sources, arranged mainly in the order in which they appear in the text, follows.

Dominion Bureau of Statistics, *Retail Trade*, annual (Ottawa), issue for 1960; *Retail Trade, 1930–1951 (Revisions to Intercensal Estimates)*, Reference Paper No. 56 (Ottawa, 1955); *A Decade of Retail Trade, 1923–1933* (Ottawa, 1935); *Retail Chain Stores*, annual since 1933 (Ottawa), various issues; *New Motor Vehicle Sales and Motor Vehicle Financing*, annual since 1935 (Ottawa), issues for 1960 and 1948; *Operating Results and Financial Structure, Retail Food Stores (Independent)*, periodic since 1938 (Ottawa), various issues; *Operating Results of Chain Food Stores*, biennial since 1947 (Ottawa), various issues; *Operating Results and Financial Structure, Retail Clothing Stores (Independent)*, periodic since 1938 (Ottawa), various issues; *Operating Results of Chain Clothing Stores*, biennial since 1947 (Ottawa), various issues; *Operating Results and Financial Structure, Retail Hardware, Furniture, Appliance, Radio and Television Stores (Independent)*, periodic since 1938 (Ottawa); *Operating Results of Chain Furniture Stores*, biennial since 1953 (Ottawa), issue for 1959; *Operating Results and Financial Structure of Filling Stations and Garages (Independent)*, periodic since 1938 (Ottawa), issues for 1959 and for individual years to which the data apply for 1938 to 1950; *Operating Results and Financial Structure of Independent General Stores*, periodic since 1952 (Ottawa), all issues; *Operating Results and Financial Structure, Independent Restaurants*, periodic since 1952 (Ottawa), all issues; *Operating Results and Financial Structure, Independent Fuel Dealers*, periodic since 1952 (Ottawa), all issues; *Operating Results and Financial Structure, Independent Drug Stores*, 1938 and periodic since 1952 (Ottawa), all issues; *Operating Results of Chain Drug Stores*, biennial since 1953 (Ottawa), issue for 1959; *Operating Results and Financial Structure Independent Jewellery Stores*, periodic since 1952 (Ottawa), all issues; *Operating Results and Financial Structure, Independent Tobacco Stores*, 1952, 1954 and 1956 (Ottawa), all issues; *Operating Results and Financial Structure, Miscellaneous Retail Stores*, periodic 1938 to 1950 (Ottawa), all issues; *Operating Results of Country General and Dry Goods Stores*, periodic 1938 to 1946 (Ottawa); *Operating Results of Chain Variety Stores*, biennial since 1953 (Ottawa), issue for 1959; *Wholesale Trade*, monthly since 1936 (Ottawa), various issues; *Wholesale Trade, 1949 (Revised Indexes)* (Ottawa, 1950); *Summary of Monthly Indexes of Wholesale Sales in Canada 1935–1943* (Ottawa, 1944); *Wholesale Trade in Canada and the Provinces, 1939* (Ottawa, 1940); *Farm Implement and Equipment Sales*, annual from 1936 (Ottawa), various issues throughout; *Operating Results of Food Wholesalers*, biennial, 1947 to 1957 (Ottawa); *Operating Results of Dry Goods, Piece Goods and Footwear Wholesalers*, biennial 1947 to 1957 (Ottawa); *Operating Results of Automotive Parts and Accessories Wholesalers*, biennial, 1953 to 1957 (Ottawa); *Operating Results of Hardware Wholesalers*, biennial, 1953 to 1957 (Ottawa); *Operating Results of Plumbing and Heating Supplies Wholesalers*, biennial, 1953 to 1957 (Ottawa); *Operating Results of Drug Wholesalers*, biennial, 1953 to 1957 (Ottawa); *Operating Results for Miscellaneous Wholesalers*, biennial, 1947 to 1951 (Ottawa); *Laundries, Cleaners and Dyers*, formerly *Power Laundries Cleaning and Dyeing Establishments*, annual (Ottawa), issues for 1960, 1939 and 1928; *Hotels*, annual since 1949 (Ottawa), issue for 1960; *Hotel Statistics, 1941* (Ottawa, 1943); *Census of Canada, 1931*, vol. XI, *Merchandising and Services, Part 2* (Ottawa, King's Printer, 1934); *Advertising Agencies, 1959* (Ottawa, 1961); *Motion Picture Theatres and Film Distributors, 1960* (Ottawa, 1962); *Motion Picture Theatres, Exhibitors and Distributors, 1955* (Ottawa, 1956).

Some of the tables on wholesale trade are based on unpublished portions of a paper prepared by J. C. Brearley and M. T. Segall of the Dominion Bureau of Statistics.

While little of the data of this section was taken directly from the publications of the decennial censuses of trade and services it is important to note these publications which contain much more detail than given in monthly, annual or periodic reports. These census publications are:

Dominion Bureau of Statistics, *Census of Canada, 1931*, vol. X, *Merchandising and Services, Part 1* (Ottawa, King's Printer, 1934) and vol. XI, *Merchandising and Services, Part 2* (Ottawa, King's Printer, 1934); D.B.S., *Census of Canada, 1941*, vol. X, *Merchandising and Services, Part I* (Ottawa, King's Printer, 1944) and vol. XI, *Merchandising and Services, Part II* (Ottawa, King's Printer, 1947); D.B.S., *Census of Canada, 1951*, vol. VII, *Distribution, Retail Trade* (Ottawa, Queen's Printer, 1954) and vol. VIII, *Distribution, Wholesale Trade, Services* (Ottawa, Queen's Printer, 1954).

In addition D.B.S., *Wholesale Trade Proper, 1958 and 1959* (Ottawa, Queen's Printer, 1961), contains data obtained in a survey of all businesses in wholesale trade proper.

General note

The collection of data on internal merchandising and services in Canada, in common with many countries, began at a relatively late date. A first attempt at obtaining such data was made by the Dominion Bureau of Statistics in 1924 to cover retail and wholesale trade in 1923. The list of establishments to whom questionnaires were mailed was based upon information collected in the decennial census of 1921 and enlarged from other sources (see the note for the decennial census of merchandising and services below). The number of returns received, however, was not sufficiently large to provide reliable results for the whole of retail and wholesale trade. No further attempt was made to collect internal trade data until the decennial census of 1931 though estimates of retail trade were later made for the period back to 1923 (see series T25–34).

Regular collection of data on wholesale and retail trade and on some services began for 1930. (Laundries and dry cleaning plants were covered earlier as noted below.) Basic to the collection of annual and monthly, retail and wholesale trade data are the complete censuses of merchandising and services taken in conjunction with the decennial population census since 1931.

The decennial census of merchandising and services is taken in two parts. At the time of the decennial Population Census enumeration, at the beginning of June in the census year, the census enumerators compile lists of wholesale, retail and service establishments in their census areas with relevant information for a later questionnaire survey. The lists prepared by census enumerators were supplemented, in 1931, by information from trade associations, trade directories, and other such sources and, in 1941, by information from the Wartime Prices and Trade Board. When the lists are complete, questionnaires are mailed to the businesses listed. The usual procedure of checking with delinquents by correspondence and, if necessary, through regional offices of the Bureau is followed in order to obtain as complete coverage as possible. The tabulations based on the returned questionnaires form benchmark data for the annual and monthly series. The years covered by the complete censuses are 1930, 1941 and 1951; a complete census for 1961 is also being taken. It has been noted already that the earlier attempt at a complete merchandising census for 1923, based on lists collected in the 1921 census, did not yield satisfactory results.

Annual figures on wholesale and retail sales have been prepared from data collected annually and/or monthly from samples, in the main, of wholesalers, independent retailers, most of the large department stores and chain stores. For chain stores the annual survey has been based on complete coverage from the beginning.

The annual surveys (as distinct from the complete census) were first taken for wholesale and retail trade and retail chain stores for 1933. At the same time data for 1931 and 1932 were obtained from the same respondents. Thereafter until 1939 such surveys were taken yearly. Monthly surveys on a sample basis of retail trade including department stores, chain stores and some independents began in the early nineteen-thirties; for wholesale trade, the monthly survey of a sample of wholesalers began in late 1934. The annual survey was distinct from the monthly survey, covered a larger sample, and in the case of retail trade obtained more information than gathered in the monthly reports which were confined to sales.

With the outbreak of war the annual surveys of both wholesale and retail trade were discontinued (except the complete annual survey of retail chain stores which was continued). Annual data were compiled from the monthly trade reports. Special efforts were made after the end of each year to complete the returns of all businesses in the monthly sample for that year, checking being done by correspondence and through the Bureau regional offices.

The system of obtaining annual intercensal sales data from monthly returns for both wholesale and retail trade was continued until 1957 for retail trade and 1960 for wholesale trade. In 1957 an annual survey of retail trade, as distinct from the monthly surveys, was begun again. In 1958 a complete census of wholesale trade proper, based on lists in the employers' index of the Unemployment Insurance Commission, was taken.

The size of the sample of independent retail stores was 3,000 for the monthly, 17,000 for the annual in 1935, 7,200 in 1945, 9,000 in 1955 and 10,000 in 1960. The sample of department stores has always taken in the larger department stores and has had a high proportion of coverage. Annual retail chain store sales are based on complete annual coverage though monthly sales are obtained from a sample. (The total number of retail stores in 1930 was 120,000; in 1941 it was 137,000; and in 1951 it was 152,000.) The number of wholesalers covered in the relevant surveys was 1,400 in 1955, and 400 in the nineteen-

forties; in 1935 it was 200 in the monthly survey and those with sales of over $100,000 in the annual survey.

For retail trade, the data obtained in the annual and monthly surveys have been used to estimate total retail sales by the application of the annual results to the data of census benchmark years. The method used was to chain from year to year. During the later nineteen-forties and nineteen-fifties, though not in the nineteen-thirties, adjustments were made to the annual sales to take account of births and deaths of retail stores, the deaths being obtained from a continuing group carried through from the last census and the births being obtained since 1946 from sample surveys in particular areas taken in connection with the Labour Force Survey. After a new complete census is taken the annual figures are revised back to the preceding census. (See D.B.S., *Retail Trade, 1930–1951* (*Revisions of Intercensal Estimates*), Reference Paper No. 56, pp. 10–11 for the method of revising the intercensal estimates 1931 to 1941 and 1941 to 1951.)

The wholesale series were not adjusted for births and deaths before 1951, though the sample was adjusted at times to take account of changes in the size of wholesalers' scale of operations. An estimate of total annual wholesale sales, apart from the complete census, has been available only for 1930 to 1939 and from 1951 onward. For 1939 to 1951 the annual series on wholesale sales are in the form of indexes, covering only some categories of wholesale trade, formed by linking each year to the preceding year; these indexes are available back to 1935. Revisions of intercensal data, based on new data of the latest census, have not been made, though data for 1952 to 1960 were revised after the complete census for 1958 was taken.

In addition to the foregoing data which, other than in decennial census years, relate mainly to sales, the Bureau has collected periodically, since 1938 for retail trade and since 1947 for wholesale trade, data on operating statistics and financial structure of samples of wholesale and retail concerns. The 1938 survey was taken with the regular annual census of retail trade. Since the end of the war these surveys have been taken mainly, though not invariably, biennially. They deal with employment, payrolls, costs of materials, trade margins, inventories, and the like. The sample sizes are given in the reports. These kinds of data are also collected in the biennial reports on chain stores, which began in 1947.

Trading concerns engaged in both wholesale and retail trade are classified according to the activity that is predominant. Those concerns for which more than 50 per cent of sales are retail are included with retail trade, those with more than 50 per cent of their sales in wholesale trade are included in wholesale trade. Business units are assigned, as a whole, to one group or another and sales of a particular concern are not split in accordance with the amounts that are wholesale or retail.

Retail sales include, in addition to the sales of retailers proper, sales of retail units, if a distinct entity, of businesses engaged in other activities. Thus retail sales branches of manufacturers are included, as are sales units of electrical utilities selling electrical appliances. The statistics do not include: door to door sales of any kind; retail sales of wholesalers and service establishments; retail sales by manufacturing bakeries, manufacturing dairies and purchasing co-operatives; sales of meals, beverages and tobacco by hotels; line elevator sales; retail sales of manufacturers other than through separate retail units; nor sales of businesses with more than 50 per cent of their receipts coming from repair work.

Annual wholesale sales are, in the main, for wholesalers proper though sales of petroleum products bulk tank stations and packing houses were included in the annual survey for 1930 to 1939. Trade by commission agents, brokers, assemblers, manufacturers' sales branches and the like are excluded except for census years.

Descriptions of the collection of data on services are given in the notes on individual tables in the remainder of the text, since methods differ somewhat among the services.

RETAIL TRADE (Series T1–96)

T1–24. Retail sales, by kind of business, 1930 to 1960

SOURCE: for 1959 and 1960, D.B.S., *Retail Trade, 1960*, table 5, pp. 10–11, except for series T3, which was provided directly by D.B.S., Industry and Merchandising Division; for 1930 to 1958, tabulation provided by D.B.S., Industry and Merchandising Division. The latter were in the main based upon *Retail Trade 1930–1951* (*Revisions to Intercensal Estimates*) for 1930 to 1951. However, series T3 alcoholic beverage outlets, and series T5 other food stores, which were included in series T24, all other retail, in the latter source, are shown separately and some gaps in other series have been filled by estimation. For 1951 to 1958 the data are based mainly on the estimates in *Retail Trade*, though alcoholic beverage outlets were not shown separately. Since 1954, series T3, T4 and T5 are given as one figure in *Retail Trade*.

See the general note to section T for the general method of obtaining these data.

For 1931 to 1940, sales of meat markets (series T4), garages and filling stations (series T10) and all other retail (series T24) were not given in *Retail Trade, 1931–1951*. Further, alcoholic beverage outlets (series T3) and other food stores (series T5) were included in all other retail (series T24). They were estimated by the Merchandising and Services Section, Industry and Merchandising Division of D.B.S. as follows:

To obtain meat market sales, 1931 to 1940, the ratio of meat store sales to sales of grocery and combination stores was calculated for each of the complete census years 1930 and 1941 and the arithmetic average taken. This average was then applied to the annual sales of grocery and combination stores, 1931 to 1940, to estimate meat store sales.

For garages and filling stations the ratios of their sales to new motor-vehicles sales were calculated for each of 1930 and 1941 and the arithmetic average taken. This average was applied to new motor-vehicle sales 1931 to 1940 to estimate garage and filling station sales for these years.

With the calculation of the above two series for 1931 to 1940, and with the total of retail sales being given, the figures for all other retail were calculated as a residual to fill in these years in the source table.

Sales of alcoholic beverage outlets were estimated by taking the ratio of sales of these outlets as shown in the complete censuses to the sales of outlets reporting annually to the Bureau in these census years. Intercensal estimates were made by applying the average ratio of the terminal years in each of the intercensal periods to the annual sales of alcoholic beverage outlets reporting to the Bureau. (These outlets do not include taverns, lounges and bars.)

Sales of other food stores (series T5) were calculated in two parts. The sales of other food chains were taken from the annual survey of chain stores. For other independent food stores the ratio of their sales to the entire all other retail item was calculated for the census years. The average of these ratios is applied to the entire all other retail group.

The estimates in series T1–24 cover sales of independent stores, retail chain stores and department stores. For retail sales not included see the general note to section T.

The following notes are largely word for word from *Retail Trade, 1960* and *Retail Trade, 1930–1951*.

T2. Grocery and combination stores (groceries and meat) include all such stores whose sales are not more than 85 per cent fresh meat.

T3. Alcoholic beverage outlets include government liquor stores, brewers' retail stores, and wine stores. Beverage sales by grocery stores in Quebec are not included.

T4. Meat markets, to remain in this classification, must not sell more than 15 per cent grocery items. Since 1954 this item is grouped with other food stores and alcoholic beverage outlets in the published sources.

T5. Other food stores include candy and nut stores, confectionary stores, dairy products stores, fruit and vegetable stores, fish markets, specialty food stores and the like.

T6. General stores, usually located in rural areas, sell over 33 per cent groceries.

T7. Department stores include mail order sales. This class does not include large departmentalized clothing stores which sell no durable goods such as furniture and appliances. For the distinction of department stores, which may have more than one outlet, from chain stores see the note to series T35–52.

T8. Variety stores sell a low-price range of goods, on a cash and carry basis. They are mainly chain stores once known as 5 and 10 cent stores.

T9. Motor-vehicle dealers include (1) authorized dealers (20 per cent or more new car sales) (2) motor-vehicle dealers with wholesale car departments (3) motor-vehicle dealers selling farm implements. Used car dealers are not included.

T10. Garages and service stations must not have repair work in excess of 50 per cent of total sales.

T11. Men's clothing stores includes men's and boys' clothing and furnishing stores, hat stores and custom tailors.

T12. Family clothing stores sell mainly men's, women's, children's and infants' clothing and may handle other dry goods not in excess of 50 per cent of their sales.

T13. Women's clothing stores do not include furriers, millinery shops and infant specialty stores all of which are included in series T24.

T14. Shoe stores include men's, women's and family shoe stores.

T15. Hardware stores include regular hardware stores and in addition some hardware stores that sell significant amounts of farm implements.

T16. Lumber and building material dealers may also sell fuel to a maximum of 50 per cent of sales but do not include specialized dealers, such as roofing suppliers, where lumber is not sold.

T17. Furniture stores include those selling at least 67 per cent furniture and also those where undertaking is part of the business but does not account for more than 50 per cent of receipts. This category was merged with series T18 in 1955 owing to the large appliance sales being made by furniture stores.

T18. Appliance and radio stores include specialty stores with more than 67 per cent sales in these commodities and also combination furniture and appliance stores other than those included in series T17. See also the note to series T17.

T19. Restaurants include eating places where people sit down, and fish and chip shops. Excluded are refreshment booths and stands, caterers, cocktail lounges and taverns.

T20. Fuel dealers include general fuel dealers as well as those selling only fuel oil mainly for household consumption. Specialized ice dealers are not included.

T21. Drug stores include those both with and without soda fountain.

T22. Jewellery stores sell mainly jewellery, silverware, time pieces and may sell additional lines such as luggage, gifts and novelties. Repairs must not exceed 50 per cent of total trade.

T23. Tobacco stores must sell more than 50 per cent tobacco products but may have a substantial newsstand business. Tobacco stores since 1955 are included in series T24.

T24. All other retail contains such major trades as farm implement dealers, farm supplies including feed and seed, used cars, tobacco stores beginning in 1955 and stores that are excluded from series T2–23 owing to not meeting the specifications for classification in these series. For example, women's millinery stores, infant specialty stores, specialized roofing dealers, specialized ice dealers and the like are included here.

T25–34. Retail sales, by kind of business, 1923 to 1933

SOURCE: D.B.S., *A Decade of Retail Trade, 1923–1933*, table 28, pp. 26–7.

The data of these series were calculated in the Bureau in 1934 and 1935. The figures for 1930 were taken from the complete census for that year. Those for 1931 to 1933 were estimated from the survey of a sample of retail stores for 1933 which also covered sales of these stores for 1931 and 1932 (see the general note to section T) and which was the first of the annual censuses of retail trade. Data for the period 1923 to 1929 were estimated in a variety of ways which are described in the notes to each series. See the source for the description of methods on which the following notes are based.

The kinds of retail trade covered are the same as for series T1–24 though the classifications differ (see the notes to T1–24 and the general note to section T).

T26. Food group includes grocery and combination stores, meat markets and some, but not all, of the stores included in other food stores (series T5). The method of calculating sales from 1923 to 1929 was to construct an index of food sales for 1923 to 1930 from the value of food products manufactured in Canada adjusted for exports and imports and then to apply this index to 1930 sales, taken from the census, to obtain dollar sales from 1923 to 1929.

T27. Country general stores roughly correspond to the classification general stores (series T6) and are located in centres of less than 10,000 population. The method used for estimating sales for 1923 to 1929 is not completely clear in the source. A number of series to which country store sales were related were used to construct sales indexes for individual provinces which were applied to the provincial sales in 1930 and totals then taken. The series used included gross agricultural revenue, trends of mail-order sales, and amounts of money orders paid which appeared related to mail-order sales. The results of the census of merchandising for 1923 were also used as a check, since country general stores were covered more fully in this census than were other groups.

T28. General merchandising group includes department stores and mail-order houses, general merchandise stores, and variety (5 and 10 cent) stores. The department store and mail-order sales make up by far the largest part of the group. Department store and mail-order sales were available for a very large proportion of stores from 1925 to 1933 and for some stores as far back as 1923 in evidence given before the select committee of the House of Commons on mass buying, a committee which was succeeded by the Royal Commission on Price Spreads, appointed in 1934. These data were used to estimate department store and mail-order sales prior to 1930. The sales of general merchandise stores, which amounted to 20 million dollars in 1930, were estimated by using the index of department store sales for 1923 to 1930. Variety store sales before 1930 were worked out on the basis of data in evidence given before the Royal Commission on Price Spreads. Sales of dry goods stores were estimated in the same manner as for the clothing group (see the note to series T30).

T29. Automotive group largely corresponds to motor-vehicle dealers and garages and filling stations, series T9 and T10.

Sales of new motor vehicles 1923 to 1930 were estimated from motor-vehicle registrations. Garage and filling stations sales were estimated from the apparent consumption of gasoline. It is not clear in the source whether indexes of new car sales and of gasoline sales were separately applied to separate 1930 census figures of the relevant sales or whether a combined index of sales 1923 to 1930 was first constructed and then applied to the total sales, in 1930, of the automotive group.

T30. Apparel group includes men's and women's specialty stores and shoe stores. An index of sales of this group for 1923 to 1930 was calculated by adding imports to domestic production and subtracting exports. This index was then applied to the 1930 census figure to obtain estimates for 1923 to 1929.

T31. Building materials group includes hardware stores, establishments selling lumber and building materials, electrical and plumbing shops and paint and glass stores. Sales of hardware in 1930 were 71 million dollars and of lumber and building materials 76 million dollars out of the total of 162 million dollars. Sales of hardware stores were carried back from 1930 to 1923 on the basis of available indexes of hardware store sales obtained from trade journals. The remainder was carried back from 1930 on the basis of revenue freight of lumber unloaded in each province.

T32. Furniture and household group includes as its main categories furniture and house furnishings stores, household appliance stores and radio and music stores. It appears from the source that separate indexes for 1923 to 1930 were calculated for furniture and house furnishing stores on one hand and household appliance and radio and music stores on the other. These indexes were obtained by adding imports to domestic production and subtracting exports. They were then applied to the 1930 census figures for the group to get dollar sales from 1923 to 1929.

T33. Restaurants and eating places cover the same activities as those of restaurants, series T19. The data for 1923 to 1929 were obtained by applying the index of sales in the food group to restaurant sales in 1930, province by province.

T34. Other retail stores include farm implement and farm supply dealers, coal and wood yards, drug stores, news dealers and tobacco stands, office appliance dealers, government and other liquor stores and some others. Liquor store sales, available in D.B.S. reports on *The Control and Sale of Liquor in Canada*, were used to estimate the liquor store sales for 1923 to 1929. Available figures for sales of farm implements were used to carry the 1930 figures of farm implement sales back to 1923. Partial figures on the amount of coal used for domestic purposes were used to carry sales of coal and wood yards back to 1923. For the remainder of the group an index, made up from production plus imports less exports for tobacco, jewellery and books and stationery, was applied to the 1930 figure to obtain sales for 1923 to 1929. Checks for some of the items were possible from material of the census for 1923.

T35–52. Retail sales, by kind of business, and number of chains and stores, chain stores, 1930 to 1960

SOURCE: D.B.S., *Retail Chain Stores*, various issues, generally from table 1 and tables 3 or 4.

A retail chain store is defined as 'an organization operating four or more retail stores in similar and related kinds of business under the same ownership' (*Retail Chain Stores, 1960*, p. 5). Chain department stores are not included as the various member stores frequently do their own buying or are operated under less central control than the regular chain stores. Voluntary groups or chains, which are made up of independent stores affiliated with suppliers for purchasing or for other reasons, are also not included.

The classifications are the same as those used for total retail trade, series T1–24.

In addition to sales figures given here the reports include data on numbers employed (in earlier years), salaries and wages, inventories and accounts outstanding at year end. These data are given for various classes of chain stores.

T53–60.　Retail sales, by province, 1923 to 1960

SOURCE: for 1930 to 1960, D.B.S., *Retail Trade, 1960*, table 1, p. 7; for 1923 to 1933, D.B.S., *A Decade of Retail Trade, 1923–1933*, table 29, pp. 26–7. See also *Retail Trade of Canada, 1930–1951*.

Movements of sales within provinces are based upon data in the decennial censuses and the annual sample returns from each province. Adjustments to intercensal estimates are made whenever a new census appears. Sales of mail-order houses in 1930 were attributed to the province in which the store was located. In 1941, mail-order sales made through local ordering offices were attributed to the province in which the office was located but mail-order sales arising from orders sent in directly by customers were attributed to the province in which the store was located. In 1951 all mail-order sales were allocated to the province of the customer. In the revision of intercensal data from 1941 to 1951 adjustments were made to put the data on the 1951 basis (see D.B.S., *Retail Trade, 1930–1951*, p. 11) but apparently no adjustment was made for 1930 to 1941. The provincial data are carried forward from 1951 on the 1951 census basis.

For methods of allocating sales to provinces in 1923 to 1929 see D.B.S., *A Decade of Retail Trade, 1923–1933*. The division of sales among provinces in 1930 provided the main basis for the division in earlier years.

See the general note to section T for kinds of retail sales included and excluded.

T61–66.　Retail sales of new motor vehicles, 1932 to 1960

SOURCE: for 1946 to 1960, D.B.S., *New Motor Vehicle Sales and Motor Vehicle Financing, 1960*, table 1, p. 8; for 1932 to 1945, D.B.S., *New Motor Vehicle Sales and Motor Vehicle Financing, 1948*, table 4, p. 7.

The annual data of retail sales, given in the annual reports, are summaries of monthly data which were collected by the Bureau beginning in 1932. The data were collected from Canadian manufacturers and assemblers, who reported their dealer sales monthly, and in the case of foreign-made cars, until the war, from head offices of companies abroad on their exports to Canada. Since the war the information on foreign cars has increasingly come from importers and Canadian distributing centres; from 1955 onward the reports stated that all Canadian sales of foreign vehicles are obtained from direct importers of foreign cars.

Until 1954 the retail value was stated as being the price paid by the individual purchaser at the Canadian point of manufacture including sales and excise taxes charges, the cost of standard accessories, dealers' commissions and the like. Duty was included in the case of imported vehicles as well as the items noted for Canadian-made cars. Freight charges from the factory or from the importer to place of purchase were excluded on both foreign and domestic vehicles. Beginning with 1955 it is stated that the data on Canadian-made cars are consolidated totals of dealers' monthly statements on sales to customers, collected by the manufacturers; the basis of valuation remains the same as that used before 1955.

T63 and 64. Passenger cars include all sales of such vehicles even if they are used for business purposes. For example, automobiles used by taxi companies are included.

T65 and 66. Commercial vehicles include both buses and trucks.

The source gives separate data for British and European vehicles. It also includes statements on motor-vehicle financing.

T67–96.　Retail trade, gross profit margins by kind of business, 1938 to 1960

SOURCE: for independent stores: series T67–71, for 1954 to 1960, D.B.S., *Operating Results and Financial Structure, Retail Food Stores, 1960*, tables 1, 6, 11, 16 and 21, for 1938 to 1952, same title but for the year 1952, p. K-8; series T72–79, for 1954 to 1960, D.B.S., *Operating Results and Financial Structure, Retail Clothing Stores, 1960*, tables 1, 9, 16 and 23, for 1941 to 1950, same title but for the year 1952, p. L-8, for 1938, D.B.S., *Operating Results of Independent Clothing and Shoe Stores in Canada, 1938*, pp. 2–3; series T80–85, for 1952 to 1959, D.B.S., *Operating Results and Financial Structure, Retail Hardware, Furniture, Appliance, Radio and Television Stores, 1959*, tables 1, 9 and 15, for 1948 and 1950 same title (word 'television' omitted), but for year 1950, pp. M10, M15 and M17, for 1938 to 1948, same title but for 1948, p. 11; series T86–87, for 1952 to 1959, D.B.S., *Operating Results and Financial Structure of Filling Stations and Garages, 1959*, tables 1 and 6, for 1938 to 1950, individual reports of the same title but for the particular year to which the data apply; series T88, for 1954 to 1960, D.B.S., *Operating Results and Financial Structure Independent General Stores, 1960*, table 1, p. 4, for 1950 and 1952, same title but for 1952, pp. O1–9, for 1945 to 1948, D.B.S., *Operating Results and Financial Structure, Miscellaneous Retail Stores, 1948*, table 1, p. 12, for earlier years, *Operating Results of Country General and Dry Goods Stores*; series T89–96, for 1952 and later years, D.B.S., separately published reports for each category under the general title *Operating Results and Financial Structure*, with the following subtitles: *Independent Restaurants, 1959*, *Independent Fuel Dealers, 1959*, *Independent Drug Stores, 1959*, *Independent Jewellery Stores, 1959*, and *Independent Tobacco Stores, 1956*, for 1938 to 1950, D.B.S., *Operating Results and Financial Structure, Miscellaneous Retail Stores*, reports for the years to which the data apply; for chain stores: series T67–69, D.B.S., *Operating Results of Chain Food Stores, 1959*, table 3, p. 7, table 5, p. 9, same title for 1957, table 8, p. H14, same title for 1947, table 1, p. 12; series T73–79, D.B.S., *Operating Results of Chain Clothing Stores, 1959*; series T83, D.B.S., *Operating Results of Chain Furniture Stores, 1959*, table 1, p. 4; series T93, *Operating Results of Chain Drug Stores, 1959*, table 1, p. 4.

See the general note to section T for a description of the manner in which these data are obtained.

In 1952 a sample of 17,000 independent stores (originally selected in 1944) was being canvassed and about 10,000 useable returns were being obtained (see D.B.S., *History, Function, Organization* (Ottawa, D.B.S., 1952), pp. 76–7). The numbers reporting in the various categories are given in the reports.

The data on retail chain stores, for the years covered, were obtained at the same time that the annual survey was taken.

Gross profit margin is the ratio of the difference between net sales and cost of goods sold to net sales. Cost of goods sold is obtained by adding the beginning inventory to net purchases of goods and deducting the ending inventory.

The gross profit margins of chain variety stores (which did not fit in with any category of independent stores) as a percentage of net sales from 1947 to 1959 were as follows.

Gross profit margins, chain variety stores, 1947 to 1959
(per cent of net sales)

Year	Gross profit margin	Year	Gross profit margin
1959	38.7	1951	37.8
1957	38.6	1949	37.5
1955	38.3	1947	37.7
1953	37.8		

SOURCE: D.B.S., *Operating Results of Chain Variety Stores, 1959*, table 1, p. 4.

The reports also give details of operating costs and balance sheet data by size classes for the various categories of stores.

WHOLESALE TRADE (Series T97–176)

T97–115. Estimated annual wholesale sales, by kind of trade, 1951 to 1960

SOURCE: for 1951 to 1958, D.B.S., *Wholesale Trade, May 1961*, pp. 2–3; for 1959 and 1960, D.B.S., *Wholesale Trade, December 1961*, p. 3.

Following the decennial census of 1951, the sample of wholesalers covered monthly was increased from 400 to 1,400 and an attempt was made to cover all types of wholesalers proper. The sample was chosen from three size classes within each trade, based on the 1951 census. The trends given by the sample are applied to expenditures by various categories obtained in the 1951 decennial census of distribution to yield estimates of total annual sales. The estimates first appeared in D.B.S., *Wholesale Trade, September and October 1955, Annual 1951–1954*. For 1951 to 1957 revised estimates were published in *Wholesale Trade, December 1958*, the revisions taking into account firms entering and leaving the various trades during 1952 to 1957 (see p. 1 of the December 1958 issue). The data were further revised after the comprehensive survey of wholesale trade for 1958 was completed and the revised estimates, which are those given here, appeared in the source.

The surveys cover wholesalers proper who are described as middlemen between the producer and retailer or producer and business, industrial or institutional user. They hold inventories and buy and sell on their own account. Not included are agents and brokers, manufacturers' sales branches, assemblers of primary products, petroleum bulk stations and certain other types of operations not included in the survey but usually considered to perform wholesale functions. (See D.B.S., *Wholesale Trade, September and October, 1955, Annual, 1951–54*.)

The nature of each trade group is described in the last cited reference as being ascertainable readily from its title with the exception of series T115, all other trades. This last group is described as including motor vehicle and grain firms, classified as wholesalers, and firms engaged in one or more of such trade lines as 'sporting goods, toys, beer and ale, books, household and office furniture, industrial chemicals, metal goods, scrap metal, rubber goods, used machinery, leather, livestock, livestock feeds, scientific equipment, optical goods, etc.' (p. 2). The classification by kind of trade is mainly that of the 1951 census. For a description of the census classification see D.B.S., *Census of Canada, 1951*, vol. VIII, *Wholesale Trade, Services*, appendix B.

See also the general note to section T.

T116–125. Index numbers of wholesale trade, by kind of business, 1930 to 1953

SOURCE: for 1950 to 1953, the index was calculated as the arithmetic average of the monthly indexes given in D.B.S., *Wholesale Trade*, monthly issues to the end of 1954; for 1941 to 1949, D.B.S., *Wholesale Trade, 1949 (Revised Indexes)*, table 2, p. B9; for 1935 to 1940, D.B.S., *Summary Monthly Indexes of Wholesale Sales in Canada, 1935–1943*; for 1930 to 1937 (basis 1930 = 100), D.B.S., *Wholesale Trade in Canada and the Provinces, 1939*, tables 1 and 2, pp. 5–7. The method noted above of obtaining the indexes for 1950 to 1953 was that used by the Bureau for 1935 to 1949.

The indexes for 1935 to 1953 were obtained as averages of monthly indexes based on the monthly surveys of a sample of wholesalers. The sample size was 200 from 1935 to 1939, became 300 in 1940 and 400 from 1944 to the end of the period covered. These indexes are for wholesalers proper (see the note to series T97–115 and the general note to section T). Only nine trades are covered and the index of total sales is based on these nine trades only. The index of trade for each month was obtained by linking with the same month a year earlier on the basis of reported sales for each of the two months.

These estimates provide the only data on annual sales available for 1940 to 1950. They have not been revised on the basis of information in the decennial censuses of 1941 and 1951.

The indexes for 1930 to 1937 (basis 1930 = 100) are from the annual survey of wholesale trade, which was conducted from 1933 to 1939, and from the decennial census of 1930. The annual survey was based on a larger sample than the monthly survey. It covered all branches of wholesale trade proper and in addition petroleum bulk tank stations and meat packing plant wholesale outlets. A classification similar to that of the 1930 census but somewhat different from that of the monthly survey was used. For this table, items were selected to correspond as closely as possible to the categories of the monthly survey. The index for all kinds of business, series T116, has a considerably wider coverage than that obtained from the monthly survey.

The types of business covered in the monthly survey are best described by reference to the classification of wholesale trade by kinds of business, given in the 1930 census of wholesale trade (D.B.S., *Census of Canada, 1931*, vol. XI, *Merchandising and Services, Part II*, p. 483). The figures in brackets in the following descriptions are those attached to the descriptions in the foregoing reference. A statement of what is included in the monthly indexes is given in D.B.S., *Current Trends in Wholesale Trade* (Ottawa, mimeographed, 1936) and in the indexes based on annual surveys in D.B.S., *Wholesale Trade in Canada and the Provinces, 1933*.

T117. Grocery trade includes groceries (general line) (48) but not specialty grocers for 1935 to 1953. For 1930 to 1937 (basis 1930 = 100) it may also contain food and grocery specialties (49).

T118. Fruit and vegetable trade includes fruits and vegetables, fresh (40) and includes wholesalers who may carry other lines of food produce but with fruits and vegetables predominating.

T119. Tobacco and confectionery include tobacco and tobacco products (general line, except leaf) (78), which contains tobacco and confectionery as a sub-category. For 1930 to 1937 (basis 1930 = 100) confectionery and soft drinks (35) is also included.

T120. Clothing includes clothing and furnishings, other than millinery and footwear (14). This covers men's, women's and children's clothing and furnishings including specialty shops. For 1930 to 1937 (basis 1930 = 100) millinery (17) and footwear (20) are also included.

T121. Dry goods trade includes dry goods (15 and 16) and piece goods of all kinds (19). For 1930 to 1937 (basis 1930 = 100) it also includes notions (18).

T122. Footwear includes shoes and other footwear (20). For 1930 to 1937 (basis 1930 = 100) this category is not shown separately but is included with clothing, series T120.

T123. Auto parts and equipment trade includes automotive equipment (accessories, radios, garage equipment and supplies and the like) (4) and automobile parts new and used (5). It does not include tires.

T124. Hardware includes general and specialty trade (50 and 51).

T125. Drugs trade includes drugs and drug sundries, general line (8) and drugs and drug sundries, specialty (9). For 1930 and 1937 (basis 1930 = 100) it also includes alcoholic beverage (10) and toilet articles and preparations (11).

The annual reports for 1933 to 1939 contain estimates of total sales in dollar terms as well as the indexes.

T126–138. Wholesale sales, by kind of business and type of operation, 1930, 1941 and 1951

SOURCE: for all series J. C. Brearley and M. S. Segall, 'Wholesale Trade in Canada, 1930–1951', an unpublished manuscript of which a somewhat different version, without these tables, appeared in Edward J. Fox and David S. R. Leighton, *Marketing in Canada* (Homewood, Illinois, Richard D. Irwin, 1958).

The data in this table include only the categories in which the largest values of sales were found. There were smaller amounts in a number of other categories. For total sales by the various categories of outlets and for sales of petroleum bulk tank stations see series T 139–152.

The content of the various kinds of business and the nature of type of operation in the 1951 census may be found in D.B.S., *Census of Canada, 1951*, vol. VIII, *Distribution, Wholesale Trade, Services*, appendix B and appendix A respectively. See also table 3 in the same volume.

T 126. Groceries and food specialties include groceries, general line, and such grocery specialties as canned foods, sugar, coffee, tea, cocoa, spices and the like.

T 127. Other food and tobacco include confectionery, soft drinks and tobacco, dairy and poultry products, fish and sea foods, frozen or frosted foods, fresh fruits and vegetables, meats and meat products and other foods except groceries.

T 128. Farm products include grain as a major item, livestock, hides, skins, wool and raw furs, flowers and nursery stock and other farm raw materials.

T 129. Chemicals, drugs and allied products are industrial chemicals, drugs and drug sundries, soaps and toilet preparations and other chemicals and allied products.

T 130. Dry goods and apparel are clothing and personal furnishings of all kinds including millinery and shoes, dry goods, piece goods and notions.

T 131. Furniture and house furnishings include household and office furniture, household furnishings of all kinds, china, glassware, crockery and pottery and musical instruments and sheet music.

T 132. Automotive includes motor vehicles, automotive parts and accessories, tires and tubes and other automotive equipment.

T 133. Electrical goods include electrical merchandise, general line, household appliances, radio and television sets, wiring supplies and construction materials and electrical apparatus and equipment.

T 134. Lumber and building materials include lumber and millwork, general construction materials, glass, paints, varnishes, lacquers and enamels, wallpaper, insulation, siding and roofing materials and the like.

T 135. Paper and paper products include newsprint, fine papers of all kinds, wrapping paper and bags and, in general, all purely paper items.

T 136. Hardware includes general and specialty hardware lines.

T 137. Machinery, equipment and supplies include commercial, industrial, farm, professional, service and sundry other machinery, equipment and supplies.

T 138. Metal and metalwork include both iron and steel and nonferrous metals and metalwork.

Export merchants are included. The export trade is particularly important, for agents and brokers, in farm products and in paper and paper products; it is particularly important for manufacturers' sales branches in lumber and building materials, paper and paper products and metal and metal works.

T 139–152. Wholesale trade, by major type of operation, 1930, 1941 and 1951

SOURCE: Brearley and Segall, 'Wholesale Trade in Canada, 1930–1951', table 3, p. 6 (see also the source to series T 126–138).

A description of the nature of the various categories of wholesale outlets may be found in D.B.S., *Census of Canada, 1941*,

vol. XI, pp. xxii to xvii. See also D.B.S., *Census of Canada, 1951*, vol. VIII, appendix B.

T 141 and 142. Wholesalers proper have been described (see the note to series T 97–115). They include separately incorporated selling organizations which are subsidiaries of manufacturing companies and sell the products of the parent company.

T 143 and 144. Manufacturers' sales branches operate as distinctive units separate from the manufacturing plant but not incorporated as subsidiaries.

T 145 and 146. Agents and brokers engage in the purchase and sale of commodities on behalf of others; they do not buy or sell outright for their own account but do their business for commissions or fees. The total value of the sales arranged by agents and brokers is given and not just their commissions.

T 147 and 148. Petroleum bulk tank stations are wholesale depots from which petroleum products, chiefly gasoline and oil, are distributed by tank wagon to retailers, industrial users, distributors, jobbers, farmers and others. The larger numbers of these stations are owned by refining companies and operated like manufacturers' sales branches under various arrangements but there are also some independent stations.

T 149 and 150. Assemblers of primary products buy farm products, fish, furs and forest products. They may buy outright, the more common practice, or act on a commission basis for a dealer. Some buyers operate very much like regular wholesalers except that they buy from primary producers. Co-operative marketing associations and sales agencies are included. Independent country grain elevator companies, line grain elevator companies and co-operative grain elevator companies are an important part of this group. In 1941 and 1951 the values included for grain elevator companies were purchases from farmers; in 1930 the value was sales of the elevator companies. Assemblers of fish products and fruit and vegetables are included but not fishermen or growers of fruits and vegetables who do their own packing.

T 151 and 152. Other types cover mainly warehouses which perform the functions of both storage and distribution. The sale of goods must account for at least 50 per cent of the revenue of these warehouses. Film exchanges which distribute motion picture films to exhibitors are also included here. In 1941 some government crown corporations engaged in accumulation, storage and sale of commodities particularly required for the war effort were also included.

T 153–166. Wholesale trade, farm implement and equipment sales, by kind, 1936 to 1960

SOURCE: D.B.S., *Farm Implement and Equipment Sales*, annual from 1936 to 1960, tables in various issues on 'Farm Implement and Equipment Sales, by major Groups, Canada' and on 'Sales of Repair Parts by Provinces'. A summary for 1936 to 1943 appears in D.B.S., *Sale of Farm Implements and Equipment in Canada, 1936–43*. The tables were entitled somewhat differently in earlier years and in some instances it was necessary to go to the more detailed tables.

These data are obtained from reports of farm implement manufacturers and importers. They give sales in the Canadian market and hence do not include value of exports of Canadian manufacturers. Duplications that might arise from importers selling to manufacturers, who in turn sell to dealers, are eliminated. Values are at wholesale prices to dealers less any discounts granted.

A number of changes in groupings and classification have occurred over the years. The groupings used in this table are those given in the report for 1957 and since. In 1957 tractor loaders were transferred from series T 158 to series T 160. Until 1948 attachments for implements were given separately and have been included in series T165 here. Beginning in 1949 attachments were included in the category of implements for which they were sold. This change in classification probably explains most of the drop in series T165 between 1948 and 1949. For years before 1957 some items have been added together to give the 1957 groupings.

Other changes have also occurred. Prior to 1957 some attempt had been made to obtain data from manufacturers with minor items of farm equipment as side lines. This practice was discontinued in 1957, since the amounts involved were small, the coverage of these other manufacturers was incomplete, and it was often difficult to determine if the sales were actually for farm use. This change would lead to some slight decline in coverage in minor lines and specially in 'other farm equipment' (series T165). Coverage of main line implements and equipment remains complete. In 1957 also, the number of units sold was changed to those sold by dealers rather than the sales of manufacturers, though the prices remained at the wholesale level. The information on numbers sold by dealers was obtained through manufacturers. Small specialty manufacturers were not able to provide this information and in their case the units sold are those disposed of by the manufacturers.

A detailed listing of the contents of the categories except for series T165 is too long to be included here. In any event the headings give a reasonable indication of content, and details may be found in any recent issue of *Farm Implement and Equipment Sales*. Other farm implements, series T165, include wagon unloaders, silo unloaders, power-driven post-hole diggers, land levellers, pull-type ditchers, poultry farm equipment, metal grain storage bins and sundry other.

Used farm machinery, motor trucks for farm use and binder twine are not included in the data of this table.

T167–176. Wholesale trade, gross profit margins by kind of business, biennially, 1947 to 1957

SOURCE: D.B.S., *Operating Results of Food Wholesalers*, biennially, 1947 to 1957, each issue, table on summary of results; D.B.S., *Operating Results of Automotive Parts and Accessories Wholesalers*, issues for 1953, 1955 and 1957, table 1; D.B.S., *Operating Results of Hardware Wholesalers*, issues for 1953, 1955, 1957, table 1; D.B.S., *Operating Results of Plumbing and Heating Supplies Wholesalers*, issues for 1953, 1955 and 1957, table 1; D.B.S., *Operating Results of Drug Wholesalers*, issues for 1953, 1955, 1957, table 1; D.B.S., *Operating Results of Miscellaneous Wholesalers*, issues for 1947, table 1, p. 9, issue for 1949, p. E7 and issue for 1951, p. O7. The last-named publication contained data for wholesalers in automotive parts and accessories, hardware, plumbing and heating supplies and drugs, which became separate publications in 1953.

See the general note to section T concerning the collection of data on operating results of retail and wholesale firms and the note to series T67–96 for a definition of gross profit margins.

The surveys were made of all wholesalers proper in ten trades which, in 1941, accounted for 35 per cent of sales of all wholesalers proper. The ten trades covered were selected for their importance in the distribution of consumer goods to retailers and in most cases a very high proportion of sales was made to retailers; the piece goods trade was a notable exception, with the dominant sales being to other wholesalers and large users; and plumbing and heating supplies were sold predominantly to contractors. The companies covered for each trade included only those with a high proportion of their trade in the designated kind of business.

The operating ratios given in this table are for all wholesalers for whom tabulations were made. In addition, in each report, profit margins were given for identical firms in the year being covered and in the previous survey two years earlier. However, the number of identical firms changed between each pair of years for which comparisons were given and for this reason their profit margins are not given here.

Descriptions of the detailed content of the various trades are not given in the sources. The descriptions of the trades covered in series T116–125 given in the notes to those series probably indicate the nature of the trades covered.

These surveys were discontinued after 1957 and will not be conducted again until after the results of the 1961 decennial census of trade are known.

A good deal of additional information is given in the source. In general it is similar to that provided in kindred reports for retail trades (see the note to series T67–96). Some separate data are provided for incorporated companies only.

In 1953, 1955 and 1957, an additional trade 'Household Appliance and Electrical Supply' was added. The gross profit margins were 19.67 per cent in 1953, 18.67 per cent in 1955 and 18.93 per cent in 1957.

SERVICE ESTABLISHMENTS
(Series T177–226)

T177–186. Power laundries, cleaning and dyeing plants, operating statistics, 1917 to 1960

SOURCE: for 1930 to 1960, D.B.S., *Laundries, Cleaners and Dyers, 1960*, tables 5 and 13; for 1917 to 1929, D.B.S., *Power Laundries and Cleaning and Dyeing Establishments in Canada, 1939*, table 7, p. 12 and table 20, p. 32; for 1917 to 1926, D.B.S., *Report on the Dyeing, Cleaning and Laundry Industry in Canada, 1928*, p. 3.

These data were collected as a part of the annual census of manufacturers from 1917 to 1936; thereafter they were collected annually by the Internal Trade Branch of the Industry and Merchandising Division of D.B.S. The same procedures were used throughout. All businesses in these industries are covered.

See the general note to series Q1–137 for description of the meaning of series T177–180 and series T182–185. Series T181 and T186 are receipts for services performed for customers.

Cost of fuel and electricity is given also in each annual report but it is not given in the historical summaries. It is not included in series T180 and T185.

The data for 1917 to 1926 are not strictly comparable with those for later years. They were not given separately for laundries and dyeing and cleaning establishments. Dyeing and finishing of textile goods was included in those years but excluded in the data for 1927 to 1960: in 1927 the value of work done on dyeing and finishing textiles was 2,871 thousand dollars; in 1928 it was 3,074 thousand dollars. Employees in 1917 to 1926 included outside piece workers. Finally in 1921 to 1924 considerable numbers of hand laundries were included, affecting mainly the number of establishments.

T187–203. Statistics of hotels, 1930, 1941 and 1949 to 1960

SOURCE: for 1949 to 1960, series T187, 188 and 199–203 from D.B.S., *Hotels, 1960*, p. 7, for series T189–198 from each individual issue of *Hotels* for the year concerned, various tables; for 1941, all data from D.B.S., *Hotel Statistics, 1941*, table 1, p. 4; for 1930, all data from D.B.S., *Census of Canada, 1931*, vol. XI, pp. 1,237–9.

Data on hotels have been collected in the decennial census, 1931 and 1941, and annually since 1949. All hotels are covered in each year. For the way in which lists of such establishments are obtained in decennial census years see the general note to section T. The lists collected in the decennial census are supplemented by lists of licensed hotels provided by provincial governments.

The data cover full year hotels and seasonal hotels. A full year hotel is one that operated for at least ten months in the year. To be classified as a hotel an establishment must have six or more rooms and provide lodging or lodging and board to transient guests. For seasonal hotels generally the establishment must have six or more rooms in the main lodge but an exception is made in the case of resort hotels where sleeping accommodation is in cabins or cottages but central dining room, entertainment and administrative facilities are provided in the main lodge. Seasonal hotels include such businesses as resort hotels, hunting or fishing lodges, ski lodges or chalets and dude ranches. (See D.B.S., *Hotels, 1960*, p. 4.) The data do not cover motels at all or tourist camps, cabins or other forms of accommodation not meeting the above requirement. Nor are public houses in Ontario included for 1949 to 1960 although they are included in the earlier decennial census figures. Seasonal hotels typically have accounted for about 5 per cent of receipts of all hotels and between 15 and 20 per cent of the rooms.

A number of changes through the years have affected the comparability of the data from year to year though probably not seriously. These changes are indicated in the footnotes but one of them needs special mention. The change in measuring occupancy rates between 1955 and 1956 makes it appear that occupancy increased in 1956. This apparent result is caused by the fact that the small hotels with 10 rooms or less had very low occupancy rates, 24 per cent in 1955 as against rates that gradually increased by size of hotel to 75 per cent for hotels with more than 500 rooms. The removal of hotels with 10 rooms or less from the calculation of occupancy rates in 1956 explains fully the apparent increase in the rate in 1956.

The principal operating expenses given as a percentage of total receipts (series T 191–198) do not cover all expenses. There are, in addition, costs such as taxes, depreciation, rent and sundry other expenses.

Receipts from all other sources (series T 203) include sales of newsstands, tobacco stands and such ancilliary operations.

T 203–212. Statistics of advertising agencies in Canada, 1941 and 1946 to 1960

SOURCE: D.B.S., *Advertising Agencies, 1960*, table 1, p. 2.

The decennial census survey of advertising agencies in 1941 and the annual surveys since 1944 cover all businesses in this particular field.

The data are collected on the basis of business units and not by establishments.

These data pertain to businesses whose main activity is placing advertising in various media, principally publications, television or radio, on a commission or fee basis. Some market surveys and research and production work may be done but printing or other production work is usually contracted out to other firms. Business concerns whose activities are confined to preparing advertising copy, commercial art or other production work are not included.

T 206. Commissionable billings include advertising outlay for space or time and production costs. From 80 to 85 per cent has been for advertising outlay.

T 207. Other billings are for market surveys, research, production work done by the agencies themselves, and other fees. In 1960, of this item, $2,018 thousand was for production services.

T 209. Gross revenue on commissionable billings is the commissions received for placing advertising or letting out production work to other businesses.

T 210. Gross revenue from other billings is receipts obtained for the services described in the note to series T 207 and, since 1957, other revenue that cannot be separated.

The source gives, in addition, data on employees and their recompense, in total and by size distribution, classification of agencies by size of billings, distribution of billings among various media and the like.

Other data on advertising may be found in D.B.S., *Advertising Expenditures in Canada, 1954*, Reference Paper No. 67 (Ottawa, Queen's Printer, 1956) in which data collected largely from various advertising media are given. It contains considerable detail on revenue of different advertising media, internal cost of advertisers, advertising costs in various industries and the like.

T 213–226. Statistics of motion picture and drive-in theatres, 1930 to 1960

SOURCE: for 1940 to 1960, D.B.S., *Motion Picture Theatres and Film Distributors, 1960*, table 1, p. 7 and table 9, p. 12; for 1930 to 1939, D.B.S., *Motion Picture-theatres, Exhibitors and Distributors, 1955*, table 1, p. R-7.

A census of all motion picture theatres was first taken with the decennial census of 1931 for the year 1930. An annual census covering all such theatres has been taken regularly since 1933. The original list of motion picture theatres was obtained by the population census enumerators in 1931 (see the general note to section T). Since then lists of licensed operators are obtained each year from the various provincial licensing authorities.

The data for 1948 to 1960 are for regular motion picture theatres and drive-in theatres. They do not cover itinerant operators who show pictures in halls or community enterprises, such as churches, lodges, boards of trade and the like which show pictures in community halls on a nonprofit basis. Prior to 1948, data for community enterprises are included. The Bureau ceased collecting information for itinerant operators and community enterprises in 1957.

The data are collected on an establishment basis.

T 214–216 and 221–223. Employment figures and salaries and wages do not include working proprietors of unincorporated businesses whether they received a stated salary or not. Nor do they include members of proprietors' families employed in the business but not receiving stated salaries. There were 1,088 working proprietors of unincorporated concerns and unpaid family workers in 1960. Employment figures are averages for the year.

These data before 1948 are not much affected by the inclusion of community enterprises since members of the latter frequently donate their services free of charge.

T 218 and 225. Receipts from admissions are what the theatres receive and do not include amusement taxes. Revenue from sales of candy, drinks, cigarettes and the like, from rental revenue of vending machines, from revenue for showing commercial films and from other sources provide additional receipts. Such revenue amounted to $11,678 thousand in 1960.

The source also gives data on seating capacity, average utilization of capacity, size of projection equipment, working proprietors and family members, provincial breakdowns of many of these data and the like. They also include statements on itinerant operators until 1956, on community enterprises, 1949 to 1956, and on film exchanges.

Material in other sections of this volume related to trade and service may be found in section C on the labour force in distribution and services, in section D on total wages and salaries by industry, in section E on distribution of national product by industry, in section F on external trade, in section J on prices, in section L on domestic disappearance of certain agricultural foodstuffs, in section P on sales of electricity and in section S on expenditure for transportation.

Series T1–24. *Retail sales, by kind of business, 1930 to 1960*
(millions of dollars)

Year[1]	Total sales	Grocery and combination stores	Alcoholic beverage outlets	Meat markets	Other food stores	General stores	Department stores	Variety stores	Motor vehicle outlets	Garages and filling stations	Men's clothing stores	Family clothing stores
	1	**2**	**3**	**4**	**5**	**6**	**7**	**8**	**9**	**10**	**11**	**12**
1960	16,502	3,474	808	447		640	1,453	350	2,551	1,145	259	235
1959	16,284	3,287	731	446		630	1,420	331	2,613	1,104	250	226
1958	15,444	3,126	684	435		625	1,345	315	2,414	1,037	238	227
1957	14,826	2,894	652	430		595	1,282	296	2,483	939	235	218
1956	14,298	2,639	649	395		568	1,242	274	2,542	822	230	215
1955	13,112	2,430	573	377		530	1,150	250	2,370	718	214	200
1954	12,066	2,279	532	154	238	515	1,062	234	2,029	632	207	191
1953	12,128	2,133	536	151	238	521	1,027	224	2,285	556	214	209
1952	11,533	2,041	516	162	226	541	991	214	2,096	507	212	210
1951	10,694	1,905	476	176	229	525	910	196	1,884	479	203	192
1950	9,617	1,615	396	165	243	480	880	175	1,505	459	175	174
1949[1]	8,532	1,474	381	162	229	483	860	168	994	451	175	168
1948	7,835	1,368	364	156	232	455	796	159	803	415	167	165
1947	6,963	1,176	352	152	221	424	699	139	725	362	156	153
1946	5,787	999	327	129	205	377	606	127	475	240	138	135
1945	4,573	849	277	110	179	324	510	113	240	109	115	111
1944	4,093	768	217	102	104	298	460	104	201	94	105	100
1943	3,786	707	191	96	164	274	420	99	180	89	98	94
1942	3,619	663	177	92	155	245	419	98	217	116	96	88
1941	3,415	567	145	80	139	215	378	85	360	205	80	74
1940	2,935	469	119	68	124	194	327	70	340	189	68	61
1939	2,578	404	103	60	120	183	291	59	294	160	60	51
1938	2,530	396	97	60	122	187	280	54	302	153	59	47
1937	2,593	398	94	62	120	189	289	53	326	170	64	51
1936	2,289	352	83	57	115	173	274	47	254	130	59	47
1935	2,105	327	73	54	116	161	259	43	212	106	55	43
1934	1,984	317	74	54	117	155	254	40	175	85	51	39
1933	1,773	317	70	56	107	137	242	37	127	61	44	32
1932	1,908	316	85	57	128	144	254	40	133	63	47	32
1931	2,305	361	109	67	171	168	313	44	184	85	59	37
1930	2,736	405	127	78	181	208	355	44	252	114	72	42

Year[1]	Women's clothing stores	Shoe stores	Hardware stores	Lumber and building material dealers	Furniture stores	Appliance and radio stores	Restaurants	Fuel dealers	Drug stores	Jewellery stores	Tobacco stores	All other retail
	13	**14**	**15**	**16**	**17**	**18**	**19**	**20**	**21**	**22**	**23**	**24**
1960	277	169	326	436	547		569	324	416	134	1,971	
1959	273	155	326	492	582		567	342	405	137	1,967	
1958	265	146	318	482	566		543	326	383	133	1,838	
1957	257	136	302	458	567		528	322	358	131	1,743	
1956	247	129	291	483	584		508	312	329	131	1,706	
1955	225	123	256	451	541		468	268	300	124	1,545	
1954	221	121	247	406	194	292	453	250	282	116	87	1,325
1953	219	122	249	417	195	284	474	225	282	121	88	1,358
1952	210	118	232	369	188	258	468	235	267	115	86	1,270
1951	193	112	228	359	148	211	438	233	249	105	79	1,164
1950	166	103	221	348	142	193	390	220	223	99	71	1,175
1949	186	104	213	277	134	169	364	201	212	91	76	961
1948	171	97	199	251	135	139	330	196	197	84	74	880
1947	143	91	180	206	131	120	298	171	179	81	71	737
1946	129	82	156	143	112	80	270	144	168	82	62	603
1945	111	69	104	100	79	37	232	137	148	71	65	482
1944	102	62	89	97	69	31	216	131	138	60	59	427
1943	94	57	85	84	62	33	196	138	128	52	56	393
1942	87	54	81	82	66	42	158	123	115	44	49	352
1941	71	44	73	80	64	46	127	99	101	38	43	301
1940	55	34	65	66	57	43	87	87	84	32	36	260
1939	40	30	59	53	46	35	69	83	76	25	31	248
1938	35	30	59	49	44	35	71	77	74	23	30	246
1937	40	32	58	51	48	37	78	80	74	24	30	226
1936	34	30	53	45	38	32	66	77	67	21	26	210
1935	29	28	49	38	33	30	55	73	63	19	24	214
1934	29	27	47	36	29	26	49	72	61	17	23	207
1933	24	26	43	29	23	23	40	70	57	15	22	172
1932	28	27	47	35	26	28	46	71	64	16	24	197
1931	41	32	59	48	35	40	61	76	71	21	27	196
1930	49	36	71	66	41	53	75	86	77	27	31	245

[1] Includes Newfoundland beginning in 1949.

Series T 25–34. *Retail sales, by kind of business, 1923 to 1933*
(millions of dollars)

Year	Total sales	Food group	Country general stores	General merchandise group	Automotive group	Apparel group	Building materials group	Furniture and household group	Restaurants and eating places	Other retail stores
	25	26	27	28	29	30	31	32	33	34
1933	1,777	431	151	313	218	147	83	51	42	341
1932	1,917	461	159	331	235	156	96	59	48	374
1931	2,326	534	185	401	298	189	129	82	62	444
1930	2,756	615	229	452	382	220	162	102	76	518
1929	3,158	668	259	495	488	268	207	120	83	570
1928	3,036	640	261	482	420	266	220	105	79	561
1927	2,783	609	255	444	366	244	207	92	75	490
1926	2,568	560	242	410	333	228	192	83	69	449
1925	2,304	514	229	380	241	205	177	73	64	421
1924	2,139	492	210	354	205	196	158	69	61	395
1923	2,179	500	205	344	222	203	168	71	62	405

Series T 35–52. *Retail sales, by kind of business, and number of chains and stores, chain stores, 1930 to 1960*
(series T 35–36 in numbers; series T 37–52 in millions of dollars)

Year[4]	Number of chains	Average number of stores	Sales of all chain stores	Grocery and combination stores	Meat markets	Variety stores	Men's and boys' clothing stores	Family clothing stores	Women's apparel and accessories stores
	35	36	37	38	39	40	41	42	43
1960	537	9,954	3,468	1,603	10	298	29	65	84
1959	507	9,491	3,280	1,481	8	283	30	50	81
1958	509	9,122	3,073	1,369	8	264	29	45	78
1957	493	8,822	2,842	1,242	8	247	28	40	71
1956	499	8,559	2,647	1,096	8	229	29	36	67
1955	496	8,274	2,354	963	8	208	27	33	62
1954	491	8,136	2,147	863	7	194	25	32	55
1953	466	7,835	2,048	773	6	188	25	36	49
1952	476	7,766	1,925	702	7	180	25	36	46
1951[4]	488	7,846	1,776	610	7	164	25	40	41
1950	423	7,155	1,560	505	6	148	20	36	39
1949	381	6,839	1,420	434	6	142	18	34	37
1948	403	6,821	1,336	387	7	134	18	34	35
1947	422	6,716	1,177	302	8	118	17	30	29
1946	422	6,559	1,015	238	7	108	13	24	23
1945	429	6,580	876	214	7	96	11	20	19
1944	431	6,560	770	199	6	86	10	18	17
1943	444	6,780	704	180	6	84	10	17	15
1942	455	7,010	687	188	5	84	8	15	14
1941	529	7,622	639	172	5	74	9	14	12
1940	451	7,131	509	141	4	61	7	10	8
1939	446	7,215	432	124	4	51	6	9	6
1938	457	7,356	414	117	5	47	7	8	6
1937	447	7,346	414	116	5	46	7	9	6
1936	457	7,588	395	107	4	41	7	9	6
1935	445	7,666	364	101	4	38	7	8	5
1934	445	7,804	347	101	4	36	6	7	5
1933	461	7,900	329	99	5	33	5	7	4
1932	486	8,066	361	104	5	35	6	4	5
1931	506	8,188	434	117	6	39	8	4	7
1930	518	8,097	487	119	8	39	10	5	9

Series T 35–52. *Retail sales, by kind of business, and number of chains and stores, chain stores, 1930 to 1960 (continuation)*
(series T 35–36 in numbers; series T 37–52 in millions of dollars)

Year[4]	Shoe stores	Hardware stores	Lumber and building material dealers	Furniture stores	Household appliance, radio and music stores	Restaurants	Drug stores	Tobacco stores and stands	Other chain stores
	44	**45**	**46**	**47**	**48**	**49**	**50**	**51**	**52**
1960	77	49	95	49	64	41	55	—[3]	949
1959	70	49	103	54	73	41	53	—[3]	904
1958	64	43	107	52	76	38	50	—[3]	850
1957	58	39	97	53	74	36	45	—[3]	804
1956	53	37	100	55	78	36	41	16	766
1955	48	20	92	48	69	35	37	15	689
1954	45	18	84	38	59	34	36	16	641
1953	43	14	91	44	53	34	35	17	640
1952	42	13	82	43	52	32	33	17	615
1951[4]	38	12	75	37	42	29	31	17	608
1950	33	11	67	36	36	23	29	16	555
1949	32	9	59	35	29	21	27	16	521
1948	31	8	56	36	27	22	27	16	498
1947	29	6	51	33	23	21	27	15	499
1946	26	6	44	22	17	21	26	14	426
1945	24	5	39	18	12	20	24	13	354
1944	21	5	37	16	9	20	23	11	292
1943	20	4	31	14	10	19	22	10	262
1942	19	4	25	14	13	16	20	8	254
1941	16	4	22	15	19	12	19	7	239
1940	12	5	17	10	15	8	16	7	188
1939	11	5	14	5	3[1]	7	14	6	167
1938	10	5	13	5	3[1]	7	14	6	161
1937	10	5	13	5	3[1]	7	14	6	162
1936	9	5	13	4	2[1]	7	13	6	162
1935	8	4	11	5	2[1]	7	12	6	146
1934	8	4	11	5	—[2]	7	12	6	135
1933	7	3	10	4	1[1]	7	11	5	128
1932	7	3	11	5	9	8	13	6	140
1931	8	4	13	8	12	11	14	7	176
1930	8	4	19	9	17	13	14	8	205

[1] Includes radio and music stores only.
[2] Figure withheld to prevent disclosure of individual operation.
[3] Included with other chain stores.
[4] Includes Newfoundland beginning in 1951.

Series T53–60. *Retail sales, by province, 1923 to 1960*
(millions of dollars)

Year	Total for Canada[1]	Atlantic[1] Provinces	Quebec	Ontario	Manitoba	Saskatchewan	Alberta	British Columbia[2]
	53	54	55	56	57	58	59	60
From Retail Trade								
1960	16,502	1,430	3,944	6,313	842	938	1,366	1,668
1959	16,284	1,362	3,878	6,218	813	951	1,355	1,707
1958	15,444	1,290	3,647	5,934	754	914	1,275	1,631
1957	14,826	1,234	3,521	5,663	726	855	1,211	1,616
1956	14,298	1,211	3,322	5,499	700	812	1,159	1,594
1955	13,112	1,127	3,006	5,115	669	748	1,035	1,412
1954	12,066	1,025	2,798	4,634	637	758	964	1,249
1953	12,128	1,018	2,756	4,616	677	845	987	1,228
1952	11,532	982	2,635	4,383	651	764	939	1,177
1951	10,693	899	2,443	4,130	610	659	854	1,100
1950	9,617	822	2,183	3,715	567	571	777	982
1949	8,532	734	1,872	3,294	523	538	697	874
1948	7,835	607	1,792	3,067	466	473	611	818
1947	6,963	564	1,621	2,721	407	410	504	737
1946	5,787	491	1,342	2,265	338	341	416	594
1945	4,573	387	1,081	1,774	269	279	329	455
1944	4,093	351	976	1,574	243	249	296	404
1943	3,786	319	913	1,488	220	219	266	362
1942	3,619	301	876	1,447	206	201	243	346
1941	3,415	279	820	1,388	193	189	228	318
1940	2,935	235	683	1,191	182	174	198	273
1939	2,578	196	602	1,039	166	154	180	242
1938	2,530	188	598	1,026	164	136	177	240
1937	2,593	199	605	1,068	165	136	165	255
1936	2,289	170	518	941	150	138	147	225
1935	2,105	157	473	875	139	124	137	200
1934	1,984	147	454	833	131	115	125	179
1933	1,773	129	419	735	121	103	109	157
1932	1,908	140	462	783	131	112	115	165
1931	2,305	172	558	945	153	133	134	210
1930	2,736	197	646	1,091	188	188	175	251
From A Decade of Retail Trade								
1933	1,777	131	421	737	120	104	108	155
1932	1,917	141	465	787	131	113	116	104
1931	2,326	173	562	951	155	138	137	210
1930	2,756	198	651	1,100	189	189	177	252
1929	3,158	215	722	1,250	227	244	216	284
1928	3,036	199	674	1,186	229	265	215	267
1927	2,783	185	625	1,081	211	246	188	247
1926	2,568	174	576	998	196	227	168	229
1925	2,304	160	515	901	180	194	148	205
1924	2,139	153	485	850	163	160	135	191
1923	2,179	157	495	863	165	173	134	192

[1] Includes Newfoundland beginning in 1949.　　[2] Includes Yukon and the Northwest Territories.

Series T61–66. *Retail sales of new motor vehicles, 1932 to 1960*
(values in millions of dollars)

Year[1]	Total vehicles Number	Total vehicles Value	Passenger cars Number	Passenger cars Value	Commercial vehicles Number	Commercial vehicles Value
	61	62	63	64	65	66
1960	523,188	1,575	447,771	1,289	75,417	286
1959	502,626	1,540	425,038	1,241	77,588	299
1958	444,769	1,365	376,723	1,111	68,046	255
1957	458,299	1,369	382,023	1,088	76,276	281
1956	499,921	1,455	408,233	1,129	91,688	327
1955	465,678	1,256	386,962	1,023	78,716	233
1954	382,628	990	310,546	798	72,082	192
1953	462,526	1,162	359,172	900	103,354	263
1952	400,777	1,004	292,095	725	108,682	278
1951	385,648	950	275,686	683	109,962	267
1950	429,695	886	324,903	662	104,792	224
1949[1]	286,341	589	202,318	412	84,023	176
1948	221,300	439	145,655	283	75,645	156
1947	230,255	416	159,205	283	71,050	133
1946	120,044	193	77,742	120	42,302	73
1945	24,356	—	4,526	—	19,830	—
1944	11,670	—	2,156	—	9,514	—
1943	4,798	8	984	1	3,814	6
1942	30,356	43	17,286	24	13,070	19
1941	118,073	152	83,642	109	34,431	43
1940	130,552	149	101,789	115	28,763	34
1939	114,747	126	90,054	97	24,693	29
1938	121,165	135	95,751	105	25,414	30
1937	144,441	149	114,275	117	30,166	32
1936	113,314	118	92,287	95	21,027	22
1935	101,461	102	83,242	83	18,219	18
1934	73,358	76	61,503	64	11,855	12
1933	45,332	45	39,568	40	5,764	6
1932	45,870	45	38,621	39	7,249	6

[1] Includes Newfoundland beginning 1 April 1949.

Series T67–96. *Retail trade, gross profit margins by kind of business, 1938 to 1960*
(per cent of net sales)

	Retail food stores					Retail clothing stores							
						Men's clothing stores		Women's clothing stores		Family clothing stores		Family shoe stores	
Year	Grocery stores	Combination stores	Meat markets	Fruit and vegetable stores	Confectionery stores	Unincorporated	Incorporated	Unincorporated	Incorporated	Unincorporated	Incorporated	Unincorporated	Incorporated
	67	**68**	**69**	**70**	**71**	**72**	**73**	**74**	**75**	**76**	**77**	**78**	**79**
	Independent stores												
1960	15.35	15.36	20.25	19.67	19.91	28.8	31.5	29.9	32.5	26.6	30.5	30.0	34.1
1959	—	—	—	—	—	—	—	—	—	—	—	—	—
1958	15.07	15.07	19.07	19.00	19.15	28.6	30.9	28.8	31.9	27.1	30.6	29.3	33.2
1956	14.76	15.40	19.61	19.39	18.98	28.2	30.8	28.3	31.8	26.5	30.3	29.4	33.5
1954	14.38	15.09	18.90	18.42	17.57	27.0	29.8	27.4	31.2	25.9	29.5	27.8	31.5
1952	13.88	14.50	17.78	17.74	18.93	26.4	29.2	26.8	29.8	24.5	29.7	27.2	30.1
1950	14.4	14.9	16.1	17.5	18.2	26.8	29.8	26.8	29.0	24.4	29.6	27.4	32.0
1948	14.0	14.6	16.6	17.5	19.1	25.9	28.6	25.8	28.5	23.4	28.8	26.6	32.1
1946	14.3	15.1	17.2	16.1	18.9	26.9	30.5	27.1	29.2	23.8	29.3	26.8	31.8
1945	14.1	14.9	16.9	16.0	20.7	27.5	31.5	27.7	30.5	24.8	29.1	27.3	31.9
1944	14.2	15.2	17.1	16.4	19.5	27.2	—	27.9	—	24.3	—	27.6	—
1941	15.2	16.9	—	—	—	27.7	—	27.5	—	—	—	26.3	—
1938	16.0	17.4	22.4	—	—	28.7	—	29.7	—	27.1	—	29.8	—
	Chain stores[1]												
1959	16.5	17.9	—	—	—	—	35.7	—	34.6	—	32.6	—	35.9
1957	15.5	17.4	20.2	—	—	—	32.1	—	34.4	—	33.0	—	34.0
1955	16.0	16.5	18.8	—	—	—	31.0	—	32.7	—	33.4	—	33.0
1953	15.0	—	—	—	—	—	30.9	—	31.5	—	31.0	—	31.6
1951	15.5	15.8	15.8	—	—	—	28.8	—	28.3	—	28.8	—	31.6
1949	16.0	15.6	17.6	—	—	—	29.1	—	29.4	—	30.2	—	30.8
1947	16.8	16.0	20.5	—	—	—	30.0	—	31.0	—	26.4	—	30.8

	Hardware, furniture, appliance stores						Other retail outlets										
	Hardware stores		Furniture stores		Appliance, radio and television stores						Fuel dealers		Drug stores		Jewellery stores		
Year	Unincorporated	Incorporated	Unincorporated	Incorporated	Unincorporated	Incorporated	Filling stations	Garages	General stores	Restaurants	Unincorporated	Incorporated	Unincorporated	Incorporated	Unincorporated	Incorporated	Tobacco stores
	80	**81**	**82**	**83**	**84**	**85**	**86**	**87**	**88**	**89**	**90**	**91**	**92**	**93**	**94**	**95**	**96**
	Independent stores																
1960	—	—	—	—	—	—	—	—	15.4	—	—	—	—	—	—	—	—
1959	27.0	27.9	27.2	26.3	29.7	25.3	22.3	33.2	—	40.3	22.4	23.7	31.6	33.0	42.0	41.1	—
1958	—	—	—	—	—	—	—	—	14.8	—	—	—	—	—	—	—	—
1956	25.8	26.9	26.1	28.0	25.6	25.5	20.8	33.6	14.8	40.8	21.1	22.1	30.3	32.8	40.8	44.2	18.7
1954	25.8	27.0	26.9	28.2	26.1	26.4	20.8	30.6	15.2	37.7	23.0	22.4	29.8	32.1	40.2	43.5	18.3
1952	25.9	27.3	27.8	—	26.4	—	20.1	29.9	14.9	38.9	20.4	22.0	29.1	34.1	39.5	41.8	16.5
1950	25.8	27.0	27.1	—	27.8	—	18.7	27.8	14.5	38.7	20.6	20.2	28.9	33.4	38.8	41.7	17.6
1948	24.7	26.2	26.7	—	27.4	—	19.0	26.2	15.1	37.1	20.4	19.9	28.4	33.1	39.1	40.8	16.5
1946	23.7	—	26.7	—	29.2	—	18.2	27.7	15.5	37.2	21.1	—	27.0	32.2	37.1	—	15.6
1945	24.6	—	28.0	—	36.4	—	17.9	27.9	15.4	36.8	20.1	—	27.2	33.9	38.6	39.8	15.9
1944	25.7	—	29.9	—	35.2	—	16.5	26.7	14.7	—	20.7	—	25.9	—	41.3	—	17.3
1941	25.7	—	—	—	—	—	17.2	—	16.0	35.8	21.2	—	27.4	—	38.9	—	—
1938	25.6	—	33.5	—	—	—	21.6	33.1	16.1	40.2	21.1	—	29.8	—	40.2	—	21.5
	Chain stores[1]																
1959	—	—	—	36.1	—	—	—	—	—	—	—	—	—	33.9	—	—	—
1957	—	—	—	36.7	—	—	—	—	—	—	—	—	—	34.4	—	—	—
1955	—	—	—	33.5	—	—	—	—	—	—	—	—	—	34.9	—	—	—
1953	—	—	—	31.8	—	—	—	—	—	—	—	—	—	33.8	—	—	—
1951	—	—	—	30.7	—	—	—	—	—	—	—	—	—	33.7	—	—	—
1949	—	—	—	35.1	—	—	—	—	—	—	—	—	—	33.3	—	—	—
1947	—	—	—	32.6	—	—	—	—	—	—	—	—	—	34.2	—	—	—

[1] See text for gross profit margins of chain variety stores.

Series T 97–115. *Estimated annual wholesale sales, by kind of trade, 1951 to 1960*

(millions of dollars)

Year	Total, all trades	Fresh fruits and vegetables	Groceries and food specialties	Meat and dairy products	Clothing and furnishings	Footwear	Other textile and clothing accessories	Coal and coke	Drugs and drug sundries	Newsprint, paper and products
	97	98	99	100	101	102	103	104	105	106
1960	8,764	288	1,650	165	116	38	205	154	222	276
1959	8,752	280	1,545	171	120	37	212	156	217	263
1958	7,906	264	1,385	175	124	34	215	164	199	242
1957	7,692	237	1,264	152	117	31	201	183	185	252
1956	7,672	238	1,158	146	114	31	199	189	174	253
1955	6,767	230	1,079	138	109	31	185	162	163	232
1954	6,033	221	1,011	150	98	28	175	160	151	217
1953	6,138	207	978	144	99	29	181	172	147	207
1952	5,971	214	952	140	95	30	183	193	139	202
1951	5,784	183	923	173	85	29	180	227	133	213

Year	Tobacco, confectionery, soft drinks	Auto parts and accessories	Commercial, institutional and service equipment and supplies	Construction materials and supplies, including lumber	Farm machinery	Hardware	Household electrical appliances	Industrial and transportation equipment and supplies	All other trades
	107	108	109	110	111	112	113	114	115
1960	741	415	137	878	73	327	183	748	2,149
1959	723	408	130	964	85	318	181	780	2,164
1958	679	364	109	825	69	309	166	709	1,876
1957	636	342	105	800	56	315	161	796	1,879
1956	585	338	105	799	69	320	165	805	1,985
1955	534	303	91	736	57	288	166	612	1,652
1954	508	270	84	603	51	265	149	488	1,407
1953	497	275	82	576	70	269	138	539	1,529
1952	500	266	76	523	72	259	125	530	1,473
1951	458	247	73	515	66	267	93	437	1,483

Series T 116–125. *Index numbers of wholesale trade, by kind of business, 1930 to 1953*

Year	All kinds of business	Grocery	Fruit and vegetable	Tobacco and confectionery	Clothing	Dry goods	Footwear	Auto parts and equipment	Hardware	Drugs
	116	117	118	119	120	121	122	123	124	125
				Annual averages of monthly indexes[1] *(1935–39 = 100)*						
1953	362.2	318.9	305.3	419.9	260.2	238.0	335.6	592.4	452.3	381.5
1952	362.5	314.7	329.1	428.9	263.0	243.3	438.9	567.2	446.9	371.4
1951	338.9	305.1	292.6	412.3	252.6	249.4	328.5	510.9	455.6	348.8
1950	306.6	274.6	272.8	395.2	247.2	246.1	283.2	429.1	396.4	312.4
1949	291.3	257.0	263.0	372.8	248.2	240.4	281.9	397.6	374.9	305.5
1948	283.2	254.0	237.2	354.8	265.1	264.7	286.8	379.9	359.7	281.8
1947	272.0	244.2	274.7	317.1	255.4	244.5	300.8	369.8	325.0	254.6
1946	244.0	208.9	291.2	296.9	229.3	197.5	279.4	334.0	277.4	245.2
1945	205.4	180.2	262.4	258.1	186.3	161.9	224.0	242.8	212.0	222.1
1944	186.0	169.3	222.0	230.1	183.1	165.9	188.8	197.2	183.8	201.9
1943	168.3	150.3	206.1	207.3	177.5	150.9	173.1	158.1	173.1	184.2
1942	156.2	146.5	158.5	172.4	170.9	160.2	161.0	147.6	170.0	165.7
1941	142.0	134.7	131.2	150.6	142.8	141.8	141.6	157.8	165.2	145.2
1940	120.7	116.2	116.2	130.6	121.1	116.5	124.2	135.3	131.9	122.7
1939	109.1	108.6	107.7	113.4	106.1	105.8	111.5	112.8	110.6	111.0
1938	101.6	101.1	103.4	106.4	95.9	96.1	93.7	106.5	103.4	104.1
1937	105.3	104.1	105.2	102.5	106.3	107.9	107.4	101.7	109.6	104.2
1936	95.6	96.3	96.0	91.0	97.7	97.4	97.0	94.5	93.9	93.5
1935	88.5	90.0	87.7	76.7	94.0	92.8	90.4	84.5	82.5	87.3
				Annual survey[1] *(1930 = 100)*						
1937	98.7	105.2	92.7	102.8	91.9	82.6	—	99.2	100.3	105.7
1936	86.2	97.3	84.0	90.3	85.3	74.8	—	88.7	85.0	95.2
1935	78.9	90.8	76.2	84.1	80.5	71.6	—	78.7	74.7	88.7
1934	74.7	87.8	72.9	77.3	75.8	70.3	—	73.1	70.1	83.4
1933	65.7	82.4	63.7	70.1	68.3	61.2	—	62.8	57.7	79.1
1932	68.7	79.4	70.1	76.5	72.4	63.0	—	64.9	59.4	85.2
1931	81.6	87.7	83.5	89.1	83.5	77.7	—	83.9	76.5	96.3
1930	100.0	100.0	100.0	100.0	100.0	100.0	—	100.0	100.0	100.0

[1] See the notes for differences in content of the annual survey and the annual averages based on monthly series.

Series T126–138. *Wholesale sales, by kind of business and type of operation, 1930, 1941 and 1951*

(millions of dollars)

Year	Groceries and food specialties	Other food and tobacco	Farm products	Chemicals, drugs and allied products	Dry goods and apparel	Furniture and house furnishings	Automotive	Electrical goods	Lumber and building materials	Paper and paper products	Hardware	Machinery, equipment and supplies	Metal and metalwork
	126	127	128	129	130	131	132	133	134	135	136	137	138
Wholesalers proper													
1951[1]	858	854	136	163	282	93	349	185	317	213	247	606	217
1941	347	404	150	94	126	28	69	44	118	140	112	208	111
1930	221	285	133	35	102	14	27	23	68	22	66	59	14
Manufacturers' sales branches													
1951[1]	323	274	—	259	274	30	316	408	303	327	16	465	428
1941	116	97	—	98	161	12	50	134	33	50	5	78	177
1930	97	85	—	36	56	11	75	112	34	25	6	57	51
Agents and brokers													
1951[1]	145	138	1,345	15	192	23	14	32	77	95	20	37	161
1941	102	83	364	20	117	15	20	8	29	5	12	43	38
1930	76	50	181	20	73	4	5	8	18	29	6	25	32
Assemblers													
1951[1]	—	—	1,160	—	—	—	—	—	—	—	—	—	—
1941	—	—	368	—	—	—	—	—	—	—	—	—	—
1930	—	—	328	—	—	—	—	—	—	—	—	—	—

[1] Includes Newfoundland.

Series T139–152. *Wholesale trade, by major type of operation, 1930, 1941 and 1951*

(sales in millions of dollars)

Year	All types		Wholesalers proper		Manufacturers' sales branches		Agents and brokers		Petroleum bulk tank stations		Assemblers of primary products		Other types	
	Number	Sales	Number	Sales	Number	Sales	Number	Sales	Number	Sales	Number	Sales	Number	Sales
	139	140	141	142	143	144	145	146	147	148	149	150	151	152
1951[1]	26,157	14,376	10,465	5,453	2,713	3,810	1,741	2,494	3,880	1,020	7,177	1,518	165	82
1941	24,489	5,235	9,417	2,358	1,622	1,207	2,106	908	3,973	216	7,366	453	5	93[2]
1930	18,576	3,141	5,137	1,255	1,546	755	1,798	572	3,602	185	6,482	374	11	—[2]

[1] Includes Newfoundland.   [2] Less than one million dollars.

Series T153–166. *Wholesale trade, farm implement and equipment sales, by kind, 1936 to 1960*

(thousands of dollars)

Year[1]	All types of machinery	Tractors and engines	Ploughs	Tilling, cultivating and weeding machinery	Planting, seeding and fertilizing machinery	Haying machinery	Harvesting machinery	Machines for preparing crops for market or for use	Farm wagons, wagon trucks and sleighs	Barn equipment	Dairy machinery and equipment	Spraying and dusting equipment	Other farm equipment	Sales of repair parts
	153	154	155	156	157	158	159	160	161	162	163	164	165	166
1960	217,465	80,093	11,635	12,650	7,873	30,544	46,485	6,262	2,025	4,095	5,766	1,637	8,400	41,313
1959	212,231	78,938	11,189	11,920	7,894	30,655	44,122	7,510	1,994	3,869	5,139	1,466	7,535	38,887
1958	172,014	63,171	9,790	9,656	7,104	26,257	29,851	6,102	1,900	3,521	6,488	1,558	6,616	33,979
1957	149,902	56,651	8,952	7,845	6,703	23,566[2]	23,984	5,556[2]	1,527	2,863	5,468	1,269	5,518[2]	33,820
1956	170,767	63,262	8,019	7,070	6,094	27,245	34,753	4,768	1,805	2,637	4,787	1,770	8,556	31,825
1955	153,124	58,760	8,225	7,016	5,341	19,820	27,564	4,933	1,433	2,671	3,953	1,996	11,412	28,452
1954	146,703	55,168	10,201	7,644	5,707	17,730	26,195	4,581	1,643	2,524	3,414	1,851	10,044	27,336
1953	238,050	85,261	16,870	10,696	8,130	19,787	69,580	7,716	2,243	2,281	3,567	1,902	10,036	31,819
1952	250,277	89,992	18,235	10,138	9,151	17,230	74,336	11,324	2,691	3,116	3,011	1,688	9,366	31,232
1951	235,620	92,662	15,454	12,508	9,516	14,844	58,641	11,382	2,484	2,314	3,398	1,986	10,431	28,773
1950	218,187	98,001	15,228	13,202	8,806	10,610	44,243	8,487	2,221	2,266	4,034	1,417	9,672	29,862
1949[1]	217,090	102,026	17,938	12,241	8,138	10,569	39,088	7,822	2,825	2,167	4,005	1,333	8,939[2]	28,105
1948	170,666	63,065	11,961	9,337	7,023	9,351	36,047	5,904	3,384	1,945	4,287	1,489	16,873	26,997
1947	122,395	42,223	8,210	6,306	5,083	5,688	23,179	5,125	3,556	1,852	4,970	1,122	15,081	23,276
1946	81,698	24,983	5,537	4,648	3,646	3,733	15,211	3,782	1,609	1,417	5,977	748	10,409	20,827
1945	64,293	20,977	4,183	3,020	2,961	2,444	13,168	2,930	889	1,254	4,348	482	7,638	18,734
1944	54,824	22,487	3,401	2,132	2,135	1,625	9,548	2,325	446	1,067	3,470	297	5,891	17,084
1943	29,562	9,172	3,246	1,847	1,639	1,104	4,789	920	442	—	2,386	187	3,830	14,768
1942	50,462	19,644	3,881	2,658	2,570	1,818	10,211	760	568	—	2,536	75	5,741	—
1941	52,106	23,188	4,668	2,727	2,129	1,836	7,587	726	608	—	2,923	77	5,637	—
1940	47,748	21,301	4,080	2,287	2,271	1,497	9,896	692	491	—	1,727	54	3,452	—
1939	34,060	14,769	2,556	1,790	1,358	1,097	6,077	533	439	—	1,600	55	3,087	—
1938	36,213	15,311	2,643	1,918	1,855	1,434	7,099	386	531	—	1,919	46	3,071	—
1937	30,775	12,523	2,990	1,754	2,209	1,294	3,884	364	656	—	1,805	62	3,234	—
1936	19,344	6,214	2,276	1,200	1,316	1,039	2,543	399	518	—	1,587	16	3,552	—

[1] Includes Newfoundland beginning in 1949.   [2] See text for changes in classification and other changes in coverage among the years.

Series T 167–176. *Wholesale trade, gross profit margins by kind of business, biennially, 1947 to 1957*

(per cent of net sales)

Year	Grocery	Fruit and vegetable	Tobacco and confectionery	Dry goods	Piece goods	Footwear	Automotive parts and accessories	Hardware	Plumbing and heating	Drugs
	167	168	169	170	171	172	173	174	175	176
1957	6.84	12.14	6.73	16.04	17.21	13.60	25.36	20.25	16.97	11.79
1955	7.20	11.50	7.33	16.43	16.44	16.40[1]	25.41	19.17	16.37	12.73
1953	7.66	11.79	7.63	16.01	16.10	13.51	24.91	19.45	16.99	12.36
1951	7.96	11.27	7.55	16.96	15.19	14.07	25.29	20.49	17.78	13.43
1949	7.73	10.57	7.14	15.73	15.93	12.78	25.18	19.26	19.07	12.48
1947	8.07	9.13	6.85	16.64	18.40	12.64	24.48	20.14	20.45	12.77

[1] This figure, for 25 businesses, seems high: the figure given in the 1955 report for 19 identical businesses in 1953 and 1955 is 13.32 per cent.

Series T 177–186. *Power laundries, cleaning and dyeing plants, operating statistics, 1917 to 1960*

	Power laundries					Cleaning and dyeing plants				
Year[1]	Number of plants	Number of employees	Salaries and wages	Cost of materials and supplies	Receipts	Number of plants	Number of employees	Salaries and wages	Cost of materials and supplies	Receipts
			(thousands of dollars)					(thousands of dollars)		
	177	178	179	180	181	182	183	184	185	186
1960	329	13,537	34,433	6,456	69,251	1,514	17,061	43,348	10,822	94,214
1959	330	13,954	33,864	6,658	68,096	1,483	17,233	42,344	10,588	92,212
1958	322	14,258	32,762	6,049	65,350	1,417	16,721	39,518	10,127	87,195
1957	320	14,557	31,870	5,747	63,106	1,381	16,701	38,286	9,711	84,282
1956	308	14,514	30,091	5,738	58,874	1,338	16,939	35,621	9,157	78,527
1955	306	13,991	28,078	4,994	54,200	1,205	15,909	32,874	7,930	70,734
1954	299	13,754	26,636	4,666	50,513	1,107	15,485	31,513	7,535	67,223
1953	310	14,164	25,802	6,511	49,121	1,029	15,234	29,898	7,255	64,029
1952	307	13,922	24,496	6,144	46,853	991	14,816	27,149	6,710	58,478
1951	317	14,079	22,249	n.a.	44,053	981	13,933	23,850	n.a.	52,798
1950[1]	323	14,310	20,976	4,812	40,587	919	13,450	21,705	5,379	46,250
1949[1]	332	14,240	20,408	4,485	38,660	905	12,886	20,107	4,940	42,574
1948	294	13,923	18,737	4,138	35,361	787	11,953	17,140	4,401	36,621
1947	244	13,950	16,357	3,560	30,459	530	10,906	14,144	3,042	28,584
1946	238	13,674	14,648	3,074	27,427	452	9,880	11,613	2,504	23,721
1945	217	13,232	13,652	2,717	25,463	385	8,147	8,848	1,952	18,618
1944	227	13,259	12,781	2,491	24,559	399	7,732	8,213	1,694	16,887
1943	225	13,209	12,339	2,530	23,436	362	7,388	7,866	1,519	15,218
1942	238	12,848	11,679	2,533	22,396	365	6,990	6,969	1,453	14,353
1941	237	11,844	10,121	2,349	19,817	363	6,554	6,126	1,434	12,678
1940	230	10,034	8,156	1,809	16,719	300	5,474	4,956	1,156	10,057
1939	234	9,217	7,466	1,617	14,268	268	4,995	4,284	1,035	8,659
1938	232	8,981	7,029	1,542	13,735	230	4,320	3,890	1,000	7,994
1937	225	8,576	6,679	1,403	13,164	193	3,976	3,493	856	7,179
1936	229	7,925	5,997	1,275	12,024	191	3,643	3,112	710	6,305
1935	237	7,644	5,668	1,118	10,983	179	3,108	2,671	621	5,328
1934	236	7,393	5,387	945	10,589	175	2,983	2,527	518	5,014
1933	239	7,616	5,501	897	10,374	172	2,912	2,881	503	4,866
1932	243	8,292	6,482	1,066	12,297	166	2,878	2,538	522	5,006
1931	250	8,807	7,710	1,350	14,380	157	2,965	2,962	618	6,145
1930	242	9,100	8,140	1,572	16,284	126	2,785	3,110	624	6,412
1929	230	8,928	7,925	1,716	16,353	127	2,811	3,002	634	6,689
1928	233	8,095	7,039	1,537	14,590	124	2,644	2,602	645	5,924
1927	223	7,290	6,350	1,350	13,088	115	1,883	1,931	445	4,340
			Power laundries, cleaning and dyeing plants[3]							
1926	350	8,975[2]	8,229	2,104	17,642	—	—	—	—	—
1925	343	8,089	7,338	2,433	15,578	—	—	—	—	—
1924	518	8,134	7,512	2,219	15,577	—	—	—	—	—
1923	605	7,969	7,156	1,825	15,552	—	—	—	—	—
1922	620	7,490	6,539	1,733	14,650	—	—	—	—	—
1921	535	6,872	6,248	1,796	13,879	—	—	—	—	—
1920	379	7,246	6,527	1,835	14,168	—	—	—	—	—
1919	366	7,240	5,321	1,665	11,841	—	—	—	—	—
1918	341	6,523	4,141	1,441	8,969	—	—	—	—	—
1917	333	6,496	3,912	1,569	8,319	—	—	—	—	—

[1] Includes Newfoundland beginning in 1949.
[2] For the period 1917 to 1926 the number of employees includes outside piece-workers.
[3] Data for 1917 to 1926 include dyeing and finishing of textiles (see the note to series T 177–186).

Series T 187–203. Statistics of hotels, 1930, 1941 and 1949 to 1960
(values in thousands of dollars)

				Principal operating expenses as a percentage of total receipts[2]								Receipts				
Number of hotels	Number of rooms	Bed capacity	Percentage of room occupancy	Salaries and wages		Cost of goods sold		Light, heat and power		Repairs and maintenance		Total	Rooms	Meals	Beer, wine and liquor	All other sources
				Incorporated	Unincorporated	Incorporated	Unincorporated	Incorporated	Unincorporated	Incorporated	Unincorporated					
187	188	189	190	191	192	193	194	195	196	197	198	199	200	201	202	203
5,294	155,538	288,007	51	25.8	18.0	45.0	50.1	2.8	3.2	2.7	3.2	545,457	120,890	98,641	283,223	42,703
5,269	154,725	282,686	52	25.9	18.1	45.3	49.9	2.8	3.4	2.8	3.7	517,483	117,396	95,139	264,087	40,861
5,088	151,362	274,483	52	25.8	19.5	45.9	51.6	2.8	3.5	3.3	3.8	480,295	111,174	87,550	243,695	37,876
5,151	151,517	278,513	54	25.3	17.9	46.1	50.8	2.8	3.4	3.4	3.9	470,069	110,505	84,049	238,210	37,305
5,067	149,625	271,182	56[2]	25.6	17.9	46.3	51.3	2.9	3.5	3.4	3.8	441,831	104,453	78,169	223,398	35,811
5,081	147,812	266,846	52	26.7	16.0	40.4	52.7	3.0	3.3	3.3	3.4	415,309	96,273	72,236	211,415	35,385
5,208	148,890	264,912	53	30.3	16.1	35.7	52.4	3.1	3.1	4.2	3.5	405,856	94,094	70,829	204,555	36,378
5,209	149,653	261,455	55	29.9	15.6	36.4	53.6	3.0	2.8	4.0	3.6	410,715	93,914	70,974	209,984	35,843
5,157	149,615	263,357	58	29.0	15.1	37.2	54.1	—	—	—	—	391,936	89,879	67,269	201,759	33,029
5,092	146,441	257,657	58	28.8	15.1	37.8	53.4	—	—	—	—	357,282	83,322	63,440	180,642	29,878
5,169	146,353	237,735	58	29.3	15.9	—	—	—	—	—	—	322,390	75,842	58,586	162,815	25,147
5,425	150,098	—	—	27.8	15.2	—	—	—	—	—	—	324,452	77,466	59,610	162,789	24,587
5,646	128,980[5]	—	—	—	—	—	—	—	—	—	—	147,488	33,188	24,519	78,696	11,086
4,958	129,462	—	—	—	—	—	—	—	—	—	—	90,519	30,154	28,124	23,942	8,299

[1] Newfoundland is included beginning in 1949.

[2] In 1956 two changes in tabulating the data were made: occupancy rates became rates for hotels with 11 or more rooms rather than for all hotels which was the practice for 1955 and earlier years; principal operating expenses as a percentage of total receipts became based on a panel of hotels with 11 to 99 rooms rather than on all hotels as in 1955 and earlier years.

[3] In both 1950 and 1955 some establishments formerly included were dropped either because it had become evident they had less than six rooms or were of the tourist home type.

[4] The decennial census data for 1941 and 1931 include public houses in Ontario which are not included for 1949 to 1960. There were 422 public houses, with 5,414 rooms in Ontario in 1949 with total receipts of 30.8 million dollars of which 26.6 million was from beer, wine and liquor sales.

[5] In addition to the 128,980 rooms, it was stated there was accommodation in cabins, etc., for 13,937 persons. This ancillary accommodation is included in other years, though the number of rooms would be less than the number of persons that can be accommodated.

Series T 204–212. Statistics of advertising agencies in Canada, 1941 and 1946 to 1960
(values in thousands of dollars)

Year[1]	Number of firms	Amount of billings			Gross revenue on			Total gross revenue as a percentage of total billings	Gross revenue on commissionable billings as a percentage of commissionable billings
		Total billings	Commissionable billings	Other billings	Total billings	Commissionable billings	Other billings[2]		
	204	205	206	207	208	209	210	211	212
1960	131	272,740	267,756	4,984	45,150	39,994	5,157	16.6	14.9
1959	122	254,146	250,080	4,066	41,127	37,679	3,448	16.2	15.1
1958	123	237,654	233,789	3,865	38,073	35,277	2,846	16.0	15.1
1957	113	226,084	222,025	4,059	35,758	33,377	2,380	15.8	15.0
1956	110	204,581	201,797	2,784	32,204	30,453	1,751	15.7	15.1
1955	104	177,240	174,295	2,315	27,690	26,469	1,221	15.6	15.1
1954	91	156,163	154,467	1,696	24,579	23,230	1,350	15.7	15.0
1953	88	144,339	142,958	1,381	22,592	21,559	1,033	15.7	15.1
1952	88	121,667	120,629	1,038	19,060	18,246	814	15.7	15.1
1951	83	108,414	107,462	952	17,015	16,255	760	15.7	15.1
1950	75	96,221	95,567	654	15,013	14,444	569	15.6	15.1
1949	74	86,742	86,451	291	13,526	—	—	15.6	—
1948	75	73,762	73,544	218	11,553	—	—	15.7	—
1947	67	64,595	64,423	172	10,092	—	—	15.6	—
1946	57	52,169	52,079	90	8,458	—	—	16.2	—
1941	49	29,224	—	—	4,824	—	—	16.5	—

[1] The source does not indicate when Newfoundland was first included; presumably it was in 1949.

[2] Beginning in 1957 figures for series T 210 contain some revenue which does not pertain to surveys, research or other agency services.

Series T213–226. *Statistics of motion picture and drive-in theatres, 1930 to 1960*

	Motion picture theatres							Drive-in theatres						
Year[1]	Number of establishments	Number of employees		Salaries and wages	Amusement taxes	Receipts from admissions	Number of paid admissions (thousands)	Number of establishments	Number of employees		Salaries and wages	Amusement taxes	Receipts from admissions	Number of paid admissions (thousands)
		Male	Female	(thousands of dollars)					Male	Female	(thousands of dollars)			
	213	214	215	216	217	218	219	220	221	222	223	224	225	226
1960	1,427	6,124	4,436	16,143	5,365	65,505	107,705	232	1,239	772	1,839	524	6,790	10,029
1959	1,515	6,825	4,712	16,506	5,960	68,370	118,633	234	1,244	795	1,702	505	7,144	10,226
1958	1,622	6,691	5,085	17,111	6,951	75,139	136,335	232	1,197	747	1,757	504	6,254	10,149
1957	1,716	7,190	5,478	17,669	7,815	76,486	146,756	229	1,276	792	1,625	520	5,725	9,946
1956	1,849	7,787	5,874	17,894	8,675	80,666	162,859	237	1,347	795	1,527	520	5,394	9,706
1955	1,950	8,378	6,073	19,448	10,264	86,374	184,968	242	1,459	756	1,600	602	5,755	10,688
1954	1,938	9,235	6,533	20,154	12,099	97,012	218,509	230	1,472	710	1,629	722	6,317	12,380
1953	1,906	9,027	6,723	20,018	12,760	100,889	241,183	174	1,325	647	1,433	685	5,863	11,135
1952	1,843	8,804	6,296	18,868	12,308	98,851	247,733	104	914	406	998	540	4,409	8,380
1951	1,808	14,034		17,137	11,374	90,986	239,132	82	933		792	407	3,348	6,555
1950	1,801	8,297	5,569	15,640	11,445	82,708	231,747	62	677	196	557	300	2,291	4,943
1949[1]	1,731	7,635	5,429	14,438	12,564	77,419	229,312	30	352	84	290	245	1,394	3,091
1948	1,604	7,340	5,047	12,986	13,583	68,694	219,289	15	243	12	171	131	659	1,596
1947	1,693	7,375	4,529	11,588	15,819	62,865	220,858	7	86	14	61	58	274	671
1946	1,477	6,813	4,143	10,466	15,053	59,889	227,539	—	—	—	—	—	—	—
1945	1,323	6,330	4,020	9,664	14,055	55,431	215,573	—	—	—	—	—	—	—
1944	1,298	6,098	4,017	9,381	13,556	53,173	208,167	—	—	—	—	—	—	—
1943	1,265	5,904	3,765	8,882	13,160	51,485	204,678	—	—	—	—	—	—	—
1942	1,247	5,655	2,990	8,205	11,557	45,720	182,846	—	—	—	—	—	—	—
1941	1,240	6,121	2,487	6,174	—	40,796	161,678	—	—	—	—	—	—	—
1940	1,229	5,691	1,979	6,331	—	37,474	151,591	—	—	—	—	—	—	—
1939	1,183	5,502	1,890	5,908	—	33,696	137,899	—	—	—	—	—	—	—
1938	1,130	5,354	1,813	5,622	—	33,346	137,381	—	—	—	—	—	—	—
1937	1,044	5,240	1,631	5,561	—	32,163	133,668	—	—	—	—	—	—	—
1936	956	4,917	1,536	4,906	—	29,440	126,914	—	—	—	—	—	—	—
1935	859	4,553	1,436	4,799	—	27,012	117,521	—	—	—	—	—	—	—
1934	796	4,224	1,341	4,277	—	25,281	107,355	—	—	—	—	—	—	—
1933	762	3,822	1,378	4,434	—	24,906	—	—	—	—	—	—	—	—
1932	—	—	—	—	—	28,585	—	—	—	—	—	—	—	—
1931	—	—	—	—	—	33,706	—	—	—	—	—	—	—	—
1930	907	4,546	1,475	6,811	—	38,130	—	—	—	—	—	—	—	—

[1] Includes Newfoundland beginning in 1949.

SECTION V: EDUCATION

R. W. B. JACKSON, *Ontario College of Education*

Series V1–108 are statistics of elementary and secondary schools in Canada since Confederation. Series V109–118 are statistics of attendance at private business colleges since 1920. Series V119–136 present statistics of schools for the blind and the deaf beginning in 1870. Series V137–157 cover some of the major statistics of teacher training in Canada, also beginning with 1870. Series V158–183 present statistics of the finance of elementary and secondary schools since 1870. Series V184–225 are statistics of higher learning in the period beginning in 1920.

A large number of federal and provincial sources have been used. They are listed here in the order of their occurrence in the text and assigned numbers; hereafter, they are cited by number. The following are publications of the Dominion Bureau of Statistics, Queen's (King's) Printer, Ottawa:

No. 1, *Dominion Bureau of Statistics, History, Function, Organization* (1952); no. 2, *Report of Conference on Education Statistics* (1921); no. 3, *Historical Statistical Survey of Education in Canada* (1921); no. 4, *Elementary and Secondary Education in Canada, 1936–38* (1940); no. 5, *Survey of Elementary and Secondary Education, 1956–58* (1960); no. 6, *Survey of Elementary and Secondary Education, 1954–56* (1959); no. 7, *Survey of Elementary and Secondary Education, 1948–50* (1956); no. 8, *Elementary and Secondary Education in Canada, 1938–40* (1942); no. 9, *Annual Survey of Education in Canada, 1935* (1937); no. 10, *Annual Survey of Education in Canada, 1925* (1926); no. 11, *Annual Survey of Education in Canada, 1930* (1932); no. 12, *Elementary and Secondary Education in Canada, 1940–42* (1944); no. 13, *Annual Survey of Education in Canada, 1934* (1936); no. 14, *Salaries and Qualifications of Teachers in Public Elementary and Secondary Schools, 1958–59* (1960); no. 15, *Teachers' Salaries and Qualifications in Nine Provinces, 1950* (1952); no. 16, *Teachers' Salaries and Qualifications in Nine Provinces, 1952–1953* (1954); no. 17, *Teachers' Salaries and Qualifications, 1953–54* (1956); no. 18, *Salaries and Qualifications of Teachers in Public Elementary and Secondary Schools, 1954–1955* (1958); no. 19, *Salaries and Qualifications of Teachers in Public Elementary and Secondary Schools, 1956–57* (1959); no. 20, *Salaries and Qualifications of Teachers in Public Elementary and Secondary Schools, 1957–1958* (1959); no. 21, *Teachers' Salaries and Qualifications in Eight Provinces, 1939* (1940); no. 22, *Teachers' Salaries and Qualifications in Eight Provinces, 1940* (1941); no. 23, *Teachers' Salaries and Qualifications in Eight Provinces, 1941* (1942); no. 24, *Teachers' Salaries in Eight Provinces, 1942* (1943); no. 25, *Teachers' Salaries and Qualifications in Eight Provinces, 1943* (1944); no. 26, *Teachers' Salaries and Qualifications in Eight Provinces, 1944* (1945); no. 27, *Teachers' Salaries and Qualifications in Eight Provinces, 1945* (1946); no. 28, *Teachers' Salaries and Qualifications in Eight Provinces, 1947* (1949); no. 29, *Teachers' Salaries and Qualifications in Eight Provinces, 1948* (1950); no. 30, *Teachers' Salaries and Qualifications in Eight Provinces, 1949* (1951); no. 31, *Survey of Elementary and Secondary Education, 1950–54* (1959); no. 32, Education Statistics Branch, *Statistical Report on Education in Canada, 1921* (1923); no. 33, *Survey of Elementary and Secondary Education, 1946–48* (1952); no. 34, *Fall Enrolment in Universities and Colleges, 1957* (1958); no. 35, *Fall Enrolment in Universities and Colleges, 1956* (1957).

The following provincial publications were also used:

No. 36, *Annual Report*, Department of Education, Newfoundland; no. 37, *Journals of the House of Assembly*, Prince Edward Island; no. 38, *Annual Report*, Department of Education, Prince Edward Island; no.

39, *Annual Report*, Department of Education, Nova Scotia; no. 40, *Annual Report*, Department of Education, New Brunswick; no. 41, *Annual Report*, Department of Education, Manitoba; no. 42, *Annual Report*, Department of Education, Alberta; no. 43, *Annual Reports of the Public Schools of Prince Edward Island*, by the chief Superintendent of Education; no. 44, *Annual Report of the Bureau of Education*, Newfoundland; no. 45, *Annual Report of the Schools of New Brunswick*; no. 46, *Annual Reports on the Common, Superior, Grammar, Normal and Model Schools of New Brunswick*; no. 47, *Report of the Chief Superintendent of Schools*, New Brunswick; no. 48, *Annual Reports of the Superintendent of Education of the Province of Quebec* (prior to 1896 designated *Sessional Papers, II* with no further title); no. 49, *Statistics of Education*, Bureau of Statistics, Province of Quebec; no. 50, Department of Education, Province of Saskatchewan, *Summary of Annual Returns of School Districts* (manuscripts in Dominion Bureau of Statistics Library); no. 53, *Annual Reports on Public Schools, of the Province of British Columbia*; no. 54, *Annual Report, Superintendent of Education, Public Schools of Nova Scotia*; no. 55, *Report of the Superintendent of Public Instruction*, Quebec; no. 56, *Statistical Yearbook*, Quebec; no. 57, *Sessional Papers*, Quebec; no. 58, *Report, Minister of Education*, Ontario; no. 59, *Sessional Papers*, Ontario; no. 60, *Annual Reports of the Normal, Model, Grammar and Common Schools of Ontario*; no. 61, *Report, Department of Education*, Northwest Territories; no. 62, *Annual Report of the Board of Education*, Prince Edward Island; no. 63, *Annual Report, Normal, Model, High and Public Schools of Ontario*; no. 64, *Annual Report of the Common, Academic and Normal and Model Schools of Nova Scotia*; no. 65, *Journal of the Proceedings of the Legislative Council of the Province of Nova Scotia*; no. 66, *Annual Reports, Department of Education*, Saskatchewan; no. 67, *Statistical Report of the Department of Education*, Northwest Territories; no. 68, *Public Accounts*, Newfoundland; no. 69, *Reports of School Corporations*, Quebec; no. 70, *Public Accounts*, Ontario; no. 71, *Public Accounts*, Yukon; no. 72, *Public Accounts*, Northwest Territories; no. 73, *Report, Department of Education*, Yukon; no. 74, *Public Accounts*, Nova Scotia; no. 75, *Municipal Affairs Report*, Nova Scotia; no. 76, Dominion Bureau of Statistics, *Fall Enrolment in Universities and Colleges*; no. 77, *Statistical Report of the Bureau of Education*, Newfoundland.

General note

The British North America Act of 1867 granted to the Canadian provinces almost complete jurisdiction over education. The federal government, however, was given the responsibility of protecting the rights of minorities and was made responsible for education in the territories and for the education of Indians and Eskimoes in all provinces.

This federated structure gave rise to a variety of educational systems. In 1958 there were eleven systems in the provinces— one in each of nine provinces and two in the province of Quebec.

This variety of educational systems has presented certain obstacles to the collection of adequate and comparable statistical information. Chief among these obstacles has been the failure of some provinces to collect and preserve the basic data in regard to pupils, teachers and schools and the lack of uniformity in the meaning given to certain terms within and among the provinces.

Provincial departments of education have collected information related to pupils and teachers from the beginnings of governmental interest in education. Quebec has certain records of importance to educational statistics which date back to the early days of the colony of New France. The data for Newfoundland, on the other hand, are very limited. Despite its early settlement, this colony lacked any agency to gather educational data for the whole island and the data on its denominational schools are far from complete.

According to the Dominion Bureau of Statistics, 'The early provincial statistics of education comprised little more than a count of the number of schools in operation, partial records of pupil enrolment, and some figures on government expenditures' (see reference no. 1, p. 42).

The inadequacy of provincial education statistics and the need for nationwide education data were stressed in the Departmental Commission, 'Such statistics should comprise the nature and variety of educational institutions, public and private, including their organization, grading and equipment, whether for primary, secondary or higher education. They should also give the number of pupils and students in the various grades, their attendance, age on entering and leaving school, the nature of the education given, whether theoretical, practical or special, and any supplementary educational facilities, including libraries, night schools, art or trade schools, etc. Particulars should be included as to the teaching staffs, their qualifications, sex, age, frequency of changes in the staffs; also the expenditure on education in the various grades, distinguished as permanent and annual expenditure' (reference no. 2, p. 5).

Two years later in 1914, an Interprovincial Convention of teachers and educational officials of the three Maritime Provinces recommended that the Dominion Bureau of Statistics collect and publish regularly the statistics on education in Canada. The result of this request was the addition of a section on education statistics to the *Canada Year Book* of 1914 and annually thereafter (reference no. 2, p. 5).

Although the statistics of the various provinces were compiled by the Dominion Bureau to make national statistics available, there were serious difficulties to be overcome before comparable and meaningful data could be obtained from the provinces. The variation in definition of terms has been mentioned, for example, the term 'classroom' did not have the same meaning in all provinces. In addition, there was no uniformity in the dates of the statistical school year, some provinces using the calendar year while others reported upon the period from 1 July to the following 30 June. Further problems in presentation of data were caused by the inconsistency in classification of elementary and secondary grades. In the Prairie Provinces, for example, 'there is a tendency to consider grade VII as the real land mark or end of elementary work, grade VIII being a transitional or intermediate state which may be considered elementary or secondary according to the institution in which it is taken up' (reference no. 3, p. 29). In the reporting of financial data on education the lack of distinction between grants from the provincial government and local assessments added to the complexity of the reporting problem. These differences in the data available from the various provinces were drawn to the attention of the provincial education authorities by the Dominion Bureau of Statistics in a memorandum, 'Statistics of Education—Their Co-ordination and Enlargement' (reference no. 2, p. 5).

In 1919 the forerunner of the Education Division of the Dominion Bureau of Statistics was set up and one of its first tasks was the preparation of schedules to be used in the collection of comparable data from the provinces.

Two years later, in 1921, the Education Statistics Branch issued its first statistical report, *Historical Statistical Survey of Education in Canada* (reference no. 3). Subsequently, annual and later biennial statistical reports on education were issued.

In addition to the provincial departments of education and the Dominion Bureau of Statistics, certain other institutions, agencies and individuals have collected statistical data on education in Canada. Among these are the Canadian Adult Education Association and the Canadian Teachers Federation.

ELEMENTARY AND SECONDARY SCHOOLS
(Series V1–108)

V1–20. Total enrolment and total average daily attendance in publicly controlled elementary and secondary schools, by province, 1867 to 1958

SOURCE: files of the Education Division, Dominion Bureau of Statistics.

In interpreting the information offered in this and the following table, one must bear in mind that the data for the various provinces are not comparable for every year. For example, there is a noticeable drop in the numbers shown for the province of Ontario between 1930 and 1935. The reason for this contradiction of fact is that, prior to 1933, Ontario calculated school enrolment for the calendar year rather than for the school year. When the change to the statistical school year was made, many thousand duplicates were eliminated. Similar changes in reporting procedures were made in other provinces at an earlier date. For this reason, it is not possible to state that a lowered enrolment according to the data presented necessarily indicates a true decrease.

Another source of possible error in the data is the lack of uniform practice in the reporting of students who transfer from one school to another within the school year. In certain cases, these students were counted twice, in other cases, they were correctly tabulated. For example, when Manitoba in 1932 adopted the practice of recording transfers as such, the year's enrolment dropped by 1,600 while the average daily attendance for the same year increased about 2,100 (see reference no. 4, p. 14).

V9 and 10. Quebec. 1930 to 1958: schools under control only, except for 1944, when independent schools are included. 1901 to 1929: includes enrolment in independent schools as well as those under control. 1892 to 1900: figures include enrolments in Roman Catholic and Protestant schools, independent as well as under control. 1891: Roman Catholic schools under control only. 1890: all schools, Roman Catholic, Protestant, under control, and independent. 1889: Roman Catholic schools under control only. 1885 to 1888: all schools both Roman Catholic and Protestant. 1882 to 1884: Roman Catholic schools under control only. 1875 to 1881: includes both Roman Catholic and Protestant schools under control. 1868 to 1874: figures include enrolment in all schools, Roman Catholic, Protestant, under control and independent.

The Quebec data for series V9 for the year 1916 are obviously incomplete and figures for some other years do not seem to be 'in series'.

V11 and 12. Ontario. Some differences in coverage among years are caused by the inclusion or exclusion of part-time students in the vocational schools. Differences may also be due to the use of two separate report forms as the basis of different tables without reconciliation. These differences within the Ontario report affect the 1925 to 1940 data.

V21–31. Number of pupils enrolled in publicly controlled elementary schools, by province and sex, selected years, 1870 to 1958

SOURCE: for Newfoundland, reference nos. 1, 36, 44 and files of the Education Division of Dominion Bureau of Statistics; for P.E.I., nos. 1, 5, 10, 38 and 43; for N.S., no. 39; for N.B., nos. 3, 4, 5, 45, 46, 47 and files of the Education Division, D.B.S.; for Que., nos. 48 and 49; for Ont., nos. 1, 58, 59 and 60; for Man., nos. 2, 4, 41 and files of Education Division, D.B.S.; for Sask., no. 50 and figures supplied by Department of Education, Saskatchewan; for Alta., no. 40; for B.C., no. 53.

Although the division of the students into elementary and secondary (series V 32–42) has been done on the basis of Grade 8's being the end of elementary school, it must be remembered that this does not apply to all provinces. See the general note.

V 28. Manitoba. No breakdown by grades is available for years prior to 1905. Grand totals are given in Minister's Report of 1904. The figures given combine both elementary and secondary. It is not known what part of this group was secondary but it was likely a very small fraction of the total.

See also the note to series V 1–20.

V 32–42. Number of pupils enrolled in publicly controlled secondary schools, by province and sex, selected years, 1870 to 1958

SOURCE: same as series V 21–31.

See note to series V 1–20 and V 21–31.

V 43–53. Number of the population at schools, by age and sex, census years, 1911 to 1951

SOURCE: prepared from census data by the Education Division, D.B.S.

The information contained in these series was obtained by the D.B.S. Education Division from the decennial census data rather than from the provincial education authorities. The data are not given by censuses previous to 1911.

V 54–67. Distribution among grades of pupils enrolled in publicly controlled elementary and secondary schools, by province, census years, 1871 to 1951 and 1958

SOURCE: the files of the Education Division, Dominion Bureau of Statistics.

V 68–78. Number of teachers in publicly controlled elementary and secondary schools, by province and sex, selected years, 1870 to 1958

SOURCE: for all provinces for 1910 to 1958, nos. 2, 3, 5, 6, 7, 10, 11 and 31; for earlier years: for P.E.I., nos. 38 and 43; for N.S., no. 54; for N.B., nos. 45 and 47; for Que., nos. 55, 56 and 57; for Ont., nos. 58 and 60; for Man., no. 61; for B.C., no. 53.

The information contained in these tables may not be entirely accurate. The sources of possible error have been set forth in the *Historical Statistical Survey of Education in Canada*, 1921: 'It must be borne in mind that the number of teachers given for any year does not mean the number teaching at one time. (A truer estimate...is...the number of classrooms in operation.) Some teachers leave the school before the end of the year and are replaced by new teachers. They may teach in one part of the province during one part of the year and in another at another; thus the same teacher may be counted more than once. For this reason the statistics of the number of teachers in a province where the staff is more or less permanent are nearer to the true number than those of a province where the teachers are continually changing' (reference no. 3, p. 65).

V 73. Quebec. There is considerable variation in what teachers were included in the figures reported over the years. The following indicates the variation by types of schools. Previous to 1885 the figures for the two systems are inseparable.

(1) Roman Catholic lay teachers: 1869 to 1874, all teachers in all schools—under control and independent, Roman Catholic and Protestant, lay and religious; 1875, Roman Catholic lay teachers in independent schools and schools under control; 1876 to 1884, teachers in Roman Catholic and Protestant independent schools and schools under control; 1887 to 1890, schools under control only; 1892 to 1943, includes teachers in independent schools as well as in schools under control; 1944 to 1958, teachers in schools under control only.

(2) Roman Catholic religious teachers: 1869 to 1874, included with lay teachers; 1875 to 1942, not reported; 1943, those in independent schools as well as in schools under control; 1944 to 1958, those in schools under control only.

(3) Protestant teachers: 1869 to 1884, included with Roman Catholic lay teachers; 1885 to 1886, includes teachers in independent schools; 1887 to 1890, teachers in schools under control only; 1891 to 1958, includes teachers in independent schools except for 1944 and 1945, which are for schools under control only.

V 79–87. Number of teachers in publicly controlled elementary and secondary schools, by province and class of certificate, selected years, 1870 to 1958

SOURCE: for Newfoundland, for 1955 and 1958, reference nos. 18 and 14, for 1950, no. 15, for 1920 and 1935 to 1945, no. 36, for 1930, no. 77, for 1925, no. 45; for P.E.I., for 1872 to 1875, no. 37, for 1876 to 1879, no. 62, for 1880 to 1920, no. 43, for 1931 to 1938, no. 38, for 1942, 1952 and 1956, nos. 38, 31 and 2, for other years, 1939 to 1959, nos. 15, 16, 17, 18, 19, 20, 21, 22, 23, 25, 26, 27, 28, 29, 30; for N.S., for 1867 to 1875, no. 65, for 1876 to 1885, no. 64, for 1886 to 1942, no. 54, for 1952 to 1958, nos. 6, 15, 16, 17, 18, 19, 20, 21, 22, 23, 24, 25, 26, 27, 30, 31; for N.B., 1867 to 1871, no. 47, for 1872 to 1879, no. 46, for 1880 to 1935, no. 45, for 1936, 1938 and 1942, no. 40, for other years, 1939 to 1958, nos. 6 and 15 to 30, inclusive; for Quebec, files of the Education Division, D.B.S.; for Ont., for 1867 to 1870, no. 60, for 1871 to 1874, no. 63, for 1885 to 1935 and 1937 to 1944, no. 58, for 1936, no. 4, for 1952, no. 31, for 1956, no. 6, for other years, 1937 to 1958, nos. 15 to 20, 21 to 25 and 27 to 30; for Man., for 1935, no. 1, for later years, nos. 18, 19 and 20; for Sask., for 1904 and 1905, no. 67, for 1909 to 1938, no. 66, for later years, nos. 6 and 21 to 31; for Alta., for 1906 to 1942, no. 42, for later years, nos. 6 and 25 to 30; for B.C., for 1910 to 1938 and for 1942, no. 53, for later years except 1942, nos. 4, 21 to 23 and 31.

'Tables of teachers classified by professional qualifications by provinces are of very little value and very misleading unless the academic standing required of each class as well as some general information on the other conditions attached to a class of certificate is given' (reference no. 3, p. 67).

In accord with the foregoing statement, the classification of teachers which is presented in series V 79–87 is based upon the academic standing required of teachers without reference to the varied classificatory systems used throughout the provinces.

In order to establish a comparable classification across all provinces and express this in terms not used by any province, yet readily interpreted, all certificates were classified in terms of years of training referred to the base of junior matriculation level designated as J. J + 1 means junior matriculation level plus one year of further education. In all cases those classified in the 'plus' categories required at least one year of professional training. J − 1 means one year short of junior matriculation level. Usually the professional training required was less than one year, sometimes as short as 6 weeks. Grade 10 at most and no professional training includes those teaching on permits. *Special* includes vocational teachers and teachers certificated to teach only special subjects or classes such as music, art, etc.

It should be noted that this is a classification of teachers *according to the certificate granted by the province*. A considerable number of teachers, particularly in some provinces, may have had more education and training than their certificates indicated.

V88–97. Number of classrooms in operation in publicly controlled elementary and secondary schools, by province, selected years, 1870 to 1958

SOURCE: see reference nos. 36, 37, 38, 39, 40, 41 and 42.

The term 'classroom' is taken to mean the smallest school unit, a school room in the charge of a teacher who keeps the register. As reported in the *Historical Statistical Survey of Education in Canada*, 'The number of classrooms in a province ...will not necessarily correspond to the number of teachers, partly because of the existence of the more or less itinerant specialists...and partly because owing to the frequent changes of teachers, the number of teachers in a province during the year will not be the number teaching at one time' (reference no. 3, p. 5).

V98–108. Number of pupils attending private elementary and secondary schools, by province, selected years, 1920 to 1958

SOURCE: for all provinces in 1925 and 1930, no. 7, for 1935 to 1958 successive *Annual Surveys of Elementary and Secondary Education* and files of the Education Division B.C.; for Quebec in same years, no. 48.

Prior to 1920 the statistics available for private schools were practically nonexistent. The *Historical Statistical Survey of Education in Canada*, 1921, reported that '...efforts are now being made to collect such figures and it is to be hoped that before very long it may be possible to give these statistics on a comparative basis with the statistics of publicly controlled schools, and that the sum total will be available to compare with a table of population of school age' (reference no. 3, p. 17).

PRIVATE BUSINESS COLLEGES
(Series V109–118)

V109–118. Number of pupils attending private business colleges, by province and sex, selected years, 1920 to 1958

SOURCE: for 1925 to 1945, nos. 8, 9, 11 and 33; for 1950 to 1958, the files of the Education Division, D.B.S.

The term 'business college' is here '...applied to a private institution teaching any or all forms of commercial work with the literary preparation for that work' (reference no. 32, p. 6).

SCHOOLS FOR THE BLIND AND THE DEAF
(Series V119–136)

V119–128. Number of pupils attending schools for the blind and deaf, by pupils' province of residence, selected years, 1870 to 1958

SOURCE: for 1905 to 1958, successive issue D.B.S., *Annual Survey of Elementary and Secondary Education* and successive *Annual Report* of the Departments of Education in the provinces; for 1957 to 1958 the files of the Education Division, D.B.S.

Because not all provinces have schools for the blind and deaf, it is necessary to categorize the data in two ways, one by location of school, the other by the pupil's province of residence.
Data for western provinces from 1905 to 1920 are not complete. Only a few figures could be separated from the figures of other provinces where the school was located.
See the note to series V129–136.

V129–136. Number of pupils attending schools for the blind and the deaf, by location of schools, selected years, 1870 to 1958

SOURCE: same as for series V119–128.

School for Blind in Nova Scotia, series V129, had students from Newfoundland, New Brunswick and Prince Edward Island and sometimes also Quebec from 1921 to 1958.
From 1875 to 1900 Ontario figures, series V132, include students from other provinces also. Manitoba, series V133, had a school for deaf and dumb from 1890, and students from British Columbia, Alberta and Saskatchewan were also registered in the Manitoba school. The blind students from the western provinces for a long time went to the Ontario school.
See note to series V119–128.

TEACHER TRAINING (Series V137–157)

V137–147. Number of students enrolled in normal schools and teachers' colleges, by province, selected years, 1870 to 1958

SOURCE: for 1925 to 1958, the files of the Education Division, D.B.S.; for 1957 and 1958, no. 80.

V148–157. Number of students enrolled in university colleges of education, by province, 1920 to 1958

SOURCE: same as series V137–147.

New Brunswick figures are not available for 1925–1945. Students in Maritime universities preparing for teaching are reported as Arts students until 1935, similarly at McGill University until 1933. The training of teachers in university began in British Columbia in 1924, Saskatchewan in 1928, Alberta in 1930, and Manitoba in 1936.

FINANCE OF
ELEMENTARY AND SECONDARY SCHOOLS
(Series V158–183)

V158–170. Receipts of boards of publicly controlled elementary and secondary schools, by province and by source of funds, selected years, 1870 to 1958

SOURCE: for Newfoundland, successive issues of no. 68; for Quebec, nos. 55, 56, 57 and 69, successive issues; for Ontario, nos. 58 and 70, successive issues; for Yukon, nos. 71 and 73, successive issues; for N.W.T., nos. 61 and 72, successive issues; for N.S., nos. 44, 74 and 75, various issues; for N.B., nos. 45 and 75, various issues, plus an estimate for Restigouche County made for this volume; for Man., no. 41, successive issues; for Sask., no. 66, successive issues; for Alta., no. 42, successive issues; for B.C., for most years, nos. 53 and 76, successive issues, for 1947 to 1953, compilations of the financial reports of school boards as reported in D.B.S., *Surveys of Elementary and Secondary Education*.

According to the *Biennial Survey of Education in Canada, Part I, 1936–38*, 'it is quite impossible to construct a uniform set of tables (showing finances of the schools) for all provinces' (reference no. 4, p. 68). Nevertheless, the record of receipts and expenditures even though incomplete, and not entirely comparable between provinces, makes possible a comparison of the extent of financial support provided by the central and local authorities within each province, as well as a comparison of the amounts spent on current and capital costs.

For Prince Edward Island from 1873 to about 1945 information was available from the Education Department report on provincial grants and from 1883 onward the amounts of tax levied for current and for building school houses separately were available. From 1880 to 1882 inclusive only the total tax was reported. As grants were given for current purposes only, it is assumed that money voted for erection of school houses was the annual capital cost, and that expenditure was approximately equal to revenue. Where reports were not available or were incomplete, public accounts were consulted for grants paid, and where public accounts were also missing, the grants were estimated by interpolation.

The assumption that the 'school-house' vote was the annual capital cost may be in error, as the current expenses other than teachers' salaries are not reported in detail, and interest on debentures, if any, may have been included in the current expenditure. If so, the capital item here may be only capital outlays from current funds.

No information is available in years prior to 1947 concerning local revenue other than taxes.

For Nova Scotia provincial grants from 1948 and following include provincial capital outlays on regional consolidated high schools.

Capital section of expenditure from 1867 to 1878 for Nova Scotia comprises capital outlays from current funds plus debt charges. From 1909 to 1924 it comprises capital outlays from current funds plus debt charges. From 1925 to 1953 no breakdown between current and capital is available.

Where total expenditure was not available in Nova Scotia, it was assumed equal to current revenue. Where capital outlays only were known the current expenditure was estimated by deducting capital outlays from total revenue. Local revenues other than tax are probably buried in tax where they are not reported. 1893 reports cover nine months only.

In New Brunswick, 'other' revenues were not reported separately, so they may be included in the tax or omitted. This is usually a small component, running, where the amount is known, not over 3 per cent of revenues.

The Department of Education of New Brunswick purports to report total expenditures and to show whether the funds were provided by grants or local tax. We have therefore assumed that grants and taxes provide all funds, and that revenues and expenditures were equal in years when accounts could be completed on these assumptions.

Quebec reported fees and other revenue separately from 1915 on. Prior to 1915, other revenue reported comprised fees only. It has not been assumed in Quebec as in other provinces that revenue and expenditure were approximately equal, because it is known that debentures were often used to raise money for current expenditures, and the school board debt over the years rose to crippling amounts until, about 1947, the provincial government assumed a large proportion of it. The sudden drop in revenue from fees (under 'other sources') in 1884 occurred only in the cities, and is assumed to result from a change of local policy.

The accounts for the years 1947 were estimated for various sources. Quebec school boards report on an academic year basis, while most other provinces report on a calendar year basis. Academic year accounts have been converted to an estimate of the calendar year from 1954 to 1958. As reports for 1958–59 were not available, the Quebec report contains an estimate for the last four months of 1958.

In Ontario, annual payments of principal and interest on debentures were included in current expenditures, and could not be separated out, from 1867 to 1927. Capital expenditure during this period represents capital outlays only.

From 1928 to 1932 capital included both capital outlays from current funds and debt charges. In 1928 secondary school debentures were not reported at all, and for this reason outlays from current funds are unknown.

From 1933 to 1939 capital included only debt charges, capital outlays from current funds being included in current expenditures.

From 1939 to 1947 capital outlays from current funds in the elementary schools could be established and this amount has been included in capital expenditure, but in the secondary schools, capital outlays were buried in current expenditures during this time.

A peculiarity of Ontario receipts has been the inclusion of balances, buried in other sources of revenue. An attempt to eliminate this was made by subtracting the previous year's surplus from other sources, in each year up to 1945, while this method of accounting was used. Elementary school balances were identifiable for various periods prior to 1945, but secondary school balances were not.

In Manitoba, prior to 1890, Protestant and Roman Catholic school systems existed side by side. On 1 May 1890 the two systems were combined in a public nondenominational system. The taxes reported here for 1884 to 1886 inclusive are known to be for the Protestant section only, and 1887 taxes probably are, also.

From 1883 to 1906 gross capital outlays only were reported, debt charges being included in current expenditure payments, and debenture sales were not identified, so that it was not possible to estimate Manitoba's capital outlays from current funds.

Saskatchewan and Alberta inherited an education system from the Northwest Territories administration when they were established as provinces in 1905. The Dominion government assumed responsibility for the administration of the Northwest Territories in 1869. The Territories then included all areas north and west of Ontario, except British Columbia. Manitoba became a province in 1870, inheriting from the Northwest Territories a dual school system, about which we have no financial data prior to 1877. Yukon became a separate territory in 1898, but records show no school system operating in the Yukon area prior to 1900, so that the Northwest Territories school board finances here reported for the years 1890 to 1904 inclusive are actually those of the area which became Alberta and Saskatchewan in 1905. These provinces inherited the Northwest Territories system leaving no public schools in Northwest Territories until 1939–40 when public school districts were set up at Yellowknife and Fort Smith followed in 1953–54 by Separate School District No. 2. No financial information about these schools is available prior to 1954, except grants, which were obtained from Northwest Territories public accounts. Grants were paid irregularly from 1940 to 1948–49, the large grants of 1947–48 and 1948–49 being for building purposes. In 1952–53 regular grants on a per pupil basis were begun.

No information is available for British Columbia prior to 1873. From 1873 to 1898 the provincial government department of education contributed to 'education proper' which in the early years meant paying teachers' salaries and providing grants for current operating expenses of schools and paying the expenses of the Department of Education office, which ran from $3,357 in 1886 to $10,016 in 1897; and the Department of Lands and Works contributed to rural school construction, the two items making the provincial contribution to education. By deducting 'education office' expenses from this, the 'grants' figure was obtained, except in 1878 and 1883 when the amount was not reported separately. Grants in 1878 and 1883 are therefore inflated by this unknown amount.

Department of Education expenditures (including education office) for the years 1873 to 1885 were, respectively, as follows: $36,764; $35,288; $34,822; $44,506; $47,130; $43,334; $22,111 ($\frac{1}{2}$ year only); $47,006; $49,961; $49,269; $50,851; $66,654; $71,152.

The cities provided the school buildings in the early years and for this reason total capital cost, and taxation are unknown.

SOURCE: Department of Education reports, provincial public accounts and, for the years 1947 to 1953, D.B.S. compilations of the financial reports of school boards as reported in the biennial Survey of Elementary and Secondary Education.

Prior to 1898 Yukon was part of the Northwest Territories. Public accounts of Yukon Territory show no expenditure for education prior to 1900. Public accounts are not available from 1900 to 1936 inclusive, and the appropriation for schools, where available, has been used, with missing years estimated by interpolation from 1916 to 1936. A superintendent's report for 1918 indicates no 'substantial' change in staff or enrolment since 1905. Enrolments were given from 1909 to 1918 with some breaks, and the appropriations from 1909 to 1915 are assumed to bear some relation to enrolment. For 1900 to 1908 capital costs must have been considerable, and therefore no attempt has been made to estimate grants or costs.

Yukon Territory performs the functions of a school board, thus territorial expenditure for schools may be considered equivalent to grants in the provinces, as all expenses were paid out of general territorial revenue until 1949. In 1950 the National Defence establishment at Whitehorse began to pay fees for children living on the station, and in 1952 a local tax for school purposes began to be levied.

Totals for Canada have been prepared only where data were complete and comparable from province to province. (See notes above on individual provinces for varying interpretations.) Fiscal years for 1954 to 1958 are calendar years, except for Yukon, which is April to March, 1957–58 being reported as 1957 and similarly for earlier years. Prior to 1954, various fiscal years are used, though Ontario and the prairie provinces have been on a calendar year basis for many years.

V171–183. Expenditures of boards of publicly controlled elementary and secondary schools, by province and type of expenditure, selected years, 1870 to 1958

SOURCE: same as series V158–170.

See the note to series V158–170.

HIGHER EDUCATION (Series V184–225)

V184–195. Full-time undergraduate enrolment in universities and colleges by province and for Canada, by sex, 1920 to 1958

SOURCE: the files of the Education Division, Dominion Bureau of Statistics.

V196–206. Full-time and part-time graduate enrolment in universities and colleges, by province and for Canada, by sex, 1920 to 1958

SOURCE: the files of the Education Division, Dominion Bureau of Statistics.

V207–214. Degrees granted by Canadian universities and colleges, by type of degree and sex, 1920 to 1958

SOURCE: the files of the Education Division, Dominion Bureau of Statistics.

V215–225. Total full-time teachers in universities and colleges, by province, selected years, 1936 to 1958

SOURCE: the files of the Education Division, Dominion Bureau of Statistics.

Series V 1–20. *Total enrolment and total average daily attendance in publicly controlled elementary and secondary schools, by province, 1867 to 1958*

(thousands of pupils)

Year	Newfoundland		Prince Edward Island		Nova Scotia		New Brunswick		Quebec[1]	
	Total enrolment	Total average daily attendance	Total enrolment	Total average daily attendance	Total enrolment	Total average daily attendance	Total enrolment	Total average daily attendance	Total enrolment	Total average daily attendance
	1	2	3	4	5	6	7	8	9	10
1958	113.2	99.5	21.9	18.7	164.3	147.3	133.5	119.3	944.5[1]	917.7
1957	108.1	96.1	22.0	18.6	160.3	144.8	131.1	118.7	893.4[1]	914.5
1956	102.6	90.1	21.5	18.0	156.8	140.4	127.1	113.7	854.2	844.3
1955	97.8	85.4	20.6	17.6	151.7	136.5	122.1	105.6	811.9	806.2
1954	92.4	80.8	20.4	16.8	146.4	129.8	117.4	100.7	761.9	718.0
1953	87.8	77.0	19.7	16.2	141.5	126.7	110.6	95.8	719.0	681.3
1952	83.7	71.1	19.1	15.3	138.0	117.3	106.5	87.7	676.4	646.0
1951	79.3	67.6	18.9	15.3	134.5	114.3	105.7	84.9	640.8	606.0
1950	78.3	66.7	18.9	15.0	130.4	111.8	104.1	87.2	619.6	587.6
1949	75.1	59.5	18.4	14.7	127.1	107.9	101.3	82.2	525.3[1]	566.5
1948	72.9	55.7	18.6	14.7	124.1	103.9	98.3	81.1	568.4	545.8
1947	71.9	54.1	18.5	14.4	122.2	102.1	96.4	78.1	554.5	535.7
1946	70.5	52.1	18.6	14.3	120.7	99.4	95.2	74.5	537.8	529.6
1945	69.7	51.2	18.3	13.0	116.6	93.8	90.1	70.7	542.9	523.7
1944	67.6	49.1	17.5	12.6	114.9	89.5	88.7	69.5	599.4	518.9
1943	66.4	48.1	16.8	12.8	114.8	86.6	89.2	69.8	545.4	515.1
1942	66.2	44.3	18.4	13.0	116.1	89.9	91.1	72.1	554.7	532.8
1941	67.2	46.1	18.5	12.9	116.9	89.4	92.0	69.3	584.4	542.9
1940	66.5	46.7	18.6	13.6	117.2	93.4	93.6	73.0	593.4	555.8
1939	65.9	45.2	18.5	13.4	117.0	93.3	94.2	73.2	608.7	560.0
1938	64.3	43.4	18.4	13.5	116.4	93.2	93.9	73.0	594.1	549.4
1937	62.5	40.9	18.3	13.3	116.7	92.7	94.2	72.7	581.3	541.7
1936	59.0	39.1	18.5	13.1	116.9	92.3	93.0	71.1	586.7	539.7
1935	57.4	37.7	18.6	13.5	116.8	90.6	92.3	70.8	575.6	539.4
1934	55.1	36.9	18.9	13.4	117.8	93.3	92.7	72.1	571.9	542.4
1933	55.3	36.7	18.8	13.8	117.2	93.9	90.9	72.2	567.3	525.2
1932	59.2	40.2	18.3	13.1	116.0	89.5	89.8	71.4	559.7	518.9
1931	60.6	40.3	17.8	12.7	115.5	87.4	88.8	70.9	538.4	502.9
1930	60.8	40.0	17.5	12.2	113.9	85.1	87.3	65.7	486.3	478.7
1929	60.6	38.7	17.3	12.1	113.2	84.3	84.4	63.3	555.2	468.5
1928	60.7	38.7	17.5	12.1	112.9	82.6	83.3	62.2	543.6	461.2
1927	60.3	38.7	17.4	11.8	112.6	81.4	81.9	61.1	540.8	452.8
1926	59.1	36.5	17.7	11.8	112.4	80.4	81.3	58.7	532.0	448.3
1925	59.4	36.0	17.7	12.3	112.4	80.3	80.4	58.4	527.5	443.7
1924	58.1	34.5	17.5	11.8	111.6	79.5	79.4	58.4	517.5	430.2
1923	56.4	34.2	18.0	11.8	114.5	83.5	78.9	53.7	516.8	426.9
1922	55.2	33.6	18.7	12.3	114.2	79.4	77.9	51.7	510.6	426.5
1921	55.6	33.8	17.8	11.4	109.5	78.2	73.8	49.7	493.1	401.7
1920	53.6	31.2	17.6	11.0	108.1	66.4	73.0	47.0	478.0	379.3
1919	—	—	17.9	10.9	107.0	65.9	71.0	45.8	452.9	370.7
1918	—	—	18.1	11.3	108.1	67.9	71.8	46.5	438.5	369.4
1917	—	—	18.5	11.3	109.0	70.1	72.0	46.9	463.4	367.9
1916	—	—	18.6	11.3	109.2	69.2	73.0	48.1	270.6[1]	373.8
1915	—	—	18.7	11.7	107.8	70.4	72.0	47.9	448.1	360.9
1914	—	—	18.4	11.2	106.4	66.6	70.6	44.5	435.9	344.7
1913	—	—	17.8	11.0	105.4	65.7	69.7	44.4	411.3	324.4
1912	—	—	17.4	10.9	104.0	63.6	69.2	43.7	400.0	314.5
1911	—	—	17.7	10.5	102.9	61.3	69.0	42.8	389.1	301.7
1910	—	—	18.2	11.6	102.0	65.6	68.2	42.6	374.6	293.0
1909	—	—	18.4	11.5	101.7	61.8	67.7	42.5	367.0	285.7
1908	—	—	18.3	11.6	100.1	58.3	66.4	40.2	352.9	271.0
1907	—	—	19.4	11.5	100.0	57.2	66.4	38.8	346.9	266.5
1906	—	—	19.2	11.9	100.3	59.2	66.6	38.5	332.6	263.1
1905	—	—	19.5	11.6	100.3	56.3	66.9	39.4	335.8	255.4
1904	—	—	19.2	11.7	96.9	54.0	65.3	37.6	329.7	246.3
1903	—	—	20.0	12.1	98.8	55.2	66.0	38.0	326.2	243.1
1902	—	—	20.8	12.9	99.1	55.4	67.4	38.7	321.2	236.9
1901	—	—	21.0	12.3	98.4	53.6	66.7	37.5	314.8	232.3
1900	—	—	21.3	13.2	100.1	56.2	67.2	37.9	302.4	—
1899	—	—	21.9	12.9	100.6	55.9	63.5	38.2	307.3	229.6
1898	—	—	22.2	13.4	101.2	57.8	63.3	38.5	304.3	227.0
1887	—	—	22.2	13.0	101.2	54.9	61.9	37.3	334.3	222.3
1896	—	—	22.4	13.4	101.0	54.0	62.2	37.8	293.7	221.0
1895	—	—	22.4	13.3	100.6	54.0	62.8	38.1	286.2	221.2
1894	—	—	22.4	12.8	98.2	51.2	61.3	37.1	274.8	206.1
1893	—	—	22.4	13.0	94.8	50.1	60.2	37.0	267.1	206.5
1892	—	—	22.3	13.0	—	51.0	60.8	35.1	263.8	205.6
1891	—	—	22.5	12.9	85.6	49.3	59.6	34.1	227.6	204.2
1890	—	—	22.7	12.5	88.2	49.6	58.7	33.5	244.0	202.4
1889	—	—	23.2	13.2	86.5	50.0	59.8	31.7	222.0	124.8
1888	—	—	22.6	12.2	86.6	48.7	59.6	32.2	291.2	192.0
1887	—	—	22.6	12.3	86.7	50.1	59.8	33.1	265.6	190.9
1886	—	—	22.5	12.6	86.9	51.1	61.8	33.0	217.0	130.0

[1] See the note on series V 9 and 10.

Series V 1–20. *Total enrolment and total average daily attendance in publicly controlled elementary and secondary schools, by province, 1867 to 1958 (continued)*

(thousands of pupils)

Year	Newfoundland Total enrolment	Newfoundland Total average daily attendance	Prince Edward Island Total enrolment	Prince Edward Island Total average daily attendance	Nova Scotia Total enrolment	Nova Scotia Total average daily attendance	New Brunswick Total enrolment	New Brunswick Total average daily attendance	Quebec[1] Total enrolment	Quebec[1] Total average daily attendance
	1	2	3	4	5	6	7	8	9	10
1885	—	—	22.1	12.2	86.6	48.4	63.0	33.6	288.8	189.8
1884	—	—	21.8	12.0	84.3	47.3	53.5	31.9	213.6	138.7
1883	—	—	21.5	11.8	81.9	45.7	50.7	31.9	207.4	132.5
1882	—	—	21.3	11.3	81.2	43.7	52.8	29.2	155.0	133.6
1881	—	—	21.6	11.9	80.2	43.5	49.6	31.1	204.0	180.4
1880	—	—	21.2	11.3	78.8	42.6	50.3	29.7	203.2	180.3
1879	—	—	19.9	10.7	84.4	45.9	53.7	30.9	206.2	183.7
1878	—	—	19.2	10.4	84.2	49.0	52.8	30.7	—	180.3
1877	—	—	16.1	9.3	83.9	46.7	51.6	28.3	212.0	176.6
1876	—	—	—	—	82.0	45.4	47.9	27.6	206.2	184.2
1875	—	—	14.8	—	81.9	44.2	46.0	24.9	202.5	193.7
1874	—	—	—	—	79.9	44.1	44.8	23.5	219.7	186.9
1873	—	—	—	—	78.3	41.4	40.4	22.5	217.0	171.2
1872	—	—	—	—	76.5	40.8	28.8	15.3	215.9	—
1871	—	—	—	—	77.2	43.6	32.0	17.7	214.5	—
1870	—	—	—	—	76.2	42.2	30.7	16.6	209.0	—
1869	—	—	—	—	75.5	43.1	32.6	16.4	207.0	—
1868	—	—	13.4	—	72.1	39.8	31.4	14.8	205.5	—
1867	—	—	—	—	70.1	36.9	28.2	14.7	—	—

Year	Ontario Total enrolment	Ontario Total average daily attendance	Manitoba Total enrolment	Manitoba Total average daily attendance	Saskatchewan Total enrolment	Saskatchewan Total average daily attendance	Alberta Total enrolment	Alberta Total average daily attendance	British Columbia Total enrolment	British Columbia Total average daily attendance
	11	12	13	14	15	16	17	18	19	20
1958	1174.6	1071.4	164.0	148.5	187.7	169.1	247.2	231.1	277.1	252.4
1957	1097.5	1040.7	164.8	148.9	182.9	164.8	234.4	220.4	260.1	234.0
1956	1037.3	980.9	160.2	144.2	181.2	161.8	223.9	209.0	240.7	218.8
1955	979.6	895.9	152.1	138.2	177.0	156.9	212.7	198.5	223.8	203.6
1954	933.1	857.5	146.6	132.3	170.4	149.0	201.4	186.5	210.2	191.2
1953	877.9	775.3	139.6	124.5	163.5	142.2	189.1	174.0	195.3	176.1
1952	814.1	710.2	132.8	117.8	168.3	139.7	179.7	163.5	183.1	163.4
1951	768.2	674.9	128.9	112.7	167.5	137.6	174.0	150.0	173.4	154.1
1950	745.3	660.2	126.5	106.0	166.7	137.0	167.8	146.4	164.2	147.6
1949	712.4	638.7	122.9	105.2	167.4	135.9	160.8	136.7	155.5	138.9
1948	690.6	613.6	120.5	103.7	168.6	135.6	156.6	133.4	146.7	129.9
1947	678.0	597.7	120.8	103.7	170.3	135.0	155.5	131.0	137.8	121.3
1946	666.5	590.8	121.3	104.7	173.6	138.3	155.5	133.2	130.6	114.6
1945	651.0	571.6	118.4	101.0	175.0	135.3	152.5	130.1	125.1	107.6
1944	645.3	559.8	119.1	99.5	179.4	136.8	152.0	128.1	119.0	103.0
1943	621.9	554.0	123.1	100.2	186.3	138.0	157.5	127.2	115.4	93.5
1942	626.8	576.7	126.6	106.6	197.0	154.2	161.6	139.9	118.4	102.1
1941	642.7	582.5	131.6	110.8	201.4	155.9	163.4	135.4	119.6	103.2
1940	663.7	607.7	134.4	114.8	205.2	163.6	163.9	139.9	120.5	108.8
1939	678.8	605.5	137.2	115.7	206.6	163.4	163.2	138.4	120.9	107.7
1938	671.3	607.9	139.3	116.7	211.3	173.2	166.7	135.2	120.4	106.5
1937	667.3	605.8	140.5	117.2	215.6	165.5	168.0	133.1	118.4	104.0
1936	673.7	601.8	142.5	115.7	217.2	164.1	167.2	132.7	116.7	101.9
1935	678.2	609.3	144.7	117.4	221.3	175.3	168.0	136.2	117.2	104.8
1934	694.6	607.7	147.3	120.3	223.5	175.5	172.0	139.2	115.8	103.4
1933	699.4	613.1	150.1	121.2	225.9	175.0	171.4	137.6	116.8	105.0
1932	690.2	606.9	151.9	122.8	229.2	176.9	170.8	136.7	115.9	103.5
1931	668.1	597.2	153.6	120.7	230.5	176.7	168.7	134.1	113.9	99.4
1930	706.4	592.3	143.1	117.0	228.4	169.9	164.5	129.4	111.0	96.2
1929	706.2	583.3	146.8	116.6	227.3	161.7	161.2	120.2	109.6	94.4
1928	686.3	535.7	150.9	114.3	223.0	157.2	155.9	116.2	108.2	91.8
1927	673.0	528.5	148.8	106.8	218.6	157.4	151.3	112.4	105.0	88.3
1926	670.6	512.2	148.3	106.8	213.4	152.4	148.2	108.9	101.7	85.3
1925	658.9	508.0	145.8	104.3	206.6	144.7	145.7	106.0	98.0	82.7
1924	650.7	496.7	145.0	103.8	204.2	139.8	145.3	104.0	96.2	79.3
1923	634.1	482.1	142.4	98.8	194.3	130.5	145.8	103.6	94.9	77.8
1922	—	475.6	136.9	95.4	183.9	119.0	142.9	100.5	91.9	75.5
1921	—	450.7	129.0	86.1	184.8	113.4	124.3	89.4	86.0	68.6
1920	—	398.3	123.5	88.6	174.9	101.4	135.8	82.4	79.2	59.8
1919	—	391.5	114.7	72.1	164.2	98.0	121.6	74.8	72.0	56.7
1918	—	382.5	109.8	70.0	151.3	91.0	111.1	68.5	67.5	54.7
1917	—	371.1	106.6	69.2	142.6	88.8	107.7	65.4	65.1	52.6
1916	—	366.9	103.8	66.6	129.4	71.5	99.2	60.3	64.6	50.9

Series V 1–20. *Total enrolment and total average daily attendance in publicly controlled elementary and secondary schools, by province, 1867 to 1958 (continued)*

(thousands of pupils)

Year	Ontario Total enrolment	Ontario Total average daily attendance	Manitoba Total enrolment	Manitoba Total average daily attendance	Saskatchewan Total enrolment	Saskatchewan Total average daily attendance	Alberta Total enrolment	Alberta Total average daily attendance	British Columbia Total enrolment	British Columbia Total average daily attendance
	11	12	13	14	15	16	17	18	19	20
1915	571.4	368.0	101.0	68.3	122.9	72.1	97.3	61.1	64.3	52.5
1914	563.9	357.5	94.0	58.8	114.0	65.0	89.9	54.6	62.0	49.1
1913	544.1	340.2	83.7	48.2	101.5	56.0	79.9	45.9	57.4	43.1
1912	527.6	323.4	—	48.0	81.9	49.9	70.4	39.2	50.0	37.4
1911	518.6	305.6	80.8	45.3	72.3	38.3	61.7	32.6	44.9	32.5
1910	510.7	299.7	76.2	43.9	65.4	34.5	55.3	29.6	40.0	28.4
1909	507.2	295.4	73.0	41.4	55.1	29.0	46.0	22.2	36.1	25.7
1908	501.6	292.1	71.0	40.7	47.1	26.1	39.7	18.9	33.2	23.5
1907	493.8	285.0	67.1	37.3	37.6	19.8	34.3	17.3	30.0	20.5
1906	492.5	285.3	64.1	34.9	31.3	15.8	28.8	14.8	28.5	19.8
1905	487.6	281.7	63.3	33.8	25.2	13.5	24.3	13.4	27.4	18.9
1904	484.4	273.8	58.5	31.3	41.0[2]	20.9[2]	—	—	25.8	17.1
1903	487.9	275.4	57.4	36.5	33.2	16.3	—	—	24.5	16.6
1902	489.9	276.0	54.2	28.3	27.4	—	—	—	23.9	16.6
1901	492.5	275.2	51.9	27.6	23.8	—	—	—	23.6	15.3
1900	495.5	275.9	50.5[3]	27.9	20.3	—	—	—	21.5	13.4
1899	504.7	282.3	48.7	25.5	18.8	—	—	—	19.2	12.3
1898	512.8	287.4	44.1	25.0	16.8	—	—	—	17.7	11.1
1897	517.9	288.4	39.8	21.5	14.6	—	—	—	15.8	10.0
1896	516.7	271.4	38.0	20.2	—	—	—	—	14.5	9.3
1895	518.7	286.6	35.4[3]	19.5	—	—	—	—	13.5	8.6
1894	516.1	282.9	32.7	16.3	—	—	—	—	12.6	7.8
1893	512.9	273.3	28.7	14.2	—	—	—	—	11.5	7.1
1892	508.5	267.5	23.2	13.0	—	—	—	—	10.8	6.2
1891	514.0	268.3	23.9	12.4	—	—	—	—	9.3	5.1
1890	516.0	262.7	23.3[3]	11.6	—	—	—	—	8.0	4.3
1889	519.5	264.7	18.4	11.2	—	—	—	—	6.8	3.7
1888	513.3	256.3	18.0	9.9	—	—	—	—	6.4	3.1
1887	510.7	255.4	16.9	9.7	—	—	—	—	5.3	2.9
1886	502.8	247.8	15.9	8.6	—	—	—	—	4.5	2.5
1885	486.7	234.1	13.1[3]	7.8	—	—	—	—	4.0	2.1
1884	479.7	229.2	11.7	6.5	—	—	—	—	3.4[4]	1.8[4]
1883	476.2	222.0	10.8	5.1	—	—	—	—	2.7	1.4
1882	484.0	220.8	7.0	3.3	—	—	—	—	2.7	1.4
1881	489.4	222.5	4.9	2.4	—	—	—	—	2.6	1.4
1880	496.0	227.3	—	—	—	—	—	—	2.5	1.3
1879	499.1	226.4	—	—	—	—	—	—	2.3	1.3
1878	499.6	230.6	—	1.3	—	—	—	—	2.2	1.4
1877	498.0	222.4	—	1.0	—	—	—	—	2.0	1.3
1876	499.1	198.6	—	.8	—	—	—	—	1.7	1.0
1875	490.0	192.9	—	.8	—	—	—	—	1.4	.9
1874	479.1	192.2	—	—	—	—	—	—	1.2	.8
1873	473.8	193.2	—	—	—	—	—	—	—	.6
1872	462.4	188.7	—	.6	—	—	—	—	—	—
1871	443.0	188.3	.8	—	—	—	—	—	—	—
1870	433.3	181.6	—	—	—	—	—	—	—	—
1869	423.9	178.1	—	—	—	—	—	—	—	—
1868	410.6	170.0	—	—	—	—	—	—	—	—
1867	389.9	167.1	—	—	—	—	—	—	—	—

[1] See notes to series V 1–20 for the coverage of the total enrolment figures for Quebec in various years.

[2] Prior to 1905 the enrolment figures include Saskatchewan and Alberta which were then part of the Northwest Territories.

[3] These figures include students in elementary schools and an unknown number of students in secondary school.

[4] Prior to 1885, the enrolment figures are for elementary schools only. In 1885 total secondary and other enrolment was 178.

Series V 21–31. *Number of pupils enrolled in publicly controlled elementary schools, by province and sex, selected years, 1870 to 1958*

Year	Total ten provinces	New-foundland	Prince Edward Island	Nova Scotia	New Brunswick	Quebec[1]	Ontario	Manitoba	Saskatchewan	Alberta	British Columbia
	21	22	23	24	25	26	27	28	29	30	31
Male and female											
1958	2,827,302	98,731	18,333	138,785	113,831	808,067	950,275	134,339	150,968	196,131	217,842
1957	2,709,290	95,081	18,462	136,096	112,289	775,842	893,577	136,114	148,073	187,867	205,889
1956	2,599,277	90,428	18,111	133,626	109,307	750,573	846,415	133,001	146,185	180,284	191,347
1955	2,486,416	86,231	17,440	129,314	105,436	721,399	803,613	128,094	144,129	171,957	178,803
1950	1,955,698	69,808	15,975	113,063	90,956	556,950	604,111	101,390	137,514	135,012	130,919
1945	1,737,641	63,413	14,987	101,594	79,618	489,994	524,973	98,840	143,794	122,498	97,930
1940	1,817,599	60,783	15,744	98,529	82,968	533,613	527,694	107,098	168,496	131,447	91,227
1935	1,876,940	53,875	15,366	99,722	80,956	539,314	552,616	115,210	185,577	139,306	94,998
1930	1,911,154	57,857	15,228	100,945	80,834	470,007	606,854[2]	136,027	203,293	145,262	94,847
1925	1,871,348	52,495	15,963	100,499	74,894	513,383	574,532[2]	132,467	188,561	131,924	86,730
1920	1,738,912	52,746	17,142	98,605	62,785	469,605	558,804	115,456	164,629	126,602	72,538[3]
1915	1,503,341[5]	—	18,020	98,291	64,998	442,462	516,517	94,576	116,072	92,053	60,352[3]
1910	1,231,408[5]	—	17,932	93,378	60,944	370,903	464,042	70,594	62,767	53,219	37,629[3]
1905	1,080,267[5]	—	19,117	92,966	58,595	332,876	442,661	60,049	24,571	23,669	25,763[3]
1900	1,023,288[5]	—	21,288	92,880	59,886	301,610	456,260	50,460[3]	19,928[4]		20,976[3]
1895	—	—	21,877	95,027	61,955	284,751	476,116	35,371[3]	—	—	13,004[3]
1890	—	—	22,523	83,893	58,250	243,147	484,181	23,256[3]	—	—	7,785[3]
1885	—	—	—	83,808	62,652	254,984	463,332	13,074[3]	—	—	3,849[3]
1880	—	—	—	78,808[3]	50,308[3]	203,189	467,914	—	—	—	2,462[3]
1875	—	—	—	81,878[3]	46,039[3]	202,544	465,451	—	—	—	1,403[3]
1870	—	—	—	76,237[3]	30,693[3]	209,013	351,248	—	—	—	—
Male											
1958	1,467,193	50,323	9,743	72,024	59,081	419,383	494,671	69,538	78,075	101,182	113,173
1957	1,404,211	48,569	9,801	70,653	58,232	402,504	463,342	70,546	76,607	97,209	106,748
1956	1,346,000	45,961	9,557	69,204	56,697	389,947	437,883	68,869	75,484	93,318	99,080
1955	1,287,530	43,879	9,235	66,898	54,563	374,674	415,733	66,408	74,374	89,065	92,701
1950	1,013,384	35,426	8,399	58,627	46,839	290,022	313,187	52,489	71,014	69,680	67,701
1945	—	—	7,777	51,834	40,062	—	270,239	50,578	73,559	62,919	50,422
1940	—	—	8,226	51,019	42,074	246,312[1]	269,404	55,026	86,621	67,518	47,182
1935	—	—	7,929	51,088	40,974	—	283,775	58,971	95,577	70,755	49,033
1930	—	—	6,896	51,756	40,668	—	313,025[2]	65,448	104,261	73,714	48,670
1925	—	—	8,297	51,229	37,224	—	294,729[2]	—	96,739	65,933	—
1920	—	—	—	49,866	—	—	—	—	—	—	36,946[3]
1915	—	—	—	50,213	—	—	—	—	—	41,707	31,215[3]
1910	—	—	—	47,737	—	—	—	—	—	—	19,432[3]
1905	—	—	—	47,929	—	—	—	—	—	—	13,671[3]
1900	—	—	—	—	—	—	—	—	—	—	10,864[3]
1895	—	—	—	—	—	—	—	—	—	—	6,610
1890	—	—	—	—	—	—	—	—	—	—	4,018[3]
1885	—	—	—	—	—	—	—	—	—	—	2,210[3]

[1] See the note to series V 1–20 for coverage of enrolment figures for Quebec. For 1940, male pupils in Quebec are Roman Catholic only.
[2] For 1930 enrolment was as of 31 May; for 1925 enrolment was as of December. See the notes to series V 1–20.

[3] Includes an unknown number of secondary students.
[4] Includes Saskatchewan and Alberta which were then part of the Northwest Territories.
[5] For 1900 to 1915, total 9 provinces; Newfoundland excluded.

Series V 32–42. *Number of pupils enrolled in publicly controlled secondary schools, by province and sex, selected years, 1870 to 1958*

Year	Total ten provinces	New-foundland	Prince Edward Island	Nova Scotia	New Brunswick	Quebec[1]	Ontario	Manitoba	Saskatchewan	Alberta	British Columbia
	32	33	34	35	36	37	38	39	40	41	42
					Male and female						
1958	585,446	14,170	3,584	24,823	19,487	133,603	214,528	29,205	35,730	51,088	59,228
1957	531,139	12,714	3,465	23,588	18,224	115,057	195,328	28,227	33,826	46,530	54,180
1956	493,243	11,844	3,388	22,535	17,084	100,579	183,807	26,735	34,279	43,665	49,327
1955	449,781	11,204	3,157	21,667	15,952	87,308	169,007	23,613	32,088	40,748	45,037
1950	348,844	8,037	2,832	17,335	11,176	60,382	134,759	19,349	28,903	32,778	33,293
1945	307,979	5,878	2,483	14,993	7,437	50,777	118,445	19,550	31,177	30,034	27,205
1940	329,316	5,360	2,564	17,638	9,467	46,704	127,255	21,990	36,661	32,445	29,232
1935	277,419	3,495	2,928	17,076	6,817	23,244	118,897	18,828	35,251	28,648	22,235
1930	213,161	2,902	1,979	12,915	4,801	16,285	98,582	15,819	24,451	19,257	16,170
1925	172,883	1,597	1,756	11,853	5,466	14,068	82,502	13,367	17,536	13,768	10,970
1920	—	823	237	9,450	2,265	8,034	—	7,996	10,296	9,148	6,636
1915	92,357[3]	—	309	9,477	2,030	5,706	52,513	6,387	6,790	5,233	3,912
1910	73,547[3]	—	239	8,057	1,935	3,651	46,658	5,653	2,625	2,088	2,041
1905	62,688[3]	—	197	7,286	1,805	2,893	44,974	3,238	620	585	1,090
1900	—	—	198	7,249	1,558	839	39,191	—	415	—	553
1895	—	—	178	5,528	853	1,429	42,598				515
1890	—	—	149	2,991	439	893	31,779	—	—	—	244
1885	—	—	121[2]	2,770	349	—	23,372	—	—	—	134
1880	—	—	108[2]	—	—	—	28,041	—	—	—	—
1875	—	—		—	—	—	24,501	—	—	—	—
1870	—	—		—	—	—	82,020[4]	—	—	—	—
					Male						
1958	288,862	6,934	1,539	11,372	8,763	64,361	108,184	14,832	17,337	25,682	29,858
1957	260,507	6,205	1,484	10,676	8,078	55,034	98,512	14,115	16,159	23,080	27,164
1956	241,870	5,798	1,483	10,308	7,467	47,967	92,928	13,330	16,290	21,669	24,630
1955	218,592	5,437	1,399	9,726	6,961	41,189	85,057	11,590	15,034	19,892	22,307
1950	165,913	3,617	1,195	7,528	4,910	30,169	65,358	8,918	13,059	15,202	15,965
1945	—	—	986	6,193	2,912	—	54,938	8,930	13,321	13,362	12,879
1940	—	—	1,056	7,315	3,846	17,236[1]	59,949	10,295	16,440	14,669	14,367
1935	—	—	1,060	7,112	2,697	—	57,502	9,018	15,722	13,186	10,956
1930	—	—	566	4,931	1,902	—	47,072	6,569	10,226	8,223	7,455
1925	—	—	557	4,696	2,278	—	38,054	—	7,255	5,917	—
1920	—	—	—	3,312	—	—	—	—	—	—	2,826
1915	—	—	—	3,436	—	—	—	—	—	523	1,844
1910	—	—	122	3,181	—	—	—	—	—	—	919
1905	—	—	101	2,732	—	—	—	—	—	—	433
1900	—	—	—	—	—	—	—	—	—	—	212
1895	—	—	—	—	—	—	—	—	—	—	238
1890	—	—	89	—	—	—	—	—	—	—	111
1885	—	—	67	—	—	—	—	—	—	—	58

[1] See the note to series V 1–20 for coverage of enrolment figures for Quebec. For 1940, male pupils in Quebec are Roman Catholic only.
[2] Figures for 1880 and 1885 do not include data of Prince of Wales College.
[3] For 1905 to 1915 total 9 provinces; Newfoundland excluded.

[4] There appears to have been a substantial reclassification of pupils in Ontario from secondary to elementary between 1870 and 1875. See also the entries for series V 27 for 1870 and 1875.

Series V 43–53. *Number of the population at school, by age and sex, census years, 1911 to 1951*

Year	Total[1]	New-foundland	Prince Edward Island	Nova Scotia	New Brunswick	Quebec	Ontario	Manitoba	Saskatchewan	Alberta	British Columbia
	43	44	45	46	47	48	49	50	51	52	53
					Male pupils 5 to 11 years						
1951	690,788	22,488	5,409	37,195	29,107	214,544	207,493	37,017	42,038	46,166	49,331
1941	568,044	—	5,252	31,162	24,720	182,179	175,532	34,184	46,284	38,695	30,036
1931	611,638	—	5,101	32,140	25,736	179,997	191,058	41,881	59,518	42,742	33,465
1921	522,643	—	4,865	29,970	21,277	156,434	162,235	38,372	49,178	34,081	26,231
1911	356,355	—	5,001	26,462	18,153	122,007	120,885	20,025	18,798	13,149	11,875
					Male pupils 12 to 17 years						
1951	482,403	15,183	4,018	26,031	20,737	136,891	146,387	26,665	34,204	36,077	36,210
1941	464,149	—	3,781	23,329	18,387	133,760	144,330	30,978	43,809	35,930	29,845
1931	430,191	—	3,597	22,913	17,187	107,421	139,744	32,714	44,781	34,444	27,390
1921	310,962	—	3,549	20,692	14,286	82,405	99,854	23,614	27,218	22,405	16,939
1911	209,943	—	3,879	16,914	12,477	58,523	76,832	13,534	11,092	8,778	7,914
					Male pupils 18 years and over[2]						
1951	95,199	1,238	443	3,597	2,648	26,561	33,755	5,219	5,466	7,101	9,171
1941	61,640	—	406	2,572	2,038	15,816	19,971	3,913	5,856	5,666	5,402
1931[2]	43,055	—	309	1,769	1,468	10,365	16,775	3,026	3,331	3,094	2,918
1921[2]	24,144	—	233	1,397	839	6,650	9,558	1,502	1,238	1,335	1,392
1911[2]	14,051	—	172	878	701	3,686	5,805	951	566	595	697
					Female pupils 5 to 11 years						
1951	667,290	22,201	5,357	36,355	28,237	207,520	199,544	35,418	40,192	44,604	47,862
1941	559,388	—	5,195	30,611	24,728	180,602	172,116	33,358	45,151	38,341	29,286
1931	602,626	—	5,182	31,863	25,234	179,421	187,275	41,001	58,086	42,008	32,556
1921	515,877	—	4,675	29,102	21,374	157,759	159,629	37,495	47,172	33,044	25,627
1911	348,617	—	4,820	26,041	17,608	122,200	116,893	19,540	17,967	12,207	11,341
					Female pupils 12 to 17 years						
1951	469,733	14,810	4,089	26,096	21,103	126,285	143,137	26,875	35,087	36,473	35,778
1941	467,935	—	4,108	24,933	19,806	129,088	146,720	31,273	44,329	36,762	30,916
1931	430,476	—	3,754	23,907	17,921	105,251	137,325	32,794	46,137	35,544	27,843
1921	316,697	—	3,527	21,613	15,224	83,758	101,715	23,900	27,032	22,252	17,676
1911	212,378	—	3,638	18,040	13,041	59,645	77,070	13,662	10,705	8,523	8,054
					Female pupils 18 years and over[2]						
1951	61,404	1,059	398	2,853	1,968	14,081	21,083	3,804	5,251	5,388	5,519
1941	53,016	—	347	2,902	2,230	8,707	16,797	3,928	6,609	6,756	4,740
1931[2]	36,709	—	258	2,184	1,488	5,281	13,900	3,025	4,074	3,678	2,821
1921[2]	20,258	—	221	1,574	931	3,275	8,347	1,560	1,505	1,473	1,372
1911[2]	12,213	—	135	1,203	735	1,912	5,588	987	558	608	487

[1] Includes Newfoundland in 1951 only.

[2] Data for 1911, 1921 and 1931 do not include persons over 24 years of age at school.

Series V 54–67. *Distribution among grades of pupils enrolled in publicly controlled elementary and secondary schools, by province, census years, 1871 to 1951 and 1958*

Year	Pre-grade 1	Grade 1	Grade 2	Grade 3	Grade 4	Grade 5	Grade 6	Grade 7	Grade 8	Grade 9	Grade 10	Grade 11	Grade 12	Grade 13
	54	55	56	57	58	59	60	61	62	63	64	65	66	67
							Newfoundland							
1958	4,232	15,983	13,629	13,236	12,530	11,882	10,805	8,801	7,615	7,388	3,931	2,807	44	—
1951	—[1]	17,212[1]	10,417	9,572	8,474	7,774	6,809	5,905	4,185	3,931	2,734	1,849	49	—
1941	—[1]	18,538[1]	8,413	8,288	7,190	6,504	5,170	3,866	3,425	2,047	1,512	1,826	—[2]	—
1931	—[1]	19,902[1]	7,715	7,932	7,500	4,406	5,077	3,522	1,226	1,917	765	628	2	—
1921	4,471	4,145	3,901	3,933	3,644	2,404	1,597	1,458		713		156	24	—
							Prince Edward Island							
1958	97	2,464	2,457	2,482	2,524	2,510	2,200	1,901	1,698	1,397	1,159	625	403	—
1951	—	2,552	2,163	2,067	1,858	2,003	1,988	1,686	1,563	1,190	1,076	563	97	—
1941	—	3,034	1,902	1,727	2,187	2,051	1,602	1,381	1,509	1,197	993	313	149	—
1931	—	2,988	1,833	2,265	2,028	1,641	1,576	1,425	1,633	931	957	162	83	—
1921	—	5,929		5,425		4,240		1,462		—			154	—
1911	—	5,790		6,563		5,044		20	7	—	—	—	—	—
1901	—	4,744		7,037		3,776		3,218	1,851	—	—	—	—	—
1891	—	5,590		6,728		4,438		4,038	1,401					
							Nova Scotia							
1958	15,384	17,455	16,357	17,165	17,244	16,659	14,496	12,925	11,100	9,618	7,892	5,222	2,091	—
1951	14,319	11,240	15,186	15,134	14,075	13,415	12,580	11,359	9,274	7,444	5,450	3,729	1,278	—
1941	12,325	8,635	12,675	13,195	12,832	12,233	10,829	9,564	7,863	6,518	5,131	3,762	1,318	—
1931	12,919	10,873	12,768	13,042	13,193	12,363	10,421	8,730	7,350	5,970	4,645	2,684	553	—
1921	7,087	24,152	12,733	11,875	11,039	10,952	8,946	7,103	5,891	4,896	3,058	1,407	289	—
1911	976	26,167	11,767	11,774	11,746	10,660	8,936	6,913	5,295	4,717	2,550	1,223	186	—
1901	663	18,522	13,089	11,975	12,655	10,590	8,700	8,292	6,628	4,461	1,850	878	107	—
1891	—	17,799	12,097	11,255	11,434	9,691	7,531	7,628	4,452	1,594	804	470	—	—

Series V 54–67. *Distribution among grades of pupils enrolled in publicly controlled elementary and secondary schools, by province, census years, 1871 to 1951 and 1958 (continued)*

Year	Pre-grade 1	Grade 1	Grade 2	Grade 3	Grade 4	Grade 5	Grade 6	Grade 7	Grade 8	Grade 9	Grade 10	Grade 11	Grade 12	Grade 13
	54	55	56	57	58	59	60	61	62	63	64	65	66	67
New Brunswick														
1958	—	16,858	15,315	15,804	15,724	15,748	13,268	11,219	9,893	7,270	5,430	3,679	3,151	615
1951	—	15,023	13,376	13,030	12,123	11,453	10,206	9,104	7,540	4,818	3,773	2,724	141	—
1941	—	14,285	11,186	11,226	11,257	10,199	9,041	7,708	6,936	4,436	2,807	1,949	65	—
1931	—	16,400	11,876	11,863	11,466	9,751	7,780	6,128	6,358	2,369	1,459	869	37	—
1921	—	16,179	11,111	11,221	10,791	8,604	3,326	2,643	1,958	1,192	686	380	12	—
1911	—	14,730	9,980	10,667	10,470	8,805	2,733	1,989	1,896	1,011	570	281	14	—
1901	—	14,936	9,321	10,049	9,795	8,494	2,521	1,894	1,721	893	454	246	18	—
1891	—	14,106	11,218	10,281	10,457	7,304	2,446	1,839	1,297	455	95	62	8	—
Quebec[3]														
1958	7,072	124,753	121,139	125,054	124,678	116,294	103,952	85,125	53,814	40,053	23,515	12,775	3,446	—
1951	4,192	97,997	95,303	93,509	87,775	77,717	66,644	50,980	28,121	18,853	9,699	5,663	1,759	—
1941	1,645	83,841	78,242	86,673	90,211	78,641	61,312	40,124	21,137	13,818	7,243	3,273	629	—
1931	92,068	90,683	95,283	89,405	64,749	39,418	24,058	13,739	8,230	4,349	2,185	1,516	—	—
1921	40,710	144,353	103,359	86,167	56,332	28,153	15,812	9,126	5,596	1,713	1,038	616	—	—
1911	—	144,845	94,206	71,555	40,697	21,513	8,585	4,005	2,705	569	405	—	—	—
1901	—	129,717	82,699	53,249	24,140	13,557	6,450	2,917	1,686	382	—	—	—	—
1892[3]	—	100,994	67,262	48,286	27,918	10,283	4,855	2,709	1,461	—	—	—	—	—
Ontario														
1958	77,073	133,705	123,707	118,891	112,554	114,862	102,534	87,457	79,492	79,402	58,633	37,177	26,769	12,547
1951	39,797	95,425	82,006	77,087	73,300	70,397	66,314	61,281	56,581	51,655	37,188	23,430	16,895	10,291
1941	21,032	76,103	66,468	62,105	62,968	62,943	58,170	52,277	57,801	41,162	31,242	20,033	14,326	8,431
1931	32,539	102,633	78,099	35,013	67,709	75,899	62,620	55,868	53,092	38,665	27,206	17,091	10,354	6,157
1921	25,959	130,312	80,132	35,792	73,198	64,522	55,989	47,760	63,589	17,983	12,644	10,433		1,491
1911	20,677	122,258	65,962	89,630		88,886		85,940		30,079		12,511		2,662
1901	11,405	108,526	69,551	86,982		92,203		84,106		17,269	14,158	6,652		1,682
1891	6,375	185,079		96,018		100,817		89,528		28,725	6,430	946		53
1881	—	161,463		107,458		120,725		73,754		—	—	—		—
1871	—	123,071		87,552		90,908		74,863		55,903	9,662	702		299
Manitoba														
1958	4,832	19,262	17,277	17,500	16,991	17,280	15,496	13,561	12,140	11,495	8,478	6,488	2,744	—
1951	—[1]	20,659[1]	15,381	14,416	13,584	13,096	11,523	10,860	9,106	7,637	6,234	4,923	1,449	—
1941	—[1]	20,765[1]	13,247	13,472	13,751	13,920	12,405	11,717	10,200	8,127	6,868	5,581	1,509	—
1931	—[1]	25,690[1]	16,532	17,079	16,667	14,950	12,467	11,116	9,569	7,004	5,094	3,784	743	—
1921	2,373	29,877	18,374	17,127	15,705	13,404	10,191	6,616	6,733	4,340	2,522	1,650	103	—
1911	—	22,828	10,594	10,053	9,477	7,254	5,740	3,660	4,886	—	—	—	—	—
Saskatchewan														
1958	2,286	21,559	20,184	20,446	19,572	19,813	17,151	15,688	14,269	13,095	9,690	7,438	5,507	—
1951	—[1]	21,961[1]	18,876	18,283	17,191	17,508	15,864	14,874	13,388	10,792	8,083	6,068	4,273	—
1941	—[1]	28,660[1]	20,608	20,893	21,649	21,634	19,333	17,125	15,762	11,751	9,448	7,893	5,869	—
1931	—[1]	39,694[1]	25,864	27,401	28,042	24,342	21,548	14,366	19,703	10,860	8,373	6,065	3,103	—
1921	1,728	45,406	21,997	24,357	24,095	18,263	13,934	9,369	12,921	5,709	3,246	3,027	770	—
1911	—	24,085	9,587	10,446	9,760	6,101	3,605	2,535	3,062	2,122		718	239	—
1901[4]	—	6,912	3,933	4,343	4,519	2,566		1,050		301		174	39	—
Alberta														
1958	—	28,955	26,679	26,291	25,859	26,026	22,799	20,309	19,213	18,114	13,738	10,780	8,456	—
1951	—	21,900	20,085	18,730	17,668	16,884	15,770	15,245	13,786	11,713	9,084	6,865	6,239	—
1941	—	20,125	16,910	17,486	17,398	16,954	15,525	14,205	12,568	11,368	7,458	6,275	7,153	—
1931[5]	—	25,527	19,269	19,644	18,920	17,949	15,851	13,598	13,706	10,024	7,242	4,894	2,106	—
1921[6]	—	31,436	16,171	16,066	14,152	12,031	10,922	8,416	7,625	3,522	2,236	1,371	380	—
1911[7]	—	18,866	8,864	10,291	10,338	6,744	4,123	—	—	1,563	607	264	—	—
1901[4]														
British Columbia[8]														
1958	3,522	31,206	29,393	28,737	28,138	28,116	24,878	22,371	21,481	20,428	16,552	12,400	9,012	836
1951	1,215	20,922	20,246	19,011	17,585	16,297	15,087	14,656	13,341	11,929	9,554	7,197	5,426	888
1941	—	12,168	10,980	11,327	11,851	11,831	11,471	11,282	9,924	9,674	7,625	5,955	4,738	808
1931	—	13,676	12,277	12,525	12,943	12,278	10,979	10,604	10,467	7,981	5,972	3,650	562	—
1921[8]	—	14,054	6,522	7,738	12,791	20,940	16,360	212	—	—	—	—	—	—
1911[8]	—	8,316	3,960	4,530	5,359	6,997	8,467	—	—	—	—	—	—	—
1901[8]	—	5,598	2,928	1,839	3,427	3,838	2,748	2,353	—	—	—	—	—	—
1891[8]	—	2,171	1,301	—	1,619	1,827	1,172	914	—	211	—	—	—	—

[1] In Newfoundland, Manitoba and Saskatchewan, for years 1931 to 1951 pre-grade 1 enrolment is included with grade 1 enrolment, series V 55.

[2] There was likely some enrolment in post-grade 11 commercial classes but the numbers were not reported.

[3] See note to series V 1–20 for coverage of enrolment figures for Quebec. For 1892 data include Roman Catholic elementary and secondary schools only. The figures for 1891 are not available.

[4] For 1901 the figures for Alberta are included with Saskatchewan.

[5] Includes enrolment in private schools of 2,944 pupils.

[6] Half year ending 30 June.

[7] Prior to 1912, school grades were known as standards 1 to 8.

[8] Prior to 1923 grades 1 to 7 were known as first and second primer followed by first to fifth readers.

Series V68–78. *Number of teachers in publicly controlled elementary and secondary schools, by province and sex, selected years, 1870 to 1958*

Year	Canada[1]	New-foundland	Prince Edward Island	Nova Scotia	New Brunswick	Quebec[2]	Ontario	Manitoba	Saskatchewan	Alberta	British Columbia
	68	69	70	71	72	73	74	75	76	77	78
						Male and female					
1958	132,803	3,527	849	5,912	4,981	42,758	40,403	6,645	8,033	9,702	9,993
1957	126,848	3,368	833	5,766	4,858	41,648	38,143	6,345	7,767	8,910	9,210
1956	120,033	3,106	822	5,586	4,636	39,689	35,560	6,080	7,624	8,391	8,539
1955	112,820	3,049	778	5,345	4,385	37,280	33,059	5,837	7,345	7,714	8,028
1950	88,599	2,375	711	4,279	3,477	28,757	25,128	4,829	7,210	6,071	5,762
1945	75,892[1]	2,227	665	3,617	2,862	26,347	21,837	4,353	6,916	5,099	4,196
1940	76,079	1,938	665	3,429	2,782	25,249	22,003	4,497	7,422	5,887	4,145
1935	74,174	1,709	652	3,649	2,622	23,132	21,427	4,396	8,443	5,911	3,942
1930	70,255	1,689	617	3,448	2,661	20,971	20,127	4,378	8,517	5,705	3,854
1925	61,881	1,529	616	3,331	2,484	19,122	17,977	4,028	7,736	4,864	3,294
1920	54,691	1,423	577	3,015	1,975	16,710	15,331	3,479	7,544	5,014	2,557
1915	48,046	—	586	2,945	2,106	14,796	13,504	2,976	4,949	4,218	1,966
1910	38,074	—	591	2,723	1,974	12,381	11,705	2,774	2,672	2,217	1,037
1905	30,455	—	570	2,566	1,866	10,943	10,598	2,272			629
1900	28,174	—	586	2,557	1,830	9,773	10,786	1,596	1,011		454
1895	25,690	—	559	2,399	1,746	8,956	10,238	1,093	592		298
1890	21,149	—	529	2,215	1,573	6,282	9,201	840	401		285
1885	—	—	494	2,055	1,659	6,773	8,036	476	224		—
1880	—	—	459	1,809	1,310	6,216	7,426	—	—		—
1875	—	—	306	1,775	1,217	—	5,425	—	—		—
1870	—	—	—	1,565	927	4,992	5,165	—	—		—
						Male					
1958	35,460	1,188	124	993	898	8,235	12,365	1,985	2,646	2,882	4,144
1957	33,475	1,119	116	970	882	7,799	11,640	1,866	2,521	2,655	3,907
1956	31,804	1,047	131	940	839	7,482	10,836	1,744	2,551	2,593	3,641
1955	29,556	1,018	107	876	720	7,081	9,983	1,668	2,369	2,409	3,325
1950	23,120	812	126	725	567	5,759	7,396	1,404	2,201	1,974	2,156
1945	15,439[1]	652	82	369	310	5,353	4,831	803	1,385	1,117	1,189
1940	20,017	711	173	542	469	5,030	6,500	1,174	2,457	2,079	1,593
1935	18,053	632	181	518	383	4,472	5,489	1,102	2,678	1,888	1,342
1930	14,064	544	135	296	267	3,751	3,971	831	2,285	1,405	1,116
1925	11,552	463	135	301	255	3,175	3,106	815	2,145	1,260	847
1920	8,852	302	91	199	141	2,548	2,248	669	1,583	1,161	572
1915	9,244	—	152	256	184	2,184	2,322	598	1,609	1,418	521
1910	7,396	—	188	339	233	1,704	2,233	621	1,074	716	288
1905	—	—	246	386	304	1,336	2,461	597	—	—	177
1900	—	—	314	616	370	1,248	2,630	592	—	—	176
1895	—	—	302	540	373	1,122	2,843	570	—	—	137
1890	—	—	276	580	394	725	2,730	451	—	—	139
1885	—	—	271	631	475	1,000	2,744	231	—	—	—
1880	—	—	263	720	526	1,154	3,264	—	—	—	—
1875	—	—	—	672	452	—	2,645	—	—	—	—
1870	—	—	—	767	399	1,096	2,753	—	—	—	—

[1] For 1945 and earlier years data for Canada do not include teachers in Newfoundland.   [2] See note to series V68–78 for coverage of teachers in Quebec.

Series V79–87. *Number of teachers in publicly controlled elementary and secondary schools, by province and class of certificate, selected years, 1870 to 1958*

Year	Total	Grade 10 at most[1]	J minus[2]	J[3]	J+1[4]	J+2 or 3[5]	J+4[6]	Special[7]	Un-classified
	79	80	81	82	83	84	85	86	87
				Newfoundland					
1958	3,575	533	—	1,271	996	495	279	1	—
1950	2,375	395	—	929	705	279	57	—	10
1940	1,938	110	—	944	588	165	131	—	—
1930	1,664	270	—	768	352	274	—	—	—
1920	1,423	298	—	666	286	173	—	—	—
				Prince Edward Island					
1958	851	100	1	24	399	277	46	4	—
1950	711	58	—	29	359	263	—	2	—
1940	665	—	—	13	376	270	—	—	6
1930	617	—	—	47	396	174	—	—	—
1920	577	6	—	133	347	91	—	—	—
1910	591	5	—	161	309	116	—	—	—
1900	586	—	—	117	349	120	—	—	—
1890	529	—	—	334	140	55	—	—	—
1880	459	—	—	358	69	32	—	—	—

Series V 79–87. *Number of teachers in publicly controlled elementary and secondary schools, by province and class of certificate, selected years, 1870 to 1958 (continued)*

Year	Total	Grade 10 at most[1]	J minus[2]	J[3]	J+1[4]	J+2 or 3[5]	J+4[6]	Special[7]	Un-classified
	79	**80**	**81**	**82**	**83**	**84**	**85**	**86**	**87**
				Nova Scotia					
1958	5,755	321	—	533	1,233	2,242	1,362	64	—
1950	4,279	511	—	479	1,224	1,332	733	—	—
1940	3,868	52	77	525	1,432	1,138	644	—	—
1930	3,448	475	410	1,026	974	293	270	—	—
1920	3,015	438	818	795	725	174	65	—	—
1910	2,723	268	853	940	567	—	95	—	—
1900	2,557	187	923	945	413	89	—	—	—
1890	2,265	—	855	1,067	297	46	—	—	—
1880	1,834	—	708	806	287	33	—	—	—
1870	1,593	—	748	597	229	19	—	—	—
				New Brunswick					
1958	4,981	422	—	146	3,552	107	483	271	—
1950	3,272	558	—	61	734	1,790	128	—	1
1940	2,782	—	—	193	780	1,746	—	52	11
1930	2,698	—	—	238	1,157	1,168	30	—	105
1920	2,054	—	—	410	945	595	25	—	79
1910	1,974	—	—	431	969	515	23	—	36
1900	1,856	—	—	472	881	455	22	—	26
1890	1,617	—	502	797	262	—	12	—	44
1880	1,333	—	446	608	242	2	12	—	23
1870	961	18	343	320	250	18	12	—	—
				Quebec					
1958	40,038	4,385	2,497	8,550	8,497	13,500	1,456	—	1,153
1950	27,226	2,988	3,367	8,426	3,412	8,027	630	—	376
1940	14,339	528	—	5,531	7,231	419	630	—	—
1930	12,107	736	7,060	2,612	1,322	—	377	—	—
1920	9,644	949	7,517	—	1,000	—	178	—	—
1910	7,500	1,453	5,435	—	491	—	121	—	—
1900	6,509	698	5,250	—	457	—	104	—	—
1890	5,440	908	4,219	—	228	—	85	—	—
				Ontario					
1958	39,706	878	—	2,051	2,983	23,950	6,801	3,043	—
1950	25,178	1,350	—	59	4,033	13,337	4,286	2,113	—
1940	22,008	—	—	78	6,958	8,660	4,398	1,914	—
1930	19,569	242	138	628	12,391	3,671	2,075	424	—
1920	14,829	766	491	1,159	9,606	1,367	1,319	121	—
1910	11,406	719	419	2,971	5,044	693	920	—	640
1900	9,901	56	4,351	3,565	524	—	568	—	837
1890	8,394	217	4,069	2,829	258	427	—	—	594
1880	6,662	474	4,268	1,001	253	—	320	—	346
1870	5,447	—	4,319	342	259	—	—	—	527
				Manitoba					
1958	6,092	322	—	—	1,440	3,159	1,063	108	—
1950	4,829	400	—	10	800	2,533	695	83	308
1940	4,262	—	—	22	1,568	2,551	—	78	43
1930	4,716	30	—	73	2,819	1,707	—	87	—
1920	3,479	376	—	816	1,758	468	—	61	—
1910	2,774	251	—	718	1,452	353	—	—	—
1900	1,596	47	—	497	767	285	—	—	—
1890	821	100	—	369	279	73	—	—	—
				Saskatchewan					
1958	7,736	167	—	—	289	6,089	1,115	76	—
1950	7,210	596	—	17	777	5,096	677	43	4
1940	7,422	—	—	5	1,243	6,022	—	34	118
1930	8,528	2	—	28	5,400	3,098	—	—	—
1920	7,007	737	2,033	3,136	903	198	—	—	—
1910	2,726	541	837	1,082	212	54	—	—	—
				Alberta					
1958	8,687	221	—	54	647	5,867	1,882	16	—
1950	6,071	297	—	10	1,722	3,284	718	8	32
1940	6,990	—	—	6	1,440	5,145	276	123	—
1930	5,705	1	—	123	3,684	1,849	—	48	—
1920	5,014	706	567	2,532	1,044	—	—	71	94
1910	2,217	366	268	1,251	332	—	—	—	—
				British Columbia					
1958	9,993	113	—	22	1,148	4,764	3,937	9	—
1950	5,762	214	—	16	752	2,699	1,836	236	9
1940	4,145	—	—	41	680	3,115	—	309	—
1930	3,854	35	—	83	1,534	1,257	730	215	—
1920	2,557	132	404	976	499	—	417	129	—
1910	1,131	192	181	323	234	—	201	—	—

[1] Grade 10 at the most and no professional training, including those teaching on permits.

[2] Training and education below Junior Matriculation level. Usually the professional training required was less than one year, sometimes as short as six weeks.

[3] Training and education up to Junior Matriculation level; includes at least some professional training.

[4] Junior Matriculation level plus one year of professional training.

[5] Junior Matriculation level plus two or three years of further education including at least one year of professional training.

[6] Junior Matriculation level plus four or more years of further education including at least one year of professional training.

[7] Special includes vocational teachers and teachers certificated to teach only special subjects or classes such as music, art and the like.

Series V88–97. *Number of classrooms in operation in publicly controlled elementary and secondary schools, by province, selected years, 1870 to 1958*

Year	New-foundland	Prince Edward Island	Nova Scotia	New Brunswick	Quebec	Ontario	Manitoba	Saskatchewan	Alberta	British Columbia
	88	89	90	91	92	93	94	95	96	97
1958	3,387	817	5,583	4,594	—	41,355	—	7,322	8,729	—
1957	3,215	817	5,361	4,432	—	37,918	—	7,240	8,267	—
1956	2,998	799	5,208	4,207	—	35,699	—	7,159	7,801	—
1955	2,878	778	5,033	4,008	—	33,761	—	7,442	7,368	—
1950	3,354	707	4,250	3,369	—	—	—	—	6,050	—
1945	2,047	670	3,593	2,759	—	—	—	—	5,419	—
1940	1,810	675	3,408	2,711	—	—	—	7,071	6,180	—
1935	1,558	652	3,286	2,558	—	—	—	6,929	5,815	—
1930	1,565	615	3,191	2,441	—	—	—	6,850	5,558	—
1925	—	614	3,062	2,277	—	—	—	6,050	4,759	—
1920	—	580	3,015	1,898	—	—	—	5,591	4,289	—
1915	—	586	2,795	1,959	14,796[1]	13,504[1]	2,727	4,135	3,082	1,897
1910	—	591	2,579	1,859	12,370[1]	11,920[1]	2,227	2,261	1,610	1,012
1905	—	570	2,429	1,751	10,948[1]	10,598[1]	1,761	821	628	663
1900	—	582	2,417	1,771	—	10,192[1]	1,352	—	—	—
1895	—	561	2,305	1,695	—	—	982	—	—	—
1890	—	521	2,243	1,565	—	—	712	—	—	—
1885	—	494	2,014	1,430	—	—	390	—	—	—
1880	—	478	—	1,408	—	—	—	—	—	—
1875	—	409	1,742	—	—	—	—	—	—	—
1870	—	373	—	888	—	—	—	—	—	—

[1] This figure represents the number of teachers; therefore, it is an overestimate of the actual number of classrooms.

Series V98–108. *Number of pupils attending private elementary and secondary schools, by province, selected years, 1920 to 1958*

Year	Total[1]	New-foundland	Prince Edward Island	Nova Scotia	New Brunswick	Quebec	Ontario	Manitoba	Saskatchewan	Alberta	British Columbia
	98	99	100	101	102	103	104	105	106	107	108
1958	138,342	105	1,403	6,023	3,031	70,569	22,876	9,085	4,371	5,353	15,526
1957	131,742	82	1,333	5,254	2,332	71,259	21,412	8,468	3,261	4,990	13,351
1956	128,398	100	1,131	5,503	1,677	72,124	20,155	7,601	3,488	3,826	12,793
1955	119,840[1]	—	1,159	5,337	1,924	69,089	17,768	8,380	2,986	4,274	8,923
1950	100,253	—	971	4,217	2,306	56,240	18,823	5,271	2,630	3,539	6,256
1945	101,294	—	754	3,913	2,843	62,000	15,911	4,593	3,544	2,032	5,704
1940	88,397	—	576	2,719	2,707	53,561	13,515	4,632	2,037	3,739	4,911
1935	86,248	—	548	2,948	3,162	53,324	11,232	5,136	1,990	3,424	4,484
1930	94,830	—	605	2,833	3,890	57,841	12,232	5,784	2,787	3,557	5,301
1925	84,146	—	552	2,846	3,494	54,959	10,149	4,086	1,939	2,104	4,017
1920	—	—	—	—	—	50,708	—	—	—	—	—

[1] For 1955 and earlier years Newfoundland not included in total.

Series V109–118. *Number of pupils attending private business colleges, by province and sex, selected years, 1925 to 1958*

Year	Total	Prince Edward Island	Nova Scotia	New Brunswick	Quebec	Ontario	Manitoba	Saskatchewan	Alberta	British Columbia
	109	110	111	112	113	114	115	116	117	118
					Male and female					
1958	44,170	95	510	907	15,864	13,248	5,032	1,797	3,014	3,703
1957	45,446	111	574	636	15,700	14,145	5,842	1,869	3,338	3,231
1956	44,347	116	525	1,003	14,160	14,440	5,717	1,613	3,563	3,210
1955	39,409	122	477	837	13,500	11,723	4,317	1,545	3,534	3,354
1950	35,802	185	1,053	1,099	9,100	11,999	3,648	1,662	2,700	4,356
1945	30,486	104	684	816	8,557	9,961	3,532	1,200	2,726	2,906
1940	21,522	179	740	404	6,102	7,749	1,858	973	1,562	1,955
1935	19,757	175	542	556	5,377	6,225	3,087	883	1,338	1,574
1930	29,120	194	787	741	3,106	13,994	3,545	1,612	2,304	2,837
1925	22,337	62	688	577	2,860	9,673	2,914	1,314	2,209	2,040
					Male					
1958	9,810	27	64	148	5,540	2,158	1,042	205	236	390
1957	—	23	61	96	—	2,201	1,475	172	306	160
1956	—	20	35	246	—	2,847	1,290	161	306	226
1955	—	26	65	226	—	1,855	863	190	352	391
1950	9,101	66	268	372	2,615	2,704	1,079	302	627	1,068
1945	—	—	—	253	—	—	—	—	—	—
1940	—	52	172	168	—	2,107	700	236	456	529
1935	—	53	162	206	—	2,049	1,046	248	421	429
1930	8,585	56	196	215	1,127	3,791	1,132	361	879	828

Series V 119–128. *Number of pupils attending schools for the blind and deaf, by pupils' province of residence, selected years, 1870 to 1958*

Year	New-foundland	Prince Edward Island	Nova Scotia	New Brunswick	Quebec	Ontario	Manitoba	Saskatchewan	Alberta	British Columbia
	119	120	121	122	123	124	125	126	127	128
1958	91	10	158	123	792	554	108	123	142	224
1957	82	9	167	118	749	529	106	106	132	203
1956	86	10	148	118	737	515	118	118	87	184
1955	92	13	155	119	722	511	105	111	114	160
1950	76	26	183	115	632	481	71	117	104	128
1945	31	15	194	95	655	378	67	115	81	89
1940	11	5	202	104	737	433	150	115	101	92
1935	3	10	198	108	756	428	128	150	72	79
1930	38	11	178	99	732	429	109	66	55	86
1925	30	14	170	95	698	438	95	70	46	80
1920	33	10	148	55	542	368	90	55	36	23
1915	27	16	157	61	580	426	8	7	2	3
1910	24	14	164	73	537	418	5	4	4	1
1905	23	14	165	69	515	403	—	2	1	1
1900	18	11	193	75	523	427	—	—	—	—
1895	15	5	104	53	504	445	—	—	—	—
1890	12	3	82	31	489	455	—	—	—	—
1885	6	6	66	40	430	444	—	—	—	—
1880	—	—	—	—	324	479	—	—	—	—
1875	—	—	—	—	—	377	—	—	—	—
1870	—	—	—	—	80	—	—	—	—	—

Series V 129–136. *Number of pupils attending schools for the blind and deaf, by location of schools, selected years, 1870 to 1958*

Year	Nova Scotia	New Brunswick	Quebec	Ontario	Manitoba	Saskatchewan	Alberta	British Columbia
	129	130	131	132	133	134	135	136
1958	300	—	917	591	32	151	126	224
1957	308	—	841	590	31	142	—	203
1956	295	—	873	559	28	171	—	175
1955	310	—	880	553	32	183	—	167
1950	338	—	769	531	17	177	—	134
1945	301	—	700	432	33	141	—	101
1940	278	—	658	457	157	154	—	92
1935	283	—	691	428	167	124	—	79
1930	300	—	732	477	183	—	—	86
1925	315	—	698	495	165	—	—	80[1]
1920	284	—	542	413	159	—	—	—
1915	273	31	579	448	—[2]	—	—	—
1910	265	36	537	436	—	—	—	—
1905	264	30	515	399	—	—	—	—
1900	227	41	523	427	—	—	—	—
1895	146	36	504	443	—	—	—	—
1890	113	22	—	455	—	—	—	—
1885	100	17	430	444	—	—	—	—
1880	—	—	324	479	—	—	—	—
1875	—	—	—	377	—	—	—	—
1870	4	—	80	—	—	—	—	—

[1] The school for the blind in British Columbia became provincial in 1920. Provincial reports have no record of it before that date.

[2] No data available in provincial reports although the school was in existence prior to 1913.

Series V 137–147. *Number of students enrolled in normal schools and teachers' colleges[1], by province, selected years, 1870 to 1958*

Year	Canada[2]	New-foundland	Prince Edward Island	Nova Scotia	New Brunswick	Quebec	Ontario	Manitoba	Saskatchewan	Alberta	British Columbia
	137	138	139	140	141	142	143	144	145	146	147
						Male and female					
1958	14,242	—	43	319	387	8,697	3,647	509	640	—	—
1957	12,989	—	46	330	397	7,643	3,442	481	650	—	—
1956	13,663	—	60	329	382	7,419	3,139	591	800	—	943
1955	11,412	—	43	229	370	6,045	2,692	551	681	—	801
1950	10,319	143	76	343	170	6,136	1,481	360	582	475	553
1945	7,056	—	41	145	147	5,028	765	246	458	—	226
1940	7,049	—	140	307	254	3,082	1,247	205	909	614	291
1935	7,334	—	118	304	319	2,607	2,103	240	865	532	246
1930	7,310	—	219	263	300	1,985	1,530	549	1,296	803	365
1925	8,913	91	297	412	430	1,771	2,412	695	1,702	631	563
1920	5,608	138	137	228	267	1,303	1,248	526	899	575	425
1915	5,945	—	299	355	351	1,312	1,160	672	911	576	309
1910	3,995	—	285	260	358	787	1,235	503	241	218	108
1905	1,907	—	197	148	285	416	306	491	—	—	64
1900	—	—	203	223	259	329	781	263	95		—
1895	—	—	171	177	282	369	442	338	40		—
1890	—	—	134	114	239	280	418	87	—		—
1885	—	—	118	205	379	298	405	124	—		—
1880	—	—	78	151	274	314	483	—	—		—
1875	873	—	—	112	149	275	337	—	—		—
1870	712	—	—	—	88	284	340	—	—		—
						Male					
1958	2,706	—	4	25	72	1,582	723	114	186	—	—
1957	2,493	—	7	42	60	1,350	757	115	162	—	—
1956	2,671	—	5	45	61	1,166	670	184	228	—	312
1955	2,401	—	13	26	68	1,044	592	157	217	—	284
1950	2,024	80	16	70	30	895	377	92	167	133	164
1945	1,000	—	5	10	20	831	92	11	—	—	31
1940	1,873	—	35	42	65	969	292	31	176	186	77
1935	2,440	—	57	66	88	1,070	614	63	254	160	68
1930	1,230	—	71	23	32	193	298	84	319	150	60
1925	1,527	—	112	63	—	202	370	—	466	221	93
1920	636	—	77	—	25	173	203	55	—	103	
1915	714	—	113	28	52	191	126	—	—	204	—
1910	458	—	—	26	63	177	121	—	—	71	—
1905	297	—	101	—	54	142	—	—	—	—	—
1900	—	—	96	—	56	101	198	—	—	—	—
1895	—	—	101	—	56	130	157	—	—	—	—
1890	—	—	84	—	49	136	119	—	—	—	—
1885	—	—	—	—	63	130	145	—	—	—	—
1880	—	—	—	—	76	121	295	—	—	—	—
1875	312	—	—	—	55	116	141	—	—	—	—
1870	319	—	—	—	26	135	158	—	—	—	—

[1] These figures do not include students enrolled in university colleges of education.

[2] For 1945 and earlier years figures for Canada do not include data for Newfoundland.

Series V 148–157. *Number of students enrolled in university colleges of education, by province, 1920 to 1958*

Year	Canada	New-foundland	Nova Scotia	New Brunswick	Quebec	Ontario	Manitoba	Saskatchewan	Alberta	British Columbia
	148	149	150	151	152	153	154	155	156	157
1958	5,331	565	157	44	1,669	285	148	377	721	1,365
1957	4,387	390	116	28	1,214	371	128	331	695	1,114[1]
1956	3,333	306	139	46	1,167	407	148	267	735	118
1955	2,804	252	111	42	738	492	109	250	697	113
1950	1,961	131	114	6	181	427	120	265	498	189
1945	648	—	19	—	228	233	15	33	99	21
1940	731	—	30	3	190	329	34	45	31	69
1935	802	—	7	10	210	435	—	46	28	66
1930	528	—	—	—	86	341	—	—	—	101
1925	382	—	—	—	25	304	—	—	—	53
1920	136	—	—	—	—	136	—	—	—	—

[1] In 1956–57 the College of Education of the University of British Columbia took over teacher training formerly done by the provincial normal schools.

Series V 158–170. *Receipts of boards of publicly controlled elementary and secondary schools, by province and by source of funds, selected years, 1870 to 1958*

(dollars)

Year	Canada	New-foundland	Prince Edward Island	Nova Scotia	New Brunswick	Quebec	Ontario	Manitoba	Saskat-chewan	Alberta	British Columbia	Yukon	North-west Terri-tories
	158	159	160	161	162	163	164	165	166	167	168	169	170
						Provincial government grants							
1958	346,874,644	11,532,995	1,219,705	12,287,299	6,829,446	58,955,000	129,551,913	13,189,945	20,579,192	48,689,837	43,216,583	726,905	95,824
1957	285,074,895	8,934,795	1,174,252	11,314,997	7,712,300	48,659,000	98,182,276	10,092,521	18,636,687	40,593,970	39,446,218	259,578	68,301
1956	232,555,506	7,715,895	1,077,575	10,748,523	7,074,623	41,048,000	80,292,926	8,928,352	12,993,200	26,742,290	35,570,755	305,627	57,740
1955	214,491,774	6,959,716	994,249	7,389,431	6,775,614	38,827,000	73,649,871	8,578,062	11,594,469	24,979,893	33,992,023	694,480	56,966
1950	108,555,133	3,430,267	595,480	6,103,265	4,803,316	17,202,000	42,661,144	4,086,810	6,919,369	7,794,234	14,794,397	164,851	—
1945	48,883,300	—	318,460	2,109,109	1,016,639	7,273,000	26,606,874	1,482,381	3,191,011	3,042,302	3,786,904	56,470	150
1940	19,387,724	—	268,899	806,086	551,999	2,203,188	6,996,354	1,247,143	2,757,386	1,870,413	2,648,133	35,723	2,400
1935	13,559,617	—	264,541	631,234	446,472	1,059,401	4,739,116	988,434	1,804,842	1,432,085	2,157,525	35,967	—
1930	16,974,640	—	249,247	449,576	449,702	1,467,502	5,598,879	1,310,587	3,126,151	1,593,995	2,681,623	47,000	—
1925	13,433,273	—	244,643	356,794	417,200	987,805	4,721,600	1,091,151	2,136,106	1,084,879	2,348,095	45,000	—
1920	8,478,223	—	179,284	260,330	207,287	617,238	2,413,896	822,186	1,344,233	885,524	1,707,245	41,000	—
1915	5,811,858	—	143,187	256,326	214,209	577,635	1,104,775	503,774	1,055,230	540,235	1,371,487	45,000	—
1910	3,919,829	—	107,864	230,871	206,139	423,140	981,568	296,115	593,595	301,239	741,298	38,000	—
1905	—	—	106,318	199,955	163,299	237,000	535,642	214,796	157,468	131,511	451,731	—	—
1900	1,815,002	—	115,658	199,220	169,305	237,000	473,101	172,339	—	—	297,723	—	150,656[1]
1895	1,476,572	—	111,099	197,834	157,532	188,000	398,420	129,099	—	—	196,114	—	98,474[1]
1890	1,254,210	—	101,776	181,140	139,063	194,650	386,211	99,257	—	—	152,113	—	—
1885	—	—	99,254	169,914	178,141	152,868	350,588	40,916	—	—	—	—	—
1880	—	—	86,000	150,094	125,643	167,000	346,359	—	—	—	—	—	—
1875	—	—	52,702	139,980	109,856	166,000	347,881	—	—	—	—	—	—
1870	—	—	—	120,133	99,606	134,088	249,703	—	—	—	—	—	—
						Local assessment							
1958	494,976,033	162,625	1,177,600	15,258,348	14,796,544	120,519,000	197,655,645	24,400,414	34,613,107	41,091,848	45,127,873	69,479	103,550
1957	451,434,559	30,000	1,000,038	13,216,498	13,453,075	106,655,000	188,721,785	23,471,538	32,269,715	35,678,196	36,766,155	60,909	111,650
1956	393,637,479	—	855,740	11,383,492	11,756,598	93,878,000	164,295,095	21,424,949	29,707,169	30,374,780	29,794,611	59,709	107,336
1955	342,255,139	—	813,918	10,724,123	10,407,409	82,402,000	140,865,761	19,250,730	25,145,782	26,904,108	25,613,837	52,193	75,278
1950	—	—	488,714	5,974,035	6,660,199	46,832,000	73,195,577	12,875,011	16,372,024	19,619,264	16,683,852	—	—
1945	—	—	250,741	4,009,024	3,124,416	26,526,005	36,666,540	8,477,203	10,780,060	10,856,052	8,661,003	—	—
1940	—	—	176,057	3,379,497	2,650,791	20,204,598	42,151,109	6,699,506	7,252,136	8,684,262	6,935,916	—	—
1935	84,196,660	—	223,922	3,087,322	2,160,875	18,127,195	35,743,806	5,635,473	6,105,128	7,489,823	5,623,116	—	—
1930	98,663,320	—	189,669	3,024,194	2,618,062	17,613,082	41,751,799	7,675,879	10,670,745	8,854,951	6,264,939	—	—
1925	85,203,336	—	167,596	3,016,118	2,948,315	15,529,353	32,476,610	7,302,044	10,460,784	8,197,098	5,105,418	—	—
1920	62,619,746	—	131,031	2,185,662	1,460,941	9,807,527	22,753,821	6,922,864	9,149,253	6,894,401	3,314,246	—	—
1915	35,654,055	—	91,258	1,217,826	859,176	5,645,915	14,060,718	3,296,667	4,439,377	3,733,323	2,309,795	—	—
1910	18,866,693	—	53,925	895,429	670,522	3,217,576	8,600,799	1,682,238	1,369,531	1,278,013	1,098,660	—	—
1905	10,794,646	—	45,666	711,702	479,148	1,949,337	5,625,367	951,911	404,131	377,463	249,891	—	—
1900	7,742,463	—	34,055	630,243	437,261	1,414,054	4,313,856	645,283	—	—	81,888	—	185,823[1]
1895	6,577,263	—	39,427	567,944	279,301	1,232,115	3,785,521	481,828	—	—	51,438	—	139,689[1]
1890	5,777,714	—	37,610	492,195	278,141	902,808	3,782,268	225,089	—	—	14,428	—	45,175[1]
1885	—	—	44,389	451,342	—	783,016	2,922,903	195,640	—	—	—	—	—
1880	—	—	34,916	388,742	—	645,266	2,544,563	—	—	—	—	—	—
1875	—	—	—	385,473	—	563,615	2,465,817	—	—	—	—	—	—
1870	—	—	—	284,626	—	447,595	1,379,981	—	—	—	—	—	—

[1] Prior to 1905, Northwest Territories included the areas that later became Alberta and Saskatchewan.

Series V171–183. *Expenditures of boards of publicly controlled elementary and secondary schools, by province and type of expenditure, selected years, 1870 to 1958*

Year	Canada	New-foundland	Prince Edward Island	Nova Scotia	New Brunswick	Quebec	Ontario	Manitoba	Saskat-chewan	Alberta	British Columbia	Yukon	North-west Terri-tories
	171	172	173	174	175	176	177	178	179	180	181	182	183
						Current							
1958	690,542,147	10,117,872	2,049,309	23,802,344	19,132,867	136,782,000	273,717,565	33,800,050	45,588,127	65,945,827	78,963,366	511,329	129,491
1957	607,410,930	8,470,331	1,876,111	21,707,197	17,245,013	123,677,000	239,281,519	30,476,475	40,059,755	56,649,807	67,363,913	489,155	114,654
1956	534,695,873	7,783,000	1,714,307	19,576,600	15,366,708	108,185,000	211,387,627	27,550,121	36,070,707	49,131,886	57,352,574	445,276	132,067
1955	474,830,045	7,186,000	1,604,260	15,838,838	13,404,560	95,039,000	187,159,999	25,181,900	33,230,476	44,146,202	51,524,919	388,853	125,038
1950	—	3,651,758	1,053,945	—	—	51,593,130	99,184,110	14,601,883	20,770,756	24,653,882	25,266,970	148,265	—
1945	—	—	558,918	—	—	28,883,495	54,147,463	9,489,073	12,748,349	12,560,154	—	56,104	—
1940	—	—	437,144	—	—	19,164,019	40,927,448	6,709,151	8,185,117	8,760,293	—	35,723	—
1935	—	—	426,382	—	—	15,529,340	36,465,040	5,848,243	6,962,366	7,596,194	—	35,967	—
1930	—	—	428,845	—	—	18,221,624	40,178,902	7,668,097	12,206,821	9,251,575	—	47,000	—
1925	—	—	384,354	—	—	13,527,975	38,888,591	7,098,496	10,235,723	7,404,701	—	45,000	—
1920	—	—	295,266	2,080,116	—	8,691,129	24,366,632	7,031,704	9,141,328	6,326,190	—	41,000	—
1915	—	—	201,279	1,331,842	—	5,380,982	12,764,455	3,099,225	3,323,958	3,534,776	—	45,000	—
1910	—	—	152,142	1,019,853	—	—	8,376,690	1,759,915	1,611,756	1,204,440	—	38,000	—
1905	—	—	144,611	843,404	—	—	5,981,872	1,001,728	445,320	398,961	—	—	—
1900	—	—	143,800	709,225	—	—	4,764,759	658,488	—	—	—	—	332,871[1]
1895	—	—	141,140	690,574	—	—	4,371,975	440,976	—	—	—	—	—
1890	—	—	130,010	622,265	—	—	4,005,876	230,091	—	—	—	—	—
1885	—	—	136,143	577,185	—	—	3,292,814	239,530	—	—	—	—	—
1880	—	—	—	499,123	—	—	2,893,327	—	—	—	—	—	—
1875	—	—	—	325,446	—	—	2,488,302	—	—	—	—	—	—
1870	—	—	—	249,249	—	—	1,584,470	—	—	—	—	—	—
						Capital							
1958	172,531,877	3,259,957	403,203	3,336,422	3,275,213	58,085,000	54,175,971	2,809,946	9,256,058	25,498,719	11,783,154	612,204	36,130
1957	147,561,008	2,876,535	326,859	2,679,559	3,621,690	46,155,000	45,369,540	3,904,465	7,985,178	21,437,342	13,170,298	4,601	29,941
1956	114,875,540	2,036,000	200,699	1,765,783	3,288,263	38,554,000	39,173,747	2,929,797	6,761,808	8,636,096	11,487,917	672	40,758
1955	101,048,165	1,769,000	214,338	1,572,411	2,139,974	31,634,000	35,533,452	3,401,242	6,241,672	7,686,378	10,374,213	467,865	13,620
1950	—	857,316	126,529	—	—	11,325,320	13,836,402	2,773,767	4,339,708	3,512,085	7,245,277	33,586	—
1945	—	—	7,501	—	—	8,540,188	7,714,005	1,274,981	1,245,922	1,674,164	—	366	—
1940	—	—	7,265	—	—	6,898,987	7,971,033	1,096,491	1,565,857	2,131,739	—	—	—
1935	—	—	62,081	—	—	6,248,567	5,693,782	1,307,854	1,201,100	1,743,576	—	—	—
1930	—	—	10,071	—	—	5,618,001	9,280,730	1,724,050	3,549,221	1,939,792	—	—	—
1925	—	—	16,885	—	—	5,027,358	2,410,056	1,304,106	2,501,005	1,795,073	—	—	—
1920	—	—	15,049	365,876	—	2,949,633	2,406,424	—	1,680,615	1,667,511	—	—	—
1915	—	—	33,166	142,310	—	3,028,663	4,284,790	1,082,043	1,580,000	1,065,437	—	—	—
1910	—	—	9,647	106,447	—	—	2,602,677	802,361	643,114	830,633	—	—	—
1905	—	—	7,403	68,253	—	—	1,183,862	—	107,373	117,202	—	—	—
1900	—	—	5,913	120,551	—	—	540,926	—	—	—	—	—	55,451[1]
1895	—	—	9,386	75,881	—	—	544,801	—	—	—	—	—	—
1890	—	—	9,376	51,460	—	—	917,011	—	—	—	—	—	—
1885	—	—	7,500	46,191	—	—	449,649	—	—	—	—	—	—
1880	—	—	—	39,781	—	—	342,656	—	—	—	—	—	—
1875	—	—	—	60,069	—	—	836,791	—	—	—	—	—	—
1870	—	—	—	47,851	—	—	265,156	—	—	—	—	—	—

[1] Northwest Territories included, in 1900, the areas that later became Alberta and Saskatchewan.

Series V 184–195. *Full-time undergraduate enrolment in universities and colleges, by province and for Canada, by sex, 1920 to 1958*

Year	Canada Total	Women	New-foundland	Prince Edward Island	Nova Scotia	New Brunswick	Quebec	Ontario	Manitoba	Saskatchewan	Alberta	British Columbia
	184	185	186	187	188	189	190	191	192	193	194	195
1958	82,380	18,300	1,000	350	4,730	3,080	27,100	23,950	4,780	3,810	4,370	9,210
1957	74,710	16,200	730	310	4,470	2,760	24,600	22,200	4,370	3,300	4,000	7,970
1956	69,410	14,765	573	263	4,385	2,497	22,892	21,088	4,215	3,007	3,873	6,617
1955	65,051	13,979	482	246	4,055	2,259	21,317	20,442	4,114	2,614	3,472	6,050
1954	61,198	13,400	421	257	3,876	1,990	20,302	19,037	4,014	2,421	3,264	5,616
1953	60,046	13,225	426	268	3,579	1,801	19,847	19,333	3,941	2,310	3,018	5,523
1952	59,849	13,247	379	258	3,504	1,916	19,468	19,495	3,895	2,317	2,945	5,672
1951	64,036	13,866	380	270	3,879	2,020	19,819	21,268	4,411	2,575	3,015	6,399
1950	69,111	14,083	324	298	4,116	2,195	19,687	23,679	4,369	3,256	3,662	7,525
1949	75,807	14,415	—	306	4,307	2,509	20,317	26,303	5,528	3,956	3,984	8,597
1948	79,346	14,615	—	307	4,165	2,723	19,721	27,648	6,321	4,700	4,442	9,319
1947	76,237	14,531	—	276	4,161	2,509	19,016	25,848	6,443	4,689	4,124	9,171
1946	61,861	12,870	—	268	3,400	2,137	16,534	20,278	5,427	3,997	2,996	6,824
1945	38,376	10,995	—	179	2,112	1,252	13,387	12,297	2,789	1,787	1,478	3,095
1944	35,132	8,911	—	179	2,104	1,102	12,144	11,364	2,433	1,617	1,572	2,617
1943	35,692	8,423	—	152	2,019	1,020	11,734	11,734	2,607	2,001	1,719	2,706
1942	34,680	8,141	—	135	1,924	911	11,271	11,040	2,418	1,950	1,733	2,698
1941	34,817	8,107	—	128	1,964	1,011	10,930	11,693	2,483	1,945	1,939	2,724
1940	35,903	8,155	—	115	2,028	1,054	11,060	12,290	2,671	2,186	1,982	2,517
1939	35,164	7,664	—	115	2,079	1,006	10,921	12,229	2,738	1,858	1,831	2,387
1938	34,460	7,547	—	108	2,075	942	10,769	11,833	2,860	1,839	1,706	2,328
1937	33,918	7,582	—	96	2,137	882	10,471	11,946	2,759	1,788	1,756	2,083
1936	33,522	7,494	—	93	2,099	863	10,249	12,066	2,670	1,776	1,745	1,961
1935	33,051	7,375	—	104	2,010	872	10,053	12,002	2,654	1,766	1,694	1,896
1934	32,596	7,210	—	117	2,130	921	9,696	11,916	2,649	1,726	1,690	1,751
1933	33,166	7,565	—	119	2,159	935	9,655	12,078	2,940	1,735	1,617	1,928
1932	32,862	7,825	—	128	2,190	944	9,174	11,810	3,125	1,752	1,539	2,200
1931	31,576	7,428	—	102	1,968	903	9,090	11,414	2,608	1,755	1,490	2,246
1930	30,209	7,113	—	107	1,854	819	8,955	10,664	2,649	1,622	1,436	2,103
1929	28,306	6,492	—	107	1,778	730	8,501	9,928	2,538	1,449	1,294	1,981
1928	26,932	6,107	—	102	1,651	627	8,263	9,621	2,358	1,165	1,213	1,932
1927	25,734	5,787	—	101	1,554	627	8,118	9,121	2,263	1,109	1,065	1,776
1926	24,852	5,272	—	108	1,561	560	8,039	8,785	2,239	878	1,085	1,597
1925	24,805	5,229	—	125	1,585	493	8,030	8,752	2,258	870	1,077	1,615
1924	24,530	4,753	—	119	1,560	508	7,986	8,738	2,215	875	1,089	1,440
1923	25,212	4,622	—	107	1,629	513	8,016	9,393	2,161	871	1,210	1,312
1922	24,114	4,405	—	108	1,660	519	7,479	9,446	1,956	702	1,021	1,223
1921	22,791	3,716	—	107	1,660	487	7,157	9,050	1,644	647	989	1,050
1920	21,869	3,170	—	127	1,463	477	6,905	8,868	1,522	641	969	897

Series V196–206. *Full-time and part-time graduate enrolment in universities and colleges, by province and for Canada, by sex, 1920 to 1958*

Year	Canada Total	Women	New-foundland	Nova Scotia	New Brunswick	Quebec	Ontario	Manitoba	Saskatchewan	Alberta	British Columbia
	196	197	198	199	200	201	202	203	204	205	206
1958	5,896	996	20	140	57	1,791	2,781	225	119	294	469
1957	5,056	854	10	99	40	1,463	2,499	256	100	193	396
1956	5,013	797	4	81	47	1,602	2,371	245	111	201	351
1955	4,854	785	4	73	62	1,629	2,180	253	115	173	365
1954	4,709	785	—	67	54	1,548	2,312	190	95	144	299
1953	4,387	615	—	88	41	1,456	2,033	151	114	204	300
1952	4,302	663	—	83	41	1,488	1,911	195	116	189	319
1951	4,559	702	—	119	32	1,465	1,939	174	168	239	423
1950	5,262	1,127	—	112	42	1,857	2,283	173	104	259	432
1949	4,857	1,124	—	80	30	1,692	2,179	95	109	220	452
1948	4,139	867	—	97	31	1,361	1,900	99	73	216	362
1947	3,674	719	—	96	33	1,206	1,682	72	74	167	344
1946	2,870	630	—	78	22	921	1,463	59	46	101	180
1945	1,689	428	—	38	7	662	663	52	33	94	140
1944	1,392	404	—	29	3	471	630	29	28	78	124
1943	1,227	287	—	37	4	376	544	48	23	87	108
1942	1,406	312	—	33	9	396	662	48	30	87	141
1941	1,569	326	—	60	9	419	717	68	49	84	163
1940	1,601	354	—	71	19	393	753	61	43	99	162
1939	1,550	341	—	70	16	364	767	59	38	88	148
1938	1,540	332	—	61	13	348	799	46	46	77	150
1937	1,635	398	—	67	13	379	792	63	54	85	182
1936	1,586	388	—	59	26	385	751	73	58	84	150
1935	1,533	399	—	60	24	396	735	76	50	88	114
1934	1,687	424	—	56	21	411	869	61	53	100	116
1933	1,698	398	—	50	27	435	837	60	64	97	128
1932	1,569	402	—	42	13	435	740	65	66	96	112
1931	1,350	352	—	40	5	369	633	50	62	84	107
1930	1,137	318	—	47	11	351	546	33	33	57	59
1929	1,010	269	—	43	5	296	487	43	27	62	47
1928	1,039	291	—	52	8	316	473	41	29	69	51
1927	929	252	—	39	4	273	419	38	25	84	47
1926	846	221	—	21	6	253	385	40	21	66	54
1925	873	228	—	24	8	259	368	40	20	108	46
1924	851	221	—	21	9	222	396	44	—	105	54
1923	714	195	—	13	8	197	322	29	13	83	49
1922	558	158	—	15	6	162	222	31	16	68	38
1921	423	108	—	18	6	113	190	30	10	41	15
1920	383	99	—	12	1	98	182	21	6	43	20

Series V 207–214. *Degrees granted by Canadian universities and colleges, by type of degree and sex, 1920 to 1958*

Year	Bachelor and first professional		Master and Licence		Doctorate (earned)		Doctorate (honorary)	
	Total	Women	Total	Women	Total	Women	Total	Women
	207	208	209	210	211	212	213	214
1958	16,080	3,810	1,521	295	272	25	245	15
1957	14,800	3,460	1,449	271	292	23	209	10
1956	12,978	2,994	1,539	303	266	17	200	15
1955	12,039	2,822	1,438	268	271	24	282	25
1954	12,083	2,893	1,468	245	242	12	249	20
1953	12,575	2,938	1,418	219	262	23	286	12
1952	13,288	3,030	1,601	248	234	21	224	10
1951	15,754	3,200	1,632	227	202	11	186	11
1950	18,081	3,245	1,699	256	226	21	192	8
1949	17,883	3,415	1,619	255	194	19	227	8
1948	13,733	3,159	1,187	159	136	10	173	11
1947	9,830	2,580	1,084	143	116	13	175	8
1946	8,192	2,200	877	99	104	12	134	6
1945	6,416	1,779	602	106	89	11	114	4
1944	6,310	1,589	520	58	88	14	89	—
1943	6,335	1,577	600	89	97	16	129	7
1942	6,263	1,539	564	59	121	10	117	8
1941	6,576	1,582	673	71	75	5	83	6
1940	6,671	1,577	666	81	82	3	85	4
1939	6,439	1,576	632	94	80	7	107	9
1938	6,299	1,585	643	91	84	11	94	5
1937	6,145	1,513	600	90	78	7	129	4
1936	6,441	1,630	485	83	68	5	100	2
1935	6,226	1,578	481	107	77	4	76	3
1934	6,272	1,585	517	107	89	11	96	—
1933	5,891	1,584	529	112	87	9	102	—
1932	5,552	1,443	493	87	80	11	78	2
1931	5,290	1,338	468	100	46	7	95	—
1930	5,185	1,346	400	83	61	7	127	1
1929	4,932	1,221	363	79	51	5	108	1
1928	4,545	1,091	400	80	41	4	119	3
1927	4,414	993	362	78	40	1	79	2
1926	4,319	976	324	67	28	4	67	—
1925	4,037	856	323	69	33	3	72	2
1924	4,467	843	341	70	35	3	78	1
1923	4,509	799	315	65	31	2	84	1
1922	3,843	734	259	50	24	1	145	—
1921	3,627	664	218	48	24	1	58	—
1920	2,889	462	213	45	24	—	66	1

Series V 215–225. *Total full-time teachers in universities and colleges, by province, selected years, 1936 to 1958*

Year[1]	Canada	New-foundland	Prince Edward Island	Nova Scotia	New Brunswick	Quebec	Ontario	Manitoba	Saskatchewan	Alberta	British Columbia
	215	216	217	218	219	220	221	222	223	224	225
1958	7,500	54	16	335	210	2,725	2,550	380	320	330	580
1957	7,000	50	15	310	200	2,550	2,365	370	300	300	540
1956	6,719	46	14	308	187	2,429	2,298	353	279	275	530
1951	5,539	26	12	262	186	2,185	1,757	275	199	242	395
1946	4,503	—	16	202	104	2,154	1,336	214	162	155	160
1941	3,169	—	14	192	87	1,121	1,179	149	157	139	131
1936	3,115	—	18	199	60	1,209	1,036	164	192	121	116

[1] For the school year ending in the year given.

SECTION W: POLITICS AND GOVERNMENT

NORMAN WARD,[1] *University of Saskatchewan*

The data in the tables of section W fall into two major divisions. Series W1–250 concern the federal scene, series W251–339 the ten provincial scenes. Within the first major division, series W1–39 contain data on executive and legislative posts and occupants; series W40–176 on elections and parliamentary sessions; series W177–217 on employees and representation abroad; and series W218–250 on disallowance of provincial acts, reservation of provincial bills and on federal Royal Commissions. Within the second division series W251–255 present provincial data on lieutenant-governors and premiers, series W256–339 the results of provincial elections.

The statistics of this section are obtained in a way that places them in two major categories: those for which there are official records, such as the data for the monarchy, for the governor general and provincial lieutenant-governors, for parliamentary terms and for elections; and those for which only unofficial records exist, including all those involving election results by political parties, and political affiliation of ministers, electoral candidates and elected members of legislatures. This distinction arises from the nature of governmental and electoral processes.

Official data become available in several ways. First, official acts of the Government of Canada are published in the *Canada Gazette*, an official publication existing specifically for this purpose, and official acts of provinces are published in similar provincial publications. Thus notices of accession of monarchs, of appointments of governors general and lieutenant-governors, of establishment of portfolios or like posts and of the appointment of occupants, of the establishment of Royal Commissions and of the appointment of the commissioners, and of proclamation of elections and dissolution of parliament are published officially. Secondly, for the Dominion government, the Parliamentary Debates (Hansard) and other parliamentary documents are published; some provinces also publish the debates of their legislatures but the practice is not general and where followed is in most cases of recent origin. Thirdly, chief electoral officers of the Dominion government and of provincial governments publish results of elections giving numbers on electoral lists, votes polled by each candidate, spoiled ballots and the like. Finally, government departmental records are the sources of data such as the numbers of employees.

Unofficial data must be relied upon for those statistics which, for one reason or another, governments do not obtain or prepare. Except rarely, the political affiliations of candidates for election are not placed on ballots; the voter is presumed to vote for individuals. Consequently the results of voting by parties must be prepared by private individuals or bodies from information collected in various ways about party affiliation of the candidates who have been officially listed. Similarly, the designation of political affiliation of members of elected bodies, of ministries and the individual members thereof, is not given officially though it is fairly easy to obtain in most cases from the official or unofficial records of actions of legislating bodies. It nevertheless remains that the exercise of personal and private judgment plays some part in the listing of matters of party affiliation. An exception to the above is the fact that beginning with the election of 1945 for the Dominion parliament a document has been sent to those members of the armed services voting under the provisions of the election act, which makes special provision for servicemen voting, giving the party affiliation of each candidate as designated by the candidate himself. Some provincial governments also in more recent periods have given party affiliation on the ballot. Even in these cases problems may arise as more than one person in an electoral district may designate himself as a candidate for a given political party.

The reliability of the data both official and unofficial may vary depending on the process by which they are made known. Data obtained from official acts of governments are quite reliable. Official election results are also reliable though there is room for error. The counting of ballots is ordinarily done at each poll. Unless a recount is necessary there is no further counting. The results are sent from the polls to returning officers for electoral districts, and from returning officers to the Chief Electoral officers. Sources of error lie in the counting at polls, in the transmission of information from one person to another and in their final publication. The errors are apt to be small and may, to some extent, offset one another. The remaining official data, on employees in the Federal Civil Service, discussed more fully below, are subject to a lesser degree of accuracy owing to problems of classification of personnel, the dates at which a count is taken, and the inadequacy of department records in earlier years.

The unofficial data vary in accuracy depending on the nature of the material and the care exercised in handling it. In earlier years, when party affiliations were loose in any event, there is considerable room for error and even more recently the element of judgment involved in designating party affiliation allows some inaccuracies. Further, the assembly of electoral district data to obtain provincial and national aggregates requires careful handling. Owing to these factors varying unofficial sources sometimes are in conflict. In such cases that source which is believed to have the greatest accuracy is used.

The following list of sources used in assembling the data includes both official and unofficial publications. Official publications may give data coming from unofficial sources and unofficial publications may give data from official sources. The list gives government publications first.

Government publications: Dominion Bureau of Statistics, *Canada Year Book*, annual since 1905 (Ottawa, Queen's Printer), various years; Public Archives of Canada, *Guide to Canadian Ministries since Confederation July 1, 1867–January 1, 1957* (Ottawa, Queen's Printer, 1957); Dominion Bureau of Statistics, *Statement of Civil Service Personnel and Salaries in the Month of January, 1912–1924* (Ottawa, King's Printer, 1925); Parliament of Canada, *Civil Service Employees: Number Total Salaries and Bonus* (Ottawa, King's Printer, 1923); G. V. LaForest, Department of Justice, *Disallowances and Reservations of Provincial Legislation* (Ottawa, Queen's Printer, 1955); *Debates of the House of Commons* (Ottawa, Queen's Printer), various years;

[1] The author of this section wishes to acknowledge particularly the contribution of J. E. Hodgetts of Queen's University, who prepared series W247–250, and of Howard Scarrow of the University of Michigan, who provided much valuable assistance on the political statistics relating to federal and provincial election results.

Journals of the House of Commons of Canada (Ottawa, Queen's Printer), various years; Chief Electoral Officer, *Report of the Chief Electoral Officer* (Ottawa, Queen's Printer), various years; *A Statistical History of all the Electoral Districts of the Province of Ontario* (Toronto, undated); Province of Quebec, Bureau of Statistics, *Statistical Year Book* (Quebec, Queen's Printer, annual since 1913); Province of Saskatchewan, *Who's Who*; Great Britain, *The Public General Acts and Church Assembly Measure, 1960* (London, Her Majesty's Stationery Office, 1961).

Non-government publications: J. M. Beck, *The Government of Nova Scotia* (Toronto, University of Toronto Press, 1957); Keith Callard, *Commissions of Inquiry 1867–1959* (available on photostat in the Parliamentary Library, Ottawa); H. McD. Clokie, 'Basic Problems of the Canadian Constitution', *Canadian Journal of Economics and Political Science*, vol. 8, no. 2, February 1942; *Canadian Parliamentary Companion*, annual 1862 to 1897 (various editors and published at various places); Copp Clark Editorial Department, *Canadian Almanac and Directory* (Vancouver, Toronto, Montreal, The Copp Clark Publishing Co. Limited), various years; R. MacGregor Dawson, *The Government of Canada*, 3rd edition (Toronto, University of Toronto Press, 1957); James G. Foley, *Resume of General Elections, 1896–1911*; *Canadian Annual Review*, beginning in 1960 (Toronto, University of Toronto Press); Paul Gérin-Lajoie, *Constitutional Amendment in Canada* (Toronto, University of Toronto Press, 1950); J. E. Hodgetts, *Royal Commissions of Inquiry in Canada* (University of Toronto, M. A. Thesis, 1939); Frank MacKinnon, *The Government of Prince Edward Island* (Toronto, University of Toronto Press, 1951); Pierre G. Normandin, editor, *Canadian Parliamentary Guide*, annual since 1898, apparently a successor to the *Canadian Parliamentary Companion* (Ottawa); John Saywell, *The Office of Lieutenant-Governor* (Toronto, University of Toronto Press, 1957); H. G. Skilling, *Canadian Representation Abroad, From Agency to Embassy* (Toronto, University of Toronto Press, 1945); Norman Ward, *The Canadian House of Commons: Representation* (Toronto, University of Toronto Press, 1950).

Important sources of information, which contain much material included in the above sources, are the federal and provincial sessional papers.

The British North America Act, 1867 and its Amendments are the main formal foundation of government in Canada. They are not complete statements however of even the formal part of the constitution. Other statutes of the United Kingdom, such as the Statute of Westminster 1931, statutes of the parliament of Canada on such matters as the houses of parliament themselves, on election procedures and the like, and statutes of provincial governments on matters such as their own electoral and legislative forms are of the more formal part of the constitutional structure. In addition the informal parts of the constitution are very important. The system of cabinet government responsible to parliament and particularly the House of Commons as developed in the United Kingdom has been adopted in Canada; and other usages have also been adopted from the British parliament. The increasing numbers of conventions that have developed within the Parliament of Canada itself and within the provincial legislative bodies are also important parts of the constitution. (See the *Canada Year Book, 1957–58*, pp. 39–41, for the short but good statement on which this paragraph is based.)

THE FEDERAL GOVERNMENT, EXECUTIVE AND LEGISLATIVE POSTS AND OCCUPANTS (Series W 1–39)

W 1–2. The monarchy, 1867 to 1960

SOURCE: *Canada Year Book, 1959*, p. 61.

W 3–5. Governors general, 1867 to 1960

SOURCE: *Canada Year Book, 1959*, p. 62; *Canadian Almanac and Directory, 1960*, p. 301.

The Governor General of Canada is now appointed by the Queen on the advice of the Prime Minister of Canada. Before 1890 the Governor General was appointed by the monarch on the advice of British authorities alone, but thereafter the Dominion government was usually (though not always) consulted; the present practice dates from the Imperial Conference of 1926 which agreed that a Governor General was not the representative or agent of the British government but of the monarch. Until 1952, when a Canadian was first appointed Governor General of Canada, the incumbent was invariably a person of title from the United Kingdom. The term of appointment of the Governor General is not fixed, though six years is considered normal. No Governor General of Canada has been removed from office, though undoubtedly the government could advise the monarch to remove her representative. The Governor General has two Deputies (both are justices of the Supreme Court of Canada) who are empowered to act in his absence and in the event of a vacancy in the office, the B.N.A. Act recognizes an Administrator who can carry on in the name of the Queen.

W 6–16. Canadian ministries, dates, numbers of portfolios, turnover of personnel, and party affiliations, 1867 to 1960

SOURCE: *Guide to Canadian Ministries since Confederation; July 1, 1867–January 1, 1957*; *Canada Year Book, 1957–8, 1959*, p. 63; *Canadian Parliamentary Guide, passim*.

The Canadian ministry at any one time consists of all those sworn to act as the monarch's confidential advisers on affairs of state. The great majority of the ministers serve as heads of departments of government (e.g. the Minister of Agriculture is said to hold the Agriculture portfolio), but it is common for the ministry to include one or more 'ministers without portfolio', who have the same responsibilities as any other minister except those of a department head. Usually in Canada the ministry and the cabinet consist of the same people, but before 1926 it was customary for the incumbents of a few junior portfolios to be outside the cabinet. The parliamentary secretaries (members of parliament assigned to assist ministers) are not officially recognized as members of the ministry, although after some initial experimentation during World War I they have been accepted as a permanent part of governmental machinery. The term of a ministry is not fixed, but coincides with the term of a prime minister, who serves as long as he has the confidence of a majority of the members of the House of Commons, and thus may continue through several general elections. During the life of one ministry, a single portfolio may be held in succession by several individuals, while a single individual may in succession hold several portfolios; it is not uncommon for a portfolio to be temporarily vacant during which period an acting minister will serve, or for one individual to hold two portfolios coincidentally. Ordinarily all members of the cabinet must have or obtain a seat in the House of Commons, except for the government leader in the Senate.

The following qualifications and definitions apply to series W 6–16.

W 7. Dates of ministry are opening and closing dates of the prime minister's term in office.

W 8. Party gives the affiliations of prime minister and cabinet members.

W 9. Number of portfolios gives the total number of separate portfolios in existence during the ministry.

W 10. Number of occupants is the turnover of personnel in the portfolios in series W 9, including acting ministers.

W 11. Ministers without portfolio, number of posts, gives the maximum number of such posts in existence at any one time in the ministry.

W 12. Ministers without portfolio, number of occupants, gives the total number of persons holding posts of series W 11 at any time in the ministry.

W 13. Non-cabinet posts are the total number of ministerial posts whose incumbents were not members of the cabinet.

W 14. Number of occupants of non-cabinet ministers posts is the total number occupying such posts at any time.

W 15. Parliamentary secretaries' posts (the term was first used in Borden's ministry of 1917–20) are non-cabinet posts held by members of parliament, and identified by the term. The figures give the maximum number of posts at any one time in the term of the ministry.

W 16. Number of occupants of parliamentary secretaries' posts gives the total number of persons holding such posts at any time in the ministry's life.

W 17–28. Growth of representation in the House of Commons and redistribution, by province, 1867 to 1960

SOURCE: *Canada Year Book, 1959*, p. 59; Ward, *The Canadian House of Commons*, p. 56.

Representation in the Canadian House of Commons is based on the single-member constituency system (with two exceptions having two members) adapted to recognize the federal principle: seats in the House of Commons are divided among the provinces after each decennial census, in accordance with a formula described in the British North America Act. At present the House of Commons has a fixed total of 263 seats (temporarily raised to 265 in 1952 because of the operations of one of the clauses designed to protect the representation of smaller provinces from sudden drastic diminution), divided among the provinces on a basis proportionate to population. No province can have fewer members of parliament in the House of Commons than it has senators. The allocation of seats among the provinces is prescribed by law, but the actual drawing of constituency boundaries within each province has been effected since 1903 by legislation prepared by a committee of the House of Commons; prior to that, constituencies were created by legislation sponsored by the cabinet. Series W 17–28 show both general redistributions (1872, 1882, 1892, 1903, 1914, 1924, 1933, 1947, 1952) and partial redistributions occasioned by the admission of one or more new provinces (1871, 1873, 1887, 1907, 1949) or a constitutional amendment (1915).

W 25–26. Saskatchewan and Alberta, for the period prior to their creation in 1905, shows the representation of the Northwest Territories from which they were formed.

W 28. Yukon gives the representation of the Yukon, the only territory represented in the House of Commons after 1905 until the creation of the constituency of Mackenzie River in 1952, since when each district has one representative in the House of Commons.

W 29–39. Growth of representation in the Senate of Canada, 1867 to 1960

SOURCE: *Canada Year Book, 1959*, p. 66.

Representation in the Senate of Canada, as prescribed by the British North America Act, was originally intended to give equal representation of 24 senators each to the three main regions of Canada: the Maritimes, Quebec and Ontario. As the four western provinces developed, the same regional equality was ultimately extended to them by a constitutional amendment in 1915. The admission of Newfoundland in 1949 marred the symmetry of representation in the Senate but it had been agreed in 1915 that, in the event of Newfoundland's admission to Canada, the province was to be given the same number of seats as the last four provinces that were brought up to the basic

principle of equality. Additional senators beyond the original 24 for each region can be appointed but only in groups of four or eight depending on whether there are one or two additional senators for each major region, and the maximum senatorial membership cannot exceed 110. Such additional senators have never been appointed.

THE FEDERAL GOVERNMENT, ELECTIONS AND PARLIAMENTARY SESSIONS (Series W 40–176)

W 40–49. Dates of general elections and sessions of Dominion parliaments, 1867 to 1960

SOURCE: *Canada Year Book, 1940*, p. 46; *1945*, p. 53; *1957–8*, p. 46; *1959*, p. 65; supplemented by information in *Journals of the House of Commons, 1959, passim*.

The parliament of Canada has no fixed term; the British North America Act sets a maximum life of five years to a parliament, the time beginning from the day on which the writs certifying each member's election are returned. In 1916 the life of the twelfth parliament was extended one year by constitutional amendment. Within the five years prescribed by law, the actual choice of the date of a dissolution, a general election, and an opening and closing (or prorogation) of each parliamentary session, are within the discretion of the government, which formally advises the Governor General to make the appropriate announcement; a dissolution terminates the life of a parliament, and is shortly followed by an election.

W 44. Days of session include some adjustments to source data to adjust for the fact that, for an unexplained reason, the official sources deduct numerous adjourned days, commonly in long sessions, from the length of the session; where they can be detected, these omitted days have been added in obtaining series W 44.

W 45. Sitting days are not available before 1936 but could be computed from the *Journals of the House of Commons* for each year. There are minor discrepancies in the sources: for example, *Canada Year Book, 1945*, p. 53, gives the length of the 18th Parliament as 4 years, 3 months, 13 days, and *ibid. 1951*, p. 61, gives it as 4 years, 2 months, 16 days.

W 50–73. General elections, number of electors on lists and votes polled, by province and election, 1896 to 1960

SOURCE: *Canada Year Book, passim*; Foley, *Resume of General Elections, 1896–1911*. No official compilations of numbers of electors on lists exists before 1911; the detailed reports of general elections, constituency by constituency, appear in the *Sessional Papers* following each general election, 1867 to 1908. The statistics compiled by Foley, *op. cit.* were accumulated by him while he was Clerk of the Crown in Chancery and thus are virtually official. For changes in the franchise see Ward, *The Canadian House of Commons*.

Lists of electors in Canada are compiled for each general election, by house to house enumeration; an urban elector must be on a list in order to vote, but rural electors can be sworn in on polling day. The franchise has since 1920 been determined by the parliament of Canada, but for two periods, 1867 to 1885 and 1898 to 1920, provincial franchises were used in Dominion elections; during most of these periods, provincial polling lists were also used. The columns entitled 'Polled' indicate the numbers of electors who cast ballots, and include wasted ballots, which are now a negligible factor in elections.

Series W 54–57 from 1896 to 1958, and series W 58–59 and W 62–63 from 1896 to 1930, are skewed by the existence of two-member constituencies. In each instance each elector had two votes, but was counted only once as an elector; thus in Prince

Edward Island in 1958, for instance, 24,930 electors cast 42,954 votes in one constituency. See *Canada Year Book, 1926*, p. 82; *1945*, p. 66; *1957–58*, p. 57; *1959*, p. 76. See *ibid.* for slight skewing of results caused by occasional acclamations. Series W 72–73 include the electoral districts of Yukon and Mackenzie River 1953 to 1958, Yukon alone 1908 to 1949, and the Northwest Territories alone (from which Alberta and Saskatchewan were formed in 1905) 1896 to 1900.

Female suffrage in Dominion elections began on a partial basis in 1917, when female relatives of members of the armed forces voted, and was general for the election of 1921.

W 74–164. Votes polled in Dominion elections, by party and province, 1896 to 1960

SOURCE: Foley, *Resume of General Elections, 1896–1911*; *Canadian Annual Review, 1917*, p. 643; *1921*, p. 509; *1925–6*, p. 45; Chief Electoral Officer of Canada. The series for 1926 to 1940 were compiled by the Canadian Press, and thereafter by the Chief Electoral Officer, who was required after 1944 to ascertain party affiliations for the convenience of electors in the armed forces.

Compilations of election results by parties are at best semi-official. The actual votes polled by individual candidates in each constituency are initially counted by the deputy returning officers in each polling division, and reported to the constituency returning officer, who in turn reports to the Chief Electoral Officer; the party affiliations of candidates do not appear on the ballots or other official papers, except those used by members of the armed forces. The series for each general election show in the left-hand column the party polling the most votes but not necessarily (as in 1926 and 1957) winning the election.

W 79. 'Others' refers more often to independents from Quebec than to any other group of candidates. A multiplicity of parties began to appear after the general election of 1917, however, and the 'Others' columns altogether include votes polled by over twenty separate groups, all of which are identified in the compilations made by the Chief Electoral Officer after 1944, and the Canadian Press, 1926 to 1940.

W 165–176. Members elected in Dominion elections, by party and province, 1867 to 1960

SOURCE: *Canadian Parliamentary Companion*; *Canadian Parliamentary Guide*; *Canadian Annual Review*; *Canadian Almanac and Directory*; all throughout their years of publication.

The series depend primarily on newspaper compilations of election results, and each Member of Parliament's own statement of his party affiliation as listed in biographical works such as the *Canadian Parliamentary Guide*.

No official statistics on election results by parties are kept, and there is room for disagreement over the classification of particular members of parliament, especially for the earlier years. There are discrepancies in the sources, and the table has been corrected where possible by other evidence. Each general election result lists the winning party first. In the series before 1930, a zero indicates that, so far as the records show, a party ran candidates without success, while an asterisk indicates no candidates.

The Liberal party has been popularly called by that name since shortly after Confederation; for earlier years, members frequently identified themselves as 'Reform' or 'Grit'. The party now called Progressive Conservative has changed its name several times: Progressive Conservative 1945 to 1960; National Government in 1940; Conservative and Liberal Conservative before 1935, except for 1917, when most Conservative candidates (and many Liberals) ran as Unionists. These various changes in name are not all shown in the series.

THE FEDERAL GOVERNMENT, EMPLOYEES AND REPRESENTATION ABROAD (Series W 177–217)

W 177–213. Dominion government employees, by department, branch and service, 1900 to 1959

SOURCE: *Canada Year Book*, various years, for 1924 to 1959; *Statement of Civil Personnel and Salaries in the month of January, 1912–1924* for 1912 to 1924 inclusive; *Civil Service Employees*, for 1900 to 1915.

A continuously reliable series of statistics on government employees classified by departments or agency does not exist. Changes in the names and internal organizations of departments, the transfer of branches from one department to another, and changes in the ways in which civil servants are classified as permanent, casual, and temporary, and in records concerning them, all make a single consistent set of series impossible, and the statistics in this series must be used with great caution. A statement of the limitations on statistics from the *Canada Year Book* can be obtained from the Dominion Bureau of Statistics. In order to enable the user to judge on the consistency of the series in the three sources, overlaps of the data are given for 1924 and for 1912 to 1915; the report on *Civil Service Employees* actually gave data running from 1900 to 1922.

For the years 1924 to 1958, the *Canada Year Book* gives tables for government employment under different headings for different years. The figures in the tables are subject to the qualifications and reservations given in the relevant years of the *Canada Year Book* in addition to those given in these notes. The series from 1925 to 1952 was originally intended to list only employees covered by the Civil Service Act, but the Dominion Bureau of Statistics is authority for the statement that there was considerable diversity among departments in reporting on their employees, so that some lists do not include all civil servants covered by the Act while others include employees not covered by the Act. A new series (explained in *Canada Year Book, 1954*, p. 98) was begun after 1954.

For 1912 to 1924, inclusive, the *Statement of Civil Service Personnel and Salaries in the Month of January, 1912–1924*, is now a scarce document. This second source is generally not comparable with the first, for it was compiled on a different basis than the tables in the *Canada Year Book* after 1924.

The source for figures prior to 1915, *Civil Service Employees*, printed by order of parliament in 1923, is also a scarce document. Here a very different basis for these statistics was used, and the figures before 1915 from this source are generally not comparable with those for later years from the other sources. Each of the three sources used employs a different time-period as the basis of selection. Further information on sizes of staffs from 1878 to 1900 (not given here because no complete figures could be compiled) can be found in the *Reports of the Auditor General of Canada* after 1878, and in the *Civil Lists* published annually from 1867.

All statistics in this table, according to the sources, show the total number of employees (permanent and temporary, casual and other, and inside and outside service which is staff at Ottawa and elsewhere) which can properly be regarded from the records as members of the staff of the departments and services named. Admittedly this compilation of totals can be misleading, especially for departments employing large numbers of casual workers. Further, it seems apparent from a comparison of the two sets of overlapping data for the years 1912 to 1915 that the figures given in *Civil Service Employees* must have omitted at least substantial numbers of 'outside' employees for certain departments such as, for example, the post office (series W 194), transport (series W 198) and others. In some instances the detailed notes in the last-mentioned source state that the figures are only for the 'inside' service. The *Canada Year Book* for the series for 1953 to 1955 and 1956 to 1958 breaks down totals into sub-totals. The table does not list separately most temporary departments and branches such as Reconstruction and Supply, and Munitions and Supply (see *Canada Year Book* for 1940 to 1950), Soldiers' Settlement Board (1918 to 1948, when its activities were absorbed into Veterans' Affairs) and Soldiers' Civil Re-Establishment (1918 to 1927), statistics of which can be found in all three sources given above. Where possible, temporary departments are tabulated with the newer departments into which they subsequently developed, and such tabulations are explained below. Other departments and services which were absorbed into new or reorganized departments are referred to below.

The series do not include the significant numbers of staff members (now around 150,000) employed by the non-departmental crown corporations and other public enterprises. Tables of employment in these institutions, showing totals only for twenty-two enterprises, appeared first in the *Canada Year Book*, *1955* (p. 112) and are now published regularly in the same source. Detailed figures by enterprises can be calculated from the annual reports of most of the separate enterprises and from evidence which some of them have given to committees of the House of Commons. Canadian National Railways, for example, is examined regularly by the House of Commons' Committee on Railways, Air Lines and Shipping.

In the following detailed notes for each series, the dates given for the establishment of departments are taken from the first annual report of the department itself.

W 177. 'Totals', owing to the way in which the series have been prepared from the source data, gives necessarily for 1924 to 1959 the grand totals of series W 178–213. The statistics for 1924 to 1959 are not, in two periods, the totals given in the relevant tables of the *Canada Year Book*. The totals for 1933 to 1936 given in the *Canada Year Book* have been adjusted to exclude employees of the Canadian Broadcasting Commission since they disappear from the figures from 1937 onward when the commission became a corporation and employees were no longer a part of the civil service. Similarly, employees of the Federal District Commission and National Capital plan have been removed from the total and from series W 210, Privy Council, for 1953 to 1955 since as far as could be determined they were not included before 1953 and again after 1955 when they are reported with Crown Corporations. The totals for 1912 to 1924 from *Civil Service Personnel in the Month of January*, as given in the source, are the sums of the figures in series W 178–213.

For 1956 to 1959 the total combines the categories of 'Classified Prevailing Rate' and 'Casuals and Others' as given in the *Canada Year Book*; for 1953 to 1955 the totals, as adjusted, combine 'Classified' and 'Exempt'.

W 178. Agriculture, created in 1867, for 1900 to 1915 includes the total of permanent and other employees.

W 179. Defence Production, created in 1951, includes statistics for Reconstruction and Supply (1945 to 1949) and Munitions and Supply (1940 to 1945). Munitions and Supply was not organized until after the fiscal year 1939–40, hence there are no statistics for 1940.

W 180. External Affairs, created in 1909, includes the staff of the Prime Minister's Office for the years prior to 1948, since when it has been included with the Privy Council. The Information Division of the Department, created in 1947, integrated the former Canadian Information Service into the Department. The employees of the Canadian Information Service for 1946–47 and its predecessor, the Wartime Information Board, 1943 to 1945, have been added to External Affairs. Since 1952 the personnel of the International Joint Commission has been included in External Affairs.

W 181. Finance, created in 1869, includes, where necessary, the staffs of Comptroller of the Treasury, Government Contracts Supervision Commission and similar groups (see e.g. *Canada Year Book*, *1938*, p. 1067). The series includes civil servants in inside and outside services throughout.

W 182. Fisheries, created in 1930, from part of the former Department of Marine and Fisheries, was formerly included in that Department. See also the notes on W 197.

W 183. Justice, created in 1868, includes the staff of the Commissioner of Penitentiaries (sometimes given separately in official statistics), and from 1952 to 1956 approximately three hundred judges, then listed as salaried employees.

W 184. Labour, created in 1900, includes only full-time employees for the data 1900 to 1915 from *Civil Service Employees* and thereafter as described in *Canada Year Book* for the several years.

W 185. Mines and Technical Surveys, created in 1949, was known by various names throughout the period. From 1936 to 1949 the department was called Mines and Resources and from 1907, when it was created, to 1935 as Mines. In 1936 the former Departments of Immigration and Colonization, Indian Affairs and Interior, were transferred to Mines and Resources (see *Canada Year Book*, *1938*, p. 1069, n. 4). For the period prior to 1936 these departments are shown separately. The series for all departments from 1900 to 1915 from *Civil Service Employees* show employees in the inside service only.

W 186. Citizenship and Immigration, created in 1949, includes employees of services previously in other departments. Citizenship and Immigration combined the Administrative Branch, Canadian Citizenship Branch and Canadian Citizenship Registration Branch previously under Secretary of State (series W 195) and those for Immigration and Indian Affairs previously under Mines and Resources. See *Canada Year Book*, *1951*, p. 1143.

For the years 1900 to 1936 this series includes statistics for the Department of Immigration and Colonization created in 1917. From 1867 to 1892 immigration was handled by the Department of Agriculture and from 1892 to 1917 by the Department of the Interior. This series, 1900 to 1915, from *Civil Service Employees* includes employees in the inside service only. See also the note on series W 185.

W 187. Indian Affairs, created in 1880, disappears in 1936, when this department was transferred to Mines and Resources, later Mines and Technical Surveys. This series, 1900 to 1915, from *Civil Service Employees* includes employees in the inside service only. See also the note on series W 185.

W 188. Interior, created in 1873, disappears in 1936 when this department was transferred to Mines and Resources, later Mines and Technical Surveys. This series, 1900 to 1915, from *Civil Service Employees* gives employees in the inside service only. See also the note on W 185.

W 189. National Defence, created in 1922, includes the former Department of Militia and Defence, the Naval Service and Air Board. The series shows permanent civilian employees only.

W 190. National Health and Welfare, created in 1944 from part of the former Department of Pensions and National Health includes also predecessor bodies. The Department of Pensions and National Health was formed in 1928 from the Department of Soldiers' Civil Re-establishment, itself created in 1918, the

Department of Health, created in 1919, The Board of Pension Commissioners, established in 1917, and the Federal Appeal Board, established in 1926. The Military Hospitals Commission, 1916 to 1918, had in turn been incorporated in Soldiers' Civil Re-establishment. From 1919 to 1928 by far the larger part of the combined employment was in Soldiers' Civil Re-establishment which had 8,121 employees in 1920, 3,823 employees in 1923 and 1,890 employees in 1928. See also the note on series W208.

W191. National Revenue, created in 1927, covers also the predecessor departments Customs and Excise (1921 to 1927) and Customs and Inland Revenue (1918 to 1921). Before 1918 customs and inland revenue acts were administered by separate departments; the statistics before 1918 combine the departments. The series for 1900 to 1915, from *Civil Service Employees*, include both inside and outside service employees. The figures for 1924 and 1925 include Income Taxation Commissioner, listed separately in *Canada Year Book, 1925*, p. 986. From 1917 to 1924 the data from *Civil Service Personnel in the Month of January* also include the Commissioner of Income Taxation.

W192. National War Services, created in 1940, but not organized for the fiscal year 1939–40 is included here separately because of its size. The series does not include the Wartime Information Board or its successor, the Canadian Information Service, which were attached to the Privy Council at the time. See *Canada Year Book 1943 to 1947* and also notes on W180.

W193. Northern Affairs and National Resources, created in 1953, prior to which it was called Resources and Development, was before 1950 part of Mines and Resources. See *Canada Year Book, 1951*, p. 1145.

W194. Post Office, created in 1867, gives data for personnel in the inside service only for the period 1900 to 1915 from *Civil Service Employees*.

W195. Secretary of State, created in 1867, contains roughly comparable statistics throughout. For 1920 to 1927 the staff of Patents and Copyrights (formerly in Agriculture), listed separately in official sources, has been added; for 1940 to 1941 the staff of Superintendent of Bankruptcy, also given separately, has been added; and for 1950 to 1955, the Office of Custodian, again listed separately, has been added.

W196. Trade and Commerce, created in 1887, has rough comparability throughout. See also the notes on series W208 and W209.

W197. Transport, created in 1936, covered varying Departments and agencies in earlier years. Transport was formed from the former Departments of Marine and of Railways and Canals, and from the Civil Aviation Branch of National Defence.

For the years 1930 to 1936 the series include employees in the Departments of Marine and of Railways and Canals and in the Board of Railway Commissioners. The Department of Marine had in turn been established in 1930, when the Department of Marine and Fisheries was separated into the Departments of Marine and of Fisheries. Prior to 1930 the fisheries personnel are included in this series. See also the note on W182.

W198. Veterans' Affairs, created in 1944, includes for 1945 to 1948 the staff of the Soldier Settlement Board, and prior to 1945 consists exclusively of that staff. The series does not include the Department of Soldiers' Civil Re-establishment (1916 to 1927), which was merged into Pensions and National Health in 1928. See also notes on W190.

W199. Public Works, created in 1867, gives only inside service for 1900 to 1915 from *Civil Service Employees*.

W200. Auditor General's Office, created in 1878, has performed the same general functions throughout its life.

W201. Chief Electoral Officer, created in 1920, contains statistics for prior years referring to the relevant staff in the office of Secretary of State. The statistics in all cases are for Ottawa staff only.

W202. Civil Service Commission, created in 1908, contains statistics on employees related to a consistent function throughout.

W203. Conservation Commission, ends in 1922 when 'the Department ceased to function on March 31st, 1922 and the majority of the employees were transferred to other Departments' (*Civil Service Personnel and Salaries in the Month of January*).

W204. Governor General and Lieutenant-Governors include figures for staff only, and exclude the Governor General or Lieutenant-Governors themselves; before 1953, the figures are for Governor General's Secretary only.

W205. Insurance, created in 1875 as a branch of Finance, is reported separately from Finance. The Department of Insurance was established separately in 1910, still under the Minister of Finance and still reported separately.

W206. International Joint Commission, created in 1909, has been included in External Affairs since 1952.

W207. Legislation, includes statistics for the House of Commons, Senate, and Library of Parliament; these three institutions are listed separately in the sources down to 1952, and together thereafter. The records of the House of Commons were destroyed by fire in 1916, and the series from 1912 to 1916 is for the Senate and Library only.

W208. National Film Board, created in 1939, is given separately though the Board has been attached in turn to several departments, and statistics of its employees have had an erratic history. The Board was not organized for the fiscal year 1939–40; statistics of its employees for 1941 were included with Trade and Commerce, and for 1945 to 1947 with National Health and Welfare.

W209. National Research Council, created in 1917, and whose first laboratories were established in Ottawa in 1928, was included in Trade and Commerce before 1934. Numbers given in the source for 1953 to 1955 included employees of the Atomic Energy Control Board. The Atomic Energy Control Board, created in 1946 and a separate body, has been added here for other years of its life; it had five employees in 1947, seven employees from 1948 to 1951, six in 1952, seven in 1956, six in 1958 and eight in 1959.

W210. Privy Council, includes 21 employees of the Royal Commission on Price Spreads in Food Products and of the Royal Commisssion on Energy Policies in 1958 (*Canada Year Book, 1959*, p. 125). The series does not include employees of the Wartime Information Board (1943–44) or the Canadian Information Service (1944 to 1946), which were attached to the Privy Council at the time but are included in W180. See also the note on W180. Nor does it include the Federal District Commission which was reported with it from 1953 to 1955. See the note on W177. The Prime Minister's Office, included with External Affairs before 1948, has been reported with the Privy Council in 1948 and since 1953; it has been added to the Privy Council for 1949 to 1952. See also the note on W180.

W211. Public Archives and National Library, created in 1872 and 1953 respectively, are combined in official sources after 1953; before that date the series is for archives only, except for 1951 and 1952, when respectively six and eight members of the staff of the Bibliographic Centre were included. Before 1913, the archives statistics were included with Agriculture.

W212. Public Printing and Stationery, created in 1886, and since then attached to Secretary of State, gives permanent employees only for 1900 to 1915 as given in *Civil Service Employees*.

W 213. Royal Canadian Mounted Police, created in 1873 as the Northwest Mounted Police, includes only the administrative staff prior to 1953; since 1953 the force itself is included in the official sources.

W 214–217. Representation of government of Canada abroad, 1867 to 1960

SOURCE: *Canada Year Book, 1960*, pp. 158–60. See also Skilling, *Canadian Representation Abroad, from Agency to Embassy.*

Prior to the Imperial Conference of 1926, Canada's sole formal representative abroad was the High Commissioner to the United Kingdom, an office created in 1880. Though Canada early began to play an important role in the negotiation of commercial treaties with other countries, the formal role of representatives of the British government, as co-signers of treaties, continued down to World War I. In the negotiation of political treaties Canadian progress was slower and it was not until Dominion status was achieved in 1926 (and confirmed in the Statute of Westminster, 1931) that Canada and the other members of the Commonwealth assumed a role as fully independent nations in external affairs; independence in internal affairs had been achieved much earlier. After 1926 Canadian representation abroad grew steadily, as is shown in series W 214–217. The status of representatives is hierarchical: high commissioner (in commonwealth countries) and ambassador (in non-commonwealth countries) rank highest; then come minister, chargé d'affaires, consul general and consul. Prior to World War II Canada had no representatives ranked as ambassadors, sending high commissioners to commonwealth countries and ministers or other representatives elsewhere.

THE FEDERAL GOVERNMENT, DISALLOWANCES OF PROVINCIAL ACTS, RESERVATIONS OF PROVINCIAL BILLS AND FEDERAL ROYAL COMMISSIONS
(Series W 218–250)

W 218–220. Formal amendments to the British North America Act, 1867 to 1960

SOURCE: no official list of amendments to the British North America Act, 1867, exists, but there is general agreement among authorities that the amendments to the Act include more than just the statutes subsequent to 1867 also entitled British North America Act. The list in series W 218–220 is from a standard monograph, Gérin-Lajoie, *Constitutional Amendment in Canada*, supplemented by data in Dawson, *The Government of Canada*, and Great Britain, *The Public General Acts and Church Assembly Measure, 1960*. There is disagreement, however, among authorities as to the number and classification of amendments to the British North America Act, 1867; for a list somewhat different from series W 218–220, see Clokie, 'Basic Problems of the Canadian Constitution', in *Canadian Journal of Economics and Political Science*, vol 8, no. 1 (February 1942), pp. 1–32. The formal citation of each statute refers to the year of the monarch's reign (e.g. 1 Elizabeth II is the first year of Elizabeth II).

Since until 1949 most relevant sections of the British North America Act could be amended formally only by the parliament of the United Kingdom, which passed the original statute, all the amendments before 1949 are statutes of the United Kingdom. In 1949 the parliament of Canada assumed jurisdiction over those parts of the British North America Act which refer only to the Dominion's part of the constitution, but important sections of the Act can still be altered formally only by the United Kingdom parliament, which since 1867 has acted to do so only when requested by Canada. Canadian authorities are currently working to bring the entire amendment process to Canada, a change which can be made as soon as the Canadian authorities can agree on how it should be done.

W 221–224. Provinces and territories, dates and processes of admission and present areas, 1867 to 1960

SOURCE: *Canada Year Book, 1959*, p. 60. The source should be consulted for more detailed information on changes in the areas of several of the provinces after their original establishment, and of the territories. See also series K 1–2.

The provinces have become parts of Canada in three ways: by original creation as provinces in 1867; by subsequent creation out of territories that were themselves part of Canada; and by the admission as provinces of new areas that were not formerly part of Canada. The Dominion's power to admit certain colonies as provinces was recognized in the British North America Act of 1867, and enlarged to include the creation of new provinces out of territories in 1871. Thus British Columbia, Prince Edward Island and Newfoundland were admitted as established entities. The prairie provinces were created from the territories which had been purchased from the Hudson's Bay Company in 1870, and then annexed to Canada. Once a new province is established, the Dominion is not competent to alter the act of creation except in regard to boundary changes, which can be made only with the province's consent.

W 225–235. Number of provincial statutes disallowed by Dominion government, by province and decade, 1867 to 1960

SOURCE: LaForest, *Disallowance and Reservation of Provincial Legislation*, pp. 83–101. The source lists each statute by citation, title, reasons for disallowance, date of report of Minister of Justice, with further references.

The Canadian government has the unqualified power to disallow any act of a provincial legislature within a year of its passage. The power was widely used in the four decades immediately following 1867, but its employment is now rare, as political, legal and economic developments have all enhanced the status of the provinces within Confederation. The power still exists in law, unrestricted, and attempts to persuade the Dominion government to use it against provincial legislation that is unpopular with various organized groups are not uncommon.

Some of the earlier statistics are in one sense misleading, for sometimes the Dominion disallowed substantially the same provincial act several times; each separate disallowance is given in the series.

W 236–246. Number of provincial bills reserved by lieutenant-governors, by province and decade, 1867 to 1960

SOURCE: LaForest, *Disallowance and Reservation of Provincial Legislation*, pp. 102–115. The source includes a detailed examination and list of reserved bills, including the disposition made of each bill, and the reasons therefor.

The Lieutenant-Governor of each province, who is appointed by the Governor General on the advice of the prime minister of Canada, has the power to reserve assent to any bill passed by the provincial legislature, and to refer it to the Dominion government for the signification of the latter's pleasure. If the Dominion government takes no action of any kind for one year, the bill dies; but the Dominion may also instruct that assent to the bill be given, or give assent itself. Generally the Dominion authorities have held that Lieutenant-Governors should reserve a provincial bill only on instructions from Ottawa, but in fact most reserved bills have been reserved without instructions, and in most cases the

Dominion has taken no action. As with disallowance, the use of the reservation power has declined, but it was employed in 1961 when the Lieutenant-Governor of Saskatchewan reserved a bill without instructions, and in due course was instructed to give his assent.

W247-249. Federal royal commissions, 1867 to 1959

SOURCE: compilation by Callard from records in Privy Council, 'Commissions of Inquiry—1867 to 1959', available on photostat in the Parliamentary Library; supplemented by a list in the appendix to Hodgetts, *Royal Commissions of Inquiry in Canada*. Fairly complete lists are to be found in: Government of Canada, *Sessional Papers*, 1892, vol. xxv, no. 84; *ibid.* 1900, vol. xxxiv, no. 64; *ibid.* 1937, no. 269; *ibid.* 1939, no. 114.

The definition of 'Royal Commission' is not at all clear. Presumably all commissions issued under Part I of Public Inquiries Act qualify; but these include many minor investigations into individual charges of political partisanship and the like. A number of these may have been omitted from the column headed 'minor commissions'. Commissions issued under Part II of the Inquiries Act do not bear the Great Seal and therefore technically fail to qualify; but again several important investigations set up as 'departmental inquiries' under Part II have been regarded as Royal Commissions. The compilation contains some of these. Several other statutes have provided for public inquiries, and commissioners appointed under these acts have often been designated royal commissioners; for example, 38 Victoria, chap. 53 (1875) to adjust claims to Manitoba lands; the Combines Act, the Judges Act (to study a case for dismissal of a judge). Pre-dating the Industrial Disputes Investigation Act there were also many commissions set up to study industrial unrest. These have been included, mainly in the column headed 'minor commissions'. The segregation into 'major' and 'minor' commissions has been based on the importance of the subject and/or the value of the report(s).

W250. Subjects of major royal commissions, 1867 to 1959

SOURCE: see series 247-249.

Series 250 lists the major federal royal commissions designated in series 247.

THE PROVINCIAL GOVERNMENTS, LIEUTENANT-GOVERNORS AND PREMIERS
(Series W251-255)

W251-252. Lieutenant-governors, by province, 1867 to 1960

SOURCE: Department of Provincial Affairs, Newfoundland; Mac-Kinnon, *The Government of Prince Edward Island*; Deputy Provincial Secretary, Nova Scotia; Beck, *The Government of Nova Scotia*; *Annuaire Statistique*, Quebec, 1958; *Saskatchewan Who's Who*; *Canada Year Book*, passim; *Canadian Parliamentary Guide*, passim; see also Saywell, *The Office of Lieutenant-Governor*.

The lieutenant-governor is nominally the chief executive officer of each province. He is appointed and paid by the Dominion government, ordinarily for a term of five years, though removable for cause, and was originally intended to be a federal official in each province; judicial decision has added to his powers a status not unlike that of the governor general—that is he is Her Majesty's representative in each province. His functions are largely ceremonial, but lieutenant-governors have made more frequent use of their powers to reserve or withhold assent to bills than have governors general of Canada or monarchs in the United Kingdom. The powers and prestige of the lieutenant-governor vary from individual to individual and from place to place, but in general have declined throughout Canada since 1867. The lieutenant-governor is still nonetheless an integral part of each provincial legislature.

W253-255. Ministries, by province and premier, 1867 to 1960

SOURCE: MacKinnon, *The Government of Prince Edward Island*; Deputy Provincial Secretary, Nova Scotia; Beck, *The Government of Nova Scotia*; *Annuaire Statistique*, Quebec, 1958; Saskatchewan Archives Board; Clerk of the Legislative Assembly, Alberta; Province of British Columbia; and *Canadian Parliamentary Companion*, passim; *Canadian Parliamentary Guide*, passim; *Canada Year Book*, passim; Deputy Provincial Secretary, British Columbia.

The office of premier, as leader of a government with a majority in the legislature, has been recognized in most provinces since their establishment, though Professor W. L. Morton has observed in *Encyclopedia Canadiana*, vol. 2, p. 45, that it is doubtful if the position of premier was recognized in Manitoba before 1874. Certainly the powers of the premier, and his views of his functions and his relations with the other parts of the provincial government, have not been identical in all the provinces since they entered Confederation.

The determination of party affiliations for earlier years is in several instances difficult, and in a few impossible; in any event, a provincial party label then, as now, did not always mean that a provincial premier of one party gave his wholehearted support to the same party at the federal level, or paid much attention to the party of the same name in other provinces.

THE PROVINCIAL GOVERNMENTS, PROVINCIAL ELECTIONS
(Series W256-339)

W256-339. Provincial government elections, party standing and size of legislature, 1867 to 1960

SOURCE: Department of Provincial Affairs, Newfoundland; Mac-Kinnon, *The Government of Prince Edward Island*; Chief Election Officer, Nova Scotia; Department of the Provincial Secretary-Treasurer, New Brunswick; *Annuaire Statistique*, Quebec, 1958; Chief Election Officer of Ontario; *A Statistical History of All the Electoral Districts of the Province of Ontario since 1867*; Saskatchewan Archives Board; Clerk of the Legislative Assembly, Alberta; Province of British Columbia; and *Canadian Parliamentary Companion*, passim; *Canadian Parliamentary Guide*, passim; *Canadian Almanac and Directory*, passim; *Canada Year Book*, passim.

Provincial election results, by parties, include some of the most elusive political statistics in Canada, and must be used with caution. The Deputy Provincial Secretary, Prince Edward Island, for example, has confirmed that information in the *Canadian Parliamentary Guide* may be considered official for the Island; the *Guide*, nonetheless, has included inconsistencies in its data, including different dates for the same election and different party affiliations for individuals. Other provinces appear to have kept official statistics of their elections since Confederation.

Several sections of series W256-339 require special qualification: (*a*) multi-member constituencies are far less common than they were. In Nova Scotia, for example, all constituencies returned at least two members from 1876 to 1916; now only three two-member constituencies remain. See *Acts of Nova Scotia*: 1914, ch. 16; 1932, ch. 19; 1948, ch. 47; 1955, ch. 7. (*b*) Series W281-287 excludes the Legislative Council of Quebec. Quebec is now the only province with a bicameral legislature, though several of the older provinces formerly were bicameral. The series throughout W256-339 refer only to the lower houses. (*c*) Party affiliations in Manitoba, series W299-311, have not always been sufficiently clear to make tabulation easy, and in earlier years (especially 1870 and 1874) the number of members whose affiliation was not known (shown in 'Other' column) is formidable. Detailed study of party results in Manitoba requires more qualification than can be provided here. The main limitations on series W 299–311 are: (1) After 1932, the column 'Liberal and Liberal Progressive' represents a combination of Liberal and Progressive forces which cannot be separated. (2) The elections of 1941, 1945 and 1949 resulted in coalition governments of a type not suggested in the statistics. See *Canadian Parliamentary Guide* for relevant years. (3) The election of 1921 is shown in the *Canadian Parliamentary Guide* as returning 21 'Government' candidates; these were Liberals according to the biographical sketches in *ibid.* 1921. However, other Liberals opposed 'Government' candidates at the polls. (*d*) The Province of British Columbia is authority for the statement that the election of 1903, in series W 331–339, was the first run on party lines, hence the gaps in the table before that date. The *Canadian Parliamentary Guide* for elections before 1903 identifies candidates as Government and Opposition only.

Series W 1–2. *The monarchy, 1867 to 1960*

	Monarch	Accession
Years of reign	**1**	**2**
1952–	Elizabeth II	6 February 1952
1936–1952	George VI	11 December 1936
1936	Edward VIII	20 January 1936[1]
1910–1936	George V	6 May 1910
1901–1910	Edward VII	22 January 1901
1837–1901	Victoria I	20 June 1837

[1] Abdicated before coronation.

Series W 3–5. *Governors General, 1867 to 1960*

Term of office	Number	Governor-General	Appointed	Assumed office
		3	**4**	**5**
1959–	19	Major-General Georges Philias Vanier, D.S.O., M.C., C.D.	1 August 1959	15 September 1959
1952–1959	18	The Right Honourable Vincent Massey, C.H.	24 January 1952	28 February 1952
1946–1952	17	Field Marshal Viscount Alexander of Tunis, K.G., G.C.B., G.C.M.G., C.S.I., D.S.O., M.C., A.D.C.	1 August 1945	12 April 1946
1940–1946	16	Major-General The Earl of Athlone, K.G., P.C., G.C.B., G.C.M.G., G.C.V.O., D.S.O.	3 April 1940	21 June 1940
1935–1940	15	Lord Tweedsmuir of Elsfield, G.C.M.G., G.C.V.O., C.H.	10 August 1935	2 November 1935
1931–1935	14	The Earl of Bessborough, G.C.M.G.	9 February 1931	4 April 1931
1926–1931	13	Viscount Willingdon of Ratton, G.C.S.I., G.C.I.E., G.B.E.	5 August 1926	2 October 1926
1921–1926	12	General The Lord Byng of Vimy, G.C.B., G.C.M.G., M.V.O.	2 August 1921	11 August 1921
1916–1921	11	The Duke of Devonshire, K.G., G.C.M.G., G.C.V.O.	19 August 1916	11 November 1916
1911–1916	10	Field Marshal, H.R.H. The Duke of Connaught, K.G.	21 March 1911	13 October 1911
1904–1911	9	Earl Grey, G.C.M.G.	26 September 1904	10 December 1904
1898–1904	8	The Earl of Minto, G.C.M.G.	30 July 1898	12 November 1898
1893–1898	7	The Earl of Aberdeen, K.T., G.C.M.G.	22 May 1893	18 September 1893
1888–1893	6	Lord Stanley of Preston, G.C.B.	1 May 1888	11 June 1888
1883–1888	5	The Marquis of Lansdowne, G.C.M.G.	18 August 1883	23 October 1883
1878–1883	4	The Marquis of Lorne, K.T., G.C.M.G.	5 October 1878	25 November 1878
1872–1878	3	The Earl of Dufferin, K.P., K.C.B., G.C.M.G.	22 May 1872	25 June 1872
1869–1872	2	Lord Lisgar, G.C.M.G.	29 December 1868	2 February 1869
1867–1869	1	Viscount Monck, G.C.M.G.	1 June 1867	1 July 1867

Series W 6–16. *Canadian ministries, dates, numbers of portfolios, turnover of personnel, and party affiliation, 1867 to 1960*

Year	Number	Prime Minister	Dates of Ministry	Party[1]	Portfolios Number	Portfolios Number of occupants	Ministers without portfolio Number of posts	Ministers without portfolio Number of occupants	Non-cabinet ministers Number of posts	Non-cabinet ministers Number of occupants	Parliamentary secretaries Number of posts	Parliamentary secretaries Number of occupants
		6	**7**	**8**	**9**	**10**	**11**	**12**	**13**	**14**	**15**	**16**
1957–	18	Rt. Hon. John George Diefenbaker	21 June 1957[2]	Cons.	22	37	3	4	—	—	19	29
1948–1957	17	Rt. Hon. Louis Stephen St. Laurent	15 November 1948 21 June 1957	Lib.	25	48	2	3	—	—	18	38
1935–1948	16	Rt. Hon. William Lyon Mackenzie King	23 October 1935– 15 November 1948	Lib.	28	87	2	4	—	—	17	26
1930–1935	15	Rt. Hon. Richard Bedford Bennett	7 August 1930– 23 October 1935	Cons.	19	33	4	5	—	—	—	—
1926–1930	14	Rt. Hon. William Lyon Mackenzie King	25 September 1926– 6 August 1930	Lib.	21	27	2	2	—	—	—	—
1926	13	Rt. Hon. Arthur Meighen	29 June 1926– 25 September 1926	Cons.	17	29	4	5	—	—	—	—
1921–1926	12	Rt. Hon. William Lyon Mackenzie King	29 December 1921– 28 June 1926	Lib.	18	39	5	8	2	2	—	—
1920–1921	11	Rt. Hon. Arthur Meighen	10 July 1920– 29 December 1921	Unionist	20	31	4	4	1	1	—	—
1917–1920	10	Rt. Hon. Sir Robert Laird Borden	12 October 1917– 10 July 1920	Unionist	23	39	4	4	1	1	3	5
1911–1917	9	Rt. Hon. Sir Robert Laird Borden	10 October 1911– 12 October 1917	Cons.	19	42	3	3	3	4	—	—
1896–1911	8	Rt. Hon. Sir Wilfrid Laurier	11 July 1896– 6 October 1911	Lib.	18	46	2	5	3	6	—	—
1896	7	Hon. Sir Charles Tupper	1 May 1896– 8 July 1896	Cons.	14	14	3	3	1	1	—	—
1894–1896	6	Hon. Sir Mackenzie Bowell	21 December 1894– 27 April 1896	Cons.	14	35	3	4	3	4	—	—
1892–1894	5	Rt. Hon. Sir John Sparrow David Thompson	5 December 1892– 12 December 1894	Cons.	12	12	2	2	3	3	—	—
1891–1892	4	Hon. Sir John Joseph Caldwell Abbott	16 June 1891– 24 November 1892	Cons.	13	21	1	2	—	—	—	—
1878–1891	3	Rt. Hon. Sir John Alexander Macdonald	17 October 1878– 6 June 1891	Cons.	15	53	2	4	—	—	—	—
1873–1878	2	Hon. Alexander Mackenzie	7 November 1873– 9 October 1878	Lib.	13	32	2	2	—	—	—	—
1867–1873	1	Rt. Hon. Sir John Alexander Macdonald	1 July 1867– 5 November 1873	Cons.	15	45	1	1	—	—	—	—

[1] See note to series W165–176 for changes in official party names through the years.   [2] As of 1 January 1961.

Series W 17–28. *Growth of representation in the House of Commons and redistribution (general and partial), by province, 1867 to 1960*

Year	Total for Canada	Newfoundland	Prince Edward Island	Nova Scotia	New Brunswick	Quebec	Ontario	Manitoba	Saskatchewan	Alberta	British Columbia	Yukon
	17	18	19	20	21	22	23	24	25	26	27	28
1952[2]	265	7	4	12	10	75	85	14	17	17	22	2[1]
1949[2]	262	7	4	13	10	73	83	16	20	17	18	1
1947	255	—	4	13	10	73	83	16	20	17	18	1
1933	245	—	4	12	10	65	82	17	21	17	16	1
1924	245	—	4	14	11	65	82	17	21	16	14	1
1915[2]	235	—	4	16	11	65	82	15	16	12	13	1
1914[2]	234	—	3	16	11	65	82	15	16	12	13	1
1907[2]	221	—	4	18	13	65	86	10	10	7	7	1
1903	214	—	4	18	13	65	86	10	10[3]	—	7	1
1892	213	—	5	20	14	65	92	7	4	—	6	—
1887[2]	215	—	6	21	16	65	92	5	4	—	6	—
1882	211	—	6	21	16	65	92	5	—	—	6	—
1873[2]	206	—	6	21	16	65	88	4	—	—	6	—
1872[2]	200	—	—	21	16	65	88	4	—	—	6	—
1871[2]	185	—	—	19	15	65	82	4	—	—	—	—
1867	181	—	—	19	15	65	82	—	—	—	—	—

[1] Includes one member for Mackenzie River.   [2] See note on series W 17–28.   [3] Northwest Territories.

Series W 29–39. *Growth of representation in the Senate of Canada, 1867 to 1960*

Year	Total for Canada	Atlantic provinces				Quebec	Ontario	Western provinces			
		Newfoundland	Prince Edward Island	Nova Scotia	New Brunswick			Manitoba	Saskatchewan	Alberta	British Columbia
	29	30	31	32	33	34	35	36	37	38	39
1949	102	6	4	10	10	24	24	6	6	6	6
1915	96	—	4	10	10	24	24	6	6	6	6
1905	87	—	4	10	10	24	24	4	4	4	3
1903	83	—	4	10	10	24	24	4	4[1]	—	3
1892	81	—	4	10	10	24	24	4	2[1]	—	3
1887	80	—	4	10	10	24	24	3	2[1]	—	3
1882	78	—	4	10	10	24	24	3	—	—	3
1873	77	—	4	10	10	24	24	2	—	—	3
1871	77	—	—	12	12	24	24	2	—	—	3
1870	74	—	—	12	12	24	24	2	—	—	—
1867	72	—	—	12	12	24	24	—	—	—	—

[1] Northwest Territories.

Series W 40–49. *Dates of general elections and sessions of Dominion parliaments, 1867 to 1960*

Year of election	Parliament	Session	Date of opening	Date of prorogation	Days of session	Sitting days of House of Commons	Date of election	Writs returnable	Dissolution	Length of parliament
40	41		42	43	44	45	46	47	48	49
1958	24	4	17 November 1960	—	—	—	31 March 1958	30 April 1958	—	—
		3	14 January 1960	10 August 1960	210	146	—	—	—	—
		2	15 January 1959	18 July 1959	185	127	—	—	—	—
		1	12 May 1958	6 September 1958	117	93	—	—	—	—
1957	23	1	14 October 1957	1 February 1958	111	78	10 June 1957	8 August 1957	1 February 1958	5 m, 25 d
1953	22	5	8 January 1957	12 April 1957	95	71	10 August 1953	8 October 1953	12 April 1957	3 y, 6 m, 5 d
		4	26 November 1956	8 January 1957	44	5	—	—	—	—
		3	10 January 1956	14 August 1956	218	152	—	—	—	—
		2	7 January 1955	28 July 1955	203	140	—	—	—	—
		1	12 November 1953	26 June 1954	227	139	—	—	—	—
1949	21	7	20 November 1952	14 May 1953	176	108	27 June 1949	25 August 1949	13 June 1953	3 y, 9 m, 20 d
		6	28 February 1952	20 November 1952	267	87	—	—	—	—
		5	9 October 1951	29 December 1951	82	56	—	—	—	—
		4	30 January 1951	9 October 1951	253	105	—	—	—	—
		3	29 August 1950	29 January 1951	154	17	—	—	—	—
		2	16 February 1950	30 June 1950	135	90	—	—	—	—
		1	15 September 1949	10 December 1949	87	64	—	—	—	—
1945	20	5	26 January 1949	30 April 1949	95	59	11 June 1945	9 August 1945	30 April 1949	3 y, 8 m, 22 d
		4	5 December 1947	30 June 1948	209	119	—	—	—	—
		3	30 January 1947	17 July 1947	169	115	—	—	—	—
		2	14 March 1946	31 August 1946	171	118	—	—	—	—
		1	6 September 1945	18 December 1945	104	76	—	—	—	—
1940	19	6	19 March 1945	16 April 1945	29	19	26 March 1940	17 April 1940	16 April 1945	5 y
		5	27 January 1944	31 January 1945	371	136	—	—	—	—
		4	28 January 1943	26 January 1944	364	120	—	—	—	—
		3	22 January 1942	27 January 1943	371	124	—	—	—	—
		2	7 November 1940	21 January 1942	441	105	—	—	—	—
		1	16 May 1940	5 November 1940	174	61	—	—	—	—

Series W 40–49. *Dates of general elections and sessions of Dominion parliaments, 1867 to 1960 (continued)*

Year of election	Parlia-ment	Session	Date of opening	Date of prorogation	Days of session	Sitting days of House of Commons	Date of election	Writs returnable	Dissolution	Length of parliament
40	41		42	43	44	45	46	47	48	49
1935	18	6	25 January 1940	25 January 1940	1	1	14 October 1935	9 November 1935	25 January 1940	4 y, 2 m, 16 d
		5	7 September 1939	13 September 1939	7	6	—	—	—	—
		4	12 January 1939	3 June 1939	143	103	—	—	—	—
		3	27 January 1938	1 July 1938	156	102	—	—	—	—
		2	14 January 1937	10 April 1937	87	62	—	—	—	—
		1	6 February 1936	23 June 1936	139	91	—	—	—	—
1930	17	6	17 January 1935	5 July 1935	170	—	28 July 1930	18 August 1930	15 August 1935	4 y, 11 m, 29 d
		5	25 January 1934	3 July 1934	160	—	—	—	—	—
		4	6 October 1932	27 May 1933	234	—	—	—	—	—
		3	4 February 1932	26 May 1932	113	—	—	—	—	—
		2	12 March 1931	3 August 1931	145	—	—	—	—	—
		1	8 September 1930	22 September 1930	15	—	—	—	—	—
1926	16	4	20 February 1930	30 May 1930	100	—	14 September 1926	2 November 1926	30 May 1930	3 y, 7 m
		3	7 February 1929	14 June 1929	128	—	—	—	—	—
		2	26 January 1928	11 June 1928	138	—	—	—	—	—
		1	9 December 1926	14 April 1927	127	—	—	—	—	—
1925	15	1	7 January 1926	2 July 1926	177	—	29 October 1925	7 December 1925	2 July 1926	6 m, 26 d
1921	14	4	5 February 1925	27 June 1925	143	—	6 December 1921	14 January 1922	5 September 1925	3 y, 7 m, 26 d
		3	28 February 1924	19 July 1924	143	—	—	—	—	—
		2	31 January 1923	30 June 1923	151	—	—	—	—	—
		1	8 March 1922	28 June 1922	113	—	—	—	—	—
1917	13	5	14 February 1921	4 June 1921	111	—	17 December 1917	27 February 1918	4 October 1921	3 y, 7 m, 6 d
		4	26 February 1920	1 July 1920	127	—	—	—	—	—
		3	1 September 1919	10 November 1919	71	—	—	—	—	—
		2	20 February 1919	7 July 1919	138	—	—	—	—	—
		1	18 March 1918	24 May 1918	68	—	—	—	—	—
1911	12	7	18 January 1917	20 September 1917	246	—	21 September 1911	7 October 1911	6 October 1917	6 y
		6	12 January 1916	18 May 1916	127	—	—	—	—	—
		5	4 February 1915	15 April 1915	71	—	—	—	—	—
		4	18 August 1914	22 August 1914	5	—	—	—	—	—
		3	15 January 1914	12 June 1914	148	—	—	—	—	—
		2	21 November 1912	6 June 1913	198	—	—	—	—	—
		1	15 November 1911	1 April 1912	139	—	—	—	—	—
1908	11	3	17 November 1910	29 July 1911	255	—	26 October 1908	3 December 1908	29 July 1911	2 y, 7 m, 28 d
		2	11 November 1909	4 May 1910	175	—	—	—	—	—
		1	20 January 1909	19 May 1909	120	—	—	—	—	—
1904	10	4	28 November 1907	20 July 1908	236	—	3 November 1904	15 December 1904	17 September 1908	3 y, 9 m, 4 d
		3	22 November 1906	27 April 1907	157	—	—	—	—	—
		2	8 March 1906	13 July 1906	128	—	—	—	—	—
		1	11 January 1905	20 July 1905	191	—	—	—	—	—
1900	9	4	10 March 1904	10 August 1904	154	—	7 November 1900	5 December 1900	29 September 1904	3 y, 9 m, 26 d
		3	12 March 1903	24 October 1903	227	—	—	—	—	—
		2	13 February 1902	15 May 1902	90	—	—	—	—	—
		1	6 February 1901	23 May 1901	107	—	—	—	—	—
1896	8	5	1 February 1900	18 July 1900	168	—	23 June 1896	13 July 1896	9 October 1900	4 y, 2 m, 26 d
		4	16 March 1899	11 August 1899	149	—	—	—	—	—
		3	3 February 1898	13 June 1898	131	—	—	—	—	—
		2	25 March 1897	29 June 1897	97	—	—	—	—	—
		1	19 August 1896	5 October 1896	48	—	—	—	—	—
1891	7	6	2 January 1896	23 April 1896	111	—	5 March 1891	25 April 1891	24 April 1896	5 y
		5	18 April 1895	22 July 1895	96	—	—	—	—	—
		4	15 March 1894	23 July 1894	131	—	—	—	—	—
		3	26 January 1893	1 April 1893	66	—	—	—	—	—
		2	25 February 1892	9 July 1892	136	—	—	—	—	—
		1	29 April 1891	30 September 1891	155	—	—	—	—	—
1887	6	4	16 January 1890	16 May 1890	121	—	22 February 1887	7 April 1887	3 February 1891	3 y, 9 m, 27 d
		3	31 January 1889	2 May 1889	92	—	—	—	—	—
		2	23 February 1888	22 May 1888	90	—	—	—	—	—
		1	13 April 1887	23 June 1887	72	—	—	—	—	—
1882	5	4	25 February 1886	2 June 1886	98	—	20 June 1882	7 August 1882	15 January 1887	4 y, 5 m, 10 d
		3	29 January 1885	20 July 1885	173	—	—	—	—	—
		2	17 January 1884	19 April 1884	94	—	—	—	—	—
		1	8 February 1883	25 May 1883	107	—	—	—	—	—
1878	4	4	9 February 1882	17 May 1882	98	—	17 September 1878	21 November 1878	18 May 1882	3 y, 5 m, 28 d
		3	9 December 1880	21 March 1881	103	—	—	—	—	—
		2	12 February 1880	7 May 1880	86	—	—	—	—	—
		1	13 February 1879	15 May 1879	92	—	—	—	—	—
1874	3	5	7 February 1878	10 May 1878	93	—	22 January 1874	21 February 1874	17 August 1878	4 y, 5 m, 25 d
		4	8 February 1877	28 April 1877	80	—	—	—	—	—
		3	10 February 1876	12 April 1876	63	—	—	—	—	—
		2	4 February 1875	8 April 1875	64	—	—	—	—	—
		1	26 March 1874	26 May 1874	62	—	—	—	—	—
1872	2	2	23 October 1873	7 November 1873	16	—	20 July 1872–12 October 1872	3 September 1872	2 January 1874	1 y, 4 m
		1	5 March 1873	13 August 1873	161	—	—	—	—	—
1867	1	5	11 April 1872	14 June 1872	65	—	7 August 1867–20 September 1867	24 September 1867	8 July 1872	4 y, 9 m, 15 d
		4	15 February 1871	14 April 1871	59	—	—	—	—	—
		3	15 February 1870	12 May 1870	87	—	—	—	—	—
		2	15 April 1869	22 June 1869	69	—	—	—	—	—
		1	6 November 1867	22 May 1868	199	—	—	—	—	—

Series W 50–73. *General elections, numbers of electors on lists and votes polled, by province and election, 1896 to 1960*

Year of election	Totals for Canada		Newfoundland		Prince Edward Island		Nova Scotia		New Brunswick		Quebec	
	Polling lists	Polled	Polling lists	Polled	Polling lists	Polled	Polling lists	Polled	Polling lists	Polled	Polling lists	Polled
	50	**51**	**52**	**53**	**54**	**55**	**56**	**57**	**58**	**59**	**60**	**61**
1958	9,131,200	7,357,139	204,778	160,928	54,200	69,302	390,196	418,479	294,387	249,706	2,576,682	2,045,199
1957	8,896,011	6,682,462	197,239	92,858	54,224	67,218	384,948	394,130	291,036	237,001	2,504,978	1,815,586
1953	8,401,691	5,701,963	194,715	111,768	55,469	66,562	380,836	334,855	287,657	225,390	2,352,619	1,565,400
1949	7,893,629	5,903,572	182,439	105,190	55,772	68,393	373,585	338,928	286,723	225,877	2,177,152	1,610,510
1945	6,952,445	5,305,193	—	—	54,794	63,807	362,754	312,954	262,261	204,273	1,956,225	1,433,591
1940	6,588,888	4,672,531	—	—	55,339	62,943	335,990	283,428	251,986	174,734	1,799,942	1,189,489
1935	5,918,207	4,452,675	—	—	53,284	61,641	304,313	275,523	229,266	177,485	1,575,159	1,162,862
1930	5,153,971	3,922,481	—	—	46,985	59,519	275,762	268,727	207,006	186,277	1,351,585	1,029,480
1926	4,665,381	3,273,062	—	—	46,208	55,569	273,712	229,846	210,028	162,777	1,133,633	809,205
1925	4,607,419	3,168,412	—	—	45,454	49,558	277,073	222,883	211,190	152,652	1,124,998	805,492
1921	4,435,310	3,119,306	—	—	46,879	52,556	294,473	260,860	204,575	156,263	1,056,792	779,591
1917	2,093,799	1,650,377[1]	—	—	28,221	32,249	133,930	106,621	94,456	84,408	396,666	301,519
1911	1,820,742	1,307,528	—	—	—	28,636	136,994	113,022	101,112	79,072	455,288	324,039
1908	1,463,591	1,174,703	—	—	—	28,782	132,914	111,138	98,026	75,651	415,076	283,132
1904	1,385,440	1,030,788	—	—	—	29,427	124,086	103,651	95,487	72,799	372,198	257,064
1900	1,167,402	950,763	—	—	—	21,026	106,451	105,194	94,877	68,267	350,250	237,320
1896	1,358,328	899,046	—	—	25,245	18,672	111,125	100,685	91,697	64,100	351,275	224,690

Year of election	Ontario		Manitoba		Saskatchewan		Alberta		British Columbia		Yukon and Northwest Territories	
	Polling lists	Polled	Polling lists	Polled	Polling lists	Polled	Polling lists	Polled	Polling lists	Polled	Polling lists	Polled
	62	**63**	**64**	**65**	**66**	**67**	**68**	**69**	**70**	**71**	**72**	**73**
1958	3,189,422	2,534,555	481,552	385,648	488,139	399,949	608,820	452,977	830,237	629,982	12,787	10,414
1957	3,100,456	2,295,033	473,802	351,827	484,318	392,266	591,043	431,184	802,017	596,424	11,950	8,935
1953	2,894,150	1,938,959	465,374	276,422	480,532	356,479	548,747	343,258	730,882	475,456	10,710	7,414
1949	2,718,118	2,042,294	451,882	324,079	472,884	375,471	492,228	341,222	673,782	464,785	9,064	6,823
1945	2,457,937	1,831,806	433,921	327,794	445,601	379,539	430,430	315,863	545,077	433,402	3,445	2,164
1940	2,340,344	1,625,439	425,066	320,860	481,931	373,376	423,609	272,418	472,584	368,103	2,097	1,741
1935	2,174,188	1,608,244	377,733	284,589	451,386	347,536	368,956	241,107	382,117	292,423	1,805	1,265
1930	1,894,624	1,364,960	328,089	235,192	410,400	331,652	304,475	201,635	333,326	243,631	1,719	1,408
1926	1,847,512	1,226,267	257,244	198,028	353,471	246,460	279,463	157,993	262,262	185,345	1,848	1,482
1925	1,821,906	1,223,027	250,505	171,124	346,791	197,246	283,529	161,423	244,352	183,748	1,621	1,259
1921	1,738,020	1,139,635	255,143	173,941	333,613	225,236	273,706	173,824	230,451	156,012	1,658	1,388
1917	904,075	710,077	138,029	109,542	133,806	99,253	140,757	107,272	122,071	97,994	1,788	1,442
1911	693,485	480,572	98,588	77,696	142,414	89,043	107,228	69,775	83,081	43,559	2,552	2,114
1908	660,340	462,280	84,537	68,047	—	59,868	—	45,972	69,827	37,368	2,871	2,465
1904	607,854	444,257	70,121	48,122	—	—	—	—	45,345	25,184	70,349	50,284
1900	482,003	427,173	64,027	41,714	—	—	—	—	38,448	26,451	31,346	23,618
1896	650,473	422,075	65,685	32,884	—	—	—	—	38,010	18,152	24,818	17,788

[1] An unusually large number of acclamations (31) affected the statistics for 1917, as did the Wartime Elections Act of that year.

Series W 74–164. *Votes polled in Dominion elections, by party and province, 1896 to 1960*

Province	Federal general election 1958						Federal general election 1957					
	Progressive Conservative[1]	Liberal[2]	Cooperative Commonwealth Federation	Social Credit[3]	Labour Progressive Party	Others	Liberal[2]	Progressive Conservative[1]	Cooperative Commonwealth Federation	Social Credit[3]	Labour Progressive Party	Others
	74	**75**	**76**	**77**	**78**	**79**	**80**	**81**	**82**	**83**	**84**	**85**
Newfoundland	72,282	86,960	240	—	—	263	56,993	34,795	321	—	—	—
Prince Edward Island	42,911	25,847	215	—	—	—	31,162	34,965	680	—	—	—
Nova Scotia	237,422	160,026	18,911	—	—	—	176,891	197,676	17,117	473	—	—
New Brunswick	133,935	107,297	4,541	1,711	—	—	112,518	114,060	2,001	2,420	—	3,159
Quebec	1,005,120	935,881	45,594	12,858	1,162	23,634	1,116,028	562,133	31,780	3,877	2,377	73,865
Ontario	1,413,730	815,524	262,120	8,386	3,035	1,718	845,308	1,104,366	274,069	38,418	1,432	978
Manitoba	216,948	82,450	74,906	6,753	1,503	—	93,258	124,867	82,398	45,803	1,579	205
Saskatchewan	204,442	78,121	112,800	1,745	458	146	118,282	90,359	140,293	40,830	212	122
Alberta	269,942	61,583	19,666	97,502	1,196	—	119,190	118,225	27,127	162,083	815	212
British Columbia	308,971	100,889	153,405	59,762	2,515	—	121,301	192,988	131,873	143,145	1,345	887
Yukon	3,069	2,340	—	—	—	—	2,422	2,358	—	—	—	—
Mackenzie River	2,080	2,782	—	—	—	—	2,686	1,253	—	—	—	—
Totals for Canada	3,910,852	2,459,700	692,398	188,717	9,869	25,761	2,796,039	2,578,045	707,659	437,049	7,760	79,428

Series W 74–164. *Votes polled in Dominion elections, by party and province, 1896 to 1960 (continuation)*

	Federal general election 1953						Federal general election 1949						
Province	Liberal[2]	Progressive Conservative[1]	Cooperative Commonwealth Federation	Social Credit[3]	Labour Progressive Party	Others	Liberal[2]	Progressive Conservative[1]	Cooperative Commonwealth Federation	Social Credit[3]	Union des Electeurs	Labour Progressive Party	Others
	86	87	88	89	90	91	92	93	94	95	96	97	98
Newfoundland	74,357	31,060	707	—	—	4,459	75,235	29,203	197	—	—	—	—
Prince Edward Island	33,874	31,836	552	—	—	—	33,480	32,989	1,626	—	—	—	—
Nova Scotia	176,554	133,498	22,357	—	794	—	177,680	126,365	33,333	—	—	—	—
New Brunswick	121,936	93,450	6,769	931	—	—	123,453	88,049	9,450	—	2,172	—	533
Quebec	1,001,655	455,688	23,833	—	10,819	54,778	984,131	397,803	17,767	—	80,990	4,868	107,741
Ontario	898,692	772,691	212,224	5,427	18,414	7,972	930,719	757,987	306,551	3,225	2,036	13,613	8,043
Manitoba	110,843	73,644	64,402	17,260	6,194	434	153,857	70,689	83,176	—	—	6,523	6,666
Saskatchewan	133,493	41,538	156,406	18,810	3,906	—	161,887	53,624	152,399	3,474	—	1,531	—
Alberta	118,941	49,450	23,573	138,847	9,155	275	116,647	56,947	31,329	131,007	—	2,201	—
British Columbia	145,570	66,426	125,487	123,700	10,340	—	169,018	128,620	145,442	2,109	—	3,887	11,992
Yukon	2,176	590	—	998	—	—	3,284	—	1,140	—	—	—	2,283
Mackenzie River	1,722	1,344	—	—	—	421	—	—	—	—	—	—	—
Totals for Canada	2,819,813	1,751,215	636,310	305,973	59,622	68,339	2,929,391	1,742,276	782,410	139,815	85,198	32,623	137,258

	Federal general election 1945							Federal general election 1940				
Province	Liberal[2]	Progressive Conservative[1]	Cooperative Commonwealth Federation[4]	Social Credit	Bloc Populaire	Labour Progressive Party	Others	Liberal[2]	Conservative[5]	Cooperative Commonwealth Federation	New Democrat[6]	Others
	99	100	101	102	103	104	105	106	107	108	109	110
Prince Edward Island	30,696	30,025	2,685	—	—	—	—	34,664	28,028	—	—	—
Nova Scotia	141,911	114,214	51,892	—	—	1,800	850	151,731	112,206	17,715	—	—
New Brunswick	100,939	77,225	14,999	2,300	—	—	6,423	97,062	74,970	761	—	—
Quebec	722,707	138,344	33,729	63,310	168,389	14,641	273,049	868,663	231,851	7,610	11,191	52,182
Ontario	745,571	757,057	260,502	3,906	5,038	36,333	6,560	834,166	687,816	61,166	786	25,480
Manitoba	111,863	80,303	101,892	10,322	—	15,984	2,451	151,480	82,240	61,448	5,831	15,884
Saskatchewan	124,191	70,830	167,233	11,449	—	3,183	—	159,530	52,496	106,267	12,106	40,735
Alberta	67,662	58,077	57,077	113,821	—	14,136	—	102,060	35,116	35,082	93,023	4,062
British Columbia	125,085	128,529	132,068	9,890	—	25,128	7,741	136,065	110,619	103,181	506	12,773
Yukon	—	849	584	—	—	687	—	793	915	—	—	—
Totals for Canada	2,170,625	1,455,453	822,661	214,998	173,427	111,892	297,074	2,536,514	1,416,257	393,230	123,443	151,116

	Federal general election 1935									Federal general election 1930								
Province	Liberal	Conservative	Reconstruction	Cooperative Commonwealth Federation	Social Credit	Independent Liberal	Communist	Others	Rejected Ballots	Conservative	Liberal	Progressive	Labour Progressive	Labour	Independent	United Farmers of Alberta	Farmer	Communist
	111	112	113	114	115	116	117	118	119	120	121	122	123	124	125	126	127	128
Prince Edward Island	35,757	23,602	2,089	—	—	—	—	—	193	29,692	29,698	—	—	—	—	—	—	—
Nova Scotia	142,334	87,893	38,175	—	—	—	5,365	—	1,756	140,513	127,189	—	—	—	—	—	—	—
New Brunswick	100,537	56,145	18,408	—	—	672	—	—	1,723	109,839	75,221	—	—	—	—	—	—	—
Quebec	623,579	323,177	103,857	7,326	—	70,504	3,385	14,693	16,341	456,037	542,135	—	—	—	21,776	—	—	313
Ontario	675,803	562,513	181,981	129,457	—	14,459	8,945	21,089	13,997	745,414	590,071	12,815	—	992	8,785	—	—	1,499
Manitoba	100,535	75,574	16,439	54,491	5,751	18,973	9,229	—	3,597	111,312	37,234	—	59,155	19,809	2,018	—	—	3,873
Saskatchewan	134,914	71,285	2,273	73,505	63,593	—	—	—	1,966	129,420	153,673	18,178	—	—	6,155	—	22,766	—
Alberta	50,539	40,236	1,785	29,066	111,627	—	2,672	2,588	2,594	67,808	60,148	—	—	8,769	2,727	60,924	—	—
British Columbia	91,729	71,034	19,208	97,015	1,796	—	1,555	6,446	3,640	119,074	98,933	—	—	15,732	7,894	—	—	—
Yukon	—	—	—	—	—	555	—	696	14	846	558	—	—	—	—	—	—	—
Totals for Canada	1,955,727	1,311,459	384,215	390,860	182,767	105,163	31,151	45,512	45,821	1,909,955	1,714,860	30,993	59,155	45,302	49,355	60,924	22,766	5,685

Series W 74–164. *Votes polled in Dominion elections, by party and province, 1896 to 1960 (continuation)*

Province	Federal general election 1926								Federal general election 1925				
	Conservative	Liberal	Progressive	Labour Progressive	Labour	Independent	United Farmers of Alberta	Rejected Ballots	Liberal	Conservative	Progressive	Labour	Independent
	129	**130**	**131**	**132**	**133**	**134**	**135**	**136**	**137**	**138**	**139**	**140**	**141**
Prince Edward Island	26,217	29,222	—	—	—	—	—	130	25,681	23,799	—	—	—
Nova Scotia	122,965	99,581	—	—	6,412	—	—	888	92,525	124,545	—	3,617	—
New Brunswick	87,080	74,465	—	—	—	—	—	1,232	61,161	90,405	—	—	84
Quebec	266,824	507,775	50,360	38,112	6,282	8,787	—	5,909	469,475	273,818	—	1,685	58,588
Ontario	680,742	441,254	50,360	38,112	6,282	5,356	—	4,161	392,039	691,365	108,051	9,552	19,104
Manitoba	83,100	36,242	22,092	38,379	17,194	—	—	1,021	34,538	70,264	45,859	18,335	—
Saskatchewan	67,524	125,849	38,324	13,413	—	—	—	1,350	82,810	51,512	62,268	—	1,914
Alberta	49,514	38,451	—	—	8,148	163	60,740	977	44,291	51,114	50,592	8,572	6,040
British Columbia	100,066	68,317	—	—	11,757	4,330	—	875	63,506	90,032	15,829	11,463	888
Yukon	823	648	—	—	—	—	—	11	508	742	—	—	—
Totals for Canada	1,504,855	1,421,804	110,776	89,904	49,793	18,636	60,740	16,554	1,266,534	1,467,596	282,599	53,224	87,618

Province	Federal general election of 1921				Federal general election of 1917				Federal general election of 1911		
					Unionist		Laurier-Liberals				
	Liberal	Conservative	Progressive	Independent	Civilian	Soldiers'	Civilian	Soldiers'	Conservative	Liberal	Other
	142	**143**	**144**	**145**	**146**	**147**	**148**	**149**	**150**	**151**	**152**
Prince Edward Island	23,950	19,504	8,990	—	10,450	2,775	12,224	434	14,638	13,998	—
Nova Scotia	136,064	87,988	35,741	—	40,985	10,699	49,831	1,474	55,209	57,462	351
New Brunswick	76,653	61,172	17,447	—	35,871	9,934	32,397	919	38,880	40,192	—
Quebec	558,056	163,743	31,790	39,477	61,808	14,206	240,504	2,927	159,299	164,281	459
Ontario	351,717	445,150	329,502	9,003	419,928	95,212	263,300	5,793	269,930	207,078	3,564
Manitoba	29,525	46,486	83,350	13,361	83,469	23,698	26,073	1,157	40,356	34,781	2,559
Saskatchewan	46,447	37,345	136,486	3,610	68,424	12,996	30,829	2,672	34,700	52,924	1,419
Alberta	27,404	35,181	104,295	6,024	60,399	19,575	48,865	1,055	29,675	37,208	2,892
British Columbia	46,249	74,226	21,786	12,739	59,944	26,461	40,050	2,059	25,622	16,350	1,587
Yukon	658	707	—	18	666	293	776	32	1,285	829	—
Totals for Canada	1,296,723	971,502	769,387	84,232	841,944	215,849	744,849	18,522	669,594	625,103	12,831

Province	Federal general election 1908			Federal general election 1904			Federal general election 1900			Federal general election 1896		
	Liberal	Conservative	Other	Liberal	Conservative	Other	Liberal	Conservative	Other	Liberal	Conservative	Other
	153	**154**	**155**	**156**	**157**	**158**	**159**	**160**	**161**	**162**	**163**	**164**
Prince Edward Island	14,496	14,286	—	14,441	14,986	—	10,887	10,139	—	9,515	9,157	—
Nova Scotia	56,638	54,500	—	56,526	46,131	994	54,384	50,810	—	49,176	50,772	737
New Brunswick	40,716	34,935	—	37,158	35,593	138	35,401	32,638	228	28,383	31,399	4,318
Quebec	162,176	115,579	5,377	144,992	111,550	522	133,566	103,253	501	120,321	102,884	1,485
Ontario	217,963	237,548	6,769	219,871	223,627	759	212,595	212,413	2,165	169,480	189,927	62,668
Manitoba	30,892	35,078	2,077	26,713	20,119	1,290	21,597	20,177	—	11,519	15,459	5,906
Saskatchewan	33,885	22,007	3,976									
Alberta	23,100	20,433	2,439	27,173[7]	19,367[7]	136[7]	13,012[7]	10,606[7]	—	8,191[7]	7,811[7]	1,786[7]
British Columbia	13,412	17,503	6,453	12,458	9,781	2,945	12,985	10,814	2,652	8,921	9,231	—
Yukon	992	265	1,208	1,495	2,113	—						
Totals for Canada	594,270	552,134	28,299	540,827	483,177	6,784	494,427	450,790	5,546	405,506	416,640	76,900

[1] Includes Independent Progressive Conservative.
[2] Includes Independent Liberal.
[3] Includes Independent Social Credit.
[4] Includes Independent Cooperative Commonwealth Federation.
[5] Includes Independent Conservative and National Government.
[6] Includes Social Credit.
[7] Northwest Territories.

Series W 165–176. *Members elected in Dominion elections, by party and province, 1867 to 1960*

Year	Party	Totals for Canada	New found-land	Prince Edward Island	Nova Scotia	New Bruns-wick	Quebec	Ontario	Mani-toba	Saskat-chewan	Alberta	British Columbia	Yukon and Northwest Territories
		165	166	167	168	169	170	171	172	173	174	175	176
1958	Progressive Conservative	208	2	4	12	7	50	67	14	16	17	18	1
	Liberal	48	5	*	*	3	25	14	*	*	*	*	1
	Cooperative Commonwealth Federation	8	*	*	*	*	*	3	*	1	*	4	*
	Liberal Labour	1	*	*	*	*	*	1	*	*	*	*	*
1957	Progressive Conservative	112	2	4	10	5	9	61	8	3	3	7	*
	Liberal	105	5	*	2	5	63	20	1	4	1	2	2
	Independent Liberal	1	*	*	*	*	1	*	*	*	*	*	*
	Cooperative Commonwealth Federation	25	*	*	*	*	*	3	5	10	*	7	*
	Social Credit	19	*	*	*	*	*	*	*	*	13	6	*
	Liberal Labour	1	*	*	*	*	*	1	*	*	*	*	*
	Independent	2	*	*	*	*	2	*	*	*	*	*	*
1953	Liberal	170	7	3	10	7	66	50	8	5	4	8	2
	Independent Liberal	2	*	*	*	*	2	*	*	*	*	*	*
	Progressive Conservative	51	*	1	1	3	4	33	3	1	2	3	*
	Cooperative Commonwealth Federation	23	*	*	1	*	*	1	3	11	*	7	*
	Social Credit	15	*	*	*	*	*	*	*	*	11	4	*
	Independent	3	*	*	*	*	3	*	*	*	*	*	*
	Liberal Labour	1	*	*	*	*	*	1	*	*	*	*	*
1949	Liberal	190	5	3	10	7	66	56	12	14	5	11	1
	Independent Liberal	3	*	*	*	1	1	1	*	*	*	*	*
	Progressive Conservative	41	2	1	2	2	2	25	1	1	2	3	*
	Cooperative Commonwealth Federation	13	*	*	1	*	*	1	3	5	*	3	*
	Social Credit	10	*	*	*	*	*	*	*	*	10	*	*
	Independent	5	*	*	*	*	4	*	*	*	*	1	*
1945	Liberal	125	—	3	8	7	54	34	10	2	2	5	*
	Independent Liberal	2	—	*	*	*	2	*	*	*	*	*	*
	Progressive Conservative	67	—	1	3	3	1	48	2	1	2	5	1
	Independent Conservative	1	—	*	*	*	1	*	*	*	*	*	*
	Cooperative Commonwealth Federation	28	—	*	1	*	*	*	5	18	*	4	*
	Independent Cooperative Commonwealth Federation	1	—	*	*	1	*	*	*	*	*	*	*
	Social Credit	13	—	*	*	*	*	*	*	*	13	*	*
	Independent	5	—	*	*	*	4	*	*	*	*	1	*
	Bloc Populaire	2	—	*	*	*	2	*	*	*	*	*	*
	Labour Progressive Party	1	—	*	*	*	1	*	*	*	*	*	*
1940	Liberal	178	—	4	10	5	61	55	14	12	7	10	*
	Independent Liberal	3	—	*	*	*	3	*	*	*	*	*	*
	Conservative	39	—	*	1	5	*	25	1	2	*	4	1
	Independent Conservative	1	—	*	*	*	1	*	*	*	*	*	*
	Social Credit	10	—	*	*	*	*	*	*	*	10	*	*
	Cooperative Commonwealth Federation	8	—	*	1	*	*	*	1	5	*	1	*
	Liberal Progressive	3	—	*	*	*	*	*	2	1	*	*	*
	Independent	1	—	*	*	*	*	*	*	*	*	1	*
	Unity	2	—	*	*	*	*	*	*	2	*	*	*
1935	Liberal	171	—	4	12	9	55	56	12	16	1	6	.
	Independent Liberal	5	—	*	*	*	5	*	*	*	*	*	*
	Conservative	39	—	*	*	1	5	25	1	1	1	5	*
	Independent Conservative	1	—	*	*	*	*	*	*	*	*	*	1
	Social Credit	17	—	*	*	*	*	*	*	2	15	*	*
	Cooperative Commonwealth Federation	7	—	*	*	*	*	*	2	2	*	3	*
	Liberal Progressive	2	—	*	*	*	*	*	2	*	*	*	*
	Reconstruction	1	—	*	*	*	*	*	*	*	*	1	*
	Independent	1	—	*	*	*	*	*	*	*	*	1	*
	United Farmers of Ontario—Labour	1	—	*	*	*	*	1	*	*	*	*	*

Series W 165–176. *Members elected in Dominion elections, by party and province, 1867 to 1960 (continued)*

Year	Party	Totals for Canada	Newfoundland	Prince Edward Island	Nova Scotia	New Brunswick	Quebec	Ontario	Manitoba	Saskatchewan	Alberta	British Columbia	Yukon and Northwest Territories
		165	166	167	168	169	170	171	172	173	174	175	176
1930	Conservative	137	—	3	10	10	24	59	11	8	4	7	1
	Liberal	88	—	1	4	1	40	22	1	11	3	5	*
	United Farmers	10	—	*	*	*	*	1	*	9	*	*	*
	Progressive	2	—	*	*	*	*	*	*	2	*	*	*
	Liberal Progressive	3	—	*	*	*	*	*	3	*	*	*	*
	Labour	2	—	*	*	*	*	*	2	*	*	*	*
	Independent Labour	1	—	*	*	*	*	*	*	*	*	1	*
	Independent	2	—	*	*	*	1	*	*	*	*	1	*
1926	Liberal	116	—	3	2	4	60	23	4	16	3	1	*
	Conservative	91	—	1	12	7	4	53	0	0	1	12	1
	United Farmers of Alberta	11	—	*	*	*	*	*	*	*	11	*	*
	Progressive	13	—	0	0	0	0	4	4	5	0	0	*
	Liberal Progressive	9	—	0	0	0	0	2	7	0	0	0	*
	Labour	3	—	*	*	*	*	*	2	*	*	1	*
	Independent	2	—	*	*	*	1	*	*	*	*	1	*
1925	Liberal	101	—	2	3	1	60	12	1	15	4	3	*
	Conservative	116	—	2	11	10	4	68	7	0	3	10	1
	Progressive	24	—	0	0	0	0	2	7	6	9	0	*
	Labour	2	—	*	*	*	*	*	2	*	*	*	*
	Independent	2	—	*	*	*	1	*	*	*	*	1	*
1921	Liberal	117	—	4	16	5	65	21	2	1	0	3	*
	Conservative	50	—	0	0	5	0	37	0	0	0	7	1
	Progressive	64	—	0	0	1	0	24	12	15	10	2	*
	Labour	3	—	*	*	*	*	*	1	*	2	*	*
	Independent	1	—	*	*	*	*	*	*	*	*	1	*
1917	Unionist	153	—	2	12	7	3	74	14	16	11	13	1
	Liberal	82	—	2	4	4	62	8	1	0	1	0	0
1911	Conservative	133	—	2	9	5	27	72	8	1	1	7	1
	Liberal	86	—	2	9	8	37	13	2	9	6	0	0
	Independent	2	—	*	*	*	1	1	*	*	*	*	*
1908	Liberal	133	—	3	12	11	53	36	2	9	4	2	1
	Conservative	85	—	1	6	2	11	48	8	1	3	5	0
	Independent	3	—	*	*	*	1	2	*	*	*	*	*
1904	Liberal	139	—	1	18	7	54	38	7	—	—	7	7
	Conservative	75	—	3	0	6	11	48	3	—	—	0	4
1900	Liberal	128	—	3	15	9	56	35	2	—	—	3	5
	Conservative	78	—	2	5	5	7	54	3	—	—	3	0
	Other (no details)	8	—	—	—	—	—	—	—	—	—	—	—
1896	Liberal	117	—	2	10	5	49	43	2	—	—	4	2
	Conservative	89	—	3	10	9	16	44	4	—	—	2	1
	Independent	7	—	*	*	*	*	5	1	—	—	*	1
1891	Conservative	123	—	2	16	13	30	48	4	—	—	6	4
	Liberal	92	—	4	5	3	35	44	1	—	—	0	0
1887	Conservative	123	—	0	14	10	33	52	4	—	—	6	4
	Liberal	92	—	6	7	6	32	40	1	—	—	0	0
1882	Conservative	139	—	4	15	10	48	54	2	—	—	6	—
	Liberal	71	—	2	6	6	17	37	3	—	—	0	—
1878	Conservative	137	—	5	14	5	45	59	3	—	—	6	—
	Liberal	69	—	1	7	11	20	29	1	—	—	0	—
1874	Liberal	133	—	6	17	11	33	64	2	—	—	0	—
	Conservative	73	—	0	4	5	32	24	2	—	—	6	—
1872	Conservative	103	—	—	11	7	38	38	3	—	—	6	—
	Liberal	97	—	—	10	9	27	50	1	—	—	0	—
1867	Conservative	101	—	—	3	7	45	46	—	—	—	—	—
	Liberal	80	—	—	16	8	20	36	—	—	—	—	—

Series W 177–213. *Dominion government employees, by department, branch and service, 1900 to 1959*

Year[1]	Totals for Canada	Agriculture	Defence Production	External Affairs	Finance	Fisheries	Justice	Labour	Mines and Technical Surveys	Citizenship and Immigration	Indian Affairs	Interior
	177	178	179	180	181	182	183	184	185	186	187	188
Federal government employees—Dominion Bureau of Statistics												
1959	197,909	8,135	1,432	1,963	5,291	1,989	2,366	10,731	2,734	4,407	—	—
1958	195,390	7,760	1,427	1,954	5,340	1,768	2,183	10,683	2,126	4,596	—	—
1957[2]	—					—					—	—
1956	182,835	7,444	1,456	1,594	4,874	1,925	2,186	9,352	2,349	3,899	—	—
1955	181,582	7,679	1,455	1,548	5,126	1,875	2,286	9,368	1,982	3,855	—	—
1954	171,065	7,544	1,522	1,474	5,176	1,847	2,263	9,531	1,919	3,462	—	—
1953	165,161	7,320	1,678	1,395	5,157	1,875	2,148	8,963	1,703	3,435	—	—
1952	131,646	6,888	1,488	1,327	4,959	1,031	1,714	7,486	1,746	3,095	—	—
1951	124,580	7,078	—	1,342	5,135	962	1,713	7,686	1,720	2,917	—	—
1950	127,196	6,667	—	1,301	5,874	883	1,556	7,793	1,661	2,657	—	—
1949	123,924	5,914	408	1,234	6,664	569	1,434	7,577	5,187	—	—	—
1948	118,370	5,381	329	1,054	6,774	533	1,326	7,760	4,211	—	—	—
1947	125,337	3,833	986	890	10,839	350	1,239	9,328	3,842	—	—	—
1946	120,557	3,535	1,925	759	14,860	361	1,113	9,836	4,361	—	—	—
1945	115,908	3,195	3,835	680	12,772	374	1,032	9,111	3,694	—	—	—
1944	112,658	3,326	4,027	571	12,707	364	996	8,365	3,601	—	—	—
1943	104,055	3,303	4,303	494	10,828	318	975	5,141	3,517	—	—	—
1942	83,781	3,202	3,219	371	6,673	332	1,048	1,716	3,307	—	—	—
1941	66,937	3,110	1,244	293	3,347	289	1,086	355	3,278	—	—	—
1940	49,656	3,362	—	219	2,103	312	1,115	303	3,177	—	—	—
1939	46,106	3,122	—	193	1,432	325	1,091	244	3,147	—	—	—
1938	44,143	2,926	—	185	1,475	301	1,044	244	3,106	—	—	—
1937	42,836	2,633	—	167	1,409	309	1,016	238	3,124	—	—	—
1936	41,001	2,344	—	172	1,399	320	1,049	200	456	615	1,029	945
1935	40,709	2,280	—	159	1,466	339	1,093	176	368	635	1,072	947
1934	40,401	2,176	—	159	1,466	310	1,064	164	354	647	1,020	969
1933	41,901	2,292	—	159	526	349	1,091	170	373	722	1,056	1,010
1932	44,002	2,385	—	160	536	362	874	197	394	781	1,077	1,125
1931	45,581	2,247	—	155	405	382	819	143	532	883	1,074	2,037
1930	44,175	2,113	—	154	419	381	707	141	383	955	1,035	2,415
1929	42,790	1,962	—	143	414	—	679	137	361	924	988	2,323
1928	41,243	1,846	—	129	421	—	675	125	343	887	934	2,229
1927	39,592	1,758	—	109	409	—	647	109	310	860	934	2,229
1926	39,154	1,698	—	102	416	—	621	102	317	884	912	2,068
1925	38,883	1,574	—	103	444	—	614	99	310	928	896	2,048
1924	40,068	1,538	—	109	503	—	600	96	298	1,119	858	2,092
Civil service personnel in the month of January—Dominion Bureau of Statistics												
1924	38,062	1,597	—	99	546	—	599	94	296	840	794	2,052
1923	38,992	1,481	—	104	589	—	592	123	282	747	784	2,153
1922	41,094	1,360	—	105	479	—	562	146	276	713	784	2,179
1921	41,957	1,178	—	131	534	—	499	139	259	706	775	2,008
1920	47,133	1,125	—	139	656	—	494	154	275	607	787	1,975
1919	41,825	1,137	—	151	713	—	454	238	276	709	788	1,904
1918	38,369	1,194	—	82	803	—	469	67	267	824	711	1,896
1917	32,435	1,137	—	65	248	—	504	45	303	674	847	1,861
1916	29,219	1,046	—	53	176	—	512	45	260	728	843	1,888
1915	28,010	995	—	41	138	—	504	44	224	718	803	1,765
1914	25,107	839	—	33	122	—	467	43	195	663	787	1,532
1913	22,621	824	—	31	113	—	443	35	182	564	731	1,386
1912	20,016	718	—	26	113	—	419	30	148	476	659	1,270
Civil service employees: number—Parliamentary Return												
1915	—	1,264	—	21	129	—	540	44	255	109	90	976
1914	—	1,181	—	18	120	—	531	42	221	100	93	909
1913	—	1,128	—	14	121	—	507	33	200	96	78	806
1912	—	1,326	—	11	121	—	477	27	170	82	78	720
1911	—	1,001	—	10	121	—	414	24	150	83	78	701
1910	—	949	—	9	110	—	387	21	115	74	76	666
1909	—	960	—	6	111	—	387	17	104	76	72	663
1908	—	799	—	—	114	—	400	14	108	61	64	578
1907	—	576	—	—	109	—	385	13	73	57	63	468
1906	—	548	—	—	110	—	360	11	57	47	63	403
1905	—	652	—	—	105	—	347	11	62	33	56	360
1904	—	646	—	—	98	—	366	11	59	33	56	335
1903	—	702	—	—	90	—	341	11	54	26	56	274
1902	—	713	—	—	80	—	341	9	54	21	52	231
1901	—	770	—	—	74	—	338	10	53	18	52	206
1900	—	471	—	—	—	—	—	—	51	14	52	194

[1] Data for 1924 to 1959 are for 31 March.   [2] No separate tabulation available.

Series W 177–213. *Dominion government employees, by department, branch and service, 1900 to 1959 (continuation)*

Year[1]	National Defence	National Health and Welfare	National Revenue	National War Services	Northern Affairs and National Resources	Post Office	Secretary of State	Trade and Commerce	Transport	Veterans' Affairs	Public Works
	189	190	191	192	193	194	195	196	197	198	199
						Federal government employees—Dominion Bureau of Statistics					
1959	54,267	4,567	14,967	—	5,164	24,739	712	4,194	13,387	13,548	8,494
1958	55,223	4,422	15,258	—	4,659	24,245	671	4,014	13,607	13,516	8,077
1957[2]	—	—	—	—	—	—	—	—	—	—	—
1956	54,805	4,077	14,657	—	2,548	21,827	592	3,665	12,166	12,905	7,718
1955	53,909	3,926	14,707	—	2,733	21,320	628	3,685	11,482	13,483	7,870
1954	45,718	3,737	14,058	—	2,335	19,789	608	3,699	12,298	13,986	7,797
1953	42,820	3,727	13,439	—	2,402	19,298	594	3,924	11,546	14,218	7,595
1952	24,175	3,239	12,540	—	1,671	19,510	579	3,686	9,073	13,822	7,183
1951	17,757	2,954	13,205	—	1,689	19,478	588	3,720	9,301	14,155	7,231
1950	16,847	2,801	16,715	—	1,570	19,096	608	3,748	9,682	15,082	6,954
1949	16,904	2,585	17,480	—	—	18,049	557	3,401	8,721	15,479	6,547
1948	15,039	2,346	16,030	—	—	17,105	528	3,500	8,000	16,851	6,574
1947	18,665	2,517	12,423	5	—	16,499	470	3,318	7,536	21,098	6,341
1946	19,228	1,830	11,771	45	—	15,256	457	2,907	7,432	14,241	6,184
1945	26,920	1,302	10,706	1,217	—	13,770	387	2,620	6,797	7,364	5,845
1944	29,625	4,998	9,285	1,176	—	13,105	361	2,657	6,833	339	5,694
1943	28,957	4,038	7,949	2,090	—	12,622	365	2,755	6,363	253	5,378
1942	22,212	3,371	6,657	709	—	12,809	426	3,302	5,705	255	4,858
1941	15,056	2,980	5,904	1,079	—	13,160	434	1,839	5,604	258	4,538
1940	3,592	2,578	5,700	—	—	12,857	421	1,801	5,414	265	4,250
1939	1,424	2,335	5,706	—	—	12,518	346	1,794	5,710	303	4,124
1938	1,306	2,288	5,784	—	—	12,122	324	1,607	4,816	307	4,027
1937	1,336	2,354	5,521	—	—	11,649	312	1,867	4,549	325	3,860
1936	1,143	2,290	5,454	—	—	10,847	294	1,685	4,662	335	3,682
1935	1,096	2,264	5,374	—	—	10,780	208	1,682	4,678	336	3,620
1934	1,103	2,266	5,360	—	—	10,842	196	1,756	4,526	343	3,594
1933	1,256	2,711	5,654	—	—	11,140	212	2,065	4,919	370	3,794
1932	1,352	2,750	6,260	—	—	11,676	214	2,632	4,970	369	3,950
1931	1,358	2,848	6,309	—	—	11,961	220	1,870	5,683	504	4,050
1930	1,244	2,518	6,131	—	—	11,739	216	1,675	5,458	528	4,030
1929	1,206	2,332	5,935	—	—	11,515	206	1,497	5,682	538	4,003
1928	1,163	2,289	5,771	—	—	10,871	197	1,363	5,611	546	3,933
1927	1,123	2,261	5,252	—	—	10,455	188	1,341	5,473	496	3,836
1926	1,113	2,452	5,137	—	—	10,240	188	1,112	5,516	489	3,897
1925	1,088	2,723	5,037	—	—	10,254	182	1,037	6,018	514	3,160
1924	1,110	3,156	5,101	—	—	10,259	195	1,236	5,956	609	3,326
			Civil service personnel in the month of January—Dominion Bureau of Statistics								
1924	1,304	3,408	5,136	—	—	10,213	236	1,403	4,327	618	3,004
1923	1,538	4,130	5,241	—	—	10,068	246	1,426	4,364	692	2,970
1922	2,398	5,194	5,308	—	—	10,007	247	1,487	4,449	770	3,020
1921	2,685	6,573	5,269	—	—	9,950	221	1,068	4,239	1,136	3,030
1920	5,547	9,466	4,719	—	—	9,740	177	1,021	4,157	1,175	3,103
1919	7,392	3,876	4,376	—	—	10,002	82	931	3,997	68	3,015
1918	5,771	3,852	4,525	—	—	9,084	77	695	4,106	2	2,189
1917	4,143	648	4,294	—	—	8,729	75	694	4,351	—	2,085
1916	2,708	47	4,225	—	—	8,057	68	499	4,549	—	2,007
1915	1,747	—	4,144	—	—	7,849	51	463	5,169	—	1,911
1914	919	—	4,037	—	—	7,171	52	437	4,784	—	1,708
1913	841	—	3,651	—	—	5,919	45	463	4,605	—	1,554
1912	725	—	3,214	—	—	5,082	38	293	4,235	—	1,481
			Civil service employees: number—Parliamentary Return								
1915	128	—	4,274	—	—	694	55	249	341	—	326
1914	130	—	4,194	—	—	727	51	292	347	—	285
1913	125	—	3,884	—	—	638	47	338	334	—	251
1912	112	—	3,464	—	—	596	39	418	320	—	234
1911	103	—	3,051	—	—	504	34	147	301	—	232
1910	94	—	2,923	—	—	497	35	145	311	—	233
1909	96	—	2,827	—	—	475	34	121	251	—	208
1908	99	—	2,749	—	—	370	34	104	164	—	203
1907	44	—	2,560	—	—	347	34	101	153	—	178
1906	39	—	2,454	—	—	329	32	90	136	—	155
1905	39	—	2,382	—	—	310	30	71	135	—	146
1904	36	—	2,314	—	—	326	32	76	134	—	159
1903	34	—	2,214	—	—	283	32	66	119	—	137
1902	36	—	2,130	—	—	271	31	45	118	—	132
1901	32	—	2,140	—	—	246	31	17	119	—	108
1900	32	—	2,087	—	—	246	32	13	48	—	—

[1] Data for 1924 to 1959 are for 31 March. [2] No separate tabulation available.

Series W 177–213. *Dominion government employees, by department, branch and service, 1900 to 1959 (continuation)*

						Branch or Service								
Year[1]	Auditor General	Chief Electoral Officer	Civil Service Commission	Conservation Commission	Governor General, Lieutenant-Governors	Insurance	International Joint Commission	Legislation	National Film Board	National Research Council	Privy Council	Public Archives, and National Library	Public Printing and Stationery	Royal Canadian Mounted Police
	200	201	202	203	204	205	206	207	208	209	210	211	212	213
					Federal government employees—Dominion Bureau of Statistics									
1959	133	16	647	—	13	94	—	925	756	2,905	135	141	1,776	7,281
1958[2]	133	89	639	—	13	89	—	521	732	2,809	113	134	1,674	6,915
1957[2]	—	—	—	—	—	—	—	—	—	—	—	—	—	—
1956	129	17	585	—	24	93	—	880	616	2,577	91	99	1,453	6,232
1955	140	18	595	—	24	92	—	873	591	2,517	107	83	1,390	6,236
1954	141	20	570	—	24	94	—	897	553	2,415	103	78	1,295	6,112
1953	145	22	578	—	28	94	—	877	558	2,268	106	79	1,199	5,969
1952	158	21	544	—	13	83	12	855	579	2,052	90	67	1,132	828
1951	163	14	536	—	10	82	11	857	565	1,898	85	65	1,041	622
1950	169	13	580	—	10	72	10	843	596	1,701	87	61	991	568
1949	173	19	572	—	10	63	4	822	547	1,531	72	55	856	490
1948	173	10	532	—	12	59	4	720	598	1,550	68	54	786	463
1947	198	12	618	—	11	54	3	711	—	2,246	43	57	783	422
1946	247	12	684	—	10	53	5	741	—	1,379	43	52	771	459
1945	263	12	560	—	10	49	5	616	—	1,385	44	50	794	499
1944	262	9	591	—	10	47	5	646	476	1,232	51	50	824	425
1943	269	10	568	—	10	47	5	696	377	1,135	32	51	817	389
1942	359	38	453	—	12	49	5	687	49	792	23	53	766	323
1941	292	16	364	—	13	53	5	716	—	585	24	55	709	251
1940	280	38	277	—	11	53	6	328	—	310	23	69	665	127
1939	231	15	235	—	14	53	6	688	—	226	19	67	652	86
1938	226	5	230	—	12	54	6	736	—	185	18	74	635	100
1937	220	6	195	—	12	49	7	690	—	171	18	69	622	108
1936	233	14	147	—	12	50	6	649	—	144	17	77	617	114
1935	221	13	133	—	11	49	6	727	—	129	17	77	627	126
1934	212	3	124	—	10	47	6	701	—	126	19	76	601	161
1933	214	3	137	—	10	45	6	627	—	—	18	80	692	200
1932	220	4	155	—	10	43	5	605	—	—	18	81	709	88
1931	211	7	176	—	10	42	5	750	—	—	18	83	721	78
1930	205	10	173	—	10	40	5	602	—	—	20	83	715	70
1929	202	4	157	—	10	40	5	652	—	—	20	83	714	58
1928	202	5	144	—	11	38	5	657	—	—	21	83	696	48
1927	206	12	143	—	12	36	5	645	—	—	21	78	690	47
1926	214	12	138	—	12	34	5	639	—	—	21	79	689	47
1925	196	4	146	—	12	35	5	632	—	—	21	76	686	41
1924	211	4	155	—	12	35	5	626	—	—	20	84	715	40
				Civil service personnel in the month of January—Dominion Bureau of Statistics										
1924	209	4	172	—	12	34	5	231	—	—	19	81	688	41
1923	199	6	176	—	13	35	5	228	—	—	20	81	663	36
1922	205	39	219	10	15	32	5	224	—	—	18	79	729	35
1921	195	8	217	46	13	31	5	218	—	—	21	80	702	21
1920	158	—	118	46	14	29	5	184	—	—	25	80	1,142	15
1919	142	—	52	34	13	27	5	136	—	—	27	76	1,192	12
1918	150	—	13	36	12	22	5	140	—	—	29	78	1,260	10
1917	142	—	12	37	11	21	5	227	—	—	26	76	1,165	10
1916	111	—	14	34	12	19	5	50	—	—	27	76	1,150	10
1915	95	—	13	32	12	18	5	52	—	—	25	74	1,106	12
1914	97	—	14	31	11	20	5	56	—	—	21	62	989	12
1913	96	—	11	27	11	18	5	54	—	—	27	59	915	11
1912	83	—	11	20	11	16	5	50	—	—	20	—	862	11
			Civil service employees: number—Parliamentary Return											
1915	101	2	16	—	—	25	—	—	—	—	30	—	42	11
1914	102	3	16	—	—	23	—	—	—	—	28	—	42	12
1913	88	12	16	—	—	19	—	—	—	—	22	—	48	10
1912	92	23	14	—	—	17	—	—	—	—	28	—	54	11
1911	87	—	13	—	—	17	—	—	—	—	24	—	58	11
1910	85	—	10	—	—	14	—	—	—	—	23	—	70	10
1909	93	—	9	—	—	12	—	—	—	—	29	—	70	7
1908	72	—	5	—	—	11	—	—	—	—	37	—	34	10
1907	71	—	—	—	—	10	—	—	—	—	30	—	30	10
1906	72	—	—	—	—	9	—	—	—	—	31	—	33	9
1905	74	—	—	—	—	9	—	—	—	—	30	—	32	9
1904	58	—	—	—	—	6	—	—	—	—	32	—	30	8
1903	54	—	—	—	—	6	—	—	—	—	30	—	27	6
1902	48	—	—	—	—	6	—	—	—	—	33	—	27	6
1901	44	—	—	—	—	8	—	—	—	—	31	—	27	6
1900	42	—	—	—	—	—	—	—	—	—	30	—	26	6

[1] Data for 1924 to 1959 are for 31 March.   [2] No separate tabulation available.

Series W 214–217. *Representation of government of Canada abroad, 1867 to 1960*

Year	Total number of places where represented	Place of representation added	Year of establishment	Status of representative at 31 January 1960
	214	**215**	**216**	**217**

		Regular diplomatic representation		
1960, 31 January	50	Austria	1952	Ambassador
		Burma	1958	Ambassador
		Ceylon	1953	High Commissioner
		Columbia	1953	Ambassador
		Dominican Republic	1954	Ambassador
		Ghana	1957	High Commissioner
		Haiti	1954	Ambassador
		Indonesia	1953	Ambassador
		Iran	1958	Minister
		Israel	1954	Ambassador
		Lebanon	1954	Ambassador
		Malaya	1958	High Commissioner
		Portugal	1952	Ambassador
		Spain	1953	Ambassador
		United Arab Republic	1954	Ambassador
		Uruguay	1952	Chargé d'Affaires ad interim
		Venezuela	1952	Ambassador
1950, 31 December	33	Argentina	1941	Ambassador
		Brazil	1941	Ambassador
		Chile	1942	Ambassador
		Cuba	1945	Ambassador
		Czechoslovakia	1943	Chargé d'Affaires ad interim
		Denmark	1946	Ambassador
		Finland	1949	Minister
		Germany	1950	Ambassador
		Greece	1943	Ambassador
		Iceland	1949	Minister
		India	1947	High Commissioner
		Italy	1947	Ambassador
		Luxembourg	1945	Minister
		Mexico	1944	Ambassador
		Norway	1943	Ambassador
		Pakistan	1950	High Commissioner
		Peru	1944	Ambassador
		Poland	1943	Chargé d'Affaires ad interim
		Sweden	1947	Ambassador
		Switzerland	1947	Ambassador
		Turkey	1947	Ambassador
		Union of Soviet Socialist Republics	1943	Ambassador
		Yugoslavia	1943	Ambassador
1940, 31 December	10	Australia	1939	High Commissioner
		Belgium	1939	Ambassador
		Ireland	1940	Ambassador
		Netherlands	1939	Ambassador
		New Zealand	1940	High Commissioner
		Union of South Africa	1940	High Commissioner
1930, 31 December	4	France	1928	Ambassador
		Japan	1929	Ambassador
		United States of America	1927	Ambassador
1920, 31 December	1	United Kingdom	1880	High Commissioner

		Special missions		
1960, 31 January	5[1]	Paris, Canadian Delegation to the North Atlantic Council	1952	Ambassador[1]
		British West Indies, Commissioner's Office	1958	Commissioner
1950, 31 December	4	Paris, Canadian Delegation to the Organization for European Economic Cooperation	1950	Ambassador[1]
		Berlin, British Sector, Canadian Military Mission	1946	Head of Mission
		New York, Permanent Delegation of Canada to the United Nations	1948	Permanent Representative
		Geneva, Permanent Delegation of Canada to European Office of the United Nations	1948	Permanent Representative

		Consulates		
1960, 31 January	12	Germany	1956	Consul
		United States of America, Los Angeles, California	1953	Consul General
		New Orleans, Louisiana	1952	Consul General
		Seattle, Washington	1953	Consul General
1950, 31 December	8	Brazil	1947	Consul
		Republic of the Philippines	1949	Consul General
		United States of America, Boston, Massachusetts	1948	Consul General
		Chicago, Illinois	1947	Consul General
		Detroit, Michigan	1948	Consul
		New York, New York	1943	Consul General
		Portland, Maine	1947	Honorary Vice-Consul
		San Francisco, California	1948	Consul General

[1] One representative, with the status of Ambassador, heads the Canadian Delegations to the North Atlantic Council *and* to the Organization for European Economic Cooperation.

Series W 218–220. *Formal amendments to the British North America Act, 1867 to 1960*

Year of amendment	Citation	Title	Subject
	218	**219**	**220**
1960	9 Elizabeth II, ch. 2 (U.K.)	The British North America Act, 1960	Tenure of office of Judges
1952	1 Elizabeth II, ch. 15 (Can.)	The British North America Act, 1952	Representation in the House of Commons
1951	14–15 George VI, ch. 32 (U.K.)	The British North America Act, 1951	Dominion jurisdiction over old age pensions
1949	13 George VI, ch. 81 (U.K.)	The British North America (No. 2) Act, 1949	Amendment of the Constitution
1949	12–13 George VI, ch. 22 (U.K.)	The British North America (No. 1) Act, 1949	Entry of Newfoundland
1946	10 George VI, ch. 63 (U.K.)	The British North America Act, 1946	Representation in the House of Commons
1943	6–7 George VI, ch. 30 (U.K.)	The British North America Act, 1943	Postponement of adjustment of representation in the House of Commons
1940	3–4 George VI, ch. 36 (U.K.)	The British North America Act, 1940	Transfer of jurisdiction over unemployment insurance to the Federal government
1931	22 George V, ch. 4 (U.K.)	The Statute of Westminster	To give effect to certain resolutions passed by Imperial Conferences of 1926 and 1930
1930	20–21 George V, ch. 26 (U.K.)	The British North America Act, 1930	Transfer of natural resources to Prairie provinces
1916	6–7 George V, ch. 19 (U.K.)	The British North America Act, 1916	To extend life of House of Commons elected in 1911
1915	5–6 George V, ch. 45 (U.K.)	The British North America Act, 1915	Representation in Senate and House of Commons
1907	7 Edward VII, ch. 11 (U.K.)	The British North America Act, 1907	Dominion–Provincial financial arrangements
1895	58 Victoria, Session 2, ch. 3 (U.K.)	The Canadian Speaker (Appointment of Deputy) Act	To remove doubts concerning Parliament's power re appointment of deputy for Speaker of Senate
1889	52–53 Victoria, ch. 28 (U.K.)	The Canada (Ontario Boundary) Act, 1889	Determination of boundaries of Ontario
1886	49–50 Victoria, ch. 35 (U.K.)	The British North America Act, 1886	Representation of territories in House of Commons and the Senate
1875	38–39 Victoria, ch. 38 (U.K.)	The Parliament of Canada Act, 1875	To remove doubts of privileges, etc., of parliament and members
1871	34–35 Victoria, ch. 28 (U.K.)	The British North America Act, 1871	Dominion's power to establish new provinces from territories

Series W 221–224. *Provinces and territories, dates and processes of admission and present areas, 1867 to 1960*

	Province, territory or district	Date of admission or creation	Process of admission	Present area (square miles)
	221	**222**	**223**	**224**
1949	Newfoundland	31 March 1949	The British North America Act, 1949, 12–13 George VI, ch. 22 (U.K.)	156,185
1920	Mackenzie[1]	1 January 1920	Order in Council, 16 March 1918	527,490[1]
	Keewatin[1]			228,160[1]
	Franklin[1]			549,253[1]
1905	Alberta	1 September 1905	Alberta Act, 1905, 4–5 Edward VII, ch. 3 (Can.)	255,285
1905	Saskatchewan	1 September 1905	Saskatchewan Act, 1905, 4–5 Edward VII, ch. 42 (Can.)	251,700
1898	Yukon Territory	13 June 1898	Yukon Territory Act, 1898, 61 Victoria, ch. 6 (Can.)	207,076
1873	Prince Edward Island	1 July 1873	Imperial Order in Council, 26 June 1873	2,184
1871	British Columbia	20 July 1871	Imperial Order in Council, 16 May 1871	366,255
1870	Manitoba	15 July 1870	Manitoba Act, 1870, 33 Victoria, ch. 3 (Can.) and Imperial Order in Council, 23 June 1870	251,000
1870	Northwest Territories	15 July 1870	Rupert's Land Act, 1868, 31–32 Victoria, ch. 105 (U.K.) and Imperial Order in Council, 23 June 1870	1,304,903[1]
1867	Ontario	1 July 1867	The British North America Act, 1867, 30–31 Victoria, ch. 3 (U.K.) and Imperial Order in Council, 22 May 1867	412,582
	Quebec			594,860
	New Brunswick			21,425
	Nova Scotia			28,354

[1] The districts of Mackenzie, Keewatin and Franklin are divisions of the present Northwest Territories.

Series W 225–235. *Number of provincial statutes disallowed by Dominion government, by province and decade, 1867 to 1960*

Decade	Totals	Newfound-land	Prince Edward Island	Nova Scotia	New Brunswick	Quebec	Ontario	Manitoba	Saskat-chewan	Alberta	British Columbia
	225	**226**	**227**	**228**	**229**	**230**	**231**	**232**	**233**	**234**	**235**
1957–1960	—	—	—	—	—	—	—	—	—	—	—
1947–1956	—	—	—	—	—	—	—	—	—	—	—
1937–1946	11	—	—	—	—	—	—	—	—	11	—
1927–1936	—	—	—	—	—	—	—	—	—	—	—
1917–1926	6	—	—	3	—	—	—	—	—	1	2
1907–1916	8	—	—	—	—	1	2	1	3	—	1
1897–1906	22	—	—	—	—	—	2	2	—	—	20
1887–1896	13	—	—	—	—	2	—	10	—	—	1
1877–1886	32	—	—	1	1	1	5	9	—	—	15
1867–1876	20	—	—	5	—	2	3	6	—	—	4
Totals	112	—	—	9	1	6	10	28	3	12	43

Series W236–246. *Number of provincial bills reserved by lieutenant-governors, by province and decade, 1867 to 1960*

Decade	Totals	Newfoundland	Prince Edward Island	Nova Scotia	New Brunswick	Quebec	Ontario	Manitoba	Saskatchewan	Alberta	British Columbia
	236	237	238	239	240	241	242	243	244	245	246
1957–1960	—	—	—	—	—	—	—	—	—	—	—
1947–1956	—	—	—	—	—	—	—	—	—	—	—
1937–1946	3	—	—	—	—	—	—	—	—	3	—
1927–1936	—	—	—	—	—	—	—	—	—	—	—
1917–1926	2	—	—	—	—	—	—	—	—	—	2
1907–1916	2	—	—	—	—	—	—	—	—	—	2
1897–1906	5	—	1	—	1	1	—	—	—	—	2
1887–1896	12	—	2	—	3	4	—	3	—	—	—
1877–1886	8	—	3	1	—	1	—	2	—	—	1
1867–1876	37	—	4	2	7	1	2	16	—	—	5
Totals	69	—	10	3	11	7	2	21	—	3	12

Series W247–249. *Federal royal commissions, 1867 to 1959*

(number)

Year appointed	Major commissions	Minor commissions	Total	Year appointed	Major commissions	Minor commissions	Total
	247	248	249		247	248	249
1959	2	2	4	1910	1	5	6
1958	1	1	2	1909	3	3	6
1957	4	—	4	1908	3	2	5
1956	—	—	—	1907	4	1	5
				1906	2	5	7
1955	3	—	3				
1954	3	3	6	1905	3	4	7
1953	—	1	1	1904	3	6	9
1952	—	1	1	1903	5	6	11
1951	1	3	4	1902	2	—	2
				1901	1	8	9
1950	—	4	4				
1949	1	—	1	1900	4	6	10
1948	2	1	3	1899	2	4	6
1947	—	2	2	1898	2	5	7
1946	3	—	3	1897	—	10	10
				1896	1	7	8
1945	2	4	6				
1944	3	2	5	1895	1	2	3
1943	2	1	3	1894	—	8	8
1942	1	2	3	1893	—	1	1
1941	—	1	1	1892	2	4	6
				1891	1	3	4
1940	—	2	2				
1939	—	2	2	1890	—	1	1
1938	2	2	4	1889	—	1	1
1937	1	2	3	1888	—	2	2
1936	6	1	7	1887	—	6	6
				1886	4	3	7
1935	2	4	6				
1934	3	4	7	1885	—	2	2
1933	2	2	4	1884	1	2	3
1932	2	7	9	1883	—	1	1
1931	3	2	5	1882	—	4	4
				1881	—	3	3
1930	1	8	9				
1929	1	1	2	1880	1	2	3
1928	2	4	6	1879	—	2	2
1927	3	4	7	1878	—	1	1
1926	3	2	5	1877	—	2	2
				1876	—	3	3
1925	—	2	2				
1924	1	1	2	1875	—	1	1
1923	3	5	8	1874	1	3	4
1922	2	—	2	1873	1	1	2
1921	1	3	4	1872	—	—	—
				1871	—	1	1
1920	1	6	7				
1919	4	6	10	1870	1	1	2
1918	3	7	10	1869	—	1	1
1917	4	7	11	1868	1	—	1
1916	5	10	15	1867	—	—	—
1915	3	7	10				
1914	2	5	7				
1913	5	5	10				
1912	7	2	9				
1911	1	1	2				

Series W250. *Subjects of major royal commissions, 1867 to 1959*

Year appointed	Subjects
	250
1959	Freight rates and transportation problems; Coal.
1958	Boxcar allocation.
1957	Diesel issue re C.P.R.; Newfoundland terms of Union; Energy; Price spreads.
1956	—
1955	Coasting trade; Long-term economic prospects; Broadcasting.
1954	Operation of Patent Act, etc.; Criminal law re sexual psychopaths; Criminal law re defence of insanity.
1953	—
1952	—
1951	South Saskatchewan river projects.
1950	—
1949	Arts, letters and sciences.
1948	Prices; Transportation.
1947	—
1946	Espionage in government service; Administrative classifications in Public Service; Indian Act and administration.
1945	Veterans' qualifications; Loyalty of Japanese.
1944	Coal; Co-operatives and Income Tax Act; Taxation of annuities.
1943	Japanese welfare in B.C.; Wages, western coal mines.
1942	Despatch of troops to Hong Kong.
1941	—
1940	—
1939	—
1938	Bren gun contract; Alaska highway.
1937	Dominion–Provincial relations.
1936	Textile industry; Penal system of Canada; National employment; Anthracite coal; Grain trade; Indian affairs.
1935	Unemployment of ex-servicemen; Canadian Performing Rights Society.
1934	Natural resources of Alberta; Price spreads and mass buying; Maritime claims.
1933	Banking system of Canada; Natural resources of Saskatchewan.
1932	Canadian Performing Rights Society; Ports of Canada.
1931	Grain futures; Chignecto Canal; Transportation.
1930	Compensation to provinces on return of natural resources.
1929	Technical and professional officials of Civil Service.
1928	Transfer of natural resources Manitoba; Radio broadcasting.
1927	Reconveyance of land to B.C.; Political partisanship in Department of Soldiers Civil Re-establishment; Fishing industry in Maritimes.
1926	Maritime claims; Customs and Excise Department; Toronto Harbour Commissioners.
1925	—
1924	Failure of Home Bank.
1923	Lake freight rates; Grain trade; Pulpwood export.
1922	Pacific fisheries; Pensions and re-establishment.
1921	Marketing of grain (no report).
1920	Uniformity in labour laws.
1919	Treatment of soldiers on 'Northland'; Reindeer and musk ox in Arctic; Relations between capital and labour; Racing and betting.

Year appointed	Subjects
	250
1918	Pilotage, Victoria, Vancouver, etc.; Pilotage, Halifax, etc.; Allegations re Chambly-Verchères election.
1917	Newsprint industry; Export of electricity; Packers' profits. Findings of Mr. Justice Galt against Rogers.
1916	Fire in Parliament Buildings; Railway development in Canada; Cost of food; Sale of small arms, ammunition; Grain, handling and marketing.
1915	Supply of munitions and raw materials; Agricultural production; War contracts.
1914	Georgian Bay Canal; Loss of *Empress of Ireland*.
1913	Better terms for B.C.; Penitentiaries; Cost of living; Coal mining disputes in Vancouver; Sale and disposal of Dominion lands since 1896.
1912	National Transcontinental Railway; Farmers Bank failure; Dominion's resources (Imperial Commission); Shell fisheries of Maritimes; State of departmental records; Indian lands in B.C.; Public departments.
1911	Public Service.
1910	Industrial and technical education.
1909	Fisheries of Manitoba and Saskatchewan; Swine industry; Trade with West Indies (Imperial Commission).
1908	Civil Service of Canada; Losses to Chinese, Vancouver; Shad fisheries of Minas Basin.
1907	Civil Service of Canada; Quebec bridge collapse; Losses to Japanese in Vancouver; Methods of inducing Oriental immigration.
1906	Insurance; Grain trade.
1905	B.C. fisheries; Georgian Bay fisheries; Employment of aliens on Père Marquette Railway.
1904	Salmon and lobster fishery; Employment of aliens on Grand Trunk Railway; Italian labourers in Montreal.
1903	Defalcation in Militia Department; Tread gold and other concessions in Yukon; Transportation; Herring and sardine fishery; Industrial disputes in B.C.
1902	Salmon fishing in B.C.; Tobacco trade.
1901	Alleged paper combine.
1900	Chinese and Japanese immigration; North West rebellion—scouts claims (2 Commissions); Election frauds.
1899	Manitoba grain trade; Mining disputes in British Columbia.
1898	Lobster fishing industry; Charges against government officials in Yukon.
1896	Manitoba school question.
1895	Sweating system.
1892	Liquor traffic; Charges against Sir A. P. Caron.
1891	Civil Service of Canada.
1886	Railways; Labour relations; Rebellion losses; Lachine Canal leases.
1884	Chinese immigration.
1880	Civil Service of Canada.
1874	Prohibition.
1873	Charges re C.P.R.
1870	Improvement inland navigation.
1869	Obstruction to William McDougall in North West.
1868	Civil Service of Canada.

Series W 251–252. *Lieutenant-governors, by province, 1867 to 1960*

Term of commission	Number	Lieutenant-governor	Date of commission
		251	**252**

Newfoundland

Term of commission	Number	Lieutenant-governor	Date of commission
1957–	3	Campbell Macpherson	16 December 1957
1949–1957	2	Lt.-Col. Sir Leonard Outerbridge	5 September 1949
1949	1	Sir Albert Joseph Walsh	1 April 1949

Prince Edward Island

Term of commission	Number	Lieutenant-governor	Date of commission
1958–	18	F. Walter Hyndman	31 March 1958
1950–1958	17	T. W. L. Prowse	4 October 1950
1945–1950	16	J. A. Bernard	18 May 1945
1939–1945	15	Bradford W. LePage	11 September 1939
1933–1939	14	George D. DeBlois	28 December 1933
1930–1933	13	Charles Dalton	19 November 1930
1924–1930	12	Frank R. Heartz	8 September 1924
1919–1924	11	Murdoch MacKinnon	2 September 1919
1915–1919	10	A. C. Macdonald	3 June 1915
1910–1915	9	Benjamin Rogers	1 June 1910
1904–1910	8	D. A. MacKinnon	3 October 1904
1899–1904	7	P. A. McIntyre	23 May 1899
1894–1899	6	George W. Howlan	21 February 1894
1889–1894	5	Jedediah S. Carvell	2 September 1889
1884–1889	4	Andrew A. Macdonald	18 July 1884
1879–1884	3	Thomas H. Haviland	10 July 1879
1874–1879	2	Sir Robert Hodgson	4 July 1874
1873–1874	1	William Robinson	10 June 1873

Nova Scotia

Term of commission	Number	Lieutenant-governor	Date of commission
1958–	22	Maj.-Gen. Edward C. Plow	15 January 1958
1952–1958	21	Alistair Fraser	1 September 1952
1947–1952	20	J. A. D. McCurdy	12 August 1947
1942–1947	19	Lt.-Col. H. Ernest Kendall	17 November 1942
1940–1942	18	Frederick F. Mathers	31 May 1940
1937–1940	17	Robert Irwin	7 April 1937
1931–1937	16	Walter H. Covert	5 October 1931
1930–1931	15	Frank Stanfield	19 November 1930
1925–1930	14	James C. Tory	14 September 1925
1925	13	J. Robson Douglas	12 January 1925
1916–1925	12	MacCallum Grant[1]	29 November 1916
1915–1916	11	David MacKeen	19 October 1915
1910–1915	10	James D. McGregor	18 October 1910
1906–1910	9	Duncan C. Fraser	27 March 1906
1900–1906	8	Alfred G. Jones	26 July 1900
1890–1900	7	Sir Malachy Bowes Daly[1]	11 July 1890
1888–1890	6	A. W. McLelan	9 July 1888
1883–1888	5	Matthew Henry Richey	4 July 1883
1873–1883	4	Sir Adams G. Archibald	4 July 1873
1873	3	Joseph Howe	1 May 1873
1867–1873	2	Lt.-Gen. Sir C. Hastings Doyle[1]	18 October 1867
1867	1	Lt.-Gen. Sir William F. Williams	1 July 1867

New Brunswick

Term of commission	Number	Lieutenant-governor	Date of commission
1958	21	J. Leonard O'Brien	6 June 1958
1945–1958	20	David Laurence MacLaren	1 November 1945
1940–1945	19	W. G. Clark	5 March 1940
1935–1940	18	Col. Murray MacLaren	5 February 1935
1928–1935	17	Maj.-Gen. Hugh H. McLean	11 December 1928
1923–1928	16	William F. Todd	24 February 1923
1917–1923	15	William Pugsley	6 November 1917
1916–1917	14	G. W. Ganong	29 June 1916
1912–1916	13	Josiah Wood	6 March 1912
1907–1912	12	L. J. Tweedie	2 March 1907
1902–1907	11	Jabez B. Snowball	30 January 1902
1896–1902	10	A. R. McClelan	9 December 1896
1893–1896	9	John A. Fraser	20 December 1893
1893	8	John Boyd	21 September 1893
1885–1893	7	Sir Samuel Leonard Tilley	31 October 1885
1880–1885	6	Robert Duncan Wilmot	11 February 1880
1878–1880	5	E. Barron Chandler	16 July 1878
1873–1878	4	Samuel Leonard Tilley	5 November 1873
1868–1873	3	L. A. Wilmot	14 July 1868
1867–1868	2	Col. F. P. Harding	18 October 1867
1867	1	Maj.-Gen. Sir C. Hastings Doyle	1 July 1867

Quebec

Term of commission	Number	Lieutenant-governor	Date of commission
1958–	20	Onésime Gagnon	14 February 1958
1950–1958	19	Gaspard Fauteux	3 October 1950
1939–1950	18	Maj.-Gen. Sir Eugène Fiset[1]	30 December 1939
1934–1939	17	E. L. Patenaude	29 April 1934
1929–1934	16	Henry George Carroll	2 April 1929
1928–1929	15	Sir Lomer Gouin	31 December 1928
1924–1928	14	Narcisse Pérodeau	8 January 1924
1923–1924	13	Louis-Philippe Brodeur	31 October 1923
1918–1923	12	Sir Charles Fitzpatrick	21 October 1918
1915–1918	11	Sir Pierre-Evariste Leblanc	9 February 1915
1911–1915	10	Sir François Langelier	5 May 1911
1908–1911	9	Sir Charles A. P. Pelletier	15 September 1908
1898–1908	8	Sir Louis-Amable Jetté[1]	20 January 1898
1892–1898	7	Sir Joseph-Adolphe Chapleau	5 December 1892
1887–1892	6	Auguste-Réal Angers	24 October 1887
1884–1887	5	L. F. R. Masson	4 October 1884
1879–1884	4	Théodore Robitaille	26 July 1879
1876–1879	3	Luc Letellier de Saint-Just	15 December 1876
1873–1876	2	René-Edouard Caron	11 February 1873
1867–1873	1	Sir Narcisse F. Belleau[1]	1 July 1867

Ontario

Term of commission	Number	Lieutenant-governor	Date of commission
1957–	19	John Keiller Mackay	30 December 1957
1952–1957	18	Louis O. Breithaupt	24 January 1952
1946–1952	17	Ray Lawson	26 December 1946
1937–1946	16	Albert Matthews	23 November 1937
1932–1937	15	Col. Herbert Alexander Bruce	25 October 1932
1926–1932	14	William Donald Ross	20 December 1926
1921–1926	13	Col. Henry Cockshutt	10 September 1921
1919–1921	12	Lionel H. Clarke	27 November 1919
1914–1919	11	Lt.-Col. Sir John S. Hendrie	26 September 1914
1908–1914	10	Sir John M. Gibson	22 September 1908
1903–1908	9	Sir William Mortimer Clark	20 April 1903
1897–1903	8	Sir Oliver Mowat	18 November 1897
1892–1897	7	Sir George A. Kirkpatrick	28 May 1892
1887–1892	6	Sir Alexander Campbell	8 February 1887
1880–1887	5	John Beverley Robinson	30 June 1880
1875–1880	4	D. A. MacDonald	18 May 1875
1873–1875	3	John W. Crawford	5 November 1873
1868–1873	2	W. P. Howland	14 July 1868
1867–1868	1	Maj.-Gen. H. W. Stisted	1 July 1867

Manitoba

Term of commission	Number	Lieutenant-governor	Date of commission
1953–	15	John Stewart McDiarmid	1 August 1953
1940–1953	14	Roland Fairbairn McWilliams	1 November 1940
1934–1940	13	William J. Tupper	1 December 1934
1929–1934	12	J. D. McGregor	25 January 1929
1926–1929	11	Theodore A. Burrows	9 October 1926
1916–1926	10	Sir James A. M. Aikins[1]	3 August 1916
1911–1916	9	Sir Douglas C. Cameron	1 August 1911
1900–1911	8	Sir Daniel H. McMillan[1]	10 October 1900
1895–1900	7	J. C. Patterson	2 September 1895
1888–1895	6	J. C. Schultz	1 July 1888
1882–1888	5	James C. Aikins	29 September 1882
1877–1882	4	Joseph E. Cauchon	8 October 1877
1872–1877	3	Alexander Morris	2 December 1872
1872	2	Francis G. Johnson	9 April 1872
1870–1872	1	A. G. Archibald	20 May 1870

Saskatchewan

Term of commission	Number	Lieutenant-governor	Date of commission
1958–	11	F. L. Bastedo	1 September 1958
1951–1958	10	W. J. Patterson	4 July 1951
1948–1951	9	J. W. Uhrich	24 March 1948
1945–1948	8	Reginald J. M. Parker	22 June 1945
1945	7	Thomas Miller	27 February 1945
1936–1945	6	A. P. McNab	10 September 1936
1931–1936	5	Lt.-Col. H. E. Munroe	31 March 1931
1921–1931	4	H. W. Newlands	17 February 1921
1915–1921	3	Sir Richard S. Lake	6 October 1915
1910–1915	2	George W. Brown	5 October 1910
1905–1910	1	A. E. Forget	24 August 1905

Alberta

Term of commission	Number	Lieutenant-governor	Date of commission
1959–	8	J. Percy Page	19 December 1959
1950–1959	7	John J. Bowlen	1 February 1950
1937–1950	6	J. C. Bowen	20 March 1937
1936–1937	5	Philip C. H. Primrose	10 September 1936
1931–1936	4	William L. Walsh	24 April 1931
1925–1931	3	William Egbert	20 October 1925
1915–1925	2	Robert George Brett[1]	6 October 1915
1905–1915	1	George H. V. Bulyea[1]	24 August 1905

British Columbia

Term of commission	Number	Lieutenant-governor	Date of commission
1960–	20	Maj.-Gen. George Pearkes	11 October 1960
1955–1960	19	Frank Mackenzie Ross	3 October 1955
1950–1955	18	Col. Clarence Wallace	1 October 1950
1946–1950	17	Col. Charles Arthur Banks	1 October 1946
1941–1946	16	Lt.-Col. William C. Woodward	29 August 1941
1936–1941	15	Eric Werge Hamber	29 April 1936
1931–1936	14	John William Fordham Johnson	18 July 1931
1926–1931	13	Robert Randolph Bruce	21 January 1926
1920–1926	12	Walter Cameron Nichol	24 December 1920
1919–1920	11	Col. Edward Gawler Prior	9 December 1919
1914–1919	10	Sir Frank Stillman Bernard	5 December 1914
1909–1914	9	Thomas Wilson Paterson	3 December 1909
1906–1909	8	James Dunsmuir	11 May 1906
1900–1906	7	Sir Henri G. Joly de Lotbinière	21 June 1900
1897–1900	6	Thomas Robert McInnes	18 November 1897
1892–1897	5	Edgar Dewdney	1 November 1892
1887–1892	4	Hugh Nelson	8 February 1887
1881–1887	3	Clement Francis Cornwall	21 June 1881
1876–1881	2	Albert Norton Richards	27 June 1876
1871–1876	1	Sir Joseph W. Trutch	5 July 1871

[1] Appointed for second term.

Series W253–255. Ministries, by province and premier, 1867 to 1960

Years of ministry	Number of ministry	Premier	Date of appointment	Party
		253	254	255

Newfoundland

Years of ministry	Number of ministry	Premier	Date of appointment	Party
1949–	1	Joseph R. Smallwood	1 April 1949	Liberal

Prince Edward Island

Years of ministry	Number of ministry	Premier	Date of appointment	Party
1959–	24	Walter Shaw	1 September 1959	Conservative
1953–1959	23	A. W. Matheson	25 May 1953	Liberal
1943–1953	22	J. Walter Jones	11 May 1943	Liberal
1936–1943	21	Thane A. Campbell	14 January 1936	Liberal
1935–1936	20	Walter M. Lea	15 August 1935	Liberal
1933–1935	19	William J. P. MacMillan	14 October 1933	Conservative
1931–1933	18	James D. Stewart	29 August 1931	Conservative
1930–1931	17	Walter M. Lea	20 May 1930	Liberal
1927–1930	16	Albert C. Saunders	12 August 1927	Liberal
1923–1927	15	James D. Stewart	5 September 1923	Conservative
1919–1923	14	J. H. Bell	9 September 1919	Liberal
1917–1919	13	Aubin Arsenault	21 June 1917	Conservative
1911–1917	12	John A. Mathieson	2 December 1911	Conservative
1911	11	H. James Palmer	16 May 1911	Liberal
1908–1911	10	F. L. Haszard	1 February 1908	Liberal
1901–1908	9	A. Peters	29 December 1901	Liberal
1898–1901	8	D. Farquharson	August 1898	Liberal
1897–1898	7	A. B. Warburton	October 1897	Liberal
1891–1897	6	F. Peters	27 April 1891	Liberal
1889–1891	5	N. McLeod	November 1889	Conservative
1879–1889	4	W. W. Sullivan	25 April 1879	Conservative
1876–1879	3	L. H. Davies	August 1876	Liberal (Coalition)
1873–1876	2	L. C. Owen	September 1873	Conservative
1873	1	J. C. Pope	April 1873	Conservative

Nova Scotia

Years of ministry	Number of ministry	Premier	Date of appointment	Party
1956–	17	Robert L. Stanfield	20 November 1956	Conservative
1954–1956	16	Henry D. Hicks	30 September 1954	Liberal
1954	15	Harold Connolly	13 April 1954	Liberal
1945–1954	14	Angus L. Macdonald	8 September 1945	Liberal
1940–1945	13	A. S. MacMillan	10 July 1940	Liberal
1933–1940	12	Angus L. Macdonald	5 September 1933	Liberal
1930–1933	11	Col. Gordon S. Harrington	11 August 1930	Conservative
1925–1930	10	E. N. Rhodes	16 July 1925	Conservative
1923–1925	9	E. H. Armstrong	24 January 1923	Liberal
1896–1923	8	George H. Murray	20 July 1896	Liberal
1884–1896	7	W. S. Fielding	28 July 1884	Liberal
1882–1884	6	W. T. Pipes	3 August 1882	Liberal
1882	5	J. S. D. Thompson	25 May 1882	Conservative
1878–1882	4	S. H. Holmes	22 October 1878	Conservative
1875–1878	3	P. C. Hill	11 May 1875	Liberal
1867–1875	2	William Annand	7 November 1867	Liberal
1867	1	H. Blanchard	4 July 1867	Conservative

New Brunswick

Years of ministry	Number of ministry	Premier	Date of appointment	Party
1960–	23	L. J. Robichaud	12 July 1960	Liberal
1952–1960	22	H. J. Flemming	8 October 1952	Conservative
1940–1952	21	J. B. McNair	13 March 1940	Liberal
1935–1940	20	A. Allison Dysart	16 July 1935	Liberal
1933–1935	19	L. P. D. Tilley	1 June 1933	Conservative
1931–1933	18	Charles D. Richards	19 May 1931	Conservative
1925–1931	17	John B. M. Baxter	14 September 1925	Conservative
1923–1925	16	Peter Veniot	28 February 1923	Liberal
1917–1923	15	Walter E. Foster	4 April 1917	Liberal
1917	14	James Murray	1 February 1917	Conservative
1914–1417	13	George G. Clarke	17 December 1914	Conservative
1911–1914	12	James K. Flemming	16 October 1911	Conservative
1908–1911	11	J. D. Hazen	24 March 1908	Conservative
1907–1908	10	C. W. Robinson	31 May 1907	Liberal
1907	9	William Pugsley	6 March 1907	Liberal
1900–1907	8	L. J. Tweedie	31 August 1900	Conservative
1897–1900	7	H. R. Emmerson	29 October 1897	Liberal
1896–1897	6	James Mitchell	July 1896	Conservative
1883–1896	5	A. G. Blair	1883	Liberal
1882–1883	4	D. L. Hannington	1882	Conservative
1878–1882	3	J. J. Fraser	1878	Conservative
1872–1878	2	G. E. King	1872	Liberal
1867–1872	1	A. R. Wetmore	1867	—

Quebec

Years of ministry	Number of ministry	Premier	Date of appointment	Party
1960–	23	Jean Lesage	5 July 1960	Liberal
1960	22	Antonio Barrette	7 January 1960	Union Nationale
1959–1960	21	Paul Sauvé	10 September 1959	Union Nationale
1944–1959	20	Maurice Duplessis	30 August 1944	Union Nationale
1939–1944	19	Adélard Godbout	8 November 1939	Liberal
1936–1939	18	Maurice Duplessis	24 August 1936	Union Nationale
1936	17	Adélard Godbout	11 June 1936	Liberal
1920–1936	16	L. Alexandre Taschereau	9 July 1920	Liberal
1905–1920	15	Sir Lomer Gouin	23 March 1905	Liberal
1900–1905	14	S. Napoléon Parent	3 October 1900	Liberal
1897–1900	13	F. Gabriel Marchand	24 May 1897	Liberal
1896–1897	12	Edmund J. Flynn	11 May 1896	Conservative
1892–1896	11	L. Olivier Taillon	16 December 1892	Conservative
1891–1892	10	Charles E. B. deBoucherville	21 December 1891	Conservative
1887–1891	9	Honoré Mercier	29 January 1887	Liberal
1887	8	L. Olivier Taillon	13 January 1887	Conservative
1884–1887	7	John J. Ross	23 January 1884	Conservative
1882–1884	6	J. Alfred Mousseau	1 August 1882	Conservative
1879–1882	5	J. Adolphe Chapleau	31 October 1879	Conservative
1878–1879	4	Henri C. Joly	8 March 1878	Liberal
1874–1878	3	Charles E. B. deBoucherville	22 September 1874	Conservative
1873–1874	2	Gédéon Ouimet	27 February 1873	Conservative
1867–1873	1	Pierre J. Chauveau	15 July 1867	Conservative

Ontario

Years of ministry	Number of ministry	Premier	Date of appointment	Party
1949–	16	Leslie M. Frost	4 May 1949	Conservative
1948	15	T. L. Kennedy	19 October 1948	Conservative
1943–1948	14	George Drew	17 August	Conservative
1943	13	H. C. Nixon	18 May 1943	Liberal
1942–1943	12	G. D. Conant	21 October 1942	Liberal
1934–1942	11	M. F. Hepburn	10 July 1934	Liberal
1930–1934	10	G. S. Henry	15 December 1930	Conservative
1923–1930	9	G. H. Ferguson	16 July 1923	Conservative
1919–1923	8	E. G. Drury	14 November 1919	United Farmers of Ontario
1914–1919	7	Sir William Hearst	2 October 1914	Conservative
1905–1914	6	Sir J. P. Whitney	8 February 1905	Conservative
1899–1905	5	G. W. Ross	21 October 1899	Liberal
1896–1899	4	A. S. Hardy	25 July 1896	Liberal
1872–1896	3	Oliver Mowat	25 October 1872	Liberal
1871–1872	2	Edward Blake	20 December 1871	Liberal
1867–1871	1	J. S. Macdonald	16 July 1867	Conservative

Manitoba

Years of ministry	Number of ministry	Premier	Date of appointment	Party
1958–	15	Dufferin Roblin	16 June 1958	Conservative
1948–1958	14	D. L. Campbell	7 November 1948	Liberal
1943–1948	13	S. S. Garson	8 January 1943	Coalition
1922–1943	12	John Bracken	8 August 1922	Coalition[1]
1915–1922	11	T. C. Norris	12 May 1915	Conservative
1900–1915	10	Sir R. P. Roblin	29 October 1900	Conservative
1900	9	H. J. Macdonald	8 January 1900	Conservative
1888–1900	8	T. Greenway	19 January 1888	Liberal
1887–1888	7	D. H. Harrison	26 December 1887	Conservative
1878–1887	6	John Norquay	16 October 1878	Conservative
1874–1878	5	R. A. Davis	3 December 1874	—[2]
1874	4	N. A. Girard	8 July 1874	Conservative
1872–1874	3	H. J. Clarke	14 March 1872	
1871–1872	2	N. A. Girard	14 December 1871	Conservative[3]
1870–1871	1	A. Boyd	16 September 1870	—[3]

Saskatchewan

Years of ministry	Number of ministry	Premier	Date of appointment	Party
1944–	8	T. C. Douglas	10 July 1944	Cooperative Commonwealth Federation
1935–1944	7	W. J. Patterson	1 November 1935	Liberal
1934–1935	6	J. G. Gardiner	19 July 1934	Liberal
1929–1934	5	J. T. M. Anderson	9 September 1929	Conservative
1926–1929	4	J. G. Gardiner	26 February 1926	Liberal
1922–1926	3	C. A. Dunning	5 April 1922	Liberal
1916–1922	2	W. M. Martin	20 October 1916	Liberal
1905–1916	1	Walter Scott	12 September 1905	Liberal

Alberta

Years of ministry	Number of ministry	Premier	Date of appointment	Party
1943–	8	E. C. Manning	31 May 1943	Social Credit
1935–1943	7	William Aberhart	3 September 1935	Social Credit
1934–1935	6	Richard G. Reid	10 July 1934	United Farmers of Alberta
1925–1934	5	John E. Brownlee	November 1925	United Farmers of Alberta
1921–1925	4	Herbert Greenfield	13 August 1921	United Farmers of Alberta
1917–1921	3	Charles Stewart	30 October 1917	Liberal
1910–1917	2	A. L. Sifton	26 May 1910	Liberal
1905–1910	1	Alex Rutherford	2 September 1905	Liberal

1 Successively United Farmers, Progressive, and then Coalition.
2 Elected as candidate of Grangers.
3 See notes on series W253–255.

Series W 253–255. *Ministries, by province and premier, 1867 to 1960 (continued)*

Years of ministry	Number of ministry	Premier	Date of appointment	Party	Years of ministry	Number of ministry	Premier	Date of appointment	Party
		253	254	255			253	254	255
		British Columbia			1902–1903	15	E. G. Prior	21 November 1902	—
1952–	26	W. A. C. Bennett	1 August 1952	Social Credit	1900–1902	14	J. Dunsmuir	15 June 1900	—
1947–1952	25	Byron Johnson	18 January 1947	Coalition	1900	13	Joseph Martin	28 February 1900	—
1947	24	Byron Johnson/ Herbert Anscomb	29 December 1947	Coalition	1898–1900	12	C. A. Semlin	12 August 1898	—
					1895–1898	11	J. H. Turner	4 March 1895	—
1941–1947	23	John Hart	9 December 1941	Coalition	1892–1895	10	T. Davie	2 July 1892	—
1933–1941	22	T. D. Pattullo	15 November 1933	Liberal	1889–1892	9	J. Robson	2 August 1889	—
1928–1933	21	Simon F. Tolmie	21 August 1928	Conservative	1887–1889	8	A. E. B. Davie	15 May 1887	—
					1883–1887	7	W. Smythe	29 January 1883	—
1927–1928	20	John D. Maclean	20 August 1927	Liberal	1882–1883	6	R. Beaven	13 June 1882	—
1918–1927	19	John Oliver	6 March 1918	Liberal					
1916–1918	18	Harlan C. Brewster	23 November 1916	Liberal	1878–1882	5	G. A. Walkem	25 June 1878	—
1915–1916	17	William J. Bowser	15 December 1915	Conservative	1876–1878	4	A. C. Elliott	1 February 1876	—
1903–1905	16	Richard McBride	1 June 1903	Conservative	1874–1876	3	G. A. Walkem	11 February 1874	—
					1872–1874	2	A. De Cosmos	23 December 1872	—
					1871–1872	1	J. F. McCreight	13 November 1871	—

Series W 256–339. *Provincial government elections, party standings and size of legislature, 1867 to 1960*

Newfoundland

Year of election	Number	Date of election	Liberal	Conservative	Other	Size of legislature
	256	257	258	259	260	261
1959	4	20 August 1959	31	3	2	36
1956	3	2 October 1956	32	4	—	36
1951	2	26 November 1951	24	4	—	28
1949	1	27 May 1949	22	5	1	28

Prince Edward Island

Year of election	Number	Date of election	Conservative	Liberal	Other	Size of legislature[1]
	262	263	264	265	266	267
1959	24	1 September 1959	22	8	—	30
1955	23	25 May 1955	3	27	—	30
1951	22	26 April 1951	6	24	—	30
1947	21	11 December 1947	6	24	—	30
1943	20	15 September 1943	10	20	—	30
1939	19	18 May 1939	3	27	—	30
1935	18	23 July 1935	—	30	—	30
1931	17	6 August 1931	18	12	—	30
1927	16	25 June 1927	6	24	—	30
1923	15	24 July 1923	25	5	—	30
1919	14	24 July 1919	4	25	1	30
1915	13	16 September 1915	16	13	1	30
1912	12	3 January 1912	27	2	1	30
1908	11	18 November 1908	14	16	—	30
1904	10	7 December 1904	8	22	—	30
1900	9	12 December 1900	9	21	—	30
1897	8	28 July 1897	10	20	—	30
1893	7	13 December 1893	7	23	—	30
1890	6	30 January 1890	15	15	—	30[1]
1886	5	30 June 1886	19	11	—	30
1882	4	1 May 1882	19	11	—	30
1879	3	2 April 1879	25	3	2[2]	30
1876	2	10 August 1876	14	9	7[2]	30
1873	1	April 1873	17	11	—	28

Nova Scotia

Year of election	Number	Date of election	Conservative	Liberal	Cooperative Commonwealth Federation	Other	Size of legislature
	268	269	270	271	272	273	274
1960	24	7 June 1960	27	15	1	—	43
1956	23	30 October 1956	24	18	1	—	43
1953	22	26 May 1953	13	22	2	—	37
1949	21	9 June 1949	7	28	2	—	37
1945	20	23 October 1945	—	28	2	—	30
1941	19	28 October 1941	4	23	3	—	30
1937	18	29 June 1937	5	25	—	—	30
1933	17	22 August 1933	8	22	—	—	30
1928	16	1 October 1928	23	20	—	—	43
1925	15	25 June 1925	40	3	—	—	43
1920	14	27 July 1920	3	29	—	11	43
1916	13	20 June 1916	13	30	—	—	43
1911	12	14 June 1911	11	27	—	—	38
1906	11	20 June 1906	5	32	—	1	38
1901	10	2 October 1901	2	36	—	—	38
1897	9	20 April 1897	3	35	—	—	38
1894	8	15 March 1894	13	25	—	—	38
1890	7	21 May 1890	10	28	—	—	38
1886	6	15 June 1886	8	29	—	1	38
1882	5	20 June 1882	14	24	—	—	38
1878	4	17 September 1878	30	8	—	—	38
1874	3	17 December 1874	14	24	—	—	38
1871	2	16 May 1871	13	25	—	—	38
1867	1	18 September 1867	2	36	—	—	38

[1] The legislature was bicameral until 1892. The series shows the assembly only before that date.

[2] Includes several members whose affiliation is not known.

Series W256–339. *Provincial government elections, party standings and size of legislature, 1867 to 1960 (continuation)*

		New Brunswick				Size of legis-lature
Year of election	Number	Date of election	Liberal	Conser-vative	Other	
	275	276	277	278	279	280
1960	23	27 June 1960	31	21	—	52
1956	22	18 June 1956	15	37	—	52
1952	21	22 September 1952	16	36	—	52
1948	20	28 June 1948	47	5	—	52
1944	19	28 August 1944	36	12	—	48
1939	18	20 November 1939	29	19	—	48
1935	17	27 June 1935	43	5	—	48
1930	16	19 June 1930	17	31	—	48
1925	15	10 August 1925	11	37	—	48
1920	14	9 October 1920	24	14	10	48
1917	13	24 February 1917	27	21	—	48
1912	12	20 June 1912	2	44	2	48
1908	11	3 March 1908	10	31	5	46
1903	10	28 February 1903	27	15	4	46
1899	9	18 February 1899	41	5	—	46
1895	8	16 October 1895	34	10	2	46
1892	7	22 October 1892	27	13	1	41
1890	6	21 January 1890	7	34	—	41
1886	5	26 April 1886	18	19	4	41
1882	4	15 June 1882	20	15	6	41
1878	3	June 1878	24	13	4	41
1874	2	June 1874	35	4	2	41
1870	1	June–July 1870	25	16	—	41

		Quebec		Union	Conser-		Size of legis-lature
Year of election	Number	Date of election	Liberal	Nationale	vative	Other	
	281	282	283	284	285	286	287
1960	26	22 June 1960	51	43	—	1	95
1956	25	20 June 1956	19	73	—	1	93
1952	24	16 July 1952	23	68	—	1	92
1948	23	28 July 1948	8	82	—	2	92
1944	22	8 August 1944	37	48	—	6	91
1939	21	25 October 1939	70	15	—	1	86
1936	20	17 August 1936	14	76[3]	—	—	90
1935	19	25 November 1935	48	—	16	26	90
1931	18	24 August 1931	79	—	11	—	90
1927	17	16 May 1927	75	—	9	1	85
1923	16	5 February 1923	64	—	19	2	85
1919	15	23 June 1919	74	—	5	2	81
1916	14	22 May 1916	75	—	6	—	81
1912	13	15 May 1912	64	—	15	2	81
1908	12	8 June 1908	58	—	13	3	74
1904	11	25 November 1904	68	—	6	—	74
1900	10	7 December 1900	67	—	7	—	74
1897	9	11 May 1897	51	—	23	—	74
1892	8	8 March 1892	21	—	51	1	73
1890	7	17 June 1890	42	—	24	7	73
1886	6	14 October 1886	31	—	28	6	65
1881	5	2 December 1881	15	—	49	1	65
1878	4	1 May 1878	30	—	33	2	65
1875	3	7 July 1875	19	—	43	3	65
1871	2	June–July 1871	20	—	45	—	65
1867	1	August–September 1867	14	—	50	1[4]	65

		Ontario	Conser-vative	Liberal	Cooperative Common-wealth Federation	Labour Pro-gressive	United Farmers of Ontario	Pro-gressive	Labour and Liberal–Labour	Other	Size of legis-lature
Year of election	Number	Date of election									
	288	289	290	291	292	293	294	295	296	297	298
1959	26	11 June 1959	71	22	5	—	—	—	—	—	98
1955	25	9 June 1955	84	11	3	—	—	—	—	—	98
1951	24	22 November 1951	79	7	2	1	—	—	1	—	90
1948	23	7 June 1948	53	13	21	2	—	—	1	—	90
1945	22	4 June 1945	66	11	8	2	—	—	3	—	90
1943	21	4 August 1943	38	15	34	2	—	—	—	1	90
1937	20	6 October 1937	23	63	—	—	1	—	—	3	90
1934	19	19 June 1934	17	66	1	—	1	—	—	5	90
1929	18	30 October 1929	91	14	—	—	1	5	1	—	112
1926	17	1 December 1926	74	17	—	—	3	13	1	4	112
1923	16	25 June 1923	77	14	—	—	17	—	3	—	111
1919	15	20 October 1919	25	29	—	—	44	—	11	3	112
1914	14	29 June 1914	84	25	—	—	—	—	1	1	111
1911	13	11 December 1911	83	21	—	—	—	—	1	—	105
1908	12	8 June 1908	86	19	—	—	—	—	1	—	106
1905	11	25 January 1905	69	29	—	—	—	—	—	—	99
1902	10	29 May 1902	46	51	—	—	—	—	—	—	97
1898	9	1 March 1898	43	49	—	—	—	—	—	1	93
1894	8	26 June 1894	27	49	—	—	—	—	—	16[5]	92
1890	7	5 June 1890	36	54	—	—	—	—	—	—	90
1886	6	28 December 1886	26	64	—	—	—	—	—	—	90
1883	5	27 February 1883	36	48	—	—	—	—	—	2	86
1879	4	5 June 1879	29	58	—	—	—	—	—	1	88
1875	3	18 January 1875	33	51	—	—	—	—	—	4	88
1871	2	21 March 1871	32[6]	41[6]	—	—	—	—	—	7	80
1867	1	August–September 1867	56[6]	23[6]	—	—	—	—	—	5	84

[3] Union Nationale formed in 1936 from Conservative and Action Liberale Nationale sources.
[4] One election (Kamouraska) annulled; seat vacant until 1871.
[5] Includes 14 Patrons of Industry.
[6] Counts Unionists as Conservatives, and Reformers as Liberals.

Series W 256–339. *Provincial government elections, party standings and size of legislature, 1867 to 1960 (continuation)*

Manitoba

Year of election	Number	Date of election	Conservative	Liberal and Liberal Progressive	Progressive	Liberal	Cooperative Commonwealth Federation	Social Credit	Labour-Progressive (Communist)	Labour	United Farmer	Other	Size of legislature
	299	300	301	302	303	304	305	306	307	308	309	310	311
1959	26	14 May 1959	36	11	—	—	10	1	—	—	—	—	57
1958	25	16 June 1958	26	19	—	—	11	—	—	—	—	1	57
1953	24	8 June 1953	12	35	—	—	5	2	1	—	—	2	57
1949	23	10 November 1949	10	29	—	—	7	—	—	—	—	11	57
1945	22	15 October 1945	13	26	—	—	10	2	1	—	—	3	55
1941	21	22 April 1941	14	25	—	—	3	3	—	—	—	8	55
1936	20	27 July 1936	16	23	—	—	7	5	1	—	—	3	55
1932	19	16 June 1932	10	—	38	—	—	—	—	5	—	2	55
1927	18	28 June 1927	15	—	29	7	—	—	—	3	—	1	55
1922	17	18 July 1922	6	—	1	7	—	—	—	6	27	8	55
1920	16	29 June 1920	7	—	—	21	—	—	—	11	12	4	55
1915	15	16 September 1915	5	—	—	40	—	—	—	—	—	2	49
1914	14	10 July 1914	28	—	—	21	—	—	—	—	—	—	49
1910	13	11 June 1910	28	—	—	13	—	—	—	—	—	—	41
1907	12	7 March 1907	28	—	—	13	—	—	—	—	—	—	41
1903	11	20 July 1903	31	—	—	9	—	—	—	—	—	—	40
1899	10	7 December 1899	26	—	—	14	—	—	—	—	—	—	40
1896	9	15 January 1896	5	—	—	32	—	—	—	—	—	3	40
1892	8	23 July 1892	14	—	—	25	—	—	—	—	—	1	40
1888	7	11 July 1888	5	—	—	28	—	—	—	—	—	4	38
1886	6	9 December 1886	19	—	—	13	—	—	—	—	—	3	35
1883	5	23 January 1883	22	—	—	7	—	—	—	—	—	2	31
1879	4	16 December 1879	18	—	—	4	—	—	—	—	—	2	24
1878	3	18 December 1878	13	—	—	4	—	—	—	—	—	7	24
1874	2	23 December 1874	8	—	—	4	—	—	—	—	—	11	24
1870	1	27 December 1870	8	—	—	1	—	—	—	—	—	13	24

Saskatchewan

Year of election	Number	Date of election	Cooperative Commonwealth Federation	Liberal	Conservative	Progressive	Social Credit	Other	Size of legislature
	312	313	314	315	316	317	318	319	320
1960	14	8 June 1960	38	17	—	—	—	—	55
1956	13	20 June 1956	36	14	—	—	3	—	53
1952	12	11 June 1952	42	11	—	—	—	—	53
1948	11	24 June 1948	31	19	—	—	—	2	52
1944	10	15 June 1944	47	5	—	—	—	3	52[7]
1938	9	8 June 1938	10	38	—	—	2	2	52
1934	8	19 June 1934	5[8]	50	—	—	—	—	55
1929	7	6 June 1929	—	28	24	5	—	6	63
1925	6	2 June 1925	—	50	3	6	—	4	63
1921	5	9 June 1921	—	45	2	6	—	10	63[7]
1917	4	26 June 1917	—	51	7	—	—	4	59[7]
1912	3	11 July 1912	—	46	8	—	—	—	54
1908	2	14 August 1908	—	27	14[9]	—	—	—	41
1905	1	13 December 1905	—	16	9[9]	—	—	—	25

Alberta

Year of election	Number	Date of election	Social Credit	Liberal	Conservative	Cooperative Commonwealth Federation	Labour	United Farmers of Alberta	Other[10]	Size of legislature
	321	322	323	324	325	326	327	328	329	330
1959	14	18 June 1959	62	1	1	—	—	—	1	65
1955	13	29 June 1955	37	15	3	—	—	—	5	61
1952	12	5 August 1952	52	4	2	2	—	—	1	61
1948	11	17 August 1948	50	3	—	2	—	—	2	57
1944	10	8 August 1944	51	—	—	2	—	—	4	57
1940	9	21 March 1940	36	1	—	—	1	—	19	57
1935	8	22 August 1935	56	5	2	—	—	—	—	63
1930	7	19 June 1930	—	11	5	—	4	39	4	63
1926	6	28 June 1926	—	7	4	—	6	43	—	60
1921	5	18 July 1921	—	13	1	—	4	39	2	59
1917	4	7 June 1917	—	33	19	—	1	1	4	58
1913	3	17 April 1913	—	39	17	—	—	—	—	56
1909	2	22 March 1909	—	36	2	—	—	—	3	41
1905	1	9 November 1905	—	23	2	—	—	—	—	25

[7] Plus 3 armed services representatives.
[8] Farmer-Labour.
[9] Known as Provincial Rights party.

[10] Includes Independent Social Credit, Independents, Armed Forces 1917 and 1944.

Series W 256–339. *Provincial government elections, party standings and size of legislature, 1867 to 1960 (continuation)*

Year of election	Number	Date of election	British Columbia						Size of legislature
			Social Credit	Cooperative Commonwealth Federation	Liberal	Conservative	Labour	Other[11]	
	331	332	333	334	335	336	337	338	339
1960	26	12 September 1960	32	16	4	—	—	—	52
1956	25	19 September 1956	39	10	2	—	1	—	52
1953	24	9 June 1953	28	14	4	1	1	—	48
1952	23	12 June 1952	19	18	6	4	1	—	48
1949	22	15 June 1949	—	7	39[12]		2	—	48
1945	21	25 October 1945	—	10	37[12]		1	—	48
1941	20	21 October 1941	—	14	21[13]	12[13]	1	--	48
1937	19	1 June 1937	—	7	31	8	1	1	48
1933	18	2 November 1933	—	7	34	—	1	5	47
1928	17	18 July 1928	—	—	12	35	1	—	48
1924	16	20 June 1924	—	—	27	16	3	2	48
1920	15	1 December 1920	—	—	26	14	—	7	47
1916	14	14 September 1916	—	—	37	9	—	1	47
1912	13	28 March 1912	—	—	—	40	—	2	42
1909	12	25 November 1909	—	—	3	36	—	3	42
1907	11	2 February 1907	—	—	13	26	—	3	42
1903	10	3 October 1903	—	—	17	21	1	2	42
1900	9	9 June 1900	—	—	—	—	—	—	38
1898	8	9 July 1898	—	—	—	—	—	—	38
1894	7	7 July 1894	—	—	—	—	—	—	33
1890	6	13 June 1890	—	—	—	—	—	—	33
1886	5	7 July 1886	—	—	—	—	—	—	26
1882	4	24 July 1882	—	—	—	—	—	—	26
1878	3	22 May 1878	—	—	—	—	—	—	26
1875	2	11 September 1875	—	—	—	—	—	—	25
1871	1	October–December 1871	—	—	—	—	—	--	25

[11] Includes Socialist party before 1924.
[12] Coalition of Liberal and Conservative parties.
[13] The Liberals and Conservatives formed a coalition to carry on as the government.

SECTION Y: JUSTICE

NICOLAS ZAY, *University of Montreal*

This section contains statistical data on crime (convictions of adults) in series Y1–73, on delinquency (appearances at court and convictions of juveniles under 16 years of age) in series Y74–155, on penal institutions (penitentiaries, reformatories, jails and training schools) in series Y156–173, on releases under the Ticket of Leave Act and on pardons in series Y174–177; it contains, furthermore, series on suicide in series Y178–201 and commercial failures dealt with under federal or provincial legislation in series Y202–216.

The sources of data for this section are nearly all federal government publications. The publications of the Dominion Bureau of Statistics used as sources are given first. They are: Dominion Bureau of Statistics, *Statistics of Criminal and Other Offences*, annual since 1926 (Ottawa, Queen's Printer); *Criminal Statistics*, annual 1876 to 1925 (Ottawa, King's Printer), published annually 1917 to 1925 by Dominion Bureau of Statistics, published annually 1876 to 1917 by various departments and found in the *Sessional Papers of Canada* until 1922; *Canada Year Book*, annual since 1905 (Ottawa, Queen's Printer), various years; *Vital Statistics*, annual since 1921 (Ottawa, Queen's Printer). Other sources of data are: *Report of the Committee to Advise upon the Revision of Penitentiary Regulations and the Amendment of the Penitentiary Act* (Ottawa, King's Printer, 1921); *Proceedings of a Special Committee on the Traffic in Narcotic Drugs in Canada*, a committee of the senate (Ottawa, Queen's Printer, 1955); *Reports of the Joint Committee of the Senate and the House of Commons on Capital Punishment, Corporal Punishment and Lotteries* (Ottawa, Queen's Printer, 1956); *Annual Report of the Directors of Penitentiaries of the Dominion of Canada*, 1867 to 1874 (Ottawa, I. B. Taylor); *Report of the Minister of Justice as to Penitentiaries of Canada*, annual 1875 to 1913 (Ottawa, King's Printer); *Report of the Inspectors of Penitentiaries*, annual 1914 to 1918 (Ottawa, King's Printer); *Report of the Superintendent of Penitentiaries*, annual 1919 to 1947 (Ottawa, King's Printer); *Annual Report of the Commissioner of Penitentiaries*, from 1948 (Ottawa, Queen's Printer); *Report of the Royal Canadian Mounted Police*, annual since 1920 (Ottawa, Queen's Printer); *Dun's Bulletin* (New York, Dun and Co.) and *Dun and Bradstreet Review* (New York, Dun and Bradstreet Inc.).

STATISTICS ON CRIME (Series Y1–73)

In Canada, basic statistics on crime have been collected and published on a nationwide basis since 1876. The Criminal Statistics Act of that year made specific provisions for the furnishing of information by the various trial courts of general jurisdiction on their 'criminal business' and by wardens of penal institutions on their inmates to the Minister of Agriculture who published until 1911 an annual report based on these returns. The first reports entitled *Criminal Statistics* show the number of charges, acquittals and convictions, by judicial district, by class of offences, and by disposition, together with other information on each convicted person and on cases in which the prerogative of mercy of the Crown had been exercised. For the years 1912 to 1916, the annual reports were published by the Minister of Trade and Commerce; subsequently, they were published by the Dominion Bureau of Statistics. The Statistics Act of 1918, which provided for the establishment of the Bureau, consolidated the dispositions of the former law concerning the centralized collection of

statistics by requiring that information on court business be transmitted to the Dominion Statistician. In 1926 the title of the annual reports was changed from *Criminal Statistics* to *Statistics of Criminal and Other Offences*.

Other data on crime collected on a nation-wide basis can be found in the annual reports of federal law enforcement and correctional agencies; they are, however, limited to some specialized aspects of the criminal field. We can mention in this connection the statistics published since 1876 on penitentiaries under federal administration (see general note for series Y156–173), the annual report of the recently created National Parole Board, and the reports of the Commissioner of the Royal Mounted Police which show figures on offences committed against federal statutes the enforcement of which is in the exclusive jurisdiction of the Force (the Opium and Narcotic Drug Act, the Excise Act, the Income Tax Act, the Customs Act, etc.), as well as statistics on all offences committed in the Northwest and Yukon Territories where the Force is the only police body.

In addition, information limited to one province or another can be found in the reports of provincial law enforcement agencies. The Quebec Bureau of Statistics has published since 1914 an annual *Yearbook* giving statistical material on criminal and civil judicial procedures. In Ontario, statistics on prisons and reformatories have been published since 1868 when the Inspector of Asylums, Prisons and Public Charities issued the first report on the subject. The Commissioner of the Ontario Provincial Police publishes annual reports on offences dealt with by the Force, on arrests, etc. In British Columbia, annual reports on provincial jails and police activities have been published from 1879 to 1937 by the Superintendent of Police and from 1938 to 1949 by the Commissioner of Provincial Police and Inspector of Gaols. In 1950, however, the task of the provincial police was taken over by the Canadian Mounted Police and data on jails have been published since that date by the Director of Corrections. In Saskatchewan, the annual reports of the Department of Social Welfare, published since 1944, include some material on adult prisoners detained in provincial jails.

Finally, some limited information on crime can be found in the proceedings and reports published by royal commissions and committees appointed, both on the federal and the provincial levels, to inquire into certain aspects of the criminal or correctional field. This material is usually obtained from the sources listed above, but in some cases it is original in the sense that it has not been published elsewhere. The most significant reports are: *Report of the Royal Commission to Investigate the Penal System of Canada* (Ottawa, King's Printer, 1938); *Reports of the Joint Committee of the Senate and the House of Commons on Capital Punishment, Corporal Punishment, Lotteries* (1956); *Proceedings of the Special Committee on the Traffic in Narcotic Drugs in Canada* (1955).

A fairly complete record of convictions for criminal and non-criminal offences extending in some cases over a period of 80 years is available, but any time series in this field has to be used with caution. Many factors contribute to diminish the comparability of data between years. Changes in such matters as the legal definition of offences and the meaning attached even to common terms, and in police and court procedures have to be taken into account. An offence is any violation of the law; if the law changes, or if it is not enforced in the same way by the group whose function is to do so, the comparability of statistics is affected. There are always new laws which accompany social changes and new laws 'create' new offences.

According to the British North America Act of 1867 (section 91), the criminal law and procedures in criminal matters are under the exclusive legislative authority of the Parliament of Canada, while the maintenance and organization of provincial courts, both of civil and criminal jurisdiction, and of procedures in civil matters in these courts are under the legislative authority of the provinces (section 92). The provincial power under section 92 of the B.N.A. Act to enforce provincial legislation by imposing penalties has resulted in the creation of an important body of law which is criminal in all but name but violation of which under existing legislation does not constitute an indictable offence. A codification of the criminal law of Canada, through a Criminal Code Bill founded on the English draft code of 1878, was brought about in 1892; it came into force on 1 July 1893 and was last revised in 1954. The revised criminal code came into force on 1 April 1955. The provisions of the Criminal Code apply throughout Canada except (a) in the Northwest Territories, in so far as they are inconsistent with the Northwest Territories Act, and (b) in the Yukon Territory, in so far as they are inconsistent with the Yukon Act. In addition, the Parliament of Canada may declare offences against other acts to be criminal acts (i.e. The Opium and Narcotic Drug Act) and put them into force throughout Canada; this fact increases the comparability of data in time series of criminal offences.

Changes and improvements in collecting and processing source data may also affect the comparability of criminal statistics between years. Identical standards of technical adequacy cannot be assumed when considering series which cover a long period of time. The figures presented in this section are based, with the exception of series Y 67, on data collected at court level. In 1876, there were 85 judicial districts reporting; in 1946, 1,729 reports were received from 159 judicial districts. The number of returns for each year affects the comparability of figures in the sense that a greater number of returns for a year may give the impression of an increase in the amount of crime or in the number of offenders, while a lesser number of returns may give the impression of a decrease. Data on criminal offences are collected by the Dominion Bureau of Statistics from registrars of the Assize and General Sessions of the Peace, clerks of county and district courts, officials of the Magistrate's and Family Courts and Justices of the Peace. The figures reported do not represent, by any means, the total number of offences nor the total number of offenders. They relate only to offences which have been prosecuted. There are offences which are known only to the offenders; others are known only, besides the offenders, to the victims themselves who do not want to report them. Further, of those known to law enforcement or social agencies, only a portion is prosecuted. However, time series of crime based on court statistics can be made, without one knowing the real amount of crime or the real number of offenders, on the assumption—challenged by a few scholars—that the proportion of recorded offences (offenders) in the unknown whole remains fairly constant and that the proportion of prosecuted offences (offenders) in the total number of known offences (offenders) also remains fairly stable. Criminologists generally agree that offences collected at police level are the closest indication of the volume of crime, but the problem of uniformity of reporting at this level, with a great number of agencies engaged in the process of collecting data, is far more acute than at any other level.

Figures in series Y 1–66 and Y 68 are tabulated on the basis of offences. When an accused person is charged and convicted for more than one offence at the same trial, each one of the offences is recorded; thus, when the accused is convicted of, say, two charges of robbery and three charges of theft, all five convictions are recorded. The offence has been the basic unit of tabulation of Canadian criminal statistics until 1948. It gives a more accurate picture of the amount of crime but, the number of charged or convicted persons not being known, uncritical use of these data in an attempt to understand and explain criminal behaviour may lead to faulty conclusions. For example, if a person aged 30 is convicted for one offence and a person aged 20 for five offences at the same trial, the total number of convictions (six) corresponds to the number of criminal acts, but tables showing the age groups of offenders may appear to indicate that one person aged 30–34 and five persons aged 20–24 have been convicted. Prior to 1893, duplication of charges for the same offence was eliminated; for example, if a person was charged and convicted for two charges of robbery, only one was recorded, but if the same person was charged and convicted, at the same trial, for 'assault' and 'robbery' both were recorded. A Dominion–Provincial Conference, held in Ottawa in May 1949, proposed that the basic unit of compilation become 'the person'. Figures based on persons are not comparable with those based on offences. However, in order to make historical comparisons possible, a limited number of tables showing figures based on offences are still published by the Dominion Bureau of Statistics. In this subsection no series are given based on persons but some figures compiled on the basis of persons are presented in the note to series Y 1–13.

Criminal offences, prosecuted under the criminal law, are made up of a wide variety of prohibited acts which range from minor breaches of the law to the most serious act of murder. The Criminal Code recognizes two types of offences: crimes which are called indictable offences and ordinary offences. The very nature of the indictable offence consists in the fact that it is a tort of so serious a nature that it is considered as an offence not only against a person but against the whole state. Indictable offences are so designated in the statute creating them and providing for their punishment; they demand a more formal hearing than an ordinary offence. Most of them are triable on indictment, the legal process by which a bill of indictment is preferred before a grand jury in provinces which have a grand jury. In the provinces of Quebec, New Brunswick (since 1959), Manitoba, Saskatchewan, Alberta, British Columbia and in the Yukon and Northwest Territories it is not necessary to prefer a bill of indictment before a grand jury. It is sufficient if the trial of an accused is commenced by an indictment in writing setting forth the offence with which he is charged. The ordinary offences are those which are not expressly made indictable; they are, as a rule, minor misdemeanours and are considered as wronging the person only and not society; they are disposed of by police magistrates or other justices of the peace. All provincial statutes and municipal by-laws are in this category (offences against traffic laws and liquor laws, breaches of the peace, etc.). However, the distinction between these two classes of 'offences' is not based on actual procedural differences; in many cases, indictable offences are heard on summary trials as are the less serious offences. A summary trial by a magistrate is either (1) a trial with consent or (2) a trial without consent. Where a trial is allowed without the consent of the accused, it is known as an absolute indictable offence and the jurisdiction of the magistrate does not depend upon the consent of the accused (theft or obtaining money or property by false pretence where its value does not exceed fifty dollars—ten until 1936, subsequently twenty-five—gaming, betting, etc.). Neither is the distinction between the indictable and the other offences based on the nature of the act, because, in some cases, the same act can be qualified as indictable or not, according to the severity or circumstances of the case or the mode of trial elected by the prosecutor. Offences have been classified under these two headings since 1884 by the Dominion Bureau of Statistics and predecessor collectors of data. Only time series relating to indictable offences are included in this section; statistics relating to the other offences can be found in the annual reports, *Statistics of Criminal and Other Offences*; they have been excluded because they seem to be subject to strong yearly fluctuations due to changes in customs and judicial procedures.

In order to facilitate the interpretation of criminal statistics, population figures with an age distribution consistent with other data in this section are given in series Y 14–26.

Y 1–13. Convictions for indictable offences of persons aged 16 years and over, Canada and the provinces, 1886 to 1960

SOURCE: D.B.S., *Statistics of Criminal and other Offences* and *Criminal Statistics*, annual report for each year.

Figures prior to 1886 are not comparable. Until 1884, no distinction was made between indictable and other offences; in 1885, the indictable offences tried summarily were classified together with the ordinary offences (see general note to series Y 1–73). These figures, tabulated on the basis of offences, do not represent the actual number of offenders. Until 1921, offences committed by adults and juveniles were tabulated together. Figures in series Y 1–13 relate only to persons aged 16 years and over; data on juveniles under 16 years are given in series Y 74–85.

For comparison with the data on number of offences, figures for the number of persons convicted for indictable offences since 1949 are given in the following table. Until 1948 the basis of the statistics of indictable crime was the offence and figures for number of persons convicted are not available on a satisfactory basis (see the general note to series Y 1–73). Even after 1949 some duplications existed in the data based on number of persons convicted; in 1953, revised processing methods eliminated some duplication. The data are given on both compilation procedures for the years 1953 to 1956.

Number of persons convicted for indictable offences,
Canada, 1949 to 1958

Year[1]	Old compilation procedure	Revised compilation procedure
1958	—	34,546
1957	—	31,765
1956	30,280	27,413
1955	31,240	28,273
1954	32,767	30,848
1953	30,839	29,567
1952	29,761	—
1951[2]	28,980	—
1950	31,385	—
1949	30,922	—

SOURCE. D.B.S., *Statistics of Criminal and Other Offences*, annual report for each year.

[1] Figures for 1949 and 1950 are for the twelve months ending 30 September; figures in 1951 and subsequently are for calendar years. In the months October to December 1950 there were 7,907 persons convicted for an indictable offence. Cases not entirely disposed of in a year, that is, tried but the sentence postponed, are included in the next year's figures.

[2] Statistics relating to Newfoundland are included in 1951 and later years.

Y 14–26. Census and estimated population aged 16 years and over, Canada and the provinces, 1881 to 1959

SOURCE: Dominion Bureau of Statistics. Census figures are those for the years 1881 to 1921 inclusive, 1931, 1941, 1951 and 1956. In the intercensal years, the Dominion Bureau of Statistics makes esti-

mates by sex and age groups; these estimates are adjusted at the next census. Figures presented in series Y 14–26 derive from the revised estimates for 1922 to 1950, D.B.S., *Population Estimates, 1921–1952*, Reference Paper No. 40, and from the revised estimates for 1952 to 1955, D.B.S., *Population Estimates 1952–1956*, Supplement to Reference Paper No. 40. Figures for 1957 to 1959 are subject to revision following the 1961 census.

Y 27–32. Convictions for indictable offences, by nature of the offence, Canada, 1886 to 1960

SOURCE: D.B.S., *Statistics of Criminal and Other Offences*, annual report for 1946, historical appendix, table II; annual report for 1952, historical appendix, table 2; for later years each annual report, part II. For the years 1907, 1934 and 1949 errors in the historical appendices were corrected to the data of the original annual reports.

Figures prior to 1886 are not comparable (see note for series Y 1–13). A historical table covering the period 1876 to 1936 making no distinction between indictable and ordinary offences can be found in the annual report for 1936, historical appendix, table I.

Figures for 1886 to 1921 include juveniles under 16 years of age and are not comparable with those for later years relating only to persons aged 16 years and over. Offences are grouped in classes which correspond roughly to the main divisions of the criminal code; offences against federal statutes other than the criminal code are classified under the heading 'other indictable offences'. Figures in series Y 32 are strongly influenced by the inclusion of new offences and of ordinary offences made indictable by new dispositions in the law, as well as by changes in judicial practices relating to offences triable as indictable or non-indictable, according to the circumstances or the severity of the case.

Y 27. Offences against the person include such crimes as abandoning child, abduction and kidnapping, abortion, various forms of assault, bigamy and polygamy, buggery or bestiality causing bodily harm (since 1951), criminal negligence and criminal negligence in operating a motor-vehicle (since 1957), nonsupport and desertion, incest, indecent assault on male and female, gross indecency, infanticide, killing unborn child, libel, manslaughter, murder (see note for series Y 61–66), neglect in childbirth, procuring, rape, seduction, sexual intercourse and attempt, etc.

Y 28. Offences against property with violence include breaking and entering (see note for series Y 42–50), robbery (see note for series Y 51–60), extortion, etc.

Y 29. Offences against property without violence include such offences as fraud, embezzlement, false pretences, receiving stolen goods and various forms of theft (prior to 1955 theft was an indictable or nonindictable offence according to the value of the stolen goods; since 1955 it is always indictable).

Y 30. Malicious offences against property include arson and other malicious damages to property.

Y 31. Forgery and offences against currency include forgery, uttering forged documents, offences against currency.

Y 32. Other offences include all other offences against the criminal code such as keeping bawdy houses (since 1916), being an inmate in a bawdy house (excluded in 1956), counselling or aiding suicide, attempt of suicide (excluded in 1956), gambling, carrying offensive weapons, escape of prison, dangerous or reckless driving (since 1939), driving car while drunk (since 1938), or failing to stop at the scene of accident (since 1940), etc. Includes also offences against federal statutes such as the Bank Act, the Bankruptcy Act (since 1919), the Canada Election Act, the Combines Investigation Act (since 1923), the Excise Act, the Opium and Narcotic Drug Act (since 1923), the Post Office Act, etc.

Y33-41. Sentences for indictable offences, Canada, 1886 to 1951

SOURCE: D.B.S., *Statistics of Criminal and Other Offences*, annual report for 1946, historical appendix, table II; annual report for 1952, historical appendix, table 3. For the years 1919 and 1929, errors in the 1946 historical appendix were corrected to the original annual reports. For 1930 figures for series Y33 and Y37 are from D.B.S. Figures prior to 1886 are not comparable (see note for series Y1–13); a historical table covering the period 1876 to 1936 making no distinction between the two categories can be found in the annual report for 1936 (historical appendix, table II).

The publication of figures in series Y33–41 tabulated on the basis of convictions was discontinued in 1951, two years after the changing of the basic counting unit from offence to person. Figures for 1886 to 1921 include juveniles under 16 years of age and are not comparable with those for later years relating only to persons aged 16 years and over. The sentence imposed by the court upon an offender is the sanction authorized by the law. It is for the court to determine in each case which one of the degrees of punishment, provided by the law, will be the most appropriate. Changes between years in each of the series reflect not only an increase or a decrease in the number of offences for which the sanction indicated in the heading is authorized, but also changes in the dispositions of the law in respect to sanctions to be applied, changes in judicial practices and changes in facilities (available institutions and services required to carry out a specific type of sentence). Figures in series Y36 and Y41 are specially affected by this last factor. Only offenders sentenced for two years of imprisonment or more can be sent to a penitentiary, Y37–39. Under the criminal code in force before 1955, treason, piracy, murder and rape were the only offences for which capital punishment was prescribed, Y40. A sentence could be suspended, Y41, only in the case of a first offender convicted for an offence punishable with not more than two years' imprisonment. If the offence were punishable with more than two years' imprisonment, a suspended sentence could not be authorized unless the Crown Counsel concurred.

Y42-50. Convictions for breaking and entering, by sentence, Canada, 1879 to 1951

SOURCE: D.B.S., *Statistics of Criminal and Other Offences*, annual report for 1935, part IV, table I; annual report for 1952, historical appendix, table 8. For 1928 the figure for series Y50 is correctly reported in the 1946 report, p. 172. For the year 1947 the figures in the source, which omitted juvenile offenders, have been corrected.

Figures prior to 1879 are not comparable; the publication of these series, tabulated on the basis of offences, was discontinued two years after the changing of the statistics of indictable crimes from offences to persons (see general note to series Y1–73). Figures relate to convictions of adults and juveniles, but since 1927 data on juveniles have been based on appearances at court while those referring to adults have been based on offences. 'Breaking and entering' includes any unlawful entry to commit an offence, to kill, to rape, or, most commonly, to steal even though force was not used to gain entrance in dwelling-house, building, railway, vehicle, vessel, aircraft, trailer, etc. See also text for series Y33–41. Corporal punishment, Y50, is imposed as part of the sentence. For data on corporal punishment, see *Reports of the Joint Committee of the Senate and the House of Commons on Capital Punishment, Corporal Punishment, Lotteries*, pp. 43–59.

Y51-60. Convictions for robbery, by sentence, Canada, 1879 to 1951

SOURCE: D.B.S., *Statistics of Criminal and Other Offences*, annual

report for 1935, part IV, table II; annual report for 1952, historical appendix, table 9.

Figures prior to 1879 are not comparable; the publication of these series, tabulated on the basis of offences, was discontinued two years after the changing of the statistics of indictable crimes from offences to persons (see general note to series Y1–73). Figures relate to convictions of adults and juveniles, but since 1927 data on juveniles have been based on appearances at court, while those referring to adults have been based on offences. Robbery is a completed theft by means of violence or threats against a person, or by using such violence or threat after the theft in order to secure the stolen goods; a person who assaults any other person with intent to steal from him or steals from any person when armed with any offensive weapon or imitation thereof also commits a robbery. For series Y52–57 and 59, see note for series Y33–41. For series Y60 see note for series Y42–50.

Y61-66. Murder: charges, dispositions, commutations and executions, Canada, 1879 to 1960

SOURCE: D.B.S., *Statistics of Criminal and Other Offences*, annual report for 1935, table XI; annual report for 1946, historical appendix, table VI; annual report for 1952, historical appendix, table 10; for later years each annual report. See also *Reports of the Joint Committee of the Senate and the House of Commons on Capital Punishment, Corporal Punishment, Lotteries*, p. 8, used to correct some figures for 1952 given in the annual report for that year, and also *Minutes of Proceedings and Evidence* of the same committee, vol. I, pp. 512–24 and vol. II, pp. 701–10.

Figures in series Y61–66 relate to adults as well as to juveniles. Murder is the unlawful act of causing the death of another person with intent to kill, or with intent to cause bodily injury through recklessness; however, a man may commit murder without any intent to cause even harm if, for an unlawful object, he does anything that he knows or ought to know is likely to cause death. Further, in committing some specified offences he may be guilty of murder even though there is no reason to say that he knew or should have known that his act was likely to cause death. Murder charges do not represent the real incidence of murder in Canada; no doubt, most deaths are recorded, but among deaths regarded as accidental or due to natural causes or suicide, there are successful murders (see series Y67). If the killer remains unknown, disappears, or is mentally incapacitated, no charge is laid. In some cases the prosecution lessens the charge to an offence easier to prove. On the other hand an offender prosecuted for murder may be convicted for the lesser offence of manslaughter. Prior to 1953 data on convictions for reduced offences are not available; therefore, they have not been included for later years in order to assure comparability. In 1953 and 1954 the number of charges of murder reduced to manslaughter approximates the number of charges of murder dealt with as such. The downward trend in series Y61 may be due to an increase in the number of cases reduced to manslaughter.

Y67. Number of homicidal deaths, Canada, 1926 to 1958

SOURCE: for the years 1930 to 1954, *Reports of the Joint Committee of the Senate and the House of Commons on Capital Punishment, Corporal Punishment and Lotteries*, pp. 8–10; for the other years, D.B.S., *Vital Statistics*, annual reports (table showing causes of death). Figures given in the sources for years after 1949 have been revised for this study (see below).

Homicidal deaths refer to deaths reported by coroners and medical examiners of official death registration as having been purposely inflicted by somebody else, following a post-mortem inquiry, investigation or inquest. Figures do not include cases of injury by intervention of police, of legal execution and of late effects, that is, deaths which occurred some time after the offence and which can be connected in some way with the offence. In the sources these cases have been included after 1949; in order to make the series homogeneous, figures after 1949 have been revised and the above-mentioned cases excluded. Time series on homicidal deaths complete the figures collected by courts relating to murders, series Y61. However, homicidal deaths do not represent all deaths caused purposely by somebody else (see note for series Y61–66). In order to use these figures for estimating the trend of murder, it has to be assumed that the proportion of murders in the total of homicidal deaths remains fairly constant. Data prior to 1926 are not comparable because the collection of vital statistics and the classification of causes of death were not standardized throughout Canada (see note for series Y178–201).

Y68. Convictions under the Opium and Narcotic Drug Act, Canada, 1921 to 1960

SOURCE: for 1921 to 1955, *Proceedings of a Special Committee on the Traffic in Narcotic Drugs in Canada*, pp. 478 ff.; for years after 1955 *Report of the Royal Canadian Mounted Police*, annual, Appendices; see also D.B.S., *Statistics of Criminal and Other Offences*.

Figures are based on offences, so that should a person be convicted for two offences, he would be counted twice. The first law prohibiting the importation, manufacture and sale of opium was enacted in 1908; in 1911, the law was extended to other drugs as defined by the Governor General in Council. According to an amendment of 1921, any person who committed an offence, under the Act, could be proceeded against either by indictment, or on summary conviction (see general note to series Y1–73), with the exception of the offence of selling, giving away, or distributing any drug to a minor; in the latter case, the proceeding had to be by indictment. Since 1920, the Royal Canadian Mounted Police have been responsible for the enforcement of the law.

Y69–73. Dispositions of appeals of indictable offences, Canada, 1937 to 1960

SOURCE: D.B.S., *Statistics of Criminal and Other Offences*, annual report for each year, part IV.

Figures relate to appeals submitted by the accused, the Crown or the informant; they include appeals that were dealt with by the Supreme Court of Canada or the provincial Supreme Courts from convictions and acquittals as well as from sentences. These statistics have been compiled only since 1937.

STATISTICS ON DELINQUENCY
(Series Y74–155)
General note

Series on delinquency relate exclusively to children under 16 years of age who have been dealt with by the courts.

The sources of statistics on juvenile delinquency are identical with those providing data on adult offenders. Since 1922, the Dominion Bureau of Statistics has tabulated delinquency cases separately and has published since 1927 an annual report entitled *Juvenile Delinquents*. Other sources are the annual reports of provincial Public Welfare Departments and, in Quebec, the *Yearbook* published by the Quebec Bureau of Statistics. The material from provincial sources is not comparable from province to province because the collecting and processing methods are different.

A 'juvenile delinquent' is, according to the law, a child who violated any provision of the criminal code or of any Dominion or provincial statute, or of any by-law or ordinance of any municipality, or who is guilty of sexual immorality or any similar form of vice, or who is liable by reason of any other act to be committed to an industrial school or juvenile reformatory under the provision of any federal or provincial statute. A commission of any of these acts constitutes an offence to be known as delinquency.

There are many other definitions of the juvenile delinquent and of delinquency based on psychological or sociological theories which can be useful for the purposes for which they have been worked out but for the specific purpose of statistical measurement, the legalistic definition is the most practical.

The Juvenile Delinquent Acts of 1929 and 1952 define a child as a boy or a girl apparently or actually under the age of sixteen years with a provision giving power to the Governor General in Council to raise the age limit in any province to 18 years. The upper age limit was set at 16 in New Brunswick, Nova Scotia, Ontario, Prince Edward Island and Saskatchewan, at 17 in Newfoundland, and at 18 in British Columbia, Manitoba and Quebec. In Alberta, the provision for the older age in effect from 1935 to 1950 was repealed in 1951, and the age under 16 years, as stated in the Juvenile Act of 1929, put into effect; subsequently, during the same year, the definition was changed again and the upper age limit of 18 re-established, but only for girls; in 1956, the age limit was set at 18 for both sexes. In Newfoundland for offences committed by young persons under 17 proceedings which would be under the criminal code and Juvenile Delinquents Act of Canada in other provinces are under a provincial statute which operates by virtue of the terms of agreement of confederation between Canada and Newfoundland. Figures relating to juvenile delinquents aged 16 and over (in the provinces where the upper age limit is higher than 16) are included in the statistics on adult offenders; their number was, from 1953 to 1958, 1,176, 1,283, 1,212, 1,526, 2,202 and 2,311 respectively (D.B.S., *Juvenile Delinquents*, report for each year).

The fact that juvenile delinquency data include violations of provincial statutes and municipal by-laws as well as violations of the criminal code makes the comparability of figures between years more vulnerable to changes in the laws.

From 1927 to 1949 offences committed by juveniles were divided into major and minor offences which correspond roughly to indictable and nonindictable offences committed by adults. Some offences, however, punishable on summary conviction if committed by an adult, were considered serious enough to be classified as major offences when committed by a juvenile; this division was somewhat arbitrary and was therefore eliminated in 1950.

With the exception of series Y74–85, all other juvenile delinquency statistics have been tabulated on the basis of appearances at court. They do not represent the actual number of children brought before the court, for a child referred to the court two or more times during the year for different reasons is counted as a different case each time. Neither do they represent the number of offences committed by the boys or girls brought before the court for more than one offence, because, for a boy charged with two or more offences at the same hearing, only the most serious offence is recorded. From 1953 to 1957, the number of appearances per hundred of the unduplicated number of boys was respectively, 109, 108, 107, 105 and 109 (D.B.S., *Juvenile Delinquents*, report for each year). The practice with respect to holding children for court hearings varies from province to province and from one period to another. At one extreme, a formal charge is laid in every case in which a delinquent act is alleged to have occurred; at the other extreme, formal charges may be withdrawn in any case where the appearance of the juvenile in court might prove damaging to him or to his family. In Saskatchewan, for instance, the chief probation officer decides whether proceedings shall be instituted or not; therefore, a smaller proportion of cases is counted. It seems that the tendency to handle cases unofficially is growing and affects the comparability of the number of recorded court cases. An attempt was made to find out the size of the group handled in this unofficial manner. Thirty-six courts supplied figures. If this small number of courts which reported is any indication of the general practice in Canada, then, for every three cases given a formal hearing, four are dealt with informally as 'occurences' and are not registered (D.B.S., *Juvenile Delinquents, 1949*, p. 5).

Series Y74–85 cover the period 1886 to 1926 while all the other series start with 1927; they are not comparable. The necessity for differentiating in the treatment of youngsters guilty of an offence was felt as early as 1894. A law was passed which amended the Criminal Code and provided for separate trials of 'young persons apparently under the age of sixteen years' and for 'their incarceration, prior to sentence, separately from older persons'. But it was only the Juvenile Delinquent Act of 1908 that provided for specially established courts under provincial statutes to deal with young offenders. During the following decade many courts were organized but, until 1922, data on juvenile delinquents were reported and tabulated together with figures on adult offenders. By 1922 a sufficient number of juvenile courts had been established, in accordance with the Juvenile Delinquent Act, to justify a separate statistical handling of juvenile delinquency cases. From 1922 to 1926 inclusive, juvenile delinquency data were tabulated on the basis of offences and it was only in 1927 that 'appearance at court' became the counting unit.

There have been many changes during the years in the reporting agencies due to the reorganization of the judicial approach to juvenile offenders. At present, statistics on juvenile delinquents are reported by the juvenile courts and by magistrates who hear children's cases where no juvenile court has been established, except in British Columbia, where the Department of the Attorney General, in Alberta, where the Juvenile Offender Branch of the Department of the Attorney General, and in Saskatchewan, where the Correction Branch of the Department of Social Welfare and Rehabilitation undertake the collection of the reports for submission to the Bureau.

In order to facilitate interpretation of juvenile delinquency statistics, estimated population figures for youngsters aged 7–15 years are presented in series Y86–109.

Y74–85. Convictions for major offences of juveniles under 16 years, Canada and the provinces, 1886 to 1926

SOURCE: D.B.S., *Criminal Statistics*, annual report for each year.

Convictions of juveniles were tabulated together with convictions of adults until 1921 (see series Y1–13). From 1922 to 1926 they were compiled separately and offences which would have been indictable if committed by adults were called 'major offences' (see general note to series Y74–155). In 1927 the basic statistical unit became the 'appearance at court'. Therefore, figures in series Y74–85 are not comparable with those in series Y110–155.

Y86–109. Census and estimated population aged 7–15 years, by sex, Canada and the provinces, 1927 to 1958

SOURCE: Dominion Bureau of Statistics, see note for series Y14–26.

Y110–118. Appearances of juveniles before the court and results, by sex, Canada, 1927 to 1960

SOURCE: D.B.S., *Juvenile Delinquents*, annual report for 1950, historical appendix, table II (*a*) and each annual report for later years, table 2 (A).

Figures prior to 1927 are not comparable (see note for series Y74–85). From 1927 to 1949 appearances before the court and results were compiled separately for major and for minor offences (see general note to series Y74–155). In the annual reports for 1950 and later the two classes of offences are grouped together and in the historical appendix of the same volume the figures for the major and minor offences were also grouped together for 1929 to 1949. The comparability of figures for 1927 to 1949 with those for later years in series Y110–113 is affected by the fact that appearances in court for minor offences which resulted in dismissal were not recorded prior to 1950 but have been from 1950 onward. Some courts consider children whose cases are adjourned *sine die* as delinquents but others do not; a few courts have changed their policy in this regard. When studying trends in series Y116 and 117, changes in series Y114 and 115 have to be taken into account: when the number of boys and girls declared delinquent goes down, the number of cases adjourned *sine die* goes up and vice versa. The practice of adjourning cases *sine die*, which decreased from 1945 to 1948, has been increasing since 1952.

Y119–140. Delinquency cases, by sex and by province, 1927 to 1960

SOURCE: D.B.S., *Juvenile Delinquents*, in each annual report, see table 1, and after 1948 table 1 (A).

Figures include only appearances in court which resulted in a finding of delinquency (see series Y116–118). Before 1950 data were tabulated separately for major and minor offences (see general note to series Y74–155); from 1950 onward the two classes of offences are grouped together (see note for series Y110–118). Data prior to 1927 are not comparable (see note for series Y74–85).

Y141–146. Delinquency cases, by nature of the offence, Canada, 1927 to 1960

SOURCE: D.B.S., *Juvenile Delinquents*, annual report for 1950, historical appendix, table 3 (*a*) and each annual report for later years, table 2 (A).

If a boy or a girl is charged with more than one offence at the same hearing, only the most serious offence is recorded. In 1952 figures for 1927 to 1949, compiled separately for major and minor offences, were revised and minor offences were redistributed in the categories established for major offences (see note for series Y110–118). Figures prior to 1927 are not comparable (see note for series Y74–85).

Y147–155. Delinquency cases, by disposition, Canada, 1927 to 1960

SOURCE: D.B.S., *Juvenile Delinquents*, annual report for 1950, historical appendix, table III (*b*) and each annual report for later years, table 2 (B). A few errors in the historical appendix of the 1950 annual report have been corrected according to the original sources.

In the 1950 annual report figures for 1927 to 1949, tabulated separately for minor and major offences, were revised and the two classes of offences grouped together. Figures prior to 1927 are not comparable (see note for series Y74–85). Indefinite detention, series Y148, represents a short period of detention, from a few days to about a month, during which the child is under observation or is awaiting his hearing. The sharp decline in the practice of detaining children is due partly to a better use of community resources. Under 'supervision of the court', series Y149, are listed those children who have been placed in foster homes by Children's Aid Societies and Provincial Child Welfare Departments or who have been placed under the care of a probation officer. There is no provision in the Juvenile Delinquent Act for the suspension of the sentence, series Y 153, or for corporal punishment, series Y 154. Figures in series Y 147–155 are inter-related, that is, upward trends in some series are accompanied by downward trends in others.

STATISTICS ON PENAL INSTITUTIONS
(Series Y 156–173)
General note

Canadian penal institutions may be classified under four headings: penitentiaries, reformatories, jails and training schools for boys and girls. According to the British North America Act, the Parliament of Canada has exclusive jurisdiction over the establishment, maintenance and management of penitentiaries. The other institutions are maintained either directly by the provincial governments, or by religious or other organizations subsidized by the provincial treasuries. Statistical material on penitentiaries and penitentiary population can be found: (1) in the annual reports published since Confederation, under various names, by the Department of Justice of Canada; (2) in the annual reports now known as *Statistics of Criminal and Other Offences*, published by D.B.S.; (3) in the reports of royal commissions or committees appointed to study the problems of the penitentiaries, for example, the *Report of the Committee to Advise upon the Revision of Penitentiary Regulations and the Amendment of the Penitentiary Act* (1921), the *Report of the Royal Commission to Investigate the Penal System of Canada* (Ottawa, King's Printer, 1938), and the *Report of a Committee appointed to Inquire into the Principles and Procedures followed in the Remission Service of the Department of Justice of Canada* (Ottawa, Queen's Printer, 1956). The Dominion Bureau of Statistics started the publication of statistics on movement of population in penitentiaries, reformatories, jails and training schools in 1918; data on penitentiaries were supplied until 1919 by each penitentiary, subsequently, by the Penitentiary Branch of the Department of Justice. These statistics were limited to the number of prisoners at the beginning of the reporting year, the number of admissions and discharges during the year, and the number of prisoners at the end of the reporting year.

Collection of statistics on convicts admitted to penitentiaries was started in 1937 through an agreement between the Dominion Bureau of Statistics and the Department of Justice. A census was taken of all prisoners on the registers of the penitentiaries, as of 31 March 1937, and an individual card reporting system was introduced. Since that time a perpetual inventory of convicts has been maintained at the Dominion Bureau of Statistics. Data on convicts admitted to Canadian penitentiaries have been published since 1938 in the annual report of the Commissioner of Penitentiaries. Admission and discharge cards are compiled by the penitentiary authorities and a copy is forwarded to the Bureau. Figures in series Y 158–165 are based on these compilations.

Statistics on reformatories, jails and training schools have been compiled since 1918 by the Dominion Bureau of Statistics on the basis of data gathered from the sheriff or the officer in charge of the various institutions, with the exception of a few provinces where the provincial government makes returns for the whole province. Provincial governmental agencies also issue reports on institutions under provincial administration. In Ontario, for example, statistics on prisons and reformatories have been published in annual reports issued since 1868. Data on provincial training schools and industrial schools have been published in the annual reports of the Department of Public Welfare, subsequently, in those of the Provincial Secretary and, since 1947, in the reports of the Department of Reform Institutions. In British Columbia, data on institutions for boys and

girls have been published since 1947 in the annual reports of the Social Welfare Branch of the Department of Health and Welfare. In Saskatchewan, the annual report of the Department of Social Welfare and Rehabilitation, published since 1944, includes data on adult prisoners in the provincial jails as well as on the Saskatchewan Boys' School. In Quebec, the annual *Yearbook* published by the Quebec Bureau of Statistics includes statistical material on prisons, reformatories, and industrial schools. Other reports are those of the Inspector of Penal Institutions in New Brunswick, the Department of Public Welfare in Nova Scotia, and the Department of Public Welfare in Newfoundland.

In addition, a census of reformatories and of training schools has been taken from time to time by the Dominion Bureau of Statistics, the latest being that of 1 June 1951.

Y 156–157. Number of prisoners in penitentiaries, by sex, Canada, 1867 to 1960

SOURCE: annual reports issued successively since 1867 by the Directors of Penitentiaries, the Minister of Justice, the Inspectors of Penitentiaries, the Superintendent of Penitentiaries and the Commissioner of Penitentiaries. In a few annual reports between 1867 and 1912 prisoners in penitentiaries have been counted together with convicts; in order to assure comparability, figures were revised and prisoners (those awaiting trial or in the penitentiary because there was no jail) were excluded. In 1868, 1869 and 1878 the two categories of inmates, in the numbers 57, 54 and 78 respectively, could not be separated at the penitentiary of Halifax. Therefore data relating to this penitentiary have been left out for these years.

Figures relate to the population at the end of each reporting year and, in spite of the fact that the turnover in penitentiaries is slow, they do not represent the whole population that went through the penitentiaries during the year. In 1867 there were three penitentiaries, Kingston, Halifax, and St. John, N.B.; Saint Vincent de Paul was established in 1873, the penitentiary in Manitoba in 1874 and the penitentiary in British Columbia in 1875. In 1880 the penitentiaries of Halifax and St. John were closed and, in 1881, the penitentiary of Dorchester was established. From 1907 to 1920 there was a penitentiary in Alberta. The penitentiary in Saskatchewan was established in 1911, Collins Bay in 1931, the Federal Training Centre (for young offenders under 25 years of age) in 1952, and the Joyceville institution as part of Kingston penitentiary in 1957.

Y 158–165. Admissions of males in penitentiaries, by age, Canada, 1938 to 1960

SOURCE: *Annual Report of the Commissioner of Penitentiaries* (from 1938 to 1947 Superintendent of Penitentiaries).

Procedures for compiling data on convicts admitted to penitentiaries were established in 1937 (see general note to series Y 156–173). In 1956 a change was made in the definition of the 'admitted convict' used as basic statistical unit, which, however, does not affect significantly the comparability of figures in each series.

Y 166–169. Penitentiaries operating costs, Canada, 1895 to 1960

SOURCE: for the years 1895 to 1919, *Report of the Committee to Advise upon the Revision of Penitentiary Regulations and the Amendment of the Penitentiary Act* (1921); for the years prior to 1895 and for the period 1920 to 1960, *Annual Report of the Commissioner of Penitentiaries* for each year. Data given in the *Report of the Committee* differ slightly from those indicated in the annual reports of the Commissioner. For series Y 166 the figures for 1912 to 1919 have been revised.

Before 1936 the average cost per convict per year, series Y 168, and the average cost per convict per diem, series Y 169, for each year were calculated on the net cost, that is, the actual cost less the value of supplies on hand at the end of the fiscal year and the estimated value of labour on production of capital and revenue. The actual cost was computed by adding the net expenditures (gross expenditures less revenues) and the value of supplies on hand at the beginning of the fiscal year. Since 1936 the operating costs for services rendered and goods consumed during the fiscal year have been used as a basis for computing the average cost per convict and per diem. This item does not include disbursements for capital equipment; on the other hand revenues are not deducted. Therefore, figures for 1936 to 1960 are not strictly comparable with those for previous years. From 1944 to 1949 the average cost given in the annual reports for these years was computed on the basis of operating costs including disbursements on capital. In order to make data comparable, the basis of computation has been revised and the average costs established accordingly. Federal prisoners in Newfoundland are incarcerated in the provincial jail at St. John's. The amount paid for their maintenance by the federal government to the province of Newfoundland is not included in the total of 'operating costs'.

Y170–173. Number of prisoners in reformatories and training schools, by sex, in jails and in all penal institutions, Canada, 1916 to 1955

SOURCE: D.B.S., *Statistics of Criminal and Other Offences*, entitled *Criminal Statistics* before 1926, annual report for each year.

Figures relate to the population at the end of the reporting year. Common jail population is made up partly of accused persons awaiting trial who may be liberated or sent to a penitentiary or reformatory. In jails the turnover of prisoners is very rapid; the difference between the number of persons registered at the end of the reporting year and the number of persons who went through the institution during the year is, therefore, far greater than in reformatories and in training schools where the turnover is relatively slow.

STATISTICS ON RELEASES UNDER THE TICKET OF LEAVE ACT AND PARDONS
(Series Y174–177)

Y174–177. Tickets of leave and pardons, Canada, 1876 to 1955

SOURCE: D.B.S., *Statistics of Criminal and Other Offences*, annual report for 1946, historical appendix, table VII; annual report for 1952, historical appendix, table 11; each annual report for later years. See also *Report of a Committee Appointed to Inquire into the Principles and Procedures followed in the Remission Service of the Department of Justice* (Ottawa, Queen's Printer, 1956), pp. 91 ff.

All releases granted under the Ticket of Leave Act of 1899, repealed in 1958, are classified under the heading 'releases under ticket of leave', series Y175. According to the Act of 1899, the Governor General had the power to grant to any convict under sentence of imprisonment in a penitentiary, jail or other public reformatory prison, a licence to be at large in Canada during such portion of his term of imprisonment and upon such conditions in all respects as it seemed fit to him. Since 1959 these releases have been granted by the National Parole Board under the Parole Act of 1958. Figures in series Y175 become more meaningful if related for each year to the population in penal institutions during that year. Comparability of data is affected by changes in processing of the material (from 1929 to 1950 figures include releases on temporary tickets of leave). Fluctuations in this series are due partly to changes in policy (re.: portion of term of imprisonment

that has to be accomplished before the release is granted), as well as to changes in practices as to under what legal disposition the prerogative of mercy of the Crown is exercised.

Other conditional and unconditional pardons, series Y176, include commutations of death sentences, presented separately in series Y65, remission of corporal punishment, granting of free pardons on the ground of innocence established and admitted by the prosecution, granting of free pardons on the ground of special considerations of an unusual character, remission of sentences of imprisonment (not to be confused with the benefit of parole under the Ticket of Leave Act), and remission in whole or in part of fines, pecuniary penalties, forfeitures and costs. These figures become more meaningful if related to the population which may benefit from conditional and unconditional pardons. Fluctuations in this series are due to changes in policy as well as to special proclamations of clemency which affect a great number of convicted persons.

STATISTICS ON SUICIDE (Series Y178–201)
Y178–201. Suicide and deaths from self-inflicted injury, by sex, Canada and the provinces, 1921 to 1960

SOURCE: D.B.S., *Vital Statistics*, for each year, see table showing causes of death; see also D.B.S., *Mortality from Suicide, 1921–1958* (April 1960).

Suicides relate to deaths reported by coroners and medical examiners of official death registration as having been due or 'probably due' to suicide following the usual post-mortem inquiry, as required by the law. Figures in series Y178–201 do not represent the real amount of suicides because many suicidal deaths are not reported as such; when there is not sufficient evidence that the death was suicidal it is classified as 'accidental'. Trend studies on suicide are necessarily based on the assumption that the proportion of registered suicides in the unknown whole remains fairly constant. Data on suicidal deaths have been available in Canada since 1921 when the first comprehensive annual report on vital statistics was issued; prior to that date, figures are available only for a few provinces and they are not comparable. Each province used its own system of reporting and processing. Since 1921 causes of death have been reported on a uniform basis and classified in accordance with the international classification of causes of death. Changes in this classification did not affect the comparability of data.

STATISTICS ON BANKRUPTCIES AND INSOLVENCIES (Series Y202–216)
General note

Commercial failures and insolvencies are dealt with under federal or provincial legislation. Federal insolvency legislation started with the Insolvency Act passed in 1869 which applied to the four original provinces. In 1875 a new Insolvency Act applying to the whole Dominion came into force, but it was repealed in 1880 and there was no federal legislation on the subject until 1919. During the interval, all commercial failures were handled under provincial legislation. In 1921 the administration of the Bankruptcy Act came under the authority of the federal Minister of Justice, and since 1952 the administration of bankruptcy estates has been carried on by the Superintendent of Bankruptcy with the object of conserving, as far as possible, the assets of bankruptcy estates for the benefit of the creditors. Data on this administration can be found in the annual reports of the Superintendent published since 1932.

Series Y202–214 present figures on insolvencies dealt with

under federal legislation; series Y215–216 include statistics on bankruptcies and insolvencies collected by a commercial agency (Dun and Bradstreet Inc., formerly Dun and Co.) and dealt with under provincial as well as federal legislation.

Y202–214. Bankruptcies and insolvencies under federal legislation, by branch of business, with estimated total assets and liabilities, Canada, 1924 to 1958

SOURCE: D.B.S., *Canada Year Book*; see also *Annual Report of the Superintendent of Bankruptcy*.

Figures relate exclusively to bankruptcies dealt with under federal legislation. Data on cases proceeded with under the Bankruptcy Act of 1919 and the Winding Up Act of 1906 have been collected by the Dominion Bureau of Statistics since 1920. However, changes made in the Bankruptcy Act which went into effect on 1 October 1923 affect the comparability of figures prior to 1924 with those for later years. In 1949 a new Bankruptcy Act was passed. It provided for proposals to be made by the insolvent persons to the creditors: if the proposal is accepted and an arrangement is made, data are not registered. Therefore, figures for 1950 and later years are not strictly comparable with those for previous years. In 1955, a major revision was made in the compilation and presentation of data by the Dominion Bureau of Statistics. Previously, although these statistics covered only failures coming under federal legislation, they included assignments of individuals; the coverage of the new series has been limited to business failures only, excluding failures of individuals such as wage earners, salesmen and executive personnel. In order to show how the new figures compare to the former ones,

figures for the year 1955 are presented both ways: figures compiled according to the old system are in italics. Figures relating to assets and liabilities are estimates made by the debtor. Figures on estimated assets have not been published since 1955.

Y215–216. Commercial failures in Canada, number and liabilities, 1885 to 1935

SOURCE: *Dun's Bulletin* and *Dun and Bradstreet Review* (reproduced in the *Canada Year Book*).

Figures published by Dun and Co. and by Bradstreet's (later Dun and Bradstreet Inc.) are the only source on commercial failures in Canada between 1875 and 1919 (see general note to series Y202–216). Series Y215–216, based on Dun's records, include bankruptcies in general, insolvencies under provincial company acts and such proceedings as bulk sales, bailiff's sales, landlord's seizures, etc., when loss to creditors results; these figures do not include assignments of individuals.

In 1936 Dun and Bradstreet Inc. adopted a new method of classification and new policy relating to what kind of failures have to be included. The principal changes consisted in setting up a new group, construction enterprise, previously included in manufacturing, and a new class for commercial service. Real estate companies, holding and other financial companies, and agents of various kinds were dropped. These changes have had the effect of confining the failure records more to industrial and commercial lines of activity. Liabilities were reduced more than in proportion to the number of failures, since the companies eliminated usually ran high in indebtedness. The new series are not comparable with the old.

Series Y 1–13. *Convictions for indictable offences of persons aged 16 years and over, Canada and the provinces, 1886 to 1960*

Year[1]	Canada	Newfoundland[2]	Prince Edward Island	Nova Scotia	New Brunswick	Quebec	Ontario	Manitoba	British Columbia	Saskatchewan	Alberta	Northwest Territories[3]	Yukon[4]
	1	2	3	4	5	6	7	8	9	10	11	12	13
1960	64,707	717	34	1,956	1,350	13,548	25,010	4,317	7,605	2,755	7,135	—	280
1959	56,204	806	98	1,771	1,122	12,361	21,695	1,770	7,280	2,054	7,080	—	167
1958	62,839	848	154	1,656	1,295	12,644	21,795	3,462	6,797	3,052	11,048	—	88
1957	54,900	1,013	119	1,504	1,051	12,304	19,227	4,272	6,569	2,027	6,727	—	87
1956	45,913	838	78	1,317	953	10,248	16,750	3,692	5,325	2,409	4,237	—	66
1955	46,239	788	142	1,802	937	10,809	18,118	3,300	4,804	1,804	3,733	—	2
1954	47,981	838	175	1,744	965	11,215	18,795	2,803	5,492	2,096	3,784	—	74
1953	45,071	584	291	1,699	820	9,932	17,771	2,734	4,994	1,993	4,170	—	83
1952	41,591	628	94	1,323	902	8,528	17,096	2,570	4,811	1,647	3,895	—	97
1951	40,289	553	111	1,359	876	8,042	16,399	2,566	4,602	1,795	3,902	—	84
1950[1]	*10,772*	—	*25*	*336*	*277*	*2,085*	*4,366*	*677*	*1,288*	*444*	*1,251*	—	*23*
1950	42,624	—	125	1,557	1,056	8,907	17,594	2,756	5,138	1,676	3,649	—	166
1949	41,661	—	130	1,590	899	9,232	17,303	2,553	4,552	1,710	3,573	—	119
1948	41,632	—	127	1,550	1,170	8,176	17,705	3,207	4,369	1,737	3,462	45	84
1947	44,056	—	177	1,843	1,468	7,279	20,178	2,808	4,125	2,172	3,850	54	102
1946	46,939	—	320	2,261	1,492	8,578	21,379	2,834	3,916	2,503	3,526	49	81
1945	41,965	—	231	2,116	1,248	9,592	17,287	2,517	3,480	2,204	3,201	5	84
1944	42,511	—	262	1,782	1,310	10,386	17,613	2,420	3,418	2,074	3,164	11	71
1943	41,752	—	174	1,725	1,211	11,669	16,779	2,060	3,092	2,213	2,787	20	22
1942	39,309	—	205	1,646	1,063	10,269	15,070	2,419	2,792	2,621	3,193	26	5
1941	42,646	—	207	1,675	1,185	11,514	15,861	2,811	2,996	3,106	3,263	22	6
1940	46,723	—	251	1,573	1,131	12,152	17,558	3,353	3,392	2,886	4,411	13	3
1939	48,107	—	268	1,635	1,107	10,804	19,804	3,220	3,701	3,450	4,087	24	7
1938	43,599	—	225	1,269	912	10,277	17,248	3,041	4,443	2,555	3,619	3	7
1937	37,148	—	98	1,081	759	7,781	14,569	2,839	3,331	3,083	3,589	10	8
1936	36,059	—	75	1,147	744	9,497	13,594	2,631	3,021	2,194	3,138	10	8
1935	33,531	—	59	1,002	576	9,354	12,653	2,382	3,088	1,976	2,424	14	3
1934	31,684	—	88	992	525	7,687	11,761	2,571	2,946	2,396	2,708	7	3
1933	32,942	—	70	1,160	479	7,713	13,152	2,667	3,094	2,049	2,544	7	7
1932	31,383	—	78	1,072	514	7,086	12,428	2,982	3,072	1,893	2,241	—	17
1931	31,542	—	57	1,184	461	5,737	12,000	3,102	3,385	2,716	2,887	5	8
1930	28,457	—	59	875	354	5,540	11,774	2,272	2,694	2,355	2,525	3	6
1929	24,097	—	55	869	358	4,780	9,489	1,988	2,425	1,918	2,201	6	8
1928	21,720	—	43	891	365	4,299	9,052	1,672	1,931	1,761	1,701	—	5
1927	18,836	—	14	680	287	3,621	7,962	1,457	1,833	1,492	1,483	4	3
1926	17,448	—	14	752	222	3,053	7,248	1,383	1,252	2,052	1,463	6	3
1925	17,219	—	3	624	244	3,084	7,751	1,215	1,385	1,654	1,254	3	2
1924	16,258	—	25	595	224	2,729	7,180	1,160	1,265	1,647	1,423	1	9
1923	15,188	—	13	400	148	2,655	6,886	1,094	1,116	1,446	1,424	5	1
1922	15,720	—	27	701	322	2,885	7,021	1,188	1,004	1,391	1,171	—	10
1921	16,169	—	15	712	313	2,654	7,548	1,159	1,282	1,220	1,263	—	3
1920	15,088	—	4	580	375	2,517	6,707	987	1,212	1,467	1,233	—	6
1919	14,520	—	14	663	241	2,960	6,605	919	951	1,134	1,028	—	5
1918	13,266	—	12	563	230	2,916	6,111	811	659	1,067	886	—	11
1917	11,953	—	21	427	228	2,667	4,824	755	1,058	1,057	894	—	22
1916	16,003	—	11	519	241	3,166	6,023	914	1,503	1,711	1,895	—	20
1915	17,575	—	12	840	206	2,427	7,112	1,362	1,517	1,993	2,082	—	24
1914	18,810	—	18	669	179	2,918	7,479	1,284	2,112	1,889	2,235	—	27
1913	16,007	—	8	598	140	2,336	6,272	1,331	1,794	1,594	1,908	—	26
1912	13,685	—	11	657	107	2,052	5,456	1,120	1,532	1,204	1,513	7	26
1911	11,188	—	19	356	123	1,865	5,067	888	1,015	957	870	4	24
1910	10,327	—	31	684	164	1,810	4,539	744	727	896	709	—	23
1909	10,299	—	18	463	156	2,136	4,524	784	799	737	645	—	37
1908	10,130	—	10	535	202	2,194	4,371	715	849	637	591	—	26
1907	8,106	—	9	402	147	1,827	3,392	773	532	587	395	—	42
1906	7,310	—	21	269	118	1,819	3,145	668	533	359	334	—	44
1905	6,824	—	35	342	110	1,861	2,805	534	574	—	—	524	39
1904	6,057	—	26	368	108	1,614	2,645	408	365	—	—	472	51
1903	5,483	—	32	393	131	1,397	2,344	318	443	—	—	369	56
1902	4,801	—	38	368	125	1,222	2,078	185	470	—	—	268	47
1901	4,621	—	14	287	100	1,222	2,169	185	401	—	—	203	40
1900	4,853	—	21	257	109	1,279	2,260	221	447	—	—	164	95
1899	4,777	—	14	210	103	1,495	2,176	185	341	—	—	253	—
1898	4,951	—	21	205	87	1,364	2,457	186	443	—	—	188	—
1897	4,998	—	29	223	87	1,528	2,451	216	294	—	—	170	—
1896	4,544	—	23	250	103	1,277	2,338	168	243	—	—	142	—
1895	4,648	—	28	226	101	1,389	2,349	133	307	—	—	151	—
1894	4,571	—	28	159	90	1,420	2,310	169	227	—	—	168	—
1893	3,962	—	22	164	101	1,205	1,889	163	283	—	—	135	—
1892[5]	3,316	—	28	110	74	1,156	1,599	78	186	—	—	85	—
1891	3,349	—	27	108	80	1,167	1,664	86	144	—	—	73	—
1890	3,340	—	16	111	68	1,038	1,759	77	179	—	—	92	—
1889	3,521	—	18	100	76	1,123	1,927	78	142	—	—	57	—
1888	3,145	—	13	72	62	1,042	1,734	54	119	—	—	49	—
1887	2,835	—	15	150	52	945	1,500	64	96	—	—	13	—
1886	3,123	—	39	85	60	911	1,734	75	168	—	—	51	—

[1] Figures for the years 1886 to 1950 are for the twelve months ending 30 September; later figures are for the calendar year. Statistics for the intervening months (October–December 1950) are given in italics. Cases not entirely disposed of within a year (i.e. tried but sentence postponed) are included in the next year's figures.

[2] The Canadian Criminal Code came in force in Newfoundland on 1 August 1950.

[3] Figures for the years 1886 to 1905 include statistics relating to that part of the Northwest Territories which became in 1905 the provinces of Alberta and Saskatchewan. Figures for the years 1886 to 1899 include statistics relating to the Yukon.

[4] For the years 1906 to 1910, 1913 to 1922, 1932 and 1949 to 1960 figures include statistics relating to the Northwest Territories.

[5] Prior to 1893, only one charge was recorded for a person charged with more than one offence of the same kind at the same trial.

Series Y 14–26. *Census and estimated population aged 16 years and over, Canada and the provinces, 1881 to 1959*

(thousands)

Year[1]	Canada[2]	New-foundland[3]	Prince Edward Island	Nova Scotia	New Brunswick	Quebec	Ontario	Manitoba	British Columbia	Saskatchewan	Alberta	Northwest Territories[4]	Yukon[4]
	14	15	16	17	18	19	20	21	22	23	24	25	26
1959	11,333.7	254.2	63.9	455.6	358.6	3,142.1	4,004.5	586.7	1,073.0	581.9	792.8	12.4	8.0
1958	11,111.5	248.6	62.8	452.5	350.6	3,070.4	3,922.6	577.8	1,061.0	574.7	770.6	11.9	8.0
1957	10,885.2	242.8	62.2	449.2	344.3	3,001.9	3,835.4	575.3	1,030.2	573.0	751.5	11.7	7.7
1956	10,607.4	238.3	62.9	447.1	339.1	2,926.5	3,713.5	572.9	974.1	579.5	733.4	12.0	8.1
1955	10,418.9	234.8	64.0	441.3	335.8	2,871.6	3,643.1	569.7	942.7	581.1	716.6	10.9	7.3
1954	10,220.2	230.3	65.2	436.2	333.4	2,809.5	3,568.0	563.2	916.9	580.9	699.4	10.5	6.7
1953	9,992.2	224.7	65.6	431.6	330.4	2,746.8	3,475.4	557.5	890.9	577.4	676.0	9.7	6.2
1952	9,787.2	220.4	64.9	427.0	327.5	2,693.4	3,394.4	552.7	867.6	568.1	655.3	9.7	6.2
1951	9,545.9	213.6	63.8	422.3	322.7	2,621.8	3,296.1	542.3	846.6	562.4	637.9	9.9	6.4
1950	9,410.3	215.9	62.8	424.4	325.1	2,582.9	3,235.0	540.6	834.5	566.6	622.5	—	—
1949	9,276.6	215.6	61.8	421.3	325.3	2,538.0	3,180.0	536.4	823.0	569.0	606.2	—	—
1948	8,918.0	—	61.9	420.8	321.6	2,489.3	3,122.0	531.7	807.3	576.6	586.8	—	—
1947	8,784.0	—	63.7	419.7	318.2	2,452.0	3,071.5	530.3	782.5	576.9	569.2	—	—
1946	8,641.5	—	64.3	416.4	314.6	2,407.8	3,023.9	522.9	757.7	575.6	558.3	—	—
1945	8,510.8	—	62.9	425.1	309.0	2,365.2	2,958.8	526.6	719.9	578.6	564.7	—	—
1944	8,425.5	—	62.1	421.2	305.2	2,327.2	2,930.1	527.0	709.1	578.1	565.5	—	—
1943	8,312.5	—	62.0	418.5	306.3	2,293.9	2,896.0	523.3	688.0	576.9	547.6	—	—
1942	8,200.7	—	60.9	407.8	306.9	2,243.7	2,871.8	522.9	668.1	579.0	539.6	—	—
1941	8,082.9	—	64.5	397.9	301.8	2,196.9	2,796.0	524.4	629.8	608.5	552.0	7.4	3.6
1940	7,963.0	—	64.8	392.5	297.9	2,148.6	2,760.9	522.5	621.6	607.4	546.9	—	—
1939	7,841.5	—	63.9	385.9	293.4	2,101.2	2,719.5	518.3	610.9	606.3	542.1	—	—
1938	7,719.0	—	64.6	380.5	289.5	2,049.2	2,683.6	510.4	597.3	607.5	536.4	—	—
1937	7,592.0	—	63.6	374.2	284.0	2,002.7	2,643.9	502.0	583.4	608.4	529.8	—	—
1936	7,473.2	—	64.1	368.0	279.9	1,956.6	2,609.4	492.7	574.2	607.9	520.4	—	—
1935	7,346.5	—	62.7	360.0	273.6	1,929.2	2,561.9	487.3	557.5	600.9	513.4	—	—
1934	7,233.2	—	61.4	353.1	268.0	1,906.2	2,520.5	482.5	545.6	591.9	504.0	—	—
1933	7,116.6	—	60.0	346.3	263.5	1,873.4	2,482.5	477.5	534.2	584.6	494.6	—	—
1932	7,001.0	—	59.0	340.3	258.8	1,840.7	2,444.1	472.3	522.9	578.4	484.5	—	—
1931	6,882.6	—	58.1	334.7	254.5	1,790.5	2,408.5	465.7	510.6	574.0	477.2	5.5	3.1
1930	6,735.1	—	58.0	334.6	253.1	1,752.3	2,371.8	453.3	495.1	558.2	458.7	—	—
1929	6,588.9	—	58.0	334.6	251.7	1,712.3	2,330.6	440.2	480.8	541.4	439.3	—	—
1928	6,429.5	—	57.8	334.0	250.0	1,670.4	2,283.8	425.9	466.1	523.4	418.1	—	—
1927	6,264.9	—	57.1	333.3	248.1	1,625.6	2,234.6	411.8	451.1	505.1	398.2	—	—
1926	6,109.0	—	57.0	332.4	246.6	1,581.2	2,189.1	398.9	437.0	487.7	379.1	—	—
1925	5,990.4	—	56.1	331.7	244.0	1,547.3	2,144.1	393.1	422.1	477.2	374.8	—	—
1924	5,871.4	—	56.2	331.7	242.7	1,509.2	2,101.1	387.1	407.0	465.9	370.5	—	—
1923	5,766.9	—	57.0	332.3	240.6	1,474.3	2,062.6	381.9	393.7	457.0	367.5	—	—
1922	5,690.7	—	58.6	334.5	240.6	1,444.9	2,035.3	378.8	381.1	450.5	366.4	—	—
1921	5,595.5	—	58.0	335.3	239.9	1,409.3	1,995.8	374.3	367.1	442.8	364.3	4.8	3.2
1911	4,693.5	—	60.9	316.0	219.8	1,192.4	1,738.7	294.0	296.2	316.9	247.2	4.0	7.2
1901	3,411.1	—	64.3	294.1	205.6	975.1	1,451.5	152.0	131.7	53.8	43.1	15.1[5]	24.8
1891	2,968.9	—	65.9	280.0	194.4	867.8	1,336.4	91.5	71.5	—	—	61.3[5]	—
1881	2,552.1	—	64.5	263.7	189.6	782.5	1,149.9	36.6	34.3	—	—	30.8[5]	—

[1] Figures for 1881 to 1921, 1931, 1941, 1951 and 1956 are census figures.

[2] Owing to rounding, totals shown for Canada do not necessarily correspond to sums of data shown for provinces and territories. Estimated totals for intercensal years 1922 to 1950 do not include figures for the Northwest Territories and Yukon.

[3] Newfoundland became part of the Confederation in 1949.

[4] Estimates for the intercensal years prior to 1951 not available.

[5] Includes figures for Saskatchewan, Alberta and the Yukon.

Series Y 27–32. *Convictions for indictable offences, by nature of the offence, Canada, 1886 to 1960[1]*

Year[1]	Offences against the person	Offences against property with violence	Offences against property without violence	Malicious offences against property	Forgery and offences against currency	Other offences
	27	28	29	30	31	32
Persons aged 16 years and over						
1960	6,145	14,776	35,040	1,078	4,036	3,632
1959	5,451	12,590	29,984	914	3,633	3,632
1958	5,857	12,320	32,172	941	3,420	8,129
1957	6,165	10,298	27,752	866	3,309	6,510
1956	5,684	8,525	22,067	808	2,906	5,923
1955	5,743	8,466	20,115	652	3,255	8,008
1954	6,460	8,450	20,117	425	2,911	9,618
1953	6,485	7,661	19,988	452	2,139	8,346
1952	6,015	6,550	18,672	710	2,232	7,412
1951[3]	5,554	6,427	18,450	686	1,980	7,192
1950[2]	*1,450*	*1,509*	*5,044*	*210*	*508*	*2,051*
1950	6,405	6,734	18,878	903	1,985	7,719
1949	6,408	5,999	18,610	993	2,024	7,627
1948	6,814	5,541	17,115	1,050	1,988	9,124
1947	7,925	5,304	17,111	1,036	1,780	10,900
1946	7,784	5,783	16,586	1,167	1,607	14,012
1945	6,197	5,297	15,552	944	985	12,990
1944	5,549	5,291	15,902	843	934	13,992
1943	5,610	4,223	15,419	863	1,044	14,593
1942	5,465	3,920	14,721	830	1,225	13,148
1941	5,142	4,217	15,779	805	1,089	15,614
1940	5,268	5,416	19,112	812	1,603	14,512
1939	5,478	6,147	21,358	755	2,126	12,243
1938	5,624	5,509	19,683	584	1,319	10,880
1937	4,824	4,604	18,494	591	1,242	7,393
1936	4,457	4,841	17,022	492	1,094	8,153
1935	3,985	4,147	16,161	439	910	7,889
1934	3,588	4,238	15,853	484	690	6,831
1933	4,019	4,347	16,349	519	825	6,883
1932	4,091	4,267	15,585	518	902	6,020
1931	4,483	4,327	16,143	568	899	5,122
1930	4,314	3,696	14,766	432	1,009	4,240
1929	4,015	2,553	12,138	381	724	4,286
1928	3,678	2,167	11,016	315	554	3,990
1927	3,209	1,910	9,928	278	477	3,034
1926	3,368	1,625	8,958	239	385	2,873
1925	2,904	1,934	8,796	195	408	2,982
1924	2,923	1,718	8,147	234	328	2,908
1923	2,574	1,325	7,303	275	311	3,400
1922	2,804	1,977	7,598	218	465	2,658
Persons of all ages						
1921	3,007	2,611	10,438	297	542	2,501
1920	2,901	2,313	10,022	328	430	2,449
1919	2,605	2,608	9,911	370	377	2,525
1918	2,526	2,051	9,602	249	256	2,686
1917	2,526	1,322	8,393	301	238	2,779
1916	3,443	1,484	9,541	264	315	4,113
1915	3,975	2,242	12,626	256	347	1,179
1914	4,428	1,810	13,000	248	519	1,433
1913	4,256	1,478	10,608	260	541	1,177
1912	3,486	1,196	9,073	273	415	1,124
1911	2,442	978	7,803	211	328	865
1910	2,632	945	6,780	214	237	892
1909	2,441	852	6,638	190	279	1,049
1908	2,413	914	6,796	164	262	786
1907	1,849	684	5,509	163	190	715
1906	1,618	649	4,570	81	220	954
1905	1,609	670	4,222	94	173	856
1904	1,603	565	3,960	100	152	374
1903	1,602	562	3,725	128	120	384
1902	1,329	419	3,443	98	70	301
1901	1,189	493	3,462	106	92	296
1900	1,235	431	3,622	80	91	309
1899	1,168	456	3,666	77	108	236
1898	1,154	555	3,654	90	85	249
1897	1,204	489	3,549	74	82	323
1896	1,099	419	3,305	76	87	218
1895	1,108	483	3,449	57	61	316
1894	1,163	467	3,270	56	37	265
1893	1,124	366	2,800	68	46	226
1892[4]	1,026	262	2,454	51	41	206
1891	905	292	2,493	59	36	189
1890	876	288	2,417	73	46	234
1889	992	307	2,617	50	41	201
1888	817	234	2,276	95	45	284
1887	737	227	1,967	59	43	220
1886	735	268	2,055	56	43	352

[1] For the total number of convictions, see series Y 1 and Y 74.
[2] Figures for the years 1886 to 1950 are for the twelve month period ending 30 September; later figures are for the calendar year; statistics for the intervening months (October–December 1950) are given in italics. Cases not entirely disposed of within a year (i.e. tried but sentence postponed) are included in the next year's figures.

[3] Statistics relating to Newfoundland included since 1951.
[4] Prior to 1893 only one charge is recorded for a person who is charged with more than one offence of the same kind at the same trial.

Series Y 33–41. *Sentences for indictable offences, Canada, 1886 to 1951*[1]

Year[2]	Jail With option of a fine	Jail Without option Under one year	Jail Without option One year and over	Committed to reformatories	Penitentiary Two years and under five	Penitentiary Five years and over	Life	Death	Suspended sentence and other disposition
	33	34	35	36	37	38	39	40	41
Persons aged 16 years and over									
1951[2,3]	9,376	12,744	2,565	3,244	4,030	812	6	15	7,497
1950	9,974	13,460	2,719	4,016	3,767	760	5	19	7,904
1949	10,397	13,454	2,754	3,672	3,482	539	4	26	7,333
1948	12,680	12,926	2,460	3,233	3,134	725	3	19	6,452
1947	15,077	13,004	2,157	3,349	2,763	417	5	18	7,266
1946	18,789	12,747	1,976	3,138	2,874	708	8	32	6,667
1945	16,900	11,189	1,664	2,912	2,389	559	2	17	6,333
1944	17,367	11,134	1,569	3,041	2,594	426	6	11	6,363
1943	17,789	10,735	1,587	2,614	2,532	356	3	9	6,127
1942	15,573	11,139	1,516	2,241	2,173	347	1	15	6,304
1941	16,828	12,354	1,578	2,596	2,119	459	7	13	6,692
1940	14,873	14,766	1,784	2,738	3,103	500	7	17	8,935
1939	13,047	16,246	1,904	3,629	3,558	497	3	14	9,209
1938	11,368	15,115	1,740	3,122	2,804	608	7	22	8,813
1937	9,310	12,224	1,506	2,519	2,434	644	2	13	8,496
1936	9,593	11,319	1,651	2,572	2,371	528	6	22	7,997
1935	9,374	10,631	2,357	467	2,191	462	3	15	8,031
1934	8,614	10,492	2,391	297	1,902	353	5	19	7,611
1933	8,973	10,132	2,656	168	2,018	451	15	24	8,505
1932	8,143	9,314	2,760	376	2,347	536	9	23	7,875
1931	8,036	8,801	2,728	597	2,551	568	10	25	8,226
1930	7,472	7,589	2,502	224	2,502	508	4	17	7,639
1929	7,050	6,423	1,715	319	1,781	374	9	26	6,400
1928	6,719	5,737	1,668	227	1,622	362	7	19	5,359
1927	5,606	5,016	1,456	195	1,370	364	5	12	4,812
1926	5,469	4,612	1,309	172	1,198	351	4	15	4,318
1925	4,712	4,385	1,336	370	1,244	278	14	18	4,862
1924	5,142	3,702	1,461	149	1,054	330	5	22	4,393
1923	4,916	3,601	1,057	105	949	223	2	15	4,320
1922	4,430	3,982	1,531	89	1,153	435	11	19	4,070
Persons of all ages									
1921	5,059	3,932	1,262	502	1,124	481	9	17	7,010
1920	5,447	3,750	886	615	873	245	7	26	6,594
1919	5,053	3,455	921	678	978	229	7	28	7,047
1918	5,106	3,284	783	678	701	185	4	20	6,609
1917	4,845	2,890	462	584	540	145	1	15	6,077
1916	6,786	3,816	666	568	799	178	5	21	6,321
1915	5,344	5,774	893	517	1,074	241	7	34	6,741
1914	5,518	6,306	946	592	967	241	8	27	6,833
1913	4,655	5,263	798	551	1,007	293	3	23	5,727
1912	4,144	4,779	738	433	931	308	9	25	4,200
1911	3,071	3,994	568	315	821	259	5	17	3,577
1910	3,088	3,621	444	433	729	151	2	21	3,211
1909	2,916	3,579	470	300	844	275	2	18	3,045
1908	3,126	3,794	497	327	779	202	6	15	2,589
1907	2,260	3,062	426	305	533	204	5	8	2,307
1906	1,878	2,685	384	253	622	180	5	2	2,083
1905	1,796	2,697	368	305	519	153	2	12	1,772
1904	1,302	2,454	367	232	501	156	—	14	1,728
1903	1,261	2,260	268	325	431	172	1	6	1,797
1902	1,130	2,149	214	245	358	116	1	11	1,436
1901	953	2,064	251	248	383	140	—	6	1,593
1900	1,067	2,170	286	256	378	157	5	10	1,439
1899	870	2,332	245	252	428	162	2	11	1,409
1898	864	2,501	323	231	369	189	1	13	1,296
1897	930	2,461	328	177	426	178	5	4	1,212
1896	723	2,384	267	205	371	162	2	6	1,084
1895	884	2,414	286	236	354	145	—	5	1,150
1894	798	2,428	263	190	388	173	9	11	998
1893	817	2,114	234	168	274	137	1	6	879
1892[4]	646	1,889	203	187	249	111	4	5	746
1891	572	1,925	184	201	299	119	2	7	665
1890	568	1,927	215	204	284	124	2	8	602
1889	592	2,109	196	271	300	138	5	8	589
1888	596	1,887	182	216	231	117	5	9	508
1887	543	1,717	201	167	249	91	3	4	278
1886	622	1,731	203	153	316	136	13	14	321

[1] For the total number of indictable offences, see series Y 1 and Y 74.

[2] Figures for the years 1886 to 1950 are for the twelve month period ending 30 September; figures for 1951 are for the calendar year; statistics for the intervening months (October–December 1950) not available. Cases not entirely disposed of within a year (i.e. tried, but sentence postponed) are included in next year's figures.

[3] Includes statistics relating to Newfoundland.

[4] Prior to 1893 only one charge was recorded for a person charged with more than one offence of the same kind at the same trial.

Series Y 42–50. *Convictions for breaking and entering, by sentence, Canada, 1879 to 1951*

| | | | Jail | | Committed to reforma-tories | Penitentiary | | | |
| | | | Without option | | | | | | |
Year[1]	Total[2]	With option of a fine	Under one year	One year and over		Two years and under five	Five years and over	Sentence suspended	Lashes[2]
	42	43	44	45	46	47	48	49	50
1951[1,3]	7,105	418	1,351	494	1,222	1,351	279	1,990	—
1950	7,295	324	1,449	632	1,578	1,180	197	1,935	—
1949	6,600	471	1,415	611	1,283	1,031	137	1,652	9
1948	6,065	435	1,329	667	1,123	920	102	1,489	1
1947	6,044	548	1,266	441	1,106	963	153	1,565	2
1946	6,360	518	1,343	525	1,183	908	276	1,607	—
1945	6,354	551	1,333	450	1,107	934	291	1,688	—
1944	6,504	515	1,246	462	1,296	899	202	1,884	—
1943	5,304	309	978	319	1,052	788	109	1,749	—
1942	5,075	244	991	350	802	680	150	1,858	—
1941	5,166	172	1,108	366	963	702	168	1,687	—
1940	6,136	80	1,451	382	1,079	1,064	221	1,859	—
1939	6,766	90	1,599	541	1,304	1,231	119	1,882	—
1938	6,190	87	1,387	459	1,015	1,106	267	1,869	—
1937	5,419	113	1,180	398	946	905	154	1,723	—
1936	5,502	94	1,279	493	872	989	189	1,586	6
1935	4,742	90	1,086	656	251	796	150	1,713	—
1934	4,919	125	1,261	780	259	685	82	1,727	2
1933	4,901	117	1,256	728	163	806	165	1,669	—
1932	4,756	99	1,149	758	215	779	237	1,519	6
1931	4,620	110	1,008	678	258	847	137	1,582	2
1930	4,212	163	882	535	158	852	169	1,453	14
1929	3,270	139	632	433	214	439	144	1,269	—
1928	2,766	140	577	328	182	430	120	989	—
1927	2,501	109	486	296	131	372	145	962	—
1926	2,075	101	433	206	113	339	111	772	7
1925	2,482	72	453	318	158	330	78	1,073	—
1924	2,369	47	325	307	128	323	161	1,078	17
1923	1,927	65	277	210	95	246	52	982	1
1922	2,560	129	423	387	118	325	97	1,081	—
1921	2,340	76	370	259	77	323	192	1,043	—
1920	2,073	65	404	167	164	202	52	1,019	4
1919	2,420	114	332	225	217	279	56	1,197	—
1918	1,932	105	276	137	154	189	45	1,026	1
1917	1,223	33	221	66	107	106	38	652	3
1916	1,369	62	193	64	147	178	51	674	—
1915	2,061	66	456	164	134	294	54	893	—
1914	1,638	44	430	186	158	204	45	571	2
1913	1,269	49	281	115	74	193	68	489	12
1912	1,033	57	231	92	60	184	92	317	—
1911	830	61	179	72	43	146	68	261	—
1910	844	30	180	49	100	134	22	329	—
1909	756	19	140	56	43	203	80	215	—
1908	792	29	194	45	64	169	45	246	—
1907	582	9	154	49	26	97	80	167	—
1906	583	25	155	25	74	112	43	149	—
1905	572	5	174	44	29	106	44	170	—
1904	460	21	115	47	29	100	37	111	—
1903	462	8	103	39	76	79	62	95	—
1902	384	—	110	22	25	83	27	117	—
1901	399	2	81	31	42	92	44	107	—
1900	322	—	66	28	35	89	41	63	—
1899	394	—	93	31	28	88	55	99	—
1898	491	1	129	59	23	106	49	124	—
1897	422	6	110	47	23	95	69	72	—
1896	333	—	116	50	11	59	35	62	—
1895	409	4	131	57	20	90	38	69	—
1894	390	1	130	50	15	88	61	45	—
1893	299	5	96	39	33	42	40	44	—
1892[4]	217	7	69	22	12	54	30	23	—
1891	229	—	89	22	13	59	22	26	—
1890	234	1	89	22	15	60	28	19	—
1889	232	—	68	23	19	56	50	36	—
1888	178	4	68	12	14	42	21	17	—
1887	200	4	67	25	15	47	27	15	—
1886	184	1	62	16	7	71	26	1	—
1885	164	2	54	15	5	43	21	24	—
1884	144	2	56	24	—	33	13	16	—
1883	106	9	27	3	6	30	25	6	—
1882	116	7	40	11	12	27	13	6	—
1881	115	6	30	8	8	44	14	5	—
1880	131	—	37	16	6	53	16	3	—
1879	176	1	59	19	1	63	21	12	—

[1] Figures for the years 1879 to 1950 are for the twelve month period ending 30 September; figures for 1951 are for the calendar year; figures for the intervening months (October–December 1950) not available.

[2] Figures in series Y 50 are not included in the totals.

[3] Includes statistics relating to Newfoundland.

[4] Prior to 1893 only one charge is recorded for a person charged with more than one offence of the same kind at the same trial.

Series Y 51–60. *Convictions for robbery, by sentence, Canada, 1879 to 1951*

Year[1]	Total[2]	Jail — With option of a fine	Jail — Without option, Under one year	Jail — Without option, One year and over	Committed to reformatories	Penitentiary — Two years and under five	Penitentiary — Five years and over	Penitentiary — Life	Sentence suspended	Lashes[2]
	51	52	53	54	55	56	57	58	59	60
1951[1,3]	864	13	126	49	105	256	257	2	56	3
1950	776	20	108	64	115	236	177	—	56	—
1949	743	4	109	78	144	237	128	—	43	—
1948	705	15	79	74	134	255	102	1	45	10
1947	614	10	101	62	114	197	101	—	29	4
1946	776	13	99	65	140	223	190	—	46	6
1945	456	16	77	53	63	144	62	—	40	1
1944	526	15	82	45	111	151	71	—	51	8
1943	469	13	82	26	47	177	85	3	36	3
1942	381	6	58	30	62	112	57	—	56	6
1941	458	8	63	34	81	148	97	1	26	4
1940	541	2	94	41	91	157	125	—	31	11
1939	588	11	89	68	101	150	130	—	39	16
1938	441	1	98	45	50	129	75	—	43	21
1937	407	4	50	32	45	100	144	—	32	28
1936	358	—	31	37	42	128	102	—	18	19
1935	436	1	47	92	5	103	159	—	29	33
1934	391	3	56	79	5	106	127	4	11	34
1933	418	4	77	35	6	131	119	3	43	62
1932	438	1	44	61	12	153	134	3	30	61
1931	668	3	77	101	16	243	187	5	36	107
1930	435	3	55	60	1	134	146	—	36	36
1929	259	7	33	53	1	101	46	—	18	30
1928	225	5	22	26	6	60	78	—	28	34
1927	170	3	35	25	1	50	44	—	12	24
1926	221	10	27	30	1	78	45	—	30	20
1925	246	6	49	44	5	54	58	—	30	27
1924	166	2	28	25	2	49	43	—	17	19
1923	149	5	28	43	2	28	22	—	21	6
1922	224	3	46	44	—	50	67	—	14	14
1921	269	11	51	30	2	67	61	—	47	5
1920	237	27	35	33	3	70	37	—	32	—
1919	186	7	50	43	3	47	19	—	17	—
1918	117	4	20	13	5	29	16	—	30	—
1917	98	11	27	11	1	18	13	—	17	—
1916	109	4	27	17	3	30	11	—	17	1
1915	173	7	43	30	—	53	23	—	17	4
1914	172	6	58	40	5	27	17	—	19	3
1913	203	18	47	43	1	42	26	—	26	3
1912	162	12	47	24	1	39	23	—	16	—
1911	147	8	57	12	1	24	28	—	17	2
1910	99	3	38	10	2	27	10	—	9	—
1909	92	5	24	11	3	12	20	—	17	—
1908	101	9	39	8	1	25	9	—	10	1
1907	99	10	33	18	—	15	11	—	12	1
1906	62	1	32	9	—	15	5	—	—	2
1905	84	—	34	18	1	19	1	—	11	—
1904	92	—	29	19	1	19	11	—	13	—
1903	81	2	20	11	7	20	10	—	11	—
1902	29	—	8	5	—	6	8	—	2	—
1901	52	—	15	4	1	16	12	—	4	—
1900	85	—	19	4	1	35	14	—	12	—
1899	50	—	9	9	—	21	10	—	1	—
1898	49	—	10	14	—	14	8	—	3	—
1897	53	2	18	10	1	14	7	—	1	—
1896	75	1	19	10	1	25	13	—	6	—
1895	53	—	30	9	2	6	3	—	3	—
1894	60	—	18	14	—	11	10	—	7	—
1893	63	2	25	12	1	12	8	—	3	—
1892[4]	34	—	16	2	1	5	4	—	6	—
1891	54	—	16	5	9	15	7	—	2	—
1890	42	—	24	1	—	12	5	—	—	—
1889	51	—	9	5	5	15	11	—	6	—
1888	47	—	24	3	2	12	3	—	3	—
1887	48	1	18	7	—	10	9	—	3	—
1886	71	—	21	6	—	28	16	—	—	—
1885	58	—	21	5	3	12	12	—	5	—
1884	67	—	21	15	1	23	4	—	3	—
1883	26	1	10	5	—	5	5	—	—	—
1882	57	2	22	2	3	17	9	—	2	—
1881	29	2	15	1	—	4	6	—	1	—
1880	45	—	26	5	3	7	4	—	—	—
1879	61	1	22	8	—	22	5	—	3	—

[1] Figures for the years 1879 to 1950 are for the twelve month period ending 30 September; figures for 1951 are for the calendar year; figures for the intervening months (October–December 1950) not available.

[2] Figures in series Y 60 are not included in the totals.

[3] Includes statistics relating to Newfoundland.

[4] Prior to 1893 only one charge is recorded for a person charged with more than one offence of the same kind at the same trial.

Series Y61–66. *Murder: charges, dispositions, commutations and executions, Canada, 1879 to 1960*

Year[1]	Charges	Ac-quittals[2]	Detained for insanity	Death sentences	Commu-tations[3]	Execu-tions[3]	Year[1]	Charges	Ac-quittals[2]	Detained for insanity	Death sentences	Commu-tations[3]	Execu-tions[3]
	61	62	63	64	65	66		61	62	63	64	65	66
1960	32	13	9	10	n.a.	n.a.	1920	57	28	3	26	14	7
1959	57	34	7	16	n.a.	n.a.	1919	79	44	7	28	7	19
1958	35	13	3	19	15	2	1918	50	23	7	20	10	6
1957	42	25	9	8	6	4	1917	48	28	3[5]	17	8	7
1956	24	8	6	10	8	4	1916	56	32	3	21	13	8
1955	34	14	4	16	5	8	1915	86	48	4	34	13	14
1954	35	16	4	15	1	4	1914	62	31	4	27	16	13
1953	36	18	8	10	10	11	1913	55	27	5	23	15	9
1952[1,4]	50	32	—	18	3	12	1912	52	24	3	25	11	8
1951[1,4]	52	30	7	15	2	6	1911	53	34	2	17	8	7
1950	29	9	1	19	6	13	1910	55	31	3	21	2	13
1949	55	27	2	26	4	13	1909	42	23	1	18	4	13
1948	56	33	4	19	4	12	1908	42	24	3	15	8	7
1947	61	30	13	18	6	10	1907	37	28	1	8	4	7
1946	66	29	5	32	8	14	1906	30	26	2	2	2	2
1945	35	10	8	17	3	6	1905	38	24	2	12	5	5
1944	33	20	2	11	3	6	1904	27	11	2	14	6	6
1943	23	10	4	9	—	7	1903	26	20	—	6	5	5
1942	41	17	9	15	4	6	1902	28	17	—	11	3	9
1941	40	19	8	13	6	9	1901	22	14	1	7	3	4
1940	40	18	5	17	6	8	1900	18	7	1	10	3	6
1939	37	20	3	14	5	7	1899	23	9	3	11	6	9
1938	45	19	4	22	7	7	1898	25	11	1	13	4	8
1937	35	16	6	13	4	12	1897	17	13	—	4	3	3
1936	48	18	8	22	3	8	1896	28	20	2	6	2	—
1935	46	22	9	15	5	17	1895	16	10	1	5	1	3
1934	46	24	3	19	1	12	1894	27	16	—	11	7	4
1933	43	11	8	24	4	16	1893	20	13	1	6	1	1
1932	47	18	6	23	6	16	1892	23	18	—	5	5	4
1931	49	14	10	25	2	22	1891	18	10	1	7	2	2
1930	54	30	7	17	5	10	1890	26	17	1	8	1	10
1929	50	17	7	26	8	11	1889	26	17	1	8	3	1
1928	42	18	5	19	8	7	1888	25	12	4	9	3	7
1927	45	23	11	11	1	9	1887	13	9	—	4	5	3
1926	51	31	5	15	5	9	1886	26	10	2	14	6	2
1925	54	32	4	18	10	6	1885	20	10	—	10	4	12
1924	61	34	5	22	6	13	1884	26	13	2	11	3	6
1923	47	27	5	15	6	13	1883	25	14	—	11	4	5
1922	56	34	3	19	7	9	1882	28	16	1	11	4	4
1921	77	55	5	17	10	8	1881	40	23	1	16	2	3
							1880	25	20	—	5	2	6
							1879	36	22	—	14	6	5

[1] Figures for the years 1879 to 1950 are for the twelve months ending 30 September; all other figures are for the calendar year. Figures for the intervening months (October–December 1950) not available. Cases not entirely disposed of within a year (i.e. tried but sentence postponed) are included in the next year's figures.

[2] Includes acquittals, jury disagreements, stay of proceedings, no bill and *nolli prosequi*.

[3] Figures represent commutations and executions that took place the year mentioned regardless of the year sentences of death were imposed. Figures are not included in the totals.

[4] Statistics relating to Newfoundland included since 1951.

[5] Figures include two Eskimos convicted of murder and exiled in the north.

Series Y67. *Number of homicidal deaths, Canada, 1926 to 1958*

Year	Number of deaths	Year	Number of deaths
	67		67
1958	198	1940	148
1957	165	1939	124
1956[1]	171	1938	127
		1937	138
1955	157	1936	137
1954	157		
1953	149	1935	153
1952	135	1934	142
1951	137	1933	147
		1932	158
1950	112	1931	172
1949[2]	172		
1948	155	1930	214
1947	146	1929	182
1946	146	1928	150
		1927	124
1945	152	1926	126
1944	106		
1943	125		
1942	113		
1941	130		

[1] Statistics relating to the Northwest and Yukon Territories included since 1956.

[2] Statistics on Newfoundland included since 1949.

Series Y 68. *Convictions under the opium and narcotic drug act, Canada, 1921 to 1960*

Year[1]	Number of convictions		Year[1]	Number of convictions
	68			**68**
1960	580		1940	173
1959	585		1939	150
1958	473		1938	155
1957	354		1937	131
1956	453		1936	102
1955	357		1935	184
1954	391		1934	271[1]
1953	381		1933	—[1]
1952	411		1932	178
1951[2]	364		1931	135
1950	407		1930	236
1949	343		1929	266
1948	320		1928	161
1947	238		1927	176
1946	142		1926	280
1945	193		1925	355
1944	151		1924	218
1943	95		1923	506
1942	190		1922	800
1941	176		1921	610

[1] Figures for the years 1921 to 1932 are for the twelve month period ending 30 September; figures for the years 1935 to 1960 are for the twelve month period ending 31 March; figures for the year 1934 are for the period 1 October 1932 to 31 March 1934 (18 months).

[2] Statistics on Newfoundland included since 1951.

Series Y 69–73. *Dispositions of appeals of indictable offences, Canada, 1937 to 1960*

Year[1]	Number of appeals disposed of during the year	Appeal dismissed	Convictions quashed	Sentence varied	New trial directed
	69	**70**	**71**	**72**	**73**
1960	2,036	1,396	79	501	60
1959	1,311	888	73	317	33
1958	1,313	876	95	290	52
1957	1,427	1,004	90	297	36
1956	1,093	751	86	198	58
1955	1,207	836	114	201	56
1954	976	646	83	205	42
1953	830	513	86	195	36
1952	847	526	87	168	66
1951[2]	839	511	115	166	47
1950	895	538	104	201	52
1949	721	429	89	164	39
1948	799	527	95	125	52
1947	662	450	80	93	39
1946	729	439	109	151	30
1945	557	351	80	100	26
1944	519	321	78	85	35
1943	354	214	48	66	26
1942	319	188	53	45	33
1941	421	257	65	74	25
1940	443[3]	245	72	89	37
1939	424[4]	233	70	84	37
1938	530	325	92	83	30
1937	428	255	85	67	21

[1] Appeals in a specific year include cases which were tried during that year as well as the years before; similarly, the results of new trials ordered by appeal courts in that specific year are included in later years depending on when the case is disposed of.

[2] Statistics relating to Newfoundland included since 1951.

[3] Include 27 cases held over from previous year.

[4] Include 20 cases held over from previous year.

Series Y 74–85. *Convictions for major offences of juveniles under 16 years, Canada and the provinces, 1886 to 1926*

Year[1]	Canada	Prince Edward Island	Nova Scotia	New Brunswick	Quebec	Ontario	Manitoba	British Columbia	Saskatchewan	Alberta	Northwest Territories[2]	Yukon[3]
	74	75	76	77	78	79	80	81	82	83	84	85
					Major offences							
1926	5,299	6	195	55	870	2,282	1,002	317	246	326	—	—
1925	5,246	18	263	77	971	2,230	915	277	280	215	—	—
1924	4,722	31	251	59	782	2,044	750	251	362	192	—	—
1923	4,165	10	253	60	864	1,633	581	268	249	246	—	1
1922	4,065	5	167	45	655	1,852	627	278	196	240	—	—
					Indictable offences							
1921	3,227	9	149	77	821	1,597	333	201	27	13	—	—
1920	3,355	15	133	59	771	1,707	436	226	1	7	—	—
1919	3,876	17	104	92	960	2,023	467	200	1	12	—	—
1918	4,104	25	154	104	831	2,202	553	200	32	3	—	—
1917	3,606	12	155	104	709	2,100	335	176	8	7	—	—
1916	3,157	3	125	55	658	1,865	312	116	18	5	—	—
1915	3,050	4	110	72	626	1,822	215	163	29	6	—	3
1914	2,628	7	97	50	668	1,453	210	101	39	2	—	1
1913	2,313	4	87	48	653	1,131	251	110	23	5	—	1
1912	1,881	—	72	28	463	992	181	121	16	8	—	
1911	1,439	2	27	23	179	844	159	134	20	49	—	2
1910	1,373	17	75	49	252	834	11	71	12	52	—	—
1909	1,150	7	69	32	228	689	30	34	8	52	—	1
1908	1,204	5	38	28	277	661	117	43	26	9	—	—
1907	1,004	5	48	16	230	499	148	54	3	1	—	—
1906	782	4	25	22	194	383	116	33	1	4	—	—
1905	800	2	42	16	204	431	75	24	—	—	3	3
1904	697	2	66	14	124	389	81	14	—	—	4	3
1903	1,038	6	51	24	279	540	63	73	—	—	1	1
1902	859	11	50	33	183	492	38	47	—	—	4	1
1901	1,017	3	42	27	268	600	17	56	—	—	4	
1900	915	6	68	28	208	509	48	42	—	—	6	—
1899	936	2	40	22	284	517	39	29	—	—	3	—
1898	836	16	35	17	239	443	14	70	—	—	2	—
1897	723	13	32	8	209	404	29	28	—	—	—	—
1896	660	11	29	13	143	445	13	4	—	—	2	—
1895	790	11	13	18	226	480	27	10	—	—	5	—
1894	687	11	23	19	233	372	17	9	—	—	3	—
1893	668	2	35	20	169	426	5	11	—	—	—	—
1892[4]	714	3	40	19	182	465	4	1	—	—	—	—
1891	615	2	16	16	189	382	7	1	—	—	2	—
1890	594	4	15	11	182	364	14	4	—	—	—	—
1889	687	4	31	4	238	391	15	4	—	—	—	—
1888	602	—	8	9	159	410	13	3	—	—	—	—
1887	418	3	20	2	78	307	6	—	—	—	2	—
1886	386	—	16	5	78	282	2	1	—	—	2	—

[1] Figures are for the twelve months ending 30 September of the year given. Cases not entirely disposed of within a year (i.e. tried but disposition postponed) are included in next year's figures.

[2] For the years 1886 to 1905 includes statistics relating to that part of the Northwest Territories which became the Provinces of Alberta and Saskatchewan. Figures for the years 1886 to 1899 include statistics relating to the Yukon.

[3] For the years 1906 to 1910 and 1913 to 1922 figures include data on the Northwest Territories.

[4] Prior to 1893 only one offence is recorded for a person who is charged with more than one offence of the same kind at the same trial.

Series Y 86–109. *Census and estimated population aged 7–15 years, by sex, Canada and the provinces, 1927 to 1958*

(thousands)

Year[1]	Canada[2] M	Canada[2] F	Newfoundland[3] M	Newfoundland[3] F	Prince Edward Island M	Prince Edward Island F	Nova Scotia M	Nova Scotia F	New Brunswick M	New Brunswick F	Quebec M	Quebec F
	86	87	88	89	90	91	92	93	94	95	96	97
1958	1,523.9	1,462.5	47.5	47.1	10.0	9.6	68.1	65.3	60.0	57.7	474.5	458.1
1957	1,458.4	1,402.4	46.0	45.7	9.9	9.5	66.6	64.1	58.6	56.4	460.6	445.5
1956	1,390.4	1,337.8	44.4	43.8	9.6	9.2	64.9	62.5	56.4	54.3	443.7	429.2
1955	1,308.1	1,255.5	43.2	41.5	10.2	9.8	62.2	59.1	54.6	52.0	421.0	404.9
1954	1,248.0	1,199.0	40.7	39.4	9.6	9.4	60.7	57.7	52.6	50.2	399.0	384.5
1953	1,191.1	1,144.9	38.7	37.3	9.8	9.2	58.7	56.2	50.6	48.4	382.7	368.5
1952	1,140.1	1,097.4	36.9	35.7	9.3	8.8	56.9	55.0	48.8	47.0	367.8	354.5
1951	1,094.5	1,055.6	34.9	34.1	8.8	8.3	55.5	53.8	47.1	45.7	352.9	341.1
1950	1,062.6	1,028.8	33.3	32.8	8.5	8.0	54.4	51.8	45.8	44.5	344.0	334.0
1949	1,041.2	1,009.9	32.4	31.9	8.4	7.8	53.0	50.1	45.3	43.7	336.1	328.3
1948	988.1	961.6	—	—	8.2	7.7	51.9	49.6	44.3	42.9	328.8	321.8
1947	973.2	947.0	—	—	8.0	7.9	51.2	49.1	43.4	42.3	322.2	316.1
1946	959.6	937.5	—	—	8.2	8.1	50.5	49.2	42.7	41.9	316.6	311.8
1945	951.2	932.6	—	—	8.2	8.1	51.4	49.7	42.0	41.2	315.1	311.6
1944	965.5	940.9	—	—	8.5	8.1	51.8	49.8	42.3	41.6	318.8	313.6
1943	971.4	950.9	—	—	8.5	8.1	51.6	49.9	42.9	42.3	321.4	317.5
1942	980.7	959.6	—	—	8.5	8.0	51.2	49.5	43.5	42.9	323.3	318.7
1941	988.4	967.1	—	—	8.7	8.5	50.7	49.2	43.3	42.9	324.0	319.8
1940	993.8	972.5	—	—	8.7	8.4	50.3	48.9	43.6	43.0	326.6	322.2
1939	1,006.8	984.4	—	—	8.8	8.5	50.5	49.0	44.1	43.4	330.6	326.0
1938	1,014.5	991.2	—	—	8.4	8.4	50.8	49.1	44.4	43.4	334.0	329.1
1937	1,017.3	995.9	—	—	8.4	8.4	50.9	49.4	44.5	43.6	332.7	328.8
1936	1,019.1	998.7	—	—	8.2	8.2	51.1	49.7	44.4	43.4	331.7	326.9
1935	1,022.4	1,002.9	—	—	8.6	8.3	51.8	50.4	44.9	44.0	321.5	318.8
1934	1,021.6	1,002.6	—	—	8.6	8.5	52.6	51.3	45.0	44.2	311.7	309.6
1933	1,013.5	993.7	—	—	8.8	8.6	52.7	51.3	44.9	43.8	302.9	301.4
1932	1,001.1	979.4	—	—	8.8	8.6	52.3	50.9	44.6	43.1	294.4	292.8
1931	991.3	969.9	—	—	8.6	8.4	51.8	50.3	43.6	42.2	293.7	292.4
1930	975.8	957.3	—	—	8.8	8.4	51.7	50.3	43.4	41.7	287.5	288.0
1929	958.3	943.6	—	—	8.8	8.4	51.7	50.1	42.9	41.2	280.1	283.3
1928	941.9	929.0	—	—	8.9	8.3	51.5	49.9	42.2	40.5	272.3	278.7
1927	925.1	914.8	—	—	8.6	8.2	51.1	49.6	41.6	39.6	266.7	272.7

Year[1]	Ontario M	Ontario F	Manitoba M	Manitoba F	Saskatchewan M	Saskatchewan F	Alberta M	Alberta F	British Columbia M	British Columbia F	Yukon and the Northwest Territories[4] M	Yukon and the Northwest Territories[4] F
	98	99	100	101	102	103	104	105	106	107	108	109
1958	474.7	453.9	76.0	72.1	81.0	77.4	106.6	101.3	122.6	117.2	2.9	2.8
1957	447.6	428.2	73.4	69.7	78.2	74.9	100.1	95.4	114.8	110.7	2.6	2.3
1956	420.0	402.3	70.8	67.4	76.7	73.5	95.1	91.1	106.0	101.9	2.6	2.5
1955	386.1	370.5	67.7	65.4	75.3	72.7	88.7	84.6	96.7	92.6	2.4	2.4
1954	368.4	353.2	64.8	62.3	73.6	71.3	85.2	81.7	91.1	87.1	2.3	2.1
1953	348.2	334.5	62.2	59.8	71.2	69.4	81.1	77.5	85.8	82.2	2.1	1.9
1952	330.6	317.3	60.4	58.2	69.6	67.4	77.1	73.7	80.7	77.8	2.0	2.0
1951	316.8	304.2	57.8	55.5	69.1	66.2	73.7	71.2	76.1	73.6	1.9	1.8
1950	306.2	295.7	56.8	54.4	69.2	66.8	71.9	69.8	72.5	71.0	—	—
1949	300.7	288.9	56.0	54.1	69.0	67.6	70.2	68.6	70.1	68.9	—	—
1948	294.0	285.0	55.3	53.5	70.0	68.0	68.5	67.0	67.1	66.1	—	—
1947	290.0	281.2	54.6	52.9	70.6	68.8	67.4	65.1	65.8	63.6	—	—
1946	286.9	279.1	54.8	53.0	71.8	69.5	65.7	64.1	62.4	60.8	—	—
1945	281.7	274.8	54.6	53.3	73.8	71.0	66.5	65.2	57.9	57.7	—	—
1944	286.1	278.0	55.8	53.9	77.1	73.2	67.4	66.3	57.7	56.4	—	—
1943	288.1	280.6	56.8	55.3	77.9	75.4	67.3	65.9	56.9	55.9	—	—
1942	292.0	284.8	58.3	56.6	80.2	77.7	67.8	66.4	55.9	55.0	—	—
1941	291.6	283.7	60.5	58.7	85.3	82.7	70.2	68.9	54.0	52.8	—	—
1940	291.3	283.5	61.5	59.5	87.7	85.0	70.1	69.0	54.0	53.0	—	—
1939	294.5	286.6	62.7	60.5	90.1	87.5	71.0	69.6	54.5	53.3	—	—
1938	295.7	287.8	63.9	61.6	92.0	89.1	70.9	69.8	54.4	52.9	—	—
1937	296.7	288.6	64.9	62.8	93.6	91.2	71.3	70.3	54.3	52.8	—	—
1936	295.6	288.6	66.1	65.0	96.2	93.3	72.7	71.7	53.1	51.9	—	—
1935	300.9	293.2	67.9	66.5	98.1	95.7	72.8	71.7	55.9	54.3	—	—
1934	304.0	296.5	69.1	67.2	99.9	97.5	73.9	72.5	56.8	55.3	—	—
1933	303.1	295.2	70.2	67.7	100.7	98.3	73.9	72.5	56.3	54.9	—	—
1932	300.1	291.4	70.0	67.6	101.0	98.8	73.9	71.7	56.0	54.5	—	—
1931	295.5	286.3	70.1	68.0	100.3	98.0	72.8	70.8	54.8	53.4	—	—
1930	290.8	283.2	70.1	67.9	98.8	96.3	71.2	69.3	53.5	52.2	—	—
1929	285.2	279.6	70.1	67.9	97.4	94.4	69.8	67.6	52.3	51.1	—	—
1928	281.8	275.2	70.2	67.9	95.8	92.8	68.3	66.2	50.9	49.5	—	—
1927	276.4	272.6	70.1	68.0	94.3	91.3	66.8	64.7	49.5	48.1	—	—

[1] Figures for 1931, 1941, 1951 and 1956 are census figures.
[2] Owing to rounding, totals shown for Canada do not necessarily correspond to sums of data shown for provinces and territories. Prior to 1951 estimated totals do not include figures for Yukon and Northwest Territories.

[3] Newfoundland became part of the Confederation in 1949.
[4] Figures prior to 1951 not available.

Series Y 110–118. *Appearances of juveniles before the court and results, by sex, Canada, 1927 to 1960*

Year[1]	Appeared before the court[2]		Dismissed[2]		Adjourned *sine die*		Found delinquent		
	Boys	Girls	Boys	Girls	Boys	Girls	Boys	Girls	Total
	110	**111**	**112**	**113**	**114**	**115**	**116**	**117**	**118**
1960	14,137	1,872	455	62	1,296	231	12,386[3]	1,579	13,965
1959	11,843	1,486	330	40	1,093	180	10,420[3]	1,266[4]	11,686
1958	11,568	1,566	360	56	1,151	176	10,057[3]	1,334[4]	11,391
1957	10,482	1,446	292	39	1,700	218	8,490	1,189	9,679
1956	9,120	1,195	200	21	952	157	7,968	1,017	8,985
1955	7,186	1,001	180	27	820	135	6,186	839	7,025
1954	6,956	795	216	21	1,057	125	5,683	649	6,332
1953	6,999	830	185	31	1,122	114	5,692	685	6,377
1952	6,465	748	168	10	879	88	5,418	650	6,068
1951[5]	6,805	716	185	10	588	94	6,032	612	6,644
1950	6,548	756	176	21	600	89	5,772	646	6,418
1949[1]	*1,623*	*199*	*39*	*3*	*141*	*16*	*1,443*	*180*	*1,623*
1949	6,362	676	146	20	606	68	5,610	588	6,198
1948	6,988	890	179	11	461	72	6,348	807	7,155
1947	7,363	902	191	6	456	67	6,716	829	7,545
1946	7,617	1,090	171	12	575	93	6,871	985	7,856
1945	8,599	1,157	150	12	582	103	7,867	1,042	8,909
1944	10,274	1,280	240	7	1,159	231	8,875	1,042	9,917
1943	10,795	1,430	246	21	1,345	317	9,204	1,092	10,296
1942	12,388	1,414	237	24	1,451	332	10,700	1,058	11,758
1941	10,812	1,325	226	4	1,330	267	9,256	1,054	10,310
1940	8,857	1,119	232	7	1,055	251	7,570	861	8,431
1939	8,514	983	224	11	1,404	245	6,886	727	7,613
1938	8,086	843	240	5	1,459	190	6,387	648	7,035
1937	8,886	789	280	5	1,512	162	7,094	622	7,716
1936	8,060	708	224	14	1,205	115	6,631	579	7,210
1935	8,645	752	180	7	1,344	187	7,121	558	7,679
1934	8,662	786	253	10	1,226	153	7,183	623	7,806
1933	8,154	708	274	9	1,036	90	6,844	609	7,453
1932	8,420	734	368	17	1,314	92	6,738	625	7,363
1931	9,183	767	345	15	1,685	137	7,153	615	7,768
1930	10,162	743	296	14	1,997	173	7,869	556	8,425
1929	9,812	697	218	19	2,318	128	7,276	550	7,826
1928	9,488	645	209	7	2,176	42	7,103	596	7,699
1927	9,520	699	237	11	1,733	53	7,550	635	8,185

[1] Figures for the years 1927 to 1949 are for the twelve months ending 30 September; later figures are for the calendar year. Statistics for the intervening months (October–December 1949) are given in italics. Cases not entirely disposed of within a year (i.e. tried but disposition postponed) are included in the next year's figures.

[2] From 1927 to 1949 figures in series Y 112–113 refer to boys and girls brought to court for major offences only. In the same period series Y 110–111 do not include boys and girls brought to court for minor offences whose cases were dismissed, although they do include those on minor charges whose cases were not dismissed.

From 1950 onward those charged with minor offences whose cases were dismissed are included in all series Y 110–113.

[3] In 1959 the figure includes 33 cases and in 1958, 892 cases 'adjourned *sine die*' compiled for statistical purposes under the heading 'found delinquent'.

[4] In 1959 the figure includes 2 cases and in 1958, 64 cases 'adjourned *sine die*' compiled for statistical purposes under the heading 'found delinquent'.

[5] The Canadian Criminal Code came in force in Newfoundland on 1 August 1950. Statistics on juvenile delinquency in this province are reported since 1951.

Series Y119–140. *Delinquency cases, by sex and by province, 1927 to 1960[1]*

Year[2]	New-foundland[3] M	New-foundland[3] F	Prince Edward Island M	Prince Edward Island F	Nova Scotia M	Nova Scotia F	New Brunswick M	New Brunswick F	Quebec M	Quebec F	Ontario M	Ontario F	Manitoba M	Manitoba F	Saskatchewan M	Saskatchewan F	Alberta M	Alberta F	British Columbia M	British Columbia F	Yukon and the Northwest Territories M	Yukon and the Northwest Territories F
	119	120	121	122	123	124	125	126	127	128	129	130	131	132	133	134	135	136	137	138	139	140
1960	383	26	34	1	612	70	406	54	2,430	262	4,650	714	875	144	219	12	910	121	1,867	175	—	—
1959	247	15	39	3	577	46	337	18	2,166	244	3,647	552	556	73	171	11	804	107	1,841	197	35	—
1958	322	21	25	—	624	52	381	50	1,989	240	3,574	534	686	104	76	9	776	130	1,594	194	10	—
1957	280	21	35	—	451	41	298	26	1,193	158	3,488	563	605	103	26	—	678	88	1,433	188	3	1
1956	329	7	47	1	381	31	287	24	1,058	126	3,441	504	524	69	41	3	601	114	1,254	137	5	1
1955	243	11	30	—	363	27	187	15	890	150	2,801	337	307	94	54	3	467	68	844	134	—	—
1954	213	5	43	—	404	36	212	12	583	95	2,637	308	287	54	56	3	391	37	857	99	—	—
1953	186	10	32	1	413	30	217	18	678	95	2,653	322	297	63	48	1	313	44	852	100	3	1
1952	197	18	29	—	326	30	243	24	591	37	2,597	292	319	90	75	6	261	56	780	97	—	—
1951	167	8	51	1	458	25	237	24	1,089	91	2,729	295	280	67	61	3	223	19	736	79	1	—
1950	—	—	10	—	320	31	249	9	1,201	168	2,753	303	344	56	76	—	181	23	632	56	6	—
1949[2]	—	—	*10*	—	*130*	*10*	*49*	*6*	*285*	*34*	*573*	*81*	*155*	*19*	*30*	*3*	*52*	*9*	*159*	*18*	—	—
1949	—	—	45	4	405	28	177	21	1,172	151	2,301	240	360	43	168	3	237	9	744	89	1	—
1948	—	—	27	1	388	33	233	30	1,607	257	2,538	261	319	45	165	4	217	20	843	156	11	—
1947	—	—	29	1	377	35	311	23	1,555	287	2,546	284	373	51	203	9	265	12	1,040	127	17	—
1946	—	—	52	3	360	24	329	53	1,765	390	2,751	353	273	25	184	11	378	27	779	99	—	—
1945	—	—	99	16	459	34	298	40	1,985	402	3,132	399	316	26	324	10	507	24	747	91	—	—
1944	—	—	98	11	442	33	444	30	1,920	339	3,984	444	374	42	399	23	543	22	671	98	—	—
1943	—	—	71	18	449	39	411	18	2,721	475	3,779	399	393	45	402	19	428	19	550	60	—	—
1942	—	—	89	12	321	32	323	27	3,523	521	4,063	331	559	43	446	20	814	21	562	51	—	—
1941	—	—	72	3	331	54	413	23	3,391	576	3,201	266	351	27	293	23	676	40	528	42	—	—
1940	—	—	41	4	281	32	299	18	2,561	505	2,732	200	310	33	235	6	542	27	568	36	1	—
1939	—	—	44	4	279	30	316	19	2,166	410	2,737	178	305	23	221	8	423	21	395	34	—	—
1938	—	—	22	1	341	46	250	7	1,980	335	2,576	190	217	17	237	4	422	18	342	30	—	—
1937	—	—	48	3	476	38	348	21	2,033	334	2,861	147	199	19	320	11	429	19	380	30	—	—
1936	—	—	19	1	391	26	255	11	1,911	270	2,761	164	281	43	225	13	391	25	397	26	—	—
1935	—	—	31	3	293	19	342	13	2,233	251	2,589	164	532	50	270	12	367	13	464	33	—	—
1934	—	—	8	2	411	32	258	19	2,234	299	2,287	140	783	59	195	21	462	11	545	39	—	1
1933	—	—	10	2	333	17	337	19	1,977	293	2,365	150	950	87	151	9	279	17	442	15	—	—
1932	—	—	4	2	236	26	257	16	1,742	231	2,415	176	1,034	109	235	21	410	22	405	22	—	—
1931	—	—	15	—	202	15	340	46	1,613	210	2,441	177	1,175	100	327	26	577	12	463	29	—	—
1930	—	—	8	2	301	24	272	29	1,427	154	2,927	181	1,281	108	437	20	638	13	578	25	—	—
1929	—	—	7	—	269	26	190	9	1,248	175	2,802	153	1,444	132	323	23	508	11	485	21	—	—
1928	—	—	11	—	302	18	208	13	1,283	176	2,516	184	1,478	139	307	25	422	4	576	37	—	—
1927	—	—	21	—	251	15	213	15	1,469	271	2,921	135	1,597	152	263	20	343	8	472	19	—	—

[1] For totals for Canada, see series Y 116–118.
[2] Figures for the years 1927 to 1949 are for the twelve months ending 30 September; later figures are for the calendar year. Statistics for the intervening months (October–December 1949) are given in italics. Cases not entirely disposed of within a year (i.e. tried but sentence postponed) are included in the next year's figures.
[3] The Canadian Criminal Code came in force in Newfoundland on 1 August 1950.

Series Y141–146. *Delinquency cases, by nature of the offence, Canada, 1927 to 1960[1]*

Year[2]	Against the person	Against property with violence	Against property without violence	Wilful offences against property	Forgery and uttering	Other offences	Year[1]	Against the person	Against property with violence	Against property without violence	Wilful offences against property	Forgery and uttering	Other offences
	141	142	143	144	145	146		141	142	143	144	145	146
1960	369	2,953	5,694	1,272	36	3,641	1940	208	1,261	3,058	762	8	3,134
1959	265	2,408	4,748	952	27	3,286	1939	190	1,207	2,926	700	13	2,577
1958	346[3]	2,268	4,436	985	36	3,320	1938	187	1,122	3,062	692	9	1,963
1957	254	2,005	3,764	994	28	2,634	1937	186	1,222	3,143	824	10	2,331
1956	250	1,888	3,572	839	39	2,397	1936	204	1,019	3,106	791	11	2,079
1955	181	1,548	2,767	629	29	1,871	1935	248	1,031	3,562	745	12	2,081
1954	184	1,444	2,489	673	32	1,510	1934	227	1,072	3,114	1,013	11	2,369
1953	169	1,416	2,415	770	19	1,588	1933	247	972	3,164	1,016	4	2,050
1952	172	1,456	2,496	633	25	1,286	1932	232	927	3,104	978	11	2,111
1951[4]	188	1,542	2,563	765	20	1,566	1931	256	961	3,150	1,041	10	2,350
1950	151	1,337	2,394	667	16	1,853	1930	199	951	3,686	972	17	2,600
1949[2]	*49*	*310*	*608*	*163*	*2*	*491*	1929	219	976	3,096	1,049	12	2,474
1949	176	1,346	2,244	600	15	1,817	1928	184	824	3,265	883	13	2,530
1948	204	1,229	2,400	729	15	2,578	1927	179	772	3,311	1,021	7	2,895
1947	189[5]	1,389	2,449	677	23	2,818							
1946	173[5]	1,353	2,594	887	23	2,826							
1945	220	1,513	2,964	1,190	29	2,993							
1944	216	1,739	3,393	1,269	22	3,278							
1943	260	1,550	3,658	1,140	21	3,667							
1942	206	1,536	4,039	1,228	11	4,738							
1941	263	1,407	3,467	1,063	14	4,096							

[1] For total delinquency cases, see series Y 116–118.
[2] Figures for the years 1927 to 1949 are for the twelve months ending 30 September; later figures are for the calendar year. Statistics for the intervening months (October–December 1949) are given in italics. Cases not entirely disposed of within the year (i.e. tried but disposition postponed) are included in the next year's figures.
[3] Beginning in 1958 this series includes criminal negligence and criminal negligence in operation of motor-vehicles, previously listed under heading 'other offences'.
[4] The Canadian Criminal Code came in force in Newfoundland on 1 August 1950. Statistics on juvenile delinquency in this province are reported since 1951.
[5] Beginning in 1946 this series includes intimidation, sodomy and bestiality previously listed under heading 'other offences'.

Series Y 147–155. *Delinquency cases, by disposition, Canada, 1927 to 1960[1]*

Year[2]	Reprimand	Indefinite detention	Release on probation		Fine or restitution	Training school	Final disposition suspended	Corporal punishment	Mental hospital[3]
			Supervision of court	Care of parents					
	147	148	149	150	151	152	153	154	155
1960	442	42	7,413	518	2,289	1,791	1,456	—	14
1959	236	9	6,151	412	2,810	1,678	1,381	—	9
1958	504	13	5,728	294	1,624	1,822	1,389	3	14
1957	460	63	3,822	300	2,261	1,563	1,202	1	7
1956	359	30	3,155	404	2,015	1,440	1,577	—	5
1955	181	50	3,067	365	1,064	1,172	1,118	—	8
1954	199	27	2,595	174	1,095	1,121	1,119	2	—
1953	227	28	2,620	186	1,147	1,107	1,062	—	—
1952	243	1	2,412	148	1,015	1,149	1,095	2	3
1951[4]	309	45	2,313	154	1,433	1,141	1,247	2	—
1950[2]	354	26	2,392	94	1,148	1,144	1,257	3	—
1949[2]	*139*	*13*	*533*	*25*	*341*	*300*	*272*	—	—
1949	196	39	2,141	98	1,655	1,036	1,029	4	—
1948	248	47	2,201	55	1,850	1,120	1,622	12	—
1947	182	40	2,273	69	2,116	1,108	1,733	24	—
1946	233	53	2,291	67	1,854	1,180	2,150	28	—
1945	352	65	2,698	109	2,367	1,348	1,947	23	—
1944	395	92	2,780	112	2,547	1,376	2,551	64	—
1943	464	101	2,854	140	1,962	1,401	3,322	52	—
1942	432	118	3,069	83	2,302	1,454	4,249	51	—
1941	422	139	5,024	130	1,397	1,332	1,831	35	—
1940	296	163	3,448	33	823	1,194	2,433	41	—
1939	404	156	2,262	28	608	984	3,143	28	—
1938	383	45	2,705	38	472	847	2,497	48	—
1937	474	48	3,862	37	608	774	1,864	49	—
1936	470	27	3,660	36	528	779	1,653	57	—
1935	482	17	4,030	61	510	743	1,705	131	—
1934	821	22	3,928	30	337	670	1,965	33	—
1933	902	15	3,592	27	426	666	1,799	26	—
1932	845	15	3,294	81	544	780	1,772	32	—
1931	902	32	3,743	62	938	629	1,438	24	—
1930	758	70	3,522	58	1,268	719	2,008	22	—
1929	652	126	3,001	196	1,835	660	1,318	38	—
1928	1,093	200	2,698	137	1,327	631	1,549	64	—
1927	825	346	2,559	158	1,639	669	1,880	109	—

[1] For total delinquency cases, see series Y 116–118.
[2] Figures for the years 1927 to 1949 are for the twelve month period ending 30 September; later figures are for the calendar year. Statistics for the intervening months (October–December 1949) are given in italics. Cases not entirely disposed of within the year (i.e. tried but disposition postponed) are included in next year's figures.
[3] Category added in 1952.
[4] The Canadian Criminal Code came in force in Newfoundland on 1 August 1950. Statistics on juvenile delinquency in this province are reported since 1951.

Series Y 156–157. *Number of prisoners in penitentiaries, by sex, Canada, 1867 to 1960*

Year[1]	Males	Females	Year[1]	Males	Females	Year[1]	Males	Females	Year[1]	Males	Females
	156	157		156	157		156	157		156	157
1960	6,220	124	1935	3,552[3,4]	34[3]	1910	1,859	—	1885	1,112	—
1959	6,181	114	1934	4,220[3,4]	—[3]	1909	1,765	—	1884	1,039	—
1958	5,682	88	1933	4,539[5]	48	1908	1,476	—	1883	1,113	—
1957	5,347	86	1932	4,112	52	1907	1,423	—	1882	1,127	—
1956	5,426	82	1931	3,670	44	1906[1]	1,439	—	1881	1,218	—
1955	5,412	95	1930	3,149	38	1905	1,367	—	1880	1,213	—
1954	5,025	95	1929	2,737	32	1904	1,328	—	1879	1,200	—
1953	4,829	105	1928	2,520	40	1903	1,250	—	1878	1,110[6]	—
1952	4,561	125	1927	2,441	39	1902	1,214	—	1877[1]	1,108	—
1951	4,712	105	1926	2,440	34	1901	1,382	—	1876	1,069	—
1950[2]	4,650	90	1925	2,318	27	1900	1,424	—	1875	848	—
1949[2]	4,173	87	1924	2,194	31[3]	1899	1,445	—	1874	679	—
1948	3,777	74	1923	2,486[3]	—[3]	1898	1,446	—	1873	567	—
1947	3,695	57	1922	2,640	—	1897	1,383	—	1872	605	—
1946	3,313	49	1921	2,150	—	1896	1,361	—	1871	692	—
1945	3,077	52	1920	1,931	—	1895	1,277	—	1870	756	—
1944	3,035	43	1919	1,689	—	1894	1,223	—	1869	745[6]	—
1943	2,917	52	1918	1,468	—	1893	1,194	—	1868	861[6]	—
1942	3,193	39	1917	1,694	—	1892	1,228	—	1867	972	—
1941	3,642	46	1916	2,118	—	1891	1,249	—			
1940	3,739	33	1915	2,064	—	1890	1,251	—			
1939	3,768	35	1914	2,003	—	1889	1,195	—			
1938	3,541	39	1913	1,970	—	1888	1,094	—			
1937	3,232	32[3]	1912	1,895	—	1887	1,159	—			
1936	3,098[3]	—[3]	1911	1,865	—	1886	1,200	—			

[1] From 1867 to 1876 the reporting year ends on 31 December; from 1877 to 1905 on 30 June and for later years on 31 March.
[2] Figures include statistics relating to Newfoundland since 1949.
[3] Figures in series Y 156 for the years 1936, 1934 and prior to 1924 include female prisoners.
[4] Figures include 531 Doukhobors in custody at Piers Island.
[5] Figures include 570 Doukhobors in custody at Piers Island.
[6] Does not include penitentiary at Halifax, see note to series Y 156–157.

Series Y 158–165. *Admissions of males in penitentiaries, by age, Canada, 1938 to 1960*[1]

		Age at admission in penitentiary						
Year[2]	Admissions	Under 16	16	17	18	19	20	21 and over
	158	159	160	161	162	163	164	165
1960	3,332	30	59	115	166	189	217	2,556
1959	2,975	22	57	101	143	156	173	2,323
1958	2,929	37	67	98	138	197	159	2,233
1957	2,266	25	66	86	101	111	113	1,764
1956	2,363	26	51	78	104	121	113	1,870
1955	2,328	14	45	75	116	115	115	1,848
1954	2,418	24	46	78	114	89	123	1,944
1953	2,101	18	48	71	90	111	116	1,647
1952	1,806	9	23	43	71	96	82	1,482
1951	1,951	5	21	49	76	67	94	1,639
1950	1,996	6	20	59	85	92	109	1,625
1949	1,843	4	18	49	64	83	91	1,534
1948	1,547	2	15	42	75	100	67	1,246
1947	1,663	4	19	44	70	113	89	1,324
1946	1,635	4	15	51	69	93	101	1,302
1945	1,335	2	12	40	68	84	75	1,054
1944	1,476	4	20	56	87	93	94	1,122
1943	1,171	10	15	49	42	71	66	918
1942	1,143	1	6	33	41	68	52	942
1941	1,489	2	20	33	56	79	71	1,228
1940	1,685	1	12	30	77	72	73	1,420
1939	1,896	3	20	38	67	97	83	1,588
1938	1,447	1	17	27	61	64	69	1,208

[1] Convicts admitted to and transferred to another penitentiary during the same year are counted only once.　　[2] Figures are for the fiscal year ending 31 March.

Series Y 166–169. *Penitentiaries operating costs, Canada, 1895 to 1960*

(series Y 166 in thousands of dollars, series Y 168 and Y 169 in dollars)

Year[1]	Operating cost (thousands of dollars)	Average population	Net cost *per capita* per year	Net cost *per capita* per diem	Year[1]	Operating cost (thousands of dollars)	Average population	Net cost *per capita* per year	Net cost *per capita* per diem
	166	167	168	169		166	167	168	169
1960	12,787	6,141	2,082	5.70	1925	1,205	2,217	544	1.48
1959	11,714	5,935	1,974	5.41	1924	1,129	2,373	476	1.30
1958	10,965	5,312	2,064	5.66	1923	1,442	2,582	558	1.53
1957	10,033	5,257	1,908	5.23	1922	1,365	2,417	565	1.55
1956	8,833	5,237	1,687	4.62	1921	1,503	2,058	731	2.00
1955	8,253	5,204	1,586	4.34	1920	1,068	1,832	583	1.60
1954	7,624	4,722	1,615	4.42	1919	901	1,530	589	1.61
1953	7,364	4,708	1,504	4.29	1918	845	1,513	559	1.53
1952	6,956	4,721	1,474	4.04	1917	794	1,938	410	1.12
1951	6,121	4,700	1,302	3.57	1916	809	2,074	390	1.07
1950	5,271	4,390	1,201	3.29	1915	777	1,989	390	1.07
1949	4,709	3,989	1,181	3.23	1914	763	1,946	392	1.07
1948	3,914	3,769	1,030	2.84	1913	678	1,911	355	.97
1947	3,394	3,541	958	2.63	1912	612	1,853	330	.90
1946	2,979	3,175	938	2.57	1911	474	1,834	258	.70
1945	2,747	3,063	897	2.46	1910	491	1,824	269	.74
1944	2,614	3,000	871	2.39	1909	488	1,620	301	.83
1943	2,541	3,028	839	2.29	1908	500	1,418	353	.97
1942	2,539	3,438	738	2.02	1907[1]	327	1,433	228	.63
1941	2,449	3,685	665	1.82	1906	411	1,407	292	.80
1940	2,508	3,736	671	1.84	1905	374	1,359	275	.75
1939	2,429	3,618	671	1.84	1904	349	1,286	272	.74
1938	2,265	3,371	672	1.85	1903	409	1,224	335	.92
1937	2,150	3,103	693	1.89	1902	343	1,294	265	.79
1936	2,243	3,148	712	1.95	1901	403	1,405	287	.79
1935	1,889	3,895	485	1.33	1900	349	1,430	244	.67
1934	2,104	4,358	483	1.32	1899	345	1,447	238	.65
1933	2,285	4,425	516	1.41	1898	279	1,415	197	.54
1932	1,984	3,931	505	1.38	1897	312	1,353	230	.63
1931	1,873	3,434	545	1.49	1896	345	1,314	263	.72
1930	1,457	2,868	508	1.39	1895	441	1,250	353	.97
1929	1,351	2,643	511	1.40					
1928	1,331	2,423	549	1.50					
1927	1,237	2,456	504	1.38					
1926	1,179	2,396	492	1.35					

[1] For the years 1895 to 1906 the figures are for the fiscal year ending 30 June of the year given. Figures for 1907 are for nine months ending 31 March 1907. From 1908 to 1960 the figures are for the fiscal year ending 31 March of the year given.

Series Y 170–173. *Number of prisoners in reformatories and training schools, by sex, in jails and in all penal institutions,*
Canada, 1916 to 1955

Year	Reformatories and training schools[1]		Jails[2]	All penal institutions[3]	Year	Reformatories and training schools[1]		Jails[2]	All penal institutions[3]
	Males	Females				Males	Females		
	170	**171**	**172**	**173**		**170**	**171**	**172**	**173**
1955	5,058	1,086	6,397	18,048	1935	2,823	722	3,419	10,550
1954	4,883	1,083	6,283	17,369	1934	2,987	734	3,958	11,899
1953	4,651	1,019	5,779	16,383	1933	3,132	764	4,174	12,657
1952	4,630	931	5,599	15,846	1932	3,528	852	4,711	13,255
1951	4,222	834	5,422	15,295	1931	3,426	932	4,477	12,549
1950	4,390[4]	892	5,990[4]	16,012	1930	3,105	648	4,283	11,223
1949	4,545	804	4,964	14,573	1929	2,846	602	3,579	9,796
1948	4,304	780	4,519	13,454	1928	2,435	437	3,129	8,561
1947	3,887	682	4,160	12,481	1927	2,409	441	2,634	7,964
1946	3,319[5]	785	4,185	11,651	1926	2,249	431	2,439	7,593
1945	3,275	949	3,981	11,334	1925	2,193	403	2,602	7,543
1944	3,818	1,024	3,292	11,212	1924	2,187	387	2,327	7,126
1943	3,671	1,020	3,202	10,862	1923	1,922	383	2,058	6,849
1942	3,012	851	3,356	10,451	1922	1,878	405	2,678	7,601
1941	3,286	973	3,816	11,763	1921	2,023	344	2,674	7,191
1940	3,883	964	4,332	12,951	1920	1,636	281	2,156	6,004
1939	3,925	879	4,267	12,874	1919	1,319	298	2,136	5,442
1938	4,023	857	4,978	13,438	1918	1,195	311	2,052	5,026
1937	3,740	792	4,412	12,208	1917	1,188	309	1,977	5,168
1936	3,420	688	3,948	11,154	1916[6]	1,198	276	1,867	5,459

[1] The reporting year ends on 30 September.
[2] From 1916 to 1948 the reporting year ends on 30 September with the exception of Ontario (31 March), Nova Scotia (30 November) and Quebec (31 December). Since 1949 the reporting year ends on 31 March with the exception of Quebec where it ends on 31 December.
[3] Includes convicts detained in penitentiaries as shown in series Y 156–157.
[4] Oakalla Prison Farm, B.C., previously classed as a reformatory for men, was changed to a jail.
[5] Figures prior to 1946 include a few women prisoners at Oakalla Prison Farm.
[6] Figures relate to the beginning of the reporting year 1917.

Series Y 174–177. *Tickets of leave and pardons, Canada, 1876 to 1955*

Year[1]	Total	Released under ticket of leave	Other conditional or unconditional pardon	Ticket-of-leave man granted further clemency	Year[1]	Total	Released under ticket of leave	Other conditional or unconditional pardon	Ticket-of-leave man granted further clemency
	174	**175**	**176**	**177**		**174**	**175**	**176**	**177**
1955	1,672	1,342	284	46	1915	1,593	1,287	231	75
1954	1,236	906	313	17	1914	1,430	1,193	175	62
1953	1,139	857	250	32	1913	1,146	980	138	28
1952	1,070	792	235	43	1912	1,035	913	94	28
1951[2]	1,127	818	243	66	1911	927	782	114	31
1950[1]	*422*	*263*	*137*	*22*	1910	740	595	121	24
1950	1,820	1,287	475	58	1909	734	578	133	23
1949	1,464	942	468	54	1908	601	396	187	18
1948	1,437	972	418	47	1907	590	419	158	13
1947	1,368	980	357	31	1906	471	306	158	7
1946	1,155	809	300	46	1905	405	219	181	5
1945	1,399	844	505	50	1904	352	192	153	7
1944	1,326	663	604	59	1903	412	189	220	3
1943	1,155	604	519	32	1902	442	247	195	—
1942	1,101	705	364	32	1901	326	169	157	—
1941	971	457	459	55	1900	302	124	178	—
1940	1,441	663	691	87	1899	240	—	240	—
1939	1,651	733	897	21	1898	153	—	153	—
1938	1,548	644	890	14	1897	163	—	163	—
1937	1,268	588	668	12	1896	143	—	143	—
1936	1,492	716	758	18	1895	193	—	193	—
1935	1,652	770	851	31	1894	159	—	159	—
1934	2,448	1,160	1,256	32	1893	107	—	107	—
1933	2,863	1,982	862	19	1892	190	—	190	—
1932	1,449	944	487	18	1891	119	—	119	—
1931	1,423	982	429	12	1890	156	—	156	—
1930	1,472	778	668	26	1889	130	—	130	—
1929	1,457	1,105	320	32	1888	147	—	147	—
1928	1,669	645	1,001	23	1887	116	—	116	—
1927	1,681	761	838	82	1886	130	—	130	—
1926	1,113	763	299	51	1885	99	—	99	—
1925	1,197	747	380	70	1884	134	—	134	—
1924	1,670	1,137	460	73	1883	126	—	126	—
1923	1,640	1,154	425	61	1882	105	—	105	—
1922	1,473	1,182	264	27	1881	103	—	103	—
1921	1,012	847	143	22	1880	123	—	123	—
1920	1,241	751	466	24	1879	117	—	117	—
1919	1,495	840	613	42	1878	153	—	153	—
1918	1,183	703	453	27	1877	122	—	122	—
1917	1,389	1,143	200	46	1876	86	—	86	—
1916	1,321	1,098	146	77					

[1] Figures for the years 1876 to 1950 are for the twelve months ending 30 September; later figures are for the calendar year; statistics for the intervening months (October–December 1950) are given in italics.
[2] Statistics relating to Newfoundland included since 1951.

Series Y178–201. *Suicide and deaths from self-inflicted injury, by sex, Canada and the provinces, 1921 to 1960*

	Canada		Newfoundland[1]		Prince Edward Island		Nova Scotia		New Brunswick		Quebec[2]		Ontario		Manitoba		Saskatchewan		Alberta		British Columbia		Yukon and the Northwest Territories[3]	
Year	M	F	M	F	M	F	M	F	M	F	M	F	M	F	M	F	M	F	M	F	M	F	M	F
	178	179	180	181	182	183	184	185	186	187	188	189	190	191	192	193	194	195	196	197	198	199	200	201
1960	1,084	266	11	1	8	—	43	15	22	5	199	57	413	115	86	15	68	7	104	15	126	36	4	—
1959	1,017	270	13	1	2	1	27	3	27	5	203	52	404	115	54	11	52	16	104	13	126	53	5	—
1958	1,022	249	11	—	6	1	28	6	23	7	182	57	396	100	68	17	67	16	95	16	143	29	3	—
1957	981	266	13	1	5	1	43	7	18	—	176	81	388	102	59	10	57	18	85	20	137	26	—	—
1956	952	274	7	2	4	—	22	5	19	5	181	62	370	97	60	20	61	15	87	28	134	39	7	1
1955	844	259	5	1	4	2	29	7	19	4	150	49	302	111	60	17	75	16	77	19	123	33	3	—
1954	841	261	6	2	8	—	18	9	12	3	150	58	314	94	46	12	63	22	83	24	141	37	2	—
1953	820	232	8	1	5	—	27	6	15	3	139	48	307	99	62	11	42	9	60	12	138	44	5	—
1952	810	240	7	1	4	1	32	10	14	3	104	35	335	105	52	10	48	13	76	18	128	44	3	—
1951	785	248	10	2	5	—	22	6	14	5	120	57	287	98	77	15	55	8	67	19	155	52	8	—
1950	823	237	7	—	3	—	34	11	25	5	103	42	306	92	69	10	54	10	67	15	125	36	2	—
1949	819	208	1	—	3	—	36	6	21	3	122	28	326	88	61	21	60	10	64	16	132	31	4	—
1948	769	231	—	—	4	—	30	8	19	6	104	27	289	102	64	17	65	24	55	12	107	34	4	—
1947	710	238	—	—	3	3	30	6	23	3	102	33	261	106	45	15	57	19	79	21	111	29	2	—
1946	758	244	—	—	1	—	27	7	19	5	110	43	309	105	45	15	57	19	79	21	111	29	2	—
1945	565	199	—	—	1	2	16	5	19	7	80	27	214	93	33	14	51	11	57	19	94	21	4	—
1944	542	189	—	—	3	1	17	7	14	1	87	25	234	84	46	18	43	15	63	16	64	24	2	—
1943	543	215	—	—	2	2	21	6	11	4	84	25	213	103	41	16	50	18	63	16	58	25	3	—
1942	621	218	—	—	2	1	21	5	16	5	90	22	252	99	42	20	51	22	66	20	81	24	2	—
1941	664	232	—	—	2	2	29	9	25	6	105	34	217	102	55	10	63	19	78	25	90	25	3	—
1940	711	237	—	—	5	—	20	8	21	7	118	38	243	97	43	18	71	23	81	15	109	31	3	—
1939	765	213	—	—	5	1	27	8	15	5	119	35	272	85	69	15	73	17	81	22	104	25	4	—
1938	749	199	—	—	1	2	35	7	16	4	104	31	274	86	68	23	68	10	83	17	100	19	5	—
1937	750	228	—	—	5	1	24	5	17	13	127	28	271	95	64	23	69	18	80	21	93	24	3	—
1936	707	221	—	—	3	1	25	8	15	9	82	32	299	99	50	19	70	18	77	10	86	25	3	—
1935	713	192	—	—	3	2	26	3	11	4	111	29	280	87	51	9	81	18	74	10	76	30	1	—
1934	725	202	—	—	3	—	21	6	12	3	95	26	267	93	56	12	82	23	79	27	110	12	2	—
1933	733	189	—	—	2	—	19	3	16	4	107	37	291	75	63	15	76	17	65	20	94	18	4	—
1932	812	212	—	—	5	—	28	6	21	7	108	25	320	103	75	19	61	13	80	16	114	23	6	—
1931	795	209	—	—	5	1	18	3	18	3	99	24	327	99	49	7	64	12	104	19	111	41	6	—
1930	805	205	—	—	1	—	16	1	13	2	94	20	301	103	59	19	101	26	104	9	116	25	2	—
1929	649	186	—	—	4	—	22	3	15	6	80	30	239	81	55	18	85	10	77	11	87	13	4	—
1928	593	158	—	—	4	—	16	5	21	5	79	18	207	78	38	14	64	14	68	9	97	9	1	—
1927	612	147	—	—	3	—	17	2	17	4	65	20	231	87	53	9	61	7	68	9	83	18	—	—
1926	543	137	—	—	4	—	29	5	11	2	65	19	209	62	44	7	44	10	54	14	83	18	—	—
1925	466	120	—	—	—	1	21	5	14	3	—	—	200	65	54	10	47	14	53	10	77	12	—	—
1924	399	136	—	—	7	—	18	5	13	1	—	—	185	74	42	17	35	9	39	12	60	18	—	—
1923	404	134	—	—	3	3	18	13	6	5	—	—	169	67	27	10	45	9	57	13	79	14	—	—
1922	376	111	—	—	2	—	19	9	7	3	—	—	169	63	35	10	47	14	42	7	55	5	—	—
1921	342	89	—	—	5	—	14	5	8	2	—	—	119	41	34	10	47	10	58	12	57	9	—	—

[1] Newfoundland entered Confederation in 1949.
[2] Figures prior to 1926 not comparable.

[3] Figures prior to 1956 relate to both males and females; they are not included in the totals for Canada; figures before 1927 not available.

Series Y 202–214. *Bankruptcies and insolvencies under federal legislation, by branch of business, with estimated total assets and liabilities, Canada, 1924 to 1958*

(series Y 213 and Y 214 in thousands of dollars)

Year	Agriculture	Forestry, fishing, trapping	Mining	Manufacturing	Construction	Transportation, communication, storage	Trade	Finance, public utilities	Services	Not classified	Total	Estimated total assets	Estimated total liabilities
	202	203	204	205	206	207	208	209	210	211	212	213	214
1958	49	9	9	356	367	105	882	42	295	11	2,125	—	72,778
1957	51	14	15	366	372	109	928	40	244	74	2,213	—	79,863
1956	45	10	3	342	375	83	782	28	246	53	1,967	—	64,254
1955[1]	59	3	4	290	309	68	772	14	250	26	1,795	—	53,776
1955[1]	52	8	8	305	287	116	882	44	454	292	2,448	—	59,138
1954	48	17	15	416	135	67	973	41	408	158	2,278	38,370	53,142
1953	37	6	10	359	124	52	650	30	286	103	1,657	21,899	32,818
1952	42	2	7	305	114	45	569	32	279	114	1,509	20,381	29,658
1951	20	8	8	269	126	42	570	27	255	74	1,399	18,238	25,912
1950[2]	24	7	5	257	97	40	502	20	273	78	1,303	17,169	24,872
1949[3]	8	10	10	232	94	46	374	19	203	70	1,066	15,549	21,356
1948	9	4	3	188	77	30	289	4	144	65	813	9,856	15,724
1947	6	7	—	152	57	20	153	5	92	53	515	5,933	10,078
1946	2	4	3	57	32	14	77	7	64	18	278	4,039	5,966
1945	2	—	3	54	39	12	58	6	70	28	272	1,864	3,995
1944	4	2	3	47	27	11	83	7	62	31	277	2,020	4,044
1943	13	1	7	61	38	14	166	11	78	32	421	3,198	5,340
1942	14	—	10	80	58	17	342	2	181	33	737	4,500	6,019
1941	34	2	14	132	64	13	482	8	188	71	1,008	7,326	9,134
1940	67	4	15	167	53	13	591	11	201	51	1,173	7,676	10,663
1939	108	6	18	210	80	22	664	12	197	75	1,392	11,186	15,089
1938	101	1	11	200	50	9	667	4	109	67	1,219	8,782	14,017
1937	104	5	21	182	46	7	584	15	123	39	1,126	10,704	14,303
1936	123	2	12	191	53	10	536	11	189	71	1,198	10,704	15,145
1935	173	3	10	180	62	11	594	16	186	79	1,314	12,174	17,567
1934	82	3	2	217	59	20	799	16	217	117	1,532	19,257	23,598
1933	92	1	5	357	57	26	1,089	12	246	159	2,044	27,033	32,954
1932	190	9	6	468	83	43	1,171	7	290	153	2,420	40,604	51,629
1931	125	5	7	464	61	42	1,102	21	255	134	2,216	46,839	52,553
1930	115	12	9	488	55	48	1,204	29	283	159	2,402	44,048	48,164
1929	125	4	11	443	61	21	1,100	5	239	158	2,167	32,064	38,748
1928	108	31	23	505	70	45	884	5	263	103	2,037	26,583	32,455
1927	116	30	26	430	63	36	818	—	243	79	1,841	23,198	30,634
1926	135	27	20	390	52	34	805	1	225	84	1,773	24,677	32,291
1925	158	14	15	403	50	21	1,026	5	220	84	1,996	26,968	32,154
1924	204	14	22	329	44	36	1,317	8	129	216	2,319	43,194	48,105

[1] Figures for 1955 to 1957 not strictly comparable with those for previous years. See note to series Y 202–214. Figures for 1955 are given on both old and new basis.
[2] Statistics on Newfoundland included from 1950 to 1958.

[3] Figures for 1924 to 1949 not strictly comparable with those for later years. See note to series Y 202–214.

Series Y 215–216. *Commercial failures in Canada, number and liabilities, 1885 to 1935*

(series Y 216 in thousands of dollars)

Year[1]	Number of failures	Liabilities	Year[1]	Number of failures	Liabilities	Year[1]	Number of failures	Liabilities	Year[1]	Number of failures	Liabilities
	215	216		215	216		215	216		215	216
1935	1,402	14,542	1920	1,078	26,494	1905	1,347	9,855	1890	1,847	18,000
1934	1,627	20,728	1919	755	16,256	1904	1,246	11,394	1889	1,747	14,529
1933	2,344	29,251	1918	873	14,502	1903	978	7,553	1888	1,667	13,975
1932	2,938	56,631	1917	1,097	18,241	1902	1,101	10,935	1887	1,366	16,071
1931	2,563	52,987	1916	1,685	25,070	1901	1,341	10,812	1886	1,233	10,171
1930	2,741	57,191	1915	2,661	41,132	1900	1,355	11,613	1885	1,247	8,743
1929	2,310	44,441	1914	2,898	34,997	1899	1,287	10,659			
1928	2,120	53,420	1913	1,719	16,979	1898	1,300	9,821			
1927	2,182	34,462	1912	1,357	12,316	1897	1,809	14,157			
1926	2,196	37,083	1911	1,332	13,491	1896	2,118	17,170			
1925	2,371	45,768	1910	1,262	14,515	1895	1,891	15,803			
1924	2,474	64,531	1909	1,442	12,983	1894	1,856	17,616			
1923	3,247	65,810	1908	1,640	14,932	1893	1,344	12,690			
1922	3,695	78,069	1907	1,278	13,221	1892	1,680	13,703			
1921	2,451	73,299	1906	1,184	9,086	1891	1,861	16,724			

[1] Statistics on Newfoundland included from 1885 to 1893 and from 1905 to 1932.

INDEX

923665